ELENCHUS OF BIBLICAL BIBLIOGRAPHY

10

ROBERT NORTH S.J.

ELENCHUS OF BIBLICA

1994

EDITRICE PONTIFICIO ISTITUTO BIBLICO
ROMA 1997

© 1997 – E.P.I.B. – Roma
ISBN 88-7653-609-4

EDITRICE PONTIFICIO ISTITUTO BIBLICO
Piazza della Pilotta, 35 - 00187 Roma

Urbes editionis – Cities of publication

AA	Ann Arbor		Lp	Leipzig
Amst	Amsterdam		Lv(N)	Leuven (L-Neuve)
B	Berlin		Lvl	Louisville KY
Ba/BA	Basel/Buenos Aires		M/Mi	Madrid/Milano
Barc	Barcelona		Mkn/Mp	Maryknoll/Minneapolis
Bo/Bru	Bologna/Brussel		Mü/Müns('r)	München/Munster
CasM	Casale Monferrato		N	Napoli
CinB	Cinisello Balsamo		ND	NotreDame IN
C	Cambridge, England		Neuk	Neukirchen/Verlag
CM	Cambridge, Mass.		NHv / Nv	New Haven / Nashville
Ch	Chicago		NY	New York
ColMn	Collegeville MN		Ox	Oxford
Da: Wiss	Darmstadt, WissBuchg		P/Pd	Paris/Paderborn
DG	Downers Grove IL		Ph	Philadelphia
Dü	Düsseldorf		R/Rg	Roma/Regensburg
E	Edinburgh		S/Sdr	Salamanca/Santander
ENJ	EnglewoodCliffs NJ		SF	San Francisco
F	Firenze		Shf	Sheffield
FrB/FrS	Freiburg-Br/Schweiz		Sto	Stockholm
Fra	Frankfurt/M		Stu	Stuttgart
Gö	Göttingen		T/TA	Torino/Tel Aviv
GR	Grand Rapids MI		Tü	Tübingen
Gü	Gütersloh		U/W	Uppsala/Wien
Ha	Hamburg		WL	Winona Lake IN
Heid	Heidelberg		Wmr	Warminster
Hmw	Harmondsworth		Wsb	Wiesbaden
J	Jerusalem		Wsh	Washington D.C.
K	København		Wsz	Warszawa
L/Lei	London/Leiden		Wu/Wü	Wuppertal/Würzburg
LA	Los Angeles		Z	Zürich

Please recall:

To separate a subtitle
from its title

we use a SEMICOLON (;)

where the original
varyingly uses
full-stop, colon, or new line

PRICE of books
is rounded off

($13 for 12.95;
less often £20 for 19.90;
DM 40 for 39,50)

to take account of
conciseness and inflation.

Note L^m 50 = Lire it. 50.000

With an annual grant from The Catholic Biblical Association of America, this ELENCHUS has been compiled from the libraries of the Pontifical Biblical Institute and Gregorian University, the Deutsches Archäologisches Institut, the École Française, and the American Academy, all in Rome; and of the Saint Louis and Milwaukee-Marquette universities, with the financial support of their Jesuit communities. The publication management has been assured by Father Pasquale PUCA for the Pontifical Gregorian University Press.

Index systematicus – Contents

Ave atque Vale!

This is the last volume of the ELENCHUS OF BIBLICA to appear in its present mode of production. For the coming years we will pass to fully computerized automation.

The 1995 materials have already been almost completely gathered. The strictly biblical sections E-F-G are foreseen to appear in a volume apart. The more peripheral areas (languages, history, theology) will hopefully follow soon after. But in both cases the computer-editing, though in many ways easier, will take a long time.

The format for 1996 and after, we cannot now exactly foresee, amid the swirl of on-line services. CD-ROM, the Network, and other yet-unforeseen technological marvels — doubtless with a follow-up printed volume somewhat like today's.

* * *

The occasion seems to call for an expression of our appreciation for the many who have in various ways contributed to make possible whatever usefulness our work may have had.

In first place and above all it seems opportune to mention here the thirty years' editorship of the German Father Peter NOBER, S.J., whose talents and selfless dedication brought this bibliography to recognition throughout the world as a useful tool of scholarship.

Also deserving of special mention are our high-quality printers: first and for many years the Scuola Tipografica Pio Decimo, and more recently the Pontifical Gregorian University Press. It is hard to resist the temptation to single out for special thanks the individuals whose collaboration was most friendly and appreciated; but these would doubtless prefer that their colleagues with whom we have had a less-immediate contact should not seem to be less needed and important.

Specifically for this year's Index, alongside the valued continuing help of Carlo VALENTINO and our colleagues Fred BRENK and Jean-Nöel ALETTI, we have been uniquely indebted to the skill and availability of Andrzej GIENIUSZ, of the Resurrectionist Fathers, whose seminarians of an earlier generation shared our philosophy formation — a pleasant memory of bygone days at Saint Louis University.

For the future, we wish all success to Father Robert ALTHANN and those who will cooperate in the continuance of Father NOBER's work.

R. N.

Acronyms: Periodica - Series (small).
8 fig. = ISSN; *10 fig.* = ISBN; *6/7* = DissA.

🅐: *arabice,* in Arabic.
AAS: Acta Apostolicae Sedis; Vaticano. 0001-5199.
AASOR: Annual of the American Schools of Oriental Research; CM.
Abh: Abhandlungen Gö Lp Mü etc.; ➤ DOG / DPV.
AbhChrJüDial: Abhandlungen zum christlich-jüdischen Dialog; Mü, Kaiser.
AbrNahr: Abr-Nahrain; Lv, Peeters.
AcAANorv: Acta ad archaeologiam et artium historiam; R, Inst. Norv.
AcAntH: Acta Antiqua; Budapest.
AcArchH/K: Acta Archaeologica; Hungarica, Budapest. 0001-5210 / København. 0065-101X.
AcArchLov: Acta archaeologica Lovaniensia; Lv.
AcClasSAfr: Acta Classica; Pretoria. 0065-1141.
Acme; Mi, Fac. Lett. Filos. 0001-494X.
AcPByz: Acta Patristica et Byzantina; Pretoria. 1022-6486 (5,1994).
AcPIB: Acta Pontificii Instituti Biblici: Roma.
AcPraeh: Acta Praehistorica/Archaeol.; B.
AcSum: Acta Sumerologica; Hiroshima Univ., Linguistics. 0387-8082.
Act: Actes/Acta (Congrès, Colloque).
ActIran: Acta Iranica; Téhéran/Leiden.
ActOrH/K: Acta Orientalia: Budapest. 0044-5975 / K (Soc. Or. Danica, Norveigica). 0001-6438.
AcTSAf: Acta theologica Bloemfontein. (15,1995).
ActuBbg: Actualidad Bibliográfica; Barcelona. 0211-4143.
ADAJ: Annual of the Department of Antiquities, Jordan; 'Amman.
ADPF: Association pour la diffusion de la pensée française; Paris ➤ RCiv.
Aeg: Aegyptus; Milano. 0001-9046.
ÄgAbh: Ägyptologische Abhandlungen; Wb.
ÄgAT: Ägypten und Altes Testament; Wiesbaden. 0720-9061.
AegHelv: Aegyptiaca Helvetica: Basel Univ. Äg. Sem. (Univ. Genève).
ÄgLev: Ägypten und Levante; Wien. 1015-5014.
AEM: Archives Épistolaires de Mari.

ÄthF: Äthiopische Forschungen; Stu.
AevA: Aevum Antiquum; Mi, Univ. Cattolica/ViPe.
Aevum; Milano [anche Univ. Catt.].
AfER: African Ecclesial Review; Eldoret, Kenya.
AfJB: African Journal of Biblical Studies; Ibadan.
AfO: Archiv für Orientforschung; Graz.
AfTJ: Africa Theological Journal; Arusha, Tanzania. 0856-0048.
AGJU: Arbeiten zur Geschichte Antik. Judentums und des Urchristentums; Leiden.
AIBL: Académie des Inscriptions et Belles-Lettres; P ➤ CRAI. – AIEMA ➤ BMosA.
AION [-Clas]: Annali (dell')Istituto Universitario Orientale [Classico] di Napoli ➤ ArchStorAnt.
AJA: American Journal of Archaeology; Princeton NJ. 0002-9114.
AJS: Association for Jewish Studies Review; CM 0364-0094.
Akkadica; Bruxelles/Brussel.
al.: et alii, and other(s).
ALASP: Abhanglungen zur Literatur Alt-Syrien-Palästinas; Münster.
Alexandria, cosmology; GR. (1,1991).
ALGHJ: Arbeiten zur Literatur und Geschichte des hellenistischen Judentums; Leiden.
Al-Kibt, The Copts, die Kopten; Ha.
Altertum (Das); Berlin. 0002-6646.
AltOrF: Altorientalische Forschungen; Berlin. 0232-8461.
AmBapQ: American Baptist Quarterly; Valley Forge PA. 0015-8992.
AmBenR: American Benedictine Review; Richardton ND. 0002-7650.
Ambrosius, bollettino liturgico; Milano. 0392-5757.
America; NY. 0002-7049.
AmHR: American Historical Rev.; NY.
AmJPg: American Journal of Philology; Baltimore. 0002-9475.
AmJTPh: American Journal of Theology and Philosophy; Lawrence.
AmMessianJ: The American Messianic Jew; Ph.
AmNumM: American Numismatic Society Museum Notes; NY.

AmPhTr: Transactions of the American Philosophical Society; Ph.

AmstCah: Amsterdamse cahiers voor exegese/bijbelse theologie; Kampen.

AmstMed ➤ Mededelingen.

AmStPapyr: American Studies in Papyrology; NHv.

AnalPapyr: Analecta Papyrologica; Messina. (1,1989).

AnáMnesis: teología, Dominicos; México. (3,1991).

AnArStorAnt: Annali di Archeologia e Storia Antica.

AnASyr: Annales Archéologiques Arabes Syriennes; Damas.

Anatolica; Istanbul. 0066-1554.

AnatSt: Anatolian Studies; London.

AnAug: Analecta Augustiniana; R.

ANaut: Archaeonautica; P. 0154-1854.

AnBib: Analecta Biblica. Investigationes scientificae in res biblicas; R. 0066-135X.

AnBoll: Analecta Bollandiana; Bruxelles. 0003-2468.

AnBritAth: Annual of the British School at Athens; London.

AnCalas: Analecta Calasanctiana; Salamanca. 0569-9789.

AnCÉtRel: Annales du Centre d'Études des Religions; Bru.

AncHB: Ancient History Bulletin; Calgary/Chicago. 0835-3638.

AnChile: Anales de la Facultad de Teología; Santiago, Univ. Católica.

AnchorB[D]: Anchor Bible [Dict]; NY. ➤ 495.

AncHRes: Ancient History Resources for Teachers; Sydney. 0310-5814.

AnCist: Analecta Cisterciensia; Roma. 0003-2476.

AnClas: Annales Universitatis, sectio classica; Budapest.

AnClémOchr: Annuaire de l'Académie de théologie 'Ochrida'; Sofya.

AnCracov: Analecta Cracoviensia (Polish Theol. Soc.); Kraków. 0209-0864.

AncSoc: Ancient Society. Katholieke Universiteit; Leuven. 0066-1619.

AndNR: Andover Newton Review; Newton Centre MA (3,1992).

AndrUnS: Andrews University Seminary Studies; Berrien Springs, Mich. 0003-2980.

AnEgBbg: Annual Egyptological Bibliography; Leiden.

AnÉPH: Annuaire ➤ ÉPHÉ.

AnÉSC: Annales Économies Sociétés Civilisations; P. 0395-2649.

AnÉth: Annales d'Éthiopie; Addis-Ababa.

AnFac: Let: Annali della facoltà di lettere, Univ. (Bari/Cagliari/Perugia).

— **Ling/T:** Annal(es) Facultat(is); linguarum, theologiae.

AnFg: Anuario de Filología; Barc.

Ang: Angelicum; Roma. 0003-3081.

AnglTR: Anglican Theological Review; Evanston IL. 0003-3286.

AnGreg: Analecta (Pont. Univ.) Gregoriana; Roma. 0066-1376.

AnHArt: Annales d'histoire de l'art et d'archéologie: Bru.

AnHConc: Annuarium Historiae Conciliorum; Paderborn.

ANilM: Archéologie du Nil Moyen; Lille. 0299-8130.

AnItNum: Annali (dell')Istituto Italiano di Numismatica; Roma.

AnJapB: Annual of the Japanese Biblical Institute; Tokyo ❶ ➤ Sei-Ron.

AnLetN: Annali della Facoltà di lettere e filosofia dell'Univ.; Napoli.

AnLovBOr: Analecta Lovaniensia Biblica et Orientalia; Lv.

AnnTh: Annales Theologici; Roma.

AnOr: Analecta Orientalia: Roma.

AnOrdBas: Analecta Ordinis S. Basilii Magni; Roma.

AnPg: L'Année Philologique; P. ➤ 7,858.

AnPisa: Annali della Scuola Normale Superiore; Pisa.

AnPraem: Analecta Praemonstratensia; Averbode.

AnRIM: Annual Review of the Royal Inscriptions of Mesopotamia Project; Toronto. 0822-2525.

AnRSocSR: Annual Review of the Social Sciences of Religion; The Hague. 0066-2062.

ANRW: Aufstieg und Niedergang der römischen Welt ➤ 496.

AnSacTar: Analecta Sacra Tarraconensia; Barcelona.

AnSemClas: Annali del Seminario di Studi del Mondo Classico; N, Univ.

AnStoEseg: Annali di Storia dell'Esegesi; Bologna. 1120-4001.

AntAb: Antike und Abendland; Berlin. 0003-5696.

AntAfr: Antiquités africaines; Paris. 0066-4871.

AnTar: Antiquité tardive (IVe-VIIe s.); Turnhout (1,1993: 2-503-50328-4).

AntClas: L'Antiquité Classique; Bru.

AntClCr: Antichità classica e cristiana; Brescia.

Anthropos; 1. Fribourg/Suisse. 0003-5572. / [2. Famiglia; Roma].

Anthropotes; Roma, Città Nuova.

AntiqJ: Antiquaries Journal; London. 0003-5815.

Antiquity; Gloucester. 0003-5982.

Ant/ka: Ⓖ Anthropologiká: Thessaloniki.

AntKu: Antike Kunst; Basel. 0003-5688.

Anton: Antonianum; Roma. 0003-6064.

AntRArch: Antiqua, Rivista d'Archeologia e d'Architettura; Roma.

AntWelt: Antike Welt; Feldmeilen.

AnuFg: Anuari de Filologia; Barc (15,1992).

Anvil, Anglican Ev. theol.; Bramcote, Nottingham. 0003-6226.

AnzAltW: Anzeiger für die Altertumswissenschaft; Innsbruck. 0003-6293.

AnzW: Anzeiger der österreichischen Akademie; Wien. 0378-8652.

AOAT: Alter Orient und Altes Testament: Kevelaer/Neukirchen.

AOtt: Univ. München, Arbeiten zu Text und Sprache im AT; St. Ottilien.

Apocrypha; Turnhout (1,1990).

Apollonia: Afro-Hellenic studies; Johannesburg, Rand Afrikaans Univ.

Appoint; Montréal. (25,1992).

ArabArchEp: Arabian Archaeology and Epigraphy; K. 0905-7916.

ArabScPh: Arabic sciences and philosophy; C (1,1991).

Aram: Oxford.

Arasaradi, journal of theological reflection; Tamilnadu, Madurai (3/2, 1990).

ArBegG: Archiv für Begriffsgeschichte (Mainz, Akad.); Bonn.

ArbGTL: Arbeiten zur Geschichte und Theologie des Luthertums, NF; B.

ArbKiG: Arbeiten zur Kirchengeschichte; B.

ArbNTJud: Arbeiten zum NT und zum Judentum: Frankfurt/M. 0170-8856.

ArbNtTextf: Arbeiten zur Neutestamentlichen Textforschung; B/NY.

ArbNZ: (Texte und) Arbeiten zum NT und seine Zeitgeschichte (non = TANZ), Neuk.

ArbT: Arbeiten zur Theologie (Calwer); Stu.

ArCalc: Archeologia e calcolatori; F, Univ. Siena [1 (1990) 88-7814-072-4].

ARCE ⤳ J [News] AmEg.

Archaeología; Wsz. 0066-605X.

Archaeology; Boston. 0003-8113.

Archaeometry; L. 0003-813X.

ArchAnz: Archäologischer Anzeiger; Berlin. 0003-8105.

ArchAth: Ⓖ Archaiología; Athēna.

ArchBbg: Archäologische Bibliographie zu JbDAI; Berlin.

ArchBW: Archaeology in the biblical world; Shafter CA (2,1992).

ArchClasR: Archeologia Classica; Roma. 0391-8165.

Archeo, attualità del passato; Milano.

Archéologia; (ex-Paris) Dijon, Faton. 0570-6270 ⤳ Dossiers.

Archéozoologie; Grenoble (4/2,1991).

ArchEph: Ⓖ Archaiologikē Ephēmeris; Athēnai.

ArchInf: Archäologische Informationen; Bonn.

ArchMIran: Archäologische Mitteilungen aus Iran, N.F.; Berlin.

ArchNews: Archaeological News; Tallahassee FL. 0194-3413.

ArchRep: Archaeological Reports; Wmr, British Sch. Athens. 0570-6084.

ArchWsz: Archaeologia; Warszawa. 0066-605X (44,1993).

Arctos, Acta Philologica Fennica; Helsinki. 0570-734X.

ArCyp: Archaeology of Cyprus (2, 1990).

ArEspArq: Archivo Español de Arqueología; Madrid. 0066-6742.

ARET/S: Archivi Reali di Ebla, Testi/Studi; Roma, Univ.

Arethusa; Buffalo NY. 0004-0975.

ArFranchHist: Archivum Franciscanum Historicum; Grottaferrata.

ArGlottIt: Archivio Glottologico Italiano; Firenze. 0004-0207.

ArHPont: Archivum Historiae Pontificiae; Roma.
ArKulturg: Archiv für Kulturgeschichte; Köln. 0003-9233.
ArLtgW: Archiv für Liturgiewissenschaft; Regensburg. 0066-6386.
ArNews: Archaeology News (16,1991).
ArOr: Archiv Orientální; Praha. 0044-8699.
ArPapF: Archiv für Papyrusforschung; Leipzig. 0066-6459.
ArRefG: Archiv für Reformationsgeschichte; Gütersloh.
ArRepAth: Archaeological Reports; Athens (JHS/BritSch). 0570-0084.
ArSSocRel: Archives de Sciences Sociales des Religions; Paris.
ArTGran: Archivo Teológico Granadino; Granada. 0210-1629.
ArztC: ➤ ZMedEth.
ASAE: Annales du Service des Antiquités de l'Égypte; Le Caire.
AsbTJ: Asbury Theological Journal; Wilmore, KY.
AshlandTJ: ... Theological J. (Ohio).
AsiaJT: Asia Journal of Theology; Bangalore. (1,1992).
ASOR: American Schools of Oriental Research; CM (diss.: Dissertation Series).
Asprenas... Scienze Teologiche; Napoli.
At[AcBol/Tor/Tosc]: Atti [dell'Accademia... di Bologna / di Torino / Toscana].
ATANT: Abhandlungen zur Theologie des Alten & Neuen Testaments; Zürich.
ATD: Das Alte Testament Deutsch. Neues Göttinger Bibelwerk; Gö.
AteDial: Ateismo e Dialogo; Vaticano.
AtenRom: Atene e Roma; Firenze. 0004-6493.
Athenaeum: Letteratura e Storia dell'antichità; Pavia.
`Atiqot; J, Dept. Ant.; from 20 (1991) Eng. + ❾. 0066-488X.
AtKap: Ateneum Kapłańskie; Włocławek. 0208-9041.
ATLA: American Theological Library Association; Evanston, IL.
Atualização; Belo Horizonte, MG.
AuCAfr: Au cœur de l'Afrique; Burundi.
Aufidus; Roma.
AugL: Augustinus-Lexikon ➤ 582.
AugLv: Augustiniana; Leuven.

AugM: Augustinus; Madrid.
AugR: Augustinianum; Roma.
AugSt: Augustinian Studies; Villanova PA.
AulaO: Aula Orientalis; Barc.
AusgF: Ausgrabungen und Funde; B.
AustinSB: Austin (TX) Sem. Bulletin.
AustralasCR: Australasian Catholic Record; Sydney. 0727-3215.
AustralBR: Australian Biblical Review; Melbourne.
AVA: ➤ BeitAVgA.
BA: Biblical Archaeologist; CM. 0006-0895.
Babel (translation); Budapest, Akad.
BaBernSt: Basler und Berner Studien zur hist./systematischen Theologie; Bern.
Babesch: Bulletin Antieke Beschaving; Haag. 0165-9367.
BaghMit: Baghdader Mitteilungen DAI; Berlin.
BAH: Bibliothèque Archéologique et Historique (IFA-Beyrouth).
BAnglsr: Bulletin of the Anglo-Israel Archaeological Soc.; L. 0266-2442.
BangTF: Bangalore Theological Forum.
BapRT: Baptist review of theology; Gormley ON (3,1993).
BaptQ: Baptist [Historical Soc.] Quarterly; Oxford. 0005-576X.
BArchAlg: Bulletin d'Archéologie Algérienne; Alger.
BarIlAn: Bar-Ilan Annual; Ramat-Gan. 0067-4109.
BAR: British Archaeology Reports; Ox.
BAR-W: Biblical Archaeology Review; Washington. 0098-9444.
BArte: Bollettino d'Arte; Roma.
BAsEsp[Or/Eg]: Boletín de la Asociación Española de Orientalistas / de Egiptología (2, 1990); Madrid.
BASOR: Bulletin of the American Schools of Oriental Research; Atlanta. 0003-097X.
BASP: Bulletin, American Society of Papyrologists; NY. 0003-1186.
BAusPrax: Biblische Auslegung für die Praxis; Stuttgart.
Bazmaveb (Pazmavep; Armenian); Venezia.
BBArchäom: Berliner Beiträge zur Archäometrie; Berlin. 0344-5098.
BBB: ➤ BiBasB & BoBB.

BbbOr: Bibbia e Oriente; Bornato BS.
BBelgRom: Bulletin de l'Institut Historique Belge; R. 0073-8530.
Bbg: Bibliographia/-y.
BBRes: Bulletin for Biblical Research; Annandale NY. (1,1991).
BBudé: Bulletin de l'Association G. Budé; Paris.
BBVO: Berliner Beiträge zum Vorderen Orient: Berlin, Reimer.
BCanadB/Mesop: Bulletin Canadian Society of Biblical / Mesopotamian Studies; Calgary / Toronto 0844-3416.
BCanMedit: Bulletin of the Canad. Mediterranean Institute.
BCentPrei: Bollettino del Centro Camuno di Studi Preistorici; Brescia. 0057-2168.
BCentProt: Bulletin du Centre Protestant d'Études; Genève.
BCH: Bulletin de Correspondance Hellénique; Paris. 0007-4217.
BCILL: Bibliothèque des Cahiers de l'Institut de Linguistique; Lv/P.
BCNH-T: Bibliothèque Copte de Nag Hammadi -Textes; Québec.
BDialRel: (Bu) Pro Dialogo; Vatican.
BEcuT: Bulletin of ecumenical theology; Enugu, Nigeria.
BeerSheva: ✪ Annual: Bible/ANE; J.
BÉF: Bibliothèque des Écoles françaises d'Athènes et de Rome; R. → MÉF.
BEgS: Bulletin of the Egyptological Seminar; NY.
BeitATJ: Beiträge zur Erforschung des Alten Testaments und des Antiken Judentums; Bern. 0722-0790.
BeitAVgArch: Beiträge zur allgemeinen und vergleichenden Archäologie; München, Beck.
BeitBExT: Beiträge zur biblischen Exegese und Theologie [ipsi: BET]; Frankfurt/M.
BeitErfAJ: Beiträge zur Erforschung des ATs und des antiken Judentums; Fra. 0722-0790.
BeitEvT: Beiträge zur evangelischen Theologie; München.
BeitGbEx: Beiträge zur Geschichte der biblischen Exegese; Tübingen.
BeitHistT: Beiträge zur Historischen Theologie; Tübingen.
BeitNam: Beiträge zur Namenforschung N. F.; Heid. 0005-8114.

BeitÖkT: Beiträge zur ökumenischen Theologie: München, Schöningh. 0067-5172.
BeitRelT: Beiträge zur Religionstheologie; Wien-Mödling.
BeitSudan: Beiträge zur Sudanforschung; Wien, Univ.
Belleten (Türk Tarih Kurumu); Ankara.
Benedictina; Roma.
Berytus (Amer. Univ. Beirut); K.
BethM: ✪ Beth Mikra; Jerusalem. 0005-979X.
BÉtOr: Bulletin d'Études Orientales; Damas, IFAO.
BFaCLyon: Bulletin des Facultés Catholiques; Lyon. 0180-5282.
Bib → Biblica; Roma. 0006-0887.
BibAfr: La Bible en Afrique [francophone]; Lomé, Togo.
BiBasB: Biblische Basis Bücher; Kevelaer/Stuttgart.
BiBeit: Biblische Beiträge, Schweizerisches Kath. Bibelwerk; Fribourg.
BibFe: Biblia y Fe; M. 0210-5209.
BibKonf: Biblische Konfrontationen; Stu.
Bible Bhashyam: Kottayam. 0970-2288.
Biblica: commentarii Pontificii Instituti Biblici; Roma. 0006-0887.
Biblos 1. Coimbra; 2. Wien.
BibNot: Biblische Notizen; Bamberg. 0178-2967.
BibOrPont: Biblica et Orientalia, Pontificio Istituto Biblico; Roma.
BibTB: Biblical Theology Bulletin; South Orange NJ, Seton Hall. 0146-1079.
BibTSt: Biblisch-Theologische Studien; Neukirchen-Vluyn. 0930-4800.
BibUnt: Biblische Untersuchungen; Regensburg.
BIFAO: Bulletin de l'Institut Français d'Archéologie Orientale; Le Caire. 0255-0962.
Bijd: Bijdragen, Filosofie en Theologie; Nijmegen. 0006-2278.
BiKi: Bibel und Kirche; Stuttgart. 0006-0623.
BInfWsz: Bulletin d'Information de l'Académie de Théologie Catholique; Warszawa. 0137-7000.
BInstArch: Bulletin of the Institute of Archaeology; London. 0076-0722.
BInterp[S]: Biblical Interpretation [series].

BIP[Br]: Books in Print, U.S., annual; NY, Bowker [British, L, Whitaker]; fr./it./dt.

BiRes: Biblical Research; Chicago. 0067-6535.

Biserica... Ortodoxă; Bucureşti.

BIstFGrec: Bollettino dell'Istituto di Filologia Greca, Univ. Padova; R.

Bits and bytes review; Whitefish MT. 0891-2955.

BJG: Bulletin of Judaeo-Greek Studies; Cambridge Univ.

BJRyL: Bulletin of the John Rylands Library; Manchester. 0301-102X.

BKAT: Biblischer Kommentar AT; Neuk.

BL: Book List, The Society for Old Testament Study. 0309-0892.

BLCéramÉg: Bulletin de liaison... céramique égyptienne; Le Caire, IFAO. 0255-0903.

BLitEc [Chr]: Bulletin de Littérature Ecclésiastique [Chronique]. Toulouse. 0007-4322 [0495-9396].

BLtg: Bibel und Liturgie; Wien-Klosterneuburg. 0006-064X.

BMB: Bulletin du Musée de Beyrouth.

BMeijiG: Bulletin Christian Research Institute Meiji Gakuin Univ.; Tokyo.

BMosA [ipsi AIEMA]: Bulletin, étude mosaïque antique; P. 0761-8808.

BO: Bibliotheca Orientalis; Leiden. 0006-1913.

BoBB: Bonner Biblische Beiträge; Königstein.

Bobolanum, teologia; Wsz. 0867-3330.

BogSmot: Bogoslovska Smotra; Zagreb. 0352-3101.

BogVest: Bogoslovni Vestnik; Ljubljana.

BonnJb: Bonner Jahrbücher.

Boreas [1. Uppsala, series]; 2. Münster, Archäologie. 0344-810X.

BProtF: Bulletin, Histoire du Protestantisme Français; Paris.

BR: Bible Review; Wsh. 8755-6316.

BRefB: Bulletin, Reformation Biblical Studies: Fort Wayne.

BritAth: Papers of the British School in Athens; L.

BritJREd: British Journal of Religious Education; London,

BRöG: Bericht der Römisch-Germanischen Kommission DAI; Mainz. 0341-9312.

BrownJudSt/StRel: Brown Judaic Studies / Studies in Religion; Atlanta.

BS ⇥ BtS.

BSAA: Boletín, Seminario Estudios Arte y Arqueología; Valladolid.

BSAC: Bulletin de la Société d'Archéologie Copte; Le Caire.

BSeptCog: Bulletin of the International Organization for Septuagint and Cognate Studies; ND.

BSignR: Bulletin Signalétique, religions; Paris. 0180-9296.

BSLP: Bulletin de la Société de Linguistique; Paris.

BSNAm: Biblical Scholarship in North America; Atlanta, SBL.

BSNEJap ⇥ Oriento.

BSO: Bulletin of the School of Oriental and African Studies; London. 0041-977X.

BSoc[Fr]Ég: Bulletin de la Société [Française] d'Égyptologie; Genève [Paris].

BSpade: Bible and Spade; Ballston NY.

BStLat: Bollettino di Studi Latini; N.

BSumAg: Bulletin on Sumerian Agriculture; Cambridge. 0267-0658.

Bt: Bibliotheca/-que.

BTAM: Bulletin de Théologie Ancienne et Médiévale; Lv. ⇥ RTAM.

BtEscB/EstB: Biblioteca Escuela Bíblica; M / de Estudios Bíblicos, Salamanca.

BtETL: Biblioteca, ETL; Leuven.

BThemT: Bibliothek Themen der Theologie; Stuttgart.

BtHumRef: Bibliotheca Humanistica et Reformatorica; Nieuwkoop, de Graaf.

BtHumRen: Bibliothèque d'Humanisme et Renaissance; Genève/Paris.

BtMesop: Bibliotheca Mesopotamica; Malibu CA.

BToday: The Bible Today; Collegeville MN. 0006-0836.

BTrans: The Bible Translator [Technical/ Practical]; Stu. 0260-0943.

BtS: Bibliotheca Sacra; Dallas. 0006-1921.

BtScRel: Biblioteca di Scienze religiose; Roma, Salesiana.

BTSt: Biblisch-theologische Studien (exBiblische Studien); Neukirchen.

BtStor: Biblioteca di storia e storiografia dei tempi biblici; Brescia.

BtTPaid: Biblioteca Teologica; Brescia.

BTT: Bible de tous les temps; Paris.

BTZ: Berliner Theologische Zeitschrift; Berlin. 0724-6137.
Bu[BbgB]: Bulletin [de Bibliographie Biblique; Lausanne].
BuBRes: Bulletin for Biblical Research; Annandale NY.
BudCSt: Buddhist-Christian Studies; Honolulu, Univ. 0882-0945.
Burgense; Burgos. 0521-8195.
BurHist: Buried History; Melbourne. 0007-6260.
BVieChr: Bible et Vie Chrétienne; P.
BViewp: Biblical Viewpoint; Greenville SC, Jones Univ. 0006-0925.
BW: Beiträge zur Wissenschaft vom Alten und Neuen Testament; Stuttgart.
BySlav: Byzantinoslavica; Praha. 0007-7712.
ByZ: Byzantinische Zeitschrift; München. 0007-7704.
Ⓔ Byzantina; Thessaloniki.
Byzantion; Bruxelles.
ByzFor: Byzantinische Forschungen; Amsterdam.
BZ: Biblische Zeitschrift; Paderborn. 0006-2014.
BZA[N]W: Beihefte zur ➤ ZAW [ZNW].
CAD: [Chicago] Assyrian Dictionary; Glückstadt. ➤ 7,9273.
CADIR: Centre pour l'Analyse du Discours Religieux; Lyon ➤ SémBib.
Cadmo: Lisboa, Univ. 0871-9257 (1,1991).
CAH: Cambridge Ancient History²; Cambridge Univ. ➤ 498.
CahArchéol: Cahiers Archéologiques; Paris.
CahCMéd: Cahiers de Civilisation Médiévale; Poitiers.
CahDAFI: Cahiers de la Délégation Archéologique Française en Iran; Paris. 0765-104X.
CahÉv: Cahiers Évangile; Paris. 0222-8741.
CahGlotz: Cahiers Centre G. Glotz; P.
CahHist: Cahiers d'Histoire; Lyon.
CahIntSymb: Cahiers Internationaux de Symbolique; Mons, Belgique.
CahLV: Cahiers voor Levensverdieping; Averbode.
CahPhRel: Cahiers de l'École des sciences philosophiques et religieuses: Bru, Fac. S. Louis.

CahRechScRel: Cahiers de Recherche en Sciences de la Religion; Québec.
Cah[Bu]Renan: Cahiers du Cercle E. Renan; Montreuil (distinct from Bulletin of same Cercle). Cah. 123 is a listing of titles 1982-92; Cah. 184 is for 1993.
CahSpIgn: Cahiers de spiritualité ignatienne; Québec.
CahSPR: Cahiers de l'École des Sciences Philosophiques et Religieuses; Bru Fac. S.-Louis (12,1992).
CahSubaq: Cahiers d'archéologie subaquatique; Fréjus. (10,1991).
CahTrB: Cahiers de traduction biblique; Pierrefitte France. 0755-1371.
CahTun: Les Cahiers (de la Faculté des Lettres) de Tunisie; Tunis.
CalvaryB: Calvary Baptist Theological Journal; Lansdale PA. 8756-0429.
CalvinT: Calvin Theological Journal; Grand Rapids MI. 0008-1795.
CalwTMg: Calwer Theologische Monographien (A: Biblisch); Stuttgart.
CamArch: Cambridge (Eng.) Archaeological Journal. 0959-7743. (1,1991).
CamCW: Cambridge Commentary on Writings of the Jewish and Christian World.
CanadCath: Canadian Catholic Review; Saskatoon.
CANAL-infos: judaïsme-christianisme anciens: P, ÉPHÉR (9,1992).
Carmel: Tilburg.
Carmelus: Roma. 0008-6673.
Carthage Conservation Bulletin; Tunis.
Carthaginensia; Murcia, Inst. Teol. 0213-4381.
CathCris: Catholicism in crisis; ND.
CathHR: Catholic Historical Review; Wsh. 0008-8080. ➤ USCatH.
Catholica (Moehler-Institut, Paderborn); Münster.
Catholicisme: Paris ➤ 499.
Catholic Studies, Tokyo ➤ Katorikku.
CathTR: Catholic Theological Review; Clayton/Hong Kong.
CathTSocAmPr: ➤ PrCTSAm [AnCTS].
CathW: Catholic World; NY.
CathWRep: Catholic World Report; SF. 1058-8159.

CATSS: Computer assisted tools for Septuagint studies: Atlanta ➤ SBL.
CBQ: Catholic Biblical Quarterly; Washington, DC. 0008-7912.
CC: La Civiltà Cattolica; R. 0009-8167.
CCAR: (Central Conference of American Rabbis); NY. 0149-712X.
CCGraec/Lat/Med: Corpus Christianorum, series graeca / latina / continuatio mediaev.; Turnhout.
CdÉ: Chronique d'Égypte; Bruxelles.
CEB: Commentaire évangelique de la Bible; Vaux/Seine ➤ Édifac.
CERDAC: (Atti) Centro di Ricerca e Documentazione Classica; Milano.
CERDIC: Centre d'échanges et de recherches sur la diffusion et l'inculturation du christianisme.
CETÉDOC: Centre de Traitement Électronique des Documents; Lv.
CGL: Coptic Gnostic Library ➤ NHS.
CGMG: Christlicher Glaube in moderner Gesellschaft; FrB.
CGrebel: Conrad Grebel Review ... Christian inquiry; Waterloo ON (Mennonite). 0829-044X (10,1992). CGST; Hong Kong.
ChCu: Church and Culture; Vatican.
CHermProt: Centre d'Herméneutique Protestante.
ChH: Church History; Indiatlantic FL.
CHH(p): Center for Hermeneutical Studies in Hellenistic & Modern Culture (protocol); Berkeley.
Chiea [ChAfC]: Nairobi, Catholic Higher Institute of Eastern Africa.
CHIran: Cambridge History of Iran ➤ 9,584*.
Chiron: Geschichte, Epigraphie; München.
CHistEI: ❻ Cathedra, History of Eretz-Israel; Jerusalem.
CHist-J: Jerusalem Cathedra.
CHJud: Cambridge History of Judaism ➤ 501.
CHLC: The Cambridge history of literary criticism; C.
Chm: Churchman 1. (Anglican); London: 0009-661X / 2. (Humanistic); St. Petersburg FL: 0009-6628.
ChrCent: Christian Century; Chicago. Christus; 1. Paris; 2. México.

ChrJRel: Christian Jewish Relations; L.
ChrLit: Christianity and Literature: Carrollton GA College. 0148-3331 (42,1992).
ChrNIsr: Christian News from Israel; Jerusalem.
ChrOost: Het Christelijk Oosten; Nijmegen.
ChrSchR: Christian Scholar's Review; Houston TX.
ChrT: Christianity Today; Carol Stream IL. 0009-5761.
ChrTW: Christ to the World; Roma ... 0011-1485.
ChSoc: Church and Society; NY.
ChSt: Chicago Studies; Mundelein IL.
Church: NY, Nat. Pastoral Life.
ChuT: Church & Theology; L. (6,1986).
ChWoman: The Church Woman; NY. 0009-6598.
Cienie i Światło [Ombres et Lumière (revue chrétienne des personnes non pleinement habiles: AtKap 491, 2+183s]; Wsz.
CistSt: Cistercian Studies; ed. Getsemani KY; pub. Chimay, Belgium.
Citeaux; Achel, Belgium. 0009-7497.
Cithara: Judaeo-Christian Tradition; St. Bonaventure (NY) Univ.
CiTom: Ciencia Tomista; S. 0210-0398.
CiuD: Ciudad de Dios; M. 0009-7756.
CivClCr: Civiltà classica e cristiana; Genova. 0392-8632.
CiVit: Città di Vita; Firenze. [0]009-7632.
Claret: Claretianum; Roma.
ClasA: [formerly California Studies in] Classical Antiquity; Berkeley.
ClasB: Classical Bulletin; Ch. 0009-8137 (ᴱAsbury Coll., Wilmore KY).˙
ClasJ: Classical Journal; Greenville SC. 0009-8353.
ClasMed: Classica et Mediaevalia; København. 0106-5815.
ClasOutl: The Classical Outlook; Ch [ed. Miami Univ. OH]. 0009-8361.
ClasPg: Classical Philology; Chicago. 0009-8361.
ClasQ: Classical Quarterly NS; Oxford. 0009-8388.
ClasR: Classical Review NS; Oxford. 0009-840X.

ClasWo: Classical World; Pittsburgh. 0009-8148.
CLehre: Die Christenlehre; Berlin.
Clio, studi storici; N. ➤ Klio.
CMatArch: Contributi e materiali di archeologia orientale; Roma, Univ.
CNRS: Conseil National de Recherche Scientifique; Paris.
CogF: Cogitatio Fidei; Paris.
ColcCist: Collectanea Cisterciensia; Forges, Belgique.
ColcFranc: Collectanea Franciscana; Roma. 0010-0749.
ColcT: Collectanea Theologica; Warszawa. 0137-6985.
ColcTFu: Collectanea theol. Univ. Fujen = *Shenhsileh Lunchi*; Taipei.
CollatVL: Collationes, Vlaams... Theologie en Pastoraal; Gent.
Colloquium; Brisbane (25,1992).
ColStFen: Collezione di Studi Fenici; Roma, Univ.
Commentary; NY. 0010-2601.
CommBras: Communio Brasiliensis: Rio de Janeiro.
CommWsh: Communio USA; Washington. 0094-2065.
CommRevue: Communio [various languages, not related to ComSev]: revue catholique internationale; Paris.
CommStrum: Communio, strumento internazionale per un lavoro teologico; Milano.
Communio deutsch ➤ IkaZ.
ComOT: Commentaar op het Oude Testament. Kampen.
CompHum: Computers and the Humanities; Osprey FL. 0010-4817.
CompNT: Compendium rerum Iudaicarum ad NT; Assen.
Compostellanum; Santiago de Compostela.
ComRatisbNT: Comentario de Ratisbona; Barc.
ComSev: Communio; Sevilla. 0010-3705.
ComSpirAT/NT: Commenti spirituali dell'Antico / Nuovo Testamento; Roma.
ComTeolNT: Commentario Teologico del NT; Brescia.
ComViat: Communio Viatorum; Praha. 0010-7133. Suspended 33 (1990).

ConBib: Coniectanea Biblica OT/NT; Malmö.
Conc: Concilium, variis linguis; P; M; Eng. now L/Ph 0010-5236 [deutsch ➤ IZT].
ConcordJ: Concordia Journal; St. Louis. 0145-7233.
ConcordTQ: Concordia Theological Quarterly; Fort Wayne.
Confer (Vida Religiosa); M. (32/121-4,1993).
ConsJud: Conservative Judaism; NY. 0010-6542.
Contacts/Orthodoxe, de théologie et spiritualité; P. 0045-8325.
Contagion [< COV&R]; Greenville NC. 1075-7201 (1,1994).
Continuum; NY. (1,1991).
ContrIstStorAnt: Contributi dell'Istituto di Storia Antica; Milano, Univ. Catt.
ConvA: Convivium assisiense. (1,1993).
Coptologia [also for Egyptology]: Thunder Bay ONT, Lakehead Univ.
CouStR: Council for the Study of Religion Bulletin; Macon GA, Mercer Univ.
CovQ: Covenant Quarterly; Chicago.
CRAI: Comptes rendus de l'Académie des Inscriptions et Belles-Lettres; P.
CreSpir: Creation Spirituality (M. Fox); San José CA. 1053-9891 (8,1992).
Cretan Studies; Amst.
CRIPEL ➤ SocUÉg.
CriswT: Criswell Theological Review; Dallas.
Criterio; Buenos Aires. 0011-1473,
CritRR: Critical Review of Books in Religion; Atlanta.
CrkvaSv: Crkva u Svijetu; Split.
CrNSt: Cristianesimo nella Storia; Bologna. 0393-3598.
CroatC: Croatica Christiana; Zagreb.
CrossC: Cross Currents; West Nyack NJ. 0011-1953.
Crux: Vancouver. 0011-2186.
CSCO: Corpus Scriptorum Christianorum Orientalium; Lv. 0070-0401.
CScrN: Corpus Sacrae Scripturae Neerlandicae Medii Aevi; Leiden.
CuadFgClás: Cuadernos de Filología Clásica; M, Univ.
CuadTeol: Cuadernos de Teología; Buenos Aires.

CuadTrad: Cuadernos de Traducción y Interpretación; Barc.
CuesT: Cuestiones Teológicas; Medellín.
CuH: Culture and History; K.
CurrAr: Current Archaeology; L (11, 1993).
CurResB: Currents in research, biblical studies; Shf. 0966-7377 (1,1993).
CurrTM: Currents in Theology and Mission; St. Louis. 0098-2113.
CyrMeth: Cyrillomethodianum; Thessaloniki.
D: director: 1. (in Indice etiam *auctor*) Dissertationis; 2. Congressus, *etc.*
DAFI: Délégation Archéologique Française en Iran (Mém); Paris.
DAI: Deutsches Archäologisches Institut; Rom (nobis utilissimum), *al.* ➤ Mi(tt).
DamaszM: Damaszener Mitteilungen, DAI;
DanTTs: Dansk Teologisk Tidsskrift; København.
DanVMed/Skr: Dansk. Videnskabornes Selskap, Hist./Fil. Meddelelser / Skriften; K.
DBS [= SDB].
DECR: Department for External Church Relations of the Moscow Patriarchate: Moskva.
DeltChr: Deltion tes christianikēs archaiologikēs hetaireias: Athēna.
DeltVM: ⊖ Deltío vivlikôn meletôn, Bulletin Études Bibliques; Athēnai.
DHGE: Dictionnaire d'Histoire et de Géographie Ecclésiastiques; P ➤ 502.
Diakonia; 1. Mainz/Wien. 0341-9592; Stu. 2. (Eastern Christianity); Scranton (26,1993).
DialArch: Dialoghi di Archeologia; Mi.
DiálEcum: Diálogo Ecuménico; Salamanca. 0210-2870.
DialHA: Dialogues d'Histoire ancienne; Besançon. 18,1 (1992): 2-251-60475-8.
Dialog; Minneapolis. 0012-2033.
DialR: Dialog der Religionen. (1,1991).
DialTP: Diálogo teológico; El Paso TX.
DictSpir: Dictionnaire/Spiritualité; P ➤ 503.
Didascalia; Rosario ARG.
Didaskalia; Lisboa.
DielB: Dielheimer Blätter zur Archäologie und Textüberlieferung; Heid.

Dionysius: Halifax. 0705-1085.
Direction; Fresno CA.
DiscEg: Discussions in Egyptology; Oxford. 0268-3083.
Disciple, the (Disciples of Christ); St. Louis. 0092-8372.
DissA: Dissertation Abstracts International; AA/L. -A [= US *etc.*]: 0419-4209 [C = Europe. 0307-6075].
DissHRel: Dissertationes ad historiam religionum (supp. Numen); Leiden.
Divinitas, Pont. Acad. Theol. Rom. (Lateranensis); Vaticano. 0012-4222.
DivThom: Divus Thomas; Bologna. 0012-4257.
DizTF: Dizionario di Teologia Fondamentale ➤ 505.
DJD: Discoveries in the Judaean Desert; Oxford.
DLZ: Deutsche Literaturzeitung; Berlin. 0012-043X.
DMA: Dictionary of the Middle Ages; NY ➤ 7,670.
DocCath: Documentation Catholique; Paris.
DoctCom: Doctor Communis; Vaticano.
DoctLife: Doctrine and Life; Dublin.
DOG: Deutsche Orient-Gesellschaft: B.
DosB: Les dossiers de la Bible; P.
DossD: Dossiers d'archéologie; Dijon.
DowR: Downside Review; Bath. 0012-5806.
DPA: Dizionario patristico e di antichità cristiane; Casale Monferrato ➤ 506.
DrevVost: ⊕ Drevnij Vostok; Moskva.
DrewG: The Drew [Theological School] Gateway; Madison NJ.
DSD: Dead Sea Scrolls Discoveries; (1,1994).
DumbO: Dumbarton Oaks Papers; CM. 0070-7546.
DutchMgA: Dutch Monographs in Ancient History and Archaeology; Amst.
E: editor, Herausgeber, *a cura di.*
EAfJE: East African Journal of Evangelical Theology; Machakos, Kenya.
EAsJT: East Asia Journal of Theology [combining NE & SE AJT]; Tokyo. 0217-3859.
EAPast: East Asian Pastoral Review; Manila. 0040-0564.

ÉchMClas: Échos du Monde Classique/Classical Views; Calgary. 0012-9356.

ÉchSM: Les Échos de Saint-Maurice; Valais, Abbaye.

EcOr: Ecclesia Orans; R, Anselm.

ÉcoutBib: Écouter la Bible; Paris.

EcuR: Ecumenical Review; Geneva. 0013-0790.

EdbR: The Edinburgh Review of theology and religion; E, Univ. (1,1995).

EDIFAC: Éditions de la Faculté libre de Théologie Évangélique; Vaux/Seine.

Editio, internationales Jahrbuch für Editionswissenschaft; Tü (7,1993).

EfMex: Efemerides Mexicana; Tlalpan.

Egb: Ergänzungsband.

ÉglT: Église et Théologie; Ottawa.

EgVO: Egitto e Vicino Oriente; Pisa.

ÉHRel: Études d'histoire des religions.

Eikasmós, Quaderni di Filologia Classica; Bologna, Univ.

Einz: Einzelband.

EkK [Vor]: Evangelischer-katholischer Kommentar zum NT; Z/Köln; Neukirchen-Vluyn ['Vorarbeiten'].

EkkT: ⑤ Ekklēsía kaì Theología; L.

Elenchos, ... pensiero antico; Napoli.

Elliniká; ⑤ Thessaloniki.

Emerita (lingüística clásica); M.

Emmanuel: St. Meinrads IN/NY. 0013-6719.

Enc. Biblica → EnṣMiqr.

EncHebr: ⓗ Encyclopaedia Hebraica; J/TA.

Enchoria, Demotistik/Koptologie; Wsb.

EncIran: Encyclopaedia Iranica; L. → 8, 755; cf. CHIran → 8,746*.

EncIslam: Encyclopédie de l'Islam. Nouvelle édition [+ Eng]; Leiden/P → 507.

EncKat: Encyklopedia Katolicka; Lublin.

Encounter (theol.); Indianapolis.

EncRel: (1) ᴱEliade M., NY. – 2. Fi.

EnṣMiqr: ⓗ *Enṣiqlopediya miqrā'ît,* Encyclopaedia Biblica; Jerusalem.

Entschluss: Wien. 0017-4602.

EnzMär: Enzyklopädie des Märchens; B.

EOL: Ex Oriente Lux → 1.Jb/2. Phoenix.

Eos, ... philologia; Wsz. 0012-7825.

EpAnat: Epigraphica anatolica; Bonn.

ÉPHÉ[H/R]: École Pratique des Hautes-Études, Annuaire [Hist.-Pg. / Sc. Rel.]; Paris.

EpHetVyz: ⑤ Ephēmeris tēs Hetaireías Vyzantinōn Spoudōn; Athēnai.

EphLtg: Ephemerides Liturgicae; R.

EphMar: Ephemerides Mariologicae; Madrid.

ÉPR: Études préliminaires aux religions orientales dans l'Empire romain; Leiden.

Eranos[/Jb]: Acta Philologica Suecana; Uppsala / Jahrbuch; Fra.

ErbAuf: Erbe und Auftrag; Beuron.

ErfTSt/Schr: Erfurter Theologische Studien/ Schriften.

ErIsr: Eretz-Israel; J. 0071-108X.

ErtFor: Ertrag der Forschung; Darmstadt, Wissenschaftliche Buchg. 0174-0695.

Erytheia, estudios biz./neogrieg.

EscrVedat: Escritos del Vedat; Valencia. 0210-3133.

EsprVie: Esprit et Vie: 1. [< Ami du Clergé]; Langres; 2. Chambray.

EstAgust: Estudio Agustiniano; Valladolid. 0425-340X.

EstBíb: Estudios Bíblicos; Madrid. 0014-1437.

EstClas: Estudios clásicos; M. 0014-1453 (34,1992).

EstDeusto: Estudios de (Universidad) Deusto; Madrid. 0423-4847.

EstE: Estudios Eclesiásticos; Madrid. 0210-1610.

EstFranc: Estudios Franciscanos; Barcelona.

EstJos: Estudios Josefinos; Valladolid.

EstLul: Estudios Lulianos; Mallorca.

EstMar: Estudios Marianos; Madrid.

EstTrin: Estudios Trinitarios; Salamanca.

EstudosB: Estudos Bíblicos; Petrópolis.

ÉtBN: Études Bibliques, Nouvelle Série; Paris. 0760-3541.

ÉtClas: Les études classiques; Namur. 0014-200X.

ÉtFranc: Études Franciscaines; Blois.

ETL: Ephemerides Theologicae Lovanienses; Leuven. 0013-9513. → Bt.

ÉtPapyr: Études [Société Égyptienne] de Papyrologie; Le Caire.

ÉtPgHist: Études de Philologie et d'Histoire; Genève, Droz.

ÉTRel: Études Théologiques et Religieuses; Montpellier. 0014-2239.

ÉtTrav: Études et Travaux; Varsovie.

Études; Paris. 0014-1941.
Euhemer (℗ hist. rel.); Wsz. 0014-2298
EuntDoc: Euntes Docete; Roma.
EurHS: Europäische Hochschulschriften /
Publ. Universitaires Européennes; Fra.
EurJT: The European journal of the-
ology: Carlisle. 0960-2720.
EurWomenT: European ... / Jahrbuch
der Europäischen Gesellschaft für
die theologische Forschung von
Frauen: Kamen (1,1993).
Eutopia: R, Quasar (1,1s, 1992s).
Evangel; Edinburgh. 0265-4547.
EvErz: Der evangelische Erzieher;
Frankfurt/M. 0014-3413.
EvJ: Evangelical Journal; Myerstown.
EvKL: Evangelisches Kirchenlexikon;
→ 595.
EvKom: Evangelische Kommentare;
Stuttgart. 0300-4236.
EvQ[RT]: Evangelical Quarterly [Re-
view of Theology]; Exeter.
EvT: Evangelische Theologie, NS;
München. 0014-3502.
EWest: East and West; 1. L / 2. R.
EWSp: Encyclopedia of World Spirituality;
NY/L.
ExAud: Ex auditu; Princeton. 0883-
0053.
Exchange, missiological/ecumenical re-
search; Leiden, IIMO. 0166-2740 (21,
1992).
ExcSIsr: Excavations and Surveys in
Israel < Ḥadašot; J. 0334-1607.
ExGG: Exegetical guide to the Greek NT;
GR.
Expedition; Ph. 0014-4738.
Explor [sic]; Evanston. 0362-0876.
ExpTim: The Expository Times; Edin-
burgh. 0014-5246.
F&M: Faith and mission; Wake
Forest NC. (10,1992).
F&R: Faith and Reason; Front Royal
VA. 0098-5449.
FascBíb: Fascículos bíblicos; Madrid.
Faventia: clásica; Barc. 0210-7570.
FemT: Feminist Theology; Shf (1,
1992).
fg./fil.: filologia/co, filosofia/co.
FgNt: Filologia neotestamentaria; Cór-
doba, Univ. 0214-2996.
FidH: Fides et Historia; Longview TX.
FilT: Filosofia e teologia; Napoli.

FirsT: First Things (religion/public
life); Denville. 1047-5141 (28,1992).
FoiTemps: La Foi et le Temps. NS;
Tournai.
FoiVie: Foi et Vie; Paris. 0015-5357.
FolArch: Folia Archaeologica; Buda-
pest. 0133-2023.
FolOr: Folia Orientalia, Polska Aka-
demia Nauk; Kraków. 0015-5675.
FonC: Fontes Christiani; FrB.
Fondamenti; Brescia, Paideia.
ForBE: Forum for bibelsk Eksegese.
(3,1992).
ForBib: Forschung zur Bibel; Wü/Stu.
ForBMusB: Forschungen und Berich-
te, Staatliche Museen zu Berlin.
ForFF: Forum, foundations and
facets; Bonner MT. 0883-4970.
ForGLProt: Forschungen zur Geschichte
und Lehre des Protestantismus; Mü.
ForJüdChrDial: Forschungen zum jüdisch-
christlichen Dialog; Neuk.
ForKiDG: Forschungen zur Kirchen- und
Dogmengeschichte; Gö.
Fornvännen; Lund. 0015-7813.
ForRel: Forum Religion; Stu (1,1994).
ForSystÖ: Forschungen zur Systemati-
schen & Ökumenischen Theologie; Gö.
ForTLing: Forum Theologiae Linguisticae;
Bonn.
Fortunatae; revista canaria de filolo-
gía; Tenerife. (1,1991).
ForumKT: Forum Katholische Theo-
logie; Münster. 0178-1626.
FOTLit: Forms of OT Literature; GR,
Eerdmans.
FraJudBei: Frankfurter Judaistische Bei-
träge: Fra.
FranBog: Franciscanum, ciencias del
espíritu; Bogotá. 0120-1468.
FrancSt: Franciscan Studies; St. Bo-
naventure, NY. 0080-5459.
FranzSt: Franziskanische Studien; Pd.
FraTSt: Frankfurter Theologische Studien;
Fra, S. Georgen.
FreibRu: Freiburger Rundbrief. ...
christlich-jüdische Begegnung; FrB.
FreibTSt: Freiburger Theologische Stu-
dien; Freiburg/Br.
FrKf: Freikirchenforschung; Münster
(1,1992).
FRL: Forschungen zur Religion und Lite-
ratur des Alten und NTs; Gö.

FrSZ: Freiburger Zeitschrift für Philosophie & Theologie; Fribourg.
Fundamentum; Basel ev. Akad. (1993).
FutUo: Il futuro dell'uomo; Firenze, Assoc. Teilhard. 0390-217X.
Ⓖ *Graece*; title/text in Greek.
GCS: Die Griechischen Christlichen Schriftsteller der ersten Jahrhunderte; B.
GdT: Giornale di Teologia; Brescia.
GeistL: Geist und Leben; Würzburg. 0016-5921.
Genava (archéologie, hist. art); Genève. 0072-0585.
GenLing: General Linguistics; University Park PA. 0016-6553.
GeogAnt: Geographia Antiqua; Firenze. 1121-8940 (1,1992).
Georgica: Jena/Tbilissi. 0232-4490.
GerefTTs: Gereformeerd Theologisch Tijdschrift; Kampen. 0016-8610.
Gerión, revista de Historia Antigua; Madrid, Univ. 0213-0181.
GGA: Göttingische Gelehrte Anzeigen; Göttingen. 0017-1549.
GItFg: Giornale italiano di filologia; Napoli. 0017-0461.
GLÉCS: (Comptes rendus) Groupe Linguistique d'Études Chamito-Sémitiques; Paris.
GLern: Glaube und Lernen; Gö.
GLeven: Geest en leven; Eindhoven.
Glotta: griech.-lat.; Gö. 0017-1298.
Gnomon; München. 0017-1417.
GöMiszÄg: Göttinger Miszellen ... zur ägyptologischen Diskussion; Göttingen. 0344-385X.
GöOrFor: Göttinger Orientforschungen; Würzburg.
GöTArb: Göttinger Theologische Arbeiten; Göttingen.
GraceTJ: Grace Theological Journal folded 12,2 (1991) p. 161.
GraecChrPrim: Graecitas Christianorum Primaeva; Nijmegen, van den Vegt.
Grail, ecumenical quarterly; Waterloo.
GreeceR: Greece and Rome; Oxford.
Greg[LA/Inf.]: Gregorianum; R, Pontificia Universitas Gregoriana [Liber Annualis / Informationes PUG].
GrOrTR: Greek Orthodox Theological Review; Boston. 0017-3894.
GrRByz: Greek, Roman and Byzantine Studies; CM. 0017-3916.

GrSinal: Grande Sinal; Petrópolis.
Gymn: Gymnasium; Heid. 0342-5231.
Ⓗ *(Neo-)hebraice*; (modern) Hebrew.
HaBeiA: Hamburger Beiträge zur Archäologie. 0341-3152.
HABES: Heidelberger Althistorische Beiträge und Epigraphische Studien: Stu.
Ḥadašôt arkeologiyôt Ⓗ [News]; J.
HalleB: Hallesche Beiträge zur Orientwissenschaft; Halle. 0233-2205.
Hamdard Islamicus [research]; Pakistan. 0250-7196.
Handes Amsorya [armen.]; Wien.
HarvSemMon/Mus: Harvard Semitic Monographs / Museum Series; CM.
HarvStClasPg: Harvard Studies in Classical Philology; CM.
HarvTR: The Harvard Theological Review; CM. 0017-8160.
HbAltW: Handbuch der Altertumswissenschaft; München.
HbAT/NT: Handbuch zum Alten/Neuen Testament; Tübingen.
HbDG: Handbuch der Dogmengeschichte; Freiburg/B.
HbDTG: Handbuch der Dogmen- und Theologiegeschichte; Göttingen.
HbOr: Handbuch der Orientalistik; Leiden.
HbRelG: Handbuch der Religionsgeschichte; Göttingen.
HbRwG: Handbuch Religionswissenschaftlicher Grundbegriffe; Stuttgart.
HDienst: Heiliger Dienst; Salzburg. 0017-9620.
HebAnR: Hebrew Annual Review; Columbus, Ohio State Univ.
HebSt: Hebrew Studies; Madison WI. 0146-4094.
Hekima; Nairobi.
Helikon (Tradizione e Cultura Classica, Univ. Messina); Roma.
Helinium; Stockholm.
Hellenika; Bochum. 0018-0084; ⇒ *Ell.*
Helios (21,1994).
Helmantica; Salamanca, Univ.
Henceforth; Lenox MA.
Henoch (ebraismo): Torino (Univ.).
Hephaistos, Theorie / Praxis Arch.; Ha.
HerdKor: Herder-Korrespondenz; Freiburg/Br. 0018-0645.
HerdTKom, NT: Herders Theologischer Kommentar zum NT; FrB.
Heresis; Carcassonne. 0758-3737.

Hermathena; Dublin. 0018-0750.
Hermes; Wiesbaden. 0018-0777.
HermUnT: Hermeneutische Untersuchungen zur Theologie; Tü. 0440-7180.
HervTS: Hervormde Teologiese Studies; Pretoria.
Hesperia: 1. (American School, Athens); Princeton. 0018-098X. - 2. Roma. (1,1990).
Hethitica. Travaux édités; Lv.
HeythJ: Heythrop Journal; London. 0018-1196.
HistJb: Historisches Jahrbuch; Mü.
L'Histoire; Paris (151-161, 1992).
Historia; 1. Baden-Baden: 0018-2311; 2. Santiago/Chile, Univ. Católica.
History: Oxford. 0018-2648 (78,1993).
HistRel: History of Religions; Chicago. 0018-2710.
HLand[S]: Das Heilige Land (Deutscher Verein) Köln [(Schw. Verein); Luzern].
Hokhma; Lausanne. 0379-7465.
HolyL: Holy Land: J, OFM. 0333-4851 ➤ TerraS.
Homiletica (para los domingos): Valladolid. 0439-4208 (5,1994).
Homoousios; Buenos Aires.
HomP: Homiletic and Pastoral Review; New York. 0018-4268.
HomRel: Homo religiosus (histoire des religions); Louvain-la-Neuve.
HorBibT: Horizons in Biblical Theology; Pittsburgh. 0195-9085.
Horizons (College Theology Society); Villanova PA. 0360-9669.
Hsientai Hsüehyüan (= Universitas); Taipei.
HSprF: Historische Sprachforschung; Göttingen. 0935-3518.
HUC|A: Hebrew Union College [+ Jewish Institute of Religion] Annual; Cincinnati.
Humanitas; 1. Brescia; 2. Tucuman.
HumT: Humanística e Teologia; Porto.
HWomenRel: History of women religious, news and notes; St. Paul MN.
Hypom: Hypomnemata; Göttingen, VR.
HZ: Historische Zeitschrift; München. 0018-2613.
IBMiss: International Bulletin of Missionary Research; Mp.

ICC: International Critical Commentary; Edinburgh.
Ichthys; Aarhus (22,1995).
IClasSt: Illinois Classical Studies; Urbana. 0363-1923.
IFA[O]: Institut Français d'Archéologie (Orientale, Le Caire / Beyrouth).
IJbFs: Internationale Jahresbibliographie der Festschriften; Osnabrück ➤ 2.
IJCR: International Journal of Comparative Religion; North York ON, Univ.
IkaZ: Internationale Katholische Zeitschrift [= Communio]; Rodenkirchen. 0341-8693.
IkiZ: Internationale kirchliche Zeitschrift; Bern. 0020-9252.
Immanuel (ecumenical); J. 0302-8127.
Impacts: Lille (NTAbs: Angers) Univ. Cath. de L'Ouest. 0019-2899 (1, 1994).
InBeitKultW/SprW/TS: Innsbrucker Beiträge zur Kulturwissenschaft / Sprachwissenschaft / Theologische Studien.
Index Jewish Studies ➤ RAMBI.
IndIranJ: Indo-Iranian Journal; (Canberra-) Leiden. 0019-7246.
IndJT: Indian Journal of Theology; Serampore.
IndMissR: Indian Missiological Review; Shillong.
IndogF: Indogermanische Forschungen; Berlin. 0019-7262.
IndTSt: Indian Theological Studies; Bangalore, St. Peter's.
InfPUG ➤ Gregoriana; R.
Interp: Interpretation; Richmond VA. 0020-9643.
IntJNaut: International Journal of Nautical Archaeology L/NY. 0305-7445.
IntJPhR: International Journal for the Philosophy of Religion; Haag.
IntJSport: International Journal of the history of sport; London.
IntRMiss: International Review of Mission; London. 0020-8582.
Iran; London. 0578-6967.
IrAnt: Iranica Antiqua; Leiden.
Iraq; London. 0021-0889.
IrBSt: Irish Biblical Studies; Belfast. 0268-6112.
Irén: Irénikon; Chevetogne. 0021-0978.

IrTQ: Irish Theological Quarterly; Maynooth. 0021-1400.
Isidorianum; Sevilla (5-6,1994).
Islam, Der: Berlin. 0021-1818.
Islamochristiana; Roma, Pontificio Istituto di Studi Arabi. 0392-7288.
IsrClasSt; Jerusalem.
IsrEJ: Israel Exploration Journal; Jerusalem. 0021-2059.
IsrJBot/Zool: Israel Journal of Botany 0021-213X / Zoology 0021-2210: J.
IsrLawR: Israel Law Review; Jerusalem. 0021-2237.
IsrMusJ: Israel Museum Journal; Jerusalem.
IsrNumJ[SocB]: Israel Numismatic Journal, J [Society Bulletin: TA].
IsrOrSt: Israel Oriental Studies; Tel Aviv.
Istina; Paris. 0021-2423.
Italoellenika, rivista di cultura greco-moderna; Napoli. (2,1989).
Itinerarium, teologico; Messina (1, 1993).
IVRA (Jura); Napoli.
IZBG ➤ 778: Internationale Zeitschriftenschau für Bibelwissenschaft und Grenzgebiete; Pd. 0074-9745.
IZT: Internationale Zeitschrift für Theologie [= Concilium deutsch].
JAAR: Journal, American Academy of Religion; Atlanta. 0002-7189.
JACiv: Journal of Ancient Civilizations: Chang-chun, Jilin (4, 1989).
JAfAs: Journal of Afroasiatic Languages; Leiden. 0894-9824 (3,1991).
JAMin: Journal of the American Academy of Ministry (1,1992: BtS 150, 109).
JAncCiv: Journal of Ancient Civilizations; Changchun, China, IHAC univ. 1004-8371 (7,1993).
JAncTop: Journal of Ancient Topography; F. 1121-5275 (3,1993).
J[News]AmEg: Journal [Newsletter] of the American Research Center in Egypt [ARCE]; Winona Lake IN.
JAmScAff: ➤ PerScCF.
JANES: Journal of the Ancient Near Eastern Society; NY, Jewish Theol. Sem. 0010-2016.
JanLing[Pract]: Janua Linguarum [Series Practica]; Haag / Paris.

JAOS: Journal of the American Oriental Society; NHv. 0003-0279.
JapJRelSt: Japanese Journal of Religious Studies; Nagoya.
JapRel: Japanese Religions; Tokyo.
JArchSc: Journal of Archaeological Science; London/New York.
JAs: Journal Asiatique; P. 0021-762X.
JAsAf: Journal of Asian and African Studies; Toronto / Leiden.
JaTop: Journal of Ancient Topography; Rome.
Jb: Jahrbuch [Heid, Mainz...]; Jaarbericht.
JbAC: Jahrbuch für Antike und Christentum; Münster im Westfalen.
JbBerlMus: Jahrbücher der Berliner Museen; Berlin.
JbBTh: Jahrbuch für biblische Theologie; Neukirchen.
JbEOL: Jaarbericht van het Vooraziatisch-Egyptisch Genootschap Ex Oriente Lux; Leiden.
JBEq: Journal of Biblical Equality; Lakewood CO.
JbEvHL: Jahrbuch des Deutschen Evangelischen Instituts für Altertumswissenschaft des Heiligen Landes; Firth.
JbKonT: Jahrbuch für kontextuelle Theologie; Fra (1993).
JBL: Journal of Biblical Literature; Atlanta. 0021-9231.
JBlackT: Journal of Black Theology; Atteridgeville SAf.
JbLtgH: Jahrbuch für Liturgik und Hymnologie; Kassel.
JbNumG: Jahrbuch für Numismatik und Geldgeschichte; Regensburg.
JbÖsByz: Jahrbuch der Österreichischen Byzantinistik; W. 0378-8660.
JBQ: Jewish Bible Quarterly (< Dor le-Dor); Jerusalem. 0792-3910.
JbRelW: Jahrbuch für Religionswissenschaft und Theologie der Religionen; FrB.
JChrB: Journal of the Christian Brethren Research Fellowship; Wellington NZ.
JChrEd: Journal of Christian Education; Sydney. 0021-9657.
JCS: Journal of Cuneiform Studies; CM. 0022-0256.

JDharma: Journal of Dharma; Bangalore.
JdU: Judentum und Umwelt; Frankfurt/M.
JEA: Journal of Egyptian Archaeology; London. 0307-5133.
JEarlyC: Journal of Early Christian Studies; Baltimore. 1067-6341.
JEcuSt: Journal of Ecumenical Studies; Ph, Temple Univ. 0022-0558.
Jeevadhara; Alleppey, Kerala.
JEH: Journal of Ecclesiastical History; Cambridge. 0022-0469.
JEmpirT: Journal of empirical theology; Kampen.
JerónMg: Institución S. Jerónimo, estudios y monografías; Valencia.
JESHO: Journal of Economic and Social History of the Orient; Leiden.
JEvTS: Journal of the Evangelical Theological Society; Lynchburg VA. 0360-8808.
JewishH: Jewish History; Leiden. 0334-701X.
JFemR: Journal of Feminist Studies in Religion; Chico CA. 8755-4178.
JField: Journal of Field Archaeology; Boston, Univ. 0093-4690.
JGlass: Journal of Glass Studies; Corning, NY. 0075-4250.
JGraceEv: Journal of the Grace Evangelical Society; Roanoke TX (4,1991).
JHiC: Journal of Higher Criticism.
JHispT: Journal of Hispanic/Latino theology; ColMn (1,1993).
JHistId: Journal of the History of Ideas; Ph, Temple Univ. 0022-5037.
JHMR: Judaica, Hermeneutics, Mysticism, and Religion; Albany, SUNY.
JhÖsA: Jahreshefte des Österreichischen Archäologischen Institutes; Wien. 0078-3579.
JHS: Journal of Hellenic Studies; London. 0075-4269.
Jian Dao ©, a journal of Bible and theology; Hong Kong (1,1994).
JIndEur: Journal of Indo-European Studies; Hattiesburg, Miss.
JIntdenom: Journal, Interdenominational Theological Center; Atlanta.
JIntdis: Journal of the Society for Interdisciplinary History; CM, MIT.
JInterp: Journal of Interpretation.
JJC: Jésus et Jésus-Christ; Paris.

JJS: Journal of Jewish Studies; Oxford. 0022-2097.
JJTht: Journal of Jewish Thought and Philosophy (1,1991).
JJurPap: Journal of Juristic Papyrology; Warszawa.
JLawA: Jewish Law Annual (Oxford).
JMeditArch: Journal of Mediterranean Archeol.; Sheffield. 0952-7648.
JMedvRenSt: Journal of Medieval & Renaissance Studies; Durham NC.
JMoscPatr: [Engl.] Journal of the Moscow Patriarchate; Moscow.
JNES: Journal of Near Eastern Studies; Chicago, Univ. 0022-2968.
JNWS: Journal of Northwest Semitic Languages; Leiden.
jNsu/jOsu: JStNT supp. 0143-5108 / JStOT supp. 0309-0787: Shf.
JOrAf: Journal of Oriental and African Studies; Athens (3,1991s).
Josephinum; Cincinnati. (1,1994).
JPentec: Journal of Pentecostal Theology; Shf (1,1992).
JPersp: Jerusalem perspective.
JPrehRel: Journal of Prehistoric Religion; Göteborg. 0283-8486.
JProgJud: Journal of Progressive Judaism; Shf. (1,1993).
JPseud: Journal for the Study of the Pseudepigrapha; Sheffield. 0951-8207.
JPsy&C/Jud/T: Journal of Psychology & Christianity; Farmington Hills MI. 0733-4273 / ... & Judaism; NY / ... & Theology; Rosemead CA.
JQR: Jewish Quarterly Review (Ph, Dropsie Univ.); WL. 0021-6682.
JRadRef: Journal from the Radical Reform; Morrow GA.
JRArch: Journal of Roman Archaeology; AA.
JRAS: Journal of the Royal Asiatic Society; London.
JRefJud: Journal of Reform Judaism; NY. 0149-712X.
JRel: Journal of Religion; Chicago. 0022-4189.
JRelAf: Journal of Religion in Africa; Leiden. 0022-4200.
JRelEth: Journal of Religion and Ethics; ND (ᴱRutgers). 0384-9694.

JRelHealth: The Journal of Religion and Health; New York.
JRelHist: Journal of Religious History; Sydney, Univ. 0022-4227.
JRelPsyR: Journal of Religion and Psychical Research; Bloomfield CT.
JRelSt: Journal of Religious Studies; Cleveland.
JRelTht: Journal of Religious Thought; Washington DC.
JRelTInf: Journal of Religious and Theological Information; Binghamton NY (1,1993).
JRit: Journal of ritual studies; Pittsburgh/Waterloo ON.
JRMilit: Journal of Roman Military Equipment Studies; Newcastle. 0961-3684 (1,1990).
JRomArch: Journal of Roman Archaeology: Ann Arbor MI (4,1991).
JRPot: Journal of Roman Pottery Studies: Oxford.
JRS: Journal of Roman Studies; London. 0075-4358.
JSArm: Journal of the Society for Armenian Studies; LA.
JSav: Journal des Savants: Paris.
JScStR: Journal for the Scientific Study of Religion; NHv. 0021-8294.
JSemant: Journal of Semantics; Oxford. 0167-5133.
JSemit: Journal for Semitics / Tydskrif vir Semitistiek; Pretoria, Unisa.
JSHZ: Jüdische Schriften aus hellenistischer und römischer Zeit; Gütersloh.
JSQ: Jewish Studies Quarterly; Tü (1/1, 1993).
JSS: Journal of Semitic Studies; Manchester. 0022-4480.
JSStEg: Journal of the Society for the Study of Egyptian Antiquities [ipsi SSEA]; Toronto. 0383-9753.
JSt[HL]JTht: Jerusalem Studies in [Hebrew literature] Jewish Thought; J.
JStJud: Journal for the Study of Judaism in the Persian, Hellenistic, & Roman Periods; Leiden. 0047-2212.
JStNT/OT: Journal for the Study of NT/OT; Sheffield, Univ. 0142-064X/0309-0892. → jN/Osu. 0143-5108/ 0309-0787.

JStRel: Journal for the study of religion [formerly Religion in Southern Africa]; Pietermaritzburg, Natal.
JTrTL: Journal of Translation and Textlinguistics; Dallas (ex-OPTAT).
JTS: Journal of Theological Studies; Oxford/London. 0022-5185.
JTSAfr: Journal of Theology for Southern Africa; Rondebosch.
Judaica; Zürich. 0022-572X.
Judaism; NY. 0022-5762.
JudTSt: Judaistische Texte und Studien; Hildesheim.
JWarb: Journal of the Warburg and Courtauld Institutes; London.
JwHist: Jewish History; Haifa.
JWomen&R: Journal of Women and Religion; Berkeley.
JyskR → RJysk.
Kadmos; Berlin. 0022-7498.
Kairos 1. (Religionswiss.); Salzburg. 0022-7757. - 2. Guatemala 1014-9341.
Karawane (Die); Ludwigsburg.
Karthago (archéologie africaine); P.
KAT: Kommentar zum AT: Gütersloh.
KatBlät: Katechetische Blätter; Mü.
KatKenk: Katorikku Kenkyu < Shingaku; Tokyo, Sophia. 0387-3005.
KBW: Katholisches Bibelwerk; Stu [bzw. Österreich, Schweiz].
KeK: Kritisch-exegetischer Kommentar über das NT; Göttingen.
KerDo: Kerygma und Dogma; Göttingen. 0023-0707.
KerkT: Kerk en Theologie; Wageningen. 0165-2346.
Kernos, religion grecque; Liège.
Kerux; Escondido CA. 0888-8513.
Kerygma (on Indian missions); Ottawa. 0023-0693.
KGaku: ❸ Kirisutokyo Gaku (Christian Studies); Tokyo, 0387-6810.
KingsTR: King's College Theological Review; London.
KirSef: ❸ Kiryat Sefer, Bibliographical Quarterly; Jerusalem, Nat.-Univ. Libr. 0023-1851. → Rambi.
KIsr: Kirche und Israel, theologische Zeitschrift; Neukirchen. 0179-7239.
KkKS: Konfessionskundliche und Kontroverstheologische Studien; Paderborn.

KkMat: Konfessionskundliches Institut, Materialdienst; Bensheim.

KleinÄgTexte: Kleine ägyptische Texte; Würzburg.

Kler: ☉ Klēronomia; Thessaloniki.

Klio: Berlin. 0075-6334.

KLK: Katholisches Leben und Kirchenreform im Zeitalter der Glaubensspaltung; Münster.

KLpJ: Kirchliche Hochschule Leipzig Forschungsstelle Judentum Mitteilungen und Beiträge; Lp (5,1992).

KölnFG: Kölner Jahrbuch für Vor- und Frühgeschichte; B. 0075-6512.

KomBeiANT: Kommentare und Beiträge zum Alten und N.T.; Düsseldorf.

Kratylos (Sprachwissenschaft); Wsb.

KřestR [TPřil]: Křest'anská revue [Theologická Příloha]; Praha.

Kristu Jyoti; Bangalore (8,1992).

KTB/KUB: Keilschrifttexte/urkunden aus Boghazköi; B, Mann/Akademie.

Ktema; Strasbourg, CEDEX.

KuGAW: Kulturgeschichte der Antiken Welt; Mainz.

KvinnerA: Kvinner i arkeologi i Norge; Bergen, Historisk Museum.

KZg: Kirchliche Zeitgeschichte; Gö.

LA: Liber Annuus; J. 0081-8933. ⇥ SBF.

Labeo, diritto romano; N. 0023-6462.

LAeg: Lingua aegyptia; Gö/LA.

Landas: Journal of Loyola School of Theology; Manila,

Language; Baltimore. 0097-8507.

LAPO: Littératures Anciennes du Proche-Orient; Paris, Cerf. 0459-5831.

Lateranum; R, Pont. Univ. Lateranense.

Latomus (Ét. latines); Bru. 0023-8856.

Laur: Laurentianum; R. 0023-902X.

LavalTP: Laval Théologique et Philosophique; Québec.

Laverna, Wirtschafts- und Sozialgeschichte; St. Katharinen. 0938-5835.

LDiv: Lectio Divina; Paris, Cerf.

LebSeels: Lebendige Seelsorge; Wü/FrB.

LebZeug: Lebendiges Zeugnis; Paderborn. 0023-9941.

Lěšonénu (Hebrew Language); J.

Levant (archeology); London.

LexMA: Lexikon des Mittelalters; Mü/Z ⇥ 509*.

LexTQ: Lexington [KY] Theological Quarterly. 0024-1628.

LFrühJ: Literatur und Religion des Frühjudentums; Wü/Gü.

LGB: Lexikon des Gesamten Buchwesens²; Stu ⇥ 571.

LIAO: Lettre d'Information Archéologie Orientale; Valbonne, CNRS. 0750-6279.

LIMC: Lexicon iconographicum mythologiae classicae; Z. ⇥ 571.

LimnOc: Limnology & Oceanography; AA.

LinceiR/Scavi/BClas: Accademia Nazionale dei Lincei. Rendiconti / Notizie degli Scavi / Bollettino Classico. 0391-8270: Roma.

LingBib: Linguistica Biblica; Bonn. 0342-0884.

Lire la Bible; P, Cerf. 0588-2257.

Listening: Romeoville IL.

LitCu: Literary currents in biblical interpretation; Louisville.

LitLComp: Literary and Linguistic Computing; Ox. 0268-1145.

LitTOx: Literature and theology; Ox.

LivLight: The Living Light (US Cath. Conf.); Huntington. 0024-5275.

LivWord: Living Word; Alwaye, Kerala.

Lᵐ: lire (ital.) × 1000.

LoB: Leggere oggi la Bibbia; Brescia, Queriniana.

LogosPh: Logos, philos.; Santa Clara.

Logotherapie; Bremen.

LOrA: Langues orientales anciennes; Lv. 0987-7738.

LPastB. Lettura pastorale della Bibbia: Bo.

LStClas: London studies in classical philology [8, Corolla Londiniensis 1]; Amst.

LtgJb: Liturgisches Jahrbuch; Münster/Wf.

LTK³: ⇥ 510.

Lucentum; prehistoria, arqueología e historia antigua; Alicante, Univ.

LumenK: Lumen; København.

LumenVr: Lumen; Vitoria.

LumièreV: Lumière et Vie; Lyon. 0024-7359.

Luther [Jb]; Ha. 0340-6210. - [Gö].

LuthMon: Lutherische Monatshefte; Hamburg. 0024-7618.

LuthTJ: Lutheran Theological Journal; North Adelaide, S. Australia.

LuthTKi: Lutherische Theologie und Kirche; Oberursel. 0170-3846.

LuthQ: Lutheran Quarterly; Ridgefield NJ.
LuxB: Lux Biblica; R, Ist. B. Evangelico (1,1990).
LVitae: Lumen Vitae; Bru. 0024-7324.
LvSt: Louvain Studies.
Ⓜ magyar: *hungarice*, en hongrois.
M: *mentio, de eo*; author commented upon.
Maarav; WL. 0149-5712.
MadMitt [B/F]: DAI Madrider Mitteilungen [Beiträge/Forschungen]; Mainz.
MAGA: Mitteilungen zur Alten Geschichte und Archäologie; B.
Maia (letterature classiche); Messina. 0025-0538.
MaimS: Maimonidean Studies; NY, Yeshiva Univ./KTAV (1,1990).
Manresa (espiritualidad ignaciana); Azpeitia-Guipúzcoa.
Manuscripta; St. Louis.
Mara: tijdschrift voor feminisme en theologie.
MarbJbT: Marburger Jahrbuch Theologie: Marburg (4,1992).
MaRg: Mitteilungen für Anthropologie und Religionsgeschichte; Saarbrücken.
MARI: Mari, Annales de Recherches Interdisciplinaires; Paris.
Marianum; Roma.
MariolSt: Mariologische Studien; Essen.
MarŠipri; Boston, Baghdad ASOR.
MarSt: Marian Studies; Washington.
Masaq, al-, Arabo-Islamic Mediterranean studies; Leeds (1,1988).
Masca: Museum Applied Science Center for Archaeology Journal; Ph.
MasSt: (SBL) Masoretic Studies; Atlanta.
MastJ: Master's Seminary Journal; Sun Valley, CA (1,1990).
MatDClas: Materiali e discussioni pero l'analisi dei testi classici; Pisa. 0392-6338.
MatKonfInst: Materialdienst des konfessionskundlichen Instituts; Bensheim.
MatPomWykBib: Materiały pomocznicze do wykładów z biblistyki; Lublin.
Mayéutica; Marcilla (Navarra).
MDAV: Mitteilungen des Deutschen Archäologen-Verbandes; Münster.
MDOG: Mitteilungen der Deutschen Orientgesellschaft; B. 0342-118X.
Meander; Wsz Akad. 0025-6285.
Med: Mededelingen [Amst,]; Meddelander.

MeditArch: Mediterranean Archaeology; Sydney. 1030-8482.
MeditHR: Mediterranean historical review Tel Aviv Univ.; L. 0951-8967.
MeditQ: Mediterranean Quarterly; Durham NC.
MedvHum: Mediaevalia & Humanistica (Denton, N. Texas U.); Totowa.
MedvSt: Mediaeval Studies; Toronto. 0076-5872.
MÉF-A [= MélÉcFrR]: Mélanges de l'École Française de Rome/Athènes, Antiquité. 0223-5102.
MélSR: Mélanges de Science Religieuse; Lille.
Mém: Mémoires ➤ AIBL... AcSc, T...
Menora: Jahrbuch deutsch-jüdische Geschichte; Mü. (1,1990).
MenQR: Mennonite Quarterly Review; Goshen, Ind.
Mensaje; Chile.
Meroit: Meroitic Newsletter / Bulletin d'informations méroitiques: Paris, CNRS.
MESA: Middle East Studies Association (Bulletin); Tucson, Univ. AZ.
MesCiv: Mesopotamian Civilization; WL.
MesopK: Mesopotamia: københavn.
MesopT: Mesopotamia; T (pub. F).
Mesorot [Language-tradition researches]; Jerusalem.
MESt: Middle Eastern Studies; L.
Metanoia; social and cultural issues; Praha, Brož.
MetB: Metropolitan Museum Bulletin; New York. 0026-1521.
MethT: Method and theory in the study of religion; Toronto.
Mêtis, Anthropologie grecque; P.
Mg: Monograph (-ie, -fia); ➤ CBQ, SBL, SNTS.
MgANE: Monographs on the Ancient Near East; 1. Leiden; 2. Malibu.
MGraz: Mitteilungen der archäologischen Gesellschaft; Graz.
MgStB: Monographien und Studienbücher; Wu/Giessen.
MHistOv: Memorias de historia antigua; Oviedo, Univ. (13s,1992s).
MHT: Materialien zu einem hethitischen Thesaurus; Heidelberg.
MichTh: Michigan Theological Journal; AA (3,1992).

MiDAI-A/K/M/R: Mitteilungen des Deutschen Archäologischen Instituts: Athen / Kairo / Madrid / Rom 0342-1287.

MidAmJT: Mid-America Journal of Theology: Orange City, Iowa.

Mid-Stream, Disciples of Christ; Indianapolis. – Midstream (Jewish); NY. 0026-332X.

Mikael; Paraná, Arg. (Seminario).

MilltSt: Milltown Studies (philosophy, theology); Dublin. 0332-1428.

Minerva: 1. filología clásica; Valladolid; 2. (incorporating Archaeology Today); L (1,1990).

Minos (Filología Egea); Salamanca. 0544-3733.

MiscArH: Miscelánea de Estudios Árabes y Hebraicos; Granada (41,1992).

MiscCom: Miscelánea Comillas, estudios históricos; M. 0210-9522.

MiscFranc: Miscellanea Francescana; Roma (OFM Conv.).

Mishkan, a theological forum on Jewish evangelism; Jerusalem.

MissHisp: Missionalia hispanica; Madrid, CSIC Inst. E. Flores.

Missiology; Scottdale PA.

Mitt: Mitteilungen [Gö Septuaginta; Berliner Museen...]; ➤ MiDAI.

Mnemosyne, Bibliotheca Classica Batava [+ Supplements]; Leiden.

ModB: Modern Believing [until 34 (1993) Modern Churchman] C. 0025-7597.

ModJud: Modern Judaism; Baltimore.

ModT: Modern Theology; Oxford.

MonSt: Monastic Studies; Montreal. 0026-9190.

MondeB: Le Monde de la Bible: 1. P. 0154-9049. – 2. Genève.

Monde Copte, Le: 0399-905X.

MondoB: Il mondo della Bibbia; T-Leumann, LDC. 1120-7353.

Month; London. 0027-0172.

Moralia; Madrid.

Mosaic (language teaching); Lewiston NY (1 c. 1993).

MsME: Manuscripts of the Middle East; Leiden. 0920-0401.

MSVO: Materialien zu den frühen Schriftzeugnissen des Vorderen Orients: B.

MüÄgSt: Münchener Ägyptologische Studien; München/Berlin.

MüBeit[T]PapR: Münchener Beiträge zur [Theologie] Papyruskunde und antiken Rechtsgeschichte; München.

MünstHand: Münsterische Beiträge zur Antiken Handelsgeschichte; St. Katharinen. 0722-4532.

MüStSprW: Münchener Studien zur Sprachwissenschaft; Mü. ➤ AOtt.

MüTZ: Münchener Theologische Zeitschrift; St. Ottilien. 0580-1400.

Mus: Le Muséon; LvN. 0771-6494.

MusHelv: Museum Helveticum; Basel.

MUSJ: Mélanges de l'Université Saint-Joseph (*rediviva*); Beyrouth [51 (1990): 2-7214-5000-X].

MuslimW: Muslim World; Hartford.

MuzTA: ❽ Muzeon Ha-Areṣ NS; TA.

NABU: Nouvelles assyriologiques brèves et utilitaires; 0989-5671.

NachGö: Nachrichten der Akademie der Wissenschaften; Göttingen.

NarAzAfr: ❽ *Narody:* Peoples of Asia and Africa; Moskva.

NatGeog: National Geographic; Washington. 0027-9358.

NatGrac: Naturaleza y Gracia; S.

NBL: Neues Bibel-Lexikon; Z ➤ 511.

NBlackfr: New Blackfriars; London. 0028-4289.

NCent: The New Century Bible Commentary (reedited); Edinburgh / GR.

NChrIsr: Nouvelles Chrétiennes d'Israël: Jérusalem.

NDizTB: Nuovo Dizionario Teol.B ➤ 9, 599.

NduitsGT: Nederduits-Gereformeerde Teologiese Tydskrif; Kaapstad. 0028-2006.

NEA: The Near East in Antiquity [1-3, German projects; 4, final issue]; Amman (3,1992).

NedTTs: Nederlands Theologisch Tijdschrift; Wageningen. 0028-212X.

Nemalah: K, Dansk Bibel-Inst. (11, 1992).

Neotestamentica; Pretoria; NTWerk.

Nestor, Classical Antiquity, Indiana Univ.; Bloomington. 0028-2812.

NesTR: Near East School of Theology Review; Beirut.

News: Newsletter: Anat[olian Studies; NHv]; Targ[umic and Cognate Studies; Toronto]; ASOR [Baltimore]; Ug[aritic Studies; Calgary]; ➤ JAmEg.
NewTR: New theology review: Ch. 0896-4297.
NHC: Nag Hammadi Codices, Egypt UAR Facsimile edition; Leiden.
NHL/S: Nag Hammadi Library in English / Studies; Leiden.
NHLW: Neues Handbuch der Literaturwissenschaft: Wsb, Athenaion.
Nicolaus (teol. ecumenico-patristica); Bari.
NICOT: New International Commentary OT; Grand Rapids, Eerdmans.
NigJT: The Nigerian Journal of Theology; Owerri.
NIGT: New International Greek Testament Commentary; Exeter/GR.
NInterp: New Interpreter's Bible ➤ 1575.
NJBC: New Jerome Biblical Commentary ➤ 1576.
NOrb: NT & Orbis Antiquus; FrS/Gö.
NorJ: Nordisk Judaistik.
NorTTs: Norsk Teologisk Tidsskrift; Oslo. 0029-2176.
NoTr: Notes on Translation; Dallas.
NOxR: New Oxford Review; Berkeley.
NRT: Nouvelle Revue Théologique; Tournai. 0029-4845.
NS [NF]: Nova series, nouvelle série.
NSys: Neue Zeitschrift für systematische Theologie und Religionsphilosophie; Berlin. 0028-3517.
NT: Novum Testamentum; Leiden. 0048-1009.
NTAbh: Neutestamentliche Abhandlungen. [N.F.]; Münster.
NTAbs: New Testament Abstracts; CM. 0028-6877.
NTDt: Das Neue Testament deutsch; Gö.
NTextUp: New Testament textual research update; Sydney, Macquarie Univ. 1320-3037 (3,1993).
NTS: New Testament Studies; C.
NTTools: Leiden. 0077-8842.
NubChr: Nubia Christiana; Wsz.
Nubica; Köln (1,1990).
NumC: Numismatic Chronicle; London. 0078-2696.
Numen (History of Religions); Leiden.

Numisma; Madrid. 0029-0015.
NumZ: Numismatische Zeitschrift; Wien. 0250-7838.
NuovaUm: Nuova Umanità; Roma.
NVFr/Z: Nova et Vetera; 1. Fribourg, Suisse. / 2. Zamora.
NZMissW: Neue Zeitschrift für Missionswissenschaft; Beckenried, Schweiz. 0028-3495. ➤ NSys.
ObnŽiv: Obnovljeni Život; Zagreb.
OBO: Orbis Biblicus et Orientalis: FrS/Gö.
OEIL: Office d'édition et d'impression du livre; Paris.
ÖkRu: Ökumenische Rundschau; Stuttgart. 0029-8654.
ÖkTbKom, NT: Ökumenischer Taschenbuchkommentar; Gütersloh / Würzburg.
ÖsterrBibSt: Österreichische Biblische Studien; Klosterneuburg.
Offa, ... Frühgeschichte; Neumünster. 0078-3714.
Ohio ➤ JRelSt: Cleveland.
OIAc/P/C: Oriental Institute Acquisitions / Publications / Communications; Ch.
OikBud: Oikumene, historia; Budapest.
Olivo (El), diálogo jud.-cr.: Madrid.
OLZ: Orientalistische Literaturzeitung; Berlin. 0030-5383.
OMRO: Oudheidkundige Mededelingen, Rijksmuseum Oudheden; Leiden
OmT: Omnis Terra [English; also French, Spanish ed.]; Roma (27, 1993).
OneInC: One in Christ (Catholic Ecumenical); Turvey, Bedfordshire.
OnsGErf: Ons Geestelijk Erf; Antwerpen. ➤ GLeven.
OpAth/Rom: Opuscula Atheniensia / Romana; Swedish Inst.
OPTAT ➤ JTrTL.
Opus, storia economica (Siena); R.
Or: ➤ Orientalia; Roma.
OraLab: Ora et Labora; Roriz, Portugal.
OrBibLov: Orientalia et Biblica Lovaniensia; Lv.
OrChr: Oriens Christianus; Wsb.
OrChrPer[An]: Orientalia Christiana Periodica [Analecta]; R, Pontificium Inst. Orientalium Stud. 0030-5375.
OrExp: L'Orient express, informations archéologiques. (1,1991).
OrGand: Orientalia Gandensia; Gent.

Orientalia (Ancient Near East); Rome, Pontifical Biblical Institute. 0030-5367.
Orientierung; Zürich. 0030-5502.
Orient-Japan: Orient, Near Eastern Studies Annual; Tokyo. 0743-3851; cf. ❹ Oriento. 0030-5219.
Origins; Washington Catholic Conference. 0093-609X.
OrJog: Orientasi, Annual ... Philosophy and Theology; Jogjakarta.
OrLovPer[An]: Orientalia Lovaniensia Periodica [Analecta]; Lv. 0085-4522.
OrMod: Oriente Moderno; Napoli. 0030-5472.
OrOcc: Oriente-Occidente. Buenos Aires, Univ. Salvador.
OrPast: Orientamenti Pastorali; Roma.
Orpheus: 1. Catania; 2. -Thracia; Sofya (1,1990).
OrSuec: Orientalia Suecana; Uppsala.
OrtBuc: Ortodoxia; Bucureşti.
OrthF: Orthodoxes Forum; München.
OrTrad: Oral Tradition; Columbia. MO.
OrVars: Orientalia Varsoviensia; Wsz. 0860-5785.
OstkSt: Ostkirchliche Studien; Würzburg. 0030-6487.
Ostraka, rivista di antichità; Napoli. 1122-259X (1,1992).
OTAbs: Old Testament Abstracts; Washington. 0364-8591.
OTEssays: Old Testament essays; Pretoria. 1010-9919.
OTS: Oudtestamentische Studiën; Leiden. 0169-9555.
OTWerkSuidA: Die Ou Testamentiese Werkgemeenskap Suid-Afrika; Pretoria.
OvBTh: Overtures to Biblical Theology; Philadelphia.
Overview; Ch St. Thomas More Asn.
OxJArch: Oxford Journal of Archaeology; Ox. 0262-5253.
❹: *polonice,* in Polish.
p./pa./pl.: page(s)/paperback/plate(s).
PAAR: Proceedings of the American Academy for Jewish Research; Ph.
Pacifica: Australian theological studies; Melbourne Brunswick East.
PacTR: Pacific theological review: SanAnselmo, SF Theol.Sem.
Palaeohistoria; Haarlem.

PalCl: Palestra del Clero; Rovigo.
PaléOr: Paléorient; Paris.
PalSb: ❹ Palestinski Sbornik; Leningrad.
PapBritSR: Papers of the British School at Rome; London.
PAPS: Proceedings of the American Philosophical Society; Philadelphia.
PapTAbh: Papyrologische Texte und Abhandlungen; Bonn, Habelt.
PapyrolColon: Papyrologica Coloniensia; Opladen. 0078-9410.
Parabola; New York.
Paradigms; Louisville KY.
ParOr: Parole de l'Orient; Kaslik.
ParPass: Parola del Passato; Napoli. 0031-2355.
ParSpV: Parola, Spirito e Vita; Bologna.
ParVi: Parole di Vita; T-Leumann.
PasT: Pastoraltheologie; Göttingen.
PastScP: Pastoral / Sciences pastorales; psych.sociol.théol.; Ottawa.
Patr&M: Patristica et Mediaevalia; BA.
PatrByz: Patristic and Byzantine Review; Kingston NY. 0737-738X.
PatrMedRen: Proceedings of the Patristic, Mediaeval and Renaissance Conference; Villanova PA.
PatrStudT: Patristische Studien und Texte; B. 0553-4003.
PBtScB: Petite bibliothèque des sciences bibliques; Paris, Desclée.
PenséeC: La Pensée Catholique; P.
PEQ: Palestine Exploration Quarterly; London. 0031-0328.
PerAz: Peredneaziatskij Sbornik; Moskva.
Peritia; Dublin (8,1994).
Persica: Leiden.
PerScCF: Perspectives on Science and Christian Faith (replacing JAmScAff since 39,1987); Ipswich MA. 0892-2675.
PerspRef: Perspectives, a journal of Reformed thought (7,1992).
PerspRelSt: Perspectives in Religious Studies (Baptist); Danville VA.
PerspT: Perspectiva Teológica; Belo Horizonte.
Pg/Ph: philolog-/philosoph-.
PgOrTb: Philologia Orientalis; Tbilisi.
Pharos; Amst, Athens Inst. 1380-2240 (1,1993).
Phase; Barcelona.

PhilipSa: Philippiniana Sacra; Manila.
Philologus; B. 0031-7985.
Phoenix; Toronto. 0031-8299.
PhoenixEOL; Leiden. 0031-8329.
Phronema: Greek Orthodox; Sydney.
Phronesis; Assen. 0031-8868.
PhTh: Philosophy and Theology; Milwaukee, Marquette Univ. [7 (1992) 0-87462-559-9].
Pneuma, Pentecostal; Pasadena.
PoeT: Poetics Today; Durham NC, Duke Univ. 0333-5372 (14,1993).
PoinT: Le Point Théologique; P.
Polin: Polish-Jewish Studies; Oxford.
PontAcc, R/Mem: Atti della Pontificia Accademia Romana di Archeologia, Rendiconti/Memorie; Vaticano.
Pontica; St. Étienne/İstanbul (1,1991).
PracArch: Prace Archeologiczne; Kraków, Univ. 0083-4300.
PraehZ: Praehistorische Zeitschrift; Berlin. 0079-4848.
PrakT: Praktische theologie; Zwolle.
PraktArch: ☉ Praktika, Archeology Society Athens.
PrCambPg: Proceedings of the Cambridge Philological Soc. 0068-6735.
PrCTSAm: Proceedings Catholic Theological Society of America; Villanova.
PredikOT/NT: De Prediking van het OT / van het NT; Nijkerk.
Premislia Christiana; Przemyśl.
Presbyteri; Trento.
Presbyterion; St. Louis.
PresPast: Presenza Pastorale; Roma.
Pre/Text, rhetorical theory; Arlington TX. 0731-0714 (13,1992).
PrêtreP: Prêtre et Pasteur; Montréal. 0385-8307.
Priest (The); Washington.
PrincSemB: Princeton Seminary Bulletin; Princeton NJ.
PrIrB: Proceedings of the Irish Biblical Association; Dublin.
Prism; St. Paul MN.
ProbHistRel: Problèmes de l'Histoire des Religions; Bruxelles (1,1990).
ProcClas: Proceedings of the Classical Association; London.
ProcCom: Proclamation Commentaries; Ph.
ProcGM: Proceedings of the Eastern Great Lakes and Midwest Bible Societies; Buffalo.

ProcIsrAc: Proceedings of the Israel Academy of Sciences & Humanities; Jerusalem.
ProEc: Pro Ecclesia; Northfield MN (2,1993).
Prooftexts; Baltimore.
PrOrChr: Proche-Orient Chrétien; Jérusalem. 0032-9622.
Prot: Protestantesimo; R. 0033-1767.
ProtokB: Protokolle zur Bibel; Klosterneuburg, ÖsKBW. (1,1992).
Proyección (mundo actual); Granada.
ProySal: Proyecto Centro Salesiano de Estudios; Buenos Aires. (4,1992).
PrPeo: Priests and People; L.
PrPg/PrehS: Proceedings of the Philological/Prehistoric Society; Cambridge.
PrSemArab: Proceedings of the Seminar for Arabian Studies; London.
Prudentia (Hellenistic, Roman); Auckland NZ. 0110-487X.
PrzPow: Przegląd Powszechny, Kraków.
PT: Philosophy/Theology: Milwaukee, Marquette Univ.
PubTNEsp: Publicaciones de la Facultad Teológica del Norte de España; Burgos.
PUF: Presses Universitaires de France; P.
Qadm: Qadmoniot ☉ Quarterly of Dept. of Antiquities; Jerusalem.
Qardom, ☉ mensuel pour la connaissance du pays; Jerusalem, Ariel.
QDisp: Quaestiones Disputatae; FrB.
Qedem: Monographs of the Institute of Archaeology: Jerusalem.
QLtg: Questions Liturgiques; Lv.
QRMin: Quarterly Review [for] Ministry; Nv. 0270-9287.
QuadCatan / Chieti: Quaderni, Catania / Chieti; Univ.
QuadSemant: Quaderni di Semantica; Bologna.
QuadSemit: Quaderni di Semitistica; Firenze.
QuadUrb: Quaderni Urbinati di Cultura Classica; Urbino. 0033-4987.
Quaerendo (Low Countries: Manuscripts and Printed Books); Amst.
QuatreF: Les quatre fleuves: Paris.
QüestVidaCr: Qüestions de Vida Cristiana; Montserrat.
QumC: Qumran Chronicle; Kraków.

Ⓡ: *russice*, in Russian.
ᴿ: *recensio*, book-review(er).
RAC: Reallexikon für Antike und Christentum; Stuttgart ⇢ 512.
Radiocarbon; NHv, Yale. 0033-8222.
RAfrT: Revue Africaine de Théologie; Kinshasa/Limete.
RAg: Revista Agustiniana; Calahorra.
RAMBI: Rešimat Ma'amarim bemadda'ê ha-Yahedût, Index of articles on Jewish Studies; J. 0073-5817.
RaMIsr: Rassegna mensile di Israel; Roma. 0033-9792.
RArchéol: Revue Archéologique; Paris. 0035-0737.
RArchéom: Revue d'Archéométrie; Rennes.
RArtLv: Revue des Archéologues et Historiens d'Art; Lv. 0080-2530.
RasArch: Rassegna di archeologia; F (9,1990).
RasEtiop: Rassegna di Studi Etiopici; R/N.
RAss: Revue d'Assyriologie et d'Archéologie Orientale; Paris.
RasT: Rassegna di Teologia; Roma [ᴱNapoli]. 0034-9644.
RazF: Razón y Fe; M. 0034-0235.
RB: Revue Biblique; J/P. 0035-0907.
RBén: Revue Bénédictine; Maredsous. 0035-0893.
RBgNum: Revue Belge de Numismatique et Sigillographie; Bruxelles.
RBgPg: Revue Belge de Philologie et d'Histoire; Bru. 0035-0818.
RBBras: Revista Bíblica Brasileira; Fortaleza.
RBibArg: Revista Bíblica; Buenos Aires. 0034-7078.
RCatalT: Revista Catalana de Teología; Barcelona, St. Pacià.
RCiv: Éditions Recherche sur les Civilisations [Mém(oires) 0291-1655]; P ⇢ ADPF.
RClerIt: Rivista del Clero Italiano; Milano. 0042-7586.
RCuClaMed: Rivista di Cultura Classica e Medioevale; R. 0080-3251.
RCuT: Revista de Cultura Teológica: São Paulo Ipiranga (1,1993).
RÉAnc: Revue des Études Anciennes; Bordeaux. 0035-2004.
RÉArmén: Revue des Études Arméniennes. 0080-2549.

RÉAug: Revue des Études Augustiniennes; Paris. 0035-2012.
REB: 1. Revista Eclesiástica Brasileira; Petrópolis. 2. ⇢ **RNEB**.
RÉByz: Revue des Études Byzantines; Paris.
RECAM: Regional Epigraphic Catalogues of Asia Minor [AnSt].
RechAug: Recherches Augustiniennes; Paris. 0035-2021.
RechSR: Recherches de Science Religieuse; Paris. 0034-1258.
RecTrPO: Recueil de travaux, Proche-Orient ancien; Montréal.
RefEgy: Református Egyház; Budapest. 0324-475X.
ReferSR: Reference Services Review; Dearborn MI, Univ.
RefF: Reformiertes Forum; Zürich.
RefGStT: Reformationsgeschichtliche Studien und Texten: Münster.
RefJ: The Reformed Journal; Grand Rapids. 0486-252X.
Reformatio; Zürich. 0034-3021.
RefR: Reformed Review; New Brunswick NJ / Holland MI. 0034-3064.
RefTR: Reformed Theological Review; Hawthorn, Australia. 0034-3072.
RefW: Reformed World; Geneva. 0034-3056.
RÉG: Revue des Études Grecques; Paris. 0035-2039.
RÉgp: Revue d'Égyptologie; Paris.
RÉJ: Revue des Études Juives; Paris. 0035-2055.
RÉLat: Revue des Études Latines; P.
RelCult: Religión y Cultura; M.
RelEdn: Religious Education (biblical; Jewish-sponsored); NHv.
Religion [... and Religions]; Lancaster. 0048-721X.
RelIntL: Religion and Intellectual Life; New Rochelle. 0741-0549.
RelPBeit: Religionspädagogische Beiträge; Kaarst.
RelSoc: Religion and Society; B/Haag.
RelSt: Religious Studies; Cambridge. 0034-4125.
RelStR: Religious Studies Review; Nv, Vanderbilt. 0319-485X.
RelStT: Religious Studies and Theology; Edmonton. 0829-2922.

RelT: Religion and Theology; Pretoria. (1,1994).

RelTAbs: Religious and Theological Abstracts; Myerstown, Pa.

RelTrad: Religious Traditions; Brisbane. 0156-1650.

RencAssInt: Rencontre Assyriologique Internationale, Compte-Rendu.

RencChrJ: Rencontre Chrétiens et Juifs; Paris. 0233-5579.

Renovatio: 1. Zeitschrift für das interdisziplinäre Gespräch; Köln: 2. (teologia); Genova.

RepCyp: Report of the Department of Antiquities of Cyprus; Nicosia.

RépertAA: Répertoire d'art et d'archéologie; Paris. 0080-0953.

REPPAL: Revue d'Études Phéniciennes-Puniques et des Antiquités Libyques; Tunis.

ResB: Reseña Biblica; Estella (1, 1994).

REspir: Revista de Espiritualidad; San Sebastián.

ResPLit: Res Publica Litterarum; Kansas.

RestQ: Restoration Quarterly; Abilene TX.

Résurrection, bimestriel catholique d'actualité et de formation.

RET: Revista Española de Teología; Madrid.

RÉtGC: Revue des Études Géorgiennes et Caucasiennes; Paris. 0373-1537 [< Bedi Kartlisa].

RevCuBíb: Revista de Cultura Bíblica; São Paulo.

RevSR: Revue des Sciences Religieuses; Strasbourg. 0035-2217.

RExp: Review and Expositor; Louisville. 0034-6373.

RFgIC: Rivista di Filologia e di Istruzione Classica; Torino. 0035-6220.

RgStTh: Regensburger Studien zur Theologie; Fra/Bern, Lang.

RgVV: Religionsgeschichtliche Versuche und Vorarbeiten; B/NY, de Gruyter.

RHDroit: Revue historique de Droit français et étranger; Paris.

RHE: Revue d'Histoire Ecclésiastique; Louvain. 0035-2381.

RheinMus: Rheinisches Museum für Philologie; Frankfurt. 0035-449X.

Rhetorica; (12,1994).

Rhetorik [Jb]; Stu / Bad Cannstatt.

RHist: Revue Historique; Paris.

RHPR: Revue d'Histoire et de Philosophie Religieuses; Strasbourg. 0035-2403.

RHR: Revue de l'Histoire des Religions; Paris. 0035-1423.

RHS ➤ RUntHö; RU ➤ ZPrax.

RHText: Revue d'Histoire des Textes; Paris. 0373-6075.

Ribla: Revista de interpretación bíblica latinoamericana; San José CR.

RIC: Répertoire bibliographique des institutions chrétiennes; Strasbourg ➤ 6,1063.

RICAO: Revue de l'Institut Catholique de l'Afrique de l'Ouest; Abidjan. (1,1992).

RICathP: Revue de l'Institut Catholique de Paris. 0294-4308

RicStoB: Ricerche storico bibliche; Bologna. 0394-980X.

RicStorSocRel: Ricerche di Storia Sociale e Religiosa; Roma.

RicT: Ricerche Teologiche; R (1,1990).

RIDA: Revue Internationale des Droits de l'Antiquité; Bruxelles.

RijT: Riječki Teološki Časopis; Rijeka (Fiume), Croatia. 1330-0377.

RIMA ➤ AnRIM.

RINASA: Rivista Ist. Nazionale di Archeologia e Storia dell'Arte; Roma.

RitFg: Rivista italiana di Filologia Classica.

RItNum: Rivista Italiana di Numismatica e scienze affini; Milano.

RivArCr: Rivista di Archeologia Cristiana; Città/Vaticano. 0035-6042.

RivArV: Rivista di Archeologia, Univ. Venezia; Roma.

RivAscM: Rivista di Ascetica e Mistica; Roma.

RivB: Rivista Biblica Italiana; Bologna, Dehoniane. 0393-4853.

RivLtg: Rivista di Liturgia; T-Leumann.

RivPastLtg: Rivista di Pastorale Liturgica; Brescia. 0035-6395.

RivScR: Rivista di Scienze Religiose; Molfetta.

RivStoLR: Rivista di Storia e Letteratura Religiosa; F. 0035-6573.

RivStorA: Rivista Storica dell'Antichità; Bologna. 0300-340X.

RivVSp: Rivista di Vita Spirituale; Roma. 0035-6638.
RJysk: Religionsvidenskapeligt Tidsskrift (Jysk/Jutland); Aarhus. 0108-1993.
RLA: Reallexikon der Assyriologie & vorderasiatischen Archäologie; B ➤ 9,601.
RLatAmT: Revista Latinoamericana de Teología; El Salvador.
RLitND: Religion and Literature; Notre Dame, Univ. 0029-1500 (24, 1992).
RNEB: revision of New English Bible.
RNouv: La Revue Nouvelle; Bruxelles. 0035-3809.
RNum: Revue Numismatique; Paris.
RoczOr: Rocznik Orientalistyczny; Warszawa. 0080-3545.
RoczTK: Roczniki Teologiczno-Kanoniczne; Lublin. 0035-7723.
RömQ: Römische Quartalschrift für Christliche Altertumskunde...; Freiburg/Br. 0035-7812.
RomOrth: Romanian Orthodox Church News, French Version [sic]; Bucureşti.
RossArkh: Rossijskaja Arkheologija [= SovArch] after 1992/2: Moskva.
RPg: Revue de Philologie, de Littérature et d'Histoire anciennes; Paris, Klincksieck. 0035-1652.
RPontAr: (Atti) Rendiconti della Pontificia Accademia Romana di Archeologia; R.
RQum: Revue de Qumrân; P. 0035-1725.
RRéf: Revue Réformée; Saint-Germain-en-Laye.
RRel: Review for Religious; St. Louis. 0034-639X.
RRelRes: Review of Religious Research; New York. 0034-673X.
RRT: Reviews in religion and theology; L, SCM. 1350-7303 (1, 1994).
RRns: The Review of Religions; Wsh. 0743-5622.
RSO: Rivista degli Studi Orientali; Roma. 0392-4869.
RSPT: Revue des Sciences Philosophiques et Théologiques; [Le Saulchoir] Paris. 0035-2209.
RStFen: Rivista di Studi Fenici: R.
RSzem: Református Szemle; Budapest.
RTAM: Recherches de Théologie Ancienne et Médiévale; Louvain. 0034-1266. ➤ BTAM.

RTBat: Revista Teológica (Sem. Batista); Rio de Janeiro.
RThom: Revue Thomiste; Toulouse/ Bru. 0035-4295.
RTLim: Revista Teológica; Lima.
RTLv: Revue théologique de Louvain. 0080-2654.
RTop: [Journal of/] Rivista di Topografia (4,1994) ➤ 438.
RTPhil: Revue de Théologie et de Philosophie; Épalinges. 0035-1784.
RuBi: Ruch Biblijny i Liturgiczny; Kraków. 0209-0872.
RUntHö: Religionsunterricht an höheren Schulen; Dü. (RU ➤ ZPrax).
RVidEspir: Revista de vida espiritual; Bogotá.
RZaïrTP: Revue Zaïroise de Théologie Protestante.
SAA[B]: State Archives of Assyria [Bulletin]; Helsinki.
SacEr: Sacris Erudiri; Steenbrugge. Saeculum; FrB/Mü. 0080-5319.
SAfBap: South African Baptist Journal of Theology; Cape Town. 1019-7990 (2,1992).
Sales: Salesianum; Roma. 0036-3502.
Salm: Salmanticensis; S. 0036-3537.
SalT: Sal Terrae; Sdr. 0211-4569. Sandalion (Sassari); R, Herder.
SAOC: Studies in Ancient Oriental Civilization: Ch, Univ. 0081-7554. ➤ OI.
Sap: Sapienza; Napoli. 0036-4711.
SapCro: La Sapienza della Croce; R.
SASTUMA: Saarbrücker Studien und Materialien zur Altertumskunde; Bonn. 0942-7392 (2,1992).
sb.: subscription; price for members.
SbBrno: Sborník praci filozoficke fakulty; Brno, Univ.
SBF Anal/Pub [min]: Studii Biblici Franciscani: Analecta / Publicationes series maior 0081-8971 [minor]; Jerusalem. ➤ LA.
SBL [AramSt / Mg / Diss / GRR / MasSt / NAm / SemP / TexTr / W]: Society of Biblical Literature: Aramaic Studies / Monograph Series / Dissertation Series / Graeco-Roman Religion / Masoretic Studies / Biblical Scholarship in North America / Seminar Papers 0145-2711 / Texts and Translations / Writings of the Ancient World. ➤ JBL; CATSS; CritRR.

SBS [KBW]: Stuttgarter Bibelstudien; Stuttgart, Katholisches Bibelwerk.
ScandJOT: Scandinavian Journal of the Old Testament; Aarhus.
ScAnt: Scienze dell'Antichità; storia archeologia antropologia; Roma (3s,1989s).
ScEsp: Science et Esprit; Montréal. 0316-5345.
SCHN: Studia ad Corpus Hellenisticum NT; Leiden.
Schönberger Hefte; Fra.
Scholars Choice; Richmond VA.
SChr: Sources Chrétiennes; P. 0750-1978.
SCompass: Social Compass, revue internat. sociologie de la religion: Lv.
ScotBEv: The Scottish Bulletin of Evangelical Theology; E. 0265-4539.
ScotJT: Scottish Journal of Theology; Edinburgh. 0036-9306.
ScotR: Scottish Journal of Religious Studies; Stirling. 0143-8301.
ScrCh: Scripture in Church; Dublin (25,1993).
ScrCiv: Scrittura [scrivere] e Civiltà; T.
ScrClasIsr: Scripta Classica Israelica; J.
ScriptB: Scripture Bulletin; London. 0036-9780.
Scriptorium; Bruxelles. 0036-9772.
ScripTPamp: Scripta theologica; Pamplona, Univ. Navarra. 0036-9764.
Scriptura; Stellenbosch. 0254-1807.
ScriptVict: Scriptorium Victoriense; Vitoria, España.
ScuolC: La Scuola Cattolica; Venegono Inferiore, Varese. 0036-9810.
SDB [= DBS]: Supplément au Dictionnaire de la Bible; Paris ➤ 602.
SDH: Studia et documenta historiae et iuris; Roma, Pont. Univ. Lateran.
SecC: Second Century ➤ JEarlyC.
Sefarad; Madrid. 0037-0894.
SEG: Supplementum epigraphicum graecum; Withoorn.
Segmenten; Amsterdam, Vrije Univ.
SelT: Selecciones de Teología; Barc.
SémBib: Sémiotique et Bible; Lyon ➤ CADIR. 0154-6902.
Semeia (Biblical Criticism) [Supplements]; Atlanta. 0095-571X.
Seminarios; Salamanca.

Seminarium; Roma.
Seminary Review; Cincinnati.
Semiotica; Amsterdam. 0037-1998.
Semitica; Paris. 0085-6037.
Sens; juifs et chrétiens; Paris.
SeptCogSt: ➤ B[ulletin].
Servitium; CasM (ᴱBergamo).
SEST: South-Eastern [Baptist] Seminary Studies; Wake Forest NC.
SetRel: Sette e religioni; Bologna (2, 1992).
Sevārtham; Ranchi. 0970-5324.
Sève = Église aujourd'hui; P. 0223-5854.
SewaneeTR: Sewanee Theological Review (ex-St.Luke's); Sewanee TN. (17, 1992).
SFulg: Scripta Fulgentina; Murcia. (1,1991s).
SGErm: ❸ Soobščeniya gosudarstvennovo Ermitaža, Reports of the State Hermitage Museum; Leningrad. 0432-1501.
SH: Social History; London.
ShinKen: ❹ Shinyaku Kenkyū, Studia Textus Novi Testamenti; Osaka.
ShMišpat: Shnaton ha-Mišpaṭ ha-Ivri, Annual of Jewish Law.
ShnatM: ❺ Shnaton la-Mikra (Annual, Biblical and ANE Studies); TA.
SicArch: Sicilia archeologica; Trapani.
SicGym: Siculorum Gymnasium; Catania.
Sidra, a journal for the study of Rabbinic literature; Ramat-Gan.
SIMA: Studies in Mediterranean Archaeology; Göteborg.
SixtC: The Sixteenth Century Journal; St. Louis (Kirksville). 0361-0160.
SkK: Stuttgarter kleiner Kommentar.
SkrifK: Skrif en Kerk; Pretoria, Univ.
SMEA: Studi Micenei ed Egeo-Anatolici (Incunabula Graeca); Roma.
SMSR: Studi e Materiali di Storia delle religioni: Roma.
SNTS (Mg.): Studiorum Novi Testamenti Societas (Monograph Series); Cambridge.
SNTU-A/B: Studien zum NT und seiner Umwelt; Linz [Periodica / Series].
Soc[An till 1993]Rel: Sociology [-ical analysis of] of religion; Chicago.

SocUÉg: Sociétés Urbaines en Égypte et au Soudan; Lille.
SocWB: The Social World of Biblical Antiquity; Sheffield.
Soundings; Nashville. 0585-5462.
SovArch: → RossArkh.
Speculum (Medieval Studies); CM. 0038-7134.
SPg: Studia Philologica. 0585-5462.
SpirC, SpirNC: La Spiritualità cristiana / non-cristiana; R → 5,907.
Spiritus; Paris. 0038-7665.
SpirLife: Spiritual Life; Washington. 0038-7630.
Sprache; Wien. 0038-8467.
SR: Studies in Religion / Sciences Religieuses; Waterloo, Ont. 0008-4298.
SSEA → JSStEg.
ST: (Vaticano) Studi e Testi.
ST: Studia Theologica; K. 0039-338X.
StAäK: Studien zur altägyptischen Kultur; Hamburg. 0340-2215.
StAChron: Studies in Ancient Chronology; London. 0952-4975.
Stadion, Geschichte des Sports; Sankt Augustin. 0178-4029.
StAns: Studia Anselmiana; Roma.
StANT: Studien zum Alten und Neuen Testament; München.
StAntCr: Studi di Antichità Cristiana; Città del Vaticano.
Star: St. Thomas Academy for Research; Bangalore.
Stauròs, Bollettino trimestrale sulla teologia della Croce: Pescara.
StBEC: Studies in the Bible and Early Christianity; Lewiston NY.
StBEx: Studies in Bible and Exegesis; Ramat-Gan.
StBib: Dehon/Paid/Leiden: Studi Biblici; Bo, Dehoniane / Brescia, Paideia / Studia Biblica; Leiden.
StBoğT: Studien zu den Boğazköy-Texten; Wiesbaden.
STBuc: Studii Teologice; Bucureşti.
StCatt: Studi cattolici; Mi. 0039-2901.
StCEth: Studies in Christian Ethics; Edinburgh. 0953-9468.
StChrAnt: Studies in Christian Antiquity; Wsh.
StChrJud: Studies in Christianity and Judaism; Waterloo ON.

StClasBuc: Studii Clasice; Bucureşti.
StClasOr: Studi Classici e Orientali; R.
StCompRel: Studies in Comparative Religion; Bedfont. 0039-3622.
StDelitzsch: Studia Delitzschiana (ᴱMünster); Stuttgart. 0585-5071.
StEbl: Studi Eblaiti; Roma, Univ.
StEC: Studies in Early Christianity; NY, Garland.
StEcum: Studi Ecumenici; Verona. 0393-3687.
StEgPun: Studi di Egittologia e di Antichità Puniche (Univ. Bo.); Pisa.
StEpL: Studi Epigrafici e Linguistici sul Vicino Oriente antico; Verona.
STEv: Studi di Teologia dell'Istituto Biblico Evangelico; Padova.
StFormSp: Studies in Formative Spirituality; Pittsburgh. 0193-2478.
StGnes: Studia Gnesnensia; Gniezno.
StHistANE: Studies in the history of the ancient Near East; Leiden. 0169-9024.
StHJewishP: Studies in the History of the Jewish People; Haifa.
StHPhRel: Studies in the History and Philosophy of Religion; CM.
StHRel [= Numen Suppl.] Studies in the History of Religions; Leiden.
StIntku: Studien zur Interkulturellen Geschichte des Christentums / Eng.; Fra.
StIran: Studia Iranica; Leiden. 0772-7852.
StIsVArh: Studii şi cercetări de Istorie Veche şi arheologie; Bucureşti. 0039-4009.
StItFgC: Studi Italiani di Filologia Classica; Firenze. 0039-2987.
StiZt: Stimmen der Zeit; FrB. 0039-1492.
StJudLA: Studies in Judaism in Late Antiquity; Leiden. 0169-961X.
StLatIt: Studi Latini e Italiani: R, Univ. (5,1991).
StLeg: Studium Legionense; León.
StLtg: Studia Liturgica; Nieuwendam.
StLuke → Sewanee TR.
StMiss: Studia Missionalia, Annual; Rome, Gregorian Univ.
StMor: Studia Moralia; R, Alphonsianum. 0081-6736.
StNT: Studien zum Neuen Testament; Gütersloh; STNT → Shin-Ken.
StNW: Studies of the NT and its World; E.

StOr: Studia Orientalia; Helsinki, Societas Orientalis Fennica. 0039-3282.
StOrL: Studi Orientali e Linguistici; Bologna, Univ. Ist. Glottologia.
StOrRel: Studies in Oriental Religions; Wiesbaden.
StOvet: Studium Ovetense; Oviedo.
StPatav: Studia Patavina; Padova. 0039-3304.
StPatrist: Studia Patristica; Berlin.
StPhilonAn: Studia Philonica Annual; Atlanta.
StPostB: Studia Post-Biblica; Leiden.
StPrace: Studia i Prace = Études, Wsz.
StRefTH: Studies in Reformed Theology and History; Princeton Sem. 1667-4268. (1,1993).
Streven: 1. cultureel; Antwerpen. 0039-2324; 2. S.J., Amst.
StRicOrCr: Studi e Ricerche dell'Oriente Cristiano; Roma.
StRom: Studi Romani; Roma.
Stromata (< Ciencia y Fe); San Miguel, Argentina. 0049-2353.
StRz: Studia Religioznawcze (Filozofii i Socjologii); Wsz, Univ.
StScT: Studies in Science and Theology; Geneva (1,1993).
StSemLgLing: Studies in Semitic Language and Linguistics; Leiden.
StSp: Studies in Spirituality; Kampen. (2,1992).
StSp (Dehoniane) ➤ 6,854*.
StSpG (Borla) ➤ 6,855.
StStoR: Studi storici e religiosi; Capua. (1,1992).
StTNeunz: Studien zur Theologie und Geistesgeschichte des Neunzehnten Jh.; Göttingen.
StudiaBT: Studia Biblica et Theologica; Pasadena CA. 0094-2022.
Studies; Dublin. 0039-3495.
StudiesBT: Studies in Biblical Theology; L.
Studium; 1. Madrid; 2. R −0039-4130.
Stulos, theological journal; Bandung, Indonesia (1,1993).
StVTPseud: Studia in Veteris Testamenti Pseudepigrapha; Leiden.
StWarm: Studia Warmińskie; Olstyn. 0137-6624. (22s, 1992 per 1985s).
STWsz: Studia theologica Varsaviensia; Warszawa.

Stylos; Buenos Aires (1,1992).
SubsBPont: Subsidia Biblica; R, Pontifical Biblical Institute.
SudanTB: Sudan Texts Bulletin; Ulster, Univ. 0143-6554.
Sumer (Archaeology-History in the Arab World); Baghdad, Dir. Ant.
SUNT: Studien zur Umwelt des NTs; Gö.
SUNY: State University of New York; Albany etc.
Supp.: Supplement ➤ NT, JStOT, SEG.
Supplément, Le: autrefois 'de VSp'; P.
SvEx: Svensk Exegetisk Årsbok; U.
SVlad: St. Vladimir's Theological Quarterly; Tuckahoe NY. 0036-3227.
SvTKv: Svensk Teologisk Kvartalskrift; Lund.
SWJT: Southwestern Journal of Theology; Fort Worth. 0038-4828.
Symbolae (graec-lat.); Oslo. 0039-7679.
Symbolon: 1. Ba/Stu; 2. Köln.
Synaxe; annuale, Catania.
Syria (Art Oriental, Archéologie); Paris, IFA Beyrouth.
SyrMesSt: Syro-Mesopotamian Studies (Monograph Journals); Malibu CA.
Szb: Sitzungsberichte [Univ.], phil.-hist. Klasse (Bayr.). Mü. 0342-5991.
Szolgalat ⓦ ['Dienst']; Eisenstadt, Ös.
ⓣ: *lingua turca*, Turkish; − ᵀtranslator - ᵗBHT ➤ 1550.
Tablet; London. 0039-8837.
TAik: Teologinen Aikakauskirja / Teologisk Tidskrift; Helsinki.
TaiwJT: Taiwan [Presbyterian Sem.] Journal of Theology; Taipei.
TAJ: Tel Aviv [Univ.] Journal of the Institute of Archaeology. 0334-4355.
TAn: Theology Annual; Hongkong.
TanturYb: Ecumenical Institute for Theological Research Yearbook; J.
TANZ: Texte und Arbeiten zum neutestamentlichen Zeitalter; Tü. non = ArbNZ.
TArb: Theologische Arbeiten; Stu/B.
Tarbiẓ ❸ (Jewish Studies); Jerusalem, Hebr. Univ. 0334-3650.
TArg: Teología; Buenos Aires.
Target, translation studies; Amst.
TAth: ❺ Theología; Athēnai.
TAVO: Tübinger Atlas zum Vorderen Orient [Beih(efte)]: Wiesbaden.
TBeit: Theologische Beiträge; Wu.

TBer: Theologische Berichte: Z/Köln.
TBR: Theological Book Review; Guildford, Surrey. (6,1993s).
TBraga: Theologica; Braga.
TBud: Teologia; Budapest, Ac. Cath.
TBüch: Theologische Bücherei. (Neudrukke und Berichte 20. Jdt.); München.
TCN: Theological College of Northern Nigeria Bulletin; Bukuru.
TContext[o]: Theology in Context; Aachen 8,1 (1991). 0176-1439 = Teología in Contexto 1,1 (1991). 0938-3468 = **TKontext,** Theologie im Kontext 12,1 (1991). 0724-1628.
TDeusto: Teología-Deusto; Bilbao/M.
TDienst: Theologie und Dienst; Wu.
TDig: Theology Digest; St. Louis. 0040-5728.
TDNT: Theological Dictionary of the NT [< TWNT]; Grand Rapids ➤ 5,811.
TDocStA: Testi e documenti per lo studio dell'Antichità; Milano, Cisalpino.
TDOT: Theological Dictionary of the Old Testament [< TWAT] ➤ 9,602*.
TEdn: Theological Education; Vandalia, Ohio.
TEdr: Theological Educator; New Orleans.
TEFS: Theological Education [Materials for Africa, Asia, Caribbean] Fund, Study Guide; London.
Téléma (réflexion et créativité chrétiennes en Afrique); Kinshasa-Gombe.
Teocomunicação.
Teresianum; Roma.
TerraS / TerreS: Terra Santa: 0040-3784. / La Terre Sainte; J (Custodia OFM). ➤ HolyL.
TEspir: Teología Espiritual; Valencia.
TEuph: Transeuphratène [Syrie perse]; P.
TEV: Today's English Version (Good News for Modern Man); L, Collins.
TEvca: Theologia Evangelica; Pretoria, Univ. S. Africa.
TExH: Theologische Existenz heute; Mü.
Text; The Hague. 0165-4888.
TextEstCisn: Textos y Estudios 'Cardenal Cisneros'; Madrid, Cons.Sup.Inv.
TextPatLtg: Textus patristici et liturgici; Regensburg, Pustet.
Textus, Annual of the Hebrew Univ. Bible Project; J. 0082-3767.

TFor: Theologische Forschung; Ha.
TGegw: Theologie der Gegenwart in Auswahl; Münster, Regensberg-V.
TGL: Theologie und Glaube; Pd.
THandkNT: Theologischer Handkommentar zum NT; Berlin.
THAT: Theologisches Handwörterbuch zum AT; München. ➤ 1,908.
Themelios; London. 0307-8388.
Theokratia, Jahrbuch des Institutum Delitzschianum; Leiden/Köln.
Théologiques; Montréal (1,1993).
Theológos, Ho; Fac. Teol. Palermo.
THist: Théologie Historique; P. 0563-4253.
This World; NY.
Thomist, The; Wsh. 0040-6325.
Thought; NY, Fordham. 0040-6457.
ThSex: Theology and Sexuality; Shf. (1,1994).
Tikkun; Oakland CA.
TimLitS: Times Literary Supplement; L.
TItSett: Teologia; Brescia (Fac. teol. Italia settentrionale).
T-Iusi: Teología, Instituto Universitario Semin. Interdioc.; Caracas.
TJb: Theologisches Jahrbuch; Leipzig.
TkLima: Theologika; Lima, Univ. Incaica.
TKontext: Theologie im Kontext; Aachen. 0724-1682. ➤ TContext[o].
TLInf: Textuswissenschaft — Theologie — Hermeneutik — Linguistik — Literaturwissenschaft — Informatik; Tü.
TLond: Theology; London. 0040-571X.
TLZ: Theologische Literaturzeitung; Berlin. 0040-5671.
TolkNT: Tolkning [commentarius] av Nya Testamentet; Stockholm.
TopO: Topoi Orient-Occident; Lyon. (1, 1991).
TorJT: Toronto Journal of Theology.
TPast: Theologie en pastoraat; Zwolle.
TPhil: Theologie und Philosophie; Freiburg/Br. 0040-5655.
TPQ: Theologisch-praktische Quartalschrift; Linz, Ös. 0040-5663.
TPract: Theologia Practica; München/Hamburg. 0720-9525.
TR: Theologische Revue; Münster. 0040-568X.
TradErn: Tradition und Erneuerung (religiös-liberales Judentum); Bern.
Traditio; Bronx NY, Fordham Univ.

Tradition, orthodox Jewish; NY.
Trajecta, geschiedenis van het katholieke leven; Nijmegen. (1.1992).
Transformation ... evangelical Mission/ Ethics; Wynnewood PA. 0265-3788.
TRE: Theologische Realenzyklopädie; Berlin ➤ 517.
TRef: Theologia Reformata; Woerden.
TRevNE: ➤ NesTR.
TRicScR: Testi e ricerche di scienze religiose; Brescia.
TrierTZ: Trierer Theologische Zeitschrift; Trier. 0041-2945.
TrinJ: Trinity Journal; Deerfield IL. 0360-3032.
TrinSemR: Trinity Seminary Review; Columbus.
TrinT: Trinity theological journal, Singapore.
TrinUn [St/Mg] Rel: Trinity University Studies in Religion, San Antonio.
Tripod; Hong Kong.
TRu: Theologische Rundschau; Tübingen. 0040-5698.
Trumah: Wsb, Reichert (3,1992).
TS: Theological Studies; Baltimore. 0040-5639.
TSard: Theologica, annali Pont. Fac. Sardegna; Cagliari (1,1992).
TsGesch: Tijdschrift voor Geschiedenis; Groningen.
TsLtg: Tijdschrift voor Liturgie; Lv.
TsMeditA: Tijdschrift voor Mediterrane Archeologie; Lv. (5,1992).
TStAJud: Texte und Studien zum Antiken Judentum; Tübingen. 0721-8753.
TsTKi: Tidsskrift for Teologi og Kirke; Oslo. 0040-7194.
TsTNijm ➤ TvT.
TStR: Texts and Studies in Religion; Lewiston NY.
TSzem: Theologiai Szemle; Budapest. 0133-7599.
TTod: Theology Today; Princeton. 0040-5736.
TU: Texte und Untersuchungen, Geschichte der altchristlichen Literatur; Berlin.
Tü [ÄgBei] ThS: Tübinger [Ägyptologische Beiträge; Bonn, Habelt] Theologische Studien; Mainz, Grünewald.
[Tü]TQ: [Tübinger] Theologische Quartalschrift; Mü. 0342-1430.

TürkArk: Türk Arkeoloji dergisi; Ankara.
TUmAT: Texte aus der Umwelt des ATs; Gütersloh ➤ 518.
TVers: Theologische Versuche; Berlin. 0437-3014: 18 (1993) letztes.
TViat: Theologia Viatorum; SAfr.
TVida: Teología y Vida; Santiago, Chile. 0049-3449.
TvT [= TsTNijm]: Tijdschrift voor Theologie; Nijmegen. 0168-9959.
TWAT: Theologisches Wörterbuch zum Alten Testament; Stu ➤ 519.
TWiss: Theologische Wissenschaft, Sammelwerk für Studium und Beruf; Stu.
TWNT: Theologisches Wörterbuch zum NT; Stuttgart (➤ GLNT; TDNT).
TXav: Theologica Xaveriana; Bogotá.
TxK: Texte und Kontexte (Exegese); Stuttgart.
Tyche, Beiträge zur alten Geschichte, Papyrologie und Epigraphik; Wien.
Tychique (Chemin Neuf); Lyon.
TyndB: Tyndale Bulletin; Cambridge.
TZBas: Theologische Zeitschrift; Basel. 0040-5741.
UF: Ugarit-Forschungen; Kevelaer/ Neukirchen. 0342-2356.
Universitas; 1. Stuttgart. 0041-9079; 2. Bogotá. 0041-9060.
UnivT: Universale Teologica; Brescia.
UnSa: Una Sancta: 1. Augsburg-Meitingen; 2. Brooklyn.
UnSemQ: Union Seminary Quarterly Review; New York.
UPA: University Press of America; Wsh/ Lanham MD.
Update [religious trends]; Aarhus.
URM: Ultimate Reality and Meaning; Toronto.
USCathH: U.S. Catholic Historian; Baltimore. 0735-8318. (10,1992).
VAeg: Varia Aegyptiaca; San Antonio. 0887-4026.
VBGed: Verklaring van een Bijbelgedeelte; Kampen.
VComRel: La vie des communautés religieuses; Montréal.
VDI: ❸ Vestnik Drevnej Istorii; Moskva. 0321-0391.
Veleia, (pre-) historia, filología clásicas; Vitoria-Gasteiz, Univ. P. Vasco.

Verbum; 1. SVD; R;-2. Nancy.
Veritas; Porto Alegre, Univ. Católica.
VerkF: Verkündigung und Forschung; München. 0342-2410.
VerVid: Verdad y Vida; M. 0042-3718.
VestB: Vestigia Biblica; Hamburg.
VetChr: Vetera Christianorum; Bari.
Viator, Medieval and Renaissance studies; Berkeley. 0083-5897.
Vidyajyoti (Theology); Ranchi.
VieCons: La Vie Consacrée; P/Bru.
VigChr: Vigiliae Christianae; Leiden. 0042-6032.
ViMon: Vita Monastica; Arezzo.
ViPe: Vita e Pensiero: Mi, S. Cuore.
VisLang: Visible Language; Cleveland.
VisRel: Visible Religion, annual for iconography; Leiden. 0169-5606.
VitaCons: Vita Consacrata; Milano.
Vivarium; Catanzaro (1,1993).
VivH: Vivens Homo, scienze rel.; F.
VizVrem: Ⓥ Vizantijskij Vremennik; Moskva. 0136-7358.
VO: Vicino Oriente; Roma.
Vocation; Paris.
VoicesTW: Voices from the Third World; Colombo, Sri Lanka. (15, 1992).
VoxEvca: Vox Evangelica; London. 0263-6786.
VoxEvi: Vox Evangelii; Buenos Aires.
VoxRef: Vox Reformata; Geelong, Australia.
VoxScr: Vox Scripturae; São Paulo. 0104-0073. (2,1992).
VoxTh: Vox Theologica; Assen.
VSp: La Vie Spirituelle; Paris. 0042-4935; ⇥ Supplément. 0083-5859.
VT: Vetus Testamentum; Leiden. 0042-4935.
WAfEc: West African Journal of Ecclesial Studies; Ibadan (3,1991).
WDienst: Wort und Dienst; Bielefeld. 0342-3085.
WegFor: Wege der Forschung; Da, Wiss.
WeltOr: Welt des Orients; Göttingen. 0043-2547.
WesleyTJ: Wesleyan Theological Journal; Marion IN. 0092-4245.
WestTJ: Westminster Theological Journal; Philadelphia. 0043-4388.
WEvent: Word + Event; Stuttgart.
WienerSt: Wiener Studien; Wien.

WisLu: Wisconsin Lutheran Quarterly; Mequon. (88,1991).
Wiss: Wissenschaftliche Buchhandlung; Da.
WissPrax: Wissenschaft und Praxis in Kirche und Gesellschaft; Göttingen.
WissWeish: Wissenschaft und Weisheit; Mü-Gladbach. 0043-678X.
WM: Wissenschaftliche Monographien zum Alten/Neuen Testament; Neukirchen.
WoAnt: Wort und Antwort; Mainz.
Word and Spirit; Still River MA.
WorldArch: World Archaeology; Henley.
World Spirituality ⇥ EWSp.
Worship; St. John's Abbey, Collegeville, Minn. 0043-9414.
WrocST: Wrocławskie Studia Teologiczne / Colloquium Salutis; Wrocław. 0239-7714.
WUNT: Wissenschaftliche Untersuchungen zum NT; Tübingen.
WVDOG: Wissenschaftliche Veröffentlichungen der Deutschen Orient-Gesellschaft; Berlin.
WWorld: Word and World; St. Paul.
WZ: Wissenschaftliche Zeitschrift [... Univ.].
WZKM: Wiener Zeitschrift für die Kunde des Morgenlandes; Wien. 0084-0076.
Xenia [latina]; R, Bretschneider. (1, 1992).
Xilotl, revista nicaraguense de teología.
Xipe-Totek, ... filosofía, ciencias, acción social; Guadalajara, Méx (1, 1992).
YaleClas: Yale Classical Studies; NHv.
Yuval: Studies of the Jewish Music Research Centre [incl. Psalms]; Jerusalem.
ZäSpr: Zeitschrift für Ägyptische Sprache und Altertumskunde; Berlin. 0044-216X.
ZAHeb: Zeitschrift für Althebraistik; Stuttgart. 0932-4461.
ZAss: Zeitschrift für Assyriologie & Vorderasiatische Archäologie; Berlin. 0048-5299.
ZAW: Zeitschrift für die Alttestamentliche Wissenschaft; Berlin. 0044-2526.
ZDialekT: Zeitschrift für dialektische Theologie; Kampen.

ZDMG: Zeitschrift der Deutschen Morgenländischen Gesellschaft; Wiesbaden.
ZDPV: Zeitschrift des Deutschen Palästina-Vereins; Stu. 0012-1169.
ZeichZt: Die Zeichen der Zeit, Evangelische Monatschrift; Berlin.
Zeitwende (Die neue Furche); Gü. Zephyrus; Salamanca. 0514-7336.
ZEthnol: Zeitschrift für Ethnologie; Braunschweig. 0044-2666.
ZEvEthik: Zeitschrift für Evangelische Ethik; Gütersloh. 0044-2674.
ZfArch: Zeitschrift für Archäologie: Berlin. 0044-233X.
ZfG: Zeitschrift für Geschichtswissenschaft; Berlin. 0044-2828.
ZGPred: Zeitschrift für Gottesdienst und Predigt; Gütersloh.
Zion: ❶; Jerusalem. 0044-4758.
ZIT: Zeitschriften Inhaltsdienst Theologie; Tübingen. 0340-8361.
ZKG: Zeitschrift für Kirchengeschichte; Stuttgart. 0044-2985.
ZkT: Zeitschrift für katholische Theologie; Innsbruck. 0044-2895.
ZMedEth: Zeitschrift für medizinische Ethik [= Arzt und Christ bis 39 (1993)]: Salzburg.

ZMissRW: Zeitschrift für Missionswissenschaft und Religionswissenschaft; Münster. 0044-3123.
ZnTg: Zeitschrift für neuere Theologiegeschichte; B/NY. 0948-3592 (1, 1994).
ZNW: Zeitschrift für die Neutestamentliche Wissenschaft & Kunde des Alten Christentums; B. 0044-2615.
ZPapEp: Zeitschrift für Papyrologie und Epigraphik; Bonn. 0084-5388.
ZPraxRU: Zeitschrift für die Praxis des Religionsunterrichts; Stuttgart.
ZRelW: Zeitschrift für Religionswissenschaft; Marburg (1,1993).
ZRGg: Zeitschrift für Religions- und Geistesgeschichte; Köln. 0044-3441.
ZSavR: Zeitschrift der Savigny-Stiftung (Romanistische) Rechtsgeschichte: Weimar. 0323-4096.
ZSprW: Zeitschrift für Sprachwissenschaft; Göttingen. 0721-9067.
ZTK: Zeitschrift für Theologie und Kirche; Tübingen. 0513-9147.
Zwingliana; Zürich.
Zygon; Winter Park FL. 0591-2385.

Below are 276ᶠ, 153 miscellanea, and 444 other compilations or Acta

I. Bibliographica

A1 *Opera collecta* .1 **Festschriften**, memorials

1 ᴱ*Begg* C.T., Festschriften and Collected Essays: OTAbs 17 (1994) 196-9.422-6.646-651; – Collected essays: CBQ 56 (1994) 167-192.393-411.615-627.814-836; – JBL 113 (1994) 165-176.361-372.551-560; Collected Studies: AJS 19 (1994) 115-125.301-316; – *Langlamet* François, Recueils et mélanges: RB 101 (1944) 130-8.288-293.428-442.
1* *Thiel* Winfried, Alttestamentliche Forschung in Fest- und Gedenkschriften: TRu 59 (1994) 225-251.
2 RIT: ᴱ*Treesh* Erica, Religion Index Two: multi-author works, (vol. 19) for 1992. – Evanston 1994, ATLA, 0149-8436. pp. xiii-xxiv, titles indexed (including Festschrifts, not separately).

2* ABRAHAM [Andrzejewski] Roy C. (1890-1963) mem. [Symposium 1990 → 9,541*] ᴱ*Jagger* Philip J. L 1992, School of Oriental and African Studies. ix-202 p. – ᴿBSO 57 (1994) 252 (N. *Skinner*); OLZ 89 (1994) 447 (Irmtraud *Herms*).

3 ACHBERGER Leopold mem.: Ökumenisches Forum: Grazer Ökumene 16. Graz 1993. 316 p. – ᴿTAth 65 (1994) 185-8 (E. A. *Theodorou*, ⊙).
4 AERTS Willem J.: Polyphonia byzantina, ᴱHokwerda H., *al.* Mdv-Groningana 13. Groningen 1993, Forsten. ix-383 p. RHE 90, 263*.
5 ALLEN Judson Boyce mem., Two uses of manuscripts in literary studies, ᴱMorse Charlotte C., *al.*: StMdvCu 31. Kalamazoo 1992, Western Mich. Univ. xxiv-338 p. 4 pl.; $35; pa. $15. – ᴿSpeculum 69 (1994) 608 (tit. pp.).
6 AVERY Peter W.: History and Literature in Iran: ᴱMelville Charles, Pembroke Papers 1. C 1994 [reissue of 1990 title Persian and Islamic studies], Univ. Centre ME Studies. iii-234 p. £39.50. – ᴿBSO 57 (1994) 650s (Isabel *Miller*).
7 BAER Klaus, 1930-1987, mem.: For his Ka, ᴱSilverman David P.: SAOC 55. Ch 1994, Univ. Oriental Inst. xviii-332 p.; portr. 0-9189-8693-1. 21 art.; ➤ vol. 9.
8 BALDERMANN Ingo: ...dann werden wir sein wie die Träumenden, 65. Gb., ᴱGreve Astrid, *Albrecht* Folker, *al.* Siegen 1994, Univ. 3-9801926-2-8. 3056; U4.
9 BALIL ILLANA Alberto [† 23.VIII.1989] mem. [not = 6,9]: Finis terrae, ᴱAcuña Castroviejo Fernando, *al.* Santiago de Compostela 1992, Univ. 438 p.
10 BARR James: Language, theology, and the Bible, ᴱBalentine Samuel E., *Barton* John. Ox 1994, Clarendon. xiv-418 p.; 3-16-26 on Barr; 398-413 bibliog. 0-19-826191-8. 25 art., infra. [BL 95,7, D. J. *Reimer*; JBL 107,364, tit. pp.; JTS 46,196-8, R. *Coggins*; RelStR 21,125, C. *Bernas*]. – ᴿNBlackf 75 (1994) 492-4 (Susan *Gillingham*).
10* BASABE TERREROS E. (1893-1977) centenario = Perficit, Estudios clásicos 2/17 (1987-93); p. 73-79, *Garcia* Bernardo, *Dal* en el AT; ➤ 9964*.
11 BATLLORI Miquel: La cultura del Renaixement: Manuscrits 1. Barc 1993, Univ. Autónoma. 194 p. [RHE 90, 263*].
11* BECK Heinrich: Sein — Erkennen — Handeln; interkulturelle, ontologische und ethische Perspektiven, 65. Gb., ᴱSchadel Erwin, *Voigt* Uwe: Triadik 7. Fra 1994, Lang. 854 p. DM 178. 3-631-46466-5.
12 BÉKÉS Gerard, OSB [= Gellert]: *a*) Miscellanea 80 ann., ᴱSzennay András, *Somorja* Ádám. Pannonhalma 1994s, Katolikus Szemle. I. 360 p.; II.; bibliog. II. 63-82; ISBN 963-00-1843-8. – *b*) Az egység szolgálatában = (Unum omnes in Christo) In unitatis servitio 1994 Hms. A Katolikus Szemle (1994, 3s) 359 p. ISSN 1218-1374 [Not a tr.; all different; Gregorianum 76, 767, M. *Szentmártoni*, on both].
12* BELARDI Walter: Miscellanea di studi linguistici, ᴱCipriano P., *al.*, R 1994, Calamo. I. xii-349 p. bibliog. p. xv-xxxii; II. 0392-9361. p. 533-1108. – 31 + 31 art. 4 infra.
13 *a*) BELLO Antonio: Studi, ᴱDe Palma L. M. Archivio dioc. quad. 14. Molfetta 1992, Mezzina. [RHE 90, 62*].
— *b*) BERNARDUS Magister... of Clairvaux; nonacentenary, ᴱSommerfeldt John R. Kalamazoo MI 1992, Cistercian. 578 p. $49. – ᴿHeythJ 35 (1994) 221 (C. *Morris*).
— *c*) BERNHARD Ludger O.S.B.: Liebe zum Wort; Beiträge zur klassischen und biblischen Philologie, 80. Gb., ᴱReiterer Friedrich V., *Eder* Petrus. Salzburg 1993, Müller. 298 p. 3-7013-0856-0 [RelStR 21,242, J. T. *Fitzgerald*].
14 BERRIOT F.: Spiritualités, hétérodoxes et imaginaires; études sur le Moyen Âge et la Renaissance. St-Étienne 1994, Univ. 420 p. F 200 [RHE 90, 62*].
14* BERTSCH Ludwig, Inkulturation und Kontextualität; Theologien im weltweiten Austausch, 65. Gb., ᴱPankoke-Schenk Monika, *Evers* Georg.

Fra 1994, Knecht. 346 p.; portr. DM 68. 3-7820-0705-0 [ZkT 117,495, H. B. *Meyer*].
15 BEYERLIN Walter: Neue Wege der Psalmenforschung [p. 1-200 < SBL-Internat. Münster, 10 art. + 10 others, all infra], ᴱSeybold Klaus, *Zenger* Erich: BibSt 1. FrB 1994, Herder. x-392 p.; 391 Beyerlin psalms-bibliog. 3-451-23151-4 [RB 102,446, tit. pp.; RBibArg 57, 239-242, A. *Ricciardi*].
15* BIANCHI Ugo: *Agathē elpis*, studi storico-religiosi in onore, ᴱSfameni Gasparro Giulia. R 1994, Bretschneider. 551 p. 88-7062-835-3. 35 art.
16 BIROT Maurice mém.: Florilegium marianum II, ᴱCharpin Dominique, *Durand* Jean-Marie: NABU 3. P 1994, SEPOA. 355 p.
16* BLÁZQUEZ José María, Homenaje, ᴱMangas J., *Alvar* J. M Ed. Clásicas. I 1993, 464 p.; 95 fig.; II 1994, 519 p.; 135 fig. [Gerión 13, 413s, F. *Corriente*].
17 BÖHLIG Alexandre; 80. Gb.: BSACopte 33 (1994) 1-23, phot. Biobibliog.
BOESSNECK Joachim mem., Archäozoologie 1993/4 ➤ 459.
18 BRANDENBURG Hugo: Bild- und Formensprache der spätantiken Kunst, 65. Gb., ᴱJordan-Ruwe Martina, *Real* Ulrich: Boreas 17 (1994). iv-307 p.; 26 pl., portr.; Bibliog. iii-iv. 0344-310X. 17 art. ➤ 3642.
18* BREGLIA Laura: AnnItNum 38-41 (1991-4).
19 BROWN Frank E. [1908-1988] mem.: Eius virtutis studiosi; classical and postclassical studies, ᴱScott Russell T. & Anne R.; StHistArt 43. Symposium 23 [Rome 6.VI.1989, Wsh 17-18.XI.1989]. Hanover 1993, Univ. Press of New England. 502 p.; ill.
19* BURGER Michael: Mélanges de philosophie et de littérature médiévales, ᴱCerquiglini-Toulrt Jacqueline, *Collet* Olivier: Publ. Romanes 208. Genève 1994, Droz. 363 p. [Speculum 70,227].
20 CAHEN Claude [1991] mém.: Itinéraires d'Orient, ᴱCuriel Raoul, *Gyselen* Rika: Res Orientales 6. Bures/Yvette 1994. 442 p. 2-9508-2660-1. – ᴿWZKM 84 (1994) 354 (Gisela *Prochàzka-Eisl*).
21 CAMPBELL Donald K.: Integrity of heart, skillfulness of hands; biblical and leadership studies, ᴱDyer Charles H., *Zuck* Roy B. GR 1994, Baker. 373 p. 0-8010-3027-5. – 27 art., 16 infra.
21* CAMPBELL George: Georgica, Greek studies, ᴱFlower M. A., *Toher* M.: BuSupp 58. L 1991, Inst. Clas. St. 192 p. – ᴿRÉG 107 (1994) 240s (J. *Irigoin*).
22 *a*) CASCIARO José M., Biblia, exégesis y cultura, ᴱAranda G., *al*.: ColTeol 42. Pamplona 1994, Univ. Navarra (EUNSA). 763 p.; bibliog. 23-35 (V. *Balaguer*). 84-313-1274-2. 46 art.; 31 infra [AcPIB 9,893; RB 102,440, tit. pp.].
— *b*) CESTARO Antonio, Studi di storia del Mezzogiorno, ᴱVolpe F.: PiccolaBtMedit 10. Genova 1993, Osanna. 442 p.
— *c*) CHANTRAINE Heinrich: E fontibus haurire; Beiträge zur römischen Geschichte und zu ihren Hilfswissenschaften, 65. Gb.: StGKuAlt mg 1. Pd 1994, Schöningh. xii-405 p. DM 54. [RHE 90,263*].
CHANTRAINE Pierre mém.: La langue et les textes 1989/92 ➤ 429, ᴱLétoublon F.
23 CHAUNU Pierre: La vie, la mort, la foi, le temps, ᴱBardet J.-P., *Foisil* M. P 1993, PUF. xxiv-760 p. F 1350 [RHE 90, 264*].
23* CHEVALLIER Raymond: Mélanges I. Présence des idées romaines dans le monde d'aujourd'hui, ᴱTernes Charles M., *al*.: Caesarodunum coll. 28 bis / BAntLux 23. Luxembourg 1994.
24 *a*) CHRIST Günther: Beiträge zu Kirche, Staat und Geistesleben, 65. Gb.,

ᴱSchröder J.; BeitReichsK 14. Stu 1994, Steiner. x-362p.; ill. DM144 [RHE 90,264*].
— b) CLARA: Centenario de Santa Clara: Las Clarisas de España y Portugal: Verdad y Vida 52 (1994) 946p.
— c) COLLINSON Patrick: Religion, culture and society in early modern Britain, ᴱFletcher A., Roberts P. C 1994, Univ. xx-372p.; 10 fig. [RHE 89,248*]. – ᴿExpTim 106 (1994s) 215 (J.A. Newton: on Puritans; high praise).
25 CONNELL Desmond, abp. Dublin: At the heart of the real; philosophical essays, ᴱO'Rourke Fran. Dublin 1992, Irish Academic. xx-427p. – ᴿTPhil 69 (1994) 434-6 (W. Löffler).
26 COOK James I.: RefR 48,3 (1994s) 165-238; portr.; bibliog. p.239-242.
27 COQUIN Marie-Georges, Christianisme d'Égypte, ᴱRosenstiehl Jean-Marc: BtCopte Cah 9. P c.1994, Peeters. xvi-169p. Fb1100. 2-87723-178-X / 90-6831-663-X [RelStR 21,331, B.A. Pearson].
28 CORMILLY-WEINBERGER Moshe: Jews in the Hungarian economy, 1760-1945, 80th b., ᴱSilber Michael K. J 1992, Magnes. 965-223-783-3 [ZIT 92, XVIII].
28* CORSARO Francesco: Studi classici e cristiani. Catania 1994, Univ. [OTAbs, 18,537].
29 CORSINI Eugenio: Voce di molte acque, present. Barberi Squaroni G. T 1994, Zamorani. xxxiv-622p.; phot.; bibliog. xxi-xxvii (i suoi disegni xxix-xxxiv). 88-7158-034-6. 51 art., 5 infra.
30 COUTURIER Guy: 'Où demeures-tu?' (Jn 1,38), 75 ans, ᴱPetit Jean-Claude. Québec 1994, Fides. vi-572p.; bibliog. 553-8. C$40. 2-7021-1065-1. [OTAbs 18, p.141 with renvoi to 17 art. summarized; RB 102,292; 29 titles pp.; ZAW 107,537, tit. pp.; JStJud 26,215, J. Duhaime]; 28 art.; 12 infra, 12 in 1995.
31 DAMME Dirk Van: Peregrina curiositas; eine Reise durch den orbis antiquus, ᴰKessler Andreas, al.: NOrb 27. FrS 1994, Univ. x-318p. 3-7278-0928-0. [RelStR 21,141, J.T. Fitzgerald; ZAW 107,362, nur 77-116, Uehlinger C., Ahab].
31* DAUTZENBERG Gerhard: Nach den Anfängen fragen. 60. Gb., ᴱMeyer Cornelius, Müller Karlheinz, Schmalenberg Gerhard. Giessen 1994, Ev.-Kath. Fak. 810p. DM60. 3-923690-07-X. [TR 90,515, tit. pp.]. – 43 art., 36 infra. – ᴿETL 70 (1994) 457s (F. Neirynck).
32 a) DAVIDSON Robert: Words at work; using the Bible in the academy, the community and the churches, ᴱCarroll Robert P., Hunter Alastair G. 1994, Trinity St. Mongo. xvi-155p. £10. 0-9522-3110-7. [BL 95,82, J. Goldingay praises Carroll on M. THATCHER's 'Sermon on the Mound'; TLond 98,303, L. Houlden]. – ᴿExpTim 106 (1994s) 86 [C.S. Rodd].
— b) DAVIS Natalie Zenon: Culture and identity in early modern Europe, 1500-1800, ᴱDiefendorf B.B., Hesse C. AA 1993. Univ. Michigan. x-280p. [RHE 90,264*; SixtC 26,254, L.H. Zuck].
— c) DETWEILER Robert: In good company, ᴱJasper David, Ledbetter Mark. Atlanta 1994, Scholars. xviii-455p. $45 [LitTOx 9,341, J.S. Fountain].
33 a) DÍAZ MERCHÁN Gabino, obispo 25 años: StOvet 22 (1994); portr. 84-404-3076-0.
— b) DÍAZ Y DÍAZ Manuel C., Evphrosyne 22 (Lisboa 1994), 518p.; portr. bibliog. 357-367 (Manuela Dominguez); 33 art.
— c) DÖRING Heinrich, Religiöse Erfahrung und theologische Reflexion, 60. Gb., ᴱKreiner Armin, Schmidt-Leukel Perry. Pd 1993, Bonifatius. 402p.; Bibliog. 395-400 (Kattner Gerda). DM58. 3-87088-772-9 [TR

91,81: 24 tit. pp. (175-194; *Beinert* W., Angst-Macht-Kirche); ZkT 117, 355, K. H. *Neufeld*]. – ᴿArTGran 57 (1994) 449s (R. *Franco*).

— *d*) DOYLE A. I.: Late-Medieval religious texts and their transmission: Woodbridge/Rochester 1994, Boydell &B. x-198 p. $63 [Speculum 70,987, tit. pp.].

DURANTE Marcello, † 1992 mem. → 450.

— *e*) ᶠEBELING Jürgen: Wahrheit der Schrift — Wahrheit der Auslegung, ein Zürcher Vertragsreihe, 80. Gb., ᴱGeisser H. F., *al.* Z 1993, Th. V. 352 p. Sf 90 [TLZ 120,218]. 3-290-10917-8.

— *f*) ECKERMANN Willigis: Traditio augustiniana, Studien über AUGUSTINUS und seine Rezeption, 60. Gb., ᴱZumkeller Adolar, *Krümmel* Achim: Cassiciacum 46. Wü 1994, Augustinus. xliii-597 p. DM 130. 3-7613-0176-6 [TR 91,361, tit. pp.; TPQ 143,307, F. *Reisinger*].

— *g*) EHRENKREUTZ Andrew S.: The Jihād and its times, ᴱDajani-Shakeel Hadja, *Messier* Ronald A. AA 1991, Univ. Michigan. iv-135 p.; biobibliog. $13 pa. – ᴿJAOS 114 (1994) 113s (R. *Amitai-Preuss*: expert in Islamic monetary history, but also Saladin; articles here mostly on Crusades).

34 *a*) Eichstätt Theol. Fak.: I. 150 Jahre; ᴱGlässer A., II. Vom Bischöflichen Lyzeum zur Katholischen Universität, ᴱMüller R. A.: Eichstätter Studien 33. Regensburg 1993, Pustet. 350 p.; 416 p. DM 68. [RHE 90,565, R. *Aubert*).

— *b*) ENGELS Odilo: Köln – Stadt und Bistum in Kirche und Reich des Mittelalters, 65. Gb., ᴱVollrath Hanna, *Weinfurter* Stefan: KölnHistAbh 39. Köln 1993, Böhlau. xiv-796 p. DM 148. 3-412-12492-3. 23 art. [TR 91,231, P. *Engelbert*].

— *c*) Les Études classiques, 60 anniv.: Miscellanea linguistica graeco-latina, ᴱIsebaert L.: ÉtClas coll. 7. Namur 1993. 358 p. – ᴿBSLP 89,2 (1994) 192-8 (A. *Blanc*).

— *d*) FANGMEIER Jürgen; Das Wort, das in Erstaunen setzt, Dankesgabe ᴱJeschke Dieter, *al.*; TVG Mg. Wu 1994, Brockhaus. 319 p. DM 58. 3-417-29395-2. 30 art.; 10 infra [TR 91,359, tit. pp.].

— *e*) FIEY Jean-Maurice mém. [1914-1995]: Univ. S. Joseph, Annales du Departement de Lettres Arabes 6B. Beyrouth 1991s, Univ. S. Joseph. → 3070*b*.

35 FREY Otto-Herman, 65. Gb., ᴱDobiat Claus: Marburger StVFrühG 16. Marburg 1994, Hitzerath. 715 p.; ill.; bibliog. 11-17, diss.ᴰ 18-21. 3-89398-159-4. 44 art.; 7 infra.

35* FRÉZOULS Edmond: Hommage: ᴱDardaine Sylvie, *Morant* Marie-José; Ktema 17 (1992) 317 p.; portr.; bibliog. 7-13.

36 FUĆAK Marian J., 1932-1992, in mem.: BogSmot 64 (1994); portr.; biobibliog. 5-17 (Z. I. *Herman*) 20 art. bibl., infra; 19 hist.-theol.

37 GALLAVOTTI Carlo, † 9.II.1993 mem.: RivCuClasMdv 36 (1994). 391 p.; v-xxx bibliog.

38 GAMPER Arnold, 70 Gb., ᴱFischer Georg, *Oesch* Josef M.: ZkT 116,4 (1994) 387-493; portr.

39 GARCIA PALAU Sebastián: Miscellanea. Palma de Mallorca 1989, Moll. 119 p. [CiuD 206 (1993) 258].

40 GEORGI Dieter: *Quid ergo Athenis et Hierosolymis?*; Religious propaganda and missionary competition in the New Testament world, ᴱBormann Lukas, *Del Tredici* Kelly, *Standhartinger* Angela: NT supp. 74. Leiden 1994, Brill. xiii-570 p.; portr.; bibliog. 551-8. *f* 225. 90-04-10049-0. 25 art., infra. [BL 95,9, D. J. *Bryan*; JBL 107,568, tit. pp.; ETL

71, 227-230, J. *Verheyden*; RelStR 21,141, F. W. *Burnett*; JTS 46,662, M. *Goulder*: some polysyllabic rhetoric conveys only anger].

41 *a*) GEROV Borisi: Studia in honorem, ᴱTaceva Margarita, *Bojadžiev* Dimitar: Univ. Serdicensis, Cathedra Thracologiae. Sofia. 266 p.; portr. Biobibliog. 7-11-16 (*Velkov* V.; *Boteva* D.). 33 art.; 2 infra.

— *b*) GIEROWSKI J. A.: The Jews in Poland, I, 70 b. Kraków 1992, Univ. 510 p. 38 art. [Judaica 50 (1994) 106-8 tit. pp.].

— *c*) Gifford Lectures [105 years, 'Glasgow centenary'], Humanity, environment and God, ᴱSpurway Neil. L 1993, Blackwell. 280 p. $41 [RelStR 21,208, Mary *Gerhart*).

42 GIGANTE Marcello: Storia, poesia e pensiero nel mondo antico, ᴱDel Franco Francisco: Saggi 46. N 1994, Bibliopolis. xxiii-640 p. 88-7088-283-3. – 57 art., 1 infra, 7 in 1995.

43 GIRARD René: A tribute; 70th b., ᴱHamerton-Kelly Robert = Contagion 1 (1994). xii-183 p. $32; individuals $8. 1075-7201. 12 art.; 3 infra.

44 GNEUSS Helmut: Words, texts and manuscripts; Studies in Anglo-Saxon culture, 65th b., ᴱKorhammer Michael, *al.* Woodbridge, Suffolk/ Rochester NY 1992, Boydell & B. xv-498 p.; 2 fig.; 11 pl. $79. – ᴿSpeculum 69 (1994) 606s (tit. pp.).

45 GOULDER Michael D.: Crossing the boundaries; essays in biblical interpretation, ᴱPorter Stanley J., *al.*: BInterp series, 8. Leiden 1994, Brill. xviii-381 p.; bibliog. 379-381. *f*145. 90-04-10131-4 [BL 95,20, J. L. *North*; TLond 98,304s (M. *Casey*)]. – 24 art., infra. – ᴿExpTim 106 (1994s) 125 (C. S. *Rodd*).

46 GUNDRY Robert B.: To tell the mystery; essays on NT eschatology, ᴱSchmidt Thomas E., *Silva* Moisés: jNsu 100. Shf 1994, Academic. 266 p.; portr.; bibliog. 17-20. £37.50. 1-85075-436-1. [JTS 46,665, J. M. *Court*].

48 HAHN István 1913-1984, Gedenkschrift, ᴱNémeth György. Budapest 1993, Univ. 293 p.; phot.; bibliog. 271-291. 19 art. 6 infra.

49 HALL Alan S. [26.X.1931-12.XII.1986], mem.: Studies in the history and topography of Lycia and Pisidia [3 by him + 3], ᴱFrench David: Mg 19. Ankara 1994, British Institute. 118 p.; 8 fig.; 62 pl.; bibliog. ix. 1-898249-03-2.

50 HAMMEL Hildebrecht: Charisteria, 85. Gb. ᴱKiefner Gottfried: Spudasmata 40. Hildesheim 1988, Olms. 301 p.; 9 pl.

51 HARLFINGER Dieter: Symbolae Berolinenses, 50. Gb., ᴱBerger Friederike. Amst 1993, Hakkert. vii-459 p.

52 HAUCK Karl: Iconologia sacra; Mythos, Bildkunst und Dichtung in der Religions- und Sozialgeschichte Alteuropas, 75. Gb., ᴱKeller Hagen, *Staubach* Nikolaus: ArbFrühMA 23. B 1994, de Gruyter. xii-667 p.; portr.; 106 phot.; Bibliog. 651-667. 3-11-013255-9. 35 art.; 3 infra.

53 HAUG Walter, WACHINGER Burghart, Fs. ᴱJanota Johannes. Tü 1992, Niemeyer. 1. ix-527 p.; 2. p. 529-1261. DM 432: ➤ 14193, HIERONYMUS' Briefe. – ᴿSpeculum 69 (1994) 931 (tit. pp.).

53* HEERS Jacques, Villes et sociétés urbaines au moyen âge, CuCivMdv 11. P 1994, Sorbonne. 315 p.; portr. F 175. 29 art. [Speculum 70,990, tit. pp.]. – ᴿRHist 292 (1994) 469s (R. *Fossier*).

54 *a*) HEINEMEYER Walter: MABILLONs Spur, 80. Gb. ᴱRock Peter. Marburg 1992, Inst. Hist. Hilfswissenschaften. ix-410 p., ill. DM 60. – ᴿHZ 259 (1994) 126s (T. *Kölzer*); Speculum 69 (1994) 882s (J. M. *McCulloch*; largely on manuscripts).

— *b*) HEMPEL Johannes: Kirche als Kulturfaktor, ᴱKühn F. (Univ. Leipzig, Theol. Fak.). Hannover 1994, Luther. 283 p. DM 24,80. 3-7859-0691-9 [TLZ 120, 1059-63, J. *Rogge*].

— c) HENZ Hubert: Gegenwart und Zukunft christlicher Erziehung, 68. Gb., EScharl W., *Poggeler* F.: Christliche Pädagogik 4. Wü 1994, Echter. 434 p. DM 56. – RHE 90,264*.
— d) HEYER Friedrich: Horizonte der Christenheit, 85. Gb. Erlangen 1994, Lehrstuhl-GTh. 629 p. 3-925-11933-X [TLZ 120,971, W. *Schwaigert*].
— e) HOULDEN Leslie: Resurrection, EBarton Stephen, *Stanton* Graham. L 1994, SPCK. xiii-233 p. £17.50. 0-281-04775-8. 19 art. [Tablet 249,226, H. *Wansbrough*; TLond 98,305s, P. *Baelz*]. – RExpTim 106 (1994s) 86 [C. S. *Rodd*].
55 HROUDA Barthel: Beiträge zur altorientalischen Archäologie und Altertumskunde; 65. Gb.; ECalmeyer Peter, *al*. Wsb 1994, Harrassowitz. ix-341 p.; Bibliog. 329-341 (I. *Gerlach*). 3-447-03503-X. – 40 art., 25 infra.
57 HÜNERMANN Peter: Kirche und Theologie im kulturellen Dialog, EFraling Bernhard, *al*. FrB 1994, Herder. 494 p.; bibliog. 476-492 (*Fliethmann* Thomas). DM 78. 3-451-23380-4 [26 art.: TR 90,511, tit. pp.]. 5 infra.
58 HUNGER Herbert: *Andrias*, 80. Gb., EHörandner Wolfram, *al*., JbÖsByz 44 (1994) [RHE 90,264*].
59 HURLEY Denis abp.: Shaping English liturgy, EFinn Peter C., *Schellman* James M. pastoral. 493 p. $40. – RCanadCath 12,5 (1994) 29 (R. K. *Sesoltz*).
59* JAHNOW Hedwig: Feministische Hermeneutik und Erstes Testament; Analysen und Interpretationen: Marburg. Stu 1994, Kohlhammer. 167 p. DM 39,80. 3-17-013047-1 [OTAbs 18,383 with reference to 8 cited items].
60 a) JAL P.:   Présence de TITE-LIVE, EChevallier R., *Poignault* R.: Caesarodunum 27 bis. Tours 1994, Univ. Centre A. Piganiol. 310 p. – RBStLat 24 (1994) 265-7 (Antonella *Borgo*).
— b) JANAKI S. S.: Felicitation volume: Madras Journal of Oriental Research 56-62 (1992). xxxvii-440 p. rs 175. – RNumen 41 (1994) 105 (D. *Shulman*: 40 art., many on or in Sanskrit).
— c) JÁRDÁNYI-PAULOVICS István 1892-1952: AcClasDebrecen 30 (1994); 121-128 bibliog. (*Nagy* Mihály).
61 JASPER Ronald mem.: Liturgy in dialogue, EBradshaw Paul, *Spinks* Bryan. L 1993, SPCK. £15. 0-281-04734-0. [JTS 46,436, K. *Stevenson*].
61* KAISER Otto: 'Wer ist wie du, Herr, unter den Göttern?'; Studien zur Theologie und Religionsgeschichte Israels, 70 Gb., EKottsieper Ingo, *al*. Gö 1994, Vandenhoeck &R. xi-508 p. 3-525-53631-3. 35 art.; infra. [TR 91,272s & ZAW 107,370, tit. pp.].
62 KALOGIROU Johannes O.: *Timētikò aphierōma*, EZissis Theodoros, *al*. Thessaloniki 1992, Univ. 34 art. – RIkiZ 83 (1993) 190-192 (P. *Amiet*; p. 173.183 sein Beitrag, Aspekte des Unglaubens).
63 KAMIN Sarah zal. 16.IX.1989, aet. 51, mem. ❸; The Bible in the light of its interpreters, EJaphet Sara. J 1994, Magnes. 232 p.: portr. $43. 965-223-854-6. 37 art. ❸ [RB 192,449, tit. pp.; OTAbs 18,621, with summaries of 20 art.].
64 KARAGEORGHIS Vassos: Kypriakai spoudai 54s (1991s). Nicosia 1992, Imprinta. 374 p. 86 pl. – RRStFen 22 (1994) 147-151 (D. *Ciafaloni*).
65 KASSER Rodolphe: Coptology, past, present, and future, EGiversen S., *Krause* M., *Nagel* P.: OrLovAnal 61. Lv 1994, Peeters. xxvi-369 p.; bibliog. xiii-xxv. 90-6831-040-X. – 28 art.; 7 infra.
65* KENNEDY Elspeth: Shifts and transpositions in medieval narrative, EPratt Karen, *al*., Woodbridge/Rochester 1994, Boydell & B. xxi-206 p.; portr. $53. [Speculum 70,989, tit. pp.].

66 KHAFAGA Mohamed Saqr, memorial, 30th anniv., Classical papers,
ᴱEtman Ahmed. Cairo 1994, Univ. 128 p. + ❹210.
67 a) KING Philip J.: Scripture and other artifacts; essays on the Bible and
archaeology, ᴱCoogan Michael D., *Exum* J. Cheryl, *Stager* Lawrence E.;
(Managing) *Greene* Joseph A. Lvl 1994, Westminster-Knox. xxvii-
452 p.; ill.; portr.; bibliog. p. xxv-xxvii. $25. 0-664-22036-3. 24 art.;
infra. [BA 58,240 & BASOR 299,132, J. C. *Moyer*; RelStR 21,225, M. A.
Sweeney].
— b) KOTTJE Raymond: Aus Archiven und Bibliotheken, 65. Gb., ᴱMordek
Hubert: FreibBeit MAG 3. Fra 1992, Lang. xi-658 p. [RHE 90,506, G.
Fransen †].
— c) KRAFT Sigisbert: Christus Spes, Liturgie und Glaube im ökumenischen
Kontext, ᴱBerlis Angela; *Gerth* Klaus D. Fra 1994, Lang. xxviii-351 p.
DM 59. 3-631-46621-8 [TR 91,166].
68 LABUSCHAGNE C. J.: Studies in Deuteronomy, 65th b., ᴱGarcía Martínez
F., *al.*: VTSup 53. Leiden 1994, Brill. xii-305 p.; portr.; bibliog. 289-
294 (A. *Hilhorst*). 90-04-10052-0. 18 art. [BL 95,85, R. E. *Clements*;
ÉTRel 70,425, T. *Römer*; JTS 46,577, J. G. *McConville*; NRT 117,907,
J.-L. *Ska*; OTAbs 18,155, T. M. *Willis*; RB 102,294 & ZAW 107,170, tit.
pp.]. – ᴿEstE 69 (1994) 531-4 (E. *Pascual*).
69 LACEY Walter K.; Nile, Ilissos and Tiber, ᴱGray V. J. = Prudentia 26,1
(1994). 165 p.; phot.; viii-ix. biobibliog. v-ix. 10 art., 3 infra.
70 LAGA Carl: Philohistôr, 70 ann., ᴱSchoors A., *Deun* P. van: OrLovAnal
60. Lv 1994, Univ./Peeters. xv-580 p.; portr. [RHE 90,63*; ETL
71,277-280, A. Van *Roey* sur la séance Lv 19.XI.1994 et CCSG dirigé par
Laga]. 35 art., infra.
71 LAPSLEY James N.: The treasure of earthen vessels; explorations in
theological anthropology, ᴱChilds Brian H., *Waanders* David W. LVL
1994, W-Knox. vii-276 p. $20 [PrincSemBu 16,349, J. N. *Poling*).
72 LA TORRE Julio de: La justicia social, ᴱÁlvarez Verdes L., *Vidal* M.:
EstÉticaTeol 11. M 1993, Perpetuo Socorro. 527 p. [RHE 88,428*]. –
ᴿETL 70 (1994) 212s (J. *Étienne*).
72* LECLANT Jean: Hommages, ᴱBerger Catherine, *Clerc* Gisèle, *Grimal*
Nicolas: BtÉt 106. Le Caire 1994, IFAO. I. Études pharaoniques,
x-548 p.; portr.; ill.; II. Nubie, Soudan, Éthiopie; [vi-]432 p.; ill.; III.
Études isiaques, 503 p.; IV. Varia, 491 p. [bibliog. 429-491]. 42 + 43
+ 49 + 42 art. 23 infra. 2-7247-0137-2; -35-6; -38-0; -39-9.
73 LE GLAY Marcel, 7.V.1920-16.VIII.1992, mém.; L'Afrique, la Gaule, la
religione à l'époque romaine, ᴱLe Bohec Yann: Coll. Latomus 226. Bru
1994. xxx-876 p.; portr. bibliog. xix-xxx.
LEHKOWICZ Nikolaus, Katholische Universität 1993 ➤ 1012.
74 LEYERLE John, The centre and its compass; studies in medieval literature,
ᴱ*Taylor* R. A., *al.*: StMdvCu 33. Kalamazoo 1993, West Michigan Univ.
xii-474 p.; ill. $40; pa. $20 [RHE 90,63*; Speculum 70,740, tit. pp.].
75 LIEBMANN Maximilian: Kirche in bewegter Zeit; Beiträge zur Geschichte
der Kirche in der Zeit der Reformation und des 20. Jahrhunderts, 60. Gb.,
ᴱZinnhobler Rudolf, *al.*, Graz 1994, Styria. 495 p. Sch 590. 3-7012-
0028-9 [TPQ 143,436, F. *Schragl*; TLZ 100,618, S. *Beilner*].
76 a) LONGENECKER Richard N.: Gospel in Paul; studies on Corinthians,
Galatians and Romans, ᴱJervis L. Ann, *Richardson* Peter: jNsu 108. Shf
1994, Academic. 412 p.; bibliog. 18-20. £40. 1-85075-505-1. – 16 art.;
infra [NTAbs 39, p. 334; RelStR 21,237, A. J. *Malherbe*]. – ᴿExpTim 106
(1994s) 344 (J. A. *Ziesler*).

— b) LUKKEN G.: Per visibilia ad invisibilia ... liturgy, sacraments, ETongeren
L. van, *Caspers* C. (Fac. Tilburg). Kampen 1994, Kok Pharos. 404 p.
[TD 42,375].

— c) MAHDI Muhsin S.: The political aspects of Islamic philosophy,
EButterworth Charles E.: MidEMg 27. CM 1992, Harvard Center MidE.
406 p. – RJAOS 114 (1994) 680-2 (F. M. *Najjar*).

77 MANASSY-GUITTON Jacqueline: Nomina rerum, EKircher-Durand Chantal:
LAMA 13, Nice 1994, Centre Langues Medit. Anc. 421 p. – RRPg 58
(1994) 258-363 (J.-P. *Levet*: 27 résumés sans pp.).

77* MARSHALL I. Howard: Jesus of Nazareth, Lord and Christ; essays on the
historical Jesus and NT Christology, 60th b., EGreen Joel B., *Turner* Max.
GR/Carlisle 1994, Eerdmans/Paternoster. xxi-536 p. $37.   0-8028-3750-6 /
UK 0-85364-560-4 [TDig 42,71; TLZ 120,411, J. *Roloff*; TLond 98,307, D.
Catchpole]. – RExpTim 106 (1994s) 185 (E. *Franklin*).

78 MARTY Martin E.:   New dimensions in American religious history, EDolan
J.P., *Wind* J.P. GR 1993, Eerdmans. xi-329 p. $30 [CathHR 81,101,
C. H. *Lippy*; RHE 90,63*].

79 MASSARI GABALLA Graziella, TOCCHETTI POLLINI Umberto: Scritti in
ricordo. Mi 1986, ET. – 419 p.

80 MAYER-OPIFICIUS Ruth: Beschreiben und deuten in der Archäologie des
Alten Orients, EDietrich M., *Loretz* O.: Altertumskunde des Vorderen
Orients 4. Münster 1994, Ugarit-Verlag. xvii-353 p.; Bibliog. xiii-xvii.
3-937120-18-0. [OIAc 11,33]. – 32 art., infra (1995). – RUF 25 (1993!)
498s (O. *Loretz*).

FMetz J. B. (Symposium) Diagnosen zur Zeit 1994 ➤ 371.

80* MEUTHEN Erich: Studien zum XV. Jh. 1994. [RHE 90,279*].

81 MEYER Léon de: Cinquante-deux réflexions sur le Proche-Orient ancien,
EGasché H., *al*.: Mesopotamian History and Environment, occas. 2. Lv
1994, Peeters. ix-561 p. 90-6831-601-X. 52 art., 17 in 1995.

82 MISCHLEWSKI Adalbert: Auf den Spuren des hl. Antonius, 75. Gb., EFriess
P. Memmingen 1994, Zeitung. x-370 p.; 21 fig.; 3 pl.; 7 maps [RHE
90,528, C. *Schmitt*].

83 MÖRNER Magnus: Agrarian society in history, ELundahl Mats, *Svensson*
Thommy. L 1990, Routledge. x-374 p. – REngHR 109 (1994) 546s
(V. G. *Kiernan*).

84 MORELAND Donald: The secret of faith; in your heart — in your mouth,
70th b., EPretorius M. W. Lv-Heverlee 1992, Ev. Theol. Fac. xi-228 p.
[< OTAbs 16, p. 399].

85 München Mariendom: 500-Jahr-Feier, Monachium Sacrum, 1. Kirchengeschichte, ESchwaiger Georg; 2. Kunstgeschichte, ERamisch Hans. Mü
1994, Deutscher Kunstverlag. 642 p.; 685 p. DM 198. – RTüTQ 174 (1994)
325s (R. *Reinhardt*).

86 MUFFS Yohanan: Comparative Studies = JANES 22 (1993).

87 NALDINI Mario: Paideia cristiana, 70 anni, EBurini Clara. R 1994,
Gruppo Int. xxiii-674 p.; bibliog. xix-xxiii. 88-8011-024-3. 47 art.; 18
infra.

88 a) NICOL Donald M.:   The making of Byzantine history, EBeaton
Roderick, *Roueché* Charlotte: L King's College Hellenic Studies 1.
Aldershot 1993, Variorum. xxvii-206 p.; bibliog. xiii-xxvii (I. *Martin*). –
12 art.; ➤ 11046.

— b) NIEBUHR Ursula M.: Associate editor 1981-6: Biblical Theology
Bulletin 24,2 (1994); 42s (-91); phot.

— c) NÚÑEZ CASTAÑEDA Emilio Antonio: Kairós 14s (Guat 1994) 175 p.; portr.; biobibliog. 13-17 (*Pérez Máximo*). 7 art. in Spanish on Catholics and Protestants in 21st century Latin America. ODENDAAL D. 1991 ➤ 327.

89) a) ÖZGÜÇ Nimet: Aspects of art and iconography, Anatolia and its neighbors, ^EMellink Machtell J., *Porada* Edith, *Özgüc* Tahsin. Ankara 1993, Türk Tarih Kurumu. xiii-730 p.; 147 pl. + 4 color.; bibliog. xi-xiii. 975-96308-0-5. 81 art.; plures infra.

— b) OLBRICHT Thomas N., 65th b., ^E*Marrs* Rick: RestQ 36,4 (1994) 193-339.

— c) OLIN John C.: Religious orders of the Catholic Reformation, 75th b., ^EDeMolen Richard L. NY 1994, Fordham. xix-290 p. $30. 0-8232-1512-1. – 9 art. [TDig 42,288].

— d) OROZ RETA José, Charisteria augustiniana [I. 1993 ➤ 9,118]; II. Theologica, ^EMerino P., *Torrecilla* J. M. = Augustinus 39 (1994), 594 p. 37 art., 4 infra.

— e) OTZEN Benedikt: In the last days; on Jewish and Christian apocalyptic and its period, ^EJeppesen Knud, *al.* Aarhus 1994, Univ. 261 p.; portr.; bibliog. 204-214 (*Carstens* P.) + 215-243, D. E. *Aune.* 87-7288-471-1 [TLZ 120,1062, M. *Frenschkowski*]. All infra.

90 a) PAGLIARO Antonino mem.: Studi latini e romanzi, ^EBelardi Walter, *al.*; BtRicLingFg 14. R 1984, Univ. Dipt. Glottoantropolog. xii-349 p. 0392-9361.

— b) PAPADOPOULOS Stephanos (1929-1992) mem.: Ellinika 43 (1993), 260 p.; portr.; résumés français 261-5. 20 art.; 5 infra.

— c) PASCUAL PASCUAL Recuero: Homenaje [† VII.1988] Granada 1991, Univ. MiscArH 37s (1988s) & 40 (1991). xxv-479 p. – ^RVT 44 (1994) 143s (N. de *Lange*: mostly Judeo-Spanish philosophy; D. *González Maeso* on biblical poetry; Guadalupe *Saíz Muñoz* on women in prophets/ wisdom).

91 PAVAN Massimiliano: In ricordo di un maestro, ^EBonamente Giorgio. Assisi 1993, Minerva. 163 p.

91* PEUKEN Helmut, Anerkennung der Anderen; eine theologische Grund-dimension interkultureller Kommunikation, ^E Arens E.: QDisp 155. FrB 1995, Herder [Orientierung 58 (1994) 233].

92 PIERACCIONI Dino [11.III.1920-9.XII.1989], Scritti in memoria di, ^EBandini Michele, *Pericoli* Federico G. F 1993, Ist. Papirologico Vitelli. 313 p.; phot.; bibliog. vi-xx. 22 art., 2 infra.

92* PIERONEK Tadeusz, bp., 60e anniv.: AnCracov 26 (1994); color. portr.; biog. ix-xx ℗ (ital. xxi-xxxiii); bibliog. xxxv-xlii. 39 art., mostly ℗ avec/con résumé.

93 PINELLI I PONS Jordí: Psallendum: StAnselm 105. R 1992, S. Anselmo. – ^RMaisD 196 (1993) 152s (J.-L. *Verstrefen*).

94 POLOTSKY Hans J. † 1991, mem.: Semitic and Cushitic studies, ^EGoldenberg Gideon, *Raz* Shlomo. Wsb 1994, Harrassowitz. x-287 p. DM 128. 3-447-03447-5. – 14 art.; 5 infra. – ^RWZKM 84 (1994) 351s (S. *Procházka*). PORAT J. 1992 ➤ 108b.

94* PORTER H. Boone: Creation and liturgy, ^EMcMichael Ralph. Wsh 1993, Pastoral. viii-320 p. $25. 1-56929-001-6. – ^RWorship 65 (1994) 278s (K. *Stevenson*).

95 POTTMEYER Hermann Josef: Kirche sein; Theologie im Dienst der Kirchenreform, ^EGeerlings Wilhelm, *Seckler* Max. FrB 1994, Herder. 461 p. DM 68. 3-451-23329-0. 26 art., 8 infra [TR 91,74, tit. pp.].

95* PRETE Sesto, mem.: ResPLitt 15s (1992s).
96 PROSDOCIMI Luigi: Cristianità in Europa, EAlzati Cesare. R 1994,
   Herder. 354 p.; p. 355-852 [RHE 90,153, † G. *Fransen*].
97 RACKMAN Menachem E.: Studies in Halakha and Jewish thought, 80th b.,
   EBeer Moshe. Ramat-Gan 1994, Bar-Ilan Univ. 324 + 66 p.; bibliog.
   11-15. 965-226-163-7; p. 49*-58* Eng. *Kellner* Menachem on Jer 9,22s.
98 RADMILLI Antonio Mario: Miscellanea archeologica, EStaduti Piero.
   Pisa 1994, ETS. xii-446 p.; ill. 20 art.; 3 infra. 3-6 attività scientifica ['180
   pubblicazioni' non nominate].
98* RANDI Eugenio [1957-1990], mem.: Filosofia e teologia nel trecento,
   EBianchi Luca: TÉtMAge 1. LvN 1994, Féd. Inst. Mdv. 575 p. [RHE
   90,638, J.-F. *Gilmont*].
99 a) RASMUSSEN Niels K. OP., mem.: Fountain of life, EAustin Gerard.
   Wsh 1991, Pastoral. ix-249 p. $25. – RSpeculum 69 (1994) 105-7 (R. E.
   Reynolds).
— b) RECIO VEGANZONES Alejandro: Historiam pictura refert; studi di
   archeologia cristiana. Vaticano 1994. – RSMSR 60 (1994) 399-408 (F.
   Bisconti, D. *Mazzoleni*).
— c) REICHMAN Shalom 1935-1992, mem.: ⊕ Studies in the Geography of
   Israel 14, EKark Ruth, *Salomon* Ilan. J 1993, Univ./Israel Expl. Soc.
   324 p. 965-221-024-2 [RB 102,292, only 19-30, *Rubin* Rehav, The desert
   marches of the Roman and Byzantine empires as a cultural crossroad; and
   31-49 *Potcher* Odel, *Tepper* Yigal, The 'Avedat cave city, an early urban
   manifestation of arid region settlement].
100 RENOIR Alain: 'De gustibus' EFoley John M.: A. B. LORD studies in oral
   tradition 11. NY 1992, Garland (RefLibHum 1482). xiv-596 p. $75. –
   RSpeculum 69 (1994) 288s.
   REUSCHEL Wolfgang mem., 3. Arab. Kolloquium 1991/4 ➤ 453.
101 REVENTLOW Henning Graf: Altes Testament, Forschung und Wirkung,
   EMommer Peter, *Thiel* Winfried. Fra 1994, Lang. xii-407 p.; Bibliog.
   395-407. 3-631-46609-9 [OTAbs 18, p. 140, with renvoi to 24 summaries;
   TLZ 120,972, S. *Wagner*; ZAW 107,344, tit. pp.]. – 25 art., infra.
102 RICHARDSON H. Neil † 1988, mem.: Discovering ancient stones, EHopfe
   Lewis N. [† 2.X.1992]. WL 1994, Eisenbrauns. xviii-270 p.; portr.;
   bibliog. xii-xviii. 0-931464-73-0. 19 art.; infra. [BL 55,15, L. L. *Grabbe*;
   OTAbs 18, p. 139, S. A. *Wiggins*, with renvoi to 16 art.; ZAW 107.547,
   tit. pp.].
103 RIET Simone, van, † 1993, mém.: Byzantion 64,1 (1994); 4-7, phot.,
   biobibliog. (J. *Grand'Henry*).
104 RIONDATO Ezio, Ethos e cultura, 70° compleanno: Miscellanea erudita
   51s. Padova 1991, Antenore. 1282 p. (2 vol.). – RSalesianum 56 (1994)
   178s (G. *Abbà*).
105 ROBINSON Donald, abp.: In the fullness of time; biblical studies, EPeterson
   David, *Pryor* John. Homebush NSW 1992, Lancer. xxxvi-317 p. A$25. 18
   art. – RCritRR 6 (1993) 598s (D. M. *Scholer*: tit. pp.); EvQ 66 (1994) 261-3
   (P. M. *Head*).
   ROSTAGNI Augusto † 1961, mém.: A cent'anni dalla nascita, incontro 1992
   ➤ 433c.
106 RUPP Alfred, 19.XI.1930-28.I.1993, in memoriam: MARG [Saarbrücken,
   Mitteilungen für Anthropologie und Religionsgeschichte] 9. Münster
   1994, Ugarit-V. xxvi-340 p.; ix-xix Bibliog., *Dietrich* M. 3-927120-23-5.
   – RUF 25 (1993) 509s (O. *Loretz*; tit. pp.).
107 RUTENBER Culbert G.: Perspectives on ethical and social issues; 85th b.,

ᴱScholer David M.: NABPR Fs 11. = PerspRelSt 21,4 (1994) 277-387; bibliog. 279-283 (J.J.J. *Leese*).

108 *a*) Sᴁʙø Magne: Text and theology; 65th b., ᴱTångberg Arvid. Oslo 1994, Verbum. 381 p. Nk 298, 82-543-0647-8 [BL 95,22, G.W. *Anderson*; OTAbs 17, p.423; ZAW 107,172 tit. pp.]. – ᴿTsTKi 65 (1994) 229s (A. *Aschim*).
— *b*) Sᴀꜰʀᴀɴ Joaeph: Pᴏʀᴀᴛ Yosef, ᴱSafran Bezalei & Eliyahu. Hoboken 1992, ᴋᴛᴀᴠ. ix-265 p. + ❿ 80 p. / 17 art.; → 2009 [JQR 84,393].
— *c*) Sᴀɴᴛɪɴᴇʟʟᴏ Giovanni: Concordia discors, studi su Niccolò Cᴜꜱᴀɴᴏ e l'umanesimo europeo, ᴱ*Piaia* G.: Medioevo e Umanesimo 84. Padova 1993, Antenore. 591 p. RHE 90,265*.
— *d*) Sᴀᴜᴇʀ Ralph: Warum Gott...? Der fragende Mensch vor dem Geheimnis Gottes, ᴱLesch K.J., *Saller* M. Kevelaer 1993. [ZAW 107,369: only 12-18, *Dohmen* C. on Ps. 22,2].

109 Sᴄʜᴀᴇɴᴅʟɪɴɢᴇʀ Anton C. † 1991, mem.: WZKM 82 (1992). 453 p.; portr.; Biobibliog. 5-14 (*Köhbach* M., *Römer* Claudia). 0084-0076. 33 art.; 3 infra.

110 Sᴄʜɪʟʟᴇʙᴇᴇᴄᴋx Edward: Temidden van de cultuur; ᴱBorgman Erik, *Häring* Hermann: Tijdschrift voor Theologie 34,4 (Nijmegen 1994) 330-438; portr.; bibliog. sinds 1982 p. 436-8.

110* Sᴄʜɪᴍᴍᴇʟ Annemarie: Gott ist schön und Er liebt die Schönheit, 70. Gb., ᴱGiese Alma, *Bürgel* J. Christoph. Fra 1994, Lang. 474 p. Fs 125. 3-906750-90-6. – ᴿWZKM 84 (1994) 348s (S. *Procházka*).

111 Sᴄʜᴍᴀᴜꜱꜱ Michael mem.: MüTZ 45,2 (1994) 115-127 portr. (Erinnerungen).

111* Sᴄʜᴍɪᴅᴛ Ernst G.: 65. Gb.: Philologus 138,2 (1994).

112 Sᴄʜᴍɪᴅᴛ Karl Horst: Indogermanica et Caucasica, 65. Gb., ᴱBielmeier Roland, *Stempel* Reinhard: StIndEur 6. B 1994, de Gruyter. xvi-560 p.; bibliog. 535-560 (217 items + ᴿ433: *Hlaváček* Klara, *Hoffmann* Ingrid). 3-11-012448-9. 40 art.

113 Sᴄʜɴᴀᴄᴋᴇɴʙᴜʀɢ Rudolf, 80. Gb.: Weltgericht und Weltvollendung; Zukunftsbilder im Neuen Testament, ᴱKlauck Hans-Josef: QDisp 150. FrB 1994, Herder. 268 p. 3-451-02150-1. 11 art., infra [TR 90,515, tit. pp.].

114 Sᴄʜʀᴏᴇᴅᴇʀ Edward H., A crossings celebration; Ed Schroeder and his ministry [St. Louis lay institute; 20 items by laymen; C.E. *Ford* on Bᴏɴʜᴏᴇꜰꜰᴇʀ and Bᴇʀᴅʏᴀᴇᴠ], ᴱKoch Irmgard, *al*. St. Charles/St. Louis 1993, Greenhorn/HomeLee. 123 p. $13. – ᴿCurrTM 21 (1994) 57 (R.W. *Klein*).

115 Sᴄʜᴜɴᴄᴋ Klaus-Dietrich: Nachdenken über Israel, Bibel und Theologie, 65. Gb., ᴱNiemann Michael, *al*., BeitErfAJ 37. Fra 1994, Lang. 498 p. portr.; Bibliog. 485-498. [OTAbs 18, p.141]. 3-631-47033-9.

116 Sᴄʜᴜꜱᴛᴇʀ A. Ildefonso card. ᴏ.ꜱ.ʙ.: Il servo di Dio ~ nel quarantesimo della morte (1954-1994): Benedictina 41,1 (1994); 309 p. [+ 2,341-375]; 10 art.; p.163-182, *Ranzato* Agostino, Uso e ruolo della S. Scrittura nel pensiero del card. Schuster; analisi esemplificativa dell'opera 'Un pensiero quotidiano sulla Regola di S. Benedetto'.

117 Sᴄʜᴡᴀʙʟ Hans: *Sphairos*, 70. Gb. = Wiener Studien 107s (1984s), 355 p., portr.; p. 357-646. 3-7001-2189-X; -90-3.

117* Sᴇɪᴅᴇʟ Hans: Gottes Ehre erzählen, 65. Gb., ᴱAlbani M., *Arndt* T. Lp 1994, Thomas. – 272 p.; portr. 3-86174-037-0 [TLZ 120,1064, E.-J. *Waschke*; ZAW 107,353, tit. pp.].

118 Sʜᴏʀᴇ A.F. ['Peter']: The unbroken reed, 70th b., ᴱEyre Christopher, *al*.; OccasP 11. L 1994, Egypt Exploration Soc. xii-401 p.; portr. 0-85698-124-9. 33 art.; 8 in Elenchus vol. 11.

118* SICHERL Martin, *Philophronēma*; von Textkritik bis Humanismusforschung, ᴱ**Harlfinger** Dieter: Görres-G. StudGKuA 4. Pd 1990, Schöningh. 389 p.; portr.; Bibliog. 11-17. 3-506-79054-4. 21 art.

119 SILLER Hermann Pius: Gottesrede – Glaubenspraxis; Perspektiven theologischer Handlungstheorie, 65. Gb., ᴱ**Arens** E. Da 1994, Wiss. v-197 p. DM 40. 3-534-11698-4 [TR 90,171, tit. pp.]. – ᴿTLZ 119 (1994) 879 (C. *Grethlein*).

119* SLOMP Jan: Muslims and Christians in Europe; Breaking new ground, ᴱ**Speelman** Gé, *al.* Kampen 1993, Kok. 211 p. – ᴿIslamochristiana 20 (1994) 315s (M. L. *Fitzgerald*).

120 SLOYAN Gerard S.: Horizons 20th Anniv. 21,1 (1994).

120* SMART Ninian: Aspects of religion ᴱ**Masefield** Peter, *Wiebe* Donald. NY 1994, Lang. xiv-417 p.; portr. 0-8204-2237-1. 6 infra (1995).

121 SMIT Erasmus Johannes: J/Tyd Sem 5,1 (1993) i-ii, portr.; 109 p. (4 infra).

123 SMITH Morton, † 11.VII.1991, mem. [< meeting San Masiato Nov. 2-5, 1992]: Josephus and the history of the Greco-Roman period, ᴱ**Parente** Fausto, *Sievers* Joseph: StPostB 41. Leiden 1994, Brill. x-392 p.; bibliog. 339-371 [on Smith 1-8, *Cohen* S.]. 90-04-10114-4. – 18 art.; infra.

123* SMITH Ronald Morton: Corolla Torontonensia [Indology], ᴱ**Robbins** Emmet, *Sandahl* Stella. Toronto 1994, Univ. xix-275 p. $30. 0-920661-22-X. – ᴿWZKM 84 (1994) 347s (S. *Procházka*).

124 STRANGE John: Fra dybet, from the depths, 60th b., ᶠ**Lemche** N. P., *Müller* M.: Forum for bibelsk eksegese 5. K 1994, Museum Tusculanum. 286 p. Dk 195. 87-7289-295-1 [BL 95,30, K. *Jeppesen*, topics sans tit. pp.].

124* STUHLMUELLER Carroll (1923-1994) mem.: BToday 32,4 (1994).

125 SUBILIA Vittorio: Il pluralismo nelle origini cristiane, ᴱ**Conte** Gino: Fac. Valdese 18. Torino 1994, Claudiana. 220 p.; bibliog. 117-207. 88-7016-190-0. – 7 art.; 6 infra. [Gregorianum 76,394, G. *Marconi*; STEv 7,86-89, L. *De Chirico*].

125* SWEENEY Leo: Greek and medieval studies, ᴱ**Carroll** William J., *Furlong* John J. NY 1994, Lang. xxviii-302 p. $47. 0-8204-1641-X [TDig 43,66].

126 SWINBURNE Richard, Reason and the Christian religion, ᴱ**Padgett** Alan. Ox 1994, Clarendon. xiii-362 p. £40. 0-19-824042-2. – ᴿExpTim 106 (1994s) 217s (W. D. *Hudson*).

127 TAVARD George H.: The Quadrilog [Catholic, Anglican, Methodist, Lutheran]: tradition and the future of ecumenism, ᴱ**Hagen** Kenneth. ColMn 1994, Liturgical/Glazier, vii-421 p.; bibliog. $29. 0-8146-5836-5. 22 art. [TDig 42,85; TBR 8/2, 26, R. *Greenacre*; ProEccl 4,246, W. G. *Rusch*].

128 TELLENBACH Gerd G.: Nobiltà e chiesa nel medioevo, ᴱ*Violante* C.: UnivPisa mdv 3. R 1993, Jouvence. 233 p., map, 3 foldouts. Lᵐ 50. [RHE 90,264, D. *Dereck*, tit. pp.].

129 THRAEDE Klaus, Panchaia, ᴱ**Wacht** Manfred. Mü 1995, Aschendorff. 260 p. DM 100. 3-402-08106-7. 23 art. [TR 91,359, tit. pp.]. 11-23, *Balch* D., Paul in Acts [21,21]; 45-50, *Dassmann* E., Gn 1,27; 121-130, *Fürst* A., Gal 2,11-14.

TOCCHETTI POLLINI U.: mem. 1986 → 78.

129* TOMBOLANI Michele [18.VII.1943-1989], mem.: Studi di archeologia della X Regio, ᴱ**Scarfi** Bianca Maria. R 1994, Bretschneider. 583 p.; 10-17, fot. biog. (Giulia *Fogolari*), 19-21 bibliog. (*Bianchin Citton* E., *Gambacurta* G. 88-7062-831-0. 50 art.

130 TRAPP J. B. [(I.) 1990 → 9,154*] (II.): England and the continental Renaissance, ᴱ**Chaney** Edward, *Mack* Peter. Woodbridge 1990, Boydell. xi-322 p. £39.50. – ᴿEngHR 109 (1994) 434s (D. *Norbrook*).

131 *a*) UNTERMANN Jürgen: Sprachen und Schriften des antiken Mittel-
meerraums, 65. Gb., ᴱHeidermanns F., *Rix* H., *Seebold* E.; InnBeitSprW
78. Innsbruck 1993. IX-512 p. – ᴿBeitNam 265 (1994s) 306-312 (J.
Ulrich); BSLP 89,2 (1994) 187-9 (P. *Flobert*).
— *b*) URBAN Günter: Architektur und Kunst im Abendland, ᴱJensen
Michael, *Winands* Klaus. R 1992, Herder. 286 p., ill.
— *c*) VELLAS Vassilios, mem. (25th anniv.): DeltioVM 13,1 (1994). 113 p.;
phot.
— *d*) VERBRAKEN Pierre-Patrick † 1992: RBén 104 (1994); portr.; biobibliog.
1-18 (E. *Dekkers*).
— *f*) VERHEUL Ambroos; QLtg 73,3 (1992); 127-145; phot.
— *g*) VISENTIN Pelagio: Amen vestrum; miscellanea di studi liturgico-pa-
storali, ᴱCatella A. Padova 1994, Messaggero. xxiv-489 p. [RHE 90,65*].
— *h*) VOGT Hermann-Josef: Lebendige Überlieferung; Prozesse der An-
näherung und Auslegung, ᴱKhoury N. el-, *Crouzel* H., *Reinhardt* R.
Ostfildern 1992, Schwaben. 389 p. [RHE 90,65*].
132 VORSTER Willem S., mem.: Critical scholarship and the NT; a dialogue
with ~, ᴱBotha Pieter J.J., *al.* Neotestamentica 28,3 (special), 1994.
288 p.; portr.; bibliog. 283-8.
132* VRYONIS Spyrosᴶ, To Hellēnikón, I. Hellenic Antiquity and Byzantium,
ᴱLangdon J.S., *al.* New Rochelle 1993, Caratzas. xlvii-474 p.; portr.
$75. [RHE 90,265*; Speculum 70,713, tit. pp.].
133 WACHOLDER Ben Zion: Pursuing the text; 70th B., ᴱReeves John C., K-
ampen John: jOsu 184. Shf 1994, Academic. 434 p. bibliog. 410-2
(*Selavan* Ida C., *Wolfson* Laurel S.). [OTAbs 18, p. 622, with renvoi to
12 items; ZAW 107,538, tit. pp.; ETL 55,195, J. *Lust*, NTAb 49 p. 323].
134 WAGNER Günter: International [Baptist] Theological Studies, 1. Bern
1994, Lang. xviii-251 p.; bibliog. 243-251.
135 WANSBROUGH John E.: BSO 57,1 (1994); phot.; 4-15 bibliog. (M. *Brett*,
G. *Hawting*).
136 WEINTRAUB Dov [18.X.1926-23.VI.1985], mem.: Studies in rural development, ᴱKahana Reuven: ScrHieros 34. J 1993, Hebrew Univ. 217 p.
0800-8369. 9 art. (all on modern Israel), 1 infra.
137 WESENER Günter: Vestigia iuris romani. 60. Gb., ᴱKlingenberg Georg, *al.*
Graz 1992, Leykam. 552 p. – ᴿZSav-R 111 (1994) 669-678 (R. *Zimmermann*).
137* WESTENFDORF Wolfhart: Quaerentes scientiam, 70. Gb., ᴱBehlmer Heike
(p. 13-26 on Panopolis). Gö 1994, Univ. Seminar für Ägyptologie und
Koptologie. 314 p.; Bibliog. (197-214), Westendorf 9-12. 14 art.; 8 infra.
138 WHYBRAY R. Norman: Of prophets' visions and the wisdom of sages,
70th b., ᴱMcKay Heather A., *Clines* David J.A.: jOsu 162, 1993 ➤ 9,170;
portr.; biobibliog. 15-20 (M.A. *Knibb*), 17 art.; infra.
139 ᶠWILDER A.N.: NewLitCrit & NT, ᴱMalbon E.S., *McKnight* E.V. jNsu
109. Shf 1994, Academic. £31.50. 1-85075-510-8 [TLZ 120,625-8, W.
Schenk].
WILLAERT Benjamin: Naming God today 1994 ➤ 410.
140 WILLIAMS J. Rodman, Spirit and renewal, 75th b., ᴱWilson M.W.:
JPentecT supp. 5. Shf 1994, Academic. 221 p. biobibliog. 203-8. £15.
1-85075-471-3 [NTAbs 38, p. 454].
141 WILLIAMS Shafer mem.: In iure veritatis; studies in canon law, ᴱBowman
Steven B., *Cody* Blanche E. Cincinnati 1991, Univ. College of Law.
xvii-199 p.; front. £29. – ᴿExpTim 106 (1994s) 23 (C.S. *Rodd*, amid 20
other JStOT titles); Speculum 69 (1994) 284s.

142 WILSON Bryan R.:   Secularization, rationalism, and sectarianism,
    EBarker Eileen, al. Ox 1993, Clarendon. xvi-322 p. $55. 0-19-827721-0.
    [TDig 42,89]. 17 art. – RTLond 97 (1994) 225s (P. B. Clarke).
143 WINDEKENS A. J., Van [†28.III.1989], mem.: Studia etymologica
    indoeuropaea: OrLovAnal 45. Lv 1991, Univ./Peeters. 90-6831-378-9.
    EIsebaert L. – RArOr 62 (1994) 452-6 (V. Blašek).
144 WINKLER Klaus: Zwischenbilanz; Pastoralpsychologische Herausforde-
    rung, EKlessmann Michael, Lückel Kurt. Bielefeld 1994, Luther. 199 p.;
    186-192 bibliog. DM 29,80. 3-7858-0359-1. 14 art. [TR 90,512, tit. pp.].
145 WINTER Erich: Aspekte spätägyptischer Kultur, 65. Gb., EMinas Mar-
    tina, Zeidler Jürgen, al.: AegTrev 7. Mainz 1994, von Zabern. ix-298 p.;
    29 fig.; 12 pl. 1-8 Bibliog. (Stöhr Simone). DM 148.   3-8053-1691-7. 27
    art., ► Elenchus 11 (1995). [ZAW 107,519, only 139-147, Haag E. Isa
    19,25].
145* WISBEY Roy, German narrative literature in the twelfth and thirteenth
    centuries [83-97, Sethites, Murdoch B.; 133-7, Apostles' journeys, Wells
    D. ...], EHanemann Volker, al. Tü 1994, Niemeyer, vi-410 p., portr. [Spe-
    culum 70,711, tit. pp.].
146 WISEMAN D. (75th b.: p. vii): He swore an oath; biblical themes from
    Genesis 12-50, EHess Richard S., al. Carlisle/GR 1993, ²1994, Pater-
    noster/Baker. 222 p. 0-85364-609-0 / GR 0-8010-2014-X. 10 art.; infra.
146* YEIVIN Israel: ⊕ Language studies V-VI: EBar-Asher Moshe. J 1992,
    Magnes. xlviii-616 p. – RAJS 19 (1994) 301s (titles in English sans pp.).
147 ZAMPETTI Pietro: Studi, 80⁰ anniv., EVarese Ranieri. Ancona 1993,
    Lavoro. 676 p.; ill.
147* ZEDDA Silverio SI, mem.: Miscellanea biblica, EMorfino Mauro M.:
    Theologica (della Sardegna) 3 (Cagliari 1994). 379 p.; phot.; bibliog. 19-33
    (Spanu Dionigi). Lᵐ 45. [ParVi 40/4, 62, A. Rolla]. 12 art., infra.
148 ZERFASS Rolf: Was die Pastoral bewegt, 60 Gb.: Bibel und Liturgie 67,2s
    (1994) 57-193; Bibliog. 187-193 (Dötterl Klaus).
149 ZIMMERMANN Albert: 'Scientia' und 'Ars' im Hoch- und Spätmittel-
    alter, ECraemer-Ruegenberg I., Speer A.: MiscMdv 22. B 1994, de
    Gruyter. xxx-513 p.; xi, p. 515-1065; ill. [RHE 90,265*; RSPT 79,189s,
    tit. pp.].

A1.2 Miscellanea unius auctoris.

150 Thiel Winfried,   Alttestamentliche Forschung in Sammelbänden [nicht
    Festschriften]: TRu 59 (1994) 1-40; 6-8, McCarthy D. J., AnBib 109.

151 a) Aguirre Rafael, La mesa compartida; estudios del NT desde las ciencias
    sociales: PresTeol 77. Sdr 1994, Sal Terrae. 242 p. 84-293-1127-0 [TLZ
    120,443].
— b) Allony Nehemya (1906-1983), ⊕ Studies in medieval philology and
    linguistics [6 vol.; 1. SAʿADIA's works], ETobi Yosef, J 1986-92, Yad
    Ben-Zvi (vol. 1-3) / Mass (4-6, 1991s). 406 p.; 606 p.; 380 p.; 528 p.; 496 p.;
    328 p. – RSefarad 53 (1993) 210s (C. del Valle).
— c) d'Alverny M.-Th., Études sur le symbolisme de la Sagesse et sur
    l'iconographie, EBurnett C.: CS 421. Aldershot 1993, Variorum. xii-332 p.
    [RHE 90,62*].
152 Angel Marc D., rabbi, Seeking God, speaking peace: Collected essays,
    EAngel Hayyim J.; Library of Sephardic... Hoboken 1994, KTAV.
    xii-303 p. bibliog. 295-303. 0-88125-241-7. 37 art.

152* **Aubert** Roger, Le Cardinal MERCIER (1851-1926), un prélat d'avant-garde [15 articles d'Aubert pour ses 80 ans], ᴱ*Hendrickx* J.-P., *al.* Lv 1994, Academia. 500 p. [NRT 117,262-5, B, *Joassart*; RHE 90,205-8, J. *Gadille*]. – ᴿETL 70 (1994) 528-532 (R. *Boudens*).

153 **Aus** Roger D., Barabbas and Esther, and other studies in the Judaic illumination of earliest Christianity: SFLJud 54. Atlanta 1992, Scholars. xii-205 p. $60; sb. $40. [CritRR 6 (1993) 578, tit. pp.] 7 art. 1973-87 + 2 inedita.

154 **Axel** Michael, The writings of Larry E. Axel (1946-1991); studies in liberal religious thought. Lewiston NY 1992, Mellen. 260 p. $70. – ᴿAmJTP 15 (1994) 221-6 (D. *Webster*).

155 **Baarda** Tjitze, [15] Essays on the Diatessaron: ContribExegT 11. Kampen 1994, Kok Pharos. 320 p. *f* 80. 90-390-0113-8.

156 **Badian** E., From Platea to Potidaea; studies in the history and historiography of the Pentacontaetia [5 art. 1987-90, revised]. Baltimore 1993, Johns Hopkins Univ. 264 p. – ᴿRÉAnc 96 (1994) 624 (P. *Brun*).

156* **Bal** Mieke, On meaning-making; essays in semiotics. Sonoma CA 1994, Polebridge. vii-312 p. $30. 0-944344-39-9 [TLZ 120,975, W. *Schenk*].

157 **Barigazzi** Adelmo † 1993, Studi su PLUTARCO: Scienze dell'antichità, Studi e Testi 12. F 1994, Univ. 330 p.

158 *a)* **Barnes** Timothy D., From EUSEBIUS to AUGUSTINE, selected papers 1982-1993: CS 438. Aldershot 1994, Variorum. xii-334 p.; portr. 0-86078-397-9. 22 reprints + 2 inedita, infra.

— *b)* **Baum** Gregory, Essays in critical theology, KC 1994, Sheed & W. viii-244 p. $17 pa. 1-55612-710-3. 11 reprints [TDig 42,355].

— *c)* **Baur** Jörg, Luther und seine klassischen Erben: Theologische Aufsätze und Forschungen. Tü 1993, Mohr. 398 p. DM 74. 3-16-146055-3 [TLZ 120, 1111-5, J. von *Lüpke*].

— *d)* **Baur** Jörg, Einsicht und Glaube: Aufsätze 2. Gö 1994, Vandenhoeck & R. 219 p. DM 48. 3-525-56187-3 [TR 91,277].

159 **Beinert** Wolfgang, Vom Finden und Verkünden der Wahrheit in der Kirche (60. Gb.; seine Art., 17 1967-81), ᴱ*Kraus* Georg. FrB 1993, Herder. 369 p. DM 78. 3-451-23083-6: ᴿTPQ 142 (1994) 422 (A. *Habichler*); ZkT 116 (1994) 103 (K. H. *Neufeld*).

160 **Betz** Hans-Dieter, Paulinische Studien [9 of the 12 Eng.]: GesAufs 3. Tü 1994, Mohr. ix-327 p. DM 128. 3-16-146204-1. [JBL 114,567, tit. pp.; RelStR 21,237, A. J. *Malherbe*]. – ᴿTLZ 119 (1994) 1075s (F. M. *Horn*).

160* **Bobrinskoy** Boris, Communion du Saint-Esprit [art. 1959-80, pas assez bien présentés], ᴱ*Clément* Olivier: Spiritualités orientales 56. Bégrolles-en-Mauges 1992, Bellefontaine. 490 p. – ᴿScEspr 46 (1994) 120s (J. *Sison*).

161 **Borg** Marcus J., Jesus in contemporary scholarship [since 'watershed year' 1980; 5 reprints, 4 inedita]. Ph 1994, Trinity. xiv-209 p. $16 pa. 1-56338-094-3 [RelStR 21,234, F. W. *Burnett*].

161* **Borrmans** Maurice, Islam e Cristianesimo; le vie del dialogo [ristampe 1976-92]. T 1993, Paoline. 240 p. – ᴿIslamochristiana 19 (1993) 321s (M. L. *Fitzgerald*).

162 **Braulik** Georg, The theology of Deuteronomy, ᵀ*Linblad* Ulrika: BIBAL Collected Essays 2. N. Richland Hills TX 1994, BIBAL. ix-302 p.; bibliog. 272-302.

162* **Bredin** Eamonn, Praxis and praise [four reprints on post-Vatican-II relation of liturgy to the radical message of Christ]. Dublin 1994, Columba. 205 p. £10. 1-85907-114-6. – ᴿExpTim 106 (1994s) 283s (B. D. *Spinks* praises and regrets only Catholics in view).

163 **Brin** Gershon, ❸ Issues in the Bible and the Dead Sea Scrolls. TA 1994, Hakibutz Hameuchad. 287 p. 19 art., ❸ only; 7 inedita [RB 102,296, tit. pp. from list furnished in English].

163* **Brin** Gershon, Studies in biblical law, from the Hebrew Bible to the Dead Sea Scrolls [1975-94], ᵀ*Chipman* Jonathan: jOsu 176. Sheffield 1994, Academic. 176 p. £45. 1-85075-484-3 [TLZ 120,324, E. *Otto*].

164 *a*) **Brueggemann** Walter, A social reading of the Old Testament, prophetic approaches to Israel's communal life [15 reprints 1975-91], ᴱ*Miller* Patrick D. Mp 1994, Fortress. 328 p. 0-8006-2734-2 [OTAbs 18, p. 392 tit. pp.].

— *b*) **Büsser** F., Die Prophezei; Humanismus und Reformation in Zürich; [seine] ausgewählte Aufsätze und Vorträge, 70. Gb., ᴱ*Schindler* A.: ZBeitRefG 17. Bern 1994, Lang. 243 p.; 12 facsim; foldout [RHE 90,263*].

— *c*) **Busi** G., Il succo dei favi; studi sull'umanesimo ebraico [3, 1984-92]: BtHebr 1. Bo 1992, Fattoadarte. 129 p. – ᴿHenoch 16 (1994) 365s (M. *Perani*).

— *d*) **Canfora** Luciano, [26] Studi di storia della storiografia romana; Univ. Dip. Ant. 15. Bari 1993, Edipuglia. 321 p. – ᴿBStLat 24 (1994) 286-8 (Valeria *Viparelli*).

165 **Casey** Michael, The undivided heart; the Western monastic approach to contemplation. Petersham MA 1994, St. Bede's. vi-217 p. $13. 1-879007-04-5 [TDig 42,158].

166 **Ceresko** Anthony R., Psalmists and sages; studies in OT poetry and religion: TheolSt supp. 2. Bangalore 1994, St. Peter's. 250 p. $5 [OTAbs 17, p. 648; RB 102,445, tit. pp.]. 15 reprints.

166* **Chilton** Bruce, Judaic approaches to the Gospels [1 ineditum, 11 already or soon published]: SFLJud 2. Atlanta 1994, Scholars. xii-321 p. 0-7885-001-5 [RB 102,453, tit. pp.; BL 95,144, C.T.R. *Hayward*].

167 **Classen** Carl J., Die Welt der Römer, ᴱ*Vielberg* Meinolf: UntAntLG 41. B 1993, de Gruyter. 279 p. – ᴿRÉLat 72 (1994) 285s (J. *Hellegouarc'h*).

167* **Crenshaw** James L., Trembling at the threshold of a biblical text [20 brief sermons & 20 prayers]. GR 1994, Eerdmans. xiii-167 p. $11. 0-8028-0720-8 [TDig 42,160].

168 *a*) **Cullmann** Oscar, Das Gebet im Neuen Testament; zugleich Versuch einer vom Neuen Testament aus zu erteilenden Antwort auf heutige Fragen. Tü 1994, Mohr. ix-194 p. 2-16-146276-5; pa. -66-1 [TLZ 120, 437-9, U. *Wilckens*].

— *b*) **Cutler** Anthony, Imagery and ideology in Byzantine art: CS 358. Aldershot 1992, Variorum. x-324 p. £69.50. – ᴿRÉByz 51 (1993) 274-6 (C. *Walter*).

— *c*) **Dassmann** Ernst, Ämter und Dienste in den frühchristlichen Gemeinden [14 art.]: Hereditas 8. Bonn 1994, Borengässer. x-246 p. 3-923946-26-0 [JTS 46,706, H. *Chadwick*: welcome].

— *d*) **Daube** David, Collected works I. Talmudic Law, ᴱ*Carmichael* Callum C. Berkeley 1992, Univ. California. xlii-527 p. – ᴿZSav-R 111 (1994) 702s (R. *Westbrook*).

— *e*) **Davidson** Clifford, On tradition; essays on the use and valutation of the past [1 ineditum]: AMS-MA 20. NY 1992, AMS. xi-240 p. 12 fig. $45. – ᴿSpeculum 70 (1995) 604s (H. *Chickering*).

169 **Dickens** A.G., Late monasticism and the Reformation. L 1994, Hambledon. xvi-222 p.; 2 fig. £35. 1-85285-091-4. – ᴿJTS 45 (1994) 771s (D. *MacCulloch*).

169* **Dinzelbacher** Peter, Mittelalterliche Frauenmystik [reprints 1978-92]. Pd 1993, Schöningh. 343 p. DM 68 [TR 91,234, Louise *Gnädinger*].

170 **Donner** Herbert, Aufsätze zum Alten Testament aus vier Jahrzehnten: BZAW 224. B 1994, de Gruyter. xii-311 p.; Bibliog. 286s. 3-11-014097-7. 15 art., 1959-92. [RB 102,444, tit. pp.; TLZ 120,1065, W. *Thiel*].

171 **Drijvers** Han J. W., History and religion in Late Antique Syria: CS 464. Aldershot 1994, Variorum. xii-305 p. 0-86078-451-7. – 21 art., with the original pagination.

172 *a*) **Fackre** Gabriel, Ecumenical faith in evangelical perspective [essays 1985-93]. GR 1993, Eerdmans. – ᴿMid-Stream 33 (1994) 485-7 (D. F. *Martensen*).

— *b*) **Filoramo** Giovanni, Figure del sacro; saggi di storia religiosa. Brescia 1993, Morcelliana. – ᴿQVidCr 174 (1994) 123 (A. *Rodríguez*).

— *c*) **Fitzmyer** Joseph A., According to Paul; [3 inedita + 4] studies in the theology of Paul the Apostle. NY 1993, Paulist. xi-177 p. $13. 0-8091-3390-3 [RB 102,143, tit. pp.].

— *d*) **Forell** George W., Martin LUTHER, theologian of the Church; collected essays, 75th b., ᴱ*Russell* William R.: Word & World supp. 2. St. Paul 1994, xiii-265 p. $15 pa. 0-9632389-1-4. [TDig 42,269]. – 27 art.

— *e*) **Forey** Alan, Military orders and crusades: CS 432. Aldershot 1994, Variorum. viii-318 p. $92. 0-86078-398-7 [RHE 90,150, J. *Richard*; Speculum 70,52 tit. pp.].

— *f*) **Forni** Giovanni, Esercito e marina di Roma antica (16 art.): Mavors 5. Stu 1992, Steiner. 455 p. – ᴿArctos 27 (1993) 188-192 (C. *Brunn*).

— *g*) **Freedman** Paul, Church, law and society in Catalonia, 900-1500: CS 440. L/Brookfield VT 1994, Variorum/Ashgate. xii-270 p. $77,50. 0-86078-414-2 [TDig 42,165].

— *h*) **Frei** Hans, Theology and narrative, selected essays, ᴱ*Hunsinger* George, *Placher* William C. NY 1993, Oxford-UP. 274 p. – ᴿModT 10 (1994) 425-7 (C. L. *Campbell*).

173 **Fridrichsen** Anton, Exegetical writings, a selection, ᵀᴱ*Caragounis* Chrys C., *Fornberg* Tord: WUNT 76. Tü 1994, Mohr. xiii-314 p. DM 168. 3-16-146268-8 [TR 91,361]. – 29 art.

173* **Fuller** Reginald H., Christ and Christianity; studies in the formation of Christology [10 reprints since 1959], ᴱ*Kahl* Robert. Ph 1994, Trinity. x-181 p. $15 pa. 1-56338-076-5 [RelStR 21,140].

174 **Gerrish** R. A., Continuing the Reformation; [12] essays on modern religious thought. Ch 1993, Univ. xv-283 p. £39.25; pa. £23. 0-226-28870-6; -1-4 [TDig 41,361; JTS 46,403, T. *Gorringe*]. – ᴿTBR 6,3 (1993) 32 (L. *Houlden*); TLond 97 (1994) 467s (G. *Ward*: invaluable).

175 **Gottwald** N., The Hebrew Bible in its social world and in ours 1993 → 9,201: [RB 102,136, tit. pp.].

175* **Greschat** Martin, 60 Gb.: Protestanten in der Zeit; Kirche und Gesellschaft in Deutschland vom Kaiserreich bis zur Gegenwart. Stu 1994, Kohlhammer. xv-243 p. DM 89. 3-17-013182-6 [TLZ 120,1057, T. *Sauer*].

176 **Griffith** Sidney H., Arabic Christianity in the monasteries of ninth-century Palestine: CS 380. Aldershot 1992, Variorum. viii-341 p. £49.50. – ᴿBSO 57 (1994) 649 [H. T. *Norris*].

177 **Grimes** Ronald L., Ritual criticism; case studies in its practice; essays on its theory. Columbia 1990, Univ. S. Carolina. xiii-270 p. $35. – ᴿCritRR 5 (1992) 501-4 (E. V. *Gallagher*: partly inedita).

178 **Gurevich** Aaron, Historical anthropology of the Middle Age, ᴱ*Howlett* Jana. Ch 1992, Univ. 280 p. $40. 0-226-31083-3. – ᴿSpeculum 69 (1994) 602.

179 **Habgood** John, [Archbishop of York, some sermons of the past five years] Making sense. L 1993, SPCK. 231 p. £10 pa. – ᴿTLond 97 (1994) 394s (D. L. *Edwards*: still merits the Olympic gold medal, barely beating out the Pope because 'he never fails to provide proof that he has thought the subject out for himself').

180 **Habicht** Christian, Athen in hellenistischer Zeit; Ges. Aufs. Mü 1994, Beck. 378 p. 3-406-38164-2. – 29 art. (classics).

180* **Haendler** Gert, Die Rolle des Papsttums in der Kirchengeschichte bis 1200 [1956-90 reprints]. Gö 1993, VR. 371 p. 3-525-58159-9. – ᴿZKG 105 (1994) 130 (H. *Zimmermann*).

181 **Harl** Marguerite, Le déchiffrement du sens; [21] études sur l'herméneutique chrétienne d'Origène à Grégoire de Nysse: ÉtAug Coll. 135. P 1993, Inst. Ét. Aug. 471 p. [RHE 90,621, J.-M. *Auwers*].

181* **Harrington** Wilfred J., God does care; the presence of God in our world. Dublin 1994, Columba. xi-104 p. £6. 1-85607-099-9. – ᴿTBR 7,3 (1994s) 38 (C. *Armstrong*).

182 **Hauerwas** Stanley, Dispatches from the front; theological engagements with the secular. Durham ɴᴄ 1994, Duke Univ. 235 p. £23,50: 0-8223-1475-4 [TDig 42,169; TS 56,388, J. *Kotva*: the essay 'why Gays (as a Group) are Morally Superior to Christians (as a Group)' is not about homosexuality but about the fact that gays take their convictions seriously and make more trouble for the military; TLond 98,377-9, M. *Northcott*]. – ᴿTBR 7,2 (1994s) 33 (M. *Northcott*: fascinating).

182* **Hauerwas** Stanley M., Christian existence today; essays on Church, world, and living in between. Durham ɴᴄ 1988, Labyrinth. x-256 p. $15. – ᴿCritRR 5 (1992) 284-6 (T. *Reynolds*); ScotJT 46 (1993) 133s (D. B. *Forrester*: essays in response to Gᴜsᴛᴀғsᴏɴ).

183 **Hempel** Johannes (65. Gb.), Kirche wird auch in Zukunft sein. Lp 1994, Ev.-V. 264 p. ᴅᴍ 29,50. 3-374-01525-5 [TLZ 120,412, M. *Kruse*].

183* **Henrici** Peter, Glauben — Denken — Leben; Gesammelte Aufsätze [< IkaZ 1980-92]. Köln 1994, Communio. 204 p. ᴅᴍ 32. – ᴿLebZeug 49 (1994) 307 (B. *Neumann*).

184 **Hill** W. J., Search for the absent God [14 art.], ᴱ*Hilkert* Mary Catherine. NY 1992, Crossroad. xv-224 p. $27.50. – ᴿExpTim 106 (1994s) (T. *Gorringe*); ZkT 116 (1994) 339s (K. H. *Neufeld*).

185 **Hoffmann** Paul, Studien zur Frühgeschichte der Jesus-Bewegung: SBAufs 17. Stu 1994, KBW. 368 p. ᴅᴍ 79 [RHE 90,266*; TLZ 120,657, B. *Roloff*]. 3-460-06171-5. – 12 reprints.

186 **Hofius** Otfried, Paulusstudien²: ᴡᴜɴᴛ 51. Tü 1994, Mohr. vi-321 p. ᴅᴍ 59. 3-16-146265-5 [RelStR 21,237, A. J. *Malherbe*: not clear why called a revision of 1989].

187 **Horst** Pieter W. van der, Hellenism – Judaism – Christianity; essays on their interaction: ContriBExT 8. Kampen 1994, Kok Pharos. 300 p. ƒ70. 90-380-0106-5. – 15 reprints + 1 ineditum infra ➤ 7380 [JBL 107,566 & RB 102,451 & ZAW 107,531, tit. pp.; TLZ 120,428, M. *Karrer*].

188 **Houlden** J. L., Bible and belief [12 mostly reprints]. L 1991, SPCK. 174 p. £11. – ᴿNBlackf 74 (1993) 50s (D. *Fergusson*).

189 **Hourani** Albert, ᴱ*Khoury* Philip S., *Wilson* Mary, The modern Middle East [27 art. 1961-1991]. L 1993, Tauris. xii-692 p. – ᴿOrChrPer 60 (1994) 697s (V. *Poggi*).

189* **Hürten** Heinz [65. Gb., Aufsätze 1963-92], Katholiken, Kirche und Staat als Problem der Historie, ᴱ*Gruber* H. Pd 1994, Schöningh. viii-342 p. 3-506-73964-6 [TLZ 120,617, K. *Nowak*].

190 **Jaspert** Bernd, Theologie und Geschichte, GesAufs 2: EurHS 23/476. Fra 1994, Lang. 486 p. DM 108 pa. 3-631-45888-6 [TR 91,79, 15 tit. pp.; 271-355 BULTMANN].

190* **Jomier** Jacques, L'Islam vécu en Égypte (1945-1975): ÉtMusulmanes 35. P 1994, Vrin. 266 p. – ᴿIslamochristiana 20 (1994) 335 (M. *Borrmans*: 9 art., tit. pp.).

191 **Jones** Charles W. [1905-1989], BEDE, the schools and the Computus, ᴱ*Stevens* Wesley M.: CS 356. Aldershot 1994, Variorum. 356 p. $99.50. 0-86078-413-4 [TDig 42,71: 11 art., including on his Gen commentary and Easter computation; also a 154 p. annotated inventory of scientific writings falsely attributed to Bede).

191* **Jung** Hans-Gernot, Rechenschaft der Hoffnung, ᴱ*Hein* M.: MarbTSt 35. Marburg 1993, Elwert. x-301 p. 3-7708-1010-4 [TLZ 120,415, J. *Rogge*).

192 **Kern** Walter, Geist und Glaube [13 art. 1959-90 + biobibliog. 397-406-438 (A. *Batlogg*) & Innsbruck (7-30) K. H. *Neufeld*)], ᴱ *Neufeld*. Innsbruck 1992, Tyrolia. 451 p. 3-7022-1839-4 [Gregorianum 76,389, E. G. *Farrugia*].

193 **Klauck** H.-J., Alte Welt und neuer Glaube; [14] Beiträge zur Religionsgeschichte, Forschungsgeschichte und Theologie des Neuen Testaments: NOrb 29. FrS/Gö 1994, Univ./VR. 314 p. Fs 88. 3-7278-0945-9 / 3-525-53931-2 [NTAbs 38, p. 450; RB 102,298, tit. pp.].

194 **Knaus** Hermann, Studien zur Handschriftenkunde; ausgewählte Aufsätze, ᴱ*Achten* Gerard; Bibliog. *Staub* Christa. Mü 1992, Saur. 297 p. DM 148. 3-598-10975-X. – ᴿTGL 84 (1994) 489s (H.-W. *Stork*).

195 **Lambrecht** Jan, Pauline studies, collected essays: BtETL 115. Lv 1994, Univ./Peeters. xiv-465 p. Fb 2500. 90-6186-623-5 / 90-6831-622-2 [NTAbs 39, p. 336; RB 102,456, tit. pp.; TLZ 120,886, E. *Lohse*]. – ᴿExpTim 106 (1994s) 213s (E. *Best*: helpful).

196 **Landau** Jacob M., Jews, Arabs, Turks; [37] selected essays. J 1993, Magnes. 491 p. – ᴿWZKM 84 (1994) 358s (Claudia *Römer*).

197 **Lapide** Pinchas, Entfeindung leben? [12 art.]. Gü 1993, Gü-V. 175 p. DM 34. 3-579-02205-9 [NTAbs 38, p. 313].

198 **Leibowitz** Yeshayahu, Judaism, human values, and the Jewish State [27 art. ⊕ 1952-86], ᵀᴱ*Coldman* Eliezer, *al.* CM 1992, Harvard Univ. xxxiv-291 p. 0-674-48775-3. – ᴿSalesianum 56 (1994) 767s (R. *Vicent*).

199 *a)* **Lloyd** G. E. R., Methods and problems in Greek science; selected papers. C. 1991, Univ. xiv-457 p. – ᴿAnzAltW 46 (1993) 116s (Monika *Lavrencic*).

— *b)* **Lobo** George, Church and social justice. Anand 1992, Gujarat. x-169 p. $8; pa. $6 [TDig 42,174].

— *c)* **Löwe** Heinz † 1991, Religiosität und Bildung im frühen Mittelalter, Aufsätze, ᴱ*Struve* T. Weimar 1994, Böhlau. xv-384 p.; portr. DM 94. 3-7400-0920-9 [TLZ 120,536, G. *Haendler*].

200 **Lohfink** Norbert, Studien zur biblischen Theologie: SBAufs 16. Stu 1993, KBW. 325 p. DM 54 (48,60).

201 **Lohfink** Norbert, Theology of the Pentateuch; themes of the Priestly narratives and Deuteronomy [11 art. from various sources indicated in his Preface], ᵀ*Maloney* Linda M. E 1994, Clark. xiii-314 p. 0-567-29251-7.

Lohfink Norbert, *Zenger* Erich, Der Gott Israels und die Völker, Isa Pss 1994 → 3402.

202 **Luttrell** Anthony, The hospitallers of Rhodes and their Mediterranean world: CS 360. Aldershot 1992, Variorum. – [R]Speculum 69 (1994) 1308 (tit. pp.).

203 *a)* **McCormick** Richard A., Corrective vision; explorations in moral theology. KC 1994, Sheed&W. viii-256 p. $16. 1-55612-601-8 [TDig 42,375].

— *b)* **McEvenue** Sean, Interpretation and Bible; essays on truth in literature [4 inedita + 10]. ColMn 1994, Liturgical. 187 p. 0-8146-5036-8 [RB 102,441, tit. pp.; BL 95,95; R.P. *Carroll*: high praise; CBQ 57,626, E. *Hensell*]. – [R]OTAbs 17 (1994) 423 (R. E. *Murphy*).

— *c)* **McEvoy** James, Robert GROSSETESTE, exegete and philosopher: CS 446, 1994 [Speculum 70,985, 9 tit. pp.].

— *d)* **McGinn** Bernard, Apocalypticism in the Western tradition: CS 430. Aldershot 1994, Variorum. x-334 p. £18.50 [RHE 90,613, D. *Bradley*].

— *e)* **Madec** Goulven, Petites études augustiniennes: Antiquité 142. Turnhout 1994, Brepols. 388 p. Fb 1365. 2-85121-142-0.

204 **Madelung** Wilferd, [CS 1. 1985; 2.] Religious and ethnic movements in medieval Islam: CS 364. Aldershot/Brookfield VT 1992. Variorum. [x-377 p.] £49.50. – [R]BSO 57 (1994) 648s (M. *Cook*).

205 **Manni** Eugenio, *Sikelikà kaì italiká*; scritti minori 1-2: Kokalos supp. 8. R 1991, Bretschneider. viii-980 p. 88-7689-054-8. – [R]AJA 97 (1993) 368s (Laura *Maniscalco*).

206 **Markus** Robert A., Sacred and secular; studies on AUGUSTINE and Latin Christianity: CS 465. Aldershot/Brookfield 1994, Variorum/Ashgate. x-324 p. $90; 0-86078-450-9 [TDig 42,280: 19 art. 1957-92].

206* **Maron** Gottfried (65. Gb.), Die ganze Christenheit auf Erden; M. LUTHER und seine ökumenische Bedeutung; [E]*Müller* Gerhard, *Seebass* Gottfried. Gö 1993, VR. 301 p. – [R]TRu 59 (1994) 455s (B. *Moeller*).

207 *a)* **Mayerson** Philip, Monks, martyrs, soldiers and Saracens; papers on the Near East in late antiquity [40 reprints, in chronological order] (1962-1993). J 1994, Israel Expl. Soc, with NYU. xi-173 p.; 20 pl. 965-221-025-0. 10 infra.

— *b)* **Mees** M. [1921-90], Die frühe Rezeptionsgeschichte des Johannesevangeliums; am Beispiel von Textüberlieferung und Väterexegese [20 art.], [E]*Scheuermann* G., *Alkofer* A.-P.: ForBi 72. Wü 1994, Echter. x-320 p. DM 48. 3-429-01604-5 [NTAbs 39, p. 509; RHE 90,306*].

— *c)* **Meier** Fritz, Bausteine, Ausgewählte Aufsätze zur Islamwissenschaft, [E]*Glassen* Erika, *Schubert* Gudrun: Beiruter TSt 53a-c. Istanbul/Stu 1992, DMG/Steiner. I. xxvi-631 p.; II. xii-p. 635-1195; III. Indices xiv-166 p. DM 280. – [R]OLZ 89 (1994) 565-7 (M. *Gronke*).

— *d)* **Meyer** H. E., Kings and lords in the Latin kingdom of Jerusalem: CS 437. 1994, Variorum. x-338 p. [RHE 90,64*].

— *e)* **Minnich** Nelson H., Collected Studies: i) Fifth Lateran council / ii) Catholic Reformation. Brookfield 1993, Ashgate. viii-342 p. / x-313 p. $90 each [RelStR 21,180, D. R. *Janz*].

— *f)* **Momigliano** Arnaldo, Essays on ancient and modern Judaism, [T]*Masella-Gayley* Maura, [E]*Berti* Silvia. Ch 1994, Univ. xxviii-242 p. $25. 0-226-53381-6 [TDig 42,179].

— *g)* **Monaco** Giusto, Scritti minori: Pan 11s. Palermo 1992, Univ. 424 p. – [R]BStLat 24 (1994) 694-701 (Carla *Lo Cicero*).

208 *a)* **Montesi** Giancarlo, Miscellanea di studi storico-religiosi, [E]*Sanzi* Ennio. R 1993, Nuova Cultura. 132 p.

— *b)* **Morgan** Michael L., Dilemmas in modern Jewish thought; the dialectics of revelation and history [12 reprints 1981-92, adapted].

Bloomington 1992, Indiana Univ. xxi-181 p. $35. [RelStR 21,154, J. *Meskin*].
— *c*) **Muffs** Yohanan, Love and joy; law, language and religion in ancient Israel [6 reprints + inedita]. NY 1992, Jewish Theological Sem. xxvi-240 p. – ᴿAJS 19 (1994) 238-240 (G. *Anderson*: a skilled craftsman).
— *d*) **Munier** C., Autorité épiscopale et sollicitude pastorale, IIᵉ-VIᵉ siècles: CS. Aldershot 1991, Variorum. – ᴿRÉAug 39 (1993) 23-35 (P. *Mattei*).
209 **Nichols** Aidan, Scribe of the Kingdom; essays on theology and culture. L 1994, Sheed & W. vi-255 p., viii-255 p., £25 each. [TR 90,510, tit. pp.]. – ᴿMonth 255 (1994) 370s (M. *O'Halloran*).
210 **Nijenhuis** Willem, Ecclesia Reformata; studies on the Reformation II. [1 ineditum + réimpriés]. Leiden 1994, Brill. 325 p. 90-04-09465-2 [TLZ 120,345, B. *Moeller*]. – ᴿRHPR 74 (1994) 343s (M. *Chevallier*).
211 **Norsa** Medea [1877-1952], Syngrammata, ricerche papirologiche, ᴱ*Capasso* M. N 1993, Ellebors. 172 p. – ᴿAegyptus 79 (1994) 199-201 (Anna *Passoni dell'Acqua*).
212 **Oberman** Heiko A., The impact of the Reformation [13 reprints 1983-93]. GR 1994, Eerdmans. xi-263 p. $50. 0-8028-0732-0 [RelStR 21,244, D.R. *Janz*].
212* **Oberman** Heiko A., The Reformation; roots and ramifications [10 publications 1967-85], ᵀ*Gow* Andrew C. GR 1994, Eerdmans. xv-232 p. $30 [RelStR 21,244, D.R. *Janz*; TDig 42,389].
213 *a*) **O'Malley** John W., Religious culture in the sixteenth century; preaching, rhetoric, spirituality, and reform: Variorum CS. Brookfield ᴠᴛ 1993, Ashgate. x-282 p. $80 [RelStR 21,150, D.R. *Janz*].
— *b*) **O'Meara** J.J., [23] Studies in AUGUSTINE and ERIUGENA, ᴱ*Halton* T. Wsh 1992, Catholic University of America. 362 p. $60. 0-8132-0768-1 [RHE 90,246, P.-A. *Deproost*].
— *c*) **Osborne** Catherine, Eros unveiled; Plato and the God of love. Ox 1994, Clarendon. xiii-246 p. £30. 0-19-826761-4 [JTS 46,683, J.M. *Rist*, an appetizer, lacking system].
 Pannenberg Wolfhart, Toward a theology of nature; essays on science and faith 1993 ➳ 7247.
— *d*) **Parkes** M.B., Scribes, scripts, and readers; studies in the communication, presentation and dissemination of medieval texts. L/Rio Grande ᴏʜ 1991, Hambledon. xxiii-325 p.; 72 pl. $65 [Speculum 70, 687, tit. pp.]. – ᴿScriptorium 47 (1993) 107-110 (Monique-Cécile *Garand*).
214 **Perlitt** Lothar, Deuteronomium-Studien: ForAT 8. Tü 1994, Mohr. viii-211 p. 3-16-146154-1. – 15 reprints [RB 102,445, tit. pp.; TLZ 120,419, E. *Nielsen*].
215 **Pinckaers** S., La parola e la coscienza [20 art < L'Evangile et la morale 1990]. T 1991, SEI. – ᴿAnnTh 7 (1993) 271 (M. Pilar *Río*).
216 **Pope** Marvin H., Probative pontificating, ᴱ*Smith* Mark E. Ug. Bab. Lit. 10. Münster 1994, Ugarit-V. xv-406 p.; bibliog. 377-386. 3-927120-15-4 [UF 25 (1993) 505]. 32 reprints.
216* **Poupard** Paul, The Church and culture; challenge and confrontation, inculturation and evangelization, ᵀ*Miller* John H. St. Louis 1994, ᴄᴄᴠᴀ. xii-153 p. $15. 0-9626257-7-9 [TDig 42,183].
217 **Ramsey** Paul, The essential Paul Ramsey, a collection; ᴱ*Werpchowski* William, *Crocco* Stephen D. NHv 1994, Yale Univ. xxv-272 p. $30. 0-300-05815-2 [TDig 42,184].
218 **Raubitschek** A.E., The school of Hellas; [46 out of 294] essays on Greek

history, archaeology, and literature. Ox 1991, UP. xvi-384 p. $45. 0-19-505691-4. – ᴿAJA 97 (1993) 176s (D.J. *Geagan*).
219 **Ravasi** Gianfranco, Mattutino [articoli c.1991s su testi biblici o altri]. CasM 1993, Piemme. 468 p. Lᵐ40. – ᴿCC 145 (1994,1) 614s (F. *Castelli*).
219* **Reynolds** Roger E., Law and liturgy in the Latin Church, 5th-12th centuries: CS 457. Aldershot/Brookfield 1994, Variorum/Ashgate. xii-318 p. $90. 0-86078-405-3 [TDig 42,288: 18 art. 1968-91].
220 **Ricœur** Paul, Lectures 3: aux frontières de la philosophie: La couleur des idées. P 1994, Seuil. 374 p. F 160. 2-02-02506-8. 18 art.; 3 in 1995 *Elenchus*. – ᴿÉtudes 381 (1994) 279 (G. *Petitdemange*).
220* **Robbins** V.K., New boundaries in old territory; form and social rhetoric in Mark, [10 art. 1973-90], ᴱ*Gowler* B.: StEarlyC. NY 1994, Lang. xx-270 p. $40. 0-8204-1911-7 [NTAbs 39, p. 144].
221 **Roberts** W. Dayton, Patching God's garment; environment and mission in the 21st century. Monrovia CA 1994, World Vision. $14. 0-912552-85-9 [TDig 42,186].
221* *a)* **Rorty** Richard, Consequences of pragmatism (essays 1972-1980). Mp 1994, Univ. Minnesota. xlvii-237 p. 0-8166-1063-0; pa. -4-9.
— *b)* **Rorty** Richard M., Contingency, irony, and solidarity [... pro-Nɪᴇᴛᴢsᴄʜᴇ]. C 1993 = 1989, Univ. xvi-201 p. 0-521-35381-3; pa. -6781-6.
222 **Rose** Peter, Sons of the gods, children of earth; ideology and literary form in ancient Greece. Ithaca 1992, Cornell Univ. $45; pa. $15. – ᴿClasJ 90 (1994s) 195-8 (S. *Goldhill*).
222* **Ruppert** Lothar, Studien zur Literaturgeschichte des Alten Testaments: SBAufs 18. Stu 1994, KBW. 312 p. DM 79. 3-460-06181-2. – 15 reprints + 1 ineditum infra. [OTAbs 18, p. 395; TLZ 120,643, H. *Seebass*].
223 **Saxer** Victor, Pères saints et culte chrétien dans l'Église des premiers siècles: CS 446 [French, 3 German, 3 Italian; 1959-65]. Aldershot 1994, Variorum. xii-298 p. $87.50. 0-86078-441-X [TDig 42,187].
224 *a)* **Schürmann** H., Jesus – Gestalt und Geheimnis; Gesammelte Beiträge, ᴱ*Scholtissek* K. Pd 1994, Bonifatius. 456 p. DM 50. 3-87088-773-7 [RB 102,455, tit. pp. and notice of earlier collections]. – ᴿETL 70 (1994) 174s (F. *Neirynck*); SNTU 19 (1994) 197s (A. *Fuchs*); TGL 84 (1994) 485-7 (J. *Ernst*); TvT 34 (1994) 444 (H. van de *Sandt*).
— *b)* **Schütte** Heinz, The primacy of Peter; essays in ecclesiology, ᴱ*Meyendorff* J. 1992. – ᴿOstKSt 43 (1994) 74s (B. *Plank*).
— *c)* **Schwartz** G. David, A Jewish appraisal of dialogue; between talk and theology. Lanham MD 1994, UPA. xiii-148 p. $42.50. 08191-9413-1 [TDig 42,290: reprinted book-previews and 4 reprinted art.; 2 inedita].
— *d)* ᴱ**Siebers** Tobin, Religion and the authority of the past [10 essays]. AA 1993, Univ. Michigan. x-294 p. $45; pa. $17 [Cithara 34/1,45, D. *Jobling*].
— *e)* **Simonetti** Manlio, Ortodossia ed eresia tra I e II secolo [11 art. 1966-92]: Armarium 5. Messina 1994, Ribbettino. 351 p. Lᵐ 28 [RHE 90,625, J.-M. *Auwers*].
— *f)* **Sobrino** Jon, The principle of mercy; taking the crucified people from the Cross. Mkn 1994, Orbis. viii-199 p. $17 pa. 0-88344-986-2 [TDig 42,292].
— *g)* **Sullivan** Richard E., Christian missionary activity in the early Middle Ages: CS 431. Aldershot/Brookfield 1994, Variorum/Ashgate. x-265 p. $79. 0-86078-402-9.

225 **Templeton** Elizabeth, The strangeness of God [11 art. since 1978]. L 1993, A. James. xv-137 p. £8 pa. – ᴿAnglTR 76 (1994) 120-2 (R. J. *Kus*).

225* **Theissen** Gerd, Lichtspuren; Predigten und Bibelarbeiten [1990-3]. Gü 1994, Kaiser. 219 p. DM 38. 3-579-03009-4. – ᴿTLZ 119 (1994) 1139-41 (J. *Hermelink*).

226 **Thomson** Robert W., [19 1964-92] Studies in Armenian literature and Christianity: CS 451. Aldershot 1994, Variorum. xii-322 p. [TDig 42,190]. – ᴿOrChrPer 60 (1994) 641s (G. *Traina*).

226* **Tsaferis** Yoram, Ancient churches revealed. J 1993, Israel Expl. Soc. xi-358 p.; 27 pl. $40. – ᴿOLZ 89 (1994) 561-4 (G. *Strohmaier-Wiederanders*).

227 **Vermeylen** A., Nova et vetera, ᴱ*Wulf* G. de: Recueil 6/41. LvN/Bru 1992, Collège Érasme/Nauwelaerts. xix-256 p. [RHE 90,265*].

227* **Vernant** Jean-Pierre, Mortals and immortals; collected essays, ᴱ*Zeitlin* Froma I. Princeton 1991, Univ. viii-341 p. $13 pa. 0-691-09131-2 [RelStR 21,50, L. J. *Alderink*).

228 **Vinay** Valdo, Commenti ai Vangeli. Brescia 1992, Morcelliana. 336 p. Lᵐ 28. – ᴿCC 145 (1994,3) 346s (D. *Scaiola*: 'non si presenta come un libro commemorativo di V. V.').

229 **Wallis** Gerhard, Mein Freund hatte einen Weinberg; Aufsätze und Vorträge zum Alten Testament: BeitErfAJ 23. Fra 1994, Lang. [viii-] 301 p.; portr. 3-8204-1174-7. 18 art.; 3 inedita infra [BL 95,23, J. W. *Rogerson*; OTAbs 18, p. 142, *dates* with tit. pp.; ZAW 107,368, tit. pp.].

230 **Ward-Perkins** J. B., a) Marble in antiquity, collected papers, ᴱ*Dodge* Hazel, *Ward-Perkins* Bryan: Mg 6. Rome 1992, British School. xii-180 p.; 141 fig.; 2 pl. £25. 0-904152-20-0. – ᴿLatomus 53 (1994) 719 (J. *Debergh*).

– b) **Ward-Perkins** J. B. (1912-1981), Studies in Roman and early Christian architecture. L 1994, Pindar. viii-532 p. 0-907132-76-6.

– c) **Watson** Wilfred G. E., Traditional techniques in classical Hebrew verse [3 inedita infra & revised reprints]: jOsu 170. Shf 1994, JStOT. 534 p. £55. 1-85075-459-4. – ᴿExpTim 106 (1994s) 157 (C. S. *Rodd*).

– d) **Watt** W. Montgomery, Early Islam; (23) collected articles. E 1990, Univ. xi-207 p. – ᴿIslamochristiana 19 (1993) 351s (J. *Lacunza-Balda*).

– e) **Weren** Wim, Intertextualiteit en bijbel [8 studies 1984-92]. Kampen 1993, Kok Pharos. 262 p. 90-242-7451-6 [RB 102,142, tit. pp.; CBQ 57,847, J. *Gillman*].

– f) **Winternitz** Moriz [1863-1937], Kleine Schriften [79, not only on Indology], ᴱ*Brinkhaus* Horst: Glasenapp-Stiftung 30. Stu 1991, Steiner. xxvi-464 p. xvii - p. 465-968. – ᴿJAOS 114 (1994) 117s (R. *Salomon*).

231 **Wise** Michael O., Thunder in Gemini and other essays on the history, language and literature of Second Temple Palestine: JPseud supp. 15. Shf 1994, JStOT. 265 p. $37.50. 1-85075-460-8 [OTAbs 17, p. 690: 2 reprints + inedita with renvoi to abstracts there; RB 102,296, tit. pp.; BAR-W 21/4,8, 231, G. J. *Brooke*].

232 **Wolf** George, Studies in the Hebrew Bible and early rabbinic Judaica. NY 1994, Moriah. vii-183 p.; bibliog. 172-8.

233 **Würthwein** Ernst, Studien zur deuteronomistischen Geschichtswerk: BZAW 227. B 1994, de Gruyter. vii-219 p. 3-11-014269-4. – 12 art. (3 inedita, infra). [OTAbs 18,158; RB 102,295, tit. pp.]. – ᴿExpTim 106 (1994s) 332s (R. *Mason*).

234 **Zobel** Hans-Jürgen, Altes Testament — Literatursammlung und Heilige Schrift; Gesammelte Aufsätze [teils inedita] zur Entstehung, Geschichte

und Auslegung des Alten Testaments: BZAW 212. B 1993, de Gruyter.
vii-306 p. DM 138. 3-11-013892-0 [BL 95,23, K.W. *Whitelam*: careful,
dated].

A1.3   *Plurium compilationes* **biblicae.**

235 Collected essays [by (or reprints of) various authors, without pp.]: JQR 84
(1993s) 118-127. 389-396.

236 *a*) **Abadie** P., *al.*, Initiation à la lecture d'un texte bibliqie. Lyon 1994,
Profac. 217 p. F 90 [NRT 117,266, J.-L. *Ska*].
— *b*) Auf der Suche nach einer neuen Christologie; von Jesus, dem Juden
erzählen. Bendorf/Rhein 1993, Hedwig-Dransfeld-Haus. 99 p. DM 10
[TR 90,519, tit. pp.].
— *c*) ^E**Bailey** R., Hermeneutics for preaching: approaches to contemporary
interpretation of Scripture [7 emerging models, each with a Scripture
example]. Nv 1992, Broadman. 223 p. $16. 1-8054-1016-3 [NTAbs 38,
p. 444].
— *d*) ^E**Beale** G.K., The right doctrine from the wrong texts? Essays on the
use of the Old Testament in the New. GR 1994, Baker. 440 p.; bibliog.
405-414. 0-8010-1088-8.
— *e*) ^e**Børresen** Kari, [*Vogt* K....] Women's studies of the Christian and
Islamic traditions; ancient, medieval and Renaissance foremothers). Dordrecht 1993, Kluwer. 368 p. $109 [TLZ 120,314, R. *Kirste*].
237 ^E**Bosman** H.I., *al.*, Plutocrats and paupers; wealth and poverty in the
OT. Pretoria 1991, van Schaik. vi-265 p. $16.60. 0-627-01778-9
[OTAbs 16, p. 437, R. *Harrison*: on everything from medieval exegesis to
Iron Age soil types, but not systematically on rich/poor]. – ^RAndrUnSem
32 (1994) 117s (P.U. *Maynard-Reid*).
238 ^E**Carson** D.A., Right with God; justification in the Bible and the world.
GR 1994, Baker. 255 p. $20. 0-8536-4516-7. – ^RKerux 9,3 (1994) 42s
(R.A. *Riesen*).
239 *a*) [➤ 251*] Chiesa e magistero: SubsBPont 17. R 1994, Pontificio
Istituto Biblico [AcPIB 9,893, 11-33 *Gilbert* M.].
— *b*) ^E**Chilton** Bruce D., *Evans* Craig A., Studying the historical Jesus;
evaluations of the state of current research: NTTools 19. Leiden 1994,
Brill. xvi-611 p. *f*250. 90-04-09982-4 [NTAbs 29, p.135, topics sans
tit. pp.; TR 91,77: 16 tit. pp.] 5 infra.
— *c*) ^E**Cohen** Shaye J.D., The Jewish family in antiquity: BrownJud 289.
Atlanta 1993, Scholars. 167 p. $41 [RelStR 21,340].
— *d*) ^E**Coulot** Claude, Exégèse et herméneutique; comment lire la Bible
[CERIT]: LDiv 158. P 1994, Cerf. 175 p. F 80. 2-204-05068-7. 6 art. [RB
102,441, tit. pp.].
240 ^E**Davis** Moshe, *Ben Arieh* Yehoshua, With eyes toward Zion III. Western
societies and the Holy Land. NY 1991, Praeger. xiv-275 p. [AJS 17 (1992)
375s; titles (18) sans pp.].
Duhaime Jean ➤ 255s, *Mainville* Odette 1994.
240* *a*) ^E**Emmerson** Grace, Prophets and poets; a companion to the prophetic books of the OT. – *b*) ^E**Parr** John, Sowers and reapers; a
companion to the four Gospels and Acts [both books are materials from
Guidelines series]. L 1994, Bible Reading Fellowship. 301 p., £9 / 446 p.,
£10. 0-7459-2599-5; -31-6. – ^RExpTim 106 (1994s) 277s (N. *Clark*).
241 *a*) ^E**Engberg-Pedersen** T., *al.*, Fra Alexander til Apokalypser: Hel-

lenismestudier 7. Aarhus 1992, Univ. 77 p. Dk 38. 87-7288-387-1. 4 art.; p. 64-77 *Hallbäck* Geert, Åbenbaring og fremdtit ['future', OTAbs 16, p. 559].
— *b*) ᴱ**Evans** Craig A., *Stegner* W. Richard, The Gospels and the Scriptures of Israel: jNsu 104. Shf 1994, JStOT. 505 p. £35. 1-85075-497-7 [NTAbs 39, p. 323].
— *c*) **Feldmeier** Reinhard, *Heckel* Ulrich, Die Heiden; Juden, Christen und das Problem des Fremden [15 art.]: WUNT 70. Tü 1994, Mohr. xviii-449 p. DM 288. 3-16-146147-9 [RB 102,451, tit. pp.].
— *d*) ᴱ**Frankel** Jonathan, Jews and messianism in the modern era: Metaphor and meaning in contemporary Jewry 7. Ox 1991, UP. xv-439 p. £30. 0-19-506690-1. – ᴿJSS 38 (1993) 157s (L. *Kochan*).
242 ᴱ**Gameson** R., The early medieval Bible; its production, decoration and use: StPalaeog 2. C 1994, Univ. xiv-242 p.; 58 fig. £40. [RHE 89,211*].
243 ᴱ**Gill** David W. J., *Gempf* Conrad, The Book of Acts in its Graeco-Roman Setting... First Century Setting 2 [1. 1993 ➤ 258*c*]. GR/Carlisle 1994, Eerdmans/Paternoster. xiii-627 p. 0-8028-2434-X / UK 0-85364-564-7. 17 art.; infra [NTAbs 39, p. 137, topics sans tit. pp.]. – ᴿExpTim 106 (1994s) 120s (C. K. *Barrett*).
244 **Gottwald** N. K., *Horsley* R. A., The Bible and liberation²ʳᵉᵛ [➤ ¹1976]; political and social hermeneutics. Mkn/L 1993, Orbis/SPCK. xxi-558 p. $22. – ᴿLvSt 19 (1994) 269-272 (Jesús *Castillo-Coronado*).
245 ᴱ**Green** Joel B., *Turner* Max, Jesus of Nazareth, Lord and Christ; essays on the historical Jesus and New Testament Christology. GR/Carlisle 1994, Eerdmans/Paternoster. xxi-536 p. £30. 0-8028-3750-6.
246 ᴱ**Hengel** Martin, *Löhr* Harmut, Schriftauslegung im antiken Judentum und im Urchristentum: WUNT 73. Tü 1994, Mohr. [ix-]282 p.
246* ᴱ**Hoerth** Alfred J., *al.*, Peoples of the Old Testament world. GR 1994, Baker. 400 p. $30. 0-8010-4383-2 [RelStR 21,126, W. L. *Humphreys*].
247 ᴱ**Holm** John, (*Bowden* John), Attitudes to nature [both cosmogony and ecology]: Themes in religious studies. L/NY 1994, Pinter/St. Martin's. xii-172 p. [RelStR 21,207, G. *Yocum*].
248 ᴱ**Jefford** Clayton N., The Didache in context; essays on its text history and transmission [ᵀ*Cody* Aelred 3-14]: NT supp. 77. Leiden 1994, Brill. 420 p. $120. 90-04-10045-8 [TR 91,275, tit. pp.].
249 ᴱ**Katz** Steven T., Interpreters of [mostly modern] Judaism in the late twentieth century: History of the Jewish People. Wsh 1993, B'nai B'rith. xv-423 p. $20; pa. $12 [RelStR 21,340, R. B. *Gibbs*].
250 ᵀᴱ**Kessler** Martin, (p. ix-xxix) Voices from Amsterdam; a modern tradition of reading biblical narrative [11 Dutch articles],ᵀ: SBL Semeia Studies. Atlanta 1994, Scholars. vii-168 p.; $30. 1-55540-897-4. 11 art. infra [OTAbs 17, p. 650, indicating number of each excerpt; CBQ 57,623, Carol J. *Dempsey*; TLZ 120,132, H. *Seebass*; RB 102,293 & ZAW 107,548, tit. pp.].
251 ᴱ**Kevers** P., Waarom en hoe de bijbel leven? Konelcahier 6. Averbode/Den Bosch 1992, Altiora / Kath. B.-Stichting. 122 p. – ᴿCollatVL 24 (1994) 433s (M. *Vervenne*).
251* **Laghi** P., *Gilbert* M., *Vanhoye* A., Chiesa e Sacra Scrittura; un secolo di magistero ecclesiastico e studi biblici: SubsBPont 17. R 1994, Pontificio Istituto Biblico. 58 p.
252 ᴱ**Laperrousaz** E.-M., *Lemaire* A., La Palestine à l'époque perse: BJér-Ét annexe. P 1994, Cerf. 329 p.; ill. – ᴿRStFen 22 (1994) 275s (E. *Acquaro*).

253 ᴱLevy Bernard S., The Bible in the Middle Ages; its influence on literature and art: MdvRenTSt 89. Binghamton 1992. xvi-208 p. [RelStR 21,41, Celia *Chazelle*: six fine big-name studies].

254 ᴱLohrbächer Albrecht, Was Christen vom Judentum lernen können. FrS 1994, Herder. 220 p. ᴅᴍ 58. – ᴿEntschluss 49,11 (1994) 42s (T. M. *Meier*).

ᴱLorenzani Massimo, La volontà di Dio nella bibbia: Studi biblici 13, 1994 → 368,

255 ᴱMainville Odette, *Duhaime* Jean, *Létourneau* Pierre, Loi et autonomie dans la Bible et la tradition chrétienne: Héritage et projet 53. Saint-Laurent 1994, Fides. 292 p. $35. 2-7621-1725-0. – 12 art. [RB 102,442, tit. pp.].

255* — ᴱDuhaime Jean, *Mainville* Odette, Entendre la voix du Dieu vivant; interprétations et pratiques actuelles de la Bible: Lectures Bibliques 41. Montréal 1994, Médiaspaul. 367 p. 2-89420-258-X. – 20 art.; 11-26, *Laberge* L., TeNaK; 117-129, *La Potterie* I. de, patrist.-médiév.

256 ᴱMartini Luciano, Mare di guerra, mare di religione; il caso Mediterraneo: Forum per i problemi della pace e della guerra. F 1994, Cultura della Pace. 206 p. 88-09-14054-1.

256* *a)* ᴱMinkoff Harvey, Approaches to the Bible; the best of Bible Review. Wsh 1994, BA[R] Soc. vii-372 p. 1-880317-16-8. – 27 reprints [OTAbs 18, p. 140, tit. pp.].

257 *a)* ᴱOchs Peter, The return to Scripture in Judaism and Christianity; [republished] essays in postcritical Scriptural interpretation. NY 1993, Paulist. 378 p. $19. 0-8091-3425-X. – ᴿExpTim 106 (1994s) 248 (F. *Morgan*).

— *b)* La pace nella Bibbia: Sussidi biblici. Reggio Emilia, c. 1993, S. Lorenzo. viii-105 p. 88-8071-055-9.

— *c)* **Porter** Stanley E., *Carson* D. A., Biblical language and linguistics; open questions in biblical research [first half: Porter-Fanning debate on verbal aspect 1-82]: jNsu 80. Shf 1993, Academic. 217 p. – ᴿFgNt 7 (1994) 215-22 (J. *Mateos*, all on first half).

— *d)* ᴱReeves John C., Tracing the threads; studies in the vitality of Jewish pseudepigrapha: SBL Early Judaism 6. Atlanta 1994, Scholars. xiii-296 p. $30; pa. $20. 1-55540-994-6; pa. -5-4. – 10 solicited essays, infra [RB 102,448, tit. pp.].

258 *a)* ᴱSchüssler Fiorenza Elisabeth, Searching the Scriptures, 1. A feminist introduction [critical homage to Elizabeth STANTON 1895 and Anna COOPER 1892]. L 1994, SCM. xiii-397 p. £17.50. 0-334-02556-7. – ᴿTvT 34 (1994) 440 (H. *Meyer-Wilmes*).

— *b)* **Seybold** Michael, *Waldenfels* Hans, La rivelazione, ᵀᴱ*Ruggieri* Giuseppe [HbDg 1971/7]: Storia delle dottrine cristiane 1. Palermo 1992, Augustinus. xviii-617 p. 88-246-1301-2 [Gregorianum 76,389, R. *Fisichella*].

— *c)* **Winter** Bruce W., The book of Acts in the first century setting: Book of Acts in its Ancient Literary Setting 1 [of 6 foreseen; → 243 supra; 9,301]. GR 1993, Eerdmans, for UK Paternoster. 479 p. $37.50. 0-8028-2433-1 [TLZ 120,1005, M. *Wolter*]. – ᴿBZ 38 (1994) 290s (R. *Schnackenburg*: series to continue and replace FOAKES-JACKSON 1992-39); CBQ 57,441, P. H. *Davids*; ExpTim 106 (1994s) 88 (C. K. *Barrett*).

— *d)* ᴱWise Michael G., al., Methods of investigation of the Dead Sea Scrolls and the Khirbet Qumran site; present realities and future projects:

Annals 722. NY 1994, Acad. Sciences. xiii-514 p. 0-89766-793-X [OIAc 11,45].

A1.4   *Plurium compilationes* **theologicae.**

259 ᴱ**Alcock** Susan E., *Osborne* Robin, Placing the gods; sanctuaries and sacred space in ancient Greece [11 authors comment on F. de POLIGNAC's Naissance de la laïcité grec 1984]. Ox 1994, Clarendon. x-271 p.; ill.; maps. $55. 0-19-814947-6 [RelStR 21,324].

259* ᴱ**Atherton** John, Christian social ethics, a reader [i. social Christianity; ii. liberation theology; iii. conservatism, M. NOVAK]. Cleveland 1994, Pilgrim. xii-410 p. $25 pa. 0-8298-0000-6 [TDig 42,159].

260 ᴱ**Barbour** R. S., The Kingdom of God and human society [14 art.]: Scripture, Theology & Society Group. E 1993, Clark. xv-289 p. £15 pa. – ᴿTLond 97 (1994) 480s (M. *Oakley*: lucid but dense).

261 ᴱ**Barkaï** R., Chrétiens, Musulmans et Juifs dans l'Espagne médiévale; de la convergence à l'expulsion. P 1994, Cerf. 334 p. [RHE 89,409*].

261* ᴱ**Basden** Paul, Has our theology changed? Southern Baptist thought since 1845. Nv 1994, Broadman. $20. 0-8054-1045-7.

262 ᴱ**Berkey** R. F., *Edwards* S. A., Christology in dialogue. Cleveland 1993, Pilgrim. viii-390 p. $25. 0-8298-0956-2. 24 art. [NTAbs 38, p. 311].

262* ᴱ**Boeft** J. den, *Hilhorst* A., Early Christian poetry; a collection of essays. Leiden 1993, Brill. 318 p. 90-04-09939-5 [RelStR 21,243, R. J. *Wilken*].

263 ᴱ**Bulman** Raymond, *Panella* Frederick J., Paul TILLICH, a Catholic assessment [13 orig. art.]. ColMn 1993, Liturgical/Glazier. 200 p. $13. 0-8146-5828-8 [TDig 42,182: *Gilkey* L., Protestant response].

264 Communio 19 (Paris 1994): **111**. Décalogue III, Le respect du sabbat; – **112**. Les nations [... Unies; Sarajevo]; – **113**. La spiritualité; – **114**. La guerre; – **115**. Médias, démocratie, Église; – **116**. La charité. c. 160 p. chaque. Autres éditions dans plusieurs langues partiellement traduites.

265 IZT – Concilium deutsch 30 (1994): **1**. Christlicher Glaube in unterschiedlichen Kulturen; – **2**. Gewalt gegen Frauen; – **3**. Islam – eine Herausforderung; – **4**. Die Mystik und die Krise der Institutionen; – **5**. Katholische Identität [ökumenisch, juridisch, Media]; – **6**. Wozu Theologie? – Similar editions in English, French etc.

266 *a*) ᴱ**Cook** Guillermo, New face of the Church in Latin America, between tradition and change: AmerMissiol 18. Mkn 1994, Orbis. xiv-289 p. $19. 0-88344-937-4 [TDig 42,379: 21 art.; half reprints].

— *b*) ᴱ**Craemer-Ruegenberg** I., *Speer* A., Scientia et ars im Hoch- und Spätmittelalter: MiscMdv 22, 1994 → 149.

— *c*) Cristianesimo e religioni in dialogo: SemQuadT 4. Brescia 1994, Morcelliana. 261 p. Lᵐ 30. 88-372-1536-3 [Gregorianum 76,774, J. *Dupuis*].

— *d*) ᴱ**Crump** Miller R., Empirical theology; a handbook. Birmingham AL 1992, Rel.Edn. vi-304 p. – ᴿAngelicum 71 (1994) 597-9 (A. *Wilder*: quite informative; the two Catholic contributions, by G. *Sloyan* and B. *Lee*, are the most specifically Christian).

— *e*) ᴱ**Delumeau** Jean, Le fait religieux [dans le monde actuel], P c. 1994, Fayard. 781 p. – ᴿCRAI (1994) 104s (*ipse*).

267 ᴱ**Dijk-Hemmes** Fokkelien van, *Brenner* Athalya, Reflections on theology and gender. Kampen 1994, Kok Pharos. 107 p. f 50. 90-390-0111-1. – p. 33-48, *Henten* J. van, Judith 7,13; p. 21-31, *Heijerman* Mieke, Prov 7.

268 ᴱ**Douglass** R. Bruce, *Hollenbach* David,   Catholicism and liberalism; contributions to American public philosophy: C Studies in Religion and American Public Life. C 1994, Univ. xv-352 p. $40. 0-521-44528-0 [TR 90,518, tit. pp.].

268* ᴱ**Erhart** Hannelore,   Frauenforschungsprojekt zur Geschichte der Theologinnen, Gö Hist.-Th. 19.-20. Jh. 7.   Neuk 1994. viii-526 p. DM 43,20. 3-7887-1477-8 [TLZ 120,161, Maike *Lauther-Pohl*].

269 ᴱ**Evans** Craig A., *Hagner* Donald A.,   Anti-semitism and early Christianity; issues of polemic and faith. Mp 1993, Fortress. xxiii-328 p. $16. 0-8006-2748-2. – ᴿTBR 7,2 (1994s) 34 (M. *Bockmuehl*).

270 ᴱ**Filoramo** Giovanni,   Storia delle religioni, 1. Le religioni antiche: Enciclopedie del sapere. Bari 1994, Laterza. 702 p. Lᵐ 75. 88-420-4488-1 [Gregorianum 76,775, G. *Marconi*].

271 ᴱ**France** R.T., *McGrath* A.E. [...Oxford Wycliffe Hall adherents] Evangelical Anglicans; their role and influence in the Church today. L 1993, SPCK. viii-183 p. £10 pa. – ᴿChurchman 107 (1993) 278-280 (C. *Idle*); TLond 97 (1994) 131s (T. *Lane*: fine 'Outsider's perspective' by 'liberal Catholic bishop', R. *Holloway*: evangelicals' Christianity may survive and become dominant; they can embrace bad taste for the sake of the Gospel).

272 ᴱ**Galvin** John P.,   Faith and the future (W. KASPER, G. O'COLLINS, R. E, BROWN). NY 1994, Paulist. 73 p. $7. 0-8091-3455-1 [Gregorianum 76,211]. – ᴿTBR 7,3 (1994s) 43 (A. *Chester*).

272* ᴱ**Gerrish** Brian A.,   Continuing the Reformation; essays on modern religious thought [12 reprints]. Ch 1993, Univ. xv-283 p. $20. 0-226-28871-4 [ZnTg 2,303-6, D. *Jodock*].

273 ᴱ**Gibellini** Rosino, *a)* Percorsi di teologia africana: GdT 226. Brescia 1994, Queriniana. 132 p. Lᵐ 35. 88-399-0726-2 [Gregorianum 76,163-5, A. *Wolanin*]. – ᴿEstE 69 (1994) 279s (J. *Madangi Sengi*). – *b)* Paths of African theology [11 art.]. Mkn 1994, Orbis. xi-202 p. $19. 0-88344-974-9.

273* ᴱ**Gilley** Sheridan, *Sheils* W.J.,   A history of religion in Britain; practice and belief from pre-Roman times to the present [26 art.]. CM 1994, Blackwell [but all except 2 from UK]. viii-590 p. $65; pa. $30. 0-631-15281-4; -9378-2 [TDig 42,169].

274 *a)* ᴱ**Gossen** Gary H., (*León-Portilla* Miguel),   South and Meso-American native spirituality; from the cult of the feathered serpent to the theology of liberation: World Spirituality 4.   NY 1993, Crossroad. xii-563 p. $49.50. – ᴿCritRR 6 (1993) 585s (tit. pp.).

— *b)* ᴱ**Haddad** Yvonne Y., *Smith* Jane I.,   Muslim communities in North America. Albany 1994, SUNY. xxx-545 p. $89.50; pa. $30. 0-7914-2019-1; -30-5 [TDig 42,180].

— *c)* ᴱ**Hallman** David G.,   Ecotheology; voices from South and North. Geneva/Mkn 1994, WCC/Orbis. ix-316 p. $17 pa. / 0-88344-993-5 [TDig 42,267].

275 ᴱ**Hill** Christopher, *Yarnold* Edward,   Anglicans and Roman Catholics; the search for unity; the ARCIC [I only] documents and their reception. L 1994, SPCK/CTS, 344 p. £20. 0-281-04745-6. – ᴿExpTim 106 (1994s) 217 (G. R. *Evans* makes clear that *prior* 'elucidations' were published *with* 'The Final Report', but not whether the 'clarifications' aimed to answer the Vatican's formal response are *these* or are also *prior*).

275* ᴱ**Hoesterey** Ingeborg,   Zeitgeist in Babel; the postmodernist controversy. Bloomington 1991, Indiana Univ. xv-269 p. $13 pa. 0-253-20611-2. – ᴿChrSchR 23s (1993s) 210s (J. E. *Horstmann*).

276 ᴱHoffman Ronald, *Albert* Peter J., Religion in a revolutionary age: Perspectives on the American Revolution. Univ. Press of Virginia for U.S. Capitol Historical Soc., 1994. xvii-350 p. $39.50. 0-8139-11485-5 [TDig 42,85].

277 ᴱHolm Joan [→ 10361], Women in religion. L/NY 1994, Pintor/St. Martin's. xii-181 p. £29.50; pa. £10. 1-85567-1085; -9-3. – ᴿTBR 7,3 (1994s) 565 (A. *Pryce*).

277* Horstmann Johannes, Ende des Katholizismus oder Gestaltwandel der Kirche? Vorträge 43. Schwerte 1993, Katholische Akademie. 147 p. 3-927382-13-2.

278 ᴱIdinopulos Thomas A., Religion and reductionism; essays on ELIADE [contested by SEGAL], and the challenge of the social sciences for the study of religion [(Oxford, ᴼᴴ) Miami Univ. Nov. 1990]. StHistRel 62. Leiden 1994, Brill. viii-238 p. 90-04-08870-4. 16 art.; 8 infra → Elenchus 11 (1995).

279 ᴱKansas John F. X., Thomistic papers VI [11 responses to MᶜCOOL Gerald, From unity to pluralism; plus a 1993 lecture]. Houston 1994, Univ. St. Thomas. x-278 p. $27; pa. $16. 0-268-01886-3; -7-1 [TDig 42,191].

280 ᴱKatz Steven T., Mysticism and language [10 art.]. NY 1992, Oxford-UP. 262 p. $38. – ᴿJAOS 114 (1994) 475s (E. *Deutsch*).

    ᴱKustermann Abraham P., Revision der Theologie – Reform der Kirche; Bedeutung des Tü Theologen J. S. DREY (1777-1853) in Geschichte und Gegenwart 1994 → 355b.

281 ᴱLaChance Albert J., *Carroll* John E., Embracing earth; Catholic approaches to ecology. Mkn 1995, Orbis. xxiv-280 p. $19 pa. 0-88344-966-8 [TDig 42,268].

282 ᴱLangan John P., Catholic universities in Church and society. Wsh c. 1994, Georgetown Univ. 261 p. $15 [NOxR 67/1, J. *Wills*, also on HESBURGH T. M.].

282* ᴱLanger Michael, Wir alle sind Fremde; Texte gegen Hass und Gewalt. Rg 1993, Pustet. 180 p. ᴰᴹ 26,80. – ᴿTPQ 142 (1994) 315-7 (Eva *Drechsler*: doubtful that such books will ever be read by those they should be aimed at).

283 ᴱNelson James B., *Longfellow* Sandra P., Sexuality and the sacred; sources for theological reflection. L 1994, Murray. xviii-406 p. 0-264-67329-8. – 36 reprints; 3 infra.

283* ᴱNeusner Jacob, *al.*, Religion, science, and magic; in concert and in conflict. Ox 1992, UP. xii-294 p. £12. – ᴿBijdragen 55 (1994) 458s (A. van *Dijk*).

284 ᴱNoll Mark, *al.*, Evangelicalism; comparative studies of popular Protestantism in North America, the British Isles and beyond 1700-1900. NY 1994, Oxford-UP. 430 p. £40; pa. £14. 0-19-508362-9; -3-6. – ᴿExpTim 106 (1994s) 58 (J. *Kent*).

284* ᴱParratt John, *Cristo in Africa oggi* [12 art. 1987], ᵀComba Aldo: PiccBtT 32. T 1994, Claudiana. 200 p. Lᵐ 25. 88-7016-195-1 [Gregorianum 76,397-9, A. *Wolanin*].

285 ᴱPašuto V. T., *Catalano* Pierangelo, L'idea di Roma a Mosca nei secoli XV-XVI; fonti per la storia del pensiero sociale russo: Univ. R., Da Roma alla Terza Roma 1. R 1993, Herder. lxxxvii-449 p.; 7 color. pl. – ᴿOrChrPer 60 (1994) 700-703 (I. *Biliarsky*).

285* ᴱPopkin Richard H., *Weiner* Gordon M., Jewish Christians and Christians; Jews from the Renaissance to the Enlightenment: HistIdeas

138.   Dordrecht 1994, Kluwer.   vi-218 p. $99.   0-7923-2452-8 [TDig 42,274]. 9 art. on period 1450-1800.
286 ᴱReid Patrick V., Readings in western religious thought, II. The Middle Ages through the Reformation. NY 1995, Paulist. xii-377 p. $25. 0-8091-3533-7 [RelStR 21,244, D. R. *Janz*].
287 a) ᴱRoozen David A., *Hadaway* C. Kirk, Church and denominational growth; what does (and does not) cause growth or decline. Nv 1993, Abingdon. 400 p. $22. 0-687-15904-0. – ᴿRExp 91 (1994) 449-452 (J. M. *Terry*: scholarly sociology).
— b) ᴱScherer James A., *Bevans* Stephen B., New directions in mission and evangelization [1. 1992] 2. Theological foundations. Mkn 1994, Orbis. xiv-215 p. $19 pa. 0-88344-953-6 [TDig 42,180; Gregorianum 76,772, J. *López-Gay*].
— c) ᴱSchlossberg Herbert, *al.*, Christianity and economics in the post-cold war era; the [1990] Oxford declaration and beyond. GR/L 1994, Eerdmans/FowlerWright. 186 p. £9. 0-8028-0798-4. – ᴿExpTim 106 (1994s) 350s (D. *Attwood*).
— d) ᴱSchumaker J. F., Religion and mental health. NY 1992, Oxford-UP. 320 p. – ᴿSvTKv 70 (1994) 82s (Eva *Johanson*).
— e) ᴱSelling Joseph A., *Jans* Jan, The splendor of accuracy; an examination of the assertions made by *Veritatis Splendor*. Kampen 1994, Kok Pharos. 182 p. 90-390-0402-1. – ᴿETL 70 (1994) 521-3 (J. *Étienne*).
— f) Sicking Thom, présent., Foi chrétienne et inculturation au Proche-Orient. Beyrouth 1992, Univ. S. Joseph, Inst. Sup. ScRel. 198 p. – ᴿPr-OrChr 43 (1993) 214s (P. *Ternant*).
288 a) ᴱSiebers Tobin, Religion and the authority of the past. AA 1993, Univ. Michigan. 294 p. $45; pa. $17. – ᴿAmHR 99 (1994) 1444 (titles sans pp.).
— b) ᴱSievernich Michael, *al.*, Conquista und Evangelisation; fünfhundert Jahre Orden in Lateinamerika. Mainz 1992, Grünewald. 486 p. – ᴿNZMiss 50 (1994) 156 (A. *Peter*).
— c) Siker Jeffrey S., Homosexuality in the Church; both sides of the debate. LvL 1994, W-Knox. xvii-211 p. $15 pa. 0-664-25545-0 [TDig 42,273].
— d) ᴱSorrentino Sergio, BARTH in discussione. Potenza 1993, Ermes. – ᴿProtestantesimo 49 (1994) 168-170 (M. C. *Laurenzi*).
289 ᴱSugirtharajah R. S., Frontiers in Asian Christian theology; emerging trends. Mkn 1994, Orbis. viii-263 p. $19. 0-88344-954-4 [TDig 42,165; a 6th anthology].
290 ᴱSwatos William H.ᴶ, Gender and religion [12 art from Sociological Analysis, called Sociology of Religion since 1993]. New Brunswick 1994, Transaction. xi-196 p. $20 pa. 1-56000-699-4 [TDig 41,169].
290* ᴱTracy Thomas F., The God who acts; philosophical and theological explorations [eight colleagues interacting: *Wiles* M., *Tanner* Kathryn, *al.*]. Univ. Park 1994, Penn. State. x-148 p. $28.50; pa. $15. 0-271-01039-8; -40-1. – ᴱExpTim 106 (1994s) 314 (A. *Freeman*).
291 ᴱWalker Andrewᴶ, Different gospels; Christian orthodoxy and modern theologies [liberationist, feminist, pluralist... built on sand]. L 1993, SPCK. 231 p. £10 pa. – ᴿTLond 97 (1994) 293s (A. *Race*: polemic directed against a moving target called the Enlightenment, as comforting assurance that somewhere once there was a 'mere Christianity', though many of us are unable to share the assumptions of the Fathers).
291* ᴱWallace M. I., *Smith* T. H., Curing violence. Sonoma 1994, Polebridge.

p. 3-24, *Hamerton-Kelly* Robert G., Religion and the thought of René GIRARD [TLZ 120,516].

292 EZagzebski Linda,   Rational faith;   Catholic responses to Reformed epistemology (9 original essays): Library of Religious Philosophy 10. Notre Dame 1993, Univ. vi-290 p. $33; pa. $15.   0-268-01643-7; -4-5. – RChrSchR 24 (1994) 344-7 (R. D. *Geivett*, also on *Holtenga* D. 1991).

A1.5   *Plurium compilationes* philologicae *vel* archaeologicae.

294 a) Apostolos-Cappadona Diane, Dictionary of Christian art. NY 1994, Continuum. 376 p.; 162 fig. $39.50.   0-8264-0779-X [TDig 32,354].

— b) Archer Léonie J., *al.*, Women in ancient societies; an illusion of the night. Basingstoke 1994, Macmillan. xx-308 p. 0-333-52397-0; excerpted].

— c) Berger Alan L.,   Judaism in the modern world: Rudolph Lectures. NYU 1994. x-297 p. $50; pa. $18 [AmHR 100,1349: 14 art. sans pp.].

— d) EBowman Alan K., *Woolf* Greg, Literacy and power in the ancient world.   C 1994, Univ. ix-249 p.   0-521-43369-X [OTAc 11,15; excerpted].

— e) EBoyd Susan A., *Mango* Marlia M.,   Ecclesiastical silver plate in sixth-century Byzantium; symposium May 16-18, 1986. Wsh 1993, Dumbarton Oaks. xxxii-243 p. $120.   0-88402-203-X. – RMuséon 107 (1994) 397-411 (Linda *Safran*).

— f) EBrunner K., *Merts* B.,   Ethnogenese und Überlieferung; angewandte Methoden der Frühmittelalterforschung: Ös.GFor. Veröff. 31. W 1994, Oldenbourg. 310 p.; 33 fig. [RHE 89,363*].

— g) EBurenhult Göran,   Old World civilizations; the rise of cities and states: American Museum Natural History 3. McMahon Point NSW 1994, Weldon Owen. 239 p.; ill. 0-06-250270-0 [OIAc 11,16].

— h) EDani A. H., *Masson* V. M.,   History of civilizations of central Asia, I. The dawn of civilization. earliest times to 700 B.C. P 1992, UNESCO, 535 p.; ill. 92-3-102719-0 [OIAc 11,19].

295 EDever William G.,   Preliminary excavation reports; Sardis, Paphos, Caesarea Maritima, Shiqmim, Ain Ghazal: AASOR 51. NHv 1994, ASOR. [iv-] 126 p.; ill. 1-55540-926-1.

296 EEdmunds Lowell, Approaches to Greek myth. Baltimore 1990, Johns Hopkins. 445 p.

297 EFoley William A.,   The role of theory in language description: Trends-Ling 69. B/NY 1993, Mouton de Gruyter. viii-467 p. – RBSLP 89,2 (1994) 50-72 (C. *Hagège*).

298 EHaug Walter, *Wachinger* Burghart,   Traditionswandel und Traditionsverhalten: Fortuna vitrea 5. Tü 1991, Niemeyer. vii-223 p.; 26 fig. DM 78. – Speculum 69 (1994) 291.

298* EHaverkamp Anselm, *al.*, Memoria – Vergessen und Erinnern: Poetik und Hermeneutik 15. Mü 1993, Fink. xxx-536 p. DM 78 pa. 3-925412-18-8 [TR 91,82, 22 tit. pp.].

299 ELaw Vivien, History of linguistic thought in the early Middle Ages: StHistLangSc 71. Amst/Ph 1993, Benjamins. 255 p. – RRÉLat 72 (1994) 248s (J. *Dangel*).

299* ELucy John A.,   Reflexive language; reported speech and metapragmatics. C 1993, Univ. x-414 p. 0-521-35164-2. – RBSLP 89,2 (1994) 136-8 (X. *Mignot*).

300 a) EMcKitterick R., Carolingian culture; emulation and innovation. C 1994, Univ. xvii-334 p.; 21 fig. £45; pa. £15 [RHE 88,401*].

— b) ᴱMathers Clay, *Stoddart* Simon, Development and decline in the Bronze Age Mediterranean: ArchMg 8. Shf 1994, Collis. viii-367 p.; ill. 0-90609-49-0 [OIAc 11,32, excerpted].

— c) ᴱMorris Ian, Classical Greece; ancient histories and modern archaeologies. C 1994, Univ. 244 p. [RelStR 21,133, Sally *Schultz*].

— d) ᴱNardocchio Elaine F., Reader response to literature; the empirical dimension [computer-contribution]. B/NY 1992, Mouton de Gruyter. 313 p. – ᴿBSLP 89,2 (1994) 151-3 (P. *Kirtchuk*).

— e) ᴱNippel Wilfried, Über das Studium der Alten Geschichte. Mü 1993, Deutscher TbV. 443 p. – ᴿHistTheor 33 (1994) 268s (W. N.).

301 a) ᴱPetöfi János E., Approaches to poetry; some aspects of textuality, intertextuality and intermediality: Researches in Text Theory 20. B 1994, de Gruyter. viii-300 p.; 5 fig. 3-11-013893-X. P. 77-93, *Holthuis* Susanne, Intertextuality and meaning-constitution.

— b) ᴱReyes Mate M., Filosofia de la historia: EncIberoAF 5. M 1993, Trotta. 308 p. – ᴿComSev 27 (1994) 109-111 (M. *Sánchez*).

— c) Sayed Abdel Monem, The Red Sea and its hinterland in antiquity [< his diss.; + reprints also from ❹]. Alexandria 1993, Dar al-Maʿarifa. 210 p.; ill. [AnEgBbg for 1993, 256].

— d) ᴱSettis Salvatore, Il rito e la vita privata: Civiltà dei Romani [3 dei 4]. Mi 1994, Electa. 328 p.; 391 fig. Lᵐ 140. – ᴿArcheo 9,113 (1994) 122s (E. *Gizzi*).

302 ᴱSpencer Nigel, Text, tradition and society in Greek archaeology; bridging the 'Great Divide'; Theoretical Archaeology Group. L c.1994, Routledge. xx-179 p.; bibliog. 150-171. 0-415-4412-8.

302* ᴱWorthington Ian, Ventures into Greek history. Ox 1994, UP. xiv-401 p. 0-19-814938-X [OIAc 11,45, excerpted].

A2 Acta *congressuum* .1 biblica [*Notitiae*, reports ⮞ Y7.2].

303 a) ᶠAarhus 50th [and] NEPPER-CHRISTENSEN Poul: New directions in biblical theology 16-19 Sept. 1992, ᴱPedersen Sigfred: VTS 76. Leiden 1994, Brill. xiv-290 p. $88.75. 90-04-10120-9 [RelStR 21,242, J. T. *Fitzgerald*]. 13 art., infra.

— b) ᴱAland Barbara, *Delobel* Joël, New Testament textual criticism, exegesis, and early Church history; a discussion of methods [Münster 25-29 July 1993]: ContribExT 7. Kampen 1994, Kok. 152 p. ƒ55. 90-390-0105-7 [RB 102,453, tit. pp.].

— c) ᴱAlexander Philip S., *Samely* Alexander, Artifact and text; the re-creation of Jewish literature in medieval Hebrew manuscripts: Manchester Univ. 28-30 April 1992: JBRyL 75 (1993). 284 p.

303* a) ᴱAmewowo W., *al.*, Les Actes des Apôtres et les jeunes églises / Communautés johanniques, Actes deuxième/quatrième congrès des biblistes africains, Ibadan août 1984/1989. Kinshasa/[W] 1990/91, Fac. Cath. / Katholische Jungschar Österreichs. 11 + 11 art., infra.

— b) ᴱAssaf David, Proceedings of the Eleventh World Congress of Jewish Studies, Jerusalem, June 22-29, 1993. J 1994, World Union. 240 p. + ❺- 158 p. 0333-9068 [6 vol.]. A – The Bible and its world, 33 art. + 21 ❺; infra.

304 a) ᴱBax Mart, *Koster* Adrianus, Power and prayer; religious and political processes in past and present [conference Amst 1990, 17 art.]: CentRePol. Amst 1993, VU. vi-308 p. $35. 90-5383-209-2 [TDig 42,287].

— b) ᴱBeattie D. R. G., *McNamara* M. J., The Aramaic Bible; Targums in

their historical context [Dublin conference 1992]: jOsu 166. Shf 1994, JStOT. 470 p. $60. 1-85075-454-3 [RelStR 21,323, L. J. *Greenspoon*: 26 splendid essays].
— *c*) ᴱ**Bergen** Robert D., Biblical Hebrew and discourse linguistics. Dallas/ WL 1993/4, Summer Linguistics/Eisenbrauns. 560 p. $40. 1-55671-007-0 [OTAbs 18, p. 391 with renvoi to 22 items cited].
— *d*) ᴱ**Bertalot** R., *Leonardi* G., *Stancari* P., Violenza e non violenza nella Bibbia, Atti del II incontro biblico ecumenico, Cosenza 30-31 maggio 1992. Cosenza 1993, Due Emme.
305 ᴱ**Beuken** W. A. M., The Book of Job, colloquium Aug. 24-26, 1993: BtETL 114. Lv 1994, Univ./Peeters. x-462 p. Fb 2500. 90-6186-622-7 / 90-6831-652-4. 14 main papers + 14 others; infra.
305* BIBLIA, Associazione laica di cultura biblica; Atti del Seminario invernale, Fortezza, tragedia e inganno; la donna all'epoca dei Giudici; Verona 28-31.I.1993. Settimello Fi 1994, Bibbia. 218 p. 10 art., infra.
306 — ᴱ**Stefani** Piero, Gli animali e la Bibbia; i nostri minori fratelli [Spoleto, 23-25 apr. 1993]: Biblia/World Nature Fund, Grande Codice 2. Roma 1994, Garamond. 134 p.; ill. Lᵐ 20. 88-86180-09-8. 11 art.; 7 infra.
306* ᴱ**Black** David A., *al.*, Linguistics and NT interpretation; essays on discourse analysis [Dallas (?) Wycliffe translators conference 1990]; largely on particles, *kaí, dé, oûn*]. Nv 1992, Broadman. 319 p. 0-8054-1509-2 [RB 102,141, tit. pp.].
307 ᴱ**Brooke** George J., (*Garcia Martínez* Florentino) New Qumran texts and studies; proceedings of the first meeting of the International Organization for Qumran Studies, Paris 1992: STDJ 15. Leiden 1994, Brill. ix-328 p.; 9 fig. ƒ145. 90-04-10093-8 [BL 95,143, P. R. *Davies*].
308 ᴱ**Brooke** G. J., *al.*, Ugarit and the Bible, Manchester Sept. 1992: Ug.-Bibl. Lit. 11. Münster 1994, Ugarit-Verlag. x-470 p. 3-927120-22-7 [ZAW 107,546, tit. pp.]. – ᴿUF 25 (1993!) 496s (O. *Loretz*, tit. pp.].
309 ᴱ**Burkert** Walter, *Stolz* Fritz, Hymnen der Alten Welt im Kulturvergleich [Schw.Ges. OrAltW/RelW 1991]: OBO 131. FrS/Gö 1994, Univ./VR. 123 p. DM 44. 3-525-53766-2. – ᴿOTAbs 17 (1994) p. 648 (S. A. *Wiggins*; also p. 483-6:) *Assmann* J., Ägypten 33-58; *Burkert* W. gr. 9-17; *Edzard* D. O., sum./akk. 19-31; Nachwort 59-77 [OTAbs reference to its Nᵒ 1687 not verified, presumably for 1987 OT]. – ᴿTüTQ 174 (1994) 241 (W. *Gross*).
309* ᴱ**Buzzetti** Carlo, *Cimosa* Mario, I giovani e la lettura della Bibbia; orientamenti e proposte [Univ. Salesiana, R 2-4.I.1992]. R 1992, LAS. 219 p. Lᵐ 25. – ᴿCC 145 (1994,1) 533s (D. *Scaiola*).
310 ᴱ**Canziani** Guido, *Zarka* Yves-Charles, L'interpretazione nei secoli XVI e XVII, Atti del convegno Milano/Parigi 1991. Mi 1993, F. Angeli. – ᴿAnStoEseg 11 (1994) 633-5 (Lisa *Ginzburg*).
312 ᴱ**Charlesworth** James H., *Weaver* Walter P., Images of Jesus today [Florida Lakeland college symposia]: Faith and scholarship colloquies 3. Ph 1994, Trinity. xxi-119 p. $14. 1-56338-082-X [TDig 42,70]. p. 42-67, *Borg* M.; 68-97, *Horsley* R.; 98-112, *Mendes* D.
313 ᴱ**Charlesworth** J. M., *al.*, The Lord's Prayer and other prayer texts from the Greco-Roman era [SBL group 1989-92]. Ph [now 'Valley Forge', 20 k NW] 1994, Trinity. ix-292 p. $18. 1-56338-080-3 [NTAbs 39, p. 135, topics sans pp.].
314 Colloquium oecumenicum paulinum 21-26 Sept. 1992. Gal 1,1-4,11. R 1993, St. Pauls. 289 p. [RB 102,299, tit. pp.].

315 CROSSAN John D.:   ᴱCarlson Jeffrey, *Ludwig* Robert A.,   Jesus and faith; a conversation [11 art. mostly from DePaul conference, Chicago 1993] on the work of Crossan [Historical Jesus 1991]. Mkn 1994, Orbis.   xi-180 p. $19. 0-88344-936-6 [TDig 41,365]. – ᴿETL 70 (1994) 455s (P. *Neirynck*); ExpTim 106 (1994s) 54s (Meg *Davies*).

316 ᴱEmmerson Richard K., *McGinn* Bernard, The Apocalypse in the Middle Ages. Ithaca NY 1993, Cornell Univ. 448 p. $50; pa. $20.   0-8014-2282-9; -9550-4. – ᴿSpeculum 69 (1994) 1305 (tit. pp.).

317 ᴱEskenazi Tamara C., *Richards* Kent H.,   Second Temple Studies 2. Temple community in the Persian period: jOsu 175.   Shf 1994, Academic. 111 p.; ill.   1-85075-472-1 [BL 95,38, D.J. *Reimer*; CBQ 57,837, J.T. *Strong*; JBL 107,565, tit. pp.].

318 ᴱEvans Craig A., *Stegner* W. Richard,   The Gospels and the Scriptures of Israel: jNsu 104. Shf 1994, Academic. 505 p.   1-85075-497-7 [RelStR 21,234, T. *Dwyer*].

319 ᴱFabiny Tibor,   Literary theory and biblical hermeneutics [Pannonhalma, July 1991]. Szeged 1992, Univ.   251 p. 16 art. [LitTOx 9,103s, D. *Jasper*].

319* ᴱFelici Sergio,   Esegesi e catechesi nei Padri (secc. IV-VII) [Pontificium Institutum Altioris Latinitatis, Roma 25-27 marzo 1993]: BtScRel 112. R 1994, LAS[alesianum]. 88-213-0285-7. 14 art. ➤ 13839*.

320 FERRARA Bible: Introducción a la Biblia de Ferrara, Actas del Simposio Sevilla 25-28 de noviembre de 1991: Encuentros. M 1994, Cons. Sup. Inv.

321 ᴱGalli G.,   Interpretazione e gratitudine; XIII Colloquio Macerata 30-31 Marzo 1992: Fac lett/fil 68, Atti 22.   Macerata 1994, Univ.   295 p., 15 fig. [RHE 90,335*].

322 ᴱHelleman Wendy E.,   Hellenization revisited; shaping a Christian response within the Greco-Roman world [Toronto 1991: 1. praeparatio evangelica; ii. spoliatio].   Lanham MD 1994, UPA. [xxii-] 544 p.; bibliog. 513-527. 0-8191-9643-X; pa. -4-8.

322* ᴱHengel Martin, *Löhr* Hermut, Schriftauslegung im antiken Judentum und im Christentum. Dü-Mickeln 16-19.V.1991: WUNT 73. Tü 1994, Mohr.   vii-282 p. DM 23.   3-16-146172-X [RB 102,452, tit. pp.; SNTU 20,202, A. *Fuchs*]. 4 art. infra + 4 1995].

323 *a)* Hengel M., *Schwemer* A.,   Die Septuaginta zwischen Judentum und Christentum [Tü 1990]. WUNT 72. Tü 1994, Mohr. 3-16-146173-8 [JTS 46,585, A. *Salvesen*; RB 102,450, tit. pp.].

— *b)* ᴱHenten Jan W. van, *Horst* Pieter W. van,   Studies in early Jewish epigraphy [Utrecht conference 1992]: AGJU 21.   Leiden 1994, Brill. iv-280 p.   98-04-09916-6 [NTAbs 38, p. 329; OTAbs 17, p. 423; RB 102,140, tit. pp.].

— *c)* [ᴱ*Hoftijzer* J. ➤ 9,9682], European Science Foundation Workshop on the semantics of classical Hebrew: ZAHeb 6,1(2) (1993) [titles in ZIT 93,259].

324 *a)* ᴱHübner Hans,   Die Weisheit Salomos im Horizont biblischer Theologie [Tagung 1991]: BThSt 22. Neuk 1993.   viii-112 p. DM 26,80. 3-7887-1447-6 [BL 94,108, R. *Mason*].

— *b)* ᴱIrsigler Hubert,   Syntax und Text; Beiträge zur 22. Internationalen Ökumenischen Hebraisch-Dozenten-Konferenz 28.IV-3.V.1993 in Bamberg: MüUniv. AOtt 40. St. Ottilien 1993, EOS. ix-174 p. DM 25.   3-88096-540-4 – 6 art.; infra.

— *c)* ᴱIzquierdo Cesar,   Dios en la Palabra y en la historia [Dei Verbum 25 años], XIII Simposio 1992. Pamplona 1993, EUNSA.   627 p. – ᴿCarthaginensia 10 (1994) 466s (F. *Chavero Blanco*); ScripTPamp 26 (1994) 280-3 (L. F. *Mateo-Seco*).

— *d*) ᴱ**Kavunkal** Jacob, *Hrangkhuma* F., Bible and mission in India today [Fellowship of Indian missiologists, Pune Union Sem. 29-31 Aug. 1992]. Bombay 1993, St. Paul's. 336 p. rs 96. – 81-7109-179-2. – ᴿMissiology 22 (1994) 384s (R. E. *Holland*); Vidyajyoti 58 (1994) 258s (J. F. *Durack*).

— *e*) [➤ 332*b*] ᴱ**Klauck** Hans-Josef, Weltgericht und Weltvollendung; Zukunftsbilder im Neuen Testament [Salzburg 29. März-2. April 1993]: QDisp 150. FrB 1994, Herder. 268 p. 3-451-02150-1.

— *f*) ᴱ**Leuba** Jean-Louis, Temps et eschatologie; données bibliques et problématiques contemporaines: Acad. Internat. Sc. Rel., Bâle 10-11.IV.1987. P 1994, Cerf. 374 p. F 150, 2-204-05040-7. 10 art. [RB 102,458, tit. pp.].

— *g*) ᴱ**Levine** Lee I., The Galilee in late antiquity [NY Jewish Theological Sem. conference 1991]. CM 1992, Harvard Univ. xxiii-410 p. $35; pa. $15. 0-674-34113-9; -4-7 [BL 95,31, J. R. *Bartlett*].

— *h*) ᴱ**Lilienfeld** Fairy von, *Ritter* Adolf M., Einheit der Kirche in vorkonstantinischer Zeit [Patrist. Arb-G. Vorträge, Bern 2.-4. Jan 1985]: Oikonomia 25. x-165 p. [TLZ 120,1013, R. *Staats*].

325 ᴱ**Lovering** Eugene H., SBL 1994 seminar papers 33 (130th annual meeting, Ch Nov. 19-22, 1994). Atlanta 1994, Scholars. ix-916 p. 0-7885-0038-4.

325* ᴱ**McKenzie** Steven L., *Graham* M. Patrick, The history of Israel's traditions; the heritage of Martin Noth [Wsh 1993 SBL Symposium]: jOsu 182. Shf 1994, Academic. 326 p. £40. 1-85075-499-3 [OTAbs 18, p. 413]. 128-159 D. N. *Freedman* on Noth.

326 ᴱ**Migliore** Daniel L., Hope for the Kingdom and responsibility for the world; 1993 F. Neumann symposium on the theological interpretation of Scripture: PrincSemB 3-supp. (1994). 152 p. $6.

326* ᴱ**Millard** A. R., *al.*, Faith, tradition, and history; Old Testament historiography in its near Eastern Context [Wheaton (IL) College symposium November 1990]. WL 1994, Eisenbrauns. xiv-354 p. 0-931464-82-X [RB 102,442, tit. pp.]. 18 art.; 10 infra ➤ 11049.

327 Odendaal Dirk H., mem. [† 27.VII.1990, auto accident], Understanding the OT in South Africa; symposium Univ. Stellenbosch 5-6 Sept. 1991, ᴱ**Bosman** Hendrik, *Olivier* Hannes = OTEssays 7 (,4, special issue, 1994). 353 p. 1010-9919. 39 art.; 29 infra.

327* ᴱ**Oort** J. van, *Wickert* U., Christliche Exegese zwischen Nicaea und Chalcedon [Tagung Berlin 1991]. Kampen 1992, Kok Pharos. 226 p. 90-242-3067-5. – ᴿZKG 105 (1994) 110-3 (M. *Vincent*).

328 ᴱ**Padovese** L., Atti del simposio di Tarso su S. Paolo Apostolo: Turchia, la Chiesa e la sua storia 7. R 1994, Antonianum. vi-191 p.

329 ᴱ**Padovese** L., Atti del IV simposio di Efeso su S. Giovanni apostolo [III. 1992/3 ➤ 9,401]: Turchia/Chiesa 6. R 1994, Pont. Ateneo Antonianum. 247 p. [RHE 90,65*]. 14 art., infra. – ᴿCompostellanum 39 (1994) 263-5 (E. *Romero-Pose*).

329* ᴱ**Patlagean** Évelyne, *Le Boulluec* Alain, Les retours aux Écritures; fondamentalismes passés et présents [colloque Collège de France 27-30 janv. 1992]: ÉPHÉR Bt 99. Lv/P 1993, Peeters. 399 p. [RHE 90,611, J.-M. *Auwers*].

330 *a*) ᴱ**Pesce** Mauro, Studi sulla letteratura esegetica cristiana e giudaica antica, Atti del X/XI seminario, Viverone, 7-9 ottobre 1992 / Sacrofano, 20-22 ottobre 1993: AnStoEseg 10,2 (1993) 275-731 / 11,2 (1994) 411-717.

— b) ᴱPippin Tina, Ideological criticism of biblical texts [DERRIDA, GIRARD...; 1990 SBL consultation]: Semeia 59. Atlanta 1992, Scholars. viii-249 p. $20. 0095-571X [RelStR 21,34, Chris A. *Franke*].

— c) ᴱPorter Stanley E., *Olbricht* Thomas H., Rhetoric and the New Testament; essays from the 1992 Heidelberg conference [WUELLNER Wilhelm & 26 others]: jNsu 90. Shf 1993, JStOT. 538 p. $75. 1-85075-449-7 [RelStR 21,34, Pheme *Perkins*: only the index clues to the doubtless lively disagreements].

— d) ᴱReventlow Henning, *Hoffman* Yair, *Uffenheimer* Benjamin, Politics and theopolitics in the Bible and postbiblical literature: jOsu 171. Shf 1994, JStOT. 216 p. £20. 1-85075-461-6. 13 art., 8 infra [OTAbs 18, p. 141, F. E. *Greenspahn*, with 9 renvois + 10 other topics; TR 90,513 & ZAW 107,363, tit. pp.].

331 ᴱRichard Earl, New views on Luke and Acts [< CBA task force since 1976]. ColMn 1990, D. L. Matson.

332 a) [ᴱSchmidinger Heinrich], Jesus von Nazaret... Salzburger Hochschulwochen 25. Juli - 6. August 1994. Graz c. 1994, Styria. 283 p. DM 40. 3-222-12283-0. [TR 91,533, tit. pp.] 11-34, *Sporschill* G., Sein Blut... über uns; 25-50, *Jüngel* E., Der historische Jesus; 117-147, *Moltmann-Wendel* Elisabeth, Frauen und Männer; 185-200, *Berger* K., Vom Verkündiger zum Verkündigten ...

— b) ꟳSCHNACKENBURG Rudolf [p. 9], Weltgericht und Weltvollendung, Zukunftsbilder im NT, 80. Gb., Tagung Salzburg 1993, ᴱKlauck Hans-J. [➤ 324e]: QDisp 150. FrB 1994, Herder. 268 p. DM 68. 3-451-02150-1.

— c) ᴱShanks Hershel, The search for Jesus; modern scholarship looks at the Gospels [Smithsonian symposium 1993]. Wsh 1994, Biblical Archaeology Soc. vii-152 p. $12 pa. 1-880317-14-1 [NTAbs 39, p. 146].

— d) ᴱShanks Hershel, The Dead Sea Scrolls after forty years; symposium at the Smithsonian Institution October 27, 1990. Wsh 1992, Biblical Archaeology Society. xv-85 p. 0-9613089-7-4. – *VanderKam* J. on Christianity; *McCarter* P. on the copper scroll; *Sanders* J., texts.

333 SOTS bulletin for 1994: 69th winter meeting, Univ. London 4-6 Jan. 1994: *Gibson* J. C. L., presidential address, The Vav consecutive, — *Fyall* R. S., Yahweh, Mot and Behemoth in Job (13,15; 40,15-24); – *Pilkington* C. M., Is 45,15. – *Auld* A. G., Joshua after Kings. – *Goldingay* J., Is 40-55 in the 1890s and the 1990s. – *Barton* J., Historical/literary criticism common ground? – P. 15 gives titles of 14 papers at the 9th Joint Meeting with Dutch-Flemish Werkegezelschap at Kampen 28-31 August 1994.

334 SOTS (1994 bulletin) 70th summer meeting, Edinburgh 18-21 July 1994: *Davidson* R., Isa 40,6-8. — Feminist criticism section: *Exum* J. C. on Judges; *McKay* H. A., Sarah's laughter silenced; *Munro* J., Metaphor in the Song of Songs; *Smith* Carol (*Goldingay* J.): Masculist Hos 1-3; Gen 1-4. – Creation theology section: *Bultmann* C., J. G. HERDER on Gen 1.; *Dell* K. J., Green ideas in the Wisdom tradition; *Forrest* R. W. E., Earthquake imagery in Amos; *Geyer* J. B., Devastation in the Zion theology. – *Butterworth* M., Zech structure. – *Davies* J., *Rogerson* J., Siloam tunnel built by Hasmoneans, not Hezekiah. – *Lawson* J. N., Dan 2,47. – *Malamat* A., Exodus Egyptian analogies. – *Provan* I. W., Ideologies in newer histories of Israel. – *Barker* Margaret, Atonement. – *Brenner* Athalya, Feminism/Humour. – *Moor* J. C de, Egypt, Ugarit – Exodus.

335 ᴱStump Eleonore, *Flint* Thomas F., Hermes and Athena; biblical exegesis and philosophical theology: StPhRel 7, ND 1993, Univ. xxvii-225 p. 0-268-01099-4.

336 ᴱVanderKam James C., Biblical interpretation in Qumran texts [SBL section (*Schuller* Eileen), Washington 1993]: DSD 1,2 (1994) 149(-237), response 229-237, G. W. E. *Nickelsburg*, Dealing with challenges and limitations [on comparative-placement techniques for reconstruction, used in four of these papers].

337 *a*) ᴱWagner Silvia, *al.*, (Anti-) Rassistische Irritationen; biblische Texte und interkulturelle Zusammenarbeit [Evangelische Studenten-Gemeinde Köln 13.-15.XI.1992]. B 1994, Alektor. 256 p. 3-88425-059-0. – ᴿDielB 28 (1992s) 274-8 (B. J. *Diebner*).

— *b*) ᴱWalker P. W. L., Jerusalem, past and present in the purposes of God [< British conferences since 1989]. Carlisle 1994, Paternoster. 200 p. £10 pa. 0-9518-354-0. – ᴿEvQ 66 (1994) 285-7 (W. *Riggans*).

— *c*) Wiles Maurice, A shared search; doing theology in conversation with one's friends [13 articles he wrote for Festschrifts and a defense of the genre]. L 1994, SCM. viii-211 p. £13. 0-334-02559-1. – ᴿExpTim 106 (1994s) 86 (C. S. *Rodd*).

338 ᴱZannoni A. E., Jews and Christians speak of Jesus [St. Paul (MN), St. Thomas Univ. 1993]. Mp 1994, Fortress. xiv-191 p. $12 pa. 0-8006-2804-7 [NTAbs 39, p. 330].

A2.3   **Acta congressuum theologica** [reports → Y7.4].

339 **Altendorf** H.-D. (concl.), Orthodoxie et hérésie dans l'Église ancienne [1983, sur BAUER]: RTPhilCah 17. Genève 1993. 144 p. – ᴿRechSR 82 (1994) 624-6 (B. *Sesboüé*).

340 **Ambrosio** G., *al.*, Cristianesimo e religione; Atti Teol. It. Sett. 25-26 febb. 1992: Disputatio 4. Mi 1992, Glossa. 233 p. Lᵐ 32. – ᴿAsprenas 41 (1994) 454-6 (A. *Russo*).

340* ᴱAssmann Jan, Die Erfindung des inneren Menschen; Studien zur religiösen Anthropologie [Heidelberg Nov. 1990]: StudVerstFremdRel 6. Gü 1993, Mohn. 200 p. DM 78. 3-579-01788-8. – ᴿTGL 84 (1994) 246s (R. *Geisen*).

341 ᴱAttfield Robin, *Belsey* Andrew, Philosophy and the natural environment [meeting Cardiff July 1993]. C 1994, Univ. 250 p. £14. 0-521-46903-1. 16 art. – ᴿExpTim 106 (1994s) 219s (D. *Gosling*: POLKINGHORNE nowhere mentioned but perhaps targeted).

341* ᴱAyris P., *Selwyn* D., Thomas CRANMER, churchman and scholar [500th b. conference, Durham 1989]. Woodbridge 1993, Boydell. xv-355 p.; portr. [RHE 88,408*].

342 ᴱBarr William R., *Yocum* Rena M., The Church in the movement of the spirit [Faith and Order group]. GR 1994, Eerdmans. xii-136 p. $13. 0-8028-0554-X [TDig 42,61].

342* ᴱBaumann Fred E., *Jensen* Kenneth M., Religion and politics [6 art.; Kenyon College conference 1985]. Charlottesville 1989, Univ. Virginia. vii-114 p. $11. – ᴿCritRR 5 (1992) 439-441 (D. E. *Owen*).

343 ᴱBerry Philippa, *Wernick* Andrew, Shadow of spirit; postmodernism and religion [1990 Cambridge conference]. L 1993, Routledge. 274 p. £35; pa. £13. – ᴿTLond 97 (1994) 43s (G. *D'Costa*: won't show you what postmodernism is, but touches intriguing shadow-areas).

343* ᴱBest Thomas F., *Gassmann* Günther, On the way to fuller koinonia; official report of the Fifth World Conference on Faith and Order: Paper 166. Geneva 1994, WCC. xxx-318 p. $21.50. 2-8254-1127-2 [TDig 42,181].

344 *a*) ^E**Bianchi** Ugo, The notion of 'religion' in comparative research; selected proceedings of the XVI congress of the Int. Asn. Hist. Rel., Rome 3-8 Sept. 1990: StRel 2. R 1994, Bretschneider.: xlviii-921 p. 88-7062-852-3. [Gregorianum 76,774, J. *Dupuis*]. The 15 invited papers infra; 10 of the 90 others in Elenchus Vol. 11.

— *b*) ^E**Birch** Charles, *al.*, Liberating life; approaches to ecological theology [WCC consultation, Annecy Sept. 1988]. Mkn 1990, Orbis. iv-293 p. $17 pa. – ^RCritRR 6 (1993) 484-6 (D. L. *Dungan*).

— *c*) ^E**Blaising** Craig A., *Block* Darrell L., Dispensationalism, Israel and the Church; the search for definition [EvTheolSoc meeting, San Francisco Nov. 19, 1992]. GR 1992, Zondervan. – ^RAndrUnSem 32 (1994) 41-46 (N. R. *Gulley*).

345 *a*) ^E**Blakely** Thomas D., *al.*, Religion in Africa: 1986 Brigham Young Univ.; Kennedy International Studies 4. Portsmouth NH / L 1994, Heinemann / Currey. xvi-512 p. $40; pa. $25. 0-435-08083-0 [TDig 42,185].

— *b*) ^E**Bonamente** G., *Fusco* F., Costantino il Grande dall'Antichità all'umanesimo; colloquio sul cristianesimo nel mondo antico, 18-20 dic. 1990: Fac. lett/f 67, Atti 21. Macerata 1992s, Univ. xxiv-497 p., p. 502-955; 77 fig., foldout [RHE 90,269*].

— *c*) ^E**Bourgeois** Henri, *Gondal* Marie-Louise, Le catéchumenat (Lyon 5-9 juillet 1993): Spiritus 35,154 (1994). 144 p.

— *d*) ^E**Breid** Franz, Busse – Umkehr – Formen der Vergebung: Linzer Priesterakademie, Aigen 1991. Steyr 1993, Ennsthaler. 256 p. Sch. 138. 3-85068-354-0 [ZkT 117,376, R. *Messner*].

346 [*Breton* S., *al.*] La Bible en philosophie, approches contemporaines [Colloque L'Arbresle 1990]. P 1993, Cerf. 165 p. F 95. – ^REsprVie 104 (1994) 338-340 (J. *Milet*).

346* ^E**Bsteh** Andreas, Der Islam als Anfrage an Christliche Theologie und Philosophie: Erste Religionstheologische Akademie St. Gabriel 1994: StRelT 1. W-Mödling 1994, St. Gabriel. 545 p. – 3-85264-457-7.

347 *a*) Budapest 22d conference on sociology of religions [19-23 July 1993]: Social Compass 37-40 (1993), first four sets of papers; 41,1 (1994) four more sets, largely on ethnicity: → 10912.

347* ^E**Byrne** James M., The Christian understanding of God today [Dublin Trinity College 1992 quatercentenary colloquium]. Dublin 1993, Columba. 174 p. £10. 1-85607-087-5. – ^RExpTim 106 (1994s) 91 (D. R. *Peel*).

348 ^E**Canobbio** Giacomo, Dio, natura e mondo nelle religioni orientali; Atti del convegno ATI, Brescia 20-22.VI.1991. Padova 1993, Messaggero. 173 p. L^m 18. – ^RBenedictina 41 (1994) 559s (Annamaria *Valli*).

349 *a*) La carità e la Chiesa, virtù e ministero [Fac. T. It. Sett, 23s.II.1993]: Disputatio 5. Mi 1993, Glossa. 188 p. – ^RTeresianum 45 (1994) 311s (M. *Caprioli*).

— *b*) La carità; teologia e pastorale, convegno 'La Carità come ermeneutica teologica e metodologia pastorale'. Bo 1988, Dehoniane [RasT 35,338].

— *c*) CTA Proc 49 (Santa Clara 1994) [NTAbs 39, p. 389: *D'Angelo* M. R., The concrete foundation of Christianity; re-membering Jesus [a prophet within a Spirit-driven prophetic movement, 135-146; response by *Phelps* J. T. 147-155; *Fiorenza* F., 96-99].

350 *a*) ^E**Chapple** Christopher K., Ecological prospects; scientific, religious, and aesthetic perspectives [Los Angeles Loyola Marymount conference 1991]. Albany 1994, SUNY. 236 p. $20 [RelStR 21,207, G. *Yocum*].

— *b*) ^E**Colpe** C., *al.*, Spätantike und Christentum [Berlin FU]. B 1992, Akademie. 280 p. DM 124. – ^RHZ 259 (1994) 459s (R. *Klein*).

— c) ᴱCosi Dario M., Mircea ELIADE e Georges DUMÉZIL; Atti del Simposio 'Dalla fenomenologia delle religioni al pensiero religioso del mondo
classico'. Padova 1994, Sargon. 120 p. – ᴿSMSR 60 (1994) 409-412 (P.
Xella).

351 Cristianesimo e specificità regionali nel Mediterraneo latino (sec. IV-VI):
XXII incontro Antichità Cr., R 6-8.V.1993: StEphAug 46. R 1994. Inst.
Patr. Aug. 640 p.; 13 fig. Lᵐ 90 [RHE 90,268*].

351* Cristianesimo latino e cultura greca sino al secolo IV: XXI incontro
antichità cr., R 7-9.V.1992: StEphAug 42. R 1993, Inst. Patr. Aug. 430 p.
[RHE 90,267*].

352 a) Crow Paul al., The Fifth World Conference on Faith and Order
[Compostela 4-14 August 1993]: Mid-Stream 33,1 (1994) 1-10 (-106).

— b) Le Défi de la modernité; conférences au Carrefour théologique,
Aix-en-Provence, février 1993: RRéf 47,178 (1993) 1-80.

— c) ᴱDel Col Andrea, Paolin Giovanna, L'Inquisizione Romana in Italia
nell'età moderna; archivi, problemi di metodo e nuove ricerche, Atti
Trieste 18-20 maggio 1988. R 1991, Ministero per i beni [uff.] ar-
chivistici. 404 p. – ᴿRivStoLR 30 (1994) 212-6 (G. Dell'Olio). [ZAW
107,349, tit. pp.].

353 ᴱDiurni G., Rerum novarum; l'uomo centro della Società e della Chiesa
[Roma Lateranense 6-9 maggio 1991]: Utrumque Ius 22. Vaticano 1992,
Editrice. xviii-729 p. – ᴿAnnTh 8 (1994) 201-4 (E. Colom).

354 ᴱDockrill D. W., Tanner R. G., Tradition and traditions; papers from a
conference, St. Patrick's Manly, 12-15 July 1990: Prudentia 26 supp.
(1994) vii-366 p. 28 art.; 8 infra. 0110-487X.

355 a) ᴱDouglass R. Bruce, Hollenbach David, Catholicism and liberalism;
contributions to American public philosophy [Wsh Georgetown Univ.
1989 &1990 meetings]: Cambridge studies in religion and American public
life. NY 1994, Cambridge-UP. xv-352 p. $60. 0-521-44528-0.

— b) ᶠDREY Johann Sebastian, 175 Gb. Symposium 1992: Revision der
Theologie, Reform der Kirche: die Bedeutung des Tübinger Theologen ∼
in Geschichte und Gegenwart, ᴱKustermann Abraham P. Wü 1994,
Echter. 351 p. DM 78. 3-426-01573-1 [TR 91,412, H. Wagner].

— c) ᴿDuke Alastair, Lewis Gillian, Calvinism in Europe, 1540-1620 [1992
Oxford conference]. C 1994, Univ. xii-283 p. 0-521-43269-3. – ᴿExpTim
106 (1994s) 215 (P. N. Brooks).

356 ᴱDurand Jean-Dominique, Histoire et théologie, Actes Histoire religieuse
contemporaine 26 sept. 1992. P 1994, Beauchesne. 180 p. F 150 [RHE
90,617, Y. Krumenacker].

356* ᴱDykema Peter A., Oberman Heiko, Anticlericalism in Late Medieval
and Early Modern Europe [colloquium Tucson 1990]: StMdvRefTht 51.
Leiden 1993, Brill. xi-704 p. ƒ 345. 90-04-09518-7. – ᴿJEH 45 (1994)
145-7 (M. Chinca).

357 ᴱEbenbauer Alfred, Zatloukal Klaus, Die Juden in ihrer mittelalterlichen
Umwelt. W 1991, Böhlau. 320 p. – ᴿIrTQ 60 (1994) 157s (M. Maher).

357* ᴱEnglish Donald, Windows on salvation. L 1994, Darton-LT. 194 p.
£9. – ᴿExpTim 106 (1994s) 216s (J. C. Saxbee, 'grateful' for this 'largely
Methodist symposium of uneven quality').

358 a) ᴱErnst W., Gerechtigkeit in Gesellschaft, Wirtschaft und Politik
[Tagung Erfurt Aug. 1991; 5 art., 3 resp,]. FrS/FrB 1992, Univ./Herder.
190 p. 3-451-22990-0. – ᴿAntonianum 69 (1994) 131-3 (L. Oviedo).

— b) ᴱFallon Timothy P., Riley Philip B., Religion in context; recent studies
in LONERGAN [1984 Santa Clara Symposium vol. 2; 1 was 1987]: CTS

Resources in Religion 4. Lanham MD 1988, UPA. xiv-201 p. $41; pa.
$19.75. – ᴿCritRR 5 (1992) 499-501 (W. E. *Conn*).
— *c*) ᴱ**Floyd** Wayne W.ᴶ, *Marsh* C., Theology and the practice of
responsibility [6th Bonhoeffer conference 1992]. Ph 1994, Trinity.
xiv-334 p. $25 [RelStR 21,313, J. S. *Scott*; TDig 42,190].
359 *a*) ᴱ**Focant** Camille, L'enseignement de la religion au carrefour de la
théologie et de la pédagogie; LvN 28.IV.1993: RTLv Cah 26. LvN 1994,
Fac. Théol. – ᴿETL 70 (1994) 532s (A. *Haquin*).
— *b*) ᴱ**Fontaine** Jacques, *al.*, Patristique et Antiquité tardive en Allemagne et
en France de 1870 à 1930; colloque franco-allemand Chantilly 1991]:
ÉtAug mod, 27. P 1993, InstÉtAug. xvi-322 p. 2-85121-130-7 [RB 102,
143, tit. pp.]. 16 art., 2 infra.
— *c*) ᴱ**Fragomeni** Richard N., *Pawlikowski* John T., The ecological
challenge; ethical, liturgical, and spiritual responses [10 essays mostly from
Chicago Catholic Theological Union seminar]. ColMn 1994, Liturgical/
Glazier. ix-140 p. $10 pa. 0-8146-5840-7 [TDig 42,267].
360 *a*) ᴱ**Galindo** A., Ecologia y creación [XXIII Semana Teol. León]:
BtSalm Est 139. S 1991. 339 p. – ᴿScripTPamp 26 (1994) 860s (J. R.
Villar).
— *b*) ᴱ**Gassmann** Günther, *Heller* Dagmar, Santiago de Compostela 1994,
Fünfte Weltkonferenz für Glauben und Kirchenfassung: ÖkRu Beih 67.
Fra 1994, Lambeck. 272 p. DM 32. 3-87476-295-5 [TR 90,520, tit. pp.].
— *c*) ᴱ**Giannoni** P., La creazione: oltre l'antropocentrismo? Atti XIV ATI
sett. 1992: Studi Religiosi. Padova 1993, Messaggero. 414 p. Lᵐ 40
[NRT 117,460, R. *Escol*].
ᴱ**Gibellini** Rosino, Percorsi di teologia africana; i teologi africani si
domandano e propongono 1994 ➤ 273.
— *d*) ᴱ**Grane** L., *al.*, Auctoritas Patrum; zur Rezeption der Kirchenväter im
XV. und XVI. Jht., Tagung Rolighed 25.-29.IX.1991: MainzEurG supp.
37. Mainz 1993, von Zabern. x-295 p.; 5 facsim. DM 68 [RHE 90,100*]:
1-13, *Burger* C., ERASMUS/AUGUSTIN/LUTHER.
361 ᴱ**Granfield** Patrick, The Church and communication [12 art. from 1989
Rome seminar]: Communication, culture and theology. KC 1994, Sheed
& W. vii-327 p. $25. 1-55612-674-3.
362 ᴱ**Halligan** Frederica R., *Shea* John J., The fires of desire; erotic energies
and the spiritual quest [1991 conference]. NY 1992, Crossroad. 208 p.;
$22. – ᴿCritRR 6 (1993) 482s (R. C. *Fuller*).
363 ᴱ**Hanson** Bradley C., Modern Christian spirituality; methodological
and historical essays [1984-8 AAR seminar]: AAR StR 62. Atlanta
1990, Scholars. viii-269 p. $35, pa. $20. – ᴿCritRR 6 (1993) 511-3
(D. S. *Ferguson*).
364 ᴱ**Haubst** Rudolf, *Kremer* Klaus, Weisheit und Wissenschaft; CUSANUS im
Blick auf die Gegenwart; Akten des Symposions in Bernkastel-Kues und
Trier, 29.-31.März 1990: Mitt. Cusanus-Ges. 20. Trier 1992, Paulinus.
286 p. DM 42. – ᴿHZ 259 (1994) 119s (E. *Meuthen*).
364* ᴱ**Hutchison** William R., *Lehmann* Hartmut, Many are chosen; divine
election and western nationalism [9 art. & Responses from 1991
conference, 'Chosen people; themes in western nationalist movements']:
HarvardTheolSt 38. Mp 1994, Fortress. 306 p. $16. 0-8006-7091-4 [TDig
42,279].
365 *a*) ᴱ**Irwin** Kevin W., *Pellegrino* Edmund D., Preserving the creation;
environmental theology and ethics: symposium 1992. Wsh 1994,
Georgetown Univ. xi-153 p. $40. 0-87840-549-0 [TDig 42,183].

— *b*) ᴱKeulman Kenneth, Critical moments in religious history [1984 Rice University conference]. Macon 1993, Mercer Univ. viii-230 p. $25. 0-86554-411-5 [TDig 42,62].

— *c*) ᴱKöpf U., Historisch-kritische Betrachtung; F.C. BAUR und seine Schüler; VIII. Blaubeurer Symposium: Contubernium 40. Sigmaringen 1994, J. Thorbecke. 247 p.

366 ᴱLamberigts M. (*Kenis* L.), L'Augustinisme à l'ancienne faculté de théologie de Louvain. BtETL 111. Lv 1994, Univ./Peeters. 455 p. 90-6186-590-5 / 90-6831-573-0 [TR 91,78, tit. pp.]. 6 infra.

366* Legionarios de Cristo, La evangelización del Nuevo Mundo, simposio Roma 6-8.IV.1992. R 1992, Romana. 348 p. – ᴿTeresianum 45 (1992) 533s (E. *Pacho*).

367 ᴱLewis Bernard, *Niewöhner* Friedrich, Religionsgespräche im Mittelalter [Symposium Juni 1989; 22 Vorträge]: Wolfenbütteler Mittelalter-Studien 4. Wsb 1992, Harrassowitz. 388 p. DM 148. – ᴿJudaica 50 (1994) 52s (S. *Schreiner*).

367* Libertà e obbedienza nella Chiesa (Seminario di Brescia, 2º lavoro interdisciplinare): QuadTeol 2. Brescia 1992, Morcelliana. 302 p. – ᴿAngelicum 71 (1994) 297-9 (G. *Grasso*).

368 ᴱLorenzani Massimo, La volontà di Dio nella Bibbia. L'Aquila 1994, Studio Biblico Teologico. xiii-235 p. 9 art., 3 infra.

368* ᴱMcGinn Bernard, *Otten* Willemien; ERIUGENA East and West; 8th colloquium Ch/ND 18-20 Oct. 1991: MdvSt 5. ND 1994, Univ. xi-290 p. $40. 0-268-00939-5 [TDig 42,163].

369 ᴱMcGregor Bede, *Norris* Thomas, The formation journey of the priest; exploring Pastores dabo vobis [Maynooth conference]. Dublin 1994, Columba. 215 p. £8. – ᴿMonth 255 (1994) 297s (F. *Turner*: consensus reflecting ecclesiastical post of participants).

370 ᴱMcInerny Ralph, Modernity and religion [Castelgandolfo symposium]. ND 1994, Univ. xi-172 p. $22. 0-268-01408-6 [TDig 42,281].

370* ᴱMensen Bernhard, Die Schöpfung [the created world] in den Religionen: Vortragsreihe St. Augustin Völker und Kulturen. Nettetal 1990, Steyler. 111 p. [RelStR 21,33, L.D. *Lefebure*).

371 ᶠMETZ J.B.: Diagnosen zur Zeit. Dü 1994, Patmos. 92 p. DM 19.80. 3-491-72307-8. – ᴿTvT 34 (1994) 450 (J. *Brok*: afscheidssymposium).

372 ᴱMeyer Ben F., One Lord, one cup; ecumenical studies of 1 Cor 11 and other Eucharistic texts [on LÉON-DUFOUR X. 1982/7]: New Gospel St. 6. Cambridge conference on the Eucharist August 1988. Lv/Macon GA 1993, Peeters/Mercer Univ. xii-149 p. $25. 0-86554-398-4 [TDig 42,59].

372* ᶠMEYJES Guillaume H.M. Posthumus: Hugo GROTIUS Theologian, ᴱNellan Henk J.M., *Rabbie* Edwin: StHistChrTht 55. Leiden 1994, Brill. xii-275 p.; portr.; 219-245. Grotius bibliog.; 247-257, Meyjes bibliog. 90-04-10000-8. 13 art.; 8 infra [BL 95,19, J.L. *North*; TLZ 120,825: 65-76 Gospels, *Jonge* Henk J. de; 77-98 ERASMUS, *Trapman* Johannes].

373 MICHEL Virgil [1890-1938], symposium; The future of the Catholic Church in America. ColMn 1988/91, Liturgical. 120 p. $8. – ᴿNewTR 7,3 (1994) 105s (Kathleen *Hughes*).

374 ᴱMigliore Daniel L. [introd. 1s], The 1993 F. Neumann symposium on the theological interpretation of Scripture: PrincSemB supp. 3 (1994). 152 p. 3 art.; infra.

375 *a*) ᴱMilitello Cettina, Chiesa e ministero [Palermo 17-19 novembre 1989]. R 1991, Dehoniane. 621 p. – ᴿTeresianum 45 (1994) 347s (J. *Castellano*).

— *b*) ᴱMoreschini Claudio, *Menestrina* Giovanni, La traduzione dei testi religiosi; atti del convegno Trento 10-11 febbraio 1993: Religione e cultura 6. Brescia 1994, Morcelliana. 254 p. 88-372-1565-7. p. 11-21, *De Benedetti* Paolo, biblica; 23-34, *Irigoin* Jean, Settanta; 35-55, *Buzzetti* Carlo, usualia.

— *c*) ᴱMottu Henry, *Dettex* Pierre-André, Le défi homilétique; l'exégèse au service de la prédication: Actes [1993] théol. pratique Suisse romande. Genève 1994, Labor et Fides. 321 p. 2-8309-0738-8 [TLZ 120,371, E. *Henau*].

376 ᴱMühlenberg E., *Oort* J. van, Predigt in der Alten Kirche [Patristische Arbeitsgemeinschaft, Herrnhut]. Kampen 1994, Kok Pharos. 134 p. 90-390-0301-7. – ᴿTvT 34 (1994) 445 (L. *Meulenberg*).

377 La mystique africaine [colloque Theresianum, Kinshasa]. Kinshasa 1993, Baobab. 373 p. – ᴿTeresianum 45 (1994) 323-5 (J. *Kalonga*).

378 ᴱNeusch Marcel, Le sacrifice dans les religions [travail pluridisciplinaire ISTS (Institut de Science et de Théologie des Religions) UER de l'Inst. Catholique 1991-3]: ScTRel 3. P 1994, Beauchesne. 310 p. F 180. 3-7010-1303-8. 12 art., 4 infra.

379 ᴱNeuser Wilhelm H., CALVINUS Sacrae Scripturae professor = Calvin as confessor [sic] of Holy Scripture [Fourth international congress on Calvin research 1990]. GR 1994, Eerdmans. xiv-277 p. $25. 0-8028-0716-X [TDig 42,70 does not say where the meeting was (Grand Rapids?), but ten of the 18 papers are in German]. – ᴿRefR 48 (1994s) 53 (D. *McKim* also has 'Confessor' in the English title).

379* ᴱNicholls Bruce J., The unique Christ in a pluralist world [evangelical conference Manila 1992). Carlisle/GR 1994, Paternoster/Baker. 288 p. £15. 0-85364-574-4 / 0-8010-2013-1. – ᴿExpTim 106 (1994s) 349 (R. *Sturch*).

380 ᴱNoll Mark A., *Bebbington* David W., *Rawlyk* George A., Evangelicalism; comparative studies of popular Protestantism in North America, the British Isles, and beyond, 1700-1990 [Wheaton conference]: Religion in America. Ox 1994, UP. 430 p. £40; pa. £14. 0-19-508363-6. – ᴿTLond 97 (1994) 472s (E. *Norman*).

381 *Pagé* Norman, présente, Les sciences religieuses au seuil du XXIᵉ siècle [McMartin Lectures 1992, University of Ottawa]: SR 23 (1994) 255-265 [-348]; 349-360, conclusion ['Oracle'] *Lapointe* Roger.

382 *Parada Navas* J.J., Variaciones sobre la Familia; VII Jornadas de Teología del I[nstituto]T[eológico Franciscano de]M[urcia] y de la EUCIF [Escuela Universitaria de Ciencias de la Familia], Murcia 22-28 febrero 1994. – ᴿCarthaginensia 10 (1994) (235-) 427-9.

383 ᴱPeden W. Christian, *Axel* Larry E., New essays in religious naturalism [Highlands Institute conference on American religious thought, 2]. Macon 1994, Mercer Univ. viii-250 p. $30. 0-86554-426-3 [TDig 41,374: 18 art. 'pertinent to the Chicago school of theology'].

384 ᴱPelchat Marc, Les approches empiriques en théologie [4ᵉ colloque pastoral 1991]: TPrat 4. Québec 1992, Univ. Laval. 390 p. – ᴿSR 23 (1994) 231 (F. *Dumont*).

384* ᴱPerry M., *Schweitzer* F., Jewish-Christian encounters over the centuries; symbiosis, prejudice, holocaust, dialogue: Baruch College, 1-3.III.1989: AmerUnivSt 9/136. NY 1994, P. Lang. x-437 p. [RHE 90,92*].

385 ᴱPestalozzi Karl, *Weigelt* Horst, Das Antlitz Gottes im Antlitz des Menschen... LAVATER [J.K., 250. Gb., Symposion Zürich 1991]: Arb-

Pietismus 31. Gö 1994, Vandenhoeck & R. 355 p. DM 138. 3-525-55815-5 [TLZ 120,907, H.-M. *Kirn*].

386 ᴱ**Phan** Peter C., Ethnicity, nationality and religious experience: College Theology Society [1991 meeting] 37 (1991) [appeared 1995: Lanham MD, UPA]. 0-98191-9524-3. 16 art., infra.

387 ᴱ**Pittau** G., *Sepe* C., Identità e missione del sacerdote. R 1994, Città Nuova.

388 ᴱ**Poewe** Karla, Charismatic Christianity as a global culture [1991 conference; 11 art.]: Studies in comparative religion. Columbia 1994, Univ. S. Carolina. xiv-300 p. $35. 0-87249-996-0 [TDig 42,262].

389 ᴱ**Poli** C., *Timmermann* P., L'etica nelle politiche ambientali [convegno Fondazione Lanzi, Borca di Cadore ag. 1990]. Padova 1991, Gregoriana. 390 p. Lᵐ 50. – ᴿAngelicum 71 (1994) 137-140 (Teodora *Rossi*).

389* ᴱ**Rae** Murray, *Regan* Hilary, *Stenhouse* John, Science and theology; questions at the interface [Dunedin NZ 1993]. GR 1994, Eerdmans. viii-260 p. $30 pa. 0-8028-0816-6 [TDig 42,387].

390 ᴱ**Reynolds** Frank, *Tracy* David, Discourse and practice [one of a series of conferences on comparative religion]. Albany 1991, SUNY. 316 p. $19. – ᴿJRel 74 (1994) 112s (S. *Biderman*).

391 ᴱ**Ricken** Friedo, *Marty* François, KANT über Religion [München PhHochschule Mai 1992; 12 art.]: MüPhSt 7. Stu 1992, Kohlhammer. 240 p. – ᴿScripTPamp 26 (1994) 1237s (J. M. *Odero*); TPhil 69 (1994) 107s (J. *Splett*).

392 [ᴱ*Rius-Camps* J.], Missió i encarnació; l'església catalana e il repte de la seva tasca evangelitzadora: Actes del Congrès 3-5 maig 1993, 25è aniversari de la Facultat de Teologia de Catalunya: RCatalT 18,2 (1993) 201-369. 19 art.; 6 infra.

393 ᴱ**Rosner** Gotthard, Cardinal LAVIGERIE: colloque Toulouse 6-8 nov. 1992: BLitEc 95,1s (1994): 5-21, *Soetens* Claude, ... le christianisme oriental et l'union des Églises; 39-54, *Borrmans* Maurice, ... et les Musulmans; 135-150, ... *Shorter* Aylward, ... et la culture [Eng. 22.55.150]; *al*.

393* **Runzo** Joseph, Is God real? [< Claremont conference]. NY 1993, St Martins. 216 p. $40 [JRel 75,138, G. L. *Goodwin*].

394 El sacerdocio en la obra y el pensamiento de Pablo VI; Salamanca 8 nov. 1991. Brescia / R 1994, Istituto Paolo VI / Studium. 172 p. Lᵐ 35. 88-382-3700-X [TR 90,518, tit. pp.].

394* ᴱ**Santiago-Otero** H., Diálogo filosófico-religioso entre Cristianismo, Judaismo e Islamismo durante la Edad Media en la Península Ibérica: Actes... El Escorial 23-26.VI.1991: RencontresPhMdv 3. Turnhout 1994, Brepols. xi-507 p. [RHE 90,93*]. 29-52 *Epalza* M. de, Islam/ adopcianismo.

395 ꟳSCHILLEBEECKX Edward [doctorat d'honneur 17.VI.1993; colloque]: LavalTP 50,2 (1994) 259-327.

395* ᴱ**Shatzmiller** Maya, Crusaders and Muslims in twelfth-century Syria [Univ. W. Ontario] 1988. Leiden 1993, Brill. xii-235 p. $80 [Speculum 70,239, tit. pp.].

396 ᴱ**Shenk** Wilbert R., The transfiguration of mission; biblical, theological and historical foundations: Institute of Mennonite Studies (annual meetings), missionary studies 12. Scottdale PA 1993, Herald. 256 p. $16. 0-8361-3610-1 [TDig 42,93].

397 ᴱ**Sigal** P. A., L'image du pèlerin au Moyen-Age et sous l'Ancien Régime [Colloque internat. 29 sept. - 3 oct. 1993]. Gramat 1994, Amis de Rocamadour. 408 p.; 32 fig.; map. [RHE 89,440*].

398 E*Snodgrass* Klyne R.,   *a*) Resurrection; Ch North Park symposium Oct.
8-10, 1983: ExAuditu 9 (1993) vii-150 p.; bibliog. 143-150. 0883-0053. –
b) The Church; Chicago North Park Sem. Symposium Oct. 14-16, 1994:
ExAuditu 10 (1994). 131 p.

399 E**Spindler** M., *Gadille* J., Sciences de la mission et formation missionnaire
au XXe siècle, Actes de la XIIe session du CREDIC à Vérone (août 1991):
CRÉDIC 10. Lyon/Bo 1992, Lyonnaises d'Art / Missionarie Italiane. 442 p.
– RNZMiss 50 (1994) 137s (J. *Baumgartner*).

400 E**Stock** Konrad, Die Zukunft der Erlösung; zur neueren Diskussion über
die Eschatologie [6 Vorträge, Jahrestagungen 1991s]: Veröff.Wiss.Ges.
Theol. 7. Gü 1994, Kaiser. 176 p. DM 68. 3-579-00258-9. – RTLZ 119
(1990) 1129 (F. *Beisser*).

401 E**Stolz** Fritz, *Mertens* Victor, Zukunftsperspektiven des Fundamentalismus; Religion – Politik – Gesellschaft in der Schweiz [Symposion
Zürich 11./12. Sept. 1989]. FrS 1991, Univ. 128 p. Fs 28. – RTPQ 142
(1994) 84 (J. *Singer*).

402 E**Tardan-Masquelier** Ysé, Les spiritualités au carrefour du monde
moderne; traditions, transitions, transmissions [Paris-Sorbonne mai 1993
sur le Yoga, seuls les 7 rapports sur relations avec le monde moderne]. P
1994, Centurion. 175 p. F 110. 3-227-31587-3. – RÉTRel 69 (1994) 567
(J. *Argaud*).

403 La théologie au risque de l'histoire: Colloque Sém. Montréal 1-3 oct.
1992: Communautés et ministères 4. Saint-Laurent QC 1994, Bellarmin.
250 p. [NRT 117,252, A. *Toubeau*].

403* E**Thompson** Thomas A., Mary and popular devotion: Mariological
Society 44th, Providence, May 27-28, 1993: Marian Studies 44. Dayton
1993, Univ. 166 p. $15 [NRT 117,472, A. *Harvengt*].

404 E**Tilley** Maureen A., *Ross* Susan A., Broken and Whole; essays on
religion and the body; College Theology Society [San Francisco meeting]
annual publication 39 (1993). Lanham MD 1994, UPA. xi-221. 0-8191-
9746-7; pa. -7-5. 14 art.; some infra.

405 E**Triacca** Achille M., Il mistero del Sangue di Cristo nella liturgia e nella
pietà popolare; Atti 3º convegno pastorale, Roma 27-30 dic. 1988: Sangue
e vita 5. R 1989, Pia unione. I. 504 p., 18 art.; II. 515 p., 11 art. Lm 50.
→ 5044 [4º 1990 → 7,563].

406 E**Valentini** Donato, L'ecclesiologia contemporanea: Atti ATI aggiornamento 3-4 I, 1992. Padova 1994, Messaggero. 253 p. 88-250-0426-5
[Gregorianum 76,604, J. *Galot*].

407 La vida consagrada hoy; carismas en la Iglesia para el mundo; realidad,
misión, comunión, identidad: Congreso Internacional Unión de Superiores
Generales, Roma 22-27 noviembre 1993: Confer 33,122s (1994) 325-653.

407* Vorbestimmung und persönliche Freiheit [22. Tagung Saarbrücken
20.-21.VI.1992]: MaRg 8. Münster 1994, Ug.-V. 3-927120-21-9. – RUF
25 (1993) 504, relevant tit. pp.

408 E**Weingartner** Paul, *Klevakina-Uljanov* Elena, *al.*, Scientific and religious
belief [Salzburg 1991]: PhilosSt 59. Dordrecht / Norwell MA 1994,
Kluwer. viii-186 p. $89. 0-7923-2595-8. – 7 art.– RTBR 7,1 (1994s) 18 (J.
Polkinghorne).

409 E**Wiederkehr** Dietrich, Der Glaubenssinn des Gottesvolkes; Konkurrent
oder Partner des Lehramts?: QDisp 151. FrS 1994, Herder. 214 p.
DM 54. 3-451-02151-X [TR 90,520].

409* FWILLAERT Benjamin, colloquium Naming God today, E**Mertens** H.-E.,
Boeve L.: Annua Nuntia Lv 38. Lv 1994, Univ./Peeters. 103 p. Fb 380.

90-6186-614-6 / 90-6831-603-6. – ᴿExpTim 106 (1994s) 219 (D. A. *Pailin*); LvSt 19 (1994) 274s (J. *Haers*).
410 ᴱ**Wright** D. F., Martin BUCER; reforming Church and community [15 quincentenary essays]. C 1994, Univ. xiv-194 p. £35. 0-521-39144-X. – ᴿExpTim 106 (1994s) 57s (G. R. *Evans*).
411 ᴱ**Ziegenaus** Anton, Maria in der Evangelisierung [Deutsche Arbeitsgemeinschaft für Mariologie, Tagung 1992]: MariolSt 9. Rg 1993, Pustet. 200 p. DM 38. – ᴿTR 90 (1994) 245s (F. *Courth*).

A2.5   *Acta philologica et historica* [reports ➤ Y7.6].

412 *a)* Actes de l'Association: RÉG 107,2 (1994) ix-lii.
— *b)* ᴱ**Alvar** J., *al.*, Héroes, semidioses y daimones: Primer encuentro Arys (Cáceres) dic. 1989. M 1992, Clásicas. 510 p. – ᴿGerión 11 (1993) 40s (Mirella *Romero Recio*).
— *c)* ᴱ**Aurell** Martin, *al.*, La sociabilité à table; commensalité et convivialité à travers les âges; Actes du colloque 14-17 nov. 1990: Ribl. 178. Rouen 1992, Univ. 393 p.; ill. – ᴿRÉAnc 96 (1994) 573 (R. *Étienne*).
413 *a)* ᴱ**Baccari** M. F., Diritto e religione da Roma a Costantinopoli a Mosca (Rendiconto dell'XI Seminario, Da Roma alla Terza Roma). R 1994, Herder. ➤ 3849 [1993: L'idea di Roma a Mosca nei secoli XV-XVI; xxxvii-441 p.; 7 color pl. – ᴿOrChrPer 60 (1994) 102s (J. *Bilinsky*)].
— *b)* ᴱ**Baslez** Marie-Françoise, *al.*, L'invention de l'autobiographie, d'Hésiode à Saint Augustin: Actes du deuxième colloque Hellénisme Post-Classique: P 14-16.VI.1990: ÉtLitAnc 5. P 1993, École Normale Supérieure. 334 p. – ᴿRÉAnc 96 (1994) 579s (Lucienne *Deschamps*).
— *c)* ᴱ**Bilde** Per, *al.*, Religion and religious practice in the Seleucid kingdom [Denmark meeting Jan. 1990]. Aarhus 1990, Univ. 269 p.; 52 fig. 87-7288-322-7. – ᴿAJA 97 (1993) 581 (Susan B. *Downey*); TopO 3 (1993) 345-354 (D. T. *Potts*).
414 ᴱ**Blumenthal** H. J., Clark E. G., The divine IAMBLICHUS, philosopher and man of gods [Liverpool Univ. 23-26 sept. 1990]. Bristol 1993, Classical. vii-215 p. £30. – ᴿPrudentia 26,2 (1994) 52-54 (Maryse *Waegeman*).
414* ᴱ**Bolelli** T. (p. 11-14), La posizione attuale della linguistica storica nell'ambito delle discipline linguistiche (Roma, 26-28 marzo 1991): Atti Convegni Lincei 94. R 1992, Accad. Lincei. 199 p. 12 art.; 3 infra.
415 ᴱ**Boussac** M.-F., Salles J.-F., Séminaire Lyon 1993 sur ᴱSHERWIN-WHITE Susan, KUHRT A., Les Séleucides (L 1993 ➤ 9,12634; 13 critiques): TopO 4 (1994) 431-610.
415* ᴱ**Carlsen** Jasper, *al.*, Alexander the Great; reality and myth: Inst. Danici. Anal. supp. 20. R 1993, Bretschneider. 206 p.
416 *a)* CASTAGNOLI Ferdinando, mem.: Bilancio critico su Roma arcaica fra monarchia e repubblica, convegno Lincei 100, Roma 3-4 giugno 1991. R 1993, Accad. Lincei. 157 p.
— *b)* [Christol A., *al.*, présente] Étymologie diachronique et étymologie synchronique en grec ancien; Actes du Colloque de Rouen 21-22 nov. 1991: RPg 65,1 (1991, apparu 1993). 253 p. – ᴿBSLP 89,2 (1994) 204-211 (J.-P. *Levet*).
— *c)* ᴱ**Connor** Peter J., Ancient Macedonia, an Australian symposium [2d, Melbourne Univ. 8-13 July 1991]: MeditArch 7 (1994) 126 p.
— *d)* ᴱ**Coulson** William, Kyrieleis Helmut, Olympic Games, symposium Athens 5-9 Sept. 1993. Athenae 1992. 190 p., 68 pl. + 25 color. $58 pa. [ClasW 89,230, S. *Lattimore*].

417 *a*) ᴱ**Darteville** P., *al.*, Blasphèmes et liberté [Ligue pour l'abolition des lois reprimant le blasphème, colloque 10 févr. 1990]. P 1993, Cerf. 144 p. – ᴿMélSR 51 (1994) 227-230 (J.-C. *Matthys*: utile).

— *b*) ᴱ**D'Ippolito** Gennaro, *Gallo* Italo, Strutture formali dei 'Moralia' di PLUTARCO: 3º Convegno, Palermo 3-5.V.1989. N 1991, D'Auria. 514 p. 88-7092-044-5. 34 art., 5 infra.

— *c*) ᴱ**Dougherty** Carol, *Kurke* Leslie, Cultu[r]al poetics in archaic Greece; cult, performance, politics [Wellesley 1990]. C 1993, Univ. 266 p. – ᴿRÉG 107 (1994) 715s (Jacqueline *Assaël*: 'cultural').

— *d*) **Étienne** R., *Le Dinaret* M.-T., L'espace sacrificiel [colloque Lyon, Maison de l'Orient 4-7 juin 1988]. P 1991, de Boccard. 346 p.; LXXXII pl. – ᴿRÉG 107 (1994) 730-2 (B. *Holtzmann*).

418 ᴱ**Filigheddu** Paolo, Circolazioni culturali nel Mediterraneo antico; Iº convegno internazionale di linguistica, Sassari 24-27 aprile 1991 (Sesta giornata camito-semitico e indoeuropea). Cagliari 1994. 278 p. 24 art.; 4 infra.

418* ᴱ**French** David H., *Lightfoot* Christopher S., The eastern frontier of the Roman Empire: colloquium Ankara Sept. 1988: Bar-Int. 553. Ox 1989. 615 p.; ill. – ᴿTopO 3 (1993) 363-7 (E. *Dąbrowa*).

419 **Gascó** F., *Alvar* J., Heterodoxos, Reformadores y marginados en la antigüedad clásica [9 conferencias Univ. La Rábida verano 1990]. Sevilla 1991. 242 p. – ᴿGerión 11 (1993) 409s (Celia *Martínez Maza*).

420 ᴱ**Giannotta** M.E., *al.*, La decifrazione del Cario; Atti del 1º Simposio, Roma 3-4 maggio 1993. R 1994, Cons. Naz. Ricerche. 253 p.; bibliog. 247-253. 88-8080-005-1.

421 ᴱ**Gill** Christopher, *Wiseman* T.P., Lies and fiction in the ancient world. Austin 1993, Univ. Texas. xviii-263 p. $30. – ᴿClasOut 71 (1993s) 142.144 (G. *Schmeling*); JRS 84 (1994) 197s (R.B. *Rutherford*).

421* ᴱ**Goulet-Cazé** Marie-Odile, *Goulet* Richard, Le cynisme ancien et ses prolongements [CNRS Paris 22-25 juillet 1990]. P 1993, PUF. 612 p. – ᴿRÉG 107 (1994) 732s (P. *Nautin*).

422 ᴱ**Graf** Fritz, Klassische Antike und neue Wege der Kulturwissenschaften: Symposium K. Meuli, Basel 11.-13.IX.1991: Beiträge zur Volkskunde 11. Ba 1992, Ges. Volkskunde. 221 p.

422* ᴱ**Grafton** Anthony, *Marchand* Suzanne L., Proof and persuasion in history [Jan 1993, Princeton]: HistTheor theme issue 33 (1994). 133 p. 5 art.

423 ᴱ**Hackens** Tony, *Miró* Marta, Le commerce maritime romain en Méditerranée occidentale, Colloque Barcelone 16-18 mai 1988: PACT 27. Strasbourg 1990, Conseil de l'Europe. 390 p. 26 art.

423* ᴱ**Hägg** Robin, Iconography of Greek cult: Kernos supp. 1. Liège 1990/2, Centre Rel. Grecque. 230 p. – ᴿOpAth 20 (1994) 271s (H.A. *Shapiro*).

424 ᴱ**Hansen** Mogens H., The ancient Greek city-state; symposium 250th anniv. Royal Danish Acad. 1-4 July 1992: Meddelelser 67. K 1993, Munksgaard. 281 p. 87-7304-242-0. 9 art.; 3 infra.

425 ᴱ**Hermon** E., Gouvernants et gouvernés dans l'Imperium Romanum (3ᵉ s. av. J.-C. - Iᵉ s. ap.): CahÉtAnc 36. Québec 1991, Univ. Laval. x-276 p. – ᴿPhoenix 48 (Toronto 1994) 85-87 (J.S. *Richardson*).

425* ᴱ**Hornblower** Simon, Greek historiography [Oxford seminar 1991]. Ox 1994, UP. xii-286 p. $55 [RelStR 21,327, D.F. *Graf*].

426 ᴱ**Hunt** Lynn, The invention of pornography; obscenity and the origins of modernity, 1500-1800 [Univ. Pennsylvania conference]. NY/CM 1993, Zone/MIT. 411 p. $27. – ᴿAmHR 99 (1994) 504s (Valerie *Steele*).

427 ᴱLaiou Angeliki E., *Maguire* H., Byzantium, a world civilization: 50th anniversary symposium Dumbarton Oaks Nov. 3, 1990. Wsh 1993, DO Research Library. 162 p. – ᴿOrChrPer 60 (1994) 257s (E. G. *Farrugia*).

428 Lepori F., *Santi* F., Il mestiere di storico del Medioevo; convegno Lugano 17-19.V.1990: Quad. Cultura Mediolatina 7. Spoleto 1994, Centro Alto Mdv. ix-124 p. [RHE 90,7*].

429 ᴱLétoublon Françoise, La langue et les textes en grec ancien; actes du Colloque P. CHANTRAINE (Grenoble, 5-8 sept. 1989). Amst 1992, Gieben. viii-369 p. – ᴿBSLP 89,2 (1994) 198-204 (A. *Blanc*); RÉAnc 96 (1994) 579-582 (Nicole *Maurice-Guilleux*); RÉG 107 (1994) 239s (A. *Wartelle*).

430 *a*) ᴱLomas F. J., *Devis* F., De Constantino a Carlomagno; disidentes, heterodoxos, marginales. Cádiz 1992, Univ. 253 p.; 10 art. – ᴿGerión 12 (1994) 315-336 (E. *Bravo*: 'La transición').

— *b*) ᴱLópez Ferez Juan Antonio, Tratados hipocráticos (estudios acerca de su contenido, forma e influencia), Actas del VIIᵉ colloque Madrid 24-29.IV.1990. M 1992, Univ. a distancia. 751 p. 84-362-2779-4. 52 art., 7 infra.

— *c*) ᴱLuce (Torrey) J., *Woodman* A. ., TACITUS and the Tacitean tradition [colloquium Princeton 1990]. Princeton 1993, Univ. xvii-207 p. – ᴿHist-Theor 33 (1994) 123 (T. J. L., sub Luce).

— *d*) ᴱMeschonnic Henri, Le langage comme défi [rencontre Paris VIII, 4-5 mai 1990]: Cahiers de Paris VIII. Presses Universitaires de Vincennes. 292 p. – ᴿBSLP 89,2 (1994) 142-9 (Annie *Montaut*).

431 *a*) ᴱMeyuhas Ginio Alisa, Jews, Christians and Muslims in the Mediterranean world after 1492 [Tel Aviv Univ. 2-6 June 1991) = MeditHistR 6 (1991). L 1992, Cass. 296 p. – ᴿSefarad 54 (1994) 423-5 (M. *Orfali*).

— *b*) ᴱPhilippaki-Warburton Irene, *al.*, Themes in [mostly modern] Greek linguistics: First conference, Reading Sept. 1993; AmstTHLing. Amst 1994, Benjamins. xx-534 p. 90-272-3620-8 / Ph 1-55639-57-0-...

— *c*) ᴰRaaflaub Kurt, (*Müller-Luckner* Elisabeth), Anfänge politischen Denkens in der Antike [Juni 1990]: Kolloquien des Historischen Kollegs 24. Mü 1993, Oldenbourg. xxiv-461 p. 3-486-55993-1 [RelStR 21,42, D. I. *Owen*).

432 Le ravitaillement en blé de Rome et des centres urbains des débuts de la République jusqu'au Haut Empire; actes du colloque international organisé par le Centre Jean Bérard et l'URA 994 du CNRS, Naples 14-16 février 1991; Coll.Éc.Fr.R 196. N/R 1994, Centre Bérard / École Française. 335 p. 2-903189-43-0 / 2-7283-0315-0. / 28 art.; 9 infra.

433 *a*) Rizzo Paolo Francesco, present., 'Nostoi' ed 'emporia'; la Sicilia punto di riferimento fino al VI sec. a. C.: Atti dell'VIII congresso internazionale di studi sulla Sicilia antica, Palermo 18-23 aprile 1993: Kokalos 39s (1993s). xxiii-397 p. 88-7889-112-9. 18 art.; 6 infra.

— *b*) ᴱRosner Michael, *Johnson* Roderick, Computational linguistics and formal semantics [Lugano workshops up to 1990]: Studies in Natural Language Processing. C 1992, Univ. xx-321 p. 0-521-41950-X; pa. -12988-0. – ᴿBSLP 89,2 (1994) 115-8 (G. *Rebuschi*).

— *c*) ROSTAGNI Augusto: A cent'anni dalla nascita (1892-1961) incontro 20.III.1992, ᴱLana Italo: AcAcad Torino 126 supp. T 1992. 146 p. – ᴿRÉAnc 96 (1994) 574 (Lucienne *Deschamps*).

— *d*) ᴱRougemont G., [*al.*] Aujourd'hui, qu'est-ce que la recherche littéraire sur les auteurs anciens [Séminaire Lyon 1994]: TopO 4 (1994) 611s [-669].

435 ᴱRück P., *Boghardt* M., Rationalisierung der Buchherstellung im Mittelalter und in der frühen Neuzeit: Wolfenbüttel 12.-14. Nov. 1990: Elementa diplomatica 2. Marburg 1994, Inst. Hist. Hilfswiss. 204 p., 70 fig. DM 80 [RHE 90].

436 ᴱRydén Lennart, *Resenqvist* Jan Olaf, Aspects of Late Antiquity and early Byzantium; Colloquium Swedish Research Inst. İstanbul, June 1992: Transactions 4. U 1993, Almqvist & W. 173 p. – ᴿOrChrPer 60 (1994) 657s (V. *Ruggieri*).

437 ᴱSamuel Raphael, *Thompson* Paul, The myths we live by [6th Oral History Conference 1989]. L 1990, Routledge. x-262 p. £35; pa. £19. – ᴿEngHR 109 (1994) 547s (P. *Burke*).

438 ᴱUggeri Giovanni, Metodologie nella ricerca topografica, Iᵒ Congresso R 13-15 maggio 1993 = J/RTop 4 (1994). 223 p. 18 art.; 215-7 English summaries.

440 ᴱVirgilio Biagio, Aspetti e problemi dell'ellenismo; Atti del Convegno di Studi, Pisa 6-7 nov. 1992: BtStAnt 73. Pisa 1994, Giardini. 247 p. 88-427-0279-X. – 10 art. ↣ Elenchus vol. 11.

442 ᴱVryonis Speros, The Greeks and the sea: Hellenism; ancient, medieval, modern 18. New Rochelle 1993, Caratzas. xii-234 p.; ill.

A2.7 *Acta* orientalistica.

443 ᴱAllam Schafik, Grund und Boden im Altägypten (Rechtliche und sozio-ökonomische Verhältnisse); Akten des internationalen Symposions, Tübingen 18.-20. Juni 1990: Untersuchungen zum Rechtsleben im alten Ägypten 2. Tü 1994, auct. [vi-]417 p. 3-924299-92-0. 28 art., 14 in our 1995 volume.

444 Ancient Near East and India; intercultural religious parallels (the Franco-Finnish symposium 10-11 Nov. 1990: StOr 10. Helsinki 1993, Soc. Orientalis Fennica. 149 p. Fm 150. 951-9380-19-1 [RelStR 21,33, D. I. *Owen*).

445 ᴱBülow-Jacobsen Adam, Proceedings of the 20ᵗʰ international congress of papyrologists, Copenhagen, 23-29 August 1992. K 1994, Univ. Museum Tusculanum. 631 p.; 37 pl. – ᴿAegyptus 79 (1994) 187-9 (S. *Daris*).

446 ᴱCameron Averil, *Conrad* Lawrence J., The Byzantine and Early Islamic Near East, I. Problems in the literary source material; First Workshop: StLAntIsl 1. Princeton 1992, Darwin. xiv-428 p. $30. – 8 art. – ᴿRÉByz 52 (1994) 296s (J.-C. *Cheynet*); RSO 68 (1994) 167-9 (L. *Capezzone*).

448 ᴱCanivet Pierre, *Rey-Coquais* Jean-Paul, La Syrie de Byzance à l'Islam (VIIᵉ-VIIIᵉ siècles), Actes du Colloque international [Maison de l'Orient Méditerranéen / Univ. Lyon II / CNRS 11-15 sept. 1990. Damas 1992, IFED 137. 369 p. – ᴿMuséon 107 (1994) 208-21 (A. de *Halleux*); PrOrChr 43 (1993) 211-4 (P. *Ternant*); RÉByz 52 (1994) 297-9 (J.-C. *Cheynet*).

449 Coptes 4 [*Rosenstehl* J. M. présent.]: quatrième journées d'études coptes, Strasbourg 26-27 mai 1988: BtCopte Cah 8. P 1994, Peeters. xi-121 p. 2-87723-199-2.

450 Durante Marcello † 1992, Giornata di studio, Roma 23 marzo 1994, ᴱMarcozzi Daria, *al.*; SMEA 33 (1994). 176 p. [... oralità omerica].

450* ᴱEid Mushira, *al.*, Perspectives on Arabic linguistics 6: papers from the 6th annual symposium: Current Issues in Linguistic Theory 115. Amst 1994, Benjamins. viii-239 p. 90-272-3618-6.

451 ᴱLavenant René, VI Symposium Syriacum 1992, Cambridge Aug. 30-

Sept. 2: OrChrAn 247. R 1994, Pont.Ist.Or. 495 p. 88-7210-205-3. 36 art., plures infra.
451* **Maxfield** V. A., *Dobson* M. J., Roman frontier studies [15th Limes Congress, Canterbury 2-10 Sept.] 1989. Exeter 1991, Univ. 512 p.; 334 fig. – 85 art. – ᴿAcArchH 46 (1994) 450-3 (I. *Bóna*, deutsch).
452 ᴱ**Menu** Bernadette, Les problèmes institutionnels de l'eau en Égypte ancienne et dans l'antiquité méditerranée: colloque aides Vogüé 1992: BtÉt 110. Le Caire 1994, IFAO. xxiv-326 p.; iv pl.; xvii-xxii bibliog. (*Bonneau* Danielle, *Bernard* Étienne). 2-7247-0150-X.
ᴱ**Porter** Stanley E., *Carson* D. A., Biblical language and linguistics 1993 ➔ 9511.
453 REUSCHEL Wolfgang [16.XI.1924-18.IX.1991] Gedenkschrift: Akten des III. Arabistischen Kolloquiums, Leipzig 21.-22. November 1991, ᴱ**Bellmann** Dieter: AbhKundeMorg 51/1. Stu 1994, DMG. 3-515-06283-3. – 27 art.
453* ᴱ**Vogelzang** Marianna E., *Vanstiphout* Herman L. J., Mesopotamian epic literature; oral or aural? Lewiston NY 1992, Mellen. xi-328 p. 0-7734-9538-X.
454 ᴱ**Wunsch** Cornelia, XXV. Deutscher Orientalistentag vom 8. bis 13.IV.1991 in München; ZDMG Supp. 10. Stu 1994, Steiner. 540 p. 3-515-06527-X. 53 art.; 2 infra.

A2.9 *Acta* **archaeologica** [reports ➔ Y7.8].

455 AIA 94th New Orleans 27-30 Dec. 1992, summaries / 95th Washington 27-30 Dec. 1993: AJA 97 (1993) 295-352; 353s index of the 300-some summaries / 98 (1994) 283-341 . 341-3.
455* ᴱ**Alvar** Jaime, *Blázquez* José M., Los enigmas de Tartessos [1991 Complutense summer course]. M 1993, Cátedra. 84-376-1138-5. – ᴿAJA 98 (1994) 369s (A. *Gilman*).
456 ᴱ**Amouretti** Marie-Claire, *Comet* G., Des hommes et des plantes; plantes méditerranéennes, vocabulaire et usages anciens [Table Ronde Aix 1992]. Aix-en-Provence 1993, Univ. 174 p. – ᴿTopO 4 (1994) 271-6 (S. *Amigues*).
456* ᴱ**Antonacci Sanpaolo** Elena, Archaeometallurgia, ricerche e prospettive, Colloquio Bologna 18-21 ott. 1988. Bo 1992, Clueb. 696 p. 50 art.; plures infra.
457 ᴱ**Barlow** Jane A., *al.*, Cypriot ceramics; reading the prehistoric record [colloquium Philadelphia 1989]: mg 74 / Lewis Found. Ph 1991, Univ. Museum. 258 p.; 90 fig. 0-924171-10-3. – ᴿAJA 98 (1994) 778s (D. W. *Rupp*).
457* ᴱ**Begley** V., *De Puma* R. D., Rome and India; the ancient sea trade [AIA 88th meeting, San Antonio 27-30 Dec. 1986]. Madison 1991, Univ. Wisconsin. 248 p. – ᴿTopO 3 (1993) 525-534 (A. *Tchernia*).
458 ᴱ**Bietak** Manfred, Trade, power and cultural exchange; Hyksos Egypt and the Eastern Mediterranean world: NY Met Symposium Nov. 3, 1993: Ägypten und Levante 5 (1994). 132 p. 3-7001-2205-5. 8 art., infra.
458* ᴱ**Bleiberg** Edward, *Freed* Rita, Fragments of a shattered visage; the proceedings of the international symposium of Ramesses the Great: Gb Inst. Eg. Art 1. Memphis TN 1991, Memphis State Univ. v-269 p. 0-9636816-0-5.
459 BOESSNECK Joachim [26.II.1925-1.III.1991] mem.: Beiträge zur Archäozoologie und prähistorischen Anthropologie; 8. Arbeitstreffen der Osteologen, Konstanz 1993, ᴱ**Kokabi** Mostafa, *Wahl* Joachim: Forschungen

Baden-W. 33. Stu 1994, Theiss. 432 p. 3-8062-1155-8. 42 art., 2 infra
➤ 13348.
460 ᴱBorchhardt Jürgen, *Dobesch* Gerhard, Akten des II. internationalen
Lykien-Symposions, Wien 6.-12. Mai 1990, Band I.: Denkschr 231-5. W
1993, Österr. Akademie. 276 p.; 321 p. + 64 pl. 3-7001-2081-8. – 24 art.;
2 infra. – ᴿRÉAnc 96 (1994) 667s (J. des *Courtils*).
461 ᴱBriend J., *al.*, La Syrie-Palestine à l'époque perse; continuités et ruptures
à la lumière des périodes néo-assyrienne et hellénistique: Actes du IIᵉ
colloque international, Inst. Cath. de Paris 3-5 oct. 1991: Transeuphratène
6 (1993) 169 p.; XIV pl.; 7 (1994) 172 p.; II pl.; 8 (1994) 184 p.; XIX pl.
462 ᴱCameron Catherine M., *Tomka* Steve A., Abandonment of settlements
and regions; ethnoarchaeological approaches: New Dir. C 1993, Univ.
xv-201 p.
462* Vere Gordon CHILDE centennial conference London Univ. Inst.
Archaeol. 8-9 May 1992, The archaeology of V. G. Childe, contemporary
perspectives. L 1994, UCL. xii-148 p. 1-85728-220-5.
463 ᴱÇilingiroğlu A., *French* D. H., Anatolian Iron Age, colloquium İzmir
4-8 May 1987: Ankara British Institute mg. 13. Ox 1991, Oxbow.
xxviii-164 p.; 67 fig.; 33 pl. $42. 0-046897-38-7. – ᴿAJA 98 (1994) 782s
(Lynn E. *Roller*).
464 ᴱCorona Raimondo, Oggetti domestici di Terra Santa al tempo di Cristo
e nel periodo bizantino: Settimana Biblica Abruzzese 9, 4-9 luglio 1994;
Atti supp. L'Aquila 1994, Curia OFM. 54 p. 16 color pl.
465 ᴱDavies Glenys, Plaster and marble; the classical and neo-classical
portrait bust: Edinburgh Albacini [1838 collection] colloquium: Journal of
the History of Collections 3. Ox 1991, UP. 0954-6650. – ᴿAJA 98 (1994)
796 (M. *Vickers*).
466 ᴱDebord Pierre, *Descat* Raymond, Fortifications et défense du territoire
en Asie Mineure occidentale et méridionale: Table Ronde CNRS. Istanbul
20-27 mai 1993: RÉAnc 96,1s (1994). 354 p.; ill. 25 art., 9 infra.
467 ᴱDewachter Michel, *Fouchard* Alain, L'Égyptologie et les Champollion:
'à l'occasion du Colloque bicentenaire de J.-F. CHAMPOLLION né 1790'.
Grenoble 1994, Univ. 382 p.; ill. F 100. 2-7061-0542-9. 31 art.
467* ᴱDietrich Walter, *Klopfenstein* Martin A., Ein Gott allein? JHWH-
Verehrung und biblischer Monotheismus im Kontext der israelitischen
und altorientalischen Religionsgeschichte: Symposium Bern Jan. 1993:
OBO 139. FrS 1994, Univ. 608 p. 3-7728-0962-0 / VR 3-525-53774-3. 28
art.; infra [JBL 107,561 & RB 102,443, tit. pp.],
Élayi J. & A. G., Trésors de monnaies phéniciennes et circulation monétaire
(Vᵉ-IVᵉ s.). Transeuphratène supp. 1 1993 ➤ 12133.
469 Fischer-Hansen Tobias, *al.*, Ancient portraiture, image and message
[Copenhagen Univ. Seminar]: Acta Hyperborea 4. K 1992, MusTusc.
395 p.; 198 fig. 87-7288-213-7. – ᴿAJA 97 (1993) 811s (Susan *Wood*).
469* ᴱGünter Ann C., Investigating artistic environments in the Ancient
Near East [Smithsonian symposium 1988]. Wsh/Madison 1990, Univ.
Wisconsin. 153 p.; 76 fig. – ᴿTopO 3 (1993) 217-245 (Margaret C. *Root*).
470 ᴱGundlach Rolf, *Buchholz* Matthias, Ägyptische Tempel – Struktur,
Funktion und Programm: Akten der Ägyptologischen Tempeltagungen in
Gosen 1990 und in Mainz 1992: ÄgBeit 37. Hildesheim 1990/2/44,
Gerstenberg. viii-331 p.; ill. 3-6067-8131-1. – 23 art., 5 infra.
470* ᴱHägg R., The iconography of Greek cult in the archaic and classical
periods: Actes du premier séminaire, Delphes 16-18 nov. 1990: Kernos
suppl. 1. Athènes-Liège 1992. – ᴿRÉG 107 (1994) 247s (C. *Mauduit*).

471 ᴱHalpern Baruch, Hobson Deborah W., Law, politics and society in the ancient Mediterranean world [11 Gerstein Lectures, York Univ. 1988]. Shf 1993, Academic. 291 p. £40. – ᴿJAOS 114 (1994) 661s (V. H. Matthews).
472 **Hoffmann** Adolf, al., Bautechnik der Antike [Berlin 15-17.II.1990; 39 art.]: Diskussionen zur archäologischen Bauforschung 5, Mainz 1991 ➤ 8,718: ᴿAJA 97 (1993) 577s (J. G. Pedley).
473 ᴱHolliday Peter J., Narrative and event in ancient art [College Art Asn 1988 meeting]. C 1993, Univ. xvi-368 p.; 95 fig. 0-521-43013-5 [RelStR 21,40, R. D. Woodard).
474 ᴱKarageorghis V., a) The civilizations of the Aegean and their diffusion in Cyprus and the Eastern Mediterranean, 2000-600 B.C.; Symposium, 18-24 Sept. 1989. Larnaca 1992, Pierides Foundation. 144 p.; 39 pl. 99-83-560-72-5. – ᴿAJA 97 (1993) 802s (D. W. Rupp). – b) Cyprus in the 13th c. B.C. Nicosia 30-31 Oct. 1993/1994 [RB 102,438, tit. pp.].
474* ᴱKlees Frank, Kuper Rudolph, New light on the Northeast African past; current prehistoric research; contributions to a symposium, Cologne 1990: Africa praehistorica 5. Köln 1992, H. Barth Inst. 248 p. 3-927688-06-1 [OIAc 11,29].
475 ᴱKroll Ellen M., Price T. Douglas, The interpretation of archaeological seasonal patterning [Toronto Society for American archaeology 1987 symposium]. NY 1991, Plenum. xiii-316 p.; 91 fig. 0-306-43645-0. – ᴿAJA 97 (1993) 168 (Pam J. Crabtree).
476 ᴱLa Regina Adriano, al., Atti del convegno internazionale 'Vox lapidum'; dalla riscoperta delle iscrizioni antiche all'invenzione di un nuovo stile scrittorio; Acquasparta/Urbino 11-13 sett. 1993: Eutopia 3,1s (1994), 357 p. 1121-1628. 9 art. (post-medieval work on classical antiquity).
476* a) ᴱLayton R., Who needs the past? Indigenous values and archaeology / b) **Shennan** S., Archaeological approaches and cultural identity: [< Southampton 1986] One World Archaeology 5.7. L 1994 = 1989, Routledge. xxiv-215 p.; xxviii-217 p. £17; £18 0-415-09558-1; -7-3 [BL 95,30, L. L. Grabbe].
477 **Le Guen-Pollet** Brigitte, Pelon Olivier, La Cappadoce méridionale jusqu'à la fin de l'empire romain: Colloque Istanbul 13-14 avril 1987. P 1991, RCiv. 90 p.; 33 pl. F 125. 2-86538-225-7. – ᴿSyria 71 (1994) 468-470 (C. Michel).
478 ᴱLeonardi Giovanni, Formation processes and excavation methods in archaeology; perspectives; Seminario internazionale Padova 15.-27.VII. 1991: Piovego Saltuarie 3. Padova 1992, Univ. 416 p.
479 ᴱMaggi R., al., Archeologia della pastorizia nell'Europa meridionale, Tavola rotonda Chiavari 23-24 sett. 1989: RStLiguri 56s. Bordighera 1990s. 328 p.; 264 p. Lᵐ 80. – ᴿAJA 98 (1994) 163 (R. J. Rowland).
480 ᴱMilano Lucio, Drinking in ancient societies; history and culture of drinks in the ancient Near East: symposium Rome May 17-19, 1990: HistANE St 6. Padova 1994, Sargon. xvi-471 p.; 12 fig.; XI pl. 25 art.
480* **Moore** Brian, al., Ages in chaos? How valid are Velikovsky's views on ancient history; Glasgow Univ. conference 7-8 April 1978, Cleveland 1982, Society for Interdisciplinary Studies [Journal 4,1-3; 0308-3276]. 84 p.; ill. [OIAc 11, p. 34].
481 ᴱMotte André, Influences, emprunts et syncrétismes religieux en Grèce ancienne, Actes du IVᵉ colloque Bru 2-4.IX.1993: Kernos 7 (1994).
481* ᴱMusti D., al., La transizione dal miceneo all'alto arcaismo, dal palazzo alla città: Roma 14-18 marzo 1988, R 1991, Cons. Naz. Ricerche. 629 p. Lᵐ 60. – ᴿAJA 97 (1993) 803 (I. Morris).

482 ᴱOrtner Donald J., *Aufderhaide* Arthur C., Human paleopathology; current syntheses and future options [symposium Zagreb July 1988]. Wsh 1991, Smithsonian. vii-311 p. $70. 1-56098-039-7. – ᴿJField 21 (1994) 239-243 (G. J. *Armelagos*).

483 ᴱPeretto Carlo, *al.*, Bollettino [2º] del [i. e. Invito per il] XIII Congresso dell'Unione Internazionale delle scienze preistoriche e protostoriche, Forlì, Italia, 1996 [8-14 sett.]; contiene storie dei congressi 1871 e 1962 e di simili imprese. Forlì 1994, Provincia. 140 p. 'Diffusione gratuita'.

484 ᴱPiérart Marcel, Polydipsion Argos; Argos de la fin des palais mycéniens à la constitution de l'état classique: FrS 7-9 mai 1987: BCH supp. 22. P 1992, de Boccard. xii-324 p.; 47 pl. Fs 75. 2-86958-041-X. – ᴿAJA 98 (1994) 784-6 (M. *Munn*, also on FOLEY A. 1988); TopO 3 (1993) 247-257 (P. *Sauzeau*).

485 ᴱPolland A. M., New developments in archaeological science; a joint symposium of the Royal Society and the British Academy: Proc 77, 1992 → 9,574: ᴿAJA 98 (1994) 774-6 (R. H. *Tykot*).

486 ᴱPostgate Nicholas, *Powell* Martin, Domestic animals of Mesopotamia I [Barcelona July 1990]: BuSumAgr 7. C 1993, Univ. Or. Fac. 258 p. – ᴿAnOr 62 (1992) 347-350 (B. *Hruška*).

486* ᴱQuaegebeur J., Ritual and sacrifice in the Ancient Near East; Leuven 17-20 April 1991: OrLovAnal 55. Lv 1994, Univ./Peeters. xxx-541 p. 90-6831-580-3 [OIAc 11,38; ᴢᴀᴡ 107,341, tit. pp.].

487 Schwartz Glenn M., [Khabur p. 19-35] *Falconer* Steven E., [Jordan valley p. 21-42] Archaeological views from the countryside; village communities in early complex societies [also p. 109-120, *Wattenmaker* Patricia, Kartan; p. 37-47, *Magness-Gardiner* Bonnie, Alalaḫ]. Wsh 1994, Smithsonian. vii-273 p. 1-56098-319-1.

488 ᴱSebasta Judith L., *Bonfante* Larissa, The world of Roman costume [1988 seminar]: Wisconsin Studies in Classics. Madison 1994, Univ. Wisconsin. xviii-272 p.; 190 fig. 0-299-13850-X. 13 art.

489 ᴱSkeates R., *Whitehouse* R., Radiocarbon dating and Italian prehistory [conference 1991, Rome British School]: mg 8. R 1994. 288 p. – ᴿOrigini 18 (R 1994) 481s (Alessandra *Manfredini*).

490 ᴱStein G., *Rothman* M. S., Chiefdoms and early states in the Near East; the organizational dynamics of complexity [Amer. Anthropological Asn. 1989]: WArch mg 18. Madison 1994, Prehistory Press. – ᴿBuCanadMesop 28 (1994) 44s (M. *Fortin*).

491 [Valbelle Dominique], Sociétés urbaines en Égypte et au Soudan: Papyrologie Cah. 16. Lille 1994, Univ. 209 p.; 28 pl. 0153-5021.

492 ᴱVandenabeele Frieda, *Laffineur* Robert, Cypriote terracottas; proceedings of the first international conference of Cypriote studies, Brussels-Liège-Amsterdam, 29 May-1 June 1989. Bru 1991, Leventis Foundation. 259 p.; 71 pl.; 2 maps. 9963-560-12-1. – ᴿAJA 97 (1993) 175s (J. P. *Uhlerbrock*).

492* ᴱWaelkens Marc, *al.*, Ancient stones; quarrying, trade and provenance [Tagung Lv 1990]: AcArchLv, Mg. 4. Lv 1992, Univ. vii-292 p.; ill.; 4 color. pl. – ᴿMusHelv 51 (1994) 182 (D. *Willers*).

493 ᴱWesterdahl C., Crossroads in ancient shipbuilding; Proceeding of the Sixth International Symposium on boat and ship archaeology, Roskilde [Denmark] 1991: Mg 40. Ox 1994, Oxbow. 290 p. £40 pa. 0-946897-70-0. – ᴿIntJNaut 23 (1994) 332.

494 ᴱYon Marguerite, Kynyras; l'archéologie française à Chypre: table-ronde Lyon 5-6 1991: TravMO 22. Lyon 1993, Maison de l'Orient Méd. 254 p.;

ill. [RB 102,132, tit. pp.; réserves sur la procédure bilingue]. – ᴿRStFen 22 (1994) 146s (E. *Acquaro*).

A3   *Opera consultationis* – **Reference works** .1 *plurium separately infra.*

495 **AnchorBD:** The Anchor Bible Dictionary, ᴱ**Freedman** David N., *al.*, 1992 ➤ 8,741; 9,580. – ᴿBiblica 75 (1994) 291-5 (R. *North*); BZ 38 (1994) 102s (J. *Schreiner*); ChrSchR 22 (1992) 418-420 (R. W. *Wall*: 'much more useful than the IDB which it replaces'); Interpretation 48 (1994) 407-410 (W. S. *Towner*); JBL 113 (1994) 299-310 (W. *Harrelson*); LavalTP 50 (1994) 223-5 (P.-H. *Poirier*); RB 101 (1994) 309-311 (J. *Murphy-O'Connor*); ScEspr 46 (1994) 115s (P.-É. *Langevin*).

496 **ANRW:** Aufstieg und Niedergang der Römischen Welt II. Principat [27,1; 34,1; 37,1 1993 ➤ 9,581], ᴱ**Haase** W., [continuing; but associate-publisher is now Boston Univ. Clas. Dept.]: 18,1; 34,2, Sprache und Literatur, Hadrianische Zeit [... Aelius Aristides, Lucianus, Apuleius] 1993, p. 873-1941. 3-41-010390-7. – 36,7, Philosophie, p. 4417-5514; 3-11-013946-4; – 37,2. – ᴿAnzAltW 46 (1993) 167-177 (M. *Erler*, 36,3s) & 177-190 (M. *Baltes*); ZSav-R 111 (1994) 684-690 (D. *Nörr* 33,5; 36,5s).

497 **AugL** [➤ 8,743]: vol. I complete, Aaron-Conversio. Ba 1994, Schwabe. 334 col. DM 74. 3-7965-0854-5 [ZkT 117,258, L. *Lies*].

498 **CAH** [5, 1992 ➤ 9,583] 9²: ᴱ**Crook** J. A., *al.*, The last age of the Roman Republic, 146-43 B.C. C 1994, Univ. xviii-929 p. £85 [ÉtClas 63,396, Véronique *Von Driessche*]. – ᴿClasR 44 (1994) 99-101 (R. A. *Knox*, 5); GreeceR 41 (1994) 233s (T. *Wiedemann*, 9).

499 **Catholicisme** [59, 1991 ➤ 9,584] XIII, 61; 62s, 513-1232, S. Germain-Sida; XIV, 64s, 1-512: Sida [= AIDS], Structure 1994s [RHE 90,590, R. *Aubert*]. – ᴿETL 70 (1994) 219s (F. *Neirynck*, 49-61); Gregorianum 75 (1994) 174s (J. *Galot*, 60); NRT 116 (1994) 782s (N. *Plumat*, 62s).

501 **CHJud:** Cambridge History of Judaism, ᴱ**Davies** W. ... 1989 ➤ 5,884 ... 9,585: ᴿJQR 84 (1993s) 365-372 (A. *Wasserstein*, 2).

502 **DHGE:** Dictionnaire d'histoire et de géographie ecclésiastiques [XXIV, 143: col. 1281-1510 + 244 p. supp. Hildesheim]. XXV, 144s, Hubert-Hyacinthe p. 1-512. P 1994. Letouzey & Âné. – ᴿEprVie 104 (1994) 555-8 (G. du *Pasquier*); NRT 116 (1994) 783 (N. *Plumat* 143).

503 **DictSpir:** Dictionnaire de spiritualité, ᴱ**Derville** A., *al.*, XVI, 104s Vide-; 106s, Vocation-Zypaeus. P 1994, Beauchesne. 1153-1680 col. [RHE 99,11*]. – ᴿFrSZ 41 (1994) 285s (S. *Pinckaers*, 104s); Gregorianum 75 (1994) 779s (M. *Ruiz Jurado*, 104s); Manresa 65 (1993) 219 & 66 (1994) 206s. 449 (I. *Iglesias*, 102-7); OrChrPer 60 (1994) 320s (V. *Poggi*, XVI, 104s; index awaited); RET 54 (1994) 477-9 (M. *Gesteira*); RHE 89 (1994) 764 (R. *Aubert*, 106s); RHPR 74 (1994) 304s (M. *Chevallier*, 102-5).

505 ᴱ**Latourelle** René [Eng. ed.], *Fisichella* Rino, Dictionary of fundamental theology. NY 1994, Crossroad. xxviii-1222 p. $75. 0-8245-1395-9 [TDig 41,356: 222 articles by over 100 collaborators]; éd. franç. 1990 ➤ 9,588: ᴿÉTRel 68 (1993) 448s (A. *Gounelle*: renseignements, défauts); RThom 94 (1994) 661-4 (G. *Narcisse*).

506 **DPA** [➤ 7,671]: **Di Berardino** Angelo, Encyclopedia of the Early Church, ᵀᴱ**Walford** E. 1992 ➤ 8,754; 9,592: ᴿPrPeo 8 (1994) 170s (P. *Parvis*); – Diccionario patristico 1991s ➤ 7,671*a* ... 9,591: ᴿCiuD 206 (1993) 241s (C. J. *Sánchez*).

507 **EncIslam:** Encyclopedia of Islam² ᴱ**Bosworth** C. E. [also of simultaneous

French edition with partly-different cue-words], Eng. [7,129s, 1992; 8,131s
➤ 9,593], now 8,137s, Rafᶜ-Rida 1994 [OIAc 11,15].
508 **EvKL:** III. Fasc. 10 after a pause, Sabbat-Taufe; much on Russia up to
1994; 3-525-50138-2 [TR 91,358; RelStR 21,210, J.P. *Galvin*]. IV
completed in 1996 [earlier parts 1994s]. – ᴿLuJb 61 (1994) 132s (H.
Junghans, 3); RBBras 10 (1993) 278s (C. *Minette de Tillesse*, 3); ZkT 116
(1994) 227s (L. *Lies*, 3).
509 **LexÄg:** VII 1992 ➤ 8,761: ᴿWZKM 84 (1994) 192-7 (E. *Winter*).
509* **LexMA:** Lexikon des Mittelalters, ᴱ**Giertz** Gernot [5,3-5 (ohne 6s) 8
➤ 7,681]: 5,6s, 6 [1s, 1992 ➤ 8,761]. Jetzt 6,5-10, Mummolus-Plantagenêt
1993, p. 897-2206 [RHE 90,*12]; 7,1-5 Plaudes-Russisch 1994, p. 1-120.
510 **LTK³:** Lexikon für Theologie und Kirche, ᴱ**Kasper** W., *Baumgartner* K.
[1. 1993 ➤ 9,597]. **2**, 1994, Barclay-Domodos; 14*-1388 p. 3-451-22002-4.
– ᴿTPQ 142 (1994) 209-211 (J. *Niewiadomski*).
511 **NBL:** Neues Bibel-Lexikon, ᴱ**Görg** M., *Lang* B., 48s Jes-Klage-Magie. Z
1992/4, Benziger. col. 317-492; 493-684. 3-545-23059-7; -60-0 [TLZ
120,979, R. *Stahl*]. – ᴿRBBras 10 (1993) 279s (C. *Minette de Tillesse*).
NJBC: New Jerome biblical commentary ➤ 1576; *NInterp* ➤ 1575.
512 **RAC:** Reallexikon für Antike und Christentum, ᴱ**Dassmann** Ernst [15/
125, 1992 ➤ 8,764]: 16,124-8; 17,129-133: 1994s [RHE 90,206]; ᴿTRu 59
(1994) 109-112 (E. *Mühlenberg*, 14s).
514 **RLA:** Reallexikon der Assyriologie, ᴱ**Edzard** Dietz O. [8,1s ➤ 9,601].
515 **SDB:** Supplément au Dictionnaire de la Bible, ᴱ**Briend** J., *al.* [12,67s
➤ 9,602] 69. – ᴿNRT 116 (1994) 112 (J. L. *Ska*, XII,66].
517 **TRE:** Theologische Realenzyklopädie, ᴱ**Müller** Gerhard, *al.* [22, 1992 ➤ 8,
768] 23. Minucius Felix – Namengebung; 24. Napoleonische Epoche-
Obrigkeit. B 1994, de Gruyter. 807 p. 788 p. 3-11-013852-3; -4596-0. –
ᴿETRel 69 (1994) 145s (B. *Reymond*, 22); JEH 45 (1994) 114s (O.
Chadwick, 22); TR 90 (1994) 107-110 (R. *Bäumer*, 22); SvTKv 70 (1994)
42-44 (B. *Hägglund*, 20-22); ZkT 116 (1994) 226s (L. *Lies*, 22).
518 **TUmAT** [➤ 9,604]: ᴿZkT 116 (1994) 95s (F. *Mohr* 2,4-6; 3,1).
519 **TWAT:** Theologisches Wörterbuch zum Alten Testament, ᴱ**Fabry** H.-J.,
Ringgren H., [VII/8, 1993 ➤ 9,605] VIII, 1-3, *šākar-šaʿar*, 1-384; 4,
šaʿar-šātāh, -512; 5-7, *šatah-Taršiš* & Register, -741 + xiv / 393-408. Stu
1994s, Kohlhammer. – ᴿNRT 116 (1994) 111s (J. L. *Ska*); TLZ 119 (1994)
1072-4 (J. *Heller*, 7).

A3.3   *Opera consultationis* **biblica** *non excerpta infra* – **not subindexed.**

520 ᴱ**Balz** H., *Schneider* G., Exegetical dictionary of the NT 2s, 1991/3
➤ 9,611: ᴿCarthaginensia 10 (1994) 181 (R. *Sanz Valdivieso*).
521 **Bauer** J.-B., *al.*, Bibeltheologisches Wörterbuch⁴ [¹1958]. Graz 1994,
Styria. 621 p. Sch. 1225. 3-222-12256-6 [NRT 117,156, J.-L. *Ska*].
522 **Bergant** Diane, The Collegeville concise dictionary of biblical terms
[partly < BToday]. ColMn 1994, Liturgical. 99 p. $8. 0-8146-2239-9
[NTAbs 38, p. 444].
523 *a)* ᴱ**Bocian** M., *al.*, Lexikon der biblischen Personen: Tb 460. Stu 1989,
Kröner. x-510 p. – *b)* ᴱ**Coggins** R., *Houlden* J., Dictionary of biblical
interpretation 1990 ➤ 6,865 ... 8,772: ᴿTAth 64 (1993) 331-3 / 524-7 (P.
Simotas).
524 [*Born* A. van den] ᵀ*Gallart* Miquel, ᴱ*Arias* Isidro, Diccionario enciclopedico de la Biblia: Maredsous 1993 ➤ 9,606: ᴿEstAg 29 (1994) 165
(C. *Mielgo*); LumenVr 42 (1993) 429 (F. *Ortiz U.*); Phase 33 (1993) 445s

(J. *Latorre*); QVidCr 170 (1994) 134 (M. *Roure*); RazF 229 (1994) 551s (R. *de Andrés*); RET 54 (1994) 83-85 (L. *Díez Merino*); ScripTPamp 26 (1994) 274-7 (G. *Aranda Pérez*); Stromata 50 (1994).

525 **Carrez** Maurice, Dictionnaire de culture biblique 1993 → 9,608: ᴿEspr-Vie 104 (1994) 47 (É. *Cothenet*); ÉTRel 69 (1994) 276s (E. *Cuvillier*).

526 — Dizionario culturale della Bibbia. T 1992, SEI. xxvi-309 p. Lᵐ 25. – ᴿCC 145 (1994, 2) 523s (D. *Scaiola*).

527 ᴱ**Coenen** L., Theologisches Begrifflexikon zum Neuen Testament [¹1971, ²1977]: Sonderausgabe. Wu 1993, Brockhaus. xxv-1536 p. 3-417-24800-0. – ᴿTvT 34 (1994) 78 (B. van *Iersel*: of high quality and usable, but not clear why reprinted, since the documentation still stops with 1977).

528 **Day** A. Colin, Roget's thesaurus of the Bible 1992 → 8,774: ᴿInterpretation 48 (1994) 216.8 (C. *Morrison*).

529 ᴱ**Galbiati** Enrico, Dizionario enciclopedico della Bibbia e del mondo biblico² [¹1986 < *Grollenberg & Corswant*]: Enciclopedie per tutti, 8. Mi 1994, Massimo. 912 p.

530 Enciclopedia illustrata della Bibbia. CinB 1991. 912 p. 88-7030-719-0.

531 **Harrison** R. K., Encyclopedia of biblical and Christian ethics² → 8,780: ᴿCanadCath 12,4 (1994) 29s (D. W. T. *Brattston*).

532 ᴱ**Green** Joel B., *McKnight* Scot, *Marshall* I. H., Dictionary of Jesus and the Gospels 1992 → 8,778; 9,612: ᴿEvQ 66 (1994) 71-73 (S. E. *Porter*: just prefix Evangelical to the title).

Metzger B. M., *Coogan* M. D., The Oxford companion to the Bible 1994 → 741.

533 **Müller** Paul-Gerhard, Lessico della scienza biblica. ᵀᴱ*Masini* Mario: LoB 3.11. Brescia 1990, Queriniana. 221 p. Lᵐ 30. 88-399-1691-1. – ᴿGregorianum 75 (1994) 203 (F.-A. *Pastor*: metalingüística, no geografía).

534 **Panimolle** S., Dizionario di spiritualità biblico-patristica I 1992 → 8,787; 9,620: ᴿAsprenas 41 (1994) 433-8 (L. *Fatica*); ParVi 38 (1993) 146s (Clara *Burini*: il volume intero è su Dio Padre, come vol. 2 già pubblicato sull'Alleanza; i volumi successivi seguono l'ordine consueto). – Vol. 3. Amore; 4. Apostoli; 5. Ascolto. R 1992s, Borla. – ᴿParVi 39,4 (1994) 54s (A. *Rolla*).

535 ᴱ**Rienecker** Fritz, Lexikon der Bibel, ²ʳᵉᵛ*Maier* Gerhard. Giessen/Wu 1994, Brunnen/Brockhaus. viii-1792 p., 6000 + Stichworte... DM 98. 3-417-24653-9 [TR 91,359].

536 ᴱ**Schoeps** Julius H., Neues Lexikon des Judentums. Gü/Mü 1992, Bertelsmann/Lexikon-V. 486 p. DM 128. – ᴿEntschluss 48,4 (1993) 39s (Maria *Neubrand*).

537 ᴱ**Wigoder** Geoffrey, ᵀᴱ*Goldberg* Sylvie Anne, *al.*, Dictionnaire encyclopédique du Judaïsme [1989], ᵀ1993 → 9,621: ᴿRÉJ 153 (1994) 449-451 (M. *Petit*).

A3.5   *Opera consultationis* **theologica** *non excerpta infra.*

538 ᴱ**Ancilli** E., *al.*, Dizionario enciclopedico di spiritualità² 1990 → 7,710; 8,791: ᴿNRT 116 (1994) 461 (L.-J. *Renard*); ZkT 116 (1994) 554s (H. B. *Meyer*).

539 **Andresen** Carl, *Denzler* Georg, Dizionario storico del cristianesimo [ed. 3], ᵀᴱ*Airoldi* Mariná, *Tuniz* Dorina 1992 → 9,622: CinB 1992, Paoline. 790 p. – ᴿLateranum 60 (1994) 176s (B. *Amata*).

540 **Atiya** Aziz S., Coptic Encyclopedia, 8 vols. 1991 → 7,712...9.622: ᴿOLZ 89 (1994) 503-520 (W. *Klein*).

541 EBautz F. W. [2], Traugott [3-7], Biographisch-bibliographisches Kirchenlexikon, 1990. – 2. Faustus-Jeanne d'Arc; 3. Jedin-Kleinschmalt; 4. Kleist-Lucas 1993 [➤ 9,624]. – 5. Leyden-Nikolaus; 6. Moenius-Patijn 1993 [7. 1994]. Hamm/Wf, Bautz; je 1600 p. [RHE 89,367*].

542 Bouyer Louis, Breve dizionario teologico [Dictionnaire 1990]ʳᵉᵛᵀ. Bo 1993, Dehoniane. 405 p. Lᵐ 50. 88-10-20551-0. – ᴿAngelicum 71 (1994) 99s (T. Stancati).

542* EBurkhardt H., Swarat U., al., Evangelisches Lexikon für Theologie und Gemeinde [1. 1992 ➤ 8,799], 2s. Wu/Z 1993s, Brockhaus. p. 661-1453; 1454-2232. 3-417-24642-3; -3-1 [TLZ 120,1030, E. Winkler].

543 Canobbio Giacomo, Pequeño diccionario de teología [1989 ➤ 6,894], ᵀOrtiz García Alfonso: Verdad e Imagen 122. S 1992, Salamanca. 314 p. 84-301-1196-4. – ᴿLumenVr 42 (1993) 96s (F. Ortiz U.); RET 53 (1993) 407s (M. Gesteira).

544 Day Peter, The liturgical dictionary of Eastern Christianity 1993 ➤ 9,628: ᴿExpTim 105 (1993s) 252 (P. Tovey: useful, but with scary minor errors).

545 EDinzelbacher Peter, Sachwörterbuch der Mediävistik: Tb 477. 1992, Kröner. xxii-941 p. DM 58. – ᴿStreven 60 (1993) 665s (F. Willaert).

546 EDouglas J. D., The new 20th century encyclopedia of religious knowledge [¹ 1955] 1991 ➤ 7,720; 9,631: ᴿJEvTS 37 (1994) 440-2 (T. P. Erdel, also on Mennonite-5).

547 EDowney Michael, The new dictionary of Catholic spirituality 1993 ➤ 9,632: ᴿHeythJ 35 (1994) 471s (P. Endean); Worship 65 (1994) 264s (Jane Burton).

547* EDwyer Judith A., The new dictionary of Catholic social thought. ColMn 1994, Liturgical. xxxi-1019 p. $79.50 [RelStR 21,316, J. J. Buckley].

548 EEncrevé André, Les Protestants: Dictionnaire du monde religieux dans la France contemporaine 5, 1993 ➤ 9,634; 2-7010-1261-9: ᴿÉTRel 69 (1994) 117 (L. Gambarotto).

549 EFiloramo Giovanni, Dizionario delle religioni. T 1993, Einaudi. – ᴿRevSR 68 (1994) 250s (F. Boespflug).

550 EFriemel Franz G., Erste Auskunft Religion in 1111 Stichworten. Lp 1991, Benno. 181 p. – ᴿTPQ 142 (1994) 100s (W. Zauner: begeistert).

551 EGössmann Elisabeth, al., Wörterbuch der feministischen Theologie. Gü 1991, Mohn. 448 p. DM 78 [TR 91,379, Beatrice A. Zimmermann].

552 EHärle Wilfried, Wagner Harald, Theologenlexicon; von den Kirchenvätern bis zur Gegenwart: BReihe 321. Mü 1994, Beck. 311 p. DM 24,80. 3-406-38570-2.

552* EJenkins Jan C., Bloock C. Vander, International biographical dictionary of religion; an encyclopedia of more than 4000 leading personalities. Mü 1994, Saur. xviii-385 p. DM 380 [TLZ 120,222, Annette Weidhas]. – ᴿNRT 116 (1994) 918 (P. Evrard).

553 EKazhdan Alexander P. The Oxford dictionary of Byzantium 1-3, 1991 ➤ 7,727 … 9,638: ᴿByzantion 64 (1994) 233s (J. Mossay); ClasJ 89 (1993s) 91-96 (A. R. Dyck); HZ 257 (1993) 418-420 (P. Schreiner); Missiology 20 (1992) 397-9 (B. Nassif).

554 Kelly J. F., Dictionnaire du christianisme ancien: ᵀPetits dictionnaires bleus. Turnhout 1994, Brepols. ix-277 p. [RHE 99,61*]. – ᴿNRT 116 (1994) 781 (A. Harvengt).

555 **Lanczkowski** Johanna, Kleines Lexikon des Mönchtums. Stu 1993, Reclam. 280 p. DM 10. – ᴿTPQ 142 (1994) 100 (R. *Zinnhobler*).
556 **McManners** John, The Oxford illustrated history of Christianity 1990 ➤ 9,640: ᴿChurchman 108 (1994) 181s (H. *Rowdon*).
557 **Mayeur** J.-M., *Hilaire* Y.-M., Dictionnaire du monde religieux dans la France contemporaine 6. Lyon–Le Beaujolais ᴱ*Moniclos* Xavier de. P 1994, Beauchesne. 461 p. F 300. – ᴿÉtudes 381 (1994) 281 (P. *Vallin*).
558 **Mondin** B., Dizionario dei teologi 1992 ➤ 9,643; Lᵐ 90; 88-7094-111-6: ᴿAnnTh 7 (1993) 533-543 (A. *Cirillo*); CC 145 (1994,3) 544s (P. *Vanzan*); Gregorianum 75 (1994) 565s (R. *Fisichella*).
559 **O'Collins** G., *Farrugia* E., Concise dictionary of theology 1991 ➤ 7, 737...9,644: ᴿScotJR 14 (1993) 127s (D. A. S. *Ferguson*).
560 ᴱ**Rotter** Hans, *Virt* Günter. Nuevo diccionario de moral cristiana, ᵀ*Gancho* Claudio. Barc 1993, Herder. 632 p. – ᴿLumenVr 43 (1994) 186s (T. *Querejazu*).
561 **Ruh** U., *Seeber* D., *Walter* R., Dizionario delle questioni religiose del nostro tempo, ᵀᴱ*Francesconi* G. Brescia 1992, Queriniana. 500 p. Lᵐ 65. – ᴿAsprenas 41 (1994) 132 (P. *Pifano*).
562 ᴱ**Schütz** Christian, Praktisches Lexikon der Spiritualität. FrB 1988, Herder. xv-1503 p. DM 78. – ᴿTR 90 (1994) 434s (H. *Wieh*).
563 ᴱ**Schwaiger** Georg, Mönchtum — Orden — Klöster; von den Anfängen bis zur Gegenwart; ein Lexikon 1993 ➤ 9,651; DM 40: ᴿTPQ 142 (1994) 97s (R. *Zinnhobler*).
564 **Vidal Manzanares** César, Diccionario de Patrística (s. I-IV) 1993 ➤ 9, 656: ᴿAngelicum 71 (1994) 97-99 (T. *Stancati*).

A3.6   *Opera consultationis* **philologica** *et* **generalia.**

565 **Barbero** Alessandro, *Frugoni* Chiara, Dizionario del Medioevo. R c. 1994, Laterza. 277 p., 26 fig. Lᵐ 29. – ᴿArcheo 9,117 (1994) 126 (Anna *Enrico*).
566 **Bonte** Pierre, *Izard* Michel, Dictionnaire de l'ethnologie et de l'anthropologie. P 1991, PUF. xii-755 p., ill. F 496. – ᴿAnthropos 88 (1993) 220s (J. F. *Thiel*).
567 ᴱ**Burguière** André, Dizionario di scienze storiche [1986], ᵀ*Coccia* Edmondo, ᴱ*Pierini* Franco, 1992 ➤ 9,667: ᴿAngelicum 71 (1994) 100-3 (T. *Stancati*, anche su ᴱANDRESEN C., *al.*, 1992); RBBras 10 (1993) 280 (C. *Minette de Tillesse*).
568 **Ferrari** Anna, Dizionario di mitologia classica. T 1990, UTET. xvii-349 p. – ᴿSalesianum 56 (1994) 139s (R. *Sabin*).
569 ᴱ**Glück** Helmut, Metzler Lexikon Sprache [...sprachwissenschaftliche Begriffe]. Stu 1993, Metzler. xx-711 p. – ᴿBeitNam 29s (1994s) 62-70 (E. *Meineke*).
570 ᴱ**Holmes** George, The Oxford illustrated history of medieval Europe. Ox 1988, UP. xvi-398 p.; 48 fig. 0-19-285220-5. – ᴿSalesianum 56 (1994) 143s (G. *Gentileschi*).
571 **LIMC** VI Kentauri-Oiax, ᴱ**Kahil** Lilly [➤ 9,664]. Z 1992, Artemis. xxx-1091 p., 152 drawings; 779 p., 718 pl. (3752 photos). 3-7608-8751-1: ᴿAJA 98 (1994) 471-3 (Brunhilde *Sismondo-Ridgway*); AntClas 63 (1994) 587s (R. *Laffineur*); Gnomon 66 (1994) 437-441 (A. H. *Borbein*, 2-3); RBgPg 72 (1994) 195-7 (R. *Lambrechts*, 6/1s).
571* **Schneider** Thomas, Lexikon der Pharaonen; die altägyptischen Könige

von der Frühzeit bis zur Römerherrschaft. Z 1994, Artemis. 328 p. 3-7608-1102-7.

A4   **Bibliographiae, computers** .1 **biblicae.**

572 *Abadie* Philippe, *Bovon* François,   Chronique de l'AT/NT: LumièreV 43,216 (1994) 95-99 / 217, 99-102.
573 **Aguado de Gea** G., Diccionario comentado de terminología informática. M 1993, Paraninfo. 431 p. – ᴿRelCu 40 (1994) 639 (J. *Muñoz*).
573* *Auneau* Joseph, Bulletin biblique [GILBERT M., GRELOT P.]: MaisD 192 (1992) 139-
574 Bible Words for Windows,   Seattle c. 1993, Hermeneutika Computer Bible Research Software. $595, $300 if you hurry. – ᴿCurrTM 21 (1994) 60s (R. W. *Klein*).
575 — Universe for Windows, Multi-lingual scholar 4.1, WYSIWYG (what you see is what you get).   Santa Monica CA c. 1993, Gamma. Arabic-Greek-Hebrew and 29 other 'standard' alphabets, plus 'supplementary' Ethiopian, Coptic, etc., all together $347.50; but Syriac $210 extra. – ᴿTPQ 142 (1994) 206 (F. *Böhmisch*).
575* **BTAM** for 1994 (p. 1-237) is vol. 16; but 1993 p. 267-341 is *not* (should be vol. 15 → 9,713).
576 ᴱ**Butler** Christopher S.,   Computers and written texts [10 art.; machine-translation, language-learning, etc.]. Ox/CM 1992, Blackwell. 306 p. 0-631-16381-6; pa. 2-4. – ᴿLitLComp 9 (1994) 254s (M. *Brown*).
577 *Claassen* W. T.,   New [computer] ways of access to Old Testament information: → 327, ODENDAAL D. mem., OTEssays 7,4 (1991/4) 333-342.
578 **Cook** Johann,   Towards an appropriate textual base for the Old Testament [SCHENKER A. ...]: JNWS 20,1 (1994) 171-7.
579 **Cutter** Charles, *Oppenheim* Micha F.,   Judaica reference sources, a selective annotated bibliographic guide [= ²Jewish reference sources (Garland) 1983] 1993 → 9,680: ᴿRÉJ 153 (1994) 449 (R. S. *Kohn*).
580 **Davis** Malcolm C.,   Catalogue of the pre-1850 books in the Cecil ROTH [† 1970] collection. Leeds 1994, Univ. Brotherton Library. vi-119 p. [BL 95,11, S. C. *Reif*]. – ᴿRÉJ 153 (1994) 453s (G. *Nahon*).
581 *a*) **Eshel** Esther, *Lange* Armin, *Römheld* K. F. D., Dokumentation neuer Texte; – *b*) *Müller* Hans-P. + 10 *al.*, Bibliographische Dokumentation; lexikalisches und grammatisches Material: ZAHeb 7 (1994) 101-121. 258-283 / 88-100 . 245-257.
581* *Girón* Luis F.,   Crítica bibliográfica [STEMBERGER-⁷STRACK, ᵀ*Pérez Fernández* Miguel, BtMidrásica 10, Estella 1990; NEUSNER; Misná 'fracaso' ...]: Sefarad 53 (1993) 377-398.
582 BL: ᴱ**Grabbe** Lester L., Society for Old Testament Study book list. 1994. Leeds 1994, SOTS [ed. Hull, Univ.; US orders: Atlanta, Scholars]). 185 p. (400 books). 0-905495-13-6.
582* **DissA:** Dissertation Abstracts [International; mostly -A (-C for Europe)]. AA, now available also on disk (with its own computer, offering printout or copy to user's disk). Most of the relevant titles are listed as 'Biblical Studies', others as 'Religion', 'Archeology'. But the actual printed volume is on disk only for 750 [out of some 2000] arbitrarily chosen titles per volume (month) in confused order.
583 **Hänsel-Hohenhausen** Markus, Vom Manuskript zur Buchhandlungsveröffentlichung; Lehrbuch für den wissenschaftlichen Autor. Egelsbach 1993, auct. DM 5. 3-89349-348-4 [TR 90,509].

584 *Harrington* Daniel J., Books on the Bible: America 170,9 (1994) 16-21.
585 *Heintz* Jean-Georges, Chronique de l'Ancien Testament, IV: RHPR 74 (1994) 281-302.
586 **Hsu** Jeffrey, *al.*, Computer Bible study; up-to-date information on the best software and techniques 1993 ➤ 9,688: ᴿAngelicum 71 (1994) 446-9 (T. *Stancati*); ArTGran 57 (1994) 426-8 (L. *Enríquez*); PerspRelSt 21 (1994) 264-7 (W. E. *Mills*).
587 **Hupper** W., Index to English periodical literature on OT-ANE [1-5, 1966-92 ➤ 8,863]; OT 6 ATLA 21, 1994. – ᴿTBR 7,2 (1994s) 7 (H. G. M.*Williamson*).
588 [Bible et] Informatique³ 1991/2 ➤ 8,450*: ᴿNRT 116 (1994) 899s (X. *Jacques*).
589 **IZBG:** Internationale Zeitschriftenschau für Bibelwissenschaft und Grenzgebiete, ᴱ**Lang** Bernhard, *al.* (Paderborn), 39 für 1992-3 Dü 1994, Patmos. xiv-469 p. 2874 items, with 100-word summary, about half each in German and English. 3-491-66039-4 or ISSN 0074-9745.
590 **Jahndel** Martin, *Henze* Klaus-Manfred, Theologische Literatur, Bibelwissenschaft, AT, NT: TR 90 (1994) 169-178. 507-517 [255-263 KG, Fund-T.; 347-352, Ök.Ltg.Soz.Past; 435-440, TGesch; 517-528, Moral, Dogma, Spir. Varia].
591 *Jaki* Stanley L., Computers; lovable but unloving: DowR 112 (1994) 185-200.
592 Jerusalem Perspective 42ss (1994) 46s: Index 1987-1993.
593 JStOT 59-62 index: JStOT 62 (1994) 123-128 [in the middle of an annual volume, not at the end].
593* *Kaestli* J.-D., Livres du NT; épîtres et Apocalypse: Bulletin de Bibliographie Biblique 10 (Lausanne 1994) 1-72 [< NTAbs 39, p. 52].
594 *Kjell* Bradley, Authorship determination using letter pair frequency features with neural network classifiers: LitLComp 10 (1994) 119-124.
595 macBible 3.0: *a)* New American Bible (including Introduction and Notes); – *b)* NRSV with Apocrypha/Deuterocanonical books; – *c)* Greek New Testament (UBS⁴); – *d)* Hebrew Bible (BHS). GR 1993, Zondervan. $130 each module (with manual, same for all). – ᴿOTAbs 17 (1994) 690s (A. A. *Di Lella*).
596 *McNamara* Martin, Hiberno-Latin bulletin: PrIrB 16 (1993) 114-122; 122-4, addendum to 12 (1989) 90-94, *Breatnach* Liam.
597 *Miller* Paul, Gramcord / *Akiyama* James, Bible Word Plus, Version 3.00 [both IBM] ... Gramcord Institute. – ᴿCalvaryB 9,1 (1993) 65-67 (L. M. *Bruffey*, also on BAIMA J., LBase, IBM.
598 **Mills** Watson E., An index to the periodical literature on the Apostle Paul: NT TSt 16. Leiden 1993, Brill. xx-345 p. ƒ125. – ᴿNT 36 (1994) 406-8 (J. K. *Elliott*).
599 NTSSA (NT Society of South Africa), list of members: Neotestamentica 28 (1994) 615-623.
600 ᴱ**Perrone** Lorenzo, Bibliografia ... A general bibliography on the history of biblical interpretation, exegesis, hermeneutics, uses of the Bible 7s (1993) / 9s (1994): AnStoEseg 10 (1993) 205-271. 645-730 / 11 (1994) 325-408 . 647-716.
601 *Pesce* Mauro, Rassegna di storia dell'esegesi 5/6: AnStoEseg 11 (1994) 293-303 / 619-631.
601* *Piñero* A., New Testament philology bulletin 13/14: FgNt 7 (1994) 91-123 . 229-254.
602 *Runia* David T., *al.*, *a)* Annotated bibliography 1991; – *b)* Provisional

bibliography 1992-4; – *c*) References to PHILO from JOSEPHUS until 1000 A.D.: StPhilonAn 6 (1994) 122-150 / 151-159 / 111-121.

603 *Sakitani* Mitsuru, A framework for the computational analysis of text in biblical studies: Jian Dao 2 (1994) 35-72; ⊙ 72.

604 *Scholer* David M., Q bibliography supplement V: ⇢ 325, SBLSem (1994) 1-8.

604* ᴱSchwantes Milton, Bibliografia biblica latino-americana. São Paulo. 5. 1992, 445 p. 6. 1993, 487 p.

605 *Tilsed* Ian, *Myhill* Martin, [The star of the east, irrelevant pre-title] Machine-based information-sources for theologians [Internet, British Janet]: TLond 97 (1994) 179-188.

606 VOEGELIN Eric, A classified bibliography: BJRyL 76,2 (1994) 3-180 (G. L. *Price*).

607 *a*) *Waschke* Jochen, Zeitschriftenschau; – *b*) *Köckert* Matthias, Bücher- schau: ZAW 106 (1994) 125-148.322-347.491-517 / 148-174.347-373. 517-543.

608 **Watson** Duane F., *Hauser* Alan J., Rhetorical criticism of the Bible; a comprehensive bibliography with notes on history and method: Bibl- InterpSer, 4. Leiden 1994, Brill. xx-208 p. $63.   90-04-09903-4 [RelStR 21,139, J. T. *Fitzgerald*].

609 ᴱ**Waxman** Ruth B., *Bodoff* Lippman, Judaism, Twenty year cumulative index [21-40] 1972-1991. 1992. 108 p.

610 **Wiskus** Kate, National association of professors of Hebrew 1993-4 members directory. Madison 1994, Univ. Wisconsin. 94 p.

611 **Zannoni** Arthur E., The OT, a bibliography OTSt 8. ColMn 1992, Liturgical/Glazier. x-377 p. $18. – ᴿCBQ 56 (1994) 129s (C. E. *Hauer*).

612 Zeitschriftenschau: ZNW 85 (1994) 159-162.292-4.

A4.2   *Bibliographiae* theologicae.

613 AVAGLIANO Faustino [1441-], biobibliografia [...Echi di Montecassino]: Benedictina 41 (1994) 477-501 [M. *Dell'Omo*].

614 BAYREUTHER Erich, aet. 90, Bibliographie 1981-1994: TLZ 119 (1994) 847-9 (D. *Blaufuss*).

615 *Bertuletti* Angelo, [22 *al.* p. 373] I problemi metodologici della teolo- gia sulle riviste del 1991/1992: TItSett 19 (1993) 371-454 / 20 (1994) 340-431.

616 **Besutti** Giuseppe M., Bibliografia mariana 1985-9. R 1993, Ed. Marianum. xix-828 p. – ᴿMarianum 55 (1993) 665-7 (S. *De Fiores*).

617 Bibliographia oecumenica: EcuR 45 (1993) 131-3.246-8.369-371. 505-7; 46 (1994) 129s.261-3.377-9.494s. – Journals contents (titles without pages) 45, 126-130.243-5.365-8.500-3; 46, 124-8.256-60. 372-6.490-3.

618 *Boespflug* François, À propos de quelques livres récents en histoire des religions: RevSR 68 (1994) 245-254, ...

619 *Borgman* Erik, Promoties in de theologie: TvT 34 (1994) 70-74. 187-190.296-9.

620 *Braaten* Carl E., *Jenson* Robert W., The youth and age of theological journals: ProEc 3,1 (Northfield MN 1994) 22-23.

621 *Bräuer* Siegfried, 'Dass die Zeitschrift eine progressivere Tendenz erhält': der Herausgeberwechsel bei der Theologischen Literaturzeitung 1958-1960; Gründe und Hintergründe: TLZ 119 (1994) 577-600.

622 ᴱ**Burini** Clara, Epistolari cristiani (secc. I-V) [*al.* latina/greca (anche)

IV-V secc.], repertorio bibliografico. R 1990, Benedictina. xxviii-131 p.,
L^m 22 pa. [➤ 7,e970]. [xxi-155 p., L^m 25; xxi-207 p., L^m 28; NTAbs
36,442].

623 *Cavarnos* Constantine, Orthodox Christian terminology. Belmont MA
1994, Institute for Byzantine and Modern Greek Studies. 80 p. $6.
0-914744-89-4 [TDig 42,261, with notice of two other items of his].

624 *Dubois* Jean-Daniel, Chronique patristique VIII: ÉTRel 68 (1993)
395-407.

625 *Duval* André, Aux origines de la RSPT [en rapport avec le centenaire de
la RThom]: RSPT 78 (1994) 31-44.

626 *Duval* Yves-Marie, Bulletin de patrologie latine: RechSR 82 (1994)
251-286.

626* Ecumenical Resources: JEcuSt 31 (1994) 211-222.427-438.

627 ^EEpp Eldon J., [JAAR-JBL] Critical review of books in religion 6.
Atlanta 1993, Scholars. v-640 p. 0894-8860 [many cited here].

627* Dissertations completed: RelStR 20 (1994) 251-7. – Cumulative Index
[entire RelStR] 1-15 (1974-89): Valparaiso IN, Univ. $35 pa. $20.

628 Evangelical Theological Society, directory of members: JEvTS 37 (1994)
285-317.

629 *Figueroa* P.M., *Miño* D., *al.*, Fichero de Revistas Latinoamericanas
[siglas]: Stromata 50 (1994) 253-295 [249-252]; ANT 277-9; Santo
Domingo 1992, p. 257-260.

630 *Grau Monrós* Vicente, Los índices de Teología Espiritual: TEspir 38
(1994) 107-155.

631 *Gy* Pierre-Marie, Bulletin de liturgie: RSPT 78 (1994) 271-300.

632 Habilitationen / Dissertationen im Akademischen Jahr 1992/3: TR 90
(1994) 79s / 80-90 [presumably including those formerly published in BZ;
none in 1994; resumed in 1995 with two-year interval foreseen].

633 HAENDLER Gert 1984-94 Bibliog.; Fortsetzung TLZ 120 (1995) 88s.

634 *Häussling* Angelus A., *al.*, Literaturbericht; der Gottesdienst der Kirche:
ArLtgW 33 (1991) 92-191.

635 *Haverals* M., Bibliographie: RHE 89 (1994) 5*-188*.189*-362*. 363*-
621* [very valuable].

636 **Henkel** W., Bibliographia missionaria 56 pro 1992. Vatican 1993, Pontifical Urban Univ. 494 p. – ^RNzMiss 50 (1994) 321s (J. *Baumgartner*).

637 *Heuchan* Valerie, Dissertations [in religion in Canadian universities]: SR
22 (1993) 535-9 / 23 (1994) 523-7.

638 Index international des dissertations doctorales en théologie et en droit
canonique présentées en [1991 (rarement)-] 1993: RTLv 25 (1994)
522-597; 952 items not indexed [except for names mentioned incidentally;
participating institutions now listed only every 5 years: 23 (1992) 524-533].
Our Elenchus volume 9 (1993) is greatly indebted to this Index for a large
number of the dissertations there cited.

639 *Junghans* Helmar, *al.*, Lutherbibliographie 1994: LuJb 61 (1994) 143-188;
Register 189-194 [130-142 (seine, 14) Rezensionen].

639* *Jossua* Jean-Pierre, Bulletin de théologie littéraire: RSPT 78 (1994)
301-322.

640 **Kenis** Leo, The Louvain faculty of theology in the nineteenth century; a
bibliography of the professors in theology and canon law: Annua Nuntia
Lv 341. Lv 1994, Univ./Peeters. 220 p. Fb 1300. 90-6186-589-1 /
90-6831-583-8 [TLZ 119,171].

641 KRAFT Heinrich, Bibliographie: TLZ 119 (1994) 567-571 (H. *Bassenge*).

642 **Lazcano** Rafael, Bibliographia missionalia augustiniana, America Latina

1533-1993. M 1992, AugM. 645 p. – ᴿEstE 69 (1994) 422s (A. *Santos Hernández*).

643 *Lobrichon* Guy,   Bulletin d'histoire des doctrines médiévales: RSPT 78 (1994) 125-137 (-144, L.-J. *Bataillon*).

644 LOTZ Johannes B. (1903-1992): Bibliographie [... Philosophie]: TPhil 69 (1994) 238-262 (J. de *Vries*, M. *Nechleba*).

645 Maison-Dieu: Tables générales 1945-1994: La Maison-Dieu 200 (1994) 55-262.

646 *Marholdt* Anka, (*Lindemann* Gerhard),   Bibliographie zur kirchlichen Zeitgeschichte: KZg 7 (1994) 402-522.

647 *Mecham* Frank,   Seventy years of the [Australasian Catholic] Record: 70,1 (1993) 3-13.

648 *Meijer* Albério de,   Bibliographie historique de l'Ordre de Saint-Augustin 1989-1993: AugLv 43 (1993) 171-407.

648* *Müller* Wolfgang, *Vorster* Hans,   Ök. Zeitschriftenschau: ÖkRu 41 (1992) 117-9 . 246-8 . 378s . 517s; 42 (1993) 121-3 . 251-3 . 380-8 . 521-4.

649 a) *Müller-Clemm* Julia,   Register für die Jahrgänge 1 (1945) bis 50 (1994); – b) *Mühling* Andreas, Anfangsjahre/K.-L. SCHMIDT; – c) *Kaye* Bruce N., Bo REICKE; – d) *Smend* R., Das AT in der TZ: Theologische Zeitschrift 50 (Basel 1994) 336-403 / 286-294 / 295-301 / 302-320.

650 *Neunheuser* Burkhard,   Liturgie im Gesamtzusammenhang der Theologie: ArLtgW 33 (1991) 306-432.

651 *Oury* G.-M.,   Bulletin de spiritualité: EsprVie 104 (1994) 72-79 . 89-94.

652 Phase: Indices 101-200 (1977-1994): Phase 34 (1994) 143-160.

653 Princeton Seminary Faculty publications 1992:   PrincSemB 14 (1993) 173-182 / 15 (1994) 186-196.

654 *Printzipa* G. T.,   Bibliographikòn deltíon: TAth 64 (1993) 826-851 / 65 (1994) 956-976.

655 *Regensburger* Dietmar,   Bibliography of literature on the [GIRARD R.] mimetic theory: COV&R 7 (1994) 3-5,

656 RivLtg: Indice 71-80 (1984-1993): RivLtg 80 (1993) (645-) 656-701.

657 **Robinson** Thomas A.,   The early Church; an annotated bibliography of literature in English: ATLA 33. Metuchen 1993, Scarecrow. xxiii-495 p. $57.50. 0-8108-2763-8 [RelStR 21,243, C. T. *McCullough*]. – ᴿTBR 7,1 (1994s) 7 (G. *Gould*: 'the best bibliography of patristic studies ever produced').

658 ᴱ**Schönberger** Rolf, *Kible* Brigitte,   Repertorium edierter Texte des Mittelalters aus dem Bereich der Philosophie und angrenzenden Gebiete. B 1994, Akademie. xii-888 p., DM 198 [TR 91,400, L. *Hödl*].

658* **Schwinger** Gerhard,   Wie finde ich theologische Literatur³ʳᵉᵛ [¹1978]. B 1994, Berlin-V. 207 p. DM 38. 3-87061-367-X [TLZ 120,974].

659 **Sheldon** Joseph K.,   Rediscovery of creation; a bibliographical study of the Church's response to the environmental crisis. Metuchen/Folkestone 1993, Scarecrow/Shelwing. xvi-282 p. £30. 0-8108-2539-2. – ᴿEvQ 66 (1994) 372s (I. *Bradley*).

660 SOBRINO Jon: MiscCom 52 (1994) 417-444 (P. *Barquero*).

661 STOEBE Hans Joachim,   Bibliog. 1989-93 [85. Gb. 24.II.1994]: TLZ 119 (1994) 182-7 (Heinz-D. *Neef*).

662 SVDVerbum,   Index generalis 1970-1994: SVDStudium 35 (1994) 435-513.

663 *Theobald* Christoph,   Bulletin de théologie dogmatique; question de Dieu et Trinité: RechSR 82 (1994) 287-308.

663* Theologische Versuche: Register für die Bände I-XVIII (letzten!): TVers 18 (1993) 263-276.

664 Travaux des enseignants 1987-1992: RICathP 47 (1993) 373 p.
664* *Tretter* H., Bibliographie: OstKSt 42 (1993) 73-96. 217-272. 347-382 /
   43 (1994) 80-104. 225-272. 349-382.
665 *Trevijano Etcheverria* R., Bibliografía patrística hispano-luso-americana,
   VIII (1991-1992): Salmanticensis 41 (1994) 83-139; 100s, NT.
666 **Van Allen** Rodger, Being Catholic; Commonweal from the seventies to
   the nineties [sequel to his 1974 dissertation Commonweal]. Ch 1993,
   Loyola. xix-203 p. $13 pa. – ᴿHorizons 21 (1994) 142-6 (Margaret M.
   Reher) & 146-8 (W. L. *Portier*) & 148-151 (Debra *Campbell*); 151-8, Van
   Allen response.
666* *Villapadierna* Isidoro de, Select news of Franciscan scientific activities in
   1993, ᵀ*Vadakkekara* Benedict: ColcFran 64 (1994) 501-519.
667 *Wéber* Édouard-Henri, Bulletin d'histoire des doctrines médiévales, de
   saint Anselme à Maître Eckhart: RSPT 78 (1994) 587-622.
668 *Wolf* Ann, Sexual abuse issues; an annotated bibliography: TDig 41
   (1994) 203-249. 331-344.
668* a) *Wright* J. Robert, The first seventy-five years of the Anglican
   Theological Review; its purpose and contents, 1918-93; – b) *Weil* Louis,
   The contribution of the AnglTR in recent liturgical perspective: AnglTR
   76 (1994) 132-159 / 184-196.

A4.3   *Bibliographiae* **philologicae** *et* **generales.**

669 **AnPg:** ᴱ[*Ernst* Juliette] **Corsetti** Pierre-Paul, L'Année Philologique 63
   pour 1992. P 1994, BLettres. xxxix-1203 p. 0184-6949.
670 [*Aulino* Francesca, schedario] Rassegna bibliografica: Ivra 43 (1992)
   293-445; indici 447-487.
671 **BAHR:** Bulletin Analytique d'histoire romaine [bibliographie alphabétique
   par auteurs p. 35-281, index 283-376; ensuite renvois par mots-clés,
   p. 377-490, pour vol. 1]: 1 (Univ. Strasbourg, 1992) / 2 (1993).
672 *Bec* P., *al.*, Bibliographie: CahCMédv 36,4 (1993) 1*-249*.
673 *Beguin* Daniel, Informatique et recherche en langues anciennes: RHText
   23 (1993) 219-241; Eng. 352.
673* a) *Bender* Henry V., 1995 survey of audio-visual materials in the classics
   [ii. Middle and Near East]; – b) *Smith* Alden, Books for teaching classics
   in English: ClasW 88 (1994s) 379-439 [381-4] / 259-358.
674 Bibliographische Beilage: Gnomon 66 (1994) 1,1-48; 3,49-92; 5,93-140;
   7,141-184.
674* **Buonocore** Marco, Bibliografia retrospettiva dei fondi manoscritti della
   Biblioteca Vaticana 1: ST 361. Vaticano 1994, Biblioteca. 568 p. 88-
   210-0654-9.
675 **Calder** W. M., *Kramer* D. J., An introductory bibliography to the history
   of classical scholarship 1992 ➛ 9,783: ᴿClasR 44 (1994) 421s (J. B.
   Trapp).
675* ᴱ*Cockshaw* Pierre, *Manning* Eugène, *al.*, Bulletin codicologique: Scriptorium 47 (1993) 1*-90*. 91*-213*; 48 (1994) 1*-96*. 97*-212*.
676 **Cupaiuolo** Fabio, Bibliografia della lingua latina (1949-1991): Studi latini
   11. N 1993, Loffredo. 592 p. Lᵐ48. – ᴿRÉLat 72 (1994) 238 (J.
   Hellagouarc'h); RFgIC 122 (1994) 222-6 (M. *De Nonno*).
677 *Cupaiuolo* Giovanni, Notiziario bibliografico (1993/4): BStLat 24 (1994)
   379-415 autori; 774-804 materie.
679 *Heraklēs*; Banca-dati bibliografici del mondo antico, Release 1-2. R
   1994, Bretschneider. – ᴿBonnJbb 194 (1994) 499-501 (G. *Bauchheuss*).

680 *Mosconi* Giuseppe, *Serafini* Maria Grazia,   Formulazione in linguaggio naturale e formulazione in linguaggio 'computeristico' di un *insight problem* (il problema dei nove punti): RLomb 128,1 (1994) 89-102 [vastly better, therefore worse: it transforms the given problem into a new one].

681 *Ostler* Nicholas, *Zampolli* Antonio,   Special section on corpora 2: Literary and Linguistic Computing 9 (1994) 21-46 (-86).

682 Quaderni Urbinati, Index 1-75 (1966-1994): QuadUrb 77 (1994) 42 p.

683 *Russo* Antonella,   SNS-Greek & Latin 1.0, una applicazione per la consultazione di banche dati su CD-ROM: AnPisa 23 (1993) 105-113.

684 **Vérilhac** Anne-Marie, *Vial* Claude,   La femme dans le monde méditerranéen, 2. La femme grecque et romaine; bibliographie [3300 titres]. Lyon/P 1990, Maison d'Orient Médit. / de Boccard.   214 p. – ᴿPhoenix 43 (Toronto 1994) 181-3 (M. Eleanor *Irwin*, also on *Pomeroy* S. & *Schmitt Pantel* T.).

685 *Schreiner* Peter, *Scholz* Cordula,   Bibliographische Notizen und Mitteilungen: ByZ 86s (1994) 160-317. 512-562.

A4.4   *Bibliographiae* orientalisticae.

686 *Acquaro* E., *al.*,   Bibliografia: RStFen 22 (1994) 281-306.

687 *Balconi* Carla, *al.*,   a) Bibliografia metodica degli studi di egittologia e di papirologia; – b) Testi recentemente pubblicati: Aegyptus 79 (1994) 213-293 / 137-181.

688 *Cahen* Claude, *Leemans* W. F., founders: ᴊᴇsʜᴏ after 35 years; ᴊᴇsʜᴏ 36 (1993) 103s (-191); table générale vol. 26-35, p. 194-210; p. 104-119, *Lightstone* Jack A., Trends or cycles? The economic history of East-West contact in the early modern world.

689 *Deller* K., *Klengel* H., *Maksen* K.,   Keilschriftbibliographie 53, 1993: Orientalia 63 (1994) 1*-111*.

690 *Felber* Heinz,   Demotistische Literaturübersicht XXI: Enchoría 21 (1994) 107-127.

691 a) *Ferone* Claudio,   Storia romana antica; – b) *Zannini Quirini* Bruno, Religione romana: Studi Romani 41,1s (1993) 83-93 / 106-113.

692 *Gilliot* Claude,   Bulletin d'Islamologie et d'études arabes: RSPT 78 (1994) 453-497.

693 Hɪɴᴛᴢᴇ Fritz,   Verzeichnis seiner Schriften: ZäSpr 121 (1994) 159-174 (P. *Wolf*).

694 **Hovestreydt** W., *Zonhoven* L. M. J.,   Annual Egyptological bibliography for 1992. Leiden 1995. 345 p. 1120 items, each with summary. Author index p. 287-338.

695 *Merçil* Erdogan,   Belleten Dizini / Index 36-51 / 141-200 [1972-87]: Belleten 58,223 (1994) 94 p.   975-16-0031-6.

696 **OIAc: Jones** Charles E.,   Oriental Institute acquisitions 11s (1994).   Final issue; hopefully to be replaced in relation to on-line service.

697 **Roper** G. J.,   Index islamicus 1981-5; a bibliography of books and articles on the Muslim world. L 1991, Mansell. xliii-643 p.; xvi + p. 644-1347. £165.   0-7201-2009-8. – ᴿJSS 38 (1993) 171s (C. E. *Bosworth*).

698 ᴱ**Saporetti** Claudio,   Assiriologia e Egittologia nell'Informatica Pisana: Geo-Archeologica 1990/1. Pisa 1991.   115 p.; ill. [OIAc 11,40].

699 *Vattioni* Francesco,   Saggio di bibliografia semitica 1992-1993: AION 54 (1994) 211-246.

700 **Zwaini** Laila al-, *Peters* Rudolph, A bibliography of Islamic law, 1980-1993: HbOr 1/18. Leiden 1994, Brill. ix-239 p. 90-04-10009-1.

A4.5 *Bibliographiae* **archaeologicae.**

701 Archäologische Dissertationen [je c. 90]: ArchAnz (1992) 147-152; (1993) 155-160; (1994) 119-123.
702 a) Ausstellungskalender; – b) Dissertationen und Magisterarbeiten: MiDAV 25,2 (1994) 3-11 / 12-54.
703 ᴱ**Bacus** Elizabeth A., *al.*, A gendered past; a critical bibliography of gender in archaeology: Technical Report 25. AA 1993, Univ. Museum of Anthropology. xix-172 p.; 7 fig. $19. 0-915703-31-9. – ᴿAJA 98 (1994) 773s (Louise *Zarmati*).
704 *Bush* Louise K., Checklist of articles and books: JGlass 35 (1993) 161-234 / 36 (1994) 126-202.
705 *Calmeyer* Peter, Archäologische Bibliographie 1992 / 1993: ArchMIran 26 (1993) 287-298 / 27 (1994) 349-357.
706 *Dollfuss* Geneviève, *Lechevallier* Monique, Bibliographie annuelle générale: Paléorient 20,2 (1994) 179-206.
707 **Korfmann** Manfred, *al.*, Anatolien in der Frühen und Mittleren Bronzezeit, 1. Frühbr.: TAVO B-73/1. Wsb 1994, Reichert. 248 p. 3-88226-692-9 [OIAc 11,29].
708 ᴱ**Reilly** Paul, *Rahtz* Sebastian, Archaeology and the information age; a global perspective [Venezuela 2d Congress One World Archaeology, Sept. 1990]. ɴʏ 1992, Routledge. xxiv-395 p.; 132 fig. 0-415-07858-6. – ᴿAJA 98 (1994) 356s (Susan S. *Lukesh*).
709 Répertoire 1-296 (1964-93), 6000 références: Archéologia (1994) 75 p.

II. Introductio

ʙ1   *Introductio* .1 *tota vel VT* – **Whole Bible or OT**

710 **Alonso Schökel** Luis, *al.*, La Bibbia nel suo contesto: IntrStB 1. Brescia 1994, Paideia. 524 p. Lᵐ 68. 88-394-0510-0.
711 **Artola Arbiza** Antonio M., *Sánchez Caro* José M., Bibbia e parola di Dio: IntrStB 2. Brescia 1994, Paideia. 382 p. Lᵐ 48. 88-394-0507-0.
712 **Balabán** Milan, Hebrejské myšlení [Hebrew (... biblical) thought]. Praha 1993, Herrmann. 144 p. Kč 56. – ᴿArOr 62 (1994) 441s (S. *Segert*).
713 **Barstad** Hans M., Det Gamle Testamente, en inføring → 9,816: ᴿSvEx 59 (1994) 171-6 (S. *Olofsson*).
714 **Barth** Christoph, God with us; a theological introduction to the OT 1991 → 7,919 ... 9,817: ᴿCritRR 6 (1993) 148s (Maribeth *Howell*); OTEssays 7 (1994) 113-5 (M. J. *Oosthuizen*).
715 **Beasley** James R., *al.*, An introduction to the Bible. Nv 1991, Abingdon. 496 p. $25. 0-687-19493-8. – ᴿRExp 91 (1994) 265 (T. G. *Smothers* commends).
716 *Beek* M. A., Saturation points and unfinished lines in the study of Old Testament literature: → 250, Amsterdam 1994, 23-35 [OTAbs 17, p. 491: the admirably full summary and cross-referencing regrettably do not indicate the original date and publication-place].
716* **Beyerlin** W., Testi religiosi AT 1992 [¹1975] → 9,817*: ᴿParVi 39,1 (1994) 51-53 (A. *Rolla*).

717 ᴱBiggar Stephen,   Creating the OT 1988 ➤ 5,1133 ... 9,818:   ᴿScotJR 11
   (1990) 47-49 (R. P. *Carroll*); ScotJT 46 (1993) 237 (S. B. *Dawes*).
718 *Bohlen* Reinhold,   Bibel (einleitungswissenschaftlich): ➤ 510, LTK³ 2
   (1994) 362-5; 365s, *Maier* Johann, Judentum; 366-370, *Kremer* Jacob,
   Kirche; 370-5 *al.*, Text(-ausgaben).
719 **Cate** Robert L.,   An introduction to the historical books of the OT. Nv
   1994, Broadman & H.   xii-175 p.   0-8054-1044-9.
720 **Ceresko** Anthony R.,   IntrOT ... Liberation 1991 also L Chapman 1991
   ➤ 8,1018*; 9,821:   ᴿPrincSemB 15 (1994) 295-7 (D. T. *Olson*); PrPeo 8
   (1994) 255 (B. P. *Robinson*).
721 **Coote** R. & M.,   Power, politics, and the making of the Bible 1990
   ➤ 6,g608 ... 8,k165:   ᴿCritRR 5 (1992) 85s (D. L. *Smith*).
721* **Duggan** Michael,   The consuming fire; a Christian introduction to the
   OT 1991 ➤ 8,1020*c*; 9,825:   ᴿRelEdn 89 (1994) 140s (J. D. *Newsome*).
722 **Fabris** Rinaldo, *al.*,   Introduzione generale alla Bibbia: Logos 1.
   T-Leumann 1994, Elle Di Ci.   564 p.   Lᵐ 55.   88-01-10334-4.
723 **Freedman** D. N.,   Unity of the Hebrew Bible 1991 ➤ 7,993; 9,828:
   ᴿCritRR 6 (1993) 159s (E. *G. Bowman*); JAOS 114 (1994) 135 (H. C.
   Brichto: overuses ambivalent in-words like 'unity' and 'scientific'); JBL
   113 (1994) 122s (R. G. *Bowman*); JRel 74 (1994) 380s (W. *Brueggemann*:
   seeks the 'canonical shape' in ways different from CHILDS); RExp 91
   (1994) 114s (J. D. W. *Watts*).
724 *Freedman* David N. (interview),   The undiscovered symmetry of the Bible:
   BR 10,1 (1994) 34-41 . 63.
725 **Gese** H.,   Alttestamentliche Studien 2., 1991 ➤ 7,204:   ᴿBO 51 (1994)
   622-8 (A. van der *Wal*).
726 **Girlanda** Antonio,   Iniziazione biblica, AT/NT.   CinB 1991s, Paoline.
   318 p.; 334 p. ill.   Lᵐ 18 ciasc. – ᴿCC 145 (1994,1) 622s (D. *Scaiola*).
727 **Goldingay** John,   Models for Scripture.   GR/Carlisle 1994, Eerdmans/
   Paternoster.   xi-420 p.   /0-85364-638-7. – ᴿTBR 7,3 (1994s) 13 (J. L.
   Houlden, the new editor, who has already converted to a larger print).
728 **González Etchegaray** J., *al.*,   La Biblia en su entorno: Intr 1, 1990
   ➤ 8,1022:   ᴿCiuD 206 (1993) 223s (J. *Gutiérrez*).
729 **González Núñez** A.,   La Biblia, los autores... el mensaje 1989 ➤ 6,1166:
   ᴿScripTPamp 26 (1994) 792s (F. *Varo*).
729* **Gower** R.,   Usi e costumi dei tempi della Bibbia [New manners 1985
   < *Wight* F. 1953],ᵀ T-Leumann 1990, Elle Di Ci.   396 p.   Lᵐ 43. –
   ᴿAsprenas 41 (1994) 439s (V. *Scippa*).
730 **Heaton** E. W.,   The school tradition of the OT; Bampton Lectures 1994.
   Ox 1994, UP.   xiii-208 p.   0-19-826362-7.
730* **Hinson** David F.,   The Books of the OT²ʳᵉᵛ.   Delhi 1993, ISPCK.
   xiii-210 p. $35.   81-7214-118-1. – ᴿVidyajyoti 58 (1994) 257 (P. *Meagher*).
731 **Howard** D. M.,   An introduction to the OT historical books 1993
   ➤ 9,833:   ᴿJEvTS 37 (1994) 596s (S. *Schultz*).
732 **Imbach** Joseph,   Come leggere e capire la Bibbia, introduzione esegetica.
   R 1992, Città Nuova.   140 p.   Lᵐ 10. – ᴿCC 145 (1994,3) 199s (D.
   Scaiola).
733 ᴱ**Jagersma** H., *Vervenne* M.,   Inleiding in het Oude Testament 1992
   ➤ 8,1037; 9,835:   ᴿOTEssays 7 (1994) 478-480 (W. *Boshoff*, Afrikaans).
734 **Josipovici** Gabriel,   Il libro di Dio [1988 ➤ 4,1073],ᵀ.   396 p.   Lᵐ 45. –
   ᴿCiVit 48 (1993) 81 (F. *Pecci*).
735 **Kaiser** Otto,   Grundriss der Einleitung [1. erzähl- 1992 ➤ 8,1028] 2. Die
   prophetischen / 3. Die poetischen und weisheitlichen Werke. Gü 1994,

Mohn. 188 p.; 163 p. je DM 68. 3-579-0005[8-6]-3-5; -4-3 [TLZ 120,878, R. *Smend*].

736 **Knauf** Ernst Axel, Die Umwelt des Alten Testaments: NStuK AT 29. Stu 1994, KBW. 288 p.; ill. 3-460-07291-1.

737 **Lombardi** Paolo, La Bibbia contesa, tra umanesimo e razionalismo. F 1992, Nuova Italia. xiv-290 p. L^m 35. - ^RCC 145 (1994,1) 93-95 (G. L. *Prato*).

738 **McKim** Donald K., The Bible in theology and preaching [= ²What Christians believe 1985]. Nv 1994, Abingdon. 250 p. $13. 0-687-44611-2. – ^RTBR 7,1 (1994s) 19 (A. *Gilmore*).

739 *Massey* James E., *al.*, Reading the Bible from particular social locations ... / as African Americans [Asian, Hispanic, native, women]: ➤ 1575, NInterp 1 (1994) 150-160 [-187].

740 **Matthews** V. H., *Benjamin* D. C., OT parallels; laws and stories from the ANE 1991 ➤ 7,947; 8,1035: ^RGregorianum 75 (1994) 160s (G. L. *Prato*); VT 44 (1994) 137-9 & 285 correction (J. *Day* cannot recommend).

741 **Metzger** B., *Coogan* M., Oxford Companion to the Bible 1993 ➤ 9,844: ^RAnnTh 8 (1994) 195-7 (B. *Estrada*); LexTQ 29 (1994) 59s (Margaret *Ralph*); Month 255 (1994) 275s (P. *Hackett*); Tablet 248 (1994) 776s (W. *Raines*); TLond 97 (1994) 375-7 (H. *Wansbrough*, certainly admiring but critical: too largely post-biblical and rather Christian-bashing).

742 ^EMulder Martin J., Mikra 1988 ➤ 4,317 ... 9,845: ^RJPseud 8 (1991) 111-5 (Carol *Newsom*).

743 *Pilch* J., Introducing the cultural context of the OT 1991 ➤ 7,947; 8,1040: ^RBA 57 (1994) 246s (W. R. *Kotter*); BL (1993) 20 (I. W. *Provan*: more interesting for US/Catholic than for UK); OTEssays 7 (1994) 156s (F. E. *Deist*: cosmological more helpful); Vidyajyoti 58 (1994) 406s (P. *Meagher*, also on his NT).

744 **Rabinowitz** Isaac *zal.*, A witness forever; ancient Israel's perception of literature and the resultant Hebrew Bible. Bethesda MD 1993, CDL. v-148 p. $20. 1-88305-302-1 [OTAbs 17, p. 657].

745 **Ramsay** William M., The Westminster guide to the books of the Bible [including revised his Layman's NT]. Lvl 1994, W-Knox. xi-564 p. $30. 0-664-22061-4 [RelStR 21,319, L. J. *Greenspoon*].

746 **Rendtorff** Rolf, The OT, an introduction, ^TBowden John. Mp 1991, Fortress. 320 p. $16. 0-8006-2544-7. – ^RNewTR 7,1 (1994) 93s (C. *Stuhlmueller*).

748 **Salles** Catherine, L'Ancien Testament: Sujets. P 1994, Belin. 356 p. – ^RÉtudes 381 (1994) 139 (J.-M. *Carrière*).

749 *a) Scholer* David M., Did you know?; little known and remarkable facts about the history of the Bible; – *b) Waltke* Bruce, How we got our Old Testament; – *c) Herklots* H. G. G., Discovering the oldest New Testaments; – *d) Thiede* Carsten P., A testament is born; could Matthew take shorthand? Christian history 13, 43 (Carol Stream IL 1994) 2s / 32s / 34-47 / 24-29.

751 **Severance** W. Murray, Pronouncing Bible names²ʳᵉᵛ [¹1983]. Nv 1994, Broadman & H. vii-167 p. $15. 1-55819-418-5.

752 **Sicre** José Luis, Introducción al Antiguo Testamento 1993 ➤ 8,1048; 9,849: ^REstE 69 (1994) 414s (E. *Olivares*); RET 53 (1993) 118-122 (P. *Barrado Fernández*: espléndido); SalT 81 (1993) 322.

753 **Smelik** K. A. D., Historische Dokumente aus dem alten Israel: Kleine Vandenhoeck-Reihe N⁰ 1528, 1987 ➤ 3,b598, 4,d108: ^RSalesianum 56 (1994) 158 (M. *Cimosa*).

754 **Soggin** J. A., Introduction to the OT 1989 ➤ 5,1170 ... 8,1049: ᴿÉTRel 69 (1994) 420s (J.-D. *Macchi*); JEvTS 37 (1994) 35s (A. E. *Steinmann*).
755 **Tarazi** Paul N., The OT, an introduction 1991 ➤ 8,1052: ᴿNewTR 7,1 (1994) 94-97 (Dianne *Bergant*, also on CERESKO A.).
757 **Trebolle Barrera** Julio, La Biblia judía y la Biblia cristiana 1993 ➤ 9,851: ᴿDSD 1 (1994) 263s (A. van der *Kooij*); NRT 116 (1994) 94s (J. L. *Ska*); RHR 211 (1994) 472s (A. *Caquot*); Salmanticensis 41 (1994) 327-330 (J. M. *Sánchez Caro*).
758 *Van Buren* Paul M., Altes Testament, Tanakh, Hebräische Bibel, ᵀ*Rendtorff* Rolf: KIsr 9 (1994) 9-20.
759 **Walton** John H., Ancient Israelite literature ... parallels 1989 ➤ 6,1186 ... 8,1054: ᴿJEvTS 37 (1994) 131-3 (B. E. *Beyer*; for grads or prof); JNES 53 (1994) 70s (Barbara *Kaiser*: helpful but with evangelical slant).
760 **Zenger** Erich, Das Erste Testament, die jüdische Bibel und die Christen 1991 ➤ 8,1055; 9,853: ᴿBiKi 48 (1993) 51s (M. *Helper*).

B1.2 'Invitations' to Bible or OT.

761 *Agenda bíblica* 1995 [... cada día un sencillo comentario]. Estella 1994, VDivino. 288 p. pt. 365.
762 *Aguirre* Rafael, Reinterpretar la Palabra hoy, cómo leer de forma creyente los textos fundantes de la fe: SalT 82 (1994) 349-360.
763 *Anderson* Bernhard W., The Bible as the shared story of a people: ➤ 9,375* ONT rel. 1993, 19-37 [< OTAbs 17, p. 367].
764 *Avril* Anne-Catherine, La lettura ebraica della Scrittura, con antologia di testi rabbinici²: Spiritualità ebraica. Magnano VC 1989, Qiqajon. 102 p. 88-85227-01-5.
764* **Barton** John, What is the Bible? 1991 ➤ 7,962; 8,1059: ᴿChurchman 108 (1994) 82s (D. *Spanner*: unacceptable presuppositions).
765 *Beauchamp* Paul, La Bible, livre d'espérance; Études 381 (1994) 69-78.
766 *Bianchi* Enzo, *a*) La parola di Dio presente nelle Scritture; – *b*) Lectio divina; proposta di un metodo: Ambrosius 69 (1993) 404-425 / 426-438 . 485-502.
767 *La Bibbia blu* [tre teologi e 30 laici, con 2 esegeti consulenti, in tedesco]ᵀ, sguardo panoramico della S. Scrittura, present. *Fabris* R. Padova 1993, Messaggero/Queriniana. 255 p. Lᵐ 10. 88-250-0241-6. – ᴿAngelicum 71 (1994) 594 (S. *Jurić*).
768 *Brown* R. E., Responses to 101 questions 1990 ➤ 6,1194 ... 9,864: ᴿAnnTh 7 (1993) 477-486 (M. A. *Tábet*).
769 **Brown** Raymond E., 101 questions sur la Bible et leurs réponses 1993 ➤ 9,865: ᴿCarthaginensia 10 (1994) 213 (J. F. *Cuenca Molina*); RTLv 25 (1994) 493 (C. *Focant*: curieux); Telema 20 (1994) 92 (W. *Okambawa*).
770 **Bundesen** Lynne, The woman's guide to the Bible. NY 1993, Crossroad. x-192 p. 0-8245-1377-8.
771 **Buzzetti** Carlo, 4 × 1; un unico brano biblico e vari 'fare'; Guida pratica di ermeneutica e pastorale biblica: Un Ponte Per 3. CinB 1994, Paoline. 287 p. 88-315-0982-9.
772 *Cansi* Bernardo, 'Ano Bíblico' e estudos sobre as leituras da Bíblia: REB 54 (1994) 677-684.
773 **Charpentier** Étienne. ❷ Czytając Stary Testament. Włocławek 1993, Diecezjalne. 168 p. – ᴿRuBi 47 (1994) 217-9 (A. *Dreja*, ❷).
774 **Chopineau** Jacques, Lire la Bible. Lillois 1993, Alliance. 55 p. F 23. 2-87300-001-5. – ᴿÉTRel 69 (1994) 413 (P. *Lehnebach*).

774* **Clare** John D., *Wansbrough* Henry, The Bible alive. L 1993, Harper Collins. 256 p. £15. 0-00-513002-6. – ᴿVidyajyoti 58 (1994) 753 (P. *Meagher*).

775 *Coleridge* Mark, Life in the crypt, or Why bother with biblical studies? [an Australian's reaction to his middle-age doctorate studies on two chapters of Luke]: BInterp 2 (1994) 139-151.

775* **Comay** John / **Brownrigg** Ronald, Who's who in the OT [➤ 9,872] / NT. L 1994 pa. = 1971, Dent. £10 each. 0-460-06194-4 [OT Dent]. – ᴿTablet 248 (1994) 710 (H. *Wansbrough*).

776 — [no evident connection] Who's Who in the Bible; an illustrated biographical dictionary. Pleasantville NY 1994, Reader's Digest. 480 p. 0-89577-618-9.

777 **Cunningham** P. J., Exploring Scripture; how the Bible came to be 1992 ➤ 8,1067: ᴿOTEssays 7 (1994) 101-3 (W. *Vosloo*).

778 **Drane** John, Unlocking the Bible. Ox 1992, Lion. 48 p. £1.35. 0-7459-2210-4. – ᴿScotBuEvT 11 (1993) 58s (W. G. *Young*).

779 ᴱ**Duhaime** Jean, *Mainville* Odette, Entendre la voix du Dieu vivant; interprétations et pratiques actuelles de la Bible: Lectures Bibliques 41. Montréal 1994, Médiaspaul. 367 p. $29. 2-89420-258-X.

780 **Fanin** Luciano, Come leggere 'il Libro'; lineamenti di introduzione biblica. Padova 1993, Messaggero. 224 p. Lᵐ 20. – ᴿAngelicum 71 (1994) 280 (S. *Jurić*).

781 *Federici* Tommaso, Il volto divino e umano; nostalgia e certezza nella Bibbia: Studium 90 (R 1994) 61-78.

782 *Futterlieb* Hartmut, Die hebräische Bibel oder Von der Einheit der Schrift: Forum Religion 1 (Stu 1994) 9-17 [< ᴢɪᴛ 94,166].

783 **Germain** Pierre, De la Genèse à l'ère nucléaire; questions à la Bible. P 1994, Foyer de l'Âme. 142 p. – ᴿRHPR 74 (1994) 467s (R. *Mehl*).

784 **Giavini** Giovanni, Verso la Bibbia, e in ascolto del suo messaggio. Mi 1993, Àncora. 200 p. 88-7610-432-1.

785 **Hauerwas** Stanley, Unleashing the Scripture; freeing the Bible from captivity to America. Nv 1993, Abingdon. 159 p. – ᴿChrTod 38,5 (1994) 52-53 (R. *Yarbrough*, also on BRUEGGEMANN) [< NTAbs 38, p. 334]; RExp 91 (1994) 631-3 (D. P. *Gushee*: Bible-reading not for the untrained!).

786 **Hill** Charles, The Scriptures Jesus knew; a guide to the Old Testament. Newtown NSW 1994, Dwyer (Harrisburg: Morehouse). xviii-232 p. $13. 0-85574-365-4 [TDig 42,272].

787 **Jeanne d'Arc,** sr., Chemins à travers la Bible, ANT 1993 ➤ 9,884: ᴿEsprVie 104 (1994) 46 (É. *Cothenet*).

788 **Lane** Robert D., Reading the Bible; intention, text, interpretation. Lanham MD 1994, UPA. [xxxii-] 209 p. 0-8191-9114-0.

789 **Lohfink** Norbert, Unsere neuen Fragen und das AT; wiederentdeckte Lebensweisung: Herder-Tb 1594, 1989 ➤ 5,301; 7,976: ᴿSalesianum 56 (1994) 152 (C. *Bissoli*).

790 ᴱ**Luz** Ulrich, La Bible, une pomme de discorde 1992 ➤ 8,479; 9,889: ᴿStPhilonAn 6 (1994) 273s (E. *Cuvillier*).

791 **Marín Heredia** Francisco, La Biblia, palabra profética: MundoB. Estella 1992, VDivino. 330 p. 84-7151-816-3. – ᴿRET 54 (1994) 85-88 (P. *Barrado Fernández*).

792 **Martini** Carlo M., dialogo con *Elkann* Alain, Cambiare il cuore. Mi 1993, Bompiani. 135 p. Lᵐ 24. – ᴿViPe 77 (1994) 152-8 (E. *Zambruno*).

792* ᴱOchs Peter, The return to Scripture in Judaism and Christianity. NY 1990, Paulist. 378 p. $19. – ᴿFirsT 43 (1994) 59s (J. D. *Levenson*).

793 **Ord** David R., *Coote* Robert B., Is the Bible TRUE? Understanding the Bible today. Mkn 1994, Orbis. xii-132 p. $10. 0-88344-948-X.

794 **Ralph** M. N., Discovering Old Testament origins; the books of Genesis, Exodus and Samuel 1992 → 9,895: ᴿOTEssays 7 (1994) 91-93 (J. H. *Breytenbach*, in Afrikaans).

795 **Ranke-Heinemann** Uta, *a)* Nein und Amen: Anleitung zum Glaubenszweifel. – *b)* Così non sia. Mi 1993, Rizzoli. – ᴿNuovaUm 16 (1994) 97-122 (G. *Rossé*).

796 **Rizzi** Giuseppe, I grandi temi della vita cristiana nella Bibbia. R 1993, Città Nuova. 518 p.; 16 color. pl. Lᵐ 48. – ᴿCC 145 (1994,1) 621s (A. *Ferrua*).

797 **Rohr** R., Grandi temi della Bibbia, Antico e Nuovo Testamento 1993 → 9,899: ᴿAsprenas 41 (1994) 117s (G. *Di Palma*).

798 ᴱSatterthwaite Philip E., *Wright* David F., A pathway into the Holy Scripture. GR 1994, Eerdmans. viii-344 p. 0-8020-4078-7.

799 *a) Schröer* H., Bibelfrömmigkeit und wissenschaftliche Schriftauslegung; über die Berechtigung verschiedener Zugänge zur Bibel; – *b) Spieckermann* H., Die Stimme des Fremden im AT: PasT 83 (Gö 1994) 38-51 / 52-57 [< ZIT 94,170].

800 **Sloyan** Gerard S., So you mean to read the Bible? 1992 → 8,1102: ᴿBL (1994) 19 (H. *McKay*: final chapter splendid; earlier three too R. C.); TBR 7,3 (1994) 14 (A. *Gilmore*: an ideal beginners' book, also for Protestants).

801 **Timmer** J., Le salut de la Genèse à l'Apocalypse [They shall be my people 1983],ᵀ.: RRéf 44,4s (1993) 184 p. [NTAbs 43, p. 315].

802 **Travis** Stephen H., The Bible as a whole [130 passages giving a sense of the developing content]. Ox/Sutherland NSW 1994, Bible Reading Fellowship / Albatross. 280 p. £8. 0-7459-2527-8 / 0-7324-0784-2. – ᴿTBR 7,3 (1994s) 14 (A. *Gilmore*).

803 **Tremblay** J., Un chemin de vie; l'Ancien Testament, guide spirituel pour notre temps 1993 → 9.909: ᴿBLitEc (1994) 239s (L. *Monloubou*).

804 *Vanhoye* Alberto, Salvezza universale nel Cristo e validità dell'antica alleanza: CC 145 (1994,4) 433-445.

805 **White** J. B., From Adam to Armageddon; a survey of the Bible³ʳᵉᵛ. Belmont CA 1994, Wadsworth. xiii-222 p.; ill.; 9 maps. 0-534-21282-4 [NTAbs 38, p. 286].

806 **Williams** Michael E., The storyteller's companion to the Bible. Nv 1992, Abingdon.

B1.3 *Paedagogia biblica* – **Bible-teaching techniques.**

807 *Bach* Ulrich, Mit behinderten Menschen das Evangelium neu entdecken: BTZ 11 (1994) 107-123.

808 **Becker** Ulrich, *al.*, Neutestamentliches Arbeitsbuch für Religionspädagogen: Urban-Tb 439, 1993 → 9,916: ᴿTLZ 119 (1994) 361-3 (J. *Lähnemann*).

809 *Berg* Horst K., Ein Wort wie Feuer 1991 → 7,991 ... 9,918: ᴿBiLtg 66 (1993) 187-190 (T. *Söding*); TLtg 66 (1993) 167-190 (T. *Söding*).

810 *Chmiel* Jerzy, Biblia w rodzinie (in the family): RuBi 47 (1994) 37-42.

811 *Boyer* Larry G., A curriculum for training the college student to lead inductive Bible studies: diss. Fuller, ᴰ*Redman* R. Pasadena 1994. 188 p. 94-33175. – DissA 55 (1994s) p. 2259.

812 **Cochran** Murray R.,   Teaching them to observe all things; a practical rationale for teaching Scripture in evangelical colleges: diss. Boston College 1994, ᴰ*Boys* Mary.   230 p.   95-09244. – DissA 55 (1994s) p. 3462.

813 **Dorph** Gail,   Conceptions and preconceptions; a study of prospective Jewish educators' knowledge and beliefs about Torah: diss. Jewish Theol. Sem.; ᴰ*Lukinsky* J.   ɴʏ 1993. – RelStR 21,251.

813* ᴱ**Eder** Monika [p. 187-211, Jesus; die Sprache der Bibel verstehen], *al.*, Abschied vom Kinderglauben; Handbuch zu Matthias Sᴄʜᴀʀᴇʀ, Miteinander unterwegs.   Salzburg 1994, Otto Müller.   337 p.   ᴅᴍ 36.   3-7013-0892-6.

814 **Giorgio** Vincenzo, *Paganelli* Rinaldo,   Il catechista incontra la Bibbia: Educatori e catechisti.   Bo 1994, Dehoniane.   283 p.   Lᵐ 21.   88-10-10343-2.

815 Grundkurs Bibel: AT, Werkbuch für die Bibelarbeit mit Erwachsenen. Stu 1993, KBW.   10 Einzelhefte in Ordner, c. ᴅᴍ 128. – ᴿBiKi 49 (1994) 113-5 (H. K. *Berg*, ohne Name irgend eines Verantwortlichen).

816 *Hagen* Markus von,   Verkündigung in Sprechblasen; zur Geschichte und Entwicklung der Bibel-Comics: Entschluss 49,12 (1994) 33-38; 9 fig.

817 **Hill** Robert C.   Breaking the bread of the Word: SubsBPont 15, 1991 ➤ 7,992:   ᴿScripB 23 (1993) 43s (Christine *Dodd*).

818 **Hurley** Robert,   Biblical interpretation in the 'Viens vers le Père' catechetical series: diss. McGill.   Montreal 1994.   > ᴜᴘᴀ. – RTLv 26, p. 529.

819 **Knecht** Lothar & Martin,   Lebendige Bibelarbeit; Beispiele für Schule und Gemeinde.   FrB 1992, Herder.   288 p. – ᴿTPQ 142 (1994) 327 (Roswitha *Unfried*).

820 **Kreeft** Peter J.,   Your questions; God's answers [for teenagers].   SF 1994, Ignatius.   111 p. $9.   0-80870-488-X [TDig 42,74].

820* ᴱ**Langer** Wolfgang.   Lavorare con la Bibbia ... per catechisti e insegnanti di religione.   T-Leumann 1994, Elle Di Ci.   288 p. – ᴿParVi 39,5 (1994) 56 (A. *Bagni*).

821 *a*) *Langer* Wolfgang,   Das Evangelium lernen; Herausforderung für die Erwachsenenkatechese; – *b*) *Nipkow* Kark Ernst,   Evangelische Erwachsenenbildung; Grundlagen, Grundsätze, Aufgaben und Herausforderungen; – *c*) *Englert* Rudolf,   Warum ist Erwachsenenkatechese so schwierig? ... aus katholischer Sicht; – *d*) *Biesinger* Albert,   Erstkommunion als Familienkatechese; zur Relevanz von 'catequesis familiar': TüTQ 174,2 (1994) 83-94 / 95-107 / 107-120 / 120-135 (-158, *al.*).

822 **Lucas** Daryl J.,   The eager reader Bible story book; Bible stories to grow on; Catholic edition.   Huntington ɪɴ 1994, Our Sunday Visitor. $16. 0-87973-252-0 [TDig 42,175].

823 ᴱ**Porter** David,   Word alive; Bible teaching at the cutting edge.   Leicester 1994, Inter-Varsity.   223 p.   £7.

824 *Ruiz* Jean-Pierre,   Listening habits; teaching, preaching, undergraduates and the Bible: Priest 50,3 (1994) 39-44.

825 **Scott** Macrina,   Picking the 'right' Bible study program: reviews of 150 recommended programs with a listing of the top 15²ʳᵉᵛ.   Ch 1994, ᴀᴄᴛᴀ. viii-376 p. $15.   0-87946-063-6 [TDig 41,382].

B2.1   **Hermeneutica.**

826 ᴱ**Abel** Oliver, *Smyth* Françoise.   Le livre de traverse 1992 ➤ 9,942: ᴿNumen 41 (1994) 205s (B. *Lang*).

827 **Aillet** M., Lire la Bible avec S. THOMAS; le passage de la *littera* à la *res* dans la Somme théologique: STFrib 80. FrS 1993, Univ. 355 p. – ᴿAnnTh 8 (1994) 173-6 (M. A. *Tábet*).

828 **Albert** Hans, Kritik der reinen Hermeneutik; der Antirealismus und das Problem des Verstehens: Einheit der Gesellschaftswissenschaften 85. Tü 1994, Mohr. xix-272 p. 3-16-146258-0.

829 **Alexander** Werner, Hermeneutica generalis; zur Konzeption und Entwicklung der allgemeinen Verstehenslehre im 17. und 18. Jahrhundert. Stu 1993, M&P WissF. 301 p. – ᴿFrSZ 41 (1994) 273-7 (K. *Petrus*).

830 **Alonso Schökel** Luis, Bravo Aragón José María, Apuntes de hermenéutica: Estructuras y procesos; religión. M 1994, Trotta. 169 p. 84-87699-90-1. – ᴿRazF 230 (1994) 111 (J. *Gómez Caffarena*).

831 **Alonso Schökel** Luis, Bravo Aragón José M., Appunti di ermeneutica [Apuntes 1994], ᵀZucchi Gabriella: StBDeh 24. Bo 1994, Dehoniane. 192 p. Lᵐ 24. 88-10-40726-1.

832 *Beauvais* Chantal, La théologie comme herméneutique selon Claude GEFFRÉ: ScEspr 46 (1994) 255-271.

833 *Beutel* Albrecht, 'Scriptura ita loquitur; cur non nos?'; Sprache des Glaubens bei LUTHER: KerDo 40 (1994) 184-202; Eng. 202: God's word 'says' then 'effects'; men's language does not.

834 *Blumrich* Rüdiger, Überlieferungsgeschichte als Schlüssel zum Text [... Vitaspatrum]: FrSZ 41 (1994) 188-222.

835 *Bodendorfer-Langer* Gerhard, 'Sie ist nicht im Himmel!'; rabbinische Hermeneutik und die Auslegung der Tora: BibNot 75 (1994) 35-47.

836 **Brewer** David I., Techniques and assumptions in Jewish exegesis before 70 C.E.: TStAJud 30, 1992, ➤ 9,10671: ᴿSalesianum 56 (1994) 781 (R. *Vicent*).

837 *Bühler* Pierre, Der Beitrag der Hermeneutik zum Thema 'Wissenschaft und Glaube': TZBas 50 (1994) 152-158.

838 **Burrows** M., Rorem P., Biblical hermeneutics in historical perspective 1991 ➤7,58; 8,1146: ᴿModT 10 (1994) 103-6 (G. *Lindbeck*); RLitND 24,2 (1992) 77-81 (Mary *Gerhart*, also on PRICKETT and DETWEILER-DOTY).

839 *Capelle* Philippe, Le Nouvel Âge herméneutique de la raison [ᴱGREISCH J. 1987-85-91]: RICathP 49 (1994) 63-72.

840 **Chidester** David, Word and light; seeing, hearing, and religious discourse. Urbana 1992, Univ. Illinois. 168 p. – ᴿScEspr 46 (1994) 97-101 (Shannon-Elizabeth *Farrell*: chiefly AUGUSTINE; 'anthropological questions making for a dialogue between biblical and patristic scholars').

841 **Colombo** Paolo, La questione della verità nel pensiero di H.-G. GADAMER; ermeneutica filosofica e teologia: diss. ᴰBertuletti A. Milano 1994. 442 p. > Glossa. – RTLv 26, p. 529.

842 ᴱ**Coulot** Claude, Exégèse et herméneutique; comment lire la Bible?: LDiv 158. P 1994, Cerf. 175 p. F 80. 2-204-05068-7.

843 **Cowley** R. W., Ethiopian biblical interpretation 1988 ➤4,1186...8,1150: ᴿOLZ 89 (1994) 62-65 (M. *Kropp*).

844 **Dawson** D., Allegorical readers and cultural revision in ancient Alexandria [diss. Yale 1988, ᴰLayton B.]. 1992 ➤ 8,1151: ᴿChH 63 (1994) 254-6 (J. W. *Trigg*).

845 *Despland* Michel, Un tournant vers l'herméneutique en France en 1806? [FAURIEL C., CABANIS G., CONSTANT B., MICHELET J., QUINET E. 1827: anticipaient les origines attribuées à SCHLEIERMACHER (-DILTHEY-HEIDEGGER-GADAMER)]: SR 23 (1994) 5-24.

846 **D'Isanto** Luca, JÜNGEL's hermeneutics. diss. ᴰ*Scharlemann* R. [? Union, Richmond] Virginia. – RTLv 26, p. 529.

847 **Dockery** David S., Biblical interpretation, then and now 1992 ➤ 8,1152; 9,963: ᴿRExp 91 (1994) 107-9 (J. P. *Newport*); WestTJ 56 (1994) 206-8 (M. *Silva*).

847* **Dormeyer** Detlev, Handlungstheoretische Hermeneutik biblischer Texte: ➤ 119, ᶠSILLER H., Gottesrede 1994, 6-28 [20-89, *al.*, application to the separate theological areas].

848 *Ebeling* Gerhard, Hermeneutik zwischen der Macht des Gotteswortes und seiner Entmachtung in der Moderne: ZTK 91 (1994) 80-96.

849 *a)* *Ebeling* Gerhard, L'herméneutique entre la puissance de la parole de Dieu et sa perte de puissance dans les temps modernes; – *b)* *Holenstein* Elmar, L'herméneutique interculturelle: RTPhil 126 (1994) 39-56 / 19-37. – Eng. 96.

850 **Edgerton** W. Dow, The passion of interpretation; Literary currents, 1992 ➤ 8,1155*; $20: ᴿCBQ 56 (1994) 371s (Elizabeth S. *Malbon*); Interpretation 48 (1994) 306s (W. A. *Kort*).

851 ᴱ**Fatum** Lone, *Nielsen* Eduard, Fortolkning some formidling [interpretation as mediation]; om den bibelske eksegeses funktion 1992 ➤ 8, 351*c*: ᴿSvEx 59 (1994) 176s (L. O. *Eriksson*).

852 **Fee** G. D., Gospel and Spirit; issues in NT hermeneutics 1991 ➤ 7,197: ᴿSvEx 59 (1994) 204s (C. C. *Caragounis*, Eng.).

  ᶠFROEHLICH Karlfried: Biblical hermeneutics in historical perspective, ➤ 838, ᴱ**Burrows** M., *Rorem* P. 1991.

854 *Gallinaro* Roberto, Ermeneutica e teologia; riesame della prospettiva di H.-G. GADAMER: Asprenas 41 (1994) 227-246.

855 *García* Mateo Rogelio, Importancia de los 'textus accommodati' para el estudio e interpretación de los 'Ejercicios Espirituales': EstE 69 (1994) 367-385.

856 *Garfinkel* Stephen, Applied *peshat*; historical-critical method and religious meaning: ➤ 86, ᶠMUFFS Y., JANES 22 (1993) 19-28.

857 **Girard** Marc, Les symboles dans la Bible 1991 ➤ 8,1162: ᴿSR 22 (1993) 126s (J. *Duhaime*).

858 **Greene-McCreight** Katherine, Ad litteram; the plain sense of Scripture: diss. Yale, ᴰ*Oden* T. NHv 1994. – RelStR 21, 253.

859 **Greisch** Jean présent., (*Bochet* I., *al.*) Comprendre et interpréter; le paradigme herméneutique de la raison: Inst. Cath. ph. 15. P 1993, Beauchesne. 430 p. F 190. 2-7010-1291-0. – ᴿRevSR 68 (1994) 368s (Y. *Labbé*); RTPhil 126 (1994) 374s (Clairette *Karakash*).

860 **Grondin** Jean, L'universalité de l'herméneutique. P 1993, PUF. 249 p. – ᴿRTPhil 126 (1994) 70s (J. *Schouwey*).

861 **Halivni** David W., Peshat and Derash 1991 ➤ 8,1165; 9,975: ᴿCritRR 5 (1992) 365-7 (G. A. *Anderson*); Prooftexts 14 (1994) 71-96 (B. J. *Schwartz*).

862 *Helm* Paul, Understanding scholarly presuppositions, a crucial tool for research?: TyndB 44 (1993) 143-154.

863 **Hoffmann** Manfred, Rhetoric and theology; the hermeneutic of ERASMUS: E. Studies 12. Toronto 1994, Univ. ix-306 p.; bibliog. 288-298. 0-8020-0579-9.

863* **Hutmacher** Hans A., Symbolik der biblischen Zahlen und Zeiten. Pd 1993, Schöningh. 232 p. DM 28 pa. 3-506-73967-0 [TR 91,76]. – ᴿTGgw 37 (1994) 155s (K. *Prenner*).

864 *Jacobsen* Douglas, The Calvinist-Arminian dialectic in evangelical hermeneutics: ChrSchR 23 (1993s) 72-89.

865 **Jeanrond** Werner G., Theological hermeneutics 1991 ➤ 7,1027 ... 9,978: ᴿScotJT 47 (1994) 122-5 (K. J. *Vanhoozer*).

866 **Jeanrond** Werner G., L'ermeneutica teologica; sviluppo e significato [1991 ➤ 7,1027], ᵀ*Volpe* Giorgio. Brescia 1994, Queriniana. 334 p. Lᵐ 38. 88-399-0727-0. – ᴿAsprenas 41 (1994) 609s (B. *Forte*); EstE 69 (1994) 554 (A. *Drake*).

867 *Jostein* Ådna, What does it mean to interpret a biblical text?: TsTKi 65 (1994) 173-183 Norwegian; 184 Eng.

868 **Kaiser** W. C., *Silva* M., An introduction to biblical hermeneutics; the search for meaning. GR 1994, Zondervan. 298 p. $25. 0-310-53090-3 [NTAbs 38, p. 449].

869 **Klein** W. W., *al.*, Introduction to biblical interpretation 1993 ➤ 9,982: ᴿAngelicum 71 (1994) 281-3 (S. *Jurić*); BibTB 24 (1994) 38s (T. R. *Hobbs*); BL (1994) 91 (G. W. *Anderson*); TrinJ 15 (1994) 251s (A. J. *Kostenberger*).

870 **Körtner** Ulrich H. J., Der inspirierte Leser; zentrale Aspekte biblischer Hermeneutik. Gö 1994, Vandenhoeck & R. 179 p. DM 28. 3-525-01618-2 [TLZ 120,982, H. *Weder*].

871 *Körtner* Ulrich H. J., Schrift und Geist; über Legitimität und Grenzen allegorischer Schriftauslegung: NSys 36 (1994) 1-17 [> TDig 41 (1994) 135-140, ᵀᴱ*Asen* B. A.].

872 *Küster* Volker, Models of contextual hermeneutics; liberation and feminist theological approaches compared: Exchange 23,2 (1994) 149-...

873 *Kuske* D. P., What in Scripture is universally applicable and what is historically conditioned?: WisLuthQ 91,2 (Mequon 1994) 83-105 [< NTAbs 38, p. 337].

874 **Larkin** William J.ᴶ, Culture and biblical hermeneutics; interpreting and applying the authoritative word in a relativistic age. Lanham MD 1993, UPA. 401 p.; bibliog. 351-381. 0-8191-9219-8.

875 *Lategan* Bernard C., Revisiting [his 1985, with Vorster] Text and reality: ➤ 132, ꟳVORSTER W., Neotestamentica 28,3 (1994) 121-135.

876 *a) Le Roux* Jurie H., A brief description of an intellectual journey; on W. Vorster's quest for understanding; – *b) Tilborg* Sjef van, Metaphorical versus visionary language: ➤ 132, ꟳVORSTER W., Neotestamentica 28,3 (1994) 1-32 / 77-91.

877 *a) Liburd* Ron, 'Like ... a house upon the sand'; African American biblical hermeneutics in perspective; – *b) Hendrichs* Osayande O., Guerrilla exegesis; a post-modern proposal for insurgent African American biblical interpretation: JIntdenom 22 (1994) 71-91 / 92-

878 **Loades** Ann, *McLain* M., Hermeneutics ... lit. crit. 1992 ➤ 8,477; 9,987: ᴿHeythJ 35 (1994) 203s (B. L. *Horne*).

879 ᴱ**McKenzie** Steven L., *Haynes* Stephen R., To each its own meaning; an introduction to biblical criticisms and their applications. LVL 1993, W-Knox. 251 p. $13. 0-664-25236-2. – ᴿBibTB 24 (1994) 144s (K. C. *Hanson*); BL (1994) 93s (H. S. *Piper*); LitTOx 8 (1994) 221 (D. *Jasper*).

880 **Maier** Gerhard, Biblische hermeneutik² 1991 ➤ 8,1175: ᴿTR 90 (1994) 281-3 (O. B. *Knoch* †).

881 ᴱ**Marcheselli-Casale** Cesare, Oltre il racconto; esegesi ed ermeneutica; alla ricerca del senso: BtTeolNapolitana. N 1994, D'Auria. 238 p.

882 *Marty* Martin E., Literalism vs. everything else; a continuing conflict: BR 10,2 (1994) 38-43 . 50.

883 **Mickelsen** A. B & A. M., Understanding Scripture 1992 ➤ 8,1037 (also under Berkeley 8,1062): ᴿRBibArg 55 (1993) 183s (A. J. *Levoratti*).

884 **Mura** Gaspare, Ermeneutica e verità; storia e problemi della filosofia dell'interpretazione. R 1990, Città Nuova. 516 p. – ᴿSalesianum 56 (1994) 596 (C. *Nanni*).

885 *Ong* Walter J., Hermeneutic forever; voice, text, digitization, and the 'I': OralT 10,1 (1995) 3-26.

886 **Opitz** Peter, Calvins theologische Hermeneutik: diss. ᴰ*Link* C. Bern 1994. 303 p. > Neuk. – RTLv 26, p. 545.

887 **Resweber** Jean-Paul, Qu'est-ce qu'interpréter? Essai sur les fondements de l'herméneutique 1988 ⇒ 4,1287; 6,1312: ᴿRTLv 25 (1994) 258s (E. *Brito*).

888 *Samuel* David, The place of private judgment: Churchman 108 (1994) 6-21.

889 **Scalise** Charles J., Hermeneutics as theological prolegomena; a canonical approach: Studies in American Biblical Hermeneutics 8. Macon 1994, Mercer Univ. xiv-155 p.; bibliog. 131-142. 1-86554-434-4.

890 *Scalise* Charles J., Canonical hermeneutics; CHILDS and BARTH: ScotJT 47 (1994) 61-88.

891 *Schneiders* Sandra M. [response *Senior* D.], Living word or dead[ly] letter; the encounter between the NT and contemporary experience: CathTProc 47 (1992) 45-60 [61-68].

892 *a) Sinclair* Melinda, Are academic texts really decontextualized and fully explicit? A pragmatic perspective on the role of context in written communication; – *b) Clayman* Steven E., Reformulating the question; a device for answering / not answering questions: Text 13 (1993) 529-558 / 159-188.

893 *a) Smit* Dirk J., A story of contextual hermeneutics and the integrity of NT interpretation in South Africa / Reading the Bible and the '(un) official interpretive culture'; – *b) Bird* Phyllis, Authority and context in the interpretation of biblical texts; – *c) Botha* Jan, How do we 'read the context'?: Neotestamentica 28 (1994) 265-289.301-321 / 323-337 / 291-307.

894 *Sparn* Walter, Stand und Aufgaben der Hermeneutik in Europa [Fremdheit und Vertrautheit, Halle 21.-24.IX.1994]: TLZ 120, 741-5.

895 **Stein** Robert H., Playing by the rules; a basic guide to interpreting the Bible. GR 1994, Baker. 219 p. 0-8010-8366-4.

896 **Streib** Heinz, Hermeneutic of metaphor, symbol and narrative in faith-development theory. Fra 1991, Lang. – ᴿZRGg 46 (1994) 183-5 (K. *Ebert*).

897 *a) Tábet* Miguel Ángel, Unidad y diversidad en la Sagrada Escritura; un tema de la hermenéutica de Santo Tomás; – *b) Estrada B.* Bernardo, La metáfora en la parábola; – *c) Viciano* Albert, Retórica, gramática y dogma en la técnica hermenéutica de la antigüedad clásica: ⇒ 22, ᶠCASCIARO J. M., Biblica 1994, 53-63 / 65-75 / 101-8.

898 **Tate** W. Randolph, Biblical interpretation; an integrated approach 1991 ⇒ 7,1056*; 9,1017: ᴿCBQ 56 (1994) 127-9 (D. *Penchansky*: finally!).

899 **Thiselton** Anthony C., New horizons in hermeneutics 1992 ⇒ 9,1020: ᴿCBQ 56 (1994) 158-160 (C. *Mercer*); ModT 10 (1994) 433s (A. K. M. *Adam*); ScotJT 47 (1994) 141s (Rosalini *Papaphilippopoulos*); WestTJ 55 (1993) 343-6 (V. S. *Poythress*).

900 **Timm** Hermann, Wahr-Zeichen; Angebote zur Erneuerung religiöser Symbolkultur. Stu 1993, Kohlhammer. 159 p. DM 29,80. 3-17-012704-7 [TLZ 120,713, K. *Lüthi*].

901 *Vedder* Ben, Een metafysische motivatie van de hermeneutik; over het

eeuwig metafysische in de mens volgens DILTHEY: Bijdragen 55 (1994) 249-267; Eng. 268.
902 *Vroom* Hendrik M., Religious hermeneutics; culture and narratives [... Ps 8]: JIntRD 4 (1994) 189-213.
903 **Zakovitch** Yair, ☉ An introduction to inner biblical interpretation. Even Yehuda 1992, Reches. 157 p. 965-403-038-1 [OIAc 11,46].

B2.4 *Analysis* **narrationis** *biblicae* (generalior ➢ J9.6).

904 **Alter** Robert, L'arte della narrativa biblica 1990 ➤ 6,1336 ... 8,1204: ᴿTeresianum 45 (1994) 316s (A. *Borrell*).
905 **Beauchamp** Paul, Le récit 1992 ➤ 8,1206; 9,1035: ᴿNRT 116 (1994) 97 (Y. *Simoens*); RTLv 25 (1994) 81 (A. *Wénin*: beau; ne se sent guère que c'est un recueil).
906 **Berman** Ruth Aronson, **Slobin** Dan I., Relating events in narrative; a crosslinguistic developmental study. Hilsdale NJ 1994, Erlbaum. xvi-748 p.; bibliog. 679-717. 0-8058-1435-3.
907 **Bradt** Kevin M., The recovery of story as a way of knowing in postmodern approches to psychotherapy and Scripture; a study of epistemologies, paradigms, theory, and practice: diss. Graduate Theological Union, ᴰ*Milgrom* J. Berkeley 1994. – RelStR 21,252.
908 **Culley** Robert C., Themes and variations; a study of action in biblical narrative: SBL Semeia Studies 1992 ➤ 8,1210; 9,1039: ᴿRelStR 20 (1994) (W. L. *Humphreys*); CBQ 56 (1994) 328s (Alice L. *Laffey*); ÉglT 25 (1994) 132s (W. *Vogels*); JRel 74 (1994) 89s (Susan *Niditch*); VT 44 (1994) 423s (P. E. *Satterthwaite*).
909 **Exum** Cheryl J., Tragedy and biblical narrative 1993 ➤ 8,1213; 9,1041: ᴿBInterp 2 (1994) 226s (R. P. *Carroll*: a joy to read a good literary critic); CBQ 56 (1994) 101s (Camilla *Burns*); Horizons 21 (1994) 179s (Kathleen M. *Gaffney*); Interpretation 48 (1994) 200 (Susan *Ackerman*); JRel 74 (1994) 90-92 (D. *Jobling*); LitTOx 8 (1994) 219s (S. E. *Porter*: beatifully produced, genuine literary feel, some reserves); OTEssays 7 (1994) 121-3 (P. J. *Nel*: a welcome contribution).
910 *Gołębiewski* Marian, ☉ La structure du récit comme une catégorie essentielle de l'exégèse et de la théologie narrative: AtKap 123 (1994) 58-66.
911 **Gunn** David M., **Fewell** Danna N., Narrative in the Hebrew Bible 1993 ➤ 9,1043: ᴿBiblica 75 (1994) 417-420 (J.-L. *Ska*); BL (1994) 88 (H. S. *Pyper*); HeythJ 35 (1994) 440s (J. *Mulrooney*); RelStR 20 (1994) 141 (W. L. *Humphreys*); TLond 97 (1994) 378-380 (Sue *Gillingham*: fine but how far really is literary from historical criticism?).
912 *Holland* Scott, How do stories save us? Two contemporary theological responses [GERTZ C.; LINDBECK G.]: CGrebel 12 (1994) 130-153 [171-188, *Weaver* J. Denny, in Anabaptism].
913 **Kaminsky** Joel S., Punishment displacement in the Hebrew Bible: diss. ᴰ*Collins* J. J. Chicago 1994. – RelStR 51,255; RTLv 26, p. 531.
914 **Kaster** Douglas L., [Gn 37; 39s] Salience [LONGACRE 1989, 1992] in biblical Hebrew narrative; diss. Texas, ᴰ*Herning* Susan C. Arlington 1994. 1359406 [DissA disk] MAI 33 (1994s) p. 725.
915 *Kozima* Hideki, *Furugori* Telji, Segmenting narrative text into coherent scenes: LitLComp 9 (1994) 13-19.
916 **Krondorfer** Bjorn, Body and Bible; interpreting and experiencing biblical narratives 1992 ➤ 8,358*b*: – ᴿRelStR 20 (1994) 141 (R. G. *Bowman*).

917 **Lescow** Theodor, Das Stufenschema ... BZAW 211, 1992 → 8,1201: ᴿBL
    (1994) 91 (H. G. M. *Williamson*); CBQ 56 (1994) 767s (M. E. *Biddle*).
918 **Meier** Samuel A., Speaking of speaking: VTS 46, 1992 → 8,1219; 9,1048;
    ᴿAJS 19 (1994) 350-2 (F. E. *Greenspahn*); BSO 57 (1994) 590s (R. S.
    Hess); CBQ 56 (1994) 558-560 (Cynthia L. *Miller*); JBL 113 (1994) 704s
    (D. *Nelson*).
919 *Maas* Jacques J. C., La narration par la narration? [résumé de sa diss.
    Tilburg 1993, Verhalen met verhalen]; (Étude sémiotique de l'approche
    contextuelle des textes bibliques pour l'enseignement religieux et la ca-
    téchèse): SémBib 73 (1994) 56-61.
919* **Navone** John, Seeking God in story [a 1979 book plus 24 reprints].
    ColMn 1990, Liturgical. xvi-335 p. $12 pa. – ᴿCritRR 6 (1993) 127-9
    (A.K.M. *Adam*: will appeal to those for whom the Christian narrative is
    simply one example of universal mythic structures).
920 *Palache* J. L., The nature of Old Testament narrative: → 250;
    VAmsterdam 1994, 3-22 [OTAbs 17, p. 493 sans original date].
921 **Powell** Mark A., What is narrative criticism? 1993 = 1990 → 6,1349 ...
    9,1049: ᴿScotJT 47 (1994) 530 (Rosalind *Papaphilippopoulos*); TLond 97
    (1994) 51 (R. *Garside*: limited to the four Gospels).
922 *Quick* Philip A., Resumptive repetition; a two-edged sword: JTrTL 6
    (1993) 289-316 [< OTAbs 17, p. 494].
923 ᴱ**Rosenblatt** Jason P., *Sitterson* Joseph C.ᴶ, 'Not in heaven'; coherence
    and complexity in biblical narrative [Georgetown Univ. April 1989] 1991
    → 7,454b: ᴿLitTOx 8 (1994) 107s (W. *Moberly*).
924 *Ruf* Frederick J., The consequences of genre; narrative, lyric, and
    dramatic intelligibility: JAAR 62 (1994) 799-818.
924* **Sellars** Michael W., The influence of literary theory upon biblical
    hermeneutics: diss. Texas A & I [*sic*], ᴰ*Sabrio* D. Kingsville TX 1992.
    vi-75;. [?93 for] 13-50664. – OIAc 11,41.
925 *Smelik* K.A.D., Vertellingen in de Hebreeuwse Bijbel; de benadering van
    het bijbelse verhaal door PALACHE, BEEK en diene leerlingen: AmstCah 9
    (1988) 18-21 [< OTAbs 16, p. 218].
926 **Swartley** Willard M., Israel's Scripture traditions and the synoptic
    gospels; story shaping story. Peabody MA 1994, Hendrickson. xv-367 p.
    1-56563-001-7 [TDig 41,385].
926* **Tertel** Hans Jürgen, Text and transmission; an empirical model for the
    literary development of Old Testament narratives [Diss. 1991] BZAW 221.
    B/NY 1994, de Gruyter. x-311 p. [OIAc 11,43] 3-11-013921-9.
927 **Vanhoozer** Kevin J., Biblical narrative / RICOEUR 1990 → 6,1356 ... 8,1052:
    ᴿCritRR 5 (1992) 492-4 (L. S. *Mudge*); ScotJT 47 (1994) 400s (A. *Wood*).
928 **Wildgen** Wolfgang, Process, image, and meaning; a realistic model of the
    meanings of sentences and narrative texts: Pragmatics and Beyond NS 31.
    Amst 1994, Benjamins. xii-281 p.; bibliog. 255-270. 90-272-5043-X.

B2.6 *Critica reactionis lectoris* – **Reader-response criticism.**

930 *Porter* Stanley E., Reader-response criticism and New Testament study; a
    response to A. C. THISELTON's New horizons in hermeneutics: LitTOx 8
    (1994) 94-102.

B3 *Interpretatio ecclesiastica* .1 **Bible and Church.**

932 *a) Abraham* William J., A theology of evangelism; the heart of the
    matter; – *b) Hunsberger* George R., Is there biblical warrant for

evangelism?; – *c*) *Guder* Darrell L., Evangelism and the debate over Church growth: Interpretation 48,2 (1994) 117-130 / 131-144 / 145-157.

933 **Alencherry** Francis, The truth of Holy Scripture, according to Vatican II and in Catholic theology, 1965-92: diss. Pontifical Gregorian Univ. – R 1994. xvi-324 p.; bibliog. 299-324.

934 *Amiet* Peter, *a*) Notizen eines Altkatholiken zum neuen römischen Katechismus; – *b*) Aspekte des Unglaubens: IkiZ 83 (1993) 33-9 [193-232, *Baumer* Ivo].

935 *a*) *Appleby* R. Scott, Religious fundamentalism as a global phenomenon; – *b*) *Phan* Peter, Might or mystery; the fundamentalist concept of God; – *c*) *McCarthy* John P., Inspiration and trust; narrowing the gap between fundamentalist and higher biblical scholarship; – *d*) *Dinges* William D. [*Schüssler Fiorenza* Francis], Catholic fundamentalism; – *e*) *Gnuse* Robert, Social inspiration; a renewed consideration; – *f*) *Walsh* J.P.M., 'Leave out the poetry'; reflections on the teaching of Scripture: ➤ 9,485, Struggle 1989/93, 3-29 / 81-102 / 123-136 / 255-279 [231-254] / 137-155 / 317-326.

936 *Arens* Eduardo, Roma y la interpretación de la Biblia: Páginas 19,128 (Lima 1994) 64-77.

937 **Bayer** Oswald, Autorität und Kritik. Tü 1991, Mohr. 225 p. – ᴿRTPhil 126 (1994) 390s (M.-A. *Freudiger*).

938 *Beentjes* Panc, Pauselijke Bibelcommissie doet van zich spreken; Collat-VL 24 (1994) 401-9.

939 ᴱ**Beinert** W., 'Katholischer' Fundamentalismus? 1991 ➤ 8,1236: ᴿAtKap 122 (1994) 594-6 (J. *Krokos*, ❷).

939* *Ben Barka* Mokhtar, Le fondamentalisme américain; une approche historico-théologique: MélSR 51 (1994) 401-423; Eng. 424.

940 **Bendroth** Margaret Lamberts, Fundamentalism and gender, 1875 to the present. NHv 1993, Yale Univ. 170 p. $22.50. 0-300-05593-5 [TDig 42,95].

941 *Bonino* Serge-Thomas, Peut-on tout dire, tout croire, tout penser? [*Donneaud* H., du Christ? *La Soujeole* B.-O. de, de l'Église?]: NVFr 69 (1994) 81-91 [14-24 / 25-32].

942 **Briese** Russell J., Foundations of a Lutheran theology of evangelism: RgStT 42. Fra 1994, Lang. xiii-304 p.; bibliog. 299-304. 3-631-46392-0.

943 *Burggraf* David L., The role of higher education in fundamentalism: CalvaryB 9,1 (1993) 13-28.

944 *Byrne* Brendan, A new Vatican document on the Bible. [OssR 28.IV. 1993]: AustralasCR 71 (1994) 325-9.

945 **Carroll** Robert P., Wolf in the sheepfold; the Bible as a problem for Christianity 1991 ➤ 7,966 ... 9,1072: ᴿScotJT 47 (1994) 274s (W. *Moberly*: hard to see any useful purpose).

946 The Catechism of the Catholic Church [➤ 9.1080] ColMn, Liturgical, 803 p. $30; pa. $20. – ᴿChrCent 111 (1994) 1115. 7-9 (Mary C. *Boys*).

947 *a*) *Cimosa* Mario, La Sacra Scrittura nel Catechismo della Chiesa Cattolica; – *b*) *Bergamelli* Ferdinando, L'uso dei Padri nel nuovo Catechismo della Chiesa Cattolica; – *c*) *Gianetto* Ubaldo, Storia della redazione del Catechismo della Chiesa Cattolica: Salesianum 56 (1994) 81-98 / 99-119 / 3-30 [*al.* 31-98 . 209-312].

948 ᴱ**Cohen** Norman J., The fundamentalist phenomenon. GR 1990, Eerdmans. viii-266 p. $15 pa. – ᴿChH 63 (1994) 166-8 (W. J. *Vinz*).

949 *Corbon* Jean, Le Catéchisme de l'Église catholique et ses lectures au Proche-Orient: PrOrChr 42 (1992) 289-312.

949* *Cortes Soriano* Agustín, La teología como supuesto y resultado de la interpretación de la Escritura, en Jaime PÉREZ de Valencia: AnVal 20 (1994) 1-97.

950 *Cothenet* Édouard, L'interprétation de la Bible dans l'Église [Vatican 15.IV.1993]: EsprVie 104 (1994) 121-6.
951 **Cunniggim** Merrimon, Uneasy partners; the college and the Church. Nv 1994, Abingdon. 201 p. $15 [TS 56, 407, T. M. *Landy*].
952 *Cunningham* Lawrence S., Theology for the Church: Church 10,3 (NY 1994) 16-20.
953 *Dayton* Donald W., 'The search for historical evangelicalism'; George MARSDEN's history of Fuller Seminary as a case study: ChrSchR 23,1 ('What is Evangelicalism?' 1993s) 12-33 (-61, responses by Marsden, FULLER D., PINNOCK C., SWEENEY D., CARPENTER J.; Dayton 62-71).
954 *a*) *Dulles* Avery, The interpretation of the Bible in the Church. a theological appraisal; – *b*) *Berg* Werner, *Volk Gottes*, ein biblisches Begriff?: ➤ 95, ᶠPOTTMEYER H., Kirche sein 1994, 29-38 / 13-20.
955 *a*) *Dumestre* Marcel J., Moving beyond fundamentalism; – *b*) *Rohr* Richard, The goal of Christian ministry; – *c*) *Fiand* Barbara, In search of a dancing God: CathW 237 (1994) 219-225 / 204-9 / 226-231.
956 *Fea* John, Understanding the changing facade of twentieth-century American Protestant fundamentalism; toward a historical definition: TrinJ 15 (1994) 181-199.
957 *Fernández* Domiciano, al. Teología y magisterio: EphMar 42 ('Mariologia y magisterio' 1992) 11-45 [-127].
958 [ᴱ*Filippi* Alfio, *Lora* Erminio] Enchiridion Biblicum, documenti della Chiesa sulla Sacra Scrittura, edizione bilingue. ᵀ*Bittasi* Stefano, *Ravaglia Luca*. Bo 1993, Dehoniane. 1296 p. 88-10-20561-8. – ᴿRivB 42 (1994) 483-5 (G. *Ghiberti*).
959 **Fitzmyer** Joseph A., Scripture, the soul of theology. NY 1994, Paulist. viii-128 p. $11. 0-8091-3509-4.
960 *Focant* Camille, L'interprétation de la Bible dans l'Église [Commission Biblique Pontificale (P 1994, Cerf) 129 p.]: RTLv 25 (1994) 348-354.
961 *Fossion* André, Über den rechten Gebrauch des 'Katechismus': TGgw 37 (1994) 162-173 [213-227, *Wess* Paul].
962 *Fox* Helmut, *Pauly* Wolfgang, Glauben lernen heute; der 'Katechismus KK' auf dem Prüfstand. Mü 1994, Ehrenwirt. 372 p. DM 30. 3-431-03348-2 [TLZ 120,488, G. R. *Schmidt*].
963 *Fretheim* T. E., Salvation in the Bible vs. salvation in the Church: WWorld 13/4 (1993) 363-372 [NTAbs 38, p. 238].
964 *a*) *Ghiberti* Giuseppe, Cent'anni di esegesi biblica; – *b*) *Ghidelli* Carlo, La dimensione pastorale dell'insegnamento della S. Scrittura: ➤ 148, Mem. ZEDDA S. Theologica 3 (1994) 35-59 / 61-84.
965 *Grisez* Germain, The ordinary magisterium's infallibility [SULLIVAN F. A.]: TS 55 (1994) 720-732.737s; Sullivan 732-7.
966 ᴱ**Hagen** Kenneth, The Bible in the churches; how various Christians interpret the Scriptures²: Marquette Studies in Theology 4. Milwaukee 1994, Marquette Univ. v-185 p. 0-87462-628-5.
967 *Hart* D. G., Presbyterians and fundamentalism [LONGFIELD B. 1991]: WestTJ 55 (1993) 331-342.
968 *Hebblethwaite* Peter, The Bible in the Church: Tablet 248 (1994) 444s.
969 **Hill** Brennan, *Madges* William, The Catechism; highlights and commentary. Blackburn 1994, Collins Dove. 155 p. – ᴿAustralasCR 71 (1994) 504s (G. *Kelly*).
970 [*Denzinger* H.] **Hünermann** P. Enchiridion³⁷ ... Kompendium der Glaubensbekenntnisse 1991 ➤ 9,15626: ᴿTLZ 118 (1993) 682s (M. *Petzoldt*); TvT 34 (1994) 83 (H. *Häring*).

971 La Interpretació de la Biblia en l'Església (1993) ᴱRaurell Frederic. Barc 1994, Claret. – ᴿQVidCr 174 (1994) 59-65 (D. *Roure*).

972 JEAN-PAUL II, *al.*, ᴱ*Vesco* J.-L. L'interprétation de la Bible dans l'Église. P 1994, Cerf. xxiii-123 p. F 45. 2-204-04997-2 [NTAbs 38, p. 449]. – ᴿÉtudes 380 (1994) 714 (Y. *Simoens*).

973 *Jericó Bermejo* Ignacio, Auctoritas Ecclesiae et auctoritas Scripturae; enseñanza de Bartolomé de CARRANZA (1540-1546): AnVal 19 (1993) 289-309.

974 *Klenicki* Leon, Der Katechismus der katholischen Kirche mit jüdischen Augen gelesen: UnSa 49 (1994) 246-255.

975 ᴱKochanek Hermann, Der verdrängte Freiheit; Fundamentalismus in den Kirchen [Tagung St. Augustin] 1991 ➤ 8,1278; 9,1116: ᴿAtKap 122 (1994) 596s (I. *Bokwa*, ◑ auch über ᴱWERBICK J.); TLZ 119 (1994) 67-69 (U. *Tworuschka*).

976 *Kremer* Jacob, Die Interpretation der Bibel in der Kirche; Marginalien: StiZt 212 (1994) 151-167.

977 **Laghi** Pio, *Gilbert* Maurice, *Vanhoye* Albert, Chiesa e Sacra Scrittura; un secolo di magistero ecclesiastico e studi biblici: SubsBPont 17. R 1994, Pontificio Istituto Biblico. 58 p. 88-7653-604-3.

977* ᴱ**Langan** John P., Catholic universities in Church and society; a dialogue on Ex corde Ecclesiae 1993 ➤ 9,463*: ᴿChrCent 111 (1994) 419-421 (C. E. *Curran*).

978 *Lanne* Emmanuel, La notion ecclésiologique de réception: RTLv 25 (1994) 30-45.

979 *a) La Potterie* Ignace de, The Catechism of the Catholic Church; the section on Sacred Scripture; – *b) Kelly* Francis D., ... its literary form, authority and catechetical implications: ComWsh 21 (1994) 450-460 / 399-408 [385-502, *al.*].

980 *Le Brun* Jacques, Autorité doctrinale, définition et censure dans le catholicisme moderne (notes critiques): RHR 211 (1994) 335-343.

981 *a) Leibrecht* John, The bishop, the university, and 'Ex corde Ecclesiae' ['the relationship should remain informal and dialogic in nature']; – *b) Malone* James, Implementing 'Ex corde Ecclesiae'; the task ahead: Origins 23,35 (Fb. 17, 1994) 605-607s / 608s (-614, responses to proposed ordinances).

982 *Loza Vera* José, La interpretación de la Biblia en la Iglesia: Anamnesis 4,2 (1994) 77-117.

983 **McBride** Alfred, Essentials of the faith; a guide to the Catechism of the Catholic Church. Huntington IN 1994, Our Sunday Visitor. 224 p. $10. 0-87973-740-9 [TDig 42,175].

984 *a) McLoughlin* David, The treasure honse of faith [new Catechism]; – *b) Häring* Bernard, A text to ponder; – *c) Küng* Hans, Yesterday's document: Tablet 248 (1994) 654-7 / 658-600s / 664 [721s *Murray* Robert, The Bible in the Church; 722, *Kelly* Kevin, The spirit and the letter].

985 ᴱ**Marty** Martin E., *Appleby* R. Scott, Fundamentalism 1. observed; 2. and society; reclaiming the science, the family, and education; 3. and state; remaking politics, economies, and militance, 1991-3-3 ➤ 9,1129: ᴿChrSchR 23 (1993s) 98-101 (D. *Jacobsen*); CritRR 6 (1993) 313-6 (M. J. *Toulouse*); PerspRelSt 21 (1994) 153-6 (J. *Fea*); TorJT 10 (1994) 230-8 (D. *Wiebe*).

986 **Marty** Martin E., *Appleby* R. Scott, The glory and the power; the fundamentalist challenge 1992 ➤ 8,1292: ᴿReligion 24 (1994) 92s (I. *Strenski*).

987 *Marucci* Corrado, L'interpretazione della Bibbia nella Chiesa: RasT 35 (1994) 587-594.
988 *Mills* Jonathan, The new Catechism of the Catholic Church; a review dialogue: Crux 30,1 (1994) 33-44.
989 *Muñoz León* Domingo, Una exégesis que llegue hasta la palabra de Dios [documento 1993]: ➤ 33c, DÍAZ MERCHÁN G., StOvet 22 (1994) 267-289.
990 **Murray** Andrew, The new catechism; analysis and commentary. Sydney 1994, Manly Catholic Inst. 105 p. A$12. – ᴿAustralasCR 71 (1994) 502-4 (T. *Kelly*).
991 **Neveu** Bruno, L'erreur et son juge; remarques sur les censures doctrinales à l'époque moderne [... Jansénisme]: Serie Studi 12. N 1993, Bibliopolis. 758 p. – ᴿBLitEc 95 (1994) 345s (J.-C. *Meyer*).
992 *a) Nossol* Alfons, ❷ Le fondamentalisme comme le défi à l'écuménie; – *b) Życiński* Józef, ❷ La genèse du fondamentalisme chrétien; – *c) Bartnik* Czesław, ❷ L'essentiel du fondamentalisme contemporain: AtKap 122 (1994) 506-517 / 467-480 / 419-430.
993 **Örsy** Ladislas, The Church, learning and teaching; Magisterium, assent, dissent, academic freedom 1987 [ch. 2s < TS 48 (1987)] ➤ 4,1346 ... 8,1298: ᴿBijdragen 55 (1994) 95 [A.H.C. van *Eijk*: sound and sensible, but we await his views on further developments: CURRAN, the Cologne declaration, the Vatican instruction(s)].
994 *Olsen* Glenn W., The university as community; community of what?: ComWsh 21 (1994) 344-362.
995 *a) Pagé* Roch, Von der tatsächlich katholischen zur im juridischen Sinn katholischen Universität, ᵀ*Albrecht* A.; – *b) Tracy* David, Die römisch-katholische Identität im Licht der ökumenischen Dialoge, ᵀ*Klenger* Susanne; – *c) Birmelé* A., ... aus der Sicht eines Partners im Dialog, ᵀ*Dehé* Astrid: IZT-Conc 30 (1994) 439-445 / 451-7 / 458-464.
996 *Paximadi* Giorgio, Il documento della Pontificia Commissione Biblica, 'L'interpretazione della Bibbia nella Chiesa': ViPe 77 (1994) 456-466.
997 **Pennock** Michael F., The seeker's catechism; the basics of Catholicism presented in the light of the new Catechism of the Catholic Church. ND 1994, Ave Maria. 132 p. $4. 0-87795-539-4 [TDig 42,182].
998 *Pittau* Giuseppe, L'Università cattolica; la sua missione nei confronti della comunità ecclesiale: ViPe 77 (1994) 642-7.
999 *Pontificia comisión biblica*, La interpretación de la Biblia en la Iglesia: RBibArg 56,1 (1994) 1-64 (entero); 56,3 (1994) 175-8 (A. J. *Levoratti*); 179-182, extracto de JUAN PABLO II, 23.IV.1993.
1000 *Potočnik* Vinko, University as coexistence of science and faith: BogVest 53 (1993) 3-9 Slovene; Eng. 9.
1001 *Prins* J.M.G., Ou-Testamentiese Riglyne vir die Kategese [against outdated 'cognitive' approach in Church catechesis]: Acta Theologica 13 (Bloemfontein 1993) 1-17 [< OTAbs 17,479].
1002 *Putney* Michael, [*al.*], The Catechism of the Catholic Church in the Australian context: AustralasCR: 71 (1994) 387-399 [-464 *al.*, one on Mary, none on Scripture].
1003 *a) Quay* Paul M., Towards a Christian understanding of academic freedom; – *b) Jaki* Stanley L., Liberalism and theology: Faith & R 20 (1994). 369-402 / 347-368.
1004 [*Ratzinger* J. document summarized] The Catholic Church and Bible interpretation; major Catholic report endorses modern critical scholarship, condemns fundamentalist biblical interpretation: BR 10,4 (1994) 32-35.

1005 *a)* **Ratzinger** Joseph, *Schönborn* Christoph, Introduction to the Catechism of the Catholic Church; – *b)* Companion to ... compendium of texts referred to in [it]. SF 1994, Ignatius. 97 p.; $10 / 975 p.; $40. 0-89870-485-5; -50-2 [TDig 42,62].

1006 *Ratzinger* Joseph, Evangelisierung, Katechese und Katechismus: TGL 84 (1994) 273-288.

1006* **Refoulé** F., *Dreyfus* F., Quale esegesi oggi nella Chiesa? Sussidi Biblici 38s, 1992 ⮞ 8,1670*: ᴿParVi 39,2 (1994) 60s (G. *Castello*).

1007 **Riesebrodt** Martin, Fundamentalismus als patriarchalische Protest-bewegung 1990 ⮞ 7,1168 ... 9,1153: ᴿTLZ 119 (1994) 941-4 (Annette *Weidhas*).

1007* *Rodríguez Carmona* Antonio, Cómo leer la Biblia; un nuevo documento...: Proyección 41 (1994) 219-226.

1008 ᵀ**Romaniuk** Kazimierz, Interpretacja Pisma Świętego w Kościele [i] przemówienie Jana Pawła II. Poznań 1994, Pallottinum. 117 p.

1009 *Ruppert* Lothar, Neue Impulse aus Rom [Die Interpretation der Bibel in der Kirche]: BiKi 49 (1994) 202-213 [181-201].

1010 *Seckler* Max, 'Lehrer des Christentums im Namen der Kirche' (J. S. DREY); Über das Wesen, die Aufgabe und die Stellung der Theologie in der Kirche sowie über einige Aspekte des Dissensproblems: TüTQ 174 (1994) 1-16.

1011 *Segundo* Juan Luis, The liberation of dogma, ᵀ*Berryman* P. 1992 ⮞ 8, 1312; 9,1158: ᴿJRel 74 (1994) 103s (R. *Haight*).

1012 ᴱ**Seybold** Michael, [ᶠLEHKOWICZ Nikolaus], Katholische Universität, Wesen und Aufgabe: Extemporalia 11. Eichstätt 1993, Franz-Sales. 183 p. DM 24. 3-7721-0144-5. – ᴿForKT 10 (1994) 145s (J. *Listl*).

1014 *Sloyan* Gerard S., A theological and pastoral critique of the Catechism of the Catholic Church: ⮞ 120, ᶠSLOYAN, Horizons 21 (1994) 159-171.

1015 *Stravinskas* Peter, The place of Mary in classical fundamentalism, Faith & R 20 (1994) 3-35.121-147.

1016 *Tábet* Miguel Angel, *a)* La Sacra Scrittura nel Catechismo della Chiesa Cattolica; – *b)* L'interpretazione della Bibbia nella Chiesa ... Pont. Comm. Biblica: AnnTh 7 (1993) 3-46 / 8 (1994) 23-68.

1017 *Vanhoye* Albert, *a)* Dopo la Divino afflante Spiritu; progressi e problemi dell'esegesi cattolica: ⮞ 251*, Chiesa e SScr 1994, 35-51; – *b)* L'interpretazione della Bibbia nella Chiesa; riflessione circa un documento della Commissione Biblica: CC 145 (1994,3) 3-15.

1018 *Veliath* Dominic, Youth and fundamentalism: Kristu Jyoti 10,1 (Bangalore 1994) 17-29.

1019 *Villiers* P.G.R. de, The Bible and the struggle (for power): Scriptura 45 (1993) 1-28 [< NTAbs 38, p. 165].

1020 *Virgoulay* René, Un texte á références; Écriture et Concile dans le Catéchisme: LumièreV 43,216 (1994) 47-59.

1021 *Vischer* Lukas, Zum neuen 'Katechismus der katholischen Kirche': EvT 54 (1994) 375-380.

1022 ᴱ**Walsh** Michael J., Commentary on the Catechism of the Catholic Church [by 25 theologians]. ColMn 1994, Liturgical. 440 p. $35 pa. [RelStR 21,317, J. J. *Buckley*].

1023 **Watson** Francis, Text, church and world; biblical interpretation in theological perspective. E 1994, Clark. viii-366 p. £25. 0-567-09700-5. – ᴿTBR 7,3 (1994s) 13s (S. *Plant*).

1024 *Westerman* Pauline C., The modernity of fundamentalism [MARTY-APPLEBY 1991 take it in the widest possible sense]: JRel 74 (1994) 77-85.

1025 *Westphal* Merold, Saving Sola Scriptura from [R.] REHM and the rationalists: Persp [Ref, 7/12, 12-17 'The book that binds us'] 8,2 (1993) 10s.

1026 *Wrenn* Michael J., *Whitehead* Kenneth D., An ugly reception for the Catechism; even before the English translation appears, a prominent group of theologians assembles to subvert its purposes: [E*Walsh* Michael, + 25 theologians' commentary on the cathechism] CWRep 4,4 (1994) 24-33.

B3.2 *Homiletica* – The Bible in preaching.

1027 **Achtemeier** Elizabeth, Nature, God and pulpit 1992 ➤ 8,1334; 9,1176: RInterpretation 48 (1994) 298-300 (P. H. *Biddle*); TorJT 10 (1994) 286 (Karen *Hamilton*).

1028 E**Bailey** Raymond, Hermeneutics for preaching; approaches to contemporary interpretations of Scripture. Nv 1992, Broadman. 223 p. 0-8054-1016-3. – RAndrUnSem 32 (1994) 253s (D. *Nelson*); ConcordJ 20 (1994) 208-211 (F. C. *Rossow*: praise); PrincSemB 15 (1994) 230s (R. A. *Rhem*); RBibArg 56 (1994) 153-5 (A. *Ricciardi*); RExp 91 (1994) 263s (T. G. *Long*).

1029 **Baron** John, Speaking the word; a historical inquiry into the nature of hieratic function: diss. Drew, D*Pain* J. Madison NJ 1994. – RelStR 21,256.

Ben Barka Mokhtar, Quand la prédication évangélique envahit la télévision américaine: MélSR 51 (1994) 253-276; Eng. 277. ➤ 939*.

1030 **Brueggemann** Walter, Finally comes the poet 1989 ➤ 6,1454 ... 9,1179: RCritRR 5 (1992) 83-85 (M. *Ragness*: for preachers; insightful but it should add a real sermon or two); Month 255 (1994) 147s (M. *Kirwan*).

1031 **Buttrick** David, A captive voice; the liberation of preaching. LVL 1994, W-Knox. xii-164 p. $13. 0-664-35540-X [TDig 42,58].

Cunningham David S., Faithful persuasion 1991 ➤ 7104.

1032 *a*) *Cameron* Charles M., Karl BARTH, the preacher; – *b*) *Rees* Frank D., The need and promise of Christian preaching: EvQ 66 (1994) 99-106 / 107-121.

1033 *Coogan* Michael B., The great gulf between scholars and the pew: BR 10,3 (1994) 44-48.55.

1035 *deSilva* David A., 'The feast in the text'; Lancelot ANDREWES on the task and art of preaching: AnglTR 76 (1994) 9-26.

1036 **Engemann** Wilfried, Semiotische Homiletik; Prämissen – Analysen – Konsequenzen: TLInf 5. Tü 1993, Francke. xviii-244 p. DM 78. – RTZBas 50 (1994) 184s (J. *Knobloch*).

1037 **Fischer** Richard, Theories of preaching; selected readings in the homiletical tradition. Durham NC 1987, Labyrinth. xii-368 p. $30; pa. $16. – RTR 90 (1994) 77s (F. *Schumacher*).

1038 **Heintz** Harry J., An integrative approach to preaching [... must always begin with Scripture]: diss. Fuller Theol. Sem. D*Redman* R. Pasadena 1994. 208 p. 95-14053. – DissA 55 (1994s) p. 3881.

1039 **Holtz** Sabine, Theologie und Alltag; Lehre und Leben in den Predigten der Tübinger Theologen 1550-1750: Spätmittelalter und Reformation NR 3. Tü 1993, Mohr. xii-479 p. – RRHE 99 (1994) 192-5 (H. *Storme*).

1039* **Hook** Dan, Effective preaching: how to prepare good homilies today. Newton NSW 1991, Dwyer. 139 p. A$17. – RAustralasCR 70 (1993) 256-8 (J. *Thornhill*, stressing the pastoral with no mention of scriptural).

1040 ^E**Klein** George L., Reclaiming the prophetic mantle; preaching the Old Testament faithfully 1992 ➤ 8,1368: ^RAndrUnSem 32 (1994) 280s (M. G. *Hasel*); TrinJ 15 (1994) 255-9 (D. M. *Howard*: high praise).

1041 *Knellwolf* Ulrich, HAMANNS Frage an die Homiletik: TZBas 50 (1994) 71-75.

1042 *Krieg* Gustav A., Der alte Text — die neue Botschaft; homiletische Theorie und volkskirchliche Wirklichkeit: TLZ 119 (1994) 195-210.

1042* **Lecoy de la Marche** A., Le rire du prédicateur [1888], ^E*Berlioz* J.: Miroir du Moyen Âge. Turnhout 1992, Brepols. 206 p.; ill. – ^RMélSR 51 (1994) 96s (H. *Platelle*: délicieux et extrêmement utile).

1043 **MacArthur** John^J, *al.*, Rediscovering expository preaching. Dallas 1992, Word. 410 p. $22. – ^RPerspRelSt 21 (1994) 81-84 (G. *Greenfield*).

1044 **McKim** Donald K., The Bible in theology and preaching^{2rev}. Nv 1994, Abingdon. 250 p. $13. 0-687-44611-2 [TDig 42,77].

1045 **Moeller** Pamela A., A kinesthetic homiletic; embodying Gospel in preaching 1993 ➤ 9,1206: ^RRefR 48 (1994s) 149s (T. *Barthe*).

Mottu H., *Dettex* P.-A., Le défi homilétique 1993/4 ➤ 375c.

1046 **Olivar** Alexandre, La predicación cristiana antígua: BtHerder 189, 1991 ➤ 7,1227 ... 9,1212: Barc 1991, 998 p. – ^RMaisD 189 (1992) 149-153 (J. *Fontaine*).

1047 The pastor's story file 10 (June 1994) / Parables etc. 14 (June 1994): BtS 151 (1994) 483 (M. T. *Hunn*: both 8-page newsletters, source not given; a third and more elaborate compilation is Quote, monthly, for public speakers in general. Las Cruces NM POB 815; $38 per year or in computer file).

1048 **Romaniuk** Kazimierz, ❷ The Bible better understood in pastoral transmission. Wsz 1994, akces. 151 p. 83-900243-4-9.

1049 *Stahl-Wert*, Wagging the tale of God; the preacher's vocation in story: CGrabel 12 (1994) 203-9 (211-6, *King* Michael A.).

1050 **Stichel** Rainer, Homiletik, Hymnographie und Hagiographie im früh-byzantinischen Palästina: ➤ 58, ^FHUNGER H., Andrias 1994, 389-406.

1051 **Theissen** Gerd, Zeichensprache des Glaubens; Chancen der Predigt heute. Gü 1994, Kaiser. 197 p. 3-579-02068-4 [TLZ 120, 718, J. *Hermelink*].

1052 **Theissen** G. The open door 1991 ➤ 8,1383b; 9,1220: ^RLuthQ 6 (1992) 439s (S. L. *McKinley*).

1053 **Theissen** Gerd, La puerta abierta; variaciones bíblicas para la predicación. S 1993, Sígueme. 260 p. – ^REstAg 29 (1994) 170s (R. A. *Díez*).

1053* **Webb** Joseph M. [revision of MACK Burton L.], Playing the gaps, a worldly theory of [biblical] preaching: diss. Claremont, ^D*Mack*, 1994. 151 p. 94-26482. – DissA 55 (1994s) p. 1271.

1054 *Wilson* Paul S., WESLEY's homiletic; law and gospel for preaching: TorJT 10 (1994) 215-225.

1055 **Windham** Neal, NT Greek for preachers and teachers; five areas of application. Lanham MD 1991, UPA. 264 p. $43.50, pa. $21.50. 0-8191-8325-3; -6-7. – ^REvQ 66 (1994) 70s (Ruth B. *Edwards*).

1056 *Wintzer* Friedrich, Homiletische Literatur: TRu 59 (1994) 410-430.

1057 *Woesthuis* Marianus M., 'Nunc ad historiam revertamur'; history and preaching in HELINAND of Froidmont (Chronicon 1204): SacrEr 34 (1994) 313-333.

B3.3   **Inerrantia, inspiratio** [Revelatio ➤ H1.7].

1058 **Allencherry** Francis, The truth of Holy Scripture according to Vatican II and in Catholic theology, 1965-92: diss. Pont. Univ. Gregoriana, ^D*Wicks* J. Roma 1994. 368 p.; extr. n. 4008, 324 p. – RTLv 26, p. 546.

1059 **Bloesch** Donald G., Holy Scripture, revelation, inspiration and interpretation: Christian foundations 2 (of 7). Carlisle/DG 1994, Paternoster/InterVarsity. 384 p. £20. 0-85364-589-2 [TDig 42,57]. – ᴿRefR 48 (1994) 57 (D. K. *McKim*); TBR 7,1 (1994s) 18 (R. *Hannaford*: evangelical but not uncritically).

1060 *Canale* Fernando L., Revelation and inspiration; the liberal model: Andr-UnSem 32 (1994) 169-195.

1061 *Casanova* José, Protestant fundamentalism — Catholic traditionalism and conservatism [MARTY-APPLEBY]: CathHR 80 (1994) 102-110.

1062 **Countryman** Larry W., Biblical authority or biblical tyranny? Scripture and the Christian pilgrimage^{2rev} [¹c. 1983]. Ph 1994, Trinity. xi-125 p. $12. 1-56338-085-4 [NTAbs 38, p. 446].

1063 **De Souza** Walter, The evangelical identity and the inerrancy of the Bible; an inquiry: diss. ᴰ*Létourneau* L. Montréal 1994. 320 p. – RTLv 26, p. 563.

1064 **Gabel** Helmut, [kath.] Inspirationsverständnis im Wandel 1991 ➤ 8,1401; 9,1231: ᴿBiKi 49 (1994) 71 (C. *Dohmen*).

1065 **Hodges** Louis I., Evangelical definitions of inspiration; critiques and a suggested definition [God's word written by Spirit concurrence with human thought processes 'complete' and 'infallible' in the original manuscripts]: JEvTS 37 (1994) 99-114.

1066 **Lohfink** Norbert, The inerrancy of Scripture and other essays 1992 ➤ 8,274: ᴿPerspRelSt 21 (1994) 169-173 (D. S. *Mynatt*).

1067 **Karpp** Heinrich, Schrift, Geist und Wort Gottes; Geltung und Wirkung der Bibel in der Geschichte der Kirche 1992 ➤ 9,1235: – ᴿTPhil 69 (1994) 271-3 (H. J. *Sieben*).

1068 **Ord** D. R., *Coote* R. B., Is the Bible true? Understanding the Bible today. Mkn 1994, Orbis. xii-132 p. $10. 0-88344-948-X [NTAbs 38, p. 452].

1069 *Purcell* Michael, The absent author; Maurice BLANCHOT and inspiration: HeythJ 35 (1994) 249-267.

1070 *Tábet* Miguel Ángel, Ispirazione, condiscendenza divina ed incarnazione nella teologia di questo secolo: AnnTh 8 (1994) 235-283.

1071 **Wenz** Armin, Das Wort Gottes, Gericht und Rettung; Untersuchungen zur Autorität der Heiligen Schrift in Bekenntnis und Lehre der Kirche: Diss. ᴰ*Slenczka* R., Erlangen-N 1994. 316 p. – RTLv 26, p. 563; TR 91,94.

B3.4 Traditio.

1072 *Achtemeier* P. Mark, The truth of tradition; critical realism in the thought of Alasdair MACINTYRE and T. F. TORRANCE: ScotJT 47 (1994) 355-374.

1073 **Boeglin** Jean-Georges, La question de la tradition dans la théologie catholique contemporaine: diss. cath. ᴰ*Winling* R. Strasbourg 1994. 834 p. – RTLv 26, p. 546.

1074 *a) Charlesworth* Max, Tradition and the foundations of knowledge; – *b) Ibbett* John, The role of tradition in GADAMER's philosophical hermeneutics; – *c) Koch* Peter, Tradition and the individual talent: ➤ 354, Prudentia supp. 1990/4, 1-16 / 38-50 / 275-288.

1075 *a) Coffey* David, CONGAR's Tradition and traditions, thirty years on; – *b) Hill* John, The Catholic tradition; some questions; – *c) Minns* D. P., The appeal to tradition and IRENAEUS of Lyons: ➤ 354, Tradition 1990 = Prudentia supp. 1994, 51-59 / 60-65 / 79-90.

1076 *Longobardo* Luigi, Tradizione e novità del cristianesimo; attualità del pensiero di VINCENZO di Lérins: Asprenas 41 (1994) 5-24.
1077 **Portier** William L., Tradition and incarnation; foundations of Christian theology. NY 1994, Paulist. ix-380 p. $15. 0-8091-3467-5. – ᴿTBR 7,2 (1994s) 24s (S.W. *Need*: Catholic, for college; clear, useful).
1078 **Schori** Kurt, Das Problem der Tradition 1992, ➤ 8,1421; 9,1255: ᴿScripTPamp 26 (1994) 848s (C. *Izquierdo*).

B3.5   Canon.

1079 *Albert* Micheline, Les 'Bet Mawtbé' [Jos-Rois, Job-Ct-Prov-Qoh-Sir] nestoriens; ➤ 415, 155-168 [169-176 Mcb éthiop., *Beylot* R.].
1080 *Artola* A.M., El canon antes del canon; los componentes conceptuales del canon bíblico: ➤ 22, ᶠCASCIARO J.M., Biblia 1994, 39-52.
1081 **Blanchard** Yves-Marie, Aux sources du canon ... IRÉNÉE 1993 ➤ 9,1259: ᴿCarthaginensia 10 (1994) 185 (R. *Sanz Valdivieso*); RBén 104 (1994) 436s (F.-M. *Bogaert*); RÉAug 40 (1994) 216-8 (B. *Pouderon*); RTLv 25 (1994) 237 (A. de *Halleux*†).
1082 **Dohmen** C., **Oeming** M., Biblischer Kanon ...: QDisp 137, 1992 ➤ 8, 1427: 9,1261: ᴿCBQ 56 (1994) 757s (B.C. *Ollenburger*).
1083 *Farmer* William R., The role of Isaiah in the development of the Christian canon: ➤ 102, Mem. RICHARDSON H., Uncovering ancient stones, 1994, 217-222.
1084 **Hahneman** Geoffrey M., The Muratorian fragment and the development of the canon 1992 ➤ 8,1428; 9,1265: ᴿBR 10,1 (1994) 12s (R.J. *Miller*); CBQ 56 (1994) 594s (M.W. *Holmes*); NT 36 (1994) 297-9 (J.K. *Elliott*); ScotJT 47 (1994) 418s (L.R. *Wickham*); WestTJ 56 (1994) 437s (C.E. *Hill*).
1085 *Haran* Menahem, Archives, libraries, and the order of the biblical books [our earliest evidence is bBaba Batra 14*b*]: ➤ 85, ᶠMUFFS Y., JANES 22 (1993) 51-61; 1 fig.
1086 *Lühr* Winrich A., Kanonsgeschichtliche Beobachtungen zum Verhältnis von mündlicher und schriftlicher Tradition im zweiten Jahrhundert: ZNW 85 (1994) 234-258.
1087 **Metzger** Bruce, Der Kanon des Neuen Testaments; Entstehung, Entwicklung, Bedeutung [1987 ➤ 3,1456; 9,1268]. ᵀ*Röttgers* Hans M. Dü 1994, Patmos. 304 p. DM 50 [TR 91,463-5, T. *Söding*].
1088 **Miller** John W., The origins of the Bible; rethinking canon history: Theological Inquiries. NY 1994, Paulist. vi-250 p. $19. 0-8091-3522-1.
1089 *Müller* Mogens, The Septuagint as the Bible of the NT Church; some reflections: ScandJOT 7 (1993) 194-207.
1090 ᴱ**Pannenberg** W., *Schneider* T., Verbindliches Zeugnis, 1. Kanon-Schrift-Tradition 1992 ➤ 8,1435; 9,1269: ᴿTLZ 119 (1993) 456-461 (A. von *Scheliha*); TPhil 69 (1994) 570s (H. *Engel*).
1091 **Rendtorff** Rolf, Kanon und Theologie 1991 ➤ 9,1272: ᴿBiKi 49 (1994) 120s (F.J. *Stendebach*, auch über DOHMEN-OEMING 1992); NewTR 7,3 (1994) 81-83 (L.J. *Hoppe*).
1092 **Sanders** James A., Canon and community; a guide to canonical criticism: Studies in Biblical Scholarship OT. Mp 1984, Fortress. xviii-78 p. 0-8006-0468-7.
1093 *Smelik* K.A.D., Text, Kanon und Tradition; einige methodische Überlegungen: AmstCah 11 (1992) 78-83 [< OTAbs 17, p. 12].
1094 ᴱ**Tardieu** Michel, La formation des canons scripturaires 1987/93 ➤ 9, 415: ᴿOrChrPer 60 (1994) 271-4 (P. *Luisier*).

1095 *Trevijano Etcheverría* R., La obra de PAPIAS y sus noticias sobre Mc y Mt: Salmanticensis 41 (1994) 181-212; Eng. 212.

1096 **Vasholz** R. I., The OT canon in the OT church 1990 ➤ 6,1573 ... 9,1278: ᴿConcordJ 20 (1994) 84-86 (H. D. *Hummel*: praise).

1097 ᴱ**Younger** K. L., *al.* Biblical Canon 1990/1 ➤ 7,334*: ᴿJAOS 114 (1994) 136 (B. *Halpern*).

1098 *Ziegenaus* Anton, Der Schriftkanon im ökumenischen Dialog: ForKT 10 (1994) 197-210.

B4 *Interpretatio humanistica* .1 **The Bible and man; health, toil. age.**

1099 *Alkire* Sabina *al.*, Biblical attitudes to work [rather anonymous section of a prize essay on this unemployment; disaster or opportunity?]: TLond 97 (1994) 403-7 [402-413].

1099* **Applebaum** Herbert, The concept of work; ancient, medieval, and modern: Anthropology of Work. Albany 1992, SUNY. xiii-645 p. $74.50; pa. $24.50. – ᴿAmHR 99 (1994) 186s (Joan *Campbell*).

1100 ᴱ**Bauer** Dieter, *Meissner* Angelika, Männer weinen heimlich; Geschichten aus dem AT: Tb 17. Stu 1993, KBW. 159 p. DM 16,80 [BiKi 49,76].

1100* **Carson** D. A., How long, O Lord? Reflections on suffering and evil. GR 1990. Baker. 275 p. $14 pa. – ᴿJEvTS 37 (1994) 450s (J. B. *Modica*: appendix on AIDS claims disturbingly and without documentation that 67 % come from *either* pimp-or-no father families *or* 'battle-ax' mother; 30 % from brutal father; the 3 % seduced, often by a male relative).

1101 *a) Chmielewski* Philip J., The changing world of work; challenging body and soul; – *b) Dreyer* Elizabeth A., Toward a spirituality of work: CathW 237 (1994) 176-183 / 156-167.

1102 **Doty** William G., Myths of masculinity. NY 1993, Crossroad. vii-225 p. $24 [RelStR 21,36. *Sun Chael*].

1103 *Jordan* Timothy R., Separation [i.e. personal decision on one's companions or course of action]: optional or essential?: CalvaryB 9,1 (1993) 1-12. [29-51, *McLachlan* Douglas R.].

1104 *Kern* Udo, '... dass ein Mensch fröhlich sei in seiner Arbeit' (Prediger 3,22); theologische Überlegungen zur Arbeit: TLZ 119 (1994) 209-222.

1105 *Köhler* Josef, Einsamkeit und gelingendes Leben; Studien zur Erscheinungsformen von Einsamkeit im AT und ihre Relevanz für Spiritualität und Ethik: kath. Diss. ᴱ*Fraling*. Würzburg 1992s. – TR 90,90.

1106 *Kolden* Marc, Work and meaning, some theological reflections: Interpretation 48 (1994) 262-271.

1107 **Kuschel** Karl-Josef, *a)* Lachen; Gottes und der Menschen Kunst. FrB 1994, Herder. 232 p. DM 36. – *b)* Laughter; a theological essay, ᵀ*Bowden* John. NY 1994, Continuum. xxi-150 p. $18. 0-8264-0660-2 [TDig 42 173]. – ᴿTR 90 (1994) 506-8 (G. *Kranz*).

1108 **Kushner** Harold S., ❸ Kiedy złe rzeczy zdarzają się dobrym ludziom, ᵀ*Koraszewska* Małgorzata. Wsz 1993, Werbistów. – ᴿRuBi 47 (1994) 64s (S. *Grzybek*).

1109 *a) Niemand* Christoph, Nationalismus in der Bibel?: – *b) Palaver* Wolfgang, Die religiöse Dimension des Nationalismus: TPQ 142 (1994) 263-275 / 225-233 (-262, *al.*).

1110 *Oates* Wayne E., A biblical perspective on [drug-] addiction: RExp 9 (1994) 71-76 [*al.* 5-69; 77-81, *Smith* Michael A., Psalms 42 and 130, Hope for the hopeless].

1111 [*Paluch*] *Staszkiel* Krystyna, ❷ The Bible in contemporary Polish art; Gdańsk, Muzeum Narodowe 22.v-30.IX.1994: PrzPow 878 (1994) 112-4.
1112 *Stordalen* Ter, Man, life and death in the Old Testament: TsTKi 65 (1994) 203-211 in Norwegian.
1113 *Suess* Paulo, Über die Unfähigkeit der Einen, sich der Andern zu erinnern I-II: Orientierung 58 (1994) 233-6, 245-9 [in ᶠPEUKERT H. 1995 zu erscheinen).
1114 *Warzecha* Julian, ❷ Les problèmes de la vie humaine dans la Bible; les aspects anthropologiques et éthiques: AtKap 123 (1994) 47-57.

B4.2 *Femina, familia;* Woman in the Bible [➤ H8.8s].

1115 **Archer** Leonie J., Her price is beyond rubies: jOsu 60, ᴰ1990 ➤ 6,1590 ... 9,1305: ᴿBZ 38 (1994) 119-122 (Christa *Schäfer-Lichtenberger*); CritRR 5 (1993) 352-4 (Kathleen E. *Corley*: useful but ignores KRAEMER and BROOTEN on Hellenistic Jewish women).
1116 *Aynard* Laure, La Bible au féminin: LDiv 138. 1990 ➤ 7,1311; 8,1466: ᴿBijdragen 55 (1994) 440s (J. van *Ruiten*).
1117 ᴱ**Bach** Alice, The pleasure of her text 1990 ➤ 6,1592 ... 9,1307: ᴿPacifica 7 (1994) 100-2 (Elaine *Wainright*).
1118 *Bach* Alice, Reading allowed; feminist biblical criticism approaching the millennium: CuRB 1 (1993) 191-215.
1119 ᴱ**Bal** Mieke, Anti-Covenant 1989 ➤ 5,625 ... 9,1308: ᴿCurrTM 21 (1994) 135 (H. M. *Niemann*).
1120 **Bal** Mieke, Femmes imaginaires; l'AT au risque d'une narratologie critique 1986 ➤ 2,1066; 3,1482; 90-6194-155-5: ᴿRB 101 (1994) 147-151 (E. *Nodet*).
1121 ᴱ**Baskin** Judith R., Jewish women in historical perspective. Detroit 1991, Wayne State Univ. 330 p. $40; pa. $20. – ᴿCritRR 6 (1993) 547-9 (Judith *Plaskow*).
1122 *Bedini* E., *al.*, Figure femminili nella Sacra Scrittura: Conversazioni bibliche. Bo 1994, Dehoniane. 96 p. 88-10-70944-6.
1123 **Bellis** Alice O., Helpmates, harlots, and heroes; women's stories in the Hebrew Bible. LvL 1994, W.-Knox. ix-281 p. $20. 0-664-25430-6 [OTAbs 17, p.651].
1124 **Bieżuńska-Malowist** I., ❷ Kobiety antyku ... Women of antiquity; talents, ambitions, passions. Wsz 1993, PWN. – 282 p.; zł 34. – ᴿEos 81 (1993) 312-8 (L. *Olzewski*).
1125 **Brenner** Athalya, *Dijk-Hemmes* Fokkelien van, On gendering texts; male and female voices in the Hebrew Bible 1993 ➤ 9,1310: ᴿBL (1994) 81s (R. P. *Carroll*); BO 51 (1994) 631-3 (A. *Verheij*); CBQ 56 (1994) 749s (Kathleen A. *Farmer*); VT 44 (1994) 420-2 (Katharine J. *Dell*).
1126 **Bronner** Leila Leah, From Eve to Esther; rabbinic reconstructions of biblical women: Gender and the Biblical Tradition: LvL 1994, W-Knox. xxiii-214 p. 0-664-25542-8.
1127 **Brown** Cheryl A., No longer be silent [PsPhilo, JosF ...] 1992 ➤ 8,1471; 9,1311: ᴿCritRR 6 (1993) 408-413 (D. T. *Stewart*).
1128 ᴱ**Bührer** Emil (*Sölle D., al.*), Great women of the Bible in art and literature. GR 1994, Eerdmans. 295 p. 0-8028-3769-7.
1129 **Butting** Klara, Die Buchstaben werden sich noch wundern; innerbiblische Kritik als Wegweisung feministischer Hermeneutik. B 1994, Alektor. 208 p. 3-88425-058-2. – ᴿDielB 28 (1992s!) 243-9 (B. J. *Diebner*).

1130 **Coles** Robert. The spiritual life of children. Boston 1990, Houghton Mifflin. xix-358 p. $23 [RelStR 21,86, Kelly *Bulkeley*, also on 8 cognates].
1131 **Cunningham** Elizabeth [Kabbala Lilith]. The wild mother. Station Hill Press 1993. – ᴿCreSp 10 (1994) 60s (Leah *Samuel*).
1132 **Davidman** Lynn, Tradition in a rootless world; women turn to Orthodox Judaism 1991 ➤ 7,a95; 8,10903: ᴿCritRR 6 (1993) 444s (Dianne *Ashton*); JRel 74 (1994) 127 (Laura J. *Praglin*).
1133 ᴱ**Day** Peggy L., Gender and difference in ancient Israel 1989 ➤ 5,391 ... 8,1473: ᴿBijdragen 55 (1994) 76s (J. van *Ruiten*).
1134 **Dennis** Trevor. Sarah laughed; women's voices in the OT. L 1994, SPCK. x-187 p. £10. 0-281-04689-1. – ᴿBL (1994) 85 (H. A. *McKay*); TLond 97 (1994) 380s (J. Cheryl *Exum*: unduly assumes that what the Bible tells about women is woman's voice).
1135 **Exum** J. Cheryl, Fragmented women: jOsu 163, 1993 ➤ 9,1320: ᴿBL (1994) 85s (R. P. *Carroll*); VT 44 (1994) 407-410 (Katharine J. *Dell*).
1136 **Fewell** Danna N., *Gunn* David M., Gender power and promise; the subject of the Bible's first story [Gn through 2 Kgs] 1993 ➤ 9,1322: ᴿTLond 97 (1994) 452 (Grace I. *Emmerson*).
1137 *Fishman* Talya, A kabbalistic perspective on gender-specific commandments on the interplay of symbols and society: AJS 17 (1992) 199-245.
1138 **Gallares** Judette A., Images of faith; spirituality of women in the Old Testament. Mkn 1992, Orbis. vii-225 p. $11. 0-88344-943-9 [OTAbs 17, p. 655].
1139 **Goldenberg** Naomi R., Returning words to flesh; feminism, psychoanalysis, and the resurrection of the body. Boston 1990, Beacon. ix-255 p. $20. – ᴿCritRR 5 (1992) 429-431 (Diane *Jonte-Pace*).
1140 **Grassi** J., Children's liberation; a biblical perspective 1991 ᴿAustralasCR 70 (1993) 123-5 (Laurie *Woods*); CritRR 5 (1992) 89-91 (Elizabeth S. *Malbon*: intriguing, strained).
1141 **Haag** Hebert, *Sölle* Dorothee, *Kirchberger* Joe H., Vrouwen in de bijbel [1993 ➤ 9,1326]ᵀ. Lv 1993, Davidsfonds. 288 p. Fb 2425. – ᴿStreven 61 (1994) 566.
1142 ᴱ**Haas** Peter J., Recovering the role of women ... rabbinic 1992 ➤ 9, 1327: ᴿJSS 39 (1994) 332-4 (Nina L. *Collins*).
1143 *Hafstad* Kjetil, Marriage in theological and Church debate: ST 24 (1994) 150-163.
1144 **Hammer** Margaret L., Giving birth; reclaiming biblical metaphor for pastoral practice. LvL 1994, W-Knox. 226 p. $15 [RelStR 21,110, Kelley *Raab*].
1145 **Hollyday** Joyce, Clothed with the sun; biblical women, social justice, and us. LvL 1994, W-Knox. xiii-241 p. 0-664-25538-8.
1146 **Jeansonne** Sharon P., The women of Genesis 1990 ➤ 6,1612 ... 9,1329: ᴿAJS 17 (1992) 281-4 (M. I. *Gruber*: disturbing inaccuracy).
1147 **Kaufman** Debra R., Rachel's daughters; newly orthodox Jewish women [149 interviewed after interracial marriage]. New Brunswick 1991, Rutgers Univ. xv-243 p. $30; pa. $12. – ᴿCritRR 6 (1993) 560s (Pamela S. *Nadell*).
1148 **LaCocque** André, The feminine unconventional 1990 ➤ 6,1614 ... 9,1332: ᴿScotJT 47 (1994) 537s (Deborah F. *Sawyer*).
1149 **Lacocque** André, Subversives, ou un Pentateuque de femmes, ᵀ*Veugelen* Claude: LDiv 148, 1992 ➤ 8,1493; 9,1333: 191 p. F 135. – ᴿCBQ 56 (1994) 114s (Barbara *Green*).

1150 *Levoratti* Armando J., Lo femenino y la Biblia: RBibArg 55 (1993) 159-182.
1151 **Ljung** Inger, Silence or suppression 1989 ➤ 7,1325 ... 9,1335: RVT 44 (1994) 131s (Katharine J. *Dell*).
1152 **McKenna** Megan, Not counting women and children; neglected stories from the Bible [she calls this 'midrash'] Mkn 1994 Orbis. v-225 p. $11 pa. 0-88344-946-3 [NTAbs 38, p. 451].
1153 **McKenzie** Jennifer J., I will love unloved; a linguistic analysis of woman's biblical importance[2rev]. Lanham MD 1994, UPA. viii-377 p.
1154 *Maltz* M. H., The Jewish view of women; gender-based and gender-biased: J/Tyd Sem 5 (1993) 186-199.
1155 *Matthews* Victor H., Female voices; upholding the honor of the household: BibTB 24 (1994) 8-15.
1156 **Merlini** C. G., Analisi lessico-semantica degli antroponimi femminili in ebraico biblico, diss. Firenze 1992s, DZatelli I. – RivB 42 (1994) 113.
1157 **Noller** Annette, Der Paradigmenwechsel der feministischen Hermeneutik: Diss. DGestrich C. Berlin 1994. – TR 91,93.
1158 **Pardes** Ilana, Countertraditions in the Bible; a feminist approach 1992 ➤ 9,1343: RCritRR 6 (1993) 565-9 (Peggy L. *Day*); PerScCF 46 (1994) 67 (Elizabeth M. *Hairfield*).
1159 **Phipps** William E., Assertive biblical women [Sarah to Junia]: CWomen'sSt 128. Westport 1992, Greenwood. 184 p. $40. 0-313-38498-0. – RInterpretation 48 (1994) 305s (Kristen E. *Kvam*).
1160 **Plaskow** Judith, Standing again at Sinai 1990 ➤ 6,1625...9,1502: RJudaism 41 (1992) 420-3 (Rebecca T. *Alpert*); RelStR 20 (1994) 13-16 (Joanne C. *Brown*) & 16-19 (Laura S. *Levitt*).
1161 EPomeroy Sarah B., Women's history 1991 ➤ 7,405; 9,1344: RPrudentia 25,1 (1993) 76-79 (P. *McKechnie*).
1162 *Prouser* O. Horn, The truth about women and lying [in the Bible, often noted with either praise or blame: but really the gender is incidental]: JStOT 61 (1994) 15-28.
1163 *Pyper* Hugh, Speaking silence; male readers, women's readings and the biblical text: LitTOx 8 (1994) 296-310.
1164 ERosenblatt Marie-Eloise, Where can we find her?; searching for women's identity in the new Church. NY 1991, Paulist. $13. 0-8091-3227-3. – RChrLit 43 (1993s) 99-101 (W. J. *Urbrock*).
1165 *Scalise* Pamela J., 'I have produced a man with the Lord' [Gen 4,1]; God as provider of offspring [and their upbringing] in Old Testament theology: RExp 91 (1994) 577-589.
1166 **Schüssler Fiorenza** Elisabeth, Searching the Scriptures; a feminist introduction I, 1993 ➤ 9,1349: also L 1994, SCM; – 2. A feminist commentary 1994. – ROTAbs 17 (1994) 429 (C. K. *Kelm*); TLond 97 (1994) 451s (Katherine J. *Dell*).
1167 **Soskice** Janet Martin, After Eve; women, theology, and the Christian tradition 1990 ➤ 7,382 (ind. Soskic!). – RHeythJ 34 (1993) 86s (Ann *Jeffers*: T. *Radcliffe* on 1 Cor 11 is stimulating; L. *Archer* on Ex 4,24 more sociological than biblical; P. *Joyce* and R. *Morgan* mainly hermeneutics).
1168 **Tannen** Deborah, Gender and discourse. NY 1994, Oxford-UP. xi-203 p. 0-19-508975-8.
1169 **Toorn** Karel van der, From her cradle to her grave; the role of religion in the life of the Israelite and the Babylonian woman [c. 1987], TDenning-Bolle S.: BibSem 23. Shf 1994, JStOT. 151 p. £12.50. 1-85075-446-2 [OTAbs 17, p. 658]. – RSMSR 60 (1994) 417-9 (P. *Merlo*).

1170 *Vanhoye* Albert, Il bambino nella Sacra Scrittura, in Il bambino è il futuro della società, Atti 8ª Conferenza pontificia, Pastorale per gli Operatori Sanitari, 18-20 nov. 1993 = Dolentium hominum 9 sp. (1994) 38-42.

B4.4 *Exegesis litteraria* – **The Bible itself as literature.**

1172 **Alter** Robert, The world of biblical literature 1992 → 8,1512; 9,1359: ᴿBInterp 1 (1993) 371s (J.F.A. *Sawyer*); JRel 74 (1994) 382-4 (J.S. *Ackerman*); PrPeo 8 (1994) 127 (B. *Robinson*).

1173 *a) Deist* F.E., The Bible as literature; whose literature?; – *b) Heerden* S.W. van, Imagination and the interpretation of the OT: OTEssays 7 (1994) 327-343 / 343-359.

1174 **Fiddes** Paul S., Freedom and limit; a dialogue between literature and Christian doctrine 1991 → 9,1362: ᴿScotJT 47 (1994) 128-130 (Francesca *Murphy*).

1175 *Fisch* Harold, Being possessed by Job: LitTOx 8 (1994) 280-291.

1176 **Frye** Northrop †, The double vision; language and meaning in religion. Toronto 1991, Univ. 124 p. $11 pa. 0-8020-6365-0. – ᴿCritRR 5 (1992) 72-74 (E.V. *McKnight*).

1177 — *a) Hamilton* A.C., Northrop FRYE on the Bible and literature; – *b) Denham* Robert D., The religious base of Northrop Frye's criticism. ChrLit 42 (Seattle Pacific 1991s) 255-276 / 241-254.

1178 **Handelman** Susan A., Fragments of redemption — Jewish thought and literary history in BENJAMIN, SCHOLEM and LEVINAS. Bloomington IN 1991, Univ. Indiana. 0-253-20679-0. – ᴿJAAR 62 (1994) 192-5 (Annette *Aronowicz*).

1179 *a) Handelman* Susan, The 'torah' of criticism and the criticism of Torah; recuperating the pedagogical moment; – *b) Hartman* Geoffrey H., Midrash as law and literature; – *c) Tracy* David, Literary theory and return of the forms for naming and thinking God in theology; – *d) Doniger* Wendy, Speaking in tongues; deceptive stories about sexual deception [Hagar and gnostic *sophia* fleetingly mentioned, but mostly on extrabiblical RgVeda etc.]: JRel 74,3 ('Religion and literature; some new directions' 1994) 356-371 / 338-355 / 302-319 / 320-337.

1180 **Jasper** David, The study of literature and religion 1989 → 7,1343...9, 1365: ᴿCritRR 5 (1992) 74-76 (L.D. *Bouchard*).

1181 *Jasper* D., Living in the reel world; the Bible in films: Modern Believing 35,1 (Leominster 1994) 29-37 [< NTAbs 38, p. 352].

1182 *Jean-Nesmy* Claude † 1994, Les deux faces de 1900: EsprVie 104 (1994) 145-154.

1183 **Jemielity** T., Satire and the Hebrew prophets 1992 → 8,3614: ᴿCBQ 56 (1994) 550s (J.L. *Sullivan*); ChrLit 43 (1993) 97 (D.E. *Ritchie*); Interpretation 48 (1994) 84.86 (G.M. *Landes*); JRel 74 (1994) 90-92 (D. *Jobling*).

1184 **Jens** W., Küng H., Literature and religion 1991 → 8,1520: ᴿChrLit 41 (Seattle 1991s) 71s (D.P. *Slattery*); CritRR 5 (1992) 76-79 (E.J. *Ziolkowski*).

1185 *Marx* Steven, Northrop FRYE's Bible: JAAR 62 (1994) 163-172: he remains the eighth most frequently cited author in the arts and humanities amid Aristotle, Shakespeare, Freud.

1186 **Norton** D., History of the Bible as literature 2, 1993 → 9,1368: ᴿChr-Lit 43 (1993s) 95s (D.J. *McMillan*) JTS 45 (1994) 282-4. 699s (S.

Prickett); RHE 99 (1994) 106s (D. *Bradley*); TLond 97 (1994) 377s (N. *Turner*, 2).
1187 **Scranton** George A., Dramatic comedy and theology; an interactive exploration (biblical poetry); diss. Graduate Theological Union, ᴰ*Empereur* J. Berkeley 1994. 272 p. 94-26255. – DissA 55 (1994s) p. 1144.
1188 ᴱ**Walhout** Clarence, *Ryken* Leland, Contemporary literary theory; a Christian appraisal. GR 1991, Eerdmans. x-304 p. $20 pa. 0-8028-0479-9. – ᴿLitTOx 8 (1994) 119s (A. C. *Thiselton*).
1189 *Walhout* Clarence, The problem of moral criticism in Christian literary theory: ChrSchR 54 (1994) 26-44.
1190 **Wilder** Amos N., The Bible and the literary critic 1992 ➤ 8,1529; 9,1373: ᴿChrLit 41 (1994) 200-2 (W. F. *Gentrup*).

B4.5 **Influxus biblicus in litteraturam profanam**, *generalia*.

1191 ᴱ**Atwan** Robert, *Wieder* Laurance, Chapters into verse; poetry in English inspired by the Bible 1993 ➤ 9,1374: ᴿCommonweal 121,5 (1994) 18.20 (Suzanna *Keen*); PrincSemB 15 (1994) 101s (L. W. *Farris*).
1192 ᴱ**Corn** Alfred, Incarnation; contemporary writers on the NT 1990 ➤ 6,1658: ᴿChrLit 41 (1991s) 204-6 (Faye P. *Whitaker*).
1193 ᴱ**Curzon** David, Modern poems on the Bible; an anthology. Ph/J 1994, Jewish Publication Soc. 377 p. $35. – ᴿBR 10,3 (1994) 12-14 (R. S. *Hendel*, also on ATWAN anthology).
1194 **Forshey** Gerald E., American religions and biblical [film–] spectaculars: Media and Society. Westport OT 1992, Praeger. xii-202 p. $45. – ᴿChH 63 (1994) 488s (Q. J. *Schultze*).
1195 *Hamilton* Christopher T., Poet versus priest; biblical narrative and the balanced portrait in English literature: ChrSchR 23 (1993s) 145-158.
1196 *Hayek* Michel, Jésus en croix dans la poésie arabe contemporaine: RICathP 50 (1994) 15-27.
1197 *a) Hayward* Douglas, Contextualizing the Gospel among the Saxons ... as found in the Heliand; – *b) Lenchak* Timothy, The Bible and intercultural communication: Missiology 22 (1994) 439-453 / 457-468.
1198 *Jasper* David, Interpretations of the Old Testament in modern fiction: *a)* TLond 97 (1994) 276-282; – *b)* ScandJT 7 (1993) 7-16.
1199 ᴱ**Jeffrey** D. L., A dictionary of biblical tradition in English literature 1992 ➤ 8,1541; 9,1380: ᴿAnnTh 8 (1994) 169s (B. *Estrada*); BL (1994) 89 (D. *Clines*: superb); ExpTim 105 (1993s) 15s (F. *Watson*); JTS 45 (1994) 267s (J. *Drury*); Speculum 69 (1994) 1186-8 (L. *Besserman*); Vidyajyoti 58 (1994) 404s (P. *Meagher*).
1200 ᴱ**Jensen** J. I., Old Testament and literature; – *b) Jasper* David, Interpretations of the Old Testament in modern fiction: ScandJOT 7 (1993) 3-6 / 7-16.
1201 ᴱ**Kamińska** Maria, *Malek* Eliza, ❷ Biblia a kultura Europy. Łódź 1992, Univ. 2 vol. – ᴿZeKUL 36 (1993) 103-5 (R. *Rubinkiewicz* ❷) & 106-8 (C. *Deptuła* ❷) & 108-116 (H. *Duda*, ❷, linguistic problems).
1202 *Krämer* Michael, '... da ist noch Brot und dort ist Wein'; die Bibel in der deutschsprachigen Literatur der Gegenwart [*al.* Kunst, Kino, Cartoons ...]: BiKi 48,2 (1993) 100-106 [60-115].
1203 **Kreitzer** Larry J., The Old Testament in fiction and film; on reversing the hermeneutical flow: Biblical Seminar 24. Shf 1994, Academic. 243 p. £12.50. 1-85075-487-X.
1204 **McCone** Kim, Pagan past and Christian present in early Irish literature:

Mg 3. Maynooth 1990, An Sagart. xii-277 p. £24. – ᴿIrTQ 60 (1994) 152-4 (M. *McNamara*).

1205 **Polhemus** Robert M., Erotic faith; being in love from Jane AUSTEN to D. H. LAWRENCE [faith in secular and physical love to bring redemption, as alternative to WORDSWORTH, TENNYSON, ARNOLD]. Ch 1990, Univ. xii-363 p. $30. 0-226-67322-7. – ᴿChrSchR 23 (1993s) 101-3 (Darlene *Erickson*: high praise).

1206 **Ryken** Leland, Realms of gold; the [largely English] classics in Christian perspective. Wheaton IL 1991, Shaw. x-230 p. $15 pa. 0-87788-717-9. – ᴿChrSchR 56 (1994) 82s (D. W. *King*).

1207 **Sabrazin** Bernard, La Bible parodiée; paraphrases et parodies. P 1993, Cerf. 235 p. F 139. 3-204-04711-2. – ᴿÉTRel 69 (1994) 144s (J. *Cottin*: passionnant, style FRYE N., JOSSUA J.-P.).

1208 SCOTT: *Donaldson* Mara E., *Harris* Max, Christian poetics and the ethos of encounter; theological criticism, theologies of culture and the work of Nathan A. Scott. Jr. [Modern literature and the religious frontier 1958; The climate of faith in modern literature 1964; and 15 cognate books in 40 years]: RelStR 20 (1994) 117-9.

1209 ᴱ**Shaw** D.W.D., Dimensions, literary and theological [7 lectures by Mary's College profs, 1991s, on TENNYSON, HARDY, *al.*] 1991, St. Andrew's Univ. 119 p. £6. 0-95161-361-8. – ᴿJStOT 64 (1994) 124 (P. R. *Davies*: high quality).

1210 **Watson** J. B., The Bible in English literature; a review article [JEFFREY D. 1992]: ExpTim 105 (1993s) 15s.

B4.6 *Singuli auctores* – **Bible-influence on individual authors.**

1211 **Arce** José P., The utilization of texts and narratives in the Gospels, the Apocalypse, and the rosary found in three twentieth-century Spanish-American novels [ROA BASTOS A., VARGAS LLOSA M., CARPENTIER A.]: diss. Texas, ᴰ*Lindstrom* Naomi. Austin 1994. 242 p. 94-28447. – DissA 55 (1994s) p. 1573.

1212 **Wood** Ralph C., The comedy of redemption; Christian faith and cosmic vision in four American novelists 1988 ➤ 4,1547 ... 8,1547*: ᴿScotJT 46 (1993) 563s (G. *Jones*).

1213 AMOROS: **Acosta** María Elena, Creation to Apocalypse; renewal in the poetry of Amparo Amoros: diss. Miami, ᴰ*Randolph* D. 203 p. – 94-26862. – DissA 55 (1994s) p. 1271.

1214 BIALIK: **Breslauer** Daniel, The Hebrew poetry of Hayyim Nahman Bialik and a modern Jewish theology. Lewiston NY 1993, Mellen. 182 p. – ᴿCCAR 41,4 (1994) 73-77 (W. *Cutter*).

1215 BUNYAN: ᴱ**Collmer** Robert G., Bunyan in our time. Kent OH 1990, Kent State Univ. viii-243 p. $26. – ᴿChH 63 (1994) 117s (T. L. *Underwood*).

1216 *Parkin-Speer* Diane, John Bunyan's legal ideas and the legal trials in his allegories: BapQ 35 (1993s) 324-331.

1217 **Wakefield** Gordon, Bunyan the Christian. SF 1992, HarperCollins. X-143 p. £18. – ᴿBapQ 35 (1993s) 52 (R. *Pooley*).

1218 BYRON: **Hirst** Wolf Z., Byron, the Bible, and religion 1982 ➤ 9,1395: ᴿRLitND 25,3 (1993) 105s (D. *Hoolsema*).

1219 CHAUCER: *East* W. G., 'Goddes pryvetee' [Chaucer shows interest not only in all other aspects of Christian teaching, but also in mysticism, 2 Cor 12,1-4]: DowR 112 (1994) 164-9.

1220 **Hadden** Barney C., Social limitations on Chaucer's knowledge of Scripture; quoting and cribbing from the Bible in 'The Canterbury tales': diss. UCLA 1994, ᴰ*Kelly* Henry A. 369 p. 95-10879. – DissA 55 (1994s) p. 3519.

1221 **Minetti Biscoglio** Frances, The wives of the Canterbury tales and the tradition of the valiant woman of Proverbs 31:10-31, SF 1993, Mellen Research Univ. v-177. – ᴿChrLit 43 (1993s) 107s, (P. T. *Piehler*; informative and stimulating, but no real nexus shown and in tough style).

1222 DANTE: *a*) **Torrens** James, Presenting Dante's 'Paradise'; translation and commentary. Scranton 1993, Univ. 268 p. $43.50; pa. $19. – *b*) **Ferrante** Joan M. Dante's Beatrice; priest of an androgynous God: MedvRenTSt. Binghamton 1992, SUNY. 0-86698-122-5. – ᴿRenLit 43 (1993s) 235-7 (P. S. *Hawkins*) 237s (M. *Vander Weele*).

1223 *a*) *Vander Waele* Michael, Mother and child in Paradiso 27; – *b*) *Franke* William, Dante's hermeneutic rite of passage, Inferno 9: RLitND 26,3 (1994) 1-19 / 26,2 (1994) 1-26.

1224 **Williams** Charles, ᴱ*Hadfield* Alice M., Outlines of romantic theology [Dante, MALORY, DONNE, PATMORE...]. GR 1990, Eerdmans. 113 p. $15. – ᴿJEvTS 37 (1994) 602s (M. *Bauman*).

1225 DONNE: **Frost** Kate G., Holy delight; typology, numerology, and autobiography in Donne's Devotions upon emergent occasions. Princeton 1990, Univ. xvi-178 p. $27.50. – ᴿCritRR 6 (1993) 359-361 (D. R. *Dickson*).

1226 FOGEL: *Alter* Robert, *Kronfeld* Chana, *al.*, David Fogel (1891-1944) and the emergence of Hebrew modernism: Prooftexts 13,1 (1993) 3-13.45-63 (-124, *al.*); 15-30 Fogel, Language and style in our young literature 1931.

1227 HOPKINS: *Allsopp* Michael E., G. M. Hopkins, narrative, and the heart of morality; exposition and critique: IrTQ 60 (1994) 287-307.

1228 KROG: *Robinson* A. S. (Rensia), The creative functioning of biblical imagery in a complex poetic text, Die Jerusalemgangers (1985) by Antjie Krog: Neotestamentica 28 (1994) 413-428.

1230 LANGLAND W.: **Harwood** Britton J., 'Piers Plowman' and the problem of belief. Toronto 1992, Univ. xii-237 p. £39. – ᴿHeythJ 35 (1994) 223s (I. *Johnson*); MedvHum 21 (1994) 187-190, (Kathryn *Kerby-Fulton*); Speculum 69 (1994) 794-6 (C. D. *Benson*).

1231 **Kerby-Fulton** Kathryn, Reformist apocalypticism and Piers Plowman. C 1990, Univ. xii-256 p. £30. – ᴿEngHR 109 (1994) 703-5 (G. *Leff*); LitTOx 8 (1994) 109s (Wendy *Scase*, also on two cognates).

1232 **Kaulbach** Ernest N., Imaginative prophecy in the B-text of 'Piers Plowman'. Woodbridge / Rochester 1993, Boydell & B. v-158 p. – ᴿSpeculum 69 (1992) 1190-3 (M. Teresa *Tavormina*).

1233 LEWIS: C. S.: *Kantra* Robert A., Undenominational satire; CHESTERTON and Lewis revisited: RLitND 24,1 (1992) 33-57.

1234 *Rossow* Francis C., Problems of prayer and their Gospel solutions in four poems by C. S. Lewis: ConcordJ 20 (1994) 106-114.

1235 LEWIS W.: **Schenker** Daniel, Wyndham Lewis, Religion and modernism. 1992, Univ. Alabama. xiv-225 p. $32.50. – ᴿRLitND 26,3 (1994) 99s (J. *Watson*).

1236 MELVILLE: *Yoder* Jonathan A., Melville's snake on the cross; justice for John Claggart: ChrLit 43 (1993s) 131-150.

1237 MERESHKOVSKII: *Davis* Glenn A., Symbol, idol and belief in Dimitri Mereshkovskii's The death of the gods: ChrLit 43 (1993s) 151-166.

1238 MILTON: **Honeygosky** Stephen R., Milton's House of God; the invisible

and visible Church. Columbia 1993, Univ. Missouri. xiv-255 p. $40. –
RChH 63 (1994) 460s (R. L. *Greaves*).
1239 **Rosenblatt** Jason P., Torah and law in 'Paradise Lost'. Princeton 1994,
Univ. x-274 p. $39.50. 0-691-03340-4 [TDig 42,186]. – RTBR 7/3 (1994s)
74 (R. *Coggins*).
1240 **Tanner** John S., Anxiety in Eden; a Kierkegaardian reading of Paradise
Lost. NY 1992, Oxford-UP. xii-209 p. £27.50. – RLitTOx 8 (1994) 330s
(J. S. *Reist*).
1241 O'CONNOR: **Gerald** Kelly Suzanne, The emblematic shoe [biblical
symbolism] in Flannery O'Connor's fiction: diss. S. Alabama 1997,
D*Walker* Sue. 152 p. 13-58492 [DissA-disk] MAI 33 (1994s) p. 344.
1242 SHAKESPEARE: E**Batson** Beatrice, Shakespeare and the Christian
tradition. Lewiston NY 1994, Mellen, xviii-189 p. $80. 0-7734-9425-1. –
RChrLit 43 (1993s) 238s (M. *Hunt*).
1243 E**Battenhouse** Roy, Shakespeare's Christian dimension; an anthology of
commentary. Bloomington 1994, Indiana Univ. xi-520 p. £25. 0-253-
31122-5. – RTBR 7,3 (1994s) 74 (B. L. *Horne*).
1244 WHITE: *a) Giffin* Michael, Between Athens, Jerusalem, and Stonehenge;
the Christian imagination in the novels of Patrick White: ChrLit 43
(1993s) 167-187; – *b*) Between torah, haskalah and kabbalah; the revealed
imagination in the novels of Patrick White: LitTOx 8,1 (1994) 64-79.
1245 WORDSWORTH: *Dabundo* Laura, The voice of the mute; Wordsworth
and the ideology of romantic silence [... Gen 2; Act 2]: ChrLit 43 (1993s)
21-35.

B4.7 *Interpretatio* psychiatrica.

1246 E**Aden** Leroy, *al.*, Christian perspectives on human development;
Psychology & Christianity. GR 1992, Baker. 274 p. $22.50 pa. 0-8010-
0225-7. – RChrSchR 24 (1994s) 238s (Troy M. *Buchanan*).
1247 *Avgustides* Adamantios, ⊕ Church ministry and preventive psychiatry:
TAth 65 (1994) 91-100; Eng. 1019 [209-230, *Theodorou* E. D.].
1248 **Baumgartner** J., *a*) Pastoralpsychologie; Einführung in die Praxis
heilender Seelsorge. Dü 1990, Patmos. – *b*) Psicologia pastorale, Introduzione alla prassi di una pastorale risanatrice, T. R 1993, Borla.
602 p. Lm 80. – RRasT 35 (1994) 621s (Concetta *Pizzuti*).
1249 **Bucher** Anton A., Bibel-Psychologie; psychologische Zugänge zu
biblischen Texten. D1992 → 8,1573*; 9,1422: RPrakT 20 (1993) 312s (ook
over DREWERMANN), TPQ 142 (1994) 103 (J. *Janda*).
1250 **Buggle** Franz, Denn sie wissen nicht, was sie glauben; oder warum man
redlicherweise nicht mehr Christ sein kann. Reinbek 1992, Rowohlt.
404 p. DM 48. – RBiKi 48 (1993) 49s (K. *Kiessling*: provokative klinische
Psychologie).
1250* **Caballero Arencibía** Agustín, Psicoanálisis y Biblia; el psicoanálisis
aplicado a la investigación de textos biblicos: BtSalmEst 161. S 1994,
Univ. 337 p.; bibliog. 27-55. 84-7299-320-5.
1251 **Clarke** J.J., JUNG and Eastern thought; a dialogue with the Orient.
L 1994, Routledge. 217 p. £35; pa. £13. – RMonth 255 (1994) 483s (M.
Barnes).
1252 *De Rosa* Giuseppe, JUNG, la religione e il cristianesimo, I. La psicologia
analitica; II. La visione religiosa: CC 145 (1994,1) 445-458; (1994,2)
129-142.
1253 **Drechsel** Wolfgang, Pastoralpsychologische Bibelarbeit; ein Verste-

hens- und Praxismodell gegenwärtiger Bibel-Erfahrung. Stu 1994, Kohlhammer. 360 p. DM 50. 3-17-012847-7 [TLZ 120,982, W. *Rebell*].

DREWERMANN:
1254 Le cas Drewermann; les documents. P 1993, Cerf. 296 p. F 125. 2-204-
04783. – ᴿÉTRel 68 (1993) 611s (A. *Gaillard*, aussi sur Fonctionnaires).
1255 ᴱCoffele Gianfranco, Colloquio su Eugen Drewermann: Ieri oggi
domani 19. R 1994, LAS(alesianum). 119 p. 88-213-0272-5.
1256 Grelot Pierre, Réponse à Eugen Drewermann: Théologies Apologique.
P 1994, Cerf. 222 p. 2-204-05104-7.
1257 **Lang** Bernhard, Eugen Drewermann, interprète de la Bible: Théologies.
P 1994, Cerf. 172 p. F 118. 2-204-04884-4 [NTAbs 38, p. 450]. –
ᴿÉTRel 69 (1994) 439s (J. *Ansaldi*).
1258 **Marcheselli-Casale** Cesare, Il caso Drewermann 1991 ➤ 7,1405; 8,1601:
ᴿAnStoEseg 11 (1994) 309-311 (G. *Coccolini*); Teresianum 45 (1994) 606s
(A. *Borrell*).
Lüdemann G., Texte und Träume ... Drewermann Mk 1992 ➤ 4772.
1259 *Minde* Hans-Jürgen van der, Eugen Drewermanns theologischer Ansatz
für Exegese, Moraltheologie und Dogmatik; eine Einführung: IkiZ 83
(1993) 162-172.
1260 *a*) *Nauta* R., De tragiek van de zonde; over het beeld van de mens
bij Eugen Drewermann; – *b*) *Meijering* E. P., De bruikbaarheid van
de dieptepsychologie voor de theologie: KerkT 45 (1994) 101-113 /
92-100.
1261 *Neuhaus* Gerd, Dürften die aus Bergen-Belsen Befreiten Gott danken?
Die Theodizeefrage im Werk Eugen Drewermanns: TrierTZ 103 (1994)
113-130.
1262 ᴱPottmeyer Hermann J., Fragen an E. Drewermann; eine Einladung zum
Gespräch: Kath.Akad. Bayern 146. Dü 1992, Patmos. 132 p. DM 19,80.
3-491-77928-6 [TR 91,75: 5 tit. pp.].
1263 **Raguse** H., Psychoanalyse und biblische Interpretation ... Drewermann,
Apokalypse 1993 ➤ 9,1436: ᴿTvT 34 (1994) 441 (P. *Vandermeersch*).
1264 *Rauglaudre* Claude de, *a*) Une lecture féminine de la 'Genèse', à propos
de Drewermann: Études 380 (1994) 389-395; – *b*) Una lectura femenina
del 'Génesis', a propósito de Drewermann: RazF 229 (1994) 309-316.
1264* *Römelt* Josef, [Drewermann] Angst und Freiheit in der Kirche; ein
theologisher Nachruf?: TGgw 37 (1994) 136-143.
1265 **Drewermann** Eugen, Glauben in Freiheit oder Tiefenpsychologie und
Dogmatik, 1. Dogma, Angst und Symbolismus. Solothurn 1993, Walter.
720 p. DM 90. 3-530-16896-3. – ᴿTGL 84 (1994) 384-6 (W. *Beinert*); ZkT
116 (1994) 504-510 (G. *Baudler*).
1266 **Drewermann** Eugen, Les structures du mal [diss. catholique Pd 1977]:
ᴿLumièreV 43,217 (1994) 103-9 (J.-J. *Meisch*).
1267 *Drewermann* Eugen, L'essentiel est invisible; une lecture psychanalytique
du Petit Prince [SAINT-EXUPÉRY]², ᵀBagot Jean-Pierre. P 1992, Cerf.
166 p. F 89. – ᴿRHPR 74 (1994) 100s (Danielle *Fischer*).
1268 **Drewermann** Eugen, Biser Eugen, Welches Credo? ᴱAlbus Michael:
Spektrum 4204. FrB 1993, Herder. 240 p. – ᴿTAth 64 (1993) 852-5 (E. A.
Theodorou).
1269 **Drewermann** E., Worum es eigentlich geht; Protokoll einer Verurteilung
1992 ➤ 8,1605; 9,1423: ᴿTvT 34 (1994) 88s (T. *Schoof*: includes 150 p.,
the 6-hour conference of D. with his bishop J. DEGENHARDT and A.
KLEIN and D. EICHER).

1270 **Sobel** Alfred, Eugen Drewermann Bibliographie. Wsb 1993, Sobel. 100 p. 3-9802928-0-0. – ᴿForKT 10 (1994) 224 (M. *Hauke*).

1271 *Gonneaud* Didier, Entre l'Évangile et le ministère, la psychanalyse?: NRT 116 (1994) 321-339.

1272 **Husser** Jean-Marie, Le songe et la parole; étude sur le rêve et sa fonction dans l'ancien Israël: BZAW 210. B 1994, de Gruyter. xii-302 p.; Bibliog. 273-294. 3-11-013719-4. – ᴿUF 26 (1994) 603 (O. *Loretz*).

1272* — **Morgenthaler** Christoph, Der religiöse Traum; Erfahrung und Deutung. Stu 1992, Kohlhammer. 204 p. DM 35. – ᴿTZBas 50 (1994) 181s (W. *Neidhart*).

1273 *Jobling* David, Transference and tact in biblical studies; a psychological approach to Gerd THEISSEN's Psychological aspects of Pauline theology [... Jobling encourages integration of psychoanalytic reading into 'a genuinely critical approach, as opposed to a pseudo-criticism that does not criticize anything']: SR 22 (1993) 451-462.

1274 **Jones** James W., Contemporary psychoanalysis and religion; transference and transcendence. NHv 1991, Yale Univ. x-144 p. $17. – ᴿCritRR 5 (1992) 431-3 (Brita L. *Gill-Austern*).

1275 **Leiner** Martin, Grundfragen einer textpsychologischen Exegese des Neuen Testaments: Diss. ᴰ*Theissen* G., Heidelberg 1994. 268 p. > Gü, Psychologie und Exegese. – RTLv 26, p. 538.

1276 **Ouaknin** Marc-Alain, Bibliothérapie; lire, c'est guérir: La couleur des idées. P 1994, Seuil. 445 p. – ᴿRTPhil 126 (1994) 402 (J. *Borel*).

1277 **Rice** E., Freud and Moses 1990 ↠ 7,1414; 8,1608: ᴿAJS 17 (1992) 127-9 (S. L. *Gilman*).

1278 — **Yerushalmi** Y. H., Freud's Moses 1991 ↠ 7,1415; 9,1458: ᴿCritRR 5 (1992) 395-7 (L. *Bregman*).

1279 **Saal** Holger, Tiefenpsychologie im Dienste der Theologie? ...: ev. Diss. ᴰ*Fraas* H.-J. München 1994. – TR 91,99.

1280 **Smit** J., *Stroeken* H., Lotgevallen; de Bijbel in psychoanalytisch perspectief. Amst 1993, Boom. 184 p. ƒ34.50. 90-5382-097-X. – ᴿTvT 34 (1994) 440s (S. *Ypma*).

1281 **Sons** Rolf, Seelsorge zwischen Bibel und Psychotherapie: Diss. ᴰ*Seitz* M. Erlangen-N. 1994. 234 p. – RTLv 26, p. 586.

1282 **Sublon** Roland, La lettre ou l'Esprit, lecture psychanalytique de la théologie: Théologies. P 1993, Cerf. 238 p. – ᴿRThom 94 (1994) 329-331 (P. *Lacas*).

1283 **Toinet** Paul † 16.VI.1991, La psychanalyse et le Saint-Esprit: Essais. P 1992, FAC. 316 p. F 198. 2-903-42241-9. – ᴿGregorianum 75 (1994) 771-3 (A. *Querault*); RThom 94 (1994) 663-7 (G. *Narcisse*).

1284 **Topp** Donald M., Interpretation of psychotherapy texts; philosophical, theoretical, and practical considerations in the application of biblical hermeneutic methods: diss. Rutgers, ᴰ*Fishman* D. New Brunswick 1994, 477 p. 95-14282. – DissA 55 (1994s) p. 5579.

1285 **Wolff** Hanna, Vino nuovo in otri vecchi; il problema dell'identità del cristianesimo alla luce della psicologia del profondo. Brescia 1992, Queriniana. 256 p. Lᵐ 28. – ᴿCC 145 (1994,1) 307s (G. *Rossi*: affrettato sulla colpa delle Chiese).

B5 **Methodus exegetica.**

1286 *Beardslee* William A., Poststructuralist criticism: ↠ 9,976, *Haynes* S. 1993, 221-235 [< OTAbs 17, p. 13s, where 16 others of the articles are cited].

1287 **Beller-McKenna** Daniel, Brahms, the Bible, and post-romanticism; cultural issues in Johannes Brahms's later settings of biblical texts, 1877-1896: diss. Harvard. CM 1994. 268 p. 95-00012. – DissA 55 (1994s) p. 2198.

1288 *a) Berger* Klaus, Exegese und systematische Theologie — aus der Sicht eines Exegeten; – *b) Alemany* José J., Gibt es eine problematische Beziehung zwischen Exegese und Dogmatik? ᵀ*Drasen-Segbers* Victoria M.: IZT- Conc 30 (1994) 533-9 / 540-5.

1289 **Berlin** Adele, Poetics and interpretation of biblical narrative. WL 1994, Eisenbrauns. 181 p. bibliog. 159-170.

1290 *a) Beuken* W.A.M., The present state of OT studies in Europe and foreseeable directions for the future; – *b) Deist* F. E., South African OT studies and the future [*al.*]; – *c) Combrink* H.J.B., The future of OT studies through NT eyes; – *d) Gruchy* J. de., ... from the perspective of systematic theology [*al.*]: → 327, ODENDAAL D. mem., OTEssays 7,4 (1994), 25-32 / 33-51 [13-24.52-61] / 269-281 / 282-5 [-313; 32-6].

1291 **Brett** Mark G., Biblical criticism in crisis? ... canonical 1991 → 7,1425*b;* ... 9,1461: ᴿCritRR 5 (1992) 116-9 (D. *Patrick*); ScotJT 47 (1994) 395s (R. P. *Carroll*: excellent, gritty).

1292 **Buckley** Geraldine M., Redemptive and prophetic television; the way to pierce the darkness [based on the communication theories of Jacques ELLUL, Clifford CHRISTIANS, Quentin SCHULTZE]: diss. ᴰ*Quicke* A. Regent, 1994. 167 p. [Diss-A disk] MAI 32 (1994s) p. 1493.

1293 ᴱ**Caquot** A. [*Vesco* J.] – Naissance de la méthode critique 1990/2 → 8,462; 9,1465: ᴿArchivScSocR 39,86 (1994) 298s (J. *Séguy*); CBQ 56 (1994) 405s (L. *Laberge*); Gregorianum 75 (1994) 795 (J. *Galot*); NRT 116 (1994) 95-97 (Y. *Simoens*); Salesianum 56 (1994) 776s (R. *Vicent*).

1294 **Crenshaw** James L., Trembling at the threshold of a biblical text. GR 1994, Eerdmans. viii-167 p. 0-8028-0720-8.

1295 *Dangl* Oskar, Skeptische Exegese: BibNot 75 (1994) 67-81.

1296 ᴱ**Dockery** David S., Foundations for biblical interpretation; a complete library of tools and resources. Nv 1994, Broadman & H. xviii-614 p. $30. 0-8054-1039-2.

1297 *Dohmen* T. (p. 13-74; *Jacob* C. p. 75-130), Neue Formen: QDisp 140, 1992 → 8,495: ᴿFrSZ 41 (1994) 300-3 (H.-J. *Venetz*).

1298 **Exum** J. C., *Clines* D., New LitCrit 1993 → 9,271. – ᴿÉTRel 69 (1994) 568s (D. *Lys*).

1299 *Fabris* Rinaldo, Problemas e perspectivas das Ciências Bíblicas, ᵀ*Gaio* Luiz João. São Paulo 1994, Loyola. 402 p. – ᴿREB 54 (1994) 991s (L. *Garmus*).

1300 ᴱ**Fewell** Danna N., Reading between texts 1992 → 8,351*d:* ᴿAndr-UnSem 32 (1994) 268-270 (Susan E. *Jacobsen*); LitTOx 8 (1994) 220s (S. B. *Plate*).

1301 **Fischer** Rainer, Die Kunst des Bibellesens; theologische Ästhetik am Beispiel des Schriftverständnisses: Diss. ᴰ*Sauter* G. Bonn 1994. – RTLv 26, p. 581.

1302 ᶠFROEHLICH K., Reading the text; biblical criticism and literary theory, ᴱPrickett S. 1991 [the ᶠ1991 → 7,58 has a different title and editor → 838 (852*) supra [< 7,324* ... 9,1491]: ᴿJStOT 63 (1994) 122s (P. R. *Davies*); LitTOx 8 (1994) 105-7 (J. W. *Rogerson*).

1303 **Goldingay** John, Models for [not 'for interpretation of' (1995)] Scripture. GR/Carlisle 1994, Eerdmans/Paternoster. xi-420 p. $20. 0-8028-0146-3.

1304 **Habermas** Jürgen, Textes et contextes; essais de reconnaissance théo-rique: Passages. P 1994, Cerf. 201 p. 2-204-05024-5.

1305 *Hess* E., Practical biblical interpretation [5 steps; 1. engaging our prejudices; starting from where we are]: RelEdn 88 (NHv 1993) 190-210 [< NTAbs 38, p. 336].

1306 ᴱHouse Paul R., Beyond form criticism; essays in OT literary criticism 1992 ➤ 8,357: ᴿCBQ 56 (1994) 402s (J. M. *O'Brien*).

1306* *Howard* David M., Rhetorical criticism in OT studies: BuBRes 4 (1994) 87-104.

1307 *Huizing* Klaas, Die Bibel nachspielen; durch ästhetische Erfahrung wird Christus lebendig: EvKomm 27 (1994) 717-9.

1308 ᴱJong Irene J. F. de, *Sullivan* J. P., Modern critical theory and classical literature: Mnemosyne supp. 130. Leiden 1994, Brill. vii-292 p.; bibliog. 281-8. 90-04-09571-3.

1309 **Kennedy** George A., A new history of classical rhetoric. Princeton 1994, Univ. xi-301 p. $30 [RelStR 21,328, W. M. *Calder*: excellent].

1310 *a) Le Roux* J. H., Historical criticism — the end of the road?; – *b) Krüger* H., The canon critical approach as a means of understanding the OT; – *c) Odendaal* M., A feminist understanding of the OT; – *d) Abrahams* S. P., A black theological perspective on the OT: ➤ 327, ODENDAAL D. mem., OTEssays 7,4 (1991/4) 198-202 / 181-197 / 254-8 / 244-253.

1311 **Levenson** Jon D., The Hebrew Bible ... Jews and Christians [6 reprints] 1993 ➤ 9,1480: ᴿBibTB 24 (1994) 145s (J. F. *Craghan*); BR 10,1 (1994) 13s (J. *Van Seters*: stimulating and provocative); Commonweal 120, 21 (1993) 18-21 (L. T. *Johnson*); PrincSemB 15 (1994) 295 (J.J.M. *Roberts*).

1312 **Linnemann** Eta, Historical criticism of the Bible; methodology or ideology [Wissenschaft 1986] 1993 ᵀ*Yarbrough* R. (1990) ➤ 5,1730 ... 9,1482; 0-8010-5662-4: ᴿConcordTQ 58 (1994) 182-4 (G. J. *Lockwood*: a call to repentance).

1313 ᴱLuz U., Zankapfel Bibel; eine Bibel — viele Zugänge. Z 1992. [➤ 4830, Mk 6,30 *Schellong*].

1314 *a) Lyons* Campbell N. D., From persuasion to subversion; a review of past and current trends in defining rhetoric; – *b) Cornelius* Elena M., The relevance of ancient rhetoric to rhetorical criticism; – *c) Vorster* Johannes M., The epistemic status of rhetoric; – *d) Botha* Pieter J.J., Moral possibility and narrative rhetoric: Neotestamentica 28 (1994) 429-456 / 457-467 / 469-493 / 495-510.

1314* **McGehee** Michael D., God's word expressed in human words; the Bible's literary forms. ColMn 1991, Liturgical. 103 p. $8 pa. – ᴿCritRR 6 (1993) 126s (A.K.M. *Adam*).

1315 *Meyer* Ben F., The relevance of 'horizon' ['horizonal' is not 'horizontal']: DowR 112 (1994) 1-14.

1316 **Meynet** Roland, L'analyse rhétorique 1989 ➤ 5,1642...8,1659: ᴿMél-SR 51 (1994) 331-3 (J.-M. *Breuvart*).

1317 *Meynet* Roland, L'analyse rhétorique; une nouvelle méthode pour comprendre la Bible [< Brotéria]: NRT 116 (1994) 641-657.

1318 *Meynet* Roland, Un nuovo modo per comprendere la Bibbia; l'analisi retorica: CC 145 (1994,3) 121-134.

1319 **Monteleone** Ciro, Stratigrafie esegetiche: Scrinia 5. Bari 1992, Edipuglia. 198 p. – ᴿOrpheus 15 (1994) 240s (F. *Corsaro*: intertestualità).

1320 *Navarro* Mercedes, Tendencias actuales de la exégesis bíblica: SalT 82 (1994) 377-386.

1321 *a) Nel* P., Philosophical presuppositions of a literary approach to the OT; – *b) Coetzee* J., Close reading of the Bible; – *c) Prinsloo* W. S., A comprehensive semiostructural exegetical approach; – *d*) *Oosthuizen* M., The narratological approach as a means of understanding the OT; – *e*) *Dyk* P.J. van, A folkloristic approach; – *f*) *Hunter* J., Literary understandings of the Bible; the deconstructionist approach; – *g*) *Lategan* B.C., Some implications of reception theory for the reading of OT texts: ➤ 327, ODENDAAL D. mem., OTEssays 8,4 (1991/4) 65-71 / 72-77 / 78-83 / 84-91 / 92-98 / 99-104 / 105-112.

1322 *Nisslmüller* Thomas, Rezeptionsästhetik und Bibellese; Wolfgang ISERS Lese-Theorie als Paradigma für die Rezeption biblischer Texte: ev. Diss. ᴰ*Volp* R. Mainz 1994s. – RTLv 26, p. 529.

1323 **Nobel** Hans, Gods gedachten tellen; numeriske structuuranalyse en de elf gedachten Gods in Genesis – 2 Koningen [ᴰ1993 ➤ 9,1487]. Coevorden 1993, auct. xii-298 + 95 pa. – ᴿCBQ 56 (1994) 774-6 (M. E. *Biddle*: inadequate improvement on SCHEDL C., LABUSCHAGNE C.).

1324 *Oden* Thomas C., After-modern evangelical spirituality; toward a neoclassic critique of criticism: ConcordJ 20 (1994) 6-24.

1325 **Patrick** Dale, *Scult* Allen, Rhetoric and biblical interpretation: jOsu 82, 1990 ➤ 6,1736 ... 9,1489: ᴿBijdragen 55 (1994) 79 (J. van *Ruiten*); BZ 38 (1994) 313-5 (J. *Scharbert*).

1326 **Piret** P., L'Écriture et l'Esprit; une lecture théologique sur l'exégèse et les philosophies. Bru 1988, Inst. Ét. Théol. 302 p. – ᴿCiuD 206 (1993) 234s (J. *Gutiérrez*).

1327 **Powell** Mark A., *al.*, The Bible and modern literary criticism 1992 ➤ 8,1666: ᴿInterpretation 48 (1994) 248 (Elizabeth A. *Castelli*).

ᴱ**Prickett** Stephen, Reading the text; biblical criticism and literary theory 1991 ➤ 1302.

1329 **Rang** Jack C., How to read the Bible aloud; oral interpretation of Scripture. NY 1994, Paulist. viii-144 p. 0-8091-3493-4.

1330 *Rendtorff* Rolf, 'Canonical interpretation' — a new approach to biblical texts: ST 48 (1994) 3-14.

1331 *Ruppert* Lothar, Die historisch-kritische Methode der Bibelexegese im deutschen Sprachraum: Vorgeschichte, gegenwärtige Entwicklungen, Tendenzen, Aufbrüche [ineditum] ➤ 222, Studien 1994, 266-307.

1332 *Shapiro* Susan E., Rhetoric as ideology critique; the GADAMER-HABERMAS debate reinvented: JAAR 62 (1994) 123-150.

1333 ᴱ**Sills** Chip, *Jensen* George H., The philosophy of discourse; the rhetorical turn in twentieth-century thought. Portsmouth NH 1992, Boynton/Cook. I. ix-270 p.; II. ix-266 p. 0-86709-286-6.

1334 *Silva* M., O uso e o abuso das linguas bíblicas: VoxScr 4,1 (São Paulo 1994) 37-49 [< NTAbs 38, p. 344].

1334* **Simian-Yofre** Horacio (p. 9-22; 79-137; 171-195), *al.*, Metodologia dell'Antico Testamento. Bo 1994, Dehoniane. 243 p. Lᵐ 32. 88-10-407-25-3 [OTAbs 19,150: *Ska* J.L., 23-38; 139-170; *Pisano* S., 39-137; *Gargano* I., 197-222].

1335 ᴱ**Sternberg** Thomas, Neue Formen der Schriftauslegung? 1992 ➤ 8,495; 9,1502: ᴿBiKi 49 (1994) 218 (F.J. *Stendebach*); TüTQ 174 (1994) 69s (W. *Gross*).

1336 *Tschuggnall* Peter, 'Das Wort ist kein Ding'; eine theologische Einübung in den literaturwissenschaftlichen Begriff der Intertextualität: ZkT 116 (1994) 160-178.

1337 ᴱ**Warner** Martin, The Bible as rhetoric 1990 ➤ 6,561 ... 8,1683: ᴿScotJT 46 (1993) 234s (Hazel *Sherman*).

1338 **Watson** Duane F., *Hauser* Alan J., Rhetorical criticism of the Bible; a comprehensive bibliography with notes on history and method: BInterp series 4. Leiden 1993, Brill. xx-206 p. ƒ110. 90-04-09903-4 [OTAbs 17,434].

1339 ᴱ**Watson** Francis, The open text? New directions in biblical study 1992/3 ➤ 9,418: ᴿJTS 45 (1994) 268s (D. *Jasper*); ScotJT 47 (1994) 421s (Rosalind *Papaphilippopoulos*).

1340 **Weren** Wim, Intertextualiteit en bijbel 1993 ➤ 9,1505; ƒ40: ᴿTvT 34 (1994) 439 (B. van *Iersel*).

1341 *Wolde* Ellen van, *Sanders* José, [1K 3,25.38; Job 42,1-6] Kijken met de ogen van anderen; perspectief in bijbelteksten: TvT 34 (1994) 221-244: Eng. 244s.

1342 ᴱ**Worthington** Ian, Persuasion; great rhetoric in action. L 1994, Routledge. xi-277 p.; bibliog. 264-273. 0-415-08138-6.

III. Critica Textus, Versiones

D1   **Textual Criticism.**

1343 **Agati** Maria Luisa, La minuscola 'bouletée': Littera antiqua 1-2: Littera antiqua 9,1s. Vatican 1992, Scuola di Paleografia. xxxiii-368 p.; vol. of 220 pl. – ᴿOrChrPer 60 (1994) 265-8 (L. *Pierelli*); RÉtByz 52 (1994) 288s (P. *Géhin*).

1344 **Alexander** Jonathan A. G., Medieval illustrators and their methods of work 1992 ➤ 9,1509: ᴿManuscripta (1993) 84; MedvHum 21 (1994) 145 (J. B. *Friedman*). Speculum 69 (1994) 1101-5 (R. *Sharpe*).

1345 **Barthélemy** Dominique, Critique textuelle de l'AT 3, 1992 ➤ 8,1689; 9,1511: ᴿBiblica 75 (1994) 242-5 (H.-D. *Neef*); CBQ 56 (1994) 746s (R. J. *Owens*); JBL 113 (1994) 113 (P. E. *Dion*); RB 101 (1994) 275-287 (G. J. *Norton*); RBBras 10 (1993) 326-8 (C. *Minette de Tillesse*).

1346 **Blanck** Horst, Das Buch in der Antike 1992 ➤ 9,1313: ᴿAntClas 63 (1994) 477s (P. van *Langenhoven*); HZ 259 (1994) 744 (M. *Fuhrmann*).

1347 *Brooks* James A., Bruce Metzger as textual critic: PrincSemB 15 (1994) 156-164.

1348 *a) Cohen-Mushlin* A., The division of labour in the production of a XIIth century manuscript; – *b) Needham* P., Res papirea; sizes and formats of the late medieval book: ➤ 435, Rationalisierung 1990/4, 51-67; 20 fig. / 123-145 [RHE 50, 17*s].

1348* *Friedman* Mordechai A., ❹ The primary dedication of the Torah scroll attributed to Moses BEN ASHER (Ms. Firkowich B 188): Tarbiz 62 (1992s) 133-5; Eng. VIII.

1349 **García Oro** J., El Cardenal CISNEROS 2. Vida y empresas 1993 ➤ 9,1523: ᴿCarthaginensia 10 (1994) 204s (P. *Riquelme Oliva*); RHE 89 (1994) 187-192 (G. M. *Colombás*).

1350 ᴱ**Gistelinck** Frans, *Sabbe* Maurits, Early sixteenth-century printed books (1501-1540) in the library of the Leuven Faculty of Theology: DocLibr 15. Lv 1994, Bt / Peeters. 18 (1994) 373s (L. *Kenis*).

1351 **Grafton** Anthony, Forgers and critics 1990 ➤ 6,1785: ᴿJHistId 52 (1991) 509-518 (J. *Hankins*, also on VEYNE J. 1988).

1352 ᴱ**Günther** Hartmut, *Ludwig* Otto, Schrift und Schriftlichkeit; ein interdisziplinäres Handbuch internationaler Forschung 1/1: Handbücher zur Sprach- und Kommunikationswissenschaft 10/1. B 1994, de Gruyter. xlviii-903 p. 3-11-011129-2.

1353 **Hall** Basil, Humanists and Protestants 1500-1900 [including ineditum 1975 Birbeck Lectures on Complutensian Bible; also an essay on ERASMUS as biblical scholar]. E 1990, Clark. x-380 p. £20. – REngHR 109 (1994) 441 (C.S.L. *Davies*).

1354 EHamesse Jacqueline, Les problèmes posés par l'édition critique des textes anciens et médiévaux: Textes 13. LvN 1992, Univ. Inst. Mdv. xiii-522 p.; 26 fig. – RRBén 104 (1994) 440s (L. *Wankenne*).

1355 EHindman Sandra, Printing the written word; the social history of books 1991 → 8,1711: RSpeculum 69 (1994) 488-500 (G. R. *Keiser*: not 17 but only 8 scribes became printers).

1356 *Johnson* W. A., Macrocollum [PLINY NH 13,80: wide-sheet roll]: ClasPg 89 (1994) 62-64 [< NTAbs 38, p. 341].

1357 FKLIJN A.F.J. [→ 4,85, there spelled Klein; 65th b.] Text and testimony ... NT/apocryphal 1988: RTR 90 (1994) 458-460 (H.C.C. *Cavallin*).

1358 **Layton** Evro, The sixteenth century Greek book in Italy; printers and publishers for the Greek world: Library 16. Venice, Inst.Byz. xxxii-611 p.; bibliog. 553-595.

1359 **Lemaire** J., Introduction à la codicologie 1989 → 5,1675 ... 8,1714: RCiuD 206 (1993) 916 (J. *Gutiérrez*).

1360 **List** Claudia, *Blum* Wilhelm, Buchkunst des Mittelalters; ein illustriertes Handbuch. Stu 1994, Reiser. 160 p. [RHE 90,279, A. *Haquin*).

1361 **Mayr-Harting** Henry, Ottonian book-illustration (1987 Slade Lectures], I. Themes; II. Books. L 1991, H. Miller. 271 p., 118 pl. + 36 colour; 299 p., 142 pl. + 25 colour. £48 each. 0-90520-389-5; -90-9. – RJEH 45 (1994) 465-473 (T. *Reuter*, with 3 other 'pre-Gregorian mentalities'); Speculum 69 (1994) 529-531 (R. *Deshman*).

1362 **Mazal** Otto, The keeper of the manuscripts, with a chapter on restoring the text [Zur Praxis des Handschriftenarbeiters 1987], TWilson Thomas J. (*McNamara* Martin): Bibliologia 11. Turnhout 1992, Brepols. 180 p. – RRÉLat 72 (1994) 239 (J.-P. *Rothschild*).

1363 *Minnen,* Peter van, The century of papyrology: BASP 30 (1993) 5-18.

1364 *Müller* Paul-Gerhard, Bibelhandschriften: → 510, LTK³ 2 (1994) 375-382.

1365 *Netzer* Nancy, Cultural interplay in the viiith century; the Trier Gospels and the making of a scriptorium at Echternach: StPalaeog 3. C 1994, Univ. xvi-258 p.; 10 p. pl. £45 [RHE 89, 196*]. 0-521-41255-2.

1366 *Ognibeni* Bruno, Varianti testuali e cuadri cubisti; ovvero sull'uso delle collezioni di KENNICOTT e DE ROSSI: RivB 42 (1994) 447-457.

1367 **Parkes** M. B., Pause and effect 1992 → 9,1531: RAevum 68 (1994) 477s (Anna Lia *Gaffuri*).

1368 **Richler** Benjamin, Guide to Hebrew manuscript collections. J 1994, Israel Acad. xvi-314 p. 965-208-112-4. – RRÉJ 153 (1994) 433-5 (G. *Nahon*; p. 435s sur le catalogue des microfilms).

1369 *Richler* Benjamin, Hebrew manuscripts, a treasured legacy (*Brody* Robert, Cairo Genizah). J 1990, Ofeq. 166 p. – RRÉJ 153 (1994) 451s (G. *Nahon*).

1370 ERoth E., *Prijs* L., Hebräische Handschriften 1B, Fra 1990 → 6,1837; 9,1538: RHenoch 16 (1994) 136-9 (B. *Chiesa*).

1371 **Rupprecht** Hans A., Kleine Einführung in die Papyruskunde: AltW. Da 1994, Wiss. xii-272 p.; 4 pl. 3-534-04493-2. – RJJurPap 24 (1994) 213s (J. K. *Winnicki*).

1372 **Sed-Rajna** Gabrielle, Les manuscrits hébreux enluminés des bibliothèques de France: Corpus of illuminated manuscripts 7, oriental 3. Lv 1994, Peeters. xxiii-390 p.; 342 fig.; 20 color. pl. 90-6831-602-8. – ᴿRÉJ 153 (1994) 437-9 (E. *Revel-Neher*).

1373 *Soloff* Rav A., Citing chapter and verse [advocates a less-polemical chapter and verse division]: JBQ 20 (1991s) 234-240.

1374 **Zatelli** Ida, La Bibbia a stampa da Gutenberg a Bodoni. F 1991, Bt. Medicea. 224 p.; ill. – ᴿAevum 66 (1992) 713s (E. *Barbieri*).

D2.1   *Biblia hebraica,*   **Hebrew text.**

1375 *Azcárraga* M. Josefa de, Las *'otiyyôt gᵉdôlôt* en las compilaciones masoréticas: Sefarad 54 (1994) 13-29; Eng. 29.

1376 **Beit-Arié** Malachi, The makings of the medieval Hebrew book; [10 1977-91] studies in paleography and codicology 1993 ⇒ 9,182: ᴿSefarad 54 (1994) 415s (Emilia *Fernández Tejero*).

1377 *Breuer* Mordekhai, ⊕ Insoluble problems [*gᵉ'ayot* in Aleppo Codex]: Lešonenu 58 (1994s) 283-296; Eng. 4/I.

1378 **Brotzman** Ellis R., Old Testament textual criticism; a practical introduction ['conservative alternative to E. Tᴏᴠ 1992']. GR 1994, Baker. 208 p. 0-8010-1065-6 [RelStR 21,319, L. J. *Greenspoon*: his Ruth shows the inadequacy].

1379 *Levit-Tawil* Dalia, The elusive, inherited symbolism in the arcade illuminations of the Moses Bᴇɴ Asʜᴇʀ codex (A.D. 894-95): JNES 53 (1994) 157-193; 27 fig.

1380 *Miletto* Gianfranco, Il testo consonantico della tradizione babilonese; Ms. Opp. Add. 4 154 della Biblioteca Bodleiana [< diss. ᴰ*Sacchi* P., mostly just the numbers of the variants from BHS]: Sefarad 54 (1994) 333-360; Eng. español 361.

1381 **Mynatt** Daniel S., The sub loco notes in the Torah of Biblia Hebraica Stuttgartensia ᴰ1992 ⇒ 8,1753]: Diss. 2. Richland Hills 1994, BIBAL. x-278 p. $19. 0-941037-33-9 [TR 91,360].

1382 **Penkower** Jordan S., New evidence for the Pentateuch text in the Aleppo Codex 1992 ⇒ 8,1754: ᴿCBQ 56 (1994) 565-7 (P. *Doron*); RivB 42 (1994) 245s (M. *Perani*).

1383 **Penkower** J. S. ⊕ *Aram-Ṣobah* ... Aleppo codex. RamatGan 1993, Bar-Ilan Univ. 144 p. – ᴿZAW 106 (1994) 365 (J. *Maier*).

1384 **Perani** Mauro, Frammenti ... ebraici a Nonantola 1992 ⇒ 8.1721; 9,1533: ᴿRB 101 (1994) 311s (P. *Garuti*); RSO 68 (1994) 166s (G. *Garhai*); Sefarad 53 (1993) 411s (Emilia *Fernández Tejero*).

1385 ᴱ**Pérez Castro** F., El códice de profetas de El Cairo 8; índice alfabético de sus masoras: TEstCisn 51, 1992 ⇒ 9,1549: ᴿCBQ 56 (1994) 125s (E. *Ben Zvi*).

1386 **Reinhardt** Klaus, *Gonzálvez* Ramón, Catálogo de códices bíblicos de la catedral de Toledo: Monumenta Ecclesiae Toletanae historica 1, regesta 2. M 1991, Fund. Areces. 513 p.; 32 pl. – ᴿSefarad 54 (1994) 429-431 (N. *Fernández Marcos*).

1387 **Richter** W., BHᵗ 1991-3: see under the separate books; here some overviews; ᴿAION 53 (1993) 473 (J. A. *Soggin*, 5-15); BL (1994) 169 (many titles); JSS 39 (1994) 290-5 (E. *Talstra*: positive); OLZ 89 (1994) 560s (R. *Stahl*: dringend empfohlen); RB 101 (1994) 416-421 (F. *Langlamet*); TRu 59 (1994) 456-8 (L. *Perlitt*: 1-16, 7391 p.; DM 870; not

just a costly, ugly, useless transcription but partly premasoretic editing);
ZkT 116 (1994) 85s (J. M. *Oesch*).
1388 **Rickert** Franz, Studien zum Ashburnham Pentateuch: Diss. Bonn 1985.
– ᴿKairos 32s (1990s) 255-260 (K. *Schubert*).
1389 **Römer** Thomas, *Macchi* Jean-Daniel, Guide de la Bible hébraïque; la
critique textuelle dans la Biblia Hebraica Stuttgartensia. Genève 1994,
Labor et Fides. 78 p. Fs 15. 2-8309-0753-1.
1390 [Sᴀssᴏᴏɴ David S., collection] Seventy-six important Hebrew and
Samaritan manuscripts. L 1994, Sotheby's. 135 p.
1391 *Schenker* Adrian, *a*) Der alttestamentliche Text in den vier grossen
Polyglottenbibeln nach dem heutigen Stand der Forschung: TR 90 (1994)
177-186; – *b*) Eine geplante Neusausgabe der hebräischen Bibel: Judaica
50 (1994) 151-5.
1393 ᴱTal Abraham, The Samaritan Pentateuch, MS 6(c) of the Shekhem
Synagogue: TStHeb 8. TA 1994, Univ. ix-220 p.
1395 ᴱTamani Giuliano, I tipografi ebrei a Soncino 1483-1490, convegno
1988/9 ➤ 8,497; 9,1551: ᴿSefarad 53 (1993) 224-6 (Emilia *Fernández
Tejero*).
1396 **Tov** Emanuel, Textual criticism of the Hebrew Bible 1992 ➤ 8,1761;
9,1553: ᴿAJS 18 (1993) 103-5 (L. H. *Schiffman*); Biblica 75 (1994)
413-420 (G. J. *Norton*); BO 51 (1994) 619-622 (E. *Talstra*); BR 9,4 (1993)
11s (E. *Ulrich*); Carthaginensia 10 (1994) 173s (R. *Sanz Valdivieso*); DSD
1 (1994) 259-262 (R. P. *Gordon*); JStJud 25 (1994) 340-7 (R. *Fuller*); JTS
45 (1994) 194-8 (S. C. *Reif*); LvSt 19 (1994) 180s (E. *Eynikel*); NT 36
(1994) 402-4 (J. K. *Elliott*: NT applications); OTEssays 7 (1994) 152-4
(P. J. *Nel*); Salesianum 56 (1994) 577s (R. *Vicent*); WestTJ 56 (1994) 425-8
(Karen H. *Jobes*); ZkT 116 (1994) 86s (J. M. *Oesch*).
1397 **Verheij** Arian J. C., Grammatica digitalis I. The morphological code in
the 'Werkgroep Informatica' computer text of the Hebrew Bible: Ap-
plicatio 11. Amst 1994, VU. 88 p. $20.
1398 *Weisberg* David B., 'Break in the middle of a verse'; some observations
on a Massoretic feature: ➤ 133, ᶠWᴀᴄʜᴏʟᴅᴇʀ B. Z., Pursuing the text
1994, 34-46.
1399 **Zipor** Moshe A., Some notes on the origin of the tradition of the
eighteen *tiqqûnê sôpᵉrîm*: VT 44 (1994) 77-102.

D2.2 Targum.

1400 ᴱ**Beattie** D.R.G., *McNamara* M.G., The Aramaic Bible; targums in
their historical context: jOsu 166. Shf 1994, JStOT. 470 p. £40. 1-
85075-454-3.
1401 **Campbell** Ronald M., A fragment-targum without a purpose? The
raison d'être of ms. Vatican Ebr 440 (Targum V) [only one-sixth of the
verses of the Pentateuch]: diss. Northwestern, ᴰ*Flesher* P. Evanston 1994.
352 p. 94-33806. – DissA 55 (1994s) p. 2345.
1402 ᴱ**Flesher** Paul V. M., Targum studies I, 1992 ➤ 8,1765: ᴿSalesianum 56
(1994) 777s (R. *Vicent*).
1403 *Gordon* R. P., Dialogue and disputation in the Targum to the prophets:
JSS 39 (1994) 7-17.
1404 **Grelot** Pierre, What are the Targums? Selected texts [Les Targoums,
CahÉv 54, 1992], ᵀ*Attanasio* Salvator: OTSt 7, 1992 ➤ 8,1766: ᴿBL
(1994) 46 (P. S. *Alexander*: severe); CritRR 6 (1993) 413s (P.V.M.
Flesher).

1405 *Hayward* Robert, Major aspects of targumic studies 1983-1993; a survey: CuRB 2 (1994) 107-122.

1406 **Kaufman** S. A., *Sokoloff* M. Key-word ... concordance Neofiti 1993 ➤ 9,1558: ᴿJStJud 25 (1994) 99s (A. S. van der *Woude*).

1407 **Klein** Michael L., Targumic manuscripts in the Cambridge Genizah collections 1992 ➤ 8,1769; 9,1559: ᴿCBQ 56 (1994) 110 (H. *Basser*); OTEssays 7 (1994) 106-8 (J. A. *Naudé*).

1408 **Margain** J., Les particules dans le Targum samaritain de Genèse-Exode; jalons pour une histoire de l'araméen samaritain: ÉPHÉ Publ. 29. Genève 1993, Droz. – ᴿHenoch 16 (1994) 353-5 (A. *Mengozzi*).

1409 *Merino Díez* L., Dos reglas de hermenéutica targúmica; traducción de topónimos y otros nombres comunes y nueva identificación: MiscArH 42,2 (Granada 1993) 19-36 [< Judaica 50 (1994) 180].

1410 **Samely** Alexander, The interpretation of speech in the Pentateuch Targums 1992 ➤ 9,1563: ᴿCritRR 6 (1993) 177s (G. A. *Anderson*); JSS 39 (1994) 326s (M. L. *Klein*); Salesianum 56 (1994) 381s (R. *Vicent*).

1411 **Shinan** Avigdor, ⊕ The embroidered targum; the Aggadah in Targum Pseudo-Jonathan of the Pentateuch. J 1992, Magnes. 234 p. – ᴿProof-texts 14 (1994) 88-94 (B. L. *Visotzky*, also on his 1993 *Miqra eḥad wᵉ-targumim harbeh*).

1412 ᴱ**Sperber** Alexander, The Bible in Aramaic (1959-73] ²*Gordon* Robert P. Leiden 1992, Brill. 4 vol. *f* 471. 90-04-09580-2. – ᴿJJS 38 (1993) 173 (J. F. *Healey*).

D3.1   *Textus graecus* – Greek NT.

1414 **Aland** Kurt, Kurzgefasste Liste der griechischen Handschriften des Neuen Testaments²ʳᵉᵛ [¹1963]: ArbNtTf 1. B 1994, de Gruyter. xiv-507 p. 3-11-011986-2. ᴿJian Dao 1 (1994) 121-5 (S. *Wong*, ⊕); TR 90 (1994) 10-20 (J. K. *Elliott*).

1415 *Nestle-Aland*²⁷ [= 26ʳᵉᵛ²] ᴱ**Aland** Barbara & Kurt, Novum Testamentum graece et latine. Stu 1994, Deutsche Bibelgesellschaft. 46*-680 double p.; p. 683-810 appendices; inside-cover maps. 3-438-05401-9. – ᴿTR 90 (1994) 10-20. 19-23 (J. K. *Elliott*).

1416 **Aland** K., K. v. TISCHENDORF 1993 ➤ 9,1465; 3-05-002459-3: ᴿNT 36 (1994) 103 (J. K. *Elliott*).

1417 (*Vaganay* L.), **Amphoux** C.-B., An introduction to NT textual criticism 1991 ➤ 7,1536 ... 9,1583: ᴿEvQ 66 (1994) 67-70 (M. *Bockmuehl*). NT 36 (1994) 287-291 (J. H. *Petzer*).

1418 *Birdsall* J. Neville, A hundred years since WESTCOTT and HORT; where have we got to in the textual criticism of the New Testament?: PrIrB 16 (1993) 7-19.

1419 **Black** D. A., NT textual criticism, a concise guide. GR 1994, Baker. 79 p. $8. 0-8010-1074-8 [NTAbs 38, p. 144].

1420 **Bover** José M., *O'Callaghan* José, Nuevo Testamento trilingüe³ [¹1976; ²1988]. M 1994, BAC. lxiii-1380 p.; map. 84-7014-121-7.

1421 **Comfort** Philip W., The quest for the original text of the NT 1992 ➤ 6,1852 ... 9,1568: ᴿAndrUnSem 32 (1994) 125s (J. *Paulien*); JBL 113 (1994) 529-531 (W. L. *Petersen*: inadequate); NT 36 (1994) 284-7 (J. K. *Elliott*).

1422 **Ehrman** Bart D., The orthodox [Christology] corruption of Scripture ... NT 1993 ➤ 9,1569: ᴿAnglTR 76 (1994) 376-9 (T.S.L. *Michael*); Churchman 108 (1994) 84-86 (G. *Bray*: conjectures compounded); IrTQ

60 (1994) 227s (D. *Brown*: fascinating); JRel 74 (1994) 562-4 (W. L. *Petersen*); JTS 45 (1994) 704-8 (D. C. *Parker*); Neotestamentica 28 (1993) 606s (M. A. *Kroger*); NT 36 (1994) 405s (J. K. *Elliott*); PrincSemB 15 (1994) 110-2 (B. M. *Metzger*); TLond 97 (1994) 460-2 (J. N. *Birdsall*: overstated).

1423 *Ehrman* Bart D., Heracleon and the 'Western' textual tradition: NTS 40 (1994) 161-179.

1424 **Elliott** J. K., Essays and studies in NT textual criticism 1992 ⇒ 8,239: REvQ 66 (1994) 169-174 (Jenny *Heimerdinger*); NT 36 (1994) 202-4 (D. C. *Parker*: 'Keith Elliott's thoroughgoing eclecticism').

1425 *Elliott* J. Keith, The New Testament in Greek; two new editions [1993: UBS⁴, Nestle-ALAND²⁷]: TLZ 119 (1994) 493.

1426 **Epp** E., *Fee* G., Theory & Method StDoc 45, 1993 ⇒ 193: RExpTim 105 (1993s) 250 (J. K. *Elliott*).

1427 **Geer** Thomas C., Family 1739 in Acts: SBL mg 48. Atlanta 1994, Scholars. vii-149 p. 0-7885-0036-8.

1428 **Hirunuma** Toshio, ❶ The papyri bearing the New Testament text I. Osaka 1994, Christian Bookshop. vii-293 p. Contents p. v-vii with title and source of 45 papyri also in English etc. (many with photo). Y 15,450. 4-900800-01-5.

1429 **Hunger** H., *al.*, Katalog der griechischen Handschriften Wien 3/3, W 1992, Hollinek. xxi-573 p. – ROrChrPer 60 (1994) 268s (L. *Pieralli*).

1430 *Lohse* Eduard, Neue Auflagen des Greek NT und des NT graece: ZNW 85 (1994) 290s.

1431 **Metzger** Bruce M., The text of the New Testament; its transmission, corruption and restoration³ʳᵉᵛ. [¹c. 1960]. Ox 1992, UP. x-310 p. £15 pa. – RNT 36 (1994) 97s (J. K. *Elliott*).

1432 **Metzger** Bruce M., A textual commentary on the Greek NT² [United Bible Societies⁴; ¹1975 was on UBA³, reasons for the critical choices]. Stu 1994, Deutsche B-Ges. xvi-16*-696 p. DM 38. 3-438-06010-8. [TLZ 120, 803s, J. K. *Elliott*, Eng.].

1433 **Parker** D. C., Codex Bezae 1992 ⇒ 8,1792; 9, 1576: RBijdragen 55 (1994) 86s (M. *Parmentier*, Eng.); Neotestamentica 28 (1994) 600s (J. H. *Petzer*); ScotJT 47 (1994) 108-110 (C. M. *Martini*, TWickham C.).

1434 **Passoni dell'Acqua** Anna, Il testo del NT; introduzione alla critica testuale. T-Leumann 1994, ElleDiCi. 238 p.; 16 color. pl. – RAegyptus 79 (1994) 206s (Orsolina *Montevecchi*).

1435 *Pickering* Stuart R., *a)* The survival and dating of Codex Bezae; - *b)* A quarter-century of NT textual research: NTUp 1 (1993) 1s / 21-25 (–53).

1436 **Ralston** Timothy J. The majority text and Byzantine [NT] texttype development; the significance of a non-parametric method of data analysis for the exploration of manuscript traditions; diss. Dallas Theol. Sem., DWallace D. 1994. 445 p. 95-01626. - DissA 55 (1994s) p. 2868.

1437 *Wallace* Daniel B., The majority-text theory; history, methods and critique: JEvTS 37 (1994) 185-215.

D3.2　*Versiones graecae* — **VT, Septuaginta etc.**

Aejmelaeus Anneli, On the trail of Septuagint translators 1993 ⇒ 9,176.
1438 EBrooke G., *Lindars* B., Septuagint-Manchester 1990/92 ⇒ 8,459: RBO 51 (1994) 629s (M. J. *Mulder*).

1439 *Chamberlain* Gary A., Method in Septuagint lexicography: ⇒ 102, Mem. RICHARDSON H., Uncovering 1994, 177-191.

1440 *Cook* J., The study of the Septuagint in South Africa: ➤ 327, ODENDAAL D. mem., OTEssays 7,4 (1991/4) 205-213.
1441 **Cousin** Hugues, La Biblia griega; los Setenta 1992 ➤ 8,1803: ᴿRBib-Arg 56 (1994) 124-6 (J. P. *Martín*).
1442 ᴱ**Cox** Claude E., VIIth Septuagint-Cognate Lv 1989/91 ➤ 7,426: ᴿBO 51 (1994) 628s (M. J. *Mulder*). ÉglT 25 (1994) 263-7 (L. *Laberge*, also on BROOKE-LINDARS).
1443 *Epstein* Marcelo, On the 'original' Septuagint: BTrans 45 (1994) 322-9.
1444 **Fernández Marcos** Natalio, Scribes and translators; Septuagint and Old Latin in the book of Kings: VTS 54. Leiden 1994, Brill. x-98 p.; 3 fig. 90-04-10043-1.
1445 *Fernández Sangrador* Jorge J., Papiros cristianos del Antiguo Testamento hallados en Egipto (siglos I y II): ➤ 33, ᶠDÍAZ MERCHÁN G., StOvet 22 (1994) 233-244.
1446 ᴱ**Hengel** Martin, *Schwemer* Anna Maria, Die Septuaginta zwischen Judentum und Christentum [Tü Seminar 1990s]: WUNT 72. Tü 1994, Mohr. xii-325 p. DM 230. – [TR 91, 76 (6 tit. pp.); TLZ 120, 340, E. *Reinmuth*], 3-16-146173-8.
1447 **Lowden** John, The octateuchs; a study in Byzantine manuscript illumination. Ph 1992, Univ. xix-140 p. $49.50. – ᴿRÉByz 52 (1994) 325s (C. *Walter*).
1448 *Mayerson* Philip, Codex Sinaiticus; an historical observation [< BA (1983) 54-56]: ➤ 207, Monks 1994, 212-5.
1449 *a) Müller* Mogens, The Septuagint as the Bible of the NT church; some reflections; – *b) Lemche* Niels Peter, The Old Testament — a Hellenistic book? [The Hebrew Bible came into existence during 193-163, a postexilic, presumably Hellenistic, age]: ScandJOT 7 (1993) 194-207/163-193.
1450 **Muraoka** Takamitsu, The Melbourne symposium on Septuagint lexicography [Aug. 17, 1987] SBLCog 28. Atlanta 1990, Scholars: 136 p. $15. VT 44 (1994) 286 (R. P. *Gordon*).
1451 **Olofson** S., The Septuagint / God is my Rock: ConBib OT 31s, 1990 ➤ 6,1887 ... 9,1592: ᴿScotJT 46 (1993) 572-4 (S. *Brock*); TR 90 (1994) 29-31 (A. *Schenker*).
1453 **Sailhamer** John H., The translational technique of the Greek ... Ps 3-41: 1991 ➤ 7,2787 ... 4,3062: ᴿÉglT 25 (1994) 267-9 (L. *Laberge*).
1454 **Salvesen** Alison, SYMMACHUS in the Pentateuch 1991 ➤ 7,1551 ... 9,1595: ᴿTLZ 119 (1994) 308-310 (A. *Aejmelaeus*).
1455 *Schaper* J.L.W., The unicorn in the messianic imagery of the Greek Bible: JTS 45 (1994) 117-136.
1456 ᶠSOISALON-SOININEN I., [seine] Studien zur Septuaginta-Syntax ᴱ**Aejmelaeus** A., *al.*, 1987 ➤ 3,305: ᴿJSS 39 (1994) 115 (T. *Muraoka*).
1457 **Taylor** Bernard A., The analytical lexicon to the Septuagint; a complete parsing guide. GR 1994, Zondervan. xix-460 p. 0-310-53540-9 [RelStR 21, 320, L. J. *Greenspoon*].
1458 **Veltri** Giuseppe, Eine Tora für den König Talmai — Untersuchungen zum Übersetzungsverständnis in der jüdisch-hellenistischen und rabbinischen Literatur [Diss. B-FU 1990]: TStAJud 41. Tü 1994, Mohr. xi-289 p. 0179-7891 [IsrClas 14, 178-184 E. *Tov*].

D4   **Versiones orientales.**

1459 *Adair* J. R., A methodology for using the versions in the textual criticism of the OT: JNWS 20,2 (1994) 111-142.

1460 **Boismard** M.-E., Le Diatessaron 1992 ➤ 8,1919; 9,1598: ᴿComSev 26 (1993) 93s (M. de *Burgos*); RB 101 (1994) 153s (J.-M. *Rousée*).

1461 ᴱ**Dirksen** P., La Peshitta dell'AT, ᵀᴱ*Borbone* Pier Giorgio: StBPaid 103, 1993 ➤ 9,1599; Lᵐ 20: ᴿRivB 42 (1994) 475-7 (M. *Perani*).

1462 **Falla** Terry C., A key to the Peshitta Gospels I a-d 1991 ➤ 7,1556 ... 9,1600: ᴿAbrNahr 31 (1993) 136s (H.J.W. *Drijvers*); ScotJT 47 (1994) 273s (J. N. *Birdsall*).

1463 **Hiebert** Robert J. V., The 'syrohexaplaric' psalter: SBL SeptCog 27, 1989 ➤ 5,3005; 7,2727: ᴿScotJT 46 (1993) 136s (D. C. *Parker*: not easy or clear but useful and thorough).

1464 **Jenner** K. D., De perikopentitels van de geillustreerde Syrische Kanselbijbel van Parijs (MS Parijs, Bibliothèque nationale, Syriaque 341); een vergelijkend onderzoek naar de oudste Syrische perikopenstelsels: diss. Leiden 1994, ᴰ*Kooij* A. van der. Leiden 1994, Peshitta Institute. x-483 p. – TvT 34 (1994) 297.

1465 **Kiraz** George A., Computer-generated concordance to the Syriac NT 1993 ➤ 9,1601: ᴿBSO 57 (1994) 648 (A. G. *Salvesen*); NT 36 (1994) 291s (J. K. *Elliott*); RB 101 (1994) 580-2 (M. *Pazzini*, ital.).

1466 **Kiraz** George A., Lexical tools to the Syriac New Testament: JSOT Manuals 7. Shf 1994, Academic. v-137 p. 1-85075-470-6.

1467 *Koster* M. D., Peshitta revisited; a reassessment of its value as a version: JSS 38 (1993) 235-269.

1468 **Lane** D. J., Lev [–Jos, *al.*] OTSyriac 1991 ➤ 7,1561; 9,1602: ᴿJTS 45 (1994) 198-203 (M. P. *Weitzman*).

1469 *Lane* D. J., Text, scholar, and church; the place of the Leiden Peshitta within the context of scholastically and ecclesiastically definitive versions: JSS 38 (1993) 33-47.

1470 **Lyon** Jeffrey P., Syriac Gospel translations; a comparison of the language and translation method used in the Old Syriac, the Diatessaron, and the Peshiṭto: CSCOr, Subsidia 88. Lv 1994, Peeters. xxiv-235 p.; bibliog. xiii-xxiv. 2-87723-167-4.

1471 *McFall* Leslie, TATIAN's *Diatessaron*; mischievous or misleading: WestTJ 56 (1994) 87-114.

1472 **Petersen** William L., TATIAN's Diatessaron; its creation, dissemination, significance and history in scholarship: VigChr supp. 25. Leiden 1994, Brill. xix-555 p. *f*220. 90-04-09469-5.

1474 *Luke* Kuriakose, The Coptic versions of the Bible (2): Living Word 99 (Alwaye 1993) 3-20. [< TContext 11/1, p. 38].

1475 *Pietersma* A., *Comstock* S.T., A Sahidic lectionary of the New Testament and Psalms: BASP 29 (1992) 57-66.

1476 **Schmitz** Franz J., *Mink* G., Die sahidischen Handschriften der Evangelien: Liste kopt. NT 1, 1991 ➤ 7,1566; 8,1831: ᴿOLZ 89 (1994) 270-2 (H.-M. *Schenke*).

1477 **Zuurmond** R., NT aethiopice: Synoptic Gospels 1989 ➤ 7,4277: ᴿRB 101 (1994) 115-7 (M.-É. *Boismard*); TR 90 (1994) 23-26 (H. *Strutwolf*).

1478 *Cowe* S. Peter, An Armenian gospelbook in the SOAS collection (ms 11521): BSO 57 (1994) 360-6.

1479 **Browne** Gerald H., Bibliorum Sacrorum versio palaeonubiana: CSCOr Subsidia 87. Lv 1994, Peeters. ix-131 p. 90-6831-655-9.

1480 *Shehadeh* Haseeb, Some reflections on the Arabic translation of the Samaritan Pentateuch: Nordisk Judaistik 14,1 (Aarhus 1993) 36-44 [< Judaica 50,62].

D5 **Versiones latinae.**

1481 **Anderson** Jeffery C., The New York cruciform lectionary: College Art Asn Mg Fine Arts 48. Univ. Park 1992, Penn State Univ. xi-105 p.; 64 fig. $42.50. – ᴿSpeculum 69 (1994) 731-3 (Mary-Lyon *Dolezal*).
1482 ᴱ**Gameson** R., The early medieval Bible; its production, decoration and use: StPalaeog. C 1994, Univ. xiv-242 p.; 68 fig. $65. 0-521-44540-X [NTAbs 38, p.447]; 1-23 *McGurk* P., Latin Bible; 223-232 *Smith* L., theology. – ᴿTS 55 (1994) 785s (J.F. *Kelly*).
1483 **Gibson** Margaret T., The Bible in the Latin West: The Medieval Book 1. ND 1993, Univ. xi-100 p.; 28 pl. $27. 0-268-99693-8. – ᴿJEH 45 (1994) 723 (P. *McGurk*).
1484 *Marsden* Richard C.J., a) The survival of GEOLFRITH's Tobit in a tenth-century insular manuscript: JTS 45 (1994) 1-23; – b) Old Latin intervention in the Old English Heptateuch: Anglo-Saxon England 23 (C 1994) 229-264 [RHE 90,33*].
1485 **Masser** Achim (*Felip-Jaud* Elisabeth de), Die lateinisch-althochdeutsche Tatianbilingue, St. Gallen Cod 56: GöAkad AltHD 25. Gö 1994, Vandenhoeck & R. 695 p. – ᴿBeitNam 29s (1994s) 105s (G. *Lohse*).
1487 **Morano Rodríguez** Ciríaca, Glosas marginales de Vetus Latina en las Biblias Vulgatas españolas, 1-2 Samuel: TEstCisn 48, 1989 ↠ 5,2716: ᴿArTGran 56 (1993) 328.
1489 *O'Loughlin* T., The Latin version of the Scriptures in Iona in the late 8th century; the evidence from ADOMNÁN's De locis sanctis: Peritia 8 (1994) 18-26 [< RHE 89,232*].
1490 *Steen* Diedrich, *Steiger* Thomas, Vetus Latina; Wurzel der abendländischen Kultur; der archäologische Beitrag: BiKi 48 (1993) 225-8 / 229.
1491 Vetus Latina Stiftung, Bericht 37 (26. des Instituts). FrB 1993, Herder. 63 p.
1492 **Wissemann** Michael, Schimpfworte in der Bibelübersetzung des HIE-RONYMUS: BtKlasAltW 2/86. Heid 1992, Winter. x-212 p. 3-533-04529-3. – ᴿLatomus 53 (1994) 682s (G.J.M. *Bartelink*).

D5.5 *Citationes apud Patres* — **the Patristic Bible.**

1493 *Deun* Peter Van, Les extraits de MAXIME le Confesseur contenus dans les chaînes sur le Nouveau Testament, abstraction faite des évangiles: OrLovPer 23 (1992) 205-217.
1494 *Dolbeau* François, À propos d'un florilège biblique traduit du grec par MOÏSE de Bergame [de Brolo, c. 1136]: RHText 24 (1994) 336-358.
1495 Lectures anciennes de la Bible [*Dorival* G. on pagan references to Septuagint, etc.]: Biblia Patristica Cah. 1. Strasbourg 1987, Centre Patristique. – ᴿJTS 41 (1990) 230s (Frances M. *Young*: some authors or subjects; no tit. pp.).
1496 **Ehrman** Bart D., *al.*, The text of the Fourth Gospel in the writings of ORIGEN I 1992 ↠ 8,5644: ᴿNT 36 (1994) 415s (J.K. *Elliott*).
1497 **Jenkins** R.G., The OT quotations of PHILOXENUS of Mabbug [often different from Peshiṭta]: CSCOr 514, Studia 84. Lv 1989, Peeters. 206 p. – ЯRechSR 82 (1994) 643s (B. *Sesboüé*).

1498 **Joest** Christoph, Bibelstellenkonkordanz zu den wichtigsten älteren Mönchsregeln: Instrumenta Patristica 9. Steenbrugge 1994, S. Pietersabdij. xiv-149 p.

1499 CYRILLUS H.: **Mullen** Roderic L., CYRIL of Jerusalem and the text of the New Testament in fourth-century Palestine: Diss. Univ. N. Carolina, *DEhrman* B. Chapel Hill 1993. 430 p. 94-29437. – DissA 55 (1994s) p. 1591; RelStR 21,256. – RJTS 44 (1993) 305-8 (J. L. *North*).

    D6 **Versiones modernae** .1 *romanicae,* **romance.**

1500 **Bogaert** Pierre-Maurice, Les Bibles en français; histoire illustrée du Moyen Âge à nos jours 1991 ➤ 7,1600 ... 9,1629: RMélSR 50 (1993) 53-56 (H. *Platelle*); RHE 89 (1994) 461-7 (J.-C. *Polet*).

1501 **Carrez** Maurice, Nouveau Testament interlinéaire grec-français [TOB + français courant] 1993 ➤ 9,1630; RÉTRel 69 (1994) 277s (É. *Cuvillier,* presqu'exclusivement sur les dangers et maux d'un tel projet); RÉG 107 (1994) 302s (A. *Wartelle*).

1502 **Chambers** Bettye Thomas, Bibliography of French Bibles, 2. Seventeenth century French-language editions of the Scriptures: TravHumRen 282. Genève 1994, Droz. 938 p.; ill. 2-600-00016-X [RHE 90,193, J.-F. *Gilmont*].

1503 **Chédozeau** B., La Bible et la liturgie en français ... (1600-1789), 1990 ➤ 6,1945 ... 9,1631: RMaisD 196 (1993) 134-9 (Monique *Beulin*).

1504 **Hurault** Bernard & Louis, *Maarsh* Jean Van Der, La Bible des communautés chrétiennes, traduite des textes originaux. P 1994, Médiaspaul. 0-89420-043-9.

1505 TJeanne d'Arc sr. Les évangiles — les quatre. P 1992, D-Brouwer. 622 p. F 32. – RFoiTemps 23 (1993) 454 (M. *Coenraets*).

1505* TEAlonso Schökel Luis, Biblia del Peregrino. Bilbao 1993, Mensajero. xiii-1732, 449 + 351 p. – RProyección 41 (1994) 63s (J. L. *Sicre*).

1506 *Fernández Tejero* Emilio, *Fernández Marcos* Natalio, La polémica en torno a la Biblia Regia de Arias Montano [Indices expurgatorios 1607 & 1612]: Sefarad 54 (1994) 259-270; Eng. 270.

1507 *a) Morreale* Margherita, La 'Bibbia di Ferrara', 450 anni dopo la sua pubblicazione: Memorie 9/4/3. R 1994, Accademia dei Lincei. 50 p. Lm 9.
– *b) Fernández Marcos* Natalio, La Biblia de Ferrara y sus efectos en las traducciones bíblicas al español: ➤ 320, Simposio 1991/4, 445-471.

1508 **Fernández Lago** José, A Biblia, ó galego²ʳᵉᵛ. Vigo 1992, Adro. xxii-1780 p. 88-7337-040-5.

1509 [Conferencia episcopal México (Colombia)], Biblia de América. M 1994, Atenas. xiii-1982 p. 84-7151-996-8.

1509* *Olivetti* Odayr (presbiteriano, préside), Nova versão internacional da Biblia em português; escorço informativo: VoxScr 3 (1993) 215-226.

1510 **Saramago** José, O evangelho segundo Jesus Cristo. São Paulo 1992, Letras. 445 p. – RVoxScr 3 (1993) 103-7 (M. L. *Carpenter*).

    D6.2 *Versiones anglicae* — **English Bible translations.**

1510* *Carson* D. A., Five Gospels, no Christ [cover: Jesus Seminar's bizarre Bible]: ChrT 38,5 (1994) 30-33.

1511 **Barnhouse** Rebecca A., Text and image in the illustrated Old English hexateuch: diss. N. Carolina, ᴰ*Wittig* J. Chapel Hill 1994. 301 p. 94-29382. - DissA 55 (1994s) p. 1554.

1512 *Barr* James, Modern English Bible versions as a problem for the Church: QRMin 14 (1994) 263-278.

1513 **Chamberlin** W. J., Catalogue of English translations; a classified bibliography ONT-apocrypha: BIndRel 21. Westport CT 1991, Greenwood. xliii-898 p. – ᴿRivB 42 (1994) 325 (M. *Pesce*).

1514 **Daniell** D., Tyndale's OT 1992 ➤ 8,1874; 9,1650; (1989, 0-300-04419-4, 429 p.); – ᴿBInterp 1 (1993) 258s (P. W. *Coxon*). BL (1993) 58 (L. *Grabbe*: important as first English from Hebrew).

1515 ᴱ**Doane** A. N., The Saxon Genesis [B + Vat] 1991 ➤ 8,1875; ᴿPgQ 71 (1992) 361-4 (R. D. *Fulk*); Speculum 69 (1994) 130-2 (Susan E. *Deskis*).

1516 **Ericksen** Janet A. S., Narration and vision in the Old English 'Genesis B': diss. Univ. Illinois, ᴰ*Wright* C. Urbana 1994. 187 p. 94-16357. – DissA 55 (1994s) p. 88.

1517 ᵀᴱ**Farstad** Arthur L., *al.*, The NKJV Greek-English interlinear New Testament. Nv 1994, Nelson. xviii-918 p. $30. 0-8407-8357-4 [TDig 41, 351].

1518 *a) Frerichs* Ernest S., The Bible in recent English translation; the Word and the words; – *b) Rogers* Robert C., Biblical hermeneutics and contemporary African theology: ➤ 102, Mem. RICHARDSON H. N., Uncovering ancient stones 1994, 237-243 / 245-260.

1519 *Jensen* Joseph, Inclusive language and the Bible: America 171,14 (1994) 14.16-18.

1520 *Knoch* Otto R., *Scholtissek* Klaus, Bibelübersetzungen: ➤ 510, LTK³ 2 (1994) 362-5. 368-396 [*al.* 385-8.397-400].

1521 *Lane* Tony, The crown of English Bibles; the King James version was the culmination of 200 turbulent years of Bible translation: Christian History 13,43 (1994) 6-11.

1522 ᴱ**Liuzza** R. M., The Old English version of the Gospels, I. Text and introduction. Ox 1994, UP. lxxviii-202 p. 0-19-722306-0.

1523 **Metzger** B., *al.*, The making of NRSV 1991 ➤ 7,1626; 9,1657: ᴿScripB 23 (1993) 44s (R. C. *Fuller*).

1524 *Metzger* Bruce M., Some curious [English printed] Bibles [and number of 'canonical' books varying from 5 (Samaritans) to 81 (Ethiopians)]: ➤ 26, ᶠCOOK J., RefR 48,3 (1994s) 230-8.

1525 ᵀ**Murphy** Conor, The New Testament: African Bible. Nairobi 1994, Paulines. 709 p. 9966-21-120-9.

1526 NET: [**Beck** W. F., *Graham* W.]: New Evangelical translation. God's word to the nations NT³ [¹1966] Cleveland 1990. – ᴿRivB 42 (1994) 247s (S. P. *Carbone*).

1527 **Orlinsky** H., *Bratcher* R., A history of Bible translation and the North American contribution 1991 ➤ 7,1629; 9,1661: ᴿCBQ 56 (1994) 123-5 (K. R. *Crim*).

1528 **Voas** David, The bad news Bible; a narrative summary drawing on the King James Version; the New Testament. L 1994, Duckworth. [vi–] 209 p. 0-7156-2605-1.

D6.3   *Versiones germanicae* — **Deutsche Bibelübersetzungen.**

1530 **Acker** Geoffrey B., The codex argenteus Upsaliensis [in Gothic], a codicological examination: diss. Illinois, ᴰ*Marchand* J. Urbana 1994. 425 p. 95-12275. – DissA 55 (1994s) p. 3878.

1531 *Strand* Kenneth A., Some significant Americana; the Saur German Bibles: AndrUnSem 32 (1994) 57-106.
1532 **Strohm** Stefan, Deutsche Bibeldrucke 1601-1800. Stu 1993, Frommann. I. 1601-1700, xxxvi-338 p.; II. 1701-1800, p. 339-880; III. Anhang p. 881-1395. DM 677. 3-7728-0845-X [TLZ 120, 634, N. *Petzoldt*].

D6.4 **Versiones nordicae** *et variae.*

1534 **Ejrnæs** Bodil, Skriftsynet igennem den Danske Bibels historie (Understanding of Scripture in the history of the Danish Bible): diss. ᴰ*Nielsen* S. H. Kopenhagen 1994. 213 p. > MusTusc. – RTLv 26, p. 544.
1535 **Astås** Reidar, An Old Norse biblical compilation; Studies in Stjörn ['guide de conduite']: AmUnivSt 7/109. NY 1991, Lang. x-251 p. – ᴿRHE 89 (1994) 786s (P.-M. *Bogaert*).
1536 ᴱ**Popowski** Remigiusz, **Wojciechowski** Michał, ᴳ❾ Grecko-polski Nowy Testament z kodami gramatycznymi. Wsz 1994, Vocatio. xlvi-1236 p. 83-85435-18-2.
1537 *Wong* Simon, ❾ Some orthographieal problems of the Chinese Bible: Jian Dao 2 (1994) 73-117; Eng. 117 (project to replace all 118 'special characters' used by and since T. C. *Chow*'s first Chinese computer Bible).
1538 **So Ki Jong**, The translation of the Bible into Korean; its history and significance: diss. Drew, ᴰ*Pain* J. Madison NJ 1992. – RTLv 26,533.

D7 *Problemata vertentis* — **Bible translation techniques.**

1538* **Abramson** Shraga, ❾ Tactics of Arabic-Hebrew translations: Lešonenu 58 (1994s) 189-199; Eng. II.
1539 **Askani** Hans-Christoph, Das Problem der Übersetzung, dargestellt an Franz ROSENZWEIG: ev. Diss. Tübingen 1994, ᴰ*Jüngel* E. 500 p. – RTLv 26, p. 528.
1540 **Buber** Martin, *Rosenzweig* Franz, Scripture and translation, ᵀ*Rosenwald* Lawrence, *Fox* Everett: StBLit. Bloomington 1994, Indiana Univ. lvi-223 p. 0-253-31272-8.
1541 **Chouraqui** André, Reflexionen über Problematik und Method der Übersetzung von Bibel und Koran, ᴱ*Abramowski* Luise: Lucas-Preis 1993. 67 p. 3-16-146202-5.
1542 *Culy* M. M., The top-down approach to translation [start from a text with exegesis]: NotTr 7,3 (1993) 28-51 [< NTAbs 38, p. 344].
1543 *Giese* Ronald L., 'A place for everything and everything in its place'; the role of range and sense in Bible translation: BTrans 44 (1993) 301-9.
1544 **Hargreaves** Cecil, A translator's freedom; modern English Bibles and their language: Biblical Seminar 22. Shf 1993, JStOT. 206 p. $18.50. 1-85075-400-4 [RelStR 21,324, L. J. *Greenspoon*: relevant beyond English]. – ᴿOTAbs 17 (1994) 430 (R. E. *Murphy*).
1545 *Kedar-Kopfstein* Benjamin, Zum lexikalischen Äquivalenzprinzip in Bibelübersetzungen; Beobachtungen und statistische Proben: ZAHeb 7 (1994) 133-140.
1546 **Laffling** John, Towards high-precision machine translation, based on contrastive textology. B/NY 1991, Foris, X-178 p. 3-11-013388-1. – ᴿBSLP 89,2 (1994) 118-122 (Rachel *Panckhurst*).
1547 **Lapide** Pinchas, Ist die Bibel richtig übersetzt? [1. c. 1986]. 2. Gü 1994, Gü-V. 94 p. 3-579-01441-2.

1548 *Merwe* C.H.J. van der, *Winckler* W. K., Training tomorrow's translators in the context of today's translations: JNWS 20,2 (1994) 79-109.
1549 *Nida* Eugene, The sociolinguistics of Bible translating: Jian Dao 2 (1994) 19-33; ☯ 33s.
1550 *Omanson* Roger L., Translating the anti-Jewish bias of the NT: BTrans 43/(1992).
1551 **Rösel** Martin, Übersetzung als Vollendung der Auslegung; Studien zur Genesis-Septuaginta [ᴰ1993 Hamburg, ᴰ*Koch* ➤ 9,1594]: BZAW 223. B 1994, de Gruyter. viii-290 p.; Bibliog. 261-282. 3-11-014234-1 [OIAc 11,39].
1552 *Taradach* Madeleine, Hommage aux traducteurs [HARL M. LXX; BOTTÉRO J., Gilgamesh; RIBERA-FLORIT J., Targum...]: RCatalT 18 (1993) 163.
1553 **Vries** J. E. de, Zuiver en unvervalscht? Een beschrijvingsmodel voor Bijbelvertalingen ontwikkeld en gedemonstreerd aan de Petrus Canisius vertaling: diss. ᴰ*Waard* J. de, Vrije Univ. Amst 1994. 233 p. – TvT 35,70; RTLv 26, p. 544.

D8 *Concordantiae, lexica specialia* – **Specialized dictionaries, synopses.**

1554 Concordance de la TOB 1993 ➤ 9,1711: ᴿÉTRel 69 (1994) 407-410 (D. *Lys*); NRT 116 (1994) 898s (X. *Jacques*); REJ 153 (1994) 445-7 (M. *Petit*).
1555 **Day** A. Colin, Roget's thesaurus of the Bible. SF 1992, Harper. 927 p. $28 (thumb-index $30). 0-06-061773-X (-2-1). – ᴿRExp 91 (1994) 267 (J. W. *Cox*).
1556 **Even Shoshan** A. New concordance 1989 ➤ 5,1868: ᴿRBibArg 55 (1993) 61-63 (P. *Andiñach*).
1557 **Flis** Jan, Konkordancja do Biblii Tysiąclecia 1991 ➤ 9,1712: ᴿAtKap 120 (1993) 389s (J. *Zalęski*, ☯).
1558 **Katz** E., Topical concordance OT 1992 ➤ 9,1713: ᴿAndrUnS 31 (1993) 147s (P. D. *Duerksen*).
1559 ᴱ**Lindsey** Robert L., (*Dos Santos* Elmar C.). A comparative Greek concordance of the Synoptic Gospels. J 1985-9, Baptist House POB 154. xiv-1078 p. – ᴿPerspRelSt 21 (1994) 267-270 (W. T. *Sawyer:* devised to support his thesis against Two-Source, but of wide usefulness).
1560 **Strong** concordance number above each word: ᵀᴱ**Green** Jay P., The interlinear Hebrew-Aramaic Old Testament. Peabody MA 1993, Hendrickson. 4 vols. c. xv-700 each. 0-913-57329-9.

| IV. ➤ K 1 | V. **Exegesis generalis VT vel cum NT** |

D9 **Commentaries on the whole Bible or OT.**

1561 ᴱ**Allen** G. *al.*, (*Sparhs* B.), The Orthodox study Bible; NT and Psalms, New King James version. Nv 1993, Nelson. 1054 p.; 8 pl.; 9 maps. $25. 0-8407-8391-4 [NTAbs 38, p. 453].
1562 ᴱ**Barker** Kenneth L., *Kohlenberger* Johnᴵᴵᴵ, The Zondervan NIV Bible commentary. GR 1994, Zondervan. I. OT, ix-1558 p.; II. NT, x-1243 p. 0-310-57850-7; -40-X [RelStR 21,319 L. J. *Greenspoon*).
1563 ᴱ**Carson** B. A., *al.*, New Bible commentary, 21st century edition [¹1970]. Leicester 1994, Inter-Varsity. xiii-1455 p.; maps. [TDig 41,374] 0-85110-615-3.

1564 *Cunningham* Lawrence S., The Bible and its companions [Oxford; Jerome handbook]: Commonweal 121,8 (1994) 25s.
1565 *Dorsey* David A., A guide to OT commentaries: EvJ 12 (1994) 29-34. 60-66.
1566 ᴱHammond Pete, *Hendricks* William D., The Word in life study Bible, as fresh as your morning paper. Nv c. 1993, Nelson. $40 (pa.) $20 [BAR-W 20,2 (1994) 1 adv.; and 68.70.72 in survey-chart of **fifty** 1994 study Bibles].
1567 Haug Helmut, *Lange* Joachim, Stuttgarter Erklärungsbibel. Stu 1992, Deutsche Bibelgesellschaft. 1626 p. – ᴿConcordiaJ 20 (1994) 82s (P. *Bohlken:* even better than Concordia Self-study Bible).
1568 *Holladay* C.R., Sorting out the NRSV study Bibles [HarperCollins (➤ 1572) far superior to the other three]: ChrCent 111 (1994) 350-2 [< NTAbs 38, p. 345].
1569 ᴱJackson Kent P., [Mormon] 1 Kings to Malachi: Studies in Scripture 4. Salt Lake City 1993, Deseret. x-533 p. $19. 0-87579-789-X [TDig 42,83].
1570 McGrath Alister E., NIV Bible commentary. L 1988, Hodder & S. 394 p. 0-340-58427-0.
1571 ᴱMays James L., Harper's Bible Commentary 1988 ➤ 4,2035 ... 8,1994 (not 'John'): ᴿJNES 53 (1994) 41-43 (G. W. *Ahlström* †).
1572 ᴱMeeks Wayne, 'by SBL' The HarperCollins study Bible with the apocryphal/deuterocanonical books. NY 1993, HarperCollins. xlii-1359 p. 0-06-065580-1. – ᴿNewTR 7,3 (1994) 79-81 (D. M. *Bossman*).
1573 ᴱMills Watson E., *Wilson* Richard F., Mercer [dictionary 1990] commentary on the Bible. Macon 1994, Mercer Univ. xxii-1547 p. 0-86554-406-9 [TDig 42,178; RelStR 21, 319, L. J. *Greenspoon*].
1574 Newsom Carol A., *Ringe* Sharon H., The women's Bible commentary 1992 ➤ 8,1945: ᴿHorizons 21 (1994) 348s (Regina A. *Boisclair*); JBL 113 (1994) 311-3 (R. *Scroggs*); JRel 74 (1994) 561s (J. Cheryl *Exum:* a commentary perforce has much that is not specifically feminist); SWJT 36,1 (1993s) 58 (D. G. *Kent*); TBR 7,3 (1994s) 15 (Deborah *Sawyer*).
1575 NInterp: New Interpreter's Bible, ᴱKeck Leander E., 1. General articles and introduction; Gen-Lev. Nv 1994, Abingdon. xx-1193 p.; 10 fig. 0-687-27814-7 [TDig 41,374]. – ᴿJHisp 2,3 (1994s) 71-74 (Christine *Esparza:* ... *Segovia* F., Reading the Bible as Hispanic Americans).
1575* NIV Quest study Bible. GR 1994, Zondervan. viii-1862 p.; 13 color maps. $38. 0-310-92411-1 [TDig 43,57; on same page NIV adapted to 3d-grade vocabulary (also in edition for adults), New International Reader's Version NT ᴱ*Youngblood* Ron, Zondervan 1995, $13; pa. $10].
1576 NJBC: New Jerome biblical commentary, ᴱBrown R.E., *al.,* 1989 ➤ 5,384 ... 9,1722: ᴿPrincSemB 13 (1991) 251-3 (J. H. *Charlesworth*).
1577 Quinzio S., Un commento alla Bibbia² [¹1972-6 in 4 vol.]. Mi 1991, Adelphi. 820 p. Lᵐ 60. – ᴿProtestantesimo 49 (1994) 78s (C. *Tron*).

VI. Libri historici VT

E1   **Pentateuchus, Torah** .1 *Textus, commentarii.*

1578 *Azzimonti* Alessandro, 'Sicut dictum vidimus'; Un anonimo commentario al pentateuco di età protocarolingia (Ambr. G 82 inf.): Aevum 68 (1994) 283-302.

1579 **Blenkinsopp** J., The Pentateuch 1992 ➤ 8,1952; 9,1728:   ᴿBR 10,6 (1994) 19 (T. R. *Dozeman*); JBL 113 (1994) 317 (W. Lee *Humphreys*).

1580 **Boorer** Suzanne, The promise of the land as oath; a key to the formation of the Pentateuch: BZAW 205, ᴰ1992 ➤ 9,1729:   ᴿÉTRel 68 (1993) 418s (T. *Römer*); ZAW 106 (1994) 352 (E. *Blum*).

1581 **Crüsemann** F., Die Tora; Theologie und Sozialgeschichte 1992 ➤ 8,229; 9,1730:   ᴿGregorianum 75 (1994) 755-9 (G. L. *Prato*); OTEssays 7 (1994) 128-131 (W. C. van *Wyk*, Afrikaans); ZAW 106 (1994) 353s (M. *Köckert*); ZkT 116 (1994) 70-73 (R. *Oberforcher*).

1582 **Green** Winifred, Ears to hear; an introduction to the first five books of the Bible: Oxford Bible Reading Fellowship (&) Sutherland NSW 1994, Albatross. 128 p. $5. 0-7459-2829-3 UK / 0-7324-08970. – ᴿTBR 7,1 (1994s) 22 (R. *Mason*).

1583 ᴱ**Haudebert** Pierre, Le Pentateuque: LDiv 151, 1991/2 ➤ 8,474: 9,1732: ᴿCarthaginensia 10 (1994) 173s (R. *Sanz Valdivieso*); ÉglT 25 (1994) 119-125 (A. *Faucher*); ÉTRel 68 (1993) 416-8 (J.-D. *Macchi*); NRT 116 (1994) 101s (J. L. *Ska*); RTLv 25 (1994) 78s (A. *Kabasele Mukenge*).

1584 **Houtman** Gees (Cornelius), Der Pentateuch; die Geschichte seiner Erforschung neben einer Auswertung [1980 updated to 1994],ᵀ: CtrbBExT 9. Kampen 1994, Kok. xxii-472 p. ƒ65. 90-390-0114-6 [OTAbs 17, p. 659]. – ᴿDielB 28 (1992s!) 225-8 (B. J. *Diebner*: not updated enough; BLUM, CRÜSEMANN ...).

1585 **McEvenue** Sean, Interpreting the Pentateuch 1990, ➤ 6,2067... 9,1735: ᴿPrPeo 8 (1994) 130 (B. *Robinson*: there is no substitute for discovering where each part of the OT comes from and when); TorJT 10 (1994) 110s (D. *Becker*).

1586 *Pollack* Meira, Alternate renderings and additions in Yeshuᶜah BEN YEHUDA's Arabic translation of the Pentateuch: JQR 84 (1993s) 209-226.

1587 **Sailhamer** John H., The Pentateuch as narrative 1992 ➤ 9,1736: ᴿAndrUnSem 32 (1994) 148-150 (R. *Gane*).

1588 **Salas** A., Un pueblo en marcha; Pentateuco y libros históricos. 1993: ᴿCiuD 206 (1993) 648s (M. A. *Keller*).

E1   *Pentateuchus* .2 **Introductio; Fontes JEDP.**

1589 **Campbell** Anthony F., O'Brien Mark A., Sources of the Pentateuch; texts, introductions, annotations 1992 ➤ 9,1743:   ᴿBL (1994) 54 (R. N. *Whybray*); OTEssays 7 (1994) 155s (F. E. *Deist* appreciates, though others may find outdated, this synopsis of Martin NOTH); TorJT 10 (1994) 107s (D. *Becker*).

1590 **Friedmann** Richard E., Chi ha scritto la Bibbia? ᵀ*Bertolino* A. T 1991, Bollati Boringhieri. 249 p. – ᴿBbbOr 35 (1993) 122-7 (E. *Jucci*).

1591 **Levin** Christoph, Der Jahwist: FRL 157, 1993 ➤ 9,1747:   ᴿBL (1994) 92 (E. W. *Nicholson*); EstAg 29 (1994) 373s (C. *Mielgo*); ExpTim 106 (1994s) 331 (R. *Mason*); OTAbs 17 (1994) 435s (C. T. *Begg*: 'one of the brightest younger stars in the Gö exegetical firmament').

1592 ᴱ**Pury** A, de, Le Pentateuque en question 1986/9 ➤ 5,601 ... 9,1749: ᴿAsprenas 41 (1994) 271-6 (G. *Castello*); TEuph 5 (1992) 164s (F. *Smyth*).

1593 **Rendtorff** R., Problem of transmission 1990 ➤ 6,2070 ... 9,1751: ᴿEvQ 66 (1994) 57s (T. D. *Alexander*); Henoch 16 (1994) 349s (A. *Catastini*).

1594 **Rofé** Alexander, ➒ Introduction to the composition of the Pentateuch. TA 1994, Academon. [iv-] 141 p. $14. 965-350-032-5.

E1.3 *Pentateuchus,* **themata.**

1595 *Anderson* Gary A., The status of the Torah before Sinai; the retelling of the Bible in the Damascus Covenant and the Book of Jubilees: Dead Sea Discoveries 1 (Leiden 1994) 1-29.

1596 ᴱ**Brekelmans** C., *Lust* J., Pentateuchal and deuteronomistic studies, 13th IOSOT: BtETL 84, 1989/90 ➤ 6,518... 9,1759: ᴿBZ 38 (1994) 113-5 (J. *Schreiner*).

1597 *Cazelles* Henri, Clans, état monarchique et tribus [J favors David and uses *šebeṭ* for 'branch (of the people)': ➤ 9,6, ᶠANDERSON George, Understanding poets and prophets 1993, 77-92 [< OTAbs 17,473].

1598 **Cohen** Raphaël, Tora au présent. P 1994, Buchet/Chastel. 200 p. F 130 [Études 381,570 adv.].

1599 *Duranti* Gian Carlo, Codici del Pentateuco e matematica egizio-platonica: BtFilOggi 2/5. Genova 1994, Arcipelago. 68 p.

1600 *Faucher* Alain, Des circuits d'hypothèses aux voies nouvelles de l'exégèse; prospectives didactiques des études sur le Pentateuque: ÉglT 25 (1994) 37-45 (+ 119-125 ACFEB 14ᵉ).

1601 **Grant** James A., A reformulated hypertext representational model and navigational schema for large multilingual bodies of literature [chiefly Pentateuch; computer hypertext to be useful for classics and religious writings must have an adapter]: diss. S. Louisiana, ᴰ*Moreau* D. 1994. 203 p. DissA-B 55 (1994s) 2848. (No AA number).

1602 *Jackson* Jared T., Whither the Pentateuch?: ProcGM 13 (1993) 1-9.

1603 **Jenson** Philip P., Graded holiness... P: jOsu 106, ᴰ1992 ➤ 8,1988; 9,1763: ᴿBL (1993) 108 (G.J. *Wenham*); CBQ 56 (1994) 551-3 (E. *Hensell*); ConcordJ 20 (1994) 69s (P.R. *Raabe*); ÉTRel 68 (1993) 269s (T. *Römer*); ETL 70 (1994) 139s (A. *Schoors*); EvQ 66 (1994) 58-60 (G. *McConville*); JBL 113 (1994) 318s (G.A. *Anderson*); JTS 45 (1994) 177s (J.G. *Snaith*); TLZ 119 (1994) 628s (K. *Zobel*); WestTJ 56 (1994) 185-8 (R.E. *Averbeck*).

1604 **Krapf** Thomas M., Die Priesterschrift... KAUFMANN: OBO 119, ᴰ1992 ➤ 8,1971: ᴿJStJud 25 (1994) 101-3 (A.S. van der *Woude*); Judaica 50 (1994) 157-9 (S. *Schreiner*); WZKM 84 (1994) 221-3 (H.U. *Steymans*).

Moberly R., The OT of the OT... Yahwism 1992 ➤ 7013.

1605 *Phillips* A., [Kindness to] Animals and the Torah: ExpTim 106 (1994s) 260-5.

1606 *Rendtorff* Rolf, The [nomad-Landnahme consensus] paradigm is changing; hopes – and fears: BInterp 1 (1993) 34-53 [> BtS 150 (1993) 493s (R.A. *Taylor*)].

1607 *Schiff* Daniel, Reimagining Torah: CCAR 41,3 (1994) 49-64.

1608 **Schmidt** Ludwig, Studien zur Priesterschrift: BZAW 214. B 1993, de Gruyter, viii-281 p. 3-11-013867-0 [Biblica 76,396-415, J.L. *Ska*]: ᴿCBQ 56 (1994) 778-780 (M.S. *Moore*: Pentateuch study has been undergoing an earthquake; Schmidt 'emerging from the rubble like some subterranean survivor, stubbornly proposes that the latest seismographs are deceptive').

1609 *Seidel* Bodo, Entwicklungslinien der neueren Pentateuchforschung im 20. Jahrhundert: ZAW 106 (1994) 476-485.

1610 **Synowiec** Juliusz S., ➒ *Na początku...* In the beginning: select problems of the Pentateuch. Wsz 1987, Akad. Teol. Katolickiej. 256 p.; map.

1611 **Van Seters** John, Prologue to history 1992 ➤ 8,1977: ᴿBibTB 24 (1994) 33s (R. *Gnuse*); BInterp 1 (1993) 259s (R. D. *Miller*: clear, effective; some reserves); BL (1993) (P. R. *Davies*: DE came first, J wrote a 'prequel'); Interpretation 48 (1994) 289-291 (R. G. *Boling*); JRel 74 (1994) 87s (L. K. *Handy*); TLZ 119 (1994) 235-7 (L. *Schmidt*); TorJT 10 (1994) 248s (D. *Becker*); ᴢᴀᴡ 105 (1993) 536s (E. *Blum*: eingehend).
1612 *Van Seters* John [Prologue to history reviewed Dec. 1993 by] *Friedman* Richard E.: Scholars face off over age of biblical stories: BR 10,4 (1994) 40-44 . 54 [10,6 (1994) 14 . 55, J. *Blenkinsopp* against Friedman].
1613 *Van Seters* John, The theology of the Yahwist; a preliminary sketch: ➤ 61, ᶠKAISER O., 'Wer ist' 1994, 219-228.

E1.4 **Genesis;** *textus, commentarii.*

1614 **Boecker** Hans Jochen [continuation of *Zimmerli* W., vol. 2, 1976], 1. Mose 25:12-37:1: Isaac und Jakob: Z BK AT 1/3. Z 1992, Theol.-V. 152 p. Fs 32. – ᴿCBQ 56 (1994) 536s (R. *Gnuse*).
1615 ᴱ**Brenner** Athalya, A feminist companion to Genesis 1993 ➤ 9,1769: ᴿBL (1994) 52 (Grace I. *Emmerson*); CBQ 56 (1994) 819-821 (Alice L. *Laffey*, also on her Song of Songs).
1616 *Fretheim* Terence E., The Book of Genesis; introduction, commentary, and reflections: ➤ 1575, NInterp 1 (1994) 319-674 (the biblical text is on an azure background).
1617 **Gartig** William G., A critical edition with English translation of the Genesis portion of 'Avdat Nefesh', a medieval supercommentary to Abraham IBN EZRA's commentary on the Pentateuch: diss. HUC, ᴰ*Cooper* A. Cincinnati 1994. 490 p. 94-27339.–DissA 55 (1994s) p. 1989.
1618 **Hamilton** V. P., Gn 1-17: NICOT 1990 ➤ 6,2082; 9,1775: ᴿConcordTQ 58 (1994) 39s (A. E. *Steinmann*).
1619 **Isabelle de la Source**, sr., La Genèse: Lire la Bible avec les Pères 1. P/Montréal 1990, Médiaspaul/Paulines. 174 p. 2-7122-0305-4.
1620 **Janzen** J. G., Abraham and all the families of the earth; a commentary on Gn 12-50. GR 1993, Eerdmans. 215 p. $18. – ᴿOTEssays 7 (1994) 309-313 (R. F. *Rhode*).
1621 **Johnson** Bo, Ursprunget; bibelteologisk kommentar till Första Moseboken. Sto 1992, Verbum. 168 p. – ᴿTsTKi 65 (1994) 142 (T. *Stordalen*, Norwegian).
1622 **Kamesar** Adam, JEROME, Greek scholarship, and the Hebrew Bible; a study of the Quaestiones hebraicae in Genesim 1993 ➤ 9,1777: ᴿChH 63 (1994) 606s (G. T. *Armstrong*); JTS 45 (1994) 333-5 (H. F. D. *Sparks*); VigChr 48 (1994) 190s (G. J. M. *Bartelink*); VT 44 (1994) 431s (P. E. *Satterthwaite*).
1623 **Korsak** Mary Phil, At the start ... Genesis made new: Lv Cah 124, 1992 ➤ 8,2008; 9,1778: ᴿBL (1994) 47 (G. L. *Emmerson*); BToday 31 (1993) 119 (C. *Stuhlmueller*).
1624 **McNamara** Martin M., Targum Neofiti I. Genesis 1992 ➤ 8,1771.2008*: ᴿAndrUnSem 32 (1994) 291-3 (J. E. *Miller*); CBQ 56 (1994) 769-771 (Z. *Garber*); CritRR 6 (1993) 168-170 (Julia A. *Foster*) all also on MAHER, Ps.-Jonathan.
1625 ᵀ**Mathews** E. G.ᴶ, *Amar* J. P., ᴱ*McVey* K., St. EPHREM the Syrian, Selected prose works: Commentary on Gen/Ex...: Fathers 91. Wsh 1994, Catholic Univ. xxx-393 p. [RHE 90,42*].
1626 **Petit** Françoise, La chaîne sur la Genèse 1991 ➤ 7,1728 ... 9,1780:

ᴿOrChrPer 60 (1994) 686-8 (L. *Pieralli*); RÉByz 51 (1993) 305s (P. *Géhin*); RTPhil 126 (1994) 171s (R. *Gounelle*); Sefarad 54 (1994) 427-9 (Beatrix *Monco Taracena*); VigChr 48 (1991) 198-201 (R. B. *ter Haar Romeny*).

1627 **Rad** Gerhard von, ❶ *Sōsēki*: Genesis 1-25,18 / 25,19-50,26 [1976], ᵀ*Yamaga* Tetsuo. Tokyo 1993, Seishochūkai Kankōkai, xvi-472 p.; xi - p. 473-848. Y 6500 + 5300. [BL 94,71].

1628 ᵀ**Rosenberg** A. J., Genesis [through ch. 22], a new English translation, with RASHI and other commentaries. NY 1993, Judaica. xix-275 p.; bibliog. 267-275. 1-880582-08-2.

1629 **Rottzoll** Dirk U., Rabbinischer Kommentar zum Buch Genesis; Darstellung der Rezeption des Buches Genesis in Mischna und Talmud. NY 1994, de Gruyter. 539 p. [BL 95,72, L. L. *Grabbe*: a useful index]. – ᴿJudaica 50 (1994) 159 (D. *Krochmalnik*).

1630 **Ruppert** Lothar, Genesis; ein kritischer und theologischer Kommentar, 1. Gen 1,11-11,26: ForBi 70, 1992 ➤ 8,2015: ᴿÉTRel 69 (1994) 98 (T. *Römer*); TR 90 (1994) 455s. (Helen *Schüngel-Straumann*).

1631 **Scullion** John J., Genesis 1992 ➤ 8,2017; 9,1783: ᴿBL (1994) 74 (E. B. *Mellor*); PrPeo 8 (1994) 298 (B. P. *Robinson*).

1632 **Soggin** J. Alberto, Genesi 1-11, 1991 ➤ 7,1729; 8,2018: ᴿCritRR 6 (1993) 278-280 (R. H. *McGrath*).

1633 **Sylwan** A., Petrus CANTOR, Glossae super Genesim 1-3, 1992 ➤ 8,2019: ᴿRÉAug 39 (1993) 272s (G. *Dohan*).

1634 **Vegas Montaner** Luis, Génesis Rabbah I, comentario midrásico al libro del Génesis. Estella 1994, VDivino. 438 p. pt. 3900. 84-8169-004-X [RB 102,466, É. *Nodet*].

1635 **Wenham** Gordon J., Genesis II, 16-50: Word Comm 2. Irving TX 1994, Word. xxxviii-517 p. $28. 0-8499-0201-0 [TDig 41,391].

1636 **Wevers** J. W., Notes on the Greek text of Genesis 1993 ➤ 9,1786: ᴿBL (1994) 48 (A. G. *Salvesen*); CBQ 56 (1994) 781-4 (J. R. *Davila*); OTAbs 17 (1994) 437 (A. A. *Di Lella*).

1637 *Zipor* Moshe A., Notes sur les chapitres I à XVII de la Genèse dans la Bible d'Alexandrie: ETL 70 (1994) 385-393.

E1.5   *Genesis, themata.*

1638 *Alexander* T. D., Genealogies, seed and the compositional unity of Genesis: TyndB 44 (1993) 255-270.

1639 **Breukelman** F. H., De theologie van het boek Genesis: Bijbelse theologie 1/2, 1992 ➤ 8,2021; 9,1788: ᴿOTEssays 7 (1994) 133-5 (M. D. *Terblanche*).

1640 **Davis** Dale R., Looking on the heart: Expositor's guide to the historical books. GR 1994, Baker. I. 144 p. $9. II. 187 p. 0-8010-3025-0; -4-2.

1641 *a)* *Elgvin* Torleif, The Genesis section of 4Q422 (4QParaGenExod); – *b)* *Brooke* George J., The genre of 4Q252; from poetry to pesher [Gn 9; 22; 28]: ➤ 337, DSD 1 (1994) 180-196 / 160-179.

1642 **Greenspahn** Frederick E., When brothers dwell together; the preeminence of younger siblings in the Hebrew Bible. NY 1994, Oxford-UP. xi-193 p. 0-19-508253-2 [OIAc 9,28].

1643 **Gunkel** Hermann, The stories of Genesis [*Sagen* not Sagas; ¹1901 appeared that year in English; here we have ³1910], ᵀ*Scullion* John J. †, ᴱ*Scott* W. R. Vallejo CA 1994, BIBAL (*Christensen* D. L.), 155 p. 0-941037-21-5 [OTAbs 17, p. 660].

1644 *Krašovec* Jože, Punishment and mercy in the primeval history (Gen 1-11): ETL 70 (1994) 5-33.
1645 **Minear** Paul S., Christians and the New Creation; Genesis motifs in the New Testament [Lk, Jn, 1 Cor]. LVL 1994, W-Knox. xvi-142 p. $15. 0-664-25531-0 [RelStR 21,332, A. B. *Scott*]. – ᴿExpTim 106 (1994s) 213 (N. *Clark*).
1646 **Moberly** R. W. L., Genesis 12-50: OT Guides 1992 ➤ 9,1796: ᴿBL (1994) 68 (P. J. *Harland*): ZAW 106 (1994) 363 (M. *Köckert*).
1647 **Moloney** Patrick F., The mirror of Paradise; language and politics in medieval and early modern political thought [drawn from Genesis]: diss. Rutgers, ᴰ*Schochet* G. New Brunswick 1994. 270 p. 95-11508. – DissA 55 (1994s) p. 3975.
1648 **Nobel** Hans, Gods gedachten tellen; numerieke struktuuranalyse en de elf gedachten in Genesis - 2 Koningen (counting God's eleven thoughts): diss. ᴰ*Labuschagne* C. Groningen 1994. 208 p.; 95 p. – RTLv 26,532.
1649 **Ohm Won Shik,** A comparative analysis of the literary structure of Genesis 1-11 to ancient Near Eastern patterns: diss. Mid-America Baptist 1992. viii-280 p. 93-23655. – OIAc 11,35.
1650 **Prewitt** Terry J. P., The elusive covenant; a structural-semiotic reading of Genesis, 1990 ➤ 6,2104: ᴿAJS 17 (1992) 89-91 (Y. *Gitay*).
1651 **Ralph** Margaret N., Discovering OT origins, Gn Ex Sam 1992 ➤ 8,2031: ᴿOTEssays 7 (1994) 91-93 (J. H. *Breytenbach*, Afrikaans); ScripB 23 (1993) 48s (M. *McNamara*); Vidyajyoti 58 (1994) 405s (P. *Meagher*).
1652 **Rashkow** Ilona N., The phallacy of Genesis [12; 20...]; a feminist-psychoanalytic approach: LitCuBInt, 1993 ➤ 9,1345: ᴿRelStR 20 (1994) 142 (W. L. *Humphreys*).
1653 **Steinmetz** Devorah, From father to son... Gn, 1991 ➤ 7,1746; 8,2033: ᴿCritRR 6 (1993) 182.4 (R. L. *Cohn*).
1654 **Syrén** Roger, The forsaken first-born: jOsu 133, 1993 ➤ 9,1801: ᴿBL (1994) 100 (J. R. *Porter*); CBQ 56 (1994) 342s (A. *da Silva*).
1655 **Turner** Laurence A., Announcements of plot in Genesis: jOsu 96, ᴰ1990 ➤ 6,2109... 9,1802: ᴿBijdragen 55 (1994) 72 (J. van *Ruiten*).
1656 **White** Hugh C., Narrative 1991 ➤ 7,1752... 9,1803: ᴿCritRR 6 (1993) 187-190 (R. S. *Hendel*).
1657 *Wolters* Albert M., Reflections on 'Primeval History' and [H.] VAN TILL's hermeneutics: MAJT 6 (1990) 117-124 [< OTAbs 18, p. 288].

E1.6 **Creatio,** *Genesis 1s.*

1658 **Arteaga Natividad** R., La creación en los comentarios de san AGUSTÍN al Génesis: Mayéutica Mg 2. Marcilla 1994, Recoletos. 374 p. – ᴿSalmanticensis 41 (1994) 450-3 (R. *Trevijano*).
1659 **Banks** Michaela, *Baumann* Gerlinde, Am Anfang war...? Gen 1,1ff und Prov 8,22-31 im Vergleich: BibNot 71 (1994) 24-52.
1660 **Bianchi** E., *Adamo, dove sei?* Commento esegetico-spirituale ai capitoli 1-11 del libro della Genesi. Magnano 1994, Qíqayon. 322 p. Lᵐ 35 [NRT 117,267, J.-L. *Ska*].
1661 *Bona* Isabella, Dipendenza e originalità nell'Esamerone di AMBROGIO [V,9,24; 10,31; 13,44; 16,33.55]: Koinonia 17 (1993) 35-47.
1662 **Boss** Jeffrey, Becoming ourselves; meanings in the creation story, with a new translation of Genesis 1-11 from the original Hebrew 1993 ➤ 9,1808: ᴿBL (1994) 52 (P. J. *Harland*).
1663 *Breukelman* Frans, Die Schöpfungsgeschichte als Unterricht in bibli-

scher Hermeneutik [ned.]ᵀ: Texte und Kontexte 17,1 (1994) 29-52.(53-64
über Gn 6,1-4) [< OTAbs 18, p. 45s].
1664 **Brown** William P., Structure, role, and ideology in the Hebrew and
Greek texts of Gen 1:1-2:3: SBL diss. 132, 1993 → 9,1810: ᴿBL (1994)
53s (P. J. *Harland*); ETL 70 (1994) 433s (J. *Lust*); Interpretation 48 (1994)
420 (J. R. *Davila*); JRel 74 (1994) 596 (R. S. *Hendel*: dubiously based on a
minor translational inconcinnity); RelStR 20 (1994) 230 (L. J. *Greenspoon*:
excellent, exciting).
1665 *Carroll* William E., S. TOMMASO, ARISTOTELE e la creazione: AnnTh
8 (1994) 365-376.
1666 ᴱ**Clifford** R. J., *Collins* J. J., Creation, 1992 → 8,346; 9,1813: ᴿBInterp 2
(1994) 224-6 (D. E. *Law*); RB 101 (1994) 291 (tit. pp.).
1667 **Coote** Robert B., *Ord* David R., In the beginning, creation and the
priestly history 1991 → 8,1757: ᴿCritRR 6 (1993) 155-7 (R. W. *Klein*);
Interpretation 48 (1994) 80 (J. H. *Adams*).
1668 **Eyjólfsson** Sigurjón, Rechtfertigung und Schöpfung in der Theologie
Werner ELERTs: ArbGTLuth 10. Hannover 1994, Luth.-V. 367p.
DM 64. 3-7859-0654-4 [TLZ 120,703-5, N. *Slenczka*].
1669 *a) Floss* Johannes P., Schöpfung als Geschehen? Von der Syntax zur
Semantik in der priesterschriftlichen Schöpfungsdarstellung Gen 1,
1-2,4a; – *b) Metzger* Martin, Ein Elfenbeinrelief aus Minet el-Bēdā; die
Gottheit, die Tiere füttert, and das Motiv des von Tieren flankierten
Baumes auf dem Berg; – *c) Wallis* Gerhard, Schöpfung oder Evolution:
→ 115, ᶠSCHUNCK K.-D., Nachdenken 1994, 311-318 / 333-355; 21 fig. /
319-332.
1670 **Frank** Richard M., Creation and the cosmic system; al-GHAZĀLĪ and
AVICENNA: AbhHeid ph/h. Heid 1992, Winter. 89p. DM 36. – ᴿBSO 57
(1994) 330s (O. *Leaman*).
1671 **Greene-McCreight** Kathryn Emily, Ad litteram; understanding of the
plain sense of Scripture in the exegesis of AUGUSTINE, CALVIN and
BARTH of Genesis 1-3: diss. Yale, ᴰ*Kelsey* D. NHv 1994. 406p.
94-28287. – DissA 55 (1994s) p. 1600.
1672 *Jaki* Stanley L., Genesis i through the ages, 1992 → 8,2049: ᴿAngelicum 70 (1993) 450s (S. *Jurič*); Faith & R 20 (1994) 309-315 (T. B.
Fowler); NBlackf 75 (1994) 283s (D. A. *Jones*: hard on others' exegesis,
weak in his own); Salesianum 56 (1994) 781s (M. *Cimosa*); ZkT 116 (1994)
87s (G. *Fischer*).
1673 *Leven* Christoph, Tatbericht und Wortbericht in der priesterschriftlichen
Schöpfungserzählung: ZTK 91 (1994) 115-133.
1674 *Lindeskog* G. †, Schöpfer und Schöpfung in den Schriften der Apostolischen Väter: → 496, ANRW 2/27/1 (1993) 588-648.
1675 **Maitland** Sara, A big-enough God. L 1994, Mowbray. 191p. £10.
0-264-67331-X. – ᴿExpTim 106 (1994s) 314 (R. G. *Jones*: 'a romp around
creation'; she says 'theology has always been on the retreat before science
and still is').
1676 *Maldamé* Jean-Michel, La création sans concordisme: Études 380
(1994) 77-87.
1677 **May** Gerhard, Creatio ex nihilo; the doctrine of 'creation out of
nothing' in early Christian thought, ᵀ*Worrall* A. E 1994, Clark. xxi-
197p. 0-567-09695-5.
Minear Paul S., [Gen 1-4 in 1Cor 15 etc.] Christians and the New Creation
1994 → 1645.
1678 *Ohly* Friedrich, Neue Zeugen des 'Buchs der Natur' aus dem Mittelalter

[CHRYSOSTOMUS, IBN GABIROL]: ➤ 52, ᶠHAUCK K., Iconologia 1994, 546-568.

1679 *Pérez de Laborda* Alfonso, El mundo como creación; comentarios filosóficos sobre el pensamiento de san AGUSTÍN en el De Genesi ad litteram: CiuD 207 (1994) 365-417.

1680 **Rad** Gerhard von, Genesi, la storia delle origini. Brescia 1993, Paideia. 189 p. Lᵐ 16. – ᴿParVi 39,2 (1994) 61s (A. *Rolla*: ristampa dei cap. 1-11 del Genesis 1972, ital. 78).

1681 *Rossi* Benedetto, La creazione nella letteratura giudaica antica extrabiblica, letteratura qumranica, targumica e rabbinica: VivH 5 (1994) 119-152; Eng. 152.

1682 *Roth* David I., Genesis [1] and the real world: Kerux 8,2 (1994) 30-54 [< OTAbs 18, p. 45].

1683 **Samuelson** Norbert M., The first seven days 1992 ➤ 8,2053: ᴿBL (1993) 68 (J. F. *Elwolde*: idiosyncratic); ÉglT 25 (1994) 125s (W. *Vogels*).

1684 **Samuelson** Norbert, Judaism and the doctrine of creation. C 1994, Univ. 362 p. £40. 0-521-46214-7. – ᴿExpTim 106 (1994s) 314 (R. G. *Jones*).

1685 **Simkins** Ronald A., Creator and creation. Peabody MA 1994, Hendrickson. xii-306 p. 1-56563-042-4 [NRT 117,903, J.-L. *Ska*; RelStR 21,128, Dianne *Bergant*].

1685* *Souzenelle* Annick de, Nouveaux regards sur la Genèse: BCentProt 46,1 ('Autour de la Kabbale' 1994) 12-19.

1686 **Vannier** Marie-Anne, Creatio... AUGUSTIN, ᴰ1991 ➤ 7,1780... 9,1832: ᴿAngelicum 71 (1994) 288-290 (B. *Degórski*); RevSR 68 (1994) 361s (J. *Garcia*); TR 90 (1994) 137-9 (C. *Müller*).

1687 *Vannier* Marie-Anne, 'Creatio' et 'formatio' chez ECKHART: RThom 94 (1994) 100-9.

1689 **Vogels** Walter, Nos origines, Genèse 1-11: Horizon du croyant, 1992 ➤ 8,2055; 9,1834: ᴿScEspr 46 (1994) 255s (M. *Roberge*).

1690 *Vorster* J. N., Creatures creating creators: the potential of rhetoric: R & T 1 (Pretoria 1994) 118-135 [< ZIT 95, p. 16].

1691 *Wächter* Ludwig, Die Aufnahme der biblischen Schöpfungsberichte in LUTHERs Katechismusschriften: TVers 18 (1993) 45-54.

1692 **Wolde** Ellen van, Words become worlds; semantic studies of Genesis 1-11: BInterpS 6. Leiden 1994, Brill. xi-213 p.; ill. 90-04-09887-9.

1693 *a*) *VanderKam* James C., Genesis 1 in Jubilees 2; – *b*) *Kugel* James, The Jubilees [23] apocalypse: DSD 1 (1994) 300-321 / 322-337.

1694 *Runesson* Anders, [Gn 1; Ps 104] Skapelsverb i aktivt particip + GT — teologiska implikationer: SvEx 59 (1994) 7-20.

1695 *Bartelmus* R., [Gn 1,1] šᵉmayim 'Himmel': ➤ 519, TWAT 8,1 (1994) 204-239.

1696 *Duchesne-Guillemin* Jacques, [Lc 3,22 < Gn 1,2: merahevet 'battant les ailes'] Vers la Trinité – et retour; CRAI (1994) 641-3.

1697 *Mainville* O., [Gn 1,1] De la *ruah* biblique au *pneûma* chrétien; le langage descriptif de l'esprit de Dieu: Théologiques 2,2 (Montréal 1994) 21-40.

1698 **Tsumura** David T., The earth and the waters in Genesis 1 and 2; jOsu 83, 1989 ➤ 5,1978... 8,2060: ᴿCurrTM 21 (1994) 133 (H. M. *Niemann*); EvQ 66 (1994) 257-9 (C. T. *Mitchell*).

1699 *Marin* Marcello, [Gn 1,5] Nomen quasi notamen; una nota su AUG. Gen. litt. impf. 6,26: ➤ 86, ᶠNALDINI M., Paideia 1994, 227-234.

Gen 1,26: imago Dei

1700 *Cottin* Jérôme,   Le regard et la Parole; une théologie protestante de l'image [diss.]. P 1994, Labor et Fides.   342 p. – ᴿRHPR 74 (1994) 273-280 (P. *Prigent*).

1701 ꟳGOLUB Ivan,   Homo imago et amicus Dei, ᴱ**Ratko** P. 1991 ➤ 7,67: ᴿOstKSt 42 (1993) 267s (H. M. *Biedermann*).

1702 *Gross* Walter,   Die Gottebenbildlichkeit des Menschen nach Gen 1,26.27: BibNot 68 (1993) 35-48.

1703 *McLeod* Frederick G.,   The Antiochene tradition regarding the role of the body within the 'image of God': ➤ 405, Broken 1993/4, 23-53.

1704 *Middleton* J. Richard,   The liberating image? Interpreting the *imago Dei* in context: ChrSchR 24 (1994) 8-26.

1705 *Schreiner* Stefan,   Partner in Gottes Schöpfungswerk; zur rabbinischen Auslegung von Gen 1,26-27:   Judaica 49 (1993) 131-145.

1706 *Vogels* Walter,   The human person in the image of God (Gn 1,26): Sc-Espr 46 (1994) 189-202.

1707 ᴱ**Coste** René, *Ribaut* Jean-Pierre,   Sauvegarde et gérance de la création [Paris Pax Christi Sept. 1990]. P 1991, Desclée.   280 p. F 155. – ᴿÉglT 25 (1994) 269s (J. R. *Pambrun*).

1708 *Gerstenberger* Erhard S.,   [Gen 1,24-31] 'Sujeitai a terra' — acerca da mitologia do poder: EstudosT 33 (1993) 227-238 [< OTAbs 17, p. 543].

1709 *a) Gerstenberger* Erhard,   'Macht euch die Erde untertan' (Gen 1,28); vom Sinn und Missbrauch der 'Herrschaftsformel'; – *b) Ruppert* Lothar, Tradition und Interpretation in Israel — aufgezeigt an der biblischen Urgeschichte: ➤ 31*, ꟳDAUTZENBERG G., Nach 1994, 235-250 / 521-538.

1710 **Rüterswörden** Udo,   Dominium terrae; Studien zur Genese einer alttestamentlichen Vorstellung: BZAW 215, 1993 ➤ 9,1863: ᴿBL (1994) 98 (P. L. *Harland*); FrSZ 41 (1994) 291-5 (C. *Uehlinger*); JBL 113 (1994) 701s (R. J. *Clifford*: good but the Bible never shows animals as enemies or competitors of humans.

1711 **Wybrow** Cameron,   The Bible, Baconianism and mastery over nature; the Old Testament and its modern misreading. NY 1991, P. Lang. vi-231 p. – ᴿPerspScCF 46 (1994) 133-5 (E. B. *Davis*, < Isis Mar. 1994, 127-9); SR 23 (1994) 237 (P. D. *Benton*: England's 17th century 'Baconians' got it right; but it is not explained why we have since gone so wrong).

1712 *Bube* Richard R.,   [Gn 1,28] Do biblical models need to be replaced in order to deal effectively with environmental issues?: PerspScCF 46 (1994) 90-97 [80-89, *De Witt* Calvin B.].

1713 **Tsumuraya** Katsuko,   A canonical reading of Genesis 1-3 [not two separate accounts]: diss. Catholic Univ., ᴰ*Di Lella* A. Wsh 1994. 374 p. 95-03615. – DissA 55 (1994s) p. 2868.

E1.7   *Genesis 1s*:   **Bible and myth** [➤ M3.8].

1714 **Adams-Leeming** David & Margaret,   Encyclopedia of creation myths. Santa Barbara CA 1994, ABC-Clio.   viii-330 p. $60. 0-87436-739-5 [TDig 42,74].

1715 *Averbeck* Richard E.,   The Sumerian historiographic tradition and its implications for Genesis 1-11: ➤ 326*, Faith 1990/4, 79-102.

1716 **Batto** Bernard F.,   Slaying the dragon — mythmaking in the biblical tradition 1992 ➤ 9,1867: ᴿBibTB 24 (1994) 146 (J. B. *Burns*); BL (1993)

71s (J. *Day*); CBQ 56 (1994) 314-6 (R. S. *Hendel*); Interpretation 48 (1994) 301 (L. *Boadt*); JBL 113 (1994) 506-8 (J. A. *Davila*); OTEssays 7 (1994) 108-110 (M. G. *Swanepoel*).

1717 **Bertrand** Guy-Marie, La révélation cosmique dans la pensée occidentale [à partir d'Égypte, Mésopotamie]: Recherches NS 28. Montréal/P 1993, Bellarmin/Cerf. 590 p. – ᴿSR 23 (1994) 88s (Catherine *Barry*).

1718 **Bickel** Suzanne, La cosmologie égyptienne, avant le Nouvel Empire: diss. Genève 1993: OBO 134. FrS/Gö 1994, Univ./VR. 346 p. 3-7278-0950-7 / VR 3-525-53769-7 [BL 95,123, K. A. *Kitchen*]. – ᴿÉTRel 69 (1994) 566 (Françoise *Smyth*).

1719 ᴱ**Biderman** Shlomo, *Scharfstein* Ben-Ami, Myths and fictions: Philosophy and religion 3. Leiden 1993, Brill. vii-397 p. ƒ185. 90-04-09838-0 [BL 95,8, N. *Wyatt*].

1720 **Bietenholz** Peter G., Historia and fabula; myths and legends in historical thought from antiquity to the modern age: StudIntelHist 59. Leiden 1994, Brill. xii-435 p. 90-04-10063-6.

1721 *Blomqvist* Jerker, The fall of Phaeton and the Kaalijärv meteorite crater; is there a connection? [probable]: Eranos 92 (1994) 1-16.

1721* **Clifford** Richard J., Creation accounts in the Ancient Near East and in the Bible: CBQ mg 26. Wsh 1994, Catholic Biblical Asn. xiii-217 p. $8, 0-915170-25-6 [BL 95,83, W. G. *Lambert*; TLZ 120,985, T. *Naumann*].

1722 **Curtis** Vesta Sarkhosh, Persian myths: The Legendary Past. L 1993, British Museum. 80 p.; ill. 0-7141-2082-0 [OIAc 11,19].

1723 *Dietrich* M., 'Wir wollen die Menschheit schaffen!' der göttliche Ursprung des Menschenwegs nach der sumero-babylonischen Mythologie: MARG 9 (1994) 40-54 [< ZIT 95, p. 276].

1724 *Dubuisson* D., Ontogenèse divine et structures énonciatives; la création illocutoire d'Agni dans le Rigveda: RHR 211 (1994) 225-... [< ZIT 95, p. 69].

1725 *Fischer* Dick, In search of the historical Adam, 2. [Adapa]: PerspScCF 46 (1994) 47-57 [69, letter of *Siemens* D. F. on part 1].

1726 **Gibert** P., Bibbia, miti e racconti dell'inizio 1993 → 9,1870: ᴿAsprenas 41 (1994) 283-5 (G. *Di Palma*); ParVi 39,5 (1994) 55s (S. *Migliasso*); RivB 42 (1994) 459-462 (G. *Segalla*).

1727 ᴱ**Hess** Richard S., *Tsumura* David T., 'I studied inscriptions from before the Flood'; Ancient Near Eastern literary and linguistic approaches to Genesis 1-11: Sources for biblical and theological study 4. WL 1994, Eisenbrauns. xvi-480 p. 0-99-1464-88-9.

1728 *Jack* R. D. S., [BARRIE James] Peter Pan as DARWINIAN creation myth: LitTOx 8 (1994) 157-173.

1729 (Lundager) *Jensen* Hans J., [Rev 21; Gen 18-22; 2 Kgs 4; 1 Kgs 17; Baucis] The cosmic wedding and the brief life on earth: → 89e, ᶠOTZEN B., In the last days 1994, 136-157.

1730 **Knappert** Jan, The encyclopaedia of Middle Eastern mythology and religion. Brisbane 1993, Element. 309 p. $30. 1-85230-427-8 [RelStR 21,320, M. A. *Sweeney*].

1731 **Kramer** Samuel N., *Meier* John, Myths of Enki, the crafty god 1989 → 5,2007 ... 8,2085: ᴿJNES 53 (1994) 322-4 (B. *Alster*).

1732 **Kreitzer** Larry J., Prometheus and Adam; enduring symbols of the human situation. Lanham MD 1994, UPA. x-214 p. 0-8191-8497-7.

1733 **Lameyre** Alain, Les philosophes de l'âge de pierre, ou la vérité de la Genèse: Pratiques théoriques. P 1992, PUF. 198 p. – ᴿRAss 88 (1994) 176s (P. *Amiet*: artificiel); RThom 94 (1994) (J. M. *Maldamé*).

1733* *Lee* Archie C.C., The Chinese creation myth of Nu Kua and the biblical narrative in Genesis 1-11: BInterp 2 (1994) 312-324.
1734 **Loh** Johannes, Mythenlogik als praktisch-theologische Herausforderung biblischer Texte, dargestellt am Paradiesmythos: Hab.-Diss. ᴰ*Schröer* H. Bonn 1994s. – RTLv 26, p. 529.
1735 *Lüdde* M.E., Mythos und Bibel im Werk Franz FÜHMANNs: ZeichZt 48 (1994) 232-... [< ZIT 95, p. 96].
1736 **Luginbühl** Marianne, Menschenschöpfungsmythen; ein Vergleich, zwischen Griechenland und dem Alten Orient [Diss. Zürich 1990]: EurHS 15/58. Fra 1992, Lang. 206 p.; 10 pl. 3-261-04533-7 [OIAc 11,31].
1737 *Mondi* Robert, *Chaos* and the Hesiodic cosmogony: HarvClasPg 92 (1989) 1-41 [ArBegG 36 (1993) 335s (*ipse*)].
1738 *Müller* Hans-Peter, Entmythologisierung und AT: NSys 35 (1993) 1-27; Eng. 27.
1739 **Niditch** Susan, Folklore and the Hebrew Bible 1993 → 9,1879: ᴿBL (1994) 96 (J.R. *Porter*); VT 44 (1994) 577 (J.A. *Emerton*, also on her 1993 War),
1740 **Nugent** Anthony, Star God; Enki/Ea and the biblical God as expressions of common Ancient Near Eastern astral-theological symbol system: diss. ᴰ*Gates* R. – RTLv 26, p. 532.
1741 *O'Malley* William J., Scripture and myth: America 171,3 (1994) 6-9.
1742 **Patai** Raphael, Robert GRAVES and the Hebrew myths; a collaboration [Hebrew myths; the book of Genesis 1975; but here we have their correspondence after Graves' 'fan letter' 1947 on Patai's Man and Temple]. Detroit 1992, Wayne State Univ. 468 p. – ᴿAJS 19 (1994) 237s (Martin *Benal*, p. 238; or *Bemal*, contents before 135, or *Bernal*?).
1743 **Penglase** Charles, Greek myths and Mesopotamia; parallels and influence in the Homeric Hymns and Hesiod. L 1994, Routledge. xii-278 p.; bibliog. 251-264. 0-415-08371-0 [OIAc 11,36].
1744 *Schmidt* Werner H., *al.*, Mythos AT: → 517, TRE 23 (1994) (597-) 625-644.
1745 *Vanstiphout* H.I.J., Enuma Elish as a systematic creed; an essay: OrLovPer 23 (1992) 37-61.
1746 **Worthen** Thomas D., The myth of replacement; stars, gods, and order in the universe 1991 → 7,1833*; 9,1882: ᴿJRel 73 (1993) 128-130 (D. *Gold*: a good try).

E1.8 *Gen 1s, Jos 10,13 ... :* **The Bible, the Church, and Science.**

1747 *Alviar* Joselito J., Towards a modern presentation of the mystery of creation: PhilipSac 29 (1994) 485-493.
1748 **Appleyard** Bryan, Understanding the present; science and the soul of modern man 1992 → 9,1885: ᴿChrCent 110 (1994) 19-22 (H. *Rolston*); CW 237,2 (1994) 96 (D. *Liderbach*); JScStRel 32 (1993) 406-8 (D.C. *Johnson*).
1749 **Artigas** Mariano, *a*) Las fronteras del evolucionismo; – *c*) El hombre a la luz de la ciencia; – *c*) Ciencia, razón y fe: M 1991-92-92, Palabra. 206 p./254 p./198 p. – ᴿScripTPamp 26 (1994) 289-292 (A. *Pardó*).
1750 **Bailey** Lloyd R., Genesis, creation and creationism 1993 → 9,1889: ᴿCW 237,1 (1994) 53-55 (Deborah *Blake*); Horizons 21 (1994) 380s (R.A. *Simkins*); Interpretation 48 (1994) 420.2 (C. *Hyers*).
1751 **Barbour** Ian, Ethics in an age of technology 1992 → 8,2099; 9,1892: ᴿEurJT 3,2 (1994) 177s; franç. deutsch 176; NBlackf 74 (1993) 373-5 (R. *Ruston*).

1752 **Barbour** Ian, Religion in an age of science 1990 → 6,2195 ... 9,1891: ᴿChurchman 108 (1994) 188s (D. *Spanner*); EurJT 3 (1994) 82-84 (R. *Sturch*).

1753 ᴱ**Bauman** Michael, Man and creation; perspectives on science and theology. Hillsdale College, 1993. 306 p. $10 pa. – ᴿJEvTS 37 (1994) 598-600 (J. K. *La Shell*).

1754 **Beukel** A. van den, More things in heaven and earth; God and the scientists; ᵀ*Bowden* J. L 1991, SCM. 188 p. £8.50. 0-334-02504-4. – ᴿChurchman 108 (1994) 274s (D. *Spanner*).

1755 **Binns** Emily, World as creation 1990 → 6,2200 = 7204: ᴿNewTR 7,1 (1994) 111s (Z. *Hayes*).

1756 ᴱ**Brandmüller** Walter, *Greipl* Egon J., Cᴏᴘᴇʀɴɪᴄᴏ, Gᴀʟɪʟᴇɪ e la Chiesa; fine della controversia (1820); gli Atti del Sant'Ufficio: Pont. Acad. Scientiarum. F 1992, Olschki. 498 p. 88-222-3997-0. – ᴿCC 145 (1994,1) 90s (M. *Chappin*); Gregorianum 75 (1994) 585s (P. *Gilbert*); QuadSto 39 (1994) 329-332 (L. *Canfora*).

1757 **Brooke** John H., Science and religion; some historical perspectives 1991 → 8,2111; 9,1899; C 1991, Univ. 422 p. £27.50; pa. £11. 0-521-23961-3; -8374-4. – ᴿAmHR 99 (1994) 191 (R. *Olson*: History of Science Society prize); Churchman 108 (1994) 281 (D. *Spanner*); Protestantesimo 49 (1994) 385s (P. *Comba*).

1758 *Brooke* John H., Between science and theology; the defence of teleology in the interpretation of nature, 1820-1876: ZnTg 1 (1994) 47-65.

1759 ᴱ**Bühler** Pierre, *Karakash* Clairette, Science et foi font système; une approche herméneutique; Travaux de l'Institut de Recherches Herméneutiques et Systématiques: Lieux théologiques 21. Genève 1992, Labor et Fides. 215 p. Fs 32. – ᴿÉglT 25 (1994) 269-272 (J. R. *Pambrun*).

1760 *Bühler* Pierre, Science et foi; l'apport de l'herméneutique: RTPhil 126 (1994) 143-153; Eng. 192.

1761 **Caleo** Marcello, Gᴀʟɪʟᴇᴏ, l'anticopernicano. Salerno-Pellezzano 1992, Dottrinari. 309 p. Lᵐ 35 [Gregorianum 76,158, R. *Fisichella*].

1762 *Chaline* Jean, *Marchand* Didier, Une révolution en paléoanthropologie! ... l'homme, accumulant un retard considérable dans son développement, se verrait par là-même incapable d'atteindre une maturité comparable à celle du singe: Archéologia 302 (1994) 19-25 [304 p. 12-15, découvertes en Éthiopie].

1763 **Chan Sing**, Concepts of the nature of science and religion in Hong Kong secondary schools: diss. Biola Univ. ᴰ*Lingenfelter* S. 1994. 311 p. 94-26469. – DissA 55 (1994) p. 1233.

1764 *Clark* James P., Fact, faith and philosophy; one step toward understanding the conflict between science and Christianity: PerspSCF 46 (1994) 242-252.

1765 *Cloots* André, Snijdt het kosmologisch argument nog hout? Over de verhouding tussen wetenschap en geloof: CollatVL 24 (1994) 133-155.

1766 **Clouser** Roy A., The myth of religious neutrality; an essay on the hidden role of religious beliefs in theories 1991 → 7,1851: ᴿAndrUnSem 32 (1994) 121-3 (M. F. *Hanna*). → 862.

1767 **Colditz** Jens D., Kosmos als Schöpfung; die Lehre von der creatio ex nihilo als Orientierungsparameter im Dialog mit der modernen Kosmologie: ev. Diss. ᴰ*Schwarz* H. Regensburg 1994. – TR 91,101.

1768 **Cole-Turner** Ronald, The new Genesis; theology and the [DNA] genetic revolution 1993 → 9,1902: ᴿPrincSemB 15 (1994) 83s (R. L. *Shinn*).

1769 *Collins* C. John, How old is the earth? Anthropomorphic days in

Genesis 1:1-2:3: Pres[-byterion St Louis?] 20 (1994) 109-130 (OTAbs 18, p. 288; abbreviation not listed).

1770 *a) Corbally* Christopher J.,   Science and faith; an astronomer's perspective; – *b) Byers* David M.,   *Pace* GALILEO; the present and future of religion/science dialogue: America 170,12 (1994) 22-25-26.

1771 **Corey** Michael A.,   Back to DARWIN; the scientific case for deistic evolution.   Lanham MD 1994, UPA.   434 p. $62.50; pa. $37.   0-8191-9306-2; -7-0 [TDig 41,355: sequel to God and the new cosmology].

1772 **Craig** William L.,   *Smith* Quentin,   Theism, atheism and big bang cosmology.   Ox 1993, Clarendon.   x-342 p. £35. – ᴿRelSt 30 (1994) 327-9 (R. *Le Poidevin*).

1773 **Crook** Paul,   Darwinism, war and history; the debate over the biology of war from the 'Origin of Species' to the First World War.   C 1994, Univ.   xii-306 p. [AmHR 100,1526s, H. L. *Kaye*].

1774 *Cunningham* Lawrence,   DARWIN et le 'transformisme des auteurs classiques':   LavalTP 50 (1994) 389-413.

1775 *a) Delsol* Michel,   Le hasard et la sélection naturelle expliquent-ils l'évolution?   Biologie ou métaphysique; – *b) Koninck* Thomas de,   La science et Dieu; – *c) Boné* Édouard,   La coupure anthropologique; – *d) Tournier* François,   Histoire ou rétrodiction scientifique: LavalTP 50 (1994) 7-41 / 43-60 (111-143) / 61-69 / 71-93 [595-600, *Artigos* Mariano; *Price* Colin].

1776 *Drees* Willem B.,   Welke vissen ontsnappen?   [Which fish escape?]   Over de relevatie van natuurwetenschap voor theologie: TvT 34 (1994) 169-183; Eng. 183.

1777 **Eccles** John C. [neurophysiology Nobel],   Evolution of the brain; creation of the self.   L 1989, Routledge.   xv-282 p. $25. – ᴿCritRR 5 (1992) 427-9 (J. B. *Ashbrook*: 'how we humans came to be').

1778 **Edwards** Denis,   Jesus and the cosmos.   ... 1991, St. Paul.   140 p. A$11. – ᴿAustralasCR 70 (1993) 256 (R. *Lennan*).

1779 **Ellul** Jacques,   The technological bluff 1990 → 7,1857* ... 9,1917: ᴿCritRR 5 (1992) 434-7 (R. R. *Reno*).

1780 *Emberger* Gary,   Theological and scientific explanations for the origin and purpose of natural evil: PerspSCF 46 (1994) 151-8.

1781 **Evans** Evelyn M.,   God or DARWIN; the development of beliefs about the origin of species: diss. Michigan, ᴰ*Wellmon* H.   AA 1994.   195 p. 95-00920. – DissA 55 (1994s) p. 2335.

1782 **Facchini** Fiorenzo,   L'uomo; origine ed evoluzione.   Mi 1994, Jaca. 40 p., ill. Lᵐ 18. – ᴿArcheo 9,111 (1994) 105s (S. *Mammini*).

1783 **Fantoli** Annibale,   GALILEO; per il copernicanismo e per la Chiesa. Vaticano 1993, Specola.   xv-447 p.; ill.   Lᵐ 60. – ᴿCC 145 (1994,2) 608s (P. *Millefiorini*).

1784 **Fantoli** Annibale,   GALILEO; for Copernicanism and for the Church, ᵀ*Coyne* George V.   R/ND 1994, Vatican Observatory.   xiv-540 p. $22 [TS 56,369, E. *McMullin*].

1785 **Ferguson** Kitty,   The fire in the equations; Science, religion and the search for God.   L 1994, Transworld.   £17. – ᴿMonth 255 (1994) 375s (C. *Moss*).

1786 **Fernández-Rañada** Antonio,   Los científicos y Dios.   Oviedo 1994, Nobel.   300 p. – ᴿRazF 230 (1994) 229s (A. *Udías*).

1787 *Fischer* Johannes,   Kann die Theologie der naturwissenschaftlichen Vernunft die Welt als Schöpfung verständlich machen?: FrSZ 41 (1994) 491-514.

1788 *Foppa* Carlo, L'analyse philosophique jonassienne de la théorie de l'évolution; aspects problématiques: LavalTP 50 (1994) 575-593.

1789 **Ford** Adam, Universe, God, man, and science, 1986 ➤ 2,1501: ᴿScot-JR 12 (1991) 56-58 (H. R. *Wilson*).

1790 **Forsthoefel** Paulinus F., Religious faith meets modern science. NY 1994, Alba. ix-146 p. $9 pa. 0-8189-0704-5 [TDig 42,165].

1791 **Gapaillard** Jacques, Et pourtant elle tourne! Le mouvement de la terre. P 1994, Seuil. 354 p. – ᴿArchivScSocR 39,88 (1994) 72 (É. *Poulat*).

1792 *García-Rivera* Alejandro, A contribution to the dialogue between theology and the natural sciences: JHispT 2,1 (1994) 51-59.

1793 *Gascoigne* Robert M., The new cosmology; science ponders divine creation: AustralasCR 71 (1994) 330-340.

1794 *a*) *Giberson* Karl, Jerusalem and the National Academy of Science; is there a Christian philosophy of science? [response, *Wilcox* David]; – *b*) *Mouw* Richard J., Creational politics; some Calvinist amendments: ChrSchR 23 (1993s) 194-202 [203-7] / 181-193.

1795 *Giberson* Karl, Intelligent design on trial; review essay [MORELAND J. 1994, *al.*]; ChrSchR 24 (1994s) 459-471; 472-8, Moreland's reply.

1796 **Gilkey** Langdon, Nature, reality and the sacred; the nexus of science and religion. Mp 1993, Fortress. xii-266 p. – ᴿTLond 97 (1994) 392s (J. *Polkinghorne*: rich and stimulating, sometimes repetitiously).

1797 **Gillies** Donald, Philosophy of science in the twentieth century; four central themes. Ox/CM 1993, Blackwell. xv-251 p. £35; pa. £12. – ᴿZkT 116 (1994) 207-212 (W. *Löffler*).

1798 **Gish** Duane C., Creation scientists answer their critics. El Cajon CA 1993, Inst. Creation Research. 451 p. $17 pa. – ᴿPerspSCF 46 (1994) 193s (J. W. *Burgeson*) & 193-5 (J. *Lippard*).

1799 **Gismondi** Gualberto, Fede e cultura scientifica: Fede e Cultura 3. Bo 1993, Dehoniane. 230 p. Lᵐ 27. 88-10-20803-X. – ᴿAntonianum 69 (1994) 338-369 (Gisella *Zigliani*, con due altri suoi libri della serie).

1800 *Gregersen* Niels H., Theology in a Neo-Darwinian world: ST 24 (1994) 125-149.

1801 *Haas* J. W.ᴶ, John WESLEY's views on science and Christianity; an examination of the charge of antiscience: ChH 63 (1994) 378-392.

1802 **Haffner** Paul, Creation and scientific creativity; a study in the thought of S. L. JAKI 1991 ➤ 9,1925: ᴿAngelicum 71 (1994) 135s (A. *Wilder*).

1803 **Harris** Errol E., Cosmos and Theos; ethical and theological implications of the anthropic cosmological principle 1992 ➤ 8,2134: ᴿÉglT 25 (1994) 274s (J. R. *Pambrun* compares to HITCHCOCK J.).

1804 **Hefner** Philip, The human factor; evolution, culture, and religion 1993 ➤ 9,1927: ᴿAmJTP 15 (1994) 210-6 (J. E. W. *Robbins*, also on MUNZ P.); ChrSchR 24 (1994s) 494-6 (B. R. *Reichenbach*); Interpretation 48 (1994) 437s (W. C. *Placher*).

1805 *Highfield* Ron, GALILEO, scientific creationism, and biblical hermeneutics: ➤ 89*, ᶠOLBRICHT T., RestQ 36 (1994) 279-290.

1806 **Hobbs** Jesse, Religious explanation and scientific ideology: Toronto Studies in Religion. NY 1993, P. Lang. xxii-234 p. $46 [RelStR 21,208, Mary *Gerhart*].

1807 **Jaki** Stanley L., Scientist and Catholic P. DUHEM 1991 ➤ 8,2142: ᴿCanadCath 12,10 (1994) 27 (M. *Daughty*).

1808 **Jaki** Stanley L., Is there a universe?... Wethersfield Inst. 137 p. $13; pa. $9. – ᴿCanadCath 12,11 (1994) 18 (J. *Hanrahan*: his 35th book).

1809 **Jaki** Stanley L., Dio e i cosmologi [1989 < Oxford 1988]: Scienza e fede 7, 1991 ➤ 9,1935: 88-209-1778-5: ᴿGregorianum 75 (1994) 195 (W. *Welten*).
1810 ᴱ**Jewett** Paul K., God, creation and evolution; a neo-evangelical theology. GR 1991, Eerdmans. xiv-535 p. $30. 0-8028-0460-8. – ᴿChrSchR 22 (1992) 435-7 (R. L. *Maddox*).
1811 *Johansson* Sverker, Är kreationismen vetenskapligt hållbar?: SvTKv 68 (1992) 19-28; Eng. 28.
1812 **Johnson** Phillip, Dᴀʀᴡɪɴ on trial² [¹1991 + new epilogue] ➤ 9,1936: ᴿChrSchR 24 (1994s) 479-488 (W. *Hasker*), 489-493, Johnson's reply.
1813 **Kaiser** Christopher B., Creation and the history of science 1991 ➤ 8, 2147; 9,1937; $18 pa.: ᴿChrSchR 23 (1993s) 487 (J.H. *Crichton*); Churchman 108 (1994) 279s (D. *Spanner*); ScripTPamp 26 (1994) 864 (J. *Morales*).
1814 *a) Kitchen* Kenneth A., Genesis 12-50 in the Near Eastern world; – *b) Wenham* Gordon, The face at the bottom of the well; hidden agenda of the Pentateuchal commentator; – *c) Alexander* T. Desmond, Abraham re-assessed theologically; the Abraham narratives and the NT understanding of justification by faith: ➤ 145c, ᶠWɪsᴇᴍᴀɴ D., He swore an oath ²1994, 67-92 / 185-209 / 7-28 [< OTAbs 18, p. 508].
1815 **Kozhamathadam** Job, The discovery of Kᴇᴘʟᴇʀ's laws; the interaction of science, philosophy, and religion. ND 1994, Univ. xi-315. $40. [AmHR 100,1555s, W. H. *Donahue*: useful within limitations].
1816 *Kozhamathadam* Job, The Gᴀʟɪʟᴇᴏ episode revisited: Vidyajyoti 58 (1994) 337-358.
1817 **Krause** Helmut, Theologie, Physik und Philosophie im Weltbild Karl Hᴇɪᴍs: ev. Diss. ᴰ*Nethöfel* W. Marburg 1994. – TR 91,99.
 Lameyre Alain, Les philosophes de l'âge de pierre ou la vérité de la Genèse: Pratiques théologiques 1992 ➤ 1733.
1818 *Lane* David H., *a)* Special creation or evolution — no middle ground; – *b)* Theological problems with theistic evolution: BtS 151 (1994) 11-31 / 155-174.
1820 **Lecourt** Dominique, L'Amérique entre la Bible et Dᴀʀᴡɪɴ: Science, histoire, société 1992 ➤ 8,2153; 9,1940: ᴿRHR 210 (1993) 494-6 (F. *Zimmermann*).
1821 **Lubenow** Marvin L., Bones of contention; a creationist assessment of human fossils. GR 1992, Baker. 295 p. $13. – ᴿBtS 151 (1994) 118s (F. R. *Howe*).
1822 **McCrady** Edward, Seen and unseen; a biologist views the universe 1990 ➤ 8,2159; 0-918769-16-7: ᴿChrSchR 23 (1993s) 454-6 (P. *Pun*).
1823 **Magnin** Thierry, Quel Dieu pour un monde scientifique? 1993 ➤ 9, 1950: ᴿÉglT 24 (1993) 450s (R. *Martínez de Pisón* L.); NRT 116 (1994) 758s (P. *Evrard*).
1824 **Maldamé** Jean-Michel, Le Christ et le cosmos; incidence de la cosmologie moderne sur la théologie 1991 ➤ 9,1951: ᴿNRT 116 (1994) 290s (P. *Evrard*); ScEspr 46 (1994) 367-9 (C. *Saint-Germain*).
1825 ᴱ**Mangum** John M., The new faith-science debate 1987/9 ➤ 5,702 ... 7,1880: ᴿRTPhil 126 (1994) 86s (Clairette *Karakash*),
1826 ᴱ**Manna** Ambrogio, L'enigma della vita; ricerca sul problema delle origini: Problemi di attualità. N 1993, Loffredo. 245 p. Lᵐ 40. – ᴿRasT 35 (1994) 507-9 (P. *Orlando*).
1827 **Martin** Russell N. D., Pierre Dᴜʜᴇᴍ; philosophy and history in the work of a believing physicist 1991 ➤ 8,2164: ᴿJRel 74 (1994) 109 (M. F. *Frampton*).

1828 **Maturana** Humberto, *Varela* Francisco, L'arbre de la connaissance; racines biologiques de la connaissance humaine. P 1994, Addison-Wesley. 272 p. – ᴿRTPhil 126 (1994) 377s (J.-J. *Ducret*).

1829 **Midgley** Mary, Science as salvation; a modern myth and its meaning 1992 → 9,1994; $25; 0-415-06271-3: ᴿChrCent 110 (1993) 269-274 (J. M. *Gustafson*); ChrSchR 24 (1994s) 498-500 (C. A. *Russell*); HeythJ 35 (1994) 335s (P. *Avis*).

1830 *Millefiorini* Pietro, GALILEO al di là delle polemiche [FANTOLI A. 1993]: RasT 35 (1994) 497-505.

1831 **Moreland** J. P., Christianity and the nature of science; a philosophical investigation 1989 → 5,2077... 8,2168: ᴿChrSchR 24 (1994) 325-7 (J. *Culp*, also on POLKINGHORNE 1991); ConcordJ 20 (1994) 346s (J. W. *Klotz*).

1832 ᴱ**Moreland** J. P., The creation hypothesis; scientific evidence for an intelligent designer. DG 1994, InterVarsity. 335 p. $13 pa. [JEvTS 38,622, P. *Copan*; RelStR 21,115, S. M. *Heim*].

1833 *Moreland* J. P., Conceptual problems and the scientific status of creation science: PerspScCF 46 (1994) 2-11 (12-18-21, replies, *Meyer* Stephen C., The use and abuse of philosophy of science; *Bube* Richard H., Is creation science an oxymoron?; 22-25, Moreland rejoinder).

1834 **Moss** Jean D., Novelties in the heavens; rhetoric and science in the Copernican controversy 1993 → 9,1959: ᴿAmHR 99 (1994) 540s (P. *Dear*).

1835 *Motta* Uberto, Sugli studi galileiani: ViPe 77 (1994) 400-455.

1836 *Muratore* Saturnino, 'Dio' nelle nuove cosmologie: CC 145 (1994,1) 553-566.

1837 *Murphy* George L., The science-theology dialogue and theological ambiguity: CurrTM 21 (1994) 246-252.

1838 **Murphy** Nancey, Theology in the age of scientific reasoning 1990 → 8,2170: ᴿCanadCath 12,1 (1994) 26s (C. *Delzell*); RTPhil 126 (1994) 87s (Clairette *Karakash*); ScotJT 47 (1994) 269-271 (P. *Avis*); ScripTPamp 26 (1994) 1248-1250 (J. *Alviar*).

1839 **Nebelsick** Harold F., Renaissance and Reformation and the rise of science 1992 → 8,2172: ᴿEvQ 66 (1994) 355-7 (C. R. *Trueman*).

1840 **Nelson** J. Robert, On the new frontiers of genetics and religion. GR 1994, Eerdmans. xii-212 p. $13 pa. 0-8028-0741-0 [TDig 42,180]. – ᴿSewaneeTR 38 (1994s) 78-80 (R. T. *Nolan*, also on COLE-TURNER R. 1993).

1841 **Nickel** James, Mathematics; is God silent? Vallecito 1990, Ross: ᴿChrSchR 56 (1994) 68 (W. D. *Laverell*: only book on the market aiming to provide a Christian perspective on mathematics).

1842 **Noll** Mark A., The scandal of the evangelical mind [... fundamentalist 'creation-science' fails to influence higher education]. GR/Leicester 1994, Eerdmans/Inter-Varsity. ix-274 p. $20. 0-8028-3715-8/.

1843 **Numbers** Ronald L., The creationists; the evolution of scientific creationism 1992 → 9,1965; 0-679-40104-0: ᴿAmHR 99 (1994) 525s (Catherine L. *Albanese*); ChrSchR 24 (1994) 98s (E. A. *Olson*); JIntdis 25 (1994s) 537s (E. L. *Larson*); JRelH 18 (1994) 110-2 (N. *Weeks*).

1843* **Patai** Raphael, The Jewish alchemists; a history of science book. Princeton 1994. $35. 0-691-03290-0.

1844 **Peacocke** Arthur, Theology for a scientific age [= 1990 + 1993 Gifford Lectures] → 9,1969; also L 1993, SCM. 438 p. £15, 0-334-03547-8 [RelStR 21,208, Mary *Gerhart*]. – ᴿExpTim 106 (1994s) 159 (C. S. *Rodd*:

major, essential); TLond 97 (1994) 199s (J. *Polkinghorne*, whose outlook is repeated all wrong but with an endnote acknowledging he told him this); TvT 34 (1994) 204 (T. *Brattinga*).

1845 **Pearcey** Nancy R., *Thaxton* Charles B., The soul of science; Christian faith and natural philosophy. Wheaton IL 1994, Crossway. viii-298 p. $11. 0-89107-766-9. – ᴿChrSchR 24 (1994s) 496-8 (Sara J. *Miles*).

1846 *Pharantos* Megas I., ᴳ Science and religion : TAth 64 (1993) 30-79. 581-652; 65 (1994) 29-79. 494-517. 679-722...

1847 **Polkinghorne** John, The faith of a physicist. Princeton 1994, Univ. 211 p. $25. 0-691-03620-9. – ᴿWorship 68 (1994) 561s (J. F. *Haught*).

1848 **Polkinghorne** John, Quarks, chaos and Christianity; questions to science and religion. L 1994, Triangle. 102 p. £5. 0-281-04779-0. – ᴿExpTim 106 (1994s) 319 [C. S. *Rodd*].

1849 **Polkinghorne** John, Reason and reality 1991 ➤ 7,1897...9,1971: ᴿScotBuEv 12 (1994) 72-75 (G. *Houston*).

1850 **Polkinghorne** John, Science and Christian belief; theological reflections of a bottom-up thinker [Gifford Lectures 1993s]. L 1994, SPCK. 211 p. £10. 0-281-04714-6 [TDig 42,83]. – ᴿExpTim 105/10 2d-top choice (1993s) 290s (C. S. *Rodd*); TLond 97 (1994) 391s (C. *Knight*).

1851 **Polkinghorne** John, The way the world is² 1992 ➤ 8,2182c; 9,1973: ᴿPerspScCF 45 (1993) 61s (D. E. *Wray*).

1852 **Poppi** Antonio, CREMONINI, GALILEI e gli inquisitori del santo a Padova. Padova 1993, Centro Studi Antoniani 15. 128 p., 8 pl. [NRT 117,181, N. *Plumat*].

1853 ᴱ**Poupard** Paul, Après Galilée. P 1994, D-Brouwer. 266 p. – ᴿArchivScSocR 39,89 (1994) 98s (É. *Poulat*).

1854 **Raven** Charles, Science, religion and the future: Library of Anglican Spirituality (reprints). L 1994, Mowbrays & M. 125 p. £8. 0-264-67374-3. – ᴿExpTim 106 (1994s) 159 [C. S. *Rodd*], with two other titles of the series.

1855 *Raymo* Chet, Science vs. religion 1. Some tough questions; 2. *Honner* John, Some possible answers: Commonweal 121,16 (1994) 11-13. 14-17.

1856 **Root-Bernstein** Robert S., Discovering, inventing, and solving problems at the frontiers of scientific knowledge. CM 1989, Harvard Univ. 502 p. $35. 0-674-21175-8. – ᴿChrSchR 23,3 ('Christianity and bioethics' 1993s) 377-9 (G. D. *Hess*).

1857 **Ross** Hugh N., Creation and time; a biblical and scientific perspective on the creation-date controversy. Colorado Springs 1994, Navpress. 187 p. $10. 0-89109-776-7 [TDig 42,186].

1858 **Ross** Hugh, The fingerprint of God. Orange 1991, Promise. $10 pa. – ᴿJEvTS 37 (1994) 600s (D. W. *Hall*: 'an astronomer prior to his conversion').

1859 ᴱ**Russell** Robert J., *Stoeger* William R., *Coyne* George V., Physics, philosophy and theology 1987/8 ➤ 5,2095... 8,2187: ᴿCritRR 5 (1992) 437-9 (J. F. *Ollom*).

1860 **Segre** Michael, In the wake of GALILEO. New Brunswick NJ 1991, Rutgers Univ. xix-192 p. $28. – ᴿAmHR 99 (1994) 1352 (W. H. *Donahue*).

1861 *Siegwalt* Gérard, La justesse fonctionnelle de la science et la question de la vérité: RHPR 74 (1994) 249-263.

1862 *Sierotowicz* Tadeusz M., L''organizzazione mitica' del mondo e il dialogo tra scienza e teologia: Asprenas 41 (1994) 533-550.

1863 **Simkins** Ronald A., Creator and creation; nature in the worldview of ancient Israel. Peabody MA 1994, Hendrickson. xii-306 p. F00915 pa. 1-456563-042-4 [TDig 42,291].

1864 *Solis Fernández* Eduardo, 'La Biblia y la ciencia' del cardenal Zeferino GONZÁLEZ: ➤ 33*a*, FDÍAZ MERCHÁN G., StOvet 22 (1994) 205-224.

1865 *Strolz* Walter, Nature as creation; some reflections on biblical cosmology, T*Jansen* Henry: JIntRD 4 (1994) 158-169.

1866 **Swimme** Brian, *Berry* Thomas, The universe story; from the primordial flaring forth to the ecozoic era [after 2000 A.D.]; a celebration of the unfolding of the cosmos 1992 ➤ 9,1982: RPerScCF 46 (1994) 143s (J. de *Koning*: not Christian but recommended).

1867 *Tanzella-Nitti* Giuseppe, Cultura scientifica e rivelazione cristiana; orientamenti per un dialogo fra scienza e fede dopo GALILEO: AnnTh 8 (1994) 133-168.

1868 **Tiffin** Lee, Creationism's upside-down pyramid; how science refutes fundamentalism. Amherst NY 1994, Prometheus. 229 p. $30. 0-87975-898-8 [BL 95,22, L. L. *Grabbe*: useful but not orderly].

1869 **Tilby** Angela [BBC-TV producer] Science and the soul; new cosmology, the self and God 1992 ➤ 8,2199: RTLond 97 (1994) 146s (Mary *Midgley*: 'since fundamentalists on both sides won't give an inch, a skeptical third force called postmodernism has arisen to send harmless bystanders into vertigo').

1870 **Tipler** Frank J., Die Physik der Unsterblichkeit; moderne Kosmologie, Gott und die Auferstehung der Toten. Mü 1994, Piper. 605 p. DM 50. 3-492-03611-2. – RTGL 84 (1994) 378-381 (D. *Hattrup*).

1871 **Torrance** Thomas F., Preaching Christ today; the Gospel and scientific thinking. GR 1994, Eerdmans. viii-71 p. [RelStR 21,316].

1872 **Toumey** Christopher P., God's own scientists; creationists in a secular world. New Brunswick 1994, Rutgers Univ. xi-289 p. $45; pa. $15. 0-8135-2043-6; -4-4 [TDig 42,191]. – RPerspSCF 46 (1994) 266-8 (J. W. *Haas*).

1873 **Villain** Noel, Ontological and gnoseological presuppositions of science in the works of Stanley L. JAKI: diss. DNubiola Aguilar J. Pamplona 1994. – RTLv 26, p. 530.

1874 **Von Fange** Erich A., Helping children understand Genesis and the dinosaur. Tecumseh MI 1992, *auct.* xii-208 p. $13 pa. – RBtS 151 (1994) 119 (J. A. *Witmer*).

1875 *Wassermann* Christoph, Une évaluation théologico-philosophique du Big Bang et de son au-delà: BCentProt 46,3 (1994) 22-32.

1876 *Wauzzinski* Robert A., Technological pessimism [ELLUL J., *al.*]: Persp-ScCF 46 (1994) 98-113.

1877 EWeingartner Paul, *al.*, Scientific and religious belief [7 art.]: Philosophical Studies 59s. Dordrecht 1994, Kluwer. viii-186 p. $89. 0-7923-2595-8 [TDig 42,89].

1878 **Wilkinson** David, God, the Big Bang and Stephen HAWKING; an exploration into origins. Tunbridge Wells 1993, Monarch. 156 p. – REv-RT 18 (1994) 385-7 (D. *Parker*).

Wybrow Cameron, The Bible, Baconianism, and mastery over nature; the Old Testament and its modern misreading: AmerUnivSt 7/112, 1991 ➤ 1711.

1879 *a*) *Young* Davis A., The antiquity and the unity of the human race revisited; – *b*) *Reichenbach* Bruce R., Justifying in principle nonproductive theories; the case of evolution; – *c*) *Baldwin* John T., The argument from sufficient initial system organization as a continuing challenge to the Darwinian rate and method of transitional evolution; – *d*) *Mills* Gordon C., Theistic evolution; a design theory at the level of genetic information: ChrSchR 24 (1994s) 380-396 / 397-422 / 423-443 / 444-458.

E1.9 *Peccatum originale,* **The Sin of Eden,** *Genesis 2-3.*

1880 **Adler** Gerhard, Die Engel des Lichts; von den Erstlingen der Schöpfung. Stein am Rhein 1992, Christina. 160 p. DM 19,80 [TR 91,263, H. *Hark*].
1881 E**Anderson** Gary A., *Stone* Michael E., A synopsis of the Books of Adam and Eve [Greek, Latin; Armenian, Georgian, Slavonic in English / French / German as originally published]: Early Judaism and its literature 5. Atlanta 1994, Scholars. xi-76 p. $30; sb./pa. $20. 1-55540-983-6; -4-4 [TDig 42,45]. ➤ 1950.
1882 *a) Bach* Alice, Slipping across borders; the Bible and popular culture; – *b) Levine* Amy-Jill, Second-temple Judaism, Jesus, and women; yeast of Eden; – *c) Elliott* John H., The evil eye and the Sermon on the Mount; contours of a pervasive belief in social scientific perspective; – *d) Busto* Rudy V., 'It really resembled an earthly paradise'; reading Motolinía's account of the [1539 Mexican religious play] Caída de nuestros primeros padres: BInterp 2 (1994) 1-7 / 8-33 / 51-84 / 111-137; 1 fig.
1883 **Balducci** Corrado, El diablo. Bogotá 1991, Paulinas. 317 p. – REfMex 11 (1993) 118-120 (M. *Ramírez* A.).
1884 **Barr** James, The garden of Eden 1992 ➤ 9,1990: RHeythJ 35 (1994) 315 (J. *Mulrooney*); JTS 45 (1994) 172-5 (W. *Moberly*); TsTKi 65 (1994) 70 (T. *Stordalen,* Norwegian).
1886 **Basset** Lytta, Le pardon originel; de l'abîme du mal au pouvoir de pardonner: Lieux Théologiques 24. Genève 1994, Labor et Fides. 500 p.; bibliogr. 479-493. 2-8309-9720-5.
1887 *Baudry* Gérard-Henry, *a)* Le retour d'Adam au Paradis, symbole du salut de l'humanité: MélSR 51 (1994) 117-146; Eng. 147; – *b)* Le salut d'Adam: EsprVie 104 (1994) 81-88; – *c)* La théorie du 'penchant mauvais' et la doctrine du 'péché originel': BLitEc 95 (1994) 271-300; Eng. 301; – *d)* Le péché originel selon TEILHARD [Centre Teilhard du Nord 35s (Omega 1993)]: EsprVie 104 (1994) 371-3 (J. *Daoust*).
1889 *a) Bird* Phyllis A., Genesis 3 in der gegenwärtigen biblischen Forschung, TRoth Wolfgang; – *b) Otto* Eckart, Vom Rechtsbruch zur Sünde; – *c) Soosten* Joachim von, Die 'Erfindung' der Sünde; soziologische und semantische Aspekte zu der Rede von der Sünde im alttestamentlichen Sprachgebrauch: JbBT 9 (1994) 3-24 / 25-52 / 87-110.
1890 *Blumreich-Moore* Kathleen, Original sin as treason in Act I of the Mystère d'Adam: PgQ 72 (1993) 125-141.
1891 *Bray* Gerald, Original sin in patristic thought: Churchman 108 (1994) 37-47.
1892 *Büsing* Gerhard, Benennung in Gen 1-3 — ein Herrenrecht?: BibNot 73 (1994) 42-49.
1893 *Cardellino* Lodovico, Abramo e il mito del paradiso terrestre: BbbOr 36 (1994) 101-128.
1894 *Carter* Roman E. A., Two glimpses of Satan [ROSE E. 1992; LEEMING B. 1951]: PhilipSac 28 (1993) 353-9.
1895 *Chappell* T. D. J., Explaining the inexplicable; AUGUSTINE on the Fall: JAAR 62 (1994) 869-884.
1896 *Chareire* Isabelle, Note sur le péché originel dans trois catéchismes: LumièreV 43,216 (1994) 61-70.

1897 **Clines** David J.A., What does Eve do to help? jOsu 94, 1990
➤ 6,213 ... 9,2001: ᴿBZ 38 (1994) 315-7 (J. *Scharbert*); CritRR 5 (1992)
121-4 (Peggy L. *Day*: playful and engaging).

1898 *Crouzel* Henri, Diable et démons dans les homélies d'ORIGÈNE: BLitEc
95 (1994) 303-351; Eng. 351: deux art. à suivre.

1899 **Delumeau** Jean, Une histoire du paradis [aussi dans la culture
postbiblique], 1,1992 ➤ 9,2004: ᴿAmHR 99 (1994) 864 (E. *Peters*).

1900 *De Maio* Mimma, Per una antropologia edenica; ermeneutica del
racconto biblico di Adamo ed Eva: Riscontri 15,1 (Avellino 1993)
101-9.

1901 *Derycke* Hugues, Le Dogme comme mode original d'affirmation dans la
culture; le Péché originel, le pardon et la temporalité: RechSR 82 (1994)
193-216; Eng. 163.

1902 *Dohmen* Christoph, Natürliche Künstlichkeit in Gottes Garten: TGL
84 (1994) 209-225.

1904 *a) Ebach* J., Die Paradiesgeschichte; Anmerkungen zu ihrer Lektüre; –
b) Baudler G., Das Paradies und seine Zerstörung; Individual- und
sozialgeschichtliche Aspekte der religionsgeschichtlichen Paradiesvor-
stellung und der biblischen Paradieserzählung; – *c) Keller* R.U., Paradies
aus psychoanalytischer Sicht; Regression oder Grundlage?: WortAnt 35
(Mainz 1994) 150-8 / 159-164 / 165-7 [< ZIT 95, p. 95].

1905 **Forsyth** Neil, The old enemy, Satan... 1987 ➤ 3,2095 ... 9,2008:
ᴿGnomon 66 (1994) 358-360 (P. *Habermehl*); RTPhil 126 (1994) 275s
(C.-A. *Keller*).

1906 *a) Fretheim* Terence E., Is Genesis 3 a Fall story?; – *b) McEvenue*
Sean, Reading Genesis with faith and reason: WWorld 14 (1994) 144-
153 / 136-143.

1907 **Garrett** Susan B., The demise of the devil... Luke 1989 ➤ 5,5036 ...
9,2011: ᴿBijdragen 55 (1994) 208s (B.J. *Koet*).

1908 — *Frankfurter* D., Luke's *mageîa* and GARRETT's 'magic': UnSemQ
47,1s (1993) 81-89 [< NTAbs 39, p. 40].

1909 *a) Gemünden* Petra von, L'arbre et son fruit; analyse d'un corpus
d'images comme méthode exégétique [< diss. Végetationsmetaphorik]; –
b) Engammare Max, Le Paradis à Genève; comment CALVIN prêchait-il
la chute aux Genevois?: ÉTRel 69 (1994) 315-327 / 329-347.

1910 *Gozzelino* Giorgio, [Catechismo CC], Il dogma del peccato originale; lieto
annuncio di una indomabile volontà di perdono: Salesianum 56 (1994)
693-715.

1911 **Grelot** Pierre, Riflessioni sui problemi del peccato originale: Letture
bibliche 9. Brescia 1994, Paideia. 112 p. Lᵐ 14. 88-394-0508-9.

1912 **Hampl** Franz, Menschen und Dämonen. Bozen 1992, Raetia. 136 p.;
160 color. pl. – ᴿAnzAltW 46 (1993) 213-5 (G. *Radke*).

1913 **Harpur** Patrick, Daimonic reality; a field guide to the Otherworld. L
1994, Viking Arkana. xxi-330 p.; 8 pl. $30. 0-670-85569-3. – ᴿTBR 7,3
(1994s) 7s (Una *Kroll*: daimons are really angel-visions; not approved).

1914 **Hauke** Manfred, Heilsverlust in Adam; Stationen griechischer Erbsün-
denlehre: KkK 58, 1992 ➤ 8,2232: ᴿJbAC 37 (1994) 182-5 (B. *Studer*);
ScripTPamp 26 (1994) 284-9 (L.F. *Mateo-Seco*); TLZ 189 (1994) 688-690
(G. *Feige*); TvT 34 (1994) 84 (F. van de *Paverd*).

1915 **Hoping** Helmut, Freiheit... Erbsündenlehre... KANT 1990 ➤ 9,2015:
ᴿTGL 84 (1994) 120-2 (D. *Hattrup*); ZkT 116 (1994) 517-9 (W. *Kern*).

1916 *Hoping* Helmut, Freiheitsdenken und Erbsündenlehre; der transzendentale Ursprung der Sünde: TGL 84 (1994) 299-317.

1917 **Hughes** Robert D.,   Satan's whispers; breaking the lies that bind us. Nv 1992, Broadman.   175 p.   0-8054-6052-7. – ᴿRExp 91 (1994) 111s (C. *Miller*).

1918 *Kelly* Brian,   Redemption and original sin: IrTQ 60 (1994) 1-16.

1919 **Ladaria** Luis F.,   Teologia del pecado original y de la gracia; antropología teológica especial. 9 BAC Sap. Fidei. M 1993, Católica. xxix-317 p. [NRT 117,135, L. *Renwart*]. – ᴿComSev 27 (1994) 193s (M. *Sánchez*); Proyección 49 (1994) 65 (C. *Granado*); Salmanticensis 41 (1994) 144s (J. L. *Ruiz de la Peña*); Teresianum 45 (1994) 318s (P. *Boyce*).

1920 *a) Launderville* Dale,   Satan and the power of evil; – *b) Nowell* Irene, Demonic forces in the OT; – *c) Sweet* Anne Marie,   The fall of the angels; – *d) Sloyan* Gerard S.,   Demons and exorcisms; – *e) Hyland* William P., Demons and early theology: BToday 32 (1994) 4-9 / 10-14 / 15-20 / 21-26 / 27-31.

1921 **Leisch-Kiesl** Monika [cf. ᴰ1991 ⇥ 7,1948],   Eva als Andere; eine exemplarische Untersuchung zu Frühchristentum und Mittelalter; Vorw. *Gössmann* Elisabeth.   Köln 1992, Böhlau.   300 p. DM 64. – ᴿBiKi 45 (1994) 75 (Helen *Schüngel-Straumann*).

1922 **Levison** John R.,   Portraits of Adam in early Judaism: JPseud supp. 1, 1988 ⇥ 4,2192 ... 9,2020: ᴿJQR 84 (1993s) 350-2 (S. E. *Robinson*).

1924 **Louys** Daniel, Le jardin d'Éden: Lire la Bible 95. P 1992, Cerf. 225 p. F 100.   2-2040-4539-X. – ᴿBL (1993) 91 (J. *Day*: idiosyncratic); ÉTRel 68 (1993) 585 (J.-L. *Klein*).

1925 *Marlé* René,   Victoire du Christ sur les forces du mal [... dramatique vétéro-testamentaire]: EsprVie 104 (1994) 465-479.

1926 *a) Morales* José,   El retorno de la creación en la teología bíblica; – *b) Sans* Isidro M.,   Iblis y el primer pecado; – *c) Iñiguez* José A.,   Una exégesis medieval de Gen. II,8-18 y III,23-24: ⇥ 22a, ᶠCASCIARO J., Biblia 1994, 175-190 / 191-9 / 565-571.

1927 *Monaci Castagno* Adele,   La demonologia degli Atti di Pietro: ⇥ 29, ᶠCORSINI E., Voci 1994, 331-343.

1928 **Morand** Georges,   Sors de cet homme, Satan 1993 ⇥ 9,2026: ᴿEsprVie 104 (1994) 95 (J. *Vernette*).

1929 ᴱMorris Paul, *Sawyer* Deborah,   A walk in the garden; jOsu 136, 1992 ⇥ 8,482; 9,2028: ᴿBibTB 24 (1994) 37s (R. A. *Simkins*).

1931 *Niehaus* Jeffrey,   In the wind of the storm; another look at Genesis III 8: VT 44 (1994) 263-7.

1932 *a) Nielsen* Kirsten,   If you loved man, why did you not kill the devil? [Apocalypse of Sedrach 5,3]; – *b) Jeppesen* Knut,   Then began men to call upon the name of Yahweh; an idea [Gen 4,26 should follow 3,24]: ⇥ 89c, ᶠOTZEN B., In the last days 1994. 54-59 / 158-163.

1933 *Nixon* Rosemary,   Images of the Creator in Genesis 1 and 2:   TLond 97 (1994) 188-197.

1934 **Nugent** Christopher, Masks of Satan; the demonic in history, KC 1984. Sheed & W. < 1899, Chr. classics. 216 p. $75.   0-87061-163-1. – ᴿLandas 8 (Manila 1994) 142s (V. *Marasigan*).

1935 **Ormerod** Neil,   Grace and disgrace; a theology of self-esteem, society and history 1992 ⇥ 8,2253: ᴿMonth 255 (1994) 65s (P. *Burns*).

1936 *Pagels* Elaine,   The social history of Satan, 2. Satan in the NT Gospels: JAAR 62 (1994) 17-58.

1937 *Pikaza* Xabier,   Principios de antropología biblica; Gen 2-3; el árbol del juicio y la caida humana: Anámnesis 5 (México 1993) 5-39 [< Stromata 49,291].

1938 **Resnick** Irven M., ODO of Tournai, On original sin & A dispute with the Jew Leo of Tournai concerning the advent of Christ, Son of God. Ph 1994, Univ. Pennsylvania. 146 p. £28.50; pa. £12. 0-8122-3288-7; -1450-0. – ᴿTBR 7,3 (1994s) 34 (T. *Gray*).

1939 *Richter* Hans Friedemann, Das Liedgut am Anfang der 'jahwistischen' Urgeschichte: WeltOr 25 (1994) 78-108.

1940 **Rolwing** Richard J., Israel's original sin; a Catholic confession. SF 1994, International Scholars. xvi-515 p.; bibliog. 487-505. $70; pa. $50. 1-883255- 61-9.

1941 *Rosset* Michèle, La logique de la génération selon Yahvé-Dieu; lecture sémiotique et anthropologique de Genèse, ch. 2 et 3: SémBib 73 (1994) 3-29; 74,3-29; 75,1-28.

1942 *Rota Scalabrini* Patrizio, Il peccato nella luce della redenzione; la rivelazione delle origini, Gen 2-3: Ambrosius 70 (1994) 302-322.

1943 **Ruiz de la Peña** Juan L., Creación, gracia, salvación. Sdr 1993, SalT. 143 p. – ᴿSalT 82 (1994) 75.

1944 *Savigni* Raffaele, Esegesi medievale ed antropologia biblica; l'interpretazione di Genesi 1-3 nei commentari carolingi ed i suoi fondamenti patristici: → 330*, X-Viverone 1992/3, 571-614; Eng. 277.

1945 **Sayés** J. A., *a)* Anthropología del hombre caído; el pecado original 1991 ➤ 7,7155* ... 9,2039: ᴿCC 145 (1994,1) 260-9 (S. *Moschetti*: attenzione forse eccessiva al diavolo). – *b)* Sobre el pecado original; respuesta a A. VILLALMONTE (NatGrac 1994, 201): Burgense 35 (1994) 539-555.

1946 **Schüngel-Straumann** Helen, Die Frau am Anfang — Eva und die Folgen 1989 ➤ 6,2345; 7,1971: ᴿBiKi 48 (1993) 168 (F. *Porsch*).

1947 *Schwager* Raymund, Neues und Altes zur Lehre von der Erbsünde: ZkT 116 (1994) 1-29.

1948 *Stefanovic* Zdravko, The great reversal; thematic links between Genesis 2 and 3: AndrUnSem 32 (1994) 47-56.

1949 **Stewart** Charles, Demons and the devil... in modern Greek culture 1991 ➤ 7,1973 ... 9,2044: ᴿHistRel 33 (1993s) 202-4 (Sarah I. *Johnston*).

1950 **Stone** Michael E., A history of the literature of Adam and Eve 1992 ➤ 8,a258; 9,2045: ᴿCBQ 56 (1994) 155-7 (R. D. *Chesnutt*); ETL 70 (1994) 150s (A. *Schoors*); JStOT 62 (1994) 118 (J. F. *Elwolde*).

1952 **Terreros** Marco T., Death before the sin of Adam, a fundamental concept of theistic evolution and its implications for evangelical theology: diss. Andrews, ᴰKiš M. Berrien Springs 1994. – AndrUnSem 32 (1994) 114; 383 p. 94-28814. – DissA 55 (1994a) p. 1299.

1953 *Te Selle* E., Serpent, Eve, and Adam; Augustine and the exegetical tradition: ➤ 9,464f, Collectanea 1990/3, 341-361.

1954 *Tornatora* Alberto, Diabolus eloquens; l'archetipo letterario di un 'nuovo' locus a factione (CIPRIANO, De opere et eleemosynis cap. 22): SMSR 59 (1993) 21-34.

1955 **Ulmer** Rivka, The evil eye in the Bible and in rabbinic literature. Hoboken 1994, KTAV. x-213 p. $29.50.

1956 **Ulrich** Kerstin, Evas Bestimmung; Studien zur Beurteilung von Schwangerschaft und Mutterschaft im Ersten Testament [attention is focused on the (male) child, not on the woman's fulfilment]: ➤ ᶠJAHNOW H. 1994, 149-164.

1957 **Unger** Michael, Die Paradies-erzählung Gen 2/3; eine exegetische Untersuchung: Diss. ᴰMarböck J. Graz 1994. 286 p. – RTLv 26,533.

1958 *Vanneste* A., Le péché originel; un débat sans issue?: ETL 70 (1994) 359-383.

1959 **Wiesel** Elie,   Adam oder das Geheimnis des Anfangs; Legenden und Porträts: Spektrum 4249. FrB 1994, Herder.   230 p. DM 15,80. – RLeb-Zeug 49 (1994) 311 (P. *Petzel*).

1960 **Zimmermann** A. F., *a*) Original Sin; where doctrine meets science. – *b*) The religion of Adam and Eve.   NY 1990s, Vantage. 264 p.; 150 p. – RSalmanticensis 41 (1994) 471 (J. R. *Flecha Andrés*).

1961 *Filigheddu* Paolo,   ʿēd (Genesi 2,6): un mitologhema sumerico? ➤ 418, Circolazioni 1991/4, 109-120.

1962 **Navarro** Mercedes, [Gen 2,7] Barro y aliento ... Gen 2,3, 1993 ➤ 9,2052: RCompostellanum 32 (1993) 341s (J. *Precedo Lafuente*); SalT 82 (1994) 499s (F. *Rivas*).

1962* *Poirier* Paul-Hubert,   Pour une histoire de la lecture pneumatique de Gn 2,7; quelques jalons jusqu'à IRÉNÉE de Lyon: RÉAug 40 (1994) 1-22.

1963 *a*) *De Benedetti* Paolo,   [Gn 2,19] Uomini e animali di fronte a Dio; – *b*) *Sierra* Sergio J.,   Il rapporto con il mondo animale e l'ebraismo; – *c*) *Spinsanti* Sandro, *al*.,   Gli animali nell'orizzonte della bioetica; solidarietà e responsabilità fra tutti i viventi: ➤ 306, Animali 1993/4, 13-26 / 27-34 / 77-86 [-113].

1964 *Federici* Tommaso, [Gn 3,1-19], Note sullo scisma 'biblico' fontale: EuntDoc 46,3 (1993) 349-360 [< NTAbs 38, p. 408].

1965 *Pickstock* Catherine, [('Did God really say') Gen 3,1] The sacred polis; language as syntactic event: LitTOx 8 (1994) 367-383.

1966 *Vasholz* Robert J., 'He (?) will rule over you'; a thought on Genesis 3:16 [rather 'your love']: Pres 20 (1994) 51s [< OTAbs 18,290].

1967 *Tsumura* David T.,   A note on *hērōnēk* (Gen 3,16):   Biblica 75 (1994) 398-400.

1968 *Arzt* Paul J.,   'Unter Mühsal wirst du von ihm essen!' (Gen 3,17); die Acker-Mensch-Beziehung der Urgeschichte und ihre ökologische Aktualisierung: ProtokB 3 (1994) 73-82.

1968* *Brandscheidt* Renate,   'Nun ist der Mensch geworden wie einer von uns...' (Gen 3,22) — Zur Bedeutung der Bäume im Garten von Eden: TrierTZ 103 (1994) 1-17.

E2.1   **Cain et Abel;**   *gigantes, longaevi; Genesis 4s.*

1969 *Deurloo* K. A.,   The scope of a small literary unity in the OT; introduction to the interpretation of Genesis 4: ➤ 250, VAmst 1994, 37-51.

1970 *Grattepanche* J.,   Caïn et Abel dans les légendes islamiques: OrLovPer 24 (1993) 133-142.

1971 **Greenspahn** Frederick E.,   When brothers dwell together; the preeminence of younger siblings in the Hebrew Bible. Ox 1994, UP. 193 p. $30. 0-19-508253-2 [OTAbs 17, p. 655; BL 95,89, W. J. *Houston*, some brief severe reserves]. – RTS 55 (1994) 584s (F. L. *Moriarty*).

1972 **Lapide** Pinchas,   Von Kain bis Judas; ungewohnte Einsichten zu Sünde und Schuld: Tb 1439. Gü 1994, Gü.-V.   128 p. DM 19,80. – REntschluss 48,9s (1994) 43s (T. M. *Meier*).

1973 *Lescow* Theodor,   Gen 4,1.25; zwei archaische Geburtsberichte; ein Nachtrag: ZAW [105 (1993) 19-26] 106 (1994) 485s.

1974 *Lewis* Jack P.,   The offering of Abel (Gen 4:4); a history of interpretation: JEvTS 37 (1994) 481-496.

1975 [Gen 4,16] *Görg* Manfred, Kain und das 'Land Nod': BibNot 71 (1994) 5-12.
1976 *Harrison* R. K. †, From Adam to Noah; a reconsideration of the antediluvian patriarchs' ages: JEvTS 37 (1994) 161-8.
1977 **Kaulins** Andis, Kings and dynasties; the dynasties of man from the days of Adam to the reigns of the Pharaohs according to the Wheel of Heaven: Origins 5. Lincoln 1994, Isandis. xii-198 p. $59.
1978 *Oosthuizen* R. D., African experience of time and its compatibility with the OT view of time as suggested in the genealogy of Genesis 5: OTEssays 6 (1993) 190-204.
1979 *Yamada* Shigeo, The editorial history of the Assyrian King List: ZAss 84 (1994) 11-37.
1980 *Savasta* Carmelo, 'Figli di Dio' e 'giganti' (Gen. 6,1-4); una proposta di identificazione: BbbOr 36 (1994) 193-215.
1980* a) *Breukelman* Frans H., [Gn 6,1-4] The story of the sons of God who took the daughters of humans as wives [< AmstCah 1 (1980) 9-21]; – b) *Deurloo* Karel A., The way of Abraham / 'Because you have hearkened to my voice' Genesis 22 [ineditum / < AmstCah 5 (1984) 41-60]: ⇒ 250, Voices from Amst 1994, 83-94 / 95-112 . 113-130.
1981 *Jacobson* Howard, (Gn 6,3; 49,10) *Beshaggam* and *Shiloh* revisited [gematria already equated both with *Moshe*]: ZAW [105 (1993) 258-261, *Rosenberg* R.] 106 (1994) 490.

E2.2 *Diluvium*, **The Flood;** Gilgameš (Atraḫasis); **Genesis 6 ...**

1982 *Abusch* Tzvi, Gilgamesh's request [1. ᶠHALLO W. ⇒ 9,3079] 2. An analysis and interpretation of an Old Babylonian fragment about mourning and celebration: ⇒ 85*, ᶠMUFFS Y., JANES 22 (1993) 3-17.
1983 *Edzard* D. O., Sumerian epic; epic or fairy tale? [... Gilgamesh]: Bu-CanadMesop 27 (1994) 7-14; franç. 7.
1984 *Ferguson* Paul, Nebuchadnezzar, Gilgamesh, and the 'Babylonian Job': JEvTS 37 (1994) 321-331.
1985 **Jackson** Danny P., The epic of Gilgamesh 1992 ⇒ 8,2309: ᴿBu-CanadMesop 26 (1993) 67-69 (D. *Matthews*, aussi en français).
1985* a) *Jakobson* Vladimir A., Folklore motifs in the epic of Gilgamesh; – b) *Hruška* Blahoslav, Die sumerischen Georgica; Dichtung und Wahrheit: ⇒ 454, XXV. Tagung 1991/4.
1986 *Krebernik* Manfred, Ein Keulenkopf mit Weihung an Gilgameš im Vorderasiatischen Museum, Berlin: AltOrF 21 (1994) 5-9; 6 fig.
1987 **Leed** Eric J., The mind of the traveler; from Gilgamesh to global tourism. NY 1991, Basic. xiii-128 p. $15 pa. 0-465-04619-3 [RelStR 21,48, A.T. *Kraabel*].
1988 *Metzler* Kai A., Restitution der Mimation im altbabylonischen Atram-ḫasis-Epos: UF 26 (1994) 369-372.
1988* [**Schörf**] **Kluger** R., The archetypal significance of Gilgamesh; a modern ancient hero. Einsiedeln 1991, Daimon. 238 p. – ᴿAulaO 12 (1994) 144s (G. del *Olmo Lete*).
1989 ᵀᴱTournay Raymond-Jacques, *Shaffer* Aaron, L'épopée de Gilgamesh: LAPO. P 1994, Cerf. 320 p. F 180. 2-204-05003-2. – ᴿAulaO 12 (1994) 145s (G. del *Olmo Lete*); RÉJ 153 (1994) 439-443 (D. *Arnaud*).
1990 *Vetta* Massimo, La saga di Gilgameš e l'epica greca fino all'arcaismo: QuadUrb 76 (1994) 7-20.

1991 *Vulpe* Nicola,   Irony and the unity of the Gilgamesh epic: JNES 53 (1994) 275-284.

1992 *Forrest* Robert W. E.,   Paradise lost again; violence and obedience in the Flood narrative: JStOT 62 (1994) 3-18.

1993 **Bailey** Lloyd R.,   Noah; the person and the story in history and tradition 1989 ➤ 5,2216 ... 8,2317*:   ᴿJQR 84 (1993s) 334s (I. M. *Kikawada*).

1994 *Glesmer* Uwe,   Antike und moderne Auslegung des Sintflutberichtes Gen 6-8 und der Qumran-Pesher 4Q252: LpJudMitt 6 (1993) 3-79 [< OTAbs 17, p. 630].

1995 **Homolka** Walter, *Friedlander* Albert H.,   Von der Sintflut ins Paradies; der Friede als Schlüsselbegriff jüdischer Theologie: Forum 78. Da 1993, Wiss. x-107 p. DM 14,80.   3-534-80147-4. – ᴿActuBbg 31 (1994) 110s (J. *Boada*).

1996 *Niccacci* Alviero,   Diluvio, sintassi e metodo: LA 44 (1994) 9-46; Eng. 611.

1997 *Eddy* G. T.,   [Gen 6,11-22] Noah's Ark: ExpTim 106 (1994s) 146s.

1998 *Lezzi* Maria Teresa,   L'arche de Noé en forme de bateau; naissance d'une tradition iconographique: CahCMédv 37,148 (1994) 301-324; 31 fig.

1999 **Yocham** Virgil, [really *Wyatt* Ron, guide of search]. Noah's Ark. Lubbock TX, 1991, Sunset Extension. 120 mm. tape. $25. – ᴿRestQ 36 (1994) 121s (D. W. *Manor*: dubious).

2000 **Wolde** Ellen van,   A text-semantic study of the Hebrew Bible, illustrated with Noah and Job: JBL 113 (1994) 19-35.

2001 *Flusser* David,   Noachitische Gebote I. Judentum [binding on non-Jews]: ➤ 517, TRE 24 (1994) 582-5 [-7, NT, *Heiligenthal* Roman].

2002 *Steinmetz* Devora,   Vineyard, farm, and garden; the drunkenness of Noah in the context of primeval history: JBL 113 (1994) 193-207.

2003 *Stander* H. F.,   The Church Fathers on (the cursing of) Ham: AcPatrByz 5 (Pretoria 1994) 113-125.

2003* **Linde** Jan M. van der,   Over Noah met zijn zonen; de Cham-ideologie en de leugens tegen Cham tot vandag: IIMO Res. 33. Utrecht 1993, Missiologie/Oecumenica. 160 p. f29,50. 90-211-7001-9 [Exchange 22,184s].

2004 *Mosis* Rudolf,   Gen 9,1-7; Funktion und Bedeutung innerhalb der priesterschriftlichen Urgeschichte: BZ 38 (1994) 195-228.

2005 *Vermeylen* J.,   La 'table des nations' (Gn 10); Yaphet figure-t-il l'Empire perse?: TEuph 5 (1992) 113-132.

2005* [Augusto] *Tavares* Antonio, 'Meshech' (Genesis 10:2), one of the Sea Peoples in the South Iberian Peninsula? [Avienus Ora Maritima (1985 p. 28) 4th c. A.D. < Greek 1st BC < Massaliote Periplus 6th BC]: ➤ 535a, *Assaf*, 11th Jewish 1993/4, 27-42.

2006 *Padilla Monge* A., [Gn 10,5...] Consideraciones sobre el Tarsis biblico: AulaO 12 (1994) 51-71 [Tarsus in Cilicia!].

2006* *Ceccherelli* Ignazio M., [Gen 10,8] Nimrod, primo re 'universale' della storia: BbbOr 36 (1994) 25-39.

2007 *Ararat* N.,   ❺ The tower of Babel as a satiric drama: BeitM 39 (1994) 224-231 [< OTAbs 18, p. 47, Y. *Gitay*].

2008 *Berges* Ulrich,   Gen 11,1-9; Babel oder das Ende der Kommunikation: BibNot 74 (1994) 37-56.

2009 *Hertzberg* David,   Genesis of the polity — an analysis of the sin of Babel: ➤ 108b, ᶠSAFRAN J., Porat 1992.

2010 *Krašovec* Jože,   De la dispersion de Babel à l'élection d'Israël: Communio 19,112 (P 1994) 48-54.

2011 *Lacambre* Denis, La tour de Babel et la recherche des cieux: DossA 191 ('Astrologie en Mésopotamie' 1994) 68-73.
2012 *Greenspahn* Frederick, [Gn 11; Dt 30,11] A Mesopotamian proverb and its biblical reverberations: JAOS 114 (1994) 33-38.
2013 **Uehlinger** Christoph, Weltreich und 'eine Rede'... Gen 11,1-9: OBO 101, 1990 ➤ 5,2238... 9,2114: ᴿBZ 38 (1994) 105-8 (E. S. *Gerstenberger*); JNES 53 (1994) 220s (D. *Pardee*).

E2.3   **Patriarchae, Abraham;** *Genesis 12s.*

2014 **Abramovitch** Henry H., The first father, Abraham; the psychology and culture of a spiritual revolutionary. Lanham MD 1994, UPA. [x-] 192 p.; bibliog. 171-183. 0-8191-9027-6.
2015 *Beauchamp* Paul, [Gen 12,10-13,4] Abram et Saraï; la sœur-épouse, ou l'énigme du couple fondateur: ➤ 239d, Exégèse 1994, 11-50.
2016 *Chamiel* C. H., ❶ Regarding the election of Abraham: BethM 39 (1994) 133-140 [OTAbs 17, p. 619].
2017 **Harrisville** Roy A.ᴵᴵᴵ, The figure of Abraham [only Gen 12-25] in the Epistles of Paul, SF 1993, Mellen. [xviii-] 314 p. $80. – ᴿCBQ 56 (1994) 375s (B. S. *Crawford*).
2018 *Kass* Leon R., Educating Father Abraham, 1. The meaning of wife; 2. The meaning of fatherhood: FirsT 47 (1994) 16-26 / 48 (1994) 32-43.
2019 *Lash* Nicholas, Hoping against hope, or Abraham's dilemma: ModT 10 (1994) 233-246.
2020 *Lof* L. J. van der, The 'Prophet' Abraham in the writings of IRENAEUS, TERTULLIAN, AMBROSE and AUGUSTINE: AugLv 44 (1994) 17-30 [< ZIT 95, p. 165].
2021 *Mandal* Paul, The call of Abraham; a midrash revisited: Prooftexts 14 (1994) 267-284.
2022 *Michaud* Robert, Les patriarches bibliques, histoire et théologie: Lire la Bible 42. P 1992, Cerf. – ᴿÉglT 25 (1994) 126s (W. *Vogels*).
2023 **Riemer** Judith, *Dreifuss* Gustav, Abramo, l'uomo e il simbolo, ᵀ*Ventura* Milka: Schulim Vogelmann 41. F 1994, Giuntina. 169 p. 88-85943-89-6.
2024 *Ruppert* Lothar [*al.*], Abraham (AT): ➤ 510, LTK³ 1 (1993) 61s [-65].
2025 **Siker** Jeffrey, Disinheriting the Jews; Abraham 1991 ➤ 7,2048... 9,2133: ᴿChH 63 (1994) 82s (J. S. *Kaminsky*); CritRR 6 (1993) 291-4 (C. W. *Hanson*).
2026 *Deurloo* Karel, *a*) The way of Abraham; routes and localities as narrative data in Gn. 11:27 - 25:11; – *b*) 'Because you have hearkened to my voice' (Genesis 22): ➤ 250, VAmst 1994, 95-112 / 113-130.
2027 **Fischer** Irmtraud, Die Erzeltern Israels; feministisch-theologische Studien zu Genesis 12-36 [diss. 1993 Graz]: BZAW 222, B 1994, de Gruyter. xii-396 p. 3-11-014232-5.
2028 **Anderson** Ronald D., [Gn 12-23] Discourse markers [SCHIFFRIN D. 1987] in the Hebrew Bible: diss. Utah. 112 p. 94-19199. – DissA 55 (1994s) p. 289.
2029 *Aleixandre* Dolores, 'Va a la terra que yo te mostraré...' (Gn 12,1): SalT 82 (1994) 431-448.
2030 *Niehoff* Maren R., ❶ [Gen 12:10-20] Associative thinking in the Midrash exemplified by the rabbinic interpretation of the journey of Abraham and Sarah to Egypt: Tarbiz 62 (1992s) 339-359.
2031 *Qimron* Elisha, Towards a new edition of the Genesis Apocryphon

[none of FITZMYER's editions reliable because he ignored criticism of his failing to use marks to distinguish the degree of plausibility of his reading]: JPseud 10 (1992) 11-18.

2032 *Gosse* Bernard,   Genèse 13,15 et le don de la terre à Abraham: RHPR 74 (1994) 395-7.

2033 *Uribarri* G.,   Las teofanías veterotestamentarias en JUSTINO, 'Dial.' 129, y TERTULIANO, 'Prax.' 11-13:   MiscCom 52 (1994) 305-320 [< ZIT 95, p. 151].

E2.4   Melchisedech, Sodoma; *Genesis 14 ... 19.*

2034 **Bindella** Francesco,   Melchisedek alla luce della rivelazione del Nome divino; sacerdozio – regalità – profezia all'origine: Praesidium assisiense. Assisi 1994, Porziuncola.   188 p.; bibliog. 87-102. L^m 15.

2035 *Bodinger* Martin,   L'énigme de Melkisédeq: RHR 211 (1994) 297-333; Eng. 297.

2036 *Loader* James A.,   Tale of two cities 1990 ➤ 6,2419 ... 9,2142:   RCritRR 6 (1993) 166-8 (G. E. *Sterling*); ScripTPamp 26 (1994) 706s (S. *Ausín*).

2037 *a*) *McConville* J. Gordon,   Abraham and Melchizedek; horizons in Genesis 14;   – *b*) *Millard* Alan R.,   Abraham, Akhenaten, Moses and monotheism: ➤ 146, FWISEMAN D., He swore an oath 1994, 93-118 / 119-129.

2038 TEMorisi Luca,   Versus de Sodoma [Gn 19,1-26c. 450 d.C.]: EdSaggi-FgClas 52, 1993 ➤ 9,2143:   RRÉLat 72 (1994) 278s (F. *Chapot*).

2039 *Thekeparampil* Jacob,   Malkizedeq according to JACOB of Sarug: ➤ 450c, Syriacum 6 (1992/4) 123-133.

E2.5   The Covenant (alliance, Bund); *Foedus, Genesis 15 ...*

2040 **Gitau** Samson N.,   A comparative study of the transmission, actualization and stabilization of oral traditions; an examination of traditions of circumcision in Africa and ancient Israel: diss. Boston Univ. DPurvis J. 1994. 462 p. 94-22451. – DissA 55 (1994s) p. 604.

2041 **Hagelia** Hallvard,   Numbering the stars; a phraseological analysis of Genesis 15 [diss. Uppsala 1994, DOttosson M.]: ConBib OT 39. Sto 1994, Almqvist & W.   252 p. Sk 204.   91-22-01591-4 [OTAbs 17, p. 660; BL 95,65, P. *Harland*; RelStR 21, 138, M. A. *Sweeney*; JTS 46,575, P. W. *Coxon*]. – RScandJOT 8 (1994) 311s (T. L. *Thompson* severely attacks not only the dissertation but the Uppsala faculty); TLZ 119 (1994) 1066-8 (T. *Naumann*).

2042 *a*) *Hess* Richard S.,   The slaughter of the animals in Genesis 15; Genesis 15:9-21 and its Ancient Near Eastern context;   – *b*) *Kitchen* Kenneth A., Genesis 12-50 in the Near Eastern world ➤ 146, FWISEMAN D., He swore an oath 1994, 55-65 / 67-92.

2043 **Nordheim** Eckhard von,   Die Selbstbehauptung Israels Gn 15 ...: OBO 115, 1992 ➤ 8,2366; 9,2148:   RCBQ 56 (1994) 575s (F. W. *Dobbs-Allsopp*).

2044 *a*) *Römer* T.,   Genèse 15 et les tensions de la communauté juive postexilique dans le cycle d'Abraham;   – *b*) *Diebner* B. J., Die Bedeutung der mesopotamischen 'Exilsgemeinde' (*galut*) für die theologische Prägung der jüdischen Bibel: ➤ 461, TEuph 7 (1991/4) 107-121 (Eng. 107) / 123-142 (franç. 123).

Canfora L., *al.*, I trattati 1986/90 ➤ 6,724: 10985.

2045 *Weitzman* Steven, [Apc. Abr. 17 on Gen 15] The song of Abraham: HUCA 65 (1994) 21-33.
2046 *Rottzoll* Dirk U., Gen 15,6 – ein Beleg für den Glauben als Werkgerechtigkeit: ZAW 106 (1994) 21-27.
2047 *Kemmler* A., *Müllner* I., [Gen 16] Frauenkonflikte in der Bibel: KatBlätt 119 (Mü 1994) 802-9 [< ZIT 95, p. 58].
2047* *Lyke* Larry L., Where does 'the boy' [Ishmael an infant, though age 13 in ch. 17] belong? Compositional strategy in Genesis 21:14: CBQ 56 (1994) 637-648.
2048 *Stancil* David C., Genesis 16:1-16; 21:8-21 — The uncherished child; a 'modern' wilderness of the heart: RExp 91,3 (children-ministries 1994) 393-400.
2049 *Wyatt* N., The meaning of El Roi and the mythological dimension in Genesis 16(,13): ScandJOT 8 (1994) 141-151.
2050 *Cardellino* Lodovico, [Gen 18,11] Computo di anni e stagioni da Abramo [età inverosimile di Sara] a Salomone: BbbOr 36 (1994) 3-24 [86, nota, *Chandler* Tertius, Dating Abraham; 188, Dating Jacob/Job].
2051 *Soggin* J. Alberto, Abraham hadert mit Gott; Beobachtungen zu Gen 18,16-32: ➤ 61, ᶠKAISER O., 'Wer ist' 1994, 214-8.
2052 *Orbe* Antonio, [Gen 19] Los hechos de Lot, mujer e hijas vistos por san IRENEO (adv. haer. IV,31,1,15/3,71): Gregorianum 75 (1994) 37-64; Eng. 64.
2052* *a*) *Leygraaf* Monique, Vreemdeling in Sodom (Genesis 19:1-11); – *b*) *Smelik* K. A. D., Lot tussen Noach en Abraham; hergebruik van een verhaalmotief in Genesis; – *c*) *Ketelaar* Saskia, De 'onvruchtbare' moeders in de Hebreeuwse Bijbel: AmstCah 12 (1993) 20-30 / 31-37 / 7-19; Eng. 131s.
2053 *Steinberg* Naomi, Kinship and gender in Genesis; the case of Sarah and Hagar: BRes 39 (1994) 46-56.
2053* *a*) *Frerichs* Terence E., The birth of Isaac; Genesis 21:1-7; – *b*) *Wenham* Gordon J., Reading Genesis today; – *c*) *Ross-Burstall* Joan, Leah and Rachel, a tale of two sisters; – *d*) *Bangsund* James C., The consolation of the firstborn in Genesis; a lesson for Christian mission: WWorld 14 (1994) 154-161 / 125-135 / 162-170 / 171-7.
2054 *Duguid* Iain M., [Gen 21,9] Hagar the Egyptian; a note on the allure of Egypt in the Abraham cycle: WestTJ 56 (1994) 419-421.

E2.6 The ʿAqedâ; Isaac, Genesis 22 ...

2055 *Abramovitch* Henry H., The relations between fathers and sone in biblical narrative; toward a new interpretation of the Akedah: ➤ 331*a*, 11th Jewish 1993/4, A-31-42 [20-30, *Rashkow* Ilona N., Daughters].
2056 *Doukhan* Jacques B., The *Aqedah* at the 'crossroad'; its significance in the Jewish-Christian-Muslim dialogue: AndrUnSem 32 (1994) 29-40.
2057 *Dulaey* M., La grâce faite à Isaac; Gn 22,1-19 à l'époque paléochrétienne: RechAug 27 (1994) 3-40 [< RHE 90,307*].
2058 *Gellman* Jerome I., The fear, the trembling, and the fire; KIERKEGAARD and Hasidic masters on the binding of Isaac. Boston 1994, UPA. 123 p. – ᴿJJS 45 (1994) 315-7 (R. A. *Cohen*: 'Boston').
2059 *Japhet* Sara, The trial of Abraham and the test of Job; how do they differ?: Henoch 16 (1994) 153-171; ital. 172.
2060 *Krupe* Michael, [Gn 22] Die Bindung Isaaks nach dem Midrash Bereschit Rabba: Texte und Kontexte 65s (1995) 3-59 [< OTAbs 18, p. 511].

2061 *Jensen* Robin M., The offering of Isaac in Jewish and Christian tradition; image and text: BInterp 2 (1994) 85-110; 13 fig.

2062 *Kunin* Seth D., The death of Isaac; structuralist analysis of Genesis 22 [compared to 37]: JStOT 64 (1994) 57-81.

2063 *a) Millet* Olivier,   Exégèse évangélique et culture littéraire humaniste; entre LUTHER et BÈZE, l'Abraham sacrifiant selon CALVIN; – *b) Higman* Francis, Calvin polémiste: ÉTRel 69 (1994) 367-389 / 340-365.

2064 *Mleynek* Sherryll, Abraham, ARISTOTLE, and God; the poetics of sacrifice: JAAR 62 (1994) 107-121.

2065 **Sassmann** Christiane K., Die Opferbereitschaft Israels; anthropologische und theologische Voraussetzungen des Opferkults: ev. Diss. ᴰ*Reventlow* H. Bochum 1994.

2066 *Moberly* R.W.L.,   Christ as the key to Scripture; Genesis 22 reconsidered: ➤ 146, ᶠWISEMAN D., He swore an oath, ᴱ*Hess* Richard S., *al.*, 1994, 143-173.

2067 *Tschuggnall* Peter, Abrahams Opfer, eine anstössige Erzählung über den Glauben? Dichterische Varianten — philosophische und psychologische Rezeption — Literaturwissenschaftliche und theologische Befragung: ZRGg 46 (1994) 289-318.

2068 [Gn 22] *Yanow* Dvora, Sarah's silence; a newly discovered commentary on Genesis 22 by RASHI's sister: Judaism 43 (1994) 398-408 [editor's reserves in note p. 398].

2069 *Renninger* W. Richard,   Seeing and believing; Gen 22,1-19: ➤ 84, ᶠMORELAND D. 1992, 133-146.

2070 *Savasta* Carmelo, Schemi e strutture in Gen 22,1-19: RivB 42 (1994) 179-192.

Levenson Jon D., Death ... transformation of child sacrifice 1993 ➤ 7766.

2071 *Frettlöh* Magdalene L., Isaak und seine Mutter; Beobachtungen zur exegetischen Verdrängung von Frauen am Beispiel von Gen 24.62-67: EvT 54 (1994) 427-452.

2072 *Teugels* Lieve, 'A strong woman, who can find?' A study of characterization in Genesis 24, with some perspectives on the general presentation of Isaac and Rebekah in the Genesis narratives: JStOT 63 (1994) 89-104.

2073 *a) Neinhard* K., Rebekka; niet zomaar een maagd; een andere kijk op Genesis 24:16; – *b) Wolde* E. van,   Ruth in de Bijlmer: Mara 6,2 ('Sporen van vrouwenteksten?' 1993) 36-45 / 8-15 [< GerefTTs 93,200].

2074 **Teugels** Godelieve, Midrasj in de bijbel of midrasj op de bijbel? [midrash concerning or inside the Bible?] Een exemplarische studie van 'de verloving van Rebekka' (Gn 24) in de Bijbel en in de rabbijnse midrasj: diss. ᴰ*Vervenne* M. Leuven 1994. 275 p. – RTLv 26,533.

2075 *a) Vall* Gregory, [*lāśûaḥ*] What was Isaac doing in the field? (Genesis XXIV 63); – *b) Wahl* Harald M., Die Jakobserzählungen der Genesis und der Jubiläen im Vergleich: VT 44 (1994) 513-523 / 524-546.

2076 **Bucher-Gillmayr** Susanne, 'Und siehe, Rebekka kommt heraus'; eine textlinguistische Untersuchung zu Gen 24: Diss. ᴰ*Gamper* A. Innsbruck 1994. 356 p. – RTLv 26, p. 530; TR 91,97.

2077 [Gn 24,10 ...] *Bucher-Gillmayr* Susanne, Begegnungen am Brunnen: BibNot 75 (1994) 48-66; 6 statistical tables.

E2.7   **Jacob** and Esau; ladder-dream; *Jacob, somnium, Genesis 25 ...*

2079 **Dicou** Bert, Edom. Israel's brother and antagonist; the role of Edom in biblical prophecy and story [< diss. 1990]: jOsu 169.   Shf 1994,

Academic. 227 p. £30. 1-85075-458-6 [BL 95,84, J. R. *Bartlett*; JTS 46, 209, R. *Mason*]. – ᴿBZ 38 (1994) 105 (J. *Becker*); DielB 28 (1992s!) 209s (B. J. *Diebner*: Jacobs Bruder wieder undifferenziert 'Völkertyp').

2080 **Meier** Levi, Jacob. Lanham MD 1994, UPA. 110 p. $36; pa. $20, 0-8191-9667-3; -8-1 [TDig 42,280].

2081 *Hayward* Robert, Targum Pseudo-Jonathan to Genesis 27:31 [Esau gives his father a cooked dog at pesaḥ]: JQR 84 (1993s) 177-188.

2082 *a*) [Gn 28,3] *Rackman* Joseph, Was Isaac deceived?; – *b*) *Elazar* Daniel J., Jacob and Esau and the emergence of the Jewish people: Judaism 43 (1994) 37-45 / 294-301.

2083 *Schmidt* Ludwig, Die Erzählung von Jakob in Bet-El, Gen 28,11-22: ➤ 61, ᶠKAISER O., 'Wer ist' 1994, 156-168.

2084 *McEvenue* Sean, A return to sources in Genesis 28,10-22?: ZAW 106 (1994) 375-389 [E. BLUM: unsatisfactory].

2085 **Kushner** Lawrence, [Gn 28,10-16] God was in this place and I did not know it. Woodstock NY 1991, Jewish Lights. 192 p. – ᴿCCAR 41,4 (1994) 77-80 (S. A. *Moss*: a kabbalistic midrash).

2086 **Kushner** Lawrence, In questo luogo c'era Dio e io non lo sapevo; sette commenti a Genesi 28,16: Schulim Vogelmann 45. F 1994, Giuntina. 179 p. 88-85943-97-7.

2087 *Tucker* Gordon, Jacob's terrible burden in the shadow of the text: BR 10,3 (1994) 20-28 . 54.

2087* *Dresner* Samuel H., [Gn 30,1] Barren Rachel [... early Church ideal of barrenness]: Judaism 40 (1991) 422-451.

2088 **Dresner** Samuel H., Rachel. Mp 1994, Fortress. xvi-256 p. $15. 0-8006-2777-6 [TDig 42,266].

E2.8   **Jacob's wrestling; the Angels;** *lucta, Angelus/malʾak Gn 31-36 & 38.*

2088* *Bezza* Dario, Farsi amico un Angelo; l'angelo imparadisa l'uomo: PalCl 73 (1994) 431-457.

2089 *Faes de Mottoni* Barbara, S. BONAVENTURA e la ministerialità degli angeli: Antonianum 69 (1994) 405-416.

2090 **Hark** Helmut, Mit den Engeln gehen; die Botschaft unserer spirituellen Begleiter. Mü 1993, Kösel. 221 p. DM 38 [TR 91,267, W. *Schildmann*].

2091 **Mach** Michael, Entwicklungsstadien des jüdischen Engelglaubens ᴰ1992 ➤ 8,2424; 9,2204: ᴿBL (1994) 145 (D. *Bryan*); JBL 113 (1994) 140s (J. J. *Collins*); JStJud 23 (1994) 103-6 (J. *Duhaime*); JTS 45 (1994) 633-8 (L. W. *Hurtado*, also on OLYAN); TR 90 (1994) 115-8 (B. *Ego*).

2092 — **Estivill** Daniel E., La imagen del ángel en la Roma del siglo IV; estudio de iconología: diss. R 1994, Pont. Inst. Orientale. xi-254 p.; 43 pl.; bibliog. 241-9.

2093 **Olyan** Saul M., A thousand thousands served him; exegesis and the naming of angels in ancient Judaism: TStAJud 36. Tü 1993, Mohr. xiv-148 p. DM 138. 3-15-146063-4 [BL 1994,148, D. *Bryan*].

2094 *Osborn* Lawrence, Entertaining angels; their place in contemporary theology: TyndB 45 (1994) 273-306.

2095 *Plathow* Michael, 'Dein heiliger Engel sei mit mir'; Martin LUTHERs Engelpredigten: LuJb 61 (1994) 45-70.

2096 **Serres** M., La légende des anges. P 1993, Flammarion [RSPT 79,283-292, C. *Boureux*].

2097 **Vorgrimler** Herbert, Wiederkehr der Engel? [1991 ➤ 9,2210] ²1994 [TR 91,264-8, T. *Sternberg* auch über 20 ähnliche].

2097* a) *Ravasi* Gianfranco,   Giacobbe lotta con Dio (Gen 32,23-33); – b) *Fanuli* Antonio, 'Il Signore cercò di far morire Mosè' (Es 4,24-26); – c) *Mello* Alberto,   'Adamo, dove sei?' (Gen 3); – d) *Mazzinghi* Luca, '... e fece loro tuniche di pelli ...' La misericordia di Dio in Gen 3:   ParSpV 30 ('Esperienza e silenzio di Dio' 1994) 29-38 / 39-48 / 11-27 — 29 ('Peccato e misericordia' 1994) 11-23.

2098 *Pennant* David F.,   Genesis 32; Lighten our darkness, Lord, we pray: ➤ 146, F WISEMAN D., He swore an oath 1994, 175-183.

2099 *Viterbi Ben Horin* Miryam,   La lotta di Giacobbe con l'angelo: Vita Monastica 46/191 (Camaldoli 1992) 82-91 [< Judaica 49,63].

2100 *Amit* Yairah, ⊕ [Gn 34] A hidden polemic in the story of the rape of Dinah: ➤ 331a, 11th Jewish 1993/4, 1-8.

2101 *Bechtel* Lyn M.,   What if Dinah is not raped? (Genesis 34): JStOT 62 (1994) 19-36.

2102 *Shapira* A., ⊕ [Gen 34,5] Be silent: an immoral behavior: BeitM 39 (1994) 232-244 [< OTAbs 18, p. 49].

2103 *Standhartinger* Angela,   'Um zu sehen die Töchter des Landes'; die Perspektive Dinas in der jüdisch-hellenistischen Diskussion um Gen 34: ➤ 40, F GEORGI D., 1994, 89-116.

2104 *Steudler* Andreas, [Gn 35,4] Eiche oder Terebinthe?: IkiZ 83 (1993) 184-6.

2105 **Lambe** Anthony J.,   Genesis 38; literary design and context: diss. Newfoundland Memorial, D *Parker* K.   1994. 196 p. MM 91650. – (DissA-disk) MAI 33 (1994s), p. 740.

2106 *Soggin* J. Alberto,   Judah and Tamar (Genesis 38): ➤ 138, F WHYBRAY N., 1993, 281-7.

2107 *Wassén* Cecilia,   The story of Judah and Tamar in the eyes of the earliest interpreters: LitOx 8 (1994) 354-366.

2108 *Wildavsky* Aaron,   Survival must not be gained through sin; the moral of the Joseph stories prefigured through Judah and Tamar: JStOT 62 (1994) 37-48.

E2.9   **Joseph**; Jacob's blessings; *Genesis 37; 39-50.*

2109 **Alonso Schökel** Luis,   Giuseppe e i suoi fratelli: Letture Bibliche 11. Brescia 1994, Paideia. 109 p. L m 13. 88-394-0511-9.

2110 E Catastini Alessandro,   Storia di Giuseppe (Genesi 37-50): Lo stilo. Venezia 1994, Marsilio. 201 p.; bibliog. 195-201. 88-317-6007-6 [Gregorianum 76,596, G. *Marconi*].

2111 *Cruz Hernández* M. [on Joseph and Moses in Egypt]: MiscArH 41,2 (1992) [< VT 44,575].

2112 *Endo* Yoshinobu,   The verbal system of classical Hebrew in the Joseph story; an approach from discourse analysis: diss. Bristol 1993, D *Wenham* C. – TyndB 44 (1993) 373-7.

2114 *Groll* Sarah,   The identical characteristics existing between the personalities of '*pr-y3* [which she transcribes 'Cpr i3' from his Saqqara tomb] and the personalities of Joseph and Moses: ➤ 331a, 11th Jewish 1993/4, A-16-22.

2115 *Morris* Gerald,   Convention and character in the Joseph narrative: ProcGM 14 (1994) 69-85.

2116 **Niehoff** Maren,   The figure of Joseph in post-biblical Jewish literature D 1992 ➤ 8,2444; 9,2225: R NT 36 (1994) 304-7 (Nina L. *Collins*).

2117 *Saporetti* Claudio,   Il messaggio nel sogno; le manifestazioni oniriche e la loro interpretazione nelle società antiche: Archeo 9,118 (1994) 118s.

2118 **Schweizer** Harald, Die Josefsgeschichte 1991 → 7,2122: ᴿCBQ 56 (1994) 126s (A. *Gianto*); WeltOr 25 (1994) 176-9 (W. *Zwickel*); ᴢᴀᴡ 106 (1994) 533s (H.-C. *Schmitt*); ZkT 116 (1994) 73-75 (J. M. *Oesch*).

2119 *a*) *Seebass* Horst, Joseph, sein Vater Israel und das pharaonische Ägypten; – *b*) *Johnson* Bo, Die Josephserzählung und die Theodizeefrage; – *c*) *Golka* Friedemann, Die biblische Josefsgeschichte und Thomas Maɴɴs Roman: → 115, ꜰScʜᴜɴᴄᴋ K.-D., Nachdenken 1994, 11-25 / 27-36 / 37-49.

2120 *Shupak* Nili, ❶ [Gn 37] The story of Joseph; legend or history?: → 331*a*, 11th Jewish 1993/4, 17-22.

2121 **Silva** Aldina da, *a*) [Gn 37-50], La symbolique des rêves et des vêtements dans l'histoire de Joseph et de ses frères: Héritage et projet 52. Québec 1994, Fides. 210 p. 2-7621-1272-5 [NRT 117,805, J. L. *Ska*; OTAbs 18, p. 633, D. B. *Sharp*]. – *b*) Le rêve comme expérience démoniaque en Mésopotamie: SR 22 (1992) 301-310.

2121* *Ska* Jean-Louis, La scoperta del disegno di Dio nella storia di Giuseppe: → 368, Volontà di Dio 1992/3, 113-132.

2122 *West* Gerald, Difference and dialogue; reading the Joseph story with poor and marginalized communities in South Africa: BInterp 2 (1994) 152-170.

2122* **Wills** L., The Jew in the court of the foreign king 1990 → 6,2518; 8,2447: ᴿAJS 17 (1992) 286-8 (F. E. *Greenspahn*).

2123 **Wood** Kathleen M., The dreams of Joseph in light of Ancient Near Eastern divinatory practice: diss. Georgia, ᴰ*Lewis* T. 1994. 115 p. 135-8824 (DissA-disk) MAI 33 (1994s) p. 362.

2124 *Endo* Yoshinobu, ❹ Who did what? An interpretation on Gen 37:28: Exegetica 5 (Tokyo 1994) 57-68: ['Ishmaelites' and 'Midianites' refer to the same group.

2125 *Kern-Ulmer* Brigitte, Zwischen ägyptischer Vorlage und talmudischer Rezeption; Josef und die Ägypterin: Kairos 34s (1992s) 75-90.

2126 *Boecker* Hans J., [Gn 39] Überlegungen zur Erzählung von der Versuchung Josephs: → 101, ꜰReᴠᴇɴᴛʟᴏᴡ H., 1994, 3-13 [< OTAbs 18, p. 50].

2127 *Görg* Manfred, [Gen 41,39s] Zu einem 'Verstehensproblem' in der Josefsgeschichte: BibNot 75 (1994) 13-17.

2128 *Hurowitz* Victor A., Joseph's enslavement of the Egyptians (Genesis 47,13-26) in light of famine texts from Mesopotamia: RB 101 (1994) 355-362; franç. 355.

2129 **Wildavsky** Aaron, Assimilation versus separation; Joseph the administrator and the politics of religion in biblical Israel. L 1993, Transaction. ix-236 p. $35. 1-56000-081-3 [OTAbs 18, p. 411, J. L. *Berquist*].

2130 *Catastini* Alessandro, Un errore significativo nella tradizione di Genesi 47:5-6: Sefarad 54 (1994) 253-8; Eng. 258: longer LXX reveals homoeoteleuton of present MT.

2131 *Rendsburg* Gary A., [ancient north-] Israelian Hebrew features in Genesis 49: Maarav 8 (1992) 161-170.

2132 *Catastini* Alessandro, Sul testo di *Genesi* 49,11: Henoch 16 (1994) 15-22.

2133 *Deurloo* K. A., 'Wer ist das eigentlich – Gott?' Over Genesis 50:15-21: Om het levende Woord 2 (1993) 62-75 [< OTAbs 17, p. 551, M. *Kessler* at length; but from the half-Dutch title it is not clear whether the article is in German].

E3.1   Exodus event and theme; *textus, commentarii.*

2134 **Binz** Stephen J., The God of freedom and life; a commentary on the Book of Exodus 1993 ➤ 9,2243:   RCanadCath 12,11 (1994) 26 (M. *Duggan*).

2135 **EBrenner** Athalya, A feminist companion to Exodus to Deuteronomy: FemB 6. Shf 1994, Academic. 269 p. £16.60.   1-85075-463-2 [JTS 46, 216, Meg *Davies*].

2136 **Brueggemann** Walter, The Book of Exodus: ➤ 1575, NInterp 1 (1994) 675-981.

2137 *Ceccherelli* Ignazio M., Gli Hyksos, la discesa in Egitto e l'Esodo degli Ebrei: BbbOr 36 (1994) 139-168.

2138 *Crocker* P.T., Exodus matters update: BurHist 30 (1994) 121-134.

2139 **Gowan** Donald E., Theology in Exodus; biblical theology in the form of a commentary. LVL 1994, W-Knox. xviii-297 p. 0-664-22057-6 [TDig 42,369; RelStR 21,224, M.B. *Phelps*].

2140 **Holladay** Carl R., Fragments from... Ezekiel the tragedian 1989 ➤ 5, b678... 9,2249:   RCritRR 5 (1992) 367-9 (B.Z. *Wacholder*).

2141 **Houtman** Cornelis, Exodus I [Eng.]: HistCommOT. Kampen 1993, Kok. xii-554 p. ƒ97,50. 90-242-6213-5 [BL 95,66, J.G. *Snaith*: includes 45 pages on fauna and flora of the whole Bible].

2142 **Hughes** Paul E., A literary reading of the Exodus story: diss. Edinburgh 1994. 276 p. – RTLv 26,531.

2143 *Jacob* Benno, The second book of the Bible, Exodus, TJacob W. 1992 ➤ 8,2468; 9,2251: RZAW 106 (1994) 524s (M. *Köckert*).

2144 *Jebaraj* D., Exodus, a paradigm of the salvation and liberation of the oppressed: EvRT 18 (Exeter 1994) 161-6 [< OTAbs 17, p. 621].

2145 **Loewenstamm** S.E., The evolution of the Exodus tradition [Ⓖ 1968, 'enlarged' 1987], TSchwartz Baruch J., 1992 ➤ 8,2469*: RVT 44 (1994) 574s (G.I. *Davies*).

2146 TMcNamara Martin; notes *Hayward* Robert, Targum Neofiti 1, Exodus [with **Maher** M., Pseudo-Jonathan p. 159-276]: Aramaic Bible 2. ColMn/E 1994, Liturgical/Clark. xiv-326 p. bibliog. 277-289.

2146* **Magnante** Antonio, La teologia dell'Esodo nei Salmi [78; 105s; 135s], D1991 ➤ 7,2147*; 8,2472: RParVi 39,2 (1994) 63 (T. *Lorenzin*).

2147 *Maher* Michael, Targum Pseudo-Jonathan, Exodus [with ➤ 2146, **McNamara**]: Aramaic Bible 2 (1994) pp. 159-276.

2148 *Pinto* León Adolfo, *Amar y las transiciones temporales en los libros Éxodo y Deuteronomio:* EfMex 12 (1994) 33-54.

2148* **Spreafico** Antonio, Il libro dell'Esodo 1992 ➤ 8,2478; 9,2258: RParVi 39,3 (1994) 59 (A. *Rolla*).

2149 **Terian** Abraham, Quaestiones et solutiones in Ex I-II: Œuvres de PHILON 14c, 1992 ➤ 8,2479; 9,2250: RJTS 45 (1994) 287-290 (D.T. *Runia*); PrOrChr 43 (1993) 201 (P. *Ternant*); ScEspr 46 (1994) 117-9 (P.-H. *Poirier*); VigChr 48 (1994) 187-9 (J.C.M. van *Winden*).

2150 *Tov* Emanuel, The Exodus section of 4Q422: ➤ 336a, DSD 1 (1994) 197-209.

2151 *Utzschneider* Helmut, Die Renaissance der alttestamentlichen Literaturwissenschaft und das Buch Exodus: ZAW 106 (1994) 197-223.

2152 **Wevers** J,W., Exodus: Gö LXX 2/1, 1991 ➤ 7,2155: RSalesianum 56 (1994) 384 (M. *Cimosa*).

2153 **Wevers** J.W.,   Text History Ex 1992 ➤ 8,2480; 9,2260:   ᴿJBL 113 (1994) 514-6 (P. W. *Flint*: fine meticulous scholarship).
2154 **Wevers** John W., Notes on the Greek text of Exodus 1990 ➤ 6,2555; 7,2154 [TR 91,310s, A. *Schenker*].
2155 **Wright** Paul A., Exodus 1-24 (a canonical study): ev. Diss. ᴰ*Sauer* G. Wien 1994. – TR 91,102.
2156 **Zakovitch** Yair, 'And you...' Exodus 1991 ➤ 7,2159; 9,2262:   ᴿCritRR 6 (1993) 193s (S. E. *Balentine*).

E3.2   **Moyses**   – Pharaoh, Goshen – *Exodus 1*...

2157 **Alonso Schökel** Luis, Mosè mediatore: Fondamenti Biblici del Presbiterato. R c.1994, Seminario Romano Maggiore.   60 p.
2158 *a) Beckerath* J. von,   Zur Datierung Ramses' II; – *b) Peden* A. J., A note on the accession date of Merenptah; – *c) Kruchten* Jean-Marie, Quelques passages difficiles de la Stèle d.Israël: GöMiszÄg 142 (1994) 55s / 140 (1994) 69 / 37-48.
2159 **Blum** Erhard, Studien zur Komposition des Pentateuch [Ex 1-14]: ʙᴢᴀᴡ 189,1990 ➤ 6,2527... 8,2487: ᴿAntonianum 69 (1994) 454s (M. *Nobile*).
2160 *[da Rocha] Couto* António J., Revelação de Deus e vocação/missão de Moisés, a que é associado Aarão [Ex 3,6]: Ho Theológos 15 (1994) 19-38 [< OTAbs 18, p. 297].
2161 **Davies** Gordon F., Israel in Egypt... Ex 1-2: jOsu 135, 1992 ➤ 8,2489: ᴿCBQ 56 (1994) 329-331 (R. B. *Robinson*).
2162 **Dörrfuss** Ernst M., Mose in den Chronikbüchern, Garant theokratischer Zukunftserwartung: ʙᴢᴀᴡ 219. B 1994, de Gruyter. xiii-302 p. ᴅᴍ 148. 3-11-014017-9 [BL 95,61s, A. G. *Auld*].
2163 *Exum* J. Cheryl, Second thoughts about secondary characters; women in Exodus 1.8-2.10 [correcting her 1983 article]: ➤ 2135, FemComp 6. Ex 1994, 75-87.
2164 *Frankemölle* Hubert, Mose in Deutungen des Neuen Testaments: KIsr 9 (1994) 70-86.
2165 *Gross* Walter, Die Position des Subjekts im hebräischen Verbalsatz, untersucht an den asyndetischen ersten Redesätzen in Gen, Ex 1-19, Jos - 2 Kön: ZaHeb 6 (1993) 170-187.
2166 *Hasel* Michael G., *Israel* in the Merneptah stela: BASOR 296 (1994) 45-61.
2167 **Hörnemann** Wolfgang, Die Figur des Moses als Typus eines Helfers und Begleiters; das Exodusbuch als Ermutigung für pastorales und diakonisches Handeln: Diss. ᴰ*Pompey* H. Freiburg/B 1994. 737 p. – TR 91,95; RTLv 26, p. 587.
2168 **Lee** Choong-Quon, The missiological approaches revealed in the post-Abrahamic covenants [Moses, David, Jeremiah] and their theological contextualization in Korea: diss. Fuller, ᴰ*Van Engen* C. Pasadena 1994. 13-57362. – [DissA-disk] MAI 32 (1994s) p. 1535.
2169 ᴱ**Martín Lunas** T. H., S. Gʀᴇɢᴏʀɪᴏ de Nisa, Vida de Moisés [y Cantar]: Ichthys 15, 1993 ➤ 9,2280: ᴿEfMex 12 (1994) 409-412 (M. A. *Flores Ramos*); EstAg 29 (1994) 181s (P. de *Luis*).
2170 ᵀᴱ**Mateo-Seco** L. F., Gʀᴇɢᴏʀɪᴏ de Nisa, Sobre la vida de Moisés. M 1993, Ciudad Nueva. 252 p. – ᴿRelCu 40 (1994) 641s (J. *Tejedor*).
2171 Die Modelle der Exoduszyklen in sphardischen [sic] Pesach-Haggadot [no ed. or other data]: ᴿKairos 34s (1992s) 245-7 (Katrin *Kogman-Appel*].
2172 **Mélèze-Modrzejewski** Joseph, Les Juifs d'Égypte de Ramsès II à Hadrien

1991 ► 7,2165; 9,2281:   ᴿRB 101 (1994) 118-129 (Sylvie *Honigman*);
ZSav-R 111 (1994) 733s (H.-P. *Benöhr*).
2173 *Nibbi* Alessandra,   Some unanswered questions on Canaan and Egypt
and the so-called Israel Stela: BibNot 73 (1994) 74-84 + 4 fig. (map);
dazu 74 (1994) 27-30, *Görg* Manfred, 'Kanaan' und 'Israel'; kein Umzug
nach Afrika.
2174 *Perlitt* Lothar, Mose als Prophet [< EvTh 31 (1971) 588-608]: ► 214,
Dt-St 1994, 1-19.
2175 *Roubey* Leston W.,   The Moïse of Alfred de VIGNY, introduction and
translation: CCAR 40,163 (1994) 45-53.
2176 *Ruiten* Jacques van, *Vandermeersch* Patrick,   Psychoanalyse en historisch-kritische exegese; de actualiteit van FREUD's boek over Mozes en het
monotheïsme; op zoek naar het 'echte feit':   TvT 34 (1994) 269-291; Eng.
291, Freud's 'topicality'.
2177 **Van Seters** John,   The life of Moses; the Yahwist as historian in
Exodus-Numbers. LVL 1994, W-Knox.   xvi-524 p. $33.   0-664-22038-X
[TDig 42,192; Biblica 76,419-422, J. L. *Ska*]. – ᴿOTAbs 17 (1994) 660s
(R. E. *Murphy*).
2178 *Zenger* Erich, Mose... [NT, *Sänger* Dieter]: ► 517, TRE 23 (1994)
330-341 [342-6 (-357, apokalypt., *Oberhänsli-Widmer* Gabrielle)].
2179 *Zivotofsky* Ari Z.,   The leadership qualities of Moses: Judaism 43
(1994) 258-269.

2180 *Pazzini* Massimo,   Senso lessicale e senso contestuale; osservazioni di
esegeti ebrei medievali a Es 1-20:   LA 44 (1994) 331-350; Eng. 614.
2181 **Davies** Gordon F.,   Israel in Egypt; reading Exodus 1-2: jOsu 135, 1992
► 8,2489; 9,2273:   ᴿInterpretation 48 (1994) 80s (J. S. *Ackerman*).
2182 **Jeammet** Nicole,   Les destins de la culpabilité; une lecture de l'histoire
de Moïse aux frontières de la psychanalyse et de la théologie: Le fait
psychanalytique. P 1993, PUF.   216 p. F 180.   2-13-045394-5. – ᴿÉTRel
69 (1994) 124s (J. *Ansaldi*).
2183 *Römer* Thomas,   Les sages-femmes du pharaon (Exode 1/15-22): ÉTRel
69 (1994) 265-270.
2184 *Brenner* Athalya, [Ex 1s...] Who's afraid of feminist criticism? Who's
afraid of biblical humour? The case of the obtuse foreign ruler in the
Hebrew Bible: JStOT 63 (1994) 38-55.
2185 *Wright* Paul A., Exodus 1,24; a canonical study: ev. Diss. ᴰ*Sauer* G.
Wien 1994. 241 p. – RTLv 26,533.
2186 *Macchi* Jean-Daniel,   La naissance de Moïse (Exode 2/1-10): ÉTRel 69
(1994) 397-403.
2187 — *Andiñach* Pablo R.,   La leyenda acádica de Sargón: RBibArg 55
(1993) 103-119.
2188 *Zakovitch* Yair, ⊕ [Ex 2,1s] Between 'have no fear, for it is another boy
for you' and 'have no fear, for you have borne a boy'; a study in parallels:
► 331*a*, 11th Jewish 1993/4, 9-16.
2189 *McNutt* Paula M., [Ex 3,1 (Jg 1,16); Ex 18,1] The Kenites, the Midianites
and the Rechabites as marginal mediators in ancient Israelite tradition
[*Benjamin* Don C., response]: Semeia 67 (1994) 109-132 [133-145].

E3.3   **Nomen divinum, Tetragrammaton; *Exodus 3,14* ... Plagues.**

2190 *Broadie* Alexander,   MAIMONIDES on the great tautology; Exodus 3,14:
ScotJT 47 (1994) 473-488.

2191 *Carroll* R.P., Strange fire; abstract of presence absent in the text [;] meditations on Exodus 3: JStOT 61 (1994) 39-58.

2192 *Daalen* A.G. van, The place where YHWH showed himself to Moses; a study of the composition of Exodus 3: ➤ 250, VAmst 1994, 133-144.

2192* *Hertog* Cok den, De naam van de god van de profeten: Exodus 3:13-15: AmstCah 12 (1993) 438-61; Eng. 132s.

2193 **Lenzen** Verena, Biblisches Leben und Sterben im Namen Gottes; Studien über die Heiligung des göttlichen Namens (*kiddush ha-shem*): kath. Hab.-Diss. ᴰ*Höver* G. Bonn 1994. – TR 91,89.

2194 *Liwak* Rüdiger, *al.*, Namen/Namengebung biblisch: ➤ 517, TRE 23 (1994) (743-) 749-754 (-764).

2195 **Mettinger** Tryggve N.D., Buscando a Dios; significado y mensaje de los nombres divinos en la Biblia, ᵀ. Córdoba 1994, Almendro. 245 p.; bibliog. 215-225.

2196 *Mianbé Bétoudji* Denis, El le dieu suprême et le Dieu des Patriarches: RelWTSt 1, 1986 ➤ 2,1652 ... 5,2270: ᴿBL (1994) 112 (N. *Wyatt*: aimed at Chad).

2197 *Motzkin* G., 'Ehyeh' and the future; 'God' and HEIDEGGER's concept of 'becoming' compared: Yearbook for religious anthropology (Berlin 1994) 173-... [< ZIT 95, p. 207].

2198 *Muller* Frank, Les premières apparitions du tétragramme dans l'art allemand et néerlandais des débuts de la Réforme: BtHumRen 56 (1994) 327-346; 12 fig.

2199 *Rendtorff* Rolf, ʾEl als israelitische Gottesbezeichnung; Appendix: Gebrauch von *Ha-Elohim*: ZAW 106 (1994) 4-21.

2200 **Rothschild** Anne, Le Buisson de Feu, roman. Lausanne 1992, Age d'homme. Fs 25. – ᴿJudaica 49 (1993) 107-9 (Gabrielle *Oberhäusli-Widmer*: 'eine moderne Fassung des brennenden Dornbuschs').

2201 *Thompson* Thomas L., Hvorledes Jahve blev Gud (how Y. became God); Exodus 3 og 6 og Pentateukens centrum: DanTTs 57 (1994) 1-18 [< OTAbs 17, p. 554; ZAW 106,498].

2202 *a) Wahl* Harald M., 'Ich bin, der ich bin'; Anmerkungen zur Rede vom Gott des AT; – *b) Schreiner* Josef, Kein anderer Gott; Bemerkungen zu Ex 34,11-26; – *c) Fritz* Volkmar, Jahwe und El in vorpriesterschriftlichen Geschichtswerken: ➤ 61, ᶠKAISER O., 'Wer' 1994, 32-48 / 199-213/ 111-126.

2203 *Yeo Khiok-Khng*, The 'Yin and Yang' of God (Exo 3:14) and humanity (Gen 1:26-27): ZRGg 46 (1994) 319-332.

2204 *Ska* Jean Louis, Note sur la traduction de *wᵉ-lōʾ* en Exode III 19ᵇ [applied to a proposition which is itself negative]: VT 44 (1994) 60-65.

2205 ᴱ**Perrone** Lorenzo, [Ex 4,21] 'Il cuore indurito del Faraone'; ORIGENE e il problema del libero arbitrio: CISEC Origini 3, 1992 ➤ 8,2526; 9,2309: ᴿOrpheus 15 (1994) 249-252 (Paola *Santorelli*).

2206 *Ashby* G.W., The bloody bridegroom; the interpretation of Exodus 4:24-26: ExpTim 106 (1994s) 203-5.

2207 **Gitau** Samson Njuguna, A comparative study of the transmission, actualization and stabilization of oral traditions; an examination of traditions of circumcision in Africa and Ancient Israel: diss. Boston 1994. – RelStR 21,251.

2208 **Leeuwen** J.H. van, De inlijving door het bloed, of het overlevingshistorische probleem van de Pentateuch in literair perspektief, aan de hand van Exodus 4:24-26: diss. Bru/Voorburg Ned 1985, Prot. Stichting. 167 p. (Eng. 4 p.) *f* 24,75. – ᴿVT 44 (1994) 129 (G.I. *Davies*).

2209 [Ex 4,21-26] *Reis* Pamela T., The bridegroom of blood; a new reading: Judaism 40 (1991) 325-331.
2210 *Römer* Thomas, De l'archaïque au subversif; le cas d'Exode 4/24-26: ÉTRel 69 (1994) 1-12; dazu DielB 29 (1992s) 199-201 (B. J. *Diebner*).
2211 **Grünwald** Klaus, Exil und Identität; Beschneidung, Passa und Sabbat in der Priesterschrift. Fra 1992, Hain. x-254 p. DM 88. 3-445-09148-X. – ᴿOTAbs 17 (1994) 435 (P. L. *Redditt*).
2212 *Gosse* Bernard, Exode 6,8 comme réponse à Ézéchiel 33,24: RHPR 74 (1994) 241-7.
2213 *Bailey* Randall C., 'And they shall know that I am YHWH'; the P recasting of the Plague narratives in Exodus 7-11: JIntdenom 22 (1994) 1-17.
2214 **Schmidt** Ludwig, Beobachtungen zu den Plagenerzählungen in Ex VII.14-XI,10: StB 4, 1990 ➤ 6,2624...9,2316: ᴿTLZ 119 (1994) 124-7 (W. H. *Schmidt*).

E3.4   *Pascha, sanguis, sacrificium:* **Passover, blood, sacrifice,** *Ex 11*...

2215 *Greenstein* Edward L., ❸ [5 options 'no dog shall...':] Ex 11,7: ➤ 62, ᶠKAMIN 1994, 587-600 [< OTAbs 18, p. 514].
2216 *Kline* Meredith G., [Ex 12 *pesaḥ*, meaning akin to 'hover over' Gen 1,2] The feast of cover-over: JEvTS 37 (1994) 497-510.
2217 *Bergant* Dianne, An anthropological approach to biblical interpretation; the Passover supper in Exodus 12:1-20 as a case study [response *Buckley* Jorunn J.]: Semeia 67 (1994) 43-62 [63-71].
2218 *Collins* Nina L., Evidence in the Septuagint of a tradition in which the Israelites left Egypt without Pharaoh's consent: CBQ 56 (1994) 442-8.
2219 *Segert* Stanislav, Crossing the waters; Moses and Hamilcar: JNES 53 (1994) 195-203.
2220 **Bauer** Uwe F. W., All diese Worte... Ex 13,17-14,31: EurHS 23/442. Fra 1992, Lang. 378 p. DM 89. – ᴿBiKi 49 (1994) 70s (M. *Helsper*).
2221 — *Vervenne* Marc, [Ex 13s] The sea-narrative revisited [BAUER U. 1992]: Biblica 75 (1994) 80-98.
2222 *Bach* Alice, [Ex 15,20s] 'With a song in her heart'; listening to scholars listening to Miriam: ➤ 2135, FemEx 1994, 243-254 [200-230 *al.*; < OTAbs 18, p. 52s].
2223 *Brooke* George J., Power to the powerless; the long-lost song of Miriam [Ex 15,21 / 4Q365]; an expanded Song of the Sea: BAR-W 20,3 (1994) 62-99.
2224 **Watts** James W., Psalm and story; inset hymns in Hebrew narrative: jOsu 138, 1992 ➤ 8,1228: ᴿBL (1993) 70 (K. J. *Cathcart*); CBQ 56 (1994) 351s (W. A. *Young*); Interpretation 48 (1994) 196.8 (J. L. *Mays*); JBL 113 (1994) 126-8 (R. *Gnuse*); WestTJ 55 (1993) 346-8 (P. *Enns*).
2225 *McEvenue* Sean, Truth and literature in Exodus 16: TPhil 69 (1994) 493-510.
2226 *Schroven* Brigitte, Religionspädagogik im AT am Beispiel von Ex 16: ➤ 34d, ᶠFANGMEIER J. 1994, 145-152.
2227 **Burden** Terry L., The kerygma of the wilderness traditions in the Hebrew Bible: AmerUnivSt 7/163. NY 1994, P. Lang. xii-259 p. 0-8204-2253-3.
2228 **López Melús** Francisco M., Desierto; una experiencia de gracia: Nueva Alianza 128. S 1994, Sígueme. 393 p. 84-301-1233-2.
2229 *Truper* M., ❸ Moses as desert guide: BeitM 39 (1994) 279-283.

2230 **Ego** Beate, Israel und Amalek; Übersetzung und Kommentierung von Targum Scheni: ev. Hab.-Diss. Tübingen 1994. – TR 91,91.

2231 *Maier* Johann, [Ex 17,8] Amalek in the writings of JOSEPHUS: ➤ 123, Mem. SMITH M., Josephus 1992/4, 109-126.

2232 *Lopasso* Vincenzo, L'esperienza religiosa di Israele al Sinai (Es 19-24): Vivarium 2 (1994) 371-390.

2233 **Renaud** Bernard, La théophanie... Ex 19-29: CahRB 30, 1991 ➤ 7, 2208... 9,2334: ᴿGregorianum 75 (1994) 549-552 (G. L. *Prato*).

2234 *Tonder* C. A. P. van, *Oberholzer* J. P.,, 'n Sosiologiese perspektief op die literêre kompositie van die Sinaikompleks (Eksodus 19-34): HervTSt 50 (1994) 730-754 [< OTAbs 18, p. 298].

Williams Larry, The mountain of Moses [in Arabia-'Midian' east of Aqaba Gulf] c. 1992 ➤ 12849.

2234* **Zenger** Erich, Am Fuss des Sinai; Gottesbilder des Ersten Testaments. Dü 1993, Patmos. 174 p. DM 29,80. – ᴿLebZeug 49 (1994) 147 (R. *Jungenitsch*).

E3.5 **Decalogus**, *Ex 20* = *Dt 5; Ex 21ss;* **Ancient Near East Law.**

2235 **Brooks** Roger, The spirit of the Ten Commandments 1990 ➤ 6,2654; 8,2543: ᴿAJS 17 (1992) 299-301 (R. *Goldenberg*); CritRR 5 (1992) 359-361 (T. *Kleven*) & 6 (1993) 406-8 (J. T. *Pawlikowski*).

2236 **Carmichael** Calum M., The origins of biblical law; the Decalogue and the Book of the Covenant 1992 ➤ 8,2543*; 9,2335: ᴿInterpretation 48 (1994) 84 (V. H. *Matthews*).

2237 *Cohen* Jeffrey M., The nature of the decalogue: JBQ 22 (1994) 173-7 [< OTAbs 18, p. 53].

2238 *Fritzsche* Helmut, Die aktuelle Bedeutung des Dekalogs in kulturgeschichtlicher und theologischer Sicht: ➤ 115, ᶠSCHUNCK K.-D., Nachdenken 1994, 411-444.

2239 *Gatti* Guido, L'utilizzazione del Decalogo nel Catechismo della Chiesa Cattolica: Salesianum 56 (1994) 121-137.

2240 *Jacquin* Françoise, Les Dix Paroles dans la pédagogie juive: ➤ 264, Communio 19,111 (1994) 43-55.

2241 *Korsvaar* Hendrik, The ten words, Ex 20,1-17: ➤ 84, ᶠMORELAND D., The secret of faith 1992, 91-99.

2242 *Kratz* Reinhard G., Der Dekalog im Exodusbuch: VT 44 (1994) 205-238.

2243 *Oeming* Manfred, Hiob 31 und der Dekalog: ➤ 304, Job 1993/4, 362-8.

2244 *Wénin* André, Le décalogue, révélation de Dieu et chemin de bonheur: RTLv 25 (1994) 145-182; Eng. 287;

2245 *Youngblood* Ronald, Counting the Ten Commandments: BR 10,6 (1994) 30-35.

2246 *Krašovec* Jože, [Ex 20,5s; Dt 7,9s; 34,6s; Jer 32,18] Is there a doctrine of 'collective retribution' in the Hebrew Bible? HUCA 65 (1994) 35-89.

2247 *Patrick* Dale, Is the truth of the First Commandment known by reason?: CBQ 56 (1994) 423-441.

2248 **Willis-Watkins** David, The Second Commandment and Church reform; the colloquy of St. Germain-en-Laye, 1562: StRefT 2/2. Princeton 1994, Theol. Sem. xii-80 p.

2249 *Loretz* Oswald, Das 'Ahnen- und Götterstatuen-Verbot' im Dekalog und die Einzigkeit Jahwes; zum Begriff des Göttlichen in altorientalischen und alttestamentlichen Quellen: → 467*, Ein Gott allein? OBO 139, 1993/4, 491-527.

2250 ᴱ**Dohmen** C., *Stemberger* T., ...kein Bildnis machen; Kunst und Theologie im Gespräch 1987 → 3,395; 7,2210: ᴿTLtg 67 (1994) 51s (A. *Demblon*).

2251 **Keel** Othmar, Das Recht der Bilder gesehen zu werden: OBO 122, 1992 → 8,2556; 9,2359: ᴿBL (1994) 28 (R. P. R. *Murray*); JBL 113 (1994) 501 (M. *Kessler*: hardly anything on the Bible; his title means that Bilder must be seen according to their own relative merit and context, not hastily forced into a biblical Procrustean bed); ZDPV 110 (1994) 190-3 (J. F. *Quack*).

2252 *Loretz* Oswald, Semitischer Anikonismus und biblisches Bilderverbot: UF 26 (1994) 209-223.

2253 **Rordorf** Bernard, Tu ne te feras pas d'image; prolégomènes à une théologie de l'amour de Dieu: CogF167, 1992 → 8,2461*; 9,2358: ᴿFoiTemps 23 (1993) 369s (G. *Harpigny*); Salesianum 56 (1994) 591s (R. *Vicent*).

2254 *Bidault* Bernard, Le travail et le sabbat dans la Bible: LumièreV 220 (1994) 37-46 [< OTAbs 18, p. 354].

2255 *Fersterer* Anton, Exegetische Notizen zum Sabbatwort, Ex 20,8-11 bzw. Dtn 5,12-15: ProtokB 3 (1994) 41-64.

2256 **Ginsburg** Elliot K., *Sod ha-Shabbat*, The mystery of the sabbath: StJudaica. Albany 1989, SUNY. xvi-264 p. – ᴿAJS 17 (1992) 123-6 (Eliot R. *Wolfson*).

2257 *Ratzinger* Joseph, *al.*, 'Keep holy the day of the Lord': CommWsh 21,1 (1994) 5-26 (-48, *al.*).

2258 **Shea** William H., Sargon's Azekah inscription; the earliest extrabiblical reference to the Sabbath?: AndrUnSem 32 (1994) 247-251.

2259 **Spier** Erich, Der Sabbat: Das Judentum 1. B 1989, Inst. Kirche und Judentum. 220 p. – ᴿJQR 84 (1993s) 321-3 (Catherine *Hezser*).

2260 *a)* *Tronina* Antoni, ⊕ De sabbato — archetypo dominicae in VT; – *b)* *Sobeczko* Helmut, ⊕ De valore theologico et pastorali dominicae celebrandae sabbato vespere: RuBi 47 (1994) 95-103 / 162-175 [268-280 in pastorali germanica, *Rojewski* Andrzej].

2261 ᴱ**Trotta** Giuseppe, Il sabato nella tradizione ebraica: Attendendo l'Aurora, 1991 → 8,2566; 9,2360: ᴿSalesianum 56 (1994) 161 (R. *Vicent*).

2262 **Marshall** Jay Wade, Israel and the Book of the Covenant; an anthropological approach to Biblical Law (SBL diss. 150) 1993 → 9,2364 [RelStR 20,230, Naomi *Steinberg*: exceedingly important]. – ᴿBL (1994) 112 (B. S. *Jackson*).

2263 **Otto** Eckhart, Rechtsgeschichte... 'Bundesbuch': OBO 85, 1989 → 7, 2219: ᴿRB 101 (1994) 449s (M. *Sigrist*); ZAss 84 (1994) 148-151 (J. *Oelsner*).

2264 **Schwienhorst-Schönberger** Ludger, Das Bundesbuch: BZAW 188, 1990 → 6,2675 ... 8,2571: ᴿBZ 38 (1994) 108s (J. *Scharbert*).

2265 **Sprinkle** Joe, [Ex 20,22-23,19] The Book of the Covenant; a literary approach [< diss.]: jOsu 171. Shf 1994, Academic. 224 p. £35. 1- 85075-467-5 [OTAbs 17, p. 661; BL 95,75, N. J. *Phillips*; TLZ 120,328, E. *Otto*].

2266 **Osumi** Yuichi, Die Kompositionsgeschichte des Bundesbuches: OBO 105, 1991 → 7,2218 ... 9,2365: ᴿWZKM 83 (1993) 149-165 (E. *Otto*: Grundpfeiler nicht tragfähig).

2267 **Bechtel** D. R., [Ex 21,22s ...] Women, choice, and abortion; another look
at biblical traditions; Prism 8,1 (St. Paul 1994) 74-89 [< NTAbs 38,
p. 236: PHILO/JOSEPHUS motivation dubious; Jesus not against).

2268 *Fuller* Russell, Exodus 21:22-23; the miscarriage interpretation and the
personhood of the fetus: JEvTS 37 (1994) 169-184.

2269 *Sprinkle* Joe M., The interpretation of Exodus 21:22-25 (lex talionis)
and abortion: WestTJ 55 (1993) 233-253.

2270 *Nel* P. J., [Ex 21,25; Ruth; Jg 13-16] The Talion principle in Old
Testament narratives: JNWS 20,1 (1994) 21-29.

2271 *Westbrook* Raymond, The deposit law of Exodus 22,6-12: ZAW 106
(1994) 390-403.

2272 **Bultmann** Christoph, [Ex 22,21] Der Fremde: FRL 153, 1992 ➤ 8,2581;
9,2374: ᴿTLZ 119 (1994) 780-2 (H. M. *Neumann*); TRu 59 (1994) 215s (C.
Westermann).

2273 **Barbiero** Gianni, L'asino del nemico ... Es 23,4s: AnBib 128, 1991 ➤ 7,
2224 ... 9,2379: ᴿBZ 38 (1994) 122 (J. *Becker*).

2274 *Stancari* Piero, [Ex 23,4; Num 22 ...] Violenza e non violenza; il caso
dell'asino [< ᴱ*Bertalot* R., al., Violenza 1992/3]: ➤ 306, Animali 1993/4,
25-49.

2275 *a) Anbar* Moshe, 'Thou shalt make no covenant with them' (Exodus
23,32); – *b) Amir* Yehoshua, Josephus on the MOSAIC 'constitution'; – *c)*
Rakover Nahum, 'The law' and the Noahides: ➤ 331*b*, Politics 1985/94,
41-48 / 13-27 / 148-159.

2276 **Bovati** Pietro, Re-establishing justice; legal terms, concepts, and procedures in the Hebrew Bible [ᴰ1985, hitherto listed under *rîb* ➤ 2,
7458 ... 8,9487]: ᵀ*Smith* Michael J.: jOsu 105. Shf 1994, JStOT. 478 p.
£47.50. 1-85075-290-7 [BL 45,110, B. S. *Jackson*: valuable; RelStR 21,
320, V. H. *Matthews*: useful on legal procedures and the history of law]. –
ᴿExpTim 106 (1994s) 157 (C. S. *Rodd*, amid 4 other jOsu and 5 jNsu:
makes a clear distinction between the *rîb* and the 'juridical process'
(*mišpat*) and relates this to NT social justice); Salesianum 56 (1994) 149s
(M. *Cimosa*).
  Brin Gershon, Studies in biblical law, from the Hebrew Bible to the Dead
Sea Scrolls: jOsu 176, 1994 ➤ 163.

2277 *Eckart* Otto, Wandel der Rechtsbegründungen 1988 ➤ 4,2543 ... 6,2677:
ᴿZSav-R 111 (1994) 707s (Z. W. *Falk*).

2278 *Fuss* Abraham M., Two bibliographies of Jewish law [RAKOVER N.;
WEISBARD Phyllis H. & SCHONBERG D.; both 1990]: JQR 84 (1993s)
99-101.

2279 **Gentry** K. L.ᴶ, God's law in the modern world; the continuing relevance
of OT law. Phillipsburg NJ 1992, Presbyterian & R. 81 p. 0-87552-296-3.
– ᴿScotBuEv 12 (1994) 67-69 (C. E. *Trueman*).

2280 *Haase* Richard, Deuteronomium und hethitisches Recht; über einige
Ähnlichkeiten in rechtshistorischer Hinsicht: WeltOr 25 (1994) 71-77.

2281 **Houten** Christiane van, The alien in Israelite law: jOsu 107, ᴰ1991
➤ 7,2231; 9,2375: ᴿJSS 38 (1993) 145-7 (S. Joy *Osgood*).

2282 **Jaruzelska** I., ❿ La propriété dans la loi biblique. Wsz 1992, PWN.
205 p. zł 25,000. 83-01-10579-8. Eng. summary [RB 102,148, L. *Rusz-
kowski*].

2283 **Lasserre** Guy, Synopse des lois du Pentateuque: VTS 59. Leiden 1994,
Brill. xxx-242 p. 90-04-10202-7.

2284 **ᴱLevinson** Bernard W., Theory and method in biblical and cuneiform
law; revision, interpolation and development: jOsu 181. Shf 1994, JStOT.
207 p. 1-85075-498-5.
2285 *Lion-Cachet* F. N., Die begrunding van geregtigheid; 'n perspektief op
die wettebundels van die Pentateug: In die Skriflig 28 (1994) 247-259
[< OTAbs 18, p. 44].
2286 *Loza Vera* José, Universalismo y particularismo en las leyes del AT:
RBibArg 55 (1993) 65-90.
2287 **Niehr** H., Rechtsprechung... SBS 130, 1987 ⇥ 3,2430... 6,2694: ᴿVT 44
(1994) 287 (G. I. *Davies*: fresh).
2289 **Rakover** Nahum, A guide to the sources of Jewish law. J 1994, Library
of Jewish law. 135 p.
2290 **Viberg** Åke, Symbols of law... OT 1992 ⇥ 8,2590; 9,2395: ᴿCBQ 56
(1994) 347-9 (D. *Patrick*).
2291 **Westbrook** Raymond, Property and the family in biblical law: jOsu 113,
1991 ⇥ 8,2592; 9,2396: ᴿBZ 38 (1994) 127s (H.-D. *Preuss*); JSS 39 (1994)
101-3 (B. A. *Levine*); Salesianum 56 (1994) 160s (R. *Vicent*).
2292 *Wyschogrod* Michael, Christianity and Mosaic law: Pro Ecclesia 2
(Northfield MN 1993) 451-9 [< Judaica 50,181].

———

2293 **Briend** Jacques, Tratados y juramentos del Antiguo Oriente Próximo:
CuadB sup. Estella 1994, VDivino. 110 p. pt. 1250.
2294 **Frymer-Kensky** Tikva S., The judicial ordeal in the Ancient Near East:
diss. Yale 1977. I. 340 p.; II. p. 314-653; bibliog. 615-653. 80-02726.
2295 *a) Haase* Richard, Drei Kleinigkeiten zum hethitischen Recht; – *b)*
Freydank Helmut, Nachlese zu den mittelassyrischen Gesetzen: AltOrF
21 (1994) 65-72 / 203-211.
2296 *Lipiński* E., Traditions juridiques des Sémites de l'Ouest à l'époque
préhellénistique: les esclaves: ⇥ 461, TEuph 8 (1991/4) 121-135; Eng. 121.
2297 **Nardoni** Enrique, La justicia en la Mesopotamia antigua / el Egipto
antiguo: RBíbArg 55 (1993) 193-214 / 56 (1994) 193-217.
2298 **Puckett** Richard A., Law and authority in ancient Israel; an analysis of
three stages in the development of Israelite jural authority [seminomadic
lineage-systems; chiefdoms; Saul to Solomon; only afterward the State]:
diss. Yale, ᴰ*Wilson* R. NHv 1994. 556 p. 94-28304. – DissA 55 (1994s)
p. 1592; RelStR 21,256.
2299 **Selb** Walter, Antike Rechte im Mittelmeerraum; Rom, Griechenland,
Ägypten und der Orient. W 1993, Böhlau. 208 p,; 12 pl. 3-205-08089-1
[OIAc 11,41].
2300 **Stone** E., *Owen* D., Adoption in Nippur 1991 ⇥ 7,2249 ... 9,2410:
ᴿJAOS 114 (1994) 94-96 (D. *Charpin*).

E3.6 **Cultus,** *Exodus 24-40.*

2301 **Koester** Craig R., The Dwelling of God; the tabernacle in the OT,
intertestamental Jewish literature, and the NT: CBQ mg 22, 1989 ⇥ 5,
2500... 9,2424: ᴿJQR 84 (1993s) 79s (W. *Adler*).
Schenker A., Studien zu Opfer und Kult 1992 ⇥ 7776.
2303 *Schenker* Adrian, Les sacrifices d'alliance, Ex XXIV,3-8 dans leur
portée narrative et religieuse; contribution à l'étude de la bᵉrît dans l'AT:
RB 101 (1994) 481-494; deutsch 481.

2304 *Nagano* Shigehiro, The elders of Israel in Exodus 24:9-11: AnJapB 19 (1993) 3-33.
2305 *Houtman* Cornelis, Wie fiktiv ist das Zeltheiligtum von Exodus 25-40?: ZAW 106 (1994) 107-113.
2306 **Brinkman** Johan, [Ex 25-31] The perception of space in the OT ᴰ1992 ➤ 8,2604: ᴿCBQ 56 (1994) 322 (F. M. *Gorman*).
2307 *Steins* Georg, Bundeslade: ➤ 510, LTK² 2 (1994) 794s.
2308 *Purvis* James D., The Tabernacle in Samaritan iconography and thought: ➤ 102, Mem. RICHARDSON H., Uncovering 1994, 223-236; 2 fig.
2309 ᴱ**Anderson** G., *Olyan* S., Priesthood and cult in ancient Israel 1991 ➤ 7,288; 8,2613: ᴿJAOS 114 (1994) 90-92 (B. A. *Levine*); JSS 39 (1994) 320s (J. *Maier*).
2310 **Nelson** Richard D., Raising up a faithful priest; community and priesthood in biblical theology. LVL c. 1994, W-Knox. 192 p. $20. – ᴿBR 10,5 (1994) 13s (J. *Milgrom*: excellent on Israel's priesthood).
2311 *Margaliot* Meshullam, The [covenant] theology of Exodus 32-34: ➤ 531*d*, 11th Jewish 1993/4, A-43-50.
2311* a) *Spreafico* Ambrogio, [Es 32-34] Peccato, perdono, alleanza; – b) *Mello* Alberto, [Es 34,6-7] Il Dio misericordioso e gli attributi della sua misericordia: ParSpV 29 (1994) 25-36 / 37-50 [51-61, *Virgulin* S., Ger; 63-71, *Monari* L., Ezech].
2312 *Frankel* David, [Ex 32,20] The destruction of the Golden Calf; a new solution: VT 44 (1994) 330-9.
2313 *Brueggemann* Walter, [Ex 32,33s; Hos 2,2-23; Isa 54,7-10] Crisis-evoked, crisis-resolving speech [of YHWH]: BibTB 24 (1994) 95-105.
2314 *Kogel* Judith, Le veau d'or dans l'exégèse juive en France du Nord (XIᵉ et XIIᵉ s.): RÉJ 153 (1994) 269-301.
2315 *Kaiser* Gerhard, Begegnung zwischen Gott und Mensch; der Brief vom 10. Mai in GOETHES 'Werther', OVIDS 'Metamorphosen' 3,2566ff und Exodus 33,17ff: ZTK 91 (1994) 97-114.
2316 **Podella** Thomas, Das Lichtkleid JHWHs; Untersuchungen zur Gestalthaftigkeit Gottes im AT und seiner altorientalischen Umwelt: Hab.-Diss. ᴰ*Janowski* B. Heidelberg 1994. – TR 91,90.
2317 *Sedgwick* Colin, [Ex 34,29-35] The glow and the glory: ExpTim 106 (1994s) 149s: the glow of holiness arouses suspicion and fear.
2318 *Scolnic* Benjamin E., [Ex 34,29] Moses and the horns of power: Judaism 40 (1991) 569-579.
2319 *Millard* Alan R., Re-creating the [stone slab] tablets of the law: BR 10,1 (1994) 48-53.

E3.7 **Leviticus.**

2320 **Gerstenberger** E. S., Das dritte Buch Mose: Lv, ATD 6, 1993 ➤ 9,2437: ᴿBL (1994) 58 (W. *Houston*: replaces NOTH, but personal interpretation, not scholarly debate); CBQ 56 (1994) 761-3 (J. *Milgrom*: his theology not sufficiently informed by philology); KerkT 45 (1994) 161 (H. *Jagersma*); TLZ 119 (1994) 977-9 (M. *Millard*); ZAW 106 (1994) 521 (G. *Metzner*).
2321 *Kaiser* Walter C.ᴶ, The Book of Leviticus: ➤ 1575, NInterp 1 (1994) 983-1195.
2322 **Lane** David J., The Peshitta of Leviticus: Monograph [to his 1991 Syriac text] 6. Leiden 1994, Brill. xv-184 p. $71.50. 90-04-10020-2 [OTAbs 17, p. 661; TLZ 120,641, W. *Schwaigert*].

2323 ᵀᴱMcNamara Martin, ᴱ*Hayward* Robert, Leviticus (p. 13-113); Targum Neofiti 1 / ᵀᴱ*Maher* Michael, Targum Pseudo-Jonathan (p. 121-211): Aramaic Bible 3. ColMn/E 1994, Liturgical/Clark. xiv-250 p. $80. 0-8146-5478-9 / E 0-567-09460-X [TDig 42,257].

2324 **Milgrom** J., Leviticus 1-16: AnchorB 3, 1991 [Gregorianum 76, 147-152, G. L. *Prato*]: ➤ 7,2270 ... 9,2440: ᴿÉTRel 68 (1993) 267-9 (D. *Lys*); IrBSt 15 (1993) 140s (T. D. *Alexander*); JSS 38 (1993) 141-3 (P. J. *Rudd*); VT 44 (1994) 142s (J. A. *Emerton*).

2325 **Péter-Contesse** René, Lévitique 1-16, 1993 ➤ 9,2442: ᴿBL (1994) 71 (G. J. *Wenham*); RÉJ 153 (1994) 456-8 (S. C. *Mimouni*).

2326 **Grabbe** Lester L., Leviticus: OT Guides. Shf 1993, JStOT. 116 p. £6. 1-85075-440-3 [TLZ 119,1065, E. S. *Gerstenberger*].

2327 **Harrington** H. K., The impurity systems of Qumran and the rabbis; biblical foundations: SBL diss. 143 (Calif. ᴰ*Milgrom* J.) 1993: ᴿDSD 1 (1994) 371-3 (P. R. *Davies*).

2328 **Neilsen** Bruce E., Earth, seed, and food; the social setting of the Levitical purity rules in the Judaism of the first four centuries C.E.: diss. Jewish Theol. Sem. ᴰ*Cohen* S. NY 1993. – RelStR 21,252.

2329 *a) Stallman* Robert C., Levi and the Levites in the Dead Sea Scrolls; – *b) Stuckenbruck* Loren T., Bibliography on 4QTgLev (4Q136): JPseud 10 (1992) 163-189 / 53-55.

2330 **Knierim** Rolf E., Text and concept in Lev 1:1-9: ForAT 2, 1992 ➤ 8,2630; 9,2450: ᴿCBQ 56 (1994) 556s (B. A. *Levine*); JBL 113 (1994) 123s (D. P. *Wright*); HeythJ 35 (1994) 317s (J. *Mulrooney*); OTEssays 7 (1994) 118-121 (M. J. *Oosthuizen*: ritual, as RENDTORFF); TLZ 119 (1994) 630s (A. *Marx*, franç.); ZAW 106 (1994) 358 (E. *Blum*).

2331 **Jagersma** H., Opbouw en functie van Leviticus 1:1-9: AmstCah 13 (1994) 7-13; Eng. 127.

2331* *Vattioni* F., Levitico 1,6 in ORIGENE: AugR 34 (1994) 223-5.

2332 *Zwickel* Wolfgang, [... 1 Sam 13,7b; in Jerusalem only after Ahaz 2 Kgs 16,10] Zur Frühgeschichte des Brandopfers in Israel: ➤ 8,105, ᶠMETZGER M., OBO 123, 1993, 231-248 [OTAbs 17, p. 482s, Deirdre A. *Dempsey*, at length].

2333 *Schenker* Adrian, Interprétations récentes et dimensions spécifiques du sacrifice *ḥaṭṭat* [non 'péché' Lv 8,15; 12; Num 6]: Biblica 75 (1994) 59-70.

2334 *Greenstein* Edward L., ❶ [Lv 10,1s] An inner-biblical midrash of the Nadab and Abihu episode: ➤ 331*a*, 11th Jewish 1993/4, 71-78.

2335 **Houston** W., [Lev 11; Dt 14] Purity and monotheism; clean and unclean animals...: jOsu 140, 1993 ➤ 9,2455: ᴿBL (1994) 107 (A. *Jeffers*); Interpretation 48 (1994) 442.4 (J. *Milgrom*); JJS 45 (1994) 131s (G. *Harvey*); JTS 45 (1994) 178s (L. L. *Grabbe*: definitive); OTAbs 17 (1994) 213-5 (M. S. *Smith*); TLZ 119 (1994) 784-6 (E. S. *Gerstenberger*).

2336 **Kitz** Anne Marie, [Lev 13s] *Saraʿat* accusations and the sociology of exclusion: diss. Johns Hopkins. Baltimore 1994. 355 p. 94-29529. – DissA 55 (1994s) p. 1591.

2337 *Wilton* Patrick, [Lev 14,9; Num 27,21; Jos 2,1; 1 Kgs 14,9; Jer 45,4; 46,25; Am 5,18.20] More cases of waw explicativum: VT 44 (1994) 125-8.

2338 **Deiana** Giovanni, [Lev 16] Il giorno dell'espiazione; il *kippur* nella tradizione biblica: RivB supp. 30. Bo 1994, Dehoniane. 218 p. Lᵐ 28. 88-10-30218-4.

2339 *Helm* Robert, [Lev 16,8] Azazel in early Jewish tradition: AndrUnSem 32 (1994) 217-226.
2340 *a) Eckart* O., Lv 17-26; – *b) Maier* J., Lv 19,16: ➤ 101, FREVENTLOW H., (1994) 65-80 / 307-311.
2341 **Joosten** Jan, People and land in the Holiness Code; an exegetical study of the ideational framework of the law in Leviticus 17-26: diss. DJagersma H. Brussel 1994. xxiii-315 p. – RTLv 26,531.
2342 *Gignac* Alain, Citation de Lévitique 18,5 en Romains 10,5 et Galates 3,12; deux lectures différentes des rapports Christ-Torah?: ÉglT 25 (1994) 367-403; 6 diagrams.
2343 **Klaassens** K. H. W., [Lv 23,15] De vijftigdagentijd; de bijbelse gegevens, de uitwerking in de vroege kerk en de hedendaagse liturgische vernieuwing: prot. diss. Bru, DNielsen J. Kockengen 1993, Shepherd. 248 p. 90-801038-37. – TvT 34 (1994) 71.
2344 *Rubenstein* Jeffrey L., The symbolism of the *sukkah*: Judaism 43 (1994) 371-387.
2345 *Chaney* Marvin J., [Lev 25,11...] Debt easement in Israelite history and tradition: ➤ 7,67, FGOTTWALD N., The Bible and the politics of exegesis 1991, 127-139.325-9 [... *Wright* C. J. H., What happened every seven years in Israel?: EvQ 56 (1984) 193-201; & God's people 1990].
2346 **Chirichigno** Gregory C., Debt slavery D1993 ➤ 9,2467 [Biblica 76, 254-261, E. *Otto*].
2347 **Fager** Jeffrey A., [Lev 25] Land tenure and the biblical jubilee; uncovering Hebrew ethics through the sociology of knowledge: jOsu 155, 1993 ➤ 9,2467: RBibTB 24 (1994) 195 (K. C. *Hanson*); BL (1994) 85 (W. J. *Houston*); CBQ 56 (1994) 758s (H. T. C. *Sun*); Interpretation 48 (1994) 428.430 (J. H. *Yoder*); JBL 113 (1994) 702-4 (R. *Gnuse*); OTAbs 17 (1994) 235s (J. J. *Pilch*).
2347* *Lage* Francisco, [Lv 25] La remisión de las deudas en la legislación del Antiguo Testamento: Moralia 15 (M 1993) 55-72.
2348 **Wright** C. J. H., God's people/land D1990 ➤ 6,2762...9,2473: RCritRR 6 (1993) 190s (Carol *Meyers*).

E3.8 *Numeri;* **Numbers, Balaam.**

2349 **Ashley** Timothy R., The Book of Numbers: NICOT 1993 ➤ 9,2475: RAntonianum 69 (1994) 383s (M. *Nobile*); BtS 151 (1994) 495s (E. H. *Merrill*); STEv 6 (1994) 87 (G. *Emetti*).
2349* **Burden** Terry L., The kerygma of the wilderness traditions in the Hebrew Bible: AmerUnivSt 7/163, NY 1994, Bern. x-259 p. Fs 33. 0-8204-2253-3 [BL 95,82, E. W. *Nicholson*].
2350 **Dorival** Gilles, *al.*, Les Nombres: Bible d'Alexandrie 4. P 1994, Cerf. 604 p. map. F 240 [NRT 117,906, J.-L. *Ska*].
2351 *Douglas* Mary, The glorious book of Numbers [highly artistic despite appearances]: Jewish Studies Q 1 (1993s) 193-226 [< OTAbs 19, p. 34].
2352 **Harrison** R. K., Numbers: Wycliffe Comm. 1992 = 1990 ➤ 9,2478: RCBQ 56 (1994) 549s (S. *Greenhalgh*: rigidly conservative); EvQ 66 (1994) 259-261 (R. S. *Hess*: not updated with MILGROM); OTEssays 7 (1994) 138s (J. H. *Breytenbach*, Afrikaans).
2353 **Levine** Baruch A., Numbers 1-20: AnchorB 4, 1993 ➤ 9,2479: RClaretianum 34 (1994) 614-6 (J. *Sánchez Bosch*); ETL 70 (1994) 140s (J. *Lust*); ÉTRel 69 (1994) 99 (T. *Römer*); Interpretation 48 (1994) 424,6 (D. T. *Olson*); PrincSemB 15 (1994) 201s (Katharine D. *Sakenfeld*).

2354 **Mainelli** Helen Kenik, Numeri [ColMn], [T]*Rusconi* Carlo: La Bibbia per tutti, 5. Brescia 1994, Queriniana, 193 p,; map. L[m] 19.5. 88-399-2105-2 [NRT 117,268, J.-L. *Ska*]. – [R]Asprenas 41 (1994) 602-4 (G. *Castello*).

2355 **Milgrom** J., Numbers: JPS Torah comm. 1990 ➤ 6,2768 ... 9,2480: [R]VT 44 (1994) 143 (J. A. *Emerton*).

2356 **Scharbert** Josef, Numeri: NEchter 27, 1992 ➤ 8,2652; 9,2484: [R]TLtg 66 (1993) 58s (C. *Frevel*).

2357 **Douglas** Mary, In the wilderness; the doctrine of defilement in the Book of Numbers: jOsu 158. Sheffield 1993, Academic. 259 p.; maps. 1-85075-444-6 [Interpretation 49,305s, J. *Neusner*].

2358 **Eddy** Mark R., The role relationship between men and women as exhibited in the Book of Numbers: diss. Concordia Sem. [D]*Judisch* D., Fort Wayne. – ConcordTQ 58 (1994) 149s.

2359 *Seebass* Horst, Einige vertrauenswürdige Nachrichten zu Israels Anfängen; zu den Söhnen Hobabs, Sichon und Bileam im Buch Numeri [SBL Münster 1993]: JBL 13 (1994) 577-585.

2360 *Ricciardi* Alberto, La bendición aarónica; una interpretación de Nm 6,22-27: RBíbArg 56 (1994) 219-230 [< OTAbs 18, p. 518].

2361 *Mohr* Friedrich, Die Kundschaftergeschichte Num 13,1-14,38; evangelisch-praktische Assoziationen im Kontext kirchlicher Jugendarbeit: ➤ 37, [F]GAMPER A., ZkT 116 (1994) 427-434.

2362 *Milgrom* Jacob, [Num 19,7-10] Confusing the sacred and the impure; a rejoinder: VT [43 (1992) 442-451, *Baumgarten* A.] 44 (1994) 554-9.

2363 *Freund* Richard A., [Nm 20, Dt 32] 'Thou shalt not go thither'; Moses and Aaron's punishments and varying theodicies in the MT, LXX and Hellenistic literature: ScandJOT 8 (1994) 105-125.

2364 *Seebass* Horst, Nm 20,1-13 und 21,4-9: ➤ 101, [F]REVENTLOW H., 1994, 219-229 [< OTAbs 18, p. 55].

2364* **Cartledge** Tony W., [Nm 21; 6; 15; 30] Vows in the Hebrew Bible and the Ancient Near East [< diss. Duke, [D]*Meyers* E.]: jOsu 147, 1992 ➤ 8,2655: [R]CBQ 56 (1992) 541s (J. R. *Spencer*); OTAbs 17 (1994) 234 (T. J. *Lewis*).

2365 [E]**Hoftijzer** J., *Kooij* G. van der, The Balaam text from Deir'Alla 1989/91 ➤ 7,440; 8,2666: [R]OrLovPer 23 (1992) 329s (A. *Schoors*); WZKM 83 (1993) 293-7 (S. *Segert*).

2366 *Shifman* J. S., [Num 22-24] ⊕ Bile'am son of Beor: VDI 208 (1994) 99-133; Eng. 134.

2367 **Greene** John T., Balaam 1992 ➤ 8,2665; 9,2503: [R]JSS 38 (1993) 314s (A. *Salvesen*).

2368 *Sasson* Victor, Once more *smr* and '*tm* in Balaam's book from Deir'Alla: UF 26 (1994) 435-442.

2369 *Savran* G., Beastly speech; intertextuality, Balaam's ass and the garden of Eden: JStOT 64 (1994) 33-55.

2370 *Schmitt* Hans-Christoph, Zum Verständnis Bileams in der Endgestalt von Num 22-24: ➤ 61, [F]KAISER O., 'Wer ist' 1994, 180-198.

2371 *McNamara* Martin, Early exegesis in the Palestinian Targum (Neofiti 1) Numbers chapter 24: PrIrB 16 (1993) 57-79.

2372 *Smelik* K. A. D., Een ezel stoot zich in't gemeen; een verkenning van Numeri 22-24: AmstCah 13 (1994) 14-30; Eng. 127.

2373 **Moore** Michael S.,   The Balaam traditions: SBL diss. 113, 1990 ➤ 6,
2790 ... 8,2667: ᴿJQR 84 (1993s) 507s (T. *Herbert*).
2374 *Shifman* J. Sh., ❸ [Nm 22,24] Bileam son of Be'or: VDI 208 (1994)
99-133; Eng. 134.
2375 *Frankel* David, ❸ [Nm 27,14] The priestly story of the waters of
Meribah; a new solution to an old problem: ➤ 331a, 11th Jewish 1993/4,
23-30.

2376 *Simotas* Panagiotis N., ❸ [Num 25,1; Ex 31,16] Israel's apostasy at
Shittim: TAth 64 (1993) 371-398; Eng. 881s.
2377 *Abma* R.,   Pioniers in het land; de dochters van Selofchad in Numeri
27:1-11: AmstCah 13 (1994) 31-47 [< OTAbs 18, p. 56].
2378 *Bernstein* Arye, ❸ [Nm 26,30; 1 Chr 7,18 ...] The inheritance of Aviezer
[RSV Iezer]; the inheritance of the first-born among his brethren: ➤ 331a,
11th Jewish 1993/4, 39-46.
2379 *Vasholz* Robert J., [Num 36:26] Israel's cities of refuge: Presbyterion 19
(1993) 115-8 [< OTAbs 17, p. 558].

        E3.9   **Liber Deuteronomii.**

2379* ᴱ**Basser** Herbert W.,   Pseudo-Rabad, Commentary to Sifre Deuteronomy: SFlaJud 92.   Atlanta c. 1994, Scholars. xliv p. Eng. + ❹ 342.
$110; sb. $75.   1-55540-925-3 [BL 95,142, S. C. *Reif*].
2380 **Bovati** Pietro,   Il libro del Deuteronomio (1-11): Guide Spirituali AT.
R 1994, Città Nuova.   168 p.   88-311-3737-9.
2381 **Braulik** Georg,   Deuteronomium II, 16,19-34,12: NEchter 28, 1992
➤ 8,2671; 9,2512:   TLtg 66 (1993) 56-58 (C. *Frevel*).
2382 **Brown** Raymond,   The message of Deuteronomy: not by bread alone
1993 ➤ 9,2513 ('in bread'): Leicester 1993, IVP. 333 p. £9. 0-85110-878-8.
– ᴿBL (1994) 53 (A. D. H. *Mayes*: 'by bread').
2383 **Cairns** Ian, Deuteronomy; word and presence: comm. 1991 ➤ 7,2321;
8,2514: ᴿOTEssays 7 (1994) 169s (W. J. *Wessels*).
2384 **Christensen** Duane L., Dt 1-11: WordComm 6A 1991: ᴿRelStR 19
(1993) 66 (C. T. *Begg*).
2385 **Dogniez** C., *Harl* M., Le Deutéronome: Septante 1992 ➤ 8,2673; 9,2515:
ᴿBiblica 75 (1994) 421-4 (Anna *Passoni Dell'Acqua*).
2386 *Fernández Marcos* Natalio, 5QDt y los tipos textuales bíblicos: ➤ 22,
ᶠCASCIARO J. M., Biblia 1994, 119-125; 1 fig.
2387 **Fraade** Steven D.,   From tradition to commentary ... Midrash Sifre to
Dt 1991 ➤ 7,2326* ... 9,2516: ᴿBijdragen 55 (1994) 436s (J. van *Ruiten*);
JQR 84 (1993s) 82-90 (H. W. *Basser*); 237-242, Fraade response; CritRR 5
(1992) 363-5 (B. E. *Nielsen*).
2388 **Hoppe** L., Deuteronomio [ColMn],ᵀ; Bibbia per tutti, 6.   148 p.; map.
Lᵐ 16.5 [NRT 117,269s, J. L. *Ska*]. – ᴿAsprenas 41 (1994) 602-4 (G.
Castello).
2389 **Labuschagne** Cas,   Deuteronomium: Belichting. Brugge 1993, Tabor.
191 p. 90-6173-556-4 [OTAbs 18, p. 413, M. *Kessler*].
2390 **Merrill** Eugene H.,   Deuteronomy: NewAmerComm 4.   Nv 1994,
Broadman & H.   477 p.   0-8054-0104-0. – ᴿOTAbs 17 (1994) 662 (C. T.
Begg: Moses author, in view of Hittite treaty affinities).
2391 **Miller** Patrick D.,   Deuteronomy: Interpretation comm. 1990 ➤ 6,
2810 ... 9,2519: ᴿChrSchR 23 (1993s) 218-220 (D. E. *Burke*).
2392 **Rose** Martin, 5. Mose: B ZK AT 5. Z 1994, Theol.-V. xi-328 p. xi-263 p.

Fs 80 [RelStR 21.128, C. T. *Begg*: not in the sequence of the chapters, but in 12 regroupings of the material].
2393 **Weinfeld** Moshe, Dt 1-11: AnchorB 5, 1991 ➤ 7,2337...9,2520 [Gregorianum 76,377, G. L. *Prato*]: ᴿAJS 19 (1994) 241-4 (D. E. *Friedman*); Biblica 75 (1994) 246-250 (L. *Perlitt*); JSS 39 (1994) 104s = 38 (1993) 143-5 (J. G. *McConville*).

2394 *Akao* J. O., In search of the origin of the Deuteronomic movement: IrBSt 16 (1994) 174-189 [< OTAbs 18,300].
2395 *Begg* Christopher T., 1994, a significant anniversary in the history of Deuteronomy research [STAERK W., STEUERNAGEL C., Numeruswechsel 1894]: ➤ 68, ꜰLABUSCHAGNE C., VTS 53 (1994) 1-11.
ᴱ**Christensen** Duane L., A song of power and the power of song [24 reprints since 1951 on Dt] 1993 ➤ 263.
2396 *Curtis* John B., *a*) Astral worship and the date of Deuteronomy: ProcGM 14 (1994) 87-93; – *b*) Some observations on Deuteronomy's 'Name-theology': ProcGM 13 (1993) 23-29.
2397 **Dangl** Oskar, Methoden im Widerstreit [SCHWEIZER H., RICHTER W.]; sprachwissenschaftliche Zugänge zur deuteronomistischen Rede von der Liebe Gottes [updated 1985 Diss. Wien]: TextwInformatik 6, 1993 ➤ 9, 2524; ᴿOLZ 89 (1994) 282-5 (R. *Stahl*).
2398 *Deist* Ferdinand E., The dangers of Deuteronomy; a page from the reception history of the book: ➤ 66, ꜰLABUSCHAGNE C. J., VTS 53 (1994) 13-29.
2399 *Dohmen* Ulrich, Weitere Fälle von Siebenergruppierungen im Buch Deuteronomium: BibNot 72 (1994) 5-11.
2400 **Gertz** Jan Christian, Die Gerichtsorganisation Israels im deuteronomischen Gesetz [Diss. Göttingen 1993, ᴰ*Perlitt* L. ➤ 9,2527]: FRL 165. Gö 1994, Vandenhoeck & R. 255 p.; Bibliog. 234-251. 3-525-53847-2.
2401 *Krašovec* Jože, *a*) Reward and punishment in Deuteronomy: BogVest 53 (1993) 143-154 Slovene; 154s Eng. – *b*) Praemium ac poena in Libro Deuteronomii: ➤ 36, Mem. FUĆAK M., BogSmot 64 (1994) 72-82.
2402 **Lohfink** N. & [on] RÖMER T., Die Väter Israels im Dt: OBO 111, 1991 ➤ 7,2336...9,2530: ᴿCBQ 56 (1994) 115 (M. C. *Lind*); ÉTRel 69 (1994) 99s (Françoise *Smyth*).
2403 **Lohfink** N., Studien zum Dt, 2: SBAufs 12, 1991 ➤ 6,265 ... 9,2531: ᴿBZ 38 (1994) 128s (H. D. *Preuss*).
2404 **McConville** J. Gordon, Grace in the end; a study in Deuteronomic theology: StOTBTh. Grand Rapids / Carlisle 1993, Zondervan/Paternoster. 170 p. $17. 0-310-51421-5. – ᴿBL (1994) 111 (I. *Provan*); ScotBuEv 12 (1994) 151s (M. *Goldsmith*).
2405 *McConville* J. Gordon, Time and place in Deuteronomy: jOsu 179. Shf 1994, Academic. 155 p. £25. 1-85075-494-2.
2406 *Merrill* Eugene H., Deuteronomy, New Testament faith, and the Christian life: ➤ 21, ꜰCAMPBELL D., Integrity 1994, 19-33.
2407 **Pressler** Carolyn, The view of women found in the Deuteronomic family laws: BZAW 216, 1993 ➤ 9,2536: ᴿTLZ 119 (1994) 983-6 (E. *Otto*).
2408 **Römer** T., Israels Väter OBO 99, 1990 ➤ 6,2817... 8,2686: ᴿTEuph 5 (1992) 184s (F. *Smyth*). ➤ 2402.
2409 *Römer* Thomas, Le Deutéronome à la quête des origines: LDiv 1994, 65-98 [DielB 28 (1992s) 203s, B. *Diebner*].
2410 *a*) *Vervenne* Marc, The question of 'Deuteronomic' elements in Genesis

to Numbers; – *b) Moor* Johannes C. de,   Poetic fragments in Deuteronomy and the deuteronomistic history; – *c) Garcia Martínez* F., Les manuscrits du désert de Juda et le Deuteronomium: ➤ 68, ᶠLABUSCHAGNE C., VTS 53 (1994) 243-268 / 183-196 / 63-82.
2411 *Westermann* Claus,   Mahnung, Warnung und Geschichte; die Paränese Deuteronomium 1-11: ➤ 115, ᶠSCHUNCK K.-D., Nachdenken 1994, 51-67.
2412 *a) Wevers* John W.,   Yahweh and its appositives in LXX Deuteronomium; – *b) Deurloo* Karel A.,   The one God and all Israel in its generations: ➤ 66, ᶠLABUSCHAGNE C., VTS 53 (1994) 269-280 / 31-46.
2413 **Zobel** K., Prophetie und Dt: BZAW 199, 1992 ➤ 8,2689; 9,2538 [BL 95,122, R. E. *Clements*]: ᴿCBQ 56 (1994) 130s (W. A. *Vogels*); JBL 113 (1994) 518s (B. O. *Long*); RelStR 19 (1993) (C. T. *Begg*); RExp 91 (1994) 113 (J. D. W. *Watts*); TR 90 (1994) 210s (Christa *Schäfer-Lichtenberger*).

2414 *Vandersleyen* C.,   [Dt 1,7...] L'Euphrate, Aram Naharaïm et la Bible [jamais limite de la Terre Promise]: Muséon 107 (1994) 5-14.
2415 *Lohfink* Norbert,   Zu *sābab et* in Dtn 2,1.3: ➤ 38, ᶠGAMPER A., ZkT 116 (1994) 435-9.
2416 *Geller* Stephen A.,   Fiery wisdom; logos and lexis in Deuteronomy 4: Prooftexts 14 (1994) 103-139.
2417 **Achenbach** Reinhard, Israel... Dt 5-11 [ᴰ1989 Gö ᴰ*Perlitt* L.] 1991 ➤ 7,2342; 8,2692: ᴿRelStR 19 (1993) 67s (C. T. *Begg*).
2419 *Hilhorst* A.,   Deuteronomy's monotheism and the Christian's — the case of Deut 6:13 and 10:20: ➤ 68, ᶠLABUSCHAGNE C., VTS 53 (1994) 83-91.
2420 *Venema* René G. J.,   Israël en de talrijke volken; Dt 7: AmstCah 13 (1994) 48-55; Eng. 128.
2421 **Braulik** Georg,   Die deuteronomischen Gesetze und der Dekalog; Studien zum Aufbau Dt 12-26, 1991 ➤ 7,2343: ᴿJBL 113 (1994) 124-6 (L. J. *Hoppe*: excellent); TLZ 119 (1994) 15-17 (E. *Otto*).
2422 *Mayes* A. D. H., Deuteronomy 14 and the Deuteronomic world view: ➤ 68, ᶠLABUSCHAGNE C., VTS 53 (1994) 165-181.
2423 [*de Noronha*] *Galvão* Henrique, [Dt 15] The messianic sabbatical year and the social mission of the Church: ComWash 21 (1994) 49-68.
2424 **Hamilton** J. M.,   Social justice and Deuteronomy; the case of Deuteronomy 15: SBL diss. 136, Atlanta 1992 ➤ 8,2706; 1-55540-747-1; -8-X [JStOT 60,124]. – ᴿInterpretation 48 (1994) 192. 4 (D. E. *Gowan*); ZAW 106 (1994) 522 (M. *Köckert*).
2425 *Mulder* M. †, [Dt 15,2] S*e*miṭṭah 'Erlass': ➤ 519, TWAT 8,1 (1994) 197-203.
2426 *Tsevat* Matityahu,   The Hebrew slave according to Dt 15:12-18; his lot and the value of his work, with special attention to the meaning of *mišnĕh*: JBL 113 (1994) 587-595.
2427 **Krinetzki** Günter,   Rechtsprechung und Amt im Deuteronomium; zur Exegese der Gesetze Dtn 15,19-20; 17,8-19,22. Fra 1994, Lang. 320 p.; Bibliog. 282-293. 3-631-46472-X.
2428 *a) Otto* Eckart,   Deuteronomistische Gestaltung und deuteronomistische Interpretation im 'Ämtergesetz' Dtn 16,18-18,22; – *b) Schmidt* Werner H., Einsichten und Ausdruckweisen des Deuteronomiums in der Priesterschrift: ➤ 61, ᶠKAISER O., 'Wer ist' 1994, 142-155 / 169-179.
2429 *Gosse* Bernard,   Deutéronome 17,18-19 et la restauration de la royauté au retour de l'exil: BbbOr 36 (1994) 129-138.

2430 *Guillemette* Yves, 'Pour vivre heureux dans le pays'; à propos de deux lois du Deutéronome (Dt 20,5; 22,8): ➤ 30, ᶠCOUTURIER G., Maison 1994, 123-137.

2431 *Noort* E., [Dt 20,10s] Das Kapitulationsangebot im Kriegsgesetz Dtn 20:10ff und in den Kriegserzählungen: ➤ 66, ᶠLABUSCHAGNE C., VTS 53 (1994) 197-232.

2432 *Davies* Eryl W. [Dt 21,15-17; Nm 27,1-11], The inheritance of the first-born in Israel and the Ancient Near-East: JSS 38 (1993) 175-191.

2433 *a) Goulder* Michael D., Ruth; a homily on Deuteronomy 22-25?; – *b) Cazelles* Henri, Les milieux du Deutéronome: ➤ 138, ᶠWHYBRAY N., 307-319 / 288-306.

2434 **Locher** C., Die Ehre einer Frau... Dt 22,13-21: OBO 70, ᴰ1986 ➤ 2,1938... 6,2839: ᴿVT 44 (1994) 132s (G. I. *Davies*).

2435 *Hiebert* Robert J. V., Deuteronomy 22:28-29 and its premishnaic interpretations: CBQ 56 (1994) 203-220.

2436 *Neudecker* Reinhold, Das 'Ehescheidungsgesetz' von Dtn 24,1-4 nach altjüdischer Auslegung; ein Beitrag zum Verständnis der neutestamentlichen Aussagen zur Ehescheidung: Biblica 75 (1994) 350-387; franç. 387.

2437 *Loader* J.A., [Dt 25,5-10] Of barley, bulls, land and levirate: ➤ 66, ᶠLABUSCHAGNE C., VTS 53 (1994) 123-138.

2438 *Janzen* J. Gerald, [Dt 26,5] The 'wandering Aramean' reconsidered: VT 44 (1994) 359-373.

2439 **Norin** Stig, [Dt 26,5] Ein Aramäer, dem Umkommen nahe — ein Kerntext der Forschung und Tradition: ScandJOT 8 (1994) 87-104.

2440 *Evans* Mary J., [Dt 27...] 'A plague on both your houses'; cursing and blessing reviewed: VoxEvca 24 (1994) 77-89.

2441 **Lenchak** Timothy A. [Dt 28,69-30,20] Choose life < ᴰ1992 Greg. ᴰ*Conroy* C.: AnBib 129. R 1993, Pont. Ist. Biblico [Biblica 76,93-98, J.-P. *Sonnet*].

2442 *Lohfink* Norbert, Moab oder Sichem — wo wurde Dtn 28 nach der Fabel des Deuteronomiums proklamiert?: ➤ 68, ᶠLABUSCHAGNE C., VTS 53 (1994) 139-148.

2443 **Steymans** Hans U., Deuteronomium 28 und die Adê zur Thronnachfolge Asarhaddons; Segen und Fluch im Alten Orient und in Israel: kath. Diss. ᴰ*Braulik* G. Wien 1994. – RTLv 26,533.

2444 **Rosenblatt** J.F., *Sitterson* J.C.ᴶ, [Dt 30] Not in heaven; coherence and complexity in biblical narrative. Bloomington 1991, Indiana Univ. xii-262 p. £29.50; pa. £12. – ᴿHeythJ 35 (1994) 64s (J. *Mulrooney*).

2445 *Peels* Hendrik G.L., On the wings of the eagle (Dtn 32,11) — an old misunderstanding: ZAW 106 (1994) 300-3.

2446 **Rossi de Gasperis** Francesco, La roccia che ci ha generato (Dt 32,18) (Tutte le nostre sorgenti sono in te, Sal 87,7), un pellegrinaggio nella Terra Santa come esercizio spirituale: Bibbia e preghiera. R 1994, ADP. 178 p. 88-7357-148-4.

2447 **Beyerle** Stefan, Der Mosesegen im Deuteronomium; eine text-, kompositions- und formkritische Studie zu Deuteronomium 33: Diss. ᴰ*Seebass* H. Bonn 1994s. – RTLv 26, p. 530.

2448 *a) Lust* J., For I lift up my hand to heaven and swear; Deut. 32;40; – *b) Ruiten* J. van, The use of Dt 32:39 in monotheistic controversies in rabbinic literature; – *c) Kooij* Arie van der, The ending of the Song of Moses; on the pre-masoretic version of Deut 32:43; – *d) Woude* A.S. van der, Erwägungen zum Rahmenpsalm von Dt 33; – *e) García López* Félix,

Deut 34, Dtr history and the Pentateuch: ➤ 68, FLABUSCHAGNE C., VTS 53 (1994) 155-164 / 223-241 / 93-100 / 281-8 / 47-61.
2449 Porter J.R., The interpretation of Deuteronomy XXXIII 24-5: VT 44 (1994) 267-270.
2450 **Olson** Dennis T., Deuteronomy and the death of Moses; a theological reading: OvBT. Mp 1994, Fortress. xvi-191 p. $14 pa. 0-8006-2639-7 [BL 95,97, J. *Goldingay*: personalized praise; TS 56,395, S. *McEvenue*].

E4.1 *Origo Israelis in Canaan; Deuteronomista;* **Liber Josue.**

2451 **Davies** Philip R., In search of 'Ancient Israel': jOsu 148, 1992 ➤ 8,2724; 9,2567: RAndrUnSem 32 (1994) 260-2 (M. G. *Hasel*: provocative).
2452 *Gottwald* Norman K., Recent studies of the social world of premonarchic Israel: CuRB 1 (1993) 163-189.
2453 *Hess* Richard S., a) Fallacies in the study of early Israel; an onomastic perspective [against facile assumption that they were insurgent Canaanites]: TyndB 45 (1994) 339-354.– b) Early Israel in Canaan; a survey of recent evidence and interpretations: PEQ 125 (1993) 125-142; map.
2454 **Jericke** Detlef, Die Landnahme im Süden; archäologische und exegetische Studie: Diss.DWelten P. Berlin 1994. – TR 91,92.
      Lemche N., The Canaanites 1991 ➤ 10997*.
2455 — *Na'aman* Nadav, The Canaanites in their land; a rejoinder [LEMCHE N. 1991]: UF 26 (1994) 397-414.
2456 *Maldonado* Robert D., ¿La conquista? Latin American (*mestizaje*) reflections on the biblical conquest: JHisp 2,4 (1994s) 5-25..
2457 **Nodet** Étienne, Essai sur les origines du judaïsme 1992 ➤ 9,2574: RCBQ 56 (1994) 336s (L. L. *Grabbe*); ÉTRel 68 (1993) 102s (Jeanne-Marie *Léonard*); RBíbArg 55 (1993) 296-8 (J. Pablo *Martín*); RevSR 68 (1994) 346-350 (F. *Blanchetière*); Salesianum 56 (1994) 573s (R. *Vicent*).
2458 *Whitelam* Keith W., The identity of early Israel; the realignment and transformation of Late Bronze-Iron Age Palestine: JStOT 63 (1994) 57-87.

2459 **Doorly** William J., Obsession with justice; the story of the Deuteronomists. NY 1994, Paulist. viii-166 p. $13. 0-8091-3487-X [BL 95,85, A. D. H. *Mayes*].
2459* *Gosse* Bernard, La rédaction deutéronomiste de Dt, 12,10 à 1 Rois 5,18 et la tranquillité devant les ennemis de l'alentour: ÉglT 25 (1992) 323-331.
2460 **McLean** Richard W., 'These are the words'; studies in the Deuteronomistic history: diss. Vanderbilt, DKnight D. Nashville 1994. – RelStR 21,251.
2461 **Noth** Martin, O deuteronomista, 1943-1993, 50 anos de crítica autoral [Überlieferungsgeschichtliche Studien Kap. I. ²1957], TEMinette de Tillesse Caetano: RBB 10 (1993) 183 p.; bibliog. 184-194; complementos 197-267.
2462 **O'Brien** Mark A., The Deuteronomistic history hypothesis: OBO 92, 1989 ➤ 5,2608 ... 9,2584: RBO 51 (1994) 394-401 (Helga *Weippert*).
2463 *Smend* Rudolf, NOTH, Martin: ➤ 517, TRE 24 (1994) 659-661.
2464 **Tausend** Klaus, Amphiktyonie und Symmachie; Formen zwischenstaatlicher Beziehungen im archaischen Griechenland: Historia Einz 73. Stu 1992, Steiner. viii-273 p. DM 120. 3-515-06137-1. – RHZ 259 (1994) 441s (W. *Günther*).

2465 **Westermann** Claus, Die Geschichtsbücher des AT; gab es ein deu-
teronomistisches Geschichtswerk?: TBü 87, Gü 1994, Kaiser. 150 p.
3-579-01810-8 [RelStR 21,44, S. L. *McKenzie*: several independent books
got a deuteronomistic overlay; BL 95,107, A. G. *Auld*; TLZ 120,332, W.
Dietrich].
2466 *Würthwein* Ernst, Erwägungen zum sogenannten deuteronomistischen
Geschichtswerk [ineditum] ➤ 233, Studien 1994, 1-11.

2467 **Fritz** Volkmar G., Das Buch Josua: HAT 7. Tü 1994, Mohr. ix-258 p.
3-16-146131-2. – REstAg 29 (1994) 587s (C. *Mielgo*).
2468 **Hawk** L. Daniel, Every promise fulfilled; contesting plots in Joshua
1991 ➤ 9,2591: RCBQ 56 (1994) 109s (H. *Basser*); CritRR 6 (1993) 160s
(P. D. *Miscall*).
2469 **Holland** Martin, Das Buch Josua: Wu Studienbibel AT. Wu 1993,
Brockhaus. 317 p. DM 38 pa. 3-417-25223-7. – ROTAbs 17 (1994) 443
(C. T. *Begg*: holds composed at latest in time of Samuel, but with later
redactional alterations).
2470 **Mitchell** Gordon, Together in the land; a reading of the Book of Joshua
[< diss. Heidelberg]: jOsu 134. Shf 1993, Academic. 239 p. £30. 1-
95075-409-8 [BL 95,70s, A. G. *Auld*].
2471 **Navarro** Mercedes. I libri di Giosuè, Giudici e Rut: Guide Spirituali
AT. R 1994, Città Nuova. 159 p. 88-311-3738-8.

2472 *Beek* M. A., Joshua the savior: ➤ 250, VAmst 1994, 145-153 [< OTAbs
17, p. 560].
2473 **Bieberstein** Klaus, LUKIAN und THEODOTION im Josuabuch, mit einem
Beitrag zu den Josuarollen von Hirbet Qumran: BibNot Beih 7. Mü
1994, Inst. B. Exeg. 107 p. DM 10.
2474 **Cohen** M., Miqraoth gedoloth 'haketer', Jos Jg Samuel 1992s ➤ 9,2587:
RRÉJ 153 (1994) 443-5 (Judith *Kogel*).
2475 **Curtis** Adrian H. W., Joshua: OTGuides. Shf 1994, Academic. 89 p.
£6. 1-85075-706-2 [BL 95,61, J. R. *Duckworth*; RelStR 21,128, C. T. *Begg*
misses 'hermeneutic', meaning actualization].
2476 *Galil* Gershon, ❸ The formation of the book of Joshua: ➤ 331a, 11th
Jewish 1993/4, 47-54.
2477 *Greenspoon* Leonard, Non-Masoretic elements in the transmission and
translation of the book of Joshua: ➤ 331a, 11th Jewish 1993/4, A-51-58.
2478 *Hertog* Cornelis den, Die invertierten Verbalsätze im hebräischen
Josuabuch; eine Fallstudie zu einem vernachlässigten Kapitel der hebräischen Syntax: ➤ 31*, FDAUTZENBERG G., Nach 1994, 277-291.
2479 *Lambert* Frith, Tribal influences in Old Testament tradition: SvEx 59
(1994) 33-58.

2480 *a)* *Noort* Edward, Josua und seine Aufgabe; Bemerkungen zu Jos 1:
1-4; – *b)* *Ringgren* Helmer, Der Landtag in Sichem; – *c)* *Otto* Eckart,
Das Kriegslager — die Wiege der altisraelitischen JHWH-Religion?
Tendenzen der Kriegsüberwindung im AT und ihre Begründungen:
➤ 115, FSCHUNCK K.-D., Nachdenken 1994, 69-87 / 89-91 / 357-373.
2481 **Felber** Anneliese, Ecclesia ex gentibus ... Jos 2: 1992 ➤ 8,2758; 9,2601:
RRB 101 (1994) 304s (F. *Langlamet*).

2482 **Fahr** Heinz, *Glessmer* Uwe, Jordandurchzug und Beschneidung als Zurechtweisung in einem Targum zu Josua 5 (Edition des Ms T.-S. B 13,12): OBChr 3. Glückstadt 1991, Augustin. 162 p. 3-87030-152-X [TR 89,166]. – ᴿBL (1993) 49 (C. T. R. *Hayward*); RelStR 20 (1994) 68 (B. *Grossfeld*).

2483 *Anbar* Moshé, La critique biblique à la lumière des Archives royales de Mari; Jos 8: Biblica 75 (1994) 70-74.

2484 **Younger** R. L., [Jos 9-12] Ancient conquest accounts: jOsu 98, 1990 ➤ 6,b404 ... 9,2608: ᴿBZ 38 (1994) 111s (N. *Lohfink*).

2485 [Jos 10s ...] *Schäfer-Lichtenberger* Christa, Bedeutung und Funktion von Herem in biblisch-hebräischen Texten: BZ 38 (1994) 270-5.

2486 *Hoffmeier* James K., The structure of Joshua 1-11 and the annals of Thutmose III; – b) *Walton* John H., Joshua 10:12-15 and the Mesopotamian celestial omen texts; – c) *Hess* Richard S., Asking historical questions of Joshua 13-19; recent discussion concerning the date of the boundary lists: ➤ 326*, Faith 1990/4, 165-179 / 181-190 / 191-205.

2487 *Santos Santos* Demetrio, [Jos 10,12] La batalla de Gabaón: Compostellanum 38,1 (1993) 47-55.

2488 **Svensson** Jan, Towns and toponyms in the Old Testament with special emphasis on Joshua 14-21: a) diss. Uppsala 1994. 160 p. [DissA-disk] DissA-C 55 (1944s) p. 1053. – b) ConBib OT 38. Sto 1994, Almqvist & W. 156 p. Sk 132. 91-22-01581-7.

2489 *Elitzur* Yoel, [Jos 15,48-60] Rumah in Judah: IsrEJ 44 (1994) 123-8.

2490 *Görg* Manfred, Gruppenschreibung und Morphologie; zur Bedeutung ausserbiblischer Nebenüberlieferungen für die Strukturanalyse biblischer Ortsnamen am Beispiel von 'Scharuhen': BibNot 71 (1994) 65-77.

2491 **Koopmans** William T., Joshua 24 as poetic narrative: jOsu 93, 1990 ➤ 6,2880 ... 9,2615: ᴿBZ 38 (1994) 317s (J. *Scharbert*).

E4.2   *Liber Judicum:* **Richter, Judges.**

2492 **Danieli** M. Ignazia, ORIGENE, Omelie sui Giudici. R 1992, Città Nuova. 172 p. Lᵐ 16. – ᴿCC 145 (1994,3) 313s (E. *Cattaneo*).

2493 ᵀᴱ**Messié** Pierre, al., ORIGÈNE/RUFIN, Homélies sur les Juges: SChr 389, 1993 ➤ 9,2621: ᴿBLitEc 95 (1994) 333 (H. *Crouzel*); Gregorianum 75 (1994) 574 (G. *Pelland*); NRT 116 (1994) 442 (A. *Harvengt*).

2494 *Trebolle Barrera* J., 4QJudgᵃ: MiscArH 40,2 (1991) ... [< VT 44,144].

2495 **Wilcock** M., The message of Judges. Grace abounding 1992 ➤ 8,2775; 9,2624: ᴿEvQ 66 (1994) 165s (G. *Millar*).

2496 **Álvarez** Miguel, Terminología deuteronomística en los libros históricos (Jueces - 2 Reyes); BtAntonianum 34. R 1994, Pont. Ath. Antonianum. 130 p.

2497 *Chisholm* Robert B.ᴶ, The role of women in the rhetorical strategy of the Book of Judges: ➤ 21, ꟻCAMPBELL D., Integrity 1994, 34-49.

2498 a) *Younger* K. Lawsonᴶ, Judges 1 in its Near Eastern literary context; – b) *Block* Daniel J., Deborah among the historians: ➤ 326*, Faith 1990/4, 207-227 / 229-253.

2499 *Neef* Heinz-Dieter, Deboraerzählung und Deboralied; Beobachtungen zum Verhältnis von Jdc IV und V: VT 44 (1994) 47-59.

2500 *Würthwein* Ernst, Abimelech und der Untergang Sichems; Studien zu Jdc 9 [ineditum]: ➤ 234, Studien 1994, 12-28.

2501 *Alonso Schökel* Luis, *a*) La figlia di Jefte; – *b*) Debora e Giaele; ➤ 305, Biblia 1993/4, 51-59 / 43-48.

2502 **Green** Michelle F., [Jg 11,30s] Jephthah's daughter [chamber music based on a poem by Nathaniel P. Willis]: diss. Columbia, ᴰ*Davidovsky* M. NY 1994. 244 p. 94-27075. – DissA 55 (1994s) p. 1734.

2503 **Bader** Winfried, Simson bei Delila; computerlinguistische Interpretation des Textes Ri 13-16: Textw-Inf 3. Tü 1991, Francke. x-468 p. DM 19,80. 3-7720-1952-8. – ᴿTLZ 119 (1994) 411-3 (A. *Verheij*).

2504 **Kim Jichan**, The structure of the Samson cycle [diss. Kampen, ᴰ*Moor* J. de]. Kampen 1993, Kok Pharos. xvii-464 p. [Biblica 76,98-101, W. *Gross*].

2505 **Mobley** Gregory, Samson, the liminal hero; a comparative study of Judges 13-16 and Ancient Near Eastern heroic tradition: diss. Harvard, ᴰ*Machinist* P. CM 1994, 204 p. 95-00190. – DissA 55 (1994s) p. 2436.

2506 *a*) *Perroni* Marinella, Le donne di Sansone; – *b*) *Gardenak* Gianna, Pietro ABELARDO e i due 'planctus'; Sansone e Dalila e la figlia di Jefte: ➤ 305, Fortezza 1993/4, 63-87 / 91-131.

2507 *Bader* Winfried, Traut LeserInnen etwas zu! Eine unnötige textkritische Ergänzung in Ri 16,13.14: BibNot 75 (1994) 5-12.

2508 *Satterthwaite* Philip E., No king in Israel; narrative criticism and Judges 17-21: TyndB 44 (1993) 75-88.

2509 *a*) *Amit* Yairah, Literature in the service of politics; studies in Judges 19-21; – *b*) *Hoffman* Yair, The concept of 'other gods' in the deuteronomistic literature / reflections on the relationship between theopolitics, prophecy and historiography; – *c*) *Frey* Christopher, The biblical tradition in the perspective of political theology and political ethics: ➤ 331*b*, Politics 1994, 28-40 / 66-84.85-99 / 55-65.

2510 *Hudson* Don M., Living in a land of epithets; anonymity in Judges 19-21: JStOT 62 (1994) 49-66.

2511 *Jones-Warsaw* Koala, Towards a womanist hermeneutic; a re-reading of Judges 19-21; JIntdenom 22 (1994) 18-35.

2512 *a*) *Tomassoni* Letizia, [Giud 19,25] La concubina del levita di Efraim; – *b*) *Soggin* J. Alberto, Introduzione storico-critica all'epoca dei Giudici; – *c*) *Flores d'Arcais* Francesco, Cronistoria fra Giosuè e Samuele: ➤ 305, Fortezza 1993/4, 135-149 / 31-39 / 9-18.

E4.3 **Liber Ruth**, '*V Rotuli*', the Five Scrolls.

2513 **Altbauer** Moshe, The five biblical scrolls in a sixteenth-century Jewish translation into Belorussian (Vilnius codex 262). J 1992, Israel Acad. 425 p. – ᴿOrChrPer 60 (1994) 300s (C. *Simon*).

2514 **Beattie** D.R.·G., The targum of Ruth [with ➤ 2754*, *McIvor* J. Chronicles]: Aramaic Bible 19. ColMn 1994, Liturgical. vi-258 p. (Ruth pp. vi-37) $65. 0-8146-5455-X [OTAbs 17, p. 663].

2515 **Frevel** Christian, Das Buch Rut: NStu 8, 1992 ➤ 8,2806: ᴿTLtg 67 (1994) 249-254 (R. *Bohlen*).

2516 *Manns* Frédéric, Le Targum de Ruth — manuscrit Urbinati I, traduction et commentaire: LA 44 (1994) 253-290; Eng. 613.

2517 **Scharbert** Joseph, Rut (p. 1-28) [➤ 2359, *Hentschel* Georg, 1 Samuel]; NEchter. Wü 1994, Echter. 160 p. DM 34. 3-429-01597-9. – ᴿÉTRel 69 (1994) 569 (Françoise *Smyth*).

2518 **Zakovitch** Yair, ❸ Ruth 1990 ➤ 9,2699: ᴿCritRR 6 (1993) 192s (F. E.
Greenspahn); Prooftexts 13 (1993) 175-181 (M. Z. Brettler).

2519 a) Bartolomei M. Cristina, Rut e Noemi; – b) Levi d'Ancona Mirella,
Figurazioni del libro di Rut; – c) Carucci Viterbi Benedetto, Le 'eroine'
dell'epoca dei Giudici: ➤ 305, Fortezza 1993/4, 151-175 / 178-190; 13 fig.
/ 207-218.

2520 **Caspi** Michael M., The book of Ruth, an annotated bibliography:
RefHum 1410 / Books of the Bible 7. NY 1994, Garland. xiv-133 p.
$22. 0-8240-4632-3 [TDig 42,260].

2521 **Fewell** Danna N., Gunn D. M., Compromising redemption ... Ruth 1990
➤ 6,2920 .. 9,2656: ᴿBZ 38 (1994) 118s (Helga Weippert).

2522 **Gow** Murray D., The book of Ruth; its structure, theme and purpose
1992 ➤ 9,2657: ᴿEvQ 66 (1994) 167s (G. Millar).

2523 Jackson Glenna S., Naomi, Ruth, and Orpah: BToday 32 (1994) 68-72.

2524 **Johnson** Robert M.ᴶ, The words in their mouths; a linguistic and
literary analysis of the dialogues in the Book of Ruth: diss. Vanderbilt,
ᴰBarr J. Nashville 1993. – RelStR 21,251.

2525 ᴱ**Kates** Judith A., Reimer Gail T., Reading Ruth; contemporary women
reclaim a sacred story. NY 1994, Ballentine. xii-386 p. $23. 0-345-
38033-9 [OTAbs 18, p. 414].

2526 Knauf Ernst A., Ruth la Moabite: VT 44 (1994) 547.

2527 Landy Francis, Ruth and the romance of realism, or deconstructing
history: JAAR 62 (1994) 285-317.

2528 Loader James A., Yahweh's wings and the gods of Ruth: ➤ 61,
ᶠKAISER O., 'Wer ist' 1994, 389-401.

2529 Loader J. A., a) [Ruth, literarily] Job's sister; undermining an unnatural
religiosity [which does not allow bitterness toward God]: OTEssays 6
(1993) 312-329 [< OTAbs 17, p. 562]; – b) David and the matriarch in the
Book of Ruth: In die Skriflig 28 (1994) 25-35.

2530 **Masini** M., 'Lectio divina' del libro di Rut: Leggere le Scritture 1.
Padova 1994, Messaggero. 383 p. Lᵐ 28. 88-250-0396-X [Gregorianum
76,761, E. Farahian; NRT 117,270, J.-L. Ska].

2531 Niehoff M., ❸ The characterization of Ruth in the Midrash: JStJTht 11
(1993) 40-78 [< JStJud 25,151].

2532 Nielsen Kirsten, Stamtavle og fortælling i Ruths Bog: DanTTs 57
(1994) 81-93 [< OTAbs 17, p. 562].

2533 **Wolde** E. van, Ruth en Noëmi, twee vreemdgangers. Baarn 1993, Ten
Have. 163 p. ƒ29,50. – ᴿTvT 34 (1994) 192 (E. Eynikel).

2534 Collins C. John, Ambiguity and theology in Ruth; Ruth 1:21 and 2:20:
Presbyterion 19 (1993) 97-102 [< OTAbs 17, p. 562].

E4.4 1-2 Samuel.

2535 **Caquot** André, Robert Philippe de, Les livres de Samuel: CAT 6.
Genève 1994, Labor et Fides. 649 p. 2-8309-0703-5 [JTS 46,580, D. F.
Murray; Biblica 76,422-6, S. Pisano; BL 95,60, R. N. Whybray]. –
ᴿArTGran 57 (1994) 425s (J. L. Sicre); CRAI (1994) 447s; OTAbs 17
(1994) 664 (C. T. Begg); RHPR 74 (1994) 364 (P. de Robert).

2536 **Chafin** Kenneth L., 1-2 Samuel: Communicator'sC. Dallas 1990, Word.
404 p. 0-8499-0413-7. – ᴿIrTQ 60 (1994) 72s (Carmel McCarthy).

2537 **Conrad** Joachim, *Bauer* Dieter, *al.*, Der gefahrvolle Weg zur Macht; Samuelbücher: BAPrax 5. Stu 1994, KBW. 152 p.; Bibliog. 148-158. 3-460-26051-8.

2538 **Davis** Dale R., Looking on the heart; exposition of the First Book of Samuel: Expositor's Guide to the historical books. GR 1994, Baker. I. 1Sam 1-14, 144 p.; II. 1Sam 15-31, 187 p. 0-8010-3025-0; -4-2.

2539 **Hentschel** Georg, 1 Samuel [mit *Scharbert* Josef, Rut] 1994 ➤ 2517: NEchter 33. p. 29-160.

2540 **Hentschel** Georg, 2 Samuel: NEchter 34. Wü 1994. 112 p. 3-429-01634-7.

2541 ᴱ**Morano Rodríguez** C., 1-2 Samuel; Glosas marginales de 'Vetus Latina' en las Biblias Vulgatas españolas: TEstCisn 48, 1989 ➤ 5,2716... 7,2466 [cf. ➤ 2639 infra, *Moreno Hernández* A., 1-2 Reyes]: ᴿArTGran 56 (1993) 328-330 (A. *Torres*).

2542 **Richter** W., BHᵗ 1991 ➤ 8,2823: ᴿOTEssays 7 (1994) 315-7 (J. A. *Naude*: on Sam and 10 others).

2543 **Robinson** Gnana, Let us be like the nations... 1-2 Samuel: IntTComm 1993 ➤ 9,2680: ᴿOTEssays 7 (1994) 306-9 (P. *Els*).

2544 **Schroer** Silvia, Die Samuelbücher: NStuK 7, 1992 ➤ 8,2824; 9,2681: ᴿBiKi 49 (1994) 218s (W. *Schwendemann*); TLtg 66 (1993) 182s (J. M. *Oesch*); TPQ 142 (1994) 410s (F. D. *Hubmann*).

2545 **Stoebe** Hans-Joachim, Das [erste 1973] zweite Buch Samuelis: KAT 8,2. Gü 1994, Kaiser. 565 p. DM 350. 3-579-04279-3 [OTAbs 18, p. 161; RelStR 21,129, C. T. *Begg*].

2546 **Taylor** B. A., The Lucianic manuscripts of 1 Reigns, 1. Majority text: HarvSemMg 50, 1992s ➤ 9,2682: ᴿBL (1993) 53 (A. G. *Salvesen*: FERNÁNDEZ-BUSTO preferable); ETL 70 (1994) 141 (J. *Lust*); VT 44 (1994) 413-8 (E. D. *Herbert*).

2547 ᴱ**Vuillaume** Christophe, GRÉGOIRE le Grand; commentaire sur le Premier Livre des Rois 2 (1 Sam 2,29-3,37): SChr 391. P 1993, Cerf. 341 p. F 145. 2-204-04899-2. – ᴿETL 70 (1994) 184 (A. de *Halleux*); NRT 116 (1994) 444 (V. *Roisel*); RÉAug 40 (1994) 250s (M. *Doucet*); RechSR 82 (1994) 276s (Y.-M. *Duval*); RHPR 74 (1994) 326s (P. *Maraval*); VigChr 48 (1994) 193s (G. J. M. *Bartelink*).

2548 ᴱ**Brenner** Athalya, A feminist companion to Samuel and Kings: FemC 5. Shf 1994, Academic. 286 p. bibliog. 272-286; £16,50. 1-85075-480-2.

2549 *Krašovec* Jože, [Eng.] Punishment and forgiveness in the First Book of Samuel: BogVest 54 (1994) 1-34.

2550 *Payne* David F., Apologetic motifs in the books of Samuel: VoxEvca 23 (L 1993) 57-66.

2551 **Rattray** Susan, The tense-mood-aspect system of biblical Hebrew, with special emphasis on 1 and 2 Samuel: diss. Univ. California. Berkeley 1992. x-152 p. – OIAc 11,38.

2552 *Shargent* Karla G., Living on the edge; the liminality of daughters in Genesis to 2 Samuel: ➤ 2548, FemSm 1994, 26-42.

2553 *Tsevat* Metitiahu, The interpretative principle *cui bono* (to whose benefit) in biblical studies; the case of the book of Samuel: ➤ 331*a*, 11th Jewish 1993/4, A59-66.

2554 **Verheij** A. J. C., Verbs and numbers... SmKgsChr 1990 ➤ 6,9176: ᴿJQR 84 (1993s) 353-5 (G. B. *Sarfati*).

2555 **Wonneberger** R., Redaktion; Studien zur Textschreibung im AT, entwickelt am Beispiel der Samuel-Überlieferung [Hab.-Diss. Mainz 1991]:

FRL 156, 1993 ➤ 8,3830; 9,2690: ᴿCBQ 56 (1994) 354s (P. D. *Miscall*); JBL 113 (1994) 516-8 (T. R. *Hobbs*); TLZ 118 (1994) 19-21 (E. *Kellenberger*); ZAW 106 (1994) 378 (M. *Köckert*).

2556 **Fokkelman** J. P.,   Vow and desire (1 Sam 1-12): Narrative art [1-3 ➤ 1981-6-90 ➤ 62,2962*d*..., 8,2884] IV. StSemNeer, 1993 ➤ 9,2684: ᴿTLZ 119 (1994) 885-8 (H. J. *Stoebe*).

2557 *Spina* Frank A.,   Eli's seat; the transition from priest to prophet in 1 Samuel 1-4: JStOT 62 (1994) 67-75.

2558 *Zyl* Danie C. van,   Hannah's share; once more 1 Samuel 1:5: OTEssays 6 (1993) 364-6 [< OTAbs 17, p. 564].

2559 **Becker-Spörl** Silvia, 'Und Hanna betete, und sie sprach ...' Literarische Untersuchungen zu 1 Sam 2,1-10: Textw/Informatik 2, 1992 ➤ 8,2640: ᴿCBQ 56 (1994) 316s (R. E. *Person*); WeltOr 25 (1994) 179-181 (W. *Zwickel*).

2560 *Lewis* Theodore J.,   The textual history of the song of Hannah, 1 Samuel II 1-10: VT 44 (1994) 18-46.

2561 *Warren* A. L.,   A trisagion inserted in the 4QSamᵃ version of the Song of Hannah, 1 Sam. 2:1-10: JJS 45 (1994) 278-285.

2562 *Duarte Castillo* Raúl,   La casa de Elí no tuvo consistencia (1 Sm 2, 27-37): EfMex 12 (1994) 181-194.

2563 *Hurowitz* Victor A.,   Eli's adjuration of Samuel (1 Samuel III 17-18) in the light of a 'diviner's protocol' from Mari (AEM 1/1): VT 44 (1994) 483-497.

2564 *Luciani* Ferdinando, [1 Sm 4,8; 14,48; 26,8; 2 Sm 8,13] Le differenze tra testo ebraico e targum in alcuni passi del libro di Samuele: Aevum 66 (1992) 5-14.

2565 *Zwickel* Wolfgang,   Dagons abgeschlagener Kopf (1 Samuel V 3-4): VT 44 (1994) 239-249.

2566 *Orel* Vladimir, [1 Sam 6,4] Textological notes 3-4; on golden mice of Philistines and King David in the Song of Songs [2,9 peering through the lattice]: Henoch 16 (1994) 147-151; ital. 151s.

E4.5   *1 Sam 7 ... Initia potestatis regiae,*   **Origins of kingship.**

2567 *Álvarez Barredo* M.,   Valoración deuteronomística de la praxis cultual del comienzo de la Monarquía: Carthaginensia 10 (1994) 1-17; Eng. iii.

2568 *Boecker* Hans Jochen,   Das Problem des Staates in der Geschichte des Alten Israel: ➤ 31*, ᶠFANGMEIER J. 1994, 117-132.

2569 *Cohen* Kenneth J.,   King Saul, a bungler from the beginning: BR 10,5 (1994) 34-39. 56.

2570 *Edelman* Diana V.,   King Saul in the historiography of Judah: jOsu 121, 1991 ➤ 7,2482; 9,2700: ᴿCBQ 56 (1994) 100s (E. T. *Mullen*: synchronic and modern-literary); JSS 39 (1994) 313s (Gwilym H. *Jones*).

2571 **Goodblatt** David,   The monastic principle; studies in Jewish self-government in antiquity: TStAJ 38. Tü 1994, Mohr. xii-336 p. DM 188. 3-16-14176-2 [NTAbs 38, p. 489].

2572 **Kessler** Rainer,   Staat und Gesellschaft im vorexilischen Juda: VTS 47, 1992 ➤ 8,k207: ᴿEstAg 29 (1994) (C. *Mielgo*); ÉTRel 69 (1994) 100s (J.-P. *Sternberger*); JBL 113 (1994) 511s (J. A. *Dearman*).

2573 **Long** V. Philips,   The reign and rejection of King Saul; a case for literary and theological coherence: SBL diss. 118, 1989 ➤ 5,2738 ... 8,2853: ᴿBiblica 75 (1994) 99-102 (A. *Wénin*).

2574 **Polish** David, Give us a king 1990 → 7,e945*; 8,2856: ᴿAJS 17 (1992) 118-120 (D. *Novak*).
2575 **Popović** Anto, The election-rejection of Saul (1 Sam 9,1-11,15; 13,7b-15a; 28,3-25): diss. Samobor, Croatia 1994. 98 p. extract [AcPIB 9,922].
2576 *a) Williams* James G., Sacrifice and the beginning of kingship; – *b) Krondorfer* Björn, response, Re-mythologizing Scriptural authority: Semeia 67 (1994) 73-92 / 93-107.

2577 *a) Long* V. Philips, [1 Sam 9,1; 10,17] How did Saul become king? Literary reading and historical reconstructing; – *b) Gordon* Robert P., [1 Sam 8-10] Who made the kingmaker; reflections on Samuel and the institution of the monarchy: → 326*, Faith 1990/4, 271-284 / 255-269.
2578 *Burkert* Walter, [1 Sam 9,22, sanctuary-appendage] Lescha-Liskah; sakrale Gastlichkeit zwischen Palästina und Griechenland: → 567, Rel-gBeziehungen 1993, 19-38 [< OTAbs 17,p. 43].
2579 *Jacobson* Howard, [1 Sam 12,11] Bedan and [=] Barak reconsidered: VT 44 (1994) 108s.
2580 *Cook* Stephen L., The text and philology of 1 Samuel XIII 20-1: VT 44 (1994) 250-4.
2581 *Craig* Kenneth M.ᴶ, Rhetorical aspects of questions answered with silence in 1 Samuel 14:37 and 28:6: CBQ 56 (1994) 221-239.
2582 *Layton* Scott C., [1 Sam 14,49...] The Hebrew personal name Merab: JSS 38 (1993) 195-207.

E4.6 *1 Sam 16... 2 Sam: Accessio Davidis.* David's Rise.

2583 **Auld** A. Graeme, Kings without privilege; David and Moses in the story of the Bible's kings. Edinburgh 1994, Clark. x-203 p.; bibliog. 176-185. 0-567-09639-4 [OIAc 11,12; BL 95,80, K. W. *Whitelam*: Chr is claimed not to have used Kgs].
2584 *Costacurta* Bruna, Con la cetra e con la fionda; l'ascesa di Davide verso il trono. R 1994, Dehoniane. 265 p. Lᵐ 28. 88-396-0552-5. – ᴿCC 145 (1994) 618s (R. *Meynet*).
2585 *Dirven* Lucinda, 'The smallest among his brethren'; origin and meaning of an early Coptic narrative cycle of David's youth [Bawit Apa-Apollo]: Boreas 16 (Münster 1993) 181-198.
2586 **Gauger** Hans-Martin, Davids Aufstieg, Erzählung. Mü 1993, Beck. 183 p. DM 34. 3-406-37378-X [RB 102,148, F. *Langlamet*: de haute qualité narrative et critique].
2587 *a) Gordon* Robert P., In search of David; the David tradition in recent study; – *b) Niehaus* Jeffrey J., The warrior and his God; the covenant foundation of history and historiography: → 326*, Faith 1990/4, 285-298 / 299-312.
2587* *Heater* Homerᴶ, Young David and the practice of wisdom: → 21, ꟳCAMPBELL D., Integrity 1994, 50-61.
2588 **Ho** Craig Y.S., The troubles of David and his house; textual and literary studies of the synoptic stories of Saul and David in Samuel-Kings and Chronicles: diss. ᴰ*Auld* A. G. Edinburgh 1994. 209 p. – RTLv 26,531.
2589 **Kohlschein** Franz, *Küppers* Kurt, 'Der grosse Sänger David, eure Muster': LtgQFor 73. Münster 1992, Aschendorff. xvii-390 p. DM 88. 3-402-03859-5. – ᴿMaisD 198 (1994) 129-133 (Monique *Brulin*).

2590 *Lemche* Niels P.,   Det Gamle Testamente; David og hellenismen [defence against NIELSEN E., WILLESEN F.]: DanTTs [55 (1992) 81-101] 57 (1994) 20-39 [< OTAbs 17,477].

2591 *a*) *Polak* Frank H.,   David's kingship — a precarious equilibrium; – *b*) *Falk* Ze'ev W.,   Religion and state in ancient Israel: ➤ 331*b*, Politics 1994, 119-147 / 49-54.

2592 *Sternberger* Jean-Pierre,   David est-il parmi les prophètes? La mention du nom de David dans les oracles des prophètes postérieurs: ÉTRel 69 (1994) 53-61.

2593 *Langlamet* François,   'David-Jonathan-Saül' ou le 'Livre de Jonathan' 1 Sam 16,14 - 2 Sam 1,27*:   RB 101 (1994) 326.

2594 *Berger* Robert D.,   [1 Sam 16,13-23] Evil spirits and eccentric grammar; a study of the relationship between text and meaning in Hebrew narrative: ➤ 303*c*, Biblical Hebrew 1993/4, 320-335.

2595 **Barthélemy** D.,   [1 Sam 17] Story of David and Goliath 1986 ➤ 2,2060... 6,2999:   ᴿTR 90 (1994) 283-5 (L. *Schwienhorst-Schönberger*).

2596 *Eaton* M. R.,   [1 Sam 17,41-47...] Some instances of flyting [stylized exchange of hostile provocations] in the Hebrew Bible: JStOT 61 (1994) 3-14.

2597 *Cook* Edward M.,   1 Samuel XX 26 - XXI 5 according to 4QSam*: VT 44 (1994) 442-454.

2598 *Reis* Pamela T.,   Collusion at Nob; a new reading of 1 Samuel 21-22: JStOT 61 (1994) 59-73.

2599 **Riepl** Christian,   Sind David und Saul berechenbar? 1 Sam 21s: AOtt 39, ᴰ1993 ➤ 9,2728:   ᴿBL (1994) 72 (J. R. *Porter*); OTEssays 7 (1994) 141-4 (L. C. *Jonker*: good but in W. RICHTER jargon); RB 101 (1994) 612-6 (F. *Langlamet*); TLZ 119 (1994) 500-4 (W. *Dietrich*).

2600 *Begg* Christopher, [1 Sam 24; 2 Chr 21; Ant 7,318-334] JOSEPHUS' version of David's census: Henoch 16 (1994) 199-225; ital. 226.

2601 *a*) *Zatelli* Ida,   Analysis of lexemes from a conversational prose text; HNH as signal of a performative utterance in 1 Sam. 25:41; – *b*) dazu: *Lipiński* Édouard, Kinship terminology in 1 Sam 25:40-42: ZAHeb 7 (1994) 5-11/12-16.

2602 **Cryer** Frederick H.,   [1 Sam 28,8] Divination in Israel and its Near Eastern environment; a social-historical investigation [diss. Aarhus/ Bochum]: jOsu 142. Shf 1994, JStOT. 367 p. $70. 1-85075-353-9 [RelStR 21,125, M. A. *Sweeney*].

2603 **Zangara** Vincenza, [1 Sam 28] Exeuntes de corpore 1990 ➤ 7,4229... 9,2729:   ᴿVigChr 48 (1994) 96s (G. J. M. *Bartelink*).

2604 *Weitzman* Steven,   David's lament and the poetics of grief in 2 Samuel: JQR 85 (1994s) 341-360.

2605 **Polzin** Robert,   David and the Deuteronomist; 2 Samuel 1993 [Biblica 76,101-3, A. *Wénin*] :   ᴿTBR 7,2 (1994s) 13 (R. *Coggins*).

2606 **Fokkelman** J. P.,   Throne and city: Narrative art... 3. II Sam 2-8 & 21-24, 1990 ➤ 6,3008... 8,2885:   ᴿBiblica 75 (1994) 102-6 (G. *Hentschel*); BO 51 (1994) 392-4 (Diana *Edelman*); CBQ 56 (1994) 104-7 (R. *Polzin*); ScripTPamp 26 (1994) 1213s (F. *Varo*).

2607 — *Beuken* Willem A. M.,   De boeken van Samuël in een nieuw licht [FOKKELMAN J. P., 1-3, 1981-90], een bespreking: PhoenixEOL 40 (1994) 109-116.

2608 *Haelewyck* J.-C., Le meurtre d'Asaël, une péripétie de la bataille de Gabaon (II Sam 2,18-32)?: ZAW 106 (1994) 27-39.

2609 *Stone* Ken, [2 Sam 3 & 16] Sexual power and political prestige; the case of the disputed concubine: BR 10,4 (1994) 28-31. 52.

2610 *Spanier* Ktziah, [2 Sam 3,3 ...] The queen mother in the Judaean royal court; Maacah – a case study: ➤ 2548, SmK 185-195 [< OTAbs 18, p. 311].

2611 *Oeming* Manfred, Die Eroberung Jerusalems durch David in deuteronomistischer und chronistischer Darstellung (II Sam 5,6-9 und I Chr 11,4-8); ein Beitrag zur narrativen Theologie der beiden Geschichtswerke: ZAW 106 (1994) 404-420; 1 fig.

2612 *Herbert* Edward D., 2 Samuel V 6, an interpretative crux reconsidered in the light of 4QSam^al: VT 44 (1994) 340-8.

2613 *Kleven* Terence, The use of *ṣnr* in Ugaritic and 2 Samuel V 8; Hebrew usage and comparative philology: VT 44 (1994) 195-204.

2614 *Jurić* S., 2 Sam 5,11 ➤ BogSmot 63 (1993) 276-300; ital. 300.

2615 **Gelander** Shamai, [2 Sam 6] David and his God 1991 ➤ 7,2512; 9,2738: RCBQ 56 (1994) 107s (B. *MacDonald*); JSS 39 (1994) 314s (A. H. W. *Curtis*); SvEx 59 (1994) 171-3 (A. *Carlson*).

2616 *Zwickel* Wolfgang, [2 Sam 6,1] David, historische Gestalt und idealisiertes Vorbild; Überlegungen zu Entstehung und Theologie von 2 Sam 6: JNWS 20,1 (1994) 79-123.

2617 *Toorn* Karel van der, *Houtman* Cees, [2 Sam 6,2] David and the Ark: JBL 113 (1994) 209-231.

2618 EClines D., *Eskenazi* T., Telling Queen Michal's story: jOsu 119, 1991 ➤ 7,295; 9,2729: RHenoch 16 (1994) 357s (A. *Catastini*).

2619 **Hentschel** Georg, Gott, König und Tempel... 2 Sam 7,1-17: 1992 ➤ 8, 2891; 9,2742: RTR 90 (1994) 26-28 (E.-J. *Waschke*).

2620 *Eslinger* Lyle, House of God or house of David; the rhetoric of 2 Samuel 7: jOsu 164. Shf 1994, JStOT. 118 p. $35. 1-85075-481-0 [JTS 46,210, D. F. *Murray*; TLZ 120,24-27, T. *Naumann*]. – RÉTRel 69 (1994) 569s (Françoise *Smyth*); OTAbs 17 (1994) 665 (J. L. *Berquist*).

2621 *Cryer* Frederick H., On the recently discovered 'House of David' inscription (Tel Dan; unwarranted claims of A. BIRAN and J. NAVEH, IsrEJ 43 (1994) 81-98; the stela is not (pure) Aramaic, nor securely dated 9th century; and 'house of David' could be not Judah but any part of his reign]: ScandJOT 8 (1994) 3-19.

2622 *Cortese* Enzo, 2 Sam 7 e 1 Cr 17; prospettive attuali dell'esegesi: Antonianum 69 (1994) 141-155 [giornata di studi 11.IV.1994; ➤ p. 322-5, *Penna* R.; 326s, *Nobile* M.].

2623 *Dietrich* Walter, [2 Sam 7...] Nathan: ➤ 517, TRE 24 (1994) 18-21.

2624 **Jones** Gwilym H., [2 Sam 7...] The Nathan narratives: jOsu 80, 1990 ➤ 7,2517... 9,2743: RJJS 45 (1994) 130s (J. G. *Campbell*).

2625 *Renaud* B., [2 Sam 7] La prophétie de Nathan; théologies en conflit: RB 101 (1994) 5-61; Eng. 5.

2626 *Schlosser* Jacques, [2 Sam 7] L'oracle de Nathan dans le NT: ➤ 31*, FDAUTZENBERG G., Nach 1994, 569-587.

2627 *Langlamet* François, Analyse formelle et numérique de 2 Samuel 7:1-17; ➤ 68, FLABUSCHAGNE C., VTS 53 (1994) 101-122.

2628 *Frolov* Serge, *Orel* Vladimir, On the meaning of 2 Sam 9,1: BibNot 73 (1994) 31s [74 (1994) 15-23, Notes on 1 Sam 9,3s; 28,20s].

2629 **Bailey** Randall C., David in love and war... 2 Sam 10-12: jOsu 75, 1990

➤ 6,3010 ... 9,2746: ᴿBZ 38 (1994) 317s (J. *Scharbert*); CritRR 5 (1992) 110-3 (R. G. *Bowman*, also on G. JONES jOsu 80).
2630 *Frisk* A., ❹ Image contrasts and literary representation through the key word *šwb* (2 Sam 15-20; 1 Kgs 12): BeitM 39 (1994) 245-257 [< OTAbs 18, p. 70].
2631 *Beek* M. A., David and Absalom; a Hebrew tragedy in prose?: ➤ 250, VAmst 155-168 [OTAbs 17, p. 567].
2632 a) *Hentschel* Georg, Die Hinrichtung der Nachkommen Sauls (2 Sam 21,1-14); – b) *Thiel* Winfried, Erwägungen zur aramäisch-israelitischen Geschichte im 9. Jh. v.C.; – c) *Seidel* Hans, Die Trägergruppen alttestamentlicher Überlieferung: ➤ 115, ᶠSCHUNCK K.-D., Nachdenken 1994, 93-116 / 117-131 / 375-386.
2633 a) [2 Sam 21] *Thiel* Winfried, Rizpa und das Ritual von Gibeon; – b) *Conrad* Joachim, Wird Gott sein Volk nochmals in Frage stellen?: ➤ 61, ᶠKAISER O., 'Wer ist' 1994, 247-262 / 265-276.

E4.7   *Libri Regum;* Solomon, Temple: 1 Kings ...

2634 **Brueggemann** Walter, Il primo libro dei Re; guida alla lettura 1993 ➤ 9,2766: ᴿParVi 39,2 (1994) 62 (A. *Rolla*); RivB 42 (1994) 488s (anche A. *Rolla*).
2636 **Fernández Marcos** Natalio, Scribes and translators; Septuagint and Old Latin in the books of [Samuel and] Kings [Oxford Grinfield lectures]: VTS 54. Leiden 1994, Brill. x-99 p.; ill. 90-04-10043-1.
2637 **Knoppers** Gary N., Two nations under God; the deuteronomistic history of Solomon and the dual monarchies; 1. The reign of Solomon and the rise of Jeroboam; 2. The reign of Jeroboam, the fall of Israel, and the reign of Josiah: HarvSemMg 52s. Atlanta 1994, Scholars. xv-302 p.; xvii-340 p. $32 each. 1-55540-913-X; -4-8 [BL 41s, A. D. H. *Mayes*).
2638 **Long** Burke O., 2 Kings: FOTLit 10, 1991 ➤ 7,2533; 8,2770: ᴿNewTR 7,1 (1994) 98-100 (L. J. *Hoppe*).
2639 **Moreno Hernández** A., Las glosas marginales de Vetus Latina en las Biblias Vulgatas españolas 1-2 Reyes 1992 ➤ 8,2911 [cf. supra ➤ 2541, *Morano Rodríguez* C., 1-2 Sam]. – ᴿMnemosyne 47 (1994) 560s (G. J. M. *Bartelink*).
2640 **Ravasi** Gianfranco, I libri dei Re: Centro Culturale S. Fedele, Milano: Conversazioni bibliche. Bo 1994, Dehoniane. 132 p. 88-10-70946-2.
2641 **Smelik** Klaus A. D., 1 Koningen: Belichting 1993 ➤ 9,2773: ᴿStreven 61 (1994) 469s (P. *Beentjes*).
ᵀᴱ**Vuillaume** Christophe, GRÉGOIRE le Grand sur 1 Rois II [1 Sam 2,11-2,21]: SChr 391, 1993 ➤ 2547.
2643 **Wiseman** Donald J., 1 and 2 Kings: Tyndale OT. 1993 ➤ 9,2774: ᴿBL (1994) 78 (G. H. *Jones*).

2644 **Lowery** R. H., The reforming kings: jOsu 120, ᴰ1991 ➤ 7,2583 ... 9,2983: ᴿBijdragen 55 (1994) 73s (J. van *Ruiten*); BZ 38 (1994) 125-7 (W. *Thiel*).
2645 **McKenzie** Steven J., The trouble with Kings: VTSup 42, 1991 ➤ 7, 2534 ... 9,2771: ᴿBInterp 2 (1994) 227s (E. R. *Salters*); CBQ 56 (1994) 119s (L. J. *Hoppe*); ScandJOT 8 (1994) 155-7 (N. P. *Lemche*); JSS 39 (1994) 315s (R. N. *Whybray*); VT 44 (1994) 135s (R. P. *Gordon*).
2646 a) *Naᶜaman* Nadav, Criticism of voluntary servitude to foreign powers; a historiographical study in the Book of King; – b) *Elgavish* David, The diplomatic envoy in the Bible and the ancient Near East; parallels; –

c) *Meitlis* Itzhak, The 'Ḥatserim'; a farmstead from the end of the First Temple: ➤ 331*a*, 11th Jewish 1993/4, 63-70 / 79-86 / 55-62.
2647 *Smelik* K. A. D., *Soest* H.-J. van, Overlijdensteksten [obituary formulas] in het boek Koningen: AmstCah 13 (1994) 56-71; Eng. 129 [continuing Smelik cah. 6 & 12].

2648 **Beyer** Rolf, König Salomo 1993 ➤ 9,2777 [TLZ 120,777, H. M. *Niemann*, unzufrieden].
2649 *Newing* Edward G., Rhetorical art of the Deuteronomist; lampooning Solomon in First Kings: OTEssays 7 (1994) 247-260.
2650 *Renaud* Bernard, Salomon, figure du Messie: RevSR (1994) 409-426.
2651 **Parker** Kim I., Wisdom and law in the reign of Solomon 1992 ➤ 8,2918: ᴿCBQ 56 (1994) 564s (L. J. *Hoppe*: helps the traditional toward the literary-critical).

2652 *Walsh* Jerome T., [1 Kgs 1-11 chiasms] Symmetry and the sin of Solomon: Shofar 12 (1993) 11-27 [< OTAbs 17, p. 568].
2653 **Moyers** Tony L., The social function of 1 Kings 1-2: diss. Baylor, ᴰ*Bellinger* W. 1994. 276 p. 94-22792. – DissA 55 (1994s) p. 996.
2654 *Reinhartz* Adela, [1 Kgs 1s] Anonymous women and the collapse of the monarchy; a study in narrative technique: ➤ 2548, FemCSam 43-65 [196-200, *Pippin* Tina, Jezebel].
2655 **Pennoyer** Raymond P.ᴵᴵᴵ, Solomonic apologetic; text and redaction in the Succession Narrative with special attention to the so-called 'Miscellanies' in 3 Reigns 2: diss. Johns Hopkins, ᴰ*McCarter* P. Baltimore 1992. 93-27648. – OIAc 11,36.
2656 *Anbar* Moshe, [1 R 2,3s] Un 'mot en vedette' et une 'reprise' introduisant une promesse conditionnelle de l'éternité de la dynastie davidique: VT 44 (1994) 1-9.
2657 *Scolnic* Benjamin E., [1 Kgs 2,5s] David's final testament; morality or expediency?: Judaism 43 (1994) 19-26.
2658 **Särkiö** Pekka, Die Weisheit und Macht Salomos in der israelitischen Historiographie; eine traditions- und redaktionskritische Untersuchung über 1 Kön 3-5 und 9-11 [diss. ᴰ*Veijola* T. – RTLv 26,532]: Schriften 69. Helsinki 1994, Finnische Exegetische Ges. vi-281 p. 951-9217-15-0 [Gö VR ᴰᴹ 68; 3-525-63630-5; RelStR 21,321, C. T. *Begg*].
2659 **Carr** David M., [1 Kgs 3,2-15] From D to Q... Solomon's dream SBL mg 44,1991 ➤ 8,2921; 9,2784: ᴿJRel 74 (1994) 118 (M. *Brettler*); JSS 39 (1994) 105-7 (T. H. *Lim*).
2660 *Fidler* Ruth, ❻ [1 Kgs 3,4] Problems of propaganda; on King Solomon's visit to Gibeon: ➤ 331*a*, 11th Jewish 1993/4, 31-38.
2661 *Heijst* Annelies van, [1 Kgs 3:16-28] Beyond dividing thinking; Solomon's judgment and the Wisdom-traditions of women: LvSt 19 (1994) 99-117.
2662 *Hurowitz* Victor, Did King Solomon violate the second commandment?: BR 10,5 (1994) 24-33.57.

Templum. 1 Reg 6s.

2663 **Bissoli** G., Il Tempio nella letteratura giudaica e neotestamentaria; studio sulla corrispondenza fra tempio celeste e tempio terrestre: SBF Anal 37. J 1994, Franciscan. xiv-299 p. [LA 44,743; Biblica 76,141]. – ᴿCiuD 207 (1994) 884s (J. *Gutiérrez*).

2664 *a*) **Bloch-Smith** Elizabeth, 'Who is the King of Glory?' Solomon's Temple and its symbolism; – *b*) *Millard* Alan, King Solomon's shields: ➤ 67, ᶠKING P., Scripture 1994, 18-31 . 286-295; 4 fig.

2665 **Edersheim** Alfred, The Temple, its ministry and service. Peabody MA 1994 = 1874, Hendrickson, xii-310 p. 1-56563-136-6; pa. -006-8.

2666 **Hurowitz** Victor, I have ... Temple building: jOsu 115, ᴰ1991 ➤ 8,2929; 9,2788: ᴿCBQ 56 (1994) 333s (A. A. *Di Vito*); Interpretation 48 (1994) 87s (S. S. *Tuell*).

2667 *Hurowitz* Victor, Inside Solomon's Temple: BR 10,2 (1994) 24-37 . 50.

2668 **Schmidt** Francis, La pensée du Temple, de Jérusalem à Qoumran; identité et lien social dans le judaïsme ancien. P 1994, Seuil. 279 p.; bibliog. p. 323-345. 2-02-021786-4.

2669 **Junco Garza** Carlos, La crítica profética ante el tempio; teología veterotestamentaria: BtMex 5. México 1994, Univ. Pontificia. 412 p.

2670 **Weinberg** Joel, The citizen-temple community [8 German articles of the 1970s], ᵀ*Smith* Christopher D. L.: jOsu 151. Shf 1992, JStOT. £35. 1-85075-395-X. – ᴿTLZ 119 (1994) 413s (T. *Krüger*).

2671 **Zwickel** Wolfgang, Der Tempelkult in Kanaan und Israel; Studien zur Kultgeschichte Palästinas von der Mittelbronzezeit bis zum Untergang Judas: ForAT 10. Tü 1994, Mohr. xvi-424 p. 3-16-146218-1.

2672 **Coogan** Michael D., [1 Kgs 7,1] The Solomonic palace: ➤ 30, ᶠCOUTURIER G., Maison 1994, 93-97.

2673 **Talstra** Epp, [1 K 8] Solomon's prayer [1987],ᵀ 1993 ➤ 9,2794: ᴿBL (1994) 101 (W. *Johnstone*); ᴢAW 106 (1994) 370 (U. *Becker*).

2674 *Irvine* Stuart A., [3 K 10,2] The southern border of Syria reconstructed: CBQ 56 (1994) 21-41.

2675 **Lassner** Jacob, Demonizing the Queen of Sheba 1993 ➤ 9,2798 [BL 95,154, A. *Jeffers*].

2676 **Boer** Roland, Jameson and Jeroboam; a Marxist reading of 1 Kings 11-14, 3 Reigns 11-14 and 2 Chronicles 10-13: diss. McGill, ᴰ*Culley* R. Montreal 1993. – RelStR 21,251; SR 23,525.

Chronologia Regum.

2677 **Barnes** W. H., Studies in the chronology of the Divided Monarchy of Israel ᴰ1991 ➤ 7,2557; 8,2944: ᴿᴢAW 106 (1994) 149s (R. *Liwak*).

2678 **Günter** W., *Ahlgrimma* E., Die Daten der Bibel: Zeitalterwechsel. Fra 1994, Fischer. 21 p. 3-89501-071-5.

2679 **Hayes** J. H., *Hooker* P. K., A new chronology for the kings of Israel and Judah 1988 ➤ 4,2931 ... 6,3058: ᴿJQR 84 (1993s) 298-300 (M. *Cogan*).

2680 *Hentschel* G., AT [*Söding* T. NT], Biblische Chronologie: ➤ 510, LTK³ (1994) 417s [-9].

2681 **Mellersh** H. E. L., Chronology of the ancient world 10,000 B.C. to A.D. 799: Chronology of world history. Ox 1994 = 1976, Helicon. x-500 p. £40, 0-09-178259-7 [BL 95,44, L. L. *Grabbe*, also on three reprints of later periods in the series).

2682 **Coote** Robert B., In defense of [Jeroboam's] revolution; the Elohist history 1991 ➤ 7,1699; 9,1745: ᴿCritRR 6 (1993) 153-5 (R. E. *Friedman* does not accept despite the admirable clarity).
Begg Christopher, Josephus' account of the early divided monarchy 1993 ➤ 12640.

2683 a) *Mommer* Peter, Das Verhältnis von Situation, Tradition und Redaktion am Beispiel von 1 Kön 12: → 101, ᶠREVENTLOW H., AT 1994, 47-64.
2684 *Herr* Bertram, Welches war die Sünde Jerobeams? Erwägungen zu 1 Kön 12,26-33: BibNot 74 (1994) 57-65.
2685 *Marcus* David, [1 Kgs 13,18] Elements of ridicule and parody in the story of the lying prophet from Bethel: → 331a, 11th Jewish 1993/4. A-67-74.
2686 **Toews** Wesley I., Monarchy and religious institution in Israel under Jeroboam I: SBL mg 47. Atlanta 1993, Scholars. x-197 p. $45; sb./pa. $28. 1-55540-876-1; -7-X. – ᴿBL (1994) 116 (K. W. *Whitelam*].
2687 *Reis* Pamela T., Vindicating God; another look at 1 Kings XIII: VT (1994) 376-386.
2689 *Jones* Gwilym H., [1 Kgs 15,1s; 2 Chr 13,1s] From Abijam to Abijah: ZAW 106 (1994) 420-434.
2690 *Puech* Émile, [1 R 15...] La stèle araméenne de Dan; Bar Hadad II et la coalition des Omrides et de la maison de David: RB 101 (1994) 215-241; 2 fig.; pl. IV; Eng. p. 161.
2691 *Naʾaman* Nadav, The campaign of Mesha (31-33) against Horonaim [Kerak]: BibNot 73 (1994) 27-30.
2692 *Pienaar* D. N., Aram and Israel during the reigns of Omri and Ahab reconsidered: J/Tyd Sem 6 (1994) 34-45.
2693 *Feldman* Louis H., [1 Kgs 15] JOSEPHUS' portrait of Asa: BuBR 4 (1994) 41-59.

E4.8   *1 Regum 17-22: Elias,* **Elijah.**

2694 ᴱ**Coote** Robert B., Elijah and Elisha in socioliterary perspective: Semeia 1992 → 8,347: ᴿCBQ 56 (1994) 396s (R. A. *Simkins*); JSS 38 (1993) 316-320 (E. W. *Davies*).
2695 *Dolbreau* F., *Poirot* E., Sur les miracles d'Élie et d'Élisée (CPL 1155c): SacrEr 34 (1994) 135-164.
2696 *Feldman* Louis H., JOSEPHUS' portrait of Elijah: ScandJOT 8 (1994) 61-86.
2697 **Hauser** Alan J., *Gregory* Russell, From Carmel to Horeb; Elijah in crisis: jOsu 85, 1990 → 6,3068... 9,2814: ᴿJBL 113 (1994) 128s (M. A. *Throntveit*); TLZ 119 (1994) 122s (G. *Hentschel*).
2698 **Masson** M., Elia – l'appello del silenzio [1992 → 8,2962]ᵀ. Bo 1993, Dehoniane. 118 p. Lᵐ 15. 88-10-203650-0. – ᴿAntonianum 69 (1994) 389s (E. *Cortese*).
2700 *Nardi* Carlo, DANTE e il profeta Elia; ancora sulla positura di Belacqua: VivH 5 (1994) 188-203; Eng. 204.
2701 **Poirot** Éliane, Élie dans la tradition monastique: cath. diss. ᴰCanevet M. Strasbourg 1994. 639 p. – RTLv 26, p. 541.
2702 *Thiel* Winfried, MENDELSSOHNs 'Elias' und der biblische Elia: → 101, ᶠREVENTLOW H., AT 1994, 337-353.
2703 **White** Marsha C., The Elijah legends and Jehu's coup; an examination of a biblical accession text: diss. Harvard, ᴰMachinist P. CM 1994, 327 p. 95-00205. – DissA 55 (1994s) p. 2437.
2704 **Woods** Fred E., Water and storm polemics against Baalism in the Deuteronomic History: AmerUnivSt 7/150. NY 1994, P. Lang. [x-] 121 p.; bibliog. 127-159. $38. 0-8204-2111-4 [TDig 42,194; BL 95,122, J. *Day*, unconvinced].
2705 **Rentrop** Jürgen, [1 Kgs 17-19] Elija aus Tischbe; eine literarische und

redaktionsgeschichtliche Untersuchung von 1 Kön 17-19: kath. Diss.
ᴰHossfeld F. Bonn 1994. – TR 91,94.

2706 **Brichto** H. C., [1 Kgs 17...] Toward... poetics/prophets 1992 ➤ 8,3115;
9,1462.2811: ᴿCBQ 56 (1994) 320s (W. L. Humphreys); Interpretation 48
(1994) 194.6 (P. D. Miller); HeythJ 35 (1994) 65s (J. Mulrooney); Salesianum 56 (1994) 565s (R. Vicent).

2707 Giannarelli Elena, [1 Re 17,6] Dalla Bibbia al PETRARCA; Elia, i corvi e
l'amicizia: ➤ 86, ᶠNALDINI M., Paideia 1994, 255-273.

2708 Chisholm Robert B.ᴶ, [1 K 17s] The polemic against Baalism in Israel's
early history and literature: BtS 151 (1994) 267-283.

2709 Würthwein Ernst, Tradition und theologische Redaktion in 1 Reg 17-18
[ineditum] ➤ 233, Studien 1994, 102-117.

2710 Kiuchi Nobuyoshi, Elijah's self-offering; 1 Kings 17,21: Biblica 75
(1994) 74-79.

2711 Carucci Viterbi Benedetto, L'esperienza di Dio sul Horeb di Elia [1 Re
19]: ParSpV 30 (1994) 49-60.

2712 Mosconi Franco, 'Camminò fino al monte di Dio' (1 Re 19,8): Presbyteri 28 (1994) 511-525.

2713 Thiel Winfried, [1 K 20] Erwägungen zur aramäisch-israelitischen Geschichte im 9. Jh. v. Chr.: ➤ 115, ᶠSCHUNCK K., Nachdenken 1994, 17-31
[OTA 18,43].

2714 **Tertel** Hans Jürgen, [1 Kgs 22 & 20] Text and transmission; an empirical
model for the literary development of OT narratives: BZAW 221. B 1994,
de Gruyter. x-311 p. DM 152. 3-11-013821-9 [BL 95,105, R. P. Carroll:
Akkadian surface, conservative agenda]. – ᴿExpTim 106 (1994s) 244 (G.
Auld).

2715 Feldman Louis H., [1 Kgs 22] JOSEPHUS' portrait of Jehoshaphat:
➤ 9,102*, ᶠMERIDOR R., ScripClasIsr 12 (1993) 159-175.

2716 Hamilton Jeffries M., [1 Kgs 22] Caught in the nets of prophecy?
The death of King Ahab and the character of God: CBQ 56 (1994)
649-663.

E4.9   2 Reg 1... Elisaeus, **Elisha**... Ezechias, Josias.

2717 Orlandi Tito, Sulla versione copta del IV (II) libro dei Re: ➤ 65,
ᶠKASSER R., Coptology 1994, 357-362.

2718 Le saint prophète Élisée 1991 ➤ 9,2828*: ᴿRThom 94 (1994) 702 (D.
Cerbelaud: aucun auteur ou responsable).

2719 Becking Bob, Elisha: 'Shaᶜ is my God'?: ZAW 106 (1994) 113-6.

2719* **Moore** Rick D., God saves; lessons from the Elisha stories: jOsu 95,
1990 ➤ 9,2834: ᴿCritRR 6 (1993) 170-2 (M. A. Throntveit).

2720 Feldman Louis H., JOSEPHUS' portrait of Elisha: NT 36 (1994) 1-28.

2721 a) Clements Ronald E., The politics of blasphemy; Zion's God and
the threat of imperialism; – b) Gerstenberger Erhard S., Andere Sitten –
andere Götter: ➤ 61, ᶠKAISER O., 'Wer ist' 1994, 231-246 / 127-141.

2722 **Kuan Kah-Jin**, Assyrian historical inscriptions and Israelite/Judean-
Tyrian-Damascene political and commercial relations in the ninth-eighth
centuries BCE: diss. Emory, ᴰHayes J. Atlanta 1993. – RelStR 21,255.

2723 Martinez Borobio Emiliano, Algunos aspectos del poder real en Aram,
siglos ix-viii a.C.: AnuFg 16,3 (1993) 29-40 [< OTAbs 17, p. 537].

2724 **Reinhold** G. G. G., Die Beziehungen Altisraels zu den aramäischen
Staaten in der israelitisch-jüdischer Königszeit [Diss. Frankfurt 1989,

ᴰ*Schottroff* W.]: EurHS 23/368, 1989 ➤ 7,2577:   ᴿRivB 42 (1994) 103-8
(G. L. *Prato*); WZKM 84 (1994) 209-211 (M. *Jeroš*).

─────────────

2725 *Feldman* Louis H., [2 Kgs 3-6] JOSEPHUS's portrait of Jehoram, king of
Israel: BJRyL 76,1 (1994) 3-20.
2726 **Baumgart** Norbert C., Gott, Prophet und Israel; eine synchrone und
diachrone Auslegung der Naamanerzählung und ihrer Gehasiepisode
(2 Kön 5) [Diss. Erfurt 1993, ᴰ*Hentschel* G.]: ErfTSt 68. Lp 1994, Benno.
xxvii-290 p. DM 78. 3-89543-028-5 [OTAbs 18,416].
2727 *Smith* W. Alan, [2 Kgs 5] Naaman and Elisha; healing, wholeness, and
the task of religious education: RelEdn 89 (1994) 205-219.
2728 *Marinkovic* Peter, 'Geh in Frieden' (2 Kön 5,19); Sonderformen legitimer
JHWHverehrung durch 'Heiden' in 'heidnischer' Mitwelt [*Umemoto* Naoto:
bei PHILON]: *Feldmeier*, Die Heiden: WUNT 70 (1994) 3-21 (22-59).
2729 **Mulzer** Martin, Jehu schlägt Joram... 2 Kön 8,25-10,36: AOtt 37, 1992
➤ 8,2978; 9,2836: ᴿBL (1994) 69 (G. H. *Jones*); OTEssays 7 (1994) 467-9
(J. H. *Breytenbach*, Afrikaans); RivB 42 (1994) 349-351 (A. *Rolla*); TLZ
119 (1994) 631-3 (G. *Hentschel*).
2729* **Barré** Lloyd M., The rhetoric of political persuasion; the narrative
artistry and political intentions of 2 Kings 9-11: CBQ Mg. 20. Wsh 1988,
Catholic Biblical Association. ix-161 p. ➤ 6,5087.
2730 **Minokami** Y., [2 Kgs 9,14] Die Revolution des Jehu: GöTArb 38, 1989
➤ 5,3851; 6,3088: ᴿVT 44 (1994) 143s (R. P. *Gordon*).
2731 *White* Marsha, [2 Kgs 9,25s] Naboth's vineyard and Jehu's coup; the
legitimation of a dynastic extermination: VT 44 (1994) 66-76.
2732 *Mulzer* Martin, Et ascenderunt eunuchi... Zur Bewertung der Vet-Lat-
Fragmente in 2(4) Kön 9,33: BibNot 73 (1994) 20-26.
2733 *Keel* Othmar, *Uehlinger* Christoph, Der Assyrerkönig Salmanassar III
und Jehu von Israel auf dem schwarzen Obelisken aus Nimrud: ➤ 38,
ᶠGAMPER A., ZkT 116,4 (1994) 391-420; 10 fig.
2734 *Lambert* W. G., [2 Kgs 10,36] When did Jehu pay tribute?: ➤ 45,
ᶠGOULDER M., Crossing 1994, 53-56 [Shalmaneser's 18th-year rather
than 21st-year Syria campaign].
2735 **Dutcher-Walls** Patricia, II Kings 11-12; narrative art and political
rhetoric: diss. Graduate Theological Union, ᴰ*Chaney* M. Berkeley 1994.
323 p. 95-11331. – DissA 55 (1994s) p. 3879; RelStR 21,254.
2735* *Gosse* Bernard, 2 Rois 14:27 et l'influence des livres prophétiques sur la
rédaction du deuxième livre des Rois: OTEssays 7 (1994) 167-174.
2736 *Macchi* J.-D., [2 R 17,24-41] Les controverses théologiques dans le
judaïsme de l'époque postexilique; l'exemple de [additions deutérono-
mistiques à] 2 Rois 17,24-41: TEuph 5 (1992) 85-93.
2737 **Hooker** Paul K., The kingdom of Hezekiah; Judah in the geo-political
context of the late eighth century B.C.E.: diss. Emory, ᴰ*Hayes* J. Atlanta
1993. xiv-389 p. 93-33167. – OIAc 11,26.
2738 **Hull** John H.ᴶ, Hezekiah – saint and sinner; a conceptual and contextual narrative analysis of 2 Kings 18-20. Diss. ᴰ*Knierim* R. Claremont
1994. 628 p. 95-02371. – DissA 55 (1994s) p. 2436. – RelStR 21,255.
2739 *Naʾaman* Nadav, ❸ Ahaz's and Hezekiah's policy toward Assyria in the
days of Sargon II and Sennacherib's early years: Zion 59 (1994) 5-30;
Eng. v.
2740 a) *Rainey* Anson F., Hezekiah's reform and the altars at Beer-sheba
and Arad; ➤ 67, ᶠKING P., Scripture 1994, 333-354; 13 fig.

2741 *a) Naʾaman* Nadav, Hezekiah and the kings of Assyria; – *b) Franklin* Norma, The Room V reliefs at Dur-Sharrukin and Sargon II's western campaigns: TAJ 21 (1994) 235-254 / 255-275; 8 fig.

2742 *Vera Chamaza* Galo W., Der VIII. Feldzug Sargons II. — Eine Untersuchung zu Politik und historischer Geographie des späten 8. Jhs. v. Chr. (I): ArchMIran 27 (1994) 91-118; 2 maps.

2743 *a) Finkelstein* Israel, [2 Kgs 21] The archaeology of the days of Manasseh; – *b) Stern* Ephraim, The eastern border of the kingdom of Judah in its last days; – *c) Mazar* Amihai, The northern Shephelah in the Iron Age; some issues in biblical history and archaeology: ⟶ 67, ᶠKING P., Scripture 1994, 169-187 / 399-409; 5 fig. / 247-267; 5 fig.

2744 *Álvarez Barredo* Miguel, [2 Reyes 22s] La reforma de Josías en la óptica deuteronomística: Antonianum 69 (1994) 417-432; Eng. 417.

2745 *Gieselmann* Bernd, [2 Kön 22s] Die sogenannte josianische Reform in der gegenwärtigen Forschung: ZAW 106 (1994) 223-242.

2746 *a) Deurloo* K. A., Chulda's profetie; een collage van woorden uit het boek Jeremia (2 Koningen 22,15-20); – *b) Smelik* K. A. D., *Soest* H.-J. van, Openingsformules in het boek Koningen; – *c) Wit* W. G. de, Voorwerpen in de tempel; en begeleidend motief in het boek Koningen: AmstCah 12 (1993) 106-115 / 62-86 / 87-105; Eng. 133s.

2746* *Edelman* Diana, [2 Kgs 22,14] Huldah the prophet — of Yahweh or Asherah? 1994 ⟶ 2548, FemSam 231-250.

2747 *Sonnet* Jean-Pierre, 'Le livre trouvé; 2 Rois 22 dans sa finalité narrative: NRT 116 (1994) 836-861.

2748 *Laato* Antti, Josiah and David redivivus 1992 ⟶ 8,2994; 9,2850: ᴿBiblica 75 (1994) 250-5 (J. *Becker*); CBQ 56 (1994) 334-6 (M. P. *Graham*); JBL 113 (1994) 519-521 (G. M. *Landes*); TsTKi 65 (1994) 142-4 (T. *Stordalen*, in Norwegian).

2749 *Tagliacarne* Pierfelice, 'Keiner war wie er' ... 2 Kön 22s: AOtt 31, 1989 ⟶ 5,2870 ... 9,2852: ᴿTR 90 (1994) 209 (Eleonore *Reuter*).

2750 **Nakasone** Shigeyuki [2 Kgs 22] Josiah's passover; sociology and the liberating Bible: Bible & Liberation. Mkn 1993, Orbis. xvi-192 p. 0-88344-849-1. – ᴿBL (1994) 95 (R. P. *Carroll*: approves help for coming revolution); JStOT 61 (1994) 124 (P. R. *Davies*); NewTR 7,3 (1994) 83-85 (L. *Boadt*).

2751 *Dever* William G., The silence of the text; an archaeological commentary on 2 Kings 23 [Josiah reform; N. LOHFINK in ᶠCROSS 1987, 459 'mired in detail': archaeology not much help]: ⟶ 67, ᶠKING P., Scripture 1994, 143-168.

2752 *Emerton* J. A., 'The high places of the gates' in 2 Kings XXIII 8: VT 44 (1994) 455-467.

2753 *Larson* Erik, [2 Kgs 24,17; Jer 34; 23] 4Q470 and the angelic rehabilitation of King Zedekiah: ⟶ 337, DSD 1 (1994) 210-228.

2753* **Milikovsky** Chaim [2 Kgs 25,8 *vs.* Jer 52,12], ❿ The date of the destruction of the First Temple according to Seder Olam, the Tosefta and the Babylonian Talmud; studies in the development of a tradition: Tarbiz 62 (1992s) 487-500; Eng. v.

E5.2   *Chronicorum libri* – **The books of Chronicles.**

2754 **Japhet** Sara, 1 & II Chronicles: OTLibrary 1993, ⟶ 9,2861: ᴿBL (1994) 63 (W. *Johnstone*); ÉTRel 69 (1994) 415-7 (J.-D. *Macchi*).

2754* ᵀᴱMcIvor J. Stanley, The Targum of Chronicles [with and after Ruth, but numbered separately 258 p.]: Aramaic Bible 519. E 1994, Clark. (37-) 258 p. [$65; 0-8146-5455-X; NTAbs 38, p. 342].
2755 **Selman** Martin J., I/II Chronicles: Tyndale OT comm. Leicester/DG 1994, Inter-Varsity. 264 p.; p. 265-551. $9.50 + $8.50, 0-85111-847-X; -8-8 [BL 95,75, G. H. *Jones*; TDig 43,87]. – ᴿTBR 7,3 (1994s) 17s (R. *Mason*).
2755* **Thompson** John A., 1,2 Chronicles: NewAmerComm 9. Nv 1994, Broadman & H. 411 p. 0-8054-0109-1.

2756 *Abadie* P., Le fonctionnement symbolique de la figure de David dans l'œuvre du Chroniste: ➤ 461, TEuph 7 (1991/4) 143-151; Eng. 143.
2756* **Ackroyd** Peter R., The Chronicler in his age: jOsu 101, 1991 ➤ 7, 2604 ... 9,2865: ᴿSalesianum 56 (1994) 148 (R. *Vicent*).
Dörrfuss Ernst M., Mose in den Chronikbüchern; Garant theokratischer Zukunftserwartung [< Diss. Berlin]: BZAW 219, 1994 ➤ 2162.
2758 **Duke** R. K., Persuasive appeal: jOsu 38, 1990 ➤ 6,3119 ... 9,2867: ᴿHenoch 16 (1994) 358 (A. *Catastini*).
2759 **Jones** Gwilym H., 1 & 2 Chronicles: OT guides. Shf 1994, JStOT. 139 p. £6.
2760 *Kalimi* Isaac, ⓗ The contribution of the literary study of Chronicles to the solution of its textual problems: Tarbiz 62 (1992s) 471-486; Eng. v.
2761 **Kleinig** John W., The Lord's song; the basis, function and significance of choral music in Chronicles: jOsu 156, 1993 ➤ 9,2873: ᴿBL (1994) 64 (G. H. *Jones*); ᴢAW 106 (1994) 357s (P. *Welten*).
2762 *Kleinig* John W., Recent research in Chronicles: CuRB 2 (1994) 43-76.
2763 **Mason** Rex, Preaching the tradition 1990 ➤ 6,3125 ... 9,2875: ᴿJBL 113 (1994) 135s (M. A. *Throntveit*: insightful).
2764 *Nel* H. W., The Davidic covenant in 1 and 2 Chronicles; a new theme for an old song: In die Skriflig 28 (1991) 429-444 [< OTAbs 18, p. 74].
2765 **Riley** William, King and cultus in Chronicles; Worship and the reinterpretation of history: jOsu 160, 1993 ➤ 9,2877 [JTS 46,217-222, J. L. W. *Schafer*]. – ᴿTBR 7,2 (1994s) 13s (R. *Mason*).
2766 *Ruffing* Andreas, Jahwekrieg als Weltmetapher ... Chr: BoBB 34, 1992 ➤ 8,3020; 9,2878: ᴿBijdragen 55 (1994) 201 (P. C. *Beentjes*).
2766* **Schniedewind** William M., History or homily; toward understanding the Chronicler's purpose; – b) **Brettler** Marc Zvi, From the Deuteronomist(s) to the Chronicler; continuities and innovations: ➤ 331a, 11th Jewish 1993/4, A 91-97 / 83-90.
2767 *Schniedewind* William M., King and priest in the book of Chronicles and the duality of Qumran messianism: JJS 45 (1994) 71-78.
2768 *Steins* Georg, König, Tempel, Leviten ... Chr: kath. diss. Münster 1993, ᴰZenger. – TR 90,86.
2769 *Van Roon* Harry V., Prophet and society in the Persian period according to Chronicles: ➤ 317, Second Temple Studies 2 (1994) 163-178 [146-162, *Willi* T.].
2769* **Weinberg** J. P., [Chr/Ezra] Die Mentalität der jerusalemischen Bürger-Tempel-Gemeinde des 6.-4. Jh. v. u. Z.: TEuph 5 (1992) 133-141.

2770 **Kartveit** Magnar, Motive und Schichten der Landestheologie in 1 Chronik 1-9: ConBib OT 28, ᴰ1989 ➤ 5,2895 ... 8,3023: ᴿTsTKi 65 (1994) 231s (A. *Aschim*, Norwegian).

2770* *Laato* Antti, The Levitical genealogies in 1 Chronicles 5-6 and the formation of Levitical ideology in post-exilic Judah: JStOT 62 (1994) 77-99.
2771 *Augustin* Matthias, [1 Chr 5,1-10] Neue territorialgeschichtliche Aspekte zu 1 Chr 1-9 am Beispiel der Rubeniten: → 115, FSCHUNCK K.-D., Nachdenken 1994, 299-309.
2771* *Heltzer* M., Some considerations about the books of Chronicles [after ch. 1-9] and the Lindos Chronicle [BLINKENBERG C. 1912... 1941]: OrLovPer 23 (1992) 127-142.
2772 *Gilad* David, ❻ The first two deeds of King David (1 Chr 11-13) [puts Temple first; 2 Sam puts his house first]: BeitM 39 (1994) 156-163 [< OTAbs 17, p. 570].
2772* *Bailey* Noel, David's innocence [denied, in the census; 1 Chr 27]; a response to J. WRIGHT; JStOT 60 (1993) 87-105; 64 (1994) 83-90.

2773 *Hognesius* Kjell, The capacity of the molten sea in 2 Chronicles IV 5; a suggestion: VT 44 (1994) 349-358.
2773* *Hobbs* T. R., [2 Chr 11:5-12] The 'fortresses of Rehoboam'; another look: → 102, Mem. RICHARDSON H., Uncovering 1994, 41-64.
2774 *Spanier* Ktziah, [2 Chr 11; 21] The Queen Mother in the Judaean royal court; Maacah and Athaliah; → 331a, 11th Jewish 1993/4, A-75-82.
2774* *Knoppers* Gary N., [2 Chr 17,7 - 19,11] Jehoshaphat's judiciary and 'the scroll of Yhwh's Torah': JBL 113 (1994) 59-80.
2775 *Beentjes* Pancratius C., King Jehoshaphat's prayer; some remarks on 2 Chr 20,6-13: BZ 38 (1994) 264-270.
2775* *Burns* John B., [2 Chr 35,22] Is Neco also among the prophets?: ProcGM 14 (1994) 113-122.
2776 *Handy* Lowell K., Josiah after the Chronicler: ProcGM 14 (1994) 95-103.
2776* *Smit* E. J., [2 Chr 36,6; Jer 36,29] So how did Jehoiakim die?: J/Tyd Sem 6 (1994) 46-56.
2777 *Kalimi* Isaac, *Purvis* James D. [2 Chr 36,9s] King Jehoiachin and the vessels of the Lord's house in biblical literature: CBQ 56 (1994) 449-457.

E5.4   *Esdrae libri* (*etiam 3-5*) – **Ezra, Nehemiah.**

2778 **Breneman** Marvin, Ezra, Nehemiah, Esther: NewAmerComm 10. Nv 1993, Broadman & H. 383 p. $28. 0-8054-0110-5 [BL 95,56, L. L. *Grabbe*].
2779 *Carrez* Maurice, Esdras Septante: RHPR 74 (1994) 13-42; Eng. 112.
2780 EHanhart Robert, Esdrae II: Gö-Septuaginta 1993 → 9,2901 [= Hebrew Ez, Neh; BL 95,50, M. A. *Knibb*]: RTAth 69 (1994) 612-4 (P. *Simotas*).
2781 **Roberts** Mark D., Ezra, Nehemiah, Esther: Communicator'sC OT 11. Dallas 1993, Word. 442 p. $20. 0-8499-941-61 [RB 102,612, É. *Nodet*].
2782 **Throntveit** Mark A., Ezra Nehemiah: Interpretation Comm. 1992 → 9,2908: RCritRR 6 (1993) 184s (J. W. *Wright*); Interpretation 48 (1994) 88.90 (R. K. *Duke*); ZAW 106 (1994) 72s (P. *Welten*).

2782* *Blenkinsopp* Joseph, The Second Temple as house of prayer: → 30, FCOUTURIER G., Maison 1994, 109-122.
2783 EDavies Philip R., Second Temple studies, 1. Persian period: jOsu 117, 1991 [108-124 textual stereotypes, *Carroll* Robert P.] → 9,2897: RBijdragen 55 (1994) 331s (J. van *Ruiten*); TEuph 8 (1994) 163-5 (A. *Sérandour*).

2784 *a) Davies* Philip R. [➤ 9,2897] Sociology and the Second Temple; – *b)* *Grabbe* Lester L., Reconstructing history from the Book of Ezra; – *c)* *Carroll* Robert P., Textual strategies and ideology in the Second Temple period: 2d Temple Studies 1 (1991) 11-19 / 98-106 / 108-124.

2785 *Eskenazi* Tamara C., Current perspectives on Ezra-Nehemiah and the Persian period: CuRB 1 (1993) 59-86.

2786 **Goodblatt** David, The monarchic principle; studies in Jewish self-government in antiquity [Persian period onward]: TStAJ 38. Tü 1994, Mohr. xii-336 p. [RelStR 21,341: M. S. *Joffee*: magisterial].

2787 **Hoglund** Kenneth G., Achaemenid imperial administration in Syria-Palestine and the missions of Ezra and Nehemiah ᴰ1992 ➤ 8,3044; 9,2903 [RB 102,466, E. *Nodet*]: ᴿBInterp 2 (1994) 229-231 (M. W. *Hamilton*); ETL 70 (1994) 141s (J. *Lust*); TEuph 8 (1994) 167-9 (A. *Lemaire*); VT 44 (1994) 429s (H. G. M. *Williamson*, also on JAPHET comm.).

2788 *a) Hoglund* Kenneth, The Achaemenid context; – *b) Smith* Daniel L., The politics of Ezra; sociological indicators of postexilic Judaean society; – *c)* response, *Halligan* John M., Nehemiah 5; – *d) Jobling* David, Texts and the world — an unbridgeable gap: ➤ 2783, ᴱ*Davies* P., Second Temple Studies 1 (1991) 54-72 / 73-97 / 146-153 / 175-182.

2789 **Maier** Johann, Zwischen den Testamenten; Geschichte ... des Zweiten Tempels: NEchter Egb 3, 1990 ➤ 7,9779; 8,a232*: ᴿCritRR 5 (1992) 99-101 (J. *Kampen*); TR 90 (1992) 118-120 (R. G. *Kratz*).

2790 **Maier** Johann [➤ 10689], Storia del Giudaismo nell'antichità 1992 ➤ 8, a464: ᴿHumBr 48 (1993) 768 (F. *Montagnini*).

2791 *Moy* R. G., [exilic, Hellenistic] Biculturalism, race, and the Bible: RelEdn 88 (1993) 415-433 [< NTAbs 38, p. 337].

2792 *Richards* R. R., National reconstruction and literary creativity in Ezra-Nehemiah; a black South African perspective: OTEssays 7 (1994) 277-301.

2793 **Sacchi** Paolo, Storia del Secondo Tempio; Israele tra VI secolo a,C. e I secolo d.C.²ʳᵉᵛ [¹1976]. T 1994, SEI. vi-529 p. 88-05-05377-5 [OTAbs 17, p. 658]. – ᴿTeresianum 45 (1994) 595s (A. *Borrell*).

2794 **Schiffman** Lawrence H., From text to tradition; a history of second temple and rabbinic Judaism 1991 ➤ 7,9970; 9,10705: ᴿCritRR 6 (1993) 427-9 (J. D. *Tabor*).

2795 *Schwartz* Seth, On the autonomy of Judaea in the fourth and third centuries B.C.E.: JJS 45 (1994) 157-168.

2796 **Stiegler** Stefan, Die nachexilische YHWH-Gemeinde in Jerusalem; ein Beitrag zu einer alttestamentlichen Ekklesiologie [diss. Halle 1987]: BeitErfAJ 34. Fra 1994, Lang. 176 p. DM 59. 3-631-45819-1 [TLZ 120,31, R. *Albertz*].

2797 ᴱ**Stone** Michael E., *Satran* David, Emerging Judaism; studies on the fourth and third centuries B.C.E. Mp 1989, Fortress. xiv-178 p. $15. 0-8006-2090-9. – ᴿBijdragen 55 (1994) 330s (J. van *Ruiten*).

2798 **Willi** Thomas, Juda – Jehud – Israel; Studien zum Selbstverständnis des Judentums in persischer Zeit: ev. Diss. ᴰ*Dietrich*. Bern 1993 [TR 90,79].

2799 *Demsky* Aaron, Who came first, Ezra or Nehemiah? The synchronistic approach: HUCA 65 (1994) 1-19.

2800 *Grabbe* Lester L., What was Ezra's mission? ➤ 317, Second Temple Studies 2 (1994) 286-299 [189-216, *Japhet* Sara, chronology; 243-285, *al.*, marriages].

2801 *Abadie* Philippe,   La rupture des mariages mixtes (Esd 7-10) et la lecture de la Loi (Ne 8): Cahiers Évangile 95.
2802 *Oorschot* Jürgen von,   [Esra 9] Nachkultische Psalmen und spätbiblische Rollendichtung: ZAW 106 (1994) 69-86.

2803 *Enomate* J.M.,   The status of Nehemiah [...eunuch]: DeltioVM 12,2 (1993) 25-34.
2804 *Redditt* Paul L.,   Nehemiah's first mission and the date of Zechariah 9-14: CBQ 56 (1994) 664-678.
2805 *Tångberg* Arvid,   Nehemia/-buch: ➤ 517, TRE 24 (1994) 242-6.
2805* *Kröker* Valdemar,   De lamentação para celebração; a mensagem de Neemias: VoxScr 4 (1994) 143-9.
2806 *Crocker* Piers, Nehemiah's wall of Jerusalem [3.1-32]; some new considerations [BAILEY C. 1990 'minimalist']: BurHist 29 (1993) 116-121 [< OTAbs 17, p. 571].
2807 **Mathys** Hans-Peter, [Neh 9 ...] Dichter und Beter; Theologen aus spätalttestamentlicher Zeit: [Hab.-Diss. Bern 1990]. OBO 132. FrS/Gö 1994, Univ./VR.   vii-374 p. DM 132. 3-525-53767-0 / 3-7278-0931-0 [BL 95,115, D.J. *Reimer*]. – ᴿExpTim 106 (1994s) 333s (R. *Mason*); OTAbs 17 (1994) 680s (P. L. *Redditt*); TüTQ 174 (1994) 162s (W. *Gross*).
2808 *Heltzer* M.,   Neh 11,24 and the Provincial Representative at the Persian royal court; ➤ 461, TEuph 8 (1991/4) 109-121; franç. 109.
2809 *Boda* M.J.,   The use of *tôdôt* in Nehemiah XII: VT 44 (1994) 387-393.

2810 *Esler* Philip F.,   The social function of 4 Esra: JStNT 53 (1994) 99-123.
2811 **Klijn** A.F.J., Die Esra-Apokalypse (IV. Esra) 1992 ➤ 8,3060:   ᴿTLZ 119 (1994) 332s (Michaela *Zelzer*).
2812 **Stone** M.E., Textual... IV Ezra 1990 ➤ 6,3168 ... 9,2917: ᴿCritRR 5 (1992) 92s (R. W. *Thomson*).

E5.5 **Libri Tobiae, Judith, Esther.**

2813 **Bonora** Antonio, Tobia; Dio è provvidenza: Comunità degli uomini. Padova 1993, Gregoriana. 150 p. 88-7706-114-6.
2814 **Cheregatti** Arrigo, Tobia; lettura spirituale: Conversazioni bibliche. Bo 1993, Dehoniane. 90 p. Lᵐ 16. 88-10-70938-1 [OTAbs 17, p. 666].
2815 **Drewermann** Eugen, Dieu guérisseur; la légende de Tobit ou le périlleux chemin de la rédemption; interprétation psychologique d'un livre de la Bible. P 1993, Cerf. 121 p. F 69. 2-204-04866-6. – ᴿBLitEc 95 (1994) 239 (J. des *Rochettes*); LavalTP 50 (1994) 415-420 (J.-J. *Lavoie*); RHPR 74 (1994) 102s (B. *Kaempf*).
2816 *Kollmann* Bernd,   Göttliche Offenbarung magisch-pharmakologischer Heilkunst im Buch Tobit: ZAW 106 (1994) 289-299.
2817 *Manfredi* Manfredo,   Un frammento del libro di Tobit LXX, Tobias 12,6-7,8-11: ➤ 86, ᶠNALDINI M., Paideia 1994, 175-9; 2 fot.
2817* *Ravasi* Gianfranco, [Tob 13] Il cantico della misericordia: ParSpV 29 (1994) 73-84.
2818 **Rabenau** Marten,   Studien zum Buch Tobit [diss. Marburg 1992, ᴰ*Kaiser*

O. ➤ 8,3072]: BZAW 220.   B 1994, de Gruyter.   viii-249 p.; Bibliog. 201-
219.   3-11-014125-6 [BL 95,165, L. L. *Grabbe*].

2819 *Bal* Mieke,   Head hunting; 'Judith' on the cutting edge of knowledge:
JStOT 63 (1994) 3-34; 13 fig.
2820 *Clayton* M.,   ÆLFRIC's Judith; manipulative or manipulated?: Anglo-
Saxon England 23 (1994) 215-227 [RHE 90,51*].
2821 **Curry** Peggy L.,   Representing the biblical Judith in literature and art;
an intertextual cultural critique: diss. Massachusetts, ᴰ*Smith* C. 1994.
214 p. 99-34470. – DissA 55 (1994s) p. 2374.
2822 **Hellmann** M.,   Judit: EurHS 23/444,   ᴰ1992 ➤ 8,3074:   ᴿZAW 106
(1994) 355 (M. *Köckert*).
2823 *Henten* Jan W. van,   Judith as a female Moses; Judith 7-13 in the
light of Ex 17, Num 20 and Dt 33,8-11: ➤ 267, RefTGender 1992/4,
33-48.
2824 **Herrmann** Wolfram, [Judith] Jüdische Glaubensfundamente: BErfAJ 36.
Fra 1994, Lang.   117 p. $27.   3-631-45187-2 [OTAbs 18, p. 162].
2825 *Roitman* Adolfo D.,   'This people are descendants of Chaldeans' (Judith
5:6); its literary form and historical setting: JBL 113 (1994) 245-263.
2825* *Schaker* Zina,   Une veuve nommée Judith: Tychique 107 (1994) 31-36.
2826 ᴱ**VanderKam** James C.,   'No one spoke ill...' Judith 1992 ➤ 8,500*;
9,2928:   ᴿJSS 38 (1993) 320-2 (G. J. *Brooke*).

2827 ᴱ**Grossfeld** Bernard,   The Targum Sheni to the Book of Esther; a critical
edition based on MS. Sassoon 282 with critical apparatus.   NY 1994,
Sepher-Hermon. xvii-195 p. $50.   0-87203-142-X.
2828 **Grossfeld** Bernard,   The two targums of Esther: Aramaic Bible 18, 1991
➤ 7,2675:   ᴿCBQ 56 (1994) 108s (D. M. *Golomb*).
2829 **Segal** Eliezer,   The Babylonian Esther midrash, a critical commentary:
BrownJud 291-3.   Atlanta 1994, Scholars.   I. xi-330 p.; bibliog. 295-309;
II.   xx-360 p. bibliog. 311-328; III. xx-308 p. bibliog. 259-286.   1-
55540-996-2; -7-0; -8-9 [BL 95,168, M. *Maher*].

2830 *Barbaglia* Silvio,   Il messaggio del libro di Ester (ebraico): RivB 42
(1994) 257-309; Eng. 310.
2831 *Heltzer* Michael,   [Esth 2,21-23] Mordekhai and Demaratos and the
question of historicity: ArchMIran 27 (1994) 119-121.
2832 *Börner-Klein* Dagmar,   Der Ester-Midrasch in Megilla 10b-17a; eine
literarische Einheit: Judaica 49 (1993) 220-7.
2833 **Brenner** Athalya,   A feminist companion to Esther, Judith and Susanna:
FCompB 7. Shf c. 1994, Academic.   336 p. $24.50.   1-85075-527-2.
2834 *Butting* Klara,   The book of Esther; a reinterpretation of the story of
Josef; innerbiblical critique as a guide for feminist hermeneutics: Amst-
Cah 13 (1994) 81-87.
2835 **Fox** Michael V.,   Character and ideology in the book of Esther 1991
➤ 7,2672 ... 9,2932:   ᴿAJS 19 (1994) 247-9 (R. L. *Cohn*); Biblica 75 (1994)
106-112 (Adèle *Berlin*, also on his Redaction 1991 ➤ 7,2673); JRel 74
(1994) 88s (J. J. *Collins*: excellent); JSS 39 (1994) 317-320 (H. G. M.
Williamson, also on his Redaction).

2836 *Horowitz* Elliott, **O** '... And it was reversal'; Jews and their enemies in the festival of Purim: Zion 59 (1994) 129-168; Eng. x.
2837 *Langenhorst* Horst G., 'Überall blickt Gott auf Ester'; literarische Deutungen der biblischen Figur in unserer Zeit: KIsr 9 (1994) 150-167.
2838 *Loewenclau* Ilse von, Apologie für Ester: → 115, FSCHUNK K.-D., Nachdenken 1994, 251-277.
2839 *Noss* Philip A., A footnote on time; the book of Esther: BTrans 44 (1993) 309-320.
2840 *Rubenstein* Jeffrey, Purim, liminality and communitas: AJS 17 (1992) 247-277.
2841 **Walfish** Barry D., Esther in medieval garb 1993 → 9,2941 [RB 102,466, E. *Nodet*]: RBL (1994) 78 (S.C. *Reif*); ZAW 106 (1994) 542 (L. *Bultmann*).

E5.8   *Machabaeorum libri*,   **1-2 [-4] Maccabees.**

2842 **Balla** George E., The four centuries between the testaments; a survey of Israel and the diaspora from 336 BC to 94 AD. Richland Hills TX 1993, BIBAL. xii-71 p.; 10 maps. $8 [TDig 42,155].
2843 **Bar-Kochva** Bezalel, Judas Maccabaeus 1989 → 5,2960 ... 9,2945: RCritRR 5 (1992) 94-97 (G. E. *Sterling*: new level); JNES 53 (1994) 314s (E. A. *Knauf*); JQR 84 (1993s) 346s (U. *Rappaport*).
2844 *Bar-Kochva* Bezalel, On JOSEPHUS and the books of the Maccabees; philology and historiography: Tarbiz 62 (1992s) 115-132 (Eng. VII), defense of his Mcb. against 60 (1990s) 443-450 by D. *Schwartz*.
2845 **Bickerman** Elias, Gli ebrei in età greca [1988], T1991 → 7,2683; 9,2946: RQuadStor 35 (1992) 165-8 (L. *Canfora*).
2846 *Efron* Joshua, Studies in the Hasmonean period [1963-76; compiled **O** 1980], T1987 → 4,3088; 5,2964: RJAOS 114 (1994) 87s (L. H. *Feldman*: restores primacy to Jerusalem over Babylonian Talmud).
    Grabbe L. L., Judaism from Cyrus to Hadrian I-II, 1992 → 9782.
2847 **Kampen** John, The Hasideans... 1-2 Mcb 1988 → 4,3093 ... 9,2957: RRB 100 (1993) 614s (É. *Nodet*).
2848 *Keller* Hagen, Machabaeorum pugnae; zum Stellenwert eines biblischen Vorbilds in WIDUKINDs Deutung der ottonischen Königsherrschaft: → 52, FHAUCK K., Iconologia 1994, 417-437.
2849 **Sievers** Joseph, The Hasmoneans and their supporters 1990 → 6,3210 ... 9,2960: RAJS 17 (1992) 284-6 (J. *Kampen*); Biblica 77 (1994) 112-5 (Angelika *Strotmann*); JSS 39 (1994) 325s (M. *Goodman*).

2850 *a*) *Nielsen* Inge, The Hellenistic palaces of the Jewish kings; – *b*) *Strange* John, Hellenism in archaeology: → 89e, FOTZEN B., In the last days 1994, 181-4 / 175-180.
2850* *Hossfeld* Frank-Lothar, Volk Israel und Diaspora; bibeltheologische Überlegungen: LebZeug 49 (1994) 10-20.
2851 *Sisti* Adalberto, L'attesa del profeta fedele al tempo dei Maccabei: LA 44 (1994) 47-82; Eng. 611.
2852 **Unnik** Willem C. van †, EHorst P. van der, Das Selbstverständnis der jüdischen Diaspora 1993 [RB 102,615, É. *Nodet*]. – RStPhilonAn 6 (1994) 192-9 (F. *Siegert*, deutsch).

2853 *Marangon* Antonio, Il primo libro dei Maccabei: RClerIt 75 (1994) 436-443.

2854 *Feldmann* Louis H.,   *a*) JOSEPHUS' portrayal of the Hasmoneans compared with 1 Maccabees: ➤ 123, Mem. SMITH M., Josephus 1992/4,
41-68; − *b*) Hebraism and Hellenism reconsidered: Judaism 43 (1994)
115-126.
2855 *Nodet* É., Mattathias, Samaritains et Asmonéens: ➤ 461, Syrie, TEuph
7 (1991/4) 93-107; Eng. 93.
2856 *González Echegaray* Joaquín, La doble expedición de Lisias a Judea,
comentando a 1 Mac 4,26-35 y 6,28-63: ➤ 22, ᶠCASCIARO J., Biblia 1994,
147-174.
2857 *Knauf* Ernst A., 1. Makk 9,35-41 oder eine transjordanische Art der
Konfliktbewältigung (Supplementa ismaelitica 15): BibNot 75 (1994)
18-20.

2858 *Gądecki* Stanisław, ⦿ Historiografia w 2 Księdze Machabejskiej: RuBi
47 (1994) 1-17.
2859 *Kalimi* Isaac, *Purvis* James D., [2 Mcb 2,7s; 2 Baruch 6,7s] The hiding of
the Temple vessels in Jewish and Samaritan literature: CBQ 56 (1994)
679-685.
2860 *Cohen* Getzel M., [2 Mcb 4,9] The 'Antiochenes in Jerusalem' again:
➤ 133, ᶠWACHOLDER B. Z. 1994, 243-259.
2861 *Parente* Fausto, *Toùs en Ierosolýmois Antiocheîs anagrápsai* (II Macc.
IV,9); Gerusalemme è mai stata una polis?: RivStoLR 30 (1994) 3-38.
2862 *Witakoski* Witold, Mart(y) Shmuni, the mother of the Maccabean
martyrs, in Syriac tradition: ➤ 450*c*, Syriacum 6 (1992/4) 153-168; color.
phot.
2863 *Storniolo* Ivo, [2 Mcb 7] Família sem pai: Vida Pastoral 174 (São Paulo
1994) 13-20 [< Stromata 50,277].
2864 *Vinson* M., Gregory NAZIANZEN's homily 15 and the genesis of the
Christian cult of the Maccabean martyrs: Byzantion 64 (1994) 166-192
[< JStJud 25,360].
2865 *Wilk* R., [2 Mcb 13,33] ⦿ The abuse of Nicanor's corpse: Sidra 8 (1992)
53-57 [< JStJud 25,167].

2866 **Kraus Reggiani** Clara, 4 Macc comm. 1992 ➤ 8,3109: ᴿStPhilonAn 6
(1994) 186-8 (N. *Walter*).

───────────

VII. Libri didactici VT

E6.1   *Poesis 1. metrica,* **Biblical** and Semitic **versification.**

2867 **Alonso Schökel** Luis, Antología de la poesía hebrea, bilingüe² 1992
➤ 8,3111; 9,2968: ᴿActuBbg 31 (1994) 37 (J. *González Faus*); LumenVr
43 (1994) 379s (F. *Ortiz de Urtaran*); RazF 228 (1993) 467s (J. M.
Vallarino).
2868 **apRoberts** Ruth, The biblical web [Hebrew poetry...]. AA 1994, Univ.
Michigan. viii-191 p. 0-472-10494-2.
2869 **Berlin** Adele, The dynamics of biblical parallelism 1985 ➤ 1,2983...
4,3110: ᴿAulaO 12 (1994) 136s (G. del *Olmo Lete*).
2870 **Berlin** Adele, Biblical poetry through medieval Jewish eyes 1991
➤ 7,2713; 9,2970: ᴿLitTOx 8 (1994) 108s (W. *Moberly*); VT 44 (1994)
417s (Meira *Pollack*).

Ceresko Anthony R., Psalmists and sages [chiasm ... Ps 21, 34, 63, 105, 146] 1994 ➤ 165.
2872 **Gillingham** S. K., The poems and psalms of the Hebrew Bible. Ox 1994, UP. xiii-311 p.; bibliog. 378-387. 0-19-213243-1. – ᴿExpTim 106,1 top choice (1994s) 1s (C. S. *Rodd*); NBlackf 75 (1994) 543-6 (G. *Moore*: some arguable points).
2873 *Gruber* Mayer I., The meaning of biblical parallelism; a biblical perspective: Prooftexts 13 (1993) 289-293.
2874 *Payne* Geoffrye, Parallelism in biblical Hebrew verse; some secular thoughts: ScandJOT 8 (1994) 126-140.
2875 **Petersen** David L., *Richards* Kent H., Interpreting Hebrew poetry 1992 ➤ 8,3121: ᴿCBQ 56 (1994) 337s (W. G. E. *Watson*); RBibArg 56 (1994) 123s (P. *Andiñach*); TorJT 10 (1994) 112s (J. L. *McLaughlin*).
2876 *Spieckermann* H., Alttestamentliche Hymnen: ➤ 310, Hymnen 1991/4, 97-108.
2877 *Watson* Wilfred G. E., Ethnopoetics and Hebrew verse; ineditum: ➤ 230c, Traditional 1994, 31-44.
Watts James W., Psalm and story; inset hymns in Hebrew narrative; jOsu 138, 1992 ➤ 2224.

E6.2 **Psalmi, textus.**

2878 *Anderson* Jeffrey C., The Palimpsest Psalter, Pantokrator Cod. 61, its content and relationship to the Bristol Psalter: DumbO 48 (1994) 199-220; 16 fig.
2879 **Auwers** Jean-Marie, Le Psautier hébraïque et ses éditeurs; recherches sur une forme canonique du Livre des Psaumes: diss. ᴰ*Bogaert* P. LvN 1994. 612 p. (3 vol.). – RTLv 25,285s; 26, p. 530; Travaux 16/1; RB 101 (1994) 242-257.
2880 **Corrigan** Kathleen, Visual polemics in the ninth century Byzantine psalters. C 1992, Univ. xvi-325 p. – ᴿChH 63 (1994) 262s (G. T. *Dennis*); RÉByz 52 (1994) 390-2 (C. *Walter*).
2881 **Gabra** Gawdat, Bemerkungen zu einigen Wörtern des oxyrhynchitischen (mesokemischen) Psalters: ➤ 65, ᶠKASSER R., Coptology 1994, 193-5.
2882 **Gibson** Margaret, *al.*, The Eadwine psalter 1992 ➤ 9,2984: ᴿJEH 45 (1994) 135s (B. C. *Barker-Benfield*); Speculum 69 (1994) 1168-71 (Marcia *Kupfer*).
2883 *Defaux* G., MAROT [Clément], traducteur des Psaumes; de nouveau sur l'édition anonyme (et genevoise) de 1543: BtHumRen 56 (1994) 59-82.

E6.3 **Psalmi, introductio.**

2884 *Anderson* R. Deanᴶ, The division and order of the Psalms: WestTJ 56 (1994) 219-241.
2885 ᴱ**Burkert** W., *Stolz* E., Hymnen der Alten Welt im Kulturvergleich: OBO 137. FrS/Gö 1994, Univ/VR. – ᴿExpTim 106 (1994s) 334 (R. *Mason*).
2886 ᴱ**Corona** Raimondo, I Salmi, lettura esegetico-esistenziale: Settimana Biblica Abruzzese 8, Tocco Casauria 6-10 luglio 1993. L'Aquila 1994, Curia Prov. OFM. 256 p.
2887 **Day** J., Psalms: OTGuides, 1990 ➤ 8,3137: ᴿRCatalT 18 (1993) 177 (F. *Raurell*).
2888 *a) Gerstenberger* Erhard S., Der Psalter als Buch und als Sammlung; –

b) Koch Klaus, Der Psalter und seine Redaktionsgeschichte: ➤ 15,
[F]BEYERLIN W., Neue Wege 1994, 3-13 / 243-277.
2889 **Girard** Marc, Les psaumes redécouverts; de la structure au sens:
Psaumes 2s. Saint-Laurent 1994, Bellarmin. 624 p.; $35; 564 p.; $32.
2-89007-557-5. – [R]ÉglT 25 (1994) 130s (W. *Vogels*).
2890 GREGORY of Nyssa, Commentary on the inscriptions of the Psalms,
[T]*McCambley* Casimir: Iakovos Library 17. Brookline MA 1987, Hellenic
College. xii-150 p. 0-917653-45-9.
2891 GREGORIO di Nissa, Sui titoli dei Salmi, [TE]*Traverso* Alberto: TPatr 110.
R 1994, Città Nuova. 236 p. 88-311-3110-9.
2892 **Hurvitz** Avi, *a)* ✡ *Šᵉqîᶜê ḥokmâh*... Wisdom language in biblical
psalmody. J 1991, Magnes. 162 p. – *b)* ✡ *Bên lāšôn la-lāšôn*... The
transition period in biblical Hebrew; a study in post-exilic Hebrew and
its implications for dating of [Wisdom] psalms. J 1972, Mosad Bialik. –
[R]JQR 84 (1993s) 319s (I. B. *Gottlieb*).
2893 **Kuntz** J. Kenneth, Engaging the Psalms; gains and trends in recent
research: CuBR 2 (1994) 77-106.
2894 **Longman** T., How to read the Psalms 1988 ➤ 4,3117; 5,3918: [R]JEvTS
37 (1994) 138s (F. C. *Putnam*).
2895 [E]**McCann** J. Clinton, The shape and shaping of the Psalter: jOsu 159,
1993 ➤ 9,395: [R]BL (1994) 68 (J. H. *Eaton*); Interpretation 48 (1994) 426
(M. *Goulder*); VT 44 (1994) 134s (P. E. *Satterthwaite*).
2896 **McCann** J. Clinton, A theological introduction to the Book of Psalms;
the Psalms as Torah [... 'God's instruction to the faithful'] also L 1994,
SPCK. £14; 0-687-41468-7: [R]ExpTim 106 (1994s) 287 [C. S. *Rodd*];
TBR 6,3 (1993s) 20 (R. *Coggins*).
2897 **Mays** James L., The Lord reigns; a theological handbook to the Psalms.
LvL 1994, W-Knox. ix-159 p.; $17 pa. 0-665-25558-2 [OTAbs 18,
p. 417, J. O. P., not listed; TDig 42,376].
2898 **Murphy** Roland E., Responses to 101 questions on the Psalms and
other Writings. NY 1994, Paulist. xii-128 p. $9. 0-8091-3630-9 [BL
95,71, A. H. W. *Curtis*; TDig 43,78].
2899 **Pleins** J. David, The Psalms; songs of tragedy, hope, and justice: The
Bible and Liberation, 1993 ➤ 9,2997: [R]TBR 7,3 (1994s) 19 (A. *Gilmore*:
in order of subject matter 'which makes it easier').
2900 *Ribera-Mariné* Ramon, Structures arithmétiques du Psautier; quelques
exemples: RCatalT 18 (1993) 151-161; Eng. 162.
[E]**Seybold** Klaus, *Zenger* Erich, Neue Wege der Psalmenforschung 1994
➤ 15, [F]BEYERLIN W.
2901 [**Solms** Élisabeth de, *Jean-Nesmy* Claude, Psautier IV [1977 =] Unité du
Psautier chrétien. P 1993, Téqui. 400 p. – [R]RThom 94 (1994) 159s (X.
Perrin: le nouveau titre, heureux, reflète l'unité même de la vie chrétienne).
2901* **Willard** Matthias, Die Komposition des Psalters; ein formgeschicht-
licher Ansatz [Diss. Heid, [D]*Rendtorff* R.]: ForAT 9. Tü 1994, Mohr.
ix-299 p. [BL 95,97, J. H. *Eaton*].
2902 **Wittstruck** Thorme, The Book of Psalms, an annotated bibliography:
Garland Ref 1413, Bible 5. NY 1994, Garland. 480 p.; p. 481-984. $145.
0-8240-4700-1 [TDig 42, p. 296].

E6.4   Psalmi, commentarii.

2903 **Alonso Schökel** Luis, *Carniti* Cecilia, Salmos (Estella) 1992s ➤ 8,3147*a;
9,3005: [R]EstE 69 (1994) 548s (J. R. *Busto Saiz*); QVidCr 170 (1994) 135s
(Hilari *Raguer*).

2904 **Alonso Schökel** L., *Carniti* C., I Salmi 1992s ⇥ 8,3147*... 9,2004; 886 p.: ᴿCC 145 (1994,1) 404-7 (G. *Borgonovo*); ParVi 39,4 (1994) 52s (T. *Lorenzin*).

2905 ᴱ**Boese** Helmut, Anonymi Glosa psalmorum ex traditione seniorum I (1-100) ⇥ 8,3149; 9,3006; II (101-150): VLat 25. FrB, Herder. I. 1992; 72* + 471 p.; II. 1994, 24* + 287 p. 3-451-22692-0; -1951-4. – ᴿJTS 45 (1994) 363s (M. *Gibson*); NRT 116 (1994) 264s (V. *Roisel*).

2906 **Booij** T., Psalmen III (81-110): PredikOT Nijkerk 1994, Callenbach. 328 p. ƒ99,50. 90-266-0734-2 [OTAbs 17, p.669; BL 95,55, J.W. *Rogerson*]. – ᴿTvT 34 (1994) 441 (B. *Standaert*).

2907 **Cattani** Luigi, KIMCHI D., Commento ai Salmi I (1-50) 1991 ⇥ 8,3151: ᴿRivB 42 (1994) 355-7 (M. *Perani*).

2908 ᵀᴱ**Coppa** Giovanni, ORIGENE-GEROLAMO, 74 omelie sul Libro dei Salmi: Letture cristiane del primo millennio 13. Mi 1993, EP. 744 p. Lᵐ45. – ᴿRasT 35 (1994) 509s (E. *Cattaneo*); RicScR 8 (1994) 235s (P. *Fragnelli*).

2909 **Dorival** Gilles, Les chaînes exégétiques grecques sur les Psaumes: SpicSLv 43-45. Lv 1986 [⇥ 3,2984]/89 [⇥ 7,2758]/92, Peeters. 328 p.; 386 p.; 570 p. – ᴿRechSR 82 (1994) 634s (B. *Sesboüé*); RHE 89 (1994) 107s (Françoise *Petit*).

2910 **Hossfeld** F.-L., *Zenger* E., Die Psalmen, 1-50: NEcht 29, 1993: ᴿTLtg 67 (1994) 250-4 (N. *Lohfink*); ZAW 106 (1994) 523 (H. *Spieckermann*).

2911 ᴱ**Kasper** Walter, *al.*, Ich lobe dich von ganzer Seele; alle 150 Psalmen mit Auslegungen. Stu 1993, Kreuz. 380 p. DM 29,80; Studienausgabe 19,80.

2912 **Kraus** H.-J., Los Salmos 1-59, 1993 ⇥ 9,3016: ᴿPhase 33 (1993) 249-253 (J. *Latorre*) [II. 1995, p. 569-883; 84-301-1170-0].

2913 **Łach** Stanisław, ❷ Księga Psalmów: PismoŚ ST 7/2. Poznań 1990, Pallottinum. 738 p. – ᴿBZ 38 (1994) 302s (J. *Scharbert*).

2913* **Levine** Herbert J., Sing to the Lord a new song; a contemporary reading of the Psalms: StBibLit. Bloomington 1995, Indiana Univ. xvii-279 p.; bibliog. 257-272. 0-253-33341-5.

2914 **Magonet** Jonathan, A rabbi reads the Psalms [19 and 12 others]. L 1994, SCM. 200 p. £13. 0-334-01364-X [BL 95,95, R. P. R. *Murray*; OTAbs 18, p. 164]. – ᴿExpTim 105 (1993s) 354s (C. S. *Rodd*).

2915 **Mays** James L., Psalms: Interp. comm. LVL 1994, W-Knox. xi-457 p. $30. 0-8042-3115-X [TDig 42,177; TS 56,355s, W. *Soll*]. – ᴿExpTim 106 (1994s) 86s (C. S. *Rodd*); TBR 7,3 (1994) 19s (A. *Warren*: more pastoral than academic).

2916 [ᴱ**Nowell** Irene], The revised Psalms of the New American Bible, authorized by Catholic Bishops' Conference. NY 1992, Catholic Book. $5. – ᴿCBQ 56 (1994) 570s (H. P. *Nasuti*: text identical with Collegeville Annotated 1991 but notes are inserted at point needed). ⇥ 2966.

2916* **Prévost** Jean-Pierre, Piccolo dizionario dei Salmi: QuadB 4. R 1991, Borla. 64 p. Lᵐ 12. – ᴿParVi 39,2 (1994) 63 (T. *Lorenzin*).

2917 ᵀ**Prinzivalli** Emanuela, ORIGENE, Omelie sui Salmi 36-38, 1991 ⇥ 8,3162; 9,3019: ᴿCompostellanum 38 (1993) 242s (E. *Romero Pose*).

2918 **Prinzivalli** Emanuela, La tradizione manoscritta e le edizioni delle Omelie sui Salmi di ORIGENE tradotte da RUFINO: VetChr 31 (1994) 155-169.

2919 **Ravasi** Gianfranco, ᴱ*Michaud* Robert, Les Psaumes [1988]. Montréa/p 1993, Paulines / Médiaspaul. 959 p. $40 [ÉglT 25, 282-4, W. *Vogels*].

2920 **Spurgeon** Charles, Psalms I-II = The treasury of David 1869-83; Wheaton IL 1993, Crossway. xvi-366 p.; xiv-374 p. £8 each. 1-85684-083-2; -4-0 [BL 95,76, J. H. *Eaton*, high praise].

2921 **Tate** Marvin E., Psalms 51-100: Word comm. 20, 1990 ➤ 6,3264*b*...
9,3024: ᴿJTS 45 (1994) 184s (G.W. *Anderson*); SvEx 59 (1994) 170s
(L.O. *Eriksson*).

2922 *Vian* Giovanni M., La tradizione esegetica alessandrina sui Salmi; alla
ricerca dell'ORIGENE perduto: ➤ 86, ᶠNALDINI M., Paideia 1994,
219-226.

2923 ᵀᴱ**Walsh** P.G., CASSIODORUS, explanation of the Psalms [I-III ➤ 9,
3025s]: AnCWr 51.52.53. NY 1990s, Newman. vi-618 p.; vi-528 p.; vi-
543 p. $35 each. 0-8091-0441-5; -4-X; -5-8. – ᴿChrSchR 24 (1994) 89-92
(A. *Ferriro*, repeated 330-2 with spelling Ferreiro).

2924 *Zorzi Pugliese* Olga, Il commento di Girolamo BENIVIENI ai salmi
penitenziali: VivH 5/2 (1994) 475-493; Eng. 494.

E6.5 Psalmi, themata.

2925 *Adutwum* Ofosu, *Batach* in the book of the Psalms: IrBSt 15 (1993)
28-38.

2926 **Avishur** Yitzhak, Studies in Hebrew and Ugaritic psalms: Perry
Foundation. J 1994, Hebrew Univ. 388 p.; bibliog. 334-368. $35. 965-
223-864-3.

2927 **Brueggemann** W., Abiding astonishment 1991 ➤ 7,2771... 9,3031: ᴿInterpretation 47 (1993) 66-68 (R.W. *Nysse*, also on his Interpretation and
Obedience 1991); Mid-Stream 32,4 (1993) 117s (R.H. *Boyte*); Vidyajyoti
58 (1994) 124s (P. *Mangal*).

2928 **Creach** Jerome F.D., The choice of Yahweh as refuge [*hasah*] and the
editing of the Hebrew Psalter: diss. Union Theol. Sem., ᴰ*Mays* J.
Richmond 1991. 228 p. 94-27921. – DissA 55 (1994s) p. 1589.

2929 **Dhanaraj** Dharmakkan, Theological significance of the motif of
enemies: OrBibChr 4, ᴰ1993 ➤ 8,3177: ᴿZAW 106 (1994) 153s (H.
Spieckermann).

2929* *Dines* Jenny, [Lament psalms] Rage against God!: PrPeo 8 (1994)
103-7.

2930 **Fischer** Irmtraud, *a*) Selig, wer auf die Tora mit Lobliedern antwortet
[Psalmen]; – *b*) Bestätigung geglückten Lebens; Seligpreisungen im AT
[Spr; 1 Kön 10,8]: TPQ 142 (1994) 192-196 / 57-62.

2931 **Gesigora** Gerd, Studium zur humanistischen Psalmenexegese des 15.
und 16. Jahrhunderts: kath. Diss. ᴰ*Riedlinger*. Freiburg/B 1994. – TR
91,95; RTLv 26, p. 544.

2932 **Girard** Marc, Les Psaumes miroir de la vie des pauvres: Lectures
Bibliques. Montréal 1993, Paulines. 118 p. F 50. – ᴿÉTRel 69 (1994)
101 (P. *Auffret*).

2933 *a*) *Girardi* Mario, Appunti per una definizione dell'esegesi allegorica di
BASILIO di Cesarea, le Omelie sui Salmi; – *b*) *Gori* Franco, Da una
compilazione medievale sui Salmi; recuperi per i commentari di GIRO-
LAMO, di PROSPERO di Aquitania e di ARNOBIO il Giovane: ➤ 330*a*,
X-Viverone 1992/3, 405-529 / 531-566 + 4pl.; Eng. 277.

2934 **Haufe** Martin, Die naturhaften Phänomene in den Psalmen: diss. Greifswald, ᴰ*Zobel*. – TR 90,85.

2935 **Hunter** Jannie H., Interpretationstheorie in der postmodernen Zeit;
Suche nach Interpretationsmöglichkeiten anhand von Psalm 144: ➤ 15,
ᶠBEYERLIN W., Neue Wege 1993/4, 45-62.

2936 **Jauss** Hannelore, Tor der Hoffnung, Vergleichsformen... Pss: EurHS
23/412, ᴰ1991 ➤ 7,2778; 8,3184: ᴿBiKi 45 (1994) 73 (E. *Bone*).

2937 **Lindström** Fredrik, Suffering and sin [psalms of complaint]. Sto 1994, Almqvist & W. 500 p. Sk 310. 91-22-0150-9 [OTAbs 17, p. 668]. – ᴿExpTim 105,12 (1993s) 354 (C. R. *Rodd*: tied with MAGONET for second place); TLZ 119 (1994) 979-981 (M. *Oeming*).
2938 *MacCoull* L. S. B., Further notes on P. Gr. Wess. Prag. 3: Greek psalm antiphons in 11th century Egypt: EphLtg 106 (1992) 167-170.
2939 *Maire* Thierry, Dieu n'échappe pas à la réalité; la réussite des impies, un défi pour la foi du Psalmiste: ÉTRel 69 (1994) 173-183.
2940 *Manicardi* Luciano, L'amore di Dio nei Salmi: ParVi 37,1 (1992) 14-25.
2941 **Mathias** D., Die Geschichtstheologie ... Summarien Pss ᴰ1993 ➤ 9,3045: ᴿTLZ 119 (1994) 982s (T. *Krüger*).
2942 *Miller* Patrick D., Dietrich BONHOEFFER and the Psalms; – b) *Duff* Nancy J., D. Bonhoeffer's theological ethic; PrincSemB 15 (1994) 274-281 / 263-273.
2943 **Neveu** Louis, Au pas des psaumes 4, 1993 (fin): CCLLR 11, ➤ 9,3018: ᴿÉglT 25 (1994) 128 (W. *Vogels*).
2944 a) *Nowell* Irene, The 'cursing' psalms; – b) *Perelmuter* Hayim, The Bible in Judaism: BToday 32 (1994) 218-222 / 247-251.
2945 *Ravasi* Gianfranco, Delitto e perdono nel Salterio: Ambrosius 70 (1994) 323-342.
2946 **Sailhamer** H. John, [Ps 3-41] Translational technique ... Greek/Hebrew verbs 1991 ➤ 7,2787; 9,2052: ᴿSalesianum 56 (1994) 380s (M. *Cimosa*).
2947 *Savage* Alan D., 'En simplicité du langage de Canaan'; Agrippa D'AUBIGNE, 'Méditations sur les Psaumes' [Huguenot]: diss. ᴰ*Desan* P. Ch 1994. 250 p. 94-25420. – DissA 55 (1994s) p. 982.
2948 **Schwager** Raymund, 'Lüge auf Lüge, Gewalt auf Gewalt'; die Rotte der Gewalttäter in den Psalmen Israels: Entschluss 49,9s (1994) 32-38.
2949 **Sperling** Uwe, Das theophanische Jahwe-Überlegenheitslied ... Zionlieder 1991 ➤ 7,2789; 9,3053: ᴿBO 51 (1994) 410-2 (P. J. *Botha*).
2950 a) *Spieckermann* Hermann, Rede Gottes und Wort Gottes in den Psalmen; – b) *Müller* Hans-Peter, Gottesfrage und Psalmenexegese; zur Hermeneutik der Klagepsalmen des Einzelnen; – c) *Greenberg* Moshe, Hittite royal prayers and biblical petitionary psalms: ➤ 15, ᶠBEYERLIN W., Neue Wege 1994, 157-173 / 279-299 / 15-27.
2951 **Sylva** Dennis D., Psalms [131; 23; 117; 107; 92; 62; 123] and the transformation of stress; poetic communal interpretation and the family: LvTPast 16. Lv c. 1993, Peeters. xv-367 p. 90-6831-634-6.
2952 **Zenger** Erich, Ein Gott der Rache?: Feindpsalmen verstehen. FrB 1994, Herder. 188 p. DM 38. 3-451-23332-0. – ᴿEntschluss 49,11 (1994) 43s (C. *Schwaiger*).

E6.6 *Psalmi: oratio, liturgia* – **Psalms as prayer.**

2953 **Arocena Solano** Félix, Orationes super Psalmos e ritu hispano-mozarabico; ad Laudes matutinas et Vesperas per quattuor hebdomadas Psalterii distributas. Toledo 1993, S. Ildefonso, Sem. Conciliar. 242 p. 84-604-5945-4.
2954 **Asensio** F., La oración en los Salmos 1991 ➤ 9,3057: ᴿRET 54 (1994) 88s (P. *Barrado Fernández*).
2955 **Craven** Toni, The Book of Psalms: MessageBSpir 6, 1992 ➤ 8,3152; 9,3059: ᴿBL (1994) 55 (J. M. *Dines*); CBQ 56 (1994) 327 (P. D. *Miller*); ExpTim 105 (1993s) 22 (J. *Eaton*).

2956 *Daschner* Dominik, Meditation oder Antwort — zur Funktion des Antwortpsalms: HDienst 48 (1994) 131-153 . 200-220.

2957 *Gerstenberger* Erhard S., Weibliche Spiritualität in Psalmen und Hauskult: OBO 139 ➤ 467*, Ein Gott allein? 1993/4, 349-363.

2958 **Gilbert** Maurice, Les louanges du Seigneur 1991 ➤ 7,2802 ... 9,3060: ᴿAtKap 121 (1993) 443s (B. *Nadolski* ❷).

2959 **Gilbert** M., Ogni vivente 1991s ➤ 7,2802; 8,3206: ᴿAsprenas 41 (1994) 137s (V. *Scippa*).

2960 **Goulder** Michael, The prayers of David [Ps 51-72]: jOsu 102, 1990 ➤ 6,3332 ... 9,3062: ᴿBZ 38 (1994) 112s (N. *Lohfink*).

2960* a) *Harman* Allan M., The Psalms and Reformed spirituality; – b) *Velema* W. H., Preaching on the Psalms: RefTR 53 (1994) 53-62 / 63-72.

2961 **Holladay** W., The psalms ... prayerbook 1993 ➤ 9,3063: ᴿBL (1994) 61 (D. J. *Bryan*); Interpretation 48 (1994) 287-9 (J. L. *Mays*); OTAbs 17 (1994) 221s (M. S. *Smith*); TS 55 (1994) 140-2 (J. C. *Endres*).

2962 **Huonder** V., Die Psalmen in der Liturgia Horarum [Hab.-Diss. FrS]: StFrib 74, 1991 ➤ 9,3065: ᴿZAW 106 (1994) 157 (J. *Henkys*).

2963 **Mowinckel** Sigmund, The Psalms in Israel's worship [Offersang og Sangoffer 1951], ᵀ*Ap-Thomas* D. R. 1962, ᴱ*Gnuse* R., *Knight* D.: The Biblical Seminar 14. Shf 1992, JStOT. xxx-246 p. + 303 p. in one vol. £25. 1-85075-333-4. – ᴿTBR 7,2 (1994s) 14s (A. L. *Warren*).

2964 *Munk* Arne, Salmernes Bog; tempel [MOWINCKEL S.] eller synagoge?: Forum for bibelsk Eksegese 3 (1992) 87-105 [< OTAbs 18, p. 80].

2965 a) *Murphy* Roland E., The Psalms; prayer of Israel and the Church; – b) *Bergant* Dianne, A lesson on prayer; the book of Jonah; – c) *Connolly* Michele A. [*al.*], Jesus at prayer: BToday 32 (1994) 133-7 / 138-143 / 145-150 [-160].

2966 **NAB**: The Psalms, Prayer edition, authorized by Catholic Bishops' Conference. ColMn 1991, Liturgical. 213 p. $7. – ᴿCBQ 56 (1994) 570s (H. P. *Nasuti*: one of three editions with identical text and Hebrew numbering). ➤ 2916.

2966* *Quecke* Hans, Psalmverse als 'Hymnen' in der koptischen Liturgie? ➤ 27, ᶠCOQUIN R.-G., Christianisme d'Égypte 1994, 101-114.

2967 **Tournay** R.-J., Voir et entendre Dieu avec les Psaumes 1988 ➤ 4,3222 ... 7,2811: ᴿTEuph 5 (1992) 185s (J. *Sapin*, aussi sur NASUTI).

2968 **Tournay** Raymond J., Seeing and hearing God with the Psalms, ᵀ*Crowley* J. E.; jOsu 118, 1991 ➤ 7,2812 ... 9,3072: ᴿBtS 151 (1994) 368s (R. B. *Chisholm* prefers several earlier datings); Interpretation 47 (1993) 76 . 78 (N. *Parker*).

E6.7 *Psalmi: versiculi* – **Psalms by number and verse.**

2969 *Koch* Dietrich-Alex, Auslegung von Psalm 1 bei JUSTIN und im Barnabasbrief: ➤ 15, ᶠBEYERLIN W., Neue Wege 1994, 223-242.

2970 **Sarna** Nahum M., Songs of the heart; an introduction to the Book of Psalms [on Ps 1 and nine others]. NY 1993, Schocken. 204 p. $25. 0-8052-0253-6. – ᴿBR 10,2 (1994) 11 (J. L. *Mays*); TTod 51 (1994s) 441 (J. *Limburg*).

2971 a) *Flint* Peter W., Translation technique in the Septuagint Psalter — as illustrated in Psalms 2 and 137; – b) *Bernstein* Moshe J., Translation technique in the Targum to Psalms; two test cases, Psalms 2 and 137; – c) *McCarthy* David P., Some useful things worth knowing about the

Vulgate and Jerome [his knowledge of Hebrew was minimal; he translated Psalms first and it became a Hebrew dictionary for him]; – *d*) *Sheppard* Gerald T., Pre-modern criticism in English translations of the Psalms during the seventeenth century: ➤ 394, SBLSem 33 (1994) 312-320 / 326-345 / 321-5 / 346-375.

2971* *Gironés* Guillem Gonzalo, [Salmo 2] La teología del humor: AnVal 20 (1994) 233-340.

2972 *Bianchi* Francesco, Il Salmo 4; una 'meditazione' su Zorobabele?: BbbOr 36 (1994) 217-230.

2973 *Lee* Stuart, [Ps 5, note on] The comet in the Eadwine Psalter; a recently discovered seventeenth century transcription: Manuscripta 37 (1993) 322-4.

2974 **Auffret** Pierre, Quatre psaumes et un cinquième; étude structurelle des psaumes 7 à 10 et 35. P 1993, Letouzey & Â. 274 p. F 340. 2-7063-0187-2. – ᴿBL (1994) 49 (J. H. *Eaton*); ÉglT 25 (1994) 128s (W. *Vogels*); ScEspr 46 (1994) 359s (M. *Girard*); ᴢᴀᴡ 106 (1994) 148s (H. *Spieckermann*).

2975 *Janowski* Bernd, Jʜᴡʜ der Richter — ein rettender Gott; Psalm 7 und das Motiv des Gottesgerichts: JbBT 9 (1994) 53-85.

2976 **Lifschitz** Daniel, Dalla bocca dei bimbi e dei lattanti (Salmi 7 e 8): La tradizione ebraica commenta i Salmi 3. T-Leumann 1991, LDC. 310 p. 88-01-11723-X.

2977 *Kaiser* Otto, Erwägungen zu Psalm 8: ➤ 15, ꟳBᴇʏᴇʀʟɪɴ W., Neue Wege 1994, 207-231.

2978 *McNamara* Martin, Psalm 8 in the Bible, in earlier and Irish tradition: MilltSt 32 (1993) 24-41.

2979 *Robert* P., [Ps 8,2] 'Ta splendeur est chantée par la bouche des enfants, des tout-petits': FoiTemps 24 (1994) 436-441 [< ᴢɪᴛ 95, p. 145].

2979* *Raurell* Frederic, The 'doxa' of man in Psalm VIII,6: Laurentianum 35 (1994) 73-90.

2980 *a*) *Brueggemann* Walter, Psalm 9-10, a counter to conventional social reality; – *b*) *Coote* Robert B., Psalm 139; – *c*) *Sheppard* Gerald T., 'Enemies' and the politics of prayer in the book of Psalms; – *d*) *Camp* Claudia V., [Prov 5,7-14] What's so strange about the strange woman? – *e*) *Meyers* Carol, To her mother's house; considering a counterpart to the Israelite *bēt āb*; – *f*) *Brown* John P., Prometheus, the Servant of Yahweh, Jesus; legitimation and repression in the heritage of Persian imperialism; – *g*) *Malina* Bruce J., Interpretation: Reading, abduction, metaphor [thanks, Norm]: ➤ 7,67, ꟳGᴏᴛᴛᴡᴀʟᴅ, Politics of exegesis 1991, 3-15 / 33-38 / 61-82 / 17-31 / 33-51 / 109-125 / 253-266.

2980* ᴱ**Lifschitz** Daniel, Tutti sono corrotti; Salmi 11-14: TradEbrCr Salmi 5. T-Leumann 1994, Elle Di Ci. xxxii-270 p. Lᵐ 24. – ᴿParVi 39/6 (1994) 54 (G. *Torta*).

2981 *Loretz* Oswald, *a*) Gottes Thron in Tempel und Himmel nach Psalm 11; von der altorientalischen zur biblischen Tempeltheologie; – *b*) Zur Zitat-Vernetzung zwischen Ugarit-Texten und Psalmen: UF 26 (1994) 245-270 / 225-243.

2982 **Dhonaraj** Dharmakkan, [Ps 12-18], Theological significance of the motif of enemies in selected psalms of individual lament [Diss. ᴰ*Otto* E., Osnabrück 1987]: OrBChr 4. Glückstadt 1992, Augustin. xii-311 p. 3-87030-153-8 [TLZ 120,780, E. S. *Gerstenberger*].

2983 *Conti* Martino, Arroganza umana e fedeltà divina secondo il Salmo 12: Antonianum 69 (1994) 156-178; Eng. 156.

2984 *Irsigler* Hubert, Psalm-Rede als Handlungs- Wirk- und Aussage-prozess; Sprechaktanalyse und Psalminterpretation am Beispiel von Psalm 13: ➤ 15, ᶠBEYERLIN W., Neue Wege 1994, 63-104.

2985 *Miller* Patrick D., Kingship, Torah obedience, and prayer; the theology of Psalms 15-24: ➤ 15, ᶠBEYERLIN W., Neue Wege 1994, 127-142.

2986 *Weinfeld* Moshe, ❿ [Ps 15; 24] Instructions for Temple visitors in ancient Israel and in ancient Egypt: Tarbiz 62 (1992s) 5-15; Eng. v.

2987 **Aparicio Rodríguez** Ángel, Tu eres mi bien; análisis exegético y teológico del Salmo 16 [tiempos de Hoseas]; aplicación a la vida religiosa 1993 ➤ 9,3100: ᴿRivB 42 (1994) 462-4 (G. *Ravasi*).

2988 *Aparicio Rodríguez* A., Datación y 'Sitz im Leben' del Sal 16: RivB 42 (1994) 385-408.

2989 *Auffret* P., 'Je serai rassasié de ton image'; étude structurelle du Psaume 17: ᴢAW 106 (1994) 446-458.

2990 *Auffret* Pierre, 'C'est un peuple humilié que tu sauves'; étude structurelle du Psaume 18 (1): ScEspr 46 (1994) 271-291.

2991 **Berry** Donald K., The psalms and their readers; interpretive strategies for Ps 18: jOsu 153. Shf 1993, Academic. 160 p. £24.50. 1-85075-399-7. – ᴿBL (1994) 50 (R. P. R. *Murray*); Interpretation 48 (1994) 426.8 (J. K. *Kuntz*).

2992 *Ben-David* Israel, ❿ 'Day to day makes utterance' (Ps 19:3): Lešonenu 57 (1993); Eng. I.

2993 *Cooper* Alan, Creation, philosophy and spirituality; aspects of Jewish interpretation of Psalm 19: ➤ 133, ᶠWACHOLDER B. Z., Pursuing 1994, 15-33.

2995 **Loretz** O., Die Königspsalmen I 20/21 ... 1988 ➤ 4,3238; 5,3105: ᴿBO 51 (1994) 407s (T. *Booij*).

2996 *Sandberger* Jörg V., Hermeneutische Aspekte der Psalmeninterpretation dargestellt an Psalm 23: ➤ 15, ᶠBEYERLIN W., Neue Wege 1994, 317-344.

2997 *Stern* Philip D., The 'bloodbath of Anat' and Psalm XXIII: VT 44 (1994) 120-125.

2998 *Botha* P. J., Psalm 24; unity in diversity: OTEssays 7 (1994) 360-9.

2999 *Lohfink* Norbert, [Ps 25; Isa], Bund und Tora bei der Völkerwallfahrt: ➤ 200, Der Gott Israels 1994, 37-83.

3000 *Human* Dirk, a) Reading the text of the Bible, with illustrative reference to Psalm 25: Scriptura 49 (1994) 88-98 [< OTAbs 18, p. 81]; – *b*) [Ps 25, 55, 79, 83], Die begrip 'berit' in 'n aantal klaagpsalmen; 'n perspektief: SkrifK 15 (1994) 280-293 [< OTAbs 18,322].

3001 *Pasquetto* Virgilio, 'Dio mio, in te confido' (Sal 25,2); la speranza del povero di Israele: RivVSp 48 (1994) 359-379.

3002 *Schenker* Adrian, Gewollt dunkle Wiedergaben in LXX? Am Beispiel von Ps 28 (29),6: Biblica 75 (1994) 546-555.

3003 **Bons** Eberhard, Psalm 31 – Rettung als Paradigma; eine synchron-le-serorientierte Analyse [Diss. 1993, Fra St. Georgen]: FraTSt 48. Fra 1994, Knecht. xii-307 p. ᴅM 68. 3-7820-0708-3.

3004 *Wendland* Ernest R., Genre criticism and the Psalms; what discourse typology can tell us about the text (with special reference to Psalm 31): ➤ 304*c*, Biblical Hebrew 1993/4, 374-414.

3005 **Moncrieffe** Orlando M., Cosmic creation and creative redemption in the OT; the witness of the hymns Ps. 33 and Ps. 136: diss. Duke, ᴰ*Bailey* L. Durham ɴᴄ 1993. 323 p. 94-05988. – DissA 54 (1993s) p. 3478; RTLv 26, p. 532.

3006 *Hossfeld* Frank Lothar, *Zenger* Erich, 'Von seinem Thronsitz schaut er nieder auf alle Bewohner der Erde' (Ps 33,14); Redaktionsgeschichte und Kompositionskritik der Psalmengruppe 25-34: ⇒ 61, FKAISER O., 'Wer ist' 1994, 375-388.

3007 **Eriksson** Lars O., 'Come, children, listen to me' Psalm 34 in the Hebrew Bible and in early Christian writings: ConBib OT 32, 1991 ⇒ 8,3255: RBL (1994) 57 (J.H. *Eaton*); ÉTRel 68 (1992) 270 (S. *Ebane Ango*); SvEx 58 (1994) 163-170 (S. *Samuelsson*); TsTKi 65 (1994) 141s (T. *Stordalen*, Norwegian).

3008 **Volgger** David, Psalm 39, die Gnadentaten JHWHs will ich für immer besingen: kath. Diss. DSeidl T. Würzburg 1994. – TR 91,104.

3009 **Wu** John, The significance of silence in the OT with particular reference to Psalm 39: diss. Knox College, DWalters S. Toronto 1994. – SR 23 (1994) 525.

3010 *Michel* Alain, AUGUSTIN et le sublime; les 'enarrationes in psalmos' 41 et 42: ⇒ 89d, FOROZ RETA J. II, AugM 39 (1994) 357-363.

3011 *Oorschot* Jürgen van, [Ps 42... 88] Der ferne *deus praesens* des Tempels; die Korachpsalmen und der Wandel israelitischer Tempeltheologie: ⇒ 61, FKAISER O. 1994, 416-430.

3012 *Zenger* Erich, [Ps 42-49; 84; 87s] Zur redaktionsgeschichtlichen Bedeutung der Korachpsalmen: ⇒ 15, FBEYERLIN W., Neue Wege 1994, 175-198.

3013 **Grünbeck** Elisabeth, Christologische Schriftargumentation und Bildersprache; zum Konflikt zwischen Metapherninterpretation und dogmatischen Schriftbeweistraditionen in der patristischen Auslegung des 44. (45.) Psalms [Diss.]: VigChr supp. 26. Leiden 1994, Brill. xxi-438 p. 90-04-10021-0 [TR 9,275; RHE 89,430*].

3014 *Eaton* J.H., [Ps 47; 93... BENTZEN A., GUNKEL H.] 'A bloodless compromise'? The question of an eschatological ritual in ancient Israel: ⇒ 45, FGOULDER M., Crossing 1994, 69-82.

3015 *Schaper* Joachim, Psalm 47 und sein 'Sitz im Leben': ZAW 106 (1994) 262-275.

3016 *Israel* Felice, [Ps 47,4] Un supposto aramaismo e il demone Deber: ⇒ 156, FTSERETELI C., Semitica 1993, 127-9; franç. 129.

3017 *Smith* Mark S., The invocation of deceased ancestors in Psalm 49:12c: JBL 112 (1993) 105-7.

3018 *Seybold* Klaus, [Ps 50; 73-83] Das 'wir' in den Asaph-Psalmen [alle (10) mit Ausnahme 73 &77 'ich']; spezifische Probleme einer Psalmgruppe: ⇒ 15, FBEYERLIN W., Neue Wege 1994, 143-155.

3019 **Brusch** Jack E., Gotteserkenntnis und Selbsterkenntnis; LUTHERs Verständnis des 51. Psalms: Hab.-Diss. DThoma Clemens. Zürich 1994. – RTLv 26, p. 543; TR 91,92.

3020 TEDonnelly John Patrick, Girolamo SAVONAROLA, Prison meditations on Psalms 51 and 31: Reformation Texts with Translation 1. Milwaukee 1994, Matquete Univ. 142 p. 0-87462-700-1 [RelStR 21,244, D.R. *Janz*: Latin and English on facing pages).

3021 *a) Würthwein* Ernst, Bemerkungen zu Psalm 51; – *b) Schmidt* Werner H., Individuelle Eschatologie im Gebet; Psalm 51: ⇒ 15, FBEYERLIN W., Neue Wege 1994, 381-8 / 345-360.

3022 *Bail* Ulrike, [Ps 55 as the cry of a woman who has been raped] 'Vernimm, Gott, mein Gebet'; Psalm 55 und Gewalt gegen Frauen: ⇒ 59*, FJAHNOW H., 1994, 67-84 [< OTAbs 18, p.323].

3023 *Jenni* Ernst, [Ps 55,14; 58,5] Pleonastische Ausdrücke für Vergleichbarkeit: ⇒ 15, FBEYERLIN W., Neue Wege 1994, 201-6.

3024 *Tropper* Josef, 'Sie knurren wie Hunde'; Psalm 59,16, Kilamuwa 10 und die Semantik der Wurzel *lyn*: ZAW 106 (1994) 87-95; 1 fig.

3025 *Garsiel* M., ❹ Psalm 60; its historical background, interpretation, literary allusions and meaning: BeitM 39 (1994) 193-209 [< OTAbs 18, p. 82].

3026 **Bellinger** W. H.ᴶ, A hermeneutic of curiosity and readings of Psalm 61: StOTInterp 1. Macon 1995, Mercer Univ.

3027 *Lienhard* J. T., 'The glue itself is charity'; Ps 62,9 in AUGUSTINE's thought: ➤ 9,464f, Collectanea 1990/3, 375-384.

3028 **Beyerlin** Walter, Im Licht der Traditionen, Ps LXVII und CXV: VTS 45, 1992 ➤ 8,3271; 9,3131: ᴿTLZ 119 (1994) 231s (H. *Spieckermann*); ZAW 106 (1994) 149 (G. *Metzner*).

3029 *Prinsloo* W. S., Psalm 67; harvest thanksgiving psalm, (eschatological) hymn, communal prayer, communal lament or...?: OTEssays 7 (1994) 231-246.

3030 *Jongeneel* Jan A. B., [Ps 67,1] Waar zijn de 'blinde heidenen' gebleven?: KerkT 45 (1994) 206-218.

3031 **Tillmann** Norbert, 'Das Wasser bis zum Hals!'; Gestalt, Geschichte und Theologie des 69. Psalms: MünsteranerTA 20. Altenberge 1993, Oros. 345 p. DM 55. [TR 90,86].

3032 *Auwers* Jean-Marie, Les psaumes 70-72; essai de lecture canonique: RB 101 (1994) 242-257; Eng. 242 [**Auwers** Psautier ᴰ1993].

3033 *Auffret* Pierre, 'Ma bouche publiera ta justice'; étude structurelle du psaume 71: ÉglT 25 (1994) 5-35.

3034 *Shaviv* Yehudah, ❹ 'We will utterly subdue them' (Ps 74:8): BeitM 39 (1994) 184-8 [< OTAbs 17, p. 581].

3035 **Weber** Beat, Psalm 77 und sein Umfeld: eine poetologische Studie: Diss. ᴰ*Seybold* K. Basel 1994. – RTLv 26,533.

3036 *Emerton* J. A., The text of Psalm LXXVII 11: VT 44 (1994) 183-194.

3037 *Meer* Willem van der, Psalm 77,17-19; hymnisches Fragment oder Aktualisierung?: ETL 70 (1994) 105-111.

3038 *Rokay* Zoltán, Vom Stadtor zu den Vorhöfen; Ps 82 – Sach 1-8, ein Vergleich: ➤ 37, ᶠGAMPER A., ZkT 116 (1994) 457-463.

3039 *Wanke* Günther, Jahwe, die Götter und die Geringen; Beobachtungen zu Psalm 82: ➤ 61, ᶠKAISER O. 1994, 445-453.

3040 *Auffret* Pierre, Qu'elles sont aimables, tes demeures: Étude structurelle du psaume 84: BZ 38 (1994) 29-43.

3041 *Booij* T., Psalm LXXXIV, a prayer of the anointed: VT 44 (1994) 433-441.

3042 *Culley* Robert C., The Temple in Psalms 84, 63, and 42-43: ➤ 30, ᶠCOUTURIER G., Maison 1994, 199-212.

3043 *Prinsloo* Willem S., Psalm 84; ''n Dag in U voorhowe...?': In die Skriflig 28 (1994) 179-197 [< OTAbs 18, p. 82].

3043* *Weiss* Meir, ❹ Psalm 88: Tarbiz 62 (1992s) 153-167; Eng. V.

3044 *Manicardi* Luciano, 'Perché, Signore, mi respingi?' (Sal 88); ParSpV 30 (1994) 61-80.

3044* *Pawlowski* Zdzisław, The reality of death and the fact of prayer; Psalm 88: FolOr 29 (1992s) 163-176 [< OTAbs 18, p. 83].

3045 **Volgger** David, Notizen zur Textanalyse von Ps 89: Univ. Mü , ArbO 45. St. Ottilien 1994, EOS. xi-258 p. 3-88096-545-5.

3046 *Krüger* Thomas, Psalm 90 und die 'Vergänglichkeit des Menschen': Biblica 75 (1994) 191-219; franç. 219.

3047 *Wahl* Harald-Martin, Psalm 90,12; Text, Tradition und Interpretation: ZAW 106 (1994) 116-123.

3048 *Gosse* Bernard,   Les introductions des Psaumes 93-94 et Isaïe 59,15b-20: ZAW 106 (1994) 303-6.

3049 *Hossfeld* Frank-Lothar,   Psalm 95; gattungsgeschichtliche, kompositionskritische und bibeltheologische Anfragen: ➤ 15, FBEYERLIN W., Neue Wege 1994, 29-44.

3050 *Auffret* P.,   Splendeur et majesté devant lui; étude structurelle du Psaume 96: OTEssays 6 (1993) 150-162 [< OTAbs 17, p. 584].

3051 **Brüning** Christian,   Mitten im Leben... Ps 102: BoBB 84, D1992 ➤ 8,3290: RRB 101 (1994) 451s (R. J. *Tournay*).

3052 *Limburg* James,   Down-to-earth theology; Psalm 104 and the environment: CurrTM 21 (1994) 340-6.

3053 *Wright* David P.,   Ritual analogy in Psalm 109: JBL 113 (1994) 385-404.

3054 *Conti* Martino,   Beatitudine del giusto e rovina dell'empio secondo il Salmo 112: Antonianum 69 (1994) 433-454; Eng. 433.

3055 *a*) *Glassner* Gottfried,   Aufbruch als Heimat; zur Theologie des 114. Psalms; – *b*) *Hubmann* Franz D., Gedanken zu Ps 103: ➤ 38, FGAMPER A., ZkT 116 (1994) 472-9 / 464-471.

3056 *Lohfink* Norbert,   Das tanzende Land und der verflüssigte Fels; zur Übersetzung von Ps 114,7: ➤ 8, FBALDERMANN I. 1994, 201-222.

3057 *Auffret* Pierre,   Louez YHWH, toutes les nations! Étude structurelle du Psaume 117: BibNot 74 (1994) 5-9.

3058 **Schröten** Jutta,   Lobt JHWH; ja, gut ist Er! Psalm 118 im Kontext des Hallel; Untersuchungen zu seiner Entstehung, Komposition und Wirkungsgeschichte: kath. Diss. DZenger E. Münster 1994. – TR 91,100.

3059 *Doignon* Jean,   Une exégèse d'HILAIRE de Poitiers [In Psalm 118,7/8] sur le désir de voir la face de Dieu: FrSZ 41 (1994) 542-5.

3060 *Toloni* Giancarlo,   Un problema di semantica; la traduzione greca di *šᵉ* in alcuni versetti del Sal 119 (118): RivB 42 (1994) 35-58; Eng. 58.

3061 *a*) *Viviers* Hendrik,   [Ps. 120-134] When was the *maᶜalot* collection written?: HervTSt 50 (1994) 798-811 [< OTAbs 18, p. 325]; – *b*) The coherence of the *maᶜᵃlot* psalms (Pss 120-134): ZAW 106 (1994) 275-289.

3062 EPerelmuter Hayim G., ❻ David BEN-MANASSEH Darshan, *Shir ha-Maᶜalot*, Song of the steps, in defense of preachers (*darshanim*): Alumnia Series. Cincinnati 1994, HUC.

3063 *Curti* Carmelo,   Due frammenti esegetici sul Salmo 123 adespoti [= anonimi] nei manoscritti poziori della Catena palestinese: ➤ 86, FNALDINI M., Paideia 1994, 131-140.

3064 *Reynolds* Carol B.,   Psalm 125; between text and sermon: Interpretation 48 (1994) 272-5.

3065 *Gallicet* Ezio,   [Ps 125,5s] Il pianto del neonato; AGOSTINO, Serm. 31,4: ➤ 86, FNALDINI M., Paideia 1994, 247-254.

3066 *a*) *Vanoni* Gottfried,   Wie Gott Gesellschaft wandelt; der theologische Grund der JHWH-Furcht nach Psalm 130,4; – *b*) *Sanders* James A., Psalm 154 revisited: ➤ 87, FLOHFINK N., BibT/Wandel 1993, 330-344 / 296-306.

3067 *Nel* Philip,   Recurrence in biblical Hebrew poetry; an analysis of Psalm 132: ➤ 331*a*, 11th Jewish 1993/4, 145-150.

3068 *Loretz* Oswald,   'An den Wassern Babels' — Psalm 137; ein Gespräch mit B. DUHM und H. GUNKEL über textologische Vorurteile: ➤ 61, FKAISER 1994, 402-451.

3069 *Hunter* Jannie H.,   Interpretationstheorie in der postmodernen Zeit; Suche nach Interpretationsmöglichkeiten anhand von Psalm 144: ➤ 15, FBEYERLIN W., Neue Wege 1994, 45-62.

3070 *Kimelman* Reuven, Psalm 145; theme, structure, and impact: JBL 113 (1994) 37-58.
3070* *Meynet* Roland, Le Psaume 145: → 34c, Mém. J.-M. FIEY = Annales du Département de Lettres Arabes, Univ. S. Joseph 6-B (Beyrouth 1991s) 213-225.
3071 *Carl* William J., Psalm 146: between text and sermon: Interpretation 48 (1994) 166-9.
3072 *Gosse* Bernard, Le Psaume CXLIX et la réinterprétation post-exilique de la tradition prophétique: VT 44 (1994) 259-263.
3073 *Qimron* Elisha, Some remarks on the apocryphal Psalm 155: JPseud 10 (1992) 57-59.

E7.1 **Job,** *textus, commentarii.*

3074 *Arduini* Maria Lodovica, Per l'autenticità rupertiana del Commentarius in Iob: Aevum 68 (1994) 303-321.
3075 ᴱ**Basser** H. W., *Walfish* B. D., ❻ Moses Kimḥi, commentary on the book of Job [1184; no ᵀ]: SFlJud 64. Atlanta 1992, Scholars. xxix-121 p. $70; sb. $45. 1-55540-779-X. – ᴿJStOT 64 (1994) 127s (J. F. *Elwolde*).
3075* **Bullinger** E. M., The Book of Job; the oldest lesson in the world; a new translation. GR 1990, Kregel. xiv-203 p.
3076 **Calvin** John, [150] Sermons on Job (facsimile of ᵀ*Golding* Arthur 1574). E 1993, Banner of Truth. 572 p. £35. 0-85151-644-0. – ᴿScotBuEvT 12 (1994) 149s (P. *Cook*).
3077 **Clines** David J. A., Job: Word Comm 17, 1989 → 5,3173 ... 8,3319: ᴿConcordTQ 58 (1994) 45-48 (H. D. *Hummel*: very thorough, but theologically 'value-free'); JEvTS 37 (1994) 136-8 (E. B. *Smick*).
3078 *a) Fernández Marcos* Natalio, The Septuagint reading of the Book of Job; – *b) Mangan* Celine, The interpretation of Job in the Targums; – *c) Vermeylen* J., Le méchant dans les discours des amis de Job; – *d*) *Weinberg* J., Job versus Abraham; the question for the perfect God-fearer in rabbinic tradition: → 304, Job 1993/4, 251-266 / 267-280 / 101-127 / 281-296.
3079 **Gentry** Peter J., Analysis of the revisor's text of Greek Job: diss. Toronto, ᴰ*Wevers* J. 1994. – SR 23 (1994) 525.
3080 **Hagedorn** Ursula & Dieter, Die älteren griechischen Katenen zum Buch Hiob 1. Einleitung, Prologe und Epiloge, Fragmente zu Hiob 1,1-8,22: PatrTStud 40. B 1994, de Gruyter. xv-457 p.; Bibliog. x-xiii. 3-11-014483-2.
3081 **Honsey** Rudolph E., Job: People's Bible. Milwaukee/St. Louis 1992, Northwestern/Concordia. 364 p. – ᴿConcordJ 20 (1994) 217s (C. W. *Mitchell* recommends without reserve).
3082 **Mangan** Céline, The targum of Job; *Healey* John F., ... of Proverbs; *Knobel* Peter S., ... of Qohelet: Aramaic Bible 15, 1991 → 7,2883 ... 9, 3189: ᴿJSS 39 (1994) 161-181 (D. M. *Stec*: proposals; careless preparation. e. g. second bracket omitted).
3082* **Mitchell** Stefan, The Book of Job. Garden City NY 1992, Harper Perennial. xxxii-131 p.
3083 ᴱ**San José Lera** Javier, Fray Luis de LEÓN, Exposición del libro de Job: Textos recuperados 8. S 1992, Univ. 929 p. (2 vol.). – ᴿTPhil 69 (1994) 599-601 (K. *Reinhardt*).
3084 **Schreiner** Susan E., Where shall wisdom be found? CALVIN's [159-sermon] exegesis of Job from medieval and modern perspectives. Ch

1994, Univ. ix-264 p. $36. 0-226-74043-9 [TDig 42,88; BL 95,74, D.
Bagchi].
3085 ᴱ**Siniscalco** P., S. GREGORIO Magno, Commento morale in Giobbe I
(1-8): Opere 1/1. R 1992, Città Nuova. 712 p. Lᵐ 90 [NRT 117,597, A.
Harvengt]. – ᴿCC 145 (1994,4) 514-6 (G. *Cremascoli*).
3086 **Stec** David M., The text of the Targum of Job [ᴰManchester 1989]:
ArbGJud 20. Leiden 1994, Brill. viii-488 p. $103. 90-04-09874-7
[OTAbs 18, p. 163; BL 95,53, C. T. R. *Hayward*].
3087 **Szpek** Heidi M., Translation technique in the Peshitta to Job: SBL diss.
137, 1992 ➤ 8,3332; 9,3192: ᴿCBQ 56 (1994) 343s (E. G. *Mathews*); JBL
113 (1994) 328-330 (J. A. *Lund*); ZAW 106 (1994) 369 (H. P. *Mathys*).
3087* *Vattioni* Francesco, Un resto dell'originale di Giobbe in un ma-
noscritto della Laurenziana: AugR 34 (1994) 467-9.
3088 *Zerafa* P., Il commento di San TOMMASO al libro di Giobbe tra esegesi
antica e esegesi contemporanea: Angelicum 71 (1994) 461-507.

E7.2   *Job: themata*, **Topics** ... *Versiculi*, **Verse-numbers.**

3089 **Chauvin** Jacques, Job l'insoumis; Dieu n'est jamais celui qu'on croit.
Aubonne 1994, Moulin. 63 p. – ᴿEsprVie 104 (1994) 333 (P. *Jay*).
3090 **Cheney** Michael, Dust, wind and agony; character, speech and genre in
Job: *a*) diss. Lund 1994. 379 p. 91-22-01603-1. – RTLv 26, p. 530. – *b*)
ConBibOT 36. Sto 1994, Almqvist & W. xii-323 p.
3091 *a*) *Clines* D. J. A., Why is there a book of Job and what does it do to
you if you read it?; – *b*) *Müller* H.-P., Die Hiobrahmenerzählung und ihre
alttestamentlichen Parallelen als Paradigmen einer weisheitlichen Wirk-
lichkeitswahrnahme: ➤ 304, Job 1993/4, 1-20 / 21-39.
3092 **Dailey** Thomas F., The repentant Job; a Ricœurian icon for biblical
theology [diss. Gregorian 1993 ➤ 9,3198]. NY 1994, UPA. xv-236 p.
0-8191-9589-8 [RelStR 21,323, J. L. *Crenshaw*: Job's silence is 'pre-ethical
listening'].
3093 *a*) *Day* J., How could Job be an Edomite? – *b*) *Begg* C. T., Comparing
characters; the book of Job and the Testament of Job; – *c*) *Hartley* J. E.,
From lament to oath; a study of progression in the speeches of Job; – *d*)
Berges Ulrich, Hiob in Lateinamerika; der leidende Mensch und der
aussätzige Gott: ➤ 304, Job 1993/4, 392-9 / 435-445 / 79-100 / 297-317.
3094 **Dell** Katharine J., The book of Job as sceptical literature 1991
➤ 5,3190 ... 9,3200: TrierTZ 103 (1994) 319s (T. *Mende*).
3095 *De Smet* Richard, Job's 'insufferable comforters' and the law of Karma:
Vidyajyoti 58 (1994) 308-318.
3096 *Fleming* Daniel E., Job, the tale of patient faith and the book of God's
dilemma: VT 44 (1994) 468-482.
3097 **Fuchs** Gisela, Mythos und Hiobdichtung 1993 ➤ 9,3201 [BL 95,87,
K. J. *Dell*; TLZ 120,27, S. *Wagner*].
3098 **García-Moreno** Antonio, Sentido del dolor en Job 1990 ➤ 7,2894 ... 9,
3202: ᴿScripTPamp 26 (1994) 790s (F. *Varo*).
3099 *Holm-Nielsen* Svend, Is Job a scapegoat? [not as GIRARD 1983;
Lundager JENSEN dansk 1990]: ➤ 89*, ᶠOTZEN B., 1994, 128-138.
3100 *Kegler* Jürgen, 'Gürte wie ein Mann deine Lenden!' Die Gottesreden
im Ijob-Buch als Aufforderung zur aktiven Auseinandersetzung mit dem
Leid: ➤ 115, ᶠSCHUNCK K.-D., Nachdenken 1994, 217-234.
3101 **Langenhorst** Georg, *a*) Hiob unser Zeitgenosse; die literarische Rezeption der biblischen Figur im 20. Jahrhundert als theologische Her-

ausforderung: kath. Diss. ^D*Kuschel* K. Tübingen 1992s. – TR 90,88; RTLv 26, p. 566. – *b*) Hiob unser Zeitgenosse; die literarische Hiob-Rezeption im 20. Jahrhundert als theologische Herausforderung. Mainz 1994, Grünewald. 448 p. DM 64. – ^ROrientierung 58 (1994) 267s (W. *Oelmüller*).

3102 *Leduc-Fayette* D., La 'clef' de Job; [diss. sur] PASCAL; la liberté/le mal: RPhil 119 (1994) 181-194.

3103 *Levoratti* Armando J., Las preguntas de Job: RBibArg 55 (1993) 1-53.

3104 *Marnewick* J. C., *Breytenbach* A. P. B., Die boek Job gelees vanuit 'n Ou-Testamentiese verbondsperspektief: HervTSt 50 (1994) 923-935 [< OTAbs 18,327].

3105 **Martini** Carlo M., [Job] Perseverance in trials 1992 → 9,3211: ^RWay 34 (1994) 159 (J. *Pridmore*: duly critical).

3106 **Mason** Mike, The Gospel according to Job, Wheaton 1994, Crossway, xiv-448 p. $16. 0-89107-785-3 [< TDig 42,77].

3107 *Mettinger* Tryggve D. N., Intertextuality; allusion and vertical context systems in some Job passages: → 138, ^FWHYBRAY 1993, 257-280.

3108 *Millard* Matthias, Das Hiobbuch; Skizzen zur Interpretation eines Buches der 'Schriften': WDienst 22 (1993) 27-38 [< OTAbs 17, p. 587].

3109 *Newsom* Carol A., The moral sense of nature; ethics in the light of God's speech to Job: PrincSemB 15 (1994) 9-17.

3110 *Parsons* Greg W., Guidelines for understanding and proclaiming the Book of Job: BtS 151 (1994) 393-413.

3111 *Penzenstadler* Joan, Teaching the Book of Job with a view to human wholeness: RelEdn 89 (1994) 223-231.

3112 **Perdue** Leo G., Wisdom in revolt... Job: jOsu 112, 1991 → 7,2905; 8,3360: ^RETL 70 (1994) 149s (A. *Schoors*).

3113 *Pleins* J. David, 'Why do you hide your face?' Divine silence and speech in the Book of Job: Interpretation 48 (1994) 229-239.

3114 **Reyburn** William D., A handbook on the Book of Job: Helps for Translators 1992 → 8,3362: ^RBL (1994) 72 (W. *McKane*); CBQ 56 (1994) 777s (Kathleen M. *O'Connor*).

3115 **Reiser** Werner, Hiob; ein Rebell bekommt Recht. Stu 1991, Quell. 208 p. – ^RTZBas 50 (1994) 88-91 (E. *Buess*).

3116 *Ruiz* Jean-Pierre, Contexts in conversation; first world and third world readings of Job: JHisp 2,3 (1994s) 5-29.

3117 **Safire** William, The first dissident; the book of Job in today's politics. NY 1992, Random. xxix-231. – ^RCCAR 41,3 (1994) 87-89 (D. *Clinton*).

3118 **Schultz** Karl A., Where is God when you need him? sharing stories of suffering with Job and Jesus; from easy answers to hard questions. Sydney 1993, St. Paul. 165 p. $18. – ^RAustralasCR 70 (1993) 525 (Teresa *Pirola*).

3119 *Unsvåg* Hilde H., The speeches of Yahweh in the Book of Job; monologue or dialogue? TsTKi [64 (1993) 21-37] 65 (1994) 81-95 Norwegian; 95 Eng.

3120 *Zobel* Hans-Jürgen, Schuld und Leiden in der Auseinandersetzung mit Gott nach der Hiob-Dichtung: TVers 18 (1993) 13-26.

3121 **Zuckerman** Bruce, Job the silent 1991 → 2,2917... 9,3231: ^RChrLit 41 (1991s) 202s (J. *Vickery*); JAAR 62 (1994) 230-3 (W. J. *Urbrock*); TR 90 (1994) 113-5 (M. *Oeming*).

3122 *a) Vogels* Walter, Job's empty pious slogans (Job 1,20-23; 2,8-10); – *b) Beuken* W. A. M., Job's imprecation as the perplexing impact of the

semantic correspondences between Job 3, Job 4-5 and Job 6-7; – c)
Perdue L. G., Metaphorical theology in the book of Job; theological
anthropology in the first cycle of Job's speeches (Job 3; 6-7; 9-10; – d)
Gorea Maria, Job 7,8; une contribution à la problématique des versets
portant astérisques dans la Septante: ➤ 304, Job 1993/4, 369-376 / 41-78 /
129-156 / 430-4.

3123 *Vogels* Walter, Job's superficial faith in his first reactions to suffering
(Job 1:20-23; 2:8-10): ÉglT 25 (1992) 343-359.

3124 a) *Hill* Robert C., Job in search of wisdom; – b) *Greenhalgh* Stephen,
Waiting for God's ʿôth [Job 2,10]: ScripB 23,2 (1993) 34-38 / 39-41.

3125 *Bezuidenhout* L. C., Semantiese ritme en beweging in Job 3; 'n Ander
benadering tot die waardering van die teks: HervTSt 50 (1994) 236-245
[< OTAbs 18, p. 86].

3126 *Burns* John B., [Job 3,1-10; Jer 20,14-19] Cursing the day of birth:
ProcGM 13 (1993) 11-22.

3127 **Course** John E., Speech and response; a rhetorical analysis of the
introductions to the speeches of the book of Job (chaps. 4-24): CBQ Mg
25. Wsh 1994, CBA. vii-184 p. $8,50. 0-915170-24-8 [BL 95,61, K. J.
Dell; OTAbs 18, p. 36; TLZ 120,636, H. M. *Wahl*].

3128 **Cotter** D. W., A study of Job 4-5, ᴰ1989/92 ➤ 8,3376; 9,3234: ᴿCBQ
56 (1994) 336s (G. *Vall*); ÉglT 25 (1994) 131s (W. *Vogels*); ZAW 106
(1994) 152s (J. van *Oorschot*).

3129 *Wolfers* David, 'Sparks flying'? Job 5:7 [rather 'pestilences prevail']:
JBQ 23 (1993) 3-8.

3130 *Szpek* Heidi M., The Peshiṭta on Job 7:6, 'My days are swifter (?) than
an *ere*': JBL 113 (1994) 287-290; rather 'more trifling than the thrum of
looms'.

3131 a) *Regt* L. J. de, Implications of rhetorical questions in strophes in Job
11 and 15; – b) *Wolfers* David †, Job 15,4.5; an exploration; – c) *Michel*
Walter L., Confidence and despair; Job 19,25-27 in the light of
Northwest Semitic studies; – d) *Holman* Jan, Does my Redeemer live or
is my Redeemer the Living God? Some reflections on the translation of
Job 19.25: ➤ 304, Job 1993/4, 321-8 / 382-6 / 157-182 / 377-381.

3132 *Wolfers* David, Reflections on Job XII: VT 44 (1994) 401-6.

3133 *Chin* Catherine, Job and the injustice of God; implicit arguments in Job
13.17-14.12: JStOT 64 (1994) 91-101.

3134 **Witte** Markus, [Job 21-27] Vom Leiden zur Lehre; der dritte Redegang
(Hi 21-27) und die Redaktionsgeschichte des Hiobbuches: a) ev. Diss.
ᴰKaiser O. Marburg 1994. – TR 91.99. – b) BZAW 230. B 1994, de
Gruyter. xi-333 p.

3135 a) *Talstra* Eep, Dialogue in Job 21; 'virtual quotations' or 'text
grammatical markers'?; – b) *Witte* Markus, Die dritte Rede Bildads
(Hiob 25) und die Redaktionsgeschichte des Hiobbuches; – c) *Wolfers*
David [31.I.1927-17.IX.1994; M.D.; Deep Things out of darkness
awaited 1995, Eerdmans], Job 26, an orphan chapter: ➤ 304, Job 1993/4,
329-348 / 349-355 / 387-391.

3136 *Michel* Walther L., Hebrew poetic devices in the service of biblical
exegesis; illustrated in a discussion of Job 25:1-6: ➤ 331a, 11th Jewish
1993/4, 151-8.

3137 **Zuck** Roy B., Sitting with Job [reprints on 28 & 19,23-29] 1992 ➤ 8,
3371; 9,3230: ᴿEvQ 66 (1994) 168s (J. B. *Job*); OTEssays 7 (1994)
469-472 (J. A. *Loader*, Afrikaans).

3138 a) *Steck* Odil Hannes, Israels Gott statt anderer Götter — Israels

Gesetz statt fremder Weisheit; Beobachtungen zur Rezeption von Hi 28 in
Bar 3,9-44; – *b*) *Spieckermann* Hermann, Die Satanisierung Gottes; zur
inneren Konkordanz von Novelle, Dialog und Gottesreden im Hiobbuch:
→ 61, ^FKAISER O., 'Wer ist' 1994, 457-471 / 431-444.

3139 *a*) *Oorschot* Jürgen van, Hiob 28; die verborgene Weisheit und die
Furcht Gottes als Überwindung einer generalisierten ḥokmâh; – *b*) *Wahl*
Harald M., Das 'Evangelium' Elihus (Hiob 32-37); – *c*) *Lévêque* Jean,
L'interprétation des discours de Yhwh (Job 38,1-42,46); – *d*) *Wolde* Ellen
J. van, Job 42,1-6; the reversal of Job: → 304, Job 1993/4, 183-201 /
356-361 / 203-222 / 223-250.

3140 *Wolfers* David, The stone of deepest darkness; a mineralogical mystery
(Job XXVIII): VT 44 (1994) 274-6.

3141 *Zimmermann* Ruben, Homo Sapiens Ignorans; Hiob 28 als Bestandteil
der ursprünglichen Hiobdichtung: BibNot 74 (1994) 90-100.

3142 **Wahl** Harald-M., Der gerechte Schöpfer... Hiob 32-37: BZAW 207,
1993 → 9,3245*b* [TLZ 120,647, S. *Wagner*]. – ^RBL (1994) 77s (J. H.
Eaton).

3143 *Wahl* H.-M., Elihu, Frevler oder Frommer? Die Auslegung des Hiobbuches (Hi 32-37) durch ein Pseudepigraphon (TestHi 41-43): JStJud 25
(1994) 1-17.

3144 *Wolfers* David, *a*) Sire? (Job XXXIV 36); – *b*) The 'neck' of Job's tunic
(Job XXX 18): VT 44 (1994) 567-9 / 570-2.

3145 **Keel** Othmar, Dieu répond à Job (38-41) 1993 → 9,3248: ^RNRT 116
(1994) 103 (J. L. *Ska*); Carthaginensia 10 (1994) 178s (R. *Sanz Valdivieso*);
VSp 148 (1994) 261 (J. *Asurmendi*).

3146 *Newsom* Carol A., [Job 38] The moral sense of nature; ethics in the light
of God's speech to Job: PrincSemB 15 (1994) 9-17.

3147 **McKirren** Bill, [Job 38,1-42,6] The comforting wind; God, Job, and the
scale of creation. GR 1994, Eerdmans. vii-95 p. $9. 0-8028-0499-3
[OTAbs 18, p. 164].

3148 *Odell* David, Images of violence in the horse in Job 39:18-25: Prooftexts 13 (1993) 163-173.

3149 *Dailey* Thomas F., The wisdom of divine disputation? On Job 40.2-5:
JStOT 63 (1994) 105-119.

3150 **Kushner** Harold, [Job 40,9-14] When bad things happen to good people.
1982, Avon (and 1983, 1989, 1990 editions): ^RHervTSt 50 (1994)
990-1004 (I. J. J. *Spangenberg*).

E7.3 *Canticum Canticorum,* **Song of Songs, Das Hohelied,** *textus, comm.*

3151 **Alonso Schökel** Luis, El cantar 1990 → 6,3492; 9,3251: ^RRBibArg 56
(1994) 115-9 (P. *Andiñach*).

3152 **Alonso-Schökel** Luis, 'Steh auf, meine Freundin, meine Schöne, und
komm!' Gedanken zum Hohenlied [1990 → 6,3492],^T. Mü 1991, Neue
Stadt. 134 p. DM 17,80. [TR 91,124, H. *Haag*; (Text-)Übersetzung,
Vorzüge und Schwächen; Kommentar, so genannt obgleich nicht gemeint].

3153 **Artola** A. M., El Cantar de los Cantares. Bilbao 1992, Pasionistas.
168 p. – ^RCiuD 206 (1993) 950s (F. *Carmona*).

3154 *Barbàra* Maria Antonietta, Progetto di edizione critica dei frammenti di
ORIGENE sul Cantico; spoglio delle catene e stato delle ricerche: → 330*a*,
X-Viverone 1992/3, 439-450; Eng. 276.

3155 *Bauer* Johannes B., Apponiana [Hoheslied 1986]: → 117, ^FSCHWABL H.,
WienerSt 108 (1994s) 523-532.

3156 **Blecua** José Manuel, Fray Luis de LEÓN, Cantar de cantares de Salomón: Bt Románica Hispánica 4, Textos 22. M 1994, Gredos. 206 p.; ill. - ᴿSefarad 54 (1994) 420s (Emilia *Fernández Tejero*).

3157 — **Reinhardt** Klaus, A propósito de la nueva edición del 'Cantar de Cantares de Salomón' de Fray Luis de LEÓN [BLECUA J.M. 1994]: RAg 35 ('750 Aniversario de la Orden de San Agustín' 1994) 989-1001.

3158 ᵀᴱ**Brésard** Luc, *al.*, ORIGÈNE Ct: SChr 375s, 1991s ➤ 8,3402; 9,3257: ᴿPrOrChr 42 (1992) 227s (P. *Ternant*); RÉByz 52 (1994) 294-6 (J. *Wolinski*); RHPR 74 (1994) 317 (D.A. *Bertrand*); RTPhil 126 (1994) 278s (E. *Junod*).

3159 **Diebner** B.J., *Kasser* R., Hamburger Papyrus Bil 1 Ct Eces 1989 ➤ 8, 3406; 9,3258: ᴿOLZ 88 (1993) 482-6 (H.G. *Bethke*).

3160 **Dünzl** Franz, Braut und Bräutigam; die Auslegung des Canticum durch Gregor von NYSSA: [kath. Diss. Regensburg 1991 ➤ 9,3959]: BeiGBEx 32. Tü 1994, Mohr. ix-419 p. DM 178. 3-16-146033-2 [TR 91,181]. - ᴿBL (1994) 57 (W.G.E. *Watson*); RechSR 82 (1994) 598s (M. *Fédou*); ScripTPamp 26 (1994) 733-6 (L.F. *Mateo-Seco*); VigChr 48 (1994) 394-8 (J.C.M. van *Winden*).

3161 **Engammare** Max, Qu'il me baise... Ct/Ren 1992 ➤ 8,3430; 9,7284: ᴿÉTRel 69 (1994) 113s (H. *Bost*); JEH 45 (1994) 731 (Ann *Moss*).

3162 **Fernández Tejero** Emilia, El Cantar más bello; cantar de los cantares de Salomón; traducción y comentario. M 1994, Trotta. 111 p. 84-8164-018-2.

3163 **Garbini** G., Cantico 1992 ➤ 8,3409; 9,3262: ᴿAsprenas 41 (1994) 441-4 (A. *Rolla*); Biblica 75 (1994) 576-582 (G. *Borgonovo*: schema ideologico per un poema lirico forse troppo rigido; influsso su Gesù-Gv innegabile); BL (1994) 58 (W.G.E. *Watson*: origin THEOCRITUS, not Mid-East); ParVi 39,1 (1994) 54-56 (A. *Rolla*); Salesianum 56 (1994) 779 (M. *Cimosa*: utilmente provocatorio).

3164 **Girón Blanc** Luis-Fernández, Midrás Cantar 1991 ➤ 7,2943; 9,3263: ᴿArTGran 57 (1994) 521s (A. *Torres*); CiTom 121 (1994) 198s (M. *García Cordero*); Sefarad 53 (1993) 406-410 (E. *Fernández Tejero*).

3165 **Girón** Luis F., Vocablos griegos y latinos en Cantar de los Cantares Rabbá: Sefarad 54 (1994) 271-305; Eng. 306.

3166 **Guérard** Marie-Gabrielle, NIL d'Ancyre, Commentaire sur le Cantique des Cantiques I: SChr 403. P 1994, Cerf. 383 p. F 169. 2-204-05141-1 [JTS 46,727, G. *Gould*; TLZ 120,1015, G. *Haendler*].

3167 **Hoyland** Gilbert de, Sermons 1-20 sur le Cantique, ᵀᴱ*Emery* Pierre-Yves: Pain de Citeaux 6. Oka 1994, N.-D. du Lac: ᴿEsprVie 104 (1994) 511s (G.-M. *Oury*).

3168 **Keel** Othmar, The Song of Songs [1986]ᵀ: Continental comm. Mp 1994, Fortress. v-308 p. 0-8006-9507-0 [OTAbs 18, p. 165; TDig 42,472; BL 95,67, W.G.E. *Watson*: 158 remarkable drawings].

3169 **König** E. Hildegard., APPONIUS, Lied 1992 ➤ 8,3412; 9,3266: ᴿNRT 116 (1994) 264 (V. *Roisel*).

3170 **Maier** Gerhard, Das Hohelied: StudB AT. Wu 1991, Brockhaus. 187 p. 3-417-25319-5; pa. -9. - ᴿBijdragen 55 (1994) 328 (J. van *Ruiten*).

3171 **Manzoni** Giuseppe, Il Cantico. 1993, Dehoniane. 432 p. - ᴿTeresianum 45 (1994) 635 (V. *Pasquetto*).

3172 **Martin-Lunas** Teodoro H., S. GREGORIO de Nisa, Comentario al Cantar de los Cantares: Ichthys 16. S 1993, Sígueme. 254 p. - ᴿEfMex 12 (1994) 428-430 (M.A. *Flores Ramos*); Proyección 41 (1994) 238 (R. *Franco*).

3173 **Morfino** Mauro M., L'elezione divina negli scritti di ORIGENE sul Cantico dei Cantici, nel Targum Shir haShirim e nel Shir haShirim Rabbah. Cagliari 1992. 92 p. [< diss.].

3174 **Müller** H.-P., Das Hohelied [+ *Kaiser* O. Lam; *Loader* J. Ester] 1992 ➤ 9,3269: ᴿZAW 106 (1994) 364 (G. *Metzner*).

3175 **Murphy** R. E., The Song of Songs: Hermeneia comm. 1990 ➤ 7,2951 ... 9,3271: ᴿScotJT 47 (1994) 396-8 (R. P. *Carroll*: judicious); TsTKi 65 (1994) 139 (M. *Sæbø*, Norwegian); VT 44 (1994) 286s (H. G. M. *Williamson*).

3176 **Ravasi** Gianfranco, Il Cantico dei Cantici, commentario e attualizzazione; Testi e commenti 4, 1992 ➤ 8,3417; 9,3273: ᴿRivB 42 (1994) 213-7 (L. *Manicardi*).

3177 ᴱ**Schulz-Flügel** Eva, GREGORIUS Eliberritanus, Epithalamium sive explanatio in Ct: VLatGesch 26, 1994 ➤ 9,3276; 3-451-21940-9 [BL 95,74, P. W. *Coxon*; JTS 46,724, L. R. *Wickham*; NRT 117,597, A. *Toubeau*].

3178 **Snaith** John G., Song of Songs: NCent 1993 ➤ 9,3277: ᴿAntonianum 69 (1994) 117s (M. *Nobile*); CalvaryB 9,2 (1993) 65-67 (S. *Horine*); ClasW 88 (1994s) 496s (S. *Mandell*); JTS 45 (1994) 185s (M. D. *Goulder*); Vidyajyoti 58 (1994) 63s (P. *Meagher*).

3179 **Stadelmann** L., Love and politics 1992 ➤ 8,3419; 9,3278: ᴿBL (1994) 75s (P. W. *Coxon*); OTEssays 7 (1994) 111-3 (H. *Viviers*: rich on Persian-era background, silent on what the Song really communicates); RivB 42 (1994) 108-110 (G. *Ravasi*: infondato).

E7.4   **Canticum**, *themata, versiculi.*

3180 **Bekkenkamp** Jonneke, Canon en Keuze, het bijbelse Hooglied en de Twenty-one love poems van Adrienne RICH als bronnen van theologie. Kampen 1993, Kok Agora. ix-318 p. *f*45. – ᴿStreven 61 (1994) 669s (P. *Beentjes*).

3181 **Clines** David J. A., Why is there a Song of Songs? and what does it do to you when you read it?: Jian Dao 1 (1994) 3-26; ☺ 27.

3182 **Deckers-Dijs** Mimi, Begeerte in bijbelse liefdespoëzie; een semiotische analyse van het Hooglied. Kampen 1991, Kok. 315 p. *f*49. 90-242-3160-4. – ᴿKerkT 45 (1994) 161s (N. den *Bok*).

3183 *Dennison* James T.ᴶ, What should I read on the Song of Solomon?: Kerux 8,2 (1993) 35-41 [< OTAbs 18,91].

3184 *Elliott* Mark W., Ethics and aesthetics in the Song of Songs: TyndB 45 (1994) 137-152.

3185 *Emmerson* Grace I., The Song of Songs; mystification, ambiguity and humour: ➤ 45, ᶠGOULDER M., Crossing 1994, 97-111.

3187 **Fulton** Rachel L., The Virgin Mary and the Song of Songs in the high Middle Ages: diss. Columbia, ᴰ*Bynum* C. NY 1994. 710 p. 94-27072. – DissA 55 (1994s) p. 1656.

3188 **Gledhill** Tom, The message of the Song of Songs; the lyrics of love. Leicester 1994. Inter-Varsity. 254 p. £9. 0-85110-967-5 [BL 95,62, C. H. *Knights*]. – ᴿTBR 7,1 (1994s) 23 (R. *Mason*).

3189 **Keel** Othmar, The symbolism [42 love songs] of the ancient world; the Song of Songs. Mp 1994, Fortress. ix-308 p. $32. 0-8006-9507-0. – ᴿExpTim 106 (1994s) 184 (C. S. *Rodd*: to replace Keel's translations with adapted NRSV was 'a stupid decision'; Keel has no use for allegory, 'an elegant way of despising the text').

3190 *Krichbaumer* Maria, Ecclesia und Synagoga; die Stellung von Sermo

super Cantica Canticorum 14 im Gesamtwerk BERNHARDs von Clairvaux: MüTZ 45 (1994) 289-300 (271-287, *Maidl* Lydia & *Bendel* Rainer).
3190* *Marin Heredia* F., La otra cara del Cantar: Carthaginensia 10 (1994) 19-26; Eng. iii.
3191 **Matter** E. Ann, The voice... 1990 ➤ 6,3528... 8,3438: ᴿConcordTQ 58 (1994) 62 (K. F. *Fabrizius*).
3192 *Müller* Hans-Peter, Menschen, Landschaften und religiöse Erinnerungsreste; Anschlusserörterungen zum Hohenlied: ZTK 91 (1994) 375-395.
3192* **Pelletier** Anne-Marie, Le Cantique: CahEv 85. P 1993, Cerf. – ᴿVSp 148 (1994) 262 (J. *Asurmendi*).
3193 *a) Ramos-Lissón* Domingo, Las tipologías de Cristo en el 'Canticum Canticorum' según el tratado ambrosiano 'De virginitate'; – *b) Mateo-Seco* Lucas F., Cristología y doctrina espiritual en GREGORIO de Nisa: ➤ 22, ᶠCASCIARO J. M., Biblia 1994, 533-541 / 511-531.
3194 *Richardson* John P., Preaching from the Song of Songs? Allegory revisited: Churchman 108 (1994) 135-142.
3195 *Watson* Wilfred G. E., A reappraisal [of gender-matched parallelism] with particular reference to the Song of Songs (ineditum): ➤ 230*c*, Traditional 1994, 226-239.

3196 *Callow* John, Units and flow in the Song of Songs 1:2-2:6: ➤ 304*c*, Biblical Hebrew 1993/4, 462-488 [< OTAbs 18, p. 333].
3197 *Rendsburg* G. A., Talpiyyot (Song 4:4): JNWS 20,1 (1994) 13-21.
3198 *Görg* Manfred, 'Kanäle' oder 'Zweige' in HLd 4,13?: BibNot 72 (1994) 20-23.
3199 *Piras* Antonio, [deutsch] At ille declinaverat atque transierat (Cant 5,2-8): ZAW 106 (1994) 487-490.

E7.5 *Libri sapientiales* – **Wisdom literature.**

3200 **Barrett** Ruth, House as a wisdom metaphor in Solomonic literature: diss. St. Michael's, ᴰ*Sheppard* G. Windsor 1993. – SR 23 (1994) 525.
3201 ᴱ**Berndt** Rainer, ANDREAS de S. Victore, Expositiones historicae in libros Salomonis: Opera 3, CCMdv 53 B, 1991 ➤ 7,2976; 8,3452: ᴿSpeculum 69 (1994) 101s (Rachel *Fulton*: rather a glossary than a commentary).
3202 *Brueggemann* Walter, James L. CRENSHAW [some 35 writings on Wisdom and credo-covenant theology]; faith lingering at the edges: RelStR 20 (1994) 103-111 [111s, Crenshaw, Reflections on three decades of research].
3203 **Clements** Ronald E., Wisdom... in theology 1992 ➤ 8,3458: ᴿBL (1994) 105 (R. J. *Coggins*); BR 10,2 (1994) 10s (R. C. *Van Leeuwen*); CBQ 56 (1994) 751-3 (J. G. *Williams*: useful but 'must be given greater scope'); Interpretation 48 (1994) 198.200 (W. P. *Brown*); NesTR 15 (1994) 193-5 (J. *Derksen*).
3204 *Crenshaw* James L., Wisdom and the sage; on knowing and not knowing: ➤ 331*a*, 11th Jewish 1993/4, A-137-144.
3205 *a) Crenshaw* James L., Wisdom literature; retrospect and prospect; – *b) Eaton* John, Memory and encounter; an educational ideal; – *c) Brenner* Athalya, Some observations on the figurations of women in wisdom literature: ➤ 138, ᶠWHYBRAY N., Of prophets/sages 1993, 161-178 / 178-191 / 192-208.

3206 *Dell* Katharine J., 'Green' [ecological] ideas in the Wisdom tradition: ScotJT 47 (1994) 423-451.

3207 **Ernst** Alexander, Weisheitliche [& Proph.] Kultkritik: ev. Diss. ᴰ*Schmidt* W. Bonn 1994. – TR 91,93.

3208 **Giudici** Maria Pia, Sulle strade della Sapienza; itinerari di Lectio Divina: Religiosi duemila 4. Mi 1994, Paoline. 329 p. 88-315-0997-7.

3209 **Goldsworthy** G., Gospel and wisdom; Israel's wisdom literature in the Christian life 1987 → 3,2326 ... 5,3282: ᴿVT 44 (1994) 427-9 (Katharine J. *Dell*).

3210 **Golka** Friedemann W., Die Flecken des Leoparden; biblische und afrikanische Weisheit in Sprichwort [The leopard's spots 1993 → 9,3312],ᵀ: ArbT 78. Stu 1994, Calwer. 176 p. ᴅᴍ 58.

3211 **Kottsieper** Ingo, Die Sprache der Ahiqarsprüche: ʙᴢᴀᴡ 194, 1991 → 6, 3563 ... 9,3317: ᴿJBL 113 (1994) 326-8 (B. *Grossfeld*).

3212 ᴱ**Lebrun** René, Sagesses de l'Orient ancien et chrétien. P 1993, Beauchesne, 246 p. F 150. – ᴿÉtudes 381 (1994) 715 (M. *Fédou*).

3213 **Lux** Rüdiger, Die Weisen Israels; Meister der Sprache, Lehrer des Volkes, Quelle des Lebens 1992 → 8,3473; ᴿᴢᴀᴡ 106 (1994) 161 (M. *Köckert*).

3214 **Morla Asensio** Víctor. Libros sapienciales y otros Escritos; Introducción al estudio de la Biblia 5. Estella 1994, VDivino. 541 p. pt. 2800. 84-7151-907-0 [OTAbs 18, p. 640: R. E. *Murphy*].

3215 *Mouhanna* Antoine, Universalismo y particularismo de la sabiduría en los escritos sapienciales: RBibArg 55 (1993) 215-224.

3216 **Müller** Hans-Peter, Mensch – Umwelt – Eigenwelt 1992 → 8,288: ᴿTLZ 119 (1994) 234s (C. *Westermann*).

3217 **Murphy** R. E., L'albero della vita; una esplorazione della letteratura sapienziale [1990 → 6,3567],ᵀ. Brescia 1993, Queriniana. 244 p. Lᵐ 32. – ᴿAsprenas 41 (1994) 583-590 (G. *Di Palma*, ma Roland, no Raymond).

3218 *Murphy* Roland E., *a*) Wisdom literature and biblical theology: BibTB 24 (1994) 4-7; – *b*) Israelite wisdom and the home: → 30, ᶠCᴏᴜᴛᴜʀɪᴇʀ G., Maison 1994, 199-212.

3219 **Nebe** G., Text und Sprache der Weisheitsschrift 1993 → 9,3321: ᴿJStJud 25 (1994) 108-112 (G. *Veltri*).

3220 **Neilly** Raymond R., Human achievement in the Wisdom literature of ancient Israel, the gift of God as attainment, piety, or simple pleasure: diss. Drew, ᴰ*Huffmon* H. Madison ɴᴊ 1994. 405 p. 94-32951. – RelStR 21,255; DissA 55 (1994s) p. 2004.

3221 **Niccacci** Alviero, La casa della Sapienza; voci e volti della sapienza biblica. Mi 1994, San Paolo. 186 p. Lᵐ 24. 88-215-3758-1 [BL 95,97, J. R. *Duckworth*; OTAbs 18, p. 416, R. E. *Murphy*].

3222 **O'Connor** Kathleen M., The Wisdom literature: MessageBSpir 5, 1988 → 4,3459 ... 6,3568: ᴿNesTR 15 (1994) 85s (J. *Derksen*).

3223 **Panikkar** Raimon, A dwelling place for wisdom. Lᴠʟ 1993, W-Knox. [JDharma 19 (1994) 104].

3224 *Perdue* Leo G., Wisdom and creation; the theology of wisdom literature. Nv 1994, Abingdon. 420 p.; bibliog. 379-390. $22. 0-687-45626-6 [OTAbs 18,160, R. E. *Murphy*].

3225 *Preuss* H. Dietrich, Einführung in die alttestamentliche Weisheitsliteratur 1987 → 3,3244 ... 7,2999: ᴿSalesianum 56 (1994) 155s (M. *Cimosa*); TR 90 (1994) 378-350 (L. *Schwienhorst-Schönberger*).

3226 **Quack** Joachim F., Die Lehren des Ani; ein neuägyptischer Weisheitstext in seinem kulturellen Umfeld: OBO 141. FrS 1994, Univ. x-331 p.; Bibliog. 221-263. 3-7278-0984-1.

3227 **Römer** Thomas, La sagesse dans l'AT: Prov. Job, Qoh: CahB 3, 1991
→ 7,3002: ᴿRTPhil 126 (1994) 180s (D. *Bodi*).

3228 **Rüger** Hans-Peter, Die Weisheitsschrift aus der Kairoer Geniza: WUNT
53, 1991 → 7,3002... 9,2331: ᴿKairos 32s (1990s) 253-5 (G. *Stemberger*);
Salesianum 56 (1994) 156s (M. *Cimosa*).

3229 **Shupak** Nili, Where can wisdom be found?...: OBO 130, 1993 → 9,
3334: ᴿBL (1994) 99 (K. A. *Kitchen*); ÉTRel 69 (1994) 272s (Françoise
Smyth-Florentin); JBL 113 (1994) 710-2 (Shannon *Burkes*).

3230 *Sneed* Mark, Wisdom and class; a survey and critique: JAAR 62 (1994)
651-672: toward a criterion of class other than mode of production.

3231 **Steiert** F.-J., Weisheit/Fremdkörper? ᴰ1990 → 6,2573; 8,2359: ᴿSalesianum 56 (1994) 158s (M. *Cimosa*); TPhil 69 (1994) 265s (R. *Scoralick*).

3232 *a*) *Swanepoel* C. F., Orality and literariness; the interface of values
[PROPP: ONG W.; Sotho African proverbs]; – *b*) *Deist* F. E., Orality,
'editure', literature — reflections on orality, literariness and First Testament literature: JNWS 20,2 (1994) 143-154 / 155-163.

3234 **Tarr** Delbert H., Double image; biblical insights from African parables.
NY 1994, Paulist. ix-209 p. 0-8091-3469-1.

3235 **Vorster** Jan H., Aspekte van die verhouding tussen heerskappij en
gemeenskap in die kritiese wijsheid van Israel: diss. ᴰ*Loader* J. Pretoria.
190 p. – RTLv 26, 533 sans date.

3236 **Weeks** Stuart, Early Israelite wisdom [did not originate in education
of administrators; diss. Oxford 1991 → 8,3487], Ox 1994, Clarendon.
xii- 212 p. £25. 0-19-826750-9 [TDig 42,295]. – ᴿBL (1994) 102 (L. L.
Grabbe); JTS 45 (1994) 630s (W. *McKane*); OTAbs 17 (1994) 447 (R. E.
Murphy: mostly disproves reigning tenets: von RAD's Solomonic 'enlightenment', LEMAIRE's school system...); TLond 97 (1994) 456s (R.
Davidson: like GOLKA, challenges many assumptions).

E7.6 **Proverbiorum liber,** *themata, versiculi.*

3237 **Ehlke** Roland C., Proverbs: People's Bible. Milwaukee 1992, Northwestern. 322 p. – ᴿConcordJ 20 (1994) 217s (C. W. *Mitchell*: series
co-published at St. Louis Concordia).

3238 **Farmer** Kathleen A., Who knows what is good? A commentary on
Prov Eces 1991 → 7,3009... 9,3343: ᴿCritRR 6 (1993) 157s (H. C.
Washington); OTEssays 7 (1994) 151s (F. N. *Lion-Cachet*, Afrikaans).

3239 **Garrett** Duane A., Proverbs, Ecclesiastes, Song of Songs: NAmerComm
14, 1993 → 9,3344; 0-8054-0114-8. – ᴿBtS 151 (1994) 496s (R. B. *Zuck*).

3240 **Hubbard** D. A., Proverbs 1989 → 5,3312... 8,3493: ᴿJEvTS 37 (1994)
140 (J. C. *Whytock*).

3241 **Lelièvre** André, *Maillot* Alphonse, Commentaire des Proverbes... de
Salomon 10-18: LDivCom 1. P 1993, Cerf. 300 p. F 180. – ᴿBL (1994)
65 (R. N. *Whybray*); Carthaginensia 10 (1994) 179 (R. *Sanz Valdivieso*);
CBQ 56 (1994) 557s (Camilla *Burns*); NRT 116 (1994) 103 (J. L. *Ska*);
RHPR 74 (1994) 196-8 (E. *Jacob*); ZAW 106 (1994) 360 (J. van
Oorschot).

3242 **Meinhold** Arndt, Die Sprüche: Z BK AT 16, 1991 → 7,3041; 8,3495:
ᴿCBQ 56 (1994) 560-3 (R. C. *Van Leeuwen*: good sense); VT 44 (1994)
141 (J. A. *Emerton*).

3243 ᵀᴱ**Visotzky** Burton L., The midrash on Proverbs: Yale Jud 27. NHv
1992, Yale. 170 p. $28.50. 0-300-05107-7. – ᴿBL (1993) 139 (S. C. *Reif*);
CritRR 6 (1993) 440s (J. S. *Kaminsky*).

3244 **Wehrle** Josef, Sprichwort und Weisheit; Studien zur Syntax und Semantik der *ṭôb... min*-Sprüche im Buch der Sprichwörter [Diss. Mü 1992, ᴰ*Görg* M. ⇒ 8,3510]: ArbO 38, 1993 ⇒ 9,3362: ᴿBL (1994) 164s (W. *McKane*); TLZ 119 (1994) 639s (R. *Bartelmus*).

3245 **Whybray** R. Norman, Proverbs, based on RSV: NCent. GR 1994, Eerdmans. xxxii-445 p.; bibliog. xiii-xxxii. 0-8028-0787-9.

3246 *Berndt* Rainer, Skizze zur Auslegungsgeschichte der Bücher Prouerbia et Ecclesiastes in der abendländischen Kirche: SacrEr 34 (1994) 5-32.

3247 **Bland** Dave L., A rhetorical perspective on the sentence sayings of the Book of Proverbs: diss. Washington, ᴰ*Campbell* J. Seattle 1994. 279 p. 94-34297. – DissA 55 (1994s) p. 2207.

3248 **Boström** Lennart, The God of the sages... Prov: ConBib OT 29, 1990 ⇒ 6,3578... 9,3350: ᴿCritRR 5 (1992) 115s (D. C. *Snell*).

3249 *Clements* Ronald E., The good neighbour in the book of Proverbs: ⇒ 138, ᶠWHYBRAY N., Of prophets/sages 1993, 200-228.

3250 **Hinds** Mark D., The Book of Proverbs; toward alternative pedagogical principles for confirmation in the P.C. (U.S.A.) Presbyterian Church: diss. Union, ᴰ*Melchert* C. Richmond 1994. 187 p. 94-31479. – DissA 55 (1994s) p. 1890.

3251 **Lelièvre** André, La sagesse des Proverbes; une leçon de tolérance: Essais bibliques 23, 1993 ⇒ 9,2372: ᴿOTEssays 7 (1994) 302-4 (F. *Deist*); RHPR 74 (1994) 198 (P. de *Robert*).

3252 **McKenzie** Alyce M., Subversive sages; preaching on proverbial wisdom in Proverbs, Qohelet and the Synoptic Jesus through the reader-response theory of Wolfgang ISER: diss. ᴰ*Long* T. Princeton Theol. Sem. 1994. 297 p. 94-30036. – DissA 55 (1994s) p. 2003.

3253 *Masenya* M.J., Wisdom meets wisdom; selected OT proverbs in a Northern Sotho setting: NederduitsGT 35 (1994) 15-23 [< OTAbs 18, p. 88].

3254 **Snell** Daniel C., Twice-told proverbs 1993 ⇒ 9,3358; 0-931464-66-8: ᴿOTAbs 17 (1994) 449 (R.E. *Murphy*: first to focus usefully the repetitions, clichés, and shapes of the collections).

3255 **Whybray** R.N., The composition of the Book of Proverbs: jOsu 168. Shf 1994, JStOT. 173 p. £30. 1-85075-457-8 [BL 95,77, K.J.A. *Larkin*; the most thorough there is; JTS 46,222, J.D. *Martin*].

3256 *Bonora* Antonio, La 'donna straniera' in Pr 1-9: RicStoB 6 (1994) 101-9 [< OTAbs 18, p. 330].

3257 **Cook** Johann, *Iššâ zārâ* (Proverbs 1-9 Septuagint); a metaphor for foreign wisdom?: ᴢᴀᴡ 106 (1994) 458-476.

3258 *a)* **Klopfenstein** Martin A., Auferstehung der Göttin in der spätisraelitischen Weisheit von Prov 1-9? – *b)* *Schroer* Silvia, Die personifizierte Sophia im Buch der Weisheit: ⇒ 467*, Ein Gott allein? 1993/4, 531-542 / 543-558 [559-564, *Lang* B.].

3259 **Ranieri** Aldo A., Studio grammaticale e semantico del parallelismo in Proverbi I-IX; un contributo alla comprensione della formula introduttiva dell'istruzione sapienziale: diss. Studium Biblicum Franciscanum; ᴰ*Niccacci* A. J 1993. – LA 44 (1994) 741-3.

3260 *Washington* Harold C., The 'strange woman' of Proverbs 1-9 and post-exilic Judean society [via mixed marriages they were getting title to all the land]: → 317, Second Temple Studies 2 (1994) 217-242 [< OTA 18, p. 331].

3261 *Fox* Michael V., The pedagogy of Proverbs 2: JBL 113 (1994) 233-243.

3262 *Precedo Lafuente* Manuel J., [Prov 6,16...] Las sentencias numerales en los libros bíblicos: Compostellanum 38,1 (1993) 9-46.

3263 *Peels* Hendrik G. L., Passion or justice? The interpretation of *beyōm nāqām* in Proverbs VI 34: VT 44 (1994) 270-4.

3264 *Heijerman* Mieke, Who would blame her? The 'strange' woman of Proverbs 7: → 267, ReflTGender (1994) 21-31 [OTAbs 18, p. 88].

3265 *Gosse* Bernard, Le sens du terme *ṭebaḥ* dans les livres prophétiques ['massacre'; ailleurs seul Prov. 7,22; 8,2; Gn 43,16 'immolation']: BibNot 73 (1994) 18s.

3266 *Williams* Daniel H., Proverbs 8:22-31: Interpretation 48 (1994) 275-9.

3267 *Hurvitz* A., *amûn* Prov 8,30 'skilled worker' rather than 'foster-parent': → 62, ᶠKAMIN S., ● Bible 1994, 647-650.

3268 **McCreesh** Thomas P., Biblical sound and sense... Proverbs 10-29: jOsu 128, 1991 → 7,7030; 9,3371: ᴿCBQ 56 (1994) 117s (A. R. *Ceresko*); RelStR 20 (1994) 142 (J. L. *Crenshaw*); JSS 38 (1993) 147-9 (J. *Eaton*).

3269 **Westermann** Claus, [Prov 10-31] Roots of wisdom [1990 → 6,3597], ᵀ*Charles* J. Daryl. LVL 1994, W-Knox. 178 p. $20. 0-664-25559-0 [OTA 14/91, nº 384; 18, p. 1248: bibliography not updated].

3270 **Parker** Don, Syntactic and poetic structures in Proverbs 10:1-22;16: diss. California, ᴰ*Segert* S. Los Angeles 1992. xxii-441 p. 93-10883. – OIAc 11,36.

3271 *Goldingay* John, The arrangement of sayings in Proverbs 10-13: JStOT 61 (1994) 75-83.

3272 *Whybray* R. N., The structure and composition of Proverbs 22:17-24:22: → 45, ᶠGOULDER M., Crossing 1994, 83-96.

3273 *Carasik* Michael, Who were the 'men of Hezekiah' (Proverbs XXV 1)?: VT 44 (1994) 289-300.

3274 *Moore* Rick D., A home for the alien; worldly wisdom and covenantal confession in Proverbs 30,1-9: ZAW 106 (1994) 96-107.

3275 *Wolters* Al, [Prov 31:19] The meaning of *kîšôr* [spindle, not distaff]: HUCA 65 (1994) 91-104.

E7.7   *Ecclesiastes* – **Qohelet;** *textus, themata, versiculi.*

3276 **Bonora** Antonio, Il libro di Qoèlet 1992 → 8,3535; 9,3380: ᴿArTGran 57 (1994) 424s (J. *Vílchez*); CBQ 56 (1994) 319s (J. F. *Craghan*); CC 145 (1994,3) 198s (D. *Scaiola*); ParVi 39,3 (1994) 58s (A. *Rolla*).

3277 **Bonora** A., El libro de Qohelet, ᵀ*Villanueva* Marciano. Barc/M 1994, Herder/CiudadNueva. 207 p. pt. 1800. 84-254-1839-9. – ᴿActuBbg 31 (1994) 216 (J. *O'Callaghan*).

3278 **Diego Sánchez** M., El comentario al Eclesiastés de DÍDIMO A. 1991 → 7,3045... 9,3384: ᴿCompostellanum 38 (1993) 264s (E. *Romero Pose*).

3279 **Géhin** P., ÉVAGRE, Scholies à l'Ecclésiaste: SChr 397, 1993 → 9,3385: ᴿNRT 116 (1994) 443 (A. *Harvengt*).

3280 ᵀᴱ**Gómez Aranda** Mariano, El comentario de Abraham IBN EZRA al libro del Eclesiastés, edición crítica: TEstCisn 56. M 1994, Cons. Sup. Inv. cxxi-220-128* p. 84-00-07402-5 [BL 95,64, S. C. *Reif*]. – ᴿRB 102 (1994) 164 (É. *Nodet*).

3281 **Labate** A., Catena hauniensis 1992 → 8,3539; 9,3390: ᴿByzantion 64 (1994) 229-231 (J. *Declerck*); OrChrPer 60 (1994) 684-6 (L. *Pieralli*);

RechSR 82 (1994) 619 (B. *Sesboüé*); SMSR 18,60 (1994) 153s (S. *Zincone*).

3282 **Murphy** R. E., Ecclesiastes Word comm. 23A, 1992 ➤ 8,3542: ᴿRelStR 20 (1994) 233 (J. L. *Crenshaw*: 'unfortunately nothing new, and much that I cannot accept').

3283 **Perry** T. A., Dialogues with [i.e. of two debaters within] Kohelet; the book of Ecclesiastes, translation and commentary: 1993 ➤ 9,3393: ᴿBL (1994) 70 (R. N. *Whybray*); JStOT 64 (1994) 125s (J. *Jarick*: inventive but overstretched).

3284 **Vílchez Líndez** José, Eclesiastes o Qohelet: NuevaBEsp sap. 3. Estella 1994, VDivino. 507 p.; bibliog. 102-9. pt. 4300. 84-7151-669-1 [OTAbs 18, p. 643; Biblica 76,565, G. *Ravasi*].

3285 **Backhaus** Franz Joseph, '... denn Zeit und Zufall trifft sie alle ...' Studien zur Komposition und zum Gottesbild im Buch Qohelet [Diss. Münster 1991]: BoBBeit 83. Fra 1993, Hain. x-490 p. DM 44. 3-445-09146-3 [TR 91,76].

3286 *Chamiel* C., ❺ Luck, destiny and prayer in the targum of Qohelet: BMikra 39 (1994) 261-8 [< OTAbs 18, p. 89].

3287 *Custer* John S., Qoheleth and the canon; the dissenting voice in dialogue: Josephinum 1 (1994) 15-24 [< OTAbs 18, p. 89].

3288 *D'Alario* Vittoria, Il libro del Qohelet; struttura letteraria e retorica: RivB supp. 27, ᴰ1992 ➤ 9,3399: ᴿCC 145 (1994,3) 347s (D. *Scaiola*); NRT 116 (1994) 102s (J. L. *Ska*); ParVi 39,6 (1994) 55s (A. *Rolla*); RivB 42 (1994) 352-5 (F. *Bianchi*); RTPhil 126 (1994) 182 (M. *Rose*).

3289 *Dell* Katharine J., Ecclesiastes as wisdom; consulting early interpreters: VT 44 (1994) 301-329.

3290 *a) Hart* Thomas M., Qoheleth looks at friendship; – *b) Harrington* Daniel J., [Sirach] Sage advice about friendship: BToday 32 (1994) 74-78 / 79-83.

3291 *Jong* Stephan de, Qohelet and the ambitious spirit of the Ptolemaic period: JStOT 61 (1994) 85-96.

3292 **Klein** Christian, Kohelet und die Weisheit Israels, eine formgeschichtliche Studie [Diss. Münster 1992, ᴰ*Müller* H.-P. ➤ 9,3402]: BW 132. Stu 1994, Kohlhammer. 227 p. DM 79. 3-17-012497-8 [TLZ 120,234, T. *Krüger*]. – ᴿOTAbs 17 (1994) 670s (R. E. *Murphy*).

3293 *Lavoie* Jean-Jacques, La pensée de Qohélet; étude exégétique et intertextuelle: Héritage et projet 49, 1992 ➤ 8,3533: ᴿSR 23 (1994) 98s (Catherine *Barry*).

3294 *Loretz* O., Jüdischer Gott und griechische Philosophie (*hokmat yewanit*) im Qohelet-Buch: MAnthropRG 8 (Münster 1994) 151-176 [< ZIT 95, p. 275].

3295 *McKenna* John F., The concept of *hebel* in the book of Ecclesiastes: ScotJT 45 (1992) 29-28.

3295* *Papone* Paolo, La presenza misteriosa di Dio (Kohelet): ParSpV 30 (1994) 93-102.

3296 *Pinto* Carlos O., Eclesiastes; uma análise introdutória: VoxScr 4 (1994) 151-166.

3296* *a) Rosendal* Bent, Popular wisdom in Qohelet; – *b) Bach-Nielsen* Carsten, Words of wisdom [... hieroglyphs]: ➤ 89e, ᶠOTZEN B., In the last days 1994, 121-7 / 164-174.

3297 *a) Scheffler* Eren, Qohelet's positive advice; – *b) Salters* R. B., Observations on the Septuagint of Ecclesiastes: OTEssays 6 (1993) 248-271 / 183-174 [< OTAbs 17, p. 590].

3298 **Schoors** Antoon, The preacher sought to find pleasing words ... Qoh: OrLovAnal 41, 1992 ➤ 8,3560: ᴿBijdragen 55 (1994) 201s (P.C. *Beentjes*); JBL 113 (1994) 524s (E.G. *Hostetter*); OTEssays 7 (1994) 97-99 (I.J.J. *Spangenberg*: a second volume co-authored by W.C. *Delsman* awaited).

3299 **Zuck** Roy B., Reflecting with Solomon; selected studies on the Book of Ecclesiastes [33 reprints]. GR 1994, Baker. 426 p. 0-8010-9939-0 [OTAbs 18,419, tit. pp.].

3300 *Japhet* Sara, 'Goes to the south and turns to the north' (Eces 1:6); the sources and history of the exegetical traditions: Jewish Studies Quarterly 1 (Tü 1993s) 289-322 [< OTAbs 18, p. 330].

3301 *Krüger* Thomas, Qoh 2,24-26 und die Frage nach dem 'Guten' im Qohelet-Buch: BibNot 72 (1994) 70-94.

3302 **Schwienhorst-Schönberger** Ludger, 'Nicht im Menschen gründet das Glück' (Koh 2,24); Kohelet im Spannungsfeld jüdischer Weisheit und hellenistischer Philosophie; Herders biblische Studien 2. FrB 1994, Herder. ix-358 p. ᴅᴍ 88. 3-451-23149-2 [Biblica 76,562, J. *Vilchez*].

3303 *Vílchez* José, Poema sobre el tiempo (Ecle 3,1-8): SalT 81 (1993) 871-877.

3304 *Bianchi* Francesco, 'Ma Dio ricerca ciò che è scomparso'? (Qo 3,15b); la storia, la memoria e il tempo nel libro di Qohelet: RivB 42 (1994) 58-73.

3305 *Tsukimoto* Akio, The background of Qoh 11:1-6 and Qohelet's agnosticism: AnJapB 19 (1993) 34-52 [< OTAbs 18, p. 90].

3306 *Niekerk* M.J.H. van, Qohelet's advice to the young of his time — and to ours today? Chapter 11:7-12:8 as a text of the pre-Christian era: OTEssays 7 (1994) 370-380.

3307 *Lavoie* Jean-Jacques, Étude de l'expression *bêt 'ôlāmô* dans Qo 12,5 à la lumière des textes du Proche-Orient ancien: ➤ 30, ᶠCOUTURIER G., Maison 1994, 213-226.

3308 a) *Backhaus* F.-J., Der Weisheit letzter Schluss: Qoh. 12,9-14 im Kontext von Traditionsgeschichte und beginnender Kanonisierung; – b) *Koenen* Klaus, Zu den Epilogen des Buches Qohelet: BibNot 72 (1994) 28-59 / 24-27.

3309 *Lohfink* Norbert, [Qoh 12,9-14] Grenzen und Einbindung des Kohelet-Schlussgedichts: ➤ 101, ᶠREVENTLOW H. 1994, 33-46.

3310 *Lavoie* Jean-Jacques, Un éloge à Qohélet (étude de Qo 12,9-10): LavalTP 50 (1994) 145-170.

E7.8 *Liber Sapientiae* – **Wisdom of Solomon.**

3311 *Horbury* William, The Wisdom of Solomon in the Muratorian Fragment: JTS 45 (1994) 149-159.
ᴱ**Hübner** Hans, Die Weisheit Salomos 1991/4 ➤ 324a.

3312 *Poniży* Bogdan, 'Mądrość Salomona' kisięga spotkania: W drodze 249 (1994) 62-72.

3313 **Schmitt** Armin, Weisheit: NEchter 23, 1989 ➤ 5,3379 ... 7, 3078: ᴿTLtg 66 (1993) 183s (L. *Schwienhorst-Schönberger*).

3314 **Sisti** A., Il libro della Sapienza. Assisi 1992, Porziuncola. – ᴿRivB 42 (1994) 351s (M. *Priotto*).

3315 **Pock** Johann I., Sapientia Salomonis; HIERONYMUS' Exegese des Weisheitsbuches im Lichte der Tradition: Diss. Graz 89, 1992 ⇒ 8,3573; 9,3419: ᴿVigChr 48 (1994) 191-3 (G. J. M. *Bartelink*).

3316 **Gilbert** Maurice, Studi sul libro della Sapienza, ᵀᴱ*De Carlo* Giuseppe; aggiornamento bibliografico. Bo 1994. vi-319 p.; bibliog. 1-35.

3317 *Poniży* Bogdan, ❷ Il libro della Sapienza sulla scelta o respinta della fede: Zeszyty karmelitańskie 3s (1994) 71-82.

3318 **Premstaller** Volkmar M., Gericht und Strafe im Buch der Weisheit; Rezeption und Neugestaltung eines alttestamentlichen Themas in hellenistischem Kontext: kath. Diss. ᴰ*Schmitt* Armin. Regensburg 1994. – TR 91,101.

3319 **Kolarcik** Michael, The ambiguity of death in the Book of Wisdom 1-6: AnBib 127, ᴰ1991 ⇒ 7,3080; 9,3427, ᴿCBQ 56 (1994) 110-2 (D. *Winston*: very useful; bypasses AMIR); RBibArg 55 (1993) 54-61 (A. *Ricciardi*); ZAW 106 (1994) 160 (F. *Bermpohl*).

3320 *Scarpat* Giuseppe, Un Hapax assoluto, *airetís* Sap. 8,4: ⇒ 28*, ꟳCORSARO F., Scritti 1994, 643-7 [< OTAbs 18,537s].

3321 **Enns** Peter E., Exodus retold; ancient exegesis of the departure from Egypt in Wis 10; 15-21 and 19:1-9: diss. Harvard, ᴰ*Kugel* J. CM 1994. 226 p. 95-00173. – DissA 55 (1994s) p. 2436.

3322 *Poniży* Bogdan, ❷ Wielka alegoria patriarchów, Sap 10,1-14: RuBi 47 (1994) 145-159.

3323 **Cheon** Samuel, An investigation of Pseudo-Solomon's interpretation of the Exodus story in the Wisdom of Solomon 11-19: diss. Graduate Theological Union, ᴰ*Endres* J. Berkeley 1994. 235 p. 95-11333. – DissA 55 (1994s) p. 3878.

3324 *Scarpat* Giuseppe, La 'buona speranza' in Sap 12,10: RivB 42 (1994) 203-8.

3325 *Dumoulin* Pierre, [Sap 16] Entre la manne et l'Eucharistie; la manne dans le livre de la Sagesse; synthèse de traditions et préparation au mystère eucharistique: AnBib 132. R 1994, Pontificio Istituto Biblico. xviii-240 p. Lᵐ 40. 88-7653-132-7 [OTAbs 18, p. 160].

3326 **Mazzinghi** Luca, Notte di paura e di luce; esegesi di Sap 17,1-18,4: diss, Pont. Ist. Biblico, ᴰ*Gilbert* M. R 1994. – AcPIB 9,10 (1993s) 923.971; RTLv 26, p. 531.

3327 **Schwenk-Bressler** Udo, SapSal 10-18, 1993 ⇒ 9,3432: ᴿJStJud 25 (1994) 122-4 (G. J. *Boiten*).

E7.9 *Ecclesiasticus, Siracides;* **Wisdom of Jesus Sirach.**

3328 **Petraglio** Renzo, Il libro che contamina le mani; Ben Sirac rilegge il libro e la storia d'Israele 1993 ⇒ 9,3447; Augustinus. 462 p. Lᵐ 60 [NRT 117,271, J. L. *Ska*]. – ᴿParVi 39,6 (1994) 54s (A. *Rolla*).

3329 **Samaan** Kamil W., Sept traductions arabes de Ben Sira [diss. Pont. Ist. Biblico 1990 ⇒ 8,3588]: EurHS 23/492. Fra 1994, Lang. 465 p. 3-631-46565-3 [AcPIB 9,922].

3330 **Bohlen** R., Die Ehrung der Eltern bei Ben Sira 1991 ⇒ 8,3592: ᴿBZ 38 (1994) 123-5 (F. V. *Reiterer*); JBL 113 (1994) 136-8 (L. J. *Hoppe*).

3331 *Foulkes* Pamela A., 'To expound discipline or judgement'; the portrait of the scribe in Ben Sira: Pacifica 7 (1994) 75-84.

3332 *Harrington* Daniel J., *a*) Sirach research since 1965 [YADIN find; ZIEGLER LXX]; progress and questions: ➤ 133, ᶠWACHOLDER B. Z. 1994, 164-176. – *b*) Ben Sira as a spiritual master: JSpForm 15 (Pittsburgh 1994) 147-157; – *c*) Sage advice about friendship; BToday 32 (1994) 79-83 [< NTAbs 38, p. 430s].

3333 **Heaton** Eric, [Sirach point of departure] The school tradition of the Old Testament [Hampton lectures]. Ox 1994, Clarendon. xiv-208 p. £25. 0-19-826362-7 [BL 95,90, K. J. A. *Larkin*]. – ᴿExpTim 106 (1994s) 183s (R. *Coggins*).

3334 *Krawczyk* Roman, ❷ Doctrina anthropologica Gen 1-3 ut motivum vitae ethicae in Siracide: RuBi 47 (1994) 176-183.

3335 *Lehmann* Manfred R., Jewish wisdom formulae; Ben Sira, the Dead Sea Scrolls, and Pirke Avot: ➤ 331*a*, 11th Jewish 1993/4, 159-162.

3336 *Marböck* Johannes, Sündenvergebung bei Jesus Sirach: ➤ 37, ᶠGAMPER A., ZkT 116 (1994) 480-6.

3337 *Reiterer* Friedrich V., Das Verhältnis Jobs und Ben Siras: ➤ 304, Job 1993/4, 405-429.

3338 *Williams* David S., The date of Ecclesiasticus [175 BCE, grandson's translation 115]: VT 44 (1994) 563-5.

3339 *Zappella* Marco, L'immagine di Israele in Sir 33 (36),1-19 secondo il ms. ebraico B e la tradizione manoscritta greca; analisi letteraria e lessicale: RivB 42 (1994) 409-446; Eng. 446.

3340 *Beentjes* Pancratius C., Ben Sira 36,26d according to Ms. C; a new proposal: EstB 52 (1994) 535-9.

3341 **Gnan** Michael, Rezeptionsgeschichtliche Beiträge zum Sirachbuch; synagogale, evangelische und katholische Musiktraditionen zu Sir 51,12a-o; 50,24-26 (Lutherbibel) 44,16.20 (Vulgata): kath. Diss. ᴰ*Marböck* J. Passau 1994. – TR 91,100.

VIII. Libri prophetici VT

E8.1 **Prophetismus.**

3342 **Aberbach** David, Imperialism and biblical prophecy, 750-500 B.C.E. 1993 ➤ 9,3454 [BL 95,79, B. P. *Robinson*; RelStR 21,224, M. A. *Sweeney*: he curiously overlooks the pre-Alexander demise of prophecy].

3343 *Alexandre* Dolores, El profetismo, cara y cruz de la ley; – *b*) *Muñoz León* Domingo, El judaismo rabínico, sublimación de la ley; – *c*) *Pikaza* Xabier, Amor versus ley; novedad mesiánica de Jesús; – *d*) *Salas* Antonio, Libertad versus ley; la nueva oferta paulina: BibFe 20,60 ('El hechizo de la ley' 1994) 384-400 / 401-425 / 426-465 / 466-485.

3344 **Alonso Schökel** Luis, *Gutiérrez* Guillermo, Io pongo le mie parole. 1992 ➤ 8,8287: ᴿLetture 48 (1993) 83s (G. *Ravasi*).

3345 **Bowen** Nancy Ruth, The role of YHWH as deceiver in true and false prophecy: diss. Theol. Sem., ᴰ*Miller* P. Princeton 1994. 160 p. 94-30029. – DissA 55 (1994s) p. 2000.

3346 *Brin* Gerson, The laws of the prophets in the sect of the Judaean Desert; studies in 4Q 275: JPseud 10 (1992) 19-51.

3347 **Brzegowy** Tadeusz, ❷ Prorocy Izraela. Tarnów 1994. 243 + 237 p. ᴿRuBi 47 (1994) 219-221 (S. *Grzybek*, ❷).

3347* **Cappelletto** G., *Milani* M., In ascolto dei profeti e dei sapienti: IntrodAT 2, 1992, ➤ 9,820: ᴿParVi 39,4 (1994) 51s (T. *Lorenzin*).

3348 *Carroll Rodas* M. Daniel, Los profetas del octavo siglo y su crítica de la economía; un diálogo con Marvin CHANEY: Kairós 13,2 (Guat 1993) 7-24 [< OTAbs 17, p. 594].

3349 **Collins** Terence, The mantle of Elijah; the redaction criticism of the prophetic books 1993 ➤ 9,3466: ᴿBL (1994) 84 (P. M. *Joyce*); ETL 70 (1994) 435s (J. *Lust*); ExpTim 105 (1993) 382 (H. *Mowvley*).

3350 **Cryer** Frederick H., Divination in ancient Israel and its Near Eastern environment; a socio-historical investigation: jOsu 142. Shf 1994, Academic. 367 p.; bibliog. 333-360. 1-85075-353-9 [OIAc 11,19].

3350* *Deissler* Alfons, 'Zerstörung des Tempels und der Häuser' bei den Propheten: ➤ 30, ᶠCOUTURIER G., Maison 1994, 153-163.

3351 **Evans** M., Prophets of the Lord. Exeter 1992, Paternoster. 267 p. 0-85364-483-7. – ᴿJStOT 62 (1994) 115 (P. R. *Davies*: clear, but mingles exegesis with actualization).

3352 **Gilbert** Pierre, Le motif imprécatoire chez les Prophètes bibliques du 8ᵉ siècle a.C. à la lumière du Proche-Orient ancien; diss. ᴰ*Couturier* G. Montréal 1994. – SR 23 (1994) 525.

3353 *Grottanelli* Cristiano, Le rituel et les prophètes bibliques: ArchivSc-SocR 39/85 (1994) 69-84; Eng. español 84.

3354 *a) Heltzer* Michael, [Emar; Neh 6] ❺ 'True' and 'false' prophecies; – *b) Barstad* Hans M., Lachish Ostracon III and ancient Israelite prophecy: ➤ 8,91, ᶠMALAMAT A., ErIsr 24 (1993) 83-86; Eng. 234* / 8*-12*.

3355 *Hilber* John W., Diversity of OT prophetic phenomena and [correspondences to] NT prophecy: WestTJ 56 (1994) 243-258.

3356 *Ibañez Arana* Andrés, Los profetas y la política: LumenVr 43 (1994) 339-361.

3357 **Jaramillo Rivas** P., La injusticia y la opresión en el lenguaje figurado de los Profetas [diss. Gregoriana 1986]: Jerón 26. Estella 1992, VDivino. xvii-328 p. – ᴿNRT 116 (1994) 106 (J. L. *Ska*); TLZ 119 (1994) 881-3 (R. *Kessler*).

3358 *Jarick* John, The seven (?) prophetesses of the OT [four by name called such, plus Isaiah's wife unnamed, plus (one or other of) four in rabbinic tradition]: LuthTJ (Adelaide 1994) 116-121 [< OTAbs 18, p. 335].

3359 **Jemielity** Thomas, Satire and the Hebrew prophets 1992 ➤ 8,3614; 9,3471: ᴿTorJT 10 (1994) 108s (J. L. *McLaughlin*).

3360 *Jeremias* Jörg, Das Proprium der alttestamentlichen Prophetie: TLZ 119 (1994) 483-494.

Junco Garza Carlos, La crítica profética ante el Templo 1994 ➤ 2669.

3361 **Koenen** Klaus, Heil den Gerechten — Unheil den Sündern [Hab.-D. Bonn 1994 ➤ 9,3473]: BZAW 229. B 1994, de Gruyter. xi-293 p. 3-11-014376-3 [TLZ 120,1068, K. *Koch*].

3362 *a) Mayes* Andrew D. H., Prophecy and society in Israel; – *b) Grabbe* Lester L., Prophets, priests, diviners and sages in ancient Israel; – *c) Gordon* Robert P., From Mari to Moses; prophecy at Mari and in ancient Israel; – *d) Coggins* Richard, Prophecy – true and false: ➤ 138, ᶠWHYBRAY R. N. 1993, 25-42 / 43-62 / 63-79 / 80-94.

3363 **Michniewicz** Wojciech, ❶ Idea zjednoczenia naroda w nauce prorockiej (unity of the nation in prophetic teaching): diss. ᴰ*Homerski*. Lublin 1994. xxx-200 p. – RTLv 26,531.

Overholt Thomas W., Channels of prophecy 1989 ➤ 10370.

3364 **Schwemer** Anna Maria, Studien zu den frühjüdischen Prophetenlegenden,

den Viten der grossen Propheten Jesaja, Jeremia, Ezechiel und Daniel: ev. Diss. ᴰ*Hengel* H. Tübingen 1994. 450 p. > TStAJ. – RTLv 26,535.
3365 **Sicre** José Luis, Profetismo 1992 → 8,3630; 9,3491: ᴿBiblica 75 (1994) 255-9 (A. *Spreafico*); RBibArg 55 (1993) 184-6 (A. J. *Levoratti*).
3366 **Sicre** J. L., *al.*, La Iglesia y los profetas: Entorno al NT 5, 1989 → 5,3447 ... 8,3631: ᴿQVidCr 172 (1994) 130 (J. *Comes*).
3367 *Simian-Yofre* Horacio, Volontà di Dio e storia degli uomini; riflessione teologica sui profeti: → 368, Volontà di Dio 1994, 59-96.
3368 **Smith** Gary V., An introduction to the Hebrew prophets; the prophets as preachers. Nv 1994, Broadman & H. iii-372 p. 0-8054-1610-2 [OTAbs 18, p. 421).
3369 **Spreafico** A., I profeti; introduzione e saggi di lettura. Bo 1993, Dehoniane. 139 p. Lᵐ 16. – ᴿParVi 39,4 (1994) 51 (A. *Rolla*).
3369* **Synowiec** Juliusz S., ⊕ *Prorocy*... Israel's prophets, their writings and teaching. Kraków 1994, Bratni Zew. 398 p. 83-900498-2-1.
3370 **Tarazi** Paul N., Prophetic traditions: OT introduction 2. Crestwood NY 1994, St. Vladimir. xiv-233 p. 0-88141-106-X.
3371 **Torrell** Jean-Pierre, Recherche sur la théorie de la prophétie au Moyen Âge, 1992 → 9,16241: ᴿRThom 94 (1994) 171 (S.-T. *Bonino*).
3372 *Tumbarello* Giacomo, Profetismo: BbbOr 36 (1994) 169-180.
3373 **Verhoef** P. A., Profete en profesie. Capetown 1993, Lux Verbi. 135 p. 0-86997-432-7 [OTAbs 17, p. 671].
3374 **Vogels** W., [Ottawa: Novalis] I profeti, saggio di teologia biblica: StrumScRel, Temi 7. Padova 1994, Messaggero. 131 p. Lᵐ 16 [NRT 117, 272, J.-L. *Ska*].
3375 *Wahl* Harald-Martin, Die Überschriften der Prophetenbücher; Anmerkungen zu Form, Redaktion und Bedeutung für die Datierung des Buches: ETL 70 (1994) 91-104.
3376 **Zucker** David J., Israel's prophets; an introduction for Christians and Jews. NY 1994, Paulist. xiv-208 p. $12.

E8.2   **Proto-Isaias,** *textus, commentarii.*

3377 **Azcárraga Servet** M. Josefa de, Minḥat Šay... de NORZI; Isaías 1993 → 9,3502: ᴿBL (1994) 43 (J. F. *Elwolde*); CBQ 56 (1994) 755s (E. *Ben Zvi*); Sefarad 53 (1993) 401s (E. *Fernández Tejero*).
3379 **Goshen-Gottstein** Moshe, (*Perez* Maᶜaravi). R. Judah ibn Balᶜam's commentary on Isaiah, Arabic Firkovitch I 1377 with a Hebrew translation. Ramat-Gan 1992, Bar-Ilan. vii + ⊕ 267 p. $28. – ᴿBR (1994) 58 (S. C. *Reif*); CritRR 6 (1993) 437 (G. A. *Anderson*: 40 years work).
3380 ᴱ**Gryson** Roger, [with *Auwers* J.-M. from fasc. 2] Esaias fasc. 1-3: [40ss]: VLat 12/2. FrB 1993s. p. 800-1040 [JTS 46,589, J. K. *Elliott*]. – ᴿVigChr 48 (1994) 97-99 (G. J. M. *Bartelink*, auch über 11/2/4 and 10/3/1).
3381 **Gryson** R., *al.*, Commentaires de Jérôme sur le prophète Isaïe I-IV: VLGesch 23, 1993 → 9,3505: ᴿBL (1994) 60 (C. T. R. *Hayward*); JTS 45 (1994) 728-731 (A. *Kamesar*); RHE 89 (1994) 117s (P. *Nautin*).. – V-VII, VLGesch 27, 1994; p. 471-872. – ᴿRPg 68 (1994) 334s (R. *Braun*).
3382 **Gummelt** Volker, Lex und Evangelium; Untersuchungen zur Jesajavorlesung von J. BUGENHAGEN: Diss. ᴰ*Leder.* Greifswald 1993. xi-209 p.; Bibliog. 197-206. [TR 90,84]. 3-11-014204-X.
3383 **Hacking** Philip, Free to suffer and to serve; Isaiah: Crossway Bible Guide. Nottingham 1994, Crossway. 213 p. 1-85684-082-4. [BL 95,65; R. J. *Coggins*: no scholarly pretensions].

3384 **Helfmeyer** F. J., Isaia; il santo d'Israele tuo redentore: Bibbia per tutti. Assisi 1989, Cittadella. 228 p. – RProtestantesimo 49 (1994) 176s (C. *Dupré*, anche su Ez-Dan).

3385 **Kilian** Rudolf, Jesaja [I. 1986 ➤ 2,2637], II: 13-39: Lfg 32. Wü 1994, Echter. P. 95-217. DM 28. 3-429-01596-0 [OTAbs 17, p. 672; BL 95,67, H. G. M. *Williamson*]. – RActuBbg 31 (1994) 218s (J. M. A.: también Dan 1 Sam, Richter).

3386 **McKenzie** David L., Isaiah 1-39 / 40-66 Communicator's comm. 16AB. Dallas 1993, Word. 381 p.; p. 387-668. 0-8499-0422-6; -1139-7 [OTAbs 17, p. 671s].

3387 **Miscall** Peter D., Isaiah: Readings 1993 ➤ 9,3510: RCBQ 56 (1994) 562s (G. J. *Polan*).

3388 TEMoraldi Luigi, Il libro di Isaia; testo ebraico a fronte, pref. *Ravasi* Gianfranco: BtUniversale Classici, L-951. Mi 1994, Rizzoli. 364 p. 88-17-16951-X.

3389 **Motyer** J. A., The prophecy of Isaiah 1993 ➤ 9,3512: RBL (1994) 68 (R. E. *Clements*, severe); VT 44 (1994) 576s (H. G. M. *Williamson*: deserves a hearing).

3391 **Ravasi** Gianfranco, Il profeta Isaia: Conversazioni bibliche. Bo 1992, Dehoniane. 132 p. Lᵐ 16. – RAsprenas 41 (1994) 604 (G. *Di Palma*, anche su Conf. Geremia).

3392 **Seitz** Christopher R., Isaiah 1-39: Interpretation comm. ➤ 9,3518. LVL 1993, W-Knox. xvi-271 p. $22. 0-8042-3131-1 [BL 95,74s, D. J. *Bryan*]. – RTS 55 (1994) 782s (Gina *Hens-Piazza*).

3393 **Stacey** David †, Isaiah 1-39: Epworth Comm., 1993 ➤ 9,3519: RExp-Tim 106 (1994s) 86 (R. *Coggins*).

3394 **Watts** J., Isa 34-66. WordC 25, 1987 ➤ 2,2632 ... 9,3520: RJEvTS 37 (1994) 143s (E. *Smick*).

3395 **Widyapranawa** S. H., The Lord is savior... comm. Isa 1-39; 1990 ➤ 6, 3762 ... 9,3521: RConcordTQ 58 (1994) 40s (A. E. *Steinmann*); JEvTS 37 (1994) 141 (J. R. *Master*, also on KNIGHT G., Is 40-56).

3396 *Wilcox* Peter, 'The restoration of the Church' in CALVIN's 'Commentaries on Isaiah the Prophet': ArRefG 85 (1994) 68-95; deutsch 95.

3397 **Williamson** H. G. M., The book called Isaiah; Deutero-Isaiah's role in composition and redaction. Ox 1994, Clarendon. xvii-306 p. £35. 0-19-826360-0 [TR 91,75; BL 95,79, G. I. *Emmerson*; TS 56,772-4, Gina *Hens-Piazza*]. – RExpTim 106 (1994s) 150 (bp. M. E. W. *Thompson*: 'Isaiah edited by Deutero-Isaiah').

E8.3   [Proto-]**Isaias 1-39**, themata, versiculi.

3398 **Bosshard** Erich, Jesaja 1-39 und das 'Zwölfprophetenbuch' in exilischer und frühnachexilischer Zeit; redaktionsgeschichtliche Untersuchungen zur literarischen Vernetzung der Prophetenbücher: Diss. ᴰSteck O. H. Zürich 1994s. – RTLv 26,530: 'Vernetzung'.

3399 **Croatto** J. Severino, Isaias... y su selectiva hermenéutica [original of Vozes Portuguese]. BA 1994, Lumen. 320 p. 950-724-403-4 [OTAbs 18, p. 433].

3400 **Darr** Katheryn P., Isaiah's vision and the family of God: LitCuB. LVL 1994, W-Knox. 280 p.; bibliog. 258-270. $22. 0-664-25537-X [BL 95,84, J. F. A. *Sawyer*: TLZ 120,990-2, H. *Reventlow*]. – RExpTim 106 (1994s) 244 (R. *Coggins*: a reader-oriented construal).

3401 **Doorly** W. J., Isaiah of Jerusalem 1992 ➤ 8,3660; 9,3527: ᴿOTEssays 7 (1994) 99-101 (S. L. *Stassen*).
3402 **Lohfink** Norbert, *Zenger* Erich, Der Gott Israels und die Völker; Untersuchungen zum Jesajabuch und zu den Psalmen: SBS 154. Stu 1994, KBW. 213 p.; Bibliog. 186-206. 3-460-04541-8.
3403 **Miller** Kenneth K., The Gospel according to Isaiah; expository sermons on every chapter of Isaiah. Ann Arbor 1992, Cushing-Malloy. – ᴿConcordTQ 58 (1994) 309s (R. *Preus*).
3404 *Morfino* Mauro M., L'escatologia del Targum di Isaia; alcuni aspetti: ➤ 148, Mem. ZEDDA S., Theologica 3 (1994) 331-370.
3405 **O'Connell** Robert H., Concentricity and continuity; the literary structure of Isaiah: jOsu 188. Shf 1994, Academic. 272 p.; bibliog. 247-254. 1-85075-521-3.
3406 *Pełczyński* Grzegorz, ℗ De theologia pacis in Proto-Isaia: RuBi 47 (1994) 183-8.
3407 **Ploch** Winfried, Jesaja-Worte in der synoptischen Evangelientradition: Diss. 64 [Mü ᴰ*Gnilka* J.]. StOttilien 1993, EOS. 296 p. DM 38. 1-88096-764-4 [OTAbs 17, p. 687; NTAbs 39, p. 143].
3408 *Sweeney* Marvin A., The book of Isaiah in recent research: CuRB 1 (1993) 141-162.
3409 ᴱ**Vermeylen** Jacques, Le livre d'Isaïe; les oracles et leurs relectures, unité et complexité de l'ouvrage: BtETL 81,1997/9 ➤ 5,614... 9,3541: ᴿBZ 38 (1994) 103-5 (J. *Schreiner*).
3410 a) *Uffenheimer* B., Isaiah's and Micah's approaches to policy and history; – b) *Reventlow* Henning, The biblical and classical tradition of 'just war': ➤ 331b, Politics 1994, 176-188 / 160-175.
3411 *Verheyden* Joseph, Some observations on the Gospel text of EUSEBIUS of Caesarea illustrated from his Commentary on Isaiah: ➤ 70, ᶠLAGA C., Philohistôr 1994, 35-70.
3412 *Weiss* Andrea L., Female imagery in the Book of Isaiah: CCAR 41,1 (1994) 65-77.
3413 **Wong Yee Cheung**, A text-centered approach to Old Testament exegesis and theology and its application to the book of Isaiah: diss. Trinity Evangelical, *Sailhamer* J. 1994. 643 p. 94-32078. – DissA 55 (1994s) p. 1594.

3414 *House* Paul R., Isaiah's call and its context in Isaiah 1-6: CriswellTR 6 (1991) 207-222 [*Oswalt* John H., ʿ*almah* in Isa 7-12; < OTAbs 18, p. 336s].
3415 **Garrett** Duane A., An analysis of the hermeneutics of John CHRYSOSTOM's commentary on Isaiah 1-8 with an English translation: StBEarlyC 12. Lewiston NY 1992, Mellen. 258 p. $70. 0-88946-612-2 [BL 95,87s, R. P. R. *Murray*].
3416 *Oesch* Josef M., Jes 1,8f und das Problem der 'wir-Reden' im Jesajabuch: ➤ 27,ᶠGAMPER A., ZkT 116 (1994) 440-6.
3417 **Uffenheimer** Benjamin, ❺ The motif of 'the day of God' in Isaiah 2-4: BethM 39 (1994) 97-132 [< OTAbs 17, p. 598].
3418 **Brenneman** James E., Canon(s) in conflict; negotiating texts in true and false prophecy; Isaiah 2:2-4/Micah 4:1-4 vs. Joel 4:9-12 (Eng. 3:9-12): diss. ᴰ*Sanders* J. Claremont 1993. 295 p. 94-22478. – DissA 55 (1994s) p. 603; RelStR 21,255.

3419 *Dobberahn* Friedrich E., Jesaja [5,8-10] verklagt die Mörder an der menschlichen Gemeinschaft; ein exegetischer Versuch zum 'erkenntnistheoretischen Privileg' der Armen Lateinamerikas: EvT 54 (1994) 400-412.

3420 *a)* *Metzger* Martin, [Jes 6] Jahwe der Kerubenthroner, die von Keruben flankierte Palmette und Sphingenthrone aus dem Libanon; – *b)* *Köckert* Matthias, Die Erwählung Israels und das Ziel der Wege Gottes im Jesajabuch; – *c)* *Vermeylen* Jacques, Isaïe et le ralliement d'Ephraïm: ➤ 61, ᶠKAISER O., 'Wer ist' 1994, 75-90 / 277-300 / 342-354.

3421 *McLaughlin* John L., Their hearts *were* hardened; the use of Isaiah 6,9-10 in the book of Isaiah: Biblica 75 (1994) 1-24; franç. 24.

3422 *Finley* Thomas J., *Payton* George, A discourse analysis of Isaiah 7-12: JTrTL 6 (1993) 317-335 [< OTAbs 17, p. 598].

3423 **Irvine** Stuart A., Isaiah, Achaz, and the Syro-Ephraimite crisis: SBL diss. 123, 1990 ➤ 6,3783; 8,3682: ᴿTR 90 (1994) 456s (A. *Schenker*).

3424 **Wegner** Paul D., [Is 7-11; 32] An examination of kingship and messianic expectation in Isaiah 1-35. Lewiston NY 1992, Mellen. xiii-397 p. 0-7734-2354-0 [RelStR 21,322, M. A. *Sweeney*].

3425 **Werlitz** J., Studien... Jes 7,1-17; 29,1-8: BZAW 204, 1992 ➤ 8,3691; 9,3555 [BL 95,77, J. F. A. *Sawyer*]: ᴿBO 51 (1994) 401-4 (P. *Höffken*); CBQ 56 (1994) 352-4 (M. A. *Sweeney*: negative); OLZ 89 (1994) 59-62 (R. *Stahl*); TLZ 119 (1994) 416-9 (H. C. *Schmitt*).

3426 *Cole* Dan P., Archaeology and the Messiah oracles of Isaiah 9 and 11: ➤ 67, ᶠKING P., Scripture 1994, 53-69; 4 fig.

3427 *Kruger* H. A. J., Isaiah 9:5-6 and peace in South Africa; an exercise in inner-biblical exegesis: NduitsGT 34 (1993) 3-14 [< OTAbs 17, p. 131].

3428 *Muñoz León* Domingo, Targum, Midrash y Talmud en la obra 'Pugio Fidei' de Raimundo MARTÍ; los nombres y atributos divinos del Niño-Hijo de Is 9,5-6: ➤ 22, ᶠCASCIARO J., Biblia 1994, 447-462.

3429 *Warzecha* Julian, ⊕ Quid significat 'mittere verbum' apud Isa 9,7?: RuBi 47 (1994) 223-234.

3430 *Haag* Ernst, Jesaja, Assur und der Antijahwe — zur Literar- und Traditionsgeschichte von Jes 10,5-15: TrierTZ 103 (1994) 18-37.

3431 *Sweeney* Marvin A., Sargon's threat against Jerusalem in Isaiah 10,27-32: Biblica 75 (1994) 457-470; franç. 470.

3432 **Fabiny** Tibor, The lion and the lamb 1992 ➤ 8,3699: ᴿRelStR 20 (1994) 46 (C. *Bernas*).

3433 *Gallagher* W. R., On the identity of Hêlēl Ben Šaḥar of Is. 14:12-15*: UF 26 (1994) 131-146.

3434 *Köszeghy* Miklós, Hybris und Prophetie; Erwägungen zum Hintergrund von Jesaja XIV 12-15: VT 44 (1994) 549-554.

3435 *Haag* Ernst, 'Gesegnet sei mein Volk Ägypten' (Jes 19,25); ein Zeugnis alttestamentlicher Eschatologie: ➤ 145, ᶠWINTER E., Aspekte 1994, 139-147.

3436 *Krašovec* Jože, *a)* Punishment of the nations and deliverance of Israel in the ['Great' 24-27, 'small' 34s] Apocalypse of Isaiah; – *b)* Deliverance of the Remnant from judgment in the prophecy of Isaiah: BogVest 54 (1994) 253-268 / 331-357; Slovene 269 / 358.

3437 *Noegel* S. B., Dialect and politics in Isaiah 24-27: AulaO 12 (1994) 177-192.

3438 *Irwin* William H., The city of chaos in Isa 24,10 and the genitive of result: Biblica 75 (1994) 401-3.

3439 **Steingrimsson** Sigurdur Örn, Gottesmahl und Lebensspende; eine literaturwissenschaftliche Untersuchung von Jesaja 24,21; 23; 25,6-10a: Mü

Univ ArbO 43. St. Ottilien 1994, EOS. 114 p.; Bibliog. 100-5. 3-
88096-543-9.
3440 a) *Anderson* Bernhard W., The slaying of the fleeing, twisting serpent;
Isaiah 27: 1 in context; – b) *Darr* Katheryn P., Two unifying female
images in the book of Isaiah: ➤ 102, Mem. RICHARDSON H., Uncovering
1994, 3-15 / 17-30.

E8.4 **Deutero-Isaias 40-52:** *commentarii, themata, versiculi.*

3441 *Agourides* S., Ⓖ Ecumenical characteristics in the prophecy of
Deutero-Isaiah: ➤ 131c, Mem. VELLAS V., DeltioVM 23,1 (1994) 7-23.
3442 **Beaucamp** Évode, Le livre de la consolation... Is 40-55, 1991 ➤ 7,
3191 ... 9,3586: ᴿRTPhil 126 (1994) 182s (G. *Lasserre*); Salesianum 56
(1994) 148 (R. *Vicent*).
3443 **Christ** Franz, Gottes Wort im Umbruch; das Evangelium des namen-
losen Propheten Jesaja 40-53 [Predigte 1990s]. Ba 1994, Reinhardt. 286 p.
DM 32,80. 3-7245-0841-3 [OTAbs 18, p. 645].
3444 *Croatto* J. Severino, La propuesta querigmática del segundo Isaías:
RBíbArg 56 (1994) 65-76 [< OTAbs 18, p. 90].
3445 a) *Detting* Wilfried, Deuterojesaja, der Prophet und sein Buch; – b)
Görg Manfred, 'Bildner von Licht' — 'Schöpfer von Finsternis'; Deu-
terojesajas Glaube im Widerspruch zum Denken; – c) *Weinberg* Zvi, Die
Gottesknechtlieder [GRIMM W., Jesaja]: Entschluss 49/4 (1994) 4-7 /
11-14 / 15-17 [18-22 . 27-30].
3446 **Echigoya** Akria, Deutero-Isaiah's polemics in communicative discourse;
the intended audiences of the trial and disputation speeches: diss. Vanderbilt, ᴰ*Knight* D. Nashville 1994. – RelStR 21,251.
3448 ᴱ**Gryson** R., Esaias 2/2, introd.; Is 40,1-41,20: Vetus Latina 12. FrB
1994, Herder. p. 881-960.
3449 *Hamlin* E. John, Deutero-Isaiah's picture of Cyrus as a key to his understanding of history: ProcGM 14 (1994) 105-111.
3450 a) *Hanson* Paul D., Second Isaiah's eschatological understanding of
world events; – b) *Peters* Ted, Eschatological sanctions and Christian
ethics: ➤ 326, Hope for the Kingdom 1993/4, 17-25 / 129-152.
3451 *Johnston* Ann, A prophetic vision of an alternative community; a
reading of Isaiah 40-55: ➤ 102, Mem. RICHARDSON H., Uncovering 1994,
31-40.
3452 *Motyer* Alec, Three [Isaiah-books] in one or one in three; a dipstick
into the Isaianic literature: Churchman 108 (1994) 22-36.
3453 **Oorschot** Jürgen Van, Von Babel zum Sion 1993 ➤ 9,2594: ᴿBL (1994)
96 (A. *Gelston*); OTEssays 7 (1994) 318-320 (M. D. *Terblanche*).
3453* *Ruppert* Lothar, Das Heil der Völker (Heilsuniversalismus) in Deu-
tero- und 'Trito-' Jesaja: MüTZ 45 (1994) 137-159.
3454 **Sommer** Benjamin D., *Leshon limmudim*; the poetics of allusion in Isaiah
40-66: diss. ᴰ*Fishbane* M. Ch 1994. 347 p. 94-25426. – DissA 55 (1994s)
p. 996.
3455 *Troxel* Ronald L., *Eschatos* and eschatology in LXX-Isaiah: BSeptCog
25 (1992) 18-27 [< OTAbs 17, p. 129].

_____

3456 *Kratz* Reinhard G., Der Anfang des Zweiten Jesaja in Jes 40,1f. und das
Jeremiabuch: ZAW 106 (1994) 243-261.

3457 *Goldingay* J. [Isa 41,1-7], You [Cyrus] are Abraham's offspring, my friend; Abraham in Isaiah 41: ↠ 146c, FWISEMAN D., 'He swore' 1994, 29-54.

3458 **Farfán Navarro** Enrique, [Isa 41,17-20] El desierto transformado ...: AnBib 130, 1992 ↠ 8,3731; 9,3601 [BL 95,117, P.J. *Harland*: thorough and stimulating]: RBiblica 75 (1994) 259-262 (R. *Merendino*); Carthaginensia 10 (1994) 180s (R. *Sanz Valdivieso*); CBQ 56 (1994) 331s (C. *Bernas*); CC 145 (1994,2) 412s (D. *Scaiola*); NRT 116 (1994) 107-9 (J.L. *Ska*).

3459 *Janzen* J. Gerald, Isaiah 41:27, reading *hnh hnwmh* in 1QIsaᵃ and *hnh hnm* in the Masoretic text: JBL 113 (1994) 597-607.

3460 *Stern* Philip, [Isa 42,19] The 'blind servant' imagery of Deutero-Isaiah and its implications: Biblica 75 (1994) 224-232.

3461 **Gunsalus González** Catherine: Isaiah 43:8-15; between text and sermon: Interpretation 48 (1994) 169-173.

3462 **Gross** W., *Kuschel*, K.-J. [Jes 45,7] Ich schaffe... Ist Gott verantwortlich für das Übel? 1992 ↠ 8,3736: RDiakonie 25 (1994) 215s (N. *Mette*).

3463 **Franke** Chris, Isaiah 46, 47, and 48; a new literary-critical reading; Biblical and Judaic Studies 3. WL 1994, Eisenbrauns. x-293 p. $32.50. 0-931464-79-X [RelStR 21,322, M.A. *Sweeney*: for all libraries].

3464 **Rechenmacher** Johann P., Jungfrau, Tochter Babel; eine Studie zur sprachwissenschaftlichen Beschreibung althebräischen Texte am Beispiel von Jes 47: *a*) kath. Diss., ᴰ*Wehrle* J. München 1994, 421 p. – RTLv 26,532. – *b*): ArbO 44. St. Ottilien 1994, EOS. ix-421 p.; Bibliog. 398-407. 3-88096-544-7.

3465 *Janzen* J. Gerald, [Isa 51,9s] On the moral nature of God's power; Yahweh and the sea in Job and Deutero-Isaiah: CBQ 56 (1994) 458-478.

E8.5   *Isaiae 53ss, Carmina Servi YHWH:* **Servant-Songs.**

3466 *a*) *Baltzer* Klaus, Jes 52,13; die 'Erhöhung' des 'Gottesknechtes'; – *b*) *Barth* Gerhard, Umstrittener Auferstehungsglaube: ↠ 40, FGEORGI D., Religious propaganda 1994, 45-56 / 117-132.

3467 **Bastiaans** J.C., Interpretaties van Jesaja; een intertextueel onderzoek naar de lijdende knecht in Jes. 53 (MT/LXX) en in Luc. 22:14-38; Hand 3:12-26; 4:23-31; 8:36-40): diss. Tilburg, ᴰ*Weren* W. Tilburg 1993, Univ. xiv-471 p. ƒ65. 90-361-9723-6. – TvT 34 (1994) 73; RTLv 25, p.528. – RStreven 60 (1993) 956 (P. *Beentjes*).

3468 *Ceresko* Anthony R., The rhetorical strategy of the Fourth Servant Song (Isaiah 52:13-53:12); poetry and the Exodus — New Exodus: CBQ 56 (1994) 42-55.

3469 *Deurloo* K.A., JHWH's koninklijke terugkeer naar Sion en de functie van zijn knecht tegenover de Gola, in Deutero-Jesaja: AmstCah 13 (1994) 72-80; Eng. 129 [< OTAbs 18, p.97].

3470 *a*) *Gelston* Anthony, Knowledge, humiliation or suffering; a lexical, textual and exegetical problem in Isaiah 53; – *b*) *Jeppesen* Knud, Mother Zion, Father Servant; a reading of Isaiah 48-55; – *c*) *Williamson* H.G.M., First and last in Isaiah: ↠ 138, FWHYBRAY N., Of Prophets 1993, 136-141 / 109-125 / 95-108.

3471 **Laato** Antti, The servant of YHWH and Cyrus, Is 40-55: ConBibOT 35, 1992 ↠ 8,3725 ... 9,3613: RCBQ 56 (1994) 112-4 (W.H. *Irwin* compares KRATZ R. 1991); JBL 113 (1994) 521s (L. *Boadt*); TLZ 119 (1994) 306-8 (R.G. *Kratz*); VT 44 (1994) 573s (H.G.M. *Williamson*); ZAW 106 (1994) 526s (H.-C. *Schmitt*).

3472 — **Kratz** Reinhard G., Kyros... Jes 40-55, 1991 ➤ 7,3199 ... 9,3593:
ᴿJBL 113 (1994) 129-131 (M. A. *Sweeney*: intriguing but problematic);
OTEssays 7 (1994) 566s (H. L. *Bosman*).

3473 *Leene* H., Kan een fictionele gestalte onze plaats innemen? Over-
wegingen bij de uitleg van Jesaja 53: GerefTTs 93 (1993) 232-253.

3474 **Steck** Odil H., Gottesknecht und Zion 1992 ➤ 9,239 [TR 91,219-221, A.
van *Wieringen*]: ᴿJBL 113 (1994) 712-4 (J. L. *McLaughlin*); JTS 45 (1994)
180-3 (R. N. *Whybray*); OTEssays 7 (1994) 103-5 (M. D. *Terblanche*).

3475 *Stuhlmacher* Peter, Der messianische Gottesknecht: JbBT 8 (1993)
131-154.

3476 **Varo** F., Los cantos del Siervo en la exégesis hispano-hebrea 1993
➤ 9,3619 [NRT 117,123, J.-L. *Ska*; TLZ 120,129, R. *Kessler*].

3477 *Wénin* A., Le poème du 'Serviteur souffrant' (Is 52,13-53,12); proposition
de lecture: FoiTemps 24 (1994) 493-508 [< ᴢɪᴛ 95, p. 146].

3478 *Stassen* S. L., Marriage (and related) metaphors in Isaiah 54:1-17: J/Tyd
Sem 6 (1994) 57-73.

3479 *Gołębiewski* Marian, ❷ De 'novo egressu' in Deutero-Isaia 55,12-13:
RuBi 47 (1994) 234-242.

E8.6   [Trito-] **Isaias 56-66.**

3480 **Emmerson** Grace I., Isaiah 56-66: OT Guides 1992 ➤ 8,3750; 9,3621:
ᴿBO 51 (1994) 634s (A. van *Wieringen*); Vidyajyoti 56 (1994) 257 (P.
Meagher).

3481 **Lau** Wolfgang, Schriftgelehrte Prophetie in Jes 56-66; eine Untersuchung
zu den literarischen Bezügen in den letzten elf Kapiteln des Jesajabuches
[➤ 9,3621*; Diss. Kiel, ᴰ*Donner* H.]: BZAW 225. B 1994, de Gruyter.
ix-357 p. 3-11-014239-2 [BL 95,68, A. *Gelston*; RelStR 21,130, M. A.
Sweeney; TLZ 129,782-6, O. H. *Steck*]. – ᴿZAW 106 (1994) 528 (G.
Metzner).

3482 *a)* *Gaiser* Frederick J., A new word on homosexuality? Isaiah 56:1-8 as
case study; – *b)* *Forde* Gerhard O., *Hultgren* Arland, Sex in Romans
1,16s: WWorld 14,2 ('Sexual orientation', social acceptance of gays, 1994)
280-293 / 305-315-325.

3482* *Dolbeau* François, Une citation d'Isaïe (57,8 LXX) [presque] non
reconnue dans les éditions d'AuɢusᴛIN Sermo 177,9: AugR 34 (1994)
395s.

3483 *Rosendal* Bent, 'Gerechtigkeit' und 'Werke' in Jesaja 57,12: ScandJOT
8 (1994) 152-4.

3484 *Stachowiak* Lech, ❷ Isa 59,1-21. L'azione salvifica di Dio ed i peccati
d'Israele: ➤ 9,71, ꜰJANKOWSKI A., Agnus 1993, 271-280; ital. 280.

3485 *Gosse* B., Sur l'identité du personnage d'Isaïe 61,1: TEuph 5 (1992)
45-48; Eng. 45: the high-priest himself, as held by CAZELLES H.

3486 *Timm* Alberto R., El lagarero [winepresser] solitario (una exegesis
de Isaías 63:1-8): Theologika 8 (Lima 1993) 128-141 [< OTAbs 17,
p. 602].

3486* *Virgulin* Stefano, [Is 63,7-64,11] 'Dov'è la tua misericordia?': ParSpV
30 (1994) 93-102.

3487 *Kaimakis* Dimitris, ❻ [Isa 65,17] There shall be a new heaven and a new
earth: ➤ 131*c*, Mem. VELLAS V., DeltioVM 23,1 (1994) 24-28.

3488 **Fung** Raymond, [Is 65,20-23] The Isaiah vision; an ecumenical strategy for congregational evangelism: Risk. Geneva 1992, WCC. 55 p. [NZMissW 49,147].

E8.7 Jeremias.

3489 *Bogaert* Pierre-Maurice, Le livre de Jérémie en perspective; les deux rédactions antiques selon les travaux en cours: RB 101 (1994) 363-406; Eng. 363.

3490 **Bonora** Antonio, Geremia uomo dei dolori 1992 ➤ 8,3758; 9,3637: ^RAngelicum 71 (1994) 277s (S. *Jurić*); CC 145 (1994,1) 620s (D. *Scaiola*); Protestantesimo 49 (1994) 89s (G. *Anziani*).

3490* **Briend** J., Geremia. R 1993, Borla. 64 p. L^m 12. – ^RParVi 39,4 (1994) 52 (A. *Rolla*: uno dei Cahiers Évangile, serie di 24 titoli in italiano).

3491 **Brueggemann** W., To pluck up, Jer 1-25 / To build, Jer 36-52, 1988/91 ➤ 4,3233 ... 9,3638: ^RCritRR 6 (1993) 151s (L. *Boadt*).

3492 *Fischer* Georg, Das Jeremiabuch 1. Vom Tod zum Leben; 2. Verkündigung, die zum Leiden führt; BLtg 67 (1994) 44-48 / 233-7 (-246).

3493 **Goldman** Yohanan, Prophétie et royauté au retour de l'exil; les origines littéraires de la forme massorétique du livre de Jérémie [diss.]: OBO 118. FrS/Gö 1992, Univ./VR. xiv-259 p. Fs 68. – ^RBO 51 (1994) 635-7 (W. L. *Holladay*); JBL 113 (1994) 522-4 (Kathleen M. *O'Connor*); RevSR 68 (1994) 108s (B. *Renaud*); ZAW 106 (1994) 521 (R. *Liwak*).

3494 **Huey** F. B., Jeremiah, [-&] Lamentations: NewAmerC 16. Nv 1993, Broadman. 512 p.

3495 **Jones** Douglas R., Jeremiah: NCent 1992 ➤ 8,3764; 9,3642: ^RBL (1994) 63 (R. P. *Carroll*: excellent, though 'completely rejecting' himself); Carthaginensia 10 (1994) 450s (R. *Sanz Valdivieso*, también sobre THOMPSON J.); JBL 113 (1994) 325s (W. L. *Holladay*); OTEssays 7 (1994) 157s (W. J. *Wessels*).

3496 **Lingen** Anton van der, Een profeet onder de profeten, Jeremia 1992 ➤ 9,3644: ^RRB 101 (1994) 463 (P. *Henne*).

3497 **Oosterhoff** B. J., Jeremia [I. 1990 ➤ 6,3870] II: 11-29. Kampen 1994, Kok. 399 p. ƒ 69.50. 90-242-6193-7 [OTAbs 17, p. 673].

3498 **Ribera Florit** Josep, Targum Jonatán de los Profetas Posteriores en tradición babilónica; Jeremías: TEstCisn 52. M 1992, Cons. Sup. Inv. Inst. Fg. 300 p. 84-00-7257-x [sic, en el libro]. ~ [Su Traducción de Targum de J. 1992 ➤ 9,3646]. – ^RRÉJ 153 (1994) 458 (J. *Margain*).

3499 **Carroll** R. P., Jeremiah: OTGuides 1989 ➤ 5,3602 ... 7,3245: ^RJNES 53 (1994) 215s (E. A. *Knauf*).

3500 *a) Domeris* William R., Jeremiah and the religion of Canaan; – *b) Jeremias* J., The Hosea tradition and the book of Jeremiah: OTEssays 7 (1994) 7-20 / 21-38.

3501 **Goldingay** John, God's prophet, God's servant; a study in Jeremiah and Isaiah 40-55: Biblical Classics. Carlisle 1994, Paternoster. 160 p. 0-85364-604-X.

3502 *Gonçalves* Francolino J., 'La maison qui est appelée du nom du Seigneur' au livre de Jérémie [7,1-15 ...]: ➤ 30, ^FCOUTURIER G., Maison 1994, 165-185.

3503 **Kilpp** Nelson, Niederreissen und Aufbau ... Jer ^D1990 ➤ 6,3883: ^RTZBas 50 (1994) 182-4 (B. *Huwyler*).

3504 **King** Philip J., Jeremiah, an archaeological companion. LVL 1993,

W-Knox. xxvi-204 p. $27. [BL 95,30, J. *Duckworth*: praise]. – ᴿBAR-W 20,3 first choice (1994) 4 (K. N. *Schoville*); ÉTRel 69 (1994) 570s (Françoise *Smyth*); RefR 48 (1994s) 60s (R. A. *Coghenour*); ᴢAW 106 (1994) 526 (G. *Wanke*).

3505 **King** Philip J., Jeremiah's polemic against idols; what archaeology can teach us: BR 10,6 (1994) 22-29.

3506 *Lamblin* Jacques-Paul, Un chemin de souffrance vers la vie; le livre de Jérémie: Sève 566 (1995) 30-35.

3507 *Le Roux* J. H., In search of CARROLL's Jeremiah (or, Good old Jerry; did he really live?); OTEssays 7 (1994) 60-90 [< OTAbs 18, p. 99, R. D. *Haak*, '1944'].

3508 **McConville** J. G., Judgment and promise... Jer 1993 ↠ 9, 3666: ᴿBL (1994) 67 (B. P. *Robinson*); CBQ 56 (1994) 768s (A. R. *Drummond*); ScotBuEv 12 (1994) 59s (R. S. *Hess*).

3509 **Mesters** Carlos, Il profeta Geremia bocca di Dio, bocca del popolo; introduzione alla lettura del libro del profeta Geremia: Figure bibliche 9. Assisi 1994, Cittadella. 180 p. 88-308-0542-4.

3510 **Pohlmann** K.-F., [Jer 11...] Die Ferne Gottes; BZAW 179, 1989 ↠ 5, 3647... 8,3801: ᴿTEuph 5 (1992) 183s (T. *Römer*).

3511 *Ribera* J., [NT parallels to Jer Targum]: MiscArH 40, (1991)... [< VT 44,144].

3512 **Römer** Thomas, Discours de Jérémie ou l'actualité permanente de la Parole de Dieu: CahB 5. Aubonne 1992, Moulin. 32 p. – ᴿRTPhil 126 (1944) 181 (L. *Wisser*).

3513 *Schenker* Adrian, La rédaction longue du Livre de Jérémie doit-elle être datée au temps des premiers Hasmonéens?: ETL 70 (1994) 281-293.

3514 **Schulz-Rauch** Martin, Die Rezeption der Verkündigung Hoseas durch Jeremias: ev. Diss. ᴰ*Jeremias* Jörg. München 1994. – TR 91,99.

3515 **Seybold** K., Der Prophet Jeremia. Leben und Werk: Urban-Tb 416. Stu 1993, Kohlhammer. 219 p. DM 29,80. 3-17-010809-3. – ᴿBL (1994) 75 (W. *McKane*); ÉTRel 69 (1994) 101s (T. *Römer*); TvT 34 (1994) 76 (A. *Schoors*); ᴢAW 106 (1994) 535s (G. *Wanke*).

3516 **Stipp** Herman-Josef, Das masoretische und alexandrinische Sondergut des Jeremiabuches; textgeschichtlicher Rang, Eigenarten, Triebkräfte: OBO 136. FrS/Gö 1994, Univ./VR. vii-186 p. 3-7278-0956-6 / 3-525-5377-9 [OTAbs 18, p. 645].

3517 *Vieweger* D., Die literarischen Beziehungen... Jer/Ezech: BErfAJ 26, ᴰ1993 ↠ 9,3673: ᴿBL (1994) 101 (P. M. *Joyce*); OTAbs 17 (1994) 228s (W. *Roth*); TLZ 119 (1994) 788-790 (K. *Zobel*); ᴢAW 106 (1994) 541 (G. *Wanke*).

3518 **Wendel** Ute, Jesaja und Jeremia; Worte, Motive und Einsichten Jesajas in der Verkündigung Jeremias: diss. ᴰ*Schmidt* W. Bonn 1994s. – RTLv 26,533.

3519 **White** R. E. O., The indomitable... Jer 1992 ↠ 8,3790; 9,3674: ᴿOTEssays 7 (1994) 126-8 (C. A. P. van *Tonder*: spirited observations free of scholarly apparatus).

3520 *Mack* C., Jer 1,11-19 *šqd*: BeitM 39 (1994) 269-73.

3521 *Fischer* Georg, 'Ich mache dich... zur eisernen Säule' (Jer 1,18); der Prophet als besserer Ersatz für den untergegangenen Tempel: ↠ 37, ᶠGAMPER A., ZkT 116 (1994) 447-450.

3522 **Cloete** Walter R.W., Versification and syntax in Jeremiah 2-25; syntactical constraints in Hebrew colometry: SBL diss. 117, 1989 ➤ 5,3634... 7,3259: ᴿJQR 84 (1993s) 91s (Adèle *Berlin*).

3523 *Bergren* Theodore A., JEROME's translation of ORIGEN's homily on Jeremiah 2,21-22 (Greek homily 2, Latin 13): ➤ 131*d*, Mem. VERBRAKEN P., RBén 104 (1994) 260-283.

3524 *Hoffman* Yair, 'Isn't the bride too beautiful?' The case of Jeremiah 6.16-21: JStOT 64 (1994) 102-120.

3525 *a*) *Scheffler* Eben, The holistic historical background against which Jeremiah 7:1-15 makes sense; – *b*) *Da Silva* A.A., Die teologie van Jeremiah 10:1-16: OTEssays 7 (1994) 381-395 / 396-416.

3526 **Jost** Renate, Frauen, Männer und die Himmelskönigin; Studien zu Jeremia 7,17-18 und Jeremia 44,15-25: ev. Diss. ᴰSchottroff W. Frankfurt 1994s. > Gü. 272 p. – RTLv 26,531.

3526* *Kellner* Menachem, MAIMONIDES and Samuel IBN TIBBON on Jeremiah 9:22-23 and human perfection: ➤ 97, ᶠRACKMAN M. 1994, 49*-55*.

3527 *Dyer* Charles H., [Jer 13,1-7] Waistbands, water, and the word of God; where did Jeremiah bury his girdle?: ➤ 21, ᶠCAMPBELL D., Integrity 1994, 62-81.

3528 *Watson* Wilfred G.E., The imagery in Jeremiah 17:1 (ineditum): ➤ 290*c*, Traditional 1994, 395-400.

3529 *Ciccarese* Maria Pia, *Perdix diabolus*; l'esegesi patristica di Ger 17,11: ➤ 86, ᶠNALDINI M., Paideia 1994, 275-296.

3530 **Cook** Robert R., [Jer 18,6] The art of God [seems to leave even human artifacts passive; R. *Nozick* whimsically on Gen 1, 'the only thing mere speaking can create is a story; ... where we live is created by and in words: a uni-verse']: VoxEvca 23 (1993) 31-38.

3531 *Swart* Ignatius, 'Because every time I speak, I must shout it out, I cry — "violence and oppression!"'; the polyvalent meaning of *ḥamas wešad* in Jeremiah 20:8: OTEssays 7 (1994) 193-204.

3532 *Pohlmann* Karl-Friedrich, Das Ende der Gottlosen; Jer 20,14-18, ein Antipsalm: ➤ 15, ᶠBEYERLIN W., Neue Wege 1994, 301-316.

3533 *a*) *Wessels* W.J., The fallibility and future of leadership according to Jeremiah 23,1-4; – *b*) *Heerden* Willie van, Preliminary thoughts on creativity and biblical interpretation with reference to Jeremiah 30:12-17: OTEssays 6 (1993) 330-8 / 339-350 [< OTAbs 17, p.604].

3534 **Epp-Tiessen** Daniel J., Concerning the prophets; true and false prophecy in Jeremiah 23.9-29.32: diss. St. Michael, ᴰSheppard G. Toronto 1994. 365 p. – RTLv 26, p.531.

3535 *a*) *Hausmann* Jutta, 'Ein Prophet, der Träume hat, der erzähle Träume, wer aber mein Wort hat, der predige mein Wort recht' (Jer 23,28) — ein Beitrag zum Verstehen der deuteronomistischen Wort-Theologie; – *b*) *Schmidt* Werner H., 'Kann ich nicht mit euch verfahren wie dieser Töpfer?' Disputationsworte im Jeremiabuch; – *c*) *Herrmann* Siegfried, Grenzen der Prophetenforschung, dargestellt am Buche Jeremia: ➤ 115, ᶠSCHUNCK K.-D., Nachdenken 1994, 163-175 / 149-161 / 133-147.

3536 *Wessels* W.J. [Jer 27s] Winds of change; an OT theological perspective [can an ancient text fit questions of our time?]: OTEssays 7 (1994) 205-230.

3537 **Fischer** Georg, Das Trostbüchlein... Jer 30-31, 1993 ➤ 9,3698: ᴿBL (1994) 57 (W. *McKane*); TLZ 119 (1994) 782-4 (R. *Liwak*).

3538 *Becking* Bob, *a*) Jeremiah's book of consolation; a textual comparison; notes on the Masoretic text and the Old Greek version of Jeremiah

XXX-XXXI: VT 44 (1994) 145-149; – *b*) 'A voice was heard in Ramah';
some remarks on structure and meaning of Jeremiah 31,15-17: BZ 38
(1994) 229-242.
3539 *Peklaj* Marijan, [Jer 31,31] *Nova zaveza*... New Covenant in the OT:
BogVest 54 (1994) 193-200.
3540 **Hardmeier** Christof, Probleme der Textsyntax, der Redeeinbettung und
der Abschnittgliederung in Jer 32 mit ihren kompositionsgeschichtlichen
Konsequenzen: ➤ 323*, Syntax 1993, 49-79.
3541 *Heyns* Daleme, History and narrative in Jeremiah 32: OTEssays 7
(1994) 261-276.
3542 *a*) *Lust* John, The diverse text forms of Jeremiah and history writing
with Jer 33 as a test case; – *b*) *Kooij* A., van der, Jeremiah 27:5,15; how
do MT and LXX relate to each other?: JNWS 20,1 (1994) 31-48 /
59-78.
3543 *Knights* C.H., *a*) The structure of Jeremiah 35: ExpTim 106 (1994s)
142-4; – *b*) The Rechabites of Jeremiah 35; forerunners of the Essenes?:
JPseud 10 (1992) 81-87; – *c*) The Nabataeans and the Rechabites: JSS 38
(1993) 227-233.
3544 *Becking* Bob, Baalis, the king of the Ammonites; an epigraphical note
on Jeremiah 40:14: JSS 38 (1993) 15-24.
3545 *Cook* Johann, The difference in the order of the books of the Hebrew
and Greek versions of Jeremiah — Jeremiah 43 (50) a case study:
OTEssays 7 (1994) 175-192.
3546 *Brueggemann* Walter, The 'Baruch connection'; reflections on Jer 43:1-7:
JBL 113 (1994) 405-420.
3547 *a*) *McKane* William, Worship of the Queen of Heaven (Jer 44) [7,18]; –
b) [Jer 35] *Levin* Christoph, Die Entstehung der Rechabiter; – *c*)
Pohlmann Karl-Friedrich, Erwägungen zu Problemen alttestamentlicher
Prophetenexegese: ➤ 61, ᶠKAISER O., 'Wer ist' 1994, 318-324 / 301-317 /
325-341.
3548 *Joosten* Jan, La macrostructure du livre de Job et quelques parallèles
(Jérémie 45, 1 Rois 19): ➤ 305, Job 1993/4, 400-4.
3549 *Luciani* Ferdinando, Il problema testuale di Ger 52,20b: RivB 42
(1994) 75-80.
3550 *a*) *Wessels* Willie J., A theology of renewal; a perspective on social
justice from the Book of Jeremiah; – *b*) *Watts* John D.W., 'The Spirit' in
the prophets; three brief studies [Isa 32,15; 57,15; Ezek 36,26]: ➤ 140,
ᶠWILLIAMS J., Spirit 1994, 92-109 / 84-91.

E8.8   **Lamentationes,** *Threni;* **Baruch.**

3551 **Dobbs-Allsopp** E.E.W., Weep... City-Lament: BOrPont 44, 1993 ➤ 9,
3719: ᴿCBQ 56 (1994) 756s (Kathleen *Farmer*); JBL 113 (1994) 708-710
(W.C. *Gwaltney*).
3552 **Droin** Jean-Marc, Le livre des lamentations 'Comment?', une traduction
et un commentaire: La Bible porte-parole. Genève 1995, Labor & Fides.
106p. Fs 29. 2-8309-0761-2 [OTAbs 18, p. 646].
3553 **Ferris** Paul W.ᴶ, The genre of communal lament in the Bible and the
Ancient Near East: SBL diss. 127. Atlanta 1992. $45; pa. $30. – ᴿCBQ
56 (1994) 103s (E.W. *Dobbs-Allsopp*).
  Michalowski Piotr, The lamentation over the destruction of Sumer 1989
➤ 9154.
3554 **Rankema** J., Klaagliederen: CommOT, 1993 ➤ 9,3726: ᴿETL 70

(1994) 142-4 (J.H. *Hunter*); Streven 61 (1994) 375 (P. *Beentjes*); TvT 34 (1994) 192 (A. *Schoors*).
3555 **Short** (Hobbs) Helen, 'Sa splendeur s'est retirée'. La symbolique de la figure de Sion dans le Livre des Lamentations: prot. diss. ᴰ*Heintz* J. Strasbourg 1994. 303 p. – RTLv 26,533.
3556 **Westermann** Claus, Lamentations; issues and interpretation, ᵀ*Muenchow* Charles. Mp/E 1994, Fortress/Clark. xvi-252 p. £12.50. 0-567-29226-6 [OTAbs 18, p. 647, M. *Bredin*; BL 95,77, I. *Provan*; TS 56,605, F.L. *Moriarty*]. – ᴿExpTim 106 (1994s) 184 (C.S. *Rodd*).

3557 *Gous* J.G.P., Exiles and the dynamics of experiences of loss; the reaction of Lamentations 2 on the loss of land: OTEssays 6 (1993) 351-363 [< OTAbs 17, p. 607].

3558 **Herzer** Jens, *a*) Tradition und Redaktion in den Paralipomena Jeremias: kath. Diss. ᴰ*Wolff* C. Berlin 1994. – TR 91,92. – *b*) Die Paralipomena Jeremias; Studien zu Tradition und Redaktion einer Haggada des frühen Judentums: TStAJud 43. Tü 1994, Mohr. xi-252 p. 3-16-146307-2 [BL 95,151, G.J. *Brooke*].

3559 **Nioku** Mark Chiaka, The image of the prophet Jeremiah in the 'so-called Baruch biography' and cognate prose texts; a theological consideration of the canonical text: diss. ᴰ*Ruppert* L. FrB 1994. 200 p. – RTLv 36,532.
3560 **Harlow** Daniel, The Greek 'Apocalypse of Baruch' (3 Baruch) in Hellenistic Judaism and early Christianity: diss. ᴰ*Collins* J. Notre Dame 1994. 385 p. 94-22393. – RelStR 21,255; RTLv 26, p. 534; DissA 55 (1994s) p. 604.
3561 *Steck* Odil H., Zur Rezeption des Psalters im apokryphen Baruchbuch: → 15, ꟳBEYERLIN W., Neue Wege 1994, 361-380.
3562 **Kabasele** Mukenge André, La supplique collective de Ba 1,15-3,8: diss. LvN 1992, ᴰ*Bogaert* P. 381 p. – ETL 70 (1994) 244.

E8.9   **Ezechiel:** *textus, commentarii; themata, versiculi.*

3563 **Allen** Leslie C., Ezekiel 20-28: Word Comm. 29. 1990 → 6,3932 … 9,3732: ᴿAsbTJ 49,1 (1994) 87s (H.T.C. *Sun*).
3564 **Blenkinsopp** Joseph, Ezekiel: InterpComm 1990 → 6,3934 … 9,3733: ᴿCritRR 5 (1992) 113-5 (Carol A. *Newsom*: superb skill and grace).
3565 **Cooper** Lamar E., Ezekiel: NewAmerC 17. Nv 1994, Broadman & H. 440 p. 0-8054-0017-2. – ᴿOTAbs 17 (1994) 674 (R.A. *Taylor*).
3566 ᵀᴱ**Foxgrover** David, *Martin* Donald, Ezekiel I: CALVIN's OT Commentaries 18. Carlisle/GR 1994, Paternoster/Eerdmans. xiii-322 p. £21, pa. $35/25. 0-85364-598-1; -9-X / US 0-8028-2468-4; -0751-8 [BL 95,59, D.V.N. *Bagchi*; RelStR 21,152, D.K. *McKim*].
3567 **Halperin** David J., Seeking Ezekiel; text and psychology [… mentally ill]. Univ. Park 1993, Penn State Univ. xv-260 p. $35; pa. $17. 0-271-00948-9 [RelStR 21,224, M.A. *Sweeney*; OTAbs 18, p. 424; BL 95,89, P.M. *Joyce*: gives psychology a bad name].
3568 **Recchia** Vincenzo, S. GREGORIO M., Omelie su Ezechiele I. R 1992, Città Nuova. 191 p. Lᵐ 55 [NRT 117,598, A. *Harvengt*]. – ᴿCC 145 (1994,4) 304-6 (G. *Cremascoli*).

3569 **Richter** Wolfgang,   Ezechiel: BH^t 9, AOtt 33, 1993 ➤ 9,3739: ^{R}Antonianum 69 (1994) 380s (M. *Nobile*).
3570 **Sàvoca** G., El libro de Ezequiel ^{T}1992 ➤ 9,2740: ^{R}AnVal 19 (1993) 230s (F. T.); SalT 81(1993) 322.
3571 ^{E}**Signer** Michael A.,   ANDREAS de S. Victore, Expositio in Ezechielem: Opera 6, 1991 ➤ 8,3856; 9,3741: ^{R}Speculum 69 (1994) 102s (E. Ann *Matter*).
3572 **Vawter** B., *Hoppe* L.,   Ezekiel; a new heart 1991 ➤ 7,3303 ... 9,3742: ^{R}ConcordTQ 58 (1994) 221 (A. E. *Steinmann*).

3573 **Auffarth** Christoph,   Der drohende Untergang/Odyssee. Ezech: Rel-gVV 39, 1991 ➤ 7,3304; 9,3743: ^{R}BiKi 48 (1993) 52s (J. *Rüpke*); ClasR 44 (1994) 2-4 (V. A. *Rodgers*: sacral kingship in the Odyssey?).
3574 **Bauer** L.,   Zeit des zweiten Tempels — Zeit der Gerechtigkeit: Beit-ErfAJ 31.   Bern 1992, P. Lang. 324 p. DM 38.   3-631-45230-6. – ^{R}JStOT 62 (1994) 115 (P. *Davies*: high praise for 'Temple ṣedeq is economics'; mentions Zech but without indicating whether Hag-Zech-Mal or Chr-Ez-Neh are the three books forming a single corpus).
3575 *Darr* Katheryn P., Ezekiel among the critics: CuRB 2 (1994) 9-24.
3576 **Duguid** Iain W.,   Ezekiel and the leaders of Israel [< diss. Cambridge 1992]: VTS 56.   xi-163 p.   90-04-10074-1 [OTAbs 18, p. 423; BL 95,85, P. M. *Joyce*].
3577 *Greenberg* Moshe, Notes on the influence of tradition on Ezekiel: ➤ 85*, ^{F}MUFFS Y., JANES 22 (1993) 29-37.
3578 **McKeating** Henry,   Ezekiel: OTGuide 1993 ➤ 9,3752 [RelStR 21,46, M. A. *Sweeney*, also on the Hosea and Jonah guides]: ^{R}BL (1994) 67 (P. M. *Joyce*); CBQ 56 (1994) 338 (J. T. *Strong*); HeythJ 35 (1994) 441 (J. *Mulrooney*).
3579 *McKeating* H.,   Ezekiel the 'prophet like Moses': JStOT 61 (1994) 87-109.
3580 **Pohlmann** Karl-F., Ezechielstudien...: BZAW 202, 1992 ➤ 8,3868; 9,3752: ^{R}Antonianum 69 (1994) 381-3 (M. *Nobile*); CBQ 56 (1994) 338s (R. W. *Klein*: brilliant insights, drastic rearrangements); OTEssays 7 (1994) 93-95 (P. M. *Venter*).
3581 *Rooy* H.-P. van,   Die wisselwerking tussen profeet en gehoor in die bock Esegiël: In die Skriflig 28 (1994) 235-246 [< OTAbs 18, p. 191].
3582 *a) Schwartz* Baruch J.,   Repentance and determinism in Ezekiel; – *b) Marquis* Galen, Allusive rhetoric in the prophecies of Ezekiel: ➤ 303*b*, 11th Jewish 1993/4, A-123-130 / 131-6.

3583 **Lieb** Michael,   The visionary mode; biblical prophecy, hermeneutics and cultural change [Ezech 1] 1991 ➤ 8,3618; 9,3756: ^{R}CritRR 6 (1993) 126 (R. W. *Klein*) &163-8 (Michael *Fishbane*: bold, ambitious, must reading).
3584 **Ohnesorge** Stefan, [Ez 11 ... 37] Jahwe gestaltet sein Volk neu: ForBi 64, 1991 ➤ 7,3318 ... 9,3759: ^{R}Biblica 75 (1994) 262-6 (L. C. *Allen*).
3585 *Davies* Graham I.,   An archaeological commentary on Ezekiel 13: ➤ 67, ^{F}KING P., Scripture 1994, 108-125.
3586 *Bodendorfer-Langer* Gerhard, *a)* 'Und die Hand des Armen und Elenden machte sie nicht stark' (Ez 16,49); zur Parteilichkeit der Bibel und der unterschiedlichen Wertung in jüdischer und christlicher Auslegung; – *b)* 'Durch dein Blut lebe' (Ez 16,6); ein Ezechielwort und die jüdische Identität: ProtokB 3 (1994) 9-23 / 83-97.

3587 **Matties** Gordon H.,   Ezekiel 18 and the rhetoric of moral discourse:
SBL diss. 126, 1990 ➤ 6,3965 ... 9,3764:   ᴿJQR 84 (1993s) 501-3 (Ellen F.
Davis).
3588 *Reiser* Werner,   'Damit ihr lebt!'; Predigt über Ezechiel 18:   TZBas 50
(1994) 169-173.
3589 **Sedlmeier** Franz,   Studien ... Ez 20: SBB 21, 1990 ➤ 6,3966 ... 9,3767:
ᴿETL 70 (1994) 146s (J. *Lust*).
3590 **Fechter** Friedrich, [Ezech 25s] Bewältigung der Katastrophe ... Fremd-
völkersprüche Ez: BZAW 208, 1992 ➤ 8,3885:   ᴿTüTQ 74 (1994) 71s (W.
Gross).
3591 *Mendecki* Norbert,   Postdeuteronomistische Redaktion von Ez 28,25-
26?:   BibNot 73 (1994) 66-73.
3591* *Schreiner* Josef,   Ezechiel 34 im Hintergrund des johanneischen Wortes
[Jn 10] vom guten Hirten: ➤ 31*, ᶠDAUTZENBERG G., Nach 1994,
589-606.
3592 *Philonenko* Marc,   De Qoumrân à Doura-Europos; la vision des os-
sements desséchés (Ézéchiel 37,1-4): RHPR 74 (1994) 1-12; 5 fig.
3592* *Mazurel* J.W.,   Het woord ʿēṣ in Ezechiël 37:16-20:   AmstCah 12
(1993) 116-121; Eng. 134s.
3593 *Hoelmer* Harold W.,   The progression of events in Ezekiel 38-39: ➤ 21,
ᶠCAMPBELL D., Integrity 1994, 82-92.
3594 *Odell* Margaret S.,   The city of Hamonah in Ezekiel 39:11-16; the
tumultuous city of Jerusalem: CBQ 56 (1994) 479-489.
3595 **Tuell** Stephen S.,   The law of the Temple in Ezek 40-48: HarvSemMg 49,
1992 ➤ 8,3893:   ᴿBL (1994) 77 (R. E. *Clements*); CBQ 56 (1994) 574s (M.
Hillmer); ETL 70 (1994) 147s (J. *Lust*); Interpretation 48 (1994) 86s (J. D.
Levenson); JBL 113 (1994) 131-3 (D. I. *Block*); JTS 45 (1994) 183s (P.
Joyce); TLZ 119 (1994) 892-4 (E. *Otto*).

3596 **Mueller** James R.,   The five fragments of the Apocryphon of Ezekiel:
JPseud supp. 5. Shf 1994, Academic. 196 p. £27.50. 1-85075-195-1. -
ᴿExpTim 106 (1994s) 311 (C. S. *Rodd*).

E9.1 Apocalyptica VT.

3596* **Althaus** H., *al.* [Germania 1985] Apocalittica e escatologia; senso e fine
della storia. Brescia 1992, Morcelliana. 176 p. Lᵐ 20. - ᴿParVi 39,3 (1994)
60s (A. *Rolla*).
3597 **Cohn** Norman, [Zoroastrian-influenced apocalyptic] Cosmos. chaos, and
the world to come 1992 ➤ 9,3782:   ᴿJJS 45 (1994) 127s (C. *Rowland*).
ᴱ**Collins** J.J.,   *Charlesworth* J.H.,   Mysteries and revelations; apocalyptic
1991 ➤ 7,425; 8,3900.
3598 *Colpe* Carsten,   *a)* Die Apokalyptik als Elementargedanke und als Dif-
fusionsphänomen [ᴱ*Hellholm* 1983/9); – *b)* Rede am 9. Nov. 1993 in der
Hochmeisterkirche; – *c)* Frühe jüdische Mystik [SCHÄFER P. 1991]: BTZ
11 (1994) 281-288 / 269-278 / 288-291.
Himmelfarb Martha, Ascents to heaven in Jewish and Christian apocalyptic
1993 ➤ 8873.
3599 *Lemche* Niels P.,   From prophetism to apocalyptic; fragments of an
article [amid the 'very little published on this change of paradigm' in
footnote p. 98 does not cite the similar title of *North* R., VTS 22 (1972)
47-71] ➤ 89*e*, ᶠOTZEN B., In the last days 1994, 98-103.

3600 **Marconcini** Benito, *al.*, Profeti e apocalittici: Logos 3. T-Leumann 1994, Elle Di Ci. 459 p. L^m 55.

3601 *Muñoz León* Domingo, Universalidad de la salvación en la apocalíptica (Daniel, 4⁰ de Esdras y 2⁰ de Baruc): RBibArg 56 (1994) 129-148.

3602 *Pilgaard* Aage, Apokalyptik als bibeltheologisches Thema: ➤ 330, New-Directions 1992/4, 180-200.

3603 **Russell** D. S., Prophecy and the apocalyptic dream — protest and promise. Peabody MA 1994, Hendrickson. 136 p. 1-56563-054-8 [NRT 117,272, J. *Grégoire*]. – ᴿExpTim 106 (1994s) 151 (J. M. *Court* misses a balanced comparison of Rev with Dan).

3604 **Russell** D. S., Divine disclosure 1992 ➤ 8,3911; 9,3788: ᴿHeythJ 35 (1994) 70s (Margaret *Barker*).

3605 **Sacchi** Paolo, L'apocalittica giudaica 1990 ➤ 6,3984 ... 9,3790: ᴿOrpheus 15 (1994) 235 (A. *Gallico*).

3606 *Sacchi* Paolo, Die Macht der Sünde in der Apokalyptic, ᵀ*Stemberger* Günter: JbBT 9 (1994) 111-124.

3607 *a) Sæbø* Magne, Old Testament Apocalyptic in its relation to prophecy and wisdom [RAD G. von]; – *b) Bilde* Per, Gnosticism, Jewish apocalypticism, and early Christianity: ➤ 89e, ꟲOTZEN B., In the last days 1994, 78-91 / 9-32.

E9.2   **Daniel:** *textus, commentarii; themata, versiculi.*

3608 *a) Asmussen* Jes P., A Judeo-Persian Daniel apocalypse; – *b) Hidal* Sten, Apocalypse, persecution and exegesis; HIPPOLYTUS and THEODORET of Cyrrhus on the book of Daniel; – *c) Cryer* Frederick H., The problem of dating biblical Hebrew and the Hebrew of Daniel: ➤ 89e, ꟲOTZEN B., In the last days 1994, 38-40 / 49-53 / 185-198.

3609 **Becquet** Gilles, *al.*, La fosse aux lions; lecture du livre de Daniel: P 1993, Ouvrières. 176 p. F 98. – ᴿVSp 148 (1994) 133 (J. *Asurmendi*).

3610 **Collins** John J., Daniel: Hermeneia 1993 ➤ 9,3794 [BL 95,60s, P. R. *Davis*; JTS 46,224, J. *Goldingay*]: ᴿRB 102 (1994) 278-290 (P. *Grelot*); TS 55 (1994) 537s (R. J. *Clifford*).

3611 **Cowe** S. Peter, The Armenian version of Daniel 1992 ➤ 8,3916; 9,3795: ᴿBtS 151 (1994) 369s (R. A. *Taylor*).

3612 **Lederach** Paul M., Daniel: [Mennonite] Believers' Church Bible Commentary. Scottdale PA 1994, Herald. 326 p. $18. 0-8361-3663-2.

3613 **McLay** Tim, Translation technique and textual studies in the Old Greek and THEODOTION versions of Daniel: diss., ᴰ*Salvesen* A. G. Durham UK 1994. – RTLv 26,531.

3614 **Miller** Stephen R., Daniel: NewAmerC 18. Nv 1994, Broadman & H. 348 p. [OTAbs 18, p. 424; BL 95,56, L. L. *Grabbe*].

3615 *Mitchell* Terence C., Shared vocabulary in the Pentateuch and the Book of Daniel: ➤ 146, ꟲWISEMAN D., He swore an oath 1994, 131-141.

3616 **Péter-Contesse** René, *Ellington* John, A handbook on the Book of Daniel. NY 1993, United Bible Societies. viii-365 p. $9. 0-8267-0126-4 [BL 95,52, P. W. *Coxon*].

3617 *Pilgaard* Aage, Apokalyptik als bibeltheologisches Thema, dargestellt an Dan 9 und Mk 13: ➤ 303a, New Directions 1992/4, 180-200.

3618 *a) Schmitt* Armin, Die Danieltexte aus Qumran und der masoretische Text (M); – *b) Koch* Klaus, Die Entstehung der Heilandserwartung in Israel und ihre kanonische Rezeption: ➤ 115, ꟲSCHUNCK K.-D., Nach-denken 1994, 279-297 / 235-250.

3620 **Taylor** Richard A.,   The Peshiṭta of Daniel [diss. Wsh Catholic Univ. ᴰ*Griffith* S.]: Peshiṭta Inst. mg 7.   Leiden 1994, Brill.   xiii-344 p.; bibliog. 326-344 [OTAbs 18, p. 425, A. A. *Di Lella*].

3621 *Taylor* Richard A.,   The Peshiṭta of Daniel; questions of origin and date: ➤ 451, Syriacum 6 (1992/4) 31-42.

3622 **Thompson** Henry C.,   The Book of Daniel; an annotated bibliography. NY 1993, Garland. li-547 p. $84.   0-8240-4873-3 [BL 95,76, L. L. *Grabbe*].

3623 *Trakatellis* Demetrios,   *Lógos agōnistikós*; Hɪᴘᴘᴏʟʏᴛᴜs' commentary on Daniel: ➤ 40, ꟳGᴇᴏʀɢɪ D., 1994, 527-550.

3624 *Zier* Mark A.,   The manuscript tradition of the Glossa ordinaria for Daniel, and hints at a method for a critical edition: Scriptorium 47 (1993) 3-25, pl. 1-8.

3625 **Husser** Jean-Marie, [Dan ... Gen 37,5; 41,1] La royauté et le songe dans le Proche-Orient ancien: diss. Sorbonne, ᴰ*Meslin* M. Paris 1994. – RTLv 26,531.

3626 *Lust* J., Cult and sacrifice in Daniel; the Tamid and the abomination of desolation: ➤ 486*, *Quaegebeur*, Ritual 1993, 283-299.

3627 *Mason* Steve,   Jᴏsᴇᴘʜᴜs, Daniel, and the Flavian house: ➤ 123, Mem. Sᴍɪᴛʜ M., Josephus 1992/4, 161-191.

3628 *Schwantes* Siegfried J.,   La fecha del libro de Daniel [antes de 500]: Theologika 8 (Lima 1993) 88-109 [< OTAbs 17, p. 609].

3629 **Stahl** Rainer,   Von Weltengagement zu Weltüberwindung; theologische Positionen im Danielbuch: ContribBExegT 4. Kampen 1994, Kok Pharos. 215 p. *f* 65.   90-390-0013-1 [OIAc 11,42].

3630 **Stefanovic** Zdravko, The Aramaic of Daniel 1992 [< diss. Correlations ➤ 8,3934; 9,3813]. – ᴿJSS 39 (1994) 299s (P. W. *Coxon*).

3631 *Verhoef* P. A.,   Die aanduiting van tijd ['time'] in die boek Daniel: In die Skriflig 28 (1994) 223-233 [< OTAbs 38, p. 223 'Designations for time'].

3632 *Woodard* Branson L.ᴶ,   Literary strategies and authorship in the Book of Daniel: JEvTS 37 (1994) 39-53.

3633 **Woude** A. S. van der,   The Book of Daniel, 40th Lv: BtETL 106, 1991/3 ➤ 9,420 [JTS 46,226, P. M. *Casey*]:   ᴿBL (1994) 79 (tit. pp.); TAth 65 (1994) 986-9 (P. *Simotas*).

────────────

3634 *Cheung* Vincent, ⓒ To do nor not to do (Dan 1,3-16) [back-cover contents has 1,4-13]: Jian Dao 1 (1994) 109-113.

3635 **Meadowcroft** Tim,   A literary critical comparison of the Masoretic text and Septuagint of Daniel 2-7 [< diss. Edinburgh 1993, ᴰ*Hayman* A. ➤ 9,3816]: TyndB 45 (1994) 195-9.

3636 *Helberg* J. L., [Dan 3,17s] Die mag van God volgens die belydenis van Daniël se vriende: In die Skriflig 28 (1994) 75-88 [< OTAbs 17, p. 609].

3637 *Chojnacki* Stanisław,   [Dan 3,20] Les trois Hébreux dans la fournaise, une enquête iconographique dans la peinture éthiopienne: RasEtiop 35 (1991) 13-40 + 10 (color.) fig.

3638 *Albertz* Rainer,   Bekehrung von oben als 'messianisches Programm'; die Sonderüberlieferung der Septuaginta in Dan 4-6: ➤ 31*, ꟳDᴀᴜᴛᴢᴇɴʙᴇʀɢ G., Nach den Anfängen fragen 1994, 33-53.

3639 **Steussy** Marti J.,   Gardens in ... Daniel ᴰ1993 ➤ 9,3819:   ᴿCBQ 56 (1994) 573s (J. T. *Walsh*).

3640 *Grelot* Pierre, [Dan 4,13] Nabuchodonosor changé en bête [< Mém. PEDREIRO DE CASTRO 1971]: VT 44 (1994) 10-17.

3641 **Margain** Jean, Le livre de Daniel [6,1-7,28]: commentaire philologique du texte araméen: *a*) Les classiques bibliques. P 1994, Beauchesne. 80 p. 2-7010-1318-6 [BL 95,70, L. L. *Grabbe*]. – *b*) LORA 4 (1993) 57-72.

3642 *Arbeiter* Achim, [Dan 6,16] Frühe hispanische Darstellungen des Daniel in der Löwengrube: → 18, ᶠBRANDENBURG H., Boreas 17 (1994) 5-12; pl. 1-2.

3643 *Woude* A. S. van der, *a*) Daniel [6] uit de kuil opgetrokken; KerkT 45 (1994) 89-91; – *b*) Zu Daniel 6,11: ZAW 106 (1994) 123s: 'on that very day'.

3644 **Burnier-Genton** Jean, Le rêve subversif d'un sage; Daniel 7: Monde B. 1993 → 9,3824: ᴿGregorianum 75 (1994) 553-8 (C. *Conroy*); JTS 45 (1994) 448 (J. *Goldingay*); NRT 116 (1994) 110 (J. L. *Ska*).

3645 ᴱ**Bader** Winfried, 'Und die Wahrheit wurde hinweggefegt'; Daniel 8 linguistisch interpretiert [Methode H. SCHWEIZER]: Textw/Informatik 9. Tü 1994, Franke. 170 p. DM 68. 3-7720-1959-5 [OTAbs 17, p. 676-8].

3646 **Owusu-Antwi** Brempong, An investigation of the chronology of Daniel 9,24-27: Diss. Andrews, ᴰ*Hasel* G. Berrien Springs MI 1994.

3647 *Hardy* Frank W., The Hebrew singular for 'week' in the expression 'one week' in Daniel 9,27: AndrUnSem 32 (1994) 197-202.

3648 *Cristofani* José R., Dor [= dolor] e resistência; jovens, mulheres e crianças na origem social do apocalipsismo judaico — relendo Daniel 11,29-35: EstudosT 34 (São Leopoldo 1994) 87-100 [< OTAbs 17, p. 610].

3649 *Wolters* Al, Zōhar hārāqīaᶜ (Daniel 12,3) and Halley's Comet: JStOT 61 (1994) 111-120.

E9.3 *Prophetae Minores,* **Dōdekaprophētōn ... Hosea, Joel.**

3650 *Coggins* R. J., The minor prophets — one book or twelve?: → 45, ᶠGOULDER M., Crossing 1994, 57-68.

3651 **Gordon** Robert P., Studies in the Targum to the Twelve Prophets; from Nahum to Malachi [< ᴰ1973]: VTSup 51. Leiden 1994, Brill. xii-177 p. *f* 110. 90-04-09987-5 [JTS 46,233-5, C. T. R. *Hayward*, high praise; Rel-StR 21,323, Z. *Garber*]. – ᴿBL (1994) 56 (A. *Gelston*).

3652 **Jacob** Edmond, *Keller* Carl-A., *Amsler* Samuel, Osée, Joël, Amos, Abdias, Jonas³; CommAT XIa, Genève 1992, Labor et Fides. xiii-295 p. 2-8309-0664-0 [Salesianum 56,571, R. *Vicent*].

3653 **Jones** Barry E., The formation of the Book of Twelve; a study in text and canon: diss. Duke, ᴰ*Meyers* E. Durham NC 1994. 392 p. 94-32470. – DissA 55 (1994s) p. 2002; RelStR 21,255.

3654 **McComiskey** T. E., The minor prophets, I. Hosea, Joel, Amos 1992 → 9,3838: ᴿAndrUnSem 32 (1994) 142-4 (B. *Taylor*); BtS 151 (1994) 498s (R. B. *Chisholm*).

Muraoka T., A Greek-English lexicon of the Septuagint (Twelve Prophets) 1993 → 9308.

3656 **Nogalski** James, *a*) Literary precursors to the Book of Twelve / *b*) Redactional procedures in the Book of the Twelve: BZAW 217s. B 1993, de Gruyter. ix-301 p.; ix-300 p. DM 138 each. 3-11-013702-X; -67-4 [BL 95,71, J. M. *Dines*]. – ᴿZAW 106 (1994) 533s (G. *Metzner*).

3657 **Tov** E., The Greek Minor Prophets scroll from Naḥal Ḥever: DJD 8, 1990 → 6,3959; 9,3842: ᴿRÉG 107 (1994) 978s (J. *Irigoin*).

3658 **Andeberhan** Waldetensao, Commentari etiopici sul libro del profeta

Osea, edizione critica da mss inediti: ÄthFor 40. Wsb 1994, Harrassowitz. [iv-] 327 p. 3-447-03605-2.
3659 **Borbone** Pier G., Il libro del profeta Osea 1990 → 6,4036 ... 9,3844:
ᴿBO 51 (1994) 637-9 (A. *Schenker*).
3660 **Carbone** Sandro P., *Rizzi* Giovanni, Il libro di Osea... masoretico,
greco, targum aramaico 1992 → 8,3962; Lᵐ 44. – ᴿCBQ 56 (1994) 750s
(S. *Pisano*); CC 145 (1994,2) 198s (D. *Scaiola*); Salesianum 56 (1994) 775s
(M. *Cimosa*).
3661 **Davies** Graham I., Hosea: NCent 1992 → 8,3964: ᴿAntonianum 69
(1994) 115-7 (M. *Nobile*); BL (1994) 55 (G. I. *Emmerson*); BtS 151 (1994)
242 (H. *Heater* welcomes); OTEssays 7 (1994) 135-8 (C. W. *Retief*:
actualization missing); Vidyajyoti 58 (1994) 468s (P. *Meagher*).
3662 *Ferrer* J., El Targum d'Osees, traducció crítica catalana del text aramen:
Anuari 14 (1991) 61-92 [< JStJud 25,141].
3663 *Perani* Mauro, Frammenti del commento originale di Yosef ben
Šimʿon QARA a Osea e Michea: → 330a, X-Viverone 1992/3, 615-625;
Eng. 278.
3664 **Simian-Yofre** Horacio, El desierto de los dioses... Oseas 1993 → 8,3975;
9,3854: ᴿBiblica 75 (1994) 572-6 (I. *Cardellini*); Eborensia 7 (1994) 153;
ÉTRel 69 (1994) 417 (T. *Römer*); Gregorianum 75 (1994) 157-160 (C.
Conroy); NRT 116 (1994) 105s (J. L. *Ska*); RevSR 68 (1994) 352-5 (B.
Renaud); Salesianum 56 (1994) 789 (M. *Cimosa*); TLZ 119 (1994) 890-2
(R. *Kessler*); ZkT 116 (1994) 89s (G. *Fischer*).
3665 — *Levoratti* Armando J., Una relettura de Oseas [SIMIAN-YOFRE 1993]:
RBíbArg 56 (1994) 77-84 [< OTAbs 18, p. 103].
3666 **Simian-Yofre** Horacio, Il deserto degli dèi; teologia e storia nel libro di
Osea, ᵀ*Cavazzuti* Tommaso: [Testi e commenti A2 (non nel libro)]. Bo
1994, Dehoniane. 236 p. Lᵐ 32. 88-10-20579-0.
3667 **Simon** Uriel, Abraham ben Ezra's... Hosea, Joel, Amos 1989 → 6,4046;
9,3855: ᴿBijdragen 55 (1994) 332s (J. van *Ruiten*).

3668 *Ausin* Santiago, La tradición de la alianza en Oseas: → 22, ᶠCASCIARO
J., Biblia 1994, 127-146.
3669 **Boshoff** Willem S., The book Hosea and the Yahweh-Baal-controversy
(in Afrikaans): diss. Pretoria 1994. – DissA 55 (1994s) p. 2067.
3670 *Carroll* Robert P., [Hos 1,2] On representation in the Bible; an *ideologiekritik* approach: JNWS 20,2 (1994) 1-15.
3671 **Davies** G. I., Hosea: OTGuides 1993 → 9,3848: ᴿBL (1994) 55s (G. I.
Emmerson); ETL 70 (1994) 436-8 (J. *Lust*, also on Jon Zeph); Vidyajyoti
58 (1994) 257s (P. *Meagher*).
3672 *Krašovec* Jože, Punishment and mercy in Hosea: BogVest 53 (1993)
193-213 Slovene, 213s Eng.
3673 **Morris** Gerald P., Prophecy, poetry, and Hosea: diss. Southern Baptist
Theol. Sem., ᴰ*Keown* G. Dallas 1994. 225 p. 94-28254. – DissA 55 (1994s)
p. 1284.
3674 *a*) *Rooy* H. E. van, The names Israel, Ephraim and Jacob in the Book
of Hosea; – *b*) *Wittenberg* Gunther H., Amos and Hosea; a contribution
to the problem of the 'Prophetenschweigen' in the Deuteronomistic
history: OTEssays 5 (1993) 135-149 / 295-311 [< OTAbs 17, p.
610 . 613].
3675 **Seifert** Brigitte, 'Ich nahm Ephraim auf meine Arme...'; metaphorisches
Reden von Gott im Hoseabuch: Diss. ᴰ*Köckert* M. Berlin 1994. – TR
91,93.

3676 **Smith** Duane A., Kinship and covenant; an examination of kinship metaphors for covenant in the book of the prophet Hosea: diss. Harvard, ᴰ*Moore* F. CM 1994. 286 p. 95-00201. – DissA 55 (1994s) p. 2437.

3677 **Stuart** Douglas, Hosea-Jonah: Word Themes 1989 ➤ 5,3795; 7,3385; ᴿJEvTS 35 (1992) 412p (B. E. *Beyer*).

3678 *Wacker* Marie Thérèse, Spuren der Göttin im Hoseabuch: ➤ 467*, Ein Gott? 1993/4, 329-348 [*Hadley* Judith W., Yahweh and 'his Asherah' 235-268; *Day* John, *Smith* M., 181-196-234].

3679 *Willis* John T., 'I am your God' and 'you are my people' in Hosea and Jeremiah: ➤ ᶠOSBORNE T., RestQ 36 (1994) 291-303 [304-315, *Marrs* R.].

3680 *Zulick* Margaret N., Rhetorical polyphony in the book of the prophet Hosea: diss. Northwestern, ᴰ*Bird* Phyllis A. Evanston 1994. 305 p. 94-33951. – DissA 55 (1994s) p. 2868.

3681 *Boshoff* Willem, Sexual encounters of a different kind; Hosea 1-2 as foreplay to the message of the book of Hosea: Religion and Theology 1 (Pretoria 1994) 329-339 [< OTAbs 18,346].

3682 *Werner* Wolfgang, Einige Anmerkungen zum Verständinis von Hos 6,1-6: ➤ 61, ᶠKAISER O., 'Wer ist' 1994, 355-372.

3683 *Swanepoel* M. G., Solutions to the crux interpretum of Hosea 6:2: OTEssays 7 (1994) 39-59 [OTAbs 18, p. 103: leaves resurrection open].

3684 *Pury* Albert de, a) Erwägungen zu einem vorexilischen Stämme-jahwismus; Hosea 12 und die Auseinandersetzung um die Identität Israels und seines Gottes; ➤ 467*, OBO 139, 1993/4, 412-462; – b) Las dos leyendas sobre el origen de Israel (Jacob y Moisés) y la elaboración del Pentateuco: Estudios Bíblicos 52 (M 1994) 95-131 [< OTAbs 17, p. 611].

3686 **Leeuwen** C. van, Joël: PredikOT. Nijkerk 1993, Callenbach. 261 p. ƒ89,50. 90-266-0318-5 [OTAbs 17, p. 678; BL 95,68, J. W. *Rogerson*]. – ᴿETL 70 (1994) 438s (J. *Lust*, also on his Obadja).

3687 *Marcus* David, Nonrecurring doublets in the book of Joel: CBQ 56 (1994) 56-67.

3688 **Simkins** Ronald, Yahweh's activity in history and nature in the book of Joel [< 1990 diss. Harvard, ᴰ*Cross* F. M.]: ANE TSt 10, 1991 ➤ 8,3411: ᴿBibTB 24 (1994) 195s (H. E. *Page*); OTAbs 17 (1994) 455s (Kathleen S. *Nash*).

3689 *Stark* Marcus, HESYCHIUS von Jerusalem, Scholien zum Propheten Joel: JbAC 37 (1994) 37-44.

E9.4 **Amos.**

3690 **Bovati** Pietro, *Meynet* Roland, Le livre du prophète Amos: Rhétorique biblique 2. P 1994, Cerf. 443 p. F 220. 2-204-05076-8 [BL 95,56, R. J. *Coggins*; OTAbs 18, p. 169; Gregorianum 76,439, *ipsi*].

3691 — **Bovati** P., *Meynet* R., La fin d'Israël; paroles d'Amos [condensation]: Lire la Bible 101. P 1994, Cerf. 238 p. F 98. 2-204-04867-4 [Gregorianum 76,440, *ipsi*].

3692 — **Bovati** Pietro, *Meynet* Roland, Il libro del profeta Amos: Retorica biblica 2. R, Dehoniane. 474 p. Lᵐ 55.

3693 **Carbone** Sandro P., *Rizzi* Giovanni, Il libro di Amos; lettura ebraica, greca e aramaica. Bo 1993, Dehoniane. 176 p. Lᵐ 27. 88-10-20563-4. – ᴿETL 70 (1994) 439 (J. *Lust*: 'hebraica'; some reserves).

3694 **Dines** Jennifer M., The Septuagint of Amos; a study in interpretation: diss. Heythrop. L 1992. 316 p. – ᴿETL 70 (1994) 439 (J. *Lust*).

3695 **Jaruzelska** Izabela, Social structure in the kingdom of Israel in the eighth century B.C. as reflected in the Book of Amos: FolOr 29 (1992s) 91-117 [< OTAbs 18, p. 104].

3696 **Mowvley** H., Amos-Hosea: Epworth comm. 1991 ⇥ 7,3423: ᴿBR (1992) 81 (G.I. *Emmerson*); VT 44 (1994) 285 (R.P. *Gordon*).

3697 **Paul** Shalom M., Amos 1991 ⇥ 7,3425...9,3882: ᴿAJS 19 (1994) 244-7 (G.A. *Rendsburg*: good).

3698 **Álvarez Barredo** Miguel, Relecturas deuteronomísticas de Amós, Miqueas y Jeremías: InstTFranc 10, 1993 ⇥ 9,3884: ᴿAngelicum 71 (1994) 591s (J. *García Trapiello*); Carthaginensia 10 (1994) 176s (F. *Marín Heredia*); ÉTRel 69 (1994) 417s (T. *Römer*); NRT 116 (1994) 105 (J.L. *Ska*).

3699 **Carroll Rodas** Mark D., Contexts for Amos; prophetic poetics in Latin American perspective [< diss.]: jOsu 132. Shf 1992, JStOT. 362 p. £40; sb. £30. 1-85075-297-4. – ᴿCBQ 56 (1994) 540s (V.H. *Matthews*); TBR 7,3 (1994s) 18s (A. *Warren*).

3700 *Clines* David J.A., Metacommenting Amos: ⇥ 138, ᶠWHYBRAY N., Of prophets 1993, 141-160.

3701 *a) Freedman* David N., *Welch* Andrew, Amos's earthquake and Israelite prophecy; – *b) Campbell* Edward F., Archaeological reflections on Amos's targets: ⇥ 67, ᶠKING P., Scripture 1994, 188-198 / 32-52; 8 fig.

3702 **Muñoz Ramírez** Guillermo, The social location of the prophet Amos in light of a cultural anthropological model: diss. Emory, ᴰ*Tucker* G. Atlanta 1993. – RelStR 21,255.

3703 *a) Valle* José Luis del, Amos; justicia 'versus' poder; – *b) Martín Juárez* Miguel A.. Esperanza y poder en Isaías: BibFe 20,58 ('El hechizo del poder' 1994) 28-42 / 43-66.

3704 *a) Vermaak* Petrus S., The meaning of *pesha* in the Book of Amos; – *b) Schmitt* John J., Samaria in the books of prophets of the eighth century BCE: ⇥ 303, 11th Jewish 1993/4, A-107-114 / 115-121.

3705 *Warwick* Frederick S., Amos and Hosea; action and reaction: ExpTim 105 (1993s) 13s.

───────────

3706 *Ceresko* Anthony R., Janus parallelism in Amos's 'oracles against the nations' (Amos 1:3-2:16): JBL 113 (1994) 485-490.

3707 *Vieweger* Dieter, [Am 1,3-2,16] Zur Herkunft der Völkerworte im Amosbuch unter besonderer Berücksichtigung des Aramäerspruchs (Am 1,3-5): ⇥ 101, ᶠREVENTLOW 1994, 103-119.

3708 *Niemann* Hermann M., Theologie im geographischen Gewand; zum Wachstumprozess der Völkerspruchsammlung Amos 1-2: ⇥ 115, ᶠSCHUNCK K.-D., Nachdenken 1994, 177-196.

3709 **Wood** Joyce, Amos; prophecy as a performing art and its transformation in book culture: diss. St. Michael's, ᴰ*Peckham* B. Windsor 1993. – SR 23 (1994) 525.

3710 *Noble* Paul R., I will not bring 'it' back (Amos 1:3); a deliberately ambiguous oracle?: ExpTim 106 (1994s) 105-9.

3710* *Meynet* Roland, [Am 3,8] 'Le lion a rugi; qui ne craindrait?' La peur dans le livre d'Amos. LVitae 49 (1994) 157-165.

3711 *Snyman* S. D., A note on Ashdod and Egypt in Amos III 9: VT 44 (1994) 559-562.
3712 **Blum** Erhard, 'Amos' in Jerusalem, Beobachtungen zu Am 6-7: Henoch 16 (1994) 23-47, ital. 47.
3713 *Mittmann* S., Der Rufende im Feuer (Amos 7:4): JNWS 20,1 (1994) 165-170.
3714 *Garcia-Treto* F. O., A reader-response approach to prophetic conflict; the case of Amos 7,10-19: ➤ 9,271, New Lit. Crit. 1993, Osu 143, pp. 114-124.
3715 *Waschke* Ernst J., Die fünfte Vision des Amosbuches (9,1-4) — eine Nachinterpretation: ZAW 106 (1994) 434-445.
3716 *Cathcart* Kevin J., *Rōʾš*, 'poison' in Amos IX 1 [support for HORST]: VT 44 (1994) 393-6.
3717 *Smith* Regina, A new perspective on Amos 9:7: JIntdenom 22 (1994) 36-47.

E9.5 **Jonas.**

3718 *Brock* Sebastian P., EPHREM's verse homily on Jonah and the repentance of Nineveh; notes on the textual tradition: ➤ 70, ᶠLAGA C., Philohistôr 1994, 71-86.
3719 ᵀ**Jundt** Pierre, M. LUTHER, Explication du prophète Jonas et du prophète Habaquq 1526: Œuvres 14, 1993 ➤ 9,3913: ᴿBL (1994) 66 (J. W. *Rogerson*: robust).
3720 **Kilpp** Nelson, Jonas. Petrópolis 1994, Vozes. 198 p. – ᴿRBíbArg 56 (1994) 250s (P. R. *Andiñach*).
3721 **Lifshitz** Zeʾev H., The paradox of human existence; a commentary on the book of Jonah, ᵀ*Goldwasser* Julie. Northvale NJ 1994, Aronson. xxv-269 p. 1-568212-19-4.
3722 **Limburg** James, Jonah; a commentary: OT Library 1993 ➤ 9,3915: ᴿBL (1994) 65 (J. M. *Dines*); ETL 70 (1994) 440s (J. *Lust*); WWorld 14 (1994) 364s (R. S. *Hanson*).
3723 *Longacre* Robert E., *Hwang Shin-Ja* J., A textlinguistic approach to the biblical Hebrew narrative of Jonah: ➤ 304c, Biblical Hebrew 1993/4, 336-358 [320-8, *Andersen* F., Micah].
3724 ᵀᴱ**Pavia** Nicoletta, GIROLAMO, Commento al libro di Giona: TPatr 96. R 1992, Città Nuova. 120 p. 88-311-3096-X. – ᴿCC 145 (1994,3) 193-5 (G. *Cremascoli*); Salesianum 56 (1994) 373 (A. *Glanc*); Teresianum 45 (1992) 326 (M. *Diego Sánchez*).
3724* *Pelletier* Marcel, Jonas: Tychique 111 (1994) 37-42.
3725 **Siegert** Folker, Ps.-Philon Jona/Simson II 1992 ➤ 8,323 ('*Folker* S.'); 9,3920: ᴿJBL 113 (1994) 527-9 (A. *Kamesar*); Judaica 50 (1994) 5052 (C. *Thoma*); Salesianum 56 (1994) 788s (R. *Vicent*).
3726 **Simon** Ulrich, Jona, ein jüdischer Kommentar (❿ 1992)ᵀ: SBS 157. Stu 1994, KBW. 163 p. DM 44 pa. 3-460-04571-X [OTAbs 18, p. 648].

3727 **Craig** K. M.ᴶ, A poetics of Jonah; art in the service of ideology 1993 ➤ 9,3925: ᴿJStOT 61 (1994) 125 (P. R. *Davies*); TTod 51 (1994s) 322.4.6 (J. *Limburg*).
3728 *Feldman* Louis H., JOSEPHUS's interpretation of Jonah: AJS 17 (1992) 1-29.
3729 *Holmgren* Frederick C., Israel, the prophets, and the book of Jonah; the rest of the story, the formation of the canon: CurrTM 21 (1994) 127-132.

3730 *Kahn* Paul, An analysis of the Book of Jonah: Judaism 43 (1994) 87-100.

3731 *Lillegard* David, Narrative and paradox in Jonah: Kerux 8,3 (1993) 19-30 [< OTAbs 18, p. 106].

3732 **Lux** Rüdiger, Jona, Prophet zwischen 'Verweigerung' und 'Gehorsam'; eine erzählanalytische Studie [Hab.-Diss. Halle 1992]: FRL 62. Gö 1994, Vandenhoeck & R. 240 p. 3-525-53844-8 [OTA 18, p. 425s].

3733 *Nordheim* Eckhard von, Das Buch Jona und die Anfänge der hellenistisch-jüdischen Mission: ➤ 31*, ᶠDAUTZENBERG G., Nach 1994, 441-460.

3734 *Mora* Vincent, Jonas, un conte théologique; MondeB 84 (1993) > Espr-Vie 104 (1994) 114-6 (J. *Daoust*).

3735 *Pell* M., ➌ Jonah as an artistic story: BeitMikra 39 (1994) 210-223 [< OTAbs 18, p. 106].

3736 **Potgieter** J. H., Narrattologiesc onderzoek... Jona 1991 ➤ 7,3448: ᴿETL 70 (1994) 441s (J. *Lust*).

3737 **Salters** Robert B., Jonah & Lamentations: OTGuides. Shf 1994, JStOT. 125 p. £6. 1-85075-719-4. [BL 95,73, P. P. *Jenson*].

3738 **Soggin** J. Alberto, Storia di un viaggiatore e di un umorista: il profeta Giona: ➤ 418, Circolazioni 1991/4, 239s.

3739 **Steffen** Uwe, Die Jona-Geschichte; ihre Auslegung und Darstellung im Judentum, Christentum und Islam. Neuk 1994, Neuk-V. x-146 p. DM 29,80. 3-7887-1492-1 [TR 91,181].

3740 **Trible** Phyllis, Rhetorical criticism; context, method and the Book of Jonah: GuidesBS. Mp 1994, Fortress. xii-264 p. $13 pa. 9-8006-2798-9 [OTAbs 18, p. 648].

3741 *Zimmermann* Frank, Problems and solutions in the Book of Jonah: Judaism 40 (1991) 580-9.

3742 *Fürst* Alfons, Kürbis oder Efeu? [gourd or ivy]: zur Übersetzung von Jona 4,6 in der Septuaginta und bei HIERONYMUS: BibNot 72 (1994) 12-19.

3743 *Crouch* Walter B., To question an end, to end a question; opening the closure of the Book of Jonah; JStOT 62 (1994) 101-112.

E9.6 *Michaeas,* **Micah.**

3744 **García Rodríguez** Miguel Ángel, Comentarios bíblicos etíopes al profeta Miqueas, edición crítica de manuscritos inéditos, traducción y exposición de su teología: diss. Pont. Univ. Gregoriana Nº 7196, ᴰ*Raineri* O. Roma 1994. 398 p.; extr. Nº 4045, 130 p. – InfPUG 26,131 (1994) 32; RTLv 26, p. 531.

3745 **Mason** Rex, Micah, Nahum, Obadiah: OT Guides 1991 ➤ 7,3457; 9,3942: ᴿVT 44 (1994) 137 (R. P. *Gordon*: excellent).

3746 **Schibler** D., Der Prophet Micha 1991 [1989 ➤ 5,3885]: ᴿOTEssays 7 (1994) 473-6 (J. A. *Naudé*: an honest attempt, despite inconsistencies).

3747 **Shaw** C. S., The speeches of Micah: jOsu 145, 1993 ➤ 9,3943: ᴿETL 70 (1994) 148s (J. *Lust*).

3748 **Bosman** Johan G., (in Afrikaans) Justice in the book of Micah; a traditional-historical analysis of the concept: diss. ᴰ*Prinsloo* W. S. Pretoria 1994. – DissA 55 (1994s) p. 1290.

3749 *Dempsey* Carol J., [*al.*] Economic injustice in Micah: BToday 32,5 ('The Bible and the economy' 1994) 272-6 [-294].

_____

3750 **Dempsey** Carol J., The interplay between literary form and technique and ethics in Micah 1-3: diss. Catholic Univ., ᴰ*Begg* C. Wsh 1994. 259 p. 94-21559. – DissA 55 (1994s) p. 603.
3751 *Beal* Timothy K., [Mi 1,8s...] The system and the speaking subject in the Hebrew Bible; reading for divine abjection: BInterp 2 (1994) 171-189.
3752 *Anbar* Moshé, Rosée et ondées ou lion et lionceau (Michée 5,6-7)?: BibNot 73 (1994) 5-8.
3753 *Snyman* S. D., A text intern and text extern investigation of Micah 6,9-16: NederduitsGT 35 (Stellenbosch 1994) 332-8 [< OTAbs 18, p. 351].

E9.7   *Abdias, Sophonias...* **Obadiah, Zephaniah, Nahum.**

3754 *Dietrich* Walter, Obadia/-buch: ➤ 517, TRE 24 (1994) 713-720.
3755 **Leeuwen** C. van, Obadja: PredikOT. Nijkerk 1993, Callenbach. 115 p. ƒ54.50. 90-266-0328-2 [BL 95,69, J. W. *Rogerson*].
3756 *McDuling* J. J. M., Obadia van af die Preekstoel: Acta Theologica 14 (Bloemfontein 1994) 111-120.

_____

3757 **Ben-Zvi** Ehud, Historical-critical study of Zephaniah: BZAW 198, 1991 ➤ 8,4069; 9,3954: ᴿBO 51 (1994) 640-5 (J. *Vlaardingerbroek*).
3758 **Berlin** Adele, Zephaniah: AnchorB 25A. NY 1994, Doubleday. xvi-165 p. $29. 0-385-26631-6 [TDig 42,356]. – ᴿUF 26 (1994) 593 (O. *Loretz*).
3759 *King* Greg A., The remnant in Zephaniah: BtS 151 (1994) 414-427.
3760 **Mason** Rex, Zephaniah, Habakkuk, Joel: OTGuides. Shf 1994, JStOT. 132 p. $10 pa. 1-85075-718-6 [OTAbs 17, p. 679; BL 95,70, K.J. *Cathcart*).
3761 **Ryou** D. H., Zephaniah's oracles against the nations: diss. VU, ᴰ*Leene* H. Amsterdam 1994. 411 p. – TvT 35,71; RTLv 26,532.
3762 ᴱ**Spreafico** Ambrogio, Sofonia 1991 ➤ 9,3956; 88-211-8011-7: ᴿGregorianum 75 (1994) 759s (C. *Conroy*: review copy received 1994); ZAW 106 (1994) 536 (J. A. *Soggin*).
3763 **Weigl** Michael, Zefanja und das 'Israel der Armen'; eine Untersuchung zur Theologie des Buches Z. [< kath. Diss. Wien 1991]: ÖBS 13. Klosterneuburg 1994, Österr. KBW. 329 p. DM 49.20. 3-85396-085-3 [OTAbs 18,170; BL 95,121, R. *Mason*].

_____

3764 *Dietrich* Walter, Nahum (/-buch): ➤ 517, TRE 23 (1994) 736-742.
3765 *Floyd* Michael H., The chimerical acrostic of Nahum 1:2-10: JBL 113 (1994) 421-437.
3766 **Roberts** J. J. M., Nahum, Habakkuk and Zephaniah 1991 ➤ 7,3477; 9,3960: ᴿBL (1994) 73 (K. J. *Cathcart*); ConcordTQ 58 (1994) 171s (T. *Trapp*); JRel 74 (1994) 552-4 (M. A. *Sweeney*).

E9.8   *Habacuc,* **Habakkuk.**

3767 *Dangl* Oskar, Habakuk – Prophet der Opfer der Gewalt: ProtokB 3 (1994) 25-40.

3768 *Dietrich* Walter, Habakuk – ein Jesajaschüler: ➤ 115, ᶠSCHUNK K.-D., Nachdenken 1994, 197-215.
3769 **Haak** Robert D., Habakkuk: VTS 44, 1992 ➤ 7,1483; 9,3966: ᴿBO 51 (1994) 405-8 (E. *Otto*); JNWS 20,1 (1994) 179-181 (P. A. *Kruger*).
3769* *Teixeira* Sayão, Habacuque e o problema do mal: VoxScr 3 (1993) 3-18.
3770 *Thompson* Michael, Prayer oracle and theophany; the book of Habakkuk: TyndB 44 (1993) 33-53.

E9.9 *Aggaeus,* **Haggai** – *Zacharias,* **Zechariah** – *Malachias,* **Malachi.**

3771 *Amsler* Samuel, Les derniers prophètes; Aggée, Zacharie, Malachie et quelques autres: CahÉv 90 (1994).
3772 **Bauer** Lutz, Zeit des Zweiten Tempels, Zeit der Gerechtigkeit 1992 ➤ 9,3974: ᴿActuBbg 31 (1994) 215 (J. *Boada*).
3773 **Reventlow** Henning, Die Propheten Haggai, Sacharja und Maleachi⁶: ATD 25/2, 1993 ➤ 9,3978: ᴿTLZ 119 (1994) 414s (A. *Meinhold*); ZAW 106 (1994) 533 (A.-C. *Wegner*).
3774 **Tidiman** B., Les livres d'Aggée et de Malachie: Comm. év. 15. Vaux-sur-Seine 1993, Edifac. 255 p. F 135 [NRT 117,125, J. L. *Ska*].
3775 **Tollington** Janet E., Tradition and innovation in Haggai and Zechariah 1-8 [diss. Oxford 1991]: jOsu 150, 1993 ➤ 9,3979: ᴿBL (1994) 76 (R. E. *Clements*); BO 51 (1994) 646s (B. *Becking*); JTS 45 (1994) 629s (D. R. *Jones*); TBR 7,2 (1994s) 16 (Katrina *Larkin*).

3776 *Bianchi* F., Le rôle de Zorobabel et de la dynastie davidique en Judée du VIᵉ siècle au IIᵉ siècle av. J.-C.: ➤ 461, TEuph 7 (1991/4) 153-165; Eng. 153.
3777 *Kessler* J., The second year of Darius and the prophet Haggai: TEuph 5 (1992) 63-84.
3778 *Meyers* Eric M., Second Temple studies in the light of recent archaeology; I. the Persian and Hellenistic periods: CuRB 2 (1994) 25.42.
3779 *a) Petersen* David L., The Temple in Persian period prophetic texts; – *b) Blenkinsopp* Joseph, Temple and society in Achaemenid Judah; – *c)* response, *Bedford* Peter R., On models and texts; & *d) Horsley* Richard A., Empire, temple, and community — but no bourgeoisie: ➤ 9,2897, ᴱ*Davies* P., Second Temple Studies 1 (1991) 108-124 / 22-53 / 154-162 / 163-174.
3780 *Carroll* Robert P., So what do we know about the [second] temple? The temple in the prophets [a period of disputed temples]: ➤ 317, Second Temple Studies 2 (1994) 34-51 [< OTAbs 18,335].

3781 **Butterworth** Mike, Structure and the Book of Zechariah: jOsu 130, 1992 ➤ 8,4087; 9,3980: ᴿJBL 113 (1994) 133-5 (R. F. *Person*).
3782 *Karavidopoulos* Jean, Ⓖ Citation de Zacharie dans le Nouveau Testament: ➤ 131*c*, Mem. VELLAS V., DeltioVM 13,1 (1994) 48-55.

3783 *Clark* David J., Vision and oracle in Zechariah 1-6: ➤ 304*c*, Biblical Hebrew 1993/4, 529-560 [< OTAbs 18, p. 353].

3784 **Tigchelaar** Eibert, Prophets of old and the day of the end; Zechariah, the Book of Watchers and apocalyptic: diss. ᴰ*Woude* A. van der. Groningen 1994. 222 p. – TvT 35,71; RTLv 26, p. 533.

3785 *Laato* Antti, Zachariah 4,6b-10a and the Akkadian royal building inscriptions: ZAW 106 (1994) 53-69.

3786 *Kline* Meredith G., By my spirit [continued; on Zech 4,7, Zerubbabel's temple]: Kerux [9/1s, 3-15; 3-22] 9/3 (1994) 20-41.

3787 **Larkin** K., The eschatology of Second Zechariah; a study of the formation of a mantological Wisdom anthology: ContribBExT 6. Kampen 1994, Kok. 267 p. ƒ70. 90-390-0101-4 [BL 95,67s, P. P. *Jenson*]. – ᴿJStJud 25 (1994) 323s (E. *Tigchelaar*).

3788 **Person** Raymond F., Second Zechariah and the Deuteronomic school: jOsu 167, ᴰ1993 → 9,3985: ᴿETL 70 (1994) 442s (J. *Lust*).

3789 **Meyers** Carol L. & Eric M., Demography and diatribes; Yehud's population and the prophecy of Second Zechariah: → 67, ᶠKING P., Scripture 1994, 268-285.

3790 **Wilbur** Kenneth C., Analysis of poetic and prose expression in Zechariah 9-11: diss. Boston Univ. ᴰ*Parker* S. 1994. 417 p. 94-15033. – DissA 55 (1994s) p. 4476.

3791 *Stiglmair* Arnold, Der Durchbohrte – ein Versuch zu Sach 12: → 37, ᶠGAMPER A., ZkT 116 (1994) 451-6.

3792 *Lauscher* Frans du Toit, Epiphany and sun mythology in Zechariah 14: JNWS 20,1 (1994) 125-138.

3793 *a) Nielsen* Eduard, A note on Zechariah 14,4-5; – *b) Barstad* Hans M., Prophecy at Qumran?; – *c)* (*Kragelund*) *Holt* Else, '... und der Ursprung der Eschatologie'; S. MOWINCKEL's thesis in W. BRUEGGEMANN's adaptation: → 89e, ᶠOTZEN B., In the last days 1994, 33-37 / 104-120 / 92-97.

─────────────

3794 *Redditt* Paul L., The Book of Malachi in its social setting: CBQ 56 (1994) 240-255.

3795 **Hugenberger** Gordon P., Marriage as covenant; a study of biblical law and ethics governing marriage, developed from the perspective of Malachi [diss. ᴰ*Wenham* G. J.]: VTS 52. Leiden 1994, Brill. xix-414 p. 90-04-09977-8 [RelStR 21,130, M. A. *Sweeney*; BL 94,62, G. I. *Davies*].

3796 **Krieg** M. Mutmassungen über Maleachi: ATANT 80, 1993 → 9,3995 [TLZ 120,236, U. *Feist*].

3797 **Kugler** Robert A., The Levi-Priestly tradition, from Malachi to Testament of Levi: diss. ᴰ*VanderKam* J. Notre Dame 1994. 401 p. 94-22404. – DissA 55 (1994s) p. 605; RTLv 26,534.

3798 **O'Brien** Julia M., Priest and Levite in Malachi ᴰ1990 → 7,3499 ... 9,3997: ᴿTEuph 8 (1994) 173s (A. *Sérandour*).

3799 *Viberg* Åke, Wakening a sleeping metaphor; a new interpretation of Malachi 1:11: TyndB 45 (1994) 297-319.

3800 *Collins* C. John, The (intelligible) Masoretic text of *Malachi* 2:16 or, How does God feel about divorce: Pres [= Presb(byterion) not listed in OTAbs 18, p. 553] 20 (1994) 36-40.

3801 *Smit* E. J., [Mal 3,24] Elia in die boek Maleagi: In die Skriflig 28 (1994) 199-212 [< OTAbs 18,108].

3802 *Alonso Díaz* José, Eclipse y extinción del profetismo en Israel: ➤ 33*a*,
FDÍAZ MERCHÁN G., StOvet 22 (1994) 225-232.

IX. NT Exegesis generalis

F1. New Testament Introduction.

3803 **Aleu** José, Jesús de Nazaret en los orígenes del cristianismo. Tarrasa 1992,
Clie. 335 p. – RCarthaginensia 10 (1994) 459s (F. *Martínez Fresneda*).
3804 *Allison* Dale C., A plea for thoroughgoing eschatology ['the humiliating
discovery that Jesus proclaimed the near end of the world'...]: JBL 113
(1994) 651-668.
3805 *a) Andersen* Øivind, *Robbins* Vernon K., Paradigms in HOMER, PINDAR,
the tragedians, and the NT; – *b) Branham* R. Bracht, Authorizing
humor; LUCIAN's Demonax and Cynic rhetoric; – *c) Avery-Peck* Alan J.,
Rhetorical argumentation in early Rabbinic pronouncement stories; – *d)*
Speight R. Marston, Rhetorical argumentation in the Hadith literature
of Islam; – *e) Dean-Otting* Miriam & *Robbins*, Biblical sources for
pronouncement stories in the Gospels: Semeia 64 (1993) 3-31 / 33-48 /
49-71 / 73-92 / 95-115.
3805* **Araújo** Vera, Gesù e l'uso dei beni 1993 ➤ 9,4005: RCC 145 (1994,4)
98 (G. *Forlizzi*).
3806 EBecker Jürgen, Christian beginnings; word and community from Jesus
to post-apostolic times [1987], TKidder Annemarie, *Krauss* Reinhard, 1993
➤ 9,4008: RChH 63 (1994) 251s (E. G. *Hinson*).
3807 *a) Behr* C. A. [*al.*], Studies on the biography of Aelius ARISTIDES; – *b)*
Ruiz Montero C., CHARITON von Aphrodisias [*al.*]: ➤ 496, ANRW 34,2
(1994) 1140-1233 [-1313] / 1006-54 [-86].
3808 **Beker** J. Christiaan, The New Testament; a thematic introduction. Mp
1994, Fortress. 152 p. $10 pa. 0-8006-2775-X [NTAbs 38, p.444]. –
RelStR 20 (1994) 236 (C. *Bernas*).
3809 **Bell** Albert A.J, A guide to the New Testament world. Scottdale PA
1994, Herald. 324 p. $16. 0-8361-3650-0 [RelStR 21,140, J. T. *Fitzgerald*;
TDig 42,55].
3810 **Berger** Klaus, Hermeneutik des NTs 1988 ➤ 4,4076... 7,3506: RZkT
116 (1994) 220-2 (R. *Oberforcher*).
3811 EBerger K., *Colpe* C., Testi religiosi per lo studio del NT 1993 ➤ 9,4010:
RTeresianum 45 (1994) 597-9 (A. *Borrell*).
3812 *Betz* Hans D., The birth of Christianity as a Hellenistic religion; three
theories of origin: JRel 74 (1994) 1-25.
3813 EBillerbeck Margarethe, Die Kyniker in der modernen Forschung:
BochumerStPhil 15. Amst 1991, Grüner. viii-324 p. – REOS 81 (1993)
125-8 (M. *Winiarczyk,* ❷).
3814 **Blair** Joe, Introducing the New Testament. Nv 1994, Broadman & H.
xv-217 p.; ill.; maps. 0-8054-2123-8.
3815 **Blasi Birbe** Ferrán, Los nombres de Cristo en la Biblia: NTReligión.
Pamplona 1993, Univ. Navarra. 219 p. – RRelCu 40 (1994) 389 (A.
Turienzo); ScripTPamp 26 (1994) 791s (P. *Varo*).
3816 *Bolyki* Janos, Die Tischgemeinschaften Jesu; Methoden und Ergebnisse;
Perspektiven für die heutige Kirche: EurJT 3,2 (1994) 164-179; Eng.,
franç. 164.

3817 **Bonanate** U., Nascita di una religione; le origini del cristianesimo. T 1994, Boringhieri. 211 p. [CC 146/4, 314, G. L. *Prato*].

3818 **Bundewald** D., Das Wahre aus den Evangelien [90 Einheiten]: die Liebesbotschaft Jesu. Fra 1994, Fischer. 76 p. DM 14,80. 3-89501-091-X [NTAbs 39, p. 501].

3819 **Carson** G. A., *Moo* D. J., *Morris* L., An introduction to the NT 1992 ➤ 8,4119; 9,4017: ᴿEvQ 66 (1994) 269s (I. H. *Marshall*); ScotJR 14 (1993) 60s (J. *Drane*).

3820 ᴱ**Cartlidge** David R., *Dungan* David L., Documents for the study of the Gospels. Mp 1994, Fortress. xiii-298 p. 0-8006-2809-8.

3821 **Childs** Brevard S., The New Testament as canon; an introduction. Ph 1994, Trinity. xxxiii-572 p. 1-56338-089-7.

3822 **Collins** Raymond F., The birth of the New Testament; the origin and development of the first Christian generation. NY 1993, Crossroad. x-324 p. $30. – ᴿLvSt 19 (1994) 374s (J. *Lambrecht*).

3823 **Court** John M. & Kathleen M., The New Testament world 1990 ➤ 6,4175 ... 9,4022: ᴿSalesianum 56 (1994) 150 (J. J. *Bartolomé*).

3824 **Crabtree** Harriet, The Christian life; traditional metaphors [servant, steward, athlete, fruit-bearing, war, pilgrim] and contemporary theologies. Mp 1991, Fortress. 193 p. $15 pa. – ᴿCritRR 6 (1993) 502-4 (D. L. *Alexander*).

3825 **Davies** Steven L., New Testament fundamentals²ʳᵉᵛ [¹NT, a contemporary introduction]. Sonoma CA 1994, Polebridge. 250 p.: ill. £13.50. 0-944344-41-0. – ᴿTBR 7,3 (1994s) 21 (R. *Morgan* finds useful but less than L. T. JOHNSON's Writings of NT).

3826 **Downing** J. G., Cynics and Christian origins 1992 ➤ 8,4131; 9,4026: ᴿCathHR 80 (1994) 554s (H. W. *Attridge*); CBQ 56 (1994) 587-9 (L. E. *Vaage*: 'begs any number of questions; fortunately the right ones'); IrBSt 16 (1994) 138-144 (F. *Williams*); JBL 113 (1994) 727-731 (R. F. *Hock*: a promising re-imagining); JEH 45 (1994) 115s (W. H. C. *Frend*); JTS 45 (1994) 209s (H. *Chadwick*); TLond 97 (1994) 53s (Loveday *Alexander*).

3827 **Evans** Craig A., Noncanonical writings and NT interpretation 1992 ➤ 9,10436: ᴿCBQ 56 (1994) 591s (R. *Doran*); Churchman 108 (1994) 84 (G. *Bray*); ETL 70 (1994) 177s (F. *Neirynck*); Interpretation 48 (1994) 307 (J. C. *Wilson*); JRelH 18 (1994) 229s (M. *Harding*); TrinJ 15 (1994) 140-2 (M. C. *Williams*).

3828 **Fee** Gordon D., Gospel and spirit 1991 ➤ 8,4135*: ᴿRBíbArg 56 (1994) 126s (A. J. *Levoratti*).

3829 **Fideler** D., Jesus Christ, Son of God; ancient cosmology and early Christian symbolism. Wheaton IL 1993, Quest. xviii-430 p. $24; pa. $16. 0-8356-0698-8; -6-1 [NTAbs 38, p. 488].

3830 *Fiensy* David A., Craftsmen as brokers [... how Jesus the artisan, whatever his gifts, could have exerted leadership]: ProcGM 14 (1994) 57-68.

3832 **Grelot** P., Homilías sobre la Escritura en la época apostólica 1991 ➤ 8,4139; 9,4035: ᴿCiuD 206 (1993) 926s (J. *Gutiérrez*); EfMex 11 (1993) 275s (C. *Zesati Estrada*).

3833 **Gundry** Robert H., A survey of the New Testament³ [¹1973, ²1978]. Carlisle 1994, Paternoster. 495 p. 0-85364-600-7.

3834 **Hock** R. F., *O'Neil* E. N., Chreia I 1985 ➤ 1,3863*; 2,2986 ...: ᴿRB 101 (1994) 468s (B. T. *Viviano*).

3835 **Horst** Pieter W. van der, *Mussies* Gerard, Studies on the Hellenistic background of the NT: ThReeks 10, 1990 ➤ 6,4191; 7,3521: ᴿTLZ 119 (1994) 135-7 (N. *Walter*).

3836 **Hultgren** Arland J.,   The rise of normative Christianity.   Mp 1994, Fortress. xiii-210 p.
3837 *Joubert* S.,   A kaleidoscope of approaches; paradigms, paradigm-changes and the Umwelt of the NT: Neotestamentica 28 (1994) 23-40.
3838 *a*) *Kelber* Werner H.,   Modalities of communication, cognition, and physiology of perception; orality, rhetoric, scribality; – *b*) *Boomershine* Thomas E.,   Jesus of Nazareth and the watershed of ancient orality and literacy [responses *Jaffee* Martin S., *Robbins* Vernon K.]; – *c*) Kelber, Jesus and tradition; words in time, words in space [responses *Foley* John M., *Scott* Brandon B.]: Semeia 65 (Kelber-inspired Orality and Textuality in early Christian literature 1994) 193-216 / 7-36 [67-73 . 75-91] / 139-167 [169-180 . 181-191].
3839 *Kieffer* R.,   En ny måde at strukturere fortællingerne om Jesus: DanTTs 57 (1994) 40-51 [< ZNW 85,292].
3840 *Klauck* Hans-Josef,   'Siehe, meine Mutter und meine Brüder'; Haus und Familie am Ursprung frühchristlicher Gemeindebildung: Entschluss 49,2 (1994) 4-9 (19, *al*.).
3841 *Koester* Helmut,   *a*) Written gospels or oral tradition?:   JBL 113 (1994) 293-7; – *b*) Jesus' presence in the early Church: CrNSt 15 (1994) 541-557.
3842 ᵀᴱ**La Garanderie** Marie-Madeleine de,   **Penham** Daniel F.,   BUDÉ Guillaume,   Le passage de l'hellénisme au christianisme [de transitu hellenismi 1535]: Classiques de l'humanisme 9.   P 1993, BLettres. lxxii-294 p.   2-251-34441-1. – ᴿÉTRel 69 (1994) 279 (H. *Bost*).
3843 **L'Éplattenier** *Charles*,   L'Évangile de Jésus.   Genève 1993, Labor et Fides. 422 p. – ᴿBrotéria 138 (1994) 230 (I. *Ribeiro da Silva*).
3844 **McCracken** David,   The scandal of the Gospels; Jesus, story, and offense.   NY 1994, Oxford-UP. xii-204 p.; bibliog. 183-191. 0-19-508428-4.
3845 *a*) *Mack* Burton J.,   Persuasive pronouncements; an evaluation of recent studies on the Chreia; – *b*) *Ledbetter* Mark,   Telling the other story; a literary response to socio-rhetorical criticism of the NT: Semeia 64 (1993) 283-7 [vii-xvii, *Robbins* Vernon K.] / 289-301.
3847 *a*) *Marguerat* Daniel,   Entrare nel mondo del racconto; la rilettura narrativa del NT; – *b*) *Destro* Adriana, *Pesce* Mauro,   Dal testo alla cultura; antropologia degli scritti proto-cristiani: Protestantesimo 49 (1994) 196-213 / ➤ 3892*.
3848 **Marshall** Colin B.,   A guide through the NT. LVL 1994, W-Knox. 143 p.; maps. $16.   0-664-25484-5. – ᴿTBR 7,3 (1994) 22 (G. B. *Miles*).
3849 *Marucci* Corrado,   Romani e diritto romano nel Nuovo Testamento: ➤ 413*a*, Diritto 1994, 37-74.
3849* **Merklein** Helmut, La signoria di Dio nell'annuncio di Gesù: StBPaid 107. Brescia 1994, Paideia. 249 p. Lᵐ 36.
3850 *Moennig* Ulrich, ☺ La prétendue traduction en grec moderne du NT par Mitrofanis KRITOPOULOS [malentendu de J. FRANZIUS 1787]: ➤ ᶠPAPADOPOULOS S., Ellinika 43 (1992) 213-6.
3851 **Moore** S. D.,   Poststructuralism and the New Testament; DERRIDA and FOUCAULT at the foot of the Cross.   Mp 1994, Fortress. vii-143 p. $12.   0-8006-2599-4 [NTAbs 38, p. 452]. – ᴿPacifica 7 (1994) 360-2 (F. J. *Moloney*).
3852 *a*) *Müller* Karlheinz,   Die Bevollmächtigung der Halacha durch die Imagination einer durchgängigen Kontinuität der Überlieferung im Frühjudentum; – *b*) *Rütten* Almut,   Überlegungen zur Entstehung des christlichen Sonntags: ➤ 31*, ᶠDAUTZENBERG G., Nach den Anfängen fragen 1994, 415-440 / 539-551.

3853 **Newsome** James D., Greeks, Romans, Jews; currents of belief in the NT world 1992 [BL 95,161s, D. J. *Bryan*]; ➤ 8,4172: ᴿAndrUnSem 32 (1994) 144s (H. R. *Treiyer*).

3854 *Oakes* Peter, EPICTETUS (and the New Testament): VoxEvca 23 (L 1993) 39-56.

3855 **Orchard** Bernard, Born to be king; the epic of the Incarnation. Ealing 1994, Abbey. £16; pa. £11. – ᴿPrPeo 8 (1994) 488 (A. *Nichols*).

3856 ᴱ**Piñero** Antonio, Fuentes del cristianismo 1993 ➤ 9,4063: ᴿBibFe 21 (1994) 152s (M. *Sáenz Galache*); Carthaginensia 10 (1994) 452s (R. *Sanz Valdivieso*); ComSev 27 (1994) 81-98! (M. de *Burgos*); FgNt 7 (1994) 87s (J. *Peláez*); Gerión 12 (1994) 391s (J. M. *Blázquez*); Proyección 41 (1994) 320 (F. *Contreras*); QVidaCr 174 (1994) 117s (D. *Roure*); RAg 35 (1994) 1203-6 (S. *Sabugal*); Teresianum 45 (1994) 603-5 (A. *Borrell*).

3857 **Piñero** A., Orígenes del Cristianismo 1990/1 ➤ 7,453... 9,4062: ᴿNRT 116 (1994) 902s (X. *Jacques*).

3858 *Placher* William C., Gospels' ends; plurality and ambiguity in biblical narratives: ModT 10 (1994) 143-163.

3859 *Porter* Stanley E., Did Jesus ever teach in Greek? TyndB 44 (1993) 199-235: only 'he had sufficient linguistic competence', against the consensus.

3860 **Puskas** Charles R., An introduction to the NT 1989: ➤ 8,4177: ᴿConcordTQ 58 (1994) 304s (G. J. *Lockwood*); EvQ 66 (1994) 66s (S. A. *Cummins*).

3861 **Reese** James M., The student's guide to the Gospels: Good News 24. ColMn 1992, Liturgical/Glazier. 150 p. $10. – ᴿBibTB 24 (1994) 32s (E. L. *Bode*).

3862 *Remus* Harold, 'Magic', method, madness (1994 presidential address); Canadian Society of Biblical Studies Bulletin and Abstracts 54 (1994s) 18-46; bibliog. 46-54 [80-91, membership list].

3863 **Russell** D. S., Poles apart; the Gospel in creative tension 1991 ➤ 8,4179: ᴿCritRR 5 (1992) 91s (K. *Snodgrass*).

3864 *a) Schlosser* Jacques, Die Vollendung des Heils in der Sicht Jesu; – *b) Müller* Karlheinz, Gott als Richter und die Erscheinungswesen seiner Gerichte in den Schriften des Frühjudentums; – *c) Mussner* Franz, Implikate der Parusie des Herrn; – *d) Dormeyer* Detlev, Metaphorik und Erzähltextanalyse als Zugänge zu apokalyptischen Texten [Lk 12,8f; Mt 10,32f; Mk 8,38]: ➤ 113, ᶠSCHNACKENBURG R., Weltgericht 1994, 54-84 / 23-53 / 225-231 / 182-205.

3865 **Schneiders** Sandra M., The revelatory text, NT 1991 ➤ 7,3555... 9,4070: ᴿCritRR 6 (1993) 287s (L. T. *Johnson*); JRel 74 (1994) 93 (Kathryn G. *McCreight*).

3866 **Schnelle** Udo, Einleitung in das Neue Testament: Uni-Tb Nr. 1830. Gö 1994, Vandenhoeck & R. 639 p. DM 49. 3-8252-1830-9 [RelStR 21,140, J. T. *Fitzgerald*].

3867 *Schweizer* E., Theologische Einleitung in das NT 1989 ➤ 5,3997... 9,4073: ᴿProtestantesimo 49 (1994) 74s (B. *Corsani*); Salesianum 56 (1994) 157 (C. *Bissoli*).

3868 *Seeley* David, Deconstructing the NT: BInterp series 5. Leiden 1994, Brill. xvi-201 p. ƒ115. 90-04-09880-1 [JTS 46,296-9, F. G. *Downing*]. – ᴿExpTim 106 (1994s) 151s (S. E. *Porter*: finds internal contradictions in the text, without carrying us much further).

3869 **Stein** R. H., The method and message of Jesus' teaching[2rev] [[1]c. 1978]. Lv 1994, W-Knox. xvi-203 p. $15. 0-664-25513-2 [NTAbs 39, p. 512].

3870 **Stein** Robert H., Difficult passages in the NT 1990 ➤ 7,3559; 8,4191: ᴿConcordTQ 58 (1994) 157s (C. A. *Gieschen*).
3871 **Stenger** Werner, Introduction to NT exegesis 1993 ➤ 9,4077: ᴿTLond 97 (1994) 382 (T. *Moritz*).
3872 **Stott** John R. W., Men with a message; an introduction to the New Testament and its writers. GR 1994, Eerdmans. 159 p. 0-8028-3720-4.
3873 **Strecker** Georg, Literaturgeschichte des NTs 1992 ➤ 8,4192; 9,4078: ᴿTRu 59 (1994) 331-4 (J. *Roloff*).
3874 **Thomas** Johannes, Der jüdische PHOKYLIDES; formgeschichtliche Zugänge zu Pseudo-Phokylides und Vergleich mit der neutestamentlichen Paränese: NOrb 23, 1992 ➤ 8,4198; Fs 120; ᴿJBL 113 (1994) 714-6 (W. T. *Wilson*: 'major repository of the ethics of Hellenistic Judaism before Philo' says J. J. COLLINS rightly); TLZ 119 (1994) 796 (T. *Holtz*).
3875 *a) Trocmé* Étienne, Pourquoi le christianisme est-il si vite devenu romain?; – *b) Bowersock* G. W., Les grecs 'barbarisés' [in Naples and Velia, STRABO 6,1: tacitly citing a source several centuries earlier in a sense not elsewhere relevant to 'barbarized']: ➤ 35*, ᶠFREZOULS E. 1992, 297-304; Eng. 316 / 249-257; Eng. 314.
3876 **Vielhauer** Philipp, Historia de la literatura... NuevoT 1991 ➤ 8,4203: ᴿPerspT 26 (1994) 403-8 (J. *Konings*).
3877 **Weder** Hans, Einblicke ins Evangelium 1980-91; 1992 ➤ 8,329a: ᴿTLZ 119 (1994) 26-28 (G. *Haufe*).
3878 **Welburn** Andrew, The beginnings of Christianity; Essene mystery, Gnostic revelation and Christian vision 1991 ➤ 8,4207 [RelStR 19 (1994) 168, B. A. *Pearson*: 'anthroposophy'].
3879 *Wiarda* Timothy, Simon, Jesus of Nazareth, son of Jonah, son of John; realistic detail in the Apostles and Acts: NTS 40 (1994) 196-209.
3880 *Wilson* Jonathan R., By the logic of the Gospel; proposal for a theology of culture; ModT 10 (1994) 401-414.
3881 *a) Wilson* Robert M., Coptic and the Neutestamentler; – *b) Funk* Wolf-Peter, Zur Frage der achmimischen Version der Evangelien: ➤ 65, ᶠKASSER R., Coptology 1994, 87-97 / 327-339.
3882 **Wilson** Walter V., The mysteries of righteousness; the literary composition and genre of the Sentences of Pseudo-PHOCYLIDES: TStAJ 40. Tü 1994, Mohr. xiv-247 p.; bibliog. 201-222. 3-16-146211-4.
3883 **Wright** N. T., The NT and the people of God 1992 ➤ 8,4209; 9,4086: ᴿCBQ 56 (1994) 164-6 (A. K. M. *Adam*); EurJT 3,1 (1994) 90-93 (D. A. *Carson*); JBL 113 (1994) 536-8 (L. T. *Johnson*); ModT 10 (1994) 313s (S. *Ford*); NewTR 7,2 (1994) 102s (J. P. *Scullion*); NT 36 (1994) 296s (P. R. *Rodgers*); SewaneeTJ 38 (1994s) 80-82 (C. *Bryan*).
3884 **Zumstein** Jean, L'apprentissage de la foi; à la découverte de Jésus et de ses lecteurs. Aubonne 1993, Moulin. 101 p. – ᴿÉTRel 69 (1994) 275 (E. *Cuvillier*).

F1.2   *Origo Evangeliorum,* **the Origin of the Gospels.**

3885 **Bovon** François, L'Évangile et l'Apôtre; le Christ inséparable de ses témoins. Aubonne 1993, Moulin. 77 p. – ᴿRHPR 74 (1994) 103 (B. *Kaempf*).
3886 *Bovon* François, La structure canonique de l'Évangile et l'apôtre: CrNSt 15 (1994) 559-576.
3887 *Bragstal* William R., The origin of the Gospels: ConcordTQ 58 (1994) 283-294.

3888 *Broadhead* Edwin K., What are the Gospels? Questioning Martin KÄHLER: Pacifica 7 (1994) 145-159.
3889 **Burridge** R. A., Four gospels, one Jesus? A symbolic reading. GR 1994, Eerdmans. xvi-191 p.; 9 fig. $13. 0-8028-0876-X [NTAbs 39, p. 502].
3890 **Burridge** R., What are the Gospels? 1992 → 8,4212; 9,4091: ᴿEurJT 3 (1994) 84-86 (Loveday *Alexander*); EvQ 66 (1994) 73-76 (also Loveday *Alexander*); Gnomon 66 (1994) 492-6 (F. E. *Brenk*); Salesianum 56 (1994) 567s (J. J. *Bartolomé*); ScotJT 47 (1994) 420s (Rosalind *Papaphilippopoulos*).
3891 **Deardorff** J. W., Problems / Glasnost approach 1992 → 8,4213: ᴿCritRR 6 (1993) 220s (R. H. *Stein*).
3892 **Delorme** Jean, Au risque de la parole; les Évangiles 1991 → 7,195: ᴿCritRR 6 (1993) 222s (D. C. *Stoutenburg*).
3892* *Destro* A., *Pesce* M., Dal testo alla cultura; antropologia degli scritti proto-cristiani: Protestantesimo 49 (1994) 214-229.
3893 *Fitzgerald* John, The ancient lives of ARISTOTLE and the modern debate about the genre of the Gospels: RestQ 36 (1994) 209-221.
3894 **Flynn** L. B., Four faces of Jesus; the uniqueness of the Gospel narratives. GR 1993, Kregel. 175 p. $10 pa. 0-8254-2638-3 [NTAbs 38, p. 460].
  Funk R. W., The five Gospels 1993 → 4226.
3895 *Görtz* Heinz, Glaube *und* Geschichte; zur Rückfrage nach Jesus Christus: TGL 84 (1994) 330-343.
3896 **Goosen** Gideon, *Tomlinson* Margaret, Studying the Gospels; an introduction. Newton NSW 1994, Dwyer. xiv-219 p. $13 (Harrisburg PA, Morehouse). 0-85574-389-1 [TDig 42,270].
3897 *Guerra Gómez* Manuel, La 'cuestión homérica' y su repercusión en la 'cuestión evangélica'; en torno a la composición y a la transmisión oral y escrita de los poemas homéricos y de los Evangelios: → 22, ᶠCASCIARO J., Biblia 1994, 255-284.
3898 *Halverson* John, Oral and written gospel; a critique of Werner KELBER [1983]: NTS 40 (1994) 180-195.
3899 *a)* *Jonge* Henk Jan de, GROTIUS' view of the Gospels and the Evangelists; – *b)* *Heering* Jan Paul, Hugo Grotius. De veritate religionis Christianae: ᶠMEYJES G., H. Grotius Theologian 1994, 65-74 / 41-52 [219-245 Grotius bibliog.].
  Kelber Werner, (The oral and the written Gospel 1983) Tradition orale et écriture (Mc) 1991) → 4770.
3900 *Kippenberg* Hans G., Mirrors, not windows; semiotic approaches to the Gospels [10 books and AnchorBD]: Numen 41 (1994) 88-97.
3901 **Klijn** A. F. J., Jewish-Christian Gospel tradition [JUSTIN and CLEMENT preserve traces of a gospel(-document) 'probably destroyed by Great Church Christians']: VigChr supp. 17, 1992 → 8,4221; 9,4100: ᴿJBL 113 (1994) 538-541 (W. E. *Petersen*: valuable but with defects making it not the definitive recovery).
3902 **Koester** H., Ancient Christian Gospels 1990 → 6,4246... 9,4101: ᴿScotJT 47 (1994) 271-3 (J. N. *Birdsall*: useful).
3903 **Moloney** F. J., Quattro Vangeli, una parola 1992 → 8,4225; 9,4105: ᴿSalesianum 56 (1994) 572s (J. J. *Bartolomé*).
3904 *a)* *Petersen* Norman R., Can one speak of a gospel genre?; – *b)* *Botha* Pieter J. J., Rethinking progress in NT scholarship; – *c)* *Boers* Hendrikus J., Context in the interpretation of the Jesus tradition: → 132, ᶠVORSTER W., Neotestamentica 28,3 (1994) 137-158 / 93-120 / 159-179.

3905 **Ralph** Margaret N., Discovering the Gospels; Four accounts of the Good News 1990 ➤ 6,4249: ᴿCritRR 6 (1993) 254s (S. L. *Cox*).

3906 **Schulz** Hans-Joachim, Die apostolische Herkunft der Evangelien. 411 p. DM 58 pa. 3-451-02145-5. – ᴿBZ 38 (1994) 131-4 (H. J. *Klauck*); FrSZ 41 (1994) 532-41 (G. *Schelbert*); TPQ 142 (1994) 202 . 204 (M. *Stowasser*).

3907 **Segalla** G., Evangelo e Vangeli: La Bibbia nella storia 10, 1993 ➤ 9,4110: ᴿAnnTh 8 (1994) 398-401 (B. *Estrada*); Lateranum 60 (1994) 173s (R. *Penna*).

3908 **Stoldt** M.-H., Aenigma fundamentale Evangeliorum; EurHS 23/416, 1982 ➤ 8,4233; 3-631-43580-0 [NTAbs 37, p. 285, does not specify whether in Latin or German].

3909 **Thatcher** Tom, The Gospel genre; what are we after?: RestQ 36 (1994) 129-138.

3910 *Vallauri* Emiliano, La nascita dei Vangeli: Laurentianum 35 (1994) 33-72.

3911 ᴱ**Wansbrough** H., Jesus and the oral gospel tradition: jNsu 64, 1991 ➤ 7,460b ... 9,4113: ᴿHeythJ 35 (1994) 67s (G. *Turner*); RHPR 74 (1994) 206s (C. *Grappe*); SvTKv 69 (1993) 85-87 (S. *Byrskog*).

F1.3 **Historicitas,** *chronologia* **Evangeliorum.**

3912 **Burkhard** D., Widersprüche und Fälschungen in der Bibel [... not from Jesus]. Mü 1992, Erd. 184 p. DM 33. 3-8138-0234-5 [NTAbs 38, p. 445].

3913 **Casciaro** José E., Las palabras de Jesús, transmisión y hermenéutica 1992 ➤ 9,4117: ᴿCarthaginensia 10 (1994) 182 (R. *Sanz Valdivieso*).

3914 *Moberly* R. B., New Testament chronology; some current ideas: TLond 97 (1994) 170-9.

3915 **Rolland** Philippe, L'origine et la date des évangiles, les témoins oculaires de Jésus. P 1994, Saint-Paul. 180 p. F 110. 2-85049-588-3. – ᴿÉtudes 381 (1994) 426s (Y. *Simoens*); NRT 116 (1994) 906-8 (X. *Jacques*); RThom 94 (1994) 694s (H. *Ponsot*).

3916 **Spila** Arnaldo, Storia di Gesù. R 1990. 477 p. – ᴿSalesianum 56 (1994) 576s (C. *Bissoli*: ricostruzione cronologica fondamentalista, sbrigativa, erronea).

3917 **Staudinger** H., Credibilità storica dei Vangeli [1988]: Grandi Religioni. Bo 1991, Dehoniane. 123 p. – ᴿAnnTh 8 (1994) 180-2 (M. A. *Tábet*).

F1.4 *Jesus historicus* – **The human Jesus.**

3918 *Aarde* Andries G. van, The epistemic status of the New Testament and the emancipatory living of the historical Jesus in engaged hermeneutics: Neotestamentica 28 (1994) 575-596.

3919 *a) Aarde* Andries G. van, Tracking the pathways opened by Willem VORSTER in historical Jesus research; – *b) Craffert* Pieter F., Through the eyes of a historian; W. Vorster on historical interpretation: ➤ 132, ꟳVorster W.: Neotestamentica 28,3 (1994) 235-259 / 51-76.

Aletti Jean-Noël, Jésus-Christ fait-il l'unité du NT?: JJC 61 1994 ➤ 4215.

3921 **Aleu** José, Jesús de Nazaret, en los orígenes del cristianismo. Terrasa 1992, Clie. 335 p. 84-7645-575-5. – ᴿActuBbg 31 (1994) 51 (J. *Boada*).

3922 *Alison* James, [GIRARD-inspired] Knowing Jesus 1993 ➤ 9,4128: ᴿPrPeo 8 (1994) 362s (F. *Kerr*).

3923 *Batdorf* Irvin W., Exercising the canonical option in the quest for Jesus [against the 'Jesus seminar' claim that the canonical Gospels are 'spinoffs']: EvJ 12 (1994) 51-59.

3924 *Bergin* Helen F.,   Biblical and cultural images of Jesus: IrTQ 60 (1994) 185-197.

3925 **Betz** Hans-Dieter,   Jesus and the Cynics; survey and analysis of a hypothesis [DOWNING F., MACK B., VAAGE L.]:   JRel 74 (1994) 453-475.

Blasi Birbe F., Les nombres de Cristo en la Biblia 1993 → 3815.

3927 **Bockmuehl** Markus,   This Jesus; martyr, Lord, Messiah.   E 1994, Clark. 242 p. £10.   0-567-29250-9. – ᴿExpTim 106,4 top choice (1994s) 97s (C. S. *Rodd*, appending presumably Bockmuehl's own answer to five objections).

3928 **Borg** Marcus,   Jesus, a new vision 1993 = 1987 → 4,4155... 9,4137: ᴿTLond 97 (1994) 384s (R. *Holloway*: encouraging).

3929 **Borg** M. J.,   Jesus in contemporary scholarship [9 aspects]. Ph 1994, Trinity. xiii-209 p. $16 pa. 1-56338-094-3 [NTAbs 39, p. 135].

3930 **Borg** M. J.,   Meeting Jesus again for the first time; the historical Jesus and the heart of contemporary faith. SF 1994, Harper Collins. ix-150 p. $16. 0-06-060916-8 [NTAbs 38, p.456]. – ᴿChrCent 111 (1994) 784-7 (L. E. *Keck*, also on CROSSAN and VERMES).

3931 **Byrskog** Samuel,   Jesus the only teacher; didactic authority and transmission in ancient Israel, ancient Judaism and the Matthean community: ConBib NT 24.   Sto 1994, Almqvist & W.   501 p. Sk 288.   91-22-01590-6 [TR 20,513]. – ᴿETL 70 (1994) 471-5 (J. *Verheyden*); ExpTim 106 (1994s) 309s (R. A. *Burridge*); RB 102 (1994) 618 (B. T. *Viviano*); SvTKv 70 (1994) 185-9 (H. *Kvalbein*).

3932 ᴱ**Carlson** J., *Ludwig* R. A., Jesus and faith [1991 De Paul meeting on CROSSAN]. Mkn 1994, Orbis.   xi-180 p. $19 pa. 0-88344-936-6 [NTAbs 38, p.458]. – ᴿJEvEth 31 (1994) 360s (D. *McCready*).

3933 ᴱ**Carrez** Maurice,   Jésus (50 mots) [2 par Carrez]. P 1993, D-Brouwer. 127 p. F 48.   2-220-03374-0. – ᴿÉTRel 69 (1994) 104s (P. *Genton*).

3934 *a) Casey* P. Maurice,   The deification of Jesus; – *b) Nickelsburg* George W. E.,   Wisdom and apocalypticism in early Judaism; some points for discussion; – *c) Horsley* Richard A.,   Wisdom justified by all her children; examining allegedly disparate traditions in Q: → 394, SBLSem 33 (1994) 697-714 / 715-732 / 753-751.

ᴱ**Charlesworth** J., *Weaver* W., Images of Jesus today 1994 → 312.

ᴱ**Chilton** Bruce, *Evans* Craig A.,   Studying the historical Jesus; evaluations of the state of current research 1994 → 239*b*.

3935 **Cooke** Bernard J.,   God's beloved; Jesus' experience of the transcendent 1992 → 8,2462; 9,4147:   ᴿJRel 74 (1994) 150 (E. *Leonard*).

3936 **Crossan** J. D.,   The historical Jesus... peasant 1991 → 7,3596... 9,4150: ᴿChH 63 (1994) 426s (P. L. *Tite*); ETL 70 (1994) 221-234 (F. *Neirynck*); HeythropJ 35 (1994) 66s (G. *O'Collins*).

3937 **Crossan** John D.,   Jesús; vida de un campesino judío. Barc 1994, Crítica-Grijalbo/Mondadori.   565 p. – ᴿComSev 27 (1994) 376-8 (M. de *Burgos*); RazF 230 (1994) 232s (A. *Echánove*).

3938 **Crossan** J. D.,   Jesus, a revolutionary biography ['Peasant' popularized]. SF 1994, Harper Collins.   xiv-209 p. $18. 0-06-061661-X [NTAbs 38, p.458].

3939 **Crossan** J. D.,   The essential Jesus; [90] original sayings and [25] earliest images. SF 1994, Harper Collins. viii-199 p.; 25 pl. $18. 0-06-251044-4 [NTAbs 39, p. 322].

3940 **DeHaven-Smith** L.,   The hidden teaching of Jesus; the political meaning of the Kingdom of God. GR 1994, Phanes.   245 p. $15. 0-933999-36-4

[NTAbs 39, p. 136: he was clearly opposed to organized religion but could not express his views because he was persecuted].

3941 *Derrett* J. Duncan M., Jesus as a seducer (*planos* = *mat'eh*): Bijdragen 55 (1994) 43-55 [> TDig 42,125-29, ᴱ*Asen* B. A.].

3942 *Dormeyer* D., Jesus as wandering prophet wisdom teacher: HervTSt 49,1 (1993) 101-117 [< NTAbs 38, p. 181].

3943 **Duquesne** Jacques, Jesus. P 1994. F 98. 2-08-067083-2 Flammarion / 2-220-03540-9 D-Brouwer [NTAbs 39, p. 503; NRT 117,580-9, P. *Deschuyteneer*; RSPT 79,71-88, R. *Rey*]. – ᴿEsprVie 104 (1994) 668-672 (E. *Cothenet*, aussi sur POTIN J., QUESNEL N.).

3944 **Eckardt** Roy, Reclaiming the Jesus of history 1992 → 8,4271; 9,4154: ᴿNewTR 7,2 (1994) 107-9 (C. M. *Williamson*).

3945 *Eckert* Jost, Anspruch und Einzigartigkeit Jesu als Grund des Christusbekenntnisses: → 31*, ᶠDAUTZENBERG G., Nach dan Anfängen fragen 1994, 179-197.

3946 **Edersheim** A. [1825-1829], The life and times of Jesus the Messiah. Peabody MA 1993, Hendrickson. xix-1114 p.; 4 maps. $30. 0-943575-83-4 [NTAbs 39, p. 323: 'slightly revised' from a not-dated original and translation; 19 appendices].

3947 **Escallier** Claude, MAURIAC et l'Évangile [Vie de Jésus 1935]: Essais. P 1993, Beauchesne. 364 p. F 195. – ᴿÉtudes 380 (1994) 126 (D. *Salin*).

3948 **Evans** Bruce D., Studying the historical Jesus: evaluations of current research: NTTools 19. Leiden 1994, Brill. xvi-350 p. £250. 90-04-09982-4 [TR 91,77. 16 tit. pp.]. 6 infra. → 241*b*.

3949 **Fabris** Rinaldo introd., I Vangeli nello specchio della creazione; gli insegnamenti di Gesù nei Vangeli di Matteo, Marco e Luca; le parabole di Giovanni. CinB 1994, Paoline.

3950 **Funk** R. W., ²*Beutner* E. F., Jesus as precursor [¹1975]. Sonoma CA 1994, Polebridge. v-150 p. $15. 0-944344-40-2 [NTAbs 39, p. 137: on Jesus as a teacher].

3951 *Galvin* John P., From the humanity to the Jesus of history; a paradigm shift in Catholic Christology: TS 55 (1994) 252-273.

3952 *García* José A., 'Yo tengo otro alimento, que vosotros no conocéis'; Jesús y la voluntad de Dios, su padre: SalT 81 (1993) 675-687.

3953 *Gherardini* Brunero, Il 'Gesù' di Vittorio SUBILIA; → 125, ᶠSUBILIA A. Pluralismo 1994, 103-110.

3954 **Gnilka** J., Jesus von Nazaret 1990 → 6,4289... 9,4160: ᴿEntschluss 49,1 (1994) 36 (R. *Oberforcher*).

3955 **Gnilka** Joaquín, Jesús de Nazaret, mensaje y historia 1993 → 9,4161: ᴿBibFe 29 (1994) 149s (A. *Salas*); Carthaginensia 10 (1994) 476s (F. *Martínez Fresneda*); ComSev 27 (1994) 375s (M. de *Burgos*); Proyección 41 (1994) 257s (A. *Jiménez Ortiz*); RelCu 40 (1994) 641 (M. A. *Martín Juárez*).

3956 **Goldsmith** Malcolm, Knowing me, knowing God [Jesus was all the different types of personality disclosed by MYERS-BRIGGS questionnaire]. L/Ph 1994, SPCK/Triangle. 119 p. £5. 0-281-04769-3. – ᴿExpTim 106 (1994s) 94 (C. S. *Rodd*).

3957 *Grünfelder* Anamaria, Theologie und Geschichtlichkeit; die Frage nach dem historischen Jesus als Testfall für den Historiker: → 36, Mem. FUĆAK M., BogSmot 64 (1994) 34-45.

3958 *Guillemette* Nil, Did Jesus side with the poor?: Landas 8 (1994) 182-207: only in the extended sense 'lacking in something important for a full life'.

3959 **Hamilton** William, A quest for the post-historical Jesus 1993 → 9,4166: ᴿChrCent 111 (1994) 1052.4 (R. *Carson*); RevRT 1,3 (1994) 20-24 (K. *Vanhoozer*) [< NTAbs 38, p.461; 39, p.204]; TLond 97 (1994) 307s (C. *Marsh*: irksomely out of date; the Quest is far from dead).

3960 **Harrington** Wilfred J., The Jesus story 1991 → 7,3603 ... 9,4167: ᴿCrit-RR 6 (1993) 253s (S. L. *Cox*).

3961 **Heiligenthal** Roman, Der Lebensweg Jesu von Nazareth; eine Spurensicherung. Stu 1994, Kohlhammer. 162 p. 3-17-012964-3.

3962 *Hengel* Martin, Wer war Jesus Christus? eine aktuelle Bilanz der neutestamentlichen Forschung: EvKomm 27 (1994) 605-8.610.

3963 **Hick** John, The metaphor of God incarnate. L 1993, SCM. x-180 p. £10. – ᴿIrBSt 16 (1994) 95s (D. J. *Templeton*).

3964 **Hill** Brennan, Jesus the Christ; contemporary perspectives 1991 → 7, 3605; 9,4169: ᴿThought 67 (1992) 353-5 (P. E. *Ritt*).

3965 *Holmberg* Bengt, En historisk vändning i forskningen um Jesus: SvTKv 69 (1993) 69-76; Eng. 76.

3966 **Hultgren** A. J., *a*) The Jesus seminar and the Third Quest: Pro Ecclesia 3,3 (Northfield MN 1994) 266-270 [< NTAbs 39, p.204]; – *b*) Jesus of Nazareth; prophet, visionary, sage, or what?: Dialog 33 (St. Paul 1994) 263-273 [< NTAbs 39, p.204].

3967 **Jeremias** Joachim † 1979, Gesù e il suo annuncio [1960-76]. ᵀ*Colao Pellizzari* M. A.: Letture bibliche 2. Brescia 1993, Paideia. 115 p. Lᵐ 13. 88-394-0493-7.

3968 **Giovanni Paolo II,** Vita di Cristo, present. *Negri* Luigi: BtUnivCr. R 1994, Logos. 389 p.

3969 **Jones** James, The power and the glory; the authority of Jesus. L 1994, Barton-LT. xiii-114 p. 0-232-52030-5.

3970 **Kaylor** R. David, Jesus the prophet; his vision of the Kingdom on earth. LvL 1994, W-Knox. xiii-227 p. $20. 0-664-25505-1 [NTAbs 38, p.462]. – ᴿExpTim 106 (1994s) 54 (L. *Houlden*: dependable, not exciting).

3971 *Keck* L. E., The second coming of the liberal Jesus?: ChrCent 111 (1994) 784-7 [< NTAbs 39, p.205].

3972 **Kee** Howard Clark [e non Klee Howar Klark], Che cosa possiamo sapere di Gesù? T 1993, Claudiana. 155 p. Lᵐ 17. – ᴿRivScR 8 (1994) 252s (A. *Resto*).

3973 **Keerankeri** George, Aspects of the historical Jesus: Bible Bhashyam 20 (1994) 165-190 [< NTAbs 39, p.391].

3974 *Koester* Helmut, Redirecting the quest for the historical Jesus: HarvDivBu 23,1 (1993) 9-11 [< NTAbs 38, p.182].

3975 *Konings* J., O 'Jesus histórico'; a nova fase e a divulgação do debate: PerspT 25 (1993) 357-370 [< NTAbs 38, p.182].

3976 **Kümmel** Werner-Georg, Vierzig Jahre Jesusforschung (1950-1990): BoBB 91. Weinheim 1994, Beltz. 706 p. DM 168. 3-89547-011-2 [TR 91,274].

3977 *Kuen* Alfred, Die Pädagogik von Jesus und von Paulus; Fundamentum (1994,1) 49-79.

3978 **Laliberté** Madeleine, Le problème de Jésus historique dans l'œuvre de Paul TILLICH: diss. Laval, ᴰ*Richard* J. 1994. 318 p. – RTLv 26, p.549.

3979 **La Potterie** Ignace de, The praying Jesus; as the Messiah... as the Servant of Yahweh... as the Son of God, ᵀ*Chianese* Joseph. Nyeri, Kenya 1994, Apostolate Prayer Africa. 141 p., ill.

3980 **Letham** Robert, The work of Christ. Leicester 1993, Inter-Varsity. 284 p. £13. 0-851-10891-7. – ᴿScotBuEv 12 (1994) 54s (R. *Calvert*: both conservative and creative; required reading for all Church leaders).

3981 **Lux** Rüdiger, Jesus, Prophet zwischen 'Verweigerung' und 'Gehorsam'; eine erzählanalytische Studie [Diss. Halle 1992]; FRL 162. Gö 1994, Vandenhoeck & R. 340 p. DM 78. 3-525-53844-8 [TLZ 120, 642-4, T. *Krüger*].

3982 **McCormick** Scott, Behold the man; re-reading Gospels, re-humanizing Jesus. NY 1994, Continuum. 216 p. 0-8264-0680-7.

3983 **Magdalen** Margaret, The hidden face of Jesus; reflections on the emotional life of Christ. L 1994, Darton-LT. xii-244 p. 0-292-51996-X.

3984 **Manaranche** A., Un amor llamado Jesús. Valencia 1991. Edicep. 206 p. ᴿSalmanticensis 41 (1994) 357 (J. *García Rojo*).

3985 **Marsh** Clive, Albrecht RITSCHL and the problem of the historical Jesus 1992 ➤ 8,4316: ᴿJRel 74 (1994) 401s (W. R. *Barnett*).

3986 **Marshall** I. Howard, The work of Christ: Biblical Classics. Carlisle 1994 = 1969, Paternoster. 129 p. 0-85364-629-5.

3987 *Merrigan* Terrence, De geschiedenis van Jezus in haar actuele betekenis; de uitdaging van het pluralisme: ➤ 110, ᶠSCHILLEBEECKX E., TvT 34,4 (1994) 407-429; Eng. 492.

3988 **Meyer** Ben F., [1 Cor 3,10 (regarding Paul)] Christus faber; Christ, the Master-Builder and the house of God 1992 ➤ 8,4160: ᴿCBQ 56 (1994) 141s (D. *Seeley*: on the historical Jesus); SR 23 (1994) 238-240 (S. *Mason*).

3989 **Moingt** Joseph, L'homme qui venait de Dieu 1993 ➤ 9,7681 [JTS 46,419, P. *Widdicombe*]: ᴿCarthaginensia 10 (1994) 195s (F. *Martínez Fresneda*); EstAg 29 (1994) 173 (C. *Morán*); ETL 70 (1994) 203s (A. de *Halleux*); RechSR 82 (1994) 87-102 (B. *Sesboüé*); RET 53 (1993) 497s (M. *Gesteira*).

3990 **Moltmann** Jürgen, Jesus Christ for today's world. L 1994, SCM. 152 p. £7. 0-334-00814-X [TDig 42,179]. – ᴿExpTim 106 (1994s) 95 [C. S. *Rodd*].

3991 **Moltmann** J., El camino de Jesucristo: Verdad y imagen 129. S 1993, Sígueme. 482 p. pt. 2000. – ᴿProyección 41 (1994) 151 (J. A. *Estrada*).

3992 *Myre* André, Jésus avait-il une maison? ➤ 30, ᶠCOUTURIER G., Maison 1994, 305-322.

3993 **Nolan** Albert, Jesus before Christianity²ʳᵉᵛ. L 1994 = 1987, ²1992 reprint, Barton-LT. xi-196 p. 0-232-52012-7.

3994 **O'Collins** Gerald, What are they saying about Jesus now?: America 171,5 (1994) 32-35 (with R. E. BROWN against CROSSAN).

3995 **O'Grady** John F., Models of Jesus [1981] revisited. NY 1994, Paulist. v-233 p. $15. 0-8091-3474-8 [Gregorianum 76,608, J. *Dupuis*].

3996 *O'Malley* W. J., The moral practice of Jesus: America 170,14 (1994) 8-11 [< NTAbs 38, p. 353: 'the only requisite is admitting one's need of forgiveness'].

3997 **Omodeo** Adolfo, Gesù il Nazoreo [1927], ᴱSciuto F. E. Soveria Mannelli 1992, Rubettino. 188 p. Lᵐ 20. – ᴿProtestantesimo 49 (1994) 75s (B. *Corsani*).

3998 **Ottati** Douglas F., Jesus Christ and the Christian vision 1989 ➤ 6, 7536... 8,7552: ᴿCritRR 5 (1992) 482-4 (W. P. *Loewe*: elegant, liberal, Calvinistic).

3999 **Patterson** Stephen, *Borg* Marcus, *Crossan* John Dominic, *Shanks* Hershel, The search for Jesus; modern scholarship looks at the Gospels [< BR]. Wsh 1994, Biblical Archaeology Soc. vii-152 p. – ᴿPerspRelSt 21 (1994) 245.

4000 **Perrot** Charles, Jésus et l'histoire²ʳᵉᵛ [¹1979]: JJC 11. P 1993, Desclée. 297 p. 2-7189-0605-7.

4001 **Potin** J., Jésus, l'histoire vraie. P 1994, Centurion. vi-538 p.; 2 maps. F 159. 2-227-43613-1 [NTAbs 39, p. 510; RSPT 79, 71-88, B. *Rey*, aussi sur DUQUESNE J.].

4002 **Reiser** William, Talking about Jesus today 1993 ➤ 9,4195: ᴿHorizons 21 (1994) 196s (T. E. *Clarke*).

4003 *Røsæg* Nils A., The historical Jesus; an overview of recent research: TsTKi 65 (1994) 45-62 in Norwegian.

4004 **Roux** Jean-Paul, Jésus 1989 ➤ 6,4322; 7,3623: ᴿRuBi 47 (1994) 65s (J. *Chmiel*, ❷).

4005 **Sanders** E. P., The historical figure of Jesus. L 1993, Lane/Penguin. xiv-337 p.; £19. 0-713-99059-7 [NTAbs 38, p. 354 (G. *Vermes*) & 39, p. 145].

4006 **Sanders** E. P., The historical figure of Jesus 1993 ➤ 9,4197: ᴿTLond 97 (1994) 122s (L. *Houlden*: relief after a silly season in this area); LTimesLitSupp (Mar 25, 1994) 4 (G. *Vermes*) [< NTAbs 38, p. 354].

4007 *Schaberg* J., A feminist experience of historical Jesus scholarship: Continuum 4 (1994) 266-285 [< NTAbs 39, p. 207].

4008 **Schnackenburg** R., Die Person Jesu 1993 ➤ 9,4200; ²ʳᵉᵛ1994: 3-451-23072-0: ᴿBZ 38 (1994) 276-8 (M. *Theobald*); Entschluss 49,7s (1994) 50 (R. *Oberforcher*); TGL 84 (1994) 115 (J. *Ernst*); ZkT 116 (1994) 214 (M. *Hasitschka*).

4009 *Schweizer* Eduard, Jesus – made in Great Britain and U.S.A. [auf deutsch: THIERING B. (Australien!), CROSSAN J., SANDERS E.; meist MEIER J.]: TZBas 50 (1994) 310-321.

4010 **Senior** Donald, Jesus, a Gospel portrait²ʳᵉᵛ. NY 1992, Paulist. 161 p. $10. – ᴿNewTR 7,1 (1994) 102s (D. J. *Harrington*).

4011 **Song** C. S., Jesus in the power of the Spirit. Mp 1994, Fortress. 335 p. [TS 56,796s, J. L. *Fredericks*: liberation from BARTH].

4012 *Sorg* Jean-Paul, Les concepts de représentation et de volonté dans les analyses de SCHWEITZER; notes en marge d'une traduction [ici 133-164]; ÉTRel 69 (1994) 165-171.

Stein Robert H., The method and message of Jesus' teaching²ʳᵉᵛ 1994 ➤ 3869.

4014 **Stuhlmacher** Peter, Jesus of Nazareth — Christ of faith, ᵀ*Schatzmann* Siegfried S. 1993 ➤ 9,4205 [RelStR 21,142, J. T. *Fitzgerald*].

4015 **Stuhlmacher** Peter, Gesù di Nazaret — Cristo della fede: StBPaid 98, 1992. – ᴿAntonianum 69 (1994) 387s (M. *Nobile*).

4016 **Swidler** Leonard, Der umstrittene Jesus [a model for moderns] 1991 ➤ 8,4410: ᴿActuBbg 31 (1994) 68-70 (J. *Boada*).

4017 *Talbert* C. H., Political correctness invades Jesus research [the (FUNK) seminar is an ideological mirror of the left-wing civil religion that dominates North American education today]: PerspRelSt 21,3 (1994) 245-52 [< NTAbs 39, p. 207].

4018 *Tanzer* S., The historically Jewish Jesus encounters one modern Catholic theologian [KÜNG H., Judaism 1992]; a cautionary tale: CTA Proc 49 (1994) 105-115 [< NTAbs 39,393].

4019 *Taylor* W. F., New Quests for the historical Jesus [FUNK R. MEIER J.; CROSSAN J.]: TrinitySemR 15,2 (Columbus 1993) 69-83 [< NTAbs 38, p. 354].

4020 *a) Telford* William R., Major trends and interpretative issues in study of Jesus; – *b) Freyne* Seán, The geography, politics and economics of Galilee and the quest for the historical Jesus: ➤ 439*b*, *Chilton* B., *Evans* C., Studying 1994, 33-74 / 75-121.

4021 *Thompson* William M., 'Distinct but not separate'; historical research in the study of Jesus and Christian faith: Horizons 21 (1994) 130-141.

4022 **Tilliette** Guy, Jésus et ses mystères, préf. *Doré* J.: Essai.   P 1992, Desclée.   215 p. F 80. – ᴿRICathP 50 (1994) 164s (J. *Blaise*).

4023 **Weinandy** T. G., In the likeness of sinful flesh 1993 → 9,4212:   ᴿPrPeo 8 (1994) 487s (A. *Nichols*).

4024 **Wenham** J.,   Christ and the Bible? [¹c. 1975]. GR 1994, Baker.   333 p.; pa. $11.   0-8010-9733-9 [NTAbs 39, p. 329].

4025 **Wolff** Hanna, ⊚ Der kollektive Schatten [< Jesus der Mann⁰, Stu 1988, Radius: Jung depth-psychology]: DeltioVM 13 [for 12], 1 (1993) 49-62.

4026 **Wright** N. T.,   Following Jesus.   L 1994, SPCK.   xi-96 p.   £5.   0-281-04805-3. – ᴿExpTim 106 (1994s) 214 (N. *Clark*: a reliable challenge; though 'dumping these college sermons on the heads of average congregations would lead to nothing but grief').

4027 *Wright* T. R., The letter and the spirit; deconstructing RENAN's Life of Jesus and the assumptions of modernity: RelLit 26,2 (ND 1994) 55-71 [< NTAbs 39, p. 208: Renan showed awareness of the limitations of modernity].

4028 *Yarborough* R. W.,   Modern wise men encounter Jesus: Christianity Today 38,14 (1994) 38-42.44s: MEIER J., WITHERINGTON B., FARMER W. [< NTAbs 39, p. 394: 'not all academic Jesus-research is useless'].

4029 **Yoder** John H.,   The politics of Jesus; vicit agnus noster² [¹1978].   GR 1994, Eerdmans.   xiii-257 p.   0-8028-0734-8.

4030 **Ziegler** Herbert, 'Wehe euch, ihr Heuchler!' Die ureigenen Worte Jesu. Dü 1993, Walter.   237 p.   DM 29,30.   3-530-98484-1. – ᴿActuBbg 31 (1994) 70s (J. *Boada*).

F1.5   *Jesus et Israel* – Jesus the Jew.

4031 **Boccara** Elia,   Il peso della memoria; una lettura ebraica del Nuovo Testamento: StBDeh 23.   Bo 1994, Dehoniane.   283 p.   Lᵐ 35.   88-10-40723-7.

4032 *Botha* P. J.,   Jesus the Jew: some reflections on current investigations: R&T 1 (Pretoria 1994) 185-209 [< ZIT 95, p. 16].

4033 ᴱBroer Ingo, Jesus und das jüdische Gesetz 1990/2 → 8,458d: ᴿJudaica 49 (1993) 236s (H. L. *Reichrath*); TPQ 142 (1994) 89s (P. *Fiedler*); TR 90 (1994) 287-9 (T. *Söding*).

4034 **Calimani** Riccardo, Gesù ebreo 1990 → 7,3644; 8,4356:   ᴿProtestantesimo 49 (1994) 348 (M. *Abbà*).

4035 **Casey** P. M.,   From Jewish prophet to Gentile God 1991 → 7,3645 ... 9,7589:   ᴿCritRR 6 (1993) 210-2 (Arland J. *Hultgren*).

4036 *Casey* Maurice,   From Jewish prophet to Gentile God; a reply to Professor O'NEILL: IrTSt [14 (1992) 192-8] 16 (1994) 50-65.

4037 ᴱCharlesworth J.,   The Messiah; first Princeton symposium on Judaism and Christian origins 1987/92 → 8,463:   ᴿTR 90 (1994) 31-33 (E. *Lohse*).

4038 **Charlesworth** James H.,   Gesù nel giudaismo del suo tempo, alla luce delle più recenti scoperte: ᵀ*Tomasetto* D.   T 1993, Claudiana.   303 p. Lᵐ 36. – ᴿRasT 35 (1994) 760s (M. *Abbà*).

4039 **Chilton** Bruce D.,   Judaic approaches to the Gospels: SFʟᴄJud 2. Atlanta 1994, Scholars.   xii-321 p.   0-7885-0001-5.

4040 **Chilton** Bruce,   The Temple of Jesus; his sacrificial program 1992 → 8,4361; 9,4231:   ᴿEvQ 66 (1994) 271-3 (I. H. *Marshall*); HeythropJ 35 (1994) 318s (M. M. *Winter*); JStNT 53 (1994) 124s (T. R. *Hatina*);

SewaneeTJ 38 (1994s) 291-4 (A. Katherine *Grieb*); TorJT 10 (1994) 252s (G. *Le Marquand*).
4041 ᴱ**Dunn** J. D. G., Jews and Christians; the parting ...: WUNT 66, 1989/92 ➤ 8,467; 9,4237: ᴿEvQ 66 (1994) 283-5 (W. *Riggans*); JTS 45 (1994) 259-261 (Judith *Lieu*); Salesianum 56 (1994) 766s (R. *Vicent*); TLZ 119 (1994) 792-4 (K.-W. *Niebuhr*).
4042 **Dunn**, Partings 1991 ➤ 7,3650 ... 9,4238: ᴿCritRR 6 (1993) 226-8 (J. S. *Sikor*).
4043 **Elliott** Mark A., The survivors of Israel; attitudes toward the national salvation among Late Second Temple Jewish protest groups, and implications for the literature and beliefs, and for the definition of pre-Christian Judaism: diss. Aberdeen 1994. 413 p. – RTLv 26,534.
4044 **Ephraim** frère, Gesù ebreo praticante: Parole di vita. Mi 1993, Àncora. 315 p. Lᵐ 35. – ᴿBenedictina 41 (1994) 538s (S. de *Piccoli*: nato ebreo, poi protestante, ora cattolico; mistico, non esegetico né storico].
4045 ᶠFʟᴜssᴇʀ David, Messiah and Christos; studies in the Jewish origin of Christianity, ᴱ**Gruenwald** I., *al*. 1992 ➤ 8,57: ᴿSalesianum 56 (1994) 786s (R. *Vicent*).
4045* *a*) *Galizzi* Mario, Fariseo e pubblicano; – *b*) *Fong Ko Ha* Maria, Un fariseo simpatizzante di Gesù: ParVi 39,6 ('I Farisei' 1994) 26-29 / 5-8.
4046 *a*) *Gallego* Epifanio, Jesús y el poder religioso; – *b*) *Quelle* Constantino, Jesús y el poder civil; – *c*) *Sáenz Galache* Mercedes, Las antinomías del poder: BibF 20,58 ('El hechizo del poder' 1994) 67-89 / 90-142 / 143-170.
4047 *Gray* D. P., Jesus was a Jew: ➤ 384*, Jewish-Christian 1989/94, 1-25.
4048 *Hauerwas* S., When the politics of Jesus makes a difference: ChrCent 110 (1993) 982-7 [< NTAbs 38, p. 182].
4049 *Hegstad* Harald, *a*) Der Erlöser der Heiden oder Israels Messias? Zur Frage der theologischen und christologischen Bedeutung des Judeseins Jesu: KuD 40 (1994) 32-46. – *b*) The saviour of the Gentiles or the Messiah of Israel? on the question of the theological and Christological significance of the Jewishness of Jesus: TsTKi 64 (1993) 81-94, Norwegian; Eng. 95.
4050 *a*) *Hofius* Otfried, Ist Jesus der Messias? Thesen; – *b*) *Zeller* Pieter, Zur Transformation des *Christós* bei Paulus; – *c*) *Schmidt* Heinz, Messianität ohne Messias? Religionspädagogische Ambivalenzen mit der Messianität Jesu: JbBT 8 (1993) 103-129 / 155-167 / 313-334.
4051 **Holtz** Gudrun, Der Herrscher und der Weise im Gespräch; Studien zu Form, Funktion und Situation der neutestamentlichen Verhörgespräche und der Gespräche zwischen jüdischen Weisen und Fremdherrschern: Diss. ᴰOsten-Sacken P. von der. Berlin 1994. – TR 91,92.
4052 *Judge* E. A., Judaism and the rise of Christianity; a Roman perspective: TyndB 45 (1994) 355-368.
4053 *Karrer* M., Der Gesalbte: FRL 151, 1991 ➤ 7,3662 ... 9,4247: ᴿActu-Bbg 31 (1994) 42s (J. *Boada*).
4054 *Kosch* Daniel, Neue Jesusliteratur [18 nicht sensationelle Bücher]: BiKi 48 (1993) 40-45.
4055 *Lapide* Pinchas, Gespräch mit *Petzold* L., Jesus – ein frommer Jude?: ZeichZt 48 (Lp 1994) 209-211 [< zit 95, p. 96].
4056 **Lenhardt** Pierre, *Collin* Matthieu, La Tora oral de los fariseos; textos de la tradición de Israël, ᵀ*Darrícal* Nicolás 1991 ➤ 8,4383; 9,10686: ᴿActu-Bbg 30 (1993) 59s (X. *Alegre*).
4057 *Lieu* Judith, 'The parting of the ways'; theological construct or historical reality?: JStNT 56 (1994) 101-119.

4058 *a*) *Lieu* Judith M., Do God-fearers make good Christians?; – *b*) *Goodman* Martin, Sadducees and Essenes after 70 C.E.: ➤ 45, ᶠGOULDER M., Crossing 1994, 329-345 / 347-356.

4059 *Longenecker* Richard N., A hermenêutica judaica no primeiro século [< seu Biblical Exegesis 1975]. ᵀ*Benigno* Lucian: VoxScr 3 (1993) 167-191.

4060 **Lunny** W. J., The Jesus option. NY 1994, Paulist. v-217 p. $13 pa. 0-8091-3445-4 [NTAbs 39, p. 140: Jesus trained his disciples to be judges of Israel itself under direct rule of God in place of the Zion tradition; Gregorianum 76,607s, J. *Dupuis*].

4060* *Macina* M. R., Jésus 'le juif' ou Jésus 'l'Hérodien'? À propos d'une thèse récente d'A. PAUL: FoiVie 93,3 (1994) 87-104 [< NTAbs 39, p. 205: 'idyllic, even hagiographic, Herod'].

4061 *McCready* Wayne O., Sadducees and ancient sectarianism: ➤ 8,26, ᶠCAHILL P. J., RelStT 12,2 (1994) 79-97.

4062 **Maier** Johann, Gesù Cristo e il cristianesimo nella tradizione giudaica antica [1994], ᵀ*Zonta* Mario: StBPaid 106. Brescia 1994, Paideia. 354 p., Bibliog. 309-332. 88-394-0512-7.

Maier Johann, Il Giudaismo del Secondo Tempio 1991 ➤ 10689.

4063 **Manns** Frédéric, Jésus Fils de David; les évangiles: leur contexte juif et les Pères de l'Église. P/Montréal 1994, Médiaspaul. 194 p. F 115. 2-7122-0476-X / Canada 2-89420-039-0 [NTAbs 39, p. 326]. – ᴿEsprVie 104 (1994) 492s (É. *Cothenet*).

4064 **Manns** Frédéric, Le Judaïsme, milieu et mémoire du NT: SBF Anal 36, 1992 ➤ 8,4385: ᴿSalesianum 56 (1994) 785s (R. *Vicent*).

4065 **Manns** Frédéric, Il giudaismo; ambiente e memoria del Nuovo Testamento [1992 ➤ 8,4385], ᵀ*Fabbri* Romeo, ᴱ*Mela* Roberto. Bo 1994, Dehoniane. 253 p. Lᵐ 35. 88-10-40727-X.

4066 **Maqsood** Ruqaiyyah W., The separated ones; Jesus, the Pharisees and Islam. L 1991, SCM. 194 p. $17.50. 0-334-02498-6. – ᴿInterpretation 48 (1994) 106 (C. A. *Kimball*).

4067 **Marquardt** Friedrich-W., Das christliche Bekenntnis zu Jesus, dem Juden, eine Christologie 2, 1991 ➤ 8,7540: ᴿRHPR 74 (1994) 441s (G. *Siegwalt*).

4068 **Meier** John P., A marginal Jew 1, 1991 ➤ 7,5667 ... 9,4254; also L, Chapman, £17: ᴿBijdragen 55 (1994) 84s (N. *Schreurs*); CurrTM 21 (1994) 56s (D. *Rhoads*); IrBSt 15 (1993) 179-185 (C. *Marsh*: magnificent, and not to be judged by the teen-age boy with halo on the cover); IrTQ 60 (1994) 70s (B. *Nolan*); JStNT 53 (1994) 124 (T. R. *Hatina*); PerspRelSt 21 (1994) 157-160 (S. D. *Harstine*); RRel 52 (1993) 153s (J. J. *Mueller*); ScotJT 47 (1994) 257s (C. J. A. *Hickling*); TLond 97 (1994) 205s (R. *Sturch* briefly: immensely stimulating).

4069 **Meier** J. P., Jesus, a marginal Jew 2, 1994; $35; 0-385-46992-6 [NTAbs 39, p. 396]. – ᴿAmerica 171,16 (1994) 25-27 (J. A. *Fitzmyer*; sound, unlike CROSSAN, MACK, FUNK): Commonweal 121,20 (1994) 33-35 (L. T. *Johnson*: too heavy from exhausting every issue; 'creeping certainty' from dubious inferences).

4070 **Moltmann** Jürgen, Jésus, le Messie de Dieu [Der Weg... in messianischen Dimensionen 1989 ➤ 5,7487]: CogF 171. P 1993, Cerf. 475 p. F 219. 2-204-04628-0. – ᴿÉTRel 69 (1994) 593-5 (P. *Geissbühler*).

4071 *Neusner* Jacob, Who needs 'the historical Jesus'?; an essay-review [CROSSAN J., MEIER J.]: BuBR 4 (1994) 113-126; response 127-134, *Evans* Craig A.

4072 **Neusner** J., Jews and Christians, the myth of a common tradition 1991
→ 7,3673 ... 9,4258: ᴿMissiology 22 (1994) 242 (C. *Hall*); TR 90 (1994)
277-9 (A. *Schenker*).

4073 **Neusner** J., A rabbi talks with Jesus 1993 → 9,4260: ᴿHomP 95,3
(1994s) 70s (W. G. *Most*); NOxR 61,7 (1994) 24-26 (G. *Buccellati*); RRel
52 (1993) 939s (Ruth *Graf*).

4074 — *Trudinger* P., The contemporary rabbi and Jesus: StMark 157
(Canberra 1994) 19-23.

4075 **Neusner** Jacob, Rabbinic literature and the New Testament; what we
cannot show, we do not know [... on Morton SMITH, MEIER, CROSSAN,
RATZINGER], Ph 1994, Trinity. xii-195 p. $17 pa. 1-56338-074-9 [TDig
42,283].

4076 **Omodeo** Adolfo, Gesù il Nazoreo [1927], ²*Sciuto* Francesco E., Armarium 2, 1992 → 8,4324: ᴿLatomus 53 (1994) 451-4 (A. *Milano*).

4077 — *Osculati* Roberto, Gesù il Nazoreo [*Omodeo* A. 1927 = 1992
ᴱ*Sciuto* F. E. → 8,4324]: Orpheus 15 (1994) 26.

4078 *Overman* J. Andrew, Recent advances in the archaeology of the Galilee
in the Roman period: CuRB 1 (1993) 35-56; map 57.

4079 **Pelletier** M., Les Pharisiens; Lire la Bible 86, 1990 → 6,4377: ᴿCiuD
206 (1993) 922s (J. *Gutiérrez*).

4080 *a*) *Perelmuter* Hayim G., Jesus the Jew; a Jewish perspective; – *b*)
Scullion James P., Pastoral implications of a Jewish Jesus and a Jewish
Paul; – *c*) *Mindling* Joseph A., 'Are they Hebrews? So am I'; the Jewish
side of the Apostle to the Gentiles: NewTR 7,2 (1994) 27-36 / 18-26 /
6-17.

4081 **Phipps** William E., The wisdom and wit of Rabbi Jesus. LVL 1993,
W-Knox. ix-254 p. $18. – ᴿCithara 33,2 (1994) 31s (D. *Swanson*).

4082 *Prockter* L. J., The blind spot; NT scholarship's ignorance of Rabbinic
Judaism: Scriptura 48 (1994) 1-12 [< NTAbs 39, p. 215].

4083 *Puech* Émile, Les Esséniens et le Temple de Jérusalem: → 30,
ᶠCOUTURIER G., Maison 1994, 263-287.

4084 **Riches** John, The world of Jesus; first-century Judaism in crisis 1990
→ 6,4379: ᴿRestQ 36 (1994) 123s (R. D. *Chestnutt*: p. 192 Chesnutt).

4085 *Sacchi* Paolo, Gli Ebrei di fronte allo Stato, con particolare riguardo al
tempo di Gesù: → 29, ᶠCORSINI E., Voce 1994, 295-304.

4086 *Safrai* C., ❸ *Kultura sporów* [The rabbinic] Culture of controversy,
applied to the Gospel tradition: ColcT 64,2 (1994) 37-42 [< NTAbs 39,
p. 201].

4087 *Safrai* Shmuel, Jesus and the Hasidim: Jerusalem Perspective 42ss (1994)
3-22; ill.

4088 **Sanders** E. P., Judaism, practice and belief 64 BCE-66 CE 1992 → 8,4403;
9,4273: ᴿAJS 19 (1994) 252-4 (S. *Isser*); JBL 113 (1994) 141s (M. J.
Cook); ScotJT 47 (1994) 89-95 (M. *Goodman*); TvT 34 (1994) 305s (M.
Poorthuis).

4089 — *Mendelson* Alan, 'Did Philo say the Shema?' and other reflections
on E. P. SANDERS' Judaism, practice and belief: StPhilonAn 6 (1994)
160-170.

4090 **Sanders** E. P., Jewish law from Jesus to the Mishnah 1990 → 6,295...
9,4272: ᴿCritRR 5 (1992) 382-4 (A. J. *Saldarini*: challenging debate with
NEUSNER); CurrTM 21 (1994) 224 (E. *Krentz*: five immensely useful
studies); JSS 38 (1993) 150-4 (R. *Bauckham*).

4091 **Schmidt** Francis, La pensée du Temple; de Jérusalem à Qumran; identité
et lieu social dans le judaïsme ancien [essence of a single Judaism, thus

against current trends, in overturning last-century's Christianity-oriented works]: Librairie du XXᵉ siècle. P 1994, Seuil. 371 p. F 170. 2-02-021786-4 [JTS 46,594, G. J. *Brooke*].

4092 **Schwartz** Daniel B., Studies in the Jewish background of Christianity: WUNT 60, 1992 → 8,4405: ᴿBAngIsr 13 (1993s) 57-59 (Joan E. *Taylor*); HeythJ 35 (1994) 74s (G. *Harvey*); Salesianum 56 (1994) 787s (R. *Vicent*); TGgw 37 (1994) 312-5 (H. *Giesen*).

4093 *Segalla* Giuseppe, Gesù, profeta escatologico della restaurazione di Israele? [BORG M.]: StPatav 40 (1993) 83-102.

4094 ᴱ**Shanks** Hershel, Christianity and rabbinic Judaism; a parallel history of their origins and early development 1993 → 9,298: ᴿBL (1994) 163s (M. *Maher*); TLond 97 (1994) 124s (Judith *Lieu*) & 125s (M. *Hilton*: brilliantly produced parallels that never meet; Jewish scholars in time-honoured fashion ignore the rise of Christianity; Christian contributors in turn ignore later Jewish thought).

4095 *a) Sherwin* Byron L., 'Who do you say that I am' (Mark 8:29); a new Jewish view of Jesus; – *b) Redman* Barbara J., One God; toward a rapprochement of orthodox Judaism and Christianity: JEcuSt 31 (1994) 255-267 / 307-331.

4096 *Silberman* Neil A., The politics of first century Judea; searching for Jesus [4Q521 'the Messiah will release the captives, ... heal the sick, and announce glad tidings to the poor']: Archaeology 47,6 (1994) 30-40.

4097 *Stegemann* Ekkehard W., Der Jude Jesus und der Glaube der Christen: Judaica 50 (1994) 92-102.

4098 **Stemberger** Günter, Farisei, sadducei, esseni: StPaid 105. Brescia 1993, Paideia. 192 p. Lᵐ 24.

4099 *Stock* Alex, Jesus, Sohn der Thora; eine Aggadische Phantasie von Huub OOSTERHUIS: TGL 84 (1994) 84-97; 2 fig.

4100 **Testa** Emmanuel, The faith of the mother church; an essay on the theology of the Judeo-Christians, ᵀ*Rotondi* Paul: SBF min 32. J 1992, Franciscan. xvii-236 p.; 41 pl. – ᴿSalesianum 56 (1994) 791s (R. *Vicent*).

4101 *Troiani* Lucio, The politeia of Israel in the Graeco-Roman age: → 123, Mem. SMITH M., Josephus 1992/4, 11-22.

4102 **Vermes** Geza, The religion of Jesus the Jew 1993 → 9,4284: ᴿBAR-W 20,3 (1994) 6-8 (A. *Segal*); JEcuSt 31 (1994) 382s (R. *Hjelm*); RefR 48 (1994s) 65s (D. W. *Jurgens*).

4103 **Vermes** G., Jesus der Jude 1993 → 9,4285: ᴿTLZ 119 (1994) 422s (G. *Schille*) [TR 91,384, E. *Bammel*].

4104 **Witherington** Benᴵᴵᴵ, Jesus the sage; the pilgrimage of wisdom. E 1994, Clark. xi-436 p.; bibliog. 388-409. £25. 0-567-09701-3 [TDig 42,394].

4105 **Zeitlin** Irving M., Jesus and the Judaism of his time 1988 → 4,4278 ... 9,4291: ᴿJQR 84 (1993s) 336-9 (H. *Merkel*).

F1.6   *Jesus in Ecclesia* – **The Church Jesus.**

4106 **Baxter** Margaret, Jesus Christ, his life and his Church; NTIntr 1. Delhi 1983 ISPCK, or 93 (SPCK 1989). x-144 p. rs 35. 81-7214-141-6. – ᴿVidyajyoti 58 (1994) 407s (P. *Meagher*).

4107 **Blough** Neal, al., Jésus-Christ aux marges de la Réforme: JJC 54 → 8,342: ᴿÉtudes 377 (1992) 138s (R. *Marlé*).

4108 **Callan** Terrance, The origins of Christian faith. NY 1994, Paulist. vii-147 p. $10. 0-8091-3459-4 [TDig 42,59].

4109 **Dunn** James D. G., Jesus' call to discipleship: Understanding Jesus today

1992 ➤ 8,4270:   ᴿCritRR 6 (1993) 208-230 (Marianne *Meye Thompson*: ch. 5, 'Would Jesus have been disappointed with the Church?').

4110 **Fernández Rodríguez** Pedro,   La humanidad de Cristo en la Iglesia: Glosas 20. S 1993, San Esteban. 268 p. – ᴿMaisD 197 (1994) 158s (J. *Ribeiro*).

4111 **Furnish** Victor P., Jesus according to Paul 1993 ➤ 9,4294:   ᴿTLond 97 (1994) 385s (J. *Barclay*).

4112 **Gisel** P.,   Le Christ de CALVIN: JJC 44, 1990 ➤ 6,7461; 7,7431: ᴿEsprVie 104 (1994) 333-5 (P. *Jay*).

4113 **Goergen** Donald J., The Jesus of Christian history: Theology of Jesus 3, 1992 ➤ 8,4417; 9,4296:   ᴿCritRR 6 (1993) 241s (C. *Brown*).

4114 **Hoffmann** Paul,   Das Erbe Jesu und die Macht in der Kirche; Rückbesinnung auf das NT: ToposTb 213, 1991 ➤ 9,4297; DM 9,80; 3-7867-1588-2: ᴿActuBbg 31 (1994) 228s (J. *Boada*).

4115 **Leclercq** J.,   Regards monastiques sur le Christ au Moyen Âge: JJC 56, 1993 ➤ 9,4299: ᴿNRT 116 (1994) 273 (L.-J. *Renard*).

4116 **Lyons** Enda, Jesus; self-portrait, by God.   Dublin 1994, Columba. 206 p. £9.   1-85607-102-2 [Gregorianum 76,166, J. *Dupuis*]. – ᴿExpTim 106 (1994s) 25s (R. J. *Sturch*: for vague lay Catholics, leaving more to be said).

4116* **McIntosh** John,   Biblical exclusivism; towards a Reformed approach to the uniqueness of Christ: RefTR 53 (1994) 13-27.

4117 **O'Carroll** Michael,   Verbum caro, an encyclopedia on Jesus, the Christ 1992 ➤ 8,4420*: ᴿHeythJ 35 (1994) 206s (J. P. *Galvin* cannot recommend).

4118 **O'Collins** Gerald,   Experiencing Jesus. NY 1994, Paulist. vi-122 p. 0-8091-3543-4.

4119 **Poulat** Émile,   La galaxie Jésus; un évangile et des Églises; deux millénaires d'expansion chrétienne. P 1994, Atelier. 158 p. F 90. – ᴿEsprVie 104 (1994) 454s (P. *Jay*).

4120 **Weber** É.-H., Le Christ selon s. THOMAS: JJC 34, 1988 ➤ 6,7485... 8,4423: ᴿÉglT 25 (1994) 298-300 (L. *Laberge*).

F1.7 *Jesus 'anormalis':* **to atheists, psychoanalysts, romance ...**

4121 *Agera* Cassian R.,   A wounded divinity; an Indian perspective on Christ: JIntRD 4 (1994) 117-132.

4122 **Alter** M. G.,   Resurrection psychology; an understanding of human personality based on the life and teachings of Jesus. Ch 1994, Loyola Univ. xxii-194 p. 0-8294-0782-0 [NTAbs 39, p. 133].

4123 **Anandam** Lourdu, Jesus Christ, the Purusha; Christology of Bede GRIFFITHS: Diss. ᴰ*Walter* P. Freiburg/B 1994. – RTLv 26, p. 559.

4124 *Artz* P.,   Don't go mistaking Paradise; Jesus in der Rockmusik am Beispiel der Lieder Bob DYLANs [believer only after 1978]: ProtokB 3,2 (1994) 129-138 [< NTAbs 39, p. 202].

4125 **Assiouty** S. A. Al-,   Révolutionnaires et contre-révolutionnaires parmi les disciples de Jésus et les compagnons de Muhammad: RechComp [1-3] 4. P 1994, Letouzey &Â. iii-310 p. F 120. 2-7063-0190-2 [NTAbs 30, p. 133].

4126 **Barnhardt** Wilton, Gospel [novel about modern scholars]. NY 1993, St. Martin's. 788 p. $25. – ᴿBR 10,4 (1994) 14 (R. J. *Schork*).

4127 **Basetti-Sani** Giulio,   Maria e Gesù figlio di Maria nel Corano. Palermo 1989, Ila Palma. 218 p. – ᴿIslamochristiana 17 (1991) 209-211 (M. *Borrmans*).

4128 **Boyer** Régis, Il Cristo dei barbari: Gesù dopo Gesù 1992 → 8,4428; 9,4305: [R]Asprenas 41 (1994) 124-6 (A. *Langella*); Protestantesimo 49 (1994) 81s (E. *Noffke*).

4129 **Cousins** Ewert, Christ of the 21st century. Rockport MA 1992, Element. xii-206 p. $15 [RelStR 21,116, J. V. *Apczynski*].

4130 **Dembowski** Hermann, *Greive* Wolfgang, Der andere Christus; Christologie in Zeugnissen aus aller Welt: Tb. 100, 1991 → 9,4311; DM 28: [R]TLZ 119 (1994) 177s (T. *Mickel*).

4131 **Denis** Ph., Il Cristo conteso; le rappresentazioni dell'uomo-Dio al tempo delle Riforme 1500-1565[T]. Brescia 1994, Morcelliana. 222 p. L[m] 25 [RHE 90,315*].

4132 *Dinter* P. E., Christ's body as male and female: CCurr 44 (New Rochelle 1994) 390... [< ZIT 95, p. 75].

4133 **Douglas** Kelly B., The black Christ: Turner Studies 9. Mkn 1994, Orbis. 130 p. $13. 0-88344-630-0 [TDig 42,64]. – [R]JHisp 2,4 (1994s) 57-59 (J. *Stowe*).

4134 *Ernst* Michael, Die Theorie der Verfremdung [B. BRECHT] als methodischer Zugang zu Jesusfilmen: ProtokB 3 (1994) 139-148.

4135 **Finger** Joachim, Jesus – Essener, Guru, Esotiker; Neue Evangelien und Apokryphen auf den Buchstaben gefühlt 1993 → 9,4317: [R]Entschluss 48,12 (1993) 36 (R. *Oberforcher* auch über BETZ-RIESNER).

4136 *Gibbs* Jeffrey A., The search for the idiosyncratic Jesus [... The Five Gospels]: ConcordJ 20 (1994) 368-384.

4137 *Gibson* G. S., The everlasting man: ExpTim 106 (1994s) 148s.

4138 *Gottwald* E., Jesus, die Jeans und das Gottesreich; Konsumreligion und Transzendenz: EvErz 46 (Fra 1994) 423... [< ZIT 95, p. 257].

4139 *Grégoire* Jean-François, Jésus dans quelques romans d'aujourd'hui [... NIEL J.]: FoiTemps 23 (1993) 342-368.

4140 **Hamilton** W., A [poets', novelists'] quest for the post-historical Jesus. NY 1994, Continuum. viii-304 p. $27.50. 0-8264-0641-6 [NTAbs 38, p. 461].

4141 **Hurth** Elisabeth, Der literarische Jesus; Studien zum Jesusroman [deutsch 1880-1945]: ThTSt 3. Hildesheim 1993, Olms. vi-231 p. DM 50 pa. 3-487-09764-8 [RelStR 21,330].

4142 *Hurth* Elisabeth, 'Christus ante portas!' Jesusromane vor der Jahrtausendwende: Entschluss 49,12 (1994) 21-24 . 29.

4143 *a*) *Juncker* Günther, Christ as angel ['sent' but also 'the message']; the reclamation of a primitive title; – *b*) *Smith* Barry D., The historical-critical method, Jesus research, and the Christian scholar: TrinJ 15 (1994) 221-250 / 201-220.

4144 **Küchler** Uwe, Die Jesusgestalt in der Erzählprosa des deutschen Naturalismus 1993 [TR 91,257-264, G. *Kranz*, 'Der literarisierte Jesus; neue Studien zum Jesus-Roman zwischen 1780 und 1945'].

4145 *Kuitse* Roelf F., Christology in the Qur'an: Missiology 20 (1992) 355-369.

4146 **Levison** Priscilla P.-& John, Jesus in global context. LVL 1992, W-Knox. 232 p. $18. – [R]Missiology 22 (1994) 105 (C. *Lacy*).

4147 *Livermore* Craig W., *al.*, Christology of response; non-Hindu interpretations of Jesus: JIntRD 4 (1994) 5-11.

4148 **Maldamé** J. M., Le Christ et le cosmos [D]1991 → 8,7539: [R]BLitEc 95 (1994) 233-8 (M.-J. *Nicolas*).

4149 **Piñero** Antonio, El otro Jesús... apócrifos 1993 → 9,4331: [R]RazF 229 (1994) 329s (M. *Alcalá*).

4150 **Robinson** Neal, Christ in Islam and Christianity; the representation of Jesus in the Qur'an and the classical Muslim commentaries. L 1991, Macmillan. xi-235 p. $20 pa. 0-7914-0559-1. – ᴿChrSchR 24 (1994) 83-85 (Lyle *Vander Werff*); Islamochristiana 17 (1991) 331s (M. L. *Fitzgerald*); RelStR 19 (1993) 45 (J. *Renard*).

4151 **Rothstein** A. M., The Jesus idea. Buffalo 1993, Prometheus. 135 p. $23. 0-87975-862-7 [NTAbs 38, p. 465 'Jesus' as an idea of salvation was personified gradually out of OT material].

4152 **Schweitzer** A., Die psychiatrische Beurteilung Jesu; Darstellung und Kritik [1913 ²1933]. Hildesheim 1994, Olm. vii-46 p. DM 19,80. 3-487-09759-1 [NTAbs 39, p. 146].

4153 **Sobrino** Jon, Jesus the liberator; a historical-theological reading of Jesus of Nazareth, ᵀ*Burns* Paul, *McDonagh* Francis. Mkn 1993, Orbis. ix-308 p. $20. 0-88344-930-7 [TDig 42,90].

4154 ᴱ**Sugirtharajah** R. S., Asian faces of Jesus 1993 → 9,302: ᴿLandas 8 (1994) 304 (J. H. *Kroeger*).

4155 *Tilliette* Xavier, [non → 9,4338] Le Christ des philosophes; du Maître de sagesse au divin Témoin: Ouvertures 10. Namur 1993, Culture et vérité. 496 p. – ᴿEsprVie 104 (1994) 137-141 (J. *Milet*); RThom 94 (1994) 309-314 (Y. *Floucat*).

4156 **Tilliette** Xavier [per dottorato d'onore], Sulla fenomenologia del Cristo: RasT 35 (1994) 15-25.

4157 **Whitworth** Eugene, The nine faces of Christ, Ⓖ ᵀ*Giannatos* C., Athena 1990, Kastaniotis. – ᴿDeltioVM 13 [for 12],1 (1993) 67s (S. *Agourides*).

4158 **Wiesel** E., Le mendiant de Jérusalem. P 1968, Seuil. – ᴿFoiTemps 23 (1993) 358s (J.-F. *Grégoire*).

F2.1   *Exegesis creativa* – innovative methods.

4159 *Bailey* James L., *Vander Broek* Lyle D., [3;] Literary forms in the NT 1992 → 8,4465; 9,4345: ᴿCritRR 6 (1993) 197-9 (E. V. *McKnight*); Interpretation 48 (1994) 90 (R. N. *Soulen*).

4161 ᶠ**Berger** Klaus, *al.*, Studien und Texte zur [NT] Formgeschichte: TANZ 7. Tü 1992, Francke. viii-232 p. DM 79 [TR 91,125, T. *Söding*]. – ᴿBZ 38 (1994) 130s (B. *Heininger*).

4162 *Combrink* H. J. B., 'n Retoriese benadering tot die Nuwe Testament: SkrifKerk 14 (1993) 146-162 [< NTAbs 38, p. 335].

4163 (*Conzelmann* H.), **Lindemann** A., Interpreting the NT 1988 → 8,4472: ᴿEvQ 66 (1994) 65-66 (S. A. *Cummins*); SvEx 59 (1994) 205-7 (T. *Fornberg*).

4164 *Covino* Deborah A., Looking at (the) Logos; hard evidence, gender dialectics, and intentional phallacies on the Body of Christ: Pre-Text 14 (1993) 253-270.

4165 *Freeman* M. K., Pursuing the 'higher criticism'; NT scholarship and library collections at the University of Chicago: Criterion 32,3 (Ch 1993) 2-11 [< NTAbs 38, p. 348].

4166 **Hengel** Martin, Aufgaben der neutestamentlichen Wissenschaft [SNTS presidential address, Chicago Aug. 1993]: NTS 40 (1994) 321-357.

4167 **Hochschild** Ralph, Sozialgeschichtliche Exegese; zur Entwicklung, Geschichte und Methodik einer neutestamentlichen Forschungsrichtung: Diss. ᴰ*Theissen* G. Heidelberg 1994. – TR 91,97.

4168 *Holtz* Traugott, Mythos NT [... BULTMANN]: → 517; TRE 23 (1994) 644-650 (-678 al.).

4169 *a*) *Horsley* Richard A., Innovation in search of reorientation; NT studies rediscovering its [sic] subject matter; – *b*) *Brown* Delwin, Believing traditions and the task of the academic theologian: JAAR 62 (1994) 1127-66 / 1167-79.

4170 **Huppenbauer** Markus, Mythos... BULTMANN/PICHT G. 1992 ➤ 8, 4146: ᴿActuBbg 31 (1994) 58s (J. *Boada*).

4171 *Kippenberg* Hans G., Mirrors, not windows [FREYNE] semiotic approaches to the Gospels [AnchorBD; ᴱBALCH; MACK; KLOPPENBORG]: Numen 41 (1994) 88-97.

4172 **Leiner** Martin, Grundfragen einer textpsychologischen Exegese des NTs: Diss. ᴰ*Theissen* G. Heidelberg 1994. – TR 91,97.

4173 **(Loiz) Macaliano** Fernando, The 'new' socio-historical method for New Testament interpretation. R 1994, Pont. Univ. Gregoriana. iv-131 p.; bibliog. 120-9.

4174 ᴱ**Malbon** Elizabeth S., *McKnight* Edgar V., The new literary criticism and the New Testament: jNsu 109. Shf 1994, Academic. 399 p. 1-85075-510-8.

4175 *a*) *Marguerat* Daniel, Entrare nel mondo del racconto; la rilettura narrativa del NT, ᵀ*Dupré* Cornelia; – *b*) *Destro* Anna, *Pesce* Mauro, Dal testo alla cultura; antropologia degli scritti proto-cristiani; – *c*) *Wuellner* Wilhelm, Critica retorica, ᵀ*Bernabei* Simona; – *d*) *Vouga* François, Analisi retorica e interpretazione esistenziale; – *e*) *Robinson* James M., Il significato dei testi gnostici di Nag Hammadi per la scienza neotestamentaria: Protestantesimo 49/3 (1994) 196-213 / 214-230 / 231-255 / 256-271 / 283-296.

4176 ᴱ**Miller** Robert J., The complete Gospels [all 20, in 5 categories: 1. (including Mt Mk Lk Jn) narrative; 2. sayings; 3. infancy; 4. fragmentary; 5. Jewish-Christian]; annotated scholars' version³ʳᵉᵛ. SF 1994, Harper-Collins. xvi-462 p. $18. 0-06-065587-9 [RelStR 21,149, J. T. *Fitzgerald*).

4177 **Moore** S. D., Poststructuralism & NT. Mp 1994, Fortress. 143 p. 0-8006-2599-4. – ᴿExpTim 106 (1994s) 309 (A. C. *Thiselton*).

4178 *Nel* G. C. J., *Aarde* A. G. van, Die 'postmoderne' stempel in die Nuwe-Testamentiese hermeneutiek: HervTSt 49 (1993) 609-620 [< NTAbs 38, p. 338].

4179 **Nikolakopoulos** Konstantinos, ⓖ *Kainē diathēkē* — NT and rhetoric... *Schēmata dianoías* (Gedankfiguren) *stà historikà bíblia*. Katerinē 1993, Tertios. 383 p. 960-7297-73-3.

4180 *a*) *Übelacker* Walter, Retorisk analys och Nya testamentet; – *b*) *Winninge* Mikael, Den intertestamentala litteraturen och Nya testamentet: SvTKv 70 (1994) 167-175 / 176-183.

4181 *Warren* W. F., Trends in NT studies today: TEdn 49 (1994) 39-48 [< NTAbs 38, p. 333].

F2.2 *Unitas VT-NT:* **The Unity of the Two Testaments.**

4182 *a*) *Alexander* T. Desmond, Abraham re-assessed theologically; the Abraham narrative and the NT understanding of justification by faith; – *b*) *Wenham* Gordon, The face at the bottom of the well; hidden agendas of the Pentateuchal commentator [von RAD and M. STERNBERG better than CALVIN, GUNKEL, WESTERMANN]: ➤ 145*c*, He swore an oath 1994, 7-28 / 185-209.

4183 ᴱ**Baldermann** Ingo, AT und christlicher Glaube: JbBT 6, 1991 ➤ 7,310: ᴿZkT 116 (1994) 217 (R.*Oberforcher*).

ᴱBeale G.K., The right doctrine from the wrong texts? Essays on the use of the Old Testament in the New 1994 ➤ 236*d*.

4184 **Beauchamp** Paul, L'un et l'autre Testament 2. Accomplir les Écritures 1990 ➤ 6,4555 ... 8,4492: ᴿCritRR 5 (1992) 81-83 (W.A. *Vogels*: very original).

4185 — *Benzi* Guido, Per una riproposizione dell'esegesi figurale secondo la prospettiva di P. BEAUCHAMP: RivB 42 (1994) 129-178; Eng. 178.

4186 *Beaude* Pierre-Marie, N'y a-t-il d'accomplissement que chrétien?: RevSR 68 (1994) 325-336.

4187 *Beyse* Karl-Martin, Das Geheimnis der Drei; die Dreizahl in den Erzählungen des Alten und Neuen Testaments: ➤ 31*, ᶠDAUTZENBERG G., Nach den Anfängen fragen 1994, 95-105.

4188 **Chalvon-Demersay** Guy, Le symbolisme du Temple et le nouveau Temple [< diss. P Inst. Cath. 1991, ᴰ*Cazelles* H.]: RechSR 82 (1994) 165-192; Eng. 161s.

4189 *Cranfield* C.E.B., Has the Old Testament a place in the Christian life? A response to Professor WESTERHOLM [Israel's Law 1988: Paul saw no continuing role for the Law in the ethical life of the Christian]: IrBSt 15 (1993) 50-64.

4190 *Dean-Otting* M., *Robbins* V.K., Biblical sources for pronouncement stories in the Gospels: Semeia 64 (1993) 95-115 [< NTAbs 39, p. 211].

4191 **Dohmen** Christoph, *Mussner* Franz, Nur die halbe Wahrheit?; für die Einheit der ganzen Bibel 1993 ➤ 9,4373: ᴿTGL 84 (1994) 115s (J. *Ernst*); TPhil 69 (1994) 268 (R. *Sebott*).

4192 **Ellis** E. Earle, The OT in early Christianity: WUNT 54, 1991 ➤ 7,198 ... 9,4375: ᴿCritRR (1992) 86-88 (J.J. *Collins*).

ᴱ**Evans** Craig A., *Stegner* W. Richard, The Gospels and the Scriptures of Israel: jNsu 104, 1994 ➤ 318.

4193 **Fruchtenbaum** Arnold G., Israelology, the missing link in systematic theology. Tustin CA 1989, Ariel. 1052 p. $30. – ᴿBtS 151 (1994) 120s (R.P. *Lightner*).

4193* *Gäde* Gerhard, 'Altes' oder 'Erstes' Testament? Fundamentaltheologische Überlegungen zu Erich ZENGERs Vorschlag einer christlichen Neubenennung der Schrift Israels: MüTZ 45 (1994) 161-177.

4194 **Görg** Manfred, In Abrahams Schoss; Christsein ohne NT 1993 ➤ 9, 4378: ᴿBiKi 45 (1994) 74 (Verena *Lenzen*).

4195 *Grenholm* Cristina, Christian interpretation of the OT in a pluralistic context: ST 24 (1994) 97-109.

4196 *Hasel* Frank M., The Christological analogy of Scripture in Karl BARTH: TZBas 50 (1994) 41-49.

Hill Charles, The Scriptures Jesus knew 1994 ➤ 786.

4197 **Holwerda** David E., Jesus and Israel; one covenant or two? GR 1994, Eerdmans. xi-133 p. 0-8028-0685-6.

4198 *a*) *Hübner* Hans, Offenbarungen und Offenbarung; philosophische und theologische Erwägungen zum Verhältnis von Altem und Neuem Testament; – *b*) *Nielsen* Kirsten, Old Testament metaphors in the New Testament; – *c*) *Pedersen* Sigfred, The concept of God as theme of biblical theology: ➤ 303*a*, Aarhus New approaches 1992/4, 10-23 / 126-142 / 243-266.

4199 **Juel** Donald, Messianic exegesis; Christological interpretation of the OT in early Christianity 1992 (1988) ➤ 3,4136 ... 9,7539: ᴿCarthaginensia 10 (1994) 182 (R. *Sanz Valdivieso*).

4200 *Kaiser* Otto, Die Bedeutung des Alten Testaments für Heiden, die manchmal auch Christen sind: ZTK 91 (1994) 1-24.

4201 **Liebers** Reinhold, 'Wie geschrieben steht'; Studien zu einer besonderen
Art frühchristlichen Schriftbezuges [27 vague NT echoes of OT] 1993
➤ 9,4383 [TR 91,472-4, H. *Hübner*]: ᴿExpTim 106 (1994s) 269 (E. *Best*).
4202 **Minear** Paul S., Christians and the new creation; Genesis motifs in the
NT. Lᴠʟ 1994, W-Knox. xxi-142 p. $15 pa. [TS 56,395, D. *Hamm*].
4203 *Molenberg* Corrie, Typos and *theoria* in Isho ʙᴀʀ ɴᴜɴ's 'Selected
Questions' on the New Testament: ➤ 450c, Syriacum 6 (1992/4) 135-143.
4204 *Muñoz León* Domingo, La relación entre Antiguo y Nuevo Testamento
en el documento de la Pontificia Comisión Bíblica (1993): MiscCom 52
(1994) 249-274.
4205 *Neale* D., Was Jesus a *mesith* [Dt 13,3 prophetic leader; rabbinically
taken as one who incites to apostasy]? Public response to Jesus and his
ministry: TyndB 44 (1993) 89-101.
4205* **Nobile** Marco, Premesse anticotestamentarie e giudaiche di Cristologia.
R 1993, Antonianum. – ᴿParVi 39,3 (1994) 64 (F. *Perrenchio*).
4206 ᴱ**Norelli** E., La Bibbia nell'antichità cristiana 1. Da Gesù a Origene: La
Bibbia nella storia 15. Bo 1993, Dehoniane. 423 p. Lᵐ 52. 88-10-
40258-8 [NTAbs 38, p. 452].
4207 **Rolla** Antonio, Ad Abramo e alla sua discendenza; Pagine altre.
Molfetta ʙᴀ 1993, Meridiana. 162 p.
4208 **Schroven** Brigitte, '... sie ist es, die von mir zeuget' (Joh 5,39);
christologische Auslegung des ATs im Kontext von Theologie und
Zeitgeschichte zwischen den beiden Weltkriegen: Diss. ᴰ*Fangmeier* J.
Wuppertal 1994. 292 p. – RTLv 26,532.
4209 *Seebass* Horst, Hat das Alte Testament als Teil der christlichen Bibel
für christliche Theologie und Kirchen grundlegende Bedeutung? TR 90
(1994) 265-277; 273-8, *Zenger* Erich, Antwort, Zum Versuch einer neuen
jüdisch-christlichen Bibelhermeneutik.
4210 **Scheurer** Erich, Die Bedeutung des ATs in der deutschsprachigen evangelischen Missionstheologie: ev. Diss. ᴰ*Beyerhaus*. Tübingen 1992s. – TR 90,88.
Swartley Willard W., Israel's Scripture traditions and the Synoptic Gospels;
story shaping story 1994 ➤ 4264.
4212 *Thaidigsmann* Edgar, Jedem das Seine; zum Thema 'Gesetz und
Evangelium': NSys 35 (1993) 237-258; Eng. 258.
4213 ᴱ**Zenger** Erich, Der Neue Bund im Alten; zur Bundestheologie der
beiden Testamente [Alttestamentler(innen)-Tagung Augsburg 1991]:
QDisp 146, 1993 ➤ 9,421: ᴿMüTZ 45 (1994) 219-222 (G. *Gäde*); ÖkRu
43 (1994) 231s (K.W. *Niebuhr*); TPQ 142 (1994) 87s (F. *Böhmisch*);
BogVest 53 (1993) 189s (M. *Peklaj*).
4214 *Zenger* Erich, Die verdrängte Wurzel; die Christen und ihr Altes
Testament: TGgw 37 (1994) 118-123.

F2.3   *Unitas interna* – NT – **Internal unity.**

4215 **Aletti** Jean-Noël, Jésus-Christ fait-il l'unité du Nouveau Testament?:
JJC 51. P 1994, Desclée. 296 p.; bibliog. 283-291. 2-7181-0644-0. –
ᴿRB 102 (1994) 620 (J. *Murphy-O'Connor*).
4216 *Hahn* Ferdinand, Vielfalt und Einheit des Neuen Testaments; zum
Problem einer neutestamentlichen Theologie: BZ 38 (1994) 161-173.

F2.5   *Commentarii* – **Commentaries on the whole NT.**

4218 **Aguirre Monasterio** Rafael, *al.*, Ev. sinópt. y Hechos: Introd 6, 1992
➤ 8,4522: ᴿActuBbg 30 (1993) 57 (X. *Alegre*).

4219 ᴱBischoff Bernhard, *Schetter* Willy, *al.*, SEVERI episcopi 'malacitani' in Evangelia libri XII; das Trierer Fragment der Bücher VIII-X: Abh ph/h 109. Mü 1994, Bayerische Akademie. 219 p.

4220 **Carson** D. A., NT commentary survey⁴ 1993 ➤ 9,4396: ᴿCurrTM 21 (1993) 372s (E. *Krentz*).

4221 **Karris** R. J., Collegeville NT 1992 ➤ 8,1939.4523: ᴿNBlackf 75 (1994) 231 (J. *Muddiman*: Mary Ann GETTY and Pheme PERKINS the liveliest).

4222 **Keener** Craig S., The IVP Bible background commentary, New Testament. DG 1993, InterVarsity. 831 + 10 p. 0-8308-1405-1.

4223 **Làconi** Mauro, *al.*, Vangeli sinottici e Atti degli Apostoli: Logos 5. T-Leumann 1994, LDC. 584 p.; bibliog. 21-30. 88-01-10474-X. – ᴿTeresianum 45 (1994) 599-601 (A. *Borrell*).

Malina Bruce J., *Rohrbaugh* R. L., Social-science commentary on the Synoptic Gospels 1992 ➤ 8,k220; 9,15339.

4224 **Rafailidis** Neofitos, Les commentaires de Georges CORESSIOS sur le Nouveau Testament; problèmes philologiques: diss. ᴰCanevet M. Strasbourg 1994. 340 + 93 p. – RTLv 26, p. 539.

X. Evangelia

F2.6 **Evangelia Synoptica;** *textus, synopses, commentarii.*

4225 ᴱFocant Camille, The Synoptic Gospels; source criticism and the new literary criticism [Lv 41ᵉ Colloquium, 18-20 août 1993]: BtETL 110. Lv 1993, Univ/Peeters. xxxix-669 p. Fb 3000   90-6186-543-3 / 90-6831-483-9 [TvT 34,193X], P. *Chatelion Counet*; TR 91,390, T. *Söding*]. – ᴿETL 70 (1994) 449-452 (G. *Van Oyen*); ÉTRel 69 (1994) 274s (E. *Cuvillier*); RivB 42 (1994) 489-491 (A. *Rolla*); TLZ 119 (1994) 800-4 (D. *Sänger*).

4226 **Funk** Robert W., *Hoover* Roy W., The five gospels 1993 ➤ 9,4098: ᴿBR 10,3 (1994) 14s (J. P. *Meier*); ETL 70 (1994) 161s (F. *Neirynck*); FirsT 43 (1994) 43-48 (R. B. *Hays*: 'The corrected Jesus'); Interpretation 48 (1994) 405-7 (Ben F. *Meyer*); Presbyterion 20,1 (1994) 8-20 (R. W. *Yarborough*); TLond 97 (1994) 457-460 (D. *Catchpole*: only 15 sayings almost-fully survived, chiefly the 'other cheek' and 'shirt also'; a majority of the 74 deciders admitted doubting Jesus' celibacy; but they warned themselves 'beware of finding a Jesus entirely congenial to you'); TLZ 119 (1994) 987-990 (O. *Betz*).

4227 — *Carson* D. A., Five Gospels, no Christ [FUNK more fundamentalist than what he opposes]: ChrTod 38,5 (1994) 30-33 [< NTAbs 38, p. 352].

4228 — *Talbert* Charles H., Political correctness invades Jesus research [FUNK R., *al.*, The Five Gospels 1993; CROSSAN J. D., Jesus; . .]: PerspRelSt 21 (1994) 245-252.

4229 *Lindemann* Andreas, Literatur zu den synoptischen Evangelien 1984-1991: TRu 59 (1994) 41-100. 113-185. 252-284.

4230 ᴱLindsey, R., A comparative Greek concordance of the Synoptic Gospels, 2s. J 1988s, Dugith. iv-327 p.; iv-300 p. $75 each [NTAbs 38, p. 294].

4231 **Neville** David J., Arguments from order in Synoptic source criticism [since Griesbach]: New Gospel Studies 3. Macon 1994, Mercer Univ. xiv-270 p. $25. 0-86554-399-2 [RelStR 21,329, L. *Cope*]. – ᴿExpTim 106 (1994s) 342 (Meg *Davies*: clear).

4232 **Poppi** Angelico,   Sinossi greca-italiana I 1992 ➤ 9,4403:   ᴿNT 36 (1994) 200-2 (J. K. *Elliott*).

F2.7   *Problema synopticum:* **The Synoptic Problem.**

4233 *Batten* Alicia,   More queries for Q; women and Christian origins: ➤ 88*, ᶠNɪᴇʙᴜʜʀ Ursula;   BibTB 24 (1994) 44-51.
4234 **Catchpole** D.,   The Quest for Q 1993 ➤ 9,4407:   ᴿETL 70 (1994) 164-7 (F. *Neirynck*); Neotestamentica 28 (1994) 260-3 (P. J. *Hartin*); NT 36 (1994) 204-7 (M. *Goulder*); SewaneeTR 38 (1994s) 287s (B. *Chilton*).
4235 *Downing* F. Gerald,   A genre for Q and a socio-cultural context for Q; comparing sets of similarities with sets of differences: JStNT 55 (1994) 3-26.
4236 ᴱ**Dungan** David L.,   The interrelations of the Gospels 1984/90 ➤ 6,524 ... 9,4399:   ᴿConcordTQ 58 (1994) 306-9 (D. P. *Scaer*: high praise for Fᴀʀᴍᴇʀ); TorJT 10 (1994) 119-121 (J. S. *Kloppenborg*).
4237 **Jacobson** Arland D.,   The first Gospel .. Q [diss. Claremont 1978] 1992 ➤ 9,4411:   ᴿCBQ 56 (1994) 376-8 (R. J. *Miller*); JBL 113 (1994) 336-6 (H. T. *Fleddermann*).
4238 **Jenkins** Geoffrey,   A written Jerusalem Gospel [before 40] 'Y'; reflections on the socio-politics of the Synoptic Problem: Pacifica 7 (1994) 309-323 [really concerning and promoting Q, which only p. 323 tells us (but not why) he calls Y].
4239 **Johnson** Sherman E.,   The Griesbach hypothesis and redaction criticism: SBL mg 41, 1994 ➤ 8,4540; 9,4412.   ᴿJBL 113 (1994) 332-4 (O. W. *Allen*).
4240 ᴱ**Kloppenborg** John S.,   The shape of Q; signal essays on the Sayings Gospel. Mp 1994, Augsburg-Fortress. vii-224 p. 0-8006-2600-1. – ᴿETL 70 (1994) 163s (F. *Neirynck*).
4241 *Kloppenborg* John S.,   The Sayings Gospel Q; recent opinion on the people behind the document: CuRB 1 (1993) 9-34.
4242 **Linnemann** Eta,   Is there a synoptic problem? 1992 ➤ 8,4545; 9,4415; ᴿCritRR 6 (1993) 252-4 (J. S. *Kloppenborg*: ignores relevant studies); EvQ 66 (1994) 266s (J. *Wenham*, praise with limited dissent); WestTJ 55 (1993) 348-350 (D. G. *McCartney*).
4243 **Mack** Burton L.,   The lost Gospel; the book of Q and Christian origins 1993 ➤ 9,4419:   ᴿChrSchR 24 (1993) 93-95 (M. R. *Fairchild*); HeythJ 35 (1994) 444-6 (M. *Barker*); NewTR 7,2 (1994) 104s (C. *Osiek*); PrincSemB 14 (1993) 302-4 (S. R. *Bechtler*).
4244 *März* Claus-Peter,   Zum Verständnis der Gerichtspredigt in Q: ➤ 113, ᶠScʜɴᴀᴄᴋᴇɴʙᴜʀɢ R., Weltgericht 1993/4, 128-148.
4245 *Mattila* Sharon L.,   A problem still clouded; yet again — statistics and 'Q':   NT 36 (1994) 313-329.
4246 *Moreland* Milton C., *Robinson* James M.,   The international Q project work sessions 6-8 August [Bamberg], 18-19 November 1993 [Washington D. C.]: JBL 113 (1994) 495-9.
4247 *Nel* G. C. J., *Aarde* A. G. van,   Die etiek van Jesus in die lig van Q; eskatologies of wysheidsteologies begrond: HervTSt 50 (1994) 936-952 [< NTAbs 39, p. 392: 'earliest layer of' Q shows no eschatology; more like Jewish wisdom tradition].
4248 **Schüling** Joachim,   Studien zum Verhältnis von Logienquelle und Mar-

kusevangelium [< Diss. Giessen 1987]: ForBi 65, 1991 → 9,4975: ᴿJBL 113 (1994) 724-6 (A. D. *Jacobson*); TPhil 69 (1994) 573s (J. *Beutler*).

F2.8 *Synoptica:* **themata.**

4249 *Bailey* Kenneth E., Middle Eastern oral tradition and the Synoptic Gospels: ExpTim 106 (1994s) 363-7.
4250 **Betz** H. D., Synoptische Studien 1992 → 8,210: ᴿTLZ 119 (1994) 21-23 (F. W. *Horn*).
4251 **Corley** Kathleen F., Private women, public meals; social conflict in the Synoptic tradition 1993 → 9,9324: ᴿRefTR 53 (1994) 146s (M. *Harding*).
4252 *Doriani* Daniel, The deity of Christ in the synoptic gospels: JEvTS 37 (1994) 333-350.
4253 **Ennulat** Andreas, Die 'minor agreements'; Untersuchungen zu einer offenen Frage des synoptischen Problems: WUNT 2/62. Tü 1994, Mohr. viii-594 p.; Bibliog. 431-467. 3-16-145775-7.
4254 — *Fuchs* A., Bevormundung oder Die Arroganz der halben Wahrheit; zu einer neuen Agreement Dissertation [ENNULAT A.]: SNTU 19 (1994) 161-172.
4255 **Farmer** W. R., The Gospel of Jesus; the pastoral relevance of the Synoptic Problem. LVL 1994, W-Knox. 240 p. $20. 0-664-25514-0. – ᴿExpTim 106 (1994s) 120 (C. *Tuckett*: outdated); TBR 7,3 (1994s) 23s (J. E. *Bardwell*: highly polemical).
4256 **Fortuna** Mariola, ❷ *Pochodzenie* ... L'origine des sémitismes dans les Évangiles synoptiques à la lumière des recherches actuelles: diss. ᴰ*Frankowski* J. Warszawa 1994. – RTLv 26,536.
4258 **Lang** M. H. de., De opkomst van de historische en literaire kritiek in de synoptische beschouwing van de evangeliën van CALVIN (1555) tot GRIESBACH (1774) [diss.]. Leiden 1992, Rijksuniv. 335 p. *f* 50. 90-9005838-9 [TLZ 120,903, O. *Merk*]. – ᴿNT 36 (1994) 102s (A. *Hamilton*: to what extent did synopses lead to doubts?).
4259 **Lohmeyer** Monika, Der neutestamentliche Apostelbegriff auf dem Hintergrund der synoptischen Aussendungsreden: Diss. ᴰ*Broer*. Siegen 1994. – TR 91,101.
4260 **Merklein** Helmut, Die Jesusgeschichte — synoptisch gelesen: SBS 156. Stu 1994, KBW. 244 p. DM 50. 3-460-04561-2 [TLZ 120,661, E. *Rau*].
4261 **New** David S., OT quotations. ᴰ1993. – ᴿETL 70 (1994) 167s (F. *Neirynck*).
4262 **Parkman** Joel W., Adam Christological motifs in the Synoptic traditions: diss. Baylor, ᴰ*Keathley* R. 1994, 221 p. 94-22757. – DissA 55 (1994s) p. 996.
4263 **Sevenich-Bax** Elisabeth, Israels Konfrontation mit den letzten Boten der Weisheit; Form, Funktion und Interdependenz der Weisheitselemente in der Logienquelle [kath. Diss. Münster 1992, ᴰ*Löning* K]: MünsteranerTAbh 21, 1993 → 9,4437: ᴿBZ 38 (1994) 278-281 (M. *Ebner*); CBQ 56 (1994) 609-611 (J. S. *Kloppenborg*); RivB 42 (1994) 224-6 (V. *Fusco*); TR 90 (1994) 289-291 (H. von *Lips*).
4264 **Swartley** Willard M., Israel's Scripture traditions and the Synoptic Gospels; story shaping story. Peabody MA 1994, Hendrickson. xii-367 p. $18 pa. 1-56563-001-7 [RelStR 21,53, F. W. *Burnett*, NTAbs 38, p. 467; BL 95,170, G. H. *Jones*]. – ᴱExpTim 106 (1994s) 121 (Meg *Davies*).
4265 *Tuilier* André, La Didache et le problème synoptique: → 248, Didache 1994, 110-130.

4266 **Vaage** L. E., Galilean upstarts; Jesus' first followers according to Q. Ph 1994, Trinity. xv-239 p. $15 pa. 1-56338-090-0 [NTAbs 38, p. 147]. – ^RRB 102 (1994) 425-8 (W. *Klassen*).

F3.1 **Matthaei evangelium:** *textus, commentarii.*

4267 **Beare** F. W., Il Vangelo secondo Mt 1990 ➤ 8,4568; 9,4442: ^RLA 44 (1994) 693-5 (G. C. *Bottini*).

4268 *Bendinelli* Guido, Un confronto; i commentari a Matteo di ORIGENE e ILARIO di Poitiers: DivThom 96,3 (numerato anche 6, 1994) 214-237.

4269 **Blomberg** Craig L., Matthew: NewAmC 22, 1992 ➤ 8,4569; 9,4443: ^RCBQ 56 (1994) 131s (D. J. *Harrington*).

4270 **Bonnard** Pierre, L'Évangile de Matthieu. Genève 1992, Labor et Fides. 423 p. – ^REsprVie 104 (1994) 43 (É. *Cothenet*).

4271 **Bovon** F., Révélations et écritures; litt. apocryphe chr. 1993 ➤ 9,259: ^RÉTRel 69 (1994) 421s (E. *Cuvillier*).

4272 **Collier** Gary D., The forgotten treasure; reading the Bible like Jesus. West-Monroe LA c. 1993, Howard. 208 p. – ^RRestQ 36 (1994) 189s (A. *Resner*; really a commentary on Mt).

4273 **Davies** Margaret, Matthew: Readings 1993 ➤ 9,4445: ^RJTS 45 (1994) 648 (J. C. *Fenton* is left with three questions).

4274 **Davies** W. D., *Allison* D. C., ICC Mt II (12-18) 1991 ➤ 9,4446: ^RConcordTQ 58 (1994) 188-190 (D. P. *Scaer*); JTS 45 (1994) 212-5 (I. H. *Jones*).

4275 **Drewermann** E., Mt 1, 1992 ➤ 8,4573; 9,4448: ^RZkT 116 (1994) 217-9 (R. *Oberforcher*).

4276 **Fabrizius** Carl F., RUPERT of Deutz on Matthew [R. HAACKE ed. 1979]; a study in exegetical method: diss. Marquette. Milwaukee 1994. 264 p. 94-33776. – DissA 55 (1994s) p. 2437.

4277 **Frankemölle** Hubert, Matthäus-Kommentar 1. Dü 1994, Patmos. 332 p. DM 55. 3-491-77948-0 [TR 91,182; NTAbs 39, p. 323; TLZ 120,883, W. *Wiefel*].

4278 **Garland** David E., Reading Matthew 1993 ➤ 9,4450: ^RCBQ 56 (1994) 795s (F. S. *Spencer*); CurrTM 21 (1994) 373 (E. *Krentz*); RExp 91 (1994) 440s (K. *Snodgrass*).

4279 **Gundry** R. M., Matthew^{2rev}; a commentary on his handbook for a mixed Church under persecution [¹c. 1982]. GR 1994, Eerdmans. xlii-685 p. $37. 0-8028-0735-6 [NTAbs 39, p. 323].

4280 **Hagner** Donald A., Mt 1-13: Word Comm. 33A, 1993 ➤ 9,4452: ^RAngelicum 71 (1994) 450s (S. *Jurič*).

4281 **Hare** Douglas R. A., Matthew: Interp 1993 ➤ 9,4452: ^RCBQ 56 (1994) 595s (G. T. *Montague*); Interpretation 48 (1994) 410.2 (D. C. *Allison*; also on GARLAND); RestQ 36 (1994) 55s (A. V. *McNicol*).

4282 **Harrington** Daniel J., The Gospel of Matthew: SacPag 1, 1991 ➤ 7,3838 ... 9,4454: ^RBiblica 75 (1994) 115-8 (D. C. *Allison*); CritRR 5 (1993) 251s (R. B. *Gardner*); DocLife 44 (1994) 509s (J. *Brennan*); RivB 42 (1994) 223-5 (M. *Làconi*).

4283 **Harrington** D., Mt: Bibbia per tutti 26 ^E*Della Vecchia* Flavio. Brescia 1992s, Queriniana. Mt. 88-399-2126-5. – ^RETL 70 (1994) 219 (F. *Neirynck*, aussi sur les autres NT 27-36, louange).

4284 **Harrington** D. J., El Evangelio de San Mateo, ^T*Alfaro* J. I., NT 1. ColMn 1994, Liturgical. 120 p. $4 ill. 0-8146-1852-9 [NTAbs 39, p. 505: Mk Lk Jn 1-3Jn also available in Spanish]. – ^RRB 101 (1994) 457 (B. T. *Viviano*).

4285 **Jones** Ivor H., The Gospel of Matthew. Epworth comm. 1994. xxii-175 p. £9. 0-7162-0496-7. – ᴿExpTim 106 (1994s) 87 (N. *Clark*: reliable, impressive).

4286 **Luz** Ulrich, Das Evangelium nach Matthäus 1-7, 1993 ➤ 9,4459: ᴿBibFe 20 (1994) 175 (A. *Salas*); TüTQ 174 (1994) 235-9 (M. *Limbeck*, auch über ᶠPᴇsᴄʜ W. 1988; ᶠVöɢᴛʟᴇ A. 1991).

4287 **Luz** Ulrich, Matthew 1-7, a commentary, ᵀ*Linss* Wilhelm C. 1994 ➤ 5,4333 ... 9,4460 [Gregorianum 76, 382-5, E. *Farahian*].

4288 **Luz** Ulrich, El Evangelio según San Mateo 1-7, ᵀ*Olasagasti Gaztel-lumendi* Manuel: BtEstB 74. S 1993, Sigueme. 589 p. 84-301-1213-8. – ᴿActuBbg 31 (1994) 220s (X. *Alegre*); EfMex 12 (1994) 263-5 (S. *Carrillo Alday*); EstAg 29 (1994) 170 (R. A. *Diez*).

4289 **Morris** Leon, Gospel according to Matthew: Pillar comm. 1992 ➤ 9, 4464; ᴰAndrUnSem 32 (1994) 294s (E. J. *Bursey*); Interpretation 48 (1994) 90.92 (M. L. *Reid*); RefTR 53 (1994) 39s (D. *Peterson*).

4290 **Nackaparampil** Michael, The Gospel of Matthew [1-7; 8-12]. Bangalore 1992s, BCC. 84 p.; 33 p. Vidyajyoti 58 (1994) 398 [-404, P. *Meagher*, also on Hᴀʀʀɪɴɢᴛᴏɴ D., Mᴇɪᴇʀ J., Dᴀᴠɪᴇs M., Lᴀᴍʙʀᴇᴄʜᴛ J., all Mt].

4291 **Powell** Enoch, The evolution of the Gospel; commentary on the first Gospel, with translation [in varying type to show editing] and introductory essay. NHv 1994, Yale. xxviii-224 p. £17. 0-300-05421-1 [TDig 42,287; Jesus died by stoning for blasphemy]. – ᴿExpTim 106 (1994s) 212 (Ivor H. *Jones'* final sentence not clear whether in support of or against the 'lucid distinguished literary critic'); Tablet 248 (1994) 1164 (J. *Ashton*).

4292 **Sand** Alexander, Il Vangelo di Matteo, tradotto e commentato. Brescia 1992, Morcelliana. 1014 p. (2 vol.) Lᵐ 100. – ᴿCC 145 (1994,1) 623s (D. *Scaiola*).

4293 **Tassin** Claude, L'évangile de Matthieu, commentaire pastoral, 1991 ➤ 7,3848; 8,4593: ᴿRB 101 (1993) 457 (B. T. *Viviano*).

4294 **Vogt** H. J., Oʀɪɢᴇɴᴇs Mt II-III, 1990/3 ➤ 8,4594: ᴿVigChr 48 (1991) 389s (J. C. M. van *Winden*).

4295 **Weren** Wim, Matteüs: Belichting. Haag/Bruges 1994, KBS/Tabor. 255 p. 90-6173-841-5 / 90-6597-070-3 [NTAbs 39, p. 330].

F3.2 **Themata** *de Matthaeo.*

4296 **Aarde** Andries van, God-with-us, the dominant perspective in Matthew's story; and other essays: HervTSt sup. 5. xviii-326 p. $50. 0-9583208-3-7. – ᴿExpTim 106 (1994s) 211s (I. H. *Jones*).

4297 *Agourides* S., ☉ Matthew as theologian of the Church of his time (tradition and renewal): DeltVM 13 (for 12), 1 (1993) 5-17 [< NTAbs 39, p. 212].

4298 **Allison** Dale C., The new Moses; a Matthean typology 1993 ➤ 9,4470 (Fortress 0-8006-2699-0) [NTAbs 38, p. 455; Biblica 76,574-8, J. *Roloff*]: ᴿExpTim 106 (1994s) 55 (C. *Tuckett*); JStJud 25 (1994) 314s (W. J. van *Bekkum*).

4299 **Anderson** Janice Capel, Matthew's narrative web; over, and over, and over again [< diss. 1985]: jNsu 91. Shf 1994, Academic. 261 p. £30. 1-85075-450-9. – ᴿExpTim 106 (1994s) 87 (N. *Clark*).

4300 ᴱ**Balch** David L., Social history of the Matthean community 1989/91 ➤ 7,415*d*: ᴿJEcuSt 31 (1994) 383s (Regina A. *Boisclair*).

4300* *Brodie* Thomas L., Vivid, positive, practical; the systematic use of Romans in Matthew 1-7: PrIrB 16 (1993) 36-55.

4301 **Byrskog** Samuel, Jesus the only teacher [didactic authority and transmission in ancient Israel, ancient Judaism and the Matthean community: diss. Lund 1994, ᴰ*Gerhardsson* B.]: ConBibNT 24. Sto 1994, Almqvist & W. 501 p. 91-22-01590-6 [NRT 117,273-5, J.-L. *Ska*; RTLv 26,535]. – Sk 188. TyndB 45 (1994) 413s (ipse).

4302 *Cavallo* Jo Ann, Agricultural imagery in the Gospel of Matthew and The Gospel of Truth: RLitND 24,3 (1992) 27-38.

4303 **Charette** Blain, The theme of recompense in Matthew's Gospel: jNsu 79,1992 ⇥ 8,4604; 9,4473: ᴿCBQ 56 (1994) 585s (R. A. *Edwards*); JTS 45 (1994) 215s (A. G. *Hunter*).

4304 *Combrink* H. J. B., Resente Matteusnavorsing in Suid-Afrika: HervTSt 50 (1994) 169-193 [< NTAbs 39, p. 212].

4305 *Combrink* H. J. Bernard, The use of Matthew in the South African context during the last few decades: Neotestamentica 28 (1994) 339-358.

4306 *Deun* Peter van, Les extraits de MAXIME le Confesseur contenus dans les chaînes sur l'Évangile de Matthieu: ⇥ 70, ᶠLAGA C., Philohistôr 1994, 295-328.

4307 *Deutsch* Celia, Christians and Jews of the first century; the Gospel of Matthew: Thought 67 (1992) 399-408 (409-419 *Cohen* Norman J., The parting of the ways).

Franklin Eric, Luke, interpreter of Paul, critic of Matthew: jNsu 92 1994 ⇥ 4882.

4309 **Fusco** V., La casa sulla roccia; temi spirituali di Matteo: SpirB. Magnano 1994, Qiqajon. 135 p. Lᵐ 20. 88-85227-62-7 [NTAbs 39, p. 504].

4310 **Grasso** S., Gesù e i suoi fratelli; contributo allo studio della cristologia e dell'antropologia nel Vangelo di Matteo: RivB supp. 29, 1993 ⇥ 9,4481; ᴿParVi 39,4 (1994) 55s (G. *Leonardi*).

4311 *a) Houlden* J. Leslie, The puzzle of Matthew and the Law; — *b) Orton* David E., Matthew and other creative Jewish writers: ⇥ 45, ᶠGOULDER M., Crossing 1994, 115-131 / 133-140.

4312 **Howard** George, The Pseudo-Clementine writings and Shem-Tob's Hebrew Matthew: NTS 40 (1994) 622-8.

4313 **Knowles** Michael, Jeremiah in Matthew: jNsu 68,1993 ⇥ 9,4487: ᴿCBQ 56 (1994) 601s (D. J. *Harrington*); TLZ 119 (1994) 652-4 (W. *Wiefel*).

4314 **Korsch** Dietrich, Glaubensgewissheit und Selbstbewusstsein; vier systematische Variationen über Gesetz und Evangelium: BeitHisT 76, 1989 ⇥ 7,5340: ᴿZevEth 37 (1993) 240-3 (F. *Wagner*).

4315 *Kozar* Joseph V., The imagery of Israel's religious history as portrayed in the story of Matthew's Gospel: ProcGM 13 (1993) 47-54.

4316 *Love* Stuart L., The place of women in public settings in Matthew's gospel; a sociological inquiry: ⇥ 88*, ᶠNIEBUHR Ursula, BibTB 24 (1994) 52-65.

4317 **Luz** Ulrich, Die Jesusgeschichte des Matthäus 1993 ⇥ 9,4490 [TLZ 120, 343, I. *Broer*]: TR 90 (1994) 381-3 (T. *Söding*).

4318 **Luz** Ulrich, Matthew in history; interpretation, influence, and effects. Mp 1994, Fortress. x-108 p. 0-8006-2833-0.

4319 **Malina** B., *Neyrey* J., Calling Jesus names ... Mt 1988 ⇥ 4,4471: ᴿRB 101 (1994) 455 (B. T. *Viviano*: appreciation with reserves).

4320 **Massaux** Édouard, The influence of the Gospel of Saint Matthew on Christian literature before Saint IRENAEUS ᵀ1990-2 ⇥ 7,3866 ... 9,4494: ᴿConcordTQ 58 (1994) 190-3 (D. P. *Scaer*: invites negating Marcan priority, 'academic self-annihilation'); ExpTim 106 (1994s) 883 (I. H. *Jones*; high praise); TBR 7,3 (1994s) 24s (A. *Chester*).

4321 **Menninger** Richard E., Israel and the Church in the Gospel of Matthew: AmerUnivSt 7/162. NY 1994, P. Lang. x-204 p.; bibliog. 173-193, 0-8204-2242-8 [TDig 43,76].

4322 **Mills** W. E., The Gospel of Matthew: BibliogNT 1. Lewiston NY 1993, Mellen. xxiii-279 p. $170. 0-7734-2347-8 [NTAbs 39, p. 141: 2000 items by verse; 1000 by subject or commentaries].

4323 **Mora** Vincent, La symbolique de la création dans l'évangile de Matthieu: LDiv 144, 1991 ➤ 7,3868 ... 9,4495: ᴿTelema 19 (1993) 92s (R. *Capoen*).

4323* *Mourlon Beernaert* Pierre [Mc 2,13; Luc 5,27], Jésus appelle Matthieu à le suivre; analyse d'un double niveau: LVitae 48 (1993) 429-440; Eng. 441.

4324 *Mowery* Robert L., The Matthean references to the Kingdom; different terms for different audiences: ETL 70 (1994) 308-405.

4325 a) *Müller* Mogens, Salvation-history in the Gospel of Matthew; an example of biblical theology; – b) *Nielsen* Helge K., Diakonia als bibeltheologisches Thema: ➤ 303a, New Directions 1992/4, 58-76 / 201-219.

4326 *Murray* Gregory, New light on St. Matthew's Gospel [RILEY H.]: DowR 112 (1994) 34-43.

4327 *Ogawa* Akira, Action-motivating faith; the understanding of 'faith' in the Gospel of Matthew: AnJapB 19 (1993) 53-86 [< ZNW 85,292].

4328 **Orton** David E., The understanding scribe; Matthew and the apocalyptic ideal: jNsu 25, 1989 ➤ 5,4374 ... 8,4621: ᴿJJS 45 (1994) 140-2 (Christine *Schams*).

4329 **Overman** J. Andrew, Matthew's Gospel and formative Judaism 1990 ➤ 6,4687 ... 9,4497: ᴿJQR 84 (1993s) 356-8 (S. P. *Saunders* faults referring stories allegorically to context); Vidyajyoti 58 (1994) 192-9 (G. *Keerankeri*).

4330 *Powell* M. A., Expected and unexpected reading of Matthew; what the reader knows: AsburyTJ 48,2 (1993) 31-51 [< NTAbs 38, p. 188].

4331 **Quesnel** Michel, Jésus-Christ selon saint Matthieu; synthèse théologique: JJC 47, 1990 ➤ 7,3837 ... 9,4499: ᴿRB 101 (1994) 139s (L. *Larroque*).

4332 **Quesnel** M., Jesucristo según San Mateo: EstB 1993 ➤ 9,4300: ᴿRET 53 (1993) 244-6 (P. *Barrado Fernández*).

4333 **Riley** Harold, The first Gospel (Mt) 1992 ➤ 8,4629; 9,4501: ᴿCBQ 56 (1994) 383-5 (E. C. *Maloney*); TorJT 10 (1994) 126s (J. S. *Kloppenborg*: presupposes what he aims to prove).

4334 *Rowland* C. C., Apocalyptic, the poor, and the Gospel of Matthew: JTS 45 (1994) 504-518.

4335 **Saldarini** Anthony J., Matthew's Christian-Jewish community. Ch 1994, Univ. vii-317 p. $63.25; pa. $30.25. 0-226-73419-6; -21-8 [TDig 42,88; BL 95,167, P. M. *Casey*; praise, queries]. – ᴿTBR 7,2 (1994s) 17 (Irina A. *Levinskaya*).

4336 a) *Saucy* Mark, The Kingdom-of-God sayings in Matthew; – b) *McLean* John A., Did Jesus correct the disciples' view of the Kingdom ?: BtS 151 (1994) 175-197 / 215-227.

4337 **Segundo** Juan Luis, El caso Mateo [¿Existe una moral cristiana diferencial?], Sdr 1994, Sal Terrae. 270 p. – ᴿRazF 230 (1994) 113 (R. de *Andrés*).

4338 **Stanton** Graham N., A gospel for a new people .. Mt 1992 ➤ 8,313; 9,4503: ᴿCBQ 56 (1994) 154s (M. A. *Powell*); Pacifica 7 (1994) 95-97

(Theresa *Angert-Quilter*, methodological survey p. 1-108); TorJT 10 (1994) 129-131 (R. S. *Ascough*).

4339 *a)* *Stanton* Graham N., Revisiting Matthew's communities; – *b)* *Kea* Perry V., Writing a *bios*; Matthew's genre choices and rhetorical situation; – *c)* *Boring* M. Eugene, The convergence of source analysis, social history, and literary structure in the Gospel of Matthew: – *d)* *Adam* A. K. M., Matthew's readers, ideology and power: ➤ 325, SBLSem 33 (1994) 9-23 / 574-586 / 587-611 / 435-449.

4340 **Stock** Augustine, The method and message of Matthew. ColMn 1994, Liturgical. iv-443 p. $27. 0-8146-5022-8 [NTAbs 38, p. 467].

4341 *Stoellger* W., Johannes CHRYSOSTOMUS bei der Predigtarbeit; Bemerkungen zu Hom. 2 in Matth.; ➤ 376, Predigt 1994, 82-119.

4342 **Tisera** Guido, Universalism according to the Gospel of Matthew: EurUnivSt 23/482 [Diss. ᴰ*Stock* K.] 1993 ➤ 9,4505: ᴿVerbumSVD 35 (1994) 215-8 (J. *Kuhl*).

4344 **Trainor** Michael, Voices from the edge, Matthew's Gospel in our world. Blackburn 1992, Collins Dove. 172 p. $15. – ᴿAustralasCR 71 (1994) 114s (C. *Thom*).

4345 **Vledder** Evert-Jan, *Aarde* Andries G. van, The social stratification on the Matthean community: Neotestamentica 28 (1994) 511-522.

4346 **Wainwright** Elaine M., Towards a feminist critical reading of the Gospel according to Matthew: BZNW 60, ➤ 7,3879; 9,4467: ᴿCritRR 6 (1993) 573-5 (Amy-Jill *Levine*); RB 101 (1994) 455s (B. T. *Viviano*).

4347 **Wouters** A., '... wer den Willen ...' Handeln im Mt-Ev 1992 ➤ 8,4649; 9,4508: ᴿCiuD 207 (1994) 516s (J. *Gutiérrez*); Salmanticensis 41 (1994) 336s (Felipe F. *Ramos*).

F3.3 *Mt 1s* (*Lc 1s* ➤ F7.5) *Infantia Jesu* – **Infancy Gospels.**

4348 **Broszio** Gabriele, Die Stammbäume Jesu in der Auslegung der christlichen Schriftsteller der ersten fünf Jahrhunderte: kath. Diss. ᴰ*Geerlings* W. Bochum 1994. DM 58,50. 3-88476-105-6 [NTAbs 39, p. 502]. – TR 91,93 [➤ 9,4517].

4349 *De Chazal* Nancy, The women in Jesus' family tree [Mt 1,1-17]: TLond 97 (1994) 413-9.

4350 *Jones* John M., Subverting the textuality of Davidic messianism; Matthew's presentation of the genealogy and the Davidic title: CBQ 56 (1994) 256-272.

4351 *a)* *Luzarraga* Jesús, Lo simbólico de la mujer en la genealogía mateana; – *b)* *Muñoz Iglesias* Salvador, Lexemas y estilemas en Mateo 1-2: ➤ 22, ᶠCASCIARO J., Biblica 1994, 295-310 / 285-294.

4352 *Bejczy* I., De infantia Salvatoris; joodse vijandigheid als Leitmotiv: Millennium 7 (1993) 116-130 [RHE 90,36*].

4353 *Norelli* Enrico, Avant le canonique et l'apocryphe; aux origines des récits de la naissance de Jésus: RTPhil 126 (1994) 304-324; Eng. 406.

4354 **Quarles** Charles L., An analysis of midrash criticism as applied to the Synoptic birth narratives: diss. Mid-America Baptist Theol. Sem. 1994. 243 p. 94-27484. – DissA 55 (1994s) p. 1592.

4355 *Buth* L., The early Roman Christmas gospel; Magi, manger or Verbum Factum: StLtg 24 (ND 1994) 214-222 [< ZIT 95, p. 128].

4356 *Adkin* Neil, How long was Christ in the womb? [nine or ten months indifferently]: ETL 70 (1994) 394-7.

4357 *Sebothoma* W. A.,   Why did Paul make so little of the birth of Jesus [?]: HervTSt 50 (1994) 655-668 [< NTAbs 39, p. 424].

4358 **Cullmann** Oscar,   L'origine della festa del Natale [¹1947 1990], [T]*Limiroli* Mariarosa: GdT 223. Brescia 1993, Queriniana.   65 p. L[m] 14.   88-399-0723-8. – [R]ActuBbg 31 (1994) 99s (A. *Borràs*).

4359 *Graffy* A., [Mt 1,22s) The coming of the Messiah: PrPeo 8 (1994) 472-5.

4360 *Engelbrecht* J. J., [Afrikaans] The virginal conception of Jesus Christ; remarks on an important debate [PATTE S., DUNN J., BROWN R. E.]: HervTSt 50 (1994) 296-310 [< NTAbs 39, p. 203].

4361 *Grelot* Pierre,   La conception virginale de Jésus et sa famille [contre DUQUESNE J. 1994]: EsprVie 104 (1994) 625-633 [< NTAbs 39, p. 294].

4362 **Kerr** Fergus,   Questioning the Virgin Birth [< NBlackf 75 (1994)]: CanadCath 12,11 (1994) 6-11.

4363 **Nodras** Krzysztof, Omelia copta attribuita a DEMETRIO di Antiochia sul Natale e Maria vergine: Unione Accademica, corpus dei Manoscritti Copti Letterari. R 1994, CIM. 241 p.

4364 **Ranke-Heinemann** Uta,   Putting away childish things; the virgin birth, the empty tomb, and other fairy tales you don't need to believe to have a living faith.   NY 1994, HarpersSF.   x-306 p.   0-06-066860-1.

4365 *Torrance* Thomas F.,   The doctrine of the Virgin Birth: ScotBuEv 12,1 (1994) 8-25 [< NTAbs 39, p. 21].

4366 *Mauny* Michel de, Histoire et légende des rois mages: PeCa 268 (1994) 42-49.

4367 *Paffenroth* Kim,   [Mt 2,9] Science or story? the star of Bethlehem: ExpTim 106 (1994s) 78s [80s, *Withers* Michael].

4368 *Quéré* Mme France,   Les mages à la clarté de l'Étoile [< MondeB 85,1993]: EsprVie 104 (1994) 442s (J. *Daoust*).

4369 *Molinari* Paolo, *Hennessy* Anne,   La famiglia di Gesù: TerraS 70,5 (1994) 7-14.

4370 *Pérez Rodriguez* Gabriel, La familia de Nazaret: Carthaginensia 10 (1994) 237-261; Eng. before 235.

4371 **Drewermann** Eugen,   De la naissance des dieux à la naissance du Christ; une interprétation des récits de la nativité de Jésus d'après la psychologie de profondeurs, [T]*Feisthauer* Joseph 1992 → 8,4652; 9,4511: [R]BiKi 48 (1993) 166s (R. *Hoppe*); RHPR 74 (1994) 101s (Danielle *Fischer*).

4372 — *a)* Bertrand G. M.,   Les récits de l'Enfance selon Eugène DREWERMANN; – *b) Mongeau* M., Saint Joseph, époux 'bien accordé' à Marie: CahJos 42 (1994) 287-292 / 173-216 [< NTAbs 39,398].

4373 *Carrasco* José A.,   La paternidad de José sobre Cristo; ¿necesita de nueva reflexion?:   Teresianum 45 (1994) 185-194.

4374 *Hunt* Alison M.,   Maculating Mary; the detractors of the N-town cycle's 'Trial of Joseph and Mary': PgQ 73 (1994) 11-29.

4375 *Królikowski* Janusz, [P] Biblijne miejsce [place of] Jósefologii: RuBi 47 (1994) 42-48.

4376 **Parrinder** Geoffrey,   Son of Joseph 1992 → 8,4669; 9,4522:   [R]ScotJR 14 (1993) 126s (H. R. *Wilson*).

4377 *Prete* Benedetto,   Il messaggio cristologico nell'annuncio a Giuseppe (Mt 1,18-25): DivThom 96,3 (numerato anche 6) 190-213.

4378 *Stramare* Tarcisio,   Sarà chiamato Nazareno; era stato detto dai Profeti: BbbOr 36 (1994) 231-249.

4379 **Quéré** France,   Jésus enfant: JJC 55, 1992 → 8,4686; 9,4548:   [R]RThom 94 (1994) 161s (Louise-Marie *Antoniotti*).

4380 **Baumann** Maurice, Jésus à quinze ans; didactique du catéchisme des adolescents; Pratique 10. Genève 1993, Labor et Fides. 261 p. – ᴿEspr-Vie 104 (1994) 41s (sr. *Valleix*).

F3.4   *Mt 3 ... Baptismus Jesu,* **Beginning of the Public Life.**

4381 **Cantalamessa** Raniero, The Holy Spirit in the life of Jesus; the mystery of Christ's baptism, ᵀ*Nearne* Alan. ColMn 1994, Liturgical. 83 p. $5. 0-8146-2128-7.

4382 **Cho Byoung-Son,** 'Mehr als ein Prophet'; Studien zum Bild Johannes des Täufers im NT auf dem Hintergrund der Prophetenvorstellungen im zeitgenössischen Judentum: Diss. ᴰ*Rese* M. Münster 1994. 229 p. – RTLv 26,534.

4383 *Cisetti* J., A man sent from God [each Gospel has its own 'Baptist-ology']: Emmanuel 100 (1994) 619-623 [< NTAbs 39, p. 201].

4384 *Cook* Randall K., A imersão judaica e o batismo cristão: VoxScr 3 (1993) 21-33.

4385 **Ernst** J., Johannes der Täufer — der Lehrer Jesu? [not = J. Interpretation c. 1988]: Biblische Bücher 2. FrB 1994, Herder. 166 p. DM 22,80. 3-451-23479-3 [NTAbs 39, p. 504]. – ᴿCrNSt 15 (1994) 137-144 (E. *Lupieri*).

4386 **Fichtner** R., Taufe und Versuchung Jesu in den Evangeliorum libri quattuor des Bibeldichters JUVENCUS (1,346-408): BeitAltK 50. Stu ᴰ1994, Teubner. 222 p. [RHE 90,39*].

4387 **Häfner** G., Der verheissene Vorläufer; redaktionskritische Untersuchung zur Darstellung Johannes des Täufers im Matthäus-Evangelium [Diss. Freiburg 1993, ᴰ*Oberlinner* L.]: SBB 27. Stu 1994, KBW. xiii-443 p. DM 49. 3-460-00271-9 [NTAbs 39, p. 505].

4388 *a) Orsatti* Mauro, Camminerà davanti al Signore; – *b) Infante* Renzo, Giovanni e Gesù al Giordano; – *c) Galizzi* Mario, La predicazione di Giovanni, il Battista; – *d) Ghidelli* Carlo, I dubbi di Giovanni, Il martirio del Battista [testimonio di Flavio Giuseppe]: ParVi 39,1 (1994) 5-9 / 9-12 / 13-16 / 17-19 / 20-23 [6s].

4389 *Pitcher* E.H.V., [Lk 1,5-25] The role of John the Baptist: ExpTim 106 (1994s) 49s.

4390 *a) Puech* Émile, Jean Baptiste était-il essénien?; – *b) Légasse* Simon, J.B. et Jésus dans les Évangiles synoptiques; – *c) Piccirillo* Michele, Ain Karim; les sanctuaires de l'enfance de Jésus [Machéronte; Sébaste]; – *d) Alliata* Eugenio, Le lieu du baptême: MondeB 89 (1994) 7s / 15-17 / 24s [32s. 34s] / 37-30.

4391 **Tatum** W.B., John the Baptist and Jesus; a report of the Jesus seminar. Sonoma 1994, Polebridge. x-182 p. $18 pa. 0-944344-42-0 [NTAbs 39, p. 147].

4392 **Tilly** Michael, Johannes der Täufer und die Biographie der Propheten; die synoptische Täuferüberlieferung und das jüdische Prophetenbild zur Zeit des Täufers [ev. Diss. Mainz 1993: → 9,4556]: BW 137. Stu 1994, Kohlhammer. 293 p. DM 98. 3-17-03180-X [TLZ 120,903-6, D. *Sänger*].

4393 **Vigne** Daniel, Christ au Jourdain; le baptême de Jésus dans la tradition judéo-chrétienne: EtBN 16, 1992 → 8,4699; 9,4565: ᴿEsprVie 104 (1994) 489-491 (É. *Cothenet*); ÉTRel 69 (1994) 581s (J.-N. *Pérès*); Gregorianum 75 (1994) 556-8 (G. *Marconi*); RevSR 68 (1994) 356-8 (C. *Munier*); RHR 211 (1994) 353-5 (A. *Méhat*).

4394 **Webb** Robert L., John the Baptizer and prophet...: jNsu 62, 1991
➤ 7,3919 ... 9,4559: ᴿRHPR 74 (1994) 204 (C. *Grappe*).
4395 *Webb* Robert L., John the Baptist and his relationship to Jesus ➤ 239*b*,
Chilton B., *Evans* C., Studying 1994, 179-200.
4396 *Wilkens* W., Die Täuferüberlieferung des Matthäus und ihre Verarbeitung durch Lukas: NTS 40 (1994) 542-557.

4397 *Garlington* Don B., [Mt 3,17] Jesus, the unique Son of God; tested and
faithful: BtS 151 (1994) 284-308.
4398 *Ito* A.Y., [> Mt 4,8 ...] Les sept montagnes de Jésus dans saint
Matthieu: LumièreV 49 (1994) 413-423 [< NTAbs 39,397: a 7-branch
candlestick with 15,29 as pivot].
4399 *Kähler* Christoph, Satanischer Schriftgebrauch; zur Hermeneutik von
Mt 4,1-11/Lk 4.1-13: TLZ 119 (1994) 857-868.

F3.5   **Mt 5... Sermon on the Mount** [... plain, Lk 6,17].

4400 **Carter** W., What are they saying about Matthew's sermon on the
mount? NY 1994, Paulist. vi-136 p. $8 pa. 0-8091-3473-X [TDig
42,359]. – ᴿTBR 7,3 (1994s) 27s (D. *Lee*).
4401 **Derrett** J.D.M., The Sermon on the Mount, a manual for living.
1994, Pilkington. 112 p. £10. 1-899041-02-7. – ᴿExpTim 106 (1994s) 54
(L. *Houlden*).
4402 **Entrich** Manfred, Der Bergpredigt als Ausbildungsordnung; der katechetische Entwurf einer 'ratio formationis' bei ALBERT dem Grossen:
StTPraxSeels 10; 1992 ➤ 8,4736: ᴿTLZ 119 (1994) 246s (P. *Heidrich*).
4403 *a)* Gerhardsson Birger, [Mt 1,18s ...] Mighty acts and the rule of man;
'God is with us'; – *b)* Goulder Michael, Already?; – *c)* Marshall I.
Howard , The synoptic 'Son of Man' sayings in the light of linguistic
study; – *d)* Hagner Donald A., Matthew's eschatology: ➤ 46, ᶠGUNDRY
R., To tell the mystery 1994, 34-48 / 21-33 / 72-94 / 49-71.
4404 **Giavini** Giovanni, Ma io vi dico; esegesi e vita attorno al Discorso della
Montagna²ʳᵉᵛ [¹1980 Tra la folla]: Parola di vita. Mi 1993, Àncora.
165 p. 88-7610-446-1.
4405 *Hanson* K.C., Transformed on the mountain; ritual analysis and the
Gospel of Matthew [*Esler* P.F., response]: Semeia 57 (1994) 147-170
[171-7].
4406 **Hughes** Michael B., The Sermon on the Mount as a paradigm for
effective Christian discipleship: DMin Diss. Fuller, ᴰ*Redman* R.
Pasadena 1994. 299 p. 95-14054. – DissA 55 (1994s) p. 3875.
4407 **Kelly** J.L., [Mt 5-7] Conscientious objectors; toward a reconstruction of
the social and political philosophy of Jesus of Nazareth: TorStT 68.
Lewiston NY 1994, Mellen. x-458 p. $110. 0-7734-1935-7 [NTAbs 39,
p. 225].
4408 **Krämer** Michael, Die Überlieferungsgeschichte der Bergpredigt; eine
synoptische Geschichte zu Mt 4,23-7,29 und Lk 6,17-49²ʳᵉᵛ: Deutsche
Hochschulschriften 433. Fra 1994, Hänsel-Hohenhausen. 270 p. DM 58.
3-89349-433-2 [TR 91,274; TLZ 120,659, K.M. *Bull*]. – ᴿBiKi 48 (1993)
239 (O. *Knoch*).
4409 **Lambrecht** Jan, Pero yo os digo ... El sermón programático de Jesús
(Mt 5-7; Lc 6,20-49) [1983, franç. 1986]ᵀ: BtEstB 81. S 1994, Sígueme. 302 p. 84-301-1238-3. – ᴿRET 54 (1994) 469s (P. *Barrado Fernández*).

4410 **Martini** Carlo Maria,   Il Vangelo alle sorgenti; meditando ad Assisi, il Discorso della Montagna; Testi spirituali 5. Mi 1990, Àncora. 114 p.

4411 **Meyer** B. F., [Mt 5-7; 10; 13; 18; 24s] Five speeches that changed the world. ColMn 1994, Liturgical. 139 p. $10 pa. 0-8146-2282-8 [NTAbs 39, p. 141].

4412 **Schnackenburg** Rudolf, Tutto è possibile a chi crede; discorso sulla montagna e Padre nostro nell'intenzione di Gesù: StBPaid 89, 1989 ➤ 5,4458:   RLateranum 57 (1991) 228s (R. *Penna*).

4413 **Segundo** J. L.,   El caso Mateo; los comienzos de una ética judeocristiana. Sdr 1994, Sal Terrae. 270 p. – RBibFe 20 (1994) 59 (A. *Salas*).

4414 **Slenczka** R.,   Die Bergpredigt Jesu; Auslegung in dreissig Andachten: Dienst am Wort 66. Gö 1994, Vandenhoeck & R. 158 p. DM 24.   3-525-59330-9 [NTAbs 39, p. 512].

4415 *Smit Sibinga* J.,   Exploring the composition of Matth. 5-7; the Sermon on the Mount and some of its 'structures': FgNt 7 (1994) 175-184; español 194.

4416 **Weder** Hans,   Die 'Rede der Reden'; eine Auslegung der Bergpredigt heute³ [¹1985 ➤ 3,4363]. Z 1994. Theol.-V. 253 p. 3-290-11565-8.

F3.6   Mt 5,3-11 (Lc 6,20-22) Beatitudines.

4417 *Bonar* C.,   The spirituality of the Beatitudes — the purgative / illuminative / unitive way: Emmanuel 100 (1994) 288-303 / 365-8 / 429-431 [< NTAbs 39, p. 27.215].

4418 *Buchanan* G. W.,   Matthaean beatitudes and traditional promises; JRadRef 3,1 (1993) 45-69 [< NTAbs 38,189].

4419 **Galloway** Kathy,   Struggles to love; the spirituality of the Beatitudes. L 1994, SPCK. viii-165 p. £8. – RTLond 97 (1994) 454s (Jane *Williams*).

4420 **Malipurathu** Thomas,   The Beatitudes according to Luke: diss. Pont. Univ. Gregoriana, DLentzen-Deis F. †, Grilli M., No 7201.   R 1994. – InfPUG 26,131 (1994) 33.

4421 **Mateos** Juan,   L'utopia di Gesù 1991 ➤ 8,4317:   RAngelicum 71 (1994) 276s (S. *Jurić*).

4422 *Mongillo* Dalmazio, [Mt 5,1-10] Les béatitudes et la béatitude; le dynamisme de la Somme de Théologie de Thomas d'AQUIN; une lecture de la Ia-IIae q. 69:   RSPT 78 (1994) 373-388.

4423 *Smith* P., [Lk 6,20-26] Beatitudes and woes: JSpForm 15,1 (Pittsburgh 1994) 35-45 [< NTAbs 38, p. 371].

4424 **Stock** Klemens, Jezus głosi błogosławienstwa. Kraków 1994, WAM. 169 p. 83-85304-97-5.

4425 *Verbraken* Pierre-P., †   Le Sermon 53 de saint AUGUSTIN sur les Béatitudes selon saint Matthieu: ➤ 116, RBén 104 (1994) 19-33.

4426 M. *Cecilia* OCD,   Dall'Antico al Nuovo Testamento; i pacifici chiamati 'beati': RivVSp 48 (1994) 8-14.

4427 *a) Pérez* Gabriel,   Bienaventurados los desprendidos (Mt 5,3); – *b*) *O'Callaghan* José,   Reflexiones críticas sobre Mt 21,7: ➤ 22, FCASCIARO J., Biblia 1994, 311-325 / 249-252.

4428 *a) Lattke* Michael,   Glückselig durch den Geist (Mt 5,3); – *b*) *Beutler* Johannes, Ihr seid das Salz des Landes (Mt 5,13); – *c*) *Giesen* Heinz, Christusnachfolge als Weg zum Heil; zum matthäischen Verständnis des Logions vom engen Tor (Mt 7,13f); – *d*) *Schweizer* Eduard,   Die Bergpredigt im Kontext des Matthäusevangeliums; – *e*) *Fiedler* Peter, Das

Matthäusevangelium und 'die Pharisäer': → 31*, FDAUTZENBERG G., Nach 1994, 363-382 / 85-94 / 251-276 / 607-617 / 199-218.

4429 *González Faus* J. I., [Mt 5,3-12] ¿Hacia una cultura del perdono? la misericordia y las bienaventuranzas como carta magna del creyente: RLatAmT 10 (1993) 171-187 [< NTAbs 38, p. 190].

4430 *Askola* Irja, [Mt 5,13; Ex 1,15-2,10; Acts 16,11-40; Jn 21,1-13; Mk 6,34-44] But I cannot see the salt! Five vignettes on biblical images of laity: EcuR 45,4 ('Laity' 1993) 388-391.

4431 *Parisi* Serafino, Mt 5,17-48; giustizia superiore e fede 'estroversa'; la morale sociale da 'un punto di vista' della Scrittura: Vivarium 2 (Catanzaro 1994) 45-62.

4432 *Kampen* John, [Mt 5,21-28] The sectarian form of the antitheses within the social world of the Matthean community: DSD 1 (1994) 338-363.

4433 **Collins** Raymond F., [Mt 5,32; 19,9] Divorce in the NT: Good News Studies 1992 → 8,4751; 9,4593: RBiblica 75 (1994) 290-3 (S. B. *Marrow*); CBQ 56 (1994) 362-4 (G. S. *Sloyan*); CritRR 6 (1993) 215-7 (C. *Keener*); Furrow 45 (1994) 257s (M. *Reidy*); Interpretation 48 (1994) 212.4 (Mary Lynn *Dell*); LvSt 19 (1994) 267s (G. van *Oyen*).

4434 *Haacker* Klaus, Ehe und Ehescheidung — Konflikte und Krisen in der Bibel: → 31d, FFANGMEIER J., Das Wort 1994, 187-194.

4435 **Keener** Craig S., [Mt 5,32] '... And marries another'; divorce NT 1991 → 8,4750: RBtS 151 (1994) 250 (J. A. *Witmer*).

4436 *Mangatt* G., [Mt 5,32] Jesus' teaching on marriage and divorce: Bible Bhashyam 20 (1994) 88-107 [< NTAbs 39, p. 391].

4437 *Broer* Ingo, [Mt 5,38] Das ius talionis im NT: NTS 40 (1994) 1-21.

4438 *Syreeni* Kari, Separation and identity; aspects of the symbolic world of Mt 6. 1-18: NTS 40 (1994) 522-541.

F3.7 *Mt 6,9-13 (Lc 11,2-4)* **Oratio Jesu,** Pater Noster, **Lord's Prayer [→** H1.4].

4439 **Biser** Eugen, Glaubensbekenntnis und Vaterunser²ʳᵉᵛ. Dü 1994, Patmos. 190 p. – RTAth 65 (1994) 981-4 (E. A. *Theodorou,* Ⓖ).

4440 ECharlesworth James R., [→ 313] The Lord's Prayer and other prayer texts from the Greco-Roman era. Ph 1994, Trinity. ix-292 p. 1-56338-080-3.

4441 *Mattam* Joseph, The Our Father, revolutionary prayer of commitment to the Kingdom of God: AfER 35 (1993) 69-78.

4442 *Mell* Ulrich, Gehört das Vater-Unser zur authentischen Jesus-Tradition? (Mt 6,9-13; Lk 11,2-4): BTZ 11 (1994) 148-180: a synagogal prayer unsuited as key to Jesus' theology.

4443 EMigliore Daniel L., The Lord's Prayer; perspectives for redeeming Christian prayer [Princeton symposium 1991] 1993 → 9,4607: RPrincSemB 15 (1994) 200s (B. *Hanson:* published also as PrincSemB supp).

4444 **Peters** Albrecht, Das Vaterunser: LUTHERS Katechismen 3, 1992 → 9, 4611: RTLZ 119 (1994) 257s (B. *Hägglund*); TZBas 50 (1994) 176s (H. J. E. *Beintker*).

4445 *Sperl* S., The literary form of prayer; Qur'ān Sura One, the Lord's Prayer, and a Babylonian prayer to the moon god: → 136, FWANSBROUGH J., BSO 57 (1994) 213-227.

4446 *Limbeck* Meinrad, [Mt 6,10] 'Es geschehe dein Wille!' Zur Verkündigung des Matthäus-Evangeliums: TLtg 66 (1993) 50-53 (111-4. 169-174. 251-6).

4447 *Elliott* John H., [Mt 6,22s] The Evil Eye and the Sermon on the Mount: contours of a pervasive belief in social scientific perspective: BInterp 2 (1994) 51-84.

4447* *Wischmeyer* Oda, Matthäus 6,25-34 par; die Spruchreihe vom Sorgen; ZNW 85 (1994) 1-22.

4448 *McEleney* Neil J., The unity and theme of Matthew 7:1-12:   CBQ 56 (1994) 490-500.

4449 *Breton* Stanislas, [Mt 7,1] Ne jugez pas; réflexions sur un impératif évangélique: RICathP 49 (1994) 41-50.

4450 *Murray* M.J., *Meyers* K., [Mt 7,7] Ask and it will be given to you; RelSt 30 (C 1994) 311-330 [< NTAbs 39, p. 215].

4451 *Hunyadi* Marc, [Mt 7,12; RICŒUR P., Soi-même 1990] La Règle d'Or; l'effet-radar: RTPhil 126 (1994) 215-222; Eng. 303.

4452 *Kellas* Carol, [Mt 8,1-4...] The healing of the leper; the accounts in the Synoptic Gospels and Papyrus Egerton 2, Papyrus Köln 255:   IrBSt 16 (1994) 161-173.

4453 *Gagnon* Robert A.J., [Mt 8,5-13] The shape of Matthew's Q text of the centurion at Capernaum; did it mention delegations?: NTS 40 (1994) 133-143.

4454 *Schwarz* Günther, 'Er berührte ihre Hand'? (Matthäus 8,15): BibNot 73 (1994) 33-35.

4455 *Gundry* Robert H., On true and false disciples in Mt 8.18-22: NTS 40 (1994) 433-441.

4456 *Schwarz* Günther, 'Ein grosses Beben entstand auf dem Meer'? (Matthäus 8,24): BibNot 74 (1994) 31s.

4457 *Van Elderen* Bastiaan, [Mt 8,28-34...], Early Christianity in Transjordan: TyndB 45 (1994) 97-117.

4458 **Vledder** Evert-Jan, Conflict in the miracle stories in Matthew 8 and 9; a sociological and exegetical study: diss. ᴰ*Aarde* A. van. Pretoria 1994. – DissA 55 (1994s) p. 3892.

F4.1   *Mt 9-12; Miracula Jesu* –   **The Gospel miracles.**

4459 *Conus* H.-T., Les miracles [... AT; NT] et la vie chrétienne: NVFr 69 (1994) 33-46.

4460 ᴱ**Dierkens** Alain, Apparitions et miracles: ProbHRel. Bru 1991, Univ. 191 p. – ᴿRBgPg 72 (1994) 921-3 (G. *Philippart*).

4461 *Dos Santos* João Ferreira, Teologia dos milagres de Jesus.   RJ 1992, JUERP.   170 p. – ᴿVoxScr 84 (1994) 226 (C. O. *Pinto*).

4462 *Engebrecht* J., Die historiese Jesus as wonderwerker: HervTSt 49,1 (1993) 119-133 [< NTAbs 38, p. 180].

4463 **Fischbach** Stephanie M., Totenerweckungen ᴰ1992 ➤ 8,4791; 9,4629: ᴿTLZ 119 (1994) 508s (G. *Haufe*).

4464 *Fossum* Jarl, Understanding Jesus' miracles: BR 10,2 (1994) 16-23. 50.

4465 **Houston** J., Reported miracles; a critique of HUME.   C 1994, Univ. xii-264 p. £35.   0-521-41549-7. – ᴿExpTim 106 (1994s) 29s (W. D. *Hudson*); TBR 7,3 (1994s) 12s (Saeed *Hamid-Khani*).

4466 **Kahl** Werner, New Testament miracle stories in their religious-historical setting; a religionsgeschichtliche comparison from a structural perspective [diss. Emory, ᴰ*Boers* H. ➤ 9,4652]: FRL 163. Gö 1994, Vandenhoeck & R. 258 p.; bibliog. 240-258.   3-525-53854-6 [NTAbs 39, p. 506].

4467 **Kee** Howard C., Medicina, milagro y magía 1992 ➤ 8,4798; 9,4633: ᴿSalesianum 56 (1994) (J. J. *Bartolomé*).

4468 *Kirschner* Estevan F., Jesus e os exorcistas de seu tempo; paralelos e distinções: VoxScr 4 (São Paulo 1994) 9-24.
4469 **Koskenniemi** Erkki, Der philostratische APOLLONIOS (von Tyana...): CommHumLitt 94, 1991 ➤ 7,3997; 9,4634: ᴿCritRR 5 (1992) 298-300 & 6 (1993) 334-6 (L. H. *Martin*).
4470 **Koskenniemi** Erkki, Apollonius von Tyana in der neutestamentlichen Exegese; Forschungsbericht und Weiterführung der Diskussion; WUNT 2/61. Tü 1994, Mohr. ix-273 p.; Bibliog. 237-256. DM 98. 3-16-145894-X [TLZ 120,801, H.-G. *Thümmel*].
4471 **Latourelle** R., The Miracles of Jesus 1988 ➤ 4,4652... 8,4902: ᴿVidyajyoti 58 (1994) 329s (P. A. *Joseph*).
4472 **Latourelle** R., Los Milagros 1990 ➤ 6,4855*b*... 8,4803: ᴿRET 53 (1993) 395-7 (E. *Tourón*).
4473 *a) Lührmann* Dieter, Neutestamentliche Wundergeschichten und antike Medizin; – *b) Schottroff* Willy, *Conclamatio* und *Profectio*; zur Veranschaulichung neutestamentlicher Wundergeschichten: ➤ 40, ᶠGEORGI D., Religious propaganda 1994, 195-204 / 257-281; 2 fig.
4474 **McClenon** James, Wondrous events, foundations of religious belief. Ph 1994, Univ. Pennsylvania. xiv-281 p. $40; pa. $18. 0-8122-3074-4 [TDig 42,375].
4475 **McCready** W. D., Signs of sanctity... miracles/GREGORY 1989 ➤ 5,4558 ... 9,4637: ᴿ ÉglT 25 (1994) 435-7 (J. K. *Coyle*); Salesianum 56 (1994) 589s (F. *Meyer*).
4476 I miracoli di Gesù: 1. Sono possibili i miracoli?; 2. Storicità e significato: CC 144 (1993) 425-438. 529-541.
4477 **Neyton** André, Le merveilleux religieux dans l'Antiquité, aspects choisis 1991 ➤ 8,4807; 2-7063-0184-8: ᴿBL (1993) 125 (J. *Barton*: outdated, rambling); PrOrChr 42 (1992) 467s (P. *Ternant*); RHPR 74 (1994) 308 (T. *Ziegler*: ni l'AT ni le NT n'échappent aux normes de 'démonstration'); ZAW 106 (1994) 167 (G. *Begrich*).
4478 **Pain** Timothy, Miracles are impossible; you decide [CERULLO M.] 1994. 88 p. £10. 1-898797-00-5. – ᴿChurchman 108 (1994) 271-4 (P. *May*).
4479 *Parmentier* Martin, Zur Theologie der Thaumaturgie: Bijdragen 55 (1994) 296-324; Eng. 324.
4480 *Phillips* D. Z., Miracles and open-ended epistemology; ScotJR 14 (1993) 33-40.
4481 *Robiano* P., Philostrate et la chevelure d'APOLLONIOS de Tyane: Pallas 41 (1994) 57-65.
4482 **Schulte** Birgit, Die Darstellungen der Wundertaten Christi in der Malerei und Graphik des 19. Jahrhunderts; eine Untersuchung zur christlichen Ikonographie [Diss. Münster 1987]: EurHS 28/81. Fra 1988, Lang. 643 p.; 242 fig. DM 232.50. – ᴿTR 90 (1994) 57 (A. *Stock*).
4483 *Sicre* José Luis, Jesús poderoso en obras (Mt 8-9), I. el problema de los milagros; II. comentario: Proyección 41 (1994) 3-17. 259-275.
4484 **Skutch** Robert, Journey without distance; the story behind A course in miracles. Berkeley CA 1994, Christian Arts. [xii-] 132 p. 0-89087-404-2.
4485 *Thomas* David, The miracles of Jesus in early Islamic polemic: JSS 39 (1994) 221-243.
4486 *Tomczak* R., ❂ Cud znakiem... Miracle as sign of the divine mission of Jesus: RoczT 40,2 (1993) 53-69 [< NTAbs 39, p. 202].
4487 **Trunk** Dieter, Der messianische Heiler; eine redaktions- und religionsgeschichtliche Studie zu den Exorzismen im Matthäusevangelium: *a)* kath. Diss. ᴰ*Klauck* H.-J. Würzburg 1994. – TR 91,104. – *b)* BStud 3. FrB

1994, Herder. xiii-457 p.; Bibliog. 436-452. DM 88. [TLZ 120,1003, J. *Becker*]. 3-451-23150-6.
4488 *Twelftree* G. H., Jesus the exorcist 1993 → 9,4647: ᴿJTS 45 (1994) 646s (Helga K. *Nielsen*).

4489 *Bordage* A., [Mc 8,22-26; 5,1-17] À propos de deux miracles de Jésus: CahRenan 185 (1994) 23-26.
4489* **Herrenbrück** Fritz, [Mt 9,10] Jesus und die Zöllner; WUNT 2/41, 1990 → 6,4873 ... 9,4649: ᴿSvEx 59 (1994) 181s (A. *Hultgård*).
4490 *Standaert* Benoît, [Mt 9,13; 12,7] 'Misericordia voglio'; ParSpV 29 (1994) 109-119.
4491 **Trummer** Peter, [Mt 9,20] Die blutende Frau 1991 → 7,4015; 8,4817: ᴿBiKi 48 (1993) 109 (R. *Russ*).
4492 **Grilli** Massimo, Comunità e missione; le direttive di Matteo ... 9,35-11,1: EurHS 23/458, 1992 → 8,4818: ᴿCBQ 56 (1994) 374s (B. T. *Viviano*); RB 101 (1994) 617 (B. T. *Viviano*).
4493 **Weaver** Dorothy J., [Mt 9,35-11,1] Matthew's missionary discourse: jNsu 38, ᴰ1990 → 6,4876 ... 8,4919: ᴿFgNt 7 (1994) 82s (J. *Mateos*).
4494 *Peterson* Robert A., A traditionalist response to John STOTT's arguments for annihilationism [Mt 10,28 ...]: JEvTS 37 (1994) 553-568.
4495 *Tabor* James D., *Wise* Michael O., [Mt 11,5] 4Q521 'On Resurrection' and the Synoptic Gospel tradition; a preliminary study: JPseud 10 (1992) 149-162.
4496 *Llewelyn* Stephen, The Traditionsgeschichte of Matt. 11:12-13 [Kingdom/violence] par. Luke 16:16: NT 36 (1994) 330-349.
4497 *Efferin* H., The Sabbath controversy based on Mt 12,1-8: StulosTJ 1,1 (Bandung 1993) 43-48 [< NTAbs 38, p. 362].
4498 *Bravo* Ernesto, [Mt 12,1-8 *al*.] Jesús y el sábado: RBibArg 56 (1994) 149-174 / 237-249.
4499 **Chow** Simon, The sign of Jonah reconsidered; Matthew 12:38-42 and Luke 11:29-32: Theology and Life 15s (Hong Kong Lutheran Theol. Sem. 1993) 53-60.
4499* *Fuchs* Albert, [Mt 12,39 ...] Das Zeichen des Jona: vom Rückfall: SNTU 19 (1994) 131-160.
4500 *Deist* F. E., [Mt 12,39] De teken van Jona en Jesus as Messias: Skrif-Kerk 14,1 (1993) 20-27 [< NTAbs 38, p. 192].

F4.3   **Mt 13 ...** *Parabolae Jesu* – **the Parables.**

4501 *Brosend* William F.ᴵᴵ, The limits of metaphor [in parable study: J. R. DONAHUE 'escalation' ... metaphors 'shattering worlds, creating new visions, and calling existence into question']: PerspRelSt 21 (1994) 23-41.
4502 *Buth* Randall, Symbols and 'diabols'; reflections upon the thought of F. W. DILLISTONE: PerspRelSt 21 (1994) 203-225.
4503 **Casciaro** José M., Parábolas de Jesús; transmisión y hermenéutica: Coll. Teológica 80. Pamplona 1992, EUNSA. 189 p. – ᴿCiuD 207 (1994) 195s (J. *Gutiérrez*).
4504 **Cocagnac** Maurice, La parole et son miroir; les symboles bibliques: Lire la Bible 102. P 1994, Cerf. 240 p. F 90.
4505 **Cuvillier** Elian, Le concept de parabolē dans le second évangile ...: ÉtBN 19, 1993 → 9,4676 [Biblica 76,118, A. *Puig*]. – ᴿBLitEc 95 (1994) 241s (H. *Crouzel*); CBQ 56 (1994) 789s (Mary R. *Thompson*); Gregorianum 75 (1994) 554s (B. *Marconi*); RHPR 74 (1994) 207s (É. *Trocmé*).

4506 — *Walter* L., Qu'est-ce qu'une parabole? [Mc: CUVILLIER E., diss. prot. Montpellier 1991]: EsprVie 104 (1994) 154-8.
4508 **Hammer** Margaret L., Giving birth; reclaiming biblical metaphor for pastoral practice. LVL 1994, W-Knox. xi-286 p. 0-664-25137-4.
4509 *Harnisch* Wolfgang, Beiträge zur Gleichnisforschung (1984-1991): TRu 59 (1994) 346-387.
4510 **Hedrick** Charles W., Parables as poetic fictions [... Coptic Thomas]; the creative voice of Jesus. Peabody MA 1994, Hendrickson. xxxix-279 p. $20. 0-913573-90-6 [TDig 42,272]. – ᴿExpTim 106 (1994s) 366 (W. G. *Morrice*).
4511 **Herzog** William R.ᴵᴵ, Parables as subversive speech; Jesus as pedagogue of the oppressed. LVL 1994, W-Knox. xi-299 p. $20 pa. 0-664-25255-5 [NTAbs 39, p.138; RelStR 21,142, T. *Dwyer*: he uses Paulo FREIRE; TS 56,571s, L. T. *Johnson*].
4512 **Lagarde** Claude & Jacqueline, Catéchèse biblique et symbolique: Séquences 3. P 1993, Centurion. 244 p. F 100. – ᴿEsprVie 104 (1994) 148 [P. *Rouillard*].
4513 **Lambrecht** J., Out of the treasure; parables/Mt 1992 ⇒ 8,4857; 9,4687: ᴿRB 101 (1994) 616s (B. T. *Viviano*).
4514 **McArthur** H. K., *Johnston* R. M., They also taught in [125 rabbinic] parables 1990 ⇒ 6,4910 ... 8,4588: ᴿConcordTQ 58 (1994) 230-2 (G. J. *Lockwood*); CritRR 5 (1992) 378-380 (B. B. *Scott*).
4515 **McCracken** David, The scandal of the Gospels. Ox 1994, UP. 204 p. £25. 0-19-508428-4. – ᴿExpTim 105 (1993s) 347s (N. *Clark*: the parables are essentially occasions for scandal, 'collision' provoking either destruction or transformation).
4516 **McKenna** M., Parables, the arrows of God. Mkn 1994, Orbis. v-170 p. $11 pa. 0-88344-975-7 [NTAbs 39, p. 508].
4517 **Maggioni** Bruno, Le parabole evangeliche 1992 ⇒ 9,4691: ᴿCC 145 (1994,4) 207s (D. *Scaiola*); Lateranum 60 (1994) 172s (R. *Penna*).
4518 **Marguerat** D., Parábola: CuadB 75. Estella 1992, VDivino. 66 p. – ᴿCiTom 121 (1994) 406 (J. L. *Espinel*, también sobre BEAUCHAMP P. 76, ABREGO J. M. 69, *al.*).
4519 **Mateos** Juan, *Camacho* F., Vangelo, figure e simboli ᵀ1991 ⇒ 7,4055; 9,4694: ᴿAngelicum 71 (1994) 277s (S. *Jurić*); Salesianum 56 (1994) 375s (C. *Bissoli*).
4520 *Nolland* J., Reading and being read; new insights into the parables of Jesus ['regularly dishonored by how people read them']: Crux 29,3 (1993) 11-17 [< NTAbs 38, p. 186].
4521 **Pérez Cotapos** Larrain E., Parábolas / DUPONT ᴰ1991 ⇒ 8,4861; 9, 4699: ᴿRBíbArg 55 (1993) 188s (A. J. *Levoratti*).
4522 **Ploeg** J. P. M. van der, Jésus nous parle; les paraboles et les allégories des quatre évangiles. P 1994, Gabalda. 242 p. 2-85021-072-2.
4523 **Rau** Eckhard, Reden in Vollmacht ...: FRL 149, ᴰ1990 ⇒ 6,4919 ... 9,4701: ᴿTR 90 (1994) 214-6 (J. *Lambrecht*).
4524 *Schmeller* Thomas, Das Reich Gottes im Gleichnis; eine Überprüfung neuerer Deutungen der Gleichnisrede und der Reich-Gottes-Verkündigung Jesu [< kath. Hab.-Vorlesung Mü 1993]: TLZ 119 (1994) 599-608.
4525 **Scott** B. B., Hear then 1990 ⇒ 5,4632 ... 9,4703: ᴿFgNt 7 (1994) 81s (J. *Mateos*).
4526 **Vallet** R. E., Stepping stones of the steward; a faith journey through Jesus' parables²ʳᵉᵛ [¹1989]: Faith's Horizons. GR / Manlius NY 1994, Eerdmans / Rose. xiv-192 p. $11. 0-8028-0834-4/. [NTAbs 39, p. 513].

4527 **Weder** Hans, Metafore del Regno [Die Gleichnisse Jesu als Metaphern 1978], ᵀ*Garra* G.: BtCuRel 60, 1991 ➤ 8,4876; 9,4707 [Orpheus 15,246, A. *Gallico*]. – ᴿSalesianum 56 (1994) 383s (C. *Bissoli*).
4528 **Wenham** D., Parables of Jesus 1989 ➤ 6,4021; 7,4067: ᴿScotJR 11 (1990) 51s (J. *Drane*).

4529 **Estrada-Barbier** Bernardo, [Mt 13...] El sembrador; perspectivas filológico-hermenéuticas de una parábola: BtSalmEst 165. S 1994, Univ. 250 p.[TLZ 120,439, C. *Stenschke*]. 84-7299-328-0. – ᴿBbbOr 36 (1994) 251 (G. *De Virgilio*); Burgense 35 (1994) 505s (A. *Martínez Sierra*).
4530 *Genuyt* François, Matthieu 13; l'enseignement en paraboles; SémBib 73 (1994) 30-44 (74, 30-41 / 75, 29-36: Mt 14/15).
4531 *McIver* Robert K., One hundredfold yield — miraculous or mundane? Mt 13.8,23; Mk 4.8,20; Lk 8.8.: NTS 40 (1994) 606-8.
4532 *Bivin* David, [Mt 13,44s] Counting the cost of discipleship; [Robert L.] LINDSEY's reconstruction of the Rich Young Ruler complex: Jerusalem Perspectives 42ss (1994) 23-36; ill.
4533 *Bauckham* Richard, [Mt 14,3...] The brothers and sisters ['sister' on page-headings!] of Jesus; an Epiphanian [EPIPHANIUS: children of Joseph by a previous marriage] response to John P. MEIER [favouring HELVIDIUS's: children of Joseph and Mary; JEROME's 'cousins' improbable]: CBQ [54 (1992) 1-28 (and A marginal Jew 1991) not available to his Jude 1990] 56 (1994) 686-700.
4534 **Grassi** Joseph A., [Mt 14,13-21] Loaves and fishes 1991 ➤ 7,4078: ᴿBibTB 24 (1994) 38 (M. *McVann*).
4535 **Madden** Patrick J., [Mt 14,25] Jesus' walking on the sea; an investigation of the origin of the narrative account: diss. Catholic Univ., ᴰ*Fitzmyer* J. Washington 1994. – RTLv 26, p. 338.
4536 *Jackson* Glenna S., 'Have mercy on me'; the Canaanite woman in Matthew 15:21-28: diss. Marquette. Milwaukee c. 1993. – BToday 32 (1994) 73.
4537 *Jackson* Glenna S., [Mt 15,21-28] A source for Matthew's story of the Canaanite Woman: ProcGM 14 (1994) 47-56.
4538 **Baudoz** Jean-François, [Mt 15,21-28] Les miettes de la table [Mc 7,24-30 ...] – a) essai sur les diverses pratiques missionnaires judéo-chrétiennes: diss. Paris, Inst. Cath. 1993, ᴰ*Perrot* C. 545 p. – RICathP 49 (1994) (C. *Perrot*); – b) Étude synoptique et socio-religieuse de Mt 15,21-28 et de Mc 7,24-30: ÉtBN ... P c. 1994, Gabalda. 451 p. F 340. 2-85021-076-5.
4539 *Monro* A., [Mt 15,22] Alterity and the Canaanite woman; a postmodern feminist theological reflection on political action: Colloquium 26,1 (Brisbane 1994) 32-43 [NTAbs 39, p. 216].

F4.5   **Mt 16...** *Primatus promissus* – **The promise to Peter.**

4540 ᴱ**Aguirre Monasterio** Rafael, Pedro en la Iglesia primitiva 1991 ➤ 7,284: ᴿRET 53 (1993) 403-5 (M. *Gesteira*); ScripTPamp 26 (1994) 1216s (J. M. *Casciaro*).
4541 *Bivin* David, Matthew 16:18; the *Petros-petra* wordplay — Greek, Aramaic, or Hebrew: Jerusalem Perspective 46s (1994) 32-38.
4542 **Claudel** G., [Mt 16,13-20] La confession de Pierre (diss. Strasbourg 1986): ÉtBN 10, 1988 ➤ 4,4741... 8,4887: ᴿCiuD 207 (1994) 196s (J. *Gutiérrez*).

4543 *Fleming* Paul, Church government [p. 88: it is unhelpful to read the developed papacy back into the NT era; it is helpful to try to understand how the present structures came about in the effort to fulfil Jesus' commands]: IrBSt 16 (1994) 87-93.

4544 **Garuti** A., S. Pietro unico titolare del primato [S. Uffizio 24.I.1647] 1993 → 9,4723:   ᴿAnnTh 8 (1994) 403-9 (J. *García de Cárdenas*); CC 145 (1994,4) 408s (M. *Fois*).

4545 **Grant** M., Saint Peter, a biography. NY 1994, Scribner. xii-212 p.; 4 pl.; 2 maps. $23. 0-684-19354-X [NTAbs 39, p. 505].

4546 **Minnerath** Roland, De Jérusalem à Rome; Pierre et l'unité de l'Église apostolique: THist 101. P 1994, Beauchesne. 616 p. 2-7010-1321-6.

4547 *Mosetto* Francesco, Conferma i tuoi fratelli: ParVi 39,3 ('Pietro' 1994) 14-18 [al. 5-48].

4548 **Nau** Arlo J., Peter in Matthew 1992 → 8,4894; 9,4731:   ᴿJBL 113 (1994) 143s (W. C. *Linss*: fascinating; not completely convincing); NewTR 7,3 (1992) 87s (Elaine M. *Wainwright*); TorJT 10 (1994) 261-3 (M. *Knowles*).

4549 **Perkins** Pheme, Peter, apostle for the whole Church: Studies on personalities of the NT. Columbia 1994, Univ. S. Carolina. vi-209 p. $35 [RelStR 21,145, C. *Bernas*]. 0-87249-974-X.

[Tavares] **De Lima** João, 'Tu serás chamado *Kēphas*; estudo exegético sobre Pedro no quarto evangelho 1994 → 5212.

4550 **Tomić** Celestin, *Poceci Crkve...* Church beginnings, Peter chief of the Apostles: Povijest spasenja 13. Zagreb 1994, OFMKonv. 216 p.

4551 *Gourdain* Jean-Louis, [Mt 17] Jᴇ́ʀᴏ̂ᴍᴇ exégète de la Transfiguration: RÉAug 40 (1994) 265-373.

4552 **Lavoie** Celine, La Transfiguration selon les Synoptiques, mystère de passion et de gloire: diss. Laval, ᴰCote P. Montréal 1994. 150 p. MM 91976. (DissA-disk) MAI 33 (1994s) p. 740.

4553 **Marshall** Rob, The transfiguration of Jesus. L 1994, Darton-LT. xiii-111 p. 0-292-52028-3.

4554 **Reid** Barbara E., The transfiguration [Lk] < diss. Catholic U., ᴰMeier J. CahRB 32, 1993 → 9,4747:   ᴿCBQ 56 (1994) 807s (C. H. *Talbert*); Gregorianum 75 (1994) 762 (G. *Marconi*); JTS 45 (1994) 772-4 (I. H. *Marshall*).

4555 *Verseput* Donald J., [Mt 17,22...] Jesus' pilgrimage to Jerusalem and encounter in the Temple; a geographical motif in Matthew's Gospel: NT 36 (1994) 105-121.

4556 *Baarda* T., Matthew 18:14c; an 'extra-canonical' addition [of Tᴀᴛɪᴀɴ] in the Arabic Diatessaron [Rᴇꜱᴄʜ A. 1894]: Muséon 107 (1994) 135-149.

4557 *Tellan* Sergio, La chiesa di Matteo e la correzione fraterna; analisi di Mt 18,15-17: Laurentianum 35 (1994) 91-132.

4558 *Weber* Beat, Vergeltung oder Vergebung? Matthäus 18.21-35 auf dem Hintergrund des 'Erlassjahres' [Lv 25; Lk 4,19]: TZBas 50 (1994) 124-151.

4559 **Buckley** Thomas W., Seventy times seven... Mt 18,22, 1991 → 7,4108... 8,4908:   ᴿRB 101 (1994) 454s (B. T. *Viviano*).

4560 *Marafioti* Domenico, Verginità e matrimonio in Mt 19 e 1 Cor 7: RasT 35 (1994) 663-686.

4561 *Beilner* Wolfgang, [Mt 19,3-12 anders als Mk 10,2-12] Ehescheidung im Neuen Testament: TPQ 142 (1994) 338-342 [-371, *al.*, in der Kirche].

4562 **Kreier** Johannes J., Eunuchie und Reich Gottes; eine Studie zum Eunuchensprach, Mt 19,12: Diss. ^D*Beilner* W. Salzburg 1994. – RTLv 26, p. 537; TR 91,101.

4563 *Cacitti* Remo, [Mt 19,16-22] 'Ad caelestes thesauros'; l'esegesi della pericopa del 'giovane ricco': Aevum 67 (1993) 129-171 [< RÉAug 40 (1994) 483s (Simone *Deléani*).

4564 *Horęzga* Stanisław, ❷ Mt 19,16-22 as source of moral teaching in Veritatis splendor: RuBi 47 (1994) 48-52.

4565 **Carter** Warren, Households and discipleship; a study in Matthew 19-20: jNsu 103. Shf 1994, Academic. 249 p.; £35. 1-85075-493-4 [NTAbs 39, p. 115]. – ^RExpTim 106 (1994s) 212 (I. H. *Jones*: clear).

F4.8   **Mt 20...** *Regnum eschatologicum* – **Kingdom eschatology.**

4566 **Hezser** Catherine, Lohnmetaphorik... Mt 20,1-16: OBO 15, 1990 ➤ 6, 4969; 8,4915: ^RTR 90 (1994) 216s (J. *Lambrecht*).

4567 *Adly* Sanaa A. El-, [Mt 20,5; Prov 23,6] Der böse Blick und der blaue Stein: GöMiszÄg 138 (1994) 7-10.

4568 *O'Callaghan* José, Discusión de dos lecturas mateanas (20,31.34): ➤ 86, ^FNALDINI M., Paideia 1994, 36.

4569 *Karividopoulos* J., [Mt 21,5...] Citation de Zacharie dans le Nouveau Testament: DeltVM 23,1 (1994) 48-55 [< NTAbs 39, p. 201].

4570 *O'Callaghan* José, Reflexiones críticas sobre Mt 21,7: ➤ 22a, ^FCASCIARO J., Biblia 1994, 249-252 [< AcPIB 9,894].

4571 **Frankovic** Joseph, [Mt 21,12, den of thieves] Remember Shiloh!: Jerusalem Perspective 46 (1994) 24-31, with two im-posing possibly-relevant drawings of a Temple mount reconstruction.

4572 **Egawa** Ken, Incredulity and judgment; disputation about the authority of Jesus in Mt 21,22-22,14: diss. ^D*Lentzen-Deis* F. R 1994, Pontificia Universitas Gregoriana. [iv-]94 p.; bibliog. 42-88.

4573 *Kinman* Brent, Jesus' 'triumphal entry' in the light of Pilate's: NTS 40 (1994) 442-8.

4574 **Del Verme** Marcello, [Mt 23,23] Giudaismo... decime 1989 ➤ 5,4687*... 9,4774: ^RKairos 32s (1990s) 255 (G. *Stemberger*).

4575 *Schwartz* Günther, 'Reinige... das Innere des Bechers'? (Matthäus 23,26): BibNot 75 (1994) 31-34.

4576 *Dubois* Jean-Daniel, [Mt 23,35] La mort de Zacharie; mémoire juive et mémoire chrétienne: RÉAug 40 (1994) 23-38.

4577 **Friedl** Alfred, Der eschatologische Bericht in Bildern aus dem Alltag; eine exegetische Untersuchung von Mt 24,20f par Lk 17,34f: kath. Diss. ^D*Kremer* J. Wien 1994. – RTLv 26,536.

4578 **Kim Ki Kon,** The signs of the Parousia; a diachronic and comparative study of the apocalyptic vocabulary of Matthew 24:27-31: diss. Andrews Univ., ^D*Johnston* R. Berrien Springs MI 1994. 491 p. 94-28813. – DissA 55 (1994s) p. 1295; AndrUnSem 32 (1994) 111; RTLv 26, p. 537.

4579 *Rosenblatt* M.-E., [Mt 25,1-13] Got into the party after all; women's issues and the five foolish virgins [from a separate parable about managing some disruptive women]: Continuum 3 (1994) 107-137 [NTAbs 39, p. 217].

4580 *Scognamiglio* R., Grazia o profitto? La parabola dei talenti (Mt 25,14-30) nell'esegesi di ORIGENE: Nicolaus 21 (1994) 239-261 [< RHE 90,308*].

4581 **Frahier** Louis-Jean, (Mt 25,31-46) Le jugement dernier; implications éthiques sur le bonheur de l'homme: Rech. morales, Synthèses, 1992 ➤ 8,

4945*b*; 9,4788 [NTAbs 38, p. 460]. – ᴿRThom 94 (1994) 712s (G. *Bavaud*: riche, parfois touffu).

4582 **Gray** Sherman W., The least of my brothers, Mt 25:31-46, a history of interpretation [diss. Wsh, Catholic Univ., ᴰ*Fitzmyer* J.]: SBL Diss. 114, 1989 ► 7,4138; 8,4946: ᴿRB 101 (1994) 453s (B. T. *Viviano*).

4583 *Wengst* Klaus, Wie aus Böcken Ziegen werden (Mt 25,32f) [Einheitsübersetzung nur in einer Erprobungsphase]: zur Entstehung und Verbreitung einer Forschungslegende oder: Wissenschaft als 'stille Post': EvT 54 (1994) 491-500.

4584 *Cranfield* C. E. B., [Mt 25,40] Who are Christ's brothers?: Metanoia 4,1s (Prague 1994) 31-39 [< NTAbs 39, p. 217: the needy, all Christians, all humans].

4585 **Weber** Kathleen, The events of the end of the age in Matthew: diss. Cath. Univ., ᴰ*Meier* J. Wsh 1994. 363 p. 94-18609. – DissA 55 (1994s) p. 299; RTLv 26, p. 540.

F5.1   *Redemptio,* Mt 26, *Ultima coena;* **The Eucharist** [► H7.4].

4586 **Bader** Günter, Die Abendmahlsfeier; Liturgik – Ökonomik – Symbolik. Tü 1993, Mohr. ix-167 p. DM 88 [TR 91,344, B. *Kranemann*]. – ᴿArTGran 57 (1994) 441 (J. M. *Rodríguez-Izquierdo*).

4587 **Bishop** Jonathan, Some bodies; the Eucharist and its implications. Macon 1992, Mercer Univ. xiv-244 p. $35. – ᴿAnglTR 76 (1994) 384s (L. L. *Mitchell*); NBlackf 75 (1994) 583-6 (G. *Moore*: insights that do not add up).

4588 *Cassidy* D. C., Is transubstantiation without substance? RelSt 30 (1994) 193-9.

4589 **Chilton** Bruce, A feast of meanings; Eucharistic theologies from Jesus through Johannine circles: NT supp 72. Leiden 1994, Brill. xi-210 p. ƒ135. 90-04-09949-2 [JTS 46,634, J. C. *O'Neill*; Biblica 76,579-582, R. F. *O'Toole*]. – ᴿNBlackf 75 (1994) 546-8 (Meg *Davies*).

4590 *a*) *Chilton* Bruce, The Eucharist – exploring its origins; – *b*) *Lang* Bernhard, The Eucharist – a sacrificial formula preserved: BR 10,6 (1994) 36-43 / 44-49.

4591 **Cocksworth** Christopher J., Evangelical Eucharistic thought in the Church of England. C 1993, Univ. xiv-283 p. £35. – ᴿAnglTR 76 (1994) 118-120 (J. N. *Morris*); TLond 97 (1994) 58s (J. *Charley*: meticulous and readable).

4592 **DeConcini** Barbara, Narrative remembering. NY 1990, UPA. xv-292 p. $36.50. – ᴿCritRR 5 (1992) 69-71 (R. C. *Wood*: a significant approach to the Eucharist, though badly printed and from a religious background not adequately clarified).

4593 **Di Noia** Gerardo, Monumenta eucharistica; la testimonianza dei Padri della Chiesa I: I-IV secolo. R 1994, Dehoniane. 945 p. 88-996-0562-2.

4594 **Fitzpatrick** P. J., In breaking of bread 1993 ► 9,4808: ᴿHeythJ 35 (1994) 468-470 (R. *Moloney*, also on McPARTLAN P.); JTS 45 (1994) 811-4 (P. *McPartlan*); NRT 116 (1994) 755s (A. *Toubeau*).

4595 *Galot* Jean, La célébration eucharistique; sa valeur dans la vie chrétienne: EsprVie 104 (1994) 161-7.

4595* *García García* Luis, La transubstanciación en la versión litúrgica española: Burgense 35 (1994) 189-207.

4596 **Gerrish** B. A., Grace / CALVIN 1993 ► 9,4811: JTS 45 (1994) 771-5 (T. H. L. *Parker*).

4597 *Gesteira Garza* Manuel,   La Eucaristía como 'memorial' en la tradición patrística: RET 53 (1993) 341-387.425-447.

4598 *Giraudo* Cesare,   Prière eucharistique et inculturation; jalons pour le Synode d'Afrique: NRT 116 (1994) 181-200.

4599 *Gubler* Marie-Louise,   Das Blut des Bundes für die Vielen (Mk 14,24): Diakonia 25 (1994) 166-177.

4600 *Hoskins* Steven T.,   Eucharist and eschatology in the writings of the WESLEYs: WeslTJ 29 (1994) 64-80.

4601 *Jobert* Philippe,   La doctrine de l'Église sur le sacrifice eucharistique du concile de Trente au deuxième concile du Vatican: EsprVie 104 (1994) 97-103.

4602 **Jones** Paul H.,   Christ's eucharistic presence; a history of the doctrine: AmerUnivSt 7/157. NY 1994, P. Lang. xv-263 p. $49.   0-8204-2174-X [TDig 42,71].

4603 **Kaufmann** Thomas,   Die Abendmahlstheologie der Strassburger Reformierten bis 1528: BeitHisT 81, 1992 ⟶ 8,4971:   RÉTRel 69 (1994) 433 (Marianne *Burkard*); RHPR 74 (1994) 265-272 (M. *Lienhard*); Zwingliana 21 (1994) 195s (P. *Opitz*).

4604 *Kilmartin* Edward J.,   The Catholic tradition of eucharistic theology; towards the third millennium: TS 55 (1994) 405-457.

4605 **Klinghardt** Matthias,   Gemeinschaftsmahl und Mahlgemeinschaft; Sozialgeschichte und Gestalt frühchristlicher Mahlfeiern: Hab.-Diss. ᴰ*Berger* K. (+ 3). Heidelberg 1994. – TR 91,90.

4606 *Lapointe* Guy,   Une présence qui demeure; l'Eucharistie et le lieu: ⟶ 30, ᶠCOUTURIER G., Maison 1994, 403-423.

4606* *LaVerdiere* E.,   [⟶ 4948] Dining in the Kingdom of God; the Eucharist in Luke's Gospel: Emmanuel 100 (1994) 260-273 [< NTAbs 39, p. 40].

4607 **McPartlan** Paul,   The Eucharist makes the Church ... de LUBAC, ZIZIOULAS 1993 ⟶ 9,4824:   [Gregorianum 76,172, A. *Antón*]:   ᴿJEH 45 (1994) 716-8 (N. *Sagovsky*); OrChrPer 60 (1994) 720 (E. G. *Farrugia*); OneInC 30 (1994) 92-98 (D. *Carter*); Pacifica 7 (1994) 105-7 (J. *Chryssavgis*); ScotJT 47 (1994) 414-6 (B. D. *Spinks*); TLond 97 (1994) 135s (R. J. *Halliburton*: fine).

4607* **Mazzarollo** Isidoro,   A Eucaristia como memorial da Nova Aliança, continuidade e rupturas (Lc 22,14-20).   Porto Alegre 1994, Edições Est. 152 p.; bibliografia: p. 147-152.

4608 **Messner** Reinhard,   Die Messreform M. LUTHERs und die Eucharistie der Alten Kirche; ein Beitrag zu einer systematischen Liturgiewissenschaft [Rahner-Preis 1989]: InTSt 25. Innsbruck 1989, Tyrolia, 240 p. DM 52. – ᴿTR 90 (1994) 67-69 (H.-C. *Schmidt-Lauber*).

4609 **Moloney** Francis J., A broken body for a broken people 1990 ⟶ 7,4141; 8,4988:   ᴿCritRR 6 (1993) 269-71 (D. E. *Smith*).

4610 **Moloney** Raymond,   The Eucharist: Problems in Theology. L 1994, G. Chapman. 224 p. £13.   0-225-66758-4. – ᴿExpTim 106 (1994s) 315s (C. *Irvine*).

4611 **Power** David N.,   The Eucharistic mystery; revitalizing the tradition 1992 ⟶ 8,4996; 9,4829:   ᴿHeythJ 35 (1994) 209s (R. *Moloney*); Horizons 21 (1994) 201s (G. *Macy*); JTS 45 (1994) 441-3 (K. *Stevenson*); LvSt 19 (1994) 79-81 (Susan K. *Roll*); Mid-Stream 33 (1994) 487-9 (P. H. *Jones*: brilliant insights but perhaps too limitedly RC); Pacifica 7 (1994) 104s (G. *O'Collins*); TLZ 119 (1994) 59s (Karen W. *Tucker*); TLond 97 (1994) 57s (C. *Cocksworth*); TorJT 10 (1994) 153s (D. *Donovan*); Worship 65 (1994) 77-80 (G. W. *Lathrop*).

4612 **Rehm** J., Das Abendmahl. Gü 1993, Kaiser. 349 p. DM 68 pa. 3-579-00230-9 [TLZ 120,834, R. *Hempelmann*].
4613 **Rempel** John D., The Lord's Supper in Anabaptism [< diss. Toronto] 1993. – ᴿArchivScSocR 39,86 (1994) 304s (J. *Séguy*).
4614 *Ryken* Philip G., The sweetness of the cup; Isa. 51:17-23; Mt 26:26-30.35-46: Kerux 9,3 (Escondido 1994) 11-19.
4615 *Sattler* Dorothea, Das Opfer Jesu Christi im eucharistischen Gedächtnis; Bemühungen um einen evangelisch-katholischen Konsens: BiKi 49 (1994) 150-5.
4616 **Slenczka** Nötger, Realpräsenz und Ontologie; Untersuchung der ontologischen Grundlagen der Transsignifikationslehre: FSystÖk 66. Gö 1993, VR. ⮕ 9,4832; 602 p.; DM 148; 3-525-56273-X: ᴿTRu 59 (1994) 449-455 (R. *Schaeffler*); TvT 34 (1994) 207s (G. M. *Lukken*, also on FITZPATRICK P.).
4617 *a*) *Smith* Ralph F., Eucharistic faith and practice; – *b*) *Theiss* Norman, The passover feast of the New Covenant; – *c*) *Lampe* Peter, The Eucharist; identifying with Christ on the Cross; – *d*) *Holper* J. Fredrick, 'As often as you eat this bread and drink the cup'; – *e*) *Burkhart* John E., Reshaping table blessings (Rev. 7:12): Interpretation 48,1 (1994) 5-16 / 17-35 / 36-49 / 61-73 / 50-60.
4618 **Sokolowski** R., Eucharistic presence; a study in the theology of disclosure. Wsh 1994, Catholic University. viii-247 p. $25. 0-8132-0788-7 [JTS 46,811-3, K. *Stevenson*].
4619 **Stevenson** Kenneth, Covenant of grace renewed; a vision of the Eucharist in the seventeenth century. L 1994, Darton-LT. xx-208 p. £13. 0-232-52061-5. – ᴿTBR 7,3 (1994s) 42 (B. R. *White*).
4620 **Stookey** Laurence H., Eucharist; Christ's feast with the Church 1993 ⮕ 9,4834: ᴿPrincSemB 15 (1994) 92s (D. *Macleod*); SewaneeTR 38 (1994s) 75s (J. N. *Alexander*).
4621 **Thönissen** Wolfgang, Gemeinschaft durch Teilhabe an Christus; eine Studie zum Verhältnis von Eucharistie und Kirchengemeinschaft im Lichte der Ekklesiologie des Zweiten Vatikanischen Konzils: kath. Hab.-Diss. ᴰ*Walter*. Freiburg/B 1994. – TR 91,90.
4622 **Tilliette** Xavier, La Settimana Santa dei filosofi, ᵀ*Sansonetti* Giuliano 1992 ⮕ 9,4838: ᴿAnStoEseg 10 (1993) 635s (G. *Coccolini*).
4623 *Vanhoye* A., O sangue da aliança no Novo Testamento: Cultura y Fe 58 (Porto Alegre 1992) 23-39 [< Stromata 50,278].
4624 *Velasco Pérez* José A., El concepto de memorial objetivo en el decreto tridentino sobre el sacrificio de la Misa: RET 54 (1994) 5-48.
4625 *Whallon* William, The *pascha* in the Eucharist: NTS 40 (1994) 126-132.
4626 *Zirkel* Patricia M., The ninth-century Eucharistic controversy; a context for the beginnings of Eucharistic doctrine in the west: Worship 68 (1994) 2-23.

F5.3 **Mt 26,30 ...** ‖ *Passio Christi;* **Passion-narrative.**

4627 *Aichele* George, Fantasy and myth in the death of Jesus [... Mark]: CCurr 44 (1994s) 85-96.
4628 *Aligan* Rodel, The biblical and folkloric elements of the first Tagalog Pasyon: PhilipSac 27 (1992) 341-394.
4629 *Allison* Dale C.ᴶ, Anticipating the Passion; the literary reach of Matthew 26:47 - 27:56: CBQ 56 (1994) 701-714.

4630 **Beardslee** William A., *al.*, Biblical preaching on the death of Jesus 1989
➤ 5,4752; 6,5048:   RAmJTP 14 (1993) 67-69 (D. E. *Corner*).

4631 **Benoit** Pierre,   Passione e risurrezione del Signore.   T 1993, Gribaudi.
492 p. Lᵐ 38. – RCiVit 48 (1993) 388s (Duccia *Camiciotti*).

4632 **Bösen** Willibald, Der letzte Tag des Jesus von Nazareth; was wirklich
geschah.   FrB 1994, Herder,   410 p.   DM 48 [TR 91,22, D. *Dormeyer*].

4633 *Braulik* Georg,   [Lk 24,35] Pilgermeditationen zu den drei österlichen
Tagen [Ös. Rundfunk 1992]: Entschluss 49,3 (1994) 32-36.

4634 **Brown** R. E., The death of the Messiah, from Gethsemane to the grave; a
commentary on the Passion narratives of the four Gospels: AnchorBible
Reference. NY 1994, Doubleday. 1595 p. (2 vol.) $75 [Gregorianum 76,
388, G. *O'Collins*). – RAmerica 170,6 (1994) 19s (Pheme *Perkins*); ChrCent
111 (1994)) 900-904 (D. *Senior*, noting Newsweek cover-story on Brown;
also articles in Time and NY Times); ChrTod 38,11 (1994) 34.37 (D.
Bock: a treasure); Churchman 108 (1994) 370-2 (R. S. *Ascough*); Commonweal 121,10 (1994) 25-27 (L. T. *Johnson*); NYTimes Book Review
(April 3, 1994) 11 (L. *Houlden*) [< NTAbs 38, p. 355]; PrPeo 8 (1994)
443s (H. *Wansbrough*, also on his Birth); TLond 97 (1994) 383s (L.
Houlden: splendid without reserve); TS 55 (1994) 739-741 (F. J. *Matera*);
UnSemQ 48,1 (1994) 187-190 (R. *Scroggs*).

4635 *Collins* Adela Y.,   From noble death to crucified Messiah: NTS 40
(1994) 481-503.

4636 *Enuwosa* J.,   ⊕ *Hē phúsē*... The nature of the death of Jesus in Lucan
soteriology: DeltVM 22,2 (1993) 49-65 [< NTAbs 39, p. 224].

4637 **Garland** David E.,   One hundred years of study on the Passion
narratives: BapBibliog 3, 1989 ➤ 6,5051... 9,4844:   RRExp 91 (1994) 110s
(J. T. *Carroll*).

4638 **Grayston** Kenneth, Dying we live... death of Christ 1990 ➤ 6,5053...
8,5012:   RChrSchR 23 (1993s) 220s (F. W. *Schmidt*); CritRR 6 (1993)
245-7 (R. B. *Hayes*).

4639 **Maggioni** Bruno, I racconti evangelici della Passione: Commenti e studi
biblici.   Assisi 1994, Cittadella.   329 p. Lᵐ 35.   88-308-0543-2 [Grego-
rianum 76,387, G. *Marconi*].

4640 *a)* **Manicardi** Ermenegildo,   Esperienza e silenzio di Dio nella morte di
Gesù secondo Marco; – *b)* *La Potterie* Ignace de, L'uso di 'rimanere in'
nella mistica giovannea; – *c)* *Zevini* Giorgio,   L'esperienza di Dio nel
prologo della I Lettera di Giovanni: ParSpV 30 (1994) 105-119 / 121-136
/ 195-214.

4641 **Messori** Vittorio,   Patì sotto Ponzio Pilato?   T 1992, SEI.   368 p.
Lᵐ 25. – RCiVit 48 (1993) 189 (F. *Pecci*: il solito successo).

4642 **Meynet** Roland,   Passion de N.-S. J.-C. selon les évangiles synoptiques:
Lire la Bible 1993 ➤ 9,4849:   REsprVie 104 (1994) 366-8 (É. *Cothenet*);
QVidCr 170 (1994) 134 (D. *Roure*); RBibArg 56 (1994) 186 (V. M.
Fernández); SR 23 (1994) 518 (J.-P. *Michaud*: questions après le texte
évangélique très intéressantes; autrement hâtif).

4643 **Moore** James F.,   Christian theology after the shoah; a reinterpretation
of the Passion narratives. Lanham MD 1993, UPA. xiii-189 p. $44.50
[RelStR 21,39, B. *Harvey*: unfavoring].

4644 **Myllykoski** Matti,   Die letzten Tage Jesu; Markus, Johannes, ihre
Traditionen und die historische Frage [I, 1991 ➤ 7,4197... 9,4850] II.:
Annales B-272. Helsinki 1994, Acad. Scientiarum.   232 p.   951-41-
0730-6 [TLZ 120,150, W. *Vogler*]. – RETL 70 (1994) 176s (F. *Neirynck*) &
467-471 (J. *Verheyden*).

4645 *a*) *Neirynck* F., Gospel issues in the Passion narratives; critical note on [BROWN R. E. 1994]; – *b*) *Senior* Donald, Revisiting Matthew's special material in the Passion narrative: ETL 70 (1994) 406-416 / 417-424.

4646 *Novo-Cid Fuentes* Alfonso, La Pasión de Cristo en los escritos de AMBROSIO de Milán: Compostellanum 39 (1994) 25-104.

4647 *Ory* Georges, Le mystère de la crucifixion de Jésus: CahRenan 185 (1994) 5-21.

4648 *Potin* Jacques, *al.*, La Passion: MondeB 87 (1994) 1-14 (-40); ill.

4649 **Reinhold** Wolfgang, Der älteste Bericht über den Tod Jesu; literarische Analyse und historische Kritik der Passionsdarstellungen der Evangelien [Diss. Gö 1993 ➤ 9,4861]: BZNW 69. B 1994, de Gruyter. xii-357 p. DM 168. 3-11-014198-1. – ᴿExpTim 106 (1994s) 270 (E. *Best*).

4650 *Richard* Lucien, The many deaths of Jesus: Way 33 (1993) 289-303.

4651 **Senior** Donald, La passione di Gesù. Mi 1993, Àncora. 182 p. Lᵐ 21. – ᴿCiVit 48 (1993) 471 (Duccia *Camiciotti*).

4652 *Farmer* Craig S., [Mt 26,51 & all 3 ‖] Wolfgang MUSCULUS [1497-1563] and the allegory of Malchus's ear: WestTJ 56 (1994) 285-301.

4653 **Anderson** Ray S., The Gospel according to Judas. Colorado Springs 1991, Helmers & H. ix-166 p. – ᴿJEvTS 37 (1994) 623s (G. L. *Nebeker*).

4654 *Berkley* Timothy W., [Mt 27,3-10; Acts 1:15-20] OT exegesis and the death of Judas: ProcGM 14 (1994) 29-45.

4655 — [sans auteur]: Spécial, lecture midrashique; Le comportement de Judas (Matthieu 27/3-10 lu à la lumière de Genese 37/17b-28, la livraison de Joseph; 2 Samuel 17/23, le suicide d'Ahitophel: Lire et dire, études exégétiques en vue de la prédication 21 (1994) [ÉTRel 69/3 couv.].

4656 *Luke* K., [Mt 26,15] The thirty pieces of silver: IndTSt 31 (1994) 156-8 [< NTAbs 39, p. 217; as in Sumerian, a trifling sum, sign of contempt].

4657 **Maccoby** Hyam, Judas Iscariot and the myth of Jewish evil 1992 ➤ 8,5021; 9,4852: ᴿBR 10,1 (1994) 14s (N. *Elliott*).

4658 ᴱ**Niemann** Raul, Judas, wer bist du? 1991 ➤ 7,4210: ᴿTGL 84 (1994) 114s (B. *Dieckmann*).

4659 *Nortjé* L., Matthew's motive for the composition of the story of Judas's suicide in Mt 27:3-10: Neotestamentica 28 (1994) 41-51.

4660 **Paillard** Jean, Broder Judas; om en märklig upprätelse av Iskariot c. 1994 [RSPT 79,549-552, J.-P. *Jossua*].

4661 **Pazzi** R., Évangile de Judas [ital.] ᵀ*Orcel* Michel. P 1992, Grasset. – ᴿFoiTemps 23 (1993) 354-8 (J.-F. *Grégoire*).

4662 **Hernon** Robert W.ᴶ, Mark's account of Peter's denial < diss. Rice ᴰ*Nelson* D., 1991: ᴿCritRR 6 (1993) 255s (C. A. *Evans*).

4663 *Dautzenberg* Gerhard, Der Prozess Jesu und seine Hintergründe; Eigenart des Konfliktes und Beurteilung: BiKi 48 (1993) 147-153.

4664 *Goudote* Benoît, Ponce Pilate procurator provinciae Judaeae: Apollinaris 59 (1986) 335-368; 66 (1993) 613-652; 67 (1994) 207-318.

4665 *Koester* Helmut, Jesus before Pilate: BR 10,1 (1994) 16.62s.

4666 **Légasse** Simon, Le procès de Jésus; l'histoire: LDiv 156. P 1994, Cerf. 196 p. F 125 pa. [NTAbs 38, p. 462; TR 91,474, R. *Pesch*]. 2-204-04944-1. – ᴿEsprVie 104 (1994) 362-4 (É. *Cothenet*); ETL 70 (1994) 458s (F. *Neirynck*); SuppVSp 148 (1994) 666 (H. *Cousin*).

4667 *Potin* P., Jérusalem, hauts lieux de la Passion; le Prétoire et le Golgotha: MondeB 87 (apr. 1994) > EsprVie 104 (1994) 647-9 (J. *Daoust*).
4668 **Romano** Davide, Il processo di Gesù: Ricerche. Bari 1992, Palomar. – ᴿQuadStor 36 (1992) 187s (M. *Bretone*: Talmud preso da COHEN-ᵀTOAFF A. 1935).
4669 **Stimpfle** Alois, Pontius Pilatus, Geschichte und Historie; ein Beitrag zur Auslegungsgeschichte als rezeptionorientierter Wirkungsgeschichte: kath. Hab.-Diss. ᴰ*Leroy* H. Augsburg 1994. – TR 91,89.
4670 **Shemesh** Aharon, ❻ The punishment of flagellation in the Tannaitic sources: diss. Bar-Ilan. Ramat-Gan 1994. 320 p. – RTLv 26,535.

4671 *Gourgues* Michel, 'Il entendit de son temple ma voix'; échos du 'cantique de David' (Ps 18 = 2 S 22) en Mt 27,50-51 et dans le NT: ➤ 30, ᶠCOUTURIER G., Maison 1994, 323-341.
4671* *Swart* G.J., Twee aardbevingen of een? Die assosiasie van literêre motiewe in die eksegese van Matteus 27:51-54 & 28:2-4]: HervTSt 49 (1993) 255-265 [< NTAbs 38, p. 194].
4672 *Knoch* O., [Mt 27,61] Die 'andere' Maria; eine von den 'Frauen um Jesus'; Bausteine 34,134 (Gersfeld 1994) 3-6 [< NTAbs 39, p. 364].

4673 **Barth** Gerhard, Der Tod Jesu 1992 ➤ 8,5046; 9,4862:   ᴿJBL 113 (1994) 721s (D. *Seeley*).
4674 **Green** Joel B., The death of Jesus; tradition and interpretation in the Passion narrative; WUNT 2/33, ᴰ1988 ➤ 4,4856 ... 7,4228:   ᴿRTLv 25 (1994) 373s (C. *Focant*).
4675 **Hooker** Morna D., Not ashamed of the Gospel; New Testament interpretations of the death of Christ: Didsbury Lectures.   Carlisle 1994, Paternoster.   143 p.   0-85364-543-4.
4676 **Pesch** Otto H., La muerte de Jesús nuestra vida: Pedal 216, 1992 ➤ 9,4860:   ᴿEfMex 11 (1993) 416s (J. *Martínez Z.*).
4677 **Sabbe** M., The Johannine account of the death of Jesus and its Synoptic parallels (Jn 19,16b-42).
4678 *Sandnes* K.O., The death of Jesus for human sins; the historical basis for a theological concept: Themelios 20,1 (1994) 20-23 [< NTAbs 39, p. 209].
4679 **Sepière** Marie-Christine, L'image d'un Dieu souffrant (IXe-Xe siècle); aux origines du crucifix: Histoire.   P 1994, Cerf.   280 p.; bibliog. 235-264. 2-204-04606-X.

Derrett J.D.M., [Mt 27,63s] Jesus as a seducer (*planos* = *mat'eh*) ➤ 3941.
4681 *Ancona* Giovanni, La 'discesa agli inferi' di Gesù Cristo; note patristiche: RivScR 8 (1994) 295-311.
4682 *Gesché* Adolphe, L'agonie de la Résurrection ou la Descente aux Enfers: RTLv 25 (1994) 5-29.

F5.6   Mt 28 ‖ :   Resurrectio.

4683 **Aejmelaeus** Lars, Jeesuksen Ylösnousemus ... (p. 355:) Die Auferstehung Jesu II. Synopt., Apg.: Suomen Eks 59.   Helsinki 1994, Finnish Exeg. Soc. [viii-] 355 p. 951-9217-14-2.
4683* ᴱ**Avis** Paul, (+ 9 Anglicans), The resurrection of Jesus Christ 1993 ➤ 9,4871: ᴿScripTPamp 26 (1994) 866s (L.F. *Mateo-Seco*); TLond 97 (1994) 462s (G. *O'Collins*: also on S. DAVIS, 'best in years' and SPONG

'errors and overkill'; it is a pity that Avis's contributors did not see or react to each other).

4684 **Brown** Raymond E., I racconti evangelici della Risurrezione. Brescia 1991, Queriniana. 145 p. L^m 15. – ^RCC 145 (1993) 202s (D. *Scaiola*).

4685 **Dalferth** Ingolf U., Der auferweckte Gekreuzigte; zur Grammatik der Christologie. Tü 1994, Mohr. ix-346 p. DM 68. 3-16-46296-3 [JTS 46, 799, G. M. *Newlands*].

4686 **Daniel** Elinor P., A rhetorical analysis of the Resurrection appearance narratives in the Christian Gospels: diss. Georgia, ^DPullman G. 1994. 125 p. 95-03500. – DissA 55 (1994s) p. 2067.

4687 **Davis** Stephen, Risen indeed; making sense of the Resurrection. GR/ L 1993, Eerdmans/SPCK. 220 p. $17. – ^RExpTim 106 (1994s) 24 (B. *Bostock*: warmly but unsuitably defends orthodoxy); RefTR 53 (1994) 90s (M. *Hill*).

4688 **Durrwell** F. X., La Risurrezione di Gesù, mistero di salvezza 1993 → 9,4879: ^RRelCu 40 (1994) 877s (R. de la *Torre*).

4689 **Essen** Georg, Historische Vernunft und Auferweckung Jesu; erkenntnistheoretische und methodologische Analysen zur theologischen Verantwortung des Osterglaubens: kath. Diss. ^DStobbe H. Münster 1994. – TR 91,100.

4690 **Hennigan** Thomas J., The Pasch in the ancient Church: diss. Angelicum, ^DFilippi Nella. Roma 1994. Extr. 95 p. – RTLv 26,537.

4691 *Hilhorst* A., Le texte sur la Résurrection de Jésus dans le ms. *k* de la 'vetus Latina' (Mc 16,3): → 131, Mem. VERBRAKEN P., RBén 104 (1994) 257-9.

4692 **Kessler** H., La resurrección de Jesús 1989 → 5,4824... 8,4883: ^RCiuD 206 (1993) 635s (J. *Gutiérrez*).

4693 *Kremer* Job [*al.*], Auferstehung Christi (NT): → 510, LTK³ 1 (1993) 1177-82 [-91].

4694 **Lolla** John J., The role of the Resurrection in creating Christian identity: diss. Princeton Theol. Sem. 1994. 166 p. 94-26124. – DissA 55 (1994s) p. 1601.

4695 **Lüdemann** G., Die Auferstehung Jesu; Historie, Erfahrung, Theologie. Gö 1994, VR. 227 p. DM 58. 3-525-53523-6 [RB 102,624-6, J. *Taylor*; TLZ 119,804-9, E. *Schweizer*]. – ^REvT 54 (1994) 476-482 (U. *Luz*: Aufregung); ExpTim 106 (1994s) 27s (E. *Best*); TR 90 (1994) 480-5 (G. *Essen*, gegen kritiklos 'Infotainment' in den Medien).

4696 — *Kremers* Helmut, Wo Beweise versagen; Überlegungen anlässlich des Auferstehungsbuches von Gerd LÜDEMANN: LuMon 33,5 (1994) 31-33.

4697 **Lüdemann** Gerd, The Resurrection of Jesus; history, experience, theology. L/Mp 1994, SCM/Fortress. viii-263 p. 0-334-02560-5 [NTAbs 39, p. 325].

4698 *McIntosh* Mark A., The Eastering of Jesus; resurrection and the witness of Christian spirituality: DowR 112 (1994) 44-61.

4699 **Marxsen** Willi, Il terzo giorno risuscitò; la risurrezione di Gesù un fatto storico? [conferenza 1988], 1993 → 9,4884: ^RScuolC 122 (1994) 500s (G. *Giavini*).

4700 **O'Collins** Gerald G., The resurrection of Jesus Christ; some contemporary issues [1993 Marquette Lecture]. Milwaukee 1993, Marquette Univ. v-50 p. $10. 0-87462-548-3 [NTAbs 39, p. 326].

4701 *Pannenberg* Wolfhart, Die Auferstehung Jesu — Historie und Theologie: ZTK 91 (1994) 318-328.

4702 **Peterson** Wendy L.,   The nature of the resurrected body; an analysis of a modern controversy: diss. *DSmith* D.   Providence (Canada) College, 1994. 125 p. MM 89169. – (DissA-disk) MAI 33 (1994s) p. 60 (no abstract).
4703 *Perkins* Pheme, The Resurrection of Jesus ➤ 239*b*, Studying 1994, 423-442 [*al.* parables, miracles, death ...].
4704 **Quenot** Michel, La résurrection et l'icône. P 1992, Mame. 314 p. – RNVFr 69 (1994) 160.
4705 **Sabugal** Santos, Anástasis; resucitó y resucitaremos: BAC 536. M 1993, BAC. 712 p. – RBiFe 20 (1994) 154s (A. *Salas*); Carthaginensia 10 (1994) 470s (F. *Martínez Fresneda*); CiTom 121 (1994) 415s (J. L. *Espinel*); CiuD 207 (1994) 528s (J. M. *Ozaeta*); EstAg 29 (1994) 577-9 (C. *Mielgo*); LumenVr 43 (1994) 283s (F. *Ortiz de Urtaran*); RThom 94 (1994) 695 (H. *Ponsot*); ScripTPamp 26 (1994) 1255-7 (L. F. *Mateo-Seco*).
4706 *Sabugal* Santos, La mateana tradición histórica sobre las apariciones del resucitado (Mt. 28,9-10.16-20), análisis historico-tradicional: EstAg 29 (1994) 217-242.
4707 **Spong** J. S., Resurrection, myth or reality? L 1994, HarperCollins. xix-320 p. £9. 0-0606-7547-0 [NTAbs 38, p. 467]. – RDocLife 44 (1944) 442s (P. *Rogers*); ExpTim 106 (1994s) 24 (G. *Bostock*: glaring weaknesses, but this much is valid: Christ must be the source of a resurrection that lies within us); Tablet 248 (1994) 529s (G. *O'Collins*).
4708 — *Barnett* Paul, The Apostle Paul, the bishop [J. Spong] of Newark, and the resurrection of Jesus: Crux 30,3 (1994) 2-11 [30,1 (1994) 45-47, review of Spong by G. M. *Porter*].
4709 *Thiel* John E., Resurrected life and God's biblical promise: Month 255 (1994) 4-11.
4710 *Welker* Michael, Resurrection and the reign of God: ➤ 326, PrincSemB supp. 3 (1994) 3-16.
4711 *Winger* J. Michael, When did the women visit the tomb? Sources for some temporal clauses in the Synoptic Gospels: NTS 40 (1994) 284-8.
4712 *Gwynne* Paul, Theological issues behind the empty tomb debate: AustralasCR 71 (1994) 45-60.

4713 *Hong Sungchul* John, [Mt 28,18-20] On the great commission: EvJ 12 (1994) 67-74.
4713* *Soares-Prabhu* George M., Two mission commands; an interpretation of Matthew 28:16-20 in the light of a Buddhist text: BInterp 2 (1994) 264-282 [comments on the Asian essays of this fascicle by *Clooney* Francis X. 367-70, *Segovia* Fernando F. 371-3, *Sakenfeld* Katharine D., 363-370; *Ringe* Sharon H. 374-6].

F6.1   **Evangelium Marci** – *Textus, commentarii.*

4714 *Aranda Pérez* Gonzalo, El evangelio de san Marcos en copto sahídico 1988 ➤ 4,4954... 6,5145: REnchoria 21 (1994) 153-5 (H.-M. *Schenke*).
4715 *Cahill* Michael, The identification of the first Markan commentary [Pseudo-Jerome PL 30,589-644: before 650 (5th cent. VICTOR of Antioch in only a catena)]: RB 101 (1994) 258-268; franç. 258.
4716 **Cole** R. Alan, The Gospel according to Mark; an introduction and commentary²rev [¹1961] 1989 ➤ 5,4856... 8,5991: RJEvTS 37 (1994) 430s (G. L. *Cockerill*: revision thorough and contemporary).
4717 **Cook** Guillermo, *Foulkes* Richard, Marcos: ComHispAm. Miami 1993, Caraibe. 407 p. – RJHisp 2,3 (1994s) 74s (S. K. *Sherwood*).

4718 **Drewermann** E., Il vangelo di Marco; immagini di redenzione [1987s
➤ 4,4956 ... 9,4903], ᵀ*Laldi* Annapaola. Brescia 1994, Queriniana. 585 p.
Lᵐ 70. 88-399-0378-X [Gregorianum 76,598, G. *Marconi*].

4719 **English** Donald, The message of Mark 1992 ➤ 8,5093: ᴱEvQ 66 (1994)
257-9 (D. J. *Thomas*).

4720 **Festugière** A. J. †, La Bonne Nouvelle de Jésus-Christ selon Marc 1992
➤ 8,5095: NRT 116 (1994) 112 (Y. *Simoens*).

4721 **González Ruiz** J. M., El evangelio según Marcos 1988 ➤ 5,4862:
ᴿCiuD 207 (1994) 197s (J. *Gutiérrez*).

4722 **Gundry** Robert H., Mark, a commentary on his apology for the Cross
1993 ➤ 8,5144; 9,4908 [Biblica 76,107-115, R. *Pesch*]: ᴿAntonianum 69
(1994) 547-580 (M. *Nobile*); BtS 151 (1994) 123 (T. C. *Constable*);
ChrSchR 24 (1994) 87-89 (C. A. *Evans*); ExpTim 106 (1994s) 122s (C. S.
Rodd: not in a series; strikes out at many current enthusiasms); JBL 113
(1994) 722-4 (Adela Y. *Collins*); JTS 45 (1994) 648-654 (J. *Marcus*).

4723 **Heil** John P., The gospel of Mark as model for action; a reader-response
commentary 1992 ➤ 8,5098: ᴿCBQ 56 (1994) 138-140 (F. J. *Matera*);
Interpretation 48 (1994) 414.6.8 (R. C. *Tannehill*, also briefly on HOOKER).

4724 **Hooker** Morna D., The Gospel according to St. Mark: Black's NT
Comm. 1991 ➤ 7,4268 ... 9,4910: ᴿIrBSt 15 (1993) 39-42 (V. *Parkin*);
JBL 113 (1994) 146-8 (A. Y. *Collins*); JTS 45 (1994) 216-9 (L. E. *Keck*);
RBíbArg 55 (1993) 186s (A. J. *Levoratti*); RefTR 53 (1994) 42s (M.
Thompson); ScotJT 47 (1994) 103-5 (E. *Best*); Vidyajyoti 58 (1994) 402s
(P. *Meagher*, also on Adela *Collins*).

4725 **Humphrey** H. M., 'He is risen' ... Mk 1992 ➤ 8,5790: ᴿRivB 42 (1994)
226s (M. *Làconi*).

4726 **Iersel** Bas van, Mk Komm. Dü 1993, Patmos. – ᴿZkT 116 (1994) 213
(M. *Hasitschka*).

4727 **Kertelge** K., Markusevangelium: NEchter NT (ᵀEinheit 2). Wü 1994,
Echter. 167 p. ᴅᴍ 34. 3-429-01550-2 [NTAbs 39, p. 139]. – ᴿBiKi 49
(1994) 168s (K. *Scholtissek*).

4728 **Luz** Ulrich, El Evangelio según San Marco I (1-7): BtEstB 74. S 1993,
Sígueme. 589 p. 84-301-1213-8. – ᴿCarthaginensia 10 (1994) 454s (R.
Sanz Valdivieso); RET 53 (1993) 493-7 (P. *Barrado Fernández*).

4729 **Mateos** J., *Camacho* F., El evangelio de Marcos, texto y comentario
[not = their awaited Marcos, análisis lingüístico y comentario exegéti-
co]. Córdoba 1994, Almendro. 285 p. 84-8005-018-7 [NTAbs 39,
p. 326]. – ᴿBibFe 29,58 (1994) 151 (A. *Salas*); V. *Fusco*].
Carthaginensia 10 (1994) 453s (J. J. *Tamayo-Acosta*).

4730 **Minette de Tillesse** C., Evangelho segundo Marcos: RevBBras 9, num.
espec. Fortaleza 1992. 240 p. – ᴿRivB 42 (1994) 492 (V. *Fusco*: da tra-
durre in italiano).

4731 **Pilgaard** Aage, Kommentar til Markusevangeliet. Aarhus 1988, Univ.
304 p. – ᴿSvTKv 69 (1993) 192 (H. *Ulfgard*).

4732 **Van Linden** P., El Evangelio de San Marcos, ᵀ*Icaza* R. M.: ComB 2.
ColMn 1994, Liturgical. 95 p. $4 pa. 0-8146-1761-1 [NTAbs 39, p. 329
(33, p. 375)].

Zuurmond R., NT aeth. Syn Mk; Äthiopist. Forschungen 27, 1989 ➤ 1477.

F6.2 *Evangelium Marci,* **Themata.**

4734 ᴱ**Anderson** Janice C., *Moore* S. D., Mark and method 1992 ➤ 8,336;
9,4918: ᴿTLond 97 (1994) 52s (Bridget *Upton*).

4735 *Bartolomé* Juan J.,   Marcos, un evangelio como manual de educación en la fe: RET 54 (1991) 49-62.

4736 **Barton** Stephen C.,   Discipleship and other ties in Mark and Matthew [diss. London 1991]: SNTS mg 80. C 1994, Univ.   261 p. $30.   0-521-4650-3. – ᴿExpTim 106 (1994s) 144s (C. S. *Rodd*: above-thesis quality, also informing well about Jesus' teaching on the family); TBR 7,3 (1994s) 17 (J. *Beer*).

4737 **Biguzzi** Giancarlo,   'Yo destruiré este templo'... Mc, 1992 ➤ 8,5120: ᴿBiblica 75 (1994) 266-270 (R. F. *O'Toole*); CiuD 206 (1993) 229 (J. *Gutiérrez*); Salesianum 56 (1994) 148s (J. J. *Bartolomé*); ScripTPamp 26 (1994) 1218s (F. *Varo*).

4738 **Black** C. Clifton, Mark; images of an apostolic interpreter. 1994, Univ. S. Carolina.   xxii-327 p. $40.   0-87249-973-1 [RelStR 21,144, G. *Eichele*; TLZ 120,436, D. *Lührmann*; TS 56,396, J. R. *Donahue*]. – ᴿETL 70 (1994) 459-461 (F. *Neirynck*); ExpTim 106 (1994s) 245 (D. *Catchpole*: the author, he or she, can scarcely have dreamed of such mind-blowing interpretations).

4739 *Blount* Brian K.,   Preaching the Kingdom; Mark's apocalyptic call for prophetic engagement: ➤ 326, Hope 1993/4, 33-56.

4740 **Boismard** M.-E.,   L'Évangile de Marc, sa préhistoire: ÉtBN 26.   P 1994, Lecoffre.   308 p.; bibliog. p. 283-300. F 195.   2-85021-075-7 [TR 91,361].

4741 **Broadhead** Edwin K.,   Teaching with authority; miracles and Christology in the Gospel of Mark: jNsu 74, 1992: ➤ 8,5325:   ᴿCBQ 56 (1994) 337s (D. *Rhoads*); EvQ 66 (1994) 76s (R. T. *France*); JBL 113 (1994) 148-151 (A. Y. *Collins*); JTS 45 (1994) 219-222 (J. *Marcus*).

4742 **Bryan** Christopher,   A preface to Mark; notes on the Gospel in its literary and cultural setting 1993 ➤ 9,4925:   ᴿClasJ 90 (1994s) 463s (Judith L. *Kovacs*); RExp 91 (1994) 617 (J. L. *Blevins*: dedicated to two pets, but not light reading).

4743 *Cahill* M.,   Is the first commentary on Mark an Irish work? Some new considerations: Peritia 8 (1994) 35-45 [< RHE 89,222*].

4744 **Camery-Hoggatt** Jerry, Irony/Mk 1992 ➤ 8,2129; 9,4026:   ᴿRExp 91 (1994) 266s (G. M. *Feagin*).

4745 **Chapman** Dean W.,   The orphan Gospel; Mark's perspective on Jesus: BibSem 16, 1993 ➤ 9,4928:   ᴿCBQ 56 (1994) 787-9 (J. T. *Carroll*); TBR 7,2 (1994s) 17 (R. *Morgan*: readable; some flaws).

4746 **Clark** Denny A.,   Reading the Markan miracle materials; the narrative functions of miracle stories and miracle references in the Gospel of Mark: diss. Iliff, Denver 1994. 607 p. 95-07878. – DissA 55 (1994s) p. 3542.

4747 **Collins** Adela Y.,   The beginning of the Gospel; probings of Mark in context 1992 ➤ 8,5131; 9,4929:   ᴿCBQ 56 (1994) 586s (Karen A. *Barta*); HeythJ 35 (1994) 442s (Bridget *Upton*); TorJT 10 (1994) 255s (Wendy *Cotter*).

4748 **Cuvillier** Élian,   Le concept de *parabolē* dans le second évangile; son arrière-plan littéraire, sa signification dans le cadre de la rédaction de Jésus: ÉtBN 19, 1993 ➤ 9,4676 [RB 102,255, P. *Garuti*]:   ᴿGregorianum 75 (1994) 584s (G. *Marconi*); JTS 45 (1994) 816 (Mary Ann *Beavis*); NRT 116 (1994) 906 (X. *Jacques*); Salmanticensis 41 (1994) 333-6 (R. *Trevijano*).

4749 **Dahm** Christof,   Israel im Markusevangelium: EurHS 23/420.   Fra 1991, Lang.   v-364 p.   DM 93. – ᴿTR 90 (1994) 291-3 (R. *Kampling*: dessen ähnliche Hab.-S. gleichzeitig erschien).

4750 **Davidsen** Ole,   The narrative Jesus; a semiotic reading of Mark's Gospel [diss. Aarhus 1993].   Aarhus 1993, Univ.   x-204 p.   87-7288-423-1. – ᴿBZ 38 (1994) 281-3 (D. *Dormeyer*); SvEx 59 (1994) 83-117 (D. *Hellholm*).

4751 **Delorme** Jean, Au risque de la parole [Mc...]: Parole de Dieu. P 1991, Seuil. – ᴿSémBib 73 (1994) 62s (Cécile *Turiot*).
4752 *Dennison* James T.ᴶ, The Gospel of Mark from beginning to end: Kerux 9,3 (Escondido 1994) 3-10.
4753 **Dunn** James D. G., Jesus, Paul and the Law ... Mk/Gal 1990 ➤ 7,4294; 9,4933: ᴿConcordTQ 58 (1994) 193-5 (G. *Lockwood*).
4754 *Edwards* James R., The authority of Jesus in the Gospel of Mark: JEvTS 37 (1994) 217-233.
4755 **Elkins** W., Learning to say Jesus; narrative, identity, and community; a study of hermeneutics of Josiah ROYCE, Hans FREI, George LINDBECK, Paul RICŒUR and the Gospel of Mark: diss. Drew, ᴰ*Ochs* P. Madison NJ 1993, – RTLv 26, p. 529.
4756 **Elliott** J. K. [*Turner* C. H. *al.*], The language and style of Mark: NT supp. 72, 1993 ➤ 9,4926 [JTS 45,659-662, E. J. *Pryke*]: ᴿSvEx 59 (1994) 177-9 (K. *Búason*); TLZ 119 (1994) 986 (P. *Pokorný*).
4757 **Fajardo Santos** Narry, The paradox of authority and servanthood in the Gospel of Mark: diss. Dallas Theol. Sem., ᴰ*Lowery* D. 1994. 405 p. 94-28962. – DissA 55 (1994s) p. 1593.
4758 **Fowler** Robert M., Let the reader... response Mk 1991 ➤ 7,4300; 9,4941: ᴿCritRR 6 (1993) 237-9 (Adela Y. *Collins*); ScotJT 47 (1994) 378s (Rosalind *Papaphilippopoulos*).
4759 *Futterlieb* H., Voran nach Galiläa; sozialgeschichtliche Lektüre nach dem Markus-Evangelium: Forum Religion (Stu 1994,4) 26-37 [< ZIT 95, p. 57].
4760 *Goulder* Michael, The pre-Marcan Gospel: ScotJT 47 (1994) 453-471.
4761 *Hamerton-Kelly* Robert G., The Gospel and the sacred; poetics of violence in Mark. Mp 1994, Fortress. xvi-175 p. $13. 0-8006-2669-9 [RelStR 20,239, T. *Dwyer*: procrustean]. – ᴿExpTim 106 (1994s) 245 (D. *Catchpole*: many fine insights but perhaps superimposes an alien scheme).
4762 *Harrington* Wilfrid J., Mark as story [with plot]: PrPeo 8 (1994) 243-7 (349-353, the Cross).
4763 **Hill** Richard M., The role of Peter in the Gospel of Mark; a study in authority in the Early Church: diss. Drew, ᴰ*Doughty* D. Madison NJ 1994. 224 p. 94-32950. – DissA 55 (1994s) p. 2002; RelStR 21,255.
4764 *Huber* Konrad, Jesus in Auseinandersetzung; exegetische Untersuchungen zu den sogenannten Jerusalemer Streitgesprächen des Markusevangeliums im Blick auf ihre christologischen Implikationen: Diss. ᴰ*Hasitschka* M. Innsbruck 1994. 302 p. > Echter. – RTLv 26,537; TR 91,97.
4765 *Iersel* Bas van, His master's voice; de impliciete verteller in Marcus; stem en literaire gestalte: TvT 34 (1994) 115-127; Eng. 127 [a second-generation Christian who had run away in the moment of trial, possibly for similar Christians in Rome who failed during Nero's persecution].
4766 *Iersel* B. M. F. van, Intertestamentaire meerstemmigheid in het Marcusjaar: Tijdschrift voor Liturgie 78,3 (Oudenaarde 1994) 130-145.
4767 *Jacobs* M. M., Mark's Jesus through the eyes of twentieth century NT scholars: Neotestamentica 28 (1994) 53-85 [63-69, as teacher].
4768 *Juel* Donald H., A master of surprise; Mark interpreted. Mp 1994, Fortress. viii-152 p. 0-8006-2594-3 [RelStR 21,235, R. M. *Fowler*].
4769 **Kampling** Rainer, Israel unter dem Anspruch des Messias; Studien zur Israelproblematik im Markusevangelium [< Hab.-Diss. Münster, ᴰ*Kertelge* K.]: SBB 25. Stu 1992, KBW. 259 p.; Bibliog. 229-259. DM 49. 3-460-00251-4. – ᴿBiKi 49 (1994) 167 (K. *Scholtissek*).

4770 **Kelber** Werner, Tradition orale et écriture [The oral and the written Gospel 1983] 1991 ➤ 7,1263; 8,1418: ᴿÉglT 25 (1994) 286s (L. *Laberge*).

Kinukawa Hisako, Women and Jesus in Mark 1994 ➤ 8738.

4771 **Lanpher** James E., The miraculous in Mark; its eschatological background and Christological function: diss. ᴰ*Collins* A. Notre Dame 1994. 359 p. 94-32872. – DissA 55 (1994s) p. 2003; RTLv 26, p. 537.

4772 **Lüdemann** Gerd, Texte und Träume; ein Gang durch das Markusevangelium in Auseinandersetzung mit Eugen DREWERMANN, 1992 ➤ 8,5133; 9,4952: ᴿAnStoEseg 11 (1994) 320 (G. *Coccolini*).

4773 *a*) *McVann* Mark, Reading Mark ritually; honor-shame and the ritual of baptism [response *LaHurd* Carol S.]; – *b*) *Gorman* Frank H.ᴶ, Ritual studies and biblical studies; assessment of the past, prospects for the future [*Pilch* John J., response; *Alexander* Bobby C., afterword]: Semeia 67 (1994) 178-198 [199-208] / 13-36 [37-42 / 209-225].

4774 **Marcus** Joel, The way of the Lord; Christological exegesis of the OT in the Gospel of Mark 1992 ➤ 8,5156; 9,4955: ᴿBiblica 75 (1994) 583-5 (V. *Fusco*); BL (1994) 146 (W. S. *Sproston*); CBQ 56 (1994) 378s (Adele Y. *Collins*); ExpTim 106 (1994s) 212 (Meg *Davies*: incoherent; neither 'high' as he aims, nor 'low'); Interpretation 48 (1994) 202,4 (W. *Shiner*); JRel 74 (1994) 554s (L. W. *Hurtado*); JStNT 54 (1994) 119 (T. R. *Hatina*); JTS 45 (1994) 222-5 (E. *Best*); PrincSemB 15 (1994) 73s (B. K. *Blount*); TrinJ 15 (1994) 135-8 (C. A. *Evans*).

4775 **Marshall** C. D., Faith as a theme in Mark's narrative: SNTU mg. pa. 1994 = c. 1989 ➤ 5,4920 ... 8,5158: $18; 0-521-47766-2 [NTAbs 39, p. 506].

4776 *Medley* Mark S., Emancipatory solidarity; the redemptive significance of Jesus in Mark: PerspRelSt 21 (1994) 5-22.

4777 **Miller** Dale & Patricia, Gospel of Mark as Midrash 1990 ➤ 6,5205 ... 8,5159: ᴿTR 90 (1994) 460 (K. *Scholtissek*: 'erfüllt in keiner Hinsicht wissenschaftliche Standards').

4778 *Miller* James, The literary structure of Mark; an interpretation based on 1 Corinthians 2:1-8: ExpTim 106 (1994s) 296-9.

4779 **Mills** Watson E., The Gospel of Mark: Bibliographies for biblical research 2. Lewiston NY 1994, Mellen. xxv-525 p. 0-7734-2349-4.

4780 **Moore** Steven D., MkLk ... Jesus begins to write 1992 ➤ 8,5164; 9,4960: ᴿInterpretation 48 (1994) 92s (J. D. *Kingsbury*: DERRIDA, LACAN, FOUCAULT; withering criticism for the 'dragon', modern exegesis); LitTOx 8 (1994) 218 (D. *Templeton*).

4781 **Myers** C., Who will roll away the stone? Discipleship queries for First World Christians. Mkn 1994, Orbis. xxxii-495 p. $32 pa. 0-88344-947-1 [NTAbs 39, p. 142, sequel to his 1988 Political reading of Mark].

4782 **Neirynck** F., *al.*, The Gospel of Mark; a cumulative bibliography 1950-1990: BtETL 102, 1992 ➤ 8,2168*; 9,4961: ᴿNeotestamentica 28 (1994) 256 (P. J. *Botha*); SvEx 59 (1994) 179-181 (L. *Hartman*).

4783 *O'Neill* J. C., [Mk 10,17-19] 'Good master' and the 'good' saying in the teaching of Jesus ['why me? none but God': taken by early Fathers to mean recognition that Jesus is God]: IrBSt 15 (1993) 167-178: our Gospels are the work of collectors, gems from varying backgrounds.

4784 **Oppel** Dagmar, Möglichkeiten synchroner Textbetrachtung zur Erschliessung der Narrativität markinischer Wundererzählungen: kath. Diss. ᴰ*Gnilka* J. München 1994. – TR 91,100.

4785 **Oyen** Geert van, De studie van de Marcusredactie in de twintigste eeuw [diss. Leuven 1993, ᴰ*Neirynck* F. – ETL 70,244] 1993 ➤ 9,4963: ᴿExpTim 106 (1994s) 186 (E. *Best*); LvSt 19 (1993) 262s (R. *Gilbert*).

4786 *Pikaza Ibarrondo* Xabier, Crisis de la familia y Trinidad en Marcos: Carthaginensia 10 (1994) 263-306 (-429, *al.*); Eng. before 235.
4787 **Reilly** John,   Praying Mark. L 1992, St. Paul. 183 p. $15. – ᴿAustralasCR 70 (1993) 391 (G. *Robinson*).
4788 **Reling** Hans-Otto,   The composition of tripolar pronouncement stories in the Gospel of Mark: diss. Andrews, ᴰ*Johnston* R. Berrien Springs ᴍɪ 1994. 291 p. – RTLv 26, p. 539.
4789 **Robbins** Vernon K.,   New boundaries in old territory; form and social rhetoric in Mark: Emory StEarlyC 3. NY 1994, Lang. xxii-270 p.; bibliog. 243-254. 0-8204-1911-7.
4790 **Schneck** Richard,   Isaiah in the Gospel of Mark I-VIII [< diss. Javeriana, Bogotá 1993]: Diss. Series 1. Vallejo ᴄᴀ 1994, BIBAL. vii-339 p. $20. 0-941037-28-2 [BL 95,103, C. J. A. *Hickling*; OTAbs 17, p. 688; NTAbs 39, p. 146].
4790* **Scholtissek** Klaus, Vollmacht im AT / Jesu (Mk) 1992s ⇒ 9,4974 / 8, 5179; 9,4973:   ᴿAntonianum 69 (1994) 384-7 (M. *Nobile*).
4791 **Schüling** Joachim,   Studien zum Verhältnis von Logionquelle und Markusevangelium [< Diss. Giessen 1987, ᴰ*Dautzenberg* G.]: ForBi 65, 1991 ⇒ 7,4333; 9,4075:   ᴿRB 101 (1994) 618s (B. T. *Viviano*).
4792 *Sellin* Gerhard,   Der Mythos nach Markus; warum Glaube und Theologie auf mythische Vorstellungen angewiesen sind: EvKomm 27 (1994) 715-7.
4793 *Shim* E. S. B.,   A suggestion about the genre or text-type of Mark: Scriptura 50 (1994) 69-89 [< NTAbs 39, p. 403].
4794 *Smit* J. A., Reading Mark as mythology 1; – 2. semiological: Scriptura 50 (1994) 41-54 / 55-67 [< NTAbs 39, p. 403].
4795 **Söding** Thomas,   Glaube bei Markus; Glaube an das Evangelium, Gebetsglaube und Wunderglaube im Kontext der markinischen Basileia-theologie und Christologie [Diss. Münster, ᴰ*Thüsing* W.]. Stu 1985, ²1987, KBW. 636 p. ᴅᴍ 49 ⇒ 3,4810 ...:   ᴿBiKi 49 (1994) 195s (K. *Scholtissek*, auch über ᴢᴡɪᴄᴋ R. 1989).
4796 *Sordi* Marta, Roma 42 ᴀ.ᴅ. Peter spoke, Mark wrote: 30 Days 7,5 (R 1994) 38-43 [< NTAbs 39, p. 33].
4797 *Staples* Peter, The cultural management of space and time in the narrative gospel of Mark: ForumFF 9,1s (1993) 19-45.
4798 **Vidović** Marinko,   Preghiera nel Vangelo di Marco; relazione con Dio e missione fra gli uomini: diss. Pont. Univ. Gregoriana, ᴰ*Stock* K. Roma 1994, 368 p.; extr. N° 4014, 116 p. – RTLv 26, p. 540.
4799 *Vogt* Theo, Angst und Identität im Markusevangelium: NOrb 36, 1993 ⇒ 9,4982:   ᴿTLZ 119 (1994) 662s (W. *Schenk*).
4800 **Warren** Michael D.,   An examination of the withdrawal motif in the Gospel of Mark: diss. Mid-America Baptist Theol. Sem. 1994. 219 p. 94-27486. – DissA 55 (1994s) p. 1594.
4801 *Welborn* Lawrence, The pursuit of concord; a political ideal in early Christianity: diss. Vanderbilt; ᴰ*Patte* D. Nv 1993. – RTLv 26, p. 540.
4802 **Williams** Joel F.,   Other followers of Jesus; minor characters as major figures in Mark's Gospel: jNsu 102. Shf 1994, Academic. 231 p. £37.50. 1-85075-489-6 [JTS 46,619, H. *Anderson*].
Young David M.,   Whoever has ears to hear; the discourses of Jesus in Mark as primary rhetoric of the Greco-Roman period: diss. Vanderbilt, ᴰ*Tolbert* M. 1993 ⇒ 4817.

F6.3 Evangelii Marci versiculi 1,1 ...

4803 **Maher** Rafael, [Mc 1,1] Il tempo è compiuto ... Armonie nella storia del piano di salvezza di Dio. Verona (S. Pietro in Cariano) 1994, Il Segno. 136 p.

4804 *Thom* J.C.,   Markus 1:4 in die Nuwe Afrikaanse Vertaling: HervTSt 49 (1993) 934-941 [< NTAbs 39, p. 34: influenced by dogma].
4805 *Kirchhevel* Gordon D.,   He that cometh in Mark 1:7 and Matt 24:30: BuBR 4 (1994) 105-111.
4806 *Gibson* Jeffrey B., [Mk 1,13] Jesus' wilderness temptation according to Mark: JStNT 53 (1994) 3-34.
4807 *a*) *Stefani* Piero, 'Stava con le fiere e gli angeli lo servivano' (Mc 1,13); – *b*) *Orselli* Alba Maria, 'Super leonem et draconem'; animali biblici tra imperatori cristiani e uomini santi: → 306, Animali 1993/4, 51-57 / 59-73.
4808 *Delorme* Jean,   L'Évangile structuré et contextualisé selon Marc 1,14-15 [< ᶠBOERS H. 1990]: SémBib 75 (1994) 37-52.
4810 **Douglass** James W., [Mk 2,1-12; 8,31; 14,53-72] The nonviolent coming of God 1991 → 7,8953 ... 9,7499: ᴿCritRR 6 (1993) 223-5 (R. F. *Wilson*: aims at impressions rather than logic, as in cover painting of Mother Intifada).
4811 *Hofius* Otfried,   Jesus Zuspruch der Sündenvergebung; exegetische Erwägungen zu Mk 2,5b: JbBT 9 (1994) 125-143.
4812 *Czajkowski* Michał, ❷ Le débat sur la communauté de la table; la structure kérygmatique Mk 2,13-17: AtKap 121 (1993) 302-325.
4813 *a*) *Parrott* Rod,   Conflict and rhetoric in Mark 2:23-28; – *b*) *Salyer* Gregory,   Rhetoric, purity, and play; aspects of Mark 7: 1-23; – *c*) *Blount* Brian K., A socio-rhetorical analysis of Simon of Cyrene, Mark 15:21 and its parallels: Semeia 64 (1993) 117-137 / 139-169 / 171-198.
4814 *Roure* Damià,   Jesús/David Mc 2,23: AnBibl 124, ᴰ1990 → 6,5238 ... 9,4999: ᴿCiuD 206 (1993) 227s (J. *Gutiérrez*); JBL 113 (1994) 144-6 (R. D. *Witherup*); RCatalT 18 (1993) 178s (A. *Puig i Tàrrech*); Teresianum 45 (1994) 313-5 (A. *Borrell*).
4815 *Parker* David, [Mk 3,17] The sons of thunder: → 45, ᶠGOULDER M., Crossing 1994, 141-7.
4816 **Yoonprayong** Amnuay,   Jesus and his mother according to Mk 3, 20.21.31-35: diss. Pont. Univ. Gregoriana Nº7210, ᴰ*Rasco* E. R 1993. – InfPUG 26,31 (1994) 33; RTLv 26, p. 540.
4817 **Young** David M., [Mk 3,20-35; 4,1-34 ...] Whoever has ears to hear; the discourses of Jesus in Mark as primary rhetoric of the Greco-Roman period: diss. Vanderbilt, ᴰ*Tolbert* Mary Ann. Nashiville 1994. 579 p. 94-31662. – DissA 55 (1994s) p. 2005; RelStR 21,251.
4818 *Syx* Raoul,   Gebruikte Marcus de Q-bron? Een onderzoek van de Beëlzebul-controverse (Mc 3,20-30 en par.): diss. ᴰ*Lambrecht* J. Leuven 1994. xlix-477p. – RTLv 26, p. 540; LvSt 17 (1992) 166-180.
4819 *Fuchs* A.,   Die Sünde wider den Heiligen Geist, Mk 3:28-30 par Mat 12:31-37 par Lk 12:10: SNTU 19 (1994) 113-130 [< NTAbs 39, p. 219].
4820 *Robbins* Vernon K., Interpreting miracle culture and parable culture in Mark 4-11: SvEx 59 (1994) 59-81.
4821 **Henaut** B.W.,   Oral tradition ... Mk 4: jNsu 82, 1993 → 9,5002: ᴿSalmanticensis 41 (1994) 330-2 (R. *Trevijano*).
4822 *Arida* R.M., [Mk 4,10-12] Hearing, receiving and entering *tò mystērion* / *tà mystēria*; patristic insights unveiling the crux interpretum (Isaiah 6:9-10) of the Sower parable: SVlad 38,2 (1994) 211-234 [< NTAbs 39, p. 35].
4823 **Rauscher** Johann,   Das Bildwort von der Öllampe in der synoptischen Tradition; eine Auslegung von Mk 4,21f par Lk 8,16f; Mt 5,15; Lk 11,33. Desselbrunn 1994. xii-416p. Sch 300.
4824 *Theissen* Gerd,   Der Bauer und die von selbst Frucht bringende Erde; naiver Synergismus in Mk 4,26-29? ᴢNW 85 (1994) 167-182.

4825 **Schmeller** Thomas, [Mk 5,1-20; 7,24-37; 8,21] Jesus im Umland Galiläas; zu den markinischen Berichten vom Aufenthalt Jesu in den Gebieten von Tyros, Caesarea Philippi und der Dekapolis: BZ 38 (1994) 44-66.

4826 *Wolmarans* J. L. P., Who asked Jesus to leave the territory of Gerasa (Mark 5:17) [owners of the destroyed animals, in accord with an existing code]: Neotestamentica 28 (1994) 87-92.

4827 *Castillo* O. C., El camino de la fe según Mc. 5,21-24a.35-43; un análisis pragmático-lingüístico: Voces 4 (Insurgentes Sur, Méx 1994) 133-153 [< NTAbs 39, p. 35].

4828 *Kinukawa* Hisako, The story of the hemorrhaging woman (Mark 5:25-34) read from a Japanese feminist context: BInterp 2 (1994) 283-293.

4829 *Clancy* Jennifer A., Unveiling masculinity; the construction of gender in Mark 6:17-29: BInterp 2 (1994) 34-50.

4830 *Schellong* Dieter, Eine Bibel — viele Zugänge; Überlegungen zum [sic] 'Zankapfel Bibel' [oder/und zur Arnoldshaimer Konferenz, 'Das Buch Gottes; elf Zugänge zur Bibel' (Neuk 1993) über Mk 6,30-44]: EvT 54 (1994) 536-544.

4831 *Mazzucco* Clementina, *a)* Il viaggio a Betsaida dei discepoli di Gesù (Mc 6,45-8,22): → 29, [F]CORSINI E., Voce 1994, 305-320; – *b)* 'E voleva oltrepassarli' (Mc 6,48): RivB 42 (1994) 311-327; Eng. 327.

4832 *Collins* Adela Y., [Mc 6,45] Rulers, divine men, and walking on the water (Mark 6:45-52); – *b)* *LaFarque* Michael, The authority of the excluded; Mark's challenge to a rational hermeneutic: → 40, [F]GEORGI D., Religious propaganda 1994, 207-227 / 229-256.

4833 **Baudoz** Jean-François, Les miettes de la table (Mc 7,24-30 et Mt 15,21-28), essai sur les diverses pratiques missionnaires judéo-chrétiennes: diss. Institut Catholique, [D]*Perrot* C. Paris 1993. 545 p. – RICathP 49,97; RTLv 26,535.

4834 *Rhoads* David, [Mk 7,25-30] Jesus and the Syrophoenician woman in Mark; a narrative-critical study: JAAR 62 (1994) 343-375.

4835 *Juel* D. H., [Mk 8-10] The way of the Cross; Markan texts for late Pentecost: WWorld 14,3 (1994) 352-359 [< NTAbs 39, p. 36].

4836 *Kellas* C., [Mk 8,1-4] The healing of the leper; the accounts in the Synoptic Gospels and Papyrus Egerton 2, Papyrus Köln 255: IrBSt 16 (1994) 161-173 [< NTAbs 39, p. 490].

4837 *Keegan* Terence J., [Mk 8,11] The parable of the sower and Mark's Jewish leaders: CBQ 56 (1994) 501-518.

4838 *Malina* Bruce J., 'Let him deny himself' (Mark 8:34); a social-psychological model of self-denial: BibTB 24 (1994) 106-121.

4839 *Wenham* David, *Moses* A. D. A., 'There are some standing here ...'; did they become the 'reputed pillars' of the Jerusalem church? Some reflections on Mark 9:1; Galatians 2:9 and the Transfiguration: NT 36 (1994) 146-163.

4840 *Witherington* Ben[III], Transfigured understanding; a critical note on Mark 9:2-13 as a parousia preview: AshlandTJ 24 (1992) 88-91 [< ZNW 85,159].

4841 *Blount* Brian K., [Mark 9:14-19] Stay close: PrincSemB 15 (1994) 173-183.

4842 **Runacher** Caroline, Croyants incrédules; la guérison de l'épileptique, Marc 9,14-29 [< diss.]: LDiv 157. P 1994, Cerf. 300 p. F 150. – [R]ETL 70 (1994) 461s (F. *Neirynck*); SR 23 (1994) 514 (J.-J. *Lavoie*).

4843 *Titrud* K., *a)* Mark 9:49 revisited; – *b)* *Larsen* L., The use of *gar*: NoTr 8,2 (1994) 30-32 / 33-39.

4844 *Eubanks* Larry L., Mark 10:13-16 [receiving the Kingdom of God as a child; expository]: RExp 91,3 (children-ministries 1994) 400-5.

4845 *La Verdiere* E., Marriage and divorce in the Gospel according to Mark (ch. 10,1-12): Way 34,1 (1994) 54-64 [< NTAbs 38, p. 366].

4846 *Meynet* Roland, Présupposés de l'analyse rhétorique, avec une application à Mc 10,13-52: → 239*d*, Exégèse 1994, 69-111.

4847 *Weir* Emmett, [Mk 11,12-21] Fruitless fig tree — futile worship: ExpTim 106 (1994s) 330.

4848 *La Verdiere* E., The cursing of the fig tree and the cleansing of the Temple, Mark 11:12-25: Emmanuel 99 (1993) 440-7 . 508s . 511-6.

4849 *Lukito* D. L., [11,15-19] The cleansing of the Temple; an analysis of the intention of Jesus: StulosTJ 1,1 (Bandung 1993) 31-41 [NTAbs 38, p. 367].

4850 **Mell** U., Die 'anderen' Winzer [vine-dressers]; eine exegetische Studie zur Vollmacht Jesu Christi nach Markus 11,27-12,34 [Hab.-Diss. Kiel]: WUNT 77. Tü 1994. xiii-438 p. DM 248. 3-16-146301-3 [NTAbs 39, p. 509].

4851 *Kowalski* Beate, [Mk 12,12, Winzergleichnis, the murderous tenants; BerR 41,3; PesK 16,9] Die Wertung von Versagen und Unheil in der Geschichte: Judaica 50 (1994) 18-33.

4852 *Herzog* William R.[II], Dissembling; a weapon of the weak; the case of Christ and Caesar in Mark 12:13-17 and Romans 13:1-7 → 107, [F]RUTENBER C., PerspRelSt 21 (1994) 339-360.

4853 *Bolt* Peter G., What were the Sadducees reading? An enquiry into the literary background of Mark 12:18-23 [1 Mcb, Tob]: TyndB 45 (1994) 369-394.

4854 *Kertelge* Karl, [Mk 12,28-34] Das Doppelgebot der Liebe im Markusevangelium: TrierTZ 103 (1994) 38-55.

4855 *Oswald* Wolfgang, [Mk 12,28-34] Das Gespräch zwischen Jesus und einem Schriftgelehrten: BibNot 75 (1994) 82-100.

4856 **Beasley-Murray** George R., [Mk 13] Jesus and the last days; the interpretation of the Olivet discourse 1993 → 9,4776 [ÉglT 25,284s, M. *Dumais*]: [R]ETL 70 (1994) 169-171 (F. *Neirynck*); JStNT 56 (1994) 121s (A. R. *Cross*); TTod 51 (1994s) 321s (D. M. *Freedholm*); WestTJ 56 (1994) 192s (D. G. *McCartney*).

4857 *a) Blount* Brian K., [Mk 13] Preaching the Kingdom; Mark's apocalyptic call to prophetic engagement; – *b) Moorhead* James H., Engineering the millennium; kingdom building in American Protestantism, 1880-1910: → 326, PrincSemB 15 (1994) 33-56 / 104-128.

4858 **Gempf** Conrad, [Mk 13; 1 Thess 5,3 ...] The imagery of birth pangs in the New Testament: TyndB 45 (1994) 119-135.

4859 *Vena* Osvaldo, La expectativa escatológica en el evangelio de Marcos; análisis literario y estructural de Marcos 13: RBibArg 56 (1994) 85-101.

4860 *Evans* C. A., [Mk 13,3] Predictions of the destruction of the Herodian Temple in the Pseudepigrapha, Qumran Scrolls, and related texts: JPseud 10 (1992) 89-147 [< NTAbs 39, p. 222].

F6.8 Passio secundum Marcum, 14,1 ... [→ F5.3].

4861 **Broadhead** Edwin K., Prophet, Son, Messiah; narrative form and function in Mark 14-16: jNsu 97. Shf 1994, Academic. 224 p. £40. 1-8505-476-4 [JTS 46,616, H. *Anderson*].

4862 **Schreiber** J., Mk-Passion ²1993 → 9,5047: [R]JTS 45 (1994) 654-7 (E. *Best*); TLZ 119 (1994) 899s (G. *Schille*).

4863 **Sommer** U.,   Die Passiegeschichte des Markusevangeliums; Überlegungen zur Bedeutung der Geschichte für den Glauben: WUNT 2/58, 1993 ➤ 9,5048: [Diss. Zürich 1989, D*Weder* H.] 1993 ➤ 9,5048: R*JTS* 45 (1994) 657-9 (M. E. *Glasswell*); TvT 34 (1994) 194 (B. van *Iersel*).

4864 *Gubler* M.-L.,   Das Blut des Bundes für die Vielen (Mk 14,24): Diakonia 25,3 (1994) 166-177 [< NTAbs 39, p. 208].

4865 *Aus* Roger D.,   The release of Barabbas (Mark 15:6-15; par.; John 18:39-40) and Judaic traditions on the Book of Esther: ➤ 153, Barabbas 1992, 1-27.

4866 *O'Collins* Gerald, *Kendall* Daniel,   [Mk 15,42-47] Did Joseph of Arimathea exist?: Biblica 75 (1994) 235-241.

4866* **Hanhart** Karel,   The open tomb; a new approach; Mark's Passover Haggadah (c. 72 C.E.).   ColMn 1994, Liturgical.   xi-865 p.; bibliog. 802-827.   0-8146-5010-4.

4867 *Helton* Stanley N.,   Churches of Christ and Mark 16:9-20: RestQ 36 (1994) 33-52.

4868 **Cox** Steven L.,   A history and critique of scholarship concerning the Markan endings [< diss. Southern Baptist Sem.]. Lewiston NY 1993, Mellen.   x-275 p. $90.   0-7734-2380-X [TDig 42.62].

4869 **Magness** J. Lee, Sense and absence... Ending of Mk 1986 ➤ 2,3858; 3,4891: R*RB* 101 (1994) 457s (B. T. *Viviano*).

XII. Opus Lucanum

F7.1   *Opus Lucanum* – **Luke-Acts.**

4870 **Alexander** Loveday,   The preface to Luke's Gospel 1,1-4 and Acts 1,1: SNTS mg 78, 1993 ➤ 9,5060: R*BZ* 38 (1994) 283-5 (W. *Radl*); EvQ 66 (1994) 373-6 (I. H. *Marshall*); JTS 45 (1994) 225-8 (P. F. *Esler*); TLond 97 (1994) 204s (E. *Franklin*: praise and queries); SvTKv 70 (1994) 196s (L. *Rydbeck*); TvT 34 (1994) 442 (W. *Weren*).

4871 **Arlandson** James M.,   'The fall and rise of many'; a socio-narratological analysis of women in Luke-Acts: diss. California, D*Barricelli* Jean-Pierre. Riverside 1994. 358 p. 95-01880. – DissA 55 (1994s) p. 2435.

4872 **Bergholz** Thomas, Der Aufbau des lukanischen Doppelwerkes; Untersuchungen zum formalliterarischen Charakter vom Lukas-Evangelium und Apostelgeschichte: Diss. D*Grässer* E. Bonn 1994s. – RTLv 26,535.

4873 *Bibb* C. Wade,   The characterization of God in the opening scenes of Luke and Acts: ProcGM 13 (1993) 275-296.

4874 **Bottini** G. Claudio,   Introduzione all'opera di Luca; aspetti teologici: SBF Anal 35, 1992 ➤ 9,5062: R*CiuD* 206 (1993) 230 (J. *Gutiérrez*); RBibArg 56 (1994) 187s (A. J. *Levoratti*).

4875 *Chrupcala* Lesław D.,   Il tema del Regno di Dio nell'opera lucana: Antonianum 69 (1994) 3-34; Eng. 3 [213-230, Chiesa e Regno di Dio].

4876 **Crump** David M.,   Jesus the intercessor... LkAc: WUNT 2/49, 1992 ➤ 8,5264; 9,5067: R*CBQ* 56 (1994) 365s (F. *Danker*); RB 101 (1994) 620s (J. *Taylor*); Salesianum 56 (1994) 568 (M. *Cimosa*); TGgw 37 (1994) 311s (H. *Giesen*); TLZ 119 (1994) 131-3 (M. *Rese*).

4877 **Cunningham** Scott S.,   'Though many tribulations'; the theology of persecution in Luke-Acts: diss. Dallas Theol. Sem., 1994, D*Bock* Darrell. 339 p. 94-03183. – DissA 55 (1994s) p. 3073.

4878 **Darr** John A.,   On character building... Lk-Ac 1992 ➤ 8,5265; 9,5069:

ᴿBInterp 2 (1994) 232-6 (P.F. *Esler*); EvQ 66 (1994) 273-5 (A.T. *Lincoln*); Interpretation 48 (1994) 204.6 (J.D. *Kingsbury*); TorJT 10 (1994) 118s (D. *Neale*).

4879 **Dauer** Anton, Beobachtungen zur literarischen Arbeitstechnik des Lukas: BoBB 79, 1990 ➤ 8,5267: ᴿJBL 113 (1994) 726s (C. *Heil*: on the speeches and dialogues; largely repeats what has already been established).

4880 **Denova** Rebecca I., 'The things accomplished among us'; prophetic tradition in the structural pattern of Luke-Acts: diss. ᴰ*Goldstein* B. Pittsburgh 1994. 291 p. 94-31514. – DissA 55 (1994s) p. 2001.

4881 *Dunn* J.D.G., Baptism in the Spirit; a response to Pentecostal scholarship on Luke-Acts: JPent 3 (1993) 3-27; responses 4 (1994) 115-136, *Menzies* R.P.; 139-143, *Shelton* J.B.

4882 **Franklin** Eric, Luke, interpreter of Paul, critic of Matthew: jNsu 92. Shf 1994, JStOT. 414 p. £42.50. 1-85075-452-7 [JTS 46,263-9, J. *Nolland*; RelStR 21,53, R.S. *Ascough*]. – ᴿExpTim 106 (1994s) 24 (N. *Clark*: no Q [!]; better than PARSONS-PERVO, KIMBALL, EVANS-SANDERS); PrPeo 8 (1994) 445s (H. *Wansbrough*: thus Q becomes superfluous).

4883 *Frein* Brigid C., Narrative predictions, OT prophecies and Luke's sense of fulfilment: NTS 40 (1994) 22-37.

4884 **Gillman** John, Possessions and the life of faith... Lk-Acts 1991 ➤ 7, 4409...9,5074: ᴿGregorianum 75 (1994) 162s (G. *Marconi*); Interpretation 47 (1993) 316. 318 (W.C. *Kaiser*).

4885 **Gowler** D.B., Host... Pharisees in Lk-Acts 1991 ➤ 7,4409... 9,5075: ᴿNeotestamentica 28 (1994) 247-9 (G.P.V. du *Ploug*).

4886 **Green** Joel B., *McKeever* Michael C., Luke-Acts and NT historiography: IBR bibliographies 8. GR 1994, Baker. 148 p. 0-8010-3872-3.

4887 **Haudebert** P., La Samarie en Luc-Actes; Lc 9.51-56 – Ac 8.4-8: Impacts 1 (Angers 1994) 25-34 [< NTAbs 39, p. 43].

4888 **Huffman** Douglas S., The theology of the Acts of the Apostles; Lukan compositional markedness as a guide to interpreting Acts: diss. Trinity Evangelical, ᴰ*Liefeld* W. 1994. 366 p. 94-32064. – DissA 55 (1994s) p. 1590.

4889 *Karris* Robert J., Women and discipleship in Luke [presidential address, Atchison August 14, 1993]: CBQ 56 (1994) 1-20.

4890 **Kim** Kyoung-Jin, Stewardship and almsgiving; Luke's theology of wealth: diss. Glasgow 1993. – TyndB 44 (1993) 383-6.

4891 **Körn** Manfred, Die Geschichte Jesu in veränderter Zeit; Studien zur bleibenden Bedeutung Jesu im lukanischen Doppelwerk [< Ev, Diss. Bern 1989]: WUNT 2/51. Tü 1993, Mohr. 319 p. DM 99. 3-16-145893-1. – ᴿBZ 38 (1994) 135s (R. *Schnackenburg*); TvT 34 (1994) 195 (J. *Bastiaens*).

4892 **Kurz** William S., Reading Luke-Acts; dynamics of biblical narrative. LvL 1993, W-Knox. x-261 p. $16 pa. 0-664-25441-1 [Biblica 76,262-5, R.I. *Pervo*]. – ᴿGregorianum 75 (1994) 761 (E. *Rasco*: acompaña bien el documento contemporáneo de la Comisión Bíblica, Escritura en Iglesia); Neotestamentica 28 (1994) 249-251 (J.J. du *Plessis*: excellent); NOxRev 61,2 (1994) 31s (B. *Kennedy*: praise with objections); RivB 42 (1994) 491s (V. *Fusco*).

4893 *Mainville* Odette, L'Esprit dans l'œuvre de Luc: Héritage et Projet 45, ᴰ1991 ➤ 9,5086: ᴿJBL 113 (1994) 341s (E. *Richard*); ScEspr 46 (1994) 256s (G. *Novotný*).

4894 *Marguerat* Daniel, *a*) Juifs et chrétiens selon Luc-Actes; surmonter le conflit des lectures [McCarthy Lecture 1993]: Biblica 75 (1994) 126-146; – *b*) Juden und Christen im lukanischen Doppelwerk: EvT 54 (1994) 241-264 (201-240, *al.*).

4895 **Menzies** Robert P., The development of early Christian pneumatology
with special reference to Luke-Acts: jNsu 54, 1991 ➤ 7,4417; 9,5088:
ᴿEvQ 66 (1994) 174-6 (J. D. G. *Dunn*); JBL 113 (1994) 342-4 (J. R.
Levison).

4896 *Merkel* Helmut, Israel im lukanischen Werk: NTS 40 (1994) 371-398.

4897 **Morgenthaler** R., Lukas und QUINTILIAN; Rhetorik als Erzählkunst. Z
1993, Gotthelf. 433 p. F 130. 3-85706-280-0 [NTAbs 38, p. 464].

4898 *Mowery* R. L., The disappearance of the Father; the reference to God
the Father in Luke-Acts [never in Acts 3-28]: Encounter 55 (1994) 353-
358 [< NTAbs 39, p. 407].

4899 ᴱ**Neyrey** J. H., The social world of Luke-Acts 1991 ➤ 7,450... 9,5093:
ᴿEvQ 66 (1994) 81-87 (J. *Nolland*); Neotestamentica 28 (1994) 251-3
(P. P. J. *Botha*: an important event); RBibArg 55 (1993) 237s (N. O.
Míguez); TorJT 10 (1994) 263s (T. *Prendergast*).

4900 **O'Toole** Robert F., L'unità della teologia di Luca; un'analisi del
Vangelo di Luca e degli Atti [The unity of Luke's theology 1984], ᵀ*Gonella*
Anna Maria: Percorsi e traguardi biblici. T-Leumann 1994, Elle Di Ci.
263 p. Lᵐ 22. 88-01-10282-8. [Gregorianum 76,386, G. *Marconi*]. –
ᴿRClerIt 75 (1994) 774s (A. *Bagni*, con 16 altri su Luca).

4901 **Pareja** Renato L., The motif of hearing in Luke-Acts; a study of the
thematic configurations: diss. Angelicum, ᴰ*Agius* J. Rome 1994. 317 p. –
RTLv 26, p. 539.

4902 **Parsons** Mikeal C., *Pervo* Richard J., Rethinking the unity of Luke and
Acts 1993 ➤ 9,5097; 0-8006-2750-4: ᴿTBR 7,1 (1994s) 26 (A. *Chester*:
same author but not one book).

4903 *Perkins* Pheme, Preaching Luke, book roundup: Church 10,4 (1994) 51-54.

4904 **Plymale** Steven F., The prayer-texts of LkAc ᴰ1991 ➤ 7,4422; 9,5099:
ᴿInterpretation 48 (1994) 94 (C. H. *Talbert*).

4905 **Prieur** Alexander, Die Verkündigung der Gottesherrschaft; exegetische
Studien zum lukanischen Verständnis von *basileîa toû theoû*: ev. Diss.
ᴰ*Jeremias* G. Tübingen 1994. 287 p. > Mohr. – RTLv 26, p. 539.

4906 *Reid* Barbara E., Reading Luke with the poor: BToday 32 (1994) 283-9
[< NTAbs 39, p. 226].

4907 **Reinmuth** Eckart, Pseudo-PHILO und Lukas; Studien zum Liber Antiquitatum Biblicarum und seiner Bedeutung für die Interpretation des
lukanischen Doppelwerks [Hab.-D. Jena 1993]: WUNT 74. Tü 1994,
Mohr. xi-284 p. DM 198. 3-16-146174-6 [TR 90,175; JTS 46,644,
Loveday *Alexander*]. – ᴿTGgw 37 (1994) 315s (H. *Giesen*).

4908 **Roth** S. John, The blind, the lame, and the poor; an audience-oriented
sequential analysis of a group of character types in Luke-Acts: diss.
Vanderbilt, ᴰ*Tolbert* M. Nashville 1994. – RelStR 21,251.

4909 *Seim* Turid K., The double message; patterns of gender in Luke-Acts
[< diss. Oslo 1990]. Nv 1994, Abingdon. viii-301 p. $30. 0-687-00240-0
[NTAbs 39, p. 511].

4910 **Sheeley** Steven M., Narrative asides in Luke-Acts: jNsu 72, 1992 ➤ 8,
5290; 9,5104: ᴿCritRR 6 (1993) 290s (J. A. *Darr*); TZBas 50 (1994) 83
(M. *Rese*).

4911 **Shelton** J. B., Mighty... Spirit in Luke-Acts ᴰ1991 ➤ 7,4426...9,5105:
ᴿSvEx 59 (1994) 182 (C. C. *Caragounis*); Neotestamentica 28 (1994)
597-600 (J. L. de *Villiers*).

4912 — *Turner* Max, 'Empowerment for mission'? the pneumatology of
Luke-Acts [SHELTON James B. 1991 < diss. Stirling 1982]: VoxEvca 24
(1994) 103-122.

4913 **Shepherd** William H.[J], The narrative function of the Holy Spirit as a character in Luke-Acts: *a*) Diss. Emory, [D]*Craddock* F. Atlanta 1993. – RelStR 21,255; RTLv 26, p. 539; – *b*) SBL diss. 147. Atlanta 1994, Scholars. vii-290 p. $35; pa. $25. 0-7885-0019-8.

4914 *Siegert* F., Communication de masse et rythmes de prose dans Luc/Actes: RHPR 74 (1994) 113-127; Eng. 229.

4915 **Squires** John T., The plan of God in Luke-Acts: SNTS mg 76, [D]1993 ➤ 9,5107: [R]Biblica 75 (1994) 425-9 (R. C. *Tannehill*); JTS 45 (1994) 230-2 (E. *Franklin*).

4916 **Stegemann** W., Zwischen Synagoge und Obrigkeit [D]1991 ➤ 7,4427 ... 9,5108: [R]JEcuSt 29 (1992) 125 (J. T. *Sanders*); TGgw 37 (1994) 310s (H. *Giesen*).

4917 **Sterling** G. H., Historiography... JOSEPHOS, Luke-Acts: NT supp 64, 1992 ➤ 8,5292; 9,5109: [R]CBQ 55 (1993) 824-6 (R. *Doran*); JBL 113 (1994) 154-7 (S. *Mason*: demanding, good); StPhilonAn 6 (1994) 206-216 (N. *Walter*, deutsch); WestTJ 56 (1994) 193-5 (D. L. *Bock*).

4918 *Stock* A., A realistic spirituality; pathos in Luke-Acts: JFormSp 15 (Pittsburgh 1994) 321-332 [< NTAbs 39, p. 226].

4919 **Tyson** Joseph B., Images of Judaism in Luke-Acts [D]1992 ➤ 8,5296; 9,5115: [R]CBQ 56 (1994) 162s (E. V. *Gallagher*); CritRR 6 (1993) 301-3 (Marilyn *Salmon*); Interpretation 48 (1994) 93s (R. A. J. *Gagnon*: implied-reader-response).

4920 **Weatherly** Jon A., *a*) Jewish responsibility for the Cross in Luke-Acts: diss. Aberdeen 1991, [D]*Turner* M. – TyndB 44 (1993) 391-4; – *b*) Jewish responsibility for the death of Jesus in Luke-Acts: jNsu 106. Shf 1994, Academic. 307 p. £40. 1-85075-503-5 [TLZ 120,1081, M. *Rese*].

F7.3 **Evangelium Lucae** – *Textus, commentarii.*

4921 **Bock** Darrell L., Luke, IVP NT comm. DG/Leicester 1994, InterVarsity. 412 p. $16. 0-8308-1803-0 / UK 0-85111-678-7 [NTAbs 39, p. 501].

4922 **Bovon** François, ÉvLc 1-9, 1991 ➤ 5,5057 ... 9,5116: [R]JBL 113 (1994) 336-8 (D. L. *Jones*); RivStoLR 30 (1994) 638s (V. *Fusco*).

4923 **Corsato** Celestino, La Expositio evangelii secundum Lucam di sant'Ambrogio; ermeneutica, simbologia, fonti: StEphAug 43. R 1993, Inst. Patristicum Augustinianum. [D]1993 ➤ 9,5117: [R]Gregorianum 75 (1994) 781s (G. *Pelland*); RechSR 82 (1994) 261s (Y.-M. *Duval*); Teresianum 45 (1994) 610s (M. *Diego Sánchez*); TPhil 69 (1994) 580s (H. J. *Sieben*).

4924 **Cousin** Hugues, L'Év. de Luc 1993 ➤ 9,5118: [R]ÉTRel 69 (1994) 423s (M. *Bouttier*).

4925 **Ernst** J., Das Evangelium nach Lukas[2] [[1]c.1984]: RgNT. Rg 1993, Pustet. 558 p. DM 98. 3-7917-1393-0 [NTAbs 39, p. 137: reduces the technical in favor of needs of preachers and teachers].

4926 **Fausti** Silvano, Una comunità legge il Vangelo di Luca[4] [imprimatur 1988]: LettPastB 18. Bo 1994, Dehoniane. 813 p. L[m] 75. 88-10-20570-7.

4928 **Johnson** L. T., Gospel of Luke: SacPag 3, 1991 ➤ 7,4446 ... 9,5123: [R]BZ 38 (1994) 136s (B. *Heininger*); JBL 113 (1994) 339s (D. L. *Tiede*); RivB 42 (1994) 229s (M. *Làconi*).

4929 **Meynet** Roland, Il vangelo secondo Luca, analisi retorica [1988 ➤ 4, 5126],[T]: Retorica biblica 1. R 1994, Dehoniane. 756 p. L[m] 85. 88-396-0551-7. – [R]Gregorianum 75 (1994) 597s (*ipse*); RClerIt 75 (1994) 783 (A. *Bagni*).

4930 **Nolland** J., Luke 1-9,20 / -18,34 / -24,53: WordComm 35A-C. Dallas 1989/93/93 [➤ 5,5071... 9,5125]. lxvi-454 p. / lix-p. 455-896 / lxi, p. 897-1293 [JTS 46,628, E. *Franklin*]. – RAngelicum 71 (1994) 452s (S. *Jurić*); AnnTh 8 (1994) 182-7 (B. *Estrada*, A-C); JEvTS 37 (1994) 431s (M. R. *Fairchild*, A).

4932 **Rossé** Gérard, Il vangelo di Luca, commento esegetico e teologico 1992 ➤ 8,5314: Lᵐ 95: RCC 145 (1994,3) 347s (D. *Scaiola*); Lateranum 60 (1994) 171s (R. *Penna*).

4933 **Schürmann** Heinz, Das Lk.-Ev [I/1, 1994]; II/1 9,51-11,54. FrB 1994, Herder. xxiv-360 p. 3-451-21858-5. – RETL 70 (1994) 171-4 (F. *Neirynck*).

4933* — *Fuchs* A., Die Sehnsucht nach der Vergangenheit [SCHÜRMANN H. Lk-Komm 9,51-11,54: 1993]: SNTU 19 (1994) 68-111.

4934 **Shanahan** G. B. W., BONAVENTURE's theology of discipleship with special reference to his commentary on Luke: diss. Oxford 1994. – RTLv 26, p. 543, 'disciplineship'.

4935 ᴱ**Sieben** Hermann Josef, ORIGENES, In Lucam homiliae / Homilien zum Lukasevangelium 1-2: FonC 4. FrB 1991s ➤ 7,4452... 9,5126: RJbAC 37 (1994) 189-191 (H.-J. *Vogt*); ZKG 105 (1994) 104 (T. *Lechner*).

4936 **Stein** Robert H., Luke: NewAmC 1992 ➤ 9,5127: RBiblica 75 (1994) 575s (R. F. *O'Toole*, also on POLHILL J. Acts); EvQ 66 (1994) 270s (I. H. *Marshall* stresses similarities in L. T. JOHNSON's Sacra Pagina Luke and Acts).

4937 **Stock** Klemens, Gesù la bontà di Dio... Luca [franç. 1992] ᵀ1992 ➤ 9, 5128: RRClerIt 75 (1994) 777 (A. *Bagni*).

F7.4   *Lucae themata*   –   **Luke's Gospel, topics.**

4938 **Aletti** Jean-Noël, El arte... de Lucas 1992 ➤ 8,5324; 9,5131: RActuBbg 31 (1994) 214s (X. *Alegre*); Carthaginensia 10 (1994) 155 (J. F. *Cuenca Molina*); CiTom 121 (1994) 197 (J. L. *Espinel*); RET 53 (1993) 246-8 (P. *Barrado Fernández*); SalT 81 (1993) 323.

4939 **Aletti** J.-N., L'arte di... Luca 1991 ➤ 7,4458... 9,5120: RRClerIt 75 (1994) 781 (A. *Bagni*).

4940 **Böhlemann** Peter, Jesus und Johannes; Motive lukanischer Theologie: Diss. Bethel, ᴰ*Lindemann* A. Bielefeld 1994. – RTLv 26,535.

4941 **Diefenbach** Manfred, Die Komposition des Lukas-Evangeliums unter Berücksichtigung antiker Rhetorikelemente [Diss. Luzern 1992 ➤ 8,5330; 9,5136]: FraTSt 43. Fra 1993, Knecht. 264 p. DM 68.

4942 **Fausti** Silvano, Una comunità legge il vangelo di Luca: LPastB 18. Bo 1994, Dehoniane. 816 p. 88-384-2235-4. – RRClerIt 75 (1994) 782 (A. *Bagni*).

4943 **Graumann** Thomas, Christus interpres; die Einheit von Auslegung und Verkündigung in die Lukaserklärung des AMBROSIUS von Mailand: PatrTSt 41. B 1994, de Gruyter. xi-477 p. DM 238. 3-11-014423-9 [TR 91,86; RHE 90,39*].

4944 *a*) *Jervell* Jacob, The Lucan interpretation of Jesus as biblical theology; – *b*) *Nissen* Johannes, Jesus, the people of God, and the poor; the social embodiment of biblical faith: ➤ 303*a*, New Directions 1992/4, 77-92 / 220-242.

4945 **Kimball** Charles A., Jesus' exposition of the OT in Luke's Gospel [diss. SW Baptist, Fort Worth 1991, ᴰ*Ellis* E.]: jNsu 94. Shf 1994, JStOT. 254 p. £37.50. 1-85075-464-0 [NTAbs 39, p. 139].

4946 **Kingsbury** Jack D., Conflicto en Lucas 1992 ➤ 8,5341; 9,5147: ᴿRBib-Arg 55 (1993) 120-6 (A. J. *Levoratti*).

4947 **Lane** Thomas, The anticipation of the Gentile mission of the Acts of the Apostles in the Gospel of Luke: diss. Pont. Univ. Gregoriana, ᴰ*Kilgallen* J. Rome 1994. 399 p.; extr. n° 4115, 94 p. – RTLv 26, p. 537.

4948 **LaVerdiere** E., Dining in the Kingdom of God; the origins of the Eucharist according to Luke [ten meals described]. Ch 1994, Liturgy Training. x-227 p.; 5 maps. $12 pa. 1-56854-022-1 [NTAbs 39, p. 140]. – ᴿChurch 10,3 (1994) 51-53 (Julia *Upton*, also on three cognates).

4949 **Lentini** Gerlando, Il Vangelo di Luca oggi. R 1994, Rogate. 332 p. 88-8075-016-X.

4950 *Morgan* Robert, Which was the Fourth Gospel? [Luke: CRIBBS F. L. - SHELLARD Barbara]; the order of the Gospels and the unity of Scripture: JStNT 54 (1994) 3-28.

4951 **Neale** David A., 'None but the sinners'... 1991 ➤ 7,4473 ... 9,5152: ᴿJStNT 58 (1991) 271-3 (Susan R. *Garrett*).

4952 **Noël** Filip, De compositie van het Lucasevangelie in zijn relatie tot Marcus; het probleem van de 'grote weglating': VerhandLett 56. Bru 1994, Academie. 291 p.; bibliog. 251-274. 90-6569-604-0.

4953 **Pasquetto** Virgilio, Dio mia salvezza; testi scelti dal Vangelo di Luca. R 1994, Dehoniane. 356 p. – ᴿTeresianum 45 (1994) 341-3 (J. *Debono*).

4954 *Perkins* Pheme, Preaching Luke: Church 10,4 (1994) 51-54 [< NTAbs 39, p. 225].

4955 *a*) *Powell* Mark A., Toward a narrative-critical understanding of Luke; – *b*) *Tannehill* Robert C., 'Cornelius' and 'Tabitha' [Lucan-sounding names for imaginary Mediterranean-world characters] encounter Luke's Jesus; – *c*) *Beavis* Mary Ann, 'Expecting nothing in return'; Luke's picture of the marginalized; – *d*) *Kingsbury* Jack D., The plot of Luke's story of Jesus; – *d*) *Moxnes* Halvor, The social context of Luke's community: Interpretation 48,4 (1994) 341-6 / 347-356 / 357-368 / 369-378 / 379-389.

4955* *Punayar* Sebastian, Salvation in the Gospel of Luke: Jeevadhara 24 (1994) 360-372.

4956 *a*) *Reid* Barbara E., Luke, the Gospel for women?; – *b*) *Culpepper* R. Alan, Seeing the Gospel of God; the metaphor of sight in the Gospel of Luke: CurrTM 21 (1994) 405-414 (-423 *al.*) / 434-441 (424-433 . 444-457, *al.*).

4957 *Riesner* R., Luke's special tradition and the question of a Hebrew gospel source: Mishkan 29 (J 1994) 44-51 [< NTAbs 39, p. 41].

4958 **Riley** Harold, Preface to Luke. Macon 1993, Mercer Univ. $25. 0-86554-433-0 [TDig 42,86: collaborator of B. ORCHARD].

4959 **Rius-Camps** Josep, L'esodo dell'uomo libero... Lc 1992 ➤ 8,5358: ᴿCC 145 (1994,4) 306s (D. *Scaiola*).

4960 *Schrock* J. H., 'I am among you as one who serves'; Jesus and food in Luke's Gospel; Daughters of Sarah 19,4 (Evanston 1993) 20-23 [< NTAbs 38, p. 201].

4961 **Verboomen** Alain, L'imparfait périphrastique dans l'Évangile de Luc et dans la Septante: Fonds Draguet 11. Lv 1992, Peeters. xiv-92 p. Fb 800. 90-6831-531-7 [Gregorianum 76,152s, G. *Marconi*]. – ᴿETL 70 (1994) 175s (F. *Neirynck*).

F7.5 *Infantia, cantica* – **Magnificat, Benedictus: Luc. 1-3.**

4962 *Baum* A. D., Die älteste Teilantwort auf die synoptische Frage (Lk 1,1-4): JbEvT 8 (1994) 9-32 [< ZIT 95, p. 10].

4963 *Dillmann* Rainer,   Das Lukasevangelium als Tendenzschrift; Leserlenkung und Leseintention in Lk 1,1-4:   BZ 38 (1994) 86-93.
4964 **Coleridge** Mark, Birth of the narrative Lk 1-2, ᴰ1993 ⇥ 9,5178:   ᴿFgNt 7 (1994) 224 (J. *Peláez*).
4965 *Green* Joel B.,   The problem of a beginning; Israel's Scriptures in Luke 1-2:   BuBR 4 (1994) 61-85.
4966 *a) Malick* David L.,   A literary approach to the narratives in Luke 1-2; – *b) Zuck* Roy B.,   How Jesus responded to questions; – *c) Pentecost* J. Dwight,   The Apostles' use of Jesus' predictions of judgment; ⇥ 21, ᶠCAMPBELL D., Integrity 1994, 93-107 / 108-133 / 134-143.
4967 **Panier** Louis,   La naissance du Fils de Dieu: CogF 164, 1991 ⇥ 7,4489 ... 9,5179 [RB 102,413-9, E. *Nodet*]:   ᴿRTLv 25 (1994) 485-7 (C. *Focant*); JTS 45 (1994) 228-230 (E. *Franklin*).
4968 *Silberman* Lou H.,   A model for the Lukan infancy narratives?:   JBL 113 (1994) 491.
4969 *a) Talbert* Charles H.,   Jesus's birth in Luke and the nature of religious language; – *b) Sim* David C.,   What about the wives and children of the disciples? The cost of discipleship from another perspective: HeythJ 35 (1994) 391-400 / 373-390.

4970 **Muñoz Nieto** J.M.,   Tiempo de anuncio; estudio de Lc 1,5-2,52 [dis. FuJen Univ. 1993, ᴰ*Ramón de Diego* J.]. Taipei 1994, Fac. Theol. Bellarmino.   vii-341 p. [NTAbs 39, p. 141].
4971 **Berlingieri** G.,   Il lieto annuncio Lc 1,5-25 [diss. Greg. ᴰ*Rasco* E.]. AnGreg 258, 1991 ⇥ 7,4480 ... 9,5183:   ᴿRB 101 (1994) 623s (J. *Taylor*).
4972 *a) Busse* Ulrich,   Die Engelrede Lk 1,13-17 und ihre Vorgeschichte; – *b) Lohfink* Norbert,   Die Lieder in der Kindheitsgeschichte bei Lukas: ⇥ 31*, ᶠDAUTZENBERG G., Nach 1994, 163-177 / 383-404.
4972* *Ó Fearghail* Fearghus,   Announcement or call? Literary form and purpose in Luke 1:26-38:   PrIrB 16 (1993) 20-35.
4973 *Ayo* N., [Lk 1,28.42] The Hail Mary; a verbal icon of Mary. ND 1994, Univ. xii-231 p. $33.   0-268-01101-X [NTAbs 39, p. 135].
4974 *Mammoottil* James, [Lk 1,31] And you shall call his name 'Yeshu': ⇥ 450c, Syriacum 6 (1992/4) 145-151.
4975 *a) Hillmer* Mark,   Luke 1:46-55; – *b) Wegener* Mark I.,   Luke 2:1-20; – *c) Klassan-Wiebe* Sheila,   Luke 3:15-17, 21-22: Between text and sermon, Interpretation 48,4 (1994) 390-4 / 394-7 / 397-401.
4976 **Kowalik** K., ❷ Le commentaire de LUTHER sur le Magnificat ᴰ1994.
4977 *Lohfink* Norbert, [Lk 1,46-55.68-79] Psalmen im Neuen Testament; die Lieder in der Kindheitsgeschichte bei Lukas: ⇥ 14, ᶠBEYERLIN W., Neue Wege 1994, 105-125.
4978 **Maaluf** Leonard,   The song of Zechariah; a study of the Benedictus Canticle in the context of Luke-Acts: diss. Pont. Univ. Gregoriana Nᵒ 7221, ᴰ*Vanhoye* A.   Rome 1994. 498 p. – InfPUG 26,131 (1994) 34; RTLv 26, p. 538.
4979 *Palme* Bernhard, [Lk 2,1-5] Neues zum ägyptischen Provinzialzensus; ein Nachtrag: ProtokB [2 (1993) 1-24] 3 (1994) 1-7.
4980 *Hirschmüller* M., [Lk 2,2] Der Zensus des Quirinius bei JOSEPHUS: JvEvT 8 (1994) 33.68 [< ZIT 95, p. 10].
4981 *Breytenbach* A.P.B.,   Lukas 2:14 vanuit 'n Joods-Christelike perspektief: HervTSt 50 (1994) 272-280 [< NTAbs 39, p. 228].
4982 *Schiffman* Lawrence H., [Lk 2,22] Pharisaic and Sadducean halakhah in light of the DSS; the case of Ṭevul Yom [last day of 'her' purification,

p. 285: but the noted cases are seminal emission, leprosy, contact with corpse or insects, food; women only Lev 15,19-24]: DSD 1 (1994) 285-299.

4983 **Simón Muñoz** Alfonso, El Mesías y la Hija de Sion; teología de la redención en Lc 2,29-35 [dis. 1986 Angelicum, Roma ^D*Salguero* J.]: StSemitNT 3. M 1994, Ciudad Nueva. 479 p.; bibliog. 17-36. pt. 3500. 84-86987-66-0 [Gregorianum 76,385s, G. *Marconi*]. – ^RClaretianum 34 (1994) 628-630 (A. *Pardilla*).

4984 *Kilgallen* John J., [Lk 2,32] Jesus, savior, the glory of your people Israel: Biblica 75 (1994) 305-328; franç. 328.

4985 **Aus** R. D., [Lk 2,41-51 < 1 Sam 1-3; Mk 6,1-6 < 1 Sam 10; Mt 27,51s < 1 Sam 28] Samuel, Saul and Jesus; three early Palestinian Jewish Christian Gospel haggadoth: SFlaJud 105. Atlanta 1994, Scholars. xvi-302 p. $70. 1-55540-969-5 [NTAbs 39, p. 134].

F7.6 **Evangelium Lucae 4,1 ...**

4985* *Tihon* Paul, [Lc 4,13] Jésus et les peurs fondamentales; un tracé inspiré de l'évangile: LVitae 49 (1994) 167-172; Eng. 173

4986 *Kimball* Charles A.^{III}, Jesus' exposition of Scripture in Luke 4:16-30; an inquiry in light of Jewish hermeneutics: PerspRelSt 21 (1994) 179-202 [< NTAbs 39, p. 229].

4987 **Mielcarek** Krzysztof, ✪ Jezus – Ewangelizator ubogich (Łk 4,16-30): studium z teologii św. Łukasza: diss. ^D*Kudasiewicz* J. Lublin 1994. xxiii-220 p. – RTLv 26, p. 538.

4988 *Prior* Michael, Isaiah, Jesus and the Liberation of the Poor (Luke 4,16-30): ScrBu 24,2 (1994) 36-45.

4989 *Karman* Y., Jesus' anointing; a study of the fulfillment of Isaiah 61:1-2 in Luke 4:18-21: Studos 2,1 (Bandung 1994) 79-89 [< NTAbs 39, p. 43].

4990 *Light* Gary W., Luke 5:15-26 [man through roof]: Interpretation 48 (1994) 279-281.

4991 *Bernardi* Jean, Des chiffres et des lettres; le texte de Luc 6,1: RB 101 (1994) 62-66; Eng. 62 [not deuteroproto but beth + aleph ('go') transcribed].

4992 **Malipurathu** Thomas, [6,20-26] The Beatitudes according to Luke; an exegetico-theological study of Luke 6,20-26 in the perspective of the Sermon on the Plain and of the designation of Luke as the 'Evangelist of the poor': diss. Pont. Univ. Gregoriana, ^D*Lentzen-Deis* F.†, *Grilli* M. Rome 1994. 492 p.; extr. N° 4044, 82 p. – RTLv 26, p. 538.

4993 *Hoffmann* Paul, Q 6,22 in der Rezeption durch Lukas: → 31*, ^FDAUTZENBERG G., Nach 1994, 293-326.

4994 *García* M. A., Committed discipleship and Jesus' lordship; exegesis of Luke 6:46-49 in the context of Jesus' discourse in the plain: African Christian Studies 9,2 (Nairobi 1993) 3-10 [NTAbs 39, p. 229].

4995 *Gagnon* Robert A. J., Luke's motives for redaction in the account of the double delegation in Luke 7:1-10: NT 36 (1994) 122-145.

4996 *Brodie* Thomas, Again not Q; Luke 7:18-35 as an Acts-orientated transformation of the vindication of the prophet Micaiah (1 Kings 22:1-38): IrBSt 16,1 (1994) 2-30.

4997 *Làconi* Mauro, [Lc 7,36-50] La misericordia verso i peccatori in Luca: ParSpV 29 (1994) 121-130.

4998 *Meynet* Roland, 'Celui à qui est remis peu, aime un peu ...' (Lc 7,36-50): Gregorianum 75 (1994) 267-279; Eng. 279.

4999 *Swartz* S. M., Hiding the light; another look at Luke 8:16-18: NoTr 8,4 (1994) 53-59 [< NTAbs 39, p. 409].
5000 *Cavalcanti* Tereza, Jesus, the penitent woman, and the Pharisee: JHispT 2 (1994) 28-40.

F7.7   *Iter hierosolymitanum* – *Lc 9,51...* – **Jerusalem journey.**

5001 **Moessner** David P., [Lk 9,51...] Lord of the banquet... travel narrative ᴰ1989 ➤ 5,5153... 8,5415: ᴿBijdragen 55 (1994) 209s (B. J. *Koet*).
5002 *Fuchs* A., [➤ 4933*; Lk 10s; SCHÜRMANN H.] Die Sehnsucht nach der Vergangenheit: SNTU 19 (1994) 69-111 [< NTAbs 39, p. 230].
5003 *Talmon* Shemaryahu, [Lk 10] 'Good Samaritan' — a 'good Israelite': ➤ 61, ᶠKAISER O., 'Wer ist' 1994, 472-485.
5004 *a) Neirynck* Frans, Luke 10:25-28; a foreign body in Luke?; – *b) Marshall* I. Howard, The Christology of Luke and the pastoral epistles: ➤ 45, ᶠGOULDER M., Crossing 1994, 149-165 / 167-182.
5005 *Terrinoni* Ubaldo, [Lc 10,41] Marta e Maria; la scelta dell'unica cosa: RivVSp 48 (1994) 211-235.
5006 *Chrupcała* Lesław D., Il dito di Dio (Lc 11,20) [|| Mt 12,28 spirito di Dio] nell'esegesi moderna e patristica: LA 44 (1994) 83-110; Eng. 612.
5007 *Schwarz* Günther, 'Gebt... den Inhalt als Almosen'? (Lukas 11,40.41]: BibNot 45 (1994) 26-30.
5008 *Belaj* Vitomir, Fructus arboris fici sterilis (Lc 13,6-9): ➤ 36, Mem. FUĆAK M., BogSmot 64 (1994) 336-345 croat.; deutsch 344.
5009 *Minor* Mitzi, Luke 13:22-30 [how many saved?] — the wrong question, the right door [expository, 'following the method of Sandra SCHNEIDERS']: RExp 91 (1994) 551-7.
5010 **Braun** Willi, The use of Mediterranean banquet traditions in Luke 14,1-24: diss. ᴰ*Kloppenborg* J. Toronto 1993. – RTLv 26,535.
5011 *Volschenk* G. J., *Aarde* A. G. van, Sistematies verwronge kommunikasie in Lukas 14:1-6; die dialekties-kritiese teorie van Jürgen HABERMAS krities bespreek: HervTSt 50 (1994) 812-840 [< NTA 39, p. 409: 'systematically distorted communication'].
5012 **Vedamuthu** Sebastian, Discipleship of the Lord Jesus, Luke 14:25-35; a biblico-theological investigation: diss. Urbaniana, ᴰ*Federici* T. R 1994, Pont. Univ. Urbaniana. Excerpt xl-70 p.; bibliog. xxi-xl.

5013 **Bailey** Kenneth E., Finding the lost; cultural keys to Luke 15, 1992 ➤ 8,5437; 9,5241: ᴿCritRR 6 (1993) 199-201 (C. L. *Blomberg*); IrBSt 15 (1993) 141-4 (J. C. *McCullough*).
5014 *LaHurd* Carol S., Rediscovering the lost women in Luke 15: ➤ 88*, ᶠNIEBUHR Ursula, BibTB 24 (1994) 66-76.
5015 *Leutzsch* Martin, Sozialgeschichtliche Bibelauslegung; Lukas 15,1-3.11b-32, Der verlorene Sohn: Junge Kirche 54 (Bremen 1993) 290... [< ZIT 93,339].
5016 **Bahr** H.-E., [Lk 15,11-32] Der verlorene Sohn, oder die Ungerechtigkeit der Liebe; das Gleichnis Jesu heute. FrB 1993, Herder. 153 p. DM 26,80. 3-451-23248-0 [NTAbs 39, p. 135].
5017 **Pöhlmann** Wolfgang, [Lk 15,11s] Der verlorene Sohn und das Haus: WUNT 68, ᴰ1993 ➤ 9,5246: ᴿBZ 38 (1994) 138 (H. J. *Klauck*); TGgw 37 (1994) 154s (H. *Giesen*); TLZ 119 (1994) 420-2 (W. *Vogler*).

5018 **Nouwen** Henri J. M.,   El regreso del hijo pródigo; meditaciones ante un cuadro de Rembrandt.   M 1994, PPC. 157 p. [SalT 82,500].

5019 *Wiederkehr* Dietrich,   Der 'grössere Vater' und der 'unterworfene Sohn'; Christologie im Horizont pluraler Religionen: ➤ 57, ^FHÜNERMANN P., Kirche 1994, 327-338.

5020 *Ball* Michael, [Lk 16] The parables of the unjust steward and the rich man and Lazarus: ExpTim 106 (1994s) 329s.

5021 **Ireland** Dennis J.,   Stewardship and the Kingdom of God, Lk 16,1-13: NT supp 70, ^D1992 ➤ 8,5446; 9,5250:   ^RETL 70 (1994) 476s (A. *Denaux*); JBL 113 (1994) 541-3 (R. L. *Brawley*); ScEspr 46 (1994) 111 (P.-É. *Langevin*).

5022 *De Silva* D. A., [Lk 16,1-8] The parable of the prudent steward and its Lucan context: CriswellTR 6 (1993) 253-268 [< NTAbs 39, p. 230].

5023 *Montevecchi* Orsolina,   Luca 16,1-8 alla luce dei papiri: ➤ 86, ^FNALDINI M., Paideia 1994, 181-8.

5024 *Villapadierna* Carlos de,   ¿Siervos inútiles o qué? (Lc 17,7-10): ➤ 22a, ^FCASCIARO J., Biblia 1994, 327-335.

5025 *Hamm* Dennis,   What the Samaritan leper sees; the narrative Christology of Luke 17:11-19:   CBQ 56 (1994) 273-287.

5026 *Holmgren* Frederick C.,   The Pharisee and the tax collector; Luke 18:9-14 and Dt 26:1-15:   Interpretation 48 (1994) 252-262.

5027 *Terrinoni* Ubaldo, [Lc 18,18-30] Un notabile ricco e il suo fallimento: RivVSp 48 (1994) 533-554.

5028 *Bivin* David,   A Hebraic nuance of *legō* ['interpret'], key to understanding Luke 18:18-19:   Jerusalem Perspective 42ss (1994) 37-45.

5029 *a) Tannehill* Robert C.,   The story of Zacchaeus as rhetoric; Luke 19:1-10; – *b) Gowler* David B.,   Hospitality and characterization in Luke 11:37-54 ['an elaborated chreia']; a socio-narratological approach; – *c) Oakman* Douglas E.,   Cursing fig trees and robbers' dens; pronouncement stories within social-systemic perspective, Mark 11:12-25 and parallels: Semeia 64 (1993) 201-211 / 213-251 / 253-272.

5030 *Rodd* C. S., [Lk 19,11-32] Is the parable for us? [a vicar gave £5 each to parishioners to raise church funds with; one buried his in the ground and organized a treasure-hunt]: ExpTim 106 (1994s) 374s.

5031 *Hall* Craig L., [Lk 19,11-27] Biblical hermeneutics and the sociology of knowledge; the parable of the pounds according to C. H. DODD and Itumeleng J. MOSALA: diss. Baylor, ^D*Parsons* M.   289 p. 95-14084. – DissA 55 (1994s) p. 3879.

5032 *Kinman* Brent R.,   The 'a-triumphal' entry (Luke 19:28-48); historical backgrounds, theological motifs and the purpose of Luke [< diss. Cambridge 1993, ^D*Hooker* Morna]: TyndB 45 (1994) 189-193.

5033 *Spurin* Richard, [Lk 19,29-44] Why did Jesus go to Jerusalem? [1. to receive a kingdom; 2. to die; 3. because he loved it]: ExpTim 106 (1994) 178s.

5034 *Kinman* Brent R.,   'The stones will cry out' (Luke 19,40) — joy or judgment?:   Biblica 75 (1994) 232-5.

5035 *Fusco* Vittorio,   Il discorso escatologico lucano; 'redazione' e 'composizione' (Lc 21,5-36 e Mc 13,1-37): ➤ 147, Mem. ZEDDA S., Theologica 3 (1994) 279-329.

5036 *Achtemeier* Elizabeth,   Luke 21:25-36, from text to sermon: Interpretation 48 (1994) 401-4.

5037 *Kinman* Brent, [Lk 13,6-9 ‖ Mk 11,12.20] Lucan eschatology and the missing fig tree: JBL 113 (1994) 669-678.

F7.8   **Passio** – *Lc 22* ...

5038 *a*) *Bottini* Giovanni C., Il valore salvifico della morte di Gesù secondo Lc 22-23; un confronto con Is 52-53; – *b*) *Rasco* Emilio, Lc 24,13-35; come riconoscere il Cristo dopo la Risurrezione; – *c*) *Làconi* Mauro, Parabole lucane, testimonianza su Cristo e sulla Chiesa; – *d*) *Testa* Emanuele, Condivisione dei beni, dei ministeri e dei carismi secondo Luca e Paolo: → 147, Mem. ZEDDA S., Theologica 3 (1994), 87-110 / 111-126 / 127-149 / 151-170.

5039 *Enuwosa* J., Ⓔ The nature of the death of Jesus in Lucan soteriology, ᵀ*Agourides* S.: DeltioVM 12,2 (1992) 49-65.

   LaVerdiere Eugene, Dining in the Kingdom of God; the origins of the Eucharist according to Luke 1994 → 4948.

5041 *Plessis* Isak J. du, The saving significance of Jesus and his death on the cross in Luke's Gospel — focusing on Lk 22:19b-20; Neotestamentica 28 (1994) 523-540.

5042 **Nelson** P. K., [Lk 22,24.30] Leadership and discipleship; a study of Luke 22:24-30: SBL diss. 138 [Bristol Trinity College ᴰ*Nolland* J.]. Atlanta 1994, Scholars. xvii-330 p. $33; pa. $22. 1-55540-900-8; -1-6 [NTAbs 39, p. 142].

5043 *Nelson* Peter K., *a*) Luke 22:29-30 and the time frame for dining and ruling [< diss. Leadership and discipleship, Bristol Trinity College 1991]: TyndB 44 (1993) 351-361; – *b*) The unitary character of Luke 22.24-30: NTS 40 (1994) 609-619.

5044 *Šagi* Janko, 'Theōria' del Cristo crocifisso in Lc 23,26-49: → 456, Sangue/Liturgia 1988/9, 171-254.

5045 *Green* Joel B., The demise of the Temple as 'culture center' in Luke-Acts; an exploration of the rending of the Temple veil (Luke 23,44-49): RB 101 (1994) 495-515; franç. 495.

5046 *Bons* Eberhard, Das Sterbewort Jesu nach Lk 23,46 und sein alttestamentlicher Hintergrund: BZ 38 (1994) 93-101.

5047 *Doble* Peter, Luke 23.47 — the problem of *dikaios*: BTrans 44 (1993) 320-331.

5048 *Slenczka* Reinhard, [Lk 24,11] 'Nonsense'; dogmatische Beobachtungen zu dem historischen Buch von Gerd LÜDEMANN, 'Die Auferstehung Jesu; Historie, Erfahrung, Theologie'. Göttingen 1994: KerDo 40 (1994) 170-181.

5049 *a*) *Dauer* Anton, Zur Authentizität von Lk 24,12; – *b*) *Neirynck* Frans, Once more Luke 24,12: ETL 70 (1994) 294-318 / 319-340.

5050 *Hölscher* Elisabeth, *Klessmann* Michael, Die Auferstehung einer Geschichte; eine bibliodramatische Bearbeitung von Lk 24,13-33 [Pilatus – die Frauen]: EvT 54 (1994) 391-9.

5051 *Rosica* Thomas M., *a*) The road to Emmaus and the road to Gaza, Luke 24:13-35 and Acts 8:26-40: Worship 65 (1994) 117-131; – *b*) Encounters with Christ; word and sacrament: Church 10,1 (NY 1994) 9-13 [< NTAbs 38, p. 372].

5052 **Just** A. A., The ongoing feast; table fellowship and eschatology at Emmaus [diss. Durham UK 1990, ᴰ*McHugh* J.]. ColMn 1993, Liturgical. xviii-307 p. $22. 0-8146-0013-4 [NTAbs 38, p. 293].

5053 *Pretot* Patrick, Les yeux ouverts des pèlerins d'Emmaüs: MaisD 195 (1993) 7-48.
5054 *Zwickel* Wolfgang, Emmaus, ein neuer Versuch [Lk 24,13]: BibNot 74 (1994) 33-36.
5055 **Schertz** Mary H., Questions of the heart; feminist inquiry and Luke's Easter texts: diss. Vanderbilt, ^D*Tolbert* M. Nashville 1993. – RelStR 21,251.
5056 **Fuller** George C., The life of Jesus after the ascension (Luke 24:50-53; Acts 1:9-11): WestTJ 56 (1994) 391-8.

XII. Actus Apostolorum

F8.1 **Acts** – *text, commentary, topics.*

5057 ^E**Aland** Kurt, *al.*, Apg: Text und Textwert 3/1,5, 1993 → 9,5276: ^REnchoria 21 (1994) 151s (H.-J. *Klauck*); TR 90 (1994) 383s (W. *Radl*).
5058 **Barrett** C. Kingsley, The Acts of the Apostles [1-14; 'preliminary introd.']: ICC. E 1994, Clark. xxv-693 p.; bibliog. xiii-xxiii. $65. 0-567-09653-X [RelStR 21,235, C. *Bernas*].
5058* **Barrett** C.K., Calvino esegeta degli Atti degli Apostoli, ^T*Comba Corsani* Mirella: Protestantesimo 49 (1994) 312-326.
5059 *Betori* Giuseppe, La strutturazione del libro degli Atti; una proposta: RivB 42 (1994) 3-33; Eng. 34.
5060 **Bittel** Michael D., Historical precedent; normativity in the writing of [Roger] STRONSTAD and [Gordon] FEE [how biblical historical narrative especially in Acts can establish Christian doctrine]: diss. Regent [no dir.]. 80 p. 1358672. [DissA disk] MAI 33 (1994s) p. 328.
5061 **Bruce** F.F., Acts 1991 [< 1951] → 6,5469; 7,4602: ^REvQ 66 (1994) 280-2 (M. *Turner*).
5062 **Coleman** Raymond S., Embedded letters in Acts and in Jewish and Hellenistic literature: diss. Southern Baptist Theol. Sem., ^D*Songer* H. Dallas 1994. 281 p. 94-28245. – DissA 55 (1994s) p. 1284.
5063 **Geer** Thomas C., Family 1739 (10th c. minuscule) in Acts: SBL mg 48. Atlanta 1994, Scholars, viii-149 p. $30; pa. $20. 0-7885-0036-8; -7-6 [RelStR 21,140, M.W. *Holmes*].
5064 [^E**Gempf** Conrad], *Hemer* Colin J.†, The book of Acts in its first century setting [1. In the setting of Hellenistic history 1989 → (243 & 258c supra) 5,5231 ... 8,5482]; 2. ^E**Gill** David W.J., The book of Acts in its Graeco-Roman setting. GR 1994, Eerdmans. xiii-627 p. £30. 0-8028-2433-1 / UK 0-85364-563-9.
5065 *Head* Peter, Acts and the problem of its texts: → 9,5310, Book of Acts 1 (1993) 415-444.
5066 *a) Hillard* T., *al.*, Acts and the Pauline corpus, I. Ancient literary parallels; – *b) Wenham* David, II. The evidence of parallels; – *c) Bauckham* Richard, The Acts of Paul as a sequel to Acts: → 283, Book of Acts 1 (1993) 183-213 / 215-258 / 105-152.
5067 **Hillier** Richard, ARATOR on the Acts of the Apostles; a baptismal commentary: EarlyChrSt 1993 → 9,5292: ^RHeythJ 35 (1994) 452 (E. *Yarnold*); JTS 45 (1994) 349-351 (G. *Jeanes*); RÉAug 40 (1994) 252-5 (R. *Bureau*).
5068 **Houghton** John W., BEDE's exegetical theology; ideas of the Church in the Acts commentaries of St. Bede the Venerable: diss. ^D*Cavadini* J. Notre Dame 1994. 365 p. 94-22403. – DissA 55 (1994s) p. 613.

5070 **Johnson** L. T., Acts: SacP 5, 1992 ➤ 8,5483: ᴿBibTB 24 (1994) 197s (D. B. *Gowler*); CBQ 56 (1994) 599s (D. *Hamm*); Furrow 45 (1994) 327s (E. *O'Reilly*); IrTQ 60 (1994) 149-151 (F. *Ó Ferghail*); LvSt 19 (1994) 265s (R. F. *Collins*); NBlackf 75 (1994) 282s (C. K. *Barrett*); Neotestamentica 28 (1994) 611-3 (R. van *Ruoven*); RB 101 (1994) 630 (J. *Taylor*); TR 90 (1994) 295s (G. *Schneider*); TS 55 (1994) 142s (R. J. *Dillon*).

5071 **Kistemaker** Simon, Exposition of the Acts 1990 ➤ 7,4617; 8,5488: ᴿChrSchR 23 (1993s) 463-5 (Catherine J. *Wright*).

5072 **Kurz** W. S., [ital. ➤ 9,5293] Los Hechos de los Apóstoles, ᵀ*Icaza* R. M. [BLatinoA text]: NT 5. ColMn 1994, Liturgical. 125 p. $4. 0-8146-1850-2 [NTAbs 39, p. 506].

5073 *Larsson* Edvin, If the Acts of the Apostles did not exist: TsTKi 64 (1993) 1-19 svensk; Eng. 19: Luke is under attack, but without it we would know very little about the early Church.

5074 **L'Éplattenier** Charles, Le livre des Actes, commentaire pastoral. P 1994, Centurion. 285 p. 2-227-36604-4.

5075 **Marconcini** Benito, Atti degli Apostoli; commento esegetico-spirituale: CommNT NS 5. T-Leumann 1994, Elle Di Ci. 348 p. 88-01-10336-0.

5076 **Marshall** I. H., Acts NT Guides, 1992 ➤ 8,5492: ᴿCritRR 6 (1993) 266s (R. J. *Karris*: superbly meets the goals of the series); TBR 7,1 (1994s) 27s (B. *Capper*).

5077 *a*) *Palmer* Darryl W., Acts and the ancient historical monograph; – *b*) *Alexander* L. C. A., Acts and ancient intellectual biography; – *c*) *Spencer* F. Scott, Acts and modern literary approaches; – *d*) *Satterthwaite* Philip E., Acts against the background of classical rhetoric: ➤ 258c, Book of Acts 1 (1993) 1-29 / 31-63 / 381-413 / 337-381.

5078 *Petersen* David, The motif of fulfilment and the purpose of Luke-Acts: ➤ 258c, Book of Acts 1 (1993) 83-104.

5079 **Polhill** John B., Acts: NewAmerComm 26, 1992 ➤ 8,5497; 9,5302: ᴱEvQ 66 (1994) 78-81 (J. *Proctor*, also on 23 & 32).

5080 **Powell** Mark A., What are they saying about Acts? 1991 ➤ 7,4632; 9,5303: ᴿCritRR 6 (1993) 278 (H. C. *Kee*: ably meets its aims); RB 101 (1994) 619 (J. *Taylor*).

5081 **(Richter)** *Reimer* Ivoni, Frauen in der Apostelgeschichte des Lukas; eine feministisch-theologische Exegese. Gü 1992 ➤ 8,9072; 3-579-00092-6: ᴿBZ 38 (1994) 291-3 (A. *Weiser*).

5082 **Rius-Camps** Josep, Comentari als Feits I-II, 1991-3 ➤ 8,5498; 9,5304: ᴿActuBbg 31 (1994) 45s (J. *O'Callaghan*); ArTGran 57 (1994) 433 (A. *Rodríguez Carmona*); FgNT 7 (1994) 85 (J. *Peláez*).

5083 *a*) *Rosner* Brian S., Acts and biblical history; – *b*) *Marshall* I. Howard, Acts and the 'former treatise'; – *c*) *Nobbs* Alanna, Acts and subsequent ecclesiastical histories: ➤ 258c, Book of Acts 1 (1993) 65-82 / 163-182 / 153-162.

5084 **Segalla** Giuseppe, Carisma e istituzione... Atti 1991 ➤ 7,4640... 9,5307: ᴿSalesianum 56 (1994) 382 (C. *Bissoli*).

5085 **Soards** Marion L., The speeches in Acts; their content, context, and concerns. LvL 1994, W-Knox. xi-218 p. $23. 0-664-25221-4. – ᴱAnglTR 76 (1994) 526s (R. I. *Pervo*); ExpTim 106 (1994s) 56 (C. K. *Barrett*: good analyses, but never really gets around to their role in Acts as a whole); TBR 7,1 (1994s) 28 (B. *Capper*).

5087 *Soards* M. L., The speeches in Acts in relation to other pertinent ancient literature: ETL 70 (1994) 65-90.

5088 **Steyn** Gert J., Septuagint quotations in the context of the Petrine and

Pauline speeches of the Acta Apostolorum: diss. ᴰ*Breytenbach* C. Pretoria 1994. – DissA 55 (1994s) p. 1285.
5089 **Strange** W. A., The problem of the text in Acts ᴰ1992 ➤ 8,5503; 9,5308: ᴱEvQ 66 (1994) 87-91 (P. M. *Head*).
5090 **Tannehill** Robert C., Acts: Narrative Unity of Lk/Acts 2, 1990 ➤ 8,5294: ᴿWestTJ 55 (1993) 157-9 (C. *Balzer*).
5091 *Taylor* J., Acts and history: Colloquium 26,2 (1994) 105-115 [< NTAbs 39, p. 431: on projected first volume (Acts 9-18) of three-volume commentary carrying forward BOISMARD 1990].
5092 *Taylor* Justin, Les Actes des deux apôtres V, Commentaire historique (Actes 9,1-18,22): ÉtBN. 23. P 1994, Gabalda. xxii-397 p. F 210. – ᴿRBén 104 (1994) 425s (D. *Misonne*); SuppVSp 148 (1994) 666s (H. *Cousin*).
5093 **Zedda** Silverio, Teologia della salvezza negli Atti degli Apostoli; studi sulla terminologia: StBDeh 20. Bo 1994, Dehoniane. 135 p. 88-18- 40722-9.
5094 **Zettner** Christoph, Amt, Gemeinde und kirchliche Einheit in der Apg [kath. Diss. Bochum]: EurHS 23/423, 1991 ➤ 8,5508: ᴿRB 101 (1994) 620 (J. *Taylor*).
5095 **Zmijewski** Josef, Die Apostelgeschichte: RgNT. Rg 1994, Pustet. 971 p. DM 98. 3-7917-1421-X [NTAbs 39, p. 330].

F8.3 *Ecclesia primaeva Actuum:* **Die Urgemeinde.**

5096 *a*) *Akpunou* Damian, The Church and churches in the Acts of the Apostles; – *b*) *Balembo Buetubela*, L'autonomie des jeunes églises dans les Actes; – *c*) *Amewowo* Wynnand, The Christian community in Acts of the Apostles; model for our days; – *d*) *Waliggo* John M., The Acts of the Apostles and a hundred years of Catholic evangelization in Africa: ➤ 303*a*, Les Actes des Apôtres et les jeunes Églises 1984/90, 52-72 / 77-104 / 105-116 / 25-45.
5097 *Alkier* Stefan, Urchristentum; zur Geschichte und Theologie einer exegetischen Disziplin: BeitHisT 83, ᴰ1993 ➤ 9,5313: DM178. – ᴿTR 90 (1994) 460s (H. *Wagner*).
5098 *Bautista* Esperanza, La mujer y los factores humanos en la formación de la primera Iglesia: RET 53 (1993) 481-492.
5099 **Becker** Jürgen, Das Urchristentum als gegliederte Epoche: SBS 155. Stu 1993, KBW. 144 p. DM 36. 3-460-04551-5 [TLZ 120,517, P. *Pokorný*].
5100 **Brown** Raymond E., Le chiese degli Apostoli; indagine esegetica sulle origini della ecclesiologia 1992 ➤ 8,5509; 9,5314: ᴿLateranum 60 (1994) 187-190 (A. *Montan*); RasT 35 (1994) 506s (M. *Semeraro*).
5101 *a*) *Caballero* J. M., Esbozo ideal de la Iglesia naciente, en los 'sumarios' de los Hechos de los Apóstoles (2,42-47; 4,32-35; 5,12-16); – *b*) *Morujão* Geraldo, Dimensão eclesiológica do conceito de *adelphós* no Novo Testamento: ➤ 22a, ᶠCASCIARO J., Biblia 1994, 395-410 / 411-420.
5102 **Campbell** K. Alastair, The Elders; seniority within earliest Christianity: StNTW. E 1994, Clark. xiv-309 p.; bibliog. 261-291. 0-567-09702-1.
5103 *Conniry* Charles J.ᴶ, Identifying apostolic Christianity; a synthesis of viewpoints: JEvTS 37 (1994) 247-261.
5104 *Driver* J., The trouble with inclusiveness [the marginalized, not feminist language]; a perspective on the Acts of the Apostles: StMark 157 (Canberra 1994) 24-31 [< NTAbs 39, p. 49].
5105 **Dumais** Marcel, Communauté... Actes 1992 ➤ 8,5478: ᴿÉglT 25 (1994) 134-7 (M. *Gourgues*).

5106 **Ferraro** Giuseppe, L'evangelizzazione nella Chiesa primitiva. CasM 1994, Piemme. 127 p. L^m 20. 88-384-2225-7 (Gregorianum 76,441, *ipse*).

5107 **Gilliéron** B., Cette Église qui vient de naître; histoire et vie quotidienne des premiers chrétiens. Poliez 1993, Moulin. 108 p. [NTAbs 38, p. 447].

5108 **Goulder** Michael, *a*) St. Paul versus St. Peter; a tale of two missions. LVL 1994, W-Knox. xxi-196 p. $16 [TS 56,812s, J.F. *O'Grady*] = *b*) A tale of two missions [Peter/Paul; there never was a single united Church]. L 1994, SCM. xii-196 p. £10 pa. – ᴱExpTim 106 (1994s) 26s (Meg *Davies*: BAUR's thesis); TLond 97 (1994) 465s (F.G. *Downing* is not convinced, but/and 800 pages more of this revised Tübingen are coming).

5109 *a*) **Grech** Prosper, Ebrei e cristiani ad Efeso; riflessi nel Vangelo di Giovanni; – *b*) **Destro** Adriana, **Pesce** Mauro, Conflitti di integrazione; la prima Chiesa e la comunità ebraica nella polis (qualsiasi, di Asia Minore) ➤ 328, Efeso 4: Giovanni 1994, 139-146 / 105-138.

5109* **Kirchschläger** W., Anfänge 1990 ➤ 6,5221... 8,5517: ᴿETL 70 (1994) 481 (J. *Verheyden*).

5110 **Kirchschläger** W., Le origini della Chiesa, una ricerca biblica [Die Anfänge der Kirche; eine biblische Rückbesinnung 1990, Styria],ᵀ. R 1994, Città Nuova. 211 p. [RHE 90,267*].

5111 **Lee Sung-Min**, The unity of word and sacrament among early Christians; biblical and historical witnesses: diss. Drew, ᴰ*Rice* C. Madison NJ 1994. 190 p. 94-32952. – DissA 55 (1994s) p. 2003.

5112 **Minnerath** Roland, De Jérusalem à Rome; Pierre et l'unité de l'Église apostolique: THist 101. P 1994, Beauchesne. 616 p. F 150.

5113 **Nagler** Norbert, Frühkatholizismus; zur Methodologie einer kritischen Debatte: RgStT 43. Fra 1994, Lang. 209 p. DM 64 [Tr 91,415, H. *Wagner*].

5114 **Rouwhorst** G.A.M., La célébration de la liturgie dans l'Église primitive: QLtg 74 (1993) 89-111; Eng. 112.

5114* **Sandner** Karl H., A new family; conversion and ecclesiology in the early Church, with cross-cultural comparisons: StIntelHChr 91. NY 1994, P. Lang. 221 p. $38 [TDig 43,86].

5115 **Schenke** Ludger, Die Urgemeinde 1990 ➤ 6,5527; 9,5323: ᴿTPhil 69 (1994) 579 (J. *Beutler*).

Stegemann W., Zwischen Synagoge und Obrigkeit... die lukanischen Christen 1991 ➤ 4916.

5116 *Taylor* Nicholas, Paul, Antioch, and Jerusalem [diss. Durham 1990]: jNsu 96, 1992 ➤ 8,5534; 9,5326: ᴿJBL 113 (1994) 545-8 (C.C. *Hill*: attack artful but not mission accomplished); TBR 7,3 (1994) 23 (D. *Wenham*).

5117 **Thurston** Bonnie, Spiritual life in the early Church; the witness of Acts and Ephesians. Mp 1993, Fortress. 115 p. $9. 0-8006-2618-8. – ᴿExpTim 106 (1994s) 88 (R. *Yates*).

5118 *Venetz* Hermann-Josef, Amt und Besoldung; Impression aus der Urkirche: TPQ 142 (1994) 113-122.

5119 *a*) *Vouga* François, *Frühkatholizismus*; osservazioni su implicazioni e conseguenze ermeneutiche di un concetto per la storiografia del cristianesimo primitivo, ᵀ*Subilia* Berta; – *b*) *Conti* Gino, Il cattolicesimo incipiente nel NT: 125, ᶠSubilia V. Pluralismo 1994, 55-70 / 81-96.

5120 *Weakland* Rembert G., Rummaging in the attic; the [early] Church and democracy: Mid-Stream 33 (1994) 151-7.

F8.5 **Ascensio, Pentecostes; ministerium Petri** – *Act 1*...

5121 *Asensio* Félix, Arranque 'evangelizador' (Hech 1-8) en la homilética del CRISÓSTOMO: Burgense 35 (1994) 9-65.

5122 *Kremer* J., [Acts 1s] Biblische Grundlagen zur Feier der fünfzig Tage: HDienst 48,1 (1994) 3-15 [< NTAbs 39, p. 51: John, Paul, and perhaps even Lk 24,50-53 show no chronological distance between resurrection-ascension-Pentecost].

5123 *O'Collins* Gerald, Revelation now [Pentecost ...]: Tablet 248 (1994) 616.

5124 *Rogers* Cleon L.[J], [Ac 1,3; Rev 5s] The Davidic covenant in Acts-Revelation: BtS 151 (1994) 71-84.

5125 **Day** Michael J., The function of post-Pentecost dream-vision reports in Acts: diss. Southern Baptist Theol. Sem., [D]*Garland* D. Dallas 1994. 193 p. 91-20732. DissA 55 (1994s) p. 603.

5126 **Brown** R. E., A once-and-coming Spirit at Pentecost; essays on the liturgical readings between Easter and Pentecost, taken from the Acts of the Apostles and from the Gospel according to John. ColMn 1994, Liturgical. v-97 p. $5 pa. 0-8146-2154-6 [NTAbs 38, p. 457].

5127 *Buzzard* Anthony, Acts 1:6 and the eclipse of the biblical Kingdom: EvQ 66 (1994) 197-215.

5128 *Niccum* Curt, A note on Acts 1:14 [against antifeminist support, *Thiele* W., zaw 53 (1962) 110]: NT 36 (1994) 196-9.

5129 *Rius-Camps* Josep, Las variantes de la recensión occidental de los Hechos de los Apóstoles (III: Hch 1,15-26): FgNt 7 (1994) 53-64.

5130 **Classen** Elaine, To you is the promise; a rhetorical-exegetical analysis of Acts 2 in the context of Luke-Acts: diss. Pont. Univ. Gregoriana N° 7202, [D]*Swetnam* J. Rome 1994. 366 p. – InfPUG 26,131 (1994) p. 32 [RTLv 26,536; Extr. N° 4085; 100 p.].

5131 *Rius-Camps* Josep, Las variantes de la recensión occidental de los Hechos de los Apóstoles (IV, Hch 2,1-13]: FgNt 7 (1994) 107-207.

5132 *Wedderburn* A. J. M., Tradition and redaction in Acts 2,1-13: JStNT 55 (1994) 27-54.

5133 *Piattelli* Daniele, [Act 2,11] Tradizioni giuridiche d'Israele; all'origine dello 'Statuto' del Proselita. T 1990, Giappichelli. 88-348-0158-X.

5134 *Murphy-O'Connor* Jerome, The cenacle and community; the background of Acts 2:44-45: ➤ 67a, [F]KING P., Scripture 1994, 296-310.

5135 *Cloete* G. D., *Smit* D. J., [Acts 2 echoes Gn 11] 'Its name was called Babel': JTSAf 86 (1994) 81-87 [< NTAbs 39, p. 51].

5136 *Everts* J., Tongues or languages? Contextual consistency in the translation of Acts 2: JPentecT 4 (1994) 71-80 [< NTAbs 39, p. 51].

5137 *Sterling* Gregory E., 'Athletes of virtue'; an analysis of the summaries in Acts (2:41-47; 4:32-35; 5:12-16): JBL 113 (1994) 679-696.

5138 **Shade** Walter R., The restoration of Israel in Acts 3:12-26 and Lukan eschatology: diss. Trinity Evangelical, [D]*Liefeld* W. 1994. 316 p. 94-32075. – DissA 55 (1994s) p. 1593.

5139 **Carrón** J., Jesús, el mesías manifestado ... Ac 3,19-46, 1993 ➤ 9,5337: [R]ActuBbg 31 (1994) 38 (J. *O'Callaghan*); Carthaginensia 10 (1994) 456s (J. F. *Cuenca Molina*); CiuD 207 (1994) 215s (J. M. *Ozaeta*); Salmanticensis 41 (1994) 344-9 (R. *Trevijano*); Studium 54 (M 1994) 355 (P. *Juan*).

5140 **Grappe** Christian, D'un Temple à l'autre... Pierre 1992 ➤ 8,5512; 9,5318: [R]BZ 38 (1994) 142-6 (J. *Roloff*); LA 44 (1994) 695-7 (G. *Bissoli*); RHR 211 (1994) 355-7 (P. *Blanchetière*); RB 101 (1994) 625-7 (J. *Taylor*); TR 90 (1994) 221s (R. *Pesch*).

5141 **Perkins** Pheme, Peter, apostle for the whole Church: StPersNT. Columbia 1994, Univ. S. Carolina. vi-201 p. $35. 0-87249-974-X [TDig 42,83].

5141* *a) Stoops* Robert F., Departing to another place; the Acts of Peter and the canonical Acts of the Apostles; – *b) Stroud* William J., Models for Petrine speeches in the Acts of Peter: ➤ 325, SBL Sem. 33 (1994) 390-404 / 405-413.

5142 *Spencer* F. Scott, Neglected widows in Acts 6:1-7: CBQ 56 (1994) 715-733.

5143 *Hill* Craig C., Hellenists and Hebrews ᴰ1992 ➤ 8,5559; 9,5345: ᴿInterpretation 48 (1994) 216 (S.G. *Wilson*); JBL 113 (1994) 543-5 (M.C. *Parsons*: fully justified); RB 101 (1994) 628s (J. *Taylor*).

5144 *Tsitsigos* S.K., ⊚ *Poîo ētan*... What was the task of the seven deacons?: DeltioVM 21,2 (1992) 52-58 [< NTAbs 39, p. 236].

5145 *Amos* Clare, [Acts 6s] Renewed in the likeness of Christ; Stephen the servant martyr: IrBSt 16,1 (1994) 31-37 [< NTAbs 38, p. 381].

5146 *Anderson* Robert T., The use of Hebrew Scripture in Stephen's speech: ➤ 102, ᶠRICHARDSON H., Uncovering 1994, 205-215.

5147 **Miller** Christopher A., [Acts 7; 10s; 15; 21] The relationship of Jewish and Gentile believers to the Law between A.D. 30 and 70 in the Scripture: diss. Dallas Theol. Sem. ᴰ*Johnson* E. 254 p. 94-22499. – DissA 55 (1994s) p. 606.

5148 *Wiens* D., [Acts 7,2-53] Luke on pluralism; flex with history: Direction 23,1 (Fresno 1994) 44-53 [< NTAbs 39, p. 52].

5149 *Balling* Jakob, [Ac 7,56; Perpetua] martyrdom as apocalypse: ➤ 89e, ᶠOTZEN B., In the last days 1994, 41-48.

5150 **Heintz** Florent, [Act 8,5] La parabole du mauvais Samaritain; Actes 8,5-25 dans ses rapports avec l'accusation de magie contre les prophètes thaumaturges: prot. diss. ᴰ*Trocmé* É. Strasbourg 1994. 243 p. – RTLv 26,537.

5151 *a)* *Berger* Klaus, [8,13] Propaganda und Gegenpropaganda im frühen Christentum; Simon Magus als Gestalt des samaritanischen Christentum; – *b)* *Bormann* Lukas, Die Verrechtlichung der frühesten christlichen Überlieferung im lukanischen Schrifttum: ➤ 40, ᶠGEORGI D., Religious propaganda 1994, 313-7 / 283-311.

5152 *Gage* W.A., *Beck* J.R., The Gospel, Zion's barren woman and the Ethiopian Eunuch: Crux 30,2 (1994) 35-43 [< NTAbs 39, p. 236].

5153 *Smith* Abraham, 'Do you understand what you are reading?' A literary critical reading of the Ethiopian (Kushite) episode (Acts 8:26-40): JIntdenom 22,1 (1994) 48-70 [< NTAbs 39, p. 420].

5154 *Thomas* U., Der Auszug des Paulus aus Jerusalem; die äthiopische Rezeption des neutestamentlichen Diskursthemas: Afrika und Übersee 76 (1993) 247-252 [< OLZ 89,618].

5155 *Williams* F. [Acts 8,26-39; 14,8-18; Lk 24,13-32 parallels] Archilochus and the eunuch [Paros inscription]; the persistence of a narrative pattern: Classics Ireland 1 (Dublin 1994) 96-112 [< NTAbs 39, p. 411].

5156 **Spencer** F. Scott, The portrait of Philip in Acts [diss. Durham 1989 ᴰ*Dunn* J.]: ᴿBibTB 24 (1994) 39s (D.E. *Gowler*); CBQ 56 (1994) 152-4 (G.E. *Sterling*); EvQ 66 (1994) 282s (S. *Travis*); JBL 113 (1994) 160-2 (C.R. *Matthews*); RB 101 (1994) 628 (J. *Taylor*).

5157 *Brenk* Frederick E., Greek epiphanies and Paul on the road to Damaskos: ➤ 344, ᴱ*Bianchi* U., Notion of 'religion' 1990/4, 413-424.

5158 **Carpinelli** Francis, A source- and redaction-critical analysis of the three accounts of Paul's Damascus experience; Acts 9,1-19; 22:3-16; 26:9-18: diss. Regis College, ᴰ*Plevnik* J. Toronto 1992. – SR 22 (1993) 537.

5159 **Reymond** Sophie, [Ac 9...22] L'expérience du chemin de Damas; approche narrative d'une expérience spirituelle [diplôme]. Lausanne 1993. 158 p.

5160 *Morgado* Joel[J], Paul in Jerusalem; a comparison of his visits in Acts [9; 15] and Galatians [1,18-34? 2,1-10?...]:   JEvTS 37 (1994) 55-68.

5161 **Henrich** Sarah,   Godfearing in Acts 10; the changing rules of hospitality in early Christianity: diss. Yale, [D]*Meeks* W.   NHv 1994. 288 p. 94-30271. – DissA 55 (1994s) p. 2002. – RelStR 21,255.

5162 *Matson* David L., [Acts 10,47...] The form and function of the household conversion narratives in the Acts of the Apostles: diss. Baylor, [D]*Parsons* M. 1994. 335 p. 94-22754. – DissA 55 (1994s) p. 995.

5163 *Taylor* Justin,   Why were the disciples first called 'Christians' at Antioch? (Acts 11,26):   RB 101 (1994) 75-94; franç. 75.

F8.7   **Act 13 ...** *Itinera Pauli;*   **Paul's Journeys.**

Franklin Eric,   Luke, interpreter of Paul ... jNsu 92, 1994 ➤ 4882.

5164 **Lentz** John C.[J], Luke's portrait of Paul: SNTS mg 77, [D]1993 ➤ 9,5369: [R]CBQ 56 (1994) 798s (V.P. *Branick*); CiuD 207 (1994) 518s (J. *Gutiérrez*); EvQ 66 (1994) 347-353 (B.M. *Rapske*); JRel 74 (1994) 555-7 (C. *Mount*); JTS 45 (1994) 239-242 (R.A. *Burridge*); NT 36 (1994) 408-410 (R.S. *Ascough*); RHR 211 (1994) 473-6 (F. *Blanchetière*); TS 55 (1994) 177 (D. *Hamm*).

5165 **Macdonald** Margaret Y.,   Las comunidades paulinas; estudios socio-históricos de la institucionalización en los estudios paulinos y deuteropaulinos [diss. Oxford],[T]. BtEstB 78.   S 1994, Sígueme.   351 p.   84-301-1221-9. – [R]EstE 69 (1994) 550s (F. *Pastor-Ramos*).

5166 **Taylor** Nicholas H.,   Paul, Antioch and Jerusalem [diss. Durham, [D]*Dunn* J.]: jNsu 56, [D]1992 ➤ 8,5534; 9,5326:   [R]BZ 38 (1994) 293s (C. *Heil*); EvQ 66 (1994) 93-95 (A. *Campbell*).

5167 *Fain* J.,   Church-Mission relationships; what we can learn from Acts 13,1-4: Stulos 2,1 (Bandung 1994) 19-39 [< NTAbs 39, p. 52].

5168 *Klauck* H.J., [Acts 13,4-12; 14,8-20] With Paul in Paphos and Lystra; magic and paganism in the Acts of the Apostles: Neotestamentica 28 (1994) 93-108.

5169 *Sandt* Huub van de,   The quotations in Acts 13,32-52 as a reflection of Luke's LXX interpretation: Biblica 75 (1994) 26-58; franç. 58.

5170 *deSilva* David A., [Ac 13,38s]   Paul's sermon in Antioch of Pisidia: BtS 151 (1994) 22-49.

5171 a) *Adinolfi* Marco, [At 14] Lo storpio di Listra e quello di Alessandria in confronto tra Paolo e Vespasiano; – b) *Destro* Adriana, *Pesce* Mauro, Paolo, la magia e l'esorcismo negli Atti degli Apostoli: ➤ 328a, Tarso 2, 1993/4, 127-134 / 90-116.

5172 **Fournier** Marianne,   The episode at Lystra (Acts 14,7-20a): a rhetorical and semiotic analysis: diss. Ottawa 1994. 328 p. – RTLv 26,536.

5173 *Sheung* Alex T.M.,   A narrative analysis of Acts 14:27-15:35; literary shaping in Luke's account of the Jerusalem council: WestTJ 55 (1993) 137-154.

5174 **Mbachu** Hilary I.,   Inculturation theology of the Jerusalem Council in Acts 15; an inspiration for the Igbo church today: diss. [D]*Weiser* A. Vallendar 1994. – TR 91,102.

5175 *Tagliaferri* Fiorino,   Discutevano animatamente ... (At 15,2):   Presbiteri 28 (1994) 275 ...

5176 **Thornton** Claus-Jürgen,   Der Zeuge ...:   WUNT 56, 1991 ➤ 7,4711 ...

9,5383: ^RCBQ 56 (1994) 160-2 (M.L. *Soards*); SvTKv 69 (1993) 28s (E. *Lövestam*) [RB 102,264-272, J. *Taylor*].

5177 *van Minnen* Peter, [Acts 16,35-39...] Paul the Roman citizen: JStNT 56 (1994) 43-52.

5178 *Papadopoulos* Nectarios D., Ⓖ A critical examination of the 17th chapter of the Acts of the Apostles: TAth 65 (1994) 904-952; Eng. 1023.

5179 *Bossuyt* P., *Radermakers* J., Rencontre de l'incroyant et inculturation; Paul à Athènes (Ac 17,16-34): NRT 117 (1995) 19-43.

5180 *a) Ukachukwu Manus* Chris, The Areopagus speech (Acts 17/16-34); a study on Luke's approach to evangelism and its significance in the African context; – *b) Monsengwo Pasinya* L., L'inculturation dans les Actes des Apôtres; – *c) Ukpong* Justin S., Mission in the Acts of the evangelized; – *d) Mbefo* L., Mission in the Acts of the Apostles; – *e) Arowele* P.J.,... in the African experience; → 303*a*, Actes et Jeunes Églises 1984/90, 197-218 / 130-133 / 165-196 / 139-164 / 219-240.

5181 *McKay* K.L., Foreign gods identified in Acts 17:18? [not any Anastasis]: TyndB 45 (1994) 411s.

5182 *Yeo Khiok-khng*, A rhetorical study of Acts 17.22-31; what has Jerusalem to do with Athens and Beijing?: Jian Dao 1 (Hong Kong 1994) 75-106; Ⓖ 107.

5182* **Kruse** I., [Act 18,26] 'Und Priska liess sich nicht beirren'; Frauengeschichten aus dem frühen Christentum: Tb 541. Gü 1994, Gü-V. 156 p.; ill. DM 19,80. – RHE 90,267*

5183 *Sedgwick* Colin, [Acts 20,7-13] One Sunday in Troas: ExpTim 106 (1994s) 274s.

5184 *Bulley* Alan D., Hanging in the balance; a semiotic study of Acts 20:7-12: ÉglT 25 (1994) 171-188.

5185 *MacDonald* D.R., Luke's Eutychus and HOMER's Elpenor: Acts 20,7-12 and Odyssey 10-12: Journal of Higher Criticism 1 (Montclair NJ 1994) 5-24 [< NTAbs 39, p.238].

5186 **Cukrowski** Kenneth L., Pagan polemic and Lukan apologetics; the function of Acts 20:17-38: diss. Yale, ^D*Malherbe* A. NHv 1994. 311 p. 94-28278. – DissA 55 (1994s) p.1589; RelStR 21,255.

5187 *Kilgallen* John J., [Acts 20,18-35] Paul's speech to the Ephesian elders; its structure: ETL 70 (1994) 112-121.

5188 *O'Toole* Robert F., What role does Jesus' saying in Acts 20,35 play in Paul's address to the Ephesian elders?: Biblica 75 (1994) 329-349; franç. 349.

5189 **Maissner** Stefan, 'Die Heimholung des Ketzers'; Studien zur jüdischen Auseinandersetzung mit Paulus: Diss. ^D*Burchard* C. Heidelberg 1994. 305 p. > Tü, Mohr. – RTLv 26, p.338.

5190 **Schwartz** Daniel R., Agrippa I, the last king of Judaea [< Ⓗ 1987]: TStAJ 23, 1990: ^RJQR 84 (1993s) 329-333 (A. *Kasher*).

5191 **Rapske** Brian M., Paul in Roman custody: Acts in its First Century Setting 4. GR/Carlisle 1994, Eerdmans/Paternoster. 512 p. $30. 0-8028-2435-8 / 0-85364-565-5. – ^RExpTim 106 (1994s) 343 (C.K. *Barrett*: unlike 1s [→ 243; 258*c*], a single author and theme).

5192 *a) Rapske* Brian M., Acts, travel and shipwreck; – *b) French* David, Acts and the Roman roads of Asia Minor; – *c) Scott* James M., Luke's geographical horizons; – *d) Porter* Stanley E., The 'we' passages; – *e) Blue* Bradley, Acts and the house church; – *f) Gill* David W.J., Acts and the urban élites: → 243, Acts Graeco-Roman 1994, 1-47 / 49-58 /

483-544 / 545-574 / 119-192 + 34 fig. / 105-118 [*al.* → infra 10518, 11350, 12499, 12877, 13029, 13473].

5193 *Cagnetta* Mariella, [Ac 24,2-8] Tertullo contro Paolo; l'accusa di *stásis*: → 86, ᶠNALDINI M., Paideia 1994, 7-15.

5194 *Hawthorne* T., A discourse analysis of Paul's shipwreck: Acts 27:1-44: JTrTLing 6 (1993) 253-273 [< NTAbs 38, p. 213].

5195 *Sandt* Huub van de, Acts 28,28; no salvation for the people of Israel? an answer in the perspective of the LXX: ETL 70 (1994) 341-358.

5196 **Wansink** Craig, 'Imprisonment for the Gospel'; the Apostle Paul and Roman prisons: diss. Yale, ᴰ*Meeks* W. NHv 1993. – RTLv 26, p. 540.

XIV. **Johannes**

G1 *Corpus johanneum* .1 **John and his community.**

5197 *Busse* U., The beloved disciple: Skrift 15 (1994) 219-227 [< NTAbs 39, p. 412].

5198 **Collins** Raymond F., John and his witness: ZacchaeusSt, 1991 → 7, 4742; 9,5408: ColMn 1991, Liturgical. – ᴿAustralasCR 71 (1993) 119-122 (J. *McSweeney*, with three others of the series).

5199 **Culpepper** R. Alan, John the son of Zebedee, the life of a legend: St-PersNT. Columbia 1994, Univ. S. Carolina. xix-376 p.; bibliog. 330-352. $50. 0-87249-962-6 [NTAbs 38, p. 459; JTS 46,274, Ruth B. *Edwards*].

5200 **Ernst** Josef, Juan, retrato teológico 1992 → 8,5618; 9,5412: ᴿRazF 229 (1994) 331 (J. M. *Vallarino*); ScripTPamp 26 (1994) 782-4 (A. *García-Moreno*).

5201 **Grassi** Joseph A., The secret identity of the beloved disciple 1992 → 8,5619; 9,5413: ᴿCritRR 6 (1993) 243s (F. *Segovia*).

5202 **Howard-Brook** Wes, Becoming children of God; John's Gospel and radical discipleship: Bible & Liberation. Mkn 1994, Orbis. xviii-510 p. $22. 0-88344-983-8 [NTAbs 39, p. 324].

5203 ᴱ**Kaestli** J. D., *Poffet* J. M., *Zumstein* J., La communauté johannique 1987/90 → 6,538* ... 9,5414: ᴿCiuD 206 (1993) 917s (J. *Gutiérrez*).

5204 **Kenney** Garrett C., Leadership in John; an analysis of the situation and strategy of the Gospel and Epistles of John: diss. Gonzaga, ᴰ*Wilson* Sandra M. Spokane 1994, 104 p. 14-24601. – DissA 55 (1994s) p. 995.

5205 *a) Okure* sr. Teresa, Witnessing in the Johannine communities; – *b) Poucouta* Paulin, Les communautés johanniques et le pouvoir impérial dans Apocalypse 13; – *c) Rwehumbiza* Rulange W. P., Presence and activity of the Holy Spirit in the Johannine community (Jn 14-16): → 303*, Communautés johanniques 1989/91, 71-85 / 242-264 / 202-241.

5206 **Painter** John, The quest for the Messiah ... Johannine community 1991 → 7,245; 9,5415 [²1993: TDig 42,83]: ᴿTPhil 69 (1994) 572s (J. *Beutler*).

5207 **Powell** E., The unfinished Gospel; notes on the quest for the historical Jesus. Westlake Village CA 1994, Symposium. 347 p. 36 fig. $24. 0-9639650-6-9 [NTAbs 39, p. 143: the Beloved Disciple was in a power-struggle with Peter, for whose side Mark wrote, including Jn 21 to terminate his own Gospel].

5208 **Rensberger** David, Johannine faith and liberating community 1988 → 4,5400 ... 8,5629: ᴿConcordiaTQ 58 (1994) 53-55 (B. *Schuchard*).

5209 **Rusam** Dietrich, Die Gemeinschaft der Kinder Gottes; das Motiv der

Gotteskindschaft and die Gemeinden der johanneischen Briefe [Diss. Neuendettelsau 1990]: BW 133 ➤ 9,5417. Stu 1993, Kohlhammer. 262 p. DM 69. 3-17-012357-2. − ᴿTLZ 119 (1994) 322-4 (W. *Vogler*).

5210 **Smalley** Stephen S., Thunder and love; John's Revelation and John's community. Milton Keynes 1994, Word-UK. 223 p.; bibliog. 185-197. £8. 0-85009-606-5. − ᴿExpTim 106 (1994s) 56 (J. M. *Court*: competent but a bit old-fashioned, and not attentive to J. J. COLLINS on genre).

5211 **Stowasser** Martin, Johannes der Täufer im vierten Ev. 1992 ➤ 8,5633; 9,5420: ᴿCBQ 56 (1994) 389s (M. C. de *Boer*); FrSZ 41 (1994) 579s (G. *Schlebert*); TLZ 119 (1994) 240s (O. *Böcher*).

5212 (**Tavares de**) **Lima** João, [Jn 1,42] Tu serás chamado *Kēphas*; estudo exegético sobre Pedro no Quarto Evangelho: diss. ᴰ*Caba* J. Nº 4030: AnGreg 265. R 1994, Pont. Univ. Gregoriana. xxxiii-392 p.; bibliog. 361-385. Lᵐ 54. 88-7652-667-6. − RTLv 26, p. 538. − ᴿExpTim 106 (1994s) 185s (E. *Best*).

5213 *Timmins* Nicholas G., Variations in style in the Johannine literature: JStNT 53 (1994) 47-64.

G1.2 **Evangelium Johannis:** *textus, commentarii.*

5214 **Albisani** Sauro, Vangelo secondo Giovanni, versione in endecasillabi. F 1994, Polistampa. 151 p.

5215 **Attinger** Daniel, Evangelo secondo san Giovanni; vedere, credere, amare. R 1993, Nuove frontiere. 140 p. − ᴿClaretianum 34 (1994) 597s (A. *Pardilla*).

5216 *Backus* I., Church, communion and community in BUCER's Commentary on the Gospel of John: ➤ 410, Bucer 1994.

5217 ᵀᴱ**Blanc** Cécile, ORIGÈNE, Commentaire sur saint Jean V (Livre XXVIII et XXXII): SChr 385, 1992 ➤ 8,5638; 9,3422: ᴿAntClas 63 (1994) 422s (J. *Schamp*); Bijdragen 55 (1994) 212s (M. *Parmentier*, Eng.); Gregorianum 75 (1994) 376s (G. *Pelland*); PrOrChr 42 (1992) 228s (P. *Ternant*); RÉAug 40 (1994) 221s (J. *Doignon*).

5218 **Bondermaker** J. P., *Monshouwer* D., Johannes, de evangelie van de feesten. Zoetermeer 1993, Boeken-C. 171 p. *f* 28,50. 90-239-0077-4. − ᴿKerkT 45 (1994) 252s (J. *Helderman*).

5219 **Brown** Raymond E., Il Vangelo e le Lettere di Giovanni; commentario breve: BtBib 14. Brescia 1994, Queriniana. 179 p. Lᵐ 25. − ᴿAsprenas 41 (1994) 444 (G. *Di Palma*).

5219* **Calvin** John, John: Crossway Classic Comm. Wheaton IL 1994, Crossway. xii-473 p. 0-89107-778-2.

5220 **Christ** Karl, *al.*, Expositio Sancti Evangelii secundum Iohannem, magistri ECKHARDT: Dts/lat Werke 3. Stu 1963-90, Kohlhammer. 3-17-001085-9.

5221 **Comfort** P. W., I am the way; a spiritual journey through the Gospel of John. GR 1994, Baker. 212 p. $16. 0-8010-2591-5 [NTAbs 39, p. 322].

5222 **Ehrman** Bart D., *al.*, The text of the Fourth Gospel in the writings of ORIGEN (1) 1992 ➤ 8,5644: ᴿCBQ 56 (1994) 790s (F. T. *Gignac*); ETL 70 (1994) 157-9 (F. *Neirynck*).

5223 **Fabris** R., Gv 1992 ➤ 8,5645; 9,5426: ᴿCC 145 (1994) 94s (D. *Scaiola*).

5224 **Fernández** Víctor (Manuel), San Juan y su mundo; comentario simple al cuarto Evangelio, 1992 ➤ 9,5438 [NTAbs 38, p. 282]: ᴿRBíbArg 55 (1993) 126s (A. J. *Levoratti*).

5225 **Fischer** Bonifatius, Varianten 4. zu Johannes; VLatGesch 18, 1991 ➤ 7, 4747 ... 9,5427: ᴿCritRR 6 (1993) 233s (C. D. *Osburn*).

5226 **Flanagan** Neal, Vangelo secondo Giovanni e Lettere di Gv: Bibbia per Tutti 29. Brescia 1992, Queriniana. 187 p. Lᵐ 15. - ᴿCC 145 (1994,1) 624s (D. *Scaiola*, anche su Nº 26-28).

5227 **González** Eugenio, Y ... no le recibieron: Nueva Alianza 127. S 1994, Sígueme. 317 p. - ᴿLumenVr 43 (1994) 410 (U. *Gil Ortega*: título con ¿ — sin?; comento literario e un tanto original de Juan).

5228 **Gourgues** Michel, Jean, de l'exégèse à la prédication, 1. Carême-Pâque: Lire la Bible 97. P 1993, Cerf. 176 p. - ᴿScEspr 46 (1994) 357s (R. *Dumais*).

5229 **Koen** Lars, The Saving Passion ... CYRIL A./John 1991 ➤ 7,4955; 9,5630; really on whole Gospel, ➤ 8,8654: ᴿRechSR 82 (1994) 606 (B. *Sesboüé*: status quaestionis abondant, mais beaucoup d'ignorances et de naïvetés); SvTKv 69 (1993) 90-92 (L. *Thunberg*).

5230 **Léon-Dufour** Xavier, Lecture III,13-17, Les adieux du Seigneur 1993 ➤ 9,5435: ᴿAngelicum 71 (1994) 595-7 (S. *Jurić*); ArTGran 57 (1994) 430s (P. *Contreras*); BLitEc 95 (1994) 243 (S. *Légasse*); BZ 38 (1994) 286s (R. *Schnackenburg*: anregend, fruchtbar); CC 145 (1994,3) 201s (D. *Scaiola*, 2); CiTom 121 (1994) 410 (J. L. *Espinel*, 3); EfMex 11 (1993) 113s (R. *López*), 265-7 (S. *Carrillo Alday*, 1s); ÉTRel 69 (1994) 424s (E. *Cuvillier*); RET 53 (1993) 389-391 (P. *Barrado Fernández*, 1s); RHPR 74 (1994) 211-3 (F. *Grob*, 1s); Telema 20 (1994) 77-79 (R. *Capoen*); TvT 34 (1994) 196 (L. *Grollenberg*).

5231 **Leone** Luigi, CIRILLO d'Alessandria, Commento al Vangelo di Giovanni: TPatr 111-3. R 1994, Città nuova. 610 p., 371 p., 569 p. 88-311-3111-7. - ᴿAnnTh 8 (1994) 426s (J. A. *Riestra*).

5232 **L'Éplattenier** Charles, L'Ev. de J 1992 ➤ 9,5437: ᴿRHPR 94 (1994) 213 (F. *Grob*).

5234 **Münch-Labacher** Gudrun, Naturhaftes und geschichtliches Denken bei CYRILL von Alexandrien; die verschiedenen Betrachtungsweisen der Heilsverwirklichung in seinem Johanneskommentar: kath. Diss. ᴰ*Vogt*. Tübingen 1994. - TR 91,102.

5235 *Norris* J. M., The theological structure of AUGUSTINE's exegesis in the Tractatus in Evangelium Iohannis: ➤ 9,4664f, Collectanea 1990/3, 385-394 [RHE 90,40*].

5236 **Pacomio** Luciano, Il Vangelo secondo Giovanni; unità del cuore, unità nella storia: Rigenerati dalla Parola 1. Mi 1994, Àncora. 144 p. Lᵐ 15. 88-7610-480-1. - ᴿCC 145 (1994,4) 524s (G. *Ferraro*).

5237 ᵀᴱ**Phillips** Jane E., ERASMUS, Collected Works 46. Paraphrase on John. Toronto 1991, Univ. 371 p. $85. - ᴿJEvTS 37 (1994) 457s (M. *Bauman*: with high praise also for volumes 9, 29, 32, and AUGUSTIJN's biography; but translator of John not indicated; here Erasmus is 'B. F. WESTCOTT, J. STAUPITZ and S. JOHNSON all wrapped in one').

5238 **Marchadour** Alain, L'Évangile de Jean, commentaire pastoral. P 1993, Centurion. 263 p. 2-227-36600-1.

5238* ᵀᴱ**Rettig** John W., AUGUSTINE, Tractates on the Gospel of John 55-111: Fathers 90. Wsh 1994, Catholic University of America. x-328 p.

5239 **Schenke** Ludger, Das Johannesevangelium 1992 ➤ 8,5663; 9,5445: ᴿRHPR 74 (1994) 209s (F. *Grob*).

5240 **Servotte** Herman, According to John; a literary reading of the Fourth Gospel. L 1994, Darton-LT. vi-104 p. 0-232-52069-0.

5241 **Speyr** Adrienne von, John. SF 1991-4, Ignatius. 4 vol.: I. ᵀ*Wiedenhöver*

Lucia, 1994, 322 p.; II. ^T*McNeil* Bryan, 1994, 444 p.; III. ...; IV. ^T*Kipp* David, also 444 p. 0-87870-411-1; -413-8; ...; -368-9.

5242 **Stibbe** Mark W. G., John: Readings 1993 ➤ 9,5447: ^RCBQ 56 (1994) 808s (J. E. *Bruns*); TBR 7,2 (1994s) 19 (R. *Morgan*).

5243 **Talbert** Charles H., Reading John 1992 ➤ 8,5667; 9,5449: ^RCBQ 56 (1994) 157s (J. *Winkler*); EvQ 66 (1994) 276-8 (R. G. *Maccini*); Horizons 21 (1994) 180s (Sandra M. *Schneiders*); WWorld 14 (1994) 95s (C. R. *Koester*).

G1.3 **Introductio** *in Evangelium Johannis.*

5244 **Ashton** John, Studying John; approaches to the Fourth Gospel. Ox 1994, Clarendon. 226 p.; bibliog. p. 208-218. £27.50. 0-19-826355-4. – ^RExpTim 106 (1994s) 343 (M. W. G. *Stibbe*).

5245 **Ashton** John, Understanding the Fourth Gospel 1991 ➤ 7,4768; ... 9,5454: ^RBR 10,4 (1994) 15.54 (Pheme *Perkins*); RechSR 82 (1994) 231-5 (X. *Léon-Dufour*).

5246 **Burge** Gary M., Interpreting the Gospel of John: Baker GuidesNT 5, 1992 ➤ 8,5676; 9,5424: ^RCBQ 56 (1992) 358s (Barbara E. *Reid*: draws rather traditional conclusions from recent tools); EvQ 66 (1994) 275s (P. *Ensor*); TrinJ 15 (1994) 138-140 (A. J. *Kostenberger*).

5247 **Comfort** Philip W., **Hawley** Wendell C., Opening the Gospel of John, Wheaton IL 1994, Tyndale. xxviii-346 p. 0-8423-4596-5 [TDig 42,61].

5248 ^E**Denaux** Adelbert, John and the Synoptics [Colloquium Lv 1990]: BtETL 101, 1992 ➤ 8,465; 9,5456: ^RCBQ 56 (1994) 397-9 (C. C. *Black*); ETL 70 (1994) 444-9 (C. *Coulot*); RHPR 74 (1994) 210s (F. *Grob*); TR 90 (1994) 211-3 (U. *Schnelle*).

5249 **Dunderberg** Ismo, Johannes und die Synoptiker; Studien zu Joh 1-9 [diss. ^D*Aejmelaeus* L.]: HumLitt 69. Helsinki 1994, Acad. Fennica. 225 p. Fm 140 [RTLv 26, p. 536; RelStR 21,235, D. M. *Smith*; NTAbs 39, p. 536; TR 91,311, Beate *Kowalskij*; TLZ 120,337, K.-M. *Bull*].

5250 **Hanson** Anthony T., The prophetic Gospel, John 1991 ➤ 7,4275... 9,5459: ^RCritRR 6 (1993) 249-251 (C. K. *Koester*); Way 33 (1993) 340 (J. *Pridmore*).

5251 **Kreitzer** L., The Gospel according to John: Regent's Study Guides 1. Ox 1990, Regent's. viii-123 p. $11 pa. 0-9518104-0-5 [NTAbs 38, p. 462].

5252 **Milne** Bruce, The message of John. Leicester 1993, Inter-Varsity. 352 p. – ^RSTEv 6 (1994) 88 (M. *Clemente*).

5253 **Pongutá** H. Silvestro, El Evangelio según san Juan; Cartas de San Juan; una presentación: CuadBíb 7. Caracas 1994, Asoc. Bib. Salesiana. xi-200 p. 980-345-027-1 [NTAbs 39, p. 327].

5254 **Quast** Kevin, Reading... Jn... introd. 1991 ➤ 7,4787; 9,5463: ^RCritRR 6 (1993) 279s (G. M. *Burge*); TorJT 10 (1994) 265s (A. M. *Osiander*).

5255 **Rand** Jan A. du, Johannine perspectives; introduction to the Johannine writings 1991 ➤ 7,4789: ^RCritRR 6 (1993) 230-2 (R. *Kysar*).

5256 **Sloyan** Gerard S., What are they saying about John? 1991 ➤ 7,4792... 9,5464: ^RConcordTQ 58 (1994) 227-9 (W. C. *Weinrich*); RB 101 (1994) 141 (P. *Buis*).

5257 **Zumstein** Jean, L'apprentissage de la foi; à la découverte de l'évangile de Jean et de ses lecteurs 1993 ➤ 9,5466: ^RRHPR 74 (1994) 212 (F. *Grob*).

Structura, analysis fontium – **source analysis.**
5258 **Barnhart** B., The good wine; reading John from the center. NY 1993, Paulist. 537 p. $20. 0-8091-3416-0. – ^RExpTim 106 (1994s) 25 (M. W. G. *Stibbe*: unexciting geometrical '*mandala* squared-circle' structure).

5259 **Belle** Gilbert van, The signs source in the Fourth Gospel; historical survey and critical evaluation of the semeia hypothesis: BtETL 116. Lv 1994, Univ./Peeters. xiv-503 p. Fb 2500. 90-6186-624-3 / 90-6831-649-4 [TR 91,361].

5260 **Boismard** M.-E., *Lamouille* A., Un évangile pré-johannique 1/1, 1993 [Biblica 76,115, C. *Amphoux*] ➤ 9,5468: [R]ÉTRel 69 (1994) 105 (P. *Genton*); RB 101 (1994) 458-461 (J. *Taylor*). RBén 104 (1994) 425 (D. *Misonne*); ScripTPamp 26 (1994) 789s (A. *García-Moreno*).

5261 — 2. Jn 2,13-4,54 1994 [TLZ 120,518-520, W. *Wiefel*]. – [R]ETL 70 (1994) 462s (F. *Neirynck*).

5262 **Brodie** Thomas L., The quest for the origin of John's Gospel 1993 ➤ 9,5469: [R]CBQ 56 (1994) 582s (U.C. von *Wahlde*: would be more convincing without too-wide generalization); JStNT 56 (1994) 122s (S.A. *Hunt*); JTS 45 (1994) 232s (B. *Shellard*: imagination); RelStR 20 (1994) 152 (D.M. *Smith*: akin to 1920s B.W. BACON, not cited; does not really disprove MARTYN/BROWN synagogue controversy); ScotJT 47 (1994) 411s (M. *Goulder*); WestTJ 56 (1994) 429-431 (M. *Silva*, also on his and TALBERT's commentaries).

5263 **Harner** P.B., Relation analysis in the Fourth Gospel; a study in reader-response criticism. Lewiston NY 1993, Mellen. xiv-182 p.; $60. 0-7734-3364-8.

5264 *Johns* Loren L., *Miller* Douglas B., The signs as witnesses in the Fourth Gospel; reexamining the evidence: CBQ 56 (1994) 519-535.

5265 **Korting** Georg, Die esoterische Struktur des Johannesevangeliums. Rg 1994, Pustet. ix-447 p.; 88 p. DM 58. 3-7917-1422-8 [TLZ 120,799, J. *Frey*]. – [R]ExpTim 106 (1994s) 186 (E. *Best*); FgNt 7 (1994) 223s (J. *Peláez*).

5266 **Ruckstuhl** Eugen, *Dschulnigg* Peter, Stilkritik und Verfasserfrage im JohEv: NOrb 17, 1991 ➤ 7,4790; 9,5472: [R]JBL 113 (1994) 151s (D.A. *Carson*).

5267 **Sinclair** S.G., The road and the truth; the editing of John's Gospel: Vallejo CA 1994, BIBAL. xi-111 p. $13. 0-941037-31-2 [NTAbs 39, p. 146].

Bibliographica – **Johannine research.**

5268 **Benedetti** Ugolino, Il Vangelo secondo Giovanni alla fine dell'epoca moderna: fede cristiana come interpretazione del senso: Paralleli. Mi 1994, ViPe. 334 p. 88-343-3969-X.

5269 *Boshoff* P.B., Walter SCHMITHALS en die Johannese geskrifte: Herv-TSt 49 (1993) 728-741 [< NTAbs 39, p. 45].

5270 *Léon-Dufour* Xavier, Bulletin d'exégèse du NT; l'Évangile de Jean: RechSR 82 (1994) 227-250.

Mees M., Die frühe Rezeptionsgeschichte des Jo.-Ev. 1994 ➤ 207b.

5271 [E]**Padovese** L., Efeso su Giovanni 3, 1992/3 ➤ 9,401: [R]Gregorianum 75 (1994) 762s (G. *Ferraro*).

5271* **Reim** Günter, Zugänge zum Evangelium des Johannes; 24 Zugänge exemplarisch; Bilder und Texte aus der Literatur. Erlangen 1994, Ev.-Luth. 147 p.

5272 **Smith** D. Moody, John among the Gospels... twentieth-century research 1992 ➤ 8,5696; 9,5481: [R]Gregorianum 75 (1994) 346s (J. *Galot*); Interpretation 48 (1994) 96 (R. *Kysar*); NRT 116 (1994) 113s (Y. *Simoens*).

5273 [E]**Stibbe** Mark W. G., The Gospel of John as literature; an anthology of twentieth-century perspectives: NT TSt 17. Leiden 1993, Brill. x-254 p.

*f*145.   90-04-09848-8. – ᴿBInterp 2 (1994) 236s (J. *Ashton*); BZ 38 (1994) 285s (H. J. *Klauck*, tit. pp.).
5274 *Untergassmair* Franz G., Das Johannesevangelium; ein Bericht über neuere Literatur aus der Johannesforschung: TR 90 (1994) 91-108.

Intuitiones de scopo auctoris – **narrative analysis.**
5275 **Bradley** Mark A., The functions of questions in the Fourth Gospel; a narrative-critical inquiry: diss. Golden Gate Baptist Theol. Sem., ᴰ*Brooks* O. 1994. 281 p. 94-31756. – DissA 55 (1994s) p. 2001.
5276 *Lincoln* Andrew T., Trials, plots and the narrative of the Fourth Gospel: JStNT 56 (1994) 3-30.
5277 **Lee** Dorothy A., The symbolic narratives of the Fourth Gospel; the interplay of form and meaning [< diss. Sydney 1991, ᴰ*Byrne* B.]: jNsu 95. Shf 1994, JStOT. 263 p. £37.50. 1-85075-468-3 [NTAbs 39, p. 140; JTS 46,640-5, Catrin *Williams*]. – ᴿExpTim 106 (1994s) 56 (J. M. *Court*).
5278 **Mannucci** Valerio, Giovanni, il Vangelo narrante 1993 ➤ 9,5486 [Gregorianum 76,203, G. *Ferraro*]. – ᴿTeresianum 45 (1994) 636s (V. *Pasquetto*).
5279 *Overstreet* R. Larry, The Gospel of John, outlined by purpose: CalvaryB 9,2 (1993) 36-54.
5280 **Stibbe** Mark, John as storyteller: SNTS mg 73, 1992 ➤ 8,5724; 9,5488: ᴿJBL 113 (1994) 733-6 (R. A. *Culpepper*); Neotestamentica 28 (1994) 245s (D. F. *Tolmie*); RelStR 20 (1994) 152 (D. M. *Smith*: insightful and provocative).
5281 **Stibbe** Mark W. G., John's Gospel [hero, plot, genre, style, polemic]. L 1994, Routledge. 153 p. £30; pa. £10. 0-415-09510-7; -1-5.
5282 **Tovey** Derek, Narrative art and act in the Fourth Gospel; aspects of the Johannine point of view: diss. ᴰ*Barton* S. Durham UK 1994. – RTLv 26, p. 540.
5283 **Welch** Christian, Erzählte Zeichen; die Wundergeschichten des Johannesevangeliums literarisch untersucht; mit einem Ausblick auf Joh 21: WUNT 2/69. Tü 1994, Mohr. xvi-377 p. 3-16-146249-1.

G1.4   *Themata de evangelio Johannis* – **John's Gospel, topics.**

5284 ᴱ**Bourg** D., al., Variations johanniques 1989 ➤ 5,381: ᴿScripTPamp 26 (1994) 784s (A. *García-Moreno*: divulgación).
5285 **Collins** R. F., These things have been written 1990 ➤ 7,193; 8,5747: ᴿConcordTQ 58 (1994) 57s (B. *Schuchard*).
5286 **Countryman** L. William, The mystical way in the Fourth Gospel; crossing over into God² [¹1987]. Ph 1994, Trinity. ix-164 p. 1-56338- 103-6.
5287 **Davies** Margaret, Rhetoric and reference in the Fourth Gospel: jNsu 69, 1992 ➤ 8,5748; 9,5492 [RelStR 20,152, D. M. *Smith*]: ᴿCBQ 56 (1994) 366s (D. *Neufeld*); TBR 7,2 (1994s) 19 (R. *Morgan*).
5288 *Harrington* W., The Johannine Jesus: Scripture in Church 24 (Dublin 1994) 233-240 [< NTAbs 38, p. 374: 'John has imposed wholly the Christ of faith upon the Jesus of history'].
5289 *Hawkin* D. J., History and faith, 6. The peripheral voice; the Gospel of John and the challenge of modernity: EpworthR 21,3 (1994) 86-93 [< NTAbs 39, p. 232].
5290 **Howard-Brook** Wes, Becoming children of God; John's Gospel and radical discipleship: Bible & Liberation. Mkn 1994, Orbis. xviii-510 p. $22 pa. 0-88344-983-8 [TDig 42,273].

5291 (Pablo) *Martín* José,   Los evangelios de JUSTINO y la nueva tesis de M.-E. BOISMARD: RBibArg 55 (1993) 91-101.
5292 *Santos* B. Silva,   *a*) A humanidade de Jesus no evangelo de São João; – *b*) O simbolismo no evangelho de João: Atualização 247 (1994) 3-37 / 22 (!) (1993) 107-131 [Stromata 50 (1994) 279].
5293 **Schuchard** Bruce G.,   Scripture within... John: SBL diss. 133, 1992: RConcordJ 20 (1994) 86-89 (P. *Raabe*); Interpretation 48 (1994) 214 (R. *Kysar*); JBL 113 (1994) 344-6 (D. *Rensberger*).
5294 **Tafi** Angelo, *Zanella* Danilo,   Evangelizzatori con Giovanni Evangelista: In ascolto. T-Leumann 1993, Elle Di Ci. 171 p. 88-01-10307-7.
5295 **Westermann** Claus,   Das Johannesevangelium aus der Sicht des Alten Testaments: ArbT 77. Stu 1994, Calwer. 112 p. 3-7668-3274-3. – RDielB 28 (1992s!) 265-8 (B. J. *Diebner*: lesbar).

Theologica
5296 **Beasley Murray** G. R.,   Gospel of life; theology in the Fourth Gospel [1990 Fuller Payton lectures] 1991 → 7,4803 ... 9,5499: RCritRR 6 (1993) 205-7 (P. N. *Anderson*); Neotestamentica 28 (1994) 246s (D. F. *Tolmie*); RBibArg 55 (1993) 239-242 (A. J. *Levoratti*); SvEx 59 (1994) 183-5 (O. *Christoffersson*).
5297 **Boismard** M.-É., Moïse ou Jésus, ... christologie johannique: BtETL 84, 1988 → 5,5416 ... 9,5500: RLvSt 19 (1994) 76 (J. T. *Gignac*); ScEspr 46 (1994) 229-238 (G. *Rochais*).
5298 **Boismard** M.-É., Moses or Jesus, T*Viviano* B.T.; BtETL 84-A, 1993 (US. Mp) → 9,5501: RETL 70 (1994) 463s (F. *Neirynck*).
5299 **Burkett** Delbert,   The Son of Man in the Gospel of John [diss. Duke]: jNsu 56, 1991 → 7,4806 ... 9,5501: RTZBas 50 (1994) 268s (E. L. *Miller*).
5300 **Cassidy** Richard J.,   John's Gospel in new perspective; Christology and the realities of Roman power 1992 → 8,5731: RGregorianum 75 (1994) 203 (G. *Ferraro*); CBQ 56 (1994) 134s (J. E. *Bruns*); JBL 113 (1994) 731-3 (P. N. *Anderson*); NewTR 7,2 (1994) 100-2 (J. *Winkler*); NRT 116 (1994) 114s (Y. *Simoens*); Pacifica 7 (1994) 353-5 (F. J. *Moloney*); TLZ 119 (1994) 419s (K. *Wengst*); TorJT 10 (1994) 251s (E. P. *Janzen*).
5301 **Collins** Raymond F.,   John and his witness 1991 → 7,4770 [RB 102,621, J. *Taylor*].
5302 **Ferraro** Giuseppe, Mio-Tuo. Teologia del possesso reciproco del Padre e del Figlio nel Vangelo di Giovanni. Vaticano 1994, Editrice. 214 p. 88-209-2090-1.
5303 **Harrington** Daniel J.,   John's thought and theology 1990 → 6,5712; 8, 5733: RConcordTQ 58 (1994) 173s (W. C. *Weinrich*).
5304 **Hasitschka** M.,   Befreiung von Sünde nach dem Joh.-ev. D1989 → 6, 5714: RCiuD 207 (1994) 198s (J. *Gutiérrez*).
5305 **Kinast** Robert L.,   If only you recognized God's gift; John's Gospel as an illustration of theological reflection 1993 → 9,5505 [TBR 7/1,26, R. *Morgan*].
5306 **Knöppler** Thomas,   Die theologia crucis des Johannesevangeliums; das Verständnis des Todes Jesu im Rahmen der johanneischen Inkarnations- und Erhöhungschristologie [diss. Mü 1993s → 9,5629]: WM 69. Neuk 1994. x-310 p.; Bibliog. 279-310. 3-7887-1501-4.
5307 **Loader** William,   The Christology of the Fourth Gospel: BeitBExT 23, 1989 → 5,5446 ... 7,4824: RRThom 94 (1994) 695-8 (L. *Devillers*).
5308 **Morgen** Michèle,   Afin que le monde soit sauvé; Jésus révèle sa mission du salut dans l'Évangile de Jean: LDiv 154, 1993 → 9,5808: RCar-

thaginensia 10 (1994) 456 (R. *Sanz Valdivieso*); EsprVie 104 (1994) 79s (É. *Cothenet*).

5309 *Rabiej* Stanisław, La signification sotériologique de *egō eimi* de Jésus-Christ: AtKap 120 (1993) 15-27.

5310 **Schnelle** Udo, Antidocetic Christology in Jn, [T]*Maloney* Linda M. 1992 → 9,5514: [R]CBQ 56 (1994) 608s (D. R. *Bauer*); Pacifica 7 (1994) 246-8 (F. J. *Moloney*); TorJT 10 (1994) 267s (A. M. *Osiander*).

5311 **Scott** Martin, Sophia and the Johannine Jesus: jNsu 71, [D]1992 → 9, 5515: [R]JBL 113 (1994) 152-4 (C. R. *Koester*).

5312 **Thompson** M. M., The Incarnate Word; perspectives on Jesus in the Fourth Gospel [= The humanity of Jesus in the Fourth Gospel 1988]. Peabody MA 1993, Hendrickson. viii-168 p. $9 pa. 1-56563-025-4 [NTAbs 39, p. 329].

5313 *Trumbower* Jeffrey A., Born from above... anthropology of Jn: HermUnT 29, 1992 → 8,5741; 9,5518: [R]Biblica 75 (1994) 270-6 (G. *Segalla*); CiuD 206 (1993) 921s (J. *Gutiérrez*); JBL 113 (1994) 157-9 (Marianne *Meye Thompson*); JRel 74 (1994) 385s (A. H. *Maynard*).

Particularia – **observations of detail.**

5314 *Canévet* Mariette, Une fausse symétrie; la venue du Christ chez les parfaits dans l'Ancien et le Nouveau Testaments selon ORIGÈNE In Joh., I,VII,37-40: Gregorianum 75 (1994) 743-9.

5314* *Carl* K. J., The idea of 'knowing' in the Johannine literature: BangaloreTF 25,1 (1993) 53-75 [< NTAbs 39, p. 45].

5315 *a*) *Edmond* Djitancar G., Jésus et les autorités juives dans l'Évangile de Jean; – *b*) *Manus* Chris U., Jesus and the Jewish authorities in the Fourth Gospel: → 303*b*, [E]*Amewowo* W., *al.*, Communautés johanniques 1989/91, 118-134 / 135-155.

5316 **Ensor** Peter, Jesus and his 'works'; the Johannine sayings in historical perspective: diss. Aberdeen 1994. – RTLv 26,536.

5317 *Ferrando* M. A., Reflexiones en torno al concepto de vida en el Evangelio según san Juan: TVida 35,1s (1994) 17-19 [< NTAbs 39, p. 232].

5318 *Ferraro* Giuseppe, La terminologia temporale (l' 'ora' e il 'giorno' di Cristo) nel commento di ORIGENE al quarto vangelo: OrChrPer 60 (1994) 363-398.

5319 **Hancock** Frank C.[III], Secret epiphanies; the hermeneutics of revealing and concealing in the Fourth Gospel: diss. Rice, [D]*Kelber* W. 1994. 199 p. 95-14180. – DissA 55 (1994s) p. 3879.

5320 **Lindars** Barnabas († 1991), Essays on John, [E]*Tuckett* C. M., 1992 → 8,271; 9,5494: [R]RivB 42 (1994) 230-3 (L. *Cilia*); RThom 94 (1994) 700s (L. *Devillers*).

5321 **Manns** Frédéric, L'évangile de Jean à la lumière du Judaïsme (21 reprints): SBF Anal 33, 1991 → 8,5138: [R]Salesianum 56 (1994) 375 (R. *Vicent*).

5321* *Pinto* Carlos O., O papel da mulher no evangelho de João: VoxScr 3 (1993) 193-213.

5322 *Sielepin* Adelajda sr., ℗ Resurrection and peace in the light of the Fourth Gospel: → 92*, [F]PIERONEK T., AnCracov 26 (1994) 237-248; Eng. 248.

5323 **Suggit** J., The sign of life; studies in the Fourth Gospel and the liturgy of the Church. Pietermaritzburg 1993, Cluster. xii-194 p. R 24 pa. 0-9583807-1-6 [NTAbs 39, p. 329: D. *Tutu* pref.].

5324 *Swanson* Tod D., To prepare a place; Johannine Christianity and the collapse of ethnic territory: JAAR 62 (1994) 241-263.
5325 *Taeger* Jens-W., 'Gesiegt! O himmlische Musik des Wortes'; zur Entfaltung des Siegesmotivs in den johanneischen Schriften: ZNW 85 (1994) 23-46.
5326 *Thatcher* Tom, A new look at asides in the Fourth Gospel: BtS 151 (1994) 428-439.
5327 **Tilborg** Sjef van, Imaginative love in John: BInterp series 2. Leiden 1993, Brill. viii-262 p. *f*115. 90-04-09716-3 [Biblica 76,266-9, G. *Segalla*); TvT 34,306, W. *Weren*].
5328 *Tilborg* Sjef van, De zelfpresentatie van Jezus in het Johannes-evangelie; een christologie tussen letterlijke en figuurlijke taal: TvT 34 (1994) 128-143; Eng. 144.
5328* *Vanni* Ugo, La volontà di Dio in Giovanni: ➤ 368, Volontà di Dio 1992/3, 159-174.
5329 **Vignolo** Roberto, Personaggi del Quarto Vangelo; figure della fede in S. Giovanni: FacTItSett. Mi 1994, Glossa. v-249 p. Lᵐ 28. 88-7105-036-8 [Gregorianum 76,761, G. *Ferraro*].
5330 **Yee** Gale A., Jewish feasts and the Gospel of John: Zacchaeus Studies 1989 ➤ 5,5470; 6,5763: ᴿRThom 94 (1994) 698-700 (L. *Devillers*).

G1.5   **Johannis Prologus 1,1 ...**

5331 **Speyr** Adrienne von, The word becomes flesh; meditations on John 1-5, ᵀ*Wiedenhöver* sr. Lucia, Dru Alexander. SF 1994, Ignatius. 322 p. $25. 0-87870-411-1.
5332 **Moloney** Francis J., Belief in the Word; reading John 1-4. Mp 1993, Fortress. xvii-230 p. Mp 1993, Fortress. xvii-230 p. $19. 0-8006-2584-6 [JTS 45,237-9, Clare *Drury*]. – ᴿCBQ 56 (1994) 802s (F. F. *Segovia*); Pacifica 7 (1994) 85-94 (J. *Painter*).
5334 *Bergmeier* Roland, Weihnachten mit und ohne Glanz; Notizen zu Johannesprolog und Philipperhymnus: ZNW 85 (1994) 47-68.
5335 **Dally** John A., The eternally begotten Son; language, desire and resurrection in the [homosexually influenced] Gospel of John and PROUST's 'Recherche': diss. ᴰ*Yu* A. Ch 1994, 287 p. 94-25374. – DissA 55 (1994s) p. 956.
5336 *a) Esda* Cornelius F., The word *logos* in Johannine writings; – *b) Monsengwo* L., La foi dans les écrits johanniques; – *c) Balembo Buetubela*, Le symbolisme et la pédagogie du signe dans le quatrième évangile; – *d) Muoneke* sr. Bibiana, Worship and sacraments in John's Gospel; – *e) Akpunonu* Damien, The celebration of feasts: ➤ 303b, Communautés johanniques 1989/91, 28-56 / 10-27 / 57-70 / 86-117 / 156-190.
5337 **Evans** C. A., Word and glory; on the exegetical and theological background of John's Prologue: jNsu 89. Shf 1993, JStOT. 243 p. £35. 1-85075-448-9 [TDig 42,64]. – ᴿExpTim 106 (1994s) 55 (J. M. *Court*).
5338 *a) Gaeta* Giancarlo, Logos, parola, sapienza; l'indagine critica sul Prologo di Giovanni; – *b) Pazzini* Domenico, ...in ORIGENE; – *c) Cristiani* Maria, ...da AGOSTINO a T. d'AQUINO; – *d) De Michelis Pintacuda* Fiorella, ... tra ERASMO e LUTERO; AnStoEseg 11 (1994) 11-44 / 45-56 / 57-72 / [dal gruppo M. MIEGGE, Forlì 1993, come BORI e MARCHETTI infra ➤ 5349] 73-94. – Eng. 5s.
5339 **Harris** Elizabeth, Prologue and Gospel; the theology of the Fourth Evangelist [diss. London King's College ᴰ*Evans* C.]: jNsu 107. Shf 1994, JStOT. 215 p. £25. 1-85075-504-3.

5340 *Heintz* M.,   The immateriality and eternity of the Word in St. AUGUSTINE's Sermons on the Prologue of John's Gospel: ➤ 9,464*f*, Collectanea 1990/3, 395-402.

5341 **Hofstra** Johan D., ISHO῾DAD von Merw, Joh 1,1-18 binnen de Syrische exegetische traditie: diss. Amst VU; 1993 ➤ 9,5541: ᴿMuséon 107 (1994) 207s (A. de *Halleux* †; title has '1933').

5342 *a*) *Ladaria* Luis F., Il prologo di Giovanni nel De trinitate di ILARIO di Poitiers; – *b*) *Grossi* Vittorino, L'utilizzo pastorale di Giovanni 19-20 nella liturgia africana secondo gli 'Ordines' d'Ippona; – *c*) *Cocchini* Francesca, TEODORETO di Cirro sulle origini della comunità di Efeso: ➤ 328, Efeso 4 Giovanni (1994) 157-174 / 175-189 / 191-8.

5343 *a*) *Weder* Hans,   Die Weisheit in menschlicher Gestalt; Weisheits-theologie im Johannesprolog als Paradigma einer biblischen Theologie; – *b*) *Lieu* Judith M., Biblical theology and the Johannine literature: ➤ 303*a*, New approaches 1992/4, 143-179 / 93-107.

5344 *Osten-Sacken* Peter von der, Logos als Tora? Anfragen an eine neue Auslegung des Johannesprologs [SCHONEVELD Jacobus]: KIsr [6 (1991) 40-52] 9 (1994) 138-149.

5345 **Reinhartz** Adele,   The Word in the world; the cosmological tale in the Fourth Gospel 1992 ➤ 8,5769: ᴿCBQ 56 (1994) 147s (C. R. *Koester*); Interpretation 48 (1994) 210 (J. M. *Scholer*).

5346 *Mojola* A. Ototsi [Jn 1,1; 2 Jn 1,1] Theories of metaphor in translation: BTrans 44 (1993) 341-7.

5347 *Minnen* Peter van,   The punctuation of John 1:3-4: FgNt 7 (1994) 33-41.

5348 **Hofrichter** Peter, Wer?... Joh 1,6: 1990 ➤ 6,5776; 7,4667: ᴿCiuD 207 (1994) 200s (J. *Gutiérrez*).

5349 *a*) *Bori* Pier Cesare,   La 'luce che illumina ogni uomo' (Gv 1,9) in George FOX e Robert BARCLAY; – *b*) *Miegge* Mario, L'Evangelo alla luce della ragione; variazioni nella lettura di Gv 1,10-11 in SPINOZA e KANT; – *c*) *Marchetti* Valerio, 'Et sermo caro fuit'; lettura sociniana di Gv 1,14: AnStoEseg 11 (1994) 119-144 / 145-160 / 95-118; Eng. 4.

5350 *Trocmé* Étienne, [Jn 1,14] 'La Parole devint chair et dressa sa tente parmi nous' — Réflexions sur la théologie du IVᵉ Évangile: RHPR 74 (1994) 399-409; Eng. 475.

5351 **Streiff** Stefan, 'Novis linguis loqui'; M. LUTHERs Disputation über Joh 1,14 [1539]: ForSysÖk 70 [Diss. 1992 ➤ 9,5552]: Gö 1993, Vandenhoeck & R. 251 p. DM 68. 3-525-56277-2 [TLZ 129,545, M. *Seils*; RelStR 20,155, R. *Kolb*: provocative but does not compare similar 1540 work].

5352 *Haręzga* Stanisław, ☉ Calling of Jn 1,35-42 in 'Pastores dabo vobis': AtKap 122 (1994) 81-94.

5353 *Walker* William O.ᴶ, John 1.43-51 and 'The Son of Man' in the Fourth Gospel: JStNT 56 (1994) 31-42.

5353* *Byron* Brian,   The storyline of the marriage feast at Cana: AustralasCR 71 (1994) 61-68.

5354 **Lütgehettmann** Walter,   Die Hochzeit Joh 2,1s, ᴰ1990 ➤ 6,5796... 8,5780: ᴿCiuD 207 (1994) 201s (J. *Gutiérrez*).

5354* *a*) *Migliasso* Secondo, Maria a Cana; – *b*) *Varaldi* Enrica, La condizione della donna ai tempi di Maria di Nazaret; – *c*) *Valentini* Alberto, [Mt 12,49] 'Chi è mia madre?'; – *d*) *Serra* Aristide, Maria accanto alla

Croce; madre dei 'dispersi figli di Dio'; suggerimenti di Giovanni Paolo II: ParVi 39,2 (1994) 14-17 / 6-8 / 18-21 / 22-25.

G1.6 Jn 3ss... Nicodemus, Samaritana.

5355 **Létourneau** Pierre, Jésus, fils de l'homme et Fils de Dieu. Jean 2,23-3,36, 1992 ➤ 8,5786 [< diss. Laval 1990 ➤ 7,4884]: ᴿJBL 113 (1994) 736-8 (D. A. *Carson*: many valuable insights and an unproved thesis); LavalTP 50 (1994) 666s (M. *Girard*).

5356 *Alana* O. E., [Jn 3...] The secret disciples of Jesus: DeltVM 22,1 (1993) 43-48.

5357 **Thoreau** V., Nicodème [roman]. Bru 1988, Didier Hatier. – ᴿFoiTemps 23 (1993) 360-2 (J.-F. *Grégoire*).

5358 *Frey* Jörg, 'Wie Mose die Schlange in der Wüste erhöht hat...'; zur frühjüdischen Deutung der 'ehernen Schlange' und ihrer christologischen Rezeption in Johannes 3,14f: ➤ 322*, Schriftauslegung 1991/4, 153-205.

5359 *Morgen* Michèle, Le Fils de l'Homme élévé en vue de la vie éternelle (Jn 3,14-15 éclairé par diverses traditions juives) [Nb 21,4-9; Gn 49,16-18]: RevSR 68 (1994) 5-17.

5360 *Fletcher* Mary-Elsie C., The role of women in the Book of John: EvJ 12,1 (Myerstown 1994) 41-48 [< NTAbs 39, p. 45].

5361 *Kahl* Brigitte, Der Fremde und die Frau am Brunnen (Joh 4); menschliche Begegnung als Gotteserfahrung: Díakonia 25 (1994) 31-37.

5362 *Maccini* Robert G., A reassessment of the woman at the well in John 4 in light of the Samaritan context: JStNT 53 (1994) 35-46.

5363 *Neyrey* Jerome H., What's wrong with this picture? John 4, cultural stereotypes of women, and public and private space: ➤ 88*, ᶠNIEBUHR Ursula, BibTB 24 (1994) 77-91.

5364 *Bridges* Linda M., John 4:5-42; between text and sermon: Interpretation 48 (1994) 173-6.

5365 **Link** Andrea, 'Was redest du mit ihr?' John 4, 1992 ➤ 9,5571: ᴿCBQ 56 (1994) 602s (J. L. *Staley*); JBL 113 (1994) 738-740 (J. E. *Botha*); JTS 45 (1994) 664-9 (F. J. *Moloney*).

5366 **Valiente Lendrino** J., [Jn 4,23] El culto en espíritu y en verdad en el IV Evangelio; aspectos bíblicos del templo y su culto [diss. Univ. Navarra 1982]. Pamplona 1990. 215 p. – ᴿCiuD 206 (1993) 919s (J. *Gutiérrez*); ScripTPamp 26 (1994) 1214s (F. *Varo*).

5367 **Landis** Stephan, Das Verhältnis des Johannesevangeliums zu den Synoptikern, am Beispiel von Mt 8.5-13; Lk 7.1-10; Joh 4.46-54 [Diss. Zürich 1992, ᴰ*Weder* H.]: BZNW 74. B 1994, de Gruyter. ix-76 p. [NTAbs 39, p. 507]. 3-11-014389-5.

5368 **Morujão** Geraldo, Relações pai-filho em S. João; subsidio para a teologia trinitária a partir do estudo de sintagmas verbais gregos (Jo 5 e 17): Investigação e cultura. Viseu 1989, Politécnico. 303 p.; bibliog. p. 225-264.

5370 **Schroven** Brigitte, '...sie ist es, die von mir zeuget' (Joh 5,39); christologische Auslegung des ATs im Kontext von Theologie und Zeitgeschichte, zwischen den beiden Weltkriegen: Diss. ᴰ*Boecker* J. Wuppertal 1994. – TR 91,102.

G1.7 Panis Vitae – Jn 6...

5371 **Caba** José, Cristo pan de vida 1993 ➤ 9,5582: ᴿActuBbg 31 (1994) 216s (J. *O'Callaghan*); Antonianum 69 (1994) 391s (M. *Álvarez Barredo*);

BibFe 20 (1994) 148 (A. *Salas*); Carthaginensia 10 (1994) 474s (R. *Sanz Valdivieso*); EstAg 29 (1994) 380 (D. *Álvarez*); RelCu 40 (1994) 877 (A. *Moral*); Salmanticensis 41 (1994) 343s (*F.F.-Ramos*); ScripTPamp 26 (1994) 1196-9 (A. *García-Moreno*, también su BOISMARD, Pré-J).

5372 *a) Pervo* Richard I., *pánta koiná*; the feeding stories in the light of economic data and social practice; – *b) Smith* Dennis E., Table fellowship and the historical Jesus: ➤ 40, ᶠGEORGI D. 1994, 163-194 / 135-162.

5373 *Roberge* Michel, La composition de Jean 6,25b-34: LavalTP 50 (1994) 171-186.

5374 *a) Zuurmond* Rochus, Vlees en bloed van de mensenzoon; opmerkingen bij Johannes 6:53; – *b) Hemelsoet* Ben, Een vader had twee zonen; de verhalten van het zaad van Abraham, op het Loofhuttenfeest (Joh. 8:30-37); – *c) Monshouwer* Dirk, 'Staat op, laten wij vahier gaan!' (Joh. 14:31). Een kleine oefening in de eenheid van het vierde evangelie: AmstCah 13 (1994) 88-96 / 97-112 / 113-126; – Eng. 130s.

5375 *Domeris* William R., The confession of Peter according to John 6,69: TyndB 44 (1993) 155-167.

5376 **Borse** Udo, Die Entscheidung des Propheten; kompositorische Streichung von Joh 7,50.(53)-8,11: SBS 158. Stu 1994, KBW. 88 p. DM 40. 3-4000-4501-2 [TR 91,75].

5377 *Colombo* Gianluigi, [Gv 7,53-8,11] La critica testuale di fronte alla pericopa dell'adultera: RivB 42 (1994) 81-102.

5377* *Zevini* Giorgio, [Gv 7,53-8,11] Gesù e la donna adultera: ParSpV 29 (1994) 131-145.

5378 *Zuurmond* Rochus, [Jn 7,53-8,11] De 'overspelige vrouw': AmstCah 12 (1993) 122-130; Eng. 135.

5379 *Baum-Resch* A., 'Liebe Frau aus Joh 8,1-11!'; Eine kreativ-feministische Bibelarbeit: EvErz 46 (Fra 1994) 452-7 [< ZIT 95, p. 257].

5380 *Heil* John P., A rejoinder to [WALLACE D., NTS 39,290; O'DAY G., JBL 111,631] 'Reconsidering "The story of Jesus and the adulteress reconsidered"' [Heil, Biblica 72,182]: ÉglT 25 (1994) 361-6.

5381 **Ball** David M., [Jn 8,12...] 'I am' in context; the literary function, background and theological implications of *egō eimi* in John's Gospel: diss. Sheffield 1992, ᴰLincoln A. – TyndB 44 (1993) 179-192.

5382 *Motyer* Stephen, The Fourth Gospel — an appeal to Jews [< John 8,31-59 and the rhetoric of persuasion, diss. London 1993 ➤ 9,5595; ᴰStanton G.]: TyndB 45 (1994) 201-5.

5383 *Vignolo* Roberto, Gv 8,31-59; la paternità di Satana e il Figlio di Dio: Ambrosius 70 (1994) 387-410.

5384 *Edwards* M.J., 'Not yet fifty years old'; John 8.57 [originally 40; influence of apocryphal Jubilees]: NTS 40 (1994) 449-454.

5385 *Derrett* J.D.M., Miracles, pools, and sight; John 9,1-41; Genesis 2,6-7; Isaiah 6,10; 30,20; 35,5-7: BbbOr 36 (1994) 71-83.

5386 **Rein** Matthias, Die Heilung der Blindgeborenen (Joh 9) — Tradition und Redaktion; a) Diss. ᴰSchnelle U. – Halle-W 1994. – TR 91,96. – b) WUNT 2/73. Tü 1995, Mohr. xii-401 p.; bibliog. 367-382. 3-16-146458-3.

5387 *Tan* Amanda Shao, Disability and Christology in the Fourth Gospel, with a special reference to John 9:1-7: diss. Westminster Theol. Sem. ᴰPoythress V. 1994. 210 p. 94-28901. – DissA 55 (1994s) p. 1593.

5388 *Derrett* J.D.M., John 9:6 read with Isaiah 6:10; 20:29 [Heb. šᶜᶜ puns 'to blind / plaster over / rejoice']: EvQ 66 (1994) 251-4 [< NTAbs 39, p. 47].

5389 *Bammel* Ernst, Johannes 9,17: NTS 40 (1994) 455s.

5390 *Hainz* Josef, 'Zur Krisis kam ich in diese Welt' (Joh 9,39); zur

Eschatologie im Johannesevangelium: ➤ 113, ᶠSCHNACKENBURG R. 1993/4, 149-163.
5391 *Bailey* Ken, The shepherd poems of John 10; their culture and style: IrBSt 15 (1993) 2-17.
5392 ᴱ**Beutler** Johannes, *Fortna* Robert T., The shepherd discourse of John 10, 1985/91 ➤ 7,417 ... 9,5598: ᴿRechSR 82 (1994) 244s (X. *Léon-Dufour*).
5393 *Guerra* L.M., El buen pastor; estudio exegético-teológico de Jn 10,11: Almogaren 10 (1992) 25-93 [< RET 53,410].
5394 **Garzonio** Marco, [Jn 11] Lazzaro; l'amicizia nella Bibbia: LettBib 4. CinB 1994, Paoline. 148 p. 88-315-0978-0.
5395 **Partyka** Jan S., La résurrection de Lazare dans les monuments funéraires des nécropoles chrétiennes à Rome (peintures, mosaïques et décors des épitaphes): PAN Arch 33. Wsz 1993, Państwowe. 198 p.; 87 fig. [ArchWsz 46,120-2, Elżbieta *Jastrzębowska*).
5396 *Stibbe* Mark W.G., A tomb with a view; John 11.1-44 in narrative-critical perspective: NTS 40 (1994) 38-54.
5397 *Kasser* Rodolphe, Lazare conté en un lyco-diospolitain d'aspect fort étrange (Jean 10,7 - 13,38): ➤ 27, ᶠCOQUIN R.-G., 1994, 21-47.
5398 *Moloney* Francis J., The faith of Martha and Mary; a narrative approach to John 11,17-40: Biblica 75 (1994) 471-493; franç. 493.
5399 *Burkett* Delbert, Two accounts of Lazarus' resurrection in John 11: NT 36 (1994) 209-232.
5400 *Beutler* Johannes, Two ways of gathering; the plot to kill Jesus in John 11,47-53: NTS 40 (1994) 399-406.
5401 *Arowele* P.J., The scattered children of God (John 11:52), a Johannine ecclesial cliché: ➤ 303*b, ᴱ*Amewowo*, Johannine 1989/91, 181-201.
5402 *Reynier* Chantal, [pages L'onction de Béthanie] Le thème du parfum et l'événement des figures en Jn 11,55 - 12,11: ScEspr 46 (1994) 203-220.
5403 *Ekenberg* Anders, 'Det var om honom han talade', Jes 53, Jes 6 och Joh 12: SvEx 59 (1994) 119-126.
5404 **Kühschelm** R., Verstockung Jn 12, 1990 ➤ 6,4940 ... 8,5829: ᴿBiKi 48 (1993) 54-56 (Juan Peter *Miranda*); TPhil 69 (1994) 575-7 (J.*Beutler*: 'Kühlschelm').
5404* *Standaert* Benoît, 'Où je suis' (Jn 12,26); au service de l'unité selon saint Jean: ➤ 12, ᶠBÉKÉS G., Unum 1994, 195-203.
5405 *Rigopoulos* G., [Jn 12,36-38] ⊕ *Paradoxótēs*... The paradox of unbelief: DeltVM 23,1 (1994) 106-123 [NTAbs 39, p. 234].
5406 *a) Rodríguez* Pedro, La 'exaltación' de Cristo en la cruz Juan 12, 32 en la experiencia espiritual del Beato Josemaría ESCRIVÁ DE BALAGUER; – *b)* *Espinel* José Luis, La cruz de Jesús como exaltación en el evangelio de San Juan; – c) *Aranda Pérez* Gonzalo, Jn 1,14 frente a 'Apocalipsis de Adán' (NHC V,5); – d) *García-Moreno* Antonio, Aspectos cultuales en el IV evangelio: ➤ 22a, ᶠCASCIARO J.M., Biblia 1994, 573-601 / 385-394 / 363-383 / 337-347.

G1.8   Jn 13... Sermo sacerdotalis et Passio.

5407 *Bammel* Ernst, The farewell discourse of the evangelist John and its Jewish heritage: TyndB 44 (1994) 103-110.
5408 **Neugebauer** Johannes, Die eschatologischen Aussagen in den johanneischen Abschiedsreden; textlinguistische Untersuchungen zu Joh 13-17: kath. Diss. ᴰ*Schenke* L. Mainz 1994. 200 p. > Kohlhammer. – RTLv 26, p. 538; TR 91,99.

5409 **Schnackenburg** Rudolf, Le parole di commiato di Gesù (Gv. 13-17), ᵀᴱ*Montagnini* Felice. StBPaid 108. Brescia 1994, Paideia. 91 p. Lᵐ 17. 88-394-0516-X.

5410 **Winter** Martin, Das Vermächtnis Jesu und die Abschiedsworte der Väter; gattungsgeschichtliche Untersuchung der Vermächtnisrede im Blick auf Joh. 13-17 [Diss. ᴰ*Stegemann*, Neuendettalsau 1991s; TR 89,76]: FRL 161. Gö 1994, Vandenhoeck & R. 370 p. DM 118. 3-525-53843-X [TLZ 120,1082-5, G. *Schille*].

5411 *Alhistur* Fernando E., Lavatorío de los pies y discipulado en San Juan: Stromata 50 (1994) 3-20.

5412 *Bowe* R. E., John 13 and Christian service: BToday 32 (1994) 223-7.

5413 *Kitzberger* Ingrid R., Love and footwashing; John 13:1-20 and Luke 7:36-50 read intertextually: BInterp 2 (1994) 190-206.

5414 **Niemand** C., Fusswaschungserzählung 1993 ➤ 9,5612: ᴿBZ 38 (1994) 287-9 (R. *Schnackenburg*); ExpTim 106 (1994s) 28 (E. *Best*); TLZ 119 (1994) 993-5 (M. *Karrer*).

5415 *Niemand* Christoph, Was bedeutet die Fusswaschung; Sklavenarbeit oder Liebesdienst? Kulturkundliches als Auslegungshilfe für Joh 13,6-8: ProtokB 3 (1994) 115-127.

5416 *Thomas* John C., Footwashing in Jn 13 ... community 1991: ➤ 7,4943 ... 9,5613: ᴿEvQ 66 (1994) 278-80 (Ruth B. *Edwards*); WesleyT 28 (1993) 207-9 (R. *Morton*).

5417 *Voicu* Sever J., L'omelia In lotionem pedum (CPG 4216) [WENGER A. 1967, testo greco non critico] di SEVERIANO di Gabala; due note: Muséon 107 (1994) 349-365.

5418 *O'Neill* J. C., John 13:10 again: RB 101 (1994) 67-74; franç. 67.

5419 **Segovia** Fernando E., The farewell of the Word 1991 ➤ 8,5835; 9,5616: ᴿCBQ 56 (1994) 150-2 (F. J. *Moloney*); ScotJT 47 (1994) 126s (G. *Jones*).

5420 **Dettwiler** Andreas, Die Gegenwart des Erhöhten: eine exegetische Studie zu den johanneischen Abschiedsreden (Joh 13,31-16,33, mit Einschluss von Joh 13,1-17) insbesondere unter Berücksichtigung ihres Relektüre-Charakters: Diss. ᴰ*Zumstein* J. Neuchâtel 1994. 282 p. > FRL. – RTLv 26,536.

5421 *Vinay* Samuel, The Holy Spirit in word and works; a study in John 14 to 16: Transformation 11,3 (1994) 12-14.

5422 *Gonzalez Faus* J. I., [Jn 14,6] Aspectos antropocéntricos de Dios en Jesús: SalT 82 (1994) 635-647.

5423 *Watt* Jan G. van der, 'Metaphorik' in Joh 15,1-8: BZ 38 (1994) 67-80.

5424 *Elliott* Susan M., John 15:15 – not slaves but friends; slave and friendship imagery and the clarification of the disciples' relation to Jesus in the Johannine farewell discourse: ProcGM 13 (1993) 31-46.

5425 *Hegstad* Harald, a) The Holy Spirit as guide into all the truth (Jn 16,13) in a systematic theological perspective; – b) Transcendens og inkarnasjon [Diss. on Leiv AALEN 1992]; objections of *Kvist* Hans-Olof, *Austad* Torleif: TsTKi 64 (1993) 95-109; Eng. 109 / [50; 110] 111-133 / 134-139, Eng. 129; replikk 131-6.

5426 **Wijngaards** John, The Spirit in John 1988 ➤ 4,5527; 6,5762: ᴿConcordTJ 58 (1994) 60s (B. *Schuchard*).

5427 *Wendland* E. R., Oral-aural dynamics of the word with special reference to John 17: NoTr 8,1 (1994) 19-43 [< NTAbs 39, p. 418].

5428 **Moioli** Giovanni, 'É giunta l'ora' (Gv 17,11): Contemplatio 10. Mi 1994, Glossa. 145 p. 88-7105-038-X.

5429 **Derrett** J. D. M., The victim; the Johannine passion narrative reconsidered 1993 → 8,5849; 9,5635: [BL 95,146, W. *Sproston*]. – ^RBibTB 24 (1994) 198s (B. J. *Malina*: a gold-mine); CBQ 56 (1994) 368s (J. T. *Carroll*: iconoclast, often unconvincing).

5431 **Senior** Donald, The Passion of Jesus in the Gospel of John 1991 → 8,4958: ^RCritRR 6 (1993) 289s (Marianne *Meye Thompson*); RelStR 18 (1993) 329 (D. M. *Smith*).

5432 **Senior** Donald, La Passione di Gesù nel Vangelo di [Mc 1988; Mt 1990; Lc 1992] Giovanni: Parola di Vita. Mi 1993, Âncora. 184 p. L^m 21. – ^RBenedictina 41 (1994) 531-3 (A. *Ranzato*); Claretianum 34 (1994) 625s (A. *Pardilla*).

5433 *Beckmann* Klaus, Funktion und Gestalt des Judas Iskarioth im Johannesevangelium: BTZ 11 (1994) 181-200.

5434 *Moloney* Francis J., John 18:15-27; a Johannine view of the Church: DowR 112 (1994) 231-248.

5435 **Urbán** A., El orígen divino del poder ... Jn 19,11, 1989 → 5,5602 ... 9,5638: ^RCiuD 206 (1993) 638-640 (J. *Gutiérrez*).

5436 *a*) *Rigato* Maria Luisa, Il titolo della Croce 'Gesù il Nazoreo il re dei Giudei' (Gv 19,19), perché Nazoreo e non Nazareno? – *b*) *Dal Covolo* Enrico, Gesù e Pilato; Giovanni 18,28-19,16 nello studio dei rapporti tra la primitiva comunità cristiana e l'impero di Roma: → 328, Efeso 4 Giovanni (1994) 41-74 / 147-156.

5437 **Cory** Catherine, The rescue of Wisdom's child; uncovering the conceptual background for understanding the death of Jesus in the Johannine tradition: diss. ^D*Attridge* H. Notre Dame 1993. – RelStR 21,255.

5438 **Steiger** Mark L., The theme of John 20: belief in the resurrected Christ, the new beginning: ProcGM 14 (1994) 21-7.

5439 **Blanquart** Fabien, Le premier jour ... Jn 20: 1991 → 7,4972 ... 9,5643: ^RMaisD 192 (1992) 146s (J. *Auneau*).

5440 *Olivera* F., El sepulcro vacío; estudio exegético de Jn 20,1-10: Mayéutica 19,47 (Marcilla 1993) 9-54 [< NTAbs 38, p. 380].

5441 *López Fernández* Enrique, El simbolismo de los 'othonia' y del 'sudario' de Jesús en el relato del sepulcro vacío de Jn 20,2-8: → 33*a*, ^FDÍAZ MERCHÁN G., StOvet 22 (1994) 245-266.

5442 **Gangemi** Attilio, I racconti post-pasquali 1989 → 5,5607 ... 9,5646: ^RAngelicum 71 (1994) 278-280 & 592-4 (S. *Jurić*); ScripTPamp 26 (1994) 787s & 1212 (A. *García-Moreno*).

5443 *Auwers* Jean-Marie, Les Écritures et la foi pascale; à propos de la traduction liturgique de Jn 20,9: QLtg 74 (1993) 112-9; Eng. 119.

5444 *Brownson* James V., John 20:31 and the purpose of the Fourth Gospel: → 26, ^FCOOK J., RefR 48,3 (1994s) 212-6.

5445 *Birdsall* J. Neville, The source of catena comments on John 21:25: NT 36 (1994) 271-9.

G2.1   Epistulae Johannis.

5446 ^E**Agaësse** Paul, Saint AUGUSTIN, Commentaire sur la première épître de S. Jean, In Johannis epistulam ad Parthos^{4rev}: SChr 75. P 1994, Cerf. 452 p. 2-204-05108-X.

5446* ^{TE}**Bavel** T. J. van, AUGUSTINUS van Hippo; Preken over de Eerste Brief van Johannes. Lv 1992, Augustijns Hist. Inst. xiv-163 p. ƒ 60. – ^RTvT 34 (1994) 445 (A. *Davids*).

5447 **Bottini** Claudio, *Adinolfi* Marco, *ᴱCorona* Raimondo, Lettere di Giovanni e Apocalisse; lettura esegetico-esistenziale — VI Settimana Biblica Abruzzese 1-6.VII.1991. L'Aquila 1993, Curia O.F.M. 296 p.
5448 **Dalbesio** Anselmo, 'Quello...' L'esperienza cristiana nella 1 Gv ᴰ1990 ⇻ 6,5912 ... 9,5664: ᴿETL 70 (1994) 478s (J. *Verheyden*); ParVi 39,1 (1994) 56 (F. *Mosetto*); RechSR 82 (1994) 245s (X. *Léon-Dufour*).
5449 **Houlden** J. Leslie, A commentary on the Johannine epistles² [¹1973]. L 1994, Black. xi-170 p. 0-7136-4012-X.
5450 **Klauck** Hans-Josef, 1-3 Joh: EkK NT 23/2, 1992 ⇻ 9,5654: ᴿJBL 113 (1994) 742s (J.A. du *Rand*); TPhil 69 (1994) 577s (J. *Beutler*); TüTQ 174 (1994) 164s (M. *Theobald*, auch über ErtFor 276).
5451 **[Meye] Thompson** M., 1-3 John 1992 ⇻ 9,5687: ᴿConcordTQ 58 (1994) 233-5 (L. *Burgland*); EvQ 66 (1994) 180s (P. *Ellingworth*: more informative and acute than STEDMAN's equally faithful Hebrews).
5452 **Rusam** Dietrich, Die Gemeinschaft der Kinder Gottes; Kindschaft und die Gemeinde der johanneischen Briefe: BW 133. Stu 1993, Kohlhammer. 262 p.; bibliog. 233-253. – ᴿTR 90 (1994) 385s (H.-J. *Klauck*).
5453 **Schnackenburg** Rudolf, The Johannine Epistles [²1984] 1992 ⇻ 8,5880; 9,5658: ᴿInterpretation 48 (1994) 100.102 (C.C. *Black*); NewTR 7,2 (1994) 99s (Patricia M. *McDonald*).
5454 — **Goulder** M., Following a false clue? [SCHNACKENBURG R. swallows 1 John as scripture, and lacks imagination]: RevRT 1,1 (L 1994) 19-24 [< NTAbs 39, p. 74].
5455 **Smith** D. Moody, 1-3 John: InterpComm 1991 ⇻ 7,4988 ... 9,5659: ᴿCritRR 6 (1993) 297s (D. *Rensberger*).
5456 **Vouga** François, Die Joh-Briefe 1990 ⇻ 5,5623 ... 8,5885: ᴿÉTRel 69 (1994) 577-9 (E. *Cuvillier*); NT 36 (1994) 410-2 (B. *Lategan*).

5457 **Beilner** Wolfgang, Exegetisches Material zu den Johannesbriefen-Johannesoffenbarung: Vermittlung 24. Salzburg 1993. 207 p.
5458 **Lieu** Judith M., The theology of the Johannine epistles 1991 ⇻ 8,5876: ᴿCritRR 6 (1993) 260-2 (Pheme *Perkins*); ScotJT 47 (1994) 277s (S.S. *Smalley*).

5459 **Fehlandt** Claudius, Struktur und Botschaft des 1. Johannesbriefes: Diss. ᴰ*Thyen* H. Heidelberg 1994. – RTLv 26,536.
5460 *a*) **La Potterie** Ignace de, Struttura letteraria e progresso teologico nella 1 Gv; – *b*) *Dalbesio* Anselmo, La mediazione salvifica dello Spirito Santo secondo la prima lettera di Giovanni: ⇻ 328, Efeso 4 Giovanni (1994) 75-90 / 91-103.
5460* **Lloyd-Jones** David M., The love of God; studies in 1 John: Life in Christ 4. Wheaton IL 1994, Crossway. ix-208 p. 1-85684-089-1.
5461 *Neufeld* D., Reconceiving texts as speech-acts; an analysis of 1 John: BInterpS 7. Leiden 1994, Brill. xi-152 p. f95. 90-04-09853-4 [NTAbs 39, p. 337].
5462 **Renoux** Charles, La chaîne arménienne sur les Épîtres Catholiques 3., La chaîne sur la Première Épître de Jean: PatrOr 46. Turnhout 1994, Brepols. 474 p.
5463 *Segalla* Giuseppe, Holos ho kosmos como figura de la humanidad salvada por Jesús en 1 Jn 2,2*b*: RBibArg 55 (1993) 129-140.
5464 *a*) *Berg* Johannes van den, [1 Jn 2,18] GROTIUS' views on Antichrist and apocalyptic thought in England; – *b*) *Cameron* James K., Some aspects of

the Scottish contribution to apocalypticism in the seventeenth century and
the reaction to Grotius: ➤ 372*, ᶠMEYJES G., 1994, 169-184 / 159-168.
5465 **Jenks** Gregory C., The origins and early development of the
Antichrist myth: BZNW 59, 1991 ➤ 7,4995 ... 9,5675: ᴿRB 101 (1994)
461s (B. T. *Viviano*); TrierTZ 103 (1994) 80 (E. *Haag*).
5466 **McGinn** Bernard, Antichrist; two thousand years of the human
fascination with evil. SF 1994, Harper. xiii-368 p. $35. 0-06-965543-7
[TDig 42,278].
5467 ᴱ**Sbaffoni** Fausto, Testi sull'Anticristo, secoli i-ii: BtPatr, 1992 ➤ 8,
5887; Lᵐ 38. 88-404-2022-3. – ᴿAngelicum 71 (1994) 95a (T. *Stancati*).
5468 *La Potterie* Ignace de, 'Dio è più grande del nostro cuore' (1 Gv 3,20):
ParSpV 29 (1994) 209-221.
5468* *a) Carson* D. A., [1 Jn 5,6s] The three witnesses and the eschatology of
John; – *b) Schmidt* Thomas F., [Rev 17s] 'And the sea was no more';
water as people, not place: ➤ 46, ᶠGUNDRY R., To tell 1994, 216-232 /
233-249.

G2.3 *Apocalypsis Johannis* – **Revelation: text, introduction.**

5469 **Agouridis** S., ⓖ John's Apocalypse: Hermeneia Kainēs Diathēkēs 18.
Thessaloniki 1994, Fournarás. 611 p. 960-242-112-6 [NTAbs 39, p. 515].
5470 **Campo Hernández** A. del, Comentario al Apocalipsis de APRINGIO 1991
➤ 7,5003; 8,5896: ᴿCompostellanum 38 (1993) 265s (E. *Romero Pose*);
RET 54 (1994) 217-9 (J. J. *Ayán*).
5471 **Charlier** Jean-Pierre, Comprendre l'Apocalypse: Lire la Bible 89s, 1991
➤ 7,5005 ... 9,5083: ᴿScEspr 46 (1994) 111-3 (J.-P. *Prévost*) repeated
257-9 with date and publisher.
5472 **Delebecque** É., L'Apocalypse 1992 ➤ 8,5899; 9,5685: ᴿRBgPg 72 (1994)
140s (J. *Schamp*).
5473 **Giblin** C. H., Apocalisse: 1993 ➤ 9,5687: ᴿRivB 42 (1994) 572-5 (C.
Doglio).
5474 **Giesen** H., *al.*, Johannes-Apokalypse ³(Auflage) 1992 (¹1986) ➤ 8,5906:
ᴿTGgw 37 (1994) 231s (O. *Bücher*).
5474* GIOACCHINO da Fiore, Sull'Apocalisse: Universale economica 2089.
Mi 1994, Feltrinelli. 413 p.; bibliog. 395-411. 88-07-82089-7.
5475 *Groote* Marc De, Die *sýnopsis scholikē* zum Apokalypse-Kommentar
des ARETHAS [und dessen] handschriftliche Überlieferung: SacrEr 34
(1994) 125-134.
5476 **Harrington** Wilfrid J., Revelation: SacPag 16, 1993 ➤ 9,5689: ᴿLvSt 19
(1994) 375s (J. *Lambrechts*).
5477 **Harrington** W. J., Revelation; proclaiming a vision of hope: Scripture
for worship and education. San José 1994, Resource. viii-160 p. $15.
0-89390-307-8 [NTAbs 39, p. 518].
5478 **Roloff** Jürgen, Revelation: Continental comm 1993 ➤ 9,5692: ᴿÉTRel
69 (1994) 428 (E. *Cuvillier*); PrincSemB 15 (1994) 207-9 (D. A. *de Silva*).
5479 **Rowland** Christopher, Revelation 1993 ➤ 9,5693: ᴿExpTim 106
(1994s) 123 (J. M. *Court*).
5480 **Schmolinsky** Sabine, Apk A. minorita 1991 ➤ 9,5694: ᴿColcFran 63
(1993) 325s (C. *Bérubé*).
5481 **Schüssler Fiorenza** Elisabeth, Revelation; vision of a just world ²1991
➤ 8,5911; 9,5695: ᴿAndrUnSem 32 (1994) 270-3 (J. *Paulien*); HeythropJ
35 (1994) 317s (M. *Barker*); TLond 97 (1994) 307 (C. *Rowland*: like the
NT-book itself, demands vigilance in the critique of all forms of ideology).

5482 **Schüssler Fiorenza** Elisabeth, Das Buch der Offenbarung; Vision einer gerechten Welt [1981 ²1991], ᵀ*Graffam-Minkus* M. Stu 1994, Kohlhammer. 176 p. DM 36. 3-17-012489-7 [NTAbs 39,155]. – ᴿEntschluss 49,11 (1994) 41s (M. *Hasitschka*); TLZ 119 (1994) 660s (K. *Wengst*).

5483 **Schüssler Fiorenza** Elisabeth, Apocalisse; visione di un mondo giusto: BtBib 16. Brescia 1994, Queriniana. 188 p. 88-399-2016-1.

5484 **Talbert** C. H., The Apocalypse; a reading of the revelation of John [for those scarred by harmful expositions, or simply ignoring]. LVL 1994, W-Knox. iv-123 p. $13. 0-664-25363-6 [NTAbs 39, p. 339; TDig 42,293; RelStR 21,240, D. E. *Aune*].

5485 **Thomas** Robert L., Revelation 1-7, an exegetical commentary. Ch 1992, Moody. xxviii-524 p. $29. – ᴿBtS 151 (1994) 245 (S. D. *Toussaint*); WestTJ 55 (1993) 154-6 (V. S. *Poythress*, 'classic dispensational approach'; three others compared).

5486 **Williams** John, *Shailor* Barbara A., A Spanish Apocalypse; the Morgan Beatus manuscript. NY 1991, Braziller. 239 p.; 130 color. pl. $175. – ᴿSpeculum 69 (1994) 271-3 (J. *Guilmain*).

G2.4 *Apocalypsis,* **Revelation, topics.**

5487 *Basilides* P., *Eikōn* and *Ekklesia* in the Apocalypse: GrOrTR 38 (1993) 103-118 [< ᴢɪᴛ 95, p. 269].

5488 **Bauckham** Richard, The climax of prophecy [some inedita, some revised] 1993 ➤ 9,5702*: ᴿExpTim 105 (1993s) 350 (J. M. *Court*); TLond 97 (1994) 387s (D. *Hill*); TLZ 119 (1994) 1074s (O. *Bücher*).

5489 **Bauckham** Richard, The theology of Rev. 1993 ➤ 9,5703: ᴿBInterp 2 (1994) 242-4 (J. P. M. *Sweet*); CBQ 56 (1994) 579s (Carolyn *Thomas*); CiuD 207 (1994) 522s (J. *Gutiérrez*); JRel 74 (1994) 560s (M. E. *Boring*).

5490 **Bauckham** Richard J., La teologia dell'Apocalisse, ᵀ*Bernardini* Paolo; *Perrera* Enzo: Letture Bibliche 12. Brescia 1994, Paideia. 200 p. Lᵐ 23. 88-394-0513-5.

5491 **Charlier** J. P., Comprender el Apocalipsis [1991 ➤ 7,5005],ᵀ. Bilbao 1993, D-Brouwer. 228 p.; 254 p. pt. 2200 cada uno. – ᴿProyección 41 (1994) 237 (F. *Contreras*).

5492 **Contreras Molina** Francisco, El señor de la vida... Apc 1991 ➤ 8,5927; 9,5711: ᴿActuBbg 31 (1994) 217s (X. *Alegre*).

5493 *Corsani* Bruno, Messaggio e coscienza profetica; le loro fonti secondo l'Apocalisse di Giovanni: Protestantesimo 49 (1994) 2-12.

5494 *a) Corsini* Eugenio, La profezia messianica di Daniele nella lettura di Mc 13 e nell'Apocalisse; – *b) Adinolfi* Marco, Il libro della Genesi nell'Apocalisse; – *c) Nobile* Marco, L'Antico Testamento di Giovanni: ➤ 328, Efeso 4 Giovanni 1994, 7-28 / 97-103 / 29-40.

5495 **Court** J. M., Revelation: NTGuides. Shf 1994, Academic. 133 p. £6. 1-85075-458-6.

5496 *deSilva* David A., The construction and social function of a counter-cosmos in the Revelation of John: ForumFF 9,1 (1993) 47-61.

5497 *Diefenbach* Manfred, Die 'Offenbarung des Johannes' offenbart, dass der Seher Johannes die antike Rhetoriklehre kennt: BibNot 73 (1994) 20-57.

5497* ᴱ**Emmerson** Richard K., *McGinn* Bernard, The Apocalypse in the Middle Ages 1993 ➤ 9,268: ᴿCathHR 80 (1994) 326-8 (D. C. *West*); Speculum 69 (1994) 1305 (tit. pp.).

5498 *Ernst* Michael, Die Offenbarung des Johannes als Beispiel eines ntl.

Buches, das Partie ergreift; Beobachtungen und Impulse aus dem Fach 'Einleitung': ProtokB 3 (1994) 65-72.

5499 **Fekkes** Jan[III], Isaiah and prophetic tradition in the book of Revelation; visionary antecedents and their development [diss. Manchester, D*Lindars* B.]: jNsu 93. Shf 1994, JStOT. 333 p. £32.50.   1-85075-456-X [NTAbs p. 461; JTS 46,293, J. P. M. *Sweet*; TLZ 120,146, J.-W. *Taeger*]. – R ExpTim 106 (1994s) 55s (J. M. *Court*).

5500 **(Fernández) Ramos** Felipe, Los enigmas del Apocalipsis: Teología en diálogo 8, 1993 → 9,5714: R CiuD 207 (1994) 886 (J. *Gutiérrez*); EstAg 29 (1994) 169s (R. A. *Díez*).

5501 *Giblin* Charles H., Recapitulation and the literary coherence of John's Apocalypse: CBQ 56 (1994) 81-95.

5502 *Giesen* H., Kirche in der Endzeit; Ekklesiologie und Eschatologie in der Johannesapokalypse: SUNT 19 (1994) 5-43 [< NTAbs 39, p. 257].

5503 **Goldsworthy** Graeme, The Gospel in Revelation; Gospel and Apocalypse: Biblical Classics [= ? Wheaton]. Carlisle 1994, Paternoster. 170 p. 0-85364-630-9.

5504 **Hélou** Clémence, Symbole et langage dans l'Apocalypse de Jean; diss. Sorbonne + Inst. Cath. 1994, D*Meslin* M. 328 p. + 184 p. – RICathP 50 (1994) 183-5 (É. *Cothenet*); RTLv 26,537; 'Georgette').

5505 *Horn* Friedrich W., Zwischen der Synagoge des Satans und dem neuen Jerusalem; die christlich-jüdische Standortbestimmung in der Apokalypse des Johannes: ZRGg 46 (1994) 143-162.

5506 *Jankowski* Augustyn, ❷ Transcendencja Chrystusa według Apokalipsy Janowej: RuBi 47 (1994) 82-95.

5507 **Kraft** Heinrich, Die Bilder der Offenbarung des Johannes. Fra 1994, Lang. 243 p. 3-631-47290-0.

5508 *Long* T. M. S., Reading the book of Revelation in South Africa; some methodological and literary observations in response to DU RAND: JTSAf 83 (1993) 78-86 [< NTAbs 38, p. 227].

5509 *a) Long* Tim M. S., A real reader reading Revelation; – *b) du Rand* Jan A., The transcendent God-view; depicting structures in the theological message of the Apocalypse of John: Neotestamentica 28 (1994) 395-411 / 557-573.

5510 **Lupieri** Edmondo, *al.*, Attualità dell'Apocalisse. Palermo 1992, Augustinus. 116 p. L^m 20. – R TR 90 (1994) 130-2 (H. *Giesen*).

5511 *Malina* B. J., The Book of Revelation and religion; how did the book of Revelation persuade? Scriptura 51 (1994) 27-50 [< NTAbs 39, p. 437].

5512 **Metzger** Bruce M., Breaking the code; understanding the Book of Revelation 1993 → 9,5727: R PrincSemB 15 (1994) 289s (R. E. *Brown*).

5513 **Michaels** J. Ramsey, Interpreting the Book of Revelation 1992 → 8, 5932; 9,5728: R RefTR 53 (1994) 51 (P. *O'Brien*).

5514 *Muñoz León* Domingo, El Apocalipsis y la universalidad de la redención en Cristo: RBibArg 55 (1993) 141-157.

5515 **Murphy** Frederick J., *a)* Apocalypses and apocalypticism; the state of the question; – *b)* The book of revelation: CuRB 2 (1998) 147-179 / 181-225.

5516 **Noe** John, The Apocalypse conspiracy. Brentwood TN 1991, Wolgemuth & H. 277 p. $10. – R BtS 151 (1994) 492 (J. F. *Walvoord*: misunderstands prophecy).

O'Leary S. D., Arguing the Apocalypse; a theory of millennial rhetoric 1994 → 5562.

5518 *Oliveira C. da Silva* João A., Os Selos de Herberto HELDER e o Apocalipse; uma leitura intertextual: Brotéria 138 (1994) 301-325. 407-420.

5519 **Pippin** Tina, Death and desire ... gender/Apc: Literary Currents BInterp 1992 ➤ 9,5733: ᴿCBQ 56 (1994) 382s (C. *Osiek*).

5520 **Prévost** Jean-Pierre, How to read the Apocalypse (Crossroad, also L-SCM) 1993 ➤ 8,5938; 9,5735: ᴿDocLife 44 (1994) 57s (W. *Harrington*); PrPeo 8 (1994) 87s (C. *Rowland*); RExp 91 (1994) 270 (W.L. *Hendricks*: 'John-Pierre' 'Crossword').

5521 **Reichelt** Hansgünter, Angelus interpres-Texte in der Johannes-Apokalypse; Strukturen, Aussagen und Hintergründe [Diss. Lp 1992]: EurHS 23/507. Fra 1994, Lang. vii-246 p. 3-631-47248-X [TLZ 120,663, O. *Böcher*].

5522 **Reynold** Edwin E., The Sodom/Egypt/Babylon motif in the Book of Revelation: diss. Andrews, ᴰ*Paulien* J. Berrien Springs 1994. 396 p. 95-09595. – DissA 55 (1994s) p. 3880.

5523 *a) Roloff* Jürgen, Weltgericht und Weltvollendung in der Offenbarung des Johannes; – *b) Kuschel* Karl-Josef. Vor uns die Sintflut?; – *c) Kitzberger* Ingrid R., 'Wasser und Bäume des Lebens' — eine feministische intertextuelle Interpretation von Apk 21/22: ➤ 113, ᶠSCHNACKENBURG R., 1993/4, 106-127 / 232-260 / 206-224.

5524 *a) Stock* Konrad, Der Geist des Gesetzes und der Geist des Evangeliums; – *b) Böcher* Otto, Johannes-Apokalypse und Hebräerbrief: ➤ 31*, ᶠDAUTZENBERG G., Nach 1994, 791-9 / 107-115.

5525 *Ruiz* Jean-Pierre, The Apocalypse of John and contemporary Roman Catholic liturgy: Worship 65 (1994) 482-504.

5526 *Smidt* J.C. de, The Holy Spirit in the book of Revelation – nomenclature: Neotestamentica 28 (1994) 229-244.

5527 *Smith* Christopher R., The structure of the Book of Revelation in light of apocalyptic literary conventions: NT 36 (1994) 373-393.

5528 *Socias* Imma, Els desenganys de l'Apocalipsis disposats i declarats amb els seus signes: AnSacTar 67 (1994) 811-821; 4 fig.

5529 *a) Stegemann* Ekkehard W., Aspekte psychoanalytischer Auslegung der Johannesoffenbarung; – *b) Karrer* Martin, Psychoanalyse und Auslegung [RAGUSE H. 1992]: EvT 54 (1994) 452-466 / 467-476.

5530 **Stuckenbruck** Loren T., 'Do not worship me; worship God'; the problem of angel veneration in early Judaism and aspects of angelomorphic Christology in the Apocalypse of John: diss. Theol. Sem. ᴰ*Charlesworth* J. Princeton 1993. 402 p. 94-30038. – DissA 55 (1994s) p. 2005; RelStR 21,256.

5531 **Sutter Rehmann** Luzia, 'Geh, frage die Gebärerin ...' Feministisch-befreiungstheologische Untersuchungen zum Gebärmotiv in der Apokalyptik: Diss. ᴰ*Schottroff* Luise. Kassel 1994. – TR 91,98.

5532 **Tresmontant** Claude, Enquête sur l'Apocalypse; auteur, datation, signification. P 1994, de Guibert. 483 p. 2-86839-305-5.

5533 *Vanni* Ugo, Lo Spirito e la Sposa dicono 'vieni'; l'Apocalisse liturgia della speranza: RivLtg 81 (1994) 193-211.

5534 **Wainwright** Arthur W., Mysterious Apocalypse [history of interpretation]. Nv/L 1993, Abingdon/SPCK. 293 p. $16. 0-687-27641-1. – ᴿExpTim 106 (1994s) 247s (J.M. *Court*); PrincSemB 15 (1994) 209s (B.M. *Metzger*); RExp 91 (1994) 611 (J.L. *Blevins*); SewaneeTR 38 (1994s) 82-84 (W.H. *Shepherd*, also on AUKERMAN D.).

5535 *Wengst* Klaus, Babylon the Great and the New Jerusalem; the visionary view of political reality in the Revelation of John: ➤ 331*b*, Politics 1994, 189-201.

5536 *Winkler* J.,   Apocalypse now; interpreting the Book of Revelation: Living Light 34,1 (Wsh 1994) 32-41 [< NTAbs 39, p. 258].

G2.5 *Apocalypsis*, **Revelation** 1,1 ...

5537 **Sieg** Franciszek,   *Hómoios uiòs anthrōpou* (Offb 1,13); Schlussfolgerungen aus der Untersuchung (Offb 1,13-16.17c.18; 2,1.8.12.18; 3,1.7.14) [< Diss. Warszawa 1981]: FgNt 13 (1994) 1-14; Eng. 15.

5538 **Lee Kwan Jin,** Die theologischen Anliegen der Gemeindebriefe in Apk 2-3: Diss. ᴰ*Berger* K. Heidelberg 1994. – TR 91,97.

5539 **Ramsay** W.M.,   [Apc 2s] The letters to the seven churches [1904], ᴱ*Wilson* M.W.   Peabody MA 1994, Hendrickson.   xiv-319 p.   35 fig.;   16 pl., 2 maps.   1-56563-059-9 [NTAbs 39, p. 337].

5540 *Fox* Kenneth A.,   [Rev 2,14.20] The Nicolaitans, Nicolaus and the early Church: SR 23 (1994) 485-496.

5541 **Thomas** Scott K.,   A sociological analysis of guilds in first-century Asia Minor as background for Rev 2:18-29: diss. Baptist Theol. Sem., ᴰ*Stevens* G.   New Orleans 1994. 180 p. 95-03444. – DissA 55 (1994s) p. 2784.

5542 **Muller** Ekkehardt,   Microstructural analysis of Revelation 4-11: diss. Andrews, ᴰ*Paulien* J.   Berrien Springs MI 1994. 801 p. 94-20015. – AndrUnSem 31 (1994) 112; DissA 55 (1994s) p. 1592; RTLv 26, p. 538.

5543 **Davis** R. Dean,   The heavenly court judgment of Revelation 4-5 [diss. Andrews, ᴰ*Strand* K.] 1992 ➤ 8,5986; 9,5750:   ᴿCritRR 6 (1993) 217-9 (R.W. *Wall*); WestTJ 55 (354-6 (R.F. *White*).

5544 *Hasitschka* Martin,   'Überwunden hat der Löwe aus dem Stamm Juda' (Offb 5,5): Funktion und Herkunft des Bildes vom Lamm in der Offenbarung des Johannes: ➤ 38, ᶠGAMPER A.,   ZkT 116 (1994) 487-493.

5545 **Afzal** Cameron C.,   Time revealed; the eschatology of the Book of Revelation ch. 6-7;   diss. Columbia, ᴰ*Scroggs* R. NY 1994. 223 p. 94-21316. – DissA 55 (1994s) p. 603.

5546 *Garuti* P.,   La morte e l'Ade in Apocalisse 6,7-8: DivThom 96,2 (1993) 167-203 [< NTAbs 39, p. 75].

5547 *Bachmann* Michael,   Himmlisch: der 'Tempel Gottes' von Apk 11.1: NTS 40 (1994) 474-480.

5547* *Day* John,   The origin of Armageddon; Revelation 16:16 as an interpretation of Zechariah 12:11: ➤ 45, ᶠGOULDER M., Crossing 1994, 315-326.

5548 *Thomas* R. L., *a*) [Rev 16,17-22,5] An analysis of the seventh bowl of the Apocalypse: Master'sSemJ 5,1 (Sun Valley CA 1994) 73-95 [< NTAbs 39, p. 75]; – *b*) [Rev 17,9-11; 11,1-13] Theonomy and the dating of Revelation: Master'sSemJ 5,2 (1994) 185-202 [< NTAbs 39, p. 258].

5549 *a*) *Boring* M. Eugene,   Revelation 19-21; end without closure; – *b*) *Moorhead* James H.,   *Bonner* Bian K., AUGUSTINE's thoughts on this world and hope for the next: ➤ 326, Hope, PrincSemB supp (1994) 57-84 / 85-103.

5550 *Rosso Ubigli* Liliana,   L'uomo e l'angelo; a proposito di Apocalisse 19,10 e 22,8-9: ➤ 29, ᶠCORSINI E. Voce 1994, 323-330.

G2.7 **Millenniarismus,** *Apc 20 ...*

5551 **Archer** Gleason L.ᴶ, *al.*,   The rapture; pre-, mid-, or post-tribulational? [< ev. Free Church meeting]. GR 1994, Zondervan. 268 p. – ᴿRefR 48 (1994s) 62 (G. *Wyper* gives date as 1984).

5552 ᴱ**Blaising** Craig A., *Bock* Darrell L., Dispensationalism, Israel, and the Church; the search for definition; 1992 ➤ 8,6003; 9,5769: ᴿRefR 48 (1994s) 55 (G. *Wyper*: the book favors its 'fourth, more progressive' type).
5553 **Blaising** Craig A., *Bock* Darrell L., Progressive dispensationalism [Rev 7 and 13,5 numbers 'not symbolic but realities in the world of the writer']. Wheaton IL 1993, BridgePoint. 336 p. $16. – ᴿTrinJ 15 (1994) 253-5 (Stephen *Nichols*).
5554 *Duling* Dennis C., BTB readers guide; millenialism: BibTB 24 (1994) 132-142.
5555 **Erwin** John S., The millennialism of Cotton MATHER; an historical and theological analysis: StAmerRel 45. Lewiston NY 1990, Mellen. 247 p. $60. – ᴿChH 63 (1994) 124s (J. A. De *Jong*).
5556 **Grenz** Stanley J., The millennial maze 1992 ➤ 8,6018: ᴿAndrUnSem 32 (1994) 273-5 (J. *McVay*).
5557 **Heid** Stefan, Chiliasmus und Antichrist-Mythos; eine frühchristliche Kontroverse um das Heilige Land: Hereditas 6, 1993 ➤ 9,5674: ᴿCathHR 80 (1994) 127s (R. B. *Eno*); ForKT 10 (1994) 148-150 (W. *Gessel*); RHE 99 (1994) 105s (M. R. *Macina*); RTLv 25 (1994) 377s (A. de *Halleux*).
5558 **Knight** George B., Millennial fever and the end of the world. Boise 1993, Pacific. 384 p. $15. – ᴿAndrUnSem 32 (1994) 281-3 (B. E. *Strayer*).
5559 *Laub* Franz, *Kehl* Medard, Chiliasmus: ➤ 510, LTK³ 2 (1994) 1045s-8.
5560 **Marasigan** Vicente, Forged prophecy ['of St. Malachy'] and millenary speculations [*Valente* G. & *Borghesi* M. in 30 Days 3 (1984) 52-61]: Landas 8 (1994) 277-280.
5561 **Mealy** J. Webb, [➤ 5568s] After the thousand years: jNsu 70, 1992 ➤ 8,6020; 9,5773: ᴿEvQ 66 (1994) 229-243 (G. K. *Beale*); Interpretation 48 (1994) 102.104 (M. *Rissi*: intriguing but unlikely).
5562 **O'Leary** Stephen D., Arguing the Apocalypse; a theory of millennial rhetoric. NY 1994, Oxford-UP. x-314 p. $35. 0-19-508045-9 [NTAbs 38, p. 471; RelStR 21,159, Sarah M. *Pike*]. – ᴿTLond 97 (1994) 474 (B. R. *Wilson*: learned, uneven); TTod 51 (1994s) 436.8.440 (J. H. *Moorhead*).
5563 **Olsen** Palle J., Was John FOXE a millenarian? [it is all a matter of definition]: JEH 45 (1994) 600-624.
5564 **Saucy** Robert J., The case for progressive dispensationalism; the interface between dispensationalism and non-dispensational theology. GR 1993, Zondervan. 306 p. $20. – ᴿBtS 151 (1994) 360s (R. A. *Pyne*).
5565 *a*) *Spencer* Stephen R., Reformed theology, covenant theology; and dispensationalism; – *b*) *Walvoord* John F., The New Covenant; – *c*) *Bailey* Mark L., Dispensational definitions of the Kingdom; – *d*) *Toussaint* Stanley D., The contingency of the coming of the Kingdom: ➤ 21, ᶠCAMPBELL D., Integrity, 238-254 / 186-200 / 201-221 / 222-237.
5566 *a*) *Underwood* Grant, Millenarianism and popular Methodism in early nineteenth century England and Canada; – *b*) *Blaising* Craig A., Changing patterns in American dispensational theology: WestTJ 29 (1994) 81-91 / 149-164.
5567 **Van Kampen** Robert, The sign. Wheaton IL 1992, Crossway. 528 p. $16. – ᴿBtS 151 (1994) 113-6 (J. A. *Witmer*: pre-wrath rapture of the Church, as in *Rosenthal* M. J. 1990; but Antichrist, not Christ, is executor of the great tribulation).

5568 *a*) *Colwell* J. D., *Webb* W. J., Revelation 20; hermeneutical considerations; – *b*) *Garlington* D., Reigning with Christ; Rev. 20,1-6 in

salvation-historical setting: BapTR 4,1 (London ONT 1994) 38-55
[< NTAbs 39, p. 76].

5569 *Webb* W.J., (*Mealy* J.W.?)   Revelation 20; exegetical considerations:
BapRT 4,2 (1994) 7-39 [< NTAbs 39, p. 438].

5570 *Smidt* K. de,   Revelation 20 [not chiliastic]; prelude to the Omega Point
— the new heaven and earth: Scriptura 49 (Stellenbosch 1994) 75-87
[< NTAbs 39, p. 259].

5571 *a) White* R. Fowler,   Making sense of Rev 20: 1-10? Harold HOEHNER
versus recapitulation; – *b) Poythress* Vern S.,   2 Thessalonians 1 supports
amillennialism: JEvTS 37 (1994) 539-551 / 529-538.

5572 *Álvarez Valdes* Ariel,   La nueva Jerusalén del Apocalipsis [21,1s] y sus
raíces en el AT; el período de la 'Jerusalén Nueva': RBibArg 56 (1994)
103-113.

> **XIII. Paulus**

G3.1   **Pauli biographia.**

5573 **Barrett** C.K. Paul,   L 1994, SCM.   xii-180 p. $13 pa.   0-664-25541-8. –
RNBlackf 75 (1994) 494s (H. *Wansbrough*).

5574 **Biser** Eugen,   Paulus, Zeuge, Mystiker, Vordenker: Piper 1477.   Mü
1992, Piper.   432 p. DM 24,80.   3-492-11477-6 [NTAbs 38, p. 469].

5575 **Biser** Eugen,   Paolo apostolo e scrittore; una sfida per i cristiani: coll.
Scr.   R 1991, Città Nuova.   231 p. Lm 18. – RProtestantesimo 49 (1994)
402s (L. *De Lorenzi*).

5576 *Bovon* F.,   L'apôtre Paul comme témoignage et comme mémoire: *a)* in
Allaz J., Chrétiens en conflit 54-65; – *b)* ⓖ [➔ 5581*b]* DeltVM 23,1 (1994)
56-68 [NTAbs 31, p. 369; 39, p. 239].

5577 *Feneberg* W.,   Paulus, der Weltbürger; eine Biographie 1992 ➔ 8,6033;
9,5788:   RSalesianum 56 (1994) 568s (J.J. *Bartolomé*); TR 90 (1994)
296-8 (F. *Mussner*).

5578 *Furnish* Victor P.,   On putting Paul in his place [presidential address
Wsh Nov 1993]: JBL 113 (1994) 3-17.

5579 **Hengel** M.,   The pre-Christian Paul 1991 ➔ 7,5119 ... 9,5790:   RConcordTQ 58 (1994) 164s (C.A. *Gieschen*).

5580 **Hengel** M.,   Il Paolo precristiano [1991]T: StBPaid 100, 1992 ➔ 8,6035;
9,5791:   RAsprenas 41 (1994) 118s (G. *Citro*); Athenaeum 82 (1992) 595-8
(L. *Troiani*); RivStoLR 30 (1994) 640s (Gabriella *Dogliani Saladini*);
Salesianum 56 (1994) 570s (J.J. *Bartolomé*).

5581 *a) Hofius* Otfried, ⓖ Paulus als Apostel und als Theologe; – *b) Bovon*
François, ⓖ L'apôtre Paul comme témoignage et comme mémoire,
T*Campagnolo-Pothitis* Maria: ➔ 131*c*, Mem, VELLAS V., DeltioVM 13,1
(1994) 69-94 / 56-68.

5582 *Horn* Friedrich W.,   Saulus; neuere Arbeiten zum vorchristlichen Paulus
[HENGEL M., 1991; NIEBUHR K., 1992]: ZRGg 46 (1994) 65-69.

5583 *Malherbe* Abraham J.,   Paulus Senex [Eng.]: ➔ 89*b*, FOLBRICHT T.,
RestQ 36 (1994) 197-207.

5584 **Martin** Raymond A.,   Studies in the life and ministry of the early Paul
and related issues.   Lewiston NY 1993, Mellen.   x-251 p. $90.   0-7734-
2368-0 [RelStR 21,145, J.T. *Fitzgerald*]. – RTBR 7,1 (1994s) 24 (R.
Morgan); TLZ 119 (1994) 1080-2 (R. *Heiligenthal*).

5585 **Martini** Carlo Maria, Paolo, en lo vivo del ministerio. Valencia 1991, Edicep. – ᴿScripTPamp 26 (1994) 1271s (E. de *la Lama*).
5586 ᴱ**Pastor-Ramos** Federico, San Pablo: Reseña Bíblica primavera 1995. Estella 1994, VDivino. 71 p. pt. 1000.
5587 **Penna** Romano, Paolo di Tarso, un cristianesimo possibile: UnivT 2, 1992 ➤ 9,5798: CinB 1992, Paoline. 190 p. – ᴿCC 145 (1994,3) 445 (D. *Scaiola*); EstE 69 (1994) 269 (P. *Ramirez Fueyo*).
5588 **Riesner** Rainer, Die Frühzeit des Apostels Paulus; Studien zur Chronologie, Missionsstrategie und Theologie: WUNT 71. Tü 1994, Mohr. xiv-509 p. ᴰᴹ 168. 3-16-145828-1 [TR 91,227, T. *Holtz*].
5589 **Sanchez Bosch** J., Nacido a tiempo; una vida de Pablo, el Apóstol. Pamplona c. 1994, VDivino. 319 p. [Claretianum 35, 546]. 84-7151-977-1.
5590 *Seifrid* M. A., Blind alleys in the controversy over the Paul of history: TyndB 45,1 (1994) 73-95 [< NTAbs 39, p. 58, C. R. *Matthews*].
5591 **Witherington** Benᴵᴵᴵ, Paul's narrative thought world; the tapestry of tragedy and triumph. Lᴠʟ 1994, W-Knox. 373 p. $25. 0-664-25433-0 [TS 56,358, B. *Fiore*].

G3.2 **Corpus paulinum;** *generalia, technica epistularis.*

5592 **Aland** K., *al.*, Text und Textwert II/1-4 Briefe 1991 ➤ 7,5158... 9,5803: ᴿBASP 30 (1993) 69-71 (J. L. *White*); 179s (T. H. *Tobin*, III Apg).
5593 **Arzt** Peter, *a)* The 'epistolary introductory thanksgiving' 1994. – *b)* Analyse der Paulusbriefe auf dem Hintergrund dokumentarischer Papyri: ProtokB 3 (1994) 99-114.
5594 *Bammel* C. P., Die Pauluskommentare des Hieronymus; die ersten wissenschaftlichen lateinischen Bibelkommentare: ➤ a23, Cristianesimo latino 1992/3, 187-207.
5595 *Bishop* Jonathan, The Gospel(s) according to Paul: AnglTR 76 (1994) 296-312.
5596 ᴱ**Bouttier** M., *Brossier* F., Vocabulaire des épîtres de Paul [87 words in alphabetical order but from eight theological domains with separate authors]: CahÉv 88. P 1994, Cerf. 72 p. F 30. 0222-9714 [NTAbs 39, p. 150].
5597 *Classen* Carl J., Philologische Bemerkungen zur Sprache des Apostels Paulus: ➤ 117, ꜰScʜwᴀʙʟ H., WienerSt 107 (1994) 321-335.
5598 *Collins* R. F., Las cartas de Pablo: Actualidad Pastoral 27,204s (Moron ᴬᴿᴳ 1994) 222-231 [< NTAbs 39, p. 240: recognition that Eph Col 2Thess 1-2Tim Tit were not written by Paul allows us to appreciate more fully the richness of the NT].
5599 *Doughty* D. J., Pauline paradigms and Pauline authenticity: JHiCr 1 (1994) 95-128 [< NTAbs 39, p. 240].
5600 **Furnish** Victor P., Jesus according to Paul: Understanding Jesus today. C 1994, Univ. vii-135 p. $30; pa. $10. 0-521-45193-0; -824-2 [TDig 42,65].
5601 **Hays** R., Echoes of Scripture in the letters of Paul 1989 ➤ 9,5815: ᴿRestQ 36 (1994) 53s (J. P. *Polland*).
5602 **Jaquette** James L., Indifferent matters in Paul's letters; the functional diversity of a Graeco-Roman topos: diss. ᴰ*Sampley* J., Boston [? Univ.] 1992. – RTLv 26,537.
5603 **Michalowski** P., Letters from Early Mesopotamia: Writings from the Ancient World 3, 1993 ➤ 9,5819: ᴿVT 44 (1994) 575 (J. N. *Postgate*).
5604 **Most** William, The thought of St. Paul; a commentary on the Pauline

epistles. Front Royal VA 1994, Christendom. 301 p. $18. 0-931888-56-5 [TDig 42,282]. – ᴿHomP 95 (1994s) 82s (K. *Baker*).

5605 **Müller** Markus, Vom Schluss zum Ganzen; der Briefkorpusabschluss als Zugang zur 'Texthermeneutik' des Apostelbriefes: diss. ᴰ*Roloff* J. Erlangen-N 1994. 249 p. – RTLv 26, p. 538.

5606 **Murphy-O'Connor** Jerome, Paul et l'art épistolaire [1995!], ᵀ*Prignaud* Jean. BJérÉtAnnexe. P 1994, Cerf. 311 p. F 130. 2-204-05056-3 [RB 102,626, J.-N. *Aletti*].

5607 **Neumann** Kenneth J., The authenticity of the Pauline epistles [... Eph Col] in the light of stylostatistical analysis: SBL diss. (Toronto) 120. Atlanta 1990, Scholars. x-267 p. $26; sb./pa. $17 [RB 102,148, J. *Murphy-O'Connor*].

5608 **Neyrey** J., Paul in other words 1990 ⮕ 6,5066; 7,5175: ᴿBapRT 4,2 (1994) 83-92 (D. *Garlington*: good except for 'unhelpful' sociology method).

5609 *Penna* Romano, L'origine del corpus paulinum; alcuni aspetti della questione: CrNSt 15 (1994) 577-607.

Probst Hermann, Paulus und der Brief... 1 Kor 8-10, ᴰ1991 ⮕ 5891.

5610 **Puskas** C., Letters of Paul 1993 ⮕ 9,5821: ᴿCBQ 56 (1994) 806s (P. *Zilonka*).

5611 **Richards** E. R., The secretary 1991 ⮕ 7,5156... 9,5822: ᴿSalesianum 56 (1994) 575s (F. *Canaccini*).

5612 **Schmid-Tempel** Ulrich, MARCION und sein Apostolos; Rekonstruktion und historische Einordnung der marcionitischen Paulusbriefausgabe: Diss. ᴰ*Aland* B. Münster 1994. 337 + 65 p. – RTLv 26, p. 539.

5613 *Strickland* G., To understand St. Paul, don't read the NEB: Faith & Worship 37 (London 1994) 21-25 [< NTAbs 39, p. 424].

5614 *Toit* Andrie du, Vilification as a pragmatic device in early Christian epistolography: Biblica 75 (1994) 403-412.

5615 **Trobisch** David, Paul's letter collection; tracing the origins [< 1989 diss.], Mp 1994, Fortress. xi-108 p. $10. 0-8005-2597-8 [RelStR 21,236, A. J. *Malherbe*]. – ᴿExpTim 106 (1994s) 151 (N. *Clark*).

5616 **Trobisch** David, Die Paulusbriefe und die Anfänge der christlichen Publizistik [Paul's letter collection 1994],ᵀ: Tb 135. Gü 1994, Kaiser. 160 p.; 7 fig. DM 26,80. 3-579-05135-0 [NTAbs 39, p. 340].

5617 **Weima** Jeffrey A. D., *a)* Pauline letter closing; analysis and hermeneutical significance: diss. St. Michael's, ᴰ*Longenecker* R. Windsor 1993. – SR 23 (1994) 525. – *b)* Neglected endings; the significance of the Pauline letter closings: jNsu 101. Sheffield 1994, Academic. 278 p.; bibliog. 240-258. £37.50. 1-85075-488-8.

G3.3 **Pauli theologia.**

5618 **Barrett** C. Kingsley, Paul, an introduction to his thought: Outstanding Christian thinkers. L 1994, Chapman. xii-180 p. 0-225-66688-X.

5619 *Barry* Catherine, Anthropologie gnostique et typologie paulinienne dans la Sagesse de Jésus-Christ (NH III,4 et Berolinensis gnosticus 3): Muséon 107 (1994) 293-297.

5620 *Beilner* Wolfgang, Weltgericht und Weltvollendung bei Paulus: ⮕ 113, ᶠSCHNACKENBURG R. 1994, 85-105.

5621 **Beker** J. Christiaan, The triumph of God; the essence of Paul's thought 1990 ⮕ 6,6009... 9,5831: ᴿConcordTQ 58 (1994) 199s (C. A. *Gieschen*).

5622 *a)* *Brecht* Volker, Der Anhalt des Bekenntnissatzes 'credo in sanctam ecclesiam catholicam' an der Theologie des Paulus; – *b)* *Redhardt* Jürgen,

Ursprungssituationen individueller religiöser Fehlentwicklungen: ➤ 31*, FDAUTZENBERG G., Nach den Anfängen fragen 1994, 117-131 / 765-775.

5623 *Campbell* D., The atonement in Paul: Anvil 11 (1994) 237-250 [< NTAbs 39, p. 239].

5624 **Capes** David B., OT Yahweh texts in Paul's Christology ᴰ1992 ➤ 8,6070; 9,5835: ᴿJBL 113 (1994) 162-4 (L. W. *Hurtado*); TR 90 (1994) 33-35 (H. *Giesen*).

5626 *Capes* D. B., YHWH and his Messiah; Pauline exegesis and the divine Christ: HorBT 16,2 (1994) 121-143 [< NTAbs 39, p. 426].

Carozzi Claude, Eschatologie et au-delà; recherches sur l'apocalypse de Paul 1994 ➤ 9639b.

5628 **Cousar** Charles B., A theology of the Cross; the death of Jesus in the Pauline letters: OvBT 1990 ➤ 6,6094... 8,6071: ᴿChrSchR 23 (1993s) 461-3 (L. R. *Helyer*); ConcordTQ 58 (1994) 59s (C. A. *Gieschen*).

5629 *Dunn* James D. G., Prolegomena to a theology of Paul: NTS 40 (1994) 407-422.

5630 *Fabris* Rinaldo, L'uomo nuovo nell'antropologia paolina: VivH 5 (1994) 105-116; Eng. 117.

5631 **Georgi** Dieter, Theocracy in Paul's praxis and theology, 1991 ['Gott auf den Kopf stellen', 1987]ᵀ in ᴱ*Taubes* J., Theokratie ᵀ1991 ➤ 7,5194; 9,5844: ᴿTLZ 119 (1994) 25s (U. *Luz*).

5632 *Girardello* Rodolfo, Teologia missionaria di S. Paolo: RivVSp 48 (1994) 117-126.

5633 **Hamerton-Kelly** R. G., Sacred violence; Paul's hermeneutic of the Cross 1992 ➤ 8,7824: ᴿJStNT 55 (1994) 124 (B. J. *Dodd*).

5634 **Horn** Friedrich W., Das Angeld des Geistes; Studien zur paulinischen Pneumatologie: FRL 154, ᴰ1992 ➤ 8,6078: ᴿBiblica 75 (1994) 287-291 (R. *Penna*).

5635 **Howell** Don N., The center of Pauline theology [title (only) echoes PLEVNIK J. 1989]: BtS 151 (1994) 50-70.

5636 **Hübner** Hans, Die Theologie des Paulus: BT NT 2; 1991 ➤ 9,9650: ᴿActuBbg 31 (1994) 40s (J. *Boada*); BZ 38 (1994) 151-3 (R. *Schnakkenburg*).

5637 **Kertelge** Karl, 'Giustificazione' in Paolo [ᴰ1967] 1991 ➤ 7,5198... 9,5852: ᴿRivStoLR 30 (1994) 641s (Gabriella *Dogliani Saladini*).

5638 **Kertelge** K., Grundthemen 1991 ➤ 7,217*; 9,5853: ᴿNRT 116 (1994) 913s (X. *Jacques*).

5639 *Klehn* Lars, Die Verwendung von *en Christō* bei Paulus; Erwägungen zu den Wandlungen in der paulinischen Theologie: BibNot 74 (1994) 66-79.

5640 *Nebe* Gottfried, Christ, the Body of Christ and cosmic powers in Paul's letters and the New Testament as a whole: ➤ 331b, Politics 1994, 100-118.

5641 **Newman** Carey C., Paul's glory-Christology; tradition and rhetoric: NT supp 69, 1992 ➤ 8,6988; 9,5856: ᴿJTS 45 (1994) 255-7 (C. J. A. *Hickling*).

5642 **Penna** Romano, L'apostolo Paolo [30 reprints] 1991 ➤ 7,247: ᴿSalesianum 56 (1994) 379 (J. J. *Bartolomé*).

5643 *Pindel* Roman, ✪ De idea evolvenda [*Model rozwoju*] Corporis Christi apud S. Paulum: RuBi 47 (1994) 188-196.

5644 **Pitta** Antonio, Sinossi paolina: UnivTeol 31. CinB 1994, Paoline. 318 p. Lᵐ 35. 88-215-2880-1.

5645 **Richardson** Neil, Paul's language about God: jNsu 99. Shf 1994, Academic. 371 p. £40. 1-85075-485-3. – ᴿExpTim 106 (1994) 344 (A. T. *Lincoln*).

5646 **Ryšková** Mireia, Jetzt gibt es keine Verurteilung mehr für die, welche in Christus Jesus sind; eine bibeltheologische und fundamentalethische Untersuchung zum paulinischen *en Christō*-Gebrauch: kath. Diss. [D]*Kleber*. Passau 1992. – TR 90,87.

5647 **Scott** James M., Adoption as sons of God ... *huiothesía* in the Pauline Corpus: WUNT 2/48, [D]1992 ➤ 8,6092: [R]Biblica 75 (1994) 28-30 (J. *Schlosser*); JBL 113 (1994) 548-550 (R. G. *Grams*).

5648 **Seifrid** Mark A., Justification by faith; the origin and development of a central Pauline theme 1992 ➤ 8,6094: [R]BZ 38 (1994) 295s (T. *Söding*); CBQ 56 (1994) 386-8 (N. *Elliott*); JTS 45 (1994) 245s (J. A. *Ziesler*); ScEspr 46 (1994) 114s (P.-É. *Langevin*); WestTJ 56 (1994) 195-7 (R. B. *Gaffin*).

5649 **Tambasco** Anthony J., A theology of atonement and Paul's vision of Christianity 1991 ➤ 7,5209: [R]CritRR 6 (1993) 283-7 (M. L. *Soards*: better than RICHARDS); IrTQ 60 (1994) 73 (B. *Nolan*).

Tarocchi S., Il dio longanime ... paolino 1993 ➤ 9349*.

5650 **Theissen** Gerd, Psychological aspects of Pauline theology [1983 ➤ 65, 5591], [T]*Galvin* John P., 1987 ➤ 3,5658 ... 6,6119; $40. 0-8006-0789-9: [R]RExp 91 (1994) 445s (S. *Southard*).

5652 *Theobald* Michael, 'Sohn Gottes' als christologische Grundmetapher bei Paulus [Vortrag Wien 1993]: TüTQ 174 (1994) 185-207.

5653 *a*) *Vanni* Ugo, Salvezza giudaica, salvezza paolina; – *b*) *Cocchini* Francesca, L'esegesi paolina di TEODORETO di Cirro; – *c*) *Di Berardino* Angelo, Saulo di Tarso e la sua cittadinanza romana: ➤ 328s, Tarso 2, 1993/4, 29-41 / 145-153 / 7-28.

5654 **Way** David V., The Lordship of Christ; E. KÄSEMANN's interpretation of Paul's theology 1991 ➤ 7,5211; 9,5861: [R]ScotJT 47 (1994) 391-3 (J. *Barclay*).

5655 **Wedderburn** A. J. M. Baptism and reconciliation/Paul [D]1987 ➤ 3,5661 ... 7,5212: [R]RTLv 25 (1994) 493s (J. *Ponthot*).

5656 *Wedderburn* A. J. M., Paul and 'Biblical Theology': ➤ 303*a*, Aarhus New approaches 1992/4, 24-46.

5657 **Witherington** Ben[III], Paul's [theology, consisting of reflections on his] narrative thought world; the tapestry of tragedy and triumph. LvL/ Carlisle 1994, W-Knox/Paternoster. 373 p. £20. 0-664-35433-0 / 0- 85364- 540-X [RelStR 21,146, J. *Peterson*]. – [R]ExpTim 106 (1994s) 247 (B. *Rosner*).

G3.4 *Pauli stylus et modus operandi* – **Paul's image.**

5658 **Aageson** James W., Written also for our sake; Paul and the art of biblical interpretation 1993 ➤ 9,5864: [R]CBQ 56 (1994) 577s (L. T. *Johnson*).

5659 **Appleton** George, Paolo interprete di Cristo [1988],[T]: Bibbia per tutti 1991 ➤ 7,5150; L[m] 16. – [R]Asprenas 41 (1994) 604s (V. *Scippa*).

5660 *Barr* James, Paul and the LXX; a note on some recent work [ELLIS E. ...]: JTS 45 (1994) 593-601.

5661 **Beaudean** Jack W., Paul's theology of preaching [D]1988 ➤ 5,5814: [R]CurrTM 21 (1994) 298 (E. *Krentz*).

5662 **Castelli** Elizabeth A., Imitating Paul 1991 ➤ 7,5112 ... 9,5866: [R]Crit-RR 6 (1993) 213-5 (C. J. *Roetzel*).

5663 **Dales** Douglas J., [2 Cor; Philp] Living through dying; the spiritual experience of St. Paul. C 1994, Lutterworth. xii-97 p. £13. 0-7188- 2898-4 [NTAbs 39, p. 516]. – [R]ExpTim 106 (1994s) 88 (J. A. *Ziesler*: a beautiful production); Month 255 (1994) 484s (D. *Robinson*).

5663* *De Lorenzi* Lorenzo, Paolo, l'esperienza di Dio; – *b*) *Barbaglio* Giuseppe, La 'via crucis' di Paolo: ParSpV 30 (1994) 137-170 / 183-194.

5664 **Elliott** Neil, Liberating Paul; the justice of God and the politics of the Apostle: Bible and Liberation. Mkn 1994, Orbis. xi-308 p. $19 pa. 0-88344-981-1 [NTAbs 39, p. 333]. – ᴿExpTim 106 (1994s) 343s (J. *Proctor*: omitting Eph Col Tim and occasionally squeezing other data, seeks to claim Paul against slavery, misogynism, oppression of Latin America and the Gulf War).

5665 ᴱ**Engberg-Pedersen** Troels, Paul in his Hellenistic context: StNTW. E 1994, Clark. xxxi-341 p. 0-567-09694-7.

5666 **Jewett** R., St. Paul at the movies 1993 ➤ 9,5871: ᴿChrCent 111 (1994) 389-391 (G. E. *Forsbey*).

5667 **Klumbies** Paul-Gerhard, Die Rede von Gott bei Paulus in ihrem zeitgeschichtlichen Kontext: FRL 155, 1992 ➤ 8,6108: ᴿExpTim 106 (1994s) 270s (E. *Best*).

5668 *Murphy-O'Connor* Jerome, Does St Paul find meaning in suffering?: PrPeo 8 (1994) 99-102.

5669 *Newell* W. R., Paul's Gospel: JGrace [not = GraceJT, terminated 1991] 7,12 (Roanoke 1994) 45-50 [< NTAbs 39, p. 55].

5670 **Pak Yeong-Sik** James, Paul as missionary; a comparative study of missionary discourse in Paul's epistles and selected contemporary Jewish texts [diss. Pontifical Biblical Institute, excerpt]: UnivSt 23/410, ᴰ1991 ➤ 7,5140; 8,8116: ᴿCBQ 56 (1994) 144s (Regina A. *Boisclair*: clear; summaries superb).

5671 **Pate** C. Marvin, The glory of Adam and the afflictions of the righteous; Pauline suffering in context. Lewiston NY 1993, Mellen. xvi-353 p.; bibliog. p. 343-357. 0-7734-2360-5.

5672 *Reid* D. G., The misunderstood Apostle: Mishkan 20 (J 1994) 3-12 [13-22, *Robinson* R.; < NTAbs 39, p. 55].

5673 (**Schiefer**) **Ferrari** Markus, [1 Cor 4] Die Sprache des Leids in den paulinischen Peristasenkatalogen ᴰ1992 ➤ 8,6164*: ᴿTR 90 (1994) 39-41 (G. *Dautzenberg*).

5674 **Stanley** C. D., Paul and the language of Scripture; citation technique in the Pauline epistles and contemporary literature: SNTS mg 74, 1992 ➤ 8,6127; 9,5878: ᴿJStJud 25 (1994) 124-8 (J. van *Ruiten*); JTS 45 (1994) 673s (R. P. *Martin*); LavalTP 50 (1994) 445-8 (A. *Gignac*); OTEssays 7 (1994) 144-7 (B. A. *Nieuwoudt*).

G3.5   **Apostolus Gentium [**➤ G4.6, Israel et Lex / Jews & Law].

5675 **Baslez** Marie-Françoise, Paolo di Tarso, l'apostolo delle genti 1993 ➤ 9,5880: ᴿAmbrosius 69 (1993) 575s (G. *Giavini*, anche su LUZI P.).

5676 **Becker** Jürgen, Paul, apostle to the Gentiles 1993 ➤ 9,5881: ᴿBInterp 2 (1994) 240-2 (L. *Houlden*: grander scale than BORNKAMM 1969); ÉTRel 69 (1994) 275s (E. *Cuvillier*); PrincSemB 15 (1994) 205-7 (C. J. *Roetzel*); TTod 51 (1994s) 307s (J. A. *Fitzmyer*); WestTJ 56 (1994) 431-3 (J. K. *Chamblin*).

5677 **Boyarin** Daniel, A radical Jew; Paul and the politics of identity: Contraversions 1. Berkeley 1994, Univ. California. xi-366 p. $35. 0-520-08592-2 [NTAbs 39, p. 332; Commentary 99/6, 57-60, J. M. *Harris*].

5678 **Comblin** José, Pablo, trabajo y misión [Paulo, trabalho e missão], ᵀ*Ortiz García* Alfonso: Alcance 47. Sdr 1994, Sal Terrae. 152 p. 84-293-1118-1. – ᴿActuBbg 31 (1994) 217 (J. *O'Callaghan*).

5679 EEvans Craig A., Sanders James A., Paul and the Scriptures of Israel [HAYES R., Echoes of Scripture 1989; 5 reviews and response]: StEJC 1. Shf 1993, JStOT. 296 p. £35. 1-85075-412-8 [TLZ 120,999, D. A. Koch]. – RTBR 7,2 (1994s) 20 (R. Morgan: hardy).

5680 Finsterbusch Karin, Thora als Lebensweisung bei Paulus; Studien zur Bedeutung der Thora für die paulinische Ethik: Diss. DBurchard C. Heidelberg 1994. 300 p. s Vandenhoeck. – RTLv 26,536; TR 91,97.

5681 Fitzmyer Joseph A., a) The spiritual journey of Paul the Apostle; – b) Paul's Jewish background and the deeds of the law; – c) St. Paul and preaching [all inedita]: → 172c, According to Paul 1993, 1-17.123s / 18-35.125-130 / 106-121.151s.

5682 Freed Edwin D., The apostle Paul, Christian Jew; faithfulness and law. Lanham MD 1994, UPA. 256 p. $32.50. 0-8191-9426-3 [RelStR 21,146, M. J. Goodwin].

5683 Frizzell L. E., Paul the Pharisee: → 384*, Jewish-Christian 1989/94, 45-60.

5684 Hagner D. A., Paul and Judaism; the Jewish matrix of early Christianity; issues in the current debate: BuBRes 3 (1993) 111-130 [< NTAbs 39, p. 54].

5685 Harrisville Roy A., The figure of Abraham in the Epistles of St. Paul. Lewiston NY 1992, Mellen. 314 p. $80. 0-7734-9841-2. – RInterpretation 48 (1994) 304 (F. D. Layman).

5686 EHengel M., Heckel U., Paulus und das antike Judentum...: WUNT 58, 1988/91 → 7,437: RRHPR 74 (1994) 214s (C. Grappe); TLZ 119 (1994) 896-8 (H. Hübner).

5687 Laato Timo, Paulus und das Judentum D1991 → 7,5127.5341; 8,6141: RJTS 45 (1994) 243-5 (J. D. G. Dunn).

5688 Légasse S., Paul fut-il un Juif apostat?: BLitEc 95 (1994) 183-196.

5689 Magnante Antonio, Aspects of biblical reflection on the missionary theme in St. Paul: Omnis Terra Eng. 28 (1994) 187-194 (25-31) 195; Eng. 196.

5690 Meissner Stefan, Die Heimholung des Ketzers; Studien zur jüdischen Auseinandersetzung mit Paulus: Diss. DBurchard C. Heidelberg 1994. – TR 91,97.

5691 Niebuhr Karl-Wilhelm, Heidenapostel aus Israel...: WUNT 62, 1992 → 8,6942; 9,5887: RCBQ 56 (1994) 143s (R. Morton); SvTKv 70 (1994) 194s (W. Übelacker).

5692 Segal Alan F., Paul the convert 1990 → 6,6048... 8,6125: RAJS 17 (1992) 291-3 (Pheme Perkins); SR 23 (1994) 87s (S. Brown: exciting, fruitful).

5693 Söding T., 'Apostel der Heiden' (Röm 11,13): LebS 45 (Wü 1994) 248-254 [< ZIT 95, p. 59].

G3.6 Pauli fundamentum philosophicum [→ G4.3] et morale.

5694 Alvarez V. Lorenzo, La estratificación social en la familia según San Pablo: Moralia 15 (M 1913) 73-96.

5694* Baumert Norbert, Frau und Mann bei Paulus 1992 → 8,6149; 9,5889: RZkT 116 (1994) 222-4 (M. Lohmeyer).

5695 — Kitzberger Ingrid R., Paulus zwischen Missverständnis und (Anti-)Feminismus [BAUMERT N., Frau und Mann / Antifeminismus, beide 1992]: BZ 38 (1994) 243-253.

5696 Hasler V., Die befreite Frau bei Paulus; Perspektiven und Bilanz: TSt

139. Z 1993, Theol.-V. 63 p. Fs 15 pa. 3-290-10910-0 [NTAbs 39, p. 152].
5697 *Haufe* Günter, Das Geistmotiv in der paulinischen Ethik: zNW 85 (1994) 183-191.
5698 **Heckel** Theo K., Der innere Mensch; die paulinische Verarbeitung eines platonischen Motivs: WUNT 2/53. Tü 1993, Mohr. x-257 p. DM 89. 3-16-146026-X. – RBZ 38 (1994) 146-8 (T. *Schmeller*); StPhilonAn 6 (1994) 303-6 (D. *Zeller*, deutsch); TLZ 119 (1994) 133-5 (H. D. *Betz*); TvT 34 (1994) 307 (H. van de *Sandt*).
5699 *Jaquette* James L., Paul, EPICTETUS and others on indifference to status: CBQ 56 (1994) 67-80.
5700 **Keener** Craig S., Paul, women and wives 1992 ➤ 8,9053; 9,5894: RJRelH 18 (1994) 98s (J. W. *Pryor*); TorJT 10 (1994) 122s (Alicia *Batten*).
5701 **Malherbe** Abraham J., Paul and the popular philosophers 1989 ➤ 5,5768 ... 7,5134: RBijdragen 55 (1994) 210s (B. J. *Koet*).
5702 *Nejsum* Peter, The apologetic tendency in the interpretation of Paul's sexual ethics: ST 24 (1994) 48-62.
5703 **O'Toole** Robert, Who is a Christian? A study in Pauline ethics 1990 ➤ 6,6158 ... 9,5897: RCritRR 6 (1993) 274-7 (S. *Fowl*, also on SAMPLEY); NewTR 7,3 (1994) 88-90 (Barbara E. *Reid*).
5704 **Sampley** J. Paul, Walking between the times; Paul's moral reasoning 1991 ➤ 7,5238 ... 9,5899: RTorJT 10 (1994) 128 (L. Ann *Jarvis*: complements W. MEEKS).
5705 **Söding** Thomas, Das Liebesgebot bei Paulus; die Mahnung zur Agape im Rahmen der paulinischen Ethik: NTAbh 26. Münster 1994, Aschendorff. x-330 p. DM 90. 3-402-04774-8 [TR 91,274].
5705* *a)* *Winter* Bruce W., Is Paul among the sophists?; – *b)* *Thompson* Mark, Personal assurance and the new perspective on Paul: RefTR 53 (1994) 28-38 / 73-86.

G3.7 *Pauli* **communitates** *et* **spiritualitas.**

5706 **Banks** R., Paul's idea of community[2rev]. [[1]c. 1982]. Peabody MA 1994, Hendrickson. xiii-233 p. 1-56563-050-5 [NTAbs 39, p. 331].
5706* *Charron* André, L'église; de la maison à la ville: ➤ 30, FCOUTURIER G., Maison 1994, 425-459.
5707 *Hainz* Josef, Koinōnía bei Paulus: ➤ 40, FGEORGI D., 1994, 375-392.
5708 **Klauck** H. J., Gemeinde zwischen Haus und Stadt; Kirche bei Paulus 1992 ➤ 9,5908: RSalesianum 56 (1994) 373s (J. J. *Bartolomé*).
5709 **Lanci** John, Building a temple of God; Paul's metaphor of the community as a temple in its Roman-Corinthian context: diss. Harvard, DBrooten B. CM 1992. – RTLv 26, p. 537.
5710 *Loubser* J. A., Wealth, house churches and Rome: JTSAf 89 (1994) 59-... [< zIT 95, p. 219].
5711 **MacDonald** Margaret Y., Las comunidades paulinas; estudio socio-histórico de la institucionalización en los escritos paulinos y deuteropaulinos: BtEstB 78. S 1994, Sígueme. 321 p. pt 1850. 84-301-1221-9. – RProyección 41 (1994) 319s (J. A. *Estrada*); RET 54 (1994) 353s (P. *Barrado Fernández*).
5712 **Pesce** Mauro, Le due fasi della predicazione di Paolo; dall'evangelizzazione alla guida della comunità: StBDeh 22. Bo 1994, Dehoniane. 278 p. Lm 35. 88-10-40721-0 [NTAbs 39, p. 153].
5713 *Sanders* D., A lived Christology in Paul: Month 27 (1994) 475-9 [< NTAbs 39, p. 424].

5715 *Theobald* M., Paulinische Basisgemeinden; ein Modell für die Kirche von heute? RUHöh 37 (1994) 279-288.

G3.8 *Pauli receptio*, **history of research.**

5716 ᴱ**Babcock** W.S., Paul and the legacy of Paul [SMU conference] 1987/90 → 6,510 ... 9,5915: ᴿChH 63 (1994) 81s (J.W. *Trigg*).

5717 **Beker** J. Christiaan, Heirs of Paul 1993 → 7,5102 ... 9,5916: ᴿCurrTM 21 (1994) 222s (E. *Krentz*); Interpretation 48 (1994) 208 (R.A.J. *Gagnon*); TR 90 (1994) 208s (T. *Söding*).

5718 **Bendemann** Reinhard von, Heinrich Schlier; eine kritische Analyse seiner Interpretation paulinischer Theologie: ev. Diss. ᴰ*Schrage* W. Bonn 1994. – TR 91,23.

5719 **Jewett** Robert, Paul the Apostle to America; cultural trends and Pauline scholarship [European (German) wrongly: authoritarian, antisemitic, antifeminist, hierarchical, zealous]. LvL 1994, Knox. xi-178. $17. 0-664-25483-7. – ᴿSewaneeTR 38 (1994s) 294-6 (W. *Hathcock*); TBR 7,2 (1994s) 21 (C. *Elliott*: strained).

5720 *a*) *Kalin* E.R., Where is Pauline scholarship today?; – *b*) *Hamerton-Kelly* R.G., Paul's hermeneutic of the Cross: Dialog 32,4 (1993) 289-296 / 247-254 [< NTAbs 38, p. 214].

5721 **Noormann** R., Irenäus als Paulusinterpret; zur Rezeption und Wirkung der paulinischen und deuteropaulinischen Briefe ...[Diss. Berlin 1993, ᴰ*Wickert* U.]: WUNT 2/60. Tü 1994, Mohr. x-585p. DM 138. 3-16-14692-4 [NTAbs 49, p. 520].

G3.9 *Themata particularia de Paulo,* **details.**

5722 **Arzt** P., Bedrohtes Christsein 1992 → 9,5926: ᴿTLtg 66 (1993) 116s (D. *Kosch*).

5723 *De Lorenzi* Lorenzo, Paolo; la misericordia di Dio e il peccato dell'uomo: ParSpV 29 (1994) 147-190.

5724 **Georgi** Dieter, Remembering the poor; the history of Paul's collection for Jerusalem 1992 → 9,5907: ᴿNewTR 7,1 (1994) 100-2 (N.A. *Beck*); TorJT 10 (1994) 260s (W. *Richards*).

5725 **Gillman** Florence M., Women who knew Paul 1992 → 8,9043: ᴿCrit-RR 6 (1993) 239-241 (Cheryl A. *Brown*).

5726 *Sporschill* Georg, 'Was ich von Paulus gelernt habe': Entschluss 49,7s (1994) 14-17.

5727 **Strack** Wolfram, Kultische Terminologie in ekklesiologischen Kontexten in den Briefen des Paulus [kath. Diss. Bonn 1993, ᴰ*Merklein* H.]: BoBB 92. Weinheim 1994, Beltz. v-441p. DM 128. 3-89547-012-0 [NTAbs 39, p. 338; TR 91,77].

5728 *Trimaille* Michel, La réconciliation selon saint Paul: Spiritus 35, 135 (1994) 227-232.

G4 **Ad Romanos** .1 *Textus, commentarii.*

5729 **Bindemann** Walther, Theologie im Dialog; ein traditionsgeschichtlicher Kommentar zu Römer 1-11, 1992 → 8,6205; 9,5936: ᴿTvT 34 (1994) 81 (P.J. *Farla*).

5730 **Black** Matthew, Romans²ʳᵉᵛ [¹1973] 1989 → 5,5881: ᴿJEvTS 37 (1994) 427 (D.T. *Williams*: all-around bargain).

5731 ᵀᴱBruyn Théodore de, PELAGIUS's commentary on ... Rom ᴰ1993 ➤ 9, 5940: ᴿÉchMClas 38 (1994) 441-3 (L. A. *Harrill*).
5732 **Buzzi** Franco, M. LUTERO, La lettera ai Romani 1991 ➤ 7,5250 ... 9,5937: ᴿAsprenas 41 (1994) 277-282 (A. *Pitta*); RivB 42 (1994) 468-472 (B. *Corsani*).
5733 **Díaz García** Gonzalo, Luis de LEÓN, In epistolam ad Romanos expositio: Opera 10. S. Lorenzo Escorial 1993, Escurialense. 329 p. – ᴿCiuD 207 (1994) 208s (J. *Gutiérrez*); RAg 35 (1994) 308 (R. *Lazcano*).
5734 **Díaz Sanchez-Cid** J. B., Justicia, pecado y filiación; sobre el comentario de Origene a los Romanos 1991 ➤ 7,5252 ... 9,5943: ᴿBurgense 34 (1993) 574-6 (M. *Guerra Gómez*); Compostellanum 38 (1993) 266-8 (E. *Romero Pose*); RET 54 (1994) 356-8 (J. J. *Ayán*).
5735 **Edwards** James P., Romans: NInternatComm 1992 ➤ 7,5254 ... 9,5944: ᴿAndrUnSem 32 (1994) 130s (S. *Kubo*); CritRR 6 (1993) 232s (D. J. *Moo*); EvQ 66 (1994) 91-93 (Mateen *Elass*); RB 101 (1994) 143 (J. *Murphy-O'Connor*); SvEx 59 (1994) 167-9 (O. *Christoffersson*).
5736 **Fitzmyer** Joseph A., Romans: AnchorB 33, 1993 ➤ 9,5945 [Biblica 76,439, J. *Lambrecht*; Gregorianum 76.743-757, M. *Lubomirski*]. – ᴿLavalTP 50 (1994) 668s (Odette *Mainville*); PrincSemB 15 (1994) 299-301 (C. B. *Cousar*); RB 101 (1994) 630s (J. *Murphy-O'Connor*); TLond 97 (1994) 304-6 (J. D. G. *Dunn*: beyond praise, though more oriented to traditional questions than to contemporary discussions).
5737 **Heither** Theresia, ORIGENES, Commentarii in Epistulam ad Romanos [1-4 ➤ 8,6217; 5s ➤ 9,5947]: 7s: FonC 2/4. FrB 1994, Herder. 344 p. DM 48. 3-451-22109-8 [TR 91,395, L. *Lies*; TLZ 120,452, G. *Haendler*]. – ᴿGnomon 66 (1994) 453s (Caroline P. *Hammond-Bammel*, 1); TPQ 142 (1994) 430s (M. *Kertsch*, 2).
5737* ᵀᴱMara Maria Grazia, AGOSTINO interprete di Paolo; commento di alcune questioni della Lettera ai Romani: Lett. 1 Mill. 16. Mi 1993, Paoline. 256 p. ➤ 9,5949; Lᵐ 30. 88-315-0867-9 [Gregorianum 76,190, G. *Pelland*].
5738 ᵀᴱPani Giancarlo, M. LUTERO, Lezioni sulla Lettera ai Romani (1515s) I (1-7) 1991 ➤ 7,5263; 8,6255: ᴿSalesianum 56 (1994) 141s (G. *Semeraro*: anche su BUZZI F., solo scholia; ambedue cattolici).
5739 **Reller** Jobst, Mose BAR KEPHA und seine Paulinenauslegung; nebst Edition und Übersetzung des Kommentars zum Römerbrief: GöOrF 1. Wsb 1994, Harrassowitz. x-377 p. 3-447-03584-6.
5740 **Schmidt-Lauber** Gabriele, LUTHERs Vorlesung über den Römerbrief 1515/16; ein Vergleich zwischen Luthers Manuskript und den studentischen Nachschriften: Werbe Archiv 6. Köln 1994, Böhlau. vii-164 p. DM 88. 3-412-11193-7 [TLZ 120,674, C. *Burger*].
5741 **Sider** Robert O., D. ERASMUS, Annotations on Romans: Works 56. Toronto 1994, Univ. xxiii-480 p. 0-8020-2803-9.
5742 **Stancari** Pino, Commentario alla Lettera ai Romani 1991 ➤ 8,6233; 9,5952: ᴿCC 145 (1994,4) 208s (D. *Scaiola*).
5742* **Stott** John R. W., The message of Romans; God's good news for the world; The Bible speaks today. Leicester/DG 1994, InterVarsity. 432 p. $20. 0-8308-1692-5 / 0-85111-143-2 [NTAbs 39, p. 522]. – ᴿSTEv 7 (1994) 194 (G. *Saina*).
5743 **Stuhlmacher** Peter, Paul's letter to the Romans; a commentary [NTD 1989], ᵀ*Hafemann* Scott J. LVL 1994, W-Knox. xxiii-269 p. [NTAbs 39, p. 155]. 0-664-25287-7.
5744 **Theobald** Michael, Röm 1-11 / 12-16: KlKomm 6, 1993 ➤ 8,6235;

9,5953s: ᴿEntschluss 49,12 (1994) 47s (H. *Brandt*); SNTU 19 (1994) 231-3 (A. *Fuchs*); TLZ 119 (1994) 1082s (W. *Vogler*).
5745 **Wilckens** Ulrich, La carta a los Romanos I (1-5) / II (6-16) 1989/92 ➤ 6,6195 ... 9,5956: ᴿCiuD 207 (1994) 262s (J. *Gutiérrez*); RET 54 (1994) 90s (P. *Barrados Fernández*).

G4.2 Ad Romanos: themata, topics.

5746 **Aletti** Jean-Noël, Comment Dieu est-il juste? Clefs pour interpréter l'épître aux Romains 1991 ➤ 7,5271 ... 9,5957: ᴿBijdragen 55 (1994) 211s (J. *Lambrecht*: indispensable); RB 101 (1994) 143s (J. *Murphy-O'Connor*).
5747 *Betz* Hans-Dieter, Christianity as religion; Paul's attempt at definition in Romans: ➤ 344, Notion of 'Religion' 1990/4, 3-9.
5748 **Boers** Hendrikus, The justification of the Gentiles. Paul's letters to the Galatians and Romans. Peabody 1994, Hendrickson. xvii-334 p. $25. 1-56563-011-4 [RelStR 21,220].
5749 **Garlington** D., Faith, obedience and perseverance; aspects of Paul's letter to the Romans: WUNT 79. Tü 1994, Mohr. xi-201 p. DM 128. 3-16-146469-6 [NTAbs 39,517].
5750 **Kertelge** Karl, Biblische Theologie im Römerbrief: ➤ 303a, New approaches 1992/4, 47-57.
5751 *Norelli* E., MARCIONE lettore dell'Epistola ai Romani: CrNSt 15 (1994) 635-675.

G4.3 Naturalis cognitio Dei... peccatum originale, Rom 1-5.

5753 *Sparn* Walter, Natürliche Theologie: ➤ 517, TRE 24 (1994) 85-98.
5754 **Wisnefske** Ned, Our natural knowledge of God; a prospect for natural theology after KANT and BARTH 1990 ➤ 8,m783: ᴿCritRR 5 (1992) 495s (S. H. *Webb*: ecology-oriented).
5755 **Garlington** Don B., [Rom 1,5] 'The obedience of faith' *a*) 1991 ➤ 7, 2304 ... 9,5981: ᴿTorJT 10 (1994) 121s (L. A. *Jervis*); – *b*) WestTJ 55 (1993) 97-112, 281-297.
5756 *Mara* Maria Grazia, [Rom 1,7] L'interpretazione AGOSTINIANA del peccato contro lo Spirito Santo nella Epistolae ad Romanos inchoata expositio: ➤ 86, ᶠNALDINI M., Paideia 1994, 235-246.
5757 *Forde* G. O., The normative character of Scripture for matters of faith and life; human sexuality in light of Romans 1:16-32: WWorld 14 (1994) 305-314 [315-325, *Hultgren* A. J.; < NTAbs 39, p. 56s].
5758 *a*) *Mason* Steve, 'For I am not ashamed of the Gospel' (Rom 1,16); the Gospel and the first readers of Romans; – *b*) *Snodgrass* Klyne, The Gospel in Romans; a theology of revelation; – *c*) *Campbell* Douglas A., Determining the Gospel through rhetorical analysis in Paul's letter to the Roman Christians; – *d*) *Weima* Jeffrey A. D., Preaching the Gospel in Rome; a study of the epistolary framework of Romans; – *e*) *Dunn* James D. G., How new was Paul's Gospel? the problems of continuity and discontinuity: ➤ 76a, ᶠLONGENECKER R., Gospel in Paul 1994, 254-287 / 288-314 / 315-336 / 337-366 / 367-388.
5759 *Campbell* Douglas A., Romans 1:17 – a crux interpretum for the *pistis Christou* debate: JBL 113 (1994) 265-285.
5760 *Bavinck* J. H. [† 1963; < Themelios 2,2 (1964)], Human religion in God's eyes; a study of Romans 1:18-32: ScotBuEvT 12 (1994) 44-52 [< NTAbs 39, p. 57].

5761 **Ndyabahika** Odomaro, Paul's evangelization approach to Gentile religions; an exegetical-theological examination based on the evidence of Rom 1:18-32: kath. Diss. ᴰ*Klauck*. Würzburg 1992s. – TR 90,90.

5762 *Porter* Calvin L., Romans 1.18-22; its role in the developing argument: NTS 40 (1994) 210-228.

5763 *Cook* John G., The logic and language of Romans 1,20: Biblica 75 (1994) 494-517; franç. 517.

5764 *Martens* John W., Romans 2.14-16; a Stoic reading: NTS 40 (1994) 55-67.

5765 *Atallah* Ramez, The objective witness to conscience; an Egyptian parallel to Romans 2:15 [did Paul know of the Osiris myth? overlooked since its publication in Themelios 10,3 (1974)]: EvRT 18 (1994) 204-213 [< NTAbs 39, p. 58].

5766 *Derrett* J. D. M., 'You abominate false gods; but do you rob shrines?' (Rom 2.22*b*): NTS 40 (1994) 558-571.

5767 *Moyise* Steve, The Catena of Romans 3:10-18: ExpTim 106 (1994s) 367-370.

5768 *Klimkeit* Paul-Gerhard, Der eine Gott des Paulus; Röm 3,21-31 als Brennpunkt paulinischer Theo-logie: ZNW 85 (1994) 192-206.

5769 **Campbell** Douglas A., The rhetoric of righteousness in Romans 3,21-26: jNsu 65, 1992 ➤ 8,6280; 9,5984: ᴿFgNt 7 (1994) 323 (J. *Peláez*); HeythJ 35 (1994) 68s (G. *Turner*); TBR 7,2 (1994s) 21 (R. *Morgan*: convincing); TorJT 10 (1994) 116-8 (G. *Le Marquand*); WestTJ 56 (1994) 434-7 (P. L. *Tite*).

5770 **Kraus** Wolfgang, [Röm 3,25s] Der Tod Jesu als Heiligtumsweihe: WM 66, 1991 ➤ 7,5306... 9,5985: ᴿBiblica 75 (1994) 428-431 (R. *Penna*); JTS 45 (1994) 247-252 (D. P. *Bailey*).

5771 *a*) *Schenk* Wolfgang, 'Sühnemittel' oder 'Gnadenort'? Zur ursprünglichen Codierung von *hilastērion* Röm 3,25; – *b*) *Pesch* Rudolf, 'Erbe der Welt' (Röm 4,14); zur Weitung der Landverheissung im NT: ➤ 31*, ꟳDAUTZENBERG G., Nach 1994, 553-567 / 501-520.

5772 *Plag* Christoph, [Röm 4,1-12] Paulus und die Gezera schwara; zur Übernahme rabbinischer Auslegungskunst [JEREMIAS J., ꟳZWAAN J. de 1953; Abba 1966, 271]: Judaica 50 (1994) 135-140.

5773 *Bailey* Kenneth E., St. Paul's understanding of the territorial promise of God to Abraham; Romans 4:13 in its historical and theological context: NesTR 15 (1994) 59-69.

5774 *a*) *O'Neill* John, Adam, who is the figure of him that was to come; a reading of Romans 5:12-21; – *b*) *Dunn* James D. G., Why 'incarnation'? A review of recent NT scholarship: ➤ 45, ꟳGOULDER M., Crossing 1994, 183-199 / 235-256.

5775 *Giavini* Giovanni, Il peccato nella luce della Redenzione; Rm 5,12-21: Ambrosius 70 (1994) 411-425.

5776 *Grelot* Pierre, Pour une lecture de Romains 5,12-21 [CatéchismeÉC 1992, 87-93]: NRT 116 (1994) 495-512.

5777 *García Cordero* Maximiliano, La doctrina paulina sobre el 'Pecado original' en el entorno de la teología judía intertestamental: CiTom 121 (1994) 235-278.

5778 **Kaiser** Otto, [Röm 5:12-21] Die Ersten und die Letzten Dinge: NSys 36 (1994) 75-91; Eng. 91: Paul and Sap. Sol. between the primal (Gn) myth and the Apocalypse myth.

5779 **Sule** Emmanuel, AUGUSTINE's doctrine of original sin as based on Romans 5:12-21: diss. ᴰ*Smith* D. – Providence (Canada) College, 1994. 130 p. MM 89-171. – (DissA-disk) MAI 33 (1994s) p. 61 (no abstract).

5780 **Lyonnet** Stanislas, Molto più [Rm 5,15s]. Civitella S. Paolo 1993, S. Scolastica. 298 p. – RCC 145 (1994,4) 209s (C. *Capizzi*).

G4.4 *Redemptio cosmica:* Rom 6-8.

5781 *Mitsunobu* I., ⊙ Union with Christ in death and resurrection; St. Paul's theology as seen in Romans 6: KatKenk 63 (1994) 131-168 [< NTAbs 39, p. 58].

5782 *Cranfield* C. E. B., [His ICC] Romans 6:1-14 revisited: ExpTim 106 (1994s) 40-43.

5782* *Korteweg* T., De betekenis van *ephápax* in Rom. VI 10; kent Paulus de vorstelling van een heilsgeschiedenis?: KerkT 45 (1994) 21-27.

5783 **Baaij** P. K., Paulus over Paulus; exegetische studie van Romeinen 7; prot. diss. Bru ᴰ*Nielsen* J. Kampen 1993, Kok. vii-520 p. 90-242-6964-4. – TvT 34 (1994) 71.

5784 *Russell* Walt, [Rom 7] Insights from postmodernism's emphasis on interpretive communities in the interpretation of Romans 7 [postmodernism as 'diverse reaction to modernism' is 'defined' with D. HARVEY (really LYOTARD) as 'incredulity toward meta-narratives, broad interpretative schemas like those employed by MARX or FREUD']: JEvTS 37 (1994) 511-527.

5785 *Earnshaw* John D., Reconsidering Paul's marriage analogy in Romans 7.3-4: RNTS 40 (1994) 68-88.

5786 **Lambrecht** Jan, The wretched 'I' Rom 7,7-35: 1992 → 8,6292; 9,5997 [JTS 45,674-6, J. D. G. *Dunn*]: RRHPR 74 (1994) 216 (C. *Grappe*); RivB 42 (1994) 237s (S. P. *Carbone*).

Díaz-Rodelas J. M., Rom 7,7-8,4, ᴰ1994 → 5803.

5787 *Krarup* K., [Rom 7,7-13] Det apologetiske sigte [aim] i Paulus' apologi for loven [the Law]: DanTTs 57 (1994) 199-216 [< NTAbs 39, p. 243].

5788 *De Virgilio* Giuseppe, Spirito e libertà nel cristiano secondo Paolo (Rom 8; Gal 5): BbbOr 36 (1994) 87-100.

5789 **Ninan** Idicheria, Jesus as the Son of God; an examination of the background and meaning of 'Son of God' in Paul's Christology with particular reference to Romans 8: diss. Coventry 1994. DissA-C 56 (1995s) p. 326.

5790 *Cranfield* C. E. B., [Rom 8,2] Paul's teaching on sanctification: → 26, ꟻCOOK J., RefR 48,3 (1994s) 217-229.

5791 **Dąbek** Tomasz M., ⊙ The law of the spirit; the Spirit of the life of Christ Jesus has freed you from the law of sin and death (Rom 8,2): → 92*, ꟻPIERONEK T., AnCracov 26 (1994) 173-189; Eng. 190s.

5792 a) *Mara* Maria Grazia, Interpretazione agostiniana di Romani 8,3; – b) *Studer* Basil, Paolo, maestro di speranza cristiana, in AGOSTINO; – c) *Ghiberti* Giuseppe, La 'radice santa' della lettera ai Romani; – d) *Pani* Giancarlo, Conversione di Paolo o vocazione? La documentazione della lettera [ai Galati e (non in Indice p. 193)] ai Romani: → 328a, 155-163 / 165-172 / 117-126 / 73-88.

5793 *Keesmaat* Sylvia C., Exodus and the intertextual transformation of tradition in Romans 8,14-30: JStNT 54 (1994) 20-56.

5794 *Beker* J. Christiaan, Vision of hope for a suffering world; Romans 8:17-30: → 326, PrincSemB supp 3 (1994) 26-32.

5795 **Christoffersson** Olle, The earnest expectation of the creature... Rom 8:18-27, 1990 → 6,6347 ... 8,6303: RTR 90 (1994) 36-39 (N. *Walter*).

5796 *Lawson* J. Mark,   Romans 8:18-25 – the hope of creation: RExp 91 (1994) 559-565.
5797 *Rossi* Benedetto,   La redenzione cosmica in Romani 8,18-25; la *ktisis* in San Paolo tra protologia e storia [< diss.]. Siena 1994. 292 p.
5798 **Giglioli** A. [Rom 8,19-22] L'uomo o il creato; *ktisis* in S. Paolo: StBDeh 21. Bo 1994, Dehoniane. 139 p. Lᵐ 15. 88-10-40724-5 [NTAbs 39, p. 151]. – ᴿLA 44 (1994) 699-705 (A. M. *Buscemi*).
5799 *Tsumura* D. T.,   An OT background to Rom 8,22:   NTS 40 (1994) 620s.
5800 *Laporte* Jean-Pierre,   [Rom 8,31 trouvé 1951 inscrit à 'Iomnium', algérien] Tigzirt; saint Paul contre l'inuidus: → 73, Mém. LE GLAY M. L'Afrique... religion romaine 1994, 285-7; pl. XIV.

G4.6   *Israel et Lex;*   **The Law and the Jews,** *Rom 9-11.*

5801 **Bell** Richard H.,   Provoked to jealousy; the origin and purpose of the jealousy motif in Rom 9-11 [Diss. Tübingen → 9,6008]: WUNT 2/63. Tü 1994, Mohr. xxii-471 p. DM 118. 3-16-146091-X [JTS 46,277, B. *Byrne*; TLZ 120, 434, C. *Landmesser*; BL 95,142, C.J.A. *Hickling*: OT usefulness]. – ᴿExpTim 106 (1994s) 121 (E. *Best*); TBR 7,2 (1994) 21 (D. *Horrell*).
5802 **Campbell** William S.,   Paul's Gospel in an intercultural context; Jew and Gentile in the Letter to the Romans [10 art. 1973-90]: StIntrcult 69, 1991 → 7,5109,5329... 9,6010: ᴿÉglT 25 (1994) 138s (N. *Bonneau*).
5803 **Díaz Rodelas** Juan Miguel,   Pablo y la ley; la novedad de Rom 7,7-9,4 en el conjunto de la reflexión paulina sobre la Ley [Diss. Pont. Ist. Biblico, ᴰ*Vanhoye* A.]: Jerón 28. Estella 1994, VDivino. 282 p. 84-7151-983-6 [Biblica 76,141].
5805 **Harrington** D.J.,   Paul on the mystery of Israel 1992 → 8,6315; 9,6014: ᴿFurrow 45 (1994) 197-9 (P. *Briscoe*); NewTR 7,1 (1994) 103-6 (D.M. *Bossman*); RivB 42 (1994) 238-241 (A. *Pitta*).
5806 *Kilgallen* J.J.,   Jesus and the Law in St. Paul's letters: MelT 45,1 (1994) 19-28 [< 39, p. 54].
5807 *Kreitzer* L.,   Romans 9-11; Albert SCHWEITZER's 1929 New Testament and the call to Christian mission: TEdr 50 (New Orleans 1994) 5-14 [< NTAbs 39, p. 59].
5808 **Nikopoulos** Vasilios,   Ⓖ *Ephetē*; St. Paul's view of law. Thessaloniki 1992, Didactic. 432 p. – ᴿTAth 65 (1994) 399-401 (E.A. *Theodorou* Ⓖ).
5809 *Penna* Romano,   Ⓖ *Nómos kaì eleuthería*... Law and freedom in the view of St. Paul: DeltVM 13 (for 12) (1993) 18-42 [< NTAbs 39,241].
5810 **Sänger** Dieter,   Die Verkündigung des Gekreuzigten und Israel; Studien zum Verhältnis von Kirche und Israel bei Paulus und im frühen Christentum [< Hab.-Diss. Kiel]: WUNT 75. Tü 1994, Mohr. xi-395 p. DM 228. 3-16-146220-3 [TLZ 120,523-7, U. *Wilckens*].
5811 **Schreiner** Thomas R.,   The Law and its fulfillment; a Pauline theology of law 1993 → 9,6023: ᴿSvTKv 70 (1994) 192-4 (D. *Mitternacht*); TrinJ 15 (1994) 272-5 (E.C. *Hock*).
5812 **Stowers** Stanley K.,   A rereading of Romans; justice, Jews and Gentiles. NHv 1994, Yale Univ. 383 p. £24. 0-300-05357-6. – ᴿExpTim 106 (1994s) 248 (R. *Morgan*: sustained attack on traditional readings, likely to be the most important Romans monograph of a decade); TBR 7,3 (1994s) 23 (D. *Horrell*).
5813 **Thielman** Frank S.,   Paul and the Law; a contextual approach. DG 1994, InterVarsity. 336 p. $20 pa. 0-8308-1854-5 [NTAbs 39, p. 339].

5814 *Thielman* Frank, Unexpected mercy; echoes of a biblical motif in Romans 9-11: ScotJT 47 (1994) 169-181.

5815 **Tomson** Peter J., Paul and the Jewish Law: CompNT 3/1, 1990 ➔ 7,5357; 9,6028: RBijdragen 55 (1994) 441s (J. van *Ruiten*); WestJT 55 (1993) 161-3 (M. *Silva*).

5816 **Westerholm** Stephen, Israel's Law and the Church's faith 1988 ➔ 4,3981 ... 9,6030: RJEvTS 37 (1994) 432-5 (D. E. *Johnson*).

5817 **Winger** Michael, By what law? The meaning of nómos in the letters of Paul: SBL diss. 128, 1992 ➔ 9,6032: RAndrUnSem 32 (1994) 157s (R. *Badenas*); CBQ 56 (1994) 163s (Patricia M. *McDonald*).

5818 **Wright** N. T., Climax of covenant 1992 ➔ 9,5862: RÉTRel 69 (1994) 107-9 (E. *Cuvillier*, aussi sur TOMSON P.); EvQ 66 (1994) 176-8 (B. S. *Rosner*); IrTQ 60 (1994) 225s (M. *Hogan*); ScotJT 47 (1994) 117-9 (H. *Räisänen*); SR 23 (1994) 232s (P. *Richardson*); TorJT 10 (1994) 131s (T. J. *Donaldson*); WestTJ 56 (1994) 197-201 (T. D. *Gordon*).

5818* **Lloyd-Jones** David M., Romans; an exposition of ch. 9, God's sovereign purpose. GR 1992, Zondervan (Regents Ref.). 336 p. $23. 0-310-27500-8 [STEv 7,75, P. *Colombo*].

5819 *a*) *Crüsemann* Frank, 'Ihnen gehören ... die Bundesschlüsse' (Röm 9,4); die alttestamentliche Bundestheologie und der christlich-jüdische Dialog; – *b*) Antwort, *Zenger* Erich, Juden und Christen doch nicht im gemeinsamen Gottesbund?; – *c*) *Stegemann* Ekkehard W., Zwischen Juden und Heiden, aber 'mehr' als Juden und Heiden? Neutestamentliche Anmerkungen zur Identitätsproblematik des frühen Christentums; – *d*) *Rendtorff* Rolf, Ein gemeinsamer 'Bund' für Juden und Christen? Auf der Suche nach einer neuen Bestimmung der christlichen Identität: KIsr 9 (1994) 21-38 / 39-52 / 53-69 / 3-8 (126-138).

5820 *Reinbold* Wolfgang, Paulus und das Gesetz; zur Exegese von Röm 9,30-33: BZ 38 (1994) 253-264.

5821 *a*) *Dewey* Arthur J., A re-hearing of Romans 10:1-5; – *b*) *Ward* Richard F., Pauline voice and presence as strategic communication; – *c*) *Dewey* Joanna, Textuality in an oral culture; a survey of the Pauline traditions: Semeia 65 (1994) 109-127 [129-135 response, *Wire* Antoinette C.] / 95-107 / 37-65.

5822 **Schreiner** Thomas R., Paul's view of the law in Romans 10:4-5 WestTJ 55 (1993) 113-135.

5823 *Bechtler* Steven R., Christ, the *télos* of the Law; the goal of Romans 10:4: CBQ 56 (1994) 288-308.

5824 *Gignac* Alain, Le Christ, *télos* de la loi (Rm 10,4); une lecture en termes de continuité et de discontinuité, dans le cadre du paradigme paulinien de l'élection: ScEspr 46 (1994) 55-81.

5825 **Kauk** Myron C., Paul's use of the OT in Romans 10:6-8: diss. Westminster Theol. Sem., D*Silva* M. 1994. 208 p. 94-28898. – DissA 55 (1994s) p. 1590.

5826 *Reichrath* Hans, [Röm 11,26] 'Der Retter wird aus Zion kommen': Judaica 49 (1993) 146-155.

G4.8 **Rom 12 ...**

5827 **Dawn** Marva, The hilarity of community, Rom 12, 1992 ➔ 8,6341: RTBR 7,2 (1994s) 22 (S. *Cherry*).

5828 *Peterson* David, Worship and ethics in Romans 12: TyndB 44 (1993) 271-288.
5829 *Hiebert* D. Edmond, [Rom 12,1s] Presentation and transformation; an exposition of Romans 12:1-2: BtS 151 (1994) 309-324.
5830 **Wilson** Walter T., Love without pretense, Rom 12,9-21, ᴰ1991 ➤ 7,5374 ... 9,6041 [RB 102,304, J. *Murphy-O'Connor*].
5831 **Botha** Jan, Subject to whose authority? Multiple readings [linguistic, literary, rhetoric, social science] of Romans 13: Emory Studies in Early Christianity 4. Atlanta 1994, Scholars. xiv-261 p. $40. 1-55540-922-9 [NTAbs 39, p. 332].
5832 *Légasse* S., Paul et César: Romains 13,1-7; essai de synthèse: RB 101 (1994) 516-532; Eng. 516.
5833 *Neufeld* M. G., Submission to governing authorities; a study of Romans 13:1-7: Direction 23,2 (Fresno 1994) 90-97 [< NTAbs 39, p. 245].
5834 *a*) *Botha* J., [Rom 13,1-7] Social values in the rhetoric of Pauline paraenetic literature; – *b*) *Vorster* J. N., The context of the letter to the Romans; a critique on the present state of research: Neotestamentica 28 (1994) 109-126 / 127-145.
5835 *Grieb* A. Katherine, The root of Jesse who rises to rule the Gentiles; Paul's use of the story of Jesus in Romans 15:7-13: ProcGM 13 (1993) 71-88.
5836 **Kraus** Wolfgang, 'Freut euch ihr Heiden mit seinem Volk!' (Röm 15,10); Untersuchungen zur Gottesvolkthematik bei Paulus: Hab.-Diss. ᴰ*Roloff* J. Erlangen-N 1994. – RTLv 26, p. 537; TR 91,89.
5837 *Dewey* Arthur J., [Rom 15,24-28] *Eis tēn Spanian*; the future and Paul: ➤ 40, ᶠGEORGI D. 1994, 321-349.
5838 *Peterman* G. W., Romans 15,26: make a contribution or establish fellowship?: NTS 40 (1994) 457-463.
5839 *Cotter* Wendy, [Rom 16,1s Phoebe, *al.*] Women's authority roles in Paul's churches; countercultural or conventional?: NT 36 (1994) 350-372.
5840 *Cervin* Richard S., A note regarding the name 'Junia(s)' in Romans 16.7: NTS 40 (1994) 464-470.
5841 *a*) *Macky* Peter W., Crushing Satan underfoot (Romans 16:20); Paul's last battle story as true myth; – *b*) *Dewey* Arthur J., The devil you say — the embodiment of symbol, rhetoric, and ethics in the Pauline letters: ProcGM 13 (1993) 121-133 / 135-149.
5842 *Borse* U., Das Schlusswort des Römerbriefes; Segensgruss (16,24) statt Doxologie (vv. 25-27): SNTU 19 (1994) 173-192 [< NTAbs 39, p. 245].

G5.1   **Epistulae ad Corinthios** I, *textus, commentarii.*

5843 **Beardslee** W. A., First Corinthians; a commentary for today. St. Louis 1994, Chalice. viii-168 p. $15 pa. 0-8272-1018-3 [NTAbs 39, p. 331].
5844 **Blomberg** C., 1 Corinthians: NIV Applications comm. GR 1994, Zondervan. 352 p. $22. 0-310-48490-1 [NTAbs 39, p. 516].
5845 **Fee** Gordon D., Primera epistola a los Corintios [(versión Reina-Valera² 1960) 1987], ᵀ(*Alonso*) *Vargas* Carlos. Buenos Aires 1994, Nueva Creación. xxvi-989 p. 0-8028-0924-3.
5846 **Merklein** Helmut, Der erste Brief an die Korinther 1-4 1992 ➤ 8,6357: ᴿBZ 37 (1993) 286-9 (G. *Dautzenberg*); RB 101 (1994) 144s (J. *Murphy-O'Connor*).
5847 **Schrage** W., 1 Kor 1991 ➤ 7,5386 ... 9,6048: ᴿBiKi 48 (1993) 163-6 (R. *Hoppe*, auch über MERKLEIN H. 1992); Entschluss 49,3 (1994) 39 (C. *Cebulj*).

5848 **Watson** Nigel M., 1 Cor: Epworth 1992 → 9,6362: ᴿPacifica 7 (1994) 249s (P. *Trebilco*).

G5.2 *1 & 1-2 ad Corinthios – themata,* topics.

5849 **Balthasar** H. U. von, Paul struggles with his congregation; the pastoral message of the letters to the Corinthians [1988], ᵀ*Bojarska* B. L. SF 1992, Ignatius. 90 p. $7. 0-89870-386-7 [NTAbs 39, p. 156].

5850 *Chapa* Juan, Is First Corinthians a letter of consolation?: NTS 40 (1994) 150-160.

5851 **Chow Kin-mau** John, Patronage and power; a study in social networks in Corinth [diss. Durham]: jNsu 75. Shf 1992, JStOT. 230 p. £32.50. 1-857075-370-9. – ᴿJTS 45 (1994) 252-4 (P. *Gardner*); RExp 91 (1994) 616 (D. E. *Garland*); SvTKv 70 (1994) 154s (A. *Eriksson*); TBR 7,2 (1994s) 22 (R. *Morgan*).

5852 *de Boer* Martinus C., The composition of 1 Corinthians: NTS 40 (1994) 229-245.

5853 *Gill* David W. J., In search of the social elite in the Corinthian church: TyndB 44 (1993) 323-337.

5854 *Giumlia-Mair* Alessandra R., *Craddock* Paul T., Corinthium aes: Ant-WeltSond. 24 (1993) 62 p.; ill.

5855 **Haykin** M. A. G., The Spirit of God; the exegesis of 1 and 2 Corinthians in the pneumatomachian controversy of the fourth century: VigChr supp. 27. Leiden 1994, Brill. xxiv-253 p. ƒ160. 90-04-09947-6 [NTAbs 39, p. 518].

5856 ᴱ**Hays** David M., Pauline theology; 1 & 2 Corinthians: SBL group. Mp 1993, Fortress. xii-300 p. $31. 0-8006-2489-0. – ᴿExpTim 106 (1994s) 25 (J. *Barclay*: KRAFTCHICK and ENGBERG-PEDERSEN most significant but demanding).

5857 *Hays* Richard B., Ecclesisology and ethics in 1 Corinthians: → 398, Church, ExAud 10 (1994) 31-43.

5858 *Hester* J., [1 Cor] Re-discovering and re-inventing rhetoric: Scriptura 50 (1994) 1-22 [< NTAbs 39, p. 427].

5859 *Kreitzer* Larry, Baptism in the Pauline epistles, with special reference to the Corinthian letters: BapQ 34 (1991s) 67-78.

5860 **Mitchell** Margaret, Paul and the rhetoric of reconciliation... 1 Cor ᴰ1991 → 7,5399 ... 9,6055: ᴿHeythJ 35 (1994) 69s (G. *Turner*); JRel 74 (1994) 558-560 (V. L. *Wimbush*); NT 36 (1994) 292-4 (J. *McGuckin*); RB 101 (1994) 425-7 (J. *Murphy-O'Connor*); RestQ 36 (1994) 187-9 (W. *Willis*); TorJT 10 (1994) 123-5 (W. *Braun*).

5861 **Murphy-O'Connor** Jerome, St. Paul's Corinth² [¹1983]. ColMn 1990, Liturgical. – ᴿRB 101 (1994) 302s (J. *Taylor*).

Probst Hermann, Paulus und der Brief; die Rhetorik des antiken Briefes als Form der paulinischen Korintherkorrespondenz; WUNT 2/45, 1991 → 5891.

5863 **Quast** Kevin, Reading the Corinthian correspondence; an introduction. NY 1994, Paulist. ix-225 p. $15. 0-8091-3481-0 [NTAbs 39, p. 154].

5864 **Ramsaran** Rollin A., The form and function of maxims in Paul's argumentation; a study of 1 Corinthians 1-10: diss. Boston Univ., ᴰ*Sampley* J. P. 1994. 283 p. 94-21882. – DissA 55 (1994s) p. 2436; (Feb.) replaced in April with a corrected text.

5865 **Robertson** Joseph M., The basis for Paul's claim to authority in 1 and 2 Corinthians; a reappraisal: diss. Golden Gate Baptist theol. sem., ᴰ*Harrop* C. 1994. 234 p. 94-31757. – DissA 55 (1994s) p. 2004.

5866 *Söding* Thomas, Das Geheimnis Gottes im Kreuz Jesu [1 Kor]; die paulinische Christologie im Spannungsfeld von Mythos und Kerygma: BZ 38 (1994) 174-194.
5867 *Vielhauer* P., Paul and the Cephas party in Corinth [< NTS],^T; JHiCr 1 (1994) 129-142 [< NTAbs 39, p. 246].
5868 **Wire** Antoinette C., The Corinthian women prophets 1990 ⇥ 6,6329 ... 9,6961: ^RPacifica 7 (1994) 97-99 (Dorothy A. *Lee*); RB 101 (1994) 151s (J. *Murphy-O'Connor*).

G5.3   **1 Cor 1-7:** *sapientia crucis ... abusus matrimonii.*

5869 **Stamps** Dennis Lee, A literary-rhetorical reading of the opening and closing of 1 Corinthians: diss. ^D*Dunn* J. Durham UK 1994. 499 p. – RTLv 26, p. 539.
5870 **Clarke** A., [1 Cor 1-6] Secular and Christian leadership in Corinth ^D1993 ⇥ 9,6062: ^RBInterp 2 (1994) 238-240 (J. M. G. *Barclay*); BZ 38 (1994) 296-8 (T. *Schmeller*); ÉTRel 69 (1994) 425s (Andrianjatovo *Rakotoharintsifa*); JTS 45 (1994) 676-9 (D. W. J. *Gill*); TorJT 10 (1994) 253s (J. S. *Kloppenborg*); Worship 65 (1994) 463s (Pheme *Perkins*).
5871 **Litfin** Duane, St. Paul's theology of proclamation; 1 Cor 1-4 and Greco-Roman rhetoric [diss. Oxford ^E*Harvey* A.]: SNTS mg 79. C 1994, Univ. xiii-302 p. $60. 0-521-45178-7 [NTAbs 39, p. 336]. – ^RExpTim 106 (1994s) 25 (H. *Guite*: locating Favorinus, but widely informative); TvT 34 (1994) 444 (J. *Smit*).
5872 *Rufiński* Grzegorz, ⊕ Problem struktury 1 Kor 1-4: RuBi 47 (1994) 73-81.
5873 *Antón* Ángel, [1 Cor 1,16; Jn 20,21; Lc 4,18s ...] La tarea 'evangelizadora' de los obispos en sus diócesis y en las respectivas conferencias episcopales: Gregorianum 75 (1994) 641-672; franç. 672s.
5874 *Dugandžić* Ivan, [1 Cor 1,17] Realitas et annuntiatio crucis in theologia vitaque Pauli apostoli: ⇥ 36, Mem. FUĆAK M., 64 (1994) 19-28 (croat.).
5875 *Hombert* Pierre-Marie, Gloriae gratiae; 1 Co 1,31 et 1 Co 4,7, aux sources de la théologie augustinienne de la grâce: diss. Institut Catholique, ^D*Wolinski* J. Paris 1993. 545 p. – RICathP 49,91: RTLv 26, p. 541.
5876 **Müller** Christoph, 'Ihr seid Gottes Pflanzung – Gottes Bau – Gottes Tempel'; die metaphorische Dimension paulinischer Gemeindetheologie in 1 Kor 3,5-17: kath. Diss. ^D*Zmijewski*. Fulda 1994. – TR 91,95.
5877 *Hollander* Harm W., The testing by fire of the builders' works; 1 Cor 3.10-15: NTS 40 (1994) 89-104.
5878 *Malan* F. E., Rhetorical analysis of 1 Corinthians 4: TViat 20 (Sovengo 1993) 100-114 [< NTAbs 38, p. 390].
5879 *Hall* David R., A disguise for the wise; *metaschēmatismós* in 1 Cor 4.6: NTS 40 (1994) 143-9.
5880 **Schiefer Ferrari** Markus, [1 Kor 4,9-12; 2 Kor 11,23-29 (Bultmann-Diss. 1910)] Sprache des Leids in Peristasenkatalogen: SBB 23, 1991 ⇥ 9,6077: ^RTLZ 119 (1994) 324-6 (A. *Lindemann*).
5881 **Rosner** Brian S., Paul, Scripture and ethics, a study of 1 Corinthians 5-7 [diss. Cambridge, ^D*Horbury* J.]: ArbGAJ 22. Leiden 1994, Brill. xii-248 p. ƒ125. 90-04-10065-2 [RelStR 21,238, A. E. *Hunt*]. – ^RExpTim 106 (1994s) 310 (J. *Barclay*: though Paul rarely cites OT in ethical passages).
5882 *Vander Broek* Lyle, Discipline and community; another look at 1 Corinthians 5: RefR 48 (1994s) 5-13.
5883 *a) Drury* John, [1 Cor 5,7] 'Christ our Passover'; – *b) Tuckett*

Christopher M.,   Jewish Christian wisdom in 1 Corinthians?: ➤ 45,
   FGOULDER M., Crossing 1994, 221-233 / 201-219.
5884 **Kirchhoff** Renate,   Die Sünde gegen den eigenen Leib; Studien zu *pornē*
   und *porneîa* in 1 Kor 6,12-20 und dem sozio-kulturellen Kontext der
   paulinischen Adressaten [< Diss. Heid. D*Burchard* C.]: SUmwNT 18. Gö
   1994, Vandenhoeck &R. 227 p. DM 274. 3-525-53372-1 [RelStR 21,238,
   R. S. *Ascough*; TLZ 120,1001, G. *Haufe*].
5885 **Delesalle** Jacques,   'Être un seul Esprit' avec Dieu (1 Co 6,17) dans les
   œuvres de GUILLAUME de Saint-Thierry: diss. Lille 1993s. 332 p. – RTLv
   26, p. 542.
5886 **Deming** W.,   Paul on marriage and celibacy; the Hellenistic background
   of 1 Corinthians 7: diss. Chicago 1991, D*Betz* H. [> SNTS mg 83;
   < NTAbs 39, p. 517].
   Collins Raymond F., [1 Cor 7] Divorce in the NT 1992 ➤ 4433.
5887 *Harril* J. Albert,   Paul and slavery; the problem of 1 Corinthians 7:21:
   BRes 39 (1994) 5-28.

   G5.4   *Idolothyta... Eucharistia:*   1 Cor 8-11.

5888 **Gardner** Paul D.,   The gifts of God and the authentication of a
   Christian; an exegetical study of 1 Corinthians 8-11:1 [diss. D*Hooker* M.].
   Lanham MD 1994, UPA. xii-217 p. $36.50. 0-8191-9519-7 [RelStR
   21,239, R. S. *Ascough*]. – RExpTim 106 (1994s) 246 (B. *Rosner: gnōsis* as
   gift of the Spirit, as MURPHY-O'CONNOR).
5889 **Saez Gonzálvez** Ramón,   El problema de las carnes inmoladas a los
   idolos y las soluciones propuestas (1 Cor. 8,1.4.7.10; 10,12; Act 15,25;
   21,25; Apc 2,14.20); un estudio teológico-bíblico sobre la unidad y la
   diversidad en el Nuevo Testamento: diss. Pont. Univ. Gregoriana, D*Vanni*
   U. R 1994. 325 p.; bibliog. p. 364-379.
5889* **You Choon-Ho** Martin, Die Starken und Schwachen in 1. Kor 8,1-11,1
   im Licht der griechisch-römischen Antithese 'Frömmigkeit/Aberglaube'
   und 'Vernunft/Emotion': Diss. D*Berger* K. Heidelberg 1994. – TR 91,97.
5890 **Wright** Richard A.,   [1 Cor 8.10] Christians, Epicureans and the critique
   of Greco-Roman religion: diss. Brown, D*Stowers* S. Providence 1994.
   204 p. 94-33469. – DissA 55 (1994s) p. 2005.
5891 **Probst** Hermann,   Paulus und der Brief; die Rhetorik des antiken Briefes
   als Form der paulinischen Korintherkorrespondenz (1 Kor 8-10): WUNT
   2/45, D1991 ➤ 8,6369.6401; 9,6086: RJTS 45 (1994) 254s (D. A. *Templeton*); FrSZ 41 (1994) 295-7 (H.-J. *Venetz*); SvEx 59 (1994) 193-203 (W.
   Übelacker, also on VOUGA F., MITCHELL M., svensk).
5892 **Söding** Thomas,   Starke und Schwache; der Götzenopferstreit in 1 Kor
   8-10 als Paradigma paulinischer Ethik: ZNW 85 (1994) 69-92.
5893 **Yeo Khiok-Khng**,   Rhetorical interaction in 1 Corinthians 8 & 10; a
   formal analysis with preliminary suggestions for a Chinese cross-cultural
   hermeneutic: diss. Northwestern, D*Jewett* R. Evanston IL c. 1993
   [> BInterpS 9, Leiden, Brill; < RelStR 21,239, A. R. *Hunt*].
5894 *Yeo Khiok-Khng*,   The rhetorical hermeneutic of 1 Corinthians 8 and
   Chinese ancestor worship: BInterp 2 (1994) 294-311.
5895 *Borgen* P., 'Yes', 'No', 'How far?' The participation of Jews and
   Christians in pagan cult: Explorations 8,1 (Ph 1994) 5s [< NTAbs 38,
   p. 416].
5896 **Heil** Christoph,   Die Ablehnung der Speisegebote durch Paulus; zur
   Frage nach der Stellung des Apostels zum Gesetz [kath, Diss. Bonn 1993,

ᴰ*Merklein* H.]: BoBB 96. Weinheim 1994, Beltz Athenäum. xv-386 p.
DM 118. 3-89547-062-7 [TLZ 120,793, F. W. *Horn*].

5897 **Gooch** P. D., Dangerous food, 1 Cor 8-10: 1993 ⇒ 9,6085 [JTS 46,279,
D. *Horrell*].

5898 **Cheung Tat-Man** Alexandre, [1 Cor 8-10] Idol food in Corinth; an
examination of Paul's approach in the light of its background in ancient
Judaism and legacy in early Christianity: diss. Westminster, ᴰ*Silva* M. Ph
1994. 310 p. 94-28897. – DissA 55 (1994s) p. 1589.

5899 *Meggitt* Justin J., [1 Cor 8.10] Meat consumption and social conflict in
Corinth: JTS 45 (1994) 137-141.

5900 *a) Witherington* Benᴵᴵᴵ, [1 Cor 8,10; Acts 15] Not so idle thoughts about
eidolothuton: TyndB 44 (1993) 237-254; – *b*) [1 Cor 10,19s] Why not idol
meat? BR 10,3 (1994) 38-43 . 54.

5901 **Sisson** Russell B., The apostle as athlete; a socio-rhetorical interpretation of 1 Corinthians 9: diss. Emory, ᴰ*Robbins* V. Atlanta 1994. 187 p.
94-24819. – DissA 55 (1994s) p. 996; RTLv 26, p. 539; RelStR 21,256.

5902 *a) Richardson* Peter, Temples, altars and living from the Gospel
(1 Cor. 9.12b-18); – *b*) *Hurd* John C., Good news and the integrity of
1 Corinthians; – *c*) *Mitchell* Margaret M., Rhetorical shorthand in
Pauline argumentation; the functions of 'the Gospel' in the Corinthian
correspondence: ⇒ 76*a*, ᶠLᴏɴɢᴇɴᴇᴄᴋᴇʀ R., Gospel in Paul 1994,
89-110 / 38-62 / 63-88.

5903 *Löhr* Hermut, 'Heute, wenn ihr seine Stimme hört ...'; zur Kunst der
Schriftanwendung im Hebräerbrief und in 1 Kor 10: ⇒ 322*, Schriftauslegung 1991/4, 221-248.

5904 *Kolenkow* Anitra B., Paul and his opponents in 1 Cor 10-13; *theîoi
ándres* and spiritual guides: ⇒ 40, ᶠGᴇᴏʀɢɪ D. 1994, 351-374.

5905 *Collier* Gary D., 'That we might not crave evil'; the structure and
argument of 1 Corinthians 10,1-13: JStNT 55 (1994) 55-75.

5906 ᴱ**Meyer** Ben F., (1 Cor 11) One Lord, one cup 1988/93 ⇒ 9,397:
ᴿJEcuSt 31 (1994) 161s (D. *Liderbach*).

5907 **Schirrmacher** Thomas, Paulus im Kampf gegen den Schleier; eine
alternative Auslegung von 1. Korinther 11,2-16: Biblia et Symbolica 4.
Bonn 1993, Kultur & W. 165 p. 3-926105-14-3 [RelStR 21,239, R. S.
Ascough].

1 Cor 11, Eucharist conference 1988/93 ⇒ 372.

5908 *Hasler* Victor, Die Gleichstellung der Gattin; situationskritische Reflexionen zu 1 Kor 11,2-16: TZBas 50 (1994) 189-200.

5909 *Perriman* A. C., The head of a woman; the meaning of *kephalē* in 1 Cor
11:3: JTS 45 (1994) 602-622.

5910 *Padgett* Alan G., The significance of *antí* in 1 Corinthians 11:15:
TyndB 45 (1994) 181-7.

G5.5 1 Cor 12s ... Glossolalia, charismata.

5911 **Basadonna** G., Sui fiumi di Babilonia ... O si è profeti o si è traditori.
Mi 1993, Àncora. 160 p. – ᴿAmbrosius 70 (1994) 96 (G. *Giavini*).

5912 *Bergant* Dianne, Would that all were prophets: RRel 52 (1993) 340-9.

5913 **Bonnke** Reinhard, Mighty manifestations [of the Spirit – but not
charismata]. Eastbourne 1994, Kingsway. 190 p. £5. 0-85476-281-X. –
ᴿTBR 7,3 (1994s) 40s (A. *Warren*).

5914 **Boring** M. Eugene, The continuing voice of Jesus 1991 ⇒ 8,6420;
9,6100: ᴿTorJT 10 (1994) 115s (R. S. *Ascough*).

5915 *a) Burgess* Stanley M.,   Cutting the taproot; the modern Pentecostal movement and its traditions; – *b) Pinnock* Clark H.,   The Holy Spirit as a distinct person in the Godhead; – *c) Sullivan* Francis A.,   The laying on of hands in Christian tradition: → 140, FWILLIAMS J., Spirit and renewal: JPentT supp. 5 (1994) 56-88 / 34-41 / 42-54.

5916 **Dawes** Stuart W.,   Vers une théologie biblique et pneumatique des responsabilités sociales du mouvement pentecôtiste: diss. Laval, DRichard J. Québec 1994. – RTLv 26, p. 583.

5917 **Deere** Jack,   Surprised by the power of the Spirit; a former Dallas seminary professor [and 'cessationist'] discovers that God speaks and heals today.   GR/Eastbourne 1993, Zondervan/Kingsway. 256 p. $17. – RBtS 151 (1994) 233s (R. A. *Pyne*); TBR 7,3 (1994s) 41 (A. *Warren*).

5918 **Gillespie** Thomas W.,   The first theologians; a study in early Christian prophecy.   GR 1994, Eerdmans. xix-286 p.; bibliog. 265-281. 0-8028-3721-2.

5919 **Hasel** Gerhard F.,   Speaking in tongues; biblical speaking in tongues and contemporary glossolalia.   Berrien Springs 1991, Adventist Theol. Soc. 175 p. $12. – RAndrUnSem 32 (1994) 137s (H. *Kiessler*).

5920 *Hilber* John W.,   Diversity of OT prophetic phenomena and NT prophecy: WestTJ [TLZ 120,425] 56 (1994) 243-258.

5921 **Hocken** Peter,   The glory and the shame; reflections on the 20th-century outpouring of the Holy Spirit.   Guildford, Surrey/Wheaton IL 1994, Eagle/Shaw. 204. $14. 0-86347-117-X [TDig 42,273: Catholic priest pro & con Pentecostals].

5922 **Ibañez** Alberto,   Lenguas I. ¿Qué enseñó San Pablo?; II. Su historia.   BA 1991, Lumen.   124 p.; 181 p. – RTArg 29 (1992) 209-212 (L. H. *Rivas*).

5923 *a) Johns* Cheryl B.,   Pentecostals and the praxis of liberation; proposal for subversive theological education; – *b) Macchia* Frank, on the Blumhardts c. 1860: Transformation 11,1 (1994) 11-15 / 1-5 + inside back cover.

5924 **Layendecker** L.,   Om de beheersing van het charisma; Heil en macht in de R. K. Kerk: KNAW lett.157. Amst 1993, North-Holland. 146 p. – RArchivScSocR 39,86 (1994) 291s (W. *Frijoff*: limpide).

5925 **Lindstrom** Lars G.,   Christian spiritual healing; a psychological study; ideology and experience in the British healing movement: Psychologia et Sociologia Religionum 7.   Uppsala 1992, Univ. 207 p. – RMélSR 51 (1994) 219-222 (R. *Dericquebourg*).

5926 *Lodahl* Michael,   Wesleyan reservations about eschatological 'enthusiasm': WeslTJ 29 (1994) 50-63.

5927 **Parmentier** Martin,   Das Zungenreden bei den Kirchenvätern: Bijdragen 55 (1994) 376-398; Eng. 398: wordless jubilation could be considered a post-Corinthians form of glossolalia.

5928 **Robertson** A. Palmer,   The final word; a biblical response to the case for tongues and prophecy today.   E 1993, Banner of Truth. 150 p. – RWestTJ 56 (1994) 423-5 (R. F. *Wright* finds him tenably opposed, in view of the confusion).

5929 **Smail** Tom, *al.*,   Charismatic renewal; the search for a theology 1993 → 9,6119: RTLond 97 (1994) 47s (T. *Christie*: Smail best).

5930 **Sullivan** Francis A., ℗ Charyzmaty i odnowa charyzmatyczna.   Wsz 1992, Archidiecezja. 151 p. – RAtKap 122 (1994) 189-191 (T. *Lubiński*, ℗).

5931 **Suurmond** Jean-Jacques,   Word and spirit at play; towards a charismatic theology.   L 1994, SCM. 244 p. £15. 0-334-02417-X. – RExpTim 106

(1994s) 125 (J. *Kent,* also on *Tidball* D. 1994, both 'in the drive to establish the respectability of Evangelicalism and Pentecostalism').

5932 *a*) *Synan* Vinson, The role of tongues as initial evidence; – *b*) *Turner* Max, The Spirit of Prophecy and the ethical/religious life of the Christian community; – *c*) *Davids* Peter H., Spirit and ethics; the Holy Spirit and the use of wealth in the New Testament: ➤ 140, ᶠWILLIAMS J., Spirit 1994, 67-82 / 166-190 / 112-128.

5933 *Wan Sze-kar,* Charismatic exegesis; PHILO and Paul compared: St-PhilonAn 6 (1994) 54-82.

5934 **Wimber** John, Power evangelism²ʳᵉᵛ [mostly = ¹1985, + Study Guide]. L 1992, Hodder &S. 0-340-56127-0: ᴿEvQ 66 (1994) 365-8 (D. *Parker*: unconvincing on evangelism within charismatic framework).

5935 *Macías* Baldomero, 1 Cor 12,13: una conjetura renacentista [CANTERO Guillermo 1548, *ephōtísthēmen* for *epotísthēmen*]: FgNt 7 (1994) 209-214.

5936 *Sigountos* James G., The genre of 1 Corinthians 13: NTS 40 (1994) 246-250.

5937 *Thomas* R. L., 1 Cor 13:11 revisited; an exegetical update: Master'sSemJ 4 (Sun Valley 1993) 187-201 [< NTAbs 38, p. 220].

5938 *Smit* Joop F. M., Tongues and prophecy; deciphering 1 Cor 14,22: Biblica 75 (1994) 175-190; franç. 190.

5939 *Nadeau* Denis J., Le problème des femmes en 1 Co 14/33b-35: ÉTRel 69 (1994) 63-65.

5940 *Busto Saiz* José Ramón, [1 Cor 14,34-35 interpolado] San Pablo y las mujeres de Corinto; ¿fué San Pablo antifeminista?: SalT 81 (1993) 211-221.

G5.6   **Resurrectio;** *1 Cor 15* ... [➤ F5.6; H9].

5941 *Bachmann* Michael, [1 Kor 15] Eulen und Fallen [zu ZIMMER C.]: LingBibl [65,25-36; 67,40-44] 68 (1993) 95-99.

5942 *Kocsis* I., [1 Cor 15] La fine della morte nel rinnovamento escatologico: Folia Theologica 3 (Budapest 1992) 75-90; 4 (1994) 147-194 [< NTAbs 39, p. 429].

5943 *Lowell* Arnold B., 1 Corinthians 15; between text and sermon: Interpretation 48 (1994) 176-180.

5944 *McCant* Jerry W., Competing Pauline eschatologies; an exegetical comparison of 1 Corinthians 15 and 2 Corinthians 5: WeslTJ 29 (1994) 23-49.

5945 *Moiser* Jeremy, 1 Corinthians 15: IrBSt 14 (1992) 10-30.

5946 *Schaefer* Markus, Paulus, 'Fehlgeburt' oder 'unvernünftiges Kind'? ein Interpretationsvorschlag zu 1 Kor 15,8: ZNW 85 (1994) 207-217.

5947 **Teani** Maurizio, Corporeità e risurrezione; l'interpretazione di 1 Corinti 15,35-49 nel novecento: Aloisiana 24. R 1994, Pont. Univ. Gregoriana. 335 p. Lᵐ 50. 88-7652-668-4 [NTAbs 39, p. 155: Morcelliana 88-372-1538-3].

5948 **Brodeur** Scott, The Holy Spirit's agency in the resurrection of the dead; an exegetico-theological study of 1 Corinthians 15:44b-49 and Romans 8:9-13 [diss. Pont. Univ. Gregoriana, Nº 7211; ᴰ*Aletti* J.-N. R 1994. – InfPUG 26,131 (1994) p. 32; RTLv 26, p. 535 (extr. Nº 4064, 68 p.)]. R 1994, Pont. Univ. Gregoriana. xiv-69 p.

5949 *Botha* S. P., 1 Korintiërs 15:49b; 'n Hortatief of futurumlesing?: Herv-TSt 49 (1993) 760-774 [< NTAbs 39, p. 62].

5950 **Schneider** Sebastian,   Vollendung des Auferstehens; eine exegetische Untersuchung zu 1 Kor 15,51-52: Diss. St. Georgen, ᴰ*Baumert* N.   Frankfurt 1994. 283 p. – RTLv 26, p. 539.

5951 **Verbrugge** Verlyn D., [1 Cor 16,1s ...] Paul's style of Church leadership illustrated by his instructions to the Corinthians on the collection [< diss. Notre Dame, ᴰ*Collins* Adela Y.].   SF 1992, Mellen Research Univ. xviii-404 p. $60. – ᴿJBL 113 (1994) 740-2 (L. Ann *Jervis*, some limitations).

G5.9   Secunda epistula ad Corinthios.

5952 ᴱ**Feld** Helmut,   Commentarii in Secundam Pauli Epistolam ad Corinthios: CALVINI Opera Exegetica 15.   Genève 1994, Droz.   lx-247 p. 2-600-00021-6 [Gregorianum 76,762, G. *Marconi*; TLZ 120,1097, J. *Rogge*].

5953 **Thrall** Margaret E.,   ICC 2 Cor 1 (1-7). E 1994, Clark.   xxxvi-501 p. $55. 0-567-09665-6 [NTAbs 39, p. 340]. – ᴿExpTim 106 (1994s) 122 (C. S. *Rodd*); TBR 7,3 (1994s) 28 (Judith *Lieu*).

5954 **Bieringer** R. [inedita mostly German], *Lambrecht* J. [mostly English reprints], Studies on 2 Corinthians: BtETL 112.   Lv 1994, Peeters/Univ. xix-632 p. Fb 3000.   90-6831-612-5 / 90-6186-612-X. – ᴿExpTim 106 (1994s) 214s (E. *Best*).

5955 **Bosenius** Bärbel,   Die Abwesenheit des Apostels als theologisches Programm; der zweite Korintherbrief als Beispiel für die Brieflichkeit der paulinischen Theologie: TANZ 11.   T 1994, Francke.   xiii-231 p. DM 84. 3-7220-1868-9 [TLZ 120,1074-7, L. *Aejmelaeus*].

Dales Douglas, [largely on 2 Cor] Living through dying 1994 ➤ 5663.

5957 **Murphy-O'Connor** Jerome, La teologia della Seconda Lettera ai Corinti: TeolNT.   Brescia 1993, Paideia.   196 p. Lᵐ 20.   88-394-0486-6. – ᴿAntonianum 69 (1994) 389s (M. *Nobile*); RB 101 (1994) 142s (Clare *Amos*).

5958 *Duff* Paul B.,   2 Corinthians 1-7; sidestepping the division hypothesis dilemma [whether 2 Cor is a composite]: BibTB 24 (1994) 16-26.

5959 *Roiné* Christophe,   Notes de lecture sur 2 Corinthiens 1-2:   SémBib 73 (1994) 43-55.

5960 **Brendle** Albert, Im Prozess der Konfliktüberwindung; eine exegetische Studie zur Kommunikationssituation zwischen Paulus und den Korinthern in 2 Kor 1,1-2.13; 7,4-16: Diss. St. Georgen, ᴰ*Baumert* N. Frankfurt/M 1994. 336 p. – TR 91,95; RTLv 26. p. 535.

5961 *Lorusso* Giacomo,   Il campo dell'apostolato in 2 Cor 1,7:   RivScR 8 (1994) 269-294.

5962 **Schröter** Jens,   Der versöhnte Versöhner, Paulus ... 2 Kor 2,14-7,4: TANZ 10, 1993 ➤ 9,6151 [TLZ 120,242, E. *Lohse*].

5963 *Barberá* Carlos, [2 Cor 3,2] 'Vosotros sois carta de Cristo': SalT 81 (1993) 631-656.

5964 *Pate* C. Marvin,   Adam Christology 2 Cor 4s 1991 ➤ 7,5506; 9,6157: ᴿJBL 113 (1994) 346-9 (S. *Hafemann*).

5965 *Lambrecht* Jan, The eschatological outlook in 2 Corinthians 4.7-15:
➤ 46, FGUNDRY R., To tell 1994, 122-139.

5966 *Gräbe* P. J., [2 Cor 4,7; 6,7; 12,9] The all-surpassing power of God
through the Holy Spirit in the midst of our broken earthly existence;
perspectives on Paul's use of *dýnamis* in 2 Corinthians: Neotestamentica
28 (1994) 147-156.

5967 *Grelot* Pierre, De la maison terrestre à la maison céleste (2 Corinthiens
4,16-5,10): ➤ 30, FCOUTURIER G., Maison 1994, 343-364.

5968 **Heckel** Theo K., [2 Cor 4,16; Röm 7,22] Der innere Mensch; die
paulinische Verarbeitung eines platonischen Motifs [Diss. Erlangen 1991]:
WUNT 2/53. Tü 1993, Mohr. x-257 p. DM 89. 3-16-146026-X [RB 102,
306, J. *Murphy-O'Connor*].

5969 *Beck* R. E., Reflections on 2 Corinthians 5:11-6:2: EpworthR 21,2
(1994) 85-92 [< NTAbs 39, p. 62].

5970 **Ghirlando** Marcello, The ministry of reconciliation (2 Cor 5,17-21): a
ministry of the New Covenant, of the Spirit and of righteousness (2 Cor
3,4-11) in the service of evangelization: diss. Pont. Univ. Gregoriana,
DRasco E. Rome 1994. 213 p. – RTLv 26,536.

5971 *Härle* Wilfried, [LUTHER zu 2 Kor 5,21] 'Christus factus est peccatum
metaphorice'; zur Heilsbedeutung der Kreuzestodes Jesu Christi: NSys
36 (1994) 301-314; Eng. 315.

5972 *Goulder* Michael, 2 Cor. 6:14-7:1 as an integral part of 2 Corinthians:
NT 36 (1994) 47-57.

5973 *Sedgwick* Colin, [2 Cor 6,14-7,1; Christian insularity goes far back] Spot
the difference: ExpTim 106 (1994s) 84s.

5974 **Webb** William J., Returning home... 2 Cor 6,14-7,1: jNsu 85, 1993
➤ 9,6168 [JTS 46,282, R. P. *Martin*]: RSalmanticensis 41 (1994) 349-352
(R. *Trevijano*).

5975 *Scott* James M., The use of Scripture in 2 Corinthians 6.16c-18 and
Paul's restoration theology: JStNT 56 (1994) 73-99.

5976 **Angstenberger** Pius, Der reiche und der arme Christus; die Rezeptionsgeschichte von 2 Kor 8,9 zwischen dem 2.-6. Jahrhundert: kath. Diss.
DVogt. Tübingen 1994. – TR 91,101.

5977 **Fung Siu-Sing**, Spiritual warfare in 2 Corinthians 10-13: diss. Westminster Theol. Sem., DPoythress V. 1994. 319 p. 94-28277. – DissA 55
(1994s) p. 1590.

5978 **Heckel** Ulrich, Kraft in Schwachheit; Untersuchungen zu 2 Kor 10-13:
WUNT 2/56, D1991 ➤ 9,6173 [BL 95,150, C. J. A. *Hickling*; JTS 46,285,
also C. J. A. *Hickling*; TLZ 120,34, W. *Vogler*]: RTvT 34 (1994) 197 (H.
van de *Sandt*).

5979 *Heckel* Ulrich, Jer 9,22f. als Schlüssel für 2 Kor 10-13; ein Beispiel
für die methodischen Probleme in der gegenwärtigen Diskussion über
den Schriftgebrauch bei Paulus: ➤ 322*, Schriftauslegung 1991/4,
206-225.

5980 *Anderson* John T., [2 Cor 11:3] The body of Satan according to Paul:
ProcGM 13 (1993) 103-120.

5981 *a*) *Fee* Gordon D., 'Another Gospel which you did not embrace';
2 Corinthians 11.4 and the theology of 1 and 2 Corinthians; – *b*) *Belleville*
Linda L., Gospel and kerygma in 2 Corinthians; – *c*) *Jervis* L. Ann,
God's obedient Messiah and the end of the Law; R. A. Longenecker's
understanding of Paul's Gospel: ➤ 76*a*, FLONGENECKER R., Gospel in
Paul 1994, 111-133 / 134-164 / 21-35.

5982 *Goulder* Michael, [2 Cor 12,1-7] Vision and knowledge: JStNT 56 (1994) 53-71.

G6.1 Ad Galatas.

5983 **Cole** R. Alan, The letter of Paul to the Galatians: Tyndale NT comm. 1989 → 5,6164: ᴿJEvTS 37 (1994) 435s (B. *Cain*: boadminded conservative; holds H. D. BETZ 'prince of commentators').

5984 **Dalton** W. J., Galatians without tears → 8,6500 NSW; also ColMn 1992, Liturgical. 75 p. $5. 0-8146-2227-5 [NTAbs 38, p. 129: aim salvation of Gentiles, not attack on Judaism]. – ᴿPacifica 7 (1994) 241-3 (P. *Trebilco*).

5985 **Dunn** James D. G., The epistle to the Galatians 1993 → 9,6180: ᴿRefTR 53 (1994) 145s (G. N. *Davies*).

5986 ᴱ**Feld** Helmut, CALVIN J., Opera exegetica XVI: Commentarii in GalEphPhlpCol. Genève 1992, Droz. lxiii-483 p. Fs 90. – ᴿBtHumRen 56 (1994) 217-9 (J. L. *Thompson*).

5987 **George** Timothy, Galatians: NAmerComm 30. Nv 1994, Broadman. 463 p. $38. 0-8054-0130-X [NTAbs 39, p. 517].

5988 **Hagen** Kenneth, LUTHER's approach to Scripture as seen in his 'Commentaries' on Galatians 1519-1538 → 8,6502; 9,6193. Tü 1993, Mohr. xii-194 p. DM 148. 3-16-145977-6 [TDig 42,67]. – ᴿRelStR 20 (1994) 155 (D. R. *Janz*: salutary correctives for Luther scholarship); Salesianum 56 (1994) 780 (F. *Meyer*); TLZ 119 (1994) 1105 (R. *Mau*).

5989 **Hansen** G. Walter, Galatians: IVP NT comm. DG/Leicester 1994, InterVarsity. 212 p. $16. 0-8308-1809-X / UK 0-85111-675-2 [NTAbs 39, p. 518]. – ᴿTBR 7,3 (1994s) 29 (G. *Stanton*: excellent).

5990 **Longenecker** R. N., Gal: WordComm 41, 1990 → 6,6492... 9,6161: ᴿWestTJ 55 (1993) 159-161 (W. *Russell*).

5991 **Lührmann** Dieter, Galatians, ᵀ*Dean* O. C.: Continental comm. 1992 → 8,6505; 9,6182: ᴿAndrUnSem 32 (1994) 141s (M. *Veloso*); CurrTM 21 (1994) 141 (E. *Krentz*: not word-comments but essays); ÉTRel 69 (1994) 109-111 (E. *Cuvillier*).

5992 **Matera** Frank J., Galatians: Sacra Pagina 9. ColMn 1992, Liturgical/ Glazier. xiii-252 p. $25. – ᴿCanadCath 12,2 (1994) 31 (W. O. *McCready*); CBQ 56 (1994) 801s (B. *Fiore*); Interpretation 48 (1994) 181-3 (C. B. *Cousar*); RB 101 (1994) 145s (J. *Murphy-O'Connor*); SNTU 19 (1994) 239s (A. *Fuchs*); TorJT 10 (1994) 96-98 (L. Ann *Jervis*, also on LÜHRMANN D.).

5993 **Metzger** Daniel P., Wendelin STEINBACH's lectures on the letter to the Galatians; a late medieval [c. 1500] approach to Pauline authority and teaching: diss. Marquette, ᴰ*Hagen* K. Milwaukee 1994. 282 p. 94-33784. – DissA 55 (1994s) p. 2439.

5994 **Tarazi** Paul N., Galatians, a commentary: Orthodox Biblical Studies. Crestwood NY 1994, St. Vladimir. xiv-351 p. 0-88141-083-7.

5995 **Wachtel** Klaus, Witte Klaus, Die paulinischen Briefe 2. Gal. Eph. Phil. Kol. 1. u. 2. Thess. 1. u. 2. Tim. Tit. Phlm. Hebr.: NT auf Papyrus 2/2: ArbNTTextf 22. B 1994, de Gruyter. 359 p. DM 208. 3-11-014612-6 [TR 91,273; RelStR 21,330, M. W. *Holmes*].

5996 **Barclay** J. M. G., Obeying the truth 1991 → 4,6165... 9,6187: ᴿNeotestamentica 28 (1994) 257-260 (P. J. *Hartin*); Protestantesimo 48 (1993) 213s (B. *Corsani*).

5997 *Bercovitz* J. Peter, Paul and Galatia: ProcGM 13 (1993) 55-69.
5998 *Blank* Rudolf H.,   Six theses concerning freedom in Christ and
   liberation; liberation in Galatians, Luther, and Liberation Theology:
   ConcordJ 20 (1994) 236-260 (261-273, for peace, *Barry* A. L.; 274-291, for
   faithfulness, *Kreiss* Wilbert).
5999 **Boers** Hendrikus, The justification of the Gentiles; Paul's letters to the
   Galatians and the Romans. Peabody MA 1994, Hendrikson. xvii-334 p.
   1-56563-011-4 [Biblica 76,437, J. *Lambrecht*: holds Paul held in tension
   both faith and works; NTAbs 39, p. 332].
6000 **Buckel** John,   Free to love; Paul's defense of Christian liberty in
   Galatians: TPastMG 15. Lv/GR 1993, Peeters/Eerdmans. xiii-240 p.
   90-6831-490-4 [NTAbs 38,127]. – ᴿCBQ 56 (1994) 786s (Kim *Paffenroth*).
6002 **Casonatto** Odalberto Domingos, A escatologia cristã na Carta aos
   Gálatas: diss. Studium Biblicum Franciscanum, ᴰ*Buscemi* A. M. J 1993.
   273 p. – LA 44 (1994) 739-741; RTLv 26, p. 536; extr. 1994, 78 p.
6003 *Corsani* Bruno, La crisi in Galazia nello sviluppo del cristianesimo
   primitivo: ➤ 125, ᶠSUBILIA V., Pluralismo 1994, 71-80.
6004 *Craffert* P. F., 'n Herdefiniering van Paulus se konflik in Galasië; die
   brief aan die Galassiërs deur die bril van die sosiale wetenskappe:
   HervTSt 50 (1994) 859-876 [< NTAbs 39, p. 430].
6005 **Dunn** J. D. G., Theology of Paul's letter to the Galatians 1993 ➤ 9,6189
   [RelStR 21,54, K. L. *Cukrowski*]. – ᴿJRel 74 (1994) 557s (H. D. *Betz*).
6006 *Fairweather* Janet, The epistle to the Galatians and classical rhetoric:
   TyndB 45 (1994) 1-38 . 213-243.
6007 *Fowl* Stephen, Who can read Abraham's story? Allegory and interpretive power in Galatians: JStNT 55 (1994) 77-95.
6008 *Greenfield* G.,   Ethical themes in Galatians: TEdr 50 (New Orleans 1994)
   127-137 [85-126, *Simmons* B. E., *al.*; < NTAbs 39, p. 63].
6009 **Hong In-gyu**, The law in Galatians [< diss. Stellenbosch]: jNsu 81, 1993
   ➤ 9,6196: ᴿCBQ 56 (1994) 598s (Patricia M. *McDonald*); JTS 45 (1994)
   455 (J. M. G. *Barclay*).
6010 *Muddiman* John,   An anatomy of Galatians: ➤ 45, ᶠGOULDER M.,
   Crossing 1994, 257-270.
6011 **O'Grady** John F., Pillars of Paul's gospel, Gal Rom 1992 ➤ 8,6520;
   9,6201: ᴿAndrUnSem 32 (1994) 297s (M. *Veloso*).
6012 **Olson** M. J.,   Galatians, in defense of love; a study guide. Macon GA
   1994, Smyth & H. viii-94 p.; map. $9 pa. 1-880837-86-1 [NTAbs 39,
   p. 153].
6013 **Parker** Floyd O.ᴶ, An examination of the Akedah in Paul's letter to the
   Galatians: diss. Drew, ᴰ*Dey* Lala. Madison NJ 1994. 442 p. 94-32960. –
   RelStR 21,255 [DissA 55 (1994s) p. 2004: 'A study of...'; Isaac typology
   refers to Galatian Christians and not to Jesus].
6014 **Pitta** Antonio, Disposizione... Gal: AnBib 131, 1992 ➤ 8,6521; 9,6202:
   ᴿBiblica 75 (1994) 280-3 (B. *Standaert*); Carthaginensia 10 (1994) 183s (R.
   Sanz Valdivieso); CBQ 56 (1994) 805s (J. G. *Lodge*); CC 145 (1994,2) 301s
   (D. *Scaiola*); ETL 70 (1994) 477s (R. F. *Collins*); NRT 116 (1994) 909s (X.
   Jacques); RB 101 (1994) 421-5 (P. *Garuti*, ital.); Salesianum 56 (1994) 574s
   (J. J. *Bartolomé*).
6015 **Rapa** Robert, The meaning of *érga nómou* (works of law) in Galatians
   and Romans: diss. ᴰ*Pretorius* E. Pretoria. 274 p. – RTLv 26,539 sans
   date.
6016 *Segalla* Giuseppe, Identità cristiana e cammino secondo lo Spirito nella
   lettera ai Galati: TItSett 19 (1993) 7-63; Eng. 63.

6017 *Winger* Michael, Tradition, revelation and Gospel; a study in Galatians: JStNT 53 (1994) 65-86.

6018 **Lambrecht** J., [Gal 1-4] The truth of the Gospel 1992/3 ➤ 9,392: ᴿRivB 42 (1994) 494-6 (P. *Iovino*).

6019 *a) Holtz* Traugott, Paulus, Jerusalem und die Wahrheit des Evangeliums; Beobachtungen zu Gal 1 and 2; – *b) Baumert* Norbert, 'Mit Gewinn ernten'; zur Paränese von Gal 5,25 - 6,10; – *c) Oberlinner* Lorenz, 'Kein anderes Evangelium!' Die Auseinandersetzung des Paulus mit seinen 'Gegnern' am Beispiel des Galaterbriefes; – *d) Klauck* Hans-Josef, 'Der Gott in dir' (ep. 41,1). Autonomie des Gewissens bei SENECA und Paulus: ➤ 31*, ᶠDAUTZENBERG G., Nach 1994, 327-340 / 55-83 / 461-499 / 341-362.

6020 *Stowasser* Martin, [Gal 1s] Konflikte und Konfliktlösungen nach Gal 1-2 — Aspekte paulinischer Konfliktkultur: TrierTZ 103 (1994) 56-79.

6021 **Urbanski** Jan Piotr, *Kaléō* nella lettera ai Galati (1,6.15-16; 5,7-8,13); studio esegetico-teologico della chiamata in Paolo: diss. Angelicum, ᴰ*Viejo* J. R 1993, Univ. S. Thomae. 112 p. (excerpt; bibliog. 11-25].

6022 *Niebuhr* Karl-Wilhelm, [Gal 1,10-2,21] 'Judentum' und 'Christentum' bei Paulus und IGNATIUS von Antiochien: ZNW 85 (1994) 218-233.

6023 **Murphy-O'Connor** Jerome, [Gal 1,17] What was Paul doing in [Nabatean] 'Arabia'?: BR 10,5 (1994) 46s.

6024 *a) Donaldson* Terence L., 'The Gospel that I proclaim among the Gentiles' (Gal 2.2); universalistic or Israel-centred?; – *b) Jewett* Robert, Gospel and commensality; social and theological implications of Gal. 2.14; – *c) Wright* N.T., Gospel and theology in Galatians; – *d) Hughes* Frank W., The Gospel and its rhetoric in Galatians; – *e) Hansen* G. Walter, A paradigm of the Apocalypse; the Gospel in the light of epistolary analysis; ➤ 76*a*, ᶠLONGENECKER R., Gospel in Paul 1994, 166-193 / 240-252 / 210-221 / 222-230 / 194-209.

6025 *Jaquette* J.L., [Gal 2,6] Paul, EPICTETUS and others on indifference to status: CBQ 56 (1994) 68-80.

6026 **Georgi** D., [Gal 2,10] Der Armen zu gedenken; die Geschichte der Kollekte des Paulus für Jerusalem² [= ¹1965 + noch 50%]. Neuk 1994. 156 p. 3-7887-1424-7 [NTAbs 39, p. 151; Eng. 37, p. 126].

6027 *Agourides* S., ⊖ The episode between Peter and Paul in Antioch (Gal 2,11-21]: DeltVM 21,2 (1992) 5-27 [< NTAbs 39, p. 249].

6028 *Drobner* Hubertus R., AUGUSTIN's *sermo Moguntinus* über Gal 2,11-14; Einleitung, Übersetzung und Anmerkungen: TGL 84 (1994) 226-242.

6029 **Hennings** Ralph, Der Briefwechsel Aug/Hieron... Streit um Gal 2,11-14 [ᴰ1994 ➤ 9,6211]: VigChr supp. 21. Leiden 1994, Brill. xi-319 p. 90-04-09840-2 [JTS 46,356, G. *Bonner*; TLZ 120,157s, G. *Haendler*]. – ᴿAug-Lv 44 (1994) 463s (T.J. van *Bavel*).

6030 **Wechsler** Andreas, Geschichtsbild und Apostelstreit... Gal 2,11-14: BZNW 62, ᴰ1991 ➤ 7,5549...9,6212: ᴿCBQ 56 (1994) 810s (M. *Prior*); JTS 45 (1994) 679-681 (G. *Stanton*); TR 90 (1994) 217-9 (F. *Mussner*).

6031 **Eckstein** Hans-Joachim, Verheissung und Gesetz; eine exegetische Untersuchung zu Gal 2,15-4,7: ev. Hab.-Diss. Tübingen 1994. – TR 91,91.

6033 **Bachmann** Michael, Sünder oder Übertreter... Gal 2,15ff: WUNT 59, 1992 ➤ 8,6538; 9,6215: ᴿRHPR 74 (1994) 216s (C. *Grappe*).

6034 *McGinn* Sheila E., Galatians 2:26-29 and the politics of the Spirit: ProcGM 13 (1993) 89-101.

6035 *Geonget* Brigitte, Chapitre 3 des Galates: SémBib 76 (1994) 48-58.
6036 *Hong In-Gyu*, Does Paul misrepresent the Jewish law? Law and covenant in Gal. 3:1-14: NT 36 (1994) 164-182.
6037 *Cranford* Michael, The possibility of perfect obedience; Paul and an implied premise in Galatians 3:10 and 5:3: NT 36 (1994) 242-258.
6038 *Sänger* Dieter, 'Verflucht ist jeder, der am Holze hängt' (Gal 3,13b); zur Rezeption einer frühen antichristlichen Polemik: ZNW 85 (1994) 279-285.
6039 *Bachmann* Michael, Jüdischer Bundesnomismus und paulinisches Gesetzesverständnis; das Fussbodenmosaik von Bet Alfa und das Textsegment Gal 3,15-29: KIsr 9 (1994) 158-191; 4 fig.
6040 *Penna* Romano, La promessa ad Abramo come testamento irrevocabile secondo Gal 3,15ss: ➤ 147, Mem. ZEDDA S., Theologica 3 (1994) 203-218.
6041 a) *Borchert* Gerald L., A key to Pauline thinking — Gal 3:23-29, faith and the new humanity; – b) *Dockery* David S., Introduction to the epistle and Paul's defense of his apostleship (Gal 1:1-2:14); – c) *Garland* David E., Paul's defense of the truth of the Gospel regarding Gentiles (Gal 2:15-3:22); – d) *Longenecker* Richard N., Graphic illustrations of a believer's new life in Christ; Gal 4:21-31: – e) *Fee* Gordon D., Freedom and the life of obedience (Gal 5:1-6:18); – f) *Marshall* Molly T., Gal 5:1,3-14, free yet enslaved; – g) *Mitchell* Henry H., Gal 5:22-23; – h) *Seifrid* Mark A., bibliog.; – j) *Blevins* J. L., preaching: RExp 91,2 (1994) 145-151 / 153-164 / 165-181 / 183-199 / 201-217 / 233-7 / 239-244 / 219-224 / 225-230.
6042 a) *Gundry-Volf* Judith, Male and female in creation and new creation; interpretations of Galatians 3,28c in 1 Corinthians 7; – b) *Silva* Moisés, Eschatological structures in Galatians: ➤ 46, ᶠGUNDRY 5, To tell 1994, 95-121 / 140-162.
6043 *Escaffre* B., 'Né d'une femme' (Gal 4,4): EphMar 44 (1994) 437-452 [< NTAbs 39, p. 431: taken by LUTHER to indicate virginal conception].
6044 **Scott** James M., [Gal 4,5...] Adoption as sons of God: WUNT 2/48, 1992 ➤ 9,6224 [BL 95,168, C. J. A. *Hickling*]: ᴿCBQ 56 (1994) 148-150 (D. M. *Sweetland*).
6045 *Meynet* Roland, Quelle rhétorique dans l'Épître aux Galates? Le cas de Ga 4,12-20: Rhetorica 12,4 (Berkeley 1994) 427-450 [< NTAbs 39,431: advocates a 'biblical rhetoric' which as against classical rhetoric is concrete, paratactic, and concentric].
6046 *Jobes* Karen H., Jerusalem, our mother; metalepsis and intertextuality in Galatians 4:21-41: WestTJ 55 (1993) 299-320.
6047 a) *Pyne* Robert A., Dependence and duty; the spiritual life in Galatians 5; – b) *Bock* Darrell J., 'The new man' as community in Colossians and Ephesians: ➤ 21, ᶠCAMPBELL D., Integrity 1994, 144-156 / 157-167.
6048 *Duvall* J. Scott, Pauline lexical choice revisited; a paradigmatic analysis of selected terms of exhortation in Galatians 5 and 6: FgNt 7 (1994) 17-31; español 31.
6049 **Saldanha** Assisi, The concept of freedom in Galatians; its subordination to the truth of the Gospel; a study of Gal 5,18-25 in the light of the rhetorical analysis of the epistle: diss. ᴰ*Delobel* J. Leuven 1994. xliii-313 p. – RTLv 26, p. 539.
6050 *Kuck* David W., [Gal 6,5] 'Each will bear his own burden'; Paul's creative use of an apocalyptic motif: NTS 40 (1994) 289-297.
6051 a) *Du Toit* A. B., Galatians 6:13; a possible solution to an old exegetical problem; – b) *Loubser* J. A., The contrast slavery/freedom as persuasive device in Galatians: Neotestamentica 28 (1994) 157-161 / 163-176.

6052 *Herman* Zvonimir I., 'Creatura nova' in contextu Epistulae ad Galatas 6,15: ➤ 38, Mem. FUČAK M., BogSmot 64 (1994) 45-60, croat.; 60 ital.
6053 *Ray* C. A., [Gal 6,16] The identity of the 'Israel of God': TEdr 50 (New Orleans 1994) 105-114 [< NTAbs 39, p. 66].

G6.2   **Ad Ephesios.**

6054 **Bouttier** Michel, L'épître de saint Paul aux Éphesiens 1991 ➤ 7,5576 ...
      9,6231: ᴿBiblica 75 (1994) 119-121 (Chantal *Reynier*); JBL 113 (1994) 349-351 (E. *Best*); Protestantesimo 49 (1994) 401s (G. *Conte*).
6056 **Hodge** Charles [† 1870], Ephesians: Classic Commentaries. Wheaton 1994, Crossway. xxiii-224 p. 0-89107-784-7 [STEv 7,194, G. *Saina*].
6057 **Kitchen** Martin, Ephesians: NT Readings. L 1994, Routledge. xi-147 p. $50; pa. $15. 0-415-09506-9; -7-7 [NTAbs 39, p. 519].
6058 **Krodel** Gerhard, Deutero-Pauline Eph Col 2 Thess 1-2 Tim Tit: Proclamation 1993 ➤ 9,6232: ᴿCurrTM 21 (1994) 298s (E. *Krentz*: good but keep on hand ¹1978 J. BURGESS Col and R. H. FULLER Pastoral).
6059 **Lincoln** Andrew T., Ephesians: WordComm 42, 1990 ➤ 6,6530 ...
      9,6233: ᴿJBL 113 (1994) 351-3 (R. A. *Wild*: splendid; several positions worth mentioning).
6060 **Montagnini** Felice, Lettera agli Efesini, intr. tr. comm.: BtB 15. Brescia 1994, Queriniana. 467 p. Lᵐ 45 pa. 88-399-2015-3 [NTAbs 39, p. 152].
6061 **Morris** Leon, Expository reflections on the Letter to the Ephesians. GR 1994, Baker. 217 p. $18. 0-8010-6312-4 [NTAbs 39, p. 153].
6062 *Motyer* Stephen, Ephesians: Free to be one: Crossway Bible Guide. Nottingham 1994, Crossway. 191 p. 1-85684-091-3.
6063 ᴱNeri Umberto, Lettera agli Efesini con brevi brani dai Padri, riformatori e moderni [gr. sir, vlg, PENNA, GNILKA, CONZELMANN, SCHLIER, SCHNACKENBURG, MASSON]: Biblia, i libri della Bibbia interpretati dalla grande Tradizione, a cura della Comunità di Monteveglio. Bo 1994, Dehoniane. xcv-191 p. Lᵐ 52. 88-10-20581-2.
6064 **Olivott** Stuart, Alive in Christ; Ephesians simply explained: Welwyn comm. Darlington 1994, Evangelical. 141 p. 0-35234-515-9. – ᴿTBR 7,3 (1994s) 29 (W. *Carr*; really four short exhortations).
6065 **Ravasi** Gianfranco, Lettere agli Efesini e ai Colossesi: S. Fedele Milano, Conversazioni bibliche. Bo 1994, Dehoniane. 142 p. 88-10-70945-4.
6066 **Schlier** Heinrich, La carta a los Efesios 1991 ➤ 7,5585 ... 9,6237: ᴿRET 54 (1994) 92 (J. *Barrada Fernández*).
6067 **Schnackenburg** R., Ephesians comm., ᵀ*Heron* Helen, 1991 ➤ 7,5586 ...
      6,6238: ᴿGregorianum 75 (1994) 345s (M. *Lubomirski*); RB 101 (1994) 146 (J. *Murphy-O'Connor*); ScotJT 47 (1994) 386-8 (M. *Goulder*).

6068 **Arnold** Clinton E., Ephesians; power and magic: SNTS mg 63, 1989 ➤ 5,6213 ... 9,6240 = GR 1992, Baker. $15: ᴿWestTJ 56 (1994) 201-3 (R. M. *Kidd*).
6069 *Best* Ernest, Ministry in Ephesians: IrBSt 15 (1993) 146-166.
6069* *Cargal* Timothy B., Seated in the heavenlies; cosmic mediators in the mysteries of Mithras and the letter to the Ephesians: ➤ 325, SBL Sem. 33 (1994) 804-821; 3 fig.
6070 **Faust** Eberhard, Pax Christi et pax Caesaris; religionsgeschichtliche ... Studien ... Eph: NOrb 24, 1993. DM 148. 3-7278-0864-0 / VR 3-525-53926-6 [JTS 46,288-293, A. T. *Lincoln*]. – ᴿBZ 119 (1994) 148-151 (R. *Schnackenburg*).

6071 *Mouton* Elna, Reading Ephesians ethically; criteria towards a renewed identity awareness: Neotestamentica 28 (1994) 359-377.

6072 **Reynier** Chantal, [Éph] Évangile et mystère: LDiv 149, 1992 → 8,6573; 9,6249: RBiblica 75 (1994) 431-3 (H. E. *Lona*: drei methodologische Fragen); CC 145 (1994,3) 200 (E. *Farahian*); EsprVie 104 (1994) 414-6 (L. *Walter*).

6073 *Stephens* P., The Church in Bucer's Commentaries on the Epistle to the Ephesians: → 410, BUCER 1994, 45-60.

6074 **Toschi** Alberto, La traduzione latina del participio greco nella lettera agli Efesini: Parma, Ist. Lat. 12. R 1993, Bulzoni. 75 p. Lm 18. – RRPg 68 (1994) 319s (F. *Biville*).

6075 *Morland* Kjell A., To partake in the power and wisdom of God; pragmatic, rhetoric and worldview in Eph. 1-3: TsTKi 64 (1993) 189-203, Norwegian; Eng. 203.

6076 *Orbe* Antonio, [Ef 1,10] Omnia in semetipsum recapitulans: Compostellanum 39 (1994) 7-24.

6077 *O'Brien* Peter T., Divine analysis and comprehensive solution; some priorities from Ephesians 2: RefTR 53 (1994) 130-142.

6078 *Sapaugh* G. P., Is faith a gift? A study of Ephesians 2:8: JGrace 7,12 (Roanoke 1994) 31-43 [< NTAbs 39, p. 56].

6079 a) *Mongillo* Dalmazio, La realtà morale in Paolo; rapporto kerigma-parenesi-consigli; riflessione ispirata da Ef 2.10 [ma in Indice p. 191 'L'agire retto e l'anticipazione della pienezza a partire da Ef. 2.10']; – b) *Niccacci* Alviero, [Ef 5s; Col 3; 1 Pt 2s] Sfondo sapienziale dell'etica dei codici domestici neotestamentari: → 328a, Tarso 2, 1993/4, 135-144 / 43-72.

6080 *Balla* Peter, Is the Law abolished according to Eph 2,15?: EurJT 3 (1994) 6-8; franç. deutsch 9.

6081 *Hiebert* D. E., [Eph 2,30: the believer:] God's creative masterpiece: Direction 23,1 [Fresno 1994] 116-124 [< NTAbs 39, p. 55].

6082 *McCarthy* C., [Eph 3,16-19] God-targeted and God-touched: DocLife 44 (1994) 459-464 [< NTAbs 39, p. 251].

6083 *Gordon* T. David, 'Equipping' ministry in Ephesians 4?: JEvTS 37 (1994) 69-78.

6084 *Kuske* D. P., Ministry according to Ephesians 4:1-16: WisLuQ 91,3 (Mequon 1994) 205-216 [< NTAbs 39, p. 67].

6085 *Harris* W. HallIII, The ascent and descent of Christ in Ephesians 4:9-10: BtS 151 (1994) 198-214.

6086 *Mopsik* Charles [Eph 4,13 'mesure'] La datation du *Chi^cour qomah* d'après un texte néotestamentaire: RevSR 68 (1994) 131-144.

6087 a) *Fee* Gordon D., Some exegetical and theological reflections on Ephesians 4.30 and Pauline pneumatology; – b) *Holman* Charles C., Paul's preaching – cognitive and charismatic: → 140, FWILLIAMS J., Spirit 1994, 129-144 / 145-156.

6088 *Gosnell* Peter W., Ephesians 5:18-20 and mealtime propriety: TyndB 44 (1993) 363-371.

6089 **Fleckenstein** K.-H., Ordnet euch einander unter in der Furcht Christi; die Eheperikope in Eph 5,21-33; Geschichte der Interpretation; Analyse und Aktualisierung des Textes [Diss. DPenna R.]: ForBi 23. Wü 1994, Echter. 331 p. DM 48. 3-429-01633-9 [NTAbs 39, p. 517].

6090 *Vellanickal* M., [Eph 5,21-6,4] Family relationship; a Pauline perspective: Bible Bhashyam 20 (1994) 108-123 [< NTAbs 39, p. 431].

6091 **Rosso** Stefano, 'Mysterium magnum'; Efesini 5,21-33 nell'attuale rito romano [diss. 199]: La parola di Dio celebrata. R 1994, Anselmianum, Pont. Inst. Liturgicum. 96 p.; bibliog. 10-37.

6092 *Best* E., The Haustafel in Ephesians (5,22-6,9): IrBSt 16,4 (1994) 146-160 [< NTAbs 39, p. 431].

G6.3 Ad Philippenses.

6093 **Lightfoot** Joseph B., Philippians: [²1869] Classic Commentaries. Wheaton 1994, Crossway. xviii-192 p. 0-89107-800-2.

6094 **Melck** Richard R., Philippians, Colossians, Philemon: NAmComm, NIV, 1991 ↠ 7,5605; 9,6270: ᴿPerspRelSt 21 (1994) 261-3 (A.D. *Hopkins*: blatant about women).

6095 **Müller** Ulrich B., Der Brief des Paulus an die Philipper: THk NT 11/1, 1993 ↠ 9,6271: ᴿTLZ 119 (1994) 654s (W. *Vogler*).

6096 **O'Brien** Peter T., The epistle to the Philippians: NIGT 1991 ↠ 7,5607 ... 9,6272: ᴿBiblica 75 (1994) 121-5 (J. *Heriban*); Salesianum 56 (1994) 376s (also J. *Heriban*, Eng.).

6097 **Silva** Moisés, Philippians: ExegComm 1992 [Wycliffe taken over by Baker] ↠ 9,6272*: ᴿTrinJ 15 (1994) 115-7 (A. *Hultberg*).

6098 **Witherington** Benᴵᴵᴵ, Friendship and finances in Philippi; the letter of Paul to the Ephesians: NT in context. Ph 1994, Trinity. x-180 p. 1-56338-102-8.

6099 *Black* D.A., Section headings in Philippians: NoTr 8,3 (1994) 27-33 [< NTAbs 39, p. 432].

6100 **Bloomquist** L. Gregory, The function of suffering in Philippians: jNsu 78, 1993 ↠ 9,6273: ᴿCBQ 56 (1994) 580-2 (J. *Plevnik*).

6101 *Cipriani* Settimio, Aspetti 'liturgico-cultuali' nella lettera ai Filippesi: ↠ 947, Mem. ZEDDA S., Theologica 3 (1994) 219-234.

6102 **Geoffrion** Timothy C., The rhetorical purpose and the political and military character of Philippians; a call to stand firm [diss. Ch Lutheran 1992 ᴰ*Krentz* E.]. Lewiston NY 1993, Mellen. iv-267 p. $70. – ᴿBibTB 24 (1994) 199 (D.F. *Watson*).

6103 *Kahler* Christopher, Konflikt, Kompromiss und Bekenntnis; Paulus und seine Gegner im Philipperbrief [Hab.-Verfahren Jena 1992]: KerDo 40 (1994) 47-64.

6104 *Peterlin* Davorin, Paul's letter to the Philippians in the light of disunity in the Church [< diss. Aberdeen 1992 ↠ 9,6279; ᴰ*Marshall* I.]: TyndB 45 (1994) 207-210.

6105 *Peterman* Gerald W., Giving and receiving in Paul's epistles [Greco-Roman conventions in Philippians and in other Pauline writings: diss. London King's College 1992, ᴰ*Stanton* G. ↠ 9,6380]: TyndB 44 (1993) 189-192.

6106 **Pilhover** Peter, Philippi, die erste christliche Gemeinde Europas; mit einem Katalog der Inschriften von Philippi: ev. Hab.-Diss. ᴰ*Koch* D.-A. Münster 1994. – TR 91,91.

6107 *Schenk* Wolfgang, Der Philipperbrief oder die Philipperbriefe des Paulus; eine Antwort an V. *Koperski*: ETL [68 (1992) 331-367] 70 (1994) 122-131.

6108 **Wick** Peter, Der Philipperbrief; der formale Aufbau des Briefs als

Schlüssel zum Verständnis des Inhalts [< Diss. Basel ➤ 9,6283]: BW 135. Stu 1994, Kohlhammer. 209 p. DM 79. 3-17-012706-3 [TLZ 120,344, W. *Schenk*; TR 90,80; NTAbs 39, p. 341].

6109 *Helewa* Giovanni, Carità, discernimento e cammino cristiano; una lettura di Fil 1,9-11: Teresianum 45 (1994) 363-404.
6110 *Jaquette* J. L., A not-so-noble death; figured speech, friendship and suicide in Philippians 1:21-26 [against DROGE A.]: Neotestamentica 28 (1994) 177-190.
6111 *Vollenweider* Samuel, Die Waagschalen von Leben und Tod; zum antiken Hintergrund von Phil 1,21-26: ZNW 85 (1994) 93-115.
6112 *Treiyer* Enrique B., S'en aller et être avec Christ (Philippiens 1/23): ÉTRel 69 (1994) 559-563.
6113 **Baron** Arkadiusz, L'inno cristologico Phil. 2,5-21 nell'esegesi di Mario VITTORINO; studio analitico; diss. ᴰ*Mara* M. Grazia. R 1994, Inst. Patristicum Augustinianum. 140 p.; bibliog. 13-29.
6114 **Fowl** Stephen E., [Phlp 2,6-11; Col 1,15-20 ...] The story of Christ in the ethics of Paul ... hymnic material: jNsu 36, 1990: ᴿCritRR 6 (1993) 234-6 (F. *Thielman*); SvTKv 69 (1993) 189-192 (A. *Eriksson*).
6115 *Gundry* Robert H., Style and substance in 'The myth of God incarnate' [Goulder in HICK J. 1977, 48-86] according to Philippians 2:6-11: ➤ 45, ᶠGOULDER M., Crossing 1994, 271-293.
6116 *Olávarri Goicoechea* Emilio, El himno cristológico de Filipenses 2,6-11: ➤ 33a, ᶠDÍAZ MERCHÁN G., StOvet 22 (1994) 285-303.
6117 *Seeley* D., The background of the Philippians hymn (2:6-11): JHiCr 1 (1994) 49-72 [< NTAbs 39, p. 251].
6118 *Tellbe* Mikael, The sociological factors behind Philippians 3.1-11 and the conflict at Philippi: JStNT 55 (1994) 97-121.
6119 a) *deSilva* David A., New confidence in the flesh; the meaning and function of Philippians 3:2-21; – b) *Silva* Moisés, Systematic theology and the Apostle to the Gentiles: TrinJ 15 (1994) 27-54 / 3-26.
6120 *Pitta* Antonio, La fede e la 'conoscenza di Cristo' (Fil 3,7-11): ParSpV 30 (1994) 171-182.
6120* *Simon* László, Example-examples; thoughts about unity (Phil 3,16-17): ➤ 12b, ᶠBEKES G., 1994, 183-194.
6121 *Neri* Paolo, Nota, Filippesi 4,4-7: BbbOr 36 (1994) 250.

G6.4 **Ad Colossenses.**

6122 **Aletti** Jean-Noël, S. Paul, Épître aux Colossiens 1993 ➤ 9,6299 [Gregorianum 76,155, J. *Galot*]. – ᴿCBQ 56 (1994) 784s (S. P. *Kealy*); EsprVie 104 (1994) 44-46 (É. *Cothenet*); ETL 70 (1990) 178s (R. F. *Collins*); ÉTRel 69 (1994) 426-8 (E. *Cuvillier*); JTS 45 (1994) 681-4 (C. F. D. *Moule*: brave claims! but compelling agreement); NRT 116 (1994) 911s (X. *Jacques*); RB 101 (1994) 631s (J. *Murphy-O'Connor*); RechSR 82 (1994) 309s (P. *Lamarche*); RThom 94 (1994) 163 (H. *Ponsot*: fond fort heureux, mesuré et passionnant; certaines expressions péremptoires, d'autres trop prudentes).
6123 **Aletti** Jean-Noël, Lettera ai Colossesi; introduzione, versione, commento, ᵀ*Torti* R.: Scritti delle origini cr. 12. Bo 1994, Dehoniane. 266 p.; bibliog. p. 240-261. Lᵐ 30. 88-10-20612-0 [NTAbs 38, p. 126; 39, p. 330].
6124 **Barth** M., *Blanke* H., Colossians: AnchorB 34B. NY 1994, Doubleday. xxi-557 p. $34. 0-385-11068-5 [NTAbs 39, p. 515].

6125 **Pokorný** Petr, Colossians, a commentary, ^T*Schatzmann* S., 1991 → 7, 5624... 9,6301: ^RRB 101 (1994) 147 (J. *Murphy-O'Connor*); SvEx 59 (1994) 189-191 (B. *Ericsson*).

6126 **Yates** Roy, Colossians: Epworth comm. 1993 → 9,6304: ^RExpTim 106 (1994s) 123 (J. M. *Court*: not so much polemic as negotiated common ground).

6127 *Aune* Nils Åge, Colossians and the world of magic [in Norwegian]: TsTKi 65 (1994) 97-105; Eng. 105.

6128 **DeMaris** Richard E., The Colossian controversy; wisdom in dispute at Colossae [< 1990 Columbia/Union diss.]: jNsu 96. Shf 1994, JStOT. 170 p. £27.50. 1-85075-473-X [RelStR 21,240, J. W. *Thompson*; TLZ 120,240, E. *Schweizer*].

6129 *Dunn* James D. G., The 'body' in Colossians: → 46, ^FGUNDRY R., To tell 1994, 163-181.

6130 *Hill* Alexander D., Christian character in the marketplace; Colossians, Philemon and the practice of business: Crux 30,3 (1994) 27-34 [< NTAbs 39, p. 252].

6131 *House* H. Wayne, a) The doctrine of salvation in Colossians; – b) The Christian life according to Colossians: BtS 151 (1994) 325-338 / 440-454.

6132 **Wink** W., Engaging the powers 1992 → 8,6624: ^RHorizons 21 (1994) 181s (W. *Brueggemann*); JHisp 2,2 (1994s) 79s (T. M. *Matovina*); RefR 48 (1994s) 55s (P. W. *Zoschke*).

6133 **Kasali** Musande D., [Col 1,5...] The concept of hope in Paul; studies in selected passages: diss. Trinity ev. ^D*Harris* M. 1994. 297 p. 94-32067. – DissA 55 (1994s) p. 1601.

6134 **Arnold** Clinton E., [Col 1,15-20] Powers of darkness 1992 → 8,6626; 9,6314; Leicester 1992, Inter-Varsity. 244 p. £9. 0-85110-966-7: ^REvQ 66 (1994) 369s (N. G. *Wright*).

6135 *Basevi* Claudio, Las características del texto de Col 1,15-20 y su doctrina cristológica: → 22a, ^FCASCIARO J. Biblia 1994, 349-362.

6136 *Helyer* Larry L., Cosmic Christology and Col 1:15-20: JEvTS 37 (1994) 235-246.

6137 *McCarthy* John, Le Christ cosmique et l'âge de l'écologie; une lecture de Col. 1,15-20: NRT 116 (1994) 27-47.

6138 *Attridge* Harold W., [2,8-19] On becoming an angel; rival baptismal theologies at Colossae: → 40, ^FGEORGI D., 1994, 481-498.

6139 *Doignon* Jean, La chair du Christ comme dépouille triomphale; une lecture de Col. 2,15 par HILAIRE de Poitiers: RevSR 68 (1994) 447-452.

6140 *Vergeer* Wim C., *skiá* and *sôma*; the strategy of contextualisation in Col 2:17; a contribution to the quest for a legitimate contextual theology today: Neotestamentica 28 (1994) 379-393.

G6.5 *Ad Philemonem* – Slavery in NT Background.

6141 *Peterson* E., [Phlm] Letter from a Roman jail: ChrToday 37,15 (1993) 38-42 [< NTAbs 38, p. 223].

6142 **Steele** Donald M., Releasing the captives — releasing the captors; the letter to Philemon and the relationship of North American Christians to the peoples of the two-thirds world: diss. Graduate Theological Union,

412   Elenchus of Biblica 10, 1994   [XIII. Pauli epistulae

ᴰ*Waetjen* H. Berkeley 1994. 204 p. 95-11337. – DissA 55 (1994s) p. 3890; RelStR 21,254.
6143 *Haykin* Michael A. G., Praying together; a note on Philemon 22: EvQ 66 (1994) 331-5.

6144 **Bieżuńska-Malowist** Iża, La schiavitù nel mondo antico: Che so? 22. R 1991, Ed. Scient. Ital. 200 p. Lᵐ 25. 88-7104-294-8. – ᴿGnomon 66 (1994) 638-640 (R. *Scholl*).
6145 **Bradley** Keith P., Slavery and rebellion 1989 ➤ 5,6293... 9,6322: Klio 75 (1993) 500s (C. *Mileta*).
6146 **de Bonfils** G., Gli schiavi degli Ebrei nella legislazione del IV secolo [d.C.]; storia di un divieto. Bari 1993, Carucci. 213 p. – ᴿIvra 43 (1992) 162-5 (D. *Piattelli*).
6147 **Fisher** N. R. E., Slavery in classical Greece 1993 ➤ 9,6327: ᴿPrudentia 26,2 (1994) 57-63 (V. J. *Gray*).
6148 **Ghottès** Mustapha, Index thématique des références à l'esclavage et à la dépendance, 5. TACITE: Ann. Litt. Besançon 488. P 1993, BLettres. 484 p.
6149 **Giles** Kevin, The biblical argument for slavery; can the Bible mislead? A case study in hermeneutics: EvQ 66 (1994) 3-17.
6150 **Kudlien** Fridolf, Sklaven-Mentalität 1991 ➤ 8,6646; 9,6332: ᴿAntClas 63 (1994) 547s (J. A. *Straus*); Gnomon 66 (1994) 600-4 (J. *Christes*); HZ 259 (1994) 167s (G. *Prachner*).
6151 **Marinović** L. P., *al.*, Die Sklaverei in den östlichen Provinzen des Römischen Reiches im 1.-3. Jt., ᵀ*Kriz* Jaroslav, *al.*: Übersetzungen ausländischer Arbeiten zur antiken Sklaverei 5, 1992 ➤ 8,6647: ᴿGnomon 66 (1994) 731s (R. *Klein*); Latomus 53 (1994) 881-3 (J. *Annequin*).

G6.6 **Ad Thessalonicenses.**

6151* **Adinolfi** Marco, La prima lettera ai Tessalonicesi nel mondo greco-romano 1990 ➤ 6,6606... 8,6662: ᴿCiuD 206 (1993) 637s (J. *Gutiérrez*); CritRR 6 (1993) 195-7 (P. *Zilonka*).
6152 **Balthasar** Hans Urs von, Thessalonicher- und Pastoralbriefe des heiligen Paulus 1992 ➤ 9,6336: ᴿTPQ 142 (1994) 411s (S. *Stahr*: wie er sagt, für Gebet, nicht Exegese).
6153 **Fausti** Silvano, La fine del tempo; prima lettera ai Tessalonicesi, commentario spirituale. CasM 1994, Piemme. 135 p. 88-384-2235-4.
6154 **Morris** León, 1-2 Thessalonians²ʳᵉᵛ 1991 ➤ 7,5661: ᴿConcordiaTQ 58 (1994) 168-170 (P. J. *Bayens*).
6155 **Müller** Peter, Anfänge der Paulusschule... 2 ThesCol 1987 ➤ 5,6312: ᴿSNTU 19 (1994) 240s (R. *Oberforcher*).
6156 **Wanamaker** C. A., The epistles to the Thessalonians: NIGT 1990 ➤ 6,6621... 9,6339: ᴿCurrTM 21 (1994) 141s (E. *Krentz*).
6156* **Bassler** Josette M., Pauline theology I Thes Phlp Gal Phlm 1991 ➤ 7,290; 8,6067: ᴿGregorianum 75 (1994) 525-533 (M. *Lubomirski*).
6157 *Crofts* M., Metaphors in the five Ts [Thess Tim Tit]: NoTr 8,4 (1994) 35-52 [< NTAbs 39, p. 433].
6158 **Donfried** Karl P., *Marshall* I. Howard, The theology of the shorter Pauline letters [Thess Phlp Phlm] 1993 ➤ 9,6346: ᴿNRT 116 (1994) 912s (X. *Jacques*).

6159 **Erlemann** Kurt, Naherwartung und Parusieverzögerung im NT; ein Beitrag zur Frage religiöser Zeiterfahrung: Hab.-Diss. ᴰ*Berger* K. (+ 3). Heidelberg 1994. – TR 91,90.

6160 *Grzymska* Urszuła, ❷ De laeto aspectu parusiae in epistulis Pauli ad Thessalonicenses: RuBi 47 (1994) 247-255.

6161 **Hong Sungkook**, Paul's efforts at consolidation; a study of First Thessalonians and Philippians: diss. Boston Univ. ᴰ*Sampley* J.P. 1994. 254 p. 95-00833. – DissA 55 (1994s) p. 2002.

6162 *Koester* Helmut, Archäologie und Paulus in Thessalonike: ➤ 40, ꟳGEORGI D. 1994, 393-404.

6163 *Teani* Maurizio, Lo stile missionario di Paolo alla luce di 1 Ts 2.1-12: ➤ 147, Mem. ZEDDA S., Theologica 3 (1994) 173-201.

6164 *Winter* Bruce W., The entries and ethics of orators and Paul (1 Thessalonians 2:1-12): TyndB 44 (1993) 55-74.

6165 *Wick* Peter, Ist 1 Thess 2,13-16 antijüdisch? Der rhetorische Gesamtzusammenhang des Briefes als Interpretationshilfe für eine einzelne Perikope: TZBas 50 (1994) 9-23.

6166 *Schlueter* Carol J., Filling up the measure; polemical highlights in 1 Thess 2.14-16: jNsu 98. Shf 1994, JStOT. 226 p. £37.50. 1-80775-479-9 [JTS 46,654-9, R. *Griffith-Jones*; NTAbs 39, p. 154; TLZ 120, 527-9, I. *Broer*].

6167 *Gilliard* Frank D., Paul and the killing of the prophets in 1 Thess. 2:15: NT 36 (1994) 259-270.

6168 **Jurgensen** Herbert, Saint Paul et la Parousie; 1 Thes 4,13-5,11 dans l'exégèse moderne et contemporaine: diss. ᴰ*Trocmé* É. Strasbourg 1992. 660 p. – RTLv 26, p. 537.

6169 *Jurgensen* H., Awaiting the return of Christ; a re-examination of 1 Thessalonians 4:13-5:11 from a Pentecostal perspective: JPentecT 4 (1994) 81-113 [< NTAbs 39, p. 68].

6170 *a) Michaels* J. Ramsey, [1 Thess 4,15] Everything that rises must converge; Paul's word from the Lord; – *b) Fee* Gordon D., Pneuma and eschatology in 2 Thessalonians 2,1-2; a proposal about 'testing the prophets' and the purpose of 2 Thessalonians: ➤ 46, ꟳGUNDRY R., To tell 1994, 182-195 / 196-215.

6171 *Cosby* Michael R., Hellenistic formal receptions and Paul's use of *apántēsis* in 1 Thessalonians 4:17: BuBR 4 (1994) 15-33.

6172 **Fung** Ronald Y.K., ❸ Commentary on II Thessalonians. Hong Kong 1990, Tien Dao. 388 p. + 15 p. index. – ᴿJian Dao 1 (1994) 126-9 (K.K. *Yeo*, Eng.).

6173 **Holland** Glenn, The tradition... 2 Thess: HermUnT 24, ᴰ1988 ➤ 4,6302 ... 7,5672: ᴿProcGM 13 (1993) 259-265 (D.F. *Watson*); reply 267-273.

6174 **Menken** Maarten J.J., 2 Thessalonians; facing the end with sobriety: [ᴱ*Court* J.] NT Readings. L 1994, Routledge. 171 p. £30; pa. £10. 0-414-09504-2; -5-0 [NTAbs 19, p. 519]. – ᴿExpTim 106 (1994s) 247 (N. *Richardson*).

6175 **Silva** Valmor da, Segunda Epístola aos Tessalonicenses (não é o fim do mundo). Petrópolis 1992, Vozes. 122 p. – ᴿREB 53 (1993) 480-5 (Maria Laura *Gorgulho*).

6176 *Barnouin* M., Un 'lieu intermédiaire' mythique en 2 Thess 2.7: NTS 40 (1994) 471.
6177 *Merk* Otto, Überlegungen zu 2 Thess 2,13-17: → 31*, ᶠDAUTZENBERG G., Nach 1994, 405-414.
6177* *Grilli* Alberto, [2 Tess 3,6-9.11] Una pagina diatribica nell'apostolo Paolo: → 42, ᶠGIGANTE M., 279-283.

G7 Epistulae pastorales.

6178 *Arichea* Daniel C., [Deutero-] Authorship and translation: BTrans 44 (1993) 331-340.
6179 **Harding** Mark, Tradition and rhetoric in the Pastoral Epistles: diss. ᴰ*Beker* J. Princeton Theol. Sem. 1994. 297 p. 94-30033. – DissA 55 (1994s) p. 2001.
6179* *Kowalski* Beate, Zur Funktion und Bedeutung der alttestamentlichen Zitate und Anspielungen in den Pastoralbriefen: SNTU 19 (1994) 45-68.
6180 **Lea** Thomas D., *Griffin* Hayne P.ᴶ, 1.2 Timothy, Titus: NAmerComm 34, 1992 → 8,6689; 9,6365: ᴿBtS 151 (1994) 499s (T. L. *Constable*).
6181 *Marshall* I. H., 'Sometimes only orthodox' — is there more to the Pastoral Epistles?: EpworthR 20,3 (1993) 12-24 [< NTAbs 38, p. 225].
6182 **Merkel** Helmaut, Die Pastoralbriefe: NTD 9/1, 1991 → 7,5679; 9,6366: ᴿSvEx 59 (1994) 191s (C. C. *Caragounis*).
6183 **Oberlinner** Lorenz, Die Pastoralbriefe 1. 1 Tim.: TheolKomm 11/2. FrB 1994, Herder. 312 p. ᴅᴍ 95. 3-451-23224-3 [TR 91,273].
6184 *Pervo* R. I., Romancing an oft-neglected stone; the pastoral epistles and the [i.e. as an] epistolary novel: JHiCr 1 (1994) 25-47 [< NTAbs 39, p. 253, C. R. *Matthews*].
6185 **Redalié** Yann, Paul après Paul [the Pastorals are non-Pauline and date from the end of the first century]. Geneva 1994, Labor et Fides. 517 p. Fs 60. 2-8309-0744-2. – ᴿExpTim 106 (1994s) 213 (E. *Best*).
6186 *Skarsaune* O., Heresy and the pastoral epistles: Themelios 20,1 (1994) 9-14 [NTAbs 39, p. 253].
6187 **Towner** Philip H., 1-2 Timothy & Titus: IVP NT comm. 14. DG/ Leicester 1994, Inter-Varsity. 271 p. $16. 0-8308-1814-6 / UK 0-85111-676-0 [NTAbs 39, p. 155]. – ᴿTBR 7,3 (1994s) 50 (G. *Stanton*).
6188 **Wagener** Ulrike, Die Ordnung des 'Hauses Gottes'; der Ort von Frauen in der Ekklesiologie und Ethik der Pastoralbriefe [ev. Diss. Münster, ᴰ*Rese* M.]: WUNT 2/65. Tü 1994, Mohr. x-293 p.; Bibliog. 247-266. 3-16-146304-8 [TR 91,273].
6188* **Young** Frances, Theology of the pastoral letters. C 1994, Univ. xi-170 p. £27, pa. £10. 0-521-37036-1; -931-4. – ᴿExpTim 106 (1994s) 213 (D. *Howell*); TBR 7,3 (1994) 29s (J. *Brox*).

G7.2 1-2 ad Timotheum.

6189 *Motyer* Steve, Expounding 1 Timothy 2:8-15: VoxEvca 24 (1994) 91-102.
6190 *McDermond* J. E., Modesty; the Pauline tradition and change in East Africa: African Christian Studies 9,2 (Nairobi 1993) 30-47 [< NTAbs 39, p. 253, C. R. *Matthews*: 1 Tim 2,8-15 defines modesty as the avoidance of braids, jewelry, etc. — which in East Africa are not associated with immorality].
6191 **Kroeger** Richard C. & Catherine C., [1 Tim 2,11] I suffer not a woman ...

1992 → 9,6384:   ᴿAndrUnSem 32 (1994) 138-140 (Beatrice S. *Neall*); ChrSchR 24 (1994) 313s (Aileen *Van Ginkel*).
6192 *Baugh* S.M.,   The Apostle among the Amazons [... allegation that 1 Tim 2,12 was meant only against radical feminists as at Ephesus]:   WestTJ 56 (1994) 153-171.
6193 *Perriman* Andrew C.,   What Eve did, what women shouldn't do; the meaning of *authentéō* in 1 Timothy 2:12 ['instigate']: TyndB 44 (1993) 129-142.
6194 *Saucy* Robert L.,   [1 Tim 2,12] Women's prohibition to teach men; an investigation into its meaning and contemporary application: JEvTS 37 (1994) 79-97.
6195 *Lieu* Judith M.,   [1 Tim 2,15] Circumcision, women and salvation: NTS 40 (1994) 358-370.
6196 *Young* Frances M.,   [1 Tim 3; Tit 5; Ign.] On *episkopos* and *presbýteros*: JTS 45 (1994) 142-8.
6197 *Campbell* R. Alastair,   [1 Tim 3,16] Identifying the faithful sayings in the Pastoral Epistles: JStNT 54 (1994) 73-86.
6198 *Marcheselli-Casale* Cesare,   Gesù di Nazaret il Risorto-Asceso centro vitale della comunità ecclesiale protocristiana; considerazioni intorno al valore pasquale di 1 Tm 3,16: → 147, Mem. ZEDDA S., Theologica 3 (1994) 235-276.

6199 **Martin** Sean C.,   Pauli testamentum; a study of 2 Timothy in the light of intertestamental legends of the last words of Moses: diss. Pont. Univ. Gregoriana, ᴰ*Vanni* U. Rome 1994. 409 p. – RTLv 26, p. 538.
6200 ᵀᴱ**Pietersma** Albert, [2 Tim 3,8] The apocryphon of Jannes and Jambres the magicians, P. Chester Beatty XVI (with new editions of P. Vindobonensis gr. 29456 inv. + 20628 verso & BL Cotton Tiberius B v.f. 87): ÉPR 119. Leiden 1994, Brill. xvii-439 p. ƒ170. 90-04-09938-7 [BL 95,164, M.A. *Knibb*].

G7.3   Ad Titum.

6201 *Elliott* J.K.,   A Greek-Coptic (Sahidic) fragment of Titus-Philemon (0205):   NT 36 (1994) 183-5; 4 fig.; 190-5, Coptic text and apparatus.
6202 **Campbell** S. Alastair,   [Tit 1,7]   The elders; seniority within earliest Christianity: diss. London 1992, ᴰ*Stanton* G. – TyndB 44 (1993) 183-7.
6203 *Thiselton* A.C.,   The logical role of the liar paradox in Titus 1:12.13; a dissent from the commentaries in the light of philosophical and logical analysis: BInterp 2/2 (1994) 207-223 [< NTAbs 39, p. 254: 'Cretans are liars' is put in the mouth of a Cretan].

G8   Epistula ad Hebraeos.

6204 **Casalini** Nello,   Agli Ebrei; discorso di esortazione: SBF Anal 54, 1992 → 9,6398:   ᴿCBQ 56 (1994) 132-4 (J. *Swetnam*).
6205 *Casalini* Nello,   Per un commento a Ebrei: LA 44 (1994) 111-214; Eng. 612.
6206 ᴱ**Corona** Raimondo,   Lettera agli Ebrei; lettura esegetico-esistenziale: Atti [*Bottini* G.C.; *Adinolfi* M.] della Nona Settimana Biblica Abruzzese, Tocco Casauria 4-9 luglio 1994. L'Aquila 1994, Curia OFM. 257 p.
6207 **Ellingworth** Paul, The epistle to the Hebrews: NIGTC, 1993 → 9,6399 [STEv 7,77s, R. *Jones*]:   ᴿCBQ 56 (1994) 589-591 (J. *Swetnam*: a

translator by profession should give a full translation); Neotestamentica 28 (1994) 601-3 (R. J. *Sim*); RefTR 53 (1994) 143-5 (D. *Robinson*).

6208 **Grässer** Erich, An die Hebräer II (7,1 - 10,18]: EkK 17.2. Z/Neuk 1993, Benziger/Neuk.-V. 3-545-23125-9 / 3-7887-1443-3 [TLZ 120,791, C.-P. *März*]. – ᴿBiKi 48 (1993) 232s (C. *März*, 1); 233s (R. *Russ* über seine Aufsätze 1992).

6208* **Hegermann** Harald, Der Brief an die Hebräer 1988 ► 4,6340: ᴿSNTU 19 (1994) 234s (R. *Oberforcher*, auch über WOLFF C., 2 Cor 1989)

6209 *Heinrich* Jean-Marie, Lecture laïque d'une lettre: aux Hébreux: ► 239*d*, Exégèse 1994, 153-171.

6210 **Lane** William L., Hebrews: Word Comm 47, 1991 ► 9,6401: ᴿWestTJ 56 (1994) 203-6 (D. G. *McCartney*).

6211 **Lane** William L., Hebrews; a call to commitment. Peabody MA 1988, Hendrickson. 183 p. $8 pa. 0-943575-03-6. – ᴿJEvTS 37 (1994) 436s (G. L. *Cockerill*).

6212 **Marconi** Gilberto, Omelie e catechesi cristiane nel I secolo; lettera agli Ebrei, Lettera di Giacomo, Prima lettera di Pietro, Lettera di Giuda, Seconda lettera di Pietro. Bo 1994, Dehoniane. 189 p. Lᵐ 22. 88-10-40259-6 [NTAbs 39, p. 337].

6213 **Weiss** H.-F., Der Brief an die Hebräer 1991 ► 7,5725... 9,6406: ᴿRHPR 74 (1994) 217s (C. *Grappe*).

6214 **Backhaus** Knut, Der Neue Bund und das Werden der Kirche; die *diathēkē*-Deutung des Hebräerbriefs im Rahmen der frühchristlichen Theologiegeschichte: kath. Hab.-Diss., ᴰ*Kertelge* K. Münster 1994. – TR 91,91.

6215 *Black* David A., Literary artistry in the Epistle to the Hebrews: FgNt 7 (1994) 43-51.

6216 *Cahill* Michael, A home for the homily; an approach to Hebrews: IrTQ 60 (1994) 141-8.

6217 *DeSilva* David A., *a*) Despising shame; a cultural-anthropological investigation of the Epistle to the Hebrews: JBL 113 (1994) 439-461; – *b*) The epistle to the Hebrews in social-scientific perspective: RestQ 36 (1994) 1-21.

6218 *Duerksen* Paul D., Images of Jesus Christ as perfect high priest for God's people: QRMin 14 (1994) 321-336.

6219 **Dunnill** John, Covenant and sacrifice... Hb: SNTS mg 75, 1992 ► 8, 6737; 9,6409: ᴿCBQ 56 (1994) 370s (C. R. *Koester*); EvQ 66 (1994) 178-180 (P. *Ellingworth*); JTS 45 (1994) 257-9 (Marie E. *Isaacs*); NT 36 (1994) 294s (R. *Williamson*).

6220 *a*) *Dussaut* Louis, Histoire et structure de l'Épître aux Hébreux; – *b*) *Schenker* Adrian, Sacrifices anciens, sacrifice nouveau dans l'Épître aux Hébreux; – *c*) *Moingt* Joseph, La fin du sacrifice; – *d*) *Massonet* Jean, Note sur la fête juive de Kippour: LumièreV 43,217 (1994) 5-13 / 71-76 / 15-31 / 77-86.

6221 **Ekem** John D. Kwamena, Priesthood in context; a study of Akan traditional priesthood in dialogal relation to the Priest-Christology of the Epistle to the Hebrews...: ev. Diss. ᴰ*Ahrens* T. Hamburg 1994. – TR 91,96.

6222 **Guthrie** George H., The structure of Hebrews; a text-linguistic analysis: NT supp. 73. Leiden 1994, Brill. xix-161 p. ƒ100. 90-04-09855-6 [Biblica 76,587-590, A. *Vanhoye*; NTAbs 39, p. 151; RB 102,428, P. *Garuti*].

6223 **Josuttis** Manfred, Über alle Engel, politische Predigten Heb 1990 ► 8,6743: ᴿBiKi 48 (1993) 234s (R. *Russe*).

6224 *Koester* Craig R., The Epistle to the Hebrews in recent study: CuRB 2 (1994) 123-145.

6225 **Henderson** John, The Christology of Hebrews in relation to Jewish literature: diss. ᴰ*McCullough* J. Edinburgh 1994. – RTLv 26,537.

6226 *Hofius* Otfried, Biblische Theologie im Lichte des Hebräerbriefes: ➤ 303a, New Directions 1992/4, 108-125.

6227 **Isaacs** Marie, Sacred space; jNsu 73, 1992 ➤ 8,6742; 9,6411: ᴿInterpretation 48 (1994) 98.100 (J.M. *Scholer*).

6228 **Leschert** D.F., Hermeneutical foundations of Hebrews; a study in the validity of the epistle's interpretation of some core citations from the . Psalms [diss. Fuller Sem. Pasadena, ᴰ*Fuller* D.P.]: NAmBapD 10. Lewiston NY 1994, Mellen. xvi-286 p. $100. 0-7734-2860-7 [NTAbs 39, p. 519].

6229 **Lindars** B., Theology of Heb 1991 ➤ 7,5712: ᴿJBL 113 (1994) 353-5 (L.D. *Hurst*).

6230 **Löhr** Hermut, Umkehr und Sünde im Hebräerbrief: BZNW 73. B 1994, de Gruyter. ix-375 p. DM 168. 3-11-014202-3 [TLZ 120,1079, H.-F. *Weiss*].

6231 *McCullough* J.C., Hebrews in recent scholarship: IrBSt 16,2/3 (1994) 66-86, 108-20 [< NTAbs 39, p. 71s].

6232 *a) März* Claus-Peter, Ein 'Aussenseiter' im NT; zur Aktualität des Hebräerbriefs; – *b) Söding* Thomas, Gemeinde auf dem Weg; Christsein nach dem Hebräerbrief; – *c) Grässer* Erich, 'Viele Male und auf vielerlei Weise...' Kommentare zum Hebräerbrief 1968 bis 1991: BiKi 48 (1993) 173-9 / 180-7 / [188-197-205 *Trummer* P.; *Fuchs* O.] / 206-215.

6233 *Matera* Frank J., Moral exhortation... and doctrinal exposition in the letter to the Hebrews: TorJT 10 (1994) 169-182.

6234 **Pentecost** J. Dwight, A faith that endures; the Book of Hebrews applied to the real issues of life. GR 1992, Discovery. xii-237 p. $10. – ᴿBtS 151 (1994) 244s (R.B. *Zuck*: clear, cogent).

6235 *Porter* Stanley E., The date of the composition of Hebrews and use of the present tense-form [not determinative]: ➤ 45, ᶠGOULDER M., Crossing 1994, 295-313.

6236 **Scholer** John M., Proleptic priests 1991 ➤ 7,5718... 9,6416: ᴿÉTRel 68 (1993) 429s (P. *Magne de la Croix*).

6237 *Stanley* Steve, The structure of Hebrews from three perspectives: TyndB 45 (1994) 245-271.

6238 *Tsangalides* Ioannis A., Ⓖ The epistle to the Hebrews [addressed to Jewish Christians of Caesarea; nautical terms...]: TAth 64 (1993) 209-217; Eng. 880.

6239 *Vogler* Werner, Johannes und der Hebräerbrief: TVers 18 (1993) 83-87.

6240 *Zani* Lorenzo, Il sacerdozio di Cristo e dei cristiani nella lettera agli Ebrei: Presbyteri 28 (1994) 621-7. 702-98. 777-786...

6241 **Franco Martínez** Cesar A., [Heb 2,9-10] Jesucristo, su persona y su obra en la carta a los Hebreos. 1992 ➤ 9,6422: M 1992, Ciudad Nueva. 421 p. – ᴿGregorianum 75 (1994) 348s (J. *Galot*); CiuD 207 (1994) 203s (J. *Gutiérrez*); RBibArg 55 (1993) 127s (A.J. *Levoratti*); ScripTPamp 26 (1994) 795s (L.F. *Mateo-Seco*).

6242 *Enns* Peter E., Creation and re-creation; Psalm 95 and its interpretation in Hebrews 3:1-4:13: WestTJ 55 (1993) 255-280.

6243 *Swetnam* James, A possible structure of Hebrews 3,7-10,39: MeliT 45,2 (1994) 127-141 [< NTAbs 39, p. 435].

6243* **Carrón** Julián, Jesús, el Mesías manifestado; tradición literaria y trasfondo judío de Heb 3,19-26: S. Justino, StSem NT 2. M 1993, Ciudad Nueva. 361 p. 88-06937-51-2. – ᴿEstAg 29 (1994) 168s (R. A. *Díez*); ScripTPamp 26 (1994) 793s (J. M. *Casciaro*).

6244 *Cowdery* Ann H., Hebrews 4:1-13 [meaning of rest]: Interpretation 48 (1994) 282-6.

6245 *Kempson* Wayne R., Hebrews 5:1-8 ['impossible to return'; but with faith, no fear]: RExp 91 (1994) 567-573.

6246 *Hasitschka* Martin, 'Er lernte an dem, was er litt'; Gedanken zu Hebr 5,7-10: Entschluss 49,1 (1994) 4-6 (-33, *al.*, über Gehorsam).

6247 *Worley* David R., Fleeing to two immutable things, God's oath-taking and oath-witnessing; the use of litigant oath in Hebrews 6:12-20: ➤ 85*b*, ᶠOLBRICHT T. RestQ 36 (1994) 223-236.

6248 *Garuti* P., Ebrei 7,1-28; un problema giuridico: DivThom 97,2 (1994) 9-105 [< NTAbs 39, p. 72].

6249 *Finney* T. J., A proposed reconstruction of Hebrews 7.28a in P⁴⁶: NTS 40 (1994) 472s.

6250 **Gilmour** Michael J., The earthly tabernacle of Hebrews 9:1-5: diss. ᴰ*Johnson* D. Providence (Canada) College 1994. 128 p. MM 89170. – (DissA-disk) MAI 33 (1995) p. 60. No abstract.

6251 *Cahill* Michael, The implications of *episynagōgē* in Hebrews 10,25; the first Eucharistic homily?: QLtg 74 (1993) 198-207; franç. 207.

6252 *Swetnam* James, Hebrews 10,30-31; a suggestion: Biblica 75 (1994) 388-394.

6253 **Rose** Christian, [Heb 10,32-12,3] Die Wolke der Zeugen; eine exegetisch-traditionsgeschichtliche Untersuchung zu Heb 10,32-12,3 [Diss. Tübingen]: WUNT 2/60. Tü 1994, Mohr. xi-445 p. DM 128. 3-16-146012-X [BL 95,166, C. J. A. *Hickling*; TLZ 120,887, H. *Löhr*].

6254 **Cosby** Michael R., The rhetorical composition and function of Hebrews 11 in light of example lists in antiquity 1988 ➤ 4,6362; 6,6721: ᴿJEvTS 37 (1994) 438 (Aida B. *Spencer*).

6255 *Tenšek* Tomislav Z., Heb 11,13; Flp 3,20; biblical-theological problem of banishment (in Croatian): BogSmot 63 ('Prognanici i izbieglice', profughi/esiliati 1993) 301-316.

6256 **Willis** Timothy M., 'Obey your leaders'; Hebrews 13 and leadership in the Church: ➤ 89*b*, ᶠOLBRICHT T., RestQ 36 (1994) 316-326.

6257 *Walker* Peter, Jerusalem in Hebrews 13:9-14 and the dating of the epistle: TyndB 45 (1994) 39-71.

G9.1 **1 Petri.**

6258 **Brox** Norbert, La primera carta de Pedro: BtEstrB 73. S 1994, Sígueme. – ᴿQVidCr 174 (1994) 119 (D. *Roure*).

6259 **Goppelt** Leonhard, A commentary on 1 Peter, ᵀ*Alsuy* J. E., 1993 ➤ 9,6433 [STEv 7,77, T. *Racca* (after Goppelt:) 'by Ferdinand Hahn' ??].

6260 **Knoch** Otto, 1-2 Pt Jud 1990 ➤ 6,6736 ... 9,6436: ᴿTR 90 (1994) 120-9 (F. R. *Prostmeier*).

6261 *Dschulnigg* Peter, *a*) Aspekte des Kirchenväterverständnisses im 1. Petrusbrief: ➤ 95, ᶠPOTTMEYER, Kirche sein 1994, 21-29; – *b*) Aspekte und Hintergrund der Theologie des 1. Petrusbriefes: TGL 84 (1994) 318-329.

6262 *Lips* Hermann von,   Die Haustafel als 'Topos' im Rahmen der ur-christlichen Paränese; Beobachtungen anhand des 1. Petrusbriefes und des Titusbriefes: NTS 40 (1994) 261-280.

6263 **Metzner** Reiner, Die Rezeption des Matthäusevangeliums im 1. Petrusbrief: Diss. D*Wolff* C. Berlin 1994. – TR 91,93.

6264 *Parker* David C.,   The eschatology of 1 Peter: BibTB 24 (1994) 27-32.

6265 *Reiser* Marius, Die Eschatologie des 1. Petrusbriefs: ➤ 113, FSCHNACKEN-BURG R., 1993/4, 164-181.

6266 *Shimada* Kazuhito, Is 1 Peter dependent on Romans? AnJapB 19 (1993) 87-137 [< ZNW 85,292].

6267 *Thompson* James W.,   The rhetoric of 1 Peter: ➤ 89*b*, FOLBRICHT T., RestQ 36 (1994) 237-250.

6268 **Thurén** Lauri, The rhetorical strategy of 1 Peter, D1990 ➤ 6,6746; 7,5762: RSvTKv 69 (1993) 29s (W. *Übelacker*).

6269 *Volf* Miroslav,   Soft difference; theological reflections on the relation between Church and culture in 1 Peter: ➤ 398, Church, ExAud 10 (1994) 15-30.

6270 **Feldmeier** Reinhard, [1 Pt 2,11] Die Christen als Fremde... 1 Pt: WUNT 64, 1992 ➤ 8,6801; 9,6449: RCBQ 56 (1994) 792s (J. H. *Elliott*); JBL 113 (1994) 743-5 (W. L. *Schutter*); RHPR 74 (1994) 218s (C. *Grappe*); TR 90 (1994) 385s (T. *Söding*).

6270* *Slaughter* James R.,   Peter's instructions to husbands in 1 Peter 3,7: ➤ 21, FCAMPBELL D., Integrity 1994, 175-185.

6271 *Busto* José Ramón, [1 Pt 4,13] 'Alegraos según compartís los padecimientos de Cristo' [... aportación de l'A.T.]: Manresa 65 (1993) 139-152.

G9.2   2 Petri.

6272 **Bénétreau** S.,   La deuxième épître de Pierre; l'épître de Jude: CommÉv 16. Vaux/S 1994, EDIFAC. 320 p. F 145. 2-904407-15-4 [NTAbs 39, p. 149].

6273 **Paulsen** Henning,   Der zweite Petrusbrief und der Judasbrief 1992 ➤ 8,6808; 9,6457: RCarthaginensia 10 (1994) 184s (R. *Sanz Valdivieso*); CBQ 56 (1994) 381s (J. C. *Turro*); JBL 113 (1994) 745s (B. A. *Pearson*: many questions different from predecessor KNOPF); SNTU 19 (1994) 246 (A. *Fuchs*).

6274 *Taeger* Jens-W.,   [2 Pt] Das Einverständnis mit den Texten: ➤ 31*, FDAUTZENBERG G., Nach 1994, 619-633.

6275 *O'Keefe* Mark, [2 Pt 1,4] Theosis and the Christian life; toward integrating Roman Catholic ethics and spirituality: ÉglT 25 (1994) 47-63.

6276 *Peterson* R. A., [2 Pt 2,20] Apostasy: Presbyterion 19,1 (1993) 17-31 [< NTAbs 38, p. 240].

6277 *Dupont-Roc* Roselyne,   Le motif de la création selon 2 Pierre 3: RB 101 (1994) 95-114; Eng. 95s.

G9.4   Epistula Jacobi... data on both apostles James.

6278 **Frankemölle** Hubert, Der Brief des Jacobus 1 / 2-5: ÖkTbK 17. Wü 1994, Echter. 365 p. DM 58 / 395 p. DM 64. 3-579-00517-0; -8-9 [RelStR 21,240, L. T. *Johnson*; TLZ 120,650, E. *Baasland*].

6279 **Hodges** Z. C., The epistle of James [Jesus' half-brother]; proven character through testing, ᴱFARSTAD A. L., *Wilkin* R. N.   Irving TX 1994, Grace Ev. Soc.   128 p.   0-9641-3920-0 [NTAbs 39, p. 151].

6280 ᵀᴱ**Schnider** Franz,   La lettera di Giacomo 1992 → 8,8817; 9,6467:   ᴿCC 145 (1994,3) 204 (D. *Scaiola*); CiuD 206 (1993) 232s (J. *Gutiérrez*).

6281 **Stulac** George M., James 1993 → 9,6468:   ᴿBtS 151 (1994) 373s (T. L. *Constable*: helpful).

6282 **Townsend** Michael J.,   The Epistle of James: Epworth Comm.   L 1994, Epworth.   xxxviii-176 p.   0-7162-0500-9.

6283 **Ahrens** Matthias, Arm und Reich im Jakobusbrief — eine sozial-geschichtliche Untersuchung: ev. Diss. ᴰ*Paulsen* H. Hamburg 1994. – TR 91,96.

6284 *Camp* Ashby L.,   Another view on the structure of James: RestQ 36 (1994) 111-9.

6285 **Cargal** Timothy B.,   Restoring the diaspora; discursive structure and purpose in the epistle of James: SBL diss. 144, 1993 [ᴰ*Patte* D., Vanderbilt]. Atlanta 1993, Scholars. xiii-245. $60; pa. $40.   1-55540-861-3 [NTAbs 38, p. 128]. – ᴿCBQ 56 (1994) 583s (P. H. *Davids*).

6286 **Chester** A., (p. 1-62) The theology of the letters of James, [*Martin* R. P.] Peter, and Jude: NTTheol.   C 1994, Univ.   xii-189 p. $45; pa. $16.   0-521-35631-8; -59-8 [NTAbs 39,333]. – ᴿExpTim 106 (1994s) 213 (D. *Horrell*); TBR 7,3 (1994s) (R. *Morgan*).

6287 *Frankemölle* Hubert,   Der Jakobusbrief; Weisung für ein gelingendes Leben: BiKi 48 (1993) 141-6 [*al.* halaka, Mt Paulus, 117-140].

6288 **Greenlee** J. H.,   An exegetical summary of James.   Dallas 1993, Summer Institute of Linguistics.   235 p. $10.   0-88312-622-2 [NTAbs 39, p. 334].

6289 **Hartin** Patrick J.,   James and the Q sayings of Jesus: jNsu 47, 1991 → 9,6471:   ᴿTLZ 119 (1994) 1078-80 (M. *Hüneberg*).

6290 **Klein** Martin, 'Ergon teleion'; Vollkommenheit, Gesetz und Gericht Gottes als theologische Themen des Jakobusbriefes: ev. Diss. ᴰ*Balz* H. Bochum 1994. 300 p. > BW. – RTLv 26, p. 537; TR 91,93.

6290* **Ludwig** Martina, Wort als Gesetz... Jakobusbrief: EurHS 23/502.   Fra 1994, Lang.   217 p. DM 64.   3-631-45437-1.

6291 *a) Pratscher* Wilhelm,   Der Herrenbruder Jakobus, seine Gestalt in Geschichte und Legende; – *b) Hahn* Ferdinand,   Paulus und Jakobus beim Apostelkonvent; die Einigung in Jerusalem als Modell für ökumenische Verständigung: Entschluss 48,9s (1994) 5-13 / 14-18.27.

6292 *Pretorius* E. A. C.,   Coherency in James; a soteriological intent?: Neotestamentica 28 (1994) 541-555.

6293 *Stander* H. F., 'n Interpretasie van die beeld van die brander [sea-wave] in Jakobus 1:6: SkrifK 15,2 (1994) 383-390 [< NTAbs 39, p. 436].

6294 *Wolmarans* J. L. P.,   Male and female sexual imagery; James 1:14-15,18: AcPatrByz 5 (Pretoria 1994) 134-141.

6295 *Camroux* Martin F., [James 1,19-27] What kind of religion do we have? ExpTim 106 (1994s) 307s: 'Nothing more foolish was ever said [than Eisenhower's] I don't care what kind of religion a man has, so long as he's religious': religion can promote good or diabolical evil.

6296 *Baker* William R., 'Above all else'; contexts of the call for verbal integrity in James 5,12: JStNT 54 (1994) 57-71.

6297 *Warrington* Keith, The significance of Elijah in James 5:13-18: EvQ 66 (1994) 217-227.
6298 *Johnston* Wendell G., Does James give believers a pattern for dealing with sickness and healing? → 21, [F]CAMPBELL D., Integrity 1994, 164-174.
6299 *Thomas* J. C., The devil; disease and deliverance; James 5:14-16: JPentec 2 (Shf 1993) 23-50 [< NTAbs 38, p. 227].
6300 *Bottini* G. C., La preghiera di Elia in Giac 5,17s; studio della tradizione biblica e giudaica: SBFAnal 16. J 1981, Franciscan. 200 p. – [R]RivB 42 (1994) 357s (G. *Marconi*).

G9.6 Epistula Judae.

6301 **Bauckham** Richard, Jude and the relatives of Jesus 1990 → 6,6788 ... 9,6480: [R]CiuD 207 (1994) 520s (J. *Gutiérrez*); RHPR 94 (1994) 220s (C. *Grappe*).
   Comm. **Bénétreau** → 6272; **Paulsen** H. → 6273.
6302 **Charles** J. Daryl, Literary strategy in the Epistle of Jude 1993 → 9,6481: [R]Biblica 75 (1994) 586-9 (R. M. *Wilson*); CBQ 56 (1994) 361s (P. H. *Davids*: enlightening); JTS 45 (1994) 818 (I. *Torrance*).
6303 **Charles** J. Daryl, The use of tradition-material in the Epistle of Jude: BuBR 4 (1994) 1-14.
6304 **Vögtle** Anton, Der Judasbrief; der 2. Petrusbrief: Ekk NT 22. Solothurn 1994, Benziger. xxii-281 p.; Bibliog. xiii-xxii. 3-545-23124-0.
6305 *Wendland* E. R., A comparative study of 'rhetorical criticism' ancient and modern — with special reference to the larger structure and function of the epistle of Jude: Neotestamentica 28 (1994) 193-228.
6306 *Landon* C. H., The text of Jude 4 [originally had *theòn* after *despótēn*]: HervTSt 49 (1993) 823-843 [< NTAbs 39, p. 74].

Hoc anno non adhibentur – N⁰ 6307-6999 – **not used this year.**

XV. Theologia Biblica

H1 **Biblical Theology** .1 [OT] **God.**

7000 **Armstrong** Karen, A history of God 1993 → 9,7001: $27.50. – [R]BR 10,6 (1994) 15s (R. E. *Friedman*: big subject, little insight); Midstream 40/5 (1994) 41-43 (R. *Patai*: without such a not-really-meant title, world not have been a NYTimes bestseller).
7001 **Birnbaum** D., God and evil; a unified theodicy (theology)/philosophy 1989 → 5,7001 ... 9,7004: [R]NRT 116 (1994) 280s (X. *Jacques*).
7002 **Blumenthal** David R., Facing the abusing God; a theology of protest. LvL 1993, W-Knox. 318 p. – [R]RTPhil 126 (1994) 291s (C. A. *Keller*).
7003 *a) Bock* Sebastian, 'Deine Treue reicht, soweit die Wolken ziehen'; Bilder der Treue Gottes im AT; – *b) Weinberg* Zwi, 'Er heisst: der Fels'; die Treue Gottes zu seinem Volk Israel: Entschluss 48,5 (1993) 4-8 / 9-11.
7003* *Bradshaw* Tim, MACQUARRIE's doctrine of God: TyndB 44 (1993) 1-32.
7004 **Briend** Jacques, Dieu dans l'Écriture 1992 → 8,7002; 9,7007: [R]CC 145 (1994,3) 200s (D. *Scaiola*); ÉTRel 68 (1993) 424 (D. *Lys*); Gregorianum 75 (1994) 344s (E. *Farahian*); LavalTP 50 (1994) 458s (J.-C. *Breton*); NRT 116 (1994) 99s (J. L. *Ska*); RB 101 (1994) 269-272 (P. *Grelot*: quatre aspects; moins que la totalité); ZAW 105 (1993) 309s (G. *Metzner*).

7004* *Brueggemann* Walter, Crisis-evoked, crisis-resolving speech [... the oracles of YHWH]: BibTB 24 (1994) 95-105.
7005 *a*) *Cohen* Shaye J. D., Can converts to Judaism say 'God of our fathers'?; – *b*) *Dorff* Elliot N., The concept of God in the conservative movement: Judaism 40 (1991) 419-428 / 429-441.
7005* *Ebach* Jürgen, Der Gott des ATs — ein Gott der Rache?: Junge Kirche 55 (1994) 130-6 [< ZIT 94,272].
7006 **Farley** Wendy, Tragic vision and divine compassion; a contemporary theodicy 1990 ► 6,7007... 9,7011: ᴿCurrTM 21 (1994) 136 (J. S. *Zell*).
7007 **Frielingsdorf** Karl, Dämonische Gottesbilder; ihre Entstehung, Entlarvung und Überwindung 1992 ► 9,7013: ᴿTPQ 142 (1994) 102 (J. *Janda*).
7008 **Geivett** R. Douglas, Evil and the evidence for God; the challenge of John HICK's theodicy. Ph 1994, Temple Univ. 276 p. $45. – ᴿFirsT 48 (1994) 54-56 (I. S. *Markham*).
7009 *Hauber* Reinhard, Die Lehre vom Zorn Gottes nach Werner ELERT: NSys 36 (1994) 117-160; Eng. 161.
7009* *Krapf* Thomas, Biblischer Monotheismus und vorexilischer JHWH-Glaube; Anmerkungen zur neueren Monotheismusdiskussion im Lichte von Yehezkel KAUFMANNS Polytheismus-Monotheismus: BTZ 11 (1994) 42-64.
7010 *Lefebure* Leo D., The wisdom of God, 1. Sophia and Christian theology; 2. Dialogue and natural theology: ChrCent 111 (1994) 951-6 / 984-8.
7011 **Lodahl** Michael E., Shekhinah Spirit; divine presence in Jewish and Christian thought 1992 ► 8,7013; 9,7021: ᴿAmJTP 15 (1994) 103-8 (Delores J. *Rogers*); NewTR 7,1 (1994) 109-111 (R. H. *Miller*); TorTJ 10 (1994) 306s (Jacoba H. *Kuikman*).
7012 *a*) *Long* Gary, Dead or alive? Literality and God metaphors in the Hebrew Bible; – *b*) *Taylor* Mark C., Discrediting God: JAAR 62 (1994) 509-537 / 603-623.
7013 **Moberly** R. W. L., The OT of the OT; patriarchal narratives and Mosaic Yahwism 1992 ► 8,7017; 9,7025: ᴿCBQ 56 (1994) 563s (G. C. *Nicol*); Interpretation 47 (1993) 422s (J. H. C. *Neeb*); JTS 45 (1994) 175s (R. *Mason*); TLond 96 (1993) 318s (R. J. *Coggins*); TorJT 10 (1994) 244s (J. L. *McLaughlin*).
  Neudecker Reinhard, Az egy Istén sok arca 1992 ► 10126.
7015 *Oomen* Palmyre M. F., Lijden als vraag naar God; een bijdrage vanuit WHITEHEAD's filosofie [largely applied to three theses of EPICURUS]: TvT 34 (1994) 246-267; Eng. 268.
7016 **Petrosillo** Orazio, *Marinelli* Emanuela, (ital. book). – *b*) Shrouded in mystery: CathWRep 3,4 (1993) 42-49.
7017 *Rizzi* Armido, Dio all'immagine dell'uomo? Il linguaggio antropomorfico e antropopatico nella Bibbia: RasT 35 (1994) 26-57.
7018 *Schmidt* Werner H., Monotheismus AT [*Starobinski-Safran* Esther, Judentum]: ► 517, TRE 23 (1994) 237-248 [249-256].
7019 *Sentis* Laurent, Saint Thomas d'AQUIN et le mal; foi chrétienne et théodicée: THist 92, 1992, ► 9,7031*; 2-7010-1271-6: ᴿTvT 34 (1994) 85 (C. *Leget*).
7020 **Streminger** Gerhard, Gottes Güte und die Übel der Welt; das Theodizeeproblem 1992 ► 9,7035; v-442 p. DM 138; pa. 84. 3-16- 145890-3: ᴿZkT 116 (1994) 75-77 (W. *Kern*).
7021 **Tarocchi** Stefano, Il Dio longanime [... Paolo]: RivB supp. Bo c. 1992, Dehoniane. 176 p. Lᵐ 24.

7022 **Zenger** Erich, Am Fuss des Sinai; Gottesbilder des Ersten Testaments. Dü 1993, Patmos. 176 p. DM 26,80. – RTPQ 142 (1994) 406-8 (F. *Böhmisch*; gegen 'den ewigen Markionismus', teils in Feministen oder 'mitschwimmenden wie BOFF' von seiten jüdischer Exegetinnen aufgedeckt, S. 31). – RProtestantesimo 49 (1994) 179s (C. *Tron*).

H1.3 *Immutabilitas* – God's suffering; process theology.

7023 **Buckley** James J., Seeking the humanity of God; practices, doctrines, and Catholic theology 1992 → 9,7047: RBibTB 24 (1994) 34 (A. K. M. *Adam*); ModT 10 (1994) 215s (D. F. *Ford*); TLZ 119 (1994) 41-43 (H. *Grote*: utterly unique).

7023* **Case-Winters** Anna, God's power; traditional understandings and contemporary challenges 1990 → 9,7027: LVL 1990, W-Knox. 246 p. $20. – RAmJTP 14 (1993) 207-212 (T. *Dozeman*, also on WARD K.); CritRR 5 (1992) 467-9 (B. L. *Whitney*).

7024 *Christensen* Peter G., Dieu, sa vie, son œuvre [1980]. Jean d'ORMESSON's attack on 'apatheia' as a quality of God: LitTOx 8 (1994) 405-420.

7024* *Cotter* Jim, Does God have boundaries?: Way 33 (1993) 91-96.

7025 *Culp* John, Modern thought challenges Christian theology; process philosophy and Anglican theologian Lionel THORNTON: AnglTR 76 (1994) 329-351.

7026 *Dombrowski* Daniel A., Thomas NAGEL as a process philosopher: AmJTP 15 (1994) 163-180.

7026* **Franklin** Stephen T., Speaking from the depths; Alfred N. WHITEHEAD's hermeneutical metaphysics of propositions, experience, symbolism, language, and religion. GR 1990, Eerdmans. xv-410 p. $27.50. – RCritRR 5 (1992) 401-3 (J. M. *Hallman*).

7027 **Helm** Paul, Eternal creation: TyndB 45 (1994) 321-338.

7027* **Ickert** Scott S., LUTHER on the timelessness of God: LuthQ 7,1 (1993) 45-66 [< ZIT 93,466].

7028 *Jansen* Henry, MOLTMANN's view of God's (im)mutability; the God of the philosophers and the God of the Bible: NSys 36 (1994) 284-301; deutsch 301.

7029 *Kelly* Brian, AQUINAS on redemption and change in God: IrTQ 58 (1992) 249-263.

7030 *Milazzo* G. Tom, To an impotent God; images of divine impotence in Hebrew Scripture: Shofar 11 (Purdue 1993) 30-49 [< OTAbs 16, p. 561].

7030* **Morris** Randall C., Process philosophy and political ideology; the social and political thought of A. N. WHITEHEAD and C. HARTSHORNE 1991 SUNY. xii-289 p. $44.50 – RCritRR 5 (1992) 409-413 (C. R. *Mesle*).

7031 **Neville** Robert C., Eternity and time's flow. Albany 1993, SUNY. xxii-268 p. $17. – RTS 54 (1993) 751s (J. A. *Bracken*).

7032 **Ngien** Dennis, The suffering of God according to Martin LUTHER's theologia crucis: diss. St. Michael's, DDemson David. Windsor 1993. – SR 23 (1994) 526.

7033 **O'Hanlon** G. F., Does God change?... BALTHASAR 1990 → [title otherwise] 6,7048 ... 9,7070: RCritRR 5 (1992) 480-2 (C. *Phan*); MilltSt 31 (1993) 158-160 (T. *O'Loughlin*).

7034 **Padgett** Alan G., God, eternity and the nature of time 1992 → 9,7071: RSR 22 (1993) 121 (S. *Brown*: brilliant).

7035 **Pailin** David A., God and the processes of reality 1989 → 5,7055*; 6,7049: RScotJT 46 (1993) 248s (D. A. S. *Fergusson*).

7036 **Placher** William C., Narratives of a vulnerable God; Christ, theology and Scripture. LVL 1994, Knox. xix-188 p. $15. 0-664-25534-5. – ᴿTBR 7,3 (1994s) 57s (Esther D. *Reed*).

7037 **Reist** Benjamin A., Processive revelation [... the expression of God's own becoming] 1992 ➤ 9,7072; $25; 0-664-21955-1: ᴿInterpretation 48 (1994) 317.320 (Cynthia M. *Campbell*).

7038 *Rikhof* Herwi, God's changeability and unchangeability; the vision of Piet SCHOONENBERG: LvSt 18 (1993) 21-37.

7039 **Sarot** Marcel, God, passibility and corporeality 1992 ➤ 9,7075*b*; ᴿJRel 74 (1994) 416s (J. *Wetzel*: infelicitously based on a 'perfect-being' theology).

7040 **Schwöbel** Christoph, God, action and revelation: Studies in Philosophical Theology 3, 1992 ➤ 9,7077: ᴿBijdragen 55 (1994) 217s (L. H. *Westra*); ÉglT 25 (1994) 301s (J. van den *Hengel*); IrTQ 60 (1994) 314s (J. *Byrne*).

7041 **Sweeney** Leo, Divine infinity in Greek and medieval thought 1992 ➤ 8,7052; 9,7079: ᴿGregorianum 75 (1994) 169 (F.A. *Pastor*); Salesianum 56 (1994) 602s (P.T. *Stella*).

7042 **Tune** Anders S., Immutable, saving God; the import of the doctrine of divine immutability for soteriology in AUGUSTINE's theology: diss. Catholic Univ. ᴰ*Bonner* G. Wsh 1994. 313 p. 95-11766. – DissA 55 (1994s) p. 3091; RTLv 26, p. 541.

7043 *Vidal* Fernando, 'Les mystères de la douleur divine' — une 'prière' du jeune Jean PIAGET pour l'année 1916: RTPhil 126 (1994) 97-118; Eng. 192.

7043* *Wandinger* Nikolaus, Zur Begriff der 'aeternitas' bei Thomas von AQUIN: ZkT 116 (1994) 301-320.

7044 **Young** Henry J., Hope in process; a theology of social pluralism 1989 ➤ 8,7056; 9,7084: ᴿAmJTP 14 (1993) 220-5 (T. *Mikelson*).

H1.4   *Femininum in Deo* – **God as father and as mother** [➤ F3.7; H8.8s].

7044* **Alonso Schökel** Luis, Dios Padre, meditaciones bíblicas: El Pozo de Siquem 63. Sdr 1994, Sal Terrae. 174 p. 84-293-1124-6.

7045 **Alonso Schökel** Luis, Dio Padre; meditazioni bibliche: Bibbia e Preghiera 19. R 1994, Apost. Preghiera. 188 p. Lᵐ 18. 88-7357-143-3.

7046 *Amato* Angelo, Dio Padre — Dio madre; riflessioni preliminari: RicT 3 (R 1992) 33-57 [< ZIT 93,405].

7046* *Boughton* Lynne C., More than metaphor; masculine-gendered names and the knowability of God: Thomist 58 (1994) 283-316.

Baudler Georg, Gott und Frau 1991 ➤ 8,7808*; 9,7972.

7047 Dios es Padre (XXV Semana de Estudios Trinitarios). S 1991, Secretariado Trinitario. 341 p. ➤ 7,488*; 84-85376-92-7: ᴿAngelicum 70 (1993) 145-7 (T. *Stancati*); Gregorianum 74 (1993) 583s (F.-A. *Pastor*).

7048 **Durrwell** F.X., Der Vater 1992 ➤ 9,7094: ᴿTGegw 36 (1993) 235s (B. *Häring*).

7049 **Durrwell** F.-X., O pai; Deus en seu misterio, [1987, español 1990 ➤ 6, 7064], ᵀ*Lemos* Benoni, ᴱ*Dalboss* R. São Paulo 1990, Paulinas. 230 p. – ᴿREB 54 (1994) 235-8 (A. *Alves de Mello*).

7050 *Edwards* Denis, Jesus – the wisdom of God [JOHNSON Elizabeth A., ETL 1985]: AustralasCR 70 (1993) 342-353.

7051 **Eilberg-Schwartz** Howard, God's phallus, and other problems for men and monotheism. Boston 1994, Beacon. xii-312 p. $27.50. 0-8070-

1224-6 [TDig 42,163: still favors masculine symbols, but of a more tender, loving sort].

7051* *Foster* Julia A., The motherhood of God; the use of *ḥyl* as God-language in the Hebrew Scriptures; ➤ 102, Mem. RICHARDSON H., Uncovering 1994, 93-102.

7052 **Galot** Jean, Fêter le Père [... par une fête liturgique]: Spiritualité. P 1993, Mame. 123 p. F 75. – REsprVie 103 (1993) 669 (P. *Jay*); NRT 116 (1994) 934 (L. V.).

7052* **Galot** J. Abba Father, T*Bouchard* M. Angeline 1992 ➤ 8,7063: RRRel 52 (1993) 940-2 (G. P. *Evans*).

7053 **Gómez Acebo** I., Dios también es madre; reflexiones sobre el AT. M 1994, S. Pablo. 196 p. – REstE 69 (1994) 549s (M. Eugenia *Rueda*).

7054 *Grigg* Richard, Enacting the divine; feminist theology and the being of God: JRel 74 (1994) 506-523.

7055 *Harper* William, On calling God ' mother ': Faith and Philosophy 11 (ND 1994) 290-7.

7056 *Hook* Donald D., *Kimel* Alvin F., The pronouns of deity; a theolinguistic critique of feminist proposals: ScotJT 46 (1993) 297-323.

7057 *Hunter* Anne Marie, Numbering the hairs of our heads; male social control and the all-seeing male God: JFemStRel 8,2 (1992) 7-26.

7058 **Johnson** Elizabeth A., She who is 1992 ➤ 9,7103: RJAAR 62 (1994) 198-201 (Pamela D. *Young*: splendid; but 'if all our language about God is analogical, p. 117, how do we know that our language applies at all?'); JRel 74 (1994) 414s (Cynthia S. W. *Crysdale*); ModT 12 (1994) 123s (Jane *Williams*); NewTR 7,2 (1994) 109s (Ann D. *Graff*); PrincSemB 15 (1994) 303-5 (Cynthia L. *Rigby*); PerspRelSt 21 (1994) 59-67 (C. *Marsh*: 'two models of trinitarian theology').

7059 *Johnson* Elizabeth A., A theological case for God-she; expanding the treasury of metaphor: Commonweal 120,2 (1993) 9-14 [17-22, L. T. *Johnson* review of her cognate book].

7059* *Jüngling* Hans-Winfried, 'Was anders ist Gott für den Menschen, wenn night sein Vater und seine Mutter?'; zu einer Doppelmetapher der religiösen Sprache: ➤ 467*, Ein Gott allein? 1993/4, 365-386 [387-390, *Becking* B.].

7060 *Keel* Othmar, Wie männlich ist der Gott Israels?: Diakonia 24 (Mainz 1993) 179-185 [< ZIT 93,370].

7061 EKimel Alvin F.J, Speaking the Christian God; the Holy Trinity and the challenge of feminism 1992 ➤ 8,398; 9,7105 also Gracewing. 0-85244-213-0. £13. – RExpTim 105 (1993s) 57 (Ruth *Page*: where feminism abrades traditional belief); ModT 10 (1994) 421-3 (Ann *Loades*); Persp [Ref] 8,3 (1994) 22 (Marchiene V. *Rienstra*); TorJT 10 (1994) 303s (Cora *Twohig-Moengengango*).

7062 *Limburg* Klaus, La paternidad divina en el AT; algunas observaciones lingüístico-formales: ➤ 22, FCASCIARO J., Biblia 1994, 201-220.

7063 **Long** Asphodel P., In a chariot drawn by lions; the search for the female in deity 1992 ➤ 9,7108: RTLond 96 (1993) 324-6 (Nicola *Slee*).

7064 **Marriage** Alwyn, Life-giving Spirit; responding to the feminine in God 1989 ➤ 6,7073: RScotJT 46 (1993) 239s (Gillian *Cooper*).

7065 *Martin* F., The God and Father of our Lord Jesus Christ: Anthropotēs 9,2 (1993) 189-209 [< NTAbs 38, p. 411].

7066 **Miller** John W., Biblical faith and fathering; why we call God 'Father' 1989 ➤ 5,7087... 9,7109: RForefront 1,2 (Crestone CO 1994) 27-29 (Juli L. *Wiley*).

7067 *Reites* James W., To speak rightly about God; feminist theology and the mystery of God: Landas 8 (Manila 1994) 54-71. 219-238.

7068 ᴱ**Roman** Camille, *al.*, The women and language debate; a sourcebook. New Brunswick 1994, Rutgers Univ. [xi-] 469 p. 0-8135-2011-8; pa. -2-6.

7069 *Ruckstuhl* Eugen, Abba, Vater! Überlegungen zum Stand der Frage: FrSZ 41 (1994) 515-525 (526-541 Antwort, *Schelbert* Georges).

7070 *a) Sattler* Dorothee, Gott in Frauengestalt; weibliche Suche nach hintergründigen biblischen Gottesbildern; – *b) Heine* Susanne, Von Mannweibern, Welterlöserinnen and Karrierefrauen; Weiblichkeitsbilder in der Moderne: TGgw 37 (1994) 256-269 / 270-283.

7071 **Sebastian** Joseph, God as feminine according to Subramania BHARATI seen in the light of Christian tradition: diss. Pont. Univ. Gregoriana, ᴰ*D-havamony* M. Rome 1994. 540 p.; extr. Nº 4048, 97 p. – RTLv 26, p. 589.

7072 *Seitz* Christopher R., Reader competence and the offense of biblical language: Pro Ecclesia 2 (1993) 143-9 [< ᴢɪᴛ 93,326].

7072* **Smith** Paul R., Is it okay to call God 'Mother'? considering the feminine face of God. Peabody ᴍᴀ 1993, Hendrickson. 278 p. $12. 1-56563-013-0. – ᴿRExp 91 (1994) 274 (Molly T. *Marshall*).

7073 **Strotmann** Angelika, 'Mein Vater bist du' 1994 ➤ 7,7044... 9,7116: ᴿRB 101 (1994) 304 (B. T. *Viviano*).

7074 *Stucky-Abbott* Leona, The impact of male God imagery on female identity meaning: Journal of Pastoral Care 47 (NY 1993) 240-252 [< ᴢɪᴛ 93,695].

Wacker M., Göttin in Hosea 1994 ➤ 3678.

7075 *Ward* Graham, In the name of the Father and of the Mother: LitTOx 8 (1994) 311-327.

7076 **Widdicombe** Peter, The fatherhood of God from ORIGEN to ATHANASIUS [< diss. Oxford, ᴰ*Wiles* M.]. Ox 1994, Clarendon. xii-290 p. £35. 0-19-826751-7 [TDig 42,193]. – ᴿTBR 7,2 (1994s) 25 (T. *Bradshaw*).

7077 **Wodtke-Werner** Verena, Der Heilige Geist als weibliche Gestalt im christlichen Altertum und Mittelalter; eine Untersuchung von Texten und Bildern: kath. Diss. ᴰ*Vogt.* Tübingen 1992s. – TR 90,88.

7077* *Young* Robin D., She who is [JOHNSON E. 1992]; who is she?: Thomist 58 (1994) 323-333.

7078 *Ziegenaus* Anton, Das Problem der geschlechtsspezifischen Gottesaussagen; Auseinandersetzung mit der feministischen Theologie: AnnTh 7 (1993) 323-346.

H1.7 Revelatio.

7079 ᴱ**Alonso Schökel** Luis, *Artola* Antonio M., La palabra... Dei Verbum 1991 ➤ 7,286... 9,7124: ᴿRTLv 25 (1994) 370 (P. M. *Bogaert*).

7080 **Bloesch** Donald G., Holy Scripture; revelation, inspiration and interpretation: Christian Foundations. DG 1994, InterVarsity. 724 p. 0-8308-1412-4.

7081 **Bockmuehl** Klaus, À l'écoute du Dieu qui parle 1989 [Eng. 1990 ➤ 7,7070]: ᴿEurJT 3 (1994) 62-90 (A. D. *Thomas*, his spirituality); franç. 62s, deutsch 63s.

7081* *Canale* Fernando J., Revelation and inspiration; the classical model: AndrUnS 12 (1994) 2-28. 169-195.

7082 **Coady** Francis E., Divine revelation according to the four Eucharistic prayers of the 1975 Roman Missal: diss. Pont. Univ. Gregoriana,

ᴰO'Collins G. Roma 1994. 401 p.; extr. nº 5057, 243 p. – RTLv 26, p. 563.
7083 **Coda** P., Dios uno y trino; revelación, experiencia y teología del Dios de los cristianos. S 1993, Secr. Trinitario. 218 p. – ᴿEstE 69 (1994) 540-3 (J. R. García-Murga).
7084 **Dool** John J., Revelation and meaning; the contributions of Bernard LONERGAN to a theology of revelation: diss. St. Michael's, ᴰDoran R. Toronto 1994. 266 p. – RTLv 26, p. 563.
7085 **Dulles** Avery, Models of revelation² 1992 [= preface + ¹1983 (→ 65, 5809)]: ᴿNRT 116 (1994) 252s (L. Renwart); RTPhil 126 (1994) 287s (K. Blaser).
7086 **Fisichella** Rino, La Révélation et sa crédibilité: Recherches 23. Montréal/P 1989, Bellarmin/Cerf. 384 p. – ᴿEsprVie 104 (1994) 449s (P. Jay).
7087 ᴿ**Gil Hellin** Francisco, Vat. II, Dei Verbum 1993 → 9,7132: ᴿBbbOr 36 (1994) 252-4 (G. De Virgilio).
7088 **Gorringe** T. J., Discerning the Spirit; a theology of revelation 1990 → 7,7079: ᴿColcT 63,4 (1993) 224s (A. P. Dziuba, ❷).
7089 **Grey** Mary, The wisdom of fools? 1993 → 9,7133: ᴿNBlackf 75 (1994) 174-6 (M. Cecily Boulding: a 'must', but jumbled).
7089* **Haught** John F., Mystery and promise; a theology of revelation: NewTheol 2. ColMn 1993, Liturgical/Glazier. 224 p. $15. – ᴿBibTB 24 (1994) 197 (Anne M. Clifford).
7090 Labbé Yves, La révélation comme manifestation et comme communication; une diversité d'usages: RThom 94 (1994) 601-624.
7091 ᵀᴱ**Marquet** J.-F., Courine J.-F., F. W. J. SCHELLING, Philosophie de la révélation: Épiméthée. P 1989-, PUF. I. introd. 208 p.; II/1, 1991, 400 p. – ᴿRThom 94 (1994) 150-2 (S. Robilliard).
7092 **Möde** Erwin, Offenbarung als Alternative zur Dialektik der Postmoderne; eine fundamentaltheologische Untersuchung: kath. Diss. ᴰPetri. Rg 1994. – TR 90.80.
7093 Mondin Battista, Il linguaggio teologico, espressione del mistero rivelato nel linguaggio umano: Sapienza 46 (1993) 241-262.
7094 **Niemann** Franz-Josef, Jesus der Offenbarer 1990 → 7,7093: ᴿForKT 10 (1994) 219s (J. Schumacher).
7095 **Rovira Belloso** Josep M., Revelación de Dios, salvación del hombre: Tratado de Dios uno y trino⁴. S 1993, Secr. Trinitario. 651 p. – ᴿEstE 69 (1994) 534-540 (J. R. García-Murga).
7096 Sala Giovanni B., La Rivelazione; la parola di Dio nella storia della salvezza: RasT 35 (1994) 283-302 . 421-444.
7097 **Schmitz** Josef, La rivelazione [Offenbarung Dü 1988, Patmos] ᵀ: GdT 206, 1991 → 7,7097* ... 9,7141; Lᵐ 25. 88-399-0706-8: ᴿGregorianum 75 (1994) 558s (R. Fisichella: fa l'esperienza normativa anziché mediazione conoscitiva; traduzione inesatta).
7097* Skottene Ragnar, Revelation and conscience according to the Norwegian philosopher and theologian Georg FASTING: TsTKi 55 (1994) 15-31 Norwegian; Eng. 31.
7098 **Swinburne** R., Revelation 1991 → 8,7103; 9,7145: ᴿHeythJ 35 (1994) 84s (G. O'Collins); ScotJT 46 (1993) 579-581 (D. Brown); ScripTPamp 26 (1994) 832 (F. Conesa).
7098* Tallach John, In order there to find God; KIERKEGAARD and objective revelation: TyndB 45,1 (1994) 153-168.
7099 **Tejerina Arias** Gonzalo, Revelación y religión en la teología antro-

pológica de Heinrich FRIES: diss. Pont. Univ. Gregoriana, ᴰ*Pastor* F. A. Roma 1994. 646 p. – RTLv 26, p. 551.
7099* *Torres Queiruga* Andrés, ¿Qué significa afirmar que Dios habla? Hacia un concepto actual de la Revelación: SalT 82 (1994) 331-348.
7100 *Watson* Francis, Is revelation an 'event'?: ModT 10 (1994) 383-399.
7100* *Williams* Stephen, Revelation and reconciliation; a tale of two concepts: EurJT 3 (1994) 35-42; franç. deutsch 35.

H1.8 Theologia fundamentalis.

7101 *Antonelli* Mario, Manuali di teologia fondamentale: ScuolC 122 (1994) 507-613.
7101* **Beeck** F. J. van, [➤ 8921] The revelation and the glory; fundamental theology 2. ColMn 1993: ➤ 9,7151: ᴿRelStR 20 (1994) 211 (J. J. *Buckley*).
7102 **Bonsor** Jack A., Athens and Jerusalem; the role of philosophy in theology. NY 1993, Paulist. vi-183 p. $12 pa. – ᴿHorizons 21 (1994) 376s (F. *Buckley*); LvSt 19 (1994) 272s (S. *Rocker*).
7103 **Corduan** Winfried, Reasonable faith; basic Christian apologetics. Nv 1993, Broadman & H. 279 p. – ᴿTrinJ 15 (1994) 266-9 (P. *Copan*).
7104 **Cunningham** David S., Faithful persuasion 1990s ➤ 8,1350; 9,7159: ᴿAmerica 171,8 (1994) 27s (M. *Royackers*); AnglTR 76 (1994) 530-2 (O. C. *Thomas*); Horizons 21 (1994) 358s (M. H. *Barnes*); Interpretation 48 (1994) 220-2 (B. E. *Starr*); JRel 74 (1994) 111 (D. *Jasper*: sound aim, strong NEWMAN influence; but a 'ringing doxological tone' puts it outside the critical and literary theory debates); Month 255 (1994) 276s (D. *Robinson*); Salesianum 56 (1994) 581s (G. *Abbà*); ScripTPamp 26 (1994) 1226s (F. *Conesa*).
7105 **Davaney** Sheila G., *Cobb* John B.ᴶ, Human historicity, cosmic creativity and the theological imagination; reflection on the work of Gordon D. KAUFMANN [In face of mystery, Harvard 1993; ➤ 8937 below]: RelStR 20 (1994) 171-4-7 [-181, Kaufmann comment].
7106 *Diniz* Edwin, The point of departure of fundamental theology [the historical revelation of God in Jesus]: Teresianum 45 (1994) 439-455.
7107 *Disse* Jörg, Fundamentaltheologie als theologische Apologetik: ZkT 116 (1994) 143-159.
7108 **Döring** Heinrich, *Kreiner* Armin, *Schmidt-Leukel* Perry, Den Glauben denken; neue Wege der Fundamentaltheologie: QDisp 147, 1993 ➤ 9, 322*: DM 48. – ᴿTR 90 (1994) 415-421 (R. *Bernhardt*: Aufbruch gelungen).
7109 ᴱ**Doré** Joseph, *al.*, Le christianisme et la foi chrétienne 1-5, 1991s: ➤ 7,350; 8,7114: ᴿÉglT 25 (1994) 425-432 (L. *Laberge*); RTLv 25 (1994) 483-5 (E. *Brito*, 1).
7110 ᴱ**Doré** Joseph, Introduction à l'étude de la théologie 1991 ➤ 7,350b ... 9,7162: ᴿScEspr 45 (1993) 239s (P.-É. *Langevin*).
7111 **Dulles** Avery, The craft of theology; from symbol to system 1992 ➤ 8,236d; 9,7164: ᴿAndrUnS 32 (1994) 266s (F. *Canale*: scientific dimension somewhat deemphasized); HeythJ 35 (1994) 204s (J. *Sullivan*); Month 255 (1994) 231s (J. *Hanvey*); NewTR 7,4 (1994) 306s (J. *Burkhard*); Studies 42 (1993) 97-100 (J. *Corkery*); SWJT 36,1 (1993s) 48s (E. E. *Ellis*); Thomist 58 (1994) 513-7 (P. *Casarella*).
7112 *Ferraro* Giuseppe, Il metodo della teologia secondo il Concilio Vaticano II: CC 145 (1994,4) 226-236.
Griffiths Paul J., An apology for apologetics 1991 ➤ 8287.

7113 [Schüssler] Fiorenza Francis [→ 8927]: Fundamentale Theologie; zur Kritik theologischer Begründungsverfahren² [¹1984]. Mainz 1992, Grünewald. 316 p. DM 48. – ᴿEntschluss 49,2 (1994) 43 (M. Brasser); ZkT 116 (1994) 77-79 (K. H. Neufeld).

7114 Fischer Johannes, Zum Wahrheitsanspruch der Theologie: TZBas 50 (1994) 93-107.

7115 Fisichella Rino, Introducción a la teología fundamental. Estella 1993, VDivino. 181 p. – ᴿCarthaginensia 10 (1994) 505s (F. Oliver Alcón); TEspir 38 (1994) 159s (M. Gelabert).

7116 Fisichella Rino, Introduzione alle discipline teologiche [Gregoriana, recentemente completata, senza ᴱ o data; commenta principalmente 'Perché studiare teologia a Roma?']: ᴿGregorianum 75 (1994) 751-4 (ipse).

7117 Ford David, A long rumour of wisdom; redescribing theology. C 1992, Univ. 28 p. – ᴿScotJT 47 (1994) 402-5 (G. Lindbeck).

7118 Gaboriau Florent, Progrès de la théologie; à quelles conditions? 1991 → 9,9172: ᴿAngelicum 71 (1994) 113-5 (A. Wilder, dubious); ScEspr 45 (1993) 360s (J.-C. Petit: ... de CHENU à RATZINGER, l'Écriture négligée).

7119 Gaffin Richard B., A new paradigm in theology? [SPYKMAN G. 1992; † 13.VII.1993]: WestTJ 56 (1994) 379-390.

7120 Gerber Uwe, Wie wird in Europa Theologie betrieben? drei Modelle...: TZBas 50 (1994) 264-7.

7121 Griffin David R., Smith Huston, Primordial truth and postmodern theology. Albany 1989, SUNY. $49.50; pa. $17. – ᴿCritRR 5 (1992) 471-3 (B. L. Whitney).

7122 Gruber Franz, Diskurs und Konsens im Prozess theologischer Wahrheit: InTSt 40. Innsbruck 1993, Tyrolia. 350 p. DM 49. 3-7022-1881-5. – ᴿTGL 84 (1994) 117s (W. Beinert); ZkT 116 (1994) 335-8 (W. Kern).

7123 Hauck Friedrich, Schwinge Gerhard, Theologisches Fach- und Fremdwörterbuch⁷: Kleine Reihe 1480. Gö 1992, Vandenhoeck & R. 240 p. 3-525-3385-7. – ᴿEstE 69 (1994) 417s (J. J. Alemany: reticencias cuanto al motivo de fundación sea de los Jesuitas que del Opus Dei).

7124 Heitink G., Ontwerp van een empirische theologie [VEN J. A. van der]: PrakT 18 (1991) 525-538.

7125 Hoitenga Dewey J.ᴶ, Faith and reason from Plato to Plantinga; an introduction to Reformed epistemology 1991 → 7,7121; 9,7174*: ᴿFaith and Philosophy 11 (ND 1994) 342-7 (J. F. Sennett).

7127 Hoye W., Gotteserfahrung? [→ 9,9175] Klärung eines Grundbegriffs der gegenwärtigen Theologie. Z 1993, Benziger. 256 p. Fs 34. 3-545-24111-4. – ᴿTGL 84 (1994) 118 (W. Beinert).

7128 Kelsey David H., To understand God truly 1992 → 9,7177: ᴿJRel 74 (1994) 581 (W. C. Spohn).

7129 Kort Wesley A., Bound to differ; the dynamics of theological discourses 1992 → 9,7180: ᴿJRel 74 (1994) 411s (M. L. Cook); ModT 10 (1994) 316-8 (S. H. Webb).

7130 ᴱKüng H., Tracy D., Paradigm change in theology 1989 → 6,637*; 7,k107: ᴿChurchman 108 (1994) 91 (E. Dowse: fascinating despite its defects).

7131 ᴱLorizio G., Galantino N., Metodologia teologica. CinB 1994, S. Paolo. 487 p. – ᴿRasT 35 (1994) 750-7 (I. Sanna).

7131* McGrath Alister, Christian theology; an introduction. Ox 1994, Blackwell. 510 p. $21. – ᴿTrinJ 15 (1994) 117-123 (T. Scheck).

7132 McGrath Alister E., Intellectuals don't need God and other modern myths; building bridges to faith through apologetics. GR 1993, Zondervan [1992 ➤ 9,7184, title variations]. 241 p. $15 pa. 0-310-59091-4. – ᴿChrSchR 24 (1994) 100-2 (J. A. *Baird*); RefR 48 (1994s) 59s (H. *Buis*).

7133 **McGrath** Alister E.,   The genesis of doctrine 1990 ➤ 7,7128 ... 9,7185: ᴿJRel 73 (1993) 264-6 (B. E. *Hinze*).

7134 *Merrigan* Terrence,   The craft of Catholic theology [DULLES A. ...]: LvSt 18 (1993) 243-257.

7135 *Moore* Sebastian,   Four steps toward making sense of theology: DowR 111 (1993) 79-101.

7136 *Muller* Richard A.,   The study of theology [Zondervan 1991; xvii-237; $15] revisited; a response to John FRAME: WestTJ 56 (1994) [133-151] 409-417.

7137 **Neufeld** K. H.,   Fundamentaltheologie 1992 ➤ 8,7138; 9,7194:   ᴿEstE 69 (1994) 552s (J. J. *Alemany*).

7138 **Nichols** Aidan,   The shape of Catholic theology 1991 ➤ 8,7139; 9,7196: ᴿScotJT 47 (1994) 279s (P. *Avis*).

7139 **O'Collins** Gerald,   Retrieving fundamental theology; the three styles of contemporary theology. NY 1993, Paulist. 225 p. $15. – ᴿCommonweal 121,5 (1994) 20s (A. *Dulles*); ZkT 116 (1994) 341s (K. H. *Neufeld*).

7140 **Pailin** David A.,   The anthropological character of theology 1990 ➤ 7, e702:   ᴿScotJT 45 (1992) 553-5 (S. *Williams*).

7141 *Pelland* Gilles,   Le phénomène des écoles en théologie: Gregorianum 75 (1994) 431-467; Eng. 467.

7142 **Roberts** J. D.,   A philosophical introduction to theology 1991 ➤ 7,7138 ... 9,7202:   ᴿAmJTP 14 (1993) 80-82 (C. *Nabe*: '1981'); TLond 96 (1993) 228s (P. *Vardy*).

7143 *Rosenau* Hartmut,   Der 'consensus gentium' — fundamentaltheologische Erwägungen zu einem vernachlässigten Gottesbeweis: TPhil 69 (1994) 481-492.

7144 *Ross* James F.,   Rational reliance [modern replacement of 'certainty lacking evidence']: JAAR 62 (1994) 769-798.

7145 ᴱ**Sanna** I.,   Il sapere teologico e il suo metodo; teologia, ermeneutica e verità. Bo 1993, Dehoniane. 296 p. Lᵐ 32. – ᴿRasT 35 (1994) 235s (G. *Lorizio*).

7146 **Thiel** John,   Imagination and authority; theological authorship in the modern tradition 1991 ➤ 8,7148; 9,7209:   ᴿJRel 74 (1994) 270s (B. E. *Hinze*); ModT 10 (1994) 123-5 (T. W. *Tilley*).

7147 **Torrell** Jean-Pierre,   La théologie catholique: Que sais-je? 1268.   P 1994, PUF. 128 p. – ᴿRThom 94 (1994) 707s (M. *Morard*).

7148 **Tracy** David,   Theologie als Gespräch; eine postmoderne Hermeneutik, ᵀ*Klinger* Susanne. Mainz 1993, Grünewald. 176 p. DM 48. – ᴿBogVest 54 (1994) 380-2 (V. *Stanovnik*, Slovene; also on his Analogical Imagination); TR 90 (1994) 63 (E. *Arens*).

7149 **Verweyen** Hansjürgen,   Gottes letztes Wort; Grundriss der Fundamentaltheologie. Dü 1994. – ᴿGregorianum 75 (1994) 165-8 (R. *Fisichella*); TüTQ 174 (1994) 272-287 (T. *Pröpper*, Anfragen: erstphilosophischer Begriff oder Aufweis letztgültigen Sinnes?; 255-303 Verweyens Antwort, Glaubensverantwortung heute).

7150 **Waldenfels** Hans,   Manuel de théologie fondamentale: ᵀ*Depré* G. 1990 ➤ 7,7147; 8,7213*:   ᴿAngelicum 71 (1994) 285-8 (A. *Wilder*); RÉAug 39 (1993) 289s (M. *Fédou*).

7151 *Wiebe* Donald,   Defense of his The irony of theology and the nature of religious thought (1991) against P. Travis *Koeker* review: SR [22 (1993) 93-103] 23 (1994) 67-79; rejoinder 81s.

H2.1 Anthropologia theologica – VT & NT.

7152 *a*) *Barnes* Michael, The evolution of the soul from matter and the role of science in Karl RAHNER's theology; – *b*) *Mooney* Christopher F., The anthropic principle in cosmology and theology: ➤ 120, FSLOYAN G., Horizons 21 (1994) 85-104 / 105-129.

7153 **Chavero Blanco** F., Imago Dei... antropologia/BONAVENTURA. Murcia 1993, Inst. Theol. Francisc. 281 p. – RCarthaginensia 10 (1994) 190s (F. *Martínez Fresneda*); VerVida 52 (1994) 549 (G. *Calvo*).

7154 **Choza** Jacinto, *Arregui* Jorge Vicente, Filosofia del hombre; una antropología de la intimidad[2]: Inst. Cienc. Familia. M 1992, Rialp. 506 p. – RScripTPamp 26 (1994) 268-277 (G. *Aranda Pérez*).

7155 **Comblin** José, Retrieving the human; a Christian anthropology [franç. 1991 ➤ 9,7226]. Mkn 1990, Orbis. ix-259 P. $30; pa. $15. – RCritRR 5 (1992) 469s (C. *Davis*); LvSt 18 (1993) 272s (V. *Neckebrouck*).

7155* *Destro* Adriana, *Pesce* Mauro, Dal testo alla cultura; antropologia degli scritti proto-cristiani: Protestantesimo 49 (1994) 214-229.

7156 **Ebeling** Gerhard, LUTHERstudien II/3 Die theologische Definition des Menschen 1989 ➤ 7,7159... 9,7228: RBijdragen 55 (1994) 89s (T. *Bell*); LuJb 60 (1993) 150-2 (H. *Junghans*); Salesianum 56 (1994) 583s (P. T. *Stella*).

7157 *Elizondo* Felisa, La antropología teológica y el pensar actual sobre lo humano; el interés actual de la antropología: RET 53 (1993) 209-240.

7157* *Forconi* Maria Cristina, Antropologia come fondamento dell'unità e dell'indissolubilità dell'Alleanza matrimoniale: diss. Nº 7205, Pont. Univ. Gregoriana, DNavarrete U. Roma 1994. – InfPUG 26/131, p. 32.

7158 *Gahbauer* Ferdinand R., Die Anthropologie des Johannes von DAMASKUS: TPhil 69 (1994) 1-21.

7159 **Galantino** Nunzio, Dire 'uomo' oggi; nuove vie dell'antropologia filosofica. CinB 1993, Paoline. 192 p. Lm 18. – RLateranum 60 (1994) 219-221 (G. *Ancona*); VivH 5 (1994) 209-211 (S. *Grossi*).

7160 *a*) *Galindo Rodrigo* José A., Bosquejo de la antropología agostiniana; – *b*) *Dolby Múgica* Mª Carmen, El humanismo teocéntrico agostiniano y el humanismo antropocéntrico ateo: ➤ 9,118, FOROZ RETA J. II = AugM 39 (1994) 257-271 / 139-148.

7161 **Gesché** Adolphe, Dieu pour penser, I. Le mal ➤ 7692; II. L'homme 1993 ➤ 9,7235: RETL 69 (1993) 481-4 (J. *Étienne*); RHPR 74 (1994) 439s (J.-F. *Collange*, 1-2).

7162 **González de Cardedal** O., Madre [... origen de la existencia] y muerte. S 1993, Sígueme. 269 p. – RSalmanticensis 41 (1994) 148-150 (J. L. *Ruiz de la Peña*).

7163 **Gozzelino** Giorgio, Il mistero dell'uomo in Cristo; saggio di protologia 1981 ➤ 8,7174; 9,7238; 88-01-13997-7: RAntonianum 69 (1994) 127-9 (V. *Battaglia*).

7164 **Hiebert** Terry G., The redemption of creation in twentieth-century eco-theologies: diss. Baylor, DChristian C. 1994. 234 p. 95-14085. – DissA 55 (1994s) p. 3886.

7165 **Hogan** Maurice P., The biblical vision of the human person; implications for a philosophical anthropology: EurUnivSt 23/504. Fra 1994, Lang. xx-394 p.; bibliog. 381-394. 3-631- 47028-X.

7166 **Kobusch** Theo, Die Entdeckung der Person; Metaphysik der Freiheit und modernes Menschenbild. FrB 1993, Herder. 300 p. DM 48. – ᴿTrierTZ 103 (1994) 157s (W. *Schüssler*).

7167 **Ladaria** Luis F., Introduzione all'antropologia teologica 1992 → 9,7242: ᴿCiuD 207 (1994) 219 (M. *García*); Salmanticensis 40 (1993) 92-94 (J.L. *Ruiz de la Peña*); TEspir 38 (1994) 160s (M. *Gelabert*).

7168 **Legrain** Michel, Le corps humain; du soupçon à l'épanouissement, une vision réconciliée de l'âme et du corps² 1992 → 9,7243*: ᴿSpiritus 34 (1993) 244 (J. *Stacoffe*).

7169 **McDonald** H.D., The Christian view of man: Foundations for faith. Westchester ɪʟ 1988 = 1981, Crossway. – ᴿConcordTQ 58 (1994) 232s (A. *Borcherding*).

7170 **McFadyen** Alister, The call to personhood 1990 → 8,7183: ᴿScotJT 46 (1993) 114-6 (T. *Gorringe*: important though rebarbative; the debate with non-Christians is not so much about God as about what it is to be human).

7170* **Meis Würmer** Anneliese, El rostro amado; aproximaciones a la antropología teológica [An Cile]. 347 p. – ᴿTVida 35 (1994) 307-311 (J. *Zañartu*).

7171 *Mildenberger* Friederich, Freiheitsverständnisse und ihre Folgen: ZTK 91 (1994) 329-345.

7172 **Millet** Louis, La psychologie, connaissance réelle de l'homme? P 1993, de Guibert. 238 p. – ᴿRThom 94 (1994) 687-9 (B. *Hubert*: panorama des écoles modernes, avec bonne connaissance d'ARISTOTE et d'AQUIN).

7173 **Mondin** B., L'uomo secondo il disegno di Dio. Bo 1992, Studio Domenicano. 397 p. – ᴿAnnTh 7 (1993) 251-3 (G. *Tanzella-Nitti*).

7174 **Mroczkowski** Ireneusz, ❷ Osoba i cieleśność... Persona e corporeità; aspetti morali della teologia del corpo. Płock 1994. 303 p. – ᴿSalesianum 56 (1994) 796s (W. *Turek* dà il contenuto dettagliatamente in italiano).

7174* **Nellas** P. † 1986, Voi siete Dei; antropologia dei Padri della Chiesa. c. 1993. – ᴿRelCu 40 (1994) 393 (J. *Tejedor*).

7175 **Nelson** James B., Body theology 1992 → 8,288*d*: ᴿChrC 110 (1994) 24.26 (Bonnie *Miller-McLemore*); PrincSemB 14 (1993) 321s (B. *Wigger*).

7176 *O'Connell* Robert J., The De Genesi contra Manichaeos and the origin of the soul: RÉAug 39 (1993) 129-141.

7177 **Pannenberg** Wolfhart, Antropología en perspectiva teológica, ᵀ*García-Baró* Miguel. S 1993, Sígueme. 709 p. – ᴿComSev 27 (1994) 99s (V.J. *Ansede*); LumenVr 43 (1994) 169s (U. *Gil Ortega*); RAg 35 (1994) 322-4 (G. *Tejerino Arias*); SalT 82 (1994) 241.

7178 **Petterson** Alvin, ATHANASIUS and the human body 1990 → 7,7183: ᴿScotJT 47 (1994) 259-261 (Kelley M. *Spoerl*).

7179 **Pikaza** Xabier, Antropología bíblica; del árbol del juicio al sepulcro de Pascua: BtEstB 80, ᴰ1993 → 9,7255: ᴿActuBbg 31 (1994) 221s (J.M.A.); BibFe 58 (1994) 176 (A. *Salas*: 'distinta de cuantas conozco; no sé si mejor o peor'); Carthaginensia 10 (1994) 458s (F. *Martínez Fresneda*); QVidCr 169 (1993) 121s (D. *Roure*); RAg 34 (1993) 741-3 (S. *Sabugal*); RET 53 (1993) 391-4 (E. *Tourón*); Salmanticensis 41 (1994) 146-8 (J.L. *Ruiz de la Peña*); SalT 81 (1993) 821-3 (J.A. *García*).

7179* *Possekel* U., Der Mensch in der Mitte; Aspekte der Anthropologie HUGOS von St. Viktor: RTAM 61 (1994) 5-21.

7180 *Quinn* Patrick, The interfacing image of the soul in the writings of AQUINAS: MilltSt 32 (1993) 70-75.

7181 *Ribeiro* Hélcion, A relação lúdica entre Deus e o homem; meditação natalina a partir da antropologia teológica: REB 53 (1993) 900-915.
7182 *Rodríguez Amenábar* S.M., El efecto tiene el 'sabor' de la causa; ¿un 'vestigio' de Dios en la naturaleza misma del hombre?: Stromata 50 (1994) 237-245.
7183 **Ruiz de la Peña** J.L., El don 1991 ⇒ 8,7194; 9,7259: ᴿRTLv 25 (1994) 261-3 (E. *Brito*); REB 53 (1993) 237s (L. *Mees*).
7184 **Ruiz de la Peña** J.L., Creación, gracia, salvación: Alcance 46. Sdr 1993, Sal Terrae. 143 p. – ᴿSalmanticensis 41 (1994) 474s (J.R. *Flecha Andrés*: resumen de su antropología).
7185 *Ruiz de la Peña Solar* Juan, El hombre es uno en cuerpo y alma; la versión zubiriana del aserto conciliar: ⇒ 33*b*, ᶠDíAZ MERCHÁN G., StOvet 22 (1994) 353-366.
7186 **Rulla** Luigi M., *al.*, Anthropology of the Christian vocation [1. 1986]; 2. Existential confirmation. R 1989, Gregorian Univ. 498 p. – ᴿTPhil 69 (1994) 633s (H. *Goller*).
7186* *Russo* Giovanni, Creazione, peccato e grazia; aspetti dell'antropologia teologica per la bioetica: Itinerarium 3 (Messina 1994) 111-128.
7187 ᴱ**Sahagún** Juan de, Nuevas antropologías del siglo XX [...ZUBIRI, PANNENBERG, GIRARD, BALTHASAR]: Hermeneia 38. S 1994, Sígueme. 307 p. – ᴿLumenVr 43 (1994) 415-7 (U. *Gil Ortega*).
7188 **Schillebeeckx** Edward, L'histoire des hommes, récit de Dieu 1992 ⇒ 8,7199; 9,7262: ᴿÉTRel 68 (1993) 446s (J.-D. *Kraege*); ScEspr 46 (1994) 132-4 (J.-C. *Petit*).
7189 **Schillebeeckx** Edward, Umanità; la storia di Dio [1989; deutsch 1990 ⇒ 7,7188], ᵀ 1992 ⇒ 9,7264: ᴿGregorianum 75 (1994) 766s (J. *Galot*: 'ne reconnaît pas la réalité du Verbe fait chair']; RThom 94 (1994) 625-638 (A. *Patfoort*: titre mieux traduit 'Des hommes racontent ce qu'est Dieu']; ces hommes sont d'abord Jésus, puis 'le mouvement de Jésus', l'ensemble de la chrétienté et probablement aussi les diverses religions); StPatav 40 (1993) 114-7 (E.R. *Tura*); ZMissRW 76 (1992) 82-86 (G. *Fuchs*, deutsch).
7190 **Schnelle** Udo, Neutestamentliche Anthropologie; Jesus – Paulus – Johannes: BibTSt 18. Neuk 1991. 206 p. DM 36. 3-7887-1394-1. – ᴿLuthTKi 17 (1993) 26s (V. *Stolle*).
7191 **Schulze** Markus, Leibhaft und unsterblich; zur Schau der Seele in der Anthropologie und Theologie des Hl. Thomas von AQUIN: StFrib NS 76; 1992 ⇒ 8,7201. FrS 1992, Univ. 186 p. – ᴿRThom 94 (1994) 716s (G. *Emery*).
7192 *Weier* Winfried, Geist und Psyche in tiefenpsychologischer und phänomenologischer Perspektive: FrSZ 41 (1994) 155-187.

H2.8 Œcologia VT & NT – saecularitas.

7192* *Álvarez Bolado* Alfonso, Mística y secularización; en medio y a las afueras de la ciudad secularizada. Sdr 1992, SalT. 40 p. – ᴿSalT 81 (1993) 77s (J.A. *García*).
7193 *Arnould* Jacques, René DUBOS, pionnier de l'écologie scientifique: RSPT 78 (1994) 81-94; Eng. 94.
7194 **Bradley** Ian, Dios es 'verde'; cristianismo y mondo ambiente: Presencia Teol. 73. Sdr 1993, Sal Terrae. 163 p. – ᴿRazF 229 (1994) 110.
7195 **Brandschuh-Schramm** Christiane, Einheit und Vielheit der Kirchen; Ökumene im konziliaren Prozess [Diss.]: PrakThH 14. Stu 1993, Kohlhammer. 210 p.; 2 fig. DM 50. 3-17-012707-1. – ᴿTLZ 119 (1994) 714s.

7196 ᴱBruce Steve,   Religion and modernization; sociologists and historians
debate the secularization thesis 1992 ➤ 9,7286:   ᴿJRel 74 (1994) 274s (F.
Kniss).

7197 ᴱBrümmer Vincent,   Interpreting the universe as creation 1990/1 ➤ 8,
516:   ᴿÉglT 25 (1994) 269-271 (J. R. *Pambrun*).

7198 *Bube* Richard H.,   Do biblical models need to be replaced in order to
deal effectively with environmental issues?:   PerScCF 46 (1994) 90-97
[81-89, *De Witt* Calvin B.].

7199 **Casciaro** J. M., *Monforte* J. M.,   Dios, el mundo y el hombre en el
mensaje de la Biblia 1992 ➤ 9,7290: ᴿCarthaginensia 10 (1994) 193s (F.
Martínez Fresneda).

7199* **Clark** Stephen R. L.,   How to think about the earth; philosophical and
theological models for ecology. L 1993, Mowbray.   168 p. – ᴿDocLife 44
(1994) 508s (D. *Carroll*).

7200 **Cooper** Tim, Green Christianity 1990 ➤ 8,7231:   ᴿScotBuEvT 11 (1993)
129s (R. G. *Gosden*).

7201 *Crijnen* Ton,   Secularization seems to be a typically (Western) European
phenomenon; an interview with Father AMALADOSS: Exchange 21 (1992)
34-48.

7201* **Cummings** Charles,   Eco-spirituality; toward a reverent life.   NY 1991,
Paulist.   164 p. $10.   0-8091-3251-4. – ᴿVidyajyoti 58 (1994) 52s (S. M. J.
Kennedy).

7202 **Dalton** Anne Marie,   Thomas BERRY's religious ecology in the light of
Bernard LONERGAN's theory of emergent probability: diss. ᴰ*Happel* S.
[Catholic Univ.] Wsh 1994. – RTLv 26, p. 529.

7203 *Disse* Jörg,   Comment fonder une éthique de la nature? Un essai de pensée chrétienne à partir de Simone WEIL: RechSR 82 (1994) 71-86; Eng. 8.

7204 **Dowd** Michael, Earthspirit; a handbook for nurturing an ecological
Christianity. Mystic CT 1991, Twenty-Third. 128 p. $8 pa. 0-89622-479-1.

7205 *a) Drane* John,   Defining a biblical theology of creation; – *b) De Witt*
Calvin,   A scientist's theological reflection on creation; – *c) Sheldon*
Joseph K.,   Christians and the environment in the 1990s; a selective
bibliography: Transformation 10,2 (1993) 7-11 / 12-16 / 21-23.

7206 *Drum* Peter,   AQUINAS and the moral status of animals: AmCPhQ 66
(1992) 483-8 [< ZIT 93,687].

7207 *Echlin* Edward P.,   Jesus, the fossil record, and all things: NBlackf 75
(1994) 141-8.

7208 **Edwards** Denis,   Creation, humanity, community — building a new
theology [faithful also to 20th century science]. Dublin 1992, Gill & M [=
Collins Dove]. 81 p. – ᴿMilltSt 31 (1993) 146s (Céline *Mangan*).

7209 *Espeja* Jesús,   Claves desde el espíritu de Jesús para una praxis eco-
liberadora: Anamnesis 4,2 (1992) 45-62.

7210 *a) French* William C.,   The world as God's body; theological ethics and
panentheism; *b) McCarthy* John P.,   A short consideration of Sallie
MCFAGUE's The body of God [response, *Ross* Susan A.]: ➤ 405, Broken
1993/4, 135-144 / 145-151 [153-6].

7211 **Ganoczy** Alexandre,   Suche nach Gott auf den Wegen der Natur 1992
➤ 9,7310:   ᴿTPhil 69 (1994) 305s (K.-J. *Grün*).

7212 *Gilbert* Paul P.,   L'homme et la nature: ScEspr 45 (1993) 235-252.

7213 *Gil Ortega* Urbano,   Los problemas ecológicos y la visión del mundo y
del hombre: LumenVr 43 (1994) 233-266.

7214 *Goralczyk* Pawel,   The formation of an attitude of ecological responsibility: ComWsh 21 (1994) 538-550.

7215 **Gore** Al, Earth in the balance; ecology and the human spirit. Boston 1993, Houghton Mifflin. 408 p. $13 pa. 0-452-26935-0. – ᴿDrewG 61,2 (1993) 97-107 (M. D. *Ryan*).

7216 **Gustafson** James M., A sense of the divine; the natural environment from a theocentric perspective [Berea Baldwin College Moll Lectures 1992]. Cleveland 1994, Pilgrim. xix-176 p. $16. 0-8298-1003-X [TDig 42,168].

7217 **Hardin** Garrett, Living within limits; ecology, economics, and population taboos. Ox 1993, UP. x-349 p. – ᴿFrSZ 41 (1994) 282-4 (H. *Stücker*: katastrophisch; 'until 1730 it was normal for parents to kill off children they couldn't feed; now that food is plentiful, this is moralized unacceptable').

7218 **Haught** John F., The promise of nature; ecology and cosmic purpose 1993 → 9,7316: ᴿPerspSCF 46 (1994) 197 (J. de *Koning* regrets that he often looks to non-Christian religions for light).

7219 ᴱ**Hervieu-Léger** D., Religion et écologie: ScHum & Rel. P 1993, Cerf. 255 p. [RHE 89,265*].

7220 **Hoedemaker** Bert, Mission und Ökumene auf dem Hintergrund der Säkularisationserfahrung: VerbumSVD 33 (1992) 395-413.

7221 *Høgenhaven* Jesper, De ti bud [+ the animal message] og den gammeltestamentlige kanon: DanTTs 56 (1993) 83-95 [< ZIT 93,325].

7222 *Irrgang* Bernhard, Christliche Umweltethik; eine Einführung: UTb 1671, 1992 → 9,7317 ('-ts-'): ᴿTR 90 (1994) 157-9 (Marianne *Heimbach-Steins*).

7223 **Jung** Shannon, We are home; a spirituality of the environment. NY 1993, Paulist. 170 p. $13 pa. 0-8091-3364-4. – ᴿInterpretation 48 (1994) 434 (J. *Limburg*).

7224 **Kearns** Laurel D., Saving the creation; religious environmentalism: diss. Emory, ᴰ*Ammerman* Nancy. Atlanta 1994. 365 p. 94-24813. – DissA 55 (1994s) p. 991.

7225 *Kohák* Erazim, Varieties of ecological experience; is deep ecology deep enough?: Forefront 1,1 [formerly Desert Call; 1994] 19-21.

7226 *Kowalski* Gary, Do animals have souls? [yes, and are part of *our* soul as well]: CreSpir 9,1 (1993) 20-23.

7227 **Kurisuthara** Varghese, Ecology in the documents of the W.C.C. and the Catholic Church, 1960-1990; a study of their contribution to an ecological ethics: diss. Alfonsiana, ᴰ*Johnstone* B. Rome 1994. 119 p. – StMor 32 (1994) no. 2; RTLv 26, p. 574.

7228 ᴱ**Land** R. D., *Moore* Louis A., The earth is the Lord's; Christians and the environment. Nv 1992, Broadman. [$11 pa., 0-8054-1627-7 in BIP, putting ᴱ*Moore* first]. – ᴿPerspSCF 46 (1994) 198s (R. H. *Bube*); RExp 91 (1994) 120s (G. C. *Garrison*).

7229 *a) Lane* Belden C., Mother Earth as metaphor; – *b) May* John D., 'Rights of the earth' and 'care for the earth'; two paradigms for a Buddhist-Christian ecological ethic; – *c) Clifford* Anne M., Postmodern scientific cosmology and the Christian God of creation: → 120, ᶠSLOYAN G., Horizons 21 (1994) 7-2 / 48-61 / 62-84.

7230 *a) Langkammer* Hugolin, ❷ Biblia a ekologia; – *b) Witaszek* Gabriel, ❷ La chiesa e l'ecologia; – *c) Ordon* Hubert, ❷ Das Verhältnis der Menschen zum Tierwelt im Lichte der hl. Schrift [*Sucha* Jerzy, Gn 1,26-28]: Zeszyty Naukowe 36 (Lublin 1993) 3-12; Eng. 12 / 43-56; ital. 56 / 25-31; deutsch 31s [13-22; Eng. 22s].

7230* *a) Leimbacher* Jörg, Die Würde von Mensch und Natur ist unteilbar; – *b) Daecke* Sigurd M., Eigeninteresse des Menschen — Eigenwert der Natur: Universitas 19 (1994) 106-118 / 133-145.

7231 *Limouris* Gennadios, Environnement en danger, natura en péril, création menacée? Moratorium eschatologique d'une perspective orthodoxe: TAth 64 (1993) 80-143; Eng. 879.

7231* **Linzey** Andrew, Christianity and the rights of animals c.1992 → 9,7324: ᴿCanadCathR 10,2 (1992) 29s (D.W.T. *Brattston*: unfavorable).

7232 *Linzey* Andrew, Liberation theology and the oppression of animals: ScotJT 46 (1993) 507-525.

7233 **Lochbühler** Wilfried, Christliche Umweltsethik; theologische und philosophisch-ethische Grundlagen und Aspekte ökologieverträglichen Wirtschaftens: Diss. ᴰ*Münk* H. Luzern 1994. 346 p. – RTLv 26,575.

7234 *McCarthy* John, Le Christ cosmique et l'âge de l'écologie: NRT 116 (1994) 27-47 > The cosmic Christ and ecology, ᵀᴱ*Jermann* Rosemary, TDig 41 (1994) 123-6.

7235 **McFague** Sallie, The body of God, an ecological theology 1993 → 9,7328: ᴿAnglTR 76 (1994) 382-4 (Deborah M. *Warner*); ExpTim 105 (1993s) 186s (M. *Palmer*: good questions inadequately answered); Horizons 21 (1994) 360s (Anne M. *Clifford*); Interpretation 48 (1994) 314.6 (Rosemary R. *Ruether*); JTS 45 (1994) 429-431 (M. *Wiles*); ModT 10 (1994) 417-9 (Kathryn *Tanner*); PrincSemB 15 (1994) 307s (M.I. *Wallace*); SvTKv 70 (1994) 85-87 (Sigurd *Bergmann*); TLond 97 (1994) 197s (Mary *Grey*).

7236 **Maldamé** Jean-Michel, Le Christ et le cosmos; incidence de la cosmologie moderne sur la théologie. P 1993, Desclée. 306 p. 2-7189-0603-0. – ᴿRHPR 73 (1993) 467s (G. *Siegwalt*).

7236* *Manzone* Gianni, Etica ed ecologia come scienza: ScuolC 122 (1994) 711-734.

7237 *Mascall* Margaret, La sacramentalidad de la creación en la teología de Edward SCHILLEBEECKX, ᵀ*Ramos* Luis: Anamnesis 4,2 (1994) 73-84.

7237* **Menozzi** Daniele, La Chiesa cattolica e la secolarizzazione: PiccBt. T 1993, Einaudi. 278 p. – ᴿRivStoLR 30 (1994) 630-3 (F. *Traniello*).

7238 *Mildenberger* Friedrich, Gott und Gaja? Anfragen an Jürgen MOLTMANN: EvT [53/5 (1993)] 54 (1994) 380-4 (-7, Antwort).

7239 **Moltmann** Jürgen, Deus na criação; doutrina ecológica da criação, ᵀ*Reimer* H. & Ivona. Petrópolis 1992, Vozes. 453 p. 85-326-0881-7. – ᴿPerspT 26 (1994) 106s (J.B. *Libânio*); REB 54 (1994) 512s (J.B. *Libânio*).

7240 **Murray** R., The cosmic covenant 1992 → 8,7226; 9,7335: ᴿAustralasCR 70 (1993) 132s (Marie *Farrell*); CBQ 56 (1994) 772-4 (L.E. *Frizzell*); CritRR 6 (1993) 172s (R.J. *Clifford* find more on covenant than on ecology); ETL 69 (1993) 187s (W.A.M. *Beuken*); Way 33 (1993) 75s (Elizabeth *Lord*).

7240* **Nennen** Heinz-Ulrich, Ökologie im Diskurs; zu Grundfragen der Anthropologie und Ökologie und zur Ethik der Wissenschaften. Opladen 1991, Westd. 362 p. DM 56. – ᴿUniversitas 47 (1992) 482-4 (P. *Nickl*).

7241 **Oelschlaeger** Max, The idea of wilderness; prehistory to the age of ecology 1991 → 9,7341: ᴿAmJTP 14 (1993) 105 (J.A. *Stone*).

7242 **Oelschläger** Max, Caring for creation; an ecumenical approach to the environmental crisis. NHv 1994, Yale Univ. x-285 p. £22.50. 0-300-05817-9 [TDig 42,82]. – ᴿTBR 7,2 (1994s) 28 (C. *Elliott*, also on same main-title by C. PARK 1992).

7243 **Oikonomou** Elias V., Ⓖ Theological ecology, theory and practice. Athenae 1994, Despoini Maurommati. 368 p. – ᴿTAth 65 (1994) 188-193 (E.A. *Theodorou*, Ⓖ).

7244 a) *Olson* Roger E., Resurrection, cosmic liberation, and Christian earth keeping [response, *Bouma-Prediger* Steven]; – b) *Newport* John P., Facing toward the millennial year 2000 under biblical guidance with a focus on the Resurrection: ➤ 399, ExAud 9 (1993) 123-132 [-136] / 109-121.

7245 **Osborn** L., Guardians of creation 1993 ➤ 9,7342: ᴿChurchman 108 (1994) 374-6 (J. *Ingleby*); ExpTim 2d-top 103,4 (1993s) 99s (C. S. *Rodd*).

7246 **Oviedo Torró** L., La secularización como problema 1990 ➤ 7,7244; 8,7271: ᴿCarthaginensia 10 (1994) 497 (M. *Moreno Villa*).

7247 **Pannenberg** Wolfhart, Toward a theology of nature; essays on science and faith, ᴱ*Peters* Ted. LvL 1993, W-Knox. x-186 p. – ᴿAnglTR 76 (1994) 538-540 (Barbara *Smith-Moran*); ExpTim 106 (1994s) 60 (J. *Stewart*).

7248 **Panteghini** G., Il gemito della creazione; ecologia e fede cristiana 1992 ➤ 9,7344: ᴿBenedictina 41 (1994) 554-6 (S. *De Piccoli*).

7248* *Pérez* Adán José, Cultura y vida; los imperativos ecológicos de un nuevo paradigma: AnVal 19 (1993) 373-390.

7249 *Peschke* Karl-Heinz, Christliche Verantwortung für die Tierwelt: Trier-TZ 103 (1994) 233-9.

7249* *Petzoldt* Matthias, Säkularisierung – eine noch brauchbare Interpretationskategorie?: BTZ 11 (1994) 65-82.

7250 *Phan* Peter C., Pope Jᴏʜɴ Pᴀᴜʟ II and the ecological crisis: IrTQ 60 (1994) 59-69.

7251 ᴱ**Pinches** C., *McDaniel* J., Good news for animals? 1993 ➤ 9,7350: ᴿNRT 116 (1994) 590 (L. *Volpe*).

7251* **Primavesi** Anne, From Apc to Gn; ecology, feminism 1991 ➤ 7, 7246*... 9,7351: ᴿÖkRu 42 (1993) 535s (Brigitte *Kahl*).

7252 ᴱ**Rockefeller** Steven C., *Elder* John C., Spirit and nature; why the environment is a religious issue [Middlebury College symposium 1990] 1992 ➤ 8,614: ᴿAmJTP 15 (1994) 89-94 (L. A. *Murray*).

7253 a) *Rolston* Holmesᴵᴵᴵ, Rights and responsibilities on the home planet; – b) *Ferré* Frederick, Persons in nature; toward an applicable and unified environmental ethics: Zygon 28 (1993) 425-439 / 441-453.

7254 *Rosenau* Hartmut, Natur [... ANT]: ➤ 517, TRE 24 (1994) 98-107 [-113 und Übernatur, *Frey* Christopher].

7255 **Ruether** R., Gaia and God 1993 ➤ 9,7358: ᴿExpTim 105 (1993s) 122 (Ann *Loades*); Interpretation 48 (1994) 188-190 (H. *Rolston*); JRel 74 (1994) 580s (Ann *Swahnberg*); PrincSemB 14 (1993) 319-321 (D. T. *Hessel*); Protestantesimo 49 (1994) 407s (Elizabeth E. *Green*); TLond 97 (1994) 197-9 (Mary *Grey*).

7256 a) *Ruppert* Lothar, Schöpfungsbilder im AT im Kontext von 'Natur als Schöpfung'; – b) *Söding* Thomas, Die Welt als Schöpfung in Christus; der Beitrag des Kolosserbriefes zum interreligiösen Dialog; – c) *Stachel* Günter, 'Schöpfungsglaube' und 'Bewahrung der Schöpfung'; eine theologische und pädagogische Aufgabe; – d) *Lüke* Ulrich, Schöpfung als Evolution — Evolution als Schöpfung? Vom faulen Frieden in einem Jahrhundertkonflikt; – e) *Hoepe* Reinhard, Die Erschaffung der Welt aus dem Nichts; das Problem des Grundes in der Schöpfungstheologie; – f) *Spiegel* Egon, Da Tiere eine Seele haben?... Ökopädagogik: RelPBeit 31 (1993) 1-19 / 20-37 / 38-55 / 56-73 / 74-89 / 110-131 [...al.; < ᴢɪᴛ 93,247].

7257 **Russell** Colin A., The earth, humanity and God [Cambridge Templeton Press lectures 1993]. L 1994, University College. 193 p. £30; pa. £10. – ᴿTLond 97 (1994) 483s (D. *Gosling*).

7257* **Santmire** H. P., The travail of nature 1985 ⇥ 4,2136...9,7360: ᴿTsT-Ki 64 (1993) 160 (J. O. *Henriksen*).

7258 **Schäfer-Guigner** Otto, Et demain la terre...: Entrée libre 11. Genève 1990, Labor et Fides. 100 p. – ᴿRTPhil 126 (1994) 392s (M. *Gallopin*).

7259 **Schlitt** Michael, Umweltethik. Pd 1992, Schöningh. 302 p. DM 48. 3-506-77897-8. – ᴿTR 90 (1994) 155-7 (Marianne *Heimbach-Steins*).

7260 **Sheldon** Joseph K., Rediscovery of creation; a bibliographical study of the Church's response to the environmental crisis: ATLA. Metuchen NJ 1992, Scarecrow. xvi-282 p. $35. 0-8108-2539-2. – ᴿTBR 7,2 (1994s) 7s (A. *Johnson*).

7261 **Simkins** Ronald A., Creator and creation; nature in the worldview of ancient Israel. Peabody MA 1994, Hendrickson. xii-306 p.; bibliog. 267-298. 1-56563-042-4.

7262 *Stackhouse* Max L., Can [COBB J. 1992] 'Sustainability' be sustained?: PrincSemB 15 (1994) 143-155.

7263 *Tavernier* Johan De, Ecology and ethics [< CollatVL 23 (1993) 393-418]: LvSt 19 (1994) 235-261.

7263* *Teutsch* Gerhard M., Tier und Mensch; Fallensteller im Garten Eden: LuMon 33,3 (1994) 8-11.

7264 **Thiele** Johannes, Una tierra para el placer de vivir; la salvación de la creación [Die Heiligkeit der Erde], ᵀ*Martínez de Lapera* Víctor A. Barc 1994, Herder. 169 p. – ᴿLumenVr 43 (1994) 367s (U. *Gil Ortega*).

7265 *Vorlaufer* Johannes, Säkularer Prozess und religiöse Sprache; ein Versuch 'Welt' zu erfahren und zu denken: ZkT 116 (1994) 54-67.

7266 *Weigel* Van B., Animal suffering revisited; creeping anthropocentrism and divine double standards [*Wenneberg* Robert, reply]: ChrSchR 22,1 (1992) 71-74 [-77; < ZIT 93,333].

7267 **Wilcken** John, God in our world [can we prevent a secularized even largely Catholic society from football on Good Friday?]. Homebush 1992, St. Paul. 182 p. – ᴿAustralasCR 70 (1993) 396s (B. *Moloney*).

7268 **Wolf** Jean-Claude, Tierethik; neue Perspektiven für Menschen und Tiere. FrS 1992, Paulus. 188 p. – ᴿFrSZ 40 (1993) 492-5 (H. *Ringeling*).

7269 **Young** Richard A., Healing the earth; a therapeutic perspective on environmental problems and their solutions. Nv 1994, Broadman & H. 333 p. $20. 0-8054-1038-4 [TDig 41,391: refuting the case against Christianity].

H3.1 *Foedus* – **the Covenant;** the Chosen People; Providence.

7270 *Beauchamp* Paul, Persona, elezione e universalità nella Bibbia [< convegno Univ. Catt. Milano], ᵀ*Piana* Gabriele: RClerIt 75 (1994) 192-207.

7270* *Ciocchi* David M., Reconciling divine sovereignty and human freedom: JEvTS 37 (1994) 395-412.

7271 **Craig** William L., Divine foreknowledge and human freedom 1991 ⇥ 8,7309: ᴿTrinJ 14 (1993) 101-4 (P. D. *Feinberg*).

7271* a) *Dragona-Monachou* M., Divine providence in the philosophy of the empire; – b) *Spanneut* M., *Apatheia* ancienne... 2. *apatheia* chretienne]: ⇥ 496, ANRW 36,7 (1994) 4417-90 / 4641-4717.

7272 **Duponcheele** Joseph, L'être de l'Alliance; 'le pouvoir de faire être' comme lien philosophique et théologique entre le judaïsme et le christianisme: CogF 170. P 1992, Cerf. 988 p. – ᴿRTAM 60 (1993) 279s (E. *Manning*).

7273 *Edwards* Francis, MOLINA, Molinismus, ᵀ*Wolf* Gerhard P.: ➤ 517, TRE 23 (1994) 199-203.

7274 **Engelsma** David J., Hyper-Calvinism [predestination incompatible with proclamation of an offer of salvation to all who hear] and the call of the Gospel; an examination of the 'well-meant offer' of the Gospel. GR 1994, Reformed Free Publ. 216 p. – ᴿRefR 48 (1994s) 57s (A. *Blok*; laudable aim).

7275 *Fergusson* David A.S., Predestination; a Scottish perspective: ScotJT 46 (1993) 457-478.

7276 *Frydman-Kohl* Baruch, Covenant, conversion and chosenness; MAIMO-NIDES and HALEVI on 'Who is a Jew?: Judaism 41 (1992) 64-79.

7277 **Gorringe** T.J., God's theatre; a theology of providence 1991 ➤ 8,7315; 9,7392: ᴿScotJT 47 (1994) 119s (Ruth *Page*).

7278 **Hanson** Paul D., Das berufene Volk; Entstehen und Wachsen der Gemeinde in der Bibel [The people called 1986 ➤ 2,6072 ... 7,7882*], ᵀ*Fischer* Maria. Neuk 1993. xiv-561 p. DM 88. 3-7887-1358-5 [TR 90,173];

7279 **Helm** Paul, The providence of God. DG 1993, InterVarsity. 241 p. $15 pa. – ᴿWestTJ 56 (1994) 438-442 (J.M. *Frame*).

7280 **Holtrop** Philip C., The Bolsec controversy on predestination, from 1551 to 1555; the statements of Jerome BOLSEC, and the responses of John CALVIN, Theodore BEZA and other Reformed theologians, I. Theological currents, the setting and mood, and the trial itself. Lewiston NY 1993, Mellen. xxviii-409 p.; p. 410-1033. 0-7734-9248-8; -50-5. – ᴿRHE 89 (1994) 486s (J.-F. *Gilmont*).

7281 *Ibáñez Arana* Andrés, Israel, el pueblo elegido: LumenVr 42 (1993) 3-29.

7281* *Jospe* Raphael, The concept of the Chosen People; an interpretation: Judaism 43 (1994) 127-148.

7282 **Langendijk** L., De weerglans der verkiezing; over Karl BARTH's Kirchliche Dogmatik II 2 9 34 'De verkiezing van de gemeente' [election, predestination], diss. Amst, ᴰ*Zuurmond* R. Gorinchem 1994, Narratio. 227 p. 90-5263-126-3. – TvT 34 (1994) 296.

7283 **Lohfink** Norbert, The covenant never revoked ... Christian-Jewish dialogue, ᵀ*Scullion* John J., 1991 ➤ 7,7279 ... 9,7393: ᴿScripB 23,2 (1993) 42s (M. *McNamara*).

7283* *Mendes Fernández* Benito, El problema de la salvación de los 'infieles' en Francisco de VITORIA: Compostellanum 38,1 (1993) 78-139.

7284 *Pang* Ann A., AUGUSTINE on divine foreknowledge and human free will: RÉAug 40 (1994) 417-431.

7285 *Pierce* Ronald W., Covenant conditionality and a future for Israel: JEvTS 37 (1994) 27-38.

7286 **Röhser** Günter, Prädestination und Verstockung; Untersuchungen zur frühjüdischen, paulinischen und johanneischen Theologie: TANZ 14. Tü 1994, Francke. xiii-279 p.; Bibliog. 258-267. 3-7720-1865-3.

7286* **Rosenau** Hartmut, Allversöhnung, ein transzendentaltheologischer Grundlegungsversuch: ThBt Töpelmann 57. B 1993, de Gruyter. x-544 p. DM 212. 3-11-013738-0. – ᴿTLZ 119 (1994) 693-6 (M. *Bieler*).

7287 **Sohn** S.T., The divine election of Israel 1991 ➤ 8,7327: ᴿBL (1993) 117 (R.E. *Clements*: thorough).

7288 **Sturch** Richard, The new deism [WILES M., God's action 1986]; divine intervention and the human condition. L 1990, Duckworth. 154 p. 1-85399-152-X. – ᴿChurchman 108 (1994) 182s (D. *Spanner*).

H3.3   *Fides in VT* –   **Old Testament faith.**

7289 **Crenshaw** James L., Old Testament story and faith; literary and theological introduction. Peabody 1992, Hendrickson. viii-472 p. $20. **Barr** J., Biblical faith 1993 ➤ 7639.

7290 **Herrmann** Wolfram, Jüdische Glaubensfundamente: BeitErfAJ 36. Fra 1993, Lang. 114 p.; 3 pl. 3-631-46817-2. – ᴿJStJud 25 (1994) 319s (A. S. van der *Woude*).

7291 *Kaiser* Walterᴶ, Salvation in the OT, with special emphasis on the object and content of personal belief: Jian Dao 2 (Hong Kong 1994) 1-18 [OTAbs 17, p. 622 gives the published abstract, without indicating whether the article is in Chinese].

7291* **Schmidt** W. H., Alttestamentlicher Glaube in seiner Geschichte. Neuk 1990. 392 p. – ᴿAtKap 122 (1994) 400-403 (J. *Warzecha*, ℗).

H3.5   *Liturgia, spiritualitas VT* –   **OT prayer.**

7292 **Balentine** S. E., Prayer in the Hebrew Bible 1993 ➤ 9,7414: ᴿExpTim 105 (1993s) 247s (J. *Eaton*); OTAbs 17 (1994) 457s (D. E. *Cox*).

7293 ᴱ**Bonora** A., Espiritualidad de l'AT, I: Nueva Alianza 120. S 1994, Sígueme. 543 p. 84-301-1229-4. – ᴿRET 54 (1994) 348-351 (P. *Barrado-Fernández*).

7294 ᴱ**Bradshaw** Paul F., *Hoffman* Lawrence A., The changing face of Jewish and Christian worship in North America 1991 ➤ 9,7419: ᴿTorJT 10 (1994) 141 (Jacoba H. *Kuikman*).

7295 ᴱ**Bradshaw** P., *Hoffman* L., The making of Jewish and Christian worship 1991 ➤ 7,474... 9,7420: ᴿTLond 97 (1994) 56s (F. G. *Downing*).

7296 **Cimosa** Mario, La preghiera nella Bibbia greca 1992 ➤ 9,10168: ᴿSefarad 54 (1994) 198-200 (N. *Fernández Marcos*).

7297 **Cohen** Jeffrey M., Prayer and penitence; a commentary on the High Holy Day Machzor [= 'cycle', i.e. Roš ha-Šanâ and Yom Kippur]. Northvale ɴᴊ 1994, Aronson. xxvii-303 p. 1-56821-046-9.

7298 **Cohen** R., (Prière d'Israel), *al.*, Prier: Chêne de Mambré. P 1992, Centurion. 187 p. F 100 [NRT 116,310].

7299 **Di Sante** Carmine, Jewish prayer; the origins of Christian liturgy, ᵀ*O'Connell* Matthew J. 1991 ➤ 8,7344; 9,7428: ᴿJEarlyC 1 (1993) 443s (G. E. *Saint-Laurent*).

7300 **Elbogen** Ismar, Jewish liturgy; a comprehensive history, ᵀ*Scheindlin* Raymond P. 1993 ➤ 9,7429: ᴿJRel 74 (1994) 586s (P. V. *Bohlman*); RelStR 20 (1994) 161 (M. *Jaffee*: a monument, but time has moved on).

7301 **Fishbane** Michael A., The kiss of God; spiritual and mystical death in Judaism (Stroum Lectures). Seattle 1994, Univ. Washington. xii-156 p. 0-295-97308-0.

7301* **Gold** Avie, The complete Artscroll Machzor. AmstLinguistic. NY 1985-1994, Mesorah. I. Rosh ha-Shanah, 1985; 710 p. V. Shavuos 1991. 0-89906-676-3; -876-6.

7302 **Harrich** Walter & *Zandberg* Danuta, Fest und Feier im Judentum – Pessach. Stu c. 1992, 2-7668-3271-9, mit 15-Min. Film und 16 S. Begleitheft. – ᴿDielB 28 (1992s) 257s (B. J. *Diebner*).

7303 **Harris** Monford, Exodus and exile; the structure of Jewish holidays

1992 ⟶ 9,7439: ᴿRExp 91 (1994) 615 (J. F. *Drinkard*: interpretation rather than description).

7304 ᴱHeide A. van der, *Voolen* E. van, The Amsterdam Mahzor 1989 ⟶ 5,1672: ᴿBijdragen 55 (1994) 334 (J. van *Buiten*); Kairos 32s (1990s) 252s (Ursula *Schubert*).

7304* **Heschel** Abraham J., ❷ Sabbath and its significance [1951], ᵀ*Hałkowski*. Gdańsk 1994, Atext. 104 p. – ᴿRuBi 47 (1994) 291 (J. *Chmiel*, ❷).

7305 **Jacobs** Louis, Hasidic prayer. L 1993, Littman Library. xxv-195 p. 1-874774-18-8.

7306 **Langer** Ruth, The impact of custom, history, and mysticism on the shaping of Jewish liturgical law: diss. HUC, ᴰ*Petuchowski* J. Cincinnati 1994. 524 p. 94-27340. – DissA 55 (1994s) p. 2007.

7307 **McKay** Heather A., Sabbath and synagogue; the question of sabbath worship in ancient Judaism: RelGrRW 122. Leiden 1994, Brill. xi-279 p.; bibliog. 252-264. 90-04-10060-1 [JTS 46,610, S. C. *Reif*].

7308 *Maier* Johann, Sühne und Vergebung in der jüdischen Liturgie: JbBT 9 (1994) 145-171.

7309 **Martin-Achard** Robert, Dieu de toutes les fidélités; les grands thèmes bibliques à travers les célébrations d'Israël. Aubonne 1992, Moulin. 117 p. Fs 14. – ᴿÉTRel 68 (1993) 424s (D. *Lys*); Protestantesimo 48 (1993) 334 (Bertha *Subilia*).

7309* **Nitzan** B., Qumran prayer and religious poetry [ᴰ1991 ❶], ᴰ*Licht* J., ᵀ*Chapman* Jonathan: StTDJD 12. Leiden 1994, Brill. xxi-415 p. ƒ165. 90-04-09658-2 [BL 45,162, M. A. *Knibb*; RB 102,505, Annette *Steudel*].

7310 *Preuss* H.-D.†, Neujahrsfest AT [*Lenhardt* Pierre, Judentum]: ⟶ 517, TRE 24 (1994) 320s [322-334].

7311 **Prijs** Leo, Worte zum Sabbat; über die jüdische Religion: Reihe 419. Mü 1990, Beck. 117 p. DM 16,80. 3-406-14011-3. – ᴿBijdragen 55 (1994) 83 (J. van *Ruiten*: not about Sabbath but thoughts for preparing interiorly for Sabbath).

7312 **Reif** Stefan C., Judaism and Hebrew prayer 1993 ⟶ 9,7452: ᴿExpTim 105 (1993s) 157 (C. H. *Middleburgh*); JStJud 25 (1994) 118s (J. *Maier*); JTS 45 (1994) 285-7 (P. *Bradshaw*).

7313 **Remaud** Michel, Le mérite des Pères dans la tradition juive ancienne et dans la liturgie synagogale: diss. Institut Catholique. ᴰ*Perrot* C. Paris 1994. 405 p. – RICathP 46,211; RTLv 26,534.

7314 **Ross** Lesli Koppelman, Celebrate! The complete Jewish Holidays handbook. Northvale NJ 1994, Aronson. xxviii-346 p. 1-56821-154-6.

7315 **Rothstein** David, From Bible to Murabbaᶜat; studies in the textual and scribal features of phylacteries and mezuzot in ancient Israel and early Judaism: diss. UCLA 1992, ᴰ*Segert* S. xxi-532 p. 93-01560. – OIAc 7,43.

7315* *Stone* Ira F., Worship and redemption; recovering our spiritual vocabulary: Judaism 43 (1994) 66-77..

Swartz Michael, Mystical prayer in ancient Judaism 1992 ⟶ 9960.

7316 ᴱTrotta Giuseppe, La via del deserto tra ebraismo e cristianesimo: Attendendo l'aurora. Brescia 1993, Morcelliana. 178 p. 88-372-1508-8.

7316* **Weinberg** Werner, Lexikon zum religiösen Wortschatz und Brauchtum der deutschen Juden [+ index 40 p. hebräischer Wörter], ᴱ*Röll* Walter. Bad Cannstatt 1994. 356 p. – ᴿREJ 153 (1994) 454s (M. R. *Hayoun*).

7317 *Weitzman* Michael P., ❶ Biblical elements in Jewish prayer: ⟶ 146, ᶠYEIVIN I. 1992.

7317* **Zahavy** Tzvee, Studies in Jewish prayer. Lanham MD 1990, UPA. vii-182 p. $34.75. – ᴿCritRR 6 (1993) 434-6 (R. *Kimelman*).

H3.7 *Theologia moralis VT* – **OT moral theology.**

7318 **Amsel** Nachum, The Jewish encyclopedia of moral and ethical issues. Northvale NJ 1994, Aronson. xi-505 p. 1-56821-174-0.
7319 **Birch** Bruce C., Let justice roll down; the Old Testament, ethics, and Christian life 1991 ➤ 7,8308 ... 9,7464: ᴿInterpretation 48 (1994) 74-77 (D. A. *Knight*).
7320 **Borowitz** Eugene B., Exploring Jewish ethics; papers on covenant responsibility. Detroit 1990, Wayne State Univ. 499 p. – ᴿAJS 17 (1992) 115-7 (S. D. *Breslauer*).
7320* *Bovati* Pietro, L'esercizio della giustizia nella Bibbia, I. Il giudizio del colpevole; II. La lite bilaterale: RClerIt 75 (1994) 487-498 . 575-586.
7321 **Cohen** Hermann, L'éthique du judaïsme; ᵀᴱ*Hayoun* M.-R.: Passages. P 1994, Cerf. 354 p. 2-204-04972-7.
7322 ᵀᴱ**Cohen** Seymour J., *Iggeret ha-Kodesh*, the holy letter; a study in Jewish sexual morality. Northvale NJ 1993 = 1976, Aronson. 187 p. 1-56821-086-8.
7322* *Dresner* Samuel H., [Lv 18,28] Homosexuality and the order of creation: Judaism 40 (1991) 309-321.
7323 **Droge** A., *Tabor* J., A noble death; suicide and martyrdom 1992 ➤ 8,7423; 9,7466: ᴿBR 10,4 (1994) 12.14 (A. Katherine *Grieb*); JBL 113 (1994) 358-360 (J. M. *White*); TorJT 10 (1994) 258s (Carolina F. *Whelan*).
7324 **Janzen** Waldemar, Old Testament ethics; a paradigmatic approach. LVL 1994, W-Knox. 236 p. $20. 0-664-25410-1. – ᴿAnglTR 76 (1994) 524-6 (S. A. *Wiggins*); TBR 7,2 (1994s) 29 (R. *Coggins*).
7325 **Koch** Robert, Die Bundesmoral im Alten Testament. Fra 1994, Lang. 92 p. 3-631-46976-4.
7326 *Lion-Cachet* F.-N., Abolition or mitigation of the death penalty; a perspective on the laws of Israel: In die Skriflig 28 (1994) 89-101 [< OTAbs 17, p. 477].
7327 ᴱ**Lorenzani** Massimo, La volontà di Dio nella Bibbia: StB 13. L'Aquila 1994, ISSRA. xiii-236 p. Lᵐ 25.
7328 **Otto** Eckart, Theologische Ethik des Alten Testaments: TWiss 3/2. Stu 1994, Kohlhammer. 298 p. DM 40. 3-17-008923-4 [Biblica 76, 560-2, A. *Schenker*].
7329 *Rodd* C. S., New occasions teach new duties? 1. The use of the OT in Christian ethics: ExpTim 105 (1993s) 100-106.
7330 *Salvatierra* Ángel, El emigrante y el extranjero en la Biblia: Lumen/Vr 42 (1993) 175-187; > Eng. ᵀᴱ*Bonness* Mary Kay: TDig 42,141-4.
7330* *Satlow* Michael L., 'Wasted seed'; the history of a rabbinic idea: HUCA 65 (1994) 137-175.
7331 **Schuman** N. A., Gelijk om gelijk; verslag en balans van een discussie over goddelijke vergelding in het Oude Testament [KOCH K. 1955: God does not punish sin, sin punishes itself]. Amst 1993, Vrije Univ. xii-590 p. ƒ 69,50. 90-5383-263-7. – ᴿOTAbs 17 (1994) 462 (C. T. *Begg*): OT supports Koch, but often adds 'hope' that God will intervene where needed).
7332 **Seeley** David, The noble death 1990 ➤ 6,6116; 7,5208: ᴿJStJud 23 (1992) 134-7 (J. W. van *Henten*).

7333 *Shulman* Harvey,   The Bible and political thought; Daniel J. ELAZAR's contribution to the Jewish political tradition: Judaism 41 (1992) 18-30.

H3.8   *Bellum et pax VT-NT* – **War and peace in the whole Bible.**

7334 **Beestermöller** Gerhard,   T. von AQUIN und der gerechte Krieg 1990
➤ 7,7325: ᴿTPhil 68 (1994) 103-5 (F. *Ricken*); TPQ 140 (1992) 314s (G. *Wildmann*).

7335 *Charlton* Mark W.,   The ethical dilemmas of armed humanitarian intervention: CGrebel 12 (1994) 1-20; 217-221, response, *Regehr* E.

7336 ᴱ**Decosse** David E.,   But was it just? Reflections on the morality of the Persian Gulf war. NY 1992, Doubleday. x-132 p. $15. – ᴿLuthQ 7 (1993) 482-4 (Faye E. *Schott*).

7337 *a*) *Delàs* Josep,   El cristianisme europeu, creador d'una teologia de la guerra; – *b*) *Panikkar* Raimon,   L'albada de la cristiania: QVidCr 161 (1991) 15-33 / 34-44.

7338 **Espinel Marcos** J.L.,   El pacifismo del NT: Paradosis 8, 1992 ➤ 8,7372; 9,7502: ᴿEstE 69 (1994) 271s (R. *Aguirre*); ETL 69 (1993) 433-5 (J. *Verheyden*); ScripTPamp 26 (1994) 888s (J.R. *Villar*).

7339 **Heim** François,   La théologie de la victoire de Constantin à Théodose 1992 ➤ 8,7376; 9,7507: ᴿByZ 86 (1994) 131 (G. *Podskalsky*); RÉAug 40 (1994) 228-231 (F. *Paschoud*); RHPR 74 (1994) 312s (P. *Maraval*); RTLv 25 (1994) 240 (A. de *Halleux*); ScEspr 46 (1994) 123-5 (P.-H. *Poirier*); TPhil 69 (1994) 275s (H.J. *Sieben*); VigChr 48 (1994) 78-83 (A. *Bastiaansen*).

7340 **Hellwig** Monika K.,   A case for peace in reason and faith. ColMn 1992, Glazier-Liturgical. 112 p. $7. 0-8146-5834-2. – ᴿExpTim 105 (1993s) 122 (J. *Johansen-Berg*).

7340* **Hobbs** T.R.,   A time for war; a study of warfare in the OT: OTSt 3, 1989 ➤ 6,7532 ... 9,7509: ᴿCritRR 5 (1992) 139-142 (H.C. *Washington*).

7341 *Joubert* S.,   Jesus van Nazaret se bevrydende visie vir 'n geweldadige samelewing: SkrifKerk 14,2 (1993) 222-235 [< NTAbs 38, p. 353].

7342 *Lambrecht* Jan,   Is active nonviolent resistance Jesus' third way? An answer to Walter WINK: LvSt 19 (1998) 350s.

7343 *Lana* Italo, [1989 ➤ 7,7338 Studi su] L'idea della pace nell'antichità: Enciclopedia della Pace 10. Fiesole 1991, Cultura della Pace. 214 p. – ᴿOrpheus 14 (1993) 184-6 (F. *Corsaro*).

7343* *Lilley* J.P.U.,   Understanding the *ḥerem*: TyndB 44 (1993) 169-177.

7344 **Lincoln** Bruce,   Death, war, and sacrifice 1991 ➤ 7,222*d*: ᴿJRit 8 (1994) 131-4 (C.S. *Littleman*).

7345 **Lingen** J. van der,   Les guerres de Y: LDiv 139, 1990 ➤ 6,7359; 7,7339: ᴿBZ 38 (1994) 115-7 (Helga *Weippert*); FrSZ 40 (1993) 476-9 (A. *Schenker*).

7346 **Kurtz** Michael R.,   A comparison of Jewish and Muslim views of religious war: diss. ᴰ*Miller* R. Regina 1994. 209 p. MM91025. [DissA-disk] MAI 33 (1994s) p. 362.

7347 *a*) *Lohfink* Norbert,   La 'guerre sainte' et le 'bannissement' dans l'AT; – *b*) *Henrici* Peter,   Deux approches philosophiques de la guerre et de la paix: ➤ 264, Communio 19,114 (P 1994) 33-44 / 13-31.

7348 **Mauser** Ulrich,   The Gospel of peace; a scriptural message for today's world 1992 ➤ 8,7395; 9,7517: ᴿCritRR 6 (1993) 257-9 (A.J. *Tambasco*).

7349 ᴱ**Miller** Richard B.,   War in the twentieth century; studies in theological ethics. LvL 1992, W-Knox. xviii-469. $22. 0-664-25323-7. – ᴿHorizons 21 (1994) 217 (J.H. *Yoder*: value despite limitations).

7350 **Miller** Richard B., Interpretations of conflict; ethics, pacifism, and the just-war tradition 1991 → 8,7396; 9,7519:   RRelStR 20 (1994) 135 (T. M. *Renick*).

7351 **Musto** Ronald G., Catholic peacemakers; a documentary history; 1. From the Bible to the era of the Crusades, NT 1993, Garland.   xli-818 p. $95.   0-8253-0604-0 [TDig 41,278].

7352 **Niditch** Susan,   War in the Hebrew Bible; a study in the ethics of violence 1993 → 9,7522:   RBInterp 2 (1994) 231s (H. C. *Washington*); BL (1994) 112 (R. J. *Coggins*); Interpretation 48 (1994) 436s (B. C. *Ollenburger*); JRel 74 (1994) 381s (J. S. *Kaminsky*); SWJT 36,3 (1993s) 65s (R. *Johnson*); TS 54 (1993) 770s (Alice L. *Laffey*); TvT 34 (1994) 77 (A. van *Iersel*).

7353 **Perretto** Elio,   La sfida aperta; le strade della violenza e della nonviolenza dalla Bibbia a Lattanzio 1993 → 9,7524*:   RCBQ 56 (1994) 803-5 (S. B. *Marrow*: difficult reading, unhelpful print); RivB 42 (1994) 500s (A. *Rolla*).

7353* *Prosperi* Adriano,   I cristiani e la guerra; una controversia fra '500 e '700 [1500-1800]: RivStorLR 30 (1994) 57-83.

7354 *Reventlow* Henning,   Das Thema 'Frieden' im AT, in EBinder G., *Effe* B., Krieg und Frieden im Altertum (Trier 1989) 110-122 [ArBegG 36 (1993) 338s (ipse)].

7355 **Ruelland** Jacques G.,   Histoire de la guerre sainte: Que sais-je? 2716. P 1993, PUF.   127 p.   2-13-045071-7. – RÉTRel 69 (1994) 285s (L. *Gambarotto*: complément de ELEFORT B. 1991/2).

Rüpke Jörg, Domi militiae, die religiöse Konstruktion des Krieges in Rom D1990 → 10542.

7356 **Sherlock** C.,   The God who fights; the war tradition in Holy Scripture: Rutherford ContempT 6.   Lewiston NY 1993, Mellen.   xiii-445 p. $80. 0-7734-1653-6 [NTAbs 38, p. 314].

7357 *Stone* G. R.,   Great Bible battles: BurHist 30,1 (1994) 11-33; 10 maps.

7357* **Swartley** W. M.,   Love of enemies/non retaliation NT 1992 → 9,7528: RBR 10,5 (1994) 18 (A. C. *Winn*).

7358 *Viaene* Vincent,   Catholic attitudes towards war and peace from the 'fin-de-siècle' to World War I; the French case: RHE 89 (1994) 390-411.

7359 *Walzer* Michael,   The idea of Holy War in ancient Israel: JRelEth 20 (1992) 215-228. 235s (229-234, *Yoder* John H., response); 237-259, *Hehir* J. Bryan, just-war theory.

7360 **Winn** Albert C.,   Ain' gonna study war no more 1993 → 9,7532: RPrincSemB 15 (1994) 74a (G. *Zerbe*).

7361 *Zenger* Klaus (*Nientiedt* Klaus, interview), 'Das Alte Testament ist eindeutig gewaltkritisch': HerdKorr 47 (1993) 505-511.

7362 **Zerbe** G. M.,   Non retaliation in early Jewish and Christian texts, D1993 → 9,7534: RTLZ 119 (1994) 1083-5 (W. *Wiefel*).

H4.1 Messianismus.

7362* *Alonso Díaz* José,   La Utopía del paraíso [... 'pacifismo' primitivo en el mundo animal; utopía del hombre transformado, de la tierra fertil; Ezec 36, Zac 9-14: BibFe 20,59 (El hechizo de la Utopía 1994) 5-45.

7363 *Blancy* A.,   Le 'fils de Dieu' au défi du messianisme juif: BCentProt 45,4 (1993) 18-33 [< NTAbs 38, p. 232].

7364 *Bock* Darrell L.,   Current Messianic activity and OT Davidic promise; dispensationalism, hermeneutics, and NT fulfillment: TrinJ 15 (1994) 55-87.

7365 ᴱ**Charlesworth** J. H., The Messiah 1987/92 → 8,463; 9,7538:   ᴿPrinc-
SemB 15 (1994) 204s (D. *Flusser*).
7366 *Collins* John J., The works of the Messiah [4Q521, *Puech* É.
RQum 15 (1992) 475]: DSD 1 (1994) 98-112.
7367 *García Cordero* Maximiliano, Las esperanzas mesiánicas judías y el
mesianismo de Jesús: → 22, ᶠCASCIARO J., Biblia 1994, 221-247.
7368 *a) García Martínez* Florentino, Los Mesías de Qumrán; problemas de
un traductor; – *b) Kenig* Évelyne, Cristóbal COLÓN, descubridor mesiánico
y compilador de profecías: Sefarad 53 (1993) 345-360 / 361-9.
7369 *a) García Martínez* Florentino, Messianische Erwartungen in den
Qumranschriften; – *b) Thoma* Clemens, Redimensionierungen des frühjüdischen Messianismus; – *c) Heid* Stefan, Frühjüdische Messianologie in
JUSTINS 'Dialog'; – *d) Stemberger* Günter, Die Messiasfrage in den
christlich-jüdischen Disputationen des Mittelalters: JbBT 8 (1993)
171-208 / 209-218 / 219-238 / 239-250.
7369* *a) Körtner* Ulrich H. J., Theologia messianica; zur Kategorie des Messianischen in der gegenwärtigen dogmatischen Diskussion; – *b) Niebuhr*
Karl-Wilhelm, Jesus Christus und die vielfältigen messianischen Erwartungen Israels; ein Forschungsbericht: JbBT 8 (1993) 347-369 / 337-345.
7370 *McGarry* Michael, The meaning of the Messiah: Thought 67 (1992)
385-398.
7370* *Mardones* José M., Funciones y tareas para un mesianismo de
resistencia y creatividad: SalT 82 (1994) 43-51.
7371 **Oegema** Gerbern S., De messiaanse verwachtingen ten tijde van Jezus;
een inleiding in de messiaanse verwachtingen en bewegingen gedurende de
hellenistisch-romeins tijd [Diss. Berlin VU 1989]. Baarn 1993, Ten Have.
214 p. *f* 40. – ᴿBijdragen 55 (1994) 442-4 (J. van *Ruiten*).
7372 **Oegema** Gerbern S., [→ 9,7543], Der Gesalbte und sein Volk; Untersuchungen zum Konzeptualisierungsprozess der messianischen Erwartungen von den Makkabäern bis Bar Koziba [< Diss. FU Berlin 1990,
ᴰ*Schäfer* P.]: Delitzschianum 2. Gö 1994, Vandenhoeck & R. 351 p.
DM 98. 3-525-54201-1 [OTAbs 17, p. 686].
7372* *Rosenthal* Gilbert S., Messianism reconsidered: Judaism 40 (1991)
552-568.
7373 *Schreiner* Stefan, Die Säkularisierung der messianischen Idee; jüdischer
und polnischer Messianismus im 19. Jahrhundert: EvT 54 (1994) 45-60.
7373* ᴱ**Stegemann** Ekkehard, Messias-Vorstellungen bei Juden und Christen
1993 → 9,7547: ᴿJudaica 49 (1993) 238s (H. L. *Reichrath*).
7374 **Thoma** Clemens, Das Messiasprojekt; Theologie jüdisch-christlicher
Begegnung. Augsburg 1994, Pattloch. 460 p. DM 42. – ᴿEntschluss 49,12
(1994) 46 (T. M. *Meier*).
7375 **Van Groningen** Gerard, Messianic revelation in the Old Testament 1990
→ 6,7388; 7,7365: TrinJ 14 (1993) 93s (G. D. *Robinson*) & 94-97 (K.
Kimble).

H4.3 *Eschatologia VT –* **OT hope of future life.**

7376 *Abogunrin* S. O., Immortality and resurrection in early Judaism: Orita
23 (Ibadan 1991) 15-34 [< OTAbs 16,354].
7377 *Alonso Díaz* José, La utopía del paraíso; reflexión a la luz del Antiguo
Testamento: BibFe 59 ('El hechizo de la utopía' 1994) 5-30 [p. 3, *Tamayo*
J.: '*Hechizo* proviene del latín *facticium* e significa atractivo natural e
intenso'; the dictionary gives also 'magic' and (in first place) 'fake'].

7378 **Bloch-Smith** Elizabeth, Judahite burial practices and beliefs about the dead: jOsu 123, 1992 ➤ 9,e275: ᴿZAW 105 (1993) 130 (M. *Köckert*).

7379 **England** Archie W., An investigation of resurrection language and imagery in the Old Testament in the light of its Ancient Near Eastern literary background: diss. Mid-America Baptist Theol. Sem. 1994. 270 p. 94-27482. – DissA 55 (1994s) p. 1590.

7380 *Horst* Pieter W. van der, 'The elements will be dissolved with fire'; the idea of cosmic conflagration in Hellenism, Ancient Judaism, and early Christianity [ineditum] ➤ 186, Hellenism 1994, 227-251.

7380* **Johnston** P. S., The underworld and the dead in the OT: diss. Cambridge 1993, ᴰ*Gordon* R. P. – TyndB 45 (1994) 415-9.

7381 *a) La Fuente* Alfonso de, La vida después de la muerte según las 'Antigüedades Bíblicas' del Pseudo-Filón; – *b) Rodríguez Carmona* Antonio, Tradiciones sobre el juicio en el targum palestinense: ➤ 22, ᶠCASCIARO J. M., Biblia 1994, 423-433 / 435-445.

7382 *a) Plieth* M., Leben und Tod im AT; – *b) Pöhlmann* W., Hinabgestiegen in das Reich des Todes: Glaube und Lernen 9 (1994) 17-29 / 30-38 [< ZAW 106,498].

7383 **Puech** Émile, La croyance des Esséniens en la vie future 1993 ➤ 8,7427c; 9,7555: ᴿBL (1994) 114 (G. J. *Brooke*); CRAI (1994) 22s (A. *Caquot*); DSD 1 (1994) 246-252 (J. J. *Collins*); JStJud 25 (1994) 114-8 (F. *García Martínez*); RivB 42 (1994) 337-348 (B. G. *Boschi*); RThom 94 (1994) 689-694 (L. *Ramlot*).

7383* *Rosenbloom* Noah H., Rationales for the omission of eschatology in the Bible: Judaism 43 (1994) 149-158.

7384 *a) Schmidt* Werner H., Aspekte der Eschatologie im AT; – *b) Sæbø* M., Zum Verhältnis von 'Messianismus' und 'Eschatologie' im AT; ein Versuch terminologischer und sachlicher Klärung: JbBt 8 (1993) 3-23 / 25-55.

7384* *Suau i Puig*, L'idea de immortalitat en el Vell Testament; el procés d'una consciència: QVidCr 173 (1994) 7-22.

7385 *Sysling* Herman, *Techiyyat ha-Metim*; de opstanding van de doden in de Palestijnse Targumim op de Pentateuch en overeenkomstige tradities in de klassieke rabbijnse bronnen [diss. Leiden 1991, ᴰ*Mulder* J.]. Zutphen 1991, Terra. xv-347 p.; bibliog. 269-300.

H4.5   *Theologia totius VT* – **General Old Testament theology.**

7386 *Anderson* Bernhard W., The changing scene in biblical theology: BR 10,1 (1994) 17 . 63.

7386* *a) Bossman* David M., The person in biblical theology; – *b) Murphy* Roland E., Wisdom literature and biblical theology: BibTB 24 (1994) 2s / 4-7.

7387 **Breukelman** F. H., Bijbelse theologie 1/2, Genesis. Kampen 1992, Kok. *f* 42,50. – ᴿOTEssays 7 (1994) 133-5 (M. D. *Terblanche*, Eng.).

7388 **Brueggemann** W., OT theology. Mp 1992, Fortress. xviii-307 p. $17. – ᴿAndrUnS 32 (1994) 119-121 (G. A. *King*); ExpTim 105 (1993s) 22 (J. *Goldingay*).

7389 **Cohen** Philip M., David EINHORN [1809-1879]; biblical theology as response and reform [... Olat Tamid]: diss. Brandeis, ᴰ*Fox* M. Boston 1994. 432 p. 94-17699. – DissA 55 (1994) p. 611.

7390 *Gnuse* Robert, New directions in biblical theology; the impact of contemporary scholarship in the Hebrew Bible: JAAR 62 (1994) 893-918.

7391 **Goldingay** John,   Theology diversity and the authority of the Old Testament [... methodology of OT theology] 1987 → 3,1415 ... 5,1454: ᴿIrTQ 58 (1992) 75s (M. *Drennan*).

7392 **Goldy** Robert G.,   The emergence of Jewish theology in America. Bloomington 1990, Indiana Univ. 149 p. – ᴿAJS 17 (1992) 352-4 (P. *Ochs*: focuses on midrash).

7393 **Gunneweg** Antonius H. J.,   Biblische Theologie des ATs, eine Religionsgeschichte Israels in biblisch-theologischer Sicht 1993 → 9,7560*: ᴿCBQ 56 (1994) 548s (W. E. *Lemke*); ExpTim 105 (1993s) 336 (I. W. *Provan*); TPhil 69 (1994) 266-8 (R. *Sebott*); TüTQ 174 (1994) 68s (W. *Gross*); TvT 34 (1994) 77 (J. *Holman*).

7394 **Hasel** G. F.,   Old Testament theology; basic issues in the current debate⁴ʳᵉᵛ 1991 → 8,7430c; 9,7561*:   ᴿOTEssays 7 (1994) 123-6 (L. C. H. *Fourie*: basic conservative position unaltered).

7395 **Kaiser** O.,   Der Gott des ATs; Theologie des ATs 1, 1993 → 9,7019: ᴿBL (1994) 109 (G. W. *Anderson*); ExpTim 105 (1993s) 336s (I. W. *Provan*); OTEssays 7 (1994) 472s (J. L. *Helberg*).

7396 **Kaufman** Gordon D.,   In face of mystery; a constructive theology. CM 1993, Harvard Univ. 509 p. $40. – ᴿAmJTP 15 (1994) 327-332 (R. C. *Neville*); JAAR 62 (1994) 201-5 (P. C. *Hodgson*: brilliant, provocative; 'for Christian and Jewish communities of faith'); ModT 10 (1994) 213s (C. M. *Wood*).

7396* **Perdue** Leo G.,   The collapse of history; reconstructing OT theology: OvBT. Mp 1994, Fortress. xvi-317 p.

7397 **Preuss** H.-D.,   Theologie des ATs 1991s → 7,7388 ... 9,7566s: ᴿBijdragen 55 (1994) 80 (P. C. *Beentjes*); BiKi 48 (1994) 121s (F. J. *Stendebach*); CBQ 56 (1994) 776s (M. C. *Lind*: insightful); CritRR 6 (1993) 174-7 (W. *Brueggemann*); TPQ 142 (1994) 86s (J. *Marböck*); VT 44 (1994) 289 (H. G. M. *Williamson*).

7398 **Schweitzer** Wolfgang,   Der Jude Jesus und die Völker der Welt; ein Gespräch mit Paul M. Vᴀɴ Bᴜʀᴇɴ [→ 9,7571]: Veröff. 19. B 1993, Inst. Kirche und Judentum. 228 p. ᴅᴍ 24,80.   3-923095-22-8. – ᴿTLZ 119 (1994) 925s (G. *Begrich*).

7399 *Scobie* Charles H. H.,   Structurer la théologie biblique [TyndaleB 42], ᵀ*Carrel-Conod* Sylvie & Serge: Hokma 52 (1993) 1-31.

7400 *Simotas* Panagiotis N.,   ⊕ The problem of the unity of biblical and dogmatic theology from an Orthodox point of view: TAth 65 (1994) 231-261; Eng. 1020.

7401 *a) Spangenberg* J. J. J.,   Paradigm change and OT theology; deathblow to a nonexistent beast? – *b) Snyman* Gerrie,   OT theology; fabulous dreams of the *other* side of time and space; – *c) Loader* J. A., Logos spermatikos; die saailinge van die teologie; of: Gedagte oor gekontroleerde teologie: OTEssays 7 (1994) 435-452 / 453-465 / 417-434.

7401* *Weinberger* Theodore,   Fructifying Solomon Sᴄʜᴇᴄʜᴛᴇʀ's traditional Jewish theology: ModT 10 (1994) 271-9.

H5.1   *Deus* – NT – God [as Father → H1.4].

7402 **Altizer** Thomas J. J.,   The genesis of God; a theological genealogy. Lᴠʟ 1993, W-Knox. 200 p. – ᴿTLond 97 (1994) 446s (D. *Cupitt*: despite the often horribly obscure prose style of avant-garde Americans, his most recent books are the most brilliant and original).

7403 **Brand** Paul, Peut-on être réaliste et croire en Dieu? Genève 1990, Labor et Fides. 340 p. – RScripTPamp 26 (1994) 345s (J. M. *Odero*).
7404 **Bray** Gerald L., The doctrine of God: Contours of Christian theology. DG 1991, InterVarsity. 281 p. $15. 0-8308-1531-7 [TDig 41,352].
7405 *Breton* Stanislas, Superlatif et négation; comment dire la transcendance?: RSPT 78 (1994) 193-202.
7406 **Gesché** Adolphe, Dieu pour penser, 3. Dieu. P 1994, Cerf. 174 p. F 95. 2-204-04861-5. – REglT 25 (1994) 437s (R. *Martínez de P. L.*); RTLv 25 (1994) 361s (E. *Boné*).
7407 **Grelot** Pierre, Dieu, le père de Jésus-Christ: JJC 60. P 1994, Desclée. 368 p. 2-7189-0620-0 [RB 102,621, R. J. *Tournay*]. – REsprVie 104 (1994) 350s (P. *Jay*); RThom 94 (1994) 708-710 (G. *Emery*).
7408 **Marguerat** Daniel, Le Dieu des premiers chrétiens 1993 ➤ 6,7426 ... 9,7578: RÉTRel 69 (1994) 273 (E. *Cuvillier*); ScEsp 45 (1993) 108-110 (J.-J. *Lavoie*).
7409 **Pikaza** X., *Silanes* N., Diccionario teológico; el Dios cristiano. S 1992, Secretariado Trinitario. 1540 p. – RLumenVr 42 (1993) 192s (F. *Ortiz de Urtaran*).
7409* **Ringleben** Joachim, Der Gott des Sohnes; christologische Überlegungen zum Verhältnis von Judentum und Christentum [i. Jesus und der Gott seiner Väter ...]: KerDo 40 (1994) 20-30; Eng. 31.

H5.2 **Christologia ipsius NT.**

7410 **Brown** Raymond E., An introduction to NT Christology. NY 1994, Paulist. xii-226 p. $10 pa. 0-8091-3516-7 [TDig 42,157]; RB 102,619, J. *Murphy-O'Connor*; TLZ 120,334, E. *Schweizer*].
7411 *Davis* P. G., Divine agents, mediators, and New Testament Christology: JTS 45 (1994) 479-503.
7411* a) *Doriani* Daniel, The deity of Christ in the synoptic Gospels; – b) *Darms* John V., The subordination of the Son: JEvTS 37 (1994) 333-350 / 351-364.
7412 **Dreyfus** François, Did Jesus know he was God? [1984]. Cork 1991, Mercier. xiii-154 p. £9. – RHeythJ 35 (1994) 319-321 (J. P. *Galvin*: lacks precision; limited too much to John).
7413 *Evans* C. Stephen, The incarnational narrative as myth and history: ChrSchR 23 (1993s) 387-407.
7414 **Habermann** Jürgen, Präexistenzaussagen im NT [Diss. Mü DHahn F.]: EurHS 23/362, 1990 ➤ 6,7434; 7,7415: RTLZ 119 (1994) 646-9 (N. *Walter*).
7414* **Harris** Murray J., Jesus as God... NT 1982 ➤ 9,7592: RAndrUnS 32 (1994) 277 (P. *Coutsoumpos*).
7415 **Jossa** Giorgio, Dal Messia al Cristo; le origini della cristologia 1989 ➤ 5,7429 ... 8,7486: RRTLv 25 (1994) 242s (A. de *Halleux*).
7416 **Kuschel** Karl-J., Geboren vor aller Zeit? 1990 ➤ 7,7473: RMüTZ 44 (1993) 129-134 (G. L. *Müller*).
7417 **Kuschel** K., Born before all time? 1992 ➤ 9,7595: RHorizons 21 (1994) 197s (M. L. *Cook*); JTS 45 (1994) 780-2 (R. *Morgan*).
7417* **Mędala** Stanisław, Ⓟ Chrystologia Ewangelii św. Jana. Kraków 1993, Inst. Misjonarzy. 400 p. – RRuBi 47 (1994) 62s (A. *Jankowski,* Ⓟ).
7418 **Moltmann** Jürgen, Jésus, le Messie de Dieu; pour une christologie messianique, THoffmann Joseph: CogF 171. P 1993, Cerf. 475 p. 2-227-04628-0. – RCarthaginensia 10 (1994) 194s (F. *Martínez Fresneda*: sistemática).

7418* *a) Reiling* J., Een eeuw christologie van het Nieuwe Testament; – *b)*
Honig A. G.,   Aziatische Christologie.   KerkT 45 (1994) 269-287 /
288-299.
7419 **Rhodes** Ron,   Christ before the manger; the life and times of the
preincarnate Christ.   GR 1992, Baker.   299 p. – $14 pa. – ᴿJEvTS 37
(1994) 442 (J. R. *LaShell*, also on cognates by M. J. ERICKSON, D. F.
SCAER, C. A. EVANS).
7420 **Schnackenburg** Rudolf,   Die Person Jesu Christi 1993 ⇥ 9,7600:   ᴿTLZ
119 (1994) 658-60 (H. *Weder*).
7421 **Schneider** Gerhard,   Cristologia del Nuovo Testamento [1971], ᵀ*Ravà*
Marcella: Letture bibliche 10.   Brescia 1994 = 1975, Paideia.   113 p.
Lᵐ 14.   88-394-0509-7.
7422 **Witherington** BenIII,   The Christology of Jesus 1990 ⇥ 6,7448 ... 9,7601:
ᴿÉTRel 68 (1993) 600s (E. *Cuvillier*); HeythJ 35 (1994) 319s (J. P. *Garvin*);
RExp 91 (1994) 116s (Molly T. *Marshall*); ScotJT 46 (1993) 264-7 (M. de
Jonge: challenging).

H5.3   *Christologia praemoderna* – patristic through Reformation.

7423 *Allen* Pauline,   Monophysiten, ᵀ*Schäferdiek* Kurt: ⇥ 517, TRE 23 (1994)
219-233.
7424 **Balthasar** H. U. v.,   Les grands textes sur le Christ: JJC 50.   P 1991,
Desclée.   315 p. F 149. – ᴿEsprVie 104 (1994) 450-2 (P. *Jay*).
7425 **Bausenhart** Guido, 'In allem...' MAXIMOS/Christologie ᴰ1992 ⇥ 8,7473;
9,7603:   ᴿÉTRel 68 (1993) 441 (J.-P. *Gabus*).
7426 **Böhm** Thomas,   Die Christologie des Arius; dogmengeschichtliche Überlegungen unter besonderer Berücksichtigung der Hellenisierungsfrage
[kath. Diss. Mü]: StT&G 7.   St. Ottilien 1991, EOS.   413 p.   DM 44.
3-88096-907-8:   ᴿJTS 45 (1994) 320-2 (M. *Slusser*); TLZ 119 (1994) 902
(A. M. *Ritter*); TPhil 69 (1994) 273-5 (J. *Ulrich*).
7427 **Bruns** Peter, Das Christusbild APHRAHATs ᴰ1990 ⇥ 7,7422 ... 9,7608:
ᴿNumen 41 (1994) 102-4 (H. J. W. *Drijvers*); TR 90 (1994) 44-48 (Corrie
Molenberg).
7428 **Butler** Michael E.,   Hypostatic union and monotheletism; the dyothelite
Christology of St. MAXIMUS the Confessor: diss. Fordham, ᴰ*Ettlinger* G.
NY 1994.   294 p. 94-25187. – DissA 55 (1994s) p. 998.
7429 **Cavadini** John C.,   The last Christology of the West; adoptionism in
Spain and Gaul 785-820.   Ph 1993, Univ. Pennsylvania.   xii-225 p.
£31,50.   0-8122-3186-4. – ᴿAmHR 99 (1994) 1669s (Julia M. H. *Smith*);
CathHR 80 (1994) 785s (J. F. *O'Callaghan*); ExpTim 105 (1993s) 219s (A.
Louth); JEH 45 (1994) 691s (R. *Collins*); JTS 45 (1994) 746s (L. R.
Wickham); TS 55 (1994) 384s (K. B. *Steinhauser*).
7430 **Cho Byoung-Ha**,   Trinitätslehre und Christologie bei AMBROSIUS: ev.
Diss. ᴰ*Abramowski* L.   Tübingen 1994.   276 p. – RTLv 26, p. 540.
7431 ᵀᴱ**Constas** Nicholas P.,   Four Christological homilies of PROCLUS of
Constantinople: diss. Catholic Univ., ᴰ*Darling-Young* R.   Wsh 1994.
269 p. 94-21500. – DissA 55 (1994s) p. 611; RTLv 26, p. 540 'Young D.'.
7433 **Dahl** Nils A.,   Jesus the Christ; the historical origins of Christological
doctrine [= The crucified Messiah + 5 inedita], ᵀ*Juel* Donald H., 1991
⇥ 7,194; 9,7609:   ᴿScotJT 46 (1993) 570s (E. *Best*); TLZ 119 (1994)
798-800 (U. *Schnelle*).
7434 ᵀᴱ**Dattrino** Lorenzo, Giovanni CASSIANO; L'incarnazione del Signore:
TPatr 94, 1991 ⇥ 7,7427: ᴿLateranum 60 (1994) 180s (O. *Pasquato*).

7435 **Fideler** David, Jesus Christ, Son of God; ancient cosmology and early Christian symbolism. Wheaton IL 1993, Quest. 429 p. $24; pa. $16 [RRelRes 36,328s; Penny E. *Becker*].

7436 *Gherardini* Brunero, Fondamento cristologico dell'ecclesiologia di LU- TERO: Divinitas 37 (1993) 11-41.

7437 **Gilbert** Peter J., Person and nature in the theological poems of St. GREGORY of Nazianzus: diss. Catholic University of America, ᴰ[*D- arling-*]*Young* R. Wsh 1994. – RTLv 26, p. 541.

7438 *González* Sergio, Hijo de Dios en Luis de LEÓN: EstAg [28 (1993) 3-56] 29 (1994) 51-95.

7439 **Grillmeier** Alois, Jesus der Christus → 5,7459: ᴿMüTZ 44 (1993) 135-7 (T. *Böhm*, 2/4); TGegw 36 (1993) 234s (A. *Schmied*, 2/2).

7440 **Grillmeier** (Aloys), Le Christ dans la tradition chrétienne 2/2, 1993 → 9,7613: ᴿCarthaginensia 10 (1994) 187s (F. *Martínez Fresneda*); RHPR 74 (1994) 325s (P. *Maraval*); RÉAug 40 (1994) 255-7 (J.-N. *Guinot*); ScEspr 46 (1994) 360s (G. *Novotný*) & 362s (P.-É. *Langevin*, 2/2, 1993).

7441 **Grillmeier** Alois, Gesù il Cristo nella fede della Chiesa 1/1s, ᴱ*Norelli* E., *Olivieri* S. Brescia 1992, Paideia. 1060 p. – ᴿProtestantesimo 49 (1994) 85s (S. *Rostagno*).

7442 *Halleux* André de, †, À propos d'une lecture cyrillienne de la définition christologique de Chalcédoine: RTLv 25 (1994) 445-471.

7443 **Hattrup** D., Ekstatik der Geschichte; die Entwicklung der chri- stologischen Erkenntnistheorie BONAVENTURAS: PdTSt 23. Pd 1933, Schöningh. 341 p. DM 74 [RHE 89,433*]. – ᴿColcFran 64 (1994) 417-431 (P. *Maranesi*).

7444 **Henne** Philippe, La christologie chez CLÉMENT de Rome et dans le Pasteur: Paradosis 33, 1992 → 9,7489: ᴿCBQ 56 (1992) 796-8 (C. *Osiek*); JTS 45 (1994) 717-9 (H. O. *Maier*); RTPhil 126 (1994) 276s (J. *Borel*).

7445 **Hever** C. D. den, De messiaanse weg, 3. De christologie van het NT. Kampen 1991, Kok. 334 p. ƒ49,50. 90-242-2750-X. – ᴿBijdragen 55 (1994) 83s (W. G. *Tillmans*).

7446 **Lyman** J. Rebecca, Christology and cosmology... ORIGEN, EUSEBIUS, ATHANASIUS 1993 → 9,7620: ᴿChH 63 (1994) 429s (P. J. *Gorday*).

7446* ᵀᴱ**McGuckin** John A., The Christological controversy; its history, theology and texts; St. CYRIL of Alexandria: VigChr supp. 23. Leiden 1994, Brill. xiii-425 p.; bibliog. p. 403-418. 90-04-09990-5.

7447 **Malingrey** Anne-Marie, Jean CHRYSOSTOME, Sur l'égalité du Père et du Fils: contre les Anoméens, Homélies VII-XII: SChr 396. P 1994, Cerf. 378 p. – ᴿRÉG 107 (1994) 310-2 (L. *Brottier*); VigChr 48 (1994) 392-4 (J. C. M. van *Winden*).

7448 *Mateo Seco* Lucas F., Adopcionismo hispánico y concilio de Frankfurt (en la conmemoración de su XII centenario): AnVal 20 (1994) 99-120.

7448* *Núñez Moreno* José M., Pascha = passio en el Tractatus IX de Gregorio de Elvira; rasgos de una cristología pascual en la iglesia bética del siglo IV: Isidorianum 6 (Sevilla 1994) 7-31.

7449 *a) Orlando* José, La circunstancia histórica del adopcionismo español; – *b) Mestra* José A. & Amalia, Bibliografia sobre el adopcionismo español del siglo VIII, 1951-1990: ScripTPamp 26 (1994) 1079-91 / 1093-1152.

7450 *Ormerod* Neil, The transcultural significance of the definition of Chalcedon: AustralasCR 70 (1993) 322-332.

7450* *Pifarré* Cebrià, ARNOBIO el Joven y la cristología del 'conflictus', 1988 → 5,7473; 6,7479: ᴿRCatalT 18 (1993) 183s (M. S. *Gros i Pujol*).

7451 [Vania] *Proverbio* Delia, CHRYSOSTOMUS adversus Chalkedon, note supplémentaire sur le codex FB [copte] du Monastère Blanc à la lumière du manuscrit éthiopien Comboniano H3: Orientalia 63 (1994) 57-67.

7451* ᵀᴱ**Roey** Albert van, *Allen* Pauline, Monophysite texts of the sixth century: OrLovAnal 56. Lv 1994, Univ./Peeters. xv-320 p. 90- 5831-539-0.

7452 **Schoot** H. J. M., Christ the name of God; Thomas AQUINAS on naming Christ; kath. diss. Utrecht, ᴰ*Grijs* F. de. Lv 1993, Peeters. 231 p. 90-6831-511-0. – TvT 34 (1994) 73.

7453 *Sciuto* Francesco E., Contributo alla datazione degli 'Scholia de Incarnatione Unigeniti' di CIRILLO d'Alessandria: Orpheus 45 (1994) 343-354.

7454 *Seguenny* André, La Christologie de Caspar von SCHWENCKFELD, 1489-1561 (non aliud sed aliter): RHPR 74 (1994) 129-151; Eng. 229.

7455 **Sesboüé** Bernard, *Meunier* Bernard, Dieu peut-il avoir un fils?... IVᵉ s. 1993 ➤ 9,7628; 2-204-04714-7: ᴿRHPR 74 (1994) 313 (P. *Maraval*); TLZ 119 (1994) 905s (A. M. *Ritter*); ZkT 116 (1994) 348s (K. H. *Neufeld*).

7455* **Sinn** Gunnar, Christologie und Existenz; R. BULTMANN's Interpretation des paulinischen Christuszeugnisses [< Diss. Erlangen, ᴰ*Merk* O.]. Tü 1991, Francke. xiv-306 p. DM 84. – ᴿCritRR 6 (1993) 294-6 (A. J. *Hultgren*).

7456 *Spoerl* Kelly M., Apollinarian Christology and the anti-Marcellan tradition: JTS 45 (1994) 545-568.

7457 **Studer** Basil, Dominus salvator... Christologie 1992 ➤ 9,241: ᴿTR 90 (1994) 48-50 (N. *Brox*).

7458 **Trakatellis** Demetrios, Ⓖ The pre-existent Christ in JUSTIN [< diss. Harvard 1976], ᵀ*Chatzinikolaou* Nikolaos. Athenae 1992, Domos. – ᴿTAth 65 (1994) 989-991 (E. A. *Moutsoulas* Ⓖ).

7459 *Triqueneaux* Sylvian, Les relations entre les deux natures du Christ; Luthériens et Réformés sur la communication des idiomes: Hokhma 53 (1993) 1-19.

7460 **Welch** Lawrence J., Christology and Eucharist in the early thought of Cyril of Alexandria [< diss. Marquette]. SF 1994, Catholic Scholars. 169 p. $60; pa. $40. 1-883255-13-9; -06-6 [TDig 42,193].

7461 *a) Yarnold* Edward, Scripture, philosophy, and liturgy; the roots of patristic Christology; – *b) Cosstick* Vicky, Christology for the people; – *c) Sanders* David, A lived Christology in Paul: Month 255 (1994) 467-471 / 472-474 / 475-9.

7462 **Zañartu Undurraga** Sergio, Historia del dogma de la encarnación desde el s. V al VII. Santiago 1994, Univ. Católica de Chile. 148 p.

H5.4   (*Commentationes de*) *Christologia* moderna.

7463 **Arias Reyero** Maximino, *González* Carlos I., *Contreras* Enrique, La cristología en el contexto de la nueva evangelización [< 10ª Semana Teología Arg. Córdoba julio 1991]. BA 1992, Paulinas. 131 p. 930-09-1034-9. – ᴿRET 53 (1993) 394s (M. *Gesteira*).

7464 *Battaglia* Vincenzo, [➤ 7449*] Gesù crocifisso icona della Gloria e dell'amore di Dio; un saggio di cristologia staurologico-agapica: RicT 3 (R 1992) 7-32 [< ZIT 7449*].

7465 *Beck* Andreas J., Die postmoderne Christologia Jürgen MOLTMANNs: Fundamentum (1994,2) 66-86.

7465* (Mellick) *Belshaw* C. P., The religion of the Incarnation: AnglTR 76 (1994) 432-443.

7466 **Berten** Ignace, Jezus, God aan de rand. Averbode/Boxtel 1992, Altiora/ KBS. 108 p. Fb 390. – RStreven 60 (1993) 87 (E. De *Smet*).

7467 **Beyschlag** Karlmann, Grundriss der Dogmengeschichte 2/1, Das christologische Dogma. Da 1991, Wiss. xli-210 p. 3-534-08088-2. – REstE 69 (1994) 404s (G. *Uríbarri*).

7468 *Boshoff* P. E., Christologie; die spanningsvolle verhouding 'Verkondigen - Verkondigde' bij Rudolf BULTMANN en Walter SCHMITHALS: HervTSt 49 (1993) 547-560 [< NTAbs 38, p. 403].

7469 **Brady** James R., Jesus Christ, divine man or Son of God? Lanham 1992, UPA. vi-146 p. $38. 0-8191-8481-0 [NTAbs 38, p. 311]. – RTBR 7,1 (1994s) 37 (C. *Gunton*).

7470 *Brito* Emilio, L'unique; chronique de Christologie [... TILLIETTE X.; BRAMBILLA sur SCHILLEBEECKX, AMATO, MOIOLO]: RTLv 25 (1994) 46-59.

7471 **Brustolín** Laomar A., A cristologia como história na obra de Bruno FORTE; diss. DPalácio C. Belo Horizonte 1993. – PerspT 26 (1994) 86.

7472 *Catalá* Vicente A., Cristología y Constituciones [S.J.]: Manresa 66 (1994) 5-18.

7473 **Coda** Piero, Dios entre los hombres; breve cristología: Teología en diálogo. M 1993, Ciudad Nueva. 190 p. 84-86987-52-0. – RBibFe 58 (1994) 173 (A. *Salas*); EstAg 29 (1994) 173s (C. *Morán*); RET 93 (1993) 499 (M. *Gesteira*).

7474 **Culpepper** Gary M., Wolfhart PANNENBERG's proleptic Christology in light of his trinitarian theology and metaphysics: diss. Catholic Univ., DLoewe W. Wsh 1994. 437 p. 94-21576. – DissA 55 (1994s) p. 611.

7475 *a*) **Dunn** James D. G., Christology as an aspect of theology; – *b*) *Baird* William, Christology and criticism; from PAULUS to KEIM; – *c*) *Wiles* Maurice, Can we still do Christology?; – *d*) *Hartman* Lars, Early baptism – early Christology; – *e*) *Scroggs* Robin, Christ the cosmocrator and the experience of believers; – *f*) *Talbert* C., 'And the Word became flesh'; when?: ➤ 74, FKECK L., Future 1993, 202-212 / 213-228 / 229-238 / 191-201 / 160-175 / 43-52.

7476 **Dupuis** Jacques, Introduzione alla cristologia 1993 ➤ 9,7651: RAntonianum 69 (1994) 125-7 (V. *Battaglia*); Asprenas 41 (1994) 293s (A. *Ascione*); CC 145 (1994,1) 407-9 (F. *Lambiasi*); RelCu 40 (1994) 639 (R. de la *Torre*).

7477 **Dupuis** Jacques, Introducción a la Cristología. Estella 1994, VDivino. 284 p. pt. 1500.

7478 **Dupuis** Jacques, Who do you say I am? Introduction to Christology. Mkn 1994, Orbis. vi-194 p. $17 pa. 0-88344-940-4 [TDig 41,357].

7479 **Eckardt** Roy, Reclaiming the Jesus of history; Christology today 1992 ➤ 8,7520; 9,7652: RInterpretation 48 (1994) 316s (D. G. *Dawe*).

7480 **Erickson** Millard J., The Word became flesh 1991 ➤ 9,7521: RAndrUnS 31 (1993) 141-3 (R. *Dederen*); CritRR 5 (1992) 470s (W. *McWilliams*).

7480* *Fuller* Reginald, Christology 1955-90: AnglTR 76 (1994) (160-) 165-7.

7481 **Gagey** H. J., Jésus dans la théologie de Bultmann. P 1993, Desclée. 386 p. – RRCatalT 18 (1993) 179-181 (F. *Raurell*).

7481* *Gagnebin* Laurent, Christologies et théologies pastorales: ÉTRel 68 (1993) 385-394.

7482 **Gironés** Gonzalo, Cristología: Siftel (Servizio Informatica Teol.). Valencia 1993. 357 p. – RScripTPamp 26 (1994) 1166-1170 (L. F. *Mateo-Seco*).

7482* **Gnilka** Joachim,   Christologie: ➤ 511, LTK³ (1994) 1164-6 (-1174, A. *Schilson*).
7483 *González Faus* José I.,   La cristología después de Vaticano II: RazF 229 (1994) 501-513.
7483* **Green** Elizabeth E.,   Indirizzi di cristologia femminista: Protestantesimo 49 (1994) 354-366.
7484 **Gronchi** Maurizio,   La cristologia di S. BERNARDINO da Siena; l'imago Christi nella predicazione volgare.   Genova 1992, Marietti.   288 p.   Lᵐ 35.
    – ᴿAntonianum 69 (1994) 122-4 (V. *Battaglia*); CC 145 (1994,1) 99s (M. *Fois*).
7484* **Gunton** C. E.,   Christ and creation 1992 ➤ 8,7693:   ᴿExpTim 105 (1993s) 88s (G. W. P. *McFarlane*: it is rightly presented as a 'summary dogmatic Christology').
7485 **Hick** John,   The metaphor of God incarnate.   L 1993, SCM.   180 p. £10 pa.   0-334-02541-9. – ᴿExpTim top choice 105,4 (1993s) 97-99 (C. S. *Rodd*); TLond 97 (1994) 128-130 (J. *Macquarrie*: echoes CUPITT's 'Myth' but less polemic; anyway inescapable; rightly 'the ultimate divine reality exceeds human conceptuality'); LvSt 19 (1994) 275s (J. *Haers*); TBR 6/3 (1993s) 41 (D. P. *Ford*).
7486 **Hünermann** Peter,   Jesus Christus – Gottes Wort in der Zeit; eine systematische Christologie.   Münster 1994, Aschendorff.   419 p.   DM 88. 3-402-03268-6. – ᴿTGL 84 (1994) 492-4 (D. *Hattrup*).
7487 **Iammarrone** G., *al.*,   Gesù Cristo, volto di Dio e volto dell'uomo: Collana (OFMConv) di Cristologia 1.   R 1992, Herder.   287 p. – *Odasso R., Penna R., Pompei A.* – ᴿCarthaginensia 10 (1994) 196-8 (F. *Chavero Blanco*); RET 54 (1994) 218s (M. *Gesteira*).
7488 *Jacobsen* Douglas, *Schmidt* Frederick,   Behind orthodoxy and beyond it; recent developments in evangelical Christology: ScotJT 45 (1992) 515-541.
7489 **Kaiser** Alfred,   Möglichkeiten... 'von unten'... SCHOONENBERG 1992 ➤ 8,7830; 9,7669:   ᴿTS 54 (1993) 757-9 (P. J. *Casarella*).
7490 **Kay** James F.,   Christus praesens; a reconsideration of Rudolf BULTMANN's Christology.   GR 1994, Eerdmans.   xii-187 p.   0-8028-0131-5.
7491 *Kelly* C. J.,   The God of classical theism and the doctrine of the Incarnation: IntJPhRel 35,1 (1994) 1-20 [< ZIT 94,185].
7492 **Kereszty** Roch A.,   Jesus Christ; fundamentals of Christology.   NY 1991, Alba.   440 p. $20 pa. – ᴿAustralasCR 70 (1993) 262s (P. *Gwynne*); HomP 93,2 (1992s) 64s (P. T. *McCarthy*: alive and exciting).
7493 **Lewis** Peter,   The glory of Christ.   L/Sydney 1992, Hodder & S.   vi-503 p.   £10 pa.   0-340-56894-1. – ᴿTBR 7,1 (1994s) 37 (G. *Cray*: evangelical Calvinist).
7493* **López Amat** Alfredo,   Jesús el ungido; Cristología: Síntesis 2/4, 1991 ➤ 9,7595*:   ᴿScripTPamp 26 (1994) 350 (L. F. *Matco-Seco*).
7494 **López Amat** Alfredo,   Gesù Cristo, kenosi e gloria: Teologia a confronto.   R 1994, Dehoniane.   384 p.   Lᵐ 38.
7495 **Lyons** Enda,   Jesus, self-portrait by God.   Dublin 1994, Columbia. £9. 1-85607-102-2. – ᴿDocLife 44 (1994) 571s (W. *Harrington*); TBR 7,1 (1994s) 36 (I. *Wallis*).
7496 **McDermott** Brian O.,   Word become flesh; dimensions of Christology: NTSt 9.   ColMn 1993, Liturgical.   302 p. $20.   8-8146-5015-5. – ᴿTBR 7,3 (1994s) 39s (C. *Gunton*).
7497 **McGrath** Alister E.,   The making of modern German christology 1750-1990² [¹1987].   Leicester 1994, Apollos.   251 p.   0-85111-427-X.
7498 **Marquardt** F.-W.,   Das christliche Bekenntnis zu Jesus, dem Juden; eine

Christologie 1990 → 7,7481... 9,7679: ᴿRTPhil 126 (1994) 177s (J.-E. *Bertholet*).
7499 *Martínez Camino* Juan A., Jesús, nuestro hermano mayor; perspectiva cristológica de la antropología cristiana: → 33*b*, ᶠDíAZ MERCHÁN G. StOvet 22 (1994) 342-352.
7499* *Meagher* P., Some glimpses of Christology [SENIOR D., SLOYAN D., COOK M., *al.*]: Vidyajyoti 58 (1994) 512-529.
7500 *Mertens* Herman-Emiel, Did the Word of God become a human person? [KAISER A. 1993 on SCHOONENBERG]: LvSt 18 (1993) 175-180.
7501 **Moltmann** Jürgen, Der Weg Jesu, unser Weg 1989 → 5,7515 / La via 1991 → 8,7545*; ᴿETL 69 (1993) 484s (E. *Brito*).
7502 **Moltmann** Jürgen, The way of Jesus Christ 1990 → 7,7487... 9,7682: ᴿCritRR 6 (1993) 518-521 (R. T. *Cornelison*).
7503 **Moltmann** Jürgen, El camino de Jesucristo; cristología en dimensiones mesiánicas, ᵀ*Olasagasti* Manuel: Verdad e Imagen 129. S 1993, Sígueme. 483 p. – ᴿComSev 27 (1994) 379-381 (V. J. *Ansede*); LumenVr 43 (1994) 162s (F. *Ortiz de U.*).
7504 **Moltmann** Jürgen, O caminho de Jesus Cristo; Cristologia em dimensões mesiánicas, ᵀ*Kayser* Ilson. Petrópolis 1993, Vozes. 485 p. – ᴿPerspT 26 (1994) 87-96 (P. Américo *Maia*) & 106-114 (J. B. *Libânio*); REB 54 (1994) 514s (J. B. *Libânio*).
7506 *Nessan* Craig L., Confessing the Gospel of Jesus faithfully; the contest over Christology: CurrTM 21 (Chicago 1994) 5-20.
7507 *Nicolas* Jean-Hervé, La foi et le questionnement; à propos de l'ouvrage de Joseph MOINGT, L'homme qui venait de Dieu: RThom 94 (1994) 639-652.
7508 **Ocariz** F., *Mateo-Seco* L. F., *Riestra* J.-A., El misterio de Jesucristo; lecciones de Cristología y Soteriología. Pamplona 1991, EUNSA. 452 p. – ᴿAnnTh 7 (1993) 247-251 (Catalina *Bermúdez*).
7509 **O'Collins** Gerald, Gesù oggi; linee fondamentali di cristologia. CinB 1993, Paoline. 323 p. Lᵐ 20. – ᴿCC 145 (1994) 195s (F. *Lambiasi*).
7510 **Ols** Daniel, Cristologia contemporanea e... AQUINAS ᴰ1991 → 8,7550; 9,7687: ᴿCiTom 120 (1993) 187s (A. *Bandera*).
7511 **Porro** Carlo, Gesù il Salvatore; iniziazione alla cristologia: TViva, 1991 → 8,7556; 9,7689*: ᴿGregorianum 75 (1994) 568s (J. *Galot*); RasT 35 (1994) 614-620 (Aldo *Moda*).
7512 **Portier** William L., Tradition and incarnation; foundations of Christian theology. NY 1994, Paulist. ix-380 p. $15. 0-8091-3467-5 [TDig 42,183].
7513 *Renwart* Léon, Le 'motif' de l'Incarnation: chronique de Christologie: NRT 116 (1994) 883-897; MOINGT J. 1993; LÓPEZ AMAT A. 1994; TILLIETTE X. 1993...
7514 **Rey** Bernard, Jesucristo [Jésus le Christ; ital. 1990 → 7,7497]. Bilbao 1989, Mensajero. 133 p. – ᴿTArg 28 (1991) 265-7 (A. *Marino*).
7515 *Runia* K., De godheid van Christus: KerkT 45 (1994) 5-20.
7516 **Samartha** S., One Christ – many religions; toward a revised Christology 1991 → 8,7559; 9,7694: ᴿCritRR 6 (1993) 526-8 (P. J. *Griffiths*: inadequately based).
7517 **Scharlemann** Robert P., The reason of following; Christology and the ecstatic 1, 1991 → 8,7560; 9,7695: ᴿÉTRel 68 (1993) 126s (A. *Gounelle*).
7518 *Schwarzweller-Madl* Gabriele, Jesus Christus – der 'Gott mit uns'; Gottsein und Menschsein Jesu Christi in der katholischen Dogmatik des 19. Jahrhunderts [< ᴰ1993 → 9,7699]: TGgw 37 (1994) 242-255.

7519 *Sesboüé* Bernard,   De la rumeur de Jésus à la génération du Verbe: du nouveau en Christologie [MOINGT J. 1993].   RechSR 82 (1994) 87-102.

7520 ᴱStevens Maryanna,   Reconstructing the Christ symbol; essays on feminist Christology.   NY 1993, Paulist.   iii-151 p. $10.   0-8091-3439-X. – ᴿTBR 7,3 (1994s) 38s (Ann L. *Gilroy*).

7520* **Thompson** William M.,   († 1996)   Christology and spirituality 1991 ➔ 7,7510 ... 9,7709:   ᴿCritRR 6 (1993) 535s (B. *Hanson*).

7521 **Tilliette** Xavier,   La cristologia idealista [da KANT a SCHLEIERMACHER, 1986],   ᵀ*Cappellotti* Francesco, *Riccardino* Gianfranco: GdT 221. Brescia 1993, Queriniana.   211 p. Lᵐ 28.   88-399-0721-1 [Greg 75,400, *ipse*].

7522 *a) Tilliette* Xavier,   Filosofia e cristologia nel contesto della filosofia; – *b) Forte* Bruno,   Filosofia e teologia; le ragioni del dialogo: Asprenas 41 (1994) 163-178 / 179-188.

7523 ᶠTORRANCE J.,   Christ in our place; the humanity of God ..., ᴱ*Hart* T. 1989 ➔ 7,154*:   ᴿScotJT 47 (1994) 539s (B. D. *Spinks*).

7524 **Ward** Keith, A vision to pursue 1991 ➔ 7,k134:   L 1991, SCM.   226 p. £10. – ᴿThemelios 17,2 (1991s) 16s (R. R. *Cook*: 'taking leave of God incarnate'; as new divinity professor of Oxford, whether he calls himself a Christian is up to him).

7525 *a) Webb* Stephen H.,   At the crossroads of Christology; – *b) Marshall* Bruce D.,   Response to Stephen Webb on Christology in conflict: TorJT 10 (1994) 19-27 / 29-33.

7526 *Wills* Elizabeth,   Shusako ENDO, Christ as eternal companion: ScotJT 45 (1992) 85-100.

7527 **Wohlmuth** Josef,   Jesu Weg – unser Weg 1992 ➔ 8,7571; 9,7714: ᴿCiTim 120 (1993) 409-412 (R. de *Luis Carballada*); HerdKorr 46 (1992) 438s (A. *S.*).

H5.5   *Spiritus Sanctus; pneumatologia* –   **The Holy Spirit.**

7528 **Clark** G. H.,   The Holy Spirit.   Jefferson MD 1993, Trinity-Foundation. viii-129 p.   0-940931-37-0 [NTAbs 38, p. 312].

7529 **Fee** Gordon D.,   God's empowering presence; the Holy Spirit in the letters of Paul.   Peabody MA 1924, Hendrickson.   xxiv-967 p.; bibliog. 917-933. $36.   0-943575-94-X [TDig 42,164].

7530 **Gisel** Pierre,   La subversion [rapport avec la création, la matière] de l'Esprit; réflexion théologique sur l'accomplissement de l'homme: Lieux théologiques 23.   Genève 1993, Labor et Fides. 222 p. – ᴿRThom 94 (1994) 323-5 (C. *Morerod*).

7531 **Kooi** A. van der,   Het heilige en de Heilige Geest bij NOORDMANS; een schetz van zijn pneumatologisch ontwerp: diss. Kampen 1991, ᴰ*Neven* G. Kampen, Kok. 342 p. 90-242-6163-5. – TvT 34 (1994) 187.

7532 **Lison** Jacques,   L'Esprit répandu; la pneumatologie de Grégoire PA- LAMAS [1276-1359; diss. Lv 1991, ᴰ*Halleux* A. de]: Patrimoines. P 1993, Cerf.   305 p. – ᴿRHPR 74 (1994) 449-451 (J.-C. *Larchet*).

7533 **Larere** Philippe,   Baptism in water and baptism in the Spirit; a biblical, liturgical, and theological exposition, ᵀ*Madigan* Patrick. ColMn 1993, Liturgical.   94 p. $8 pa.   0-8146-2225-9 [TDig 41,368].

7534 **McDonnell** Kilian, *Montague* George T.,   Baptême dans l'Esprit et initiation chrétienne; témoignage des huit premiers siècles [1991 ➔ 7,7536],ᵀ. P 1993, D-Brouwer.   374 p. F 143.   2-220-03343-0. – ᴿÉTRel 68 (1993) 602s (J.-N. *Pérès*); RechSR 82 (1994) 123-4 (H. *Bourgeois*).

7535 **Moltmann** Jürgen,   The Spirit of life; a universal affirmation 1992
➤ 9,7741:   ᴿAsbTJ 49,1 (1994) 88-90 (J. C. *Cooper*); CurrTM 21 (1994)
220s (G. *Hansen*); HeythJ 35 (1994) 325s (J. *O'Donnell*); Horizons 21
(1994) 359s (Nancy A. *Dallavalle*); JRel 74 (1994) 267s (M. S. *Brocker*);
JTS 45 (1994) 787-790 (C. *Gunton*); Month 255 (1994) 105s (Gwen G.
Dickson); NBlackf 75 (1994) 331-3 (T. *Williams*); RExp 91 (1994) 116
(W. L. *Hendricks*); TorJT 10 (1994) 309-311 (H. *Wells*); TS 54 (1993)
755-7 (Catherine M. *LaCugna*).
7536 *Moltmann* Jürgen,   L'esprit donne la vie; ᵀ*Molle* Xavier: Tychique 95
(1992) 25-37 (38-40, réponse, *Cantalamessa* R. 38-40, ᵀ*Moire* Régine).
7537 **Müller-Fahrenholz** Geiko,   Erwecke die Welt; Unser Glaube an Gottes
Geist in dieser bedrohten Zeit.   Gü 1993, Kaiser.   276 p. DM 68.   3-579-
01941-4. – ᴿTvT 34 (1994) 452 (R. *Cornelissen*).
7537* **Paprocki** Henryk,   La promesse du Père; l'expérience du Saint-Esprit
dans l'Église Orthodoxe.   1990. – ᴿScEspr 46 (1994) 119s (J. *Lison*).
7538 **Plathow** Michael,   Der Geist hilft unserer Schwachheit; ein aktuali-
sierender Forschungsbericht zu M. LUTHERs Rede vom Heiligen Geist:
KerDo 40 (1994) 143-169; Eng. 169.
7538* *Sobrino* Jon,   El Espíritu, memoria y imaginación de Jesús en el
mundo; 'supervivencia' y 'civilización de la pobreza': SalT 82 (1994)
181-196.
7539 **Thompson** John,   The Holy Spirit in the theology of Karl BARTH 1991
➤ 8,7661; 9,7746:   ᴿScotJT 46 (1993) 389s (B. D. *Burton*).
7540 **Toinet** Paul,   La psychanalyse et le Saint-Esprit 1992 ➤ 9,7748:   ᴿBrotéria 137 (1993) 239 (F. *Pires Lopes*); Gregorianum 75 (1994) 771-3 (A.
Queralt).
7541 *Wegman* Herman,   Achtmaal de Geest gedenken; schriftlezinger in de
paastijd volgens recente leesroosters: TvT 34 (1994) 145-168: proposes
eight three-reading Scripture alternatives to those of seven lectionaries
since 1570, none of which reflect an on-going remembrance of the Holy
Spirit.

H5.6   *Spiritus et Filius;*   **'Spirit-Christology'**, Filioque.

7542 *Badcock* Gary D.,   The anointing of Christ and the *Filioque* doctrine:
IrTQ 60 (1994) 241-258.
7543 **Del Colle** Ralph G.,   Christ and the Spirit; Spirit-Christology in
Trinitarian perspective [diss. Union, NY 1991 ➤ 9,7753].   Ox 1994, UP.
viii-240 p. $35.   0-19-507776-8 [TDig 41,263]. – ᴿLexTQ 29 (1994) 68s
(W. R. *Barr*); TS 55 (1994) 371s (R. *Haight*).
7544 *Galot* Jean,   Le Christ et l'Esprit: EsprVie 104 (1994) 657-667. 673-682.
7545 *McDade* John,   Jesus and the Spirit: Month 255 (1994) 498-503.
7546 *Margerie* Bertrand de, L'Esprit vient du Père par le Fils: réflexions sur le
monopatrisme catholique: OrChrPer 60 (1994) 337-362.
7547 **O'Keeffe** Michael E.,   Contemporary Spirit Christologies; an examination of G. W. H. LAMPE, Walter KASPER, and Piet SCHOONENBERG:
diss. ᴰ*LaCugna* Catherine M. – Notre Dame 1994.   289 p. 94-24348. –
DissA 55 (1994s) p. 1005; RTLv 26, p. 567.
7548 **Schoonenberg** Piet,   De Geest, het Woord en de Zoon; theologische
overdenkingen over Geest-Christologie, Logos-Christologie en Drieëen-
heidsleer.   Averbode/Kampen 1991, Altiora/Kok. 258 p. – ᴿStreven 60
(1993) 177-9 (Herwi *Rikhof*).
7549 **Schoonenberg** Piet,   Der Geist, das Wort und der Sohn; eine Geist-

Christologie [1991], ᵀ*Immler* W., 1992 → 9,7756: ᴿETL 69 (1993) 211-3 (A. de *Halleux*); MüTZ 44 (1993) 125-9 (G. L. *Müller*).

7550 **Simon** Reinhard, Das Filioque bei Thomas von AQUIN; eine Untersuchung zur dogmengeschichtlichen Stellung, theologischen Struktur und ökumenischen Perspektiven der thomanischen Gotteslehre ['Contra errores Graecorum'; Diss. Berlin 1992]: Kontexte 14. Fra 1994, Lang. 182 p. – ᴿRThom 94 (1994) 717-9 (G. *Emery*).

7551 **Song** C. S., Jesus in the power of the Spirit. Mp 1994, Fortress. 335 p. – ᴿEcuR 46 (1994) 487s (A. J. van der *Bent*).

H5.7 *Ssma Trinitas* – **The Holy Trinity.**

7552 **Allison** C. FitzSimons (bp.), The cruelty of heresy; an affirmation of Christian orthodoxy [with GUNTON, 'we take seriously the doctrine of the Trinity']. L 1994, SPCK. v-197 p. £10. – ᴿAnglTR 76 (1994) 534-6 (D. F. *Winslow*); TLond 97 (1994) 445s (D. *Coggan*).

7553 *Arnold* Johannes, Zur Geschichtlichkeit der Rede von Gott; Einflüsse zeitgenössischer Königsideologie auf die Trinitätslehre Wilhelms von AUXERRE: TPhil 69 (1994) 342-372.

7555 *Barrachina Carbonell* Adolfo, La Trinidad en la anáfora bizantina de San BASILIO: AnVal 19 (1993) 1-19.

7556 **Beck** Heinrich, Die Lebensetappen als Trinitätssymbol: Symbolon 11 (1993) 53-74.

7557 **Bergin** Helen F., The triune God as liberating God; Edward SCHILLEBEECKX's recent theology of the Trinity: diss. Catholic Univ. ᴰ*Phan* P. Wsh 1994. 378 p. 94-24292. – DissA 55 (1994s) p. 1000.

7557* **Böhler** H., I consigli evangelici in prospettiva trinitaria; sintesi dottrinale. CinB 1993, Paoline. 245 p. – ᴿVConsacr 30 (1994) 379 (S. *Becchi*).

7558 *Boespflug* François, *Załuska* Yolanta, Le dogme trinitaire et l'essor de son iconographie en Occident de l'époque carolingienne au IVᵉ Concile du Latran (1215): CahCMédv 37 (1994) 181-240; 14 fig. VIII pl.

7558* **Bonanni** Sergio P., Parlare della Trinità; lettura della 'Theologia Scholarium' di ABELARDO: diss. ᴰ*Gilbert* P., Pont. Univ. Gregoriana Nᵒ 7218. R 1994. – InfPUG 26,121 (1994) 34.

7559 *Boulnois* Marie-Odile, Le paradoxe trinitaire chez CYRILLE d'Alexandrie; herméneutique, analyses philosophiques et argumentation théologique: ÉtAug.Antiq 143. P 1994, Inst.ÉtAug. 681 p.; bibliog. 603-626. 2-85121-146-3.

7560 **Ciola** Nicola, La crisi del teocentrismo trinitario nel Novecento teologico 1993 → 9,7765: ᴿAntonianum 69 (1994) 555-561 (V. *Battaglia*); OrChrPer 60 (1994) 713-6 (E. *Farrugia*); RasT 35 (1994) 103-110 (G. *Lorizio*).

7561 **Courth** Franz, Il mistero del Dio Trinità 3/6. Mi 1993, Jaca. 280 p. Lᵐ 36. – ᴿCC 145 (1994,3) 192s (G. *Ferraro*).

7562 *Downey* Michael, Trinitarian spirituality; participation in communion of persons [*LaCugna* Catherine L., 1991]: ÉglT 24 (1993) 109-123.

7563 *Elders* L. J., El carácter misterioso y la racionalidad en la doctrina trinitaria, según Tomás de AQUINO: ScripTPamp 26 (1994) 681-695.

7564 *Emery* Gilles, Creatrix Trinitas; la Trinité créatrice dans le commentaire de saint THOMAS sur les Sentences: diss. ᴰ*Torrell* J. P. FrS 1994. – RTLv 26, p. 542.

7565 *Ferrando* Miguel Ángel, El Dios confiable; la revelación del Padre, del Hijo y del Espíritu Santo en la Biblia: Textos Universitarios. Santiago 1993, Univ. Católica de Chile. 164 p. 956-14-0319-6.

7566 *Galot* Jean, Il volto autentico della Trinità: CC 145 (1994,2) 346-358.

7566* *Gerlitz* Peter, 'Trinität' und 'Matriarchat'; zur Herkunft polytheistischer Triasspekulationen in matrilinearen Gesellschaften: ➤ 11, [F]Beck, Sein 1994, 119-126.

7567 *Gresham* John L.[J], The social model of the Trinity and its critics: ScotJT 46 (1993) 325-345.

7568 **Gunton** Colin, The one, the three, and the many [Oxford 1992 Bampton Lectures] 1993 ➤ 9,7772: [R]ExpTim 105 (1993s) 219 (D. *Brown*: his most impressive work to date, but simplifies history); Horizons 21 (1994) 361s (J. A. *Bracken*); JTS 45 (1994) 787 (M. *Wiles*); RelStR 20 (1994) 211 (P. C. *Hodgson*: one of the most imaginatively creative works of our time); TLond 97 (1994) 444s (J. *Clayton*).

7569 **Gunton** Colin E., The promise of trinitarian theology 1991 ➤ 8,7637; 9,7771: [R]ScotJT 47 (1994) 379-381 (J. *Thompson*).

7570 *Gutenson* Chuck, Father, Son and Holy Spirit — the one God; an exploration of the trinitarian doctrine of Wolfhart Pannenberg: AsbTJ 49,1 (1994) 5-22.

7571 *Huculak* Benedykt, Costituzione della persona divina secondo S. Giovanni Damasceno: Antonianum 68 (1994) 179-212; Eng. 179.

7572 *Kotiranta* Matti, Das trinitarische Dogma als verbindender Faktor für das liturgische Erbe der Kirchen: KerDo 40 (1994) 115-142.

7573 **LaCugna** Catherine M., God for us; the Trinity ➤ 8,7643; 9,7776: [R]Commonweal 120,2 (1993) 23-26 (R. P. *Imbelli*); Gregorianum 75 (1994) 311-341 (E. *Muller*: a radical idea of what theology is); ScotJT 47 (1994) 135-7 (C. *Gunton*).

7574 **Lash** N., Believing three ways 1992 ➤ 9,7777: [R]LvSt 18 (1993) 270s (H.-E. *Mertens*: satisfying).

7575 *a) Loughlin* Gerard, Writing the Trinity; – *b) Thompson* Ross, Christian initiation as a Trinitarian process; – *c) Schroten* Egbert, What makes a person?: TLond 97 (1994) 82-89 / 90-98 / 98-105.

7576 *McDermott* John M., Person and nature in Lonergan's De Deo trino: Angelicum 71 (1994) 153-185.

7577 **Marsh** Thomas A., The triune God; a biblical and theological study. Dublin 1994, Columba. 201 p. £10. 1-85607-106-5 [TS 56,401s, P. G. *Crowley*: also Mystic CT, Twenty-Third, $13]. – [R]TBR 7,3 (1994s) (N. *Sagovsky*).

7577* *Maurer* Ernstpeter, Tendenzen nuerer Trinitätslehre: VerkF 39,2 (1994) 3-24.

7578 **Moltmann** J., History and the Triune God 1992 ➤ 8,7648; 9,7783: [R]LvSt 18 (1993) 73-75 (H.-E. *Mertens*); NewTR 7,1 (1994) 108s (R. *Viladesau*).

7578* **Moltmann** J., Nella storia del Dio trinitario [In der Geschichte... 1991 ➤ 7,7572], [T]*Pezzeta* Dino, 289 p. L[m] 35. 88-399-0374-7. – [R]ActuBbg 31 (1994) 28-30 (J. *Vives*).

7579 *Ortiz de Urtaran* Félix, El Vaticano II, un Concilio trinitario: LumenVr 43,5 (1994) 289-337.

7580 **Peters** Ted, God as Trinity; relationality and temporality in divine life 1993 ➤ 9,7785: $15. 0-664-25402-0. – [R]CurrTM 21 (1994) 138.140 (R. *Hütter*); ExpTim 105 (1993) 88 (R. *Butterworth*: inspired by Claude Welch); JRel 74 (1994) 575s (J. A. *Bracken*: problems about temporality); TLond 97 (1994) 44s (A. *Thatcher*).

7581 **Pikaza** Xabier, 'Deus specialiter est in sanctis per gratiam'; el misterio de la inhabitación de la Trinidad en los escritos de Santo Tomás. R 1993,

Pont. Univ. Gregoriana. xxxiv-484 p. – ᴿCarthaginensia 10 (1994) 471s (F. *Chavero Blanco*).

7582 **Plantinga** Alvin, Does God have a nature? Milwaukee 1980, Marquette Univ. – ᴿTArg 28 (1991) 267s (H. *Bonsembiante*).

7583 **Prokes** Mary Timothy sr., Mutuality, the human image of trinitarian love. NY 1993, Paulist. iv-167 p. $13. 0-8091-3443-8. – ᴿTBR 7,3 (1994s) 37 (Una *Kroll*).

7584 *Quesada García* Francisco, Forma y modas de la revelación del misterio trinitario: RET 54 (1994) 63-81.

7584* **Reumann** John, Trinity and unity in NT theology. Ox 1991, UP. xiv-330 p. $55; pa. $20. – ᴿCritRR 6 (1993) 282-4 (J. D. G. *Dunn*).

7585 *Schmidinger* Heinrich, [Paradigmenwechsel] Von der Substanz zur Person: TPQ 142 (1994) 383-394.

7586 ᴱ**Schwöbel** C., *Gunton* C., Persons, divine and human ⇥ 9,7786: ᴿHeythJ 35 (1994) 465s (P. *Hebblethwaite*, also on God, Action 1992); IrTQ 60 (1994) 73-75 (D. *Leader*); JTS 44 (1993) 801-3 (A. McFadyen: title echoes R. J. ILLINGWORTH 1894 'Personality – human and divine').

7587 *Sentis* Laurent, Penser la personne [*prósōpon*, hypostase; dignité]: NRT 116 (1994) 679-700 ...

7588 **Sesboüé** B., *Meunier* B., Dieu peut-il avoir un fils? 1993 ⇥ 9,7628: ᴿZkT 116 (1994) 347s (K. H. *Neufeld*).

7589 *Špidlík* Tomáš, Il mistero della Ss. Trinità nella spiritualità dell'Oriente cristiano: RasT 35 (1994) 58-89.

7590 **Splett** Jörg, La dottrina della Trinità in HEGEL [¹1865;³]: GdT 222, Brescia 1993, Queriniana. 303 p. 88-399-0722-X. – ᴿEstE 69 (1994) 415s (J. J. *Alemany*).

7591 *Studer* Basil, Trinity and Incarnation; the faith of the early Church ⇥ 9, 7631: ᵀ*Westerhoff* Matthias, ᴱ*Louth* Andrew. ColMn 1993, Liturgical/ Glazier. xvii-270 p. $20. 0-8146-5506-8 [TDig 42,91].

7592 *Szczurek* Jan Daniel, ❷ Posto del mistero della Trinità nella teologia contemporanea: ⇥ 93, ᶠPIERONEK T., AnCracov 26 (1994) 249-262; ital. 262.

7593 **Thompson** John, Modern trinitarian perspectives. NY 1994, Oxford-UP. vi-165 p. $32; pa. $14. 0-19-508898-0; -9-9 [TDig 42,190: Belfast Presbyterian prof.].

7594 **Tobler** S., Analogia caritatis; Kirche als Geschöpf und Abbild der Trinität: Diss. ᴰ*Egmond* A. van. Amsterdam VU 1994. 256 p. – TvT 35, 71; RTLv 26, p. 568.

7595 **Uribarri Bilbao** Gabino, Monarquía y Trinidad; el concepto teológico de *monarchia* en la controversia 'monarquiana': diss. Comillas, ᴰ*Losada* J. Madrid 1994. – EstE 69,343-366; RTLv 26, p. 541.

H5.8 *Regnum messianicum, Filius hominis* – **Messianic kingdom, Son of Man.**

7596 *Burkett* Delbert, The nontitular Son of Man; a history and critique: NTS 40 (1994) 504-521.

7597 *Chrupcala* Leslaw D., *a)* La Chiesa e il Regno di Dio; il rapporto definito nella Lumen Gentium; – *b)* Il tema del Regno di Dio nell'opera lucana: Antonianum 69 (1994) 213-230; Eng. 213 / 3-34; Eng. 3.

7598 *Draper* Jonathan A., The development of 'the sign of the Son of Man' in the Jesus tradition: NTS 39 (1993) 1-21.

7599 *a) Floristán* Casiano, La utopía de Jesús; su visión del reino de Dios; –

b) Tamayo Juan José, Religión bíblica; utopías históricas y esperanza cristiana: BibFe 59 (1994) 31-45 / 46-68.

7599* **Hell** Leonhard, Reich Gottes als Systemidee der Theologie [GALURA B., BRENNER F.] 1993 → 9,16649: RTGL 84 (1994) 374s (A. *Schilson*).

7600 **Hare** D. R. A., The Son of Man tradition 1990 → 6,7625 ... 9,7806: RScotJT 45 (1992) 546s (B. *Lindars*).

7601 **Harper** Bradley J., The Kingdom of God in the theology of George Eldon LADD; a reflection of twentieth century American Evangelicalism: diss. St. Louis Univ. 1994, DLane B. 211 p. 95-02971. – DissA 55 (1994s) p. 2869.

7602 **Hempel** Völker, Menschensohn und historischer Jesus 1990 → 6,7624 ... 8,7667: RTR 90 (1994) 35s (F. *Mussner*).

7603 EHengel M., *Schwemer* Anna M., Königsherrschaft Gottes 1991 → 7, 438 ... 9,7807: RAnnTh 7 (1993) 499 (K. *Limburg*).

7604 **Hunt** Boyd, Redeemed! eschatological redemption and the Kingdom of God. Nv 1993, Broadman & H. 384 p. – RTrinJ 15 (1994) 269-272 (T. *Ascol*).

7605 **Ireland** Dennis J., Stewardship and the Kingdom of God ... Lk 16: 1-13: NT supp. 70, 1992 → 8,5446.

7606 **Knapp** Markus [*Knap*, → 9,7812], Gottes Herrschaft als Zukunft der Welt: BoDogmSt 15. Wü 1993, Echter. 736 p. DM 80. 3-429-01507-3. – REurJT 3,2 (1994) 180-3 (E. J. *Schnabel*) franç. 101, Eng. 100 ['Knapp Martin'].

7606* *Kniazeff* A., The kingdom of Caesar and the reign of Christ: GrOrTR 38 (1993) 41-46.

7607 *Koch* Klaus, Messias und Menschensohn; die zweistufige Messianologie der jüngeren Apokalyptik: JbBT 8 (1993) 73-102.

7608 *Krainz* Howard P., Democracy and the 'kingdom of God': Studies in philosophy and religion 17. Boston 1993, Kluwer. viii-251 p. $115. 0-7923-2106-5 [TDig 41,367].

7609 *McCartney* Dan G., Ecce homo; the coming of the Kingdom as the restoration of human vicegerency: WestTJ 56 (1994) 1-21.

7610 **Merklein** Helmut, La Signoria di Dio nell'annuncio di Gesù [Jesu Botschaft 1983 ³1989], TGarra Giovanni, EMontagnini Felice: StBPaid 107. Brescia 1994, Paideia. 249 p.; bibliog. 215-249. Lm 36. 88-394-0515-1.

7611 *Quesnel* Michel, *al.*, Évangile et Règne de Dieu: CahÉv 84 (1993). 68 p. F 30.

7612 *Rubinkiewicz* R., Królestwo Boże... God's kingdom in apocrypha [1 Henoch, Jubilees, Test.Mos.]: RoczT 38s (1991s) 59-94.

7613 **Schürmann** Heinz, Worte des Herrn; Jesu Botschaft vom Königtum Gottes, auf Grund der synoptischen Überlieferung zusammengestellt⁵ʳᵉᵛ [¹1955]. Lp 1994, Benno. 432 p. 3-7452-1022-4.

7614 **Snyder** Howard A., Models of the Kingdom 1991 → 8,7677; 9,7819: RLvSt 18 (1993) 75-77 (R. *Michiels*).

7615 **Song Choan-Seng**, Jesus and the reign of God 1993 → 9,7821: RGregorianum 75 (1994) 362s (J. *Dupuis*); Interpretation 48 (1994) 430.2.4 (D. J. *Adams*); RExp 91 (1994) 117 (W. L. *Hendricks*).

7616 **Subilia** Vittorio, Il regno di Dio; interpretazioni nel corso dei secoli: Sola Scriptura 15, 1993 → 9,7822: RBenedictina 41 (1994) 557 (S. *De Piccoli*); RivB 42 (1994) 501s (V. *Fusco*).

7617 **Viviano** Benedict T., Le royaume de Dieu dans l'histoire 1992 → 9,7823: RBrotéria 137 (1993) 117s (F. *Pires Lopes*).

7618 **Vögtle** Anton, Die 'Gretchenfrage' des Menschensohnproblems; Bilanz und Perspektiv [Lk 12,8s...]: QDisp 152. FrB 1994, Herder. 182 p. DM 24,80. 3-451-02152-8.

7618* *Wallbrecht* Friedrich, Zur Eigenart der Rede vom 'Reich Gottes' bei Jesus: TVers 18 (1993) 63-82.

7619 **Weder** Hans, Metafore del Regno; le parabole di Gesù, ricostruzione ed interpretazione. ᵀ*Garra* G., ᴱ*Fusco* V.: BtCuRel 60. Lᵐ 58. 88-394-0468-6. – ᴿRivB 41 (1993) 352-4 (S. *Carbone*).

7620 *Welker* Michael, Resurrection and the reign of God: → 326, Hope 1993/4, 3-16.

H6.1 *Creatio, sabbatum NT* [→ E3.5]; **The Creation** [→ E1.6; H2.8].

7621 **Anderson** Bernhard W., From creation to new creation; Old Testament perspectives: OvBT 34. Mp 1994, Fortress. xxi-256 p. 0-8006-2847-0.

7622 **Arnould** J., *al.*, Bulletin de théologie de la création: RSPT 78 (1994) 95-124.

7622* **Bidaut** Bernard, Le travail et le sabbat dans la Bible: LumièreV 43, 220 ('Le travail' 1994) 37-46.

7623 *Brambilla* Franco G., Teologia della creazione: ScuolC 122 (1994) 615-659.

7623* **Brinkman** M. E., Schepping en sacrament 1991 → 8,7856: ᴿBijdragen 55 (1994) 93s (A. van *Eijk*).

7624 *Drane* John, Defining a biblical theology of creation: Transformation 10,2 (1993) 7-12.

7625 ᴱ**Eskenazi** Tamara C., *al.*, The sabbath 1991 → 7,431; 9,7835: ᴿAtKap 121 (1993) 447-450 (L. *Politowski*, ❷).

7626 **Fox** Matthew, Schepping en spiritualiteit; gaven tot bevrijding. Zoetemeer 1993, Meinema, 176 p. ƒ29,50. – ᴿGerefTTs 93 (1993) 267s (M. E. *Brinkman*: 'de Amerikaanse Benedictijnse priester').

7626* **Haag** E., Vom Sabbat zum Sonntag 1991 → 7,7629; 9,7835: ᴿZkT 116 (1994) 213s (M. *Hasitschka*).

7627 **Kaiser** Jürgen, Ruhe der Seele und Siegel der Hoffnung; die Sabbatdeutungen der Reformation: Diss. ᴰ*Seebass* G. Heidelberg 1994. – RTLv 26, p. 544.

7628 *Lange* Dietz, Schöpfungslehre und Ethik: ZTK 91 (1994) 156-188.

7629 **Link** Christian, Schöpfung 1-2: [ᴱ*Ratschow* Carl H.] Handbuch syst. Theol. 7. Gü 1991, Gü-V. 349 p.; 305 p. Fs 80 + 49. 8-579-04921-6; -2-4. – ᴿÉTRel 68 (1993) 297s (J.-D. *Kraege*); RHPR 73 (1993) 457-9 (G. *Siegwalt*).

7630 *McCormick* Frances R., Sabbath rest; a theological imperative according to Karl BARTH: JAAR 62 (1994) 530-552.

7631 *Martínez de Pisón* Ramón, Création et liberté: ScEspr 45 (1993) 181-211.

7632 *Minear* Paul S., Christians and the new creation; Genesis motifs in the NT [Lk 1Cor Jn]. LvL 1994, W-Knox. xvi-42 p. $15. Minear bibliog. 141-8 [TS 56,395, D. *Hamm*] 0-664-25531-0.

7633 *Pannenberg* Wolfhart, Die Kontingenz der geschöpflichen Wirklichkeit: TLZ 119 (1994) 1049-1058.

7634 a) *Sales* Michel, L'accomplissement du sabbat; de la sainte septième journée au repos de Dieu en Dieu; – b) *Winogradsky* Alexandre A., Shabbat et Trinité: Communio 19,111 (P 1994) 11-30 / 31-41.

7635 *Schneider* Michael, Die theologische Ausdeutung von Schöpfung und Heiliger Schrift bei BONAVENTURA: TPhil 69 (1994) 373-389.

7636 *a) Sobeczko* Helmut, ❷ De valore theologico ac pastorali dominicae celebrandae sabbato vespere; – *b) Tronina* Antoni, ❷ De sabbato – archetypo dominicae in Vetere Testamento: RuBi 47 (1994) 162-175 / 85-103.
7636* *Vermaak* J. M., Sabbats- en Sondagsviering in die erste vier eeue n.c.: AcPatrByz 2 (1991) 85-95 [JStJud 25,354: up to 400 Sunday was not a Christian sabbath].
7637 *Wilkinson* Loren, The new story of creation [ARC 22, 1994]; a trinitarian perspective: Crux 30,4 (1994) 26-36.

H6.3   *Fides, veritas in NT* – **Faith and truth.**

7638 **Ansaldi** Jean, L'articulation de la foi, de la théologie et des Écritures 1991 → 7,7642; 8,7707: ᴿRTPhil 126 (1994) 89s (M.-A. *Freudiger*); ScEspr 45 (1993) 357s (J.-C. *Petit*: influence de LACAN).
7639 **Barr** James, Biblical faith and natural theology [Edinburgh 1991 Gifford Lectures]. Ox 1993, Clarendon. xii-244 p. $48. – ᴿCBQ 56 (1994) 578s (A. K. M. *Adam*: 'a gift for unmasking [BARTH's] fallacies with verve'); JRel 74 (1994) 417-9 (P. E. *Devenish*: against Barth, witheringly); ModT 10 (1994) 219-221 (W. *Brueggemann*); PrincSemB 15 (1994) 301-3 (R. R. *Ollenburger*); TLond 97 (1994) 48-50 (J. *Draper*: to reject natural theology leads to standing rather aloof from the Bible, p. 200); TS 54 (1993) 754s (J. H. *Wright*).
7640 **Berger** Peter L., Una gloria lejana; la búsqueda de la fe en época de credulidad [1992 → 8,7710],ᵀ. Barc 1994, Herder. 267 p. – ᴿEstE 69 (1994) 407s (E. *Casarotti*); LumenVr 43 (1994) 164s (Felix *Ortiz de Urtaran*).
7641 ᴱ**Berthold** George C., Faith seeking understanding; learning and the Catholic tradition 1991 → 7,470: ᴿAngelicum 71 (1994) 123s (A. *Wilder*).
7642 **Biser** Eugen, Glaubenskonflikte; Strukturanalyse der Kirchenkrise: Tb 1687. FrB 1989, Herder. 127 p. – ᴿTPhil 67 (1992) 618s (W. *Löser*).
7643 **Bourgeois** H., Identité chrétienne: Petite encyclopédie moderne du christianisme 1990 → 9,7856: ᴿNRT 116 (1994) 434 (L.-J. *Renard*).
7644 **Bryant** David J., Faith and the play of imagination. Macon 1989, Mercer Univ. 217 p. – ᴿJAAR 62 (1994) 182-4 (Theresa *Sanders*).
7645 **Buber** Martin, Deux types de foi; foi juive et foi chrétienne, ᵀ*Delattre* Bernard; présent. *Werblowsky* R.: Patrimoines Judaïsme. P 1991, Cerf. 169 p. 2-204-04081-9. – ᴿSalesianum 56 (1994) 162 (R. *Vicent*).
7646 *Callan* T., The origins of Christian faith [... Resurr.]. NY 1994, Paulist. vii-147 p.; 2 fig. $10. 0-8091-3459-4 [NTAbs 38, p. 473].
7647 ᴱ**Collantes** Justo, La fede della Chiesa; le idee e gli uomini nei documenti dottrinali del magistero [1983],ᵀ. Vaticano 1993, Editrice. 1084 p. Lᵐ 85. – ᴿAngelicum 71 (1994) 103-5 (T. *Stancati*).
7648 **Cox** James L., Changing beliefs and an enduring faith. Gweru, Zimbabwe 1993, Mambo. 211 p. 0-86-922-539-1. – ᴿExpTim 105,1 top choice (1993s) 1-2 (C. S. *Rodd*).
7649 *Dalferth* Ingolf U., Subjektivität und Glaube; zur Problematik der theologischen Verwendung einer philosophischen Kategorie: NSys 36 (1994) 18-58; Eng. 58.
7650 **Davies** Hugh, Freeing the faith. L c. 1993, SPCK. 129 p. £8. – ᴿIrTQ 60 (1994) 75s (T. *Gillen*).
7651 *Delahoutre* Michel, Croyance et foi [DALMAIS I., TILLARD J., PANIKKAR R.]: EsprVie 104 (1994) 289-301.

7652 **Dulles** Avery R.,   The assurance of things hoped for; a theology of Christian faith.   NY 1994, Oxford-UP.   xii-299 p. $35.   0-19-508302-4 [TDig 41,357].
7653 **Dykstra** Craig, *Parks* Sharon,   Faith development and FOWLER [James W., Stages of faith, Harper 1981]. 1986, RelEdn. 322 p. $15. – ᴿDrewG 60,1 (1990s) 84-87 (H. O. *Thompson*).
7654 *Esquiza* Jesús,   La doble dimensión de la fe: LumenVr 43 (1994) 211-232.
7655 *Fournier* Keith A.,   Evangelical Catholics [... Catholic via curious faith-ventures back to Catholic]. Nv 1990, Nelson. 223 p. $16. – ᴿSWJT 36,1 (1993s) 60 (J. L. *Garrett*).
7656 *González Faus* J. I.,   El misterio de Jesús y la confesión de fe en él: RCatalT 18 (1993) 99-116; Eng. 117.
7657 **Hall** Douglas J.,   Professing the faith.   Mp 1993, Fortress.   x-566 p. – ᴿSR 23 (1994) 506s (D. *Schweitzer*: Hall 'Christians should not claim to know too much about God' and other inadequacies).
7658 **Harris** Robert W.,   Christian certainty and historical knowledge; a critical survey and a constructive proposal: diss. ᴰ*Gilkey* L.   Chicago 1993. – RTLv 26, p. 529.
7659 **Hart** David A.,   Faith in doubt; non-realism and Christian belief [CUPITT D.].   L 1993, Mowbray.   xiv-146 p. – ᴿPrPeo 8 (1994) 169s (J. *Rist*); TLond 97 (1994) 200s (Alan *Race*: lucidly and refreshingly expresses the view 'Our beliefs are only myths, approaches that attempt to illuminate our situation').
7660 ᴱ**Heim** S. Mark,   Faith to creed 1989/91 → 7,510:   ᴿJEarlyC 1 (1993) 100-2 (Kelly M. *Spoerl*).
7661 *Jericó Bermejo* Ignacio,   La obligación universal de creer según [† 1576 Bartolomé] CARRANZA; la necesidad y el precepto de fe explícita: ScripTPamp 26 (1994) 79-107; Eng. 108.
7662 **Johnson** Alan F., *Webber* Robert E.,   What Christians believe; a biblical and historical summary 1989 → 5,7664: ᴿConcordTQ 58 (1994) 219-221 (J. T. *Pless*).
7663 *Korsch* Dietrich,   Bildung und Glaube; ist das Christentum eine Bildungsreligion?: NSys 36 (1994) 190-213; Eng. 214.
7664 **Küng** H.,   Credo, das apostolische Glaubensbekenntnis⁴.   Mü 1993, Piper.   254 p. DM 29,80.   3-492-03009-2 [Eng. → 9,7874]: ᴿCiTom 120 (1993) 632s (R. de *Luis Carballada*); Streven 61 (1994) 565 (H. *Roeffaers*).
7664* **Küng** Hans,   Credo. M 1994, Trotta.   196 p. – ᴿEfMex 12 (1994) 420-2 (M. *Ramírez Ayala*).
7665 **Kuitert** Harry M.,   Ich habe meine Zweifel; eine kritische Auslegung des christlichen Glaubens [1992 → 8,7727].   Gü 1993, Mohn.   309 p. DM 48. – ᴿHerdKorr 47 (1993) 374s (U. *Rush*); TZBas 50 (1994) 272s (W. *Neidhart*).
7666 **Kuitert** H. M.,   I have my doubts. L/Ph 1993, SCM/Trinity.   xiv-286 p. £10 → 9,7875b: ᴿTLond 97 (1994) 50 (A. *Freeman*).
7666* *Lørning* Inge,   'Den allmänneliga kristna tron' —? Refleksjoner omkring 'Befrielsen' [Liberation (of the Church)] — stora boken om kristen tro: SvTKv 70 (1994) 10-16 [-34, *Stendahl* Kriste, *Selander* Sven-Åke]; Eng. 16.24.34.
7667 **McBrien** Richard P.,   Catholicism³ʳᵉᵛ. SF 1994, Harper. xlviii-1286 p. $60; pa. $35. 0-06-065404-X; -5-8 [TDig 41,275].
7668 **Martínez García** Jesús,   Hablemos de la fe: Patmos. M 1992, Rialp. 336 p. – ᴿCiuD 206 (1993) 654s (T. *Arregui*).

7669 *Martínez de Pisón Liébanas* Ramón,   La dialectique de la foi aujour-d'hui; entre la subjectivité 'sauvage' et le traditionalisme 'intégriste": ÉglT 25 (1994) 405-423.

7670 **Miegge** Giovanni,   Per una fede. T 1991 = 1952, Claudiana.   ix-230 p. – ᴿScripTPamp 26 (1994) 346 (J. M. *Odero*); JEvTS 37 (1994) 586s (D. *Bruce*, very severe; 'liberating love *ad nauseam*'; misunderstands or ignores alternative views).

7671 **Migliore** Daniel L.,   Faith seeking understanding 1992 ➤ 7,7130 ... 9,7189*:   ᴿÉTRel 69 (1994) 118s (J. *Gabus*: ch. 1s moins bien).

7671* **Mitchell** Basil,   Faith and criticism: 1992 Sarum lectures.   Ox 1994, Clarendon.   173 p. $30.   0-19-826758-4 [TDig 42,377].

7672 **Montefiore** Hugh,   Credible Christianity; the Gospel in contemporary culture.   L 1993, Mowbray.   287 + xii p. $17. – ᴿTLond 27 (1994) 201 (P. *Avis*: just the thing: except that many people do not want to think more truthfully about their faith — though he avoided inclusive God-terms to placate them).

7673   *a) Müller* Peter,   Der Glaube aus dem Hören; über das gesprochene und das geschriebene Wort bei Paulus; – *b) Brooten* Bernadette J.,   Is belief the center of religion?:   ➤ 40, ᶠGEORGI D., 1994, 405-442 / 471-9.

7674 **Neuhaus** Gerd,   Theodizee – Abbruch oder Anstoss des Glaubens.   FrB 1993, Herder.   400 p. DM 68.   3-451-23237-5. – ᴿTPhil 69 (1994) 609-613 (J. *Splett*).

7674* **Norris** Frederick W.,   The Apostolic faith, Protestants and Roman Catholics.   ColMn 1992.   175 p. £14.30. – ᴿDocLife 44 (1994) 56s (P. J. *Neill*).

7675 **O'Collins** G., *Venturini* Mary, Believing.   L 1993, HarperCollins.   178 p. £8. – ᴿTablet 247 (1993) 859 (D. L. *Edwards*).

7676 **Odero** José M.,   La fe en KANT: Col.Filos. 77.   Pamplona 1992, Univ. Navarra.   621 p. – ᴿScripTPamp 26 (1994) 265-8 (C. *Izquierdo*).

7677 *Osborn* Eric, Arguments for faith in CLEMENT of Alexandria: VigChr 48 (1994) 1-24.

7678 **Principe** Walter H.,   Faith, history and cultures; stability and change in Church teachings.   Milwaukee c. 1993, Marquette Univ. 63 p. $8. – ᴿCanadCath 12,2 (1994) 29s (J. *Rose*).

7679 ᴱ**Radcliffe** Elizabeth S., *White* Carol I.,   Faith in theory and practice; essays on justifying religious belief.   Ch 1993, Open Court.   xix-235 p. $35; pa. $17.   0-8126-9246-2; -7-0.

7680 **Ratzinger** J., *Henrici* P.,   Credo: Communio. Köln 1992. 398 p. DM 42.   3-921204-08-9. – ᴿTPhil 69 (1994) 615s (J. *Splett*).

7681 *Salvatierra* Ángel,   Fe, ideologías y utopías; salvación e historia: LumenVr 43 (1994) 323-343.

7682 **Sauer** Hanjo,   Erfahrung und Glaube; die Begründung des pastoralen Prinzips durch die Offenbarungskonstitution II.Vat: WüFundT 12.   Fra 1993, Lang.   802 p.   3-631-44779-5. – ᴿAntonianum 69 (1994) 552-4 (L. *Oviedo*).

7683 **Sessions** William L.,   The concept of faith; a philosophical investigation.   Ithaca 1994, Cornell Univ.   x-298 p. $37 [TS 56,174].

7684 *Smith* Joseph J.,   Hansjürgen VERWEYEN and the ground of Easter faith [... faith adequately grounded in the life and *death* of Jesus]: Landas 8 (1994) 147-181.

7685 **Thielicke** Helmut,   Modern faith and thought, ᵀ*Bromiley* Geoffrey W. GR 1990, Eerdmans. – ᴿJEvTS 36 (1993) 537-9 (T. K. *Johnson*).

7686 **Thiselton** Anthony C., BARR [Biblical faith 1991/3 ➤ 7639] on BARTH and natural theology; a plea for hermeneutics in historical theology: ScotJT 47 (1994) 519-528.

7687 **Westphal** Merold, Suspicion and faith; the religious uses of modern atheism [Freud, Marx, Nietzsche]. GR 1913, Eerdmans. xi-296 p. £15. 0-8028-0643-0. – ᴿTBR 7,1 (1994s) 48 (Don *Cupitt*: unique confidence that USA Protestant Christianity is simply true, and not seriously threatened).

H6.6   Peccatum NT – Sin, Evil [➤ E1.9].

7688 ᴱ**Adams** M.&R., The problem of evil: Readings. Ox 1990. UP. viii-230 p. 0-19-824866-0. – ᴿBijdragen 55 (1994) 92s (P. *Vermeer*).

7689 **Bassett** Lytta, Le pardon originel; de l'abîme du mal au pouvoir de pardonner. Genève 1994, Labor et Fides. 500 p. Fs 35. – ᴿÉtudes 381 (1994) 140 (Gwendoline *Jarczyk*).

7690 **Capps** Donald, The depleted self; sin in a narcissistic age. Mp 1993, Fortress. xiv-176 p. $13. – ᴿPrincSemB 15 (1994) 197-9 (Kathleen *Bilman*).

7691 a) *Colzani* Gianni, Il male; ricognizione di un tema antropologico e teologico; – b) *Marcheselli-Casale* Cesare, Dio l'uomo il male; l'interpellante prospettiva di E. DREWERMANN; – c) *Grossi* Stefano, Paul RICŒUR e il problema del male: VivH 5 (1994) 31-48 / 73-102 / 49-72; Eng. 48.102.72.

7691* *Dekker* Eef, *Veldhuis* Henri, Freedom and sin; some systematic observations: EurJT 3,2 (1994) 154-161; franç. deutsch 153.

7692 *Flora* J., NT perspektives on evil: AshlandTJ 24 (1992) 88s [< ZNW 85,159].

7692* **Gesché** Adolphe, Dieu pour penser, 1. Le mal, 1993 ➤ 9,7902: ᴿÉTRel 68 (1993) 409-413 (J.-P. *Gabus*); FoiTemps 23 (1993) 281-3 (G. *Harpigny*).

7693 *Grey* Mary, Falling into freedom; searching for new interpretations of sin in a secular society: ScotJT 47 (1994) 223-243.

7694 **Griffin** David Ray, Evil revisited; responses and reconsiderations 1991 ➤ 9,7746: ᴿCritRR 6 (1993) 509-511 (J.K. *Robbins*).

7695 *Janowski* Bernd, Die Tat kehrt zum Täter zurück; offene Fragen im Umkreis des 'Tun-Ergehen-Zusammenhangs' [i. Vergeltung; ii. als soziale Interaktion (Prov. 28,18); iii. als göttliche Intervention]: ZTK 91 (1994) 247-271.

7696 *Keenan* James F., The problem with Thomas AQUINAS's concept of sin: HeythJ 35 (1994) 401-420.

7697 **Millás** José M., Pecado... BULTMANN 1989 ➤ 6,7703: ᴿRTLv 25 (1994) 101s (E. *Brito*).

7698 a) *Neugebauer* Fritz, Die biblische Rede von der Schuld; Hilfe in den Wirrnissen unserer Tage; – b) *Beintker* Michael, Schuld und Verstrickung in der Neuzeit; – c) *Fuchs* Ottmar, In der Sünde auf dem Weg der Gnade: JbBT 9 ('Sünde und Gericht' 1994) 329-345 / 219-234 / 235-259.

7699 **Peters** Ted, Sin; radical evil in soul and society. GR 1994, Eerdmans. ix-339 p. 0-8028-3764-0; pa. -0013-7.

7700 ᴱ**Peterson** Michael L., The problem of evil; selected readings 1992 ➤ 8,7752: ᴿAmJTP 15 (Dayton 1994) 199-201 (B. *Mesle*).

7701 **Plantinga** Cornelius, Not the way it's supposed to be; a breviary of sin. GR/Leicester 1994, Eerdmans/Apollos. xiv-202 p. £15.

7701* *Reig Pla* Juan A., El proyecto de Dios sobre el hombre y el misterio del pecado: AnVal 20 (1994) 379-398.
7702 **Schwarz** Hans, Im Fangnetz des Bösen; Sünde – Übel – Schuld: BTheolSchwerpunkte 10, 1993, ➤ 9,7908*; DM 52. 3-525-61291-5: ᴿTvT 34 (1994) 481s (H. *Häring*).
7702* *Ubbiali* Sergio, [*al.*], Il peccato: ScuolC 122 (1994) 369-387 [-411].
7703 **Van de Beek** A., WHY? On suffering, guilt and God 1990 ➤ 7,7677: ᴿScotJT 46 (1993) 116s (T. *Gorringe*: some helpfulness, but not enough).
7704 *Wyman* Walter E.ᴶ, Rethinking the Christian doctrine of sin; Ernst TROELTSCH and the German Protestant liberal tradition: NtZg 1 (1994) 226-250.

H7 **Soteriologia NT.**

7705 **Bavard** Georges, La justification par la foi; quelle est la racine de la divergence entre catholiques et protestants?: NVFr 68 (1993) 250-262.
7705* **Braaten** Carl E., Justification 1990 ➤ 6,7714; 9,7916: ᴿScotJT 46 (1993) 229-231 (R. R. *Redman*).
7706 **Dillow** Joseph C., The reign of the servant kings; a study of eternal security and the final significance of man². Hayesville NC 1993, Schoettle. 649 p. $20. – ᴿBtS 151 (1994) 486-8 (T. L. *Constable*: good).
7706* **Dunn** James D. G., *Suggate* Alan M., The justice of God; a fresh look at the old doctrine of justification by faith. GR 1994, Eerdmans [< Carlisle 1993, Paternoster. 0-85364-562-0 ➤ 9,7919]. 87 p. $10. 0-8028-0797-6. – ᴿTBR 7,3 (1994s) 46 (T. J. *Gorringe*).
7707 *Dupuis* Jacques, Alleanza e salvezza [...la salvezza per mezzo dell'Alleanza; LOHFINK N.]: RasT 35 (1994) 148-171.
7708 ᴱ**Feenstra** Ronald J., *Plantinga* Cornelius, Trinity, incarnation and atonement 1989 ➤ 5,612: ᴿScotJT 46 (1993) 123-5 (J. *Thompson*).
7709 *Fretheim* T. E., Salvation in the Bible vs. salvation in the Church: WWorld 13 (St. Paul 1993) 363-372 [< NTAbs 38, p. 238].
7710 **Führer** Werner, Rechtfertigung und Heiligung bei Hans Joachim IWAND: KerDo 40 (1994) 272-281.
7711 **Garrison** Roman, Redemptive almsgiving: jNsu 77, 1993 ➤ 9,7925: ᴿCBQ 56 (1994) 592s (Sheila E. *McGinn*).
7712 *Gomes* Alan W., De Jesu Christo servatore; Faustus SOCINUS on the satisfaction of Christ: WestTJ 55 (1993) 209-231.
7713 *Hahn* Ferdinand, Is er een ontwikkeling in de uitspraken over de rechtvaardiging bij Paulus? ᴿ*Spijkerboer* A. A.: KerkT 45 (1994) 180-205.
7714 **Haight** Roger, Jesus and Salvation: on essay in interpretation: TS 55 (1994) 225-251.
7715 **Hultgren** Arland J., Christ and his benefits; Christology and redemption in the NT 1987 ➤ 3,7364... 6,7724: ᴿBijdragen 55 (1994) 85 (J.-J. *Suurmond*, Eng.).
7716 *Jenssen* Paul, Forgiveness and atonement: ScotJT 46 (1993) 141-159.
7717 **Joubert** Jacques, Le corps sauvé 1991 ➤ 7,7713; 8,7769: ᴿRTPhil 126 (1994) 396 (L. *Rumpf*).
7718 *Kaiser* Walter C.ᴶ, Salvation in the Old Testament, with special emphasis on the object and content of personal belief: Jian Dao 2 (1994) 1-18; ☯ 18. [p. 152-8; 159-162, expository articles in Chinese, with no further English clue, by KWONG Andrew and TSANG Rennie].
7719 **Kettler** Christian D., The vicarious humanity of Christ and the reality

of salvation 1991 ➤ 8,7771; 9,7931:   ᴿScotJT 46 (1993) 419s (B. D. *Spinks*).

7720 **Kühn** Ulrich, *Pesch* Otto H., Rechtfertigung... zu BAUR Jörg über 'Lehrverurteilungen' 1991 ➤ 8,8048*:   ᴿTLZ 119 (1994) 263-6 (T. *Mahlmann*).

7720* **Letham** Robert, The work of Christ. DG 1993, InterVarsity. 244 p. $15 pa. – ᴿWestTJ 56 (1994) 442s (M. J. *Klauber*: 'a classic defense of the Reformed position on the Atonement').

7721 **MacArthur** John F., Faith works; the Gospel according to the Apostles [... justification plus]. Dallas 1993, Word. 276 p. $18.   0-8499-0841-8. – ᴿRExp 91 (1994) 444s (J. M. *Terry*).

7722 **McDonald** H. D., NT concept of atonement; the Gospel of the Calvary event. C/GR 1994, Lutterworth/Baker. 144 p. £10 [NTAbs 38, p. 447]. 0-7188-288-7; 0-8010-6309-4. – ᴿTBR 7,3 (1994s) 39 (C. *Gunton*).

7723 **McGlasson** Paul, God the redeemer; a theology of the Gospel 1993 ➤ 9,7935:   ᴿJEvTS 37 (1994) 601s (G. L. *Nebeker*).

7724 **McIntyre** John, The shape of soteriology 1992 ➤ 9,7937:   ᴿHeythJ 35 (1994) 205s (M. M. *Winter*, also on MERTENS N. 1992); JTS 45 (1994) 431-3 (V. *White*).

7725 **Martens** Gottfried, Die Rechtfertigung des Sünders — Rettungshandeln Gottes oder historisches Interpretament; Grundentscheidungen... im Ökumenischen Kontext: FSysÖkT 54, 1992 ➤ 9,7939:   ᴿLuthTKi 17 (1993) 175-186 (T. *Mahlmann*).

7726 **Menke** Karl-Heinz, Stellvertretung 1991 ➤ 8,7777; 9,7941:   ᴿMüTZ 44 (1993) 120-4 (G. L. *Müller*); RTPhil 126 (1994) 286s (R. *Blaser*).

7727 *a) Moltmann* Jürgen, Justice for victims and perpetrators; – *b) Brueggemann* Walter, Justice, the earthly form of God's holiness: RefW 44 (1994) 2-12 / 13-27 [-48, *al.*].

7728 *Remy* Gérard, La substitution; pertinence ou non-pertinence d'un concept théologique: RThom 94 (1994) 559-600.

7728* *Richard* Ramesh P., Soteriological inclusivism and dispensationalism: BtS 151 (1994) 85-108.

7729 **Rosenau** Hartmut, Allversöhnungsversuch; ein transzendentaltheologischer Gründungsversuch: ThBt Töpelmann 57. B 1993, de Gruyter. x-544 p. DM 212.   3-11-013738-0.

7730 **Sattler** Dorothea, Gelebte Busse; das menschliche Busswerk (satisfactio) im ökumenischen Gespräch 1992 ➤ 8,7290; 9,7950:   ᴿRTLv 25 (1994) 388s (A. de *Halleux*); TRu 59 (1994) 218-222 (M. *Obst*).

7731 *Strehle* Stephen, Imputatio iustitiae; its origin in MELANCHTHON, its opposition in OSIANDER: TZBas 50 (1994) 201-219.

7732 **Swinburne** Richard, Responsibility and atonement 1989 ➤ 6,7749 ... 9,7958:   ᴿFaith and Philosophy 11 (ND 1994) 321-8 (Eleonore *Stump*); ScotJT 46 (1993) 548-550 (P. S. *Fiddes*).

7734 **Tamez** Elsa, The amnesty of grace; justification by faith from a Latin American perspective [Contra toda condena 1991 ➤ 9,7960], ᵀ*Ringe* Sharon H. Nv 1993, Abingdon. 208 p. $15.   0-687-00934-0. – ᴿTBR 7,1 (1994s) 39s (Anne *Murphy*).

7735 *a) Tate* Marvin E., The comprehensive nature of salvation in biblical perspective; – *b) Mueller* David L., Karl BARTH in dialogue on the foundation of salvation; – *c) Grenz* Stanley J., Salvation and God's program in establishing community; – *d) Escobar Donoso* S., Salvation according to liberation theology; – *e) Chancellor* James D., Christ and religious pluralism: RExp 91,4 (1994) 469-485 / 487-503 / 505-520 / 521-533 / 535-549.

7736 **Ternant** Paul,   Le Christ est mort pour tous 1993 ➔ 9,7962:   ᴿCarthaginensia 10 (1994) 476 (R. *Sanz Valdivieso*); PrOrChr 42 (1992!) 465-7 (V. *Mora*).
7737 **Tiessen** Terrance L., IRENAEUS on the salvation of the unevangelized: ATLA Mg 31. Metuchen NJ 1993, Scarecrow. 320 p. – ᴿRechSR 82 (1994) 429s (B. *Sesboüé*).
7738 **Torrance** Thomas F., The mediation of Christ 1992 ➔ 9,7964: ᴿScotJT 47 (1994) 115-7 (B. D. *Spinks*).
7739 **Vandevelde** Guy,   Expression de la cohérence du mystère de Dieu et du salut [... AQUIN/LEVINAS]: AnGreg 263. R 1993, Pont. Univ. Gregoriana. xxvi-178 p. – ᴿRevSR 68 (1994) 514s (Y. *Labbé*); RThom 94 (1994) 710s (G. *Bavaud*).
7739* *Vanhoye* Albert,   *a*) Salut universel dans le Christ et validité de l'ancienne alliance: NRT 116 (1994) 815-835; – *b*) Salvezza universale nel Cristo e validità dell'Antica Alleanza: CC 145 (1994,4) 433-445.
7740 *Vorgrimler* Herbert, Historische und theologische Aspekte zum Thema Sühne: Diakonia 25 (1994) 178-184.
7741 **Werbick** Jürgen, Soteriología, ᵀ*Gancho* Claudio: BtT 17, 1992 ➔ 9,7967: ᴿCiuD 206 (1993) 239 (J. M. *Ozaeta*); LumenVr 42 (1993) 195s (F. *Ortiz* U.); ScripTPamp 26 (1994) 856s (L. F. *Mateo-Seco*).
7742 **Werbick** Jürgen, Soteriologia: GdT 220, Brescia 1994, Queriniana. 353 p. Lᵐ 35. – ᴿAsprenas 41 (1994) 294-6 (P. *Cacciapuoti*).
7743 *Wood* Ralph C., What ever happened to Baptist Calvinism? A response to Molly MARSHALL and Clark PINNOCK on the nature of salvation in Jesus Christ and in the world religions: RExp 91 (1994) 593-608.

H7.2   *Crux, sacrificium;*   **The Cross; the nature of sacrifice.**

7744 *a*) *Adams* Rebecca, Violence, difference, sacrifice; a conversation with René GIRARD; – *b*) *Ong* Walter J., Mimesis and the following of Christ: RLitND 25,2 (1993) 11-33 / 26,2 (1994) 73-77.
7745 *Aguirre* Rafael, Sociología de la cruz en el NT: RLatAmT 10 (1993) 127-141.
7746 **Alison** James, Knowing Jesus [with René GIRARD; Blackfriars lectures]. L 1993, SPCK. 116 p. £8. – ᴿTLond 97 (1994) 70s (S. S. *Smalley*).
7747 *Bader* Günter, Die Ambiguität des Opferbegriffs: NSys 36 (1994) 59-74; Eng. 74 [MELANCHTHON on the Eucharist].
7748 **Barbaglio** Giuseppe, Dieu est-il violent? Une lecture des Écritures juives et chrétiennes [1991 ➔ 7,7744], ᵀ*Caldiroli* Daniela, *Arrighi* Renza: Parole de Dieu. P 1994, Seuil. 344 p. 2-02-030795-8.
7748* **Barbaglio** G., ¿Dios violento? 1992 ➔ 8,7806: ᴿRBibArg 55 (1993) 115-120 (A. J. *Levoratti*).
7749 *Barth* Hans-Martin, Stellvertretendes Opfer? UnSa 49 (1994) 29-36.
7749* **Battaglia** Vincenzo, Gesù crocifisso figlio di Dio 1991 ➔ 7,7745: ᴿAnnTh 8 (1994) 188-190 (A. *Ducay*).
7750 **Baudler** Georg, Töten oder lieben; Gewalt und Gewaltlosigkeit in Religion und Christentum ...?: ᴿTR 90 (1994) 355-364.367 (E. *Biser*); 363-8 Baudler Antwort.
7751 **Becker** William M., The historical Jesus in the face of his death; his comprehension of its salvific meaning in the writings of E. SCHILLEBEECKX and H. U. von BALTHASAR: diss. N°4046, Pont. Univ. Gregoriana, ᴰ*Fisichella* R. Rome 1994. 368 p. – 94-34995. DissA 55 (1994s) p. 2010; InfPUG 36,131 (1994) 32 (N° 7207); RTLv 26, p. 564.

7751* **Beers** William, Women and sacrifice; male narcissism and the psychology of religion [... analysis of ritual blood sacrifice]. Detroit 1992, Wayne State Univ. 205 p. $29. – ᴿJRel 74 (1994) 129s (Diane *Jonte-Pace*).

7752 *Berghe* Erik Van den, Hij is gestorven voor ons; over de heilsbetekenis van Jezus' dood: CollatVL 24 (1994) 5-24.

7753 *Berquist* Jon L., What does the Lord require? Old Testament child sacrifice and New Testament Christology [Mi 5,6-8 affirms life; Abraham failed his test; he should have struggled to save life]: Encounter 55 (Indianapolis 1994) 107-128 [< OTAbs 17, p. 618].

7753* **Bonnechère** Pierre, Le sacrifice humain en Grèce ancienne: Kernos supp. 3. Liège 1994, Centre Rel. Grecque Antique. vii-423 p.

7754 *a*) *Chauvet* Louis-Marie, Le 'sacrifice' en christianisme; une notion ambiguë; – *b*) *Neusch* Marcel, Une conception chrétienne du sacrifice; le modèle de saint Augustin; – *c*) *Tassin* Claude, L'apostolat, un 'sacrifice'? Judaïsme et métaphores pauliniennes; – *d*) *Lenhardt* Pierre, La valeur des sacrifices pour le judaïsme d'autrefois et d'aujourd'hui [al. Afrique, Islam, Inde, Chine]: → 379*, Le sacrifice 1991/4, 139-155 (277-304) / 117-138 / 85-116 / 61-84 [21-56. 157-273].

7755 **Chilton** Bruce, The Temple of Jesus; his sacrificial program 1992 → 8,4361; 9,7978: ᴿInterpretation 48 (1994) 206.8 (R. G. *Hamerton-Kelly*: unwisely against R. GIRARD); JTS 45 (1994) 204-7 (W. *Houston*).

7756 **Dinkler** E., Im Zeichen des Kreuzes 1992 → 9,236*a*: ᴿTLZ 119 (1994) (K. *Klumbies*).

7757 **Drummond** Lewis A., The word of the Cross; a contemporary theology of evangelism. Nv 1992, Broadman. 383 p. $23. – ᴿAndrUnS 32 (1994) 265 (N. R. *Gulley*); TrinJ 15 (1994) 130-5 (J. W. *Nyquist*).

7758 **Girard** René, A theater of envy, W. SHAKESPEARE. Ox 1991, UP. 366 p. $30. – ᴿLitTOx 8 (1994) 422s (H. J. Lundager *Jensen*: a masterpiece of gratefulness to his predecessor in psychological and anthropological perspicacity); RLitND 24,3 (1993) 85 (J. D. *Cox*: he finds as everywhere mimesis and scapegoating).

7759 **Hamerton-Kelly** R. G., Sacred violence; Paul's hermeneutic of the Cross 1992 → 8,7824; 9,7986: ᴿCBQ 56 (1994) 137s (S. B. *Marrow*: good on Paul, but GIRARD 'a tyrannous master of obfuscation'); Interpretation 48 (1994) 96.98 (C. *Mabee*: rightly 'if we are all scapegoats (Paul), then nobody is a scapegoat').

7760 *a*) *Hasitschka* Martin, Zugang zum lebendigen Gott; das Opferverständnis im Hebräerbrief; – *b*) *Schwager* Raymund, Lieblos und unversehrt; will Gott Opfer? – *c*) *Sandler* Willibald, Das Opfer Christi und unsere Opfer; Unterscheidungen und Zusammenhänge; – *d*) *Hell* Silvia, Hingabe und Darbringung; 'Opfer' in der ökumenischen Diskussion: Entschluss 48,1 (1993) 19s. 25s / 4-7 / 8-13 / 14-18.

7761 **Hooker** Morna B., Not ashamed of the Gospel; NT interpretations of the death of Christ [< 1988 Cambridge Didsbury lectures]. Carlisle 1994, Paternoster. 141 p. £7. 0-85364-543-4. – ᴿTBR 7,3 (1994s) 40 (D. *Lee*).

7762 **Hughes** Dennis, Human sacrifice in ancient Greece [diss. on SCHWENN F., Die Menschenopfer, Giessen 1915] 1991 → 7,7759; 8,7829: ᴿGnomon 66 (1994) 97-100 (W. *Burkert*).

7763 **Jay** Nancy, Throughout your generations forever; sacrifice, religion and paternity 1992 → 9,7991: ᴿJRel 74 (1994) 439 (Kay A. *Read*: though female data are usually unavailable rather than unused, sacrifice can mean much more than male descent); TLond 96 (1993) 227s (Malory *Nye*).

7764 **Kittel** Gisela, Die biblische Rede vom Sühnopfer Christi und ihre unsere Wirklichkeit erschliessende Kraft; eine didaktische Reflexion: JbBT 9 (1994) 285-314 [315-328, *Müller* Winnibald].

7765 **Lascaris** André, Het soevereine slachtoffer; een theologisch essay over geweld en oderdrukking 1993 ➤ 9,7997: *f* 45.   90-259-4551-1:   ᴿTvT 34 (1994) 206s (A. van *Iersel*).

7766 **Levenson** Jon D., Death / child sacrifice 1993 ➤ 9,7998: ᴿBL (1994) 110 (C. S. *Rodd*); ChrCent 111 (1994) 791s (W. T. *Stevenson*); ExpTim 105 (1993s) 282s (G. L. *Jones*); JTS 45 (1994) 643-7 (J. *Swetnam*); TS 55 (1994) 538-540 (A. J. *Saldarini*).

7767 **Lincoln** Bruce, Death, war and sacrifice [< 15 published articles & 6 inedita] 1991 ➤ 7,222*d*; 9,7999:   ᴿHorizons 21 (1994) 222s (G. *Benavides*).

7767* *a*) *Löning* Karl, Der gekreuzigte Jesus — Gottes letztes 'Opfer'; zur Bedeutung der Kultmetaphern im Zusammenhang der urchristlichen Soteriologie; – *b*) *Werbick* Jürgen, Ein Opfer zur Versöhung der zürnenden Gottheit?; – *c*) *Steymans* Hans U., Die Opfer im Buch Deuteronomium; ihre Funktion im Leben des Gottesvolkes; – *d*) *Limbeck* Meinrad, Wer Dank opfert, der preiset mich: Ps 50,23; Möglichkeiten und Grenzen kultischer Opfer: BiKi 49,2 ('Opfer und Sühne' 1994) 138-143 / 144-9 / 126-131 / 132-7 [.169, *Vanoni* G. über ᴱSCHENKER A. 1992].

7768 *Marshall* Molly T., On a hill too far away? Reclaiming the cross as the critical interpretive principle of the Christian life: RExp 91 (1994) 247-259.

7769 **Mertens** Herman-Emiel, Not the Cross, but the Crucified; an essay in soteriology 1992 ➤ 9,8001*b*: ᴿLvSt 19 (1994) 77-79 (W. M. *Thompson*: liberationist).

7770 **Marx** Alfred, Les offrandes végétales dans l'Ancien Testament; du tribut d'hommage au repas eschatologique: VTSup 57. Leiden 1994, Brill. xiii-186 p.; bibliog. 170-175.   90-04-10136-5.

7771 *Moore* Sebastian, 'Why did God kill Jesus?': DowR 112 (1994) 15-25.

7772 ᴱ**Neusch** M., Le sacrifice dans les religions: ScTRel 3. P 1994, Beauchesne. 310 p. [RHE 89,428*].

7773 ᴱ**Niewiadomski** J., Palaver W., Dramatische Erlösungslehre [SCHWAGER R. & GIRARD R., Symposion] 1992 ➤ 9,602: ᴿHerdKor 47 (1993) 106 (A. *Foitzik*); TR 90 (1994) 371s (H. G. *Türk*); TvT 34 (1994) 206 (N. *Schreurs*).

7773* *Pattery* George, Mimetic desire and sacred violence; understanding René GIRARD from the Indian context: Vidyajyoti 58 (1994) 15-32.

7774 *Rives* James B., TERTULLIAN on child sacrifice: MusHelv 51 (1994) 54-63.

7774* **Rodríguez Garrapucho** Fernando, La Cruz de Jesús y el ser de Dios; la teología del Crucificado en Eberhard JÜNGEL: BtSalm 148. S 1992, Univ. 286 p. – ᴿSalmanticensis 41 (1994) 157-9 (X. *Pikaza*).

7775 **Sassmann** Christiane K., Die Opferbereitschaft Israels, anthropologische und theologische Voraussetzungen des Opferkultes: ev. Diss. ᴰ*Reventlow* H. Bochum 1994. 275 p. – RTLv 26,532.

7776 ᴱ**Schenker** Adrian, Studien zu Opfer und Kult im AT 1990/2 ➤ 9,297: ᴿOTEssays 7 (1994) 147-151 (G. H. *Wittenburg*); RB 101 (1994) 289s (tit. pp.); TLZ 119 (1994) 633-6 (H. M. *Niemann*).

7777 *Schenker* Adrian, Les sacrifices dans la Bible: RICathP 50 (1994) 89-105.

7778 *Schwager* Raymund, Suffering, victims, and poetic inspiration, ᵀ*O'Liddy* Patrick: ➤ 43, ᶠGIRARD R., Contagion 1 (1994) 63-72.

7778* *Scullion* Scott, Olympian and Chthonian [sacrifice-attitudes]: ClasAnt 25,1 (1994) 75-119.
7779 *Seidl* T., *šᵉlāmîm* 'Heilsopfer': ➤ 519, TWAT 8,1 (1994) 101-111.
7780 ᴱ**Sykes** S.W., Sacrifice and redemption 1991 ➤ 7,384: ᴿBijdragen 55 (1994) 216s (H. *Rikhof*); JRel 73 (1993) 98s (Linda Lee *Nelson*: puzzling that the meaningfulness of the death of Christ has been treated as if critical and constructive feminist offerings were nonexistent); ScotJT 47 (1994) 398-400 (G. *Jones*).
7782 **Toniolo** Andrea, La 'teologia crucis' nel contesto della modernità; il rapporto tra croce e modernità nel pensiero di E. JUNGEL, H.U. von BALTHASAR e G.W.F. HEGEL: diss. Pont. Univ. Gregoriana, ᴰ*Salmann* E. Roma 1994. 285 p. – RTLv 26, p. 551.
7783 **Varga-Berta** József, Opfer als Weg und Wesen ökumenischer Theologie: diss. Innsbruck. 290 p. – RTLv 26,568 sans date.
7784 *Vos* J.S., Vragen rondom de plaatsvervangende zoendood van Jezus in het Nieuwe Testament: GerefTTs 93 (1993) 210-231.
7785 *Webb* Eugene, The new social psychology of France; the Girardian school: Religion 23 (L 1993) 255-264 [< zɪᴛ 93,578].
7786 **Williams** James G., The Bible, violence, and the sacred; liberation from the myth of sanctioned violence 1991 ➤ 8,7847; 9,8008: ᴿAnglTR 61 (1994) 115-7 (B.O. *Brown*); JAAR 62 (1994) 226-230 (N. *Elliott*).
7787 *Wypustek* Andrzej, The problem of human sacrifices in Roman North Africa: Eos 81 (1993) 263-280.
7787* *Zunino* Maddalena L., Del buon uso del sacrificio: QuadSto 40 (1994) 33-57.

H7.4 Sacramenta, *Gratia.*

7788 *Baudry* Gérard-Henry, Un symbole oublié du baptême; 'les deux voies': EsprVie 104 (1994) 353-363.
7788* **Benoît** André, *Munier* Charles, Le baptême dans l'Église ancienne (Ier-IIIe siècles): Traditio christiana 9. Bern 1994, Lang. xcv-276 p.; bibliog. lxxvi-xciv. 3-906752-42-9.
7789 **Bernardo** Bonifacio, Simbologia e tipologia do Baptismo. Lisboa 1989, Didaskalia. 453 p. – ᴿMaisD 195 (1993) 161s (J. *Ribeiro*).
7789* *Bourgeois* Henri, Bulletin de théologie sacramentaire: RechSR 82 (1994s) 103-131.
7790 **Buchanan** Colin, Infant baptism and the Gospel; the Church of England's dilemma. L 1993, Darton-LT. vii-204 p. £10 pa. – ᴿTLond 97 (1994) 223s (P.B. *Clarke*: confident, lively and hard hitting, with footnotes both endearing and infuriating, little on infant baptism and less on Gospel; mostly chronicles his 25 years' controversies).
7791 **Cañardo Ramírez** Santiago, Los obispos españoles ante el sacramento de la penitencia (diss. Pont. Univ. Gregoriana). S 1993, Univ. Pont. 414 p. – ᴿRelCu 40 (1994) 160s (R. del *Olmo Veros*).
7792 **Cattenoz** Jean-Pierre, Le baptême, mystère nuptial; théologie de s. Jean CHRYSOSTOME: NDVie 5. Venasque 1993, Carmel. 357 p. F 195. 2-900424-20-8. – ᴿETL 69 (1993) 450s (A. de *Halleux*).
7793 *a) Dacquino* Pietro, La confirmación desde la presencia del Espíritu Santo en la Iglesia naciente; – *b) Ibáñez Arana* A., Penitencia y reconciliación en Israel; – *c) Miguel González* J.M. de, Perspectiva trinitario-redentora de la Eucaristía; EstTrin 27 (1993) 3-20 [-350 *al.*] / 351-398 / 399-422.

7794 **Duffy** Stephen J.,   The graced horizon 1992 → 8,7865; 9,8026:   ᴿHeythJ 35 (1994) 467s (P. *Endean*).
7795 **Duffy** Stephen J.,   The dynamics of grace; perspectives in theological anthropology: NewTheolSt 3.   ColMn 1993, Liturgical/Glazier.   398 p. $23 pa.   0-8146-5790-7 [TDig 41,357].
7796 **Finn** Thomas M.,   Early Christian baptism and the catechumenate; *a*) West and East Syria; – *b*) Italy, North Africa, and Egypt: Message of the Fathers,   1992 → 8,7869; 9,8029;   £14.50; pa. £12. – ᴱExpTim 105 (1993s) 59s (K. *Stevenson*: high praise); RelStR 20 (1994) 243 (Verna E. F. *Harrison*); SR 23 (1994) 89s (P. *Jefferson*).
7796* **Fontbona i Missè** Jaume,   Comuniôn y sinodalidad; la eclesiologia eucaristica después de N. Afanasiev en I. Zizioulas y J. M. R. Tillard: diss. Pont. Univ. Gregoriana, Theol. Nº 7186; ᴰ*Vercruysse* J. R 1994. – InfPUG 26,121 (1994) p.32.
7797 *Forte* Bruno,   L'eternità nel tempo [... antropologia ed etica sacramentale]: RivScR 8 (1994) 17-35.
7797* *Freyer* Thomas, Sakrament – Instrument der Gesellschaftsveränderung; eine Auseinandersetzung mit Franz Schupp [1974]: TGgw 37 (1994) 2-21.
7798 **Galindo Rodrigo** José A.,   Compendio de la gracia 1991 → 8,7871; 9,8031: ᴿTeresianum 45 (1994) 306-8 (M. *Caprioli*).
7799 **Ganoczy** Alexandre,   Dalla sua pienezza noi tutti abbiamo ricevuto; lineamenti fondamentali della dottrina della grazia [1989]ᵀ: BtContemp 67. Brescia 1991, Queriniana.   334 p. Lᵐ 40. – ᴿGregorianum 75 (1994) 359s (M. *Lubomirski*).
7800 **Groen** Basilius J.,   'Ter genezing van ziel en lichaam' [ᴰ1990] 1992 → 8,7873; 9,8036:   ᴿBijdragen 55 (1994) 335s (L. van *Tongeren*).
7801 **Hamilton** David S. M.,   Through the waters; baptism and the Christian life 1990 → 8,7875:   ᴿScotJT 46 (1993) 119s (J. B. *Walker*).
7802 *Hofius* Otfried,   Glaube und Taufe nach dem Zeugnis des NTs: ZTK 91 (1994) 134-156.
7803 **Holeton** David R.,   Growing in newness of life; Christian initiation in Anglicanism today [1991 Consultation]. Toronto 1993, Anglican Book Centre.   256 p. $15.   1-55126-45-X. – ᴿExpTim 105 (1993s) 95 (J. *Frederick*: how can communion be refused to the baptized?).
7804 *Holland* Scott,   Signifying presence; the ecumenical sacramental theology of George Worgul: LvSt 18 (1993) 38-55.
7805 *a*) *Hultgren* Arland J.,   Baptism in the NT: origins, formulas, and metaphors; – *b*) *Teig* Mons A.,   Baptism, evangelism, and being Church: Word & World 14 (St. Paul 1994) 6-11 / 28-35.
7806 **Klär** Karl-Josef,   Das kirchliche Bussinstitut von den Anfängen bis zum Trienter Konzil [Diss. ᴰOhlig K. ..., Saarbrücken]: EurHS 23/413.   Fra 1991, Lang.   254 p. DM 70. – ᴿTR 90 (1994) 466s (H. *Lutterbach*).
7807 **Larrabe** José Luis,   El sacramento como encuentro de salvación. Vitoria 1993, Eset.   321 p. – ᴿLumenVr 43 (1994) 158-160 (J.-O. *Alonso Álvarez*).
7808 *Larrabe* José Luis,   Sacramentos en la Iglesia de Oriente y Occidente: LumenVr 43 (1994) 345-366.
7808* *Lathrop* Gordon W.,   The origin and early meanings of Christian baptism; a proposal: Worship 65 (1994) 504-522.
7809 **Légasse** Simon,   Naissance du baptême: LDiv 153, 1993 → 9,8047: ᴿÉTRel 68 (1993) 599s (E. *Cuvillier*); LA 44 (1994) 697-9 (A.-M. *Buscemi*); RevSR 68 (1994) 109-111 (C. *Munier*); RTLv 25 (1994) 236 (A. de *Halleux* †).
7810 *a*) *Leipold* Heinrich,   Die Bedeutung der Taufe für das Christsein;

lutherische Perspektiven; – *b*) *Lorenzen* Thorwald, ... baptistische; – *c*)
Neuner P., ... katholische: UnSa 48 (1993) 3-13 / 14-24 / 25-34.
7811 **Maloney** George A.,   Your sins are forgiven you; rediscovering the
sacrament of reconciliation.   NY 1994, Alba.   xv-127 p. $8 pa.   0-8189-
0691-X [TDig 42,176].
7812 *Martín Rodríguez* Francisco,   Realizan lo que significan; la eficacia en
los sacramentos cristianos: Isidorianum 6 (Sevilla 1994) 33-54.
7813 **McDonnell** Kilian, *Montague* George T., Iniziazione cristiana e battesimo
dei primi otto secoli [1990 ➤ 7,7536],ᵀ.   R 1993, Dehoniane.   451 p. –
ᴿTeresianum 45 (1994) 610 (M. *Diégo Sánchez*).
7814 **Morton** Mark,   Personal confession reconsidered; making forgiveness
real: Spirituality 50. Bramcotte Notts 1994, Grove.   24 p.   £2.   1-85174-
274-8. – ᴿTBR 7,3 (1994s) 42s (Dorothy *William*).
7815 **Old** Hughes O.,   The shaping of the Reformed baptismal rite 1992
➤ 8,7891; 9,8055:   ᴿRefR 48 (1994) 66 (M. *Van Hameesveld*); WestTJ 56
(1994) 210-2 (R. E. *Otto*).
7816 **Peters** Albrecht,   Kommentar zu LUTHERs Katechismen 4. Die Taufe,
das Abendmahl, ᴱ*Seebass* Gottfried.   Gö 1993, VR.   202 p.   DM 38.
3-525-56183-0. – ᴿRHPR 74 (1994) 335s (M. *Arnold*).
7817 *Philias* G. N., ⊙ The 'Release of evil defilement of body and soul';
aspects of the relationship between the mysteries of unction and
repentance: TAth 65 (1994) 171-184; Eng. 1020.
7818 **Prades** Javier,   'Deus ... per gratiam'; inhabitación de la Trinidad:
AnGreg B-87.   R 1993, Pont. Univ. Gregoriana.   xxxiv-486 p. –   ᴿAngelicum 71 (1994) 603-6 (C. S. *Vansteenkiste*); RThom 94 (1994) 719-722
(G. *Emery*).
7819 **Rocchetta** Carlo, Os sacramentos da fe, ᵀ*Cunha* Alvaro A. São Paulo
1991, Paulinas.   453 p.   85-05-01116-3. – ᴿPerspT 26 (1994) 103-6 (F.
Taborda; REB 54 (1994) 238-242 (F. *Taborda*).
7820 **Sayés** José A., La gracia de Cristo: BAC 535.   M 1993, Católica.
xvi-503 p.   84-7914-101-8. – ᴿGregorianum 75 (1994) 560s (L. F. *Ladaria*); Teresianum 45 (1994) 309s (M. *Caprioli*).
7820* *Seils* Martin, Sakramentenlehre: VerkF 39,2 (1994) 24-44.
7821 *Stancil* Bill, Rebaptisms in the Southern Baptist convention; a theological and pastoral dilemma: PerspRelSt 21 (1994) 127-141.
7822 *Tovey* Phillip, 'Matrimony; an excellent mystery': TLond 97 (1994)
163-170 [the title is given as a quotation; it is hard to see from what,
though Mark SEARLE is thrice praised].
7822* *Turnšek* Marian, *Teologovo 'dleto'* ... Theologian's 'chisel' participates
in shaping the picture of Church and sacraments: BogVest 54 (1994)
35-60
7823 **Van Roo** W. A., The Christian sacrament [1967],ᵀ 1992 ➤ 8,7905; 9,8069:
ᴿRechSR 82 (1994s) 106-8 (H. *Bourgeois*; peu soucieux des sciences
humaines ou des traditions non catholiques); TLZ 119 (1994) 474 (K. H.
Kandler).
7824 **Vorgrimler** H., Teologia dei sacramenti: GdT 121, 1992 ➤ 9,8071:
ᴿNRT 116 (1994) 254 (A. *Toubeau*).
7825 **Yates** T., Why baptize infants? A study of the biblical, traditional and
theological evidence. ... 1993, Canterbury.   xii-290 p.   £15.   1-85311-061-2.
– ᴿExpTim 104 (1992s) 381s (K. *Stevenson*).
7826 *Zietlow* Paul H., Martin LUTHER's arguments for infant baptism: ConcordJ 20 (1994) 147-171.
7827 **Žitnik** Maksimilian,   Sacramenta, bibliographia internationalis 1992

➤ 8,7908; 9,8072:   ᴿAnnTh 7 (1993) 254s (A. *Miralles*); Asprenas 41 (1994) 451s (P. *Cacciapuoti*); BogVest 54 (1994) 95s (M. *Smolik*); ÉglT 25 (1994) 292s (L. *Laberge*); EstE 69 (1993) 369s (J. L. *Larrabe*: buen cerebro, mucho tiempo); MaisD 194 (1993) 151s (P. De *Clerck*); NRT 116 (1994) 782 (L. *Volpe*); PerspT 26 (1994) 100-2 (F. *Taborda*); RTLv 25 (1994) 231-4 (A. *Haquin*); Salesianum 56 (1994) 173s (A. *Cuva*); ScEspr 45 (1993) 352-4 (P.-É. *Langevin*); Worship 65 (1994) 75-77 (R. K. *Seasoltz*).

H7.6   *Ecclesiologia, theologia missionis, laici* – **The Church.**

7828 *Aguirre* Rafael,   La comunidad de iguales y diferentes que Jesús quería: SalT 81 (1993) 197-210.

7829 *Alberigo* Giuseppe,   La koinonia, voie et âme de l'Église une, ᵀ*Attinger* Daniel: RevSR 68 (1994) 47-71.

7830 *Alves Martins* Antonio M.,   A sacramentalidad da Igreja na teologia actual: Eborensia 6,11s (Évora 1993) 3-29.

7830* *Anderlini* Gianpaolo,   Gesù, apostoli, chiesa: BbbOr 36 (1994) 41-61.

7831 **Bean** Alan G.,   'A fine spiritual imperialism'; the idea of world Christianity in the thought of William O. CARVER: diss. Southern Baptist Sem. 1994, ᴰ*Weber* T. 304 p. 94-28242. – DissA 55 (1994s) p. 1286.

7832 *a) Bergant* Dianne,   Violence and God; a Bible Study; – *b) Lederach* John P.,   Missionaries facing conflict and violence; problems and prospects: Missiology 20 (1992) 45-54 / 11-19.

7833 **Bermejo** Luis M.,   Infallibility on trial; Church, conciliarity and communion,   1992 ➤ 9,8079; also Westminster MD 1992, Christian Classics.   xiii-402 p. – ᴿTPhil 69 (1994) 616-9 (K. *Schatz*).

7834 *Betz* Otto, Mission NT: ➤ 517, TRE 23 (1994) 23-31 [18-23 . 31-80 *al.*]; 88-98 Missionswissenschaft, *Ustorf* Werner.

7835 ᴱ**Bianchi** E. C.,   *Ruether* R. R.,   A democratic Catholic Church 1993 ➤ 9,8080:   ᴿRefR 48 (1994s) 141s (M. A. *Danner*).

7836 **Bosch** David J.,   Transforming mission 1992 ➤ 7,7851 ... 9,8086:   ᴿBInterp 1 (1993) 386s (A. *Le Grys*); Mid-Stream 33 (1994) 125-130 (W. J. *Nottingham*); ModT 53 (1993) 372-4 (J. *Plut*).

7837 *a) Bovon* François,   The Church in the NT; servant and victorious [*Liefeld* Walter, response]; – *b) Braaten* Carl, Jesus and the Church; – *c) Miller* Donald G.,   The nature of the Church; – *d) Walters* Stanley,   The voice of God's people in exile; – *e) Carlson* Richard,   The transfiguration of power; – *f) Graff* Ann O.,   The practice of compassion and the discipleship of equals: ➤ 399, ExAud 10 (1994) 45-54 [55-57] / 59-71 / 1-14 / 73-86 / 87-103 / 104-112.

7838 **Bradshaw** Tim,   The olive branch; an evangelical Anglican doctrine of the Church. ➤ 9,8239:   Carlisle 1992, Paternoster for Latimer House. 306 p. £13.   0-85364-512-4. – ᴿExpTim 105 (1993s) 312s (K. *Mason*: imaginative competence); TLond 97 (1994) 370s (P. *Avis*).

7839 *Breshears* Gerry, [The Church as] Body of Christ: prophet, priest, or king? : JEvTS 37 (1994) 3-26.

7840 *a) Burke* Bruno, L'Église, lieu d'une communauté célébrante; – *b) Debuyst* Frédéric, ... un lieu que la foi vient habiter: MaisD 197 (1994) 9-23 / 25-38.

7841 **Canobbio** Giacomo,   Laici o cristiani; elementi socio-sistematici per una descrizione del cristiano laico. Brescia 1992, Morcelliana. 322 p. Lᵐ 30. – ᴿLetture 48 (1993) 757s (Susanna *Invernizzi*).

7842 *Canobbio* Giacomo,   Sulla cattolicità della Chiesa; – *b) Colombo*

Giuseppe, Il mistero della Chiesa e la missione; – c) *Laiti* Giuseppe, La chiesa 'cattolica' nei Padri: RClerIt 75 (1994) 6-22 / 166-178 / 355-365.

7842* *Caprioli* Mario, Il sacerdozio diocesano e le missioni; in margine al n. 39 del decreto Ad Gentes del Vaticano II: Teresianum 45 (1994) 3-32.

7843 *Chadwick* Henry, Anglican ecclesiology and its challenges: AnglTR 76 (1994) 274-284.

7843* **Christiansen** Ellen Juhl, The covenant and its ritual boundaries in Palestinian Judaism and Pauline Christianity; a study of ecclesiological identity and its markers; diss. Durham UK 1993. 334 p. – RTLv 26,536.

7844 **Cornwall** Robert D., Visible and apostolic; the constitution of the Church in High-Church Anglican and non-juror thought. Newark/ Toronto 1993, Univ. Delaware/Assoc.Univ.P. 215 p. $36.50. – ᴿAnglTR 76 (1994) 379-381 (Rowan A. *Greer*).

7844* **Crane** James J., The ministry of all believers: DMin diss. Fuller, ᴰ*Redman* R. Pasadena 1994. 199 p. 94-24849. – DissA 55 (1994s) p. 1002.

7845 *Czaja* Andrzej, ℗ Una mistica persona... [H. MÜHLEN, ecclesiologia pneumatologica]: ColcT 63,4 (1993) 79-94; franç. 94s.

7846 ᴱ**Dal Covolo** Enrico, *Triacca* Achille M., La missione del Redentore; studi sull'enciclica missionaria di GIOVANNI PAOLO II. T 1992, Elle Di Ci. 320 p. – ᴿSalesianum 56 (1994) 167s (E. M. *Vannoni*: 'ISBN 80-01-14005-3').

7847 **D'Atteo** Fedele, Appunti di storia e teologia del laicato. Foggia S. G. Rotondo 1993, Sollievo. 222 p. Lᵐ 15. – ᴿCiVit 49 (1949) 274s (B. *Farnetani*).

7848 **Denis** H., L'Église; les quatre portes du Temple. P 1991, D-Brouwer. 185 p. – ᴿAtKap 120 (1993) 575-8 (A. *Nowicki*, ℗).

7849 **Descy** Serge F., The Melkite Church; an historical and ecclesiological approach, ᵀ*Mortimer* Kenneth J. Newton Centre MA 1993, Sophia. 106 p. $7 [TDig 42,45: how its 1724 origins hardened Orthodox aloofness; how it faced the steady advance of Romanization].

7850 *Dhavamony* Mariasusai, *a*) Le sfide teologiche all'impegno missionario oggi: ViPe 77 (1994) 426-439; – *b*) Les défis théologiques à l'engagement missionnaire aujourd'huiᵀ: EsprVie 104 (1994) 481-8.

7851 *Díez del Río* Isaías, Posmodernidad y comunidad: RelCu 40 (1994) 727-756.

7852 *Drilling* Peter, The genesis of the trinitarian ecclesiology of Vatican II: ScEsp 45 (1993) 61-78.

7853 **Dujarier** Michel, L'église fraternité *adelphótēs* 1991 ➤ 8,7933: ᴿRÉAug 39 (1993) 226s (Simone *Deléani*).

7854 **Elberti** Arturo, El sacerdocio regale dei fedeli...: AnGreg 254, 1989 ➤ 5,7864... 9,8104: ᴿRET 53 (1993) 126-8 (M. *Gesteira*).

7855 **Famerée** Joseph, L'ecclésiologie d'Yves CONGAR avant Vatican II [chrétiens désunis 1937]: Histoire et Église; analyse et reprise critique 1992 ➤ 8,7937; 9,8109: ᴿÉtudes 380 (1994) 281 (M. *Fédou*).

7856 **Forte** Bruno, La Iglesia icono de la trinidad; breve eclesiología: Pedal 215. S 1992, Sígueme. 98 p. – ᴿCiTom 119 (1992) 606-8 (L. *Lago Alba*).

7857 *Foitzik* Alexander, Autonomie gegen Institution; neuere Jugendstudien zum Thema Religiosität und Kirche [... Shell-Studie 1992]: HerdKorr 47 (1993) 411-7.

7858 **Garijo-Guembe** Miguel M., Communion of the saints; foundation, nature, and structure of the Church, ᵀ*Madigan* Patrick. ColMn 1994, Liturgical-Glazier. xii-266 p. $17. 0-8146-5496-7 [TDig 42,166].

7859 **Gittins** Anthony J.,   Bread for the journey; the mission of transformation and the transformation of mission.   Mkn 1993, Orbis. xx-187 p. – ᴿLandas 8 (1994) 300s (J. H. *Kroeger*).

7859* **Greive** Wolfgang,   Die Kirche als Ort der Wahrheit ... BARTHS 1991 ➤ 8,7950; 9,8119:   ᴿÖkRu 41 (1992) 187-9 (R. *Schäfer*).

7860 *Haight* Roger,   Systematic ecclesiology [... none since Vatican II]: ScEspr 45 (1993) 253-281.

7861 *a) Hamm* Richard L.,   A white babyboomer's perspective on the disestablishment of the mainline churches; – *b) Bondi* Roberta,   House churches and alternative communities as congregations: Mid-Stream 33,4 ('The Church and the congregation; crisis and creativity' 1994) 443-458 / 435-441 (377-434, *Zizioulas* J., *al.*).

7861* *Healy* Nicholas M.,   The logic of Karl BARTH's ecclesiology; analysis, assessment and proposed modifications: ModT 10 (1994) 253-270.

7862 *a) Hearne* Brian,   Modèles de la mission; écumène – écologie – économie; – *b) Jaouen* René,   La formation continue dans l'évolution de l'Église et de sa mission: Spiritus 34 (1993) 17-24 / 44-53.

7863 **Hebblethwaite** Margaret,   Basic [community] is beautiful. L 1993, HarperCollins. £10. – ᴿPrPeo 8 (1994) 86s (Mary *Cullen*: 'how many clergy will cooperate in dismantling structures which are the source of much of their power?').

7864 **Hedlund** Roger E.,   The mission of the Church in the world; a biblical theology.   GR 1991, Baker. 304 p. $17. 0-8010-4349-2. – ᴿMissiology 20 (1992) 527 (M. *Veloso*).

7865 **Hernández Ruiz** Justo,   La razón de la Iglesia (Qué es creible y qué no es creible).   Soria c. 1994, auct. 444 p. – ᴿLumenVr 43 (1994) 417-9 (U. *Gil Ortega*).

7866 *Hilberath* Bernd J.,   Kirche als communio; Beschwörungsformel oder Projektbeschreibung?: TüTQ 174 (1994) 45-65.

7867 *Kasper* Walter,   La Iglesia en el mundo de hoy; sobre las posibilidades de una enseñanza eclesial en un mundo pluralista [conferencia 7.X.91]: TArg 28 (1991) 147-159.

7868 **Kehl** Medard,   Die Kirche 1992 ➤ 8,7961; 9,8139: ᴿHeythJ 35 (1994) 462-5 (M. J. *Parker*: recommends highly).

7868* *Kelly* Kevin T.,   Do we believe in a church of sinners?: Way 33 (1993) 106-116.

7869 **Kesel** J. de,   Omwille van zijn Naam; een tegendraads pleidooi voor de Kerk.   Tielt 1993, Lannoo. 188 p. Fb 595. – ᴿCollatVL 24 (1994) 101s (W. Van *Soom*).

7869* *Kok* Marinus,   Kirche; woher — wohin?: IkiZ 84 (1994) 193-202.

7870 *Kraabel* A. Thomas,   Immigrants, exiles, expatriates, and missionaries: ➤ 40, ᶠGEORGI 1994, 71-88.

7871 *Kremer* Jacob,   Was Jesus eigentlich wollte und heute will; Überlegungen zum Grundanliegen Jesu und dessen Rezeption in der Kirche: StiZt 212 (1994) 507-525.

7872 **Kroeger** J. H.,   Living mission; challenges in evangelization today. Manila/Mkn 1994, Claretian/Orbis. xii-184 p. – ᴿLandas 8 (1994) 301s (F. X. *Clark*).

7873 *Lanne* Emmanuel,   La notion ecclésiologique de réception: RTLv 25 (1994) 30-45 [> Eng. TDig 42,13, ᵀᴱ*Jermann* Rosemary].

7874 **Lehmann** R., *Schnackenburg* R.,   Brauchen wir noch Zeugen? 1992 ➤ 9,8152: ᴿFrSZ 41 (1994) 298s (H.-J. *Venetz*).

7875 *Lennan* Richard, Challenging and challenged; the Chuch as institution: AustralasCR 70 (1993) 434-442.

7876 **Luzbetak** Louis J., Chiesa e culture; nuove prospettive di antropologia della missione [1988], ᵀ*Ghirardi* Orlando. Bo 1991, Ed. Missionaria. 524 p. – ᴿAngelicum 71 (1994) 108-111 (G. *Phan Tan Thanh*).

7877 **Madrid** Teodoro C., La Iglesia Católica según san AGUSTÍN. M 1994, RAg. 319 p. – ᴿEstE 69 (1994) 564s (L. *Vela*).

7878 *Madrid* Teodoro C., La doctrina de San AGUSTÍN sobre la Iglesia: RAg 34 (1993) 547-603.

7879 **Marquart** Kurt E., The Church and her fellowship, ministry, and governance: Confessional Lutheran Dogmatics 9. Fort Wayne 1990, Foundation. – ᴿConcordTQ 58 (1994) 52s (G. S. *Krispin*).

7880 **Martínez Díaz** Felicísimo, Iglesia sacerdotal, Iglesia profética; la comunidad cristiana entre dos tradiciones: Verdad e Imagen 124, 1992 ➤ 9,8158: ᴿLumenVr 42 (1993) 308s (U. *Gil Ortega*); RelCu 40 (1994) 161s (J. C. *Martín*).

7881 **Mead** Loren, The once and future church; reinventing the [sacred and secular united] congregation for a new mission frontier. Wsh 1993, Alban. 92-vii p. – ᴿCCAR 41,4 (1994) 88-90 (E. S. *Schonberg*, Cathy *Felix*: an all-time Protestant best-seller).

7882 **Meyer zu Schlochtern** Josef, Sakrament Kirche; Wirken Gottes im Handeln der Menschen 1992 ➤ 8,7982; 9,8159: ᴿMüTZ 44 (1993) 387s (C. *Meuffels*); TR 90 (1994) 66 (H. *Wagner*).

7883 *Michiels* Robrecht, Church of Jesus Christ, an exegetical-ecclesiological consideration: LvSt 18 (1993) 297-317.

7884 **Migliore** R. Henry, *al.*, Church and ministry; strategic planning from concept to success. NY 1994, Haworth. xi-161 p. $35 (if 5 + copies, $20). 1-56024-346-5 [TDig 42,178].

7885 *Mondin* Battista, L'ecclesiologia di San TOMMASO: CiVit 49 (1994) 289-296.

7886 **Montserrat** José, El desafío cristiano; las razones del perseguidor. M 1992, Muchnik. 352 p. – ᴿLumenVr 42 (1993) 433-457 (J. *Andonegui*: 'como desafío al cristianismo').

7886* *Moyer* R. Larry, Assimilating new converts into the local church: BtS 151 (1994) 339-349.

7887 **Mudge** Lewis S., The sense of a people; toward a church for the human future. Ph 1992, Trinity. 258 p. $20. 1-56338-040-4. – ᴿEcuR 46 (1994) 368s (A. *Houtepen*); Interpretation 48 (1994) 320.2 (Dawn *DeVries*); Mid-Stream 33 (1994) 363-6 (G. H. *Tavard*).

7888 **Müller** Hans M., Neues zum Gemeindeaufbau: TRu 59 (1994) 431-441.

7889 **Müller** Karl, Teologia della missione; un'introduzione [1985], ᵀ*Fabbri* Romeo. Bo 1994, EMI. 283 p. – ᴿAngelicum 71 (1994) 105-8 (G. *Phan Tan Thanh*).

7889* *Neufeld* Karl H., Kirche zum Leben [H. de LUBAC, Geheimnis 1967, deutsch 1990]: ZkT 116 (1994) 188-192.

7890 *Neuner* J., Mission theology after Vatican II; magisterial teaching and missiological approaches in India: Vidyajyoti 58 (1994) 201-214 [-226, *Mattam* J.].

7890* *O'Flaherty* Colin, Church as sacrament; the need for self-questioning. Dublin 1994, Columba. 94 p. – ᴿStudies 83 (1994) 352s (Edel *O'Kennedy*).

7891 **Pagé** Jean-Guy, Primavera della Chiesa; ecclesiologia del NT. CinB 1993, Paoline. 376 p. Lᵐ 28. – ᴿCC 145 (1994,3) 445s (A. *Ferrua*).

7892 **Piper** John, Let the nations be glad! The supremacy of God in missions. Leicester 1994, Inter-Varsity. 230 p. £9.
7893 **Ratzinger** J., Église et théologie 1992 ➤ 8,8003; 9,8170: ᴿScEspr 45 (1993) 358-360 (G. *Novotný*).
7894 *Rodríguez Garrapucho* Fernando, 'Modelos de Iglesia'; perspectiva histórica y problemática actual: Salmanticensis 41 (1994) 365-394; Eng. 395.
7895 **Roloff** Jürgen, Die Kirche im NT 1993 ➤ 9,8174: ᴿBZ 38 (1994) 288-300 (R. *Schnackenburg*); ExpTim 105 (1993s) 298s (E. *Best*); TLZ 119 (1994) 655-8 (E. *Schweizer*: hilfreich); TRu 59 (1994) 216-8 (E. *Lohse*).
7896 *Runia* Klaas, The challenge of the modern world to the Church: EurJT 2,2 (1993) = EvRT 18 (1994) 301-321.
7897 *Salvatierra* Ángel, Problemas y perspectivas de la misionología actual: LumenVr 42 (1993) 313-336.
7898 **Sanks** T. Howland, Salt, leaven and light; the community called Church 1992 ➤ 8,8008: ᴿJRel 74 (1994) 419s (D. M. *Doyle*).
7898* **Schäfer** Rolf, Gotteslehre und kirchliche Praxis 1991 ➤ 7,257*: ᴿTRu 59 (1994) 325-7 (R. *Slenczke*).
7899 **Schillebeeckx** E., Church, the human story of God 1993 ➤ 9,8188: ᴿNewTR 7,3 (1994) 90s (D. *Donovan*).
7899* *Schnackenburg* Rudolf, Die Kirche als empirische Grösse und als Heilsgemeinschaft: MüTZ 44 (1993) 313-325.
7900 *Schultenover* David G., The Church as Mediterranean family: America 171,10 (1994) 9-13.
7901 *Seweryniak* Henryk, ❷ What does that mean, 'I believe in the Church?': PrzPow 858 (1993) 178-190.
7902 **Slenczka** Reinhard, Kirchliche Entscheidung in theologischer Verantwortung. Gö 1991, Vandenhoeck & R. 290 p. – ᴿTRu 59 (1994) 327-330 (R. *Schäfer*).
7902* *Smith* T. Allan, The local church in a multicultural society; an orthodox solution for an unorthodox dilemma: TorJT 10 (1994) 183-195..
7903 *Solberg* Mary M., Working on the Church; a contribution to Lutheran ecclesiology: JHispT 2,1 (1994) 60-77.
7903* **Spaemann** H., Was macht die Kirche mit der Macht? FrB 1993, Herder. 142 p. – ᴿModT 53 (1993) 381s (A. *Mlinar*).
7904 **Stolle** Volker, Kirchenmission nach lutheranischem Verständnis: LuthTKi 17 (1993) 17-21.
7904* *Taltavull i Anglada* Sebastià, L'Església en la crisi de les institucions: QVidaCr 170 (1994) 26-47.
7905 **Tavard** George H., The Church, community of salvation; an ecumenical ecclesiology 1992 ➤ 8,8020; 9,8196: ᴿETL 69 (1993) 487-9 (J. E. *Vercruysse*); ExpTim 105 (1993s) 56 (R. *Butterworth*: impeccable credentials, splendid rethinking); Gregorianum 75 (1994) 361s (A. *Antón*); Studies 42 (1993) 207-210 (Gesa *Thiessen*); TLZ 119 (1994) 266-8 (M. *Plathow*).
7906 *Theodorou* Evangelos D., ❹ The Church as a 'communion of saints': TAth 64 (1993) 545-564; Eng. 883.
7907 *a)* *Tillard* J.-M., La catholicité de l'Église locale; – *b)* *Torrella* R., L'Església catalana actual devant la societat i el conjunt de la vita eclesial europea i universal; – *c)* *Blázquez* Ricardo, Iglesia particular y 'nuevos movimientos'; – *d)* *Conway* Martin, Questions raised by the contemporary ecumenical movement; – *e)* *Dianich* Severino, Sulle condizioni di dicibilità del Vangelo in una società democratica: ➤ 392, Missio 1993, RCatalT 18,2 (1993) 205-215 / 315-318 / 261-273 / 227-233 / 321-335.

7908 *Vallin* Pierre, Bulletin d'ecclésiologie: RechSR 82 (1994) 445-481.

7909 *Vergottini* Marco, La teologia e i 'laici'; una ipotesi interpretativa e la sua recezione [convegno Milano 1986] nella letteratura: TItSett 19 (1993) 166-186.

7910 **Wess** Paul, Gemeindekirche, Ort des Glaubens; die Praxis als Fundament und als Konsequenz der Theologie. Köln 1989, Styria. 716 p. – ᴿTüTQ 174 (1994) 248-250 (B. J. *Hilberath*).

7911 **Wiedenhofer** Siegfried, Das katholische Kirchenverständnis; ein Lehrbuch der Ekklesiologie 1992 ⇒ 8,8034; 9,8212: ᴿGregorianum 75 (1994) 773s (A. *Antón*).

7912 *a*) *Wiedenhofer* Siegfried, Kirche, Geld und Glaube; ekklesiologische Überlegungen; – *b*) *Zinnhobler* Rudolf, Zur Geschichte und Praxis von Kirchensteuer und Kirchenbeitrag: TPQ 142 (1994) 169-179 / 180-185.

7913 **Wirsching** Johannes, Kirche und Pseudokirche; Konturen der Häresie 1992 ⇒ 7,7954: ᴿLuthTKi 17 (1993) 29-31 (K. H. *Kandler*).

7914 *Wright* N. T., The NT and the People of God: Christian Origins 1. L/Mp 1992, SPCK/Fortress. xx-535. £15. / 0-8006-2681-8. – ᴿHeythJ 35 (1994) 324s (G. *Turner*).

7915 *Wright* N., 'Koinonia' and Baptist ecclesiology; self-critical reflection from historical and systematic perspectives: BapQ 35 (1993s) 363-375.

7916 **Yates** Timothy, Christian mission in the twentieth century. C 1994, Univ. xvi-275 p. $60. 0-521-434939 [TDig 42,194].

H7.7 Œcumenismus – The ecumenical movement.

7917 *Aguirre* José M., Perplejidades de la tolerancia: LumenVr 43 (1994) 44-68.

7918 ᴱ**Alberigo** Giuseppe, Christian unity Ferrara/Florence 1989/91 ⇒ 7,462*a* ... 9,8291: ᴿQVidCr 160 (1992) 123s (E. *Vilanova*); RTLv 25 (1994) 366-8 (A. de *Halleux*).

7919 *Amaladoss* Michael, Inter-religious dialogue; a view from Asia: Landas 8 (1994) 208-218.

7920 *a*) *Ansaldi* Jean, Le Protestantisme; son indépassable principe unitaire, l'indécidabilité théologique de ses divisions; – *b*) *Blocher* Henri, Quel devoir d'unité entre Protestants?; – *c*) *Boutinon* Jean-Claude, L'unité du Protestantisme et le Nouveau Testament: Colloque Pomeyrol 1993, Hokhma 54 (1993) 31-41 / 43-57 / 59-74.

7921 *Anschütz* Kurt, 'Der ökumenische Glaube ist primär...' Georges CASALIS in Berlin 1946-1956 — Einblicke in seine Korrespondenz: EvT 54 (1994) 79-100.

7921* **Arbuckle** Gerald A., Refounding the Church. Mkn 1993, Orbis. 226 p. $19 pa. – ᴿOneInC 30 (1994) 296s (J. *Gros*).

7922 **Ariarajah** S. Wesley, Gospel and culture; an ongoing discussion with the ecumenical movement. Geneva 1994, WCC. xv-51 p. 3-8254-1140-X.

7923 *a*) *Arx* U. von, Der ekklesiologische Charakter der Utrechter Union [Ph 1993]; – *b*) *Baktis* Peter A., Old Catholic – Orthodox agreed statements on ecclesiology; reflections for a paradigm shift in contemporary ecumenism: IkiZ 84 (1994) 20-37 (-61, Dokument) / 229-235.

7924 *a*) *Atkinson* David W., Religious dialogue and critical possibilities; – *b*) *Smith* Huston, Universities, seminarians, and the main line churches: ⇒ 8,26*, ᶠCAHILL P. J., RelStT 12,2 (1992) 13-29 / 74-78; N. B. Cahill bibliog. p. 129-133.

7925 **Augustin** Georg, Gott eint – trennt Christus? Die Einmaligkeit und Universalität Jesu Christi als Grundlage einer christlichen Theologie der Religionen ausgehend vom Ansatz Wolfhart PANNENBERGS: kath. Diss. ᴰ*Kasper* W. Tübingen 1992. 400 p. > KkKSt 79. – RTLv 26, p. 564.

7926 **Barlow** Bernard F., A brother knocking at the door; the Malines conversations 1921-1925: diss. ᴰ*Lovegrove* D. St. Andrews 1993. 360 p. – RTLv 26, p. 562.

7927 *Bergjan* Silke-Petra, Ecclesiology in Faith and Order texts: EcuR 46 (1994) 45-77.

7928 *Black* Alan W., Ironies of ecumenism: EcuR 45 (1993) 469-481.

7929 [*Blancy* Alain → 9,8234] Dombes, groupe des, For the conversion of the churches, ᵀ*Greig* James. Geneva 1993, WCC. $11. 2-8254-1123-X [TDig 41,362]. – ᴿMid-Stream 33 (1994) 493-7 (B. W. *Robbins*).

7930 *Bonhôte* Françoise, Réflexions sur la tolérance: RTPhil 126 (1994) 1-18; Eng. 96.

7931 **Bosch** Juan, Para comprender el ecumenismo 1991 → 9,8237: ᴿCiTom 119 (1992) 603s (L. *Lago Alba*).

7932 *Bouwen* Frans, [*Corbon* Jean], Balamand 1993; VIIᵉ session de la Commission internationale pour le dialogue théologique entre l'Église catholique et l'Église orthodoxe: PrOrChr 43 (1993) 91-112; Eng. 112 [113-137; Eng. 137].

Bradshaw Tim, The olive branch; an evangelical Anglican doctrine of the Church 1993 → 7838.

7934 **Brandner** Tobias, Der kirchliche Diskurs über die Einheit; zur Tiefenstruktur ökumenischer Rationalität: Diss. ᴰ*Geisser* H. Zürich 1994s. – RTLv 26, p. 562.

7935 **Bremer** Thomas, Ekklesiale Struktur und Ekklesiologie in der Serbischen Orthodoxen Kirche im 19. und 20. Jahrhundert: Das östliche Christentum 41. Wü 1992, Augustinus. 293 p. DM 112. – ᴿTR 90 (1994) 487s (A. *Nichols*, Eng.; poorly constructed but extremely important).

7936 **Bria** Ion, The sense of ecumenical tradition; the ecumenical witness and vision of the Orthodox 1991 → 8,8056*: ᴿRTLv 25 (1994) 249s (A. de *Halleux*).

7937 *Brinkman* Martien E., The will to common confession; the contribution of Calvinist Protestantism ...: LvSt 19 (1994) 118-137.

7938 **Bundschuh-Schramm** C., Einheit und Vielheit der Kirchen; Ökumene im konziliaren Prozess: Punkt. Theol. heute 14. Stu 1993, Kohlhammer. 210 p. DM 50. 3-17-012707-1. – ᴿTvT 34 (1994) 315s (Teije *Brattinga*).

7939 *Calais* Yves, L'œcuménisme, vœu pieux ou réalité?: EsprVie 104 (1994) 273-9.

7940 **Calian** Carnegie S., Theology without boundaries... Eastern Orthodoxy 1992 → 8,8063; 9,8245: ᴿRefR 48 (1994s) 67 (R. W. *Vunderink*).

7941 ᴱ*Cambon* Enrique, Ecumenismo, crisi o svolta? dialogo RATZINGER/ RICCA: NuovUm 15,88 (1993) 101-121.

7942 **Carey** George, Spiritual journey; 1000 young adults share the reconciling experience of Taizé with [himself,] the Archbishop of Canterbury. Harrisburg PA 1994, Morehouse. viii-148 p. $11 pa. 0-8192-1505-3 [TDig 42,59].

7943 *Cereti* Giovanni, Molte chiese cristiane; un'unica Chiesa di Cristo (corso di ecumenismo 1987) 1992 → 9,8252: ᴿETL 69 (1993) 485s (J. E. *Vercruysse*).

7944 **Clutterbuck** Ivan, Marginal Catholics; Anglo-Catholicism, a further chapter of modern Church history. Leominster 1993, Gracewing. 281 p.

£10. 0-85244-234-3. – ᴿExpTim 105 (1993s) 221 (J. *Kent*: seems to ask 'Must Catholicism be Roman?' but tacitly answer 'yes').

7945 ᴱ**Collet** Giancarlo, Theologien der Dritten Welt; EATWOT als Herausforderung westlicher Theologie und Kirche: NZMissW Supp. 37, 1990 ➤ 6,399; 3-85824-069-9: ᴿTLZ 119 (1994) 79s (H.-J. *Prien*).

7946 **Cordes** P.J., Communio – Utopie oder Programm?: QDisp 148. FrB 1993, Herder. 182 p. DM 38. 3-451-02148-X. – ᴿTvT 34 (1994) 207 (R. *Cornelissen*).

7947 **Cragg** Kenneth, Life studies in inter-faith concern [13 exponents explored]. ... 1993, Pentland. viii-216 p. £14.50. – ᴿTLond 97 (1994) 149-151 (M. *Ingrave* perceives a special affinity with R. PANIKKAR except in Cragg's awareness of the shadow-side of all religions, patterns of acquiescence in the world's sin).

7948 **Cragg** Kenneth, To meet and to greet; faith with faith. L 1992, Epworth. viii-320 p. £12.50 pa. – ᴿTLond 97 (1994) 150s (M. *Ingrave*: 'we are all in transit camp').

7949 **Cullmann** Oscar, Le vie dell'unità cristiana [= ultimo cap. < Einheit durch Vielfalt² 1991; franç. 1992 ➤ 8,8071],ᵀ: GdT 224. Brescia 1994, Queriniana. 97 p. 88-399-9724-6. – ᴿEstE 69 (1994) 416 (J.J. *Alemany*).

7950 **Dallari** Carlo, Chiamati all'unità. Padova 1993, Messaggero. 160 p. Lᵐ 13. – ᴿCiVit 49 (1994) 537s (Duccia *Camiciotti*).

7951 **Davies** Horton, Bread of life and cup of joy; newer ecumenical perspectives on the Eucharist. GR/Leominster 1993, Eerdmans/ Gracewing. – ᴿPrincSemB 15 (1994) 93s (G. *Wainwright*).

7952 *Davis* Kortright, Let not the gods put asunder; can mature Christians rescue the cause of unity from the jaws of social division? (Wsh 12th Ainslie lecture): Mid-Stream 33 (1994) 131-149.

7953 **Eber** Jochen, Einheit der Kirche als dogmatisches Problem bei Edmond SCHLINK: ForSÖkT 67. Gö 1993, VR. 196 p. DM 88. 3-525-56274-8. – ᴿTLZ 119 (1994) 1143-5 (G. *Gassmann*).

7953* **Fackre** Gabriel, Ecumenical faith in evangelical perspective 1993 ➤ 9,8269: ᴿModT 10 (1994) 429s (C.A. *Hall*).

7954 **Fahey** Michael A., Ecumenism; a bibliographical overview. Westport CT 1992, Greenwood. 384 p. $69.50. – ᴿEcuR 45 (1993) 339s (J. *Gros*).

7955 *Fatui* I., *al.*, Pour sortir l'œcuménisme du purgatoire. Genève 1993, Labor et Fides. 93 p. – ᴿRHPR 74 (1995) 442s (A. *Birmelé*).

7955* **Felmy** Karl C., Die Orthodoxe Theologie der Gegenwart 1990 ➤ 7, 8011; 8,8083: ᴿÖkRu 42 (1993) 257s (N. *Thom*).

7956 *Fjedorow* Wladimir, Was bedeutet 'Ökumenismus' für die russische orthodoxe Kirche heute?: UnSa 49 (1994) 132-140.

7957 *a) Frankemölle* Hubert, Biblische Grundlagen einer Ökumene der Weltreligionen; – *b) Peter* Anton, Die Mission der Kirche angesichts der vielen Religionen; – *c) Brück* Michael von, Kommunikation und Kommunion des Christentums mit anderen Religionen: Diakonia 25 (1994) 79-91 / 91-101 / 102-110.

7958 **Frieling** Reinhard, Der Weg des ökumenischen Gedankens, eine Ökumenekunde 1992 ➤ 8,8085; 9,8273; DM 25,80: ᴿHerdKorr 47 (1993) 321s (U. *Ruh*).

7959 ᶠFRIES Heinrich, In Verantwortung für den Glauben, ᴱNeuner P., *Wagner* H. 1992 ➤ 8,59: ᴿTPhil 69 (1994) 308-310 (P. *Knauer*).

7960 **Galitis** Georg, *Mantzaridis* Georg, *Wiertz* Paul, Glauben aus dem Herzen; eine Einführung in die Orthodoxie³ʳᵉᵛ. Mü 1994, TR-Verlagsunion. 268 p. – ᴿTAth 65 (1994) 608-610 (E.A. *Theodorou*, ●).

7961 *a) Gallego* Epifanio, Jesús y el poder religioso; – *b) Quelle* Constantino, Jesús y el poder civil; – *c) Cañellas* Gabriel, Teología bíblica del poder; – *d) Gracio das Neves* Rui M., Evangelio y dialéctica del poder, hoy; – *e) Sáenz Galache* Mercedes, Las antinomías del poder: BibFe 58 (1994) 67-89 / 90-117 / 5-27 / 118-142 / 143-170.

7962 *Gassmann* Günther, Baptism, Eucharist and ministry [(Lima) 5 papers by him, Beirut 28 Sept. - 2 Oct. 1993]: NesTR 15 (1994) 133-159.

7962* *a) Geldbach* Erich, Die Taufe in zwischenkirchlichen Gesprächen; – *b) Palener-Friedrich* Götz, Kirchenmitgliedschaft und Taufe: TVers 18 (1993) 179-197 / 157-177.

7963 *Gilkey* Langdon, Through the tempest; theological voyages in a pluralistic culture, ᴱPool Jeff B. Mp 1991, Fortress. xx-252 p. $15. – ᴿTorJT 10 (1994) 150s (Emily B. *John*).

7964 **Gonnet** Domingue, La liberté religieuse à Vatican II; la contribution de J. C. MURRAY: CogF 183. P 1994, Cerf. 420 p. F 170. 2-204-05050-4. – ᴿArchScSocR 39,88 (1994) 72s (É. *Poulat*).

7965 **González Montes** A., Enchiridion œcumenicum 2. [ed. ital. ...] ed. española. S 1993, Univ. 890 p. – ᴿSalmanticensis 41 (1994) 141s (J.-R. *Flecha*).

7966 **Goosen** Gideon, Bringing churches together — an introduction to ecumenism 1993 → 9,8284: ᴿPacifica 7 (1994) 233-5 (R. *Treloar*: favors 'political correctness' over 'making distinctions').

7967 ᴱGort Jerald D., On sharing religious [... intellectual, cultural] experience; possibilities of interfaith mutuality [1990 Dutch workshop]: Currents of Encounter 4, 1992 → 8,554a: ᴿRelStR 20 (1994) 214 (J. V. *Apczynski*).

7968 *Greinacher* Norbert, Praktische Theologie und die ökumenische Frage; sieben Thesen: TüTQ 174 (1994) 17-22.

7969 *Griffiths* Paul J., Why we need interreligious polemics: FirsT 44 (1944) 31-37.

7970 *a) Gruber* Franz, Wahrheit im Dialog — für ein kommunikatives Wahrheitsverständnis im interreligiösen Gespräch; – *b) Schwager* Raymond, Kontraproduktive Folgen? — Gefahren beim Streben nach einem schnellen Konsens; – *c) Harnoncourt* Philipp, Dialog und Ökumene der Kirchen: TPQ 142 (1994) 12-22 / 23-31 / 52-56; → 10416.

7971 **Guelzo** Allen C., For the union of evangelical Christendom; the irony of the Reformed Episcopalians. Univ. Park 1994, Penn State. xi-404 p. $45; pa. $15. 0-271-01002-9; -3-7 [TDig 42,168].

7972 *Hammerschmidt* Ernst, † 16.XII.1993, Die Orthodoxen Kirchen 106: IkiZ 83 (1993) 65-100 [84 (1994) 130-155 **107** by *Stricker* Gerd].

7973 **Haudel** Matthias, Die Bibel und die Einheit der Kirchen [Diss. Münster 1992, ᴰLessing E.] 1993 → 9,8292 [NTAbs 38, p. 448]: ᴿExpTim 105 (1993s) 370 (G. *Wainwright*); TLZ 119 (1994) 261 (H. *Grote*); TR 90 (1994) 423s (G. *Wenz*); TZBas 50 (1994) 271s (K. *Blaser*).

7974 *a) Henn* William, An evaluation of 'The Church as communion in Christ' [Disciples-Catholic 1983-1992 report here p. 219-239]; – *b) Meyer* Harding, Christian world communions; identity and ecumenical calling; – *c) Kessler* Dionne C., Does the ecumenical movement have or need a viable ecclesiology?: Mid-Stream 33 (1994) 159-172 / 173-189 / 191-204.

7975 *Huppertz* Hubert, Normierte Ökumene; kritische Würdigung des neuen römisch-katholischen Ökumenischen Direktorium: IkiZ 83 (1993) 129-161.

7976 *Irvin* Dale T., Contextualization and catholicity; looking anew for the unity of the faith: ST 48 (1994) 83-96.

7977 *a) Jacobs* J., From being one to becoming one; the efforts of Belgian and Dutch Catholics for the unity of the churches, 1919-1965; – *b) Houtepen* Anton, A God without frontiers; ecumenism and criticism of nationalism: Exchange 22 (Leiden 1993) 206-234 / 235-249.

7978 **Jenson** Robert W., Unbaptized God; the basic flaw in ecumenical theology 1992 ➤ 9,8301: ᴿÉTRel 68 (1993) 459s (J.-M. *Prieur*); Mid- Stream 32,1 (1993) 85-88 (W. G. *Rusch*); ModT 10 (1994) 415-7 (G. *Wainwright*); Thomist 58 (1994) 677-682 (J. J. *Buckley*); TS 54 (1993) 608 (J. A. *Saliba*).

7979 ᴱ**John** Jeffrey, Living tradition [9,8303]: affirming Catholicism in the Anglican church [movement's first conference 1991] 1992: ᴿTLond 96 (1993) 162s (R. *Bomford*).

7980 *Kahle* Wilhelm, Tausend Jahre Christentum in Russland und der Ukraine: TRu 59 (1994) 285-324.

7981 *Kater* John L.ᴶ, Whose church is it, anyway? Anglican 'catholicity' re-examined: AnglTR 76 (1994) 44-60.

7982 **Keshishian** Aram, Conciliar fellowship; a common goal 1992 ➤ 8,8107; 9,8306: ᴿRTLv 25 (1994) 389s (A. de *Halleux*).

7982* **Kilcourse** George, Double belonging; interchurch families and Christian unity. NY/L 1992, Paulist / Fowler Wright. 129 p. $12. – ᴿOneInC 30 (1994) 83-92 (Ruth *Reardon*).

7983 *Klein* Alois, Die ökumenischen Lehrgespräche zwischen Krise und Verheissung: TGL 84 (1994) 289-298.

7984 **Kowalik** Krzysztów, ❷ Le commentaire de LUTHER sur le Magnificat; étude de théologie œcuménique: diss. ᴰ*Napiórkowski* S. Lublin 1994. 287 p. RTLv 26, p. 562.

7984* *Kraft* Sigisbert, Anglican — Old Catholic full communion as a vision for the unity we seek: IkiZ 84 (1994) 181-192.

7985 *Kroeger* James H., Encountering the world of dialogue [Faith meets faith, 20 volumes 1987-91]: JIntRD 31 (1993) 71-92.

7985* **Kühn** Ulrich, *Ullrich* Lothar, Die Lehrverurteilungen des 16. Jhts. im ökumenischen Gespräch, gemeinsame Stellungnahme und Beiträge ... ev.-k. Theologen. Lp 1992, Benno. 160 p. DM 15,80. 3-7462-7015-1. – ᴿZkT 116 (1994) 231s (K. H. *Neufeld*).

7986 **Kuttianimattathil** Jose, Practice and theology of interreligious dialogue; the trajectory undertaken by the Indian Church since Vatican II: diss. nᵒ 7197, Pont. Univ. Gregoriana. Rome 1994. – InfPUG 25/131, p. 33.

7987 *Legrand* Hervé, Catholiques et luthériens; d'un regard sur l'autre à un regard commun: PosLuth 41 (1993) 110-123 [< ZIT 93,654].

7987* *a) Legrand* Hervé, Church fellowship; Oslo doctoral theses on the Lutheran-Roman Catholic dialogue; – *b) Dahl* Otto C., St. Paul on the relations between different groups of Christians; – *c) Tjørhom* Ola, Ecumenical dialogue and theological method: TsTKi 65 (1994) 243-255 in Norwegian / 33-44, Norwegian; Eng. 44 / 267-271 in Norwegian.

7988 *Legrand* Hervé, Le dialogue catholique-orthodoxe; quelques enjeux ecclésiologiques de la crise actuelle autour des Églises unies: Centro pro Unione 43 (1993) 3-16; > Eng. Uniatism and Catholic-Orthodox dialogue, ᵀᴱ*Jermann* Rosemary: TDig 42,127-133.

7989 ᴱ**Lehmann** K., Lehrverurteilungen II, 1989 ➤ 6,8026: ᴿLuthQ 6 (1992) 223-6 (B. D. *Marshall*).

7989* ᴱ**Lehmann** K., *Pannenberg* W., Condemnations... still divide? 1990 ➤ 7,8063; 9,8316: ᴿCritRR 5 (1992) 337s (J. T. *Ford*).

7990 **Leonardi** Leonardo, La riflessione ermeneutica in prospettiva ecumenica. Bari 1992, Centro s. Nicola. 122 p. – ᴿCiVit 48 (1993) 468s (A. *Pellegrini*).

7992 *Leuba* Jean-Louis, Papauté – Protestantisme – Œcuménisme: FrSZ 41 (1994) 259-268.
7993 *Limouris* Gennadios, Being as koinonia in faith; challenges, visions and hopes for the unity of the Church today: EcuR 45,1 ('Toward the Compostela 5th World Conference' 1993) 78-92.
7994 **Lobet** B., Tolérance et vérité. P 1993, Nouvelle Cité. 152 p. – ᴿRevSR 68 (1994) 122s (R. *Mengus*).
7995 **Lochbrunner** Manfred, Über das Priestertum; historische und systematische Untersuchung zum Priesterbild des Johannes CHRYSOSTOMUS 1993 → 14091 [TR 90 (1994) 79].
7996 *Lord* Elizabeth, The Church and the churches; recent Roman Catholic ecclesial trends: Way 34 (1994) 221-231.
7997 **Lossky** Nicholas, *al.*, Dictionary of the ecumenical movement 1991 → 8,8121*; 9,8323: ᴿPrOrChr 43 (1993) 218-230 (F. *Gruber*); WWorld 14 (1994) 96s (T. *Nichol*).
7997* *Lossky* Nicolas, Conciliarité; que pourrait être la contribution orthodoxe à l'œcuménisme?: RevSR 68 (1994) 481-8.
7998 **McGrath** Alister E., The renewal of Anglicanism. L 1993, SPCK. 170 p. £10. 0-281-04724-3. – ᴿTBR 7,1 (1994s) 70s (J. *Heer*); TLond 97 (1994) 372-4 (M. *Nazir-Ali*: little concern for the *thought* of third-world Anglicans).
7999 *Maristany* Joachim, Actualitat de l'Ortodòxia a Europa després de l'esfondrament dels països de l'Est: QVidCr 167 (1993) 31-38.
8000 **Meyendorff** John, Unité de l'Empire et divisions des chrétiens 450-680, ᵀ*Lhoest* Françoise: Théologies. P 1993, Cerf. 427 p. 2-204-04646-9. – ᴿAnBoll 112 (1994) 181-3 (U. *Zanetti*).
8000* *Michalon* P., Le directoire des questions œcuméniques [8.VI.1993: DocCath 4.VII.1993]: EsprVie 104 (1994) 33-39.
8001 *Miranda* Mario de França, O encontro das religiões: PerspT 26 (1994) 9-26.
8002 *Neuhaus* R.J., *Dulles* A., *al.*, Evangelicals and Catholics together; the Christian mission in the third millennium: FirsT 43 (1994) 15-22.
8003 ᴱ**Neuner** Peter, *Ritschl* Dietrich, Kirchen in Gemeinschaft – Gemeinschaft der Kirche; Studie des DÖSTA [Deutscher Ökumenischer Studienausschuss] zu Fragen der Ekklesiologie: ÖkRu Beih 66. Fra 1993, Lembeck. 223 p. DM 32. 3-87476-291-2. – *Hossfeld* F., Biblische Grundlagen 43-49 (148-154) – *Kertelge* K., Zu DÖSTA, 39-42 (163-7). – ᴿTLZ 119 (1994) 1145-7 (G. *Krusche*); TR 90 (1994) 486s (W. *Beinert*) + 347 (tit. pp.).
8004 **Nichols** Aidan, The panther and the hind; a theological history of Anglicanism. E 1993, Clark. xxi-186 p. £10 pa. – ᴿTablet 247 (1993) 342 (H. *Chadwick*); TLond 97 (1994) 66s (P. *Baelz* asks 'is the heart of revealed truth something that God has *done* for the world rather than our human grasp of what he has done?').
8005 *Nicole* Jacques, Désapprendre pour apprendre; vers une formation théologique œcuménique: ÉTRel 69 (1994) 549-557.
8005* *a) Nicole* Jacques, L'unité de l'Église; modèles et perspectives; – *b) Gallopin* Marc, Trois domaines de conflit et quelques pistes de réflexion; – *c) Pella* Gérard, Pour la kénose des églises: Hokhma 54 ('L'unité, source de divisions?' Colloque Crêt-Bérard 1992: 1993) 5-11 / 13-20 / 21-24.
8006 **Nossol** Alfons bp., ℗ Ecumenical implications of the changes in Eastern-Central Europe: RoczT 41,7 (1994) 5-17; Eng. 17s.

8006* *Örsy* Ladislas, *Nawrócenie Kościołów* ... [The conversion of the churches, condition of unity < America (1992) 479-487], [T]*Cieślak* Tadeusz, *Ignasiak* Roman: PrzPow 869 (1994) 11-40.

8007 **Ried** Martin, Kirchliche Einheit und kulturelle Vielfalt; zum Verhältnis von Kirche und Kultur, ausgehend vom II. Vat.: kath. Diss. Frankfurt Goethe-Univ. 1993. – TR 90 (1994) 82.

8007* **Roberson** Ronald G., The Eastern Christian churches, a brief survey[3rev] → 9,8355, varyingly Robertson. R 1992, Pont.Inst.Stud.Orientalium. xi-129 p. – [R]OstKSt 42 (1993) 343s (B. *Plank*).

8008 *Romanides* John S., *a)* Orthodox and Vatican agreement, Balamand, Lebanon, June 17-24, 1993; – *b)* An Orthodox progress-report on the Lutheran-Orthodox dialogue: TAth 64 (1993) 570-580 / 65 (1994) 25-28.

8009 **Rosenstein** Gustav, Die Stunde des Dialogs [< Diss. Regensburg 1990]. Ha 1991. 265 p. – [R]ColcT 65,1 (1993) 192-5 (W. *Kamiński*, ❷).

8010 [E]**Rowell** G., The English religious tradition and the genius of Anglicanism [12 biographical lectures for an Oxford KEBLE bicentenary]. ... 1992, Ikon. 256 p. £10. – [R]TLond 97 (1994) 65s (R. *Runcie*).

8011 *Saarinen* Risto, Ökumenische Theologie; Texte und Untersuchungen: TRu 59 (1994) 388-400.

8012 **Scheidler** Monika, Christliche Communio und kommunikatives Handeln; eine Lehrperspektive für die Schule [Diss. [D]*Emeis*]: MThA 27. Altenberge 1993, Oros. xii-423 p. DM 70. – [R]TR 90 (1994) 346-8 (J. *Hofmeier*).

8013 *Schlüter* Richard, Konfessionalität und Ökumene im Religionsunterricht: TGL 84 (1994) 430-443.

8014 *Schreiter* Robert J., Christian identity and interreligious dialogue; the parliament of world religions at Chicago, 1993: JIntRD 4 (1994) 62-75. [3 (1993) 101-137, *al.*].

8014* *a) Schreiter* Robert J., The theological meaning of a truly Catholic church; – *b) Knitter* Paul F., Christian salvation; its nature and uniqueness, an interreligious proposal: NewTR 7,4 (1994) 5-17 / 33-46.

8015 **Sell** Alan P. F., A Reformed, Evangelical, Catholic Theology 1991 → 8,8152; 9,8365: [R]EcuR 45 (1993) 497-9 (E. *Brand*).

8016 *Selling* Joseph A., A Catholic theological perspective on Europe: EcuR 45 (1993) 158-168.

8017 *Sevilla* Pedro C., Ecumenism at Santiago de Compostela; how far has it come? [WCC 3-14 Aug. 1993]: Landas 8 (1994) 111-123.

8018 **Sgarbossa** Rino, La Chiesa come mistero di comunione nei documenti del dialogo internazionale luterano-cattolico (1967-1984): diss. Pont. Univ. Gregoriana, N°4075; [D]*Wicks* J. Roma 1994. – RTLv 26, p. 562.

8019 **Simioni** Claudio, Chiesa-sacramento; analisi di una categoria conciliare in prospettiva ecumenica: diss. Antonianum, [D]*Puglisi* J. Roma 1994. 101 p. – RTLv 26, p. 563.

8020 **Speelman** H. A., Calvijn en de zelfstandigheid van de Kerk: diss. [D]*Augustijn* C. Amst VU 1994. – TvT 34,295; RTLv 26, p. 545.

8021 **Spiteris** Yannis, La teologia ortodossa neo-greca 1992 → 9,8369: [R]OrChrPer 60 (1994) 327-9 (E. G. *Farrugia*).

8022 **Sullivan** F. A., Salvation outside? 1992 → 8,8157; 9,8373: [R]CathHR 79 (1993) 89s (G. H. *Tavard*); ETL 69 (1993) 198-200 (J. E. *Vercruysse*); LvSt 19 (1994) 186s (Lieven *Boeve*); PrPeo 8 (1944) 42 (R. *Esteban*); RTLv 25 (1994) 104s (G. *Thils*); ScripTPamp 26 (1994) 1258s (J. B. *Villar*); TorontoJT 10 (1994) 281-3 (R. *Haight*).

8023 **Suttner** Ernst C., Church unity... uniatism 1991 → 9,8375: ᴿPrOrChr 42 (1992) 474-6 (F. *Bouwen*).

8023* **Swidler** Leonard, Die Zukunft der Theologie, im Dialog der Religionen und Weltanschauungen [nur die Hälfte von After the Absolute 1990], 1992 → 9,8376: ᴿTR 90 (1994) 423 (H. *Waldenfels*).

8024 *Tavard* George H., [*Root* Michael & *Rush* William G.], A Catholic [Lutheran] reflection on the [Finland 1922] Porvoo Statement: Mid-Stream 33 (1994) 351-8 [358-362].

8025 *Theissen* Gerd, Die Einheit der Kirche; Kohärenz und Differenz im Urchristentum: Zeitschrift für Mission 20,2 (Stu 1994) 70-86; > Eng. TDig 42,117-126, ᵀᴱ*Asen* B. A.

8026 **Tillard** J. M. R., Church of Churches 1992 → 8,8163; 9,8379: ᴿHeythJ 35 (1994) 211 (G. R. *Evans*).

8027 **Tillard** J.-M. R., Iglesia de Iglesias, ᵀ*Ortiz* A. 1991 → 8,8164; 9,8379*: ᴿCiTom 119 (1992) 613s (A. *Bandera*); EfMex 11 (1993) 261-5 (J. M. *Crespo Garduño*); RET 53 (1993) 397-400 (M. *Gesteira*).

8028 **Tillard** J. M. R., 'Chair de l'Église, chair du Christ' 1992 → 8,8165; 9,8380: ᴿÉTRel 68 (1993) 139 (J.-M. *Prieur*); ScEspr 46 (1994) 130-2 (G. *Routhier*); Téléma 19 (1993) 89s (R. *de Haas*).

8029 *Tillard* Jean-Marie, The primacy-conciliarity tension [< Nicolaus 19 (1992) 275-283], ᵀᴱ*Jermann* Rosemary: TDig 41 (1994) 41-45.

8030 *a*) *Tillard* Jean-Marie R., L'impact du mouvement œcuménique sur les doctrines et les institutions chrétiennes; – *b*) *O'Toole* Roger, Theological ideas and their sociological implications; Tillard on ecumenism, doctrine and ecclesiastical institutions: → 381, SR 23 (1994) 293-307 / 309-314.

8031 **Tjørhom** Ola, Church fellowship — visible structured unity and essential ecclesial diversity [Catholic-Lutheran documents 1973-1984: diss. Oslo, ᵀ*Person* Morton, 1993]: ᴿTsTKi 65 (1994) 241-255 (Hervé *Legrand*, at the defense; also 257-265, I. *Asheim*; 267-271, her reply; all in Norwegian).

8032 *Torbet* Robert G., BRACKREY William H., [on ecumenism] AmBapQ 13,2 (1994) 122-198.

8033 **Tracy** David, Dialogue with the other; the inter-religious dialogue: LvTPastMg 1, 1990 → 9,8384: ᴿTvT 34 (1994) 457s (P. *Valkenberg*, ook over 9, CORNILLE-NECKEBROUCK; & 12, GILLIS).

8034 **Vercruysse** J., Introduzione alla teologia ecumenica: Intr.Discipl.T 11. CasM 1992, Piemme. 154 p. Lᵐ 25. – ᴿAsprenas 41 (1994) 452s (D. P-*acelli*); NRT 116 (1994) 590s (A. *Harvengt*).

8035 *Vercruysse* Jos E., Introducción a la Teología Ecuménica. Estella 1993, VDivino. 185 p. – ᴿIsidorianum 6 (Sevilla 1994) 257s (F. *Martín Rodríguez*); ScripTpamp 26 (1994) 1259 (J. R. *Villar*).

8035* *Vischer* Lukas, [Canberra] Ist das wirklich die 'Einheit, die wir suchen'?: ÖkRu 41 (1992) 7-22.

8036 *Wanegffelen* Thierry, La reconnaissance mutuelle du baptême entre confessions catholique et réformée au XVIᵉ siècle: ÉTRel 69 (1994) 185-201.

8037 **Webb** Henry E., In search of Christian unity; a history of the Restoration Movement. Cincinnati 1990, Standard. 492 p. – ᴿRestQ 34 (1992) 56s (B. J. *Humble*) & 58s (J. B. *North*) & 59s (D. N. *Williams*).

8038 *Wiles* Maurice, Christian theology and interreligious dialogue 1992 → 9,8400: ᴿEcuR 45 (1993) 238s (J. *Lipner*); ScotJT 46 (1993) 558s (L. *Ayres*).

8039 *a*) *Wolter* Michael, Das frühe Christentum und die Vielfalt der Konfessionen; – *b*) *Schmidt* Werner H., Exegetische Anmerkungen zum

Thema 'Pluralismus und Identität'; Momente von Spannung, Vielfalt und Einheit im Alten Testament: Glaube und Lernen 8 (Gö 1993) 120-132 / 106-119 [< ZIT 93,693].

8040 **Yannaras** Christos, Elements of faith; an introduction to Orthodox theology. E 1991, Clark. xii-167 p. £12.50. - RScotJT 46 (1993) 564s (A. *Louth*).

8041 **Yarnold** Edward, In search of unity. Middlegreen 1989, St. Paul = ColMn 1990, Liturgical. 144 p. $7. 0-85439-309-9 / 0-4146-1920-7. - RCanadCath 12,2 (1994) 30 (J. *Kelliher*).

H7.8 Amt – *Ministerium ecclesiasticum.*

8042 **Allan** Peter, *al.*, The fire and the clay; the priest in today's [Anglican] church. L 1993, SPCK. x-142 p. £9 pa. - RTLond 97 (1994) 310s (R. *Greenwood*).

8043 **Antón** A., Le conferenze episcopali, istanze intermedie? 1992: RLateranum 60 (1994) 183-6 (M. *Semeraro*).

8044 *Antón* Ángel, [Juan Pablo II: 22.V.1994] Ordinatio sacerdotalis; algunas reflexiones de 'gnoseología theológica': Gregorianum 75 (1994) 723-741; franç. 742.

8045 **Areeplackal** Joseph, Spirit and ministries; perspectives of East and West [diss. Gregorian 1988, DRosato P. (partly pneumatological dimension ... CONGAR, ZIZIOULAS)] ► 7,8104; 8,8182: Bangalore 1990, Dharmaram. x-350 p. - RRTLv 25 (1994) 229-31 (R. *Turner*).

8046 *Aumont* Michel, Homme et femme dans le dessein de Dieu (Deux sacerdoces en un). Crozon 199.., Edigrafic. 188 p. F 110. - EEsprVie 104 (1994) 610 (R. *Coste*).

8047 **Avis** Paul, Authority, leadership and conflict in the Church [a man-made social institution (*Popper*) p. 85] 1992 ► 9,8409: RTLond 96 (1993) 163 (H. *Montefiore*).

8048 **Baron** John B., Speaking the Word; a historical inquiry into the nature of hieratic function: diss. Drew, DPain J. Madison NJ 1994. 155 p. 94-32945. - DissA 55 (1994s) p. 2010.

8049 **Barral-Baron** N., Le ministère pour l'Église; ses nouveaux visages. P 1991, D-Brouwer. 182 p. - RAtKap 120 (1993) 390-3 (A. *Nowicki*, ❷).

8050 *Barruffo* Antonio, La spiritualità dei presbiteri tra le nuove sfide: RasT 35 (1994) 193-215.

8051 **Beaudette** Paul J., Ritual purity in Roman Catholic priesthood; using the work of Mary DOUGLAS to understand clerical celibacy: diss. Graduate Theological Union, Berkeley 1994. 456 p. 94-26242. - DissA 55 (1994s) p. 1289.

8052 **Bernier** Paul, Ministry in the Church; a historical and pastoral approach 1992 [NTAbs 37, p. 292]. ► 8,8186; 9,8415: RChurch 10 (1994) 55 (W. J. *Belford*).

8053 *Berquist* Jon L., 'Who do you say that I am?' Biblical images and ministerial identity: LexTQ 29 (1994) 17-36.

8054 *Bourgeois* D., L'un et l'autre sacerdoce 1991 ► 7,8108 ... 9,8418: RZkG 105 (1994) 93s (R. *Haacke*).

8055 *a) Bouwman* Walter R., In support of the threefold ordering of ordained ministry; – *b) Hütter* Reinhard, The Church's public ministry in her Babylonian captivity; – *c) Chadwick* Henry, Blocked approaches: Pro Ecclesia 2/1 (Northfield MN 1993) 12-17 / 18-20 / 5-11 [< ZIT 93,191].

8056 EBowering Michael, Priesthood here and now [anecdotes and insight of

20 presumably Anglican priests]. Newcastle 1994, Diocese. 183 p. £6 pa.
– ᴿTLond 97 (1994) 479 (W. *Carr*).

8057 **Brent** Allen,   Cultural episcopacy and ecumenism; representative ministry in church history from the age of Ignatius of Antioch to the Reformation with special reference to contemporary ecumenism: Studies in Christian Mission 6, 1992 ⇒ 8,8191; 9,8421: ƒ110. 90-04-09432-6. – ᴿJEH 45 (1994) 685s (bp. Eric *Kemp*).

8058 *a)* **Burghardt** Walter J., The priest as prophet; – *b)* *Thomas* Carolyn, Priesthood as servant-leadership: Priest 50,11 (1994) 10-13 / 20-22.

8059 **Burtchaell** James T.,   From synagogue to Church; public services and offices 1992 ⇒ 8,8192: xviii-375 p. – ᴿBR 10,2 (1994) 11s (J. *Gutmann*); CathHR 80 (1994) 321 (E. J. *Kilmartin*); CBQ 56 (1994) 359-361 (R. A. *Wild*: detects problems, adds others); ÉTRel 69 (1994) 278s (A. *Massini*); HeythJ 35 (1994) 446s (S. G. *Hall*); Horizons 21 (1994) 183s (D. N. *Power*); Interpretation 48 (1994) 310.312 (A. T. *Kraabel*); JEH 45 (1994) 333 (D. *Nineham*: current 'unstructured' consensus is largely Protestant, but the known facts against as well as for are few); ModT 12 (1994) 120-2 (M. *Root*); TLond 97 (1994) 55s (C. J. A. *Hickling*: sounds brilliantly innovative but leaves hesitancies); TLZ 119 (1994) 61-64 (W. *Wischmeyer*); Worship 65 (1994) 80s (G. S. *Sloyan*).

8060 *Butler* Sara,   Quaestio disputata 'in persona Christi' [AQUINAS, meaning the priest at Mass 'effaces himself before Christ']: TS [55 (1994) *Ferrara* Dennis M.] 56 (1995) 61-80; 81-91, Ferrara response.

8061 Catholic Church, Congregation for the clergy, Directory on the ministry and life of priests.   Vaticano 1994, Editrice / Wsh U.S. Catholic Conference. 116 p. $8. 1-55586-791-X [TDig 42,60].

8062 *Chapman* Mark D.,   Catholicity, unity and provincial autonomy; on making decisions unilaterally: AnglTR 76 (1994) 313-328.

8063 **Cholij** Roman,   Clerical celibacy 1988 ⇒ 6,8094: ᴿScotJT 46 (1993) 118 (N. *Paxton*).

8064 **Collins** J. N., *al.*,   Are all Christians ministers? 1992 ⇒ 9,8531*: ᴿAustralasCR 10 (1993) 395 (J. *Wilcken*); TorJT 10 (1994) 257 (Leona M. *Irach*).

8065 **Countryman** L. William,   The language of ordination; ministry in an ecumenical context 1992 ⇒ 9,8434: ᴿTorJT 10 (1994) 144s (D. *Donovan*).

8066 *Dawes* Gregory W.,   Analogies, metaphors, and women as priests: Pacifica 7 (1994) 47-58.

8067 **Dibie** Pascal,   Les tribus sacrées; ethnologie des prêtres. P 1993, Grasset. 297 p.; 16 fig. – ᴿArchivScSocRel 35,86 (1994) 278s (J. *Chevronneaud*: ignore la formation actuelle des séminaristes, psychologie et sociologie universitaires).

8068 **Donovan** Daniel,   What are they saying about the ministerial priesthood 1992 ⇒ 8,8204; 9,8442: ᴿCanadCathR 12,1 (1994) 28 (J. A. *Ihnatowicz*); Gregorianum 75 (1994) 563s (J. *Galot*: leaves various models open); TorJT 10 (1994) 288s (C. F. *Starkloff*).

8069 **Drewermann** Eugen,   Fonctionnaires de Dieu [Kleriker 1989] 1993 ⇒ 9, 8443: ᴿRHPR 74 (1994) 99s (Danielle *Fischer*); VSp 147 (1993) 614s (J.-P. *Jossua*: important).

8070 **Dunn** Joseph,   No lions in the hierarchy. Dublin 1994, Columba. 326 p. £8. – ᴿMonth 255 (1994) 278s (D. *Howard*: offensive beyond the inevitable).

8071 **Faivre** Alexandre,   Ordonner la fraternité 1992 ⇒ 8,239*c*; 9,8447: ᴿÉTRel 69 (1994) 584s (J.-N. *Pérès*); NRT 116 (1994) 611s (B. *Joassart*); RTLv 25 (1994) 83s (A. de *Halleux*); TPhil 69 (1994) 585s (H. J. *Sieben*).

8072 *Famerée* Joseph, Collégialité et communion dans l'Église: RTLv 25 (1994) 199-203 [< Eng. TDig 42,9-11, ^{TE}*Jermann* Rosemary].

8073 **Favale** A., Il ministero presbiterale; aspetti dottrinali, pastorali, spirituali: StSpir 7, 1989 → 5,8064*... 8,8211. R 1989, LAS. 376 p. – ^RAt-Kap 121 (1993) 436-8 (T. *Fitych*, ❷).

8073* **Felici** Sergio, La formazione al sacerdozio ministeriale... nei Padri 1992 → 8,545: ^RBenedictina 41 (1994) 534s (S. *de Piccoli*).

8074 ^E**Felici** Sergio, Sacerdozio battesimale e formazione teologica nella catechesi e nella testimonianza di vita dei Padri 1992 → 8,545*: ^RBenedictina 41 (1994) 533s (S. *de Piccoli*).

8074* **Ferwerda** Tineke, Sister Philothea; relationships between women and Roman Catholic priests [Netherlands case studies; 14 of the 23 cohabiting], ^T*Bowden* J. L 1993, SCM. xii-208 p. £12.50. 0-334-01526-X. – ^RExpTim 105 (1993s) 253 (Susan S. *Smalley*: the women fare worse).

8075 **Forestell** J. Terence, As ministers of Christ; the Christological dimension of ministry in the NT: an exegetical and theological study 1991 → 7,8128... 9,8452: ^RScEspr 45 (1993) 348-351 (J.-V. *Thériault*); SR 23 (1994) 105 (J. R. C. *Cousland*); TorJT 10 (1994) 259s (T. M. *Bosica*).

8076 *France* R. T., 'It seemed good to the Holy Spirit and to us'... decision-making, ordaining women: Churchman 108 (1994) 234-241; reply 242-6, *Tinker* Melvin.

8077 **Freiwald** Jan, Das Verhältnis von allgemeinem Priestertum und besonderem Amt bei LUTHER: diss. ^D*Seebass* G. Heidelberg 1994. – RTLv 26, p. 544.

8078 **Garuti** Adriano, Il Papa patriarca d'Occidente? 1990 → 6,234...8, 8216: ^RTArg 28 (1991) 261-5 (A. H. *Zecca*).

8078* **Gatto** Joseph C., The theology of ordained ministry in the writings of Karl RAHNER: ^D*Rosato* P., diss. Pont.Univ.Gregoriana 1994 N° 7203, InfPUG 26 / 131 (1994).

8079 ^E**Goergen** Donald J., Being a priest today 1992 → 9,8456; 0-8146-5032-5: ^RGregorianum 75 (1994) 767s (J. *Galot*: fondé sur la christologie, à bon droit).

8080 **González Faus** José I., 'Ningun obispo impuesto' (San CELESTINO, Papa), las elecciones episcopales en la historia de la Iglesia: PresTeol 70. Sdr 1992, Sal Terrae. 159 p. 84-293-1067-3. – ^RPerspT 26 (1994) 272-4 (F. *Taborda*); REB 53 (1993) 993-5 (F. *Taborda*); RET 53 (1993) 256s (M. *Gesteira*); SalT 81 (1993) 392-4 (María *Tabuyo*).

8081 **Goyret** Philip, La specificità del sacerdozio ministeriale: AnnTh 7 (1993) 157-179.

8082 **Gozzelino** Giorgio, Nel nome del signore; teologia del ministero ordinato: CorsoStT, 1992 → 9,8457; L^m 23; 88-01-14282-X: ^RGregorianum 75 (1994) 562 (J. *Galot*: vasta informazione, chiara esposizione).

8083 *a) Greenacre* Roger, Comprendre qui se passe chez les Anglicans [à propos de leur décision d'ordonner les femmes]; – *b) MacDade* John, Les ministères féminins: EsprVie 104 (1994) 209-219 / 219-223.

8084 **Groome** Thomas H., Toward a theory/method of liberation catechesis: Columbia Ed. diss. NY 1975 [cf. Lumen Vitae 31, 1976]. – ^RTrinJ 15 (1994) 89-113 (Miriam *Charter*: a priest, though married 1986; influential and doubtless acceptable in Roman Catholic circles but dubious on Scripture/revelation).

8085 *Gunten* A. F. von, Je vous donnerais des pasteurs [JEAN-PAUL II]: NVFr 68 (1993) 81-92.

8086 **Hammann** Gottfried, L'amour retrouvé; la diaconie chrétienne et le ministère du diacre: Histoire. Neuchâtel/P 1994, Univ. Fac. Théol 13 / Cerf. 291 p.; bibliog. 281-8. 2-204-05067-9.

8087 *Hauser-Borel* Sylvia, Algunos testimonios neotestamentarios sobre la diaconia, ᵀ*Quintero* Salvador: Anamnesís 4,2 (1994) 85-94.

8088 *Herms* Eilert, Obrigkeit: ➤ 517, TRE 24 (1994) 723-759.

8089 **Hill** Edmund, Ministero e autorità nella Chiesa cattolica [1988 ➤ 4, 9171],ᵀ. Padova 1994, Messaggero. 176 p. Lᵐ 18. – ᴿCiVit 49 (1994) 537 (Duccia *Camiciotti*).

8090 **Houssiau** A., Sacerdoce du Christ 1990 ➤ 6,8125 ... 9,8468: ᴿMaisD 192 (1992) 155-8 (J. *Puglisi*).

8090* *Illanes* José Luis, El cristiano 'alter Christus — ipse Christus'; sacerdocio común y sacerdocio ministerial en la enseñanza del beato Josemaría ESCRIVÁ DE BALAGUER: ➤ 22, ᶠCASCIARO J. M., Biblia 1994, 605-622.

8091 **Iori** Renato, Autorità, carisma e ministero nelle prime comunità cristiane. R 1993, Dehoniane. 125 p. – ᴿTeresianum 45 (1994) 308s (M. *Caprioli*).

8092 **Jäger** Alfred, ['Managementberatung'] Konzepte der Kirchenleitung für die Zukunft; wirtschaftsethische Analysen und theologische Perspektiven. Gü-V. 1993. 477 p. – ᴿTPQ 142 (1994) 201s (M. *Lehner*).

8093 *Jüngel* Eberhard, Was ist die theologische Aufgabe evangelischer Kirchenleitung?: ZTK 91 (1994) 189-209.

8094 *a)* *Kesel* Josef de, Herders en voorgangers in de Kerk; over de zending van de priester; – *b)* *Thévenot* Xavier, Het celibaat en de roeping van de seculiere priester: CollatVL 24 (1994) 157-174 / 175.

8095 *Kowalski* Jan, ❸ Ordination sacerdotale des [tzw. 'viri probati'] hommes mariés et célibat: ➤ 92*, ᶠPIERONEK T., AnCracov 26 (1994) 213-227; franç. 227s.

8096 *Krenn* Kurt, Wenn wir wollen, was Jesus Christus mit seiner Kirche wollte, wird es immer und überall Priester geben: ForKT 10 (1994) 293-8.

8096* *Krüger* Friedhelm, Zölibat und Ehe in protestantischer Sicht; kein unauslösliches Prägemal: LuMon 32,5 (1993) 2-4 [32/6, 13-15, *Untergassmair* Franz-G., in katholischer Sicht].

8097 **Lane** Thomas, A priesthood in tune; theological reflections on ministry 1993 ➤ 9,8476: ᴿExpTim 105 (1993s) 312 (B. L. *Horne*: solid post-Vatican-II instruction); PrPeo 8 (1994) 211 (J. *O'Brien*).

8098 *a)* *Lederhilger* Severin, Kooperative Seelsorge und die Frage nach dem Amt; kirchenrechtlich-dogmatische Probleme; – *b)* *Lehner* Markus, Zwischen den Stühlen — Laie im Hauptberuf: TPQ 142 (1994) 123-136 / 137-144 (-167, *al.*).

8099 *McAreavey* John, Priestly celibacy: IrTQ 59 (1993) 22-43.

8100 ᴱMaccarrone Michele, Il primato 1985/91 ➤ 7,523; 9,8479: ᴿTPhil 69 (1994) 284-7 (K. *Schatz*).

8101 — Noble Thomas F. X., Michele Maccarrone on the medieval papacy [Romana ecclesia 1991 ➤ 9,8480]: CathHR 80 (1994) 518-533 [546-8, P. *Granfield* on ᴱMaccarrone symposium 1989/91].

8102 **Maffeis** A., Il ministero della Chiesa; uno studio del dialogo cattolico-luterano (1967-1984): 82R, Pont. Sem. Lombardo, 1991 ➤ 9,8483: ᴿNRT 116 (1994) 594s (A. *Harvengt*).

8103 **Manaranche** André, Vouloir et former des prêtres. P 1994, Fayard. 310 p. F 139. – ᴿÉtudes 380 (1994) 860 (C. *Flipo*: un battant).

8104 **Martelet** G., Deux mille ans ... Sacerdoce 2s, 1990 ➤ 6,8141 ... 9,8484: ᴿSalesianum 56 (1994) 390-2 (O. *Pasquato*).

8105 **Mason** Kenneth, Priesthood and society 1992 → 9,8485: ᴿTLond 96 (1993) 164 (W. *Carr*).

8106 *May* J. D., Ministry re-considered [COLLINS J. N., Diakonia]: DocLife 44,3 (1994) 150-2.

8107 *Mucci* Giandomenico, Riflessioni sul celibato sacerdotale: NuovUm 15,87 (R 1993) 41-52.

8108 **Nelson** R. D., Raising up a faithful priest [→ 9,8498]: community and priesthood in biblical theology 1993 [NTAbs 38, p. 314]: ExpTim 105 (1993s) 346s (J. R. *Bartlett*).

8108* **Neuhaus** Richard J., Freedom for ministry²ʳᵉᵛ [¹1979]. GR 1992, Eerdmans. xiv-257 p. $18 pa. – ᴿHomP 93,4 (1992s) 765 (J. R. *Sheets*: inspiring).

8109 **Noll** Ray R., Christian ministerial priesthood; a search for its beginnings in the primary documents of the Apostolic Fathers [< French diss. Strasbourg c. 1974). SF 1994, Catholic Scholars. xv-406 p. $60; pa. $40. 1-883255-07-4; -00-7 [TDig 41,279].

8109* *a) Nowak* Stanislaw abp., ● La formation des prêtres en face des défis de la fin du deuxième millénaire; – *b) Słomka* Walerian, ● La nature et la mission du sacerdoce servile [p. 197]: AtKap 120 (1993) 201-9 / 210-222.

8110 **O'Grady** John F., Disciples and leaders; the origin of Christian ministry in the NT 1991 → 7,8152*; 9,8500: ᴿCritRR 6 (1993) 272 (K. *Giles*).

8110* *Pieris* Aloysius, Chastity as total consecration to service: Vidyajyoti 58 (1994) 545-558..

8111 ᴱ**Pittau** Giuseppe, *Sepe* Crescenzio, Identità e missione del sacerdote. R 1994, Città Nuova. 246 p. 88-311-7275-1.

8111* **Poling** James N., The abuse of power; a theological problem. Nv 1991, Abingdon. 224 p. $16. – ᴿTorJT 10 (1994) 295s (R. A. *Repicky*).

8112 **Ranke-Heinemann** Ute, Eunucos por el reino de los cielos; Iglesia católica y sexualidad [1990 → 8,8258],ᵀ: Estructuras/rel. M 1994, Trotta. – ᴿQVidCr 174 (1994) 129s (A. *Olivar*).

8113 **Rausch** T. P., Priesthood today; an appraisal 1992 → 8,8259; 9,8508: ᴿPrPeo 8 (1992) 256 (M. *Robson*); TorJT 10 (1994) 296 (D. *Donovan*).

8114 *Rebeiro* Manuel, The ongoing debate on infallibility; Hans KÜNG's contribution: LvSt 19 (1994) 307-337.

8115 ᴱ**Reese** Thomas J., Episcopal conferences; historical, canonical and theological studies 1989 → 6,445; 8,8260: ᴿRTLv 25 (1994) 107s (M. *Simon*).

8116 *Reumann* John, The case for twofold [rather than either 'threefold' or ordained-only] ministry: CurrTM 21 (1994) 197-212.

8117 *Richardson* John P., Need ministers be theologians?: Churchman 108 (1994) 306-314.

8118 ᴱ**Ries** Julien, Le sacerdoce du Christ et de ses serviteurs selon les Pères: Cerfaux-Lafort 8. LvN 1990. CentreHistRel. 267 p. – ᴿScEspr 45 (1993) 240s (G. *Novotný*).

8119 **Rolland** Philippe, Les ambassadeurs du Christ: Lire la Bible 92, 1991 → 9,8513: ᴿMélSR 50 (1993) 70s (M. *Huftier*: guide du prêtre).

8120 **Sabourin** Léopold, Protocatholicisme et ministère; commentaire bibliographique 1989 → 6,8157: ᴿÉglT 25 (1994) 289-291 (M. *Dumais*).

8121 **Schatz** Klaus, La primauté du Pape 1992 → 9,4898: ᴿRevSR 68 (1994) 383 (R. *Minnerath*); RHPR 74 (1994) 306 (A. *Benoît*); RHR 211 (1994) 102-5 (M. *Zimmermann*); RTLv 25 (1993) 387s (A. de *Halleux*: première histoire catholique de la primauté: non des papes ni de l'Institution romaine).

8122 *Scheffczyk* Leo, Der Zölibat; Formkraft priesterlicher Existenz und priesterlichen Denkens: Seminarium 33 (Vatican 1993) 48-59.

8123 **Schillebeeckx** Edward, Plaidoyer [1985 ➤ 1,7680] ministères dans l'Église 1987 ➤ 3,8008...: ᴿÉglT 25 (1994) 441-4 (J. K. *Coyle*).

8124 **Schimmelpfennig** Bernhard, The papacy 1992 ➤ 9,8516: ᴿJEvTS 37 (1994) 603s (G. *Crutsinger*); JRel 74 (1994) 566-8 (I. M. *Resnick*: no map or notes; numerous errors).

8125 *Schunck* Rudolf, Amtspriestertum und allgemeines Priestertum: ForKT 10 (1994) 177-196.

8126 **Schuster** Raymond, Das kirchliche Amt bei John H. NEWMAN; eine historisch-systematische Untersuchung der Genese seines Priesterbildes im Kontext: Diss. ᴰ*Biemer* G. FrB 1994. 325 p. > Lang. – RTLv 26, p. 551.

8126* **Smith** Jay E., Can fallen leaders be restored to leadership? [yes, if both his life and (what is less likely) his reputation are rehabilitated]: BtS 151 (1994) 455-480..

8127 *Soom* Willy van, Ordinatio sacerdotalis [... fem.] en die argumenten in het debat: CollatVL 24 (1994) 341-361.

8128 ᴱStenico Tommaso, Il sacerdozio ministeriale nel magistero ecclesiastico; documenti (1908-1993). Vaticano 1993, Editrice. 637 p. – ᴿTeresianum 45 (1994) 303-6 (M. *Caprioli*).

8129 *Stevens* Clifford, The law of celibacy; some historical corrections [objects to the view that celibacy has to be 'decreed from on high' i.e. 'enforced from the beginning': COCCHINI C., CHOLIJ R.]: Priest 50,5 (1994) 42-47.

8130 **Stickler** Alfons M., Il celibato ecclesiastico; la sua storia e i suoi fondamenti teologici: CuRel 3. Vatican 1994, Editrice. – ᴿPeCa 273 (1994) 10-13 (D. *Vibrac*).

8130* *Stickler* Alfons M., El celibato eclesiástico; su historia y sus fundamentos teológicos: ScripTPamp 26 (1994) 13-78; Eng. 78.

8131 *Thompson* Augustine, HILDEGARD of Bingen on gender and the priesthood: ChH 63 (1994) 340-364.

8131* *Tieleman* D., Pastoraat en zingeving [... signaal van een andere tijd]: GerefTTs 93 (1993) 1-22.

8132 **Tolhurst** James, Men, women and priesthood [7 interfaith art.]. Leominster/Bloomington 1989, Gracewing/Fowler Wright. xvi-225 p. £8. – ᴿScotJT 46 (1993) 122s (Ruth B. *Edwards*).

8133 **Torrance** T. F., Royal priesthood; a theology of ordained ministry. E 1993 = 1955. xvii-108 p. £9. 0-567-29222-3. – ᴿExpTim 105 (1993s) 312 (B. L. *Horne*); TBR 7,1 (1994s) 59 (J. *Beer*).

8134 **Vacca** Salvatore, Prima sedes a nemine iudicatur: Miscellanea Hist. Pont. R 1993, Pont. Univ. Gregoriana. 269 p. – ᴿTPhil 69 (1994) 592-4 (K. *Schatz*).

8135 *Vanhoye* Albert, Il sacerdozio nella Bibbia ➤ 387, Sacerdote 1994, 13-25.

8136 ᴱVischer Lukas, The ministry of the Elders in the Reformed Church. ... 1992, Alliance of Reformed Churches. – ᴿExpTim 105 (1993s) 61 (G. *McFarlane*: useful more broadly on Church authority).

8137 ᴱWind James P., *al.*, Clergy ethics in a changing society; mapping the terrain [Chicago Univ. group meeting 1991 ➤ 8,428: $19 [RelStR 20 (1994) 135 (R. B. *Connors*).

8138 *a) Yaacoub* Abdo, Les prêtres mariés selon le Code des Canons de l'Église Orientale; – *b) Leduc* Francis, Vocation et formation des prêtres mariés; – *c) Lingot* Jean-Louis, Vie familiale, sociale et matérielle des prêtres mariés; – *d*) *Leduc*, Comment sont perçus les prêtres mariés?; – *e*) *Sicking* Thomas, Identité du prêtre marié dans un contexte socio-pastoral en mutation [statistique]; – *f*) *Khairallah* Mounir, Éclairage historique; – *g*) *Corbon* Jean, Les enjeux ecclesiastiques; prospectives: PrOrChr 44 ['Prêtres mariés ... étude du contexte libanais' 1994] 91-108 / 109-144 / 145-173 / 193-222 / 223-246 [63-79] / 17-62 / 245-257. 258-271; English summaries 346-349.

8139 **Ysebaert** Joseph, Die Amtsterminologie im NT und in der Alten Kirche; eine lexikographische Untersuchung. Breda 1994, Eureia. viii-238 p. *f* 55. 90-7502-703-6.

H8.0 **Oratio,** *spiritualitatis personalis.*

8140 **Alonso Schökel** Luis, Piantata in terra, toccava il cielo 1993 ➤ 9,8540: ᴿAsprenas 41 (1994) 297s (G. *Di Palma*).

8140* **Alonso Schökel** L., Io pongo le mie parole sulla tua bocca 1992 ➤ 8,9287: ᴿCC 145 (1994,1) 620s (D. *Scaiola*).

8141 **Azevedo** Marcello de, Vivir la fede en un mondo plural; discrepancias y entrechoques: Horizonte. 277 p. 1300 pt. – ᴿActuBbg 31 (1994) 52 (J. *Boada*).

8142 **Barnes** Andrew E., The social dimension of piety: Theological Inquiries. NY 1994, Paulist. x-285 p. $13. 0-8091-3395-4 [TDig 42,155].

8143 **Barry** William A., Spiritual direction and the encounter with God; a theological inquiry. NY 1992, Paulist. 123 p. $8. – ᴿHomP 93,8 (1992) 78s (J. R. *Sheets*).

8143* **Bennàssar** B., Proclamar el resucitado y seguir al crucificado. S 1993, Sígueme. 150 p. – ᴿBibFe 20 (1994) 146 (A. *Salas*).

8144 **Bianchi** Enzo, Suivre Jésus le Seigneur; le radicalisme chrétien, ᵀ*Macina* M. R.: Spiritualité. P 1993, Mame. 136 p. – ᴿRThom 94 (1994) 347 (H.-F. *Rovarino*: base biblique).

8145 **Brown** Laurence B., *al.*, The human side of prayer; the psychology of praying. Birmingham AL 1994, Rel.Edn. 325 p. $20 pa. 0-89135-092-6 [TDig 42,157].

8147 *Burton-Christie* Douglas, Mapping the sacred landscape; spirituality and the contemporary literature of nature: ➤ 120, ᶠSLOYAN G., Horizons 21 (1994) 22-47.

8148 *a) Burton-Christie* Douglas, Scripture, self-knowledge and contemplation in CASSIAN's Conferences; – *b) Stewart* Columba, Scripture and contemplation in the monastic spiritual theology of John Cassian: ➤ 8,465, StPatr (11th 1991) 25 (1993) 339-345 / 457-461.

8149 *Cannon* Dale W., Different ways of Christian prayer; different ways of being Christian; a rationale for some of the differences between Christians: Mid-Stream 33 (1994) 309-334; 3 diagrams.

8150 **Cantalamessa** Raniero, Jésus-Christ le Saint de Dieu [1990 ➤ 7,8186],ᵀ: Spiritualité. P 1993, Mame. 192 p.

8150* *Cassese* Michele, 'Religione del cuore' e devozione al sangue del costato di Cristo nel pietista luterano Nikolaus L. von ZINZENDORF: RivStoLR 30 (1994) 263-297.

8151 **Cencillo** Luis, La comunicación absoluta; antropología y práctica de la oración. M 1994, San Pablo. 279 p. 84-285-1637-5. – ᴿEstE 69 (1994) 413 (P. *Cebollada*).

8152 *Chapman* Mark E., Early Christian mystagogy and the formation of modern Christians: CurrTM 21 (1994) 284-293.

8153 a) *Clendenin* Daniel B., Partakers of divinity; the Orthodox doctrine of theosis: – b) *Carson* D. A., When is spirituality spiritual? reflections on some problems of definition: JEvTS 37 (1994) 365-379 / 381-394.

8154 **Contegiacomo** Luigi, Il culto al preziosissimo sangue di N. S. Gesù Cristo; nei suoi fondamenti biblici, patristici, teologici; nella sua storia; nel suo contenuto: Sangue e Vita 7. R 1991, Pia Unione P. Sangue. 214 p. Lᵐ 20.

Cullmann Oscar, Das Gebet im NT 1994 ➤ 168.

8155 **Diego Sánchez** Manuel, Historia de la Espiritualidad patrística. M 1992, Espiritualidad. 386 p. – ᴿBurgense 34 (1994) 577s (A. *Álvarez Suárez*).

8156 *Dowd* Sharyn, Spirituality and the Bible: LexTQ 29 (1994) 37-44.

8157 ᴱ**Downey** Michael, The new dictionary of Catholic spirituality 1993 ➤ 9,8562: ᴿLexTQ 29 (1994) 66-68 (Maria *Lichtman*, very favorable); PrPeo 8 (1994) 489s (Jackie *Hawkins*).

8158 **Dreitcer** Andrew D., Roles of the Bible in Christian spirituality; a study of seven congregations: diss. Graduate Theol. Union, ᴰ*Mudge* L. Berkeley 1993. – RTLv 26, p. 557.

8159 a) *Dubuisson* Daniel, Parler aux dieux; – b) *Deremetz* Alain, La prière en représentation à Rome; – c) *Boulnois* Olivier, Quand la réponse precède la demande; la dialectique paradoxale de la prière chrétienne; – d) *Solère* Jean-Luc, De l'orateur à l'orant; la 'rhétorique divine' dans la culture chrétienne occidentale: RHPR 211 (1994) 131-9 / 141-165 / 167-186 / 187-224.

8159* ᴱ**Favale** Agostino, Vocazione comune e vocazioni specifiche² [¹1981]. R 1993, LAS. 538 p. – ᴿScripTPamp 26 (1994) 860 (J. L. *Illanes*).

8160 a) *Federici* Tommaso, La santa mistagogía permanente de la Iglesia; – b) *Castellano* Jésus, Orar con los íconos: Phase 33 (1993) 9-34 / 35-52.

8160* **Feuerstein** Georg, Spirituality by the numbers [Nos. 1-14 and 22 others (worldwide) considered sacred]. NY 1994, Putnam's. xix-252 p. 0-87477-765-8.

8161 **Friend** Stanley E., Activity in the spiritual arena (God's rules) [as found in Scripture]: diss. Fuller Theol. Sem., ᴰ*Redman* Robert R., Pasadena 1994. 129 p. 94-15210. – DissA 54 (1993s) p. 4471.

8162 a) *Galot* Jean, Problemi dottrinali della vita consacrata; – b) *Zago* Marcello, L'inculturazione, sfida per la vita consacrata: VConsacr 30 (1994) 294-304 / 331-8.

8163 *Gerlitz* P., *al.*, Mystik: ➤ 517, TRE 23 (1994) 533-547 (-597).

8164 **Giachi** Gualberto, Chiamati a collaborare con Cristo; Esercizi spirituali di S. Ignazio alla luce del Catechismo della Chiesa Cattolica. T-Leumann 1994, LDC. 124 p. Lᵐ 10. – ᴿCC 145 (1994,3) 439s (I. *Castellani*).

8165 **Holt** Bradley P., Thirsty for God; a brief history of Christian spirituality. Mp 1993, Augsburg. x-150 p. 0-8066-2640-2 [TDig 42,69].

8166 **Koenig** John T., Rediscovering NT prayer; boldness and blessing in the name of Jesus 1992 ➤ 8,8351; 9,8581: ᴿLexTQ 29 (1994) 60-62 (E. *Parrish*).

8167 **Land** Steven J., Pentecostal spirituality; a passion for the Kingdom: JPent supp. 1. Shf 1993, Academic. 239 p. £15. 1-85075-442-X. – ᴿTBR 7,1 (1994s) 66 (J. *Pemberton*: not just a jazzed-up fundamentalism: right; not assimilable into other Christian systems: wrong).

8168 **La Potterie** Ignace de, La preghiera di Gesù Messia – Servo di Dio – Figlio di Dio. R 1991, Apost. Preg. 165 p. Lᵐ 18. – ᴿCC 145 (1994,1) 520s (I. M. *Ganzi*); RivVSp 46 (1992) 550 (A. *Pigna*).

8169 **Larchet** Jean-Claude, Thérapeutique des maladies spirituelles; une introduction à la tradition ascétique de l'Église orthodoxe[2] [[1]1991]: Suresnes Arbre de Jessé. P 1993, Cerf. 948 p. – [R]NRT 116 (1994) 928s (L.-J. *Renard*); OrChrPer 60 (1994) 313s (V. *Poggi*); RThom 94 (1994) 703-5 (D. *Cerbelaud*).

8170 *Lethel* François-Marie, La théologie des saints dans le Catéchisme de l'Église Catholique: Teresianum 45 (1994) 55-80.

8171 **López Melús** Francisco M., Desierto, una experiencia de gracia: Nueva Alianza 128, 1994 → 9,8586: [R]LumenVr 43 (1994) 413-5 (U. *Gil Ortega*).

8172 **Luibl** H. J., Des Fremden Sprachgestalt; Beobachtungen zum Bedeutungswandel des Gebets in der Geschichte der Neuzeit [Diss. Zürich]: HermUnT 30. Tü 1993, Mohr. xiv-332 p. DM 108. 3-16-145978-4. – [R]TvT 34 (1994) 317 (F. *Maas*: belangwekkend).

8173 *Luz* Ulrich, *al*., Nachfolge Jesu: → 517, TRE 23 (1994) 678-686 (-713).

8174 [E]**McGinn** Bernard, *al*., Geschichte der christlichen Spiritualität [1985 → 1,371*], [TE]*Sudbrack* Josef. Wü 1993, Echter. 488 p. – [R]TPhil 69 (1994) 222-4 (G. *Switek*).

8175 *McGinn* Bernard, Ocean and desert as symbols of mystical absorption in the Christian tradition: JRel 74 (1994) 155-181.

8176 *McGrath* Alister, Reformation spirituality; historical resources, contemporary possibilities [Tipple Lecture]: DrewG 60,2 (1990s). 191 p.

8177 **McGrath** Joanna & Alister, The dilemma of self-esteem; the cross and Christian confidence. ... 1992, Crossway. – [R]TLond 97 (1994) 71s (Elaine *Graham*).

8178 **Martini** Carlo Maria, Letting God free us; meditations on the Spiritual Exercises [to bishops], [T]*Arnandez* Richard. Hyde Park NY 1993, New City, 128 p. $9. 1-56548-053-8 [TDig 41,276].

8178* [TE]**Messana** Vincenzo, EVAGRIO Pontico, La preghiera: TPatr 117. R 1994, Città Nuova. 181 p. 88-311-3117-6.

8179 **Miller** Patrick D., They cried to the Lord; the form and theology of biblical prayer. Mp 1994, Fortress. xvi-464 p. 0-8006-2762-8.

8180 **Miquel** P., Le vocabulaire latin de l'expérience spirituelle... 1050-1250: 1989 → 8,8371; 9,8395: [R]CrNSt 14 (1993) 413-5 (Silvana *Vecchio*); TorJT 8 (1992) 343s (K. E. *Anatolios*).

8181 **Ochs** Carol, Song of the self; biblical spirituality and human holiness. Ph 1994, Trinity. ix-109 p.

8182 *Panikkar* Raimun, Action and contemplation as categories of religious understanding: Forefront 1,3 (formerly Desert Call; 1994) 15-...

8183 *Ricœur* Paul, L'economia del dono; amore e giustizia: Protestantesimo 49 (1994) 13-24.

8184 **Rossi de Gasperis** Francesco, *Pacomio* Luciano, A pregare s'impara pregando, I: Dalla Parola alla vita 1. CinB 1994, Paoline. 195 p. L[m] 14. 88-315-1017-7.

8185 **Ryan** Thomas P., Disciplines for Christian living; interfaith perspectives. NY 1993, Paulist. 274 p. $13. – [R]Mid-Stream 33 (1994) 242-4 (J. D. *May*).

8186 *Sheldrake* Philip, Spirituality and history; questions of interpretation and method. NY 1992, Crossroad. 238 p. $15. 0-8245-1148-4. – [R]RExp 91 (1994) 273s (C. J. *Scalise*).

8187 **Smith** Martin L., The Word is very near you; a guide to praying with Scripture. Boston 1989, Cowley. 217 p. $20. 0-936384-81-6. – [R]Weavings 9,3 (Nv 1994) 44-46 (Elizabeth J. *Canham*).

8188 **Subilia** P., La parola che brucia; meditazioni bibliche 1991 → 9,8616*: [R]Protestantesimo 48 (1993) 224s (G. *Conte*).

8189 **Thompson** William M., Christology and spirituality 1991 ➤ 8,7569; 9,8619*: ᴿIrTQ 59 (1993) 237 (J. *Rafferty*).

8190 **Toon** Peter, The art of meditating on Scripture; understanding your faith, renewing your mind, knowing your God. GR 1993, Zondervan. 168 p. $10. 0-310-57761-6 [TDig 41,291].

8191 **Viller** Marcel, *Rahner* Karl, Ascetica e mistica nella Patristica² [¹1939 ➤ 6,k22], ᵀᴱ*Zani* Antonio. Brescia 1991, Queriniana. 314 p. Lᵐ 38. – ᴿCC 145 (1994,1) 91-93 (G. *Cremascoli*).

8192 *Waaijman* Kees, Toward a phenomenological definition of spirituality: Studies in Spirituality 3 (Kampen 1993) 5-57 [< ᴢɪᴛ 94,16].

8193 *Waltke* Bruce K., Exegesis and the spiritual life: Crux 30,3 (1994) 28-35.

8194 *Ward* Thomas R.ᴶ, Etched in the heart; listening to God in Scripture and in our lives: Weavings 9,3 (Nv 1994) 30-36.

8195 **Wells** David F., God in the wasteland; the reality of truth in a world of fading dreams. GR/Leicester 1994, Eerdmans/Inter-Varsity. x-278 p. £13.

8196 **Whelan** Michael, Living strings; an introduction to biblical spirituality. Newton ɴsᴡ 1994, Dwyer. 189 p. £8. 0-85574-373-5.

H8.1 *Spiritualitas publica:* **Liturgia, vita communitatis, Sancti.**

8197 **Bouyer** Louis, Liturgie und Architektur [1967]; Bedeutung des Kirchenbaus für die Gestaltung eines lebendigen Gottesdienstesᵀ: Theologia romanica 18. Einsiedeln 1993, Johannes. 117 p. ᴅᴍ 27. – ᴿTR 90 (1994) 488s (K. *Richter*).

8197* **Bowe** Barbara, Silent voices, sacred lives; readings for the liturgical year. ɴʏ 1992, Paulist. vi-464 p. $23. 0-8091-3335-9. – ᴿVidyajyoti 58 (1994) 290 (P. *Meagher*).

8198 **Bradshaw** Paul F. [➤ 7294s], The search for the origins of Christian worship 1992 ➤ 8,8303; 9,8627: ᴿCathHR 80 (1994) 546-8 (R. F. *Taft*); Manuscripta 36 (1992) 235s (E. A. *Diederich*); RExp 91 (1994) 621 (P. A. *Richardson*); Worship 65 (1994) 87-90 (D. *Tripp*).

8199 *Büchli* Otto, Das Gebet der Gemeinde; ein Beitrag zur Homiletik von Karl Bᴀʀᴛʜ: TZBas 50 (1994) 24-40.

8200 **Cantalamessa** Raniero, Easter in the early Church; an anthology of Jewish and early Christian texts. ColMn 1993, Liturgical. xii-254 p.; bibliog. p. 223-239.

8200* **Chavasse** Antoine, La liturgia de la ville de Rome du Vᵉ au VIIIᵉ siècle: AnalLtg 18. R 1993, S. Anselmo. 356 p. – ᴿRevSR 68 (1994) 366-8 (M. *Metzger*: aussi sur son Lectionnaires).

8201 *Costa Silva* Carlos A. da, Orações, bênçãos e a Bíblia: REB 53 (1993) 428-435.

8201* *Crawford* Janet, *Best* Thomas F., Praise the Lord with the lyre... and the gamelan? Towards koinonia in worship: EcuR 46 (1994) 78-96.

8202 **Deiss** Lucien, Celebration of the Word, ᵀwith *Burton* Jane. ColMn 1993, Liturgical. vi-145 p. $12 pa. 0-8146-2090-6 [TDig 41,263].

8203 **Doran** Carol, *Troeger* Thomas H., Trouble at the table; gathering the tribes for worship. Nv 1993, Abingdon. 160 p. $11. 0-667-42656-1. – ᴿRExp 91 (1994) 634s (P. A. *Richardson*: skilful; 'back to David!').

8204 *Drobner* Hubertus R., Wurzeln und Verbreitung des Mesopentecoste-Festes in der Alten Kirche: RivArCr 70 (1994) 203-245.

8204* **Faley** Roland T., Footprints on the mountain; preaching and teaching the Sunday readings. ɴʏ c. 1994, Paulist. $30. 1-201-825-730.

8205 *Gy* Pierre-Marie, *al.*, Bible et liturgie en dynamique œcuménique: MaisD 189 (1992) 7-18 (-147).
8205* *Hahn* Ferdinand, Le culte dans l'Église primitive, ᵀ*Sabourin* Léopold: ScEspr 46 (1994) 309-332. ...
8206 *a) Huerre* Denis, Une liturgie imprégnée par l'Écriture; – *b) Beauchamp* Paul, La lecture typologique du Pentateuque: MaisD 190 ('Quand l'Écriture devient parole' 1992) 7-24 / 51-73.
8206* *Jordan* Timothy R. [*al.*], Definition of worship: CalvaryB 9,2 (1993) 1-16 [-35].
8207 *Kleinig* John W., The biblical view of worship: ConcordiaTQ 58 (1994) 245-254.
8208 *Lukken* Gérard, Les transformations du rôle liturgique du peuple, in ᴱ*Caspers* C., *Schneider* M., Omnes circumadstantes; contributions toward a history of the role of the people in the liturgy (Kampen 1990, Kok) 15-30; ensuite SémBib 76 (1994) 27-48.
8209 *Mankowski* Paul V., p. 1 (but *Skeris* Robert A. p. 51) Ideology and liturgy; worship as the cult of the community: F & R 20 (1994) 51-66.
8210 *a)* **Messner** Reinhard, Feiern der Umkehr und Versöhnung; – *b)* **Kaczynski** Reiner, Feier der Krankensalbung: Gottesdienst der Kirche, HbLtgWiss 7/2/1s. Rg 1992, Pustet. 375 p. DM 48. – ᴿTüTQ 174 (1994) 329-333 (G. *Winkler*).
8211 **Monshouwer** Dirk, Vieren vol verwachting; de plaats van Israël in de eredienst van de christelijke gemeente: Verkenning en bezinning 5. Kampen 1992, Kok. 77 p. 90-242-6660-2. – ᴿDielB 28 (1992s) 273 (B. J. *Diebner*).
8212 **Olst** E. H. van, The Bible and liturgy [Bijbel...], ᵀ*Vriend* J., 1991 ➜ 7,8239*; 9,8650: ᴿTBR 6/5 (1993) 68 (Mary E. *Barr*).
8213 **Perry** Michael, Bible praying; Scripture prayers for worship and devotion. L 1992, Harper Collins. 353 p. $19. – ᴿEcuR 46 (1994) 369s (M. E. *Chapman*).
8214 **Peterson** David, Engaging with God; a biblical theology of worship 1993, Eerdmans ➜ 9,8651; also Leicester 1992, Apollos: ᴿEvRT 18 (1994) 289-292 (D. *Parker*), repeated 383-5.
8214* *Pickstock* Catherine, Asyndeton, syntax and insanity; a study of the revision of the Nicene Creed [Alternative Service Book 1980]: ModT 10 (1994) 321-340
8215 ᴱ**Roberts** Paul, *al.*, Something understood; a companion to ['the recent Franciscan Office Book'] Celebrating common prayer. L 1993, Hodder & S. 102 p. £7 pa. – ᴿTLond 97 (1994) 60s (C. *Read*: praised on p. 121 for detecting an absurdity which crept into Martin KITCHEN's contribution).
8216 **Salzmann** Jörg Christian, Lehren und Ermahnen; zur Geschichte des christlichen Wortgottesdienstes in den ersten drei Jahrhunderten [Diss. 1990, ᴰ*Hengel* M.]: WUNT 2/58. Tü 1994, Mohr. ix-536 p. 3-16-145971-7.
8217 **Senn** Frank, The witness of the worshiping community; liturgy and the practice of evangelism. NY 1993, Paulist. 177 p. $13. – ᴿConcordJ 20 (1994) 211-3 (J. L. *Brauer*: author an Evanston Lutheran pastor).
8218 **Skelley** Michael, The liturgy of the world; Karl RAHNER's theology of worship; pref. *Weakland* R. G., 1992 ➜ 8,8389; 9,8653: ᴿTLZ 119 (1994) 60 (W. V. *Dych*, Eng.).
8219 **Taft** Robert F., The Byzantine rite; a short history: American Essays in Liturgy. ColMn 1992, Liturgical. 84 p. $6. 0-8146-2163-5. – ᴿExpTim

105 (1993s) 222 (K. *Stevenson*: erudite, clear); OrChrPer 60 (1994) 298-300 (A. A. *Thiermeyer*); PrOrChr 43 (1993) 206s (P. *Ternant*).

8220 **Taft** Robert, La liturgie des Heures en Orient et en Occident; origine et sens de l'Office divine, ᵀ*Passelecq* Georges: Mysteria, 1991 → 8,8392; Fb 1750: ᴿETLv 25 (1994) 265s (A. *Haquin*).

8220* *Templeton* D. J., Sssh! — silence in worship: IrBSt 15 (1993) 86-90 [< BtS 151 (1994) 110s (T. J. *Ralston*)].

8221 **Vanhoye** Albert, Il pane quotidiano della Parola; commento alle letture feriali della Messa, ciclo I & II. CasM 1994, Piemme. 1022 p. 88-384-2258-3.

8221* *Volp* R., Die Kunst, Gott zu feiern. Gü 1992/4, Mohn. xx-682 p.; p. ix-683-1325. – ᴿProtestantesimo 49 (1994) 390-2 (E. *Genre*).

8222 **West** Fritz, An annotated bibliography on the three-year lectionaries; part 1, the Roman-Catholic lectionary: StLtg 23 (Rotterdam 1993) 223-... [< ZIT 93,699].

8223 **Abou Zayad** Shafiq, *Iḥidayutha*, life of singleness 1993 → 9,8659: ᴿAulaO 12 (1994) 133-6 (A. *Desreumaux*); OrChrPer 60 (1994) 325 (G. *Nedungatt*).

8224 *Bianchi* Enzo, La vita religiosa è profetica?: RasT 35 (1994) 517-533.

8225 *Biffi* Inos, Teologia monastica: TItSett 19 (1993) 64-75.

8226 **Brown** Peter, Die Keuschheit der Engel 1991 → 9,8418: ᴿZRGg 45 (1993) 282s (V. *Krech*).

8227 *Burrus* Virginia, Word and flesh; the bodies and sexuality of ascetic women in Christian antiquity: JFemStR 10,1 (1994) 27-51.

8228 **Burton-Christie** Douglas, The Word in the desert; Scripture and the quest for holiness in early Christian monasticism 1993 → 9,8664: ᴿCathHR 80 (1994) 559s (G. *Gould*); Horizons 21 (1994) 182 (E. G. *Hinson*: very fine; but has the time come to mention 'desert mothers' or at least sexlessly 'desert ascetics or monks'?); RExp 91 (1994) 442s (C. J. *Scalise*).

8229 *Camps Gaset* Montserrat, Com fan de Jesús norma vivent les comunitats cristianes d'avui: QVidCr 165 (1993) 77-98.

8231 **Decloux** Simon, Inactualité de la vie religieuse. Namur 1993. 166 p. – ᴿManresa 65 (1993) 311s (I. *Iglesias*).

8232 *Duggan* George H., Cyanide in wineskins [SCHNEIDERS Sandra, New wineskins; re-imagining religious life for today 1986]: HomP 93,1 (1992s) 49.

8233 **Elm** Susanna, 'Virgins of God'; the making of asceticism in late antiquity: ClasMG. Ox 1994, Clarendon. xvii-444 p.; bibliog. 387-429.

8234 *Galot* Jean, Valeur et nécessité de la vie consacrée dans l'Église: EsprVie 104 (1994) 401-8 (417-423, problèmes doctrinaux).

8235 *Goehring* James E., The encroaching desert; literary production and ascetic space in early Christian Egypt: JEarlyC 1 (1993) 281-296.

8236 *González de Cardedal* Olegario, Soledad y solidaridad; sentido de la vida monástica en el cristianismo: Salmanticensis 41 (1994) 213-259; Eng. 260.

8237 **Gould** Graham, The Desert Fathers on monastic community 1993 → 9,8675: ᴿExpTim 105 (1993s) 183 (G. *Bostock*: their avoidance of individual responsibility is like their fear of sex); HeythJ 35 (1994) 214-6 (R. M. *Price*); TLond 97 (1994) 62 (Mary Charles *Murray*).

8238 ᵀᴱ**Harb** Paul, *Graffin* François, *al.*, Joseph HAZZĀYĀ, Lettre sur les trois étapes de la vie monastique: PatrOr 45/2, Nº 202. Turnhout 1992, Brepols. p. 253-442. – ᴿRB 101 (1994) 305s (M.-J. *Pierre*).

8239 **Hawel** Peter, Das Mönchtum im Abendland; Geschichte – Kultur – Lebensform. FrB 1993, Herder. 480 p. DM 98. 3-451-23082-8. – ᴿTrier-TZ 103 (1994) 240 (E. *Souser*); TvT 34 (1994) 308 (J. van *Laarhoven*).

8240 *Hidalgo de la Vega* M. José, Mujeres, carisma y castidad en el cristianismo primitivo: Gerión 11 (1993) 229-244.

8241 **Joest** Christoph, Bibelstellenkonkordanz zu den wichtigsten älteren Mönchsregeln: InstrPatr 9. Brugge/Haag 1994, S. Petri/Nijhoff. xlv-149 p.

8242 **Kanior** Marian, ❷ Historia monastycyzmu chrześciańskiego, 1. Starożytność (saec. III-VIII). Kraków 1993. 398 p. – ᴿAtKap 123 (1994) 130s (K. *Rulka,* ❷).

8243 *Koonammakhal* K. R. Thomas, Early Christian monastic origins; a general introduction in the context of the Syrian Orient: [Buddhist] Dialogue 18 (1991) 14-48.

8244 *Lilienfeld* Fairy von, Mönchtum, christlich [*Klein* Wassilius, religionsgeschichtlich]: ↠ 517, TRE 23 (1994) [143-] 150-193.

8245 **López Amat** Alfredo, La vita consacrata, le varie forme dalle origini ad oggi 1991 ↠ 8,8434; 9,8683: ᴿSalesianum 56 (1994) 140s (O. *Pasquato*).

8246 *Maccise* Camillo, Le radici bibliche della spiritualità carmelitana: RivVSp 47 (1993) 318-329.

8247 *Pardilla* Ángel, Gli aspetti 'biblici' della vita consacrata nei Lineamenta: VConsac 29 (1993) 534-557.

8248 *Renwart* Léon, Théologie de la vie religieuse; Chronique: VieCons 65 (1993) 48-58 [258-267, Écr.S., *Luciani* Didier].

8249 **Rouiller** Grégoire, Choisir la meilleure part? Ou comment situer aujourd'hui le débat; baptême, mariage, vie religieuse: Cah 3. FrS 1994, Assoc. Biblique Catholique. 200 p.

8250 **Rufe** Joan B., Early Christian fasting; a study of creative adaptation: diss. Virginia, ᴰ*Gamble* H. 1994. 328 p. 94-24472. – DissA 55 (1994s) p. 993.

8250* **Shaw** Teresa M., The 'burden of the flesh'; fasting and the female body in early Christian ascetic thought: diss. Duke, ᴰ*Clark* Elizabeth A. Durham NC 1992. 361 p. (4 microfiches). 92-37879 [OIAc 11,41].

8251 **Simón Palmer** José, El monacato original en el Pratum Spirituale de Juan MOSCO. M 1993, Fund. Univ. 500 p. – ᴿJTS 45 (1994) 759s (H. *Chadwick*).

8252 *Thélamon* Françoise, Sociabilité, travail et loisir dans le monachisme antique [+ Capucins, Trappistes]: ArchivScSocR 39,86 (1994) 183-197; Eng. 197.

8253 *Theodorou* Evangelos D., ❸ Sketches of the phenomenology of Eastern and Western monasticism: TAth 65 (1994) 7-24; Eng. 1018.

8254 **Vervoorn** Aat, Men of the cliffs and caves; the development of the Chinese eremitic tradition to the end of the Han dynasty. Hong Kong 1990, Chinese Univ. xii-356 p. $29. – ᴿJAOS 113 (1993) 575-584 (A. *Berkowitz*: 'reclusion'; groundbreaking).

8255 *a) Vilanova* Evangelista, El monaquismo como utopía; – *b) Tamayo* Juan José, Religión bíblica; utopías históricas y esperanza cristiana: BibFe 20,58 (El hechízo de la Utopía 1994) 69-84 / 46-68.

8256 ᵀᴱ**Vivian** Tim, PAPHNUTIUS, Histories of the monks of upper Egypt and the Life of Onnophrius: CistSt 140. Kalamazoo MI 1993, Cistercian. 179 p. / $35; pa. $17. – ᴿÉglT 25 (1994) 139s (K. C. *Russell*).

8257 **Vogüe** Adalbert De, Histoire littéraire du mouvement monastique dans l'Antiquité 1991 ➤ 7,8223 ... 9,8693: ᴿREAug 40 (1994) 232-6 (M. *Milhau*); RTAM 60 (1993) 278s (E. *Manning*).
8258 **Wenzelmann** Gottfried, Nachfolge und Gemeinschaft; eine theologische Grundlegung des kommunitären Lebens: Calwer TMg C 21. Stu 1994, Calwer. 304 p. DM 78.
8259 ᴱ**Wimbush** V. L., Ascetic behavior 1990 ➤ 7,8296: ᴿJEarlyC 1 (1993) 222-4 (E. *Sellner*).
8260 *a)* *Zēsē* Theodōros, Ⓖ Monasticism an imitation of Christ and the Apostles; – *b)* *Kadá* Sōtēros N., The signatures (*sēmeiōmata*) of the manuscripts of the Holy Mountain, Monē Zōgraphou: Byzantiná 17 (Thessaloniki 1994) 177-187 / 141-176; 4 fig.

8261 **Abou-el-Haj** Barbara F., The medieval cult of saints; formations and transformations. C 1994, Univ. xviii-456 p. $90. 0-521-39316-7 [TDig 42,153].
8262 **Angenendt** Arnold, Heilige und Reliquien; die Geschichte ihres Kultes vom frühen Christentum bis zur Gegenwart. Mü 1994, Beck. 470 p. DM 68. – ᴿTPhil 69 (1994) 588-590 (K. *Schatz*); TR 90 (1994) 389s (W. *Beinert*).
8263 **Barth** Hans-Martin, Sehnsucht nach den Heiligen? Stu 1992, Quell. 167 p. – ᴿProtestantesimo 48 (1993) 342s (E. *Genre*: 'boccone duro da digerire ... anche i protestanti hanno i loro santi', ... martiri).
8264 **Brown** Peter, Die Heiligenverehrung; ihre Entstehung und Funktion in der lateinischen Christenheit 1991 ➤ 7,8267*... 9,8698: ᴿAltertum 39 (1993) 149-151 (F. M. *Kammel*); TR 90 (1994) 390s (A. *Angenendt*).
8265 *a)* *Klaiber* Walter, Gelebte Gnade; – *b)* *Wenz* Gunther, Evangelisches Heiligenverständnis; – *c)* *Voss* Gerhard, Heiligenlegenden mit mythischen Wurzeln; Zeugnisse von Erlösung oder von Verfremdung weiblichen und männlichen Menschseins: UnSa 49,3 ('Wiederkehr der Heiligen' 1994) 180-187 / 188-194 / 195-210.
8266 **Kleinberg** Aviad M., Prophets in their own country; living saints and the making of sainthood in the later Middle Ages. Ch 1992, Univ. x-189 p. 0-226-43971-2. – ᴿTBR 7,1 (1994s) 40 (Veronica *Laurence*).
8267 **Woodward** Kenneth L., Making saints 1991 ➤ 9,8705 [ital. ➤ 8,8451; deutsch 8452]: ᴿCanadCath 12,5 (1994) 28s (D. H. *Farmer*).

H8.2 Theologia moralis NT.

8267* *Albacete* Lorenzo, The Pope against moralism and legalism: Anthropotes (1994,1) 81-86.
8268 *Almond* Brenda, Seven moral myths [relativism, toleration, neutrality, theory & commitment, majority, morality & law, liberalism: we fail by R. M. HARE's standard, 'What are we to teach our children?']: ExpTim 105 (1993s) 164-7.
8269 **Arens** Edmund, Christopraxis; Grundzüge christlicher Handlungstheorie: QDisp 139, 1992 ➤ 9,8709: ᴿMüTZ 44 (1993) 134s (O. *Meuffeln*).
8270 **Barry** Robert L., Breaking the thread of life; on rational suicide. New Brunswick 1994, Transaction. xxii-353 p. $35. 1-56000-142-9 [TDig 42,156].
8271 **Basevi** C., E saranno una sola carne. Mi 1993, Ares. 150 p. – ᴿAnnTh 8 (1994) 176-9 (M. A. *Tábet*: antropologia biblico-paolina).

8272 *a) Bein Ricco* Elena, L'etica contemporanea tra comunitarismo e universalismo; – *b) Berlinguer* Giovanni, Per un'etica della salute; – *c) Genre* Ermanno, L'esigenza di unità nella teologia pratica; un'utopia?: Protestantesimo 49 (1994) 129-141 / 98-106 / 25-40.

8273 **Berge** Roger van den, Veritatis splendor; voorstelling en evaluatie: CollatVL 24 (1994) 79-100.

8274 **Berkman** John R., The politics of moral theology; historicizing neo-Thomist moral theology, with special reference to the work of Germain GRISEZ: diss. Duke, ᴰ*Hauerwas* S. Durham NC 1994. 331 p. 95-00516. – DissA 55 (1994s) p. 2440.

8275 *a) Boughton* Lynne C., Biblical texts and homosexuality; a response to John BOSWELL [1980]; – *b) White* Leland J., Biblical texts and contemporary gay people; a response to Boswell and Boughton: IrTQ 58 (1992) 139-153 / 286.

8276 *Brattston* David W. T., Abortion in the Bible: Churchman 108 (1994) 353-6.

8277 *Brawley* Robert L., To have, to hold, and in time – let go; ethics and interpreting the Bible: CurrTM 21 (1994) 113-6.

8278 *a) Bretzke* James T., Scripture; the 'soul' of moral theology? – the second stage; – *b) Pleins* J. David, How ought we to think about poverty? – Re-thinking the diversity of the Hebrew Bible: IrTQ 60 (1994) 259-271 / 280-6.

8279 **Bristow** John T., What the Bible really says about love, marriage, and family. St. Louis 1994, Chalice. vii-152 p. 0-8272-4232-8.

8280 *a) Browning* Peter, Homosexuality, ordination, and polity; – *b) Hughes* Sheila H., Homosexuality and group boundaries in contemporary evangelical feminism; a historical perspective; – *c) Halsey* Betsy L., Ministry to gays and Lesbians: QRMin 14 (1994) 161-179 / 135-159 / 181-195.

8281 *Bruguès* Jean-Louis, Veritatis splendor, une encyclique de combat: Communio 19,112 (P 1994) 135-152.

8282 **Bucks** Johannes R., A Biblia e a ética: diss. ᴰ*Palácio* C. Belo Horizonte 1993. – PerspT 26 (1994) 86.

8283 *Burke* Cormac, La vérité de l'amour matrimonial et la contraception: Angelicum 71 (1994) 259-274.

8284 **Byrne** Peter, The philosophical and theological foundations of ethics; an introduction to moral theory and its relation to religious belief. L 1992, Macmillan. 168 p. – ᴿTLond 97 (1994) 137s (P. *Ballard*).

8285 *Cameron* Nigel M., Soundings in a theology of medicine: TrinJ 14,2 (1993) 123-141 (-214, *al.*).

8286 *Caspar* Philippe, Approche biologique et métaphysique du statut anthropologique de l'œuf fécondé humain: NVFr 68 (1993) 304-9.

8287 *Clemons* James T., Interpreting biblical texts on suicide: QRMin 14 (1944) 17-28.

8288 **Comstock** Gary D., Gay theology without apology. Cleveland 1993, Pilgrim. 183 p. – ᴿWWorld 14 (1994) 360s.364 (R. A. *Nelson*).

8289 **Cornes** Andrew, Divorce and remarriage; biblical principles and pastoral practice 1993 → 9,8729; also Eerdmans; 0-340-57434-8: $25; ᴿChurchman 108 (1994) 283s (R. *Combes*); SWJT 36,3 (1993s) 74 (B. E. *Adams*: rigor aiming to be biblical but not succeeding).

8289* *Cottier* Georges, L'encyclique 'Veritatis splendor': NVFr 69 (1994) 1-13.

8290 *a) Countryman* L. William, NT sexual ethics and today's world; – *b) Ricœur* Paul, Wonder, eroticism, and enigma; – *c) Boswell* John,

Homosexuality and religious life; a historical approach: ➤ 283, Sexuality and the sacred 1994, 28-53 / 80-84 / 361-373.
8291 *Cunningham* L., *Komonchak* J., *Curran* C., *Cahill* Lisa S., *Hauerwas* S., *al.*, Veritatis splendor: Commonweal 120,18 (1993) 3.11-18.
8292 **Curran** Charles E., The Church and morality; an ecumenical and Catholic approach [Lutheran Hein-Fry Lectures]. Mp 1994, Fortress. 122 p. $10. 0-8006-2756-3. – ᴿCanadCath 12,10 (1994) 24s (R. *Grecco*); ChrCent 110 (1994) 119s.122 (M.G. *Long*); TBR 7,1 (1994s) 41 (N. *Adams*).
8293 *Demel* Sabine, Was für ein: Wesen ist der Fötus?: TPhil 69 (1994) 224-237.
8294 **Demmer** Klaus, Gottes Anspruch denken; die Gottesfrage in der Moraltheologie. FrS/FrB 1993, Univ./Herder. 179 p. 3-7278-0863-2. – ᴿAntonianum 69 (1994) 554s (L. *Oviedo*); ZkT 116 (1994) 521-4 (H. *Gleixner*).
8295 **Drewermann** Eugen, La peur et la faute 1992 ➤ 8,8475: ᴿFoiTemps 23 (1993) 374s (H. *Thomas*).
8296 **Drewermann** Eugen, Psychanalyse et morale 1992 ➤ 8,8477; 9,8737: ᴿÉTRel 68 (1993) 453s (J. *Ansaldi*, 2-3); NRT 116 (1994) 579-582 (J.-P. *Prévost*, 1-3).
8297 *Duquoc* Christian, L'encyclique Veritatis splendor; présentation critique: RTPhil 126 (1994) 325-332; Eng. 406.
8298 *Eenigenburg* E.M., Biblical foundations and a method for doing Christian ethics. Lanham MD 1994, UPA. xi-166 p. $36.50. 0-8191-9283-X [NTAbs 38, p.474].
8299 *Eibach* Ulrich, Der Wandel moralischer Werte — eine Herausforderung für die Kirchen: KerDo 40 (1994) 80-100; Eng. 100.
8299* *a) Fantini* Maria Grazia, Natura idest Deus; il 'luogo' nel diritto nella cultura basso-medievale; – *b) Fay* Thomas A., La teoria della legge naturale di San Tommaso; alcune recenti interpretazioni [GRISEZ G., FINNIS J.]: DivThom 97,2 (1994) 106-208 / 209-216.
8300 **Finance** Joseph de, An ethical inquiry [Éthique générale 1967],ᵀ. R 1991, Pontificia Universitatis Gregoriana. 575 p. 88-7652-632-3. – ᴿBijdragen 55 (1994) 340s (L. *Fonteyn*; touches almost all important issues).
8301 *Finnis* John, Veritatis splendor in focus, 10. Beyond the encyclical [its concerns are far more critical than the sex-problems focused by the media]: Tablet 248 (1994) 8-10 [46, 148, critical letters; 144, response].
8301* *Finnis* John, Reason, relativism and Christian ethics: Anthropotes 2 (1993s) 211-230.
8302 *Flecha Andrés* J.-R., Panorama de estudios morales: Salmanticensis 41 (1994) 291-326.
8303 *Fletcher* Verne H., What manner of man is this? the central paradigm for Christian ethics [< Indonesian]: NesTR 15 (1994) 93-132.
8304 *Fonteyn* Luc, De theoloog en het embryo [DUNSTAN G.R. 1988]: Streven 60 (1993) 227-236.
8305 *a) Forcano* Benjamin, Ley y conciencia, hoy; – *b) Estal* Gabriel del, Ley y sistema en la naturaleza y en la sociedad: Biblia y Fe 60 (1994) 152-167 / 5-49.
8306 *Ford* Norman M., When did I begin? Conception of the human individual in history, philosophy and science ➤ 8,8488: ᴿRTPhil 126 (1994) 393s (J.-M. *Thévoz*).
8307 **Fowl** S., *Jones* G., Reading in common, Scripture and ethics 1991 ➤ 7,8331 ... 9,8749: ᴿScotJT 47 (1994) 110-2 (A.I. *McFadyen*).

8308 **Fuchs** Éric, L'Éthique protestante 1990 → 7,8333 ... 9,8751: ᴿTLZ 119 (1994) 353s (H. *Kress*).

8309 **Fuchs** É., La morale selon Jean-Paul II, réponse protestante à une encyclique: Entrée libre 31. Genève 1994, Labor et fides. 65 p. F 55. – ᴿEsprVie 104 (1994) 496 (P. *Daubercies*).

8310 *Fuchs* Éric, Actualité de l'éthique protestante: ÉTRel 68 (1993) 203-212 [ital. → 9,8751*].

8311 *Fuchs* Joseph, Gibt es in sich schlechte Handlungen? Zum Problem des 'intrinsece malum': StiZt 212 (1994) 291-304 (75-86 Das Problem Todsünde).

8312 *Fuchs* Josef, 'Wer euch hört, der hört mich'; bischöfliche Moral-weisungen: StiZt 117 (1992) 723-731 > 'Whoever hears you hears me'; episcopal moral instruction [ᵀᴱ*Asen* B. A.]: TDig 41 (1994) 3-7 [several bishops' pastorals on obligation to persons in permanent coma came to conclusions different from 1992 Pennsylvania bishops' pastoral].

8313 *a) Gafo* Javier, Una lectura escolástica de la 'Veritatis Splendor'; – *b) Vidal* Marciano, ... su marcado acento tomista: MiscCom 52 (1994) 3-21 / 23-38.

8313* *Gelas* Bruno, *al.*, Du mensonge: LumièreV 43,218 (1994) 5-16 (-85, *al.*).

8314 *Greenman* Jeffrey P., Veritatis splendor and/as evangelical ethics: Crux 30,2 (1994) 17-26.

8315 **Grenz** Stanley J., Sexual ethics, a biblical perspective. Dallas 1990, Word. 269 p. $15. – ᴿJEvTS 37 (1994) 637s (D. K. *Clark*).

8316 **Grisez** Germain, The way of the Lord Jesus; living a Christian life 2. 1993 → 9,8760: ᴿAngelicum 71 (1994) 124-7 (B. *Cole*; & 291-7 on vol. 1-2); Gregorianum 75 (1994) 535-548 (Kevin *Flannery*); NBlackf 75 (1994) 225-8 (A. *Fisher*).

8317 **Grisez** G., *Shaw* R., Fulfillment in Christ; a summary of Christian moral principles, 1991 → 8,8501: ᴿAnnTh 7 (1993) 258-265 (A. *Ansaldo*).

8318 *Grisez* Germain, *Sullivan* Francis A., The ordinary magisterium's infallibility (2 queries, 2 replies): TS 55 (1994) 720-737.

8319 **Hagstrum** Jean H., Esteem enlivened by desire: the couple from Homer to Shakespeare. Ch 1992, Univ. xvi-518 p. $36. – ᴿJRel 74 (1994) 372-8 (D. *Bevington*: 'the difficult ideal of companionate marriage').

8320 *Harrington* Donal, Moral theology; a critical analysis: IrTQ 59 (1993) 1-21.

8321 **Hart** Archibald D., The sexual man. Dallas 1994, Word. xv-223 p. $20. 0-8499-1076-5. – ᴿCrux 30,3 (1994) 45s (J. *Mills*).

8322 **Harvey** A. E., Strenuous ... ethics of Jesus 1990 → 7,8374; 8,8510: ᴿJTS 45 (1994) 207-9 (J. I. H. *McDonald*).

8323 **Hauerwas** Stanley, After Christendom? 1991 → 9,8770: ᴿSWJT 36,3 (1993s) 71s (R. E. *Higgins*: powerful theses but overstated).

8325 **Hennaux** J.-M., Le droit de l'homme à la vie de la conception à la naissance. Bru 1993, Inst.Ét.Théol. 198 p. Fb 990. – ᴿNRT 116 (1994) 246-250 (M. *Schooyans*).

8326 **Holmes** Stephen, The anatomy of antiliberalism [... the moral law]. CM 1993, Hervard Univ. xvi-330 p. 0-674-03180-6. – ᴿSalesianum 56 (1994) 593-5 (G. *Abbà*).

8327 *Irving* Diane N., Scientific and philosophical expertise; an evaluation of the arguments on 'personhood' [... of embryo]: LinacreQ 60,1 (1993) 18-46.

8328 *Jans* Jan, Moraltheologisch crisismanagement ... Veritatis splendor: TvT 34 (1994) 49-66; Eng. 67 (portions from Tablet: *Grisez* G.; rejects all dissent; *Häring* B.: it distrusts moral theologians; *Fuchs* J.: it misunderstands 'fundamental option'; — concludes: shadowed by Humanae Vitae.

8329 *a) Janssens* Louis, Theology and proportionality; thoughts about the encyclical Veritatis splendor; – *b) Taels* Johan, Ethik en subjectiviteit; een omkering van perspectief: Bijdragen 55 (1994) 118-131; Eng. 132 (not accurately represented) / 133-153; Eng. 153.

8330 **John Paul II**, Veritatis splendor. L 1993, Catholic Truth Soc. 183 p. £4.50 pa. – ᴿTLond 97 (1994) 141-3 (M. *Northcott*: ironically his limiting moral creativity and authority to the Pope and his advisers bespeaks a totalitarianism like the ones he combated).

8331 — JOHN PAUL II, *al.*, Understanding Veritatis Splendor [Tablet essays republished]. L c. 1994, SPCK. – ᴿTLond 97 (1994) 321s (Ann *Loades*).

8332 **Koenig** John, New Testament hospitality; partnership with strangers as promise and mission. 1985 ↠ 1,7891; 0-8006-1543-3: ᴿWeavings 9,1 (Nv 1994) 39s (T. R. *Ward*).

8333 **Küng** H., Projekt Weltethos 1990 ↠ 8,8525; 9,a23: ᴿEvKomm 26 (1993) 354s (M. *Welker*); LuMon 32,12 (1993) 4-6 (P. F. *Knitter*, 'Stimme der Stummen') & 7s (R. *Hummel*, Küngs goldene Regel).

8334 **Küng** Hans, Global responsibility; in search of a new world ethic 1991 ↠ 7,k4; 9,8789: ᴿJEvTS 37 (1994) 618s (G. *Crutsinger*); LuthQ 6 (1992) 108-110 (Stephen *Pope*).

8335 **Küng** Hans, Proyecto de una ética mundial 1991 ↠ 9,8790: ᴿSalmanticensis 41 (1994) 162s (J.-R. *Flecha*).

8336 **Küng** Hans, Projet d'éthique planétaire; la paix mondiale par la paix entre les religions. P 1991, Seuil. 252 p. F 120. – ᴿFoiTemps 23 (1993) 456s (H. *Thomas*).

8337 ᴱ**Küng** Hans, *Kuschel* Karl-Josef, A global ethic; the declaration of the parliament of the world's religions [Chicago Sept. 1993], ᵀ*Bowden* John. L 1993, SCM. 124 p. £6 pa. – ᴿEurJT 3,2 (1994) 172s (Eng. D. *Attwood*); ExpTim 105 (1993s) 383 (also D. *Attwood*: a modest claim, graciously presented); TLond 97 (1994) 297-9 (Ursula *King*: even if controversially prescriptive and unworkable, a forceful and logical historic document).

8338 *Lahidalga Aguirre* J. M., La 'Veritatis splendor' o la no suficiente valoración de la conciencia personal: LumenVr 43 (1994) 177-210.

8339 **Lange** Dietz, Ethik in evangelischer Perspektive; Grundfragen christlicher Lebenspraxis 1992 ↠ 9,8791: ᴿSalesianum 56 (1994) 387s (G. *Abbà*).

8340 *Lell* Joachim, Mischehe, Christentum [*Falk* Zeev W., Judentum]: ↠ 517, TRE 23 (1994) 7-13 [3-7].

8341 *Lepargneur* Hubert, Os conceitos da 'Veritatis splendor': REB 54 (1994) 5-35.

8342 **Linnane** Brian F., RAHNERIAN Christology as an anthropological foundation for a theocentric ethic [better than J. GUSTAFSON's own]: diss. Yale, ᴰ*Farley* Margaret. NHv 1994. 270 p. 94-30278. – DissA 55 (1994s) p. 2013.

8343 **Lohse** Eduard, Theological ethics of the NT [1988], ᵀ*Boring* M. Eugene 1991 ↠ 4,9394 ... 9,8798: ᴿCurrTM 21 (1994) 58s (J. L. *Bailey*); Interpretation 48 (1994) 211.3 (A. K. M. *Adam*); ScotJT 47 (1994) 550-2 (M. *Keeling*).

8344 **Lohse** Eduard, Etica teologica del NT 1991 ↠ 7,8361; 9,8799: ᴿSalesianum 56 (1994) 152-4 (G. *Abbà*).

8345 *López Azpitarte* Eduardo, La Veritatis Splendor ¿condena la ética teleológica? [moderada, no]: Stromata 50 (1994) 175-188.

8346 **McAdoo** Henry, First of its kind; Jeremy TAYLOR's life of Christ; a study in the functioning of a moral theology [The great exemplar 1649). 1994, Canterbury. xii-136 p. £10 pa. – ᴿTLond 97 (1994) 469s (R. *Askew*; a holy romance, accentuating the positive, confidently uncritical).

8347 *McClure* Michael [priest; member:] Is the Homosexual Movement to be condemned? [response to Ramsey Colloquium critique]: Month 255 (1994) 431-5 [260-5].

8348 **McCormick** Richard A., The critical calling; reflections on moral dilemmas since Vatican II. Wsh 1989, Georgetown Univ. 401 p. $30; pa. $17. 0-87840-463-5; -4-3. – ᴿJRelEth 20 (1992) 209 (E.C. *Vacek*).

8349 *McCormick* Richard A., Some early reactions to Veritatis Splendor: TS 55 (1994) 481-506.

8350 **McDonald** J.J.H., Biblical interpretation and Christian ethics. C 1993, Univ. 305 p.; $35. 0-521-43059-3. – ᴿExpTim 105,7 2d-top choice (1993s) 194s (C.S. *Rodd*); TLond 97 (1994) 302s (L. *Houlden*); TS 55 (1994) 746s (W.C. *Spohn*).

8351 **McLaren** Angus, A history of contraception from antiquity. Ox 1990, Blackwell. 256 p. £25; pa. £13. 0-631-16711-0. – ᴿEngHR 109 (1994) 674s (P. *Biller*).

8352 ᴱ**Mainville** Odette, *al.*, Loi et autonomie, dans la Bible et dans la tradition chrétienne [rencontre Montréal]: Héritage et projet 53. Québec 1994, Fides. 292 p. 2-7621-1725-9.

8353 *Margerie* B. de, Saint CYPRIEN donnait-il l'Eucharistie aux divorcés-remariés?: RTAM 60 (1993) 273-5.

8354 **Markham** Ian S., Plurality and Christian ethics. C 1994, Univ. xiv-221 p. $50. 0-521-45328-3 [TDig 42,176].

8355 *Marshall* I. Howard, New occasions teach new duties? The use of the New Testament in Christian ethics: ExpTim 105 (1993s) 131-5.

8356 **Marxsen** Willi † 1993, New Testament foundations for Christian ethics ['Christliche' und ... 1989 ➤ 5,8334], ᵀ*Dean* O.C. ➤ 9,8808; also Mp 1993, Fortress. xvi-319. $17. 0-8006-2749-0: ᴿExpTim 105,11 2d-top choice (1993s) 323s (C.S. *Rodd*: exciting, rich; but not guidance on modern problems).

8357 *Masia Clavel* Juan, [Juan Pablo II, Veritatis splendor], ¿Moral de diálogo o moral de recetas?: EstE 69 (1994) 225-253.

8358 **May** William E., An introduction to moral theology²ʳᵉᵛ [¹1991]. Huntington IN 1994, Our Sunday Visitor. 288 p. $10. 0-87973-453-1 [TDig 42,177]. – ᴿLinacreQ 60,1 (1993) 91-93 (J.D. *Mindling*).

8359 *May* William E., Los actos intrínsecamente malos y la enseñanza de la encíclica 'Veritas splendor': ScripTPamp 26 (1994) 199-219 (123-197, 249-262, *al.*).

8360 **Meeks** Wayne A., The origins of Christian morality; the first two centuries. NHv 1994, Yale Univ. 275 p. $35. 0-300-05640-0. – ᴱChrCent 111 (1994) 989-993, V.P. *Furnish*, also on MARXSEN W.); Churchman 108 (1994) 368s (R.S. *Ascough*); ExpTim 105,8 top choice (1993s) 225s (C.S. *Rodd*).

8361 **Melina** L., Morale, tra crisi e rinnovamento. Mi 1993, Ares. 106 p. – ScripTPamp 26 (1994) 1163-6 (M.P. *Río*).

8362 *a) Merks* Karl-Wilhelm, Das Recht anders zu sein; eine Chance für die Moral; Pluralismus zwischen Freiheit und Verantwortlichkeit; – *b) Vos*

H. M., Pluralisme, geweten en verantwoordelijkheid: Bijdragen 55 (1994) 2-22; Eng. 23 / 24-41, Eng. 42.

8363 *Młotek* Antoni, Alla ricerca della particolarità della teologia morale polacca: Angelicum 71 (1994) 187-202.

8364 **Mouw** Richard J., The God who commands; a study in divine command ethics, ND 1990 ➤ 7,8374: ᴿWestTJ 55 (1993) 176-8 (W. *Edgar*).

8365 *Müller* Denis, Chronique d'éthique théologique; chassez le naturel... ambiguité et permanence d'un retour: ÉTRel 69 (1994) 89-94.

8366 **Murdoch** Ian, Metaphysics as a guide to morals. NY 1992, Lane/ Penguin. 520 p. $35. – ᴿJRel 74 (1994) 278-280 (Maria *Antonaccio*: metaphysics, but along with religion... and art).

8367 *Neuhaus* Richard J., *Burrell* D., *Hauerwas* S., *al.*, The splendor of truth, a symposium: FirsT 39 (1994) 14-29.

8368 *Nieuwenhove* Jacques Van, *Klein Goldewijk* Berma, Mensenrechten als rechten van God: TvT 34 (1994) 3-22; 23, Human rights as God's right; a profile of Paulo E. card. ARNS (for honorary doctorate).

8369 **O'Donovan** Oliver, Résurrection et expérience morale; esquisse d'une éthique théologique, ᵀ*Lacoste* Jean-Yves: Théologies. P 1992, PUF. 346 p. – ᴿRThom 94 (1994) 670-5 (G. *Narcisse*).

8370 **Olasky** Marvin, Abortion rites; a social history of abortion in America. Wheaton 1992, Crossway. 318-xiii p. $25; pa. $14. – ᴿTrinJ 14 (1993) 215-8 (C. B. *Mitchell*); WestTJ 55 (1993) 364-6 (J. L. *Marshall*).

8371 *a) Penna* Romano, Nuovo Testamento ed esigenza morale; – *b) Cozzoli* Mauro, La verità principio normativa della morale nella Veritatis Splendor: Lateranum 60,1 (L'enciclica 'Veritatis Splendor' 1994) 5-26; Eng. 27 / 69-97; Eng. 97.

8372 **Pinckaers** Servais, Le fonti della morale cristiana; metodo, contenuto, storia [1985 ➤ 2,6548],ᵀ: Ragione e fede 14. Mi 1992, Ares. 608 p. Lᵐ 48. – ᴿAnnT 7 (1993) 505-8 (E. *Colom*); Asprenas 41 (1994) 132s (R. *Russo*); CC 145 (1994,2) 610s (F. *Cultrera*).

8373 **Pizzorni** Reginaldo M., Giustizia e 'carita' nel pensiero (greco-)romano / nella dottrina dei Padri: Sapienza 46 (1993) 121-179 / 361-406.

8374 *Que* Nemesio S., / *Roche* Joseph L., ... on Veritatis Splendor: Landas 8 (1994) 237-254, to be continued / 255-276.

8375 **Ranke-Heinemann** Uta, Eunucos por el reino de los cielos; la Iglesia católica y la sexualidad [1988 ➤ 5,8353], ᵀ*Abelardo Martínez* Víctor. M 1994, Trotta. 334 p. 84-876-9986-3. – ᴿEstE 69 (1994) 280s (A. *Verdoy*: insufrible a parte la traducción eccelente).

8375* *Rasmussen* Douglas B., Reclaiming liberalism: Thomist 58 (1994) 109-139.

8376 *a) Ratzinger* Joseph, Christian faith as 'the Way'; an introduction to Veritatis Splendor; – *b) May* William E., An overview of the encyclical; – *c) Martin* Francis, The integrity of Christian moral activity... 1 Jn: ComWsh 21 (1994) 199-207 / 229-251 [208-243, *al.*] / 265-285.

8377 **Riddle** J. M., Conception and abortion from the ancient world to the Renaissance 1992 ➤ 8,8558; 9,8823: ᴿNYRevB 40,19 (1993) 52s (W. V. *Harris*: 'Old Wives' Tales').

8378 *Ruiz de la Peña* Juan L., La verdad, el bien y el ser; un paseo por la ética de la mano de la 'Veritatis splendor': Salmanticensis 41 (1994) 37-54; Eng. 65 [261-271, *Rodríguez* Leonardo].

8379 *Russo* Giovanni, (*al.*), Sulla Veritatis splendor: Itinerarium 2 (Messina 1994) 161-170 (-202).

8380 *Schlögel* Herbert, Euthanasia and theology [... how one defines the human person (SINGER P. 1979); < ZkT 114 (1992) 425-439]; TE*Asen* B. A.: TDig 41 (1994) 15-19.
8381 **Schnackenburg** R., El mensaje moral del NT 1991 ⟶ 7,8365; 8,8563: RCiuD 206 (1993) 224-7 (J. *Gutiérrez*, 1s).
8382 FSCHNACKENBURG R., EMerklein H., NT & Ethik 1989 ⟶ 5,173: RCiuD 206 (1993) 645 (J. *Gutiérrez*).
8382* *Schrijver* Georges de, Veritatis splendor; reacties van theologen: Streven 61 (1994) 127-140.
8383 **Schürmann** Heinz, Studien zur neutestamentlichen Ethik [13 art.], ESöding T. 1990 ⟶ 6,299; 9,8831: RSalesianum 56 (1994) 576 (G. *Abbà*).
8384 *Schützeichel* Harald, Homosexualität, ein Diskussionsbeitrag: StiZt 119 (1994) 489-497 [> TDig 42,47-51, TE*Asen* B.].
8384* *Segalla* Giuseppe, Introduzione all'etica biblica del NT 1989 ⟶ 6, 300 ... 8,8566: RProtestantesimo 49 (1994) 161-7 (B. *Corsani*, anche su SCHRAGE W., SCHNACKENBURG R.; LOHSE E.).
8385 ESelling Joe, *Jans* Jan, The splendor of accuracy. Kampen/GR 1994, Kok/Eerdmans. 181 p. DM 49,50. – RDocLife 44 (1994) 510-2 (S. *Fagan*; good).
8385* *a*) *Selling* Joseph A., Veritatis splendor and the sources of morality; – *b*) *Rigali* Norbert J., Christian morality and universal morality; the one and the many: LvSt 19 (1994) 3-17 / 18-33.
8386 *Simon* René, Morale commune et thééologie face à la vie et à la mort: RechSR 82,4 ('Problèmes de la vie' 1994) (497-)565-586 (Eng. 491-5).
8387 *Simonds* Thomas A., AQUINAS and early term abortion: Linacre Q 61,3 (1994) 10-...
8388 **Sleeper** C. Freeman, The Bible and the moral life 1992 ⟶ 8,8568; 9,8834; 0-664-25375-X: RExpTim 105 (1993s) 59s (R. G. *Jones*: Church statements cite the Bible but not competently); PrincSemB 14 (1993) 315-7 (B. R. *Reno*: thin); RefR 48 (1994s) 139 (S. *Mathonnet-VanderWell*); RelStR 20 (1994) 47 (Pheme *Perkins*); RExp 91 (1994) 625s (D. P. *Gushee*).
8389 **Storkey** Alan, The meanings of love. Leicester 1994, Inter-Varsity. 171 p. £7.
8390 **Szostek** Andrzej, Natur-Vernunft-Freiheit; philosophische Analyse der Konzeption 'schöpferischer Vernunft' in der zeitgenössischen Moraltheologie: EurHS 23/447. Fra 1992, Lang. vi-296 p. Fs 73. 2-631-43861-3. – RZkT 116 (1994) 510-3 (K. H. *Neufeld*).
8391 *Tavernier* Johan de, Vraagt ethiek om geloof?: TvT 34 (1994) 24-47; 47s, Is faith a presupposition of ethics? Ethical explorations in the works of E. *Schillebeeckx*.
8392 *Thornhill* John: AustralasCR 71 (1994) 131-144 / 145-162.
8393 FUFFENHEIMER B., Justice & righteousness, EReventlow H., *Hoffmann* Y., 1990/2 ⟶ 8,499: RCBQ 56 (1994) 184 (J. T. *Walsh*).
8394 *Ureña Pastor* Manuel, obispo, Contexto, contenidos y alcance de la carta-encíclica de JUAN PABLO II, 'Veritatis splendor': AnVal 29 (1993) 233-265.
8395 *Weber* Helmut, Zur Enzyklika 'Veritatis splendor' — Erinnerungen an Fundamente oder Stolpersteine?: TrierTZ 103 (1994) 161-197.
8396 *Weibel* Rolf, Glanz der Wahrheit; Licht und Schatten: HerdKorr 47 (1993) [569-580 Kernpassagen] 623-630.
8397 **Wogaman** J. Philip, Christian Ethics, a historical introduction 1993 ⟶ 9,8846; also L 1993, SPCK. 340 p., £15; 0-281-04733-2. – RExpTim

105,7 top choice (1993s) 193s (C. S. *Rodd*); TLond 97 (1994) 136s (R. *Gill*).

H8.4   *NT ipsum de reformatione sociali* – **Political action in Scripture.**

8398 **Amante Castasus** Alex R., The biblical basis of the Church's social doctrine; Christian exegesis of the Bible in the social encyclicals of Pope John Paul II: diss. ᴰ*Ausín* S. Pamplona 1994. 397 p. – RTLv 26, p. 563.
8399 **Andrade** Paulo F. C., de, Capitalismo e socialismo. São Paulo 1993, Loyola. 85-15-00751-7. – ᴿPerspT 26 (1994) 125 (J. B. *Libanio*).
8400 **Assmann** Hugo, *Hinkelammert* Franz, Götze Markt [1989 ⇒ 8,8587], ᵀᴱ*Goldstein* Horst: BtBefreiung 16 (aus 50). Dü 1992, Patmos. 230 p. ᴅᴹ 45. – ᴿTR 90 (1994) 159s (J. *Wiemeyer*).
8401 ᴱ**Atherton** John, Social Christianity; a reader. L 1994, SPCK. xii-410 p. £20 pa. – ᴿTLond 97 (1994) 388s (A. *Suggate*: good).
8402 **Bauckham** Richard, The Bible in politics; how to read the Bible politically 1989 ⇒ 6,8415... 8,8590: ᴿChrSchR 22 (1993s) 101s (R. *Zwier*); CritRR 6 (1993) 121s (B. *Birch*).
8403 *Bayer* Richard C., Christian personalism and democratic capitalism [*Novak* M. ...]: Horizons 21 (1994) 313-331.
8404 *Berlie* Emilio, Hacia una comunidad socio-económica mundial: Ecclesia 8 (México 1994) 6-18.
8405 *Bertelloni* Francisco, Politologische Ansichten bei den Artisten um 1230/1240; zur Deutung des anonymen Pariser Studienplans Hs Ripoll 108: TPhil 69 (1994) 34-73.
8406 *Berten* Ignace, Espérance chrétienne et réalités économiques aujourd'hui: FoiTemps 23 (1993) 293-310 (-332).
8407 *Bivin* David, Jesus' attitude toward riches: JPersp 45 (1994) 9-11 . 13.
8408 *a) Brennan* Geoffrey, Freedom, government and economics [response *Loomis* Ralph]; – *b) Hawtrey* Kim, Work; four prevalent challenges to the biblical view: Transformation 9,1 (1992) 15-19 [-20] / 1-5.
8409 **Burns** Gene, The frontiers of Catholicism; the politics of ideology in a liberal world. Berkeley 1992, Univ. California. 269 p. – ᴿArchivScSocR 39,88 (1994) 54s (Danièle *Hervieu-Léger*).
8410 *Calvez* Jean-Yves, El humanismo marxiano ['de Marx mismo', non 'marxista']: Stromata 50 (1994) 127-133.
8411 **Camacho** Ildefonso, Doctrina social de la Iglesia; una aproximación histórica. M 1991, Paulinas. 619 p. 84-285-1140-2. – ᴿEstE 69 (1994) 255-9 (G. *Higuera*).
8412 **Carol i Hostench** A., Hombre, economía y ética. Pamplona 1993, EUNSA. 230 p. – ᴿAnnTh 8 (1994) 197-200 (E. *Colom*).
8412* *Carol i Hostench* Antoni, Economía, ética y fe [Fᴀʟɪsᴇ M.]: ScripTPamp 26 (1994) 697-712.
8413 *Cassano* Angelo, L'etica politica delle prime comunità anabattiste: Protestantesimo 40 (1994) 372-382.
8414 ᴱ**Chewning** Richard C., Biblical principles and business. Colorado Springs 1989, Navpress. 304 p. $16. 0-8910-9556-X. – ᴿChrSchR 23 (1993s) 216-8 (D. B. *Newton*).
8415 Christian faith and the world economy today; a study document. Geneva 1992, WCC. – ᴿProtestantesimo 48 (1993) 227s (G. *Guelmani*).
8416 *Cobb* John B., A challenge to American theology and philosophy ['strengthening of neo-liberal economic theory and practice' by the

collapse of communism 'is a disaster']: (responses *Pederson* Ann M., *Soneson* Jerome P.): AmJTP 15 (1994) 123-136 (137-151 / 153-161).

8417 *Dal Covolo* Enrico, C'è salvezza per il ricco? Il problema della povertà e della ricchezza alle origini della Chiesa: RicT 3 (R 1992) 125-141 [< ZIT 93,405].

8418 *de Gruchy* John W., Christianity and democratization: RefW 44 (1994) 135-160.

8419 **Dölken** Clemens, Katholische Sozialtheorie und liberale Ökonomik. Tü 1992, Mohr. 3-15-145900-8. – ᴿAntonianum 69 (1994) 129-131 (L. *Oviedo*).

8420 **Duchrow** U., Alternativen zur kapitalistischen Weltherrschaft; biblische Erinnerung und politische Ansätze zur Überwindung einer schwerbedrohenden Ökonomie. Gü/Mainz 1994, Gü/Grünewald. 316 p. DM 29,80. 3-579-02282-2 / 3-7867-1752-4. – ᴿTvT 34 (1994) 453 (B. Van *Driessche*).

8421 *a) Duchrow* Ulrich, Biblical perspectives on empire; a view from western Europe: EcuR 46 (1994) 21-27; – *b) Ondra* J. N., Some biblical reflections on the changes in Europe: EcuR 45 (1993) 146-150.

8422 **Ellingsen** Mark, The cutting edge; how Churches speak on social issues. Geneva/GR 1993, WCC/Eerdmans. xxiii-370 p. £18 pa. – ᴿMid-Stream 33 (1994) 491-3 (G. C. *West*); TLond 97 (1994) 295s (K. *Clements*: invaluable catalogue; and the differences shown can hardly ever be traced to dogma-divergences).

8423 **Enderle** Georg, *al.*, Lexikon der Wirtschaftsethik. FrB 1993, Herder. 704 p. – ᴿBrotéria 137 (1993) 451-5 (B. da *Graça*).

8424 **Fabris** Rinaldo, La opción por los pobres en la Biblia, ᵀ*Ortiz* A., 1992 ↝ 9,8607: ᴿRelCu 40 (1994) 879 (A. *Moral*).

8425 **Garaudy** Roger, Les fossoyeurs [gravediggers], un nouvel appel aux vivants. P 1992, L'archipel. 262 p. – ᴿEcuR 45 (1993) 122s (A. van der *Bent*: successfully relates politics to faith).

8426 **Gelm** Richard J., Politics and religious authority; American Catholics since the Second Vatican Council: ContribStRel 36. Westport CT 1994, Greenwood. xiii-151 p. $50. 0-313-28903-4 [TDig 42,60].

8427 *a) González* Carlos Ignacio, Fundamentos bíblicos del destino universal de los bienes; – *b) Vélez* C. Jaime, La Rerum Novarum, una encíclica profética: TXav 42,101 ('Profetismo social, cien años' 1992) 55-74 / 7-16.

8428 **Gonzalez** Justo L., Faith and wealth; a history of early Christian ideas on the origin, significance and use of money 1990 ↝ 6,8436... 9,8892: ᴿScotJT 47 (1994) 125s (S. G. *Hall*).

8429 **Gordon** Barry, The economic problem in biblical and patristic thought 1989 ↝ 7,8434; 8,8617: ᴿAugM 37 (1992) 211s (J. *Oroz*); Judaism 41 (1992) 106-8 (M. *Perlman*).

8430 **Gottwald** Norman K., The Bible as nurturer of passive and active worldviews [political economy and religion in the Bible; liberation hermeneutics presupposed...]: ↝ 107, ᶠRᴜᴛᴇɴʙᴇʀ C., PerspRelSt 21,4 (1994) 313-327.

8431 *Habisch* André, Christliche Anthropologie und Ethos der Marktwirtschaft: StiZt 212 (1994) 605-617.

8432 **Halteman** Jim, Market capitalism and Christianity. GR 1998, Baker. 176 p. $10. 0-8010-4327-1. – ᴿChrSchR 23 (1993s) 476-8 (P. L. *Morgan*).

8433 **Harries** Richard, Is there a gospel for the rich? The Christian in a capitalist world 1992 ↝ 8,8619*: ᴿTLond 97 (1994) 232s (G. *Vinten*).

8434 **Hart** Stephen, What does the Lord require? 1992 ↝ 9,8895: ᴿJRel 74 (1994) 583s (D. A. *Krueger*).

8435 *Hauerwas* S., When the politics of Jesus makes a difference [valorizing J. YODER 1972]: ChrCent 110 (1993) 982-7.

8436 **Hawken** Paul, The ecology of commerce; a declaration of sustainability. NY 1993, HarperBusiness. – ᴿCreSp 10 (1994) 29s (M. *Fox*: powerful).

8437 *a*) *Hay* Donald, What does the Lord require? Three statements on Christian faith and economic life; – *b*) *Beisner* E. Calvin, Justice and poverty, two views contrasted [response *Mott* Stephen C.', The partiality of biblical justice]; – *c*) *Snyder* Howard, Models of the Kingdom; sorting out the practical meaning of God's reign: Transformation 10,1 (1993) 11-15 / 16-22 [23-29] / 1-8.

8438 *a*) *Hoksbergen* Roland, Is there a Christian economics? Some thoughts in light of the rise of postmodernism; – *b*) *Ballard* Bruce, On the sin of usury; a biblical economic ethic; – *c*) *Abou-Zeid* Bassem, The North American free trade agreement with Mexico; a biblical perspective: ChrSchR 24 (1994s) 126-142 / 210-228 / 196-209.

8439 *Honecker* Martin, Sozialethische Diskurse: TRu 59 (1994) 442-8.

8440 **Jüngel** Eberhard, Christ, justice and peace [Barmen 1934]. E 1992, Clark. 93 p. £9. 0-567-29212-6. – ᴿExpTim 105 (1993s) 58s (E. *Robertson*: powerful).

8441 **Jeremy** David J., Capitalists and Christians; business leaders and the Church in Britain, 1900-1960. Ox 1990, Clarendon. xviii-491 p. £45. – ᴿEngHR 109 (1994) 524s (G. I. T. *Machin*).

8442 *Kroeker* P. Travis, The humanization of production; a critique of [U.S. bishops'] Economic justice for all: ÉglT 25 (1994) 65-83.

8443 **Lewis** James W., Christianity and capitalism; a critique of selected Roman Catholic and Protestant accounts of economic ethics: diss. Duke, ᴰ*Hauerwas* S. Durham NC 1994, 479 p. 95-00501. – DissA 55 (1994s) p. 2442.

8444 *Maddox* Randy J., WESLEYAN resources for a contemporary theology of the poor?: AsbTJ 49,1 (1994) 35-47.

8445 *Manenschijn* Gerrit, The quest for a just economy in a new Europe; ethical implications of the social market economy: LvSt 58 (1993) 159-174.

8446 **Manzone** G., La libertà cristiana e le sue mediazioni sociali nel pensiero di J. ELLUL. Mi 1993, Glossa. 286 p. Lᵐ 45. – ᴿRasT 35 (1994) 622s (B. *Marra*).

8447 *Manzone* Gianni, Libertà cristiana e società tecnologica nel pensiero di J. ELLUL: RasT 35 (1994) 445-463.

8848 **Marsden** John, Marxism and Christian utopianism; toward a socialist political theology. NY 1991, Monthly Review. $16. – ᴿHeythJ 35 (1994) 356s (P. *Surlis*).

8449 *May* Collin, Bernard LONERGAN and political theory: ⇒ 8,26*, ꟼCAHILL P. J., RelStT 12,2 (1992) 43-68.

8450 **Milbank** John. Theology and social theory 1991 ⇒ 8,8641; 9,8921: ᴿJRel 74 (1994) 113s (R. *Lovin*); NOxR 61,3 (1994) 31s (P. E. *Devine*: argument rich but failed); ScotJT 46 (1993) 527-535 (R. H. *Roberts*).

8451 **Misner** Paul, Social Catholicism in Europe, from the onset of industrialization to the first World War 1991 ⇒ 9,8924: ᴿHeythJ 35 (1994) 339-341 (P. *Burns*: Darton-LT); JRel 74 (1994) 100 (S. *Pope*).

8452 *Moltmann* Jürgen, Covenant or Leviathan?; political theology for modern times, ᵀ*Bedford* Nancy E.: ScotJT 47 (1994) 19-44.

8453 **Mott** Steven C., A Christian perspective on political thought. Ox 1993, UP. 338 p. $55. – ᴿWWorld 14 (1994) 102.106 (W. *Sundberg*).

8454 *Musella* Marco, I vescovi italiani e i problemi economici del paese; riflessioni sul recente documento della Commissione episcopale per i problemi sociali e il lavoro: RasT 35 (1994) 555-568.

8455 *Negrut* Paul, The world after the collapse of Marxism and the failure of secularism (Laing Lecture 1993): VoxEvca 22 (1993) 25-33 (-40) responses).

8456 **Nelson** Robert H., Reaching for heaven on earth; the theological meaning of economics. Savage MD 1991, Rowman & L. xxvii-378 p. $25; pa. $17. 0-8476-7664-1; -226-3024-9. – ᴿChrSchR 24 (1994s) 229 (R. A. *Black*).

8457 **Novak** Michael, The Catholic ethic and the spirit of capitalism 1993 ➤ 9,8936: ᴿCathSchR 24 (1994s) 232-5 (B. R. *Dalgaard*); ChrC 110 (1994) 58s (I. *Hexham*).

8458 ᴱO'**Brien** David J., *Shannon* Thomas A., Catholic social thought; the documentary heritage. Mkn 1992, Orbis. viii-688 p. $50; $25. – ᴿMidStream 33 (1994) 121-4 (H. *Hatt*).

8459 O'**Brien** John, Theology and the option for the poor: Theology & Life 22. ColMn 1992, Liturgical. 167 p. 0-8146-5787-7.

8460 **Peschke** Karl-Heinz, Wirtschaft aus christlicher Sicht: Ordo socialis 2. Trier 1992, Paulinus. 96 p. DM 9,80. – ᴿTR 90 (1994) 430-2 (F. *Furger*).

8461 *Pawlas* Andreas, Ist 'Kaufhandel' immer 'Wucher'? LUTHER zu kaufmännischen Handel und Wucher als Beitrag zu einer evangelischen Wirtschaftsethik: KerDo 40 (1994) 282-304; Is bargain always usury? [... and is Kaufhandel always bargain?].

8462 **Peters** Tiemo R., Mystik, Mythos, Metaphysik; die Spur des vermissten Gottes; Forum politische Theologie 10. Mainz/Mü 1992, Grünewald/ Kaiser. 170 p. DM 28,50. – ᴿTR 90 (1994) 62s (J. *Werbick*: Weggefährte von METZ).

8463 *Pieris* Aloysius, Three inadequacies in the social encyclicals: Vidyajyoti 57 (1993) 73-94.

8464 **Preston** Ronald H., Religion and the ambiguities of capitalism 1991 ➤ 8,8652; 9,8946: ᴿChrSchR 24 (1994s) 235s (S. M. *Lee*); ScotJT 46 (1993) 414-6 (T. S. *Torrance*).

8465 *Prien* Hans-Jürgen, LUTHERs Wirtschaftsethik 1992 ➤ 9,8947: ᴿDLZ 114 (1993) 98-102 (G. *Wendelborn*); HZ 259 (1994) 207-9 (P. *Blickle*).

8466 **Rasmussen** Arne, The Church as 'polis'; from political theology to theological politics as exemplified by Jürgen MOLTMANN and Stanley HAUERWAS: diss. Lund 1994. 91-7966-363-3. – RTLv 26, p. 562.

8467 *Rheenen* Gailyn van, Cultural conceptions of power in biblical perspective: Missiology 21,1 (1993) 41-54 [< ZIT 93,192].

8468 **Rich** Arthur, Éthique économique [1990 ➤ 9,8949],ᵀ. Genève 1994, Labor et Fides. 705 p. F 220. – ᴿRHPR 74 (1994) 461-4 (G. *Vahanian*).

8469 **Rich** David, Myths of the tribe: when religion, ethics, government, and economics convergence. Buffalo 1993, Prometheus. 296 p. £25. 0-87975-824-4. – ᴿTBR 7,2 (1994s) 43s (G. *Howes*: odd proposal of a new more humane adult religion).

8470 *Robinson* Simon, Prophecy [Church's role stereotyped and undervalued by J. *Mahoney*] and modern business ethics: Month [254 (1993) 56.112] 255 (1994) 307-310.

8471 *Rossé* Gérard, L'insegnamento della Scrittura come premessa all' 'economia di comunione': NuovUm 14,80 (1992) 21-31.

8472 *Santa Ana* Julio de, About faith, economics and something else: RefW 44 (1994) 50-58 (-88, on economic reform for African women).

8473 **Schmitz** Philipp, Wohin treibt die Politik? Über die Notwendigkeit von Ethik: QDisp 149, 1993 → 9,8957: FrB 1993, Herder. 280 p. DM 50. – ᴿTR 90 (1994) 429s (J. *Wiemeyer*).

8474 **Segura** Joseba, *al.*, Economía de mercado, crisis industrial y sabiduría cristiana: Inst. Dir. Bilbao. Bilbao 1992, D-Brouwer. 130 p. – ᴿScrip-TPamp 26 (1994) 890s (V. *Ferrero*).

8475 **Sicker** Martin, What Judaism says about politics; the political theology of the Torah. Northvale NJ 1994, Aronson. xiv-252 p.; bibliog. 225-245. 0-87668-778-1.

8476 **Sider** Ronald J., Rich Christians in an age of hunger[3rev]. Dallas 1990, Word. 261 p. – ᴿSWJT 36,3 (1993s) 74s (R. E. *Higgins*).

8477 **Tanner** Kathryn, The politics of God; Christian theologies and social justice 1992 → 9,8966: ᴿJTS 45 (1994) 809-811 (D. B. *Forrester*).

8477* *Uthemann* K.-H., Eine christliche Diatribe über Armut und Reichtum (CPG 4969); handschriftliche Überlieferung und christliche Edition: VigChr 48 (1994) 235-290.

8478 **Veerkamp** Ton, Autonomie und Egalität; Ökonomie, Politik und Ideologie in der Schrift: Im Lehrhaus 4. B 1993, Alektor. 380 p. 3- 88425-057-4. – ᴿDielB 28 (1992s) 216-8 (B. J. *Diebner*).

8479 *Voulgarakis* Élie, Saint Jean CHRYSOSTOME et l'éthique sociale: TAth 65 (1994) 80-90.

8480 **Yoder** John H., The politics of Jesus; vicit Agnus noster[2] [[1]1972 with epilogue]. GR/Carlisle 1994, Eerdmans/ Paternoster. xiii-257 p. $17 pa. 0-8028-0734-8/ [TDig 42,195].

8481 *Żebrok* Józef, ❷ Conception de l'économie et ressources de la nature: PrzPow 859 (1993) 438-450.

H8.5 Theologia liberationis latino-americana.

8482 **Agudelo Giraldo** Guillermo, La gran gesta apostólica de la Iglesia (V Centenario): Bogotá-Santafé 1992, Verdad y Vida. 256 p. – TXav 42 (1992) 283 (A. *Echeverri*).

8483 **Altmann** Walter, LUTHER and liberation; a Latin American perspective, ᵀ*Solberg* Mary M. 1991 → 8,8674*; 9,8977: ᴿCurrTM 20 (1993) 221s (Luis H. *Dreher*).

8484 *a) Altmann* Walter, Europa; Überlegungen eines lateinamerikanischen Christen; – *b) Sundermeier* Theo, Pluralismus, Fundamentalismus, Koinonia [Suh Kwang-Sun, in Korea]: EvT 54 (1994) 362-374 / 293-310 [-316].

8485 **Aquino Vargas** Maria Pilar, Nuestro clamor por la vida 1992 → 9,8980: ᴿPerspT 26 (1994) 286s (J. de *León*).

8486 *Avendaño* F., La teología de la liberación; ¿una teología todavía vigente?: Senderos 43 (Costa Rica) 1993) 63-77 [44 (1993) 43-68,... y Postmodernidad, *Robles Robles* J. A.: < Stromata 50 (1994) 254s].

8487 **Bastian** Jean-Pierre, Le Protestantisme en Amérique latine; une approche socio-historique. Genève 1994, Labor et Fides. 324 p. – ᴿRHPR 74 (1994) 226s (*ipse*).

8488 **Bastian** Jean-Pierre, Historia del protestantismo en América Latina [franç. 96 p. 1991 → 9,8982*]. México [2]1990, CUPSA. 307 p. – ᴿNZMiss 48 (1992) 72 (J. *Baumgartner*).

8489 **Batstone** David, From conquest to struggle... Latin America 1991 → 7,8494... 9,8983: ᴿCritRR 6 (1993) 495-7 (J. R. *Sibley*); ÉglT 24 (1993) 448s (J. Van den *Hengel*).

8490 *Berganza* Carlos,   Teología [amer-]india: CiTom 120 (1993) 79-100.

8490* *Berger* Marc,   Mexique; l'Église et la cause des pauvres; la solidarité controversée de Mgr RUIZ avec les Indiens du Chiapas: Sève 556 (1994) 53-57.

8491 *Berzosa Marínez* Raúl,   La teología de la liberación; apuntes históricos, representantes, métodos, perspectivas: LumenVr 42 (1993) 200-241.

8491* **Bigó** Pierre,   Debate en la Iglesia; teología de la liberación.   Santiago de Chile 1991, Ilades.   168 p. – ᴿEfMex 12 (1994) 134s (E. *Bonnín*).

8492 **Boff** Leonardo,   New Evangelization; good news to the poor 1992 ➤ 9, 8993b: ᴿLvSt 18 (1993) 77s (Lieven *Boeve*).

8493 **Boff** Leonardo,   La nouvelle évangélisation dans la perspective des opprimés [1990 ➤ 9,8993a],ᵀ. P 1992, Cerf. 176 p. F 120.   2-204-04573-X. – ᴿÉTRel 68 (1993) 461s (M. *Müller*).

8494 *a) Boff* Leonardo,   Une alternative de pouvoir dans l'Église; – *b) Parker Gumucio* Cristián,   The sociology of religion in Latin America; teaching and research: Social Compass 41 (Lv 1994) 503-511 / 332-354.

8495 **Borges** Pedro,   Historia de la Iglesia en Hispanoamérica y Filipinas (siglos XV-XIX),ᵀ,   1992 ➤ 9,8994:   ᴿCarthaginensia 9 (1993) 456-8 (R. *Sanz Valdivieso*, también sobre 12 semejantes); Hispania Sacra 46 (1994) 386s (J. *Goñi Gaztambide*).

8496 *a) Borges* Pedro,   Evangelización y conflicto cultural en América; – *b) García García* Antonio,   Los problemas del Nuevo Mundo en los precursores de [Francisco de] VITORIA: StOvet 21 ('Asturias en América' 1993) 41-49 / 29-40 [5-276 al.].

8497 **Borobio** Dionisio,   Evangelización y sacramentos en la Nueva España (s. XIV) según Jerónimo de MENDIETA; lecciones de ayer para hoy. Marcia 1992, Inst.Teol.Franciscano.   191 p. – ᴿEstE 68 (1993) 268-270 (A. *Santos Hernández*: 's. XIV').

8497* **Brighenti** Agenor,   Raíces de la epistemología y del método de la teología latinoamericana [< diss. Lv 1993]: Medellín 20 (1994) 207-254 [< TContext 12,86].

8498 **Casaldáliga** Pedro, *Vigil* José M.,   *a)* Espiritualidad de la liberación. BA 1992, Centro Nueva Tierra. 286 p. – ᴿPáginas 18 (1993) 103s (A. *Gispert-Sauch*). – *b)* Espiritualidade da libertação, ᵀ*Clasen* Jaime A. São Paulo 1993, Vozes.   247 p. 85-326-0932-5. – ᴿPerspT 26 (1994) 118-121 (F. *Taborda*); REB 54 (1994) 225-9 (F. *Taborda*).

8499 ᴱ**Collet** Giancarlo,   Der Christus der Armen, ᵀ*Berz* A. 1988 ➤ 5,452; 8,8695: ᴿTR 90 (1994) 57s (M. *Sievernich*).

8500 *Delgado* Mariano,   Inkulturation oder Transkulturation; der missionstheologische Charakter der Evangelisierung der altamerikanischen Kulturen am Beispiel des abendländisch geprägten trinitarischen Gottesbegriffs: NZMiss 48 (1992) 161-190.

8501 ᴱ**Dunnavant** Anthony L.,   Poverty and ecclesiology; nineteenth century evangelicals in the light of liberation theology 1992 ➤ 8,350; 9,9006: ᴿExpTim 105 (1993s) 90 (J. *Kent*: 'gradual collapse of the conservative R. C. church'); Mid-Stream 33 (1994) 366-9 (R. E. *Osborn*: for 20 years the politically-correct watchword 'God's preferential option for the poor' has arrogantly oriented young seminary Christians toward sophisticated well-to-do theologians, ignoring what has been done by poor clergy for poor backwoodsmen).

8502 ᴱ**Düssel** Enrique, The Church in Latin America, 1492-1992: A history of the Church in the Third World 1, 1992 ➤ 9,9007: ᴿCurrTM 21 (1994) 134s (Guillermo *Hansen*); LvSt 19 (1994) 383s (L. *Kenis*); NRT 116 (1994) 618s (N. *Plumat*).

8503 ᴱ**Ellacuria** I., *Sobrino* J., Mysterium liberationis; i concetti fondamentali della teologia della liberazione [1990 ➤ 7,8513 ... 9,9008]. – ᴿRasT 34 (1993) 586s (G. *Mattai*).

8504 **Ellacuria** Ignazio, *Sobrino* Jon, Mysterium liberationis; fundamental concepts of liberation theology [1990 ➤ 7,8513: abridged],ᵀ. Mkn/North Blackburn, Australia 1993, Orbis / CollinsDove. xv-252 p. $45. – ᴿPrinc-SemB 15 (1994) 310s (R. *Shaull*: magnificent; not quite adequate).

8505 *Galli* Carlos M., Evangelización, cultura y teología; el aporte di J.C. Scannone a una teología inculturada: TArg 28 (1991) 189-202.

8506 **García Oro** José, Prehistoria y primeros capítulos de la evangelización de América. Caracas 1988, Tripode. 432 p. – ᴿVerVida 50 (1992) 451s (G. *Calvo*).

8507 ᴱ**Garrard-Burnett** Virginia, *Stoll* David, Rethinking Protestantism in Latin America. Ph 1993, Temple Univ. vi-234 p. $40; pa. $19. 1-56639-102-4; -3-2 [TDig 42,86: some juggling of religious identities].

8508 **González Faus** J.I., Vicarios de Cristo; los pobres en la teología y espiritualidad cristiana. M 1991, Trotta. 366 p. – ᴿCarthaginensia 9 (1993) 470 (P. *Martínez Fresneda*).

8509 *Ganzález Faus* J.I., Poder, or, alteritat i Evangeli: QVidCr 166 (1993) 6-25.

8510 **Gossen** Gary H., *León-Portilla* Miguel, South and Meso-American native spirituality; from the cult of the feathered serpent to the theology of liberation: EncWSp. L 1993, SCM. 563 p. £35. 0-334-02542-7 [Exp-Tim 105,191].

8511 **Greenleaf** Floyd, The Seventh-day Adventist church in Latin America and the Caribbean; 1. Let the earth hear his voice; 2. Bear the news to every land. Berrien Springs MI 1992, Andrews Univ. iv-470 p.; ii-542 p. $40. – ᴿAndrUnS 32 (1994) 135-7 (A.R. *Timm*).

8512 **Gutiérrez** Gustavo, The God of life 1991 ➤ 8,8722; 9,9015: ᴿEcuR 45 (1993) 496s (H. *Malschitzky*).

Gutiérrez Gustavo, Dieu ou l'or 1992 / En busca de los pobres 1992 ➤ Las Casas 16510s.

8513 *Hallencreutz* Carl F., Third World Church History — an integral part of theological education: ST 47 (1993) 29-47.

8514 *Hanks* Tom, Liberation theology after 25 years; passé or mainstream?: Anvil 10 (1993) 197-208 [< zIT 93,643].

8515 **Hewitt** Marsha A., From theology to social theory; Juan Luis Segundo and the theology of liberation: AmUnivSt 7/73. NY 1990, Lang. x-184 p. $42. – ᴿCritRR 6 (1993) 513s (C. *Cadorette*).

8516 *Hewitt* Marsha, Liberation theology and the emancipation of religion: ScotJR 13 (1992) 21-38.

8517 **Hoornaert** Eduardo, La mémoire du peuple chrétien [portugais; point de vue brésilien],ᵀ [avec préface dure de C. *Munier*: 'fausses notes', 'lacunes inquiétantes']. P 1992, Cerf. 295 p. F 175. 2-204-04391-5. – ᴿÉTRel 69 (1994) 111 (F. *Zorn*: quand même rend aussi fidèlement la tradition avec ses a priori).

8518 ᴱ**Hünermann** Peter, *Eckholt* Margit, Katholische Soziallehre – Wirt-schaft – Demokratie; ein lateinamerikanisch-deutsches Dialogprogramm 1: Entwicklung und Frieden 51. Mainz/Mü 1989, Grünewald/ Kaiser. 346 p. – ᴿTPhil 69 (1994) 315-320 (F. *Hengsbach*, auch über *Fornet-Betancourt* R. 1991).

8519 *James* Leslie R., Towards an ecumenical liberation theology; a critical exploration of common dimensions in the theologies of Juan L. Segundo and Rubem A. ALVES: diss. [D]*Charles* H. St. Louis Univ. 1994. 228 p. 95-02980. – DissA 55 (1994s) p. 2872.

8520 **Kern** Bruno, Fundamental-Theologie im Horizont des Marxismus 1992 ➤ 7,8538; 8,8728: [R]TR 90 (1994) 160-2 (J. *Wiemeyer*).

8522 *Londoño* Luis A., La cultura universitaria colonial de Hispanoamérica: FranBog 34 ('V Centenario de la Evangelización en América Latina', 1992) 91-124.

8523 *López-Gay* Jesús, Boletín de publicaciones sobre la Historia de la Iglesia en América Latina (1989-1992): Burgense 34 (1993) 417-457.

8524 **Lynch** Edward A., Religion and politics in Latin America; liberation theology and Christian democracy 1991 ➤ 7,8547 ... 9,9030: [R]CritRR 6 (1993) 514-6 (H. M. *Goodpasture*).

8525 *McGlone* Mary M., Toribio de MONGROVEJO, shepherd amidst butchers [second archbishop of Lima, 1591-1606]: JHispT 1,2 (1993s) 64-79.

8526 **McKelway** Alexander J., The freedom of God and human liberation. L/Ph 1990, SCM/Trinity. 128 p. $11 pa. 0-334-02466-8. – [R]Interpretation 47 (1993s) 328 (Shirley C. *Guthrie*: rightly refuses to identify God's work with right or left, but shows ideological presuppositions against feminist theology).

8527 **Martin** David, Tongues of fire; the explosion of Protestantism in Latin America 1992 ➤ 7,8554; 0-631-17186- P[?]: [R]Crux 27,3 (1991) 38-41 (P. *Freston*, also on STOLL D.).

8528 *Müller* Max, 1492-1992; l'évangélisation au risque de l'histoire de l'Amérique latine [*Bastian* J., 1991]: ÉTRel 68 (1993) 89-98.

8529 *a) Murad* Afonso, A 'teologia inquieta' de Juan Luis SEGUNDO; – *b) Vigil* José María, O que fica da opção pelos pobres: PerspT 26 (1994) 155-186 / 187-212.

8530 *a) Nicholls* Bruce, Priorities in our common task; ministry to and with the poor [New Delhi consultation opening 17 Oct. 1993]; – *b) Harris* Dorothy, Incarnation as relocation among the poor [Manila, Bangkok ...]: EvRT 18 (1994) 101-116 / 117-127.

8531 *a) Nickoloff* James B., Indigenous theology and Andean resistance to Spanish colonial rule; the rebellion of Túpac Amaru [Peru] (1780-2); – *b) Feliciano* Juan G., Suffering; a Hispanic epistemology: JHispT 2,1 (1994s) 5-27 / 41-50.

8532 *O'Meara* Thomas P., The school of Thomism at Salamanca and the presence of grace in the Americas: Angelicum 71 (1994) 321-370.

8533 **Palomino Lopez** Salatiel, Toward Reformed-Liberating hermeneutics; a new reading of Reformed theology in the Latin American context: diss. Princeton 1993, [D]*Migliore* D. – RelStR 20,253.

8534 **Persaud** Winston D., The theology of the Cross and MARX's anthropology; a view from the Caribbean [< diss. St. Andrew's]: AmerUnivSt [D]1991 ➤ 9,9043: [R]TorJT 9 (1993) 301s (G. A. *Jensen*).

8535 *Pope* Stephen J., Christian love for the poor; almsgiving and the 'preferential option': Horizons 21 (1994) 288-312.

8536 **Pottenger** John R., The political theory of liberation theology; toward a reconvergence of social values and social science. Albany 1989, SUNY. x-264 p. $44.50; pa $17. – [R]RRelRes 32 (1990s) 285s (E. *Woodrum*).

8537 **Rivera** Luis N., Evangelización y violencia; la conquista de América. San Juan PR 1991, CEMI. – [R]JEH 45 (1994) 509-511 (F. *Cervantes*).

8538 **Rivera** Luis N., A violent evangelism; the political and religious conquest of the Americas, [T]*Rivera Pagán* Luis N. 1992 ➤ 9,9050; 0-664-25367-8. – [R]AmHR 99 (1994) 1287s (R. E. *Greenleaf*); ChH 63

(1944) 97s (L. E. *Schmidt*); ChrSchR 24 (1994) 334s (D. R. *Miller*: shows many theologians fought for justice, and the monarchy impeded worse cruelties; but ultimately the local people were treated as expendable resources by the local colonists); PrincSemB 15 (1994) 81s (A. *Neely*).

8539 *a) Robra* Martin, Theological and biblical reflection on diakonia; a survey of discussion within the WCC; – *b) Padilha* Sanivaldo, Diakonia in Latin America; our answers should change the questions: EcuR 46 (1994) 276-286 / 287-291.

8540 *Ruiz García* Samuel, Caminos pastorales hacia una Iglesia Autóctona: → Congreso 1992, EfMex 10 (1992) 443-462.

8541 **Schmeller** Thomas, Das Recht der Anderen; Befreiungtheologische Lektüre des Neuen Testaments in Lateinamerika: NT Abh 27. Münster 1994, Aschendorff. x-301 p.; Bibliog. 291-9. DM 92. 3-402-04775-6 [TLZ 120,664, H. *Brandt*].

8541* **Schmitz** Stefan, Der Revolutionär Gottes; Befreiende Begegnungen mit Jesus. Olten 1992, Walter. 226 p. DM 31,50. 3-530-75681-4. – ᴿActuBbg 31 (1994) 46s (J. *Boada*).

8542 **Schubeck** Thomas L., Liberation ethics; sources, models and norms [of 12 leading liberation theologians]. Mp 1993, Fortress. x-266 p. – ᴿTLond 97 (1994) 482s (T. *Gorringe*: good within limits of the genre).

8543 *Schwantes* Milton, (interview) Die Bibel ist ein Gedächtnisbuch der Armen: Junge Kirche 54,1 (Bremen 1993) 17-21 [< ᴢɪᴛ 93,70].

8543* **Segundo** Juan Luis, ¿Qué mundo? 1993 → 9,9062: ᴿActuBbg 31 (1994) 50-54 (J. I. *González-Faus*).

8544 **Segundo** J. L., The liberation of dogma 1992 → 9,9063: ᴿAmerica 170,17 (1994) 24-26 (P. *Crowley*).

8545 *Seibold* Jorge R., La Sagrada Escritura en la evangelización de América Latina I. Buenos Aires 1993, Paulinas. 172 p. [Stromata 49 (1993) 224].

8546 *Sievernich* Michael, Quellen zur Christianisierung Lateinamerikas; ein Forschungsbericht über neuere Editionen [Päpste; LAS CASAS, *al.*]: TPhil 69 (1994) 74-89.

8547 **Sigmund** Paul E., Liberation theology at the crossroads; democracy or revolution 1990 → 6,8597... 9,9070: ᴿCritRR 5 (1992) 488-490 (Anselm K. *Min*); HeythJ 34 (1993) 90-92 (Elisabeth *Lord*, also on HEWITT's SEGUNDO).

8548 *Simian-Yofre* Horacio, Epistemología y hermenéutica de la liberación: → Biblia y cultura II (1993) 421-437.

8549 **Sobrino** J., Jesucristo liberador 1991 → 8,8772; 9,9072: ᴿCarthaginensia 9 (1993) 423 (F. *Martínez Fresneda*); Salmanticensis 41 (1994) 142s (J.-R. *Flecha*).

8550 **Sobrino** Jon, Jesus the liberator; a historical-theological reading of Jesus of Nazareth [1991 → 8,8772], ᵀ*Burns* Paul, *McDonagh* Francis. Mkn 1993, Orbis. ix-308 p. $20. – ᴿIrTQ 60 (1994) 308-310 (E. *Breden*); LvSt 19 (1994) 390-3 (J. *Castillo Coronado*).

8551 *Sobrino* Jon, Theology in a suffering world [< TPQ (1993) 253-262 < RLatAmT (1988) 243-266], ᵀᴱ*Asen* B. A.: TDig 41 (1994) 25-30.

8552 **Stoll** David, Is Latin America turning Protestant? The politics of evangelical growth 1990 → 6,8602... 9,9075: ᴿChrSchR 23 (1993s) 488s (D. L. *Parkin*: 'because it's better or because it's easier ??').

8553 *Suess* Paulo, A história dos outros escrita por nós; apontamentos para uma autocrítica da historiografía do cristianismo na América Latina: REB 53 (1993) 853-871.

8554 **Taylor** Mark K., Remembering Esperanza 1990 → 9,8781: RPacifica 6 (1993) 228-231 (I. S. *Williams*).

8555 *Wriedt* Markus, Gott und Geld; die Rolle der Kirche bei der Eroberung des lateinamerikanischen Kontinents: EvT 53 (1993) 231-251.

H8.6 *Theologiae emergentes* – 'Theologies of' emergent groups.

8556 **Abraham** Kanjarathara U., Liturgical life; a vision for religious education in the churches of India with reference to Mar Thoma church: diss. Boston Univ. 1993. 195 p. 93-12292. – DissA 54 (1993s) 878.

8557 **Acheampong** Stephen, Inculturation and African theology; indigenous and western approaches to medical practice: diss. St. Michael's, DCormie L. Toronto 1994. 298 p. – RTLv 26, p. 582; cf. **Berinyuu** A. there.

8558 E**Ahanotu Austin** Metumara, Religion, state and society in contemporary Africa: Nigeria, Sudan, South Africa, Zaire and Mozambique: AmerUnivSt 7/111. NY 1992, Lang. 208 p. $40; pa. $30. 0-8204-1755-6. – RChrSchR 24 (1994) 105-7 (J. C. *Yoder*).

8558* *Amaladoss* M., An emerging Indian theology; some exploratory reflections: Vidyajyoti 58 (1994) 473-484 . 559-572.

8559 *Arens* Edmund, Kultur, Praxis, Kritik; Anliegen einer kontextuellen Theologie in Europa: ZkT 116 (1994) 288-300.

8559* *Auza* Bernardito, The turning of the dead; death and afterlife in the Malagasy system of beliefs: PhilipSac 29 (1994) 5-32.

8560 *Awino* James A., Towards an analytical African theology; the Luo concept of God as a case in point: AfER 36 (1994) 171-180.

8560* **Barkun** Michael, Religion and the racist right. Chapel Hill 1994, Univ. N. Carolina. 290 p. $40; pa. $16. – RChrCent 111 (1994) 1019 (J. *Kaplan*: on 'Christian identity' sect claiming Anglo-Saxons are heirs of Israel's tribes).

8561 *Bediako* Kwame, Cry Jesus! Christian theology and presence in modern Africa [1993 Laing lecture] (responses *Oladipo* Emmanuel, *Cotterell* Peter): VoxEvca 23 (1993) 7-25 (27s, 29s).

8562 *Ballhatchett* Kenneth, The East India Company and Roman Catholic missionaries: JEH 44 (1993) 273-288.

8563 **Baldwin** Lewis V.J, There is a balm in Gilead; the cultural roots of Martin Luther KING jr. Ph 1991, Fortress. 339 p. – RAsbTJ 49,1 (1994) 90-96 (L. Susan *May*: claims King has been interpreted as if part of the white tradition).

8564 **Bascio** Patrick, The future of white theology; a black theological perspective: MLKing studies. NY 1994, P. Lang. 160 p. $38. 0- 8204-2257-6 [TDig 42,54: Grenada Catholic priest].

8565 **Berryman** Phillip, Stubborn hope; religion, politics, and revolution in Central America. Mkn/NYC 1994, Orbis / New Press. viii-276 p. $23. 0-88344-862-5 / 1-56584-136-0 [TDig 42,55].

8566 **Bevans** Stephen B., Models of contextual theology 1992 → 9,9102: RGregorianum 75 (1994) 354s (J. *Dupuis*); LvSt 18 (1993) 264s (J. *Ball*); NRT 116 (1994) 255s (A. *Toubeau*); TorJT 10 (1994) 149s (G. A. *Jensen*).

8567 *Botha* J. E., Contextualization; locating threads in the labyrinth: Scriptura 9-spec. (1991) 29-46 [< NTAbs 38, p. 164].

8568 E**Brennan** Frank, Reconciling our differences. Melbourne 1992, Aurora/ Lovell. vii-117 p. $A 15. Includes briefly two aborigines; also Brendan *Byrne* 'Homecoming'. – RPacifica 7 (1994) 111-4 (J. *Kaliba*).

8569 **Bujo** Bénézet,   African theology in its social context 1992 ➤ 8,8794; 9,9107: ᴿETL 69 (1993) 202-4 (V. *Neckebrouck*).

8570 *Bujo* Bénézet,   Auf dem Weg zu einer afrikanischen Ekklesiologie: StiZt 119 (1994) 254-266 [> Toward an African ecclesiology, ᵀᴱ*Asen* B. A.], TDig 42,3-8.

8571 **Carrier** Hervé,   Evangelizing the culture of modernity: Faith and Cultures. Mkn 1993, Orbis. viii-168 p. $19. 0-88344-898-X. – ᴿGregorianum 75 (1994) 799s (*ipse*).

8572 **Carrier** Hervé,   Lexique de la culture, pour... l'inculturation 1992 ➤ 9, 8800: ᴿRThom 94 (1994) 346 (H.-F. *Rovarino*).

8573 *Chapman* Mark D.,   A theology for Europe; universality and particularity in Christian theology: HeythJ 35 (1994) 125-139.

8574 *Charentenay* Pierre de, A proposito d'inculturazione [... fa vivere in mezzo alla povertà]: CC 145 (1994,2) 240-8.

8575 *Chepkwony* Adam K. A.,   Theological trends in Africa: AsbTJ 49,1 (1994) 22-34.

8576 *Cheza* Maurice,   Le rôle des missions chrétiennes dans la formation des identités nationales: CREDIC 14ᵉ colloque, Lyon 25-27 août 1993: ᴿRTLv 25 (1994) 277-9.

8577 **Coakley** J. F.,   The church of the East... Canterbury's Assyrian mission 1992 ➤ 8,8067; 9,9113: ᴿAmHR 99 (1994) 561 (J. *Cox*); HeythropJ 35 (1994) 335-7 (A. *Hamilton*); OstKSt 42 (1993) 213 (E. C. *Suttner*).

8578 *Cottier* Georges,   L'unité de la foi dans le pluralisme des cultures: NVFr 68 (1993) 161-171.

8579 **Cummins** J. S.,   A question of rites; Friar Domingo NAVARRETE and the Jesuits in China. Aldershot 1993, Scolar. xv-349 p. £39.50. – ᴿBSO 57 (1994) 245s (D. E. *Mungello*).

8580 *a) Davies* John R.,   Biblical precedents for contextualisation; – *b) Maggay* Melba P.,   Communicating the Gospel in the Philippine context: Asia Theol.Asn.J 2,1 (Bangalore 1994) 10-35 / 36... [< ZIT 94,673].

8581 *a) Davis* Cyprian,   The future of African-American Catholic studies; – *b) Fichter* Joseph H.,   The white church and the black sisters: CathH 12,1 (1994) 1-9 / 31-48 (-141, *al.*).

8582 ᴱ**[Figueroa] Deck** Allan,   Frontiers of Hispanic theology in the US 1992 ➤ 8,389; 9,9123: ᴿPrincSemB 14 (1993) 322s (C. F. *Cardoza Orlandi*: a form of Catholic popular religion; nothing about Protestant sector); Worship 65 (1994) 86s (T. M. *Matovina*).

8583 **de Gruchy** John W.,   Liberating Reformed theology; a South African contribution to an ecumenical debate 1991, 0-8028-0536-1 ➤ 8,8074 [cf. ➤ 8,8745]: ᴿWestTJ 55 (1993) 183-5 (R. E. *Otto*).

8584 **Dinh Duc Dao** Joseph,   Preghiera rinnovata per una nuova era missionaria in Asia [diss. Pont. Univ. Gregoriana]: Inculturation, testi di lavoro su fede e cultura. R 1994, Gregoriana. 214 p. Lᵐ 24. – ᴿRasT 35 (1994) 761 (Lorena *Corradino*).

8585 *Duarte Castillo* Raúl,   Inculturación en la Revelación: EfMex 11 (1993) 331-344.

8586 **Dyrness** William A.,   Invitation to cross-cultural theology; case studies in vernacular [China, Maya, Manila...] theologies. GR 1992, Eerdmans. 194 p. – ᴿJEvTS 37 (1994) 632s (G. *Crutsinger*).

8587 **Dyrness** William,   Learning about theology from the Third World 1990 ➤ 7,8614; 9,9132: ᴿJEvTS 37 (1994) 591-3 (D. B. *Clendenin*: high praise).

8588 *Eggen* Wiel,   African roads into the theology of earthly reality: Exchange 22 (Leiden 1993) 91-169.

8589 *England* John C., Epilogue: analogies of faith, signs of the way: Japanese Religions 19,1s (Kyoto 1994) 126-142 [< TContext 12,85].

8590 **Evans** James H.ᴶ, We have been believers; an African-American systematic theology 1992 → 9,9135: ᴿInterpretation 48 (1994) 296-8 (J. E. *Gilman*).

8591 *Evers* Georg, Trends and developments in contextual theologies [Kerk en Theologie in Context, 8 vol. 1991-4]: JIntRD 5 (1995) 100-111.

8592 **Felder** Cain H., Afrocentrism, the Bible, and the politics of difference: PrincSemB 15 (1994) 131-142.

8593 **Fernández** Eduardo: U.S. Hispanic theology (1968-1993), context and praxis: diss. Pont. Univ. Gregoriana, ᴰ*Roest-Crollius* A. Rome 1994, 248 p.; extr. nᵒ 4107, 109 p. – RTLv 26, p. 549.

8594 **Fujita** Neil S., Japan's encounter with Christianity; the Catholic mission in pre-modern Japan. NY 1991, Paulist. viii-294 p. $14. – ᴿAndrUnS 32 (1994) 132s (B. L. *Bauer*).

8595 *Giraudo* Cesare, Madagascar; spazio sacro e inculturazione: RasT 35 (1994) 131-147; 3 fig.

8596 **Goizueta** Roberto S., We are a people! 1990/2 → 8,564*b*: ᴿRefR 47 (1993s) 169s (D. E. *Timmer*).

8597 *a) Gómez Fregoso* Jesús, Historia de la evangelización de la cultura y de la inculturación del Evangelio en América Latina; – *b*) *Mora Lomelí* Raúl, La conquista evangelizadora en la literatura latinoamericana: Xipe-Totek 1 (1992) 260-... / 2 (1993) 3-34.

8598 **González** Justo, Out of every tribe and nation; Christian theology at the ethnic roundtable. Nv 1992, Abingdon. 244 p. $17. – ᴿCurrTM 21 (1994) 458 (E. *Pérez-Álvarez*).

8599 *González* Nazario / *Bentué* Antoni, Xoc de cultures i evangelització: enfocament històric / presentació antropológico-teológica: QVidCr 157 (1992) 7-18 / 19-37.

8600 *Gordon* J. Dorcas, The richness of cultures; how it enriches our faith: RefW 44 (1994) 117-121.

8601 **Hall** Douglas J., Thinking the faith; Christian theology in a North American context 1989 → 5,8611... 9,9149: ᴿCritRR 5 (1992) 473-5 (Anna *Case-Winters*).

8601* **Hillman** Eugene, Toward an African Christianity. NY 1993 → 9,9151: ᴿAfER 36 (1994) 195s (L. *Magesa*).

8602 *Hinga* T. M., (fem., Nairobi) Christology and various African contexts: QRMin 14 (1994) 345-357.

8603 **Hood** Robert E., Must God remain Greek? Afro cultures and God-talk 1990 → 7,8631*... 9,9153: ᴿLuthQ 6 (1992) 209-211 (S. *Gustafson*).

8604 *Hovland* Thor H., [in Norwegian] Black Theology as hermeneutics of liberation: TsTKi 64 (1993) 241-254; Eng. 254.

8605 *Hume* Lynne, Delivering the Word the aboriginal way; the genesis of an Australian aboriginal theology: Colloquium 25,2 (Sydney 1993) 86-95.

8606 **Hunter** Alan, *Chan Kim-Kwung*, Protestantism in contemporary China. C 1993, Univ. xx-291 p. 0-521-44116-7. – ᴿChrSchR 24 (1994) 342-4 (H. *Wong*).

8607 **Johnson** Jeff G., Black Christians; the untold Lutheran story 1991 → 9,9160: ᴿConcordTQ 58 (Fort Wayne 1994) 303s (H. H. *Buls*).

8608 *Kabasile Mukenge* André, Les enjeux du Synode africain: NRT 116 (1994) 161-180.

8608* *a) Kasper* Walter, Kirche und Kultur; Evangelisierung und Inkultu-ration; – *b*) *Delfor Mandrione* Héctor, Beziehungen zwischen Kirche und

Kultur; Dialog und Kreativität; – *c*) *Pérez Valera* Víctor M., Kirche, Kultur und Gesellschaft im Denken von Bernard LONERGAN; – *d*) *Fraling* Bernhard, Berufung und Institution; eine bibeltheologische Reflexion: ➤ 57, ᶠHUNERMANN 1994, 157-162 / 91-118 / 111-124 / 220-236.

8609 **Küng** Hans, *Ching* Julia, Christianity and Chinese religions [1988],ᵀ. L 1993, SCM. xix-309 p. £15 pa. – ᴿTLond 97 (1994) 227s (P. L. *Wickeri*).

8610 **Küster** Volker, Theologie im Kontext; zugleich ein Versuch über die Minjung-Theologie: Diss. ᴰ*Sundermeier*. Heidelberg 1994. 212 p. – RTLv 26, p. 529.

8610* *Lies* Lothar, The theologies of Europe in dialogue with the South-(East-) Asian theologies: Vidyajyoti 58 (1999) 369-378.

8611 **Mabee** Charles, Reading sacred texts through American eyes; biblical interpretation as cultural critique: Studies in American biblical hermeneutics 7. Macon 1991, Mercer Univ. [ix-]128 p. $25; pa. $17. – ᴿCBQ 56 (1994) 116s (J. J. *Pilch*: good on modern American, less on ancient Mediterranean).

8611* *Mana Kä*, L'Église africaine et la théologie de la reconstruction; réflexions sur les nouveaux appels de la mission en Afrique: BCentProt 46,4s (1994) 5-44.

8612 *a*) *Martin* K. John, An ashram as a space in the heart; Fr. Bede GRIFFITHS' view on ashram life; – *b*) *Chethimattam* John B., Parameters for an Indian theology: Kristu Jyoti 10,2 (Bangalore 1994) 33-40 / 1-19.

8612* **Marzal** M. M., *Robles* J. R., *al.*, Il volto indio di Dio [1991 ➤ 9,9180], ᵀᴱ*Pompei* G., *Del Bianco* A.: TeLib 7. Assisi 1993, Cittadella. 382 p. Lᵐ 30. – ᴿAsprenas 41 (1994) 449-451 (A. *Langella*).

8613 *Matthews* Donald, Proposal for an Afro-centric curriculum: JAAR 62 (1994) 885-892.

8614 **Mattiello** Cristina, Le chiese nere negli Stati Uniti; dalla religione degli schiavi alla teologia nera della liberazione. T 1993, Claudiana. Lᵐ 9,5. – ᴿProtestantesimo 49 (1994) 62s (M. *Rubboli*, anche su KING M. L. 1993).

8615 **Maw** Martin, Visions of India; fulfilment theology, the Aryan race theory, and the work of British Protestant missionaries in Victorian India. Fra 1990, Lang. xv-393 p. DM 38 pa. – ᴿEngHR 109 (1994) 495s (J. *Wolffe*).

8616 **Mbiti** John S., Oltre la magia [African religions 1969 ²1990],ᵀ. T 1992, SEI. xi-320 p. Lᵐ 35. – ᴿCC 145 (1994,1) 101s (A. *Seumois*).

8616* *Mercado* Leonardo N., The Filipino face of Christ: PhilipSac 27 (1992) 91-103.

8617 **Mesa** José M. de, Maginhawa; den Gott des Heils erfahren; theologische Inkulturation auf den Philippinen: T3Welt 17. FrB 1992, Herder. 240 p. DM 38 pa. – ᴿTPQ 142 (1994) 84s (J. *Janda*).

8618 *Meyer* Hans B., Die Instruktion 'Varietates legitimae' über die römische Liturgie und Inkulturation: HDienst 48 (1994) 186-192.

8619 **Moffett** Samuel H., A history of Christianity in Asia 1. to 1500: 1992 ➤ 8,8865; 9,9183: ᴿAmHR 99 (1994) 617 (E. M. *Yamauchi*); ChrSchR 24 (1994) 107-9 (A. H. *Winquist*); JRel 74 (1994) 429-431 (*Song Choan-Seng*); SWJT 36,2 (1993s) 53s (Justice C. *Anderson*).

8620 **Molyneux** K. Gordon, African Christian theology; the quest for selfhood. Lewiston NY 1993, Mellen. 422 p. $60. 0-7734-1946-2 [TDig 42,179: Zaïre-based].

8621 ᴱ**Mukonyora** Isabel, *al.*, 'Re-writing' the Bible; the real issues [*Banana* C. S.]; perspectives from within biblical and religious studies in Zimbabwe. Gweru 1993, Mambo. 309 p. 0-86922-538-3. – ᴿExchange 22 (1992) 87s.

8622 **Murphy** Joseph M., Working the spirit; ceremonies of the African diaspora [voodoo, condomblé, sandería, U.S. Black]. Boston 1994, Beacon. xiii-263 p. $25. 0-8070-1220-3 [TDig 41,278].

8623 **Mveng** Engelbert, Identità africana e cristianesimo 1990 ➤ 7,8860: ᴿRasT 34 (1993) 462-7 (Antoniette Maria *Mansi*).

8624 **Nedungatt** George, The spirit of the Eastern [new canon law] code. R/Bangalore 1993, Centre for Indian and Interreligious Studies / Dharmaram. xiv-261 p. – ᴿOrChrPer 60 (1994) 261-3 (J. *Abbass*).

8625 **Nemet** Ladislav, Inculturation in the Philippines; a theological study of the question of inculturation in the documents of CBCP and selected Filipino theologians in the light of Vatican II and the documents of FABC: diss. Nº 7215, Pont.Univ.Gregoriana, ᴰ*Dupuis* J. Rome 1994. – InfPUG 26/131, p. 34.

8626 **Nkabahona** Alex, Towards an African reception of Jürgen MOLTMANN's theology of suffering and resurrection: diss. ᴰ*Schrijver* G. De. Leuven 1994. 310 p. – RTLv 26, p. 567.

8627 *Nyamiti* Charles, *a)* The Incarnation viewed from the African understanding of person (5); – *b)* African ancestor veneration and its relevance to the African churches: CUEA African Christian studies 8,2 (1992) 1-28 / 9,3 (1993) 14-37 [< TContext 11/1,147; 12/1,82].

8628 **Nyimi** Modeste Malu, Inversion culturelle du déplacement de la pratique chrétienne africaine; préface à une théologie périphérique: diss. ᴰ*Camps* A. Nijmegen 1994. 216 p. > Kampen, Kok. – TvT 34,298; RTLv 26, p. 529.

8629 *Piepke* J. G., Die afro-brasilianischen Kulte; Herausforderung des Heilsmonopols der Katholischen Kirche in Lateinamerika: TGegw 36 (1993) 196-204.

8630 **Pieris** Aloysius, El rostro asiático de Cristo; notas para una teología asiática de la liberación 1991 ➤ 8,8877; 9,9197: ᴿCiTom 119 (1992) 612 (L. *Lago Alba*).

8631 *Prior* John M., From headhunting to the return of the child; Christian mission and cosmic religion: Pacifica 7 (1994) 217-227.

8632 *Prowse* Christopher, Reconciliation with the aboriginal community; some theological reflections: Pacifica 7 (1994) 31-45.

8633 **Ralston** Helen, Christian Ashrams. Lewiston NY c.1992, Mellen. 154 p. $49.45. – ᴿCanadCathR 11,3 (1993) 31 (J. F. *Baker*).

8634 **Renek** Günther, Contextualization of Christianity and Christianization of language (Papua New Guinea); Mg 5. Erlangen 1990, Ev.-Luth. Mission. xvi-316 p. – ᴿNZMiss 48 (1992) 151s (J. D. *May*).

8635 **Ried** Martin, Kirche und Kultur. – TR 90,82.

8636 **Roberts** J. Deotis, The prophethood of black believers; an African American political theology for ministry. LvL 1994, W-Knox. xv-160 p. $15 pa. 0-664-25488-8 [TDig 42,87].

8637 *Salomon* Esaúl, Biblical evangelism in Hispanic ministry: ConcordTQ 58 (1994) 113-141: US is fourth-largest Spanish-speaking country in the world, more than all Central America.

8638 *Salvatierra* Ángel, Inculturación y teología: LumenVR 42 (1993) 504-547.

8639 **Sanneh** Lamin, Encountering the West; Christianity and the global cultural process; the African dimension. Mkn/L 1993, Orbis/Marshall Pickering. 286 p. $25. 0-88344-029-3 [TDig 41,381]. – ᴿTLond 97 (1994) 226s (A. *Shorter*).

8640 *Sanneh* Lamin, World Christianity from an African perspective, interview with *Burrows* Wm. E.: America 170,12 (1994) 16-21.

8641 **Schreiter** Robert J.,   Faces of Jesus in Africa 1992 ⇒ 8,8891; 9,9211:
ᴿExpTim 104 (1992s) 28 (G. T. *Eddy*); Missiology 21 (1993) 101s (J. G.
Donders).

8642 *a) Schroer* Silvia, Dokumente interkulturellen Lernens in der Bibel; – *b)
Schreiter* Robert, Inkulturation des Glaubens oder Identifikation mit der
Kultur?; – *c) Baum* Gregory, Inkulturation und multikulturelle Gesellschaft; zwei Fragezeichen, ᵀ*Kett* Andrea: ⇒ 265, IZT-Conc 30 (1994)
4-11 / 12-18 / 67-73.

8643 **Schüttke-Scherle** Peter,   From contextual to ecumenical theology? A
dialogue between Minjung theology and 'theology after Auschwitz'
[Dublin Masters dissertation]: Studies in the intercultural history of
Christianity 60.   Fra 1989, Lang.   xii-232 p. – ᴿIrTQ 58 (1992) 75 (T.
Corbett).

8644 **Shorter** Aylward,   Toward a theology of inculturation 1988 ⇒ 4,9753...
8,9213: ᴿColcT 63,4 (1993) 221-4 (A. F. *Dziuba*, ❷).

8644* **Sindima** Harvey J.,   Dreams of redemption; an introduction to African
Christianity: ContribStRel 35.   Westport CT 1994, Greenwood.   xix-
211 p. $55.   0-313-29088-1 [TDig 42,291].

8645 **Smith** Theophilus H.,   Conjuring culture; biblical formations of black
America: Religions in America.   NY 1994, Oxford-UP.   xvi-287 p. $32.
0-19-506740-1 [TDig 41,383].

8646 **Song Choan-Seng**,   La teologia del terzo occhio; teologia in formazione
nel contesto asiastico [Third-Eye theology ¹1979 ²1991],ᵀ: StrumScRel,
Temi 5.   Padova 1993, Messaggero.   412 p. Lᵐ 35.   88-250-0185-1. –
ᴿAsprenas 41 (1994) 129s (G. *Mattai*); Gregorianum 75 (1994) 566 (J.
Dupuis).

8647 *Spijker* Gerard van 't,   Liberating the Church from its northern captivity;
dialogue with traditional religion in Africa: JIntRD 4 (1994) 170-188.

8648 **Stanley** Brian,   The history of the Baptist Missionary Society 1792-1992,
E 1992, Clark.   xix-564 p. £40. – ᴿBSO 57 (1994) 249s (A. *Porter*).

8649 *Starkloff* Carl H.,   Considering the problem of syncretism [... does not
exclude learning from God's people of other faiths]: TorJT 10 (1994)
98-100.

8650 *Starkloff* Carl,   Inculturation and cultural systems: TS 55 (1994) 66-
81. 274-294 / Way 34 (1994) 293-304.

8651 **Stirrat** R. I.,   Power and religiosity in a post-colonial setting; Sinhala
Catholics in contemporary Sri Lanka.   C 1992, Univ. 231 p. $60. – ᴿJRel
74 (1994) 431s (J. S. *Walters*; informative analysis reaching far beyond the
'Kudagama Marian shrine and its charismatic healing priest').

8652 *Suess* Paulo,   No Verbo que se faz carne, o Evangelho se faz cultura
[... inculturação; Fulni-ô, Karipuna]: REB 54 (1994) 36-49.

8653 ᴱ**Sugirtharajah** R. S., Voices from the margin 1991 ⇒ 8,8902; 9,9222:
ᴿOTEssays 7 (1994) 115-8 (M. J. *Oosthuizen*).

8654 *a)* ᴱ**Sugirtharajah** R. S., *Hargreaves* Cecil,   Readings in Indian Christian
theology 1.   L 1993, SPCK.   261 p. £8 pa.   81-7214-139-4. – ᴿTLond 97
(1994) 46s (Rajinder *Daniel*: essays since 1922, from India mostly south,
'which tells its own story'; Sister VANDANA on John glitters; for vol. 2
items are foreseen of greater length and depth). Vidyajyoti 58 (1994) 326s
(M. *Joseph*).

8655 *Taborda* Francisco,   Cristianismo e culturas indígenas; impasses e dile-
mas de uma prática evangelizadora: REB 53 (1993) 259-282.

8656 **Takenaka** Masao, *O'Grady* Ron,   The Bible through Asian eyes.

Auckland 1991, Asian Christian Art Asn. 198 p.; 100 color. pl. $25. 0-9597971-0-6.– ᴿÉTRel 68 (1993) 144s (J. *Cottin*).

8656* **Tardieu** Jean-Pierre, L'Église et les noirs au Pérou, XVIe et XVIIe siècles: Univ. Réunion. P 1993, L'Harmattan. 1033 p. – ᴿRHist 291 (1994) 219-221 (J.-P. *Blancpain*).

8657 Mother *Teresa* [Wsh National Prayer Broadcast 3.II.1994] Whatever you did unto one of the least, you did unto me: ComWsh 21 (1994) 145-150.

8658 **Ter Haar** Gerrie, Spirit of Africa ... MILINGO 1992 → 8,8906: ᴿHeythJ 35 (1994) 103s (M. F. C. *Bourdillon*).

8659 **Tinker** George E., Missionary conquest; the Gospel and native American cultural genocide. Mp 1993, Fortress. ix-182 p. $10. 0-8006-2575-5 [TDig 41,291: not against the Gospel but against imposing along with it European culture and discipline].

8660 **Tirumanywa** Cyprian, Christian religion on trial; the Good News is justice and peace for all on earth. Dar es Salaam, c. 1993, Univ. 104 p.

8661 *a*) *Tshibangu* T., Un concile africain est-il opportun?: BThA V.10 (1983) 154-73; – *b*) *Hünermann* Peter, Afrikanische Themen in Rom; theologische Reflexionen aus europäischer Sicht: TüTQ 174 (1994) 177-184.

8661* *Ukpong* Justin S., Inculturation and evangelization; biblical foundations for inculturation: Vidyajyoti 58 (1994) 298-307.

8662 **Van Rheenen** Gailyn, Communicating Christ in animistic contexts [... nowadays rather 'traditional religions']. GR 1991, Baker. 342 p. $15 pa. – ᴿAndrUnS 32 (1994) 154-6 (R. *Staples*).

8663 **Walker** Theodoreᴶ, Empower the people 1991 → 8,8914; 9,9230: ᴿETL 69 (1993) 493-5 (V. *Neckebrouck*).

8664 *Wilfred* Felix, The challenge of folklore to Indian theologizing: Jeevadhara 24 (1994) 60-80 [< TContext 12,84].

8665 **Williams** Lewin L., Caribbean theology: Research in Religion and Family, Black Perspectives 2. NY 1994, P. Lang. xiii-231 p. $44. 0-8204-1859-4 [TDig 42,193].

8666 *Wilson* Henry S., One faith and several theologies; a plea for contextualization: NesTR 15 (1994) 70-84.

H8.7 *Mariologia* – **The mother of Jesus in the NT.**

8667 **Adamiak** Elżbieta, ❷ Maryja w feministycznej teologii Cathariny HALKES: diss. ᴰNapiórkowski S. Lublin 1994. 255 p. – RTLv 26, p. 563.

8667* *Averintsev* Sergei S., The image of the Virgin Mary in Russian piety [McCarthy Lecture 1994]: Gregorianum 75 (1994) 611-622.

8668 **Baumer** R., *Scheffczyk* L., Marienlexikon [→ 5,917*... 9,9236] 3. Greco-Lail; 4. Laytha – Orangenbaum; 5. Orante – Scherer. St. Ottilien 1991/2/3, EOS. je 704 p. DM 148. 3-88096-894-2. – ᴿColcFran 64 (1994) 351s (R. *Vadakkekara*); EsprVie 104 (1994) 302 (G. de *Martel*, 1-6); TLZ 119 (1994) 278-282 (R. *Frieling*).

8669 *Baraz* Daniel, BARTOLOMEO da Trento's Book of Marian miracles; a new insight into the Arabic collections of Marian legends: OrChrPer 60 (1994) 69-85.

8670 **Benko** S., The virgin goddess 1993 → 9,9239: ᴿEphMar 43 (1993) 477-500 (J. C. R. *Garcia Paredes*); JTS 45 (1994) 711-5 (Christine *Trevett*).

8671 **Buby** Bertrand, Mary of Galilee, 1. Mary in the NT. [awaited. 2. in the Hebrew Scriptures; III. in the Apocrypha and the Sub-Apostolic writers]. NY 1994, Alba. 216 p. $12. 0-8189-0692-8.

8672 **Bur** Jacques,   How to understand the Virgin Mary [1992 ➤ 8,8932], ^T*Bowden* John, *Lydamore* Margaret. L 1994, SCM.   ix-134 p. £10. 0-334-02106-3. – ^RExpTim 105 (1993s) 350 (K. *Mason*); TBR 6,3 1993s) 41 (Jill *Pinnock*: unlike the other lively, clear, informative books of the series: badly written and edited, not the translators' fault).

8673 **Carroll** Michael P.,   Madonnas that maim 1992 ➤ 8,8936 … 9,9244: ^RCathHR 79 (1993) 505s (T. *Kselman*: title refers to a belief that Mary has sometimes caused harm as a sign of her power); JIntdis 25 (1994s) 311-3 (R. C. *Trexler*).

8674 *a*) *Cavalcoli* Giovanni,   Maria come modello della Chiesa e della donna; – *b*) *Selva* Agostino,   Maria immagine della Chiesa nel commento al Magnificat di LUTERO: SacDoc 38 (1993) 866-925 / 719-750.

8675 *Courth* Franz, Marienerscheinungen im Widerstreit [Tagung Augsburg 14.-16. März 1994]: ForKT 10 (1994) 216-8.

8676 **Cuvillier** Élian,   Qui donc es-tu, Marie? Les différents visages de la Mère de Jésus dans le NT. Poliez c. 1993; Moulin. – ^REsprVie 104 (1994) 493s (E. *Cothenet*).

8677 **De Fiores** Stefano,   Maria nella teologia contemporanea³ [²1987 ➤ 4, 9794; 5,8705]. R 1991, Centro Madre della Chiesa.   620 p. – ^RAtKap 121 (1993) 181-3 (J. *Królikowski*, ❷).

8678 **De Fiores** S.,   María en la teología contemporánea, ^T*Ortiz* A.,   1991 ➤ 7,8738: … 9,9255: ^RCiTom 120 (1993) 395-7 (A. *Bandera*).

8679 **De Fiores** Stefano, Maria Madre di Gesù … sintesi storico salvifica 1992 ➤ 8,8941; 9,9254:   ^RTGL 84 (1994) 253s (W. *Beinert*).

8679* **D'Sa** Thomas,   Mary the contrary; a reflection on the Annunciation and Visitation as models of commitment and evangelization: Vidyajyoti 58 (1994) 623-635.

8680 **Eggemann** Ina,   Die 'ekklesiologische Wende' in der Mariologie des II. Vatikanums und 'konziliare Perspektiven' als neue Horizonte für das Verständnis der Mittlerschaft Marias: MünstTAbh 22. Altenberge 1993, Oros.   xvi-381 p. DM 65. 3-89375-073-8. – ^RTGL 84 (1994) 491s (W. *Beinert*); TR 90 (1994) 246s (F. *Courth*).

8681 ^E**Felici** Sergio,   La mariologia nella catechesi dei Padri (età postnicena): Pont. Inst. Altioris Latinitatis 1989-91 ➤ 5,8711 … 8,8947: ^RAugR 32 (1992) 453-6 (E. *dal Covolo*); RasT 34 (1993) 468 (E. *Cattaneo*); Salesianum 56 (1994) 169-171 (anche E. *dal Covolo*).

8682 **Forte** B.,   María, la mujer icono del misterio [²1989 ➤ 5,8712], ^T. S 1993, Sígueme.   287 p. – ^RREspir 52 (1993) 539 (S. *Castro*).

8683 **Gambero** Luigi,   Maria nel pensiero dei padri della Chiesa 1991 ➤ 7,8744 … 9,9265:   ^RAugR 32 (1992) 450-3 (E. *Saglio*); EstJos 47 (1993) 245s (J. A. *Carrasco*).

8684 **García Paredes** José,   María y las diosas; nuevos horizontes para la mariología [BENKO S.]: EphMar 43 (1993) 477-500.

8685 **Gharib** Georges, *al.*,   Testi mariani del primo millennio, 4. Padri e altri autori orientali 1991 ➤ 8,8955; 9,9266:   ^RSalesianum 56 (1994) 171s (R. *Sabin*).

8686 **Gherardini** Brunero,   Dignitas terrae; note di mariologia agostiniana. CasM 1992, Piemme.   235 p. – ^RMarianum 55 (1993) 668 (S. *Folgado Flórez*).

8687 **González-Dorado** Antonio,   Mariologia popular latino-americana; da Maria conquistadora a Maria libertadora [1988 ➤ 4,9810], ^T*Gaio* Luiz J. São Paulo 1992, Loyola. 123 p. 85-15-00645-6. – ^RPerspT 26 (1994) 415-7 (F. *Taborda*).

8688 **Kudasiewicz** Józef, ❷ Mother of the Redeemer 1991 ➤ 8,8967*: ᴿColcT 63,1 (1993) 188-190 (J. W. *Rosłon*).
8689 **Langkammer** Hugolin, ❷ Maryja w Nowym Testamencie. Gorzów 1991, Wielkopolski. 203 p. – ᴿAtKap 123 (1994) 323-5 (H. *Ordon,* ❷).
8690 **La Potterie** I. de, Maria nel mistero dell'alleanza 1988 ➤ 4,9834 ... 8,8969: ᴿBibFe 59 (1994) 153 (M. *Sáenz Galache*).
8691 **La Potterie** Ignace de, María en el misterio de la Alianza. M 1993, BAC. 315 p. – ᴿCarthaginensia 10 (1994) 508 (P. *Chavero Blanco*); ComSev 27 (1994) 135 (M. *Sánchez*); ScripTPamp 26 (1994) 1177-83 (J. L. *Bastero*).
8692 **Laurentin** René, The meaning of consecration today; a Marian model for a secularist age [Retour à Dieu avec Marie 1991], ᵀ*Whitehead* Kenneth D. SF 1992, Ignatius. – ᴿDivinitas 37 (1993) 304-8 (A. B. *Calkins*).
8693 *Meinardus* Otto F. A., Carlo DOLCI[']s 'Mater dolorosa' in der koptischen Mariologie: OrSuec 41s (1992s) 155-165; 13 fig.
8694 **Michaud** Jean-Paul, María de los evangelios: CuadBib 77. Estella 1992, VDivino. 74 p. – ᴿEphMar (1993) 503s (A. *Aparicio*).
8695 **Militello** Cettina, Mariologia: Manuali di base 27. CasM 1991, Piemme. 117 p. – ᴿScripTPamp 26 (1994) 1252s (J. L. *Bastero*).
8696 *Mimouni* Simon C., Les *Transitus Mariae* sont-ils vraiment des apocryphes?: ➤ 9,465, StPatr (11th 1991) 25 (1993) 122-8.
8697 *Molette* C., *al.*, Le mystère de Marie et la femme d'aujourd'hui, Session 47ᵉ franç. Ét. Mariales, Blois 1991 ➤ 7,536: ᴿNRT 115 (1993) 312 (A. *Harvengt*).
8698 *Moorsel* Paul Van, Une annonciation faite à Marie au monastère des Syriens [Natroun] (une découverte de l'IFAO faite en mai 1991): BSocFÉg 124 (1992) 5-23; 8 fig.; 3 pl.
8699 **Mussner** Franz, Maria, die Mutter Jesu im NT, Vorw. *Ratzinger* J. St. Ottilien 1993, EOS. 156 p. DM 14. 3-88096-717-2 [TR 90,176]. – ᴿTüTQ 174 (1994) 322s (M. *Theobald*: sonst gute Marienbücher von katholischen Exegeten gibt es kaum).
8700 **Napiórkowski** Stanisław C., ❷ Mariologie et œcuménisme après Vaticanum II: ColcT 63,4 (1993) 45-65; franç. 66: i. les faits; ii. dodécalogue des objectifs.
8701 *Napiórkowski* Stanisław C., *al.*, Mariologie et écuménisme après le Concile Vatican II: EphMar 42 ('María en el diálogo ecuménico' 1992) 215-236 (-315) [317-362, en la liberación latinoamericana].
8702 *O'Donnell* C., Mary as prophet: StSp 1 (Kampen 1991) 181-198 [< ZIT 93,282].
8703 *Pasquetto* Virgilio, Maria di ascolto per la Chiesa nel vangelo di Luca: RivVSp 46 (1992) 272-285.
8704 *Perrella* Salvatore M., Percorsi della mariologia postconciliare; il contributo della teologia italiana (1964-1992): Asprenas 41 (1994) 85-96.
8705 *Ricca* Paolo, Maria di Nazareth nella riflessione di alcuni teologi contemporanei della Riforma: Marianum 55 (1993) 473-493.
8706 **Schillebeeckx** E., *Halkes* Catharina, Mary, yesterday, today and tomorrow, ᴱ*Bowden* J. 1993 ➤ 9,9291*b*: ᴿExpTim 105 (1993s) 186s (Sheridan *Gilley*: rejected as dogma, embraced as symbol; no real engagement with traditional Marian piety).
8707 *Sedgwick* Colin J., Mary – human like us: ExpTim 105 (1993s) 48s.
8708 **Serra** A., Maria según el Evangelio, ᵀ: Biblia y Catequesis 10, 1988 ➤ 4,9869: ᴿCiuD 206 (1993) 646 (J. *Gutiérrez*).
8709 **Serra** A., Nato di donna 1992 ➤ 8,309: ᴿAsprenas 41 (1994) 119s (A. *Rolla*); RivB 42 (1994) 465-8 (E. *Della Corte*).

8710 **Sirota** Ioann B., Ikonographie der Gottesmutter in der russischen Orthodoxen Kirche; Versuch einer Systematisierung. Wü 1992, Augustinus / Chr.Osten. 315 p.; 115 fig. - ᴿOrChrPer 60 (1994) 285s (E. G. *Farrugia*).
8711 **Testa** Emanuele, Maria terra vergine, 1. I rapporti della Madre di Dio con la Ss. Trinità (sec. I-IX); 2. Il culto mariano palestinese (sec. I-IX); 1984 ➤ 1,8447: ᴿMarianum 55 (1993) 555-578 (G. *Rossetto*).
8712 **Winter** Miriam T., The Gospel according to Mary 1993 ➤ 9,9302: ᴿCathW 237 (1994) 241 (Jacqueline *Martin*).

H8.8 *Feminae NT* - **Women in the NT and Church history.**

8713 **Aspegren** Kerstin, The male woman; a feminine ideal in the early Church 1990 ➤ 6,8827 ... 9,9308: ᴿRTPhil 126 (1994) 380s (Isabelle *Chappuis-Juillard*).
8714 **Bautista** Esperanza, La mujer en la Iglesia primitiva. Estella 1993, VDivino. 171 p. 84-7151-877-5. - ᴿActuBbg 31 (1994) 19s (H. *Vall*); EstE 69 (1994) 410 (María *Tabuyo*); RET 54 (1994) 212-4 (P. *Barrado Fernández*).
8715 *Bavel* Tarcisio Van, La mujer en san AGUSTÍN: EstAg 29 (1994) 3-49.
8716 **Bernabé Ubieta** Carmen, Maria Magdalena; tradiciones en el cristianismo primitivo: Jeron 1/27. Estella 1994, VDivino. 305 p. 84-7151-982-8. - ᴿRET 54 (1994) 471-3 (P. *Barrado Fernández*).
8717 ᴱ**Børresen** Kari E., Image of God and gender models 1991 ➤ 7,341*a*; 9,9311: ᴿRTLv 25 (1994) 75-77 (Alice *Dermience*).
8718 *Bremmer* J. N., Tussen pauper en patrones; de weduwe in de vroeg-christelijke kerk: KerkT 45 (1994) 27-47.
8719 *Büttner* Gerhard, *Maier* Joachim, Maria aus Magdala - Ester - Debora; Modelle für den evangelischen und katholischen Religionsunterricht. Stu 1994, Calwer. 96 p.; 4 Farb-Folien. 3-7668-3269-7. - ᴿDielB 28 (1992s!) 263-5 (B. J. *Diebner*).
8720 *Burrus* V., Word and flesh; the bodies and sexuality of ascetic women in Christian antiquity: JFemRel 10,1 (1994) 27-51 [< NTAbs 38, p. 440].
8721 **Byrne** Brendan, Paul and the Christian woman 1989 ➤ 5,8791 ... 7, 8805: CanadCathR 12,5 (1994) 27s (Marie E. *Bouclin*).
8722 **Carr** Anne, La femme dans l'Église; tradition chrétienne et théologie féministe [Transforming grace],ᵀ: CogF 173, 1993 ➤ 9,9320: ᴿCarthaginensia 10 (1994) 494s (F. *Oliver Alcón*); ÉTRel 69 (1994) 119-122 (F. *Beydon*).
8723 *Castelli* Elisabeth A., Heteroglossia, hermeneutics and history; a review essay of recent feminist studies of early Christianity: JFemStR 10,1 (1994) 73-98.
8724 **Corley** Kathleen E., Private women - public meals; social conflict in the Synoptic tradition ᴰ1993 ➤ 9,9324: ᴿExpTim 105 (1993s) 348 (Ruth B. *Edwards*); NRT 116 (1994) 905 (X. *Jacques*).
8725 **Corrington** Gail P., Her image of salvation; female saviors and formative Christianity: Gender and biblical tradition 1992 ➤ 9,9405: ᴿCBQ 56 (1994) 364s (S. L. *Love*); ClasB 70 (1994) 58s (Judith L. *Sebesta*); ExpTim 105 (1993s) 56 (Ruth B. *Edwards*: 'Why is the Christian savior male?').
8725* **Crawford** Patricia, Women and religion in England 1500-1720: Christianity and society in the modern world. NY 1993, Routledge. x-268 p. $50. 0-415-01696-7 [TDig 41,355].
8726 ᴱ**Delumeau** Jean, La religion de ma mère; le rôle des femmes dans la

transmission de la foi 1992 → 9,9327: ^RArchivScSocR 82 (1993) 267 (Danièle *Hervieu-Léger*).

8727 **Demers** Patricia, Women as interpreters of the Bible 1992 → 8,9030; 9,9328: ^RHorizons 21 (1994) 184s (Marie Anne *Mayeski*).

8728 *a*) *Dresen* G., Het betere bloed; heilige mannen en het bloed van vrouwen in de katholieke kerk; – *b*) *Borgman* E., Mannen en hun voormoeders; een reactie op Frèda DROËS; – *c*) *Grey* M., Afgesleten woorden, gedane zaken? Wat hebben begrippen als zonde en genade, schuld en vergeving te zeggen in deze tijd; – *d*) *Haardt* M. de, Een passie voor transcendentie; Anne-Marie KORTE over Mary DALY en het moderne denken: Mara 6,1 (1992) 28-40 / 23-27 / 3-11 / 12-22 [GerefTTs 93,67].

8729 **Erickson** Victoria L., Where silence speaks; feminism, social theory and religion. Mp 1993, Fortress. 219 p. $16, 0-8006-2635-4. – ^RExpTim 105 (1993s) 188 (N. *Slee*: damning critique of the sociology of religion).

8730 **Evdokimov** Paul † 1970, Women and the salvation of the world; a Christian anthropology on the charisms of women: ^T*Gythiel* Anthony P. Crestwood NY 1994, St. Vladimir. 285 p. $13 pa. 0-88141-093-4 [TDig 42.163].

8731 **Felber** Anneliese, Harmonie durch Hierarchie? Das Denken der Geschlechter-Ordnung im frühen Christentum [1. Jeder Ranghöhere hat einen Helfer; 2. Es schickt sich nicht, dass Frauen lehren; ... 4. Jungfräulichkeit versus Ehe; 5. In jeder Frau ist Eva; ... 7. Die Frau muss zum Mann werden]: Frauenforschung 26. W 1994, Frauenverlag. 188 p. 3-900399-94-8.

8732 *Freyer* Thomas, Die Stellung der Frau bei Thomas von AQUIN: TGL 84 (1994) 65-83.

8733 **Gillman** Florence, Women who knew Paul 1992 → 8,9043; 9,9333: ^RRB 101 (1994) 153 (J. *Taylor*).

8734 **Haskins** Susan, Mary Magdalen 1993 → 9,9339: ^RTablet 247 (1993) 1296 (M. *Walsh*).

8735 **Hebblethwaite** Margaret, Six new gospels; NT women tell their stories. L 1994, G. Chapman. 154 p. £5 pa. – ^RTLond 97 (1994) 453s (Nicola *Slee*: combines creative updated fiction with critical exegesis).

8736 **Hollis** Stephanie, Anglo-Saxon women and the early Church; sharing a common fate. 1992, Boydell & B. 288 p. $79. 0-85115-317-8. – ^RAmHR 99 (1994) 214 (JoAnn *McNamara*).

8737 **Jensen** Anne, Gottes selbstbewusste Töchter 1992 → 9,9342: ^RDielB 28 (1992s) 295-7 (C. *Nauerth*); NRT 116 (1994) 609-611 (A. *Harvengt*); OstkSt 42 (1993) 70s (Eva M. *Synek*); StiZt 212 (1994) 640-2 (Elisabeth *Gössmann*); TPhil 69 (1994) 280-2 (T. *Hainthaler*); TPQ 142 (1994) 92s (Monika *Leisch-Kiesl*).

8738 **Kinukawa** Hisako, Women and Jesus in Mark; a Japanese feminist perspective: Bible and Liberation. Mkn 1994, Orbis. xi-156 p. $16 [TDig 42,172]. 0-88344-945-5.

8738* *Levine* Amy-Jill, Second temple Judaism, Jesus, and women; yeast of Eden: BInterp 2 (1994) 8-33.

8739 **Lindboe** Inger M., Women in the NT... bibliog. 1990 → 6,8864...8, 9060: ^RRB 101 (1994) 151 (J. *Murphy-O'Connor*).

8740 *a*) *Lynch* James R., Baptist women in ministry through 1920; – *b*) *Morris* S.L., Why do freewill Baptists send out ordained women to preach the Gospel? [c. 1910]: AmBapQ 13 (1994) 304-318 (-371, name-list) / 395-9.

8741 **Maillot** Alphonse, Marie ma sœur; étude sur la femme dans le NT 1990
→ 6,8866: ᴿEphMar 43 (1993) 504 (S. *Blanco*).

8742 [*Mattioli* U., sintesi conclusiva], La donna nel pensiero cristiano antico. Genova 1992, Marietti. 399 p. – *Sfameni Gasparro* G. su S. Paolo;
Anselmetto C. sulla maternità come una delle vie di liberazione della
donna in Cristo; *Militello* C. su amicizie con asceti; + 8.

8743 ᴱ**Milano** Andrea, Misoginia; la donna vista e malvista nelle culture
occidentali. R 1992, Dehoniane. 612 p.; ill. Lᵐ 55. – ᴿCC 145 (1994s)
91-93 (P. *Vanzan*).

8744 *Nientiedt* Klaus, Von den ursprünglichen Ansätzen ist wenig geblieben
[After 8 years' effort, the fourth draft on women's pastoral submitted to
U.S. bishops conferrence failed of a two-thirds majority]: HerdKorr 47
(1993) 87-92.

8745 ᴱ**Oden** Amy, In her words; women's writings in the history of Christian
thought [36 selections]. Nv 1994, Abingdon. 347 p. $19. 0-687-45972-9
[TDig 42,70].

8746 ᴱ**Pomeroy** Sarah, Women's history and ancient history 1991 → 7,405 ...
8,9163: ᴿClasR 44 (1994) 367-9 (Edith *Hall*).

8747 *Porter* Jean, At the limits of liberalism; Thomas AQUINAS and the
prospects for a Catholic feminism [St. Louis University Aquinas Lecture
1994, unabridged]: TDig 41 (1994) 315-330.

8748 **Rapley** Elizabeth, The dévotes 1990 → 6,8880 [not 'devotees']: ᴿAmHR
99 (1994) 576 (S. *Hanley*).

8749 **Ricci** Carla, Mary Magdalene and many others; women who followed
Jesus [1991 → 9,9358], ᵀ*Burns* Paul. Mp 1994, Fortress. 237 p. $15 [TS
56,357, S. A. *Quitslund*].

8750 a) *Rossi* Mary Ann, The legitimation of the abuse of women in Christianity; – b) *Thiering* Barbara, Jesus the man – thoughts of the writer; –
c) *Green* Elizabeth E., Women's words; sexual difference and biblical
hermeneutics: FemT 4 (Shf 1993) 56-63 / 39-55 / 64-78.

8751 **Schottroff** Luise, Lydias ungeduldige Schwestern; feministische Sozialgeschichte des frühen Christentums. Gü 1994, Kaiser. 348 p. ᴅᴍ 68.
3-579-1837-X. – ᴿTLZ 119 (1994) 1116-9 (W. *Wischmeyer*).

8752 **Schottroff** Luise, Let the oppressed go free; feminist perspectives on the
NT: Gender and Biblical Tradition. LvL 1993, W-Knox. 208 p. 0-
664-25426-8. – ᴿExpTim 105 (1993s) 56 (Ruth B. *Edwards*: finds in Acts
16,13s a synagogue run entirely by women).

8752* *Schüssler Fiorenza* Elisabeth, Mujer y ministerio en el cristianismo
primitivo [< TüTQ 173 (1993) 173-185, Neutestamentliche frühchristliche
Argumente], ᵀᴱ*Torres* María J. de: SelT 33 (1994) 327-337 [-340 TüTQ
242-4 < *Mieth* Dietmar].

8753 **Schüssler Fiorenza** Elisabeth, In memory of her; a feminist theological
reconstruction of Christian origins; tenth anniversary edition (new
introduction p. xiii-lv). NY 1994, Crossroad. ʟᴠ-357 p. 0-8245-1357-6.

8754 **Schüssler Fiorenza** Elisabeth, In memoria di lei; una ricostruzione
femminista delle origini cristiane, ᵀᴱ*Corsani Comba* M. 1990 → 6,8888;
8,9075: ᴿSicGymn 44 (1991) 359s (R. *Osculati*).

8754* **Sebastiani** Lilia, Tra/Sfigurazione ... M. Magdala 1992 → 8,9076;
9,9364: ᴿAsprenas 41 (1994) 135s (V. *Scippa*); CiVit 48 (1993) 314 (P.
Montini).

8755 *Shaw* B., Women and the early Church: History Today 44,2 (L 1994)
21-28 [< NTAbs 38, p. 442].

8756 *Sneeton* Donald, Marriage, motherhood and ministry; women in the dispute between Thomas MORE and William TYNDALE: Churchman 108 (1994) 197-212.

8757 *Stevenson-Moessner* Jeanne, Elizabeth Cady STANTON, reformer to revolutionary; a theological trajectory: JAAR 62 (1993) 673-697.

8758 **Symonds** Richard, Far above rubies; the women uncommemorated in the Church of England. ... 1993, Gracewing. 287 p. £10. 0-85244-244-0. – ᴿExpTim 105 (1993s) 224 (C. S. *Rodd*).

8759 *Torjesen* Karen Jo, When women were priests; women's leadership in the early Church and the scandal of their subordination to the rise of Christianity. SF 1993, HarperCollins. x-278 p. $22. 0-06-068297-3 [NTAbs 38, p. 500]. – ᴿChrSchR 24 (1994) 365s (Susie C. *Stanley*).

8760 **Tsames** Demetrios G., Ⓖ 'Matrology' [mēterikon]; expositions, apophthegms and lives of the holy desert mothers and other Orthodox women, I-3. Thessaloniki 1991-3, St. Makrina. 384 p. – ᴿTAth 65 (1994) 395-8 (E. A. *Theodorou,* Ⓖ).

8761 **Tuana** Nancy, The less noble sex; scientific, religious, and philosophical conceptions of woman's nature. Bloomington 1993, Indiana Univ. xii-172; $30; pa. $13. – ᴿChrSchR 24 (1994) 351-4 (Helen M. *Sterk*); TBR 7,2 (1994s) 45s (Carrie *Pemberton*).

8762 *Valerio* Adriana, L'esperienza profética femminile nei sec. XIV-XVI [> ᴱ*Valerio* A., Donna e profezia; N. D'Auria]: RasT 35 (1994) 713-731.

8762* *Vandoren* María, La iglesia patriarcal; problema eclesiológico y teológico: Christus 59,1 (Méx 1994) 26-29.

8763 *White* Robert, Women and the teaching office according to CALVIN: ScotJT 47 (1994) 489-509.

H8.9 *Theologia feminae* – **Feminist theology.**

8763* *Ackermann* D., Liberating the word; some thoughts on feminist hermeneutics: Scriptura 44 (1993) 1-18 [< NTAbs 38, p. 333].

8764 *a) Allen* John, The debate on the ordination of women in the Church of England and its implications for the whole Church; – *b) Braaten* Carl E., Lutheran dilemmas on the doctrine of ministry; – *c) Reumann* John, The case for threefold ministry; – *d) Turner* Philip, Communion, order and the ordination of women: Pro Ecclesia 2 (Northfield MN 1993) 285-295 / 261-4 / 265-270 / 275-284 [< ᴢɪᴛ 93,509].

8765 **Anatrella** Toni, El sexo olvidado. Bilbao 1994, Sal Terrae. – ᴿPáginas 19,130 (Lima 1994) 105-107 (C. *Castillo*).

8766 *Axt-Piscalar* Christine, Trinitarische Entzauberung des patriarchalen Vatergottes; eine Verständigung über die Bedeutung der Trinitätslehre als Beitrag zum Gespräch mit der feministischen Theologie: ZTK 91 (1994) 476-486.

8767 *Beinert* Wolfgang, Priestertum der Frau; der Vorhang zu, die Frage offen?: StiZt 212 (1994) 723-738.

8768 **Borrowdale** Anne, Distorted images; Christian attitudes to women, men and sex. L 1991, SPCK. vii-150 p. £7. – ᴿScotJT 47 (1994) 97-101 (Susan *Dowell*).

8769 *a) Botella Cubells* V., ¿Escritura versus feminismo? – *b) Spitzlei Sabine* B., La literatura teológica femenina de la edad media y sus paralelos en Latinoamérica; – *c) Porcile Santiso* M. Teresa, Teología desde 'lo femenino': sobre la misión de la mujer en la Iglesia: TEspir 37 (1993) 463-9 / 403-416 / 319-359.

8770 ᴱBrennan Patricia,   Changing women, changing Church, ᴱ*Uhr* Marie
     Louise. Newton NSW, Millennium. 154 p. A$ 17. – ᴿAustralasCR (1994)
     395 (Maria *Farrell*).
8771 ᴱBrooke George J.,   Women in the biblical tradition: Studies in women
     and religion 31, 1992 ➤ 9,373: ᴿTBR 7,1 (1994s) 20 (Katrina *Larkin*: of
     the 31, only third in the biblical field).
8772 Buse Gunhild, Macht – Moral – Weltlichkeit; eine feministisch-theolo-
     gische Auseinandersetzung mit Carol GILLIGAN und Frigga HAUG 1993
     ➤ 9,9392: ᴿTvT 34 (1994) 318s (G. *Dresen*).
8773 Carmody Denise L.,   Virtuous woman; reflections on Christian feminist
     ethics 1992 ➤ 9,9395: ᴿNRT 116 (1994) 585 (L. *Volpe*); Pacifica 7 (1994)
     235-7 (Liz *Hepburn*).
8774 Chopelin N.,   Hommes et femmes; l'identité relationnelle de l'être hu-
     main. Lyon 1994, Profac. 80 p. [NRT 117,759, A. *Mattheuws*].
8775 *Conway* Martin, Frauen im Priesteramt; die kurzfristigen Konsequenzen
     der Entscheidung der Kirche von England für die Frauenordination:
     KkMatD 45,1 (1994) 3-5 [< ZIT 94,119].
     ᴱDijk-Hennes Fokkelien van, *Brenner* Athalya, Reflections on theology and
     gender 1994 ➤ 267.
8776 Dumais Monique,   Diversité des utilisations féministes du concept
     'expérience des femmes' en sciences religieuses: Document 33. Ottawa
     1993, Institut Rech. sur les Femmes. 54 p. – ᴿLavalTP 50 (1994) 660-2
     (G. *Bouchard*).
8776* Fatum Lone, Kvinde teologi og arven frå Eva. K 1992, Gyldendal.
     98 p. – ᴿSvTKv 70 (1994) 44-46 (Anna Karen *Hammer*).
8777 *Ferrara* Dennis M., The ordination of women; tradition and meaning:
     TS 55 (1994) 706-717.
8778 *Fricke* T.J., What is the feminist hermeneutic? An analysis of feminist
     interpretation of the Bible: [Wis]LuthQ 91 (Mequon 1994) 45-59
     [< NTAbs 38, p. 335].
8779 Fulkerson Mary M.,   Changing the subject; women's discourses and
     feminist theology, Mp 1994, Fortress. xi-142. $18. 0-8006-2747-4 [TDig
     42,166: how to cope with the little interest shown by women who are in a
     stable position other than teaching feminism].
8780 *Gamberini* Paolo,   La comunione anglicana e l'ordinazione delle donne:
     RasT 35 (1994) 172-192.
8781 García Viñó M.,   La nueva Eva; el principio femenino de la era post-
     cristiana. M 1993, 'Prodhufi'. 190 p. – ᴿBibFe 58 (1994) 173s (A. *Salas*).
8781* Gössmann Elisabeth, *al.*,   Wörterbuch der feministischen Theologie
     1991 ➤ 7,8882 … 9,9428: ᴿActuBbg 31 (1994) 54-56 (J. *Boada*).
8782 *Green* Chris, Gender and ministry: Churchman 108 (1994) 328-352.
8783 Guzzetti G. Battista,   La condizione della donna; storia e principi,
     dall'inferiorità alla reciproca complementarietà con l'uomo. Mi 1991,
     Massimo. 142 p. Lᵐ 18. – ᴿAngelicum 72 (1994) 140-3 (Margherita M.
     Rossi).
8784 Haardt M. A. C. de,   Dichter bij de dood; feministisch-theologische
     aanzetten tot een theologie van de dood [death]: diss. Tilburg 1993.
     ᴰ*Schreurs* N. Zoetermeer, Boeken-C. 284 p. 90-239-04435. – TvT 34,73.
8785 ᴱHaas Peter J.,   Recovering the role of women; power and authority in
     rabbinic Jewish society [Vanderbilt graduate sem.; 6 art.]: SFlStJud 59,
     1992 ➤ 8,471: ᴿRelStR 20 (1994) 69 (Lynn R. *LiDonnici*: for whom?).
8786 *Hallensleben* Barbara, Unerwartete kirchliche Perspektiven für Frauen:
     TGL 84 (1994) 355-360.

8787 **Hampson** Daphne, Theology and feminism 1990 ➤ 6,8760...9,9442: ᴿScotJR 13 (1992) 128-130 (Marsha *Hewitt*: she recognizes that Christianity has outgrown its historical forms).
8788 *Hampson* Daphne, response to critique of her 1990 Theology and Feminism by Pamela *Anderson*: LitTOx [7 (1993) 78-86] 209-217.
8789 **Haubert** Katherine M., Women as leaders; accepting the challenge of Scripture. Monrovia CA 1993, MARC. 101 p. $9. 0-91252-81-6. – ᴿRExp 91 (1994) 634 (Mary B. *Zimmer*).
8789* **Hauke** Manfred, Women in the priesthood? a systematic analysis in the light of the order of creation and redemption [Problematik 1980], ᵀ*Kipp* David 1988 ➤ 5,8896... 7,8885; 0-89870-165-1: ᴿCanadCathR 12,5 (1994) 27 (Agnes *Cunningham*).
8790 *Henking* Susan E. [and comments], Rejected, reclaimed, renamed; Mary DALY on psychology and religion: JPsy&T 21,3 (1993) 199-207.223-7 [208-222].
8791 *Hewitt* Marsha, The redemptive power of memory; Walter BENJAMIN and Elisabeth SCHÜSSLER FIORENZA: JFemStR 10,1 (1994) 73-89.
8792 ᴱ*Holloway* R., Who needs: feminism? 1991 ➤ 7,359a; 8,9128*: ᴿScotJT 47 (1994) 264-6 (Susan *Parsons*).
8793 **Hunt** Mary E., Fierce tenderness; a feminist theology of friendship 1991 ➤ 8,9130: ᴿRExp 93 (1994) 271s (Molly T. *Marshall*: careful but hardly Christian).
8794 *Jensen* Anne, Ist Frauenordination ein ökumenisches Problem? Zu den jüngsten Entwicklungen in den anglikanischen, altkatholischen und orthodoxen Kirchen: IkiZ 84 (1994) 210-228.
8795 *a) Joy* Morny, LEVINAS; alterity, the feminine and women – a meditation; – *b) Tomm* Winnie, Otherness in self-disclosure; a woman's perspective: SR 22 (1993) 463-485 / 467-502.
8796 ᴱ**King** Ursula, Feminist theology from the Third World; a reader. L/Mkn 1994, SPCK/Orbis. 434 p. £17.50 pa. 0-88344-963-3 [TDig 42,165]. – ᴿTLond 97 (1994) 449-451 (Esther D. *Reed*).
8796* **King** Ursula, Women and spirituality; voices of protest and promise² [¹1989]: Women in Society. xii-273 p. $16 pa. 1993, PennStateUniv. 0-271-01069-X [TLZ 120,566, J. Christine *Janowski*].
8797 *a) King* Ursula, Voices of protest and promise; women's studies in religion, the impact of the feminist critique on the study of religion; – *b) Slater* Peter, response, Winnipeg 1980: ➤ 381, SR 23 (1994) 315-329 / 339-346.
8798 *Köstenberger* Andreas J., Gender passages in the NT: hermeneutical fallacies critiqued: WestTJ 56 (1994) 259-283.
8799 *Korte* Anne-Marie, De religieuze bronnen van de compassie; feministische theologie als kritische cultuurtheologie: ➤ 110, ᶠSCHILEEBEECKX E., TvT 34,4 (1994) 361-383; Eng. 384.
8800 ᴱ**La Cugna** Catherine M., Freeing theology; the essentials of theology in feminist perspective. SF 1994, Harper. 266 p. $18 pa. – ᴿChrCent 111 (1994) 121-3 (Maureen D. *Kemeza*).
8801 **Lerner** Gerda, The creation of feminist consciousness from the Middle Ages to Eighteen-Seventy. Ox 1993, UP. xii-195 p. $27.50. – ᴿHZ 259 (1994) 720s (H. *Röckelein*).
8802 **Long** Grace D. Cumming, Passion and reason; womenviews of Christian life [...domestic creativity, addiction, AIDS]. LVL 1993, W-Knox. ix-150 p. £13. 0-664-25408-X. – ᴿTBR 7,1 (1994s) 31 (Anne *Murphy*).

8803 *Manus* U.C., E. SCHÜSSLER FIORENZA's theoretical method: WAfEcQ
3 (Ibadan 1991) 67-73.
8803* *Marinelli* Giovanni, La donna nella Chiesa, 'ministra' o mediatrice:
Sacra Doctrina 3s (1994) 284 p.
8804 **Militello** C., Donna in questione 1992 ➤ 9,9469: ᴿLateranum 60 (1994)
206s (Eva C. *Rava*); RasT 35 (1994) 113s (Cloe *Taddei Ferretti*).
8805 *Militello* Cettina, La questione femminile in alcune recenti pubblicazioni: RicT 3 (R 1992) 411-429 [< ᴢɪᴛ 93,406].
8806 *Moingt* J., Sur un débat clos [Jean-Paul II, 22.V.1994 sur l'ordination
des femmes]: RechSR 82 (1994) 321-333: p. 323: 'il ne suffit pas qu'il le
dise, encore doit-il *montrer où* cette vérité est contenue').
8807 ᴱNavarro Mercedes, Diez mujeres escriben teología: Diez palabras
clave. Estella 1993, VDivino. 388 p. 84-7151-904-6. – ᴿRET 53 (1993)
400-403 (P. *Barrado Fernández*).
8808 **Nowak** Antoni J., ❷ *Kobieta... kapłanem?* (Woman... priest?). Lublin
1993, Norbertinum. – ᴿAtKap 122 (1994) 610-3 (I.S. *Ledwoń*, ❷).
8809 *Nowak* Susan, The Girardian theory and feminism; critique and appropriation: ➤ 43, ꟳGIRARD R., Contagion 1 (1994) 19-30.
8810 **Öchsner** Iris, Arbeit am Mythos der Weiblichkeit; Kritik und Konstruktion feministischer Weisheitstheologie: ev. Diss. ᴰTimm H. München
1994s. – RTLv 26, p. 569.
8811 *a) Paton* Margaret, Representation in Eucharistic theology; its relevance
for women's ordination to the priesthood; – *b) Behr-Sigel* Elisabeth, The
ordination of women; an ecumenical problem; – *c) Brett-Crowther*
Michael, An equal ministry: TLond 97 (1994) 2-8 / 9-26 / 26-38.
8812 **Purvis** Sally B., The power of the Cross; foundations for a Christian
feminist ethic of community. Nv 1993, Abingdon. 115 p. $15. 0-687-
32606-0. – ᴿRExp 91 (1994) 618 (Molly T. *Marshall*: anchored in Paul;
'0-687-332606-0').
8813 *Raming* Ida, Endgültiges Nein zum Priestertum der Frau?: Orientierung [> TDig 42,43, ᵀᴱ*Asen* B.A.: John PAUL II May 22, 1994 bypasses
the socio-cultural context of Jesus' time and historico-critical methods].
8814 *Ratzinger* Joseph, [Su] La lettera apostolica 'Ordinatio sacerdotalis':
CC 145 (1994,3) 61-70.
8814* **Reis** Patricia, Through the [phallic] goddess; a women's way of
healing. NY 1991, Continuum. 235 p. $25. – ᴿCritRR 6 (1993) 571-3
(Carroll *Saussy*).
8815 **Rolnick** Philip A., Analogical possibilities; how women refer to God:
AAR. Atlanta 1993, Scholars. xxi-316 p. $30; sb. $20. – ᴿTS 55 (1994)
392s (G.P. *Rocca*).
8816 **Russell** Letty M., Church in the round; feminist interpretation of the
Church 1993 ➤ 9,9497; 0-664-25070-X: ᴱExpTim 105 (1993s) 188
(Nicola *Slee*); Horizons 21 (1994) 198-200 (F.J. *Farrella*).
8817 *Russo* Raffaella, Differenza e reciprocità; per una teologia del rapporto
uomo-donna: Asprenas 41 (1994) 483-510.
8818 **Saffar** Ruth A. Eli, Rapture engaged; the suppression of the feminine in
western culture. L 1994, Routledge. 168 p. £30. – ᴿMonth 255 (1994)
482s (H.S. *Lim*).
8819 **Sands** Kathleen M., Escape from Paradise; evil and tragedy in feminist
theology. Mp 1994, Fortress. xii-212 p. [TS 56,403, Irena *Makarushka*).
8820 *Scherzberg* Lucia, Sünde und Gnade in der feministischen Theologie:
JbBT 9 (1994) 261-283.
8821 *a) Schmid* Peter F., Neue Manns-Bilder? Auf dem Weg zu einer

Emanzipation der Männer; – b) *Fuchs* Gotthard, Theologische Männerforschung, ein Gebot der Stunde: Diakonia 24 (Mainz 1993) 145-150 / 159-169 [< ZIT 93,170].

8822 **Schmidt** Eva R., *al.*, Riletture bibliche al femminile; 27 saggi di interpretazione biblica femminista, ᵀ*Gandolfo* Giuliana: PiccBtT 33. T 1994, Claudiana. 255 p. 88-7016-196-X.

8823 *Schneider-Flume* Gunda, Frauensünde? Überlegungen zu Geschlechtsdifferenz und Sünde: ZTK 91 (1994) 299-317.

8824 **Schneiders** Sandra M., Beyond patching 1991 ↠ 7,8923... 9,9510: ᴿIrTQ 59 (1993) 232-4 (Linda *Hogan*).

8824* **Schottroff** Luise, Let the oppressed go free; feminist perspectives on the NT: ᵀ*Kidder* Annemarie S. Lᴠʟ 1993, Knox. 208 p. $18 pa. – ᴿAnglTR 76 (1994) 375s (Joanna *Dewey*).

8825 **Schüssler Fiorenza** Elisabeth, But she said 1992 ↠ 8,8173; 9,9512: ᴿChrSchR 24 (1994) 323-5 (R. L. *Maddox*); JAAR 62 (1994) 215-7 (Amy-Jill *Levine*: 'she choreographs corrective models... All readers would do well to put on their dancing shoes'); JRel 74 (1994) 92s (C. *Osiek*).

8826 *Schüssler Fiorenza* Elisabeth, *al.*, Gewalt gegen Frauen: ↠ 265, IZTConc 30 (1994) 95-107 (-188).

8827 **Schüssler-Fiorenza** Elisabeth, Discipleship of equals... ekklesia-logy [art. 1964-91]. NY 1993, Crossroad. xii-372 p. $20 pa. – ᴿAmerica 171,10 (1994) 265 (Susan A. *Ross*); Horizons 21 (1994) 195s (Ann O. *Graff*); Protestantism 48 (1994) 349-351 (Elizabeth E. *Green*); Worship 65 (1994) 460-2 (Sara *Butler*).

8828 *a) Sjørup* Lene, Are women's religious experiences mystical experiences?; – *b) Lundgren* Eva, 'I am endowed with all power in heaven and on earth'; when men became men through 'Christian' abuse: ST 48 (1994) 15-32 / 33-47.

8829 *Spanner* Douglas, Men, women and God: Churchman 108 (1994) 101-118.

8830 *Stanley* Susie C., Women called to ministry: EvJ 12 (1994) 35-40.

8831 *Taylor* Marion Ann, Feminist biblical scholarship; recent studies [*Brenner* A.; *Frymer-Kensky* T., *Pace* S. ...]: TorJT 10 (1994) 93-96.

8832 **Webster** Margaret, A new strength, a new song; the journey to women's [1992 Anglican] priesthood. 212 p. £10. – ᴿTLond 97 (1994) 478s (Susan *Dowell*).

8833 **Welch** Sharon D., A feminist ethic of risk 1990 ↠ 6,9028 ... 9,9533: ᴿScotJT 47 (1994) 145-7 (Elaine *Graham*).

8834 **Williams** D. S., Sisters in the wilderness; the challenge of womanist God-talk 1993 ↠ 9,9535: ᴿNRT 116 (1994) 436 (L.-J. *Renard*).

H9 Eschatologia NT, *spes, hope.*

8834* **Accattoli** L., *al.*, Quando tornerà il Figlio dell'uomo; conversazioni sui 'Novissimi'. Mi 1994, Àncora. 77 p. Lᵐ 9. – ᴿAsprenas 41 (1994) 452 (P. *Pifano*).

8835 **Aka** Christine, Tot und vergessen? Sterbebilder als Zeugnis katholischen Totengedenkens: Schr 10. Detmold/Wf 1993, Freilichtmuseum. 3-9261-6016-0 [TR 90,518].

8836 **Almeder** Robert, Death and personal survival; the evidence for [reincarnation] life after death. Lanham MD 1992, Littlefield Adams. xii-285 p. £45; pa. £16. 0-8476-7728-1; pa. 0-8226-3016-8. – ᴿTBR 7,2 (1994s) 9 (Margaret *Yee*: sequel to his 1987 Beyond death).

8837 **Almond** Philip C., Heaven and hell in Enlightenment England. C 1994,
Univ. viii-218 p.; 16 pl. $50. 0-521-45371-2 [TDig 42,153].
8838 *Bacq* Philippe, Après la mort, résurrection ou réincarnation?: Foi-
Temps 23 (1993) 63-75.
8839 *Bakker* J. T., Jan BONDA, Het ene doel van God; een antwoord op de
leer van de eeuwige straf [Baarn 1993, Ten Have; ƒ40; 90-259-4528-7]:
GerefTTs 93 (1993) 254.
8840 **Beisser** Friedrich, Hoffnung und Vollendung: HbSysT 15. Gü 1993,
Mohn. 351 p. DM 98. – ᴿTR 90 (1994) 148 (H. *Vorgrimler*).
8841 **Beker** Johan Christiaan, Suffering and hope; the biblical vision and the
human predicament. GR 1994, Eerdmans. xii-132 p. 0-8028-0722-4.
8842 ᴱ**Beltz** Walter, Lexikon der letzten Dinge. Augsburg 1993, Pattloch.
522 p. DM 68. 3-629-00671-X. – ᴿTGL 84 (1994) 386s (W. *Beinert*).
8843 **Bernstein** Alan E., The formation of Hell; death and retribution in the
ancient and early Christian worlds 1993 → 9,9545: ᴿGreeceR 41 (1994)
248 (P. *Walcot*: a compilation); Month 255 (1994) 442s (D. *Howard*);
TLond 97 (1994) 367s (M. *Goulder*).
8844 **Blanchard** John, Whatever happened to Hell? Darlington 1993, Evangelical. 336 p. 0-85234-303-5. – ᴿChurchman 108 (1994) 270 (G. *Bray*).
8845 **Boggs** Arthur M., [1 Thes 4,13-18; 1 Cor 15,15-35] With what sort of
body; pastoral concerns with and Pauline perspectives on the nature of life
after death: diss. ᴰ*Droge* A. – Chi 1994. 94-25359. – DissA 55 (1994s)
p. 997.
8846 **Bowker** John, The meanings of death 1993 → 9,9545: ᴿMonth 255
(1994) 317s (Mary Anne *Traylen*).
8847 **Brantschen** Johannes B., Hoffnung für Zeit und Ewigkeit; der Traum
vom wachen Christenmenschen. FrB 1992, Herder. 158 p. – ᴿFrSZ 40
(1993) 481-3 (G. *Bachl*).
8848 *Brattston* David, Hades, Hell and Purgatory in ante-Nicene literature:
Churchman 108 (1994) 68-79.
8849 **Bühlmann** Walbert, Gottes grosse Überraschung; was nach dem Tode
auf uns wartet [= Fragen um Tod und Jenseits 1985 verkürzt]: Topos Tb
233. Mainz 1993, Grünewald. 222 p. DM 16.80. – ᴿBiKi 49 (1994) 67 (R.
Russ).
8850 *Bynum* Caroline W., Images of the Resurrection body in the theology of
late antiquity: CathHR 80 (1994) 215-237.
8851 ᴱ**Cameron** Nigel D., Universalism and the doctrine of Hell [10
evangelical art.]. 1991/3 → 9,434c: ᴿExpTim 105 (1993s) 316s (P.
Badham); RefR 48 (1994s) 68s (H. *Buis*); TLond 97 (1994) 369s (D. F.
Wright).
   Carozzi Claude, Eschatologie et au-delà; recherches sur l'*Apocalypse de
Paul* 1994 → 5627.
8852 *Chadwick* Henry, Anglican eschatology and its challenges: AnglTR 76
(1994) 274-284.
8853 *Chan* Simon, The logic of hell; a response to [STOTT J.] annihilationism:
EvRT 18 (1994) 20-32; 33s rejoinder.
8854 **Colvin** Howard, Architecture and the after-life 1991 → 9,9552: ᴿSpeculum 69 (1994) 446s (J. F. *O'Gorman*).
8854* *Colzani* Gianni, L'escatologia nella teologia cattolica degli ultimi 30
anni: ScuolC 122 (1994) 447-477.
8855 **Couture** André, La réincarnation: L'Horizon du Croyant 2, 1992
→ 8,9218; 9,9555: ᴿNRT 116 (1994) 607 (L. *Volpe*); RHPR 74 (1994) 440
(G. *Siegwalt*; aussi sur 1 et 3); SR 23 (1994) 96s (M. *Boisvert*).

8856 **Daley** Brian E., The hope of the early Church 1991 ➤ 7,8950... 9,9560: ᴿJEarlyC 1 (1993) 444-6 (F. W. *Norris*); ScotJT 47 (1994) 375s (A. *Louth*); TR 90 (1994) 132-4 (M.-Barbara von *Stritzky*).

8857 ᴱ**Davies** Jon, Ritual and remembrance; response to death in human societies. Shf 1994, Academic. 284 p. 1-85075-469-1.

8858 *Detweiler* Robert, Thanatopoiesis; imagining death: CGrebel 12 (1994) 155-169.

8859 **Di Sante** C., Il futuro dell'uomo nel futuro di Dio; ripensare l'escatologia: Teologia per giovani animatori 7. T-Leumann 1994, Elle Di Ci. 175 p. Lᵐ 12. – ᴿAsprenas 41 (1994) 610 (P. *Pifano*).

8860 **Dixon** Larry, The other side of the Good News... Hell 1992 ➤ 9,9563: ᴿJEvTS 37 (1994) 624-6 (E. *Fudge*: ascribes evil motives to F. F. BRUCE, J. WENHAM, and other more lenient evangelicals).

8861 ᴱ**Doore** Gary, *a)* What survives? Contemporary explorations of life after death. 1990, Tarcher. $13. 0-87477-583-3. – *b)* ᵀ*Schaup* Susanne. Mü 1994, Kösel. 269 p. DM 38. 3-466-34303-8 [TR 90,510, tit. pp.].

8861* *a) Duquoc* Christian, Progrès et espérance; – *b) Robert* Sylvie, Dieu attendu et inespéré; objet de l'espérance chrétienne: LumièreV 219 (1994) 21-32 / 63-75.

8862 **Durrwell** François-X., Le Christ, l'homme et la mort. P/Montréal 1991, Médiaspaul/Paulines. 112 p. F 69. – ᴿFoiTemps 23 (1993) 185s (H. *Thomas*).

8863 **Durrwell** F.-X., Im Tod ist das Leben; Christus, der Mensch und der Tod. Mü 1993, Neue Stadt. 116 p. DM 9. 3-87996-30-2. – ᴿForKT 10 (1994) 233s (A. *Ziegenaus*).

8863* **Durrwell** F. X., Cristo, el hombre y la muerte. 1993. – ᴿScripTPamp 26 (1994) 1205s (E. *Parada*).

8864 **Egmond** D. van, Body, subject and self; the possibilities of survival after death: diss. Utrecht Rijksuniv. ᴰ*Brümmer* V. 1993. 281 p. 90-72235-23-1. – TvT 34 (1994) 73.

8864* **Eicher** Peter, ¿Hay una vida antes de la muerte? reflexiones bíblicas, ᵀ*Martínez de Lapera* Abelardo. Barc 1993, Herder. 256 p. pt. 2136. 84-254-1819-4. – ᴿActuBbg 31 (1994) 241 (J. M. *Fondevila*); EfMex 11 (1993) 423s (C. *Delpero*).

8865 **Ferrer Iñarata** Ana, El retorno del Cristo ¿mito o realidad? Barc 1993, KFM. 96 p. 84-604-7945-5.

8866 *Fuchs* Gotthard, Die Wiederentdeckung der Grenze(n); Lebenswelt und Todesbilder: Diakonia 25 (1994) 368-376.

8867 **Fudge** Edward W., ²*Cousins* Peter [¹1982], The fire that consumes; the biblical case for conditional immortality. Carlisle 1994, Paternoster. xiv-226 p. 0-85364-587-6.

8868 ᴱ**Galvin** J. P., Faith and the facts; studies in Christian eschatology. NY 1994, Paulist. iv-75 p. $7. 0-8091-3455-1 [NTAbs 38, p. 275].

8869 **Girard** Jean-Michel, La mort chez S. AUGUSTIN: Paradosis 34, 1992 ➤ 8,9235; 9,9574: ᴿEstAg 29 (1994) 694s (F. de *Luis*); JTS 45 (1994) 741-5 (G. *Bonner*).

8870 **Gozzelino** Giorgio, Nell'attesa della beata speranza; saggio di escatologia cristiana: CorsoStTeol. T-Leumann 1993, Elle Di Ci. 504 p. Lᵐ 45. 88-01-10269-0. – ᴿGregorianum 75 (1994) 769s (L. *Ladaria*).

8871 **Gustafson** Janie, The mystery of death; a Catholic perspective. Dubuque 1994, Brown. vi-230 p. $13. 0-697-17757-2.

8872 **Hill** Charles E., Regnum caelorum; patterns of future hope in early Christianity 1992 ➤ 9,9581: ᴿCompostellanum 38 (1993) 277-9 (E. *Ro-*

mero Pose); JRel 74 (1994) 564s (L. J. *Thompson*); JTS 45 (1994) 298-302 (B. E. *Daley*); TBR 5,1 (1992s) 22 (G. *Gould*); WestTJ 55 (1993) 359s (R. A. *Muller*).

8873 **Himmelfarb** Martha,   Ascents to heaven in Jewish and Christian apocalypses. Oxford 1993, UP.   xii-171 p. $30.   0-19-508203-6 [BIP; BL 95,151, D. J. *Bryan*; NTAbs 38, p. 320]. – ᴿCBQ 56 (1994) 764s (P. L. *Redditt*: 'ascent to').

8874 **Horvath** Tibor,   Eternity and eternal life; speculative theology and science in discourse.   Waterloo ON 1993, W. Laurier Univ.   ix-174 p. – ᴿBLitEc 95 (1994) 350s (J.-M. *Maldamé*).

8875 International theological commission,   Some current questions in eschatology: IrTQ 58 (1992) 209-243.

8876 *Janowski* J. Christine,   Eschatologischer Dualismus? Erwägungen zum 'doppelten Ausgang' des Jüngsten Gerichts: JbBT 9 (1994) 175-218.

8877 ᴱ**Jeppesen** Knud, *Nielsen* Kirsten, *Rosendal* Bent,   In the last days; on Jewish and Christian apocalyptic and its period. 1994 → 89*e*, ᶠOᴛᴢᴇɴ B. 261 p. Dk 198.

8878 **Kehl** Medard, Escatología, ᵀ*Olasagasti* M.: Lux Mundi 70, 1992 → 8, 9253; 9,9586:   ᴿLumenVr 42 (1993) 95a (F. *Ortiz* U.).

8879 *Kennedy* Emmanuel,   Unsterblichkeit; das Selbst als die post-mortale Belohnung [Tagung Walberberg Apr. 1991]: Symbolon 11 (1993) 11-34.

8880 Recent eschatologies, by Ph.D. candidates: sᴡᴊᴛ 36,2 (1993) 22s, *Kennedy* Henry A., on Sᴄʜʟᴇɪᴇʀᴍᴀᴄʜᴇʀ; 23, *McConnell* Russell, on Tɪʟʟɪᴄʜ; 24, *Stine* Robert C., on Bᴜʟᴛᴍᴀɴɴ; 25, *Mwakitwile* Charles, on Bᴀʀᴛʜ; 25s, *Boutwell* W. Stacey, on Pᴀɴɴᴇɴʙᴇʀɢ; 26s, *David* Joe, on Mᴏʟᴛᴍᴀɴɴ; 27s, *Daugherty* K., on Tʀᴀᴄʏ; 28s, *Vang* Preben, on Oɢᴅᴇɴ; 29s, *Rankin* R. Andrew, on G. Kᴀᴜꜰᴍᴀɴɴ; 30s, *Patrick* Rick D., on E. Fᴀʀʟᴇʏ; 31s, *Roberts* Laeron A., on Sᴄʜᴀʀʟᴇᴍᴀɴɴ.

8881 *Khatchadourian* Haig,   Death and the meaning of life: ScotJR 13 (1992) 5-20.

8882 *Kirkpatrick* William D.,   Christian hope: sᴡᴊᴛ 36,2 (1993s) 33-43.

8882* *Kremer* Jacob,   Tod und Auferstehung aus der Sicht neuerer Bibelwissenschaft: → 36, Mem. Fᴜᴄᴀᴋ M., BogSmot 64 (1994) 83-95.

8883 **Kselman** Thomas A.,   Death and the afterlife in modern France 1993 → 9,9588:   ᴿAmHR 99 (1994) 248 (P. N. *Stearns*); CathHR 79 (1993) 547s (R. *Gibson*).

8884 **Kvanvig** Jonathan L.,   The problem of Hell.   Ox 1993, UP.   viii-128 p. $30.   0-19-508487-X [TDig 41,367]. – ᴿChrLit 43 (1993s) 98s (Diana *Culbertson*); ChrSchR 24 (1994) 361-3 (L. *Lacy*); ExpTim 105,10 top choice (1993s) 289s (C. S. *Rodd*: the Good News is only one side of the story); Month 255 (1994) 442s (R. *Schniertshauer*); TLond 97 (1994) 368s (P. *Helm*).

8884* *a) Lang* Bernhard,   Das biblische Jenseits in neuer Sicht; – *b) Görg* Manfred,   Ägyptische Totentexte als Wegweiser; – *c) Kehl* Medard,   Seelenwanderung und Reinkarnation: BiKi 49,1 ('Das Leben nach dem Tod' 1994) 2-10 / 28-34 /35-42.

8885 **LeMasters** Philip,   The import of eschatology in John H. Yᴏᴅᴇʀ's critique of Constantinianism.   SF 1992, Mellen.   245 p. – ᴿPerspRelSt 21 (1994) 76-81 (J. W. *McClendon*).

8886 **Lewis** James R.,   Encyclopedia of afterlife beliefs and phenomena.   Detroit 1994, Gale.   xxi-420 p. $38.   0-8103-4879-9 [TDig 42,174].

8887 *Linfield* Alan M.,   Sheep and goats; current evangelical thought on the nature of Hell and the scope of salvation [...those who still believe in hell are an endangered species]: VoxEvca 24 (1994) 63-75.

8887* **Lona** Horacio, Uber die Auferstehung des Fleisches 1993 → 9,9596: ᴿRBíbArg 55 (1993) 245-8 (J. *Pablo Martín*).

8888 *Magnelli* Luigi, Rinnovamento dell'escatologia contemporanea e conseguenze per l'evangelizzazione: Vivarium 2 (1994) 391-412.

8889 **Marquardt** F. W., Was dürfen wir hoffen, wenn wir hoffen dürfen; eine Eschatologie 1, 1992 → 9,9601; 3-579-01925-2: ᴿTvT 34 (1994) 316s (W. *Logister*).

8890 **Martínez de Pisón** Ramón, L'au-delà: L'horizon du croyant. Ottawa 1993, Novalis. 204 p. – ᴿÉglT 25 (1994) 297s (M. *Lefebvre*).

8891 **Moder-Frei** Elfi, Reinkarnation und Christentum; die verschiedenen Reinkarnationsvorstellungen in der Auseinandersetzung mit dem christlichen Glauben: kath. Diss. ᴰ*Ziegenaus*. Augsburg 1993. – TR 90 (1994) 80.

8892 **Moioli** G., L' 'escatologico' cristiano; proposta sistematica: Lectio 2. Mi 1994, Glosas. 267 p. Lᵐ 40 [NRT 17,751, A. *Pighin*].

8893 **Ngayihembako** Samuel, Le temps de la fin; approche exégétique de l'eschatologie du NT [diss. Genève, ᴰ*Bovon* F.]: Monde B 29. Genève 1994, Labor et Fides. 430 p. F 135 [NTAbs 38, p. 478]. – ᴿEsprVie 104 (1994) 491s (É. *Cothenet*).

8894 *O'Collins* Gerald, Alla fine... l'amore [...malgrado il poco posto che tiene nelle escatologie]: RasT 35 (1994) 645-662.

8895 **O'Connor** James T., Land of the living; a theology of the last things 1992 → 9,9608: AnnTh 8 (1994) 190-3 (T. J. *McGovern*).

8896 *Peterson* Robert A., A traditionalist response to John STOTT's arguments for annihilationism: JEvTS 37 (1994) 553-568. → 4494.

8897 *Phan* Peter C., Contemporary context and issues in eschatology: TS 55 (1994) 507-538.

8898 **Pozo** Cándido, La venida del Señor en la gloria; escatología: ManTCat 22. Valencia 1993, Edicep. 228 p. 84-7050-335-9. – ᴿEstE 69 (1994) 403 (G. *Uríbarri*); ForumKT 10 (1994) 156s (A. *Ziegenaus*: mehr als Neuauflage seiner 1980 Teología del más allá, 16000 verkauft); ScripTPamp 26 (1994) 750-6 (L. F. *Mateo-Seco*).

8899 **Ratzinger** Joseph, La mort et l'au-delà, ᵀ*Rochais* Henri: Communio. P 1994, Fayard. F 120. – ᴿÉtudes 381 (1994) 282 (Gwendoline *Jarczyk*).

8900 **Riessen** Renée van, Erotiek en dood, Met het oog op transcendentie in de filosofie van LEVINAS: diss. Kampen 1991, Kok Agora. 262 p. ƒ 45. 90-391-0013-6. – ᴿBijdragen 55 (1994) 223 (A. van de *Paverd*).

8901 ᵀᴱ**Roth** Catherine P., GREGORY of Nyssa, The soul and the resurrection. Crestwood NY 1993, St. Vladimir. 130 p. $7. 0-88141-120-5 [TDig 42,168].

8902 *Roukema* R., Reïncarnatie in de Oude Kerk [...ORIGENES: J.-B. & Elias]: GerefTTs 93 (1993) 33-56.

8903 *Runia* Klaas, Eschatology and hermeneutics: EurJT 3 (1994) 17-33.

8904 *Ryan* Thomas, Resurrection and reincarnation: Forefront 1,3 (Crestone CO 1994) 8-14.

8905 *Sabugal* S., Anastasis 1993 → 9,9617: ᴿRET 54 (1994) 358-362 (E. *Tourón*).

8906 *Schenk* Richard, Tod und Theodicee; Ansätze zu einer Theologie der Trauer bei Thomas von AQUIN: ForumKT 10 (1994) 161-176.

8907 *Schmidt* Helmut, Was kommt nach dem Tod? Biblische Jenseitsvorstellungen und Grenzerfahrungen: Zeitwende 64 (1993) 196-212 [< ZIT 93,665].

F SCHNACKENBURG Rudolf, Weltgericht und Weltvollendung, Tagung 1993, E Klauck H.-J.: QDisp 150, 1994 ➤ 332b.
8907* **Schuman** Nick A., Gelijk om gelijk; verslag en balans van een discussie over goddelijke vergelding in het Oude Testament: diss Amsterdam VU 1993, D*Schuman* N. xii-590 p. 90-5383-263-7. – TLZ 120,421.
8908 *Seweryniak* Henryk, ❷ Métempsycose et foi en résurrection: PrzPow 867 (1993) 186-196.
8909 *Shaw* D. W. D., 'The undiscover'd country'; an exploration – 'The life everlasting': ScotJT 47 (1994) 149-168.
8910 **Sopata** Marian, Zur Theologie des Todes: Diss. D*Ganoczy* A. Würzburg 1992s. – TR 90,90.
8911 **Stock** K. [ev. Wissenschaftliche Gesellschaft für Theologie], Die Zukunft der Erlösung; zur neueren Diskussion um die Eschatologie: Veröff. 7. Gü 1994, Kaiser. 175 p. DM 68. 3-579-00258-9. – R TvT 34 (1994) 317 (C. *Leget*).
8912 *a*) *Stuhlmacher* Peter, The resurrection of Jesus and the resurrection of the dead, T*Whitlock* Jonathan M., – *b*) *Meyer* Ben F., Resurrection as humanly intelligible destiny; – *c*) *Ollenburger* Ben C., If mortals die, will they live again?; – *d*) *Peters* Ted, Resurrection; what kind of body? – *e*) *Osiek* Carolyn, The women at the tomb; what are they doing there? – *f*) *Pinnock* Clark H., Salvation by resurrection; – *g*) *Harakas* Stanley S., Resurrection and ethics in CHRYSOSTOM: ➤ 398, ExAud 9 (1993) 45-56 / 13-27 / 29-44 / 57-76 / 97-107 / 77-95.
8913 **Tamayo-Acosta** J. J., Para comprender la escatología cristiana. Estella 1993, VDivino. 327 p. – R BibFe 59 (1994) 157 (A. *Salas*).
8914 *Tourón del Pie* Eliseo, Ideas y creencias escatológicas en los apócrifos asuncionistas: RET 54 (1994) 125-179.
8915 **Varone** François, Ce Juge qui nous attend [Ce Dieu 1, 1981; 2, 1984; 3:]: Apologiques. P 1993, Cerf. 134 p. F 79. – R ÉglT 25 (1994) 146 (R. *Martínez de P. L.*); RThom 94 (1994) 325s (G. *Bavaud*: défend l'universalité du salut).
8916 **Vorgrimler** Herbert, Geschichte der Hölle 1992 ➤ 9,9631: R TGL 84 (1994) 105s (W. *Beinert*).
8917 **Walls** Jerry L., Hell; the logic of damnation. ND 1992, Univ. 177 p. $27; pa. $13. 0-268-01095-1; -6-X. – R ChrSchR 24 (1994) 102-5 (K. P. *Kinghorn*).
8918 *Weymann* Volker, Bilder der Hoffnung angesichts von Sterben und Tod: EvT 54 (1994) 501-519.
8919 **Wheeler** Michael, Death and the future life in Victorian literature and theology. C 1990, Univ. 456 p. $54.50. – R JAAR 62 (1994) 223-8 (K. *Lewis*: 19-p. bibliog.); RLitNT 24,1 (1992) 95s (G. B. *Tennyson*: magisterial).
8920 **Witherington** Ben III, Jesus, Paul, and the end of the world; a comparative study in NT eschatology. DG 1992, InterVarsity. – R ConcordiaTQ 58 (1994) 165-7 (J. *Gibbs*).

H9.5 *Theologia totius [V-] NT* – **General [O-] NT theology.**

8921 **Beeck** Franz J. van, God encountered [1, 1989 ➤ 5,9067 ... 9,9635] (2,1 1993: 2. God encountered; a contemporary Catholic systematic theology. ColMn 1994, Liturgical-Glazier. 400 p. $20 pa. 0-685-65631-4 [BIP]. – R TBR 7,3 (1994s) 33 (B. *Quash*, 1, 2/1).
8922 **Berger** Klaus, Theologiegeschichte des Urchristentums; Theologie des

Neuen Testaments: UTb-Wiss.   Tü 1994, Francke.   xxiii-746 p.   3-7720-1752-5 / UTb 3-8852-8028-9.
8923 **Caird** George B. † 1984,   ᴱ*Hurst* L. D., NT theology. Ox 1994, Clarendon.   xix-488 p.   £45.   0-19-82660-X [TDig 42,58]. – ᴿTBR 7,3 (1994s) 31 (J. E. *Burkwell*).
8924 **Childs** Brevard S., Biblical theology of the Old and New Testaments; theological reflection on the Christian Bible 1992 → 8,9322; 9,9638: ᴿBibTB 24 (1994) 92 (A. K. M. *Adam*); BR 10,6 (1994) 17-19 (R. S. *Hendel*); CBQ 56 (1994) 324-6 (T. E. *Fretheim*); Dialog 33,2 (St. Paul 1994) 94-98 (D. *Juel*) & 85-88 (T. F. *Lull*) & 89-93 (C. R. *Seitz*) [< NTAbs 38, p. 401s]; JbBT 9 (1994) 359-369 (R. *Rendtorff*) & 349-358 (U. *Mauser*, mit teilhaften HÜBNER H.; STUHLMACHER P.); LvSt 18 (1993) 372s (R. F. *Collins*); PerspRelSt 21 (1994) 143-152 (R. A. *Spencer*); PrincSemB 14 (1993) 196-8 (D. T. *Olson*); SWJT 26,3 (1993s) 58s (R. *Johnson*); TrinJ 14 (1993) 222-6 (C. *Vlachos*).
8925 **Childs** Brevard S., Die Theologie der einen Bibel, I. Grundstrukturen [1992], ᵀ*Oeming* Christiane. FrB 1994, Herder.   411 p.   DM 88.   3-451-23291-X.
8926 *Chopp* Rebecca S., *Fackre* Gabriel, Recent works in Christian systematic theology [EVANS J.; PETERS J. 1992; JEWETT P., MIGLIORE D., NEVILLE R. 1991 ...]: RelStR 20 (1994) 3-12.
8927 ᴱ[**Schüssler**] **Fiorenza** Francis, *Galvin* John P., Systematic theology 1991 → 7,379 ... 9,9642:   ᴿCritRR 6 (1993) 528-530 (J. F. *Puglisi*); JRel 74 (1994) 268-270 (W. P. *Loewe*); JTS 45 (1994) 425-8 (N. *Lash*).
8928 **Garrett** James L., Systematic theology; biblical, historical and evangelical 1, 1990 → 7,9032 ... 9,9644:   ᴿScripTPamp 26 (1994) 349s (L. F. *Mateo-Seco*).
8929 **Gnilka** Joachim, Theologie des Neuen Testaments (HTK NT Supp. 5. FrB 1994, Herder.   470 p.   DM 88.   3-451-23307-X. – ᴿTGL 84 (1994) 487s (J. *Ernst*).
8930 **Gnilka** Joachim, Teologia del NT 1992 → 8,9329; 9,9646:   ᴿCC 145 (1994,2) 513s (D. *Scaiola*).
8931 **Grudem** Wayne, Systematic theology; an introduction to biblical doctrine. Leicester/GR 1994, Inter-Varsity/Zondervan.   1264 p.   0- 85110-652-8 / US 0-310-28670-0.
8931* *Güttgemanns* Erhard, Die Darstellung einer Theologie des Neuen Testaments als semiotisches Problem: LingBib 68 (1993) 5-93; Eng. 93 s.
8932 **Guthrie** Shirley C., Christian doctrine²*ʳᵉᵛ* [¹1868]. LVL 1994, W-Knox.   434 p. $18.   0-664-35368-7 [TDig 42,168].
8932* *Haag* Ernst AT [*Kertelge* Karl NT]: Biblische Theologie: → 510, LTK³ 2 (1994) 423-430 [-433].
8933 **Hasel** Frank M., Scripture in the theologies of W. PANNENBERG and D. G. BLÖSCH; an investigation and assessment of its origin, nature and use: diss. Andrews, ᴰ*Canale* F. Berrien Springs 1994. 369 p. – RTLv 26, p. 563.
8934 *Hasel* Gerhard F. [† 31.VIII.1994], The nature of biblical theology; recent trends and issues: AndrUnS 32 (1994) 203-215.
8935 **Hübner** Hans, Biblische Theologie des NTs 2,1993 → 9,9650:   ᴿCritRR 6 (1993) 256-260 (G. F. *Hasel*, 1); Entschluss 49,12 (1994) 44s (M. *Brasser*); Protestantesimo 49 (1994) 180s (B. *Corsani*, 2); TLZ 119 (1994) 310-322 (K. *Niederwimmer*); TR 90 (1994) 279-281 (H. *Reventlow*, 1).
8936 **Jewett** Paul K., God, creation, and revelation; a neo-evangelical theology 1991 → 8,7087: ᴿÉTRel 69 (1994) 291 (J.-P. *Gabus*: une dogmatique

réformée néo-orthodoxe, plutôt qu'une doctrine fondamentaliste de la création).

8937 **Kaufman** Gordon D., In face of mystery; a constructive theology. CM 1993, Harvard Univ. 528 p. $40. 0-674-44575-9. – RCGrebel 12 (1994) 327-340 (H. V. *Froese*).

8938 **Klein** Hans, Leben neu entdecken; Entwurf einer biblischen Theologie 1991 → 7,9036: RTLZ 119 (1994) 513-6 (H. *Hübner*).

8939 **McGrath** Alister E., Christian theology, an introduction. Ox 1994, Blackwell. xviii-510 p. £13 pa. [TDig 41,275]. – RTLond 97 (1994) 440-2 (L. *Ayres*: despite his book-of-the-month pace, sets a standard of erudition and clarity that will not be broken for a long time).

8940 **Mildenberger** Friedrich, Biblische Dogmatik; eine biblische Theologie in dogmatischer Perspektive 1-2, 1991s → 7,9042... 9,9653: REstE 69 (1994) 553 (J. J. *Alemany*); TGL 83 (1993) 387 (W. *Beinert*).

8941 **Mildenberger** Friedrich, Biblische Dogmatik [1-2, 1991s → 7,9042... 9,9653], 3. Theologie als Ökonomie. Stu 1993, Kohlhammer. 496 p. DM 59. 3-17-011083-7. – RZkT 116 (1994) 201-3 (K. H. *Neufeld*).

8942 **Oden** Thomas C., Life in the Spirit: Syst 3, 1992 → 9,9654: RInterpretation 48 (1994) 183-5 (G. *Fackre*).

8943 **Pannenberg** Wolfhart, Systematische Theologie III, 1993 → 7,9655: RCarthaginensia 10 (1994) 443-7 (L. *Oviedo Torró*); ExpTim 105 (1993s) 368 (G. *Wainwright*, 3); NRT 116 (1994) 432 (L. *Renwart*); TGL 84 (1994) 387s (W. *Beinert*, 3); TR 90 (1994) 1-10 (G. L. *Müller*, 3).

8944 **Pannenberg** Wolfhart, [An introduction to (his)] Systematic theology 1. 1991 → 7,9045; 2 → 9,9656. GR/E 1994, Eerdmans/Clark. $40. 0-8028-3707-7 / 0-567-09598-3. – RAndrUnS 32 (1994) 146s (F. *Canale*, 1); EcuR 45 (1993) 358s (C. *Scouteris*, 1); HeythJ 35 (1994) 82s (P. *Avis*); PerspRelSt 21 (1994) 165s (M. E. *Deal*, 1).

8945 **Pannenberg** Wolfhart, Systematic theology, vol. 2, T*Bromiley* Geoffrey W. GR 1994, Eerdmans. xvi-499 p. $40. 0-8028-3707-7 [TDig 42,191]. – RTBR 7,3 (1994s) 32 (N. *Sagovsky*).

8945* — *Molnar* Paul D., Reflections on PANNENBERG's Systematic Theology: Thomist 58 (1994) 501-512.

8946 **Räisänen** Heikki, Beyond NT theology a story and a programme 1990 → 6,9149... 8,9342: RScotJT 46 (1993) 237-9 (A. J. M. *Wedderburn*).

8947 *Raurell* Frederic, Canon i teología biblica; ambigüitats: RCatalT 18 (1993) 1-23; Eng. 23: since the canon has its own historical context, criticizes CHILDS-style biblical theology for not incorporating historico-critical results.

8948 EReumann John, The promise and practice of biblical theology 1991 → 7,326... 9,9662: RCurrTM 21 (1994) 372 (E. *Krentz*: first 5 art. from Ph Lutheran Sem. 125th); LuthQ 6 (1992) 342-4 (C. D. von *Dehsen*); Neotestamentica 28 (1994) 607-610 (B. A. *Williams*).

8949 *Riches* John, A future for New Testament theology?: LitTOx 8 (1994) 343-353.

8950 *Segalla* Giuseppe, Quattro modelli di 'uomo nuovo' nella letteratura neotestamentaria: TItSett 19 (1993) 113-164; Eng. 165.

8951 **Siegwalt** G., La réalisation de la foi 1-2: Dogmatique 2. P/Genève 1991s, Cerf / Labor et Fides. 450 p.; 401 p. F 220 + 240. – RÉTRel 68 (1993) 295-7 (A. *Gounelle*, 2/1); ExpTim 105 (1993s) 368s (G. *Wainwright*, 2/2); NRT 116 (1994) 251s (L. *Renwart*, 2/1s); RThom 94 (1994) 320-3 (G. *Remy*, 2/2).

8952 **Stuhlmacher** Peter, BibT NTs 1 Jesus zu Paulus 1992 ≯ 8,9346; 9,9666:
RActuBbg 31 (1994) 47-49 (J. *Boada*); CBQ 56 (1994) 390-2 (C. *Bernas*);
KerkT 45 (1994) 254s (H.W. de *Knijff*); TLZ 119 (1994) 241-5 (E.
Roloff).

8953 **Weiser** A., Theologie des Neuen Testaments, II. Die Theologie der
Evangelisten: StudienbuchTheol 8. Stu 1993, Kohlhammer. 337 p.
DM 34. – RTvT 34 (1994) 445 (W. H. *Berflo*).

| XVI. Philologia biblica |

J1 **Hebraica** .1 *grammatica.*

8954 **Andersen** F. I., *Forbes* A. D., Spelling in the Hebrew Bible: BibOrPont
41, 1986 ≯ 2,2742... 5,9094: RBZ 38 (1994) 310s (J. *Maier*); Henoch 16
(1994) 100s (B. *Chiesa*).

8954* *Avishur* Yitzḥak, ⊕ The reversed construct structure in the Bible,
Qumran Scrolls and early Jewish literature: Lešonenu 57 (1993) 279-288;
Eng. II.

8955 **Barr** James, The variable spellings of the Hebrew Bible (Schweich
Lectures 1986) 1989 ≯ 5,9095... 7,9053: RRExp 91 (1994) 113s (J. D. W.
Watts: no reason; not much comfort).

8956 *a*) *Barr* James, Scope and problems in the semantics of classical
Hebrew; – *b*) *Swiggers* P., Recent developments / Paradigmatical
semantics; – *c*) *Zatelli* Ida, Pragmalinguistics and speech-act theory as
applied to classical Hebrew; – *d*) *Fronzaroli* Pelio, Componential analysis;
– *e*) *Petőfi* J. S., Logical semantics; – *f*) *Hospers* J. H., Polysemy and
homonymy; – *g*) *Greenfield* Jonas C., Etymological semantics: ≯ 383*e*,
ZAHeb 6 (1993) 3-14 (-20, response) / 21-25.44-55 (-60) / 60-74 (-78) /
79-91 / 92-108 (-113) / 114-123 (-127) / 26-37 (-43).

8957 *a*) *Barr* James, Three interrelated factors in the semantic study of
ancient Hebrew [homonymy or polysemy...]; – *b*) *Muraoka* Takamitsu,
Response: ZAHeb 7 (1994) 33-44 / 44-50.

8957* **Bartelmus** Rüdiger, Einführung in das biblische Hebräisch — ausgehend von der grammatischen und (text-)syntaktischen Interpretation des
althebräischen Konsonantentextes des ATs durch die tiberische Maso-
reten-Schule des BEN ASCHER — mit... Aramäisch. Z 1994, Theol.-V.
287 p.

8958 *a*) *Ben-David* Israel, ⊕ The alternation Šewa/Ṣere in the present
participle; – *b*) *Offer* Yoseph, ⊕ The notation of Šewa at the end of a
word in the Tiberian vocalization system: Lešonenu 57 (1993) 103-7 /
109-118; Eng. I/II.

8958* *Ben-David* Israel, ⊕ Biblical nouns vocalized in the construct state
where the following word is not a genitival attribute: Lešonenu 58 (1994)
25-48; Eng. III.

8959 EBergen Robert D., Biblical Hebrew and discourse linguistics. Dallas
1994, Summer Institute of Linguistics. 560 p. 1-55671-007-0.

8960 *Buth* Randall, *a*) The Hebrew verb in current discussions; – *b*) Language
use in the first century; the place of spoken Hebrew in a trilingual society:
JTrTL 5 (1992) 91-104 / 299-312 [< OTAbs 16, p. 261].

8961 *Chiesa* Bruno, Strumenti e studi di linguistica e lessicografia ebraica e
semitica: Henoch 16 (1994) 95-126.

8962 **Ciprotti** Pio, Introduzione pratica allo studio dell'ebraico 1993 ➔ 9, 9673: ᴿRasT 35 (1994) 236s (R. *Scibona*).
8963 **Dawson** David A., Text-linguistics and biblical Hebrew [diss. Edinburgh 1993 ➔ 9,9675]: jOsu 177. Shf 1994, Academic. 242 p. £37.50. 1-85075-490-X.
8964 **Doukhan** Jacques B., Hebrew for theologians; a textbook for the study of biblical Hebrew in relation to Hebrew thinking. Lanham MD 1993, UPA. xxxii-245 p. 0-8191-9269-4.
8965 **Fassberg** Steven E., Studies in biblical syntax. J 1994, Hebrew Univ. Perry Foundation. 208 p. $12.50. 965-223-816-3. – ᴿLešonenu 58 (1994) 167-9 (J. *Blau* ❸); V Eng.
8966 **Freedman** D. N., *Forbes* A. D., *Andersen* F. J., Studies in Hebrew and Aramaic orthography 1992 ➔ 8,9354: ᴿJBL 113 (1994) 313-5 (G. A. *Rendsburg*).
8967 **Garbini** Giovanni, *Durand* O., Introduzione alle lingue semitiche: StVOAnt 2. Brescia 1994, Paideia. 191 p. Lᵐ 29. 88-394-0506-2. – ᴿHenoch 16 (1994) 95s (B. *Chiesa*); Protestantesimo 49 (1994) 176 (J. A. *Soggin*).
8968 *Gross* Walter, Zur syntaktischen Struktur des Vorgeldes im hebräischen Verbalsatz: ZAHeb 7 (1994) 203-214.
8969 **Hadas-Lebel** Mireille, Storia della lingua ebraica [L'hébreu, trois mille ans d'histoire 1992], ᵀ*Lucattini Vogelmann* Vanna, F 1994, Giuntina. 146 p. Lᵐ 28. 88-85943-94-2. P. 13s 'la lingua [già] dei Patriarchi era quella di Canaan'.
8970 ᶠHOFTIJZER J., Studies in Hebrew and Aramaic syntax, ᴱ**Jongeling** K. *al.* 1991 ➔ 7,77; 9,9681: ᴿAbrNahr 31 (1993) 137-141 (S. E. *Fassberg*).
8971 *Hoftijzer* Jacob, Überlegungen zum System der Stammesmodificationen im klassischen Hebräisch: ZAHeb 5 (1992) 117-134.
8972 *Israel* Felice, Inventaire préliminaire [avec 117 + 45 textes entiers transcrits] des sceaux paléo-hébreux (Études de lexique paléo-hébraïque III): ZAHeb 7 (1994) 51-74; bibliog. 75-80.
8973 **Jagersma** H., Bijbels Hebreeuws [1. Basiskursus 1991 ➔ 9,9683]; Vervolgekursus. Kampen 1992, Kok.
8973* **Jamieson-Drake** David W., Scribes and achools in monarchic Judah jOsu 109, ᴰ1991 ➔ 8,9360; 9,9684: ᴿCritRR 6 (1993) 140-2 (Paula M. *McNatt*); ScripB 23,1 (1993) 20 (W. G. E. *Watson*); WestTJ 55 (1993) 155-7 (J. A. *Danies*).
8974 **Joüon** P., *Muraoka* T., A grammar of biblical Hebrew 1991 ➔ 7,9063; 9,9086: ᴿSefarad 53 (1993) 215-7 (L. F. *Girón*).
8975 a) *Kedar-Kopfstein* Benjamin, On the decoding of polysemantic lexemes in biblical Hebrew; – b) *Müller* Hans-Peter, Antwort: ZAHeb 7 (1994) 17-25 / 26-32.
8976 **Kelley** Page H., Biblical Hebrew; an introductory grammar 1992 ➔ 8,9363; 9,9687: Eerdmans. – ᴿCritRR 6 (1993) 162s (Z. *Garber*); RuBi 47 (1994) 66 (María *Kantor,* ❸); RExp 91 (1994) 263 (J. *Nogalski*); WestTJ 56 (1994) 190-2 (R. C. *Stallman*).
8977 *Khan* Geoffrey, The historical background of the vowel ṣere in some Hebrew verbal and nominal forms: ➔ 126, ᶠWANSBROUGH J., BSO 57 (1994) 133-144.
8977* a) *Knauf* Ernst A., Die Höchstzahl möglicher zweiradikaliger Würzeln des Ursemitischen [1008, anstatt 1428 (RÖSSLER)]; – b) *Schindele* Martin, Darstellung morphologischer Zerlegungen hebräischer Wörter: BibNot 75 (1994) 20s / 22-35.

8978 **Kogut** Simcha, ❸ Correlations between biblical accentuation and traditional Jewish exegesis; linguistic and contextual studies. J 1994, Hebrew Univ. Perry Foundation. 270 p. $17. 965-223-855-4.

8979 *a) Kroeze* J. H., Underlying syntactic relations in construct phrases of biblical Hebrew; – *b) Lübbe* J. C., The use of syntactic data in dictionaries of classical Hebrew: ↠ 121, ᶠSmit E., J/Tyd Sem 5,1 (1993) 68-88 / 89-96.

8980 **Lambdin** Thomas O., Lehrbuch Bibel-Hebräisch, ᵀᴱ*Siebenthal* Heinrich von. Giessen/Neuhausen 1990, Brunnen/Hänssler. xxviii-349 p. – ᴿTü-TQ 174 (1994) 240s (W. *Gross*).

8981 **Lettinga** Jan P., Grammatik des biblischen Hebräisch 1992 ↠ 9,9688*: ᴿFundamentum (1994,2) 117-9 (W. C. D.).

8982 *Longacre* Robert E., The analysis of preverbal nouns in biblical Hebrew narrative; some overriding concerns [defense against N. Bailey, S. Levinson]: JTrTL 5 (1992) [179-207] 208-224 [< OTAbs 16, p. 262].

8983 **Malone** Joseph L., Tiberian Hebrew phonology. WL 1993, Eisenbrauns. x-204 p. $45. 0-931464-75-7. – ᴿOTAbs 17 (1994) 430 (A. *Fitzgerald*: difficult but rewarding linguistic jargon).

8984 *Marlowe* W. Creighton, A summary evaluation of OT Hebrew lexica, translations, and philology in light of developments in Hebrew lexicographic and Semitic linguistic history: GTJ [OTAbs 17, p. 47, not in listing after p. 244] 12 (1992) 3-20.

8985 *Michel* Diethelm, Probleme des Nominalsatzes im biblischen Hebräisch: ZAHeb 7 (1994) 215-224.

8986 *Niccacci* Alviero, Simple nominal clause (SNC) or verbless clause in biblical Hebrew prose: ZAHeb 6 (1993) 216.227.

8987 *Ólafsson* Sverrir, On diglossia in ancient Hebrew and its graphic representation [Rendsburg's examples not definitive]: FolOr 28 (1991) 193-205.

8988 **Price** James D., The syntax of Masoretic accents in the Hebrew Bible: StBEC 27. Lewiston NY 1990, Mellen. 323 p. $100. 0-88946-510-X. – ᴿRExp 91 (1994) 612 (J. D. *Nogalski*: valuable, but only on Pentateuch and 3 poetic books).

8989 **Prudky** Martin, Cvidebnice [exercises] biblické hebrejštiny. Praha 1992, Scriptum. 336 p. – ᴿArOr 62 (1994) 441 (S. *Segert*).

8989* ᶠRichter Wolfgang, Text, Methode und Grammatik, 65. Gb., ᴱ**Gross** W., *al.* 1991 ↠ 7,126: ᴿLA 44 (1994) 667-692 (! A. *Niccacci*).

8990 **Sáenz-Badillos** Ángel, A history of the Hebrew language. C 1993, Univ. 371 p. £25. 0-521-43157-3. – ᴿExpTim 105 (1993s) 307s (L. L. *Grabbe*: needed; overenamoured of Dahood); JStJud 25 (1994) 333-8 (T. *Muraoka*); Lešonenu 58 (1994) 87-93 (J. *Blau* ❸); Eng. VI.

8991 **Siebesma** R. A., The function of the Niph'al 1991 ↠ 7,9079 ... 9,9701: ᴿCBQ 56 (1994) 571-3 (S. A. *Kaufman*); JSS 39 (1994) 107s (W. G. E. *Watson*); Salesianum 56 (1994) 157s (R. *Vicent*).

8992 *Sivan* Daniel, *Yona* Shamir, Style and syntax; pivotal use of extrapositional syntagms in biblical Hebrew: UF 26 (1994) 443-454.

8993 ᴱ**Smith** Diana R., *Salinger* Peter S., Hebrew Studies, Colloquium London Univ. School of Oriental and African Studies, 11-13 Sept. 1989: OccasP 13, L 1991, ↠ 8,493c: ᴿBL (1994) 163 (J. F. *Elwolde*); HebSt 33 (1992) 155-8 (H. C. *Zafren*).

8994 **Smith** Mark S., Origins and development of the waw-consecutive: HarvSemSt 39, 1991: ↠ 7,9080 ... 9,9702: ᴿBL (1994) 16s (J. C. L. *Gibson*); JSS 38 (1993) 135s (W. G. E. *Watson*); Syria 61 (1994) 255s (A. *Caquot*).

8994* *Szerwiniack* Olivier,   Des recueils d'interprétation de noms hebréux chez les Irlandais et le Wisigoth THÉODULF;   Scriptorium 48 (1994) 187-258.

8995 *Talstra* Epp,   Text grammar and biblical Hebrew; the viewpoint of Wolfgang SCHNEIDER [Heb. Grammatik 1974]: JTrTL 5 (1992) 269-297 [< OTAbs 16, p. 272].

8995* *Thorion* Yochanan, Studien zur klassischen hebräischen Syntax: Marb-StAfr As B/6.   B 1984, Reimer.   [vi-]127 p.

8996 *Tropper* Josef,   a) Dualistische Personalpronomina und Verbalformen im Althebräischen: ZAHeb 5 (1992) 201-8; – b) Nominative dual *yariḫau* im Gezer-Kalender: ZAHeb 6 (1993) 228-231.

8997 a) *Vanoni* Gottfried,   Fragen der Syntax und Semantik von Verbvalenzen im Althebräischen; – b) *Gross* Walter,   Das Vorfeld als strukturell eigenständiger Bereich des hebräischen Verbalsatzes; syntaktische Erscheinungen am Satzbeginn: → 323*, Syntax 1993, 25-47 / 1-24.

8998 **Verheij** A. J. C.,   Verbs and numbers [statistic of verb-forms in] Sm-Kgs-Chr, ᴰ1990 → 6,9176... 9,9703:   ᴿOrLovPer 24 (1993) 281s (A. *Schoors*).

8999 **Volgger** David,   Notizen zur Phonologie des Bibelhebräischen [Diplomarbeit]: AOtt 36, 1992 → 9,9704:   ᴿBL (1994) 164 (J. C. L. *Gibson*); OTEssays 7 (1994) 313-5 (J. A. *Naudé*); RivB 42 (1994) 219-222 (C. *Balzaretti*).

9000 *Waltke* Bruce K.,   How I changed my mind about [35 years'] teaching Hebrew (or retained it) [< National Association of Hebrew Professors, Wsh Nov. 1993]: Crux 29,4 (1993) 10-15 [< OTAbs 17, p. 281].

9001 **Waltke** B. K., *O'Connor* M.,   An introduction to biblical Hebrew syntax 1990 → 6,9178... 9,9705:   ᴿJNES 53 (1994) 150-3 (D. *Pardee*).

9002 *Young* Ian,   Diversity in pre-exilic Hebrew: ForAT 5, 1993 → 9,9708: ᴿOTAbs 17 (1994) 209s (M. S. *Smith*).

9003 **Zadok** Ran,   The pre-Hellenistic Israelite anthroponomy and proposopography: OrLovAnal 28, 1988 → 5,9160:   ᴿJNES 53 (1994) 71-75 (S. *Layton*).

9003* a) *Żewi* Tamar,   The nominal sentence in biblical Hebrew; – b) *Khan* Geoffrey,   The pronunciation of the verbs *hāyāh* and *ḥāyāh* in the Tiberian tradition of biblical Hebrew; – c) *Dolgopolsky* Aron,   Some Hamito-Semitic names of body parts: → 123, Mem. POLOTSKY H. J., Semitic 1994, 145-167 / 133-144 / 267-287.

J1.2 **Lexica et inscriptiones hebraicae;**   later Hebrew.

9004 **Alonso Schökel** Luis,   Diccionario biblico hebreo-español 1990-3 → 7, 9089 ... 9,9710:   ᴿHenoch 16 (1994) 115s (B. *Chiesa*); ZAW 106 (1994) 147 (M. *Calovi*).

9004* **Atlan-Sayag** Scoshana,   Itamar; les noms et prénoms hébreux d'hier et d'aujourd'hui.   P 1994, Cerf.   143 p.   2-204-04906-9.

9005 **Cano** María José, *Magdalena* José Ramón,   Epigrafía y paleografía hebrea, desde los orígenes hasta la difusión de la imprenta hebrea; introducción a la codicología hebrea medieval; textos, láminas y bibliografía.   Barc 1993, Publ. universitarias.   166 p. – ᴿSefarad 54 (1994) 421 (Lola *Ferre*).

9006 ᴱ**Clines** David J. A.,   The dictionary of classical Hebrew, vol. 1 aleph 1993 → 9,9718:   ᴿBL (1994) 159 (J. F. A. *Sawyer*: impeccable); CurrTM

21 (1994) 221s (R. W. *Klein* praises but misses the etymologies); ETL 70 (1994) 425-9 (J. *Lust*); ExpTim 105,10 (1993s) 291 (C. S. *Rodd*: high praise, except for the neither alphabetical nor logical order of the 'syntagmatic' sections, where it is hard to discover whether a noun is used with a particular verb); Henoch 16 (1994) 116-8 (B. *Chiesa*).

9006* *Cook* Johann,   Towards an appropriate textual base for the Old Testament [incorporating Qumran; ... SCHENKER A. 1992 Text und Sinn; 'was übersetzen wir?']: JNWS 10,1 (1994) 171-7.

9007 **Davies** G. J., *al.*,   Ancient Hebrew inscriptions 1991 ⇒ 7,9097... 9,9719: ᴿBA 57 (1994) 247 (J. R. *Adair*); Bijdragen 55 (1994) 78 (P. C. *Beentjes*); OLZ 89 (1994) 152-5 (R. G. *Lehmann*); VT 44 (1994) 277-9 (J. F. *Healey*).

9008 **Deutsch** R., *Heltzer* M.,   Forty new ancient West Semitic inscriptions. TA 1994, Archaeological Center.   101 p.;   bibliog.   p. 91-98.   965-225-551-8 [BL 95,25, A. R. *Millard*].

9009 *Dobbs-Allsopp* P. W.,   The genre of the Meṣad Ḥashavyahu ostracon [as R. WESTBROOK: extrajudicial appeal to king]: BASOR 295 (1994) 49-55.

ᴱ**Henten** Jan W. van, *Horst* Pieter W. van der, Studies in early Jewish epigraphy 1992/4 ⇒ 323.

Horbury William, *Noy* David,   Jewish inscriptions of Greco-Roman Egypt 1992 ⇒ 9395.

9010 *Horvath* Julia, *Wexler* Paul,   Unspoken languages and the issue of genetic classification; the case of Hebrew [modern not a real descendant of biblical]: Linguistics 32,2 (1994) 241-269.

9011 **Kaddari** Menaḥem Zevi, ❺ Post-biblical Hebrew syntax and semantics; Studies in diachronic Hebrew [1. 1991 ⇒ 9,9725] 2. Ramat-Gan 1994, Bar-Ilan Univ. p. 425-786.   965-2276-143-2.

9012 [**Koehler** L., *Baumgartner* W.] The Hebrew and Aramaic lexicon of the Old Testament³, ᵀᴱ*Richardson* M. E. J. [the first two editions were in both German and English], I.   Leiden 1994, Brill.   368 p. $129.75 [BAR-W 20/6,8; BL 95,178, L. L. *Grabbe*].

9013 **Layton** Scott C.,   Archaic features of Canaanite personal names in the Hebrew Bible: HarvSemMg 47, ᴰ1990 ⇒ 6,9202... 8,9407:   ᴿSalesianum 56 (1994) 783s (R. *Bracchi*).

9013* *Lemaire* André,   Épigraphie palestinienne; nouveaux documents, 1. Fragment de stèle araméenne de Tell Dan (IXe s. av. J.-C.): Henoch 16 (1994) 87-93.

9014 **Murtonen** Aimo, Hebrew in its West-Semitic setting 1988-90 ⇒ 2,7306... 8,9411:   ᴿWZKM 84 (1994) 211-221 (S. *Segert*).

9014* *Naudé* J. A.,   a) The asymmetry of subject pronouns and subject nouns in Qumran Hebrew and cognates; – b) Towards a typology of Qumran Hebrew: JNSW 10,1 (1994) 139-163 / 10,2 (1994) 61-78.

9015 **Ognibeni** Bruno,   Index biblique à la 'Ochlah w' ochlah' de S. FRENSDORFF: Henoch Quad 5. T 1992, Zamorani.   118 p. – ᴿSefarad 54 (1994) 206s (M. J. de *Azcárraga*).

9016 **Pérez Fernández** Miguel, [Hebraico mísnico] La lengua de los sabios, 1. Morfosintaxis 1992 ⇒ 8,9414; 9,9733:   ᴿSefarad 53 (1993) 412-4 (L. F. *Girón*).

9017 *Powels* Sylvia,   Indische Lehnwörter in der Bibel: ZAHeb 5 (1992) 186-200.

9018 **Renz** Johannes, Die althebräischen Inschriften; ev. diss. Kiel, ᴰ*Donner* 1992s. – TR 90,85.

9019 **Ridzewski** Beate, Neuhebräische Grammatik 1992 ⇒ 9,9736: ᴿJStJud 25 (1994) 120 (M. *Pérez Fernández*).

9019* *Rooker* Mark F., Diachronic analysis and the features of late biblical Hebrew: BuBR 4 (1994) 135-144 [p. 144, 14 commonly proposed Late Hebrew features].

9020 **Silva** Moisés, Biblical words and their meaning; an introduction to lexical semantics²*rev*. GR 1994, Zondervan. 224 p.

9021 *Soden* Wolfram von, Zur Verwendung des Narrativs *wăj-jiqtol* im nachexilischen Hebräisch: ZAHeb 7 (1994) 196-202.

9022 **Glinert** Lewis, Modern Hebrew; an essential grammar² [¹1989 ➤ 5, 9132]. L 1994, Routledge. xvi-174 p. 0-415-10190-5.

9023 **Glinert** Lewis, The joys of Hebrew 1992 ➤ 8,9356: ᴿSalesianum 56 (1994) 569s (R. *Vicent*).

9024 *Rosenhouse* Judith, On the use of construct forms and nominal compounds in modern Hebrew: JAfrAs 2 (1989) 54-72.

9025 **Stern** Naftali, Dictionary of [1430 modern] Hebrew verbs [alphabetically by first letter of the *form*, not radical]. Ramat Gan 1994, Bar Ilan Univ. 321 p. – ᴿLešonenu 58 (1994s) 347-361 (Esther *Borochovsky*).

9026 **Harris** Tracy K., Death of a language; the history of Judeo-Spanish. Newark 1994, Univ. Delaware. 354 p.; bibliog. 323-9.

J1.3 **Voces** ordine alphabetico *consonantium* **hebraicarum.**

Here should really be included all the 200-some Hebrew terms of the ZAHeb Bibliographische Dokumentation 1994 ➤ 693*.

9027 *adôm: Massey-Gillespie* Kevin, A new approach to basic Hebrew colour terms: JNWS 10.1 (1994) 1-11.

9028 *ap:* **Baloian** Bruce E., Anger in the OT [diss. Claremont 1988, ᴰ*Knierim* R.]: AmerUnivSt 7/99, 1992 ➤ 9,9752: ᴿAndrUnS 32 (1994) 253-5 (F. M. *Hasel*).

9029 *ašīšâ:* Recipientes bíblicos V: Sefarad 54 (1994) 47-53 (C. *Herranz*, G. *Seijas*).

9029* *ereṣ:* *Schlossberg* Eliezer, ❸ The meanings of biblical *ereṣ* as reflected in R. SAADIA Gaon's translation of the Pentateuch: Lešonenu 57 (1993) 203-214; Eng. III.

9030 *beᵉ;* **Jenni** Ernst, Die Präposition beth 1992 ➤ 8,9435; 9,9755: ᴿJBL 113 (1994) 315 (S. A. *Meier*: high praise); Salesianum 56 (1994) 618 (R. *Bracchi*).

9030* *baka:* **Anderson** Gary A., A Time to mourn, a time to dance; the expression of grief and joy in Israelite religion 1991 ➤ 9,9758: ᴿInterpretation 47 (1993) 80 (D. L. *Peterson*: joy just the reverse of sorrow? 2500-year-long rituals?).

9031 *bar: Zatelli* Ida, *bar* [pure, bright']: a sample entry for a database of the semantics of classical Hebrew: F Univ QuadLing 5 (1994) 149-155.

9032 *bārak: Artson* B. S., *Barukh ha-Shem*, God is 'bountiful': ConsJud 46,2 (1994) 32-43 [< NTAbs 398, p. 427].

9033 **Crawford** Timothy G., Blessing and curse in Syro-Palestinian inscriptions of the Iron Age [< diss. Southern Baptist sem., ᴰ*Drinkard* J.]: AmerUnivSt 7/120. NY 1992, Lang. xvii-259 p. – ᴿCBQ 56 (1994) 543s (B. F. *Batto*).

9034 *gêr:* **Bultmann** Christoph,   Der Fremde im antiken Juda; eine Untersuchung zum sozialen Typenbegriff 'ger' und seinem Bedeutungswandel in der alttestamentliche Gesetzgebung: FRL 153,   Gö 1992, VR. 235 p. DM 118. – ᴿCBQ 56 (1994) 538s (J. *Limburg*); JBL 113 (1994) 321-3 (D. *Patrick*).

9035 *Salvatierra* Ángel,   El emigrante y el extranjero en la Biblia: LumenVr 42 (1993) 175-187.

9036 *Steins* G., 'Fremde sind wir'... Zur Wahrnehmung des Fremdseins und zur Sorge für die Fremden in alttestamentlicher Perspektive: Jahrbuch für Christliche Sozialwissenschaften 35 (1994) 133-150 [< ᴢAW 106,501].

9037 *dam:* ↠ 9,493, ᴱVattioni F., Sangue 8, 1991/3, 247-264 (M. *Cimosa*).

9037* [*deror*] **andurarum*: Glosa a Al[alakh] T[ablets] *65, 6-7: AulaO 11,1 (1993) 116s (J. C. *Oliva Mompeán*).

9038 *hûn:* *Tournay* Raymond J.,   À propos du verbe *hūn / hīn* [Dt 1,11; Hab 2,5]: RB 101 (1994) 321-5.

9039 *wᵉ:* *Müller* Hans-Peter,   Nicht-junktiver Gebrauch von *w-* im Althebräischen: ZAHeb 7 (1994) 141-174.

9040 *ḥadal:* *Jenni* Ernst,   Lexikalisch-semantische Strukturunterschiede: hebräisch *ḥedl* — deutsch 'aufhören / unterlassen': ZAHeb 7 (1994) 124-132.

9041 *yādaᶜ:* **Sciumbata** M. P.,   Il campo lessicale dei verbi della 'conoscenza' nella Bibbia ebraica; valori semantici e implicazioni epistemologiche: diss. Firenze 1992s, ᴰ*Zatelli* I. – RivB 42 (1994) 113.

9042 *yᵉšurun* e *yadîd* [Dt 32s] le eccezioni alla traduzione di *aḥab* con *agapáō* nel Pentateuco dei LXX: Aevum 68 (1994) 9-26 (G. *Toloni*).

9043 *kî:* *Classen* W. T., ❶ Speaker-oriented functions of *kî* in biblical Hebrew: Exegetica 4 (Tokyo 1993) 89-108 [< OTAbs 17,274].

9043* **Jenni** Ernst,   Die Präposition Kaph: Präp. 2.   Stu 1994, Kohlhammer. 195 p. DM 98.   3-17-012688-1 [TLZ 120,876, Jutta *Körner*].

9044 *lᵉ:* **Pinto León** Adolfo,   Lamed y sus relaciones; indicaciones para su traducción [< diss. Roma, Pont. Inst. Biblico, ᴰ*Alonso Schökel* L.]. R 1990, auct. vi-126 p. – ᴿCBQ 56 (1994) 567s (M. *O'Connor*).

9044* *lōʾ / hᵃ-lōʾ:* *Sivan* Daniel, *Schniedewind* William,   Letting your 'yes' be 'no' in ancient Israel; a study of the asseverative *lōʾ* and *hᵃ-lōʾ*: JSS 38 (1993) 209-226.

9045 *nepeš:* *Michel* Diethelm,   *næpæš* als Leichnam?: ZAHeb 7 (1994) 81-84 [Num 6,6 '*nefeš* eines Toten', nicht 'eine tote Seele'].

9046 *sôd:* **Neef** Heinz-Dieter,   Gottes himmlischer Thronrat; Hintergrund und Bedeutung von *sôd*-ᴊᴴᴡᴴ im AT: ArbT 79. Stu 1994, Calwer. 96 p.; Bibliog. 81-901. DM 58.

9047 *ᶜibri:* *LaGrand* James, 'Hebrews' in the Tanak [always suitably 'outsider']: ProcGLM 11 (1991) 1-8 [< OTAbs 16, p. 35].

9047* *ᶜegel:* *Koenen* Klaus,   Der Name *ᶜglyw* auf Samaria-Ostrakon Nr. 41: VT 44 (1994) 396-400.

9048 *ᶜôd:* *Richter* Wolfgang,   Zum syntaktischen Gebrauch von Substantiven im Althebräischen am Beispiel von *ᶜōd*; ein Beitrag zur Partikelforschung: ZAHeb 7 (1994) 145-195.

9049 *ᶜôlām:* *Neusner* J., Eternity in Judaism: ScotJT 45 (1992) 29-44.

9049* *piskin, bibar* [Latin piscina and vivarium confused in Talmud with Aramaic roots]: Lešonenu 57 (1993) 191-202, ❶; Eng. II (A. *Kosman*).

9050 *ṣedeq:* **Ho** Ahuva, Ṣedeq and ṣedaqah 1991 ↠ 7,9180: ᴿCBQ 56 (1994) 765s (W. *Janzen*: ṣādîq excluded).

9051 *qārob:* **Schweizer** Harald,   Sprachkritik als Ideologiektitik; zur Grammatikrevision am Beispiel von QRB, 1991 → 7,9188: ᴿTR 90 (1994) 110-113 (J. P. *Floss*).

9052 *rûaḥ:* *Poulsen* Hartvig, Gods and i GT: Nemalah 11 (K 1992) 120-130 [< OTAbs 16,359].

9053 **Sekki** A. E., The meaning of ruaḥ at Qumran: SBL diss. 110, 1989 → 5,9239 ... 8,9486: ᴿJPseud 9 (1991) 117s (J. C. *Reeves*).

9054 *rîb:* **Bovati** Pietro, Ristabilire la giustizia ᴰ1986 → 2,7458 ... 8,9487: ᴿSalesianum 56 (1994) 149s (M. *Cimosa*). – Eng. → 2276.

9055 **Bovati** Pietro, [→ 2276], Re-establishing justice; legal terms, concepts and procedures in the Hebrew Bible, ᵀ*Smith* Michael J.: jOsu 105. Shf 1994, Academic. 478 p.; bibliog. p. 394-427. 3-85075-290-7.

9056 *šbᶜ:* *Vattioni* Francesco, La radice *šbᶜ*, 'giurare', in neopunico: AION 53 (1993) 451-5 (456-468, iscrizioni e varia).

9057 *šᵉkînâ:* **Ernst** Hanspeter, Die Schekina in rabbinischen Gleichnissen: Diss. Luzern 1992, ᴰ*Thoma* C. – TR 90,85.

9057* *Šekina* in litteratura iudaica; Christus et *šekina*: RuBi 47 (1994) 159-162, ℗ (N. *Mendecki*).

9058 *šākar* 'Wein': → 519, TWAT 8,1 (1994) 1-5 (M. *Oeming*).

9059 *šeleg* 'Schnee': → 519, TWAT 8,1 (1994) 6-8 (A. *Ernst*).

9060 *šālaḥ* 'schicken': → 519, TWAT 8,1 (1994) 46-70 (F.-L. *Hossfeld, al.*).

9061 *šulḥan* 'Tisch': → 519, TWAT 8,1 (1994) 71-79 (A. *Ernst*).

9062 *šalaṭ* 'herrschen': → 519, TWAT 8,1 (1994) 79-84 (M. *Sæbø*).

9063 *šālak* 'werfen': → 519, TWAT 8,1 (1994) 84-94 (W. *Thiel*).

9064 *šālem* 'Ganzheit, entgelten': → 519, TWAT 8,1 (1994) 93-101 (- *Illman*).

9065 *šālôm:* → 519, TWAT 8,1 (1994) 42-46 (F. J. *Stendebach*).

9066 *šālôš* 'drei': → 519, TWAT 8,1 (1994) 114-122 (K.-M. *Beyse*).

9067 *šēm* 'Name': → 519, TWAT 8,1 (1994) 122-176 (F. V. *Reiterer, al.*).

9068 *šmd* (Nif. Hif.) 'vernichten': → 519, TWAT 8,1 (1994) 176-198 (N. *Lohfink*).

9069 *šᵉmayim:* **Houtman** Cornelis, Der Himmel im AT; Israels Weltbild und Weltanschauung: OTS 30, 1993 → 9,9813: ᴿRExp 91 (1994) 267s (J. D. W. *Watts*); TR 90 (1994) 457s (H. *Reventlow*).

9070 *šāmam* 'erstarren': → 519, TWAT 8,1 (1994) 241-251 (I. *Meyer*).

9071 *šemen* 'Öl': → 519, TWAT 8,1 (1994) 251-5 (H. *Ringgren*).

9072 *šāmaᶜ* 'hören': → 519, TWAT 8,1 (1994) 255-279 (U. *Rüterswörden*).

9073 *šāmar* 'bewachen': → 519, TWAT 8,1 (1994) 280-306 (F. *García López*).

9074 *šemeš* 'Sonne': → 519, TWAT 8,1 (1994) 306-314 (E. *Lipiński*).

9075 *šānāh* 'ändern'/ 'Jahr': → 519, TWAT 8,1 (1994) 318-324 / 324-340 (T. *Kronholm* / F. J. *Stendebach*).

9076 *šen* 'Zahn': → 519, TWAT 8,1 (1994) 315-8 (A. S. *Kapelrud* †).

9077 *šānî* 'Karmesin' [purple dye]: → 519, TWAT 8,1 (1994) 340-3 (K.-M. *Beyse*).

9078 *šaᶜar* 'Tor': → 519, TWAT 8,3s (1994) 358-386 (E. *Otto*).

9079 *šapaṭ, mišpaṭ* 'richten, Rechtsprechung': → 519, TWAT 8,4 (1994) 408-428 (H. *Niehr*).

9080 *šāfak* '(Blut)vergiessen': → 519, TWAT 8,4 (1994) 428-438 (R. *Liwak*).

9081 *šāpal, šᵉpēlāh* 'niedrig': → 519, TWAT 8,4 (1994) 438-443 (K. *Engelken*).

9082 *šāqal* 'wägen': → 519, TWAT 8,4 (1994) 454-8 (M. *Oeming*).

9083 *šāqar* 'lügen': → 519, TWAT 8,4 (1994) 466-472 (H. *Seebass, al.*).

9084 *šᵉrîrût* 'Verstockung': → 519, TWAT 8,4 (1994) 477-483 (H.-J. *Fabry*, N. van *Meeteren*).

9085 *šōreš* 'Wurzel': → 519, TWAT 8,4 (1994) 483-495 (J. *Renz*).

9086 *šātāh* 'trinken; Gastmahl': → 519, TWAT 8,4s (1994s) 507-535 (J. *Gamberoni*).

9087 *twk: Nebe* Wilhelm, Zwei vermeintliche Ableitungen von twk 'Mitte' im Qumran-Hebräischen: ZAHeb 5 (1992) 218-223.

J1.5   *Phoenicia, ugaritica* – **North-West Semitic** [→ T5.4].

9088 *Adams* J.N., Latin and Punic in contacts? The case of the Bu Njem ostraca: JRS 84 (1994) 87-112.

9089 *Althann* Robert, Approaches to prepositions in Northwest Semitic studies (no *mn*; *b* and *l* have to serve): JNWS 10,2 (1994) 179-191.

9090 **Aufrecht** Walter E., A corpus of Ammonite inscriptions 1989 → 6,9367 ... 8,9533: ᴿSefarad 53 (1993) 399-401 (E. *Martínez Borobio*); ZDPV 110 (1994) 82-87 (U. *Hübner*, E. A. *Knauf*).

9091 *Briquel-Chatonnet* Françoise, Hébreu du nord et phénicien; étude comparée de deux dialectes cananéens [< diss. Relations 1992]: OrLovPer 23 (1992) 89-126.

9092 *Cook* Edward M., On the linguistic dating of the Phoenician Ahiram inscription (KAI 1) [BERNAL M., 1990: before 1200 B.C.]: JNES 53 (1994) 33-36.

9093 *Cross* Frank M., Newly discovered inscribed arrowheads of the eleventh century B.C.E.: IsrMusJ 10 (1992) 57-62; 5 fig.

9094 *Cunchillos* Jesús-Luis, Inscripciones fanicias del Tell de Doña Blanca (V): Sefarad 53 (1993) 17-24.

9095 *Cunchillos* Jesús-Luis, *Vita* Juan-Pablo, Banco de datos..1/1 ugaríticos [1993 → 9,9822*]: suplemento 1993: Sefarad 54 (1994) 143-9; Eng. 150.

9096 *Cunchillos* Jesús-Luis, *Vita* Juan-Pablo, Crónica de la destrucción de una ciudad del reino de Ugarit (Tu 00-2.61) [numeración propuesta nel Banco, M 1993]: Sefarad 53 (1993) 243-7.

9097 *Dietrich* M., *Loretz* O., *a)* Ugaritisch *it, tynde* und hebräisch *'šh, šy* (KTU 1.14 IV 38; 2.13:14-15; 2.30:12-14a); – *b)* Rasuren und Schreibfehler in den keilalphabetischen Texten aus Ugarit; Anmerkungen zur neuen Auflage von KTU; – *c)* Neue Tafelfunde der Grabungskampagne 1994 in Ugarit: UF 26 (1994) 64-72 / 23-61 / 20 nur.

9098 *Dietrich* M., *Mayer* W., Hurritische Weihrauch-Beschwörungen in ugaritischer Alphabetschrift: UF 26 (1994) 73-113; 1 pl.

9099 *Dijkstra* Meindert, The myth of Astarte, the Huntress (KTU 1,92), new fragments: UF 26 (1994) 113-126.

9100 *Greaves* S.W., Wordplay and associative magic in the Ugaritic snake-bite incantation RS 24,244: UF 26 (1994) (1994) 165-7.

9101 *Krahmalkov* Charles R., *a)* 'When he drove out Yrirachan'; a Phoenician (Punic) poem, ca. A.D. 350 [150 k S Leptis Magna, Libya]: BASOR 294 (1994) 69-82; – b) Notes on Tripolitanian Neo-Punic: JAOS 114 (1994) 453-6.

9101* *a) Krebernik* Manfred, Verbalformen mit suffigierten n-Morphemen; Überlegungen zur Morphologie des Energikus im Ugaritischen und in anderen semitischen Sprachen; – *b) Irsigler* Hubert, Grosssatzformen im althebräischen und die syntaktische Struktur der Inschrift des Königs Mescha von Moab: → 323*, Syntax 1993, 123-150 / 81-121.

9102 *Margalit* B., Studies in NWSemitic inscriptions [i. Moabitica; ii. Deir'Alla Balaam; iii. Samaliana]: UF 26 (1994) 271-315.

9103 *Muchiki* Yoshi, Spirantization in fifth-century B.C. North -West Semitic: JNES 53 (1994) 125-130.

9104 *Olmo Lete* Gregorio del, Un conjuro ugarítico contra el 'mal ojo': AnuFg 15 (1992) 7-16 [OTAbs 16, p. 267].

9105 *Pitard* Wayne T., The reading of KTU 1.14: III.41; the burial of Aqhat: BASOR 294 (1994) 31-38; 4 fig.

9106 *Sanmartín* Joaquín, *a*) Ugarítico entre la filología y la lingüística; – *b*) Grafemática fenicia y proto-alfabetos: AnuFg 14 (1991) 9-38 / 15 (1992) 17-31 [< OTAbs 16, p. 269s].

9106* *Sarfatti* Gad B., ❺ The origin of vowel letters in West-Semitic writing — a tentative recapitulation: Lešonenu 58 (1994) 13-24; Eng. 1s.

9107 **Smith** Mark S., The Ugaritic Baal cycle, I. Introduction with text, translation and commentary of KTU 1.1-1.2: VTSupp 55. Leiden 1994, Brill. xxxviii-447 p.; bibliog. p. 363-401. 90-04-09995-6: corrections in UF 26 (1994) 455.

9108 *Tropper* Josef, Das ugaritische Konsonanteninventar: JNWS 10,2 (1994) 17-59.

9109 **Тяоррея** Josef, *a*) Zur Grammatik der ugaritischen Omina; – *b*) Die enklitische Partikel –y im Ugaritischen; – *c*) Ugaritisch *palt* und hebräisch *pa'rôt*: UF 26 (1994) 457-472 / 473-482 / 483-6.

9110 **Tropper** Josef, Die Inschriften von Zincirli 1993 → 9,9833: ᴿUF 26 (1994) 606 (P. *Xella*).

9111 *Watson* W. G. E., *a*) Ugaritic *p* again; – *b*) The Ugaritic PN *krt*: UF 26 (1994) 493-5 / 497-500; – *c*) Ugaritic [personal] onomastica: AulaO 11 (1993) 213-222.

9112 *Woudhuizen* Fred C., Tablet RS 20.25 from Ugarit; evidence of maritime trade in the final years of the Bronze Age: UF 26 (1994) 509-538; 6 fig.

9113 *Wright* Richard M., Egyptian *np3p3*: a cognate for Ugaritic *mpr* 'convulsion': UF 26 (1994) 539-541.

J1.6 Aramaica.

9114 **Beyer** Klaus, Die aramäischen Texte → 65,7925 ... 6,9394: [= ¹1985 (= 1986)+ Ergänzungsband] Gö 1994, Vandenhoeck & R. 450 p. 3-525-53099-6. – ᴿTüTQ 174 (1994) 319s (W. *Gross*).

9114* *Casey* Maurice, The use of the term *br (a)nš(a)* in the Aramaic translations of the Hebrew Bible: JStNT 54 (1994) 87-118.

9115 **Fitzmyer** J., *Kaufman* S., Aramaic Bibliography 1, 1992 → 8,9573; 9,9845: ᴿBO 51 (1994) 411-4 (B. *Grossfeld*); CBQ 56 (1994) 544s (E. G. *Clarke*: some details); RB 101 (1994) 582-8 (É. *Puech*).

9115* *Friedman* Shamma, ❺ Brief notes on Babylonian Aramaic [*mar, eyma, (1)alter*]: Lešonenu 58 (1994) 49 . 57; Eng. IV..

9116 *Fox* Samuel E., The phonology and morphology of the Jilu dialect of Neo-Aramaic [SE Turkey, Hakkari mt. before 1915]: JAfrAs 3 (1991s) 35-57.

9117 **Garbini** Giovanni (*Manfredi* Lorenza-Ilia), Aramaica [→ 9,200a]: StSemit NS 10. R 1993, Univ. 230 p.

9118 *Garbini* Giovanni, L'iscrizione aramaica di Tel Dan: LinceiR 9,5,1 (1994) 461-471; 3 facsim.

García a Martínez Florentino, Qumran and ... Aramaic [55 of the 800 texts] 1992 → 9738.

9118* *Gropp* Douglas M., The 3 f.s. inflection of the perfect in Onqelos-Jonathan Aramaic and related problems: JSS 39 (1994) 153-9.

9119 *Hoberman* Robert D., Parameters of emphasis; autosegmental analysis of emphasis; autosegmental analyses of pharyngealization in [Aramaic, Kurdish, and two dialects of Arabic]: JAfrAs 2 (1989s) 73-97.

9120 **Jastrow** Otto, Der neuaramäische Dialekt von Hertevin 1988 ➤ 4, a369 ... 9,9851*: ᴿJAfrAs 3 (1991s) 77-81 (M. *Tosco*).

9121 *Kaswalder* Pietro, *Pazzini* Massimo, La stele aramaica di Tel Dan: RivB 42 (1994) 193-201; facsim.

9122 *Lemaire* André, Épigraphie palestinienne; nouveaux documents, 1, Fragment de stèle araméenne de Tell Dan (IXᵉ s. av. J.-C.): Henoch 16 (1994) 87-93.

9123 *Lipiński* Edward, Aramaic clay tablets from the Gozan-Harran area: JbEOL 33 (1993s) 143-150.

9124 **Maraqten** Mohammed, Die semitischen Personennamen ᴰ1988 ➤ 4, a371* ... 8,9245: ᴿWZKM 84 (1994) 199-201 (Esther & H. *Eshel*).

9125 **Margain** Jean, Les particules dans le targum samaritain de Genèse-Exode; jalons pour une histoire de l'araméen samaritain: ÉPHÉH 2/29, 1993 ➤ 9,9855: ᴿAulaO 11 (1993) 265s (J. *Ribera*); OTAbs 17 (1994) 430s (J. A. *Fitzmyer*).

9126 *a) Margalit* B., The Old-Aramaic inscription of Hazael from Dan; – *b) Tropper* Josef, Paläographische und linguistische Anmerkungen zur Steleninschrift aus Dan: UF 26 (1994) 317-320 / 487-492.

9127 **Nakano** Akiʾo, Ethnographical texts in modern western Aramaic 1 (dialect of Jubbᶜadin: StCulturaeIslam 49. Tokyo 1994, Inst.AsiaAfrica. vi-65 + 26 p.; 44 fig.

9128 *Naudé* J. A., The verbless clause with pleonastic pronoun in Biblical Aramaic: J/Tyd Sem 6 (1994) 74-93.

9129 **Naveh** Joseph, *Shaked* Saul, Magic spells and formulae; Aramaic inscantations of late antiquity 1993 ➤ 9,9860; $28: ᴿOTAbs 17 (1994) 656s (Deirdre A. *Dempsey*: adds to their 1985 ²1987: Amulets 12, bowls 14, and Geniza texts 21].

9130 **Odisho** Edward Y., The sound system of modern Assyrian (Neo-Aramaic): Semitica Viva 2, 1988 ➤ 6,9407; 9,9864: ᴿJAfrAs 3 (1991s) 260-3 (M. *Tosco*).

9131 **Porten** D., *Yardeni* Ada, Textbook of Aramaic 1986 ➤ 2,7829 ... 8,9590: ᴿBSO 56 (1993) 355-7 (F. M. *Fales*).

9131* *Qimron* Elisha, ❹ The use of *šᵉyēš bî* 'which is in'; an Aramaism in the Bar Kokhba documents: Lešonenu 58 (1994s) 313-5; Eng. 4/III.

9132 *Ribera* Josep, El arameo del Targum de los profetas (Isa, Jer); morfología de los pronombres: AnuFg 14 (1991) 39-54 [< OTAbs 16, p. 269].

9133 **Rubba** Johanna E., Discontinuous morphology in modern Aramaic: diss. California, ᴰ*Langacker* R. San Diego 1994. 548 p. 94-14747. – DissA 55 (1994s) p. 4426.

9134 **Schiffman** L., *Swartz* M., Hebrew and Aramaic incantation texts ... Geniza 1992 ➤ 9,9868*: ᴿCritRR 6 (1993) 439s (E. M. *Yamauchi*).

9135 **Sokoloff** Michael, A dictionary of Jewish Palestinian Aramaic 1990 ➤ 6,9414 ... 9,9869*: ᴿAJS 17 (1992) 296-9 (G. A. *Rendsburg*); BO 51 (1994) 525-533 (J. W. *Wesselius*); CritRR 5 (1992) 386s (M. J. *Bernstein*); Lešonenu 57 (1993) 58-65 (J. *Blau* ❹) & 67-94 (M. A. *Fridman* ❹; Salesianum 56 (1994) 789s (R. *Vicent*).

9136 *Wasserstein* A., A note on the phonetic and graphic representations of Greek vowels and the spiritus asper in the Aramaic transcription of Greek loanwords: ➤ 90, ᶠMERIDOR R., ScrClasIsr 12 (1993s) 200-6 [< JStJud 25,167].

9136* *Watson* W. G. E., Final -m in Ugaritic again: AulaO 12 (1994) 95-103.

9137 *Yadin* Y., *Greenfield* J.C., *Yardeni* Ada, Babatha's *ketubba*: IsrEJ 44 (1994) 75-101; 6 fig.

J1.7 Syriaca.

9138 *Contini* Riccardo, Gli inizi della linguistica siriaca nell'Europa rinascimentale: RSO 68 (1994) 15-29; Eng. 30.

9138* *Desreumaux* Alain,   *a)* Un manuscrit syriaque de Téhéran contenant des apocryphes: Apocrypha 5 (Turnout 1994) 137-164. – *b)* Repertoire 1991 ➤ 7,890 ... 9,9878: ᴿJSS 38 (1993) 154-7 (J.F. *Coakley*).

9139 *Falla* Terry C.,   Questions concerning the content and implications of the [his I. 1991] lexical work, A key to the Peshitta Gospels: ➤ 450c, Syriacum 6, 1992/4, 85-99.

9139* **Gignoux** Philippe, Incantations magiques syriaques 1987 ➤ 3,9543 ... 8,9600: ᴿJNES 53 (1994) 43-47 (M.O. *Wise*).

9140 *Joosten* Jan,   On ante-position of the attributive adjective in classical Syriac and biblical Hebrew: ZAHeb 6 (1993) 188-192.

9140* *a) Joosten* Jan,   West Aramaic elements in the Syriac Gospels; methodological considerations; – *b) Sokoloff* Michael, Jewish Babylonian Aramaic and Syriac; mutual elucidation: ➤ 450c, Syriacum 6 (1992/4) 101-9 / 401-8.

9141 **Muraoka** Takamitsu,   Classical Syriac for Hebraists 1987 ➤ 3,9550 ... 7,9262: ᴿJAfrAs 3 (1991s) 76s (G. *Krotkoff*).

9142 ᵀᵉ**Palmer** Andrew, The seventh century in the West Syrian Chronicles; 2 texts, *Brock* S.; intr. *Hoyland* R.: Translated Texts for Historians 15. Liverpool 1993, Univ. 305 p. – ᴿOrChrPer 60 (1994) 710s (V. *Ruggieri*).

9142* *a) Rompay* Lucas Van,   Some preliminary remarks on the origins of classical Syriac as a standard language; the Syriac version of EUSEBIUS of Caesarea's Ecclesiastical History; – *b) Polotsky* H.J.,   Incorporation in modern Syriac: ➤ 123, Semitic 1994, 70-89 / 90-102.

9143 *Schrier* Omert J.,   Syriac evidence for the Roman-Persian war of 421-422: GrRByz 33 (1992) 75-86.

9144 *Tubach* J.,   Der Weg des Prinzen im Perlenlied: OrChrPer 24 (1993) 87-101; Bibliog. 102-111.

J2.1 Akkadica (sumerica).

9145 **Attinger** Pascal,   Éléments de linguistique sumérique ... 'dire' 1993 ➤ 9,9886: ᴿOLZ 89 (1994) 42-46 (A. *Foxvog*); OTAbs 17 (1994) 199 (C.T. *Begg*).

9146 **CAD** 'S' 1984 ➤ 65,758 ... 9,9887: ᴿAfO 40s (1993s) 1-23 (D. *Charpin*); OLZ 89 (1994) 534-8 (W. von *Soden*).

9147 *Dandamayev* Muhammad A.,   The Neo-Babylonian [official] *zazakku*: AltOrF 21 (1994) 34-40.

9147* *Feliu* L., *Millet* A.,   La transcripción de la onomástica asiriológica al español: AulaO 11 (1993) 243-7.

9148 *Fincke* Jeannette,   Noch einmal zum mittelassyrischen *šiluḫli* [land-renter]: AltOrF 21 (1994) 339-351.

9148* **Gianto** A.,   Word order variation in the Akkadian of Byblos: StPohl 159, ᴰ1990 ➤ 6,9448 ... 8,9613: ᴿAulaO 11 (1993) 253-5 (J. *Sanmartín*).

9149 **Gong** Yushu,   Studien zur Bildung und Entwicklung der Keilschriftzeichen: Antiquates [sic] 7. Ha 1993, Kovač. ix-154 p.; Bibliog. 150-4. 3-86064-144-1.

9149* **Groneberg** Brigitte R. M., Syntax, Morphologie und Stil der jung-babylonischen 'hymnischen' Literatur; 1. Grammatik. 2. Belegsammlung und Textkatalog: FrAltorSt 14, 1987 ➤ 4,a400...6,9449: ᴿOLZ 89 (1994) 140-2 (I. *Gebhardi*).

9150 **Hayes** John L., A manual of Sumerian grammar and texts 1990 ➤ 8,9615; 9,9894: ᴿAfO 40s (1993s) 96-98 (Inge & J. *Bauer*).

9151 *a*) *Huÿssteen* P.J.J. van, The genitive construction in the Emar testaments; – *b*) *Westhuizen* J.P. van der, Morphology and morphosyntax of the noun in the Amqi Amarna letters: ➤ 121, ꜰSMIT E., J/Tyd Sem 5,1 (1993) 1-17 / 18-56.

9151* **Jacobsen** Thorkild, The harps that once... Sumerian poetry in translation 1987 ➤ 3,9580; 5,9454: ᴿOLZ 89 (1994) 546-9 (B. *Hruška*).

9152 **Kienast** Burkhart, Glossar zu den altakkadischen Königsinschriften: FrAltorSt 8. Stu 1994, Steiner. ix-406 p. 3-515-04249-9 [BL 25,29, M.J. *Geller*].

9153 **Leong Tien Fock**, Tense, mood, and aspect in Old Babylonian; diss. UCLA, ᴰ*Buccellati* G. 1994. 429 p. 95-02937. – DissA 55 (1994s) p. 2808.

9154 **Michalowski** Piotr, The lamentation over the destruction of Sumer and Ur 1989 ➤ 5,3671: ᴿJNES 53 (1994) 63-66 (B. *Alster*).

9155 *Moortgat-Correns* Ursula, (*Böck* Barbara), Die Rosette – ein Schriftzeichen? Die Geburt des Sterns aus dem Geiste der Rosette: AltOrF 21 (1994) 359-371; 8 fig.

9156 **Moran** William L., Les lettres d'El-Amarna 1987 ➤ 3,c766... 9,9901: ᴿCdÉ 69 (1994) 97s (R.J. van der *Spek*).

9157 **Platt** James H., Eblaite scribal tendencies; graphemics and orthography: diss. UCLA 1993, ᴰ*Buccellati* G. 727 p. 93-24577. – DissA 54 (1993s) 1338.

9158 *Rainey* A.F., Triptotic plurals in the Amarna texts from Canaan: UF 26 (1994) 427-434.

9159 **Robertson** Anne F., Word dividers, spot markers and clause markers in Old Assyrian, Ugaritic, and Egyptian texts; sources for understanding the use of red ink points in the two Akkadian literary texts, Adapa and Ereshkigal, found in Egypt: diss. NYU 1994, ᴰ*Levine* B. 470 p. 94-22943. – DissA 55 (1994s) p. 947.

9160 *Römer* W.H.P., Beiträge zum Lexikon des Sumerischen (5): AfO 40s (1993s) 24-38.

9161 *Schretter* Manfred, Sumerische Phonologie; zu Konsonantenverbindungen und Silbenstruktur: AcOrK 54 (1993) 7-30.

9162 **Sjöberg** Åke W., Sumerian Dictionary I. Ph 1992, Pennsylvania University Museum. xlv-209 p. 0-924171-21-9. – ᴿBO 51 (1994) 593-8 (M. *Schretter*).

9163 **Soden** Wolfram von, The ancient Orient; an introduction to the study of the Ancient Near East [1985 Einführung ➤ 1,9116], ᵀ*Schley* Donald. GR 1994, Eerdmans. 262 p. $15. 0-8028-0142-0 [BL 95,139, W.G. *Lambert*; OTAbs 17,433, C.T. *Begg*: the translator put in some parenthetical OT references].

9164 *Streck* Michael P., Funktionsanalyse des akkadischen Št₂-Stamms: ZAss 84 (1994) 161-197.

9164* *Testen* David, The East Semitic precative paradigm: JSS 38 (1993) 1-13.

9165 ᴱ**Vogelzang** Marianna E., *Vanstiphout* H.L.J., Mesopotamia, epic literature; oral or aural 1990/2 ➤ 8,9641: ᴿBO 51 (1994) 587-590 (B.R. *Foster*); BSO 57 (1994) 459s (A.S. *George*).

9165* *Wiseman* Donald J., *Hess* Richard S.,   Alalakh text 457:   UF 26 (1994) 501-8.
9166 *Zeidler* Jürgen, Einige neue keilschriftliche Entsprechungen ägyptischer Personennamen [JACOBSEN 68]: WeltOr 25 (1994) 36-56.

J2.7 Arabica.

9167 *Åkesson* Joyce, The strong verb and infinitive noun in Arabic: AcOrK 52 (1991) 35-48.
9168 **Bar-Asher** Moshe, La composante hébraïque du judéo-arabe algérien (Tlemcen, Aïn-Temouchent). J 1992, Magnes. 184 p. – ᴿBSO 57 (1994) 372s (Farida *Abu-Haidar*); Sefarad 53 (1993) 402-4 (M. *Abu-Malham*).
9169 **Blau** Joshua, Studies in Middle Arabic and its Judaeo-Arabic variety 1988 → 7,9297: ᴿRJAfrAs 3 (1991s) 67-71 (B. *Hary*).
9170 *Blau* Joshua, A Melkite Arabic lingua franca from the second half of the first millennium: → 136, ᶠWANSBROUGH J., BSO 57 (1994) 14-16.
9171 **Blau** J., *Reif* S.C., Genizah... Judaeo-Arabic 1987/92 → 8,457; 9,9917: ᴿJTS 45 (1994) 284s (Meira *Pollack*).
9172 **Bloch** Ariel A., Studies in Arabic syntax and semantics 1986 → 3,9611; 5,9369: ᴿJAfrAs 2 (1989-91) 227-9 (E. *McCarus*: excellent).
9173 *a) Bloch* Ariel A., On attractional pronouns in classical Arabic; a contribution to general syntax; – *b) Rosenhouse* Judith, The occurrence of the passive in some Bedouin dialects: JAfrAs 3 (1991s) 1-8 / 9-21.
9174 *Dichy* Joseph, La pluriglossie de l'arabe ['diglossie' MARÇAIS W. 1930, FERGUSON C. 1959]: BÉtOr 46 (1994) 19-42.
9175 **Durand** Olivier, Profilo di arabo marocchino; varietà urbane centro-meridionali: StSemit 11. R 1994, Univ. x-158 p.
9176 ᴱ**Eid** M., *Holer* C., Perspectives on Arabic linguistics 5, 1991/3 [1s, 1987s/92] → 9,543: ᴿBO 51 (1994) 715-7 (M. *Kossmann*).
9177 **Gruendler** Beatrice, The development of the Arabic scripts from the Nabatean era to the first Islamic century according to dated texts: HarvSemMg 43, 1993 → 9,9922: ᴿBL (1994) 27 (J.C.L. *Gibson*: of interest for Hebrew writing, but no photos); BO 51 (1993) 723s (M.H. *Thung*); Orientalia 63 (1994) 294-7 (Fiorella *Scagliarini*).
9178 **Hary** Benjamin H., Multiglossia in Judaeo-Arabic... Cairene Purim scroll: ÉtJudMdv 14, 1992 → 9,9923; $57: ᴿBSLP 89,2 (1994) 344-7 (Dominique *Caubet*); BSO 57 (1994) 328s (J. *Blau*).
9179 **Haywood** – *Naḥmad*, Nueva gramática arabe, ᵀ*Ruiz Girela* F. M 1992, Coloquio. 638 p. – ᴿCiuD 206 (1993) 285s (B. *Justel*).
9180 *a) Johnson* C. Douglas, Preclusteral shortening in Levantine Arabic; – *b) Ehret* Christopher, The origin of third consonants in Semitic roots; an internal reconstruction (applied to Arabic): JAfrAs 1 (1988) 1-25 / 2 (1989) 109-202.
9181 *Langhade* Jacques, Études linguistiques au Moyen-Âge, un regard interculturel; le silence des sources sur la science lexicographique arabe: BÉtOr 46 (1994) 99-110.
9182 ᴱ**Larcher** Pierre, De la grammaire de l'arabe aux grammaires des arabes: BÉtOr 43, 1991. – ᴿBSLP 89,2 (1994) 347-358 (A. *Lonnet*).
9183 **Mahdi** Muhsin, The thousand and one nights, [1-2, 1984 → 8,9664], 3. Introduction and Indexes. Leiden 1994, Brill. vii-276 p. – ❶ index 105 p. 90-04-10106-3.
9184 **Mansour** Jacob, The Jewish Baghdadi dialect [< ❶ 1974-7, some few things to add to BLANC]. Or-Yehuda 1991, Babylonian Jewry Heritage

Center. 329 p. + **❶**xxi. – ᴿAJS 19 (1994) 297-9 (B. *Hary*); BSO 57 (1994) 371s (Farida *Abu-Haidar*).
9185 *Noja* Sergio, *Hubal* = Allah: RLomb 128,1 (1994) 283-295.
9186 **O'Fahey** Rex S., Arabic literature of Africa, 1. Eastern Sudanic to c. 1900: HbOr 1/13, Leiden 1994, Brill. xv-434 p. 90-04-09450-4.
9187 **Owens** J., A short reference grammar of Eastern Libyan Arabic. Wsh 1984, Harrassowitz. – ᴿJAfrAs 2 (1989-91) 318-321 (Judith *Rosenhouse*).
9188 **Ratcliffe** Robert R., The broken plural problem in Arabic, Semitic, and Afroasiatic; a solution based on the diachronic application of prosodic analysis: diss. Yale. NHv 1992, 667 p. – DissA 54 (1993s) p. 164.
9189 **Roman** André, Grammaire de l'arabe: Que sais-je? 2531, 1990 → 9,9932 ('Nᵒ 1275'): ᴿJAfrAs 3 (1991s) 256-9 (M. *Tosco*).
9190 *Schimmel* Annemarie, Islamic calligraphy: MetBu (1993) 56 p., color. ill.
9190* *Şişmanian* A. A., L'orientalisme au carrefour; réflexions en marge d'une 'Nouvelle pratique de l'Orientalisme' [colloque Société Asiatique, Institut du Monde Arabe, Paris 10 janvier 1992]: OrLovPer 24 (1993) 251-277.
9191 **Suleiman** Saleh M., Jordanian Arabic. Amst/Ph 1985, Benjamins. xvi-131 p. 90-272-2530-8. – ᴿJSS 38 (1993) 357-9 (Y. *Suleiman*).
9191* *Tietze* Andreas, Überlegungen über die lautliche Form der arabischen und persischen Lohnwörter im älteren Osmanischen: → 109, Mem. SCHAENDLINGER A., WZKM 82 (1992) 349-358.

J3 Aegyptia.

9192 *Barta* Winfred, Zum Gebrauch des Verbums *wnn* im Alt- und Mittelägyptischen: GöMiszÄg 132 (1993) 13-18.
9192* *Beaux* Nathalie, La *douat* ['aube' / 'souterrain'] dans les Textes des Pyramides; espace et temps de gestation: BIFAO 94 (1994) 1-6.
Beinlich H., *Saleh* M., Corpus der hieroglyphischen Inschriften aus dem Grab des Tutanchamun 1989 → 12726.
9193 **Bradshaw** Joseph, The imperishable stars of the northern sky in the Pyramid texts. L 1990, auct. v-38 p.; 15 fig. £1.50. – ᴿJEA 80 (1994) 231s (J. G. *Griffiths*).
9194 *Castle* Edward W., The dedication formula *ir. n.f. m mnw.f*: JEA 79 (1993) 99-120.
9195 *Clarus* Ingeborg, Des Menschen und der Sonne Weg durch Nacht und Tod [Amduat]: Symbolen 11 (1993) 89-120; 12 fig.
9195* *Crozier-Brelot* Claude, Sirius index des citations des textes des pyramides. P 1994, auct. I. 388 p.; II. p. 389-838. 2-9509-1061-0.
9196 ᴱ**Dassow** Ewa von, *Wasserman* J., *al.*, ᵀ*Faulkner*; *Goelet* O.], The Egyptian Book of the Dead; the book of going forth by day, being the Papyrus of Ani. SF 1994, Chronicle. 175 p.; ill. from 1890 E. Wallis *Budge*. 0-8118-0767-3.
9197 *Depuydt* Leo, A demotic table of terms (astrological; Yale, from Tebtunis): Enchoria 21 (1994) 1-9; 1 pl.
9198 ᵀᴱ**DuQuesne** Terence, At the court of Osiris; Book of the Dead spell 1994: OxCommEg 4. L 1994, Darengo. 75 p. 1-871266-11-4.
9199 ᴱ**Frandsen** Paul J., The Carlsberg papyri, I. Demotic texts 1991 → 7,9345*; 9,9954: ᴿBO 51 (1994) 282-9 (F. *Hoffmann*); JEA 80 (1994) 258-260 (M. *Smith*).
9200 **Gaskell** G. A., Egyptian Scriptures interpelled through the language of symbolism present in all inspired writings. L 1991, (Daniel, reprinted by) Banton. 245 p.; ill. 1-85652-023-4 [OIAc 9,27].

9201 *Goldwasser* Orly,   An Egyptian scribe from Lachish and the hieratic tradition of the Hebrew kingdoms: TAJ 18 (1991) 248-253 [< OTAbs 17, p. 37].

9202 **Graefe** Erhart, *⁴ʳᵉᵛKahl* Jochem, Mittelägyptische Grammatik für Anfänger. Wsb 1994, Harrassowitz. xix-249 p. 3-447-03445-9.

9203 *a) Hafemann* Ingelore, Lexikalische Datenbank contra Wörterbuch; – *b) Nebe* Ingrid, Bibliographie zu den Negationen: GöMiszÄg 137 (1993) 31-38 / 9-29.

9204 *Heerma van Voss* M.,   Een egyptische Dodenpapyrus in Antwerpen: JbEOL 33 (1993s) 21-30; pl. I-VIII.

9205 **Hoch** James E., Semitic words in Egyptian texts of the New Kingdom and Third Intermediate Period. Princeton 1994, Univ. xxi-572 p.; bibliog. p. 513-532. 0-691-03761-2 [BL 95,176, K. A. *Kitchen*]. – ᴿUF 26 (1994) 602 (O. *Loretz*).

9206 *Ignatov* Sergei, Some notes on the Story of the shipwrecked sailor: JEA 80 (1994) 195-8.

9207 **Jansen-Winkeln** Karl, Text und Sprache in der 3. Zwischenzeit; Vorarbeiten zu einer spätmittelägyptischen Grammatik: ÄgAT 26. Wsb 1994, Harrassowitz. xx-152 p. 3-447-03577-3.

9208 *Jansen-Winkeln* Karl, a) Das ägyptische Pseudopartizip: OrLovPer 24 (1993) 5-28; – b) Das futurische Verbaladjektiv im Spätmittelägyptischen: StÄäK 21 (1994) 107-129.

9209 **Jasnow** Richard, A late period hieratic wisdom text (P. Brooklyn 47.218.135): SAOC 52. Ch 1992, Univ.Or.Inst. – ᴿEnchoria 21 (1994) 156-9 (C. *Burkard*).

9210 *Jong* Aleid de, Coffin Texts Spell 38, the case of the father and the son: StÄäK 21 (1994) 141-157.

9211 *Jürgens* Peter, Möglichkeiten der Stemmakonstruktion bei Texten aus lebendiger Überlieferung (am Beispiel der Sargtexte): GöMiszÄg 132 (1993) 49-65.

9212 **Kahl** Jochem, Das System der ägyptischen Hieroglyphenschrift in der 0.-3. Dynastie: GöOrF 4/29. Wsb 1994, Harrassowitz. xiii-1051 p.; Bibliog. p. 1022-1051. 3-447-03499-8.

9213 **Koch** R., Die Erzählung des Sinuhe 1990 ⇒ 6,9534; 8,9710: ᴿOLZ 89 (1994) 29s (Elke *Blumenthal*).

9214 *Kruchten* J.-M., ir wnn *śḏm.f* (*śḏm.n.f.*) et ir *śḏm.f* (*śḏm.n.f*); une approche structuraliste: JEA 80 (1994) 97-108.

9215 **Leitz** Christian, Tagewählerei; das Buch *ḥ3t nḥḥ pḥ.wy ḏt* und verwandte Texte: ÄgAbh 55. Wsb 1994, Harrassowitz. xiv-525 p.; vol. of. 79 pl. 3-447-03515-3.

9215* **Lichtheim** Miriam, Maat: OBO 120, 1992 ⇒ 8,9711: ᴿOrientalia 63 (1994) 279s (A. *Roccati*) also on PARKINSON R., Voices 1991.

9216 *Limme* Luc, Derechef le 'nom du propriétaire' du Papyrus Vandier (verso): CdÉ 69 (1994) 5-8.

9217 *Loprieno* Antonio, On the typological order of constituents in Egyptian: JAfrAs 1 (1988) 26-57.

9218 *Mayer* Walter, *Mayer-Opificius* Ronald, Die Schlacht bei Qadeš [Ramesseum]; der Versuch einer neuen Rekonstruktion: UF 26 (1994) 321-368; 2 fig.

9218* *Moreno Garcia* J.C., *Ḥwt* ['work and stock center', not 'funerary domain'] y la retribución de los funcionarios provinciales en el Imperio Antiguo; el caso di *Jbj* de Deir el-Gebrawi (Urk. I 144:3-145:3): AulaO 12 (1994) 29-50; 1 facsim.

9219 **Munro** Irmtraut, Untersuchungen zu den Totenbuch-Papyri der 18. Dynastie; Kriterien ihrer Datierung 1987 ➤ 6,9538; 7,9153:   ᴿCdÉ 69 (1994) 102-6 (A. De *Caluwe*).

9220 *Nibbi* Alessandra, Shat of the nine bows; a speculative note: DiscEg 26 (1993) 59-70; 13 fig.

9221 **Parkinson** R. B., Voices from ancient Egypt; anthology 1991 ➤ 8,9719*: ᴿCdÉ 69 (1994) 260-63 (M. *Malaise*).

9222 *Quack* Joachim F., Gefangene oder Edelfrau? Zu einem semitischen Fremdwort der ägyptischen Soldatencharakteristik: WeltOr 25 (1994) 17-20.

9223 *Rochette* Bruno, Traducteurs et traductions dans l'Égypte gréco-romaine: CdÉ 69 (1994) 313-322.

9224 *Sabbahy* K., Evidence for the titulary of the Queen from Dynasty One: GöMiszÄg 135 (1993) 81-86; 4 fig.

9225 **Sadek** A., Contribution... Amdouat: OBO 65, 1985 ➤ 1,a647*... 7, 9363: ᴿWeltOr 25 (1994) 129-132 (U. *Luft*).

9226 **Schenkel** Wolfgang, Einführung in die altägyptische Sprachwissenschaft 1990 ➤ 6,9548: ᴿAcOrK 54 (1993) 175-8 (R. H. *Pierce*).

9227 **Schlott** Adelheid, Schrift und Schreiber im alten Ägypten 1989 ➤ 5, 9446... 8,9732: ᴿSalesianum 56 (1994) 369, F. *Canaccini*, anche su HUNGER H., Byzanz; BLACK H.).

9228 **Schneider** Thomas, Asiatische Personennamen in ägyptischen Quellen: OBO 114, 1992 ➤ 8,9734: ᴿAfO 40s (1993s) 163-6 (G. *Vittmann*); HistSpr 107 (1994) 313s (M. *Mayrhofer*).

9229 *Spalinger* Anthony, Dated texts from the Old Kingdom: StAäK 21 (1994) 275-319.

9230 *Sternberg - el Hotabi* Heike, Der Untergang der Hieroglyphenschrift; Schriftverfall und Schrifttod im Ägypten der griechisch-römischen Zeit: CdÉ 69,138 (1994) 218-245 + 3 facsim.

9231 **Sturtewagen** C., The funerary papyrus Palau rib. or. 450, 1991 ➤ 7, 9371 ... 9,9992: ᴿArOr 61 (1993) 321s (L. *Bareš*).

9232 **Vleeming** S. P., The gooseherds of Hou. 1991. – ᴿEnchoria 21 (1994) 176-185 (G. *Vittman*).

9233 **Vycichl** Werner, La vocalisation de la langue égyptienne 1. La phonétique. BtÉt 16, 1990 ➤ 6,9556: ᴿJAmEg 31 (1994) 229s (J. P. *Allen*: careless); OLZ 89 (1994) 27s (W. *Schenkel*).

9234 **Wilkinson** Richard H., Reading Egyptian art; a hieroglyphic guide to ancient Egyptian painting and sculpture. NY 1992, Thames & H. 224 p.; 450 fig. $25. – ᴿAJA 97 (1993) 359s (W. H. *Peck*).

9234* **Winand** Jean, Études de néo-égyptien I. La morphologie verbale 1992 ➤ 8,9741; 9,9998: ᴿOLZ 89 (1994) 525-8 (J. *Hallof*).

9235 **Zonhoven** L., POLOTSKY, Sinuhe, negation and the sḏm.n=f; on the existence of an indicative sḏm.n=f in Middle Egyptian: JbEOL 33 (1993s) 39-109.

_____

9236 **Browne** Gerald M., Old Nubian texts from Qaṣr Ibrim II, 1989 ➤ 5,9463 ... 8,9744: ᴿJEA 79 (1993) 321s (J. D. *Ray*); OLZ 89 (1994) 97-100 (P. *Werner*, also on 1 & 3, 1988/91).

9237 **Browne** Gerald M., The Old-Nubian Miracle of saint Menas: BeitSudan Beih 7. W-Mödling 1994, Univ. Inst. Afrikanistik. iii-108 p.

9237* *Browne* M., Miscellanea Nubiana: Orientalia 63 (1994) 257-9.

9238 *Hummel* Siegbert,   Meroitisch-türkische Äquivalente: Anthropos 88 (1993) 190-4.

J3.4 Coptica.

9239 **Albert** Micheline, *al.*,   Christianismes orientaux... langues/littératures 1993:   ᴿPrOrChr 43 (1993) 210s (P. *Ternant*).

9240 **Elanskaya** Alla I.,   The literary Coptic manuscripts in the A. S. Pushkin State Fine Arts Museum in Moscow: VigChr supp. 16.

9241 ᴱ**Godlewski** W.,   Coptic Studies 1984/90 ⇥ 8,690:   ᴿBO 51 (1994) 357-361 (P. *Luisier*).

9242 **Hasitzka** Monika R. M.,   Neue Texte... zum Koptisch-Unterricht 1990 ⇥ 8,9752; 9,10016:   ᴿEos 81 (1993) 321s (J. *Prostko-Prostyński*).

9243 ᴱ**Hasitzka** Monika R. M., Koptisches Sammelbuch I, 1993 ⇥ 9,10017: ᴿWZKM 84 (1994) 183-192 (G. *Vittmann*).

9243* *Kasser* Rodolphe, *a)* Voyelles et syllabes toniques, mi-toniques et atones en copte; − *b)* Prééminence de l'alphabet grec dans les divers alphabets coptes, II. spécimens textuels; III. déductions et conclusions: BSocÉg 17 (Genève 1993) 49-55 / 16 (1992) 51-59 . 60-64.

9244 *Kasser* Rodolphe, *a)* Le Djinkim en usage dominant dans l'orthographie 'classique' de la langue bohaïrique: BSACopte 33 (1994) 109-142; − *b)* Démonstratifs et possessifs en copte: BIFAO 94 (1994) 287-301.

9244* *MacCoull* Leslie S. B.,   *a)* A Nativity hymn from Egypt in the Coptic Museum: ArPagF 40 (1994) 127-139; − *b)* Notes on some Coptic hagiographical texts [many Syriacists, no Coptologists for the new Hagiographic Society]: PrOrChr 42 (1992) 11-18.

9245 ᵀᴱ**Meyer** Marvin, **Smith** Richard, *Kelsey* Neal, *al.*, Ancient Christian magic; Coptic texts of ritual power. SF 1994, Harper. xiii-407 p. $25. 0-06-065578-X [TDig 42,154: 135 texts].

9246 ᴱ**Rassart-Debergh** M., *Ries* J., Actes du 4ᵉ Congrès Copte 1992 ⇥ 9, 694*b*: ᴿBO 51 (1994) 572-584 (R.-G. *Coquin*).

9247 *Samir Khalil* Samir,   Un texte de la Philocalie sur la 'Prière à Jé-sus' dans un manuscrit arabo-copte médiéval: PrOrChr 43 (1993) 5-37; Eng. 37s.

9248 *Vittmann* Günther, Zum koptischen Sprachgut im Ägyptisch-Arabischen: WZKM 81 (1991) 197-227.

9249 **Young** Dwight W.,   Coptic manuscripts from the White Monastery (Ahmim); works of Shenute: Mitt. ÖstNatBt Papyrussammlung NS 22. W 1993, Hollinek. 200 p.; 66 pl.

9250 *Zakrzewska* Ewa D.,   The inner-verbal subject in Bohairic Coptic, on the example of the Martyrs' legends: DiscEg 26 (1993) 71-90.

J3.8 Æthiopica.

9251 **Bernand** E., *al.*,   Recueil des inscriptions de l'Éthiopie 1991 ⇥ 7,9400*; 9,10030*: ᴿAfO 40s (1993s) 180s (W. W. *Müller*).

9252 **Haile** Getatchew, Catalogue of Ethiopian manuscripts 10, 4000-4501. ColMn 1993, St. John's. xii-512 p.; 5 pl. − ᴿOrChrPer 60 (1994) 641s (O. *Raineri*).

9253 **Leslau** Wolf, Arabic loanwords in Ethiopian 1990 ⇥ 7,9402*: ᴿBSO 56 (1993) 138s (A. K. *Irvine*).

9254 **Leslau** Wolf, *a)* Concise dictionary of Geᶜez 1989 ⇥ 6,9584; 8,9765: ᴿAfO 40s (1993s) 186s (H. *Eisenstein*); − *b)* Comparative etymological dictionary of Geez 1987 ⇢ 3,8734 ... 7,9405: Lešonenu 57 (1993) 351-65 (J. *Blau* ✪, Eng. IV).

9255 ᶠLESLAU Wolf, Semitic Studies, 85th b., ᴱ**Kaye** Alan S.; I-II 1991 ⇢ 7,93; 8,118: ᴿArOr 62 (1994) 428-435 (V. *Blašek*).

9256 **Stoffregen-Pedersen** Kirsten, Les Éthiopiens: Fils d'Abraham 1990 ⇢ 7,e855; ital. 1993 ⇢ 9,10037: ᴿBSO 57 (1994) 385s (A. K. *Irvine*, also on *Kaplan* S., Falashas).

9257 **Uhlig** Siegbert, Introduction to Ethiopian paleography: AethF 28, 1990 ⇢ 9,10038: ᴿAcOrK 53 (1992) 169s (K.-G. *Prasse*).

9258 **Ullendorff** Edward, From the Bible to E. CERULLI... Ethiopian 1990 ⇢ 6,313; 8,9771: ᴿAcOrK 52 (1991) 169-171 (K.-G. *Prasse*).

J4 Anatolica.

9259 **Boley** Jacqueline, The Hittite particle -z / -za /: InBeitSprW 79. Innsbruck 1993, Univ. Inst. SprW. 262 p. 3-85124-644-6.

9260 *Brown* Edwin L., The Linear-A signary; tokens of Luvian dialect in Bronze Age Crete: Minos 27s (1992s) 25-54; 4 fig.

9261 *a) Girbal* Christian, *šummi* im Boğazköy-Hurritischen; – *b) Wegner* Ilse, Hurritische verba dicendi mit einfacher und doppelter Absolutiv- Rektion: AltOrF 21 (1994) 171-5 / 161-170.

9262 *Hoffner* Harry A., The Hittite word for 'oil' and its derivatives: HistSpr 107 (1994) 222-230.

9263 **Jie Jin**, A complete retrograde glossary of the Hittite language: Publ. 71. Leiden 1994, Nederlands Inst. Istanbul. [x-] 100 p. 90-6258-072-6.

9264 *Mayrhofer* Manfred, Hethitisch und Laryngaltheorie [*Puhvel* J., Dictionary 3., Words beginning with H]: AfO 40s (1993s) 67-70.

9265 **Melchert** H. Craig, Cuneiform Luvian lexicon: Lexica Anatolica 2. Chapel Hill, NCarolina 1993. vi-298 p.

9266 *a) Neu* Erich, Modusbildungen im Hurritischen; – *b) Lindeman* Frederik O., 'Laryngeal' colouring and lengthened grade in Indo-European: ⇢ 112, ᶠSCHMIDT K., Indoeuropean 1994, 122-137 / 110-121.

9267 **Puhvel** Jean, HOMER and Hittite: InBeitSprW 47. Innsbruck 1991, Univ. 29 p. – ᴿRPg 67 (1993) 122 (J.-L. *Perpillou*).

9268 **Rüster** C., *Neu* E., Konträr-Index der hethitischen Keilschriftzeichen 1993 ⇢ 9,10059: ᴿZAss 84 (1994) 301s (M. *Giorgieri*).

9268* **Werner** Russell, Kleine Einführung im Hieroglyphisch-Luwisch: OBO 106, 1991 ⇢ 7,9428; 9.10061: ᴿOrientalia 63 (1994) 287-290 (Natalia *Bolatti-Guzzo*).

J4.4 Phrygia, Lydia, Lycia.

9269 *Börker-Klähn* Jutta, Ein Phryger in Kargamiš: AltOrF 21 (1994) 198 nur.

9270 **Hodot** René, Le dialecte éolien 1990 ⇢ 7,9439 ... 9,10070: ᴿRPg 66 (1992) 144s (A. *Christos*).

9271 *Liebig* Michael, Lyker und Achäer — ein Beitrag zur Aḫḫijawa-Frage: Historia 42 (1993) 492s.

J4.8 Armena, georgica.

9271* *Adiego* I. J., Licio epewētlm̃mēi: AulaO 11 (1993) 139-145; Eng. 139.

9272 **Clackson** James, The linguistic relationship between Armenian and

Greek: PgSocPubl 30.   Ox 1994, Blackwell.   x-272 p.; bibliog. p. 238-255.
£20.   0-631-19197-6.
9273 **Cowe** S. Peter,   Catalogue of the Armenian manuscripts in the
Cambridge University Library: CSCOr 546, subsidia 86.   Lv 1994,
Peeters.   xiii-232 p.   90-6831-644-3.
9274 *a) Diahukian* Gevork B.,   Indoeuropäische phonetisch-grammatische
Dialekt-Isoglossen, die vom Hethitisch-Luvischen und Armenischen geteilt
werden; – *b) Gamkrelidze* Thomas V.,   Proto-Indo-European as a language of stative-active typology; – *c) Lehmann* Winfred P.,   Modifications
in syntactic change from SOV to VSO structure: ➤ 112, ᶠSCHMIDT K.,
Indoeuropean 1994, 12-24 / 25-34 / 97-109.
9275 **Jungman** Paul, *Weitenberg* J. J. S.,   A reverse analytical dictionary of
classical Armenian: TrLingDoc 9.   B 1991, Mouton de Gruyter.   viii-
836 p.   DM 398. – ᴿLinguistics 32,2 (1994) 366s (B. *Comrie*).
9276 **Kévorkian** R. H.,   Catalogue des 'incunables' arméniens (1511-1695)
1986 ➤ 3,9774... 6,9625:   ᴿRivStoLR 29 (1993) 450-5 (S. *Voicu*).
9276* *Russell* James R.,   On the origins and invention of the Armenian script:
Muséon 107 (1994) 317-333.

9277 **Fähnrich** Heinz,   Grammatik der altgeorgischen Sprache.   Ha 1994,
Buske.   ix-269 p.; Bibliog. 261-5.   3-8758-065-1.
9278 *a) Müller* C. Detlef,   Die Georgier in Palästina; – *b) Boeder* Winfried,
Kartvelische und indogermanische Syntax; die altgeorgischen Klitika; – *c)*
Lomtatidze Ketevan, On the imperative mood: ➤ 112, ᶠSCHMIDT K. H.,
Indogermanica 1994, 489-499 / 447-471 / 479-484.

J5   **Graeca**   .1 *grammatica, onomastica* (Inscriptiones ➤ J5.4).

9279 **Adrados** F. R.,   Diccionario 3, apoikoitéō - basileús 1991 ➤ 2,7689 ...
9,10083:   ᴿRPg 66 (1992) 353s (P. *Monteil*).
9280 *Agusta-Boularot* Sandrine,   Les références épigraphiques aux *Gramma-*
tici et *grammatikoí* de l'empire romain (Iᵉʳ s. av. J.-C. - IVᵉ s. ap. J.-C.):
MÉF 106 (1994) 653-746.
9281 **Biville** Frédérique,   Les emprunts du latin au grec 1990 ➤ 7,9542;
9,10088:   ᴿKratylos 38 (1993) 92-102 (J. *Niehoff-Panagiotidis*); RPg 66
(1992) 144-6 (J.-L. *Perpillou*).
9282 **Black** David A.,   Learn to read NT Greek: Nv 1993, Broadman.   xii-
211 p. $20. – ᴿCBQ 56 (1994) 785s (H. V. *Parunak*).
9283 **Bouttier** Michel,   Mots de passe; tentatives pour saisir quelques termes
insaisissables du NT: Parole présente 1993 ➤ 9,10090:   ᴿRHPR 74 (1994)
203s (C. *Grappe*).
9284 ᴱ**Brixhe** Claude, La koiné grecque antique, I. Une langue introuvable?:
TravMémAnc 10. Nancy 1993, Presses Univ.   143 p.   2-86480-810-2. –
ᴿBSLP 89,2 (1994) 213s (A. *Christol*).
9285 **Brooks** James A.,   A morphology of New Testament Greek; a review
and reference grammar.   Lanham MD 1994, UPA.   [x-]468 p.   0-8191-
9491-3.
9286 **Calzecchi Onesti** Rosa, Leggo Marco e imparo il greco.   CasM 1993,
Piemme.   235 p.   Lᵐ 40. – ᴿAsprenas 41 (1994) 285s (G. *Di Palma*).
9287 *Cignelli* Lino, *Bottini* G. Claudio,   La diatesi del verbo nel greco biblico:
LA 44 (1994) 215-252.

9288 **Countryman** L. W., The NT is in Greek; a short course for exegetes 1993 ➤ 9,10097: ᴿScotJT 47 (1994) 414 (S. *Moyise*).

9289 **Daris** Sergio, Il lessico latino nel greco d'Egitto² [¹1971] 1991 ➤ 9, 10099: ᴿLatomus 53 (1994) 438s (A. *Martin*).

9290 *Davies* Andrew M., The prosody of Greek speech. NY 1994, Oxford-UP. xvii-565 p. 0-19-508546-9.

9291 **Duhoux** Yves, Le verbe grec ancien 1992 ➤ 8,9827; 9,10101: ᴿRBgPg 72 (1994) 111-121 (M. *Delaunois*); RPg 66 (1992) 351s (J.-L. *Perpillou*).

9292 **Easley** Kendell H., User-friendly Greek; a common sense approach to the Greek New Testament. Nv 1994, Broadman & H. viii-167 p. 0-8054-1043-0.

9292* *Ehrenstrasser* Irene, Schafe in Hosen? Die lateinischen Lohnwörter in der Sprache der griechischen Papyri Ägyptens; ein Forschungsprojekt: Biblos 43 (1994) 103-9.

9293 **Fanning** Buist M., Verbal aspect 1990 ➤ 6,9659 ... 9,10102: ᴿSalesianum 56 (1994) 372s (R. *Bracchi*).

9294 *Floor* S., [*dé, mèn oûn* + 5 of the 12] Emphasis markers in Greek discourse; a study in Louw and Nida's lexicon: NotTr 7,1 (1993) 40-48 [< NTAbs 38, p. 342].

9294* *Fraser* P. M., *Matthews* E., A lexicon of Greek personal names 2, Attica ᴱ*Osborne* M. J., *Byrne* S. G. Ox 1994, Clarendon. xxi-510 p. 0-19-814990-5. – ᴿBeitNam 29s,4 (1994s) 456-9 (Rüdiger *Schmitt*).

9295 ᴱ**Gély** Suzanne, Sens et pouvoirs de la nomination dans les cultures hellénique et romaine. II. Le nom et la métamorphose [séminaires CNRS et tables rondes 1988-90] 1992 ➤ 8,654*: ᴿRÉLat 72 (1994) 240 (J. *Dangel*).

9295* *Hajnal* Ivo, Neue Aspekte zur Reconstruktion des frühgriechischen Phonemsystems: IndogF 98 (1993) 108-129.

9296 *Hammond* Nicholas G. L., Evidence for Macedonian speech: Historia 43 (1994) 131-142.

9297 *Horsley* G. H. R., The origin and scope of Moulton and Milligan's Vocabulary of the Greek NT and Deissmann's planned NT lexicon; some unpublished letters of G. A. Deissmann to J. H. Moulton: BJRyL 76,1 (1994) 187-216.

9298 **Jacquinod** B., Le double accusatif en grec 1989 ➤ 7,9464; 8,9832: ᴿRÉG 107 (1994) 281-3 (Catherine *Dobias-Lalou*).

9299 **Jay** Eric G., Grammatica greca del NT, ᵀᴱ*Calzecchi Onesti* Rosa. CasM 1993, Piemme. 448 p. Lᵐ 55. – ᴿCC 145 (1994,2) 310s (A. *Ferrua*).

9300 **Lambin** Gérard, L'origine du *skolion* [completion of Teodorsson M. from his own 1986 Lille dissertation]: Eranos 91 (1993) 32-37.

9301 *Lignani* Antonella, L'articolo greco: Aufidus 22 (1994) 111-127.

9302 **Lloyd-Jones** Hugh, Greek in a cold climate 1991 ➤ 7,9469: ᴿPhoenix 48 (Toronto 1994) 186-8 (T. G. *Rosenmeyer*).

9303 **Lust** J., *Eynikel* E., *al.*, Greek-English lexicon of the Septuagint, 1. A-I. Stu 1992, Deutsche Bibelgesellschaft ➤ 8,9839; 9,10112; liv-218 p.: ᴿBiblica 75 (1994) 434-9 (T. *Muraoka*); JJurPap 24 (1994) 215s (M. *Moraoski*); ZkT 116 (1994) 83-85 (J. M. *Oesch*).

9304 **McKay** Kenneth L., A new syntax of the verb in New Testament Greek; an aspectual approach: Studies in Biblical Greek 5. NY 1994, P. Lang. xv-203 p. 0-8204-2123-5.

9305 **Mastronarde** Donald J., Introduction to Attic Greek. Berkeley 1993, Univ. California. $35. 0-520-07843-8; pa. -4-6. – ᴿClasO 72 (1994s) 38 (C. J. *Zabrowski*).

9306 **Meier-Brügger** Michael,   Griechische Sprachwissenschaft: Göschen...
1992 ➤ 9,10117:   ᴿJHS 114 (1994) 199 (W. F. *Wyatt*: remarkably
thorough); Minos 27 (1992s) 344s (E. *Sikkenga*).

9307 **Mounce** William D.,   Basics of biblical Greek. GR 1993, Zondervan.
xiii-446 p. $25 (workbook vi-186 p. $11). – ᴿAndrUnS 32 (1994) 255-8
(Nancy Y. *Vyhmeister*, also on BEETHAM F., BLACK D., 1992).

9308 **Muraoka** T.,   A Greek-English lexicon of the Septuagint, Twelve
Prophets 1993 ➤ 9,10120:   ᴿAegyptus 79 (1994) 129-135 (Anna *Passoni
dell'Acqua*); Asprenas 41 (1994) 440s (G. *Di Palma*); BL (1994) 48 (S. P.
Brock); CBQ 56 (1994) 771s (J. A. *Fitzmyer*: pilot-text for a larger
project); ETL 70 (1994) 132-4 (J. *Lust*: more 'fully fledged' than his own,
ampler); JTS 45 (1994) 631s (A. G. *Salvesen*).

9309 *Piñero* Antonio, Boletín de Filología Neotestamentaria: FgNt 7 (1994)
91-124.229-254. Apart from this meaty survey, all in English, it is
interesting to note that the whole volume contains only two articles and
one review which fit into our 'Philology' section, while on exegesis of
specific Bible passages there are 9 articles and 14 reviews: as distinct from
ZAHeb, of which more than half fits in this section Philology.

9310 **Porter** S. E.,   *Carson* D. A.,   Biblical Greek... open questions 1993
➤ 9,10123:   ᴿExpTim 105 (1993s) 23 (H. *Guite*).

9311 **Porter** Stanley E., Idioms of the Greek New Testament 1992 ➤ 9,10125:
ᴿBiblica 75 (1994) 440-4 (C. *Buzzetti*); JBL 113 (1994) 534-6 (D. D.
Schmidt).

9312 **Porter** S.,   Verbal aspect 1989 ➤ 5,9581... 9,10122*: ᴿJEvTS 37 (1994)
145-7 (R. A. *Young*).

9313 ᴱ*Radici Colace* Paola, *Caccamo Caltabiano* Maria, ... Lessici tecnici greci
e latini 1990/1 ➤ 7,579:   ᴿOrpheus 14 (1993) 217-222 (Elena *Scuotto*).

9314 **Rehkopf** Friedrich,   Griechisch-deutsches Wörterbuch zum NT 1992
➤ 8,9855; 9,10126:   ᴿNRT 116 (1994) 903 (X. *Jacques*); NT 36 (1994)
280s (J. K. *Elliott*).

9315 **Rijksbaron** Albert, The syntax and semantics of the verb in classical
Greek. Amst 1984, Gieben. xi-176 p. $24. 90-70265-36-2. – ᴿAntClas
63 (1994) 431s (Sylvie *Vanséveren*).

9316 **Rosłon** Józef W. L., ❷ Gramatyka języka greckiego... SNT. Wsz 1990,
Akad.Teol.Kat. 384 p. – ᴿEos 81 (1993) 122-4 (M. *Bednarski*, ❷).

9317 **Spicq** Ceslas, Lexique théologique du NT 1991 ➤ 7,9488...9,10132: ᴿÉT-
Rel 68 (1993) 105 (É. *Cuvillier*); Salesianum 56 (1994) 382s (R. *Bracchi*).

9318 **Spicq** Ceslas,   Theological dictionary of the New Testament. Peabody
MA 1994, Hendrickson.   I. lxiv-492 p.; II. xiv-603 p.; III. x-691 p. $100.
1-56563-035-1 [TDig 42,189].

9319 **Spicq** Ceslas,   Note di lessicografia neotestamentaria: GLNT supp. 4.
Brescia [I. 1988-94. ➤ 4,a640] II. 1994, Paideia.   924 p. 88-394-0514-3.

9320 **Stoy** W.,   *Haag* K., Bibelgriechisch leicht gemacht³ [¹c. 1986 + 80 p.
Lösungsbuch DM 17,80]. Giessen 1993, Brunnen.   349 p. DM 49. 3-7655-
9312-5 [-8-4; < NTAbs 38, p. 285].

9321 **Swetnam** James,   An introduction to the study of NT Greek: SubsB-
Pont 16, 1992 ➤ 8,9861; 9,10133:   ᴿCBQ 56 (1994) 611s (E. *Hensell*:
user-friendly without gimmicks; some typos); ColcT 23,4 (1993) 211-3 (W.
Chrostowski, ❷).

9322 **Trenchard** Warren C.,   The student's complete vocabulary guide to the
Greek NT. GR 1992, Zondervan.   352 p. $13. – ᴿAndrUnS 32 (1994)
153s (W. *Richardson*).

9323 **Tusa Massaro** Laura, ˙ Sintassi del greco antico e tradizione gram-

maticale: Subsidia philologica 2. Palermo 1993, Epos. 253 p.; bibliog. p. 209-218. L^m 43.
9324 **Verboomen** A., L'imparfait périphrastique Lc/LXX 1992 → 8,9866: ^RRTLv 25 (1994) 375s (P.-M. *Bogaert*).
9325 **Vincenzi** Giuseppe C., Il greco; preistoria e storia di una lingua medioeuropea 1991 → 7,9492: ^RSalesianum 56 (1994) 200 (R. *Bracchi*).
9326 *Voelz* James W., Semitic influence on the Greek of the NT: ConcordJ 20 (1994) 115-129.
9327 *Whale* P. R., More efficient teaching of NT Greek: NTS 40 (1994) 596-605.
9328 *a) Winter* Werner, Griechisch *-men & -mes;* – *b) Campanile* Enrico, Bemerkungen zu den idg. Multiplikativa und den griechischen Bildungen auf -aki(s); – *c) Hamp* Eric P., The laryngeal heteroclites [*hýdōr hýdatos, iter itineris*]; – *d) Knobloch* Johann, Grundformen subkultureller Wortbildungen und Begriffsprägungen in den klassischen Sprachen; – *e) Szemerényi* Oswald, Etyma graeca VII.: → 112, ^FSCHMIDT K., Indogermanica 1994, 265-271 / 3-11 / 35-40 / 63-66 / 211-222.
9329 *Wong* Simon, Leftovers of LOUW-NIDA's Lexicon; some considerations towards 'A Greek-Chinese lexicon': FgNt 7 (1994) 137-174.
9330 *Wong* S., What case is this case? An application of semantic case in biblical exegesis: JianDao 1,1 (Hong Kong 1994) 49-73 [< NTAbs 38, p. 344, not indicating if ◉].
9331 **Young** Richard A., Intermediate New Testament Greek; a linguistic and exegetical approach. Nashville 1994, Broadman & H. xi-308 p. 0-8054-1059-7.
9332 **Zuntz** Günther, Greek; a course in classical and post-classical Greek grammar from original texts, ^EPorter Stanley E. Biblical Languages 4. Shf 1994, Academic. I. 704 p.; II. 433 p. £55; pa. £25. 1-85075-341-5; pa. -720-8.

J5.2 Voces graecae (ordine alphabetico graeco).

9333 *agros:* *Mauduit* Christine, Remarques sur les emplois de l'adjectif *agróteros* dans l'épopée et la poésie lyrique: RÉG 107 (1994) 47-67.
9334 *aidōs:* **Cavins** D. I. Aidōs ^D1993 → 9,10145: ^RAntClas 63 (1994) 468s (Marie-Christine *Leclerc*); ÉchMClas 38 (1994) 407-9 (J.A.S. *Evans*); Prudentia 25,2 (1993) 75-78 (V. J. *Gray*).
9335 *anankē:* **Ostwald** Martin, *ananke* in Thucydides 1988 → 5,9661; 6,9720: ^RArBegG 36 (1993) 336-8 (*ipse*).
9336 *antērēs:* *Blanc* Alain, À propos de l'adjectif *antērēs*; une origine méconnue du second membre de composé *-ērēs*: RPg 66 (1992) 247-254.
9337 *apaitētēs:* **Palme** B., Amt des *apaitētēs* 1989 → 7,b138; 8,b963: ^RBO 51 (1994) 354-7 (J. G. *Keenan*).
9338 *apeithéō:* *Thibaut* André, L'infidélité ... *apeithô* 1988 → 4,a657 ... 8,9893: ^RBL (1993) 158 (A. G. *Salvesen*); Sefarad 53 (1993) 417-420 (N. *Fernández Marcos*).
9339 *argyrion:* **Caccamo Caltabiano** Maria, *Radici Colace* Paola, Dalla premoneta alla moneta; lessico monetale greco tra semantica e ideologia. Pisa 1992, ETS. xix-218 p.; 6 pl. L^m 28. 88-7741-666-1. – ^RAntClas 63 (1994) 509s (F. de *Callatay*).
9339* *Vasiliu* Anca, Le mot et le verre; une définition médiévale du **diaphane**: JSav 94 (1994) 135-162.
9340 *dikē:* *Theodorou* Evangelos D., ◉ *a)* The meaning of righteousness in

the Holy Scriptures; - b) Justification according to the Three Hierarchs and St. AUGUSTINE. TAth 65 (1994) 417-436 / 625-658; Eng. 1021s.

9341 *ekklēsia:* Bolognesi Pietro, L'uso biblico del termine ekklesia: BbbOr 36 (1994) 181-4.

9342 *exousia:* Scholtissek Klaus, [< Vorarbeiten zur Diss. 1992] Vollmacht im Alten Testament und Judentum; begriffs- und motivgeschichtliche Studien zu einem bibeltheologischen Thema [kein hebräisches Äquivalent; auch LXX kaum vor Dan]: PdTSt 24. Pd 1993, Schöningh. 186 p. DM 36. - ᴿJTS 45 (1994) 669-672 (M. *Mayordomo-Marín*); TPQ 142 (1994) 327s (G. *Stemberger*).

9343 *epieikés:* AnPisa 24 (1994) 1-18 (M. *Durán López* sobre HERÓDOTO 3,53).

9344 *érchesthai:* Toribio Cuadrado J.F., El viniente 1993 ➤ 9,10158: ᴿAntonianum 69 (1994) 392s (M. *Alvarez Barredo*); Carthaginensia 10 (1994) 457s (R. *Sanz Valdivieso*); NRT 116 (1994) 115 (Y. *Simoens*); Salmanticensis 41 (1994) 340-2 (R. *Trevijano*); Lateranum 60 (1994) 174-6 (R. *Penna*); ScripTPamp 26 (1994) 1155s (V. *Balaguer*).

9345 *euchē:* Cimosa Mario, La preghiera nella Bibbia greca 1992 ➤ 9,10162: ᴿÉglT 25 (1994) 432 (L. *Laberge*).

9346 *thánatos:* Létoublon Françoise, Ce qui n'a plus de nom dans aucune langue [... le tabou de la mort et l'expression euphémique]: RPg 66 (1992) 317-335.

9346* *thermós:* a) López Férez Juan Antonio, Thermós y derivados en el Corpus Hippocraticum; - b) Martínez Hernández Marcos, *Santana Henríquez* Germán, Los compuestos con *dys-* en el Corpus Hippocraticum: ➤ 430b, Tratados 1990/4, 365-380 / 381-407.

9347 *Italía:* Gély Suzanne, Le nom de l'Italie, mythe et histoire, d'Hellanicos à VIRGILE: BtViaggiItal 37. Genève 1991, Slatkine [➤ 8,9914]: 534 p.; 5 fig. 088-7760-037-3. - ᴿLatomus 53 (1994) 655-7 (G. *Freyburger*).

9347* *kamásion / kamision:* AnPapF 40 (1994) 132-142 (J. *Kramer*).

9348 *katallássō:* Porter Stanley E., *Katallassō* in ancient Greek literature, with reference to the Pauline writings: FgNt Est 5. Córdoba 1994, Almendro. 199 p. 84-8005-011-X [TDig 42,83].

9348* *koimáō:* Rebillard Éric, *Koimētērion* et *coemeterium*; tombe, tombe sainte, nécropole; MÉF 105 (1993) 975-1001.

9349 a) *Kybernētēs*; a helmsman from the east [< Lycian *kbar* < Luwian/ Hittite *dabar* 'rule']: AulaO 12 (1994) 5-28 (Y.L. *Arbeitman*).

— b) *lektikōs:* Barré Véronique, Laks André, Le sens de *lektikōs* dans la définition stoïcienne de l'ambiguité (Diogène LAËRCE VII, 62 = SVF III, 23): RÉG 107 (1994) 708-712.

9349* *makrothymia:* Tarocchi Stefano, La fortuna della 'longanimità' oltre il Nuovo Testamento: VivH 5 (1994) 213s; cf. Protestantesimo 49 (1994) 179 (C. *Tron*).

9350 *metanoia:* Witherup Ronald D., Conversion in the NT: Zacchaeus Studies. ColMn 1994, Liturgical/Glazier. ix-126 p. $10 pa. 0-8146-5837-7 [TDig 92,95].

9351 *metis:* Raphals Lisa, Knowing words; wisdom and cunning (*mētis*, as against *phrònesis*) in the classical traditions of China and Greece. Ithaca 1992, Cornell Univ. xviii-273 p. $40. - ᴿJRel 74 (1994) 285 (R.F. *Campany*: subtle and supple).

9352 *misos:* Kendall Daniel, O'*Collins* Gerald, On not neglecting hatred [nothing in biblical encyclopedias which have so much about love]: ScotJT 47 (1994) 511-8.

9353 *mystērion:* **Bouyer** Louis, The Christian mystery 1990 ➤ 6,9750 ...
9,10176: ᴿScotJT 46 (1993) 429s (G. S. *Wakefield*).
9354 *óchlos:* **Park Tae-Sik,** Ochlos im NT: diss. ᴰ*Strecker* G. Göttingen
1994s. – RTLv 26, p. 530.
9355 *paideía:* *Theodorou* Evangelos D., The Greek Orthodox ideal of
paideía [for honorary doctorate at Boston Holy Cross]: TAth 64 (1993)
361-370.
9356 *pálin* en el NT: FgNt 7 (1994) 65-80: con lema (entry) for D(iccionario)
G(riego) E(spañol del)NT; Eng 81 (J. *Mateos*).
9357 *pápyros:* *Lanszweert* René, *pápyros,* ein mykenisches Schimpfwort?:
➤ 112, ᶠSCHMIDT K., Indoeuropean 1994, 77-96.
Cuvillier E., Le concept de *parabolē* 1993 ➤ f43.
9358 *pistis:* **Lindsay** Dennis R., JOSEPHUS and ... *pistis* 1993 ➤ 9,10182: ᴿBL
(1994) 144 (R. *Mason*); StPhilonAn 6 (1994) 216-8 (D. M. *Hay*). — *pistis
Christou,* witness of the Fathers: NT 36 (1994) 233-241. (R. A. *Harrisville*ᴵᴵᴵ).
9358* *politeia, políteuma:* a) *Lévy* Edmond, chez POLYBE; – b) *Casevitz*
Michel, chez DIODORE de Sicile: Ktema 15 (1990) 13-26 / 27-33.
9359 *skýzesthai:* **Lamberterie** Charles de, Grec *skyzan, skýzesthai* et les
grognements d'Héra: RÉG 107 (1994) 15-46.
9360 *synagōgē:* *Kee* Howard C., The changing meaning of synagogue; NTS
[39,2 (1993) *Oster* R. E.] 40 (1994) 281-3.
9361 *syngnōmē:* **Metzler** Karin, Der griechische Begriff des Verzeihens:
WUNT 2/44, 1991 ➤ 7,9539 ... 9,10187: ᴿTR 90 (1994) 387-9 (W.
Wolbert).
9362 *tyrannís:* **Giorgini** Giovanni, La città e il tiranno, il concetto di tirannide
nella Grecia del VII-IV secolo a.C.: Arcana imperii 29. Mi 1993, Giuffré.
ix-437 p. Lᵐ 50. – ᴿClasR 44 (1994) 327 (C. J. *Smith*).
9363 — **Barceló** Pedro, Basileia, monarchia, tyrannis; Untersuchungen zu
Entwicklung und Beurteilung von Alleinherrschaft in vorhellenistischen
Griechenland: Hist Einz 79. Stu 1993, Steiner. 346 p. – ᴿClasR 44 (1994)
326s (D. *Ogden*), Gerión 12 (1994) 340-2 (A. J. *Domínguez Monedero*);
MusHelv 51 (1994) 257 (L. *Burckhardt*).
Fisher N.R.E., HYBRIS 1992 ➤ 13599.
9364 *hypó:* **Villey** Lucile, Soumission ... *hypò* 1992 ➤ 9,10191: ᴿÉglT 25
(1994) 433-5 (L. *Laberge*).
9365 *phantasía:* **Watson** G., Phantasia in classical thought. Galway 1988,
Univ. xiii-176 p. £ 15. – ᴿClasR 44 (1994) 79-81 (Anne *Sheppard*).
9366 *phthónos:* **Bulman** Patricia, *Phthonos* in Pindar: Berkeley ClasSt 35.
1992, Univ. 122 p. – ᴿRPg 67 (1993) 129s (P. *Hummel*).
9366* *phoinix:* **Stulz** Heinke, Die Farbe Purpur im frühen Griechentum
beobachtet in der Literatur und in der bildenden Kunst: BeitAltK 6. Stu
1990, Teubner. 205 p. DM 44. – ᴿClasR 44 (1994) 97s (D. *Bain:* not
concerned with color-shades).
9367 *phrēn, noûs: Sullivan* Shirley D. a) The mind and heart of Zeus in
HOMER and the Homeric hymns; – b) Psychological terminology in the
Greek archaic age [presentation of several of her researches]: ArBegG 37
(1994) 101-126 / 36 (1993) 340-3.
9367* *charássō: Blanc* Alain, *Chárax, charássō* et *kárcharos;* homophonie
radicale ou parenté étymologique: RÉG 107 (1994) 686-693.
9368 *cháris:* **MacLachlan** Bonnie, The age of grace; *charis* in early Greek
poetry. Princeton 1993, Univ. xxii-192 p.; 4 pl. 0-691-06974-3. – ᴿAnt-
Clas 63 (1994) 340s (H. Van *Looy*); ClasR 44 (1994) 393 (S. *Instone*).

9369 *psychē:* *Vernant* Jean-Pierre, *Psuchē*, simulacre du corps chez Homère, image du divin pour Plotin: → 9,51, [F]GENTILI B., Tradizione 1993, 91-99.

J5.4 *Papyri et inscriptiones graecae* – **Greek epigraphy.**

9370 [E]**Adorno** Francesco, *al.*, Corpus dei papiri filosofici greci e latini (CPF): testi e lessico nei papiri di cultura greca e latina: Acc. Toscana. F 1989-92, Olschki. I. pl. lv-469; II. p. xliv-497. 88-222-3638-6; -918-0.

9371 **Baccani** Donata, Oroscopi greci; documentazione papirologica: Univ. Messina. Messina 1992, Sicania. 192 p. – [R]CdÉ 69 (1994) 185s (C. *Harrauer*).

9372 **Bagnall** Roger S., *al.*, Columbia papyri 8: AmerStPapyr 28. Atlanta 1990, Scholars. 238 p.; 57 pl. 1-55540-396-4. – [R]JEA 80 (1994) 261-3 (R. *Coles*: mainly Greek; the first item is a 6th century copy of an already-known discourse of Abbot ISAIAS).

9373 **Bernand** Étienne, Inscriptions grecques d'Égypte et de Nubie au Louvre 1992 → 9,10196; F 480: [R]BO 51 (1994) 565-571 (A. *Lajtar*).

9374 **Bertrand** Jean-Marie, Inscriptions historiques grecques: La Roue à Livres. P 1992, BLettres. 273 p. F 135. 2-251-33915-8. – [R]AntClas 63 (1994) 400s (F. *Colin*).

9375 *Bingen* Jean, Épigraphie grecque en Égypte; la prose sur pierre: CdÉ 69 (1994) 152-167.

9376 **Bingen** Jean, *Clarysse* Willy, Elkab III, Les ostraca grecs 1989 → 6,9639; 8,9965: [R]BO 51 (1994) 83-87 (G. *Wagner*).

9377 **Bingen** J., *al.*, Mons Claudianus, ostraca 1992 → 8,9964; 9,10199: [R]CdÉ 69 (1994) 370-3 (P. *Heilporn*).

9378 [E]**Blümel** Wolfgang, Die Inschriften von Mylasa [Caria], I, Inschriften der Stadt: Inschr. Kleinas. 34. Bonn 1987, Habelt. xii-271 p. – [R]Gnomon 66 (1994) 25-40 (T. *Drew-Bear*).

9379 **Boffo** Laura, Iscrizioni greche e latine per lo studio della Bibbia: Bt Storia e Storiografia dei Tempi Biblici 9. Brescia 1994, Paideia. 459 p. 88-394-0517-8.

9380 **Brodersen** Kai, *al.*, Historische griechische Inschriften in Übersetzung, I. Die archaische und klassische Zeit: Texte zur Forschung 59. Da 1992, Wiss. xviii-150 p. DM 45. 3-534-02243-2. – [R]AntClas 63 (1994) 401s (A. *Martin*).

9381 *Brunsch* Wolfgang, 27 Mumienschilder aus der Papyrussammlung Ös.Nat.-Bt: WZKM 81 (1991) 107-146; 25 pl.

9382 *Brunsch* Wolfgang, Koptische und griechische Inschriften aus Alexandria: WZKM 84 (1994) 9-33; 28 pl.

9383 [E]**Capasso** M., *al.*, [[F]SCHOW N.] Miscellanea papyrologica ... bicentenario Charta Borgiana 1990 → 6,160a: [R]Aegyptus 79 (1994) 195-9 (Orsolina *Montevecchi*).

9384 [E]**Capasso** Mario, Papiri documentari greci: Papyrologica Lupiensia 2, 1993 → 9,10203: [R]CdÉ 69 (1994) 186-8 (G. *Nachtergael*).

9385 **Clarysse** W., Petrie papyri 1991 → 9,10206: [R]BO 51 (1994) 337-342 (Gabriella *Messeri Savorelli*).

9386 **Coles** R. A., *al.*, The Oxyrhynchus papyri **60**, Mem. 80. L 1994, Brit. Acad. for Eg. Expl. Soc. [xiii-]258 p.; XII pl.

9386* *Cook* John G., The protreptic power of early Christian language; from John to AUGUSTINE [... (&) papyri]: VigChr 48 (1994) 105-134.

9387 *Cotton* Hannah, A cancelled marriage contract from the Judaean desert (XHev/Sc.Gr.2): JRS 84 (1994) 64-86.

9388 *Drew-Bear* Thomas, *al.*, Nouvelles inscriptions de Dokimeion [carrières Afyon-Bacakale]: MÉF 106 (1994) 747-844; 30 fig.

9389 **Frösén** J., *Hagedom* D., Die verkohlten Papyri aus Bubastos I, 1990 → 6,e705 ... 9,10210: ᴿAnzAltW 46 (1993) 110-2 (R. H. *Price*, Eng.); BO 51 (1994) 347-351 (Francisca A. J. *Hoogendijk*).

9390 **Gascou** Jean, Un codex fiscal hermopolite (P. Sorb. II 68): Amer-StPapyrol 32. Atlanta 1994, Scholars. xxvi-289 p. 1-55540-936-9.

9391 ᴱ**Handley** E. U., Oxyrhynchus Papyri **59**, Mem. 79, 1992 → 9,10212: ᴿClasR 44 (1994) 386-8 (J.M.S. *Cowey*).

9392 **Haslam** M.W. *al.*, Oxyrhynchus Papyri **57** (3876-3914), Memoir 77,1990 → 7,9565; 8,9979: ᴿCdÉ 69 (1994) 169-172 (J. *Lenaerts*).

9393 **Hoogendijk** F.A.J., Berichtigungsliste 8. Leiden 1992, Brill. x-626 p. *f* 350. 90-04-09621-3. – ᴿBO 51 (1994) 550s (J. *Bingen*) [JAOS 114 (1994) 517s (R. S. *Bagnall*) reviews a Berichtigungsliste 1992 by ᴱ**Pestman** P. W., *Rupprecht* H.-A.].

9394 ᴱ**Hoogendijk** F.A.J., *Minnen* P. van, Papyri ... Leiden 1991 → 9,10215: ᴿBO 51 (1994) 551-5 (J. *Gascou*).

9395 **Horbury** W., *Noy* D., Jewish inscriptions of Graeco-Roman Egypt 1992 → 8,9982; 9,10216: ᴿBijdragen 55 (1994) 307 (P. C. *Beentjes*); JJurPap 24 (1994) 57-70 (A. *Lajtar*); JStJud 25 (1994) 300-3 (P. W. van der *Horst*); OTEssays 7 (1994) 131-3 (P.J.J. *Botha*); StPhilonAn 6 (1994) 183-5 (G. E. *Sterling*).

9396 **Horst** Pieter van der, Ancient Jewish epitaphs 1991 → 8,9402; 9,10218: ᴿZion 59 (1994) 97-103 (Z. *Safrai*, ❸).

9397 **Jördens** Andrea, Suppl. [1, 1971, *Kiessling* E.] 2 (1967-76) zum Wörterbuch der griechischen Papyrusurkunden [(PREISIGKE L.) ᴱRUP-PRECHT H.]: Mainz Akad. Wsb 1991, Harrassowitz. xii-335 p. – ᴿGno-mon 66 (1994) 723 (G. *Weber*).

9398 **Jameson** Michael H., *al.*, A lex sacra from Selinous: GrRByz mg 11. Durham NC 1993, Duke Univ. xiii-171 p.

9399 *Kasher* Aryeh, ❸ A second-century BCE inscription from Iamnia: CHistEI 63 (1992) 3-21; 8 fig.; Eng. 190.

9400 **Kayser** François, Recueil des inscriptions grecques et latines (non funéraires) d'Alexandrie impériale (Iᵉʳ-IIIᵉ s. apr.J.-C.: BtÉt 108. Le Caire 1994, IFAO. xxii-419 p. 2-7247-0145-2.

9400* *Le Dinaret* Marie-Thérèse, *al.*, ... *Feissel* Denis, Bulletin épigraphique: RÉG 107 (1994) 480-620.

9401 ᴱ**Llewelyn** S. R., New documents illustrating early Christianity 7. a review of the Greek inscriptions and papyri published in 1982-83. Sydney 1994, Macquarie Univ. AncHist Centre. v-287 p. A$55; pa. A$35.

9402 *Lőrincz* Barnabás, Die epigraphische Forschung in Ungarn seit 1979: → 60, ᶠJÁRDÁNYI-PAULOVICS I. 1994, 5-17.

9402* **Malay** Hasan, Greek and Latin inscriptions in the Manisa museum: Tituli Asiae Minoris Egb 19, Denkschr. 217. W 1994, Österr. Akad. 192 p.; 39 pl.; 2 maps. – ᴿRÉG 107 (1994) 723s (O. *Masson*).

9403 *a) Manganaro* Giacomo, Iscrizioni, epitaffi ed epigrammi in greco della Sicilia centro-orientale di epoca romana; – *b) Felle* Antonio E., Recenti acquisizioni epigrafiche da catacombe romane: MÉF 106 (1994) 78-118; 34 fig. / 43-69; 27 fig.

9403* **Manganaro** Giacomo, Nuovo manipolo di documenti 'magici' della Sicilia tardoantica: LinceiR 9,5,1 (1994) 485-517; 27 fig.

9404 **[Messeri] Savorelli** Gabriella, Griechische Texte XI: Rainieri XV 1990

[➤ 8,9994 '16,1990'; ➤ 9,10227 '15,1991']s   Aegyptus 79 (1994) 190-2 (Orsolina *Montevecchi*).

9405 **Migliardi Zingale** Livia, Papyri dell'Università di Genova 3. Papyrologica Florentina 20. F 1991, Gonnelli. viii-93 p.; 36 pl. Lᵐ 120. – ᴿCdÉ 69 (1994) 172-4 (J. *Bingen*).

9406 *Mossakowska* Maria, Les huiles utilisées pour l'éclairage (d'après les papyrus grecs): JJurPap 24 (1994) 109-131.

9407 *Nicolaou* Ino, Inscriptiones Cypriae alphabeticae XXIII, 1993: RepCyp (1994) 181-196; 5 fig.; pl. XXXIX-XLV.

9408 **Oates** John F., *al.*, Checklist of editions of Greek and Latin papyri, ostraca, and tablets⁴: BASP supp. 7. Atlanta 1992, Scholars. viii-94 p. 1-55540-782-X.

9409 **Perpillou-Thomas** Françoise, Fêtes d'Égypte ptolémaïque et romaine d'après la documentation papyrologique grecque: Studia hellenistica 31. Lv 1993. xxix-292 p.

9410 *Peseley* G. E., How many copies of the Hellenica Oxyrhynchia have been found?: AncHB 8 (1994) 38—...

9411 *a*) *Peterman* Glen L., Découverte sensationnelle des manuscrits byzantins à Pétra [pas encore déroulés]; – *b*) *Puech* Émile, Les manuscrits de la grotte aux lettres [Ḥever, rapport avec les Nabatéens]: MondeB 88 (1994) 40 / 10 [1-41 *al.*].

9412 *Rapin* Claude, Un parchemin gréco-bactrien d'une collection privée: CRAI (1994) 261-294; 2 fig. (map).

9413 **Rea** J. R., Oxyrhynchus Papyri **58**, Graeco-Roman memoirs 78, 1991 ➤ 8,a4: ᴿIVRA 43 (1991) 220-5 (G. *Foti Talamanca*); CdÉ 69 (1994) 366-370 (J. *Lenaerts*, **56** ➤ 9416); Gnomon 66 (1994) 273-5 (D. *Montserrat*, Eng. on his **51**, 1984).

9414 *Sickinger* James P., Inscriptions and archives in classical Athens: Historia 43 (1994) 286-296.

9415 *Sijpesteijn* P. J., Two tantalizing papyri [P. Mich inv. 6304 & 2320a: CdÉ 69 (1994) 297-304.

9416 **Sirivianou** M. G., Oxyrhynchus **56**, Mem. 76, 1989 ➤ 6,9700*: ᴿVDI 201 (1992) 204-210 (V. N. *Yarkho*, ☉, also on Haslam **57**).

9417 ᵀᴱ**Smith** Martin F., Diogenes of Oinoanda, The Epicurean inscription. N 1993, Bibliopolis. – ᴿRÉG 107 (1994) 267-272 (A. *Laks*).

9418 **Thür** Gerhard, *Täuber* Hans, Prozessrechtliche Inschriften der griechischen Poleis; Arkadien (IPArk): Szb ph/h 607. W 1994, Akad. xxiv-363 p. 3-7001-2141-9.

9419 **Worp** K., Die Archive der Aurelii 1991 ➤ 9,10245: ᴿBO 51 (1994) 342-7 (D. P. *Wehoe*).

9419* **Yadin** Y. *al.*, [Babatha] Greek/Aramaic papyri: Judaean Desert Studies 2, 1989 ➤ 5,9552; 7,9252; 8,9597: ᴿPEQ 126 (1994) 175s (N. *Kokkinos*).

J5.5   Cypro-Minoa [➤ T 9.1-4].

9420 **Auro Jorro** Francisco, Diccionario micenico [–español anejo 2]. ᴹ1993, Cons. Sup. Inv. 478 p. – ᴿRPg 67 (1993) 121s (N. *Maurice*).

9421 *Boëlle* Cécile, Po-ti-ni-ja à Mycènes [titre de la plus grande déesse]: Minos 27s (1992s) 283-301.

9422 **Chadwick** J., *al.*, Corpus of Mycenaean inscriptions from Knossos 1986-90 ➤ 8,a21; 9,10250: ᴿClasB 69 (1993) 98-100 (J. G. *Younger*); JHS 114 (1994) 199-201 (J. *Bennet*).

9423 **Dürr** Friedrich,   Tonspuren; ein Beitrag zur Entzifferung der altkretischen Schrift: BibNot Beih 6. Mü 1991, Görg. [iv] 184 p.

9424 **Egetmeyer** Markus,   Wörterbuch / kyprisch 1992 ➤ 8,a24; 9,20251: ᴿGnomon 66 (1994) 481-4 (O. *Masson*).

9425 *Firth* Richard J.,   A statistical analysis of the Greekness of men's names on the Knossos Linear B tablets: Minos 27s (1992s) 83-100.

9426 *Godart* Louis,   *a)* Les écritures crétoises et le bassin méditerranéen: CRAI (1994) 707-730; 6 fig., map.; – *b)* La scrittura di Troia [two rocks with 5 characters each in Linear A published by SCHLIEMANN in 1875 but ignored]: LinceiR 9,5,1 (1994) 457-460.

9427 **Godart** Louis,   Il disco de Festos; l'enigma di una scrittura.   T 1994, Einaudi. 154 p. Lᵐ 40. – ᴿArchViva 13,46 (1994) 92 (P. *Pruneti*).

9428 *Godart* Louis, *al.*,   175 raccords de fragments dans les tablettes de Knossos: Minos 27s (1992s) 55-70.

9429 *Melena* José L.,   167 joins of fragments in the Linear-B tablets from Pylos: Minos 27s (1992s) 71-82 (+ 307-424).

9430 *Michailidou* Anna,   'Ostrakon' with Linear-A script from Akrotiri (Thera); a non-bureaucratic activity?   Minos 27 (1993) 7-24; 3 fig.; 4 pl.

9431 *Mile* Monique,   Singulier et pluriel dans les lois de Gortyne; essai d'interprétation: Cretan Studies 4 (1994) 45-63.

9432 *Nikolidaki* Kalliope, *Owens* Gareth,   The Minoan libation formula; practical considerations: Cretan Studies 4 (1994) 149-153: pl. XVI-XIX.

9433 *a) Olivier* J.-P.,   **ᴳ** Cretan scripts of the 2d millenarium B.C.; – *b) Neroznak* V.P., *Sharypkin* S.Y.,   **ᴳ** Ancient Greek etymology in the light of data of Cretan-Mycenaean inscriptions: VDI 211 (1994) 107-118; Eng. 118 / 118-122; Eng. 123.

9434 *Sakellarakis* Yannis, *Olivier* Jean-Pierre,   Un vase en pierre avec inscription en linéaire A du sanctuaire du sommet minoen de Cythère: BCH 118 (1994) 343-351; 7 fig.

9435 *a) Scafa* Enrico,   A-mo-ra-ma e il reclutamento del personale nel regno miceneo di Cnosso; – *b) Bonanni* Eleonora,   Nota alle tavolette di Pilo, AN. 35.5, UN 443 (+) 998 e Tirinto X 6: ➤ 36, Mem. GALLAVOTTI C., RivCuClasMdv 36 (1994) 41-64 / 65-68.

9436 *Smith* Joanna S.,   The Pylos Jn series: Minos 27s (1992s) 167-259; 36 fig.

9437 *Sucharski* Robert A.,   Ko-ma-we-te-ta: Eos 81 (1993) 177-181.

9438 *Witczak* Krzysztof T.,   'Gold' in Mycenaean Greek and Indo-European: Orpheus-Thrac 4 (1994) 55-58.

J6   Indo-Iranica.

9438* **[Bayevskih] Baevskij** S.,   **ᴳ** *Rannyaya* ... Early Persian lexicography XI-XV cent. Moskva 1989, Nauka. 165 p. 5-02-016411-9. – ᴿBSO 57 (1994) 393s (A. *Burton*); OrLovPer 24 (1993) 283s (W. *Skalmowski*).

9439 *Cantera Glera* N.A.,   Reflexiones acerca de la oposición diatética activa-media en antiguo persa: AulaO 11 (1993) 147-154; Eng. 147.

9440 *Cereti* Carlo G.,   Osservazioni sul pronome enclitico in mediopersiano ed in alcuni testi neopersiani: AION 53 (1993) 374-410.

9441 *Daalen* L.A. van,   'The husband is a god and a lord to a living woman'; on Ramayana, critical edition, 2.21.17:   OrLovPer 24 (1993) 79-86.

9442 *Day* John V.,   The concept of the Aryan race in the nineteenth-century scholarship: OrpheusThrac 4 (1994) 13-48.

9443 *Fagan* Sarah M. B., The syntax and semantics of middle constructions [sp. German]. C 1992, Univ. x-300 p. – ᴿBSLP 89,2 (1994) 107s (P. *Flobert*).

9444 *Lambton* Ann, [Persian] *Pīshkash*, present or tribute?: ➤ 136, ꜰWANS-BROUGH J., BSO 57 (1994) 145-158.

9445 ᴱ**Mayrhofer** M., *Schmitt* R., Iranisches Personennamenbuch 5. Iranische Namen in Nebenüberlieferungen indogermanischer Sprachen; 6a ... in den griechischen Dokumenten Ägyptens, vor Philip *Huyse*. W 1990, Akad. 72 p. Schr. 168 – ᴿOLZ 89 (1994) 581-3 (S. *Zimmer*).

9445* **Pirart** J., *Kellens* F., Les textes vieil-avestiques, [I. 1988] II. Répertoires grammaticaux et lexique; III. Commentaire. Wsb 1990s. – ᴿAulaO 11 (1993) 223-232 (N. A. *Cantera Glera*).

9446 **Schmitt** R., Bisitun Old Persian: Corpus Inscriptionum Iranicarum 1/1/1, 1991 ➤ 9,10274: ᴿAcOrK 53 (1992) 177-9 (F. *Thordarson*).

9447 *Shaked* Shaul, Two Parthian ostraca from Nippur: ➤ 136, ꜰWANS-BROUGH J., BSO 57 (1994) 208-212; III pl.

9448 *Skalmowski* W., Two Old Persian names [Kambaujiva 'intrepidus'; Martiya 'notabilis']: OrLovPer 24 (1993) 74-77.

9449 **Stève** M.-J., Syllabaire élamite 1992 ➤ 8,a44; 9,10276: ᴿAfO 40s (1993s) 125s (Heidemarie *Koch*); RB 101 (1994) 297 (M. *Sigrist*).

9449* **Weber** Dieter, Ostraca (Vol. 4), Papyri und Pergamente (Vol. 6): Corpus inscriptionum iranicarum 3, Pahlavi, 1992 ➤ 8,a45: ᴿOLZ 89 (1994) 576-581 (M. *Macuch*).

9450 *Yusifov* Yu. B., *Alimirzoev* A. N., ❻ On the decipherment of numerical signs of the proto-Elamite script: VDI 206 (1993) 3-19; Eng. 20.

9450* *Zimmer* Stefan, Zwei neue Gatha-Ausgaben [HUMBACH H. 1991; KELLENS F., *Pirart* J. 1990]: OLZ 89 (1994) 239-253; Bibliog. 253-7.

J6.5 **Latina.**

9451 **Baratin** M., La naissance de la syntaxe à Rome 1989 ➤ 8,a47: ᴿMnemosyne 47 (1994) 123-132 (Ineke *Sluiter*).

9451* **Edgeworth** R. J., The colors of the Aeneid 1992 ➤ 9,10278: ᴿClasR 44 (1994) 277s (S. *Harrison*).

9452 *Gaide* Françoise, Les substantifs 'diminutifs' latins en ...lus, ...la ou ...lum: RPg 66 (1992) 15-27.

9453 **Giovè Marchioli** Nicoletta, Alle origini delle abbreviature latine; una prima ricognizione (I secolo a.C. – IV secolo d.C.): RicPapirol 2. Messina 1993, Sicania. 213 p.; bibliog. 145-158.

9454 **Keller** Madeleine, Les verbes latins à infectum en -sc; étude morphologique à partir des formations attestées dès l'époque préclassique: Coll. Latomus 216. Bru 1992. 564 p. – ᴿBSLP 89,2 (1994) 232-8 (Hélène *Vairel*).

9455 *Salway* Benet, What's in a name? A survey of Roman onomastic practice from c. 700 B.C. to A.D. 700: JRS 84 (1994) 124-145.

9456 **Sblendorio Cugusi** M. Teresa, I sostantivi latini in -tudo. Bo 1991, Pàtron. 508 p. Lᵐ 45. – ᴿGnomon 66 (1994) 362-4 (Jacqueline *Dangel*).

9457 **Solin** Heikki, Namenpaare; eine Studie zur römischen Namengebung: CommHumLit 90. Helsinki 1990, Soc. Scientiarum Fennica. 92 p. – ᴿSalesianum 56 (1994) 624 (R. *Bracchi*).

9457* **Solin** Heikki, *Salomies* Olli, Repertorium nominum gentilium et cognominum latinorum: AO-Reihe A 80. Hildesheim 1994, Olms. x-508 p.

J8.1 Philologia generalis.

9458 ^E**Bar-Asher** Moshe, Massorot; Studies in language traditions. 1991. – ^RJSS 39 (1994) 297-9 (A. *Shivtiel*).

9459 *Berardinelli* Lucia, Tra oralità e scrittura; urlo, voce, parola; Acme 47 (1994) 43-66.

9459* *Borochovski* Esther, *Trommer* Polna, **☉** A semantic-pragmatic study of the sense relation called opposition: Lešonenu 57 (1993) 215-249; Eng. IIIs.

9460 ^E**Blackshire-Belay** Carol A., Current issues in second language acquisition and development. L 1994, UPA. vi-206 p.

9460* **Brack** John, The shape of biblical language; chiasmus in the Scriptures and beyond. Crestwood NY 1994, St. Vladimir. x-387 p.; bibliog. 368-376. 0-88141-139-6.

9461 **Campbell** George L., Compendium of the world's languages. L 1991, Routledge. xxiv-1574 p. (2 vol.) – ^RMedvHum 20 (1994) 208-210 (O. W. *Robinson*).

9461* **Cumming** Alister H., Bilingual performance in reading and writing. AA 1994, Language learning. vi-378 p.

9462 **Danker** F. W., A century of Greco-Roman philology featuring the American Philological Asn and SBL. Atlanta 1988, Scholars. xviii-299 p. $27. – ^RVT 44 (1994) 424 (G. J. *Davies*: personal rather than systematic).

9462* **Fordyce** Rachel, *Marello* Carla, Semiotic and linguistics in [Lewis CARROLL's]. Alice's worlds: Research in text theory 19. Berlin 1994, de Gruyter. viii-277 p. 3-11-013894-8.

9463 ^E**Galinsky** Karl, The interpretation of Roman poetry; empiricism of hermeneutics: StKlasPg 67. Fra 1992, Lang. x-219 p. 3-631-44741-8.

9463* **Giacobbe** Jorge, Acquisition d'une langue étrangère; cognition et intéraction. P 1992, CNRS. 256 p. – ^RBSLP 89,2 (1994) 43s (L. *Danon-Boileau*).

9464 **Leirbukt** Oddleif, *Lindemann* Beate, Psycholinguistische und didaktische Aspekte des Fremdsprechenlernens. Tü 1992, Narr. – ^RBSLP 89,2 (1994) 44-49 (J. *Feuillet*).

9465 **Mannis** Rebecca T., Sight word learning in word families; a study of strategy acquisition and transfer to a second language [English-to Hebrew]: diss. Columbia, ^D*Corno* Lyn. NY 1994. 123 p. 94-27103. – DissA 55 (1994s) p. 2420.

9466 ^E**Müller** C. W., *Sier* K., *Werner* I., Zum Umgang mit fremden Sprachen in der griechisch-römischen Antike [15 art.] 1992 → 8,672: ^RJHS 114 (1994) 201 (S. C. *Colvin*).

9467 **Rodrigue-Schwarzwald** Ora, *Sokoloff* Michael, A Hebrew dictionary of linguistics and philology. Even-Yehuda 1992, Reches. [v–] 288 p. – ^RBSO 57 (1994) 461s (L. *Glinert*: with appendix of Hebrew, some 2500 terms not in Hebrew-English dictionaires; for Israelis and others seeking Hebrew explanations for English linguistic terminology).

9468 *Runggaldier* Edmund, Menschliches Handeln und Indexikalität [= terms like 'I', 'here', 'yesterday' which have no place in scientific writing]: TPhil 69 (1994) 211-223.

9469 **Schweizer** Harald, Sprachkritik als Ideologiekritik; zur Grammatikrevision am Beispiel von ORB [... 'Ortsveränderung' ...]: TLInf 1. Tü 1990, Francke, xii-173 p. DM 68. – ᴿTZBas 50 (1994) 76-83 (R. *Bartelmus*, also on Schweizer's Josef and BADER's Simson in TLInf; does not really 'uncode' ORB).

9470 ꟳSZEMERÉNYI Oswald, Historical philology, ᴱ**Brogyanyi** Bela, 1992 ➤ 8,180*b* [only the first volume there noted; there were two more, 1992s; Curr.Ling.Theory 87 & 97]: Salesianum 56 (1994) 816s (R. *Bracchi*).

9471 **Stone** M. E., Rock inscriptions Is [Sinai-Juda] 1992 ➤ 9,10296: ᴿZAW 105 (1993) 535 (M. *Köckert*).

9472 ᴱ**Vetters** Carl, (*Vet* Co), Tense and aspect in discourse: TrendLing 75. Berlin 1994, Mouton de Gruyter. vi-295 p. 3-11-013813-1.

9473 *Wylin* Koen, Una grammatica psicologico-linguistica [VERGOTE J. 1951] ed un'applicazione eventuale al verbo etrusco: RBgPg 72 (1994) 78-85.

ᴊ8.2 **Grammatica comparata.**

9474 *Alonso Schökel* Luis, Hebreo + español, notas de semántica comparada 3: Sefarad [47 (1987) 245-254; 49 (1989) 11-20]; 54 (1994) 3-11; Eng. 11.

9474* ᴱ**Bammesberger** A., Die Laryngaltheorie, I. 1988. II, Register, *Ziegler* Sabine. Heid 1990, Winter. 67 p. DM 50. – ᴿMnemosyme 47 (1994) 390-3 (F.M.J. *Waanders*).

9475 *Besserman* Lawrence, The Hebrew roots of the English language [MOZESON Isaac E., The word; the dictionary that reveals the source of English (NY 1989, Shapilsky)]: Judaism 41 (1992) 409-415: unconvincing, except in raising again E. ROSENSTOCK-HUESSY's question of how and why humans first began to speak.

9475* *Boekels* Klaus, Dreiradikalität als 'Fascinosum' in dem semitischen Sprachen; Sprache und Schrift als Kulturerbe des Orients: ➤ 11, ꟳBECK H., Sein 1994, 135-148.

9476 **Bomhard** Allan R., The nostratic macrofamily; a study in distant linguistic relationship: TrendsLing 74. B 1994, Mouton de Gruyter. xi-932 p. 3-11-013900-6.

9476* **Cohen** David, *al.*, Dictionnaire des racines sémitiques ou attestées dans les langues sémitiques, fasc. 3 GLD-DHML/R & 4 –DRR. Lv 1993, Peeters. x + p. 119-227 / x + p. 228-342. – ᴿHenoch 16 (1994) 347-9 (R. *Bertolino*).

9477 *Edzard* Lutz E., The obligatory contour principle and dissimilation in Afroasiatic: JAfrAS 3 (1991s) 151-173.

9478 ᴱ**Gvozdanović** Jadranka, Indo-European numerals: TrendsLinguistic 57, 1992 ➤ 8,g76: ᴿBSLP 89,2 (1994) 164-7 (C. de *Lamberterie*).

9479 **Khan** Geoffrey, Studies in Semitic syntax 1988 ➤ 4,8757 ... 9,10305: ᴿWZKM 84 (1994) 227s (A. *Zaborski*).

9480 **Klimov** Goergij A., Einführung in die kaukasische Sprachwissenschaft, ᵀᴱ*Gippert* Jost. Ha 1994, H. Buske. 405 p.; bibliog. 317-355. 3-87548-060-0.

9481 **Mayrhofer** Manfred, *a*) Etymologisches Wörterbuch des Altindoarischen I., 1986-9 ➤ 6,9823; 8,a83: ᴿAevum 66 (1992) 149s (G. *Bonfanti*). – *b*) Etymologisches Wörterbuch des Altindoarischen, II. Lfg. 1. IndGBt 2/1. Heid 1992, Winter. 80 p. – ᴿBSO 57 (1994) 321-8 (P. *Thieme*: really Vedic Sanskrit; and a new attempt, not just an expansion of his barely-finished Kurzg. EW).

9482 ᴱ**Perrot** Jean, Les langues dans le monde ancien et moderne, 3. Les langues chamito-sémitiques. P 1988, CNRS. [vi–] 318 p.; bibliog. 297-310. 2-222-04057-4.

9482* *Scott* Nathan A., J? A ramble on a road taken [response to kudos of Modern Language Association 29 Dec. 1993]: ChrLit 43 (1993s) 205-212; interview with Ralph C. *Wood*, 213.

9483 **Swan** Toril, *al.*, Language change and language structure; older Germanic languages in a comparative perspective: TrendsLing 73. B 1994, Mouton de Gruyter. xi-346 p.; ill. 3-11-013538-8.

9484 **Szemerényi** Oswald, Einführung in die vergleichende Sprachwissenschaft[4rev] [³1989 → 7,9640]. Da 1990, Wiss. xxv-370 p. – ᴿSalesianum 56 (1994) 624s (R. *Bracchi*).

9484* *Tropper* Josef, Present **yaqtulum* in central Semitic: JSS 39 (1994) 1-6.

9485 *a*) *Zaborski* Andrzej, Archaic Semitic in the light of Hamito-Semitic; – *b*) *Jungraithmayr* Hermann, Was ist am Tschadischen hamitosemitsch?: ZAHeb 7 (1994) 234-244 / 225-233.

J8.3 Linguistica generalis.

9486 **Akmajian** Adrian, *al.*, Linguistics, an introduction to language and communication³ [¹1990]. CM 1992, MIT. xiv-508 p.; ill. 0-262-01109-3; pa. -51-042-1.

9487 **Atchison** Jean, Language change; progress or decay?² [¹1981]: Approaches to Linguistics. C 1991, Univ. xi-258 p.; ill.; bibliog. 237-252. 0-521-41101-7; pa. -2283-3.

9488 *Babut* Jean-Marc, La linguistique au secours de l'exégète et du traducteur: RHPR 74 (1994) 431-7.

9490 ᴱ**Black** David A., Linguistics and NT interpretation; essays on discourse analysis 1992 → 8,a99: ᴿAndrUnS 32 (1994) 258-260 (E. *Müller*); CBQ 56 (1994) 817s (D. *Neufeld*: enjoyable reading despite dispensable jargon).

9491 **Blake** Barry J., Case: TextbLing. C 1994, Univ. xvii-229 p.; ill.; bibliog., 209-219. 0-521-44114-5; pa. -661-9.

9492 ᴱ**Brogyányi** Bela, Prehistory, history and historiography of language, speech, and linguistic theory: THistLing 64. Amst/Ph 1992, Benjamins. – ᴿClasB 69 (1993) 177s (H. *Liebel-Weckowicz*).

9493 ᴱ**Brown** Gillian, *al.*, Language and understanding. Ox 1994, UP. vii-208 p.; bibliog. 191-200. 0-19-437191-3.

9494 **Cann** Ronnie, Formal semantics; an introduction. C 1993, Univ. xvii-344 p. 0-521-37610-6. – ᴿBSLP 89,2 (1994) 110-4 (C. *Touratier*).

9495 **Chiesa** Curzio, Semiosis; essai sur les théories de signe de PLATON et d'ARISTOTE. Bern 1991. Land. 374 p. – ᴿRTPhil 126 (1994) 47s (S. *Imhoof*).

9496 **Coseriu** Eugenio, Textlinguistik, ³rev*Albrecht* Jörn: Uni-Tb 1808. Tü 1994, Francke. xvi-252 p. – ᴿBeitNam 29s (1994s) 181 (R. *Schützeichel*).

9497 **Crowley** Terry, An introduction to historical linguistics². Auckland, 1992 = 1983, Oxford-UP. 331 p. 0-19-558247-0. [Linguistics 33/1, 135-7, Jean *Atchison*].

9498 **Dixon** Robert M. W., Ergativity; StLing 69. C 1994, Univ. xxii-271 p.; bibliog. 237-258. 0-521-44896-2; pa. -8-0.

9499 **Duran** Jane, Knowledge in context; naturalized epistemology and sociolinguistics: New Feminist Perspectives. Lanham MD 1994, Rowman & L. xiii-238 p. 0-8476-7831-8; pa. -2-6.

9500 **Ellis** John M., Language, thought, and logic. Evanston 1994, Northwestern Univ. x-163 p. $30. [Language 71, 351,9, J.D. *McCawley*].

9501 ᴱ**Engemann** W., *Volp* R., Gib mir ein Zeichen; die Bedeuting der

Semiotik für theologische Praxis und Denkmodelle: ArbPrakT 1, 1993
→ 9,10323: ᴿTvT 34 (1994) 204s (F. *Jespers*).

9502 **Fuchs** Catherine, *Le Goffic* Pierre, Les linguistiques contemporaines;
repères théoriques: Langue Linguistique Communications. P 1992,
Hachette. 158 p. 2-0101-6009-3. – ᴿBSLP 89,2 (1994) 10s (X. *Mignot*).

9502* **Hödl** Ludwig. Textwissen und Sprachwissenschaft der scholastischen
Theologen: ZkT 116 (1994) 129-142.

9503 **Hopper** Paul J., *Traugott* Elisabeth C., Grammaticalization: Textb-
Linguist, 1993 → 9,10331: ᴿBSLP 89,2 (1994) 72-81 (C. *Hagège*).

9503* **La Matina** Marcello, Il testo antico; per una semiotica come filologia
integrata: CircSemiolSic 1. Palermo 1994, Epos. 186 p.; bibliog. 165-174
Lᵐ 24.

9504 **Lerot** Jacques, Précis de linguistique générale: Propositions. P 1993,
Minuit. 448 p. – ᴿBSLP 89,2 (1994) 29-31 (A. *Lemaréchal*).

9505 **Macaulay** Ronald K. S., The social act; language and its uses. Ox
1994, Univ. P. viii-241 p.; ill.; bibliog. p. 225-31. 0-19-508392-2.

9506 **McMahon** April M. S., Understanding language change. C 1994, Univ.
xi-361 p.; bibliog. 341-352. 0-521-44119-6; -565-1.

9507 **Marmoudian** Mortéza, Modern theories of language; the empirical
challenge. Durham NC 1993, Duke Univ. xx-233 p. 0-8223-1278-6. –
ᴿBSLP 89,2 (1994) 11s (X. *Mignot*).

9508 **Matthews** P. H., Grammatical theory in the United States from Bloomfield to Chomsky. StLinguistic 67, 1993 → 9,10340: ᴿBSLP 89,2 (1994)
22-26 (P. *Kirtchuk*).

9508* **Miller** Patricia C., Dreams in Late Antiquity; studies in the imagination of a culture. Princeton 1994, Univ. xii-273 p. $39.50. 0-691-
97422-4 [BL 95,134, L. L. *Grabbe*: dreams as semiotics].

9509 **Mounin** Georges, Dictionnaire de la linguistique: Quadrige. P 1993 =
1974, PUF. xxxvii-341 p. F 78. 2-1304-4881-X. – ᴿBSLP 89,2 (1994) 9s
(X. *Mignot*: réimpression plus maniable).

9510 **Palmer** Frank R. Grammatical rules and relations: TextbLing. C 1994,
Univ. xv-259 p.; bibliog. 241-252.

9511 ᴱ**Porter** Stanley E., *Carson* D. A., Biblical language and linguistics; open
questions in currect research: jNsu 80. Shf 1993, JStOT. 217 p. – ᴿFgNt
7 (1994) 215-222 (J. *Mateos*: sobre (también) *Fanning* B., *Schmidt* D.,
Silva M.; por lo demás, aplicaciones al NT).

9512 **Renkens** Jan, Discourse studies; an introductory textbook. Amst 1993,
Benjamins. ix-224 p.; bibliog. p. 205-217. 90-272-2136-7; pa. -7-5 / US
1-55619-492-7; -3-5.

9513 **Romaine** Suzanne, Language in society; an introduction to sociolinguistics. Ox 1994, UP. xv-235 p.; ill. 0-19-875133-4; pa. -4-0.

9514 **Ruhlen** Merritt, The origin of language; tracing the evolution of the mother tongue. NY 1994, Wiley. xi-239 p.; bibliog. p. 216-224. 0-471-58426-6.

9515 **Saussure** Ferdinand de, Cours de linguistique générale, notes de
CONSTANTIN [seul, ᵀᴱ*Harris* Ray. Ox 1993, Pergamon] et RIEDLINGER,
ᴱ*Komatsu* Eisuke. Tokyo 1993, Gakushuin. 368 p. – ᴿBSLP 89,2 (1994)
12-16 (G. *Bergounioux*).

9515* ᴱ**Schmitter** Peter, Sprachtheorien der abendländischen Antike: Geschichte der Sprachtheorie 2. Tü 1991, Narr. xii-430 p. DM 136. –
ᴿÉtClas 62 (1994) 72s (H. *Seldeslachts*).

9516 **Sebeok** Thomas A., Signs; an introduction to semiotics: StSemiotics.
Toronto 1994, Univ. xvii-154 p.; bibliog. p. 129-147. 0-8020-2958-2; pa.
-7780-3.

9517 ᴱSeiler Hansjakob, *Premper* Waldfried, Partizipation; diss.: sprachliche Erfassen von Sachverhalten: Language Universals 6. Tü 1991, Narr. 697 p. – ᴿBSLP 89,2 (1994) 92-100 (G. *Lazard*).

9518 **Sell** Mark, A study to identify and evaluate the proper and improper use of modern linguistics in confessional Lutheran hermeneutics based upon the intersecting relationship of the modern linguistic principle of 'synchronic semantic value' and the traditional linguistic principle known as the usus loquendi: diss. Concordia Sem, Fort Wayne, ᴰ*Marquart* K.-ConcordiaTQ 58 (1994) 151s.

9519 *Weismann* Francisco J., Primera aproximación al lenguaje: Stromata 50 (1994) 105-117.

9520 *Wong* Simon, What case is this case? An application of semantic case [in C. FILLMORE's sense of sense-role independent of surface inflection] in biblical exegesis: Jian Dao 1 (Hong Kong 1994) 49-73; ⊜ 73.

9521 *Zilberberg* Claude, Analyse discursive et énonciation: SémBib 69 (1993) 3-36.

J8.4   *Origines artis scribendi* – **The origin of writing.**

9522 **Azevedo** Joaquim, The origin and transmission of the alphabet: diss. Andrews, ᴰ*Storfjell* J. Berrien Springs MI 1994. 139 p. [DissA-disk] MAI 33 (1994s) p. 335.

9523 **Bernal** Martin, Cadmean letters 1990 ⇥ 6,9859 ... 9,10351: ᴿSyria 61 (1994) 254s (O. *Masson*).

9524 *Colless* Brian E., The syllabic inscriptions of Byblos Text D [emendations to MENDENHALL G. 1985]: AbrNahr 31 (1993) 35.

9524* *Friberg* Joran, Preliterate counting and accounting in the Middle East [SCHMANDT-BESSERAT D. 1992]: OLZ 89 (1994) 477-502; ill.

9525 **Green** Margaret W., **Nissen** Hans J., *al.*, Zeichenliste der archaischen Texte aus Uruk 1987 ⇥ 3,a49; 6,9376: ᴿOLZ 89 (1994) 380-5 (M. *Krebernik*).

9525* **Harris** William V., Ancient literacy 1989 ⇥ 6,9869 ... 8,a151: ᴿHZ 256 (1993) 145-7 (H. *Kloft*).

9526 **Hinüber** Oskar von, Der Beginn der Schrift und frühe Schriftlichkeit in Indien: MainzAbh g/soz 11, 1989 ⇥ 7,9683; 9,10364: ᴿGGA 246 (1994) 207-224 (Petra *Kieffer-Pülz*).

9527 *Hoch* James E., The Byblos syllabary: bridging the gap between Egyptian hieroglyphs and Semitic alphabets [MENDENHALL largely convincing]: JSSEg (SSEA) 20 (1990) 115-124.

9528 **Khan** Majeed, The origin and evolution of ancient Arabic scripts. Riyadh 1993, Riyadh Ministry of Education. 26 p. + 31 ❹; 22 pl. [OIAc 9,33).

9529 *Marek* Christian, Euboia und die Entstehung der Alphabetschrift bei den Griechen: Klio 75 (1993) 27-43; Eng. 43s.

9530 **Miller** D. Garry, Ancient scripts and philological knowledge: StTheoryHistLing 116. Amst 1994, Benjamins. xvi-139; bibliog. p. 117-135. 90-272-3619-4 / US 1-55619-570-2.

9531 ᴱNissen Hans J., *al.*, *a)* Frühe Schrift und Techniken 1990 ⇥ 7,e794: ᴿJAOS 114 (1994) 549-661 (Denise *Schmandt-Besserat*); – *b)* Die Entstehung der Schrift im frühen Babylonien: Altertum 39 (1993) 181-196.

9531* **Powell** Barry B., HOMER and the origin of the Greek alphabet 1991 ⇥ 7,9686 ... 9,10371: ᴿRPg 66 (1992) 161-3 (J. L. *Perpillou*) Salesianum 56 (1994) 622s (R. *Bracchi*).

9532 **Schmandt-Besserat** D., Before writing 1992 → 9,10374: ^RBuCanad-Mesop 26 (1993) 61s (Eng. franç.; ?M. *Fortin*); Minos 27 (1992s) 334s (E. L. *Bennett*).
9533 **Warner** Julian, From writing to computers. L 1994, Routledge. xi-159 p.; bibliog. 142-152. 0-415-09612-X.

J9.1   Analysis linguistica loquelae de Deo – God-talk.

9534 *Anderson* Pamela Sue, Agnosticism and attestation; an aporia concerning the other in RICŒUR's Oneself as another [^T*Blamey* Kathleen, Ch Univ. 1992; 'remains adamant in bracketing the question of the existence of God']: JRel 74 (1994) 65-76.
9535 *Arregui* José, La teología como lenguaje histórico: LumenVr 43 (1994) 363-379.
9536 **Bertuletti** Angelo, Teoria etica e ontologia ermeneutica nel pensiero di P. RICŒUR [Soi-même comme un autre 1990]. TItSett 19 (1993) 283-318. 331-369 Eng. 318.370.
9537 *Brandt* Reinhard, QUINES Tranchiemesser zu einigen ontologischen Voraussetzungen der Theologie: ZTK 91 (1994) 210-229.
9538 **Brantzen** Hubertus. Gemeinde als Heimat; integrierende Seelsorge unter semiotischer Perspektive: Praktische Theologie im Dialog 7. FrS 1993, Univ. 503 p. Fs 78. – ^RTR 90 (1994) 432s (A. *Wollbold*).
9539 **Brümmer** Vincent, Speaking of a personal God; an essay in philosophical theology. C 1992, Univ. 158 p. $45; pa. $15. – ^RPerspRelSt 21 (1994) 253-8 (J. *Wallhausser*).
9539* *Bucher* Rainer, Gott, das Reden von ihm und das Leben in der späten Moderne: BiLtg 67 (1994) 195-202.
9540 **Cooke** Bernard J., The distancing of God 1990 → 6,9884 ... 9,10383: ^RCritRR 6 (1993) 499-502 (P. E. *Devenish*: bold, constructive).
9541 **Cupitt** Don, Creation out of nothing 1990 → 6,2115; 8,a171: ^RScotJT 46 (1993) 111 (C. D. *Wiltshire*: everything is made out of words, including God).
9542 *Duda* Henryk, ❷ Some problems concerning the relationship between language and religion: ZeKUL 35,1s (1992) 85-93; Eng. 93.
9543 *Fischer* Rainer, Von Gott reden im Zusammenhang von Glaube und Sprachdenken; das Andenken Johann G. HAMANNs als Anregung für die gegenwärtige Theologie: VerkF 39 (1994) 44-60.
9544 *García Matarranz* Félix, Carlos BOUSOÑO, demiólogo de lo divino desde la obscuridad: LumenVr 42 (1993) 336-366.468-503.
9545 ^E**Greisch** Jean, *Kearney* Richard, Paul RICŒUR, Les metamorphoses de la raison herméneutique 1991 → 8,a213; 9,10409: ^RRTPhil 126 (1994) 373 (Sylvie *Bonzon*); ScEspr 45 (1993) 365-8 (C. *Saint-Germain*).
9546 *Hempelmann* Heinzpeter, Gottes Wort — unsere Ant-wort; sprach-theologische und sprachphilosophische Aspekte der Verkündigung des Evangeliums: EurJT 3 (1994) 44-69; franc. 43; Eng. 43s.
9547 *Hughes* C. T., MARTIN on the meaninglessness of religious language: IntJPhRel 34 (Dordrecht 1993) 95-... [< ZIT 93,575].
9548 ^E**Katz** Steven T., [→ 280] Mysticism and language 1992 → 9,10392: ^RBijdragen 55 (1994) 449 (F. *Vervooren*); JRel 74 (1994) 413s (W. J. *Wainwright*: inadequacy of the ineffability thesis).
9549 **Kraft** Charles H., Communication theory for Christian witness. Mkn 1991, Orbis. xi-180 p. £15. – ^RHeythJ 35 (1994) 86s (D. C. *Weber*).
9550 **Losee** John, Religious language and complementarity [against FLEW's

claim of 'doublethink']. NY 1992, UPA.   273 p. $46.50. – RJRel 74 (1994)
412s (G. L. *Goodwin*: dismisses a bit hastily the alternative strategy).
9550* **Marc'hadour** Germain, Le lexique chrétien 2: permanences et avatars.
Angers 1993, Univ. Cath. de l'Ouest, Langues Vivantes, Cah. 12.
iv-187 p.
9551 *Molari* Carlo, La funzione della analogia nel linguaggio teologico: RasT
35 (1994) 403-420.
9552 **Neville** Robert C., Behind the masks of God 1991 → 7,7635; 8,a189:
RAmJTP 14 (1993) 317-326 (C. D. *Hardwick*).
9553 **Niedballa** Thomas, Christliches Sprachspiel und religiöse Erfahrung;
WITTGENSTEIN und die Theologie: StSysTEth 3. Münster 1993, Lit.
291 p. DM 58. 3-89473-661-5 [TR 90,282].
9554 *Norris* Richard A.J, Theology and language in IRENAEUS of Lyon:
AnglTR 76 (1994) 285-295.
9555 *Ortiz* Gustavo, Lenguaje religioso y racionalidad argumentativa: Stromata 50 (1994) 189-220.
9556 *Power* William L., Our knowledge of God [BAILLIE John, The sense of
the presence of God (Gifford lectures 1961s, 1992) revising his 1939 ²1959,
Our knowledge of God in view of linguistic analysis]: PerspRelSt 21
(1994) 213-243.
9557 *Proudfoot* Wayne, Inquiry and the language of the divine [response,
Frankenberry Nancy (*Ford* L., on her)]: AmJTP 14 (1993) 247-255 [257-
262 (287-300)].
9558 **Reitsema** Gaathe W., Vom Winken der Wörter; Wege des Denkens über
religiöse Sprache 1992 → 9,10400: RJRel 74 (1994) 577s (D. G. *Murphy*:
usefully and widely makes Dutch data available, but disjointedly and
without fair discussion of views contrary to his own, e.g. BARTHIAN
hermeneutics is a pious fraud); ZkT 116 (1994) 199-201 (K. H. *Neufeld*).
9559 *Sauter* Gerhard, Oswald BAYERS Plädoyer für eine sprachkritische
Theologie: EvT 54 (1994) 296-8.
9560 **Stoker** W., Is vragen naar zin vragen naar God? Een godsdienst-
wijsgerige studie over godsdienstige zingeving in haar verhouding tot seculiere zingeving. Zoetermeer 1993, Meinema. 311 p. ƒ45. 90-211-3594-
9. – RTvT 34 (1994) 325 (B. *Vedder*).
9561 **Stromberg** Peter G., Language and self-transformation; a study of the
Christian conversion narrative: Publications of the Society for Psychological Anthropology 5. C 1993, Univ. xvi-148 p. 0-521-44077-7.
9562 **Strub** Christian, Kalkulierte Absurditäten; Versuch einer historisch
reflectierten sprachanalytischen Metaphorologie. FrB 1991, Alber. –
RZRGg 46 (1994) 183-5 (K. *Ebert*).
9563 **Templeton** Elizabeth, The strangeness of God. L 1993, A. James. 137 p.
£8. 0-85305-296-4. – RExpTim 105 (1993s) 187s (W. D. *Horton*: literate).
9564 **Timm** Hermann, Wahr-Zeichen; Angebote zur Erneuerung religiöser
Symbolkultur. Stu 1993. Kohlhammer. 159 p. DM 29,80. – RTR 90
(1994) 348 (J. *Sudbrack*).
9564* **Tracy** David, Theologie als Gespräch; eine postmoderne Hermeneutik
[Plurality and ambiguity], ᵀ*Klinger* Susanne: Welt der Theologie. Mainz
1993, Grünewald. 172 p. DM 48. 3-7867-1651-X. – RActuBbg 31 (1994)
236s (J. *Boada*).
9565 ᴱ*Vedder* B., *al.*, Zin tussen vraag en aanbod; theologische en vijsgerige
beschouwingen over zin [Twintig jaar ontwikkelingen, Theologische
faculteit Tilburg 1992]. Tilburg 1992, Univ. – RTvT 34 (1994) 449 (H.-E.
Mertens).

9565* **Watts** Fraser, *Williams* Mark, The psychology of religious knowing 1988 ➤ 7,9732: ᴿScotJR 13 (1992) 60s (A. *Kee*).

9566 *Yusta Sainz* Jesús, Filosofía del lenguaje y su impacto en la teología actual: Burgense 34,1 (XXV años de la facultad, 'Perspectivas de teología posconciliar' 1993) 73-94.

J9.2   *Hermeneutica paratheologica* – **wider linguistic analysis.**

9567 **Dicenso** James, Hermeneutics ... HEIDEGGER, GADAMER, RICŒUR 1990 ➤ 7,1015*: ᴿJEvTS 37 (1994) 597s (J. *Morrison*).

9568 **Flew** Anthony, Atheistic humanism. Buffalo NY 1993, Prometheus. 302 p. £25.50. 0-87975-847-3. – ᴿTBR 7,2 (1994s) 12 (H. *Dawes*).

9569 **Lovekin** David, Technique, discourse, and consciousness; an introduction to the philosophy of Jacques ELLUL. Bethlehem PA 1991, Lehigh Univ. 254 p. $38.50. – ᴿCritRR 6 (1993) 461s (M.C.E. *Peterson*).

9570 **Nida** E. A., *Louw* J. F., Lexical semantics 1992 ➤ 8,a129: ᴿJBL 113 (1994) 532s (F. W. *Danker*).

9571 **Ong** Walter J., Conversazione sul linguaggio [Why talk? 1973], ᵀ*De Veris* Gabriele [diss. 1988, Ong, parola tra oralità e scrittura], R 1993, Armando. 78 p. – ᴿCC 145 (1994,2) 623 (E. *Baragli*) Lᵐ 12.

9572 **Potts** Timothy C., Structures and categories for the representation of meaning. C 1994, Univ. xv-308; p. ; bibliog. p. 289-299. 0-521-43481-5.

9572* **Putnam** Hilary, Von einem realistischen Standpunkt; Schriften zu Sprache und Wirklichkeit, ᵀᴱ*Müller* Vincent C. Reinbek 1993, Rowohlt. 315 p. Sch. 210. 3-499-55539-5. – ᴿZkT 116 (1994) 528-531 (W. *Löffler*).

9573 **Ricœur** Paul, Oneself as another [8 of the 10 1986 Gifford Lectures Soi-même comme un autre 1990], ᵀ*Blamey* Kathleen, Ch 1992, Univ. x-363 p. F 34.50. – ᴿLitTOx 8 (1994) 328-310 (Pamela *Anderson*).

9574 **Simms** Norman, The humming tree; a study in the history of mentalities. Urbana 1992, Univ. Illinois. 271 p. $45. – ᴿJRel 74 (1994) 288s (C. *Koelb*: undecipherable reflections on the untextualizable).

9575 **Steiner** George, Real presences; is there anything in what we say? L 1898, Faber & F. 236 p. $13. – ᴿScotJT 46 (1993) 100-3 (R. P. *Carroll*).

9576 *Wilder* A. N., *Stendahl* K., Imagining the real: HarvardDivBu 23,2 (1994) 13-15.

9577 **Zemach** Eddy M., The reality of meaning and the meaning of 'reality'. Hanover NH 1992, Univ. Press. vii-220 p. $45. 0-87451-574-2. – ᴿTBR 7,2 (1994s) 8 (Margaret M. *Yee*).

J9.4   **Structuralismus,** deconstructio.

9578 **Bazerman** Charles, Constructing experience. Carbondale 1994, S. Illinois Univ. x-267 p.; bibliog. 245-258. 0-8093-1906-3.

9578* **Hart** Kevin, The trespass of the sign; deconstruction, theology and philosophy 1989 ➤ 6,9939; 8,1198: ᴿRTLv 25 (1994) 260s (E. *Brito*).

J9.6   *Analysis narrationis* – **Narrative-analysis.**

9579 **Bradt** Kevin M., The recovery of story as a way of knowing in postmodern approaches – to psychotherapy and scripture; a study of epistemologies, paradigms, theory, and practice: diss. Graduate Theological Union, ᴰ*Milgrom* Jo. Berkeley 1994. 389 p. 94-26243. – DissA 55 (1994s) p. 1290.

9580 ᴱStegman P.D.D., *Visser* J., Zin in verhalen; over de betekenis van verhalen bij de overdracht van geloof, waarden en normen. Zoetermeer 1993, Boekcn-C. 134 p. *f* 32.50. 90-239-1459-7. – ᴿTvT 34 (1994) 214s (L. van der *Tuin*).

J9.8 *Theologia narrativa* – **Story-theology.**

9581 **Navone** John, Seeking God in story 1990 ⇥ 7,9763; 9,10430: ᴿIrTQ 60 (1994) 310-2 (J. *McDonagh*).
9582 *Rocchetta* Carlo, Teologia narrativa; 2. Per una rilettura della nozione teologica di efficacia sacramentale: RicT 3 (R 1992) 235-274.
9583 *Sesboüé* Bernard, De la narrativité en théologie [... FESSARD, RICŒUR]: Gregorianum 75 (1994) 413-429; Eng. 429.
9584 **Stegner** William R., Narrative theology in early Jewish Christianity. Lᴠʟ 1989, W-Knox. x-141 p. $12. – ᴿJEvTS 37 (1994) 429-430 (D. T. *Williams*).

(IV). Postbiblica

ᴷ1 **Pseudepigrapha** [= catholicis 'Apocrypha'] .1 *VT, generalia.*

9585 *Bic* H. J. de, Op onderzoek in de intertestamentaire periode: TRef 36 (Woerden 1993) 327-346 [< ᴢɪᴛ 94,17].
9585* **Cavalletti** S., Il giudaismo intertestamentario: LoB 3.14, 1991 ⇥ 7, 9767; 9,10433: ᴿRivB 42 (1994) 243-5 (M. *Perani*).
9586 *Charlesworth* James H., In the crucible; the pseudepigrapha as biblical interpretation: ⇥ 9,262, JPseud supp. 14 (1993) 20-43 [44-64, *Kee* H.; < OTAbs 17, p. 417s].
9587 **Cimosa** Mario, La letteratura intertestamentaria 1992 ⇥ 8,a239; 9,10434: ᴿCC 145 (1994,4) 411s (G. L. *Prato*); RasT 35 (1994) 239s (Cloe *Taddei Ferretti*).
9588 **Denis** Albert-Marie, Concordance latine des Pseudépigraphes de l'AT: CCLat sup. Turnhout 1993, Brepols. xvi-631 p. – ᴿNRT 116 (1994) 914s (X. *Jacques*).
9588* *García Martínez* Florentino, ¿Fin del mundo o transformación de la historia?: ComSev 27 (1994) 3-33.
9589 **Keur** Jacob & Pieter, Apocriefen van het Oude Testament; inleiding *Unnik* W. C. van. Kampen 1958, Kok. 400 p. 90-242-0090-4.
9590 ꟳKʟɪᴊɴ A.F.J., Text and testimony, ᴱ**Baarda** T., *al.*, 1988. – ᴿTR 90 (1994) 458-460 (H.C.C. *Cavallin*).
9591 **Mędala** S., ➒ Wprowadzenie ... Introduction to intertestamental literature: Kraków 1994, Enigma/ITKS. 392 p. 83-861100-0-7 [OTAbs 17, p. 685]. – ᴿJStJud 25 (1994) 323s (Z. J. *Kapera*).
9592 **Montero Carrión** D., Literatura apocalíptica e intertestamental. M c. 1992, PPC/Casa de Biblia. 171 p. – ᴿLaurentianum 34 (1993) 389s (B. de *Armellada*).
9593 *a*) *Nickelsburg* George W.E., Why study the extra-canonical literature; a historical and theological essay; – *b*) *Horst* Pieter W. Van der, Sex, birth, purity and asceticism in the Protevangelium Jacobi: ⇥ 132, ꟳVORSTER W., Neotestamentica 28,3 (1994) 181-204 / 205-218.
9593* *Prockter* L., Intertestamental studies; problems and prospects: ⇥ 327, ODENDAAL D. mem., OTEssays 7,4 (1991/4) 214-220.

9594 *a) Reeves* John C., Jewish pseudepigrapha in Manichaean literature; the influence of the Enochic library; – *b) Kraft* Robert A., The pseudepigrapha in Christianity; – *c) Wasserstrom* Steven M., ... in Muslim literature: ➤ 256* Tracing 1994, 173-203 / 55-86 / 87-114.
9594* **Weidinger** Erich, *Jucci* Elio, Gli apocrifi 1992 ➤ 8,a347:   ᴿCC 145 (1994,4) 88-90 (G. L. *Prato*).

ᴋ1.2 Henoch.

9595 **Albani** Matthias, Astronomie und Schöpfungsglaube; Untersuchungen zum astronomischen Henochbuch [Diss. Lp 1992, ᴰ*Seidel* H. ➤ 8,a248]: WM 68. Neuk 1994. xi-386 p.; Bibliog. p. 351-365. 3-7887-1482-4.
9595* *a) Reeves* John C.,   An Enochic citation in Barnabas 4.3 and the Oracles of Hystaspes; – *b) Walter* Nikolaus, Kann man als Jude auch Grieche sein? Erwägungen zur jüdisch-hellenistischen Pseudepigraphie: ➤ 133, ᶠWACHOLDER B. Z., Pursuing 1994, 260-277 / 148-163.
9596 *Renner* Lucie, Das Ende der Welt in der Tiervision; quellenkritische Bemerkungen zu Kapitel 90 des äthiopischen Henoch: FraJudBeit 20 (1993) 1-22 [< Judaica 50,60].
9596* **Tiller** Patrick A., Commentary on the animal apocalypse 1 Enoch ᴰ1992 ➤ 10446*: ᴿBL (1994) 155 (M. A. *Knibb*); JStJud 25 (1994) 339s (E. *Tigchelaar*).

ᴋ1.3 Testamenta.

9597 **Ulrichsen** Jan H., Die Grundschrift der Testamente der Zwölf Patriarchen; eine Untersuchung zu Umfang, Inhalt und Eigenart der ursprünglichen Schrift 1991 ➤ 7,9785:   ᴿCritRR 6 (1993) 185-7 (D. *Slingerland*); RB 101 (1994) 463s (P. *Henne*).
9598 *Philonenko* M., Son soleil éternel brillera (4 Q TestLeviᶜ⁻ᵈ II 9): RHPR 73 (1993) 405-8.

ᴋ1.5 Salomonis psalmi et odae.

9599 **Franzmann** Majella, Odes of Solomon: NOrb 20, 1991 ➤ 9,10457: ᴿÉTRel 68 (1993) 109s (A. *Frey*); JTS 45 (1994) 278-280 (Susan A. *Harvey*);; RB 101 (1994) 464 (P. *Henne*).
9600 ᵀᴱ**Pierre** Marie-Joseph, Les Odes de Salomon: Apocryphes 4. Turnhout 1994, Brepols. 224 p.

ᴋ1.6 Jubilaea, Adam, Aḥiqar, Asenet.

9601 *Amaro* Betty H., The first woman, wives, and mothers in Jubilees: JBL 113 (1994) 609-626.
9601* *a) Himmelfarb* Martha, Some echoes of Jubilees in medieval Hebrew literature; – *b) Adler* William, Jacob of Edessa and the Jewish pseudepigrapha in Syriac chronography: ➤ 256*, Tracing the threads 1994, 115-141 / 143-171.
9602 ᴱ**Anderson** Gary K., *Stone* Michael E., A synopsis of the books of Adam and Eve: SBL EarlyJud 9. Atlanta 1994, Scholars. xi-76 p. 1-55540-964-4.

9603 **Bohak** Gideon, 'Joseph and Aseneth' and the Jewish temple in Heliopolis: diss. Princeton Univ. 1994. 309 p. 95-09541. – DissA 55 (1994s) p. 3878.

9603* *O'Neill* John C., What is Joseph and Aseneth about?: Henoch 16 (1994) 189-198; ital. 198.

9604 **Standhartinger** Angela, Der Beitrag von 'Joseph und Aseneth' zur Diskussion um das Frauenbild in jüdisch-hellenistischer Zeit: ev. Diss. ^D*Georgi* D. > Brill: Frauenbild. – RTLv 26,535.

9604* (*Jagoda*) *Luzzatto* Maria, Grecia e Vicino Oriente; tracce della 'Storia di Ahiqar' nella cultura greca tra VI e V secolo a.c.: QuadStor 36 (1992) 5-48.

9605 *Whitney* K. William, The place of the 'wild beast hunt' of Sibylline Oracle 3,806 in biblical and rabbinic tradition: JStJud 25 (1994) 68-81.

9606 *O'Neill* J. C., The man from Heaven; SibOr 5.256-259: JPseud 9 (1991) 87-102.

9607 **Johnston** Sarah I., Hekate Soteira; a study of Hekate's roles in the Chaldean oracles and related literature: AmerClasSt 21. Atlanta 1990, Scholars. 192 p. – ^RJAAR 61 (1993) 605-7 (Deborah *Lyons*: fresh; a real service).

9608 **Mueller** James R., The five fragments of the Apocryphon of Ezekiel; a critical study: JPseud supp. 5. Shf 1994, Academic. 198 p. £27.50.

K1.7 Apocalypses, ascensiones.

9609 **Tromp** Johannes, The Assumption of Mosee, a critical edition with a commentary: StVTPseud 10, 1993 → 9,10465: ^RBL (1994) 156 (L. L. *Grabbe*); CBQ 56 (1994) 612-4 (T. A. *Bergren*).

9610 **Frankfurter** David, Elijah in Upper Egypt; Apc 1992 → 8,a261: 9,10466: ^RCBQ 56 (1994) 793-5 (T. *Wilfong*); JTS 45 (1994) 695-7 (R. M. *Wilson*).

9610* *Frankfurter* David, The cult of the martyrs in Egypt before Constantine; the evidence of the Coptic Apocalypse of Elijah: VigChr 48 (1994) 25-47.

9611 *Hall* Robert G., Isaiah's ascent to see the beloved; an ancient Jewish source for the Ascension of Isaiah?: JBL 113 (1994) 463-484.

9612 **Norelli** Enrico, L'Ascensione di Isaia; studi su un apocrifo al crocevia dei cristianesimi [excursus troppo estesi per l'edizione CCApocr → 8,a264; 9,10467]: Bo 1994, Dehoniane. 359 p. L^m 42. 88-10-20701-7.

K2.1 Philo judaeus alexandrinus.

9613 *a) Calvert* Nancy L., Philo's use of Jewish traditions about Abraham; – *b) Kraus* Matthew A., Philosophical history in Philo's In Flaccum; – *c) Reydams-Schils* Gretchen J., Stoicized readings of PLATO's Timaeus in Philo of Alexandria: → 325, SBLSem 33 (1994) 463-476 / 477-495 / 450-462.

9614 **Dawson** David, Allegorical readers and cultural revision in ancient Alexandria 1992 → 9,10471: ^RCritRR 6 (1993) 332-4 (G. E. *Sterling*); StPhilonAn 6 (1994) 199-203 (D. T. *Runia*).

9615 **Fernández Sangrador** Jorge J., Los orígenes de la comunidad cristiana de Alejandría: Plenitudo Temporis 1. S 1994, Univ. Pontificia. 233 p. pt 1900.

9616 *Gilat* J. D., ☉. The Sabbath and the halakhot in the writings of Philo: BethM 134 (1993) 216-228 [< JStJud 25,141].

9617 *Graesholt* G.,   Philo of Alexandria; some typical traits of his Jewish identity: ClasMedv 43 (1992) 97-110 [< JStJud 25,362].

9618 a) *Hay* David M., Defining allegory in Philo's exegetical world; – *b)* *Dillon* John,   Philo and the Greek tradition of allegorical exegesis: ⇒ 325, SBLSem 33 (1994) 55-68 / 69-80.

9618* *Kamesar* Adam,   Philo, *grammatikē*, and the narrative Aggada: ⇒ 133, ᶠWACHOLDER B. Z., Pursuing 1994, 216-242.

9619 a) *Levison* John R.,   Two types of ecstatic prophecy according to Philo; – *b)* *Runia* D. T.,   Philonic nomenclature; – *c)* *Terian* Abraham,   Notes on the transmission of the Philonic corpus; – *d)* *Hoek* Annewies van den, Philo in the Alexandrian tradition; – *e)* *Wilken* Robert L., Philo in the fourth century; – *f)* *Winston* David,   Philo's Nachleben in Judaism: StPhilonAn 6 (1994) 83-89 / 1-27 / 91-95 / 96-99 / 100-102 / 103-110.

9619* *Mazzanti* Angela Maria,   *Sōtēr* e *sōtēria* nell'esegesi di Filone d'Alessandria: ⇒ 330, X-Viverone 1992/3, 355-366; Eng. 276.

9620 **Murphy** Frederick J.,   Pseudo-Philo; rewriting the Bible 1993 ⇒ 9,10486: [BL 95,159, S. P. *Brock*]: ᴿJJS 45 (1994) 302-311 (H. *Jacobson*); LexTQ 29 (1994) 62-64 (R. J. *Miller*).

9621 *Parente* Fausto,   Il Liber antiquitatum biblicarum e i falsi di ANNIO di Viterbo: ⇒ 86, ᶠNALDINI M., Paideia 1994, 153-172.

9622 **Riedweg** Christoph,   Mysterienterminologie 1987 ⇒ 3,a284 ... 9,10490: ᴿÉtClas 61 (1993) 77 (R. *Bodéüs*).

9623 **Runia** D. T.,   Philo: CompRerNT 3/3, 1993 ⇒ 9,10494:   ᴿCiuD 207 (1994) 880-2 (J. *Gutiérrez*); ClasR 44 (1994) 317s (M. J. *Edwards*); Prudentia 26,2 (1994) 71-73 (P. *McKechnie*); JStJud 25 (1994) 330-3 (A. *Hilhorst*).

9624 *Schaller* Berndt,   Philo, JOSEPHUS und das sonstige griechisch-sprachige Judentum: TRu 59 (1994) 186-214.

Siegert F., Ps.Philon, Über Jona/Simson II, 1992 ⇒ 3725.

9625 **Sly** Dorothy,   Philo's perception of women 1990 ⇒ 7,9825; 8,a287: ᴿAJS 17 (1992) 288-291 (Naomi G. *Cohen*).

9626 **Williamson**, R., Philo, Jews in the Hellenistic world 1989 ⇒ 6,a61 ... 9,10500;   ᴿRThom 93 (1993) 339s (Y.-M. *Lequin*).

9627 **Yonge** C. D., The works of Philo complete and unabridged, pref. *Scholer* David M. 1993 ⇒ 9,10504: ᴿStPhilonAn 6 (1994) 171-182 (D. T. *Runia*, 'Philo in a single volume' — as already, but cumbersome: *Turnebus* A. 1552; bilinguals 1613, 1640, 1691).

κ2.4   *Evangelia apocrypha* – **Apocryphal Gospels.**

9628 ᴱ**Elliott** J. K., The apocryphal NT 1993 ⇒ 9,10505:   ᴿETL 70 (1994) 464-6 (F. *Neirynck*: replacing M. R. JAMES 1924); ÉTRel 69 (1994) 579-581 (E. *Cuvillier*) ; ExpTim 105,8 2d-top choice (1993s) 226s (C. S. *Rodd*: replaces M. R. JAMES, more usably than SCHNEEMELCHER); JTS 45 (1994) 691-5 (R. M. *Wilson*).

9628* **Geerard** Mauritius, Clavis Apocryphorum Novi Testamenti 1992 ⇒ 8, a291: ᴿNT 36 (1994) 307-9 (J. K. *Elliott*); RivStoLR 30 (1994) 606-8 (C. *Gianotto*); NT 36 (1994) 307-9 (J. K. *Elliott*).

9629 Apocryphes AELAC 1993, 1s: Barthélemy - Abgar; – ᴿNRT 116 (1994) 915-7 (X. *Jacques*).

9629* *Junod* Éric,   'Apocryphes du NT' une appellation erronée et une collection artificielle; discussion de la nouvelle définition proposée par W. SCHNEEMELCHER: Apocrypha 3 (1992) 17-46; Eng. p. 278.

9630 ᴱ**Moraldi** Luigi, Apocrifi del NT, I. Vangeli; II. Atti degli Apostoli; III. Lettere, Dormizione di Maria, Apocalissi. CasM 1994, Piemme. I. 910 p.; II. 747 p.; III, 553 p.

9630* **Rebell** Walter, Neutestamentliche Apokryphen und Apostolische Väter. Mü 1992, Kaiser. 287 p. ᴅᴍ 49. – ᴿCritRR 6 (1993) 280-2 (C. A. *Evans*: counter-current on Egerton 2).

9631 ᴱ**Schneemelcher** Wilhelm, NT Apocrypha 2⁶, ᵀ*Wilson* R. M. (2 ed., i.e. replacing his ᵀ*Hennecke-Schneemelcher*³) 1993 → 9,10511: ᴿCBQ 56 (1994) 385s (Adela Y. *Collins*); JTS 45 (1994) 270-8 (R. *Bauckham*); NT 36 (1994) 309s (J. K. *Elliott*); sᴡᴊᴛ 36,3 (1993s) 61s (H. A. *Brehm*).

9632 **Onuki** Takashi, Gnosis und Stoa ... Apocr.Joh. 1985 → 5,9978; 7,9843: ᴿArchivScSocR 39,88 (1994) 91s (J.-D. *Dubois*).

9633 *Kirk* Alan, Examining priorities: another look at the Gospel of Peter's relationship to the NT Gospels: NTS 40 (1994) 572-595.

9633***Alcalá** M., El evangelio copto de Felipe 1992 → 9,10521: ᴿRAg 34 (1993) 1120s (J. *Sepulcre*); RBíbArg 55 (1993) 248s (J. *Pablo Martín*).

9634 ᵀᴱ**Norelli** Enrico, Ascension d'Isaïe; *Desreumaux* Alain, Histoire du roi Abgar et de Jésus; *Kaestli* Jean-Daniel, *Cherix* Pierre, L'évangile de Barthélemy: Apocryphes. Brepols 1993, Turnhout. 186 p.; 184 p.; 281 p. – ᴿOrChrPer 60 (1994) 680-4 (P. *Luisier*).

9634* *Izydorczyk* Zbigniew, Manuscripts of the Evangelium Nicodemi; a census: SubsMdv 31. Toronto 1993, Pont.Inst.Mdv. x-282 p. [RHE 89,365*].

9635 *Gounelle* René, a) À propos d'une refonte de la Narratio Iosephi [Arimatheae] jadis confondue avec les Acta Pilati, et d'un drame religieux qu'elle a inspiré; – b) Sens et usage d'*apocryphus* dans la Légende Dorée [J. de *Voragine*]: Apocrypha 5 (Turnhout 1994) 165-188 / 189-210.

9635* *Mimouni* Simon C., Les Vies de la Vierge, état de la question: Apocrypha 5 (Turnhout 1994) 211-248.

K2.7 Alia apocrypha NT.

9636 **Leloir** E., Écrits aprocyphes sur les apôtres; traduction de l'édition arménienne de Venise [I. 1986] II. Philippe ...: CCApocr 4, 1992 → 8, a302; 9,10530: ᴿJTS 45 (1994) 709-711 (S. Peter *Cowe*); NT 36 (1994) 100s (J. K. *Elliott*); RHPR 74 (1994) 315 (D. A. *Bertrand*); RivStoLR 30 (1994) 179-181 (W. *Schneemelcher*).

9637 **Longstreet** Christopher S., The romance of the apocryphal Acts of the Apostles: diss. Carleton, ᴰ*Wilson* S. (Canada) 1994. 131 p. 0-315-92990-1. – (DissA-disk) MAI 33 (1994s) 740.

9637* a) *Cartlidge* David R., Evangelist leaves wife, clings to Christ; an illustration in the Admont 'Anselm' and its relevance to a reconstruction of the Acta Ioannis; – b) *Zervos* George T., Dating the Protevangelium of James; the Justin Martyr connection: → 325, SBLSem 33 (1994) 376-389 / 415-434.

9638 *Pervo* Richard I., Johannine trajectories in the Acts of John: Apocrypha 3 (1992) 47-68.

9638* *Plümacher* Eckhard, Paignion und Bibesfabel; zum literarischen und popularphilosophischen Hintergrund von Acta Iohannis 60f. 48-54: Apocrypha 3 (1992) 69-109; Eng. 280; – b) Apostolische Missionsreise und statthalterliche Assisetour — eine Interpretation von Acta Iohannis c. 37.45 und 55: ZNW 85 (1994) 259-278.

9639 a) *Brock* Ann G., Genre of the Acts of Paul; one tradition enhancing another; – b) *Bovon* François, Une nouvelle citation des Actes de Paul chez Origène: Apocrypha 5 (Turnhout 1994) 119-136 / 113-7; – c) Ca-rozzi Claude, Eschatologie et au-delà; recherches sur l'apocalypse de Paul. Aix 1994, Univ. Provence. 137 p. F 220. 2-85388-348-5.

9639* *Hayne* Léonie, (Acts of Paul and] Thecla [decanonized 1969] and the Church Fathers: VigChr 48 (1991) 209-218.

9640 *a) Thomas* Christine M., Word and deed; the Acts of Peter and orality; – *b) Bauckham* Richard, The Apocalypse of Peter; a Jewish-Christian apocalypse from the time of Bar Kokhba: Apocrypha 3 (1992) 125-169 / 5 (1994) 7-111.

9640* **Amsler** Frédéric, Les Actes apocryphes de Philippe; commentaire: diss. ᴰ*Bovon* F. Genève 1994. 377 p. > Brepols. – RTLv 26, p. 540.

9641 *Frey* Albert, L'"Éloge de Philippe, saint apôtre et évangeliste du Christ' (BHG 1530b): Apocrypha 3 (1992) 105-209; Eng. p. 281.

9641* *Pérès* Jacques-Noël, L'épître des apôtres accompagnée du Testament de notre Seigneur et notre Sauveur Jésus-Christ [éthiopiens]: Apocryphes 5. Turnhout 1994, Brepols. 149 p. 2-503-50400-0 [TLZ 120,1080, H. *Bietenhard*].

9642 *Pérès* Jacques-Noël, [Épître des apôtres ch. 27]. Le baptême des patriarches dans les enfers: ÉTRel 68 (1993) 341-6.

9642* ᵀ**Desreumaux** A. (syriaque; *Palmer* A. grec; *Beylot* R. éthiop.), Histoire du roi Abgar et de Jésus 1993 ➤ 9,10542: ᴿByzantion 65 (1995) 266s (Jacqueline *Lafontaine-Dosgne*).

9643 *Dolbeau* François, Listes latines d'apôtres et de disciples, traduites du grec; Apocrypha 3 (1992) 259-279; Eng. 282s.

9643* ᴱ**Pietersma** Albert, The Apocryphon of Jannes and Jambres the magicians, P. Chester Beatty XVI [+ W Gk 29456 + 29828, Brit.Lib. Cotton TiberiusB v f. 87; all 3 in full facsimile]: RelGrRW 119. Leiden 1994, Brill. xvii-349 p. *f* 170. 90-04-09938-7. – ᴿJStJud 25 (1994) 328-330 (P. W. von der *Horst*).

ᴋ3 **Qumran** .1 *generalia.*

9644 **Baigent** M., *Leigh* R., La Bible confisquée; enquête sur le détourne-ment des manuscrits de la Mer Morte [1991], 1992 ➤ 9,10549; F 130: – ᴿÉTRel 68 (1993) 430s (C.-B. *Amphoux*).

9645 **Baigent** M., *Leigh* R., Verschlusssache 1991 ➤ 7,9855*...9,10550: ᴿAc-tuBbg 30 (1993) 34-40 (J. *Boada*); HerdKorr 46 (1992) 98s (K. *Nientiedt* 'Baignant').

9646 *Broshi* Magen, The Dead Sea Scrolls, discovery and identification: Isr-MusJ 9 (1990) 31-41.

9647 **Charlesworth** J. H., Graphic concordance DSS 1991 ➤ 7,9857; 9,10554: ᴿArTGran 57 (1994) 508s (A. *Torres*); BASOR 293 (1994) 88s (Deirdre *Dempsey*); Biblica 75 (1994) 445s (J. L. *Ska*); BiLtg 67 (1994) 254s (F. *Böhmisch*); CritRR 6 (1993) 133-5 (M. O. *Wise*: a puzzling answer to 'cui bono'); RB 101 (1994) 588-590 (É. *Puech*); Salesianum 56 (1994) 151s (R. *Vicent*); TR 90 (1994) 374-6 (U. *Dahmen*).

9648 *Charlesworth* James H., The Princeton Theological Seminary DSS project: JPseud 10 (1992) 5-10.

9649 *Charlesworth* James H., *Whitaker* Richard E., The Dead Sea Scrolls; the new critical edition and translation prepared on computers: ZAHeb 6 (1993) 239-242.

9650 **Cook** Edward M., Solving the mysteries of the Dead Sea Scrolls; new light on the Bible. ɢʀ 1994, Zondervan. 191 p. $13 pa. 0-310-38471-0

[OTAbs 17, p. 682; NTAbs 38, p. 485]. – ^RBAR-W 10,5 first place (1994) 6.8 (J. *Kampen*).

9651 *Cook* J., The dawning of a new era in the study of the Dead Sea Scrolls: J/Tyd Sem 5 (1993) 138-152.

9652 ^E**Dimant** D., *Rappaport* U., The Dead Sea Scrolls, forty years of research 1988/92 → 8,460*: ^RDSD (1994) 130-3 (T. H. *Lim*); JStJud 25 (1994) 315-8 (M. A. *Knibb*); TLZ 119 (1994) 497s (R. *Bergmeier*); TR 90 (1994) 376-8 (U. *Dahmen*).

9653 **Eisenman** Robert, *Wise* Michael, The DSS uncovered, first complete translation 1992 → 8,a326; 9,10556: ^RDSD 1 (1994) 238-241 (J. *Kampen*); JSS 39 (1994) 108-112 (G. J. *Brooke*); PEQ 126 (1994) 76s (Charlotte *Hempel*); TLZ 119 (1994) 23-25 (S. *Holm-Nielsen*).

9654 *Fau* Guy, Les énigmes de la Mer morte: CahRenan 186 (1994) 31-40.

9655 **Fitzmyer** Joseph A., Responses to 101 questions on the Dead Sea Scrolls 1992: → 8,a329: 9,10559: ^RBL (1994) 137 (P. R. *Davies*: the later responses dilute fact with opinion; and Fitzmyer himself 'bootlegged' a text from a lecture by MILIK); CBQ 56 (1994) 332s (J. *Duhaime*); Interpretation 48 (1994) 307s (P. W. *Flint*); JEarlyC 1 (1994) 111-3 (K. R. *Calvert*).

9656 **Fitzmyer** Joseph A., Qumran, die Antwort; 101 Fragen zu den Schriften vom Toten Meer: StuTb 18. Stu 1993, KBW. 285 p. DM 19,80. – ^RTPQ 142 (1994) 408.410 (G. *Bodendorfer-Langer*: von enormer Wichtigkeit).

9657 **Fitzmyer** J. A., Qumran; le domande e le risposte essenziali sui Manoscritti del Mar Morto; ^T*Giordano* Mauro. GdT 230. Brescia 1994, Queriniana. 288 p. 88-399-0730-0.

9658 **Fitzmyer** J. A., Dödhavsrollarna; 101 frågor och svar, ^T*Hörnlund* Brigitta. Sto 1994, Verbum. 230 p. 91-526-2161-8.

9659 **García Martínez** F., Textos de Qumran 1992 → 8,a331; 9,10563: ^RCBQ 56 (1994) 545s (J. C. *VanderKam*: amazingly complete and helpful); DSD 1 (1994) 241-6 (L. *Vegas Montaner*); JTS 45 (1994) 193s (R. *Hayward*); QVidCr 165 (1993) 135 (D. *Roure*); Sefarad 54 (1994) 203-6 (también L. *Vegas Montaner*).

9661 **García Martínez** Florentino, The Dead Sea Scrolls translated; the Qumran texts in English. Leiden 1994, Brill. lxvii-513 p. 90-04-10088-1; pa. -48-2.

9662 *Haustein* Jörg, Verdrusssache Qumran; konfessionskundliche Überlegungen zum neuen Streit um alte Rollen: KkMatD 44 (Bensheim 1993) 45-47 [< ZIT 93,379].

9663 **Humbert** Jean-Baptiste, *Chambon* Alain, Fouilles de Khirbet Qumrân et de Aïn Feshkha; album de photographies; répertoire du fonds photographique; synthèse des notes de chantier du Père Roland de VAUX; au nom de l'École Biblique et archéologique française de Jérusalem: NOrb arch. 1. FrS 1994, Univ. xv-421 p. 3-7278-0940-X / VR 3-525-53970-3.

9664 *Humbert* J.-B., L'espace sacré à Qumrân; propositions pour l'archéologie: RB 101 (1994) 161-214; 7 fig. III pl.; Eng. 161.

9665 *Humbert* Jean-Baptiste, Qumrân; une hypothèse nouvelle sur les fameuses ruines ['maison de campagne' des Esséniens pour les fêtes]: MondeB 86 (1994) 12-23 [34-41, *Puech* É, NT; crucifixion; 1-33, *al.*, plan à couleurs].

9666 *Jones* T. [with *Yamauchi* E.], Scroll hype: ChrTod 37,11 (1993) 28-31 [< NTAbs 38, p. 252].

9667 *Klinghardt* Matthias, Qumran nowhere? Symposium Graz 17s.X.1992 [→ 9,10570]: QumC 2 (1992) 31-37 [OTAbs 17, p. 180 gives titles of the papers by *Talmon* S., *Dexinger* F. and 4 others].

9668 **Lange** Armin,   Computer-aided text-reconstruction and transcription [flatbed-scanner contribution to 'digitizing' obscure texts].   Tü 1993, Mohr.   xii-160 p.   3-16-146149-5. – ᴿDSD 1 (1994) 373-5 (G. *Bearman*).

9669 **Maass** Hans,   Qumran; Texte kontra Phantasien.   Stu 1994, Calwer. 240 p. DM 24,80.   3-7668-3917-0.

9670 *Milevski* Ianir, Los manuscritos del mar Muerto 46 años despues: RArq 15,153 (1994) 20-35; color. ill.; 36s, *Tov* E., Jefe de la edición.

9671 a) *Perrot* Jean, La découverte des manuscrits; – b) *Tov* Emanuel, Les manuscrits bibliques; – c) *Puech* Émile,   Esséno-zélotes chrétiens de Judée; une position originale [BAIGENT-LEIGH, EISENMAN] sur les manuscrits de la mer Morte: DossiersA 189 (1994) 4-41 (49-57. 62s. 80-83, 88-96.102s) / 42-48 (86s) / 97-101.

9671* ᴱ**Piñero** Antonio, *Fernández-Galiano* Dimas,   Los manuscritos del Mar Muerto; balance de hallazgos y de cuarenta años de estudios: En torno al NT 18.   Córdoba 1994, Almendro.   206 p.   84-8005-017-9.

9672 *Puech* Émile, [Événement du jeudi ... 12-18 août 1993] > Terre Sainte (janv. 1994) [et MondeB 86 (1994)]; EsprVie 104 (1994) 642-4-6 (J. *Daoust*).

9673 **Reed** Stephen A. *al.*, The Dead Sea Scrolls catalogue; documents, photographs and museum inventory numbers: SBL Resources 32. Atlanta 1994, Scholars. xlvi-558 p. $90; pa. $65.   0-7885-0017-1; -8-X [TDig 42,85].

9673* *Rodley* G. A.,   An assessment of the radiocarbon dating of the Dead Sea Scrolls: Radiocarbon 35 (1993) 335-8 [< BAR-W 20/2,24].

9674 *Rohrhirsch* Ferdinand,   Wissenschaftliche Begründungsstrukturen in der neueren Qumran-Literatur: StiZt 212 (1994) 267-278.

9675 *Safrai* Baruch, ❶ A new observation on the findings of the caves in the Judean desert: BethM 39 (1994) 164-172 [< OTAbs 17, p.633: Naḥal Ḥever 1953, remains of a man in a white gown with girdle tied in knot].

9676 **Schiffman** Lawrence H.,   Reclaiming the Dead Sea Scrolls; the history of Judaism, the background of Christianity, the lost library of Qumran. Ph 1994, Jewish Publication.   xxviii-528 p.; bibliog. p. 471-511.   0-8276-0530-7.

9676* ᴱ**Shanks** H., *al.*,   The Dead Sea Scrolls, after forty years; 1991 symposium.   Wsh 1992, BASoc.   x-85 p.; ill.; maps.   0-9613-0897-4. – ᴿDeltioVM 13,1 (1993) 63-66 (S. *Agourides*, ❻).

9677 *Silberman* N. A.,   Operation Scroll: Archaeology 47,2 (1994) 27s: new Israel search results meager [< NTAbs 38, p. 421].

9678 **Skehan** P. *al.*, Qumran Cave IV, 1992 ➜ 8,a367; 9,10581:   ᴿAbrNahr 31 (1993) 133-5 (T. *Muraoka*); CBQ 56 (1994) 780s (J. R. *Davila*); DSD 1 (1994) 140-6 (Zipora *Talshir*); JRel 74 (1994) 293 (J. J. *Collins*); JTS 45 (1994) 191s (T. H. *Lim*); PEQ 126 (1994) 172s (E. D. *Herbert*).

9679 *Stone* G. R.,   Setting the record straight; a correction and more on the Dead Sea Scroll datings; BurHist 28 (1992) [20s] 109-122.

9679* *Strugnell* John, a) interview with *Shanks* H.; Ousted chief Scroll editor makes his case; – b) Yigael Yadin, 'hoarder and monopolist': BAR-W 20,4 (1994) 40-47.57 (says he was and still is under manic-depressive treatment) / 48-53.47.

9680 **Sussmann** Ayala, *Peled* Ruth,   Scrolls from the Dead Sea, an exhibition 1993 ➜ 9,10582:   ᴿDSD 1 (1994) 253-5 (D. *Dimant*).

9681 **Tov** Emanuel, *al.*,   DSS on microfiche & Companion Volume & Inventory 1993 ➜ 9,10583; *f* 1600. 90-04-09733-3; 892-5; -891-7. – ᴿBL (1994) 33s (P. R. *Davies*); DSD 1 (1994) 255-9 (M. A. *Knibb*); JBL 113 (1994) 138s (J. J. *Collins*; indispensable for libraries, though printed Facsimile Edition retains its many advantages).

9682 ᴱTrebolle Barrera J., *Vegas Montaner* L., Madrid Qumran Congress 1991/2 ➤ 8,498; 9,10584: ᴿCiuD 207 (1994) 882s (J. *Gutiérrez*); JStJud 25 (1994) 130-5 (M. A. *Knibb*).

9683 VanderKam James C., The Dead Sea Scrolls today. GR 1994, Eerdmans. xiii-208 p. $13 pa. 0-281-04774-X [OTAbs 17, p. 689]. – ᴿOTEssays 7 (1994) 476-9 (P. J. *Nel*: most reliable introduction available today).

9683* a) *Vermes* Geza, The present state of Dead Sea Scrolls research; – b) *Reed* Stephen A., What is a fragment? [only the actual ancient piece; not combination of several pieces, as in editors' usage]: JJS 45 (1994) 101-110 / 123-5.

9684 *Vermes* Geza, The war over the scrolls [EISENMAN, BAIGENT-LEIGH, THIERING, FITZMYER]: New York Review of Books 11/1,14 (Aug. 11, 1994) 10-13.

9684* *Vermes* G., *Alexander* P., Norman GOLB and modern history: QumChr 2,3 (1993) 153-6: unfair [< NTAbs 37, p. 405; 38, p. 254].

9685 ᶠWOUDE A. S. van der, The Scriptures and the Scrolls, ᴱGarcía Martínez F.: VTSup 49, 1992 ➤ 8,198: – ᴿDSD 1 (1994) 133-6 (Eileen *Schuller*, in detail); JStJud 25 (1994) 89-95 (G. J. *Brooks*).

9686 YADIN Yigael mem., Archaeology and history in the DSS, NYU conference, ᴱSchiffman Lawrence H., 1985/90 ➤ 6,554: ᴿSefarad 53 (1993) 223s (F. *Sen*).

K3.4   *Qumran,* **Libri biblici** [➤ singuli] **et pseudo-biblici.**

9687 [ᴱVanderKam James], (*Attridge* Harold, *al.*), Qumran Cave 4, VIII, Parabiblical texts, 1: DJD 13. Ox 1994, Clarendon. x-470 p. 0-19-826760-6.

9688 *Bernstein* Moshe J., a) Introductory formulas for citation and re-citation of biblical verses in the Qumran Pesharim; observations on a Pesher technique: DSD 1 (1994) 30-70; – b) 4Q252: from re-written Bible to biblical commentary [Gn 6 ... 36]: JJS 45 (1994) 1-27.

9689 *Brin* Gershon, The laws of the prophet in the sect of the Judaean Desert; studies in 4Q375: JPseud 10 (1992) 19-51.

9690 *Dimant* Devorah, Apocrypha and pseudepigrapha at Qumran: ➤ 334, DSD 1 (1994) 151-9.

9691 *Fitzmyer* Joseph A., Preliminary publication of pap4QTobᵃ ar, fragment 2 [< DJD in press]: Biblica 75 (1994) 220-224; 1 pl.

9692 *Mędala* Stanisław, ❷ The Qumran Peshers and the midrashim of ancient Judaism: ➤ 9,410, Sympozjum 1992, ColcT 63,3 (1993) 27-48.

9692* *Puech* Émile, Notes sur le fragment d'apocalypse 4Q246 – 'le Fils de Dieu': RB 101 (1994) 533-556 + 2 fig.; Eng. 533.

9693 Qimron Elisha, *Strugnell* John (*Sussmann* Ya'akov, *al.*), Qumran Cave 4-V: Miqsat Ma'ase ha-Torah: DJD 10. Ox 1994, Clarendon. 235 p.; 8 pl. $80. 0-19-826344-9. – ᴿBAR-W 20,6 (1994) 48-51, 80-62 (H. *Shanks*, 'MMT as the Maltese Falcon') & 52-54; 82 [*Abegg* Martin, Paul, 'Works of the Law' and MMT) & 56-62, (reconstructed) Hebrew and English text]; BL (1995) 165 (L. L. *Grabbe* reproaches chiefly Sussmann).

9693* — a) **Kapera** Zdzisław J., Qumran Cave 4, special report, 4QMMT 1991 ➤ 7,9873*. – ᴿBZ 38 (1994) 305s (J. *Maier*: trotz allem nützlich); – b) *Gratseas* G., ❸ The Qumran manuscript 4QMMT: publication, content, diary: ➤ 131c, Mem. VELLAS V., DeltioVM 13,3 (1994) 85-123 ....

9694 Steudel Annette, Der Midrasch zur Eschatologie aus der Qumrangemeinde (4QMidrEschat[a.b]); materielle Rekonstruktion, Textbestand, Gattung und traditionsgeschichtliche Einordnung des durch 4Q174 ('Florilegium') und 4Q177 ('Catena A') repräsentierten Werkes aus den Qumranfunden [< Diss. Gö 1990, ᴰ*Stegemann* H.]; StudDJ 13. Leiden 1994, Brill. vi-235 p. $85.75. 90-04-09763-5 [BL 95,169, M.A. *Knibb*].

9694* *Stone* Michael E., *Greenfield* Jonas C., The first manuscript of Aramaic Levi document (4QLevi[a] aram) [4Q213]: Muséon 107 (1994) 257-280 + 1 pl.

9695 ᴱ*Ulrich* Eugene, *al.*, Qumran Cave 4, VII, Genesis to Numbers: DJD 12. Ox 1994, Clarendon. xv-272 p. 0-19-826365-1.

9696 *Ulrich* Eugene, An index of the passages in the biblical manuscripts from the Judean Desert (Genesis-Kings): DSD 1 (1994) 113-129.

9697 **Wacholder** Ben Zion, *Abegg* Martin G., A preliminary edition of the unpublished Dead Sea Scrolls; the Hebrew and Aramaic texts from Cave Four. Wsh 1992, Biblical Archaeology Society. fasc. 1 fasc. 2. I. xiii-118 p. 0-9163089-9-0. II. xix-309 p. 1-880371-04-4.

K3.5 *Qumran* – **Varii rotuli et fragmenta.**

9698 ᵀᴱ**Charlesworth** James H., The Dead Sea Scrolls; Hebrew, Aramaic, and Greek texts with English translation, I. Rule of the Community and related documents: Princeton Project. Tü 1994, Mohr. xxiii-189 p. 3-16-146199-1.

9698* — *Martone* Corrado, Nuovi testimoni qumranici della Regola della Comunità: Henoch 16 (1994) 173-187; Eng. 187.

9699 ᴱ**Brooke** J., Temple scroll studies 1987/9, ᴿColcT 63,1 (1993) 182-5 (W. *Chrostowski* ❷, also on ᶠMILIK).

9699* *a)* *Kampen* John, The eschatological temple of 11QT; – *b)* *Brooke* George J., The Deuteronomic character of 4Q252; – *c)* *Abegg* Martin G.ᴶ, 4Q471; a case of mistaken identity?: ➤ 133, ᶠWACHOLDER B. Z., Pursuing 1994, 85-97 / 121-135 / 136-147.

9700 *Dahmen* Ulrich, The publication(s) of the remaining fragments of 11 Q Temple: ZAHeb 7 (1994) 85-87.

9700* *a)* *Schiffman* Lawrence H., Laws concerning idolatry in the Temple Scroll; – *b)* *Kennedy* Charles A., The semantic field of the term 'idolatry': ➤ 102, Mem. RICHARDSON H., Uncovering 1994, 159-175 / 193-204.

9701 **Molin** Georg, Das Gehemnis von Qumran; wiederentdeckte Lieder und Gebete [= Lob Gottes 1957], ²ʳᵉᵛ*Betz* Otto, *Riesner* Reiner. FrB 1994, Herder. 128 p. DM 19,80. 3-41-23324-X. – ᴿTGL 84 (1994) 487 (J. *Ernst*).

9702 *Abegg* Martin G.ᴶ, Messianic hope and 4Q285: a reassessment: JBL 113 (1994) 81-91.

9703 *Martone* Corrado, Un testo qumranico che narra la morte del Messia? a proposito del recente dibattito su 4Q285: RivB 42 (1994) 329-332.

9704 *Broshi* Magen, *Yardeni* Ada, ❹ [4Q338s] On *netînîm* and false prophets: Tarbiz 62 (1992s) 45-54; 4 pl.; Eng. VI.

9704* *Eshel* Esther, 4Q477; the rebukes by the overseer: JJS 45 (1994) 111-122.

9705 *Eshel* Esther, *Stone* Michael E., ❹ The holy language at the end of days [4Q464]: Tarbiz 62 (1992s) 169-177; Eng. V.

9705* *Falk* Daniel, 4Q393, a communal confession: JJS 45 (1994) 184-207.

9706 *Nebe* G. Wilhelm, Qumranica 1: zu unveröffentlichten Handschriften aus Höhle 4 von Qumran: ZAW 106 (1994) 307-322.

9707 *a) Schiffman* L. H.,   New halakhic texts from Qumran: – *b) VanderKam* J. C., The Scrolls, the apocrypha and the Pseudepigrapha: HebSt 34 (Madison WI 1993) 21-33 / 35-51 [< NTAbs 38, p. 253s].

9708 *Wise* Michael O.,   Thunder in Gemini, an Aramaic brontologion (4Q318) from Qumran: ⇒ 231, 1994, 13-50 [152-185, 4Q174; 186-221, 4Q332-4; 222-239, 4Q321; 51-102, J. NAVEH's Masada sherd: all abstracted by P. D. *Sansone* in OTAbs 17, p. 635s].

9709 *Muchowski* Piotr,   ⊕ *Zwój miedziany* (3Q15), The copper scroll; implications of the controversial linguistic problems. Poznań 1993, Inst. Ethnolinguistic.   vii-130 p. – RJStJud 25 (1994) 326-8 (Z. J. *Kapera*).

K3.6   Qumran et NT.

9710 **Berger** Klaus,   *a)* De Dode-Zeerollen en Jezus; een achtergehouden waarheid? Kampen 1994, Kok.   139 p. *f* 27,50.   90-242-8228-4. – RTvT 34 (1994) 439 (J. *Negenman*: BAIGENT/EISENMAN onjuist). – *b)* Qumran und Jesus; Wahrheit unter Verschluss[5]? Stu 1993, Quell.   137 p.   3-7918-1929-1. – RActuBbg 31 (1994) 54s (H. *Vall*, auch über BETZ-RIESNER).

9711 **Betz** O., *Riesner* R.,   Jesus, Qumran und der Vatican 1993 ⇒ 9,10617: RBiKi 48 (1993) 236s (Ingo *Broer*); DSD 1 (1994) 364-6 (S. *Talmon*: also on the English; and against EISENMAN, THIERING, WISE, LAPIDE).

9712 **Betz** Otto, *Riesner* Rainer,   Jesus, Qumran and the Vatican; clarifications. L/NY 1994, SCM/Crossroad.   x-187 p. £12.50.   0-334-01209-X [NTAbs 38, p. 482]. – RBL (1994) 134 (G. J. *Brooke*); Church 10,3 (1994) 55 (Karen S. *Smith*); ExpTim 105 (1993s) 348s (P. R. *Davies*: lively and factual, though no more dispassionate than its targets; respectable misgivings not distinguished from wild ideas like THIERING's).

9712* **Eisenman** R. H., *Wise* M.,   Jesus und die Urchristen; die Qumran-Rollen entschlüsselt. Mü 1994, Goldmann '12550'.   288 p., ill. DM 14,90 [RHE 90,239*].

9713 *García Martínez* Florentino,   Nuevos textos mesiánicos de Qumrán y el Mesías del Nuevo Testamento: ComSev 26 (1993) 3-31.

9714 *Garhammer* Erich,   Von der Fiktionalität zur Faktizität; Analyse momentaner Kirchenkritik am Beispiel des Qumran-Themas: TGL 84 (1994) 37-46.

9715 *Geller* M. J.,   Early Christianity and the Dead Sea Scrolls: ⇒ 136, FWANSBROUGH J., BSO 57 (1994) 82-92.

9715* *a) Lichtenberger* Hermann,   Die Texte von Qumran und das Urchristentum; – *b) Nebe* G. Wilhelm, Vom Umgang mit den Photo- und Konkordanztext-Veröffentlichungen der Handschriften vom Toten Meer; – *c) Deines* Roland, Zur Qumranforschung (BURGMANN H. 1992): Judaica 50 (1994) 68-82 / 83-86 / 87-91.

9716 EMayer Bernhard,   Christen und Christliches in Qumran? 1992 ⇒ 9,396*; RBiKi 48 (1993) 45-47 (B. *Then*); DSD 1 (1994) 137-140 (U. *Glessmer*); EstAg 28 (1993) 586-9 (R. A. *Díez*); ForKT 10 (1994) 320 (D. *Kinet*); RB 101 (1994) 291 (tit. pp.); RHPR 74 (1994) 205s (C. *Grappe*); TLZ 119 (1994) 137-139 (M. *Bockmuehl*); TPhil 69 (1994) 268-270 (R. *Sebott*).

9717 **Miller** Douglas,   The Dead Sea Scrolls and Jesus Christ; a discussion of the views of Dr. Barbara THIERING. ... Uniting Church in Australia. $5. 1-875749-42-X. – RBurHist 30 (1994) 143s (J. *Snow*).

9718 *a) Norton* Gerard J.,   Qumran and Christian origins: PrIrB 16 (1993) 99-113. – *b) Rodríguez Carmona* Antonio, Sensacionalismo sobre Qumrán: Proyección 42 (1994) 135-148.

9719 *O'Callaghan* José, El papir de Marc a Qumran; incògnites i con-seqüències: Teologia Actual 2 (1993) 47-56 [< AcPIB 9,894].

9720 *Pazzini* Massimo, I manoscritti di Qumran e il Nuovo Testamento: TerraS 69,6 (1993) 37-43.

9721 *Pazzini* Maximo, *Domingos Casonatto* Odalberto, Os manuscritos de Qumrã e o Novo Testamento: RBBras 10 (1993) 269-277.

9722 *a*) *Riesner* Rainer, Jesus, Qumran und der Vatikan [BAIGENT ...]; – *b*) *Garhammer* Erich, Qumran und die Vermarktungsmechanismen der Medien; – *c*) *Berger* Klaus, Qumran und das NT; – *d*) *Stegemann* Hartmut, Qumran und das Judentum zur Zeit Jesu: TGL 84 (1994) 139-150 / 151-8 / 159-174 / 175-194.

9722* **Rudolf** Paul F., Jesus und Qumran — War der Nazarener ein Essener? Dü 1993, Walter. 363 p. DM 40. – ᴿBiLtg 66 (1993) 177-180 (K. *Schubert*).

9723 *Schiffman* L. H., Judaism and early Christianity in the light of the DSS: → 384*, Jewish-Christian 1989/94, 27-44.

9723* *Semmelink* J.-W., THIERING's use of Qumran Pesher: Ekklesiastikos Pharos 4,2 (1993) 7-18 [< JStJud 25,364].

9724 **Silberman** Neil A., The hidden scrolls; Christianity, Judaism, and the war for the Dead Sea Scrolls. ... 1994, Putnam. xiv-306 p.; bibliog. p. 285-298 [Archaeology 47/6,40]. 0-389-13982-6.

9725 **Stegemann** Hartmut, Die Essener, Qumran, Johannes der Täufer und Jesus; ein Sachbuch[4rev]: Spektrum 4128. FrB 1994, Herder. 381 p. 3-451-04128-6. – ᴿDielB 28 (1992s!) 258-261 (B. J. *Diebner*).

9725* *Stegemann* Hartmut, Jesus and the Teacher of Righteousness; simi-larities and differences: BR 10,1 (1994) 42-47, 63.

9726 *a*) *Stegemann* Hartmut, Die Bedeutung der Qumranfunde für das Verständnis Jesu und des frühen Christentums; – *b*) *Maier* Johann, ... des Judentums; – *c*) *Fitzmyer* Joseph A., Ein Nachruf auf die 'Verschlusssache Jesus' [< America 100,5 (1992) 119-122]: BiKi 48,1 ('Qumran' 1993) 10-19 / 2-9 / 19-24.

9727 *Stegemann* Wolfgang, Qumran, Jesus und das Urchristentum; Bestseller und Anti-Bestseller [BAIGENT, EISENMAN, THIERING; fünf zentrale Thesen durchgehend erörtert]: TLZ 119 (1994) 387-408.

9728 *a*) *Tabor* James D., *Wise* Michael O. 4Q521 'On Resurrection' and the Synoptic Gospel tradition; a preliminary study; – *b*) *Evans* Craig A., Predictions of the destruction of the Herodian Temple in the Pseudepigrapha, Qumran Scrolls, and related texts [Lk 13 ...]: JPseud 10 (1992) 149-162 / 89-147.

9729 *Thiede* Carsten P., Das unbeachtete Qumran-Fragment 7Q19 und die Herkunft der Höhle 7: Aegyptus 74 (1994) 123-8.

9729* **Thiede** Carsten P., Qumran et les évangiles; les manuscrits de la grotte 7 et la naissance du Nouveau Testament. P 1994, de Guibert. 135 p.; bibliog. 127-134. 2-86839-286-5 [RB 102,589, P. *Grelot*: ne convaincra jamais que les journalistes].

9730 **Thiede** C. P., The earliest Gospel manuscript? The Qumran fragment 7Q5 and its significance for NT studies [1986]. Carlisle 1992, Paternoster. £5. 0-85364-507-8. – ᴿExpTim 105 (1993s) 249 (J. K. *Elliott*: 1984 *Biblica* article puffed up with extraneous matter); NT 36 (1994) 98-100 (J. K. *Elliott*: adds nothing to his 1984 Biblica article or to the previous contrary consensus); swjt 36,1 (1993s) 58s (E. E. *Ellis*).

9730* *Thiede* Carsten P., Greek fragment 7Q5; possibilities and [SPOTTORNO] impossibilities: Biblica 75 (1994) 394.

9731 **Thiering** Barbara,   *a*) Jesus and the riddle 1992 → 8,a400:   ᴿCritRR 6 (1993) 298-301 (W. *Wink*: mischievous, calling for aggressive antidote); – *b*) Jesus von Qumran; sein Leben neu geschrieben 1993 → 9,10632:   ᴿProtestantesimo 49 (1994) 398s (P. *Castelluccio*).

9731* *Ulfgard* Hakan,   Le mouvement de Qumrân et le christianisme primitif [< SvTKv 69 (1993) 161-173]: Études 381 (1994) 637-648.

K3.8   **Historia et doctrinae Qumran.**

9732 **Ausin Olmos** S., Moral y conducta en Qumran ... *halak* 1991 → 7,9895; 8,a403:   ᴿCiuD 206 (1993) 924s (J. *Gutiérrez*).

9732* *Baumgarten* Joseph M.,   Zab impurity [Lev 15; Num 5,2] in Qumran and rabbinic law: JJS 45 (1994) 273-7.

9733 *Bondí* Sandro F., Monaci al tempo di Gesù: Archeo 9,115 (1994) 47-53.

9734 **Burgmann** H.,   Weitere lösbare Qumranprobleme 1992 → 8,a407: PEQ 126 (1994) 74 (G. J. *Brooke*: all his work deserves to be read).

9734* *Chazon* Esther G.,   Prayers from Qumran and their historical implications: DSD 1 (1994) 265-284.

9735 *a*) *Crown* Alan D., *Cansdale* Lena,   Qumran; was it an Essene settlement?; – *b*) *Goranson* Stephen,   Qumran, a hub of scribal activity?: BAR-W 20,5 (1994) 24-35.53 / 36-39.

9736 **Davies** Philip R. Behind the Essenes; history and ideology in the DSS: BrownJud 94. Atlanta 1987, Scholars. 160 p. – ᴿSefarad 53 (1993) 214 (F. *Sen*).

9737 *Davies* P. R.,   'Age of wickedness' or 'end of days'? Qumran scholarship in prospect: HebSt 34 (Madison WI 1993) 7-19 [< NTAbs 38, p. 250].

9737* *Eshel* Esther & Hanan, *Yardeni* Ada.,   Rare DSS text mentions King Jonathan; who was he?:   BAR-W 10,1 (1994) 75-78.

9738 **García Martínez** Florentino,   Qumran and Apocalyptic; studies in the Aramaic texts from Qumran: StTDJ 8, 1992 → 8,244*a*; 9,10641:   ᴿCBQ 56 (1994) 400s (J. W. *Wright*: does not prove his perhaps-true thesis that the Aramaic texts significantly reveal Qumran origins and development; very badly proofread, especially the foreword); RB 101 (1994) 272-5 (P. *Grelot*); Sefarad 53 (1993) 404-6 (J. J. *Alarcón Sainz*).

9738* **García Martínez** F., *Trebolle Barrera* J.,   Los hombres de Qumrân 1993 → 9,10642:   ᴿActuBbg 31 (1994) 38 (J. *O'Callaghan*); QVidCr 173 (1994) 127s (D. *Roure*); RET 54 (1994) 211s (P. *Barrado Fernández*).

9739 **Harrington** Hannah K.,   The impurity systems of Qumran and the rabbis; biblical foundations: SBL diss. 143. Atlanta 1993, Scholars. xvi-313 p. $30; sb./pa. $19. 1-55540-844-3; -5-1. – ᴿBL (1994) 107 (P. S. *Alexander*: follows MILGROM).

9739* *Knoll* Israel, *Naeh* Shlomo,   Ⓗ Ordination (-week) and Yom Kippur (-week): Tarbiz 62 (1992s) 17-44; Eng. v.

9741 *Loader* Bill,   The new Dead Sea scrolls [EISENMAN-WISE]; new light on messianism and the history of the community: Colloquium 25 (Queensland 1993) 67-85 [< OTAbs 17, p. 632].

9741* *Martone* Corrado,   Un calendario proveniente da Qumran recentemente pubblicato: Henoch 16 (1994) 49-75, Eng. 76.

9742 *Mattila* Sharon Lee,   Two contrasting eschatologies at Qumran (4Q246 vs. 1QM): Biblica 75 (1994) 518-538; franç. 538.

9743 **Nitzan** Bilhah,   Qumran prayer and religious poetry; ᵀ*Chipman* Jonathan: StTDJ 12. Leiden 1994, Brill. xxi-413 p.; bibliog. p. 371-380. 90-04-09658-2.

9744 *Penney* Douglas J., *Wise* Michael O., By the power of Beelzebub; an Aramaic incantation formula from Qumran (4Q560): JBL 113 (1994) 627-650.

9744* **Schiffman** L. H., The eschatological community 1989 → 5,a30 ... 7,9888: ᴿJSS 38 (1993) 149s (G. J. *Brooke*).

9745 **Schmidt** Francis, La pensée du Temple, de Jérusalem à Qoumrân; identité et lien social dans le judaïsme ancien. P 1994, Seuil. 370 p. F 170 2-02-021786-4 [OTAbs 17, p. 688]. – ᴿÉtudes 381 (1994) 713 (P. *Gibert*).

9746 *Stegemann* Hartmut, Ein neues Bild des Judentums zur Zeit Jesu; zum gegenwärtigen Stand der Qumran- und Essener-Forschung: HerdKorr 46 (1992) 175-180.

9747 *Stemberger* Günter, Il Giudaismo classico 1991 → 9,10708: ᴿProtestantesimo 49 (1994) 179s (B. *Corsani*).

Steudel Annette, Der Midrasch zur Eschatologie aus der Qumrangemeinde (4QMidrEschatᵃ⁻ᵇ); materielle Rekonstruktion, Textbestand, Gattung und traditionsgechichtliche Einordnung des durch 4Q174 ('Florilegium') und 4Q177 ('Catena A') repräsentierten Werkes aus den Qumranfunden: StTDJ 13 1994 → 9694.

9748 *Wacholder* Ben Zion, Geomessianism; why did the Essenes settle at Qumran?: → 9,84, ᶠLEVEY S., Bits of honey 1993, 131-8.

9748* *Wise* Michael O., Second thoughts on DWQ ['observance'?] and the Qumran synchronistic calendars [4Q321]: → 133, ᶠWACHOLDER B. Z., Pursuing 1994, 98-120.

K4.1   Esseni, Zelotae.

9749 **Bergmeier** Roland. Die Essener-Berichte des Flavius JOSEPHUS 1993 → 9,10651: ᴿBO 51 (1994) 649-651 (P. R. *Davies*); JBL 113 (1994) 525s (J. J. *Collins*); OTEssays 7 (1994) 304-6 (J. A. *Naudé*); TLZ 119 (1994) 507 (W. *Vogler*).

9750 *Bojesen* Sanne, Essæerne, Dodehavs-skrifterna og Khirbet Qumran: Nemalah 13 (K 1994) 21-29 [< OTAbs 17, p. 627: the Qumranites could not have been Essenes].

9751 **Burgmann** Hans †, Die Geschichte der Essener von Qumran und Damaskus: Qumranica Mogilanensia 5, 1990 → 7,9909: ᴿBL (1994) 133 (P. R. *Davies*: distillation of his earlier eccentricities); BZ 32 (1994) 311 (J. *Maier*, kurz); DSD 1 (1994) 369s (Charlotte *Hempel*); PEQ 125 (1993) 158-160 (G. J. *Brooks*, also on Burgmann QMogil 1; and → 9734).

9751* *Campserveux* Max, Méditation sur les Esséniens exclus [... de Qoumran]: Cah Renan 190bis (1995). 42 p.

9752 *Elder* Linda B., The woman question and female ascetics among the Essenes: BA 57 (1994) 220-234.

9752* *Goranson* Stephen, POSIDONIUS, STRABO and Marcus Vipsanius Agrippa as sources on Essenes: JJS 45 (1994) 295-8.

9753 **Stemberger** Günter, Farisei, sadducei, esseni [1991] ᵀ1993 → 8,a428*; 88-394-0499-6: ᴿTeresianum 45 (1994) 596s (A. *Borrell*).

9754 **Vermes** G., *Goodman* M. The Essenes 1989 → 5,a63 ... 9,10654: ᴿRB 101 (1994) 590-3 (É. *Puech*).

9755 *Williams* David S., JOSEPHUS and the authorship of War 2.119-161 (on the Essenes): JStJud 25 (1994) 207-221.

K4.3   Samaritani.

9756 **Crown** Alan D., *al.*, A companion to Samaritan studies 1993 → 9,10655: ᴿBL (1994) 134 (L. L. *Grabbe*); JStJud 25 (1994) 82s (F. *García Martínez*).

9757 **Crown** A., The Samaritans 1989 → 5,389 ... 9,10657: ^RJPseud 8 (1991) 120s (J. C. *VanderKam*).
9758 *Crown* Alan D., Samaritan literature and its manuscripts: BJRyL 76,1 (1994) 21-49.
9759 *Florentin* Moshe, [**❂**]. An observation on the name of the Samaritan Midrash *Tībât Marqe*: Lešonenu 58 (1994s) 309-312; Eng. 4/II: perhaps not 'box' but Arabic *safînâ*, 'boat'.
9760 *Horst* P.W. van der, Samaritans and Hellenism; StPhilonAn 6 (1994) 28-35.
9761 **Macchi** J.-D., Les Samaritains; histoire d'une légende; Israël et la province de Samarie: MondeB 30. Genève 1994, Labor et Fides. 191 p. 7 fig. 4 maps. 2-8309-0712-4 [NTAbs 38, p. 492]. – ÉTRel 69 (1994) 574s (Françoise *Smyth*).
9762 *Sela* Shulamit, The head of the Rabbanite, Karaite and Samaritan Jews; on the history of a title: BSO 57 (1994) 255-267.
9763 *Weiss* Herold, The Sabbath among the Samaritans: JStJud 25 (1994) 252-273.
9764 **Zangenberg** Jürgen, Samareia; antike Quellen zur Geschichte und Kultur der Samaritaner in deutscher Übersetzung: TANZ 15. Tü 1994, Francke. xxvii-345 p. 3-7720-1866-1.

K4.5 *Ṣadoqitae, Qaraitae* – **Cairo Genizah; Zadokites, Karaites.**

9765 ^E**Blau** Joshua, *Reif* Stefan C., Genizah research after ninety years ... Judaeo-Arabic 1987/92 → 8,457: ^RJJS 43 (1992) 325-7 (D. *Frank*).
9766 ^E**Broshi** Magen, The Damascus document reconsidered 1992 → 8,a440; 9,10661: ^RNRT 116 (1994) 278s (X. *Jacques*); PEQ 125 (1993) 158 (G. J. *Brooke*).
9767 *a) Chmiel* Jerzy, Genisa — verborgenes Erbe; die Kairoer Genisa und die Genisot der neuzeitlichen Synagogen: → 92*, ^FPIERONEK T., AnCracov 26 (1994) 169-172; ❂ 172; – *b) Khan* Geoffrey, The orthography of Karaite Hebrew Bible manuscripts in Arabic transcription: JSS 38 (1993) 49-70.
9767* *Davies* Philip R., The 'Damascus' sect and Judaism: → 133, ^FWACHOLDER B. Z., Pursuing 1994, 70-84.
9768 *Harviainen* Tapani, Abraham FIRKOVITSH, Karaites in Hīt, and the provenance of Karaite transcriptions of biblical Hebrew texts into Arabic script [under same influences as Yemenite]: FolOr 28 (1991) 179-191 [< OTAbs 17, p. 10].
9768* **Hempel** Charlotte, A literary critical and comparative analysis of the laws of the Damascus Document: diss. ^D*Knibb* M. London 1994. 200 p. > DSD. – RTLv 26,534.
9769 **Miller** Philip E., Karaite separation in nineteenth-century Russia; J. S. LUTSKI's Epistle of Israel's deliverance: Mg 16. Cincinnati 1993, HUC. xix-252 p. $50. – ^RJJS 45 (1994) 146-8 (D. *Frank*).
9769* ^ESchäfer Peter, *Shaked* Saul, Magische Texte aus der Kairoer Geniza I.: TStAJ 42. Tü 1994, Mohr. xi-329 p.; Bibliog. 243-8. 3-16-146272-6.
9770 **Schur** Nathan, History of the Karaites: BeitErfAJ 29. Fra 1992, Lang. 207 p.; bibliog. 161-173. 3-631-44435-4.
9770* *Szyszman* Simon, Zum Niedergang des Karäertums und seiner Zentren: Judaica 49 (1993) 200-205.

K5 **Judaismus prior vel totus.**

9771 **Aus** Roger D., Samuel, Saul and Jesus; three early Palestinian Jewish Christian gospel haggadoth: SFlJud 105. Atlanta 1994, Scholars. xvi-202 p.; bibliog. 189-197.

9772 **Ben-Sasson** Haim H., Geschichte des jüdischen Volkes, von den Anfängen bis zur Gegenwart [< ❹ TA 1969; Eng. 1976]^{revT}. Mü 1992, Beck [= 1978-80 3 vol.] ix-1404 p. 3-406-36626-0. – ^{R}Salesianum 56 (1994) 779s (R. *Vicent*).

9773 **Boccaccini** Gabriele, Middle Judaism 1991 ➤ 8,a450; 9,10669: ^{R}CritRR 5 (1992) 354-6 (D.J. *Harrington*); ÉTRel 68 (1993) 427s (Françoise *Smyth*); RestQ 36 (1994) 190-2 (R.D. *Chesnutt*); RivStoLR 30 (1994) 603-6 (C. *Martone*).

9774 **Boccaccini** G., Il medio giudaismo 1993 ➤ 9,10670*: ^{R}RasT 35 (1994) 363-371 (Cloe *Taddei Ferretti*).

9775 **Brewer** David I., Techniques and assumptions in Jewish exegesis before 70 CE 1992 ➤ 8,a451; 9,10671: ^{R}DSD 1 (1994) 366-8 (G.J. *Brooke*); JBL 113 (1994) 719s (A.J. *Saldarini*); Judaica 50 (1994) 170s (M. *Kreuzer*); RExp 91 (1994) 114s (J.D. *Watts*); VT 44 (1994) 422 (S.A. *Reif*).

9776 **Buxbaum** Yitzhak, The life and teachings of HILLEL. Northvale NJ 1994, Aronson. ix-376 p. 1-56821-049-3.

9777 **Cohen** S., The three crowns 1990 ➤ 8,a454; 9,10673: ^{R}CritRR 5 (1992) 361-3 (Tz. *Zahavy*).

9778 **Cohn-Sherbok** Dan, The Jewish faith. L/Ph 1993, SPCK, Trinity. x-258. £15. /1-56338-083-8 [TDig 42,61]. ^{R}TLond 97 (1994) 300s (B. *Ettlinger*: excellent summary of Jewish defined as 'anyone born of a Jewish mother, irrespective of beliefs or observance'; with many small errors like 'God and Magog', "Rashbam", 'firstborn only' in Ex 1,22).

9779 *Danshin* D.I., ❹ Phanagorian community of Jews [51 C.E., earliest Bosporus mention]: VDI 204 (1993) 59-72: Eng. 72.

9780 **Faur** José, Golden doves with silver dots; semiotics and textuality in rabbinic tradition 1986 ➤ 2,7289 ... 5,a91: ^{R}Sefarad 53 (1993) 214s (J.J. *Alarcón Sainz*).

9781 *Fernández Marcos* Natalio, Exégesis e ideologia en el judaïsmo del siglo I; héroes, heroínas y mujeres: Sefarad 53 (1993) 273-288; Eng. 288: drawn largely from pseudepigrapha.

9781* ^{E}**Goodman** Lenn E., Neoplatonism and Jewish thought 1992 ➤ 8,433*b*: ^{R}JSS 49 (1994) 334s (O. *Leaman*).

9782 **Grabbe** Lester L., Judaism from Cyrus to Hadrian 1s, 1992 ➤ 8,a456; 9,10681: ^{R}Interpretation 48 (1994) 291-3 (J.C. *VanderKam*); JAAR 62 (1994) 190-2 (J. *Kampen*: valuable handbook of Second Temple era history); JNWS 19 (1993) 178-182 (J. *Cook*).

9783 *Gurevitch* Zali, *Aran* Gideon, Never in place; ELIADE and Judaic sacred space [... Canaan as place]: ArchivScSocR 39,87 (1994) 135-151; Eng 151; español 152.

9784 *Horst* Pieter W. van der, The Birkat ha-Minim in recent research: ExpTim 105 (1993s) 363-8.

9785 *Ilan* Tal, Matrona and Rabbi Jose; an alternative interpretation: JStJud 25 (1994) 18-51.

9786 *Jensen* Jørgen S., God-fearers or sympathizers — a special social group: Temenos 28 (Helsinki 1992) 188-208 [< ZIT 93,387].

9786* *Kern-Ulmer* Brigitte (Rivka), Die Bewertung der Proselyten im rabbinischen Schrifttum: Judaica 50 (1994) 1-17.

9787 ^{TE}**Kravitz** Leonard, *Olitzky* Kerry M., Pirke Avot, a modern commentary on Jewish ethics. NY 1993, Union.Amer.Heb.Congr. xiv-114.

9788 **Kusche** Ulrich, Die unterlegene Religion; das Judentum im Urteil deutscher Alttestamentler [1850-1950]: KIsr Studien 12. B 1991, Inst.

Kirche und Judentum. 209 p. DM 24,80. – ᴿJBL 113 (1994) 120s (W. *Harrelson*: fair; title justifiably bivalent, 'underlying' / 'put down').

9789 *Levey* Samson H., AKIBA, sage in search of the Messiah; a closer look: Judaism 41 (1992) 334-345.

9790 **Levine** Lee I.,   The rabbinic class of Roman Palestine in late antiquity 1989 ➤ 5,a103* ... 8,a460:   ᴿCritRR 5 (1992) 373-6 (J. *Neusner*: an anthology 'of no scholarly value whatsoever' for 3 reasons).

9791 *McKnight* Scot, A light among the Gentiles; Jewish missionary activity in the Second Temple period 1991 ➤ 7,9953 ... 9,10688:   ᴿJBL 113 (1993) 330-2 (S. *Westerholm*).

9792 **Maier** Johann,   Il giudaismo del Secondo Tempio; storia e religione [➤ 7,9971], ᵀᴱ*Chiesa* Bruno: BtCuRel 59. Brescia 1991, Paideia. 380 p. [➤ 7,9954; 9,10659]:   ᴿEstE 68 (1993) 386s (J. *Alonso Díaz*); Gregorianum 74 (1993) 383-5 (G. L. *Prato*); Orpheus 14 (1993) 405-8 (Beatrice *Marotta Mannino*); RivB 42 (1994) 358-360 (M. *Perani*).

9793 **Maier** J., Storia del Giudaismo nell'antichità: StBPaid 99. Brescia 1992, Paideia. 197 p. – ᴿRivB 42 (1994) 358 (M. *Perani*).

9793* **Mansoor** M.,   Jewish history and thought 1991 ➤ 9,10690:   ᴿHeythJ 35 (1994) 73s (L. *Jacobs*).

9794 ᴱ**Mello** A., Detti di rabbini; Pirqè Avot con i loro commenti tradizionali. Magnano 1993, Qiqajon. 232 p. – ᴿHenoch 16 (1994) 359s (P. *Capelli*).

9794* **Meyer** Johann F. von (1830), Das Buch Jezira, ᵀ*Goodman-Thau* Eveline, ᴱ*Schulte* Christoph: Jüdische Quellen 1. B 1993, Akademie. – ᴿJudaica 50 (1994) 159-161 (D. *Krochmalnik*).

9795 *Milikowski* H., ❺ The symmetry of history in rabbinic literature; the special numbers of Seder Olam ch. 2: JStJTht 11 (1993) 37-48 [< JStJud 25,151].

9796 *Neudecker* Reinhard,   Il rapporto maestro-discepolo nel giudaismo rab-binico: ➤ 535, DizSpir biblico-patr 1993, 4,57-73.

9797 *Neudecker* Reinhard,   Nächster II. Judentum [*Noort* Edward AT, *Balz* Horst NT]: ➤ 517, TRE 23 (1994) 716-9 [713-6. – 720-723 (–731 *al.*)].

9798 *Neusner* Jacob,   The academic study of Judaism, the religion; progress in thrity-five years?: JAAR 62 (1994) 1047-1068; 'special issue', also an Islam, Buddhism.

9799 **Neusner** Jacob,   Androgynous Judaism; masculine and feminine in the dual Torah. Macon GA 1993, Mercer Univ. xiv-202 p. $30. 0-86554-428-X.

9800 **Neusner** Jacob,   Classical Judaism; Torah, learning, virtue; an anthology of the Mishnah, Talmud and Midrash, I. Torah: JudUmw 36. Fra 1993. Lang. 258 p. DM 79. 3-631-45061-3 [TR 90,174].

9800* **Neusner** J.,   I fondamenti del Giudaismo [1985], ᵀ*Stefani* Piero: Schulim Vogelmann 31. F 1992, La Giuntina. – ᴿRivB 42 (1994) 243-5 (M. *Perani*).

9801 **Neusner** Jacob,   How Judaism reads the Torah 1-4 (1. Ten Command-ments; 2-3 Sifra Lv/Nm; 4 Sifre Dt): JudUmw 41s. Fra 1993, Lang. 214 + 217 p. DM 68 + 69. 3-631-45640-9; -1-7 [TR 90,174].

9802 **Neusner** J., An introduction to Judaism 1991 ➤ 8,a468:   ᴿJEvTS 37 (1994) 590s (L. *Helyer* curiously doubts that before 586 BCE Jews lived in various countries).

9803 **Neusner** Jacob,   Introduction to rabbinic literature: AnchorB Ref. NY 1994, Doubleday. xxxi-720 p. 0-385-47093-2.

9804 **Neusner** Jacob,   Judaism and story; the evidence of The Fathers ac-cording to Rabbi Nathan: StHistJud, 1992 ➤ 8,a470 ... 9,10696:   ᴿCrit-

RR 6 (1993) 423s (A. J. *Saldarini*, also on his Form-analytical 1992
→ 9,10695).

9805 **Neusner** Jacob, Symbol and theology in early Judaism 1991 → 7,9961*;
9,10693: ᴿCritRR 6 (1993) 418-420 (H. W. *Basser*: an important book, to
be studied again and again from every angle).

9806 *Neusner* Jacob, Politics to anti-politics; the transformation of Judaism
between ca. AD. 200 and 400: ThisWorld 27 (Elizabethtown PA 1992)
56-63 [< NT 16s 38, p. 258].

9807 *Noam* Vered, ❺ The scholion to the Megillat Taanit; towards an
understanding of its stemma: Tarbiz 62 (1992s) 55-99; Eng. VI.

9808 *Noam* Vered, ❺ The seventeenth of Elul [Roman withdrawal from
Jerusalem] in Mehillat Taʿanit: Zion 59 (1994) 433-444; Eng. XXVII.

Nodet Étienne, Essai sur les origines du Judaïsme 1992 → 2457.

9810 **Noy** D., Jewish inscriptions I (before 70 228 items, 68 not in Frey).
C 1993, Univ. xxii-385 p.; 32 pl. £60. – ᴿJTS 45 (1994) 701-4 (P. W. *van
der Horst*).

9810* **Otzen** B. Judaism in antiquity 1990 → 6,a155.b733*b*; 7,9967: ᴿBZ 38
(1994) 318s (J. *Maier*).

9811 **Paul** André, Il giudaismo antico e la Bibbia. Bo 1993, Dehoniane.
358 p. – ᴿTeresianum 45 (1994) 634 (V. *Pasquetto*).

9812 **Porton** Gary D., The stranger within your gates; converts and conversion in rabbinic literature: HistJud. Ch 1994, Univ. xiii-410. 0-226-
67586-6.

9813 *Rajak* Tessa, *Noy* David, Archisynagogoi; office, title, and social status
in the Greek-Jewish synagogue: JRS 83 (1993) 75-93.

9813* **Sacchi** Paolo, Storia del Secondo Tempio; Israele tra VI secolo a.C. e I
secolo d.C.: Storia. T 1994, SEI. xvii-529 p. Lᵐ 60. 88-05-05377-5.

9814 **Sanders** E. P., Judaism, practice and belief 63 B.C.E. – 66 C.E. 1992
→ 8,a480; 9,10702: ᴿTorJT 10 (1994) 113-5 (W. O. *McCready*).

9815 **Schiffman** Lawrence H., From text to tradition; a history of Second
Temple and rabbinic Judaism. 1991 → 7,9970; 9,10705 ... ᴿRB 101 (1994)
593-605 (E. *Nodet*), 605-8 sur *Cohen* S., *Will-Orrieux*.

9816 **Schubert** Kurt, Die Religion des Judentums 1992 → 8,a482; 9,10706:
ᴿEntschluss 48,5 (1993) 44 (Clara *Wilflinger*); KIsr 9 (1994) 97 (Julie
Kirchberg); LebZeug 47 (1992) 154 (B. *Neumann*).

9817 *Schultz* Joseph P., From sacred space [ELIADE M.; SMITH J. Z.] to sacred
object [Temple, Ark] to sacred person [rabbinic, mystical] in Jewish
antiquity: Shofar 12 (Purdue 1993) 28-37 [< OTAbs 17, p. 479].

9818 **Sperber** Daniel, Magic and folklore in rabbinic literature [in Eng.]:
StNELCu. Ramat Gan 1994, Bar-Ilan Univ. 256 p. 965-236-165-3.

9819 **Stemberger** Günter, Il giudaismo classico 1991 → 8,a484; 9,10709:
ᴿProtestantesimo 49 (1994) 179s (B. *Corsani*).

9820 **Stemberger** Günter, Studien zum rabbinischen Judentum: SBAufs 10.
Stu 1990, KBW. 416 p. DM 48. 3-460-06101-4. – ᴿBZ 38 (1994) 319s (J.
Maier); TLZ 119 (1994) 316s (L. *Wächter*).

9821 **Stern** Sacha, Jewish identity in early rabbinic writings: ArbGJU 23.
Leiden 1994, Brill. xxxix-269 p. 90-04-10012-1 [BL 95,169, N. de
Lange].

9821* *Trautner-Kromann* Hanne, Moderne Judaistik: SvTKv 70 (1994) 106-
113; Eng. 113.

9822 ᴱ**Trigano** Shmuel, La société juive à travers l'histoire. P 1992s, Fayard.
I. 782 p.; II. 633 p.; III, 1993: 594 p. IV. 791 p. – ᴿArchivScSocR 39,86
(1994) 310s (Régine *Azria*).

9823 **Will** É., *Orrieux* C., 'Prosélytisme' ... erreur 1992 ➤ 8,2486; 6,10710; ᴿAmHR 99 (1994) 867s (W.C. *Jordan*); Biblica 75 (1994) 295-8 (D.J. *Harrington*); RBgPg 72 (1994) 187s (J. *Klener*).

K6   **Mišna,** *tosepta; Tannaim.*

9824 *a) Cohen* Shaye J.D., Is 'proselyte baptism' mentioned in the Mishnah? [Pes 8,8; Eduyot 5,2]; – *b) Goldenberg* Robert, Did the Amoraim see Christianity as something new?; – *c) Neusner* Jacob, What the Rabbis thought; a method and a result; one statement on prophecy in rabbinic Judaism; – *d) Washofsky* Mark, Responses and rhetoric; on law, literature and the rabbinic decision; – *e) Adler* William, Ad verbum or ad sensum; the Christianization of a Latin translation formula in the fourth century: ➤ 133, ᶠWACHOLDER B.Z. 1994, 278-292 / 293-302 / 303-320 / 360-409 / 321-348.

9824* *Friedman* Shamma, The primacy of Tosefta in Mishnah-Tosefta parallels; Shabbat 16,1 *kol kitbe ha-qodeš*: Tarbiz 62 (1992s) 313-338; Eng. V-VI.

9825 ᵀᴱ**Kirschner** Robert, Baraita de-Melekhet ha-Mishkan: HUC mg 15. Cincinnati 1992, HUC. xiii-318 p. – ᴿCritRR 6 (1993) 416s (G.A. *Anderson*).

9826 *Langer* Gerhard, Zum Vermögensrecht von Frauen in der Ehe am Beispiel der Mischna- und Tosefta-Traktates Ketubbot: Kairos 34s (1992s) 27-63.

9827 **Lapin** Hayim, Text, money and law; the social and literary background of Mishnah tractate Baba⁵ Meṣiᵃ⁵: diss. Columbia, ᴰ*Halivni* D. NY 1994. 492 p. 94-21367. – DissA 55 (1994s) p. 688.

9828 *Mayer* Günter, Mischna: ➤ 517, TRE 23 (1994) 13-18.

9829 *Morfino* Mauro M., Appunti per una metodologia di approccio alla letteratura rabbinica: TSard 2 (1993) 31-59.

9830 **Neusner** Jacob, The Judaism behind the texts; the generative premises of rabbinic literature, 1. The Mishnah; A. the division of agriculture: SFLJud 89. Atlanta 1993, Scholars. xlviii-192 p. 1-55540-915-6 [B: -6-4].

9831 **Neusner** Jacob, Judaism without Christianity; an introduction to the system of the Mishnah 1991 ➤ 7,7981 ... 9,10720: ᴿBtS 150 (1993) 369s (R.A. *Taylor*).

9832 **Neusner** Jacob, The Mishnah; introduction and reader. Ph 1992, Trinity. xii-226 p. $17 pa. – ᴿCritRR 6 (1993) 424-6 (R.A. *Kugler*: not for the uninitiated; typos).

9833 **Neusner** Jacob, Rabbinic political theory; religion and politics in the Mishnah 1991 ➤ 7,9985; 8,a495: ᴿCritRR 5 (1992) 380-2 (R.A. *Kugler*).

9834 *a) Neusner* Jacob, The Greco-Roman philosophy of Judaism; the Mishnah in context; – *b) Porton* Gary G., Gentiles and Israelites in Mishnah-Tosefta': a study in ethnicity: ➤ 9,84, ᶠLEVEY S., Bits of honey 1993, 63-92 / 93-111.

9835 *Perani* Mauro, *Stemberger* Günter, Nuova luce sulla tradizione manoscritta della Tosefta; i frammenti rinvenuti a Bologna: Henoch 16 (1994) 227-250; Eng. 251; foto 252.

9835* *Perani* Mauro, Un frammento della *Mišnâ* (*Ketubbôt*) nell'archivio di stato di Modena: Sefarad 54 (1994) 363-372; español Eng. 373; 374s, 2 fot.

9836 **Pettit** Peter A., 'As it is said'; the place of Scripture citation in the Mishna: diss. ᴰ*Sanders* J. Claremont 1992. – RTLv 26,534.

9837 **Schlüter** M., Auf welche Weise wurde die Mishna geschrieben? Das Antwortschreiben des Rav Sherira Gaon [Hab. B Freie Univ. 1990]: TStMdvJ 9. Tü 1993, Mohr. x-389-70*p. DM 198. 3-16-146064-2 [NTAbs 38, p.498].

9837* *Sicker* Martin, A political metaphor in biblical and rabbinic literature [HANINA in Mishna Avot, 'welfare of the government']: Judaism 40 (1991) 208-214.

9838 **Zeidman** Reena L., A view of celebrations in early Judaism; Tosefta Avodah Zarah: diss. Toronto, ᴰFox H. 1992. – SR 22 (1993) 538.

9838* **Zlotnick** Dov, The iron pillar — Mishnah; redaction, form and intent. J 1985, Bialik. – ᴿJudaism 40 (1991) 125-8 (A. *Goldberg*: 'for the non-Hebrew reader as well as for one who reads unpointed Hebrew easily').

K6.5 **Talmud; midraš.**

9839 *Abrams* J. Z., Incorporating Christian symbols into Judaism; the case of Midrash Eleh Ezkerah: CCAR 40,3 (1990) 11-20 [< NTAbs 38,254].

9839* **Ben-Menahem** Hanina, Judicial deviation in talmudical law; governed by men, not by rules: Boston Univ. Law School, Jewish Law in Context 1. Chur/L/NY 1991, Harwood. xi-220 p. $52. – ᴿJJS 45 (1994) 144s (L. *Jacobs*, also on cognates).

9840 ᴱ**Bialik** H., *Ravnitzky* Y., Book of legends ... Talmud, Midrash 1992 →9,10728: ᴿMidstream 40,1 (1994) 41s (J. *Sloan*).

9841 **Boyarin** Daniel, Intertextuality and the reading of midrash 1990 →7, 9988; 9,10729: ᴿCritRR 5 (1992) 356-9 (Tz. *Zahavy*); JRel 74 (1994) 426s (R. S. *Sarason*); RLitND 24,1 (1995) 75-80 (G. J. *Bruns*).

9842 *Cohen* Raphaël, Le Talmud, clef de la Tora: Études 381 (1994) 525-533.

9843 **Elman** Yaakov, Authority and tradition; Toseftan baraitot in Talmudic Babylonia [*Epstein* J.; *Albeck* C.]. Hoboken 1994, KTAV. xiv-328 p. $39.50. 0-88125-425-8. – ᴿOTAbs 17 (1994) 683 (L. H. *Feldman*: could not have been drawn from an already redacted Tosefta).

9843* [(*Feldman* S.) on SNYDER Graydon F., Chicago United Church of Christ seminary prof. condemned by a faculty committee] Unintended sex leads to unintended fall [vice versa in Baba Kamma 27s]; how a story from the Talmud tainted a Bible professor with a charge of sexual harassment: BR 10,4 (1994) 36-39.

9844 **Fishbane** Simcha, The method and meaning of the [I. KAGAN 1993] midrash Berurah. Hoboken 1991, KTAV. 183 p. – ᴿAJS 19 (1994) 106-8 (M. *Washofsky*).

9845 **Fraenkel** Yonah, ❶ *Darkhei* ... Ways of Haggada and Midrash. Givatayim 1991, Yad ha-Talmud. 777 p. – ᴿProoftexts 14 (1994) 189-204 (R. *Kalmin*).

9846 *Gero* Stephen, The stern master and his wayward disciple; a 'Jesus' story in the Talmud and in Christian hagiography: JStJud 25 (1994) 297-311.

9847 **Gilat** Yitzhak D., ❶ Studies in the development of the Halakha. Ramat-Gan 1994=1992, Bar-Ilan Univ. 420 p. 965-226-123-8.

9848 *Goshen-Gottstein* Alon, Testaments in rabbinic literature; transformations of a genre: JStJud 25 (1994) 222-251.

9849 **Heller** Marvin J., Printing the Talmud; a history of the earliest printed editions of the Talmud. Brooklyn 1992, Am hasefer xvi-448 p. 0-9626445-0-1. – ᴿJStJud 25 (1994) 95s (J. *Neusner*: magnificent erudition).

9850 **Hezser** C., Form, function, and historical significance of the rabbinic story in Yerushalmi Nezīqīn: TStAJud 37. Tü 1993, Mohr. xi-437 p. DM 228. 3-16-146148-7 [NTAbs 38, p. 490].

9851 **Jacobs** Louis, Structure and form in the Babylonian Talmud 1991 → 9,10736: RBijdragen 55 (1994) 437 (J. van *Ruiten*); CritRR 5 (1992) 369-371 (J. *Neusner*: slipshod) & 6 (1993) 416-8 (R. *Kalmin*: expert up to 1975).

9852 *Kalmin* Richard, Talmudic portrayals of [disputative] relationships between rabbis; Amoraic or pseudepigraphic?: AJS 17 (1992) 165-197.

9852* *a) Kister* Menahem, Observations on aspects of exegesis, tradition, and theology in Midrash, pseudepigrapha, and other Jewish writings; – *b) Visotzky* Burton L., The conversation of palm trees; – *c) Bowley* James E., The compositions of Abraham; – *d) Dalley* Stephanie, The tale of Bulūqiya and the Alexander Romance in Jewish and Sufi mystical circles; – *e) Urowitz-Freudenstein* Anna, Pseudepigraphic support of pseudepigraphical sources; the case of Pirqe de Rabbi Eliezer: → 256*. Tracing the threads 1994, 1-34 / 203-214 / 215-238 / 239-269 / 35-53.

9853 *Kamesar* Adam, The evaluation of the narrative aggada in Greek and Latin patristic literature: JTS 45 (1994) 37-71.

9854 **Kraemer** David, The mind of the Talmud 1990 → 7,9996 ... 9,10739: RCritRR 5 (1992) 371-3 (R. A. *Kugler*).

9855 *Kraemer* David, The intended reader as a key to interpreting the Bavli: Prooftexts 13 (1993) 125-140.

9856 **Lachs** S. T., Humanism in Talmud and Midrash. Rutherford/Toronto 1993, F. Dickinson Univ. / Assoc. Univ. Pr. 150 p. 0-8386-3468-0 [NTAbs 38, p. 322].

9857 *Levenson* Alan T., Joseph B. SOLOVEITCHIK's 'The halachic mind' [1944, published 1986]; a liberal critique and appreciation: CCAR 41,1 (1994) 55-63.

9858 **Licht** Chaim, Ten legends of the sages; the image of the sage in rabbinic literature. Hoboken 1991, KTAV. xiv-221 p. $25. – RCritRR 6 (1993) 417s (Naomi *Janowitz*).

9859 **Lightstone** Jack N., The rhetoric of the Babylonian Talmud, its social meaning and context: St/Ét ChrJud 6. Waterloo ON 1994, W. Laurier Univ. xix-317 p.; bibliog. 297-307. 0-88920-238-9.

9860 **Loopik** Marcus van, The way of the sages 1991 → 7,9998; 9,10742: RCritRR 5 (1992) 376-8 (M. S. *Jaffee*: admirable toil, badly edited); Salesianum 55 (1993) 179s (R. *Vicent*).

9861 *Nador* Georg, Paradox: ein Fachbegriff der griechischen Logik im Midrasch [...fehlt im Stichwort des Hist. Wörterbuch der Philosophie. E*Ritter* J. & G.]: Sefarad 53 (1993) 371-5.

9861* *Neusner* Jacob, The documentary history of Judaism and the problem of dating sayings: Religion 23 (K 1993) 295-314 [< Judaica 50,181].

9862 **Neusner** Jacob, Judaism states its theology, the Talmudic re-presentation: SFLJud 88. Atlanta 1993, Scholars. xiii-286 p. $75. 1-55540-890-7. [NTAbs 38, p. 495].

9863 *Neusner* Jacob, Das Problem des Babylonischen Talmud als Literatur; der Bavli und seine Quellen: Kairos 34s (1992s) 64-74.

9864 **Neusner** Jacob, Scripture and Midrash in Judaism I: JudUmw (= Realms of Judaism) 47. Fra 1994, Lang. 307 p. 3-631-46461-4.

9865 **Neusner** Jacob, The Talmud of Babylonia, an American translation: since the complete listing given in → 9,10758 has appeared 18-C Brown-Jud 269.

9866 **Neusner** Jacob, The Talmud; a close encounter 1991 ➤ 8,a529: ᴿCritRR 6 (1993) 420-2 (P.V.M. *Flesher*); Henoch 16 (1994) 361-5 (M. *Pesce*, 11-22).

9866* *Rovner* Jay, Rhetorical strategy and dialectical necessity in the Babylonian Talmud; the case of Kiddushin 34a-35a: HUCA 65 (1994) 177-231.

9867 *a*) *Rubinkiewicz* Ryszard, ❷ Midrash as exegesis; – *b*) *Ołów* Antoni J., ❷ The meaning of *qara' bᵉ-šem* YHWH in the OT and the intertestamental literature; – *c*) *Pisarek* Stanisław, ❷ The Jewish criticism of Christian Bible manuals: ➤ 9,410, ᴱ*Stachowiak* L, Sympozjum 1992, ColcT 63,3 (1993) 11-26 / 79-83 / 69-78.

9868 ᵀᴱ**Salzer** Israël, Le Talmud, traité Ḥaguiga: Les Dix Paroles, 1991 ➤ 7,a6*: ᴿRTPhil 126 (1994) 75 (J. *Borel*).

9868* *Samely* Alexander, Is Targumic Aramaic rabbinic Hebrew? A reflection on midrashic and targumic rewording of Scripture: JJS 45 (1994) 92-100.

9869 ᴱ**Schäfer** Peter, *al.*, Synopse zum Talmud Yerushalmi 1/1s Zera'im: Berakhot, Pe'a: TStAntJ 31, 1991 ➤ 8,a538; 9,10763: ᴿHenoch 16 (1994) 133-6 (B. *Chiesa*); JSS 39 (1994) 328-330 (Annelies *Kuyt*); Salesianum 56 (1994) 159s (R. *Vicent*).

9870 **Schäfer** Peter, **Becker** Hans-Jürgen, Synopse zum Talmud Y 1/3-5 1992 ➤ 8,a538; 9,10764: ᴿSalesianum 56 (1994) 790 (R. *Vicent*, también sobre 1/6-11).

9871 **Sky** H. I., Redevelopment of the office of Hazzan through the talmudic period. SF 1992, Mellen Research Univ. xiii-216 p. $70. 0-7734-9823-0 [NTAbs 37, p. 476].

9872 **Stemberger** G., Einleitung in Talmud und Midrasch⁸ʳᵉᵛ 1992 ➤ 8,a542; 9,10769: ᴿRivB 42 (1994) 479s (M. *Perani*).

9873 (*Strack*) **Stemberger**, Introduction to the Talmud, ᵀ*Bockmuehl* M. 1991 ➤ 7,a9*; 8,a544: ᴿCritRR 6 (1993) 429-432 (A. J. *Saldarini*); ScotJT 47 (1994) 276 (P. *Joyce*); ScripB 23,1 (1993) 15s (A. *Gelston*).

9874 **Stemberger** Günter, Midrasch; vom Umgang der Rabbinen mit der Bibel 1989 ➤ 5,al93 ... 8,a544: ᴿBijdragen 55 (1994) 82s (J. van *Ruiten*).

9875 **Stemberger** Günter, Il midrash; uso rabbinico della Bibbia; introduzione, testi, commenti: StRel. Bo 1992, Dehoniane. 336 p. Lᵐ 50. 88-10-40790-3. – ᴿCC 145 (1994,4) 621-3 (G. L. *Prato*).

9876 *a*) *Stern* Sacha, Attribution and authorship in the Babylonian Talmud; – *b*) *Kamesar* Adam, The narrative Aggada as seen from the Graeco-Latin perspective: JJS 45 (1994) 28-51 / 52-70.

9876* **Taradach** Madeleine, Le Midrash 1991 ➤ 7,a13 ... 9,10772: ᴿSalesianum 55 (1993) 185s (R. *Vicent*).

9877 **Taradach** M. El Mídrash, Barc 1989 ➤ 5,a195; 6,a231: ᴿQVidCr 160 (1992) 117s (D. *Roure*).

9878 *Tendler* M. D., *Rosner* F., Quality and sanctity of life in the Talmud and the Midrash: Tradition 28,1 (1993) 18-27 [< NTAbs 38, p. 435].

9879 *Ulmer* Rivka, Postmoderne talmudische Hermeneutik: ZRGg 46 (1994) 352-365.

9880 **Wald** Stephen G., ❸ The Babylonian Talmud, Masechet Pesahim 3, a critical edition and comprehensive commentary: diss. Jewish Theol. Sem. ᴰ*Friedman* S. NY 1994. 664 p. 95-11743. – DissA 55 (1994s) p. 3851.

9881 ᵀᴱ **Zahavy** Tzvee, Talmud 6, An American ᵀ[➤ 9866] 30A Hullin 1-2 1992 ➤ 9,10776: ᴿJSS 39 (1994) 330-2 (L. *Jacobs*).

ᴋ7.1 Judaismus mediaevalis, *generalia*.

9881* **Blasco Martínez** Asunción, La judería de Zaragoza en el siglo XIV. Zaragoza 1988, Inst. Fernando. 322 p. – ᴿSefarad 54 (1994) 195s (D. *Romano*).

9882 **Brann** Ross, The compunctious poet 1991 → 9,10782: ᴿJAOS 113 (1993) 125-7 (R. P. *Scheindlin*).
9883 **Carrete** C., El judaísmo español y la Inquisición: Sefarad 7. M 1992, Mapfre. 338 p. – ᴿComSev 26 (1993) 398s (M. *Sánchez*).
9884 ᴱ**Casanovas Miró** Jordi, Haggadah de Poblet. Barc 1993, Ripedras. 74 p.; 76 facsim. – ᴿSefarad 54 (1994) 196 (M. José *Cano*).
9885 **Cohen** J. Simcha, The 613th commandment; an analysis of the Mitzvah to write a Sefer Torah Derush VeChiddush). Northvale NJ 1994, Aronson. [viii-] 162 p. 1-56821-249-6.
9886 **Cohen** Mark R., Under crescent and cross; the Jews in the Middle Ages. Princeton 1994, Univ. xxi-280 p. $30 [TS 56, 398, W. V. *Hudon*; RelStR 21,158, M. R. *Shapiro*].
9887 **Cohen Sarano** Matilde, Le storie del re Salomone, e le leggende del profeta Elia; e racconti di re e sultani, e di ricchi e mendicanti, ecc.ecc.: Il filo rosso. Mi 1993, Sansoni. xiv-171 p. 88-383-1497-3.
9888 **Faur** José, In the shadow of history; Jews and conversos at the dawn of modernity 1992 → 9,a551: ᴿAJS 19 (1994) 263-5 (Renée L. *Melammed*: admirably bold and provocative); Sefarad 54 (1994) 201-3 (N. *Roth*, in Spanish; intrigued despite the errors and overassurance).
9889 **Funkenstein** Amos, Perceptions of Jewish history: Centennial. Berkeley 1993, Univ. California. xiii-390 p. $35. – ᴿAmHR 99 (1994) 866 (J. M. *Harris*).
9890 **Gampel** B., Last Jews ... Iberian 1989 → 8,a617; 9,10858: ᴿEngHR 109 (1994) 423s (J. *Edwards*).
9891 **Gay** Ruth, Geschichte der Juden in Deutschland von der Römerzeit bis zum zweiten Weltkrieg, ᵀ*Spiel* Christian. Mü 1993, Beck. 280 p.; 274 fig.; 20 color. pl. DM 78. – ᴿEntschluss 49,9s (1994) 41 (H. *Brandt*).
9891* **Gay** Ruth, The Jews of Germany [c. 345-1945]; a historical portrait, ᵀ*Spiel* Christian. NHv 1992, Yale Univ. xiii-297 p. 277 fig.; 20 color pl. $35. – ᴿCritRR 6 (1993) 445-7 (Harriet *Friedenreich*: beautiful but also readable, accentuating the positive); Judaica 50 (1994) 164s (J. *Kurz*).
9892 **Graboïs** Arieh, Les sources hébraïques médiévales II. Les commentaires exégétiques: Typologie des Sources du Moyen Âge occidental. Turnhout 1993, Brepols. 65 p. Fb 750. 2-503-36066-1. – ᴿBL (1994) 59s (N.R.M. *de Lange*).
9893 *a*) *Gross* Abraham, The expulsion and the search for the ten tribes; – *b*) *Lasker* Daniel J., Judaism Jewish-Christian polemics in light of the expulsion from Spain; – *c*) *Melammed* Renée L., Woman in (post-1492) Spanish crypto-Jewish society; – *d*) *Nahon* Gérard, The impact of the expulsion from Spain on the Jewish community of pre-revolutionary France, 1550-1791; ᵀ*Greif* Deborah; – *e*) *Schachter* Jacob J., Echoes of the Spanish expulsion in eighteenth century Germany; the Bᴀᴇʀ thesis revisited; Judaism 41 (1992) 130-148 / 149-155 / 136-168 / 169-179 / 180-9.
9894 **Hayoun** Maurice-Ruben, L'exégèse philosophique dans le judaïsme médièval: TStMdvJ 7. Tü 1992, Mohr. xii-312 p. 3-16-145816-8. – ᴿRTPhil 126 (1994) 282 (J. *Borel*); Salesianum 56 (1994) 593 (P. T. *Stella*).
9895 **Idel** Moshe, Le Golem, ᵀ*Aslanoff* Cyrille. P 1992, Cerf. 426 p. F 275. 2-204-04583-7. – ᴿÉTRel 68 (1993) 429 (Jeanne M. *Léonard*).
9896 *Jiménez Garnica* Ana M., La coexistencia con los judíos en el reino de Tolosa [siglo v]: Gerión 12 (1994) 269-278.
9897 **Kanarfogel** Ephraim, Jewish education and society in the Middle Ages 1992 → 9,10790; ᴿRHR 211 (1994) 105s (S. *Schwarzfuchs*).
9898 ᴱ**Kedourie** E., Los judíos de España, la diaspora sefardi desde 1492. Barc 1992, Critica. 250 p. – ᴿComSev 26 (1993) 149 (M. *Sánchez*).

9899 a) *Lacave* José Luis, The final disposition of the synagogues and other Jewish communal property after the expulsion, ᵀ*Morales* Wilfredo; – b) *Popkin* Richard H., Jewish Christians and Christian Jews in Spain, 1492 and after; – c) *David* Benjamin, An introduction to the economic history of the Iberian diaspora in the Mediterranean; – d) *Stow* Kenneth R., Ethnic rivalry or melting pot; the 'edot' in the Roman ghetto: Judaism 41 (1992) 241-7 / 248-267 / 268-285 / 286-296.

9900 ᴱ**Menascé** Esther Fintz, L'ebreo errante; metamorfosi di un mito: Acme Quad 21. Mi 1993, Ed. Universitario. 410 p. 88-205-0745-5.

9901 **Minty** Mary, ❶ Kiddush ha-Shem [as alternative to conversion after 1096, martyrdom, including killing of themselves, their families, other Jews] in German Christian eyes in the Middle Ages: Zion 59 (1994) 209-266 (513s) Eng. XII-XIV [*Fleischer* E., *Breuer* M., 267-316.317-324 against I. YUVAL's interpretation in 58 (1993) 33-90].

9902 **Newby** Gordon D., A history of the Jews of Arabia 1988 → 7,a28 ... 9,10794: ᴿAJS 17 (1992) 314-6 (N. A. *Stillman*); JSS 38 (1993) 161-4 (S. *Firestone*).

9903 **Pagis** Dan, Hebrew poetry of the Middle Ages and the Renaissance (Taubman Lectures, 2). Berkeley 1991, Univ. California. xvi-84 p. $22.50. – ᴿSpeculum 69 (1994) 231-4 (Judith A. *Kates*).

9904 *Perani* Mauro, I manoscritti ebraici della 'Genîzâ italiana' [p. 103-118]; frammenti di una traduzione sconosciuta del *Sefer ha-Šorašim* di Yônâ IBN ĞANAḤ [p. 118-141]: Sefarad 53 (1993) 103-141; 6 pl.; Eng. 142.

9905 ᴱ**Rodríguez de Coro** F., Los judíos: Besaide 3. Vitoria 1992, Fund. Sancho. 478 p. – ᴿComSev 26 (1993) 398 (M. *Sánchez*).

9906 **Romano** David, La ciencia hispanojudía: Sefarad col. 17/2. M 1992, Mapfre. 264 p. – ᴿSefarad 53 (1993) 414s (J. L. *Lacave*).

9907 **Schippers** Arie, Spanish Hebrew poetry and the Arabic literary tradition; Arabic themes in Hebrew Andalusian poetry: MdvIberianTSt 7. Leiden 1994, Brill. xiv-376 p. 90-04-09869-0.

9908 **Scheindlein** Raymond P., The gazelle; medieval Hebrew poems on God, Israel, and the soul. Ph 1991, Jewish Publ. Soc. xi-274 p. – ᴿSpeculum 69 (1994) 561-3 (R. *Brann*).

9908* *Schwarz* Howard, The quest for the lost princess; transition and change in Jewish lore: Judaism 43 (1994) 240-257.

9909 **Sirat** Colette, La filosofia ebraica medievale [1983], ᵀᴱ*Chiesa* B. 1990 → 8,a558; 9,10798: ᴿSefarad 54 (1993) 437s (C. del *Valle*).

9910 **Stow** Kenneth R., Alienated minority; the Jews of medieval Latin Europe 1992 → 9,10800: ᴿAmHR 99 (1994) 210 (G. I. *Langmuir*); CathHR 80 (1994) 133 (E. A. *Synan*); JJS 46 (1994) 313s (D. J. *Lasker*); Speculum 69 (1994) 893-5 (S. *Bowman*); TS 54 (1993) 598 (J. T. *Pawlikowski*).

9910* *Teodor* Pompilu, The history of Jews in Romanian historiography: Studia Judaica (Cluj-Napoca 1993) 36-43 [< Judaica 50,63].

9911 *Yuval* I., ❶ defense of his 'Blood libel' explanation against E. *Fleischer*, M. *Breuer*, J. *Cohen*, A. *Grossman*: Zion 59 (1994) 351-414 [267-317-325-343-350]; Eng. XVII-XX [XIV-XVII].

K7.2 Maimonides.

9912 *Benor* Ehud Z., a) Petition and contemplation in Maimonides' conception of prayer: Religion 24,1 (L 1994) 59-66 [< ZIT 94,258]: – b) Perspectives on Maimonides [6 books 1988-91]: RelStR 20 (1994) 189-195.

9913 **Ben-Šem** Meir D., ❶ *Torat ha-Rambam*; Maimonides, Commentary on the Bible. J 1987-, H. Vagshel.

9914 *Bland* Kalman P., Medieval Jewish aesthetics; Maimonides, body, and Scripture in Profiat DURAN [1360-1414]: JHistId 54 (1993) 533-559.

9914* **[Debenedetti] Stow** S., Jehudàh ben Mošèh ben Danie'èl ROMANO, la chiarificazione in volgare delle 'espressioni difficili' ricorrenti nel Mišnèh Toràh di Mosè Maimonide: RicGiudItal 2/1. R 1990, Carucci; xi-277 p. — 2/2. T 1993, Zamorani; 368 p. – ᴿHenoch 16 (1994) 366-9 (M. *Zonta*).

9915 **Fox** M., Interpreting Maimonides 1990 → 6,a259 ... 9,10806:   ᴿMidstream 39,2 (1993) 46-48 (A. *Ages*).

9916 **Harris** Jay M., Nachman KROCHMAL, Guiding the perplexed of the modern age. NYU 1991. xvi-336 p.

9917 *Herrera* Robert A., El entendimiento agente en Maïmonides y Santo TOMÁS; secuelas para la interpretación de la profecía: CiuD 206 (1993) 859-871.

9918 ᴱ**Hyman** Arthur, Maimonidean studies 1990 → 7,a38 [2. 1991 → 9, 10809]: ᴿSefarad 54 (1994) 422s (C. del *Valle*).

9919 **Iglesias** Antelo, [Maimonides; BEN EZRA más diez] Judíos españoles de la Edad de Oro (siglos XI-XII); semblanzas, antología y glosario: Amigos de Sefarad. M 1991, Univ. Distancia. 436 p. – ᴿSefarad 53 (1993) 399 (M. *Gómez Aranda*).

9919* *Kaplan* Lawrence, The love of God in Maimonides and Rav KOOK: Judaism 43 (1994) 227-239.

9920 **Kellner** M., Maimonides 1991 → 9,10811:   ᴿCritRR 6 (1993) 437-9 (J. A. *Buijs*).

9921 *Kreisel* Howard, Imitatio Dei in Maimonides' Guide of the Perplexed: AJS 19 (1994) 169-211.

9922 *Laurenti* Joseph L., La colección de Mošeh ben Maimón en la Biblioteca Universitaria de Illinois, Urbana; ediciones de los siglos XVI y XVII: Sefarad 54 (1994) 387-397; Eng. 398.

9923 **Leibovitz** Yechayahou, La foi de Maïmonide, ᵀᴱ*Banon* D. P 1992, Cerf. 131 p. – ᴿÉTRel 68 (1993) 431s (Jeanne M. *Léonard*); NRT 116 (1994) 282s (L.-J. *Renard*); ScripTPamp 26 (1994) 838s (J. M. *Odero*).

9924 *Loopik* M. van, Maimonides over de Tora; Israël en de volkeren: Ter Herkenning 21,1 (1993) 16-34 [< GerefTTs 93,201].

9925 *Maier* Johann, Mose ben Maimon (1138-1204): → 517, TRE 23 (1994) 357-362.

9926 *Pangallo* Mario, Il posto della metafisica nel sapere umano; il pensiero di Maimonide e il suo influsso su S. Tommaso d'AQUINO: Gregorianum 74 (1993) 331-352; Eng. 352.

9926* ᴱ**Pelaez del Rosal** Jesús, Sobre la vida y obra de Maimonidés 1995/91 → 8,a41:   ᴿJSS 39 (1994) 123-5 (S. C. *Reif*).

9927 *Sagal* Paul T., Maimonides, natural law and medieval Jewish philosophy: ScotJR 12 (1991) 29-45.

9928 **Seeskin** Kenneth, Maimonides; a guide for today's perplexed. West Orange NJ 1991, Behrman. 141 p. – ᴿCCAR 41,4 (1994) 91-94 (R. C. *Klein*).

9928* *Tamani* Giuliano, La versione ebraica del Compendio della logica di al-FARABI [pensatore stimato da Maimonide]; la retorica e la poetica: Henoch 16 (1994) 253-268; Eng. 269.

9929 **Weiss** Raymond L., Maimonides' ethics 1991 → 8,a578; 9,10819:   ᴿCrit-

RR 6 (1993) 441-4 (T. *Kleven*); JRel 74 (1994) 117s (D. H. *Frank*); Speculum 69 (1994) 581-3 (H. *Kreisel*).

K7.3 Alii magistri Judaismi mediaevalis.

9929* SAADYA: *a*) *Schlossberg* Eliezer, Ten observations on rhetoric and expression by Saadia Gaon: JSS 38 (1993) 269-277; – *b*) *Sysling* Harry, Saadya's portrayal of the Messiah Ben Joseph: Nordisk Judaistik 13 (Åbo 1992) ['73-72' in Judaica 49,61].

9930 RASHI: URBACH E. E., mem. Rashi 1040-1990, ᴱSed-Rajna Gabrielle 1990/3 ➤ 9,417: ᴿBL (1994) 152s (R. *Loewe*); Sefarad 54 (1994) 431-7 (M. *Gómez Aranda*).

9931 *Heide* Albert van der, Der Verschwundene Drasch — Züge zur Raschiforschung in zwei Jahrhunderten: Kairos 32s (1990s) 238-246.

9932 *Malherbe* J. S., Medieval Jewish exegesis; an introduction to six forgotten colleagues [RASHI, RASHBAM, IBN EZRA, KIMHI, NAHMANIDES, ABRAVANEL]: ➤ 327, ODENDAAL D. mem., OTEssays 7,4 (1991/4) 221-235.

9933 GERSONIDES; *Rothschild* Jean-Pierre, Autour de Gersonide: RÉJ 153 (1994) 303-326.

9934 *Kellner* Menachem, Gersonides on the role of the active intellect in human cognition: HUCA 65 (1994) 233-259.

9934* *Zonta* Mauro, Gersonides, 'philosopher-scientist'; some recent books [WEIL O. 1991; ᴱDAHAN G. 1988/91; ᴱFREUDENTHAL G. 1988/92]: Henoch 16 (1994) 335-345.

9935 NACHMANIDES; RAMBAN: *Kravitz* Leonard S., Mose ben Nachman (1194-1270): ➤ 517, TRE 23 (1994) 362-5.

9935* **Novak** David, The theology of Nachmanides systematically presented. Atlanta 1993, Scholars. 149 p. $60. – ᴿJudaism 43 (1994) 320-5 (A. J. *Yuter*).

9936 RADAK: **Cohen** Mordechai Z., Radak's contribution to the tradition of figurative biblical exegesis [KIMHI, BEN EZRA]: diss. ᴰ*Maori* Y. Yeshiva Univ. NY 1994. 346 p. 95-09708. – DissA 55 (1994s) 3878.

9936* Roš 1250-1327: **Richter** Daniel, Die Responsen des Rabbi Ascher ben Jechiel (Rosch) [Diss.]: Studien zur Rechtsgeschichte 23. Z 1992. xv-116 p. Fs 36. – ᴿJudaica 50 (1994) 53s (S. *Schreiner*).

9937 IBN EZRA: ᴱ**Levin** M., Itzhaki Masha, ❻ Studies in the works of Abraham ibn Ezra: Te'uda 8. TA 1992, Univ. Rosenberg School. xviii-214 p.; 5 pl. – ᴿBO 51 (1994) 651-4 (R. *Kasher*); VT 44 (1994) 574 (S. C. *Reif*).

9938 **Netzer** Nissan, ❻ 'The patterns of the nouns vary' — a principle and its usage in Ben-Ezra's commentary on the Bible: HUCA 65 (1994) ❻ 1-22.

9939 IBN GABIROL *Scheindlin* Raymond P., Ibn Gabirol's religious poetry and Sufi poetry: Sefarad 54 (1994) 109-141; Eng. 142 [his innovations cannot be traced to Sufi influence].

9940 FALAQUERA: **Jospe** Raphael, Torah and Sophia ... ibn Falaquera 1988 ➤ 7,a54: ᴿAJS 17 (1992) 100-4 (S. *Harvey*).

9941 *Chiesa* Bruno, *Rigo* Caterina, La traduzione manoscritta del *seper ha-ma'alot* di Shem Tob ibn Falaquera e una citazione ignorata della *Risāl fī ism al-falsafa* di Al-Fārābī: Sefarad 53 (1993) 3-15; Eng. 15.

9942 *Zonta* Mauro, Shem Tob ibn Falaquera e la filología ebraica medievale; a proposito di [HARVEY S. 1987; ᴱDROSSAART LULOFS H. & POORTMAN E., Nicolaus DAMASCENUS (De plantis ᵀ*Qalonymos* & Falaquera) 1989]: Sefarad 53 (1993) 321-342; Eng. 343.

9943 *Einbinder* Susan E., [1345 Shem Tov ARDUTIEL, The battle of the] Pen and scissors; a medieval debate: HUCA 65 (1994) 261-278.

K7.4 *Qabbalâ, Zohar, Merkabâ* — Jewish mysticism.

9944 *Benaïm-Ouaknine* Esther, *Elbaz* Robert, [KALONYMOS 1322] *Eben Bohan* ou l'émergence d'un nouvel espace discursif: Sefarad 54 (1994) 31-40.

9944* *Davila* James R., Prolegomena to a critical edition of the Hekhalot Rabbati: JJS 45 (1994) 208-226.

9946 *a*) *Davila* James R., The Hekhalot literature and shamanism; – *b*) *Lindbeck* Kristen H., Non-rabbinic sources for Elijah legends in rabbinic literature: ➤ 394, SBLSem 33 (1994) 767-789 / 752-766.

9946* **Deleon-Jones** Karen F., Prophets, magicians and rabbis; Giordano BRUNO and the Kabbalah: diss. ᴰ*Culianu* I. Ch 1994. 446 p. 95-13969. – DissA 55 (1994s) p. 3860.

9947 ᵀᴱ**Goodman** Martin & Sarah, Johann REUCHLIN, On the art of the Kabbalah, De arte cabalistica. Lincoln 1994, Univ. Nebraska. xxiv-376 p. 0-8032-8946-4.

9948 ᵀᴱ**Herrmann** Klaus, *Massekhet Hekhalot*, Traktat von den himmlischen Palästen: TStAJ 29. Tü 1994, Mohr. xi-363 + 103 p.; Bibliog. 341-350. 3-16-146150-9.

9948* **Herrmann** Klaus, 'Feuer aus Wasser'; zum Fortleben eines unbekannten 'Sefer-Yeṣira-'Kommentars in der 'Hekhalot-'Literatur: FraJudBeit 20 (1993) 49-96 [< Judaica 50,60].

9949 **Libes** Yehuda, Studies in Jewish myth and Jewish messianism [4, one unpublished], ᵀ*Stein* Batya: Judaica. Albany 1992, SUNY. ix-226 p. [AJS 19 (1994) 121s titles & dates sans pp.].

9950 ᵀᴱ**Mopsik** Charles, Le Zohar 3. [Gn 37-44]: Dix Paroles. Lagrasse 1991, Verdier. 403 p. – ᴿRTPhil 126 (1994) 75s (J. *Borel*).

9951 **Mopsik** C, Les grands textes de la Cabale 1993 ➤ 9,10840: ᴿÉTRel 69 (1994) 141s (Jeanne Marie *Léonard*).

9952 **Mopsik** Charles, Le corpus zoharique, ses titres et ses amplifications: ➤ 9,415, ᴱ*Tardieu* M., Formation des canons 1987/93, 75-105.

9953 ᵀᴱ**Robinson** Ira, Moses CORDOVERO, *Or Ma'arav*, his introduction to Kabbalah: SStKabHasid 3. NY 1994, Yeshiva Univ. Scharf Trust. xxxiv-238 p.; bibliog. 225-232. 0-88125-439-8.

9954 *Rosenwald* Laurence, For [ALTER R.] and against [HANDELMAN S.] Gershon SCHOLEM: Prooftexts 14 (1994) 285-296.

9955 **Schäfer** Peter, Der verborgene und offenbare Gott 1991 ➤ 7,a66 ... 9,10843: ᴿCritRR 6 (1993) 426s (A. F. *Segal*: good, but beating a dead horse, SCHOLEM); HeythJ 35 (1994) 75s (C.R.A. *Morray-Jones*); Judaica 49 (1993) 237s (S. *Schreiner*); Salesianum 56 (1994) 367s (R. *Vicent*).

9956 **Schäfer** Peter, The hidden and manifest God 1992 ➤ 8,a602: ᴿAJS 19 (1994) 254-7 (D. J. *Halperin*).

9957 **Schäfer** Peter, Le Dieu caché et révélé, ᵀ*Aslanoff* Cyrille: Patrimoines Judaïsme. P 1993, Cerf. 181 p. F 160. 2-204-04466-0. – ᴿÉTRel 69 (1994) 139 (Jeanne Marie *Léonard*); NRT 116 (1994) 920s (S. *Hilaire*).

9958 *Segal* Eliezer, The exegetical craft of the Zohar; toward an appreciation: AJS 17 (1992) 31-50.

9959 **Shoham** Shlomo G., The bridge to nothingness; gnosis, Kabbala, existentialism and the transcendental predicament of man. Cranbury NJ 1994. Dickinson Univ. 433 p. £43.50. 0-8386-3396-X. – ᴿTBR 7,1 (1994s) 9 (G. *Pattison*: some insights, highly personal rather than scholarly).

9960 **Swartz** Michael D., Mystical prayer in ancient Judaism ... Merkavah 1992 ➤ 8,a605; 9,10848: ᴿCritRR 6 (1993) 432-4 (R. A. *Kugler*); JStJud 25 (1994s) 128s (N. A. van *Uchelen*); Salesianum 56 (1993) 371 (R. *Vicent*).

9961 *Swartz* Michael D., 'Like the ministering angels'; ritual and purity in early Jewish mysticism and magic: AJS 19 (1994) 135-167.

9962 ᴱ**Tishby** Isaiah, The wisdom of the Zohar, an anthology of texts, ᵀ*Goldstein* David: Littman Library. Ox 1989, pa. 1991, UP. xxxi-443 p.; xiv – p. 447-863; ix-867-1596. £60. – ᴿBSO 57 (1994) 368s (S. B. *Leperer*).

K7.5 Judaismus saec. 14-18.

9963 **Battenberg** Friedrich, Das europäische Zeitalter der Juden, I. Von den Anfängen bis 1650; 2. Von 1650 bis 1945. Da 1990, Wiss. 307 p.; 361 p. ᴿZRGg 46 (1994) 94s (L. *Heid*).

9964 **Carpi** D., ⊕ Between Renaissance and Ghetto: essays on the history of the Jews in Italy in the 14th and 17th centuries. TA 1989, Univ. 303 p. + 2 Eng. – ᴿHenoch 16 (1994) 139s (B. *Chiesa*).

9965 *Sanz* Enrique, Los Laínez y la limpieza de sangre [< dis. Salamanca 1990, Limpieza de sangre y conversos; prácticas judaizantes de los Laínez de Almazán]: Perficit, Estudios Clásicos 2/17 ➤ 10*, Centenario E. BASABE TERREROS 1893-1977 (1987-1993) 65-71.

9966 *Zoggia* Stefano, Die deutsche Synagoge in Padua 1603-1779: ZRGg 46 (1994) 44-58; 9 fig.

9967 **Uchmany** Eva A., La vida entre el judaismo y el cristianismo en la Nueva España 1580-1606. Méx 1992, Archivo General. 477 p. – ᴿAmHR 99 (1994) 1006s (Judith L. *Elkin*).

9968 **Attias** J.-C., [1437-1503] Isaac ABRAVANEL. La mémoire et l'espérance 1992 ➤ 8,a586: ᴿNRT 116 (1994) 282 (S. *Hilaire*).

9968* **Gaon** S., Influence of TOSTADO on Abravanel. Hoboken 1993, KTAV. x-120 p. $20. – ᴿVT 44 (1994) 426 (N. de *Lange*).

9969 **Segal** Lester S., Historical consciousness and religious tradition in Azariah DE' ROSSI's 'Me'or Einayim' [1573] 1989 ➤ 7,a80; 8,a631: ᴿAJS 17 (1992) 319-321 (Joanna *Weinberg*).

9970 *Estruch Tobella* Joan, Francisco Manuel de MELO, el último estudioso de la Cábala [c. 1650]: Sefarad 53 (1993) 25-39; Eng. 39.

9970* ᴱ**Herzig** Arno *al.*, REUCHLIN und die Juden. Sigmaringen 1993, Thorbecke. 360 p. 20 fig. DM 68. 3-7995-6029-7. – ᴿJudaica 50 (1994) 162s (S. *Schreiner*).

9971 **Rozen** Minna, Jewish identity and society in the seventeenth century; reflections on the life and work of Rafael Mordekhai MALKI [Livorno physician; in Jerusalem from 1677], ᵀ*Wachsmann* Goldie: TStMdvJud 6. Tü 1992, Mohr. x-190 p. – ᴿAJS 19 (1994) 265-8 (D. B. *Ruderman*: stimulating on his medical, messianic, and converso identities); Judaica 50 (1994) 54 (S. *Schreiner*).

9971* **Jung** Martin, Die Württembergische Kirche und die Juden in der Zeit des Pietismus (1675-1780) [ev. Diss. Tübingen 1990]: B 1992, Institut Kirche und Judentum. 395 p. DM 29,80. – ᴿJudaica 50 (1994) 56 (H. L. *Reichrath*).

9972 **Hayoun** Maurice-Ruben, Mémoires de Jacob EMDEN [1697-1776] ou l'anti-Sabbataï Zewi: Patrimoines Judaïsme, 1992 ➤ 9,10861; 2-204-04415-6: ᴿSalesianum 56 (1994) 769s (R. *Vicent*).

9972* *Goldish* Matt, Jews, Christians and conversos; Rabbi Solomon

Aailion's struggles [d. 1728] in the Portuguese community of London: JJS 45 (1994) 227-257.

9973 **Meitlis** Jacob, Das Ma'assebuch [altjüdische Aggada], seine Entstehung und Quellengeschichte. Hildesheim 1987 = 1933, Olms. xxii-152 p.; ill., Bibliog. 149-152. 3-487-07833-3.

9974 ᴿᴱ**Stillman** Yedida K. & Norman A., Samuel ROMANELLI, Travail in an Arab land [4 years in Morocco before 1800; ᴱ*Schiller-Szinessy* S., Cambridge 1986]. Tuscaloosa 1989, Univ. Alabama. xiii-222 p. – ᴿAJS 17 (1992) 321-4 (D. J. *Schroeter*).

9975 **Tollet** Daniel, Histoire des Juifs en Pologne du XVIᵉ siècle à nos jours. P 1992, PUF. 331 p. F 178. – ᴿHZ 259 (1994) 420s (F. *Golczewski*); RHR 211 (1994) 366-370 (M. J. *Rosman*).

9976 **Berg** Roger, Histoire du rabbinat français (XVIᵉ-XXᵉ siècle): Patrimoines Judaïsme. P 1992, Cerf. 274 p. 2-204-04252-8. – ᴿSalesianum 56 (1994) 759s (R. *Vicent*).

9977 **Tirosh-Rothschild** Hava, Between worlds ... Messer León 1991 ⮕ 9, 10870: ᴿAJS 17 (1992) 316-9 (K. F. *Bland*); Judaism 43 (1994) 110-2 (M. *Saperstein*).

9978 *Goetschel* Roland, Langage et écriture dans la Jérusalem [1783] de Moïse MENDELSSOHN: RÉJ 153 (1994) 491-500.

9978* *Breuer* Edward, ⊕ Haskalah and Scripture in the early writings of Moses MENDELSSOHN: Zion 59 (1994) 445-463.

9979 **Hagy** James W., This happy land; the Jews of colonial and antebellum Charleston. Tuscaloosa 1993, Univ. Alabama. xi-450 p. $50. – ᴿAmHR 99 (1994) 1387s (H. L. *Feingold*: then the largest and best integrated Jewish community).

K7.7   Hasidismus et Judaismus saeculi XIX.

9980 *Assaf* David, ⊕ 'The causeless hatred is ongoing'; the struggle against Bratslav Hasidism in the 1860s: Zion 59 (1994) 465-506; Eng. XXVIII.

9981 **Bering** Dietz, The stigma of names; antisemitism in German daily life, 1812-1933, ᵀ*Plaice* Neville: Social History in Germany. AA 1992, Univ. Michigan. xii-345 p. – ᴿAmHR 99 (1994) 921s (M. *Berkowitz*).

9982 **Berkowitz** J. R., The shaping of Jewish identity in nineteenth-century France 1989 ⮕ 9,10874: ᴿAJS 17 (1992) 110-3 (Paula E. *Hyman*).

9983 **Boyarin** J., Polish Jews in Paris, the ethnography of memory. Bloomington 1991, Indiana Univ. x-195 p. – ᴿAJS 19 (1994) 278-281 (S. *Gutman*).

9984 **Carlebach** Elisheva, The pursuit of heresy; Rabbi Moses HAGIZ and the Sabbatian controversies. NY 1990, Columbia Univ. 164 p. – ᴿZion 59 (1994) 521-3 (J. *Katz*).

9985 ᴱ**Carlebach** Julius *al.*, Second chance; two centuries of German-speaking Jews in the UK (36 art.). Tü 1988/91, Mohr. xii-654 p. DM 128. – ᴿEngHR 109 (1994) 1021s (G. *Alderman*).

9986 *a) Cohen* Martine, De l'emancipation à l'intégration; les transformations du judaïsme français au XIXᵉ siècle; – *b) Azria* Régine, Israël, l'invention de la nation à l'examen de conscience; la morale à l'épreuve de la politique [DIECKOFF A., GREILSAMMER I., 1993]; – *c) Storper-Perez* Danielle, Les Harédim [ultra-orthodoxe] en perspective 1988-92: ArchivScSocR 39,88 (1994) 5-22 / 23-31 / 33-41.

9987 **Endelman** Todd M., Radical assimilation in English Jewish history 1656-1945. Bloomington 1990, Indiana Univ. viii-246 p. – ᴿAJS 17 (1992) 324-7 (T. *Kushner*).

9987* ᴱEnglander David, A documentary history of Jewish immigrants in Britain, 1840-1920. London 1994, Leicester Univ. xv-380 p. £45; pa. £15. – ᴿJJS 45 (1994) 330s (R. *Liedtke*, also on KUSHNER T. 1992 cognate).

9988 Epperson Steven, Mormons and Jews; early Mormon theologies of Israel. Salt Lake City 1992, Signature. ix-228 p. $19. – ᴿAmHR 99 (1994) 971s (K. H. *Winn*).

9989 Feldman David, Englishmen and Jews; social relations and political culture, 1840-1914. NHv 1994, Yale. xii-401 p. £35. – ᴿEngHR 109 (1994) 970-2 (G. *Alderman*, also on CESARINI D.).

9990 Foxbrunner Roman A., Habad, the Hasidism of R. Shneur Zalman of Lyday [1745-1813]. Tuscaloosa 1992, Univ. Alabama. xi-307 p. – ᴿJJS 45 (1994) 142-4 (L. *Jacobs*, also on five cognates).

9990* — Loewenthal Naftali, Communicating the infinite; the emergence of the Habad school. Ch 1990, Univ. xi-336 p. $46. – ᴿJJS 45 (1994) 142s (L. *Jacobs*).

9991 Frankel Jonathan, Gli ebrei russi, tra socialismo e nazionalismo (1862-1917). T 1990, Einaudi. xvi-894 p. – ᴿOrChrPer 60 (1994) 303-5 (C. *Simon*).

9991 ᴱFrankel J., *Zipperstein* S., Assimilation and community; the Jews in nineteenth-century Europe. C 1992, Univ. 384 p. $55. – ᴿJIntdis 24 (1993s) 315s (J. *Jacobs*).

9992 ᵀᴱGourévitch Édouard, JEHUDAH BEN CHEMOUEL le Hassid, Sefer Hassidim, le guide des hassidim: Patrimoines Judaïsme. P 1988, Cerf. iv-555 p. 2-204-02827-4.

9992* — a) *Borchers* Susanne, Hexen im Sefer Hasidim: Henoch 16 (1994) 271-293; Eng. 293; – b) *Ghini* Emanuela, Il magistero dei Chassidim; positività e bellezza della vita: RivVSp 45 (1991) 143-151 / 256-266 / 557-568.

9993 — a) *Baskin* Judith R., From separation to displacement; the problem of women in Sefer Hasidim; – b) *Deshen* Shlomo, Bagdad Jewry in Late Ottoman times; the emergence of social classes and of secularization: AJS 19 (1994) 1-18 / 19-44.

9993* Kaplan Marion A., The making of the Jewish middle class; women, family and identity in imperial Germany. Ox 1991, UP. xvi-351 p. £35. – ᴿJJS 45 (1994) 329s (R. *Liedtke*).

9994 — Schiper Ignacy, [1884-1943; Ms. gefunden 1985] ℗ *Przyczynki* ... Beiträge zur Geschichte des Chassidismus in Polen, ᴱ*Targielski* Zbigniew. Wsz 1992, PWN. 139 p. – ᴿJudaica 50 (1994) 55 (M. *Galas*).

9994* *Koerrenz* Ralf, 'Geheimnis' und 'Gebot'; die dynamische Polarität des Judentums nach Leo BAECK: ZRGg 46 (1994) 31-43.

9995 Lipman Vivian D. †, A history of the Jews in Britain since 1858. NY 1990, Holmes & M. xvi-274 p. – ᴿAJS 17 (1992) 330-3 (T. M. *Endelman*).

9996 Lucas Franz D., *Frank* Heike, Michael SACHS — der konservative Mittelweg; Leben und Werk des Berliner Rabbiners zur Zeit der Emanzipation. Tü 1992, Mohr. 161 p. DM 98. – ᴿJRel 74 (1994) 427s (T. *Vehse*).

9997 McCagg William O.ᴶ, A history of Habsburg Jews 1670-1918 [ten million in 1918]. Bloomington 1989, Indiana Univ. xi-289 p. – ᴿAJS 17 (1992) 327-330 (Marsha I. *Rozenblit*).

9998 Quirin James, The evolution of the Ethiopian Jews; a history of the Beta Israel (Falasha) to 1920; Ethnohistory. Ph 1992, Univ. Pennsylvania. xviii-336 p. $37. – ᴿAmHR 99 (1994) 278s (M. M. *Laskier*).

9998* **Rohrbacher** Stefan,   Gewalt im Biedermeier; antijüdische Ausschreitungen in Vormärz und Revolution (1815-49) [Diss. Berlin 1990]: CentrumAntisemF 1. Fra 1993, Campus. 344 p. DM 68. 3-593-34886-1. – RJudaica 50 (1994) 56s (H. L. *Reichrath*).

9999 *Rubio* Javier, La derogación del edicto de expulsión de los Judíos de 1492 [1868]: Sefarad 53 (1993) 143-155; Eng. 156.

10000 **Serels** M. Mitchell, A history of the Jews of Tangier in the nineteenth and twentieth century. Brooklyn 1991, Sepher Hermon. 324 p. – RAJS 19 (1994) 91-103 (Susan G. *Miller*).

10001 *Sherwin* Byron L., Corpus Domini; traces of the New Testament in East European Hasidism?: HeythJ 35 (1994) 267-280.

K7.8   Judaismus contemporaneus.

10002 **Auerbach** Jerold S., Rabbis and lawyers [US. 1840-1950]; the journey from Torah to constitution. Bloomington 1990, Indiana Univ. xix-272 p. – RAJS 17 (1992) 104-7 (I. *Robinson*).

10003 **Alderman** Geoffrey, Modern British Jewry. Ox 1992, Clarendon. ix-397 p. $89. – RAmHR 99 (1994) 566 (T. M. *Endelman*).

10004 *Bayfield* Tony, Mission — a Jewish perspective: TLond 96 (1991) 180-190.

10005 **Beth-Hallahmi** Benjamin, Despair and deliverance; private salvation in contemporary Israel 1992 → 8,a662; 9,10894: RJRel 74 (1994) 124s (S. *Sharot*).

10006 *Beit-Hallahmi* Benjamin, Identità giudaica e nuovi movimenti religiosi in Israele: SetRel 2 (1992) 343-367 [< ZIT 93,385].

10007 **Benbassa** Esther, Une diaspora sépharade en transition. P 1993, Cerf. 260 p. F 200. – RÉtudes 381 (1994) 269s (M. *Yaèche*).

10008 **Benbassa** Esther, *Rodrigue* Aron, Juifs des Balkans; espaces judéo-ibériques, XIVe-XXe siècles. P 1993, Découverte. 416 p. – RArchivScSocR 39,86 (1994) 265s (M. *Löwy*).

10009 **Ben Chlomo** Iosef, Introduction à la pensée de Rav KOOK, TChalier Catherine: Patrimoines Judaïsme. P 1992, Cerf. 177 p. F 150. 2-204-04564-0. – RÉTRel 68 (1993) 440 (Jeanne M. *Léonard*).

10010 **Bidussa** David [genero di], LUZZATTO Amos e figlia, Oltre il ghetto; momenti e figure della cultura ebraica in Italia tra l'Unità e il fascismo. Brescia 1992, Morcelliana. 287 p. Lm 30. – RRasT 34 (1993) 235s (A. *De Meo*).

10011 *a)* *Blidstein* G. J., Biblical models in the contemporary thought of Rabbi J. B. SOLOVEITCHIK; – *b)* *Goshen-Gottstein* Alon, Love as a hermeneutic principle in rabbinic literature: LitTOx 8 (1994) 236-246 / 247-267.

10012 **ECohen** Martin A., *Peck* Abraham J., Sephardim in America; studies in culture and history. Tuscaloosa 1993, Univ. Alabama (for American Jewish Archive). ix-550 p. $33. – RAmHR 99 (1994) 1013 (titles sans pp.).

10013 **Cohen** Naomi W., Jews in Christian America 1992 → 9,10901: RAJS 19 (1994) 290-2 (R. *Polenberg*).

10014 **Cohn-Sherbok** Dan, The future of Judaism. E 1994, Clark. xviii-227 p. £12.50. 0-567-29267-3. – RTBR 7,3 (1994s) 70 (B. *Capper*).

10015 **Cohn-Sherbok** Dan, Issues in contemporary Judaism 1991 → 8,a667: RCCAR 41,2 (1994) 75-77 (Judith A. *Bluestein*).

10016 **Danzger** Herbert M., Returning to tradition; the contemporary revival of orthodox Judaism 1989 → 7,a94; 8,a668: RCritRR 5 (1992) 388-390 (Natalie *Inser*); Judaism 40 (1991) 251s (Livia *Bitton-Jackson*).

10017 **Ehrlich** Leonard H., Fraglichkeit der jüdischen Existenz; philosophische Untersuchungen zur modernen Schicksal der Juden: Fermenta philosophica. Mü 1993, Alber. 366 p. DM 78. 3-495-47750-0. – ᴿUniversitas 48 (1993) 1214 (S. *Wirth*).

10018 **Eisenstadt** S. N., Jewish civilization; the Jewish historical experience in a comparative perspective; Israeli Studies. Albany 1992 SUNY. ix-314 p. $74.50; pa. $25. – ᴿAmHR 99 (1994) 193s (Vicki *Caron*: polemical and badly edited).

10019 **Elazar** Daniel J., The other Jews; the Sephardim today. NY 1989, Basic. xii-236 p. – ᴿAJS 17 (1992) 364-7 (Yedida K. *Stillman*).

10019* ᴱ**Feingold** Henry J., The Jewish people in America. Baltimore 1993, Johns Hopkins Univ. 5 vols. [data in JJS 45 (1994) 328, with a non-reference to NYTimesLit 'last June'].

10020 **Fishman** Aryei, Judaism and modernization in the religious kibbutz. C 1992, Univ. xv-202 p. $50. – ᴿJRel 74 (1994) 123s (S. *Sharot*).

10021 **Friedlander** Judith, Vilna on the Seine; Jewish intellectuals in France since 1968. NHv 1990, Yale Univ. xv-249 p. – ᴿAJS 17 (1994) 347-350 (D. *Weinberg*); Judaism 41 (1992) 297-300 (Maud S. *Mandel*).

10021* *Galchinsky* Michael, Glimpsing *Golus* in the golden land; Jews and multiculturalism in America: Judaism 43 (1994) 360-9.

10022 **Gillman** Neil, Sacred fragments; recovering theology for the modern Jew 1990 ➤ 7,a101; 8,a673: ᴿCritRR 5 (1992) 390-2 (T. *Weinberger*: philosophy is theology is religion).

10023 **Goldberg** Harvey E., Jewish life in Muslim Libya; rivals and relatives. Ch 1990, Univ. x-181 p. – ᴿAJS 17 (1992) 107-110 (Rachel *Simon*).

10024 **Gutwein** Daniel, The divided elite; economics, politics and Anglo-Jewry, 1882-1917: Jewish Studies. Leiden 1992, Brill. 501 p. $125. – ᴿAJS 19 (1994) 275-8 (T. M. *Endelman*: informative, but even the Rothschilds can't afford it).

10025 **Handelman** Susan A., Fragments of redemprion ... BENJAMIN ... 1991 ➤ 9,10912: ᴿJSS 39 (1994) 125-7 (L. J. *Yudkin*); RLitND 25,3 (1993) 87-92 (Krzysztof *Ziarek*).

10026 **Hartman** David, Conflicting visions; spiritual possibilities of modern Israel 1990 ➤ 8,a676: ᴿCCAR 41,1 (1994) 97-100 (B. D. *Cytron*).

10027 **Heilman** Samuel, Defenders of the faith; inside ultra-orthodox Judaism. NY 1992, Schocken. xxi-394 p. $27.50. – ᴿJRel 74 (1994) 125s (H. E. *Goldberg*).

10027* *Klein* Birgit, Warum studieren in Deutschland Nichtjüdinnen und Nichtjüden Judaistik?: Judaica 49 (1993) 31-45 (-49, *Hart* Judith).

10028 **Kochan** Lionel, Jews, idols and messiahs; the challenge from history [... modernity]. Ox 1990, Blackwell. 231 p. £35. – ᴿAJS 17 (1992) 367-9 (M. A. *Meyer*); JJS 45 (1994) 326s (G. *Alderman*).

10028* *Kopnick* Sandford R., Justifying the move; confirmation [bar mitzvah] in the twelfth grade [nearer age 18 than 14]: CCAR 41,2 (1994) 57-60.

10029 *a)* *Krapf* Thomas M., Jüdische Identität und Neuhebräisch; Anmerkungen zu Yehezkel KAUFMANNS Verhältnis zur Wissenschaft des Judentums; – *b)* *Schmelzer* Hermann I., Hermann Leberecht STRACK; die Wissenschaft des Judentums als Dialog [+ unveröffentlichter Brief]; – *c)* *Völker* Heinz-H., Franz DELITZSCH als Förderer der Wissenschaft vom Judentum: Judaica 49 (1993) 69-80 / 81-89 [84-87; 2 phot.] / 90-100 (-106, *Wiefel* W.].

10029* *Krochmalnik* Daniel, Die Symbolik des Judentums nach Moses MENDELSSOHN, Isaac BERNAYS und Samson Raphael HIRSCH: Judaica 49 (1993) 206-219.

10030 *Kronholm* Tryggve, Jewish studies in Sweden [< 5th Nordic congress for Jewish studies, Lund 10-12 May 1993]: OrSuec 41s (1992s) 119-125.

10031 *Lenzen* Verena, Leben mit der Tora; eine Auseinandersetzung mit dem jüdischen Denker Jeshajahu LEIBOWITZ [geb. 1903; Chefredakteur der Hebräischen Enzyklopädie']: LebZeug 47 (1992) 296-306.

10032 **Levine** Robert M., Tropical diaspora; the Jewish experience in Cuba [from Germany, East Europe, Middle East; 20th cent.]. Gainesville 1993, Univ. Florida. xvii-398 p. $35. – ᴿAmHR 99 (1994) 1785s (M. E. *Crahan*).

10033 **Liebman** Charles S., *Cohen* Steven M., Two worlds of Judaism; the Israeli and American experiences ⇒ 6,a359; 9,a684: ᴿCritRR 5 (1992) 392-4 (B. *Kraut*).

10033* **Meyer** Michael A., Response to modernity; a history of the Reform movement in Judaism. NY 1988, Oxford-UP. 494 p. – ᴿJudaism 40 (1991) 369-377 (S. D. *Temkin*).

10034 **Mirelman** Victor A., Jewish Buenos Aires 1890-1930; in search of an identity. Detroit 1990, Wayne State Univ. 300 p. – ᴿAJS 17 (1992) 334-6 (G. *Böhm*).

10035 **Mittleman** Alan L., Between KANT and Kabbalah; Isaac BREUER's [1883-1946] philosophy of Judaism. Albany 1990, SUNY. x-227 p. – ᴿAJS 17 (1992) 336-9 (R. S. *Schine*).

10036 ᴱMor Menachem, Jewish... parties, Omaha symposium 1990-2 ⇒ 9, 299 [BL 95,158s, S. C. *Reif*].

10036* **Neusner** Jacob, Fortress introduction to American Judaism; what the books say, what the people do. Mp 1994, Fortress. xii-179 p. $11. 0-8006-2670-2. [TDig 41,374]. – ᴿTBR 7,1 (1994s) 77 (N. de *Lange*).

10037 **Oppenheim** Michael, Mutual upholding; fashioning Jewish philosophy through letters [his own, to a colleague or friend; implicitly in defense of BUBER-HESCHEL-ROSENZWEIG 'modern Bible-philosophy' against G. SCHOLEM]. NY 1992, Lang. x-186 p. – ᴿSR 23 (1994) 108s (L. *Greenspahn*).

10038 **Petuchowski** Jakob J., Mein Judesein; Wege und Erfahrungen eines deutschen Rabbiners: Spektrum 4092. FrB 1992, Herder. 160 p. – ᴿLebZeug 47 (1992) 317s (B. *Neumann*).

10039 **Ravitzky** Aviezer, ⊕ *Ha-Qeṣ, ha-Megula* ... Messianism, Zionism and Jewish radicalism. TA 1993, AmOved. 399 p. – ᴿTarbiz 62 (1992) 463-6 (A. *Funkenstein*).

10039* *Reich* S., Jodendom en internationaal recht; een onderzoek naar de mogelijke invloed van het Jodendom op de vorming en de ontwikkeling van het volkenrecht en het internationaal privaatrecht: Ter Herkenning 20 (1992) 84-94 [< GerefTT 93,67].

10040 ᴱRo't Yaacov, *Beker* Avi, Jewish culture and identity in the Soviet Union. NYU 1991. xxii-482 p. $62. – ᴿJJS 45 (1994) 332s (G. *Estraikh*).

10040* **Sachar** Howard M., A history of Jews in America. NY 1992, Knopf. 1051 p. $40. – ᴿAmHR 98 (1993) 934s (J. S. *Gurock*: unresearched on Orthodox); JIntdis 25 (1994s) 335s (R. J. *Weiner*).

10041 **Sarna** Jonathan D., JPS [Jewish Publication Society], the Americanization of Jewish culture, 1888-1988. Ph 1989, JPS. 430 p. $30. – ᴿJudaism 40 (1991) 252-2 (M. N. *Dobkowski*).

10041* **Schwartz** Shuly R., The emergence of Jewish scholarship in America; the publication of the Jewish Encyclopedia: HUC mg. 13. Cincinnati 1991 ⇒ 8,a695: ᴿAJS 19 (1994) 112-4 (H. D. *Shapiro*); CritRR 6 (1993) 449-451 (E. S. *Shapiro*).

10042 **Shmueli** Efraim, Seven Jewish cultures; a reinterpretation of Jewish

history and thought, ᵀ*Shmueli* Gila, 1990 ➤ 6,a163 ... 8,a696: ᴿCritRR 5
(1992) 350-2 (Alice E. *Eckardt*); ScotJT 45 (1992) 544-6 (N. *Solomon*).
10043 **Staiman** Mordechai, *Niggun*; stories behind the chasidic songs that
    inspire Jews. Northvale NJ 1994, Aronson. xvii-293 p. 1-56821-047-7.
10044 **Steinsaltz** Adin, The sustaining utterance; discourses on Chasidic
    thought. Northvale NJ 1989, Aronson. xiv-129 p. 0-87668-845-8.
10045 **Stillman** Norman A., The language and culture of the Jews of Sefrou,
    Morocco: an ethnolinguistic study: JSS mg 11. Manchester 1988, Univ.
    xv-172 p. – ᴿAJS 17 (1992) 362-4 (R. D. *Hoberman*).
10046 **Temkin** Sefton D., Isaac Mayer Wɪsᴇ; shaping American Judaism:
    Littman Library. NY 1992, Oxford-UP. viii-318 p. – ᴿAJS 19 (1994)
    284-8 (G. L. *Berlin*); AmHR 99 (1994) 1388 (B. *Kraut*).
10047 **Tolédano** Joseph, Les Sépharades: Fils d'Abraham. Turnhout 1992,
    Brepols. 218 p.
10047* ᴱ**Tomaszewski** Jerzy, ❷ Najnowsze dzieje ... Updated history of Jews
    in Poland to 1950. Wsz 1993, PWN. 499 p. – ᴿJudaica 50 (1994) 165s
    (S. *Schreiner*).
10048 **Trepp** Leo, Die amerikanischen Juden; Profil einer Gemeinschaft. Stu
    1991, Kohlhammer. 150 p. DM 32. – ᴿProtestantesimo 49 (1994) 58-61
    (G. *Conte*); TPQ 142 (1994) 73s (J. *Lettl*).
10049 **Varela** María Encarnación, Historia de la literatura hebrea contem-
    poránea. Barc 1992, Mirador. 346 p. – ᴿSefarad 53 (1993) 226s (L. F.
    Girón).
10050 *a*) *Wertheimer* Jack, Amerikanisches Judentum in der Gegenwart; – *b*)
    Della Pergola Sergio, Neue Daten zur Demographie und Selbstiden-
    tifikation unter Juden in den USA [both ᵀ*Albrecht-Roth* Marianne]; – *c*)
    Shekel Michal, Frauen und Rabbinat in Amerika; – *d*) *Kaufmann* Uri R.,
    Auswahlbibliographie: Judaica 50 (1994) 187-210 / 211-238 / 239-251 /
    251-4.
10051 **Wertheimer** Jack, A people divided; Judaism in contemporary America.
    NY 1993, Harper Collins (Basic). xix-267 p. $25. 0-465-00165-3 [TDig
    42,95]. – ᴿAmHR 99 (1994) 1388s (S. E. *Knee*).

K8 *Philosemitismus* – **Judeo-Christian rapprochement.**

10051* *a*) *Abrams* Judith Z., Recognizing, and repudiating, anti-Christian
    polemic in classic Jewish sources; – *b*) *Fisher* Eugene J., Jewish-Christian
    relations 1989-1993; a bibliographic update; CCAR 41,163 (1994) 37-43 /
    7-35.
10052 **Adorno** T. W., Contro l'antisemitismo, ᵀ*Petrucciani*. R 1994, Mani-
    festolibri. 94 p. Lᵐ 22. – ᴿRasT 35 (1994) 511 (B. *Marra*).
10053 **Almog** Shmuel, Nationalism and antisemitism in modern Europe
    1815-1945. NY 1990, Pergamon. ix-159 p. – ᴿAJS 17 (1992) 341-3 (J. F.
    Harris).
10054 **Arnoldi** Udo, Pro Iudaeis; die Gutachten der hallischen Theologen
    im 18. Jh. zu Fragen der Judentoleranz: KIsr Studien 14, 1993 ➤ 9,
    10947: ᴿTR 90 (1994) 310s (M. *Brecht*).
10055 **Barkun** Michael, Religion and the racist right; the origins of the
    Christian Identity movement [not Jews but white Aryans are descendants
    of the biblical tribes of Israel]. Chapel Hill 1994, N. Carolina Univ.
    xiii-290 p. $40; pa. $16. 0-8078-2145-4; -4451-0 [TDig 42,155].
10056 **Beck** Norman A., Mature Christianity in the 21st century; the
    recognition and repudiation of the anti-Jewish polemic of the New

Testament[2rev]: Shared ground 5. NY 1994, Crossroad. 372 p.; bibliog. 334-352.

10056* **Bernardini** P., La questione ebraica nel tardo illuminismo tedesco; studi intorno allo 'Über die bürgerliche Verbesserung der Juden' di C. W. DOHM (1781 su richiesta di Moses MENDELSSOHN). F 1992, Giuntina. 191 p. – [R]Henoch 16 (1994) 374-6 (C. *Martone*).

10057 *Breuning* Wilhelm, Grundzüge einer nicht antijüdischen Christologie: JbBT 8 (1993) 293-311.

10057* **Bruder** Judith, Convergence; a reconciliation of Judaism and Christianity in the life of one woman. NY 1993, Doubleday. 229 p. $20. – [R]RRel 52 (1993) 631s (J. L. *Casteel*).

10058 **Chazan** Robert, Barcelona ... 1263 and its aftermath. Berkeley 1992, Univ. California. 257 p. $40. – [R]CathHR 79 (1993) 488-495 (R. I. *Burns*); JRel 74 (1994) 121-3 (M. *Saperstein*); Sefarad 54 (1994) 196-8 (M. *Orfali*); Speculum 69 (1994) 758s (M. D. *Meyerson*).

10059 *(Chorão) Lavajo* Joaquim, A controvérsia Judio-Cristã de 1263 em Barcelona, no contexto do diálogo religioso medieval: Eborensia 7,13s (1994) 1-44.

10060 **Chrostowski** Waldemar, The Catholic-Jewish dialogue in Poland 1993-94: Religion in Eastern Europe 14,2 (1994) 22-28 [13,6 (1993) 36-48].

10061 [E]**Chrostowski** Waldemar, ℗ Jews and Christians in dialogue, Kraków-Tyniec 24-27 IV 1988: Kościół a Żydzi 3, 1992 ➤ 8,523d: – [R]ColcT 63,2 (1993) 181-9 (M. *Horoszewicz*, ℗).

10062 [E]**Cohen** Jeremy, Essential papers on Judaism and Christianity in conflict 1991 ➤ 8,346b, 9,10966*: [R]ChH 63 (1994) 105s (O. *Roynesdal*).

10063 **Cohn-Sherbok** Dan, The crucified Jew; twenty centuries of Christian anti-Semitism 1992 ➤ 8,a720: [R]BapQ 35 (1993s) 101; TLond 96 (1993) 66s (B. *Ettlinger*: clear but undocumented, and in a tone unlikely to be read by those who need it).

10064 **Cohn-Sherbok** Dan, A dictionary of Judaism and Christianity 1991 ➤ 7,711*: [R]ColcT 63,2 (1993) 189-193 (M. *Horoszewicz*, ℗).

10065 **Cohn-Sherbok** Dan, Exodus; an agenda for Jewish-Christian dialogue ... 1992, Bellew. vii-131 p. £15. – [R]TLond 96 (1993) 220s (A. E. *Harvey*, also on BAYFIELD-BRAYBROOKE).

10066 **Conzelmann** Hans, Gentiles-Jews-Christians 1992 ➤ 8,a722; 9,10968: [R]RB 101 (1994) 467s (B. T. *Viviano*).

10067 **Crombie** K., For the love of Zion. L 1991, Hodder & S. vii-278 p. £7. – [R]PEQ 25 (1993) 161 (Gillian *Webster*: history of the London Society for promoting Christianity among the Jews in Palestine).

10068 **Dahan** G., Inghetto CONTARDO 1993 ➤ 9,10972: [R]RHE 89 (1994) 692-5 (Bat-Sheva *Albert*).

10069 **De Benedetti** Paolo, Ciò che tarda, avverrà. Vercelli 1992, Qiqayon. 142 p. L[m] 15. – [R]StCattMi 37 (1993) 149 (F. *Ciccolo Fabris*).

10070 *Dudley* Martin, The Jews in the Good Friday liturgy: AnglTR 76 (1994) 61-70.

10071 [E]**Dunn** James D. G., Jews and Christians; the parting 1989/92 ➤ 8,467: [R]RCatalT 18 (1993) 181s (G. *Veltri*).

10072 **Duponcheele** Joseph, L'être de l'Alliance ... lien entre le Judaïsme et le Christianisme: CogF 170, 1992 ➤ 9,10977: [R]NRT 116 (1994) 418-429 (P. *Favraux*).

10073 *Duponcheele* Joseph, 'L'être de l'Alliance'; brève contribution au débat sur l'enjeu d'une philosophie première: NRT 116 (1994) 874-882.

10074 **Egger** Manfred, Die 'Deggendorfer Gnad' [Judenmord 1338 wegen Hostienschändung]; Entstehung und Entwicklung einer Hostienwallfahrt im Kontext von Theologie und Geschichte; Vorw. *Mussner* F. Passau 1992, Passavia. 775 p. DM 48. – ᴿTR 90 (1994) 50-52 (F. *Mussner*).

10075 ᶠEHRLICH Ernst L.: Israel und Kirche heute, ᴱMarcel M., *al.*, 1991 ➤ 7,46*; 9,10980: ᴿTPQ 142 (1994) 74s (J. *Lettl*).

10076 **Elukin** Jonathan M., The eternal Jew in medieval Europe; Christian perceptions of Jewish anachronism and racial identity: diss. Princeton 1994 ᴰ*Jordan* W. 286 p. 94-29177. DissA 55 (1994s) p. 1656.

10077 **Everett** Robert A., Christianity without antisemitism; James PARKES and the Jewish-Christian encounter: Sassoon Center Studies in Antisemitism ... 1993, Pergamon (now called Elsevier Science). xiv-346 p.; $80. 0-08-041040-5 [TDig 42,163]. – ᴿJRelH 18 (1994) 252-4 (B. *Leadbetter*).

10078 **Fabre-Vassas,** Claudine, La bête singulière; les juifs, les chrétiens et le cochon [... en mangeant du porc, les chrétiens d'Europe, consomment du juif de leur passé]: BtScHum. P 1994, Gallimard. 423 p. – ᴿArchivSc-SocRel 39,88 (1994) 66-68 (J. *Lambert*).

10079 **Feldman** Egal, Dual destinies; the Jewish encounter with Protestant America. Urbana 1990, Univ. Illinois. xi-339 p. – ᴿAJS 17 (1994) 350-2 (R. T. *Handy*).

10080 **Foschepoth** Josef, Im Schatten der Vergangenheit; die Anfänge der Gesellschaften für christlich-jüdische Zusammenarbeit; Vorw. *Jochmann* Werner. Gö 1991, Vandenhoeck & R. 250 p. DM 28. – ᴿKIsr 9 (1994) 100s (Julie *Kirchberg*).

10081 **Freudmann** Lilian C., Antisemitisms in the NT. Lanham MD 1994, UPA. xiii-344 p. $47.50; pa. $28. 0-8191-9294-5; -5-3 [NTAbs 38, p. 312].

10082 **Gilmar** Sander, The Jew's body. NY 1991, Routledge. 256 p. $45; pa. $16. 0-415-90458-7; -9-5. – ᴿJIntdis 23 (1992s) 758-760 (Laura *Engelstein*: too sweeping).

10083 **Goodhart** Sandor, Isaiah 52-3, René GIRARD, and the innocent victim [... presupposing uniqueness of Christianity; replies by SCHWAGER Raymond and NIEWIADOMSKI Jósef, both ᵀ*Palaver* B.]: COV & R 7 (1994) 11s.

10084 **Grayzel** Solomon, The Church and the Jews in the XIIIth century 2. 1254-1314, ᴱ*Stow* Kenneth R. 1989 ➤ 6,a399: – ᴿAJS 19 (1994) 88-90 (R. C. *Stacey*); CathHR 79 (1993) 99s (E. A. *Synan*); HZ 259 (1994) 189s (J. F. *Battenberg*).

10084* *Gröner* Eberhard, Christlicher Antijudaismus und psychologische Deutungsmuster [gegen D. W. WINNICOTT]: Judaica 50 (1994) 34-42.

10085 **Hägler** Brigitte, Die Christen und die 'Judenfrage', am Beispiel der Schriften OSIANDERS und ECKS zum Ritualmordvorwurf [Diss.]: Erlanger Studien 97. Erlangen 1992, Palm & Enke. 274 p. DM 48. – ᴿTR 90 (1994) 309s (R. *Bäumer*).

10086 **Hall** Sidney G.ᴵᴵᴵ, Christian anti-Semitism and Paul's theology, 1993 ➤ 9,11000: ᴿJHisp 2,3 (1994s) 77s (Steven *McMichael*); WWorld 14 (1994) 213-5 (W. *Frerichs*).

10087 **Harrelson** Walter, *Falk* Randall M., Jews and Christians; a troubled family 1990 ➤ 7,a168; 8,a737: ᴿCCAR 41,1 (1994) 94-97 (J. *Monti*).

10088 ᴱ**Haverkamp** Alfred, *Ziwes* Franz-Josef, Juden in der christlichen Umwelt während des späten Mittelalters [4 art.]: Z HistFor Beih 13, 1991 ➤ 8,a739: ᴿRHE 99 (1994) 279 (B. S. *Albert*).

10089 *Hemker* Elisheva, Die Wiederbegegnung der Christen mit dem Hebräischen in der Kirche: BiLtg 66 (1993) 233-6.

10089* ᴱHenrix Hans H., 500 Jahre Vertreibung der Juden Spaniens 1992
→ 9,326: ᴿZkT 116 (1994) 360s (J. M. *Oesch*).

10090 **Hoffmann** Christhard, Juden im Werk deutscher Althistoriker 1988
→ 5,a389; 8,a745: ᴿArKulturG 74 (1992) 489-492 (E. *Pack*).

10091 **Isser** Natalie, Antisemitism during the French Second Empire: Amer-
UnivSt 9/100. ɴʏ 1991, Lang. 149 p. – ᴿAJS 19 (1994) 96-99 (Vicki
Caron).

10092 *Joyce* Paul, Israelites and Canaanites, Christians and Jews; studies in
self-definition: NewBlackf 75/878 ('Knowing the other', Proc. Cath.
Theol. Soc. GB: 1994) 31-37.

10093 **Kamykowski** Łukasz, *a*) Izrael i Kościół według Charlesa JOURNETA.
Kraków 1993. – *b*) Qu'est-ce qu'Israël? Examen de l'approche de Charles
Journet [< ❷ Kraków 1993]: → 92* ᶠPIERONEK T., AnCracov 26 (1994)
193-211; ❷ 211s.

10094 **Katunarich** Sergio M., Ebrei e cristiani; storia di un rapporto dif-
ficile. T-Leumann 1993, SEI. 184 p. Lᵐ 14. – ᴿCC 145 (1994,1) 310s (G.
Giachi).

10095 **Kinzig** Wolfram, Philosemitismus I. Zur Geschichte des Begriffs, II.
Zur historischen Verwendung des Begriffs: ZKG 105 (1994) 202-228.
361-383.

10096 ᴱKlenicki Leon, Toward a theological encounter; Jewish understandings of Christianity 1991 → 9,11016: ᴿCCAR 41,1 (1994) 91-93 (R. M.
Falk; PrincSemB 15 (1994) 77s (J. *Marcus*).

10097 *Kloft* Matthias T., Dürfen Juden öffentlich Gottesdienst feiern? Das
Religionsexerzitium der Juden in Nassau-Hadamar im 17. Jt. in der
Beurteilung der Jesuiten und der gräflichen Regierung: ArchivMittel-
rheinKG 45 (Speyer 1993) 393-406 [< ᴢɪᴛ 94,30].

10098 *Körner* Ulrich H. J., Volk Gottes — Kirche-Israel; das Verhältnis der
Kirchen zum Judentum als Thema ökumenischer Kirchenkunde und
ökumenischer Theologie: ZTK 91 (1994) 51-79.

10098* *Kratzert* Thomas, 'Antijudaismus' nur ein westliches Übersetzungs-
problem?: ÖkRu 41 (1992) 190-202.

10099 *Kratz-Ritter* Bettina. Konversion als Antwort auf den Berliner An-
tisemitismusstreit? Nahida Ruth LAZARUS und ihr Weg zum Judentum:
ZRGg 46 (1994) 15-30.

10100 **Kraus** Hans-Joachim, Rückkehr zu Israel 1991 → 7,321; 9,11020:
ᴿTLZ 119 (1994) 43-45 (T. *Arndt*).

10101 **Küng** H., Das Judentum 1991 → 8,a757; 9,11022: ᴿTPQ 141 (1993)
307s (J. *Niewiadomski*).

10102 **Küng** Hans, Judaism, between yesterday and tomorrow; the religious
situation of our time 1992 → 8,a758; 9,11023: ᴿHeythJ 35 (1994) 71-73
(L. *Jacobs*); Horizons 21 (1994) 219s (Susannah *Heschel*); Interpretation
48 (1994) 77-79 (D. G. *Dowe*); IrTQ 60 (1994) 158 (Carmel *Niland*); LvSt
18 (1993) 265-7 (M. *Rebeiro*); PrincSemR 14 (1993) 89s (J. *Marcus*);
ScotJT 47 (1994) 532s (N. *Solomon*: well constructed but too long, and E.
Shmueli or G. *Cohen* better); Worship 65 (1994) 83-85 (H. G. *Perelmuter*).

10103 **Küng** Hans, El judaismo; pasado, presente, futuro, ᵀ*Martínez de
Lapera* V. A. M 1993, Trotta. 724 p. – ᴿRazF 229 (1994) 328s (M.
Alcalá).

10104 *a*) *Langer* Gerhard, Zwei Religionen — ein Glaube; zum jüdisch-christlichen Dialog aus biblisch-theologischer Sicht; – *b*) *Kamykowski* Ł., ❷
Apologia nell'epoca del dialogo: → 47*, ᶠFLORKOWSKI E., AnCracov
191-205; 1 fig. / 170-9; ital. 180.

10105 **Langer** Michael, Zwischen Vorurteil und Aggression; zum Judenbild in der deutschsprachigen Volksbildung des 19. Jahrhunderts [Hab.-Schr Mü 1993]: Lernprozess Christen Juden 9. FrB 1994, Herder. xiii-587 p. DM 78 pa. [TR 90,518].

10106 **Langmuir** Gavin J. Definition / History ... Antisemitism, both 1990 → 7,222a ... 9,11026s: ᴿAJS 17 (1992) 308-313 (J. *Cohen*); CritRR 6 (1993) 403-6 (Sandra B. *Lubarsky*, definition).

10107 *La Vopa* Anthony J., Jews and Germans; old quarrels, new departures [ROSE P. 1990; SORKIN D. 1987]: JHistId 54 (1993) 675-695.

10107* **Levine** Hillel, Economic origins of antisemitism; Poland and its Jews in the early modern period. NHv 1991, Yale Univ. xiii-271 p. – ᴿAJS 19 (1994) 90-93 (D. *Engel*).

10108 **Lipson** Juliene G., Jews for Jesus; an anthropological study. NY 1990, AMS. 178 p. $42.50. – ᴿThought 67 (1992) 344s (J.T. *Pawlikowski*).

10108* *Littell* Franklin H., The future of anti-Semitism: Judaism 40 (1991) 511-520.

10109 *Llamas* Román, Conflicto judaismo-cristianismo: REspir 52 (1993) 167-201.

10110 *Lowe* S., What Jesus did and did not say; a new scholarly portrait reveals the roots of antisemitism: Moment 19,2 (Wsh 1994) 40-43. 72-75 [R. FUNK Seminar results suggest that NT antisemitism started after, not with, Jesus].

10110* **Lubac** H. de, Christian resistance to anti-Semitism 1990 → 7,a193; 8,a764: ᴿThought 67 (1992) 92s (J.T. *Pawlikowski*).

10111 **Lucas** Leopold † 1943, The conflict between Christianity and Judaism; a contribution to the history of the Jews in the fourth century. L 1993 = 1910, Aris & P. 134 p. £20; pa. £10. 0-85668-586-0; -72-0 [TDig 42,175]. – ᴿBLitEc 95 (1994) 249s (J. *Dutheil*); ExpTim 105 (1993s) 318 (J. *Davies*, also on WILLIAMSON C. 1993); JRelH 18 (1994) 233s (R.A. *Kearsley*).

10113 **MacLennan** Robert S., Early Christian texts on Jews 1990 → 6,a429; 9,11035: ᴿAJS 17 (1992) 301-5 (A. *Terian*).

10114 ᴱ**Maduro** Otto, Judaism, Christianity, and liberation – an agenda for dialogue 1991 → 7,365: ᴿCCurr 43 (1993s) 125-7 (Annette *Aronowitz*: unfounded generalizations of M. *Lerner*, R. *Ruether*, M. *Ellis*).

10115 **Manuel** Frank, The broken staff; Judaism through Christian eyes 1992 → 8,a765; 9,11040: ᴿAJS 19 (1994) 260-3 (A. *Arkush*); Salesianum 56 (1994) 363s (R. *Vicent*).

10116 *Margerie* Bertrand de, Réflexions bibliques et chrétiennes sur la 'Shoah': NVFr 68 (1993) 172-192 . 272-296.

10117 *a)* *Martini* Carlo M., Il popolo, l'esilio, il cammino; – *b)* *Stefani* Piero, 'Vi è stato detto ... ma io vi dico': Studi Fatti Ricerche 67 (1994) 3-7 / 8-12.

10118 *Marx* Tzvi, The issues of Jewish-Christian dialogue today: JIntRD 3 (1993) 5-11.

10119 **Mattenklott** Gert, Über Juden in Deutschland. Fra 1992, Jüdischer-V. 202 p. – ᴿArchivScSocR 39,86 (1994) 295 (M. *Löwy*).

10120 *Mehlhausen* Joachim, Assimilation — Integration — Taufe; Hoffnungen und enttäuschte Erwartungen deutscher Staatsbürger jüdischen Glaubens von der Romantik bis zum Jahr 1933: EvT 54 (1994) 23-44.

10121 *Mendes Drumond Braga* Isabel M., Os Mouriscos perante a Inquisição de Évora: Eborensia 7,13s (1994) 45-76.

10122 *Metz* Johann Baptist, The Church after Auschwitz [< KIsr 5 (1990) 99-108], ᵀᴱ*Asen* B.A.: TDig 41 (1994) 21-24.

10123 **Miller** Ronald H., Dialogue and disagreement; Franz ROSENZWEIG's relevance to contemporary Jewish-Christian understanding. Lanham MD 1989, UPA. xix-213 p. – ᴿAJS 17 (1992) 339-341 (A. *Mittleman*: lay-Catholic oriented like P. VAN BUREN toward R.).

10124 **Modras** Ronald, The Catholic Church and antisemitism; Poland 1913-1939: Sassoon Center Studies in Antisemitism. ... 1994, Harwood for [J] Hebrew Univ. xvi-429 p. $48. 3-7186-5568-3 [TDig 42,179].

10124* **Mushkat** Marian, Philosemitic and anti-Jewish attitudes in post-holocaust Poland: Symposium series 33 [not a symposium]. Lewiston NY 1992, Mellen. vi-441 p. £50. – ᴿJudaica 50 (1994) 225s (S. *Schreiner*).

10125 **Mussner** F., Dieses Geschlecht 1991 → 7,242 ... 9,11047: ᴿFrSZ 40 (1993) 478-481 (G. *Schelbert*).

10126 **Neudecker** Reinhard, Ⓜ Az egy Istén sok arca [Die vielen Gesichter 1989 → 6,a435; ital. 8,a769], ᵀKerényi Gabor. Budapest 1992, Keresztény-Zsidó Tanács. 126 p. Ft 195. 963-00-1513-7.

10127 **Neusner** Jacob [→ 4258, Myth of common tradition 1991], Telling Tales 1993 → 9,11052: ᴿExpTim 105 (1993s) 254 (M. *Braybrooke*); Mid-Stream 33 (1994) 369-371 (Sandra M. *Halperin*).

10128 *Newman* Amy, The death of Judaism in German Protestant thought from Luther to Hegel: JAAR 61 (1993) 455-484.

10129 *Oesterreicher* Johannes, Rassenhass ist Christushass 1993 = 1938 → 9, 11058: ᴿTPQ 142 (1994) 317s (J. *Niewiadomski*).

10130 *Omanson* Roger L., Translating the anti-Jewish bias of the NT [now admitted by all Christian NT scholars]: BTrans 43 (1992) 301-313.

10131 *a) Orfali* Moshe, Judaïsme et marranisme; la question juive en Espagne en 1450 selon le hiéronymite Alonso de OROPESA; – *b) Dupuy* Bernard, Deux contemporains de Spinoza, Abraham PEREYRE et Isaac ORABIO DE CASTRO: Istina 38 (1993) 262-286 / 287-304.

10132 **Paul** André, Leçons paradoxales sur les Juifs et les Chrétiens. P 1992, D-Brouwer. 257 p. F 135. 2-220-03260-4. – ᴿÉTRel 68 (1993) 107s (E. *Cuvillier*).

10133 *Pesce* Mauro, Il cristianesimo e la sua radice ebraica; con una raccolta di testi sul dialogo ebraico-cristiano: Ecumenismo. Bo 1994, Dehoniane. 237 p. 88-10-40119-0.

10133* *Poorthuis* Marcel, The improperia and Judaism: QLtg 72 (1991) 1-24.

10134 **Rausch** David A., Communities in conflict; evangelicals and Jews 1991 → 9,11063: ᴿJEvTS 37 (1994) 616s (A. J. *Petrotta*).

10135 *Renner* Augustin U., Form und Inhalt der 'Grossen Fürbitten' des Karfreitags in den ältesten uns erhaltenen Handschriften: HDienst 48 (1994) 154-168; p. 165s for Jews (already 'perfidi/s-a' twice, properly 'unbelieving' but pejorative-sounding; *De Clerck* irrelevant on large number of Jews in Rome).

10136 ᴱRittner Carol Ann, *Roth* John K., Memory offended; the Auschwitz convent controversy. NY 1991, Praeger. xiv-289 p. – ᴿColcT 53,2 (1993) 194-201 (M. *Horoszewicz*, Ⓟ).

10137 ᴱRittner Carol, *Roth* John, Different voices; women and the holocaust. ... 1993, Paragon. xiv-435 p. $27. – ᴿTLond 97 (1994) 73s (Isabel *Wollaston*).

10138 **Röhm** Eberhard, *Thierfelder* Jörg, Juden, Christen, Deutsche 1933-1945, 1-2/1, 1990/2 → 9,11067: ᴿTR 90 (1994) 311s (K. *Novak*).

10139 *Roth* Norman, Bishops and Jews in the Middle Ages: CathHR 80 (1994) 1-17.

618   Elenchus of Biblica 10, 1994   [IV. Postbiblica

10140 ᴱRothschild Fritz, Jewish perspectives on Christianity. NY 1990
➤ 7,e378; Crossroad. x-365 p. – ᴿCCAR 41/163 (1994) 103-5, (P. J.
Haas).
10141 Rousmaniere J., A bridge to dialogue; the story of Jewish-Christian
relations. NY 1991, Paulist. – ᴿOTEssays 7 (1994) 95s (J. J. Burden).
10143 Schöppner Lothar, Begegnungsmodel jüdisch-christlicher Dialog; empirische Analyse der Würzburger Lernprojektes: Lernprozess 7. FrB 1993,
Herder. 480 p. DM 78. – ᴿTPQ 142 (1994) 77s (Silvia Hagleitner).
10144 Schor Ralph, L'antisémitisme en France pendant les années trente:
Questions au XXᵉ siècle. P 1992, Complexe. 381 p. – ᴿArchivScSocR
39,86 (1994) 306 (Régine Azria).
10145 Schreckenberg Heinz, Die christlichen Adversus-Judaeos-Texte 1988 [3
vol.] 1-2²ʳᵉᵛ: EurHS 72/172.335. Fra 1990/4, P. Lang. I. 1-11. Jh., 1990,
746 p. + 1 corrigenda; II. 11.-13. Jh., 710 p. III. 15.-20. Jh., 774 p.
3-631-42603-8; 3-8204-1436-3; 3-631-46763-X. – ᴿTPhil 69 (1994) 298s (R.
Berndt).
10145* Smelik K. A. D., Anti-judaisme in de Kerk; een Verkenning. Baarn
1993, Ten Have. 152 p. ƒ24.50. – ᴿStreven 61 (1994) 854s (E. de Smet).
10146 Smiga George M., Pain and polemic; anti-Judaism in the Gospels 1992
➤ 8,a788; 9,11080: ᴿCBQ 56 (1994) 152 (M. Cahill); RivB 42 (1994)
233-7 (V. Fusco); Worship 65 (1994) 182-4 (J. A. Melloh).
10147 Stacey Robert C., History, religion, and medieval antisemitism; a
response to Gavin LANGMUIR 1990 + Towards a definition 1990]: RelStR
20 (1994) 94-101.
10148 ᴱStrauss Herbert A., Hostages of modernization; studies on modern
antisemitism 1670/1939, Austria-Hungary-Poland-Russia: Current Research on Antisemitism 3/2. NY 1993, de Gruyter. xi-p. 670-1416, DM
268. – ᴿAmHR 99 (1994) 705 (tit. sans pp.).
10149 ᴱSwidler Leonard, al., Bursting the bonds? 1990 ➤ 7,560 ... 9,11085:
ᴿGregorianum 74 (1993) 367-9 (J. Dupuis).
10150 Swidler Leonard, Heutige Implikationen des jüdisch-christlichen Dialogs
über Jesus Christus: ZRGg 46 (1994) 333-351.
10150* Thoma Clemens, Das Messiasprojekt; Theologie jüdisch-christlicher
Begegnung. Augsburg 1994, Pattloch. 478 p.; Bibliog. 439-464. 3-629-
00626-4.
10151 Ucko Hans, Common roots, new horizons; learning about Christian
faith from dialogues with Jews: Risk 61. Geneva 1994, WCC. xi-100 p.
Fs 12.50. 2-8254-1128-0. [TDig 42,191]. – ᴿTBR 7,1 (1994s) 50 (A. R.
Brockway).
10152 Vanhoye Albert, Salut universel par le Christ et validité de l'Ancienne
Alliance: NRT 116 (1994) 815-835.
10152* Whitfield Stephen J. [in footnote Steven], An anatomy of black
anti-Semitism [not a passing phenomenon, as seemed to I. F. STONE in
1968]: Judaism 43 (1994) 341-359.
10153 Wiese Christian, Vom 'jüdischen Geist'; Isaak HEINEMANNs Auseinandersetzung mit dem akademischen Antisemitismus innerhalb der
protestantischen Theologie in der Weimarer Republik: ZRGg 46 (1994)
211-234.
10154 Williamson C. M., A guest in the house of Israel; post-holocaust
Church theology. LVL 1993, W-Knox. vii-374 p. $20 pa. 0-664-25454-3
[NTAbs 38, p. 315].
10154* Wirth Wolfgang, Solidarität der Kirche mit Israel; die theologische
Neubesinnung des Verhältnisses der Kirche zum Judentum nach 1945

anhand der offiziellen Verlautbarungen: EurHS 23/312. Fra 1987, Lang. 232 p. Fs 50. – ᴿJudaica 49 (1993) 241s (H. L. *Reichrath*).
10155 ᴱ**Zannoni** Arthur E., Jews and Christians speak of Jesus. Mp 1994, Fortress. xiv-191 p. 0-8006-2804-7.

XVII,3 Religiones parabiblicae

M1.1 **Gnosticismus classicus.**

10156 *Bianchi* Ugo, Le origini dello gnosticismo; nuovi studi e ricerche: AugR 32 (1992) 205-216.
10157 *Buckley* Jorunn J., Libertines or not; fruit, bread, semen and other body fluids in Gnosticism: JEarlyC 2 (1994) 15-31.
10158 **Couliano** Ioan P., The tree of gnosis 1992 ➤ 8,a801; 9,11106: ᴿInterpretation 48 (1994) 104.105 (Pheme *Perkins*).
10159 *Dacouras* Dionysios G., ⊖ Religion and heresy: TAth 64 (1993) 144-199; Eng. 879s.
10160 **Filoramo** Giovanni, A history of Gnosticism 1990 ➤ 6,a474 ... 9,11108: ᴿClasB 69 (1993) 107-9 (D. *Gilman:* < L'attes[t]a del[la] fine); CritRR 5 (1992) 296-8 (Karen *King*).
10160* *Holzhausen* Jens, Gnosis und Martyrium; zu VALENTINS viertem Fragment: ZNW 85 (1994) 116-122.
10161 **Jones** Peter R., The Gnostic Empire strikes back; an old heresy for the new age. Phillipsburg NJ 1992, Presbyterian & R. 112 p. $7 0-87552-285-8. – ᴿScotBuEvT 11 (1993) 140s (P. C. *Buchanan*).
10162 *Klauck* Hans-Josef, Gnosis als Weltanschauung in der Antike: *a)* WissWeis 56 (1993) 3-15; – *b)* ➤ 36, Mem. FUĆAK M., BogSmot 64 (1994) 61-71.
10162* *Lebedev* Andrei V., Orpheus, Parmenides or Empedocles? The Aphrodite verses in the Naassene treatise of HIPPOLYTUS' Elenchos: Philologus 138 (1994) 24-31.
10163 *Luttikhuizen* Gerard, Early Christian Judaism and Christian gnosis, and their relation to emerging mainstream Christianity: ➤ 132, ᶠVORSTER W., Neotestamentica 28,3 (1994) 219-234.
10163* **McBride** Daniel R., The Egyptian foundations of Gnostic thought: diss. ᴰ*Redford* D. Toronto 1994. – SR 23 (1994) 525.
10164 *Magris* Aldo, Die gnostische Umdeutung des Platonismus; die Lehre vom Bild: GrazB 20 (1994) 165-194.
10165 **Merkur** Daniel, Gnosis; an esoteric tradition of mystical visions and unions. Albany 1993, SUNY. x-387 p.; bibliog. 339-377. 0-7914-1619-4.
10165* *a) Montserrat-Torrents* Josep, Sociologie et métaphysique de la Gnose; – *b) Müller* Daniela, Cosmologie et rédemption; le modèle valentinien: Heresis 23 (1994) 57-73 / 75-96.
10166 **O'Brien** Denis, Théodicée plotinienne, théodicée gnostique: PhAnt 57. Leiden 1993, Brill. 117 p. $45.75. – ᴿFrSZ 41 (1994) 269-273 (A. *Étienne*).
10167 **Pearson** Birger A., Gnosticism, Judaism, and Egyptian Christianity 1990 ➤ 6,281; 8,a808: ᴿScotJT 46 (1993) 400-3 (A. B. *Logan*).
10168 **Perkins** Pheme, Gnosticism & NT 1993 ➤ 9,11121: ᴿExpTim 105 (1993s) 380 (C. *Tuckett*: clear, up-to-date and informative).
10169 **Pétrement** Simone, A separate God; the Christian origins of Gnosticism 1990 ➤ 7,a250; 8,a809: ᴿCritRR 5 (1992) 300-3 (M. A. *Williams*).

10170 **Scopello** Madeleine, Les Gnostiques 1991 ➤ 8,a813:   ᴿAugR 32 (1993) 447s (P. *Grech*); CritRR 5 (1992) 306s (Deirdre *Good*).

10171 **Simonetti** Manlio,   *Jonas* Hans,   Lo gnosticismo² (The Gnostic religion⁴ 1972). T 1991, SEI. 438 p. – ᴿLateranum 60 (1994) 181s (O. *Pasquato*).

10171* ᵀᴱ**Simonetti** Manlio,   Testi gnostici in lingua greca e latina [1993 ¹1970] ➤ 9,11127: ᴿCompostellanum 38 (1993) 246s (E. *Romero Pose*).

10172 **Stroumsa** G. G.,   Savoir et salut 1992 ➤ 8,316; 9,11128: ᴿBO 51 (1994) 654-7 (J. van *Amersfoort*); ÉTRel 68 (1993) 442s (A. *Gaillard*); JEarlyC 1 (1994) 109-111 (R. *Doran*); RÉAug 39 (1993) 239-241 (A. *Le Boulluec*).

10173 *a)* **Turner** John D.,   Ritual in gnosticism: – *b)* **Evans** Nancy A., Diotima, Eros, Cherubim and the sources of divine knowledge; – *c)* **Gieschen** Charles A.,   The angel of the prophetic spirit; interpreting the revelatory experiences of the Shepherd of Hermas in light of Mandate XI: ➤ 394, SBLSem 33 (1994) 136-181 / 822-846 / 790-803.

10173* ᴱ**Wallis** R. T.,   *Bregman* I.,   Neoplatonism and Gnosticism [21 art.]. Albany 1992, SUNY. xi-531 p. $20 pa. – ᴿJHS 114 (1994) 174s (J. *Dillon*).

10174 **Welburn** Andrew,   Gnosis, the mysteries and Christianity; an anthology of Essene, Gnostic and Christian writings. E 1994, Floris. 348 p. 0-86315-183-3.

10175 **Desjardins** M. R.,   Sin in Valentinianism ᴰ1990 ➤ 6,a496; 8,a818: ᴿCritRR 5 (1992) 291-3 (Deirdre *Good*).

10176 **Holzhausen** Jens,   Der 'Mythos vom Menschen' im hellenistischen Ägypten; eine Studie zum Poimandres (C.H. 1) zu VALENTIN und dem gnostischen Mythos [Diss. Berlin]: Theophaneia 33. Hain 1993, Hanstein. – ᴿVigChr 48 (1994) G. *Quispel*) 300-307.

10177 **Markschies** Christoph,   Valentinus gnosticus ? ᴰ1992 ➤ 8,a820: ᴿArchivScSocR 39,88 (1994) 89s (J.-D. *Dubois*); CBQ 56 (1994) 605-7 (Pheme *Perkins*); JAOS 114 (1994) 277s (M. *Desjardins*); JTS 45 (1994) 310-3 (A.H.B. *Logan*).

10178 ᶠ**RUDHART** Jean,   Orphisme et Orphée, ᴱ**Borgeaud** Philippe 1991 ➤ 8,675*b*: ᴿRicStoLR 30 (1994) 175-9 (P. *Scarpi*); JHS 114 (1994) 175-7 (M. J. *Edwards* in text says that of its '86 pages' many are scanty).

M1.5 **Mani,** *Dualismus;* **Mandaei.**

10179 *Adkin* Neil, [JEROME distinguishes] 'Heretics and Manichees': Orpheus 14 (1993) 135-140.

10180 ᴱ**Bauer** Johannes B.,   S. A. AUGUSTINI Opera 6/7, De moribus ... Manichaeorum: CSEL 90. W 1992, Hoelder-PT. xxx-224 p. 3-209-0122-9! – ᴿTLZ 119 (1994) 328s (G. *Haendler*).

10181 **Böhlig** Alexander, *Markschies* Christoph,   Gnosis und Manichäismus; Forschungen und Studien zu Texten von Valentin und Mani sowie zu den Bibliotheken von Nag Hammadi und Medinet Madi: BZNW 72. B 1994, de Gruyter. xi-116 p. 3-11-014294-5.

10181* *Böhlig* Alexander, Synkretismus in der Überlieferung von Manis Passion: ZRGg 46 (1994) 235-246.

10182 *Brenon* Anne,   Mort et effacement du catharisme; à propos de [JAS Michel, Braises cathares (Toulouse 1992, Loubatières)]: ÉTRel 69 (1994) 67-79.

10183 *Dubois* Jean-Daniel, Le Manichéisme vu par l'Histoire ecclésiastique d'EUSÈBE de Césarée; ÉTRel 68 (1993) 333-9.

10184 **Fontaine** P.F.M., The light and the dark; a cultural history of Judaism 7. Dualism in the Palestinian-Syrian region during the first century A.D. until *ca.* 140. Amst 1992, Gieben. xxxii-310 p. 90-5063-085-5. – RSalesianum 56 (1994) 778s (R. *Vicent*).

10185 **Giversen** S., Manichaean Coptic papyri Beatty 1-4, 1986-8 ➤ 2,7643 ... 6,a516: RAegyptus 79 (1994) 203-5 (S. *Pernigotti*).

10186 TEHutter Manfred, Manis kosmogonische Šābuhragān-Texte ... mittelpersisch M 98/99 I und M 7980-7984: StOrRel 21, 1992 ➤ 8,a833: RNumen 41 (1994) 204s (W. *Klein*); VigChr 48 (1994) 94s (J. van *Oort*).

10186* **Jehoschua** Abraham, Die Manis [Roman ● 1990], T*Achlama* Ruth. Mü 1993, Piper. – RJudaica 50 (1994) 43-49 (Gabrielle *Oberhäusli-Widmer*).

10187 *Kasser* Rodolphe, Le premier homme (celui du commencement); troisième chant de Thôm le Manichéen: AcOrK 53 (1992) 76-85.

10188 EKoenen Ludwig, *Römer* Cornelia, [Kölner-Kodex] Mani, auf der Spur einer verschollenen Religion. FrB 1993, Herder. 106 p. DM 32. – RTPQ 142 (1994) 79s (J. *Janda*).

10189 **Lieu** S.N.C., Manichaeism... China² 1992 ➤ 8,a887 ... 9,11156: RCath-HR 80 (1994) 323s (D. *Johnson*); JEarlyC 2 (1994) 103-5 (J. E. *Goehring*); RivStorLR 30 (1994) 611-3 (C. *Gianotto*); ZRGg 46 (1994) 285 (W. *Klein*).

10190 **Lieu** Samuel N.C., Manichaeism in Mesopotamia and the Roman East: RelGrRWorld 118. Leiden 1994, Brill. xiv-325 p. 90-04-09742-2. RArchivScSocR 39,88 (1994) 123s (J. D. *Dubois*).

10192 **Reeves** John C., Jewish lore in Manichaean cosmogony 1992 ➤ 8,a842; 9.11162: RVigChr 48 (1994) 92-94 (J. van *Oort*).

10193 **Richter** Siegfried, Exegetisch-literarkritische Untersuchungen von Herakleidespsalmen des koptisch-manichäischen Psalmenbuches: ArbSp-KoptÄg 5. Altenberge 1994, Oros. [xii-] 351 p.; Bibliog. p. 224-244. 3-89375-091-6.

10194 **Ries** Julien, Les études manichéennes 1988 ➤ 4,b456 ... 7,a277: RRT-Phil 126 (1994) 386s (C.-A. *Keller*: immense érudition).

10194* *a*) *Ries* Julien, La figure prophétique de Mani et les origines de sa doctrine à la lumière des Kephalaia coptes et du codex de Cologne; – *b*) *Wurst* Gregor, Bemerkungen zum manichäischen Festkalender: ➤ 65, FKASSER R., Coptology 1994, 109-121 / 151-163.

10195 **Römer** Cornelia Eva, Manis frühe Missionsreisen nach der Kölner Manibiographie: Textkritischer Kommentar und Erläuterungen zu p. 121 – p. 192 des Kölner Mani-Kodex: Abh NRhein/Wf Akad, PapColon 24. Opladen 1994, Westdeutscher V. xix-178 p. 3-531-09938-8.

10196 *Smagina* Ye. B., ● Sources and formation of the conception of the king of demons in the Manichaean religion: VDI 204 (1993) 40-57; Eng. 57s.

10197 *Teske* Roland J., WILLIAM of Auvergne and the Manichees: Traditio 48 (1993) 63-75.

10197* **Van Lindt** Paul, [➤ 8,a838] The names of Manichaean mythological figures; a comparative study on terminology in the Coptic Sources: StOrRel 26. Wsb 1992, Harrassowitz. XXVII-247 p. DM 138. 3-447-03312-6. – REnchoria 21 (1994) 173-5 (D. *Montserrat*); OLZ 89 (1994) 174-183 (A. *Böhlig*).

10198 **Villey** André, Psaumes des errants; écrits manichéens du Fayyūm: Sources Gnostiques et manichéennes 4. P 1994, Cerf. 527 p.; bibliog. 477-481. F 260. 2-204-04767-8.

10199 ᴱWiessner Gernot, *Klimkeit* Hans-J., Studia manichaica, 6.-10. Aug. 1989: StOrRel 23, 1992 ➤ 8,636: ᴿOLZ 89 (1994) 413-8 (I. *Colditz*); ZDMG 143 (1993) 406s (A. *Böhlig*); ZRGg 46 (1994) 285s (P. *Pachis*).

10200 *Fernández* Enrique L., La figura de 'Maria' en el Mandeismo a la luz de los escritos de Nag‘ Hammadi: RET 54 (1994) 181-210.

10200* **Gündüz** Şinasi, The knowledge of life; the origins and early history of the Mandaeans and their relation to the Sabians of the Qur'an and to the Harranians: JSS supp. 3. Ox 1994, UP. vii-256 p.; bibliog. 237-250. 0-19-922193-6.

10201 *Gündüz* Şinasi, The problems of the nature and date of Mandaean Sources: JStNT 53 (1994) 87-97.

10202 *Kruisheer* Dirk, Theodore Bar Koni's *Kᵉtābâ d'-'eskolyon* as a source for the study of early Mandaeism: Jb EOL 33 (1993s) 151-169.

10203 **Lupieri** Edmondo, I mandei 1993 ➤ 9,11157: ᴿOrpheus 15 (1994) 248 (F. E. *Sciuto*).

M2.1   Nag‘ Ḥammadi, *generalia*.

10204 *Barry* Catherine, Les textes de Nag Hammadi et le problème de leur classification; chronique d'un colloque [Univ. Laval, 15-19 sept. 1993]: LavalTP 50 (1994) 421-432.

10205 **Charron** Régine, Concordance des textes de Nag Hammadi; le Codex VII, 1992 ➤ 8,a849: ᴿJEarlyC 2 (1994) 107-9 (E. M. *Yamauchi*).

10205* ᴱ**Evans** Craig A., *al.*, Nag Hammadi texts and the Bible; a synopsis and an index: NT TSt 19. Leiden 1993, Brill. xxii-551 p. ƒ220. 90-04-09902-6. – ᴿBZ 38 (1994) 300s (H.-J. *Klauck*).

10206 *Myszor* Wincenty, ℗ Biuletyn patrystyczny, 1. Gnostycyzm; Nag Hammadi Studies: ColcT 63,1 (1993) 107-111 (-3, Fontes Christiani).

10207 ᴱ**Parrott** Douglas M., Nag Hammadi Codices III, 3-4 and V. 1 ...: NHS 27, 1991 ➤ 7,a287 ... 9,11173: ᴿCritRR 6 (1993) 336-8 (Deirdre *Good*).

10208 ᴱ**Robinson** James M., The Nag Hammadi library in English³ʳᵉᵛ[¹1977] 1988 ➤ 4,b460 ... 7,a284: ᴿJEvTS 37 (1994) 438s (M. R. *Fairchild*: 'thee' struck only in The prayer of thanksgiving).

10209 *Robinson* James M., Die Bedeutung der gnostischen Nag-Hammadi Texte für die neutestamentliche Wissenschaft [Gastvorlesung 1993 Gö & Bamberg]: ➤ 40, ꟳGᴇᴏʀɢɪ D., Religious propaganda 1994, 23-41.

10210 *Schenke* Hans-Martin, Nag Hammadi: ➤ 517, TRE 23 (1954) 731-6.

M2.2   Evangelium etc. Thomae – The Gospel (etc.) of Thomas.

10211 *Baars* W., *Helderman* Jan, Neue Materialien zum Text und zur Interpretation des Kindheitsevangeliums des Pseudo-Thomas: OrChr 77 (Wsb 1993) 191-226 [< ZIT 94, 323].

10212 *Cameron* Ron, Alternate beginnings, different ends; Eᴜsᴇʙɪᴜs, [Gospel of] Thomas, and the construction of Christian origins: ➤ 40, ꟳGᴇᴏʀɢɪ D., Religious propaganda 1994, 501-525.

10212* *Clarysse* Willy, Gospel of Thomas Logion 13, 'the bubbling well which I myself dug': ➤ 70, ꟳLᴀɢᴀ C., Philohistôr 1994, 1-9.

10213 **De Conick** April D., 'Seek to see him'; the influence of early Jewish mysticism and Hermeticism [but not Gnostic traditions] on the Gospel of Thomas: diss. Michigan, ᴰ*Fossum* J. AA 1994. 349 p. 94-23172. – DissA 55 (1994s) p. 995.

10214 **Patterson** Stephen J., The Gospel of Thomas and Jesus 1993 ➤ 9,11183.
– ᴿCBQ 56 (1994) 379-381 (R. L. *Mowery*); JTS 45 (1994) 262-7 (R. M.
Wilson).

10214* *Riley* G. J., The Gospel of Thomas in recent scholarship: CurResB 2
(1994) 227-252.

M2.3   *Singula scripta* – **Nagᶜ Ḥammadi, various titles.**

10215 ᵀᴱ**Barry** Catherine, La sagesse de Jésus-Christ [Barhebraeus Gnosticus
8502; NH III, 4]: BCNH-T 20, 1993 ➤ 9,11187: ᴿSR 23 (1994) 501s
(J. K. *Coyle*).

10216 **Turner** Martha Lee, The sources and organization of the [NH] 'Gospel
according to Philip': diss. ᴰ*Attridge* H.   Notre Dame 1994. 310 p.
94-32877. – DissA 55 (1994s) p. 2005; RTLv 26, p. 340.

10216* *Schenke* Hans-Martin, Zur Exegese des Philippus-Evangeliums: ➤ 65,
ꟳKASSER R., Coptology 1994, 123-137.

10217 ᴱ**Orlandi** Tito, Evangelium veritatis 1992 ➤ 8,a877; 9,11192: ᴿOr-
ChrPer 60 (1994) 662 (V. *Ruggieri*).

10218 **Gianotto** Claudio, La testimonianza veritiera: TVO 8.   Brescia 1990,
Paideia.   205 p. – ᴿRTPhil 126 (1994) 379s (Françoise *Morard*: interprétation splendide, texte mauvais).

10219 **Zandee** M. J. The teaching of Sylvanus (NHC VII, 4) 1991 ➤ 7,a324 ...
9,11198: – ᴿCdÉ 68 (1994) 313-7 (W. *Myszor*); Enchoria 21 (1994)
196-210 (H.-M. *Schenke*); JBL 113 (1994) 356-8 (M. A. *Williams*).

M3.1   *Quid est religio? Inquisitiones speculativae.* – **What is religion?**

10220 ᴱ**Agnoletto** Attilio, La 'religione popolare'; tre interpretazioni: la cattolica, la protestante, la sociologica.   Mi 1991, IPL.   318 p. – ᴿRivStoLR
30 (1994) 363-5 (C. *Prandi*).

10221 ᴱ**Arthur** Chris, Religion and the media; an introductory reader ... 1993,
Univ. Wales. 302 p. – ᴿTLond 97 (1994) 145s (A. *Tilby*: they grimly
maintain that a Christian can approve media only purified of fun, money,
violence, sex, and entertainment; but rightly 'the media world is not an
alien world, only the world of the popular imagination', Catholic Jim
McDonnell and similarly Colin *Morris*, Rachel *Viney*).

10222 *Audinet* Jacques, Théologie et sciences religieuses; réflexions sur quelques décennies de recherche: RICathP 50 (1994) 39-57.

10223 **Clarke** Peter B., *Byrne* Peter, Religion defined and explained 1993
➤ 9,11200; £40: ᴿTLond 97 (1994) 42s (I. *Markham*: the truth of religion
will forever haunt us but should not dominate the study of religion).

10224 ᴱ**Despland** Michel, *Vallée* Gérard, Religion in history; the word, the
idea, the reality [Colloque McMaster 1989]: SR ed. 13, 1992 ➤ 8,534:
ᴿLavalTP 50 (1994) 229-231 (G. *Tissot*).

10225 **Driver** Tom F., The magic of ritual; our need for liberating rites 1991
➤ 7,a338; 9,11204: ᴿCritRR 6 (1993) 506-8 (W. W. *Schroeder*); JRit 8,2
(1994) 134s (Marjorie *Procter-Smith*).

10226 *Gruenwald* Ithamar, The study of religion and the religion of study:
➤ 40, ꟳGEORGI D., Religious propaganda 1994, 3-21.

   Hervieu-Léger Danièle, La religion pour mémoire 1993 ➤ 10312.

10226* ᴱ**Guerrière** Daniel, Phenomenology of the truth proper to religion
1990 ➤ 7,357: ᴿThought 67 (1992) 139s (D. J. *Casey*).

10227 **Hjelde** Sigurd, Die Religionswissenschaft und das Christentum; eine historische Untersuchung über das Verhältnis von Religionswissenschaft und Theologie: Numen supp. 61. Leiden 1994, Brill. x-355 p.

10227* *Hull* John M., Atheism and the future of religious education [a product of the Enlightenment (p. 357; 'the atheism of the social sciences ... more value-laden than that of sciences or ... philosophy; ... an atheism of hope' p. 374]: → 45, ᶠGOULDER M., Crossing 1994, 357-375.

10228 *Levinskaya* Irina A., Syncretism — the term and phenomenon: TyndB 44 (1993) 117-128.

10228* **Mouw** Richard J., Consulting the faithful; what Christian intellectuals can learn from popular religion. GR 1994, Eerdmans. vi-84 p. 0-8028-0738-0.

10229 *Neusner* Jacob, Can you be 'religious in general'? [no, but we can accept others]: → 8,26*, ᶠCAHILL P. J., RelStT 12,2 (1992) 69-73.

10230 *Taber* Charles R. & Betty J., A Christian understanding of 'religion' and 'the religions': Missiology 20 (1992) 69-78.

10231 *Wyschogrod* Edith, Facts, fiction, ficciones; truth in the study of religion [1993 presidential address]: JAAR 62 (1994) 1-16.

M3.2   **Historia comparationis religionum:** *centra, scholae.*

10232 **Ackerman** R., Myth and ritual school ... FRAZER 1991 → 10,11221*: ᴿZygon 28 (1993) 120-2 (D. *Wiebe*).

10232* **Ahlstrand** Kajsa, Fundamental openness; an enquiry into Raimundo PANIKKAR's theological vision and its presuppositions. U ᴰ1993, Swedish Inst. Missionary Research. 209 p. – ᴿNZMiss 50 (1994) 325s (A. *Peter*).

10233 *Anderson* Douglas R., SMITH [John E., here] and DEWEY on the religious dimension of experience; dealing with Dewey's half-God: AmJTPh 14 (Dayton 1993) [119-146] 161-176 [< ZIT 94,160].

10234 ᴱAstley Jeff, *Francis* Leslie, Christian perspectives on faith development. Leominster/GR 1992, Gracewing/Eerdmans. xxiv-411 p. $25 pa. 0-85244-220-3 / 0-882-0578-7. – ᴿChrSchR 24 (1994) 327-9 (H. Newton *Maloney*: notable continuation of J. FOWLER, Stages of Faith 1961; and C. DYKSTRA, S. PARKS 1986).

10235 *Begzos* Marios, Die Religionsphilosophie in Griechenland (1916-1986): NSys 35 (1993) 215-229; Eng. 229.

10235* **Belier** Wouter, Decayed gods ... DUMÉZIL 1991 → 7,a390: ᴿLatomus 53 (1994) 669-671 (D. *Briquel*).

10236 *a) Belier* Wouter W., Arnold van GENNEP and the rise of French sociology of religion; – *b) Ay* Karl-Ludwig, Geography and mentality; some aspects of Max WEBER's Protestantism thesis: Numen 41 (1994) 141-162 / 163-194.

10237 **Brewer** Kenneth W., Hans KÜNG's theology of religions; a historical-semantic analysis and evaluation: diss. Drew, ᴰ*Oden* T. Madison NJ 1994. 387 p. 94-32947. – DissA 55 (1994s) p. 2010.

10238 *Burnside* Carol E., Jane Ellen HARRISON's contribution to the study of religion: Religion 24,1 (L 1994) 67-72 [< ZIT 94,259].

10238* — **Peacock** Sandra J., Jane Ellen HARRISON, The mask and the self. NHv 1988, Yale Univ. – ᴿReligion 24 (1994) 67-72 (Carol E. *Burnside*).

10239 — *Carpentier* Martha C., Jane Ellen HARRISON and the ritual theory: JRit 8 (1994) 11-26.

10239* *Chapman* Mark D., Religion, ethics and the history of religion school: ScotJT 46 (1993) 43-78.

10240 **Cohen** Hermann, La religion dans les limites de la philosophie [Der

Begriff der R. im System der P. 1915],[T] P 1990, Cerf. 172 p. –
[R]ScripTPamp 26 (1994) 1227s (F. *Conesa*).

10241 *Cornille* Catherine, De elf stellingen van Frank de GRAEVE voor een
theologie van de godsdiensten; tussen inclusivisme en pluralisme: Bijdragen 55 (1994) 234-247; Eng. 247s.

10242 *Delahoutre* Michel, Bulletin d'histoire des religions: EsprVie 104 (1994)
17-30.129-137; – (Islam) 424-431.531-554.

10243 **Demange** Pierre, L'essence de la religion selon SCHLEIERMACHER 1991
↠ 9,11232: [R]ScEspr 45 (1993) 125-7 (G. *Pelland*).

10244 **Desroche** Henri, (*Clévenot* Michel), Hommes et religions; histoires
mémorables. P 1992, Quai Voltaire. 176 p. – [R]RThom 94 (1994) 346 (R.
Bergeret).

10245 **Eliade** Mircea, Geschichte der religiösen Ideen 3/2, Vom Zeitalter der
Entdeckungen bis zur Gegenwart, 1991 ↠ 8,a911*: [R]TPQ 142 (1994) 72s
(J. *Janda*).

10246 **Eliade** M. *al.*, The Eliade guide to world religions 1991 ↠ 9,11233:
[R]ChH 63 (1994) 172s (R. S. *Ellwood*).

10247 **Eliade** Mircea, *Pettazzoni* Raffaele, L'histoire des religions a-t-elle un
sens? Correspndance 1926-1959: Patrimoines. P 1994, Cerf. 310 p.
F 149. 2-204-05005-9.

10248 — **Cave** David, Mircea ELIADE's Vision for a new humanism 1993
↠ 9,11234: [R]ChrC 110 (1994) 23s (G. D. *Atkins*); JRel 74 (1994) 591s (D.
Allen).

10249 — **Eyenga Liongo** On'asi Emmanuel, Dialectique du sacré et modernité; contribution de Mircéa Éliade à la problématique contemporaine
d'une philosophie de la religion: diss. [↠ 9,11237 [D]Greisch']. [D]*Michel*
M., Paris Inst.Cath. 1993. 273 p. – [R]RICathP 49 (1994) 105-8 (J. *Greisch*).

10250 — **Olson** Carl, The theology and philosophy of Eliade; a search for
the centre 1992 ↠ 9,11236: [R]JRel 74 (1994) 438s (D. *Allen*: challenging,
useful).

10251 *Fleischer* Margot, NIETZSCHE, Friedrich: ↠ 517, TRE 24 (1994)
506-524.

10252 **Gelpi** Donald L., Endless seeker ... EMERSON 1991 ↠ 7,g729; 8,m522:
[R]CritRR 5 (1992) 403-5 (A. D. *Hodder*: fills a need).

10253 **Hak** D. H., Stagnatie in de Nederlandse godsdienstwetenschap
1920-1980; de bijdragen van Gerardus van der LEEUW, Fokke SIERKSMA
en Theo P. van BAAREN aan de godsdienstwetenschap; diss. Groningen;
[D]*Bremmer* J. Amst 1994, Thesis. vi-283 p. – TvT 34 (1994) 297.

10253* *Heran* François, Rite et méconnaissance; notes sur la théorie religieuse de l'action chez [Vilfredo] PARETO et WEBER: ArchivScSocR 39,85
(1994) 137-151; Eng. español 152.

10254 **Hick** John, Disputed questions in theology and the philosophy of
religion 1993 ↠ 9,11240: [R]TLond 97 (1994) 127s (I. *Markham*: elegant,
stimulating, courteous; but the pluralist hypothesis is too high a price to
pay).

10255 *Hick* John [+ 8 others], On Wilfred Cantwell SMITH; his place in the
study of religion: Method and Theory in the Study of Religion 4,1s
(Toronto 1992) 5-20 (-130) [< ZIT 93,577].

10255* — **Geivitt** R. Douglas, Evil and the evidence for God; the challenge
of John Hick's theodicy. Ph 1994, Temple Univ. xii-276 p. $45. 1-
56639-094-X [TDig 42,65].

10256 **Hjelde** S., Die Religionswissenschaft und das Christentum; eine historische Untersuchung über das Verhältnis von Religionswissenschaft und

Theologie: Numen supp. 61. Leiden 1994, Brill. x-355 p.; ƒ 195. 90-04-9922-0 [NTAbs 38, p. 449].

10257 **Hopper** Stanley R. [1907-1991], The religious way of transfiguration; religious imagination as theopoiesis [essays 1951-89 interwoven with his biography], ᴱ*Keiser* R. Melvin, *Stoneburner* Tony, Lᴠʟ 1992, W-Knox. ix-323 p. $25. – ᴿJRel 74 (1994) 146s (S. *Happel*).

10258 **Jeanrond** Werner G., *Rike* Jennifer L., Radical pluralism and truth; David Tʀᴀᴄʏ and the hermeneutics of religion. NY 1991, Crossroad. 350 p. $34.50. 0-8245-1118-2. – ᴿLitTOx 8 (1994) 118s (W. G. *Doty*).

10258* *Karokaram* Anto, Raymond Pᴀɴɪᴋᴋᴀʀ's theology of religions [1964-70 ...], a critique: Vidyajyoti 58 (1994) 663-672.

10259 *Kondrat* Kazimierz, ❷ Theological consequences of the theory of religious language in John Hɪᴄᴋ's philosophy: ColcT 63,1 (1993) 91-105; Eng. 105.

10260 *MacKinnon* Donald M., Cᴏʟʟɪɴɢᴡᴏᴏᴅ on the philosophy of religion: ScotJR 13 (1992) 73-83.

10261 *Mahlmann* T., Was genau verstand Sigmund Fʀᴇᴜᴅ unter 'Illusion' oder wie weit reicht die Religionskritik ?: – *b*) *Auchter* T., Aggression als Zeichen von Hoffnung — oder der entgleiste Dialog: WegMensch 46 (1992) 79-101 / 53-71 [< zɪᴛ 94,247].

10262 ᵀᴱ**Malherbe** Michel, David Hᴜᴍᴇ, Dialogues sur la religion naturelle. P 1987, Vrin. 158 p. – ᴿLavalTP 50 (1994) 433-6 (L. *Langlois*).

10263 *Pailin* David A., Natürliche Religion [I. Antike, *Wissmann* Hans] II. Religionsphilosophie vom 17. Jh. bis zur Gegenwart, ᵀ*Thurm* Rüdiger; ➤ 517, TRE 24 (1994) [78-]80-85. [185-188, *Greschat* Hans-J., Natur-religionen].

10264 **Peden** W. Creighton, The philosopher of free religion, Francis Ellingwood Aʙʙᴏᴛ, 1836-1903: AmerUnivSt 133. ɴʏ 1993, P. Lang. 207 p. $40. – ᴿAmJTP 15 (1994) 201-5 (T. E. *Graham*).

10265 **Pfleiderer** Georg, Theologie als Wirklichkeitswissenschaft; Studien zum Religionsbegriff bei G. Wᴏʙʙᴇʀᴍɪɴ, R. Oᴛᴛᴏ, H. Sᴄʜᴏʟᴢ und Max Sᴄʜᴇʟᴇʀ: BeitHisT 82, 1992 ➤ 9,11262: ᴿJRel 74 (1994) 415 (W. F. *Wyman*).

10266 *Polka* Brayton, Fʀᴇᴜᴅ, science, and the psychoanalytic critique of religion; the paradox of self-referentiality: JAAR 62 (1994) 59-83.

10267 **Pradines** Maurice, Esprit de la religion [1941], ᴱ*Guyot* Roland. Guéret 1992, Verso. 553 p. – ᴿArchivScSocR 39-88 (1994) 99s (É. *Poulat*).

10268 **Ramsey** Bennett, Submitting to freedom; the religious vision of William Jᴀᴍᴇꜱ: Religion in America. Ox 1993, UP. 177 p. $25. – ᴿAmHR 99 (1994) 980s (T. D. *Hamm*); AmJTP 15 (1994) 231-5 (D. A. *Crosby*).

10269 — **Ruf** J., The creation of chaos; William Jᴀᴍᴇꜱ and the stylistic making of a disorderly world. Albany 1991, sᴜɴʏ. xviii-185 p. $60; pa $20. – ᴿAmJTP 14 (1993) 332-6 (M. L. *Raposa*); CritRR 6 (1993) 469s (J. A. *Stone*).

10270 — *Lamberth* David D., Jᴀᴍᴇꜱ's Varieties reconsidered; radical empiricism, the extra-marginal and conversion: AmJTP 15 (1994) 257-267.

10271 — *Spohn* William C., William Jᴀᴍᴇꜱ on religious experience; an elitist account ?: American Journal of Theology and Philosophy 15,1 (1994) 27-42 (3-14, *Miller* R. C.; – 15-26, *Dean* W.); – (& Wɪᴛᴛɢᴇɴꜱᴛᴇɪɴ) *Tarbox* E. J. 43-58; (& Dʜᴀʀᴍᴀᴋɪʀᴛɪ), *Powers* J. 59-85.

10272 ᴱ**Ries** J., Traité d'anthropologie du sacré, 1. Les origines et le problème de l'homo religiosus 1992 ➤ 9,11279: ᴿNRT 116 (1994) 597 (J. *Scheuer*); RTLv 25 (1994) 60-64 (J. *Étienne*).

10273 **Ries** Julien, The origins of religions, T*Singleton* Kate. GR 1994, Eerdmans. 158 p. $40. 0-8028-3767-0.

10273* **Ries** Julien, Le origini delle religioni. Mi c. 1994, Jaca. 214 p., (color) ill. Lᵐ 62. – RArcheo 9,109 (1994) 122 (S. *Moscati*).

10274 E**Rossi** Philip J., *Wreen* Michael, KANT's philosophy of religion reconsidered 1987/91 → 9,11272: RChrSchR 23 (1993s) 458s (J. R. *Wilson*).

E**Ricken** F., *Marty* F., KANT über Religion 1992 → 391.

10275 **Rudolph** Kurt, Geschichte und Probleme der Religionswissenschaft 1992 → 9,11276: RScripTPamp 26 (1994) 839s (J. M. *Odero*).

10276 *Schmidt* Francis, Des inepties tolérables; la raison des rites de John SPENCER (1685) à W. Robertson SMITH (1889): ArchivScSocR 39,85 (1994) 121-135; Eng. español 136.

10277 E**Seager** Richard H., The dawn of religious pluralism; voices from the world's parliament of religious 1893 ... 1993, Open Court. $60; pa. $29. 0-8126-9222-5; -3-3. – RChH 63 (1994) 149s (R. C. *Fuller*).

10278 E**Swatos** William H.ᴶ, Time, place, and circumstance; Neo-WEBERIAN studies in comparative religious history: ContrbStRel 24. NY 1990, Greenwood. xiii-229 p. $40. – RChH 63 (1994) 173s (R. L. *Petersen*).

10279 *Thomas* E. Vaughan, D. Z. PHILLIPS and religious belief as perspective on life: ScotJR 14 (1993) 112-124.

10279* *Thompson* Curtis L., The end of religion in HEGEL and KIERKEGAARD: Sophia 33,2 (Australia 1994) 10- ...

10280 **Vis** Jeroen, Ervaringen van het Absolute; de kritiek van de religieuse ervaringen in HEGELS Fenomenologie van de geest [diss. Amst VU]. Amst 1991, Thesis. xiv-120 p. – RBijdragen 55 (1994) 338 (L. de *Vos*).

10281 **Wach** Joachim, Introduction to the history of religions [1924 Hab.Diss. + RGG² items] TE*Kitagawa* J. M., *Alles* G. D. L c. 1993, Macmillan. xxxiv-234 p. 0-02-933530-2. – RReligion 24 (1994) 93s (D. *Wiebe*).

10282 — *Segal* Robert A., Joachim WACH [2 works Eng. 1989] and the history of religions: RelStR 20 (1994) 197-201.

10283 *Wheeler-Barclay* Marjorie, Victorian evangelism and the sociology of religion; the career of William Robertson SMITH: JHistId 54 (1993) 59-78.

10284 *Woelfel* James, Religious empiricism as '-ism'; the critical legacy of Walter KAUFMANN: AmJTP 15 (1994) 181-6.

10285 **Yandell** Keith E., HUME's 'inexplicable mystery'; his views on religion. Ph 1990, Temple Univ. xvii-360 p. $40. – RCritRR 6 (1993) 473-5 (H. *Zorn*).

M3.3 **Investigationes particulares religionum.**

10286 **Acquaviva** Salvino, *Pace* Enzo, La sociologie des religions, problèmes et perspectives [Pace, Sociologia delle religioni, presentée par Acquaviva] T*Michel* Patrick: ScHumRel. P 1994, Cerf. 202 p. – RSR 23 (1994) 509 (J.-P. *Rouleau*).

10287 **Alessi** Adriano, Filosofia della religione 1991 → 8,a939; 9,11289: RCiVit 49 (1994) 189 (A. *Pellegrini*).

10287* **Alston** William P., Perceiving God; the epistemology of religieus experience. Ithaca 1991, Cornell Univ. 336 p. $37. – RAmJTP 14 (1993) 227-232 (T. D. *Parker*).

10288 *Ansaldi* Jean, Une discipline ancienne et nouvelle; la psycho-anthropologie religieuse: ÉTRel 69 (1994) 39-52.

10289 ᴱ**Assmann** Jan,   Die Erfindung des inneren Menschen; Studien zur religiösen Anthropologie [Heidelberg Nov. 1990]. Gü 1993, Mohn. 300 p. DM 78. 3-579-01788-8. – ᴿTGL 84 (1994) 246s (R. *Geisen*).

ᴱ[**Auneau** J.], Enseigner l'histoire des religions, colloque Besançon 20-21 nov. 1991 [EsprVie 103,524] ➤ 8,448.

10290 **Batson** C. Daniel, *al.*, Religion and the individual; a social-psychological perspective. NY 1993, Oxford-UP. viii-427 p. $50; pa. $25. 0-19-506208-6; -9-4 [TDig 41,155].

10291 **Bell** Catherine,   Ritual theory, ritual practice 1992 ➤ 9,11298: ᴿJap-JRel 21 (1994) 118-120 (R. *Gardner*).

10292 **Belmont** Nicole, *Lautman* Françoise,   Ethnologie des faits religieux en Europe: Le regard de l'ethnologue 4.   P 1993, Ministère de l'éducation. 540 p. – ᴿArchivScSocR 39,88 (1994) 48-50 (Françoise *Loux*).

10293 ᴱ**Biderman** Shlomo, *Scharfstein* Ben-Ami,   Interpretation in religion [TelAviv June 1990] 1992 ➤ 9,11300: ᴿScripTPamp 26 (1994) 831 (F. *Conesa*).

10294 **Boyer** Pascal,   The naturalness of religious ideas; a cognitive theory of religion.   Berkeley 1994, Univ. California.   xv-324 p. $35.   0-520-07559-5 [TDig 41,352].

10295 **Brockelman** Paul,   The inside story; a narrative approach to religious understanding and truth.   Albany 1992, SUNY.   xii-204 p. $47.50; pa. $16. – ᴿJRel 74 (1994) 578s (S. *Kepnes*).

10296 *a) Chaim* Władysław, ❷ Acceptance of religious beliefs and the structure of needs; – *b) Makselon* Józef,   The fear of death and religiousness: ➤ 92*, ꟳPIERONEK T., AnCracov 26 (1994) 3-21; Eng. 21 / 63-67; ❷ 68.

10297 **Cumpsty** John S.,   Religion as belonging; a general theory of religion.   Lanham MD 1991, UPA. £64; pa. $35.50. 0-8191-8353-X; -9-8. – ᴿJAAR 62 (1994) 184-6 (E. T. *Lawson*).

10298 **Cupitt** Don,   After all; religion without alienation. L 1994, SCM. 124 p. £10. 0-334-00036-X. – ᴿTBR 7,1 (1994s) 14s (P. *Helm*).

10299 **Daleiden** Joseph L.,   The final superstition; a critical evaluation of the Judeo-Christian legacy.   Buffalo 1994, Prometheus.   490 p. 0-87975-896-7 [TBR 7/3, 11, no comment].

10300 **Davis** Charles,   Religion and the making of society.   C 1993, Univ. 208 p. £32.50; pa £11. 0-521-44310-5; -789-5. – ᴿExpTim 105 (1993s) 316s (R. J. *Elford*, also on RASMUSSEN L. 1994).

10301 *DiCenso* James J.,   Symbolism and subjectivity; a LACANIAN approach to religion: JRel 74 (1994) 45-64.

10302 **Falk** Nancy A., *Gross* Rita M., La religion par les femmes [anthologie de 24 études] 1993 ➤ 9,11312: ᴿÉTRel 69 (1994) 405s (J. *Argaud*); RHPR 74 (1994) 95s (I. *Grellier*).

10302* ᴱ**Filoramo** Giovanni,   Le religioni antiche: Storia delle religioni 1. Enciclopedia del Sapere.   R 1994, Laterza. 202 p. 88-420-4488-1.

10303 **Fizzotti** Eugenio,   Verso una psicologia della religione I. Problemi e protagonisti. T-Leumann 1992, LDC. 268 p. Lᵐ 25. – ᴿCC 145 (1994,1) 306s (G. *Rossi*).

10304 **Flanagan** Kieran,   Sociology and history, representations of the holy. L 1991, Macmillan.   xii-411 p. £50. – ᴿHeythJ 35 (1994) 85s (G. *Loughlin*).

10305 **Freeman** Anthony,   God in us; a case for Christian humanism. L 1993, SCM. 87 p. £6 pa. – ᴿTLond 97 (1994) 130s (M. *Wiles*: prayer? no; Church Jesus? no; immortality? no; questions the Church ought to be

discussing more openly than it does; he expresses some important things very clearly, but more than the evidence justifies).
10306 **Grabner-Haider** A., Kritische Religionsphilosophie; europäische und aussereuropäische Kulturen 1993 → 9,11320: [R]NRT 116 (1994) 918s (J. *Masson*); TLZ 119 (1994) 114-6 (G. *Keil*).
10307 **Grabner-Haider** Anton, Kritische [rel.-wiss.] Anthropologie: RWSt 29. Wü/Altenberge 1993, Echter/Oros. 371 p. DM 65. 3-429-01523-5 / 3-89375-082-7. – [R]ZkT 116 (1994) 515-7 (K. H. *Neufeld*).
10308 **Grom** Bernhard, Religionspsychologie; auch Mü, Kösel 1992 → 9, 11323; [R]TG1 84 (1994) 106s (J. *Schwermer*); TüTQ 174 (1994) 169-171 (A. *Biesinger*).
10309 **Hatzfeld** Henri, Les racines de la religion; tradition, rituel, valeurs 1993 → 9,11327; 2-02-017303-4: [R]ÉTRel 69 (1994) 567s (A. *Gaillard*); RHPR 74 (1994) 81-91 (G. *Vincent*: Formes et fonctions de la religion).
10311 **Hefner** Philip, The human factor; evolution, culture, and religion; pref. *Peacocke* A. Mp 1993, Fortress. XVIII-317 p. $18. – [TS 56,176; J. H. *Wright*].
10312 **Hervieu-Léger** Danièle, La religion pour mémoire: ScHumRel 1993 → 9,11328: [R]ÉglT 25 (1994) 451-3 (P.-A. *Turcotte*); ÉTRel 69 (1994) 305s (J.-M. *Prieur*); Études 380 (1994) 121s (C. *Flipo*: question posée par les pères fondateurs de la sociologie; définition de la religion); NRT 116 (1994) 759s (P. *Evrard*).
10313 **Hill** William J., Search for the absent God; tradition and modernity in religious understanding 1992 → 8,253: [R]Angelicum 71 (1994) 118-120 (A. *Wilder*).
10314 **Kakar** Sudhir, The analyst and the mystic; psychoanalytic reflections on religion and mysticism [... Ramakrishna case-history]. Ch 1991, Univ. 83 p. $16. – [R]JRel 74 (1994) 130s (W. B. *Parsons*).
10315 **Kenny** Anthony, What is faith? 1992 → 9,1131: [R]HeythJ 35 (1994) 233s (Sonya *Sikka*).
10316 **Lawson** E. T., *McCauley* T. Rethinking religion 1990 → 9,11335: [R]Zygon 28 (1993) 115-120 (T. F. *Godlove*).
10317 **Libiszowska-Żółtowska** Maria, **℗** *Postawy*, Situations of intelligence in face of religion; sociological study. Wsz 1991, PAN, Instytut Filozofii i Socjologii. 229 p. – [R]ColcT 23,4 (1993) 226-8 (J. *Mariański*, **℗**: 3 merits).
10318 *Maesschalck* Marc, Religion attestée et religion institutionalisée; la question anthropologique de l'appartenance religieuse: CahSPR 12 (1992) 73-106.
10319 **Magnani** Giovanni, Filosofia della religione (parte 3)². R 1991, Pont. Univ. Gregoriana. 200 p. L[m] 25.
10320 *Makrakis* Michael, **ⓖ** The psychology of religion and literature: TAth 64 (1993) 653-682; Eng. 883.
10321 **Milanesi** Giancarlo, *Bajzek* J., Sociologia della religione: StCatech 12. T 1990, LDC. 174 p. – [R]ScripTPamp 26 (1994) 1242s (J. M. *Odero*).
10321* *Miller* Richard B., *Patton* Laurie L., *Webb* Stephen H., Rhetoric, pedagogy, and the study of religions: JAAR 62 (1994) 819-850.
10322 [E]**Neusner** Jacob, World religions in America, an introduction. LvL 1994, W-Knox. x-308 p. $22; pa. $13. 0-664-22053-3; -5300-8 [TDig 41,391].
10322* **Pailin** David A., Groundwork of philosophy of religion. Ph 1986, Epworth. 258 p. $19 pa. – [R]AmJTP 14 (1993) 225-7 (C. *Nabe*).
10323 **Panikkar** R. Cosmotheandric experience 1993 → 9,11348: [R]RelStR 20 (1994) 41 (P. C. *Hodgson*: his Gifford Lectures awaited).

10324 **Peterson** Michael. *al.*, Reason and religious belief; an introduction to the philosophy of religion 1991 ➤ 9,11351: ᴿChrSchR 23 (1993s) 214-6 (A. O. *Roberts*); JEvTS 37 (1994) 593-5 (B. *Stetson*).

10325 **Pike** Nelson, Mystical union; an essay on the phenomenology of mysticism. Ithaca 1992, Cornell Univ. xiv-239 p. $30. − ᴿJRel 74 (1994) 98s (B. *McGinn*: if target W. T. STACE had not existed, they would have had to invent him).

10325* *Rodríguez Panizo* Pedro, La religión y las religiones; una aproximación fenomenólogica: RET 54 (1994) 389-412.

10326 *a) Schilbrack* Kevin, Problems for a complete naturalism; − *b) Huyssteen* J. Wentzel van, Is there still a realist challenge in postmodern theology? [STONE J. 1992]; − *c) Driskill* Todd A., Beyond the text; ecstatic naturalism and American pragmatism: AmJTP 15 (1994) 269-291 / 293-304 / 305-323.

10326* **Schwarzenau** Paul, Das nachchristliche Zeitalter; Elemente einer planetarischen Religion: Entwürfe. Stu 1993, Kreuz. 255 p. 3-7831-1258-3. − ᴿActuBbg 31 (1994) 207-211 (J. *Boada*).

10327 ᴱ**Siebers** Tobin, Religion and the authority of the past. AA 1993, Univ. Michigan. [x-] 204 p. 0-472-10489-8.

10327* *a) Smith* John E., Experience, God, and classical American philosophy; − *b) Corrington* Robert S., Beyond experience; pragmatism and nature's God; − *c) Anderson* Douglas R., Smith and Dewey on the religious dimension of experience; dealing with Dewey's half God; − *d) Robbins* J. Wesley, Neo-Pragmatism and the philosophy of experience: AmJTP 14,2 (1993) 119-145 / 147-160 / 161-176 / 177-187.

10328 **Sorrentino** Sergio, Filosofia ed esperienza religiosa. Mi 1993, Guerini. 227 p. Lᵐ 34. − ᴿRasT 35 (1994) 372-4 (P. *Vanzan*).

10329 **Stone** Jerome A., The minimalist vision of transcendence; a naturalist philosophy of religion. Albany 1992, SUNY. xiii-262 p. $49.50; pa. $17. − ᴿAmJTP 14 (1993) 82-89 (D. A. *Crosby*); & 43-50 (L. *Gilkey* to 35-42, Stone); (& 97s Stone's review of Gilkey's Tempest 1991) further on Stone 15 (1994) 293-304 (Van *Huyssteen*); JRel 74 (1994) 107s (K. *Schilbrack*).

10330 **Strenski** Ivan, Religion in relation; method, application and moral location 1993 ➤ 9,11370; also Columbia 1993, Univ.S. Carolina; $36. 0-87294-066-2. − ᴿNumen 41 (1994) 98-101 (D. *Wiebe*).

10331 **Tessier** Robert (*Prades* José A.), Le sacré: Bref 34, 1991 ➤ 7,a368; 9,11372: ᴿÉglT 25 (1994) 147 (J.-M. *Larouche*); ScEspr 45 (1993) 127s (J.-M. *Archambault*).

10333 **Tilghman** B. R., An introduction to the philosophy of religion. Ox/CM 1994, Blackwell. xi-235 p. £35; pa. £11. 0-631-18937-8; -8-6. − ᴿTBR 7,1 (1994s) 17 (Rory *Fox*).

10334 *Timm* Hermann, [*Nientiedt* Klaus, interview], 'Religion ist eine fortschrittsresistente Gestalt menschlicher Lebensführung': HerdKorr 46 (1992) 167-171.

10335 *Tomka* Miklos, The sociology of religion in Eastern and Central Europe: SocComp 41,3 (1994) 379-392 (367-378.413-433 *al.*; 339-365 Latin America; 313-338 US).

10336 ᴱ**Tworuschka** Monika & Udo, Religionen der Welt; Grundlagen, Entwicklungen und Bedeutung in der Gegenwart. Mü 1992, Bertelsmann. 480 p. DM 98. − ᴿEntschluss 49,1 (1994) 37s (H. *Brandt*).

10338 **Waardenburg** Jacques, Des dieux qui se rapprochent; introduction systématique à la science des religions: Religions en perspective 7.

Genève 1993, Labor et Fides.   210 p.   2-8309-0721-3. – ᴿÉTRel 69 (1994) 95s (J. *Argaud*).

10339 **Webb** Stephen H., Blessed excess; religion and the hyperbolic imagination: Rhetoric and Theology series. Albany 1993, SUNY. xviii-203 p. $44.50; pa. $15. – ᴿJRel 74 (1994) 576s (D. S. *Cunningham*: without criterion, 'not all excesses are equal' p. 126; BONHOEFFER and WEIL acceptable).

10340 ᴱ**Weger** K. H., Religionskritik: [170] Texte zur Fundamentaltheologie 1, 1991 ➤ 8,b2: ᴿTvT 34 (1994) 89 (H. *Häring*).

10341 **Weier** Winfried, Religion als Selbstfindung 1991 ➤ 8,b3; 9,11377: ᴿFrSZ 40 (1993) 483-7 (B. J. *Schulte*).

10342 **Whittaker** John H., The logic of religious persuasion: AmerUnivSt 7/71. NY 1990, P. Lang. 116 p. $29. – ᴿCritRR 5 (1992) 423-5 (C. *Creegan*).

10343 ᴱ**Williams** Michael A., *al.*, Innovation in religious traditions: Religion and Society 51, 1992 ➤ 8,636*: ᴿJapJRel 21,1 (1994) 115-8 (M. A. *O'Sullivan*).

10344 **Wulff** David M., Psychology of Religion; classical and contemporary views 1991 ➤ 8,b5; 9,11380: ᴿLexTQ 28 (1993) 268s (M. R. *Nichols*).

10345 **Wuthnow** Robert, Producing the sacred; an essay on public religion. Urbana 1994, Univ. x-181 p. $25; pa. $13. 0-252-01820-2; -6401-1. – ᴿTBR 7,3 (1994s) 47 (D. B. *Forrester*).

10346 **Zdybicka** Zofia J., Person and Religion; an introduction to the philosophy of religion. NY 1992 Lang. XXV-410 p. – ᴿScripTPamp 26 (1994) 841s (F. *Conesa*).

M3.4 Aspectus particulares religionum mundi.

10347 ᴱ**Bellebaum** Alfred, Vom guten Leben; Glücksvorstellungen in Hochkulturen. B 1994, Akademie. P. 59-83, *Lang* Bernhard, Religion und menschliche Glückserfahrung; zur alttestamentlichen Theorie des Glücks.

10348 *Borgeaud* Philippe, Le couple sacré/profane: genèse et fortune d'un concept 'opératoire' en histoire des religions: RHR 211 (1994) 387-418; Eng. 387.

10349 — **Hagstrum** Jean H., Esteem enlivened by desire; the couple from Homer to Shakespeare. Ch 1992. Univ. xvi-518 p.; 31 fig. $41.50. – ᴿClasR 44 (1994) 215 (T. J. *Winnifrith*).

10350 **Boyer** Alain, Le droit des religions en France: Politique d'aujourd'hui. P 1993, PUF. 262 p. – ᴿRHPR 74 (1994) 469-471 (R. *Mehl*).

10351 **Carman** John B., Majesty and meekness; a comparative study of contrast and harmony in the concept of God. GR 1994, Eerdmans. ix-453 p. $25. 0-8028-0693-7. – ᴿTBR 7,3 (1994s) 67s (R. *Hooker*).

10352 **Carmody** Denise L. & John T., In the path of the masters; understanding the spirituality of Buddha, Confucius, Jesus, and Muhammad. NY 1994, Paragon. 232 p. $23. 1-55778-409-4 [TDig 42,60].

10352* **Carmody** Denise & John, Prayer in world religions 1990 ➤ 6,a660; 8,b11: ᴿScotJR 12 (1991) 58-63 (C. *Williams*).

10353 **Casanova** José, Public religions in the modern world. Ch 1994, Univ. x-320 p. $50; pa. $18. 0-226-09534-7; -5-5.

10353* *Casasús Rodó* Josep M., *al.*, Deu en la història de les religions: QVidCr 163s ('Parlar de Deu' 1991) 9-14 (-113).

10354 **Cohn-Sherbok** Dan, World religions and human liberation: Faith meets Faith. Mkn 1992, Orbis. $40; pa. $17. 0-88344-796-7; -5-9. – ᴿRExp 90 (1993) 441s (D. J. *Berry*: good).

10354* **Collins** John E.,   Mysticism and New Paradigm psychology.   Savage MD 1991, Rowman & L.   xxiv-258 p. $42.50. – RCritRR 6 (1993) 480-2 (J. D. *Driskill*).

10355 **Coward** Howard,   Sacred word and sacred text; Scripture in world religions 1988 → 4,b517 ... 9,11391:   RCritRR 5 (1992) 271-4 (G. T. *Sheppard*).

10356 EDenny Frederick M., *Taylor* Rodney L. [10 art.],   The Holy Book in comparative perspective.   Columbia 1993 pa. [= 1985 → 1,561], Univ. S. Carolina.   viii-252 p.   0-87249-453-5.

10357 EEastman Roger,   The ways of religion; an introduction to the major traditions²ʳᵉᵛ [¹1975; anthology].   Ox 1993, UP.   xiii-489 p. £18.   0-19-507596-X. – RExpTim 105 (1993s) 319 (G. *Parrinder*).

10358 **Ellwood** R.,   History & future of faith 1988 → 7,a431:   RCritRR 5 (1992) 496-9 (D. W. *Johnson*).

10358* **Fernhout** Rein,   Canonical texts, bearers of absolute authority; Bible, Koran, Veda, Tipiṭaka; ᵀ*Jansen* Henry & Lucy J.:   Currents of Encounter 9.   Amst 1994, Rodopi.   xvi-337 p.; bibliog. 303-319.

10359 *Gerlitz* Peter,   Muttergottheiten: → 517, TRE 23 (1994) 497-503.

10360 EGriffiths Paul,   Christianity through non-Christian eyes 1990 → 6, a689; 7,a470:   RScotJR 14 (1993) 53-56 (C. G. *Williams*).

10361 EHolm Jean,   [→ 277]   Attitudes to nature.   L/NY 1994, Pinter/ St. Martin's.   xii-172 p. £29.50; pa. £9. – 1-85567-092-5; -3-3. – RTBR 7,3 (1994s) 67 (A. *Pryce*).

10362 **Johnson** Wayne G.,   The possibility of revelation in non-Christian religions in the thought of Paul KNITTER; an evangelical analysis and critique: diss. Trinity, ᴰ*Feinberg* P. 1994. 360 p. 94-32066. – DissA 55 (1994s) p. 1600.

10363 **Kepel** Gilles,   La revanche de Dieu; Chrétiens, Juifs et Musulmans à la reconquête du monde: L'épreuve des faits.   P 1991, Seuil.   283 p. – RPrOrChr 43 (1993) 220-4 (L. *Boisset*: douteux).

10363* **Kepel** Gilles,   The revenge of God; the resurgence of Islam, Christianity and Judaism in the modern world, ᵀ*Bealey* Alan. Univ. Park 1994, Penn State Univ.   215 p. $35; pa. $15.   0-271-01313-3; -4-1. [TDig 41,366].

10364 **Krieger** David J.,   The new universalism; foundations for a global theology 1991 → 8,a969; 9,11408:   RCritRR 6 (1993) 311-3 (C. *Gillis*).

10365 **Liddy** Richard M.,   Transforming light; intellectual conversion in the early LONERGAN.   ColMn 1993, Liturgical.   xxi-225 p. – RLandas 8 (1994) 292-8 (V. *Marasigan*, 'Dialogue of religions', also on HABITO R.).

10366 **Lubarsky** Sandra B.,   Tolerance and transformation; Jewish approaches to religious pluralism.   Cincinnati 1990, HUC.   x-149 p. – RAJS 19 (1994) 295-7 (M. *Wyschogrod*); CCAR 41,1 (1994) 100-2 (H. *Kasimov*); CritRR 5 (1992) 395 (P. M. *Van Buren*: she means *liberal* Jewish approaches, but has a vaulable insight).

10367 *Martin Velasco* Juan,   El Mal en las religiones: RET 51 (1991) 177-213.

10368 **Mooren** Thomas,   Auf der Grenze; die Andersheit Gottes und die Vielfalt der Religionen: EurHS 23/434.   Fra 1991, Lang. 201 p.   3-631-44213-0. – RVerbumSVD 35 (1994) 317-320 (J. *Kuhl*).

10369 **Nigosian** S. A.,   World faiths²ʳᵉᵛ.   NY 1994, St. Martin's.   xxiv-529 p. $40.   0-312-08414-5 [TDig 42,82].

10370 **Overholt** Thomas W.,   Channels of prophecy; the social dynamics of prophetic activity 1989 → 5,3438; 6,3717 ... RCritRR 6 (1993) 317s (N. C. *Habel*: cross-cultural, including Amerindian and Australian aborigine).

10371 ᴱPakoczy Susan,   Common journey, different paths; spiritual direction in cross-cultural perspective.   Mkn 1992, Orbis.   175 p. $19. – ᴿConcordJ 20 (1994) 75-77 (H. A. *Moellering*).

10372 *Panikkar* Raimon,   Les religions i la cultura de la pau: QVidCr 169 (1993) 13-38 [-64, *al.*].

10373 **Rambo** Lewis R.,   Understanding religious conversion 1993 ➤ 9,11414: ᴿExpTim 105 (1993s) 222s (D. *Atkinson*).

10374 **Reat** N. Ross, *Perry* Edmund F.,   A world theology; the central spiritual reality of humankind 1991 ➤ 8,a989; 9,11415: ᴿCritRR 6 (1993) 318-321 (M. D. *Woodhouse*).

10375 **Sered** Susan S.,   Priestess, mother, sacred sister; religions dominated by women. NY 1994, Oxford-UP.   330 p. $27.50.   0-19-508395-4 [TDig 42,89].

10376 ᴱSharma Arvind,   Religion and women: McGillHistRel.   Albany 1993, SUNY.   x-291 p. $59.50; pa. $20.   0-7914-1689-5; -90-9 [TDig 42,85].

10377 *Sievers* Joseph,   Amore divino in alcune religioni non cristiane: Nouv-Um 16 (1994) 71-92 [< AcPIB 9,897].

10378 **Smith** Huston,   The illustrated world's religions [completely revised edition of the 2-million-sold ⁵Religions of Man].   SF 1994, Harper.   255 p. $30. 0-06-057453-9 [TDig 42,90].

10379 **Smith** Wilfred C.,   What is Scripture? 1993 ➤ 9,11418:   ᴿExpTim 105 (1993s) 281s (P. D. *Bishop*); JIntRD 4 (1994) 104-8 (R. *Fernhout*); LexTQ 29 (1994) 261-3 (P. N. *Dare*); TLond 97 (1994) 301s (G. *D'Costa*: not just Bible since Max MÜLLER's 50-volume Sacred books of the East 1879-94).

10380 ᴱSundermeier Theo,   Die Begegnung mit dem Anderen; Plädoyers für eine interkulturelle Hermeneutik [Tagung Tübingen 1990]: Studien zum Verstehen fremder Religionen 2.   Gü 1991 Mohn.   205 p. DM 68. – ᴿTPQ 142 (1994) 82 (J. *Janda*).

10381 **Thompson** Sue Ellen, *Carlson* Barbara W. [1400] Holidays, festivals, and celebrations of the world.   Detroit 1994, Omnigraphics.   lxii-536 p. $48. 1-55888-768-7 [TDig 41,290].

10382 **Thorpe** S. A.,   Primal religions worldwide [without either judging or romanticizing them].   Pretoria 1992, Univ. S. Africa.   viii-126 p. – ᴿSR 23 (1994) 503s (D. *Turner*).

10383 **Van Voorst** Robert E.,   Anthology of world scriptures [by topic], Belmont CA 1994, Wadsworth.   xvi-344 p.; ill. – ᴿRelStR 20 (1994) 207 (L. E. *Nelson*: 'use with caution'; despite a bit on social justice and women, still 'the elite, literate, male tradition').

10384 *Wagner* Falk,   'Nämlich zu Haus ist der Geist nicht im Anfang'; systematisch-theologische Erwägungen zum Synkretismus [taken not just from *keránnumi*, 'mix' but with implications of Cretanism by PLUTARCH and then ERASMUS]: NSys 36 (1994) 236-257; Eng. 267.

10385 **Waltner-Kallfelz** Isolde,   Die Schatzsuche als religiöses Motiv; Schatz, Pretiosen, Kostbarkeiten: StOrRel 28.   Wsb 1993, Harrassowitz.   252 p. DM 128. 3-447-03451-2 [OTAbs 17, p. 659: texts from world religions on seeking spiritual treasure].

10386 **Ward** Keith,   Religion and revelation.   Ox 1994, Clarendon.   350 p. £14. 0-19-826375-8. – ᴿChurchman 108 (1994) 377-9 (B. *Cook*).

M3.5   **Religiones mundi ex conspectu christianismi.**

10387 **Augustin** Georg,   Gott eint – trennt Christus? Die Einmaligkeit Jesu Christi als Grundlage einer christlichen Theologie der Religionen aus-

gehend vom Ansatz Wolfhart PANNENBERGS. Pd 1993, Bonifatius. 400 p.
DM 50. 3-87088-768-0. – ᴿEntschluss 49,12 (1994) 45 (M. *Bresser*); TGL
84 (1994) 377s (D. *Hattrup*).

10388 *Barnes* Michael, Theology of religions in a post-modern world: Month
255 (1994) 270-4. 325-330.

10388* **Bernhardt** Reinhold, Der Absolutheitsanspruch des Christentums
ᴰ1990 ➤ 7,a455; 8,b24: ᴿTR 90 (1994) 421s (H. *Waldenfels*).

10389 *a) Bernhardt* Reinhold, Aufbruch zu einer pluralistischen Theologie der
Religionen: – *b) Fischer* Johannes, Pluralismus, Wahrheit und die Krise
der Dogmatik: ZTK 91 (1994) 230-246 / 487-539.

10389* *Bernhardt* Reinhold, Der Absolutheitsanspruch des christlichen Glaubens: ZeichZt 47 (1993) 52-57 [< ᴢɪᴛ 93,289].

10390 **Braaten** Carl E., No other Gospel! Christianity among the world's
religions 1992 ➤ 8,b26; 9,11430: ᴿInterpretation 48 (1994) 317 (K.
Hamilton); sᴡᴊᴛ 36,1 (1993s) 60 (H. N. *Smith*).

10391 *Cantalamessa* Raniero, La fede in Gesù Cristo unico salvatore, nel
contesto del dialogo interreligioso odierno: RasT 35 (1994) 259-282.

10392 **Catoir** John T., World religions 1992 ➤ 8,b29: ᴿAustralasCR 71
(1994) 117s (W. A. *Mullins*: Catholic viewpoint).

10393 ᴱ**Clarke** A. D., *Winter* B. M., One God, one Lord ... pluralism ²1991
➤ 7,485: ᴿEvRT 18 (1994) 81-84 (S. *Humphrey*).

10394 *Cottier* Georges, Liberté et vérité: RThom 94 (1994) 179-194.

10395 ᴱ**D'Costa** Gavin D., Christian uniqueness reconsidered; the myth of a
pluralistic theology of religion 1990 ➤ 6,402* ... 9,11434: ᴿCritRR 6
(1993) 504-6 (M. D. *Bryant*); RTPhil 126 (1994) 397s (A. *Nayak*); ScotJT
47 (1994) 261-4 (J. *Lipner*); TsTKi 64 (1993) 159s (A. *Romarheim*, also on
six cognates, in Norwegian).

10396 *a) D'Costa* Gavin, Christian theology and other religions; an evaluation of John HICK and Paul KNITTER; – *b) Dhavamony* Mariasusai, The
Cosmic Christ and world religions; – *c) Newbigin* Lesslie, Religious
pluralism; a missiological approach: StMiss 42 ('Theology of world
religions' 1993) 161-178 / 179-226 / 227-244.

10397 *D'Costa* Gavin, Discerning Christ in the world religions: Month 255
(1994) 486-490.

10398 **DiNoia** Joseph A., The diversity of religions; a Christian perspective
1992 ➤ 8,b37; 9,11437: ᴿInterpretation 48 (1994) 107s (F. W. *Norris*).

10399 **Dupuis** Jacques, Jesus Christ at the encounter of world religions, ᵀ*Barr*
Robert R., 1991 ➤ 7,a464 ... 9,11439: ᴿCritRR 6 (1993) 305-7 (G. A.
Largo); Missiology 20 (1992) 405 (J. H. *Kroeger*).

10400 **Dupuis** Jacques, Gesù Cristo incontro alle religioni². 1991. – ᴿREB 54
(1994) 984-991 (F. L. *Couto Teixeira*).

10400* **Dupuis** Jacques, Jesucristo al encuentro de las religiones 1991 ➤ 9,
11441: ᴿEfMex 11 (1993) 120-4 (U. *Sánchez*).

10401 *Fergusson* David A. S., The absoluteness of Christianity? [TROELTSCH
coinage 1901]: ScotJR 13 (1992) 114-125.

10402 **Friedli** Richard, Le Christ dans les cultures ... essai de théologie des
religions ➤ 6,a686*; 9,11447: ᴿScEsp 45 (1993) 242s (J.-M. *Archambault*).

10403 **Gillis** Chester, Pluralism; a new paradigm for theology. Lv/GR 1993,
Peeters/Eerdmans. 192 p. Fb 695. 90-6831-468-8. – ᴿExpTim 105
(1993s) 255 (E. *Hulmes* compares to CHAPMAN C.).

Griffiths Paul J., An apology for apologetics [incompatibilities should not be
soft-pedaled] 1991 ➤ h17.

10404 **Guarino** Thomas G., Revelation and truth; unity and plurality in contemporary theology 1993 → 9,11453: ᴿHorizons 21 (1994) 357s (Phyllis H. *Kaminski*).

10405 *Hahn* Eberhard, The uniqueness of Christ; au evangelical position: EurJT 3,2 (1994) 137, also French; German 138-144 (-145-162, Latin America).

10405* **Hefner** Robert W., Conversion to Christianity; historical and anthropological perspectives on a great transformation. Berkeley 1993, Univ. California. 336 p. $95; pa. $45. – ᴿJRel 74 (1994) 275s (R. J. *Parmentier*).

10406 *a*) *Henau* Ernst, Der zerbrochene Generation-Vertrag; die Kontinuität der christlichen Überlieferung in einer pluralistischen Gesellschaft; – *b*) *Blasberg-Kuhnke* Martina, Intergenerationalität; die Beziehung zwischen den Generationen als Praxis der Koinonia christlicher Gemeinde: → 148, ᶠZERFASS R., BiLtg 67 (1994) 94-98 / 148-155.

10406* *a*) *Herms* Eilert, Vom halben zum ganzen Pluralismus; einige bisher übersehenen Aspekte im Verhältnis von Staat und Kirche; – *b*) *Huber* Wolfgang, Öffentliche Kirche in pluralen Öffentlichkeiten; – *c*) *Welker* Michael, Der Mythos 'Volkskirche': EvT 54 (1994) 134-157 / 157-180 / 180-193.

10407 **Hjelde** S., Die Religionswissenschaft und das Christentum; eine historische Untersuchung über das Verhältnis von Religionswissenschaft und Theologie: StHistRel 61. Leiden 1994, Brill. x-355 p. ƒ195. 90-04-09922-0 [NTAbs 38, p. 449].

10408 **Jeanrond** Werner G., *Rike* Jennifer L., Radical pluralism and truth ... TRACY 1991 → 8,183*: ᴿChrSchR 22 (1992) 434s (T. *Linafelt*); IrTQ 60 (1994) 228s (Mary *Love*).

10409 **Kekes** John, The morality of pluralism. Princeton 1993, Univ. 227 p. $30. – ᴿAmJTP 15 (1994) 205-210 (Nancy R. *Howell*).

10410 **Küng** Hans, *al.*, Christianity and the world religions² [1984, Eng. ¹1986]. L/Mkn 1993, SCM / Orbis. xx-460 p. £12.50. – ᴿConcordJ 20 (1994) 79s (T. *Manteufel*); Month 255 (1994) 318s (J. *Pridmore*, as if Küng were sole author; along with ᶠKüngᴿ; 'uniquely important Catholic theologian', Rome notwithstanding).

10410* *Kuttianimattathil* Jose, An introduction to the relationship between Jesus Christ, Christianity and other religions in the thought of M. M. THOMAS: Kristu Jyoti 10,2 (Bangalore 1994) 20-32.

10411 *McFadyen* Alistair, The Christian claim to universal truth in a pluralist public world: ScotJT 46 (1993) 437-456.

10412 *Miranda* Mario de França, A configuração do cristianismo num contexto pluri-religioso: PerspT 26 (1994) 373-387.

10412* **Moran** Gabriel, Uniqueness 1992 → 8,b65: ᴿGregorianum 75 (1994) 353s (J. *Dupuis*).

10413 ᴱ**Müller** Karl, *Prawdzik* Werner, Ist Christus der einzige Weg zum Heil? [6.-9. Juni 1990, St. Augustin]: Veröff. 40, 1991 → 7,370; 9,11467: ᴿTrierTZ 103 (1994) 158s (H. *Schützeichel*).

10414 **Netland** Harold A., Dissonant voices; religious pluralism and the question of truth 1991 → 7,a447 ... 9,11480: ᴿChrSchR 22 (1992) 437s (S. M. *Powell*); EvRT 18 (1994) 70-72 (R. *Richard*); JEvTS 37 (1994) 593 (B. *Stetson*: courageous, valuable); TrinJ 14 (1993) 226-9 (R. S. *Greenway*).

10415 **Newbigin** Lesslie, The Gospel in a pluralist society 1989 → 6,a797 ... 9,11470: ᴿScotJT 46 (1993) 257s (J. C. *Puddefoot*: pluralism yes; without Jesus, no).

10416 a) *Niewiadomski* Józef, Einmaligkeit und Anspruch; jüdisch-christliche Tradition in einer multikulturellen Welt [die 'Gleichheit aller Religionen' fordert]; – b) *Hutter* Manfred, Vom Versuch einer 'Oberreligion' ... Baha'i: TPQ 142 (1994) 3-11 / 32-39 (-51, *al.*) ➤ 7970.

10417 **Ogden** S., Is there only one true religion? 1992 ➤ 9,11471: ᴿTLZ 119 (1994) 975s (H. *Ott*).

10417* *Pannenberg* Wolfhart, Angst um die Kirche; zwischen Wahrheit und Pluralismus: EvKomm 26 (1993) 709-713 [< NSys 36 (1994) 215s].

10418 *Peter* Anton, Die Mission der Kirche angesichts der vielen Religionen: Diakonia 25 (1994) 91-101.

10419 **Pinnock** Clark, A wideness in God's mercy; the finality of Christ in a world of religions 1992 ➤ 9,11474: ᴿEvRT 18 (1994) 73-77 (R. *Richard*: optimistic, apparently unduly).

10420 **Ruokänen** Miikka, The Catholic doctrine of non-Christian religions 1992 ➤ 8,b79; 9,11477: ᴿAngelicum 71 (1994) 111-3 (G. *Phan Tan Thanh*); CritRR 6 (1993) 388-390 (K. R. *Trembath*); Exchange 22 (1993) 179 (Karel *Steenbrink*); JIntRD 4 (1994) 101-4 (A. *Camps*); ScripTPamp 26 (1994) 840s (F. *Conesa*).

10421 **Sanders** John, No other name 1992 ➤ 9,11478: ᴿEvRT 18 (1994) 77-79 (R. *Richard*); JEvTS 37 (1994) 615s (E. *Fudge*); Missiology 21 (1993) 357 (J. *Triebel*).

10422 *Sanders* John, Evangelical responses to Salvation outside the Church: ChrSchR 56 (1994) 45-58.

10423 a) *Schillebeeckx* Edward, Universalité unique d'une figure religieuse historique nommée Jésus de Nazareth; – b) *Ménard* Camil, L'universalité du salut en Jésus le Christ d'après E. S., – c) *Petit* Jean-Claude, La portée théologique d'un principe herméneutique; – d) *Fortin-Melkevik* Anne, De l'expérience religieuse à la narrativité; parcours critique: ➤ 395, LavalTP 50,2 (1994) 265-281 / 283-296 / 305-316 / 317-325.

10424 **Smith** Jonathan Z., Drudgery divine; on the comparison of early Christianities and the religions of late antiquity 1990 ➤ 6,a706 ... 9,11483: ᴿCritRR 5 (1992) 275-9 (L. H. *Martin*); SvTK 70 (1994) 77-80 (J. P. *Södergård*).

10425 a) *Spivey* Jim, Separation no myth; religious liberty's biblical and theological bases; – b) *Johnson* Robert E., Free to believe; Anabaptists and American Baptists in the history of religious liberty; – c) *Pierard* Richard V., The expansion of religious liberty in Europe since World War II; – d) *Deiros* Pablo A., Latin American expressions of religious liberty; – e) *Linden* Robert D., Shall the accommodationists win? – f) *McBeth* H. Leon, Challenges to religious liberty; – g) *Dilday* Russell H., No other name, Acts 4:12: ➤ 9,45, ᶠEsᴛᴇᴘ W., swjᴛ 36,3 (1993s) 10-16 / 17-24 / 25-31 / 32-36 / 37-44 / 45-51 / 52-57.

10426 **Swidler** Leonard, The meaning of life at the edge of the third millennium [religions dialogue]. NY 1992, Paulist. 116 p. $9 pa. – ᴿPerScCF 46 (1994) 141s (J. de *Koning*).

10427 a) *Thiel* J. E., Pluralismus und theologische Wahrheit; – b) *Haight* R., Die Kirche als Ort der Theologie: ➤ 265, IZT-Concilium 30 (1994) 515-525 / 483-491.

10427* *Thompson* Geoffrey, Christianity and World religions; the judgment of Karl Bᴀʀᴛʜ: Pacifica 7 (1994) 185-206.

10428 **Tirumanywa** Cyprian, Christian religion on trial; the Good News is justice and peace for all on earth. Dar es Salaam c. 1993, Univ. 104 p.

10428* **Waldenfels** Hans, Phänomen Christentum; eine Weltreligion in der

Welt der Religionen. FrB 1994, Herder. 187 p. – ᴿEntschluss 49,12 (1994) 43 (Clara *Wilflinger*).

10429 **Waldenfels** Hans,   Die Spannungen ehrlich aushalten; christliche Identität im Pluralismus der Religionen: HerdKorr 47 (1993) 30-34.

10430 **Wells** David F.,   No place for truth 1993   → 9,11493:   ᴿNOxR 61,5 (1994) 28s (G. *Mar*); Pacifica 7 (1994) 243-6 (J. N. *Hewitt*); RelStR 20 (1994) 41 (G. *Fackre*: very fine, not only for evangelicals); SWJT 36,3 (1993s) 58 (M. J. *Erickson*); TrinJ 14 (1993) 234-8 (J. H. *Armstrong*).

10431 ᴱ**Werbick** Jürgen, **Brück** Michael von,   Der einzige Weg zum Heil?: QDisp 143, 1993 → 9,432*:   ᴿNRT 116 (1994) 209 (A. *Toubeau*); TPQ 142 (1994) 80 (J. *Janda*).

10432 **Whitmore** Todd D.,   Immunity or empowerment? John Courtney MUR-RAY and the question of religious liberty: JRelEth 21 (1993) 247-273.

M3.6 *Sectae*, **Cults.**

10433 **Abzug** Robert H.,   Cosmos crumbling; American reform and the religious imagination. NY 1994, Oxford-UP. ix-285 p. $30.   0-19-503752-9 [TDig 41,349].

10434 **Anglarès** Michel,   Nouvel Âge et foi chrétienne. P 1992, Centurion. 176 p. F 69. – ᴿCC 145 (1994,3) 339s (E. *Baragli*).

10435 **Baggio** Antonio M.,   Il New Age come ideologia: NuovUm 15,88 (R 1993) 3-33.

10436 **Barlow** Philip L.,   Mormons and the Bible 1991 → 8,g884; 9,11503: ᴿChR 63 (1994) 163-5 (R. M. *Payne*); ModT 9 (1993) 103s (M. A. *Noll*).

10437 **Bednarowski** Mary F.,   New religions and the theological imagination in America. Bloomington 1989, Indiana Univ. 175 p. $25. – ᴿJAAR 62 (1994) 179-182 (Carol S. *Anderson*: Mormons, Christian Science, New Age...).

10438 **Bergeron** Richard, *al.*,   Le Nouvel Âge en question. Montréal/P 1992, Paulines / Médiaspaul. 182 p. – ᴿCC 145 (1994,3) 340s (E. *Baragli*).

10439 **Binder** Andreas,   Wie christlich ist die Anthroposophie? Standortbestimmung aus der Sicht eines evangelischen Theologen. Stu 1989, Urachhaus. 217 p. DM 26. – ᴿTR 90 (1994) 441-6 (G. *Scherer*) + 445-454 (H. *Zander* über 6 ähnliche Neuerscheinungen).

10440 ᴱ**Bromley** David G., **Hammond** Phillip E.,   The future of new religious movements. Macon 1987, Mercer Univ. 278 p. – ᴿArchivScSocR 82 (1993) 258s (Françoise *Champion*).

10441 **Bulkeley** Kelly,   The wilderness of dreams; exploring the religious meanings of dreams in modern western culture. Albany 1994, SUNY. xiii-309 p. $20. – ᴿRelStR 20 (1994) 208 (Diane *Jonte-Pace*).

10442 **Burkhardt** Helmut,   Ein Gott in allen Religionen? Wiederkehr der Religiosität — Chance oder Gefahr?¹²ʳᵉᵛ [¹1990]. Giessen 1993, Brunnen. 112 p. – ᴿEurJT 3,2 (1994) 185s; Eng. franc. 185 (H. *Egelkrout*).

10443 **Clark** David K., **Geisler** Norman L.,   Apologetics in the New Age; a Christian critique of pantheism 1990 → 9,11512: ᴿJEvTS 37 (1994) 587s (M. I. *Klauber*).

10443* *Contri* Antonio,   Cenni sugli orientamenti teologici di alcuni 'movimenti religiosi alternativi' [New Age, Mormoni, Testimoni di Geova, Scientologia]: RivScR 8 (1994) 445-464 [*al.* 399-444.465-481; bibliog. 483-7].

10444 *Cox* Harvey,   Healers and ecologists; Pentecostalism in Africa: ChrCent 111 (1994) 1042-6.

10445 **Crews** Mickey, The Church of God [name claimed by several denominations]; a social history. Knoxville 1990, Univ. Tennessee. xvi-252 p. $32.50. – ᴿCritRR 6 (1993) 356s (C. H. *Lippy*).

10446 **Ferguson** Duncan S., New Age spirituality; an assessment 1993 → 9, 11521: ᴿHorizons 21 (1994) 366s (D. S. *Toolan*).

10447 *Gallagher* Eugene V., A religion without converts? Becoming a neo-pagan: JAAR 62 (1994) 851-867.

10448 **Gassmann** Lothar, Das anthroposophische Bibelverständnis; eine kritische Untersuchung unter besonderer Berücksichtigung der exegetischen Veröffentlichungen von Rudolf STEINER, Friedrich RITTELMEYER, Emil BOCK und Rudolf FRIELING [Diss.Tü 1988]. Wu 1992, Brockhaus. 267 p. DM 40. – ᴿTR 90 (1994) 450s (H. *Zander*).

10449 **Geisen** Richard, Anthroposophie und Gnostizismus; Darstellung, Vergleich und theologische Krikik [... STEINER R.]: PdTSt 22. Pd 1992, Schöningh. 504 p. DM 68. – ᴿTR 90 (1994) 445-8 (H. *Zander*).

10450 *Gerlitz* Peter, Neue Religionen: → 517, TRE 24 (1994) 299-315.

10450* **Gomes** Michael, Theosophy in the nineteenth century; an annotated bibliography: RefLibSocSc 532. NY 1994, Garland. vi-582 p. $88. 0-8240-8094-7 [TDig 43,66].

10451 **Haack** Friedrich-Wilhelm, Europas neue Religion; Sekten — Gurus — Satanskult: Spektrum 4221. FrB 1993, Herder. 208 p. DM 16,80. – ᴿTPQ 142 (1994) 85 (Eva *Drechsler*).

10452 *a)* *Hanegraaf* W. J., Esoterie, occultisme en (neo)gnostiek; historische en inhoudelijke verbanden; – *b)* *Gibbels* M., Mediums, Meesters en astrale vibratie; geschiedenis van de Theosofische Vereniging in Nederland 1880-1930; – *c)* *Hoekstra* E. G., Wegwijzer in esoterische en okkult Nederland ... Rozekruizers, antroposofie: Religieuze bewegingen in Nederland 25 (1993) 1-28 / 29-60 / 89-146 [< GerefTTs 93,201].

10453 **Hassan** Steven, Ausbruch aus dem Bann der Sekten; psychologische Beratung für Betroffene und Angehörige [1988]ᵀ: rororo 9391. Ha 1993, Rowohlt. 342 p. DM 19,90. – ᴿTPQ 142 (1994) 85s (Eva *Drechsler*).

10454 **Hébrard** Monique, Entre Nouvel Âge et christianisme; dix témoins racontent. P 1994, D-Brouwer. 223 p. F 125. – ᴿArchivScSocR 39,88 (1994) 75 (Martine *Cohen*); Études 381 (1994) 142 (C. *Flipo*).

10455 *a)* *Hilhorst* Henri W. A., De New-Age-beweging als levensbeschouwelijk zingevingssysteem in de geseculariseerde samenleving; – *b)* *Hoogen* A.J.M. van den, *Jonker* E. R., [*al.*]. De pastorale uitdaging van New Age: PrakTheol 19 (1992) 31-51 / 20 (1993) 329-349 [-463].

10456 *Hoheisel* Karl, New Age: → 517, TRE 24 (1994) 411-6.

10457 **Kollmar** Edgar, Herausforderung Anthroposophie. Wu 1992, Brockhaus, Tb 477. 126 p. DM 13. 3-417-20477-1. – ᴿLuthTKi 17 (1993) 35s (H. *Schätzel*).

10458 **Manzanara** César Vidal, Dicionario de seitas e ocultismo. Coimbra 1992, Gráfica. 276 p. – ᴿBrotéria 137 (1993) 115s (F. *Peres Lopes*).

10458* **Mather** George A., *Nichols* Larry A., Dictionary of cults, sects, religions and the occult. GR 1993, Zondervan. 384 p. $25. 0-310-53100-4. – ᴿRefR 48 (1994s) 140 (D. H. *Wacome*).

10459 **Martín Estalayo** C., A nuestra imagen y semejanza; en torno a la religiosidad sectaria: RelCu. M 1983. 265 p. – ᴿBibFe 58 (1994) 175s (A. *Salas*).

10459* **Mauss** Armand L., The angel and the beehive; the Mormon struggle with assimilation. Urbana 1994, Univ. Illinois. xviii-257 p. 0-252-02071-5 [TDig 42,56, along with (largely reprints) of same press and date on

Mormons: BITTON Davis, ᴱCORNWALL Marie, ᴱLAUNIUS R., NEWELL L. & AVERY V., UNDERWOOD G.].
10460 ᴱMiller Timothy, When prophets die; the postcharismatic fate of new religious movements 1991 ⇥ 8,b126; 9,11547:   ᴿCritRR 6 (1993) 453s (R. L. *Moore*).
10461 *Mucci* Giandomenico, Le radici gnostiche del 'New Age': CC 145 (1994,3) 470-481.
10462 **Nash** Ronald H., Worldviews in conflict; choosing Christianity in a world of ideas [New Age, naturalism...]. GR 1992, Zondervan. 176 p. $10 pa. 0-310-57771-3. – ᴿChrSchR 24 (1994) 363s (P. C. *Nnoromele*).
10463 *Oro Ari* Pedro, Évaluation de l'émergence des sectes en Amérique Latine: SR 23 (1994) 211-225.
10464 **Pawłowicz** Zygmunt, bp. ℗ Kościół (Church) i sekty w Polsce. Gdańsk 1992. 254 p. – ᴿAtKap 122 (1994) 600-3 (L. *Fic*, ℗).
10465 **Perry** Michael, Gods within; a critical guide to the New Age 1992 ⇥ 9,11551: ᴿTLond 96 (1993) 240s (G. *Harvey*).
10466 **Piette** Albert, Les religiosités séculières: Que sais-je? P 1993, PUF. 128 p. – ᴿArchivScSocR 39,86 (1994) 300s (E. *Maigret*: comble un vide).
10467 *Prévost* Jean-Pierre, Le Nouvel Âge, approche historique, sociologique et psychologique: FoiTemps 23 (1993) 18-48 (-62, *Lobet* B.).
10468 **Quillo** Ronald, Companions in consciousness; the Bible and the New Age movement. Liguori MO 1994, Triumph. 192 p. $19. – ᴿHorizons 21 (1994) 375s (J. *Martos*: balanced).
10469 ᴱ**Quinn** D. Michael, The new Mormon history; revisionist essays on the past. Salt Lake City 1992, Signature. xx-310. $19. – ᴿCritRR 6 (1993) 382-4 (P. L. *Barlow*).
10470 *Randall* Ian M., Spiritual renewal and social reform; attempts to develop social awarenss in the early Keswick [1873, 'Holiness'] movement: VoxEvca 23 (L 1993) 67-86.
10471 *Rossano* Pietro, La libertà religiosa nel magistero della Chiesa: Sette e religioni 2 (Bo 1992) 195-205 [< zɪᴛ 93,384].
10472 **Steiner** Rudolf, Theosophy, an introduction to the spiritual processes in human life and in the cosmos, ᵀ*Creeger* Catherine E. Hudson NY 1994, Anthroposophic. xxxi-220 p. $13. 0-88010-372-8 [TDig 42,91, also on his How we know].
10473 *Strenski* Ivan, response to *Rosenfeld* Jean E., Understanding Waco, (KORESH David) [her LATimes title 21 April 1993 said 'fight' where she had written 'understand'] and *Stange* Mary Zeiss: JAAR 62 (1994) [919-931 / 931-937] 838-946.
10473* *Ström* Åke V., Mormonen: ⇥ 517, TRE 23 (1994) 311-8.
10474 *Tedeschi* Enrica, Il fuoco; culti e misteri: Oikia 8. F 1994, Pontecorboli. 107 p.
10474* ᴱ**Trompf** G. W., Cargo cults and millenarian movements; transoceanic comparisons of new religious movements: RelSoc 29. B 1990, Mouton de Gruyter. xviii-456 p. DM 168. 3-11-012186-2 [BL 95,47, L. L. *Grabbe*].
10475 **Wangerin** Ruth, The Children of God; a make-believe revolution [BERG D. against capitalism 1960s]. Westport CT 1993, Grenwood. x-233 p. $50. 0-89789-352-2 [TDig 42,94].
10476 ᴱ**Wessinger** Catherine, Outside the mainstream; women's leadership in marginal religions in America. Urbana 1993, Univ. Illimois. 0-252-42025-1; -6332-5.

10477 **Wilson** Brian R., The social dimensions of sectarianism 1990 ➤ 7,a496 ... 9,11537: ᴿScotJT 45 (1992) 543s (R. *Gill*).
10478 **Wynia** Elly M., The Church of God and Saints of Christ; the rise of Black Jews: Cults and nonconventional religious groups. NY 1994, Garland. xi-129 p. $39. 0-8153-1136-2 [TDig 42,95].

M3.8 **Mythologia.**

10479 **Akoun** André, Mythes et croyances du monde entier, I. Le monde indo-européen. P 1985, Lidis-Brepols. 486 p.; ill. – ᴿSalesianum 56 (1994) 355 (R. *Bracchi*).
10480 **Biderman** Shlomo, *Scharfstein* Ben-Ami, Myths and fictions: PhRel 3. Leiden 1993, Brill. *f* 185. 90-04-09838-0. – ᴿTBR 7,3 (1994s) 66 (J. *Pemberton*).
10480* **Blumenberg** Hans, Work on myth [1975] ᵀ*Wallace* Robert [➤ 3,b19], CM 1990 = 1985, MIT. 685 p. – ᴿPhilipSac 29 (1994) 537-9 (N. M. *Castillo*).
10481 *Dukova* Ute, Der leuchtende Himmel und die dunkle Erde; Ergänzungen zur Etymologie eines indoeuropäischen Mythologems: Orpheus-Thrac 4 (1994) 5-12.
10482 ᴱ**Graf** Fritz, Mythos in mythenloser Gesellschaft [Augst 28.-30.VIII.1991]: Rauricum 3. Stu 1993, Teubner. 335 p. – ᴿRÉLat 72 (1994) 279s (G. *Freyburger*).
10483 **Harwood** W., Mythology's last gods, Yahweh and Jesus [diss. Columbia Pacific 1978] 1992 ➤ 9,11596: ᴿPerspScCF 46 (1994) 270.272 (R. M. *Bowman*).
10484 **Knappert** Jan, Indian mythology; an encyclopedia of myth and legend. L 1991, Aquarian. 288 p. 1-85538-040-4.
10485 *Kroeber* Karl, Religion, literary art, and the [Amerindian] retelling of myth: RLitND 26,1 (1994) 9-30.
10486 *Kunert* Günter, Von der Gegenwart der Mythen: Neue Rundschau 105,2 (1994) 29-32 [Zusammenfassung NSys 36,321].
10487 **López** Jesús, *Sanmartín* Joaquín, Mitologia y religión del Oriente Antiguo, I. Egipto y Mesopotamia. Sabadell 1993, AUSA. 563 p. – ᴿGerión 12 (1994) 339s (F. *Lara Peinado*).
10488 ᴱ**Noel** Daniel C., Paths to the power of myth ... CAMPBELL 1990 ➤ 6,a742 ... 9,11606: ᴿHorizons 21 (1994) 381 (C. K. *Chapple*).
10489 **Reinwald** Heinz, Mythos und Methode; zum Verhältnis von Wissenschaft, Kultur und Erkenntnis. Mü 1991, Fink. 539 p. DM 98. – ᴿAmHR 99 (1994) 517s (J. *McCole*).
10490 **Šijaković** Bogoljub, Mythos-physis, psyche: *Ogledanie* ...: Aletheia 1. Beograd 1991, Nikšić. – ᴿArBegG 36 (1993) 339s (ipse).
10490* **Sprug** Joseph W., Index to fairy tales, 1987-1992, including 310 collections of fairy tales, folktales, myths, and legends [+ pre-1987]. Metuchen NJ 1994, Scarecrow. xiii-587 p. 0-8108-2750-6.
10491 **White** David G., Myths of the dog-man 1991 ➤ 7,a530*: ᴿCritRR 6 (1993) 321s (J. R. *Phillips*).

M4 **Religio romana.**

10492 **Aberson** Michel, Temples votifs et butin de guerre dans la Rome républicaine: Bt Helvetica Romana 26. R 1994, Inst. Suisse. 284 p.
10493 **Anderson** Graham, Holy men and their associates in the early Roman

Empire. L 1994, Routledge. xii-289 p. £40. 0-415-02732-6 [TDig 42, 154]. – ᴿTBR 7,1 (1994s) 75 (Jill *Harriès*).

10494 **Anderson** Graham, The second sophistic; a cultural phenomenon in the Roman Empire. L 1993, Routledge. xiii-303 p. – ᴿRÉLat 72 (1994) 306s (L. *Pernot*).

10495 **Bakker** Jan T., Living and working with the gods; studies of evidence for private religion and its material environment in the city of Ostia (100-500 AD): DutchMgHist 12. Amst 1994, Gieben. ix-313 p.; 100 pl. 90-5063-056-1.

10496 **Beagon** Mary, Roman nature; the thought of PLINY the Elder 1992 ➤ 9,11613: ᴿAntClas 63 (1994) 409-411 (Liliane *Bodson*); ClasB 69 (1993) 47-50 (A. P. *MacGregor*); ClasR 44 1994) 54s (J. F. *Healey*); Gnomon 66 (1994) 681-4 (P. V. *Cova*); Prudentia 25,2 (1993) 72-74 (P. *McKechnie*).

10497 — **Citroni Marchetti** Sandra, PLINIO il Vecchio e la tradizione del moralismo romano: MatDiscBt 9, 1991 ➤ 8,b177; 9,11624: ᴿLatomus 53 (1994) 460 (J. *Hellegouarc'h*); Orpheus 15 (1994) 177-9 (Rosanna *Valenti*).

10497* — **Oliveira** Francisco de, Les idées politiques et morales de PLINE l'Ancien: EstudosCuClas 5. Coimbra 1992, Univ./InstNacInvCi. xi-438 p. $20. – ᴿClasR 44 (1994) 54s (J. F. *Healey*).

10498 *Beck* Roger, Cosmic models; some uses of Hellenistic science in Roman religion: Apeiron 27,4 (1994) 99-117.

10498* **Bergemann** C., Politik und Religion in spätrepublikanischen Rom: Palingenesia 38, 1992 ➤ 9,11545: ᴿRivStoAnt 22s (1992s) 299-301 (S. *Tramonti*).

10499 *Billows* Richard, The religious procession of the Ara Pacis Augustae; Augustus' supplicatio in 13 B.C.: JRomArch 6 (1993) 80-92.

10500 **Blázquez** José M., Religiones en la Hispania antigua 1991 ➤ 8,b170 ('en la España'): ᴿSefarad 54 (1994) 416s (G. *López Monteagudo*, also on two of his cognates).

10501 **Boëls-Janssen** Nicole, La vie religieuse des matrones dans la Rome archaïque: Coll.ÉFR 176. R 1993, École Française. – ᴿRÉLat 72 (1994) 349-351 (Jacqueline *Champeaux*).

10502 ᵀᴱ**Burr** E., The Chiron [= 1981 Herder-Lexikon] dictionary of Roman mythology; gods and goddesses, heroes, places, and events of antiquity. Wilmette IL 1994, Chiron. V-312 p. $15 pa. 0-933029-82-9 (NTAbs 38, p. 484].

10502* *Campanile* Enrico †, [Indo-European religion] Today, after DUMÉZIL: StClasOr 44 (1994) 13-21.

10503 **Campanile** Maria Domitilla, I sacerdoti del Koinon d'Asia (I sec. a.C. -III sec. d.C.); contributo allo studio della romanizzazione delle élites provinciali nell'Oriente greco: StEllenistici 7. Pisa 1994, Giardini. 231 p. 88-427-0278-1.

10503* **Capaldo** Lello, Misteri svelati; immagini, forme e riti misteriosi a Pompei, Paestum e in Magna Grecia. N 1994, Fiorentino. 146 p. Lᵐ 25. 88-85346-14-6.

10504 **Dal Covolo** Enrico, *a)* La religione a Roma tra 'antico' e 'nuovo'; l'età dei Severi: RivStoLR 30 (1994) 237-246; – *b)* Il sacro in un'età di crisi; l'ideologia religiosa severiana tra monoteismo e sincretismo: RicT 4,1 (1993) 197-237 [< ZIT 93,472].

10505 *Delgado* José A., El culto a Júpiter, Juno y Minerva entre las élites béticas durante el Alto Imperio Romano: Gerión 11 (1993) 337-362 + 2 fig. (map).

10506 **Dodds** Eric R., Pagani e cristiani in un'epoca di angoscia; aspetti dell'esperienza religiosa da Marco Aurelio a Costantino: Strumento ristampe. F 1993 [= 1965, ital. 1970], ᵀ*Lanata* Giuliana. La Nuova Italia. xi-145 p.

10507 **Dorcey** Peter F., The cult of Silvanus; a study in Roman folk religion 1992 ➤ 8,b182; 9,11627: ᴿAmJPg 115 (1994) 467-470 (D. L. *Thurmond*); JRomA 7 (1994) 475-9 (Valerie H. *Pennamen*).

10508 **Dowden** Ken, Religion and the Romans: ClasWorld 1992 ➤ 9,11628: ᴿGreeceR 41 (1994) 247 (P. *Walcot*: pungent).

10509 *Durand* Jean-Louis, *Scheid* John, 'Rites' et 'religions'; remarques sur certains préjugés des historiens de la religion des Grecs et des Romains: ArchivScSocR 39/85 (1994) 23-42; Eng. español 43.

Edwards Catharine, The politics of immorality in ancient Rome 1993 ➤ 11389.

10510 *Edwards* M.J., Aeternus lepos; Venus, LUCRETIUS, and the fear of death: GreeceR 40 (1993) 68-78.

10511 **Eingartner** Johannes, Isis und ihre Dienerinnen ... röm. Kunst 1991 ➤ 7, a543; 9,11630: ᴿEos 81 (1993) 131-3 (T. *Wujewski*, ❷); Latomus 53 (1994) 454-6 (M. *Malaise*).

10512 ᵀᴱ**Esolen** Anthony M., LUCRETIUS, On the nature of things. Baltimore c. 1994, Johns Hopkins Univ. $15 pa. [ClasW 88,472 adv.].

10513 **Fishwick** Duncan, The imperial cult: ÉPR 108, 1991s ➤ 8,b186: ᴿAntClas 63 (1994) 428s (M.-Thérèse *Raepsaet-Charlier*); AnzAltW 46 (1993) 53-57. 57-59 (G. *Dobesch*); Latomus 53 (1994) 230s (J.-C. *Richard*); Phoenix 48 (Toronto 1994) 87-89 (W. *Liebeschuetz*).

10514 **Flacelière** R., *Irigoin* J.; texte *Sirinelli* J. *Philippon* A. PLUTARQUE, Œuvres morales 1/1. Introduction générale ...: P 1990, BLettres. 281 p. 2-251-00359-2. – ᴿÉTRel 69 (1994) 295-7 (F. *Siegert*).

10515 **Frank** Hansgerd, Ratio bei CICERO: StKlasPg 75. Fra 1992, Lang. 424 p. Fs 90. 3-631-45109-1. – ᴿLatomus 53 (1994) 424s (C. *Moussy*).

10516 **Gale** Monica R., *a)* Myth in the *De rerum natura* of Lucretius: diss. Cambridge c. 1992. – ᴿBInstClass 38 (1991-3) 302. – *b)* Myth and poetry in LUCRETIUS. C 1994, Univ. 260 p. – ᴿRÉLat 72 (1994) 289s (J. *Kany-Turpin*).

10517 ᴿᴱ**Giancotti** Francesco, Tito LUCREZIO Caro, La natura: I grandi libri. Mi 1994, Garzanti. lxxvi-573 p. – ᴿRÉLat 72 (1994) 267s (Lucienne *Deschamps*).

10518 *a)* *Gill* David W.J., Acts and Roman religion; religion in a local setting; – *b)* *Winter* Bruce W., ... the imperial cult: ➤ 247, Acts Graeco-Roman 1994, 79-92 / 93-103.

10519 *Gire* Pierre, Le Stoïcisme, quelle actualité?: EsprVie 104 (1994) 185-192.

10520 ᴱ**Godwin** John, LUCRETIUS, De rerum natura VI (5 years after his IV), 1991 ➤ 9,11641: ᴿGreeceR 40 (1993) 85 (D. *Fowler*).

10521 **Goodman** Martin, Mission and conversion; proselytizing in the religious history of the Roman Empire [Oxford Wilde Lectures 1992]. Ox 1994, Clarendon. xiv-194 p.; bibliog. 175-188. 0-19-814941-7.

10522 *Grandazzi* Alexandre, Les mots de la divination chez Verrius FLACCUS: RPg 67 (1993) 57-71.263-285.

10523 **Grimal** Pierre, MARCO AURELIO. Mi c. 1993, Garzanti. 367 p. Lᵐ 60. – ᴿArcheo 9,108 (1994) 119 (S. *Moscati*).

10524 — **Hadot** Pierre, La citadelle intérieure; introduction aux Pensées de MARC AURÈLE. P 1992, A. Fayard. 386 p. – ᴿOrpheus 15 (1994) 511-6 (M. Laura *Astarita*).

10525 **Gross** Nikolaus, SENECAS Naturales quaestiones; Komposition, natur-
philosophische Aussagen und ihre Quellen: Palingenesia 27.   Stu 1989,
Steiner. 335 p. – ᴿGnomon 66 (1994) 120-3 (Carmen *Codonier*).

10526 **Hodapp** William F., The goddess Minerva in [Hebrew wisdom
literature and other early sources and] late medieval English dream
visions: diss. Iowa, ᴰ*Chamberlain* D. 1944. 319 p. – 94-33636. – DissA 55
(1994s) p. 2404.

10527 **Irby-Massie** Georgia L., Military cult in Roman Britain: diss. Colorado,
ᴰ*Konrad* C. Boulder 1994. 459 p. 95-06345. – DissA 55 (1994s) p. 3286.

10528 ᵀᴱ**Kany-Turpin** José, LUCRÈCE, De la nature. P 1993, Aubier. 551 p.
– ᴿRÉLat 72 (1994) 266s (Mayotte *Bollack*).

10528* — *a*) *Salem* Jean, Comment traduire *religio* chez Lucrèce?; – *b*)
Havelange M., L'univers et l'homme; lectures intertextuelles à partir de
Lucrèce: ÉtClas 62 (1994) 3-26 / 229-240.

10529 ᴱ**Knox** Bernard, The Norton book of classical literature. NY 1993,
Norton. 866 p. $30. 0-393-03426-7. – ᴿClasW 88 (1994s) 505 (J. *Clack*:
anthology pleasingly showing Greek/Roman literature as a continuum).

10530 **Köves-Zulauf** T., Römische Geburtsriten 1990 → 8,b196; 9,11646:
ᴿGnomon 66 (1994) 9-13 (R. *Turcan*).

10531 **Konstan** David, Sexual symmetry; love in the ancient novel and related
genres.   Princeton 1994, Univ. xiii-270 p.; bibliog. 233-261.   0-691-
03341-2.

10532 **Korten** Christine, OVID, Augustus und der Kult der Vestalinnen ...:
StKlasPg 72, 1992 → 9,11648: ᴿHZ 259 (1994) 172-4 (W. *Schubert*).

10533 **Mathieu** Vittorio, Tipologia dei sistemi e origine della loro unità: Atti
Lincei mor 9/4/2. R 1994, Accad. Lincei. P 93-169.

10534 **Mora** Fabio, Prosopografia isiaca [outside Egypt: Delos, Italy,
Danube, Africa]: ÉPR 113, 1990 → 8,b201; 9,11662: ᴿJEA 80 (1994)
265s (J. G. *Griffiths*).

10535 **Mueller** Hans-F. O., Exempla tuenda; religion, virtue, and politics in
Valerius Maximus: diss. North Carolina, ᴰ*Linderski* J. Chapel Hill 1994.
323 p. 9508232. – DissA 55 (1994s) p. 3500.

10535* *North* John A., Roman [religious] reactions to empire: → 9,102,
ᶠMERIDOR R., ScrClasIsr 12 (1993) 127-138.

10536 *Ockinga* Boyo, Thoughts on the nature of the divinity of the ruler in
ancient Egypt and imperial Rome: → 69, ᶠLACEY W., Prudentia 26,1
(1994) 17-34.

10537 **O'Hara** James J., Death and the optimistic prophecy in Vergil's
'Aeneid' 1990 → 8,b203: ᴿClasPg 88 (1993) 258-265 (A. *Schiesaro*).

10538 *Papi* Emanuele, Un'attestazione del culto imperiale a Capena [Etruria]
in un'epigrafe mal conosciuta: MÉF 106 (1994) 139-166; 7 fig.

10538* *Perelli* Luciano, SENECA e HEIDEGGER: BStLat 24 (1994) 45-61;
Eng. 61.

10539 *Porte* Danielle, Fas est [permis par les autorités religieuses] ... fasti:
RÉLat 72 (1994) 122-137.

10540 *Rives* James, Venus Genetrix outside Rome: Phoenix 48 (Toronto
1994) 294-306.

10541 **Romano** Domenico, SENECA, La Speranza (De spe). Palermo 1988,
Accad. Naz. 84 p. – ᴿOrpheus 15 (1994) 500-8 (A. *Bisanti*).

10542 **Rüpke** Jörg, Domi militiae; die religiöse Konstruktion des Krieges in
Rom ᴰ1990 → 7,b725; 8,b205: ᴿTLZ 119 (1994) 617s (H. *Zinser*).

10543 *Sabbah* Guy, Castum, incestum; éléments d'une éthique sexuelle dans
l'Histoire d'AMMIEN Marcellin: Latomus 53 (1994) 317-339.

10543* *Samonà* Giuseppe A., Chi ha pensato l'incesto?: SMSR 59 (1993) 133-150.

10544 **Sauron** Gilles, Quis Deum? L'expression plastique des idéologies politiques et religieuses à Rome à la fin de la république et au début du principat: BÉF 285. R 1994, École Française. [vi-] 735 p.; bibliog. 651-670; 14 fig.; 72 pl. 2-7283-0313-4.

10545 **Scheid** John, Romulus et ses frères; le collège des Frères Arvales 1990 ➤ 8,b211: ᴿAntClas 63 (1994) 456-8 (M. Thérèse *Raepsaet-Charlier*); Salesianum 56 (1994) 773s (S. *Felici*).

10546 *Scheid* John, a) Die Parentalien für die verstorbenen Caesaren als Modell für den römischen Totenkult: Klio 75 (1993) 188-200; Eng. 201. – b) Myth cult, and reality in Oᴠɪᴅ's Fasti: PrCPg 38 (1992s) 118-131.

10547 **Schmidt** Jürgen, Lᴜᴋʀᴇᴢ, der Kepos und die Stoiker; Untersuchungen zur Schule Eᴘɪᴋᴜʀs und zu den Quellen von 'De rerum natura'. Fra 1990, Lang. 283 p. – ᴿEos 81 (1993) 304-6 (M. *Wesoły*).

10548 *Schowalter* Daniel N., The emperor and the gods; images from the time of Trajan: HarvDisRel 28, 1993 ➤ 9,11677: ᴿLvSt 19 (1994) 77 (J. *Verheyden*).

10549 *Schrijvers* P. H., Intertextualité et polémique dans le De rerum natura (V 925-1010); Lᴜᴄʀᴇ̀ᴄᴇ vs. Dicéarque de Messène: Philologus 138 (1994) 288-304.

10550 *Serres* Michel, One god or a trinity? [Jupiter directs kings and priests; Mars armies; Quirinus presides over producers, agriculture, commerce; same functions with different names among Hindus, Iranians, Celts] ᵀ*Bandera* Cesáreo, *Arias* Judith: ➤ 43, ᶠGɪʀᴀʀᴅ R., Contagion 1 (1994) 1-17.

10551 *Simon* Erika, Die Götter der römischen Plebs: ArchAnz (1994) 149-158; 1 fig.

10552 *Sirks* A. J. R., Sacra, succession and the lex Voconia: Latomus 53 (1994) 273-296.

10553 *Spaeth* Barbette S., The goddess Ceres in the Ara Pacis Augustae and the Carthage relief: AJA 98 (1994) 65-100; 20 fig.

10554 a) *Speidel* M. P., Commodus the god-emperor and the army; – b) *Athanassiadi* Polymnia, Dreams, theurgy and freelance divination: the testimony of Iᴀᴍʙʟɪᴄʜᴜs: JRS 83 (1993) 109-114 / 115-131.

10555 *Spickermann* Wolfgang, Priesterinnen im römischen Gallien, Germanien und den Alpenprovinzan (1.-3. Jht. n. Chr.): Historia 43 (1994) 189-240.

10556 **Versnel** H. S., Inconsistencies in Greek and Roman religion [1. 1990 ➤ 6,a867]; 2. Transition and reversal in myth and ritual: StudGrRRel 6/2, 1993 ➤ 9,11686: ᴿClasR 44 (1994) 315-7 (J. G. *Griffiths*); CritRR 5 (1992) 307-9 (L. H. *Martin*, 1); Numen 41 (1994) 101s (C. *Auffarth*, 1) RelStR 20 (1994) 52 (J. S. *Pendergast*, 2).

10557 *Vincent* Gilbert, La problématisation philosophique de la croyance à l'âge classique: ArchivScSocRel 38 (1993) 17-46 [< ᴢɪᴛ 93,450].

10558 **Watson** Alan, International law in archaic Rome; war and religion: AncSocH, 1993 ➤ 9,11688; 0-8018-4506-8: ᴿClasW 88 (1994s) 207 (J. D. *Harrington*).

10559 **Watson** Alan, The state, law and religion; pagan Rome 1992 ➤ 9, 11689: ᴿJRel 74 (1994) 285s (H. D. *Betz*).

10560 **Watson** Lindsay, ARAE, the curse poetry of antiquity: ➤ 8,b291; 9,11680: ᴿGnomon 66 (1994) 1-3 (Christa *Waser*: chiefly Hellenistic).

10560* ᴱ**Winterbottom** M., M. Tulli Cɪᴄᴇʀᴏɴɪs De officiis: ScrClasBtOx. Ox 1994, Clarendon. xviii-272 p. 0-19-814693-6.

10561 ᵀᴱWright M.R., CICERO, On Stoic good and evil; De finibus 3 & Paradoxa Stoicorum 1991 ⇢ 9,11692: ᴿAntClas 63 (1994) 390s (D. *Knecht*).

10562 **Ziolkowski** Adam, The temples of mid-republican Rome and their historical and topographical context: Saggi di Storia Antica 4. R 1992, Bretschneider. 341 p. 88-7062-798-5. – ᴿJRS 84 (1994) 220s (D.S. *Levene*); Latomus 53 (1994) 717s (J. *Debergh*); Salesianum 56 (1994) 147s (B. *Amata*).

M4.5 **Mithraismus.**

10563 *Alvar* Jaime, Cinco lustros de investigación sobre cultos orientales [Isis ... Mitra] en la Península Ibérica: Gerión 11 (1993) 313-326.

10564 *Blomart* Alain, Mithra et Porphyre; quand sculpture et philosophie se rejoignent: RHR 211 (1994) 419-441; Eng. 419.

10565 **Brashear** W.M., A Mithraic catechism 1992 ⇢ 8,b226; 9,11698: ᴿClasR 44 (1994) 181s (J.G. *Griffiths*).

10566 **Claus** Manfred, Cultores Mithrae 1992 ⇢ 8,b228; 9,11699: ᴿBonnJbb 194 (1994) 595s (H. *Freis*); Gerión 11 (1993) 466-470 (J. *Alvar*); JRomA 7 (1994) 459-474 (R. *Gordon*); Phoenix 48 (Toronto 1994) 173-8 (R. *Beck*).

10567 ᴱ**Devoti** Luigi, Il mitreo di Marino. Velletri 1994, 'Tra 8 & 9'. 95 p.; bibliog. 87-94.

10567* *Hopfe* Lewis M. †, Archaeological indications on the origins of Roman Mithraism: ⇢ 102, Mem. RICHARDSON H., Uncovering 1994, 147-156.

10568 **Merkelbach** Reinhold, Mithras; ein persisch-römischer Mysterienkult² (Auflage). Weinheim 1994, Beltz. xvi-412 p. 3-89547-045-7.

10569 **Painter** Robert J., Mithraism and the religious context at Caesarea Maritima: diss. Southern Baptist Theol. Sem., ᴰ*Borchert* G. 293 p. 89-28255. – DissA 55 (1994s) p. 1287.

10570 **Turcan** Robert, Mithra et le Mithriacisme. P 1993, BLettres. 192 p.; 10 fig.; 16 pl. F 100. 2-251-38023-X. – ᴿGreeceR 41 (1994) 248 (P. *Walcot*: common-sense).

M5.1 *Divinitates Graeciae* – **Greek gods and goddesses.**

ᴱ**Alcock** Susan E., *Osborne* R. [on POLIGNAC F. de 1984], Placing the gods; sanctuaries and sacred space 1994 ⇢ 259.

10570* **Antonetti** Claudia, Les étoliens; image et religion: AnLittBesançon 405. P 1990 BLettres. 470 p. – ᴿRHR 211 (1994) 348-350 (P. *Ellinger*).

10571 *Assael* Jacqueline, L'Héraclès d'EURIPIDE et les ténèbres infernales: ÉtClas 62 (1994) 313-326.

10571* *Aubriot* Danièle, Sur la valeur religieuse de quelques prières dans la tragédie grecque: JSav 94 (1994) 1-18.

10572 **Aubriot-Sévin** Danièle, Prière et conceptions religieuses en Grèce ancienne [diss. Sorbonne 1990]: Coll.Or.Médit. 22, 1992 ⇢ 9,11712: ᴿAntClas 63 (1994) 450-2 (Vinciane *Pirenne-Delforge*); RÉG 107 (1994) 243-7 (J. *Laborderie*); RPg 67 (1993) 149-151 (J.-L. *Perpillou*: beau).

10573 **Avagianou** Aphrodite, Sacred marriage [here only as solemnized between gods] in the rituals of Greek religion [diss. Zürich, ᴰ*Burkert* W.]: EurUnivSt 15/54, 1991 ⇢ 9,11835; Fs 23: ᴿClasR 44 (1994) 88s (E.M. *Craik*).

10574 **Baring** Anne, *Cashford* Jules, The myth of the goddess 1992, the

evolution of an image. NY 1992, Viking Penguin. 800 p. $40. 0-14-019292-1. – ᴿClasW 88 (1994s) 225s (Catheryn L. *Cheal*).
10575 *Bermejo* Juan C., Mito e historia; Zeus, sus mujeres y el reino de los cielos: Gerión 11 (1993) 37-74.
10575* **Bierl** Anton F. H., Dionysos und die griechische Tragödie; politische und 'metatheatralische' Aspekte im Text: ClasMonacensia 1. Tü 1991, Narr. xi-288 p. 3-8235-4861-2.
10576 — *Henrichs* Albert. Der rasende Gott; zur Psychologie des Dionysos und des Dionysischen in Mythos und Literatur: AntAb 40 (1994) 31-49.
10576* *Bing* Peter, *Uhrmeister* Volker, The unity of CALLIMACHUS' hymn to Artemis: JHS 114 (1994) 19-34.
10577 ᴱ**Bonnet** C., *Jourdain-Annequin* C., Héraclès d'une rive à l'autre de la Méditerranée; bilan et perspectives: Table Ronde Rome 15-16 sept. 1989 / 1992 → 8,645: ᴿRÉG 107 (1994) 250-2 (Christine *Mauduit*).
10578 *Bonnet Xella* Corinne, Le grandi fatiche di Ercole [... il doppio culto; i viaggi]: Archeo 9,107 (1994) 58-101; ill.
10579 **(Bruit) Zaidman** L., *Schmitt Pantel* P., Religion in the ancient Greek city, ᵀ*Cartledge* Paul. C 1992, Univ. xx-278 p.; 2 maps. 0-521-41262-5. – ᴿÉchMClas 38 (1994) 409s (J.A.S. *Evans*).
10580 **(Bruit) Zaidman** Louise, *Schmitt Pantel* Pauline, Die Religion der Griechen; Kult und Mythos, ᵀ*Wittenburg* Andreas. Mü 1994, Beck. 256 p.; Bibliog. 235-242. 3-406-38146-4.
10581 **Buxton** Richard G. A. Imaginary Greece; the contexts of mythology. C 1994, Univ. xvi-250 p.; bibliog. 221-235. 0-521-32978-7; pa. -3865-4.
10582 **Casadio** Giovanni, Storia del culto di Dionisio in Argolide: Fg & Critica 71. R 1994, Gruppo Internaz. xv-371 p.; 8 pl. 88-8011-026-8.
10583 **Chuvin** Pierre, La mythologie grecque; du premier homme à l'apothéose d'Héraclès: L'Esprit de la Cité 1992 → 9,11719; F 170; 2-213-02976-8: ᴿÉTRel 69 (1994) 96s (M. *Bouttier*).
10584 ᵀᴱ**Chuvin** P., [NONNOS] Dionysiaques [I. → 8,b368] III. 1992. – ᴿAntClas 63 (1994) 380 (F. *Colin*); ClasR 44 (1994) 12s (A. S. *Hollis*); RBgPg 72 (1994) 148s (A. *Wouters*); RPg 67 (1993) 127-9 (T. *Duc*).
10585 — ᴱ**Gerbaut** Joelle, NONNOS P., Dionysiaques 7. Coll. Budé. P 1992. xiii-149 (d.) p. – ᴿClasR 44 (1994) 14s (A. S. *Hollis*).
10586 **Cohen** David J., Law, sexuality and society; the enforcement of morals in classical Athens. C 1994, Univ. xii-259 p.; bibliog. 241-255. 0-521-37447-2; pa. -46642-3.
10587 **Dawson** Doyne, Cities of the gods; communist utopias in Greek thought 1992 → 9,11722; 0-19-506983-8: ᴿClasB 69 (1993) 103s (A. *Papalas*); ClasW 88 (1994s) 215 (A. *Drozdek*).
10588 **Dee** James H., The epithetic phrases for the Homeric gods; a repertory of the descriptive expressions for the divinities of the Iliad and the Odyssey: Lord Studies in Oral Tradition 14 / RefHum 1850. NY 1994, Garland. xxix-165 p. 0-8153-1727-1.
10589 **Dowden** Ken, The uses of Greek mythology 1992 → 9,11727: ᴿClasR 44 (1994) 221 (Jennifer R. *March*); ClasW 88 (1994s) 236s (S. *Scully*).
10590 **Feeney** D.C., The gods in epic; poets and critics of the classical tradition 1991 → 7,a612 ... 9,11735: ᴿPrudentia 25,2 (1993) 78-81 (W.J. *Dominik*: an instant classic).
10591 ᴱ**Filoramo** Giovanni, Storia delle religioni, I. Le religioni antiche. R c.1994, Laterza. 702 p. Lᵐ 75.
10592 ᵀᴱ**Foley** Helene P. The Homeric hymn to Demeter. Princeton 1994, Univ. xvi-297 p.; bibliog. 267-281. 0-691-06843-7; pa. -1479-5.

10593 [Forbes] **Irving** Paul M. C.,   Metamorphoses in Greek myths 1990
➤ 7,a614; 8,b254:   ᴿSalesianum 56 (1994) 140 (R. *Della Casa*).

10594 **Frontisi-Ducroux** Françoise,   Le dieu-masque ... Dionysos d'Athènes
1991 ➤ 7,a615:   ᴿGnomon 66 (1994) 40-51 (Cornelia *Isler-Kerényi*); RÉG
107 (1994) 252s (P. *Brunet*).

10595 **Gantz** T.,   Early Greek myth 1993 ➤ 8,11736:   ᴿClasOut 71 (1993s)
104 (J. *Peradotto*).

10596 **Garland** Robert,   Introducing new gods 1992 ➤ 8,b257; 9,11738:
ᴿAmHR 99 (1994) 1293 (J. *Wickersham*).

10597 *a*) *Gentili* Bruno,   Riflessioni su mito e poesia nella Grecia antica; – *b*)
Graf Fritz,   L'iniziazione nel mondo mediterraneo: Aufidus 22 (1994)
7-21 / 23-35.

10598 **Gershenson** Daniel E.,   Apollo the Wolf-god: JIndEur Mg 8, 1991
➤ 9,11740:   ᴿAnzAltW 46 (1993) 39-41 (W. *Pötscher*); Athenaeum 82
(1994) 613-5 (F. *Roscalla*); Orpheus 14 (1993) 338-345 (M. *Morani*); RÉG
107 (1994) 253s (Yvonne *Vernière*).

10599 ᴱ**Hägg** Robin, *Nordquist* Gullog C.,   Celebrations of death and divinity
in the Bronze Age Argolid; Proceedings of the Sixth International
Symposium at the Swedish Institute of Athens, 11-13 June, 1988 [100th b.
PERSON Axel W., 1888-1951].   ➤ 7,641*; 8,656*a*, Acta-Ath 4/40.   Sto 1990,
Åström. 246 p.; ill.; map 91-7916-021-2. 23 art.; infra. – ᴿOpAth 19 (1992)
177-180 (S. *Hiller*).

10599* **Halm-Tisserant** Monique,   Cannibalisme et immortalité; l'enfant dans
le chaudron en Grèce ancienne. P 1993, BLettres. xii-312 p.; 8 pl.; map.
F 195. – ᴿRBgPg 72 (1994) 173s (L. *Jerphagnon*: musée d'horreurs; 'pon-
cifs' lents à s'effacer).

10600 **Hamilton** Richard,   Choes and Anthesteria; Athenian iconography and
ritual. AA 1992, Univ. Michigan. xii-250 p.; 18 fig. $37.50.   0-472-
10280-X. – ᴿAJA 97 (1993) 578s (M. W. *Padilla*).

10601 **Heitsch** E.,   Die Welt als Schauspiel; Bemerkungen zu einer Theologie
der Ilias: Abh Mainz g/soz 1993/10.   Stu 1993, Steiner.   32 p. – ᴿGrazB
20 (1994) 237s (K. *Korus*).

10602 **Hoffmann** Geneviève,   La jeune fille, le pouvoir et la mort dans l'Athènes classique: Coll. de Archéologie à l'Histoire.   P 1992, de Boccard.
386 p.; 15 pl., ➤ 9,12566:   ᴿRÉG 107 (1994) 286-8 (H. *Cassimatis*).

10603 **Jouan** François, *Motte* André,   Mythe et politique; Actes du colloque
de Liège, 14-16 sept. 1989: Bt. Univ. Liège 257, 1990 ➤ 8,857:   ᴿRHR
210 (1993) 215-7 (P. *Payen*: Mesopotamia, Scandinavia ... but more than
half Greece).

10604 **Kemper** Claudia,   Göttliche Allmacht und menschliche Verantwortung;
sittlicher Wert bei archaischen Dichtern der Griechen: Bochumer Alt-W.
14. Trier 1993, Wiss.   183 p. DM 36,50. – ᴿClasR 44 (1994) 397s (R. J.
Winton).

10604* *a*) *Laffineur* Robert,   De Cnossos à Mycènes; emprunts et syncrétisme
en Grèce préhistorique; – *b*) *Lebrun* R.,   Syncrétismes et cultes indigènes
en Asie Mineure méridionale: ➤ 481, Kernos 7 (1994) 131-143 / 145-157.

10605 **Larson** Jennifer,   Greek heroine cults: StClassics.   Madison 1994, Univ.
Wisconsin. xv-236 p.; bibliog. 205-214.   0-299-14370-8.

10606 **Lonsdale** Steven H.,   Dance and ritual play in Greek religion.   Baltimore
1993, Johns Hopkins Univ. xxiii-352 p.; bibliog. 325-333.   0-8018-4594-7.

10607 **Lo Schiavo** Aldo,   Charites [daughters of Zeus and Eurynome in
Hesiod]; il segno della distinzione: Saggi 44.   N 1993, Bibliopolis. 252 p.
– ᴿRFgIC 122 (1994) 217-222 (Manuela *Mari*).

10608 *Marengo* Silvia M., Sacerdoti di Apollo a Cirene; nuove letture di iscrizioni già note: AnnMacerat 24 (1991) 489-512; 1 pl.

10609 **Marinatos** Nanno, Minoan religion 1993 ➤ 9,11755: $50; 0-87249-779-5; ᴿClasW 88 (1994s) 133s (P. *Rehak*).

10610 *Metzger* Henri, Les légendes des dieux et des héros de la Grèce dans l'art des primitifs: RÉG 107 (1994) 172-6.

10610* *Mora* Fabio, L'interpretazione delle collettività divine in STRABONE (X,3) e la fenomenologia religiosa di POSIDONIO: SMSR 59 (1993) 7-29.

10611 ᴱMotte A., [+ 120 *al.*], Mentor; guide bibliographique de la religion grecque; Kernos supp 2. Liège 1992, Univ. 781 p. – ᴿRÉG 107 (1994) 242s (C. *Mauduit*); RStFen 22 (1994) 152s (S. *Ribichini*).

10612 **Neils** Jenifer, *al.*, Goddess and polis; the Panathenaic festival ['greater', held every four years for nearly 1000; there was also a 'lesser'] in ancient Athens: Hood Museum display catalogue of 71 objects; 1992 ➤ 8,b268: $49.50; pa. $20; – ᴿClasR 44 (1994) 91s (M.P.J. *Dillon*); RelStR 20 (1994) 53 (D. D. *Hughes*).

10613 **Parry** Hugh, Thelxis [temporary alteration of consciousness]; magic and imagination in Greek myth and poetry. Lanham MD 1992, UPA. xi-332 p. $44.50. 0-8191-8657-0. – ᴿClasW 88 (1994s) 134s (D. *Lateiner*). – Phoenix 48 (Toronto 1994) 359s (P. *Holt*).

10614 **Penglase** Charles, Greek myths and Mesopotamia; parallels and influence in the Homeric Hymns and HESIOD. L 1994, Routledge. ix-278 p.

10615 **Pötscher** Walter, Hera; eine Strukturanalyse im Vergleich mit Athena 1987 ➤ 3,b171: ᴿHZ 259 (1994) 156s (W. *Schuller*).

10616 *Pötscher* Walter, Der Termin des Festes auf dem Sarkophag von Hagia Triada: Klio 76 (1994) 67-77; 2 fig.; Eng. 77.

10616* *Pulleyn* Simon, The power of names in classical Greek religion: ClasQ 44 (1994) 17-25.

10617 **Reid** John D., The Oxford guide to classical mythology in the arts 1300s-1900s. NY 1993, Oxford-UP. xxiii-1310 p. (2 vol.). $195. 0-19-504998-5 [ClasW 89,235s, F. *Mench*].

10617* **Ruck** Carl A. P., *Staples* Danny, The world of classical myth; gods and goddesses, heroines and heroes. Durham NC 1994, Carolina Academic. xvi-366 p. $26 pa. – ᴿClasB 70 (Wauconda 1994) 97-99 (Laurie *Haight*).

10618 **Rudhart** Jean, Notions fondamentales de la pensée religieuse et actes constitutifs du culte dans la Grèce classique² [= 1]. P 1992, Picard. 344 p. + préf. F 180. – ᴿOrpheus 15 (1994) 230-2 (A. *Gallico*: réimpression plutôt: même les 4 pages apportées arrêtent la bibliographie 1953); RBgPg 72 (1994) 181s (E. *Guillaume*); RivStoLR 30 (1994) 177 (P. *Scarpi*: ristampa non giustificata).

10619 ᴱ**Schachter** A., Le Sanctuaire grec: Entretiens 37, 1992 ➤ 8,b274: ᴿClasR 44 (1994) 381-3 (R.C.T. *Parker*: first of the 37 on archeology).

10619* *Scullion* Scott, Olympian [feasting?] and chthonian [other? rituals]: ClasAnt 13 (1994) 75-119.

10620 **Sourvinou-Inwood** Christiane, 'Reading' Greek culture; texts and images, rituals and myths. Ox 1991, Clarendon. viii-315 p. £40. – ᴿGnomon 66 (1994) 484-492 (G. J. *Baudy*).

10621 **Spariosu** Mihai I. God of many names; play, poetry and power in Hellenic thought from Homer to Aristotle 1991 ➤ 9,11769; ᴿClasOut 71 (1993s) 105 (Karelisa *Hatigan*).

10621* *Steiner* Deborah T., Stoning and sight; a structural equivalence in Greek mythology: ClasAnt 14 (1995) 193-211.

10622 *Suys* Véronique,   Le culte de Déméter Achaia en Béotie; état actuel des connaissances: AntClas 63 (1994) 1-20.

10622* **Triomphe** Robert,   Prométhée et Dionysos ou La Grèce à la lueur des torches. Strasbourg 1992, Univ. 312 p.; 23 fig. F 150. – ᴿRBgPg 72 (1994) 184s (Sylvie *Vilatte*).

10623 *Valdés Guía* Miriam, El cult de Apolo Patroos en las fratrias: Gerión 12 (1994) 45-61; Eng. 45.

10623* **Veyne** Paul, Les Grecs ont-ils cru à leurs mythes? [1988 ➤ 6,a868]. P 1992, Seuil. 171 p. – ᴿRPg 66 (1992) 181s (P. *Flobert*).

10624 *Vian* Francis,   Théogamies et sotériologie dans les Dionysiaques de NONNOS; JSav 94 (1994) 197-233.

10624* **Winkler** John J., *Zeitlin* Froma A.,   Nothing to do with Dionysus? Princeton 1990, Univ. 422 p. $45. – ᴿMnemosyne 47 (1994) 529-531 (S. *Wiersma*).

M5.2   *Philosophorum critica religionis;* **Greek philosopher-religion.**

10625 ᵀᴱAllen Reginald E., PLATO, The symposium: Dialogues 2. NHv 1991, Yale Univ. ix-178 p. – ᴿPhoenix 48 (Toronto 1994) 75s (D. K. *House*).

10626 *Balleriaux* Omer,   Les dialogues de PLATON et les *agrapha dogmata*; le Parménide et le Sophiste à la lumière des doctrines non écrites: AntClas 62 (1994) 299-307.

10627 **Barnes** Jonathan,   The toils of [Sextus EMPIRICUS] scepticism. C 1990, Univ. 192 p. $34.50. – ᴿCurrTM 21 (1994) 223s (E. *Krentz*).

10628 *Bitsakis* Antonios E., ⊜ The immortality of the soul according to PLATO: TAth 65 (1994) 330-354.562-588.843-903 ...

10629 **Brandwood** Leonard,   The chronology of PLATO's dialogues (ᴰ1958) 1990 ➤ 8,b305*: ᴿRFgIC 121 (1993) 204-211 (M. *Tulli*); Mnemosyne 47 (1994) 539-541 (S. B. *Slings*).

10629* *a*) **Brenk** Frederick E., Tempo come struttura nel dialogo 'Sul daimónion di Socrate' di Plutarco; – *b*) *Albini* Francesca, Osservazioni sul 'Non posse suaviter vivi secundum Epicurum'; – *c*) *Borghini* Alberto, La presenza del mito come struttura formale nel 'De Iside et Osiride' [*Chiodi* Silvia M.; *Casadio* Giovanni] ➤ 417*b*, Strutture di Plutarco 1989/91, 69-82 / 63-67 / 121-143 [145-150; 257-271].

10630 **Burnyeat** Myles,   The Theaetetus of PLATO. ... 1990, Hackett. 366 p. $35; pa. $13. 0-915144-82-4; -1-6. – ᴿPhronesis 38 (1993) 321-336 (M. *McPherran*); TPhil 69 (1994) 100s (F. *Ricken*).

10630* ᴱCalame Claude,   Metamorphoses du mythe en Grèce antique 1988 ➤ 4,b718 ... 8,b308: ᴿAnzAltW 46 (1993) 35-38 (C. *Auffarth*).

10631 **Chevalier** Jacques,   Histoire de la pensée, 1. Des Présocratiques à Platon; 2. D'Aristote à Plotin 1991 ➤ 9,11783: ᴿRPg 67 (1993) 133s (P. *Louis*).

10632 *Dalfer* Joachim,   Philologia und Vertrauen (über PLATONS eigenartigen Dialog Phaidon): GrazB 20 (1994) 35-57.

10633 **Denyer** Nicholas,   Language, thought and falsehood in ancient Greek philosophy 1993 ➤ 9,11789; 0-415-09184-5: ᴿClasW 88 (1994s) 494s (Louise *Pratt*).

10633* ᵀᴱDorandi T., FILODEMO, Storia dei filosofi, PLATONE e l'Academia (PᶜHerc 1021 e 164); Testi ercolanesi 12. N 1991, Bibliopolis. 293 p. – ᴿAegyptus 79 (1994) 209-211 (G. *Milanese*).

10634 *Edwards* Mark,   Cybele among the philosophers; Pherecydes to Plato: Eranos 91 (1993) 65-74.

10634* *Fatouros* Georgios, HERAKLITs Gott: Eranos 92 (1994) 65-72.

10635 **Gerson** L.P., God and Greek philosophy; studies in the early history of natural theology 1990 → 7,a665; 8,b322: ᴿJHS 114 (1994) 192s (Catherine *Osborne*).

10636 **Giannantoni** Gabriele, Socratis et Socraticorum reliquiae: Elenchos 18/1-4, 1990 → 7,a666: ᴿGnomon 66 (1994) 201-211 (K. *Döring*).

10637 ᴱ**Gower** Barry S., *Stokes* Michael C., Socratic questions; new [1989] essays on the philosophy of SOCRATES and its significance. L 1992, Routledge. viii-228 p.; 5 fig. £35. – ᴿClasR 44 (1994) 81s (H.J. *Blumenthal*).

10638 ᵀᴱ**Halliwell** S., Republic. Wmr 1993, Aris & P. x-228 p. 0-85668-535-6; pa. -6-4.

10639 *Heitsch* Ernst, Argumentation und Psychagogie; zu einem Argumentationstrick des platonischen SOKRATES; Philologus 138 (1994) 219-234.

10640 **Heuser** Harro, Als die Götter lachen lernten; griechische Denker verändern die Welt. Mü 1992, Piper. 330 p. – ᴿTPhil 69 (1994) 425-8 (H.-L. *Ollig*).

10640* *Holzhausen* Jens, Zur Inspirationslehre PLUTARCHs in De Pythiae oraculis: Philologus 137 (1993) 72-91.

10641 *Inglessis-Margellos* Cécile, SOCRATE et son double: RÉG 107 (1994) 85-106.

10642 **Jeannière** Abel, Platon: Écrivains de toujours. P 1994, Seuil. 223 p. 2-02-019786-3.

10643 *Joyal* Mark A., SOCRATES and the Sicilian expedition: AntClas 63 (1994) 21-33.

10644 **Kardaun** M., Der Mimesisbegriff in der griechischen Antike; Neubetrachtung eines umstrittenen Begriffs als Ansatz zu einer neuen Interpretation der platonischen Kunstauffassung: VerhandNedAkad Lett NR 153. Amst 1993. 78 p. – ᴿGrazB 20 (1994) 239-242 (C. *Wagner*); Mnemosyne 47 (1994) 694-6 (D.M. *Schenkeveld*).

10645 **Kenney** John P., Mystical monotheism; a study in ancient Platonic theology. Hanover NH 1991, Univ.Press. xiii-216 p. $40. – ᴿCritRR 6 (1993) 459-461 (G.M. *Gurtler*).

10645* ᴱ**Kraut** Richard, The Cambridge companion to Plato 1992 → 9, 11805: ᴿPhilipSac 29 (1994) 171-9 (N. *Castillo*).

10646 **Kristeller** Paul O., Greek philosophers of the Hellenistic age [1991 ital.], ᵀ*Woods* Gregory. NY 1993, Columbia Univ. xiv-191 p. $35. – ᴿLavalTP 50 (1994) 246-8 (L. *Valcke*); Manuscripta 37 (1993) 216.

10647 *Lamoureux* Françoise, La prière de PLATON: NVFr 68 (1993) 142-153.

10648 **Luce** J.V., An introduction to Greek philosophy. L 1992, Thames & H. 174 p.; map. £11 pa. – ᴿClasR 44 (1994) 75s (M.R. *Wright*).

10649 **Magnard** Pierre, Le Dieu des philosophes. P 1992, Mame. 334 p. – ᴿRBgPg 72 (1994) 176s (L. *Jerphagnon*).

10650 **Morgan** M.L., Platonic piety; philosophy and ritual in fourth-century Athens 1990 → 8,b344: ᴿJHS 114 (1994) 192-4 (Catherine *Osborne*).

10651 *Murray* James S., Interpreting PLATO on sophistic claims and the provenance of the 'Socratic method': Phoenix 48 (Toronto 1994) 115-134.

10651* ᴱ**Murray** O., Sympotica 1988/90 → 6,758*: ᴿMnemosyne 47 (1994) 268s (S.R. *Slings*).

10652 **Naddaff** Ramona, Alien pleasures; the exile of the poets in PLATO's Republic [book 10]: diss. Boston Univ. 1994, ᴰ*Brinkman* K. 184 p. 94-04445. – DissA 54 (1993s) 3065.

10653 *Ostenfeld* Erik N., The physicality of God in the [PLATO] Politicus myth and in the later dialogues: ClasMedv 44 (K 1993) 97-108.

10654 **Richard** Marie-Dominique, La question de la genèse du corpus platonicien au début du XIXᵉ siècle: → 415, Formation des canons 1993, 7-46.

10654* *Rowe* Christopher, PLATO [bulletin]: Phronesis 39 (1994) 214-224.

10655 **Sánchez Manzano** Maria-Asunción, *Rus Rufino* Salvador I., Introducción al movimiento sofistico griego. León 1991, Univ. 194 p. – ᴿRPg 67 (1993) 155s (L. *Pernot*).

10656 **Saunders** Trevor J., PLATO's penal code; tradition, controversy and reform in Greek penology. Ox 1994, Clarendon. xvii-414 p.; bibliog. 362-373. 0-18-814960-3.

10657 ᵀᴱ**Smith** Martin F., DIOGENES of Oinoanda, The Epicurean inscription. N 1993, Bibliopolis. 660 p.; 18 pl. – ᴿRPg 67 (1993) 122-5 (J. *Bouffartigue*).

10658 **Strycker** Émile de [S.J., Nachlass], ᴱ*Slings* S. R., PLATO's Apology of Socrates, commentary: Mnemosyne supp. 137. Leiden 1994, Brill. xvii-405 p. 90-04-10103-9.

10659 **White** Stephen A., Sovereign virtue; ARISTOTLE on the relation between happiness and prosperity: Philosophy 8. Stanford 1992, Univ. xiv-337 p. $35. 0-8047-1694-3. – ᴿClasW 88 (1994s) 125 (J. *Bussanich*).

10660 *Yoshitake* Sumio, Disgrace, grief and other ills; Herakles' rejection of suicide: JHS 114 (1994) 135-155.

M5.3 *Mysteria Eleusinia; Hellenistica;* Mysteries, Hellenistic cults.

10661 **Annas** Julia E., Hellenistic philosophy of mind: Hellenistic Culture and Society 8, 1992 → 8,b362; 9,11832: ᴿGnomon 66 (1994) 581-5 (Margherita *Isnardi Parente*).

10662 **Atherton** Catherine, The Stoics on ambiguity: ClasSt. C 1993, Univ. xix-563 p.; bibliog. 507-527. 0-521-44139-0.

10663 ᵀᴱ**Becchi** Francesco, PLUTARCO, La virtù etica 1990 → 8,b362: ᴿGnomon 66 (1994) 73-75 (Barbara *Scardigli*).

10664 **Bernand** André, Sorciers grecs. P 1993, Fayard. 513 p.; bibliog. 409-432. F 180. 2 ... -35-8435-6.

10665 **Burkert** Walter, Les cultes à mystères dans l'antiquité [Ancient Mystery cult 1987] ᵀ*Deforge* B. *al.* P 1992, BLettres, 161 p. – ᴿGerión 11 (1993) 470s (F. *Diez de Velasco*); RechSR 82 (1994) 124-6 (H. *Bourgeois*: fait réfléchir la théologie chrétienne).

10666 **Clinton** Kevin, Myth and cult; the iconography of the Eleusinian mysteries [Nilsson Lectures 1990]: Athens Swedish Institute 11. Sto 1992, Åström. 209 p. 91-7916-025-5.

10667 **D'Anna** Nuccio, La disciplina del silenzio; mito, mistero ed estasi nell'antica Grecia: Homo Absconditus. Rimini c. 1990, il Cerchio. 207 p.

10668 ᵀᴱ**Dillon** John, *Hershbell* Jackson, IAMBLICHUS, On the Pythagorean way of life 1991 → 8,b371; 9,11846: ᴿRB 101 (1994) 469s (B. T. *Viviano*).

10669 **Dowden** Ken, Death and the maiden; girls' initiation rites 1989 → 6, a937 ... 9,11847: ᴿCritRR 5 (1992) 293-5 (Allaire *Brumfield*); ÉchMClas 37 (1993) 72-74 (Mary B. *Lefkowitz*).

10670 **Erler** Michael, *Flashar* Michael, *al.*, Die Hellenistische Philosophie: Grundriss/Ant 4. Basel 1994, Schwabe. I. p. xxvi-490; II. 493-1272. 3-7965-0930-4.

10671 *García Sanz* Oscar, Cristianismo y dionisismo: RAg 34 (1993) 537-546.

10671* **Graf** Fritz,   La magie dans l'antiquité gréco-romaine; idéologie et pratique: Histoire. P 1994, BLettres. 372 p.; bibliog. 308-313. F 140. 3-251-38027-2.

10672 **Gruen** Erich S., Studies in Greek culture and Roman policy [< 1985 Cincinnati Semple Lectures] 1990 → 6,241*; 8,b380: ᴿGnomon 66 (1994) 131-4 (Linda-Marie *Günther*).

10672* ᵀᴱ**LeGuen-Pollet** Brigitte,   La vie religieuse dans le monde grec du Vᵉ au IIIᵉ siècle avant notre ère; choix de documents épigraphiques. Toulouse 1991, Mirail. 256 p. 2-85816-165-8.

10673 **Malkin** Irad,   Religion and colonization in ancient Greece: StGRRel 3. Leiden 1987, Brill. xiii-298 p. – ᴿAncAltW 46 (1993) 134-7 (C. *Ulf*).

10673* *Mimbu* Kilol H.,   Structure et thèmes initiatiques de l'Âne d'Or d'AᴘuʟÉᴇ: AncSoc 25 (1994) 303-330.

10674 ᴱ**Moreau** Alain,   L'initiation [adolescent, myste, professionel], Actes du Colloque international de Montpellier 1991/2 → 8,670: ᴿAntClas 63 (1994) 452s (Catherine *Lecomte*); JHS 114 (1994) 209 (D. *Montserrat*); RPg 67 (1993) 367s (D. *Arnould*).

10675 **O'Meara** Dominic J.,   Pʟoᴛɪɴus, an introduction to the Enneads.   Ox 1993, Clarendon. xi-142 p.; bibliog. 127-136. 0-19-875121-4.

10676 **Sissa** Giulia,   Greek virginity 1990 → 6,a946; 7,a645: ᴿPhoenix 48 (Toronto 1994) 76-79 (Bonnie *MacLachlan*).

10676* ᵀᴱ*Valgiglio* Ernesto,   Plutarco, Gli oracoli della Pizia: Moralium 10. N 1992, D'Auria. 109 p. 88-7092-053-4.

10677 *Zeller* Dieter, Mysterien (-religionen): → 517, TRE 23 (1994) 504-526.

M5.5 **Religiones anatolicae.**

10678 *Arutunyan* R. S., ➌ Some peculiarities of Hittite domestic ceremonies [to the storm-god of Kuliwisna]: VDI 200 (1992) 119-135; Eng. 135.

10679 *Buchholz* Hans-Günter,   Eine hethitische Schwertweihung: JPrehRel 8 (1994) 21-41; 8 fig.

10680 **Haas** Volkert,   Geschichte der hethitischen Religion: HbOr 1/15. Leiden 1994, Brill. xxi-1031 p.; Bibliog. 977-1023.

10681 **Hoffner** H. A.,   Hittite myths 1990 → 6,a960 ... 9,11867: ᴿRB 101 (1994) 296 (M. *Sigrist*).

10682 **Hutter** Manfred,   Behexung ... mittelheth.: OBO 82, 1988 → 4,b815 ... 7,a713: ᴿAfO 40s (1993s) 122-5 (A. *Ünal*); JNES 53 (1994) 139-142 (T. van den *Hout*).

10682* **Loon** Maurits N. van, Anatolia in the earlier first millennium B.C.: IconRel 15/13, 1991 → 8,b405: ᴿÉtClas 62 (1994) 88s (J. *Vanschoonwinkel*).

10683 *a) Müller* Gerfrid G. W.,   Ein hethitisches Ritualfragment aus Privatbesitz; – *b) Hout* Theo P. J. van den,   Träume einer hethitischen Königin: KUB LX 97 + XXXI 71: AltOrF 21 (1994) 372-5; Facsimile / 305-327.

10684 **Pecchioli Daddi** Franca,   *Polvani* Anna Maria, La mitologia ittita 1990 → 9,11875: ᴿAthenaeum 82 (1994) 569s (Clelia *Mora*); Salesianum 56 (1994) 365 (R. *Bracchi*).

10684* *Schuol* Monika,   Die Terminologie des hethitischen SU-Orakels: AltOrF 21 (1994) 73-124.247-304.

10685 *a) Ünal* Ahmet,   Zur Beschaffenheit des hethitischen Opfertisches aus philologischer und archäologischer Sicht; – *b) Kammenhuber* Annelies, Einige Bemerkungen zum hethitischen Zeichenlexikon von Christel Rüsᴛᴇʀ und Erich Nᴇu (1989): → 55, ᶠHʀouᴅᴀ B., Beiträge 1994, 283-291; 4 fig.; pl. XXVI / 117-123.

10686 *a) Weinfeld* Moshe, Traces of Hittite cult in Shiloh, Bethel and in Jerusalem; – *b) Wright* David P., Analogy in biblical and Hittite ritual; – *c) Podella* Thomas, Notzeit-Mythologem und Nichtigkeitsfluch [from Luwian eclipse of a deity and of that human area for which it was responsible]: → 9,567 Beziehungen 1993, 455-472 / 473-500 / 427-454 [OTAbs 17, p. 8s].

M6 Religio canaanaea, syra.

10687 **Ackerman** Susan, Under every green tree 1992 → 8,b411; 9,11876: ᴿBO 51 (1994) 375-7 (M. J. *Mulder*); CBQ 56 (1994) 311s (Deborah *Klee*); JBL 113 (1994) 705-8 (T. J. *Lewis*).

10688 **Albertz** Rainer, Religionsgeschichte Israels in alttestamentlicher Zeit 1992 → 8,b412; 9,11878: ᴿBijdragen 55 (1994) 326s (P. C. *Beentjes*); Carthaginensia 10 (1994) 174s (R. *Sanz Valdivieso*); CBQ 56 (1994) 312-4 (M. E. *Biddle*); JBL 113 (1994) 116-120 (W. *Brueggemann*: enormous potential for German/US interaction); OLZ 89 (1994) 159-163 (U. *Hübner*); Protestantesimo 49 (1994) 396s (J. A. *Soggin*).

10689 — *Thiel* Winfried, Gesellschaft und Religion; zur neuen 'Religionsgeschichte Israels' von Rainer ALBERTZ: TLZ 119 (1994) 3-14.

10690 **Albertz** Rainer, A history of Israelite religion in the OT period, 1. From the beginning to the end of the monarchy; 2. From the exile to the Maccabees; ᵀ*Bowden* John: OT Library. LvL/L 1994, W-Knox/SCM. xvi-740 p. $33 + 32. 0-664-21846-6; -7-4 / [TDig 42,53]. – ᴿCurrTM 21 (1994) 458s (R. W. *Klein*: book of the decade); TLond 97 (1994) 455s (R. *Coggins*: displaces RINGGREN and FOHRER).

10691 **Arbeitman** Yoel C., Detecting the god who remained in Dan: Henoch 16 (1994) 9-14.

10692 **Barker** Margaret, The great angel 1992 → 8,b414; 9,11881: ᴿJTS 45 (1994) 187-191 (J. *Fossum*).

10693 **Barker** M., The older Testament 1988 → 3,b327 ... 9,11887: ScotJR 11 (1990) 57s (N. *Wyatt*).

10694 **Bonnet** Corinne, Melqart 1988 → 4,b839 ... 9,11887: ᴿWeltOr 15 (1994) 173s (W. *Röllig*).

10695 *a) Boshoff* W., Variety is a sign of life; thoughts on the history of Israelite religion; – *b) Krüger* P. A., The comparative religious approach; – *c) Scheffler* E. H., The psychological approach to the (Hebrew) Bible; – *d) Potgieter* A. H., A Semitic perspective on OT studies: → 327, ODENDAAL D. mem., OTEssays 7,4 (1991/4) 121-131 / 115-120 / 148-159 / 317-320.

10696 **Cauvin** Jacques, Naissance des divinités, naissance de l'agriculture; la révolution des symboles au Néolithique. P 1994, CNRS. 304 p. – ᴿPaléorient 20,2 (1994) 172-4 (C. *Renfrew*).

10697 **Chase** Debra A., Baʿl Samem; a study of the early epigraphic sources (Phoenicia): diss. Harvard, ᴰ*Cross* F. CM 1994. 336 p. 95-00171. – DissA 55 (1994s) p. 2362.

10698 *Cogan* Mordechai, ❶ Religion and cult in the kingdom of Judah under Assyrian hegemony; a new examination: CHistEI 69 (1993) 3-17; ill.; Eng. 183.

10699 **Cornelius** Izak, The iconography of the Canaanite gods Reshef and Baʿal; Late Bronze and Iron Age I periods (c. 1500 – 1000 B.C.E.): OBO 140. FrS/Gö 1994, Univ./VR. 298 p.; Bibliog. 265-291. 3-7278-0983-3 / VR 3-525-53775-1.

10700 **Cryer** Frederick H., Divination in ancient Israel and its Near Eastern environment; a socio-historical investigation: jOsu 142. Shf 1994, JStOT. 167 p. £45.

10701 *Daviau* P. M. Michèle, *Dion* Paul E., El, the god of the Ammonites? The Atef-crowned head from Tell Jawa [12k S Amman], Jordan: ZDPV 110 (1994) 158-167; 2 fig.; pl. 10.

10702 *a) Day* John, Yahweh and the gods and goddesses of Canaan; – *b) Smith* Mark S., Yahweh and other deities in ancient Israel; observations on old problems and recent trends; – *c) Hadley* Judith M., Yahweh and 'his Asherah'; archeological and textual evidence for the cult of the goddess; – *d) Keel* O., *Uehlinger* C., Yahweh und die Sonnengottheit von Jerusalem; – *e) Niehr* Herbert, JHWH in der Rolle des Baalšamem: ➤ 467*, Ein Gott 1993/4, 181-196 / 197-234 / 235-268 [99-104, *Meshel* Ze'ev] / 269-306; 11 fig. / 307-326.

10702* **Day** J., Molech 1989 ➤ 5,a948 ... 8,b422: ᴿAJS 17 (1992) 98-100 (M. Z. *Brettler*); ScripB 23 (1993) 45s (J. *Duckworth*).

10703 **Dearman** S. Andrew, Religion and culture in ancient Israel 1992 ➤ 8, b424; 9,11892 [BL 95,111, W. J. *Houston*]: ᴿCBQ 56 (1994) 753s (F. S. *Frick*); JRelHist 18 (1994) 97s (N. *Weeks*); NRT 116 (1994) 100 (J. L. *Ska*); ᴢAW 106 (1994) 153 (U. *Becker*).

10703* *a) Deist* Ferdinand, Speaking about 'Yahweh and the gods'; some methodological observations; – *b) Müller* Hans-Peter, Alttestamentliche Theologie und Religionswissenschaft: ➤ 61, ᶠKAISER O., 'Wer ist' 1994, 3-19 / 20-31.

10704 *a) Dietrich* Walter, Über Werden und Wesen des biblischen Monotheismus; Religionsgeschichtliche und theologische Perspektiven; – *b) Stolz* Fritz, Der Monotheismus Israels im Kontext der altorientalischen Religionsgeschichte; Tendenzen neuerer Forschung; – *c) Albertz* Rainer Der Ort des Monotheismus in der israelitischen Religionsgeschichte; – *d) Lemche* Niels P., Kann von einer 'israelitischen' Religion' noch weiterhin die Rede sein? Perspektiven eines Historikers: ➤ 467*, Ein Gott 1993/4, 13-30 / 33-50 / 77-96 / 59-75.

10704* ᴱ**Dietrich** Walter, *Klopfenstein* Martin A., Ein Gott allein? JHWH-Verehrung und biblischer Monotheismus im Kontext der israelitischen und altorientalischen Religionsgeschichte: OBO 139. FrS/Gö 1994, Univ./ VR. 616 p. DM 146. ➤ 467*.

10705 **Eilberg-Schwartz** Howard, The savage in Judaism 1990 ➤ 6,a985 ... 9,11896: ᴿAJS 17 (1992) 91-93 (R. *Patai*); Judaism 43 (1994) 101-9 (E. L. *Greenstein*).

10706 *Eilberg-Schwartz* Howard, reply to *Gabriel* Ayala H., review of his Savage in Judaism 1990 ➤ 6,a985 ... 9,11896: JAAR [60 (1992) 153-8] 62 (1994) 173-7; no rejoinder opted.

10707 **Fleming** D. E., The installation of Baal's high priestess at Emar ᴰ1992 ➤ 8,b421; 9,11899: ᴿBASOR 293 (1994) 87s (G. *Beckman*); JTS 45 (1994) 627-9 (A.H.W. *Curtis*); Orientalia 63 (1994) 144s (R. *DiVito*, named on p. iv).

10708 *a) Fleming* Daniel E., 'The storm-god of Canaan' at Emar; – *b) Good* R. McClive. The sportsman Baal: UF 26 (1994) 127-130 / 147-163.

10708* **Frankfort** Henri † 1954, Il dio che muore; mito e cultura nel mondo preclassico, ᵀ*Scandone Matthiae* Gabriella: Lezioni 3. F 1992, Nuova Italia. xxi-145 p. 88-221-1122-2.

10709 **Garbini** Giovanni, La religione dei Fenici in occidente: StSemit 12. R 1994, Univ. 127 p.

10710 *Garbini* Giovanni, La dea di Tharros: RStFen 21 (1993) 99-110.
10711 *Geller* Stephen A., Goddesses and women in biblical religion [FRYMER-KEMSKY Tikva 1992]: Prooftexts 13 (1993) 295-8.
10712 **Handy** Lowell K., Among the host of heaven; the Syro-Palestinian pantheon as bureaucracy. WL 1994, Eisenbrauns. xvii-281 p.; bibliog. 175-203. $27.50. 0-931464-84-6.
10713 *Heller* Birgit, Die altorientalische Göttin — Aspekte einer 'Thealogie': Kairos 34s (1992s) 91-107.
10714 **Husser** Jean-Marie, Le songe et la parole; étude sur le rêve et sa fonction dans l'ancien Israël: BZAW 230. B 1994, de Gruyter. xii-302 p.; Bibliog. 273-294.
10715 [Avigdor] *Hurowitz* Victor, Ancient Israelite cult in history, tradition, and interpretation [*Milgrom* J., AnchorB Lev 1-16, 1991]: AJS 19 (1993) 213-236.
10716 **Hvidberg-Hansen** Finn G., Kana'anæiske myter 1990 → 8,b438; 9, 11902: ScandJOT 7 (1993) 156-160 (T. *Kronholm*).
10717 *a) Ikeda* Yutaka, Because their shade is good — Asherah in the early Israelite religion; – *b) Tsumura* David Toshio, The interpretation of the Ugaritic funerary text KTU 1.161: → 9,571* Official Cult 1992/3, 56-80; 17 fig., mostly of Bible plants / 40-55.
10718 ᴱ**Janowski** B., *al.*, Religionsgeschichtliche Beziehungen... Kleinasien, Syrien, AT: OBO 129, 1990/3 → 9,567: ᴿExpTim 105 (1993s) 344s (I. *Provan*).
10719 **Keel** O., *Uehlinger* C., Göttinnen ... QDisp 134 1992 → 8,b439; 9, 11906: ᴿBiblica 75 (1994) 298-302 (E. A. *Knauf*); Bijdragen 55 (1994) 325s (J. van *Ruiten*); BO 51 (1994) 377-382 (A. *Caquot*); CBQ 56 (1994) 553s (W. E. *Aufrecht*: data rather than answers); ÉTRel 68 (1993) 592s (Françoise *Smyth*); Streven 60 (1993) 373s (P. *Beentjes*); SvTK 70 (1994) 39-41 (T. *Mettinger*).
10720 *a) Keel* Othmar, Sturmgott - Sonnengott - Einziger; ein neuer Versuch, die Entstehung des jüdischen Monotheismus historisch zu verstehen; – *b) Assmann* Jan, Zur Spannung zwischen Poly- und Monotheismus im alten Ägypten; – *c) Schroer* Silvia, Zeit für Grenzüberschreitungen; die göttliche Weisheit im nachexilischen Monotheismus; – *d) Balz-Cochois* Helgard, Magna Mater; feministische Göttinnensuche und Weibliches in einem christlichen Gottesbilde: BiKi 49,2 ('Der eine Gott und die Götter' 1994) 82-92 / 78-82 / 103-7 / 108-112.
10721 **Koh** Sejin, An archaeological investigation of the snake cult in the southern Levant; the chalcolithic period through the Iron Age (Palestine): diss. ᴰ*Esse* D. Ch 1994. 214 p. 95-01511. – DissA 55 (1994s) p. 2448.
10722 **Korpel** Marjo Christina A., A rift in the clouds; Hebrew and Ugaritic descriptions of the divine 1990 → 6,a995 ... 9,11907: ᴿAJS 17 (1992) 279-281 (D. *Marcus*); Bijdragen 55 (1994) 75s (J. van *Ruiten*).
10723 *a) Lang* Bernhard, Der monarchische Monotheismus und die Konstellation zweier Götter im Frühjudentum; ein neuer Versuch über Menschensohn, Sophia und Christologie; – *b) Fritz* Volkmar, Die Bedeutung der vorpriesterschriftlichen Vätererzählungen für die Religionsgeschichte der Königszeit; – *c) Dietrich* Walter, Der eine Gott als Symbol politischen Widerstands; Religion und Politik im Juda des 7. Jahrhunderts; – *d) Lemaire* André, Déesses et dieux de Syrie-Palestine d'après les inscriptions (c. 1000-500 av.J.-C.): → 467*, Ein Gott 1993/4, 559-564 / 403-411 / 463-490 / 127-158.

10723* **Lewis** Theodore J., Cults of the dead in ancient Israel and Ugarit 1989
→ 5,a961 ... 8,b441: ᴿJNES 53 (1994) 153s (D. *Pardee*).

10724 *Loretz* Oswald, Opfer- und Leberschau in Israel; philologische und
historische Aspekte: → 9,567, Rel-WBeziehungen 1993, 509-529 [< OTAbs
17, p. 168].

10724* *Margalith* Othniel, A new type of Asherah-figurine?: VT 44 (1994)
109-113; 1 fig.

10725 **Moor** J.C. de, An anthology of religious texts from Ugarit 1987
→ 3,b265a ... 7,a749. – ᴿScotJR 13 (1992) 66-68 (N. *Wyatt*: his excellent
updated translation will gain harmful exposure for his 'seasons' interpretation).

10726 **Moor** Johannes C. de, The rise of Yahwism: BtETL 91, 1990 → 6,7022
... 8,b442: ᴿBijdragen 55 (1994) 77 (J. van *Ruiten*).

10727 **Niehr** Herbert, Der höchste Gott...: ʙᴢᴀᴡ 190, 1990 → 6,b3 ... 9,11916:
ᴿBiKi 49 (1994) 72s (F.J. *Stendebach*); ZkT 116 (1994) 93s (R. *Oberforcher*).

10728 *Niehr* Herbert, Zur Frage der Filiation des Gottes Ba'al in Ugarit:
JNWS 10,2 (1994) 165-177.

10729 **Olmo Lete** G. del, La religión cananea según la liturgia de Ugarit 1992
→ 9,11918: ᴿAulaO 11,1 (1993) 120-2 (W.G.E. *Watson*); BO 51 (1994)
611-3 (K. *Spronk*).

10729* **Olyan** S., Ashera 1988 → 4,b871 ... 7,a753: ᴿVT 44 (1994) 410-2
(Judith M. *Hadley*).

10730 **Schmidt** Brian B., Israel's beneficent dead; ancestor-cult and necro-
mancy in ancient Israelite religion and tradition: ForAT 11. Tü 1994,
Mohr. xv-400 p. 3-16-146221-1.

10731 **Smith** Mark S., The early history of God 1990 → 6,b11 ... 9,11924:
ᴿAJS 17 (1992) 93-97 (Z. *Zevit*); ConcordTQ 58 (1994) 318s (W.A.
Meier: helpful); JIntdenom 18 (1990s) 157-164 (T.J. *Lewis*).

10732 *a)* **Soisson** Pierre, Jahveh et le Jahvisme; – *b)* *Fau* Guy, Moïse et le
monothéisme juif; – *c)* *Trèves* Marco, Combien de dieux dans l'ancien
Israël?: CahRenan 185 (1994) 113-122 / 187 (1994) 5-15 / 42-51

10733 *Taylor* Glen J., Was Yahweh worshiped as the sun? Israel's God was
abstract, but he may also have had a consort: BAR-W 20,3 (1994)
52-61.90s.

10734 **Ulmer** Rivka, The evil eye in the Bible and in rabbinic literature.
Hoboken 1994, ᴋᴛᴀᴠ. x-213 p.; bibliog. 193-204. 0-88125-463-0.

10735 **Vry** Silke, Zeus und Tyche in der Dekapolis: Diss. Kiel. — MiDAV
25,2 (1994) 32.

10736 ᴱWacher J., *Zenger* E., Der eine Gott und die Göttin ... Fem.Theol.:
Tagung Aug. 1990: QDisp 135, FrB 1991. – ᴿTPQ 142 (1994) 88s (R.
Frick-Pöder).

10737 *Wallis* Gerhard, *a)* Aufnahme und Überwindung kanaanäischer Vor-
stellungen und Eigenarten durch Alt-Israel; – *b)* Gottesvorstellung und
Gotteserfahrung der alttestamentlichen Weisheitsliteratur; – *c)* Hermann
Gᴜɴᴋᴇʟ zum 100. Geburtstag am 23. Mai 1962 [3 inedita]: → 229, Mein
Freund 1994, 89-99 / 189-205 / 241-253.

10738 **Walls** Neal H., The goddess Anat in Ugaritic myth: SBL diss 135
(Hopkins 1991), 1992 → 8,b854: ᴿCBQ 56 (1994) 349-351 (M. *Pope*);
JBL 113 (1994) 505s (D. *Pardee*: highly credible); RelStR 20 (1994) 139
(S.B. *Parker*); TüTQ 174 (1994) 242s (H. *Niehr*); ᴢᴀᴡ 106 (1994) 542 (M.
Köchert).

10738* *Weippert* Helga, Zu einer neuen ikonographischen Religionsge-

schichte Kanaans und Israels [KEEL-UEHLINGER 1992]: BZ 38 (1994) 1-28.
10739 **Wiggins** Steve A., A reassessment of 'Asherah'; a study according to the textual sources of the first two millennia B.C.E. [diss. Edinburgh]: AOAT 235, 1993 ➤ 9,11930: ᴿBL (1994) 116s (W.G.E. *Watson*); TüTQ 174 (1994) 320s (H. *Niehr*).

M6.5   Religio aegyptia.

10740 **Assmann** J., Ma'at; Gerechtigkeit 1990 ➤ 6,b20 ... 9,11934: ᴿJEA 80 (1994) 219-231 (S. *Quirke*); Muséon 107 (1994) 391-4 (C. *Vandersleyen*).
10741 **Bickel** Susanne, La cosmogonie égyptienne avant le Nouvel Empire [diss. Genève 1993]: OBO 134. FrS/Gö 1994, Univ/VR. 345 p. 3-7278-0950-7 / VR 3-525-53769-7.
10741* **Brashear** William M. (*Bülow-Jacobsen* Adam), Magica varia: Papyrol-Brux 25. Bru 1991, Fond. Reine Élisabeth. 84 p.; 15 pl.
10742 **Champdor** A., Das ägyptische Totenbuch; vom Geheimnis das Jenseits im Reich der Pharaonen [ᵀ1977] ᴱ*Lurker* Manfred: Spektrum 4183. FrB 1993, Hered. 208 p.; 110 (color) fig. DM 16,80. 3-457-04183-9. – ᴿZkT 116 (1994) 109s (K. H. *Neufeld*).
10743 **Chiodi** Silvia Maria, La religione dell'antico Egitto: Orizzonti della storia. Mi 1994, Rusconi. 207 p. 88-18-88042-X.
10744 *Cortés Martín* Juan, El clero de Amón durante las dinastías XVIII y XIX en el antiguo Egipto: Gerión 12 (1994) 309-313.
10745 ᶠDERCHAIN P., Religion und Philosophie im Alten Ägypten, ᴱVerhoeven U. ... 1991 ➤ 7,43; 9,11950: ᴿDiscEg 25 (1993) 95-104 (Renate *Müller-Wollermann*).
10746 **Derchain-Urtel** M.-Theresia, Priester im Tempel ... Edfu, Dendera 1989 ➤ 5,a996; 7,a782: ᴿBO 51 (1994) 536-544 (A. *Egberts*).
10747 **Drewermann** Eugen, La barque du soleil, la mort et la resurrection dans l'Égypte ancienne et dans l'Évangile. P 1994, Seuil. – ᴿQVidCr 174 (1994) 125 (L. *Duch*).
10748 **DuQuesne** Terence, [Anubis] Jackal at the Shaman's gate: Oxfordshire Egyptology 3. Thame 1991, Darengo. 136 p.; 8 fig. 1-871266-13-0. – ᴿJEA 80 (1994) 257s (H. D. *Betz*).
10749 **Eschweiler** Peter, Bildzauber im alten Ägypten; die Verwendung von Bildern und Gegenständen in magischen Handlungen nach den Texten des Mittleren und Neuen Reiches [Diss. Heid. 1991]: x-371 p.; Bibliog. 319-342. 3-7278-0957-4 / VR 3-525-53772-7.
10750 **Franco** Isabelle, Petit dictionnaire de mythologie égyptienne: Mythologies. P 1993, Entente. 252 p.; ill. 2-7266-0104-9.
10751 **Gallorini** Carla, Formule magiche dell'Antico Egitto: Verso Antiochia. Mi 1994, EDIS. 106 p. 88-86316-06-2.
10752 **Görg** Manfred, Mythos, Glaube und Geschichte; die Bilder des christlichen Credos und ihre Wurzeln im alten Ägypten. Dü 1992, Patmos. 189 p. DM 29,80. – ᴿBiKi 48 (1993) 241 (C. *Dohmen*); ZkT 116 (1994) 111s (R. *Oberforcher*).
10753 *Golovina* V. A., The institution of *ḥmw-k'* [funerary priest] in ancient Egypt of the Middle Kingdom: VDI 200 (1992) 3-20; Eng. 20.
10754 *Graf* Fritz, La magie dans l'antiquité gréco-romaine; idéologie et pratique: Histoire. P 1994, BLettres. 322 p.
10755 **Graindorge-Héreil** Catherine. Le dieu Sokar à Thèbes au Nouvel Empire, I. Textes; II. Planches: GöOrF 4/28. Wsb 1994, Harrassowitz. I.

xxxvi-555 p.; bibliog. 497-545; II. xvi-140 p.; 137 pl.; 57 textes. 3-447-03476-9.
10756 **Grimm** Alfred, Die altägyptischen Festkalender in den Tempeln der griechisch-römischen Epoche [Diss. München 1986]. AOAT 15. Wsb 1994, Harrassowitz. 477 p.; 6 pl. 3-447-02824-6.
10757 **Guglielmi** W., Die Göttin Mr.t; Entstehung und Verehrung einer Personifikation: Probleme der Ägyptologie 7, 1991 ⇒ 7,a789; 9,11956: ᴿBO 51 (1994) 40-42 (J.-C. *Goyon*).
10758 ᵀᴱ**Hornung** Erik, Ägyptische Unterweltsbücher³. Z 1992 = 1989, Artemis. 525 p. DM 58. – ᴿBiKi 49 (1994) 68 (R. *Russ*, auch über CHAMPDOR A. 1993).
10759 *a) Kákosy* László, Zeus in Egypt; – *b) Riad* Henry, The goddess Nemesis; her worship in Alexandria and other parts of Egypt: ⇒ 9,2, ᶠABOU DAOUD A. (1993) 173-5; pl. XXIX / 261-4, pl. XLV-XLVII.
10760 *Kákosy* L., Three decrees of gods from Theban tomb 32: OrLovPer 23 (1992) 311-328; pl. IV-VII.
10761 *Kingsley* Peter, From Pythagoras to the turba philosophorum; Egypt and the Pythagorean tradition: JWarb 57 (1994) 1-13.
10762 **Kruchten** Jean-Marie, Les annales des prêtres de Karnak 1989 ⇒ 7,a803; 8,b490: ᴿJEA 79 (1993) 308s (K.A. *Kitchen*); JNES 53 (1994) 58s (A.R. *Schulman*).
10763 **Lapp** Günter, Die Opferformel des Alten Reiches 1986 ⇒ 2,9034; 8,b491: ᴿJNES 53 (1994) 147s (Ann M. *Roth*).
10764 *Lorton* David, The invocation hymn at the temple of Hibis [Khargeh]: StÄäK 21 (1994) 159-217; 3 fig.
10765 **Luckert** Karl W., Egyptian light and Hebrew fire 1991 ⇒ 8,a806: ᴿCritRR 6 (1993) 545-7 (D. *Wiebe*).
10766 **Mora** Fabio, Prosopographia Isiaca: ÉPR 113, 1990 ⇒ 8,b201: ᴿNumen 41 (1994) 198-202 (J. *Rüpke*).
10767 **Munro** Irmtraut, Die Totenbuch-Handschriften der 18. Dynastie im Ägyptischen Museum Cairo: ÄgAbh 54. Wsb 1994, Harrassowitz. I. xiv-247 p.; 80 (color.) pl.; II. 160 pl. 3-447-03433-5.
10768 *Ockinga* Boyo, Thoughts on the nature of the divinity of the ruler in ancient Egypt and imperial Rome: ⇒ 69, ᶠLACEY W., Prudentia 26,1 (1994) 17-34.
10769 *a) Pamminger* Peter, Zur Göttlichkeit Amenophis' III; – *b) Berlandini* Jocelyne, Amenotep III et le concept de Heh [nom d'un dieu complexe ...]: BSocÉg 17 (Genève 1993) 83-92 / 11-28; 19 fig.
10770 *Pamminger* Peter, Das 'Schedsunefertem [memphitischer Hohepriester] – Problem': CdÉ 69 (1994) 9-42.
10771 **Perpillou-Thomas** Françoise, † 21.X.1993, Fêtes d'Égypte ptolémaïque et romaine d'après la documentation papyrologique grecque [diss. Rouen 1991]: StHellenistica 31. Lv 1993, Univ. xxix-293 p.; bibliog. xxi-xxix.
10772 **Pinch** Geraldine, Magic in ancient Egypt. L 1994, British Museum. 191 p.; 95 fig. 0-7141-0979-1.
10773 **Quirke** Stephen, Ancient Egyptian religion 1992 ⇒ 8,b501: ᴿBO 51 (1994) 289-294 (V.A. *Tobin*).
10774 **Römer** Malte, Gottes- und Priesterherrschaft in Ägypten am Ende des Neuen Reiches; ein religionsgeschichtliches Phänomen und seine sozialen Grundlagen [Diss. 1989, Berlin FU, ᴰFecht G.]: ÄgAT 21. Wsb 1994, Harrassowitz. xxxvii-621 p.; Bibliog. xiii-xxix. 3-447-03217-0.
10775 *Roth* Ann Macy. Fingers, stars and the 'opening of the mouth'; the nature and function of the *nṯrwj*-blades: JEA 79 (1993) 57-79; 12 fig.

10776 *Saady* Hassan el-, Reflections on the goddess Tayet: JEA 80 (1994) 213-7; 1 fig.

10777 **Schumacher** Inke W., Der Gott Sopdu: OBO 79, ᴰ1988 ➤ 5,b141 ... 9,11987: ᴿJNES 53 (1994) 59-61 (H. *Goedicke*).

10778 **Shafer** Byron E., Religion in ancient Egypt; gods, myths, and personal practice [symposium 1987] 1991 ➤ 7,625 ... 9,11989: – *Silverman* D., p. 7-87; *Lesko* L. 88-122; *Barnes* J. 123-200 [ᴢᴀᴡ 105, 323]. – ᴿCritRR 5 (1992) 66-68 (Susan T. *Hollis* compares with Tᴏʙɪɴ T. 1989).

10779 ᴱ**Simpson** W. K., Religion and philosophy in ancient Egypt 1989. – ᴿCdÉ 69 (1994) 101s (P. *Derchain*).

10780 **Smith** Mark, The liturgy of opening the mouth for breathing. Ox 1993, Ashmolean Griffith. x-131 p.; bibliog. 81-90; 11 (foldout) pl. 0-900416-62-9.

10781 *Sternberg-el Hotabi* Heike, Die mensa isiaca und die Isis-Aretalogien: CdÉ 69 (1994) 54-86; 8 fig.

10782 **Stricker** B. H., De geboorte van Horus 1989 ➤ 5,b45; ᴿDiscEg 26 (1993) 97-105 (T. *DuQuesne*).

10783 *Sweeney* Deborah, Henuttawy's guilty conscience; gods and grain in Late Ramesside Letter No. 37: JEA 80 (1994) 208-212.

10784 *Thompson* Stephen E., The anointing of officials in ancient Egypt: JNES 53 (1994) 15-25.

10785 *Winnicki* Jan K., Carrying off and bringing home the statues of the gods; on an aspect of the religious policy of the Ptolemies tpwards the Egyptians: JJurPap 24 (1994) 149-190.

10786 *Zeidler* Jürgen, Zur Frage der Spätentstehung des Mythos in Ägypten: GöMiszÄg 132 (1993) 85-109.

10787 **Griggs** C. Wilfred, Early Egyptian Christianity ...: Coptic Studies 2, 1991 ➤ 8,b519; 9,11999: ᴿBO 51 (1994) 362-5 (H. M. *Schenke*); JEarlyC 1 (1993) 91s (J. O. *Gooch*); TLZ 119 (1994) 140-3 (H. M. *Schenke*).

10787* *Minnen* Peter van, The roots of Egyptian Christianity: ArPapF 40 (1994) 71-85.

M7 **Religio mesopotamica.**

10788 **Badali** Enrico, *Zinko* Christian ²*Ofitsch* Michaela, Der 16. Tag des AN.TAḤ.ŠUM-Festes: Univ. Innsbruck InstSprW; Scientia 20. Graz 1994. 218 p.

10789 **Bjorkman** Judith K., Hoards and [votive] deposits in Bronze Age Mesopotamia: diss. Pennsylvania, ᴰ*Muhly* J. Ph 1994, 711 p. 94-27503. – DissA 55 (1994s) p. 1302.

10790 *Block* Daniel, Chasing a phantom; the search for the historical Marduk: ArchBW 2 (1992) 21-43 [< OTAbs 16, p. 207].

10791 *a)* *Bottéro* Jean, L'exorcisme et le culte privé en Mésopotamie; – *b)* *Cooper* Jerrold S., Sacred marriage and popular cult in early Mesopotamia; – *c)* *Finet* André, Les dieux de l'ombre; intégrés, intrus et médiateurs; – *d)* *Edzard* Dietz O., Private Frömmigkeit in Sumer; – *e)* *Livingstone* Alasdair, The case of the hemerologies; official cult, learned formulation and popular practice: ➤ 9,571*, Official cult 1992/3, 31-39 / 81-96 / 126-134 / 195-209 [220-2] / 97-113; 3 fig.

10792 **Braun-Holzinger** Eva A.,   Mesopotamische Weihgaben der frühdynastischen bis altbabylonischen Zeit [Hab.-Diss. Heidelberg 1987]: Heid-StAO 3, 1991 → 7,a820:   ᴿAfO 40s (1993s) 127-130 (A. *Spycket*).

10793 *Cole* Steven W., The crimes and sacrileges of Nabû-Šuma-iškun: ZAss 84 (1994) 220-252; 2 fig. (*map*).

10793* *Dietrich* Manfried, 'Kein schlechtes Gewissen hatte ich'; einige babylonische Texte zum Thema Unheil als Symbol der Gottesferne: → 61, ꟳKAISER O., 'Wer ist' 1994, 51-64.

10794 **Fleming** Daniel E., The installation of Baal's high priestess at Emar: HarvSemSt 42, 1992 → 8,b431:   ᴿRB 101 (1994) 450s (J. M. de *Tarragon*).

10795 **Green** Tamara M., The city of the Moon-God; religious traditions of Harran: RelGrRWorld 114. Leiden 1992. Brill. viii-232 p. ƒ 110. – ᴿTR 90 (1994) 502s (P. *Heinz*).

10796 *Hirsch* Hans, Die Vergangenheit im Šamaš-Hymnus (BWL 121 ff.); Interpretationsversuche 3: AfO 40s (1993s) 46-51 (p. 45, Hirsch über SEVER H., Belleten 56,667).

10796* **Kraus** F. R., The role of the temples from the Third Dynasty of Ur to the First Dynasty of Babylon: MgANE 2/4, 1990 → 8,b538: ᴿJESHO 37 (1994) 183-5 (K. R. *Veenhof*).

10797 *Krebernik* M., Zur Einleitung der z à - m e - Hymnen aus Tell Abū Ṣalābīḫ: → 55, ꟳHROUDA B., Beiträge 1994, 151-7.

10798 **Lawson** Jack N., The concept of fate in ancient Mesopotamia of the first millennium; toward an understanding of *Simtu*: OrBibChr 7. Wsb 1994, Harrassowitz. xiii-143 p.; bibliog. 135-143. 3-447-03541-2.

10799 **Maul** Stefan M., Zukunftsbewältigung; eine Untersuchung altorientalischen Denkens anhand der babylonisch-assyrischen Löserituale (Namburbi): BaghFor 18. Mainz 1994, von Zabern. xxiii-555 p.; Bibliog. xiii-xxii. 3-8053-1618-6.

10799* *Michel* Cécile, Innāya 1991 → 8,b545*: ᴿRAss 88 (1994) 81-85 (B. *Lion*).

10800 *a*) *Nel* P. J., The conception of righteousness and the Mesopotamian gods; – *b*) *Vermaak* P. S., Die rol van die tempel binne die Mesopotamiese gemeenskap: J/Tyd Sem 6 (1994) 1-14 / 15-33.

10801 *Pongratz-Leisten* Beate, *Ina Šulmi Irub*; die kulttopographische und ideologische Programmatik der *akītu*-Prozession in Babylonien und Assyrien im I. Jts. v. Chr.: BagFor 16. Mainz 1994, von Zabern. XXVII-289 p.; 5 pl.; 12 facsim. 3-8053-1594-5.

10802 *Richter* Thomas, Untersuchungen zum Opferschauwesen [I. Orientalia 62 (1993) 121s] II. Zu einigen speziellen Keulenmarkierungen: AltOrF 21 (1994) 212-246.

10803 **Starr** Ivan, Queries to the Sungod: SAA 4, 1990 → 6,b102; 8,b554: ᴿRB 101 (1994) 447s (M. *Sigrist*); WeltOr 25 (1994) 132-4 (W. von *Soden*).

10804 *Toorn* Karel van der, Gods and ancestors in Emar and Nuzu: RAss 84 (1994) 38-59.

10805 *Veldhuis* N. C., The fly, the worm, and the chain; Old Babylonian chain incantations: OrLovPer 24 (1993) 41-64.

10807 **Wilson** E. Jan, 'Holiness' and 'purity' in Mesopotamia: AOAT 237. Neuk/Kevelaer 1994, Neuk/Buxton & B. x-121 p. 3-7666-9895-X.

10808 **Zettler** Richard L., The Ur III temple of Inanna at Nippur; the operation and organization of urban religious institutions in Mesopotamia

in the late third millennium B.C.: BBVO 11. B 1992. Reimer.   xiv-303 p.
DM 78. – [R]ZAss 84 (1994) 136-144 (W. *Sallaberger*).

M7.4   *Religio persiana*,   **Iran.**

10809 *Bier* Carol,   Piety and power in early Sassanian art: ➤ 9,571*, Official
cult 1992/3, 173-188 + 7 fig.
10810 **Boyce** Mary,   Zoroastrianism; its antiquity and constant vigour: Columbia Lectures on Iranian studies 7.   Costa Mesa CA 1992, Mazda.
xix-204 p.   0-939214-89-X; pa. -90-3. – [R]JAOS 194 (1994) 498s (W. W.
Malandra).
10811 **Boyce** Mary, *Grenet* Frantz,   A history of Zoroastrianism 3.   under
Macedonian and Roman rule: HbOr 1/8/1, 1991 ➤ 7,a842*; 8,b563: [R]BO
51 (1994) 372-5 (K. *Schippmann*); BSO 57 (1994) 388-391 (P. G.
Kreyenbroek); Numen 41 (1994) 202-4 (M. *Hutter*); VDI 210 (1994)
239-245 (K. *Abdullayev* ❾).
10812 [E]**Gignoux** Philippe,   Recurrent patterns in Iranian religions; from
Mazdaism to Sufism: Proceedings of the Round Table, Bamberg Oct.
1991.   P 1992, Soc. Iranologica Europaea, Cah. 11. / Peeters.   173 p.; ill.
[R]BSO 57 (1994) 235s (W. *Madelung*).
10813 *Herrenschmidt* Clarisse, *Kellens* Jean,   La question du rituel dans le
Mazdéisme ancien et achéménide: ArchivScSocR 39/85 (1994) 45-66;
Eng. español 67.
10814 **Maneck** Susan,   The death of Ahriman; culture, identity, and theological change among the Parsis of India: diss. Arizona 1994, [D]*Eaton* R. –
446 p. 94-26587. – DissA 55 (1994s) p. 1359.
10815 **Nigosian** S. A.,   The Zoroastrian faith; tradition and modern research
1993 ➤ 9,12038:   0-7735-1133-4; [R]TBR 7,1 (1994s) 76 (R. *Hooker*).
10816 **Shaked** Saul,   Dualism in transformation; varieties of religion in
Sasanian Iran (1991 Jordan Lectures). L 1994, Univ. School of Oriental
and African Studies.   [vi-] 176 p.; bibliog. 161-176.   0-7286-0233-4.
10817 **Waldmann** Helmut,   Der kommagenische Mazdaismus: DAI IstMitt
Beih 37, 1991 ➤ 7,465* ... 9,12039:   [R]Gnomon 66 (1994) 134-140 (G.
Ahn); OLZ 89 (1994) 520-5 (J. *Tubach*).
10818 **Williams** Ron G., *Boyd* James W.,   Ritual art and knowledge; aesthetic
theory and Zoroastrian ritual 1993 ➤ 9,12040:   [R]JRel 74 (1994) 434s
(W. R. *Darrow*).

M 8.1   *Religio proto-arabica* – **Early Arabic religious graffiti.**

10819 *a*) *Arbach* Mounir,   Inscriptions sudarabiques; – *b*) *Avanzini* Alessandra, *al.*,   Materiali per il corpus qatabanico; – *c*) *Robin* Christian J.,
Documents de l'Arabie antique III: Raydan 6 (1994) 5-16 / 17-36 / 69-90
(-137) [❹ *Bafaqîh* M. 6-103, *al.*].
10820 GHUL Mahmud al-, mémorial, [his photos of 32 Sayhadic texts], [E]**Bron**
François: L'Arabie préislamique 2.   P 1992, Geuthner. 123 p.
10820***Gnoli** Gherardo,   Shaqab al-Manassa: Inventario delle iscrizioni sud-
arabiche 2.   P 1993, de Boccard.   129 p.; 18 pl.; bibliog. 113-126. L[m] 45.
10821 *Hazim* Rafat,   Eine Gattung altsüdarabischer theophorer Namen: Muséon 107 (1994) 367-374.
10821* *Korotayev* Andrej,   Middle Sabaic *bn z*; clan group or [BEESTON A.
1980] head of clan?:   JSS 39 (1994) 207-216; 216-9 bibliog.
10822 **Krone** S., ... al-Lat 1992 ➤ 8,b580: [R]ZAW 106 (1994) 359 (M. *Köckert*).

10822* **Müller** Walter W., Adler und Geier als altarabische Gottheiten: → 61, ᶠKAISER O., 'Wer ist' 1994, 91-107.

10823 *Muzzolini* A., Le profane et le sacré dans l'art rupestre saharien: BSocFÉg 124 (1992) 24-61; 9 pl.

10824 *Papathanasiou* Athanasios, Christian missions in pre-Islamic South Arabia: TAth 65 (1994) 133-140.

10825 **Ryckmans** Jacques *al.*, Textes du Yémen antique inscrits sur bois: Publ. 42. LvN 1994, Univ. Inst. Orientaliste. ix-106 p. + 60; 16 pl. 90-6831-546-3.

10826 *Snir* Reuven, The inscription of 'En 'Abdat; an early evolutionary stage of ancient Arabic poetry: AbrNahr 31 (1993) 110-125.

M8.2   *Muḥammad et asseclae* – **Qur'ān and early diffusion of Islam.**

10827 **Ayoub** Mahmoud M., The Qur'ān and its interpreters; 2. The house of 'Imran. Albany 1992, SUNY. x-433 p. 0-7914-0994-5 pa. – ᴿReligion 24 (1994) 82 (I. R. *Netton*).

10828 **Bell** Richard, A commentary on the Qur'an I (1-24) II (25-145) [→ 8,b584]: JSS Mg 14. Manchester 1991, Univ. xxii-608 p.; 603 p. £60. – ᴿJSS 39 (1994) 127-9 (R. B. *Serjeant* †).

10829 *a) Erck* Cristina, Ergeben in den Willen Gottes; Ursprung und Entwicklung des Islam; – *b) Hunke* Sigrid, Wer nach Wissen Strebt, betet Gott an; das arabische Erbe europäischer Wissenschaften: Universitas 48 (1993) 106-119 / 120-9.

10830 **Ess** Josef van, Theologie und Gesellschaft im 2. und 3. Jahrhundert Hidschra; eine Geschichte des religiösen Denkens im frühen Islam I [c. 1990] II [Iraq; half on Basra]. B/NY 1992, de Gruyter. xii-742 p. DM 400. 3-11-012212-X. – ᴿBO 51 (1994) 21-33 (M. *Cook* treats 3 pages!); Speculum 69 (1994) 907-10 (R. S. *Humphreys*).

10831 **Gil** Moshe, A history of Palestine, 634-1099: 1992 → 8,b591; 9,12072: ᴿBSO 57 (1994) 233 (H. *Kennedy*); OLZ 89 (1994) 166-9 (J. F. *Healey*); Speculum 69 (1994) 1172s (S. *Bowman*).

10832 **Gil'adi** Avner, Children of Islam; concepts of childhood in medieval Muslim society. NY 1992, St. Martin's. xii-176 p. $50. – ᴿSpeculum 69 (1994) 780s (J. P. *Berkey*).

10833 *Griffith* Sidney H., ⊕ Holy Land history from the archive of old South Palestinian Arabic texts: CHistEI 69 (1993) 57-78; Eng. 182.

10834 *Monnot* Guy, Le corpus coranique → 9,415, Formation des canons 1987/93, 61-73.

10835 **Nagel** Thomas, Geschichte der islamischen Theologie, von Mohammed bis zur Gegenwart. Mü 1994, Beck. 313 p. – ᴿRSO 68 (1994) 183s (L. *Capezzone*).

10836 *O'Shaughnessy* Thomas J., A note on sorrow for sin in the Qur'ān [13,128-135]: Landas 8 (Manila 1994) 124-7.

10837 **Peters** Francis E., Muhammad and the origins of Islam. Albany 1994, SUNY. xiii-334 p. $59.50; 0-7914-1875-8; -6-6 [TDig 42,182]. – ᴿTS 56 (1995) 397s (D. A. *Madigan*).

10838 ᴱ**Peters** Francis, A reader of classical Islam [188 items with commentary]. Princeton 1994, Univ. xvi-420 p. $35; pa. $20. 0-691-03394-7; -0040-9. [TDig 41,94].

10838* **Pouzet** Louis, Les *madrasa*-s de Damas et leurs professeurs au VII-XIIIème siècle: MUSJ 52 (Beyrouth 1991s) 123-196; foldout map.

10839 *Rippin* A., The poetics of Qur'ānic punning: ➤ 136, ᶠWANSBROUGH J., BSO 57 (1994) 193-307.
10840 **Simon** Robert, Meccan trade and Islam 1989 ➤ 7,a875: ᴿJNES 53 (1994) 154-6 (M. *Morony*).
10841 **Thomas** David, Anti-Christian ... al-WARRĀQ 1992 ➤ 8,b614: ᴿHeythJ 35 (1994) 220s (I. R. *Netton*).
10842 *Vitestam* Gösta, Zu Einflussen des Paternosters in der islamischen Tradition: OrSuec 41s (1992s) 299-306.

M8.3 Islam, *evolutio recentior* – later history and practice.

10843 **Abu-Izzeddin** Nejla M., The Druzes, a new study of their history, faith and society [corrected reprint]. Leiden 1993, Brill. xii-259 p.
10844 **Arié** Rachel, Études sur la civilisation de l'Espagne musulmane: MdvIb 6. Leiden 1990, Brill. viii-386 p. ƒ160. – ᴿJSS 39 (1994) 134-6 (J. D. *Latham*).
10845 **Barkai** R., Cristianos y musulmanes en la España medieval: El enemigo en el espejo. M 1991, Rialp. 301 p. – ᴿCiuD 206 (1993) 959s (T. *Arregui*).
10846 **Berkey** Jonathan, The transmission of knowledge in medieval Cairo; a social history of Islamic education 1992 ➤ 9,12095: ᴿJRel 74 (1994) 283s (R. C. *Martin*); JSS 39 (1994) 361-4 (A. *Allouche*).
10847 *Brett* Michael, The mīm, the ʿayn, and the making of Ismāʿīlism: ➤ 136, ᶠWANSBROUGH J., BSO 57 (1994) 35-39.
10848 **Bürgel** Johann C., Allmacht und Mächtigkeit; Religion und Welt im Islam 1991 ➤ 8,b630; 9,12100: ᴿJSS 38 (1993) 164-6 (W. *Madelung*).
10849 **Bürgel** Johann C., The feather of Simurgh 1988 ➤ 4,b989... 7,a879c: ᴿBO 51 (1994) 737-9 (J. T. P. *de Bruijn*).
10850 **Burckhardt** John L., Notes on the Bedouins and Wahabys [1831]. L 1992, Garnet. – ᴿArchivScSocR 39,86 (1994) 269s (C. *Hames*: notes infiniment précieuses).
10851 **Carré** Olivier, L'Islam laïque ou le retour à la Grande Tradition. P 1993, Colin. 167 p. – ᴿArchivScSocR 35,86 (1994) 270s (J.-L. *Triaud*).
10852 *Chehayed* Jamal, La modernité dans la conscience culturelle arabe: BÉtOr 45 (1993) 9-2; Eng. ➍ 279.
10853 **Corbin** Henry, History of Islamic philosophy [1964], ᵀ*Sherrard* L. & P. L 1993, Kegan Paul. 445 p. £55. – ᴿBSO 57 (1994) 593s (O. *Leaman*: needed; *ḥikma* beyond *falsafa*).
10854 **Daftary** Farhad, The Ismailis 1992 = 1990 ➤ 6,b174; 8,b634: ᴿWeltOr 25 (1994) 189s (J. *Danecki*).
10855 **Fakhry** Majid, Histoire de la philosophie islamique: Patrimoines Islam 1989 ➤ 9,12109: ᴿNRT 116 (1994) 602s (J. *Scheuer*).
10855* *Forstner* Martin, Die wohlgeordnete Welt — das Verhältnis zwischen Muslimen und Nichtmuslimen nach neoislamischer Rechtslehre: ➤ 109, Mem. SCHAENDLINGER A.: ᴿWZKM 82 (1992) 129-147.
10856 ᵀᴱ**Gramlich** Richard, Das Sendschreiben al-QUŠAYRĪs über das Sufitum: FreibIslSt 12, 1989 ➤ 5,b147*: ᴿJNES 53 (1994) 66s (G. *Böwering*).
10857 **Halm** Heinz, Shiism: Islamic surveys. E 1991, Univ. vi-218 p. – ᴿOrChrPer 60 (1990) 288s (V. *Poggi*).
10858 **Harvey** L. P., Islamic Spain, 1250 to 1500. Ch 1990, Univ. xvi-370 p. £47. – ᴿEngHR 109 (1994) 998s (J. *Edwards*); JSS 38 (1993) 334-9 (J. D. *Latham*).

10858* **Knysh** Alexander, A medieval scholar at work, IBN TAWUS and his library: Islamic Philosophy 12. Leiden 1992, Brill. ix-471 p. ƒ210. 90-04-09549-7. – ᴿJSS 38 (1993) 382-4 (A. J. *Newman*).

10859 **Madelung** Wilferd, Religious and ethical movements in medieval Islam: CS 364. Aldershot 1992, Variorum. – ᴿJSS 39 (1994) 130-4 (A. K. S. *Lambton*).

10860 **Pinault** David, The Shiites; ritual and popular piety in a [Hyderabad] Muslim community. NY 1992, St. Martin's. 224 p. $35. – ᴿJRel 74 (1994) 143 (Katherine C. *Kolstad*).

10861 **Renard** John, All the king's falcons; [1207-73 Jalal ad-Din] RUMI on prophets and revelation. Albany 1994, SUNY. xviii-216 p. $49.50; pa. $17. 0-7914-2221-6; -2-4 [TDig 42,86].

10862 *Renard* John, Der Islam, das Eine und das Viele; Einheit und Verschiedenheit in einer weltweiten Tradition, ᵀ*Ahlbrecht* Ansgar: IZT-Conc 30 (1994) 211-7.

10863 **Rippin** Andrew, Muslims; their religious beliefs and practices [1. The formative period] 2. The contemporary period. L 1993, Routledge. xxi-172 p. – ᴿOrChrPer 60 (1994) 290s (V. *Poggi*).

ᴍ8.4 *Alter philosemitismus* – **Islamic-Christian rapprochement.**

10864 **Adang** Camila, Islam frente a Judaismo; la polémica de IBN ḤAZM de Córdoba. M 1994, Aben Ezra. 156 p. – ᴿSefarad 54 (1994) 413s (Esperanza *Alfonso Carro*).

10865 **Anees** Munawar A., *al.*, Christian-Muslim relations; yesterday, today, tomorrow. L 1991, Grey Seal. v-96 p. £6. 1-85640-021-2. – ᴿTBR 7,1 (1994s) 50 (J. A. *Bond*: dialogue not seen as helpful).

10866 ᴱ**Antoun** Richard T., *Hegland* Mary E., Religious resurgence; contemporary cases in Islam, Christianity, and Judaism 1987 → 4,415 ... 8,b670: ᴿCritRR 5 (1992) 263s (R. *Comstock*)

10867 *Arnaldez* Roger, Chronique d'islamologie: RechSR 82 (1994) 133-155: JAMBET C., TIBI B., KHOURY A. T., KERBER W.

10868 **Assiouty** Sarwat A. al-, Révolutionnaires et contre-révolutionnaires parmi les disciples de Jésus et les compagnons de Muḥammad; Jésus, disciples grecs, romains, égyptiens, nabatéens, syriens, juifs; Muḥammad, compagnons arabes, grecs, coptes, éthiopiens, syriens, persans; l'égyptien Mary-ʿIsa auteur du quatrième évangile: RechComp ChrIslam 4. P 1994, Letouzey & A. 310 p. F 120. 2-7063-0190-2.

10869 *Bernand* Marie, La gnose islamique ou la nostalgie d'une connaissance salvatrice: Heresis 23 (1994) 99-120.

10870 *Borrmans* Maurice, Messie, messianisme et Islam: Communio 19,113 (1994) 137-157.

10871 **Bouman** Johan, Il Corano e gli ebrei; la storia di una tragedia [1990],ᵀ: GdT 208. Brescia 1992, Queriniana. 136 p. Lᵐ 18. 88-399-0708-4. – ᴿGregorianum 75 (1994) 580-2 (E. *Farahian*).

10872 ᴱ**Bsteh** Andreas, Friede für die Menschheit; Grundlagen, Probleme und Zukunftsperspektiven aus islamischer und christlicher Sicht: BeitRelTheol 8. W-Mödling 1994, St Gabriel. 331 p. DM 46. 3-85264-456-9.

10873 ᴱ**Butterworth** Charles E., *Kessel Blake* Andrée, The introduction of Arabic philosophy into Europe: StTGgMA 39. Leiden 1994, Brill. viii-149 p. 90-04-09842-9.

10874 **Campisi** Antonio, Lessico della teologia islamica. Soveria Mannelli CZ 1994, Rubbettino. 145 p. Lᵐ 22. 88-7284-238-7.

10875 *Cracco* Giorgio, GREGORIO Magno e Maometto: RivStoLR 30 (1994) 246-261.
10876 **Daniel** Norman, Islam and the West; the making of an image[2] [¹1960]. Ox 1993, One World. 467 p. $34. – ᴿConcordJ 20 (1994) 215s (*Won Yong Ji*).
10877 **Daniel** Norman, † 1992, Islam et l'Occident [1960, ³1980 = 1966], ᵀ*Spiess* Alain, revue par l'auteur (= éd. 4). P 1994, Cerf. 458 p. – ᴿRHE 89 (1994) 779 (G. *Basetti-Sani*).
10878 **Fitzgerald** Michael L., *Caspar* Robert, Signs of dialogue; Christian encounter with Muslims. Zamboanga 1992, Silsilah. xiv-245 p. – ᴿLandas 8 (1994) 299s (T. J. *O'Shaughnessy*).
10879 *Flori* Jean, La caricature de l'Islam dans l'Occident médiéval; origine et signification de quelques stéréotypes concernant l'Islam: Aevum 66 (1992) 245-256.
10880 *a) Gaffney* P. D., Warum wenden sich Christen dem Islam zu? ᵀ*Berz* A.; – *b) Esposito* John L., Islamische Bedrohung – Mythos oder Realität? ᵀ*Schmidt* W.; – *c) Arkoun* Muhammad, Ist der Islam durch das Christentum bedroht? ᵀ*Himmelsbach* A.: IZT-Conc 30 (1994) 198-202 / 217- 223 / 224-236.
10881 ᴱ**Galimberti** Sergio, L'Islam tra noi, una sfida per il diálogo. Trieste 1994. LINT. 97 p. Lᵐ 18. – ᴿCC 145 (1994s) 617s (P. *Vanzan*).
10881* *Galvache Valero* Francisco, El fenómeno islamista en el Mogreb: Proyección 41 (1994) 171-184.
10882 *Goldziher* Ignácz, ᵀᴱ*Payne* Jerry, *Sadgrove* Philip, Muhammadan public opinion: JSS 38 (1993) 97-133.
10883 *Griffith* Sidney H., Kenneth CRAGG [14 books] on Christians and the call to Islam: RelStR 20 (1994) 29-35.
10884 *Hamilton* Audrey, Moses versus Mohammed: ScotJRel 15,1 (Stirling 1994) 44-... [< ZIT 94,260].
10884* [Jordan crown-prince, Bin-Talal] **Hassan,** Christianity in the Arab World: Amman 1994, Institute for Inter-Faith Studies. 120 p. – ᴿIslamochristiana 20 (1994) 307s (M. L. *Fitzgerald*).
10885 *a) Honecker* Martin, Gottes- und Weltverständnis im Islam und Christentum; – *b) Khoury* Adel T., Muslime in einer pluralistischen Gesellschaft: UnSa 48 (1993) 106-116 . 132 / 117-126.
10886 **Hourani** Albert, Islam in European thought 1991 ➤ 7,a922; 8,b689: ᴿJAAR 62 (1994) 195-7 (E. H. *Waugh*).
10887 *Jacob* P. Xavier, Christians in Turkey and their relations with Moslems: JIntRD 4 (1994) 42-61.
10888 *Jaoudi* Maria, Christian and Islamic spirituality; sharing a journey. NY 1993, Paulist. iii-103 p. $8 pa. 0-8091-3426-8 [TDig 42,170].
10889 **Jomier** Jacques, Islamismo; historia e doutrina, ᵀ*Baraúna* Luiz J. Petrópolis 1993, Vozes. 318 p. 85-326-0852-3. – ᴿPerspT 26 (1994) 420-2 (J. B. *Libanio*).
10890 *Jomier* Jacques, Ouvrages sur l'Islam: RThom 94 (1994) 132-144.
10891 **Kelsay** John, Islam and war; a study in comparative ethics. LvL 1992, W-Knox. ix-149 p. $15 pa. – ᴿHorizons 21 (1994) 374s (D. B. *Burrell*).
10892 **Khoury** Adel T., Der Islam; sein Glaube, seine Lebensordnung, sein Anspruch: Spektrum 4167. FrB 1992, Herder. 238 p. DM 16,80. – ᴿTPQ 142 (1994) 78 (J. *Janda*, auch über sein '... kommt uns näher' 1992).
10893 **Kimball** Charles, Striving together; a way forward in Christian-Muslim relations 1991 ➤ 7,a927; 8,b699: ᴿRelStR 20 (1994) 37 (I. *Yusuf*).
10894 **Landau** Jacob M., The politics of Pan-Islam; ideology and organiza-

tion. Ox 1990, Clarendon. 438 p. £45. – ᴿEngHR 109 (1994) 271s (J. B. *Kelly*).

10894* *Lelong* Michel, L'Église catholique et l'Islam. P 1993, Maisonneuve & L. 126 p. – ᴿCiuD 207 (1994) 237 (B. *Justel*).

10895 ᵀᴱ**Le Coz** Raymond, Jean DAMASCÈNE, Écrits sur l'Islam: SChr 383, 1992 ➤ 8,b703.k781: ᴿÉTRel 68 (1993) 415s (G. *Firmin*).

10896 **Lewis** Bernard, Les Arabes dans l'histoire, ᵀ*Canal* Denis-Armand. 1993, Aubier. 260 p. F 130. – ᴿÉtudes 380 (1994) 130 (H. *Loucel*).

10897 **Lewis** Bernard, Islam and the West 1993 ➤ 9,12181: ᴿChrCent 111 (1994) 994-6 (C. E. *Bush*).

10898 *Mallat* Chibli, Readings of the Qur'ān in London and Najaf; John WANSBROUGH [received threats after his Quranic studies 1977s] and Muḥammad BĀQIR al-Ṣadr [executed without trial by Baghdad authorities after his 1979 *Madrasa*]: ➤ 136, ᶠWANSBROUGH, BSO 57 (1994) 159-173.

10899 **McAuliffe** Jane D., Qur'anic Christians 1991 ➤ 7,a931 ... 9,12184: ᴿIslamochristiana 20 (1994) 312s (M. L. *Fitzgerald*); SR 23 (1994) 94s (E. H. *Waugh*).

10900 *Mandivenga* Ephraim C., Resurgence of Islam; implications for African spirituality and dialogue: Religion in Malawi 3 (1991) 12-16 [< TContext 12,92].

10901 ᴱ**Meyuhas Ginio** Alisa, Jews, Christians, and Muslims in the Mediterranean world after 1492. Portland OR 1992, Cass. 295 p. – ᴿAmHR 99 (1994) 341 (titles sans pp.).

10901* ᴱ**Nettler** R. L., Studies in Muslim-Jewish relations I. Chur 1993, Harwood. xi-205 p. £25. – ᴿJJS 45 (1994) 148-150 (A. H. *Jones*).

10902 *Nispen* Christiaan van, *Farahian* Edmond, È possibile un rinnovamento del pensiero islamico?: CC 145 (1994,1) 220-232.

10903 ᴱ**Peters** Francis E., Judaism, Christianity and Islam ... texts 1990 ➤ 7,1219.8152; 9,12191: JSS 39 (1994) 344-6 (J. van *Ess*, deutsch).

10904 *Pfeifer* Christiane B., [H.] HEINE und der islamische Orient: Mizān 1. Wsb 1990, Harrassowitz. xiv-124 p. DM 44. – ᴿWZKM 83 (1993) 381-3 (L. *Hellmuth*: FENDRI M. 1981 weit besser).

10905 *Pierucci* Armando, P. [Giulio] BASETTI SANI, ofm: TerraS 70,5 (1994) 17-19; 20-23, risposta a un commento del Card. *Biaggio* sui Musulmani.

10906 *Podet* Allen H., Patterns of classical Islam and some American 'Black Muslims': RelEdn 89 (1994) 338-356.

10907 *Reeber* Michel, Die Grenzen das Laizismus; zur Situation der islamischen Gemeinschaft in Frankreich: HerdKorr 47 (1993) 255-260.

10908 *Rejwan* Nissim, Islam and Judaism and the Bible: Midstream 40,3 (1994) 42-44.

10909 **Renard** John, Islam and the visual image; themes in literature and the visual arts 1993 ➤ 9,12194: ᴿJAAR 62 (1994) 212s (D. *Beaumont*).

10910 **Rizzardi** Giuseppe, Introduzione all'Islam: Intr & Tr 3, 1992 ➤ 9, 12195: ᴿScripTPamp 26 (1994) 1236s (J. M. *Odero*).

10911 ᴱ**Samir** Samir Khalil, *Nielsen* Jorgen S., Christian Arabic apologetics during the Abbasid period (750-1258): StHistRel 63. Leiden 1994, Brill. xii-250 p.; 4 fig. 90-04-09568-3. – 11 art.

10912 *Samir* S. K., Notes sur la 'lettre à un musulman de Sidon' de PAUL d'Antioche: OrLovPer 24 (1993) 179-195.

10913 *Samir* S. K., Une lecture de la foi chrétienne dans le contexte arabo-musulman: PrOrChr 42 (1992) 57-125.

10914 *Schwartländer* J., Freiheit der Religion; Christentum und Islam unter dem Anspruch der Menschenrechte: Forum Weltkirche 2. Mainz 1993,

Grünewald.   474 p.   DM 64.   3-7867-1392-8 [TLZ 120,320, G. *Krusche*]. –
ᴿTvT 34 (1994) 458 (J. R. *Peters*).
10915 **Sibony** Daniel, Les trois monothéismes. P 1992, Seuil. 301 p. F 145.
2-02-015379-3. – ᴿÉTRel 68 (1994) 265 (J. *Ansaldi*).
10916 *Suleiman* M. Yasir, 'The Arabs are different from you and I' [*Albricht*
apud *Kreinan* T. 1980 p. 33]: ArOr 61 (1993) 241-260.
10917 **Thyen** J.-D., Bibel und Koran, eine Synopse gemeinsamer Überliefe-
rungen 1989 ➤ 5,b219... 9,12209: ᴿNRT 116 (1994) 601s (J. *Scheuer*);
OrChrPer 60 (1994s) 292 (C. W. *Troll*).
10918 **Waardenburg** Jacques, Islamisch-christliche Beziehungen; geschicht-
liche Streifzüge: RelWst 23, 1992 ➤ 9,12211: ᴿNZMiss 50 (1994) 323s
(P. *Antes*).
10919 *a*) *Waardenburg* Jacques, L'Islam et l'articulation d'identités musulmanes; – *b*) *Rex* John, The political sociology of multiculturalism and the
place of Muslims in West European societies; – *c*) *Lacoste-Dujardin*
Camille, Transmission religieuse et migration; l'Islam identitaire des filles
de maghrébins immigrés en France; – *d*) *Bastenier* Albert, Migrations,
choc de cultures et religions; – *e*) *Motta* Roberto, Ethnicité, nationalité et
syncrétisme dans les religions populaires brésiliennes: ➤ Budapest 22d
1993, SocComp 41,1 (1994) 21-33 / 79-92 / 163-170 / 185-192 / 67-78.
10920 **Watt** William M., Muslim-Christian encounters; perceptions and
misperceptions 1991 ➤ 7,a939*; 9,12213: NY 1991, Routledge. 164 p.
$16 pa. 0-415-05411-7. – ᴿChrSchR 24 (1994) 85-87 (L. *VanderWerff*).
10921 *a*) *Yoder* Jason J., The Trinity and Christian witness to Muslims; – *b*)
Cockerill Gareth Lee, To the Hebrews [11,1-40] / to the Muslims; Islamic
pilgrimage as a key to interpretation: Missiology 22 (1994) 339- 346 /
347-359.
10922 *Zahniser* A. H. Mathias, Close encounters of the vulnerable kind;
Christian dialogical proclamation among Muslims: AsbTJ 49,1 (1994)
71-78.

M8.5   **Religiones Indiae** *et Extremi Orientis*.

10923 *Argaud* Jacky, La notion de Nirvana: ÉTRel 68 (1993) 83-87.
10924 ᴱ**Canobbio** Giacomo, Dio, mondo e natura nelle religioni orientali:
Studi religiosi. Padova 1993, Messaggero. 173 p. Lᵐ 18. 88-250-0192-4.
10925 **Ching** Julia, Chinese religions. Mkn 1993, Orbis. 275 p. $19. – ᴿCon-
cordJ 20 (1994) 214s (*Won Yong Ji*).
10926 **Codecasa** Maria Silvia, Sette serpenti; sulle tracce di un culto ignorato
[India...]: La società narrata. R 1994, Manifestolibri. 295 p. 88-7285-
085-4.
10927 **Eck** Diana L., Encountering God; a spiritual journey from Bozeman
[Montana] to Banaras. Boston 1993, Beacon. 259 p. $24. – ᴿJRel 74
(1994) 592-4 (M. N. *Schmalz*); LexTQ 29 (1994) 267-9 (P. N. *Dare*).
10928 **Gyatso Tendsin** (Dalai Lama 14), Einführung in den Buddhismus; die
Harvard-Vorlesungen 1981: Spektrum 4148. FrB 1993, Herder. 309 p.
DM 19,80. – ᴿTPQ 142 (1994) 79 (M. *Hutter*).
10929 **Harvey** Peter, An introduction to Buddhism; teachings, history and
practices. C 1990, Univ. xvii-374 p. £11. – ᴿScotJT 46 (1993) 99s (Linda
Woodhead).
10930 **Klostermaier** Klaus K., A survey of Hinduism². Albany 1994, SUNY.
xii-715 p.; 23 fig.; 22 phot.; 3 maps; bibliog. 58 p. $59.50; pa. $20.
0-7914-2109-0; -10-4 [TDig 42,172].

10931 **Lipner** Julius, Hindus; their religious beliefs and practices: Library of RelBP. NY 1994, Routledge. xiii-375 p. $70. 0-415-05181-9 [TDig 42,174].

10931* **Oberoi** Harjot, The construction of religious boundaries; culture, identity, and diversity of the Sikh tradition. Ch 1994, Univ. xxii-494 p. $50; pa. $18. 0-226-61592-8; -3-6 [TDig 42,381].

10932 **Prebish** Charles S., Historical dictionary of Buddhism: HistDRel 1. Metuchen NJ 1993, Scarecrow. xxxiii-387 p. $42.50. 0-8108-2698-4 [TDig 42,84].

10933 **Reader** Ian, *al.*, Japanese religions, past and present. Honolulu 1993, Univ. Hawaii. 189 p. $36; pa. $16. 0-8248-1545-9; -6-7 [TDig 42,85].

10934 **Zhang Longxi**, The Tao and the Logos; literary hermeneutics, east and west. Durham 1992, Duke Univ. 288 p. $35; pa. $17. – ᴿJRel 74 (1994) 132-4 (*Li Wai-Yee*).

M8.7 *Interactio cum religione orientali;* **Christian dialogue with the East.**

10935 **Angel** Leonard, Enlightenment East and West. Albany 1994, SUNY. x-388 p. $64.50; pa. $22. 0-7914-2053-1; pa. -4-X [TDig 42,154].

10936 **Ariarajah** Wesley, Hindus and Christians; a century of Protestant ecumenical thought: Currents of Encounter 5. Amst/GR 1991, rodopi/ Eerdmans. 244 p. – ᴿJIntRD 3 (1993) 93s (F.J. *Hoffman*).

10937 **Balagangadhara** S.N., 'The heathen in his blindness..'; Asia, the West and the dynamic of religion: StHistRel 64. Leiden 1994, Brill. xii-563 p.

10938 **Berthrong** John H., All under heaven; transforming paradigms in Confucian-Christian dialogue: Chinese ph/culture. Albany 1994, SUNY. viii-273 p. $65.50; pa. $22. 0-7914-1857-X; -8-8 [TDig 41,351].

10939 *Bevir* Mark, The West turns eastward; Madame Blavatsky and the tranformation of the occult tradition: JAAR 62 (1994) 747-767.

10940 **Carman** John B., Majesty and meekness; a comparative study of contrast and harmony in the [Buddhist/Hindu...] concept of God. GR 1994, Eerdmans. iv-453 p. $25 pa. 0-8028-0693-7 [TDig 42,158; TS 56, 393s, F.X. *Clooney*].

10941 **Carmody** Denise L. & John T., In the path of the masters; understanding the spirituality of Buddha, Confucius, Jesus, and Muhammad. NY 1994, Paragon. 232 p. $23. 1-55778-409-4 [TDig 42,59].

10942 *Catret* Juan, ¿ Dar ejercicios espirituales con 'paradojas bíblicas'? (a la luz de la 'espiritualidad oriental'; los 'koan' del zen-budismo japonés): Manresa 65 (1993) 63-77.

10943 *a) Clémentin-Ojha* Catherine, *Gaboriau* Marc, La montée du prosélytisme dans le sous-continent indien; – *b) Županov* Ines, Prosélytisme et pluralisme religieux; deux expériences missionnaires en Inde aux XVIᵉ et XVIIᵉ siècles: ArchivScSocR 39,87 (1994) 13-31; Eng. 32; español 32s / 34-55; Eng. español 66.

10944 ᴱ**Cobb** John B.ᴶ, *Yves* Christopher, The emptying God; a Buddhist-Jewish-Christian conversation 1990 → 3,798 ... 9,12264: ᴿCritRR 5 (1992) 268-270 (D.J. *Fasching*); Missiology 20 (1992) 83s (S.T. *Franklin*).

10945 **Cole** W. Owen, *Sambhi* Piara Singh, † 1992, Sikhism and Christianity; a comparative study. L/NY 1993, Macmillan/St.Martin's. xii-221 p. $40. 0- 333-54107-3 / 0-312-10365-4 [TDig 41,354]. – ᴿExpTim 105 (1993s) 319 (G. *Parrinder*).

10947 *Courtright* Paul B., Recent developments in the study of Hinduism: CritRR 6 (1993) 77-95.

0948 *a*) **Culligan** Kevin, *al.*, Purifying the heart; Buddhist insight meditation for Christians; – *b*) **Meadow** Mary Jo, Gentling the heart; Buddhist loving-kindness practice for Christians. NY 1994, Crossroad. 239 p.; $15 pa. / 178 p. $14 pa. 0-8245-1420-3; -34-3 [TDig 42,63].

0949 *Deal* William E., Postmodern and new historical perspectives in recent Western scholarship on Japanese religion: CritRR 6 (1993) 1-39.

0950 *Dehn* Ulrich, Geschichte und Eschatologie im Gespräch zwischen Buddhismus und Christentum: EvT 54 (1994) 347-361.

0951 *Dhavamony* Mariasusai, Sacro e valori umani secondo la Bhagavad-Gītā: RasT 35 (1994) 303-315.

0952 *Dreuille* Mayeul de, Communauté et personne dans le bouddhisme et le christianisme: NRT 116 (1994) 658-678.

0953 **Dumoulin** Heinrich, Begegnung mit dem Buddhismus; eine Einführung²ʳᵉᵛ: Bücherei 642. FrB 1991, Herder. 205 p. DM 15,80. – ᴿTPQ 142 (1994) 73 (J. *Janda*).

0954 *Dupuis* Jacques, La fede cristiana in Gesù Cristo in dialogo con le grandi religioni asiatiche: Gregorianum 75 (1994) 217-240; franç. 240.

0955 *Griffiths* Paul J., Recent work on classical Indian Buddhism: CritRR 6 (1993) 41-75.

0956 **Huber** Friedrich, Die Bhagavadgita in der neueren indischen Auslegung und in der Begegnung mit dem christlichen Glauben: Mg Mission & Ök 12, 1991 → 8,b786; 3-872143-12-3: ᴿTLZ 119 (1994) 971-3 (U. *Tworuschka*).

0957 **Jackson** Carl T., Vedanta for the West; the RAMAKRISHNA movement in the United States: RelNAm. Bloomington 1994, Indiana Univ. xiv-185 p. $30. 0-253-33098-X [TDig 42,170].

0958 **Jaini** Padmanabh, Gender and salvation [in the Jaina tradition]. Berkeley 1991, Univ. California. 229 p. – ᴿJAAR 62 (1994) 197s (C. *Chapple*).

0959 ᴱ**Jones** Kenneth W., Religious controversy [Hindus, Muslims...] in British India; dialogues in South Asian languages. Albany 1992, SUNY. xi-291 p. $20. – ᴿHZ 259 (1994) 254-6 (D. *Rothermund*).

0960 **Küng** Hans, *al.*, Christianity and the world religions; paths of dialogue with Islam, Hinduism and Buddhism² [adds only in a brief preface 'there can no longer be a credible Christian theology which does not take seriously the challenge of the world religions']. L 1993, SCM. xx-460 p. £12.50 pa. – ᴿTLond 97 (1994) 299 (M. *Barnes*: needed, but ultimately liberal-Christian dialogue with the history of religions, not with living faiths).

0961 *Lamb* Matthew L., Inculturation and Western culture; the dialogical experience between gospel and culture: ComWsh 21 (1994) 125-144.

0962 *Lefebure* Leo D., The Buddha and the Christ 1993 → 9,12285: ᴿExpTim 105 (1993s) 318 (D. *Keown*: the China-Japan rather than mainstream SE-Asia variety).

0963 *Leung Ka-lun*, ☉ The doctrine of the goodness of human nature in Confucianism; a Christian appraisal: Jian Dao 1 (1994) 29-47; Eng. 47s.

0964 *May* John D., What do socially engaged Buddhists and Christian liberation theologians have to say to one another?: Dialogue 21 (Colombo 1994) 1-...

0965 *Means* Laurel, The 'Orient-ation' of Eden; Christian/Buddhist dialogues in the poetry of Shirley GEOK-LIN LIM. ChrLit 43 (1993s) 189-204.

0966 **Olivelle** Patrick, The ašrama system; the history and hermeneutics of a religious institution. NY 1993, Oxford-UP. xiii-274. $50 [TS 56,149s, W *Cenkner*].

10967 **Panikkar** Raimon,   Gottes Schweigen; die Antwort des Buddha füi unsere Zeit [1970, Eng. 1989 ➤ 5,b269],ᵀ. Mü 1992, Kösel.   374 p. DM 48. – ᴿTPQ 142 (1994) 71s (J. *Janda*).

10967* **Picken** Stuart D. B.,   Essentials of Shinto; an analytical guide tc principal teachings: Resources in Asian ph/rel.   Westport CT 1994, Greenwood.   xxxiii-400 p. $85.   0-313-26431-7 [TDig 42,382].

10968 **Siepen** Wolfgang,   Weg der Erkenntnis — Weg der Liebe; das spirituelle Meister-Schüler-Verhältnis beim Buddha und PACHOMIUS [Diss. Tübingen 1991]. Mainz 1992, Grünewald.   535 p. DM 52.   3-7867-1648-X. – ᴿÉTRel 68 (1993) 266 (J. *Argaud*).

10969 *Stadler* Karin,   Méditation chrétienne et techniques de méditatioɲ orientale: EsprVie 104 (1994) 593-608. 619-623.

10970 **Stoeber** Michael F.,   Theo-monistic mysticism; a Hindu-Christian comparison. NY 1994, St. Martin's. x-135 p. $50.   0-312-10746-3 [TDig 42,91].

10971 **Stutley** Margarete,   Was ist Hinduismus? Eine Einführung in die grosse Weltreligion [1985 Eng.], ᵀ*Dahme* K.   Bern 1994, Barth.   224 p. DM 36.   3-502-65590-1. – ᴿTLZ 119 (1994) 976s (K. *Dockhorn*).

10972 *Wong* Joseph H.,   Anonymous Christians; Karl RAHNER's PneumaChristocentrism and an East-West dialogue: TS 55 (1994) 609-638.

M8.9   **Religiones Africae** (maxime ➤ H8.6) **et Amerindiae**.

10973 **Carmody** Denise L. & John T.,   Native American religions; an introduction.   NY 1993, Paulist.   viii-270 p. $15.   0-8091-3404-7 [TDig 42,59]. – ᴿHorizons 21 (1994) 382s (L. J. *Biallas*: useful, sympathetic; some reserves).

10974 *Chidester* David,   Religions of South Africa 1992 ➤ 8,8803:   ᴿJRel 74 (1994) 436s (R. *Petersen*: the so-called 'history of religions' rarely gives so much historical narrative).

10974* **Hultkranz** Åke,   Shamanic healing and ritual drama; health and medicine in native American religious tradition.   NY 1992, Crossroad. xv-107 p. – ᴿSR 23 (1994) 375s (T. *Parkhill*).

10975 *Hutter* Manfred, Die biblisch-orientalische Deutung [Amer-]indianischer Mythologie; der Versuch, Fremdes zu kategorisieren; ZRGg 46 (1994) 163-171.

10976 *Mazzoleni* Gilberto,   Il Candomblé a São Paulo (transe e divinazione iɲ una moderna metropoli):   SMSR 59 (1993) 125-131.

10977 **Merkur** Daniel,   Powers which we do not know; the gods and spirits of the Inuit [-speaking, also Yup'ik-speaking people Alaska to Greenland]. Moscow ID 1991, Univ. Idaho.   280 p. $35; pa. $20. – ᴿJAAR 62 (1994) 205-7 (R. *Ridington*).

10978 *a*) *Monaco* Emanuela,   Un approccio storico-religioso alla cultura azteca;   Quetzalcoatl di Tollan; – *b*) *Visca* Danila,   Il Mugwe [Kenya], il profeta che scompare: SMSR 59 (1993) 35-86 / 87-124.

XVII,1. Historia Medii Orientis Biblici

Q1   *Syria prae-islamica, Canaan,* **Israel Veteris Testamenti.**

10979 **Ahlström** Gösta W.,   History of Ancient Palestine: jOsu 146, 1993 ➤ 9,12326: ᴿBA 57 (1994) 246s (P. S. *Ash*); Biblica 75 (1994) 556-567

(W. *Thiel*: merits respect – and queries); CBQ 56 (1994) 743-5 (T. R. *Hobbs*: massive in scope, rigorous in scholarship); CurrTM 21 (1994) 145 (R. W. *Klein*: negative, sometimes cynical, view of Scripture); JTS 45 (1994) 171s (A. D. H. *Mayes*).

10980 [*Arata*] **Mantovani** Piera, L'archeologia siro-palestinese e la storia di Israele; rassegna di studi archeologici, VII: Henoch 16 (1994) 7-86. Åström Paul, High, middle or low ... chronology 1987/9 ≯ 12177.

10981 **Bartolomé** Juan J., *Chávez* Pascual, Panorama bíblico [date-chart on 14 colored pages folded into one long one to put on a wall]. Caracas 1994, Asociación Bíblica Salesiana / Paulinas.

10982 **Becking** Bob, The fall of Samaria 1992 ≯ 8,2991; 9,12327: ᴿCBQ 56 (1994) 317s (Marilyn M. *Schaub*); ÉTRel 68 (1993) 591 (J.-D. *Macchi*); JBL 113 (1994) 115s (R. S. *Boraas*); JSS 39 (1994) 324s (A. F. *Rainey*: justifiably critical survey but his own conclusions unsound); OLZ 89 (1994) 53-58 (S. *Timm*).

10983 *Bird* Phyllis, Women in the ancient Mediterranean world, *a*) Ancient Israel; – *b*) *Osiek* Carolyn, State of the question-NT: BRes 39 (1994) 31-45 / 57-61.

10984 **Bock** S., Kleine Geschichte des Volkes Israel 1989 ≯ 5,b291; 7,b4: ᴿAtKap 120 (1993) 175-7 (J. *Warzecha*, ❷).

10985 ᴱ**Canfora** L., *al.*, I trattati 1990 ≯ 6,724; 8,b817: ᴿAevum 66 (1992) 155-7 (Anna *Passoni dell'Acqua*); BO 51 (1994) 275-8 (H. *Freydank*).

10985* **Coggins** Richard, What future for the history of Israel? (1994 Wood Lecture). L 1994, Univ. 23 p. 0-7187-1207-2 [BL 95,38, P. R. *Davies*].

10986 **Davies** Philip R., In search of 'Ancient Israel', 1992 ≯ 8, b818; 9,12332: ᴿCBQ 56 (1994) 99s (R. D. *Nelson*: to be taken seriously even if wrong); Interpretation 48 (1994) 191s (R. B. *Coote*).

10987 **Dournoy** Simon, Précis d'histoire juive [R ᵀ1936]. P 1992, Cerf. 320 p. F 95. 2-204-04580-2. – ᴿÉTRel 68 (1993) 440s (A. *Gaillard*).

10988 **Dus** Jan, Theokratische Demokratie 1992 ≯ 8,237: ᴿWeltOr 25 (1994) 174s (E. A. *Knauf*: negativ).

10989 **González Lamadrid** Antonio, Las tradiciones históricas de Israel 1993 ≯ 9,12338: ᴿCBQ 56 (1994) 763s (C. *Bernas*: more successful than most similar efforts in English); NRT 116 (1994) 102 (J. L. *Ska*); RBibArg 55 (1993) 235 (A. J. *Levoratti*); RET 53 (1993) 241-4 (P. *Barrado Fernández*); TLZ 119 (1994) 499s (E. S. *Gerstenberger*).

10990 ᵀᴱ*Hayoun* Maurice-R., Heinrich GRÄTZ, La construction de l'histoire juive [1845] 1992 ≯ 8,b821: ᴿÉTRel 68 (1993) 103s (Jeanne Marie *Léonard*).

10991 **Higginbotham** Carolyn R., The Egyptianization of Ramesside Palestine: diss. Johns Hopkins, ᴰ*McCarter* P. Baltimore 1994. 568 p. 94-19984. – DissA 55 (1994s) p. 605.

10992 **Hughes** Jeremy, Secrets of the times; myth and history in biblical chronology [diss. Oxford, ᴰ*Barr* J.]: jOsu 66, 1990 ≯ 8,b8: ᴿBO 51 (1994) 630-2 (S. *de Vries*); CritRR 5 (1992) 97-99 (L. K. *Handy*: rewarding).

10993 **Jagersma** H., A history of Israel to Bar Kochba. L 1994, SCM. 0-334-02577-X.

10994 **Jelonek** Tomasz, ❷ *Biblijna* ... salvation-history^{2rev} [¹1987]. Kraków 1991, Maszachaba. 196 p. – ᴿAtKap 123 (1994) 165-7 (J. *Warzecha*, ❷).

10995 **Kessler** Rainer, Staat und Gesellschaft im vorexilischen Juda 1992 ≯ 8,b824; 9,12342: ᴿBiblica 75 (1994) 568-571 (J. L. *Sicre*).

10996 **Kuan Kah-Jin** Jeffrey, Assyrian historical inscriptions and Israelite/

Judean–Tyrian–Damascene political and commercial relations in the 9th-8th centuries B.C.: diss. Emory, ᴰHayes J. Atlanta 1994. 434 p. 94-24814. – DissA 55 (1994s) p. 995.
10997 Lemaire André, 'House of David' restored in Moabite inscription [line 31, bt...wd]: BAR-W 20,3 (1994) 30-37.
10997* Lemche N., The Canaanites: jOsu 110, 1991 ➤ 7,b17; 8,2734: ᴿVT 44 (1994) 120s (H. G. M. Williamson).
10998 ᴱMcKenzie Steven L., Graham Patrick, The history of Israel's traditions; the heritage of Martin NOTH: jOsu 182. Shf 1994, Academic. 325 p.
10999 Mazar B. †, ᴱAhituv S., Biblical Israel 1992 ➤ 8,283; 9,12348: ᴿBASOR 293 (1994) 95s (O. Borowski); VT 44 (1994) 139s (J. A. Emerton).
11000 Mazzinghi L., Storia d'Israele: Manuali di base 4, 1991 ➤ 8,b831: ᴿNRT 116 (1994) 473 (V. Roisel).
11001 Medvedskaya I. N., ❸ rejoinder to Kurochkin G. N. †, The chronology of the Near East war expeditions according to written sources and archaeological data: RossArkh (1994,1) [117-122] 123-133.
11002 Mielgo Constantino, La enseñanza escolar en el antiguo Israel [ninguna palabra para esa en hebreo (VOLTAIRE)]: EstAg 29 (1994) 429-453.
11003 Miller J. M., Hayes J. H., A history of ancient Israel and Juda 1986 ➤ 2,9232... 6,b332: ᴿRuBi 46 (1993) 47-49 (M. Wojciechowski).
11004 Müller Hans-Peter, Babylonien und Israel; historische, religiöse und sprachliche Beziehungen: WegF 633. Da 1991, Wiss. vii-544 p.
11005 Redford D., Egypt, Canaan 1992 ➤ 8,b836; 9,12352: ᴿBASOR 294 (1994) 102s (S. E. Thompson) & 295 (1994) 81-83 (A. F. Rainey); JEA 80 (1994) 242s (K. A. Kitchen); Gnomon 66 (1994) 419-423 (W. Helck); OLZ 89 (1994) 258-269 (S. Timm); PEQ 126 (1994) 171s (E. P. Uphill).
Reinhold Gotthard G. G., Die Beziehungen Altisraels zu den aramäischen Staaten 1989 ➤ E4.9.
11006 Soggin J. Alberto, Einführung in die Geschichte Israels und Judas 1991 ➤ 7,b32*; 8,b845: ᴿBiKi 48 (1993) 238 (F. J. Stendebach).
11007 Soggin J. Alberto, An introduction to the history of Israel and Judah²ʳᵉᵛ [¹1984]. L 1993, SCM. xxii-474 p. £20. 0-334-02534-6. – ᴿBL (1994) 41 (A. D. H. Mayes).
11008 Szpet Jan, ❷ Historia biblijna... Polish manuals compared with German. Poznań 1992. 181 p. – ᴿAtKap 120 (1993) 600s (J. Bagrowicz, ❷).
11008* ṬABARI ➤ 7,b34 ... 9,12358: 12, ᵀᴱFriedman Yohannan 1992: ᴿJSS 39 (1994) 388s (M. Ibrahim); – 31, Fishbein M., The war between brothers, 809-813: 1992: ᴿJAOS 114 (1994) 282s (E. L. Daniel).
11009 Thompson Thomas L., Early history of the Israelite people 1992 ➤ 8,b848; 9,12366: ᴿCBQ 56 (1994) 346s (J. Van Seters: challenging; badly edited, disappointing); JBL 113 (1994) 508-510 (J. M. Miller: well shows the weaknesses of all current reconstructions, and adds one more, no more and no less speculative); JRel 74 (1994) 546s (J. A. Dearman); OLZ 89 (1994) 156-8 (K.-D. Schunck: a great achievement, though not all will agree on details); RBBras 10 (1993) 316s (C. Minette de Tillesse); TLZ 119 (1994) 127-131 (R. Liwak: provokativ); ZAW 106 (1994) 539s (M. Köckert: radikal).
11010 Vlachos Konstantinos S., ❹ Semeiosis... Biblical history from the divided kingdom to the decree of Cyrus. Athenae 1994. 179 p.; 2 maps. – ᴿTAth 65 (1994) 984-6 (P. Simotas).
11011 Wellhausen Julius, Prolegomena to the history of Israel [E 1885]

Encyclopedia Britannica [9th ed.] article Israel: ReprT.   Atlanta 1994,
Scholars. xvi-552 p. $45; sb. 30. 1-55540-938-5.

Q2 Historiographia – *theologia historiae.*

11012 **Angehrn** Emil,   Geschichtsphilosophie: GrundkursPh 15, 1991 ➤ 9,
12373: ᴿTPhil 69 (1994) 124-7 (H. G. *Ollig*).

11012* *Beards* Andrew,   Reversing historical skepticism; Bernard LONERGAN
on the writing of history: HistTheor 33 (1994) 198-219.

11013 **Bebbington** David,   Patterns in history² 1990 ➤ 8,b855:   ᴿConcordTQ
58 (1994) 48-50 (T. *Maschke*).

11013* *a) Bevin* Mark,   Objectivity in History; – *b) Lorenz* Christ,   Historical
knowledge and historical reality; a plea for 'internal realism': HistTheor
33 (1994) 328-344 / 297-327.

11014 **Blanke** Horst W.,   Historiographiegeschichte als Historik. Stu-Bad-
Cannstatt 1991, Frommann-Holzboog. 809 p. – ᴿHistTheor 33 (1994)
249-265 (D. A. J. *Telman*).

11014* *Bost* Hubert,   Histoire et théologie; une cartographie de la grâce:
ÉTRel 68 (1993) 63-72.

11015 *Brennecke* Hanns C.,   Geschichte als Lebensgeschichte; die Alte Kirche
im Spiegel biographischer Darstellungen: VerkF 39,1 (1994) 4-25 (-81,
Biographie neuerer Theologen).

11016 *Brueggemann* Walter,   The prophetic Word of God and history: Interpretation 48 (1994) 239-252.

11017 *Büchsel* Elfriede,   [J. G.] HERDER und [E.] ROSENSTOCK-HUESSY; uni-
versalhistorische Orientierungen: NSys 36 (1994) 223-236; Eng. 236.

11018 **Burke** Peter,   History and social theory. Ithaca NY 1993, Cornell
Univ. ix-198 p. $37.50; pa. $14.95. – ᴿAmHR 99 (1994) 519s (R. T.
Vann).

11019 *Buske* Thomas,   Die via moderna; Geschichte zwischen Sein und
Werden: TZBas 50 (1994) 108-123.

11020 **Campbell** Richard,   Truth and historicity 1992 ➤ 9,12380;   £48:
ᴿHeythJ 35 (1994) 234s (F. *Kerr*).

11021 *Cascajero* Juan,   Escritura, oralidad e ideología; hacia una reubicación
de las fuentes escritas para la Historia Antigua: Gerión 11 (1993) 95-144.

11021* *Christ* Matthew R.,   HERODOTEAN kings (non-Greek, portrayed as
inquirers) and historical inquiry: ClasAnt 13 (1994) 167-202.

11022 **Clark** G. H.,   Historiography, secular and religious² [¹1971]. Jefferson
MD 1994, Trinity. xii-366 p. $14. 0-940931-39-7 [NTAbs 38, p. 445].

11023 ᴱ**Clarke** Graeme,   Reading the past in late antiquity 1990 ➤ 7,b50;
9,12384: ᴿEngHR 109 (1994) 401s (J. D. *Frendo*).

11024 **Coleman** Janet,   Ancient and medieval memories; studies in the reconstruction of the past. C 1992, Univ. xx-646 p. $85. – ᴿSpeculum 69
(1994) 759-761 (Rita *Copeland*).

11025 **Cunico** Gerardo,   Da LESSING a KANT; la storia in prospettiva esca-
tologica: Saggi e Ricerche. Genova 1992, Marietti. 250 p. Lᵐ 30. 88-
211-9470-1. – ᴿGregorianum 75 (1994) 791 (X. *Tilliette*).

11026 *Desouche* Marie-Thérèse,   L'histoire comme lieu théologique et fon-
dement de la théologie pastorale: NRT 116 (1994) 396-417.

11027 **Doran** Robert M.,   Theology and the dialectics of history 1990 ➤ 6,
b361; 7,b56: ᴿJAAR 62 (1994) 186-190 (T. W. *Tilley*).

11028 ᴱ**Edelman** Diana V.,   The fabric of history; jOsu 127, 1991 ➤ 7,428 ...
9,12390: ᴿPEQ 126 (1994) 75s (J. R. *Bartlett*).

11029 **Forte** Bruno,	Teologia della storia; saggio sulla rivelazione, l'inizio e il compendio: Simbolica ecclesiale, una teologia come storia 7, 1991 ➤ 7,b61; 8,b869; 88-215-2095-1: ᴿRTLv 25 (1994) 227 (A. de *Halleux*).

11030 **Füredi** Frank,	Mythical past, elusive future; history and society in an anxious age. Concord MA 1992, Pluto. ix-310 p. $22. – ᴿAmHR 99 (1994) 518s (F. *Weinstein*).

11031 *Gambarotto* Laurent,	Quel usage assigner à l'histoire?: ÉTRel 69 (1994) 203-211.

11032 *Gehrke* Joachim,	Mythos, Geschichte, Politik – antik und modern: Saeculum 45 (1994) 239-264.

11033 *Golubtsova* E. S., *al.*, - 31.V.1993: ❻ Problems of methodology in the study of the ancient world: VDI 208 (1994) 33-44; Eng. 44.

11034 **Green** William A.,	History, historians, and the dynamics of change. Westport CT 1993, Praeger. x-260 p. $50; pa. $19. – ᴿAmHR 99 (1994) 514s (G. G. *Iggers*).

11035 **Gross** David,	The past in ruins; tradition and the critique of modernity: Critical perspectives on modern culture. Amherst 1992, Univ. Massachusetts. xi-175 p. $25. – ᴿAmHR 99 (1994) 514 (R. *Wolin*).

11036 **Günther** Horst,	Zeit der Geschichte, Weiterfahrung und Zeitkategorien in der Geschichtsphilosophie. Fra 1993, Fischer. – ᴿZRGg 46 (1994) 369s (C. *Schulte*).

11037 *Guerra Pratas* Maria Helena da,	Elementos para una teoria general tomista sobre el valor revelador de la historia: AnnTh 7 (1993) 71-100 . 395-427.

11037* **Hall** Robert G.,	Revealed histories: 1991 ➤ 7,b68; 9,12400:	ᴿCritRR 6 (1993) 138-140 (R. *Doran*).

11038 *Hansen* Mogens H.,	The battle exhortation in ancient historiography; fact or fiction?: Historia 42 (1993) 161-180.

11039 **Hinchliff** Peter, God and history 1992 ➤ 8,b877; 9,12402:	ᴿAmHR 99 (1994) 234s (C. D. *Cashdollar*); JRel 74 (1994) 404s (D. L. *Pals*).

11040 **Hughes** Glenn,	Mystery and myth in the philosophy of Eric VOEGELIN. Columbia 1993, Univ. Missouri. vi-131 p. $38.50. – ᴿÉglT 25 (1994) 456-8 (K. R. *Melchin*).

11041 **Kirkpatrick** Frank G.,	Together bound; God, history, and the religious community. Ox 1994, UP. xiii-195 p. $35. 0-19-508342-3 [TDig 41,366].

11042 **Kleingeld** Pauline,	Geschichtsphilosophie bei KANT; Rekonstruktion und Analyse: Diss. ᴰ*Adriaanse* H. J. Leiden 1994. – RTLv 26, p. 529.

11043 *Kosso* Peter,	Historical evidence and epistemic justification; THUCYD-IDES as a case study: HistTheor 32 (1993) 1-13.

11044 *Liverani* Mario,	History as a war game [DREWS R. 1993]: JMeditArch 7 (1994) 241-8.

11045 **Long** V. Philips,	The art of biblical history: Foundations of contemporary interpretation 5. Leicester 1991, Apollos. xvii-223 p. [BL 95,42s, D. J. *Reimer*].

11046 *Magdalino* Paul,	The history of the future and its uses; prophecy, policy and propaganda: ➤ 88, ᶠNICOL D. Byzantine history 1993, 3-34.

11047 *Makita* Etsuro,	Der Begriff des historischen Bewusstseins bei GA-DAMER: ArBegG 36 (1993) 317-331.

11047* **Martínez Lacy** Ricardo,	Dos aproximaciones a la historiografía de la antigüedad clásica. Acatlan 1994, Univ.Nac.Méx. 173 p. 968-36-3551-2.

11048 *Megill* Allan,	Jörn RÜSEN's theory of historiography between modernism and rhetoric of inquiry: HistTheory 33 (1994) 39-60.

11048* *Mayes* A. D. H.,   The place of the OT in understanding Israelite history and religion [J. BRIGHT, 'emic' approach, judges data by Israel's view; N. GOTTWALD, 'etic', rather from observer's view]: ➤ 8,6, ᶠANDERSON George, Understanding poets and prophets 1993, 242-257 [< OTAbs 17,478].

11049 *a) Millard* A. R.,   Story, history, and theology; – *b) Yamauchi* Edwin, The current state of OT historiography; – *c) Chavalas* Mark,   Genealogical history as 'charter'; a study of Old Babylonian period historiography and the OT; – *d) Arnold* Bill T.,   The Weidner Chronicle and the idea of history in Israel; – *e) Niehaus* Jeffrey J.,   The warrior and his God; the covenant foundation of history and historiography; – *f) Martins* Ebner A.,   The oscillating functions of 'history' within OT theology: ➤ 326*, Faith 1994, 1-36 / 37-64 / 79-102 / 129-148 / 299-312 / 313-340.

Moltmann Jürgen, History and the triune God 1991 ➤ 9,7783.

11050 **Momigliano** A.,   Classical foundations 1990 ➤ 6,386... 9,12414: ᴿRBgPg 72 (1994) 131 (Dominique *Briquel*).

11051 **Morrissey** Michael P.,   Consciousness and transcendence; the theology of Eric VOEGELIN.   ND 1994, Univ.   xiii-353 p. $42.   0-368-00793-4 [TDig 42,179]. – ᴿTBR 7,3 (1994s) 11 (P. A. *Monaghan*).

11052 **Moseley** James G.,   [Puritan] John WINTHROP's world; history as a story, the story as history.   Madison 1992, Univ. Wisconsin.   192 p. $42.50; pa. $15. – ᴿJRel 74 (1994) 571s (T. D. *Bozeman*).

11053 **Müller** Christof, Geschichtsbewusstsein bei AUGUSTINUS ᴰ1993 ➤ 9, 12415: ᴿTLZ 119 (1994) 912-4 (K.-H. *Kandler*); TPhil 69 (1994) 582-4 (H. J. *Sieben*).

11054 *Müller* Hans-Peter, König Mešaᶜ von Moab und der Gott der Geschichte: UF 26 (1994) 373-395.

11055 **Muhlack** Ulrich, Geschichtswissenschaft im Humanismus und in der Aufklärung; die Vorgeschichte des Historismus.   Mü 1991, Beck.   450 p. DM 98. – ᴿHistTheor 33 (1994) 113-121 (J. van der *Zande*); HZ 259 (1994) 410-2 (A. *Schindling*); RBgPg 72 (1994) 548s (Jo *Tollebeck*).

11056 **Murrmann-Kahl** Michael, Die entzauberte Heilsgeschichte; der Historismus erobert die Theologie 1880-1920: ᴰ1992 ➤ 8,b895; 9,12416: ᴿBijdragen 55 (1994) 446s (A. L. *Molendijk*); ZRGg 46 (1994) 190s (V. *Krech*).

11057 *Naddaf* Gerard, The Atlantis myth; an introduction to PLATO's later philosophy of history: Phoenix 48 (Toronto 1994) 189-209.

11058 **Nicolai** Roberto, La storiografia nell'educazione antica: MatDiscClas 10, 1992 ➤ 9,12417: ᴿAntClas 63 (1994) 478s (M.-Thérèse *Isaac*); Anz-AltW 46 (1993) 216-9 (R. *Klein*); GGA 246 (1994) 173-183 (M. *Vielberg*); Klio 76 (1994) 469 (H. *Leppin*); RFgIC 121 (1993) 331-3 (Stefania *Montecalvo*).

11059 **Nippel** Wilfried, Über das Studium der Alten Geschichte.   Mü 1993, Deutscher-Tb. 443 p. – ᴿGrazB 20 (1994) 314-7 (H. *Grassl*).

11059* *Nippel* Wilfried, Vom Nutzen und Nachteil Max WEBERS für die Althistorie: AntAb 40 (1994) 160-180.

11060 **Nnamdi** Reginald Nnadozie, Offenbarung und Geschichte; zur hermeneutischen Bestimmung der Theologie W. PANNENBERGS [Diss. Würzburg, ᴰ*Ganoczy* A.]: WüStFundT 13.   Fra 1993, Lang.   473 p. DM 108. – ᴿTR 90 (1994) 64s (J. *Schmid*).

11061 **Nunes Carreira** José, História antes de HERÓDOTO; historiografia e ideia de história na antiguidade oriental: Orientália Lusitana 1.   Lisboa 1993, Cosmos.   257 p.

11061* *Ott* Heinrich, Die Theologie vor dem Problem der Geschichte: TZBas 50 (1994) 252-263.

11062 *a*) *Ottosson* Magnus, Ideology, history and archaeology in the OT [*Sollamo* Raija, *Skjeggestad* Marit, responses]; – *b*) *Laato* Antti, History and archaeology in the OT prophetic books [responses, *Nielsen* Kirsten, *Steingrimsson* Sigurdur Ø.]; – *c*) *Lemche* Neils P., Is it still possible to write a history of ancient Israel? [responses *Berge* Norin C., *Berge* K.]; – *d*) *Barstad* Hans M., The understanding of the prophets in Deuteronomy [*Jeppesen* K., *Tengström* Sven]: ScandJT 8,2 (1994) 206-223 [224.228-235] / 267-297 [298-301.302-5] / 165-190 [191-7.198-205] / 236-251 [252-6.257-266].

11063 *a*) *Philipp* Thomas, Geschichtswissenschaft und die Geschichte des Nahen Ostens; – *b*) *Freitag* Ulrike, Entwicklung und Probleme arabischer Geschichtsschreibung am Beispiel syrischer Historiker: Saeculum 45 (1994) 166-178 / 179-194.

11064 *Polichetti* Antonio, Rassegna di studi OROSIANI: Koinonia 18 (1994) 179-197...

11065 *Pyper* Hugh S., Surviving writing; the anxiety of historiography in the Former Prophets: ➤ 9,271, New Lit. Crit. 1993, 227-249 [< OTAbs 17, p. 311].

11066 *Quezada del Rio* J., La filosofía de la historia del Antiguo Testamento: LogosMéx 61 (1993) 91-108 [< Stromata 50,277].

11067 *Rabb* Theodore K., *Rotberg* Robert I., History and religion; interpretation and illumination: JIntdis 23,3 (1992s) 445-451 [-660, meeting].

11068 *Ronconi* Lucia, ERODOTO; da Alicarnasso a Turi: Hesperia 4 (Venezia 1994) 135-149.

11069 **Sakellariou** M. B., Between memory and oblivion 1990 ➤ 8,b901; 9,12425: ᴿRÉG 107 (1994) 259s (J.-N. *Corvisier*); RPg 67 (1993) 138-143 (É. *Wills*).

11070 *Schüssler Fiorenza* Elisabeth, The rhetoricity of historical knowledge; Pauline discourse and its contextualizations: ➤ 40, ᶠGEORGI D., Religious propaganda 1994, 443-469.

11071 **Shute** Michael, The origins of LONERGAN's notion of the dialectic of history; a study of Lonergan's early writings on history. Lanham MD 1993, UPA. 232 p. $46.50 [TS 56,404, J. *Dool*]. – ᴿHistTheor 33 (1994) 124 (*ipse*).

11072 **Smelik** Klaas A. D., Converting the past; studies in ancient Israelite and Moabite historiography [5 reprints + inedita]: OTS 28, 1992 ➤ 8,110: ᴿÉTRel 68 (1993) 425 (J. P. *Stemberger*); JBL 113 (1994) 699-701 (Sara J. *Denning-Bolle*); JTS 45 (1994) 446s (R. P. *Gordon*).

11073 *Uspenskij* Boris A., Semiotik der Geschichte: Szb ph/h 579. W 1992, Österr. Akad. 313 p. DM 60. – ᴿSpeculum 69 (1994) 905-7 (D. C. *Waugh*).

11074 **Wes** A. Marinus, M. ROSTOVTZEFF 1990 ➤ 8,b913: ᴿLatomus 53 (1994) 706s (P. *Salmon*); VDI 210 (1994) 246-9 (K. A. *Avestisyan*, K. O. *Bitukov*, ⊕).

11075 **Woodman** A. J., Rhetoric in classical historiography. L 1988, Croom Helm. 236 p. – ᴿRPg 67 (1993) 171s (J.-L. *Ferrary*).

11076 ᶠWOUDE A. van der, Sacred history and sacred texts, ᶠ**Bremmer** J. 1992 ➤ 8,504: ᴿHenoch 16 (1994) 1330-3 (C. *Martone*).

Q3 *Historia Ægypti* – Egypt.

11077 **Anagnostou-Canas** Barbara, Juge et sentence dans l'Égypte romaine [diss. d'Etat Paris II 1983]. P 1991, L'Harmattan. xii-390 p. – ᴿCdÉ 69 (1994) 191-4 (H. *Melaerts*); RÉG 107 (1994) 726s (A. *Blanchard*).

11078 **Beckerath** Jürgen von,   Chronologie des ägyptischen Neuen Reiches: HildÄgBeit 39. Hildesheim 1994, Gerstenberg. xv-129 p. 3-8067-8132-X.

11079 **Bryan** Betsy M.,   The reign of Thutmosis IV 1991 → 7,b112; 8,b930: ᴿBL (1994) 117s (K. A. *Kitchen*); JAmEg 31 (1994) 225s (E. S. *Meltzer*); JEA 80 (1994) 247-251 (A. *Dodson*: only innovation a rather disappointing rhetoric); OLZ 89 (1994) 129-132 (S. *Bickel*).

11080 *Cannuyer* Christian,   Encore la date de l'accession au trône de Ramsès XI: GöMiszÄg 132 (1993) 19s.

11080* *Cervelló Autuori* J.,   Azaiwo, Afyewo, Asoiwo; reflexiones sobre la realeza divina africana y los orígenes de la monarquía faraonica: AulaO 11,1 (1993) 5-55; bibliog. 56-64; + 15 fig.; Eng. p. 5.

11081 **Cimmino** Franco,   Hašepsowe e Tuthmosis III; una regina ambiziosa e un grande faraone. Mi c. 1994, Rusconi. 254 p. Lᵐ 15. – ᴿArcheo 9,118 (1994) 122 (S. *Pernigotti*).

11082 *Clarysse* Willy,   Nephorites, founder of the 29th dynasty and his name [not Nepherites as MANETHO]: CdE 69,138 (1994) 215-7.

11083 **Clayton** Peter A.,   Chronicle of the Pharaohs; the reign-by-reign record of the rulers and dynasties of ancient Egypt.   L 1994, Thames & H. 224 p.; 220 fig. + 130 colour. 0-500-05074-0.

11084 *Collins* John J.,   The Sibyl and the power; political propaganda in Ptolemaic Egypt: → 40, ꟳGEORGI D., 1994, 57-69.

11085 *Crocker* Piers T.,   Recent discussions on the identity of King 'So' of Egypt: BurHist 29 (1993) 68-74.

11086 **Der Manuelian** Peter,   Living in the past; studies in archaism of the Egyptian twenty-sixth dynasty: StEg. L 1994, Kegan Paul. xv-467 p.; 20 pl. 0-7103-0461-7.

11087 *Dijk* J. van,   Horemheb en de strijd over de troon van Toetanchamon: PhoenixEOL 40 (1994) 62-78.

11088 ᴱ**Eide** Tormod, *al.*,   Textual sources for the history of the middle Nile region between the eighth century BC and the sixth century AD: FontesNub 1. Bergen 1994, Univ.Dept.Classics. 343 p. 82-991411-6-8.

11089 **Ellis** Walter M.,   Ptolemy of Egypt. L 1994, Routledge. xix-104; 24 pl.; 3 maps. £30. 0-415-10020-8. – ᴿGreeceR 41 (1994) 231 (J. *Salmon*: no hero).

11090 *Fay* Biri,   Custodian of the seal, Mentuhotep: GöMiszÄg 133 (1993) 19-28; 7 pl.

11090* **Gagos** Traianos, *Minnen* Peter van,   Settling a dispute; toward a legal anthropology of late antique Egypt: New Texts from Ancient Cultures 1. AA 1994, Univ. Michigan. x-151 p. 0-472-06590-4.

11091 **Galan** José M.,   Victory and border; terminology related to Egyptian imperialism in the 18th dynasty: diss. Johns Hopkins. Baltimore 1994. 395 p. 94-19972. – DissA 55 (1994s) p. 68.

11092 *Greenberg* Gary,   MANETHO rehabilitated; a new analysis of his Second Intermediate period: DiscEg 25 (1993) 21-27; 2 fig.

11093 **Grimal** Nicolas,   A history of ancient Egypt [1988], ᵀ*Shaw* Ian.   CM 1992, Blackwell. ix-512 p.; 24 pl. $35. 0-631-17472-9. – ᴿAmHR 99 (1994) 204s (K. W. *Butzer*); ClasW 88 (1994s) 212s (R. S. *Bianchi*).

11094 **Huss** Werner,   Der makedonische König und die ägyptischen Priester; Studien zur Geschichte des ptolemäischen Ägypten: HistEinz 85.   Stu 1994, Steiner. 238 p. DM 80 [BL 95,39, L. L. *Grabbe*]. – ᴿCdÉ 69 (1994 374-8 (F. *Colin*); MusHelv 51 (1994) 259s (P. *Borgeaud*).

11095 *Jasnow* Richard,   A lexicographical note on the Medinet Habu inscription of Year 11 [Ramesses III, 2d Libyan war]: JEA 80 (1994) 201s.

11096 **Johnson** Carl G., Ptolemaic royal titulature in royal and civil documents (304-116 B.C.). Diss. ᴰ*Samuel* A. Toronto 1994. 417 p. NN92650. DissA 55 (1994s) p. 3955.

11097 **Kaulins** Andis, Kings and dynasties; the dynasties of man from the days of Adam to the reigns of the Pharaos according to the Wheel of Heaven. Lincoln NE 1994, Isandis. [xviii-] 197 p.; ill.

11098 **Kitchen** K. A., Ramesside inscriptions 1990-93 → 9,12452: ᴿCdÉ 69 (1994) 263 (H. *De Meulenaere*: 7,1.16; 8,1.10); JEA 79 (1993) 302s (M. L. *Bierbrier*, 7s).

11099 **Kozloff** Arielle P., *Bryan* Betsy M., Egypt's dazzling sun, Amenhotep III and his world 1992 → 9,12453: ᴿAJA 98 (1994) 362-4 (P. F. *Dorman*).

11100 *Krauss* Rolf, a) Was wäre, wenn der altägyptische Kalendertag mit Sonnenaufgang begonnen hätte?: BSocÉg 17 (Genève 1993) 63-71; – b) Zur Chronologie des Mittleren Reiches [*Luft* U., (Illahun) 1992]: OLZ 89 (1994) 5-19.

11101 **Lichtheim** Miriam, Ancient Egyptian autobiographies: OBO 84, 1988 → 4,210* ... 8,b958: ᴿÉTRel 69 (1994) 271s (Françoise *Smyth-Florentin*, aussi sur son Maat, OBO 120, 1992).

11102 **Luft** Ulrich, Die chronologische Fixierung des ägyptischen Mittleren Reiches nach dem Tempelarchiv von Illahun: SzbÖsAkad p/h 598, 1992 → 9,12456: 3-7001-1988-7: ᴿJAOS 114 (1994) 663s (W. A. *Ward*); WZKM 84 (1994) 180-2 (K. A. *Kitchen*).

11103 *Lukaszewicz* Adam, Remarques sur les rapports entre les élites urbaines de l'Égypte et la dynastie des Sévères: JJurPap 24 (1994) 87-95.

11104 ᴱ**Malek** Jaromir, Egypt; ancient culture, modern land: Cradles of civilization. Norman 1993, Univ. Oklahoma. 192 p.; 450 (color.) fig. $40. 0-8061-2526-8. – ᴿClasW 88 (1994s) 212s (R. S. *Bianchi*: despite its lavish illustration, more critical than readable GRIMAL).

11105 a) *Ohlhafer* Klaus, Zum Thronbesteigungsdatum Ramses' XI. und zur Abfolge der Grabräuberpapyri aus Jahr 1 und 2 *wḥm-mswt*; – b) *Dautzenberg* M., Bemerkungen zur Dynastie der Grossen Hyksos bei MANETHO: GöMiszÄg 135 (1993) 59-72 / 9-26.

11106 *Oosterhout* G. W. van, Sirius, Venus and the Egyptian calendar: DiscEg 27 (1993) 83-96.

Palme B., Amt des *apaitētēs* 1989 → 9337.

11107 **Peden** A. J., Egyptian historical inscriptions of the twentieth dynasty: DocMundiAeg 3. Jonsered 1994, Åström. xix-296 p.; bibliog. 281-5. 91-7081-065-6.

11108 **Peden** A. J., The reign of Ramesses IV. Wmr 1994, Aris & P. xxviii-130 p.; bibliog. xiii-xxvi. 0-9510704-2-8.

11109 *Pérez Lagarcha* Antonio, a) Some suggestions and hypotheses concerning the Maadi culture and the expansion of Upper Egypt; – b) Relations between Egypt and Mesopotamia at the end of the fourth millennium: GöMiszÄg 135 (1993) 41-52 / 137 (1993) 59-76.

11110 **Quirke** Stephen, The administration of Egypt in the Late Middle Kingdom; the hieratic documents 1990 → 6,b450: ᴿJEA 80 (1994) 240-2 (A. *Spalinger*).

11111 a) *Robins* Gay, Queens and queenship in 18th dynasty Egypt before the Amarna period; – b) *Redford* Susan, Ramesses III and the women of the royal harim (sic): BuCanadMesop 26 (1993) 53-58 / 39-51; 6 fig.

11112 **Rössler-Köhler** Ursula, Individuelle Haltungen zum ägyptischen Königtum 1991 → 7,b143 ... 9,12465: ᴿArOr 61 (1993) 320s (L. *Bareš*).

11113 *Rose* Lynn E., The astronomical evidence for dating the end of the

Middle Kingdom of Ancient Egypt to the early second millennium: a reassessment [inconclusive but not incompatible]: JNES 53 (1994) 237-262.

11114 **Roth** Ann M., Egyptian phyles in the Old Kingdom 1991 ➤ 7,b143; 9,12466: ᴿDiscEc 26 (1993) 91-96 (J. *Baines*).

11115 **Skeat** Theodore C., The reign of Augustus in Egypt; conversion tables for the Egyptian and Julian calendar, 30 B.C. - 14 A.D.: MüBeitPapF 84. Mü 1993, Beck. viii-44 p. DM 28. 3-406-37384-4. – ᴿAegyptus 79 (1994) 189s (G. *Casanova*); BASP 31 (1994) 171s (J. F. *Oates*).

11116 *Skeat* T. C., The beginning [26 B.C.] and end of the *Kaísaros krátēsis* era in Egypt: CdÉ 69 (1994) 308-312.

11117 **Strouhal** Eugen, Life of the ancient Egyptians, ᵀ*Viney* Deryck. Norman 1992, Univ. Oklahoma. – ᴿClasB 70 (1994) 31-33 (J. H. *Johnson*).

11118 **Trigger** Bruce G., Early civilizations; ancient Egypt in context. Cairo 1993, American Univ. x-150 p.; bibliog. 123-146.

11119 **Tyldesley** Joyce, Daughters of Isis; women of ancient Egypt. L 1994, Viking. xvii-318 p.; ill.; map. 0-970-84838-7.

11120 **Valbelle** Dominique, Les neuf arcs 1990 ➤ 7,b149: ᴿDiscEg 25 (1993) 107-115 (E. P. *Uphill*: Egypt's foreign relations throughout its history).

11121 **Vercoutter** Jean, L'Égypte et la vallée du Nil, I. Des origines à la fin de l'Ancien Empire, 12000-2000 av. J.-C. P 1992, PUF. 382 p.; 51 fig.; 16 maps. F 220. 2-13-044157-2. – ᴿDiscEg 25 (1993) 107-112 (J. *Malek*).

11122 *Vliet* E. van der, Verdwijnen de 'Dark Ages'? [JAMES P. ➤ 13759]: PhoenixEOL 40 (1994) 94-108.

11123 **Weber** Gregor, Dichtung und höfische Gesellschaft; die Rezeption von Zeitgeschichte am Hof der ersten drei Ptolemäer: Hermes-Einz 62. Stu 1993, Steiner. xii-492 p. DM 148. – ᴿCdÉ 69 (1994) 183s (D. *Marcotte*); ClasR 44 (1994) 289-291 (A. *Erskine*).

11124 **Welsh** Frances, Tutankhamun's Egypt: Shire Eg 18. Princes R. Bucks 1993, Shire. 80 p. 0-7478-0196-7.

11125 **Bagnall** Roger S., Egypt in late antiquity 1993 ➤ 9,12473: ᴿBAR-W 20,6 (1994) 8s (Georgia *Frank*); RÉG 107 (1994) 725 (A. *Blanchard*).

Q4 Historia Mesopotamiae.

11126 **Aaboe** A., *al.*, Saros cycle dates and related Babylonian astronomical texts: Tr 81/6. Ph 1991, American Philosophical Soc. [iv-] 75 p. 0-87169-816-1.

11127 **Algaze** G., The Uruk world system; the dynamics of expansion of early Mesopotamian civilization 1993 ➤ 9,12476: ᴿBuCanadMesop 27 (1994) 65; RAss 88 (1994) 92s (P. *Amiet*).

11128 *a) Cooper* Jerrold S., Paradigm and propaganda; the dynasty of Akkade in the 21st century; – *b) Nissen* Hans J., Settlement patterns and material culture of the Akkadian period; continuity and discontinuity; – *c) Weiss* Harvey, *Courty* Marie-Agnès, The genesis and collapse of the Akkadian empire; the accidental refraction of historical law: ➤ 570, Akkad 1990/3, 11-23 / 91-106 / 131-151 + 5 maps.

11129 ᴱ**Curtis** J., Early Mesopotamia and Iran 1991/3 ➤ 9,571: ᴿBSO 57 (1994) 460 (Harriet *Crawford*).

11130 *a) Foster* Benjamin R., Management and administration in the Sargonic period; – *b) Westenholz* Aage, The world view of Sargonic officials;

differences in mentality between Sūmerians and Akkadians: ➤ 570, Akkad 1990/3, 25-39 (bibliog. 171-182) / 157-169

11131 *Fouts* David M., Another look at large numbers in Assyrian royal inscriptions: JNES 53 (1994) 205-211.

11132 **Frame** G., Babylonia 689-627 B.C.; a political history: Ned. Uitgaven 69, 1992 ➤ 8,b992; 9,12485: ᴿBuCanadMesop 26 (1993) 69s (A. K. *Grayson*, aussi en français); WeltOr 25 (1994) 150-2 (R. *Zadok*).

11133 **Freydank** Helmut, Beiträge zur mittelassyrischen Chronologie und Geschichte 1991 ➤ 7,b181: ᴿOLZ 89 (1994) 549-552 (G. *Wilhelm*).

11134 *Gerardi* Pamela, Prism fragments from Sippar; new Esarhaddon inscriptions: Iraq 55 (1993) 119-133; 4 fig.

11135 **Glassner** Jean-Jacques, Chroniques mésopotamiennes: La Roue à Livres (Documents) 1993 ➤ 9.12486: ᴿÉTRel 68 (1993) 425s (Françoise *Smyth*).

11136 ᴱ**Klengel** Horst, Kulturgeschichte des Alten Vorderasien 1989 ➤ 6, b498...8,d5: ᴿWeltOr 25 (1994) 145s (W. *Röllig*).

11137 **Krajčí** Jaroslav (& Anna), The civilizations of Asia and the Middle East before the European challenge. L 1990, Macmillan. xiii-348. £37.50. – ᴿEngHR 109 (1994) 125 (D. *Sinor*: highly competent; largely pre-Christian).

11138 **Liverani** Mario, Guerra e diplomazia nell'Antico Oriente 1600-1100 a.C.: Collezione Storica. R 1994, Laterza. vii-318 p.; ill. 88-420-4457-1.

11139 *a) Liverani* Mario, Model and actualization; the kings of Akkad in the historical tradition; – *b) Michalowski* Piotr, Memory and deed; the historiography of the political expansion of the Akkad state: ➤ 9,570, Akkad, 1990/3, (1-10) 41-67 / 69-90.

11140 **Melville** Sarah C., The role of Naqia-Zakutu [... Sennacherib's wife, Sargonid woman about whom there is more evidence than for all others combined] in Sargonid politics: diss. Yale, ᴰ*Hallo* W. NHv 1994. 204 p. 94-30282. – DissA 55 (1994) p. 2100.

11140* **Millard** Alan R., The eponyms of the Assyrian Empire 910-621 BC: SAA St 2. Helsinki 1994, Univ. Neo-Assyrian Project. xvi-155 p. 951-45-6715-3.

11141 **Nemet-Nejat** Karen R., Cuneiform mathematical texts as a reflection of everyday life in Mesopotamia: AmerOrSeries 75. NHv 1993, American Oriental Soc. xii-335 p. 0-940490-75-7.

11142 **Onasch** Hans-Ulrich, Die assyrischen Eroberungen Ägyptens, 1. Kommentare und Anmerkungen; 2. Texte in Umschrift: ÄgAT 27. Wsb 1994, Harrassowitz. I. xix-264 p.; X pl., bibliog. xi-xvii; II. 191 p. Texte in Umschrift. 3-447-03581-1.

11143 *Pomponio* Francesco, Re di Uruk, 're di Kiš': RSO 68 (1994) 1-13; Eng. 14.

11144 **Porter** Barbara M., Images, power, and politics; figurative aspects of Esarhaddon's Babylonian policy: Mem 208. Ph 1993, American Philosophical Society. xv-230 p. 0-87169-208-2.

11145 *Postgate* J. N., In search of the first empires: BASOR 293 (1994) 1-13.

11146 **Rollinger** Robert, HERODOTS Babylonischer logos; eine kritische Untersuchung der Glaubwürdigkeitsdiskussion an Hand ausgewählter Beispiele; historische Parallelüberlieferung — Argumentation — archäologischer Befund — Konsequenzen für eine Geschichte Babylons in persischer Zeit: InBeitKuW 84. Innsbruck 1993, Univ. Inst SprW. 249 p. Bibliog. 230-249. 3-85124-165-7.

11147 **Sack** Ronald H.,   Neriglissar, king of Babylon: AOAT 236.   Kevelaer/
Neuk 1994, Butzon &B/.   xiii-270 p.   3-7666-9694-X / Neuk 3-7887-
1480-8.

11148 *Simpson* S.,   Gazelle-hunters and salt-collectors; a further note on the
[Late Assyrian, early Islamic] Solubba: BASOR 293 (1994) 79-81.

11149 **Soden** Wolfram von,   The ancient orient; an introduction to the study
of the Ancient Near East.   GR 1994, Eerdmans.   xx-263 p.   0-85244-
252-1.

11149* ᵀᴱ**Tadmor** Hayim,   The inscriptions of Tiglath-Pileser III king of
Assyria.   J 1994, Israel Acad.   xv-319 p.

Q4.5   *Historia Persiae* – **Iran.**

11150 **Brosius** Maria,   Royal and non-royal women in Achaemenid Persia:
diss. Oxford c. 1992. – BInstClas 37 (1991-3) 306.

11150* **Dandamaev** M. A.,   Political history... Achaemenid 1989 ➤ 5,b503...
9,12509: ᴿCritRR 5 (1992) 65s (J. W. *Wright*).

11151 **Högemann** Peter,   Das alte Vorderasien und die Achämeniden...
HERODOT: TAVO B-98, 1992 ➤ 8,d38: ᴿBO 51 (1994) 608-611 (R.
Schmitt).

11152 **Jacobs** Bruno,   Die Satrapienverwaltung im Perserreich zur Zeit Darius' III: TAVO Beih B-87.   Wsb 1994, Reichert.   ix-320 p.   3-88226-
618-2.

11153 **Koch** Heidemarie,   Es kündet Dareios der König...; Vom Leben im
persischen Grossreich: KuGaW 55.   Mainz 1992, von Zabern. – ᴿHZ
259 (1994) 746-8 (J. *Wiesehöfer*); JAOS 114 (1994) 519s (Maria *Brosius*:
superficial, uncheckable assumptions); ZRGg 46 (1994) 370-2 (M.
Stausberg).

11154 **McNellen** Brad E.,   Persian *nómos* and *paranomia* in HERODOTUS: diss.
Michigan, ᴰ*Koenen* L. AA 1994.   377 p. 94-23266. – DissA 55 (1994s)
p. 954.

11155 **Petit** T.,   Satrapes et satrapies 1990 ➤ 7,b196... 9,12514: ᴿRFgIC 121
(1993) 318-322 (M. *Mari*).

11155* **Quintana** *Cifuentes* E.,   Los gobernantes elamitas: AulaO 12 (1994)
73-94.

11156 **Sancisi-Weerdenburg** H., Kuhrt A.,   Achaemenid history 4-5-6, 1990s
➤ 8,d45; 9,12516: ᴿAJA 97 (1993) 170-2 (O. W. *Muscarella*).

11156* **Vogelsang** W. J.,   The rise and organisation of the Achaemenid empire
1992 ➤ 8,d47... 9,12516: ᴿÉtClas 62 (1994) 407s (T. *Petit*).

11157 **Weiskopf** Michael,   The so-called 'Great Satraps Revolt' 1989 ➤ 5,b519
... 8,d48: ᴿJAOS 114 (1994) 99-101 (D. F. *Graf*).

11157* **Yamauchi** Edwin, Persia and the Bible 1990 ➤ 6,b553... 8,d50: ᴿChr-
SchR 24 (1994) 92s (E. J. *Collins* admires the 'preternatural way in which
Y. identifies troublesome Scripture references'); CritRR 5 (1992) 109s
(J. W. *Wright*: a useful reference despite limited aim); JAOS 114 (1994)
499-504 (P. Oktor *Skjærvø*: considerable acumen, but not to be used
without checking the sources; and many improvements suggested).

Q5   *Historia Anatoliae:* **Asia Minor, Hittites** [➤ T8.2], **Armenia** [➤ T8.9].

11158 **Astour** Michael C.,   Hittite history and absolute chronology of the
Bronze Age: SIMA pocket 73.   Partille 1989, Åström.   152 p.   91-
86098-86-1. – ᴿRB 101 (1994) 295 (M. *Sigrist*).

11159 *Balcer* Jack M., HERODOTUS, the 'Early State', and Lydia [SANCISI-WEERDENBURG H., Was there ever a Median empire? 1988]: Historia 43 (1994) 246-9.

11160 ᴱ**del Monte** Giuseppe F., L'annalistica ittita: TVOAnt 4. Brescia 1993, Paideia. 153 p. Lᵐ 30.

11161 *Hout* Theo van den, Der Falke und das Kücken; der neue Pharaoh [Ay] und der hethitische Prinz [in einem Brief von Šuppiluliuma über sein angemeldeten Tod]?: ZAss 84 (1994) 60-88.

11161* *Houwink Ten Cate* P.H.J., Urhi-Tessub revisted: BO 51 (1994) 233-259.

11162 *Lipiński* E., Gyges [roi de Lydie] et Lygdamis [Tugdamme de l'invasion Cimmérienne] d'après les sources hébraïques et néo-assyriennes: OrLovPer 24 (1993) 65-71.

11163 **Popko** Maciej, ❷ Huryci. Wsz 1992, PNW. 207 p.; ill., map. zł 29.000. – ᴿOLZ 89 (1994) 279-282 (P. *Taracha*).

11164 **Popko** Maciej, Zippalanda, ein Kultzentrum im hethitischen Kleinasien: Texte der Hethiter 21. Heid 1994, Winter. xiii-335 p. 3-8253-0829-X.

11165 *a) Ünal* Ahmet, Ritual purity versus physical impurity in Hittite Anatolia; public health and structures for sanitation according to cuneiform text and archaeological remains; – *b) Hagenbuchner* Albertine, Schütz- und Loyalitätsverpflichtungen in hethitischen Staatsverträgen: ➤ 9,358, ᴱ*Mikasa* T., Anatolian Studies 1993, 119-139 / 99-118.

Q6.1   Historia Graeciae classicae.

11166 *Alonso-Nuñez* José M., Die Weltgeschichte bei POSEIDONIOS: GrazB 20 (1994) 87-108.

Barceló P., Basileia, monarchia, tyrannis; Untersuchungen zur Entwicklung und Beurteilung von Alleinherrschaft im vorhellenistischen Griechenland: HistEinz 79, 1993 ➤ 9363 supra .

11167 **Baslez** Marie-Françoise, Histoire politique du monde grec antique: Fac-Histoire. P 1994, Nathan. 316 p. – ᴿRÉG 107 (1994) 713 (Véronique *Boudon*).

11168 **Bernal** M., Black Athena II 1991 ➤ 7,b214* ... 9,12539: ᴿJIntdis 24 (1993s) 518-521 (L. H. *Lesko*).

11168* — *Burstein* S.M., The challenge of Black Athena; an interim assessment: AncHB 8 (1994) 11- ... (correction 49).

11169 **Burkert** W., The orientalizing revolution [in] Greek culture 1º, ᵀwith *Pinder* Margaret E., 1992 ➤ 9,12546: ᴿAmHR 99 (1994) 204s (Carol G. *Thomas*).

11170 *Boulogne* Jacques, Mythe et construction du réel chez HÉRODOTE: RPg 66 (1992) 255-266.

11171 **Bowen** A.J., PLUTARCH, The malice of HERODOTUS 1992 ➤ 9,12545: ᴿClasB 69 (1993) 112s (W. *Seavey*); JHS 114 (1994) 214-6 (E.J. *McQueen*).

11172 *Brodersen* Kai, Männer, Frauen und Kinder in Grossgriechenland; Quellen und Modelle zur frühen Siedler-Identität: Mnemosyne 47 (1994) 47-63.

11173 *Burton* Joan, Why the ancient Greeks were obsessed with heroes and the ancient Egyptians were not: ClasB 69 (1993) 21-34.

11174 **Cartledge** Paul, The Greeks; a portrait of self and others: Opus. Ox 1993, UP. xv-232 p.; bibliog. 197-223. £8 pa. 0-19-288147-2.

11175 **Cole** Thomas,   The origins of rhetoric in ancient Greece 1991 ➤ 8,d73; 9,12549:   ᴿPhoenix 48 (Toronto 1994) 262-4 (J.S. *Murray*).

11176 *a*) *Edmunds* Lowell,   THUCYDIDES in the act of writing; – *b*) *Musti* Domenico,   *Sôma* in Tucidide e in Gorgia: ➤ 9,51, ᶠGENTILI B., Tradizione 1993, 831-852 / 853-864.

11177 **Fuchs** Elfriede,   Pseudologia; Formen und Funktionen fiktionaler Trugrede in der griechischen Literatur der Antike: diss. Düsseldorf 1992: BtKlasAltW 91. Heid 1993, Winter. v-295 p.

11178 **Garrity** Thomas F.,   The experience of history; reading THUCYDIDES' prose [he uses complexity to aid the reader to re-live the ambiguity of the events]: diss. California, ᴰ*Stroud* R.   Berkeley 1994, 212 p.   95-04806. – DissA 55 (1994s) p. 2815.

11178* *Gehrke* Hans J.,   THUKYDIDES und die Rekonstruktion des Historischen: AntAb 39 (1993) 1-19.

11179 **Georges** Pericles,   Barbarian Asia and the Greek experience, from the archaic period to the age of Xenophon: Ancient Society and History. Baltimore 1994, Johns Hopkins Univ.   xxii-358 p.; bibliog. 325-345. 0-8018-4734-6.

11180 **Grant** Michael,   The rise of the Greeks 1987 ➤ 4,d340; 5,b563:   ᴿKlio 76 (1994) 171s (D. *Lotze*).

11181 *Haehling* Raban von,   Furcht und Schrecken in HERODOTS Darstellung und Deutung der Perserkriege: Klio 75 (1993) 85-98; Eng. 98.

11181* *Hölkeskamp* Karl J.,   Written law in ancient Greece: PrCPg 38 (1992s) 87-117.

11182 **Hornblower** S.,   A commentary on THUCYDIDES 1-3, 1991 ➤ 8,d91; 9,12567:   ᴿGnomon 66 (1994) 196-201 (O. *Lendle*).

11183 **Hornblower** S.,   THUCYDIDES 1987 ➤ 4,d352 ... 6,b594:   ᴿMnemosyne 47 (1994) 395-400 (H. *Verdin*).

11184 **Hunt** Peter A.,   Slaves and [= surprisingly widely] soldiers in classical ideologies: diss. ᴰ*Treggiari* Susan M.   Stanford 1994.   354 p.   95-08377. – DissA 55 (1994s) p. 3286.

11185 **Jehne** Martin,   Koine Eirene; Untersuchungen zu den Befriedigungs- und Stabilisierungsbemühungen in der griechischen Poliswelt des 4. Jh.v.Chr. [Hab.-Diss. Passau 1991]: Hermes Einz 63.   Stu 1994, Steiner. 320 p. – ᴿMusHelv 51 (1994) 258s (L. *Burckhardt*).

11186 *Johnson* William A.,   Oral performance and the composition of HERODOTUS' Histories: GrRByz 35 (1994) 229-254.

11187 **Kennedy** George A.,   A new history of classical rhetoric [= ²ʳᵉᵛArt of persuasion in Greece / Art of rhetoric in the Roman world / Greek rhetoric under Christian emperors].   Princeton 1994, Univ.   xii-301 p.; bibliog. 285-295.   0-691-00059-X.

11188 **Kennelly** James,   THUCYDIDES' knowledge of HERODOTUS: diss. Brown. Providence 1994.   158 p.   94-33383. – DissA 55 (1994s) p. 1938.

11189 *Koenen* Ludwig,   Greece, the Near East and Egypt; cyclic destruction in HESIOD and the Catalogue of Women (1993 Presidential Address, Wsh): AmPgTr 124 (1994) 1-34.

11190 **Lévêque** P.,   Las primeras civilizaciones; de los despotismos orientales a la ciudad griega: Pueblos y Civilizaciones I.   M 1991, Akal.   520 p. – ᴿGerión 11 (1993) 407s (Mirella *Romero Recio*).

11191 *L'Homme-Wery* Louise-Marie,   Solon, libérateur d'Éleusis dans les 'histoires' d'HÉRODOTE: RÉG 107,2 (1994) 362-380.

11192 **Manville** Philip P.,   The origins of citizenship in ancient Athens 1990 ➤ 8,d110:   ᴿKlio 75 (1993) 494s (U. *Walter*).

11193 ᴱMarazzi Massimiliano, La società micenea: RicMedit 2. R 1994, Bagatto. 590 p. Lᵐ 75. 88-7806-081-X.

11194 *Mattingly* H. B., The practice of ostracism at Athens: Antichthon 25 (1991) 1-26.

11195 ᶠMᴇᴜʟɪ Karl, Symposium, Klassische Antike und neue Wege der Kulturwissenschaft (Basel, 11.-13. Sept. 1991), ᴱGraf Fritz: BeitVolkskunde 11. Basel 1992. 221 p. – ᴿGrazB 20 (1994) 322-8 (W. *Pötscher*).

11196 *Milanezi* Silvia, Pratiques et censures de rire et de la comédie en Grèce ancienne: EurRH 2,1 (1995) 7-18.

11197 *Moggi* Mauro, Scrittura e riscrittura della storia in Pᴀᴜsᴀɴɪᴀ: RFgIC 121 (1993) 396-419.

11198 *Nagy* Blaise, Alcibiades' second 'profanation' [return from exile during Plynteria]: Historia 43 (1994) 275-285.

11199 *Perrin* Éric, Héracleidès le crétois à Athènes; les plaisirs du tourisme culturel: RÉG 107 (1994) 192-202.

11200 *Petzold* Karl-E., Die Gründung des Delisch-Attischen Seebundes, Element einer 'imperialistischen' Politik Athens? II. Zielsetzung des Seebundes und die Politik der Zeit: Historia 43 (1994) 1-31.

11201 ᵀᴱPritchett W. Kendrick, Dɪᴏɴʏsɪᴜs of Halicarnassus, On Tʜᴜᴄʏᴅ-ɪᴅᴇs. Berkeley 1975, Univ. California. XXXIV-164 p.

11202 ᶠRᴀᴅᴋᴇ G., Présence de Tᴀᴄɪᴛᴇ [➤ 8,150b], Colloque Paris oct. 1991, ᴱChevallier R., *Poignault* R.; Caesarodunum 26 bis. Tours 1992, Centre Péganiol. 293 p. – ᴿBStLat 23 (1993) 455-8 (Rossana *Valenti*).

11203 **Reinsberg** Carola, Ehe, Hetärentum und Knabenliebe im antiken Griechenland, ²*Steuben* Hans von. Mü 1993, Beck. 242 p.; 120 fig. DM 48. 3-406-33911-5. – ᴿGrazB 20 (1994) 300-2 (W. *Pötscher*).

11204 *Rhodes* P. J., In defence of the Greek historians: GreeceR 41 (1994) 156-171.

11205 **Robb** Kevin, Literacy and paideia in ancient Greece. Ox 1994, UP. x-310 p.; bibliog. 287-299. 0-19-505905-0.

11206 **Rouillard** P., Les Grecs et la péninsule ibérique: Centre P. Paris 21. P 1991, de Boccard. – ᴿGerión 11 (1993) 475-7 (F. *Diez de Velasco*).

11207 ᴱRussell Donald A., Dɪᴏ Cʜʀʏsᴏsᴛᴏᴍ, Orations VII, XII and XXXVI [Greek]. C 1992, Univ. viii-266 p.

11207* *Sakellaridou-Sotiroudi* A., Ⓖ Hᴇ́ʀᴏᴅᴏᴛᴇ dans les *Parekbolai* d'Eustathios de Thessalonique chez Dᴇɴɪs le Périégète: ➤ 90b, ᶠPᴀᴘᴀᴅᴏᴘᴏᴜʟᴏs S., Ellinika 43 (1993) 12-28; franç. 261.

11208 **Samuel** A. E., The Greeks in history. Toronto 1992, Univ/Kent. xii-208 p.; 2 maps. $18 pa. – ᴿClasR 44 (1994) 101s (H. *Bowden*).

11209 **Scanlon** Thomas F., Echoes of Hᴇʀᴏᴅᴏᴛᴜs in Tʜᴜᴄʏᴅɪᴅᴇs; self-sufficiency, admiration, and law: Historia 43 (1994) 143-176.

Schmitt-Pantel Pauline, A history of women in the West 1992 ➤ 9,1347.

11210 **Schubert** Charlotte, Die Macht des Volkes und die Ohnmacht des Denkens; Studien zum Verhältnis von Mentalität und Wissenschaft im 5.Jh. v.Chr.: HistEinz 77. Stu 1993, Steiner. 210 p. DM 76. – ᴿClasR 44 (1994) 329s (Lorna *Hardwick*).

11211 **Schüller** Wolfgang, Griechische Geschichte³ʳᵉᵛ: Grundriss der Geschichte 1. Mü 1991, Oldenbourg. xi-247 p. DM 36. – ᴿHZ 259 (1994) 152s (P. *Siewert*: best available survey).

11212 **Shimron** Binyamin, Politics and belief in Hᴇʀᴏᴅᴏᴛᴜs: HistEinz 1989 ➤ 6,b620 ... 8,d131: ᴿAntClas 63 (1994) 356s (H. *Verdin*).

11213 **Shrimpton** Gordon S., Tʜᴇᴏᴘᴏᴍᴘᴜs the historian 1991 ➤ 6,b620 ... 8,d131: ᴿPhoenix 48 (Toronto 1994) 271-3 (I.A.F. *Bruce*).

11214 *Sordi* Marta,   La svolta del 465/4 e la data della battaglia dell'Eurimedonte: Gerión 12 (1994) 63-68.
11214* **Starr** Chester G.,   Lo spionaggio politico nella Grecia antica, ᵀᴱ*Petrocelli* Conrado. Palermo 1993, Sellario. 185 p. – ᴿResPLitt 17 (1994) 222-4 (P. *Fornaro*).
11215 **Steiner** D.T.,   The tyrant's writ; myths and images of writing in ancient Greece. Princeton 1994, Univ. 279 p. – ᴿRÉG 107 (1994) 714s (A. *Billault*).
11216 *Stroud* Ronald S.,   THUCYDIDES and Corinth: Chiron 24 (1994) 267-304.
11217 **Tausend** K. Amphiktyonie und Symmachie; Formen zwischenstaatlicher Beziehungen im archaischen Griechenland: HistEinz 73. Stu 1992, Steiner. 273 p. DM 120. 3-515-06137-1. – ᴿAntClas 63 (1994) 520s (F. *Lefèvre*).
11218 **Thomas** Rosalind,   Literacy and orality in ancient Greece: Themes in ancient history 1992 ➤ 8,d138; 9,12591: ᴿAntClas 63 (1994) 331s (J. *Labarbe*).
11219 **Vandiver** Elizabeth,   Heroes in HERODOTUS: StKlasPg 56, 1991 ➤ 7, b271: ᴿGnomon 66 (1994) 360 (D. *Fehling*).
11220 **Vernant** J.P., *al.*, El hombre griego [1991 ➤ 9,12593]. M 1993, Alianza. 340 p.; 10 fig. – ᴿGerión 11 (1993) 419-422 (C. *Fornis*).
11221 **Vilatte** Sylvie,   L'insularité de la pensée grecque: Ann. Besançon Hist. 106, 1991 ➤ 8,d843: ᴿRBgPg 72 (1994) 186s (P. *Salmon*).
11222 *Whitehead* David,   Cardinal virtues; the language of public approbation in democratic Athens. ClasMedv 44 (K 1993) 37-75.
11223 **Whitley** James, Style and society in Dark Age Greece; the changing face of a pre-literate society 1100-700 B.C. C 1991, Univ. xix-225 p. $55. – ᴿHZ 259 (1994) 153s (Barbara *Patzek*).

Q6.5   **Alexander, Seleucidae; historia Hellenismi.**

11224 **Bearzot** Cinzia,   Storia e storiografia ellenistica in PAUSANIA il periegeta: Ricerche Univ. Venezia. Venezia 1992, Cardo. 311 p.
11225 **Bengtson** Hermann,   Die hellenistische Weltkultur 1988 ➤ 5,b542... 9,12602: ᴿRBgPg 72 (1994) 170 (H. *Verdin*).
11226 ᴱ**Bilde** P., *al.*, Ethnicity in Hellenistic Egypt [1990]: StHCiv 3. Aarhus 1992, Univ. 210 p. Dk 158. 87-7288-359-6. – ᴿAntClas 63 (1994) 253-262 (F. *Colin*).
11227 ᴱ**Bilde** Per, *al.*, Centre and periphery in the Hellenistic world: Studies in Hellenistic Civilization 4. Aarhus 1993, Univ. 357 p. 87-7288-317-0.
11228 *Bloedow* Edmund F.,   Alexander's speech on the eve of the siege of Tyre: AntClas 63 (1994) 65-76.
11229 **Borza** Eugene N.,   In the shadow of Olympus; the emergence of Macedon 1990 ➤ 6,b642 ... 9,12604: ᴿEngHR 109 (1994) 675s (S. *Hornblower*).
11230 **Bowersock** G.W.,   Hellenism in Late Antiquity 1990 ➤ 6,b645... 9,12606: ᴿJRomArch 6 (1993) 461-6 (S. *Swain*).
11231 **Buckler** J.,   Philip II and the Sacred War: Mnemosyne supp. 109. Leiden 1989. 212 + xvi p.; 12 pl.; 4 maps. – ᴿEos 81 (1993) 301-4 (S. *Sprawski*).
11232 *Frazier* Françoise,   À propos de la dispositio du Sur l'ambassade infidèle; strategie rhetorique et analyse politique chez DÉMOSTHÈNE: RÉG 107 (1994) 414ss.
11233 *Gabrielsen* Vincent,   *a)* Subdivisions of the state and their decrees in

Hellenistic Rhodes; – *b*) The Rhodian association honouring Diony-
sodoros from Alexandria: ClasMdv 45 (1994) 117-135 / 137-160.
11234 *Gauthier* Philippe, Les rois hellénistiques et les juges étrangers; à
propos de décrets de Kimôlos et de Laodicée du Lykos: JSav 94 (1994)
165-193.
11235 **Green** Peter, Alexander of Macedon, 356-323 B.C.: a historical biography 1991 ► 7,b289 ... 9,12615:   ᴿMedvHum 20 (1994) 233s (D.
Bevington).
11236 ᴱ**Green** Peter, Hellenistic history and culture [symposium Univ. Texas,
Austin 20-22.X.1988]: Hellenistic culture and society 9. Berkeley 1993,
Univ. California. xvi-293 p.; 39 fig. 0-521-07564-1.
11237 *Grignaschi* M., La figure d'Alexandre chez les Arabes et sa genèse:
ArabScPh 2 (C 1992) 205-234.
11238 **Grzybek** Erhard, Du calendrier macédonien ... [diss. Genève 1987] 1990
► 7,b291; 8,d163:   ᴿBO 51 (1994) 5-20 (A. *Spalinger*); Mnemosyne 47
(1994) 287s (R. A. *Worp*); Gnomon 66 (1994) 325-331 (W. *Ameling*).
11239 **Günther** R., *Müller* R., Das goldene Zeitalter; Utopien der helleni-
stich-römischen Antike 1988 ► 9,12618: ᴿGrazB 20 (1994) 302-8 (F. F.
Schwarz).
11240 **Hammond** N. G. L., Sources for Alexander the Great 1993 ► 9,12619:
ᴿAntClas 63 (1994) 524 (J.-M. *Bertrand*); ClasR 44 (1994) 344s (J.
Moles); Gnomon 66 (1994) 320-5 (M. *Zahrnt*); MusHelv 51 (1994) 259 (U.
Hackl).
11241 **Hansen** Mogens H., The Athenian democracy in the age of De-
mosthenes 1991 ► 9,12622: ᴿHZ 259 (1994) 159-162 (K.-J. *Hölkeskamp*).
11242 **Heckel** Waldemar, The marshals of Alexander's empire 1992 ► 9,
12623; Routledge. map.; £45; 0-415-05053-7: ᴿAntClas 63 (1994) 525s
(J.-M. *Bertrand*); ÉtClas 62 (1994) 411s (H. *Leclercq*); HZ 259 (1994) 162s
(P. *Högemann*: improved updating of BERVE H. 1926).
11244 *a*) *Hiescu* V., Alexander der Grosse und Dromichaites; – *b*) *Vidman* L.,
Ägypter ausserhalb Ägypten in der Kaiserzeit: ► 41, ᴱGEROV B., 1990,
101-113 / 250-266.
11245 **Hölbl** Günther, Geschichte des Ptolemäerreiches; Politik, Ideologie und
religiöse Kultur von Alexander dem Grossen bis zur römischen Eroberung. Da 1994, Wiss. xxxii-402 p.; Bibliog. xv-xxxii. 3-534-10422-6.
11246 **Huss** Werner, Der makedonische König und die ägyptischen Priester;
Studien zur Geschichte des ptolemäischen Ägypten: HistEinz 85. Stu
1994, Steiner. 230 p.; Bibliog. 187-211. 3-515-06502-4.
11247 ᴱ**Leyton-Brown** Kenneth B., *Cleveland* Ray L., Alexander the Great,
an exercise in the study of history: Perspectives in history 2, 1992 ► 9,
12626; 0-932626-02-5: ᴿClasW 88 (1994s) 496 (Sally *Rackley*; an excellent exercise, though not a biography).
11248 I Macedoni da Filippo II alla conquista romana [CNRS 1993], ᵀ*Rohr*
Francesca, ᴱ*Bearzot* Cinzia. Mi 1993, Jaca. 256 p.; 200 color. fot.
Lᵐ 160. – ᴿCC 145 (1994,3) 337 (A. *Ferrua*).
11249 *McKechnie* Paul, Early Hellenistic history; nineties approaches [GRAIN-
GER J., LUND H., BILLOWS R., SHERWIN-WHITE R.]: Prudentia 26,2
(1994) 29-46.
11250 **Meissner** Burkhard, Historiker zwischen Polis und Königshof; Studien
zur Stellung der Geschichtsschreiber in der griechischen Gesellschaft in
spätklassischer und frühhellenistischer Zeit: Hypomnemata 99, 1992
► 9,12628; 3-525-25198-8: ᴿAntClas 63 (1994) 370 (Véronique *Krings*).
11251 *Muccioli* Federicomaria, Considerazioni generali sull'epiteto *philádel*-

phos nelle dinastie ellenistiche e sulla sua applicazione nella titolatura degli ultimi Seleucidi: Historia 43 (1994) 402-422.
11252 **O'Brien** J. M.,   Alexander... the invisible enemy 1992 ➤ 8,d169; 9, 12629:   RAmHR 99 (1994) 206s (F. L. *Holt*).
11253 *Podes* Stephan, POLYBIUS and 'induction'; commonsense reasoning in Hellenistic historiography: Eos 81 (1993) 47-56.
11254 *Riginos* Alice S.,   The wounding of Philip II of Macedon; fact and fabrication: JHS 114 (1994) 103-119.
11254* *Schmaltz* Bernhard,   Ein triumphierender Alexander?:   MiDAI-R 101 (1994) 121-9.
11255 **Sherwin-White** Susan, **Kuhrt** Amélie,   From Samarkand to Sardis... Seleucid 1993 ➤ 9,12634 [ClasW 89,76, T. R. *Martin*]:   RBL (1994) 128 (L. L. *Grabbe*); BSO 57 (1994) 367s (R. J. van der *Spek*); ClasR 44 (1994) 107-9 (S. *Mitchell*); JHS 114 (1994) 211s (F. W. *Walbank*); JIntdis 25 (1994s) 664 (F. L. *Holt*).
11256 **Shtaerman** Y. M., ⊕ Hellenism in Rome: VDI 210 (1994) 3-12; Eng. 13 (supplementing his Hellenism 1992, 140-176).
11257 **Sirinelli** Jean,   Les enfants d'Alexandre... littérature et pensée 1993 ➤ 9,12635:   RRÉG 107 (1994) 297s (V. *Boudon*).
11258 *Stoneman* Richard,   Jewish traditions on Alexander the Great: St-PhilonAn 6 (1994) 36-53.
11259 *White* John,   The improved status of Greek women in the Hellenistic period: BuBRes 39 (1994) 62-79.

Q7   Josephus Flavius.

11259* *Bammel* E.,   Von Josephus zu Hegesipp: ➤ 351*, Cristianesimo Latino e cultura greca sino al sec. IV 1992/3, 37-49.
11260 *Baumgarten* A. J., Josephus on Essene sacrifice: JJS 45 (1994) 169-183.
11261 **Begg** C.,   Josephus' account of the early divided monarchy (A.J. 8,212-420); rewriting the Bible: BtETL 108. Lv 1991, Univ. ix-377 p. Fb 2400 [NRT 117,120, J.-L. *Ska*]. – RETL 70 (1994) 151-4 (J. *Verheyden*); JJS 45 (1994) 300s (H. G. M. *Williamson*; valuable); LvSt 19 (1994) 75 (J. *Verheyden*).
11262 [*Pucci*] *Ben Zeev* Miriam, [Ant 14,217-222] Marcus Antonius, Publius Dolabella and the Jews: Athenaeum 82 (1994) 31-40.
Bergmeier Roland,   Die Essener-Berichte des Flavius 1993 ➤ 9749.
11263 *a*) *Bowley* James E.,   Josephus's use of Greek sources for biblical history; – *b*) *Feldman* Louis H.,   Josephus's portrait of Ehud [Jg 3,12-30; Ant 5,185-197]; – *c*) *Bowman* Steven,   Dates in *Seper Yosippon*: ➤ 133, FWACHOLDER B. Z., Pursuing 1994, 202-215 / 172-201 / 349-359.
11264 *a*) *Cohen* Shaye J. D., Ioudaîos tò génos and related expressions in Josephus; – *b*) *Hadas-Lebel* Mireille, Flavius Josephus, historian of Rome; – *c*) *Hata* Gohei, Imagining some dark periods in Josephus' life; – *e*) *Rajak* Tessa, [in English] Ciò che Flavio Giuseppe vide; Josephus and the Essenes: ➤ 123, Mem. SMITH M., 1992/4, 23-28 / 99-106 / 309-328 / 141-160.
11265 *Edwards* Douglas R.,   The social, religious, and political aspects of costume in Josephus: ➤ 489, World 1988/94, 153-9.
11266 *Feldman* Louis,   Josephus' portrait of Gedaliah [2 Kgs 25,22-26; Jer 40,6-41,18]: Shofar 12 (1993) 1-10 [OTAbs 17, p. 638s, with his Korah, OTEssays 6 (1993) 399-426; Gideon, RÉJ 152 (1993) 5-28; Joab, EstBib 51 (1993) 323-351; Elisha, NT 36 (1994) 1-28; Elijah, ScandJOT 8 (1994) 61-86; Jehoram, BRyl 76 (1994) 3-20].

11267 **Fenn** Richard, The death of Herod 1992 → 8,d179; 9,12646: ᴿCBQ 56 (1994) 372s (R. L. *Rohrbaugh*).
11268 *Fischer* Moshe L., *Stein* Alla, Josephus on the use of marble in building projects of Herod the Great: JJS 45 (1994) 79-85.
11269 **Gray** Rebecca, Prophetic figures in late Second Temple Palestine... Josephus 1993 → 9,12648: ᴿBL (1994) 138 (C. J. A. *Hickling*); ExpTim 105 (1993s) 345s (J. *Snaith*); IrTQ 60 (1994) 308 (W. *Riley*); JTS 45 (1994) 632s (L. L. *Grabbe*).
11270 **Hadas-Lebel** Mireille, Flavio... el judío de Roma [1989 → 5,b635], ᵀ*Colom de Llopis* María. Barc 1994, Herder. 256 p. – ᴿLumenVr 43 (1994) 377-9 (F. *Ortiz de Urtaran*).
11271 *Iamim* Anna, The right to reign [Josephus genealogy of Agrippa II pivots on women]: Jerusalem Perspective 46s [new slick color format, 1994] 10-17.
11272 ᵀᴱ**Jossa** Giorgio, Flavio Giuseppe, Autobiografia: StGiudCr 3. N 1992, D'Auria. 212 p. – ᴿRivB 42 (1994) 360-3 (Anna *Passoni dell'Acqua*).
Kottek Samuel S., Medicine and hygiene in the works of Flavius Josephus 1994 → 13500.
11272* *a) Jossa* Giorgio, Josephus' action in Galilee during the Jewish War; – *b) Rappaport* Uriel, Where was Josephus lying — in his Life or in the War?; – *c) Schwartz* Seth, Josephus in Galilee; rural patronage and social breakdown; – *d) Thoma* Clemens, John Hyrcanus I as seen by Josephus and other early Jewish sources; – *e) Schwartz* Daniel R., Josephus on Hyrcanus II; – *f) Goodman* Martin, Josephus as Roman citizen: → 123, Mem. SMITH M., 1992/4, 265-278 / 279-289 / 290-306 / 127-140 / 210-232 / 329-338.
11273 *Krieger* Klaus-Stefan, War Flavius Josephus ein Verwandter des hasmonäischen Königshauses?: BibNot 73 (1994) 58-65.
11273* **Mason** Rex, Flavius Josephus on the Pharisees: StPostB 39, 1991 → 7,b314; 8,d188: ᴿJJS 45 (1994) 134-6 (L. L. *Grabbe*); TLZ 119 (1994) 704-6 (H.-F. *Weiss*).
11274 **Mason** Steve, Josephus & NT 1992 → 8,d187; 9,12656 [BL 95,156, J. R. *Bartlett*]: ᴿCBQ 56 (1994) 607 (J. S. *Siker*); Interpretation 48 (1994) 308.310 (Marilyn *Salmon*); JRel 74 (1994) 251s (G. E. *Sterling*: praise); JRelH 18 (1994) 230-3 (M. *Harding*); NT 36 (1994) 302-4 (Nina L. *Collins*); OrChrPer 60 (1994) 269s (G. *Traina*); TLond 97 (1994) 54 (P. J. *Esler*: too concerned with first-century personalities instead of 'bedrock economic and social realities'); TorJT 10 (1994) 109s (G. *Boccaccini*).
11275 *Millar* Fergus, Taking the measure of the ancient world (Presidential address, Durham 1993): ProcClasAsn 90 (1993) 11-34: Josephus on Daniel; 4 Mcb, JEROME's Vulgate...
11276 *Neyrey* Jerome H., Josephus' Vita and the encomium; a native model of personality: JStJud 25 (1994) 177-206.
11277 **Schreckenberg** Heinz, **Schubert** Kurt, Jewish historiography and iconography: CompRerNT 3/2, 1992 → 8,d195: ᴿJStJud 25 (1994) 121 (L. L. *Grabbe*).
11277* *Schunck* Klaus-D., Hoherpriester und politiker? die Stellung der Hohenpriester von Jaddua bis Jonatan zur jüdischen Gemeinde und zum hellenistischen Stadt: VT 44 (1994) 498-512.
11278 **Schwartz** Seth, Josephus and Judaean politics 1990 → 6,b695...9, 12664: ᴿJRS 84 (1994) 263s (N. *Kokkinos*).
Sterling Gregory E., Historiography and self-definition; Josephos... 1992 → 4917.

11280 *Williams* David S., Josephus, stylometry, and Jewish studies [frequency of certain particles validates authorship and style-comparison with STRABO and others]: Shofar 11 (Purdue 1993) 16-34 [< OTAbs 17, p. 194].

11281 *Williams* D. S., On Josephus' use of NICOLAUS of Damascus; a stylometric analysis of BJ 1, 225-273 and AJ 14,280-369: ↠ 9,102*, FMERIDOR R., ScrClasIsr 12 (1993s) 176-187 [< JStJud 25,166].

Q8.1   *Roma Pompeii et Caesaris*   – Hyrcanus to Herod.

11282 *Achard* Guy, Bellum iustum, bellum acceleratum sous les rois et dans la République: BStLat 24 (1994) 474-486.

11283 *Ameling* Walter, Augustus und Agrippa; Bemerkungen zu PKöln VI 249: Chiron 24 (1994) 1-28.

11284 *Bauman* R. A., Tanaquil-Livia and the death of Augustus: Historia 43 (1994) 177-188.

11285 *Bell* Albert A.J, Fact and *exemplum* in the deaths of Pompey and Caesar: Latomus 53 (1994) 824-836.

11286 *Bell* R., The language of classical Latin poets as an indication of familiarity with Jewish institutions: AcClas 35 (1992) 61-71.

11287 **Belli** Carlo, Antipatia per POLIBIO; il greco storico della grandezza di Roma (200 a.C.-120 a.C.). Lecce/Cavallino 1992, Capone. 43 p.

11287* **Bergemann** Claudia, Politik und Religion in spätrepublikanischen Rom: Palingenesia 18. Stu 1992, Steiner. 166 p. – RGnomon 66 (1994) 560-3 (C. *Radke*).

11288 *Bertrand-Ecanvil* Estelle, Présages et propagande idéologique; à propos d'une liste concernant Octavien Auguste: MÉF 106 (1994) 487-531.

11289 *Blois* Lukas de, SUETON., Aug. 46 und die Manipulation des mittleren Militärkaders als politisches Instrument: Historia 43 (1994) 324-345.

11290 **Boldán** J. M., El imperialismo romano; Roma y la conquista del mondo mediterraneo (264-133 a.C.): HistUnivAnt 11. M 1994, Sintesis. 240 p. 84-7738-327-1. – RGerión 12 (1994) 359-362 (D. *Plácido*).

11291 *Bonnefond-Coudry* Marianne, Le *princeps senatus*; vie et mort d'une institution républicaine: MÉF 105 (1993) 103-134.

11292 **Christ** Karl, Krise und Untergang der römischen Republik³ (mit Nachtrag). Da 1993, Wiss. xv-550 p.

11293 EClemente Guido, *Gabba* Emilio, L'impero mediterraneo, 1. La repubblica imperiale: Storia di Roma 2. T 1990, Einaudi. xi-1044 p.; ill. Lm 130. 88-06-11741-6. – RLatomus 53 (1994) 468s (J. *Debergh*).

11294 **Cluett** Ronald G. A., The posthumous reputation of Pompey the Great: diss. Princeton Univ. 1994. 271 p. 94-10112. – DissA 54 (1993s) 4217.

11295 *Cordier* Pierre, M. Caelius Rufus [17 lettres à CICÉRON, ECavarzere A. 1983]; le préteur récalcitrant: MÉF 106 (1994) 533-577.

11296 **David** J.-M., Le patronat judiciaire au dernier siècle de la république romaine: BÉF 277. R 1992, École Française de Rome. xxi-952 p.; 8 fig.; 8 pl. 2-7283-0237-1. – RJRS 84 (1994) 212s (A. *Lintott*: erudite); VDI 210 (1994) 58-77 (G. S. *Knabe* ❸, Eng. 78).

11297 *David* Jean-Michel, Conformismo et transgression; à propos du tribunal de la plèbe à la fin de la République romaine: Klio 75 (1994) 210-227; Eng. 227.

11298 **De Libero** Loretana, Obstruktion: politische Praktiken im Senat und in der Volksversammlung der ausgehenden römischen Republik (70-49 v.Chr.) [Diss. Gö 1991]: Hermes Einz 59. Stu 1992, Steiner. 142 p. DM 58. 3-515-06180-0. – ᴿAntClas 63 (1994) 539s (Marianne *Bonnefond-Coudry*).

11299 **Dettenhofer** Maria H., Perdita iuventus; zwischen den Generationen von Caesar und Augustus: Vestigia 44. Mü 1992, Beck. xii-360 p. DM 138. 3-406-35856-X. – ᴿLatomus 53 (1994) 442s (C. *Edwards*); RÉLat 72 (1994) 336-8 (P. M. *Martin*).

11300 *Dreher* Martin, ❻ Pompey in the Caucasus; Colchis, Iberia, Albania, ᵀ*Vilogradov* Yu. G.: VDI 208 (1994) 20-32; Eng. 32.

11301 ᴱ**Eder** Walter, Staat und Staatlichkeit 1988/90 ➤ 6,732: ᴿLatomus 53 (1994) 657-660 (J. *Poucet*).

11302 Rufus Festus, Abrégé des hauts faits du peuple romain: Coll. Budé. P 1994, BLettres. xliv-83 p.

11303 **Freber** Philipp-Stephan G., Der hellenistische Osten und das Illyricum unter Caesar: Palingenesia 42, 1993 ➤ 9,12677: ᴿClasR 44 (1994) 350s (A. *Erskine*); Gerión 12 (1994) 350-2 (A. J. *Dominguez Monedero*).

11304 **Fuhrman** Manfred, CICERO and the Roman republic, ᵀ*Yuill* W. E. CM 1992, Blackwell. viii-249 p. $35. – ᴿAmHR 99 (1994) 532s (K. S. *Sacks*: 'we know more about Cicero than about any other person from antiquity').

11305 *Girardet* Klaus-M., 'Traditionalismus' in der Politik des Oktavian/ Augustus — mentalitätsgeschichtliche Aspekte: Klio 75 (1993) 203-218.

11306 **Goodblatt** S., The monarchic principle; studies in Jewish self-government in antiquity: TStAJ 38. Tü 1994, Mohr. xii-366 p. DM 188. 3-16-146176-2 [NTAbs 38, p. 489].

11307 **Gowing** Alain M., The triumviral narratives of APPIAN and CASSIUS [DIO]: MgClas. AA 1992, Univ. Michigan. xiii-374 p.; 9 fig. $42.50. 0-472-10294-2. – ᴿGreeceR 41 (1994) (T. *Wiedemann*: how their tastes dictated selection among the same sources); JRS 84 (1994) 225s (C. *Pelling*: praise).

11308 *Gray-Pov* Michael J. G., Qui mare teneat (Cic. Att. 10,8); Caesar, Pompey, and the waves [sea-war 49-46 B.C.]: ClasMedv 44 (K 1993) 141-179.

11309 **Gruen** Erich S., Culture and national identity in republican Rome: StClasPg 52, 1992 ➤ 9,12679; 0-8014-2759-2: ᴿAJA 98 (1994) 174-7 (K. *Galinsky*); Athenaeum 82 (1994) 586-8 (E. *Gabba*); JRS 84 (1994) 208s (Catharine *Edwards*).

11310 **Hinard** François, La République romaine: Que sais-je? 686. P 1992, PUF. 125 p. 2-13-044546-2. – ᴿAntClas 63 (1994) 537 (P. *Simelon*); Latomus 53 (1994) 439s (R. *Combès*); Mnemosyne 47 (1994) 272s (P. J. J. *Vanderbroeck*).

11311 ᴱ**Hunink** Vincent, Julius CAESAR, Bellum Civile 3. Amst 1991. xxiii-305 p. £75. – ᴿGnomon 66 (1994) 593-6 (M. G. *Schmidt*).

11312 *Jacobson* David M., King Herod, Roman citizen and benefactor of Kos: BAngIsr 13 (1993s) 31-35.

11313 **Kokkinos** N., Antonia Augusta (daughter of Mark Antony). L 1992, Routledge. xviii-254 p.; 111 fig. £35. – ᴿClassR 44 (1994) 129s (B. *Campbell*).

11314 **Liberman** Saul, ❻ Greek and Hellenism in Jewish Palestine. J 1994, Bialik/Yad Ben Zvi. xvi-328 p. [OIAc 7,33].

11314* **McLaren** James S., Power and politics 1991 ➤ 7,b339 … 9,12685: ᴿCritRR 6 (1993) 142-4 (J. C. *VanderKam*).

11315 *Martin* Paul M., 'Imperator > Rex', recherche sur les fondements républicains romains de cette inadéquation idéologique: Pallas 41 (1994) 7-26.

11315* *Pina Polo* Francisco, Ideología y práctica política en la Roma tardorrepublicana: Gerión 12 (1994) 69-94; Eng. 69.

11316 **Potter** David S., Prophets and emperors; human and divine authority from Augustus to Theodosius: Revealing Antiquity 7. CM 1994, Harvard Univ. x-281 p. 0-674-71565-9.

11317 ᴱ**Raaflaub** K. A., *Toher* M., Between republic and empire; Augustus 1987/90 ➤ 6,764; 8,d251: ᴿAnzAltW 46 (1993) 50-56 (G. *Dobesch*); EngHR 109 (1994) 199s (A. *Lintott*); Gnomon 66 (1994) 237-246 (M. G. *Schmidt*).

11318 **Rosenstein** Nathan S., Imperatores victi 1990 ➤ 8,d227: ᴿGnomon 66 (1994) 332-341 (K.-J. *Hölkeskamp*).

11319 [ᴱ*Schiavone* Aldo *al.*], Storia di Roma 2. L'impero mediterraneo, 1. La repubblica imperiale. T 1990, Einaudi. xxxix-1044 p. – ᴿAthenaeum 82 (1994) 260-2 (D. *Asheri*).

11320 **Schwartz** Daniel R., Agrippa I 1990 ➤ 8,d259: ᴿCritRR 5 (1992) 101-3 (H. W. *Hoehner*).

11321 **Simon** Barbara, Die Selbstdarstellung des Augustus in der Münzprägung und in den Res Gestae: Antiquitates 4. Ha 1993, Kovač. vii-212 p.

11322 **Sullivan** Richard D., Near Eastern royalty and Rome, 100-30 BC 1990 ➤ 6,b741 ... 9,12702: ᴿCdÉ 69 (1994) 184s (J. *Bingen*); JRomA 7 (1994) 447-453 (K. *Butcher*).

11323 **Vollmer** Dankward, Symploke 1990 ➤ 7,b353: ᴿHZ 259 (1994) 168-170 (P. *Barceló*).

11324 **Wallace-Hadrill** Andrew, Augustan Rome: ClasWorld. L 1993, Bristol Classical. xii-105 p.; 35 fig. £7 pa. – ᴿClasR 44 (1994) 414s (A. T. *Fear*); GreeceR 41 (1994) 234 (T. *Wiedemann*); Prudentia 26,2 (1994) 60-63 (V. J. *Gray*).

11325 *Wardle* D., [Vipsanius] Agrippa's refusal of a triumph in 19 B.C.: Antichthon 28 (1994) 58-64.

11326 *Warszawski* Abraham, *Peretz* Abraham, ❻ [Herod] Building the Temple mount; organization and execution: CHistEI 66 (1992) 3-46; Eng. 191.

11327 **Will** W., Der römische Mob; soziale Konflikte in der späten Republik 1991 ➤ 7,b354: ᴿMnemosyne 46 (1993) 423-5 (P. J. J. *Vanderbroeck*).

Q8.4   Zeitalter Jesu Christi: particular/general.

11328 *a) Arnaud* Pascal, Transmarinae provinciae; réflexions sur les limites géographiques et sur la nature des pouvoirs en Orient des 'corégents' sous les règnes d'Auguste et de Tibère; – *b) Hurlet* Frédéric, Recherches sur la durée de l'*imperium* des 'co-régents' sous les principats d'Auguste et de Tibère: CahGlotz 5 (1994) 221-253 / 255-289.

11329 *Geiger* Joseph ❻ [Second Sophistic] Greek orators in Palestine: CHistEI 66 (1992) 47-50; Eng. 191.

11330 *Herz* Peter, Die Adoptivsöhne des Augustus und der Festkalender; Gedanken zu einer Inschrift aus Messene [SEG 23 (1968) 206]: Klio 75 (1993) 272-288; Eng. 288.

11331 **Millar** Fergus, The Roman Near East, 31 B.C.-A.D. 337: 1993 ➤ 9, 12718: ᴿBAR-W 20,6 (1994) 9 . 74 (L. H. *Feldman*: masterful); ClasB 70 (Wauconda 1994) 113-6 (J. G. *Keenan*); EngHR 109 (1994) 1223s (B.

Campbell: a remarkable synthesis); JRS 84 (1994) 244-6 (M. *Gawlikowski*: standard reference).

11332 **Niswonger** Richard L., New Testament History. GR pa. 1992 = 1998 [➤ 6,b674 ... 9,12719], Zondervan. 332 p. $15. – ᴿSWJT 36,3 (1993s) 64 (H. A. *Brehm*).

11333 **Pani** M., Potere e valori a Roma fra Augusto e Traiano². Bari 1993, Edipuglia. 280 p. Lᵐ 50. 88-7228-674-5. – ᴿAthenaeum 82 (1994) 607-9 (A. *Marcone*).

11334 ᴱ**Pani** Mario, Continuità repubblica/principato 1989/91 ➤ 8,672*e*: ᴿLatomus 53 (1994) 472 (J.-G. *Richard*).

11334* *Silberman* Neil A., Searching for Jesus; the politics of first-century Judea: Archaeology 47,6 (1994) 30-40.

11335 **Vouga** François, Geschichte des frühen Christentum: Uni-Tb 1733. Tü 1994, Francke. xiv-287 p. 3-8252-1733-7.

Q8.7 *Roma et Oriens,* **prima decennia post Christum.**

11336 ᴱ**Alexander** Loveday, Images of empire: jOsu 122, 1991 ➤ 7,412 ... 9,12727: ᴿBInterp 1 (1993) 383s (R. A. *Burridge*).

11337 **Baudy** G., Die Brände Roms 1992 ➤ 8,d269; 9,12733: ᴿGnomon 66 (1994) 40-43 (J. *Rüpke*).

11337* *Benario* Herbert W., Recent work on Tacitus, 1984-1993: ClasW 89 (1995s) 91-162.

11338 **Ben-Shalom** I. ❶ *The Beth Shammai,* school of Shammai and the Zealots' struggle against Rome. J 1994, Yad Ben Zvi / Negev Univ. 366 p. – ᴿZion 59 (1994) 515-520 (M. *Schwartz,* ❶).

11338 *Blänsdorf* Jürger, Die Kunst der historischen Szene in den Annalen des TACITUS: Latomus 53 (1994) 761-778.

11339 *Bollansée* Jan, P. Fay. 19 [from Umm el-ʿAtl, now in Chicago Or. Inst.] Hadrian's memoirs and imperial epistolary autobiography [his letter to 'Dear Antoninus' Pius, his successor]: AncSoc 25 (1994) 279-302.

11340 **Devillers** Olivier, L'art de la persuasion dans les Annales de TACITE: Latomus coll. 223. Bru 1994. 390 p.

11341 ᴱ**Borzsák** S., (*Wellesley* K.). TACITI I, 1991s ➤ 9,12734: ᴿGnomon 66 (1994) 216-221 (A. J. *Woodman*).

11342 *Cizek* Eugène, À propos de la guerre parthique de Trajan: Latomus 53 (1994) 376-385.

11343 ᵀᴱ**Edmondson** Jonathan, Dio, the Julio-Claudians; selections from Books 58-63 of the Roman History of CASSIUS DIO: Lactor 15. L 1992, Asn. Classical Teachers. 275 p.; 2 maps. £5.50. – ᴿGreeceR 41 (1994) 96s (T. *Wiedemann*).

11344 *Follet* Simone, Lettres d'Hadrien aux Épicuriens d'Athènes: RÉG 107 (1994) 158-171.

11345 *Gys-Devic,* —, SUÉTONE face à Chrestus: CahRenan 184 (1993) 33-59 [pp. 41-84 unexplainably after p. 123]; 187 (1994) 63-93 (Clément).

11346 **Hadas-Lebel** Mireille, Jérusalem contre Rome 1990 ➤ 6,b792 ... 9,12745: ᴿRHR 211 (1994) 470-2 (M. *Benarou*).

11347 *Heil* Matthäus, Die orientalische Aussenpolitik des Kaisers Nero: Diss. Würzburg 1993 [> Mü tuduv]. – Chirōn 24 (1994) 443.

11348 **Hurley** Donna W., An historical and historiographical commentary on SUETONIUS' Life of C. Caligula: AmerClasSt 32, 1993 ➤ 9,12745*: ᴿGreeceR 41 (1994) 235 (T. *Wiedemann*).

11349 **Jones** Brian W., The emperor Domitian 1992 ➤ 9,12747: L 1992, Routledge. xi-292 p. £30. – ᴿHZ 259 (1994) 456-8 (K. *Strobel*).

11350 a) *Kearsley* R.W., The Asiarchs; – b) *Horsley* G.H.R., The politarchs; – c) *Clarke* Andrew D., Rome and Italy: ➤ 247, Acts Graeco-Roman 1994, 363-376 / 419-431 / 455-481.

11351 **Levick** Barbara, Claudius 1990 ➤ 6,b794*...8,d282: ᴿGnomon 66 (1994) 143-7 (E. *Flaig*).

11352 (Santoro) *L'hoir* Francesca, TACITUS and women's usurpation of power: ClasW 88 (1994s) 5-25.

11353 *Lindsay* Hugh, SUETONIUS as *ab epistulis* to Hadrian and the early history of the imperial correspondence: Historia 43 (1994) 454-468.

11354 ᵀ**McGushin** Patrick, SALLUST, The Histories [1,1992 ➤ 8,d283] 2, books 3-4. Ox 1994, UP. x-259 p. £30. – ᴿGreeceR 41 (1994) 254 (T. *Wiedemann*: since the Press allowed no Latin text, MAURENBRECHER is preferable to REYNOLDS but with problems of changed numbering). – ᴿÉtClas 62 (1994) 81s (P. *Hamblenne*, 1).

11355 **Marks** R.G., The image of Bar Kokhba in traditional Jewish literature; false Messiah and national hero: Hermeneutics. Univ. Park 1994, Penn. State. xiii-226 p. $35; pa. $16. 0-271-00939-X; -40-4 [NTAbs 38, p.493].

11356 **Mellor** Ronald, TACITUS. NY 1993, Routledge. xii-211 p. £25. – ᴿAmHR 99 (1994) 1665 (A.M. *Ward*); ClasR 44 (1994) 282s (J.W. *Rich*).

11357 **Millar** Fergus, The emperor in the Roman World (31 B.C.-A.D. 337). Ithaca NY 1992 = 1977, Cornell Univ. xii-673. $22 pa. [Manuscripta 36,254, high praise].

11359 *Morgan* M. Gwyn, Vespasian's fears of assassination (TACITUS, Histories 2, 74-75): Philologus 138 (1994) 118-128.

11360 **Paltiel** Eliezer, Vassals and rebels in the Roman Empire; Julio-Claudian policies in Judaea and the kingdom of the East: Coll. Latomus 212, 1991 ➤ 7,b402...9,12754: ᴿBStLat 24 (1994) 687-690 (Anna *D'Arrigo*); RÉtClas 62 (1994) 413s (O. *Devillers*); BgPg 72 (1994) 180 (J.A. *Straus*).

11361 **Price** Jonathan J., Jerusalem under siege 1992 ➤ 8,d292; 9,12755: ᴿCBQ 56 (1994) 145-7 (C.R. *Kazmierski*); ÉtClas 62 (1994) 311s (H. *Leclercq*); Latomus 53 (1994) 883s (J.-M. *Bertrand*); NT 36 (1994) 299-302 (Nina L. *Collins*).

11362 *Richard* Jean-Claude, Sur une source possible de TACITE, Annales XI, 23, 2-3: Latomus 53 (1994) 594-604.

11363 **Rudich** Vasily, Political dissidence under Nero; the price of dissimilation. L 1993, Routledge. xxxiv-354 p. £35. 0-415-06951-3. – ᴿAntClas 63 (1994) 542s (J.-P. *Martin*); ClasR 44 (1994) 348-350 (B. *Campbell*); HZ 259 (1993) 771-3 (Maria H. *Dettenhofer*).

11363* *Rutgers* Leonard V., Roman policy toward the Jews; expulsions from the city of Rome during the first century C.E.: ClasAnt 13 (1994) 56-74.

11364 **Schwartz** Daniel B., Agrippa I ᵀ1990 (Tü, Mohr; xviii-233 p.) ➤ 9, 12757: ᴿCiuD 207 (1994) 194s (J. *Gutiérrez*).

11364* *Schwier* Helmut, Tempel und Tempelzerstörung... 66-74 n.Chr.: NOrb 11, 1989 ➤ 5,b723...9,12758: ᴿCritRR 5 (1992) 384s (L. *Gaston*).

11365 **Setzer** Claudia J., Jewish responses to early Christians; history and polemics, 30-150 C.E. Mp 1994, Fortress. viii-254 p.; bibliog. 221-243. 0-8006-2680-X.

11366 ᵀᴱ**Shotter** David, SUETONIUS [VII], The lives of Galba, Otho, Vitellius. Wmr 1993, Aris & P. xx-199 p. – ᴿRÉLat 72 (1994) 275s (T. *Vernet*).

11367 *Sordi* Marta, Il De vita sua di CLAUDIO e le caratteristiche di Claudio come storico di se stesso e di Roma: RLomb 127 (1993) 213-9.

11368 **Urner** Christina, Kaiser Domitian im Urteil antiker Quellen und moderner Forschung: Diss. Augsburg 1993. – Chiron 24 (1994) 445.

Q9.1   *Historia Romae generalis et* **post-christiana.**

11369 *Angiolani* Stefano, Alessandro Severo e i cristiani nell'Historia Augusta: AnMacerata 27 (1994) 9-31.

11370 **Becher** Armin, Rom und die Chatten [Germanen]. Da 1992, Hess. Hist. Komm. 414 p.; 7 maps. – ᴿKlio 76 (1994) 528s (Gerda von *Bülow*).

11371 ᴱ**Blagg** Thomas, *Millett* Martin, The early Roman Empire in the west. Ox 1990, Oxbow. iv-250 p.; 66 fig. £18. - ᴿClasR 44 (1994) 132s (C. M. *Wells*).

11372 **Blockley** R. C., East Roman foreign policy; formation and conduct from Diocletian to Anastasius: ARCA 30. Leeds 1992, Cairns. viii-283 p.; 4 maps. £35. 0-905205-83-9. – ᴿAthenaeum 82 (1994) 605s (A. *Marcone*); ByZ 86 (1994) 139-141 (Linda-M. *Günther*); ClasR 94 (1994) 134s (M. *Whitby*); ClasW 88 (1994s) 127 (S. A. *Stertz*); HZ 259 (1994) 176s (R. *Schulz*); JRS 84 (1994) 282s (J. D. *Howard-Johnston*).

11373 ᴱ**Boeft** J. den, *al.*, Cognitio gestorum; the historiographic art of AMMIANUS Marcellinus. Amst 1992, Ned. Akad. ix-130 p. – ᴿClasR 44 (1994) 60s (M. J. *Edwards*).

11374 **Briscoe** John, Titi LIVI 31-40 (I. 31-35; II. 36-40]: BtScrGR. Stu 1991, Teubner. xxxvi/xvi-820 p. 3-519-01492-0; -3-9. – ᴿLatomus 53 (1994) 178-180 (J. *Hellegouarc'h*).

11375 — **Jal** Paul, Tite-Live, Histoire romaine, Tome XI, Livre XXIʳᵉᵛ. P 1991, BLettres. lxxxii-140 (d.) p.; 2 maps. 2-251-01345-8. – ᴿLatomus 53 (1994) 635s (L. *Bussone*).

11376 *Bujskich* Sergei, Zum Limes im nördlichen Schwarzmeerraum, ᵀ*Heinen* Heinz: BonnJbb 194 (1994) 165-174; 3 fig.

11377 **Burck** Erich, Das Geschichtswerk des Titus LIVIUS: BtKlasAltW 2/87. Heid 1992, Winter. xx-290 p. 3-533-04559-5. – ᴿLatomus 53 (1994) 427s (P. *Jal*).

11378 ᴱ**Caiazza** Antonio, PLUTARCO, Monarchia, democrazia, oligarchia: Moralium 15. 85 p. 88-7092-056-9.

11379 ᵀᴱ**Callu** J.-P., Histoire Auguste I/1, Introd., Vies d'Hadrien, Aelius, Antonin: Coll. Budé. P 1992, BLettres. cxiv-177 (d.) p. – ᴿAntClas 63 (1994) 418-420 (M.-Thérèse *Raepsaet-Charlier*); RÉLat 72 (1994) 259-265 (J.-L. *Charlet*).

11380 **Cantarella** E., I suplici capitali in Grecia e a Roma; origini e funzioni della pena di morte nell'antichità classica. Mi 1991, Rizzoli. 439 p. – ᴿIVRA 42 (1991) 153-8 (M. *Balzarini*).
CASTAGNOLI Ferdinando mem.: Bilancio critico su Roma arcaica 1991 → 416.

11381 ᵀᴱ**Chamoux** F., *Bertrac* P., ᵀ*Vernière* Y., DIODORE de Sicile, Bibliothèque historique I: Coll. Budé. P 1993, BLettres. clxvi-231 p.; 2 maps. – ᴿClasR 44 (1994) 272-4 (J. *Moles*).

11382 — ᵀᴱ**Bommelaer** Bibiane, DIODORE de Sicile, Bibliothèque historique III: Coll. Budé. P 1989, BLettres. lxxi-152 (d.) p. – ᴿRBgPg 72 (1994) 141-3 (Liliane *Bodson*).

11383 **Cunliffe** Barry, Rome and her empire. L 1994, Constable. 320 p., mostly color photos. 0-09-473500-X.

11384 ᴱ**Dagron** G., *al.*, Évêques, moines et empereurs: Histoire du Christianisme 4. P 1993, Desclée. 1050 p. – ᴿEsprVie 104 (1994) 104-110 (P. *Ourliac*).

11385 ^E**D'Anna** Giovanni, [anon.] Origine del popolo romano: ScrittoriGL. Mi 1992, Mondadori. li-129 p. 88-04-34223-4.

11386 *Debru* Armelle,   La phrase narrative d'AMMIEN Marcellin: RPg 66 (1992) 267-287.

11387 ^E**Demandt** Barbara & Alexander, T. MOMMSEN, Römische Kaisergeschichte. [*Hensel* S. & P., Vorlesungs-Mitschriften 1882-6]. Mü 1992, Beck. 634 p. DM 98. – ^RGrazB 20 (1994) 308-314 (W. *Nippel*); HZ 259 (1994) 109-118 (C. *Gizewski*).

11388 ^E**Dodgeon** Michael H., *Lieu* Samuel N.C., The Roman Eastern frontier and the Persian wars A.D. 226-363; a documentary history 1991 ➤ 7,b195; 8,d36: ^RPrudentia 15,1 (Auckland 1993) 83s (P. *McKechnie*).

11389 **Edwards** Catharine, The politics of immorality in ancient Rome 1993 ➤ 9,12784: ^RJRS 84 (1994) 186-8 (Miriam *Griffin*: Latin moralizing rhetoric of the immoral).

11390 *Erskine* Andrew, The Romans as common benefactors: Historia 43 (1994) 70-87.

11391 **Filoramo** Giovanni, *Roda* Sergio, Cristianesimo e società antica. R 1992, Laterza. xii-294 p. L^m 46. – ^RCC 145 (1994,1) 97s (A. *Ferrua*).

11392 **Flaig** Egon, Den Kaiser herausfordern, die Usurpation im Römischen Reich: HistSt 7. Fra 1992, Campus. 605 p. DM 98 pa. – ^RClasR 44 (1994) 130-132 (A. *Lintott*).

11393 *Fox* Matthew, History and rhetoric in DIONYSIUS of Halicarnassus: JRS 83 (1993) 31-47.

11394 **Freyburger** M.-Laure, *Roddaz* J.-M., DION CASSIUS, Histoire romaine 48s. [50s.]: Coll.Budé, P 1994 [1991], BLettres. clxvii-213 p. [xcix-176]; bibliog. vii-xviii. 2-251-00441-6 [-16-5]. – ^RAntClas 63 (1994) 178s (M.-Thérèse *Raepsaet-Charlier*).

11395 *Fromentin* Valérie, Les manuscrits récents du Livre I et l'épitomé des Antiquités Romaines de DENYS d'Halicarnasse: RHText 21 (1994) 93-115.

11396 *Galsterer* Hartmut, Regionen und Regionalismus im römischen Italien: Historia 43 (1994) 306-323.

11397 **Gardner** Jane F., Being a Roman citizen. L 1993, Routledge. vii-244 p.

11398 ^E**Giardina** Andrea, The Romans [ital. 1989], ^T*Cochrane* Lydia G. Ch 1993, Univ. x-393 p. $63; pa $20. – ^RClasR 44 (1994) 414 (D. *Noy*: about men).

11399 *Gordon* Richard, *al.*, Roman inscriptions 1986-90; JRS 83 (1993) 131-158.

11400 ^E**Gottlieb** Günther, *Barceló* Pedro, Christen und Heiden in Staat und Gesellschaft des 2. bis 4. Jahrhunderts; Gedanken und Thesen zu einem schwierigen Verhältnis: Univ. Augsburg hist./soz. 44, 1992 ➤ 8,392*: ^RAnStoEseg 11 (1994) 641s (F. *Ruggiero*); AntClas 63 (1994) 460 (J. *Wankenne*); BonnJbb 194 (1994) 596-8 (R. *Klein*); Klio 76 (1994) 515 (E. *Heck*); Latomus 53 (1994) 667-9 (M. *Sordi*); RHE 89 (1994) 779s (Nicole *Zeegers*).

11401 **Grant** Michael, The Antonines; the Roman Empire in transition. L 1994, Routledge. xiii-210 p.; 27 fig. 0-415-10754-7.

11402 *Honoré* Tony, Lawyers and government in the 'Historia Augusta': IVRA 42 (1991) 13-41.

11403 **Jacks** Philips, The antiquarian and the myth of antiquity; the origins of Rome in Renaissance thought. C 1993, Univ. 368 p. 0-521-44152-8. – ^RÉchMClas 38 (1994) 455-8 (J. *Osborne*).

11404 ^E**Jenkyns** R., The legacy of Rome; a new appraisal [14 authors] 1992 ➤ 8,656d; 0-19-821917-2: ^RJRS 83 (1993) 266s (D. *West*).

11405 *Johne* Renate, Griechische und barbarische Frauengestalten bei HE-
LIODOR [von Emesa, Aethiopika, Liebesroman 3. Jh. n. Chr.]: Altertum 38
(1992) 177-185; 5 fig.

11406 **Jundzili** Juliusz, ⊘ Rzymianie a morze [the sea]. Bydgoszcz 1991.
188 p., 66 fig. – ᴿEOS 81 (1993) 135-7 (T. *Łoposzko* † ⊘).

11407 **Kienast** Dietmar, Römische Kaisertabellen 1990 ➤ 6,b838: ᴿBonnJbb
194 (1994) 580s (G. *Wirth*).

11408 *a*) *Kuhoff* Wolfgang, Zur Titulatur der römischen Kaiserinnen während
der Prinzipatszeit; – *b*) *Raepsaet-Charlier* M.-Thérèse, Nouvelles recherches sur les femmes sénatoriales du Haut-Empire romain: Klio 75 (1993)
244-255; Eng. 256 / 257-271; Eng. 271.

11409 **Lane Fox** R., Pagans and Christians 1986 ➤ 3,d87; also Ringwoord
VA 1998, Penguin. 799 p. A$25: ᴿAustralasCR 71 (1994) 251-3 (F. A.
Mecham).

11410 **Le Glay** Marcel, *al.*, Histoire romaine. P 1991, PUF. xiv-594 p.; ill.
F 129. – ᴿRBgPg 72 (1994) 175s (P. *Salmon*: pour les étudiants).

11411 **Lieu** Judith, *North* John, *Rajak* Tessa, The Jews among pagans and
Christians in the Roman Empire 1992 ➤ 8,476: ᴿAthenaeum 82 (1992)
599-602 (L. *Troiani*); JTS 45 (1994) 290-2 (R. L. *Wilken*); Prudentia 25,1
(1993) 79-82 (P. *McKechnie*).

11412 **Lindskog** C., ²*Ziegler* Konrat, ³*Gärtner* Hans, PLUTARCHI Vitae pa-
rallelae. Lp 1994, Teubner. X-152 p. DM 110. – ᴿKoinonia 18 (1994)
211 (A. *Garzya*).

11413 **Lintott** Andrew, Imperium romanum, politics and administration. L
1993, Routledge. xv-247 p.; bibliog. 232-241. £35; pa. £11. 0-4150-
1594-4; -9375-9 [BL 94,125, L. L. *Grabbe* briefly: a useful summary].
– ᴿClasR 44 (1994) 351s (G. P. *Burton*); Gerión 12 (1994) 362-4 (T.
Ñaco).

11414 **Lomas** Kathryn, Rome and the Western Greeks, 350 B.C. - A.D. 200;
conquest and acculturation in southern Italy. L 1993, Routledge. xiv-
244 p.; 12 pl.; 2 maps. £35. – ᴿClasR (1994) 354s (A. *Erskine*).

11415 **McClain** T. Davina, Gender, genre, and power; the depiction of
women in LIVY's Ab urbe condita: diss. Indiana, ᴰ*Leach* Eleanor.
Bloomington 1994. 314 p. 95-07649. — DissA 55 (1994s) p. 3181.

11416 ᴱ**Manfredini** Maria, *Piccirilli* Luigi, PLUTARCO, Vita di Nicia e di
Grasso, ᵀ*Angeli Bertinelli* M. Gabriella, *al.*: Fondazione Valla, Vite
Parallele 5. M 1993, Mondadori. 441 p. Lᵐ 45. 88-04-34496-2.

11417 *Méthy* Nicole, *a*) DION CHRYSOSTOME et la domination romaine:
AntClas 63 (1994) 173-192; – *b*) Une signification nouvelle pour le nom de
Rome au second siècle de notre ère; a propos d'une phrase de Marc-
Aurèle: RBgPg 72 (1994) 98-110.

11418 **Mrozewicz** Leszek, Municipal aristocracy in Roman provinces on the
Rhine and the Danube in the period of the Early Empire. Poznań 1989.
321 p. – ᴿClasB 69 (1993) 61 (Krystyna *Stebnicka*).

11419 ᴱ**Müller** Carl W., *al.*, Zum Umgang mit fremden Sprachen in der
griechisch-römischen Antike, Lp/Saarbrücken 21.-22. Nov. 1989: Pa-
lingenesis 1992 ➤ 8,672a; DM 76; 3-515-05852-4: ᴿAntClas 63 (1994)
430s (D. *Donnet*).

11420 **Mustakallio** Katarina, Death and disgrace; capital penalties with post
mortem sanctions in early Roman historiography: DissHumLitt 72. Helsinki 1994, Akad.Sc.Fennica. 96 p. 951-41-0739-X.

11421 **Nicolet-Croizat** Fabienne, TITE-LIVE, Histoire romaine Tome XV,
livre XXV, 1992 ➤ 9,12824: ᴿOrpheus 15 (1994) 174-7 (F. *Corsaro*).

11422 **Pallottino** Massimo,   Origini e storia primitiva di Roma: Orizzonti della storia.   Mi 1993, Rusconi.   417 p.; 32 pl.

11423 **Perelli** Luciano,   La corruzione politica nell'antica Roma.   Mi c. 1994, Rizzoli.   323 p.   L^m 15. – ^{R}Archeo 9, 116 (1994) 127 (S. *Moscati*).

11424 *Poucet* Jacques,   La fondation de Rome; croyants et agnostiques [GRANDAZZI A. 1991]: Latomus [52 (1993) 936] 53 (1994) 95-104.

11425 **Quint** David,   Epic and empire; politics and generic form from Virgil to Milton.   Princeton 1992, Univ.   x-433 p.   £35; pa. £14.50.   0-6910-6942-5; -1520-1. – ^{R}JRS 84 (1994) 202-4 (Estelle *Hahn*, also on cognate BOYLE A. 1993).

11426 **Rawson** Elizabeth † 1988,   Roman culture and society 1991 ⟶ 7,251*: ^{R}ClasR 44 (1994) 119-121 (T. P. *Wiseman*).

11427 ^{E}**Rosen** Klaus,   Macht und Kultur im Rom der Kaiserzeit: StUniv 16.   Bonn 1994, Bouvier.   190 p.

11428 *a) Rüpke* Jörg,   LIVIUS, Priesternamen und die annales maximi; – *b) Evans* Richard J., The structure and source of Livy 38.44.9 -39.44.9: Klio 75 (1993) 155-178; Eng. 179 / 180-7; deutsch 187.

11429 ^{E}**Russell** D. A.,   DIO CHRYSOSTOM, Orations VII, XII, XXXVI, 1992 ⟶ 9,12831; viii-266 p.   £37.50; pa. £15.   0-521-37348-7; -606-3: ^{R}JRS 84 (1994) 265s (H. *Sidebottom*).

11430 **Rutgers** Leonard.   The Jews in late ancient Rome; an archaeological and historical study on the interaction of Jews and non-Jews in the Roman diaspora: diss. Duke, ^{D}*Meyers* E. Durham NC, 1993. – RTLv 26,534.

11430* *a) Santirocco* Matthew S.,   HORACE and Augustan ideology; – *b) Jaeger* Mary,   Reconstructing Rome; the Campus Martius and Horace, Ode 1,8: Arethusa 28 (1995) 225-243 / 177-191.

11431 **Strobel** Karl,   Das Imperium Romanum im 3 Jhdt.; Modell einer historischen Krise? Zur Frage mentaler Strukturen breiterer Bevölkerungsschichten in der Zeit von Marc Aurel bis zum Ausgang des 3 Jh.: HistEinz 75. Stu 1993, Steiner, 408 p. – ^{R}MünstHand 13,1 (1994) 114-7 (N. *Ehrhardt*); RÉLat 72 (1994) 342-4 (G. *Sabbah*).

11432 **Sullivan** J. P.,   MARTIAL 1991 ⟶ 9,12838: ^{R}Gnomon 66 (1994) 597-600 (N. *Holzberg*); Latomus 53 (1994) 430-3 (H. D. *Jocelyn*).

11433 **Sventsitskaya** I. S.,   ❸ The religious life in Asiatic provinces of the Roman Empire 2-3 cent. A.D.; paganism and Christianity: VDI 201 (1992) 54-71; Eng. 71.

11434 **Trombley** F. R.,   Hellenic religion and Christianization, c. 370-529, II: Religions in the Graeco-Roman world 115.   Leiden 1994, Brill.   xv-430 p. *f*175 [RHE 88, 427*].

11435 **Trzaska-Richter** Christine,   Furor teutonicus; das römische Germanenbild in Politik und Propaganda von den Anfängen bis zum 2. Jahrhundert n.Chr.: Bochumer Alt-Wiss Colloquium 8.   Trier 1991, Wiss.V.   262 p. DM 42.   3-88476-014-9. – ^{R}Latomus 53 (1994) 693s (O. *Devillers*).

11436 *Tsirkin* Ju. B.,   Romanisation of Spain; socio-political aspect, II: III. Romanisation during the Early Empire, ^{T}*Chistonogova* L.: Gerión 11 (1993) 271-312; 12 (1994) 217-253.

11437 **Vidén** Gunhild,   Women in Roman literature; attitudes of authors under the early Empire. StGrL 57. Göteborg 1993, Univ.   194 p. Sk 160. – ^{R}ClasR 44 (1994) 292s (Gillian *Clark*); Gerión 12 (1994) 355s (J. L. *Posadas*); GreeceR 41 (1994) 249s (P. *Walcot*, tame but good).

11438 **Wallinger** Elisabeth,   Die Frauen in der Historia Augusta: AltHEpig 2, 1990 ⟶ 9,12884: ^{R}Gnomon 66 (1994) 275-7 (A. *Lippold*).

11439 ᵀWaterfield Robin, ᴱKidd Ian, PLUTARCH, Essays. L 1992, Penguin.
ix-430 p. 0-14-044564-1.
11440 Weeber Karl-Wilhelm, Panem et circenses; Massenunterhaltung als
Politik im antiken Rom: Bildband 15. Mainz 1994, von Zabern. 180 p.;
257 (color.) fig. DM 58. 3-8053-1580-5. – ᴿNikephoros 7 (1994) 304-310
(Augusta Hönle).
11440* Wes Marinus A., Michael ROSTOVTZEFF 1990 → 8,d371: ᴿVDI 210
(1994) 246-9 (K. A. Avetisyan, K. O. Bitukov).

Q9.5   Constantinus, Julianus, Imperium Byzantinum.

11441 Athanassiadi P., Julian² [¹1981] 1992 → 8,d375: ᴿMnemosyne 47
(1994) 411s (J. den Boeft).
11442 Barnes Timothy D., Athanasius and Constantius 1993 → 9,12850:
ᴿCathHR 80 (1994) 561-5 (C. Kannengiesser); JRS 84 (1994) 280s (Theresa Urbainczyk); Prudentia 26,2 (1994) 47-51 (M. L. Sharp); RechSR 82
(1994) 589s (B. Sesboüë); VigChr 48 (1994) 398-401 (T. M. Teeter).
11443 Bleicken Jochen, Constantin der Grosse und die Christen; Überlegungen zur konstantinischen Wende: HZ Beih. 15, 1992, → 9,12854; 3-
486-64415-7: ᴿAnStoEseg 11 (1994) 637s (F. Ruggiero); Athenaeum 82
(1994) 611s (A. Marcone); Klio 76 (1994) 535-7 (G. Weber); HZ 259
(1994) 178s (R. Klein); Latomus 53 (1994) 925s (F. Ruggiero).
11444 ᴱBonamente Giorgio, Fusco Franca, Costantino il Grande dall'Antichità all'Umanesimo, Macerata 18-20 dic. 1990. Macerata 1993, Univ.
xxiv-500 p.; p. 501-964. – ᴿOrChrPer 60 (1994) 275-9 (G. Traina).
11445 Bouffartigue Jean, L'empereur Julien et la culture de son temps 1992
→ 9,12855: ᴿAthenaeum 82 (1994) 604s (A. Marcone); Euphrosyne 24
(1994) 491s (A. do Nacimento Pena); JHS 114 (1994) 197s (Polymnía
Athanassiadi); JRS 84 (1994) 276 (R. B. E. Smith); RÉByz 52 (1994) 293
(P. Géhin); RHR 211 (1994) 351-3 (R. Turcan).
11446 Brown Peter, Power and persuasion in late antiquity; towards a
Christian empire (1988 Curti lectures) 1992 → 9,12856: ᴿAmHR 99
(1994) 532s (C. Haas); Commonweal 120,7 (1993) 28s (C. L. Bankston);
GreeceR 41 (1994) 250 (P. Walcot: he has pulled it off again; every
example counts); Horizons 21 (1994) 185s (Maureen A. Tilley); JRS 83
(1993) 258s (R. A. Markus); PerspRelSt 21 (1994) 69-76 (R. Giannone);
RÉAug 40 (1994) 241-7 (S. Rabenich); Speculum 69 (1994) 1129-31 (J. E.
Lendon).
11447 a) Caltabiano Matilde, Un decennio di studi sull'imperatore Giuliano
(1981-1991; fine); – b) Criscuolo U., L'Orazione 13 Förster di Libanio
per Giuliano: Koinonia 18 (1994) 141-163 / 117-140.
11448 ᴱCameron Averil, Conrad Lawrence J., The Byzantine and early
Islamic near east; problems in the literary source material 1989/92
→ 8,682: ᴿClasR 44 (1994) 135-7 (D. Frendo).
11449 Cameron Averil, The Later Roman Empire 1993 → 9,12859; also L,
Fontana; 0-00-686172-5: ᴿCathHR 80 (1994) 128s (R. A. Markus);
HeythJ 35 (1994) 451s (R. M. Price, also on MURRAY O.² and DAVIES J.²
Greece of the 7-volume series); JRS 83 (1993) 257s (G. Woolf).
11449* Chantraine Heinrich, Die Kreuzesvision von 351 — Fakten und
Probleme: ByZ 87 (1994) 430-441.
11450 Chuvin Pierre, Chronique des derniers païens 1990 [Eng. ᵀ1990 → 6,
b865 ... 8,d836]: ᴿGnomon 66 (1994) 147-151 (P. Bruggisser).
11451 Clark Gillian, Women in late antiquity; pagan and Christian lifestyles.

Ox 1993, Clarendon. 155 p.; 5 pl. £32.50. – ᴿClasR 44 (1994) 369s (M. *Harlow*); JRel 74 (1994) 565s (Amy-Jill *Levine*).

11451* **Demandt** Alexander, Die Spätantike römische Geschichte 1989 ➤ 5, b757 ... 8,d387: ᴿAnzAltW 46 (1993) 63-67 (P. W. *Haider*).

11452 **Dodgeon** M., *Lieu* S., Roman eastern frontier 1992 ➤ 7,b195 ... 9, 12511: ᴿBSO 57 (1994) 336 (A. D. H. *Bivar*).

11453 **Eleuteri** P., *Rigo* A., Eretici, dissidenti, musulmani ed Ebrei a Bisanzio; una raccolta eresiologica del XII secolo: Univ. Fac. Lett. Venezia 1993, Cardo. 164 p.

11454 **Feldman** L. H., Jew and Gentile ... Alexander to Justinian 1993 ➤ 9, 12786: ᴿAmHR 99 (1994) 878s (J. E. *Seaver*); BL (1994) 136 (M. *Goodman*); CBQ 56 (1994) 759-761 (H. *Basser*: laden with learning); JBL 113 (1994) 716-8 (J. J. *Collins*); JRel 74 (1994) 438s (D. J. *Harrington*: a maximalist view of 'prosélytisme juif'); JRS 84 (1994) 206s (S. *Mason*); JTS 45 (1994) 638-643 (Catherine *Hezser*); Judaism 43 (1994) 328-330 (Martha *Himmelfarb*); RHE 89 (1994) 643-8 (Nicole *Zeegers*); StPhilonAn 6 (1994) 188-192 (G. H. *Sterling*); VigChr 48 (1991) 291-6 (D. T. *Runia*, also on LIEU J. *al.* 1992).

11455 **Fowden** G., Empire to commonwealth; consequences of monotheism in late antiquity 1993 ➤ 9,12865; $18: ᴿJRS 84 (1994) 296s (R. A. *Markus*).

11456 *Fowden* Garth, The last days of Constantine; oppositional versions and their influence: JRS 84 (1994) 146-170.

11457 **Fuhrmann** Manfred, Rom in der Spätantike; Porträt einer Epoche. Z 1994, Artemis & W. 416 p.; Bibliog. 395-403. 3-7608-1088-8.

11458 **Giard** Jean-B., Lorenzo VALLA, La donation de Constantin. P 1993, BLettres. xxiv-147 p. – ᴿRÉLat 72 (1994) 387 (J.-C. *Richard*).

11458* *Goodman* Martin, Mission and conversion; proselytizing in the religious history of the Roman Empire [1992 Oxford Wilde Lectures in Natural and Comparative Religion]. Ox 1994, Clarendon. 194 p. £25. 0-19-814941-7. – ᴿExpTim 106 (1994s) 89 (C. H. *Middleburgh*).

11459 **Grant** Michael, Constantine the Great; the man and his times. NY 1994, Scribner's. xii-267 p.; 19 phot.; maps. $27.50. [TDig 42,167].

11460 **Heim** François [➤ 7507], Virtus; idéologie politique et croyances religieuses au IVᵉ siècle: UnivEur 15/49, 1991 ➤ 8,d398; Fs 84,50; 3-261-043296: ᴿLatomus 53 (1994) 884-6 (H. *Le Bonniec*).

11461 **Kaegi** Walter E., Byzantium and the early Islamic conquests 1992 ➤ 9,12874: ᴿByZ 86 (1994) 141s (K. *Belke*); HZ 259 (1994) 180s (R.-J. *Lilie*).

11462 **Kaplan** Michel, Les hommes et la terre à Byzance du VIᵉ au XIᵉ siècle; propriété et exploitation du sol 1992 ➤ 9,12875: ᴿAmHR 99 (1994) 1296s (W. *Treadgold*).

11463 **Krech** Volkhard, 'Was hat Athen mit Jerusalem zu schaffen?' Sammelbesprechung neuerer Literatur zum Thema 'Spätantike und Christentum' [COLPE C., GOTTLOB G., DODDS E., ROSENTHAL J. 1992]: ZRGg 46 (1994) 59-64.

11464 **Lançon** Bertrand, Le monde romain tardif, IIIᵉ-VIIᵉ siècle av. J.-C. P 1992, Colin. 192 p. 2-200-21235-6. – ᴿLatomus 53 (1994) 667 (R. *Delmaire*).

11465 **Lech** R., Konstantin und Christus ... Repräsentation 1992 ➤ 8,d408: ᴿTLZ 119 (1994) 145-7 (C. *Markschies*).

11466 **Lee** A. D., Information and frontiers; Roman foreign relations in late antiquity. C 1993, Univ. xxii-213 p.; 4 maps. £30. 0-521-39256-X. – ᴿPrudentia 26,2 (1994) 65-68 (N. *Austin*).

11467 **Leeb** Rudolf, Konstantin und Christus; die Verchristlichung der imperialen Repräsentantion unter K.: ArbKG 58, 1992 ➤ 8,d408: ᴿJEH 45 (1994) 167s (T. D. *Barnes*).

11468 **Maas** M., J. Lydus 1992 ➤ 8,12880: ᴿHZ 259 (1994) 171s (G. *Wirth*).

11469 **Masaracchia** Emanuela. GIULIANO, Contra Galilaeos [risponde a U. *Criscuolo* 1990 ➤ 7,b886; 9,12883]: Orpheus [13 (1992) 426-433] 14 (1993) 312-9.

11470 *a) Matthews* John, Constantine and the second Roman revolution; – *b) Morpeth* Neil, Jack LINDSAY [autobiog.] and Greco-Roman antiquity: Prudentia 25,1 (Auckland 1993) 24-41 / 42-68.

11471 **Meyendorff** John, Imperial unity and Christian division; the Church 450-650 A.D. 1988 ➤ 6,b887 ... 8,d413: ᴿSalesianum 56 (1994) 770s (F. *Meyer*).

11471* *Micallela* Dina, Impegno e disimpegno; Giuliano imperatore e la letteratura: ➤ 29, ᶠCORSINI E. 1994, 129-140.

11472 **Neel** V., Medius princeps; Storia e immagine di Costantino nella storiografia latina pagana. Bo 1992, Clueb. xvi-365 p. – ᴿAthenaeum 82 (1994) 609s (A. *Marcone*).

11473 **Neri** Valerio, Medius princeps; Storia e immagine di Costantino nella storiografia latina pagana, 1992 ➤ 9,12886: ᴿRÉLat 72 (1994) 340-2 (G. *Sabbah*).

11474 *Nicholson* Oliver, The 'pagan churches' of Maximinus Daia and Julian the Apostate: JEH 45 (1994) 1-10.

11475 **Rabello** Alfredo M., Giustiniano, Ebrei e Samaritani 1988 ➤ 5,b787 ... 9,12891: ᴿSefarad 53 (1993) 220s (J. J. *Alarcón Sainz*).

11475* **Radke** Gerhard, Fasti romani; Betrachtungen zur Frühgeschichte des römischen Kalenders 1990 ➤ 8,d354; 9,12827 (not 'Günther'): ᴿAnzAltW 46 (1993) 41-44 (T. *Köves*).

11476 **Rosenthal** Jos, *Dexinger* Ferdinand, Als die Heiden Christen wurden: zur Geschichte des frühen Christentums. W 1991, Ueberrheiner.

11477 *Rota* Simona, AMMIANO e Libanio; l'epistola 1063 Först. di Libanio [FORNARA C. W.]: Koinonia 18 (1994) 165-177.

11477* ᴱSolin H., *Kajava* M., Roman Eastern policy 1988/90 ➤ 6,768* ... 9,12837: ᴿAnzAltW 46 (1993) 61-63 (P. W. *Haider*).

11478 ᴱSordi Marta, L'impero romano-cristiano; problemi politici, religiosi, culturali. R 1991, Città Nuova. 214 p. Lᵐ 23. 8 art. – ᴿAsprenas 41 (1994) 122-4 (E. *Dovere*).

11479 **Thrams** Peter, Christianisierung im Römerreich und heidnischer Widerstand, 1992 ➤ 8,d422; 9,12898: ᴿCritRR 6 (1993) 338-340 (D. *Schowalter*).

11480 **Trombley** Frank R., Hellenic religion and Christianization 1993 ➤ 9, 12899: ᴿRHE 87 (1994) 660-3 (Nicole *Zeegers*).

11481 ᴱUgenti V., GIULIANO imperatore, Alla madre degli dei 1992 ➤ 9, 12900: ᴿKoinonia 18 (1994) 214-6 (U. *Criscuolo*); VigChr 48 (1994) 86s (J. der *Boeft*).

| XVIII. Archaeologia terrae biblicae |

T1.1   **General biblical-area archeologies.**

11482 *Alagna* Sergio, Profili civilistici del ritrovamento e della scoperta di beni aventi valore culturale: ➤ 9,46*a*, ᶠFALZEA A. 1987, 7-

11483 [Arata] **Mantovani** Piera,   Introduzione all'archeologia palestinese 1991
→ 9,12909:   ᴿCC 145 (1994,3) 546s (G. L. *Prato*); RivB 42 (1994) 223s
(B. G. *Boschi*); RSO 68 (1994) 165s (G. *Garbini*).

11483* *a*) *Atkinson* Kenneth,   Diggers; from paid peasants to eager volun-
teers; – *b*) *David* Jo,   Eight not-so-obvious questions to ask before joining
your first dig; – *c*) Summer in the sand; [Israel] 1994 excavation op-
portunities: BAR-W 20,1 (1994) 66-71.80 / 64s / 50-59 [chart 60-63;
BAR dig scholarships 72].

11484 **Ben-Tor** Ammon,   The archaeology of ancient Israel [❸ 1991],
ᵀ*Greenberg* R.   NHv/TA 1992, Yale Univ./Open Univ.   xxi-398 p.;
[→ 9,12910] 268 fig.; 47 color. pl.; 20 maps. $45.   0-300-04768-1 [BL
95,24, J. R. *Duckworth*]. – ᴿAJA 98 (1994) 568s (Sharon R. *Keller*);
Antiquity 68 (1994) 179s (E. *Marcus*, also on AHLSTRÖM G. 1993);
BAR-W 20,5 (1994) 8 (M. D. *Coogan*); PEQ 126 (1994) 164s (P.
Bienkowski: accurate); SWJT 36,2 (1993s) 46 (T. V. *Brisco*, also on
McRAY J.).

11485 **Biers** William R.,   Art, artefacts and chronology in classical archaeology: Approaching the ancient world. L 1992, Routledge.   105 p.;
26 fig.   0-415-06319-1. – ᴿAJA 97 (1993) 804-6 (Martha S. *Joukowsky*).

11485* ᴱ**Biran** A.,   Biblical Archaeology today, Pre-congress symposium
1990/3 → 9,555:   ᴿTLZ 119 (1994) 770-7 (D. *Vieweger*).

11486 **Bottema** S.,   East is east and west is west?: JbEOL 33 (1993s) 5-20.

11486* **Bracco** V.,   La lunga illusione dell'archeologia. Brindisi-Fasano 1993,
Schena.   vii-413 p. – ᴿBStLat 24 (1994) 291-3 (Antonella *Borgo*).

11487 **Cambi** Franco, *Terrenato* Nicola,   Introduzione all'archeologia dei
paesaggi: Studi Superiori 203. R 1994, Nuova Italia Scientifica.   313 p.;
ill. – ᴿVetChr 31 (1994) 400-4 (G. *Volpe*).

11488 ᶠCATLING Hector: Philolakon, Lakonian studies, ᴱ**Sanders** Jan M. 1992
→ 9,30*:   ᴿAntClas 63 (1994) 533s (D. *Viviers*).

11488* ᴱ**Charlesworth** J. H., *Weaver* W. P.,   What has archaeology to do
with faith?   1992 → 8,705:   ᴿBAR-W 20,6 first place (1994) 6.8 (Ben
Witherington).

11489 **Clark** Grahame,   Space, time, and man; a prehistorian's view. C 1992,
Univ. xiii-165; 48 fig. $40.   0-521-40065-1. – ᴿAJA 97 (1993) 571s (P. S.
Wells, also on his 1989 CS).

11490 **Cole** R. D.,   Recent developments in biblical archeology: TEdr 40 (New
Orleans 1994) 51-64.

11491 **Deichmann** Friedrich W., ❷ Archeologia chrześcijańska [Einführung],
ᵀ*Jastrzębowska* Elżbieta.   Wsz 1994, Naukowe. 345 p.; ill.

11492 **Dever** William G.,   Recent archaeological discoveries and biblical
research 1990 → 6,b908 ... 8,d438:   ᴿJNES 53 (1994) 148-150 (Diana
Edelman).

11492* *Dever* William G.,   Archaeology, texts, and history-writing; toward
an epistemology: → 102, Mem. RICHARDSON H. N., Uncovering ancient
stones 1994, 105-117.

11493 **Duval** Noël,   Actes du XIᵉ congrès international d'archéologie chrétienne: StAntCr 41, Vaticano 1989 → 5,827; 7,b482:   ᴿAJA 98 (1994)
351-4 (Caroline J. *Hemans*).

11494 **Dyson** Stephen L.,   From New to New Age archaeology; archaeological
theory and classical archaeology — a 1990s perspective: AJA 97 (1993)
195-206.

11494* *Fiedler* Lutz,   Sprache archäologisch verstanden: → 35, ᶠFREY O.
1994, 213-7.

11495 **Finegan** Jack, Archeology of NT²ʳᵉᵛ 1992 → 9,12916*:   ᴿBibTB 24 (1994) 145 (V. H. *Matthews*); CBQ 56 (1994) 135-7 (L. J. *Hoppe*: revision insufficient).

11496 **Fritz** Volkmar, An introduction to biblical archaeology [1985 → 1, b421], ᵀ*Mänz-Davies* B.: jOsu 172. Shf 1994, JStOT. 223 p. $37.50. 1-85075-426-8 [OTAbs 17, p. 654].

11497 **Gądecki** Stanisław, Archeologia biblijna. Gniezno 1994, Gaudentinum. I. 462 p. II. p. 465-617, bibliog. 551-617; 147 color. phot. 83-85654-24-8; -5-1.

11498 ᴱ*Gawlikowski* Michał, *Daszewski* Wiktor A., Polish archaeology in the Mediterranean 6, Reports 1994. 117 p.

11499 *Gerstel* Sharon E. J., Liturgical scrolls [held by bishops portrayed on walls] in the Byzantine sanctuary: GrRByz 35 (1994) 195-204.

11500 **González Echegaray** Joaquín, Arqueología y Evangelios. Estella 1994, VDivino. 291 p. 84-7151-941-0. – ᴿEstE 69 (1994) 546-8 (F. *Pastor-Ramos*); RET 54 (1994) 351-3 (P. *Barrado Fernández*).

11501 **Grimal** Nicolas, Fouille et préservation; quelques éléments de réflexion... IFAO/Karnak: BSocFÉg 127 (1993) 20-37; 8 fig.

11501* **Guzzo** Pier Giovanni, Antico e archeologia; scienza e politica delle diverse antichità. Bo 1993, Nuova Alfa. 165 p. Lᵐ 38. – ᴿArcheo 9,113 (1994) 127s (D. *Manacorda*).

11502 ᴱ**Knapp** A. B., Archeology, Annales and Ethnohistory [Baltimore 1989]: New Directions, 1992 → 8,437. d453:   ᴿAntClas 63 (1994) 577s (G. *Raepsaet*); JESHO 37 (1994) 328-331 (Gina L. *Bames*).

11503 **McRay** J., Archaeology and NT 1991 → 7,b495... 9,12922:   ᴿConcordTQ 58 (1994) 187s (L. *Burgland*); CritRR 6 (1993) 144-6 (R. *Osher*); CurrTM 21 (1994) 133s (W. C. *Linss*); RExp 91 (1994) 613s (J. F. *Drinkard*).

11503* **Magall** M., Archäologie und Bibel; wissenschaftliche Wege zur Welt des ATs. Köln 1989, DuMont. 290 p. – ᴿCiuD 207 (1994) 193s (J. *Gutiérrez*).

11504 **Maisels** Charles K., The Near East; archaeology in the 'cradle of civilization' 1993 → 9,12923:   ᴿBL (1994) 29 (A. R. *Millard*); PEQ 126 (1994) 167-9 (E. P. *Uphill*); RAss 88 (1994) 71s (J.-L. *Huot*).

11505 **Malina** Jaroslav, *Zdeněk* Vešiček, Archaeology yesterday and today; the development of archaeology in the sciences and humanities. ᵀᴱ*Zvelebil* Marek. C 1990, Univ. xiv-320 p.; 50 fig. £44. 0-521-26621-1. – ᴿAJA 98 (1994) 564s (Tracey *Cullen*).

11506 ᶠMIKASA T. 65th b., ᴱ**Mori** M., al., Near Eastern Studies 1991 → 7,102c: ᴿOLZ 89 (1994) 39-42 (J. *Glücker*: 6 on OT).

11507 **Moorey** P. R. S., A century of biblical archaeology 1991 → 9,12928: ᴿCBQ 56 (1994) 122s (P. F. *Jacobs*); ClasB 69 (1993) 95-98 (Sara *Mandell*); CritRR 6 (1993) 147s (J. A. *Dearman*); HeythJ 34 (1993) 429s (J. *Mulrooney*); JSS 38 (1993) 313s (A. H. W. *Curtis*: much more than its history).

11508 *a)* **Pienaar** D. N., Palestinian 'biblical' archaeology; – *b)* *Cornelius* I., Communicating the OT world of ideas by way of ancient Near Eastern iconography: → 327, ODENDAAL D., mem., OTEssays 7,4 (1991/4) 132-8 / 327-332.

11508* **Rast** Walter E., Through the ages in Palestinian archaeology; an introductory handbook 1992 → 8,d471; $16 [BL 95,33, G. I. *Davies* commends warmly]. – ᴿWestTJ 56 (1994) 188-190 (P. *Enns*).

11509 ᴱ**Renfrew** Colin, *Zubrow* Ezra B. W., The ancient mind; elements of cognitive archaeology: New Directions. C 1994, Univ. xiv-195 p.; ill.; p. 169-176-234, writing systems. 0-521-43488-2; pa. -620-7.

11510 **Rice** T. Douglas, *Feinman* Gary M., Images of the past. Mountain View CA 1992, Mayfield. xii-529 p. $40 pa. 0-87484-814-8 [Antiquity 68,646: two cognate textbooks have identical illustrations].

11511 **Schnapp** A., La conquête du passé; aux origines de l'archéologie. P 1993, Carré. – ᴿBuCanadMesop 27 (1994) 67 (français seul, non signé).

11511* *Shanks* Hershel, Archaeology's dirty secret; archaeologists love to dig, but hate to write publication reports [chart shows percentage of sites unpublished rose from near zero in 1921 to 90% 1985]: BAR-W 20,5 (1994) 63s . 79.

11512 *Shanks* Hershel, Peace, politics and archaeology [15 years' Sinai excavation results to be turned over to Egypt; & Israel 'Operation Scroll' (*Wolff* Sam)]: BAR-W 20,2 (1994) 50-57.94 [(2). p. 40-45, *Rabinovich* Abraham, Inside the Israel Antiquities authority].

11512* **Shanks** Michael, Experiencing the past; on the character of archaeology. L 1992, Routledge. vii-251 p. £35. 0-415-05584-9. – ᴿAnt-Clas 63 (1994) 576s (F. *Verhaeghe*).

11513 **Stiebing** William H.ᴶ, Uncovering the past; a history of archaeology. Buffalo 1993, Prometheus. 315 p. $25. – ᴿBAR-W 20,3 (1994) 8 (O. *Borowski*).

T1.2   Musea, organismi, expositiones.

11514 *a)* Activités de l'École française de Rome, section antiquité: MÉF 105 (1993) 419-492; 38 fig. / 106 (1994) 431-486; 33 fig. – *b)* Recherches sur l'Adriatique antique II (1986-90) MÉF 105 (1993) 307-417.1015-1122; 5 maps.

11515 *Alfano* Carla (*Luzi* Adriano), Nefertari, luce d'Egitto; in mostra a Roma la tomba restaurata: Archeo 9,118 (1994) 46-63.

American Institute of Archaeology, AIA annual meeting 94 (1992) & 95 (1993) ➤ 455.

11515* *Andreae* Bernard, Kurze Geschichte des Deutschen Archäologischen Instituts in Rom, dargestellt im Wirken seiner leitenden Gelehrten: MiDAI-R 100 (1993) 5-41.

11516 *a)* *Berger* Klaus, 'Griechische Altertümer' im Römisch-Germanischen Museum Köln; – *b)* *Ritter* Stefan, Die antiken Bronzen ... Statuetten aus Köln; – *c)* *Wigg* David G., *Seiler* Sven, Ein Fund römischer Falsch-münzerförmchen aus Köln: KölnJb 27 (1994) 7-86; 209 fig. / 317-403; 178 fig. / 611-6; 7 fig.

11516* *Bernard* Paul, Rapport sur l'École Française d'Athènes: CRAI (1994) 581-9.

11517 ᴱ**Blomberg** Mary, From the Gustavianum collections in Uppsala, 3. The collection of classical antiquities (Antiksamlingen): Boreas 22. U 1993, Almqvist & W. 120 p.

11517* *Butcher* Kevin, *Gill* David W.J., The director, the dealer, the goddess, and her champions; the acquisition of the Fitzwilliam [fake] goddess: AJA 97 (1993) 383-401.

11518 *Delange* E., Egypt's dazzling sun; Amenhotep III and his world, Cleveland: BSocFEg 125 (1992) 29-46; 11 fig.

11519 **Effenberger** Arne, *Severin* Hans-Georg, Das Museum für spätantike und byzantinische Kunst: Staatliche Museen zu Berlin. Mainz 1991, von Zabern. 268 p.; ill. – ᴿByZ 86 (1994) 154s (Barbara *Schellewald*).

11519* *Feldman* Steen, Turmoil at the Harvard Semitic Museum [F. M. CROSS calls 'libel' Harvard lecturer and *New Republic* Editor Martin PERETZ's claim of anti-Semitism against Director L. E. STAGER for decision to replace the museum's ten employees with two new ones and disperse its Mid-East photo collection]: BAR-W 20,2 (1994) 64-66.

11520 ᴱ**Grapp** Gerd, Zarathustra und die Mithras-Mysterien, Sonderausstellung, Ha-Reinbek 1993, Museum Rade. Bremen 1993, Temmen. 96 p.; ill.

11521 *Grimal* Nicolas, Travaux de l'Institut français d'archéologie orientale en 1993-94: BIFAO 94 (1994) 383-490.

11521* *Hägg* Robin, The Swedish Institute at Athens; report for the academic years 1900-91 and 1991-92: OpAth 20 (1994) 247-250.

11522 ᴱ**Harper** F. O., *al.*, The royal city of Susa; ancient Near Eastern treasures in the Louvre. NY 1992, Abrams. xx-316 p.; 204 fig. + 76 color. $60. – ᴿJESHO 37 (1994) 185s (K. R. *Veenhof*).

11522* **Janssen** Rosalind M., The first hundred years; Egyptology at University College London 1992 ➤ 9,12975: ᴿDiscEg 25 (1993) 87s (T. *DuQuesne*).

11523 **Kitchen** Kenneth, *al.*, Catálogo / Egito, Museo Rio 1990 [Eng. 1988 ➤ 6,b981]: ᴿDiscEg 25 (1993) 89-94 (J. *Malek*); Orientalia 63 (1994) 302 (A. R. *Shulman*).

11524 ᴱ**Langdon** Susan, From pasture to polis; art in the age of Homer [exhibit of 100 objects from US collections]. Columbia 1993, Univ. Missouri. 241 p.; 16 color. pl. – ᴿRelStR 20 (1994) 234 (Sally *Schultz*).

11524* **Martiniani-Reber** M., Lyon, Musée historique des tissus; soieries sassanides, coptes et byzantines Vᵉ-XIᵉ siècles. P 1986. 131 p.; 109 fig. 9. – ᴿVizVrem 53 (1992) 203s (A. Ya. *Kakovkin*, ❸).

11525 *Meulenaere* Herman De, Les antiquités égyptiennes de la collection Charles Bogaert [... Leiden; Liverpool]: BSocFÉg 127 (1993) 6-19; 2 fig.; 3 pl.

11526 Mitglieder des Deutschen Vereins zur Erforschung Palastinas: ZDPV 110 (1994) 92-100; p. 91 'die Vereinsbibliothek wurde von Kiel nach Heidelberg verlagert'; 104-110, Hinweise für den Schriftsatz.

11527 *Moorey* Roger, Archaeology: from site to sight: IsrMusJ 9 (1990) 17-24.

11528 **Moorsel** Paul van, *al.*, Catalogue général du Musée Copte: The icons. Leiden 1994, Antiquities. [iv] 190 p.; 48 pl. + 16 color.

11528* **Moscati** Sabatino, Quegli uomini venuti dal Nord; mostra civiltà del Normanni, R febbr.-apr. 1994: Archeo 9,108 (1994) 46-55.

11529 **Nissen** H. J., *al.*, Archaic bookkeeping 1993 [Berlin exposition], ᵀ*Larsen* Paul. – ᴿAntiquity 68 (1994) 671s (Harriet *Crawford*).

11530 [ᴱ**D'Inzillo Carranza** Giuliana] Oxus; tesori dell'Asia centrale: R Palazzo Venezia 1993s. R 1993, de Luca. xii-147 p.; 159 (color.) fig. 88-8016-016-8.

11530* *a*) **Pernigotti** Sergio, Una nuova collezione egiziana al Museo Civico Archeologico di Bologna: EgAntP mg min. 6. Pisa 1994, Giardini. 101 p.; bibliog. 7-11. Lᵐ 30. – *b*) *Morigi Govi* Cristina, *Pernigotti* Sergio, Faraoni a Bologna; aperta la nuova sezione egiziana del museo civico archeologico: Archeo 9,113 (1994) 48-57; ill.

11531 **Quirke** Stephen, Owners of funerary papyri in the British Museum: OccasP 92. L 1993, British Museum Dept. Egyptian Antiquities. viii-115 p. 0-86159-092-9.

11531* **Rosensaft** Jean B., Chagall and the Bible; exhibition of Chagall's etchings at the Jewish Museum, New York. NY 1987, Universe. 159 p. 0-87663-653-9; pa. -518-4.

11532 ᴱRuprechtsberger Erwin M., Syrien, von den Aposteln zu den Kalifen, Ausstellung: Linzer Archeol. 21. Linz-Nordica 1993, Stadtmuseum. 520 p.; ill.

11532* Satzinger Helmut, Das kunsthistorische Museum in Wien; die ägyptisch-orientalische Sammlung: Bildbände zur Archäologie 14. Mainz 1994, von Zabern. [iv-] 120 p. 3-8053-1600-3.

11533 Smits Jan, De Verenigde Nederlanden op zoek naar het oude Egypte (1580-1780) — de traditie gevolgd en gewogen. Culemborg 1988, auct. 310 p.; 36 fig. ƒ42,50. – ᴿCdÉ 69 (1994) 87s (C. Cannuyer).

11534 Studium biblicum Franciscanum 1993-4; 4 dissertazioni, infra; 8 tesi di licenza; attività: LA 44 (1994) 739-747.

11534* Toubert Pierre, Rapport sur l'état et l'activité de l'Ecole Française de Rome 1993-4: CRAI (1994) 759-775.

11535 Varga E., Le passé, le présent et l'avenir de la collection égyptienne de Budapest: BSocFEg 131 (1994) 19-97; 4 fig.; 2 pl.

11535* Will Ernest, [Sigrist Marcel], Rapport sur l'état et l'activité de l'École biblique et archéologique française de Jérusalem, 1993-4: CRAI (1994) 853-8.

11536 Ziegler Christiane, Humbert Jean-Marcel, Egyptomania; propos sur une exposition [Louvre]: BSocFÉg 128 (1993) 30-40 + 4 pl.

T1.3 Methodi, Science in archeology.

11537 Buck C. E., Litton C. D., Scott E. M., Making the most of radiocarbon dating; some statistical considerations: Antiquity 68 (1994) 252-263.

11538 Eibisch J., Die werkstoffkundliche Klassifizierung von frühen Bronzewerkzeugen mit mathematisch-statistischen Methoden: BBArchäom 11 (1992) 67-91.

11539 Ferrara Giorgio, Le datazioni radiometriche applicate all'archeologia: → 98, ᶠRADMILLI A., 1994, 127-136.

11540 Fielder Lutz, Sprache archäologisch verstanden [... Statistik]: → 35, ᶠFREY O., 1994, 213-7.

11540* Gunneweg J., al., 'Edomite', 'Negbite' and 'Midianite' pottery from the Negev Desert and Jordan; instrumental neutron activation analysis results: Archaeometry 33 (1991) 239-253; map.

11541 Hatcher Helen, al., Chemical classification and provenance of some Roman glazed ceramics: AJA 98 (1994) 431-456; 4 fig. (map).

11542 Hutchinson T. F., Essentials of statistical methods, 2. History and archaeology 1993 → 9,13002: ᴿPrudentia 26,2 (1994) 63-65 (G. J. Tee).

11543 Lanting J. N., Plicht J. van der, ¹⁴C-AMS [radiocarbon dating]: pros and cons for archaeology: Palaeohistoria 35s (1993s) 1-12; 3 fig.

11544 ᴱMook W. G., Waterbolk H. T., Proc. 2d Int. symp.; 14C and Archaeology Groningen 1987: PACT 29. Strasbourg 1990, Conseil de l'Europe. 459 p. Fb 4000. 0257-8727. – ᴿAntClas 63 (1994) 582 (F. Verhaeghe).

11545 ᴱPayton Robert, Retrieval of objects from archaeological sites. L 1992, Archetype. 166 p. 1-873-13230-1. – ᴿAJA 98 (1994) 355s (Catherine Skase).

11545* Reedy T. J. & C. L., Statistical analysis in conservation science: Archaeometry 36 (1994) 1-23.

11546 ᴱTaylor Royal E., Radiocarbon after four decades; an interdisciplinary

perspective: Conference Univ. California, Lake Arrowhead 4-8.VI.1990. NY 1992, Springer. xviii-596 p.; 148 ill.
11546* *Tite* M. S., Archaeological science — past achievements and future prospects: Archaeometry 33 (1991) 139-151.
11547 **Weaver** Graham, *al.*, An introduction to materials: Science for Conservators 1. NY 1992, Routledge. 120 p. $20. 0-415-07166-6. – ᴿAJA 98 (1994) 164 (C. *Skase*, also on 2. Cleaning; 3. Coatings).

T1.4   *Exploratores* – **Excavators, pioneers.**

11548 **Åström** Paul, *al.*, 'The fantastic years on Cyprus'; the Swedish Cyprus expedition and its members: SIMA pocket 79. Jonsered 1994, Åström. 55 p.; portraits. 91-7081-059-1.
11549 **Baruffa** Antonio, Giovanni Battista DE ROSSI, l'archeologo esploratore delle catacombe. Vaticano 1994, Editrice. 223 p.; 18 pl. 88-209-20 [00-7 dentro; 10-7 fuori]. – ᴿRivArCr 70 (1994) 525-7 (V. *Fiocchi Nicolai*); SMSR 18,1 (1994) 57s (Myla *Perraymond*).
11550 **Bottini** G. Claudio, Padre Virgilio C. CORBO; una vita in Terra Santa [excavator's work and testimonies]: SBF museum 12. J 1994, Franciscan. 142 p.; ill.; bibliog. 13-26.
11550* **Bowden** Mark, Augustus PITT RIVERS, life and archaeological work. C 1991, Univ. xv-182 p.; ill. 0-521-40077-5. – ᴿAJA 98 (1994) 159s (S. L. *Dyson*).
11551 **Cannon** Garland, The life and mind of Oriental [Wm] JONES, the father of modern linguistics. C 1990, Univ. 400 p. £55. – ᴿKratylos 38 (1993) 164-6 (Rosane *Rocher*).
11551* **Chauvet** Michel, Frédéric CAILLIAUD; les aventures d'un naturaliste en Égypte et au Soudan, 1815-1822. S.-Sebastien 1989, ACL-Crocus. 371 p.; ill.; foldout map. F 295. – ᴿCdÉ 69,138 (1994) 249-251 (S. H. *Aufrère*).
11552 *Curtis* John, William Kennett LOFTUS and his excavations at Susa: IrAnt 28 (1993) 1-35; fig.; + 20 pl.
11552* *Dyson* Stephen L., Archaeological lives [WOOLLEY L., HAWES Harriet, KIDDER Alfred, DANIEL Glyn + 2 infra], 'all unsatisfactory': AJA 98 (1994) 159-161.
11553 *a)* *Evers* Sheila M., George SMITH and the Egibi tablets; – *b)* *Reade* Julian, Hormuzd RASSAM and his discoveries: Iraq 55 (1993) 107-117 / 39-62; 26 fig.
11554 **Fischer** Hans, Der Ägyptologe Georg EBERS; eine Fallstudie zum Problem Wissenschaft und Öffentlichkeit im 19. Jahrhundert: ÄgAT 25. Wsb 1994, Harrassowitz. xvi-447 p.; (foldout) ill. 3-447-03458-0.
11554* ᴱ**Harle** Diane, *Lefebvre* Jean, Nestor L'HÔTE [1804-42]. Sur le Nil avec CHAMPOLLION; letters, journaux et dessins inédits; premier voyage en Égypte 1828-30. Orléans/Caen 1993, Paradigma. 334 p.; ill. 2-86878-114-4. → 467, ᴱ*Dewachter* M.
11555 *Maier* Franz G., *al.*, Von Winckelmann zu Schliemann — Archäologie als Eroberungswissenschaft des 19. Jhts.: AntWelt 25 (Jubiläumsausgabe 1994) (3-) 35-59.
11555* **Meritt** Lucy S., History of the American School of Classical Studies at Athens 1939-1980. Princeton 1984, Am.Sch.A. xv-411 p. 0-87661- 942-1.
11556 **Metzger** Henri, La correspondance passive d'Osman HANDI bey: AIBL mém. NS 11. P 1990, Institut de France. 100 p. – ᴿRAss 88 (1994) 65s (B. *Lafont*).

11557 **Moreh** Shmuel, NAPOLEON in Egypt; ['Abd al-Rahman] Al-JABARTI's chronicle of the French occupation 1798. Princeton 1993, Wiener. [vi-] 186 p.; ill. 1-55876-069-5; pa. -70-9.

11558 **James** T. G. H., Howard CARTER; the path to Tutankhamun 1992 → 8,d346: ᴿAJA 97 (1993) 576s (W. H. *Peck*); DiscEg 27 (1993) 117-9 (Henrietta *McCall*).

11559 **Lehmann** Reinhard G., Friedrich DELITZSCH und der Babel-Bibel-Streit: OBO 133. FrS/Gö 1994, Univ./VR. 472 p. 12 pl. 3-7278-0932-9 / VR 3-529-93768-0. – ᴿÉTRel 69 (1994) 503 (Françoise *Smyth*).

11560 **Nichtweiss** Barbara, Erik PETERSON; neue Sicht auf Leben und Werk. Fr 1992, Herder. c. 1000 p. – ᴿRivArCr 70 (1994) 515-524 (L. *Dattrino*).

11561 **Rainey** Froelich, Reflections of a digger; fifty years of world archaeology. Ph 1992, Univ. Museum. xx-309 p.; 16 pl. – ᴿAJA 98 (1994) 161 (S. L. *Dyson*).

11562 *Ridley* R. T., Four unpublished letters by or relating to Bernardino DROVETTI: CdÉ 69,138 (1994) 203-214.

11563 *Samerski* Stefan, Richard DELBRUECK (1875-1957); ein Archäologe als Aussenpolitiker: MiDAI-R 101 (1994) 19-31.

11564 SCHLIEMANN; *Easton* D. F., Priam's gold; the full story: AnSt 44 (1994) 221-243 [now in Moscow Pushkin museum; Russia (as well as Germany and Turkey) has a legal claim].

11565 — *Robinson* Marcello, Pioneer scholar, and victim [Schliemann!]; an appreciation of Frank CALVERT (1828-1908): AnSt 44 (1994) 153-168.

11566 — **Traill** D. A., Excavating Schliemann 1993 → 9,13023: ᴿAntiquity 68 (1994) 455s (D. F. *Easton*: obsessional).

11567 *a) Shchavelev* S. P., ❺ Episodes from the history of Russian archaeology [D. Ya. SAMOKVASOV 15.V.1843 - 5.VIII.1911]; – *b) Dzhaparidze* O. M., ❻ On the centenary of academician B. A. KUFTIN (1892-1953): – *c) Formozov* A. A., A. S. UVAROV (1825-1884) and his place in the history of Russian archaeology: RossArkh (1993,1) 221-235 / (1993,3) 246-9; photo / (1993,3) 228-245.

11567* **Silberman** Neil A., A prophet from amongst you; the life of Yigael YADIN, soldier, scholar, and mythmaker of modern Israel. Reading MA 1993, Addison-Wesley. 423 p. $30. – ᴿArchaeology 47,2 (1994) 59-61 (W. G. *Dever*); BAR-W 20,2 (1994) 6.8.10 (A. *Malamat*).

11568 *Stucky* Rolf A., Johann Ludwig BURCKHARDT alias Scheich Ibrahim, ein Forscher zwischen zwei Welten and zwei Epochen: AntWelt 24 (1993) 90-100; 12 fig.

11568* [*Donadoni Roveri* Anna M., present.; *La Guardia* Rina, *al.*] **Vassalli** Luigi [1812-1887], egittologo, disegni e documenti nei Civici Istituti Culturali Milanesi. Mi 1994, ET. 197 p.❹199-8 bibliog. 189-195.

11569 **Webster** Graham, Archaeologist at large → 8,328 [mostly Romano-British since 1956; 3 inedita + 11]. L 1991, Batsford. 216 p. 0-7134-6803-3. – ᴿAJA 97 (1993) 815 (R. L. *Pitts*).

T1.5   *Materiae primae – **Metals, glass.***

11570 *Rybatzki* Volker, Bemerkungen zur türkischen und mongolischen Metallterminologie: StOr 73 (1994) 194-251.

11570* **Scott** David A., Metallography and microstructure of ancient and historic metals. Malibu 1991, Getty Museum. xvii-155 p., 212 fig. 20 color. pl. 0-89236-195-6.

11571 *Aes*, BRONZE: **Andrews** Tamsey K., Bronzecasting at geometric period

[900-700] Olympia and early Greek metals sources: diss. Brandeis, ᴰ*Mitten* D. Boston 1994. 247 p. 94-25843. – DissA 55 (1994s) p. 1301.

11572 *Consolo Langher* Sebastiana M., Il doppio ruolo del bronzo nella Sicilia preistorica e arcaica; asce e lance come strumenti e come moneta: RitNum 96 (1994s) 11-17.

11572* *Giumla-Mair* Alessandra R., *Craddock* Paul T., Corinthium aes; das schwarze Gold der Alchimisten: AntWelt 24 Sondernummer 1 (1993) 62 p.; 33 fig.

11573 **Pirzio Biroli Stefanelli** Lucia, Il bronzo dei Romani 1990 → 7,b688; 8,d566: ᴿBabesch 69 (1994) 226-8 (S. *Mols*). – *b*) Il bronzo dei Romani: Archeo 9,113 (1994) 58-93; ill.

11574 *Alabastrum:* **Casanova** M., La vaisselle d'albâtre de Mésopotamie, d'Iran et d'Asie centrale aux IIIᵉ et IIᵉ millénaires av.J.-C. 1991 → 8, d568: ᴿBuCanadMesop 25 (1993) 75 (Eng. franç., no author).

11574* AMBER: **Mastrocinque** Attilio, L'ambra e l'Eridano 1991 → 8,d569: ᴿArcheo 9,107 (1994) 117 (A. *Naso*).

11575 *Argentum,* SILVER: **Pirzio** B.S., L., L'argento dei Romani 1991 → 7, b688: ᴿLatomus 53 (1994) 675s (F. *Baratte*).

11575* *Aurum,* GOLD: *Quattrocchi* Giovanna, L'oro dei Greci, dai Micenei al regno di Macedonia: Archeo 9,111 (1994) 54-68; ill.

11576 *a) Klemm* Rosemarie & Dietrich M., Chronologischer Abriss der antiken Goldgewinnung in der Ostwüste Ägyptens: MiDAI-K 50 (1994) 189-222; 11 fig.; pl. 29-35.

— *b) Vercoutter* Jean, Or et politique dans l'Égypte des origines: → 73, ᶠLECLANT J. 2 (1994) 403-410; 5 fig.

11576* *Ferrum,* IRON: *Kassianidou* Vasiliki, Could iron have been produced in Cyprus?: RepCyp (1994) 73-81.

11577 *Obsidian: Bader* N.O., *al.*, L'obsidienne dans le Sinjar (Iraq): Paléorient 20,2 (1994) 6-34 [20/1, 61-68].

11577* — *Gratuze* B., *Barrandan* J.N., *al.*, Non-destructive analysis of obsidian artefacts using nuclear techniques: investigation of provenance of Near Eastern artefacts: Archaeometry 35 (1993) 11-21; 4 fig.

11578 — *Nishiaki* Yoshihiro, Anatolian obsidian and the neolithic obsidian industries of North Syria; a preliminary review: → 9,358, Anatolian 1993, 140-155 + 7 fig. (maps).

11578* *Plumbum,* LEAD: *Mossman* S., The use of lead in the Mycenaean period: diss. Birmingham UK c.1992. – BInstClas 38 (1991-3) 302.

11579 *Saxum,* STONE: **Putter** Thierry de, *Karlshausen* Christina, Les pierres utilisées dans la sculpture et l'architecture de l'Égypte pharaonique; guide pratique illustré. Bru 1992, Connaissance de l'Égypte ancienne. 176 p.; 9 fig.; 64 pl. Fb 3800. – ᴿRBgPg 72 (1994) 188-190 (P.P. *Koemoth*).

11579* *Harrell* J.A., Ancient Egyptian limestone quarries; a petrological survey: Archaeometry 34 (1992) 195-211.

11580 *Stannum,* TIN: *a) Yener* K. Aslihan, *Vandiver* Pamela B., Tin processing at [Taurus mt., 150 k N Tarsus] Göltepe, an Early Bronze site in Anatolia; – *b) Muhly* J.D., Early Bronze Age tin and the Taurus: AJA 97 (1993) 207-229; fig. (& 255-264; 2 fig., reply to Muhly) / 239-259; 3 fig.; map.

11580* — *Pernicka* E., *al.*, Tin in Anatolia [HALL Mark E., *Steadman* Sharon R.]: JMeditArch 5 (1992) 77-103.

11581 *Vitrum,* GLASS: **Dayton** John, The discovery of glass; experiments in the smelting of rich, dry silver ores, and the reproduction of Bronze

Age-type cobalt bleu glass as a slag: American School of Prehistoric Research Bulletin 41. CM 1993, Harvard Peabody Museum. xiv-47 p. 0-87365-544-3.
11582 **Lilyquist** C., *Brill* R. H., Studies in early Egyptian glass 1993 ⇥ 9, 13042; $20: ᴿArOr 62 (1994) 429s (L. *Bareš*).
11583 ᴱ**Newby** Martine, *Painter* Kenneth, Roman glass; two centuries of art and invention 1991 ⇥ 8,b609: ᴿBonnJbb 194 (1994) 643-7 (Mara *Sternini*).
11584 **Nicholson** Paul T., Egyptian faience and glass: Shire Egyptology 18. Princes R. 1993. 80 p.

T1.6   *Silex, os:* 'Prehistory' flint and bone industries.

11585 *Abdarrazak* Aḥmad R., ❾ On the patinization of the Neolithic tools of South Arabia (al-Abr region): RossArkh (1993,2) 24-32; Eng. 33.
11586 *Anderson* Patricia C., *Inizan* Marie-Louise, Utilization du tribulum au début du IIIᵉ millénaire; des lames 'cananéennes' lustrées à Kutan (Ninive V) dans la région de Mossoul, Iraq: Paléorient 20,2 (1994) 85-103.
11587 **Cauvin** Jacques, Naissance des divinités, naissance de l'agriculture; la révolution des symboles au Néolithique: Empreintes. P 1994, CNRS. 304 p. 2-271-05151-7.
11588 *a) D'Errico* Francesco, La vie sociale de l'art mobilier paléolitique; manipulation, transport, suspension des objets en os, bois de cervidés, ivoire; – *b) Bradley* Richard, *al.*, A field method for investigating the distribution of rock art: OxJArch 12 (1993) 145-174; 17 fig. / 129- 143; 9 fig.
11588* **Dibble** Harold L., *Mellars* Paul, The Middle Paleolithic; adaptation, behaviour, and variability: Mg. 78. Ph 1992, Museum. x-216 p. $50. 0-924171-07-3. – ᴿJField 20 (1993) 237s (R. G. *Klein*).
11589 **Golan** Ariel, Myth and symbol; symbolism in prehistoric religions [30 paleolithic motifs like bull's-head, birds, hands, star, cross, reinterpreted in neolithic, and surviving in later folktales and games]. J 1991, auct. 346 p. $50. – ᴿJRel 74 (1994) 149 (M. *Fishbane*).
11589* **Leakey** Richard, *Lewin* Roger, Le origini dell'uomo; lo stato attuale delle ricerche e dell'interpretazione. Mi 1994, Bompiani. 380 p. Lᵐ 38. – ᴿArcheo 9,111 (1994) 105 (M. *Piperno*).
11590 **Luedtke** Barbara E., An archaeologist's guide to chert and flint: Research Tools 7. UCLA Archeol. Inst. 1992. iv-172 p., 38 fig. $18.75. 0-917956-75-3. – ᴿAJA 98 (1994) 566s (F. N. *Kardulian*).
11591 *Mithen* Steven, *al.*, Technology and society during the Middle Pleistocene; hominid group size, social learning and industrial variability: CamArch 4 (1994) 3-32; 3 fig.
11592 *Neeley* Michael P., *Barton* C. Michael, A new approach to interpreting Late Pleistocene microlith industries in southwest Asia: Antiquity 68 (1994) 275-288; 10 fig.
11592* *Rowan* Y. M., *Levy* T. E., Proto-Canaanean blades of the chalcolithic period: Levant 26 (1994) 167-174; 3 fig.
11593 **Stringer** Christopher, *Gamble* Clive, In search of the Neanderthals; solving the puzzle of human origins. L 1993, Thames & H. 247 p.; 83 fig. $19. 0-500-05070-8. – ᴿAntiquity 68 (1994) 656s (P. M*ellars*, also on Tʀɪɴᴋᴀᴜs E. 1993); CamArch 4 (1994) 95-119 (M. *Wolpoff, al.*).

11593* *Atlit: Galili* Ehud, *al.*, Atlit-Yam, A prehistoric site on the sea-floor off the Israeli coast: JField 20 (1993) 133-157; 20 fig.

11594 **Qadeš-Barnea:** *Gilead* Isaac, *Bar-Yosef* Ofer, Early Upper Paleolithic sites in the Qadesh Barnea area, NE Sinai: JField 20 (1993) 268-280; 10 fig.

T1.7 Technologia antiqua.

11594* **Amouretti** Marie-Claire, *Comet* Georges, Hommes et techniques de l'Antiquité à la Renaissance: Cursus. P 1993, Colin. 188 p.; ill. 2-200-21390-5. – ᴿLatomus 53 (1994) 470s (R. *Chevallier*); RHist 290 (1993) 597s (J.-L. *Fray*).

11595 **Balthazar** Judith W., Copper and bronze working in Early through Middle Bronze Age Cyprus: SIMA pocket 84, 1990 ➤ 6,d105: ᴿAJA 97 (1993) 174s (Veronica *Tatton-Brown*: a corpus).

11595* ᴱ**Bonghi Jovino** Maria, Produzione artigianale ed esportazione nel mondo antico, il bucchero etrusco. Mi c. 1994, ET. 237 p.; 125 fig. Lᵐ 80. – ᴿArcheo 9,117 (1994) 125 (G. M. *Della Fina*).

11596 *Cesarini* Giuliano, *Lundborg* Gun, Il carico sulla testa; la donna come 'mezzo di trasporto' dalle radici antichissime: Archeo 9,107 (1994) 108-110; ill.

11597 ᴱ**Curtis** John E., Bronze-working centres 1988 ➤ 6,796: ᴿJNES 53 (1994) 142-5 (Eleanor *Guralnick*).

11598 **Evely** R. D. G., Minoan crafts; tools and techniques: SIMA 92. Gö 1993, Åström.

11599 **Fleury** Philippe, La mécanique de VITRUVE. Caen 1993, Univ. 378 p.; 80 fig. F 240. 2-905461-78-0. – ᴿAJA 98 (1994) 791s (Nancy L. *Klein*); RHist 292 (1994) 188 (M. C. *Amouretti*).

11600 **Hagermann** D., *Schneider* H., Technik-Geschichte: 1 [aus 5] Landbau und Handwerk 750 v.Chr. bis 1000 n.Chr. B 1991, Propyläen. 544 p.; 328 pl. – ᴿGerión 11 (1993) 413s (S. *Montero*).

11601 **Heltzer** Michael, Die Organisation des Handwerks 1992 ➤ 9,13072: ᴿWeltOr 25 (1994) 171s (R. *Haase*).

11602 **Leroi-Gourhan** André, Gesture and speech [... technology], ᵀ*Bostock-Berger* Anna. CM 1993, MIT. $40. 0-262-12173-5. – ᴿAntiquity 68 (1994) 438-441 (P. *Graves*).

11602* *a)* *Lévy* Edmond, La dénomination de l'artisan chez PLATON et ARISTOTE; – *b)* *Frézouls* Edmond, Les noms de métiers dans l'épigraphie de la Gaule et de la Germanie romaines: Ktema 16 (1991) 7-18 / 33-72.

11603 *Lierke* Rosemarie, 'aliud torno teritur'; Rippenschalen und die Spuren einer unbekannten Glastechnologie; heisses Glas auf der Töpferscheibe: AntWelt 24 (1993) 218-234; 38 (color.) fig.

11603* **McNutt** P. M., The forging of Israel ᴰ1990 ➤ 5,b998... 8,d620: ᴿPEQ 125 (1993) 169s (J. F. *Merkel*); VT 44 (1994) 136s (Joan *Oates*).

11604 *McNutt* Paula, The development and adoption of iron technology in the Ancient Near East: ProcGLM 12 (1992) 47-66 [< OTAbs 16, p. 239].

11604* *a)* *Petersmann* Hubert, Les dieux anciens et leurs professions; – *b)* *Jacquemin* Anne, Arkhitekton–ergolabos–ergones; – *c)* *Pavis d'Escurac* Henriette, Dénominations des organisations artisanales dans l'Occident romain: Ktema 15 (1990) 75-80 / 81-88 / 109-120.

11605 *Pusch* Edgar B., Divergierende Verfahren der Metallverarbeitung in Theben und Qantir? Bemerkungen zu Konstruktion und Technik: Äg-Lev 4 (1993) 145-170.

11605* *Raepsaet* Georges, Le renouveau de l'histoire des techniques; quelques jalons récentes [LEMONNIER P. + 7]: AntClas 63 (1994) 325-9.

11606 *Schmidt* Hartmut, Übersicht zur wissenschaftlichen Literatur über das 'Löten und Schweissen in der Antike/Altertum': BBArchäom 12 (1993) 5-53.
11606* *Shalev* Sariel, The change in metal production from the Chalcolithic period to the Early Bronze Age in Israel and Jordan: Antiquity 68 (1994) 630-7; 16 fig.; map p. 1 shows Ghassul as 'metal-producing', but the text (also p. 636) speaks of 'Ghassulian' only as a type-name.
11607 **Shepherd** Robert, Ancient Mining. L 1993, Elsevier Applied Science [& Andover Hamps, Chapman & H.]. xv-494; 69 fig. £65. 1-85861-011-7. – ᴿAntiquity 68 (1994) 188.190 (P. T. *Craddock*: confused, not recommended).
11607* *Tate* Georges, Les métiers dans les villages [rom.-byz.] de la Syrie du Nord: Ktema 16 (1991) 73-78.
11608 **Traina** G., La tecnica in Grecia e a Roma. R 1994, Laterza. 155 p. 16 fig. Lᵐ 15. – ᴿOpus 11 (1992!) 143-6 (G. *Pucci*).
11608* ᴱ**Wartke** Ralf-B., Handwerk und Technologie im Alten Orient; ein Beitrag zur Geschichte der Technik im Altertum. Mainz 1994, von Zabern. viii-151 p. 3-8053-1598-8.

T1.8 **Architectura.**

11609 *Bakhuizen* Simon C., The study of Greek fortifications [ᴱLERICHE P., *Trézing* P., 1982/6]: Babesch 69 (1994) 199-210.
11610 *Blaauw* Sible de, Architecture and liturgy in late antiquity and the Middle Ages: ArLtgW 33 (1991) 1-34.
11611 **Bloom** Jonathan, Minaret, symbol of Islam: Studies in Islamic Art 7. Ox 1989, UP. 216 p.; 136 fig. $55. – ᴿRelStR 20 (1994) 73 (Monique *Seefried*).
11612 **Byun** Tae Ho, Mythos of poiēsis and poiēsis of mythos; towards a mythopoetic configuration of tectonic form for architectural representation ['Architecture is a poetic act to build "the house of God" on earth']: diss. Pennsylvania, ᴰ*Rose* D. Ph 1993. 328 p. 93-21367. – DissA 54 (1993s) 710.
11612* **Çelik** Zeynep, Displaying the Orient; architecture of Islam at nineteenth-century world's fairs: CompMuslimSoc 12. Berkeley 1992, Univ. California. xv-245 p.; 128 fig. $40. – ᴿJAOS 114 (1994) 103s (W. B. *Denny*).
11613 **Clarke** J. R., The houses of Roman Italy 1991 → 8,d640; 9,13091: ᴿAJA 97 (1993) 587s (Penelope *Allison*); Gnomon 66 (1994) 543-550 (R. *Förtsch*).
11614 **Danner** Peter, Griechische Akrotere 1989 → 7,b657; 8,d644: ᴿAntClas 63 (1994) 601s (D. *Viviers*).
11615 *De Bernardi* Attilio, Due esempi di architettura euclidea (il Martyrion di S. Filippo a Hierapolis; il teatro di Segesta): AnPisa 24 (1994) 467-489.
11616 *a) Dourthe* Pierre, Les déplacements liturgiques dans une basilique paléochrétienne, Casa Herrera en Espagne; – *b) Schwebel* Horst, Espace liturgique et expérience humaine: MaisD 197 (1994) 63-69 / 39-61.
11617 DUNAYEVSKY I., mem.: The architecture of ancient Israel, ᴱ**Kempinski** A., *Reich* R. 1992 → 8,48; 9,13095: ᴿBAR-W 20,1 (1994) 8-10 (J. D. *Seger*); BASOR 293 (1994) 89s (O. *Borowski*); PEQ 126 (1994) 82s (G. R. H. *Wtight*); Syria 71 (1994) 448-452 (P. *Braemer*); VT 44 (1994) 432 (G. I. *Davies*).
11618 **Eichmann** Ricardo, Aspekte prähistorischer Grundrissgestaltung in Vor-

derasien ... 9.-4. Jh., ᴰ1991 ➤ 7,b613 ... 9,13098: ᴿBO 51 (1994) 426 (Ö. *Tunca*); OLZ 89 (1994) 47-49 (E. *Lindemeyer*).

11619 **Fleury** P., VITRUVE, De l'architecture I, 1990 ➤ 7,b660 ... 9,13101: ᴿMnemosyne 47 (1994) 137-140 (P. H. *Schrijvers*); RÉLat 72 (1994) 251s (G. *Serbat*).

11619* — ᴱ**Gros** P., Vitruve, De l'architecture IV, 1992 ➤ 8,d652: ᴿAthenaeum 82 (1994) 617s (P. *Frassinetti*).

11620 **Freyberger** K. S., Stadtrömische Kapitelle 1990 ➤ 7,b662; 8,d654: ᴿGnomon 66 (1994) 261-7 (L. *Sperti*, ital.).

11621 **Gans** Ulrich-Walter, Korinthisierende Kapitelle der römischen Kaiserzeit; Schmuckkapitelle in Italien und den nordestlichen Provinzen. Köln 1992. 232 p.; 103 fig. – ᴿBSAA 60 (1994) 549 (M. Ángeles *Gutiérrez Behemerid*).

11622 **Ginouvès** René, Dictionnaire [1. 1986 ➤ 2,9915] 2. Éléments constructifs; supports, couvertures, aménagements intérieurs: Coll. ÉcFr 54. P/R 1992, ÉcFr Athènes/Rome. viii-352 p.; 90 pl. – ᴿClasR 44 (1994) 415 (R. *Ling*); ClasW 88 (1994s) 213s (W. B. *Biers*).

11622* *Griesheimer* M., *Naccache* A., Les hypogées enclos par des chancels (Deir Sunbul, Ğebel Zāwiye, Syrie du Nord): MUSJ 52 (1991s) 75-94 + 42 fig. [➤ 12512*].

11623 **Hellmann** Marie-Christine, Recherches sur le vocabulaire de l'architecture grecque, d'après les inscriptions de Délos: BtÉcFrAR 278. P 1992, de Boccard. 471 p.; 24 pl. – ᴿAntClas 63 (1994) 591 (J.-Y. *Marc*); RÉAnc 96 (1994) 661-3 (M. *Brunet*).

11624 ᴱ**Hoffmann** Adolf, *al.*, Bautechnik der Antike: Kolloquium Berlin 1990/1 ➤ 8,718; 9,13110: ᴿArchWsz 44 (1993) 136-9 (Angela *Dworakowska*); JHS 113 (1993) 226s (R. A. *Tomlinson*); MusHelv 51 (1994) 182 (D. *Willers*).

11625 **Izenour** George C., Roofed theaters of classical antiquity. NHv 1992, Yale Univ. 216 p. $110. 0-300-04685-5. – ᴿClasR 44 (1994) 178s (I. M. *Barton*).

11625* **Kleinbauer** W. Eugene, Early Christian and Byzantine architecture; an annotated bibliography and historiography. Boston 1992, Hall. cxxiii-779 p. – ᴿRÉByz 51 (1993) 331s.

11626 **Krafeld-Daugherty** Maria, Wohnen im Alten Orient [Diss. Wien 1992: ArchAnz (1993) 157]. 1994: ᴿUF 26 (1994) 603-6 (W. *Zwickel*).

11626* **Kramer** Joachim, Korinthische Pilasterkapitelle in Kleinasien und Konstantinopel: IstMitt Supp. 39. Tü 1994. 160 p.; 15 pl. – ᴿByzantion 65,2 (1995) 533s (Catherine *Vanderheyde*).

11627 **Larkin** Diana W., The broken-lintel doorway of ancient Egypt [in use 1700 B.C. - A.D.] and its decoration: diss. NYU 1994, ᴰ*Bothmer* B. 894 p. 94-22936. – DissA 55 (1994s) p. 774.

11628 *Larson*-Miller Lizette, A return to the liturgical architecture of northern Syria: StLtg 24 (1994) 71-83; Kritik, *Renhart* Erich, HDienst 48 (1994) 318-321 (im Text 'Larsen-M.').

11629 **Meinecke** Michael, Die mamlukische Architektur in Ägypten und Syrien 648/1250 bis 923/1317): DAI-K, Abh. Islam. 5, 1992 ➤ 9,13114: ᴿBÉtOr 45 (1993) 289-291 (Marie-Odile *Rousset*).

11630 *Meyer* Jan-Waalke, Tempel- und Palastbauten im eisenzeitlichen Palästina und ihre bronzezeitlichen Vorbilder: ➤ 567, RelG-Beziehungen 1993, 325-8 [< OTAbs 17, p. 29].

11631 *Miglus* P. A., Das neuassyrische und das neubabylonische Wohnhaus; die Frage nach dem Hof: ZAss 84 (1994) 262-276 + 17 fig.

11632 **Nigro** Lorenzo, Ricerche sull'architettura palaziale della Palestina nell'età del bronzo e del ferro; contesto archeologico e sviluppo storico [< diss. Roma, 1992]: Contributi e materiali di archeologia orientale 5. R 1994, Univ. xi-493 p.; 73 fig.; 63 pl. L^m 90. 1120-9631.

11633 **Normann** Alexander von, Architekturtoreutik in der Antike: Diss. Frankfurt. – MiDAV 25,2 (1994) 20.

11634 *Novak* Mirko, Eine Typologie der Wohnhäuser von Nuzi: BaghMitt 25 (1994) 341-410 + 39 fig.

11634* **O'Connor** Colin, Roman bridges. C 1993, Univ. xviii-235 p.; 153 fig.; 11 maps. £65. 0-521-39326-4 [Antiquity 68,432].

11635 **Pevsner** Nicolaus, *al.*, Lexikon der Weltarchitektur³ [¹1971 < Penguin 1966]. Mü 1992, Prestel. 880 p.; 2920 items; 3480 fig.

11635* *Schoep* Ilse, 'Home sweet home'; some comments on the so-called house models from the prehellenic Aegean: OpAth 20 (1994) 189-200; 22 fig.

11636 *Soren* David, *Aylward* William, Dazzling spaces; indulging in architectural fantasies was one way for a rich Roman to keep up with the Julio-Claudians: Archaeology 47,4 (1994) 24-28; ill.

11637 *Spanos* P.Z., Ein Architektur-Modell der Habūr-Keramik; eine Weihgabe?: ⇒ 55, ᶠHROUDA B., Beiträge 1994, 265-8; 1 fig.

11637* **Steible** Horst, Die neusumerischen Bau- und Weihinschriften 1991 ⇒ 8,d676: ᴿAfO 40s (1993s) 93-96 (J. *Bauer*); WZKM 83 (1993) 265s (B. R. *Foster*).

11638 **Thornton** M.K. & R.L., Julio-Claudian building programs; a quantitative study in political management 1989 ⇒ 6,d185 ... 9,13132: ᴿArchWsz 44 (1993) 144s (J. *Kolendo*).

11638* **Tybout** Rolf A., Aedificiorum figurae [VITRUV], Untersuchungen zu den Architekturdarstellungen des frühen [pompeianischen] zweiten Stils [< diss. Leiden]: DutchMgArch 7. Amst 1989, Gieben. ix-462 p.; 21 fig.; 112 pl. $127. 90-5063-042-1. – ᴿJRomArch 6 (1993) 341-7 (Ann *Kutner*).

11639 **Wallace-Hadrill** Andrew, Houses and society in Pompeii and Herculaneum. Princeton 1994, Univ. xix-244 p.; bibliog. 233-240. 0-691-06987-5.

11640 **Ward-Perkins** J.B., Studies in Roman and early Christian architecture. L 1994, Pindar. 530 p.; ill.

11641 **Weber** Margo, Baldachine und Statuenschreine 1990 ⇒ 8,d682: ᴿGnomon 66 (1994) 648-650 (Charlotte *Schreiter*).

11642 **Werner** Peter, Die Entwicklung der Sakralarchitektur in Nordsyrien und Südostkleinasien, vom Neolithikum bis in das 1. Jt. v.Chr.: Mü Univ.Vorderas.St. 15. Mü 1994, Profil. 203 p.; bibliog. p.179-193; 78 pl.; map. 3-89019-351-X.

11642* *Wurster* Wolfgang W., Die Architektur des griechischen Theaters: AntWelt 24 (1993) 20-42; 54 fig.

T1.9 *Supellex;* **furniture; objects of daily life.**

11643 **Cholidis** Nadja, Möbel in Ton 1992 ⇒ 8,d689: ᴿAfO 40s (1993s) 126s (P. *Amiet*); BO 51 (1994) 683-5 (P.R.S. *Moorey*); UF 26 (1994) 594-7 (W. *Zwickel*); ZAss 84 (1994) 294-7 (Agnès *Spycket*).

11644 ᴱ**Corona** Raimondo, (*Piccirillo* M., *Loffreda* S.), Oggetti domestici di Terra Santa al tempo di Cristo e nel periodo bizantino; supplemento agli Atti della Nona Settimana Biblica Abruzzese, Tocco Casauria 4-9 luglio 1994. L'Aquila 1994, Prov. OFM. 51 p.; (color.) fot.

11645 **Daviau** P. M. M., Houses and their furnishings in Bronze Age Palestine 1993 ➤ 9,13136: ᴿJAOS 114 (1994) 667s (W. G. *Dever*); OTAbs 17 (1994) 201 (Elizabeth *Bloch-Smith*).
11646 **Gubel** Eric, Phoenician furniture; a typology based on Iron Age representations with reference to the iconographical context: StPhoen 7, 1987 ➤ 4,d915 ... 8,d695: ᴿZDPV 110 (1994) 193-7 (U. *Hübner*).
11647 **Killen** Geoffrey, Egyptian woodworking and furniture: Egyptology 21. Princes Risborough 1994, Shire. 64 p.; ill. 0-7478-0239-4.
11647* **Killen** Geoffrey, Ancient Egyptian furniture II. Boxes, chests and footstools. Wmr 1994, Aris & P. xii-105 p.; 72 pl. 0-85668-511-9.
11648 **Mols** Stephanus, Houten Meubels in Herculaneum; vorm, techniek en functie; diss. Kath. Univ. Nijmegen 1994: Indagationes Noviomagenses 10. ix-460 p.
11648* *Pilch* John J., House and hearth: BToday 31 (1993) 292-9.
11649 **Thompson** J. A., Hirten, Händler und Propheten; die lebendige Welt der Bibel 1992 ➤ 8,d701: ᴿBL (1994) 20 (J. R. *Porter*: this is a translation of Handbook of Life in Bible times 1986) ➤ 2,9994; 3,d381.

ᴛ2.1   *Res militaris;* **weapons, army activities.**

11650 *Alston* R., Roman military pay from Caesar to Diocletian: JRS 84 (1994) 113-123.
11651 **Arlağan** Çetin, *Bilgi* Önder, ➊ (&) Weapons of the prehistoric age. İstanbul 1989, Sadberk Museum. 119 p.; ill.
11651* *Bayet* Thomas, L'iconologie des enceintes et des portes de camp sur les monnaies du bas-empire romain: RBgNum 40 (1994) 5-17; 9 fig.
11652 *Bettalli* Marco, Il controllo di città e piazzeforti in ᴛᴜᴄɪᴅɪᴅᴇ; l'arte degli assedi nel V secolo a.C.: AnPisa 23 (1993) 825-845.
11653 **Bishop** M. C., *Coulston* J. C. N., Roman military equipment 1993 ➤ 9,13148: ᴿClasR 44 (1994) 137s (B. *Rankov*); Gerión 12 (1994) 366-9 (J. M. *Casillas*); JRomA 7 (1994) 491-5 (H. *Elton*).
11654 **Bol** Peter C., Argivische Schilde: OlympF 17, 1989 ➤ 8,d705: ᴿArch-Wsz 44 (1993) 139s (Maria *Nowicka*).
11654* *Brentjes* Burchard, Waffen der Steppenvölker I. – Dolch und Schwert: ArchMIran 26 (1993) 3-45; 50 fig.; pl. 1-3.
11655 **Brownstone** David, *Franck* Irene, Timelines of war; a chronology of warfare from 100,000 B.C. to the present. Boston 1994, Little Brown. [x-] 562 p. 0-316-11403-0.
11655* *Bruun* Christer, 'Berichtigungsliste' to G. ꜰᴏʀɴɪ's posthumous new list of the provenances of the Roman legionaries [Esercito e marina di Roma antica 1992 ➤ 11667: p. 64-115 supplement to I 1974 p. 11-63]: Arctos 27 (1993) 11-18.
11656 **Campbell** Brian, The Roman army, 31 BC-AD 337; a sourcebook. L 1994, Routledge. xix-272 p.
11657 ᴱ**Chudskij** Yu. C., *Plotniki* Yu. A., ➋ Military practices of the ancient and mediaeval population of northern and central Asia. Novosibirsk 1990, Akad. Nauk. 192 p. – ᴿRossArkh (1994,1) 211-4 (A. R. *Artomyov*).
11658 **Colbow** Gudrun, Die kriegerische Ištar — zu den Erscheinungsformen bewaffneter Gottheiten 1991 ➤ 7,a823: ᴿAfO 40s (1993s) 130s (D. *Collon*).
11659 *Cornik* Pierre, Guerre et armées hittites: RIDA 41 (1994) 99-109.
11660 *Cosme* Pierre, Les légions romaines sur le forum; recherches sur la colonnette mafféienne: MÉF 106 (1994) 167-196; 3 fig.

11661 **Dąbrowa** E., Legio X Fretensis; a prosopographical study of its officers: HistEinz 676, 1993 → 9,13155: ᴿArctos 27 (1993) 196s (O. *Salomies*); Gerión 12 (1994) 372-4 (G. *Bravo*).

11662 **Devijver** H., The equestrian officers of the Roman imperial army 2, 1992 → 9,13156: ᴿClasR 44 (1994) 226 (L. *Keppie*).

11663 **Dixon** K. R., *Southern* P., The Roman cavalry, from the first to the third century A.D. 1992 → 9,13157. 0-7134-6306-1: ᴿJRS 84 (1994) 239 (H. *Sidebottom*).

11664 **Drews** Robert, The end of the Bronze Age; changes in warfare and the catastrophe ca. 1200 B.C. Princeton 1993, Univ. - ᴿJMeditArch 7 (1994) 241s (M. *Liverani*); VT 44 (1994) 425s (J. A. *Emerton*).

11665 *Eck* Werner, Ein Militardiplom für die Auxiliareinheiten von Syria Palaestina aus dem Jahr 160 n.Chr.: KölnerJb 26 (1993) 451-9; 2 fig.

11666 **Flemberg** J., Venus armata 1991 → 8,d717; 9,13159: ᴿGnomon 66 (1994) 705-711 (Wiltrud *Neumer-Pfau*); OpAth 20 (1994) 288s (Olga *Palagia*) & 289-293 (Siri *Sande*).

11667 **Forni** Giovanni †, Esercito e marina di Roma antica: Mavors 17. Stu 1992, Steiner. → 11655*. - ᴿJRS 84 (1994) 237s (Margaret M. *Roxan*, also on SPEIDEL M.).

11667* **Franke** Thomas, Die Legionslegaten der römischen Armée in der Zeit von Augustus bis Traian: AltGesch 9. Bochum 1991, Univ./Brockmeyer. iii-457 p.; p. 458-692. - ᴿRÉAnc 96 (1994) 642s (Y. *Le Bohec*).

11668 **Gagsteiger** Gerti, Die ptolemäischen Waffenmodelle aus Memphis: ÄgBeit 36, 1993 → 9,13160: ᴿArOr 62 (1994) 440s (K. *Smolárikova*).

11668* **González-Conde** Maria Pilar, La guerra y la paz bajo Trajano y Adriano. M 1991, Fund. Pastor. 206 p. 84-404-9012-7. - ᴿLatomus 53 (1994) 698-700 (J. *Gascon*).

11669 **Gopher** Avi, Arrowheads of the Neolithic Levant; a seriation analysis: ASOR diss. 10. WL 1994, Eisenbrauns. xviii-325 p.; bibliog. 303-322. 0-931464-76-5.

11670 **Hanson** Victor D., Le modèle occidental de la guerre; la bataille d'infanterie dans la Grèce antique, ᵀ*Billault* Alain: Histoire. P 1990, BLettres. 298 p. F 135. - ᴿGnomon 66 (1994) 457s (P. *Ducrey*).

11671 **Hyland** A., Training the Roman cavalry; from ARRIAN's Ars tactica. Stroud 1993, Sutton. xiv-197 p.; 35 fig. £26. 0-86299-984-7. - ᴿJRS 84 (1994) 288s (H. *Sidebottom*, also on her Equus 1990).

11672 **Isaac** B., The limits of empire; the Roman army 1990 → 8,d726; 9,13165: ᴿAJA 98 (1994) 792-4 (Susan F. *Alcock*, also on KENNEDY-RILEY); IsrEJ 44 (1994) 129-135 (I. *Shatzman*).

11672* **James** S., The arms and armour from Dura-Europos, Syria: diss. London Univ. College Inst. Arch. c. 1992. - BInstClas 38 (1991-3) 304.

11673 *Kocsis* László, Pannonian weaponry; history of research: → 60, ᶠJÁRDÁNYI-PAULOVICS I. 1994, 63-71.

11674 **Kolias** T., Byzantinische Waffen 1988 → 5,d95* ... 7,b715: ᴿArKulturG 74 (1992) 229s (G. *Jaritz*).

11675 **Kostial** Michaela, Über die Vermeidbarkeit und Unvermeidbarkeit von Kriegen; die Einstellung der Römer zu Krieg und Frieden in der Zeit der Republik: Diss. Augsburg 1993. - Chiron 24 (1994) 443.

11676 **Kunze** Emil, Beinschienen: OlympF 21: 1991 → 9,13168: ᴿAntClas 63 (1994) 599-601 (Sophie *Descamps*); ArchWsz 44 (1993) 135s (P. *Taracha*).

11677 *Landucci Gattinoni* Franca, I mercenari nella politica ateniese dell'età di Alessandro: AncSoc 25 (1994) 33-61.

11678 *Lazenby* J. F., The defence of Greece 490-479 B.C. Wmr 1993, Aris &

P. ix-294; 24 pl.; 8 maps. £24. – ᴿClasR 44 (1994) 413 (T.J. *Quinn*); GreeceR 41 (1994) 94 (J. *Salmon*); Klio 76 (1994) 473s (K.-W. *Welwei*).

11679 a) *Leriche* Pierre, L'étude archéologique des fortifications urbaines grecques; – b) *Winter* Frederick E., Problems of tradition and innovation in Greek fortifications in Asia Minor 5-3c. B.C.; – c) *Debord* Pierre, Le vocabulaire des ouvrages de défense, occurrences littéraires et épigraphiques confrontées aux *Realia* archéologiques: ➤ 466, Fortifications: ᴿRÉAnc 96 (1993/4) 9-27; 6 fig. / 29-42 + 21 fig. / 53-60 + 3 fig.

11680 **Liberati** Anna Maria, *Silverio* Francesco, Legio; storia dei soldati di Roma. R c. 1993, Rivista militare. 224 p.; color. ill. Lᵐ 60. – ᴿArcheo 9,107 (1994) 120 (S. *Moscati*).

11681 **Lissarague** François, L'autre guerrier 1990 ➤ 7,b722...9,13173: ᴿRHR 211 (1994) 97-101 (P. *Ellinger*).

11682 *McKechnie* Paul, Greek mercenary troops and their equipment: Historia 43 (1994) 297-305.

11683 **Mielczarek** Mariusz, Cataphracti and Clibanarii; studies on the heavy armoured cavalry of the ancient world: Art of Warfare 1. Łódź 1993, Naukowa. 145 p.; ill.

11684 **Munn** Mark H., The defense of Attica; the Dema wall ᴰ1993 ➤ 9, 13176: ᴿAJA 98 (1994) 374s (Josiah *Ober*); RÉAnc 96 (1994) 625s (P. *Brun*).

11685 **Rosenberger** Veit, Bella et expeditiones; die antike Terminologie der Kriege Roms: HABES 12, 1992 ➤ 9,13182: ᴿGerión 12 (1994) 347 (M. Pilar *González-Conde Puente*).

11686 *Roth* Jonathan, The size and organization of the Roman imperial legion: Historia 43 (1994) 346-362.

11686* a) *Salvatore* John P., Roman tents 'replicated' in stone-built barracks of the 2d century B.C. in Spain; – b) *Woods* David, The ownership and disposal of military equipment in the Late Roman army: JMilRom 4 (1993) 23-31; 5 fig. / 55-65.

11687 a) *Scafa* Enrico, L'epica omerica e l'organizzazione militare micenea; – b) *Belardi* Walter, Il requisito tecnico primario di una cultura orale: ➤ 450, Mem. DURANTE M., SMEA 33 (1994) 55-67 / 13-24.

11688 **Shaw** Ian, Egyptian warfare and weapons: Egyptology 16. Princes Risborough 1991, Shire. 72 p. 0-7478-0342-8.

11689 **Speidel** Michael P., Riding for Caesar; the Roman emperors' horse guards. L 1994, Batsford. 223 p.

11690 **Speidel** M.P., Roman army studies 2, 1992 ➤ 8,d745: ᴿClasR 44 (1994) 138s (N. *Purcell*); Gerión 11 (1993) 460s (S. *Perea Yébenes*).

11691 **Spence** I.G., The cavalry of classical Greece; a social and military history with particular reference to Athens. Ox 1993, Clarendon. xxiv-344 p. – ᴿAmHR 100 (1995) 1540s (R.M. *Berthold*).

11691* *Taracha* Piotr, Weapons in the shaft graves of Mycenae; aspects of the relative chronology of Circle A and B burials: ArchWsz 44 (1993) 734.

11692 *Woods* D., The Christianization of the Roman army: diss. Belfast c. 1992. – BInstClas 38 (1991-3) 302.

11692* **Worley** J. Leslie, *Hippeis*; the cavalry of ancient Greece. Ox 1994, Westview. 241 p. – ᴿRÉAnc 96 (1994) 623s (P. *Brun*).

T2.2 *Vehicula,* **transportation.**

11693 *Bernabé* A., *al.*, Estudios sobre el vocabulario micénico 2; términos referidos a los carros: Minos 27s (1992s) 125-166; 3 fig.

11694 *Bollweg* Jutta, Mesopotamisch-syrische Terracottawagen: Diss. Köln. – MiDAV 25,2 (1994) 33.
11695 *a*) *Nagel* W., *Strommenger* E., Der frühsumerische Kultschlitten — ein Vorläufer des Wagens?; – *b*) *Buchholz* H.-G., Einige kyprische Pferde-Stirnbänder und Scheuklappen: ➤ 55, ᶠHROUDA B., Beiträge 1994, 201-209; 8 fig.; pl. XIX-XX / 43-59; 8 fig.; pl. IX.
11696 *Spruytte* J., Étude technologique; la roue du char royal assyrien: RAss 88 (1994) 37-46; 12 fig.

T2.3 Nautica.

11697 *Bolshakov* Andrey O., The scene of the boatmen jousting in Old Kingdom tomb representations: BSocÉg 17 (Genève 1993) 29-39.
11697* *Brottier* Laurence, Le port, la tempête et le naufrage; sur quelques métaphores paradoxales employées par Jean CHRYSOSTOME: RevSR 68 (1994) 145-158.
11698 ᴱCasson Lionel, *Steffy* J. Richard, *al.*, The Athlit ram: Nautical Archaeology 3. 1991, Texas A & M. xiii-91 p.; 83 fig. map. $72.50. – ᴿJNES 53 (1994) 213s (D. I. *Owen*).
11698* *Chaffin* Christopher E., The *tessarakonteres* reconsidered [Ptolemy IV's oared warship, largest known]: BInstClas 38 (1991-3) 213-228.
11699 **Duchêne** Hervé, La stèle du port: ÉtThasiennes 14, 1992 ➤ 8,g595*: ᴿAntClas 63 (1994) 495s (A. *Martin*).
11699* *Gagsteiger* Gerti, *Woehl* Anja, Neue Untersuchungen am Schiffswrack von Mahdia [Tunis 100 v.C.; 1907 entdeckt]: AntWelt 24 (1993) 284s; 4 fig.
11700 **Haldane** Cheryl W., Ancient Egyptian hull construction: diss. Texas A & M 1993, ᴰ*Bass* G. 299 p. 93-28731. – DissA 54 (1993s) p. 2629.
11701 *Hesnard* Antoinette, Une nouvelle fouille du port de Marseille: CRAI (1994) 197-216; 9 fig.
11702 **Jones** Dilwyn, A glossary of ancient Egyptian nautical titles and terms 1988 ➤ 4,d142*... 9,13215: ᴿCdÉ 69 (1994) 254-260 (D. *Meeks*).
11702* *Laronde* André, Nouvelles recherches archéologiques dans le port de Lepcis Magna: CRAI (1994) 991-1006; 10 fig.
11703 *Lass* Egon H. E., Quantitative studies in flotation [chiefly plants on the surface of the water] at Ashkelon, 1986 to 1988: BASOR 294 (1994) 23-38; 7 fig.
11703* *McAllister* M., Ancient ship architecture: diss. Dublin Trinity c. 1992. – BInstClas 38 (1991-3) 303.
11704 *Moortel* Aleydis van de, Un graffito de bateau de l'âge du bronze à Malia: BCH 118 (1994) 389-397; 2 fig.
11705 *Moreos* Selim A., Submarine archaeology and its future potential; Alexandria casebook: ➤ 9,2, ᶠABOU DAOUD A. (1993) 199-213; pl. XXXI-XXXII.
11706 *Paoletti* Maurizio, La nave di Porticello; una rotta siciliana: Klearchos 136 (1992) 119-142 + 6 fig.
11707 **Parker** A. J., Ancient shipwrecks of the Mediterranean and the Roman provinces: BAR-Int 580, 1992 ➤ 9,13222: ᴿJRS 84 (1994) 192 (S. *McGrail*).
11708 *Pisarevsky* N. P., ⊕ The 5th international symposium on the history of ships and ship-building in ancient times (Nauplia, 26-29.VIII.1993): VDI 209 (1994) 213-5.
11709 **Rice** Rob S., The Rhodian navy; the proper application of limited

force: diss. Pennsylvania ᴰ*Graham* A. J. Ph 1994. 617 p. – 94-27604. – DissA 55 (1994s) p. 1355.

11710 ᴱ**Shaw** Timothy, The trireme project; operational experience 1987-90; lessons learnt: Oxbow Mg 31, 1993 ➤ 9,13223; £18 pa.: ᴿAntiquity 68 (1994) 429s (C. *Broodbank*).

11711 *Stern* Ephraim, A Phoenician-Cypriote votive scapula from Tel Dor; a maritime scene: IsrEJ 44 (1994) 1-12; 12 fig.

11712 *Tilley* Alec, Sailing to windward in the ancient Mediterranean: IntJ-Naut 23 (1994) 309-313; 1 fig.

11712* **Unger** Richard W., The art of medieval technology; images of Noah the Shipbuilder 1991 ➤ 9,2098: ᴿSpeculum 70 (1995) 973s (T. J. *Runyan*).

11713 **Vinson** Steve, Egyptian boats and ships: Egyptology 20. Princes Risborough 1994, Shire. 56 p. 0-7478-0222-X.

11714 **Wallinga** H. T., Ships and sea-power 1993 ➤ 9,13225: ᴿAmHR 99 (1994) 203 (C. G. *Starr*); BL (1994) 42 (J. R. *Bartlett*); ClasR 44 (1994) 115s (B. *Rankov*); HZ 259 (1994) 745s (D. *Lotze*); JHS 114 (1994) 206-8 (J. S. *Morrison*); Mnemosyne 47 (1994) 709-717 (F. *Meijer*: highly original); TEuph 8 (1994) 177-180 (J. *Elayi*).

11715 *Wedde* Michael, Schiffe der ägäischen Bronzezeit: Diss. Mannheim 1992. – ArchAnz (1993) 160.

11715* *Wigg* David G., Die griechische Triere im archäologischen Experiment: AntWelt 24 (1993) 179-185; 18 fig.

11716 *Yardeni* Ada, Maritime trade and royal accountancy in an erased customs account from 475 B.C.E. on [= erased from] the Aḥiqar scroll from Elephantine: BASOR 293 (1994) 67-78; 4 fig.

11717 *a*) *Zevi* Fausto, Le grandi navi mercantili, Puteoli e Roma; – *b*) *Camodeca* Giuseppe, Puteoli porto annonario e il commercio del grano in età imperiale; – *c*) *Andreau* Jean, Pompéi et le ravitaillement en blé et autres produits de l'agriculture (Iᵉʳ s. ap.J.-C.) [*al.*, area vesuviana]; – *d*) *Johannowsky* Werner, Canali e fiumi per il trasporto del grano: ➤ 432, Ravitaillement 1991/4, 61-67 / 103-128, foldout map / 129-136 [-158] / 159-165.

T2.4 *Athletica,* sport, games.

11718 *Auberger* Janick, Cryptographie ou natation? (*notare/natare*) Qu'apprenaient donc les petits-fils d'Auguste [Suétone 64]: RPg 66 (1992) 209-215.

11719 **August** Roland, Cruelty and civilization; the Roman games. L 1994, Routledge. 222 p. 0-415-10452-1; pa. -3-X.

11720 **Barton** Carlin A., The sorrows of the ancient Romans; the gladiator and the monster 1993 ➤ 9,13226: ᴿAmHR 99 (1994) 531s (R. E. *Mitchell*: politics as struggle); ClasR 44 (1994) 117s (P. de *Souza*); JRS 84 (1994) 188s (J. *Davidson*: she says it is about how their emotional lives were expressed, in the extreme cases).

11721 **Beachem** Richard C., The Roman theatre and its audience 1992 ➤ 9,13228: ᴿClasB 69 (1993) 121-3 (B. S. *Hook*); ClasOut 71 (1993s) 108s (Anne H. *Groton*).

11722 **Bennett** Michael J., The belted hero in early Greece [attribute of seniority and wealth, not skill in war or sport]: diss. Harvard, ᴰ*Vermeule* Emily. CM 1994. 314 p. 94-34857. – DissA 55 (1994s) p. 2019.

11723 *Crowther* Nigel B., *a*) Reflections on Greek equestrian events; violence and spectator attitudes; – *b*) The role of heralds and trumpeters at Greek athletic festivals: Nikephoros 7 (1994) 121-133 / 135-155.

11724 **Davis** Whitney, Masking the blow... in Egyptian art 1992 → 8,d788:
ᴿAntiquity 67 (1993) 457s (I. *Shaw*); JAOS 114 (1994) 664s (Elizabeth
Finkenstaedt: largely on Narmer Palette).

11725 **Decker** Wolfgang,   Sports and games of ancient Egypt [1987], ᵀ*Guttmann* Allen 1992 → 9,13237: ᴿAmHR 99 (1994) 205 (D. G. *Kyle* dubious
about 'athletics', prizes and records); ClasB 69 (1993) 125s (A. J. *Papalas*).

11726 *DeLaine* Janet,   Roman baths and bathing [Nɪᴇʟsᴇɴ I. 1990; Mᴀɴ-
ᴅᴇʀsᴄʜᴇɪᴅ H. 1988; Yᴇɢüʟ F. 1992; Rome Table Ronde 1988/91]:
JRomArch 6 (1993) 348-358.

11727 **Delavaud-Roux** Marie-Hélène,   Les danses armées en Grèce antique
[< diss.]. Aix-en-Provence 1993, Univ.   210 p. (dessins Irigoyen A.;
photos). – ᴿRÉG 107 (1994) 263 (D. *Delattre*: agréable).

11728 **Di Donato** Michele, *Teja* Angela, Agonistica e ginnastica nella Grecia
antica: Qualità della vita 15, 1992 → 5,d175... 8,d771: ᴿNikephoros 7
(1994) 282-4 (W. *Decker*).

11729 ᴱ**Domergue** Claude, *al.*,   Spectacula I, Gladiateurs et amphithéâtres:
colloque 1987/90 → 8,686*: ᴿLatomus 53 (1994) 473s (R. *Chevallier*).

11730 **Gallo** Italo,   Ricerche sul teatro greco: Univ. Salerno, FgClas 2. N
1992, Ed. Scientif. 216 p. – ᴿOrpheus 15 (1994) 165-8 (Maurizia *Mat-
teuzzi*).

11731 **Golvin** J.-C., L'amphithéâtre romain 1988 → 5,d30... 8,d794: ᴿJRom-
Arch 6 (1993) 375-390 (D. L. *Bomgardner*).

11732 *Hall* Alan †, *Milner* Nicholas,   Education and athletics; documents
illustrating the festivals of Oenoanda [100 K W Antalya]: → 49, Mem.
Hᴀʟʟ 1994, 7-47.

11733 *Horsmann* Gerhard,   Die Bescholtenheit der Berufssportler im römischen Recht; zur Bedeutung von 'artem ludicram facere' und 'in scaenam
prodire' in den juristichen Quellen: Nikephoros 7 (1994) 207-227.

11734 **Hübner** Ulrich, Spiele und Spielzeug im antiken Palästina: OBO 121,
1992 → 8,d797; 9,13247: ᴿBL (1994) 28 (A. R. *Millard*); Nikephoros 7
(1994) 279-281 (P. S. *Vermaak*); WZKM 84 (1994) 201s (K. *Jaroš*); ᴢᴀᴡ
106 (1994) 523s (M. *Köckert*).

11735 *Jouanna* Jacques,   La roue tourne et le sportif court... avec une couronne
sur la tête (Aʀɪsᴛᴏᴘʜᴀɴᴇ, Nuées 1005-7): BCH 118 (1994) 35-49; 6 fig.

11736 *Maróti* Egon,   Zur Problematik des Wettlaufes und der Reihenfolge der
einzelnen Disziplinen beim altgriechischen Pentathlon: AcAntH 35 (1994)
1-24.

11737 *Masson* Olivier,   À propos de Théogénès, athlète et héros thasien:
RÉG 107 (1994) 694-7.

11738 **Morgan** Catherine,   Athletes and oracles 1990 → 6,d329 ... 9,13254:
ᴿAntClas 63 (1994) 519s (P. *Bonnechère*).

11739 **Mouratidis** John, ☉ History of physical *agōgē*. Thessaloniki 1990,
xi-596 p.; 70 fig. + 42 color. – ᴿNikephoros 7 (1994) 277s (C. A. *Forbes*).

11740 **Nielsen** Inge, Thermae et balnea, architectural and cultural history 1990
→ 8,d813; 9,13255: ᴿAJA 97 (1993) 185s (F. K. *Yegül*); JRS 84 (1994)
190s (Hazel *Dodge*, also on Lᴇɴᴏɪʀ M. 1991, Lɪᴄʜᴛ K. 1990); RÉLat 72
(1994) 326s (J.-M. *André*).

11741 **Prebish** Charles S.,   Religion and sport; the meeting of sacred and
profane: Contributions to the study of popular culture 36, 1993
→ 9,13258: ᴿChrSchR 24 (1994s) 241-3 (J. A. *Mathisen*).

11742 *Raschke* Wendy J., A red-figure kylix in Malibu [Getty museum Bareiss
collection]; the iconography of female charioteers: Nikephoros 7 (1994)
157-179; pl. 7s.

11743 a) *Rollinger* Robert, Aspekte des Sports im alten Sumer; sportliche Betätigung und Herrschaftsideologie im Wechselspiel; – b) *Vermaak* Petrus S., The Sumerian GEŠPÚ-LIRÙM-MA [game-board]: Nikephoros 7 (1994) 7-64 / 65-82; 7 fig.

11743* *Salza Prina Ricotti* Eugenia, Giocare nel mondo antico: Archeo 9,112 (1994) 48-85; ill.

11744 *Serwint* Nancy, The female athletic costume at the [Olympia] Heraia and prenuptial initiation rites: AJA 97 (1993) 403-422; 5 fig.

11745 *Spadoni Cerroni* Maria Carla, Donne e spettacoli a Roma ed in Italia in età imperiale: RLomb 128,1 (1994) 215-250; 4 fig.

11746 Les thermes romaines [ÉcFr 11-12 Nov. 1988]: Coll.ÉcFrR 142, 1988/91: ᴿBonnJbb 194 (1994) 603-8 (I. *Nielsen*).

11747 ᴱ**Vanhove** Doris, Le sport dans la Grèce antique; du jeu à la compétition: exposition 1992. Bru 1992, Palais des Beaux Arts. 424 p.; ill.

11748 *Visa* Valerie, a) Une image cynégétique et sportive pour le triomphe de Cypris (Hippolyte, 1268-1271): RÉG 107,2 (1994) 381-390; – b) L'image de l'athlète dans la Collection hippocratique: ➤ 430b, Tratados 1990/2, 273-283.

11749 **Wiedemann** Thomas, Emperors and gladiators 1992 ➤ 8,d827: ᴿAmHR 99 (1994) 877 (G. M. *Woloch*); ClasR 44 (1994) 127s (D. *Shotter*); JRS 84 (1994) 229-231 (D. *Potter*: best in English, synthesizing and adding to though not aiming to replace ROBERT, VILLE, GOLVIN).

11750 **Wistrand** Magnus, Entertainment and violence in ancient Rome; the attitudes of Roman writers of the 1st century A.D.: StGrLatG 56. Göteborg 1992, Acta Univ. 133 p. Sk 150. – ᴿArctos 27 (1993) 163s (Eva *Nyman-Kaarakka*).

11751 **Yegül** Fikret, Baths 1992 ➤ 9,13267: ᴿAJA 98 (1992) 380s (Ann O. *Koloski-Ostrow*); ClasO 72 (1994s) 68 (J. C. *Anderson*).

T2.5 **Musica**, dance.

11751* **Adler** Israel, (*Shalem* Lea), Hebrew notated manuscript sources up to circa 1840; a descriptive and thematic catalogue with a checklist of printed sources: Répertoire internationale des sources musicales B-IX,1. Mü 1989, Henle. lxxx-900 p. – ᴿSefarad 53 (1993) 209s (M. *Sánchez*).

11752 **Badalì** Enrico, Strumenti musicali ... delle feste ittite [< diss. 1980] 1991 ➤ 7,b806; 9,13269: ᴿBO 51 (1994) 606-8 (C. *Zinko*); WZKM 83 (1993) 276-284 (J. *Klinger*).

11752* *Barker* Andrew, Greek musicologists in the Roman Empire: Apeiron 27,4 (1994) 53-74.

11753 *Caredou* Giorgio, L'étui à hautbois du Musée Égyptien de Turin [avec scène de musique]: CdÉ 69 (1994) 43-53; 2 fig.

11753* **Duchesne-Guillemin** Marcelle, Les instruments de musique dans l'art sassanide: IrAnt supp. 6. Gent 1993, (Lv) Peeters. vi-127 p. Fb 900. 90-6831-469-6. – ᴿMesopT 29 (1994) 342s (A. *Invernizzi*).

11754 **Eichmann** Ricardo, Koptische Lauten; eine musikarchäologische Untersuchung von sieben Langhalslauten des 3.-9. Jh. n.Chr. aus Ägypten: DAI-K Sond. 27. Mainz 1994, von Zabern. xxiv-157 p.; 24 pl.; 8 foldouts.

11754* **Flashar** Martin, Apollon Kitharodos, statuarische Typen des musischen Apollon. Köln 1992, Böhlau. 244 p.; 186 fig. – ᴿMusHelv 51 (1994) 184 (L. E. *Baumer*).

11755 **Gorali** Moshe, The Old Testament in music 1993 ➤ 9,13277c: ᴿAriel 98 (J 1994) 89ss (E. *Schleifer*: for 20 years he made controversial reconstructions of biblical instruments and music-sounds, but this book is rather on 5740 compositions by later Jewish and Christian music-composers, lavishly illustrated).

11755* *Gurney* O. R., Babylonian music again: Iraq 56 (1994) 101-6.

11756 **Haïk-Vantoura** Suzanne, The music of the Bible 1991 ➤ 7,b813 ... 9,13279: ᴿSWJT 36,1 (1993s) 50s (D. W. *Music, sic*).

11757 **Idelsohn** A. Z., Storia della musica ebraica, ᵀᴱ*Jona* A. F 1994, Giuntina. 392 p. Lᵐ 56. – ᴿRasT 35 (1994) 507 (Cloe *Taddei Ferretti*).

11758 **Lonsdale** Steven H., Dance and ritual play in Greek religion: Ancient Society and History. Baltimore 1993, Johns Hopkins Univ. xxi-352 p.; 20 fig. £33. – ᴿGreeceR 41 (1994) 247 (P. *Walcot*: daring).

11758* *McKinnon* J., Music in early Christian literature. C 1989, Univ. 180 p. [cf. ➤ 9,13228]: ᴿCompostellanum 38 (1993) 261 (E. *Romero Pose*).

11759 *Saadé* Gabriel, Histoire de la musique arabe: BÉtOr 45 (1993) 201-219; Eng.; ❍ 286.

11760 *Seidel* Hans, Musik und Religion ANT: ➤ 517, TRE 23 (1994) 441-6 [-495 al.].

11761 *Taddei Ferretti* Cloe, Interdipendenza liturgica e musicale nella Sinagoga e nella Chiesa [... WERNER E., 1983]: RasT 35 (1994) 220-4.

11762 *Ulanowska* Agata, The gold ring from Mycenae; some remarks about dance: ArchWsz 44 (1993) 113-7.

11762* *Vandersleyen* Claude, Emheb, le prince nubien qui jouait du tambour: ➤ 73, ᶠLECLANT J., 2 (1994) 399-400.

11763 **Werner** Eric, The sacred bridge [1. 1959 ➤ 1,6628]; 2. The interdependence of liturgy and music in synagogue and church during the first millennium. NY 1994, KTAV. xviii-271 p.; music plates.

11763* **West** M. L., Ancient Greek music 1992 ➤ 8,d859; 9,13302; £50: ᴿÉtClas 62 (1994) 283 (D. *Donnet*).

T2.6 **Textilia,** *vestis.*

11764 **Barber** Elizabeth Wayland, Women's work the first 20,000 years; women, cloth, and society in early times. NY 1994, Norton. 334 p. $23 [BAR-W 20/5,8].

11764* *Blakolmer* Fritz, Ikonographische Beobachtungen zu Textilkunst und Wandmalerei in der bronzezeitlichen Ägäis: JbÖsA 63-B (1994) 1-28; 13 fig.

11765 *Freydank* Helmut, Gewänder für ein Dolmetscher: AltOrF 21 (1994) 31-33.

11766 **Germer** Renate, Die Textilfärberei 1992 ➤ 8,d865; 9,13309: ᴿDiscEg 26 (1993) 113s (Gillian *Vogelsang-Eastwood*).

11767 *Goldman* Bernard, The later pre-Islamic riding costume: IrAnt 28 (1993) 201-232; 41 fig.; VII pl.; bibliog. 232-9.

11768 a) *Goldman* Norma, Roman footwear; – b) *Goldman* Bernard, Graeco-Roman dress in Syro-Mesopotamia [*Roussin* Lucille A., Mishnah]: ➤ 488, World of Roman costume 1988/94, 101-127; 31 fig. / 163-181; 21 fig. [182-190].

11768* *Green* Lyn, More than a fashion statement; clothes and hairstyles as indicators of social status in ancient Egypt: BuCanadMesop 26 (1993) 29-38.

11769 *Hägg* Inga, Über quantitative Bearbeitung und Deutung eines archäologischen Textilmaterials: AcArchK 65 (1994) 197-202; 4 fig.

11770 **Hooft** P. P. M., van 't, *al.*, Pharaonic and early medieval Egyptian textiles: Collections 8. Leiden 1994, Rijksmuseum van Oudheden. xviii-199 p.

11771 *Kakovkine* Alexandre, a) Une étoffe copte avec l'image au sujet d'une parabole du Livre de Barlaam et Josaphat: GöMiszÄg 134 (1993) 55-61; – b) D'un tissu copte du musée allemand des tissus à Krefeld: GöMiszÄg 132 (1993) 67-72; 1 fig.

11773 **Kühnel** Harry, Bildwörterbuch der Kleidung 1992 → 8,d871; 9,13312: ᴿByZ 86 (1994) 150s (Gabriella *Schubert*).

11774 **Losfeld** Georges, L'art grec et le vêtement. P 1994, de Boccard. 550 p.; 30 pl. 2-7018-0086-2.

11775 **Losfeld** Georges, Essai sur le costume grec 1991 → 7,b840; 9,13314: ᴿLatomus 53 (1994) 691s (M.-L. *Freyburger-Galland*).

11776 **Martiniani-Reber** Marielle, Tissus coptes 1991 → 8,d872: ᴿBO 51 (1994) 584-6 (Patrice *Cauderlier*).

11776* **Nauerth** Claudia, Koptische Stoffe. Fra 1986, Liebighaus. 47 p.; 35 fig. – ᴿVizVrem 53 (1992) 202s (A. Ya. *Kakovkin*, ❸).

11777 *Pilch* John J., Why do you worry about clothing?: BToday 31 (1993) 353-360.

11778 **Potthoff** Anne, Lateinische Kleidungsbezeichnungen 1992 → 9,13318: ᴿAnzAltW 46 (1993) 190s (F. *Lochner von Hüttenbach*); Gnomon 66 (1994) 559s (J. *André*); RPg 67 (1993) 160s (P. *Flobert*).

11779 **Renner-Volbach** Dorothee, Spätantike und koptische Textilien ... Köln 1992 → 8,d878: ᴿOLZ 89 (1994) 530-4 (P. *Linscheid*, C. *Fluck*).

11780 **Scharf** Ursula, Römische Frauenkleidung; Texte und Dokumentation: Diss. Fra 1992. – ArchAnz (1993) 159.

11781 **Schmidt** Doris, Kleidung in der Antike, 1. Griechen; 2. Römer. Hohengehren 1992, Schneider. [3. Äg-Bab. 1992 → 9,13321].

11782 **Scholz** Birgit, Untersuchungen zur Tracht der römischen Matrona 1992 → 9,13322; DM 98; 3-412-01491-5: ᴿJRS 84 (1994) 192-7 (N. *Hannestad*, briefly amid five other sculpture surveys).

11783 a) *Stone* Shelley, The toga, from national to ceremonial costume; – b) *Sebesta* Judith L., Symbolism in the costume of the Roman woman (colors) [bride, *La Folette* L.]: → 488, World of Roman costume 1988/94, 13-45; 20 fig. / 46-53 (65-76) [54-64, 6 fig.].

11784 *Taverna* Donatella, Il cavallo alato; elementi per uno studio iconologico di un tessuto orientale dalla teca del Santo Volto in Genova: Mesop-T 28 (1993) 195-221; 2 fig.

11785 Tissus d'Égypte, témoins du monde arabe VIIIᵉ-XVᵉ siècles, collection Bouvier. Genève/P 1993, Musée d'art / Inst. Monde Arabe. 351 p.; 132 fig. + 143 color.; 2 maps. Fs 65. – ᴿCdÉ 69 (1994) 397-9 (A. *Mekhitarian*).

11785* *Trinkl* Elisabeth, Ein Set aus Spindel, Spinnwirtel und Rocken aus einem Sarkophag in Ephesus: JbÖsA 63-B (1994) 81-86; 2 fig.

11786 **Vogelsang-Eastwood** G., Pharaonic Egyptian clothing: Studies in Textile and Costume History 2, 1993 → 13325; 44 pl. *f* 140; 90-04-09744-9: ᴿJStOT 64 (1994) 121 (P. R. *Davies* looked in vain for a coat of many colours); ᴢAW 106 (1994) 371 (B. *Arnst*).

11787 **Vogelsang-Eastwood** Gillian, Patterns for ancient Egyptian clothing. Leiderdorp 1992, auct. 49 p.

11788 **Walters** Elizabeth J., Attic graves ... women/dress 1988 ➤ 5,d543 ...
8,d885:   ᴿGnomon 66 (1994) 351-4 (K. *Parlasca*).

T2.7   *Ornamenta corporis,* **jewelry, mirrors.**

11789 **Amorai-Stark** S., Engraved gems and seals from two collections in
Jerusalem: SBF museum 11. J 1993, Franciscan. 178 p.; 54 pl. [Liber
Annuus 44,743].
11790 *Buffa Giolito* M. Franca, Lapis e gemma in Pᴸɪɴɪᴏ il Vecchio:
BStLat 24 (1994) 93-100; Eng. 100.
11791 *Formigli* Edilberto, *Heilmeyer* Wolf-Dieter,   Einige Fälschungen
antiken Goldschmucks im 19. Jahrhundert: ArchAnz (1993) 299-332;
44 fig.
11791* **Gesenhoff** Georgia,   Untersuchungen zum griechischen Schmuck an
Beispielen des 7. und 6. Jahrhunderts v.Chr. [Diss. Münster 1992]. Engelbach 1994, Hansen. 286 p. auf 3 Microfiches. – ᴿMusHelv 51 (1994)
183 (D. *Willers*).
11792 **Fellner** Hans-Jörg, Gürtelbleiche aus Urarṭu 1991 ➤ 7,b862; 9,13337:
ᴿAcArchH 46 (1994) 443s (M. *Szabó*); AfO 40s (1993s) 109s (J.
Borchhardt); BO 51 (1994) 445-7 (M. *Wäfler*); OLZ 89 (1994) 50-52 (R. B.
Wartke).
11793 **Musche** Brigitte, Vorderasiatischer Schmuck: HbOr 7/1/2/7, 1992 ➤ 8,
d896; 9,13340:   ᴿAcArchH 46 (1994) 439-441 (J. *Makkay*); MesopT 29
(1994) 295-8 (P. *Brunasco*); OLZ 89 (1994) 149-152 (Ellen *Rehm*).
11794 **Pfrommer** Michael, Untersuchungen zur Chronologie früh- und hoch-
mittelhellenistischen Goldschmucks: IstFor 37, 1990 ➤ 9,13342; 3-8030-
1758-0:   ᴿAJA 97 (1993) 580s (Stella G. *Miller*); Syria 71 (1994) 472-5 (G.
Nicolini).
11795 **Pirzio Biroli Stefanelli** Lucia, Oro/gioielli 1992 ➤ 8,d888; 9,13331:
ᴿAntClas 63 (1994) 643 (J. C. *Balty*).
11796 *Postgate* J. N., Rings, torcs and bracelets: ➤ 55, ᶠHʀᴏᴜᴅᴀ B., Beiträge 1994, 235-245; 4 fig.
11796* **Rehm** Ellen, Der Schmuck der Achämeniden: Altertumskunde des
Vorderen Orients 2. Münster 1992, Ugarit. xii-468 p.; bibliog. 306-335;
120 fig. 3-927120-11-1.
11797 **Rehm** Ellen, Untersuchungen zum achämenidischen Schmuck: Diss.
Münster 1992. – ArchAnz (1993) 159.
11797* *Rehm* Ellen, Inkrustation bei achämenidischen Armreifen [bracelets]:
ArchMIran 26 (1993) 105-7; pl. 16-17.
11798 *Richthofen* Jasper von, Gebrauchsspuren an Silber- und Bronzefibeln
der älteren römischen Kaiserzeit Norddeutschlands: Offa 51 (1954) 49-
98; 47 fig.; 2 pl.
11799 *Shaw* Ian, *Jameson* Robert, Amethyst mining in the Eastern Desert; a
preliminary survey at wadi el-Hudi: JEA 79 (1993) 81-97; 4 fig.; pl. V.
11800 *Skrzhinskaya* M. V., ❸ On the history of classic jewelry [Greece from
200 B.C.: to N. Pontus]: RossArkh (1994,1) 18-25; 2 fig.; Eng. 25.
11801 *Stout* Ann M., Jewelry as a symbol of status in the Roman empire:
➤ 489, World of Roman costume 1988/94, 77-100; 34 fig.
11802 *Sweeney* Deborah, Egyptian masks in motion: GöMiszÄg 135 (1993)
101-4; 1 fig.
11803 *Szilágyi* Janos G., *Bouzek* Jan, Corpus Speculorum Etruscorum;
Hongrie-Tchécoslovaquie. R 1992, Bretschneider. 156 p.; 79 pl. Lᵐ 250.
– ᴿRBgPg 72 (1994) 214-6 (R. *Lambrechts*).

11804 *Völling* Thomas, Studien zu Fibelformen der jüngeren vorrömischen Eisenzeit und ältesten römischen Kaiserzeit: Bericht der röm.-germ. Komm. 75 (1994) 147-282; 37 fig.

11804* *Weiss* Carina, Virgo, Capricorn und Taurus; zur Deutung augusteischer Symbolgemmen: JbDAI 109 (1994) 353-369; 9 fig.

11805 **Williams** Dyfri, *Ogden* Jack, Greek gold; jewellery of the classical world. L 1994, British Museum. 256 p.

11806 **Wiman** Ingela M. B., Malstria-malena; metals and motifs in Etruscan mirror craft: SIMA 91. Göteborg 1990, Åström. 264 p.; ill. – ᴿLatomus 53 (1994) 961-3 (J.-R. *Jannot*).

11807 *Wiseman* T. P., The she-wolf mirror; an interpretation: PBritSR 61 (1993) 1-6; 2 fig.

T2.8   **Utensilia.**

11808 *Buchholz* Hans-Günter, Sakralschaufeln im antiken Zypern: RepCyp (1994) 129-154; 10 fig.; pl. XXV-XXVIII.

11809 **De Tommaso** Giandomenico, Ampullae vitreae, contenitori 1990 ➤ 9, 13352: ᴿJRomArch 6 (1993) 409 (D. *Whitehouse*); Latomus 53 (1994) 200s (M. *Vanderhoeven*).

11810 **Gillis** Carole, Minoan conical cups: SIMA 89, 1990 ➤ 9,13354: ᴿAntClas 63 (1994) 585s (R. *Laffineur*); OpAth 20 (1994) 263-6 (J. L. *Davis*).

11811 **Klein** Harald, Untersuchung... Nadeln ᴰ1992 ➤ 9,13359: ᴿAfO 40s (1993s) 193 (Erika *Bleibtreu*).

11812 **Lalou** E., Les tablettes à écrire: CNRS 1991/92 ➤ 9,527: ᴿRÉG 107 (1994) 273s (Geneviève *Husson*).

11812* *Miller* Margaret C., Adoption and adaptation of Achaemenid metalware forms in Attic black-gloss ware of the fifth century: ArchMIran 26 (1993) 109-146; pl. 38-42.

11813 **Miron** Eli [d. 1990], Axes and adzes from Canaan 1992 ➤ 9,13362: ᴿBASOR 296 (1994) 81 (W. G. *Dever*); BO 51 (1994) 692-5 (P. R. S. *Moorey*).

11814 **Müller-Karpe** Michael, Metallgefässe im Iraq I (von den Anfängen bis zur Akkad-Zeit): PrähBronzefunde 2/14. Stu 1993, Steiner. 352 p.; 181 pl. dessins, 18 pl. phot. – ᴿAulaO 12 (1994) 140s (E. *Olávarri*); BuCanadMesop 28 (1994) 43s (M. *Fortin*); Paléorient 20,2 (1994) 174-6 (Françoise *Tallon*).

11814* **Pfrommer** Michael, Metalwork [rhyta, ornaments] from the Hellenized East. Malibu CA 1993, Getty Museum. xii-244 p.; 45 fig.; 8 pl. 0-89236-218-9. – ᴿMesopT 29 (1994) 333-7 (A. *Invernizzi*).

11815 **Sakowski** Anja, Darstellungen von Dreifusskesseln des 6. und frühen 5. Jhs. v.Chr.: Diss. Berlin, Freie Univ. – MiDAV 25,2 (1994) 13.

11815* *Selz* Gebhard, Drei Beobachtungen zur 'Silbervase' des Entemena: AulaO 11,1 (1993) 107-111; Eng 107.

11816 *Shefton* Brian B., The Waldalgesheim situla; where was it made? [south Italy]: ➤ 35, ᶠFREY O., 1994, 583-593; 3 fig.

11817 **Vickers** Michael, *Gill* David, Artful crafts; ancient Greek silverware and pottery. Ox 1994, Clarendon. xiii-255 p.; bibliog. 205-238.

11818 **Ward** Rachel, Islamic metalwork. L 1993, British Museum. 128 p.

T2.9   *Pondera et mensurae* – **Weights and measures.**

11819 *Eran* A., Weights from excavations 1981-1984 at Shiloh: ZDPV 110 (1994) 151-157; pl. 9.

11820 *Gatier* Pierre-Louis,   Poids inscrits de la Syrie hellénistique et romaine (III): Syria 61 (1994) 143-9; 4 fig.

11821 ᴱ**Gyselen** Rika,   Prix, salaires, poids et mesures: Res Orientales 2, 1990 ➤ 8,d924:   ᴿMesopT 29 (1994) 314-7 (P. *Mollo*).

11821* *Jursa* Michael,   Zweierlei Mass: AfO 40s (1993s) 71-73.

11822 *Kletter* Raz,   Phoenician (?) weights from Horvat Rosh Zayit [W Galilee]: Atiqot 25 (1994) 33-43; 3 fig.

11823 *Lafont* Bertrand,   Normes, normativité, diversité dans le Proche Orient ancien [calendrier, mesures]:   CahGlotz 5 (1994) 1-20; 3 pl.

11823* *Marazzi* Massimiliano,   Tarife und Gewichte in einem althethitischen Königserlass: Orientalia 63 (1994) 88-92.

11824 *Parise* Nicola F.,   Unità ponderali orientali in occidente ➤ 433: Kokalos 39s (1993s) 135-141.

11824* *Rottländer* Rolf C. A.,   Das neue Bild der antiken Metrologie: JbÖsA 63 (1994) 1,16; 13 fig. [17-47, *Raster*].

11825 **Romano** David G.,   Athletes and mathematics in archaic Corinth; the origin of the Greek stadion: Mem. 306.   Ph 1993, Am.Phil.Soc. xiv-117 p.; 53 fig. $25 pa.   0-87169-206-6. – ᴿAntiquity 68 (1994) 429 (C. *Broodbank*); Nikephoros 7 (1994) 285-9 (W. *Decker*).

11826 *Zwarte* R. de,   Der ionische Fuss und das Verhältnis der römischen, ionischen und attischen Fussmasse zueinander: Babesch 69 (1994) 115-143; 9 fig.

T3.0   **Ars antiqua,** *motiva, picturae* [icones ➤ T3.1 infra].

11827 *Amedick* Rita,   Herakles im Speisesaale: MiDAI-R 101 (1994) 103-119; 3 fig. pl. 43.

11828 **Arafat** K. W.,   Classical Zeus 1990 ➤ 6,814.d471 ... 8,d931:   ᴿBabesch 69 (1994) 214-6 (J. M. *Hemelrijk*).

11829 **Bahnassi** Afif,   Das alte Syrien und seine Kunst.   Lp 1987, Seemann. 139 p.; ill. [? =   ➤ 3,d583, Die Kunst des alten Syrien, Stu 1987, Kohlhammer; 140 p.].

11830 *Baines* John,   On the status and purposes of ancient Egyptian art: CamArch 4 (1994) 67-94; 19 fig.

11830* *Bednarik* Robert G.,   The earliest known art: AcArchK 65 (1994) 221-232; 5 fig.

11831 **Belting** Hans,   Bild und Kult; eine Geschichte des Bildes vor dem Zeitalter der Kunst 1990 ➤ 6,d878 ... 8,d932: ᴿTZBas 50 (1994) 269s (C. *Dohmen*).

11831* **Belting** Hans,   Likeness and presence; a history of the image before the era of art [1990   ➤ 6,d478], ᵀ*Jephcott* Edmond.   Ch 1994, Univ. xxiv-651 p. $65.   0-226-04214-6 [TDig 42,55].

11832 **Benelli** Gian Carlo,   Arte, memoria, utopia; antropologia dell'arte e fenomenologia della verità: Ippogrifo 14.   R 1993, Bonacci.   257 p.

11832* **Böhm** Stephanie,   Die nackte Göttin 1990 ➤ 8,d936:   ᴿGnomon 66 (1994) 441-5 (W. *Schiering*); OpAth 20 (1994) 266-9 (J. *Flemberg*).

11833 ᴱ**Buitron-Oliver** Diana,   New perspectives in early Greek art. Wsh/ Hanover 1991, National Gallery/Univ. Press NE. 308 p.; 289 fig.; 16 pl. 0091-7338. – ᴿAJA 98 (1994) 168s (Mary *Stieber*).

11834 **Castriota** David,   Myth, ethos and actuality; official art in fifth-century B.C. Athens 1992 ➤ 8,d940:   ᴿClasR 44 (1994) 157s (R. A. *Tomlinson*); GreeceR 41 (1994) 101 (B. A. *Sparkes*).

11835 **Chevallier** Raymond,   L'artiste, le collectionneur et le faussaire; pour

une sociologie de l'art romain 1991 → 9,13388:   ᴿLatomus 53 (1994) 487s
(J. *Debergh*).

11835* **Dierichs** Angelika,   Erotik in der Kunst Griechenlands: AntWelt 24
Sondernummer 2 (1993) 136 p.; 221 fig.

11836 ᴱ**Eaton-Krauss** Marianne, *Graefe* Erhart,   Studien zur ägyptischen
Kunstgeschichte 1990 → 6,484:   ᴿCdÉ 69 (1994) 266-271 (R. *Tefnin*).

11837 *Fayard-Meeks* C.,   Face et profil dans l'iconographie égyptienne: Or-
LovPer 23 (1992) 15-36; 2 pl.

11838 ᴱ**Gazda** Elaine K.,   Roman art in the private sphere; new perspectives
on the art and decor of the domus, villa and insula.   AA 1991, Univ.
Michigan.   260 p. $42.50.   0-472-10196-X. – ᴿBonnJbb 194 (1994) 623-8
(V. M. *Strocka*); ClassJ 89 (1993s) 312-8 (W. C. *Archer*).

11839 ᴱ**Goldhill** Simon, *Osborne* Robin, Art and text in ancient Greek culture.
C 1994, Univ. xiv-341 p.; 34 fig. £40.   0-521-41185-8. – ᴿAntiquity 68
(1994) 650-5 (J. *Tanner*, also on Boardman J. 1993).

11840 **Goodenough** Erwin,   Jewish symbols in the Greco-Roman period
[1953-68, 13 vol.], abridged, ᴱ*Neusner* Jacob: Bollingen Series.   Princeton
1988, Univ. xlvi-274 p.; 91 fig. $44.50.   0-691-09967-7. – ᴿJSS 39 (1994)
120-3 (Gabrielle *Sed-Rajna*).

ᴱ**Hägg** R.,   Iconography of Greek cult 1990/2 → 423*.

11840* **Hamilton** Richard,   Choes and Anthesteria; Athenian iconography
and ritual.   AA 1992, Univ. Michigan. xv-266 p.; 18 pl. $37.50. – ᴿClas-
Pg 89 (1994) 372-5 (T. H. *Carpenter*).

11841 **Haskell** F.,   History and its images; art and the interpretation of the
past.   NHv 1993, Yale Univ.   558 p.; ill. – ᴿNumC 154 (1994) 283-5 (L.
Syson).

11841* **Karageorghis** V.,   The coroplastic art of ancient Cyprus II.   Late
Cypriote II – Cypriote Geometric III.   Nicosia 1993, Leventis. xii-112 p.
£C 20. – ᴿClasR 44 (1994) 148-151 (H. W. *Catling*); JHS 114 (1994) 222
(Veronica *Tatton-Brown*); RStFen 22 (1994) 276s (D. *Ciafaloni*).

11842 *Holl* Augustín,   Pathways to elderhood; research on past pastoral
iconography from the Tikadouine (Tassili-n-Ajjer) [Sahara]: Origini 18 (R
1994) 69-112; 13 fig.; Eng. 113.

11842* ᴱ**Holliday** Peter J.,   Narrative and event in ancient art: New
Art Hist/Crit.   C 1993, Univ. xvi-368 p.; bibliog. 330-357.   0-521-
430-13-5.

11843 **Ling** Roger,   Roman painting 1991 → 8,d964; 9,13397: ᴿAntClas 63
(1994) 638-640 (Janine *Balty*); ClasR 44 (1994) 165-7 (M. A. R. *Colledge*);
Gnomon 66 (1994) 256-281 (V. M. *Strocka*); Latomus 53 (1994) 953-6 (H.
Eristov).

11843* *Mettinger* Tryggve N. D.,   Aniconism – a west-Semitic context for the
Israelite phenomenon: → 467*, Ein Gott allein? 1993/4, 157-178.

11844 **Milde** H., Vignettes / Neferrenput 1991 → 9,13399: ᴿJAmEg 31 (1994)
226-8 (L. H. *Lesko*).

11845 **Miller** Stella G.,   The tomb of Lyson and Kallikles; a painted
Macedonian tomb.   Mainz 1993, von Zabern. xlv-129 p., 27 pl. + 5
colour. DM 120. – ᴿGreeceR 41 (1994) 102 (B. A. *Sparkes*: high praise).

11845* *Morris* Sarah P.,   Daidalos and the origins of Greek art 1992 → 8,
d967; 9,13401 [Arethusa 28,113, M. *Bernal*]. Princeton 1992, Univ.
xxx-411 p.; 62 fig.

11846 *Neureiter* Sabine,   Eine neue Interpretation des Archaismus: StÄK 21
(1994) 219-254.

11847 **Nowinski** Andrzej, Studies on the illustrated Theban funerary papyri:

OBO 86.   FrS/Gö 1989, Univ./VR.   xxxii-402 p.; 90 fig.   DM 170.   3-7278-0613-... / 3-525-53716-6. – ᴿJEA 79 (1993) 309-315 (S. *Quirke*).
11848 **Paglia** Camille,   Sexual personae; art and decadence from Nefertiti to Emily Dickinson 1991 ⇒ 9,13403:   NY 1991, Random. 736 p. $15 pa. – ᴿPersp[Ref] 8,1 (1993) 20-22 (Jane *Bach*).
11849 **Pairault-Massa** Françoise-H.,   Iconologia e politica nell'Italia antica; Roma, Lazio, Etruria dal VII al I sec. a.C.: BtArch 18. Mi 1992, Longanesi. 259 p.; 229 fig.
11849* **Potts** Alan,   Flesh and the ideal; WINCKELMANN and the origins of art history. NHv 1994, Yale Univ. vii-224 p. 0-300-05813-6.
11850 **Reid** Jane D. (*Rohmann* Chris),   The Oxford guide to classical mythology in the arts, 1300-1990s, 1. Achelous-Leander; 2. Leda-Zeus. NY 1993, Oxford-UP. xxiii-1310 p.
11850* **Robertson** Morton,   A shorter history of Greek art. C 1994 = 1981, Univ. xi-240 p. 0-521-28084-2.
11851 **Robins** Gay,   Proportion and style in ancient Egyptian art. L 1994, Thames & H. ix-283 p.; 208 fig.; 19 pl. £24.   0-500-23680-1. – ᴿAntiquity 68 (1994) 431 (C. *Broodbank*).
11852 *Robins* Gay,   On supposed connections between the 'canon of proportions' and metrology: JEA [79 (1993) 157-177, SIMON C.] 80 (1994) 191-4.
11853 **Rosenberg** Silvia,   Enchanted landscapes; wall paintings from the Roman era [77 of the 93 from Naples bay; Jerusalem Bible Lands museum exposition]. J 1993, R. Sirkis. 176 p. $40. – ᴿBAR-W 20,4 (1994) 10 (Bettina *Bergmann*).
11854 **Sakellarakis** J.A.,   The Mycenaean pictorial style in the National Archaeological Museum of Athens. Athens 1992, Kapon. 152 p. £37.50. – ᴿJHS 114 (1994) 221 (J.H. *Crouwel*).
11855 *Schadler* Ulrich,   Ikonologie und Archäologie: AntAb 39 (1993) 162-187.
11856 **Shapiro** H.A.,   Personifications in Greek art; the representation of abstract concepts 600-400 B.C. [< diss. 1976]. Kilchberg 1993, Akanthos. 301 p.; 186 fig. 3-905083-05-1. – ᴿAJA 98 (1994) 373s (Ruth *Cohen*).
11857 **Shapiro** Harvey A.,   Myth into art; poet and painter in classical Greece. L 1994, Routledge. xxii-196 p.; bibliog. 183-191.
11858 *Simon* Claire,   Le *nbi* et le canon de proportions: JEA 79 (1993) 157-177.
11859 **Van Keuren** Frances,   Guide to research in classical art and mythology. Ch 1991, American Library Asn. x-307 p. $35. 0-8389-0564-1. – ᴿAJA 98 (1994) 783 (Jennifer *Neils*).
11860 **Woodford** Susan,   The Trojan war in ancient art. L 1993, Duckworth. 134 p.; 113 fig.; map. £10. – ᴿGreeceR 41 (1994) 239 (B.A. *Sparkes*: she is a great communicator).

T3.1   *Theologia iconis,* **ars postbiblica.**

11861 The Bible [AV] OT, illustrated selections [famous European paintings with relevant text]. L 1994, Ebury. 352 p. £16. 0-09-178364-X. – ᴿTBR 7,3 (1994s) 16 (A. *Warren*).
11861* **Bigham** Stéphane,   Les chrétiens et les images; les attitudes envers l'art dans l'Église ancienne: Brèches théologiques.   Montréal/P 1992, Paulines/Médiaspaul. 194 p. – ᴿSR 23 (1994) 104s (Vicki *Bennett*).
11862 **Brend** Barbara,   Islamic art. L 1991, British Museum. 240 p. £15. – ᴿBSO 57 (1994) 374s (A. *Northedge*).

11862* **Castellano** Jesús, Oración ante los íconos; los misterios de Cristo en el año litúrgico: Dossier 56. Barc 1993, Centro Pastoral Litúrgica. 184 p.; 19 color. pl. – ᴿPhase 33 (1993) 247-9 (J. *López*).

11863 **Cavarnos** Constantine, Guide to Byzantine iconography I. Boston 1993. 264 p. – ᴿTAth 65 (1994) 1004s (P. V. *Paschos*, Ⓖ).

11864 **Cottin** J., Le regard et la Parole; une théologie protestante de l'image [diss.]. Genève 1994, Labor et Fides. 342 p. [RHPR 74, 273-280, P. *P-rigent*].

11864* *Dale* Thomas E. A., Inventing a sacred past; pictorial narratives of St. Mark the Evangelist in Aquileia and Venice, ca. 1000-1300: DumbO 48 (1994) 53-104; 50 fig. [229-242, E. *Hawkins* †: on Venice St. Mark's E dome].

11865 ᴱ**Di Castro** Daniela, Arte ebraica a Roma e nel Lazio. R 1994, Palombi. 197 p. – ᴿRivOrCr 70 (1994) 528-532 (Simona *Frascati*).

11866 ᴱ**Dunand** Françoise, *al.*, L'image et la production du sacré. P 1991 Klincksieck. 270 p. 2-86563-394-6. – ᴿÉTRel 69 (1994) 605s (J. *Cottin*).

11867 ᴱ**Duval** Noël, Naissance des arts paléochrétiens 1991 → 8,e2; 9,13431: ᴿBonnJbb 194 (1994) 647-650 (K. *Painter*); Byzantion 64 (1994) 509-513 (Janine *Balty*); Gnomon 66 (1994) 446-9 (V. H. *Elbern*).

11868 **Estivill** Daniele E., La imagen del ángel en la Roma del siglo IV; estudio de iconología, diss. Pont. Inst. Or. ᴰ*Amato* P. Roma 1994. 329-lxxx p. – RTLv 26, p. 556.

11869 **Finney** Paul C., The invisible God; the earliest Christians on art. Ox 1994, UP. xxviii-319 p. $45. 0-19-508252-4 [TDig 42,65; TS 56,190, B. *Ramsey*].

11870 **Fontana** Maria Vittoria, Iconografia dell'Ahl al-Bayt; immagini di arte persiana dal XII al XX secolo: AION supp. 78. N 1994, Ist. Univ. Orientale. vi-87 p.; bibliog. 57-69.

11871 **Gambone** Robert L., Art and popular religion in evangelical America 1915-1940. Knoxville 1989, Univ. Tennessee. xvii-278 p. – ᴿJEvTS 37 (1994) 461 (D. T. *Williams*, also on DILLENBERGER).

11872 **Heldman** Marilyn E., The Marian icons of the painter Frē Ṣeyon; a study in fifteenth-century Ethiopian art, patronage and spirituality: OrBChr 6. Wsb 1994, Harrassowitz. 220 p.; bibliog. 201-214; 78 fig. 3-447-03540-4.

11873 **Jochum** Herbert, Ecclesia und Synagoga; das Judentum in der christlichen Kunst; Ausstellungskatalog Alte Synagoge Essen/Saarbrücken 1993 → 9,13441: ᴿKIsr 8 (1993) 195s (Julie *Kirchberg*).

11873* *Kakavas* George, Venetian mannerism and Cretan school; the case of a Cretan icon with an unusual representation of the Nativity: Byzantion 63 (1993) 116-153; 9 fig.

11874 ᴱ**Keller** Hagen, *Staubach* Nikolaus, Iconologia sacra; Mythos, Bildkunst und Dichtung in der Religions- und Sozialgeschichte Alteuropas: Univ. Münster, Inst. Frühmittelalterforschung Arb. 23. B 1994, de Gruyter. xii-667 p.

11875 **Kitzinger** Ernst, Il culto delle immagini; l'arte bizantina dal cristianesimo delle origini all'Iconoclastia. Scandicci FI 1992, Nuova Italia. xiv-210 p.; 28 pl. Lᵐ 28. – ᴿCC 145 (1994,3) 332s (C. *Capizzi*).

11875* *a) Krause* Martin, Die Bedeutung alter Dokumentation für die koptische Kunst; – *b) Rassart-Debergh* Maggy, Le Christ et la croix dans l'art copte: → 65, ꟳKASSER R., Coptology 1994, 17-33; 7 fig. / 45-69; 11 fig.

11876 **Künzl** Hannelore, Jüdische Kunst, von der biblischen Zeit bis zur

Gegenwart.   Mü 1992, Beck.   266 p.; 91 fig.   3-406-36799-2. – ᴿSalesianum 56 (1994) 782s (R. *Vicent*).

11876* **Lafontaine-Dosogne** Jacqueline, Histoire de l'art byzantin et chrétien d'Orient: Inst. Mdv. 7, 1987 → 4,e384 ... 7,b982: ᴿVizVrem 52 (1991) 293-6 (V. N. *Zalesskaya*, ❸).

11877 **Lafontaine-Dosogne** Jacqueline, Iconographie de l'enfance de la Vierge. Bru 1992 = c. 1965, Académie Belge, reprinted with notes. 1247 p.; 211 p. + 74 fig. Fb 2650. – ᴿByzantion 64 (1994) 224-8 (A. *Booren*).

11877* **Lawrence** Kenneth T., *al.*, Imaging the word; an arts and lectionary resource 1.   Cleveland 1994, United Church Press.   272 p. $40; pa. $30. 0-8298-0970-8; -1-6. [TDig 41,274].

11878 **Malaspina** Fortunato, L'Hakathistos, icona del mistero di Cristo e della Chiesa nella semprevergine Madre di Dio.   Messina 1994, Ignatianum, Ist. Superiore scienze umane e religiose.   vii-367 p.

11879 **Mathews** Thomas F., The clash of gods a reinterpretation of early Christian art → 9,13453 [AmHR 100, 1518s, Annabel *Wharton*; Speculum 70, 937-940, W. *Kleinbauer*]: ᴿOrChrPer 60 (1994) 645-7 (E. G. *Farrugia*).

11879* **Mathews** Thomas F., **Sanjian** Avedis K., Armenian Gospel iconography; the tradition of the Glajor Gospel: Studies 29. Wsh 1991, Dumbarton Oaks Research Library.   xxii-246 p. $50. – ᴿRÉByz 51 (1993) 299s (A. *Failler*).

11880 *Metzger* Marcel,   Peintures 'placées haut' et images 'placées bas': RevSR 68 (1994) 453-464.

11880* *Nasrallah* Joseph, † 19.XI.1993,   Icônes mariales melchites de la Diaspora: PrOrChr 43 (1993) 39-50; Eng. 50.

11881 *Oegema* Gerbern S.,   Zur Erforschung der Geschichte des Davidsschildes; eine kritische Betrachtung: FraJudBeit 20 (1993) 175-210 [< Judaica 50,60].

11881* *Olster* David,   Byzantine hermeneutics after iconoclasm; word and image in the Leo Bible (940): Byzantion 64 (1994) 419-458; 12 fig.

11882 **Palazzo** Eric,   Les sacramentaires de Fulda; étude sur l'iconographie et la liturgie à l'époque ottonienne: LitWissQF 77.   Münster 1994, Aschendorff.   xix-260 p.; 153 pl.   3-402-04050-5.

11882* **Parker** Elizabeth C., *Little* Charles T., The Cloisters Cross; its art and meaning [99 figures, 66 inscriptions].   NY 1994, Metropolitan Museum.   316 p.; $60.   0-8109-6434-1 [NY, Abrams; TDig 41,290].

11883 **Parnes** Stephan O.,   The art of Passover. NY 1994, H. L. Levin. 119 p. 0-88363-494-5. Printed in China; an example from there on p. 59.

11884 *Paupert* Catherine, *al.*,   Thèmes apocryphes de l'iconographie des églises de Tarentaise et de Maurienne (Savoie): Apocrypha 5 (1994) 249-268.

11885 **Pelikan** Jaroslav,   Imago Dei, the Byzantine apology for icons 1987 → 6,d544 ... 8,e22: ᴿChH 63 (1994) 261s (J. W. *Trigg*); CritRR 5 (1992) 343-5 (D. J. *Sahas*).

11886 **Pillinger** Renate,   Der Apostel Andreas; ein Heiliger von Ost und West im Bild der frühen Kirche (ikonographisch-ikonologische Studie): Szb ph/h 612. W 1994, Österr. Akad. 40 p.

11887 *Quacquarelli* Antonio,   Catechesi patristica e iconografia fra III e IV secolo: VetChr 31 (1994) 5-22; 16 fig.

11888 **Radley** Lyn,   Byzantine art and architecture; an introduction. C 1994, Univ. xiv-380 p.; ill.

11889 **Revel-Neher** Elisabeth,   The image of the Jew in Byzantine art. Ox 1992, Pergamon.   133 p.; 89 fig. + 10 color [ByZ 88,174-7, D. *Jacoby*]. –

ᴿJSS 38 (1993) 325-7 (N. R. M. *de Lange*); Kairos 34s (1992s) 243 (K. *Schubert*).

11890 *Revilla* Federico, Los niños Jesús feos: BSAA 60 (1994) 297-300.

11891 **Scavizzi** Giuseppe, The controversy on images from Calvin to Baronius. NY 1992, P. Lang. 301 p. – ᴿSR 23 (1994) 512s (B. K. *Ward*).

11892 **Schrenk** Sabine, Untersuchung zu biblisch-typologischen Darstellungen in frühchristlicher Zeit: Diss. Bonn 1992. – ArchAnz (1993) 159.

11893 *a) Schubert* Kurt, Die jüdische Wurzel der frühchristlichen Kunst; – *b) Maser* Peter, Synagoge und Ecclesia — Erwägungen zur Frühgeschichte des Kirchenbaus und der christlichen Bildkunst; – *c) Kogman-Appel* Katrin, Die alttestamentlichen Szenen im Langhaus von Santa Maria Maggiore und ihr Verhältnis zu jüdischen Vorlagen; – *d) Keggler* Herbert L., Through the Temple veil; the holy image in Judaism and Christianity; – *e) Revel-Neher* Elisabeth; Some remarks on the iconographical sources of the Christian Topography of Cosmas INDICOPLEUSTES: Kairos 32s (1990s) 1-8 / 9-26 / 37-52 / 53-77 / 78-97.

11893* *Sed-Rajna* Gabrielle, Chronique d'art juif: RÉJ 153 (1994) 403-8 (415-427, *Sigal-Klagsbald* Laurence, sur Samuel HIRSZENBERG).

Sirota Ioann B., Ikonographie der Gottesmutter in der russischen ortho-doxen Kirche 1992 → 8710.

11894 **Tandeckl** Daniela, Die Bibel in der Kunst; das 19. Jahrhundert [ᴱ*Schwebel* Horst]; Die Bibel in der Kunst. Stu 1993, Deutsche Bibelges. 144 p. 50 (foldout) color. pl. DM 78. – ᴿBiKi 49 (1994) 162 (H. *Fendrich*).

11895 **Taylor** Mark C., Disfiguring; art, architecture, religion. Ch 1992, Univ. xiv-346 p. $45. 0-226-79132-7. – ᴿAnglTR 76 (1994) 107-114 (J. W. *Dixon*); TorJT 10 (1994) 243s (P. *Richardson*).

11896 *Theodorou* Evangelos D., Die theologische Ästhetik der Ikonen und ihre ökumenische Bedeutung: TAth 64 (1993) 7-29; Eng. 879.

11897 *Thiessen* Gesa, Religious art is expressionistic; a critical appreciation of Paul TILLICH's theology of art: IrTQ 59 (1993) 302-311.

11898 **Thümmel** H. G., Bilderlehre und Bilderstreit 1991 → 7,d2; 9,13480: ᴿByZ 86 (1994) 132-4 (P. *Speck*, polemisch).

11899 **Thümmel** H. G., Die Frühgeschichte der ostkirchlichen Bilderlehre; Texte und Untersuchungen zur Zeit vor dem Bilderstreit 1991 → 8,e35: ᴿByZ 86 (1994) 132 (P. *Speck*).

11899* *Todić* Branislav, [Gn 49,9; Num 24,9] *Anapesôn*, iconographie et signification du thème: → 103, Mem. Simone VAN RIET: Byzantion 64 (1994) 134-165; 12 fig.

11900 **Urbaniak-Walczak** Katarzyna, Die 'conceptio per aurem'... Bagawat 1992 → 8,e40; 9,13482: ᴿOrChrPer 60 (1994) 647s (V. *Ruggieri*); TR 90 (1994) 470s (T. *Baumeister*).

11901 ᴱ**Wood** Diana, The Church and the arts 1990/2 → 8,638*... 9,13484: ᴿHeythJ 35 (1994) 218-220 (M. E. *Williams*); JTS 45 (1994) 443-5 (J. *Drury*); TLond 96 (1993) 238-240 (T. D. *Jones*).

11902 **Zaloscer** Hilde, Zur Genese der koptischen Kunst: IkonBeit 1991 → 8,e41: ᴿEnchoria 21 (1994) 192-5 (M. *Ruprechtsberger*).

11903 *Zaloscer* Hilde, Die koptische Kunst; der heutige Stand ihrer Erfor-schung (ein Problem der Methodik): Enchoria 21 (1994) 73-89; pl. 36-38.

T3.2 **Sculptura.**

11904 **Abdalla** Aly, Graeco-Roman funerary stelae from Upper Egypt: MgArchaeolOr. Liverpool 1992, Univ. 153 p.; 85 pl. £35. – ᴿCdÉ 69 (1994) 382s (J. *Bingen*).

11905 **A Campo** Anna Laetitia,   Anthropomorphic representations in prehistoric Cyprus; a formal and symbolic analysis of figurines, c. 3500-1800 B.C.: SIMA pocket 109. Jonsered 1994, Åström. 257 p.

11906 **Amedick** R.,   Die Sarkophage mit Darstellungen aus dem Menschenleben; Vita Privata, 1991 → 8,e42*:   RJRS 84 (1994) 254s (Janet *Huskinson*, also on JONGSTE R. 1992).

11907 **Beer** Cecilia,   Temple-boys; a study of Cypriote votive sculpture 1: SIMA 113. Jonsered 1994, Åström.

11908 *Bejor* Giorgio,   I ventun anni dei bronzi di Riace: → 98, FRADMILLI A. 1994, 21-30 + 5 fig.

11908* *Bigler* Robert R.,   *Geiger* Benjamin,   Eine [Medamud?] Schenkungsstele Thutmosis' IV: ZägSpr 121 (1994) 11-17; 2 fig.

11909 *Bolshakov* Andrey O.,   Two Old Kingdom relief fragments in the Hermitage Museum: GöMiszÄg 134 (1993) 13-26; 4 fig.

11910 *Boschung* Dietrich,   Die Bildnistypen der julisch-claudischen Kaiserfamilie; ein kritischer Forschungsbericht: JRomArch 6 (1993) 39-79; 69 fig.

11911 **Byrne** Michael,   The Greek geometric warrior figurine 1991 → 9,13494: RAntClas 63 (1994) 598s (Sophie *Descamps*).

11912 *Chamoux* François,   Réflexions sur la sculpture grecque: RÉG 107 (1994) 1-14.

11913 *Colbow* Gudrun, Zur Rundplastik des Gudea 1987 → 3,d670... 7,d19: RAfO 40s (1993s) 187 (Erika *Bleibtreu*).

11913* *Compostella* Carla,   La scultura funeraria della X regio tra romanizzazione e primo Impero; alcune note su tipi, modelli e cronologia: Acme 46,2s (1993) 117-150 + 47 fig.

11914 *Coquin* René-Georges, *Rutschowskaya* Marie-Hélène,   Les stèles coptes du Département des antiquités égyptiennes du Louvre: BIFAO 94 (1994) 107-126 + 7 fig.

11915 **Czichon** Rainer M.,   Die Gestaltungsprinzipien der neuassyrischen Flachbildkunst...: MüVorderasSt 13, 1992 → 8,e56: RMesopT 29 (1994) 298-301 (R. *Viviani*); Orientalia 63 (1994) 285-7 (J.E. *Reade*); RAss 88 (1994) 72s (J.-L. *Huot*).

11916 **Denti** Mario,   Ellenismo e romanizzazione nella X regio [Venezia]: la scultura delle élites locali dall'età repubblicana ai Giulio-Claudi: Arch 97. R 1991, Bretschneider. 377 p.; 102 pl. Lm 880. – RArctos 27 (1993) 213s (O. *Salomies*); ClasR 44 (1994) 384-6 (J.J. *Wilkes*).

11916* **Edlund-Berry** Ingrid E.M.,   The seated and standing statue acroteria from Poggio Civitate (Murlo): Archaeologica 96. R 1992, Bretschneider. 256 p.; 28 pl. – RRÉAnc 96 (1994) 657-660 (J.R. *Jannot*).

11917 **Faraone** Christopher A.,   Talismans and Trojan horses; guardian statues in ancient Greek cult.   Ox D1992 → 8,b251:   RAmHR 99 (1994) 530s (R.L. *Pounder*); CamArch 4 (1994) 270-289 (S. *Goldhill, al.*).

11918 **Fleischer** R.,   Studien zur seleukidischen Kunst I. Herrscherbildnisse 1991 → 8,d849.e63; 9,13502: RBO 51 (1994) 460-3 & 695s (A. *Stamatiou*); BonnJbb 194 (1994) 565s (H.F. *Mussche*).

11919 *Flourentzos* Pavlos,   A workshop of Cypro-classical terracottas from Marion: RepCyp (1994) 161-5; pl. XXX-XXXVI.

11920 *Galán* José M.,   The stela of Hor in context [Wadi al-Hudi, 35 k SE Aswan]: StAäK 21 (1994) 65-79; 1 fig.

11921 *Gazda* Elaine K., *Haenckl* Anne E.,   Roman portraiture; reflections on the question of context [ANDERSON M., NISTA A. 1988; EBONACASA N., RIZZA A. 1984/8].

11922 *Ghoneim* Wafik, Eine Statue des Prinzen und Hohepriesters von Heliopolis, Ahmes (Cairo JE 36412): StAäK 21 (1994) 95-106; pl. 10-14.

11923 **Grassinger** Dagmar, Römische Marmorkratere: Monumenta Artis Romanae 18. Mainz 1999, von Zabern. 334 p.; 63 fig.; 257 phot. DM 168. – ᴿRBgPg 72 (1994) 206-8 (F. *Baratte*).

11923* *Grossmann* Eva, The bronze figurine of the goddess Minerva from Apollonia, Israel: TAJ 20 (1993) 225-7; 4 fig.

11924 **Hafner** G., Die Laokoon-Gruppen 1992 ➤ 9,13506: ᴿAntClas 63 (1994) 602s (D. *Viviers*); Babesch 69 (1994) 218-220 (J. M. *Hemelrijk*); BonnJbb 194 (1994) 566-9 (Thuri *Lorenz*).

11925 **Haynes** Denis, The technique of Greek bronze statuary 1992 ➤ 9, 13508; DM 65: ᴿGreeceR 41 (1994) 100 (B. A. *Sparkes*).

11925* **Hermary** A., Catalogue Louvre ... Chypre, sculptures 1989 ➤ 8,g447: ᴿTEuph 5 (1992) 171s (A.-M. *Collombier*).

11926 **Höghammar** Kerstin, Sculpture and society ... Kos: Boreas 23. U 1993, Univ. 227 p.; 28 fig. 91-5543136-4. – ᴿAJA 98 (1994) 787s (M. D. *Fullerton*); MusHelv 51 (1994) 184s (D. *Willers*).

11927 **Hölzl** Regina, Die Giebelfelddekoration von Stelen 1990 ➤ 6,d607: ᴿBO 51 (1994) 305-310 (R. *Leprohon*).

11928 **Karageorghis** Vassos, The coroplastic art of ancient Cyprus 1993 [1. 1991 ➤ 8,g449; 9,13513]; II. 1993 ➤ 11928.

11929 **Kleiner** Diana E. E., Roman sculpture 1992 ➤ 9,13514; 0-300-04631-6: ᴿAJA 97 (1993) 813 (Nancy H. *Ramage*); AmHR 99 (1994) 208 (J. R. *Clarke*); ClasW 88 (1994s) 143s (E. *Bartman*); JRomA 7 (1994) 345-9 (R. *Ling*).

11930 **Kreikenbom** Detlev, Bildwerke nach Polyklet 1990 ➤ 7,d37; 9,13516: ᴿGGA 246 (1994) 165-173 (Michaela *Fuchs*).

11931 **Kreikenbom** Detlev, Griechische und römische Kolossalporträts bis zum späten 1. Jh. n.Chr.:[< Diss. 1987], 1992 ➤ 9,13517; 3-11-013253-2: ᴿAJA 98 (1994) 789-791 (Susan *Wood*); ArchWsz 44 (1993) 140s (Z. *Kiss*).

11932 *La Rocca* Eugenio, Ferocia barbarica; la rappresentazione dei vinti tra Medio Oriente e Roma: JbDAI 109 (1994) 1-40; 39 fig.

11932* **Machaira** Vassiliki, Les groupes statuaires d'Aphrodite et d'Eros; étude stylistique des types et de la relation entre les deux divinités pendant l'époque hellénistique: BtSaripolos 85. Athenae 1993, Univ. 228 p.; 60 pl.

11933 **Magen** Ursula, Assyrische Königsdarstellungen: BaghFor 9, 1986 ➤ 3, b742: AulaO 11 (1993) 130s (G. del *Olmo Lete*).

11933* **Malbon** E., Iconography of ... Bassus 1990 ➤ 7,d42; 9,13519*: ᴿCritRR 5 (1992) 79 (J. *Gutmann*).

11934 **Mathiesen** Hans E., Sculpture in the Parthian empire; a study in chronology 1992 ➤ 9,13520; DK 302: ᴿMesopT 29 (1994) 337-9 (A. *Invernizzi*).

11935 *Matsushima* Eiko, Divine statues in ancient Mesopotamia; their fashioning and clothing and their interaction with the society: ➤ 9,571*, Official cult 1992/3, 209-219.

11936 *Maule* Quentin, The strong-jaw master [34 Etruscan bronzes]: MiDAI-R 101 (1994) 33-42; pl. 1-8.

11937 **Mikocki** Tomasz, Les sculptures mythologiques et décoratives dans les collections polonaises: Corpus Signorum Imperii Romani 3/1. Wsz 1994, Univ. Inst. Archéologie. 116 p.. 83-903062-0-4.

11938 **Moreno** Paolo, Scultura ellenistica. R 1994, Ist. Poligrafico. I. p. xi-530; 655 fig.; II. xvi-xxi, p. 531-969; fig. 656-952.

11938* *Mostafa* Doha M.,   A propos d'une particularité [un seul oeil] dans la décoration des tympans des stèles cintrées du Nouvel Empire: GöMiszÅg 133 (1993) 85-94 + 10 fig.

11939 **Moustaka** Aliki,   Grossplastik aus Ton: OlympF 22.   B 1993, de Gruyter.   xiv-180 p.; 2 fig.; 118 pl. + 4 color.   DM 260.   3-11-013485-3. – ᴿNikephoros 7 (1994) 290-5; 1 fig. (H.-V. *Herrmann*).

11940 *Nenna* Marie-Dominique,   *Seif el-Din* Mervat,   La petite plastique en faïence du musée gréco-romain d'Alexandrie: BCH 118 (1994) 291-320; 8 fig.; 4 color. pl.

11941 *Özyar* Aslı,   Architectural relief sculpture at Karkamish, Malatya and Tell Halaf; a technical study: diss. Bryn Mawr 1991. 231 p.; ill.

11942 **Pollini** John,   The portraiture of Gaius and Lucius Caesar. NY 1987, Fordham.   xvi-133 p.; 42 pl.   0-8232-1127-4. – ᴿJRomArch 6 (1933) 303.

11943 **Pollini** John,   The Cartoceto bronzes; portraits of a Roman aristocratic family of the late first century B.C.: AJA 97 (1993) 423-446; 20 fig.

11943* **Rolley** Claude,   La sculpture grecque des origines au milieu du Vᵉ siècle: Manuels d'art/arch.   P 1994, Picard.   438 p.; bibliog. 410-5.   2-7084-0448-2.

11944 **Russmann** Edna R.,   Egyptian sculpture, Cairo and Luxor.   Austin 1989, Univ. Texas / L 1990, British Museum.   xi-230 p.; colour ill. *Finn* David. .. / £25; 0-292-70402-X. – ᴿJEA 80 (1994) 236s (C. *Vandersleyen*).

11945 **Schlögl** Hermann A.,   **Brodbeck** Andreas,   Ägyptische Totenfiguren: OBO arch. 7, 1990 ➤ 6,d631; 8,e90:   ᴿCdÉ 69 (1994) 292-4 (H. De *Meulenaere*).

11946 **Schmidt** Rüdiger,   Philistäische Terrakottafigurinen; archäologische, ikonographische und religionsgeschichtliche Beobachtungen zu einer Sondergruppe palästinischer Kleinplastik der Eisenzeit: Diss. ᴰNoort E. Groningen 1994. – TvT 34,296; RTLv 26,532.

11947 **Schmidt** Stefan,   Hellenistische Grabreliefs; ... typologische und chronologische Beobachtungen.   Köln 1991, Böhlau.   viii-164 p.; 23 pl. DM 98.   3-412-05090-3. – ᴿGnomon 66 (1994) 468-470 (A. *Linfert*).

11948 **Schulz** Regine,   Die Entwicklung und Bedeutung des kuboiden Statuentypus 1992 ➤ 8,e92:   ᴿOLZ 89 (1994) 36-39 (R. S. *Bianchi*).

11949 **Seidl** Ursula,   Die babylonischen Kudurru-Reliefs: OBO 87, 1989 ➤ 5,d442; 7,d60:   ᴿRB 101 (1994) 448s (M. *Sigrist*).

11949* *Settis* Salvatore,   Dalle rovine al museo; il destino della scultura classica: QuadStor 37 (1993) 45-64.

11950 **Sguaitamatti** Michel,   L'offrande du porcelet dans la coroplathie géléenne; étude typologique.   Mainz 1984, von Zabern.   193 p. 44 pl. – ᴿRÉG 106 (1993) 653s (Hélène *Cassimatis*).

11951 *Sinn* Ulrich,   Apollon und die Kentauromachie im Westgiebel des Zeustempels in Olympia; die Wettkampfstätte als Forum der griechischen Diplomatie nach den Perserkriegen: ArchAnz (1994) 585-602; 9 fig.

11952 **Spycket** Agnès,   Les figurines de Suse I 1992 ➤ 8,e96; 9,13531:   ᴿRAss 88 (1994) 68-70 (P. *Amiet*); WeltOr 25 (1994) 154-160 (Nadja *Wrede*).

11952* *Stafford* Emma,   Aspects of sleep in Hellenistic sculpture: BInstClas 38 (1991-3) 105-120; pl. 10-11.

11953 *Steible* Horst,   Versuch einer Chronologie der Statuen des Gudea von Lagaš: MDOG 126 (1994) 81-104; 6 fig.

11954 *Steiner* Andreas M.,   Operazione 'Bronzi di Riace'; un viaggio all'interno delle famose statue: Archeo 9,107 (1994) 46-57; ill.

11954* **Todisco** Luigi,   Scultura greca del IV secolo; maestri e scuole di statuaria tra classicità ed ellenismo.   Mi 1993, Longanesi. 507 p.; 427 pl.;

41 fig. Lᵐ 360. 88-304-1111-6. – ᴿAJA 98 (1994) 759-769; bibliog. 770-2 (Brunilde S. *Ridgway*).

11955 *Trunk* Markus, Pompeius Magnus; zur Überlieferung und 'Zwiespältigkeit' seines Porträts: ArchAnz (1994) 473-487; 14 fig.

11956 *Tunca* Ö., Essai sur le rythme statuaire à la période protohistorique en Mésopotamie: ⇥ 55, ᶠHROUDA B., Beiträge 1994, 273-281; 5 fig.

11957 **Uhlenbrock** Jaimée P., The terracotta protomai from Gela ... Sicily. R 1989, Bretschneider. 170 p.; 30 fig. 56 pl. Lᵐ 240. 88-7062-650-1. – ᴿAJA 97 (1993) 367s (Rebecca M. *Ammerman*).

11957* **Vincent** Jacques, Sur les premières images historiques dans la production grecque: RHist 290 (1993) 3-13.

11958 **Viviers** Didier, Recherches sur les ateliers de sculpteurs et la Cité d'Athènes à l'époque archäique; Eudoios, Philergos, Aristoklès. Mém. Beaux-Arts 8/3/1. Gembloux 1992, Acad. Belg. 263 p.; 59 fig. Fb 950. 2-8031-0094-0. – ᴿAJA 98 (1994) 786s (Janet B. *Grossman*); ClasR 44 (1994) 128s (A. *Johnston*); RBgPg 72 (1994) 208-210 (R. *Chevallier*); RPg 67 (1993) 154s (Mary-Ann *Zagdoun*).

11959 **Wegner** Max, Gebälkfriese römerzeitlicher Bauten: OrbAnt 33. Münster 1992, Aschendorff. vii-55 p.; 23 fig. DM 29,80. 3-402-05411-6. – ᴿBonnJbb 194 (1994) 614s (G. *Schörner*).

11960 **Weis** Anne, The hanging Marsyas and its copies; Roman innovation in a Hellenistic sculptural tradition: Archaeologica 103. R 1992, Bretschneider. 244 p.; 52 pl. – ᴿRBgPg 72 (1994) 210-2 (F. *Baratte*).

ᴛ3.3 *Glyptica:* **stamp and cylinder seals,** scarabs, amulets.

11961 *Amiet* Pierre, *a*) Un sceau trans-élamite à Suse: RAss 88 (1994) 1-4; – *b*) Un sceau-cylindre syrien de Naucratis: RAss 88 (1994) 169-173.

11962 **Andrews** Carol, Amulets of ancient Egypt. L 1994, British Museum. 112 p. 0-7141-0976-2.

11963 *a*) *Archi* Alfonso, A seal impression from El-Qitar/Til-Abnu (Syria) [35 k SE Aḥmar]; – *b*) *Gorny* Ronald L., The biconvex seals of Ališar Höyük: AnSt 43 (1993) 203-7; 1 fig. / 163-191; 4 fig.

11964 *Ben-Tor* Ammon, Early Bronze Age cylinder seal impressions and a stamp seal from Tel Qashish [Qišon N-bank]: BASOR 295 (1994) 15-29; 21 fig.

11965 *Ben-Tor* Daphna, The historical implications of [67] Middle Kingdom scarabs found in Palestine bearing private names and titles of officials: BASOR 294 (1994) 7-22.

11966 *Blöcher* Felix, Probleme der Bearbeitung altbabylonischer Siegelabrollungen: ZAss 84 (1994) 89-129.

11967 **Bordreuil** Pierre, Le répertoire iconographique des sceaux araméens inscrits et son évolution: ⇥ 577, NWS seals 1991/3, 74-100 [101-129, *Gubel* E., Phoenician; 130-160, *Hübner* J., Ammonite].

11967* **Buchanan** R., *Moorey* P., Catalogue of ANE seals in the Ashmolean 3, 1988 ⇥ 5,d549 ... 7,d78: ᴿTEuph 5 (1992) 155-7 (A. *Lemaire*).

11968 **Christoph** James, The yehud stamped jar handle corpus ᴰ1993 ⇥ 9, 2914 [RTLv 26,530].

11968* — [Yehud stamps] *Rappaport* U., *al.*, Land, society and culture in Judea: ⇥ 461, Syrie, TEuph 7 (1991/4) 73-82; franç. 73.

11969 **Collon** D., Interpreting ... seals 1990 ⇥ 6,d662 ... 9,13553: ᴿAfO 40s (1993s) 151-5 (G. *Colbow*).

11970 *Dickers* Aurelia, Die Siegel aus der nachpalastzeitlichen Nekropole von Armeni/Westkreta: ⇒ 35, ᶠFREY O. 1994, 139-147; 11 fig.

11970* *Dittmann* Reinhard, Glyptikgruppen am Übergang von der Akkad- zur Ur III-Zeit: BaghMitt 25 (1994) 75-119; 11 fig.; pl. 1-3.

11971 **Doumet** Claude, Sceaux... Chiha OBO arch 9, 1992 ⇒ 8,e122; 9,13554: ᴿBO 51 (1994) 678-682 (E. *Gubel*); RAss 88 (1994) 68 (P. *Amiet*); Syria 71 (1994) 475s (D. *Collon*).

11972 *Eder* Christian, Kampfsport in der Siegelkunst der Altlevante: Nikephoros 7 (1984) 83-120; 6 fig.; pl. 1-6.

11973 *Falkovitch* Julia, L'usage des amulettes égyptiennes: BSocÉg 16 (1992) 19-26.

11974 *Feig* Nurit, A Byzantine bread stamp from Tiberias; – *b*) *Piccirillo* Michele, Uno stampo per eulogia trovato a Gerusalemme: LA 44 (1994) 591-4; 1 fig. / 585-590; 3 + 2 fig.; pl. 47-50; Eng. 617.

11975 **Franke-Vogt** Ute, Die Glyptik aus Mohenjo-Daro ᴰ1991 ⇒ 8,e124; 9,13556: ᴿAfO 40s (1993s) 140-2 (D. T. *Potts*); OLZ 88 (1993) 317 (W. von *Soden*, auch über MUSTAFA/PARPOLA); ZAss 84 (1994) 299-301 (D. O. *Edzard*).

11976 *Garlan* Yvon, Nouvelles remarques sur la chronologie des timbres amphoriques thasiennes: JSav 93 (1993) 149-181; 113 fig.

11977 *Gibson* McGuire, Parthian seal style; a contribution from Nippur: MesopT 29 (1994) 89-105; 4 fig.

11977* *Görg* Manfred, Zum Personennamen ʾbš [KEEL O. OBO 135 (1994) 214 overlooks that GIVEON already published it 1983]: BibNot 73 (1994) 9-12.

11978 **Herrmann** Christian, Ägyptische Amulette aus Palästina/Israel, mit einem Ausblick auf ihre Rezeption durch das Alte Testament (Diss. FrS 1993, ᴰ*Keel* O.): OBO 138. FrS/Gö 1994, Univ./VR. xxiv-830 p.; Bibliog. 821-7; 80 + 77 pl. 3-7278-0933-7 / 3-525-53775-5.

11979 *Jefremow* Nikolai, Bemerkungen zu einigen Emblemen altgriechischer Keramikstempel: Klio 75 (1993) 103-9; 2 fig.; Eng. 109.

11980 **Keel** O., *al.*, Studien zu den Stempelsiegeln: OBO 100, 1990 ⇒ 6,d682... 8,e134: ᴿAfO 40s (1993s) 178s (K. *Jaroš*, auch über KEEL-LEU); TR 90 (1994) 207-9 (R. *Wenning*); WZKM 83 (1994) 284-9 (E. *Porada*).

11981 **Keel** Othmar, Studien zu den Stempelsiegeln aus Palästina/Israel IV, mit Register zu I-IV: OBO 135. FrS/Gö 1994, Univ./VR. xi-227 p.; bibliog. 301-325. 3-7278-0952-3 / 3-525-53777-0.

11982 *Keel* Othmar, Philistine 'anchor' seals: IsrEJ 44 (1994) 21-35; 21 fig.

11983 **Keel-Leu** Hildi. Vorderasiatische Stempelsiegel...: OBO 110, 1991 ⇒ 7,d94; 9,13564: ᴿWeltOr 25 (1994) 167s (Beate *Salje*).

11984 *Marichal* R., Les ostraca de Bu Njem [Golan]: LibyaAnt supp. 7. Tripoli..., Jamahira. 284 p.; 151 fig.; 15 pl. F 300. – ᴿJRS 84 (1994) 261s (A. K. *Bowman*).

11985 **Matthews** Donald M., Principles of composition in Near Eastern glyptic of the late second millennium B.C.: OBO arch. 8, 1990 ⇒ 6,d686; 9,13570: ᴿWeltOr 25 (1994) 160-6 (Gudrun *Selz*); WZKM 84 (1994) 159-173 (D. L. *Stein*).

11986 **Matthews** Donald M., The Kassite glyptic of Nippur; inscriptions, *Lambert* W. G.: OBO 116, 1992 ⇒ 8,e143; 9,13572: ᴿRB 101 (1994) 445 (M. *Sigrist*).

11987 **Matthews** Roger J., Cities, seals and writing; archaic seal impressions from Jamdet Nasr and Ur: Materialien zu den frühen Schriftzeugnissen des Vorderen Orients. B 1993, Mann. 104 p.; 20 fig.; 4 pl. DM 98. – ᴿBO

51 (1994) 676 (P. *Amiet*); BuCanadMesop 26 (1993) 59-61 (Eng. franç. M. *Fortin*); JESHO 37 (1994) 186-9 (K. R. *Veenhof*).

11988 *Melaerts* Henri, Timbres amphoriques d'Égypte: CdÉ 69 (1994) 332-352 [25 avec photo].

11989 **Møller** Eva, Ancient NE seals in a Danish collection: Niebuhr 11, 1992 ► 8,e146; 9,13574: ᴿJSS 38 (1993) 310-3 (R. *Bauckham*).

11990 *Mora* Clélia, L'étude de la glyptique anatolienne; bilan et nouvelles orientations de la recherche: Syria 61 (1994) 207-215.

11991 *Otto* Adelheid, Acht Siegel einer Privatsammlung: AfO 40s (1993s) 64-66; 11 fig.

11992 a) *Porada* Edith (*Hallo* W. W.), Cylinder of Kurigalzu I?; – b) *Karg* Norbert, Das Rollsiegel AO 22298 aus der Sammlung Louis de Clercq; – c) *Colbow* G., Einige bemerkenswerte Abrollungen aus der Zeit Kaštiliašus von Ḫana: ► 55, ᶠHROUDA B., Beiträge 1994, 229-234; pl. XXIIIb-XXIV / 125-132; 3 fig. / 61-66; 9 fig.

11993 *Pullen* Daniel J., A lead seal from Tzoungiza, ancient Nemea, and Early Bronze Age Aegean sealing systems: AJA 98 (1994) 35-52; 7 fig. (map).

11994 **Richards** Fiona V., [53] Scarab seals from a Middle to Late Bronze Age tomb at Pella, Jordan. OBO 117, FrS/Gö 1992 ► 8,e151; 9,13884: ᴿJAOS 114 (1994) 97s (J. *Weinstein*); Orientalia 63 (1994) 129-192 (A. *Niccacci*); ZAW 105 (1993) 534 (D. *Vieweger*).

11995 **Salje** Beate, Der 'common style' der Mitanni-Glyptik 1990 ► 7,d108; 8,e152: ᴿOLZ 89 (1994) 306-9 (S. *Herbordt*).

11996 ᴱ**Sass** B., *Uehlinger* F., Studies in the iconography of NW Semitic inscribed seals [FrS Apr. 17-20, 1991]: OBO 125. FrS 1993, Univ. xxiii-336 p.; ill. – ᴿRStFen 24 (1994) 274 (E. *Acquaro*).

11997 *Sax* M., *Collon* D., *Leese* M. N., The availability of raw materials for Near Eastern cylinder seals during the Akkadian, post Akkadian and Ur III periods: Iraq 55 (1993) 77-90; 9 fig. (map).

11997* *Sax* M., *Meeks* N. D., The introduction of wheel cutting as a technique for engraving cylinder seals; its distinction from filing: Iraq 56 (1994) 153-166; 8 fig.

11998 **Shah** S., *Parpola* A., Corpus of Indus seals 2. Pakistan 1991 ► 8,e155: ᴿZAss 84 (1994) 297-9 (D. O. *Edzard*).

11999 **Stein** Diana, The seal impressions; Text / Catalogue: Das [Nuzi-] Archiv des Šilwa-Teššup 8s. x-282 p.; bibliog. 274-282 / [viii-] 587 p. 3-447-03200-4; -317-7.

12000 *Stern* Ephraim, Notes on the development of stamp-glyptic art in Palestine during the Assyrian and Persian periods: ► 102, Mem. RICHARDSON H., Uncovering 1994, 135-146; 19 fig.

12000* *Teissier* Beatrice, Sealing and seals on texts from Kültepe Karum level 2: Uitgaven 70. Leiden 1994, Nederlands Instituut te Istanbul. xiii-278 p.; bibliog. 93-100. – ᴿRAss 88 (1994) 183s (P. *Amiet*).

12001 *Varalis* Yannis D., Un sceau paléochrétien de pain eucharistique de l'agora d'Argos: BCH 118 (1994) 331-342; 3 fig.

12002 **Wallenfels** Ronald, Uruk, Hellenistic seal impressions in the Yale Babylonian collection; 1. Cuneiform tablets: Endb 19. Mainz 1994, von Zabern. xii-207 p.; 62 pl.; bibliog. p. 193-200. 3-8053-4726-3.

12003 *Ward* William A., Beetles in stone; the Egyptian scarabs: BA 57 (1994) 186-202; ill.

12004 *Wasserman* Nathan, BM 78613, a Neo-Babylonian imposture of an Old-Babylonian amulet?: RAss 88 (1994) 49-57; 2 fig.

12004* *Yamada* Masamichi,   The dynastic seal and Ninurta's seal; preliminary
remarks on sealing by the local authorities of Emar: Iraq 56 (1994)
59-62.
12005 *Zorn* Jeffrey B.,   Two rosette stamp impressions from Tell en-Nasbeh:
BASOR 293 (1994) 81s; 2 fig.

T3.4   **Mosaica.**

12006 *Bairrão Oleiro* João M.,   Les mosaïques romaines de Conimbriga:
DossA 198 ('Le Portugal' 1994) 42-47.
12007 **Balty** Janine,   La Mosaïque de Sarrīn (Osrhoène): IFAO-BAH 140. P
1990, Geuthner. 111 p.; 47 pl.
12008 *a) Ciancio* Angela,   Documenti di arte musiva in Puglia; mosaici della
Villa di Mola di Bari; – *b) Ennaïfer* Mongi,   La mosaïque aux chevaux
d'El Mahrine près de Thuburbo Minus, l'actuel Tébourba);   MÉF 106
(1994) 259-302; 21 fig. / 303-318; 13 fig.
12008* *Coarelli* Filippo,   La *pompé* di Tolomeo Filadelfo e il mosaico nilotico
di Palestrina: Ktema 15 (1996) 225-251; 5 fig.; 4 pl.
12009 **Donceel-Voûte** Pauline,   Les pavements des églises byzantines de Syrie
et du Liban 1988 ➤ 9,13668:   ᴿBonnJbb 194 (1994) 672-4 (B. *Brenk*).
12010 **Donderer** M.,   Mosaizisten 1989 ➤ 7,d121 ... 9,13599:   ᴿArctos 27
(1993) 197s (Heikki *Solin*).
12011 *Green* Connie Kestenbaum,   King David's head from Gaza synagogue
[mosaic] restored: BAR-W 20,2 (1994) 58-63 . 94.
12012 *Hunt* Lucy-Anne,   The Byzantine mosaics of Jordan in context; remarks
on imagery, donors and mosaicists: PEQ 126 (1994) 106-126; 10 fig.
12013 *Liverani* Paolo,   Navalia in mosaico [Museo Vaticano dalla via
Ardeatina 1842]: ArchViva 13/45 (1994) 26-29; ill.
12014 *Ness* Lester,   Astrology [... mosaic floors; Beit-Alpha ...]: ArchBW 2
(1992) 44-53 [< OTAbs 16, p. 204].
12015 *Netzer* Ehud, *Weiss* Zeev,   Byzantine mosaics at Sepphoris; new finds:
IsrMusJ 10 (1992) 76-80; 8 fig.
12016 **Piccirillo** Michele,   The mosaics of Jordan, ᴱ*Bikai* P. M., *Dailey* T. A.:
Publ. 1. Amman 1993, ACOR. 383 p.; 787 fig.; 2 plans. – ᴿBASOR 296
(1994) 84s (R. *Schick*).
12017 *Russell* James,   The mosaic inscriptions of Anemurium 1987 ➤ 4,e399
... 6,d722:   ᴿMuséon 107 (1994) 218-220 (Pauline *Donceel-Voûte*).
12017* *Saïd* Dorreya,   Deux mosaïques hellénistiques [chien, lutteurs] ré-
cemment découvertes à Alexandrie: BIFAO 94 (1994) 377-9 + map; color
pl. p. 487-489.
12018 *Waliszewski* Tomasz,   La mosaïque de Deir el-Asfur [trouvée 1924 près
de Beth-Shemesh] retrouvée [dans deux photos de l'École Biblique]; le
motif des 'rinceaux habités' en Judée et dans le Shéphéla: RB 101 (1994)
562-579; 3 fig. (map); pl. V-VI; 562 Eng. 'inhabited scroll'.
12019 *Waterhouse* Helen,   The Knossos 'town mosaic' [faience plaques] reconsidered: Cretan Studies 4 (1994) 165-174; pl. XXI-XXVI.

T3.5   *Ceramica,* **pottery** [➤ *singuli situs,* infra].

12020 **Adams** William Y. & Ernest W.,   Archaeological typology and practical
reality; a dialectical approach to artifact classification and sorting. C
1991, Univ. xxiii-427 p.; 11 fig. 0-521-39334-5. – ᴿAJA 97 (1993) 357s
(M. *Fotiadis*).

12021 **Adan-Bayewitz** David, Common pottery in Roman Galilee 1993
➤ 9,13610: ᴿAJA 98 (1994) 794s (M. *Lawall*); BL (1994) 21s (A. H. W.
Curtis).

12022 *Ballet* Pascale, Un atelier d'amphores; Late Roman Amphora 5/6 à
Kôm Abou Billou [Terana, latitude de w. Natroun]: CdÉ 69 (1994)
353-365; 14 fig. (map).

12023 *Barlow* Jane A., Notes on decoration of red polished ware: RepCyp
(1994) 45-50; 3 fig.

12023* *Bémont* Claudette, Chronique de céramologie de la Gaule: RÉAnc
96 (1994) 549-558 [559-572, *Lavagne* Henri, Chronique gallo-romaine].

12024 **Bey** George Jᴵᴵᴵ, **Pool** Christopher A., Ceramic production and
distribution; an integrated approach. Boulder 1992, Westview. xviii-
342 p.; 66 fig. $65. 0-8133-7920-2. – ᴿAJA 97 (1993) 572s (C. C. *Kolb*).

12025 *Cook* R. M., A Carian wildgoat (-style-vase-painting) workshop
[Mylasa]: OxJArch 12 (1993) 109-115; 8 fig.

12026 **Cuomo di Caprio** Ninina, Morgantina Studies 3: Fornaci e officine da
vasaio tardo-ellenistiche 1992 ➤ 9,13622; 0-691-04014-1: ᴿAJA 97 (1993)
810s (Susan I. *Rotroff*: successful); ClasR 44 (1994) 151-5 (J. *Papadopoulos*).

12027 *Dehl-von Kaenel* Christiane, Keramik als Handelsware — zum Vertrieb
korinthischer Keramik in das [Eng. to; franç, dans, p. 82s] Malo-
phoros-Heiligtum in Selinunt: MünstHand 13,1 (1994) 55-82; 6 fig.

12028 **Eriksson** Kathryn O., Red lustrous wheel-made ware: SIMA 103;
ᴰ1993 ➤ 9,13624: ᴿAJA 98 (1994) 570s (Jane A. *Barlow*).

12029 *Fisher* Susan M., *al.*, A pictorial stirrup-jar from the Mycenaean
citadel of Midea: JPreh 8 (1994) (4-) 8-19; 2 fig.

12030 **Gabler** Dénes, Die Terra Sigillata–Forschung seit I. PAULOVICS: ➤ 60,
ᶠJÁRDÁNYI-PAULOVICS 1994, 83-105 (107-110 *Bónis* Éva B., glasierte
Keramik).

12031 *Gophna* Ram, The Egyptian pottery 'En Beşor: TAJ 17 (1990) 144-
162 [< OTAbs 17, p. 23].

12032 *Hedreen* Guy, Silens, nymphs, and maenads [in vase-paintings]: JHS
114 (1994) 47-69.

12033 **Helck** W., Thinitische Topfmarken 1990 ➤ 6,d679: ᴿBO 51 (1994)
50-54 (G. *Godron*).

12033* *Isler* Hans-Peter, Der Töpfer Amasis und der Amasis-Maler; Bemerkungen zur Chronologie und zur Person: JbDAI 109 (1994) 93-114.

12034 *a*) *Jefremow* N. W., ❹ The initial period of the stamping with the
astynom names in Sinope; – *b*) *Ynukov* S. Yu., New types of the Late
Synop amphorae: RossArkh (1993,1) 31-38; Eng. 38; (1993,3) 204-213;
Eng. 213.

12035 *Karstens* Karsten, Allgemeine Systematik der einfachen Gefässformen:
Mü Univ VorderasSt 15. Mü 1994, Profil. [x-] 281 p. 3-89019-352-8.

12036 *Kenrick* Philip, Italian terra sigillata; a sophisticated Roman industry:
OxJArch 12 (1993) 235-242; 2 fig. (map).

12037 **Kilmer** Martin F., Greek erotica ... vases 1993 ➤ 9,13635: ᴿClasR 44
(1994) 383s (E. *Moignard*).

12038 *Kunow* J., *al.*, Vorschläge zur systematischen Beschreibung von Keramik; Führer des Rheinischen Landesmuseums Bonn 124. Köln 1986.
71 p.; 6 fig. DM 28. – ᴿPraehZts 69 (1994) 224-7 (Brigitte *Kull*).

12039 **Kunze-Götte** Erika, Der Kleophrades-Maler unter Malern schwarz-
figuriger Amphoren; eine Werkstattstudie. 1992 ➤ 9,13636: ᴿRBgPg 72
(1994) 212 (R. *Chevallier*).

12040 **Lehmann** Gunnar, Die Keramik der 'Perser-Zeit' in Syrien-Palästina: Diss. FU Berlin 1993. – ArchAnz (1994) 121.

12041 **Leonard** Albert, An index to the Late Bronze Age Aegean pottery from Syria-Palestine: SIMA 114. Jonsered 1994, Åström. 251 p.; 38 maps.

12041* *Maniatis* Y., New evidence for the nature of the Attic black gloss: Archaeometry 35 (1993) 23-34; 6 fig.

12042 **Medri** M., Terra sigillata tardo italica decorata; StudArch 60. R 1992, Bretschneider. 416 p.; ill.; 2 maps. 88-7062-771-3. – ᴿJRS 84 (1994) 255s (P. M. *Kenrick*).

12043 **Neeft** C. W., Addenda et corrigenda to D. A. AMYX, Corinthian vase-painting 1988: 1991 ≯ 8,e219: ᴿGnomon 66 (1994) 466-8 (M. *Tiverios*: helpful).

12044 **Orton** Clive, *al.*, Pottery in archaeology 1993 ≯ 9,13648: ᴿPraehZts 69 (1994) 222-4 (Brigitte *Kull*).

12045 **Porat** Naomi, Composition of pottery; application to the study of the interrelationships between Canaan and Egypt during the 3d millennium B.C.: diss. Hebrew Univ., ᴰ*Heller-Kallai* Liza, *Amiran* Ruth. J 1989. ix-101 pp.; appendices [OIAc 7,40].

12046 *Raepsaet* Georges, Du tesson à l'histoire; recherches récentes de céramologie antique [*Orton* C. + 26]: AntClas 63 (1994) 315-324.

12046* *Reinholdt* Claus, 'Nostos Odyssei' oder vita humana; zu einem Vasenbild des Schweine-Malers in Cambridge: OpAth 20 (1994) 163-177; 19 fig.

12047 **Robertson** Martin, The art of vase-painting in classical Athens 1992 ≯ 9,13650: ᴿAJA 98 (1994) 169s (Mary B. *Moore*); ClasW 88 (1994s) 131s (Birgitte *Ginge*); JHS 114 (1994) 227 (J. H. *Oakley*).

12048 *a) Rosen* Steven A., *Goodfriend* Glenn A., An early date for Gaza ware from the Northern Negev; – *b) Vilders* Monique M. E., Some remarks on the production [... firing] of cooking pots in the Jordan valley [Saʿidiyeh, Deir ʿAlla]; PEQ 125 (1993) 143-8; 2 fig. / 149-156; 6 fig.

12049 *Rossi* Marco, Vasi egizi invetriati importati in Italia (I secolo a.C. - I secolo d.C.): MÉF 106 (1994) 319-351; 24 fig.

12050 *Schauenburg* Konrad, Zur Mythenwelt des Baltimoremalers: MiDAI-R 101 (1994) 51-68 pl. 13-36.

12051 **Seifert** Martina, Zur Herkunftsbestimmung milesischer Keramik — Archäologie und Archäometrie: Diss. Bochum. – MiDAV 25,2 (1994) 17.

12052 **Sgourou** Marina, Attic *lebētes gamikoí* [necked bowl on tall conical stand; or ovoid pyxis with vertical handles: portraying or used for weddings]: diss. ᴰ*Miller-Collett* Stella. Cincinnati 1994. 473 p. 95-02582. – DissA 55 (1994s) p. 2611.

12053 **Skibo** James M., Pottery function; a use-alteration perspective [< diss. Arizona] 1992 ≯ 9,13654: ᴿAJA 97 (1993) 800s (Karen D. *Vitelli*).

12054 *Sparkes* Brian A., Greek pottery, an introduction 1991 ≯ 8,e234; 9, 13656: ᴿAJA 97 (1993) 178s (W. R. *Biers*: well organized and presented).

12055 *Tutundžić* Sava P., A consideration of differences between the pottery showing Palestinian characteristics in the Maadian and Gerzean cultures: JEA 79 (1993) 33-55; 12 fig.; pl. IV.

12056 *Vallerin* Michèle, Pelves estampillés de Bassit: Syria 61 (1994) 171-204; 20 fig.

12057 **Venit** Marjorie S., Greek painted pottery from Naukratis in Egyptian museums 1988 ≯ 4,e457; 6,d772: ᴿCdÉ 69 (1994) 295s (T. van *Compernolle*).

12058 *Waldbaum* Jane C.,   Early Greek contacts (chiefly Palestine pottery) with the southern Levant, ca. 1000-600 B.C.);   the eastern perspective: BASOR 294 (1994) 53-66; 12 pl. (map).
12059 **Wood** B. G.,   The sociology of pottery in ancient Palestine 1990 ➤ 6,d777; 8,e239:   ᴿBAngIsr 13 (1993s) 47-50 (Pamela *Magrill*).

T3.6 Lampas.

12060 **Bailey** Donald M.,   A catalogue of the lamps in the British Museum, 1. Roman provincial lamps. L 1988, BM. xv-560 p.; 161 fig.; 160 pl. £150. 0-7141-1278-X. – ᴿJRomArch 6 (1993) 420-6 (C. *Pavolini*, ital.).
Barag Dan, Masada IV Lamps 1994 ➤ 12272.
12061 **Barbera** Mariarosaria, *Petriaggi* Roberto,   Le lucerne tardo-antiche di produzione africana: Mus. Naz. Roma. R 1993, Ist. Poligrafico. 434 p.; 3 foldouts.
12062 **Fitch** Cleo R., *Goldman* Norma W.,   Cosa; the lamps: Memoir 39. R 1994, (AA Univ. of Michigan for) American Academy. xviii-265 p.; 142 fig.; IX pl. 0-472-10518-3.
12063 *Loffreda* Stanislao,   Dieci lucerne con iscrizioni: LA 44 (1994) 595-607; 16 fig.; Eng. 618.
12064 **Mackensen** M.,   Die spätantiken Sigillata- und Lampentöpfereien von El-Makrine (Nord-Tunisien): BeitVFG. Mü 1993, Beck. 679 p.; 138 fig.; 90 pl. DM 138. 3-406-37015-2. – ᴿJRS 84 (1994) 290s (P. M. *Kenrick*).
12065 **Paleani** Maria Teresa, Le lucerne paleocristiane: Monumenti Musei e Gallerie Pontificie, Cataloghi 1. R 1993, Bretschneider. 121 p.; ill.
12066 *Pollino* Alex,   Les lampes de Caius Clodius: Cahiers d'Archéologie Subaquatique 12 (Fréjus 1994) 137-202; 8 pl. (+ *al*.).
12067 **Tran Tam Tinh**, *Jentel* Marie-Odile,   Corpus des lampes à sujets isiaques du Musée gréco-romain d'Alexandrie: Hier pour aujourd'hui 6. Québec 1993. xxiii-399 p.; 132 pl. – ᴿRÉLat 72 (1994) 351s (R. *Turcan*).

T3.7 Cultica [➤ M4-7 et singuli situs].

12068 ᴱ**Boyer** P.,   Cognitive aspects of religious symbolism. C 1993, Univ. 246 p. – ᴿCamArch 4 (1994) 149-155 (A. *Peatfield*).
12068* ᴱ**Bonanno** A., Archaeology and fertility cult, Malta 1985 / Amst 1986 ➤ 3,e92: ᴿAulaO 12 (1994) 137-9 (G. del *Olmo Lete*).
12069 **Brouquière-Reddé** Véronique,   Temples et cultes de Tripolitaine: Ét. Ant. Afr. P 1992, CNRS. 352 p.; 113 fig. F 440. – ᴿRBgPg 72 (1994) 204-6 (R. *Lambrechts*).
12069* *Dever* William G.,   Ancient Israelite religion; how to reconcile the differing textual and artifactual portraits? ➤ 467*, Ein Gott allein? 1993/4, 105-125.
12070 a) *Duval* Noël,   L'espace liturgique dans les églises paléochrétiennes; – b) *Metzger* Catherine,   Le dispositif ancien de l'autel; – c) *Sodini* Jean-Pierre,   L'ambon dans l'Église primitive: MaisD 193 (1993) 7-29; 5 fig. / 31-38; 2 fig. / 39-51; 2 fig.
12071 *Fernández Marcos* Natalio,   Sinagoga e Iglesia primitiva; arquitectura e institución: Sefarad 53 (1993) 41-57; Eng. 58.
12072 *Garfinkel* Yosef,   Ritual burial of cultic objects; the earliest evidence: CamArch 4 (1994) 159-188; 7 fig.
12072* ᴱ**Hachlili** R.,   Ancient synagogues in Israel, 3d-7th c.: BAR-Int 490, 1989 ➤ 5,845: ᴿPEQ 125 (1993) 165-7 (Fanny *Vitto*).

12073 **Hoppe** Leslie J.,   The synagogues and churches of ancient Palestine. ColMn 1994, Liturgical.   v-145 p.; 39 fig. 0-8146-5754-0 [BL 95,28, J. R. *Duckworth*]. – ᴿLA 44 (1994) 719s (P. *Kaswalder*).

12074 *Hutter* Manfred,   Kultstelen und baityloi; die Ausstrahlung eines syrischen religiösen Phänomens nach Kleinasien und Israel: ➤ 388, Beziehungen 1993, 86-108.

12075 **Lacave** José Luis,   Juderías y sinagogas españolas: Sefarad col. 16/3. M 1992, Mapfre.   448 p. – ᴿSefarad 53 (1993) 410s (D. *Romano*).

12076 ᴱ**Marinatos** Nanno, *Hägg* Robin,   Greek sanctuaries.   L 1993, Routledge.   xvi-245 p.; 42 fig. £35.   0-415-05384-6. – ᴿAntiquity 68 (1994) 457-9 (Susan E. *Alcock*).

12077 *Nakhai* Beth Alpert,   What's a *bamah*? How sacred space functioned in ancient Israel: BAR-W 10,3 (1994) 9-29 . 77.

12078 **Peláez del Rosal** Jesús,   La sinagoga: Estudios de cultura hebrea 7. Córdoba 1988, Almendro.   180 p. – ᴿSefarad 54 (1994) 207-210 (M. José *Cano*, also on nine other volumes of this series edited by Peláez).

12079 **Ruggieri** Vincenzo,   Byzantine religious architecture (582-867); its history and structural elements: OrChrAnal 237. R ᴰ1991, Pont. Inst. Or. 287 p.; fig.; 23 pl. – ᴿByzantion 63 (1993) 463-5 (Jacqueline *Lafontaine-Dosogne*).

12080 ᴱ**Schlette** Friedrich, *Kaufmann* Dieter,   Religion und Kult in ur- und frühgeschichtlicher Zeit: Tagung XIII., Halle 4-6 Nov, 1989 ➤ 7,656a: ᴿBonnJbb 193 (1993) 437-442 (G. *Mansfeld*).

12081 ᴱ**Tsafrir** Yoram,   Ancient churches revealed 1993 ➤ 9,13683:   ᴿLA 44 (1994) 722-5 (P. *Kaswalder*); PEQ 126 (1994) 174s (T. *Axe*); PhoenixEOL 40 (1994) 124s (C. de *Geus*).

12081* *Vivante* Anna,   The sacrificial altar in Assyrian temples; a suggested new interpretation of the term *maškittu*:   RAss 88 (1994) 163-8; 3 fig.

12082 **Werner** Peter,   Die Entwickung der Sakralarchitektur in Nordsyrien und Südostkleinasien vom Neolithikum bis in das I. Jt. v.Chr.: Diss. München. – MiDAV 25,2 (1994) 41.

T3.8   **Funeraria**; *Sindon,* **The Shroud.**

12083 **Abdalla** Aly,   Graeco-Roman funerary stelas 1992 ➤ 8,e270*:   ᴿBO 51 (1994) 315-8 (H. J. A. De *Meulenaere*).

12084 *Amedick* Rita,   Die Sarkophagen mit Darstellungen aus dem Menschenleben 4, Vita privata, 1991 ➤ 8,8e42*:   ᴿArchWsz 44 (1993) 145-8 (T. *Mikocki*).

12085 *Antonaccio* Carla M.,   Contesting the past; hero cult, tomb cult, and epic in early Greece: AJA 98 (1994) 380-410; 10 fig.

12086 **Bloch-Smith** Elizabeth,   Judahite burial practice and beliefs about the dead 1992 ➤ 8,e275; 9,13688:   ᴿBAR-W 20,4 (1994) 56 (W. E. *Rost*); CBQ 56 (1994) 748s (P. J. *King*); JESHO 37 (1994) 331s (C. H. J. de *Geus*); PEQ 126 (1994) 73s (J. R. *Bartlett*); VT 44 (1994) 419s (P. S. *Johnston*).

12087 *Bolshakov* Andrey O.,   Unusual late period cartonnage mummy case in the Hermitage Museum: BSocÉg 16 (Genève 1992) 5-18; 13 fig.

12088 *Branigan* Keith,   The corbelling controversy [*thólas* tomb roofs]; another contribution: Cretan Studies 4 (1994) 65-68; 1 fig.; pl. I-II.

12089 **Brier** Bob,   Egyptian mummies; unraveling the secrets of an ancient art. NY 1994, Morrow.   357 p. 0-688-10272-7.

12090 *Briese* Christoph, *Docter* Roald,   The Lambros group; a Late Geometric grave group between Attica and the East: Babesch 69 (1994) 1-47; 51 fig.

12091 **Bruwier** Marie-Cecile, Les coffres a viscères humains en Égypte (de la 30e dynastie à l'époque romaine); diss. Lv. 1991, ᴰ*Vandersleyen* C. – RArtLv 24 (1991) 207s.

12092 **Celier** Odile, Le signe du linceul 1992 → 8,13690: ᴿBLitEc 95 (1994) 265 (D. *Vigne*); ÉTRel 69 (1994) 611 (J. *Cottin*); NRT 116 (1994) 607-9 (X. *Jacques*).

12093 **Colvin** Howard, Architecture and the after-life 1991 → 8,e278: ᴿAJA 97 (1993) 594s (F. S. *Kleiner*).

12094 **Dodson** Aidan M., The Canopic equipment of the King of Egypt: Studies in Egyptology. L 1994, Kegan Paul. xxii-215 p.; bibliog. 191- 202. 0-7103-0460-9.

12095 **Eickhoff** Tilman, Grab und Beigabe… Tell Ahmed al-Hattu: Mü- VorderasSt 14, 1993 → 9,13962: ᴿMesopT 29 (1994) 292-5 (P. *Fiorina*); RAss 88 (1994) 189-191 (J.-L. *Huot*); Orientalia 63 (1994) 283-5 (E. *Rova*).

12096 *a) Gasuli* Pepa, El sistema rituale fenicio; inhumación e incineración: MadMitt 34 (1993) 71-82; – *b) Bartoloni* P., A proposito di riti funerari fenici: RStFen 22 (1994) 57-61.

12097 *Heidorn* Lisa A., Historical implications from the earliest tombs at El Kurru [15 k N Jabl Barkal]: JAmEg 31 (1994) 115-131; 5 fig.

12098 **Hesberg** Henner von, Römische Grabbauten. Da 1992, Wiss. xii- 246 p.; 146 fig. – ᴿBonnJbb 194 (1994) 608-614 (W. K. *Kovacsovics*).

12099 **Hitzl** Ingrid, Die griechischen Sarkophage der archaischen und klassischen Zeit: SIMA pocket 104. Jonsered 1991, Åström. – ᴿClasR 44 (1994) 380s (A. *Johnston*); Gnomon 66 (1994) 571s (A. *Linfert*).

12100 **Hodel-Hoenes** Sigrid, Leben und Tod im alten Ägypten 1991 → 8, d200*: ᴿOLZ 89 (1994) 377-9 (F. *Kampp*).

12100* *Horbury* William, The 'Caiaphas' ossuaries and Joseph Caiaphas: PEQ 126 (1994) 32-48; map.

12101 *Le Mort* Françoise, *Rabinovich* Rivka, L'apparat de l'étude tapho- nomique des restes humains à la connaissance de pratiques funéraires; exemple du site chalcolithique de Ben Shemen [Lod] (Israel): Paléorient 20,1 (1994) 69-98.

12102 **Lüscher** Barbara, Untersuchungen zu ägyptischen Kanopenkästen 1990 → 6,d835: ᴿBO 51 (1994) 77-80 (D. N. E. *Magee*).

12103 ᴱ**Maloney** Paul C., The shroud of Turin; a case study in document authentication. Binghamton NY 1993, Haworth. $25. 1-56024-105-5 [JRelTInf 1,1 adv.].

12104 **Mattsson** Bengt, The ascia symbol on Latin epitaphs: SIMA pocket 70. Göteborg 1990, P. Åström. 154 p. 91-86098-83-7. – ᴿLatomus 53 (1994) 433s (M. *Christol*).

12105 **Miller** Barbara B., Women, death, and mourning in the ancient eastern Mediterranean world: diss. Michigan, ᴰ*Milne* Pamela. AA 1994, 360 p. 95-00999. – DissA 55 (1994s) 2453.

12106 **Morris** Ian, Death ritual and social structure 1992 → 8,e293; 9,13703: ᴿAJA 98 (1994) 574s (C. A. *Walz*); AmHR 99 (1994) 1666s (M. *Toher*); Arctos 27 (1993) 184s (Maijastina *Kaklos*).

12107 **Niklasson** K., Early prehistoric burials in Cyprus: SIMA 96, 1991 → 7,e126; 9,13704: ᴿOpAth 20 (1994) 251s (R. S. *Merrillees*); PEQ 126 (1994) 169 (Louise *Steel*).

12108 *a) Olkhovski* V. S., ⊕ Funeral rite (content and structure); – *b) Melnik* V. I., ⊕ Funeral custom and funeral monument; – *c) Kizlavov* I. L., ⊕

The ideological foundation of funeral rite: RossArkh (1993,1) 78-93;
Eng. 93 / 94-97; Eng. 97 / 98-111; Eng. 111s, all with diagrams.

12109 *a*) *Pekary* Thomas,   *Mors perpetua est*; zum Jenseitsglauben in Rom; –
b) *Drexhage* Hans-Joachim, Einige Bemerkungen zum Mumientrasport
und den Bestattungskosten im römischem Ägypten: Laverna 5 ('Tod,
Bestattung und Jenseits in der griechisch-römischen Antike' 1994) 87-103 /
167-175.

12110 *a*) *Pischikova* E. V.,   Representations of ritual and symbolic objects in
late XXVth dynasty and Saite private tombs; – *b*) *Wilkinson* Richard A.,
Symbolic location and alignment in New Kingdom royal tombs and their
decoration: JAmEg 31 (1994) 63-77; 43 fig. / 79-86.

12111 **Rahmani** L. Y.,   A catalogue of Jewish ossuaries in the collections of
the state of Israel.   J 1994, Antiquities Authority.   xi-309 p.; bibliog.
264-280; 135 pl. 965-406-016-7.

12112 *Richer* Nicolas,   Aspects des funerailles à Sparte: CahGlotz 5 (1994)
51-96.

12113 ᴱ**Richter** Klemens,   Der Umgang mit den Toten; Tod und Bestattung in
der christlichen Gemeinde 1989 ➤ 7,8997*:   ᴿTR 90 (1994) 148-152 (T.
Mass-Ewerd).

12114 *Rodante* Sebastiano,   La scienza convalida la Sindone; errata la datazione medievale.   Mi 1994, Massimo.   99 [+ iv] p.; 29 color. fig. Lᵐ 18.
88-7030-488-4.

12115 **Sanders** Gabriel,   Lapides memores; païens et chrétiens face à la mort
1991 ➤ 8,e299:   ᴿSalesianum 56 (1994) 144s (R. *Della Casa*).

12116 *Sannibale* Maurizio,   Le urne cinerarie di età ellenistica [Museo Vaticano etrusco].   R c. 1994, Bretschneider.   245 p.; ill. Lᵐ 280. – ᴿSrcheo
9,117 (1994) 125s (S. *Moscati*).

12116* *Schauenburg* Konrad,   Zu Gottheiten und Heroen im und am Grab:
JbOSA 63 (1994) 71-94; 24 fig.

12117 **Schmidt** Andrea B.,   Kanon der Entschlafenen; das Begräbnisrituale der
Armenier; der altarmenischer Bestattungsritus für die Laien: OrBChr 5.
Wsb 1994, Harrassowitz.   307 p.; bibliog. 20-29. 3-447-03539-0.

12118 **Strömberg** Agneta,   Male or female? A methodological study of
grave-gifts as sex indicators in Iron Age burials from Athens: SIMA
123. Jonsered 1993, Åström.   217 p.; 15 fig. – ᴿBO 51 (1994) 708-710 (I.
Morris); ClasR 44 (1994) 379s (A. M. *Snodgrass*).

12119 *Talatinian* Basilio,   La Sindone di Torino ... due francescani la salva-
rono dalle fiamme [1538]: TerraS 70,5 (1994) 33-38.

12119* **Taylor** John H.,   Egyptian coffins. Eg 11.   Bucks 1989, Shire.   68 p.
0-85263-977-5.

12120 **Walker** Cameron J. M.,   Bronze age burial customs on Crete: diss.
California State, ᴰ*Joesink-Mandeville* V. L.   Fullerton 1994.   127 p.
13-55531. (DissA-disk) MAI 32 (1994s) p. 821.

12121 **Willems** Harco,   Chests of life; a study of the typology and conceptual
development of Middle Kingdom standard class coffins 1988 ➤ 5,d645:
ᴿCdÉ 69 (1994) 291s (O. D. *Berley*); WeltOr 25 (1994) 21-35; 7 fig. (J.
Kahl).

T3.9   *Numismatica,* **coins.**

12122 ᴱ**Acquaro** E.,   Monete puniche nelle collezioni italiane 1.   R 1989,
BNum mg 6/1.   141 p.; 27 color. pl. – ᴿNumC 154 (1994) 304-6 (P. *Visonà*, also on MANFREDI L., Riconiazione 1991).

12123 **Alfaro Asins** C., Sylloge Nummorum Graecorum España 1/1 Gadir y Ebusus. M 1994. 163 p.; ill. – ᴿRStFen 22 (1994) 278s (Lorenza-Ilia *Manfredi*).

12124 **Arnold-Biucchi** Carmen, The Randazzo hoard 1990 → 9,13715: ᴿGnomon 66 (1994) 20-23 (Aldina *Cutroni Tusa*).

12125 **Balbi De Caro** Silvana, Roma e la moneta, I. Mi c. 1994, Silvana. 240 p.; 217 (color.) fig.; maps. Lᵐ 100. – ᴿArcheo 9,115 (1994) 125 (S. *Moscati* anche su II, medioevo).

12126 **Bastien** Pierre, Le buste monétaire des empereurs romains. Wetteren 1992s, Numismatique romaine 19. 328 p.; vol. of 266 pl. [RBgNum 139 (1993) 343-5, P. *Naster*]. Fb 5950.

12127 *Bickford-Smith* Roger A., The imperial mints in the East for Septimius Severus; it is time to begin a thorough reconsideration: RitNum 96 (1994s) 53-69 + II pl.

12128 **Borearachchi** O., Monnaies gréco-bactriennes et indo-grecques; catalogue raisonné. P 1991. 459 p.; 69 pl. – ᴿVDI 208 (1994) 220-5 (V. A. *Gaibov*, G. A. *Koshelenko*, ⓑ).

12129 *Botrè* Claudio, *Fabrizi* Enrico, La monetazione aurea nella Roma repubblicana (250-50 a.C.): RitNum 96 (1994s) 37-44 + 12 fig.

12130 **Burnett** Andrew, *al.*, Roman provincial coinage I to 69AD 1992 → 9,13720: ᴿAntClas 63 (1994) 510-2 (F. de *Callatay*); ArEspArq 66 (1993) 341-5 (M. P. *García Bellido*); NumC 153 (1993) 292-9 (K. E. T. *Butcher*); RBgNum 139 (1993) 345-9 (J. van *Heesch*).

12131 *Buttrey* T. V., Calculating ancient coin production; 1. facts and fantasies; 2. Why it cannot be done [presidential address]: NumC 153 (1993) 335-351 / 154 (1994) 341-352.

12131* **Callatay** François de, *al.*, L'argent monnayé d'Alexandre le Grand à Auguste: ÉtNum 12. Bru 1993, CercleÉtNum. 117 p. Fb 975. – ᴿRBgNum 40 (1994) 141-3 (P. *Naster*); RNum 36 (1994) 336s (G. *Le Rider*).

12132 **Casey** P. J., Roman coinage in Britain³ [¹1980]. Princes Risborough, Bucks 1994, Shire. 64 p. 0-7476-0231-9.

12132* *Coarelli* Filippo, Moneta; le officine della zecca di Roma tra repubblica e impero: → 18*, ᶠ*Breglia* Laura, AnnItNum 38-41 (1994) 23-66; 14 fig.

12133 **Elayi** J. & A. G., Trésors de monnaies phéniciens... 1993 → 9,13723: ᴿRBgNum 139 (1993) 341-3 (P. *Naster*); CRAI (1994) 73s (G. *Le Rider*).

12133* *Elayi* J. & A. G., *a*) La première monnaie de ʾTR/Tripolis (Tripoli, Liban) [Bru Hirsch 1759 4 s. av.-J.-C.]: TEuph 5 (1992) 143-151. – *b*) Un nouveau trésor de tétradrachmes athéniens et pseudo-athéniens: RNum 36 (1994) 26-33; 1 fig.

12134 *Ermatinger* James W., The fourth century follis [term for an actual sack of silver coins changed to a unit of monetary value]: MünstHand 13,1 (1994) 84-88; deutsch franç. 88.

12135 *Fusi-Rossetti* Anton G., Moneta e non moneta; l'aes signatum e i multipli [successore di pecunia (= pecus, bestiame) sotto influsso etrusco]: RitNum 96 (1994s) 19-32 + IV pl.

12136 **Grierson** P., *Mays* M., Catalogue of late Roman coins. Dumbarton Oaks 1992, Whittemore. 499 p.; 37 pl. – ᴿAntClas 63 (1994) 512s (F. de *Callatay*); RPg 67 (1993) 182-5 (J.-P. *Callu*).

12137 *Hazzard* Richard A., *a*) The composition of Ptolemaic silver: JSSEg (SSEA) 20 (1990, issued 1993) 89-107; – *b*) Two hoards of Ptolemaic silver, IGCH 1713 and 1722: NumC 154 (1994) 53-66.

12138 **Heipp-Tamer** Christine, Die Münzprägung der lykischen Stadt Phaselis

in griechischer Zeit: StArchG 6. Saarbrücken 1993. 182 p.; 32 pl. – ᴿRBgNum 40 (1994) 139-141 (F. de *Callatay*).
12139 **Hollstein** Wilhelm., Die stadtrömische Münzprägung der Jahre 78-50 v.Chr. zwischen politischer Aktualität und Familienthematik: QForAntW. Mü 1993, Tuduv. 424 p.; 8 pl. – ᴿNumC 154 (1994) 317-9 (J. H. C. *Williams*).
12140 **Işık** Erdoğan, Elektronstatere aus Klazomenai; der Schatzfund von 1989. Saarbrücken 1992, StArchAGesch 5, → 9,13728: 59 p. 9 fig.; 8 pl. – ᴿNumC 154 (1994) 300-2 (J. *Seier*).
12140* [Melville] **Jones** John R., Testimonia numaria; Greek and Latin texts concerning ancient Greek coinage, 1. Texts and translations. L 1993, Spink. 544 p. – ᴿNumC 154 (1994) 297-300 (T.S.N. *Moorhead*: prodigious).
12141 *Kagan* Jonathan H., An archaic Greek coin hoard from the eastern Mediterranean and early Cypriot coinage: NumC 154 (1994) 17-52; pl. 1-9.
12142 **Koch** H., A hoard of coins from Eastern Parthia: NumNMg 165. NY 1990, Am. Num. Soc. x-64 p.; 12 pl. – ᴿNumC 153 (1993) 311s (D. *Sellwood*).
12143 *Le Rider* Georges, *a)* Antiochos IV (175-164) et le monnayage de bronze séleucide: BCH 118 (1994) 17-34; – *b)* Un curieux trésor de monnaies d'electrum trouvé à Clazomènes: CRAI (1994) 945-953; 2 fig.
12144 *Lönnqvist* Kenneth, A metallurgical and chemical analysis of the procuratorial coinage of Roman Judaea: BBArchäom 11 (1992) 13-34.
12145 **MacDonald** Donald, The coinage of Aphrodisias. L 1992, Royal Numismatic Soc. xi-169 p. £30. 0-901405-30-2. – ᴿJRS 84 (1994) 256-8 (K. *Butcher*).
12145* **Malek** Hodge M., A survey of research on Sasanian numismatics: NumC 153 (1993) 227-269; pl. 37.
12146 **Martini** Rodolfo, Monetazione provinciale romana I: Glaus 5. Mi 1991, Ennerre. 181 p. – ᴿNumC 153 (1993) 300-3 (Susanne *Frey-Kupper*).
12147 **Merkelbach** R., Die Bedeutung des Geldes für die Geschichte der griechisch-römischen Welt. Stu 1992, Teubner. 79 p. – ᴿNumC 154 (1994) 296s (J. H. C. *Williams*).
12148 **Meshorer** Yaʿakov, **Qedar** Shraga, The coinage of Samaria in the 4th century B.C.E. 1991 → 8,e342: ᴿNumC 154 (1994) 312-5 (M. J. *Price*); TEuph 8 (1994) 171-3 (A. *Lemaire*).
12149 *Meshorer* Yaʿaqov, The 'black silver' coins of the Babatha papyri; a reevaluation: IsrMusJ 10 (1992) 67-74.
12150 *Metcalf* D. M., *a)* The Galini hoard concealed c. 1373-1374 [341 coins acquired by Cyprus Museum in 1945]: RepCyp (1994) 269-288; pl. LXXIV-LXXVIII [309-313, *al.*, ⊖ Ottoman coins]; – *b)* A hoard of early Tripolitan Crusader bezants: NumC 154 (1994) 214-7; pl. 28.
12151 *Michaelidou-Nicolaou* Ino, Four Ptolemaic/Roman hoards from Cyprus: NumC 153 (1993) 11-29; pl. 2-8.
12152 *Mildenberg* Leo, Über das Münzwesen im Reich der Achämeniden: ArchMIran 26 (1993) 55-79; pl. 6-13.
12152* *Mildenberg* L., On the money circulation in Palestine from Artaxerxes II till Ptolemy I; preliminary studies of the local coinage in the fifth Persian satrapy [4. Gaza mint] 5: → 461, Syrie, TEuph [2 (1990) 137-146] 7 (1994) 63-71; II pl.; franç, 63.
12153 **Mørkholm** Otto †1983, Early Hellenistic coinage, ᴱ*Grierson* Philip, *Westermark* Ulla 1991 → 7,d265... 9,13737: ᴿAJA 97 (1993) 809s (G. *Reger*).

12154 **Morrisson** Cécile,   La numismatique: Que sais-je... P 1992, PUF. 128 p.; 21 fig. – ᴿNumC 153 (1993) 271 (P. *Grierson*).

12155 *Mosig-Walburg* K.,   Sonderprägung des Xysro II. vom Typ Göbl V/6 und VI/7:   IrAnt 28 (1993) 169-191; 10 fig.

12156 *Mostecky* Helmut,   Ein spätrömischer Münzschatz aus Karthago: NumZ 102 (1994) 5-166; 2 pl.

12157 *Munro-Hay* S. C.,   Coins of ancient South Arabia.   NumC 154 (1994) 191-203; pl. 22-27.

12157* *Nicolet-Pierre* H., *Amandry* M.,   Un nouveau trésor de monnaies d'argent pseudo-athéniennes venu d'Afghanistan: RNum 36 (1994) 34-54; 2 fig.

12158 **Perez** Christine,   La monnaie de Rome à la fin de la République; un discours en images.   P 1989, Errance.   132 p.; ill. – ᴿLatomus 53 (1994) 244s (R. *Chevallier*).

12159 **Potts** B. T.,   Supplement to The Pre-Islamic Coinage of Eastern Arabia [1991 ➤ 7,d270; 9,13740]: Niebuhr 16.   K 1994, MusTusc.   88 p.; 425 fig.; map.   87-7289-172-4.

12160 **Price** M. J.,   The coinage in the name of Alexander the Great and Philip Arrhidaeus 1991 ➤ 8,e351:   ᴿNumC 153 (1993) 276-280 (R. *Ashton*).

12161 *Savio* Adriano,   Intorno ai medaglioni talismanici di Tarso e di Aboukir [c. 274 d.C.]: RitNum 96 (1994s) 73-100 + 3 pl.

12162 *Schmitt-Korte* Karl, *Price* Martin,   Nabataean coinage, 3. The Nabataean monetary system: NumC 154 (1994) 67-132; pl. 10-12.

12163 *Soheir* Bakhoum,   Trajan en Égypte d'après les documents de l'atelier monétaire d'Alexandrie: ➤ 9,2, ᶠABOU DAOUD D., 10 (1993) 7-16 + 16 fig.

12164 **Thompson** Margaret,   Alexander's drachm mints, 2. Lampsacus and Abydos: NumSt 19.   NY 1911, AmNum Soc. 77 p.; 34 pl. $55. – ᴿNumC 153 (1993) 280-7 (M. J. *Price*).

12164* **Touratsoglou** Yannis,   The coin circulation in ancient Macedonia: Bt 1. Athènes 1993, Soc. Numismatique Grecque.   88 p.; XIII pl. 960-220-374-9. – ᴿRBgNum 40 (1994) 143-5 (F. de *Callatay*).

12165 *Vin* J. P. van der,   Two new Roman hoards; Zoutkamp and Ried: Babesch 68 (1993) 247-253; 15 (× 2) fig.

12166 *Volk* Terence,   Retroconversion and the numerical analysis of Roman republican coin-hoards: RitNum 96 (1994s) 105-186; 2 maps.

12167 ᶠWESTERMARK Ulla, Florilegium numismaticum; 65 b. ᴱNilsson H., 1992 ➤ 8,194:   ᴿRitNum 96 (1994s) 351 (D. *Foraboschi*).

12168 **Williams** R. T.,   The silver coinage of Velia. L 1992, Royal Num. Soc. xi-152 p.; 47 pl. – ᴿNumC 154 (1994) 303s (K. *Rutter*).

T4   *Situs*, **excavation-sites** I. *Chronica, bulletins.*

12168* *De Vries* Bert, *Bikai* Pierre, Archaeology in Jordan: AJA 97 (1993) 457-520; 47 fig.

12169 *González Echegaray* J.,   Investigaciones arqueológicas en Levante, IV [1989s]; AulaO 11,1 (1993) 73-100.

12171 *Lafontaine-Dosogne* Jacqueline, Chronique [CahArch 37 (1989); 38 (1990) / 39 (1991); 40 (1993)]: Byzantion 63 (1993) 466-472 / 64 (1994) 518-526.

12172 *Piccirillo* Michele,   Ricerca storico-archeologica in Giordania XVI: LA 94 (1994) 619-666, map 618.

12173 *Vattioni* Francesco, Antichità archeologiche del Levante inedite o poco note: Henoch 16 (1994) 3-7.
12175 *Wolff* Samuel R., Archaeology in Israel: AJA 97 (1993) 135-163; 35 fig. (map); 98 (1994) 481-519; 46 fig.

T4.2 *Situs effossi,* syntheses.

12177 ᴱÅström P., High, midde, or low [chronology]? 3, SIMA 80, 1987/89 → 5,831*; 7,d284: ᴿPEQ 126 (1994) 164s (T. *Watkins*).
12178 **Bierling** N., Giving Goliath his due; new archaeological light on the Philistines 1992 → 8,e365; 9,13748: ᴿOTEssays 7 (1994) 140s (G. E. *Olivier*).
12179 *Bunimovitz* Shlomo, Problems in the 'ethnic' identification of the Philistine material culture [hybrid of modern research]: TAJ 17 (1990) 210-222 [< OTAbs 17, p. 19].
12180 *Cagni* Luigi, Interconnessioni culturali nel Vicino Oriente durante il periodo achemenide (539-511 a.C.): → 418, Circolazioni 1991/4, 55-65.
12181 **Dickinson** Oliver, The Aegean bronze age: World Archaeology. C 1994, Univ. xxi-342 p.; ill.; bibliog. 310-332. 0-521-242800; pa. -45664-9.
12182 **Dothan** Trude & Moshe, People of the sea; the search for the Philistines 1992 → 8,a368*; 9,13754: ᴿAJA 98 (1992) 304s (S. *Brown*); JAOS 114 (1994) 668s (W. G. *Dever*).
12183 **Drews** Robert, The end of the Bronze Age; changes in warfare and the catastrophe c. 1200 B.C.: 1993 → 9,13755: ᴿBAR-W 20,4 (1994) 10.56 (W. H. *Stiebing*); RÉG 107 (1994) 257s (J.-N. *Corvisier*).
12184 **Elayi** Josette, *Sapin* Jean, Nouveaux regards sur la Transeuphratène 1991 → 8,e747: ᴿGregorianum 75 (1994) 343s (G. L. *Prato*).
12184* **Finkelstein** Israel, The archaeology of the Israelite settlement 1988 → 4,e629; 6,d291; 7,2366: ᴿRBibArg 56 (1994) 119-122 (P. *Andiñach*).
12185 **Gal** Zvi, Lower Galilee during the Iron Age: ASOR diss. 8, 1992 → 7,d290*; 9,12758: WL 1992, Eisenbrauns. ix-118 p. – ᴿLA 44 (1994) 716-9 (P. *Kaswalder*); PEQ 126 (1994) 77s (B. *Isserlin*).
12186 *Hajman* Mordechai, The Iron Age II sites of the Western Negev highlands: IsrEJ 44 (1994) 36-61; 16 fig.
12187 **James** P., *al.*, Centuries of darkness 1992 → 7,d293 ... 9,13759: ᴿAJA 98 (1994) 362s (W. A. *Ward*: cavalier, haphazard methodology); AmHR 99 (1994) 872s (B. C. *Trigger*); DiscEg 25 (1993) 105s (G. W. van *Oosterhout*: the jump should be 480 instead of 240 years) & 27 (1993) 101-4 (D. A. *Aston*: unconvincing; alternatives ignored; no charts).
12188 **James** P. J., *al.*, Bronze to Iron Age chronology in the Old World; time for a reassessment? Studies in Ancient Chronology 1 [no more up to 1995]. L 1987, Univ. College Inst. Archaeology. iv-143 p.; bibliog. 116-143. 0952-4975.
12190 **Kohl** Philip L., Central Asia palaeolithic beginnings to the Iron Age: R Synthèse 14. P 1994, RCiv. 315 p.; bibliog. 271-282.
12191 **Kolbus** Susanne, Zur Funktion der frühbronzezeitlichen umwallten Plätze Palästinas: Diss. Münster 1992. – ArchAnz (1993) 157.
12192 **Kuhnen** Hans-Peter, Palästina in griechisch-römischer Zeit: HbArch, Vorderas 2/2, 1990: → 6,d926 ... 9,13761: ᴿAntClas 63 (1994) 610 (J. C. *Balty*); BO 51 (1994) 456-9 (K. *Vriezen*); BonnJbb 194 (1994) 549-553 (T. *Weber*).
12193 ᴱ**Laperrousaz** Ernest-Marie, *Lemaire* André, La Palestine à l'époque perse: BJér Ét. annexe. P 1994, Cerf. 329 p. F 198. 2-204-04987-5.

12193* **Lund** J., The archaeological evidence for the transition from the Persian period to the Hellenistic age in northwestern Syria: ⇒ 461, TEuph 6 (1993) 27-45; 5 fig.

12194 **Margalith** Othniel, The Sea Peoples in the Bible [*Goyye ha-Yam* 1988] Twith *Margalith* S. Wsb 1994, Harrassowitz. 354 p.; bibliog. 233-245. 3-[447 or 477 on same page]-03516-1.

12194* **Meimaris** E. Yiannis, *al.*, Chronological systems in Roman-Byzantine Palestine and Arabia; the evidence of the dated Greek inscriptions: Meletemata 17. Athens 1992. 432 p.; 3 maps. – RRÉAnc 96 (1994) 631s (M. *Sartre*).

12195 *Naᵓaman* Nadiv, The Hurrians and the end of the Middle Bronze Age in Palestine: Levant 26 (1994) 175-188.

12196 **Noort** Ed, Die Seevölker in Palästina: Palestina antiqua 8. Kampen 1994, Kok Pharos. 238 p.; bibliog. 213-223. *f* 69.

12197 **Randsborg** K., The first millennium A.D. in Europe and the Mediterranean 1991 ⇒ 7,d299; 9,13767: RJRS 84 (1994) 239s (S. T. *Loseby*).

12197* *Stern* Ephraim, Assyrian and Babylonian elements in the material culture of Palestine in the Persian period: ⇒ 461, Syrie, TEuph 7 (1991/4) 51-58 + 4 fig.; franç. 51.

12198 FTESTA E., Early Christianity in context, EMannss F., *Alliata* A, SBF maior 38, 1993: ⇒ 9,150: RBAngIsr 13 (1993s) 50-52 (S. *Mimouni*, T*Dauphin* Claudine); RivB 42 (1994) 496-500 (G. *Ravasi*).

12199 **Weippert** Helga, Palästina in vorhellenistischer Zeit 1988 ⇒ 4,e639 ... 9,13770: RJNES 53 (1994) 37-41 (G. W. *Ahlström* †).

T4.3 **Jerusalem,** *archaeologia et historia.*

12200 **Acquaviva** Giorgio, La Chiesa-madre di Gerusalemme; storia e risurrezione del giudeocristianesimo. CasM 1994, Piemme. 208 p.

12201 *Adler* Stephen J., Israeli court finds Muslim council destroyed [mostly 'covered over'] ancient remains on Temple Mount: BAR-W 20,4 (1994) 30 only.

12202 *Alliata* Eugenio, Il kathisma [via di Betlemme]; 'luogo del riposo' della Vergine: TerraS 69,5 (1993) 38-41.

12203 **Ariel** D. T., [*Groot* A. de] Excavations at the City of David II. [III. 1992] Imported stamped amphora handles, coins, worked bone and ivory, and glass: Qedem 30, 1990 ⇒ 8,e395; 9,13772: RAJA 48 (1994) 569s (J. F. *Dessel*); PEQ 126 (1994) 71s (G. *Finkielsztejn*) [74s Margaret *Steiner*].

12204 *Avni* Gideon, *Greenhut* Zvi, Scoperte a Gerusalemme; lo splendore delle grotte di Aceldama: Archeo 9,115 (1994) 54-61.

12205 *Bear* Doron, ❸ The southern boundary of Aelia Capitolina and the location of the Tenth Roman Legion's camp: CHistEI 69 (1993) 37-56; ill.; Eng. 181.

12206 *Ben-Shammai* Haggai, ❸ The location of the Karaite quarter in medieval Jerusalem: CHistEI 70 (1994) 59-74 (in part response to 29-58, *Gil* Moshe); Eng. 201.

12207 **Bermejo Cabrera** Enrique, La proclamación de la escritura en la liturgía de Jerusalén; estudio terminológico del 'Itinerarium Egeriae': SBF maior 37. J 1993, Franciscan. 534 p.; ill. – RAntonianum 69 (1994) 396s (T. *Larrañaga*).

12208 *Bieberstein* Klaus, Der Gesandtenaustausch zwischen Karl dem Grossen und Hārūn ar-Rašīd und seine Bedeutung für die Kirchen Jerusalems: ZDPV 109 (1993) 152-173.

12209 **Bieberstein** Klaus, *Bloedhorn* Hanswulf, Jerusalem; Grundzüge der Baugeschichte vom Chalkolithikum bis zur Frühzeit der osmanischen Herrschaft: TAVO B-100. Wsb 1994, Reichert. 1. 239 p.; 2. 456 p.; 3. 554 p. 3-88226-671-6 all [ByZ 88,458s, R. *Reich*].

12210 **Borgehammer** Stephan, How the Holy Cross was found 1991 → 7, d309; ... 9,13779: ᴿCritRR 6 (1993) 347-9 (H. A. *Pohlsander*); PEQ 125 (1993) 161-3 (G. S. P. *Freeman-Greenville*, with an astute comment on the cover caption; and also on *Drijvers'* Helena); Speculum 69 (1994) 425s (K. G. *Holum*).

12211 **Bunte** Wolfgang, Die Zerstörung Jerusalems in der mittelniederländischen Literatur: Judentum und Umwelt 33. Fra 1992, Lang. 802 p. Fs 125. – ᴿKairos 34s (1992s) 243s (G. *Stemberger*).

12211* *Calabi* Francesca, Aʀɪsᴛᴇᴀ e il tempio di Gerusalemme: QuadStor 38 (1993) 47-64.

12212 *Chyutin* Michael, The New Jerusalem [Aramaic; DJD 3,184-192, Mɪʟɪᴋ J.]; ideal city: DSD 1 (1994) 71-97; 10 fig.

12213 **Drijvers** J. W., Helena Augusta, the mother of Constantine 1992 → 8, e389; 9,13787: ᴿRHR 211 (1994) 477-9 (J. *Doignon*); CathHR 79 (1993) 508s (H. A. *Drake*); HZ 259 (1994) 174-6 (W. *Kuhoff*).

12214 *Edelstein* Gershon, *Milevski* Ianir, The rural settlement of Jerusalem re-evaluated; surveys and excavations in the Reph᾽aim valley and Mevasseret Yerushalayim: PEQ 126 (1994) 2-23; 16 fig. (map).

12215 **Flusin** Bernard, Saint Anastase le Perse et l'histoire de la Palestine au début du VIIᵉ siècle, I. Les textes; II. Commentaire; les moines de Jérusalem et l'invasion perse: Le Monde Byzantin. P 1992, CNRS. 420 p.; 437 p. – ᴿSpeculum 69 (1994) 1161-3 (Carmilla V. *Franklin*).

12216 **Franken** H. J., *Steiner* Margarete L., Excavations in Jerusalem 1961-7, II, 1990 → 8,e391; 9,13791: ᴿBO 51 (1994) 691s (V. *Fritz*); Levant 26 (1994) 225-9; 3 fig. (F. *Zayadine*).

12217 *Galil* Gershon, ❹ Parathon, Timnatha, and the fortifications of Bacchides [to isolate Jerusalem]: CHistEI 63 (1992) 22-30; Eng. 190.

12217* ᴱ**Geva** Hillel, Ancient Jerusalem Revealed. J 1994, Israel Exploration Society. xvi-336. $40 [BL 95,26, A. R. *Millard*: completes Jerusalem revealed].

12218 *a) Geva* H., ❹ A summary of 25 years of archaeological research in Jerusalem — achievements and evaluations; – *b) Mazar* E., Excavations in the Ophel — the royal quarter of Jerusalem during the First Temple period: Qadmoniot 26 (1993) 2-24 / 25-32 [-63, *al.* on Jerusalem].

12218* **Gibson** Shimon, *Taylor* Joan E., Beneath the church of the Holy Sepulchre, Jerusalem; the archaeology and early history of traditional Golgotha: PEQ Mg 1. L 1994. xx-102 p.; ill. £19.50. 0-903526-53-0. – ᴿLA 44 (1994) 725-9 (E. *Alliata*, ᵀ*Boettcher* J.).

12219 *a) Gill* Dan, Jerusalem's underground water systems; how they met; geology solves long-standing mystery of Hezekiah's tunnelers; – *b) Klever* Terence, Up the waterspout; how David's general Joab got David's Jerusalem; – *c) Parker* Simon B., Siloam inscription memorializes engineering achievement: BAR-W 20,4 (1994) 20-33. 64 / 34s / 36-38.

12220 *Grego* Igino, Martirio, monaco [monastero di Maᶜale Adummim sulla via di Gerico] e patriarca di Gerusalemme [non 'Costantinopoli' come coperta]: Asprenas 41 (1994) 209-226.

12221 *Greenhut* Z., ❹ New archaeological discoveries from the periphery of Jerusalem: Ariel ❺ 100s (1994) 133-147 [< JStJud 25,355].

12222 *Hamilton* Bernard, The impact of Crusader Jerusalem on western Christendom: CathHR 80 (1994) 695-713.

12223 *Kloner* Amos, *Stark* Harley, A burial cave on Mount Scopus, Jerusalem: BAnglsr 11 (1991s) 7-17 [< OTAbs 17, p. 26].

12224 **Kroyanker** Paul, Jerusalem architecture. NY 1994, Vendome (St. Martin's). 210 p. $65. 0-86565-147-7 [TDig 42,173].

12225 **Lückhoff** Martin, Das protestantische Bistum in Jerusalem (1841-1886): diss. ᴰ*Schneider* H. Marburg 1994. – RTLv 26,550.

12226 *Meinster* M. J., A short study of the image of Jerusalem in selected Arabic and Hebrew poems: J/Tyd Sem 6 (1993) 200-222.

12227 **Magness** Jodi, Jerusalem ceramic chronology 1993 [BAR-W 10/1.10]. ➤ 9,13643.

12228 *Murphy-O'Connor* Jerome, The location of the Capitol[line Temple] in Aelia Capitolina [FʟᴜsɪN J. 1992]: RB 101 (1994) 407-415.

12229 *Nadelman* Yonatan, a) The identification of Anathoth and the soundings at Khirbet Deir es-Sidd [1162 . 1353]: IsrEJ 44 (1994) 62-74; 6 fig.; – b) Vessels from a *favissa* of the First Temple [... reconstructing *qdš* on an inscription]: BAnglsr 11 (1991s) 18-21.

12230 **Pellistrandi** Christine, Jérusalem épouse et mère: Lire la Bible 87, 1989 ➤ 5,d766 ... 7,d331: ᴿSalesianum 56 (1994) 378 (M. *Cimosa*).

12231 *Peters* F. E., The distant shrine; the Islamic centuries in Jerusalem: AMS StModSoc 22. NY 1993, ᴀᴍs. 275 p. $39.50. – ᴿSpeculum 69 (1994) 875-7 (R. B. *Rose*).

12231* *Plank* Peter, Sabas von Kaisareia; ein Beitrag zur Geschichte der melkitischen orthodoxen Patriarchate von Jerusalem und von Alexandrien zur Komnenen-Zeit: OstKSt 43 (1994) 23-40.

12232 ᴱ**Raby** Julian, *Johns* Jeremy, *Bayt al-Maqdis*; 'Abd al-Mᴀʟɪᴋ's Jerusalem, I, 1992 ➤ 13804: ᴿLA 44 (1994) 730 (M. *Piccirillo*).

12233 *Ritmeyer* Leen & Kathleen, Akeldama; a) Potter's field or High Priest's tomb?; – b) *Avni* Gideon, *Greenut* Zvi, Resting place of the rich and famous: ᴿBAR-W 20,6 (1994) 22-35 . 76 / 36-46.

12233* *Saulnier* Christiane †, La cité hellénistique de Jérusalem à l'époque du grand-prêtre Jason: ➤ 461, Syrie, TEuph 7 (1991/4) 83-92; Eng. 83.

12234 *Shanks* Hershel, The tombs of Silwan: BAR-W 20,3 (1994) 38-51.

12235 *Shurman* Michael M., Wɪʟsoɴ bench-marks in the Old City of Jerusalem: PEQ 126 (1994) 49-51.

12236 a) *Sievers* Joseph, Jerusalem, the Akra, and Josephus; – b) *Levine* Lee I., Josephus' description of the Jerusalem Temple: War, Antiquities, and other sources: ➤ 123, Mem. Sᴍɪᴛʜ M., Josephus 1992/4, 195-209 / 243-6.

12236* *Spolsky* Bernard, *Cooper* Robert L., The languages of Jerusalem: Oxford Studies in Language Contact. Ox 1991, Clarendon. xiv-166 p. £30. – ᴿBSO 57 (1994) 229 (L. *Glinert*); JSS 39 (1994) 146-150 (A. *Shivtiel*).

12237 *Steiner* Margaret L., Re-dating the terraces of Jerusalem: IsrEJ 44 (1994) 13-20; 7 fig.

12238 *Stone* G. R., The fall of Jerusalem: BurHist 28,4 (1992) 100-108; 29 (wrongly numbered 30),1 (1993) 4-17 and continued 29,2 (1993) 45-61; Part 3: 35,4; 24 pl.

12239 *Storme* Albert, La casa di Caifa, ᵀsr. M. Roberta *della Chiesa*: TerraS 70,3 (1994) 16-23.

12240 **Sublet** Jacqueline, Les trois vies du sultan Baybars; choix de textes: Coll. Orientale.   P 1992, Impr. Nat.   256 p.; ill. F 450. – ᴿJAOS 114 (1994) 104-6 (R. *Irwin*: lavish, pleasing; sometimes puzzling, not academically reliable); OLZ 89 (1994) 289-292 (L. *Haarmann*: resplendent, too hasty).

12241 *Talatinian* Basile,   Les 11 Églises de Jérusalem: TerreS mars 1994 > EsprVie 104 (1994) 514-6.

12242 **Thorau** P., The lion of Egypt, Baybars, ᵀ*Holt* P. M.   L 1992, Longmans. xiii-321 p. £13.50.   0-582-06823-3. – ᴿJSS 38 (1993) 340-8 (D. P. *Little*); WeltOr 25 (1994) 205-7 (Anne-Marie *Eddé*).

12243 **Ussishkin** David, The village of Silwan 1993 ⇢ 9,13809: ᴿBiblica 75 (1994) 582s (R. *North*: 'squallor' crept in); PhoenixEOL 40 (1994) 123s (Margaret *Steiner*).

12244 **Yossi** Levi,   Jerusalem in the First and Second Temple period; tour routes. J 1988, Yad Ben-Zvi. 124 p.

ᴱ**Walker** P.,   Jerusalem past and present 1989/94 ⇢ 337*b*.

12245 **Wightman** G. J., The walls of Jerusalem, from the Canaanites to the Mamluks: MeditArch supp. 4. Sydney 1993. x-331 p.; 89 fig.; 31 pl. 0-646-16008-7.

12246 *Wilkinson* John, [Delphicae] Stone tables in Herodian Jerusalem: BAngIsr 13 (1993s) 7-21; 18 fig.

12247 ***Dawwara*** 1050-900 B.C.E: TAJ 17 (1990) 163-209 (I. *Finkelstein*) [< OTAbs 17, p. 22].

12248 ***Gabaon,*** Jîb: *Briend* J., Gabaon à l'époque perse: TEuph 5 (1992) 9-20; Eng. 9.

12249 ***Miṣpa:*** *Gunneweg* J., *al.*, Interregional contacts between Tell-en-Nasbeh and littoral Palestine centres in Canaan during Early Bronze Age I: Archaeometry 36 (1994) 227-239: 2 fig.

12249* *Liwak* Rüdiger, Mizpa: ⇢ 517, TRE 23 (1994) 121-4; 1 fig. (Nasbé plan).

12250 ***Qubayba*** 9 k NW: *Bagatti* Bellarmino, Emmaus-Qubeibeh; the results of excavations at Emmaus-Qubeibeh and nearby sites (1873; 1887-90; 1940-44), ᵀ*Bonanno* R.; SBF 4. J 1993. xiii-258 p.; 40 pl. [LA 44,243].

12251 ***Ras Abu Maʿaruf*** [4 k NW Damascus Gate], Iron Age winepress: Atiqot 25 (1994) 63-75; 9 fig. (J. *Seligman*).

T4.4   *Situs alphabetice:* **Judaea, Negeb.**

12252 ʿ***Ajrûd:*** *Hadley* Judith M., Kuntillet ʿAjrud; religious centre or desert way station? PEQ 125 (1993) 115-124; 3 fig.

12253 ***Arad:*** *Mendecki* Norbert, ❷ Świątynia [templum] Jahwe – sensacyjne wykopaliska [effossiones 1962-] na wzgórzu [tell] Arad: RuBi 47 (1994) 103-6.

12253* *Hartung* Ulrich, Bemerkungen zur Chronologie der Beziehungen Ägyptens zu Südkanaan in spätprädynastischer Zeit [Abydos: En Beşor, Halif, Arad, Lachish]: MiDAI-K 50 (1994) 107-111; foldout chart.

12254 ***Beersheba,*** Ramot Nof 1991; Atiqot: 25 (1994) 157-177; 18 fig.

12255 *Gilead* Isaac, The history of the chalcolithic settlement in the Nahal Beer Sheva area; the radiocarbon aspect: BASOR 296 (1994) 1-13.

12255* ***Bethlehem:*** *Jotischky* Andrew, Manuel Comnenus and the reunion of the churches; the evidence of the conciliar mosaics in the Church of the Nativity in Bethlehem: Levant 26 (1994) 207-223; 7 fig.

12256 *En Boqeq:* **Gichon** Mordechai, En Boqeq 1993 → 9,13828: ᴿAfO 40s (1993s) 187s (Erika *Bleibtreu*); MesopT 29 (1994) 347-350 (C. *Lippold*); Orientalia 63 (1994) 297-9 (M. *Piccirillo*).

12256* ᶜ*En-Gedi: a) Shalev* S., *Northover* J.P., The metallurgy of the Nahal Mishmar hoard reconsidered: Archaeometry 35 (1993) 35-47; 5 fig. – *b) Hadas* Gideon L., Nine tombs: Atiqot 24 (1994) 1-14, ➊ 1-75.

12257 *Erani* N-Shephelah 1985-8, EB: TAJ 18 (1991) 164-191 (A. *Kempinski*, I. *Gilead*) & 192-204 (Arlene M. *Rosen*).

12258 *Gaza:* **Sadek** Mohamed-Moain, Die mamlukische Architektur der Stadt Gaza: IslamkUnt 144. B 1991, Schwarz. 700 p.; 401 fig.; foldout plan. DM 158. 3-922968-76-7. – ᴿWZKM 84 (1994) 271-4 (S. *Procházka*).

12258* *Katzenstein* H.J., Gaza in the Neo-Babylonian period (626-539 B.C.E.): → 461, Syrie, TEuph 7 (1991/4) 35-49; franç. 35.

12259 *Halif* Iron Age cemetery 1988: Atiqot 25 (1994) 45-62; – Halif 10th 1993: Israel 44 (1994) 152-6; 5 fig. (P. *Jacobs*).

12260 *Ḥaṣeva:* **Cohen** Rudolph, The fortresses at ᶜEn Ḥaṣeva: BA 57 (1994) 203-214.

12261 *Hebron:* **Chadwick** Jeffrey R., The archaeology of biblical Hebron in the Bronze and Iron Ages; an examination of the discoveries of the American Expedition to Hebron: diss. Utah. 1992, ᴰ*Hammond* P. xvi-191 p.; ill.

12262 *Hesi:* **Dahlberg** B., *O'Connell* K.G., Tell el-Hesi (4) 1989 → 6,e18: ᴿJAOS 114 (1994) 98s (H. A. *Leibowitz*); JBL 113 (1994) 697-9 (C. *Meyers*).

12263 **Bennett** W.J., *Blakely* J.A., Tell el-Hesi: The Persian period 1989 → 8,e451: ᴿBASOR 295 (1994) 87-92 (Nancy *Lapp*); TEuph 8 (1994) 159-162 (J. *Sapin*).

12264 *Jericho:* **Binns** John, Ascetics and ambassadors of Christ; the monasteries of Palestine 314-631: Early Christian Studies. Oxford 1994, Clarendon. xi-274 p.; bibliog. 264-269. 0-19-826465-8.

12264* *Hachmann* Rolf, Die 'Befestigungen' das akeramischen Jericho: BaghMitt 25 (1994) 19-74; 11 fig.

12265 **Hirschfeld** Yizhar, The Judean Desert monasteries in the Byzantine period ᴰ1992 → 9,13841; $35. – ᴿAJA 97 (1993) 188-190 (Claudine M. *Dauphin*); BAR-W 10,2 (1994) 6 (D. E. *Grob*); RB 101 (1994) 472s (J. *Murphy-O'Connor*); ScrClasIsr 12 (1993) 210-3 (Averil *Cameron*).

12266 [*Compagnani*] di Segni Leah, Choziba, TerreS (VII 1993) > EsprVie 104 (1994) 57-59 (J. *Daoust*).

12267 *Mauny* Michel de, Jéricho dans l'Antiquité [PeCa 267 (1993) 78-83]: EsprVie 104 (1994) 310-312 (J. *Daoust*).

12268 *Judeideh* archive reappraisal: TAJ 21 (1994) 194-234; 20 fig. (S. *Gibson*).

12269 *Lachish:* **Krauss** Rolf, Ein wahrscheinlicher Terminus post quem für das Ende von Lachisch VI [Ramses IV, nicht Merneptah]: MDOG 126 (1994) 123-130; 7 fig.

12269* *Parker* Simon B., The Lachish Letters and official reactions to prophecies: → 102, Mem. RICHARDSON H., Uncovering 1994, 65-78.

12270 **Ussishkin** David, The Assyrian attack on Lachish; the archaeological evidence from the southwest corner of the site: TAJ 17 (1990) 53-86 (3-52, *Zimhoni* Orna, pottery) [< OTAbs 17, p. 34].

12271 *Masada:* **Netzer** E., Masada III. The buildings; stratigraphy and architecture 1991 → 7,e378: ᴿJRomArch 6 (1993) 473-5; 1 fig. (J. *Patrich*); ᴢAW 106 (1994) 361s (J. *Zangenberg*).

12272 **Barag** Dan, *Hershkovitz* Malka, *al.*, Masada IV, the Yigael Yadin excavations 1963-5 final reports: Lamps, textiles, basketry... wood, ballistic balls, human skeletal remains. J 1994, Israel Exploration Soc. [xii-] 388 p.; ill.; portr. 965-221-026-9.

12273 **Cotton** H., *Geiger* J., Masada II (inscriptions) 1989 ➤ 5,9552: ᴿBO 51 (1994) 414-7 (J. W. van *Henten*).

12274 **Miqne:** *Allen* Susan H., Trojan grey ware at Tel Miqne-Ekron: BASOR 294 (1994) 39-51; 6 fig.

12275 **Negeb: Shereshevsky** J., Byzantine urban settlements in the Negev desert: Beer-Sheva 5. Beersheba 1991, Ben-Gurion Univ. xvi-277 p.; 70 fig.; 7 plans. – ᴿPEQ 126 (1994) 68-70 (Claudine *Dauphin*).

12276 **Avni** Gideon, Early mosques in the Negev highlands; new archaeological evidence on Islamic penetration of southern Palestine: BASOR 294 (1994) 83-100; 12 fig. (map).

12277 **Nizzanim** [3 k W, 1136 . 1283] EB: TAJ 21 (1994) 162-185; 18 fig. (Y. *Yekutieli*, R. *Gophna*).

12278 **Cadesbarnea:** *Meskel* Zeev, The 'Aharoni fortress' near Quseima and the 'Israelite fortresses' in the Negev: BASOR 294 (1994) 39-67; 20 fig.

12279 **Ramat Matred 3** [15 k SW Sde Boqer] 1979, EB: Atiqot 25 (1994) 23-32; 8 fig. (Mordechai *Haiman*).

12279* **Reved:** *Rosen* Steven A., A Roman–period pastoral tent camp in the Negev, Israel: JField 20 (1993) 441-451; 10 fig.

12280 **Sajur** [Druze, 1823 . 2608] rock-cut tomb c. 100 C.E.: Atiqot 25 (1994) 103-115; 6 fig. (E. *Braun*, al.).

12280* **Šiqmîm:** *a*) ➤ 295, ASOR 1994, 87-106 (Levy *Tal*); – *b*) *Shalev* S., al., A chalcolithic macehead from the Negev, Israel; technological aspects and cultural implications: Archaeometry 34 (1992) 63-71; 4 fig.

12281 **Yarmut** (160 . 120) 10th 1993: IsrEJ 44 (1994) 145-151; 3 fig. (P. de *Miroschedji*).

T4.5 Samaria, Sharon.

12282 ᴱ**Finkelstein** I., *Magen* Y., Archaeological survey of the hill country of Benjamin (sites 1-544). J 1993, Survey of Israel.

12283 **Bethel:** *Livingston* David, Further considerations on the location of Bethel at el-Bireh: PEQ 126 (1994) 155-9; map.

12284 **Caesarea,** *a*) ➤ 295, ASOR report 1994, 63-86 (R. *Ball*); – *b*) Herod's amphitheatre 1992: Atiqot 25 (1994) 11*-19* ⊕; Eng. 188 (Y. *Porath*).

12285 **Blakely** J. A., Caesarea M. Excavation Report 4: The pottery and dating of Vault I, 1987 ➤ 3,e159... 6,g70: ᴿZDPV 109 (1993) 182s (U. *Hübner*).

12286 **Shremer** Adiel, *Ziv* Yehuda, ⊕ The tetrapylon of Caesarea and the burial site of Rabbi Aᴋɪᴠᴀ: CHist EI 68 (1993)188-193; 2 fig.

12287 **Oleson** J. F., *Raban* A., The harbours of Caesarea Maritima 1989 ➤ 5,d862; 6,e69: ᴿPEQ 126 (1994) 169s (A. *Flinder*).

12288 **Carmel:** *Weinstein-Evron* Mina, *Tsatskin* Alexander, The Jamal cave is not empty; recent discoveries in the Mount Carmel caves, Israel: Paléorient 20,2 (1994) 119-128.

12289 **Lissovsky** Nurit, The [Carmel] landscape of time: diss. Harvard. CM 1994. 245 p. 94-29018. – DissA 55 (1994s) p. 2182.

12290 **Dor:** **Stern** Ephraim, Dor, ruler of the seas; twelve years of excavation at the Israelite-Phoenician harbour town on the Carmel coast, ᵀ*Shadur* Joseph. J 1994, Israel Expl. Soc. 348 p. 243 fig.; VIII color. pl. $36. 965-221-127-7 [BL 95,35, T. C. *Mitchell*]. – ᴿBbbOr 36 (1994) 189-191 (D. *Sardini*).

12290* *Kingsley* Sean A., *Raveh* Kurt, A reassessment of the northern harbour of Dor, Israel: IntJNaut 23 (1994) 289-295; 5 fig.

12291 *Dothan:* *Cooley* Robert E., *Pratico* Gary D., Gathered to his people; an archaeological illustration from Tell Dothan's western cemetery: ➤ 67, ᶠKING P. 1994, 70-92; 8 fig.

12292 **Geva, 'edge of Galilee':** *Safrai* Zeev, *Lin* Micha, ❹ Geva in the Hasmonean period: CHistEI 69 (1993) 18-36; ill.; Eng. 183.

12293 **Gezer:** *Shanks* Hershel, [in favor of] Re-restoring Gezer: BAR-W 20,3 (1994) 66-68.

12294 *a)* *Yanai* Eli, A Late Bronze Age gate at Gezer?; – *b)* *Finkelstein* Israel,... Iron II wall: TAJ 21 (1994) 283-7; 1 fig. / 276-282; 1 fig.

12295 **Haquzim:** *Nadel* Dani, *Vald* Eli, Haquzim – a prehistoric occurrence in the central coastal plain: Atiqot 25 (1994) 1-22; 14 fig.

12296 **Jaffa:** *Harvey* Paul B.ᴶ, The death of mythology; the case of Joppa [Andromeda; Jonah; Peter]: JEarlyCS 2 (1994) 1-14.

12297 **Lydda:** **Schwartz** J.J., Lod 1991 ➤ 8,e495; 9,13875: ᴿPEQ 125 (1993) 177s (D. M. *Jacobson*).

12297* **Michal:** **Herzog** Z., al., Excav. t. Michal 1988 ➤ 7,d413*: ᴿTEuph 5 (1992) 172-6 (J. *Sapin*).

12298 **Modiin:** *Schwartz* Joshua, *Spanier* Yossi, On Matthias the Hasmonean and the desert of Samaria: CHistEI 65 (1992) 3-30; Eng. 190.

12299 *Netiv Hagdud* (12 k N Jericho), Early Neolithic: JFA [OTAbs 17, p. 18, not in listing after p. 144] 18 (1991) 405-424 (O. *Bar-Yosef*).

12300 *Nisya* (1718.1449 2 k SE Bireh) 10th 1993: IsrEJ 44 (1994) 142-5; 2 fig. (B. *Wood*, D. *Livingston*).

12301 '*Ofrat*/Ṭaiyiba [1692.2434] 1972: BAngIsr 13 (1993s) 37-46; 3 fig. (D. *Urman*).

12302 **Samaria-Sebasté** [➤ 10982]: **Tappy** Ron E., The archaeology of Israelite Samaria 1, 1992 ➤ 8,e500: 9,13880: ᴿBL (1994) 32 (T. C. *Mitchell*); CBQ 56 (1994) 345s (R. *North*); ÉTRel 68 (1993) 426s (J.-D. *Macchi*); JSS 39 (1994) 322s (P. R. S. *Moorey*: Kenyon chronology based on assumptions).

12302* **Dar** S., Landscape... Samaria 1986 ➤ 3,e175... 7,d421: ᴿTEuph 5 (1992) 161-4 (J. *Sapin*).

12303 **Šekem:** **Campbell** E., Shechem 2, 1991 ➤ 7,d423: ᴿCBQ 56 (1994) 120-2 (Elizabeth *Bloch-Smith*).

12304 *Wright* G. R. H., *a)* Section drawing at Shechem: AfO 40s (1993s) 321-7; 7 (foldout) fig.; – *b)* Mensuration and monuments at Shechem: ➤ 55, ᶠHROUDA B., Beiträge 1994, 321-8; 6 fig.; – *c)* The mythology of pre-Israelite Shechem [< VT 20 (1970) 75-82]: ➤ 223, Obiter 1992, (1-) 10-21.

12305 *Mor* M., ❹ The Samaritan temple on Mt. Garizim [one, not two as H. ESHEL]: BethM 135 (1993) 313-337 [< JStJud 25,141].

T4.6   **Galilaea; pro tempore Golan.**

12306 *Hartin* P. J., Galilee in the first century C.E.: J/Tyd Sem 5 (1993) 153-169.

12307 **Hennessy** Anne, sr., The Galilee of Jesus. R 1994, Pont. Univ. Gregoriana. ix-77 p. Lᵐ 15. 88-7652-666-8 [BL 95,35, J. R. *Bartlett*: lavish praise].

12308 ᴱ**Levine** Lee I., The Galilee in late antiquity 1992 ➤ 8,e511: ᴿNT 36 (1994) 414s (Nina L. *Collins*).

12309 *Overman* J.A.,   Recent advances in the archaeology of the Galilee in the Roman period: CurResB 1 (Shf 1993) 35-57 [< NTAbs 38, p.420].

12310 **Bet She'an** paved street (1953; 1983): Atiqot 25 (1994) 139-155; 15 fig. + 4 coins (M. *Peleg*).

12311 **James** Frances, *McGovern* Patrick E.,   The Late Bronze Egyptian garrison at Beth-Shan; a study of levels VII and VIII: Mg 85.   Ph 1993, Univ. Museum.   xxix-272 p.; xv + 168 fig.; 63 pl. – ᴿLA 44 (1994) 715s (L.J. *Hoppe*).

12312 *Kaswalder* Pietro A.,   Bet Shean splendida città: TerraS 69,2 (1993) 36-40; 2 fot.

12313 *Tsafrir* Yoram, *Foerster* Gideon, ❻ From Byzantine Scythopolis to Arab Baysan; changing urban concepts: CHistEI 64 (1992) 3-30; Eng. 183.

12314 *Wimmer* Stefan, 'Der Bogen der Anat' in Bet-Schean?:   BibNot 73 (1994) 36-41; 2 fig.

12315 **Bet-Yeraḥ: Esse** D.I.,   Subsistence, trade and social change in EB Palestine: SAOC 50, 1991 ➤ 7,d289; 8,e527:   ᴿPEQ 125 (1993) 163s (G. *Philip*).

12316 *Ohalo* [Kh. Kerak]: Paléorient 20,1 (1994) 113-121 (D. *Nadel*).

12317 **Capharnaum: Tzaferis** Vassilios,   Excavations at Capernaum I, 1978-82: 1989 ➤ 6,e122... 8,e518:   ᴿCritRR 4 (1922) 104-7 (D.R. *Edwards*: rarely exquisite color plates).

12318 **Loffreda** Stanislaus,   Die Heiligtümer von Tabgha, ᵀ*Grab* Olaf: Heilige Stätten Palästinas.   J 1978, Franciscan.   67 p.

12319 **Dan: Biran** Avraham,   Biblical Dan [❻ 1982ʳᵉᵛ] J 1994, Israel Exploration.   280 p. $32.   965-221-020-X [OTAbs 17, p.651: 1966-91, neolithic through Roman; RB 102,458, T. *Axe*: back to "the bad old days of 'Biblical Archaeology'"; BL 95,24, G.I. *Davies*: frustrating but useful]. – ᴿBAR-W 10,4 first choice (1994) 6.8 (J. *Laughlin*); VT 44 (1994) 418s (J.A. *Emerton*: pushes biblical correlations).

12319* *Biran* A., *Naveh* J., ❻ An Aramaic inscription of the First Temple period from Tel Dan: Qadmoniot 25 (1993) 74-81; 12 fig.

12320 *Biran* Avraham, [Gn 14,14; Jos 19,47; Jg 18,29] Tel Dan; biblical texts and archaeological data: ➤ 67, ꟳKɪɴɢ P., Scripture 1994, 1-17; 14 fig.

12321 [*Biran* Avraham], 'David' found at Dan: BAR-W 20,2 (1994) 26-39; ill. [but the cover photo of David as Orpheus playing the lyre is from the restoration of a Gaza mosaic, here *Green* C. p.58].

12322 — BAR-W 20,4 (1994) 54s, *Davies* Philip R., 'House of David' built on sand; the sins of the biblical maximizers. & 20,6 (1994) 57, *Rainey* Anson, The 'house of David' and the house of the deconstructionists; Davies is an amateur who 'can safely be ignored'.

12323 *Chapman* Rupert L.ᴵᴵᴵ, The Dan stele and the chronology of Levantine Iron Age stratigraphy: BAnglsr 13 (1993s) 23-29.

12323* *Dijkstra* Meindert,   An epigraphic note on the stela of Tel Dan: BibNot 74 (1994) 10-14.

12324 *Halpern* Baruch, The ['house of David'] stela from Dan; epigraphic and historical considerations: BASOR 296 (1994) 63-80; 2 fig.: latest rather than early 9th century.

12325 *Kaswalder* Pietro, Scoperta una iscrizione aramaica a Tel Dan; è il primo testo extra-biblico che parla della Dinastia di Davide: TerraS 70,3 (1994) 44-49; 6 fig.

12325* *Knauf* E. A., *Pury* A. de, *Römer* T., 'BaytDawīd' ou 'BaytDōd'? une relecture de la nouvelle inscription de Tel Dan: BibNot 72 (1994) 60-69.

12326 *a) Lemche* Niels P., *Thompson* Thomas L., Did Biran kill David? The Bible in the light of archaeology; – *b) Davies* Philip R., *Bytdwd* and *swkt dwyd*; a comparison; – *c) Ben Zvi* Ehud, On the reading 'bytdwd' in the Aramaic stele from Tel Dan: JStOT 64 (1994) 3-22 / 23s / 25-32.

12326* *Moscati* Sabatino, È falsa l'iscrizione del re Davide? [Dan... ve ne sono indizi... imitazione della stele di Mesha]: Archeo 9,111 (1994) 22.

12327 **Uehlinger** Christoph, Eine anthropomorphe Kultstatue des Gottes von Dan?: BibNot 72 (1994) 85-96 + 6 fig.

12327* *Yellin* J., *Maeir* A., The origin of the pictorial krater from the 'Mycenaean' tomb at Tel Dan: Archaeometry 34 (1992) 31-36; 1 fig.

12328 **Gesher Haziv** [W. Galilee] Roman cemetery: Atiqot 25 (1994) 77-93; 18 fig. (Eilat *Mazar*); 94-102 (*al.*; coins etc.).

12329 **Guš Ḥalav:** Meyers E. & C., *Strange* J., Excavations at the ancient synagogue of Gush Halav 1990 ➤ 7,d436; 8,e524: ᴿCritRR 5 (1992) 107-9 (D. R. *Edwards*); PEQ 125 (1993) 170s (R. K. *Falkner*).

12330 **Hadar** [E Lake Tiberias] 6th, 1991: IsrEJ 44 (1994) 136-141; 4 fig. (M. *Kochavi*).

12331 **Hazor** 2s; 4,1993 1s/3: Sefarad 53 (1993) 193-202 + 8 fig. / Sefarad 54 (1994) 151-3 (M. Teresa *Rubiato Díaz*).

12332 **Rubiato Díaz** Maria Teresa, El edificio de pilares de Hatsor. M 1993, Univ. Complutense. 132 p. – ᴿSefarad 54 (1994) 431 (M. Victoria *Spottorno*).

12333 *Beck* Pirhiya, A note on the 'schematic statues' from the stelae temple at Hazor [standard LB]: TAJ 17 (1990) 91-95 [< OTAbs 17, p. 18].

12334 *Lipschitz* Oded, The date of the Assyrian resistance at Ayyelet ha-Shaḥar [between 732 and 716]: TAJ 17 (1990) 96-99.

12335 **Hermon: Dar** Shimon, Settlements and cult sites on Mount Hermon, Israel; Ituraean culture in the Hellenistic and Roman periods [✪],ᵀ: BAR-Int 589. Ox 1993. xxii-325 p.

12336 **Ruprechtsberger** Erwin M., *al.*, Von Mount Hermon zum Djebel Burqush. Linz 1994. 40 p.

12337 *Jezreel* 2d 1992s: Levant 26 (1994) 1-48; 61 fig. (D. *Ussishkin*, J. *Woodhead*) & 49-65 *al.*

12338 *Jiddîn:* Pringle D., *al.*, Qalᶜat Jiddîn, a castle of the Crusader and Ottoman periods in Galilee: Levant 26 (1994) 135-166; 36 fig.

12339 **Kafr Misr** [S. En-Dor, 1900.2280] Umayyad-Mamluk synagogue: Atiqot 25 (1994) 117-134; 17 fig. (A. *Onn*).

12340 *Keisan: Gunneweg* Jan, *Perlman* Isadore, The origin of a Mycenaean III C:1 stirrup jar from Tell Keisan: RB 101 (1994) 559-561: Kouklia (Cyprus).

12341 **Kinneret: Fritz** V., Kinneret 1990 ➤ 7,d445: ᴿBO 51 (1994) 447-9 (H. J. *Franken*).

12342 **Megiddo: Kempinski** Aharon, Megiddo 1989 ➤ 5,d927... 7,d447 [1991 ➤ 8,a581]: ᴿTR 90 (1994) 373s (R. *Wenning*).

12343 *a) Finkelstein* Israel, *Ussishkin* David, Back to Megiddo; a new expedition will explore the jewel in the crown of Canaan/Israel; – *b) Davies* Graham I., King Solomon's stable: still at Megiddo?: BAR-W 20,1 (1994) 26-43.44-48.

12343* *Macchi* J.-D., Megiddo à l'époque assyrienne; remarques à propos du dossier archéologique: ➤ 461, Syrie perse 1991,   TEuph 7 (1994) 9-31 + 2 fig.; Eng. 9.

12344 *Nigro* Lorenzo, The 'Nordburg' of Megiddo; a new reconstruction on the basis of SCHUMACHER's plan: BASOR 293 (1994) 15-29; 4 fig.

12345 *a) Ussishkin* David, Gate 1567 at Megiddo and the seal of Shema, servant of Jeroboam; – *b) East* Walter E., Priestly families and the cultic structure at Taanach: ➤ 67, [F]KING P., Scripture 1994, 410-428; 7 fig. / 355-365; 1 fig.

12345* *Munḥata:* **Garfinkel** Yosef, The pottery assemblages of the Shaʿar hagolan and Babah (text Rabah) stages of Munhata: Centre FrançaisJ; 6. P 1992, Faton. 360 p.; 145 fig. 13 pl. F 240. 0243-0258. – [R]Syria 71 (1994) 453 (H. de *Contenson*).

12346 *Nabratein: Magness* Jodi, The dating of the black ceramic bowl with a depiction of the Torah Shrine from Nabratein [Galilee?]: Levant 26 (1994) 199-206; 4 fig.

12347 *Nazareth: Heid* Stefan, Das Heilige Land; Herkunft und Zukunft der Judenchristen: Kairos 34s (1992s) 1-26.

12348 *Qazrin: Kaswalder* Pietro A., Qazrin sulle alture del Golan: TerraS 69,4 (1993) 36-41.

12349 *Qiri:* **Ben-Tor** A., *Portugali* Y., Tell Qiri: Qedem 24, 1987 ➤ 4,a809... 6,e159: [R]PEQ 126 (1994) 72s (S. *Gibson*).

12350 *Sepphoris:* **Netzer** Ehud, *Weiss* Zeev, Zippori. J 1994, Israel Exploration Soc. 71 p.; (color.) ill. $16.

12350* **Batey** Richard A., Jesus and the forgotten city 1991 ➤ 7,d456... 9,13926: [R]CritRR 6 (1993) 201-4 (R. E. *Oster*: defense of National Geographic origins and style).

12351 *Taanak: Nigro* Lorenzo, The 'Nordostburg' at *Tell Taʿannek*; a re-evaluation of the Iron Age II B defence system: ZDPV 110 (1994) 168-180; 4 fig.

12352 *Tiberias: Adinolfi* Marco, Il lago di Tiberiade a le sue città nella letteratura greco-romana: LA 44 (1994) 375-9; Eng. 615.

12353 **Nun** Mendel, Sea of Galilee; newly discovered harbours from New Testament days[2rev]. Ein Gev 1989, Kinnereth Sailing Co. 32 p.

T4.8   *Transjordania:* **East-Jordan.**

12354 [E]**Homès-Fredericq** Denyse, *Hennessy* J. B., Archaeology of Jordan II. Field reports, surveys and sites, 1. A-K; 2. L-Z: Akkadica supp. 7. Lv 1989. – [R]TEuph 5 (1992) 176s (J. *Elayi*).

12354* **Kareem** Jumʿa, The settlement patterns in the Jordan Valley in the mid-late Islamic period: diss. Berlin Freie Univ. 1993. – ArchAnz (1994) 120.

12355 *Kuijt* Ian, Pre-Pottery Neolithic–A settlement variability; evidence for sociopolitical developments in the southern Levant [chiefly Jordan Valley]: JMeditArch 7 (1994) 165-192; 6 fig.

12356 *a) Lemaire* André, Les transformations politiques et culturelles de la Transjordanie au VIe siècle av. J.-C.; – *b) Muheisin* Z. Al-, L'archéologie de la période hellénistique dans le nord de la Jordanie; problèmes et prospectives: ➤ 461, Syrie, TEuph 8 (1991/4) 9-27; Eng. 9 / 29-33 + 2 maps; Eng. 29.

12356* *MacDonald* Burton, Ammon, Moab and Edom; early states/nations of Jordan in the biblical period (end of the 2nd and during the 1st millennium B.C.). Amman 1994, Kutba. 83 p. $12 [OTAbs 17, p. 656]; [R]LA 43 (1993!) 515s (F. M. *Benedettucci*).

12357 ᴱMarino Luigi, Siti e monumenti della Giordania; rapporto sullo stato di conservazione: Restauro Archeologico 2. F 1994, Alinea. 111 p. – ᴿLA 43 (1993) 495s (E. *Alliata*).

12358 *Olivier* Hannes, Archaeological discoveries in Jordan; their impact on biblical studies: In die Skriflig 26 (Potchefstroom 1992) 53-64 [< OTAbs 16, p. 23].

12358* *Palmaitis* M.-L., ❻ Trans-Jordan [fear of Edomite attack] in the light of the paleographical data from Tell-Arad: VDI 203 (1992) 99-105; 1 fig.; Eng. 105.

12359 *Peterman* Glen L., Archaeology in Jordan: AJA 98 (1994) 521-559; 29 fig.

12360 *Abata* (deir ʿain; Ghor es-Safi) 1994, St. Lot monastery: LA 44 (1994) 629s; pl. 53s (K. D. *Politis*).

12361 *Abila* 1994, EB, Roman theater, Byz church: LA 44 (1994) 630-4; pl. 55s (W. Harold *Mare*).

12362 **Barbet** Alix, *Vibert-Guigue* Claude, Les peintures des nécropoles romaines d'Abila et du Nord de la Jordanie I. Texte: IFAPO-BAH 130. Beyrouth 1994. xiv-375 p.; 117 fig. – ᴿLA 44 (1994) 654s (M. *Piccirillo*).

12363 *ʿAmman:* Najjar Mohammad, Saʿid Fatima, A new Umayyad church at Khilda/Amman: LA 44 (1994) 547-550; 3 + 3 fig.; pl. 31-40.

12364 **Hübner** H., Die Ammoniter: AbhDAV 16. Wsb 1992, Harrassowitz. xi-430 p. – ᴿPEQ 126 (1994) 79s (J. R. *Bartlett*: needed); TLZ 119 (1994) 777-780 (Maria Giulia *Amadasi Guzzo*); ᴢAW 106 (1994) 355s (M. *Köckert*).

12365 *Wenning* Robert, Die Dekapolis [... Amman, Gerasa] und die Nabatäer: ZDPV 110 (1994) 1-35; map.

12366 **Northedge** A., Studies on Roman and Islamic Amman 1992 ➔ 9,13942: ᴿAJA 98 (1994) 795s (Jodi *Magness*).

12367 *ʿAqaba:* **Pratico** Gary D., N. GLUECK's 1938-1940 excavations at Tell el Kheleifeh, a reappraisal: ASOR report 3. Atlanta 1993, Scholars. xx-223 p. – ᴿCBQ 56 (1994) 568-570 (P. F. *Jacobs*).

12368 *Arraq* Basin 1987s: Levant 26 (1994) 73-109; 13 fig. (A. *Garrard, al.*).

12369 *Deir ʿAlla:* **Franken** H. J., Excavations at Tell Deir ʿAlla; the Late Bronze Age sanctuary. Lv 1992, Peeters. xxii-196 p.; 110 fig.; 12 pl. – ᴿBASOR 295 (1994) 94s (B. G. *Wood*); BL (1994) 26 (G. I. *Davies*).

12370 *Dharih:* Muheisin Zeidoun al-, *Villeneuve* François, Découvertes nouvelles a Khirbet edh-Dharih (Jordanie), 1991-1994; autour du sanctuaire nabatéen et romain: CRAI (1994) 735-757; 10 fig.

12371 *Dibon,* Hebron, Qishon: *Krahmalkov* Charles R., Exodus itinerary confirmed by Egyptian evidence: BAR-W 20,5 (1994) 54-62 . 79.

12372 *Niccacci* Alvieri, The stele of Mesha and the Bible; verbal system and narrativity: Orientalia 63 (1994) 226-249.

12373 *Feinan,* Pounon: *Fritz* Volkmar, Vorbericht über die Grabungen in Barqā el-Hetīye im Gebiet von Fēnān, Wādi el-ʿAraba (Jordanien) 1990: ZDPV 110 (1994) 125-150; 13 fig. (map); pl. 2-9.

12374 *Gazal,* ain, 1993s, neo: LA 44 (1994) 621-3; pl. 51 (Z. *Kafafi,* G. *Rollefson*); BA 57 (1994) 239-241 (Zeidan *Kafafi,* G. *Rollefson*), also ➔ 295, ASOR report 1994, 107-126).

12375 *Gerasa:* Martin-Bueno Manuel, *Uscatescu* Alexandra, El macellum de Gerasa (Ŷaras, Jordania); la transformación de un edificio público romano en un area artesanal bizantina: BSAA 60 (1994) 171-185; 6 fig.

12376 *Z'ubi* Ibrahim, *al.*,   Note sur une mosaïque à scène bacchique dans un palais d'époque byzantine à Jérash: LA 44 (1994) 539-546; 2 fig.; pl. 27-30; Eng. 616.
12377 **Hasa:** *Olszewski* Deborah I., *al.*,   The 1993 excavations at Yutil al-Hasa (WHS 784), an upper/epipaleolithic site in west-central Jordan: Paléorient 20,2 (1994) 129-141.

12378 *Hesban:* **Mitchel** Larry A.,   Hellenistic and Roman strata; a study of the stratigraphy of Tell Hesban from the 2d century B.C. to the 4th century A.D.: Hesban 7.   Berrien Springs MI 1992, Andrews Univ. xv-189 p.
12378* ᴱ**Geraty** L., *al.*, Hesban 2-3-5, 1986/9/7 ➤ 5,d988; 7,d495: ᴿTEuph 5 (1992) 179-181 (J. *Sapin:* manque l'intégration des champs divers).
12379 *Umeiri,* Jalul 1994, Iron Age: LA 44 (1994) 623-9; pl. 52 (Eng., unsigned).
12380 *Piccirillo* Michele, Hesban, [sede episcopale] Esbus in Giordania; il presbiterio della chiesa nord: TerraS 70,6 (1994) 35-39; 5 fig. (mosaici).

12380* '*Iraq al-Amir:* Ginouvès René,   Le château du Tobiade Hyrcan à 'Iraq al-Amir: Syria 71 (1994) 433-442; 1 fig.
12381 *Jawa* E: **Betts** A. V. G., Excavations at Jawa 1972-1986:   1991 ➤ 9, 12972: ᴿPaléorient 20,1 (1994) 135s (P. de *Miroschedji*).
12382 *Jawa* (S Amman) 1993: ADAJ 38 (1994) 173-193; 18 fig. (P. M. M. *Daviau*).
12383 *Daviau* P. M. Michèle, *Pietersma* Albert,   Inscribed artifacts at Tell Jawa [west], Jordan; Naoumas' jug: BASOR 295 (1994) 73-80; 4 fig.
12384 *Kerak* Moab: *Kanaʾan* Ruba, *McQuitty* Alison,   The architecture of Al-Qaṣr on the Kerak plateau; an essay in the chronology of vernacular architecture: PEQ 126 (1994) 127-153; 19 fig. (map).
12385 *Kerak-Shihan* 1994, Byz church: LA 44 (1994) 636-8; pl. 58 (Rula *Qusus*, R. *Schick*).
12386 ᴱ**Miller** J. Maxwell,   Archaeological survey of the Kerak plateau: ASOR report 1991 ➤ 7,d500; 9,13957: ᴿBO 51 (1994) 449-456 (Helga & M. *Weippert*); CBQ 56 (1994) 120-2 (Elizabeth *Bloch-Smith*); JAOS 114 (1994) 133 (W. E. *Aufrecht*); PEQ 125 (1993) 175-7 (Kay *Prag*).
12387 **Timm** Stefan,   Moab zwischen den Mächten 1989 ➤ 5,d963 [N. B. Moab (non Micha) zwischen ...] ... 8,4053.e564: ᴿScandJOT 8 (1994) 158-160 (N. P. *Lemche*).
12388 **Hahn** Joachim,   Moab und Israel: ➤ 517, TRE 23 (1994) 124-9.
12389 **Wyk** Koot van,   Squatters in Moab; a study in iconography, history, epigraphy, orthography, ethnography, religion and linguistics of the ANE: MgCrossCu. Berrien Springs MI 1993, Hester.   108 p. $75. 0-963-8377-0. – ᴿBL (1994) 130 [J. R. *Bartlett*].
12389* *Mendecki* Norbert, ❷ Adnotationes in historiam Moab: RuBi 47 (1994) 242-7.

12390 *Kharaz* (t. Abu el) 1992: ADAJ 38 (1994) 127-145; 12 pl. (P. M. *Fischer*).
12391 *Machaerus:*   Mekawer chapel: LA 44 (1994) 640s; pl. 61s (M. *Piccirillo*).

12392 *Madaba* Elijah church and decumanus 1992-4:   LA 44 (1994) 640-3 (C. J. *Lenzen*); 643-6-651 mosaic school (C. *Cimino* / L. *Miranda*).

12393 *Piccirillo* Michele, Jordanie; l'église des Sunna à Madaba: MondeB 88 (1994) 45s.

12394 *a) Piccirillo* Michele, La chiesa del profeta Elia a Madaba; nuove scoperte; – *b) Acconci* Alessandra, *Gabrieli* Eva, Scavo del cortile Bajali a Madaba: LA 44 (1994) 381-414; 10 fig.; pl. 1-10; Eng. 615 / 405-520; 60 fig.; pl. 13-18; Eng. 615.

12395 *Piccirillo* Michele, Per la conservazione di un patrimonio d'arte [Madaba]: TerraS 70,1 (1994) 40-42; 3 fig.

12396 *Nebo: Piccirillo* Michele, *Alliata* Eugenio, Sessanta anni di presenza francescana sul Monte Nebo, Giordania, 1933-1993: TerraS 70,2 (1994) 21-36; color. ill.

12397 *Piccirillo* M., Le due iscrizioni della cappella della Theotokos nel Wadi ʿAyn al-Kanisah sul Monte Nebo: LA 44 (1994) 521-538; 4 + 2 fig.; Eng. 615s.

12398 Nebo-Siyagha: LA 44 (1994) 638-40; pl. 59s (E. *Alliata*).

12399 *Nimrin:* 1993: ADAJ 38 (1994) 205-265; 22 + 265 fig. (J. W. *Flanagan*).

12400 *Pella*-Fahil: **Smith** R. H., *Day* L. P., Pella 2, 1989 ⟶ 9,13989: RBASOR 293 (1994) 83s (J. A. *Sauer*).

12401 Pella (Sydney 14th) 1992: ADAJ 38 (1994) 81-126; 21 fig. (S. *Bourke*).

12402 **Knapp** A. B., Society and polity at Bronze Age Pella. Shf 1993, Academic. xii-117 p.; 17 fig. £22.50. 1-85075-347-4. – RAntiquity 68 (1994) 456s (G. *Philip*: valuable).

12403 *Hayyat* [SW Fahil]: *Magness-Gardiner* Bonnie, *Falconer* Steven E., Community, polity, and temple in a Middle Bronze Age Levantine village: JMeditArch 7 (1994) 127-164; 10 fig.

12404 *Petra* ACOR 1994, Byz church; Nabataean structure: LA 44 (1994) 634-6; fig. 57 (Patricia & Pierre *Bikai*).

12405 **Laborde** Léon de [21 ans], *Linand de Bellefonds* L.-M. A. [28 ans, carnet de voyage], Pétra retrouvée [1828]. P 1994, Watelet. 285 p. – RLA 44 (1994) 657 (M. *Piccirillo*).

12406 **McKenzie** Judith, The architecture of Petra 1990 ⟶ 6,e235 ... 9,13992: RAJA 97 (1993) 369s (Shelley C. *Stone*); Syria 61 (1994) 248-251 (M. *Griesheimer*: 'McEnzie' after title).

12407 **Taylor** Jane, Petra. L 1993, Aurum. 80 p. £20 [BAR-W 20/2,10].

12408 *Piccirillo* Michele, Papiri scoperti in una chiesa bizantina di Petra: TerraS 70 (1994) 30-32.

12408* *Moscati* Sabatino, Antichi rotoli a Petra ... [e/o] papiri liturgici in greco e siriaco: Archeo 9,111 (1994) 17.

12409 **Negev** A., Personal names in the Nabataean realm: Qedem 32, 1991 ⟶ 8,9551: RBAngIsr 13 (1993) 59s (A. R. *Millard*); VT 44 (1994) 576s (J. F. *Healey*).

12409* *Roche* M.-J., Les débuts de l'implantation nabatéenne à Petra: ⟶ 461, Syrie, TEuph 8 (1991/4) 35-46.

12410 *Wenning* Robert, Eine neuerstellte Liste der nabatäischen Dynastie: Boreas 16 (Münster 1993) 25-38.

12411 *Theeb* Solaiman Al-, Two new dated Nabataean inscriptions from al-Jawf [Saudi Arabia]: JSS 39 (1994) 33-40; 2 pl.; 2 fig.

12412 *Vickers* Michael, Nabataea, India, Gaul, and Carthage; reflections on Hellenistic and Roman gold vessels and red-gloss pottery: AJA 98 (1994) 231-246; 10 fig.

12413 *Lindner* Manfred, *al.*, Ez-Zantur at Petra – tower, palace or temple?

Observations, finds and preliminary conclusions: AfO 40s (1993s) 307-319: palace or more likely temple.

12414 a) *Lapp* Nancy, 'Who is this that comes from Edom?'; – b) *MacDonald* Burton, Early Edom; the relation between the literary and archaeological evidence: ➤ 67, [F]KING P., 1994, 216-229; 3 fig. / 230-246; map.

12414* **Bartlett** John R., Edom: 1989 ➤ 5,g242...7,e615: [R]JSS 39 (1994) 321s (Kay *Prag*).

12415 *Saʿidiya: Tubb* Jonathan N., *Dorrell* Peter G., Tell es-Saʿidiyeh 7th 1993 interim report: PEQ 126 (1994) 52-67; 20 fig.

12416 *Šuna*-N 3d 1993: Levant 26 (1994) 111-133; 13 fig. (D. *Baird*, G. *Philip*).

12417 *Umm Ḥammād:* **Betts** A.V.G., Excavations at Tell Um Hammad 1982-1984; the early assemblages (EB I-II). E 1992, Univ. xv-425 p.; 283 fig.; 8 pl. – [R]Paléorient 20,1 (1994) 137s (P. de *Miroschedji*).

12418 *Umm Jimāl: de Vries* Bert, What's in a name; the anonymity of ancient Umm el-Jimal: BA 57 (1994) 215-9.

12418* *Umm Raṣāṣ:* **Piccirillo** Michele, *Alliata* Eugenio, Umm al-Rasas Mayfaʿah I, Gli scavi del complesso di Santo Stefano: SBF Publ. 28. J 1994, Franciscan. 376 p.; bibliog. 355-364; 35 (color.) ill.; 4 foldout plans.

12419 *Yasileh* [N-Jordan, not on map p. 620], 5th 1994: LA 44 (1994) 651-3 (pl. 64-66) [Z. Al-*Muheisin*].

12419* *Ziqlab:* **Banning** Edward B., *al.*, The Late Neolithic of the southern Levant; hiatus, settlement shift or observer bias? The perspective from Wadi Ziqlab (N. Jordan): Paléorient 20,2 (1994) 151-164.

T5.1 **Phoenicia** – *Libanus*, **Lebanon.**

12420 **Briquel-Chatonnet** Françoise, Les relations entre les cités de la côte phénicienne et les royaumes d'Israel et de Juda: OrLovAnal 46, [D]1992 ➤ 8,e636: [R]BASOR 293 (1994) 92-94 (P. *Dion*); CBQ 56 (1994) 537s (C.G. *Romero*); JBL 113 (1994) 323-5 (L.K. *Handy*); OLZ 89 (1994) 285-8 (G. *Begrich*); Orientalia 63 (1994) 290-3 (Corinne *Bonnet*); OrLovPer 24 (1993) 279s (E. *Lipiński*). RÉJ 153 (1994) 447s (J. *Margain*).

12420* [E]**Lipinski** Edward, Phoenicia and the Bible 1990/1 ➤ 7,445: [R]BL (1994) 125s (A.R. *Millard*).

12421 *Baʿalbek: Tubach* Jürgen, Der Kalender von *Baʿalbek*-Heliopolis: ZDPV 110 (1994) 181-9.

12421* *Byblos: Elayi* J. & A.G., Nouveau trésor de monnaies de Byblos: RBgNum 139 (1993) 17-30; pl. I-V.

12422 **Acquaro** Enrico, *al.*, Biblo, una città e la sua cultura [Colloq. Roma 5-7.XII.1990]: StFen coll 34. R 1994, ConzNazRic. 230 p. 15 art., 6 infra.

12422* a) *Helck* W. †, Byblos and Ägypten; – b) *Loretz* O., Mari, Ugarit and Byblos; – c) *Bondì* S.F., Il ruolo di Biblo nell'espansione fenicea: ➤ 12416, Biblo (1990/4) 105-111 / 113-124 / 137-143.

12423 a) *Margueron* J.-C., L'urbanisme à Byblos, certitudes et problèmes; – b) *Scandone* Gabriella, La cultura egiziana a Biblo attraverso le testimonianze materiali; – c) *Amadasi Guzzo* M.G., Lingua e scrittura a Biblo: ➤ 12422, Biblo 1990/4, 13-27; 8 color. maps; / 37-45 / 179-195 [168-177, *Snycer* M.].

12423* *Kāmid/Loz:* **Adler** Wolfgang, Kāmid el-Loz [7. 1991 ➤ 8,e645] 11. Das 'Schatzhaus' im Palastbereich; Die Befunde des Königsgrabes 1994.

12424 **Metzger** M., Kāmid el-Lōz 7. Tempelanlagen 1991 ➤ 8,e645; 9,14022: [R]AfO 40s (1993s) 149-151 (Ö. *Tunca*).

12424* *Sidon:* **Stucky** Rolf A., Die Skulpturen aus dem Echmun–Heiligtum bei Sidon: AntKu Beih 17. 1993. – ᴿMesopT 29 (1994) 331-3 (A. *Invernizzi*).
12425 *Puech* É., Un cratère phénicien inscrit [Ittobaᶜal (marché de Zurich) prob. Sidon 750]: ➤ 461, Syrie, TEuph 8 (1994) 47-69 + 4 fig.; Eng. 47.
12425* *Naᵓaman* N., Esarhaddon's treaty with Baal and Assyrian provinces along the Phoenician coast: RStFen 22 (1994) 3-8.

12426 *Tyrus:* ᴱ**Schmeling** Gareth, Historia Apollonii regis Tyri, Teubner 1988 ➤ 4,e942... 8,e651: ᴿGnomon 66 (1994) 304-320 (J. M. *Hunt*).
12426* *Schmeling* G., Notes on the text of the Historia Apollonii regis Tyri: Latomus 53 (1994) 132-154. 386-403.
12427 **Archibald** Elisabeth, Apollonius of Tyre; medieval and Renaissance themes and variations [with] text + ᵀ. C 1991, Brewer. xiii-350 p. – ᴿMedvHum 20 (1994) 199-203 (P. F. *Dembowski*); Speculum 69 (1994) 411-3 (R. J. *Hexter*: Boydell & B $70).
12427* *Lipiński* É., La Tharsis de l'Histoire d'Apollonius roi de Tyr: Latomus 53 (1994) 605-7.

T5.2   *Situs mediterranei* **phoenicei et punici.**

12428 *Asolati* M., L'emissione vandala con il palmizio; prototipi punici e l'evidenza dei ripostigli: RitNum 96 (1994s) 187-201; 1 pl.
12428* **Baurain** C., *Bonnet* C., Les Phéniciens marins de trois continents 1992 ➤ 8,e655: ᴿAION 53 (1993) 478-480 (F. *Vattioni*); ÉtClas 62 (1994) 406s (Vinciane *Pirenne-Delforge*); Orientalia 63 (1994) 154 (M. Giulia *Amadasi Guzzo*).
12429 **Blázquez Martínez** J. M., Fenicios, Griegos y Cartaginenses en Occidente 1992 ➤ 8,e656; 9,14029: ᴿArEspArq 66 (1993) 347 (A. J. *Domínguez Monedero*, tambien sobre sus Religiones / Urbanismo 1991); JAOS 114 (1994) 274s (R. J. *Harrison*); Sefarad 53 (1993) 213s (J. *Carretero*).
12429* **Delz** J., SILI Italici, Punica, Teubner 1987 ➤ 5,e49: ᴿGnomon 66 (1994) 499-524 (J. *Kuppers*).
12430 **Gras** M., *al.*, L'univers phénicien 1989 ➤ 5,e51... 8,e662: ᴿTEuph 5 (1992) 166-171 (J. *Elayi*: nombreux défauts).
12430* *Jones* Donald W., Phoenician unguent factories in Dark Age Greece; social approaches to evaluating the archaeological evidence: OxJArch 12 (1993) 293-303.
12431 **Lipiński** Édouard, Dictionnaire de la civilisation phénicienne et punique 1992 ➤ 8,e664: ᴿBASOR 293 (1994) 94s (G. *Markoe*); TEuph 8 (1994) 169-171 (J. *Elayi*); TüTQ 174 (1994) 72 (H. *Niehr*).
12432 ᴱ**Mazza** Federico, *al.*, Fonti classiche per la civiltà fenicia e punica I. greche: StFen coll. 27, 1988 ➤ 5,e55... 7,d560: ᴿAfO 40s (1993s) 162s (Luciana *Aigner-Foresti*); TEuph 5 (1992) 181-3 (J. *Elayi*).
12433 Numismática hispano-púnica: Museo 1992, Trabajo 31. Ibiza 1993. 168 p.; 2 pl.
12434 **Ribichini** Sergio, *Xella* Paolo, La religione fenicia e punica in Italia: Itinerari 14. R 1994, Ist. Poligrafico. 143 p.; bibliog. 139-141. Lᵐ 20. 88-240-0355-9.
12435 *Teichner* Felix, Neue Funde iberischer Henkelattachen mit stilisierten Handflachen: RStFen 22 (1994) 35-49; pl. I.

12436 *Abul:* Mayet Françoise, *Tavares* Carlos, L'établissement phénicien d'Abul (Portugal): CRAI (1994) 171-188; 5 fig., 2 pl.

12437 *Moscati* Sabatino, I Fenici in Portogallo: LinceiR 9,5,1 (1994) 473-483; map.

12438 *Algeria:* a) Lipiński Edward, Sites phénico-puniques de la côte algérienne: Reppal 7s (1992) 287-324; – b) *Moscati* S., I fenici sulla costa nord-africana: RStFen 22 (1994) 67-69.

12439 *Agrigentum:* Schmitz Philip C., The name 'Agrigentum' in a Punic inscription (CIS I 5510.10): JNES 53 (1994) 1-13: ʾagrgnt.

12439* *Cartagena:* Martín Camino M., *Belmonte Marín* J.A., La muralla púnica de Cartagena; valoración arqueológica y análisis epigráfico de sus materiales: AulaO 11 (1993) 161-167 + 5 fig.; Eng. 161.

12440 *Cyprus:* Lipiński E., Les Phéniciens à Chypre et dans l'Égee: OrLovPer 23 (1992) 63-87.

12440* *Cyrene:* Levi della Vida G., ᴱ*Amadasi Guzzo* M.G., [96] Iscrizioni puniche della Tripolitania (1927-1967): MgArcheolLibica 22, 1987 ➤ 3,e371: ᴿAulaO 11,1 (1993) 129s (G. del *Olmo Lete*).

12441 *Ibiza:* a) Gómez Bellard Carlos, Die Phönizier auf Ibiza: MadMitt 34 (1993) 83-107; 19 fig.; pl. 12; – b) *Moscati* S., La funzione di Ibiza: RStFen 22 (1994) 51-56.

12441* *Málaga:* Giumlia-Mair A.R., The composition of copper-based small finds from a West Phoenician (Málaga) settlement site and from Nimrud compared with that of Mediterranean small finds: Archaeometry 34 (1992) 107-119; 3 fig.

12442 *Melita:* Hölbl G., Ägyptisches Kulturgut... Malta/phön Museum Valletta 1989 ➤ 5,e74 ... 8,e680: ᴿAnzAltW 46 (1993) 73s (P.W. *Haider*).

12443 *Monte Sirai* I, 1900-2: RStFen 22 (1994) 75-144 ; 4 (foldout) + 8 + 4 fig. (P. *Bartoloni, al.*).

12444 *Mozia:* Moscati Sabatino, Il VI secolo a Mozia [*Ciasca* E. VO 8 (1992) 113-135]: RStFen 22 (1994) 173-8.

12445 Ciasca Antonia, *Tori* M.P., Scavi a Mozia; le terracotte figurate: StFen coll. 33. R 1994, Cons. Naz. Ric. 87 p.; 1 foldout; 43 pl.

12446 *Roš Zayit:* Gal Zvi, A Phoenician bronze seal from ḥurbat Rosh Zayit [25 k E Acco, 1990 excavation]: JNES 53 (1994) 27-31; 3 fig.

12447 Raban A., *al.*, Phoenicians on the northern coast of Israel in the biblical period: Hecht Museum Catalogue 8. Haifa 1993. 44 p. + ❹42. – ᴿPEQ 126 (1994) 171 (Carole *Mendleson*).

12448 *Sardinia:* a) Bernardini P., La Sardegna e i Fenici; appunti sulla colonizzazione; – b) *Moscati* S., Nuovi studi sull'artigianato tardo-punico in Sardegna: RStFen 21 (1993) 29-81; pl. I-VI / 83-98.

12449 ꟻBALMUTH Miriam S., Sardinia, ᴱTykot R. 1992 ➤ 9,12: ᴿBASOR 295 (1994) 93s (R.R. *Holloway*).

12450 *Mattazzi* M. [*Costa* A.M.], La tomba 'dell'Ureo' [Cagliari Monte Luna], note a margine: RsTFen 22 (1994) 15-30; 6 fig. [31-35, fig. 7-12].

12451 *Taglīt:* Alfaro Asins Carmen, Una nueva ciudad púnica en Hispania: *tglyt* – Res Publica Tagilitana, Tíjola (Almería): ArEspArq 66 (1993) 229-243; 11 fig.; Eng. 229.

12452 *Tarraco:* Gimeno Javier, PLINIO, Nat. Hist. III,3,21; reflexiones acerca de la capitalidad de Hispania Citerior [Tarraco]: Latomus 53 (1994) 39-79 [rival of Carthago Nova].

12453 *Taršiš:* ᴱFernández Jurado J., Tartessos y Huelva: Huelva Arqueológica 10s (1988s); 3 vol. Huelva 1990, Diputación. 310 p.; 288 p.; 274 p. 0214-1187. – ᴿOrLovPer 23 (1992) 330 (E. *Lipiński*: solide; feuilles depuis 1960).

12454 **Tharros** 1993: RStFen 22 (1994) 185-8 (P. *Bernardini*, lo scavo) 189-194 (L.-I. *Manfredi*, progetto Melqart); 195-262 (*al.*).
12454* **Moscati** Sabatino, I gioielli di Tharros; origini, caratteri, confronti: CollStFen 26; CNR 59 p., 25 fig., XXXII pl. 1988 ➤ 4,e117: ᴿAulaO 11,1 (1993) 131-4 (G. del *Olmo Lete*, también sobre otros 3 de Tharros y 2 de Sulcis).

T5.3 **Carthago.**

12455 *a*) *Acquaro* Enrico, Note di archeologia punica; da Cartagine a Tharros; – *b*) *Fantar* M'Hamed [*al.*], Présence égyptienne à Carthage: ➤ 73, ᶠLECLANT J. 3 (1994) 1-4; 2 fig. / 203-211; 5 fig. [391s; 423s].
12455* **Ameling** Walter, Karthago; Studien zu Militär, Staat und Gesellschaft: Vestigia 45. Mü 1993, Beck. xi-289 p.
12456 **Brown** Shelby, Late Carthaginian child sacrifice 1991 ➤ 8,d586: ᴿBASOR 293 (1994) 84-87 (T. N. D. *Mettinger*); JRomA 7 (1994) 325-8 (H. *Hurst*).
12457 **Chelbi** F., Céramique à vernis noir de Carthage. Tunis 1992, Fond. Nat. Rech. 279 p.; 611 fig.; 634 pl. – ᴿRStFen 22 (1994) 155-9 (P. *Bartoloni*).
12458 *a*) *Docter* R. F., Karthagische Amphoren aus Toscanos; – *b*) *Maass-Lindemann* G., *Maass* M., Ägyptisierende Amulett-Blechbänder aus Andalusien: MadMit 35 (1994) 123-139; 5 fig.; pl. 7 / 140-156; pl. 9-12; 1 foldout.
12458* **Ennabli** Liliane, Carthage intra et extra muros: Inscriptions funéraires chrétiennes 3, 1991 ➤ 8,e692; 9,14064: ᴿLatomus 53 (1994) 688s (M. *Rassart-Debergh*).
12459 *Euzennat* Maurice, Le péricle d'Hannon [roi des Carthaginois]: CRAI (1994) 559-579; 6 fig.
12460 **Ferjaoui** Ahmed, Recherches sur les relations entre l'Orient phénicien et Carthage: OBO 124, 1993 ➤ 9,14066: Univ. – ᴿBL (1994) 119s (L. *Grabbe*); Orientalia 63 (1994) 150-3 (M. Giulia *Amadasi Guzzo*; RBBras 10 (1993) 304-6 (C. *Minette de Tillesse*).
12461 *Ferron* Jean, Un événement religieux capital à Carthage au début du IIIᵉ siècle avant notre ère: Muséon 107 (1994) 229-253 + 2 pl.
12462 *Fouture* Bruno, *Fantar* M'Hamed H., Cartagine, la capitale fenice del Mediterraneo. Mi c. 1993, Jaca. Ill. non numerate. Lᵐ 35. – ᴿArchéo 9,107 (1994) 117 (S. *Moscati*).
12462* **Gous** Klaus, Prosopographie der literarisch bezeugten Karthager: OrLovAn 58 / StPhoen 13. Lv 1994, Univ./Peeters. [x-] 267 p.; bibliog. 235-265. 90-6831-643-5.
12463 *Günther* Linda-Marie, Die karthagische Aristokratie und ihre Überseepolitik im 6. und 5. Jh. v. Chr.: Klio 75 (1993) 76-83; Eng. 84.
12464 **Hurst** H. R., Excavations at Carthage; the British mission: British Acad. Mg Arch 4s. Ox 1994, Univ. II,1: xi-335 p.; ill.; 8 color pl.; bibliog. 326-331; II,2: viii-115 p.; ill. 0-19-727003-4; -4-2.
12465 *Hurst* Henry, Le port militaire de Carthage: DossArch 183 (1993) 42-51.
12466 **Huss** Werner, Los cartagineses, ᵀ*Díaz Regañón* J. M. M 1993, Gredos. 431 p. – ᴿCiuD 206 (1993) 962s (T. A. *Turienzo*).
12467 *Lancel* Serge, Carthage 1992 ➤ 9,14067: ᴿHZ 259 (1994) 759s (W. *Ameling*); Klio 76 (1994) 483s (Linda-M. *Günther*).
12468 *Lipiński* E., ❸ Carthaginian pantheon: VDI 202 (1992) 29-51; Eng. 51.

2469 *Mertens-Hoen* Madeleine, Das Gesicht der Göttin Tanit?: MiDAI-R 101 (1994) 43-49; pl. 9-12.

2470 **Moscati** Sabatino, Introduzione alle guerre puniche; origine e sviluppo dell'impero di Cartagine. T c. 1994, SEI. 172 p.; 26 fig.; 44 pl. Lᵐ 30. – ᴿArcheo 9,118 (1994) 124s (S. F. *Bondi*).

2471 **Moscati** S., Il tramonto di Cartagine 1993 → 9,14070: ᴿArchViva 13,46 (1994) 92.

2472 *Moscati* Sabatino, Il tramonto di Cartagine; nuove scoperte in Sardegna e nel mondo punico: Archeo 9,110 (1994) 63-96; color. ill.

2473 **Niemeyer** H. G., Das frühe Karthago im Mittelmeerraum, 1989 → 6,e297: ᴿAnzAltW 46 (1993) 70 (P. W. *Haider*).

2474 *Norman* Naomi J., *Haeckl* Anne E., The Yasmina necropolis at Carthage, 1992: JRomArch 6 (AA 1993) 238-250; 9 fig. (251-62 *al.*, cryptoporticus/bath).

2475 **Storz** Sebastian, Tonröhren im antiken Gewölbebau... Karthago. DAI-R Sond. 10. Mainz 1994, von Zabern. ix-110 p.; 32 pl.; 19 foldouts.

2476 *Verga* F., Tharros e Cartagine; due metropoli a confronto; note topografiche: RStFen 22 (1994) 263-8.

2477 *Bertrandy* F., Les représentations du 'signe de Tanit' sur les stèles votives de Constantine (IIIᵉ-Iᵉ siècles av. J.-C.): RStFen 21 (1993) 3-22 + 6 fig.

2478 *Vattioni* Francesco, Maghrāwa [Tunisia centrale]: AION 54 (1994) 207-210.

T5.4 Ugarit – Ras Šamra.

2479 **Aboud** J., Die Rolle des Königs und seiner Familie nach den Texten von Ugarit; FARG [nicht unter den Abkürzungen UF 25, p. 530] 27. Münster 1994, Ugarit-Verlag. xi-217 p. 3-927120-20-0. – ᴿUF 25 (1993!) 494 (F. *Zeeb*).

2779* **Bordreuil** R., *al.*, Bibliothèque au Sud 1973, RS-Oug 7, 1991 → 8,e708; 9,14080: ᴿJSS 39 (1994) 289s (N. *Wyatt*).

2480 **Callot** Olivier, Ras Shamra-Ougarit; la tranchée 'Ville Sud'; études d'architecture domestique. P 1994, RCiv. 230 p. 2-86538-249-4.

2480* **Contenson** Henri de, Préhistoire de Ras Shamra: RSOug 8. P 1992, RCiv. 283 p.; 35 fig.; map. + vol. of 240 fig.; 97 pl. F 401. 2-86538-232-X. – ᴿArOr 62 (1994) 350s (P. *Charvát*); BuCanadMesop 26 (1993) 63s (? M. *Fortin*, also in French); Syria 91 (1994) 447-9 (P. *Amiet*); PEQ 126 (1994) 165s (L. *Copeland*).

2481 **Cunchillos** J.-L., La trouvaille épigraphique 2. RS-Ou 5, 1990 → 6,e305; 9,14082: ᴿJSS 39 (1994) 100s (A. H. W. *Curtis*).

2482 *Grenz* Hermann, Zur Datierung der Frühbronzezeit in *Rās eš-Šamra*: ZDPV 110 (1994) 113-124.

2483 *Niehr* Herbert, Überlegungen zum El-Tempel in Ugarit: UF 26 (1994) 419-426.

2484 **Whitt** William D., Archives and administration in the royal palace of Ugarit: diss. Duke, ᴰVan Seters J. Durham NC 1993. 353 p. 94-14113. – DissA 54 (1993s) p. 4551; RTLv 25,557.

2485 *Yon* Marguerite, Arts et industries de la pierre: RS-Oug 6, 1991 → 7,d605 ... 9,14090: ᴿAbrNahr 31 (1993) 126-8 (A. *Betts*); BO 51 (1994) 442-4 (R. *Eichmann*); OLZ 89 (1994) 552-4 (L. *Martin*); RHR 211 (1994)

93-95 (Françoise *Briquel-Chatonnet*, aussi sur 7); WeltOr 25 (1994) 169
171 (M. *Heinz*).
12485* *Yon* Marguerite, Ras Shamra-Ugarit: ➤ 12500, AJA 98 (1994
156-159; fig. 21s.

T5.5 Ebla.

12486 *Archi* Alfonso, Studies in the pantheon of Ebla: Orientalia 63 (1994
249-256.
12486* *a) Astour* Michael C., An outline of the history of Ebla (Part I); – *b*
Buccellati Giorgio, Ebla and the Amorites; – *c) Hallo* William W.
Ebrium at Ebla: Eblaitica 3 (1992) 3-82 / 83-102; 6 maps / 139-150.
12487 *a) Buccellati* Giorgio, The Ebla electronic corpus; onomastic analysis
– *b) Gordon* Cyrus H., The Ebla exorcisms; – *c) Rendsburg* Gary A.
Eblaite *sa-su-ga-lum* = Hebrew *ssᶜgr* [as in both Isa 38,14 and Jer 8,7, ɨ
colorful small bird, perhaps golden oriole]: Eblaitics 3 (1992) 105-126
127-137 / 151-3.
12487* **Fronzaroli** Pelio, (*Catagnosti* Amalia), Testi rituali della regalità
(Archivio 1.2769: ARET 11). R 1993, Univ. Missione Archeologica ir
Siria. xxi-185 p., xix-pl.
12488 *Mazzoni* Stefania, Tell Afis [... Ebla]: ArchViva 13,44 (1994) 66-69.
12488* *a) Matthiae* Paolo, A stele fragment of Hadad from Ebla; – *b*
Mazzoni Stefania, Cylinder seal impressions on jars at Ebla; new
evidence: ➤ 89*a*, ᶠÖZGÜÇ Nimet, Aspects 1993, 389-397 / 399-414.
12489 *Matthiae* Pablo, Mardikh-Ebla: ➤ 12500, AJA 98 (1994) 127-129
fig.14s.
12490 *Matthiae* Paolo, Old Syrian basalt furniture from Ebla palace
and temples: ➤ 55, ᶠHROUDA B., Beiträge 1994, 167-177; 4 fig.; pl
XV*b*-XVII.
12491 **Pagan** Joseph M., A morphological and lexical study of persona
names in the Ebla texts: diss. UCLA 1991, ᴰ*Buccellati* G. 1273 p
95-11123. – DissA 55 (1994s) p. 1273.
12492 **Platt** James H., Eblaite scribal tendencies; graphemics and ortho
graphy: diss. UCLA 1993, ᴰ*Buccellati* G. 727 p. 93-24577. – DissA 5⁴
(1993s) p. 1338.
12493 *Viganò* Lorenzo, *a)* Mari and Ebla; of time and rulers [*dam* 'woman'
nar 'singers', *nedi* 'dances' ...]: LA 44 (1994) 351-373; – *b)* On the Ebla
reports dealing with Mari: AulaO 11 (1993) 178-211.

T5.8 Situs effossi Syriae in ordine alphabetico.

12494 **Chavalas** M. W., *Hayes* John L., New Horizons in the study of ancien
Syria [Amer.Hist.Asn., Ch 1991]: BtMesop 25. Malibu 1992, Undena
vii-232 p. $30. – ᴿZAss 84 (1994) 158s (D. O. *Edzard*).
12495 **Klengel** H., Syria 1992 ➤ 8,b825: ᴿPEQ 126 (1994) 83s (Amélie *Kuhrt*)
RStFen 22 (1994) 273s (S. *Ribichini*).
12496 **Meijer** Diederik J. W., A survey in northeastern Syria 1986 ➤ 6,a337
7,d628: ᴿJNES 53 (1994) 136-8 (T. *McClellan*).
12497 **Rouault** O. & M., L'Eufrate e il tempo 1993 ➤ 9,14116: ᴿCC 14⁵
(1994,3) 311s (S. *Votto*).
12498 *Schlor* Ingrid, Kulturbeziehungen während der Frühbronzezeit zwi
schen Mitteleuropa und Syrien; ein Kulturvergleich anhand der Ösen
halsringen: Klio 76 (1994) 7-41 + 21 fig.; 4 maps; Eng. 31.

12499 *Tracey* Robyn,   Syria: ➤ 243, Acts Graeco-Roman 1994, 223-277.
12500 *Weiss* Harvey,   Archaeology in Syria: AJA 98 (1994) 101-158; 39 fig.

12501 *ʿAin Dārā: Abū Assaf* Ali,   Der Tempel von Ain Dārā in Nordsyrien: [50 k NW Aleppo]: AntWelt 24 (1993) 151-171; 30 fig.
12502 **Abu Assaf** Ali,   Der Tempel von Ain Dara: DamaszF 3, 1992:   ᴿBonn-Jbb 194 (1994) 542-9 (P. *Neve*).
12503 *Aḥmar:*   **Bunnens** G., Tell Ahmar, 1988 season, 1990 ➤ 7,d632…9, 14120*:   ᴿSyria 61 (1994) 233-5 (C. *Castel*).
12504 *ʿAgig* [? Atij: Iraq frontier east of Khabur]: *a)* **Bernbeck** R.,   Steppe als Kulturlandschaft; das ʿAgig-Gebiet Ostsyriens vom Neolithikum bis zur islamischen Zeit: BBVO Ausg. 1.   B 1993, Reimer. – ᴿBuCanadMesop 28 (1994) 45s (M. *Fortin*); – *b)* Atij 4th (Nineve 5), Gudeda 3d, 1992: Syria 71 (1994) 396; 29 fig. (M. *Fortin*). ➤ 12510.
12505 *Amrit: a) Yon* M., *Caubet* A., Arouad et Amrit VIIIᵉ-Iᵉʳ siècles av. J.-C.; documents; – *b) Jourdain-Annequin* C., Héraclès-Melqart à Amrith? Un syncrétisme gréco-phénicien à l'époque perse: ➤ 461, TEuph 6 (1993) 47-66 + 4 fig.; pl. I-VII / 69-83; 3 fig.; pl. VIII-XII.
12506 **Jourdain-Annequin** C.,   Héraclès-Melqart à Amrith; recherches iconographiques; contribution à l'étude d'un syncrétisme: IFAPO-BAH 142.   P 1992, Geuthner.   92 p.; 20 pl. – ᴿRStFen 22 (1994) 145s (S. *Ribichini*).
12507 *Apameia:*   **Balty** Jean C., *Rengen* Wilfried van, Apamée de Syrie; quartiers d'hiver de la IIᵉ Légion parthique; monuments funéraires de la nécropole militaire: Ausstellung.   Bru 1993, Vrije Univ. 55 p.; ill.
12508 **Balty** Jean-Charles,   Grande colonnade et quartiers nord d'Apamée à la fin de l'époque hellénistique: CRAI (1994) 77-101; 10 fig.
12509 **Sanlaville** Paul, *al.*,   Le paléolithique de la vallée moyenne de l'Oronte: BAR-Int 587.   Ox 1993, Tempus Reparatum. – ᴿPaléorient 20,2 (1994) 169s (Liliane *Meignen*).
12510 *Atij* 1992s: BuCanadMesop 27 (1994) 33-50; 22 fig.; franç. 33 (M. *Fortin*, Lisa *Cooper*). ➤ 12504.
12511 *Biʿa* 1993: MDOG 126 (1994) 11-30; 27 fig. (Eva *Strommenger*; 33-36 Schriftfunde, *Krebernik* Manfred).
12512 *Damascus: Will* Ernest, Damas antique: Syria 61 (1994) 1-43; 16 fig.
12512* *Deir Sunbul: Tate* G., *Naccache* A., Le village antique de Deir Sunbul: MUSJ 52 (Beyrouth 1991s) 371-423 + 122 fig. (map). ➤ 11622*.
12513 *Dura: Bounni* Adnan, Un nouveau bas-relief palmyrénien de Doura-Europos: CRAI (1994) 11-18; 2 fig.
12514 *Kelley* Christopher C., Who did the iconoclasm [gouged eyes] in the Dura synagogue? [Romans, as KRAELING; not Jews, as GOODENOUGH]: BASOR 295 (1994) 57-72; 6 fig.
12515 *Leriche* Pierre, *Mahmoud* Asʿad Al-, Doura-Europos; bilan des recherches récentes: CRAI (1994) 395-420; 11 fig.
12516 *Leriche* Pierre, *Mahmud* Asad al-, Dura-Europos: ➤ 12500, AJA 98 (1994) 154-6; fig. 36s.
12517 **Weitzmann** Kurt, *Kessler* Herbert L., The frescoes of the Dura synagogue and Christian art 1991 ➤ 7,d653 … 9,14131: ᴿKairos 32s (1990s) 247-250 (Ursula *Schubert*) + 250-2 (K. *Schubert*).

12518 *Emar: Adamthwaite* M. R., Emar's window on the OT; a preliminary view: BurHist 29,3 (1993) 75-94 (half-page addition to p. 80 furnished with fasc. 4).

Fleming Daniel E., The installation of Baal's high priestess at Emar 1992 ➤ 10707.

12519 *Margueron* Jean-Claude, Émar au XIVᵉ siècle: DossA 193 (1994) 62-67.

12519* *Zaccagnini* Carlo, Feet of clay at Emar and elsewhere [ARNAUD D. 1985-7]: Orientalia 63 (1994) 1-4.

12520 *Ḥama:* **Riis** Paul L., *Buhl* Marie-Luise, *al.*, Hama 2/2, Objets syro-hittites. K 1990. 87-89438-00-0. – ᴿSyria 71 (1994) 452s (M. al-*Maqdisi*).

12520* *Ḥamidiya:* ᴱ**Eichler** S., *al.*, Tell el-Hamidiya 2. Symposium [Berne Dec. 9-11, 1986] + excavations 1985-7: OBO arch 6, 1990 ➤ 6,a369 ... 9,14143: ᴿArOr 62 (1994) 351s (P. *Charvát*); Syria 71 (1994) 227-233 (L. *Bachelot*).

12521 *Haradum* (90 k SE Mari): **Képinski-Lecomte** Christine, Haradum ... une ville nouvelle sur l'Euphrate (XVIIIᵉ-XVIIᵉ s. av. J.-C.) 1992 ➤ 8,e779: ᴿRAss 88 (1994) 77s (P. *Amiet*).

12522 *Hassake* 1988-92: Mesop-T 29 (1994) 5-48; 42 fig. (R. M. *Munčaev*, N.-J. *Merpert*).

12523 *Rad Shaqrah* (Hassake): Polish (Reports 1994) 109-117; 2 fig. (P. *Bieliński*).

12523* *Kazel* (trouée de Ḥomṣ-Akkar = ? Simyra) 4ᵉ-8ᵉ 1988-92 LB - Iron - Persian: Syria 71 (1994) 259-359 (Leila *Badré*, *al.*).

12524 *Khabur:* **Courty** M.-A., Le cadre paléographique des occupations humaines dans le bassin du Haut-Khabour, premiers résultats: Paléorient 20,1 (1994) 21-59.

12524* *Morandi Bonacorsi* Daniele, Paesaggio rurale e popolamento del territorio della bassa valle del fiume Ḫābūr (Siria nord-orientale) in età tardo-assira (VIII-VII sec. a.C.): GeogAnt 3s (1994s) 3-28 + 15 (color.) fig. (maps).

12525 *Khalid:* a) *Clarke* G. W., Jebel Khalid on the Euphrates; the Acropolis building; – b) *Connor* P. J., Terracottas from Seleucid Jebel Khalid: ➤ 416d, MeditArch 7 (1991/4) 69-75; 5 fig. (map); pl. 1-3 / 77-81; pl. 4-7.

12525* *Vandersleyen* Claude, L'Euphrate; Aram Naharaim et la Bible: Muséon 107 (1994) 5-14.

12526 *Kowm:* ᴱ**Cauvin** J., Cahiers de l'Euphrate 5s. P 1991, RCiv. – ᴿBuCanadMesop 26 (1993) 62s (unsigned; also on Cafer in Turkey in 5s or? 6 alone).

12526* *Leilan:* *Mieroop* Marc Van De, The Tell Leilan tablets 1991; a preliminary report: Orientalia 63 (1994) 305-344; 24 fig.

12527 *Marí:* **Malamat** A., Mari and the early Israelite experience (Schweich 1984) 1992 ➤ 5,b307 ... 9,14152: ᴿPEQ 126 (1994) 160-3 (W. G. *Lambert*: further updating in the 1992 ⊕).

12528 **Malamat** Abraham, ⊕ Mari and Israel; two west-Semitic cultures. J 1991, Magnes. 240 p.; 10 pl. – ᴿCHistEI 70 (1994) 193-8 (S. *Ahituv*, ⊕).

12529 **Anbar** M., Les tribus amurrites de Mari: OBO 108, 1991 ➤ 7,d669 ... 9,14146: PEQ 125 (1993) 157s (Harriet *Crawford*); RB 101 (1994) 445-7 (M. *Sigrist*).

12530 **Birot** M., Correspondance des gouverneurs de Qattarum: ARM 27. P 1993, RCiv. 225 p.; 1 microfiche. 2-86538-242-7. – ᴿRAss 88 (1994) 88s (A. *Malamat*).

12530* *Cavigneaux* Antoine, Magica mariana [en français]: RAss 88 (1994) 155-161.

12531 *Nakata* Ichiro, Popular concerns reflected in Old Babylonian Mari theophoric personal names: ➤ 571*, Official cult 1992/3, 114-125.
12532 [F]FLEURY Michel: Florilegium marianum, [E]**Durand** J.-M. 1992 ➤ 8,56: [R]JSS 39 (1994) 285-9 (Stephanie *Dalley*).

12533 *Mozan:* **Milano** Lucio, *al.*, Mozan[2], 1991 ➤ 8,e806: [R]OLZ 89 (1994) 46s (K. *Kessler*).
12534 *Msayké* (Leja, S. Syria) 1, 1993: BÉtOr 45 (1993) 33-45 + XII pl. (Alexandrine *Guérin*); Eng. ❹ 281.
12535 *Mohammed Diyab* tell near Leilan 3d 1990, 4th 1991: [E]**Durand** J.-M., Recherches en Haute Mésopotamie: NABU mém. 2. P 1992, SEPOA. – [R]BuCanadMesop 25 (1993) 71s (Eng./franç.).
12536 *Munbaqa* 1992/3: MDOG 126 (1994) 51-62; foldout plan / 63s (D. *Machule, al.*).

12536* *Palmyra:* **Bounni** Adnan, *As ʿad* Khalad Al-, Palmyra; Geschichte, Denkmäler, Museum[2], [T]*Klengel* Horst. Damaskus 1990. 152 p.; ill.; map.
12537 *Dentzer* Jean-Marie, Khāns ou casernes à Palmyre? À propos des structures visibles sur des photographies aériennes anciennes: Syria 61 (1994) 45-112; 22 fig.; 1 dépliant.
12538 **Dentzer-Feydy** J., *Teixidor* L., Antiquités de Palmyre, Louvre 1993: [R]MesopT 28 (1994) 343s (A. *Invernizzi*).
12539 **Schmidt-Colinet** Andreas, *al.*, Das Tempelgrab Nr. 36 in Palmyra: DamaszF 4. Mainz 1992, von Zabern. – [R]ArchWsz 44 (1993) 151s (M. *Gawlikowski*); JRomA 7 (1994) 437-446 (Sarah *Cormack*); MesopT 29 (1994) 344-7 (A. *Allara*).
12540 **Stoneman** Richard, Palmyra and its empire 1992 ➤ 9,14163*: [R]AmHR 94 (1994) 1294s (G. M. *Rogers*); ClasB 70 (1994) 118s (A. J. *Papalas*); JRS 84 (1994) 242s (D. *Kennedy*).
12541 **Simiat** Bernard, *Degeorge* Gérard, Zenobia di Palmira. Mi c. 1993, Ricci. 192 p., 50 tavole a colori applicate a mano. L[m] 330. – [R]Archeo 9,107 (1994) 117s (S. *Moscati*).

12541* *Qara Quzaq* [20 k SE Jerablus]: [E]**Olmo Lete** G. del, Tell Qara Quzaq I, campañas I-III (1983-1991): AulaO supp. 4. Sabadell-Barc 1994, AUSA. 323 p.; 21 color. fot.; 7 plans. 84-605-0359-3 (BL 95,32, W. G. E. *Watson*].
12542 *Qaṭna:* **Hult** Gunnel, Qatna and Nitovikla [Cyprus, similar fortress-gates]: Levant 26 (1994) 189-197; 8 fig.
12543 [? *Qudeda* ➤ 12504] Gudeda 1992s: BuCanadMesop 27 (1994) 51-63; 17 fig., 51 franç. (M. *Fortin*, B. & C. *Routledge*).
12544 *Šamseddin*, Djerniye 1991 (Gräber ➤ 12548) 2. 170 p.; 25 pl. – [R]OLZ 89 (1994) 392-6 (J.-W. *Meyer*).
12545 *Sergilla:* **Charpentier** Gérard, Les bains de Sergilla: Syria 61 (1994) 113-142; 27 fig.
12546 *Suweida:* **Dentzer** J. M., *Dentzer-Feydy* Jacqueline, Le djebel al-ʿArab; histoire et patrimoine au Musée de Suweida; catalogue *Hatoum* H.: Guides IFAPO 1. P 1991, RCiv. 134 p.; 36 pl.
12547 **Besançon** J., *al.*, Prospection géomorphologique et préhistorique dans la région de *Tartous* (Syrie): Paléorient 20,1 (1994) 5-19.
12548 *Wreide* (Syrian Euphrates): **Orthmann** W., *Rova* E., Gräber des 3.

Jahrtausends im syrischen Euphrattal. Saarbrücken 1991, Dr. 179 p.; ill.
– ᴿOLZ 89 (1994) 387-392 (E. *Rova*, S. *Mazzoni*).

T6.1 **Mesopotamia:** *generalia.*

12549 ᶠABDEL-MESSIH Ernest T.: Studies in Near Eastern culture and history
➤ 8,3: ᴱ**Bellamy** James A. AA 1990, Univ. Michigan. xii-225 p.; portr.
– ᴿOLZ 89 (1994) 163s (H. *Preissler*).

12550 *a*) *Albenda* Pauline, Babylonian art and architecture of the late period; –
b) *Roth* Martha T., The Neo-Babylonian family and household; – *c*)
Beaulieu Paul-Alain, Antiquarianism and the concern for the past in the
Neo-Babylonian period; – *d*) *Lee* Thomas G., Propaganda and the verse
account of Nabonidus' reign: BuCanadMesop 28 (1994) 13-18; 6 fig. /
19-30 / 37-42 / 31-36 (tous précédés de résumé français).

12551 **Algaze** G., The Uruk world system; the dynamics of expansion of early
Mesopotamian civilization 1993 ➤ 9,14174: ᴿBO 51 (1994) 665-71 (R. J.
Matthews); Origini 18 (1994) 491-4 (Franca *Trufelli*).

12552 **Baffi Guardata** Francesco, *Dolce* Rita, Archeologia... cassita e me-
dio-assira 1990 ➤ 8,e835: ᴿBO 51 (1994) 674-6 (Ö. *Tunca*).

12553 **Barton** Tamsyn, Ancient astrology: Sciences of antiquity. L 1994,
Routledge. xxv-245 p.; bibliog. 229-234. 0-415-08066-5; pa. -11029-7.

12554 **Bottéro** Jean (avec *Monsacré* Hélène), Babylone et la Bible. P 1994,
BLettres. xvi-319 p. 2-231-44026-7. – ᴿRAss 88 (1994) 91 (D. *Charpin*).

12555 ᴱ**Bottéro** J., Initiation à l'Orient ancien; de Sumer à la Bible: Points
l'Histoire H-170. P 1992, Seuil. – ᴿBuCanadMesop 25 (1993) 73s (Eng.
français.; no author).

12556 **Bottéro** Jean, Mesopotamia, writing, reasoning and the gods [1987],
ᵀ*Mieroop* Z. & M. van de 1992 ➤ 9,14175: ᴿScEspr 46 (1994) 237-247
(M. *Spicer*, Eng.).

12557 *a*) *Chadwick* Robert, Goddesses, queens, and housewives; women in
ancient Egypt and Mesopotamia; – *b*) *Beaulieu* Paul-Alain, Women in
Neo-Babylonian society; – *c*) *Silva* Aldina da, La symbolique des vêtements dans les rites du mariage et du divorce au Proche-Orient ancien et
dans la Bible; – *d*) *Morrissette* Josée, La place des femmes dans la
famille; succession et héritage à Émar: BuCanadMésop 26 (1993) 5s /
7-14 / 15-22 / 23-28 / 29-38.

12558 **Charvát** Petr, Ancient Mesopotamia 1993 ➤ 9,14176: ᴿArOr 62
(1994) 341-3 (B. *Hruška*).

12559 ᴱ**Curtis** John, Early Mesopotamia and Iran 3500-1600 B.C., LUKONIN V.
mem. seminar 1993 ➤ 9,571: ᴿAJA 98 (1994) 777s (P. L. *Kohl*).

12560 *Dąbrowa* Edward, Dall'autonomia alla dipendenza; le città greche e
gli Arsacidi nella prima metà del I secolo d.C.: MesopT 29 (1994) 185-198.

12560* *Dalley* Stephanie, Nineveh, Babylon and the Hanging Gardens;
cuneiform and classical sources reconciled: Iraq 56 (1994) 45-58.

12561 *a*) *Durand* Jean-Marie, Les cieux, premier livre de lecture; – *b*) *Charpin*
Dominique, Les recueils de présages astrologiques; – *c*) *Villard* Pierre,
Astrologie et politique à la cour de Ninive; – *d*) *Maneveau* Bernard,
Positions stellaires et éclipses au service de l'histoire; – *e*) *Michel* Cécile,
La géographie des cieux; aux origines du zodiaque: DossA 191 (1994) 2-7
/ 8-15 / 18-26 / 32-35 / 36-47.

12561* ᴱ**Finkbeiner** Uwe, Materialien zur Archäologie der Seleukiden- und
Partherzeit im südlichen Babylonien und im Golfgebiet, Symposien DAI
Blaubeuren 1989/9. Tü 1993, Wasmuth. xv-294 p.; 7 pl.

12562 *Frame* Grant, Mesopotamia in the Neo-Babylonian period: BuCanad-Mesop 28 (1994) 7-11.

12562* ^FGARELLI P., Marchands... ^E**Charpin** D., *al.* 1991 ➤ 7,61: ^RJSS 38 (1993) 309s (J. N. *Postgate*); OLZ 89 (1994) 142-4 (H. *Freydank*).

12563 **Huot** Jean-Louis, Les Sumériens, entre le Tigris et l'Euphrate: Néréides. P 1989, Errance. 257 p.; ill. 2-903442-96-7. – ^RSyria 71 (1994) 463-6 (J. *Margueron*).

12563* ^FLOON Maurits N. van: To the Euphrates and beyond 1991, ^E**Haere** O., *al.* 1989 ➤ 5,122 [Haex, index Haes]: ^RSyria 71 (1994) 460-2 (H. de *Contenson*).

12564 **Matthiae** Paolo, Il sovrano e l'opera; arte e potere nella Mesopotamia antica: Grandi opere. R 1994, Laterza. [iv-]203 p. 88-420-4537-3.

12565 *Mazza* M., Strutture sociali e culture locali nelle Provincie sulla frontiera dell'Eufrate (II-IV sec. d.C.): SicGymn 45 (1992) 159-236.

12566 **Moorey** Peter R. S., Ancient Mesopotamian materials and industries; the archaeological evidence. Ox 1994, Clarendon. xxiii-414 p.; bibliog. 363-405. 0-19-814921-2.

12567 *Munchaev* R. M., *Merpert* N. Ya., ❻ New discoveries and archaeological problems of Upper Mesopotamia: VDI 207 (1993) 127-136; 4 fig.; Eng. 136.

12568 **Postgate** J. H., Early Mesopotamia 1992 ➤ 9,14188: ^RAJA 97 (1993) 573s (B. R. *Foster*).

12569 **Roux** G., Ancient Iraq^{3rev}. Penguin 1992 ➤ 8,e849: ^RBuCanadMesop 26 (1993) 66s (A. K. *Grayson*, aussi en français).

12570 **Soden** W. von, The Ancient Orient; an introduction to the study of the Ancient Near East, ^T*Shley* Donald G. GR 1994, Eerdmans. – ^RBuCanadMesop 28 (1994) 43 (A. K. *Grayson*: culture, agriculture, commerce, music duly stressed, but no charts).

12570* *Sürenhagen* Dietrich, Relative chronology of the Uruk period; new evidence from Uruk-Warka and northern Syria: BuCanadMesop 25 (1993) 57-70.

T6.3 *Mesopotamia, scripta effossa* – **Excavated Tablets.**

12571 **Arnaud** D., Altbabylonische Rechts- und Verwaltungsurkunden: BBVO Texte 1, 1989 ➤ 6,e430... 9,14193: ^RRAss 88 (1994) 78-81 (D. *Charpin*).

12572 **Arnaud** Daniel, Texte aus Larsa; die epigraphischen Funde der 1. Kampagne in Sankereh-Larsa 1933: BBVO T3. B 1994, Reimer. [iv-]25 p. 3-496-02510-7.

12573 **Beaulieu** Paul-Alain, Late Babylonian texts in the Nies Babylonian collection; Catalogue BabYale 1. Bethesda MD 1994, 'CDL'. xi-91 p. 1-8830-5304-8.

12574 *Borger* Rykle, Zum neuen Korpus der altbabylonischen Königsinschriften [FRAYNE D., RIM 4, 1990]: OLZ 89 (1994) 357-370.

12574* *Datsow* E. von, Archival documents of Borsippa families [*Joannès* F. 1989]: AulaO 12 (1994) 105-120.

12575 **Dekiere** Luc, Old Babylonian real estate documents from Sippar in the British Museum: MesopHistEnv 3/2. Ghent 1994, Univ. 4 vol.

12576 **Dijk** Jan van, Literarische Texte aus Babylon 1987 ➤ 3,e553... 9,14197: ^ROLZ 89 (1994) 272-6 (J. *Klein*: highly accurate).

12577 *Dsharakian* Rusan, Akkadische Wirtschaftstexte aus den Archiven von Awal und Gasur (III. Jt. v.Chr.): ZAss 84 (1994) 1-10.

12578 **Eidem** Jesper, The Shemshāra archives, 2. The administrative texts. 1992 ➤ 8,e862: ᴿAfO 40s (1993s) 109-111 (B. *Lafont*); JAOS 114 (1994) 497s (M. van de *Mieroop*); Orientalia 63 (1994) 140-3 (Stephanie *Dalley*); RelStR 20 (1994) 224 (D. I. *Owen*); Syria 71 (1994) 456-460 (D. *Charpin*); ᴡᴢᴋᴍ 84 (1994) 224-6 (Michaela *Weszeli*).

12579 **Englund** Robert K., *Grégoire* Jean-Pierre, The Proto-Cuneiform texts from Jemdet Nasr 1991 ➤ 7,d710; 9,14199: ᴿZAss 84 (1994) 130-5 (J. *Friberg*).

12580 **Englund** Robert K., Archaic administrative texts from Uruk; the early campaigns: Uruk-Warka 15, T 5. B 1994, Mann. 232 p. 3-7861-1745-4.

12581 ᵀᴱ**Fales** F. Mario, Lettere dalla corte assira. Venezia 1992, Marsilio. 184 p. [con testo a fronte]. 88-317-5496-3.

12582 ᴱ**Fales** Frederick M., *Postgate* J. N., Imperial administrative records 1. palace and temple administration: SAA 7, 1992 ➤ 8,e863: ᴿOrSuec 41s (1992s) 314s (T. *Kronholm*, auch 6).

12583 **Frayne** D., RIM 2 1993 ➤ 12587 [OTA 17, p. 654: 4th to appear, renvois to the other 3].

12584 **Freydank** Helmut, Mittelassyrische Rechtsurkunden und Verwaltungstexte III: WVDOG 92. B 1994, Mann. 82 p.; 86 facsim. 3-7861-1746-2.

12585 *Freydank* Helmut, Drei [Assur-] Tafeln aus der Verwaltung des mittelassyrischen Kronlandes: AltOrF 21 (1994) 13-30.

12586 **Fuchs** Andreas, Die Inschriften Sargons II. aus Khorsabad. Gö 1994, Cuvillier. [iv-] 475 p.; map. 3-930340-42-9.

12587 **Grayson** A. Kirk, Assyrian rulers 1114-859: RIMA-2 1991 ➤ 9,14203: ᴿBO 51 (1994) 365-372 (O. *Pedersén*); WeltOr 25 (1994) 143-5 (W. *Röllig*).

12588 **Hunger** H., Astrological reports to Assyrian kings. Helsinki 1992, Univ. – ᴿArOr 61 (1993) 323s (J. *Pečírková*); BuCanadMesop 26 (1993) 64s (R. *Chadwick*, aussi en français); ZAss 84 (1994) 308-310 (S. *Zawadzki*).

12589 **Kwasman** T., *Parpola* S., Legal/Nineveh I: SAA 6, 1991 ➤ 7,d723: ᴿBL (1993) 122s (A. R. *Millard*); WeltOr 25 (1994) 136-8 (W. v. *Soden*, auch über SAA 7).

12590 **Lafont** B., *Yıldız* F., Tablettes de Tello 1989 ➤ 5,e194; 9,14207*: ᴿArOr 62 (1994) 346s (B. *Hruška*).

12590* a) *Lafont* Bertrand, [4 tablettes et 1 inédite sur] L'avènement de Šu-sīn; b) *Michel* Cécile, Règlement de comptes du défunt Huraşānum; – c) *Lion* Brigitte, Un contrat de vente de maison daté du règne d'Enlil-bāni d'Isin: RAss 88 (1994) 97-119; Eng. 119 / 121-128 / 129-133.

12591 **Lanfranchi** G., *Parpola* S., Correspondence of Sargon II, 2; SAA 5, 1990 ➤ 6,e454; 8,e882: ᴿWeltOr 25 (1994) 134s (W. von *Soden*).

12591* **Leichty** Erle, *al.*, Sippar 3: BM catalogue of Babylonian tablets 8, 1988 ➤ 4,g103 ... 8,e883: ᴿJAOS 114 (1994) 666s (M. *Dandamayev*).

12592 **Maidman** Maynard P., Two hundred Nuzi texts from the Oriental Institute of the University of Chicago I: StNuziHur 6. Bethesda MD 1994, CDL. xvi-443 p. $50. 1-883053-05-6.

12593 **Muhamed** Ahmad K., Old Babylonian cuneiform texts from the Hamrin Basin, Tell Haddad: 'ᴇᴅᴜʙʙᴀ' 1. L 1992, 'ɴᴀʙᴜ'. [viii-] 69 p. 1-897750-02-1.

12594 *Neumann* Hans, *Hruška* Blahoslav, Die Ur-III-Texte aus ... Prag: ArOr 62 (1994) 227-249.

12595 **Parpola** S., Correspondence of Sargon: SAA 2/1, 1987 ➤ 3,e570 ... 7,d732: ᴿAulaO 11 (1993) 257-263 (J. *Sanmartín*, 1s. 5s); JSS 39 (1994) 97-100 (A. *Livingstone*).

12596 **Pomponio** Francesco, *Visicato* Giuseppe,   Early dynastic administrative tablets of Šuruppak: StAsiatici 6.   N 1994, Ist. Univ. Orientale.   xix-479 p.

12596* **Pomponio** Francesco,   Testi cuneiformi neo-sumerici da Drehem. Mi 1990, Ist. Ed. Univ. 235 p.; 67 pl. – ᴿJAOS 114 (1993) 278-282 (W. *Heimpel*).

12597 **Postgate** N.,   Archive of Urad Šerua 1988 ➤ 6,e461 ... 9,14210:   ᴿAfO 40s (1993s) 117-122 (S. W. *Cole*).

12598 **Sack** Ronald H.,   Cuneiform documents from the Chaldean and Persian periods.   Selinsgrove 1994, Susquehanna Univ.   x-131 p.   0-945636-67-9.

12598* *Sanati-Müller* Shirin, Texte aus dem Sinkašid-Palast [Warka] 7 [*al.*, andere Texte]: BaghMitt 25 (1994) 309-340 [447-459-472].

12599 **Snell** Daniel C., *Lager* Carl H., Economic texts from Sumer [125 copies c. 1940] 1991 ➤ 8,e893; 9,14217:   ᴿRB 101 (1994) 442 (M. *Sigrist*); ZAss 84 (1994) 305-8 (W. *Sallaberger*).

12600 ᴱ**Spar** Ira,   Tablets, cones and bricks 1988 ➤ 4,g112 ... 7,d739:   ᴿJNES 53 (1994) 61-63 (H. *Neumann*, deutsch).

12601 **Steinkeller** Peter, *Postgate* J. N.,   Third millennium legal and administrative texts in the Iraq Museum 1982 ➤ 9,14219:   ᴿBO 51 (1994) 598-600 (F. *Pomponio*: splendid); BSO 57 (1994) 588-590 (R. K. *Englund*); ZAss 84 (1994) 144-7 (W. *Sallaberger*).

12602 **Stolper** Matthew W.,   Late Achaemenid, early Macedonian, and early Seleucid records of deposit and related texts: AION supp. 77 to 53,4 (1993).   N 1993, Ist. Univ. Orientale.   99 p.; facsimiles.

12602* *Stolper* Matthew W.,   A Late-Achaemenid lease from the Rich collection [K 8133]: JAOS 114 (1994) 625s; facsim. 627.

12603 **Watson** P.,   Catalogue of cuneiform tablets in Birmingham ... 2. Neo-Sumerian from Umma *al.*   Wmr 1993, Aris & P. ix-263 p. £15. – ᴿOLZ 89 (1994) 538-545 (W. *Sallaberger*).

12604 **Weiher** Egbert von, Uruk, spätbabylonische Texte 1993 ➤ 4,g117 ... 9,14224:   ᴿMesopT 29 (1994) 302-4 (L. *Cagni*); WeltOr 25 (1994) 138-145 (Antoine *Cavigneaux*).

12605 **Weisberg** D. B.,   The Late Babylonian texts of the [Ch] Or. Inst.: BtMesop 24 1991 ➤ 9,14225:   ᴿJAOS 114 (1994) 435-9 (R. *Wallenfels*); WeltOr 25 (1994) 152-4 (R. *Zadok*); ZAss 84 (1994) 283-8 (M. P. *Streck*).

12606 **Wilhelm** Gernot,   Das Archiv des Šilwa-Teššup [2, 1983 ➤ 7,d744]; 4. Darlehensurkunden und verwandte Texte.   Wsb 1992, Harrassowitz.   ix-158 p.   3-447-03269-3.

12606* **Yang Zhi,**   Sargonic inscriptions from Adab: AncCiv 1.   Changchun 1989, Inst. Anc. Civ.   xxi-449 p. – ᴿJAOS 114 (1994) 93s (J. J. *Glassner*, franç.).

T6.5   **Situs effossi ʿIraq** in ordine alphabetico.

12607 *Akkad:* ᴱ**Liverani** Mario,   Akkad, the first world empire; structure, ideology, traditions [< Akkad, il primo impero universale, Univ. Roma 5-7.XII.1990]: HistANE/Studies 5.   Padova 1993, Sargon.   xiv-182 p.; 6 pl. 1120-4680: *a*) *Cooper* Jerrold S.,   Paradigm and propaganda; the dynasty of Akkade in the 21st century; – *b*) *Foster* Benjamin R.,   Management and administration in the Sargonic period [general bibliography]; – *c*) *Liverani*,   Model and actualization; the kings of Akkad in the historical tradition; – *d*) *Michalowski* Piotr,   Memory and deed; the historiography of the political expansion of the Akkad state; – *e*) *Nissen* Hans J., Settlement patterns and material culture of the Akkadian period; continuity and discontinuity; – *f*) *Steinkeller* Piotr, Early political development in Mesopotamia and the origins of the Sargonic empire; – *g*) *Weiss* Harvey, *Courty* Marie-Agnès, The genesis and collapse of the Akkadian empire; the accidental refraction of historical law; – *h*) *Westenholz* Aage, The world view of Sargonic officials; differences in mentality between Sumerians and Akkadians. – ᴿRAss 88 (1994) 181-3 (D. *Charpin*).

12607* **Ana Qalʿa: Northedge** A., *al.*, Excavations at ʿAna Qalʿa Island 1988 ➤ 7,d748; 8,e901: ᴿBO 54 (1994) 419-421 (D. *Whitehouse*); Syria 61 (1994) 256s (P. *Leriche*).

12608 **Babylon:** *Marzahn* Joachim, Zum sogenannten Stadtschloss-Grundriss von Babylon [UNGER E. 1931]: AltOrF 21 (1994) 41-49; 3 fig.

12609 **Brak:** *a*) *Matthews* Roger, Imperial catastrophe or local incident? An Akkadian hoard from Tell Brak, Syria: CamArch 4 (1994) 290-302; 14 fig.; – *b*) Brak 1992s: Iraq 55 (1993) 155-199; 54 fig. (David and Joan *Oates*); – *c*) Brak 1976-93/1994: Iraq 56 (1994) 167-176; plan (D. & J. *Oates*) / 177-194 (R. & W. *Matthews*, H. *Mc-Donald*).

12610 **Diyala:** **Auerbach** Elise, Terra cotta plaques from the Diyala and their archaeological and cultural contexts: diss. ᴰ*Gibson* M. Chicago 1994. 564 p. 94-25354. – DissA 55 (1994s) p. 2019.

12611 *Dzharakyan* R. V., ❺ Ethnic structure of the population north of the Diyala Valley (Iraq) in the IIId millennium B.C.: VDI 209 (1994) 3-15; Eng. 16.

12612 [**Hill** H. D.] *Delougaz* Pinhas T., ᴱ*Holland* T. A., *McMahon* Augusta, Khafajah Mounds B, C, and D; OIP 98. Ch 1989, Univ. Or. Inst. xxxiii-235 p.; 31 fig.; 68 pl. $50. – ᴿJNES 53 (1994) 131-3 (P. R. S. *Moorey*).

12613 **Fara: Martin** Harriet P., Fara; a reconstruction... of Shuruppak 1988 ➤ 6,e485; 7,d753: ᴿZAss 84 (1994) 151-8 (N. *Karg*).

12614 **Haaki** (ʿUsaimi and two nearby tells): *Rawi* F. N. H. Al-, *Black* J. A., A rediscovered Akkadian city: Iraq 55 (1993) 147s.

12615 **Ḥatra:** *Aggoula* Basile, L'institution royale à Hatra: Syria 61 (1994) 159-169.

12616 *Gawlikowski* Michał, Fortress Hatra; new evidence on ramparts and their history: MesopT 29 (1994) 147-184; 38 fig.

12617 **Larsa: Wright** Paul H., The city of Larsa in the Neo-Babylonian and Achaemenid periods; a study of urban and intercity relations in antiquity: diss. HUC, ᴰ*Weisberg* D. Cincinnati 1994. 284 p. 94-27341. – DissA 55 (1994s) p. 1544.

12618 **Maškan-Šapir:** *Stone* Elizabeth C., The anatomy of a Mesopotamian city; the Mashkan-shapir project: BuCanadMesop 27 (1994) 15-23; 2 fig.; franç. 15.

12618* **Mohammed Diyab:** ᴱ*Durand* J. M., Recherches... t. M. Diyab 1992: ᴿBuCanadMesop 25 (1993) 71.

12619 **Nimrud: Herrmann** Georgina, Nimrud Ivories 5, 1992 ➤ 8,e931: ᴿBO 51 (1994) 671-4 (E. *Gubel*); Orientalia 63 (1994) 146-150 (Serena M. *Cecchini*); RAss 88 (1994) 73s (P. *Amiet*).

12620 *Brentjes* Burchard, Sebstverherrlichung oder Legitimitätsanspruch?

Gedanken zu dem Thronrelief von Nimrud-Kalaḫ: AltOrF 21 (1994) 50-64; 7 fig.

12620* *Reade* J.E., Revisiting the north-west palace, Nimrud: Orientalia 63 (1994) 273-8; pl. IV-VI.

12621 *Sobolewski* Richard P., Rekonstruktion des Nordwestpalastes in Nimrud; Bemerkungen zu einigen *in situ* gefundenen architektonischen Elementen: → 55, ᶠHROUDA B., Beiträge 1994, 255-264; 6 fig.

12622 **Paley** Samuel M., *Sobolewski* Richard P., Reconstruction of the relief... Kalkḫu III: BaghFor 14, 1992 → 9,14246: ᴿMesopT 29 (1994) 290-2 (A. *Invernizzi*); RAss 88 (1994) 184-6 (B. *Muller*).

12623 *Ninive:* **Kwasman** T., *Parpola* S., Legal transactions of the royal court of Nineveh I: SAA 6. Helsinki 1991, Univ. 369 p.; 2 pl.; 44 items. – ᴿArOr 61 (1993) 324s (J. *Pečirková*); WZKM 84 (1994) 204-9 (M. *Jaroš*).

12624 **Russell** John M., Sennacherib's palace without rival at Nineveh ᴰ1991 → 7,d767*: ᴿZAss 84 (1994) 303s (J.E. *Reade*).

12625 *Nippur:* ᴱ**Ellis** Maria D., Nippur, 35ᵉ Rencontre 1988/92 → 8,687: ᴿBO 51 (1994) 590-3 (H. *Limet*).

12625* *Hunter* Erica C.D., Two Mandaic incantation bowls from Nippur: BaghMitt 25 (1994) 605-619; 1 fig.; pl. 25-26.

12626 **Zettler** Richard L., The Ur III temple of Inanna at Nippur: BBVO 11, 1992 → 8,e938*; 9,14249: ᴿJAOS 114 (1994) 494s (J.N. *Postgate*); OLZ 89 (1994) 144-6 (J. *Oelsner*).

12627 **Zettler** Richard I., Nippur III. Kassite: OIP 111. Ch 1993, Univ. xxxviii-347 p.; ill. 0-918986-91-5. – ᴿZAss 84 (1994) 310-2 (U. *Seidl*).

12628 **Stone** E., *Owen* D., Adoption in... Nippur 1991 → 7,2349: ᴿRB 101 (1994) 443-5 (M. *Sigrist*).

12629 *Salābīḫ:* **Moon** Jane, Catalogue of early dynastic pottery: Abu Salabikh 3, 1987 → 5,e242... 7,d771: ᴿJNES 53 (1994) 67-69 (Karen *Wilson*).

12629* ᴱ**Green** Anthony, Abu Salabikh 4, The 6G ash tip 1993 → 9,14254: ᴿRAss 88 (1994) 187-9 (J.-L. *Huot*).

12630 *Seleucia:* **Invernizzi** Antonio, Capitelli smaltati dal teatro di Seleucia sul Tigri: MesopT 29 (1994) 107-146; 38 fig.

12631 *Sippar:* **Lerberghe** T. van, On storage in Old-Babylonian Sippar: OrLovPer 24 (1993) 29-40; 1 facsim.

12632 **MacGinnis** John, The royal establishment at Sippar in the 6th century B.C.: ZAss 84 (1994) 198-216 + 6 facsim.

12633 **Warka** / Uruk: *Nagel* Wolfram, *Strommenger* Eva, Die Ausgrabungen in Uruk-Warka, Endberichte 1.7.9: Orientalia 63 (1994) 261-272.

12634 **Becker** Andrea, Uruk, Endb 6, 1993 → 9,14265: ᴿMesopT 29 (1994) 286-290 (A. *Invernizzi*, anche su 7).

12635 **Ess** Margarete van, *Pedde* Friedhelm, Kleinfunde II: Uruk Endb 7, 1992 → 8,e963; 9,14266: ᴿOLZ 89 (1994) 385-7 (E. *Lindemeyer*); RAss 88 (1994) 74s (P. *Amiet*).

12636 **Finkbeiner** U., *al.*, Uruk 35-37, 1982-4: Endb 4, 1991 → 9,14269: ᴿBuCanadMesop 25 (1993) 76 (Eng. franç., no author, or? ᴱ*Fortin* M.); ZAss 84 (1994) 291-4 (J.N. *Postgate*).

12637 **Finkbeiner** Uwe, Uruk, Register 1912-1977: 1993 → 9,14268: ᴿMesopT 29 (1994) 284-6 (A. *Invernizzi*); RAss 88 (1994) 89s (J.-L. *Huot*).

T6.7   **Arabia.**

12637* *During Caspers* Elisabeth C. L.,   Further evidence for 'central Asian' materials from the Arabian Gulf: JESHO 37 (1994) 33-53; 17 fig.

12638 ᴱInvernizzi Antonio, *Salles* Jean-François,   Arabia antiqua; Hellenistic centres around Arabia: Serie Or. 70/2.   R 1993, Ist. MEOr. xi-289 p.

12639 *Korotayev* Andrey,   *a)* The Sabaean community (*sbᵓ*, *ᵓsbᵓn*) in the political structure of the Middle Sabaean cultural area: Orientalia 63 (1994) 68-93; – *b)* Middle Sabaean cultural-political area; *Qayls*, their *bayt* and *shaᶜb*:   AulaO 11 (1993) 155-160; – *c)* Some features of Middle Sabaean political culture; clan-alliances: AulaO 12 (1994) 124-8.

12640 **Rice** Michael,   The archaeology of the Arabian Gulf [= 1984 Search for the Paradise land²]. L 1994, Routledge. xvii-369 p.; 71 fig.; 5 maps. £50.   0-415-03268-7. – ᴿAntiquity 68 (1994) 674s (D. T. *Potts*: a fount of misinformation).

12641 **Shahid** Irfan,   Byzantium and the Arabs 1989 ➤ 7,b467; 8,e975: ᴿJNES 53 (1994) 47-50 (W. E. *Kaegi*); WeltOr 25 (1994) 181-4 (J. van *Ess*).

12642 *Šabwa:* ᴱ*Breton* Jean-François,   Fouilles de Shabwa: IFAPO hors série 19, 1992 ➤ 9,14279*:   ᴿBASOR 293 (1994) 90-92 (G. W. *Van Beek*).

T6.9   **Iran,** *Persia;*   Asia centralis.

12643 *Balcer* Jack M.,   The ancient Persian satrapies and satraps in western Anatolia: ArchMIran 26 (1993) 81-90.

12643* **Carter** Elizabeth,   Elam and the Elamites: BuCanadMesop 25 (1993) 51-56; 3 fig.

12644 **Dandamayev** Muhammad A.,   *a)* Iranians in Achaemenid Babylonia: Columbia Iranian 6.   Costa Mesa CA 1992, Mazda.   xi-241 p. – ᴿJAOS 114 (1994) 617-624 (M. W. *Stolper*: numerous corrections); Kratylos 39 (1994) 82-89 (Rüdiger *Schmitt*). – *b)* A political history of the Achaemenid Empire 1989 ➤ 5,b503; 8,d35:   ᴿTEuph 5 (1994) 157-161 (J. *Elayi*).

12644* *Jamzadeh* Parivash,   Few remarks on the significance of the idea of four corners to the Achaemenids [... totality of their empire]: IrAnt 28 (1993) 137-140.

12645 **Koch** Heidemarie,   Achämeniden-Studien. Wsb 1993, Harrassowitz. [iv-] 140 p.   3-447-03328-2.

12646 **Komaroff** Linda,   The golden disk of heaven; metalwork of Timurid Iran: Persian Art 2.   Costa Mesa CA / NY 1992, Mazda / BtPersica.   xi-301 p. $65. – ᴿBSO 57 (1994) 397s (R. *Ward*).

12647 ᶠPERROT Jean,   Contribution à l'histoire de l'Iran, ᴱVallat F. 1990 ➤ 6,138:   ᴿAION 54 (1994) 247-250 (L. *Cagni*).

12647* **Vogelsang** W. J.,   The rise and organization of the Achaemenid empire; the eastern Iranian evidence 1992 ➤ 8,d47:   ᴿTEuph 8 (1994) 176s (M. *Dandamayev*).

12648 *Young* T. Cuylerᴶ,   Architectural developments in Iron Age Western Iran: BuCanadMesop 27 (1994) 25-32; 7 fig.; franç. 25.

12649 *Haft: Herrero* P. †, *Glassner* J. J.,   Haft-Tépé; choix de textes III: IrAnt 28 (1993) 97-135.

12650 *Hajji Firuz:* **Voigt** Mary M.,   Hajji Firuz Tepe, Iran, the neolithic settlement: MusMg 50, Hasanlu report 1. Ph 1983, Univ. Museum. xxviii-431 p.; bibliog. 325-336. 0-934718-49-0.

12653 ***Luristan:*** [*Schmidt* Erich F. †], **Loon** Maurits N. van, *al.*, The Holmes expeditions to Luristan 1989 ➛ 5,e282; 8,e995: RJNES 53 (1994) 133-6 (P. R. S. *Moorey*).

12654 ***Persepolis:*** *a*) *Calmeyer* Peter, Die Gefässe auf den Gabenbringer-Reliefs in Persepolis; – *b*) *Kleiss* Wolfram, Flachensteinbrüche und Einzelsteinbrüche in der Umgebung von Persepolis und Naqsh-i Rustam: ArchMIran 26 (1993) 147-160; 6 fig.; pl. 43-50 / 91-103; 26 fig.; pl. 14-15.

12656 ***Tang-e Qandil:*** *Levit-Tawil* Dalia, Re-dating the Sasanian reliefs at Tang-e Qandil and Barm-e Dilat: composition and style as dating criteria: IrAnt 28 (1993) 141-168; 17 fig.

12657 ***Taq-e Bustan:*** *a*) *Musche* B., Römische Einflüsse auf den Taq-e Bustan; – *b*) *Kroll* S., Ḥabur-Ware im Osten, oder: Der TAVO auf Irrwegen im Iranischen Hochland; – *c*) *Kleiss* Wolfram, Ein Bauwerk im Hügel — in Zentral-Iran: ➛ 55, FHROUDA B., Beiträge 1994, 193-199; 2 fig. / 159-166; map / 143-6; 2 fig.; pl. XIV.

12658 ***Vakilabad:*** *Kerner* Susanne, Vakilabad [130 k SE Shiraz] – Keramik: BBVO 13. B 1993, Reimer. 256 p.; 91 fig.; 71 pl. DM 88. – RArOr 62 (1994) 352s (P. *Charvát*).

12659 E**Dani** A. H., *Masson* V. M., History of civilization of Central Asia, I. The dawn of civilization; earliest times to 700 B.C. P 1992, UNESCO. 535 p.; 108 fig.; 14 maps. £27. 92-3-102719-0. – RAntiquity 68 (1994) 672-4 (S. *Simpson*).

12660 *During Caspers* Elisabeth C. L., Widening horizons; contacts between Central Asia (the Murghabo-Bactrian culture) and the Indus Valley civilization towards the close of the third and early centuries of the second millennium B.C.: AION 54 (1994) 171-198, IV pl.

12661 **Hiebert** Fredrik T., Origins of the Bronze Age Oasis civilization in Central Asia: AmerSchPrehRBu 42. CM 1994, Harvard Peabody Museum. xxxvii-200 p.; bibliog. 178-180. 0-87365-545-1.

12662 **Holt** Frank L., Alexander the Great and Bactria; the formation of a Greek frontier in central Asia: Mnemosyne supp 104. Leiden 1988, Brill. x-144 p. $29. 90-04-08612-9. – RSyria 71 (1994) 470-472 (P. *Leriche*).

12663 *Lamberg-Karlovsky* C. C., *al.*, The Oxus civilization; the Bronze Age of central Asia [... Bactria]: Antiquity 68 (1994) 353-427; ill.

12664 **Pitschikjan** Igor R., Oxos-Schatz und Oxos-Tempel; Achämenidische Kunst in Mittelasien. B 1992, Akademie. xii-155 p.; 40 fig. DM 136. 3-05-002145-4. – RMesopT 29 (1994) 328-330 (A. *Invernizzi*).

12665 E**Possehl** Gregory L., Harappan civilization, a recent perspective 2rev. [1 1979]. New Delhi 1993, American Institute of Indian Studies / Oxford-IBH. xix-595 p. 0-8364-2871-4.

12666 *Possehl* G. L., Ⓡ The Harappan civilization and its hunter-gatherer neighbours: VDI 207 (1993) 119-126; Eng. 126s.

12667 *Winkelmann* Sylvia, Elam-Beluchistan-Baktrien; wo liegen die Vorläufer der Hockerplastiken der Induskultur? Erste Gedanken: IrAnt 28 (1993) 57-8 + 13 fig.

T7.1 **Aegyptus,** *generalia.*

12668 **Arnold** D., Building in Egypt; pharaonic stone masonry. Ox 1991, UP.

ix-316 p.; 336 fig. $69.   0-19-506350-3. – ᴿAJA 98 (1994) 359s (E. P. *U-phill*: best since S. CLARKE/E. ENGELBACH 1930).

12669 **Beaucour** Fernand, *Laissus* Yves, *Orgogozco* Chantal,   The discovery of Egypt; artists, travellers and scientists [Napoleon to Lepsius].   P 1993, Flammarion.   272 p. 'wonderfully illustrated'. $50 [BAR-W 20,1 (1994) 10].

12670 ᶠBECKERATH Jürgen von, ᴱ**Eggebrecht** Arne, *al.* 1990 ⇥ 6,16; 9,14306: ᴿCdÉ 69 (1994) 251-4 (D. *Berg*).

12671 *Cherpion* Nadine,   Le 'cône d'onguent', gage de survie: BIFAO 94 (1994) 79-91 + 27 fig.

12672 *Cruz-Uribe* Eugene,   A model for the political structure of ancient Egypt: ⇥ 7 supra, ᶠBAER K., For his Ka 1994.

12672* **Davis** Whitney,   The canonical tradition in ancient Egyptian art: New ArtHistCrit, 1989 ⇥ 7,b907; 8,d944: ᴿAJA 97 (1993) 168-170 (Florence D. *Friedman*).

12673 *Dykstra* Darrell,   Pyramids, prophets, and progress; ancient Egypt in the writings of ʿAlī Mubārak [1823-93]: JAOS 114 (1994) 54-65.

12673* **Fazzini** R. A., *Bianchi* R. S., Cleopatra's Egypt, Brooklyn museum exhibition 1988 ⇥ 5,b862*: ᴿGnomon 66 (1994) 165-171 (Jutta *Fischer*).

12674 **Fischer** Jean-Jacques,   La moisson des dieux; P 1994, Julliard. [xix-] 289 p.; 24 pl. F 125. 2-260-01131-4.

Görg Manfred, Mythos ... Credo ... Ägypten 1992 ⇥ 10752.

12675 **Herbin** François R.,   Le livre de parcourir l'éternité; diss. Lille, ᴰ*Valbelle* D.: OrLovAnal 58. Lv 1994, Peeters. xxi-584 p.; XXXV + 18 pl. 90-6831-508-0.

12675* **Henein** Nessim H.,   Poteries et proverbes d'Egypte 1992 ⇥ 9,13629: ᴿJAmEg 31 (1994) 241s (J. *Meloy*).

12676 **Hornung** Erik,   Idea into image; essays on ancient Egyptian thought, ᵀ*Bredeck* Elizabeth, 1992 ⇥ 9,143330*: ᴿAJA 97 (1993) 575 (W. *Davis*).

12677 ᶠIVERSEN Erik: The heritage of ancient Egypt, ᴱ**Osing** J., *Nielsen* E. K.: Niebuhr 13, 1992 ⇥ 8,94: ᴿAegyptus 79 (1994) 185s (Patrizia *Piacentini*); JAOS 114 (1994) 100-2 (R. S. *Bianchi*).

12678 **Iversen** E.,   The myth of Egypt and its hieroglyphs in European tradition: Bollingen Mythologies. Princeton 1993. 178 p.; 24 pl. – ᴿAegyptus 79 (1994) 183-5 (Patrizia *Piacentini*).

12679 **Jacobsohn** Helmuth, Gesammelte Schriften, ᴱ*Jungraithmayr* H.: Collectanea 43, 1992 ⇥ 8,257: ᴿOLZ 89 (1994) 257s (R. S. *Bianchi*).

12680 **Jacobsson** Inga,   Aegyptiaca from Late Bronze Age Cyprus: SIMA 112. Jonsered 1994, Åström. iv-125 p.; 18 charts; 95 pl.; 3 maps. 91-7081-053-2.

12681 **Karenga** Maulana,   The moral ideal in ancient Egypt; a study in classical African ethics: diss. Univ. 8. California, ᴰ*Clark* H. LA 1992. – RTLv 26, p. 574.

12682 *Leclant* Jean, *Clerc* Gisèle, Fouilles et travaux en Égypte et au Soudan, 1992-3: Orientalia 63 (1994) 345-473; pl. VI-XLV.

12682* **Lesko** Leonard H.,   [Computer hieroglyphic] High tech projects for research and distribution: ZägSpr 121 (1994) 117-122.

12683 **Masi** Giuseppe,   Lo spiritualismo egiziano antico; il pensiero religioso egiziano classico. Bo 1994, CLUEB. 339 p.; bibliog. 325-330; 16 color. pl.

12684 **Metwally** Emad El-,   Entwicklung der Grabdekoration in den altägyptischen Privatgräbern; ikonographische Analyse der Totenkultdarstellungen von der Vorgeschichte bis zum Ende der 4. Dynastie [Diss. Gö

1991]: GöOrF 4/24. Gö 1992. xxvi-251 p.; 183 fig. DM 98. – ᴿWZKM 84 (1994) 175-180 (P. *Jánosi*).

12685 **Morley** Jacqueline,   Sapresti vivere come un antico egizio?   Novara 1994, De Agostini. 68 p.; color. ill. Lᵐ 23. – ᴿArcheo 9,114 (1994) 126s (S. *Moscati*: anche su 'Azteco' 'Vichingo' 'Romano').

12686 *Pruneti* Piero,   Thomas MANN e l'Egitto: ArchViva 13,47 (1994) 58-61 . 64.

12687 **Quirke** Stephen, *Spencer* Jeffrey,   The British Museum book of ancient Egypt [a revision of JAMES T. ²1979] 1992 ➤ 8,g40: £15.   0-7141-0965-7. – ᴿBO 51 (1994) 318-320 (Emily *Teeter*).

12688 **Robins** Gay,   Proportion and style in ancient Egyptian art.   Austin 1994, Univ. Texas.   283 p.; drawings *Fowler* Ann S.

12689 *a*) *Robins* Gay,   Some principles of compositional dominance and gender hierarchy in Egyptian art; – *b*) *Bochi* Patricia A.,   Images of time in ancient Egyptian art: JAmEg 31 (1944) 33-40 / 55-62; 6 fig.

12690 **Schott** Siegfried †, ᴱ*Schott* Erika,   Bücher und Bibliotheken im Alten Ägypten 1990 ➤ 6,e591:   ᴿOLZ 89 (1994) 133 (U. *Luft*); WeltOr 25 (1994) 128s (H. W. *Fischer-Elfert*).

12691 **Seidlmayer** Stephen J.,   Gräberfelder aus dem Übergang vom Alten zum Mittleren Reich,   Heid 1990, Orientverlag. 465 p.; 173 fig.   3-927552-01-1.

12692 **Shorkova** T.A.,   ❽ The study of archaeological cultures of Lower Egypt. 1994: ᴿRossArkh (1994,1) 200-4 (*ipse*).

12693 **Siliotti** Alberto,   Egypt; splendours of an ancient civilization.   L 1994, Thames & H.   291 p.   0-500-01647-X.

12694 **Springborg** Patricia,   Royal persons; patriarchal monarchy and the feminine principle.   L 1990, Unwin Hyman.   xv-326 p.; 32 fig. $(sic)30. 0-04-445376-0. – ᴿJEA 80 (1994) 237-9 (J. G. *Griffiths*: largely on Egypt, despite her L. KOLAKOWSKI formation and her Sydney lectureship on Government).

12695 *Westendorf* Wolfhart,   Ägypten und das Alte Testament: TRu 59 (1994) 337-345.

12695* **Wilkinson** Richard H.,   Reading Egyptian art; a hieroglyphic guide to ancient Egyptian painting and sculpture. L 1994, Thames & H.   224 p.; 450 fig.   0-500-27751-6.

12696 **Ziegler** Christiane, Catalogue de stèles, peintures et reliefs ég. [avant 2040] 1990 ➤ 6,d5; 8,g56:   ᴿBO 51 (1994) 73-76 (K. *Martin*).

т7.2   **Luxor,** *Karnak* [East Bank]   –   **Thebae** [West Bank].

12697 **La Fur** Daniel,   La conservation des peintures murales des temples de Karnak.   P 1994, RCiv.   211 p.   2-86538-245-1.

12698 *Cruz-Uribe* Eugene,   The Khonsu cosmogony: JAmEg 31 (1994) 169-189.

12698* *Grimal* Nicolas, *Larché* François, *al.*,   Cahiers de Karnak 4.   P 1993, RCiv.   xx-263 p.; ill.   2-86538-227-3. 11 art. on 1989-92 seasons.

12699 **Jacquet-Gordon** H.,   Karnak-Nord VI. Le trésor de Thoutmosis Ier; la décoration: Fouilles 32,   Le Caire 1988, IFAO. I. vi-301 p.; 34 fig., 1 colour pl.; II. xii-74 pl.   2-7247-0073-2.

12700 **Gohary** Jocelyn,   Akhenaten's *Sed*-festival at Karnak 1992 ➤ 8,g66: ᴿClasW 88 (1994s) 129s (W. H. *Peck*).

12701 **Redford** Donald,   The excavation of Kom el-Aḥmar and environs: Akhenaten Temple Project 2.   Toronto 1994. xvi-125 p.; 16 fig. 128 pl.   0-921428-11-1.

12702 **Redford** Susan & Donald,   The tomb of Reʿa (TT 201): Akhenaten Temple Project 4.   Toronto 1994.   iv-35 p.; 34 pl.   0-921428-10- 3.
12703 **Sternberg-el Hotabi** Heike, Der Propylon des Month-Tempels 1993 ➤ 9,14359:   ᴿArOr 62 (1994) 438s (L. *Bareš*).

12704 *Der Manuelian* Peter, *Loeben* Christian E.,   New light on the recarved sarcophagus of Hatshepsut and Thutmose I in the Museum of Fine Arts, Boston: JEA 79 (1993) 121-155; 18 fig.; pl. VI-XIV.
12705 **Niwiński** Andrzej, Studies on the illustrated Theban funerary papyri: OBO 86, 1989 ➤ 6,e625; 9,14361:   ᴿCdÉ 69 (1994) 264-6 (*Saphinaz-Amal* Naguib).
12706 **Reeves** Nicholas, The complete Tutankhamun 1990 ➤ 6,e627 ... 8,g76: ᴿJEA 80 (1994) 253-6 (Marianne *Eaton-Krauss*: the tomb; only 5% on the man; inaccuracies).
12707 **Reeves** C. N.,   After Tutʾankhamūn; research and excavation in the royal necropolis at Thebes [conference Kent, June 15-17, 1990].   L 1992, Kegan Paul.   xvi-211 p.; 40 fig.; 24 pl. $95.   0-7103-0406-1. – ᴿAJA 97 (1993) 801s (W. H. *Peck*); DiscEg 27 (1993) 105-110 (A. *Dodson*); OLZ 89 (1994) 370-4 (M. *Eaton-Krauss*).
12708 **Reeves** Carl N.,   Valley of the Kings; the decline of a royal necropolis. L 1990, Kegan Paul.   xliii-376 p.; 15 pl.   0-7103-0368-8. – ᴿCdÉ 69 (1994) 271-8 (A. *Dodson*); JEA 80 (1994) 243-7 (Hartwig *Altenmüller* & Christiane *Preuss*, deutsch); OLZ 89 (1994) 375-7 (M. *Stoof*).
12709 *Romer* J. & E., The rape of Tutankhamun 1993 ➤ 9,14397:   ᴿAntiquity 68 (1994) 663s (F. A. *Hassan*: does more harm than good).
12710 *Ryan* Donald P.,   Exploring the Valley of the Kings [... the less glamorous tombs]: Archaeology 47,1 (1994) 52-59; color. ill.
12711 **Dorman** Peter F.,   The monuments of Senenmut [TT 71 & 353] 1988 ➤ 7,d871; 8,g84*:   ᴿCdÉ 69 (1994) 278-282 (J.-L. *Chappaz*).
12712 **Dziobek** Eberhard,   Die Gräber des Vezirs Ueer-Amun Theben Nr. 51 und 131: ArchVeröff 84.   Mainz 1994, von Zabern.   107 p.; 48 pl. + 49-95 foldouts + 14 plans.   3-8053-1495-7.
12713 *Dziobek* Eberhard,   Das Grab des Ineni, Theben Nr. 81: DAI-K 68, 1992 ➤ 8,g87:   ᴿArchWsz 44 (1993) 133s (A. *Niwiński*); BO 51 (1994) 544 (A. *Mekhitarian*).
12714 *Kákosy* László,   Ninth preliminary report on the Hungarian excavation in Thebes, tomb no. 32: AcArchH 46 (1994) 21-31; 10 fig.
12715 *Russmann* Edna R.,   Relief decoration in the tomb of Mentuemhat (TT 34): JAmEg 31 (1994) 1-19; 11 fig.
12716 **Barthelmess** Petra,   Der Übergang ins Jenseits in den thebanischen Beamtengräbern der Ramessidenzeit [Diss. Heid. 1989]: StArGAä 2. Heid 1992, Orient-V. [➤ 8,g83]; xvi-200 p.; 50 fig.; 4 pl.:   ᴿArOr 61 (1993) 320 (L. *Bareš*); Orientalia 63 (1994) 123-6 (K.-J. *Seyfried*).
12716* *Seyfried* Karl-J.,   Bestattungsdarstellung und Begräbnisort in thebanischen Privat-Gräbern der Ramessidenzeit: BibNot 71 (1994) 11-19.

12717 Deir el-Bahari epigraphy 1994: ➤ 11498 (Reports 1994) 48-53 (V. *Karkowski*) -66 (*al.*).
12718 *Sowada* Karin N.,   A relief fragment from the temple of Tuthmosis III at Deir el-Bahari: MeditArch 7 (1994) 175-183; 3 fig.
12719 ᴱ**Lesko** Leonard H.,   Pharaoh's workers; the villagers of Deir

el-Medina. Ithaca 1994, Cornell Univ. x-197p.; (color.) ill. 0-8014-2915-3; pa. -8143-0.

12720 *Meskell* Lynn, Deir el Medina in hyperreality; seeking the people of pharaonic Egypt: MeditArch 7 (1994) 193-216; 7 fig.

12721 *Gabolde* Luc, *al.*, Le 'tombeau suspendu' de la 'Vallée de l'Aigle' [Deir el Médina]: BIFAO 94 (1994) 173-235; 90 fig.; + XXIV pl.

12721* **Shedid** Abdel Ghaffar, Das Grab des Sennedjem; ein Künstlergrab der 19. Dynastie in Deir el Medineh. Mainz 1994, von Zabern. 55p. 3-8053-1756-5.

12722 **Tosi** Mario, La cappella di Maia; un pittore a Deir el-Medina: QuadMusEgTorino. T 1994, Artema. 84p. Lm 30. – RArchViva 13,48 (1994) 91 (A. *Bongioianni*).

12723 *Jaritz* Horst, *Bickel* Susanne, Une porte monumentale d'Amenhotep III; second rapport préliminaire sur les blocs réemployés dans le temple de Merenptah à Gourna: BIFAO 94 (1994) 277-285; 3 fig.; color. pl. p.483.485.

T7.3   Amarna.

12724 TEMoran William L., The Amarna letters 1992 → 8,9627; 9,9901: RBAR-W 20,1 (1994) 6-8 (A. F. *Rainey*); RAss 88 (1994) 87s (D. *Charpin*).

12725 **Moran** W., Les lettres d'El Amarna 1987 → 2,e766... 9,14378: RWZKM 80 (1990) 273-7 (H. *Hirsch*).

12725* — *Gianto* Agustin, Subject fronting in the Jerusalem Amarna letters: Orientalia 63 (1994) 209-225.

12726 **Beinlich** Horst, *Saleh* Mohammed, Corpus der hieroglyphischen Inschriften aus dem Grab des Tutanchamun 1989 → 5,e342; 7,d869: RCdÉ 69 (1994) 98-101 (C. *Vandersleyen*).

12727 **Bomann** Ann E., Private chapel... Amarna... Deir/Medina 1991 → 7, a776; 9,14389*: RBO 51 (1994) 72s (A. I. *Sadek*).

12728 **Cimmino** Franco, Tutankhamun; la fine di una dinastia. Mi c.1993, Rusconi. 350p.; 20 fig.; 8 pl. Lm 34. – RArcheo 9,108 (1994) 118 (S. *Pernigotti*). → 12706.

12729 *Davoli* Paola, Un rilievo postamarniano del Museo Civico di Bologna: Aegyptus 74 (1994) 39-49; II pl.

12729* *a) Decker* Wolfgang, Ein Amarna-Block mit Wagendarstellung; – *b) Redford* Donald B., East Karnak and the Sed-Festival of Akhenaten: → 37, FLECLANT J., 1 (1994) 437-447; 11 fig. / 485-492; 3 fig.

12730 **Endruweit** Albrecht, Städtischer Wohnbau in Ägypten; klimagerechte Lehmarchitektur in Amarna. B 1994, Mann. 221p.; 11 pl.; Bibliog. 205-214. 3-7861-1671-7.

12731 *Gabolde* Marc, Baketaton fille de Kiya [tombe de Houya, Amarna]: BSocÉg 16 (1992) 27-40; 10 fig.

12732 **Hess** Richard S., Amarna personal names: ASOR diss. 9, 1993 → 9, 14392; $37.50. – ROTAbs 17 (1994) 430 (M. S. *Smith*).

12733 **Kemp** B., Amarna reports 5, 1989 → 7,d895b; 8,g116: RCdÉ 69 (1994) 286-8 (J.-L. *Chappaz*).

12733* *a) Krauss* Rolf, Piktogramme des jüngeren Goldhorusnamens von Achenaten; – *b) Pflüger* Kurt, Beiträge zur Amarnazeit: ZägSpr 121 (1994) 106-117; 4 fig. / 123-132.

12734 **Martin** Geoffrey T., The royal tomb at el-ʿAmarna 2, 1989 → 6,e646; 8,g120: RCdÉ 69 (1994) 282-4 (A. R. *Schulman*); JEA 79 (1993) 300-2 (R. *Krauss*).

12735 **Murnane** J. William, *Van Siclen* Charles C.[III], The boundary stelae of Akhenaten. L 1993, Kegan Paul. xv-227 p.; 32 pl. £75. – [R]Orientalia 63 (1994) 121-3 (J. von *Beckerath*).

12736 *Owen* Gwil, *Kemp* Barry, Craftsmen's work patterns in unfinished tombs at Amarna: CamArch 4 (1994) 121-129; 3 fig.

12737 *Podzuweit* Christian †, Bemerkungen zur mykenischen Keramik von Tell el-Amarna: ↠ 35, [F]FREY O., 1994, 457-474; 7 fig.

12738 *Schofield* L., *Parkinson* R. B., Of helmets and heretics; a possible Egyptian representation of Mycenaean warriors on a papyrus from el-Amarna: AnBritAth 89 (1994) 157-170; 5 fig.; pl. 21s + color. front.

12739 *Shaw* Ian, Balustrades, stairs and altars in the cult of the Aten at el-Amarna: JEA 80 (1994) 109-127; 9 fig.

12740 *Weatherhead* Fran, Wall-paintings from the North Harim in the great palace at Amarna: JEA 80 (1994) 198-201; 3 fig.

T7.4 **Memphis, Ṣaqqara – Pyramides, Giza** (Cairo).

12741 Saqqara 1993, Inuia tomb: JEA 79 (1993) 1-9; pl. I-III (H. D. *Schneider, al.*); Memphis 1992, 11-16 (Lisa *Giddy*, D. *Jeffreys*).

12742 **Cherpion** Nadine, Mastabas 1989 ↠ 5,e387 ... 8,g132: [R]JNES 53 (1994) 55-58 (Ann M. *Roth*).

12743 *Daoud* Khaled, Ramose, an overseer of the chamberlains at Memphis: JEA 80 (1994) 202-7.

12744 *Devauchelle* Didier, Un archétype de relief cultuel en Égypte ancienne [Pharaon massacrant les ennemis; 12 stèles de la région memphite]: BSocFrÉg 131 (1994) 38-57; 8 fig.; III pl.

12744* a) *Ghaly* Holeil, Ein Friedhof von Ziegelmastabas des Alten Reiches am Unasaufweg in Saqqara; – b) *Jeffreys* David, *Tavares* Ana, The historic landscape of Early Dynastic Memphis: MiDAI-K 50 (1994) 57-69; 5 fig.; pl. 6-8 / 143-159 + 15 fig.

12745 *Giddy* Lisa, Memphis and Saqqara during the Late Old Kingdom; some topographical considerations: ↠ 37, [F]LECLANT J. 1 (1994) 189-200; foldout plan.

12745* **Giddy** Lisa L., The Anubieion at Saqqāra II. The cemeteries 1992 ↠ 9,14405: [R]ArOr 62 (1994) 436s (L. *Bareš*).

12746 — **Jeffreys** D. G., *Smith* H. S., The Anubieion at Saqqara I, 1998 ↠ 5,g320: [R]CdÉ 69 (1994) 289-291 (H. De *Meulenaere*).

12747 *Harpur* Yvonne, Stone pillaging for the New Kingdom tombs at South Saqqara: ↠ 69, [F]LACEY W., Prudentia 26,1 (1994) 1-15; 13 fig.

12748 **Khouli** Ali el-, *Kanawati* Naguib, Excavations at Saqqara north-west of Teti's pyramid II 1988 ↠ 5,e391; 8,g135: [R]BO 51 (1994) 58-61 (Eva *Martin-Pardey*).

12749 **Kromer** Karl, Nezlet Batran ... Mastaba/Giseh 1991 ↠ 7,d926: [R]BO 51 (1994) 61-63 (A. O. *Bolshakov*).

12750 **Lloyd** A. B., *al.*, Saqqara tombs [... epigraphic] II 1990 ↠ 6,e659: [R]BO 51 (1994) 54-58 (H. *Altenmüller*); JEA 80 (1994) 239s (N. *Kanawati*; his review of I was in BO 43,409).

12751 **Martin** G. T., The Memphite tomb of Horemheb 1989 ↠ 5,e349; 6,e660: [R]OLZ 89 (1994) 30-36 (P. *Pamminger*).

12752 **Martin** Geoffrey T., Auf der Suche nach dem verlorenen Grab; neue Ausgrabungen verschollener und unbekannter Grabanlagen aus der Zeit des Tutanchamun und Ramses II. in Memphis [The hidden tombs 1991 ↠ 7,d910], [T]*Winter* Ute: KuGaW 60. Mainz 1994, von Zabern. 293 p. 3-8053-1615-1.

12753 **Maystre** C., Les grands prêtres ... Memphis: OBO 113, 1992 ➤ 8,b493: ᴿZAW 105 (1994) 532 (O. *Kaiser*).

12754 **Raven** Maarten J., *al.*, The tomb of Iurudef 1991 ➤ 7,d913; 9,14401: ᴿJEA 80 (1994) 256s (R. van *Walsem*).

12755 **Vos** R.L., The Apis embalming ritual [< Diss. Amst. 1984]: Or-LovAnal 50. Lv 1993, Peeters. 423 p. + ill. apart. Fb 3250. – ᴿArOr 62 (1994) 437s (L. *Bareš*); Enchoria 21 (1994) 186-191 (F. *Quack*).

12756 **Wietheger** Cäcilia, Der Jeremias-Kloster zu Saqqara 1992 ➤ 9,14407: ᴿTR 90 (1994) 478s (T. *Baumeister*).

12757 **Zivie** Alain, Découverte à Saqqarah: le vizir [Aperia] oublié 1990 ➤ 6,e666: ᴿJEA 80 (1994) 251-3 (G.T. *Martin*).

12758 **Hawass** Zahi, *Lehner* Mark, *a*) The passage under the Sphinx: ➤ 73, ᶠLECLANT J. 1 (1994) 201-216; 9 fig.; – *b*) The great sphinx of Giza; who built it, and why? Can the sphinx be saved?: Archaeology 47,5 (1994) 30-47; ill.

12759 **Yoshimura** Sakuji, *Tanimoto* C., *Tonouchi* S., Monitoring plan and practical design concept for the restoration of the Great Sphinx; through the First International Symposium [28 Febr.-3 Mar. 1992] towards global treatment of the Sphinx: Studies in Egyptian culture 9. Tokyo 1992, Maseda Univ. 41 p.; 12 fig.

12759* **Dauval** Robert, *Gilbert* Adrian, The Orion mystery; unlocking the secrets of the pyramids. L 1994, Heinemann. xix-325 p. bibliog. 308-314. 0-434-00074-4.

12760 *a*) *Allen* James P., Reading a pyramid [... importance of the location and order of the pyramid texts]; – *b*) *Englund* Gertie, La lumière et la répartition des textes dans la pyramide; – *c*) *Edwards* I.E.S., Do the Pyramid Texts suggest an explanation for the abandonment of the subterranean chamber of the Great Pyramid?; – *d*) *Crozier-Brelot* Claude, Supplément à une concordance informatisée des Textes des Pyramides: ➤ 37, ᶠLECLANT J. 1 (1994) 5-28; 1 fig. / 169-180 / 159-160 / 141-6.

12761 *a*) *Berger* Catherine, À la quête de nouvelles versions des Textes des Pyramides; à propos des reines de la fin de l'Ancien Empire; – *b*) *Cour-Marty* Marguerite-Anne, Les Textes des Pyramides témoignent du souci de normalisation des anciens Égyptiens; – *c*) *Pantalacci* Laure, Les noms composés dans les Textes des Pyramides; essai d'évaluation; – *d*) *Heerma van Voss* Matthieu, Spruch 659; – *e*) *Osing* Jürgen, Spruch 534; – *f*) *Assmann* Jan, Spruch 23: ➤ 37, ᶠLECLANT J. 1 (1994) 73-80; fig. 5 / 123-139; 3 fig. / 285-291 / 217-220 / 279-284 / 45-59.

12761* ᶠEDWARDS I.E.S., Pyramid studies, ᴱBaines J., *al.* 1988 ➤ 4,41: ᴿCdÉ 69 (1994) 89-93 (N. *Strudwick*).

12762 **Stadelmann** Rainer, Die sogenannten Luftkanale der Cheopspyramide, Modellkorridore für den Aufstieg des Königs zum Himmel: MiDAI-K 50 (1994) 285-294; 4 fig.; pl. 53-56.

12762* **Arnold** Dieter, The south cemeteries of Lisht [I. 1988 ➤ 5,e415], III. 1992 ➤ 8,6161.

12763 **Arnold** D., Pyramid of Senwosret I, Lisht 1988 ➤ 8,g161: ᴿBO 51 (1994) 63-68 (J. *Brinks*) [69-72, U. *Luft* on the control-marks].

12764 *McGovern* Patrick R., *al.*, The archaeological origin and significance of the [List] dolphin vase as determined by neutron activation analysis: BASOR 296 (1994) 31-43; 8 fig.

12765 *Grossmann* Peter, *al.*,   Zur römischen Festung von Babylon – Alt-Kairo: ArchAnz (1994) 271-287; 12 fig.
12766 **MacKenzie** Neil D.,   Ayyubid Cairo; a topographical study.   Cairo 1992, American Univ. vii-209 p. 977-424-275-0.
12767 **Raymond** André,   Le Caire [642-..]. P 1993, Fayard. 428 p.; cover map. F 150. – ᴿBSO 57 (1994) 594 (P. M. *Holt*: erudite, of major importance); JESHO 37 (1994) 191-3 (I. M. *Lapidus*).
12768 **Rizkana** Ibrahim, *Seeher* Jürgen, Maadi I-IV: DAI-K Veröff. 64s. 80s. Mainz 1987-8-9-90, von Zabern. 112 p., 9 fig., 89 pl., 1 plan; 115 p., 17 fig., 123 pl.; 141 p., 39 fig., 43 pl.; 178 p., 268 fig., 98 pl. 3-8053-0925-2; -0980-5; -1050-1; -1156-7. – ᴿAJA 98 (1994) 357-9 (J. M. *Weinstein*).

T7.5 Delta Nili.

12769 *Alamein* Marina: ➤ 11498, Polish 6 (Reports 1994) 28-36; 4 fig. (W. *Daszewski*).
12770 *Damiano-Appia* Maurizio,   Sulle tracce di Alessandro [... Siwa, Mersa Matruh]. ArchViva 13,44 (1994) 18-31.

12771 *Alexandria* 1994:   ➤ 11498, Polish 6 (Reports 1994) 11-20 (B. *Majcherek*; preservation W. *Kołątaj* 5-50).
12772 Alexandrie 1992s: BCH 118 (1994) 503-519; 15 fig. (J.-Y. *Empereur, al.*).
12773 *a) Barry* William D.,   Popular violence and the stability of Roman Alexandria, 30 B.C. - A.D. 215; – *b) Fraser* P. M., Byzantine Alexandria, decline and fall: ➤ 9,2, ꜰABOU DAOUD D. (1993) 19-34 / 91-105; pl. XVI.
12774 *Daszewski* A. Wiktor,   Notes sur la trame urbaine de l'ancienne Alexandrie: CRAI (1994) 423-9; 3 fig. (plans).
12775 **Delia** Diana,   Alexandrian citizenship 1991 ➤ 8,g172; 9,14426:   ᴿBO 51 (1994) 352s (J. *Whitehorne*).
12776 *a) Fernández-Galiano* Dimas,   Un monasterio pitagórico; los Terapeutas de Alejandría; – *b) Blázquez* J. M.,   La alta sociedad de Alejandría según el Pedagogo de Clemente: Gerión 11 (1993) 245-269; 1 fig. / 185-227.
12777 **Fernández Sangrador** J. J.,   Las origines de la comunidad cristiana de Alejandría: Plenitudo temporis 1.   S 1994, Univ. Pontificia. 233 p.; bibliog. 191-215; 88-7299-310-8. – ᴿArTGran 57 (1994) 435 (C. *Granado*); RechSR 82 (1994) 210 (P. *Vallin*); RET 54 (1994) 216s (J. J. *Ayán*); Salmanticensis 41 (1994) 457-9 (E. *Romero-Pose*).
12778 *Horbury* William,   A personal name in a jar-inscription in Hebrew characters from Alexandria [Kom ed-Dikka 1985; *Fiema* Z. T. 1985]: VT 44 (1994) 103-7.
12779 *a) Nibbi* Alessandra,   Some remarks about the ancient inhabitants of the Alexandria region; – *b) Pearson* Birger A.,   The Acts of Mark and the topography of ancient Alexandria.
12780 **Blum** Rudolf, KALLIMACHOS [303-240 B.C.]; the Alexandrian library and the origins of bibliography [1977], ᵀ*Willisch* Hans M.   Madison 1992, Univ. Wisconsin. ix-282 p. $37.50. – ᴿJAOS 114 (1994) 102s (A. *Kamesar*).
12780* **Pakrasi** Minoti,   The world of libraries in antiquity and in the Renaissance; the heritage of libraries and library science: diss. San José State 1994, ᴰ*Main* Linda. 105 p. [DissA-disk: MAI 33 (1994s) p. 6.
12781 *Salcedo Garces* Fabiola,   ¿Alejandría o África? ambigüedad y ambivalencia: ArEspArq 67 (1994) 71-78.

12782 *Atrib* (Benha) 1994: ➤ 11498, Polish (1994) 37-47; 3 fig. (K. *Myśliwiec*).

12783 *Dabᶜa:* Bietak Manfred, *a)* Des fresques minoennes dans le delta oriental du Nil [Dabᶜa]: MondeB 88 (1994) 42-44; – *b)* ..., *al.*, Neue Grabungsergebnisse aus Tell el-Dabᶜa und ᶜEzbet Ḥelmi im östlichen Nildelta 1989-91: ÄgLev 4 (1993) 9-58; 20 fig. + 22 pl.

12783* Dabᶜa 1992/1993: JbÖsA 62-B (Grabungen 1993) 5-8 / 63-B (Grabungen 1994) auch 5-8 (J. *Dorner*).

12784 *Mashuṭa:* Crawford Patricia L., Man-land relationships in the Wadi Tumilat of Egypt at Tell el-Maskhuta; a paleoethnobotanical perspective: diss. ᴰ*Hansen* Julie. Boston Univ. 1994. 335 p. 94-17315. – DissA 55 (1994s) p. 106.

12785 **Schneider** Thomas, [Maskhuta] Asiatische Personennamen in ägyptischen Quellen des Neuen Reiches; OBO 114, 1992 ➤ 8,9734: ᴿOrientalia 63 (1994) 127-9 (J. E. *Hoch*).

12786 *Merimdé:* Eiwanger J., Merimdé-Benisalam III. Kairo 1992, DAI Veröff. 59. 143 p. – ᴿArchWsz 44 (1993) 131 (M. *Kobusiewicz*).

12787 *Naukratis:* Muhs Brian, The great temenos of Naukratis: JAmEg 31 (1994) 99-113; 8 fig.

12788 *Tuk/Qaramus:* Zauzich Karl-T., Philologische Bemerkungen zum Schatz von Tuch el-Qaramus [Ostdelta]: Enchoria 21 (1994) 101-6 (90-100).

12789 *Tanis:* Brissaud Philippe, Tanis, cité des énigmes: MondeB 87 (1994) 41-45; ill.

12790 *Yahudiyya:* Parente Fausto, Onias III's death and the founding of the temple of Leontopolis: ➤ 123, Mem. SMITH M., Josephus 1992/4, 69-98.

T7.6 *Alii situs Aegypti* **alphabetice.**

12791 *Abu Mina* 1993: BSACopte 33 (1994) 91-104; 8 fig.; pl. XII-XV (P. G-*rossmann, al.*).

12792 *Abu Shaᶜar* (Red Sea coast S of Sinai tip): JAmEg 31 (1994) 133-168; 29 fig. (S. E. *Sidebotham*); DumbO 48 (1994) 263-275; 23 fig.; map (also S. E. *Sidebotham*).

12792* *Abydos:* Brovarski Edward, Abydos in the Old Kingdom and First Intermediate Period, Part I: ➤ 37, ᶠLECLANT J. 1 (1994) 99-126 + 7 fig.

12793 *Adaïma:* Midant-Reynes Béatrix, *al.*, [Esna], Le site prédynastique d'Adaïma; rapport de la cinquième campagne de fouilles [1993]: BIFAO 94 (1994) 329-348 [359-375, *Poupet* Pierre, sédiments].

12794 *Ašmunein:* Bailey D. M., Hermopolis Magna, buildings of the Roman period: Ashmunein excav. 4. L 1991, British Museum. – ᴿBonnJbb 194 (1994) 670-2 (P. *Grossmann*); CdÉ 69 (1994) 384-7 (Marie *Drew-Bear*); JEA 80 (1994) 266-8 (T. F. C. *Blagg*); JRS 84 (1994) 251s (N. *Pollard*).

12795 **Spencer** A. J., Ashmunein 2. The temple area 1989 ➤ 5,e445: ᴿCdÉ 69 (1994) 288s (H. *De Meulenaere*).

12796 *Aswan:* Krekeler A., Excavations and restoration on Elephantine Island [since 1969]: NEAnt 3 (1992) 69-83 [< JStJud 25,160].

12796* *Burkard* Günter, Literarische Tradition und historische Realität; die persische Eroberung Ägyptens am Beispiel Elephantine: ZäSpr 131 (1994) 93-105...

12797 *a)* Bommas Martin, Eine hieratische Aufschrift auf einem Türpfosten aus Elephantine; – *b)* Jaritz Horst, *Rodziewicz* Mieczysław, Syene — review of the urban remains and its pottery: MiDAI-K 50 (1994) 23-30; 1 fig.; pl. 1 / 116-122 + 12 fig.; pl. 16-22.

12797* **Bakchias** (Fayûm): **Pernigotti** Sergio, *Capasso* Mario, Bakchias una
città del deserto egiziano che torna a vivere: Univ. Bologna & Lecce, 1ᵃ
campagna. N 1994, Procaccini. 142 p.; 81 color. pl. Lᵐ 40. – ᴿAegyptus
79 (1994) 207-9 (Orsolina *Montevecchi*); Archeo 9,114 (1994) 122 (S.
Moscati).

12798 **Bersheh** (Mellawi): **Silverman** David P., Bersheh reports 1992 ⇢ 9,
14452: ᴿOLZ 89 (1994) 139s (J. *Bareš*).

12798* **Dair Abu Fana:** *Buschhausen* Helmut, *al.*, Ausgrabungen von Dair
Abu Fana in Ägypten im Jahr 1990: ÄgLev 4 (1993) 95-137; 33 fig.; + 16
(color.) pl.

12799 **Dendara:** **Daumas** François, (*Lentheric* Bernard), Le temple de Dendara
9, 1987 ⇢ 6,e734: ᴿCdÉ 69 (1994) 285 (H. De *Meulenaere*).

12800 **Dûš:** **Reddé** Michel, Douch IV, Le trésor: DocFouilles 28, 1992
⇢ 9,14461: ᴿCdÉ 69 (1994) 388-392 (M. *Malaise*); JAmEg 31 (1994) 230s
(R. S. *Bianchi*).

12801 **Elkab:** **Hendricks** Stan, Elkab V, the Naqada III cemetery. Bru 1994,
Musée Art/Histoire. 259 p.; bibliog. 243-252.

12801* **Hagara:** **Fayard-Meeks** C., Le temple de Behbeit al-Hagara; essai de
reconstitution [diss. ᴰ*Goyon* J.]: StAäK Beih 6. Ha 1991, Buske.
xvii-525 p.; 36 pl.; bibliog. 493-500. 3-87548-000-7.

12802 **Hagarsa** [10 k S Sohag]: *Kanawati* Naguib, El-Hagarsa mummies:
BurHist 30,1 (1994) 4-7; 1 fig.

12803 **Ḥammāmāt:** *Farout* Dominique, La carrière du *wḥmw* Ameny et
l'organisation des expéditions au ouadi Hammamat au Moyen Empire:
BIFAO 94 (1994) 143-168 + 4 facsim.

12803* **Bongrani Fanfoni** L., **Israel** F., Documenti achemenidi nel deserto
orientale egiziano (Gebel Abu Queh – Wadi Hammamat): ⇢ 461, Syrie,
TEuph 8 (1991/4) 75-92 + map & pl. XII-XIX; franç. 75.

12804 **Tuna/Gebel,** Hermopolis: *Menu* Bernadette, Le tombeau de Pétosiris;
nouvel examen: BIFAO 94 (1994) 311-327.

12805 **Idfu:** ᴱ**Kurth** Dieter, *a*) Edfu; Studien zu Ikonographie, Textgestal-
tung, Schriftsystem, Grammatik und Baugeschichte: Inschriften des
Tempels, Begleitheft 1. Wsb 1990, Harrassowitz. viii-84 p. DM 40. 3-
447-02999-4. – ᴿBO 51 (1991) 35-7 (D. *Devauchelle*); – *b*) Edfu: Ein
ägyptischer Tempel, gesehen mit den Augen der alten Ägypter. Da 1994,
Wiss. xi-83 p. 3-534-12092-2.

12806 **Jeme:** **Wilfong** Terry G., 'The woman of Jeme'; women's roles in a
Coptic town in late antique Egypt: diss. ᴰ*Johnson* Janet. Ch 1994. 206 p.
95-14037. – DissA 55 (1994s) p. 3955.

12807 Les **Kellia,** Ermitages coptes en Basse-Égypte, Genève Musée d'art et
d'histoire 1989s. Genève 1990, Tricorno. 111 p. – ᴿVizVrem 53 (1992)
204s (A. Ya. *Kakovkin,* ⊕).

12808 **Kasser** Rodolphe, Kellia, Quṣur/Rubâʿîyât EK 8184 projet international
de sauvetage 1992/3: Univ. Genève. Lv 1994, Peeters. 90-6831-647-8.

12809 **Naga^c/Der:** **Podzorski** Patricia V., Their bones... Naga ed-Der 1990
⇢ 6,e748; 8,g235: ᴿJEA 79 (1993) 287 (J. C. *Rose*).

12809* **Philae:** *a*) *Dietze* Gertrud, Philae und die [südlich-liegende] Dode-
kaschoinos in ptolemäischer Zeit; – *b*) *Huss* Werner, Das Haus des
Nektanebıs und das Haus des Ptolemaios: AncSoc 25 (1994) 63-110 /
111-7.

12810 *Pagoulatos* Gerassimos, The destruction and conversion of ancient
temples to Christian churches 4th-6th cent. [... Philae]: TAth 65 (1994)
152-170; 6 fig.

12811 **Vassilika** Elena, Ptolemaic Philae 1989 ➤ 5,e483; 6,d965: [R]JEA 79 (1993) 316s (J. G. *Griffiths*).
12812 *Qous:* Quaegebeur J., *Traunecker* C., Een 'grenstempel' te Sjenhoer bei Qoes: PhoenixEOL 40 (1994) 79-93.
12813 *Quseir* (Red Sea): *a*) *Brun* Jean-Pierre, Le faciès céramique d'Al-Zarqa [route Quft-Quseir]; observations préliminaires; – *b*) *Bülow-Jacobsen* Adam, *al.*, The identification of Myos Hormos [Quseir]; new papyrological evidence: BIFAO 94 (1994) 7-26; 12 fig. / 27-38 + 9 phot.
12814 *Peacock* D. P. S., The site of Myos Hormos, a view from space [Quseir Qadīm on Red Sea, 100 k E Koptos, 150 k S Sinai point]: JRomArch 6 (AA 1993) 226-232; 4 maps.
12815 *Salwit:* **Zivie** Christiane M., *al.*, Le temple de Deir Chalouit [2-3, 1983-6 ➤ 64,b879 ... 4,g429]; IV. Étude architecturale. 1992: [R]JAmEg 31 (1994) 231s (R. S. *Bianchi*).
12816 *Zawyet Sultan* [8 k S Minya]: **Osing** Jürgen, Das Grab des Nefersechem im Zawyet Sultan: DAI-K 88, 1993: [R]ArchWsz 44 (1993) 131-3 (A. *Niwiński*); RossArkh (1994,3) 227-230 (G. A. *Belova*).

т7.7   Antiquitates Nubiae et aegyptiae alibi.

12817 [E]**Morigi Govi** Cristiano, *al.*, L'Egitto fuori dell'Egitto 1990/1 ➤ 7,618: [R]BO 51 (1994) 279-282 (M. J. *Raven*).
12818 **Payne** Joan C., Catalogue of the predynastic Egyptian collections in the Ashmolean Museum. Ox 1993, Clarendon. xiii-303 p. 0-19-951355-4.
12819 **Bruwier** Marie-Cécile, Présence de l'Égypte dans les collections de la Bibliothèque Universitaire H. Plantin: Publ. 6. Namur 1994, Univ. 266 p. 2-87037-199-3.
12820 **Mastino** A., L'Africa romana 1991/2 ➤ 8,726: [R]AION 53 (1993) 474-8 (F. *Vattioni*); Latomus 53 (1994) 700-2 (J. *Diederich*, tit. pp.).
12821 *Pernigotti* Sergio, Le città del deserto; alla scoperta dell'Egitto sconosciuto: Archeo 9,109 (1994) 55-93; ill.
12822 *Ronca* Italo, Ex Africa semper aliquid noui; the ever surprising vicissitudes of a pre-Aristotelian proverb: Latomus 53 (1994) 570-593.
12823 **Skon-Jedele** Nancy J., 'Aigyptiaka'; a catalogue of Egyptian and Egyptianizing objects excavated from Greek archaeological sites, ca. 1100-525 B.C. [updating PENDLEBURY J. 1930]: diss. Pennsylvania, [D]*Muhly* J. Ph 1994. 2887 p. (sic). 94-27613. DissA 66 (1994s) p. 1356.

12824 *Cyrene:* **Bacchielli** Lidiano, Cirene; risorge l'Atene d'Africa; ottant'anni di scavi e restauri: Archeo 9,116 (1994) 63-109; (color.) ill.
12825 *Bacchielli* Lidiano, Sulla collina di Zeus; i restauri del tempio di Zeus a Cirene e dell'arco severiano a Leptis Magna: Archeo 9,111 (1994) 46-53.
12826 *Bacchielli* Lidiano, Alla scoperta di Cirene: Antiqua 18 (R 1993) 22-25.
12827 **Brouquier-Reddé** Véronique, Temples et cultes de Tripolitaine 1992 ➤ 9,14493*: [R]AJA 98 (1994) 178s (W. E. *Mierse*); RStFen 22 (1994) 153-5 (S. *Ribichini*).
12828 [E]**Gentili** Bruno, Cirene; storia, mito, letteratura 1988/90 ➤ 8,g256: [R]AnzAltW 46 (1993) 68s (P. W. *Haider*).
12829 *a*) **White** Donald [*al.*], The extramural sanctuary of Demeter and Persephone at Cyrene [2. 1985; 3. 1987 ➤ 5,e513] 1. Background and introduction to the excavations: Mg 52. Ph 1994, Univ. Museum.

xx-143 p.   0-934718-77 [-6; on back -8]. – ᴿGnomon 66 (1994) 347-351 (Emanuela *Fabbricotti*). – *b*) **Schaus** Gerald P., 2. The East Greek island, and Laconian pottery: mg 55, 1995. xxii-141 p.   0-934718-55-5.

12830 **Dongola** 1993s ➤ 11498, Polish (Reports 1994) 84-92 (S. *Jakobielski*), *al*. 93-108.

12831 *Ḥamra Dom:* *Säve-Söderbergh* Torgny, The Old Kingdom cemetery at Ḥamra Dom (El-Qaṣr wa es-Saiyad. Sto 1994, Royal Academy. 78 p.; 75 pl.   91-7402-248-2.

12832 *Hibernia: Carey* John,   The sun's night journey; a Pharaonic image in medieval Ireland: JWarb 57 (1994) 14-34.

12833 *Kerma:* **Ahmed Salah ed-Din** M., L'agglomération napatéenne de Kerma; enquêtes archéologique et ethnographique en milieu urbain.   P 1992, RCiv: ᴿCRAI (1994) 116s (J. *Leclant*).

12834 *a*) *Bonnet* Charles, Les fouilles archéologiques de Kerma au nord du Soudan; – *b*) *Gratien* Brigitte, Les citadelles de Nubie au Moyen Empire; – *c*) *Hinkel* Friedrich W., Les pyramides de Meroé; – *d*) *Edwards* David N., La forteresse de Qasr Ibrim: DossA 196 (1994) 16-21 / 12-15 / 60-63 / 64-49.

12835 *Leptiminus:* **Ben Lazreg** N., *Mattingly* D. J., Leptiminus (Lamta), a Roman port city in Tunisia, 1: JRArch supp. 1. AA 1992, Univ.   138 p.; ill. $79.30. – ᴿJRS 84 (1994) 252s (M. *Fulford*).

12836 *Niger* flumen: *Moscati* Sabatino, E il tempo si fermo sul fiume [Niger], una grande mostra d'arte africana: Archeo 9,109 (1994) 29-47 [48-93, *Fattovich* Rodolfo, Missione a Aksum].

12837 *Nubia:* *Damiano-Appia* Maurizio,   Il sogno dei faraoni pari; Alta Nubio una terra tra due imperi. ArchViva. F 1994, Giunti.   159 p.   88-09-20524-3.

12838 **Davies** W. V.,   Egypt and Africa; Nubia from prehistory to Islam.   L 1991, British Museum [➤ 9,14501*]; also Egypt Exploration Soc.   320 p.; 105 fig.; 16 pl.; 7 foldouts. £30. 0-7141-0962-2. – ᴿJEA 80 (1994) 268s (J. *Alexander*).

12839 **O'Connor** David,   Ancient Nubia, Egypt's rival in Africa.   Ph 1993, Univ. Museum.   xiv-178 p.   0-924171-28-6.

12840 *Roma:* **Alföldy** G.,   Der Obelisk auf dem Petersplatz in Rom 1990 ➤ 6,e753; 8,g229:   ᴿGrazB 20 (1994) 338-340 (Florens *Felten*).

12841 **Cipriani** Giovanni,   Gli obelischi egizi; politica e cultura nella Roma barocca: Acc. Toscana, Studi 131.   F 1993, Olschki.   205 p.

12842 ᴱ**Meyer** Hugo, [*Grimm* Alfred, *al*.],   Der Obelisk des Antinoos. Mü 1994, Fink. 208 p.; ill.

12843 *Qustul:* **Williams** Bruce, Qustul [etc. 1-9, 1985-92 ➤ 8,g273-8], 2. Nubian Exped. 6.   Ch 1992, Or.Inst.   xxxv-479 p.; 206 fig.; 53 pl. $75. – ᴿOrientalia 63 (1994) 132-6 (W. Y. *Adams*).

12844 *Serra* [Sudan]: **Williams** Bruce B.,   Excavations at Serra-East 1-5: Nubian Exp. 10, 1993 ➤ 9,14509:   ᴿOLZ 89 (1994) 528-540 (A. J. *Mills*); Orientalia 63 (1994) 281-3 (W. Y. *Adams*).

ᴛ7.9 Sinai.

12845 **Anati** Emmanuel,   Spedizione Sinai; nuove scoperte ad Har Karkom: Studi Camuni 11.   Valcamonica ʙs 1994, Centro Preistoria. 112 p.; 97 fig.

12846 *Digbasonis* Demetrios, ⒼThe Sinaite library [1702-8 + bibliog. +: TAth 64 (1993) 255-282.

12847 *Hershkovitz* Israel, *al.*, The pre-pottery neolithic populations of South Sinai and their relations to other circum-Mediterranean groups; an anthropological study: Paléorient 20,2 (1994) 59-84.

12847* *Rilliet* Frédéric, La bibliothèque de Ste-Catherine du Sinaï et ses membra disiecta; nouveaux fragments syriaques à la Bibliothèque Vaticane: ➤ 450c, Syriacum 6 (1992/4) 409-418.

12848 **Stewart** Frank H., Texts in Sinai bedouin law, I. English [II, Arabic, in press]: MeditLangCu 5. Wsb 1988, Harrassowitz. xvii-232 p. DM 78. – ᴿBSO 57 (1994) 383-6 (B. *Ingham*).

12849 **Williams** Larry, The mountain of Moses [not on 'Sinai' peninsula but across the nearby 'Aqaba Gulf strait, in a Saudi Arabia area vaguely corresponding to Ptolemaeus' Midian]. Solana Beach CA c. 1992, CIT. 223 p. $21 [BAR-W 10/3,79 adv.].

T8.1 **Anatolia,** *generalia.*

12850 *Alexeev* Andrei J., [*al.*] La Scythie ou les Scythes?: DossA 194 (1994) 8-11 [-88].

12851 *Bartl* Karin, *a)* Neuere archäologische Forschungen in der Ost-Türkei: Altertum 39 (1993) 163-180; – *b)* Die frühe Eisenzeit in Ostanatolien und ihre Verbindungen mit den benachbarten Regionen: BaghMitt 25 (1994) 473-518; 20 fig.

12852 **Belke** Klaus, **Mersich** Norbert, Phrygien und Pisidien: Tabula Imperii Byzantini 7, 1990 ➤ 7,d999; 9,14520: ᴿAevum 66 (1992) 461-3 (C. M. *Mazzucchi*); Gnomon 66 (1994) 78s (Barbara M. *Levick*); VizVrem 54 (1993) 205s (V. P. *Stepanenko*, ⊕ also on Kilikien-Isaurien, HEILENKAMPER H.).

12853 *Börker-Klähn* Jutta, Neues zur Geschichte Lykiens: Athenaeum 82 (1994) 315-330 + 4 pl. (maps).

12854 **Briquel** D., L'origine lydienne des Étrusques 1991 ➤ 8,g298: ᴿGnomon 66 (1994) 514-7 (Marta *Sordi*); RBgPg 72 (1994) 170-2 (C.-M. *Ternes*).

12855 *a) Descat* Raymond, Les forteresses de Théra et de Kallipolis de Carie [SW Muğla]; – *b) Pedersen* Poul, The fortifications of Halikarnassos: ➤ 466; ᴿRÉAnc 96 (1993/4) 205-9 + 11 fig. / 215-223 + 21 fig.

12856 ᴱ**Dobesch** Gerhard, *Rehrenböck* Georg, Die epigraphische und altertumskundliche Erforschung Kleinasiens; hundert Jahre Kleinasiatische Kommission der Öst. Akad. Wiss.: Tituli Asiae Minoris Egbd 14; Akad. Denkschr. 236. W 1993, Österr. Akad. 372 p.

12857 **Dräger** Michael, Die Städte der Provinz Asia in der Flavierzeit; Studien zur kleinasiatischen Stadt- und Regionalgeschichte [Diss. Kiel 1992]: EurHS 3/574. Fra 1993, Lang. 438 p.

12858 *Drews* Robert, Myths of Midas and the Phrygian migration from Europe: Klio 75 (1993) 9-26.

12858* *Foss* Clive, The Lycian coast in the Byzantine age: DumbO 48 (1994) 1-52; 40 fig.

12859 **Francovich** Géza de, Santuari e tombe rupestri dell'antica Frigia e un'indagine sulle tombe della Licia: Mdv 3. R 1990, Bretschneider. 202 p. + vol. of 512 fig. Lᵐ 350. [Gnomon 66,378-380, F. *Prayon*].

12860 *Gates* Marie H., Archaeology in Turkey: AJA 98 (1994) 249-252; 29 fig.

12861 *Hall* Alan S., Ladislav ZGUSTA's contribution to modern research; the indigenous names of Asia Minor: ➤ Mem. Studies 1994, 1-6.

12862 **Ivantchik** Askold I., Les Cimmériens: OBO 127. FrS/Gö 1993, Univ./ VR. – RMesopT 29 (1994) 529-531 (A. M. *Jasink*).

12863 — [Gade] **Kristensen** Anne K., Who were the Cimmerians? and where ded they come from? Sargon II, the Cimmerians, and Rusa I, TLæssøe Jørgen. K 1988, Munksgaard. 141 p. Dk 220. – RJNES 53 (1994) 51-53 (P. *Zimansky*).

12864 **Kolars** J. F., *Mitchell* W. A., The Euphrates river and the Southeast Anatolia development project: Carbondale 1991, S. Illinois Univ. – RBCanadMesop 25 (1993) 72s (French and English, no author).

12865 **Korfmann** Manfred, *al.*, Anatolien in der Frühen und Mittleren Bronzezeit I: Bibliographie zur Frühbronzezeit: TAVO Beih B-73,1. Wsb 1994, Reichert. 248 p. 3-88226-692-9.

12866 **Marek** C., Stadt, Ära und Territorium in Pontus-Bithynia und Nord-Galatia: IstFor 39. Tü 1993, Wasmuth. xvii-259 p.; 56 pl.; 6 maps. 3-8030-1760-2. – RJRS 84 (1994) 247s (S. R. F. *Price*).

12867 *a*) *Marksteiner* Thomas, Befestigte Siedlungen Lykiens in vorrömischer Zeit; – *b*) *Konecny* Andreas, Militärisches Formengut — zivile Nutzung; die lykischen Türme: → 11498, RÉAnc 96 (1993/4) 299-308 + 15 fig. / 315-321; 4 fig. + 6 Zeichnungen.

12868 *Mellink* Machteld J., Archaeology in Anatolia: AJA 97 (1993) 105-133; 31 fig.; map.

12869 *Nollé* Margret, Denkmäler vom Satrapensitz Daskyleion; Studien zur graeco-persischen Kunst: Antike in der Moderne. B 1992, Akademie. xvi-179 p.; 15 pl. DM 148. 3-05-002146-2. – RMesopT 29 (1994) 325-8 (A. *Invernizzi*).

12870 **Prayon** Friedhelm, *Wittke* Anna-Maria, Kleinasien vom 12. bis 6. Jh. v.Chr.; Kartierung und Erläuterung archäologischer Befunde und Denkmäler: TAVO Beih. B82. xvi-170 p.; vol. of 18 maps. 3-88226-819-0.

12871 *Ritter* Eugen J., Erdjias Dağ, der 'Mons Argäus', der Alten über der anatolischen Wüstensteppe: Zts d/öst. Alpenvereins 62 (1931) 124-148.

12872 **Scheer** Tanja S., Mythische Vorväter; zur Bedeutung griechischer Heroenmythen im Selbstverständnis kleinasiatischer Städte [Diss. Mü 1992]: ArbAltG 7. Mü 1993, Maris. 369 p.; 6 pl.; map.

12873 EShankland David, The year's work (signed items): AnSt 44 (1994) 3-25.

12874 **Sinclair** T. A., Eastern Turkey 1987/9 → 3,e920 ... 7,e22: RJRomArch 6 (1993) 467-472 (O. *Nicholson*).

12875 **Steadman** Sharon R., Isolation vs. interaction; prehistoric Cilicia and its role in the Near Eastern world system: diss. California, DTringham Ruth. Berkeley 1994. 311 p. 95-05014. – DissA 55 (1994s) p. 2879.

12876 **Trebilco** Paul, Jewish communities in Asia Minor, SNTS mg. 60, 1991 → 7,e24 ... 9,14542: RScEspr 46 (1994) 116s (P.-É. *Langevin*).

12877 *a*) *Trebilco* Paul, Asia; – *b*) *Hanson* G. Walter, Galatia: → 243, Acts Graeco-Roman 1994, 291-362 / 377-395.

12878 *Tretser* Michail J., *Vinogradov* Yurt G., Archaeology on the northern coast of the Black Sea: AJA 97 (1993) 521-563; 30 fig.

12879 *Tsetskhadze* Gocha R., Colchians, Greeks and Achaemenids in the 7th-5th centuries B.C.; a critical look: Klio 76 (1994) 78-101; deutsch 101.

12880 **Zimmermann** M., Untersuchungen zur historischen Landeskunde Zentrallykiens. Bonn 1992, Habert. 282 p. – RGerión 12 (1994) 342-4 (A. *Lozano*).

12881 *Zimmermann* Martin, Bemerkungen zur rhodischen Vorherrschaft in Lykien (189/88-167 v.Chr.): Klio 75 (1993) 110-129; Eng. 129; maps 130.

T8.2 Boğazköy, *Hethaei* – The Hittites.

12881* *Börker-Klähn* Jutta, Der hethitische Areopag: [Boğazköy-] Yerkapi, die Bronzetafel und der 'Staatsstreich': AltOrF 21 (1994) 131-160; 9 fig.

12882 **Edel** Elmar, Die ägyptisch-hethitische Korrespondenz aus Boghazköi in babylonischer und hethitischer Sprache: AbhRh/Wf Akad 77. Opladen 1994, Westd.-V. I. 240 p.; 48 pl. – II. Kommentar. 382 p. 3-531-05091-5.

12883 *Hansen* O., A Mycenaean sword from Boğazköy-Ḫattuša found in 1991: AnBritAth 89 (1994) 213-5.

12884 **Klengel** H., Texte verschiedenen Inhalts: KaB 60, 1990 ➤ 6,e832: ᴿZAss 84 (1994) 229-290 (S. *Košak*).

12885 *a) Masson* Emilia, À la découverte des Hittites; – *b) Sergent* Bernard, Les Hittites et la diaspora indo-européenne; – *c) Donbaz* Veysel, Chez les marchands assyriens d'Anatolie; – *d) Freu* Jacques, Histoire d'un peuple et d'un empire; – *e) Temizer* Raci, Le musée des civilisations anatoliennes à Ankara: DossA 193 (1994) 2-11 (40-61.68-81) / 12-19 / 20-25 / 26-39 / 82-87.

12886 **Neve** Peter, Ḫattuša – Stadt der Götter und Tempel; neue Ausgrabungen in der Hauptstadt der Hethiter: Bildband 8. Mainz 1993, von Zabern. [iv-] 88 p. 3-8053-1478-7.

12887 *Neve* Peter, Die Ausgrabungen in Boğazköy-Ḫattuša 1992: ArchAnz (1993) 621-652; 28 fig.

12888 *Otten* Heinrich, Die hethitische Grosskönigin Ḫenti in ihren Siegeln: ZAss 84 (1994) 253-261; 7 fig.

12889 *Otten* H., *Rüster* C., Hethitische Texte... Büyükkale: KaB 34, 1991 ➤ 7,e31: ᴿOLZ 89 (1994) 276-9 (V. *Haas*, I. *Wegner*).

12890 **Wilhelm** Gernot, Medizinische Omina aus Ḫattuša in akkadischer Sprache: Studien zu den Boğazköy-Texten 36. Wsb 1994, Harrassowitz. xi-107 p.; 9 pl. 3-447-03414-9.

12891 *Alaca: Ünal* Ahmet, The textual illustration of the 'Jester Scene' on the sculptures of Alaca Höyük: AnSt 44 (1994) 207-220; pl. XLVII.

T8.3 Ephesus.

12891* *Bammer* Anton, *a)* Die Geschichte des Sekos im Artemision von Ephesos: JbÖsA 62-B (1993) 145-168; 26 (foldout) fig.; – *b)* Geschichte — neu geschrieben; Mykene im Artemision von Ephesos: JbÖsA 63-B (1994) 29-40; 3 fig.

12892 **Erdemgil** Selahattin, Ephesus, ruins and museum. İstanbul 1992, Turistik. 156 p.; ill.

12892* *Friesen* Stephen J., Twice neokoros, Ephesus 1993 ➤ 9,14567: ᴿJRS 84 (1994) 246s (G. M. *Rogers*).

12893 *a) Hölbl* Günther, Archaische Aegyptiaca aus Ephesos; vorläufige Beobachtungen zu den Neufunden aus dem Artemision; – *b) Knibbe* Dieter, Geschichte und Stand der epigraphischen Forschung in Ephesos: ➤ 460, Lykien-Symposium I 1990/3, 227-253 / 265-8. pl. XVII-XXII.

12893* *Karwiese* Stefan, *al.*, Ephesos 1993: JbÖsA 63-B (Grabungen 1994) 9-31; 26 fig. [62-B, 9-32: 1992].

12894 *Mackowski* Richard M., La porta di Mazeo e Mitridate in Efeso nel quadro evergetico dell'ideologia augustea: Antonianum 69 (1994) 97-106 + 7 fig.

12894* *Oberleitner* Wolfgang, Die Apollon-Heliosplatte des Partherdenkmals — ein Neufund: JbÖsA 64 (1995) 39-61; 23 fig.

12895 ᴱ**Padovese** L., Efeso II 1992/3 ➤ 8,485: ᴿGregorianum 75 (1994) 762s (G. *Ferraro*); Salesianum 56 (1994) 154s (B. *Amata*); ScripTPamp 26 (1994) 781s (A. *García-Moreno*).

12896 **Rogers** Guy M., The sacred identity of Ephesus 1991 ➤ 7,e44... 9,14570: ᴿAJA 97 (1993) 589s (Susan G. *Cole*); Klio 76 (1994) 518-521 (Claudia *Schulte*); Latomus 53 (1994) 926s (R. *Chevallier*); Phoenix 48 (Toronto 1994) 89-91 (Mary E. H. *Walbank*).

12897 **Schulte** Claudia, Die grammateis von Ephesus; Schreiberamt und Sozialstruktur in einer Provinzhauptstadt des römischen Kaiserreiches [thesis Lic. Heidelberg 1992]: Habes 15.   Stu 1994, Steiner.   234 p. [Gerión 13, 384-7 (M. I. *Castillo Pascual*]. – ᴿRÉAnc 96 (1994) 633s (S. *Dmitriev*).

12898 **Soldan** Ute, Artemiskult und Stadtgesellschaft in Ephesus; ein Beitrag zur Sozialgeschichte der römischen Kaiserzeit: Diss. Bielefeld 1993. – Chiron 24 (1994) 444.

12899 **Thür** Hilke, Das Hadrianstor in Ephesos: ForschungenE 11/1 1989 ➤ 6,e843... 9,14572: ᴿAnzAltW 46 (1993) 98-101 (D. *Feil*).

12900 *Wohlers-Scharf* Traute, Forschungsgeschichte von Ephesos: Diss. Wien. – MiDAV 25,2 (1994) 50.

T8.4 **Pergamum.**

12901 **Andreae** Bernard, Phyromachos–Probleme 1990 ➤ 7,e48... 9,14573: ᴿAJA 97 (1993) 582s (Beryl *Bars-Sharrar*).

12902 *Gaitzsch* Wolfgang, Hellenistische Geschützteile aus Pergamon: ➤ 35, ꟳFʀᴇʏ O. 1994, 235-242; 8 fig.

12903 **Hübner** Gerhild, Die Applikenkeramik von Pergamon; eine Bildersprache im Dienst des Herrscherkultes: PergFor 7.   B 1993, de Gruyter. 231 p.; 40 fig.; 84 pl. – ᴿMusHelv 51 (1994) 185 (C. *Reusser*).

12904 **Kunze** Max, Der Pergamonaltar; seine Geschichte, Entdeckung und Rekonstruktion: Staatliche Museen Berlin.   Mainz 1992, von Zabern. 48 p.; 37 color. fig. 3-8053-1314-4.

12905 **Mandel** Ursula, Kleinasiatische Reliefkeramik der mittleren Kaiserzeit: PergFor 5, 1988 ➤ 5,e565: ᴿBonnJbb 194 (1994) 675-682 (Gioia *de Luca*).

12906 *Radt* Wolfgang, Die archaische Befestigungsmauer von Pergamon und zugehörige Fortifications–Aspekte: ➤ 466, REÁnc 96 (1994) 63-71 + 18 fig.

12907 *a*) *Radt* Wolfgang, Pergamon, Vorbericht über die Kampagne 1992 [1991; 1993]; – *b*) *Raeck* Wulf, Zeus Philios in Pergamon; – *c*) *Salzmann* Dieter, Mosaiken: ArchAnz (1993) 347-379; 36 (foldout.) fig. [auch (1992) 339-368; 31 fig.; (1944) 403-432; 25 fig.] / 381-7 / 389-400; 14 fig.].

12908 **Rheidt** K., Die byzantinische Wohnstadt; Altertümer von Pergamon 15/2, 1991 ➤ 9,14579: ᴿByZ 86 (1994) 151-4 (U. *Peschler*).

12909 *Schmidt-Dounas* Barbara, Anklänge an altorientalische Mischwesen im Gigantomachiefries des Pergamonaltares: Boreas 16 (Münster 1993) 5-17; pl. 1-3.

12910 **Virgilio** Biagio, Gli Attalidi di Pergamo; fama, eredità, memoria: BtStudi Antichi 70, ellenistici 5.   Pisa 1993, Giardini.   138 p.; 32 pl.; 3 maps. – ᴿRivStoAnt 24 (1994) 289s (G. *Susini*).

12911 *Virgilio* Biagio,   La città ellenistica e i suoi 'benefactores'; Pergamo e Diodoro Pasparos: Athenaeum 82 (1994) 299-314.
12912 *a) Wulf* Ulrika,   Der Stadtplan von Pergamon; zur Entwicklung und Stadtstruktur von der Neugründung unter Philetairos bis in spätantike Zeit; – *b) Müller-Wiener* Wolfgang †,   Eine unterirdische Grabanlage am Burgberg von Pergamon: IstMitt 44 (1994) 135-175; 6 fig.; pl. 22-32; 177-180; 1 fig.; pl. 33. [397 *Radt* W. Nachtrag zu 42,163].

T8.6   *Situs Anatoliae,*   **Turkey sites** in alphabetical order.

12913 *Aḥmar:* ᴱ**Bunnens** Guy,   Tell Ahmar, 1988 season: AbrNahrain supp. 2. Lv 1990. 151 p.; 64 fig. – ᴿBelleten 58 (1994) 469-471 (A. *Özfirat,* ❶).
12914 *Aizanoi* 1987-90; ArchAnz (1993) 437-473; 32 fig. (A. *Hoffmann, al.*): 475-507, 35 fig., Topographie (K. *Rheidt*).
12915 *Alalaḥ:* Hess Richard S.,   Alalakh studies and the Bible; obstacle or contribution?: ➤ 67, ᶠKɪɴɢ P., 1994, 199-215.
12916 *Amorium*-Hisarköy, 6th 1993: AnSt 44 (1994) 106-128; pl. XVII-XXIV (C. S. *Lightfoot*); Minerva 5/1, 14-16.
12917 *Antakya:* ᴱ**Brodersen** Kai,   Appians Antiochike: Syriake 1,1-44,232, 1991 ➤ 9,14587: ᴿClasR 44 (1994) 33s (A. *Erskine*).
12918 *Poccardi* Grégoire,   Antioche de Syrie; pour un nouveau plan urbain de l'île de l'Oronte (ville neuve), du IIIᵉ au Vᵉ siècle: MÉF 106 (1994) 993-1023; 9 fig.

12919 **Aphrodisias:** *Jones* C.P., *Smith* R.R.R.,   Two inscribed monuments of Aphrodisias: ArchAnz (1994) 455-472; 10 fig.
12920 **Smith** R.R.R.,   The monument of C. Julius Zoilas: Aphrodisias NYU excavations 1.   Mainz 1993, von Zabern.
12921 *Edwards* Douglas R.,   Defining the web of power in Asia Minor; the novelist Chariton and his city Aphrodisias: JAAR 62 (1994) 699-717.
12922 **Rouché** Charlotte,   Performers and partisans at Aphrodisias [graffiti-covered theatre, odeon, stadium] in the Roman and Late Roman periods: JRS mg 6. L 1993.   xi-284 p.; 24 pl.   0-907-76417-7. – ᴿClasR 44 (1994) 356-9 (N.P. *Milner*); JRS 84 (1994) 285s (C.P. *Jones*); Nikephoros 7 (1994) 296-303 (J. *Ebert*); Prudentia 25,2 (1993) 83-86 (P. *McKechnie*).
12923 **MacDonald** David,   The coinage of Aphrodisias.   L 1992, Royal Numismatic Soc. 23.   xii-170 p.; 320 fig. – ᴿNumC 154 (1994) 306-310 (Ann *Johnston*).

12924 *Aslanapa:* Johnson Gary J.,   A Christian business [tombstones, Gɪʙsᴏɴ E. 1978] and Christian self-identity in third.fourth century Phrygia: VigChr 48 (1994) 341-366.
12925 *Bahçehisar:* Efe Turan,   EB III pottery from Bahçehisar; the significance of the pre-Hittite sequence in the Eskişehir plain, NW Anatolia: AJA 98 (1994) 5-34; 26 pl.
12926 *Balboura* [N. Lycia]: AnSt 44 (1994) 27-46; 9 fig.; pl. I-IV (L. *Bier*); regional survey 8-10 (J.J. *Coulton*).
12927 *Belevi:* Hoepfner Wolfram,   Zum Mausoleum von Belevi [Pʀᴀsᴄʜɴɪᴋᴇʀ Camillo, *Theuer* Max 1979]: ArchAnz (1993) 111-123; 16 (foldout) fig.
12928 *Carchemish:* Jasink Anna M.,   Il medio Eufrate; continuità e innovazioni tra il secondo e il primo millennio a.C.: Mesop-T 29 (1994) 73-88.

12929 **Çatal** Höyük 1993: AnSt 44 (1994) 10-13 (I. *Hodder*); 13-15 regional survey (*al.*).

12930 **Chersonesus:** *Zolotarev* Mikhail I., *Bujskikh* Alla V., The temenos of ancient Chersonesos; an attempt at an architectural reconstruction: Ancient Civilizations from Scythia to Siberia 2 (Leiden 1993) 125-156; 14 fig.

12931 **Corycus** [coastal Cilicia]: *Williams* Margaret H., The Jews of Corycus – a neglected Diaspora community from Roman times: JStJud 25 (1994) 274-286.

12932 Cilician coast [Ceyhan], 1991 chalco-EB: AnSt 44 (1994) 85-105; 6 fig. (Sharon R. *Steadman*).

12933 **Cnidus:** *Berges* Dietrich, Alt-Knidos [? Datça] und Neu-Knidos: IstMitt 44 (1994) 5-16; pl. 1-3.

12934 **Cretopolis,** Panemoteichos, ? Kodrula (Pisidia): AnSt 44 (1994) 129-148; 2 maps (S. *Mitchell*).

12935 **Demirci:** ᴱ**Korfmann** Manfred, Demircihüyük 1988 → 5,e588...9, 14593: ᴿPraehZts 69 (1994) 102-7 (H.-G. *Buchholz*).

12935* **Didyma:** AntWelt 25 (1994) 2-31; 91 fig. (K. *Tuchelt*).

12936 **Göreme:** *Volanakis* John, ⑤ The church of El-Nazar at Göreme, Cappadocia: TAth 65 (1994) 802-842; Eng. 1023.

12937 **Jolivet-Lévy** Catherine, Les églises byzantines de Cappadoce; le programme iconographique de l'abside et de ses abords 1991 → 8,g374: ᴿSpeculum 69 (1994) 508s (A. *Grishin*).

12938 **Castellani** Vittorio, Evidence for hydrogeological planning in ancient Cappadocia [Nevşehir]: JAncTop 3 (1993) 207-216; 10 fig.

12938* **Thierry** Nicole, De la datation des églises de Cappadoce: ByZ 88 (1995) 419-455; 10 pl.; map.

12939 **Türkmenoğlu** A. G., *al.*, The deterioration of tuffs from the Cappadocia region of Turkey: Archaeometry 33 (1991) 231-8; 8 fig.

12939* **Gülnar: Davesne** A., *Le Rider* G., Gülnar (Trésor, Coins) II 1989 → 6,d874 ... 8,e321: ᴿGnomon 66 (1994) 458-460 (P. *Weiss*).

12940 **Halicarnassus-**Bodrum: *Pedersen* Poul, The fortifications of Halicarnassus: → 466, RÉAnc 94,1s (1993/4) 215-223 + 21 fig.

12941 **Scarre** Chris, A tomb to wonder at [Mausolus's at Halicarnassus, variously reconstructed from discovered portions and PLINY's description]: Archaeology 46,5 (1993) 32-38; ill.

12942 **Ḥarran** (Urfa): **Green** Tamara M., The city of the moon-god... Harran RelGRW 14, 1992 → 8,g426: ᴿNumen 41 (1994) 197s (K. *Dijkstra*).

12943 **Hassek** [Turkish Lower Euphrates]: **Behm-Blancke** M. R., Hassek-Hüyük; naturwissenschaftliche Untersuchungen und lithische Industrie: DAI IstFor 38, 1992 → 8,g381; 9,14602: ᴿOLZ 89 (1994) 146-9 (L. *Martin*).

12944 **Hierapolis-**Pamukkale: **Bejor** Giorgio, Hierapolis 3, Le Statue: Archaeologica 99, 1991 → 9,14603; Lᵐ 280. 88-7689-063-7: ᴿBabesch 69 (1994) 222s (E. M. *Moormann*, ital.); ClasR 44 (1994) 418s (J. J. *Wilkes*); Latomus 53 (1994) 951 (R. *Chevallier*); MusHelv 51 (1994) 185s (D. *Willers*).

12945 **Höyücek** 1990: Belleten 58,223 (1994) 725-743; 40 pl. (Refik *Duru*); Eng. 745-8.

12946 **İstanbul: Dagron** Gilbert [1974], Costantinopoli, nascita di una capitale (330-451), ᵀ*Serafini* Aldo: BtCuStor 186. T 1991, Einaudi. – ᴿLateranum 60 (1994) 179s (O. *Pasquato*).

12947 **Harrison** R. Martin, A temple for Byzantium 1989 ➤ 6,e878; 9,14605: ᴿJNES 53 (1994) 50s (W. E. *Kaegi*).

12948 *İzmit: Boulhol* Pascal, L'apport de l'hagiographie à la connaissance de la Nicomédie paléochrétienne (toponymie et monuments): MÉF 106 (1994) 921-992.

12949 *Kaman*-Kalehöyük 3d 1988: ➤ 9,358, Anatolian 1993, 43-57 + 13 fig. (maps); 5 pl. (M. *Mori*, S. *Omura*).

12950 *Kaunos* 1988-91: ArchAnz (1994) 185-237; 33 fig. (B. *Schmaltz, al.*).

12951 *Kültepe: a) Özgüç* Tahsin, A cult vessel discovered at Kanish; – *b) Özgüç* Nimet, Notes on cylinder seals of Level 1ᵃ⁻ᵇ from Karum-Kaniš: ➤ 55, ꟳHROUDA B., Beiträge 1994, 221-7; pl. XXII-XXIII / 219-220; pl. XXb-XXI.

12952 *Kurban:* **Wilkinson** T. J., *Algaze* Guillermo, Town and country in southwestern Anatolia 1990 ➤ 8,g395: ᴿJAOS 114 (1994) 662 (G. M. *Schwartz*).

12953 *Limyra: Marksteiner* Thomas, Kastell oder Herrensitz? Zur Besiedlung der Chora der befestigten Siedlung Zëmuri/Limyra im Lykien der klassischen Zeit: JbÖsA 63 (1994) 95-120; 26 fig.

12954 *Miletus: a) Herrmann* Peter, Milet unter Augustus; C. Iulius Epikrates und die Anfänge des Kaiserkults; – *b) Köster* Reinhard, Der sogenannte Tabernakelbau in Milet; Reste eines Grabbaus der frühen Kaiserzeit?: IstMitt 44 (1994) 203-236 pl. 36-39 / 237-301; pl. 40-51.

12955 *Kossatz* A., Milet 5/1, die megarischen Becher 1990 ➤ 8,g402; 9,14614: ᴿAcArchH 46 (1994) 444s (A. *Bugán*).

12956 *Ragone* Giuseppe, Da Mileto a Iasos; toponomastica antica, itinerari antiquari, ricognizioni moderne: AnPisa 23 (1993) 871-902 (847-998 *al*. Il territorio di Iasos) pl. 128, foldout map.

12957 *Nemrud Dağ: Waldmann* Helmut, Der Nemrud-Dağ, seine Terrassen und das indische Somaopfer: IstMitt 44 (1994) 107-124; 2 fig.

12958 *Nisibis: Drijvers* Hendrik J. W., Nisibis; ᵀ*Schäferdiek* Knut: ➤ 517, TRE 24 (1994) 573-6.

12959 *Oinoanda* [upper Şeki Çay, Xanthos R.]: AnSt 44 (1994) 59-64; pl. IX-XIII (M. F. *Smith*, Demostheneia inscription); 65-76; pl. XIV-XVI (N. P. *Milner*, M. F. *Smith*, votive reliefs).

12960 *Olbasa: Kearsley* R. A., The Milyas and the Attalids; a decree of the city of Olbasa [Pisidia (map p. 131)] and a new royal letter of the second century B.C.: AnSt 44 (1994) 47-57; pl. VI-VIII.

12961 *Olbia: Randsborg* Klavs, A Greek episode; the early Hellenistic settlement on the western Crimea [Olbia]: AcArchK 65 (1994) 171-196; 23 fig.

12962 *Priene:* **Raeder** Joachim, Priene, Funde aus einer griechischen Stadt im Berliner Antikenmuseum: Bilderheft. B 1984, Mann. 45 p. – ᴿGnomon 66 (1994) 162-5 (D. *Graepler*).

12963 *Sagalassos* (Pisidia) 4th 1993: An St 44 (1994) 169-186; 2 fig. (M. *Waelkens*, E. *Owens*).

12964 ᴱWaelkens Marc, Sagalassos [Pisidia] I. survey (1986-89) and excavations (1990-1991): AcArchLov mg. 5. Lv 1993, Univ. 238 p.; 146 fig. 90-6186-529-8. – ᴿAJA 98 (1994) 577s (Sarah *Cormack*).

12965 *Samandağ: Morray* D. W., The defences of the monastery of St Simeon the Younger on Samandağ: OrChrPer 60 (1994) 625-633.

12966 *Sardis: a) Greenewalt* C., *al.*, ➤ 295, ASOR reports 1994, 1-43; – *b)*

Ratté Christopher, Arthemion stelae from Sardis: AJA 98 (1994) 593-607; 15 fig.

12967 **Sinop:** *Garlan* Yvon, Les premières des ateliers amphoriques de Sinope: CRAI (1994) 687s.

12968 **Smyrna:** *Hilhorst* A., Heidenen, joden en christenen in Smyrna; de verdedigingsrede van de martelaar Pionius in de vervolging van Decius: Hermeneus 66 (1994) 160-6 [< JStJud 25,366].

12969 **Troja:** *Bryce* Trevor, The Trojan war in its Near Eastern context: JAncCiv 6 (1991) 1-21.

12970 **Kriesch** Elli G., Der Schatz von Troia und seine Geschichte. Hamburg 1994, Carlsen. 238 p.; ill. DM 38. [Archäologie in Deutschland 95/2, 60].

12971 *a*) *Meyer* Karl E., The hunt for Priam's treasure; – *b*) *Rose* Mark, What did Schliemann find — and where, when, and how did he find it?; – *c*) *Hoffman* Barbara, The spoils of war; how the law interprets ownership of plundered artifacts: Archaeology 46,6 (1993) 26-32 / 33-36 / 37-40.

12972 **Moorehead** Caroline, The lost treasures of Troy. L 1994, Weidenfeld & N. xiv-306 p. 0-297-81500-8.

12973 *Schiering* Wolfgang, Heinrich SCHLIEMANN in Troja: Thetis 1 (Mannheim 1994) 7-15; 8 fig.; pl. 1. ➤ 11564s.

12974 ᴱ**Gamer-Wallert** Ingrid, Troia, Brücke zwischen Orient und Occident (14 Univ. lectures for Schliemann centenary 1992 ➤ 8,g420; 9,14627: 3-89308-150-X. – ᴿAJA 98 (1994) 364-6 (D. A. *Traill* condemns for bypassing him).

12975 *Gindin* L. A. T. †, *Tsymburski* V. L., ❸ The proto-Greeks in Troy: VDI 211 (1994) 19-38; Eng. 38s.

12976 *Godart* Louis, Troia, dal mito alla storia: ArchViva 13,46 (1994) 18-23; 24-27, La riscoperta del tesoro.

12977 *Hansen* O., The Ilissos river and Hittite Wilusa (Ilios): AntClas 63 (1994) 263s.

12978 *Zangger* Eberhard, PLATO's Atlantis account — a distorted recollection of the Trojan War: OxJArch 12 (1993) 77-87.

12979 **Yalvaç** ('Pisidian' Antioch): *Taşlialan* Mehmet, Pisidian Antioch; 'the journeys of St. Paul to Antioch' [Excavations since S. MITCHELL 1982]. İstanbul c. 1992, Cem Offset. 74 p.; many color. phot. and plans.

12980 **Yanartaş:** *Ruggieri* V., *Giordano* F., *Furnari* A., Un complesso iconoclastico a Chimera (Yanartaş) [83 k da Antalya]; rapporto preliminare; OrChrPer 60 (1994) 471-502; 35 fig., 2 foldout plans; map.

12981 **Yılanlı:** AnSt 44 (1994) 187-206; 2 plans; pl. XLI-XLVI (H. *Barnes*, M. *Whittow*: medieval castles survey).

12982 **Zeugma** [10 k Nizip (Gaziantep)] 1st, 1993: AnSt 44 (1994) 18-20 (D. *Kennedy*, P. *Freeman*).

12983 **Zincirli:** *Lehmann* Günnar, Zu den Zerstörungen in Zincirli während des frühen 7. Jahrhunderts v.Chr.: MDOG 126 (1994) 105-122; 24 fig.

т8.9 **Armenia, Urarţu.**

12984 *Areshyan* G. E., ❸ Archaeology and historical synthesis (B. B. PIOTROVSKY's heritage in the field of Urartu, Caucasian and Armenian studies): VDI 203 (1992) 16-24; Eng. 27.

12985 **Brjusov** Valerij J.,   Annali del popolo armeno, ᴱ*Ferrari* Aldo.   Mi
1993, Greco & G.   220 p. – ᴿOrChrPer 60 (1994) 255s (G. *Traina*).
12986 ᴱ**Burchard** Christoph, Armenia and the Bible, International Symposium
Heidelberg, July 16-19, 1990: ArmTSt 12. Atlanta 1993, Scholars. x-251 p.
– ᴿBL (1994) 43 (J. G. *Snaith*); JTS 45 (1994) 357-9 (R. W. *Thomson*);
OrChrPer 60 (1994) 540s (G. *Traina*).
12986* *a*) *Harrak* Amir,   The survival of the Urartian people; – *b*) *Brown*
Stuart C.,   Other voices; Indo-Europeans, Urartians and Elamites on the
Mesopotamian periphery: BuCanadMesop 25 (1993) 43-49; 3 fig. /
7s(-18).
Kellner H.,   Gürtelbleiche aus Urarṭu 1991 → 13337.
12987 *Tuğrul* A. Beril, *Belli* Oktay,   Cuneiform inscriptions made visible on
bronze plates from the [c. 800 B.C. Urartu, 11 k NW Van] Upper Anzaf
fortress, Turkey: Antiquity 68 (1994) 347-9; 3 fig.
12988 *a*) *Ussishkin* David,   On the architectural origin of the Urartian
standard temples; – *b*) *Merhav* Rivka,   Gold and silver pins from Urartu;
typology and methods of manufacture; – *c*) *Dinçol* Ali M.,   Cultural and
political contacts between Assyria and Urartu: TAJ 21,1 ('Eastern
Anatolia in the Iron Age' 1994) 144-155 / 129-143 / 6-21.
12989 *Wilhelm* Gernot,   Bemerkungen zum urartäischen Paläographie: Alt-
OrF 21 (1994) 352-8; 3 fig.
12990 *Zahlhaas* Gisela,   Zwei neue urartäische Inschriften: ArchMIran 26
(1993) 47-54; 1 fig.; pl. 3, 2-5.

12991 *Muş* [(pre-)Urartian pottery]: AnSt 44 (1994) 77-84; 5 fig. (D. H.
French, G. D. *Summers*).

12991* **Braund** David E.,   Georgia in antiquity; a history of Colchis and
Transcaucasian Iberia 550 B.C.-A.D. 562.   Ox 1994, Clarendon. xviii-
359 p.; bibliog. p. 315-348. 0-19-814473-3.
12992 **Lordkapanidze** Otar, Archäologie in Georgien, von der Altsteinzeit zum
Mittelalter. Weinheim 1991, VCH Acta Humaniora. x-347 p.; 76 fig.;
58 pl. DM 228. – ᴿOLZ 89 (1994) 296-300 (W. *Orthmann*); PraehZts 69
(1994) 252-6 (Carola *Metzner-Nebelsick*).
12993 *Tsetskhladze* Gocha R.,   Archaeological investigations in Georgia in the
last ten years and some problems of the ancient history of the eastern
Black Sea region: RÉAnc 96 (1994) 385-414; 16 fig.; franç. 385.

T9.1   Cyprus.

12994 *Bolger* Diane L.,   Engendering Cypriot archaeology; female roles and
statues before the Bronze Age: OpAth 20 (1994) 9-17.
12995 *Eames* S., A re-examination of the definition, distribution, and relative
chronology of proto base ring ware [... Late Cypriote IA]:   MeditArch 7
(1994) 129-140.
12996 **Jennings** Ronald C., Christians and Muslims in Ottoman Cyprus and
the Mediterranean world; Studies NE. NY 1993, NYU. xii-428 p. – ᴿBSO
57 (1994) 387s (C. *Finkel*).
12997 ᴱ**Karageorghis** V., The civilisations of the Aegean and their diffusion
in Cyprus and the Eastern Mediterranean, 2000-600 B.C., Larnaca 18-24
sept. 1989 → 7,645*: ᴿRÉG 106 (1993) 245s (J.-N. *Corvisier*).
12997* **Karageorghis** V.,   Les anciens cypriotes, entre Orient et Occident

[Ⓖ]ᵀ: Les Néréides, 1991 ➤ 8,g448; 9,14652: ᴿTEuph 5 (1992) 177-9 (A.-M. *Collombier*: no plans; 15 photos already republished and twice here).

12998 *Knapp* A. Bernard, *al.*, Sydney Cyprus survey (2d, 1993): RepCyp (1994) 329-343; 1 fig.; pl. XC-XCIV.

12999 **Reyes** A. T., Archaic Cyprus; a study of the textual and archaeological evidence: MgClasArch. Ox 1994, Clarendon. xxiii-200 p.; ill. £50. 0-19-813227-1 [BL 95,45, J. F. *Healey*].

13000 ᴱ**Wallace** Paul W., *Orphanides* Andreas G., Sources for the history of Cyprus I. Albany 1990, SUNY. xxiv-287 p. – ᴿGnomon 66 (1994) 180 (F. G. *Maier*).

13001 *Alasia:* **Merrillees** R. N., Alashia revisited 1987 ➤ 3,f64... 7,e131: ᴿJNES 53 (1994) 138s (T. van den *Hout*).

13001* **Lagarce** Jacques & Élisabeth, Alasia IV. Deux tombes du Chypriote Récent d'Enkomi 1985 ➤ 2,b309: ᴿAulaO 11 (1993) 256s (C. *Valdés*).

13002 *Amathous:* **Hermary** Antoine, La tombe du sanctuaire d'Aphrodite à Amathonte: RepCyp (1994) 197-210; 13 fig.; pl. XLVI-XLVII (XLVIII, p. 211-4 plaque, *Pralong* Annie).

13003 *Hermary* Antoine, La date du temple d'Aphrodite à Amathonte: ᴿBCH 118 (1994) 321-330; 7 fig.

13004 **Chavanne** Marie-José, La nécropole d'Amathonte 1990 ➤ 14661: ᴿAntClas 63 (1994) 606s (Francine *Blondé*).

13005 *Pralong* Annie, La basilique de l'Acropole d'Amathonte (Chypre): RivArCr 70 (1994) 413-455; 21 fig.

13006 *Aupert* Pierre, *Leriche* Pierre, Fortifications et histoire à Amathonte: ➤ 466, Fortifications, RÉAnc 96 (1993/4) 337-342 + 13 fig.

13007 Amathonte 1993: BCH 118 (1994) 479-501; 35 fig. (A. *Hermary, al.*).

13008 *Idalion:* **Stager** Lawrence E., *Walker* Anita M.. The American expedition to Idalion, Cyprus 1973-1980: OIC 24, 1989 ➤ 9,14666: ᴿJNES 52 (1994) 53-55 (M. *Given*); PEQ 125 (1993) 172-4 (G. D. *Thomas*).

13009 **Senff** Reinhard, Das Apollon-heiligtum von Idalion; Architektur und Statuenausstattung eines zyprischen Heiligtums: SIMA 94. Jonsered 1993, Åström. 99 p.; 64 pl. 91-7081-070-2. – ᴿThetis 1 (1994) 175-8 (R. *Stupperich*).

13010 *Cross* Frank M., A Phoenician inscription from Idalion; some old and new ideas relating to child sacrifice: ➤ 67, ᶠKING F., Scripture 1994, 91-107; 2 fig.

13011 *Kalavasos*-Kopetra: Report Dept. Ant. Cyprus (1994) 289-307; 10 fig.; pl. LXXVIII-LXXXIII. (*McClellan* M. C., *Routman* M. I.).

13012 *Steel* Louise, Representations of a shrine on a Mycenaean chariot krater from Kalavasos-Ayios Dhimitrios, Cyprus: AnBritAth 89 (1994) 201-211; 4 fig.; pl. 37-38.

13013 *Kanto*-Kouphovoun: RepCyp (1994) 1-37; 15 fig.; pl. I-V (Eleni *Mantzourani,* Ⓖ).

13014 *Kholetria:* **Simmons** Alan H., Early Neolithic settlement in western Cyprus; preliminary report on the 1992-3 test excavations at Kholetria Ortos: BASOR 295 (1994) 1-14; 5 fig.

13015 *Kissonerga:* **Peltenburg** Edgar J., A ceremonial area at Kissonerga:

SIMA 70/3, 1991 → 7,e140; 9,14668:   ᴿAntClas 63 (1994) 583 (Frieda *Vandenabeele*); OpAth 20 (1994) 252-8 (R. S. *Merrillees*); Paléorient 20,1 (1994) 138 (A. *Le Brun*); PEQ 126 (1994) 170s (Louise *Steel*).

13016 *Kition*-Bamboula; Paphos... Chypre 1993: BCH 118 (1994) 647-693; 68 fig. (D. *Christou*).

13016* **Salles** J.-F., Kition-Bamboula IV. Les niveaux hellénistiques. P 1993, RCiv. 354 p.; ill. – ᴿAulaO 12 (1994) 142s (C. *Valdés Pereira*); RÉG 107 (1994) 265s (O. *Masson*).

13017 *Kourion:* **Sinos** S., *al.*, The temple of Apollo Hylates at Kourion 1990 → 8,g463:   ᴿGnomon 66 (1994) 573-5 (P. *Grossmann*).

13018 **Flourentzos** Pavlos, Excavations in the Kouris valley, 1. The tombs 1991 → 8,g464; 9,14671; 9963-36-416-0;   ᴿRB 101 (1994) 609 (R. S. *Merrillees*).

13019 *Lefkandi:* ᴱ**Popham** M. B., *al.*, Lefkandi II. The protogeometric building at Toumba, 2. The excavation, architecture, and finds: BrSch supp. 23. Athens 1993, British School. x-101 p.; 38 fig. 0-904887-11-1. – ᴿAJA 98 (1994) 573s (I. *Morris*).

13020 *Marki*-Alonia 1993s: RepCyp (1994) 51-72; 10 fig.; pl. VII-X (D. *Frankel*, Jennifer M. *Webb*).

13021 *Maroni:* **Manning** Sturt W., *al.*, Maroni valley survey 1992s: RepCyp (1994) 345-367; 6 fig.; pl. XC-XCIV.

13022 *Paphos*, Kouklia 17th, 1991s: RepCyp (1994) 115-128; 6 fig.; pl. XXII-XXIV (F. G. *Maier*, M.-L. von *Wartburg*).

13023 Paphos Garrison's camp 1990: RepCyp (1994) 215-268; 17 fig.; 3 plans; pl. XLIX-LXXIII (F. *Giudice, al.*).

13024 Alt-Paphos 16th 1989s: AnchAnz (1992) 585-597; 19 (foldout) fig. (F. G. *Maier*, Marie-Louise von *Wartburg*).

13025 **Nicolaou** Ino, Paphos 2, The coins from the house of Dionysus 1990 → 8,g471; 9,14673:   ᴿGnomon 66 (1994) 76-78 (W. *Leschhorn*); JEA 80 (1994) 265s (M. *Price*).

13025* **Hohlfelder** R., Paphos 1991 → 295, ASOR reports 1994, 45-62.

13026 Nea Paphos 1994 → 11498, Polish (Reports 1994) 67-74 (W. *Daszewski*), 75-83 (H. *Meyra*).

13027 *Giudice* F., Gli scavi del santuario di Apollo a Toumballos a Paphos (Cipro): SicGymn 45 (1992) 153-8.

13028 **Karageorghis** V., Tombs at Palaipaphos 1990 → 7,e142*; 8,g468: ᴿSyria 61 (1994) 245-8 (Valérie *Cook*).

13029 *Nobbs* Alanna, Cyprus: → 243, Acts Graeco-Roman 1994, 279-289 [p. 288, unlikely that because of Sergius Paullus the person until then called Saul takes the name of Paul].

13030 *Masson* Olivier, Amargetti, un sanctuaire rural près de Paphos: BCH 118 (1994) 261-275.

13031 *Salamis:* **Monloup** Thérèse, Les terres cuites classiques; un sanctuaire de la grande déesse: Salamine de Chypre 14. P 1994, de Boccard. 215 p. 2-903264-92-9.

13032 *Toumba/Skourou:* **Vermeule** Emily D. T., *Wolsky* Florence Z., Toumba tou Skourou, a Bronze Age potters' quarter on Morphou Bay in Cyprus 1990 → 8,g473*:   ᴿBASOR 296 (1994) 81-83 (Ellen *Herscher*).

13033 *Tsaroukkas* 1993, Mycenaeans and trade project: RepCyp (1994) 83-100; 13 fig.; pl. XI-XIII (S. W. *Manning, al.*).

13034 *Vounos: Ross* James F., The Vounos jars revisited: BASOR 296 (1994) 15-30.

T9.3   *Graecia,* Greece – mainland sites in alphabetical order.

13035 *Aellen* C., *Maffre* J.-J., *Metzger* H., Bulletin archéologique: RÉG 107 (1994) 621-685.

13036 Excavation reports [Rhamnous, Gla(s), Mycenae...]: PraktArch for 1991 (Athenai 1994) 1-396.

13037 **Forsén** Jeannette, The twilight of the Early Helladic; a study of disturbances in east-central and southern Greece towards the end of the Early Bronze Age: SIMA pocket 116. Jonsered 1992, Åström. 297 p. 17 fig. 91-7081-031-1. – ᴿOpAth 20 (1994) 260-3 (J. B. *Rutter*).

13038 **Pearson** Anne, L'antica Grecia. Novara c. 1993, De Agostini. 64 p.; 300 color. ill. Lᵐ 24. – ᴿArcheo 9,107 (1994) 118 (S. *Moscati*).

13039 **Ridgway** David, The first western Greeks 1992 → 8,g480; £32,50; pa. £11: ᴿAntiqJ 73 (1993) 201s (G. B. *Shepherd*); Antiquity 67 (1993) 461s (R. *Osborne*: updating of his 1984 L'alba della Magna Grecia).

13040 *Rutter* Jeremy B., Review of Aegean prehistory 2. The prepalatial Bronze Age of the southern and central Greek mainland: AJA 97 (1993) 745-797; 16 fig. (maps).

13041 a) *Tomlinson* R. A., Archaeology in Greece 1994-5; – b) *Ridgway* David, Archaeology in Sardinia and South Italy (1989-94): ArRepAth (1994s) 1-74; 40 fig. / 75-96; 30 fig.

13042 ꟳTRENDALL A. D., Greek colonists and native populations [First Australian Congress of classical archaeology, Sydney 1985], ᴱ**Descoeudres** Jean-Paul 1990 → 8,679; 0-19-81469-0: ᴿAJA 97 (1993) 364-6 (R. R. *Holloway*); RossArkh (1994,1) 232-9 (O. N. *Usacheva*).

13043 *Achaea: Gill* David W. J., a) Achaia; – b) Macedonia: → 243, Acts Graeco-Roman 1994, 433-453 / 397-417.

13044 ᴱ**Rizakis** A. D., Achaia und Elis in der Antike; Akten des Symposiums 1989/91 → 8,733: ᴿClasR 44 (1994) 109-111 (R. *Brock*); RPg 67 (1993) 143s (É. *Will*).

13045 *Aegae: Faklaris* Panayotis B., Aegae; determining the site of the first capital of the Macedonians: AJA 98 (1994) 609-616; map.

13046 *Aegina: Weisshaar* Hans-Joachim, Keramik des Südwest-Ägäischen Chalkolithikums von Ägina: → 35, ꟳFREY O. 1994, 675-689; 7 fig.

13047 *Aidonia: Rose* Mark, Greece sues [N. Y. Ward art gallery] for Mycenaean gold [illegally taken, from Aidonia]: Archaeology 46,5 (1993) 26-30.

13048 *Akarnia: Gehrke* Hans-Joachim, Die kulturelle und politische Entwicklung Akarniens vom 6. bis zum 4. Jahrhundert v.Chr.: GeogAnt 3s (1994s) 41-48.

13049 *Argos: Marchetti* Patrick, Recherches sur les mythes et la topographie d'Argos; II. Présentation du site; III. Le témenos de Zeus: BCH [117 (1993) 211-223] 118 (1994) 131-160; 7 fig.

13050 **Dietz** Søren, The Argolid at the transition to the Mycenaean age 1991 → 7,e149 ... 9,14683: ᴿGnomon 66 (1994) 533-7 (Imma *Kilian*).

13051 *Athenae:* **Aleshire** Sara B., The Athenian Asklepieion; the people, their dedications, and the inventories 1989 → 9,14699: Gnomon 66 (1994) 251-6 (K.-V. von *Eickstedt*).

13051* *Knell* Heiner,   Der jüngere Tempel des Apollon Patroos auf der
Athener Agora: JbDAI 109 (1994) 217-237; 8 fig.
13052 *a) Korras* Manolis,   Wilhelm DÖRPFELDS Forschungen zum Vor-
parthenon und Parthenon; – *b) Kürze-Götbe* Erika, Zwei attisch rot-
figurige Pyxiden aus Gräbern des Kerameikos [*al.* auch Kerameikos]:
MiDAI-A 108 (1993) 59-78; 15 fig. / 79-99; 2 fig.; pl. 11-15 [151-181;
49-58].
13052* **Lalonde** Gerald V., *al.*, Inscriptions, Horas...: Athenian Agora 19,
1991 → 9,14696: ᴿAntClas 63 (1994) 492s (A. *Martin*); Gnomon 66
(1994) 695 (A. *Chaniotis*); Phoenix 48 (Toronto 1994) 274-6 (D. M.
Lewis).
13053 *Palagia* O., The pediments of the Parthenon 1993 → 9,14689: ᴿJHS
114 (1994) 224s (I. *Jenkins*).
13054 *Hoff* Michael C.,   The so-called Agoranomion and the imperial cult in
Julio-Claudian Athens: ArchAnz (1994) 93-117; 18 fig.
13055 Kerameikos 1990s: ArchAnz (1993) 125-140; 20 fig. (Ursula *Knigge*).
13056 *Tobin* Jennifer,   Some new thoughts on Herodes Atticus's tomb, his
stadium of 143/4, and Philostratus VS 2.550: AJA 97 (1993) 81-89.
13057 **Welwei** Karl-W.,   Athen: vom neolithischen Siedlungsplatz zur archaischen Grosspolis. Da 1992, Wiss. vi-300 p. DM 54. – ᴿHZ 259 (1994)
442s (Maria H. *Dettenhofer*).
13058 *Conwell* David H.,   Topography and toponyms between Athens and
Piraeus: JAncTop 3 (1993) 49-62; 4 fig. (maps).

13059 *Beroea: Markle* Minor M.,   A shield monument from Veria: → 416c,
MeditArch 7 (1991/4) 83-97; 12 fig.; pl. 8.
13060 *Corinthus: Antonelli* Luca,   Corinto, Olimpia e lo spazio ionico; il
problema della *phiale* di Boston: Hesperia 3 (Venezia 1993) 35-44.
13060* *Romano* David G., *Schoenbrun* Benjamin C.,   A computerized
architectural and topographical survey of ancient Corinth: JField 20
(1993) 177-190; 7 (color.) fig.
13061 **Slane** Kathleen W., Corinth 18/2, 1990 → 8,g510: ᴿGnomon 66 (1994)
472-4 (Christa *Schauer*).

13062 *Delphes* 1993: BCH 118 (1994) 423-434; 13 fig. (V. *Deroche, al.*).
13063 *Croissant* Francis,   Le Dionysos du fronton occidental de Delphes;
histoire d'un faux problème: BCH 118 (1994) 353-360; 2 fig.
13063* **Maass** Michael,   Das antike Delphi; Orakel, Schätze und Monumente.
Da 1993, Wiss. ix-315 p.; Bibliog. 291-308. 3-534-10940-6.
13064 **Musielak** M.,   The city-state of Delphi in the fourth century B.C.; a
study in the history of Greek society. Poznań 1989. 141 p. – ᴿClasB 69
(1993) 61s (Krystyna *Stebnicka*).
13065 *Lefèvre* François,   Un document amphictionique inédit du IVᵉ siècle
[...Delphes]: BCH 118 (1994) 99-112; 2 fig.
13066 *Nenci* Giuseppe,   I donativi di Creso a Delphi: AnPisa 23 (1993)
319-331.
13067 ᴱPicard O., *Pentazos* E.,   La redécouverte de Delphes. P 1992, de
Boccard. 295 p.; 181 fig. F 350. 2-86958-050-9. – ᴿAJA 98 (1994) 170s
(M. F. *Arnush*).
13068 **Vatin** Claude, Monuments votifs de Delphes 1991 → 8,g523*; 9,14722:
ᴿKlio 76 (1994) 472s (W. *Ameling*).

13069 *Goritsa: Bakhuizen* S. C.,   A Greek city of the fourth century B.C.: Bt-

Arch 10. R 1992, Bretschneider. 327 p.; 113 fig.; 54 pl. 88-7062-720-9.
– ᴿAJA 97 (1993) 579s (Barbara *Tsakirgis*).
13070 *Kalamakia* (grotte, S. Péloponnèse) 1993: BCH 118 (1994) 535-559; 2(
fig. (H. de *Lumley*, A. *Dablas*).
13071 **Krini:** *Papazoglou-Manioudaki* Lena, A Mycenaean warrior's tomb at
Krini near Patras: AnBritAth 89 (1994) 171-200; 25 fig.; pl. 23-36.
13072 **Lavda** (Theisos in Arcadia): Pharos 2 (Amst 1994) 49-89; 6 fig.; XVI pl.
(J. *Feije*).
13073 **Lebadeia:** **Turner** Lee Ann, The history, monuments and topography
of ancient Lebadeia in Boeotia: diss. Pennsylvania, ᴰ*White* D. Ph 1994.
696 p. 94-27631. – DissA 55 (1994s) p. 1356.
13074 **Fossey** John M., Boeotia Antiqua II: McGill MgArchClass. Amst
1992, Gieben. x-63 p.; 17 fig.; 27 pl. 90-5063-083-9. – ᴿAntClas 63
(1994) 534s (C. *Müller*).
13075 **Effenterre** Henri van, Les Béotiens 1989 ➤ 8,g503*: ᴿAJA 98 (1994)
371 (D. W. *Roller*).
13076 **Lefkandi:** ᴱ**Popham** M. R., *al.*, Lefkandi 2/2, protogeometric building
at Toumba. L 1993, British School at Athens. x-101 p.; 38 pl. £26. –
ᴿClasR 44 (1994) 377-9 (J. *Whitley*).
13077 **Macedon:** *a*) *Hammond* N. G. L., Macedonia before Philip and Philip's
first year in power; – *b*) *Borza* Eugene N., The ancient Macedonians; a
methodological model; – *c*) *Londey* Peter, Philip II and the Delphic
amphiktyony; – *d*) *McKenzie* Lea, Patterns in Seleucid administration;
Macedonian or Near Eastern: ➤416*c*, MeditArch 7 (1991/4) (7-)13-15 /
17-24 / 25-34 / 61-68.
13078 **Marathon:** *Whitley* James, The monuments that stood before
Marathon; tomb cult and hero cult in archaic Attica: AJA 98 (1994)
213-230; 8 fig.
13078* *Marsch* Andrea, Archäologischer Kommentar zu den 'Gräbern der
Athener und Platäer' in der Marathonia [i.e. Anspielungen bei HERODOT,
NEPOS, PAUSANIAS]: Klio 77 (1995) 55-64.

13079 **Mycenae:** *Andreev* Yu. V., ❸ Awaiting the Greek miracle (spiritual
world of Mycenaean society): VDI 207 (1993) 14-32; Eng. 32s.
13080 *a*) *Farnoux* Alexandre, Actualités du monde mycénien; – *b*) *Touchais*
Gilles, Les origines du monde mycénien; – *c*) *Carlier* Pierre, Histoire et
institutions; – *d*) *Poursat* Jean-Claude, Les ivoires mycéniens; – *e*)
Effenterre Henri van, Effondrements et continuités; – *f*) *Crielaard*
Jean-Paul, Les Mycéniens et les poèmes épiques d'Homère: DossA 195
(1994) 6-17 (94-119) / 18-33 / 34-49 / 84-93 / 120-5 / 126-135.
13081 ᴱ**Musti** D., La transizione dal Miceneo all'Alto Arcaismo; dal palazzo
alla città: convegno SMEA 14-19.III.1988/1991 ➤ 7,649*d*: ᴿREG 106
(1993) 637 (P. *Faure*).
13082 **Ozanne** Isabelle, Les Mycéniens; pillards, paysans et poètes: Civilisations-
U. P 1992, A. Colin. 280 p. – ᴿMusHelv 51 (1994) 181 (Sylvie *Müller*).
13083 **Nemea:** ᴱ**Miller** S. G., *al.*, Excavations at Nemea I, 1992 ➤ 8,g531:
ᴿJHS 114 (1994) 223 (R. A. *Tomlinson*).

13084 **Olympia:** *Brulotte* Eric L., The 'pillar of Oinomaos' and the location
of Stadium I at Olympia: AJA 98 (1994) 53-64; 7 fig.
13085 **Schiering** W., Die Werkstatt des Pheidias in Olympia 2: OlFor 5. B
1991, de Gruyter. xiv-277 p.; 72 fig.; vol. of 95 pl. ᴅᴍ 78. 3-11-001228-6.
– ᴿJHS 114 (1994) 226s (Carol C. *Mattusch*, OlFor 18).

13086 *Siewert* Peter,   Parallelen zwischen der Entstehung des argivischen Heraions und der des Zeusheiligtums von Olympia: ArchAnz (1993) 509s.

13087 *Sinn* Ulrich, *al.*, Olympia Forschungsprojekt 1994: Nikephoros 7 (1994) 229-250; pl. 9-10 (254, Nachtrag zu Band 6, *Herrmann* H.

13087* *Philipp* Hanna,   Olympia, die Peloponnes und die Westgriechen: JbDAI 109 (1994) 77-93.

13088 *Philippes* 1993: BCH 118 (1994) 435 + 3 fig. (M. *Sève*).

13089 *Phokis:*   ᴱKase E. W. †, *al.*, The great Isthmus corridor route 1, 1991 ➤ 8,k140:   ᴿAJA 98 (1994) 575s (Susan E. *Alcock*).

13090 *Sicilia:*   *a) Martorana* Giuseppe,   I *nostoi* e la Sicilia, tra mito e storia; Troia, Roma, imperium romanum; – *b) Braccesi* Lorenzo, La Sicilia, l'Africa e il mondo dei nostoi: ➤ 433, Kokalos 39s (1993s) 363-390 (-395 discussione) / 183-210.

13091 *Sparta:*   Cartledge P., *Spawforth* A., Hellenistic and Roman Sparta 1989 ➤ 6,e988 ... 9,14740:   ᴿAnzAltW 46 (1993) 46-48 (G. *Dobesch*).

13092 *a) Dettenhofer* Maria H.,   Die Frauen von Sparta; gesellschaftliche Position und politische Relevanz; – *b) Parker* Viktor,   Some dates in early Spartan history: Klio 75 (1993) 61-75; Eng. 75 / 45-60.

13092* *Thermos* (Thermon in Aetolia?), *Klein* Gerhard,   Bau B und Tempel C in Thermos: MiDAI-A 108 (1993) 29-47; 3 fig.; pl. 1-7.

13093 *Tiryns: Zangger* Eberhard,   Landscape changes around Tiryns during the Bronze Age: AJA 98 (1994) 189-213; 14 fig.

13094 *Torone: Cambitoglou* Alexander, *Papadopoulos* John K.,   Excavations at Torone [Chalcidice] 1990:   MeditArch 7 (1994) 141-163; 42 fig.; pl. 15-21.

13095 *Ustica: Holloway* R. Ross, Ustica; the development of a Middle Bronze Age town in the Tyrrhenian basin [... Mycenean influence]: JAncTop 3 (1993) 1-16; 12 fig.

13096 *Volos* gulf: **Maren** Joseph,   Die deutschen Ausgrabungen auf der Pevkakia-Magoula in Thessalien, 3. Die Mittlere Bronzezeit. Bonn 1992, Habelt.   xii-413-84 p. 190 fig.; 30 pl. + 1 color.; 13 plans; 2 microfiches. – ᴿClasR 44 (1994) 374s (C. *Mee*).

T9.4   Creta.

13097 *Ager* Sheila L.,   Hellenistic Crete and *koinodikion*:   JHS 114 (1994) 1-18.

13098 **Castleden** Rodney,   Minoans: Life in Bronze Age Crete 1990 ➤ 6,e995; 8,g543. L 1990, pa. 1993, Routledge.   xii-210 p.; 58 fig.; 20 pl.   0-415-08833-X. – ᴿAJA 98 (1994) 572s (J. S. *Soles*); ÉtClas 62 (1994) 303s (J. *Vanschoonwinkel*); Minos 27 (1992s) 325-9 (J. *Bennet*).

13099 *Chaniotis* Angelos,   Von Hirten, Kräutersammlern, Epheben und Pilgern; Leben auf den Bergen im antiken Kreta: Ktema 16 (1991) 93-109.

13100 ᴱCunliffe Barry,   The Oxford illustrated prehistory of Europe [... Crete, Mycenae].   Ox 1994, U.P.   xii-532 p.; 300 pl. + 24 colour. £30. – ᴿGreeceR 41 (1994) 244 (P. *Walcot*: high quality).

13101 *a) Driessen* Jean,   La Crète mycénienne; – *b) Olivier* Jean-Pierre, L'économie des royaumes mycéniens d'après les tablettes en Linéaire B: DossA 195 (1994) 66-83 / 50-65.

13102 *Faure* Paul,   Cavernes sacrées de la Crète antique: Cretan Studies 4 (1994) 77-83; pl. IV-V.

13103 *Faure* Paul, Des chiffres et des lettres [furthering Sinclair HOOD's claim of fitting the Minoan 'palaces' into a series of Mid-East and Egyptian 'religious-administrative' buildings]: Cretan Studies 4 (1994) 85-89.

13104 **Marinatos** Nanno, Minoan religion; ritual, image, and symbol. Columbia 1993, Univ. S. Carolina. xii-306 p. $49.75. – ᴿAnzAltW 46 (1993) 129s (W. *Pötscher*); JRel 74 (1994) 435s (G. D. *Allen*: effectively follows BURKERT, but bypasses positivist statistics, I. HODDER & J. THOMAS).

13105 **Mastorakis** Michel, *Effenterre* Micheline van, Les Minoens; l'âge d'or de la Crète: Néréides, 1991 ➤ 7,e196* ... 9,14751: ᴿAevum 66 (1992) 150s (Celestina *Milani*); ÉtClas 62 (1994) 89 (J. *Vanschoonwinkel*); MusHelv 51 (1994) 180 (Sylvie *Müller*).

13106 *Mercereau* Rebecca, Cretan cylindrical [architecture-] models: AJA 97 (1993) 1-47; 35 fig.

13107 *Myers* J. & E., *Cadogan* G., The aerial atlas of ancient Crete 1992: ᴿClasB 70 (1994) 49s (P. *Rehak*).

13108 **Quinlan** Angus R., Toward an archaeology of religion [anthropology, rather, except for exemplifications in Crete]: diss. Southampton 1993. DissA 54 (1993s) p. 1060.

13109 *Tofanari* Susanna, Atlantide e Creta; ➤ 98, ᶠRADMILLI A. 1994, 345-357 [p. 345 'circa 10.0000 (sic)' scritti in proposito].

13110 *Watrous* J. Vance, Review of Aegean prehistory III. Crete from the earliest prehistory through the protopalatial period: AJA 98 (1994) 695-753; 31 fig.

13111 **Willets** R. F., The civilization of ancient Crete. Amst 1991, Hakkert = 1977 (Batsford). 283 p.; 25 fig.; 23 pl. 90-256-0980-5. – ᴿAntClas 63 (1994) 516 (Didier *Viviers*).

13112 *Hierapytna:* *Bowsky* M. W. Baldwin, Cretan connections; the transformation of Hierapytna [SE Crete]: Cretan Studies 4 (1994) 1-44; 8 maps.

13113 *Knossos:* **Castleden** Rodney, The Knossos labyrinth; a new view of the 'Palace of Minos' at Knossos. L 1990, Routledge. xiii-205 p.; 54 fig.; 20 pl. 0-415-03315-2. – ᴿAJA 98 (1994) 572s (J. S. *Soles*).

13114 **Doab** Penelope R., The idea of the labyrinth from classical antiquity through the Middle Ages. Ithaca 1990, Cornell Univ. xvii-355 p. – ᴿPhoenix 48 (Toronto 1994) 83-85 (C. C. *Chiasson*).

13115 **Driessen** Jan, An early destruction in the Mycenaean palace at Knossos 1990 ➤ 8,g556; 9,14758: ᴿAJA 97 (1993) 172-4 (J. *Bennet*); AntClas 63 (1994) 586s (R. *Laffineur*); Gnomon 66 (1994) 246-250 (S. *Hiller*).

13116 *a*) *Hood* Sinclair, *al.*, Excavations at Knossos; – *b*) *Musgrave* J. H., *al.*, The priest and priestess from Archanes-Anemospilia; reconstructing Minoan faces; – *c*) *Wilson* D. E., *Day* P. M., Ceramic regionalism in prepalatial central Crete; the Mesara imports at EM I to EM IIA Knossos: AnBritAth 89 (1994) 101-156; pl. 15-20 / 89-100; 8 fig.; pl. 14 / 1-87; 10 fig.; pl. 1-13.

13117 **Raison** Jacques, Le palais du second millénaire à Knossos; 2. Le front ouest et ses magasins: Ét. crétoises 29. Athenes 1993, École Française.

13118 ᴱ**Sackett** L. H., *al.*, Knossos ... unexplored mansion 2, 1992 ➤ 8,g560; 2,14759: ᴿAJA 97 (1993) 815s (G. W. M. *Harrison*).

13119 *Kommos:* **Watrous** L. V., Kommos 3: LB pottery. Princeton 1992, Univ. 238 p.; 76 fig.; 58 pl. $75. 0-691-03607-1. – ᴿAJA 98 (1994) 781s (Mervyn *Popham*); BO 51 (1994) 710-4 (J. J. *Herman*); JHS 114 (1994) 219s (P. *Warren*).

13119* *Korakomouri* (E Crete): JbÖsA 64 (1995) 1-24; 13 fig. (N. *Schlager*).

13120 *Malia* 1993: BCH 118 (1994) 471-7; 11 fig. (J. *Driessen*, A. *Farnoux*).

13121 *Mochlos:* **Soles** Jeffrey S., The prepalatial cemeteries at Mochlos and Gournia and the house tombs of Bronze Age Crete: Hesperia supp. 21. Princeton 1992, Amer. Sch. Athens. xxi-266 p.; 81 fig.; 40 pl.; 4 plans. 0-87661-524-8. – ᴿAJA 98 (1994) 167s (C. *Ten Wolde*).

13122 *Nekrokourou:* **Vagnetti** L., *al.*, Scavi a Nekrokourou (W. Creta) Kydonias I: IncunabGr 91. R 1989, Ateneo. 339 p. – ᴿAJA 97 (1993) 360s (J. A. *MacGillivray*).

13123 *Kavousi:* *Haggis* Donald C., *Mook* Margaret S., The Kavousi coarse wares; a Bronze Age chronology for survey in the Mirabello area, East Crete: AJA 97 (1993) 265-292; 27 fig.

13124 *Sicilia:* a) *La Rosa* Vincenzo, Influenze di tipo egeo e paleogreco in Sicilia; – b) *Bianchetti* Serena, Motivi delle saghe cretesi nelle tradizioni sulle *poleis* greche: ↠ 433*a*, Kokalos 39s (1993s) 9-65; 2 fig.; discussione 66-69 / 181-210.

T9.5   Insulae graecae.

13125 ᴱ**Acquaro** Enrico, Momenti precoloniali nel Mediterraneo antico 1985/8 ↠ 5,811 ... 9,14766: ᴿJNES 53 (1994) 221s (E. *Guralnick*).

13126 **Catling** H. W., Some problems in Aegean prehistory [Oxford Myers Lecture 14]. 1987; Leopard's Head Press. – ᴿAthenaeum 82 (1994) 235-7 (O. *Carruba*).

13127 **Cosmopoulos** Michael B., The Early Bronze 2 in the Aegean: SIMA 98. Jonsered 1991, Åström. xi-327 p.; 52 fig.; 12 pl. Skr 450. 91-7081-019-2. – ᴿAJA 98 (1994) 780s (D. C. *Haggis*); OpAth 20 (1994) 258-260 (Jeannette *Forsén*).

13128 **Dickinson** Oliver, The Aegean Bronze Age: Cambridge World Archaeology. C 1994, Univ. xxii-342 p.

13129 ᴱ**Kardulias** P. Nick, Beyond the site; regional studies in the Aegean area. Lanham MD 1994, UPA. xxvii-417 p. 0-8191-9633-9.

13130 *Claros:* *Marcadé* Jean, Rapport préliminaire sur le groupe cultuel du temple d'Apollon à Claros (état de mai 1995): RÉAnc 96 (1994!) 447-454 + 29 fig.; Eng. 447.

13131 *Délos* 1993: BCH 118 (1994) 465-470; 5 fig. (P. *Fraisse*, Isabelle *Bourger*).

13132 **Ekschmitt** Werner, Die Kykladen; Bronzezeit, geometrische und archaische Zeit. KuGaW Sdb. Mainz 1993, von Zabern. 304 p.; 152 fig.; 118 pl. 3-8053-1533-3.

13133 *Gill* David W. J., *Chippendale* Christopher, Material and intellectual consequences of esteem for Cycladic figures: AJA 97 (1993) 601-659; 3 fig.

13134 *Godart* Louis, La civiltà delle Cicladi: Archeo 9,108 (1994) 56-99; color. ill.

13135 *Reger* Gary, The political history of the Kyklades 360-200 B.C.: Historia 43 (1994) 32-69.

13136 *Icaria:* **Papalas** Anthony J., Ancient Icaria. Wauconda 1992, Bolchazy Carducci. 215 p. $39; pa. $24. – ᴿClasB 70 (1994) 45-47 (J. E. *Rexine*).
13137 *Keos:* **Cherry** J. F., *al.*, Landscape archaeology... N. Keos 1991 ➤ 9,14780: ᴿAJA 97 (1993) 301-3 (L. V. *Watrous*); JHS 114 (1994) 204s (M. *Wagstaff*).
13138 *Papageorgiadou-Banis,* Koinon of the Keians? [westernmost Cycladic]; the numismatic evidence: RBgNum 139 (1993) 9-16.

13139 **Lesbos:** *Williams* Hector, Secret rites of Lesbos; scholars probe the ruins of a Greek sanctuary where women held religious rituals once a year: Archaeology 47,4 (1994) 34-40; ill.
13140 *Schaus* Gerald P., *Spencer* Nigel, Notes on the topography of Enesos [SW Lesbos]: AJA 98 (1994) 411-430; 12 fig.
13141 *Labarre* Guy, *Koinon Lesbion* [cult around Messa sanctuary before 200 B.C.]: RÉAnc 96 (1994) 415-446 en français; Eng. 415.

13142 **Rhodos,** Thera, Kos; Crète... Grèce 1993: BCH 118 (1994) 695-843 (Anne *Pariente*); 169 fig.; index des sites 844-866.
13143 **Benzi** M., Rodi e la civiltà micenea. R 1992, Gruppo Internaz. xxiii-482 p.; 186 pl. – ᴿJHS 114 (1994) 220s (C. *Mee*).
13144 *Samos:* **Kreuzer** Bettina, Überlegungen zum Handel mit bemalten Keramik im 6. Jh, v.Chr. unter besonderer Berücksichtigung des Heraion von Samos: Klio 76 (1994) 103-118; Eng. 119.
13145 *Thasos* 1993: BCH 118 (1994) 447-464; 25 fig. (Y. *Grandjean*, F. *Salviat,* le rempart; Z. *Bonias*, *al.*, le théâtre; F. *Blondé, al.*, agora NE). **Duchêne** Hervé, Études thasiennes 14, 1992 ➤ 11699.
13146 *Herrmann* John J.ᴶ, *Barbin* Vincent, The exportation of marble from the Aliki quarries on Thasos: cathodoluminescence of samples from Turkey and Italy: AJA 97 (1993) 91-103; 13 fig.

13147 **Thera:** ᴱHardy D. A., Thera III,1, Archaeology 1990 ➤ 7,642...9, 14790: ᴿAJA 97 (1993) 363s (Karen P. *Foster*).
13148 **Morgan** Lyvia, The miniature wall paintings of Thera 1988 ➤ 6,g43; 9,14792: ᴿClasR 44 (1994) 146-8 (Christiane *Sourvinou-Inwood*).
13149 a) *Negbi* Ora, The 'Libyan landscape' from Thera; a review of Aegean enterprises overseas in the Late Minoan IA period; – b) responses *Manning* Sturt W., *al.*, The fatal shore, the long years and the geographical unconscious; considerations of iconography, chronology, and trade; – c) *Sherratt* Susan: JMeditArch 7 (1994) 73-112 / 219-225 / 237-240.

T9.6   Urbs Roma.

13150 *Chavasse* Antoine, Sur le sol de Rome; les lieux anciens habités par les chrétiens: RevSR 68 (1994) 2-4; map.
13151 a) *Claridge* Amanda, Hadrian's column of Trajan; – b) *Jones* Mark W., One hundred feet and a spiral stair; the problem of designing Trajan's Column: JRomArch 6 (1993) 5-22; 9 fig. / 23-38; 13 fig.
13152 **D'Ambra** Eve, Private lives, imperial virtues; the frieze of the [Domitian] Forum Transitorium in Rome. Princeton 1993, Univ. xviii-157 p.; 91 pl. $35. – ᴿAmHR 99 (1994) 1665s (R. *Brilliant*).
13153 **Denti** Mario, Ellenismo e romanizzazione nella X regio. R 1991,

Bretschneider. 377 p.; 102 pl. L^m 880. 88-7699-065-1. – ^RBabesch 69 (1994) 220-2 (E. M. *Moormann*, ital.).

13154 *Desnier* Jean-Luc, Omina [p. 547; 'omnia', index] et realia; naissance de l'Urbs Sacra sévérienne (193-204 ap. J.-C.): MÉF 105 (1993) 547-620; 12 fig.

13155 ^E**Di Castro** Daniela, Arte ebraica a Roma e nel Lazio. R 1994, Palombi. [iv-] 197 p.; 88-7621-240-X.

13156 *Fridh* Åke, Mons and collis: Eranos 91 (1993) 1-12.

13157 ^E**Giardina** Andrea, Der Mensch der römischen Antike [L'uomo romano]. Fra/NY 1991, Campus. 429 p.

13158 *Gibson* Sheila, *al.*, The triclinium of the Domus Flavia, a new reconstruction: PapBritR 62 (1994) 67-97; 29 fig.; 1 foldout.

13159 *Grandazzi* Alexandre, La Roma quadrata; mythe ou réalité?: MÉF 105 (1993) 493-545.

13160 **Hesberg** Henner von, *Panciera* Silvio, Das Mausoleum des Augustus; der Bau und seine Inschriften: Abh ph/h 108. Mü 1994, Bayerische Akad. viii-201 p.; 17 pl. 3-7696-0103-3.

13161 **Hinard** François, *Royo* Manuel, Rome, l'espace urbain et ses représentations 1991 ➤ 8,g612; 9,14797: 2-904315-89-6: ^RLatomus 53 (1994) 471s (J. *Debergh*).

13162 **Holloway** R. Ross, The archeology of early Rome and Latium. L 1994, Routledge. xx-203 p. 0-415-08065-7.

13163 *Kaestli* Jean-Daniel, Le rapport entre les deux Vies Latines [Pass. Ioh. & Virt. Ioh.] de l'Apôtre Jean [*Schäferdiek* K., AnBoll 103 (1985) 337-382]: Apocrypha 3 (1992) 111-123; Eng. 280.

13164 *Lange* Judith, Un dono per Domiziano; un monumento tra Roma e gli States: ArchViva 13,46 (1994) 28-33.

13165 **Luciani** Roberto, Il Colosseo. Novara c. 1993, De Agostini. 240 p., 300 (color.) ill. L^m 80. – ^RArcheo 9,107 (1994) 122s (S. *Moscati*).

13166 **Meyer** H., Antinoos; die archäologischen Denkmäler 1991 ➤ 8,g618: ^RAJA 98 (1994) 377s (Mara D. *Fullerton*).

13167 **Neumeister** Christoff, Roma antica; guida letteraria alla città [1991 ➤ 7,e256]^T. R c. 1993, Salerno. 314 p.; 25 fig.; 50 pl. L^m 42. – ^RArcheo 9,108 (1994) 119 (S. *Moscati*).

13167* *Packer* James E., Trajan's Forum again; the Column and the Temple of Trajan in the master-plan attributed to Apollodorus(?): JRomA 7 (1994) 163-182; 15 fig.

13168 *Peacock* D. P. S., *al.*, Mons Claudianus and the problem of the 'granito del foro'; a geological and geochemical approach: Antiquity 68 (1994) 209-230.

13169 *a) Purcell* Nicholas, Atrium libertatis [under Palazzo Senatorio); – *b) Bird* Joanna, *al.*, Porta Pia excavations and survey in an area of suburban Rome I: PBritR 61 (1993) 123-155; 4 fig. / 51-111; 27 fig.

13170 **Richardson** L., A new topographical dictionary of ancient Rome 1992 ➤ 9,14801: ^RAJA 98 (1994) 376s (P. G. *Warden*); ClasB 69 (1993) 113-5 (R. A. *Hornsby*); ClasOut 71 (1993s) 112s (Katherine A. *Geffcken*); ClasR 44 (1994) 167-9 (J. *Carter*).

13171 *Royo* Manuel, Le palais dans la ville: formes et structures topographiques du pouvoir impériale d'Auguste à Néron: MÉF 106 (1994) 219-245; 7 plans.

13171* *Sear* Frank B., The scaenae frons of the theatre of Pompey: AJA 97 (1993) 687-701; 13 fig.

13172 *Steiner* Andreas M., Incontro con *Melucco Vaccaro* Alessandra: Chi costruì l'arco di Costantino?: Archeo 9,111 (1994) 38-45.

13173 *Tomei* Maria Antonietta, La Roma quadrata e gli scavi palatini di ROSA [P., 1865]: MÉF 106 (1994) 1025-1072; 13 fig.

13174 *Ulrich* Roger B., Julius Caesar and the creation of the Forum Iulium: AJA 97 (1993) 49-80; 11 fig.

13175 **Yarden** L., Spoils of Jerusalem on the Arch of Titus 1991 → 8,g633; 9,14804: ᴿGnomon 66 (1994) 620-4 (R. *Wenning*).

13176 *Ziolkowski* Adam, Was Agrippa's Pantheon the temple of Mars *in campo*?: PapBritR 62 (1994) 261-277.

13177 *Chevallier* Raymond, Ostia antica; la città e il suo porto: Archeo 9,118 (1994) 66-108; (color.) ill.

13178 *Chevallier* R., Dix années de travaux récents sur Ostie antique: Latomus 53 (1994) 543-563.

T9.7 *Roma*, **Catacumbae.**

13179 *Baglioni* P., Peter is here [Margherita GUARDUCCI's defense of her claim to have identified the bones]: 30 Days 1 (Rome 1994) 50-54 [< NTAbs 38, p. 347].

13180 **Bargebuhr** F. P., Paintings... Via Latina 1991 → 8,g633*; 9,14806: ᴿAntClas 63 (1994) 641s (Janine *Balty*).

13181 *Berg* Beverly, Alcestis and Hercules in the catacomb of Via Latina: VigChr 48 (1994) 219-234.

13182 *Carletti* Carlo, Nuove iscrizioni dalla catacomba della ex vigna Chiaraviglio sulla Via Appia: MÉF 106 (1994) 29-41; 6 fig.

13183 *De Santis* Paola, Elementi di corredo nei sepolcri delle catacombe romane; l'esempio della regione di Leone e della galleria Bb nella catacomba di Commodilla: VetChr 31 (1994) 23-51; 16 fig.

13184 *Felle* Antonio, *Del Moro* Maria Paola, *Nuzzo* Donatella, Elementi di 'corredo-arredo' delle tombe del cimitero di S. Ippolito sulla Via Tiburtina: RivArCr 70 (1994) 89-158; 43 fig.

13185 *Giordani* Roberto, Riflessioni sulla decorazione absidale della Basilica di San Giovanni in Laterano: RivArCr 70 (1994) 271-311; 11 fig.

13186 ᴱMazzoleni D., *Carletti* C., Inscriptiones christianae urbis Romae septimo saeculo antiquiores NS 10, Coemeteria Viae Salariae Veteris et Viae Flaminiae. Vaticano 1992, Pont. Ist. Arch. Cr. 262 p.; XXXVII pl. – ᴿSMSR 59 (1993) 175-181 (G. *Cuscito*).

13187 *Thümmel* Hans Georg, Die Archäologie der Petrusmemorie in Rom: Boreas 16 (Münster 1993) 97-113; 11 fig.; pl. 8.

T9.8 *Roma*, **Ars palaeochristiana.**

13188 **Blaauw** Sible de, Cultes et décor; liturgia e architettura nella Roma tardoantica e medievale; Basilica Salvatoris, Sanctae Mariae, Sancti Petri: ST 355s. Vaticano 1994, Bt. I. 447; II. p.449-921; 26 fig.; bibliog. 759-802. 88-21000-656-5; -8-1.

13189 *Carletti* Carlo, Inscriptiones christianae urbis Romae, nova series; una banca dati: VetChr 31 (1994) 357-368.

13190 *Fabbri* Marco, La basilica paleocristiana di Siponto; nuove acquisizioni: VetChr 31 (1994) 189-196; 4 fig.

13191 *Fantò* Gabriella, *Mennella* Giovanni, Topografia ed epigrafia nelle

ultime indagini su Vercelli paleocristiana: RivArCr 70 (1994) 339-410; 27 fig.
13192 *Risconti* F.,   Materiali epigrafici dal cimitero dei ss. Pietro e Marcellino; spunti e conferme per la cronologia della regione I; RivArCr 70 (1994) 7-42(-60); 27 fig.
13193 *Smiraglia* Edvige,   I graffiti sulla mensa della Basilica anonima della via Ardeatina :   VetChr 31 (1994) 171-183 + 4 pl.

T9.9   *(Roma) Imperium occidentale*, **Europa**.

13194 ᴱ**Bassaldare** I., Pompei, pitture e mosaici. R 1990 (I-II; III 1992), Enc. Italiana. – ᴿJRS 84 (1994) 253s (Joanne *Berry*).
13195 **De Caro** Stefano,   Alla ricerca di Iside; analisi, studi e restauri dell'Iseo pompeiano nel museo di Napoli: Soprintendenza N/Caserta.   R 1992, ARTI. xii-149 p.; bibliog. 135-147. Lᵐ 80.
13196 *Dobbins* John J.,   Problems of chronology, decoration, and urban design in the forum at Pompeii: AJA (1994) 629-694; 61 fig.
13197 *Funari* Pedro P. A.,   El carácter popular de la caricatura pompeyana: Gerión 11 (1993) 153-173; 10 fig.
13198 **Hoffmann** Peter,   Der Isis-Tempel in Pompeji [Diss.]: Charybdis 7. Münster 1993, Lit. 270 p.; ill.
13199 **Laurence** Ray,   Roman Pompeii; space and society. NY 1994, Routledge. xi-158 p.; 13 fig.; 13 pl.; 31 maps. $45. 0-415-09502-6. – ᴿClasO 72 (1994s) 108s (R. I. *Curtis*).
13200 **Iappolo** Giovanni,   Le terme del Sarno a Pompei: Soprintendenza mg. 5.   R 1992, Bretschneider.   191 p.; 130 fig. (34 colour.); map. 88-7062-784-5. – ᴿAJA 97 (1993) 813 (Ann O. *Koloski-Ostrow*).
13201 **Ohr** Karlfriedrich, Die Basilika in Pompeji. B 1991, de Gruyter. x-87 p. 63 pl. DM 198. 3-11-012283-9. – ᴿAJA 97 (1993) 586s (L. *Richardson*); AntClas 63 (1994) 627s (J. C. *Balty*); ArchWsz 44 (1993) 143 (Maria *Nowicka*).
13202 **(Koloski) Ostrow** A., The [Pompeii] Sarno bath complex 1990 ➤ 8,e288: ᴿLatomus 53 (1994) 235s (L. *Foucher*).

13203 *Barford* Paul,   Rome and Barbaricum; recent work on the Roman period in Poland [20 books]: Antiquity 68 (1994) 165-172.
13204 *Cabanas* P., *al.*, Apollonia d'Illyrie (Albanie) 1993: BCH 118 (1994) 521-9; 4 fig.
13205 *Ferrua* Antonio,   Le iscrizioni antiche di Aquileia di G. B. BRUSIN [1887-1976]: RivArCr 70 (1994) 161-180.
13205* *Hauschild* Theodor [*Teichner* Felix], Évora, Vorbericht über die Ausgrabungen am römischen Tempel 1986[?]-1992: MadMit 35 (1994) 314-336 [-358], 7 [+10] (foldout) fig.; pl. 30-39 [40].
13206 **Pontrandolfo** Angela, *Rouveret* Agnès,   Le tombe dipinte di Paestum 1992 ➤ 8,g672; 9,14831:   ᴿArchWsz 44 (1993) 141s (Maria *Nowicka*).
13207 *Pontrandolfo* Angela,   Le pitture di Paestum: Archeo 9,114 (1994) 48-97.
13208 — *Greco* Emmanuel, L'agora de Poseidonia; une mise au point: CRAI (1994) 227-237; 2 fig.
13209 — *La Genière* Juliette de, *Greco Maiuri* Giovanna,   Note sur le sanctuaire de Héra au Sèle (8 k NW Paestum): CRAI (1994) 305-313; 2 fig.; 2 pl.
13210 *a) Raviola* Flavio,   La tradizione letteraria sulla fondazione di Nea-

polis; – *b) Cordiaro* Giuseppe, STRABONE ed i Messeni di Reggio; – *c)*
Luraghi Nino, Fonti e tradizioni nell'*archaiología* siciliana (per una
rilettura di THUC. 6,2-5): Hesperia 2 (Venezia 1992) 19-40 / 63-77 /
41-62.
13211 **Greco** Emanuele, Archeologia della Magna Grecia: Manuali 29. Bari
1992, Laterza. xi-398 p.; 254 fig. L^m 55. 88-420-3989-6. – ᴿAJA 97 (1993)
806s (B. E. *McConnell*).
13212 **Holloway** R. Ross, The archaeology of ancient Sicily. L 1991,
Routledge. xix-211 p.; 322 fig. (drawings by Anne L. Holloway); 2 maps.
£45. 0-41501-909-5. – ᴿAJA 97 (1993) 366 (M. *Bell*); ClasR 44 (1994)
175-8 (J. R. *Patterson*, also on WILSON R. 1990).
13213 *Salza Prina Ricotti* Eugenia, [Tivoli] Villa Adriana; un sogno fatto
pietra]: Archeo 9,117 (1994) 65-109.

XIX. Geographia biblica

U1   **Geographies.**

13214 **Alcock** Susan E., Graecia capta... landscapes 1993 ➤ 9,14839: ᴿAJA
98 (1994) 576s (G. *Reger*); AmHR 99 (1994) 876s (A. *Burford*); AntClas
63 (1994) 596-8 (M. *Sartre*); GreeceR 41 (1994) 100 (B. A. *Sparkes*: a
brilliant synthesis); JRomA 7 (1994) 417-420 (G. *Woolf*); JRS 84 (1994)
240-2 (A. J. S. *Spawforth*).
13215 ᴱ**Allen** K. M. S., *al.*, Interpreting space; G[eographical] I[nformation]
S[ystem] and archaeology. L 1990, Taylor & F. 398-xiv p.; 108 fig.; 14
colour. pl. 0-85066-824-7. – ᴿAJA 97 (1993) 357-9 (J. L. *Davis*).
Cornelius Jack, Visual representation of the world 1994 ➤ Gen 1, e16.
13216 ᴱ**Dalongeville** R., *al.*, Paysages d'Achaie, 1. le bassin du Peiros et
la plaine occidentale: Meletemata 15. Athena/P 1992, de Boccard.
299 p.; 19 fig.; 17 pl., 20 maps. F 280. – ᴿClasR 44 (1994) 111s (D. W. J.
Gill).
13217 ᵀᴱ**Fornara** Charles W. (from *Jacoby* Felix, Nachlass), Die Fragmente
der griechischen Historiker 3. Geschichte von Städten und Völkern
(Horographie und Ethnographie). Leiden 1994, Brill. [vi-]113 p. (in
English). 90-04-09975-1.
13218 *Gergel* Richard A., Costume as geographic indicator; barbarians and
prisoners on cuirassed statue breastplates: ➤ 489, World 1988/94, 191--
209; 20 fig.
13219 **González Echegaray** J., Creciente fértil 1991 ➤ 7,e302; 9,14843: ᴿRET
53 (1993) 122s (P. *Barrado Fernández*).
13220 **Gyselen** Rika, Géographie... sassanides 1989 ➤ 8,g684: ᴿMesopT 29
(1994) 311-4 (A. *Gabutti Roncalli*).
13221 *Hostetter* Edwin C., Geographic distribution of the pre-Israelite
peoples of ancient Palestine: BZ 38 (1994) 81-86.
13222 **Jacob** C., Géographie et etnographie en Grèce ancienne. P 1991,
Colin. 183 p. – ᴿGerión 11 (1993) 422-5 (G. *Cruz Andreotti*).
13223 *Limet* H., La perception de l'espace [essentiellement linéaire] dans le
Proche-Orient du 1ᵉʳ millénaire av. J.-C.: ➤ 461, Syrie, TEuph 8 (1991/4)
95-107; Eng. 95.
13224 *Olivier* J. P. J., The historical understanding of the OT; the perspective
of historical geography: ➤ 327, ODENDAAL D. mem., OTEssays 7,4
(1991/4) 139-147.

13225 **Page** Charles R.[II], *Volz* Carl A., The land and the book; an introduction to the world of the Bible 1993 ➔ 9,14850: [R]BL (1994) 38 (C. *Smith*); RExp 91 (1994) 612 (J. F. *Drinkard* commends, though brief on archeology).

13226 [E]**Barker** Graeme, *Lloyd* John, Roman landscapes; archaeological survey in the Mediterranean region: ArchMg 2. L 1991, British School at Rome. xv-240 p.; 101 fig. 0-904152-16-2. – [R]AJA 98 (1994) 347-351 (E. B. *Hitchner*); Klio 75 (1993) 508s (H.-J. *Gehrke*).

13227 **Pritchett** W. K., Studies in ancient Greek topography 5-7, 1985-89/91 ➔ 8,g690: [R]Gnomon 66 (1994) 227-231 (H.-J. *Gehrke*).

13227* **Pritchett** W. Kenrick, Studies in ancient Greek topography 8. Amst 1992, Gieben. – [R]ClasR 44 (1994) 114 (D. W. J. *Gill*).

13228 *Sapin* J., La géographie, outil de recherche sur la Syrie-Palestine achéménide: ➔ 461, TEuph 5 (1992) 95-110 + 2 maps.

13228* **Scott** Jamie, *Simpson-Housley* Paul, Sacred places... geographics of Judaism, Christianity and Islam 1991 ➔ 7,329; 8,g698: [R]JRel 74 (1994) 281-3 (D. *Carrasco*).

13229 *Sergent* Bernard, Les petites nodules et la grande Béotie I [géographie mycénienne différente de classique]: REAnc 96 (1994) 365-384; Eng. 365.

13230 *Sutherland* Denis, The interface between theology and historical geography: ScotBuEvT 11 (1993) 17-30.

13231 **Tsafrir** Yoram, *Di Segni* Leah, *Green* Judith, *al.*, Tabula imperii romani, Judaea-Palaestina; Eretz Israel in the Hellenistic, Roman and Byzantine periods; maps and gazetteer. J 1994, Israel Academy. x-263 p. – [R]IsrClas 14 (1994) 191s (B. *Isaac*); LA 44 (1994) 720-2 (M. *Piccirillo*: in attesa dell'Onomastico).

13232 *VanderKam* James C., Putting them in their place; geography as an evaluative tool: ➔ 133, [F]WACHOLDER B. Z., Pursuing 1994, 46-69.

13233 **Wang Minhua,** Modelling errors for remote sensing image classification: diss. [D]*Howarth* P. Waterloo, Canada 1994. 188 p. NN89590. – DissA 55 (1994s) p. 2518.

u1.2 **Historia geographiae.**

13234 *Arias* P. E., *Paoletti* M., La ricerca sulla 'Periegesi' di PAUSANIA e i suoi problemi: ➔ 496, ANRW [2,34,2 (1994)] Nachtrag in 2,34,4.

13235 *Baladié* Raoul, La géographie historique de la Grèce antique, au XVIIe Siècle, à Caen: JSav 93 (1993) 287-331.

13236 *Bearzot* C., Storia e storiografia ellenistica in PAUSANIA il Periegeta. Venezia 1992, Cardo. 311 p. – [R]Athenaeum 82 (1994) 583-5 (D. *Ambaglio*).

13237 *Bilde* Per, The geographical excursuses in JOSEPHUS: ➔ 123, Mem. SMITH M., Josephus 1992/4, 247-262.

13238 *Bonner* Michael, The naming of the frontier; 'AWĀṢIM, THUGHŪR, and the Arab geographers: ➔ 136, [F]WANSBROUGH J., BSO 57 (1994) 17-24.

13239 **Britton** John P., Models and precision; the quality of PTOLEMY's observations and parameters. NY 1992, Garland. xvii-202 p.

13239* **Burkert** Walter, Orientalische und griechische Weltmodelle von Assur bis ANAXIMANDROS: ➔ 117, [F]SCHWABL H., WienerSt 107 (1994) 179-186.

13240 [E]**Casevitz** M., *al.*, PAUSANIAS, Grèce 1,1 L'Attique: Coll. Budé, 1992: [R]ClasR 44 (1994) 28s (R. *Hawley*).

13241 *Cordano* Federica, Mari e arcipelaghi (STRABONE X, 4 e 5): Ann-Macerat 24 (1991) 77-92.

13242 *Desanges* Jehan, La face cachée de l'Afrique selon Pomponius MÉLA: GeogAnt 3s (1994s) 79-88; 4 fig. [109-174 + 15 (color.) fig. *Ragone* Giuseppe su Mela].

13243 **Donner** Herbert, The mosaic map of Madaba, an introductory guide 1992 ⇒ 8,g712; 9,14864: ᴿRB 101 (1994) 610-2 (T. *Axe*); RelStR 20 (1994) 242 (R. L. *Wilken*: add Y. TSAFRIR, DumbO 1986).

13244 **Frazer** James G. [1854-1941] Sulle tracce di PAUSANIA. Mi 1994, Adelphi. 384 p. Lᵐ 38. – ᴿArcheo 9,114 (1994) 123 (G. M. *della Fina*).

13245 ᵀᴱ**García Blanco** J., *García Ramón* J. L., ESTRABÓN, Geografía, libros I-II: BtClas 159. M 1991, Gredos. – ᴿGeogAnt 3s (1994s) 255s (G. *Aujac*).

13246 *Gavish* Dov, French cartography of the Holy Land in the nineteenth century: PEQ 126 (1994) 24-31; 3 fig.

13247 **Harley** J. B., *Woodward* David, Cartography in the traditional Islamic and South Asian societies: History of Cartography 2/1. Ch 1992, Univ. xxiv-579 p.; 395 pl. $125. – ᴿAmHR 99 (1994) 1286 (J. L. *Berggren*).

13248 *Husslein* Gertrud, Konrad MILLER: OrbT 1 (1994) 213-234.

13249 *a) Jacquemin* Anne, Les curiosités naturelles chez PAUSANIAS; – *b) Pavis d'Escurac* Henriette, Nature et campagne à travers la correspondance de PLINE le Jeune; – *c) Ritter* Adolf M., Natur und Landschaft bei BASIL und AUGUSTIN: Ktema 16 (1991) 123-130 / 185-194 / 195-200.

13250 *Janvier* Yves, VITRUVE et la géographie: GeogAnt 3s (1994s) 49-78.

13251 *Kornrumpf* Hans-Jürgen, Zur historischen Kartographie von Anatolien im 19. Jahrhundert: ⇒ 109, Mem. SCHAENDLINGER A., WZKM 82 (1992) 235-243; map 244.

13252 *Lacroix* Léon, Traditions locales et légendes étiologiques dans la Periégèse de PAUSANIAS: JSav 94 (1994) 75-99.

13253 *Lafond* Yves, PAUSANIAS et les paysages d'Achaie [topographie religieuse plutôt que physique/humaine]: RÉAnc 96 (1994) 485-497; Eng. 485.

13254 *Leylek* Henry, La vignetta di Antiochia e la datazione della Tabula Peutingeriana: JAncTop 3 (1993) 203; 4 fig.: under Julian or just before.

13255 *Longo* Oddone, TOLOMEO redivivo: GeogAnt 3s (1994s) 237-244.

13256 ᵀᴱ**Marcotte** Didier, Le poème géographique [Grèce] de DIONYSIOS, fils de Calliphon: Acad. Fonds Draguet 6. Lv 1990, Peeters. 220 p.; 10 maps. – ᴿÉtClas 62 (1994) 80s (M. *Huys*); RBgPg 72 (1994) 147s (M.-P. *Loicq-Berger*: chef-d'œuvre d'édition d'un ouvrage sans valeur); RÉAnc 96 (1994) 589s (P. *Counillon*); RÉG 107 (1994) 301s (D. *Rousset*).

13257 ᵀᴱ**Musti** Domenico, PAUSANIA, Guida della Grecia: Fond. Valla. Mi 1992-, Mondadori. 88-04-33898-9; -4694-9 (vol. 3-4).

13257* *a) Pingree* David, The teaching of the [PTOLEMAEUS] Almagest in antiquity; – *b) Jones* Alexander, The place of astronomy in Roman Egypt: Apeiron 27,4 ('The Sciences in Greco-Roman society' 1994) 75-98 / 25-51.

13258 *Radt* S. L., Aus der Arbeit an der neuen [Groninger], STRABON-ausgabe: Pharos 2 (Amst 1994) 31-35; 3 maps.

13259 **Radtke** Bernd, Weltgeschichte und Weltbeschreibung im mittelalterlichen Islam: BeiruterTSt 51. Stu 1992, Steiner. xi-544 p. DM 160. – ᴿWZKM 84 (1994) 239-241 (H. *Eisenstein*).

13260 **Romm** James S., The edges of the earth in ancient thought 1992 ⇒ 9,14887: ᴿAntClas 63 (1994) 488s (F. *Colin*); ClasB 69 (1993) 50-53 (Helen *Liebel-Weckowicz*).

13261 **Simek** Rudolf, Erbe und Kosmos im Mittelalter; das Weltbild vor

Kolumbus. Mü 1992, Beck. 219 p.; 32 fig.; 3 maps. DM 40. – RSpeculum 69 (1994) 885s (Valerie I. J. *Flint*).
13262 *Stone* Jon R., The medieval mappaemundi; toward an archaeology of sacred cartography: Religion 23 (L 1993) 197-216 [< ZIT 1993) 578].
13263 *Walker* Bethany J., New approaches to working with old maps [... Cairo Fusṭaṭ]; computer cartography for the archeologist: JAmEg 31 (1994) 191-202.
13264 *Woloch* G. Michael, AMMIANUS; Alpine passes and maps: Arctos 27 (1993) 149-154.

U1.4 **Atlas – maps.**

13265 **Aharoni** Y., *Avi-Yonah* M., [3]*Rainey* A., *Safran* Z. The Macmillan Bible Atlas 1993 → 9,14900: RCurrTM 21 (1994) 299s (E. *Krentz*).
13266 [*Bimson* J. J., *al.*] TEBurkhardt H., *al.*, Der neue Bibelatlas. Wu/Giessen 1992, Brockhaus/Brunnen. 128 p. DM 40. – RZAW 106 (1994) 365 (M. *Köckert*); ZkT 116 (1994) 222 (R. *Oberforcher*).
13267 **Chaliand** Gérard, *al.*, Atlas historique des migrations. P 1994, Seuil. 141 p. 2-02-013223-0.
13268 **Cohn-Sherbok** Dan, Atlas of Jewish history. NY 1994, Routledge. xii-218 p.; 120 maps; 5 photos. $55. 0-415-08684-1 [TDig 41,161].
13269 EFlon C., Der grosse Bildatlas der Archäologie, TCarstens A. Mü 1991, Orbis. 424 p.; 105 Farbzeichnungen, 550 Farbphotos, 106 maps. DM 68. – RAltertum 39 (1993) 237s (R. *Bernbeck*).
13269* **Gaube** Heinz, *Leisten* Thomas, Die Kernländer des Abbasidenreiches im 10./11. Jh.; Materialien zur TAVO-Karte B VII 6: TAVO B-7. Wsb 1994, Reichert. iv-195 p. 3-88226-2133.
13270 **Halvorson** Peter L., *Newman* William M., Atlas of religious change in America, 1952-1990 [57 denominations]. Atlanta 1994, Glenmary. x-226 p. $50 pa. 0-914422-23-5 [TDig 41,269].
13271 **Hours** François †, *Aurenche* Olivier, *Cauvin* J. & M., *al.*, Atlas des sites du Proche-Orient (14.000-5700 BP). Lyon/P 1994, Maison de l'Orient Méditerranéen. II. Cartes V + 25 [20-25 a-b(c-e)].
13272 **Hunter** Erica C. D., First civilizations; cultural atlas for young people. NY 1994, Facts on File. 96 p.; photos, maps, charts ['hundreds': BAR-W 20/5,8].
13272* EKopp Horst, *Röllig* Wolfgang, Tübinger Atlas des Vorderen Orients, Register zu den Karten, General Index. Wsb 1994, Reichert. I. A-G, 50 + 626 p.; II. H-P, p. 627-1265; III. Q-Z, p. 1267-1894. 3-8826-800-X (all 3)
13273 EMoseley Christopher, *Asher* R. E., Atlas of the world's languages. L 1994, Routledge. viii-373 p. 0-415-01925-7.
13274 **Oliphant** Margaret, The atlas of the ancient world. NY 1992, Random. 0-09-182750-7. – RBurHist 29,3 (1993) 94s (P. T. *Crocker*).
13275 EPiccirillo Michele, La terra del messaggio; per un atlante di geografia biblica. T-Leumann 1991, ElleDiCi. 248 p. L[m] 85. – RAsprenas 41 (1994) 601s (V. *Scippa*).
13276 **Riley-Smith** J., Grosser Bildatlas der Kreuzzüge [1990] T1993 → 9, 14909: RWissWeis 56 (1993) 212s (C. *Auffarth*).
13277 **Roaf** Michael, Atlas de la Mésopotamie et du Proche Orient Ancien, TTalon Philippe 1991 → 7,e336 ... 9,14910: 237 p.; 468 fig.; 53 maps. 2-503-50046-3. – ROrLovPer 24 (1993) 282s (J. *Spaey*); RAss 88 (1994) 186s (B. *Lafont*).

13278 **Stoneman** Richard,   Ancient Greece and the Aegean / Roman Italy (maps 97 × 137 cm). L 1989, Routledge. £17.25 each. – ᴿMnemosyne 47 (1994) 283s (A. J. L. van *Hooff*).

Tsafrir Yoram, *Di Segni* Leah, *Green* Judith,   Tabula imperii romani, Iudaea-Palaestina, maps and gazetteer 1994 ➤ 13231.

13280 **Wajntraub** Eva & Gimpel, Hebrew maps of the Holy Land. W 1992, Hollinek. 277 p. 3-85119-248-6. – ᴿBL (1994) 41 (J. W. *Rogerson*); TRu 59 (1994) 334-6 (L. *Perlitt*).

∪1.5 **Photographiae.**

13281 **Amiet** P., *al.*,   Mémoires d'Euphrate et d'Arabie; art et archéologie du Proche-Orient (photos *Nou* Jean-Louis †). P 1991, Hatier.   270 p.   2-218-024-594. – ᴿSyria 61 (1994) 256s (F. *Braemer*).

13282 **Hossaini** Ali A.ᴶ,   Archaeology of the photograph [... origins in Sumer, Egypt, Euclid]: diss Texas, ᴰ*Kellner* D.   Austin 1994. 390 p. 99-28550. – DissA 55 (1994s) p. 1502.

13283 **Howe** Kathleen S.,   Excursions along the Nile; the photographic discovery of ancient Egypt. Santa Barbara 1993, Museum of Art.   175 p. 0-89951-088-4; pa. -9-2.

13284 ᴱMyers J. W. & Eleanor E., *Cadogan* G., The aerial atlas of ancient Crete. Berkeley 1992, Univ. California.   XIX-319 p.; 252 fig. $110.   0-520-07382-7. – ᴿAJA 97 (1993) 360 (L. V. *Watrous*); Minos 27 (1992s) 329-333 (J. *Bennet*).

13285 **Öztuncay** Bahattin, James ROBERTSON, pioneer of photography in the Ottoman empire 1992 ➤ 9,14924;   128 p.; $50:   ᴿPEQ 126 (1994) 85 (Gillian *Webster*).

13286 ᴱRammant-Peeters Agnes,   Palmen en tempels; la photographie en Égypte au XIXᵉ siècle. Lv 1994, Peeters. 286 p. (255-293 Eng., J.-B. van *Moer* Account). 90-6831-627-3.

13287 **Taylor** J.,   High above Jordan; aerial photographs. L 1989, Threes. 64 p.; 56 color. pl. – ᴿPEQ 126 (1994) 86 (S. *Gibson*).

13288 **Wansbrough** Henry, La Biblia, historia viva, ᵀ*Iglesias* Juan A.   Barc 1994, Herder.   256 p., color. ill. (*Clarke* John D.) – ᴿLumenVr 43 (1994) 377 (F. *Ortiz de Urtaran*).

∪1.6 **Guide books,** *Führer.*

13289 ᴱAcquistapace Paolo,   Guida biblica e turistica di Terra Santa, ²*Turri* Ernani (*Galbiati* Enrico) 1992 ➤ 9,14926:   ᴿRivB 42 (1994) 368-370 (G. *Gilberti*).

13290 **Ball** Warwick,   Syria, a historical and architectural guide. Essex 1994, Serapion. 216 p.; 34 fig.; 96 color pl.; map. 0-905906-96-9.

13291 **Burns** Ross,   Monuments of Syria, an historical guide. L 1992, Tauris. xvii-297 p. £49.50. – ᴿBSO 57 (1994) 375s (M.C.A. *Macdonald*: dull, inaccurate; and paperback available inside Syria for £5).

13292 **Murphy-O'Connor** Jerome, The Holy Land; an archaeological guide from earliest time to 1700³ʳᵉᵛ: 1992 ➤ 8,g785; 9,14930:   Ox 1992, Univ. xxi-471 p.; 129 fig. – ᴿPEQ 126 (1994) 84s (G.S.P. *Freeman-Grenville*).

∪1.7 **Onomastica.**

13293 *Aydın* Nafız, ❶ Une tablette de Kültepe relative à la vente de maison et les noms de lieux existant sur les tablettes: Belleten 58 (1994) 29-38; deutsch 39-49; 4 p. facsimiles; 3 maps.

13293* *Di Segni* Leah,   A new toponym [Kefaranaya] in southern Samaria: LA 44 (1994) 579-584.

13294 *Ephratt* Michal, ❸ Is there a grammar of place-names?: Lešonenu 58 (1994s) 367s; no English summary.

13295 ᴱ**Branigan** K., *al.*, Lexicon of the Greek and Roman cities and place names in antiquity, ca, 1500 B.C. - ca. A.D. 500 [1. 1992 ➤ 9,14934]; fasc 2 Ad Novas; 3. Agia minor.

13295* *Israel* Felíce,   Note di onomastica semitica 8: l'onomastica della regione filistea ed alcune sue possibili sopravvivenze nell'onomastica fenicio-punica: ➤ 498, Circolazioni 1991/4, 127-188.

13296 *Litinas* Nikos,   Villages and place-names of the Cynopolite nome: ArPapF 40 (1992) 157-164.

13297 **Maʿani** Sultan *al.*,   Nordjordanische Ortsnamen; eine etymologische und semantische Untersuchung: TStOr 7. Hildesheim 1992, Olms. 326 p. – ᴿWZKM 84 (1994) 269-271 (S. *Procházka*).

13298 *Naʾaman* Nadav,   Assyrian Chronicle fragment 4 and the location of Idu [on Tigris N Nineveh]: RAss 88 (1994) 33-35.

13299 *Schepers* Anne,   Anthroponymes et toponymes du récit d'Ounamon: ➤ 9,14014, Phoenicia 1990/1, 17-83 [< OTAbs 16,211].

13299* *Schoors* Anton,   Biblical [geographical but mostly personal] onomastics in MAXIMUS Confessor's Quaestiones ad Thalassium: ➤ 70, ᶠLAGA C., Philohistôr 1994, 257-272.

13300 **Tånberg** Karl A.,   Der geographische Horizont der Texte aus Ebla; Untersuchungen zur eblaitischen Toponymie: MüUniv AOtt 42. St.Ottilien 1994, EOS. [vi-] 94 p. – 3-88096-542-0.

13301 **Vallat** François,   Les noms géographiques des sources suso-élamites: RepGeogCun, TAVO B 7/11, 1992 ➤ 9,14948: ᴿCRAI (1994) 116s (J. *Leclant*).

13302 **Wilhelm** Gernot, Kumme und *Kumar; zur hurritischen Ortsna-men-bildung: ➤ 55, ᶠHROUDA B., Beiträge 1994, 315-9.

U2.1   **Geologia:** soils, mountains, volcanoes, earthquakes.

13304 *Koch* Klaus, Ḥazzi-Ṣafôn-Kasion; die Geschichte eines Berges und seine Gottheiten: ➤ 9,388, Beziehungen 1993, 171-223.

U2.2   *Hydrographia:* **rivers, seas, salt.**

13305 *Amit* David,   What was the source of Herodion's water?:   LA 44 (1994) 561-578; 3 fig.; pl. 41-46.

13306 *Baxendale* J.W.,   HERODOTUS and the missing Nile *aûrai* [mist-wind]: Mnemosyne 47 (1994) 433-453.

13307 *Belli* Oktay,   Urartian dams and artificial lakes recently discovered in Eastern Anatolia: TAJ 21 (1994) 77-116; 36 fig.

13308 **Berg** Deena,   Fountains and artistic water-displays in classical antiquity; origins and development from 700 to 30 B.C.: diss. Texas, ᴰ*Edlund-Berry* Ingrid. Austin 1994. 278 p. 94-28456. – DissA 55 (1994s) p. 1608.

13309 **Bonneau** Danielle,   Le regime administratif de l'eau du Nil dans l'Égypte grecque, romaine et byzantine: Probleme der Ägyptologie 8/8, 1993 ➤ 9,14959: ᴿCdÉ 69 (1994) 378-381 (P. *Lecoq*).

13310 **Bruun** Christer, The water supply of ancient Rome 1991 ➤ 8,g814; 9,14960: ᴿGnomon 66 (1994) 431-7 (M. *Hainzmann*); Klio 76 (1994) 492 (K. *Wachtel*).

13311 *Cadell* Hélène, Vocabulaire de l'irrigation: la Septante et les papyrus: ➤ 452, L'eau en Égypte 1994, 103-117.

13312 *Cole* Steven W., Marsh formation in the Borsippa region and the course of the lower Euphrates: JNES 53 (1994) 81-111; 5 fig.

13313 **Crouch** Dora P., Water management in ancient Greek cities 1993 ➤ 9,14961: ᴿAmHR 99 (1994) 874s (J. D. *Hughes*); GreeceR 41 (1994) 240s (B. A. *Sparkes*).

13314 *Dorrell* Peter G., The spring at Jericho [2 Kgs 2,21s] from early photographs: PEQ 125 (1993) 95-114; 26 fig.

13315 **Evans** Harry B., Water distribution in ancient Rome; the evidence of FRONTINUS. AA 1994, Univ. Michigan. xii-168 p. + 15 fig. 0-472-10464-0.

13316 *Evans* Harry B., *In Taburtium usum*; special arrangements in the Roman water system (Frontinus, *Aq.* 6.5): AJA 97 (1993) 447-455; map.

13317 **Garbrecht** Günther, *Manderscheid* Hubertus, Die Wasserbewirtschaftung römischer Thermen; archäologische und hydrotechnische Untersuchungen, A. Forschungsbericht; B. Katalog der Befunde; C. (*Manderscheid*) Bilddokumentation. Braunschweig 1994, Univ. Inst. Wasserbau. 412 p.; 385 p.; 194 p. (279 fig.) 0343-1223.

13318 *Görler* Woldemar, Tiberaufwärts nach Rom; ein Thema und seine Variationen [Aeneas; Ovidius; Lateranobelisk 357 n.Chr.]: Klio 75 (1993) 228-243; Eng. 243.

13319 **Guilaine** Jean, La mer partagée; la Méditerranée avant l'Écriture, 7000-2000 av. J.-C. P 1994, Hachette. 455 p.; bibliog. 437-445; (color.) ill. 2-01-235067-4.

13320 **Hodge** A. Trevor, Roman aqueducts and water supply 1992 ➤ 8,g824; £55: ᴿAJA 98 (1994) 176 (H. B. *Evans*); ClasW 88 (1994s) 498s (J. P. *Oleson*).

13321 **Jansen** Gemma, Systeem van watervoorziening en sanotair in de woonhuizen van Herculaneum: diss. kath. Univ. Nijmegen. 1989. 185 p.

13322 *Kutlu* Emre, The Hittite dam of Karakuyu: ➤ 9,358, Anatolian Studies 1993, 1-17 + 12 fig. (maps); 26 phot.

13323 **Lowi** Miriam R., Water and power; the politics of a scarce resource in the Jordan River basin: ME Library 31. C 1993, Univ. xix-219 p. £35. – ᴿBSO 57 (1994) 597s (T. *Allan*).

13323* *Malamat* Abraham, Das heilige Meer: ➤ 61, ᶠKAISER O., 'Wer ist' 1994, 65-74.

13324 *Marín Heredia* Francisco, Torrente; temas bíblicos: InstTFran 13. Murcia 1994, Espigas. 261 p. 84-86042-16-X.

13325 *Mayerson* Philip, Choricius of Gaza on the watersupply system of Caesarea [< IsrEJ 36 (1986) 269-272]: ➤ 207, Monks 1994, 267-270.

13326 **Ravasi** Gianfranco, Il Giordano, un fiume fra i due Testamenti: Attorno alla Bibbia 1. CinB 1993, Paoline. 221 p.; map.

13327 *Strange* John, The Arabian Gulf in antiquity: AcOrK 53 (1992) 7-20.

13328 *Thomas* Robert, *Wilson* Andrew, Water supply for Roman farms in Latium and South Etruria: PapBritR 62 (1994) 139-196; 14 fig.

13329 **Tölle-Kastenbein** R., Antike Wasserkultur 1990 ➤ 7,e416: ᴿGrazB 20 (1994) 341-3 (M. *Hainzmann*).

13330 **Tölle-Kastenbein** Renate, Archeologia dell'acqua; la cultura idraulica nel mondo classico. Mi 1993, Longanesi. 280 p. Lᵐ 40. – ᴿArchViva 13,48 (1994) 91.

13331 *Ussishkin* David, ❸ The water-systems of Jerusalem during Hezekiah's reign: CHistEI 70 (1994) 3-28; ill.; Eng. 201.

13332 *Vollkommer* Rainer, Vater Rhein und seine römischen Darstellungen: BonnJbb 194 (1994) 1-42; 46 fig.

13333 *Wiedler* Simone, Einige Bemerkungen zur Wasserversorgung antiker Badeanlagen in Ägypten: GöMiszÄg 132 (1993) 75-82 + 4 fig.

13334 *Younger* K. Lawson, The Siloam tunnel inscription, an integrated reading: UF 26 (1994) 543-556.

U2.3 **Clima, pluvia.**

13335 *Brown* John P., Yahweh, Zeus, Jupiter; the high god and the elements: ZAW 106 (1994) 175-187.

13336 **Dehon** Pierre J., Hiems latina; études sur l'hiver dans la poésie latine des origines à l'époque de Néron: Coll. Latomus 219. Bru 1993. 385 p. – ^RBStLat 24 (1994) 261-3 (Antonella *Borgo*).

13337 ^FLOON M. Van, ^E**Meijer** D.J.W., Natural phenomena 1992 ➤ 8,727: ^RRAss 88 (1994) 95s (D. *Charpin*).

13338 **Panessa** Giangiacomo, Fonti greche e latine per la storia dell'ambiente e del clima nel mondo greco: Pisa Pubbl. Let/Fil 8s, 1991: ➤ 9,14979: ^RRÉAnc 96 (1994) 575 (P. *Counillon*).

13339 *Sauer* James A., A new climatic and archaeological view of the early biblical traditions: ➤ 67, ^FKING P., Scripture 1994, 366-398; 11 fig.

13340 *Stieting* William H.^J, Climate and collapse [LB Palestine]: BR 10,4 (1994) 18-27.54.

13341 *Wardy* Robert, Aristotelian rainfall or the lore of averages: Phronesis 38 (1993) 18-30.

U2.5 *Fauna*; **Animals.**

13342 **Abdel Hamid** Hussam el Din, Survey study of animal bones from Mit-Rahena [Badrashein]: Travaux Médit. 31, 1990 ➤ 8,g842: ^RBO 51 (1994) 80s (A. *Gautier*).

13343 *Albada* Anne-Michelle & Axel van, Un riche bestiaire néolithique: DossA 197 ('Art rupestre du Sahara' 1994) 34-45.

13344 *Baldacci* Massimo, Some Eblaite bird names and biblical Hebrew [...*peres* Lv 11,13; *šaqap* 'seagull'; *'eber, 'brāh* 'eagle']: WeltOr 25 (1994) 57-65.

13345 ^{TE}**Balme** D.M., †, ^E*Gotthelf* A., ARISTOTLE, History of animals 7-10: Loeb 439, 1991 ➤ 8,g846; 9,14983: ^RClasR 44 (1994) 26s (J. *Longrigg*).

13346 *a*) *Bartosiewicz* L., Late neolithic dog exploitation; chronology and function [1. food, fur; 2. guard, transport; 3. sacrifice, pet]; – *b*) *Zalalgaál* I., Betrachtungen über die kultische Bedeutung des Hundes im mitteleuropäischen Neolithikum: AcArchH 46 (1994) 59-71; 4 fig./33-57; 12 fig.

13347 *Becchi* Francesco, Istinto e intelligenza negli scritti zoopsicologici di PLUTARCO: ➤ 92, Mem. PIERACCIONI D. 1993, 59-83.

13348 *a*) *Becker* Cornelia, Elfenbein aus der syrischen Steppen? Gedanken zum Vorkommen von Elefanten in Nordostsyrien im Spätholozän; – *b*) *Chaix* Louis, Das Rind; eine wichtige und allgegenwärtige Komponente der Kerma-Kultur (N.Sudan, zwischen 3000-1500 v. Chr.): ➤ 459, Mem. BOESSNECK J., 1993/4, 169-181; 5 fig. / 263-8; 4 fig.

13349 ^E**Bodson** Liliane, (*Libois* Roland) Contributions à l'histoire des connaissances zoologiques: Journée d'étude, Univ. Liège 17 mars 1990: Zool. 2 (1,1989). 1991 ➤ 8,702*c*: ^RLatomus 53 (1994) 694s (S. *Byl*).

13350 *Bucher Gillmayr* Susanne, *Wᵉhinneh* ... Kamele kommen: ➤ 38, ᶠGAMPER A., ZkT 116 (1994) 421-6.

13350* *Capelle* Torsten, Vollplastische Tierstile im frühen Mittelalter: ➤ 52, ᶠHAUCK K., Iconologia 1994, 166-170; Abb. 68-73.

13351 **Capponi** F., Entomologia pliniana (N. H. XI. 1-120). Genova 1994, D.AR.FI.CL.ET. 233 p. – ᴿBStLat 24 (1994) 674-6 (Carmela *Laudani*).

13351* *a) Chaix* Louis, Nouvelles données de l'archéozoologie au nord du Soudan; – *b) Grzymski* Krzysztof, A statue of Nefertem on a lion; – *c) Lenoble* Patrice, Le sacrifice funéraire de bovinés de Méroé à Qustul et Nallana: ➤ 72*, ᶠLECLANT J. 2 (1994) 105-110; 2 fig. / 199-202; 3 fig. / 269-283.

13352 **Charbonneau-Lassay** Louis † 1946, Il bestiario del Cristo; la misteriosa emblematica di Gesù Cristo [1975 ➤ 6,g252*; Eng. 1991 ➤ 7, e437], ᵀ*Palamidessi* Silvestra, *Lunghi* Pietro (I); *Paluzzi* M. Rita, *Marinese* Luciana (II): La Via dei Simboli. R 1994, Arkeios. I. 685 p.; II. 710 p.; 1157 fig.

13353 *Churcher* Charles S., The vertebrate fauna from the Natufian level at Jebel es-Saaïdé (Saaïdé II), Lebanon: Paléorient 20,2 (1994) 35-58.

13354 ᵀᴱ**Clarke** Willene B., The medieval book of birds; HUGH of Fouilloy's Aviarium [c. 1140]: MdvRenTSt 80. Binghamton 1992, SUNY MdvCenter. xvii-341 p.; ill. $30. – ᴿManuscripta 37 (1993) 87.

13354* *Clutton-Brock* Juliet, *Davies* Sophie, [Five skeletons] More donkeys from Tell Brak: Iraq 55 (1993) 209-221; 8 fig.

13355 *Coleman* K. M., The 'upside-down-animal' at Palestrina [chamaeleon]: ArchAnz (1994) 255-260; 3 fig.

13355* *Collon* Dominique, Bull-leaping in Syria [Atchana...]: ÄgLev 4 (1993) 81-85 + 13 fig. [89-93 *Marinatos* Nanno].

13356 *Eidevall* Göran, Lions and birds as literature; some notes on Isaiah 31 and Hosea 11: ScandJOT 7 (1993) 78-87.

13357 **Englund** Robert K., Organisation und Verwaltung der Ur-III-Fischerei [< diss. Mü 1987]: BBVO 10. B 1990, Reimer. xvii-253 p. – ᴿArOr 62 (1994) 343-6 (B. *Hruška*).

13358 **Epstein** Mark M., Medieval Jewry and the allegorization of the animal world; a textual and iconographic study: diss. Yale, ᴰ*Ruderman* D. ➤ 8,g874; NHv 1993. – RelStR 20,256.

13359 *Galán* José M., Bullfight scenes in ancient Egyptian tombs: JEA 80 (1994) 81-96; 8 fig.; pl. IX.

13360 **Georgoudi** Stella, Des chevaux et des boeufs dans le monde grec ... Géoponiques 16s, 1990 ➤ 8,g878; 7,15001: ᴿMnemosyne 47 (1994) 702-4 (H. J. *Lirb*); RBgPg 72 (1994) 129-131 (Liliane *Bodson*); RÉAnc 96 (1994) 597s (M.-C. *Amouretti*).

13361 *Goren-Inbar* N., *al.*, A butchered elephant skull and associated artifacts from the Acheulian site of Gesher Benot Ya'aqov, Israel: Paléorient 20,1 (1994) 99-112.

13361* *Gouin* P., Bovins et laitages en Mésopotamie méridionale au 3ème millénaire: Iraq 55 (1993) 135-145; 3 fig..

13362 **Gundel** H. G., Zodiakos, Tierkreisbilder 1992 ➤ 9,15004: ᴿAltertum 39 (1993) 151s (G. *Strohmaier*).

13363 *Gury* Françoise, Principes de composition de l'image zodiacale: Latomus 53 (1994) 528-542; 16 fig.

13364 **Hamoto** Azard, Der Affe in der altorientalischen Kunst: Diss. Münster. – MiDAV 25,2 (1994) 44.

13364* *Hasitzka* Monika R. M., Das Schaf in Ägypten; Gedanken zu einer koptischen Liste über Schafe: Biblos 43 (1994) 133-9; 3 fig.; pl. I.

13365 *a*) *Haussperger* M., Die Darstellung des Hundes auf Rollsiegeln; – *b*) *Amiet* P., Une statuette susienne d'équidé; – *c*) *Spycket* A., Un naos à divinité bovine; *d*) *Driesch* Angela von den, Viehhaltung, Jagd und Fischfang in der bronzezeitlichen Siedlung von Shimal bei Ras al-Kaimah/U.A.E.: ➤ 55, FHROUDA B., Beiträge 1994, 103-110; 10 fig.; pl. XXV / 7-9; 4 fig.; pl. II-III / 269-272; 2 fig. / 73-85; 2 fig.; pl. X-XI.

13366 **Hicks** Carola, Animals in early medieval art. E 1993, Univ. X-309 p.

13367 **Hyland** Ann, Equus 1990 ➤ 6,g290: ... 9,15009: RGnomon 66 (1994) 712-5 (J. *Bergemann*, auch über MAUL-MANDELARTZ E.).

13368 **Janowski** Bernd, *al.*, Gefährten und Feinde des Menschen, das Tier ... 1993 ➤ 9,287: RTüTQ 173 (1993) 139-141 (W. *Gross*).

13369 **Janssen** Rosalind M. & Jack, Egyptian household animals: Egyptology 12. Bucks 1989, Shire. 68 p. 0-7478-000-6.

13370 *Karageorghis* Vassos, Monkeys and bears in Cypriote art: OpAth 20 (1994) 63-73; 14 fig.

13371 *Killen* John F., *a*) The oxen's names on the Knossos Ch Tablets; – *b*) Ke-u-po-da e-sa-re-u and the exemptions on the Pylos Na tablets: Minos 27s (1992s) 101-7 / 109-123.

13372 *Koenen* Klaus, '... denn wie der Mensch jedes Tier nennt, so soll es heissen' (Gen 2,19); zur Bezeichnung von Rindern im Alten Testament: Biblica 75 (1994) 539-546.

13373 **Koh** Sejin, An archaeological investigation of the snake cult in the southern Levant, the chalcolithic period through the Iron Age: diss. DEsse D. Chicago 1994. 214 p. 95-01511. – DissA 55 (1994s) p. 2448.

13374 *Kyle* Donald G., Animal spectacles in ancient Rome; meat and meaning; Nikephoros 7 (1994) 181-205.

13375 *Le Gall* Joël, Un mode de transport méconnu; les animaux de bât: ➤ 432, Ravitaillement 1991/4, 69-72; Eng. 79: pack-animals, to deliver to ba[c]kers.

13376 **Lentacker** An, La faune romaine et carolingienne de la Place Saint-Pierre à Tournai: AcArchLov 33 (1994) 55-66 [67-89(-91) *al.*, Erps-Kwerps (DNA)].

13377 **Leone** Aurora, Gli animali da lavoro, da allevamento e gli *hippoi* nell'Egitto greco-romano e bizantino. N 1992, Athens. 216 p. Lm 24. – RCdÉ 69 (1994) 196s (J. A. *Straus*).

13378 *a*) *Letellier* Bernadette, La 'mascarade des bœufs gras' de Thoutmosis IV; une désignation originale des animaux; – *b*) *Altenmüller* Hartwig, Das 'Fest des weissen Nilpferds' [5 Belege: *Kaiser* W., MiDAI-K 44 (1988) 125] und das 'Opfergefilde': ➤ 72*b*, FLECLANT J., 1 (1994) 471-7; 1 fig. / 29-44; 1 fig.

13379 **Lonsdale** Steven H., Creatures of speech; lion, herding, and hunting similes in the Iliad 1990 ➤ 8,g897; 9,15021: RÉchMClas 38 (1994) 393-6 (Ingrid E. *Holmberg*).

13379* *Maeir* Aren M., Hyksos, horses, and hippopotami: Levant [25 (1993) 208-212, *Keel* O.] 26 (1994) 231.

13380 **Michel** Simone, Der Fisch in der skythischen Kunst, zur Deutung skythischer Bildinhalte: Diss. Hamburg. – MiDAV 25,2 (1994) 27.

13381 *Nicholson* Paul T., Preliminary report on work at the sacred animal necropolis, North Saqqara, 1992: JEA 80 (1994) 1-11.

13382 *Potts* D. T., A Sasanian [cast-]lead [plomb] horse from Northeastern Arabia: IrAnt 28 (1993) 194-8 + 5 fig. (map).

13383 **Pury** Albert de, Homme et animal 1993 → 9,15035: ᴿÉTRel 69 (1994) 413s (D. *Lys*); LavalTP 50 (1994) 664 (L. *Ponton*).

13385 *Qimron* Elisha, *Talshir* David, ❸ The birds in the Deir ʿAlla inscription: Lešonenu 58 (1994s) 339-345; Eng. 4/V: of the twelve birds, the smaller ones (owl, sparrow) challenge the larger (eagle, vulture, falcon — but also two kinds of dove).

13386 **Rommelaere** Catherine, Les chevaux du Nouvel Empire égyptien; origines, races, harnachement. Bru 1991, Conn.Ég.Anc. 278 p.; 113 fig.; 8 color. pl. Fb 3400. – ᴿJAmEg 31 (1994) 228s (J. R. *Hoffmeier*); RBgPg 72 (1994) 193-5 (R. *Chevallier*).

13387 **Schouten van der Velden** Adrian, Tierwelt der Bibel [Dieren uit de Bijbel, Nieuwkoop 1992]. Stu 1992, Deutsche Bibelgesellschaft. 160 p.; 50 fig.; 68 color. pl. DM 58. – ᴿBiKi 48 (1993) 230s (H. *Haug*, auch über HEPPER, Pflanzenwelt 1992).

ᴱ**Stefani** Piero, Gli animali e la Bibbia; i nostri minori fratelli, raduno Biblia 1994 → 306.

13388 *Stone* Garry R., The camels of Abraham: BurHist 27,4 (1991); 28,1 (1992) 3-14; 10 fig.

13389 **Terian** Abraham, PHILON, Alexandre, Bruta animalia 1988 → 4,b64... 8,g923: ᴿAntClas 63 (1994) 373-5 (Liliane *Bodson*).

13390 *Zeder* Melinda A., *Arter* Susan R., Changing patterns of animal utilization at ancient Gordion: Paléorient 20,2 (1994) 105-118.

13391 **Ziolkowski** Jan M., Talking animals; medieval Latin beast poetry, 730-1150. Ph 1993, Univ. Pennsylvania. xii-354 p. $40. – ᴿMedvHum 21 (1994) 205-7 (E. *Wheatley*); Speculum 69 (1994) 589-591 (M. *Wolterbeek*).

U2.7   **Flora;** *plantae biblicae et antiquae.*

11391* *Albenda* Pauline, Assyrian sacred trees in the Brooklyn museum: Iraq 56 (1994) 123-133; 8 fig.

13392 ᵀᴱ**Amigues** Suzanne, THEOPHRASTE, plantes 3, 1993 → 9,15050: ᴿRPg 67 (1993) 313s (A. *Blanc*).

13393 **Barakat** A., *Baum* N., La végétation antique de Douch: Doc. Fouilles 27. Le Caire 1992, IFAO. x-106 p. 2-7247-0113-5. – ᴿBO 51 (1994) 327s (Renate *Germer*).

13393* *Belmonte* J.A., Los productos vegetales de KTU 1.100: 64-67: AulaO 11,1 (1993) 114s.

13394 *a)* *Beyer* Dominique, Jardins sacrés d'Émar au Bronze Récent; – *b)* *Farnoux* Alexandre, Image et paysage; l'exemple des fresques de la Maison Ouest de Théra: Ktema 15 (1990) 123-131; 6 fig. 2 pl. / 133-142; 2 color. pl.

13395 *Bottena* Sytze, *Woldring* Henk, *Aytuğ* Burhan, Late quaternary vegetation history of northern Turkey: Palaeohistoria 35s (1993s) 13-72; 23 fig.

13396 **Carroll-Spillecke** Maureen, *Kêpos*, der antike griechische Garten 1989 → 6,g340: ᴿOpAth 20 (1994) 277-9 (Espen B. *Andersson*).

13397 **Caseau** Beatrice A., Euodia; the use and meaning of fragrances in the ancient world and their Christianization (100-900 A.D.): diss. Princeton Univ. 1994. 337 p. 9433011. – DissA 55 (1994s) p. 2100.

13398 **Dittmar** Johanna, Blumen und Blumensträusse als Opfergabe im Alten Ägypten 1986 → 2,b690; 3,f502: ᴿJNES 53 (1994) 145-7 (Ann M. *Roth*).

13399 ᵀᴱ**Einarson** G., *Link* G.K.K., THEOPHRASTUS, De causis plantarum 2s: Loeb 474s. CM 1990, Harvard. vi-561 p.; vii-465 p. – ᴿAthenaeum 82 (1994) 271s (Daniela *Manetti*).

13400 **Gemünden** Petra van, Vegetationsmetaphorik im NT und seiner Umwelt; eine Bildfelduntersuchung: NOrb 18. FrS/Gö 1993, Univ./VR. xi-541 p. DM 155. 3-7278-0741-5. – ᴿTR 90 (1994) 213s (T. *Söding*).

13401 ᴱ**Gyselen** Rika, Jardins d'Orient: Res Orientales 3. 1991; 1142-2831: ➔ 8,g942: ᴿMesopT 29 (1994) 317-9 (A. *Gabutti Roncalli*).

13402 **Hansen** Julie M., Palaeoethnobotany / Franchthi 1991 ➔ 8,g947: ᴿAJA 98 (1994) 571s (Joy *McCorriston*).

13403 **Hepper** F. Nigel, Pflanzenwelt der Bibel [Illustrated encyclopedia of Bible Plants, Leicester/GR 1992, Inter-Varsity/Baker 1992 ➔ 9,15060],ᵀ. Stu 1992, Deutsche Bibelges. 192 p.; color. ill. DM 78. – ᴿBiKi 48 (1993) 231 (H. *Haug*).

13404 *Hepper* F. Nigel, *Gibson* Shimon, Abraham's oak of Mamre; the story of a venerable tree: PEQ 126 (1994) 94-105; 5 fig.

13405 **Koemoth** Pierre, Osiris et les arbres; contribution à l'étude des arbres sacrés de l'Égypte ancienne: Aegyptiaca Leodiensia 3. Liège 1994, Univ. Centre Informatique ph/lett. xxxii-336 p.; bibliog. 319-330.

13406 *Koemoth* Pierre P., Hathor et le buisson *kk* comme lieu de renaissance d'Osiris: WeltOr 25 (1994) 7-16.

13407 ᵀᴱ**König** R., PLINIUS S., Naturkunde 17, Botanik, Nutzbäume. Da 1994, Wiss.

13408 **Krauss** Christel, ...und ohnehin die schönen Blumen; Essays zur frühen christlichen Blumenssymbolik. Tü 1994, Narr. 235 p.; ill. 3-8233-4134-0.

13409 *Lewis* Naphtali, Olyra = *triticum* [not oats, *avena*]: CdÉ 69 (1994) 138s.

13410 **Manniche** Lise, An ancient Egyptian herbal ➔ 8,g957: ᴿJNES 54 (1994) 295s (J. G. *Manning*).

13411 ᴱ**Mastroroberto** M., Archeologia y botanica, Atti del convegno, Pompei apr. 1989/90 ➔ 7,649: ᴿGerión 11 (1993) 410-3 (J. *Cascajero*).

13411* a) *Murray* O., ❻ The ecology and agrarian history of ancient Greece, ᵀ*Semenchenko* L. V.; – b) *Boardman* J., ❻ Problems and prospects in the history and archaeology of colonization in the Black Sea area down to the 3d century B.C., ᵀ*Saprikin* S. Yu.: VDI 209 (1994) 87-96 / 97-99; Eng. 96.99.

13412 *Nazzaro* Antonio V., La tamerice nella letteratura classica e nella simbologia biblico-patristica: ➔ 86, ᶠNALDINI M., Paideia 1994, 439-450.

13413 Phytonymes grecs et latins, 1992/3: ᴿRPg 67 (1993) 315-7 (J.-L. *Perpillou*).

13413* *Ramelli* M. Enrico, A proposito di alcuni fitonimi greci di origine indomediterranea [*cicer* < **kakû*]: Acme 47,1 (1994) 39-41.

13414 *Ringgren* Helmer, *šāmîr* (*šayiṭ*) 'Dorngestrüpp' ➔ 519, TWAT 8,1 (1994) 239s.

13415 *Rosenberger* Veit, Trügerische Gerüche – Verfälschungen von Gewürzen und Duftstoffen bei dem älteren PLINIUS: Münst Hand 13,1 (1994) 40-52; Eng. 53; franç. 54.

13416 **Sallares** Robert, The ecology of the ancient Greek world 1991 ➔ 8,k27: ᴿJIntdis 23 (1992s) 133s (J. D. *Hughes*).

13417 *Shaw* Maria C., The Aegean garden: AJA 97 (1993) 661-685; 23 fig.

13418 *Suess* Gloria E. M., 'Lilies of the field' [color photos of mostly red alternatives, also on back cover]: Jerusalem Perspective 46s (1994) 18-23.

13419 **Tekbali** Ali O., Palynostratigraphy of the mesozoic continental clastics in western and southeastern Libya: diss. Texas, ᴰ*Cornell* W. El Paso 1994. 380 p. 95-03518. DissA-B 55 (1994s) p. 4305.

13419* ᴱ**Zeist** Willem van, *al.*, Progress in Old World palaeoethnobotany

1991 → 8,740*: ᴿAntiquity 68 (1994) 452-4 (Janneke *Buurman*, J. P. *Pals*; also on BROOKS R. 1990, RENFREW J. 1991).
Zonta M., NICOLAUS DAMASCENUS De plantis ᴱ*Drossaart Lulofs* H. 1989.
13420 *Zwickel* Wolfgang. Gat-Karmel [Amarna 288s]: BibNot 71 (1994) 20-23.

U2.8   Agricultura, alimentatio.

13420* *Amouretti* Marie-Claire, L'agriculture de la Grèce antique; bilan de recherches de la dernière décennie: TopO 4 (1994) 69-94.
13421 ᴱ**Behrends** O., *Capogrossi Colognesi* L., Die römische Feldmesskunst 1988/92 → 9,14853: ᴿArEspArq 66 (1993) 345s (M. J. *Castillo Pascual*); JRS 84 (1994) 205s (B. *Campbell*).
13422 *Bell* Malcolmᴵᴵᴵ, An imperial flour mill on the Janiculum: → 432, Ravitaillement 1991/4, 73-89; 15 fig.; ital. 73.
13423 *Ben-David* H., ⊕ Olive tree culture and production of oil in the Jewish settlements of Golan in the period of the Mishna and the Talmud: Ariel ⊕ 100s (1994) 148-156 [< JStJud 25,355].
13424 ᶠBERCHEM Denis Van, Nourrir la plèbe, ᴱ**Giovannini** A. 1989/91 → 8,645; 9,15101: ᴿAntClas 63 (1994) 567-570 (J.-M. *Carré*); Latomus 53 (1994) 224s (C. *Bossu*).
13425 *Castillo Pascual* M. José, Ager arcifinius; significado etimológico y naturaleza real: Gerión 11 (1993) 145-151.
13426 **Chouquer** G., *Favory* F., Les arpenteurs romains, théorie et pratique. P 1992, Errance. 183 p. – ᴿGerión 12 (1994) 370-2 (M. J. *Castillo Pascual*).
13427 **Civil** Miguel, The farmer's instructions; a Sumerian agricultural manual: AulaO supp. 5. Barc-Sabadell 1994, AUSA. xiii-268 p. 84-88810-03-2.
13428 *Cohen* Dan, ⊕ On viticulture and wine — in Israel and the ancient world: BethM 27 (1991s) 59-69 [< OTAbs 16, p. 18].
13428* *Corcella* A., ⊕ Scythians *arōtēres* and Scythians *geōrgoi*, ᵀ*Muraviev* A. V., VDI 208 (1994) 82-88; Eng. 89. → 13546.
13429 *Costantini* Lorenzo, *Stancanelli* Mauro, La preistoria agricola dell'Italia centro-meridionale; il contributo delle indagini archeobotaniche: Origini 18 (R 1994) 149-273; 3 fig. Eng. 244.
13429* **Cowan** C. Wesley, *Watson* Patty Jo, The origins of agriculture, an international perspective 1992 → 9,15086: ᴿAJA 98 (1994) 152 (C. *Edens*).
13430 *Criniti* Nicola, La Tabula alimentaria di Veleia. Parma 1991: ᴿRBgPg 72 (1994) 165s (R. *Duthoy*: de grand intérêt).
13430* *de Grummond* W. W., The animated implement; a CATULLAN source for VIRGIL's plough: Eranos 91 (1993) 75-80.
13431 *Dorman* Peter F., A note on the royal repast at the jubilee of Amenhotep III: → 72*b*, ᶠLECLANT J. 1 (1994) 455-466; 466-470, charts of the provisioning staff.
13432 ᵀᴱ**Dumont** Jean-Christian, COLUMELLE, De l'agriculture 3, 1993 → 9, 15093: ᴿRÉLat 72 (1994) 256s (P. *Flobert*).
13433 *Dunbabin* Katherine M. D., Wine and water at the Roman convivium: JRomArch 6 (1993) 116-141; 31 fig.
13433* **Durliat** Jean, De la ville antique à la ville byzantine; le problème des subsistances 1990 → 8,g987: ᴿHZ 259 (1994) 179s (F. *Winkelmann*).
13434 *Eyre* C. J., The water regime for orchards and plantations in Pharaonic Egypt: JEA 80 (1994) 57-81; 3 fig.; pl. VIII.

13435 *Fantasia* Ugo, Grano siciliano in Grecia nel V e IV secolo: AnPisa 23 (1993) 9-31.

13435* *Fantham* Elaine, Ceres, Liber and Flora; georgic and anti-georgic elements in OVID's Fasti: PrCPg 38 (1992s) 39-56.

13436 **Flach** Dieter, Römische Agrargeschichte: HbAw 3/9, 1990 → 7,a517 ... 9,15905: ᴿBonnJbb 194 (1994) 586-594 (P. *Herz*); EngHR 109 (1994) 399 (G. *Woolf*); Latomus 53 (1994) 441 (R. *Martin*).

13437 **Forsén** Björn, Lex Licinia Sextia de modo agrorum [limiting landowning to 500 iugera in 367, as Gracchus in 133]; fiction or reality?: CommHumLitt 96. Helsinki 1991, Soc. Scientiarum Fennica. 88 p. − ᴿGnomon 66 (1994) 232-7 (D. *Flach*); RÉAnc 96 (1994) 635s (R. *Étienne*).

13438 *a*) *Frayne* Joan, The Roman meat trade; − *b*) *Solomon* Jon, The Apician sauce: → vol. 11,a25, Food 1992/5, 107-114 / 115-131.

13439 **Gelb** I. J., *al.*, Earliest land-tenure ... kudurrus: OIP 104, 1989-91 → 7,d698: ᴿRAss 88 (1994) 85-87 (D. *Charpin*).

13439* *Giacomelli* Roberto, Lingua quotidiana e grecismo nel lessico culinario latino: Acme 47,2 (1994) 24-49.

13440 **Gowers** Emily, The loaded table 1993 → 9,15102: ᴿClasW 88 (1994s) 211 (C. F. *Natunewicz*); JRS 84 (1994) 198s (A. *Laird*).

13441 ᴱ**Gyselen** Rika, Banquets d'Orient: Res Orientales 4. Bures sur Yvette 1992, Groupe Moyen-Orient (Lv, Peeters). 150 p.; ill. − ᴿMesopT 29 (1994) 320-2 (A. *Invernizzi*).

13442 **Habbe** Joachim, Die Landwirtschaft in Palästina zur Zeit Jesu und ihr Niederschlag im Zeugnis der synoptischen Evangelien: Diss. ᴰMerk O. Erlangen-N 1994. 155 p. − RTLv 26,537.

13443 **Hadjisavvas** Sophocles, Olive oil processing in Cyprus EB-Byz: SIMA 99, 1992 → 8,g997: ᴿOpAth 20 (1994) 279-281 (Ö. *Wikander*).

13444 *Hermon* Elia, Coutumes et lois dans l'histoire agraire républicaine: Athenaeum 82 (1994) 496-505.

13445 *Hochmann* Eitan, *Zilberman* David, The agricultural settlement of the Arava; evidence for economic theory: → 188, Mem. WEINTRAUB D.N Rural development 1993, 71-79.

13445* *Houston* G. W., What uses might Roman farmers have made of the loans they received in the Alimenta program?: RivStoAnt 22s (1992s) 97-105.

13446 **Isager** Signe, *Skydsgaard* Jens Erik, Ancient Greek agriculture, an introduction 1992 → 9,15106: ᴿAntClas 63 (1994) 590 (Marie-Claire *Amouretti*); ClasW 88 (1994s) 68s (V. D. *Hanson*, also on BURFORD A.); HZ 259 (1994) 748s (K.-W. *Welwei*).

13447 **Kehoe** Dennis P., *a*) The economics of agriculture on Roman imperial estates in North Africa 1988 → 4,h176 ... 6,g420: ᴿEos 81 (1993) 138s (Małgorzata *Pawlak* ❷); − *b*) Management and investment on estates in Roman Egypt during the early Empire: PapyrTAbh 40. Bonn 1992, Habelt. xiv-188 p. 3-7749-2532-1. − ᴿJRomA 7 (1994) 432-6 (D. *Rathbone*).

13448 *Kehoe* Dennis P., Economic rationalism in Roman agriculture [RATHBONE D. Heroninos 1991]: JRomArch 6 (1993) 476-484.

13448* *Kilaniotis* A., A commentary on PHILO of Alexandria's De agricultura: diss. Dublin Trinity c. 1992. − BInstClas 38 (1991-3) 303.

13449 **Lavrencic** Monika, Spartanische Küche; das Gemeinschaftsmahl der Männer in Sparta: Alltag und Kultur im Altertum 2. W 1993, Böhlau. 147 p.; 10 fig. − ᴿKlio 76 (1994) 470s (K.-W. *Welwei*).

13450 **Lenzen** Dieter, Alla ricerca del padre; dal patriarcato agli alimenti. R c. 1994, Laterza. 338 p.; 44 pl. L^m 30. – ^RArcheo 9,118 (1994) 129 (S. *Moscati*).

13451 *Litvinenko* Y. N.,   ❺ Greek colonists and mysteries of Egyptian agriculture: VDI 209 (1994) 119-123.

13452 **Marasco** Gabriele,   Economia e storia [e geografia, della 'stele dei cereali di Cirene']. Viterbo 1992.   133 p. – ^RRÉAnc 96 (1994) 630 (P. *Brun*).

13453 **Marinone** Nino,   Il riso [rice] nell'antichità greca.   Bo 1992, Pàtron. 156 p.; ill. – ^RRFgIC 121 (1993) 230-3 (I. *Mazzini*: alimentazione, anche farmacologia).

13454 *Mayerson* Philip,   *a)* Wheat in the Roman world; an addendum [< ClasQ 34 (1984) 243-5]; – *b)* Agricultural evidence in the Colt Papyri (the ancient agricultural regime of Nessana in the central Negev) [< Excavations at Nessana 1 (1962) 224-269]; – *c)* A note on demography and land use in the ancient Negeb [< BASOR 185 (1967) 30-43]: ➤ 207, Monks 1994, 222s / 21-39 / 100-4.

13455 *Miller* Robert L.,   *Daajs*, peganum harmala L.:   BIFAO 94 (1994) 349-357.

13456 **Moatti** C.,   Archives et partage de la terre dans le monde romain (IIe s. av.-I^e ap.):   Coll. ÉFR 173.   R 1993, Éc. Française. – ^RRÉLat 72 (1994) 324-6 (J. P. *Vallat*).

13457 ^EMurray Oswyn,   Sympotica [Oxford 1994] 1990 ➤ 6,758*... 8,k20: ^RAJA 97 (1993) 177s (T. N. *Habiner*, also on SLATER W., LISSARAGUE F.).

13458 *Murray* O.,   ❺ The ecology and agrarian history of ancient Greece: VDI 209 (1994) 87-96; Eng. 96.

13459 *Naeh* S.,   *Weitzman* M. P.,   Tīrōš – wine or grape? A case of metonymy: VT 44 (1994) 115-120.

13460 *Negri* Mario,   I criteri di distribuzione delle razioni a base cerealicola negli archivi micenei: AnnMacerat 24 (1991) 9-29.

13461 *Nesbitt* Mark,   Ancient crop husbandry at Kaman-Kalehöyük; 1991 archaeobotanical report: ➤ 9,358, Anatolian 1993, 75-97; 6 fig. (map).

Neusner Jacob, Mishnah agriculture 1993 ➤ 9830.

13462 *Newmyer* Stephen T.,   PLUTARCH on the moral grounds for vegetarianism: ClasO 72 (1994s) 41-43.

Le ravitaillement en blé de Rome 1991/4 ➤ 432.

13463 *a)* *Rossi* Pasquale,   Sulla geografia agraria in età romana; una conferma storica al modello di von THÜNEN; – *b)* *Mazzini* I.,   Alimentazione, gastronomia, dietetica nel mondo classico: Aufidus 23 (1994) 57-66 / 35-56.

13464 **Schmitt Pantel** Pauline, La cité au banquet; histoire des repas publiques dans les cités grecques: Coll. ÉcFrR 157, 1992 ➤ 9,15127; 2-7283-0234-7: ^RAntClas 63 (1994) 526-8 (L. *Migeotte*); JHS 114 (1994) 208s (O. M. Van *Nijf*); Phoenix 48 (Toronto 1994) 177-9 (W. J. *Slater*); RBgPg 72 (1994) 182-4 (P. *Salmon*); RHR 211 (1994) 468-470 (Françoise *Frontisi Ducroux*).

13465 **Sijpesteijn** P. J.,   What happened to tax-grain upon arrival at Alexandria?:   CdÉ 69 (1994) 132.

13466 **Sirks** Boudewijn,   Food for Rome 1991 ➤ 7,e545... 9,15129: ^RGnomon 66 (1994) 369 (H. *Crassl*).

13467 ^ESlater William J.,   Dining in a classical context 1991 ➤ 9,15130: ^RGnomon 66 (1994) 423-431 (Elke *Stein-Hölkeskamp*).

13468 *Steinhauer* Georges,   Inscription agoranomique du Pirée [... aliments]: BCH 118 (1994) 51-68; 3 fig.

13469 *Sweeney* Deborah, Henutasowy's guilty conscience; gods and grain in Late Ramesside Letter no. 37: JEA 80 (1994) 208-212.

13470 **Toussaint-Samat** Maguelonne, A history of food [1987], ᵀ*Bell* Anthea. CM 1992, Blackwell. xix-801. $40. – ᴿAmHR 99 (1994) 198s (H. *Lewenstein*: an unorganized anthology); JIntdis 25 (1994) 459-461 (T. *Brennan*: superficial).

13471 *a*) *Virlouvet* Catherine, Les lois frumentaires d'époque républicaine; – *b*) *Garnsey* Peter, L'approvisionnement des armées et de la ville de Rome; – *c*) *Coarelli* Filippo, Saturnino, Ostia e l'annona; il controllo e l'organizzazione del commercio del grano tra II e I secolo a.C.: ➤ 432, Ravitaillement 1991/4, 11-29 / 31-34 / 35-46.

13472 ᴱ**Wells** Berit, Agriculture in ancient Greece [7th symposium] 1992 ➤ 9,540: ᴿMinos 27 (1992s) 341-3 (T. G. *Palaima*).

13473 *Winter* Bruce W., Acts and food shortages: ➤ 243, Acts Graeco-Roman 1994, 59-78.

13474 **Zeder** Melinda A., Feeding cities 1991 ➤ 9,15136: ᴿAJA 97 (1993) 574s (B. R. *Foster*).

13475 *Zvelebil* Marek, Plant use in the Mesolithic and its role in the transition to farming: PrPrehSoc 60 (1994) 35-74; 8 (foldout) fig.; (maps).

U2.9 **Medicina** *biblica et antiqua.*

13476 **Aleshire** Sara B., Asklepios at Athens 1991 ➤ 7,172: ᴿAntClas 63 (1994) 497s (A. *Martin*).

13477 **Althoff** Jochen, Warm, kalt, flüssig und fest bei ARISTOTELES; die Elementarqualitäten in den zoologischen Schriften [Diss. Freiburg ᴰ*Kullmann*]: Hermes Einz 57. Stu 1992, Steiner. 311 p. DM 96. – ᴿMnemosyne 47 (1994) 547-550 (P. J. van der *Eijk*).

13478 **Barkai** Rom, Les infortunes de Dinah... gynécologie 1991 ➤ 8,k44; 9,15140: ᴿArchivScSocR 82 (1993) 251 (L. *Podselver*); Speculum 69 (1994) 416-9 (Helen R. *Lemay*, Jane *Yahil*).

13479 **Beagon** Mary, Roman nature... PLINY (p. 202-240 on medicine) 1992 ➤ 9,14984: ᴿPrudentia 25,2 (1993) 72-74 (P. *McKechnie*).

13480 *Beckman* Gary, From cradle to grave; women's role in Hittite medicine and magic: JAncCiv 8 (1993) 25-39.

13481 *Bellemore* Jane, *Plant* Ian M., THUCYDIDES, rhetoric and plague in Athens: Athenaeum 82 (1994) 385-401.

13482 *Burkard* Günter, Medizin und Politik; altägyptische Heilkunst am persischen Königshof: StÄäK 21 (1994) 35-57.

13483 ᴱ**Campbell** Sheila, *al.*, Health, disease and healing in medieval culture. NY 1992, St. Martin's. xxiv-205 p. $60. 14 art. [Speculum 69,285, tit. pp.].

13484 **Cantarella** Eva, Bisexuality in the ancient world. NHv 1992, Yale Univ. xii-284 p. 0-300-04844-0. – ᴿClasJ 90 (1994s) 204s (J. F. *Makowski*).

13485 **Cootjans** Gerrit, La stomatologie [... noms des dents] dans le Corpus aristotélicien: Mém. 69/3. Bru 1991, Académie. 242 p.; 1 fig. Fb 800. – ᴿRBgPg 72 (1994) 139s (Danielle *Gourévitch*).

13486 **Curtis** Robert I., Garum et salsamenta 1991 ➤ 7,e562... 9,15151: ᴿLatomus 53 (1994) 930s (L. *Foucher*).

13487 *a*) **Dean-Jones** Lesley Ann, Women's bodies in classical Greek science. Ox 1994, Clarendon. xiii-293 p.; bibliog. 255-276. 0-19-814767-8.

— *b*) **de Filippis Cappai** Chiara, Medici e medicina in Roma antica. T 1993. 248 p.; 26 fig. – ᴿRivStoAnt 22s (1992s) 297s (G. *Susini*).

— c) *Desclos* Marie-Laurence, Autour du 'Protagoras'; SOCRATE médecin et la figure de Prométhée: QuadStor 36 (1992) 105-140.
— d) **Durling** Richard J., A dictionary of medical terms in GALEN: Studies in Ancient Medicine 5. Leiden 1993, Brill. xiii-344 p. f200. – ᴿÉtClas 62 (1994) 397 (S. *Byl*).
13488 **Gabriel** Richard A., *Metz* Karen S., A history of military medicine, 1. From ancient times to the Middle Ages; Military Studies 124. NY 1992, Greenwood. xxi-247 p., $75. – ᴿAmHR 99 (1994) 187s (H. J. *Cook*: takes poetry as statistics and Leviticus as 'organized sanitary corps').
13489 **Geroulanos** Stephanos, *Bridler* René, Trauma; Wund-Entstehung und Wund-Pflege im antiken Griechenland: KuGaW 56. Mainz 1994, von Zabern. 172 p.; ill.
13490 **Grandet** Pierre, Le Papyrus Harris I (BM 9999): BtÉt 109. Le Caire 1994, IFAO. I. xxix-342 p.; bibliog. xix-xxix; II. xvi-352 p.; 80 pl. 2-7247-0141-0; -2-9.
13491 *Heymer* Armin, Der etho-kulturelle Werdegang apotropäischer Verflechtungen von Pygmäen, Chondrodystrophen und Zwergenfiguren: Saeculum 44 (1993) 116-178.
13492 *Hogan* Larry P., Healing in the Second Temple period: NOrb 21, 1992 → 8,k59; 9,15166: ᴿCritRR 6 (1993) 122-4 (T. *Donaldson*: ailing prose, but informed and judicious); ETRel 69 (1994) 410-2 (F. *Siegert*); Kairos 34s (1992s) 244s (G. *Stemberger*: many typos – and the review also spells 'Günther').
13493 *Hopkins* Simon, A new autograph fragment of MAIMONIDES' Epitomes of GALEN (de locis affectis): → 136, ꟳWANSBROUGH J., BSO 57 (1994) 126-132; II pl.
13493* **Johnson** Fiona, The Hippocratics and women; a whole sex of patients: M. A. diss. London KCL c. 1992. – BInstClas 38 (1991-3) 305.
13494 **Jouanna** J., HIPPOCRATE 1992 → 8,k65; 9,15170: ᴿAmHR 99 (1994) 1661 (J. *Scarborough*).
13495 a) *Jouanna* Jacques, La naissance de la science de l'homme chez les médecins et les savants à l'époque d'HIPPOCRATE; problèmes de méthode; – b) *Singer* P. N., Some Hippocratic mind-body problems; – c) *Byl* Simon, Le traitement de la douleur dans le Corpus hippocratique; – d) *Guillén* Luis F., Hipócrates y el discurso científico; – e) *Kollesch* Jutta, Zur Mündlichkeit hippokratischer Schriften; → 13507, Tratados 1990/2, 91-111 / 131-143 / 203-213 / 319-333 / 335-342.
13496 *Jouanna* Jacques, HIPPOCRATE et la Collection hippocratique dans l'Ars Medicinae: RHText 23 (1993) 95-112; Eng. 353.
13497 *Kahl* Oliver, ꜤĪSĀ IBN MĀSSA on medicinal weights and measures: OrLovPer 23 (1992) 275-9.
13498 *Kinnier Wilson* J. V., The *sāmānu* disease in Babylonian medicine: JNES 53 (1994) 111-5.
13499 *Kollesch* Jutta, Die Sprache von Ärzten nichtgriechischer Herkunft im Urteil GALENS: Philologus 138 (1994) 260-3.
13500 **Kotter** Samuel S., Medicine and hygiene in the works of Flavius JOSEPHUS: Studies in Ancient Medicine 9. Leiden 1994, Brill. xii-217 p. $68.75. 90-04-09941-7 [OTAbs 17, p. 684].
13501 ᴱ**Kudlien** Fridolf, *Durling* R. J., GALEN's method of healing 1982/91 → 8,660; 9,15175: ᴿLatomus 53 (1994) 225s (S. *Byl*).
13502 **Langholf** Volker, Medical theories in HIPPOCRATES; early texts and the 'Epidemics'; UntAntLG 34, 1990 → 7,e578 ... 9,15177; DM 166. 3-11-011956-0: ᴿAntClas 63 (1994) 484 (Marie-Hélène *Marganne*).

13503 ᴱ**Lanternari** Vittorio, Medicina, magia, religione, valori [Perugia, apr. 1985]: Anthropos 25. N 1994, Liguori. 312 p. 88-207-2322-0.

13504 **Lloyd** Geoffrey E.R., Metodi e problemi della scienza greca [1979 → 9,15182*],ᵀ. Bari c.1994, Laterza. 787 p. Lᵐ85. – ᴿArcheo 9,110 (1994) 108 (C. *Zaccagnini*).

13505 **Lloyd Davies** M. & I.A., The Bible; medicine and myth². C 1993, Silent. x-278 p. £13. 1-85183-053-7. – ᴿBL (1994) 16s (R.J. *Coggins*: desupernaturalized).

13506 ᴱ**López Férez** Juan Antonio, GALENO; obra, pensamiento e influencia; coloquio Madrid 22-25 de marzo de 1988/1991 → 8,666*: ᴿMnemosyne 47 (1994) 121-3 (J. *Croonen*); RBgPg 72 (1994) 146s (B. *Vancamp*).

13507 ᴱ**López Férez** Juan A., Tratados hipocráticos [→ 9,527*] (estudios acerca de su contenido, forma e influencia; Actas del 7. Colloque international hippocratique, Madrid 24.-29.IX.1990, M 1992 → 430*b*, Univ. 751 p.

13508 **Marganne** Marie-Hélène, L'ophtalmologie dans l'Égypte gréco-romaine d'après les papyrus littéraires grecs: Studies in Ancient Medicine 8. Leiden 1994, Brill. xii-209 p.; 19 fig. 90-04-09907-7.

13509 *Martínez Saura* Fulgencio, Frontón; la enfermedad en el siglo II [a.C.]: Gerión 12 (1994) 103-111; Eng. 103.

13510 *Mayerson* Philip, *a*) The use of Ascalon wine in the medical writers of the fourth to the seventh centuries [< IsrEJ 43 (1993) 169-173]; – *b*) The Gaza 'wine' jar and the 'lost' Ashkelon jar (*askalōnion*) [< IsrEJ 42 (1992) 76-80]; – *c*) The wine and vineyards of Gaza in the Byzantine period [< BASOR 257 (1985) 75-80]: → 207, Monks 1994, 367-371 / 347-351 / 250-5.

13511 ᴱ**Meulenbeld** G. Jan, *Wujastyk* Dominik, Studies on Indian medical history... Wellcome Institute 2-4 Sept. 1985: GronOrSt 2. Groningen 1987, Forsten. x-247 p. ƒ65. – ᴿJAOS 114 (1994) 478-480 (F. *Zimmermann*).

13512 *Musche* Brigitte, Zur altorientalischen Rosette; ihr botanisches Vorbild und dessen pharmaceutische Verwertung: MesopT 29 (1994) 49-70; Eng. 71: chrysanthemum.

13513 **North** Robert, Medical discoveries of biblical times: → 67, ᶠKING P., Scripture and other artifacts 1994, 311-332; 6 fig.

13514 **Rechenauer** Georg, THUKYDIDES und die hippokratische Medizin; naturwissenschaftliche Methodik als Modell für Geschichtsdeutung: Spudasmata 47, 1991 → 9,15197: ᴿGnomon 66 (1994) 177 (H. *Patzer*).

13515 **Reeves** Carol, Egyptian medicine 1992 → 9,15198: ᴿBurHist 30,1 (1994) 34s (H.S.S.).

13516 *Richardson* W.F., First find your part, then name it [medical terminology for the heart: ARISTOTLE, GALEN, VESALIUS]: Prudentia 25,2 (Auckland 1993) 29-46.

13517 *Riddle* John M., *al.*, Ever since Eve... birth control [plants] in the ancient world; Archaeology 47,2 (1994) 29-35; 7 color. phot.

13518 **Riethmüller** Jürgen, Heiligtümer des Asklepius: Diss. Heidelberg. – MiDAV 25,2 (1994) 29.

13519 **Ritner** Robert K., The mechanics of ancient Egyptian magical practice: SAOC 54. Ch 1993, Univ. Or. Inst. xviii-322 p.; 22 fig. – ᴿJAmEg 31 (1994) 223-5 (L. *Kákosy*).

13519* **Romano** Elisa, Medici e filosofi; letteratura medica e società altoimperiale: Sisyphos 2. Palermo 1991, Grifo. 203 p. – ᴿOrpheus 14 (1993) 198-200 (M. Laura *Astarita*).

13520 *Salazar* C. F., The treatment of war wounds in Greco-Roman antiquity: diss. Cambridge c. 1992. – BInstClas 38 (1991-2) 303.

13520* **Sanford** J. A., Healing body and soul 1992 ➤ 8,k97: ᴿBR 10,5 (1994) 16 . 18 (Elisabeth *Johnson*).

13521 *a*) *Scarborough* John, [*al.*] Roman medicine to GALEN; – *b*) *Andorlini Marcone* Isabella, L'apporto dei papiri alla conoscenza della scienza medica antica: ➤ 496, ANRW 2,37,1 (1993) 3-48 [-456] / 458-562.

13522 *Scheidel* Walter, Libitina's bitter gains; seasonal mortality [September deaths double normal] and endemic disease in the ancient city of Rome: AncSoc 25 (1994) 151-167 + 17 fig.

13523 *a*) *Skoda* Françoise, Le marasme ['consomption'] dans les textes médicaux; sens et histoire du mot; – *b*) *Corvisier* Jean-Nicolas, Médecine et biographie; l'exemple de PLUTARQUE: RÉG 107 (1994) 107-128 / 129-157.

13523* *Sluiter* Ineke, Two problems in ancient medical commentaries: ClasQ 44 (1994) 270-3.

13524 *Swain* Simon, Man and medicine in THUCYDIDES: Arethusa 27 (1994) 303-327.

13525 *Taborelli* Luigi, Aromata e medicamenta exotica in PLINIO II: Athenaeum [I, 79 (1991) 527-562] 82 (1994) 111-151.

13526 **Temkin** O., HIPPOCRATES in a world of pagans and Christians 1991 ➤ 7,e599; 8,k107: ᴿMnemosyne 47 (1994) 537-9 (G. J. M. *Bartelink*).

13527 *Touwaide* Alain, L'histoire des sciences pharmaceutiques en Grèce et à Byzance: Byzantion 63 (1993) 451-4.

13527* *Tsekourakis* D., PLATO's *Phaedrus* and the holistic viewpoint in HIPPOCRATES' Therapeutics: BInstClas 38 (1991-3) 162-173.

13528 **Wilhelm** Gernot, Medizinische Omina aus Ḫattuša in akkadischer Sprache [mit Übersetzung]: StBoǧT 36. Wsb 1994, Harrassowitz. xi-106 p.; ix pl. 3-447-03414-9.

13529 **Wilkinson** Lise, Animals and disease; an introduction to the history of comparative medicine. C 1992, Univ. x-272 p. $70. – ᴿAmHR 99 (1994) 1288s (Ann G. *Carmichael*).

13530 *Wolska* Wanda, Zwei Fälle von Trepanation aus der altbabylonischen Zeit Syriens: MDOG 126 (1994) 37-50; 7 fig.

U3 *Duodecim Tribus:* **Israel Tribes;** Land-Ideology.

13531 **Akenson** Donald H., God's people; covenant and land in South Africa, Israel, and Ulster 1991 ➤ 9,15214: ᴿSR 23 (1994) 220s (D. *Hempton*: the other two have been undermined from within, but not Israel); TorJT 10 (1994) 269s (Elizabeth M. *Davies*).

13532 **Chapman** Colin, Di chi è la Terra promessa? Il conflitto arabo-israeliano alla ricerca di una soluzione, ᵀ*Vitti* P. Padova 1992, Messaggero. 319 p. Lᵐ 30. – ᴿProtestantesimo 48 (1993) 218-220 (J. A. *Soggin*).

13533 **Davies** William D., The Gospel and the land; early Christianity and Jewish territorial doctrine: Biblical Seminar 75. Shf 1994, JStOT. xviii-521 p.; ill.; bibliog. 439-471. 1-85075-478-0.

13534 *a*) *Grosby* Steven, Sociological implications of the distinction between 'locality' and extended 'territory' with particular reference to the OT; – *b*) *Piveteau* Jean-Luc, L'AT et la territorialisation de la Suisse: SocComp 40 (1993) 179-198 / 152.

13535 *Helberg* J. L., Die Verhouding tussen land en ekumene in die Ou

Testament en die betekenis daarvan vir vandag: In die Skriflig 26 (1992) 523-536 [< OTAbs 17, p. 166].

13536 *Kahana* Menahem, ❼ The importance of dwelling in the land of Israel, according to the Deuteronomy Mekhilta: Tarbiz 62 (1992s) 501-513; Eng. vi-vii.

13537 *Lambert* Frith, The tribe/state paradox in the Old Testament: Scand-JOT 8 (1994) 20-44.

13538 **Law** David A., From Samaria to Samarkand; the ten lost tribes of Israel 1992 ➤ 9,15255;   0-8191-8409-8:   ᴿBL (1994) 36 (L. L. *Grabbe*: worthless).

13539 **March** Wallace Eugene, Israel and the politics of land; a theological case study. LvL 1994, W-Knox. xiii-104 p. $13.   0-664-25121-8 [TDig 42,77; BL 95,96, J. *Goldingay*]. – ᴿTBR 7,1 (1994s) 54 (D. B. *Forrester*).

13540 **Neef** Heinz-D., Ephraim; Studien zur Geschichte des Stammes Ephraim von der Landnahme bis zur frühen Königszeit: ev. Diss. Tübingen, ᴰ*Mittmann* 1993. – TR 90,80.

13541 **Simoens** Yves, La Bible et la terre; réflexions sur une lettre pastorale de Jérusalem [DocCath 2086 (1994) 73-83]:   Études 381 (1994) 649-659.

13542 **Smyth-Florentin** Françoise, Les mythes illégitimes; essai sur la 'Terre promise': Entrée libre 30.   Genève 1994, Labor et Fides.   64 p.   2-8309-0735-3.

13543 **Wolff** Katherine E., 'Geh..' Das Land ᴰ1989 ➤ 6,g564 ... 9,15230: ᴿBijdragen 55 (1994) 80s (J. van *Ruiten*).

U4   *Limitrophi*, **adjacent lands.**

13544 *a) Boardman* J., ❼ Problems and prospects in the history and archaeology of colonization in the Black Sea area down to the 2d century B.C.; – *b) Shelov* D. B. †, ❼ Problem of Graeco-Barbarian contacts in the period of Greek colonization of the north Black Sea area: VDI 209 (1994) 97-99; Eng. 99 / 100-105; Eng. 105.

13545 *a) Brown* Stuart C., Other voices; Indo-Europeans, Urartians, and Elamites on the Mesopotamian periphery / Indo-European origins and the West Asian neolithic; – *b) Frayne* Douglas, Indo-Europeans and Sumerians; evidence for their linguistic contact; – *c) Harrak* Amir, The survival of the Urartian people; – *d) Carter* Elizabeth, Elam and the Elamites: BCanadMesop 25 (1993) 7s. 9-18 / 19-42 / 43-49 / 51-56.

13546 *a) Corcella* A., [➤ 13428*] ❼ Scythians *arōtēres* and *geōrgoi* (Herod. 4,17s); – *b) Pogrebova* M. N., *Raevsky* D. S., ❼ Early Scythians in the light of the written tradition and archaeological data; – *c) Melyukova* A. I., *al.*, ❼ Diskussiya: VDI 208 (1994) 82-88; Eng. 89 / Eng. 81s / ❼ 64-81.

13547 *Dyakonov* I. M., ❼ The Cimmerians and the Scythians in the Ancient Near East: RossArkh (1994,1) 108-116.

13548 **Ivantchik** Askold I., Les Cimmériens au Proche-Orient [< diss. Moscou]: OBO 127, 1993 ➤ 9,15236: ᴿBL (1994) 124 (A. R. *Millard*).

13549 *Knappert* J., The East African coast; some notes on its history: Or-LovPer 23 (1992) 143-178.

13550 *Lebrun* R., Aspects de la présence louvite en Syrie au VIIIᵉ s. av. J.-C.: ➤ 461, TEuph 6 (1993) 13-25.

13551 *a) Rayevsky* D. S., ❼ On the logic of study of the early Scythian chronology; – *b) Pogrebova* M. N., ❼ On the principles of dating the Scythian archaic period; – *c) Tokhtasyev* S. R., ❼ The chronology and

ethnic attribution of the Scythian type sites in the Near East and Middle Asia: RossArkh (1993,2) 79-84-89-97.
13552 **Wilhelm** Gernot, The Hurrians 1989 ➤ 63,9778: ᴿJNES 53 (1994) 225-230 (M. C. *Astour*).

U4.5   *Viae* – **Routes, roads.**

13553 **Caselli** Giovanni, Guida alle antiche strade 'di Roma' [coperta: 'Romane']. Novara 1994, De Agostini. 320 p.; 200 color. fig. Lᵐ 42. – ᴿArcheo 9,114 (1994) 124 (S. *Moscati*).
13554 *Graf* D. F., The Persian royal road system in Syria-Palestine: ➤ 461, TEuph 6 (1993) 149-166 + 2 maps.
13555 **Jansen** Anton, Stations along the roads in the area of Mycenae; an analysis of the Mycenaean road system and its relation to the Mycenaean state: diss. Pennsylvania, ᴰ*Iakovidis* S. Ph 1994. 280 p. 95-03776. – DissA 55 (1994s) p. 2877.
13556 **Kase** Edward W., *al.*, The great [Phokis-Doris] Isthmus corridor route 1991 ➤ 7,e633 ... 9,15245: ᴿAcArH 35 (1994) 205-7 (Dolores *Hegyi*).
13557 *Kleiss* Manfred, Bauten an Karawanenstrassen [Shiraz-Isfahan and eastward]: ArchMIran 26 (1993) 269-286; 18 fig.; pl. 76-88.
13558 *Mayerson* Philip, The Clysma-Phara-Haila road on the Peutinger Table [< ꟻTRELL B., Coins (Detroit 1981) 167-176]: ➤ 207, Monks 1994, 173-182; 3 maps.
13559 *Müller* Dietram, Von Kritalla nach Doriskos; die persische Königs-strasse und der Marschweg des Xerxesheeres in Kleinasien: IstMitt 44 (1994) 17-38; 11 fig.; pl. 4-8.
13560 ᴱ**Quilici** Lorenzo & Stephania – *Gigli*, Strade romane, percorsi e infrastrutture. R 1994, Bretschneider, 249 p. Lᵐ 170. 88-7062-855-8. 16 art. – ᴿArcheo 9,114 (1994) 124 (S. *Moscati*).
13561 **Tardieu** Michel, Les paysages reliques; routes et haltes 1990 ➤ 6,g585 ... 9,15247: ᴿAntClas 63 (1994) 489 (Janine *Balty*); JSS 39 (1994) 117-120 (S. E. *Humans*); Syria 61 (1994) 217-226 (T. *Bauzou*).

U5   *Ethnographia*, **sociologia** [servitus ➤ E3.5; G6.5].

13562 ᴱ**Abel** Olivier, *Smyth* François, Le livre de traverse; de l'exégèse biblique à l'anthropologie [symposium]: Patrimoines 1992 ➤ 8,334: ᴿCBQ 56 (1994) 167 (J. *Kaltner*); ÉTRel 68 (1993) 308-310 (*Abel*); Numen 41 (1994) 205s (B. *Lang*: Paris Protestant conspiracy); RTPhil 126 (1994) 289 (A. *Buhlmann*); Salesianum 56 (1994) 784s (R. *Vicent*).
13563 **Abraham** Gary A., Max WEBER and the Jewish question; a study of the social outlook of his sociology 1992 ➤ 9,15249: ᴿAJS 19 (1994) 281-4 (Christa *Schäfer-Lichtenberger*); AmHR 99 (1994) 592s (A. *Edelstein*); ArchivScSocR 84 (1993) 245s (M. *Löwy*).
13564 *Arnaoutoglou* Ilias, Associations and patronage in ancient Athens: AncSoc 25 (1994) 5-17: 3 of 4 needed conditions not present to support GALLANT T.
13565 **Bard** Kathryn A., From farmers to pharaohs; mortuary evidence for the rise of complex society in Egypt. Shf 1994, Academic. vii-144 p.; bibliog. 125-140. 1-85075-387-3. – ᴿOrigini 18 (1994) 430s (M. Carmela *Gatto*).
13566 **Bauman** Richard A., Women and politics / Rome 1992 ➤ 9,15251: ᴿClasR 44 (1994) 558s (R. *Seager*); HZ 259 (1994) 450s (Maria H. *Dettenhofer*).

13567 *Bechtel* Lyn M., The perception of shame within the divine-human relationship in biblical Israel: → 102, Mem. RICHARDSON H., Uncovering 1994, 79-92.

13568 **Bell** Andrew J., Spectacular power in the ancient city: diss. ᴰ*Treggiari* Susan M. Stanford 1994. 278 p. 95-08320. – DissA 55 (1994s) p. 3286.

13569 **Bennett** David W., Biblical images for leaders and followers. Ox 1993, Regnum Lynx. 207 p. 0-7459-2779-3. – ᴿTBR 7,1 (1994s) 58s (B. *Kinsey*: not sufficient advertence to NT social context).

13570 **Berger** Klaus, Historische Psychologie des NTs: SBS 146s. Stu 1991, KBW. 303 p. DM 50,20. 3-460-04231-1. – ᴿZkT 116 (1994) 221 (R. *Oberforcher*).

13571 **Berger** Klaus, Psicologia storica del Nuovo Testamento: Parola di Dio 2/14. CinB 1994, S. Paolo. 340 p. 88-215-2792-1. 88-215-2792-1.

13571* *a) Blasi* Anthony J., The more basic method in the sociology of early Christianity; – *b) Hanson* K. C., Greco-Roman studies and the social-scientific study of the Bible; a classified periodical bibliography: Forum 9,1s (1993) 7-... / 63-....

13572 **Bosch** Gudrun, Zur Struktur der Gesellschaft des Königreichs Arraphe: HeidAO 5. Heid 1993, Orientverlag. xiii-169 p. 3-927552-08-9.

13573 **Bravo** Gonzalo, Poder político y desarrollo social en la Roma antigua: Universitaria historia. M 1989, Taurus. 291 p.

13573* *Brock* Roger, The labour [toil, not childbirth] of women in classical Athens: ClasQ 44 (1994) 336-346.

13574 **Broughton** T. R. S., Candidates defeated in Roman elections 1991 → 9, 12774.

13575 *Burden* J. J., Social science and recent trends in OT research; its relevance for South African OT scholarship: OTEssays 6 (1993) 205-232 [< OTAbs 17,473].

13576 *Burford* Alison, Land and labor in the Greek world: Anc. Soc. & Hist. Baltimore 1993, Johns Hopkins Univ. x-290 p. – ᴿAmHR 99 (1994) 1293s (I. *Morris*).

13577 *Burstein* S. M., The challenge of Black Athena; an interim assessment: AncHB 8,1 (1994) 11-17.

13578 **Burton** John W., An introduction to EVANS-PRITCHARD: Anthropos St. 45, 1992 → 9,15262: ᴿNZMiss 50 (1994) 141s (O. *Bischofberger*).

13579 **Cairns** Douglas L., *Aidōs*, the psychology and ethics of honour and shame 1993 → 9,15263: ᴿClasJ 90 (1994s) 451-5 (A. W. H. *Adkins* compares FISHER and WILLIAMS).

13580 **Carrier** Hervé, Lexique de la culture pour l'analyse culturelle et l'inculturation 1992 → 9,15264: ᴿAnnTh 8 (1994) 212s (A. *Byrne*).

13580* *Castillo Solano* Enrique, La infrastructura antropológica de la salvación cristiana: EfMex 12 (1994) 195-206.

13581 *Cerutti* Maria V., Antropologia e apocalittica: StRel 7, 1990 → 7,3331: ᴿRHR 211 (1994) 89-93 (P. *Gignoux*).

13582 *Chausa* Antonio, Modelos de reservas de indígenas en el África romana: Gerión 12 (1994) 95-101; map; franç. 95.

13583 *Chelhod* Joseph, Parti pris pour un évolutionnisme social multilinéaire [... surtout arabe]: Anthropos 88 (1993) 1-4; Eng. 1.

13584 ᴱClements R. E., The world of ancient Israel; sociological ... 1989 → 5,387 ... 9,15265: ᴿBASOR 294 (1994) 101s (J. M. *Miller*); JSS 38 (1993) 138-141 (R. *Tomes*).

13585 *Coldstream* J. N., Mixed marriages at the frontiers of the Early Greek world: OxJArch 12 (1993) 89-107; 5 fig.

13586 *Cotton* Hannah, The guardianship of Jesus son of Babatha; Roman and local law in the province of Arabia: JRS 83 (1993) 94-108.

13587 *Craffert* P. F., Taking stock of the emic-etic distinction in social-scientific interpretations of the NT ['emic', falsifiable logico-empirical statements significant to those involved; 'etic', non-falsifiable phenomenal-distinction statements of the scientific community (HARRIS M.)]: Neotestamentica 28 (1994) 1-21.

13588 *Crone* Patricia, 'Even an Ethiopian slave' [can be caliph; SHAHRASTANI 'a black slave can be imam']; the transformation of a Sunnī tradition: → 136, ᶠWANSBROUGH J., BSO 57 (1994) 59-67.

13589 *Deniaux* Élisabeth, Clientèles et pouvoir à l'époque de CICÉRON: Coll. ÉFR 182. R 1993, École Française. x-628 p. – ᴿRÉLat 72 (1994) 330-2 (P. M. *Martin*).

13590 **Dixon** Suzanne, The Roman family 1992 → 8,k171; 9,15267: ᴿClasB 70 (1994) 43s (T. *Fleming*); HZ 259 (1994) 761 (Marieluise *Deissmann-Merten*).

13591 *a) Domeris* W., Anthropological and socio-historical readings of the OT; – *b) Snyman* S. D., Political reading as a means of understanding the OT: – *c) Wittenberg* G., Ideological/materialist approach to the OT: → 327, ODENDAAL D. mem, OTEssays 7,4 (1991/4) 160-6 / 173-180 / 167-172.

13592 **Dyson** Stephen L., Community and society in Roman Italy 1992 → 9,15275: ᴿLatomus 53 (1994) 194s (J.-C. *Dumont*: titre inspiré de TÖNNIES 1887).

13593 **Eder** Birgitta, Staat, Herrschaft, Gesellschaft in frühgriechischer Zeit; eine Bibliographie 1978-1992: MykenKomm 14, Szb ph/j 611. W 1994, Österr. Akad. 248 p. 3-7001-2140-7.

13594 **Edgerton** Robert B., Sick societies; challenging the myth of primitive harmony. NY 1992, Free Press. 278 p. $25. 0-402-90825-5. – ᴿChrSchR 24 (1994) 96-98 (W. *Hasker*: small-scale societies have not been so harmonious; and it is not improper to evaluate cultures other then one's own).

13595 **Esler** Philip F., The first Christians in their social worlds; social-scientific approaches to NT interpretation. L 1994, Routledge. x-164 p.; bibliog. 147-156. 0-415-11121-8.

13596 **Evans** J. K., War, women and children 1991 → 8,k176; 9,15278: ᴿGnomon 66 (1994) 460-2 (Ines *Stahlmann*); HZ 259 (1994) 449s (Rosmarie *Günther*).

13597 **Eyben** Emiel, Restless youth in ancient Rome, ᵀ*Daly* P., 1993 → 9, 15279: ᴿClasR 44 (1994) 223s (D. *Noy*).

13598 **Fayer** Carla, La familia romana; aspetti giuridici ed antiquari, I: ProbRicStA 16. R 1994, Bretschneider. 728 p.; bibliog. 613-652. 88-7062-875-2.

13598* **Fiensy** David A., The social history of Palestine in the Herodian period; the land is mine; StBEarlyC 20, 1991 → 8,k181; 9,15281: ᴿCritRR 6 (1993) 135-7 (J. *Kampen*).

13599 **Fisher** N. R. E., Hybris 1992 → 9,15283: ᴿAntClas 63 (1994) 441 (B. *Vancamp*); ClasR 44 (1994) 76-79 (D. L. *Cairns*).

13600 *Frier* Bruce W., Natural fertility and family limitation in Roman marriage: ClasPg 89 (1994) 318-333.

13601 **Gardner** Jane F., *Wiedemann* T., The Roman household [social, emotional]; a sourcebook. L 1991, Routledge. xviii-210 p. £35; pa. £11. – ᴿMnemosyne 47 (1994) 561-5 (F. G. *Naerebout*).

13602 **Ginestet** Pierre,   Les organisations de la jeunesse 1991 ➤ 9,15293: ᴿAntClas 63 (1994) 550-2 (R. *Duthoy*).

13603 **Golden** Mark,   Children / Athens 1990 ➤ 8,k187; 9,15294:   ᴿJIntdis 23 (1992s) 134-6 (I. *Morris*).

13604 **Goldman** Harvey,   Politics, death, and the devil; self and power in Max WEBER and Thomas MANN.   Berkeley 1992, Univ. California.   386 p. $35. – ᴿJRel 74 (1994) 594s (C. *Koelb*).

13605 *Grassi* Herbert,   Hohe Berge – wilde Frauen; Betrachtungen zur antiken Sozialanthropologie: GrazB 20 (1994) 195-211.

13606 **Grassi** P.,   Secolarizzazione e teologia; la questione religiosa in Peter L. BERGER.   Urbino 1992, Quattro Venti.   134 p. Lᵐ 22. – ᴿRasT 35 (1994) 242-4 (Giuseppina *De Simone*).

13607 **Hamel** Gildas,   Poverty and charity in Roman Palestine 1990 ➤ 6,g407; 8,g998:   ᴿAJS 17 (1992) 293-6 (S. *Schwartz*: mostly on Rome, poor on poverty).

13608 *Harris* W. V.,   Child-exposure in the Roman Empire: JRS 84 (1994) . 1-22.

13609 *Heine* Susanne,   'Hanging' between heaven and earth; remarks on biblical anthropology: EcuR 45,3 (Hong Kong consultation, 1993) 304-315.

   Hoffmann Paul,   Studien zur Frühgeschichte der Jesus-Bewegung 1994 ➤ 185.

13610 **Hoornaert** Eduardo,   O movimento de Jesus. Petrópolis 1994, Vozes. 160 p. 85-326-1159-1. – ᴿPerspT 26 (1994) 417-420 (J. R. *Libanio*).

13611 **Horsley** Richard A.,   Sociology and the Jesus Movement 1989 ➤ 7,e673 ... 9,15307: ᴿJEvTS 37 (1994) 427-9 (M. R. *Fairchild*).

13612 **Hutton** Rodney R.,   Charisma and authority in Israelite society. Mp 1994, Fortress.   x-229 p.; bibliog. 211-9. 0-8006-2832-2 [BL 95,40, J. R. *Porter*].

13613 **Jamieson-Drake** D. W.,   Scribes and schools 1991 ➤ 7,e676; 8,k200: ᴿHenoch 16 (1994) 350s (J. A. *Soggin*).

13614 **Janssen** R. & J.,   Growing up in ancient Egypt 1900 ➤ 6,d196; 8,d697: ᴿJEA 80 (1994) 232-5 (G. *Robins*: circumcision, toys; should have indicated sources).

13615 **Joshel** Sandra R.,   Work, identity and legal status in Rome 1992 ➤ 9,15510:   ᴿClasJ 90 (1994s) 445-450 (K. *Bradley*, also on EDWARDS C.); ClasR 44 (1994) 359-361 (Margaretha D. *Hall*).

13616 *Kämmerer* T.,   Zur sozialen Stellung der Frau in Emar und Ekalte als Witwe und Waise: UF 26 (1994) 169-208.

13617 **Kaufmann** Franz-Xaver,   Religion und Modernität; sozialwissenschaftliche Perspektiven: Tü 1989, Mohr.   vii-286 p. DM 58 pa. – ᴿTüTQ 174 (1994) 168s (P. *Hünermann*).

13618 **Kessler** Rainer,   Staat und Gesellschaft im vorexilischen Juda, vom 8. Jahrhundert bis zum Exil: VTSup 47, 1992 ➤ 8,k207; 90-04-09646-9: ᴿBL (1994) 36 (J. R. *Porter*); CBQ 56 (1994) 554s (R. S. *Moore*); JTS 45 (1994) 179s (R. *Coggins*); RelStR 20 (1994) 230 (M. S. *Sweeney*).

13619 **Kleijwegt** Marc,   Ancient youth 1991 ➤ 7,e685 ... 9,15320:   ᴿClasR 44 (1994) 370-2 (T. *Wiedemann*); JIntdis 23 (1992s) 312-4 (M. *Golden*); JRS 83 (1993) 223s (Sarah *Currie*).

13620 *Knebel* Sven K.,   Vom Ursprung der Soziologie aus der posttridentinischen Theologie: FrSZ 41 (1994) 463-490.

13621 **Krause** Jens-Uwe,   Witwen und Waisen im römischen Reich, 1 [Hab. Diss. Heid. 1993]: Heid AltHBeit. Stu 1994, Steiner.

13621* *Krause* Jens-Uwe, Die gesellschaftliche Stellung von Witwen im römischen Reich: Saeculum 45 (1994) 71-104.

13622 a) *Kreuzer* Siegfried, Grundfragen der sozialgeschichtlichen und soziologischen Forschung am Alten Testament; – b) *Langer* Gerhard, Bemerkungen zum sozialgeschichtlichen Hintergrund der Entwicklung der Synagoge. ProtokB 2 (1993) 25-40 / 47-59.

13623 **Kühnert** Barbara, Die plebs urbana der späten römischen Republik; ihre ökonomische Situation und soziale Struktur: Abh SächsAkad 73/2. Lp 1991, Akademie. 112 p. DM 42. 3-05-001782-1. – ᴿAnzAltW 46 (1993) 226-8 (Ingomar *Weiler*).

13624 a) *Laffey* Alice L., 'Love the stranger; remember when you were strangers in Egypt'; – b) *Cooke* Bernard, The historical relativity of Jesus' experience of God; – c) *Reynolds* Sally A., Toward an understanding of prejudice; contributions from Paul: ➤ 386, Ethnicity 1991, 31-45 / 47-55 / 103-127.

13625 **Larouche** Jean-Marc, Eros et thanatos sous l'œil des nouveaux clercs [... comme les professeurs de l'Université Québécoise de Montréal se présentaient]; essai socio-historique sur la sexologie et la thanatologie dans la société québécoise: Études québécoises. Montréal 1991. 290 p. [SR 22 (1993) 525].

13626 **Link** S., Landverteilung und sozialer Frieden im archaischen Griechenland: Historia Einz 69. Stu 1991, Steiner. 189 p. – ᴿGerión 11 (1993) 425s (A. *Lozano*).

13627 ᵀᴱ**Lintott** A., Judicial reform and land reform in the Roman republic [Urbino bronze tablet c. 130 B.C.]. C 1992, Univ. xxv-293 p.; 4 fig.; 8 pl. £60. 0-5214-0373-1. – ᴿJRS 84 (1994) 211s (B. W. *Frier*).

13628 **Loraux** Nicole, The children of Athena; Athenian ideas about citizenship and the division between the sexes [1984] Princeton 1993, Univ. xvii-271 p.; 10 pl.; 3 maps. £25. – ᴿGreeceR 41 (1994) 248 (P. *Walcot*: the cream appeared in Arethusa 1978].

13629 *Lyon* David, Whither shall I flee? surveillance, omniscience and normativity in the Panopticon [name coined for an aspect of prison architecture, actually characterizing social institutions like factory and school, according to Michel FOUCAULT, Discipline and punish]: ChrSchR 24 (1994) 302-312.

13630 **Macalinao** Fernando L., The 'new' socio-historical method for New Testament interpretation: diss. Pont. Univ. Gregoriana, ᴰ*Wicks* J. Rome 1994. 338 p.; extr. N° 4041, 131 p. – RTLv 26, p. 538.

13631 a) *Maffesoli* Michel, L'imaginaire et le sacré dans la sociologie de DURKHEIM; – b) *Martelli* Stephano, MAUSS et Durkheim; un désaccord sur la question du sacré et une perspective relationniste sur SIMMEL et la société post-moderne; – c) *Thompson* Kenneth, Durkheim, ideology and the sacred: Social Compass 40 (1993) 389-398 / 375-388 / 451-461 [< ZIT 93,620].

13632 **Malina** Bruce J., Windows on the world of Jesus 1993 ➤ 9,15340: ᴿRExp 91 (1994) 614s (D. E. *Garland*: 'an enjoyable read', best of its genre).

13633 ᴱ**Malina** Bruce J., *Rohrbaugh* Richard L., Social science commentary on the Synoptic Gospels 1992 ➤ 8,k220; 9,15339: ᴿBibTB 24 (1994) 35s (T. R. *Hobbs*); CBQ 56 (1994) 603-5 (F. W. *Burnett*); Churchman 108 (1994) 81s (R. *Ascough*); LvSt 19 (1994) 182-4 (R. F. *Collins*); RExp 91 (1994) 627s (S. *Southard*: M. HENGEL, included, shows a better sense of the numinous than the editors); TorJT 10 (1994) 227-230 (D. E. *Oakman*).

13634 **Malina** Bruce J., The New Testament world; insights from cultural anthropology[2rev], 1993 → 9,15338: [R]TBR 7,1 (1994s) 24 (A. *Chester*: 'important and reasonably-priced'; also on his Windows 1993).

13635 *Marra* Bruno, Aspetti antropologici dell'esperienza di fede: Asprenas 41 (1994) 189-206.

13636 [E]**Martin** Jochen, *Quint* Barbara, Christentum und antike Gesellschaft: WegFor 649, 1990 → 7,319*: [R]TR 90 (1994) 481-4 (B. *Studer*).

13637 **Matthews** V. H., *Benjamin* D. C., The social world of ancient Israel 1250-587 B.C.E. 1993 → 9,15342: [R]BR 10,5 (1994) 15s (P. J. *King*); JNWS 10,2 (1994) 210-222 (F. E. *Deist*); JRelH 18 (1994) 227-9 (V. *Eldridge*); JStOT 64 (1994) 122 (P. R. *Davies*).

13638 **May** David M., Social scientific criticism of the NT, a bibliography → 8,k234: [R]CBQ 55 (1993) 810 (F. W. *Burnett*).

13639 **Meeks** Wayne A., Urchristentum und Stadtkultur; die soziale Welt der paulinischen Gemeinden [1983 → 2,b908],[T]. Gü 1993, Gü.-V. 459 p. DM 148. – [R]Entschluss 49,4 (1994) 42 (Maria *Neubrand*).

13640 **Meeks** Wayne A., I cristiani dei primi secoli 1992 → 9,15344: [R]CiVit 48 (1993) 188s (S. *Spera*).

13641 **Mieroop** Marc Van, Society and enterprise in Old Babylonian Ur 1992 → 8,e954: [R]Syria 71 (1994) 466-8 (D. *Collon*).

13642 **Mitterauer** Michael, A history of youth, [T]*Dunphy* Graeme. CM 1992, Blackwell. ix-256 p. $50; pa. $20. – [R]AmHR 99 (1994) 197s (R. *Wegs*: dated).

13643 **Mödritzer** Helmut, Stigma und Charisma im Neuen Testament und seiner Umwelt; zur Soziologie des Urchristentums: NOrb 28. FrS/Gö 1994, Univ./VR. [iv-] 335 p.; Bibliog. 285-326. 3-7278-0938-8 / VR 3-525-53030-4.

13644 **Morris** Ian, Death-ritual and social structure in classical antiquity 1991 → 8,e293; 9,13703: [R]BL (1994) 127s (M. *Goodman*); ClasB 70 (1994) 50-52 (Billie Jean *Collins*); MusHelv 51 (1994) 253 (J.-J. *Aubert*).

13645 **Mratschek-Halfmann** Sigrid, Divites 1993 → 9,15349: [R]ClasR 44 (1994) 361s (Jane F. *Gardner*); Gerión 12 (1994) 352-5 (G. *Bravo*).

13646 **Müller** R., Polis und res publica; Studien zur antiken Gesellschafts- und Geschichtsdenken. Weimar 1987, H. Böhlau. 384 p. – [R]GrazB 20 (1994) 295-300 (F. F. *Schwarz*).

13647 **Neu** Rainer, Von der Anarchie zum Staat; Entwicklungsgeschichte Israels vom Nomadentum zur Monarchie im Spiegel der Ethnosoziologie. Neuk 1992. 350 p. – [R]JBL 113 (1994) 319-321 (B. *Lang*); OTAbs 17 (1994) 204 (T. M. *Willis*).

13648 **Newsome** James D., Greeks, Romans, Jews; currents of culture and belief in the NT world. Ph 1992, Trinity. 475 p. $27. 1-56338-633-4. – [R]Interpretation 48 (1994) 200,2 (J. D. *Kingsbury*).

13649 **Nippa** Annegret, Haus und Familie in arabischen Ländern, vom Mittelalter bis zur Gegenwart. Mü 1991, Beck. 241 p., ill. DM 44. – [R]Anthropos 88 (1993) 267s (K. *Hackstein*, E. A. *Knauf*).

13650 **Ober** J., Mass and élite in democratic Athens; rhetoric, ideology, and the power of the people. Princeton 1989. xviii-390 p. 0-691-02864-8. – [R]OpAth 20 (1994) 272-6 (L. *Karlssen*).

13651 **Osiek** Carolyn, What are they sayng about the social setting of the NT?[2] NY 1992, Paulist. 125 p. $8. – [R]BibTB 24 (1994) 36s (C. *Seeman*); Church 10,4 (1994) 55 (E. J. *Ciuba*); RivB 42 (1994) 373 (A. *Pitta*).

13652 *Paredes* Tito, Fe cristiana, antropología y las ciencias sociales: Kairós 12 (Guatemala 1993) 63-82.

13653 **Penna** Romano, Ambiente histórico-cultural de los orígines del
cristianismo; textos y comentarios: Cristianismo y sociedad 39. 402 p.;
map; 84-330-1015-8.
13654 ᴱ**Pilch** J.J., *Malina* B.J., Biblical social values and their meaning 1993
→ 9,15357: ᴿBA 57 (1994) 348 (V.H. *Matthews*); RBibArg 56 (1994)
188s (A.J. *Levoratti*); RefTR 53 (1994) 147.
13655 *a) Pilch* John J., Secrecy in the Mediterranean world; an anthropological perspective; – *b) Jacobs-Malina* Diane, Gender, power, and
Jesus' identity in the Gospels; – *c) Malina* Bruce J., John's, the maverick
Christian group — the evidence of sociolinguistics; – *d) Hanson* K.C.,
Kinship: BibTB 24 (1994) 151-7 / 158-166 / 167-182 / 183-194.
13656 *Prades* José A., Éthique et sociologie; le développement des so-
lidarités humaines dans la pensée d'Émile DURKHEIM: SR 22 (1993)
3-19.
13657 **Quass** Friedemann, Die Honoratiorenschicht in den Städten des
griechischen Ostens; Untersuchungen zur politischen und sozialen Entwicklung in hellenistischer und römischer Zeit [Diss. Gö]. Stu 1993,
Steiner. 451 p. – ᴿGerión 12 (1994) 345-7 (A. *Lozano*); HZ 259 (1994)
758s (R. *Bernhardt*); RÉLat 72 (1994) 315-7 (M. *Sartre*).
13658 *Quedraggo* Jean-Martin, La réception de la sociologie du charisme de
Max WEBER: ArchivScSocR 83 (1993) 141-152; Eng. español 157; bibliog.
152-6.
13659 *Raepsaet-Charlier* Marie-Thérèse, La vie familiale des élites dans la
Rome impériale; le droit et la pratique: CahGlotz 5 (1994) 165-197.
13660 **Rawson** Beryl, Marriage, divorce 1991 → 7,600; 9,15360: ᴿJRS 84
(1994) 178-185 (T.G. *Parkin*, also on 8 cognates); Klio 75 (1993) 498-500
(Christiane *Kunst*).
13661 *Reekmans* T., The behaviour of consummers in the Zenon papyri:
AncSoc 25 (1994) 119-140.
13661* **Reviv** Henoch, *al.*, ❶ *Ha-ḥebra...* Society in the kingdoms of Israel and
Judah: EnṣM Library 8, 1993 → 9,15361: ᴿBL (1994) 39 (G.I. *Davies*).
13662 *Rivière* Yann, *Carcer* et *uincula*; la détention publique à Rome (sous la
République et le Haut-Empire): MÉF 106 (1994) 579-652.
13663 *Rosivach* Vincent, *Anus* [usually negative, unlike *senex*]; some older
women in Latin literature: ClasW 88 (1994s) 107-117.
13664 **Salzman** Michèle R., On Roman time 1991 → 7,e713... 9,15365:
ᴿAntClas 63 (1994) 558s (J. *Balty*).
13665 *Schille* Gottfried, Die Jesusbewegung und die Entstehung der Kirche:
TLZ 119 (1994) 99-112.
13666 **Segal** Robert A., Religion and the social sciences (13 1976-87 reprinted
essays on the confrontation) 1989 → 5,355; 9,15371: ᴿNumen 40 (1993)
185-7 (E.A. *Yoman*).
13667 **Sicari** E., Prostituzione e tutela giuridica della schiava 1991 → 8,k253*;
9,15374: ᴿGnomon 66 (1994) 181-3 (Jane F. *Gardner*); IVRA 42 (1991)
209-213 (D. *Dalla*).
13668 **Spickard** Paul R., *Cragg* Kevin M., God's peoples; a social history of
Christians. GR 1994, Baker. 486 p. 0-8010-2385-0.
13669 **Stambaugh** John E., *Balch* David L., Das soziale Umfeld des NTs,
ᵀ*Lüdemann* Gerd 1992 → 8,k254; 9,15378: ᴿTR 90 (1994) 222s (R.
Pesch).
13670 **Stambaugh** John, *Balch* David, Het Nieuwe Testament in zijn soziale
omgeving. Kampen 1992, Kok. 222 p. ƒ49,50. – ᴿStreven 61 (1994) 470
(P. *Beentjes*).

13671 *Stavrianopoulou* Eftychia,   Die Wiederverheiratung auf Kos: Historia 43 (1994) 119-125.

13672 **Strauss** Barry S.,   Fathers and sons in Athens; ideology and society in the era of the Peloponnesian War. L 1993, Routledge. xv-283 p. £37.50. – ᴿGreeceR 41 (1994) 245s (P. *Walcot*: he takes time to get going but offers much).

13672* **Svenbro** Jesper, Phrasikleia; an anthropology of reading in ancient Greece, ᵀ*Lloyd* Janet, 1993: ᴿClasPg 89 (1994) 367-372 (A. *Ford*).

13673 ᴱ*Tentori* Tullio, Bronisław MALINOWSKI, Giornale di un antropologo [postumo 1967]. R 1992, Armando. – ᴿSMSR 59 (1993) 163s (Rita di *Reda*).

13674 **Theissen** Gerd, Social reality and the early Christians; ethics and the world of the NT [3 inedita + 7], ᵀ*Kohl* Margaret 1992 → 8,k258; 9,15380: ᴿHeythJ 35 (1994) 324s (G. *Turner*); JEH 45 (1994) 333 (D. *Nineham*).

13675 **Thomas** Rosalind,   Literacy and orality in ancient Greece. 1992 → 8,d138: ᴿClasW 88 (1994s) 136s (Elinor J. M. *West*: illiterate does not mean uncultured).

13676 *a*) *Thompson* Kenneth, DURKHEIM, ideology and the sacred; – *b*) *Maffesoli* Michel, L'imaginaire et le sacré dans la sociologie de Durkheim; – *c*) *Tomasi* Luigi, Social differentiation and the current significance of anomie: SocComp 40 (1993) 451-461 / 389-398 / 363-374.

13677 *Treggiari* Susan,   Putting the bride to bed: ÉchMClas 38 (1994) 311-331.

13678 **Wagner-Hasel** Beate, Matriarchatstheorien der Altertumswissenschaft: WegF 651. Da 1992, Wiss. 403 p. DM 98. – ᴿHZ 259 (1994) 438-440 (Rosmarie *Günther*).

13679 *Walcot* Peter, Separatism and the alleged conversation of women [... PLUTARCH; AUGUSTINE, JEROME]: ClasMdv 45 (1994) 27-50.

13681 **Wallace-Hadrill** Andrew, Houses and society in Pompeii and Herculaneum,   Princeton 1994, Univ. xix-284 p.; 135 fig.; 8 pl. $49.50. – ᴿClasO 72 (1994s) 144 (J. C. *Anderson*).

13682 ᴱ**Wallace-Hadrill** A., Patronage in ancient society 1990 → 5,808 ... 8,k264: ᴿJRS 84 (1994) 185s (J. K. *Davies*).

13683 **Whale** Sheila, The family in the eighteenth dynasty of Egypt: Studies 1. Sydney 1988, Australian Centre for Egyptology. x-308 p.; 13 pl.   0-85837-670-9. – ᴿJEA 79 (1993) 294-7 (Gay *Robins*).

13684 **Whitley** James,   Style and society in Dark Age Greece; the changing face of a pre-literate society 1100-700 B.C. 1991 → 8,k266: ᴿGnomon 66 (1994) 537-543 (Berit *Wells*); TopO 3 (1993) 259-264 (P. *Ruby*).

13685 **Winter** Bruce W.,   Seek the welfare of the city; Christians as benefactors and citizens: First-Century Christians in the Greco-Roman World. GR/Carlisle 1994, Eerdmans/Paternoster. ix-245 p.; bibliog. 211-224. 0-8028-4091-4 / 0-85364-633-3.

u5.3   **Commercium, oeconomica.**

13686 Amphores romaines et histoire économique, Actes du colloque de Siène 1986/9 → 7,e748: ᴿAJA 98 (1994) 580-2 (N. K. *Rauh*).

13687 *Andreau* Jean, Affaires financières à Pouzzoles au Iᵉʳ siècle ap. J.-C.; les tablettes de Murécine: RÉLat 72 (1994) 39-55.

13688 *a*) *Aruz* Joan, Imagery and interconnections; – *b*) *Arnold* Dorothea & Felix, *Allen* Susan, Canaanite imports at Lisht, the Middle Kingdom capital of Egypt; – *c*) *Karageorghis* Vassos, Relations between Cyprus and Egypt: Trade, ÄgLev 5 (1993/4) 33-48; 44 fig. / 13-32; 7 fig. / 73-78 + 6 fig.

13688* **Baloglou** Christos P., *Constantinidis* Anestis, Die Wirtschaft in der Gedankenwelt der Alten Griechen: EurHS 5/1412. Fra 1993, Lang. 197 p.

13689 **Baloglou** Christos P., *Peukert* Helge, Zum antiken ökonomischen Denken der Griechen (800 v. u. Z. - 31 n. u. Z.), eine kommentierte Bibliographie. Marburg 1992, Metropolis. 121 p. DM 32,80. – ᴿHZ 259 (1994) 155s (L. *Wierschowski*).

13690 ᴱ**Begley** Vimala, *Puma* R. P. de, Rome and India; the ancient sea trade [< colloquium AIA 1986]. Madison 1991, Univ. Wisconsin. – ᴿPhoenix 48 (Toronto 1994) 91-94 (T. D. *Barnes*).

13691 **Bogaert** Raymond, Trapezitica aegyptiaca; recueil de [20] recherches sur la banque en Égypte gréco-romaine: PapFlor 25. F 1994, Gonnelli, xi-439 p.; 4 pl. Lᵐ 400. – ᴿAegyptus 79 (1994) 194s (Orsolina *Montevecchi*); CdÉ 69 (1994) 381s (J. *Birgen*).

13692 **Brandt** Hartwin, Gesellschaft und Wirtschaft Pamphyliens und Pisidiens im Altertum: Asia Minor Studien 7. Bonn 1992. 223 p. – ᴿMünst-Hand 13,1 (1994) 102-113 (B. *Tenger*).

13693 **Budde** Michael L., The two churches, Catholicism and capitalism in the world system. Durham 1992, Duke Univ. vi-172 p. $30. – ᴿJRel 74 (1994) 100-2 (T. H. *Sanks*).

13694 *a)* **Bunimovitz** Sh., The problem of human resources in Late Bronze Age Palestine and its socioeconomic implications; – *b)* *Zwickel* Wolfgang, Wirtschaftliche Grundlagen in Zentraljuda gegen Ende des 8. Jhts. aus archäologischer Sicht — mit einem Ausblick auf die wirtschaftliche Situation im 7. Jh. UF 26 (1994) 1-20 / 557-592; 7 plans.

13694* **Capogrossi-Colognesi** Luigi, Economie antiche e capitalismo moderno; la sfida di Max WEBER: BtCuMod. Bari 1990, Laterza. xvi-391 p. – ᴿTopO 3 (1993) 23-38 (E. *Will*).

13695 ᴱ**Charpin** D., *Joannès* F., La circulation des biens, 38ᵉ Renc 1991/2 ➤ 8,683: ᴿAfO 40s (1993s) 103-6 (W. von *Soden*); JESHO 37 (1994) 332-4 (S. *Koshurnikov*); RB 101 (1994) 299 (tit. pp.).

13696 **Cline** Eric H., Sailing the wine-dark sea; international trade and the Late Bronze Age Aegean: BAR-Int 591. Ox 1994. xxii-316 p.; bibliog. 278-316. 0-86054-765-5.

13697 **Cohen** Edward E., Athenian economy and society 1992 ➤ 9,15396: ᴿAmHR 99 (1994) 875s (J. R. *Love*); ClasPg 89 (1994) 351-366 (I. *Morris*); ClasW 88 (1994s) 123 (D. C. *Mirhady*); MusHelv 51 (1994) 257s (L. *Burckhardt*); RÉG 107 (1994) 261s (J.-N. *Corvisier*).

13698 **Cozzo** A., Le passioni economiche nella Grecia antica 1991 ➤ 8,k282; 9,15397: ᴿRBgPg 72 (1994) 172 (J. P. *Callu*).

13699 **De Salvo** L., Economia privata e pubblici servizi nell'Impero Romano; i corpora naviculariorum: Kleio 5. Messina 1992, Samperi. 797 p.; 33 pl.; 3 maps. – ᴿGerión 12 (1994) 365 (Mirella *Romero Recio*); Koinonia 17 (1993) 223s (S. *D'Elia*).

13699* **Drexhage** Hans-Joachim, Einflüsse des Zollwesens auf den Warenverkehr im römischen Reich — handelshemmend oder handelfördernd? MünstHand 13,2 (1994) 1-15.

13700 **Drexhage** Hans-J., Preise, Mieten... im römischen Ägypten 1991 ➤ 9,15400: ᴿAntClas 63 (1994) 566s (J. A. *Straus*).

13700* **Dudley** Dennine L., The Nabataeans and trade; contribution elements: diss. MA Univ. Victoria, ᴰ*Oleson* J. Melbourne 1992. xi-162 p. 0-315-76060-5.

13701 **Duncan-Jones** R. P., Structure and scale in the Roman economy 1990
➤ 6,g734...9,15401: ᴿJRS 84 (1994) 231-3 (J. K. *Davies*: a quiet revolutionary).

13702 **Durliat** Jean, Les rentiers de l'impôt; recherches sur les finances
municipales dans la 'Pars Orientis' au IVᵉ siècle: ByzVindob 21. W 1993,
Österr. Akad. 150 p. ᴅᴍ 70. 3-7001-2011-7. – ᴿMuséon 107 (1994) 395-7
(B. *Coulie*).

13703 **Elayi** J., Économie des cités phéniciennes sous l'Empire perse 1990
➤ 7,d531: ᴿTEuph 8 (1994) 165-7 (J. *Sapin*).

13704 *Foster* Benjamin R., Early Mesopotamian land sales [Gᴇʟʙ I., *al.*,
Kudurrus 1991 ➤ 8,9614]: JAOS 114 (1994) 440-452; 2 facsim.

13705 **Frayn** Joan M., Markets and fairs in Roman Italy; their social and
economic importance from the 2d century ʙ.ᴄ. to the 3d century ᴀ.ᴅ. Ox
1993, Clarendon. viii-183 p.; 11 fig. £28. 0-19-814799-6. – ᴿAmHR 99
(1994) 1663s (Phyllis *Culham*); ClasR 44 (1994) 121s (Helen M. *Parkins*);
ClasW 88 (1994s) 232 (Anne *Weis*); JRS 84 (1994) 235s (Kathryn *Lomas*).

13706 — **Ligt** L. de, Fairs and markets in the Roman empire; economic and
social aspects of periodic trade in pre-industrial society. Amst 1993,
Gieben. x-315 p. ƒ140. 90-5063-146-0. – ᴿJRS 84 (1994) 236s (J. M.
Frayn).

13707 **Freyberg** H. U. von, Kapitalverkehr und Handel im römischen
Kaiserreich (27 v.Chr.-235 n.Chr.). Fr 1989! ➤ 8,k289: ᴿRitNum 96
(1994s) 356-8 (D. *Foraboschi*).

13708 ᴱ**Gale** Noel H., Bronze Age trade in the Mediterranean; Oxford Dec
1989: SIMA 90, 1991 ➤ 7,637: ᴿAntClas 63 (1994) 584s (Sylvie *Müller*).

13708* *Gawlikowski* M., Palmyra as a trading centre: Iraq 56 (1994) 27-33.

13709 **Gehlken** E., Uruk, Spätbabylonische Wirtschaftstexte 1990 ➤ 8,e867:
ᴿJSS 38 (1993) 136-8 (J. *MacGinnis*).

13710 ᴱ**Gyselen** Rika, Circulation des monnaies, des marchandises et des
biens: ResOr 5, Lv 1993. 187 p. Fb 1800. 1142-2831. – ᴿMesopT 29
(1994) 323-5 (A. *Invernizzi*); StOr 73 (Helsinki 1994) 321s (K. *Karttunen*).

13710* *Halstead* Paul, The Mycenaean palatial economy; making the most of
the gaps in the evidence: PrCPg 38 (1992s) 57-86.

13711 ᴱ**Harris** W. V., The inscribed economy; production and distribution
in the Roman Empire in the light of *instrumentum domesticum*: JRArch
supp. 6. AA 1993. 192 p.; 25 fig. £25. – ᴿJRS 84 (1994) 233-5 (D. J.
Mattingly).

13711* *Howgego* Christopher, Coin circulation and the integration of the
Roman economy: JRomA 7 (1994) 5-21.

13712 *Jankowskaya* N. B., ❾ 'The day of salvation — the day of mercy'
[warning of overall harm to the business community when the Pušuken
firm of Kaniš switched from textiles to copper-cutting]: VDI 208 (1994)
1-19; Eng. 19.

13712* *Janssen* J. J., Debts and credit in the New Kingdom: JEA 80 (1994)
129-136.

13713 *Joannès* F., Métaux précieux et moyens de paiement en Babylonie achéménide et hellénistique: ➤ 461, Syrie, TEuph 8 (1991/4) 137-144; Eng. 137.

13714 *Johnston* Alan W., Emporia, emporoi and Sicilians; some epigraphical
aspects: ➤ 433, Kokalos 39 (1993s) 155-169; 2 fig.

13715 **Joshel** Sandra R., Work identity and legal status at Rome; a study
of the occupational inscriptions. Norman 1992, Univ. Oklahoma. xvi-
239 p. £25.50. 0-8061-2413-2; pa. -44-5. – ᴿJRS 84 (1994) 258s (Hanne
S. *Nielsen*).

13716 **Kangas** Steven E., Social and economic organization during the chalcolithic period in the northern Negev, Israel; a study of ceramic variability: diss. Brandeis, ᴰGILEAD I. Boston 1994. 366 p. 94-17710. – DissA 55 (1994s) p. 620.

13717 **Karimali** Evangelia, The neolithic mode of production and exchange reconsidered; lithic production and exchange patterns in Thessaly Greece, during the transitional late neolithic-bronze age period: diss. ᴰ*Runnels* C. Boston Univ. 1994. 561 p. 94-22506. – DissA 55 (1994s) p. 1302.

13717* **Kehoe** Dennis P., Management and investment on estates in Roman Egypt during the Early Empire: PapTAbh 40, 1992 ➤ 8,k303: ᴿBASP 30 (1993) 127-135 (R. S. *Bagnall*).

13718 *Kudlien* Fridolf, Die Rolle der Konkurrenz im antiken Geschäftsleben: MünstHand 13,1 (1994) 1-38; Eng. franç. 39.

13719 *Lessnoff* Michael, Catechisms, capitalism and Max WEBER: ScotJR 12 (1991) 5-28 . 75-87.

13720 ᴱ**Linders** Tullia, *Alroth* Brita, Economics of cult in the ancient Greek world 1990/2 ➤ 8,664: ᴿAntClas 63 (1994) 528-530 (L. *Migeotte*); ClasR 44 (1994) 411s (H. van *Wees*).

13721 *Link* Stefan, Anachoresis; Steuerflucht im Ägypten der frühen Kaiserzeit: Klio 75 (1993) 306-319; Eng. 319s.

13721* *Lipiński* Edward, Économie phénicienne; travaux récents et desiderata: JESHO 37 (1994) 322-5.

13722 *a) Lyapustin* B. F., ❻ Family craft in the structure of ancient Roman economy; – *b) Koptev* A. V., ❻ The antique form of property and the state in ancient Rome: VDI 202 (1992) 52-66; Eng. 66s / 3-27; Eng. 28.

13723 **Maresch** Klaus, Nomisma und nomismata; Beiträge zur Geldgeschichte Ägyptens im 6. Jh. n.Chr.: Rh/Westf.. Akad. Abh/PapyrColon 21. Opladen 1994, Westd.-V. 3-531-09935-3.

13723* *Márquez Rowe* I., Evidence of the trade between Ugarit and Byblos; once more on RTU 4,338: 10-18: AulaO 11,1 (1993) 101-6.

13724 *Martin-Kilcher* Stefanie, Verbreitungskarten römischer Amphoren und Absatzgebiete importierter Lebensmittel: MünstHand 13,2 (1994) 95-113 + 12 fig.

13724* *Mause* Michael, Der Kaiser als Fachmann in ökonomischen Fragen? Bemerkungen zu wirtschaftlichen Aspekten in der lateinischen Panegyrik: MünstHand 13,1 (1994) 89-101; Eng. franç. 101.

13725 **Meijer** Fik, *Nijf* Onno van, Trade, transport and society in the ancient world; a sourcebook 1992 ➤ 8,k308: ᴿClasW 88 (1994s) 66s (L. *Casson*); HZ 259 (1994) 440s (P. *Herz*).

13726 *Meikle* Scott, ARISTOTLE on money: Phronesis 39 (1994) 26-44.

13727 **Meyer** Carol, Glass from Quseir al-Qadim and the Indian Ocean trade: SAOC 53, 1992 ➤ 8,d581: ᴿCdÉ 69 (1994) 197s (H. *Melaerts*); JAmEg 31 (1994) 232s (Susan H. *Auth*).

13728 **Mieroop** Marc van de, Society and enterprise in Old Babylonian Ur: BBVO 12, 1992 ➤ 9,15423: ᴿRAss 88 (1994) 65s (B. *Lafont*).

13729 **Millett** Paul, Lending and borrowing in ancient Athens 1991 ➤ 7, e784 ... 9,15424: ᴿEtClas 62 (1994) 409s (H. *Leclercq*); Gnomon 66 (1994) 17-20 (R. *Bogaert*).

13730 *a) Minnen* Peter von, Taking stock; declarations of property from the Ptolemaic period; – *b) Nielsen* Bruce E., A woman of property, Aurelia Techosous alias Eudaimonis: BASP 31 (1994) 89-101; pl. 20-21 / 129-137.

13731 *Moscati* S., Flotte e commerci nel Tirreno: RStFen 22 (1994) 9-14.

13732 **Ohrenstein** Roman A., *Gordon* Barry, Economic analysis in Talmudic literature; rabbinic thought in the light of modern economics: StPostB 40. Leiden 1992, Brill. xxii-152 p. ƒ75. 90-04-09540-3. – ᴿJStJud 25 (1994) 113s (D. *Sperber*).

13733 *Olivier* J.P.J., Money matters; some remarks on the economic situation in the kingdom of Judah during the seventh century B.C.: BibNot 73 (1994) 90-100.

13734 ᴱ**Paroli** Lidia, *Delogu* Paola, La storia economica di Roma alla luce dei recenti scavi archeologici: BtArchMdv 10. F 1993, Insegna del Giglio. 368 p.; ill. – ᴿVetChr 31 (1944) 404-8 (G. *Volpe*).

13735 *a) Perea* Alicia, Proceso de mercantilización en sociedades premonetales; – *b) Cabrera Bonet* Paloma, Comercio internacional mediterraneo en el siglo VIII a.C. ArEspArq 67 (1994) 3-14; 2 fig. (map) / 15-30.

13736 **Petrucci** A., Mensam exercere; studi sull'impresa finanziaria romana: Univ. Roma, 1991 ➤ 9,15432: Ist. dir. Rom./Medit., N 1991, Jovene. ix-419 p. – ᴿIVRA 42 (1991) 200-4 (M. J. *García Garrido*).

13737 **Rathbone** Dominic, Economic rationalism... Egypt, Heroninos 1991 ➤ 8,k324; 9,15434: ᴿAntClas 62 (1993) 445s (J. A. *Straus*); HZ 259 (1994) 165s (R. *Scholl*).

13738 *Renger* Johannes, On economic structures in ancient Mesopotamia: Orientalia 63 (1994) 157-208.

13739 **Safrai** Ze'ev, The economy of Roman Palestine. L 1994, Routledge. xii-500 p. – ᴿIsrClas 14 (1994s) 186-190 (I. *Shatzman*).

13740 *Schüle* Wilhelm, *Deimling* Irmgard von, Feldbewässerung, Vieh und Fernhandel; zur ökonomischen Trias der Erbauer von Megalith- und Kuppelgräbern am Mittelmeer und im atlantischen Europa: ➤ 35, ᶠFREY O. 1994, 549-562.

13741 **Selz** G. Altsumerische Verwaltungstexte aus Lagaš 1989 ➤ 5,e202; 7,d736*: ᴿWZKM 83 (1993) 289-291 (M. A. *Powell*).

13742 **Silver** Morris, Talking ancient mythology economically 1992 ➤ 8,k329; 9,15442: ᴿBL (1994) 19 (L. L. *Grabbe*: absurd); GreeceR 41 (1994) 112 (P. *Walcot*: wild); ZRGg 46 (1994) 191 (W. *Beltz*).

13743 **Tortorici** Edoardo, Argiletum, commercio... 1991 ➤ 8,k334*; 9,15450: ᴿAntClas 63 (1994) 541s (P. *Simelon*: passionnant).

13744 **Whittaker** C. R., Frontiers of the Roman Empire; a social and economical study. Baltimore 1994, Johns Hopkins Univ. xviii-341 p.; bibliog. 307-330. 0-8108-4677-3.

U5.7   Nomadismus; ecology.

13745 **Cribb** Roger, Nomads in archaeology: NewStudies. C 1991, Univ. xiv-253 p.; 73 fig. 0-521-32881-0. – ᴿAJA 97 (1993) 167 (T. J. *Wilkinson*); JESHO 37 (1994) 67s (B. D. *Shaw*).

13746 ᴱ**Galaty** John G., *Johnson* Douglas L., The world of pastoralism; herding systems in comparative perspective. NY 1990, Guilford. x-436 p.; ill. $32.50. – ᴿAnthropos 88 (1993) 242-5 (M. *Bollig*).

13747 **La Bianca** Ø. S., Sedentarization and nomadization: Hesban 1, 1990 ➤ 9,15457: ᴿPEQ 125 (1993) 167-9 (A. *McQuitty*); BAnglsr 13 (1993s) 52-54 (S. *Dar*).

13748 *Lemche* Niels P., Nomadentum im AT: ➤ 517, TRE 24 (1994) 587-9.

13749 **Peters** Emrys L., The bedouin of Cyrenaica; studies in personal and corporate power, ᴱ*Goody* Jack, *Marx* Emanuel: StSocCAnthrop 73. C 1990, Univ. xi-310 p.; ill. – ᴿAnthropos 88 (1993) 273s (J. *Chelhod*).

13749* ᶠPUGLISI Salvatore M., Studi di paletnologia, ᴱLiverani M., *al.*, 1985
➤ 2,89 (Puglese); xvi-920 p.; ᴿAulaO 11,1 (1993) 124-9 (C. *Valdés*).
13750 **Sallares** Robert, The ecology of the ancient Greek world 1981
➤ 7,e821 ... 9,15465: Ithaca 1991, Cornell Univ. x-588 p. – ᴿPhoenix 48
(Toronto 1994) 81-83 (R. *Develin*); WZKM 84 (1994) 202s (K. *Jaroš*).
13751 **Staubli** Thomas, Das Image der Nomaden OBO 107, 1991 ➤ 7,a821 ...
9,15466: ᴿAfO 40s (1993s) 174-7 (S. *Kreuzer*).

U5.8 Urbanismus.

13752 **Álvarez Bolado** A., Mística y secularidad, en medio y a las afueras de
la Ciudad secularizada: Aquí y ahora 20. Sdr 1992, Sal Terrae. 40 p. –
ᴿREspir 52 (1993) 359s (T. *Polo*).
13753 *Asensio Esteban* José Angel, Primeras manifestaciones del urbanismo
romano-republicano en el Valle Medio del Ebro: Zephyrus 47 (S 1994)
219-255; 4 fig.; 2 pl. (243 'headers-stretchers').
13754 *Aujac* Germaine, Les très grandes villes chez les géographes grecs:
MÉF 106 (1994) 859-899 [845-858, *Prontera* Francesco; 901-919 latine,
Desanges Jehan].
13755 ᶠBROOKE C., Church and city ᴱ*Abulafia* D., *al.* 1992➤ 8,23: ᴿHeythJ
35 (1995) 222 (B. N. *Swanson*); JTS 44 (1993) 750 (C. *Morris*).
13756 **Castel** Corinne, Habitat urbain néo-assyrien et néo-babylonien: de
l'espace bâti... à l'espace vécu: BAH 143. P 1992, Geuthner. I. xix-135 p.;
bibliog. 119-132; II. 271 p.; 78 pl.
13757 *Curty* Olivier, *a*) À propos de la syngéneia entre cités: RÉG 107
(1994) 698-707; – *b*) La notion de la parenté entre cités chez THUCYDIDE:
MusHelv 51 (1994) 193-7.
13758 **Davoli** Paola, Città e villaggi dell'antico Egitto: PiccBtEg 1. Imola 1994,
Mandragora. 103 p. 88-86123-15-9.
13759 *Domínguez Monedero* Adolfo J., La Polis y la expansión colonial
griega, siglos VIII-VI, 1991 ➤ 8,k634; 9,15474: ᴿAntClas 63 (1994) 518s
(F. de *Polignac*).
13759* **Dougherty** Carol, The poetics of colonization; from city to text in
archaic Greece. NY 1993, Oxford-UP. x-209 p. $40 [RelStR 21,325,
D. F. *Jackson*].
13760 **Erath** Gabriele, Das Bild der Stadt in der griechischen Flächenkunst:
Diss. Graz. – MiDAV 25,2 (1994) 26.
13761 **Frosini** G., Babele o Gerusalemme: per una teologia della città 1992
➤ 9,15477: ᴿAngelicum 71 (1994) 619s (G. *Grasso*); CC 145 (1994,1)
198s (P. *Vanzan*).
13761* *Garcin* Jean-Claude, La ville pré-moderne: JESHO 37 (1994) 103-6
(-146, *Reimer* Michael J., Ottoman Alexandria).
13762 **Grainger** J., Cities of Seleukid Syria 1990 ➤ 7,e829; 9,15479: ᴿJAOS
11 (1994) 267-270 (M. C. *Astour*).
13763 **Hoepfner** Wolfram, *Schwandner* Ernst-Ludwig, Haus und Stadt im
klassischen Griechenland: Wohnen in der klassischen Polis, 1. Mü 1994,
Dts. Kunst-V. xx-356 p.; ill. 3-422-06024-3.
13763* **Huot** Jean-Louis, Les premiers villages de Mésopotamie; du village à
la ville: Civilisations. P 1994, A. Colin. 224 p.; ill. – ᴿRAss 88 (1994)
175s (P. *Amiet*).
13764 *a*) *Jacobson* Diane, The city in the Bible; implications for urban
ministry; – *b*) *Brueggemann* Walter, Remembering Rachel's children; an

urban agenda for people who notice: WWorld 14,4 ('The City' 1994) 395-401 / 397-383.

13765 *Jähne* Armin, Die Städtegründungen Alexanders des Grossen in Asien: Altertum 38 (1992) 161-175; 9 fig.

13766 *Kuhnen* Hans-Peter, Kirche, Landwirtschaft und Flüchtlingssilber; zur wirtschaftlichen Entwicklung Palästinas in der Spätantike: ZDPV 110 (1994) 36-50; 8 fig. (maps); pl. 1.

13766* **Laurence** Ray, Roman Pompeii; space and society. NY 1994, Routledge. xi-158 p.; ill. 0-415-09502-6 [RelStR 21,328, T. *Brauch*: methods of urban geography].

13767 **Lonis** Raoul, La cité dans le monde grec; structures, fonctionnement, contradictions: Fac. Histoire. P 1994, Nathan. 320 p.; maps. – ᴿRÉAnc 96 (1994) 622 (P. *Brun*).

13768 *Maisels* Charles K., The emergence of civilization 1990 → 7,e836; 8,k378: ᴿAJA 98 (1994) 776s (P. M. *Fischer*).

13769 *Mayerson* Philip, Urbanization in Palaestina Tertia; pilgrims and paradoxes [< ❻ Cathedra 45 (1987) 19-40]: → 207, Monks, martyrs, soldiers and Saracens 1994, 232-240.

13770 ᴱMeyers Eleanor S., Envisioning the new city; a reader on urban ministry. LvL 1992. W-Knox. 363 p. $23. – ᴿPrincSemB 15 (1994) 89s (A. *Neely*).

13771 **Molho** Antony, *Raaflaub* Kurt, *Emlen* Julia, City-states in classical antiquity and medieval Italy: Athens and Rome, Florence and Venice. Stu 1991, Steiner. 662 p.; 40 fig. DM 118. 3-515-05873-7. – ᴿLatomus 53 (1994) 695s (R. *Chevallier*).

13772 **Murray** Oswyn, La città greca [Univ. San Marino] 1990 → 6,799 ᵀ]. T 1994, Einaudi. 166 p. Lᵐ 22. – ᴿArcheo 9,112 (1994) 107 (P. G. *Guzzo*).

13773 ᴱMurray Oswyn, *Price* Simon, La cité grecque d'Homère à Alexandre [Oxford 1986], ᵀRegnot F.: Textes à l'appui. P 1992, Découverte. 432 p.; 19 fig. F 220. – ᴿRBgPg 72 (1994) 177-9 (J.-M. *Hannick*); RÉAnc 96 (1994) 623 (P. *Brun*).

13774 **Racine** Jean-Bernard, La ville entre Dieu et les hommes. Genève 1993, Presses Bibliques Universitaires. 354 p. 2-88264-009-9. – ᴿÉTRel 69 (1994) 462s (J.-M. *Prieur*).

13775 **Reed** Jonathan L., Places in early Christianity; Galilee archaeology, urbanization, and [their impact on] Q: diss. Claremont 1991. 172 p. 94-05374. – DissA 54 (1993s) p. 3478.

13776 ᴱRich J., The city in late antiquity 1992 → 8,675a: ᴿÉchMClas 38 (1994) 443-6 (R. C. *Buckley*); HZ 259 (1994) 777s (A. *Kneppe*); JRS 84 (1994) 284s (M. *Whittow*).

13777 ᴱRich J., *Wallace-Hadrill* A., City and country 1991 → 8,k389: ᴿJRS 84 (1994) 189s (J. R. *Davies*: also on the very different though similarly titled *Owens* E. 1991).

13778 **Robertson** Noel, Festivals and legends; the formation of Greek cities in the light of public ritual: Phoenix supp. 31. Toronto 1993, Univ. xvi-287 p.; 6 maps. $83. – ᴿClasR 44 (1994) 341 (C. *Smith*); ÉchMClas 38 (1994) 409-411 (J. A. S. *Evans*); Phoenix 48 (Toronto 1994) 365-8 (M. H. *Jameson*).

13779 **Robinson** Olivia F., Ancient Rome, city planning 1992 → 8,k390; 9,15492: ᴿAntClas 63 (1994) 545-7 (J. *Gadeyne*); Ivra 43 (1992) 226-230 (F. *Milazzo*); JRS 83 (1993) 224s (Susan D. *Martin*).

13780 **Schofield** Malcolm, The Stoic idea of the city. C 1991, Univ. xii-

164 p. – ᴿEos 81 (1993) 295-300 (M. *Winiarczyk,* ❺); Mnemosyne 47 (1994) 717-720 (D. T. *Runia*).
13781 *a) Snodgrass* Anthony, The rise of the *polis*; the archaeological evidence; – *b) Gauthier* Philippe, Les cités hellénistiques; – *c) Millar* Fergus, The Greek cities in the Roman period: ➤ 424, City-State 1992/3, 30-40 / 211-231 / 232-260.
13782 *Sharon* Ilan, Demographic aspects of the problem of the Israelite settlement: ➤ 102, Mem. RICHARDSON H., Uncovering 1994, 119-134.
13784 **Stambaugh** John E., The ancient Roman city 1988 ➤ 4,h557 ... 9,15457: ᴿClasB 69 (1993) 54-56 (J. E. *Rexine*: a guide to ancient Rome; also on VANCE L.).
13785 *Stockwell* Clinton E., The enchanting city; theological perspectives on the city in post-modern dress (... J. ELLUL overdoes it, 'the city stands in rebellion against God'; Paul established churches in all the cities]: Transformations 9,2 (1992) 10-14.
13786 **Tomlinson** R., From Mycenae to Constantinople 1992 ➤ 8,k398: ᴿClasOut 71 (1993) 141s (Karelisa *Hartigan*).
13787 **Uphill** Eric P., Egyptian towns and cities: Eg 8. Bucks 1988, Shire. 72 p. 0-85263-939-2.

u5.9 *Demographia,* **population-statistics.**

13788 **Bagnall** Roger S., *Frier* Bruce W., The demography of Roman Egypt: Studies in Population 23. C 1994, Univ. xix-354 p. 0-521-46123-5. – ᴿJJurPap 24 (1994) 214s (T. *Derda*).
13789 *Bagnall* Roger S., *a)* Census declarations from the British Library: CdÉ 69 (1994) 109-126; 4 fig.; – *b)* Notes on Egyptian census declarations V: BASP 30 (1993) 35-56.
13789* *Cantarella* E., Famiglia romana e demografia sociale: Ivra 43 (1992) 99-111.
13790 *Felosova* V. K., ❺ The development of modern palaeodemography (methodological problems): RossArkh (1994,1) 67-76.
13791 *Hansen* Mogens H., The number of Athenian citizens secundum SEKUNDA [N., BtS(tud)A 87 (1992) 311-355]: ÉchMClas 38 (1994) 299-310: well over 30,000.
13792 *Lo Cascio* Elio, The size of the Roman population; BELOCH [K., Bevölkerung] and the meaning of the Augustan census-figures: JRS 84 (1994) 23-41.
13792* **McCarthy** Justin, The population of Palestine; population history and statistics of the Late Ottoman period and the Mandate: InstPalSt. NY 1990, Columbia Univ. xxix-242 p. $55. – ᴿJAOS 114 (1994) 106s (R. *Khalid*).
13793 *Parkin* Tim G., Demography and Roman society 1992 ➤ 9,15504: ᴿClasB 69 (1993) 100s (M. C. *Alexander*); ClasPg 89 (1994) 188-192 (P. D. *Shaw*); NYRevB 40,19 (1993) 52-54 (W. V. *Harris*) [NTAbs 37, p. 472; 38, p. 1243]; Prudentia 25,2 (1993) 81-83 (P. *McKechnie*).
13794 *Postgate* Nicholas, How many Sumerians per hectare? Probing the anatomy of an early city [Salabikh]: CamArch 4 (1994) 47-65; 10 fig.
13795 *a) Reed* Jonathan L., Population numbers, urbanization, and economics; Galilean archaeology and the historical Jesus; – *b) Oakman* Douglas E., The archaeology of first-century Galilee and the social interpretation of the historical Jesus: ➤ 394, SBLSem 33 (1994) 203-219 / 220-252.

13796 *Rosivach* Vincent,   The distribution of population in Attica: GrRByz 34 (1993) 391-407.

13797 *Scheidel* Walter, COLUMELLAS privates *ius liberorum*; Literatur, Recht, Demographie; einige Probleme: Latomus 53 (1994) 513-527.

13798 *Wierschowski* Lothar,   Die historische Demographie — ein Schlüssel zur Geschichte? Bevölkerungsrückgang und Krise des Römischen Reiches im 3. Jh. n.Chr.:   Klio 76 (1994) 355-379; Eng. 380.

13799 *Zorn* Jeffrey R.,   Estimating the population size of ancient settlements; methods, problems, solution, and a case study [Nasbeh]: BASOR 295 (1994) 31-48; 8 fig.

U6   **Narrationes peregrinorum et exploratorum;** *Loca sancta.*

13800 TEArrowsmith-Brown J. H., *Pankhurst* Richard, PRUTKÝ's travels 1991 ➤ 8,k407; 9,15505:   REngHR 109 (1994) 1284s (M. *Krasa, J. Polisensky*).

13801 **Bachofen** Johann Jakob,   Viaggio in Grecia, TBaroni Anselmo, ECesana Andrea: Saggi 289. Venezia 1993, Marsilio.   219 p. – RGeogAnt 3s (1994s) 245-8 (P. *Janni*).

13801* EBetrò Maria Carmela,   Racconti di viaggio e di avventura dell'antico Egitto: Testi del Vicino Oriente Antico 1/1, 1990 ➤ 8,k411: RAthenaeum 82 (1994) 237-9 (Clelia *Mora*).

13802 EBianchini Walter,   Faostino di Toscolano, Itinerario di Terra Santa; Univ. Perugia Centro Mdv 6.   Spoleto 1992, Centro Alto Medioevo. xii-614 p.; ill.; maps. – RColcFran 63 (1993) 370-2 (Isidoro de *Villapadierna*).

13802* **Brefeld** J.,   A guidebook for the Jerusalem pilgrimage in the late Middle Ages; a case for computer-aided textual criticism: Middeleeuwse-StB 40.   Hilversum 1990, Verloren.   243 p.; 22 fig. *f* 45 [RHE 90,43*; avec deux R].

13803 **Casson** Lionel,   Travels in the ancient world²rev [¹1974]. Baltimore 1994, Johns Hopkins Univ. 391 p. $16. 0-8014-4808-3 [RelStR 21,133, W. M. *Calder*].

13803* TECunz Martin,   Die Fahrt des Rabbi NACHMAN von Bratzlaw ins Land Israel (1798-99), ein Beitrag zur Geschichte und Hermeneutik des Bratzlawer Chasidismus Diss. DClemens T. Luzern 1994. 488 p. – RTLv 26,534.

13804 EDavis Moshe, *Ben-Arieh* Yehoshua,   With eyes toward Zion, 3. Western societies and the Holy Land.   NY 1991, Praeger.   xiv-275 p. $35. – RJRel 74 (1994) 293s (J. T. *Pawlikowski* does not mention 'pilgrims' among the nine categories cited); PEQ 126 (1994) 166s (Gillian *Webster*; July 1990 Symposium 'Jerusalem in the mind of the western world 1800-1948').

13804* **Eisner** Robert,   Travelers to an antique land; the history and literature of travel to Greece. AA 1991, Univ. Michigan.   304 p.; 17 fig. $25; pa. $15. 0-462-10241-9. – RJField 21 (1994) 362-9 (J. *Bennet*).

13805 *a) Ferrari* Silvio, *Margiotta Broglio* Francesco,   Laicità, libertà di culto e carattere sacro dei Luoghi Santi; – *b) Fröhlich* Elisabetta,   La condizione giuridica di Gerusalemme: ➤ 256, Mare di guerra 1994, 67-79 / 80-101.

13806 **Häselhoff** Rudolf,   Sinn unterwegs; eine Grundlegung zur Wallfahrt: kath. Diss. DRotter. Innsbruck 1994. – TR 91,97.

13806* **Harpur** James,   The atlas of sacred places; meeting points of heaven and earth [Ephesus, Catacombs, Lourdes; Mecca, but Jerusalem only as

Dome of the Rock; 28 of interest beyond Judeo-Christian]. NY 1994, Holt. 240 p. $45. 0-5050-2775-0 [TDig 42,69].

13807 **Kalfatovic** Martin R., Nile notes of a Howadji; a bibliography of traveler's tales from Egypt, from the earliest times to 1918: 1992 ➤ 8,k434: ᴿBO 51 (1994) 33s (H. De *Meulenaere*).

13808 *Kaschani* Re'uven, Die Reisen des Benjamin von TUDELA: Ariel 87 (1992) 38-50 [< Judaica 49,59].

13809 — *Kupczyg-Lewin* L., Benjamin fra TUDELA, Rejsedagbog: Nordisk Judaistik 14,1 (Aarhus 1993) 71-78 [< Judaica 50,62].

13810 — *Schmitz* [p. 295 Schimtz] Rolf, Benjamin von TUDELA, 'Das Buch der Reisen', Realität [doch] oder Fiktion: Henoch 16 (1994) 295-314; ital. 314.

13811 *Klimkeit* Hans-J., Zwischen Nil und Kaukasus; Bemerkungen zum Werk von Paul SCHOTZ (Reisebericht ⁴1991]: ZRGg 46 (1994) 270-5 [al. 247-269; Bibliog. 283].

13811* **Loewenthal** Elena, *Sefer...* Il libro di Eldad il Danita; viaggio immaginario di un Ebreo del Medioevo: BtHeb 2. Bo 1993, Fattoadarte. 91 p.; bibliog. 71-81. 88-86150-01-6.

13812 ᴱMcNeal R. A., Nicholas BIDDLE in Greece; the journal and letters of 1806. Univ. Park 1994, Penn. State Univ. vii-243 p. $35 [RelStR 21,132, W. M. *Calder*].

13812* **Magallón García** A. I., Concordancia lematizada de los Itinerarios de EGERIA y ANTONINO. Zaragoza 1993, Univ. vii-434 p. – ᴿArTGran 57 (1994) 509 (G. M. *Verd*).

13813 ᵀᴱ**Marino** L., Johann Ludwig BURCKHARDT, Viaggio in Giordania [1812; Eng. 1822]. Verona 1994, CIERRE. 245 p. – ᴿLA 44 (1944) 656s (M. *Piccirillo*).

13813* *Mulder* Nicole F., Abu Mena; how the early Christian pilgrimage was given shape: Boreas 16 (1993) 149-164; 5 fig.

13814 ᴱ**Natalucci** Nicoletta, EGERIA, Pellegrinaggio in Terra Santa: BtPatristica, 1991 ➤ 7,e875; 9,15524: Lᵐ 38: F 1991, Nardini. – ᴿGnomon 66 (1994) 272s (Veikko *Väänänen*; la 15ᵉᵐᵉ éd.).

13815 *Natalucci* Nicoletta, Grecismi-esotismi nell'Itinerarium di EGERIA: ➤ 86, ᶠNALDINI M., Paideia 1994, 103-113.

13816 — *Bermejo Cabrera* E., La proclamación de la Escritura en la liturgia de Jerusalén; estudio terminológico del 'Itinerarium Egeriae': SBF 37. xi-534 p.; ill. [LA 44,743].

13817 — **Giannarelli** Elena, EGERIA, diario di viaggio. Mi 1992, Paoline. 306 p. Lᵐ 30. – ᴿCC 145 (1994,3) 90s (G. *Cremascoli*).

13818 — ᵀᴱ**Janeras** Sebastià, EGÈRIA, Pelegrinatge à Terra Santa: Clásics del Cristianisme 35. Barc 1993. – ᴿQVidaCr 170 (1994) 105-111 (Montserrat *Camp Gaset*).

13819 ᴱ**Paolella** Alfonso, PETRARCA Francesco (1304-1374). Itinerarium breve de Ianua usque ad Ierusalem et Terram Sanctam: Scelta di rare 284. 1993, Commissione per i testi di lingua. cv-171 p.

13820 **Pixner** Bargil, Wege des Messias und Stätten der Urkirche, ᴱ*Riesner* Rainer 1991 ➤ 7,248*: ᴿPrOrChr 43 (1993) 200s (F. *Gruber*).

13821 ᴱ**Rasmussen** Stig T., [NIEBUHR C.], Den Arabiske Reise 1761-7; ein dansk ekspedition set i videnskabs-historisk perspektiv. K 1993, Munksgaard. 414 p. – ᴿBSO 57 (1994) 595-7 (H. T. *Norris*: splendid, outshining 1986s German preliminary; vaguely awaited in English).

13822 **Ravasi** Gianfranco, La città del Dio vivente; viaggio all'interno di sette chiese del NT: Pastorale oggi. Mi 1985, Àncora. 153 p. 88-7610-140-1.

13823 *Raynaud* C., Les pèlerins à Jérusalem dans quelques représentations du XIIIᵉ au XVᵉ siècle: ➤ 397, Image 1993/4, 159-181; 8 fig.

13824 *Starowieyski* Marek, Catechesi biblica dei pellegrini in Terra Santa, secoli II-IU): ➤ 319*, Esegesi 1993/4, 147-161.

13824* **Taylor** Joan E., Christians and the Holy Places; the myth of Jewish-Christian origins 1993 ➤ 9,15533; £45: ᴿAmHR 99 (1994) 873s (W. H. *Stiebing*: corrective to Tᴇꜱᴛᴀ); BAngIsr 13 (1993s) 54-57 (E. D. *Hunt* rejects, as also S. *Mimouni* p. 52); ChH 63 (1994) 253s (S. *Borgehammar*: too fierce); HeythJ 35 (1994) 447-9 (W. H. C. *Frend*, good; some observations); JEH 45 (1994) 334-6 (R. A. *Marcus*); JRS 84 (1994) 264s (O. *Irshai*); JTS 45 (1994) 304-8 (J. D. *Wilkinson*); PEQ 126 (1994) 173s (G. S. P. *Freeman-Grenville*: Bᴀɢᴀᴛᴛɪ and Tᴇꜱᴛᴀ 'were subjected to more than one deliberate and intentional fraud'); TorJT 10 (1994) 140s (J. S. *Kloppenborg*: overall convincing); VigChr 48 (1994) 84-86 (J. W. *Drijvers*).

13825 ᴱ**Vatin** Jean-Claude, Dᴇɴᴏɴ Vivant, Voyage... Égypte 1989s ➤ 8,k451: ᴿAJA 98 (1994) 567s (L. H. *Lesko*).

13826 **Wilken** Robert L., The land called holy 1992 ➤ 9,15536: ᴿAmHR 99 (1994) 273s (H. C. *Kee*); BR 10,6 (1994) 19 (F. E. *Peters*); CBQ 56 (1994) 811-3 (L. E. *Frizzell*); ChH 63 (1994) 435s (R. T. *Handy*); ClasW 88 (1994s) 503 (Shawn *Pollett*); JRel 74 (1994) 387s (W. *Kaegi*); JTS 45 (1994) 302-4 (P. *Walker*); RB 101 (1994) 471s (J. *Murphy-O'Connor*); TLond 97 (1994) 123s (S. W. *Need*); TS 55 (1994) 145-7 (J. A. *McGuckin*).

U7 *Crucigeri* – The Crusades.

13827 **Armstrong** Karen, Holy war; the Crusades and their impact on today's world. L 1991, Papermac. xxvi-628 p.; bibliog. 601-610. 0-333-56729-3.

13828 **Balard** M., Les Croisades. P 1988. – ᴿVizVrem 54 (1993) 193s (C. D. *Karpov*, ❹).

13829 **Barber** Malcolm, The new knighthood; a history of the Order of the Temple. C 1993, Univ. xxi-441 p.; 14 fig.; 17 pl. £35. 0-521-42041-5 [TDig 41,350]. – ᴿJEH 45 (1994) 696s (A. J. *Forey*).

13830 *Boas* Adrian J., The import of western ceramics to the Latin Kingdom of Jerusalem: IsrEJ 44 (1994) 102-122; 15 figs. (incl. maps).

13831 *Cohen* Geremy, ❹ The 'persecutions of 1096' — from martyrdom to martyrology; the sociocultural context of the Hebrew Crusade chronicles: Zion 59 (1994) 169-208; Eng. XI-XII.

13831* *De Sandoli* Sabino, Ritrovata la bolla di Roberto [primo], arcivescovo di Nazareth (1138-1154): TerraS 70,2 (1994) 42s; 2 phot.

13832 **Edbury** Peter W., The Kingdom of Cyprus and the Crusades, 1191-1374: 1991 ➤ 7,e889; 8,k457: ᴿChH 63 (1994) 442s (G. T. *Dennis*); EngHR 109 (1994) 994s (P. *Jackson*); Speculum 69 (1994) 138s (Sylvia *Schein*).

ꟳEʜʀᴇɴᴋʀᴇᴜᴛᴢ A., articles on Crusades and Saladin 1991 ➤ 33j.

13832* **Forey** Alan., The military orders... 1992 ➤ 8,k462: 9,15541: ᴿSpeculum 69 (1994) 470-2 (J. F. *Powers*).

13833 *France* J., Victory in the East; a military history of the First Crusade. C 1994, Univ. xv-425 p.; 18 fig. £35 [RHE 89,242].

13833* *Friedenthal* James-Francis, Dominican involvement in the Crusader states: NBlackf 75 (1994) 429-436.

13834 ᴱ**Gervers** Michael, The Second Crusade and the Cistercians 1992 ➤ 8,k462* (BIP 'Gevers'): ᴿJEH 45 (1994) 340s (J. P. *Phillips*); Speculum 69 (1994) 290 (tit. pp.).

13834* *Hehl* Ernst-Dieter, Was ist eigentlich ein Kreuzzug?: HZ 259 (1994) 297-336.

13835 **Hoch** Martin, Jerusalem, Damaskus und der zweite Kreuzzug; konstitutionelle Krise und äussere Sicherheit des Kreuzfahrerkönigreiches Jerusalem, A.D. 1136-1154: EurHS 3/560, 1993 ➤ 9,15543: ᴿRHE 99 (1994) 167s (J. *Richard*).

13835* ᴱ**Kedar** B. Z., The horns of Hattin... Crusades 1987/92 ➤ 8,692; 9,15545: ᴿSpeculum 69 (1994) 604 (tit. pp.).

13836 *Ligato* Giuseppe, Saladino e i cristiani: TerraS 70,1 (1994) 43-47.

13836* — ᵀᴱ[Rodhe] **Lundquist** Eva, Saladin and the Crusaders, selected annals from *Masālik*... by UMARI. Lund 1992, Univ. 128 p. Sk 125. – ᴿJAOS 114 (1994) 114 (R. *Amitai-Preiss*); JSS 39 (1994) 356-9 (G. R. *Smith*: attractively produced; but he adds many proposals).

13837 **Marshall** Christopher, Warfare in the Latin East, 1192-1291. C 1992, Univ. xiv-290 p. – ᴿRHist 292 (1994) 167-9 (A. *Demurger*).

13837* **Nicholson** Helen, Templars, Hospitallers and Teutonic Knights; images of the military orders, 1128-1291. NY 1993, Leicester Univ./St. Martin's. xii-207 p. – ᴿAmHR 99 (1994) 881s (W. *Urban*).

13838 *Plank* Peter, Patriarch Symeon II. von Jerusalem und der erste Kreuzzug, eine quellenkritische Untersuchung: OstKSt 43 (1994) 275-327.

13838* **Platelle** Henri, Les Croisades: BtHistChr. 33. P 1994, Desclée. 197 p.; 5 maps. [NRT 117,789, L. *Renwart*]. – ᴱEsprVie 104 (1994) 348-350 (P. *Ourliac*).

13839 **Powell** James, Muslims under Latin rule 1990 ➤ 7,e902... 9,15549: ᴿEngHR 109 (1994) 688s (C. J. *Tyerman*).

13839* **Pringle** D., The churches of the Crusader Kingdom I. A-K 1993 ➤ 7,e902... 9,15549: ᴿPEQ 126 (1994) 85s (P. *Edbury*); ZDPV 110 (1994) 88-90 (H. E. *Mayer*).

13840 *Reeth* Jan M. E. van, Les patriarches d'Orient de l'hégire aux croisades, selon la Chronique universelle de Dirk Frankenszoon PAUWELS (Theodoricus Pauli) [† 1493]: ➤ 70, ᶠLAGA C., Philohistôr 1994, 529-551.

13840* **Rheinheimer** Martin, Das Kreuzfahrerfürstentum Galiläa. Fra 1990, Lang. 199 p. DM 34. – ᴿEngHR 109 (1994) 135 (J. *Riley-Smith*: most ambitious project so far of the conspicuous Hans MEYER school).

13841 **Schein** Sylvia, Fideles crucis; the papacy, the West, and the recovery of the Holy Land, 1274-1314: 1991 ➤ 7,e911*a*... 9,15552: ᴿEngHR 109 (1994) 995s (P. *Edbury*); Speculum 69 (1994) 252s (J. R. E. *Bliese*).

13841* ᴱ**Shatzmiller** Maya, Crusaders and Muslims in twelfth-century Syria: MdvMedit 1. Leiden 1993, Brill. xii-235 p. *f* 140. – ᴿBSO 57 (1994) 594s (P. M. *Holt*); OrChrPer 60 (1994) 673s (V. *Poggi*).

13842 *Vogtherr* Thomas, Die Regierungsdaten der lateinischen Könige von Jerusalem: ZDPV 110 (1994) 51-81.

ᵁ8   *Communitates Terrae Sanctae* – **The Status Quo.**

13842* **Ateck** Naim S., Justice... Palestinian 1989 ➤ 5,g595... 8,k495: ᴿNVFr 68 (1993) 70-72 (J. *Stern*).

13843 **Bat Yeor**, Les Chrétientés d'Orient... Dhimmitude 1991 ➤ 8,k497: ᴿIslamochristiana [17 (1991) 312] 20 (1994) 297-9 (J.-M. *Gaudeul*); JSS 38 (1993) 166s (W. M. *Watt*); Speculum 69 (1994) 419s (S. H. *Griffith*).

13843* **Beit-Hallahmi** Benjamin, Original sins; reflections on the history of Zionism and Israel. L 1993, Pluto. £30; pa. £10. – ᴿTablet 247 (1993) 309 (M. *Adams*).

13844 **Ben-Rafael** Eliezer, *Sharot* Stephen, Ethnicity, religion, and class in Israeli society [based on 800 Beersheba Jews]. C 1991, Univ. x-287 p. $39.50. – ᴿJRel 74 (1994) 125s (H. E. *Goldberg*).

13845 [ᴱ*Bouwen* Frans] Chroniques: Iraq, Liban: PrOrChr 43 (1993) 138-194.

13845* *Burrell* David, Israel, a critical view: Thought 67 (1992) 430-7.

13846 **Cohen** Mitchell, Zion and state; nation, class and their shaping of modern Israel. CM 1987, Blackwell. 322 p. $25. – ᴿJudaism 40 (1991) 116-123 (J. P. *Sternstein*).

13847 *a) Corral Salvador* Carlos, El acuerdo básico de 30 Diciembre de 1994 entre la Santa Sede y el estado de Israel; desde la perspectiva de la Santa Sede; – *b) Toledano* Samuel, ... un punto de vista judío; – *c) Gil Coria* Eusebio, ... y el procuro de paz en el Próximo Oriente; perspectiva teológica: EstE 69 (1994) 145-173 / 175-179 / 181-201.

13848 **Cragg** Kenneth, The Arab Christian 1992 ⮕ 7,e925 ... 9,15568: ᴿIslamochristiana 18 (1992) 326s (A. *Ferrê*); ScotBuEvT 11 (1993) 56s (R. W. *Thomas*).

13849 **Devereux** David R., The formulation of British defence policy towards the Middle East, 1948-56. L 1990, King's College/Macmillan. xi-241 p. £35. – ᴿEngHR 109 (1994) 813s (J. *Marlowe*).

13849* **Ferrari** Silvio, Vaticano e Israele (dal secondo conflitto mondiale alla guerra del Golfo). F 1991, Sansoni. 348 p. – ᴿIslamochristiana 19 (1993) 325s (M. *Borrmans*).

13850 **Fishman** Aryei, Judaism and modernisation on the religious kibbutz. C 1992, Univ. 202 p. – ᴿArchivScSocR 39,88 (1994) 69s (Martine *Cohen*).

13851 **Foran** John, Fragile resistance; social transformation in Iran from 1500 to the revolution. Boulder 1993, Westview. xiv-452 p. $45. – ᴿAmHR 99 (1994) 1730 (E. *Abrahamian*).

13852 *Frizzell* Lawrence E., The Bible and the Holy Land; [SABBAH's] pastoral letter from Jerusalem: NBlackf 75 (1994) 303-311.

13853 *Gelvin* James L., Demonstrating communities in post-Ottoman Syria: JIntdisc 25 (1994s) 23-44.

13854 **Golan** Maidie R., Religion in social life among Jewish Israelis; cultural borders constructed and real: diss. Stanford 1994, ᴰ*Rosaldo* R. 339 p. 94-29926. – DissA 55 (1994s) p. 1612.

13855 **Heenen-Wolff** Susann, Erez Palästina, Juden und Palästinenser im Konflikt um ein Land. Fra 1990, Luchterhand. 254 p. DM 18,80. – ᴿKIsr 9 (1994) 98 (Julie *Kirchberg*).

13856 **Hunter** F. Robert, The Palestinian uprising; a war by other means. Berkeley 1991, Univ. California. xx-292 p. $25. – ᴿAmHR 99 (1994) 1370s (Julie *Peteet*).

13857 **Jennings** Ronald C., Christians and Muslims in Ottoman Cyprus and the Mediterranean World 1571-1640: NECiv 18. NYU 1993. 430 p. ᴿAmHR 99 (1994) 957 (Madeline C. *Zilfi*); OrChrPer 60 (1994) 289s (V. *Poggi*).

13858 **Kaleh** Hala, *Calderini* Simonetta, The intifada; the Palestinian uprising in the West Bank and Gaza Strip; a bibliography of books and articles 1987-1992: Research Guide 6. Ox 1993, Middle East Libraries. [vi-] 59 p. £24. – ᴿBSO 57 (1994) 649s (Ulrike *Freitag*).

13859 **Khoury** Adel T., Was ist los ... 1991 ⮕ 7,e934; 9,15580: ᴿEntschluss 48,7s (1993) 42 (H. *Brandt*).

13860 *a) Kienzler* Klaus, Der Vatikan und der Staat Israel; – *b) Brunswick* Wilhelm, Israel — einer von 179 (?) Staaten dieser Welt? – *c) Rendtorff* Rolf, Identifikation mit Israel?; – *d) Ehmann* Johannes, Solidarität mit dem Staat Israel? – *e*) *Jochum* Herbert, Ecclesia und Synagoga; Materialien zu einer ikonographischen Christologie: KIsr 7 (1992) 161-170 / 145-8 / 136-144 / 148-160 / 171-190; 5 fig.

13861 **Kimmerling** Baruch, *Migdal* Joel S., Palestinians; the making of a people 1993 ➤ 9,15581: ᴿAmHR 99 (1994) 947s (R. I. *Khalidi*); Midstream 39,4 (1993) 32-34 (Joel *Carmichael*: scholarship as fraud).

13862 *Kreutz* Andrej, The Vatican and the Palestinians; a historical overview: Islamochristiana 18 (1992) 109-125; franç. 123 [17 (1991) 325s, T. *Michel* review of his Vatican Policy on the Palestinian-Israeli Conflict (NY 1994, Greenwood) 196 p.].

13863 **Krupp** Michael, Die Geschichte der Juden im Land Israel, vom Ende des Zweiten Tempels bis zum Zionismus: Tb 785. Gü 1993. 176 p. DM 22,80. – ᴿKIsr 9 (1994) 97s (Julie *Kirchberg*, Rubrik 'zum jüdisch-palästinensischen Konflikt': 'knapp und präzise').

13864 **Landau** Jacob M., The Arab minority in Israel [1. 1948-1966: 1969] 2. 1967-1991; political aspects 1993 ➤ 9,15583: ᴿBSO 57 (1994) 369-371 (P. J. *Vatikiotis*).

13865 **Leibowitz** Yeshayahu, Judaism, human values, and the Jewish State, ᵀ*Goldman* Eliezer. CM 1992, Harvard Univ. xxxiv-291 p. $48. 0-674-48775-3. – ᴿBijdragen 55 (1994) 204 (F. De *Meyer*. Eng.: at 90 a Zionist but sharp thinker, living in Israel amid many friends and many enemies).

13866 **Lesch** David W., Syria and the U. S.; EISENHOWER's cold war in the Middle East. Boulder CO 1992, Westviews. xvii-242 p. $45. – ᴿAmHR 99 (1994) 1002 (B. R. *Kuniholm*).

13867 — **Alteras** Isaac, Eisenhower and Israel; U. S. - Israeli relations, 1953-1960. Gainesville 1993, Univ. Florida. xvi-387 p. $45; pa. $20. – ᵀᴿAmHR 99 (1994) 1424 (P. L. *Hahn*).

13868 **Libois** Charles, MonHistSJ 145, Proximi-Orientis 2, Égypte (1547-1563). R 1993, InstHistSJ. 138*-348 p. – ᴿOrChrPer 60 (1994) 318s (V. *Poggi*).

13869 *Macchi* Angelo, L' 'accordo fondamentale' tra la Santa Sede e lo Stato d'Israele: CC 145 (1994,1) 288-297.

13870 **Madfai** Madiha R. al-., Jordan, the US, and the Middle East peace process, 1974-1991: MELibrary 28. C 1993, Univ. xix-279 p. £60. – ᴿAmHR 99 (1994) 1369s (S. Z. *Freiberger*).

13871 **Marcus** Abraham, The Middle East on the eve of modernity: Aleppo 1989 ➤ 9,15588*: ᴿBSO 57 (1994) 378s (P. *Sluglett*).

13872 **Masalha** Nur, Expulsion of the Palestinians; the concept of 'transfer' in Zionist political thought 1882-1945. Wsh 1992, Institute for Palestine studies. iii-235 p. $25; pa. $12. – ᴿAmHR 99 (1994) 274 (C. S. *Kamen*).

13872* *Mazawi* André E., Palestinian local theology and the issue of Islamo-Christian dialogue; an appraisal: Islamochristiana 19 (1993) 93-114; français 115.

13873 **Melman** Billie, Women's Orient; English women and the Middle East, 1718-1918; sexuality, religion and work. AA 1992, Univ. Michigan. xix-417 p. $39.50. – ᴿAmHR 99 (1994) 556s (Dorothy O. *Helly*).

13874 **Menashri** David, Education and the making of modern Iran. Ithaca / TA 1992, Cornell Univ. / Dayan Center. xvii-352 p. $47.50. – ᴿAmHR 99 (1994) 615s (C. *Chaqueri*).

13875 **Morris** Benny, 1948 and after; Israel and the Palestinians 1990 ➤ 9, 15590: ᴿEngHR 109 (1994) 813 (L. *Kochan*: less Arab documentation available).

13875* *Nessim* Youssef Y., Les fêtes d'été et d'hiver dans le calendrier copte: AulaO 11 (1993) 173-8; Eng. 173.

13876 *O'Mahony* Anthony, The Copts of Egypt: Month 255 (1994) 298-303.
13877 **Owen** Roger, State, power and politics in the making of the modern Middle East. L 1992, Routledge. xviii-302 p. £40; pa. £13. – ᴿBSO 57 (1994) 381s (W. *Hale*).
13878 **Perthes** Volker, Staat und Gesellschaft in Syrien 1970-1989. Ha 1990, Deutsches Orient-Institut. 340 p. – ᴿOLZ 89 (1994) 169-172 (Ulrike *Freitag*).
13879 **Raheb** Mitri [luth. Pfarrer], Ich bin Christ und Palästinenser; Israel, seine Nachbarn und die Bibel. Gü 1994, Gü.-V. 126 p. DM 19,80. – ᴿEntschluss 49/12 (1994) 42 (M. *Brasser*).
13880 **Reinharz** Jehuda, Chaim WEIZMANN; the making of a statesman. NY 1993, Oxford-UP. xii-536 p. $40. – ᴿAmHR 99 (1994) 1368s (Anita *Shapira*).
13881 *Sanua* Victor D., The vanished world of Egyptian Jewry: Judaism 43 (1994) 212-9.
13882 **Schoenbaum** David, The United States and the State of Israel. NY 1993, Oxford-UP. xiv-404 p. $40; pa. $17. – ᴿAmHR 99 (1994) 692s (P. L. *Hahn*).
13883 ᴱ**Stöhr** Martin, Lernen in Jerusalem — lernen mit Israel; Anstösse zur Erneuerung in Theologie und Kirche; Verhöff. 20. B 1993, Inst. Kirche und Judentum. 470 p. DM 39. 3-923095-20-1. – ᴿJudaica 49 (1993) 185 (F. von *Hammerstein*).
13884 **Tauber** Eliezer, The emergence of the Arab movements / The Arab movements in World War I. L 1993, Cass *al*. 406 p.; 322 p. $20 each. – ᴿAmHR 99 (1994) 1730s (P. S. *Khoury*).
13885 **Tincq** Henri, L'Étoile et la Croix; Jean Paul II - Israël; l'explication. 1993, Lattès. 392 p. F 139. – ᴿÉtudes 380 (1994) 263s (J.-Y. *Calvez*).
13886 **Wahlin** Lars, Back to settled life? Rural change in the 'Allan [N as-Salt] area of Jordan, 1867-1980, diss. Stockholm 1994. 280 p. (DissA-disk) DAI-C 1955 (1994s) p. 1071.
13887 **Warburg** Gabriel R., Historical discord in the Nile Valley [Sudan]. L 1992, Hurst. xviii-210 p. £27.50. – ᴿBSO 57 (1994) 382s (H. *Bleuchot*: very useful).
13887* **Watt** W. Montgomery, Muslims and Christians after the Gulf War: Islamochristiana 17 (1991) 35-51; franç. 51.
13888 ᴱ**Waxman** Chaim I., Israel as a religious reality: Orthodox Forum. Northvale NJ 1994, Aronson. xx-153 p. 1-56821-077-9.
13889 **Winter** Michael, Egyptian society under Ottoman rule 1517-1798: TA studies in Islamic culture. L 1992, Routledge. xv-323 p. £40. – ᴿBSO 57 (1994) 377s (P. M. *Holt*).
13890 **Wolffsohn** Michael, Wem gehört das Heilige Land? Die Würzeln des Streits zwischen Juden und Arabern. Mü 1993, Bertelsmann. 288 p. – ᴿKairos 34s (1992s) 241-3 (K. *Schubert*).
13891 **Yapp** M. E., The Near East since the first World War. L 1991, Longman. xvii-526 p. £32; pa. £15. – ᴿEngHR 109 (1994) 1037s (J. S. F. *Parker*).

XX. Historia Scientiae Biblicae

Y1   **History of Exegesis 1. General.**

13892 ᴱ**Alberigo** Giuseppe, Les Conciles œcuméniques; histoire et decrets, ᵀ*Mignon* J. P 1994, Cerf. I: 410 p., II,1: 1340 p., II,2: 1140 p. F 1700 –

ᴿArchivScSocR 39,88 (1994) 43s (Ysabel de *Andia*); NRT 116 (1994) 750s (P. *Evrard*).

13893 ᴱ**Alberigo** Giuseppe, Geschichte der Konzilien; vom Nicaenum bis zum Vaticanum II. Dü 1993, Patmos. 482 p. DM 90. 3-491-71105-3. – ᴿTvT 34 (1994) 199 (J. van *Laarhoven*).

13894 ᴱ**Alberigo** Giuseppe, Historia de los Concilios ecuménicos: El peso de los días 25. S 1993, Sígueme. 397 p. – ᴿEfMex 12 (1994) 133s (R. *Jaramillo*).

13895 **Andresen** C., *Ritter* A. M., Geschichte des Christentums 1/1. Altertum: TheolWiss 6, 1993 ➤ 9,15614: Stu 1993, Kohlhammer. xiv-217 p. DM 29,80. 3-17-011710-6. – ᴿTvT 34 (1994) 198s (A. *Davids*).

13896 ᴱ**Beatrice** P. F., L'intolleranza cristiana 1993 ➤ 9,15616: ᴿCathHR 80 (1994) 560s (L. J. *Swift*); Compostellanum 38 (1993) 254s (E. *Romero Pose*); OrChrPer 60 (1994) 274s (K. *Douramani*); Orpheus 15 (1994) 253-7 (Beatrice *Marotta Mannino*); ZkT 116 (1994) 357 (K. H. *Neufeld*: gedruckt 1993).

13897 **Børresen** Kari E., Le madri della chiesa; Il Medoevo. N 1993, D'Auria. 223 p. – ᴿRasT 35 (1994) 116-8 (Cloe *Taddei Ferretti*).

13898 **Bosio** Guido, *al.*, Introduzione ai Padri; III., secoli III e IV 1993 ➤ 9,15618; Lᵐ 45: ᴿBenedictina 41 (1994) 535-8 (G. *Trettel*); CC 145 (1994,2) 410s (F. *Bergamelli*); JRS 84 (1994) 281s (M. J. *Edwards*).

13899 *Cameron* Averil, Christianity and the rhetoric of empire 1991 ➤ 7, e971 ... 9,15621: ᴿChrLit 41 (1991s) 198-200 (W. J. *Vande Koppie*).

13900 *Canevet* Mariette, La Bible et les Pères; jeunesse et impatience: NRT 116 (1994) 48-60: 'il ne faut pas confondre [leurs] principes théologiques avec les méthodes culturelles, donc contingentes, qu'ils ont utilisées' p. 60.

13901 **Carcione** Filippo, Le eresie; Trinità e Incarnazione nella Chiesa antica. CinB 1992, Piemme. 230 p. Lᵐ 15. – ᴿCC 145 (1994,3) 442s (G. *Ferraro*).

13902 **Clouse** Robert G., *Pierard* Richard V., *Yamauchi* Edwin M., Two kingdoms; the Church and culture through the ages. Ch 1993, Moody. 600 p. 0-8024-8590-1. – ᴿChrSchR 24 (1994) 370s (D. A. *Yerxa*).

13903 **Comby** Jean, Deux mille ans d'évangélisation; histoire de l'expansion chrétienne: BtHistChr 29, 1992 ➤ 8,k549: Desclée. 327 p. – ᴿNRT 116 (1994) 614s (J. *Masson*); ScEspr 46 (1994) 275 (P.-É. *Langevin*: texte magistral avec documents-sources vis-à-vis).

13904 **Contreras** E., *Peña* R., Introducción al estudio de los Padres — período preniceno 1991 ➤ 7,e973 [no como:] 8,k550: ᴿSalesianum 56 (1994) 164s (J. *Checinski*).

13905 **Conzelmann** Hans, Gentiles, Jews, and Christians; polemics and apologetics in the Graeco-Roman era, ᵀ*Boring* Eugene. Mp 1992, Fortress. $40. – ᴿCurrTM 21 (1994) 57 (D. *Rhoads*).

13906 **Dal Covolo** Enrico, Chiesa società politica; area di 'laicità' nel cristianesimo delle origini. R 1994, LAS. 187 p. – ᴿVetChr 31 (1994) 397-400 (C. *Tibiletti*).

13907 *Dal Covolo* Enrico, Lo stato attuale degli studi di patristica greco-latina: RicT 3 (1992) 397-410 [< ZIT 93,406].

13908 **Dassmann** Ernst, Kirchengeschichte I 1991 ➤ 7,e976 ... 9,15625: ᴿTPhil 49 (1994) 273 (K. *Schatz*).

13908* *Dassmann* Ernst, Beobachtungen der Kirchenväter im neuen 'Katechismus der katholischen Kirche': ➤ 95, ᶠPOTTMEYER F., Kirche sein 1994, 373-382.

(*Denzinger* H.) ³⁷**Hünermann** P., Enchiridion symbolorum 1991 ➤ 970.

13909 ᴱDi Berardino Angelo, *Studer* Basil,   Epoca patristica: Storia della teologia 1, 1993 ➤ 9, 15626: ᴿAngelicum 71 (1994) 453-5 (T. *Stancati*); Gregorianum 75 (1994) 183-6 (G. *Pelland*); LA 44 (1994) 711-5 (M. C. *Paczkowski*); Lateranum 60 (1994) 190-2 (B. *Amata*); RasT 35 (1994) 112s (E. *Cattaneo*).

13910 **Drobner** Hubertus R.,   Lehrbuch der Patrologie. FrB 1994, Herder. xliv-452 p.; bibliog. xxxiv-xliv.   3-451-23498-X [TLZ 120,807, G. *Haendler*].

13910* *Fédou* Michel,   Les Pères de l'Église dans la culture contemporaine: Études 381 (1994) 629-636.

13911 ᵀᴱ**Feiertag** Jean Louis, (*Steinmann* Werner), Questions d'un païen à un chrétien (consultationes Zacchei christiani et Apolloni philosophi):   SChr 401s.   P 1994, Cerf.   2-204-05125-X.

13911* **Felber** Anneliese,   Harmonie durch Hierarchie? Das Denken der Geschlechter-Ordnung im frühen Christentum: Frauenf 26.   W 1994, Frauen-V. 188 p.   3-800399-94-8 [TLZ 120,808, Ina *Praetorius*].

13912 ᴱ**Felici** S.,   Esegesi e catechesi nei Padri (sec. II-IV) 1992/3 ➤ 9,448*: ᴿAnnTh 7 (1993) 523-6 (M. A. *Tábet*); RivScR 8 (1994) 223-5 (G. *Lorusso*).

13913 **Gibert** Pierre,   Petite histoire de l'exégèse biblique: Lire la Bible 94, 1992 ➤ 8,k559; 9,15634: ᴿRTLv 25 (1994) 369s (C. *Focant*); RTPhil 126 (1994) 296s (P.-Y. *Ruff*).

13913* **Gnilka** Christian,   *Chrêsis*, die Methode der Kirchenväter im Umgang mit der antiken Kultur, [I. 1984 ➤ 65,d393] II. Kultur und Conversion: Univ. Münster. Ba 1993, Schwabe.   201 p. 3-7965-0951-7 [NRT 117,275, A. *Harvengt*; TLZ 120, 155, G. *Haendler*]. IV. **Becker** Maria, 1994 ➤ 14217.

13914 **Gottlieb** G.,   Christentum und Kirche in den ersten drei Jahrhunderten: Studienhefte. Heid 1991, Winter. ix-118 p. – ᴿRevSR 68 (1994) 117 (B. *Pouderon*).

13914* **Grant** R. M.,   Heresy and criticism; the search for authenticity in early Christian literature 1993 ➤ 9,15637 [NTAbs 37, p. 465]: ᴿChH 63 (1994) 427-9 (H. *Patrick*); JRel 74 (1994) 388s (E. V. *Gallagher*: Christian appropriation of literary critical methods); JTS 45 (1994) 295-8 (A. H. B. *Logan*).

13915 *Haendler* Gert,   Fortschritte bei der Vetus Latina, den Fontes Christiani und Sources Chrétiennes 1993: TLZ 119 (1994) 953-964.

13916 **Hall** S. G.,   Doctrine and practice in the early Church 1991 ➤ 7,e983 ... 9,15638: ᴿPacifica 7 (1994) 102-4 (I. *Breward*); ScotJT 47 (1994) 401s (L. R. *Wickham*).

13917 **Hartmann** Karl,   Zwanzig Jahrhunderte Kirchengeschichte; vom Anfang bis zur Gegenwart erzählt. Lahr 1992, E. Kaufmann. 262 p. ᴅᴍ 48. 3-7806-2281-5. – ᴿRHPR 74 (1994) 303s (M. *Lienhard*).

13918 *Hill* Charles,   The fathers on the biblical Word: Pacifica 7 (1994) 255-272.

13918* **Hamman** Adalbert G.,   Études patristiques; méthodologie ... 33 art., 1991 ➤ 7,209c: ᴿZKG 105 (1994) 94 (G. *Kaspar*).

13919 *Hultgren* Arland J.,   The rise of normative Christianity. Mp 1994, Fortress. xiii-210 p.; bibliog. 167-188. 0-8006-2645-1.

13919* *Juel* Donald, Messianic exegesis; Christological interpretation of the OT in early Christianity. 1992: ᴿCarthaginensia 10 (1994) 182 (R. *Sanz Valdivieso*).

13920 *Karageorgoudes* Emmanuel, Ⓖ The contribution of K. Gᴇᴏʀɢᴏᴜʟɪs to the correct evaluation of patristic thought: TAth 65 (1994) 141-151; Eng. 1019.

13920* **Kennel** Gunter, Frühchristliche Hymnen? Gattungskritische Studien zur Frage nach den Liedern der frühen Christenheit: ev. Diss. ᴰ*Hahn* F. München 1994. – TR 91,99.

13921 **Kinzig** Wolfram, *Novitas christiana*; die Idee des Fortschritts in der Alten Kirche bis EUSEBIUS: ForKDg 58. Gö 1994, Vandenhoeck & R. 702 p. 3-525-55166-5 [TLZ 120,809-814, C. *Markschies*].

13921* *Kinzig* Wolfram, L'idée de progrès dans l'église ancienne jusqu'à l'âge constantinien: ÉTRel 68 (1993) 43-60.

13922 ᴱ**Klein** Richard, Das frühe Christentum bis zum Ende der Verfolgerungen; eine Dokumentation, I. Die Christen im heidnischen Staat; II. Die Christen in der heidnischen Gesellschaft, ᵀ*Guyot* Peter: Texte zur Forschung 60.62. Da 1994, Wiss. xii-412 p. ᴅᴍ 84. 3-534-11451-5 [RelStR 21,242, J. T. *Fitzgerald*].

13922* **Kraft** Heinrich, Einführung in die Patrologie 1991 ➤ 7,e989 ... 9, 15648: ᴿRHPR 74 (1994) 308s (T. *Ziegler*).

13923 *Kreider* Alan, Worship and evangelism in pre- [Constantine] Christendom (1994 Laing lecture]: VoxEvca 24 (L 1994) 7-38 (responses 39s *Pearse* Meic; 41s *King* Philip).

13924 **Lafont** Ghislain, Histoire théologique de l'Église catholique; itinéraire et formes de la théologie: CogF 179. P 1994, Cerf. 474 p. F 190. 2-204-04887-9 [NRT 117,126, L. *Renwart*]. – ᴿArTGran 57 (1994) 447-9 (P. *Franco*); RHPR 74 (1994) 445s (G. *Siegwalt*); RSPT 78 (1994) 520-8 (B. *Rey*).

13924* **Lee Sung-Min**, The unity of word and sacrament among early Christians; biblical and historical witnesses: diss. Drew, ᴰ*Rice* C. Madison ɴᴊ 1994. – RelStR 21,252.

13925 **Lattke** Michael, Hymnus; Materialien zu einer Geschichte der antiken Hymnologie: NOrb 19, 1991 ➤ 7,8219; 8,8358: ᴿCritRR 6 (1993) 123s (D. M. *Parrott*).

13925* ᴱ**Livingstone** Elizabeth A., Studia Patristica [24 ➤ 9,465] 23, 1987/9 ➤ 5,696: ᴿRHR 210 (1993) 225-230 (J. *Doignon*).

13926 **McGinn** B., The foundations of mysticism 1991 ➤ 8,k567; 9,15650: ᴿHeythJ 35 (1994) 76-78 (P. *Sheldrake*); Speculum 69 (1994) 214-7 (W. H. C. *Frend*).

13926* **McGinn** Bernhard, Die Mystik im Abendland, I. Ursprünge, ᵀ*Maass* Clemens. FrB 1994, Herder. 527 p. ᴅᴍ 128 [TR 91,354-7, J. *Sudbrack*].

13927 *Méndez Fernández* Santiago, La búsqueda de una nueva metodología en los pensadores cristianos del siglo II: Compostellanum 38,1 (1993) 57-77.

13928 **Ostriker** Alicia S., The nakedness of the Fathers; biblical visions and revisions. New Brunswick 1994, Rutgers Univ. xv-260 p. 0-8135-2125-4.

13929 **Padovese** Luigi, Introduzione alla teologia patristica 1992 ➤ 8,k573: ᴿLA 44 (1994) 708-710 (M. C. *Paczkowski*).

13930 **Peinado Peinado** Miguel, La predicación del Evangelio en los Padres de la Iglesia; antología: BAC 519. 1992 ➤ 9,15654: ᴿAngelicum 71 (1994) 283-5 (A. G. *Fuente*).

13931 **Pelikan** Jaroslav, Christianity and classical culture; the metamorphosis of natural theology in the Christian encounter with Hellenism [Gifford Lectures 1992s]. NHv 1993, Yale Univ. 416 p. $40. 0-30-05554-4. – ᴿHeythJ 35 (1994) 449-451 (A. *Meredith*); JTS 45 (1994) 725-7 (C. *Stead*).

Piñero Antonio, Orígenes 1990/1 / Fuentes 1993 del Cristianismo ➤ 3856s.

13932 **Poulat** Émile,   La galaxie Jésus; un Évangile et des Églises; deux millénaires d'expansion chrétienne. P 1994, Ouvrières. 160 p. F 90. – RÉtudes 381 (1994) 428 (P. *Vallin*).

13933 **Quacquarelli** Antonio,   Esegesi biblica e patristica fra tardoantico e medioevo: VetChr Quad 21 (ristampe) 1991, Edipuglia.   176 p. Lᵐ 40. 88-7228-094-X. – ROrpheus 15 (1994) 252s (M. Rosaria *Petringa*).

13934 **Reventlow** Henning,   Epochen der Bibelauslegung I-II 1990 → 6,k10 ... 9,15659:   RIkiZ 84 (1994) 255s (C. *Führer*).

13935 *a*) *Ricca* Paolo, 'Un Dio non clericale?' Appunti sulla vittoria dei chierici nella Chiesa antica; – *b*) *Sciuto* Francesco E., 'Solus Christus' e teologia apofatica: → 125, FSUBILIA V., Pluralismo 1994, 43-54 / 97-102.

13935* **Rosenthal** Jos, *Dexinger* Ferdinand,   Als die Heiden Christen wurden; zur Geschichte des frühen Christentums.   W 1992, Ueberreuter.   350 p. DM 69.   – REntschluss 48,9s (1993) 38 (W. *Feneberg*: Bilder hoher Qualität).

13936 **Ruggiero** Fabio,   La follia dei cristiani; su un aspetto della 'reazione pagana' 1991 → 8,k577:   RCC 145 (1994,3) 310s (G. *Cremascoli*); Orpheus 15 (1994) 247 (F. *Paschoud*, franç.).

13937 **Ruh** Kurt, Geschichte der abendländischen Mystik, 1. Kirchenväter 1990 → 9,15661:   RJRel 74 (1994) 94-96 (B. *McGinn*).

13938 **Schmithals** Walter, Theologiegeschichte des Urchristentums; eine Problemgeschichtliche Darstellung. Stu 1994, Kohlhammer. 332 p.; bibliog. 303-312. DM 50.   3-17-012965-1 [TLZ 120, 666-9, J. *Roloff*].

13939 **Seif** Jeffrey L., The evolution of a revolution; reflections on ancient Christianity in its Judaistic, Hellenistic and Romanistic expressions. Lanham MD 1994, UPA. 194 p. 0-8191-9682-7.

13940 **Simonetti** Manlio,   Biblical interpretation in the Early Church; an historical introduction to patristic exegesis, THughes John A.   E 1994, Clark. ix-154 p.; bibliog. 138-144. $34.   0-567-09557-6 [TS 56,397, J. J. *O'Keefe*].

13941 **Smend** Rudolf,   Die Epochen der Bibelkritik [GesSt 3]. Gü 1991, Kaiser. 254 p. DM 98. 3-579-01804-3. – RTsTKi 64 (1993) 226s (T. *Stordalen*).

13942 **Smith** Robert W.,   'Araba haeresium ferax?'; a history of Christianity in the Transjordan to 395 C.E.: diss. Miami 1994, DYamauchi E.   310 p. 95-03085. DissA 55 (1994s) p. 2879.

13943 **Stead** Christopher, Philosophy in Christian antiquity [not 8,k582]. C 1994, Univ. xii-251 p.; bibliog. 245-257.   0-521-46553-2.

13943* *Thom* Johan C.,   'Don't walk on the highway'; the Pythagorean *akousmata* and early Christian literature: JBL 113 (1994) 93-112.

13944 **Trevijano Etcheverría** R., Patrologia: Sapientia fidei 16, BAC Manuales 5. M 1994, Católica.   xviii-277 p. [NRT 117,602, A. *Harvengt*]. – RArTGran 57 (1994) 437s (C. *Granado*); Salmanticensis 41 (1994) 455s (E. *Romero-Pose*).

13945 **Vaneigem** Raoul,   Les hérésies: Que sais-je? 2838.   P 1994, PUF. 128 p. – RRThom 94 (1994) 706s (N.-J. *Porret*).

13946 **Vilanova** E.,   Historia de la teología cristiana 1987-92 → 9,15672: RCiuD 206 (1993) 235s (J. M. *Ozaeta*, 3).

13947 **Volz** Carl A.,   Pastoral life and practice in the early Church; a historical look at the pastoral role. Mp 1990, Augsburg.   240 p. $16 pa. 0-8066-1961-9. – RConcordTQ 58 (1994) 64-68 (W. C. *Weinrich*).

13948 **Vouga** François,   Geschichte des frühen Christentums: UTb 17433. Tü 1994, Francke.   xiv-287 p. DM 32,80.   3-8252-1733-7 [TLZ 120,244, W. *Vogler*].

13949 **Young** Frances, The making of the creeds 1991 → 7,g17 ... 9,15677*:
ᴿConcordTQ 58 (1994) 176-8 (W. C. *Weinrich*).
13950 *a*) *Young* Norman H., The sectarian tradition in early Christianity; –
b) *Ryan* P. J., The secret gnosis of Alexandria; medium or message?:
→ 354, Tradition, Prudentia supp. 1990/4, 178-197 / 166-177.

Y1.4   *Patres apostolici et saeculi II* – **First two centuries.**

13951 ᴱ**Becker** Jürgen, Christian beginnings; word and community from Jesus
to post-apostolic times [1987], ᵀ*Kidder* Annemarie; *Kraus* Reinhard. Lᴠʟ
1993, W-Knox. 359 p. 0-664-25195-1.
13952 *a*) *Di Marco* A.-S., La recezione del NT nei padri apostolici; – *b*)
Derrett J. D. M., Scripture and norms in the Apostolic Fathers: → 496,
ARNW 2/27/1, 724-762 / 649-699.
13953 **Gillespie** Thomas W., The first theologians; a study in early Christian
prophecy. GR 1994, Eerdmans. xiv-286 p.; bibliog. 265-281. $25. 0-
8028-3721-2.
13954 **Grant** Robert M., Jesus after the Gospels; the Christ of the second
century 1990 → 6,k35 ... 8,k594: ᴿConcordTQ 58 (1994) 178-180 (W. C.
Weinrich); JEvTS 37 (1994) 446s (B. *Nassif*: original, enriching).
13955 *Kytzler* Bernhard, Minucius Felix: → 517, TRE 23 (1994) 1-3.
13955* ᴱ**Lindemann** A., *Paulsen* H., Die apostolischen Väter 1992 → 8,k592:
ᴿSvEx 59 (1994) 207s (R. *Kieffer*).
13956 **Neymeyr** U., Die christlichen Lehrer im zweiten Jahrhundert: VigChr
supp. 4, 1989 → 6,k30 ... 8,k595*: ᴿJPseud 8 (1991) 115s (W. *Adler*).
13956* **Pilhofer** Peter, *Presbyteron kreitton*; der Altersbeweis ...: WUNT 2/39,
1990 → 6,k32 ... 8,k597: ᴿCritRR 5 (1992) 303-6 (G. E. *Sterling*).
13957 *Prinzivalli* Emanuela, Incontro e scontro fra 'classico' e 'cristiano' nei
primi tre secoli; aspetti e problemi: Salesianum 56 (1994) 543-556.
13958 **Rizzi** Marco, Ideologia e retorica negli 'exordia' apologetici; il problema dell'Altro 1993 → 9,15687: ᴿVetChr 31 (1994) 247-9 (Silvia
Bettocchi).
13959 **Wagner** Walter R., After the Apostles; Christianity in the second century. Mp 1994, Fortress. xv-287 p. $16. 0-8006-2567-6 [TDig 42,193]. –
ᴿTBR 7,3 (1994s) 55 (G. *Stanton*).

13960 ATHENAGORAS: **Pouderon** B., Athénagore, Supplique: SChr 379, 1992
→ 8,k603; 9,15688: ᴿAnnTh 7 (1993) 271-3 (M. *Bandini*); AntClas 69
(1944) 420s (J. *Schamp*); JbAC 37 (1994) 185-7 (S. G. *Hall*); RÉAug 40
(1994) 215s (R. *Braun*); RÉByz 52 (1994) 343s (Marie-Hélène *Congourdeau*); RHPR 74 (1994) 316s (D. A. *Bertrand*); ScEspr 46 (1994) 260s
(G. *Novotný*).
13961 *Pouderon* Bernard, *a*) Les citations scripturaires dans l'œuvre d'Athénagore; leurs sources et leur statut: VetChr 31 (1994) 111-153; – *b*)
L'utilisation des manuscrits grecs dans les éditions et traductions d'Athénagore au XVIᵉ siècle: RHText 23 (1993) 31-56; Eng. 352.
13962 ARISTIDES: *Dummer* Jürgen, Epiphanius von Constantia und die
Apologie des Aristides; eine quellenkritische Untersuchung: Philologus
138 (1994) 267-287.
13962* BARNABAS: *Paget* James C., The epistle of Barnabas; outlook and
background: WUNT 2/64. Tü 1994, Mohr. xi-319 p.; bibliog. 265-285.
3-16-146161-4.

13963 CLEMENS A.: *Blázquez* José M., El empleo de la literatura greco-romana en el Pedagogo (I-II) de Clemente de Alejandría: Gerión 12 (1994) 113-132.
13964 *Maier* Harry O., Clement of Alexandria and the care of the self: JAAR 62 (1994) 719-745.
13965 TE**Merino** Marcelo, *Redondo* Emilio, Clemente de Alejandría, El pedagogo: Fuentes Patrísticas 5. M 1994, Ciudad Nueva. 746 p. 84-86987-69-5. – RComSev 37 (1994) 378s (M. *Sánchez*); Salmanticensis 41 (1994) 443-5 (R. *Trevijano*).
13966 *Palucki* Jerzy, ❷ Reception of the Hellenic ideals in Clement of Alexandria's teaching: RoczT 41,4 (1994) 5-26; Eng. 27.
13966* *Termini* Cristina, Il profilo letterario delle sezioni storiografiche del primo libro degli Stromata di Clemente Alessandrino: SMSR 60 (1994) 219-242.

13967 CLEMENS R.: TE**Ayan Calvo** J.J., Clemente Romano, Carta a los Corintios; homilía anónima (Secunda Clementis): Fuentes patrísticas 4. M 1994, Ciudad Nueva. 236 p. 84-86987-58-X. – RSalmanticensis 41 (1994) 441-3 (R. *Trevijano*).
13968 **Colson** J., Clément de Rome: Église d'hier et d'aujourd'hui. P 1994, Atelier/Ouvrières. 109 p.; map. F 70 [RHE 89,61*].
13969 **Lindemann** Andreas, Die Clemensbriefe 1992 ➤ 8,k616; 9,15701: RCBQ 56 (1994) 799-801 (Barbara E. *Bowe*).
13970 *Lona* Horacio E., Die Zahl der Auserwählten; ein Versuch über 1 Clem 2,4: ZNW 85 (1994) 151-158.
13971 *Martín* José P., Prima Clementis; ¿estoicismo o filonismo?: Salmanticensis 41 (1994) 5-35; Eng. 36.
13971* TE**Schneider** Gerhard, Clemens von Rom, Epistola ad Corinthios, Brief an die Korinther: FontesC 15. FrB 1994, Herder. 276 p. DM 44 [TR 91,317, A. *Lindemann*].
13972 *Jones* F. Stanley, Evaluating the Latin and Syriac translations of the Pseudo-Clementine Recognitions: Apocrypha 3 (1992) 237-257.
13973 **Rehm** Bernhard †, ²*Strecker* G., Die Pseudoklementinen II. Rekognitionen in RUFINs Übersetzung: GCS. B 1992, Akademie. cxxi-388 p. DM 280. 3-05-001002-9 [RelStR 21,243, R.L. *Wilken*]. – RGregorianum 75 (1994) 780s (G. *Pelland*); JTS 45 (1994) 735s (R.P. *Vaggione*).
13974 *Wehnert* Jürgen, Abriss der Entstehungsgeschichte des pseudoklementischen Romans: Apocrypha 3 (1992) 211-235; Eng. 281s.

13975 DIDACHE etc.: *a*) *Del Verme* M., The Didache and Judaism; the *aparché* of Didache 13:3-7; – *b*) *Tuilier* André, La liturgie dans la Didachè et l'Essénisme: ➤ 9,465, StudPatr (11th 1981) 26 (1993) 113-120 / 200-210.
13975* *Hartman* Lars, Obligatory baptism – but why? On baptism in the Didache and in the Shepherd of Hermas: SvEx 59 (1994) 127-143 [p. 143, neither 'Christ' nor 'Jesus' occurs in Hermas].
13976 *Milavec* Aaron, Distinguishing true and false prophets; the protective wisdom of the Didache: JEarlyC 2 (1994) 117-136.
13976* **Niederwimmer** Kurt, Die Didache 1989 ➤ 6.k62... 9,15707: RJTS 45 (1994) 306-310 (S.G. *Hall*).
13977 ESchöllgen G., Didache 1991 ➤ 7,g42... 9,15708: RJEarlyC 2 (1994) 226-9 (C.N. *Jefford*).
13977* **Urbán** Ángel, Concordantia in Patres apostolicos I. ... Diognetum: II.

Didache. Lexika klas. Pg. 135, 1993 ⇥ 9,15710: ᴿArTGran 37 (1994) 438s (C. *Granado*); RHPR 74 (1994) 315s (D. A. *Bertrand*); SMSR 60 (1994) 154s (S. *Zincone*).

13978 HERMAS: **Brox** Norbert, Der Hirt 1991 ⇥ 7,g46 ... 9,15714: ᴿCritRR 6 (1993) 353s (D. E. *Aune*); ÉTRel 68 (1993) 282s (M. *Bouttier*).
13979 ᴱ**Carlini** Antonio, Papyrus Bodmer XXXVIII, Erma 1991 ⇥ 7,g47 ... 9,15715: ᴿRTPhil 126 (1994) 277s (R. *Gounelle*).
13979* *Dekkers* E., Les traductions latines du Pasteur d'Hermas ⇥ 33d, ᶠDíAZ Y DíAZ, Evphrosyne 22 (1994) 13-26.
13980 **Henne** Philippe, L'unité du 'Pasteur' 1992 ⇥ 8,k639; 9,15717: ᴿCBQ 56 (1994) 596s (D. E. *Aune*); Gregorianum 75 (1994) 375 (G. *Pelland*); RB 101 (1994) 632s (F. *Blanchetière*).
13981 **Miller** Patricia C., Dreams in late antiquity; studies in the imagination of a culture [... Hermas' dream-book]. Princeton 1994, Univ. xii-273 p. $39.50. 0-691-07422-4 [TDig 42,178].
13982 *Osiek* Carolyn, The Shepherd of Hermas; an early tale that almost made it into the New Testament: BR 10,5 (1994) 48-54.
13983 ᵀᴱ**Vezzoni** Anna, Il Pastore di Erma: Nuovo Melograno 13. F 1994, Lettere. 280 p. Lᵐ 32. 88-7166-161-3.

13984 IGNATIUS A.: *Gilmour* Calum, Ignatius of Antioch; aspects of faith: ⇥ 69, ᶠLACEY W., Prudentia 26,1 (1994) 105-137.
13985 *Munier* C., Où en est la question d'Ignace d'Antioche? Bilan d'un siècle de recherches (1870-1988): ⇥ 496, ANRW 2/27/1 (1993) 359-484.
13985* *Gilmour* Calum, Ignatius of Antioch, Aspects of faith: ⇥ LACEY W., Prudentia 26 (1994).
13986 **Haley** Judy R., The politics of unity; envoy and audience in Ignatius' letters to Smyrna: Th.D. diss. Harvard, ᴰ*Koester* H. CM 1994. 181 p. 95-13751. – DissA 55 (1994s) 3883.
13987 *Macdonald* Margaret Y., The ideal of the Christian couple; Ign. Pol. 5, 1-2 looking back to Paul: NTS 40 (1994) 105-125.
13988 *Rius-Camps* Josep, Carta d'Ignasi als Efesis: Epistolari 5: RCatalT 18 (1993) 25-75.
13988* IOSEPPOS: **Menzies** Glen W., Interpretative traditions in the 'Hypomnestikon biblion Iosepppou' [c. 100]: diss. Minnesota, ᴰ*Sellew* P. Mp 1994. 459 p. 94-22304. – DissA 55 (1994s) p. 555.

13989 IRENAEUS L.: **Algorta del Castillo** Juan M., La estructura de la vida moral en San Ireneo: diss. Montevideo 1994, Instituto Teológico del Uruguay. 172 p.; bibliog. 11-17.
13990 ᵀᴱ**Brox** Norbert, Irenaeus von Lyon, Epideixis, Darlegung der apostolischen Verkündigung — Adversus Haereses 1s: FontesC 8/1s. FrB 1990, Herder. 387 p.; 320 p. DM 64 + 50. – ᴿTR 90 (1994) 464-6 (H.-J. *Jaschke*).
13991 **Fantino** Jacques, La théologie d'Irénée, lecture des Écritures en réponse à l'exégèse gnostique; une approche trinitaire [diss. Lille]: CogF 180. P 1994, Cerf. vii-456 p. 2-204-04862-2. – ᴿCompostellanum 39 (1994) 272s (E. *Romero-Pose*); RThom 94 (1994) 702s (D. *Cerbelaud*); VigChr 48 (1994) 409-413 (G. *Quispel*: triumph of DANIÉLOU & Nouvelle Théologie).
13992 *Leśniewski* Krzysztof, The Adam-Christ typology in St. Irenaeus of Lyons: RoczT 41,7 (1994) 63-73.

13993 **MacKenzie** Iain M., [Irenaeus ... AUGUSTINE; BARTH] The anachronism of time; a theological study into the nature of time. Norwich 1994, Canterbury. xvi-191 p. £17.50. 1-85311-089-2. – RChurchman 108 (1994) 379s (D. *Spanner*); TBR 7,2 (1994s) 34s (T. *Bradshaw*).

13994 **Minns** Denis, Irenaeus: Outstanding Christian thinkers. L/Wsh 1994, Chapman/Georgetown Univ. xvi-143 p. 0-87840-553-4 [TDig 42,376]. – RNBlackf 75 (1994) 586-8 (A. *Meredith*).

13995 **Noormann** Rolf, Irenäus als Paulusinterpret: zur Rezeption und Wirkung der paulinischen und deuteropaulinischen Briefe im Werk dea Irenäus von Lyon: WUNT 2/66. Tü 1994, Mohr. x-585 p.; Bibliog. 533-560. 3-16-146092-8.

13996 **Orbe** Antonio, Espiritualidad de S. Ireneo; AnGreg 256, 1989 ⮞ 5, g698 ... 9,15729: RRET 53 (1993) 123-6 (J. J. *Ayán*).

13997 *Smith* Christopher R., Chiliasm and recapitulation in the theology of Irenaeus: VigChr 48 (1994) 313-331.

13998 **Tiessen** Terrance L., Irenaeus on the salvation of the unevangelized: ATLA mg. 31. Metuchen NJ 1993, Scarecrow. xii-317 p. $39.50. 0-8108-3682-8.

13999 *Tortorelli* Kevin M., a) BALTHASAR and the theodramatic interpretation of St. Irenaeus: DowR 111 (1993) 117-126; – b) Two sketches in Irenaeus [one is rather 'on' Irenaeus as seen by F. LOOFS 1930]: VetChr 31 (1994) 369-382.

14000 JUSTINUS M.: a) *Bergada* Mercedes, San Justino, pionero y modelo de inculturación; – b) *Cassagne* Inés de, Los Padres en diálogo con las culturas; critério y crítica: TArg 29,59 (Primer Encuentro Argentino de Patrología 1991: 1992) 7-20 / 65-75 [76-111 bibliog.; 21-55, *Zañartu* Sergio, MÁXIMO C., *phýsis*].

14001 T*Archambault* G., *al.*, EDubois Jean-D., Justin martyr, oeuvres complètes: Bt 1. P 1994, Migne. 431 p. F 190. 2-908587-17-3.

14002 *Girau* Anna Maria, La coerenza cristiana nella 'Prima Apologia' di san Giustino Martire: TSard 1 (1992) 39-80.

14002* EMarcovich Miroslav, Justinus Martyr, Apologiae pro christianis: PatrTSt 38. B 1994, de Gruyter. xii-211 p. 3-11-01480-9.

14003 **Munier** Charles, L'apologie de saint Justin, philosophe et martyr: Paradosis 38. FrS 1994, Univ. xxv-174 p.; bibliog. ix-xxv. 2-8271-0678-7.

14003* *Pouderon* Bernard, [Justin, De resurrectione] Apologetica II: RevSR 68 (1994) 18-38; ms.-photo.

14004 *Uríbarri* Gabino, Las teofanías veterotestamentarias en Justino, 'Dial.' 128, y TERTULLIANO, 'Prax.' 11-13: MiscCom 52 (1994) 305-319.

14005 EHanson Richard P. C., *al.*, Hermias [pseudo-Justin c. 200] Satire des philosophes païens, T*Joussot* Denise: SChr 388. P 1993, Cerf. 149 p. F 131. 2-204-94857-7. – RGregorianum 75 (1994) 782 (G. *Pelland*); OrChrPer 60 (1994) 691s (E. G. *Farrugia*); PrOrChr 43 (1993) 203s (P. *Ternant*); RivStoLR 30 (1994) 642s (Anna Maria *Berruto*).

14006 POLYCARPI martyrium: **Buschmann** Gerd, Martyrium Polycarpi; eine formkritische Studie; ein Beitrag zur Frage nach der Entstehung der Gattung Märtyrerakte: BZNW 70. B 1994, de Gruyter. xiii-363 p. 3-11-014199-X.

14006* *Dehandschutter* R., The Martyrium Polycarpi; a century of research: ⮞ 496, ANRW 2/27/1 (1993) 485-522.

14007 **Weidmann** Frederick W., The Martyrdom of Polycarp, bishop of

Smyrna, in early Christian literature; a re-evaluation in light of previously unpublished Coptic fragments: diss. Yale, ^D*Layton* B. NHv 1993. – Rel-StR 21,256.

14008 *Prostmeier* Ferdinand R., Zur handschriftlichen Überlieferung des Polykarp- und des Barnabasbriefes; zwei nicht beachtete Deszendenten des Cod. Vat. Gr. 859: VigChr 48 (1994) 48-64.

Y1.6 Origenes.

14009 **Alviar** J. J., *Klesis*... vocation, Origen 1993 ➤ 9,15750: ^RSalmanticensis 41 (1994) 445-8 (R. *Trevijano*); ScripTPamp 26 (1994) 761-4 (J. *Morales*).

14010 **Benjamins** Hendrik S., Eingeordnete Freiheit; Freiheit und Vorsehung bei Origenes: VigChr supp. 28. Leiden 1994, Brill. x-225 p. 90-04- 10117-9.

14011 *Canévet* Mariette, Une fausse symétrie; la venue du Christ dans l'Ancien et Nouveau Testaments selon Origène, In Joh. 1, VII, 37-40 [d'après *Blanc* Cécile, SChr 120 (1966) 80]: Gregorianum 75 (1994) 743-9.

14012 **Clark** Elizabeth, The Origenist controversy; the cultural construction of an early Christian debate 1992 ➤ 8,k669; 9,15752: ^RHeythJ 35 (1994) 327s (A. *Meredith*); Horizons 21 (1994) 349s (J. C. *Cavadini*); JRel 74 (1994) 389s (J. W. *Trigg*); JTS 45 (1994) 732-5 (C. P. *Bammel*); NRT 116 (1994) 924s (V. *Roisel*); RelStR 20 (1994) 243 (P. M. *Blowers*).

14013 **Cocchini** Francesca, Il Paolo di Origene 1992 ➤ 9,15753: ^RCC 145 (1994,3) 312s (G. *Pani*).

14014 **Crouzel** Henri, Origène et Plotin 1992 ➤ 9,15756: ^RGregorianum 75 (1994) 151-6 (G. *Pelland*); RThom 94 (1994) 164-6 (D. *Cerbelaud*).

14015 *Crouzel* Henri, Chronique origénienne: BLitEc 95 (1994) 333-342.

14016 ^E**Daly** Robert J., Origeniana Quinta 1989/92 ➤ 8,531; 9,15759: ^RJb-AC 37 (1994) 187s (sr. Theresia *Heither*); TR 90 (1994) 42s (M.-Barbara von *Stritzky*); VigChr 48 (1994) 101s (tit. pp.).

14017 *Edwards* M. J., Euphrates [known to Origen], Stoic and Christian heretic: Athenaeum 82 (1994) 196-201.

14018 **Fédou** Michel, *a)* Christianisme... CELSE 1989 ➤ 5,g708... 8,k677: ^RJEarlyC 2 (1994) 219-221 (P. M. *Blowers*); – *b)* Bulletin de théologie patristique grecque; Origène, PLOTIN: RechSR 82 (1994) 432-4. 597-601.

14019 **Fernández Lago** J., La montagna... Orígenes 1993 ➤ 9,15764: ^RAnStoEseg 10 (1993) 632s (Francesca *Cocchini*); Burgense 34 (1993) 576s (E. *Bueno*); NRT 116 (1994) 940s (V. *Roisel*); RET 53 (1993) 248-250 (J. J. *Ayán*); ScripTPamp 26 (1994) 297s (A. *Garcia-Moreno*).

14020 *Haras* (Rubin) E., The Jewish origin of Julius Africanus [best known for the letter he got from Origen]: JJS 45 (1994) 86-91.

14021 **Küng** Hans, Great Christian thinkers. L 1994, SCM. 235 p.; bibliog. 217-235; Origen p. 41-67. 0-334-02558-3.

14022 **Lies** Lothar, Origenes' Peri archon, eine undogmatische Dogmatik 1992 ➤ 8,k687; 9,15770: ^RBLitEc 95 (1994) 338s (H. *Crouzel*); JbAC 37 (1994) 193-5 (Herwig *Görgemanns*).

14023 *McDonnell* Kilian, Does Origen have a trinitarian doctrine of the Holy Spirit? [yes despite subordinationist aspects]: Gregorianum 75 (1994) 5-34; franç. 35.

14024 **Neuschäfer** Bernhard, Origenes als Philologe: BeitAW 18, 1987 ➤ 3, g177... 8,k690: ^RZKG 105 (1994) 101-3 (U. *Kühneweg*).

14024* *Perrone* I., 'Quaestiones et responsiones' in Origene; prospettive di un'analisi formale; CrNSt 15 (1994) 1-50 [< TR 91,72].

14025 *Prinzivalli* Emanuela, Per un'indagine sull'esegesi del pensiero origeniano nel IV secolo: ➤ 330*a*, XI-Sacrofano 1993/4, 433-460; Eng. 411.
14025* *Sciuto* F. E., Un altro detrattore di Origene; TEODOTO d'Ancira: SicGymn 45 (1992) 255-266.
14026 **Scott** Alan, Origen and the life of the stars 1991 ➤ 7,g88; 8,k696: ᴿJTS 45 (1994) 317-320 (Catherine *Osborne*).
14027 *Scognamiglio* Rosario, La vita cristiana come esodo; tematiche origeniane: RivScR 8 (1994) 129-140.
14028 *Stok* Fabio, CELSO e VIRGILIO: Orpheus 15 (1994) 280-301.
14029 **Witte** Bernd, Das Ophitendiagramm nach Origenes Cels VI 22-38: ArbSpKÄg 6, 1993 ➤ 9,15788: ᴿTüTQ 174 (1994) 323s (H. J. *Vogt*).
14029* *Ziebritzki* Henning, Heiliger Geist und Weltseele; das Problem der dritten Hypostase bei Origenes, PLOTIN und ihren Vorläufern: BeitHisT 84. Tü 1994, Mohr. vii-286 p. DM 128. 3-16-146087-1 [TLZ 120,1018, H. G. *Thümmel*].

Y1.8 Tertullianus.

14030 *Aveling* Harry, 'The flesh, instrument of salvation'; the body in the theology of Tertullian: AustralasCR 70 (1993) 221-232.
14031 ᵀᴱ**Braun** René, Tertullien, contre MARCION I. II: SChr 365/8, 1990s ➤ 6,k122 ... 9,15792: ᴿClasR 44 (1994) 212s (Catherine *Osborne*, 2); Latomus 53 (1994) 180-2 (G. *Scarpat*).
14031* ᵀᴱ**Braun** R., Tertullien, Contre Marcion, tome III (livre III): SChr 399. P 1994, Cerf. 363 p. 2-204-05069-5 [NRT 117,591, A. *Harvengt*; JTS 46,707, M. *Winterbottom*].
14032 **Braun** R., Approches de Tertullien 1992 ➤ 9,15793: ᴿBLitEc 95 (1994) 251s (H. *Crouzel*); JTS 45 (1994) 315-7 (T. D. *Barnes*); RivStoLR 30 (1994) 643s (P. A. *Gramaglia*).
14033 *Braun* René, *al.*, Chronica Tertullianea et Cyprianea: RÉAug 40 (1994) 273-488 (c. 40, signés).
14034 **Daniélou** Jean † 1974, Le origini del cristianesimo latino 1993 ➤ 9, 15624*: ᴿAntonianum 69 (1994) 118s (M. *Nobile*).
14035 **Eckert** Günter, Orator christianus; Untersuchungen zur Argumentationskunst in Tertullians Apologeticum [diss. Saarbrücken 1992]: Palingenesia 46. Stu 1993, Steiner 278 p.
14036 *Frend* William H. C., Montanismus, ᵀ*Schäferdiek* Kurt: ➤ 517, TRE 23 (1994) 271-9.
14037 *García MacGaw* Carlos G., El donatismo, ¿religión o política [MANDOUZE A. 1976, résistance à Rome de l'Afrique tardive?]: Gerión 12 (1994) 133-153.
14038 **Georgeot** J.-M., Marcion suivi de La stratégie apostolique: De Saint-Marc jusqu'a Tertullien 12. ... 1994. 122 + 50 p.
14039 **Georgeot** J.-M., Dictionnaire A-K / L-Z: De Saint Marc jusqu'à Tertullien 13.
14039* *Haendler* Gert, Antike und Christentum bei den älteren lateinischen Kirchenvätern [(und) Tertullian, als Katholik, als Montanist]: TVers 18 (1993) 88-115.
14040 *Head* Peter, The foreign God and the sudden Christ; theology and Christology in MARCION's gospel redaction: TyndB 44 (1993) 307-321.
14041 *Kessler* Andreas, Tertullian und das Vergnügen in De spectaculis: FrSZ 41 (1994) 313-353.
14042 *Lugaresi* Leonardo, Tra evento e rappresentazione; per un'interpre-

tazione della polemica contro gli spettacoli nei primi secoli cristiani: Riv-
StoLR 30 (1994) 437-463.
14043 *McVey* Kathleen E.,   Christianity and culture, dead white European
males, and the study of patristics [Tertullian, CLEMENT A. ...; inaugural
address]:   PrincSemB 15 (1994) 103-130.
14043* **Marin Orenes** Avelino,   Cristo, siervo de Yahvé en las controversias
judía y gnóstica de Tertuliano: diss. ᴰ*Varo Pineda* F. Pamplona 1994.
326 p. – RTLv 26,531.
14044 *Markschies* Christoph,   Nochmals: Wo lag Pepuza? Wo lag Tymion?
Nebst einigen Bemerkungen zur Frühgeschichte des Montanismus: JbAC
37 (1994) 7-28; 3 maps.
14045 *Mattei* Paul,   Du divorce, de Tertullien, et de quelques autres sujets...
Perspectives nouvelles et idées reçues: RÉAug 39 (1993) 23-35.
14045* **Munier** Charles, introd., ᵀᴱ*Micaelli* Claudio, Tertullien, La pudicité
I-II: SChr 394. P 1993, Cerf. 284 p.; p. 285-467. 2-204-04981-6; -2-4. –
ᴿVigChr 48 (1994) 385-8 (J. C. M. van *Winden*).
14046 **Osborn** Eric,   The emergence of Christian theology [... essentially
rational up to CLEMENT A. and Tertullian]. C 1993, Univ. xviii-334 p. –
ᴿTLond 97 (1994) 126s (S. G. *Hall*).
14047 *Rebenich* Stefan,   Insania circi; eine Tertullianreminiszenz bei HIERO-
NYMUS und AUGUSTIN: Latomus 53 (1994) 155-8.
14047* ᴱ**Resta Barrile** A.,   Tertulliano, Apologetico: ClasGrL 55.   Mi 1994,
Mondadori. xxx-239 p.; bibliog. xxi-xxviii. 88-04-38004-7.
14048 **Ruggiero** Fabio,   Tertulliano, De corona: ClasGrL 30, 1992 → 9,
15804*:   ᴿAnStoEseg 10 (1993) 633-5 (N. *Pancaldi*); JbAC 37 (1994)
196-8 (J. *Fontaine*); RivStoLR 30 (1994) 370-2 (P. A. *Gramaglia*).
14049 *Testard* Maurice,   ... Carmenque Christo quasi Deo dicere [comme en
l'honneur d'un Dieu, Tert.]:   RÉLat 72 (1994) 138-158.
14050 ᵀᴱ**Uglione** R., Q. S. F. Tertulliano, Le uniche nozze, De monogamia:
Corona Patrum 15. T 1993, SEI. 348 p. – ᴿBStLat 24 (1994) 271-5 (C.
Magazzù); Salesianum 56 (1994) 557-560 (P. *Varalda*); SMSR 60 (1994)
389-398 (E. *Rapalino*).

Y2   *Patres graeci* – The Greek Fathers.

14051 **Aubin** Paul,   PLOTIN et le christianisme 1992 → 8,k716; 9,15808:
ᴿGregorianum 76 (1994) 384s (P. *Gilbert*); RTLv 25 (1994) 239 (A. de
Halleux, †).
14052 **Droge** Arthur J.,   Homer or Moses? 1989 → 5,g629 ... 8,k555:   ᴿSalesianum 56 (1994) 583 (E. *Fontana*).
14052* *Economou* E.,   ⑤ The Hebrew language and the Greek Fathers:
→ 131*c*, Mem. VELLAS V., DeltioVM 23,1 (1994) 29-47.
14053 ᴱ**Finan** Thomas, *Twomey* Vincent,   The relationship between Neoplatonism and Christianity [Maynooth patristic conference 1990] 1992
→ 8,547; 9,15815:   ᴿIrTQ 60 (1994) 154-6 (N. *Madden*); JEH 45 (1994)
719s (S. G. *Hall*); JTS 45 (1994) 292-5 (A. *Meredith*).
14054 *Hager* Fritz P.,   Neuplatonismus: → 517, TRE 24 (1994) 341-363.
14055 **Lorenz** Rudolf,   Das vierte Jahrhundert (Der Osten): [ᴱ*Moeller* Bernd]
Die Kirche 1, Lfg C-2.   Gö 1992, Vandenhoeck &R. vi-133 p. – ᴿRÉAug
40 (1994) 225s (M. *Figura*).
14056 **Papadopoulos** Stylianos G.,   ⑤ Patrologie [I, 1987] II. (le 4ᵉ siècle).
Athen 1990 auct. → 9,15822:   ᴿTLZ 119 (1994) 147-9 (F. *Winkelmann*).
14057 **Pelikan** Jaroslav,   Christianity and classical culture; the metamorphoses

of natural theology in the Christian encounter with Hellenism [Aberdeen Gifford Lectures 1992-3]. NHv 1993, Yale Univ. xvi-368 p. – RAnglTR 76 (1994) 527-9 (F. W. *Norris*); Phoenix 48 (Toronto 1994) 179s (Wendy E. *Helleman*); TLond 97 (1994) 210 (Averil *Cameron*: erudite but not up-to-date on what 'classical culture' is).

14058 *Sesboüé* Bernard, Bulletin de theólogie patristique grecque: RechSR 82 (1994) 417-432 . 587-629.

14059 **Studer** Basil, La riflessione teologica nella Chiesa Imperiale (sec. IV e V): Sussidi Patristici 4, 1989 → 5,g752 ... 9,15828: RAnnTh 7 (1993) 530-3 (V. *Reale*).

14060 **Trombley** Frank R., Hellenic religion and Christianization c. 370-529: RelGrRW 115 (= ÉPR). Leiden 1993s, Brill. xii-344; xv-430 p. – RMus-Helv 51 (1994) 255 (F. *Graf*).

14061 **Watson** Gerard, Greek philosophy and the Christian notion of God. Dublin 1994, Columbia. 153 p. £9. 1-85607-113-X. – RTBR 7,3 (1994s) 48s (N. *Sagovsky*).

14062 **Werner** Martin, Aspetti dell'evoluzione storico-dogmatica dopo l'età apostolica, T*Sciuto* F. con premessa: Orpheus 15 (1994) 477-487.

14063 **White** Carolinne, Christian friendship in the fourth century [Fathers]. C 1992, Univ. 274 p. – RJEH 45 (1994) 116-8 (P. *Rousseau*'s misgivings suggest an alternative approach); Orpheus 14 (1993) 402-4 (F. *Corsaro*).

14064 — *Bonner* Gerald, Friendship in Christ; a fourth-century change of perspective [WHITE C. 1992]: CathHR 80 (1994) 97-101.

14065 APOLLINARIUS: *Cattaneo* Enrico, Le traité d'Apollinaire *Contre Plotin* et les *Homélies pascales* pseudo-chrysostomiennes: OrChrPer 60 (1994) 233-7.

14066 APOPHTHEGMATA: TE**Guy** Jean-Claude, Les apophtegmes des Pères; collection systématique, I-IX: SChr 387 → 9, 15831: RJTS 45 (1994) 749-755 (G. *Gould*); RHPR 74 (1994) 318s (J.-C. *Larchet*); PrOrChr 43 (1993) 202s (P. *Ternant*).

14067 **Stewart** Columba, 'Working ...' the Messalian controversy [Apophthegmata, Ps-Macarius] to 431: 1991 → 7,g156; 9,15898: RCritRR 6 (1993) 395s (J. P. *Amar*: Messalian means in Syriac 'those who pray'); PrOrChr 43 (1993) 204s (P. *Gruber*); ScotJT 47 (1994) 382s (L. R. *Wickham*).

14068 ARIUS: E**Barnes** Michael R., *Williams* Daniel H., Arianism after Arius 1993: RExpTim 105 (1993s) 380s (R. *Butterworth*: patient theological archaeology; 11 art.; two 'reassuring' Britons amid Americans); TLZ 119 (1994) 997-9 (H.-G. *Thümmel*).

14069 *Groh* Dennis E., The Arian controversy; how it divided early Christianity: BR 10,1 (1994) 20-32.

14070 **Hanson** R. P. C., Search for the Christian doctrine of God: → 4,8475 ... 9,15834: RScotJT 45 (1992) 101-111 (R. *Williams*).

14071 *Stead* Christopher, Arius in modern research: JTS 45 (1994) 24-36.

14071* *Williams* Rowan D., Arius, Arianismus: → 510, LTK³ 1 (1993) 981-9.

14072 ATHANASIUS: **Arnold** D. W., The early episcopal career of Athanasius 1991 → 7,g122 ... 9,15839: RCritRR 6 (1993) 343-5 (R. *Valantasis*).

14073 **Barnes** T. D., Athanasius and Constantius 1993 → 9,15841: RChH 63 (1994) 450s (R. M. *Grant*); JEH 45 (1994) 686-8 (W. H. C. *Frend*); JTS 45 (1994) 722-5 (C. *Stead*).

14074 ᵀᴱBartelink G. J. M., Athanasius, Vie d'Antoine; SChr 400. P 1994, Cerf. 432 p. F 275. 2-204-04985-9 [TLZ 120,444, G. *Haendler*].

14074* — *Lanne* Emmanuel, The life of St. Anthony by St. Athanasius the Great; a link between eastern and western Christianity: PrOrChr 42 (1992) 243-259; franç, 259.

14075 — *Brakke* David, The authenticity of the Ascetic Athanasiana [JEROME: 'many books on virginity']: Orientalia 63 (1994) 17-56.

14076 *Meijering* E. P., Die Echtheit der dritten Rede des Athanasius gegen die Arianer (3, 59-67): VigChr 48 (1994) 135-156.

14077 *Sánchez Navarro* Luis Antonio, El campo semántico de 'ver' en el tratado Contra Gentes de Atanasio de Alejandria; estudio estructural: RAg 34 (1993) 467-535.

14078 BASILIUS M.: **Backus** Iréna, Lectures de Basile 1990 ⇒ 7,g129... 9,15849: ᴿJTS 45 (1994) 393s (K. *Jensen*).

14079 **Fedwick** Paul J., BtBasiliana I. The letters: CCGr 1993 ⇒ 9,15850: ᴿVigChr 48 (1994) 95s (J. C. M. van *Winden*).

14080 *Girardi* Mario, *a)* Il lavoro nell'omiletica di Basilio di Cesarea: VetChr 31 (1994) 70-110; – *b)* *Erotapokriseis* neotestamentarie negli Ascetica di Basilio di Cesarea; evangelismo e paolinismo nel monachesimo delle origini: AnStoEseg 11 (1994) 461-490.

14081 **Hauschild** Wolf Dieter, Basilius von Caesarea, Briefe [I. 1990 ⇒ 9, 15851]; 3: BtGrLit 37. Stu 1993, Hiersemann. xii-307 p. – ᴿRHE 89 (1994) 657-660 (J.-R. *Pouchet*).

14081* *Kannengiesser* Charles, Basilius von Caesarea (der Grosse); ⇒ 510, LTK³ 2 (1994) 67-69.

14082 **Koschorke** Klaus, Spuren der alten Liebe... Basilius C. 1991 ⇒ 7, 7894*: ᴿTLZ 119 (1994) 143-5 (W.-D. *Hauschild*).

14083 *Nautin* Pierre, L'éloge funèbre de Basile [SChr 384] par Grégoire de Nazianze: VigChr 48 (1994) 332-340.

14084 *Paczkowski* Mieczysław C., Esegesi prosopografica di S. Basilio Magno: LA 44 (1994) 291-330; Eng. 613.

14085 **Rousseau** Philip, Basil of Caesarea: TransfClasHer 20. Berkeley 1994, Univ. California. xx-412 p.; map; bibliog. 365-389 [RHE 90,95*]. 0-520-08238-9.

14086 **Sterk** Andrea, Basil of Caesarea and the rise of the monastic episcopate; ascetic ideals and episcopal authority in fourth-century Asia Minor: diss. ᴰMcVey Kathleen. Princeton 1994. 314 p. 94-30037. – DissA 55 (1994s) p. 2100; RelStR 21,256.

14087 *Zappalà* Olga, Le litterae commendaticiae di Basilio di Cesarea: Koinonia 17 (1993) 49-60.

14088 CHRYSOSTOMUS: **O'Roark** Douglas A., Urban family structure in late antiquity as evidenced by John Chrysostom: diss. Ohio State, ᴰGregory T. 1994. 234 p. 94-27765. – DissA 55 (1994s) p. 1656.

14089 **Klasvogt** P., Leben zur Verherrlichung Gottes; Botschaft des Johannes Chrysostomos 1992 ⇒ 8,k764*; 9,15866: ᴿBLitEc 95 (1994) 252s (H. *Crouzel*).

14090 *Krupp* Robert A., Chrysostom, Golden tongue and iron will: Christian History 13,44 (1994) 6-11 (-38, *al.*).

14091 ᵀᴱLochbrunner Manfred, [⇒ 7995] Über das Priestertum: Hereditas 5. Bonn 1993, Borengässer. xliv-386 p. DM 78. 3-92-394619-8. – ᴿForKT 10 (1994) 311s (A. *Keller*); TrierTZ 103 (1994) 320 (E. *Sauser*).

14091* ᵀᴱ**Malingrey** Anne-Marie, Jean Chrysostome, Sur l'égalité du Père et du Fils; Contre les Anoméens VII-XII: SChr 396. P 1994, Cerf. 378 p. F 224. 2-204-04852-6 [NRT 117, 593, A. *Harvengt*]. – ᴿMélSR 51 (1994) 333-6 (M. *Spanneut*).

14092 **Rau** Eckhard, Von Jesus zu Paulus; Entwicklung und Rezeption der antiochenischen Theologie im Urchristentum. Stu 1994, Kohlhammer. 121 p.; Bibliog. 118-124. 3-17-012966-X.

14093 **Taft** Robert F., A history of the liturgy of St. John Chrysostom 4: OrChrAnal 228 → 7,g142*... 9,15877: ᴿMaisD 194 (1993) 156s (L. H. *Dalmais*); RÉByz 51 (1993) 314 (B. *Flusin*).

14094 ᴱ**Uthemann** Karl-H., *al.*, Homiliae pseudo-chrysostomicae I. Turnhout 1994, Brepols. 307 p. [cf. → 9,15880].

14095 **Walsh** Efthalia M., Overcoming gender; virgins, widows and barren women in the writings of St. John Chrysostom, 386-397: diss. Catholic Univ. of America, ᴰ*Young* R. Wsh 1994. 329 p. 94-18581. – DissA 55 (1994s) p. 302.

14096 CYRILLUS A.: **Rosa** Pietro, Gli occhi del corpo e gli occhi della mente; Cirillo Alessandrino, testi ermeneutici. Bo 1994, Dehoniane. 175 p. Lᵐ 25. 88-10-40226-X.

14097 ᴱ**Éviaux** Pierre, Cyrille d'Alexandrie, Lettres festales VII-XI, tome 2: SChr 392. P 1993, Cerf. 327 p. 2-204-04801-1.

14097* CYRILLUS H.: ᵀᴱ**Maestri** Gabriella, *Saxer* Victor, Cirillo e Giovanni di Gerusalemme, Catechesi prebattesimali e mistagogiche: LettCPrimoM 13. CinB 1994, Paoline. 670 p. 88-315-0994-2.

14098 DAMASCENUS: *Huculak* Benedykt, Costituzione della persona divina secondo S. Giovanni Damasceno: Antonianum 69 (1994) 179-212; Eng. 179.

14099 **Le Coz** Raymond, J. Damascène, Écrits sur l'Islam: SChr 383, 1992 → 8,k781; 9,15888: ᴿRHR 211 (1994) 363-5 (G. *Monnot*).

14100 DIDYMUS: ᵀᴱ**Doutreleau** L., Didyme l'Aveugle, Traité du S.-Esprit: SChr 386. P 1992, Cerf. 449 p. 2-204-4611-6. – ᴿJTS 45 (1994) 326s (L. R. *Wickham*); RÉAug 40 (1994) 223s (C. *Kannengiesser*); ScEspr 46 (1994) 259s (C. *Barry*).

14100* DIOSCORUS A.: **Kuehn** Clement A., Channels of imperishable fire; the Christian mystical allegories of Dioscorus of Aphrodito: diss. Loyola, ᴰ*Keenan* J. Chicago 1993, xx-405 p. 93-26168. – OIAc 11,29.

14101 EPIPHANIUS S.: **Amidon** Philip R., The Panarion of Epiphanius [without the refutations] 1990 → 6,k192... 9,15896: ᴿSWJT 36,1 (1993s) 65 (E. E. *Ellis*).

14102 ᵀᴱ**Williams** Frank, The Panarion of Epiphanius of Salamis, I (Sects 1-46), IIs (Sects 47-80; De fide): Nag Hammadi & Manichean 24,5. Leiden 1987/94, Brill. xxx-359 p.; xviii-p. 361-677. 90-04-07926-2 [NTAbs 38, p. 50].

14103 **Pourkier** Aline, L'hérésiologie chez Épiphane: Christianisme Antique 2, 1992 → 9,15897: ᴿByZ 86 (1994) 135s (K.-H. *Uthemann*); RHPR 74 (1994) 319s (A. A. *Bertrand*); RTLv 25 (1994) 86s (A. de *Halleux*).

14104 EUSEBIUS C.: ᵀᴱ**Places** Édouard des, Eusèbe, Préparation évangélique 8-10: SChr 369, 1991 → 7,g610... 9,15905: ᴿPrOrChr 42 (1992) 224 (P. *Ternant*); RTPhil 126 (1994) 173 (É. *Junod*).

14104* *Manns* F., Une tradition chrétienne rapportée par Eusèbe de Césarée: CrNSt 15 (1994) 145-8 [< TR 91,73].

14105 *Orlandi* Tito, La traduzione copta di Eusebio di Cesarea; Hist. Eccl.: LinceiR 9,5,1 (1994) 399-456.
14105* *Barnes* T. D., a) The two drafts of Eusebius' Life of Constantine; – b) The religious affiliation of consuls and prefects, 317-361 [both inedita]: ➤ 158, From Eusebius 1994, XII (11 p.) / VII (also 11 p.).
14106 *Calderone* Salvatore, *Mē makarízein ándra prò tês teleutês*, da Solone ad Eusebio di Cesarea: ➤ 9,51, FGENTILI B., Tradizione 1993, 301-327.
14106* **Gain** Benoit, Traductions latines des Pères grecs... San Marco 584, Eusèbe: Eur 15/64. Bern 1994, Lang. xiii-536 p. F 352 [RHE 90,116, J.-R. *Pouchet*].
14107 EVAGRIUS: *Géhin* Paul, Nouveaux fragments grecs des lettres d'Évagre: RHText 24 (1994) 117-147.
14108 TE**Driscoll** Jeremy, The mind's long journey to the Holy Trinity; the Ad monachos of Evagrius Ponticus. ColMn 1993, Liturgical. vi-138 p. $10 [RelStR 21,148, R. D. *Young*: OT proverbs offered as modern spiritual reading].
14109 *Joest* Christoph, Die Bedeutung von *akedia* und *apatheia* bei Evagrios Pontikos: StMon 35 (1993) 7-53.

14110 GREGORIUS NAZ.: *Coulie* Bernard, L'édition critique des versions arméniennes de textes grecs; réflexions sur le cas de Grégoire de Nazianze: ➤ 118, FSICHERL M., *Philophronēma* 1990, 59-72.
14111 **Fipps** Bradford L., Gregory of Nazianzus' Orations 4 and 5 [really one, his longest; crowing over Julian and promoting Christianity]: diss. Drew, D*Stroker* W. Madison NJ 1994. 354 p. 94-32948. – DissA 55 (1994s) p. 2012; RelStR 21, 255.
14112 E**Lugaresi** Leonardo, Gregorio di Nazianzo, contro Giuliano l'Apostata orazione IV: BtPatr 23, 1993 ➤ 9,15913: F 1993, Nardini. 456 p. Lm 54. – RMuséon 107 (1994) 213-5 (Anna *Sirinian*); VetChr 31 (1994) 409s (Silvia *Bettocchi*).
14113 *Milovanović-Barham* Čelica, Three levels of style in Gregory of Nazianzus; the case of Oration 43: ClasMdv 45 (1994) 193-210.
14114 E**Moreschini** Claudio, *Menestrina* Giovanni, GREGORIO Nazianzeno teologo e scrittore [Trento 24-25 ott. 1990]: IstScRel 17, 1992 ➤ 8,596: RAevum 67 (1993) 242-4 (F. *Luciani*).
14115 **Norris** Frederick W., Faith gives fullness to reasoning... Nazianzen 1991 ➤ 7,g168; 8,k803: RScotJT 46 (1993) 568s (A. *Louth*).
14116 *Panagyotou* Eugénie, Le trouble [agitation] chez Saint Grégoire de Nazianze: TAth 64 (1993) 753-820; 65 (1994) 101-132. 293-529. 538-561. 843-862...
14117 *Sirinian* Anna, Sulla riproduzione dei nomi propri nella versione armena dell'Orazione 4 di Gregorio di Nazianzo: RLomb 128,1 (1994) 251-262.
14118 *Starowieyski* Marek, Les apocryphes dans la tragédie Christus patiens [attribuée au (temps de) Nazianze; EBLADUS A. 1552]: Apocrypha 5 (1994) 269-288.

14119 GREGORIUS NYSS.: **Böhm** Thomas, Die Konzeption der Mystik bei Gregor von Nyssa: FrSZ 41 (1994) 45-64.
14120 E**Drobner** H. R., *Klock* C., [ESPIRA A.] Studien zu Gregor von Nyssa 1990 ➤ 6,695: RTLZ 119 (1994) 330-2 (F. *Winkelmann*); TR 90 (1994) 135-6 (W.-D. *Hauschild*).
14122 *Dünzl* Franz, Formen der Kirchenväter-Rezeption am Beispiel der

sogenannten physischen Erlösungslehre des Gregor von Nyssa: TPhil 69 (1994) 161-181.

14123 *Marxer* Fridolin, Gregor von Nyssa – Vater der christlichen Mystik: Geist und Leben 67 (1994) 347-358; > Eng. TE*Asen* B.A.: TDig 42, 145-151.

14124 **Meissner** Henriette M., Rhetorik und Theologie; der Dialog Gregors von Nyssa, De anima et resurrectione [Diss. Mainz] Patrologia 1, 1991 → 8,k812; 9,15926: ROrChrPer 60 (1994) 315 (G. *Podskalsky*).

14125 **Stains** David R., Gregory of Nyssa's ethic of slavery and emancipation: diss. D*Wilson* J. Pittsburgh 1994. 555 p. 94-31551. – DissA 55 (1994s) p. 2008.

14126 **Völker** W., Gregorio di Nissa filosofo e mistico [1955], TE*Moreschini* C.: Platonismo e filosofia patristica. Mi 1993, ViPe. 472 p. – RVetChr 31 (1994) 410s (Immacolata *Aulisa*).

14127 MARCELLUS A.: *Vincent* Markus, Die Gegner im Schreiben Markells von Ankyra an Julius von Rom: ZKG 105 (1994) 285-328.

14128 MAXIMUS C.: **Blowers** P. M., Exegesis and spiritual pedagogy in Maximus the Confessor; an investigation of the Quaestiones ad Thalassium → 8,k821; 9,15935: RBLitEc 95 (1994) 255s (H. *Crouzel*); ChH 63 (1994) 263s (J. F. *Kelly*); JTS 45 (1994) 760 (A. *Louth*).

14129 **Jeauneau** A., Maximi Confessoris ambigua ad Iohannem, TERIUGENA CCGr 18, 1988: RVizVrem 53 (1992) 177-9 (A. I. *Sidorov*, ❸).

14129* **Karayiannis** Vasilios, Maxime le Confesseur, Essence et énergies de Dieu [diss. 1991 FrS D*Schönborn* C. von]: THist 93, 1993 → 9,15936: RRHPR 74 (1994) 446-9 (J.-C. *Larchet*: une contribution capitale, malgré pas mal d'inexactitudes).

14130 **Schoors** A., Biblical onomastics in Maximus Confessor's Quaestiones ad Thalassium: → 70, FLAGA C., Philohistôr 1994, 295-328.

14130* ROMANOS M.: *Dobrov* Gregory W., A dialogue with death; ritual lament and the *thrênos theoktónou* of Romanos Melodos: GrRByz 35 (1994) 385-405.

14131 SERAPION von Thmuis: E**Fittschen** Klaus, Echte und unechte Schriften sowie die Zeugnisse des Athanasius und anderer: PatrTSt 37. B 1992, de Gruyter. xl-226 p. [→ 8,k830]; Bibliog. 205-214. 3-11-012886-1.

14131* SEVERIANUS: **Regtuit** Remco F., Severian of Gabala, Homily on the Incarnation of Christ (CPG 4204). Amst 1992, V. Univ. 337 p. – ROrChrPer 60 (1994) 316s (S. *Voicu*).

14132 *Regtuit* Remco F., Severian of Gabala and John CHRYSOSTOM; the problem of authenticity: → 70, FLAGA C., Philohistôr 1994, 135-149.

14132* THEODORETUS C.: *Romanides* John F., LEO of Rome's support of Theodoret, DIOSCORUS of Alexandria's support of EUTYCHES and the lifting of the anathemas [hoped for in 1993 Geneva meeting from evidence he had already presented in 1964]: TAth 65 (1994) 479-493.

14133 **Bergjan** Silke-Petra, Theodoret von Cyrus und der Neunizänismus; Aspekte der altkirchlichen Trinitätslehre [Diss. München]: ArbKG 60. B 1994, de Gruyter. x-246 p. DM 148. 3-11-013955-3 [TLZ 120, 445-7, H. *Ziebritzki*].

14133* THEODORUS M.: **Bruns** Peter, Den Menschen mit dem Himmel verbinden — eine Studie zu den katechetischen Homilien des Theodor von Mopsuestia: kath. Hab.-Diss. Ruhr-Univ., D*Geerlings* W. Bochum 1994. – TR 91,89.

14134 *Carrara* Paolo, Un presunto attacco a Basilio di Cesarea nel Commento alla Genesi di Teodoro di Mopsuestia: ➤ 86, FNALDINI M., Paideia 1994, 595-611 [569-594 . 613-627 *al.*, su Basilio].

14135 ᵀᴱ**Guida** Augusto, Teodoro di Mopsuestia, Replica a Giuliano Imperatore... con nuovi frammenti: BtPatr 24. F 1994, Nardini. 260 p.; bibliog. 247-258. 88-404-2026-6.

14136 *Guida* Augusto, Per un'edizione della Replica di Teodoro di Mopsuestia al Contro i Galilei dell'imperatore Giuliano; note testuali: ➤ 86, FNALDINI M., Paideia 1994, 87-102.

14137 **Zaharopoulos** D. Z., Theodore of M. on the Bible 1989 ➤ 5,g818... 8,k838: ScripB 23 (1993) 47s (J. *McGuckin*).

14138 THEODOTUS A.: ᵀᴱ**Lo Castro** G., Teodoto di Ancira, Omelie cristologiche e mariane: TPatr 97'. R 1992, Città Nuova. 167 p. Lᵐ 16. – ᴿAsprenas 41 (1994) 605s (L. *Fatica*).

14138* THEOLEPTOS: **Sinkewicz** R. E., Theoleptos, ST 211, 1992 ➤ 9,15947: ᴿSpeculum 69 (1994) 1282-4 (A. *Papadakis*).

Y2.4 Augustinus.

14139 *a) Ando* Clifford, Augustine on language; – *b) D'Oignon* Jean, Un faisceau de métaphores platoniciennes dans les écrits d'Augustin de 386: RÉAug 40 (1994) 45-78 / 39-43.

14140 *Beckley* Frederic A., Why pears? The role of little sins in Augustine's Confessions: AugLv 43 (1993) 53-75.

14141 ᵀᴱ**Bettetini** Maria, Sant'Agostino, Ordine, musica, bellezza: Classici del Pensiero. Mi 1992, Rusconi. lxv-325 p. – ᴿAnnTh 7 (1993) 527-530 (V. *Reale*).

14142 **Brown** Peter, Augustinus van Hippo, ᵀ*Verheijen* Carla, *Dorsselaer* Karin van, Amst 1992, Agon. 472 p. – ᴿStreven 60 (1993) 89s (G. *Groot*).

14143 *Burnell* Peter, The problem of service to unjust regimes in Augustine's City of God: JHistId 54 (1993) 177-188.

14144 *Cambronne* Patrice, Unde malum? Augustin et les questions sur le mal; des philosphies classiques à la théologie: RÉAnc 96 (1994) 511-535; Eng. 511.

14145 **Clark** G., Augustine, The Confessions. C 1993, Univ. 110 p. [TDig 41,353]. – ᴿRÉG 107 (1994) 313s (A. *Billault*).

14146 ᴱ**Coyle** J. Kevin, *al.*, Aug. De moribus... Manichaeorum 1991 ➤ 7, 461... 9,15965: ᴿOrpheus 14 (1993) 207-210 (A. *Gallico*); RÉAnc 96 (1994) 615-7 (P. *Mattei*); TR 90 (1994) 138s (C. *Müller*); ZKG 105 (1994) 115s (A. *Zumkeller*).

14147 *Cutino* Michele, Scetticismo e anticristianismo nei 'Dialoghi' di Agostino: Orpheus 15 (1994) 46-75.

14148 **Dassmann** E., Augustinus, Heiliger und Kirchenlehrer. Stu 1993, Kohlhammer. 185 p. ᴅᴹ 29,80. 3-17012468-4. – ᴿTvT 34 (1994) 309 (T. J. van *Bavel*).

14149 *Dawson* David, Transcendence as embodiment; Augustine's domestication of gnosis: ModT 10 (1994) 1-26.

14150 *Dolbeau* François, Mentions de textes perdus de S. Augustin extraites des archives Mauristes I: RHText 23 (1993) 143-158; Eng. 154.

14151 ᵀᴱ**Drobner** Hubertus R., 'Für Euch bin ich Bischof'; die Predigten Augustins über das Bischofsamt (Sermones 335, 339, 340a, 383, 396): AugHeute 7. Wü 1993, Augustinus. 138 p. ᴅᴹ 28. – ᴿTR 90 (1994) 391s (C. *Mayer*).

14152 *Ferrari* Leo C.,   Doorways of discovery in Augustine's Confessions:
➤ 89*d*,   ᶠOROZ RETA II (1994) 149-164.

14153 *Ferrari* Leo C.,   Saint Augustine's various conversions; some insights of
modern science [eclipses at Carthage]:   RelStT 12,1 (1992) 24-35; 36-41
response, *Firth* Francis.

14153* *Folliet* Georges,   L'Édition princeps des lettres de Saint Augustin
parue à Strasbourg chez Mentelin vers 1471: SacrEr 34 (1994) 33-58.

14154 ᵀᴱ**García de la Fuente** Olegario,   Agustín, escritos bíblicos: BAC, Opera
28. M 1989, Católica.   737 p. – ᴿREspir 52 (1993) 355s (S. *Fernández*).

14154* **Geerlings** Wilhelm, Augustini Psalmus contra partem DONATI; ein
Versuch zur Überwindung der Kirchenspaltung: ➤ 95, ᶠPOTTMEYER H.,
Kirche sein 1994, 39-66.

14155 *Geerlings* Wilhelm,   Augustinus: ➤ 510, LTK³ 1 (1993) 1239-45 (-47).

14156 *Hallman* Joseph M.,   Am I born a sinner? Augustine of Hippo and
René GIRARD: IrTQ 59 (1993) 81-93.

14157 **Harrison** Carol, Beauty and revelation... Aug. 1992 ➤ 8,k863; 9,15980:
ᴿDowR 111 (1993) 73-76 (D. *Foster*); TPhil 69 (1994) 279s (J. *Lössl*).

14158 ᵀᴱ**Hoffmann** Andreas,   Augustinus, De utilitate credendi; Über den
Nützen des Glaubens: Fontes christiani 9, 1992 ➤ 9,15983:   DM 36;
3-451-22117-9: ᴿLatomus 53 (1994) 639-641 (S. *Deléani*); TPhil 69 (1994)
581 (H. J. *Sieben*).

14159 *a*) *Hoffmann* Andreas,   Der junge Augustinus; erst Feind, dann Ver-
fechter der katholischen Lehre; – *b*) *Lössl* Josef, Augustinus – Exeget
oder Philosoph? Schriftgebrauch und biblische Hermeneutik in De uera
religione: WissWeis 56 (1993) 16-28 / 97-114.

14160 *a*) *Hoffmann* Andreas,   Young Augustine – enemy, then advocate
[< WissWeis 56,1 (1993) 16-29]; – *b*) *Lössl* Josef, Augustine – exegete or
philosopher? [< WissWeis 56 (1993) 97-114]: > TDig 42, 30-34 [ᵀᴱ*Asen*
B.] / 35-41 [ᵀᴱ*Steinhauser* Kenneth B.].

14160* **Im Seung-An**,   John WESLEY's theological anthropology; a dialectic
tension between the Latin Western patristic tradition (Augustine) and the
Greek Eastern patristic tradition (GREGORY of Nyssa): Diss. Drew, ᴰ*Pain*
J.   Madison NJ 1994. – RelStR 21,253.

14161 *Kaufman* Peter Ivan,   Augustine, martyrs and misery: ChH 63 (1994)
1-14.

14162 **Kotila** Heikki,   Memoria mortuorum; commemoration of the departed
in Augustine: St. Inst. Aug. 38.   R 1992, Augustinianum.   230 p. – ᴿJEH
45 (1994) 118s (H. *Chadwick*).

14163 **Kranz** Gisbert,   Augustinus, sein Leben und Werken: ToposTb 244.
Mainz 1994, Grünewald.   164 p. DM 14,80.   3-7867-1795-8 [TR 91,80].

14163* *Krümmel* Achim,   Die Herausgabe von Werken Augustins in Wien im
Umkreis der 'Neueren Augustinerschule' (1760-1782): AnalAug 56 (1992)
247-265.

14164 *Lamberigts* Mathus [➤ 366],   Augustine as translator of Greek texts; an
example (De haeresibus, 'Augustine's only work which was based on a
translation from the Greek'): ➤ 70, ᶠLAGA C., Philohistôr 1994, 151-161.

14164* *Langa* Pedro,   La ordenación sacerdotal de san Agustín: ➤ 8,185,
ᶠTURRADO A., RAg 33 (1992) 51-93.

14165 *Madec* Goulven,   Bulletin augustinien pour 1993/1994 et compléments:
RÉAug 40 (1994) 501-582; index 584-8.

14165* **Mallard** William,   Language and love; introducing Augustine's
religious thought through the Confessions story. Univ.Park 1994, Penn.
State.   xii-252 p. $35; pa. $17 [TDig 42,376; RelStR 21,319, H. *Booth*].

14166 *a) Markus* Robert A., Augustine on magic; a neglected semiotic theory; – *b) Horn* Christoph, Augustins Philosophie der Zahlen: RÉAug 40 (1994) 375-388 / 389-415.

14167 *Miles* Margaret R., Desire and delight; a new reading of Augustine's Confessions: ➤ 405, Broken 1993/4, 3-16 [17-22 response, *Joy* Morny].

14168 **Mohler** James A., A speechless child is the word of God ... Augustine. New Rochelle 1992, New City. 174 p. $10. – ᴿJEarlyCS 2 (1994) 105s (T. F. *Martin*: popularized Catholic teaching, not really on Augustine).

14169 **Morgenstern** Frank, Die Briefpartner des Augustinus von Hippo; prosopographische, sozial- und ideologiegeschichtliche Untersuchungen: HistStAlt 11. Bochum 1993, Brockmeyer. v-390 p. DM 50 [TR 91,29, C. *Mayer*].

14170 **Morrison** Karl F., Conversion and text; the cases of Augustine of Hippo, HERMAN-JUDAH [1150] and Constantine TSATSOS [president of Greece 1975]. Charlottesville 1992, Univ. Virginia. xx-192 p.; 1 pl. $35; pa. $15. – ᴿSpeculum 69 (1994) 1235-7 (W. H. C. *Frend*, also p. 846 on his Understanding conversion).

14171 *Müller* Hildegrund, *Dispensio, dispensator, dispensatio* im Werk Augustins: ➤ 117, ᶠSCHWABL H., WienerSt 108 (1994s) 495-521.

14172 **O'Connell** Robert J., Soundings in St. Augustine's imagination. NY 1994, Fordham Univ. x-309 p. $40; pa. $20. 0-8232-1347-1, -8-X [TDig 41,376].

14173 **O'Donnell** James J., Augustine, Confessions 1992 ➤ 8,k881; 9,15998: ᴿClasPg 89 (1994) 293-9 (T. D. *Barnes*); JRel 74 (1994) 389-391 (Paula *Fredriksen*); JTS 45 (1994) 335-341 (Carol *Harrison*); Speculum 69 (1994) 857-9 (G. *Bonner*: a century's work drawn together).

14174 **Oort** J. van, Jerusalem and Babylon ᴰ1991 ➤ 7,g284 ... 9,15999: ᴿCiuD 206 (1993) 661s (S. *Álvarez Turienzo*); Salesianum 56 (1994) 146s (P. T. *Stella*).

14175 *Oort* Joahnnes van, AUGUSTIN und der Manichäismus: ZRGg 46 (1994) 126-142.

14176 *Pelland* G., al., Lectio Augustini Pavese 5 (Gn Manich/Litt) 1992 ➤ 9,16000:   ᴿCC 145 (1994,2) 611-3 (G. *Cremascoli*); RHR 211 (1994) 476s (J. *Doignon*).

14177 ᴱ**Piccolomini** R., Interiorità e intenzionalità nel DeCivD di S. Agostino; Atti del III Seminario Perugia. R 1991, Ist. Patr. Augustinianum. 209 p. – ᴿAsprenas 41 (1994) 120s (L. *Fatica*).

14178 **Pendergast** John S., St. Augustine and the rhetoric of obscurity: diss. Missouri, ᴰ*Camargo* M. Columbia 1994. 259 p. 95-11681. – DissA 55 (1994s) p. 3880.

14179 ᵀᴱ**Rees** B. R., Letters of Pelagius 1991 < 8,k890; 9,16004: ᴿDowR 111 (1993) 77s (D. *Foster*).

14180 **Rist** John M., Augustine; ancient thought baptized. C 1994, Univ. xix-334 p. $60. 0-521-46084-0 [TDig 42,86; TS 56,361-3, R. J. *Teske*].

14181 **Ruokanen** Miikka, Theology of social life in Augustine's 'De civitate Dei': ForKDG 53, Gö 1993, Vandenhoeck & R. 179 p. DM 68. 3-525-55161-4. – ᴿEstAg 29 (1994) 178-180 (P. de *Luis*).

14182 **Schimpf** David M., Bible, Christ, and human beings; the theological unity of St. Augustine's 'Confessions': diss. Marquette, ᴰ*Lienhard* J. Milwaukee 1994. 330 p. 94-33788. – DissA 55 (1994s) p. 2444.

14183 ᴱ**Simonetti** Manlio, al., ᵀ*Chiarini* Gioacchino, Sant'Agostino, Confessioni I (libri 1-3): ScrGrL. Mi 1992, Mondadori. clxi-264 p. – ᴿOrpheus 14 (1993) 360-5 (Daniela P. *Taormina*).

14184 *a) Speigl* Jakob,   Der Ökumenismus Augustins zwischen Anpassung und Distanz zum Staat; – *b) Teske* Roland J.,   Augustine, Maximinus and imagination: AugLv 43 (1993) 5-25 / 27-41.

14185 **Starnes** Colin, Augustine's conversion 1990 ⇒ 6,k286... 9,16012: ᴿClasR 44 (1994) 286s (Anna *Wilson*).

14186 **Studer** Basil, Gratia Christi – gratia Dei bei Augustinus von Hippo; Christozentrismus oder Theozentrismus?: StEphAug 40, 1993: ᴿGregorianum 75 (1994) 572s (G. *Pelland*); JTS 45 (1994) 341-4 (G. *Bonner*); RTLv 25 (1994) 341 (A. de *Halleux*: auraient dû constituer les articles 'Christus' et 'Deus' d'AugL).

14187 **Sumruld** William A., Augustine and the Arians; the bishop of Hippo's encounters with Ulfilan Arianism. Selingsgrove PA 1993, Susquehanna Univ. 196 p. $35. 0-945636-46-6. – ᴿTBR 7,3 (1994s) 58 (R. *Fox*).

14187* *Teske* R. J.,   The link between faith and time in St. Augustine: ⇒ 9,464*f*, Collectanea 1990/3, 195-206.

14188 **Thompson** Christopher J., Augustine and narrative ethics: diss. Marquette, ᴰ*Rossi* P.   Milwaukee 1994. 168 p. 95-05913. – DissA 55 (1994s) p. 2873.

14189 *Troxel* A. Craig, What did Augustine 'confess' in his Confessions?: TrinJ 15 (1994) 153-179.

14190 **Wetzel** James, Augustine and the limits of virtue 1992 ⇒ 9,16021: ᴿClasW 88 (1994s) 142s (R. D. *Sider*); ModT 10 (1994) 217-9 (J. *Cavadini*); TPhil 69 (1994) 277s (J. *Lössl*).

Y2.5   Hieronymus.

14191 *Adkin* Neil,   *a)* The date of John CHRYSOSTOM's *De virginitate*; OrChrPer 60 (1994) 611-7; 4 fig.; 1 plan; – *b)* The date of the dream of Saint Jerome (Ep. 22:7 & 30): StClasOr 43 (1993) 263-273; – *c)* Falling asleep over a book; Jerome, letter 60, II, 2: Eos 81 (1993) 227-230; – *d)* Hierosolymam militaturus pergerem; a note on the location of Jerome's dream [ep. 22,30,1: unclear; no proof for Antioch]: Koinonia 17 (1993) 81-83; – *e)* Juvenal and Jerome: ClasPg 89 (1994) 69-72; – *f)* Orientius and Jerome: SacrEr 34 (1994) 165-174; – *g)* 'Alii discunt — pro pudor! — a feminis', Jerome, Epist. 53.7.1: ClasQ 44 (1994) 559-561.

14192 **Allegri** Giuseppina, I damna della mensa in san Girolamo 1989 ⇒ 6,k295; 8,k903: ᴿRÉLat 72 (1994) 370s (P. *Jay*).

14192* *Bastiaensen* A. A. R., Jérôme hagiographe: in ᴱ**Philippart** G., Corpus christianorum, Hagiographies [Turnhout 1994, Brepols; 512 p.] 97-123 [RHE 90,39*. 44*].

14193 *Bauer* Erika, Zur Geschichte der Hieronymus-Briefe: ⇒ 53, ꟻHAUG/ WACHINGER 1992, 1, 305-321.

14193* *a) Bocciolini Palagi* Laura, Girolamo e le insidie del canto; alcuni aspetti del mito di Orfeo nel mondo cristiano; – *b) Sfameni Gasparro* Giulia, Dialogus sub nomine Hieronymi et Augustini de origine animarum (Ps. Girolamo, ep. 37, PL 30,270-280); per la storia della tradizione origeniana in Occidente: ⇒ 86, ꟻNALDINI M., Paideia 1994, 467-476 / 115-130.

14194 ᵀᴱ**Brady** James F., *Olin* John C., ERASMUS, The [1516] edition of St. Jerome: Collected Works 61. Toronto 1992, Univ. 336 p. $85. – ᴿTrinJ 14 (1993) 79-85 (T. *Scheck*).

14195 **Brown** Dennis, Vir trilinguis 1992 ⇒ 8,k906: ᴿCBQ 56 (1994) 323s (E. *Nardoni*); NorTTs 65 (1994) 140s (T. *Stordalen*, Norwegian); Salesianum 56 (1994) 566s (R. *Vicent*).

14195* *Fontaine* Jacques, Nouvelles perspectives sur saint Jérôme et sur les origines du monachisme occidental [VOGÜÉ A. de 1991; REBENICH S. 1992]: Revue Mabillon 65 (1993) 291-300 [< TR 91,78].

14196 *Frye* David,   Rusticus, ein gemeinsamer Freund von Athaulf und Hieronymus? A response: Historia [40 (1991) 507s; 42 (1993) 118-122, *Rebenich* S.] 43 (1994) 504-6.

14197 *Fürst* Alfons,   *Veritas latina*; AUGUSTINs Haltung gegenüber Hieronymus' Bibelübersetzungen: RÉAug 40 (1994) 105-126.

14198 *Grace* Madeleine sr.,   Jerome's Lives of illustrious men [... liked ORIGEN, not AMBROSE]: Priest 50,2 (1994) 44-47.

14199 *Hamblenne* Pierre,   L'apprentissage du grec par Jérôme; quelques ajustements: RÉAug 40 (1994) 353-364.

14200 **Hennings** R.,   Der Briefwechsel Aug-Hieron... Gal 2, 11-14: VigChr supp. 21, Leiden 1994, Brill. − ᴿEstAg 29 (1994) 395s (P. de *Luis*).

14201 *a) Horbury* W.,   Jews and Christians on the Bible; demarcation and convergence; − *b) Hennings* R., Rabbinisches und Antijüdisches bei Hieronymus Ep. 121,10: ᴱOort J. van, *Wickert* U., Christliche Exegese zwischen Nicaea und Chalcedon. Kampen 1992, Kok Pharos. (226 p.) ...

14201* *Horn* Jürgen,   Tria sunt in Aegypto genera monachorum; die ägyptischen Bezeichnungen für die 'dritte Art' des Mönchtums bei Hieronymus und Johannes CASSIANUS: → 137, ᶠWESTENDORF W. 1994, 63-82.

14202 **Lardet** Pierre,   L'apologie de Jérôme contre RUFIN, un commentaire 1993 → 9,16033: ᴿBLitEc 95 (1994) 339s (H. *Crouzel*).

14203 *Milazzo* Vincenza,   L'utilizzazione della Scrittura nell''Adversus Helvidium' di Gerolamo; tra grammatica ed esegesi biblica: Orpheus 15 (1994) 21-45.

14204 **Moreschini** Claudio,   Hieronymus, Dialogus adversus Pelagianos: Opera 3/2, CChL 80, 1990 → 7,g254 ... 9,16036: ᴿOrpheus 14 (1993) 158-160 (B. *Clausi*).

14205 *Oppel* John,   Saint Jerome and the history of sex: Viator 24 (1993) 1-22.

14206 **Petersen-Szemerédy** Grier,   Zwischen Weltstadt und Wüste; römische Asketinnen [...(Hieron.) Ep. 46]...: ForKDg 54. Gö 1993, Vandenhoeck & R. 240 p. − ᴿVigChr 48 (1994) 413s (G. J. M. *Bartelink*).

14207 **Rebenich** S.,   Hieronymus und sein Kreis 1992 → 9,16040: ᴿAthenaeum 82 (1994) 602-4 (A. *Marcona*); HZ 259 (1994) 460s (H. R. *Seeliger*); Klio 75 (1993) 521s (H. *Leppin*); RechSR 82 (1994) 263-5 (Y.-M. *Duval*, aussi sur LARDET P., BROWN D.).

14208 **Scourfield** J. H. D.,   Consoling Heliodorus... Jerome letter 60, 1993 → 9,16043: ᴿClasR 44 (1994) 61s (R. P. H. *Green*); ClasW 88 (1994s) 65s (P. B. *Harvey*); JRS 84 (1994) 295s (Jo-Marie *Claassen*); Latomus 53 (1944) 679 (G. J. M. *Bartelink*).

14209 **Serrato** Garrido M., Ascetismo femenino en Roma; estudios sobre San Jerónimo y San AGUSTÍN. Cadiz 1993, Univ. 148 p. 84-7286-128-5. − ᴿJRS 84 (1994) 276s (Veronica *Grimm*).

14210 ᶠᴱ**Valero** Juan B., S. Jerónimo, Epistolario, bilingüe: BAC 530. M 1993, Católica [Stromata 50 (1994) 144]. xxiv-910 p. − ᴿCompostellanum 38 (1993) 249s (E. *Romero Pose*); ComSev 27 (1994) 101 (M. *Sánchez*: al lugar de BAC 1962, RUIZ BUENO D.); EstAg 29 (1994) 394s (S. *González*); TEspir 38 (1994) 517s (A. *Velasco*).

14211 **Valgimogli** Lorenzo, Ricezione teorica e pratica della Bibbia ebraica

presso i Padri della Chiesa, Gerolamo ed EUSEBIO di Emesa: diss. ᴰZ-
atelli I. Firenze 1994, Univ. – RivB 43/1, 307.

Y2.6   Patres Latini in ordine alphabetico.

14211* **Canali** Luca, Ritratti dei Padri latini; sedici scrittori latini e cristiani:
BtTContemporanea 3. Pordenone 1993, Studio Tesi. [iv-] 175 p.   88-
7692-421-3.

14212 **Contreras** E., Peña R.,   El contexto histórico eclesial de los Padres latinos, siglos IV-V, 1993 ➤ 9,16048:   ᴿRÉAug 40 (1994) 224s (M.
Poirier).

14212* **Contreras** E., Peña R.,   Introducción al estudio de los Padres Latinos
de Nicea a Calcedonia, siglos IV y V.   Azul 1994, Trapense. xx-766 p. –
ᴿSalmanticensis 41 (1994) 453-5 (R. Trevijano).

14213 Dekkers E., Les Pères grecs et latins dans les florilèges patristiques
latins: ➤ 70, ᶠLAGA C., Philohistôr 1994, 569-576 [RHE 90,36*].

14214 ᴱOdahl Charles,   Early Christian Latin literature; readings from the
ancient texts.   Ch 1993, Ares. vi-209 p. $30. – ᴿClasO 72 (1994s) 107 (H.
Pohlsander).

14214* **Ulrich** Jörg,   Die Anfänge der abendländischen Rezeption des Ni-
zänums [< Diss. Erlangen 1993, ᴰBrennecke H.]: PatrTSt 39. B 1994,
de Gruyter.   x-327 p.   3-11-014405-0 [TLZ 120,453; RHE 90,114, J.
Doignon].

14215 AMBROSIASTER: Heggelbacher Othmar,   Beziehungen zwischen Ambrosiaster und MAXIMUS von Turin?   Eine Gegenüberstellung: FrSZ 41
(1994) 5-44.

14215* Perrone Lorenzo,   Echi della polemica pagana sulla Bibbia negli scritti
esegetici ... Ambrosiaster: AnStoEseg 11 (1994) 161-185; Eng. 5.

14216 AMBROSIUS: **Jacob** Christoph,   'Arkandisziplin', Allegorese, Mysta-
gogie; ein neuer Zugang zur Theologie des Ambrosius von Mailand:
Athenäum 1990 ➤ 6,k314 ... 8,k932: DM 98.   3-445-09129-3. – ᴿChH 63
(1994) 433s (J. F. Kelly); TLZ 119 (1994) 250-2 (A. M. Ritter).

14216* Jacob Christoph, Ambrosius von Mailand: ➤ 510, LTK³ 1 (1993) 495-7.

14217 **Becker** Maria,   Die Kardinaltugenden bei CICERO und Ambrosius:
Chresis 4 [➤ 13913*]. Ba 1994, Schwabe.   298 p.; Bibliog. 277-288.   3-
7965-0953-3.

14217* **McLynn** Neil B., Ambrose of Milan; Church and court in a Christian
capital: TransfClasHer 22. Berkeley 1994, Univ. California. xxiv-486 p.;
bibliog. 379-395.   0-520-08461-6.

14218 Maier Harry O.,   Private space as the social content of Arianism in
Ambrose's Milan: JTS 45 (1994) 72-93.

14219 **Oberhelman** Stephen M.,   Rhetoric and homiletics 1991 ➤ 8,k935;
9,16052:   ᴿClasW 88 (1994s) 132 (R. P. H. Greenfield).

14219* Rosen Klaus,   Fides contra dissimulationem; Ambrosius und Symmachus in Kampf um den Victoriaaltar: JbAC 37 (1994) 29-36.

14220 ᵀᴱFontaine Jacques, Ambroise, Hymnes 1992 ➤ 8,k931; 9,16050:   ᴿJb-
AC 37 (1994) 198-200 (E. Dassmann); Latomus 53 (1994) 859-865 (G.
Sanders †); RBgPg 72 (1994) 159-161 (J. Schamp); RivStoLR 30 (1994)
609-611 (M. Simonetti); VigChr 48 (1994) 157-169 (A. Bastiaensen).

14221 ᵀᴱBanterle Gabriele, al., Ambrogio, Opere 22: inni, iscrizioni, opere
poetiche e frammenti. Mi 1994, BtAmbros. 274 p. 88-311-9175-6.

14221* CAESARIUS A. [502-542]: **Klingshorn** William E.,   Caesarius of Arles;

the making of a Christian community in late antique Gaul: StMdvLife.
C 1994, Univ.   xix-317 p. $60.   0-521-43095-X [TDig 42,73].
14222 ᵀᴱKlingshorn W. E.,   Caesarius of Arles; life, testament, letters: Translated Texts for Historians 19.   Liverpool 1994, Univ.   ix-155 p.; maps.
$16.   0-85323-368-3 [RelStR 21,328, W. G. *Rush*].
14222* CASSIANUS: **Summa** Gerd, Geistliche Unterscheidung bei Johannes
Cassian: StSysSpT 7. Wü 1992, Echter. xi-266 p. DM 34 [TR 91,230, M.
Albert].
14223 CASSIODORUS: *Kennell* Stefanie A. H., Hercules' invisible basilica (Cassiodorus, Variae I,6): Latomus 53 (1994) 159-175.

14224 CYPRIANUS C.:   **Drążek** Darius, ❾ *Pojęcie*... La notion de 'discipline'
dans les écrits de saint Cyprien: diss. ᴰ*Drączkowski* F.   Lublin 1994.
199 p. – RTLv 26, p. 541.
14225 ᵀᴱPlazanet-Siaret N., *Mazières* J.-P.,   Trois vies, Cyprien, AMBROISE,
AUGUSTIN, par trois témoins [Pontus, Paulin, Possidius]: Les Pères dans
la foi 56.   P 1994, Migne.   197 p. F 90. – ᴿÉtudes 381 (1994) 282s (M.
Fédou).
14226 **Seagraves** Richard,   Pascentes cum disciplina; a lexical study of the
clergy in the Cyprianic correspondence: Paradosis.   FrS 1993, Univ.
xii-344. Fs 66 [TS 56,360, R. R. *Noll*].
14227 ᵀᴱBurini Clara,   Pseudo-Cipriano, I due monti, Sinai e Sion; De
duobus montibus: BiblPatr 25. Fiesole 1994, Nardini.   330 p.   88-404-
2027-4.

14228 GREGORIUS M.: **Astell** Ann W.,   Job, BOETHIUS, [GREGORY] and epic
truth.   Ithaca 1994, Cornell.   xx-240 p. $34. 0-8014-291-0. – ᴿChrLit 43
(1993s) 231s (J. F. *Cotter*).
14229 *a*) *Baltrusch* E.,   Gregor der Grosse und sein Verhältnis zum römischen
Recht am Beispiel seiner Politik gegenüber den Juden; – *b*) *Girardet* Klaus
M.,   Gericht über den Bischof von Rom; ein Problem der kirchlichen und
der staatlichen Justiz in der Spätantke (4.-6. Jht.): HZ 259 (1994) 39-58 /
1-38.
14230 **Marcus** R. A.,   The end of ancient Christianity 1990 ➤ 6,g379...9,
16074: ᴿCiuD 206 (1993) 927s (J. *Gutiérrez*); ConcordTQ 58 (1994) 212-4
(C. R. *Hogg*).
14231 **Motta** Carlo,   La 'lectio divina' in S. Gregorio Magno; presupposti,
pratica e apporti esistenziali: diss. Pont. Univ. Gregoriana, ᴰ*Padovese* L.
Roma 1994. 420 p. – RTLv 26, p. 541.
14231* ᵀᴱParonetto Vera, Gregorio Magno,   Lettere.   R 1992, Studium.
258 p. Lᵐ 26. – ᴿCC 145 (1994,2) 514 (G. *Cremascoli*).
14232 **Schulte** Wolfgang,   Die althochdeutsche Glossierung der Dialoge Gregors des Grossen: StAltHD 22.   Gö 1993, Vandenhoeck & R.   1013 p. –
ᴿBeitNam 29s (1994s) 301-3 (A. *Masser*).

14233 HILARIUS P., ᵀᴱLongobardo Luigi, Ilario di Poitiers, Sinodi e fede
degli Orientali: TestPatr 105. R 1993, Città Nuova. 125 p. Lᵐ 12.   88-
311-3106-2.
14234 HIPPOLYTUS: **Mansfeld** Jaap, Heresiography ...Hippolytus 1992 ➤ 8,
k958; 9,16079:   ᴿAntClas 63 (1994) 448s (B. *Colin*); ClasR 44 (1994)
307-9 (S. *Leggatt*); VigChr 48 (1994) 307-9 (J. *Dillon*).
14235 *Osborne* Catherine,   Sources of significance in Hippolytus' account of
Greek philosophy: Apeiron 27 (1994) 225-242.

14236 Lactantius: *Digeser* Elizabeth D., Lactantius and Constantine's letter to Arles; dating the Divine Institutes: JEarlyC 2 (1994) 33-52.

14237 *Rambaux* Claude, Christianisme et paganisme dans le livre I des Institutions divines de Lactance: RÉLat 72 (1994) 159-176.

14238 Salvianus M.: ᵀᴱCola Silvano, Salviano de Marsiglia, Il Governo di Dio: TestPatr 114. R 1994, Città Nuova. 258 p. 88-311-3114-1.

14239 Vincentius L.: *Guarino* Thomas, Vincent of Lerins and the hermeneutical question: Gregorianum 75 (1994) 491-523; franç. 524: 'en vue des défis de... Heidegger, Gadamer'.

Y2.8 Documenta orientalia.

14240 **Albert** Micheline, *al.*, Christianismes orientaux... langues, littératures 1993 → 9,16090: ᴿJTS 45 (1994) 755-7 (S. *Brock*).

14241 **Beggiani** Seely, Introduction to Eastern Christian spirituality; the Syriac tradition 1991 → 8,k972: ᴿRelStR 20 (1994) 234 (Susan A. *Harvey*: 'London').

14242 **Brock** Sebastian, Studies in Syriac Christianity [1. 1984; 2] CS 357, 1992 → 8,218: ᴿBSO 57 (1994) 460s (R. P. R. *Murray*).

14242* **Browne** Gerald M., The Old Nubian Miracle of Saint Menas: BeitSud 7. W 1994, Univ. Inst. Afrikanistik. iii-108 p.; 18 pl. [OIAc 11,16]. – *b*) Ad Ps.-Chrys. in Raphaelem II (Eng.): Orientalia 63 (1994) 93-97.

14243 **Cuming** Geoffrey J. †, The liturgy of St Mark edited from the manuscripts with a commentary: OrChrAn 234. R 1990, Pont. Inst. Or. xliii-155 p. – ᴿMaisD 194 (1993) 138s (I. H. *Dalmais*); OrChrPer 60 (1994) 292-8 (H. *Quecke*).

14243* *Fiey* Jean-Maurice, Une page oubliée de l'histoire des églises syriaques à la fin du XVᵉ - début du XVIᵉ siècle: Muséon 107 (1994) 123.

14244 *Gaudemet* Jean, La sauvegarde de la foi chrétienne (doctrine et législation du IIIème au VIème siècle): Islamochristiana 20 (1994) 29-40; Eng. 40.

14244* **Hausherr** Irénée, Spiritual direction in the early Christian East [OrChrAnal 144, 1955], ᵀ*Gythiel* Anthony P. 1990 → 6,8206: ᴿRelStR 20 (1994) 154 (M. *Foat*).

14245 **Junod** Éric, Les sages du désert 1991 → 9,16100: ᴿRTPhil 126 (1994) 76s (Françoise *Morard*).

14246 **Kannookadan** Paul, The East Syrian lectionary 1991 → 8,k980; 9,16101: ᴿHeythropJ 35 (1994) 330s (S. *Brock*); MaisD 194 (1993) 155s (I.-H. *Dalmais*).

14246* ᵀᴱ**Kropp** Manfred, Der siegreiche Feldzug des Königs 'Amda-Seyon gegen die Muslime in Adal im Jahre 1332 n.Chr.: CSCOr 538s aeth. 99s. Lv 1994, Peeters.

14247 *Naguib* Saphinaz-Amal, The martyr as witness; Coptic and Copto-Arabic hagiographies as mediators of religious memory: Numen 41 (1994) 223-254.

14247* **Roey** Albert Van, *Allen* Pauline, Monophysite texts of the sixth century: OrLovAnal 56. Lv 1994, Univ./Fathers. xv-317 p. 90-6831-539-0 [OIAc 11,44].

14248 Addai: **Gelston** A., The Eucharistic prayer of Addai and Mari 1992 → 8,k985: ᴿCritRR 6 (1993) 369s (B. M. *Metzger*); HeythJ 35 (1994) 78s (B. D. *Spinks*); Speculum 69 (1994) 777-9 (G. W. *Woolfenden*).

14249 ANTONIUS: *Brakke* David, The Greek and Syriac versions of the Life of Antony: Muséon 107 (1994) 29-53.
14250 APHRAATES: **Bruns** Peter, *a*) Aphrahat, Demonstrationes: FontesC 5, 1991 ➤ 7,g315... 9,16107: ᴿTPQ 142 (1994) 418s (M. *Hutter*); TR 90 (1994) 43s (Corrie *Molenberg*); ZKG 105 (1994) 113-5 (R. *Hanig*). – *b*) Das Christusbild Aphrahats ᴰ1990 ➤ 6,k181; 7,g316: ᴿNumen 41 (1994) 102-4 (H. J. W. *Drijvers*); VigChr 48 (1994) 89-92 (L. van *Rompay*).
14250* *Afinogenov* D. Ye., ⑧ The covenant and the kingdom (historiosophy of Afraat): VDI 210 (1994) 176-186; Eng. 187
14251 **Koltun** Naomi, [Aphrahat] Jewish-Christian polemics in fourth-century Persian Mesopotamia; a reconstructed conversation: diss. Stanford 1994, ᴰ*Zipperstein* S. 192 p. 94-14598. – DissA 55 (1994s) p. 4550.
14251* ᵀᴱ**Pierre** Marie-Joseph, Aphraate, Exposés Is (1-10): SChr 349. 359, 1988s ➤ 4,b935... 8,k988: ᴿBijdragen 55 (1994) 88s (G. *Rouwhorst*, 1); JTS 45 (1994) 322-6 (R. P. R. *Murray*).
14252 APOPHTHEGMATA: *Quecke* Hans, Zum koptischen Text des Apophthegmas sy.gr. X 47: ➤ 65, ᶠKASSER R., Coptology 1994, 363-9.
14252* BARDESANES: **Teixidor** J., Bardesane 1992 ➤ 8,k989: ᴿJbAC 37 (1994) 204-7 (A. *Böhlig*); RHR 211 (1994) 357s (Françoise *Briquel-Chatonnet*).
14253 BARHEBRAEUS: *Teule* Herman G. B., Barhebraeus' Ethicon, al-GHAZÂLI and IBN SINÂ: Islamochristiana 18 (1992) 73-85; franç. 84s.
14253* DEMETRIUS A.: **Madras** Krzysztof, Omelia copta attribuita a Demetrio di Antiochia sul Natale e Maria Vergine. R 1994, Unione Accademica Naz., CorpCopt. 241 p. 88-85354-04-1.
14254 ELIAS N.: *Samir Khalil Samir*, Langue arabe, logique et théologie chez Élie de Nisibe: MUSJ 52 (Beyrouth 1991s) 229-367.
14254* EPHRAIM: *a*) *Koonammakkal* Thomas, St. Ephrem and 'Greek wisdom'; – *b*) *Watt* John W., The philosopher-king in the 'Rhetoric' of Antony of Tagrit: ➤ 450c, Syriacum 6 (1992/4) 169-176 / 245-258.
14255 GREGORIUS NAZ.: *Sirinian* Anna, La versione armena dell'Orazione 7 di Gregorio di Nazianzo: Muséon 107 (1994) 55-106 (Armenian text and apparatus).
14255* ISAAC Jacques, Taksa d'ḥussayā, le rite de pardon: OrChrAnal 233, 1989 ➤ 5,g904... 7,g308: ᴿMaisD 194 (1993) 139s (I. H. *Dalmais*); TR 90 (1994) 462-4 (G. *Winkler*).
14256 JOHANNES D.: *Beulay* Robert, L'enseignement spirituel de Jean de Dalyatha 1990 ➤ 6,k403... 9,16119: ᴿÉglT 25 (1994) 438-440 (L. *Laberge*); RHE 99 (1994) 267s (J. *Hatem*); RTPhil 126 (1994) 78 (J. *Borel*).
14256* JOHANNES E.: **Harvey** Susan A., Asceticism and society in crisis; John of Ephesus and the lives of the eastern saints. Berkeley 1990, Univ. California. xvi-226 p. 0-520-06523-9 [OIAc 11,25].
14257 JOHANNES S.: ᵀᴱ**Martikainen** Jouko, Johannes I Sedra, Syrische Texte: GöOrF 1/34, Wsb 1991, x-292 p. DM 88. 3-447-03114-X. – ᴿBO 51 (1994) 614-6 (Heleen *Murre-Van den Berg*); CritRR 5 (1992) 325-7 (J. *Meyendorff*); JTS 45 (1994) 364-8 (S. *Brock*).
14257* JOHANNES III: *Youssef* Y. Nessim, Des allusions polémiques [coptes] du pape Jean III: AulaO 12 (1994) 128-131.
14258* KORIWM: ᵀᴱ**Winkler** Gabriele, Koriwms Biographie des Mesrop Maštoc'; OrChrAnal 245. R 1994, Pont. Inst. Orientalium Studiorum. 452 p.; Bibliog. 10-43. 88-7210-298-7.
14259 MAXIMUS T.: ᴱ**Trapp** Michael B., Maximus Tyrius, Declarationes. Lp 1994, Teubner. lxxii-377 p. 3-8154-1535-7.

14259* PAULUS A.: ᴱKhoury Paul, Paul d'Antioche, Traités théologiques: Corpus Islamo-Christianum 1. Wü/Altenberge 1994, Echter/Oros. 345 p. DM 90. 3-429-01593-6 / 3-89375-088-6 [TLZ 120,317, W. *Kinzig*].
14260 PETRUS A.: **Pearson** Birger, *Vivian* Tom, Two Coptic homilies attributed to Saint Peter of Alexandria; on riches, on the Epiphany. R 1993, Unione Accad., Corpus copt. 176 p.; 2 pl. 88-85354-01-7 [OIAc 11,36].
14260* PETRUS C.: *Roey* Albert Van, Un florilège trinitaire syriaque tiré du Contra Damianum de Pierre de Callinique, patriarche d'Antioche (581-591): OrLovPer 23 (1992) 189-203.
14261 SEVERUS: ᴱ**Bischoff** Bernhard, *Schetter* Willy, Severi episcopi 'Malacitani (?)' in evangelia libri XII; das Trierer Fragment der Bücher VIII-X: Abh ph/h 109. Mü 1994, Bayrische Akad. 219 p.; ill. 3-7696-0104-1.
14262 SHENUTE: *Foat* M. E., Shenute, discourse in the presence of Eraklammon: OrChrPer 24 (1993) 113-131.
14263 *Morard* F., La légende copte de Simon et Théonoé: LORA 4 (1993) 139-183 [toponyme Siflâq/Aḥmim), *Roquet* Gérard 185-9].
14263* **Young** Dwight W., Coptic manuscripts from the White Monastery; works of Shenute: MittPapRainer 22. W 1993, Hollinek. 199 p.; vol. of 66 pl. 3-85119-254-0.

Y3 **Medium aevum**, generalia.

14264 ᴱ**Affeldt** Werner, Frauen in Spätantike 1987/90 ➤ 6,715...9,16131: ᴿEngHR 109 (1994) 683 (Miri *Rubin*).
14265 ᴱ**Altenburg** Detlef, *al.*, Feste und Feiern im Mittelalter [Symposium Paderborn]. Ha 1991, Thorbecke. 551 p. 13 fig. + 7 color. 3-7995-5402-5. – ᴿEngHR 109 (1994) 1250s (F. R. H. *Du Boulay*: good).
14266 *Andonegui* Javier, Filosofía y teología; inversión de sus relaciones en el paso del medioevo a la modernidad: LumenVr 42 (1993) 201-219.
14267 **Angenendt** Arnold, Das Frühmittelalter; die abendländische Christenheit von 400 bis 900: 1990 ➤ 7,g340; 8,m5: ᴿZKG 105 (1994) 116s (Claudia *Märtl*).
14267* **Arnaldez** Roger, À la croisée des trois monothéismes; une communauté de pensée au Moyen-Âge. P 1993, A. Michel. 447 p. – ᴿIslamochristiana 20 (1994) 296 (M. *Lagarde*).
14268 **Baldwin** John W., The language of sex; five voices from northern France around 1200. Ch 1994, Univ. xxviii-332 p. $37.50 [TS 56,366, E. C. *Vacek*).
14269 **Bañeza Román** Celso, Las fuentes bíblicas, patrísticas y judaicas del libro [clásico medieval] de Alexandre. Las Palmas 1994. 235 p.; bibliog. 187-221. pt 2800.
14270 **Banning** Josef H. A. van, 'Buchstabe und Geist', zur Rezeption des 'Opus imperfectum in Matthaeum' im Mittelalter: Hab.-Diss. ᴰ*Bauer*. Innsbruck 1994. – TR 91,90.
14271 **Baumann** Karin, Aberglaube für Laien; zur Programmatik und Überlieferung mittelalterlicher Superstitionskritik 2: Quellen und Forschungen zur Europäischen Ethnologie 6/2. Wü 1989, Königshausen & N. xiv + p. 483-904. 3-88479-399-3. – ᴿSalesianum 56 (1994) 793 (P. T. *Stella*).
14272 ᴱ**Biller** P., *Hudson* A., Heresy and literacy: StMdvLit 23. C 1994, Univ. xxv-313 p.; 10 fig. [RHE 89,269*].

14273 **Bischoff** Bernhard † 1991, Manuscripts and libraries in the age of Charlemagne: StPalaeog 1. C 1994, Univ. xvii-193 p. 0-521-38346-3.

14273* **Bischoff** Bernhard, *Lapidge* Michael, Biblical commentaries from the Canterbury school of Theodore and Hadrian: StAngSax 10. C 1994, Univ. xiv-612 p. bibliog. 572-587. 0-521-33089-0 [TDig 42,356].

14274 *Blaauw* Sible De, Architecture and liturgy in late antiquity and the Middle Ages: ArLtgW 33 (1991) 1-34.

14274* **Borgolte** Michael, Die mittelalterliche Kirche: EnzDtG 17. Mü 1992, Oldenbourg. viii-159 p. DM 94, pa. 64 [TR 91,325, H. *Lutterbach*].

14275 **Boswell** John, Same-sex unions in pre-modern Europe. Villard. 412 p. $25. – [R]FirsT 47 (1994) 43-48 (R. D. *Young*).

14276 **Boureau** Alain, L'événement sans fin; récit et christianisme au Moyen Âge: Histoire. P 1993, BLettres. 392 p. F 140. 2-251-38021-3.

[E]**Brady** Thomas A., *Oberman* Heiko A., *Tracy* James D., Handbook of European history 1400-1600; 1994 ➤ 14451.

14277 *Bratu* Anca, Du pain pour les âmes du Purgatoire, à propos de quelques images de la fin du Moyen Âge: Revue Mabillon 65 (1993) 177-213 [< TR 91,78].

14278 **Bredero** Adriaan H., Christendom and Christianity in the Middle Ages [²1986], [T]*Brandsma* Reinder. GR 1994, Eerdmans. xiii-402 p. $30 [RelStR 21,140, T. F. X. *Noble*: really about *Christians* in the Middle Ages].

14279 **Buc** Philippe, L'ambiguité du livre; prince, pouvoir et peuple dans les commentaires de la Bible au Moyen Âge [1100-1350; < diss.]: THist 95. P 1994, Beauchesne. 427 p. F 85. – [R]EsprVie 104 (1994) 552-4 (P. *Ourliac*); QVidCr 174 (1994) 120 (D. *Roure*); SR 23 (1994) 515 (J.-J. *Lavoie*: excellent).

14280 **Burton** Janet, Monastic and religious orders in Britain 1000-1300: Medieval Textbooks. C 1994, Univ. xi-354 p. $70; pa. $19. 0-521-37441-3; -797-8 [TDig 42,260; TS 56,364, J. F. *Kelly*].

14281 **Bynum** Caroline W., Fragmentation and redemption; essays on gender and the human body in medieval religion 1991 ➤ 9,16150: [R]CritRR 6 (1993) 551-3 (Sharon *Elkins*).

14282 **Bynum** Caroline, Jeûnes et festins sacrés; la femme et la nourriture dans la spiritualité médiévale [Holy feast and holy fast 1987]. P 1994, Cerf. 449 p. – [R]RHist 292 (1994) 170-3 (M. *Pacaut*).

14283 *Cahill* P. Joseph, Celtic Christianity, a different drum: RelStT 12,1 (1992) 9-23.

14283* *Cantor* Norman, The civilization of the Middle Ages. NY 1993, HarperCollins. 604 p. – [R]PhilipSac 29 (1994) 180-3 (N. *Castillo*).

14284 **Carroll** Warren H., The glory of Christendom: History 3. Front Royal VA 1993, Christendom. [1. 1985; 2. 1987]; 3. 1100-1517. 774 p. $30; pa. $20. 0-931888-55-7; -4-9 [TDig 42,60].

14285 **Carruthers** Mary J., The book of memory; a study of memory in medieval culture 1990 ➤ 9,16152: [R]EngHR 109 (1994) 689s (Alison *Peden*: challenges the assumption that memory is undervalued as orality gives place to literacy); JIntdis 23 (1992s) 310-321 (P. J. *Geary*).

14286 [E]**Catto** J. I., *Evans* Ralph, Late Medieval Oxford: History of the University of Oxford 2. Ox 1992, Clarendon. lxxiv-823 p. £90. – [R]EngHR 109 (1994) 663s (N. *Orme*).

14287 **Ceccaroni** S., Il culto di S. Michele Arcangelo nella religiosità medievale del territorio spoletino: Spoletium quad. 6. Spoleto 1993, Accad. x-104 p. – [R]VetChr 31 (1994) 235-240 (A. E. *Felle*); p. 315-333-355, due art. sul culto di S. Michele.

14288 **Chélini** Jean, L'aube du Moyen Âge; naissance de la chrétienté occidentale; la vie religieuse des laïcs dans l'Europe carolingienne, 750-900: 1991 ➤ 9,16153; F 350: ᴿEngHR 109 (1994) 986s (Rosamund *McKitterick*: a book completed and available in typescript since 1974).

14289 **Chevalier** Jacques, Histoire de la pensée 3. De s. Augustin à s. Thomas; 4. de Duns Scot à Suárez. P 1992, Éd. Universitaires. 354 p.; 304 p. 2-7113-0499-X / -0500-7. – ᴿÉTRel 68 (1993) 110 (H. *Rost*: réédition).

14290 **Cobhan** Alan B., The medieval English universities Oxford and Cambridge to c. 1500: 1988 ➤ 5,g949: ᴿRHist 290 (1993) 661s (J. *Verger*).

14291 *a*) *Coleman* R. G., Vulgar Latin and proto-Romance; minding the gap; – *b*) *Kirkness* A. C., Logology; aspects of the lexicographical description of Euroclassical word-formation items: Prudentia 25,2 (Auckland July 1993 'Language growth and transition', 1993) 1-14 / 15-28.

14292 *a*) *Constable* Giles, The language of preaching in the twelfth century; – *b*) *Emery* Kentᴶ, DENYS the Carthusian and the invention of preaching materials: Viator 25 (1994) 131-152 / 377-409.

14293 **Cramer** Peter, Baptism and change in the early Middle Ages 1993 ➤ 9,16157: ᴿJTS 45 (1994) 747-9 (E. J. *Yarnold*).

14294 ᴱ**Dagron** G., Évêques, moines et empereurs (610-1054), ᵀBoshof Egon: [ᴱ**Mayeur** J., ᵀBrox N.], HistChr 4, 1993 [ByZ 88, 463-5, G. *Podskalsky*; NRT 117, 276-7, N. *Plumat*]. – ᴿTPhil 69 (1994) 590-2 (K. *Schatz*).

14295 **Dahan** Gilbert, Les intellectuels chrétiens et les Juifs au moyen âge 1990 ➤ 6,k430 ... 9,16159: ᴿAJS 17 (1992) 305-8 (R. *Chazan*).

14296 **Davidson** Linda K., *Dunn-Wood* Maryjane, Pilgrimage to the Middle Ages, a research guide: MedvBbg 16. NY 1993, Garland. xiv-480 p.: ᴿMedvHum 21 (1994) 177s (C. K. *Zacher*).

14297 **Deane** A. N., *Pasternak* Carol B., Vox intexta; orality and textuality in the Middle Ages. Madison 1991, Univ. Wisconsin. xiv-289 p. – ᴿMedvHum 20 (1994) 216s (J. M. *Dean*).

14298 *Del Zotto Tozzoli* Carla, La predicazione in volgare nell'Inghilterra anglosassone e normanna; Aelfric e Orm [autore del poema Ormulum 1200]: Antonianum 69 (1994) 34-68; Eng. 34.

14298* **Dörfler-Dierken** Angelika, Die Verehrung der heiligen Anna in Spätmittelalter und früher Neuzeit: ForKDg 50. Gö 1992, VR. 387 p. DM 108 [TLZ 120, 346, H.-P. *Hasse*].

14299 *a*) *Evans* G. R., Exegesis and authority in the thirteenth century; – *b*) *Bataillon* L.-J., Early scholastic and mendicant preaching as exegesis of Scripture: ➤ 8,475*a*, Ad litteram 1992 [< Manuscripta].

14300 ᴱ**Fabris** Rinaldo, La Bibbia dell'amore; commentata dai Padri della Chiesa; miniature del XV-XVI secolo: Bellezza e fede. Mi 1994, Paoline. 318 p.

14301 **Flasch** Kurt, Introduction à la philosophie médiévale [Einführung 1982, ²1989: Vestigia], ᵀBourgknecht Janine de: Vestigia 8. FrS/P 1992, Univ./VR. – ᴿETRel 68 (1993) 285s (H. *Bost*); RTPhil 126 (1994) 253-262 (A. *Étienne*: une autre vision).

14302 **Flint** Valerie I. J., The rise of magic in early medieval Europe 1991 ➤ 9,16172: ᴿHeythJ 35 (1994) 91s (C. *Burnett*); JRelH 18 (1994) 103-5 (Hilary M. *Carey*).

14303 ᴱ**Fontaine** Jacques, *Hillgarth* N., The seventh century; change and continuity [Warburg colloquium 8-9 July 1988]: Studies 42. L 1992, Warburg Inst. xxi-288 p. £45. – ᴿSpeculum 69 (1994) 1305s (tit. pp.).

14304 **Gandillac** Maurice de, Genèses de la modernité. P 1992, Cerf. 675 p.
— ᴿScEspr 46 (1994) 365-7 (R. *Toupin*).

14305 **Gilbert** Paul P., Introducción a la teología medieval [1992 ⇥ 9,16176],
ᵀ*Ortiz-García* Alfonso. Estella 1993, VDivino. 196 p. — ᴿCarthaginensia
10 (1994) 460 (F. *Chavero Blanco*); LumenVr 43 (1994) 166s (U. *Gil
Ortega*).

14306 *Gilbert* Paul, La ragione teologica nel secolo XIII; a proposito di
figure medievali della teologia: TItSett 19 (1993) 187-208.

14307 *Greatrex* Joan, The English cathedral priories and the pursuit of
learning in the Late Middle Ages: JEH 45 (1994) 396-411.

14308 ᴱ**Härdelin** Alf, In quest of the kingdom; ten papers on medieval
spirituality, ᵀ*Searby* Denis. Sto 1991, Almqvist & W. 284 p. — ᴿChH 63
(1994) 439s (K. J. *Egan*).

14309 **Hage** W., Das Christentum im frühen Mittelalter (476-1054); vom
Ende des weströmischen Reiches bis zum West-östlichen Schisma: Zu-
gängeKG 4. Gö 1993, Vandenhoeck & R. 192 p. ᴅᴍ 24,80. 3-525-
33590-3 [TR 91,324, H. *Lutterbach*]. — ᴿTvT 34 (1994) J. van *Laarhoven*).

14309* **Harmening** Dieter, Zauberei im Abendland; Vom Anteil der Gelehrten
am Wahn der Leute: QuelForEurEthn 10. Wü 1991, Königshausen & N.
141 p.; 3 fig. ᴅᴍ 29,80 [TR 91,323].

14310 **Harvey** Margaret, England, Rome and the papacy, 1417-1464; the
study of a relationship. Manchester 1993, Univ. viii-295 p. £40. 0-
7190-3459-0 [TDig 42,168]: ᴿJEH 45 (1994) 346-8 (R. B. *Dobson*).

14311 **Horowitz** Jeanine, *Menache* Sophia, L'humour en chaire; le rire dans
l'Église médiévale; Histoire et société 28. Genève 1994, Labor et fides.
288 p. F 150. 2-8309-0734-5. — ᴿÉTRel 69 (1994) 585s (Dominique *Viaux*).

14312 ᴱ**Humphreys** K. W., The friars' libraries; British Academy Corpus of
British medieval library catalogues [first to appear] 1990: ᴿEngHR 109
(1994) 696s (B. C. *Barker-Benfield*).

14313 *Imbach* Ruedi, Notabilia IV; Hinweise auf wichtige Neuerscheinungen aus dem Bereich der Mittelalterlichen Philosophie: FrSZ 41 (1994)
229-251.

14314 **Irvine** Martin, The making of textual culture; grammatical and literary
theory, 350-1100: StMdvLit 19. C 1994, Univ. xix-604 p.; ill.; bibliog.
553-598. 0-521-41447-4.

14315 **Jacobelli** M. C., Il risus paschalis e il fondamento teologico del piacere
sessuale³, 4. Brescia 1991, Queriniana ⇥ 8,8518 (deutsch): ᴿRasT 35
(1994) 114-6 (Cloe *Taddei Ferretti*: atti osceni di officianti alla Messa.

14315* ᴱ**Jedin** Hubert, The medieval and Reformation Church, vol. 4-6
(1962-79) ᵀ*Dolan* John, abridged by *Holland* D. Larrimore. NY 1993,
Crossroad. xviii-1054 p. $50 [RelStR 21,58, D. R. *Janz*).

14316 **Jussen** Bernhard, Patenschaft und Adoption im frühen Mittelalter;
künstliche Verwandtschaft als soziale Praxis: Planck-Gesch. 98. Gö 1991,
Vandenhoeck &R. 342 p. ᴅᴍ 74. — ᴿTR 90 (1994) 223-6 (R. *Kaiser*).

14317 *Kingsley* Peter, The Christian Aʀɪsᴛᴏᴛʟᴇ; theological interpretation
and interpolation in mediaeval versions of 'On the heavens': Muséon 107
(1994) 195.

14317* ᴱ**Klapisch-Zuber** Christiane, A history of women in the west, 2.
Silences of the Middle Ages 1992 ⇥ 8,m28; 9,16195: ᴿJIntdis 25 (1994s)
464s (Judith M. *Bennett*).

14318 **Kleinberg** Aviad M., Prophets in their own country; living saints and
the making of sainthood in the Late Middle Ages. Ch 1992, Univ.
x-189 p. $27.50. — ᴿJRel 74 (1994) 568-570 (M. *Goodich*).

14319 **Körntgen** Ludger,   Studien zu Quellen der frühmittelalterlichen Buss-
bücher: Quellen und Forschungen zum Recht im Mittelalter 7.   Sigmaringen 1993, Thorbecke.   292 p.   DM 98. – ᴿTR 90 (1994) 225s (H.
Lutterbach).
14320 ᴱ(Blumenfeld) **Kosinski** R., *Szell* T.,   Images of sainthood in medieval
Europe [Barnard College 1987]. Ithaca 1991, Cornell Univ.   vi-315 p. –
ᴿRivStoLR 30 (1994) 198-205 (Anna *Benvenuti Papi*).
14321 **Leisch-Kiesl** Monika,   Eva als Andere; eine exemplarische Untersuchung zu Frühchristentum und Mittelalter.   Köln 1992, Böhlau.
xiv-300 p.; ill. DM 64.   3-412-03591-2. – ᴿZkT 116 (1994) 354-6 (Elke
Fahrner).
14322 ᴱ**Leonardi** Claudio,   Il Cristo 5: Testi teologici e spirituali da Riccardo
di San Vittore a Caterina da Siena: Fond. Valle 1992 → 9,16198: ᴿCC
145 (1994,2) 298-300 (A. *Orazzo*).
14323 *Lerner* Robert E.,   Himmelsvision oder Sinnendelirium? Franziskaner
und Professoren als Traumdeuter im Paris des 13. Jahrhunderts: HZ 259
(1994) 337-367; 2 fig.
14324 ᴱ**Lewis** Bernard, *Niewöhner* Friedrich,   Religionsgespräche im Mittelalter [25. Wolfenbütteler Symposion 11.-18. Juni 1989]: MASt 4, 1992
→ 8,475d: ᴿTGL 84 (1994) 365s (Barbara *Hallensleben*); TR 90 (1994)
303-6 (W. A. *Euler*).
14325 **Libera** Alain de,   La philosophie médiévale: Premier cycle. P 1993,
PUF.   528 p. F 149.   2-13-046000-3. – ᴿÉTRel 69 (1994) 297s (H. *Bost*).
14326 *a*) *Lobato* Abelardo,   Filosofía y 'Sacra Doctrina' en la escuela dominicana del s. xiii; – *b*) *Merino* José A.,   Filosofía y teología en la
escuela franciscana medieval; – *c*) *Barbour* Hugh, Tra 'lectio' e 'disputatio'. negli studi monastici del XIII secolo: Angelicum 71 (1994) 3-42 /
43-64 / 65-76.
14327 **Lohrmann** Klaus,   Judenrecht und Judenpolitik im mittelalterlichen
Österreich.   W 1990, Böhlau.   354 p. Sch 620. – ᴿKairos 32s (1990s)
255-8 (K. *Schubert*: '1890').
14328 ᴱ**Lomas** Francisco J., *Devís* Federico,   De Constantino a Carlomagno,
dissidentes, heterodoxos, marginales.   Cadiz 1992, Univ.   253 p.; 2 pl. –
ᴿRÉAnc 96 (1994) 617s (J. *Fontaine*).
14329 **Lynch** Joseph H.,   The medieval Church; a brief history.   L 1993,
Longman.   xiv-335 p. – ᴿTLond 97 (1994) 211s (G. *Huelin*: could have
been the needed replacement of 1930 Margaret DEANESLY if it did not
show such unconcern for England).
14330 ᴱ**McKitterick** Rosamund,   Carolingian culture; emulation and innovation.   C 1994, Univ.   xviii-334 p.; 21 pl. [RHE 90,134, M. *Tylor*, Eng.].
14331 **McLeod** Glenda,   Virtue and venom; catalogs of women from antiquity
to the Renaissance: Women and Culture.   AA 1991, Univ. Michigan.   ix-
168 p. $25. – ᴿSpeculum 69 (1994) 257s (Thelma *Fenster*).
14332 *McNamara* Martin,   Sources and affiliations of the Catechesis celtica
(MS Vat. Reg. lat. 49): SacrEr 34 (1994) 185-237.
14333 *Macy* Gary,   The doctrine of transubstantiation in the Middle Ages:
JEH 45 (1994) 11-41.
14333* *Magnou-Nortier* Élisabeth,   Charlemagne, l'Église franque et l'État:
MélSR 51 (1994) 359-373; Eng. 373.
14334 **Marini** Alfonso,   Storia della Chiesa medievale: Manuali di base 6.
CasM 1991, Piemme.   215 p. [Benedictina 51,586].
14335 *Martin* Dennis D.,   The *via moderna*, humanism, and the hermeneutics
of late medieval monastic life: JHistId 51 (1990) 179-197.

14336 **Massa** Eugenio, L'eremo, la Bibbia e il Medioevo in umanisti veneti del primo cinquecento: Nuovo Medioevo 36. N 1992, Liguori. 406 p. 88-207-1813-8. – ᴿSalesianum 56 (1994) 768s (S. *Felici*).

14337 *Matthews Grieco* Sara F., Finzione o *anima*? [ᴱZᴀʀʀɪ Gabriella, Finzione e santità tra medioevo ed età moderna (Torino 1991, Rosenberg & S.) 570 p.]: RivStoLR 30 (1994) 102-110.

14337* ᴱ**Mayeur** Jean-Marie, *al.*, ᵀᴱ*Brox* Norbert, *al.*, 5, Machtfülle des Papsttums (1054-1274), ᵀᴱ*Engels* Odilo. Fr 1994, Herder. xl-968 p. 3-451-22255-8 [RHE 90, 71-79, J. *Seiler*, aussi sur vol. 4 et 6).

14338 *Merdrignac* B., La vie religieuse française au Moyen Âge: Synthèse/ histoire. P 1994, Ophrys. 326 p. – ᴿRHist 242 (1994) 467s (M. *Pacaut*).

14339 **Milis** Ludo J. B., Angelic monks 1992 ⮕ 8, m63: ᴿTorJT 10 (1994) 278s (Kate P. C. *Galen*).

14340 **Muralt** André de, L'enjeu de la philosophie médiévale; études tho- mistes, scotistes, occamiennes et grégoriennes: StTGgM 24. Leiden 1993, xvi-448 p. – ᴿRTPhil 126 (1994) 243-252 (F.-X. *Putallaz*: pourquoi penser au Moyen âge?).

14341 **Nineham** Dennis, Christianity mediaeval and modern; a study in religious change 1993 ⮕ 9,16216: ᴿHeythJ 35 (1994) 454s (M. J. *Walsh*); JTS 45 (1994) 374-8 (C. *Morris*); TLond 97 (1994) 62-64 (R. A. *Markus*: 'same'? yes? no? a bit baffling; cf. C. *Read* p. 61, N's 'cultural gap grows ever wider').

14342 **Nodes** Daniel J., Doctrine and exegesis in biblical Latin poetry: ᴀʀᴄᴀ 31. Leeds 1993, Cairns. x-147 p. £20. – ᴿClasR 44 (1994) 406s (P. *Burton*); Latomus 53 (1994) 70s (N. *Askin*).

14343 *Olsen* Birger Munk, Chronique des manuscrits classiques latins (IXᵉ- XIIᵉ siècles) II: RHText [I. 21 (1991) 37-76] 24 (1994) 199-249.

14344 *Orme* Nicholas, Children and the Church in medieval England: JEH 45 (1994) 563-587.

14345 **Palazzo** Éric, Le Moyen Âge; des origines au XIIIᵉ siècle: Histoires des Livres Liturgiques. P 1993, Beauchesne. 255 p.; 12 fig. F 180 pa. 2-7010-1280-5. – ᴿJTS 45 (1994) 769s (K. *Stevenson*).

14346 **Parisse** Michel, *a*) Atlas de la France de l'an mil; état de nos connaissances. P 1994, Picard. 130 p.; 36 maps. – *b*) Portrait de la France autour de l'an mil: CahCMédv 37,148 (1994) 325-340 (-346 *Vergneault* Françoise).

14347 **Paxton** Frederick S., Christianizing death; the creation of a ritual process in early medieval Europe 1990 ⮕ 7,8994; 8,9283. m70: ᴿEngHR 109 (1994) 681-3 (Janet L. *Nelson*); RelStR 20 (1994) 202s (C. *Leyser*).

14348 **Payer** Pierre J., The bridling of desire; views of sex in the later Middle Ages. Toronto 1993, Univ. ix-285 p. – ᴿHeythropJ 35 (1994) 331-3 (J. F. *Keenan*).

14349 *Pelland* Gilles, Incidence de l'exégèse sur l'évolution du droit cano- nique durant la première partie du Moyen Âge: Periodica de re canonica 82,1 (R 1993) 9-25.

14350 **Petroff** Elizabeth A., Body and soul; [eleven] essays on medieval women and mysticism. NY 1994, Oxford-UP. xii-235 p. $35; pa. $15. 0- 19-508454-3; -5-1.

14351 **Reynolds** Philip H., Marriage in the Western Church; the Christianiza- tion of marriage during the patristic and early medieval periods: VigChr supp. 24. Leiden 1994, Brill. xxx-434 p.; bibliog. 420-7. 90-04-10022-9.

14351* **Robles Sierra** Adolfo, La predicación dominicana en el contexto me- dieval: ComSev 27 (1994) 187-270.

14352 **Rubin** Miri, Corpus Christi; the Eucharist in late medieval culture 1991
→ 9,16226: ᴿJTS 45 (1994) 386-9 (R. E. *Reynolds*).

14353 *Ruello* Francis, Bulletin d'histoire des idées médiévales: RechSR 82
(1994) 371-416.

14353* **Russell** James C., The Germanization of early medieval Christianity;
a sociohistorical approach to religious transformation. Ox/NY 1994,
UP/St. Peter's College. ix-258 p. $33.50. 0-19-507696-6 [TDig 42,88].

14354 **Russell** Jeffrey B., Dissent and order in the Middle Ages; the search for
legitimate authority: StIntCuHist 3, 1992 → 9,16228: ᴿManuscripta 37
(1993) 93.

14355 ᴱ**Salisbury** Joyce E., Sex in the Middle Ages: RefLibrHum 1360. NY
1991, Garland. xv-258 p. $36. – ᴿSpeculum 69 (1994) 301.

14355* **Sawyer** B. & P., Medieval Scandinavia; from conversion to Reformation, ca. 800-1500: Nordic 17. Mp 1993, Univ. Minnesota. xvi-
265 p. $20 [Speculum 70,420-3, F. *Amory*; RHE 90,67*].

14356 *Schäferdiek* Kurt, Mittelalter: → 517, TRE 23 (1994) 110-121.

14356* **Schmitt** J.-C., Une histoire religieuse du moyen âge est-elle possible?
(Jalons pour une anthropologie historique du christianisme médiéval):
→ 428, Mestiere 1990/4, 73-83.

14357 *Schumacher* J., Breaking the bread of Scripture; on the medieval
interpretation of the Bible: Collegium Medievale 6 (1993) 107-131 [RHE
90,34*].

14357* **Schwarz** Heinz W., Der Schutz des Kindes im Recht des frühen Mittelalters: BonnHistF 56. Siegburg 1993, F. Schmitz. xxxix-237 p. DM 78
[TR 91,31, H. *Lutterbach*].

14358 **Shahar** Shulamith, Childhood in the Middle Ages. L 1990, Routledge.
x-342 p. £35. – ᴿEngHR 109 (1994) 149 (J. *Goody*).

14358* **Siems** Harald, Handel und Wucher im Spiegel frühmittelalterlicher
Rechtsquellen: MonGHist Schriften 35. Hannover 1992, Hahn. cxvi-915 p.
DM 198 [TR 91,484, J. *Eckert*].

14359 **Spencer** H. Leith, English preaching in the late Middle Ages. Ox
1993, Clarendon. xvi-542 p. $72. 0-19-811203-3 [RelStR 21,244, P. S.
Seaver: perceptive; revises OWST G., BLENCH J.].

14360 **Tellenbach** Gerd, The Church in Western Europe from the tenth to
the early twelfth century [1988 → 9,16239], ᵀ*Reuter* Timothy; Medv-
Textbooks. C 1993, Univ. xix-403 p. $80; pa. $23. – ᴿChurchman 108
(1994) 86s (H. *Bowden*); JRel 74 (1994) 568 (I. M. *Resnick*: very fine).

14361 *Tamayo-Acosta* Juan-José, Movimientos proféticos en el siglo XIV;
desafio a la Iglesia y a la sociedad: Carthaginensia 10 (1994) 27-50;
Eng. IV.

14362 **Taylor** Larissa, Soldiers of Christ; preaching in Late Medieval and
Reformation France. Ox 1992, UP. xiv-352 p. $55. – ᴿAmHR 99 (1994)
574 (D. S. *Lesnick*).

14363 *Todisco* Orlando, L'esperienza linguistica medievale; AGOSTINO, AN-
SELMO e BONAVENTURA: Sapienza 7 (1994) 31-50.

14364 *Uña Juárez* Agustín, La modernidad del siglo XIV: CiuD 206 (1993)
703-758.

14365 *Uytfanghe* Marc Van, La Bible et l'instruction des laïcs en Gaule
mérovingienne; des témoignages textuels à une approche langagière de la
question: SacrEr 34 (1994) 67-123.

14366 **Vauchez** André, *Bornstein* Daniel E., The laity in the Middle Ages,
ᵀ*Schneider* Margery 1993 → 9,16245: ᴿCathW 237 (1994) 242-3 (T. J.
Donaghy).

14367 ᴱVauchez André, Apogée et expansion de la chrétienté (1054-1274): Histoire du christianisme 5, 1993 ➤ 9,16243: ᴿRThom 94 (1994) 343s (P.-A. Amargier).

14368 ᴱVerger Jacques, Éducations médiévales: HistÉduc 50 num. spécial. P 1991, INRP. 158 p. F 65. 2-7342-0290-1. – ᴿÉTRel 68 (1993) 111 (D. Viaux).

14369 Weijers Olga, Dictionnaires et répertoires au Moyen Âge; une étude du vocabulaire: CIVICIMA 4. Turnhout 1991, Brepols. 212 p. – ᴿSpeculum 69 (1994) 270s (Marcia L. Colish).

14370 Wieland Georg, Wissenschaft und allgemeiner Nutzen; zur kulturellen Bedeutung der mittelalterlichen und neuzeitlichen Universität: Saeculum 45 (1994) 308-315.

14371 a) Winfried Eberhard, Klerus- und Kirchenkritik in der spätmittelalterlichen deutschen Stadtchronistik; – b) Sarnowsky Jürgen, England und der Kontinent im 12. Jahrhundert: HistJb 114 (1994) 349-380 / 47-75.

14371* ᴱ[Acklin] Zimmermann Beatrice, Dankmodelle von Frauen im Mittelalter: Dokimion 15. FrS 1994, Univ. 208 p. Fs 36. 3-7278-0942-6 [TLZ 120,530, K.-V. Selge].

Y3.4   Exegetae mediaevales [Hebraei ➤ K7].

14372 ABELARDUS: Jolivet Jean, Abélard ou la philosophie dans le langage. P 1994, Cerf. – ᴿEstE 69 (1994) 555s (C. Fernández).

14373 Lemoine Michel, Abélard et les Juifs: RÉJ 153 (1994) 253-267.

14374 AELRED: McGuire Brian P., Brother and lover; Aelred of Rievaulx. NY 1994, Crossroad. xviii-186 p. 0-8245-1405-X [TDig 42.176].

14375 ALBERTUS M.: Entrich Manfred, Die Bergpredigt als Ausbildungsordnung; der katechetische Entwurf einer 'ratio formationis' bei Albert dem Grossen: StSeelsorge 10. Wü 1992, Echter. xxiv-347 p. DM 48 [TR 91,38, H. Ansulewicz].

14376 Lohrum Meinolf, Albert der Grosse, Forscher – Lehrer – Anwalt des Friedens: ToposTb 216. Mainz 1991, Gruenewald. 144 p. DM 9,80 [TR 91,404, H. Ansulewicz].

14377 ALCUIN: Veyrard-Cosme Christiane, Littérature latine du haut Moyen Âge et idéologie politique; l'exemple d'Alcuin: RÉLat 72 (1994) 192-207.

14378 ANDREAS S. V.: Berndt Rainer, André de Saint-Victor [† 1175], exégète et théologien ᴰ1991 ➤ 7,g410; 8,m98: ᴿJTS 45 (1994) 385s (C. Holdsworth); RB 101 (1994) 465s (P. Henne).

14379 ANGELOMO: Cantelli Silvia, Angelomo e la scuola esegetica di Luxeuil: Medioevo Latino Bt. Spoleto 1990, Centro Medioevo. vi-530 p.; xxiv p., 250 pl. – ᴿRHE 99 (1994) 137s (D. Poirel).

14380 ANSELMUS: Corbin Michel, Prière et raison de la foi; ... Anselme 1992 ➤ 8,m101; 9,16247: ᴿRHR 211 (1994) 358s (J. Jolivet).

14380* Meinhardt Helmut, Anselm von Canterbury [... von Laon]: ➤ 510, LTK³ 1 (1993) 711s [713s].

14381 Morscher Edgar, Anselms Gottesbeweis und was Uwe MEIXNER daraus gemacht hat: TPhil 69 (1994) 22-33.

14382 Southern R. W., St Anselm 1990 ➤ 7,g416 ... 9,16249: ᴿLatomus 53 (1994) 198s (J. Meyers); RHR 211 (1994) 482-7 (A. Galonnier); ZKG 105 (1994) 126 (L. Hödl).

14383 AQUINAS: Aersten Jan A., Thomas van Aquino/Utrecht: Bijdragen 55 (1994) 56-71; 71, Thomas Aquinas and the Thomas of Utrecht

[University group hypothesis; the Summa does not begin with an informative doctrine of God, but with an inquiry into the rules, chiefly negative, for speaking about God: this hypothesis is declared to be unfounded].

14383* **Basse** Michael, Certitudo spei; T. von Aquins Begründung der Hoffnungsgewissheit und ihre Rezeption bis zum Konzil von Trient als ein Beitrag zur Verhältnisbestimmung von Eschatologie und Rechtfertigungslehre: ForSysÖk 69. Gö 1993, Vandenhoeck & R. 261 p. 3-525-56276-4 [TLZ 120,271, C. *Schröer*].

14384 **Baumgarth** William R., *Regan* Richard J., T. Aquinas, God and creation [I, 1-23, 25, 44-49, 103-105]. Scranton/Mississauga 1994, Univ./ Asn. Univ. Pr. 310 p. £38. 0-940866-27-7. – RTBR 7,3 (1994s) 35s (A. *McCoy*).

14385 **Davies** Brian, The thought of T. Aquinas 1992 ➤ 8,m106; 9,16252: RGregorianum 75 (1994) 171s (T. *Kennedy*).

14386 **Di Maio** Andrea, Il concetto di comunicazione in Tommaso d'Aquino e la 'communicatio spiritualis sapientiae' (indagine lessicale e dottrinale): diss. Pont. Univ. Gregoriana, DHenrici P. Roma 1994. 635 p.; extr. No 4106, 71 p.

14387 **Fatula** sr., Thomas Aquinas, preacher and friend 1993 ➤ 9,16254: 0-8146-5031-7. – RExpTim 105 (1993s) 350 (Carol *Harrison*).

14388 **Geisler** Norman L., T. Aquinas 1991 ➤ 7,g420... 9,16255: RBtS 151 (1994) 500s (S. R. *Spencer* would show even much more favor in this well-deserved appraisal); JEvTS 37 (1994) 604-6 (D. L. *Russell*: he had to plow through lots of evangelical disdain).

14388* **Ingardia** Richard, Thomas Aquinas, international bibliography, 1877-1990. Bowling Green OH 1993, Philosophy Documentation. 482 p.

14389 EKretzmann Norman, *Stump* Eleonore, The Cambridge companion to Aquinas. C 1993, Univ. viii-302 p. [RelStR 21,149, D. R. *Janz*].

14389* **McCool** Gerald A., From unity to pluralism... Thomism ➤ 6,m147... 8,m890 (ROUSSELOT): CanadCath 12,2 (1994) 24s (J. A. *Buijs*).

14390 **Mondin** Battista, Dizionario enciclopedico d'Aquino 1991 ➤ 7,735b... 9,16261: RGregorianum 75 (1994) 564s (R. *Fisichella*: only he could do it); Lateranum 60 (1994) 196-9 (N. *Ciola*); StPatav 40 (1993) 415s (A. *Da Re*).

14391 **Pesch** Otto H., Thomas d'Aquin, limites et grandeur de la théologie médiévale; une introduction [1988 ➤ 4k6], THoffmann J.: P 1994, Cerf. 576 p. F 200. 2-204-04743-0. – RBrotéria 139 (1994) 256ss (I. *Ribeiro de Silva*); EsprVie 104 (1994) 225-9 (P. *Jay*, bulletin); Études 380 (1994) 715 (R. *Marlé*); RHE 89 (1994) 460s (M. de *Paillerets*); RHPR 74 (1994) 443s (G. *Siegwalt*).

14392 **Pesch** Otto H., T. de Aquino, límites y grandeza 1992 ➤ 8,m113; 9,16262: RRCatalT 18 (1993) 184s (E. *Vilanova*).

14392* *Principe* W. H., 'Tradition' in Thomas Aquinas' scriptural commentaries: ➤ 128, FTAVARD G. 1994, 43-60.

14393 *a) Santi* Francesco, L'esegesi biblica di Tommaso d'Aquino nel contesto dell'esegesi biblica medievale; – *b) Rossi* Margherita Maria, La 'divisio textus' nei commenti scritturistici di S. Tommaso d'Aquino; un procedimento solo esegetico? – *c) Paretsky* A., The influence of Thomas the exegete on Thomas the theologian; the tract on law (Ia-IIae, qq. 98.108) as a test case; – *d) Bataillon* Louis-Jacques, La diffusione manoscritta e stampata dei commenti biblici di san Tommaso d'Aquino: Angelicum 71 (1994) 511-535 / 537-548 / 549-577 / 579-590.

14394 **Selman** Francis J., St. Thomas Aquinas, teacher of truth. E 1994, Clark. x-103 p. £9. 0-567-29245-2. – ᴿTBR 7,3 (1994s) 35 (A. *McCoy*).
14395 **Torrell** J.-P., Initiation à s. Thomas d'Aquin, sa personne et son œuvre. FrS/P 1993, Univ./Cerf. 592 p. Fs 120. – ᴿTS 56 (1995) 162-4 (T. F. *O'Meara*).
14396 **Wohlman** Avital, Thomas d'Aquin et MAÏMONIDE; un dialogue exemplaire 1988 ➤ 4,k10 ... 6,k499: ᴿRÉAug 40 (1994) 275s (G. *Dahan*).

14397 AUGUSTINUS C.: *Wood* Ian, The mission of Augustine of Canterbury to the English: Speculum 69 (1994) 1-17.
14398 BEDA V.: ᵀᴱ**Martin** Lawrence T., *Hurst* David, Bede, Homilies on the Gospels I-II: Cistercian Studies 110s. Kalamazoo 1991, Cistercian. xxx-252 p.; vii-290 p. $60, pa. $25 each. – ᴿManuscripta 36 (1992) 149s.
14399 *Robinson* Bernard P., The venerable Bede as exegete: DowR 112 (1994) 201-226.

14400 BERNARDUS C.: ᴱ**Bertrand** D., *Lobrichon* G., Bernard de Clairvaux; histoire, mentalité, spiritualité; colloque de Lyon-Cîteaux-Dijon: SChr 380, 1992 ➤ 8,513: ᴿGregorianum 75 (1994) 186-191 (Maria Cecilia *Zoffi*); MélSR 51 (1994) 436 (J. L. *Solère*); NRT 115 (1993) 436 (L. J. *Renard*).
14400* **Bell** T., Divus Bernardus; Bernhard von Clairvaux in M. LUTHERS Schriften: Inst.Eur.G., Rel 148. ix-418 p. DM 98. 3-8053-1329-2. 1993 [TLZ 120,817, Ute *Menneche-Haustein*].
14401 ᵀᴱ**Callerot** Françoise, *al.*, Bernard de Clairvaux; L'amour de Dieu; La grâce et le libre arbitre. SChr 393. P 1993, Cerf. 389 p. 2-2040-4960-3.
14401* **Heller** Dagmar, Schriftauslegung und geistliche Erfahrung bei Bernhard 1990 ➤ 7,g427; 8,m126: ᴿTPhil 69 (1994) 287s (R. *Berndt*).

14402 BONAVENTURA: *Bonino* Serge-Thomas, Bulletin; l'École franciscaine médiévale [... Bonaventura, LULLE]: RThom 94 (1994) 110-123.
14403 *Bougerol* Jacques Guy, La nouvelle édition critique des sermons de saint Bonaventure; un bilan: RMabillon 65 (1993) 49-82.
14403* *Murphy* Anthony, Bonaventure's synthesis of Augustinian and Dionysian mysticism; a new look at the problem of the one and the many: ColcFran 63 (1993) 385-398; ital. 398.
14404 [Zorzi] *Pugliese* Olga, [1453-1542 Girolamo] BENIVIENI's Commento and Bonaventure's Itinerarium; autobiography and ideology: RivStoLR 30 (1994) 347-362.

14404* CUSANUS: **Lücking-Michel** Claudia, Konkordanz und Konsens; zur Gesellschaftstheorie in der Schrift 'De concordantia catholica' des Nicolaus von Cues [kath. Diss. Tübingen 1992, ᴰ*Hünermann* P.]: BonnerDogmSt 16. 242 p. DM 39. 3-429-01602-9 [TLZ 120,1092, K.-H. *Kandler*].
14405 *Senger* Hans G., Nikolaus von Kues: ➤ 517, TRE 24 (1994) 554-564.
14405* **Offermann** Ulrich, Christus – Wahrheit des Denkens; eine Untersuchung zur Schrift 'De docta ignorantia' des Nicolaus von Kues [kath. Diss. Tübingen 1991, ᴰ*Hunermann* P.]: BeitGPhThMA 33. Münster 1991, Aschendorff. vi-226 p. DM 50. 3-402-03928-1 [TLZ 120,1093, K.-H. *Kandler*].
14406 **Hopkins** J., A miscellany on Nicholas of Cusa. Mp 1994, Banning. 312 p. 0-938060-43-0 [RHE 90,173, J.-M. *Counet*].

14406* **Haubst** Rudolf, Streifzüge in die cusanische Theologie 1991 ➤ 7, g431 ... 9,16279: ᴿActuBbg 31 (1994) 47s (E. *Colomer*).
14407 DANTE: *a*) **Barolini** Teodolinda, The undivine comedy; detheologizing Dante. Princeton 1992, Univ. xi-356 p. $49.50; pa. $17. – ᴿSpeculum 69 (1994) 1106-9 (G. G. *Baranski*: author of the influential 1984 Dante's poets = Il miglior fabbro 1993).
— *b*) **Botterill** Steven, Dante and the mystical tradition; BERNARD of Clairvaux in the Commedia [Paradiso 31]: StMdvLit 22. C 1994, Univ. v-269 p. $60. 0-521-43454-8 [TDig 42,258].
14407* DIONYSIUS E.: *Gómez Pallarès* Joan, Hacia una nueva edición de los 'argumenta paschalia' de Dionisio el Exiguo: Hispania Sacra 46 (1994) 13-31; Eng. 3.

14408 DIONYSIUS Pseud-A.: **Louth** Andrew, Denys the Areopagite 1989 ➤ 5,k16; 7,g153: ᴿScotJT 46 (1993) 541s (J. *McGuckin*: lucid).
14408* **Martín** Teodoro H., Obras completas del pseudo Dionisio Areopagita: BAC 511. M 1990, Católica. 1990 ➤ 7,g154; 8,k783*: ᴿEfMex 12 (1994) 245-9 (P. M. *Gasparotto*: objeciones a p. 3-115, nuevo 'neoplatonismo').
14409 *Pharantos* Megas L., Ⓖ The philosophical substructure of the theology of Pseudo-Dionysius the Areopagite [nowhere deals with revelation in Christ; cites Scripture confusingly]: TAth 64 (1993) 399-427 [479-515, *Paschos* P. B.]; Eng. 882.
14410 **Rorem** Paul, Pseudo-Dionysius; a commentary on the [Greek (Suchla)] texts and an introduction to their influence. Ox 1993, UP. xiii-267 p. $40. – ᴿCathHR 80 (1994) 780-4 (K. *Emery*); JTS 45 (1994) 354-7 (G. *Gould*); Manuscripta 37 (1993) 222 [–: closely related to C. *Luibeid*'s 1987 English); PrincSemB 14 (1993) 294-8 (J. M. *Rist*); ModT 10 (1994) 727s (A. *Louth*); ScotJT 47 (1994) 416s (also A. *Louth*); Worship 65 (1994) 175-7 (Jane *Burton*).
14411 ᴱ[*Heil* Günter] **Ritter** Adolf-M., **Dionysius**: De coelesti hirerarchia; de ecclesiastica hierarchia: de mystica theologia; epistulae: Corpus 2, PatrTSt 36. B 1991, de Gruyter. xv-300 p. 3-11-012460-2.
14411* ᴱ**Simon** Paul, *Kübel* Wilhelm, ALBERTI Magni Super Dionysium de caelesti hierarchia: Opera 36/1. Münster 1993, Aschendorff. x-276 p. ᴰᴹ268 pa. [TR 91,35, L. *Hödl*].
14412 ᵀ**Suchla** Beate R.., Pseudo-Dionysius A., Die Namen Gottes 1988 ➤ (5,g782) 6,k190: ᴿByZ 86 (1994) 136-9 (D. *Gotteschall*).

14413 ECKHART: *Corduan* Winfried, A hair's breadth from pantheism; Meister Eckhart's God-centered spirituality: JEvTS 37 (1994) 263-274.
14414 FLODOARD: **Sot** Michel, Un historien et son église au Xᵉ siècle: Flodoard de Reims. P 1993, Fayard. 832 p. – ᴿRBén 104 (1994) 435s (D. *Misonne*).
14414* GANSFORT, 'devotio moderna': ᴱ**Akkerman** F., *al.*, Wessel Gansfort (1419-1489) and northern humanism [< 1989 Groningen conference]: StIntelHist 40. Leiden 1993, Brill. xiv-425 p. $128.75 [RelStR 21,149, D. R. *Janz*: only 8 of the 15 essays treat Gansfort, but very well].
14415 GROSSETESTE: **McEvoy** James, Robert Grosseteste, exegete and philosopher: CS 446. Aldershot 1994, Variorum. x-295 p. 0-86078-433-9 [TDig 92,176]. 9 art.
14416 HILDEGARD: *Oroz Reta* José, La sibila del Rhin; misión profética de santa Hildegarda de Bingen: Latomus 53 (1994) 608-634.

14417 HUGO S.-V.: **Illich** Ivan, Du lisible au visible; sur l'art de lire de Hugues de Saint-Victor. P 1991, Cerf. 150 p. – ᴿRTPhil 126 (1994) 59s (P.-Y. *Ruff*).

14417* *Possekel* U., Der Mensch in der Mitte; Aspekte der Anthropologie Hugos von St. Viktor: RTAM 61 (1994) 5-21.

14418 HUGOLINUS: *Marcolino* Venicio, Die Wirkung der Theologie Hugolins von Orvieto im späten Mittelalter: AnAug 56 (1993) 5-124.

14418* ISIDORUS H.: **Codoñer** Carmen, Isidoro de Sevilla, Diferencias I: AutLatMA. P 1992, BLettres. iv-538 p. F 375. 2-251-33633-8. – ᴿLatomus 53 (1994) 865-7 (Lucienne *Deschamps*).

14419 **Cazier** Pierre, Isidore de Séville et la naissance de l'Espagne catholique: THist 96. P 1994, Beauchesne. 329 p. F 195. – ᴿArTGran 57 (1994) 469s (M. *Sotomayor*); RechSR 83 (1995) 640s (P. *Vallin*).

14419* JANOV: ᴱ**Nechutová** Janá, (*Krmíčková* Helena), Matthiae de Janov dicti Magistri Parisiensis Regularum Veteris et Novi Testamenti [1.-5.]; 6. Liber V. De Corpore Christi; Collegium Carolinum 69. Mü 1994, Oldenbourg. xliv-290 p. DM 129 [TR 91,487, L. *Hödl*].

14420 JULIANA N.: **Palliser** Margaret A., Christ our mother of mercy... in the Shewings of Julian of Norwich 1992 ➤ 8,m158*: ᴿTLond 97 (1994) 64s (G. R. *Evans*: no mean feat).

14420* ᴱ**Windeatt** Barry, English mystics of the Middle Ages [Julian + 4]. C 1994, Univ. xi-311 p. $60. 0-521-32740-7 [TDig 42,365].

14421 JULIANUS Tol. († 690): *O'Loughlin* Thomas, Julian of Toledo's *Antikeimenon* ['Book of oppositions' c. 670, ML 96, 583-704]: and the development of Latin exegesis: PrIrB 16 (1993) 80-98.

14421* LULLIUS: ᴱ**Bonner** Anthony, Doctor illuminatus; a Ramon Llull reader. Princeton 1993, Univ. xvii-380 p.; ill. $18 pa. 0-691-00091-3 [TLZ 120,532, H. G. *Thümmel*].

14422 LYRANUS: **Bunte** Wolfgang, Rabbinische Traditionen bei Nikolaus von Lyra; ein Beitrag zur Schriftauslegung des Spätmittelalters: JudUmw 58. Fra 1994, Lang. 324 p. 3-631-48015-6.

14423 *Schmidt* Martin A., Nikolaus von Lyra: ➤ 517, TRE 24 (1994) 564-6.

14424 MARSILIUS F.: *a*) *Allen* Michael J. B., Marsilio Ficino, Socrates and the daimonic voice of conscience; – *b*) *Hankins* James, Marsilio Ficino as a critic of scholasticism: VivH 5/2, ('Teologia a Firenze nell'età di G. Pico della Mirandola, V centenario' 1994) 301-323; ital. 324 / 325-333; ital. 334 [335-356 *Trinkaus* Charles].

14425 OCKHAM: **Pellegrini** Angelo, Lo statuto epistemologico della teologia secondo Guglielmo di Occam: diss. n° 4121, Pont. Univ. Gregoriana, ᴰ*Huber* C. R 1994. 365 p. – RTLv 26, p. 529.

14425* PÉREZ: **Peinado Muñoz** Miguel, Jaime Pérez de Valencia (1408-1490) y la Sagrada Escritura (dis,): Granada 1992, Fac.Teol.: BtTGran 26, 1992 ➤ 8,m164: ᴿCiuD 207 (1994) 207s (J. *Gutiérrez*).

14426 PETRUS A.: **Smoller** Laura A., History, prophecy and the stars; the Christian astrology of Pierre d'Ailly. Princeton 1994, Univ. xii-233 p. $35 [TDig 42,188; TS 56,399s, I. *Murdoch*].

14427 MIRANDOLA: *Mahoney* Edward P., Giovanni Pico della Mirandola and ORIGEN on humans, choice and hierarchy: VivH 5/2 (Pico centenary 1994) 359-376; ital. 376.

14427* SCOTUS: *Mathieu* Luc, La primauté universelle du Christ selon le Bienheureux Jean Duns Scot: RICathP 49 (1994) 9-18 [5-38, *al.*, sur sa béatification 20.III.1993].

14428 *a*) *Calvo Moralejo* Gaspar, El beato Juan Duns Escoto, 'maestro de pensamiento y de vida'; – b) *Pijoan* José, Escoto, el hombre; Verdad y Vida 51, 202s (Beatificación de Escoto, 1993) 149-161 / 163-9 [al.].

14428* SEDULIUS: *Favreau* Robert, Épigraphie et miniatures; les vers de Sedulius et les Évangélistes: JSav 93 (1993) 63-78 + 11 pl.

Y4.1 Luther.

14429 *Andreatta* Eugenio, Una virtù pagana [*epicikeia*] che piaceva a Lutero: Protestantesimo 49 (1994) 143-160.

14430 **Brecht** M., M. Luther (3.) The preservation of the Church, 1532-1546, T*Schaff* J. 1993 ⇒ 9,16324: RConcordTQ 58 (1994) 315-7 (K. *Schurb*); JEH 45 (1994) 703-5 (M. U. *Edwards*).

14431 **Buchholz** Armin, Schrift Gottes im Lehrstreit; Luthers Schriftverständnis und Schriftauslegung in seinen drei grossen Lehrstreitigkeiten der Jahre 1521-28 [EMSER, LATOMUS, KARLSTADT]: EurHS 23/487. Fra 1993, Lang. 275 p. 3-631-46389-8. – RRHPR 74 (1994) 338 (M. *Lienhard*: trop contre une modernisation hâtive).

14432 *Cameron* Euan, The search for Luther's place in the Reformation [BRECHT M. al.]: JEH 45 (1994) 475-485.

14433 EDelius Hans-Ulrich, al., M. Luther Studienausgabe 5. B 1992, Ev.-V. 638 p. 3-374-013888-0. – RGregorianum 75 (1994) 171s (J. E. *Vercruysse*: completes the works; three volumes of translation and glossary will follow).

14434 *Gahbauer* Ferdinand R., M. Luther und der päpstliche Primat: Renovatio 49 (Köln 1993) 118-121 [< ZIT 93,204].

14434* *Geese* U., Sprache und Buchdruck als kultisches Instrumentarium in Luthers Brief an die Ratsherren von 1524: Imprimatur, ein Jahrbuch für Bücherfreunde NF 14 (Fra 1991) 123-142; 5 fig. [RHE 90,29*].

14435 *Hattrup* Dieter, Die Philosophie in der Theologie Luthers: TGL 84 (1994) 195-208.

14436 EHutter Ulrich, al., M. Luther und die Reformation in Ostdeutschland und Südosteuropa [Vortragsreihe Ostdeutscher Kulturrat 1983]: JbSchlesKG Beih 8. Sigmaringen 1989, Thorbecke. 144 p.; 9 fig. – RZKG 105 (1994) 237s (P. *Maser*).

14437 *Jenson* Robert W., An ontology of freedom in the De servo arbitrio of Luther: ModT 10 (1994) 247-252.

14438 **Junghans** Helmar, Martin Luther in two centuries, the sixteenth and the twentieth, TGustavs K., al., St. Paul 1992, Lutheran Brotherhood. v-99 p. – RTLZ 119 (1994) 1085 (L. *Grane*).

14439 *Kennedy* Leonard A., Martin Luther and scholasticism: AugLv 42 (1992) 339-349.

14440 **Lienhard** Marc, L'Évangile et l'Église chez Luther 1989 ⇒ 5,k75... 8,m192: RSalesianum 56 (1994) 794s (F. *Meyer*: dettagli sulle parti previamente pubblicate).

14441 *Lienhard* Marc, La liberté selon Luther et selon la Révolution Française: RHPR 74 (1994) 67-79; Eng. 112.

14442 **Messner** Reinhard, Die Messreform M. Luthers und die Eucharistie der Alten Kirche: InTSt 25. Innsbruck 1989, Tyrolia. 240 p. 3-7022-1699-5. – RSalesianum 56 (1994) 795s (F. *Meyer*).

14443 a) *Metzger* Pierre E.S., La raison chez Luther; – b) *Causse* Jean-Daniel, Luther et l'angoisse de l'enfer; – c) *Bühler* Pierre, La 'Dispute au sujet de l'être humain' de Luther, hier et aujourd'hui: ÉTRel 69 (1994) 491-513 / 515-528 / 529-548.

14444 **Nelson** Timothy, 'O du armer Luther...' Sprichwörtliches in der antilutherischen Polemik des [Franziskaners] Johannes NAS (1534-1590): Sprichwörterforschung 15. Bern 1992, Lang. 334 p. – ᴿRHPR 74 (1994) 336s (M. *Lienhard*).

14444* **Peura** Simo, Mehr als ein Mensch? Die Vergöttlichung als Thema der Theologie Martin Luthers von 1513 bis 1519: Mainz. Inst. SurG, Rel 152. Mainz 1994, von Zabern. ix-325 p. [RHE 90,293, R. *Stauffenberger*].

14445 **Roynesdal** Olaf, Luther's polemics [mostly in old age and ill-health]: LuthQ 6 (1982) 235-249.

14446 *Russell* William R., Martin Luther's understanding of the Pope as the Antichrist: ArRefG 85 (1994) 32-44; deutsch 44.

14447 *Sackness* Brent W., Luther's Two Kingdoms revisited; a response to Reinhold NIEBUHR's criticism of Luther: JRelEth 20 (1992) 93-110.

14448 ·ᵀ*Sbrozi* M., ᴱ*De Michelis Pintacuda* F., M. LUTERO, Il servo arbitrio; risposta a ERASMO (1525): Opere scelte 6. T 1993, Claudiana. 471 p. Lᵐ 49. – ᴿVivH 5 (1994) 207-9 (S. *Dianich*).

14448* **Thompson** Terry D., Biographies of Luther; converging on a whole man: ConcordTQ 58 (1994) 25-38.

14449 **Trigg** Jonathan D., Baptism in the theology of Martin Luther: StHistChrTht 56. Leiden 1994, Brill. vii-234 p. ƒ120. 90-04-10016-4 [TLZ 120,1120, R. *Slenczka*].

14449* **White** Graham, Luther as nominalist; a study of the logical methods used in ML's disputations in the light of their medieval background: Agricola 30. Helsinki 1994, Luther-Agricola. 418 p. 951-9047-28-X [TLZ 120,611-6, F. *Hoffmann*].

Y4.3   **Exegesis et controversia saeculi XVI.**

14450 **Allison** Anthony F., *Rogers* D. M., The [then] contemporary printed literature of the English Counter-Reformation between 1558 and 1640; an annotated catalogue, I. works in English; 2. works not in English. Aldershot 1989/94, Scolar. xxviii-291 p., $130. xxxv-250 p., $122 [both $200]. 0-85967-852-0; -640-4.

14450* **Bagchi** David V. N., Luther's earliest opponents; Catholic controversialists 1518-1525: 1991 → 7,g503; 9,16353: ᴿÉTRel 68 (1993) 434 (H. *Bost*); JRel 74 (1994) 255s (Mary T. *Stimming*: elegant and challenging); TorJT 10 (1994) 132s (G. A. *Jensen*).

14451 ᴱ**Brady** Thomas A.ᴶ, *Oberman* Heiko A., *Tracy* James D., Handbook of European History; late Middle Ages, Renaissance and Reformation. Leiden 1994, Brill. xxv-704 p. 90-04-09762-7.

14452 **Bujanda** J. M., Index de l'Inquisition espagnole 1583-1584: Index 6. Sherbrooke 1993, Centre Renaissance. 1246 p. – ᴿSalmanticensis 41 (1994) 462s (J. I. *Tellechea Idígoras*).

14453 **Cameron** Euan, The European Reformation 1991 → 8,m223; 9,16358: ᴿConcordTQ 58 (1994) 181s (C. A. *MacKenzie*); ScotJT 46 (1993) 577-9 (R. *Rex*).

14454 **Campi** Emidio, Protestantesimo nei secoli; fonti e documenti I. Cinquecento e seicento 1991 → 7,g508... 9,16359: ᴿJEH 45 (1994) 371s (R. *MacKenney*); Zwingliana 21 (1994) 151s (F. *Ferrario*).

14454* **Chang Yang-en**, The theology of the Calvinist resistance movement; a theological study of the French Calvinist resistance literature (1572-1579): diss. Theol. Sem., ᴰ*McKee* E. Princeton 1994. – RelStR 21,256.

14455 **Christian** Olivier, Une révolution symbolique; l'iconoclasme huguenot

et la reconstruction catholique. P 1991, Minuit. 350 p. F 145. 2-707-
31391-1. – ᴿÉTRel 68 (1993) 117-9 (J. *Cottin*).
14456 **Crouzet** Denis, Les guerriers de Dieu; la violence... 1585-1610. Seyssel
1990, Champ Vallon. 793 p.; 738 p. F 490. – ᴿRHR 211 (1994) 108-116
(G. *Audisio*).
14457 *Currie* H. M., The significance of the Renaissance for the Europe of
today; some reflections: HeythJ 35 (1994) 140-155.
14458 **Dittrich** Christoph, Die vortridentinische katholische Kontroverstheologie und die Täufer [diss. FrB 1989] 1991 ➤ 8,m230: EurHS... Fra
1991, Lang. vii-457 p. – ᴿFrSZ 41 (1994) 287-291 (C. *Morerod*).
14458* ᴱ**Drobesch** W., Katholische Reform und Gegenreformation in Inner-
österreich 1564-1628. Klagenfurt/Graz 1994, Hermagoras/Styria. 795 p.;
27 fig.; 6 maps. [RHE 90,72*].
14459 **Duffy** Eamon, The stripping of the altars; traditional religion in
England 1400-1580: 1992 ➤ 8,m232; 9,16367: ᴿCommonweal 120,5
(1993) 27s (E. T. *Oakes*); DowR 111 (1993) 228-231 (D. *Lunn*); EngHR
109 (1994) 111-4 (M. *Astor*); JRel 74 (1994) 240-9 (R. *Kieckhofer*: 'church
reformed though not deformed'); Speculum 69 (1994) 766-8 (P. M.
Soergel); Tablet 247 (1993) 211s (J. J. *Scarisbrick*).
14460 **Evans** Gillian R., Problems of authority in the Reformation debate 1992
➤ 8,234; 9,16370: ᴿScotJT 47 (1994) 419s (A. *Ford*).
14461 **Fumagalli** Vito, L'alba del Medioevo. Bo 1993, Mulino. 99 p. Lᵐ 15.
– ᴿRasT 35 (1994) 376-8 (G. *Caccavale*, A. *Orazzo*).
14462 **Galtier** Jean, Protestants en révolution; préf. *Baubérot* J.: Entrée libre
5. Genève 1989, Labor et Fides. 95 p. – ᴿRTPhil 126 (1994) 383 (P.
Wurz: histoire du protestantisme dans sa relation au politique).
14463 **Garstein** Oskar, Rome and the counter-reformation in Scandinavia 4,
1992 ➤ 8,m236; 9,16374: ᴿTLZ 119 (1994) 276-8 (E. *Koch*).
14464 ᴱ**Grafton** Anthony, Rome reborn; the Vatican Library and Renaissance culture 1993 ➤ 9,16378:   ᴿCathHR 80 (1994) 120-3 (J.
Mc Manamon).
14465 ᴱ**Guggisberg** H. R., *Krodel* G. G., Die Reformation in Deutschland
und Europa; Interpretationen und Debatten. Heid 1993, Verein Ref.-G.
(Gü-V.). 703 p. [RHE 90,72*].
14465* ᴱ*Guggisberg* Hans R., *al.*, La liberté de conscience (XVIᵉ-XVIIᵉ
siècles) [Mülhouse-Basel 1989, 18 art.]. 1991 ➤ 8,556: ᴿArRefG 22-Beih
(1993) 47s (P. *Benedict*, Eng.).
14466 **Haigh** Christopher, English Reformations; religion, politics, and society
under the Tudors. Ox 1993, Clarendon. ix-367 p. £30; pa. £12. 0-19-
822163-0; -2-2. – ᴿJEH 45 (1994) 319-324 (D. *MacCullogh*, also on
Skeeters Martha and *Crawford* Patricia 1993); Tablet 248 (1994) 112 (D.
Edwards: as seen by a mildly-religious chameleon for those who favor a
religious background to social life).
14467 **Hall** Basil, Humanists and Protestants 1500-1900: 1990 ➤ 8,m244;
9,16381: ᴿConcordTQ 58 (1994) 158-160 (K. *Schurb*).
14468 **Higman** Francis, La diffusion de la Réforme en France 1520-1565:
Univ. Publ. 17. Genève 1992, Labor et Fides. 247 p. – ᴿÉTRel 68 (1993)
434s (H. *Bost*); MélSR 51 (1994) 347-9 (J.-C. *Matthys*).
14469 **Hill** Christopher, The English Bible and the seventeenth century
revolution. ... 1993, Penguin. 480 p. $30. 0-7139-9078-3. – ᴿChrCent
111 (1994) 285s (W. *Wink*).
14470 **Hsia Po-Chia** Ronald, Social discipline in the Reformation; central
Europe 1550-1750: Christianity and Society in the Modern World. L

1989, Routledge. vi-218 p. £30. 0-415-01148-5. – ᴿJEH 45 (1994) 673-684 (J. *Bossy*, on Bernd *Moeller* 1962).

14471 **Jas** Michael, Braises cathares; filiation secrète à l'heure de la Réforme. Portet 1992, Loubatières. 207 p. F 130. 2-86266-164-3. – ᴿÉTRel 68 (1993) 113 (Dominique *Viaux*).

14471* **Kamen** Henry, The phoenix and the flame; Catalonia and the counter-reformation 1993 ➤ 9,16386: ᴿCommonweal 121,1 (1994) 31s (C. L. *Bankston*: Reformation without Protestants); JEH 45 (1994) 514-7 (J.-P. *Rubiés*); TBR 7,1 (1994s) 69 (H. M. *Höpfl*).

14472 **Keith** Graham, Issues in religious toleration from the Reformation to the present day: EvQ 66 (1994) 307-329.

14472* **Klaassen** Walter, Living at the end of the ages; apocalyptic expectation in the radical Reformation 1992 ➤ 9,16389: ᴿJRel 74 (1994) 304s (J. H. *Yoder*: only his last paragraph seems to reject the apocalyptic phenomenon as a built-in human pathology).

14473 **Kolb** Robert, Confessing the faith; Reformers define the Church, 1530-1580: 1991 ➤ 9,16392: St. Louis 1991, Concordia. – ᴿConcordiaTQ 58 (Fort Wayne 1994) 311s (E. F. *Klug*: 'within Christendom Lutherans and Lutheran theology are unique in that they are confessional').

14474 **Liechty** Daniel, Sabbatarianism in the sixteenth century; a page in the history of the Radical Reformation. Berrien Springs MI 1993, Andrews Univ. x-94 p. $14 pa. 0-943872-99-5 [TDig 42, 174].

14475 **McGrath** Alister, The intellectual origin of the European reformation 1987 ➤ 3,g536... 6,k620: ᴿJRelH 18 (1994) 240-3 (Z. *Zlatar*).

14476 **McGrath** Alister E., Reformation thought² (1993 ¹1988) ➤ 4,k107*; 5,k125; 6,k621: ᴿÉTRel 68 (1993) 435s (H. *Bost*).

14477 **McGrath** Alister E., Il pensiero della Riforma: Lutero, Zwingli, Calvino, Bucero; una introduzione, ᵀᴱ*Comba* Aldo: PiccolaBtT 24, 1991 ➤ 7,g530; 9,16398: 88-7016-146-3. – ᴿSalesianum 56 (1994) 796 (P. T. *Stella*).

14478 ᴱ**McKim** Donald K., Major themes in the Reformed tradition 1992 ➤ 8,402; 9,16400: ᴿPersp[Ref] 8,9 (1993) 21s (M. I. *Klauber*).

14479 **Manchester** William, A world lit only by fire; the medieval mind and the Renaissance; portrait of an age. Boston 1992, Little Brown. 289 p. – ᴿWWorld 14 (1994) 225s.228 (R. *Jacobson*: errors on Luther and Calvin; 'one could hardly find a worse book').

14480 **Martín** Melquiades A., Historia de la mística de la Edad de Oro en España y América: BAC Maior 44. M 1994, Católica. 490 p. 84-7914-120-4. – ᴿRET 54 (1994) 335-347 (*ipse*).

14481 ᴱ**Mayeur** J.-M., *al.*, Histoire du christianisme 8, ᴱ*Venard* Marc, Le temps des confessions (1530-1620). P 1992, Desclée. 1236 p. F 450. 2-7189-0574-3. – ᴿÉTRel 68 (1993) 287s (H. *Bost*).

14482 — Die Zeit der Konfessionen (1530-1620/30), deutsch ᴱ*Smolinsky* Heribert. FrB 1991, Herder. xx-1260 p.; 32 color. pl. DM 248. 3-451-22258-2. ➤ 14484. – ᴿHistJb 114 (1994) 107-124 (W. *Reinhard*).

14483 **Michalski** Sergiusz, The Reformation and the visual arts; the Protestant image question in western and eastern Europe. NY 1993, Routledge. xii-232 p. $50. – ᴿAmHR 99 (1994) 1308s (C. C. *Christensen*).

14484 ᴱ**Mollat du Jourdin** M., *Vauchez* André, Die Zeit der Zerreissproben: Christentum 6, ᵀᴱ*Schimmelpfennig* B. FrB 1991, Herder. xx-912 p.; 32 col. pl. DM 248. 3-451-22256-6. – ᴿTPhil 69 (1994) 290s (K. *Schatz*).

14485 **Müller** Gerhard, Zwischen Reformation und Gegenwart II [19 Bei-

träge]. Hannover 1988, Luther-V.   194 p.   3-7859-0554-8. – ᴿZKG 105 (1994) 238s (H. *Klueting*).
14486 **Oehlke** Harry,   Die Konfessionsbildung des 16. Jhts. im Spiegel illustrierter Flugblätter: ArbKg 57.   NY 1992, de Gruyter.   x-474 p. DM 178. – ᴿAmHR 99 (1994) 586s (Susan C. *Karant-Nunn*).
14487 *Pangritz* Andreas,   Der 'maskierte Christus'; Nikodemismus und Antinikodemismus in der italienischen Reformation: EvT 54 (1994) 8-22.
14487* **Raitt** Jill,   The colloquy of Montébeliard [BEZA T., ANDREAE J.]; religion and politics in the sixteenth century.   NY 1993, Oxford-UP. xii-226 p. $45 [RelStR 21,151, R. *Kolb*].
14488 ᴱ**Robinson-Hammerstein** Helga,   The transmission of ideas in the Lutheran reformation.   Dublin 1989, Irish Academic. 192 p.   £30.   0-7165-2376-0. – ᴿJEH 45 (1994) 673s (J. *Bossy*).
14489 **Rummel** Erika, Scheming papists and Lutheran fools 1993 ➤ 9,16417: ᴿBtHumRen 56 (1994) 588s (J. L. *Flood*).
14490 **Saenz Badillos** Ángel, La filología bíblica / Alcalá 1991 ➤ 7,g664; 8,m275:   ᴿScripTPamp 26 (1994) 1217s (A. *Barragán Ortiz*).
14491 *Schilling* Heinz,   Luther, Loyola, Calvin und die europäische Neuzeit: ArRefG 85 (1994) 5-30; Eng. 31.
14491* **Schulze** Manfred,   Fürsten und Reformation; geistliche Reformpolitik weltlicher Fürsten vor der Reformation: SpätMARef 2.   Tü 1991, Mohr. viii-291 p. DM 138. – ᴿHeythJ 35 (1994) 458s (Bob *Scribner*).
14492 **Soergel** Philip M.,   Wondrous in his saints; Counter Reformation propaganda in Bavaria.   Berkeley 1993, Univ. California. xv-239 p. [RelStR 21,152, R. *Kolb*].
14493 *Stackhouse* Ian, The native roots of early English Reformation theology: EvQ 66 (1994) 19-35.
14493* **Stephens** John,   The Italian Renaissance; the origins of intellectual and artistic change before the Reformation.   L 1990, Longman.   xviii-248 p. £22.50; pa. £11. – ᴿEngHR 109 (1994) 423 (R. *Black*).
14494 **Tazbir** Janusz,   Reformacja w Polsce.   Wsz 1993, Książka i Wiedza. 264 p. 83-05-12613-7. – ᴿJEH 45 (1994) 352-4 (P. *Brock*).
14495 *Wagner* Christine,   *a*) L'inquisition de Tolède face au Protestantisme au XVIᵉ siècle: RHPR 74 (1994) 153-169; Eng. 229; – *b*) Los Luteranos ante la inquisición de Toledo en el siglo XVI: Hispania Sacra 46 (1994) 473-507; Eng. 397s.
14496 **White** Peter,   Predestination, policy and polemic; conflict and consensus in the English Church from the Reformation to the Civil War 1992 ➤ 9,16437: ᴿJTS 45 (1994) 403-9 (S. F. *Hughes*).
14497 **Williams** George H.,   The radical Reformation³ʳᵉᵛ 1992 ➤ 9,14639; $125: ᴿCritRR 6 (1993) 401-3 (D. *Liechty*).
14498 ᴱ**Zinger** Ilana,   L'hébreu au temps de la Renaissance: BSJS 4.   Leiden 1992, Brill. 260 p. F 125.   90-04-09557. – ᴿÉTRel 69 (1994) 112s (Jeanne Marie *Léonard*); RHR 211 (1994) 365s (S. *Schwarzfuchs*).

Y4.4   Periti aetatis reformatoriae.

14499 BELLARMINO, **Galeota** G., R. Bellarmino, Capua 1988/90 ➤ 7,e496*; 8,m302:   ᴿRivStoLR 30 (1994) 216-9 (G. *Jori*).
14500 **Biersack** Manfred,   Initia Bellarminiana ... Prädestinationslehre 1989 ➤ 7,g553 ... 9,16445:   ᴿSalesianum 56 (1994) 385s (P. T. *Stella*).
14501 *a*) *Ceyssens* L., Bellarmin et Louvain (1569-1576); – *b*) *Biersack* M.,

Bellarmin und die 'Causa BAII': ➤ 366, Augustinisme 1994, 179-205 / 267-278.

14501* DE BILLY; **Backus** Irène, La Patristique et les guerres de religion en France [J. de *Billy*] 1993 ➤ 9,16445*: ᴿBtHumRen 56 (1994) 856-9 (C. *Mouchel*).

14502 BUCER: **Greschat** M., M. Bucer 1990 ➤ 7,g557; 8,m308: ᴿTZBas 50 (1994) 175s (T. F. *Kuhn*).

14502* *Hamman* Gottfried, Die ekklesiologischen Hintergründe zur Bildung von Bucers 'Christlichen Gemeinschaften' in Strassburg (1546-8), ᵀ*Wolf* Gerhard P.: ZKG 105 (1994) 344-360.

14503 *Krüger* Friedhelm, Bucer and ERASMUS: MennoniteQR 68,1 (Goshen IN 1994) 11-23 [24-100, 5 others on Bucer < ZIT 94,180].

14504 *Lienhard* Marc, Bucer en son temps et pour notre temps: ÉTRel 69 (1994) 475-489.

14505 *Short* Howard E., Bucer's hand in the Reformation of Augsburg: LexTQ 28 (1993) 281-298.

14506 BUGENHAGEN: **Gummelt** Volker, Lex et evangelium; Untersuchungen zur Jesajavorlesung von Johannes Bugenhagen (Diss.): ArbKG 62. B 1994, de Gruyter. xi-209 p. [RHE 89,232*].

14507 *Gummelt* Volker, Bugenhagens Tätigkeit an der Wittenberger Universität: ZKG 105 (1994) 191-201.

14508 **Kötter** Rolf, J. Bugenhagens Rechtfertigungslehre und der römische Katholizismus: ForKDgG 59. Gö 1994, Vandenhoeck & R. 489 p. DM 193. 3-525-55167-3 [TLZ 120,43, V. *Gummelt*: RHE 90,288, P. *Denis*].

14509 BULLINGER: **McCoy** C.S., *Baker* J.W., Foundations of federalism... Bullinger 1991 ➤ 7,g561... 9,16452: ᴿJEvTS 37 (1994) 451s (D.W. *Hall*); Zwingliana 21 (1994) 155-7 (E. *Campi*).

14510 CALVIN: **Beeke** Joel R., Assurance of faith: Calvin, English Puritanism, and the Dutch second Reformation. NY 1991, P. Lang. xvi-518. £26. – ᴿScotJT 47 (1994) 383-386 (B. D. *Spinks*).

14511 **Butin** Philip W., Reformed ecclesiology; trinitarian grace according to Calvin: StRefT 2/1. Princeton 1994, Theol. Sem. vii-52 p.

14512 ᵀᴱ**Fuhrmann** Paul T., John Calvin, Instruction in faith (1537). LVL 1992, W-Knox. 93 p. $9. 0-664-25314-8. – ᴿRExp 91 (1994) 620 (C.J. *Scalise*).

14513 **Gisel** Pierre, Le Christ de Calvin: JJC 4, 1990 ➤ 6,7461; 7,7431: ᴿIstina 38 (1993) 424s (B. *Dupuy*).

14513* **Greef** Wulfert de, The writing of John Calvin, an introductory guide, ᵀ*Bierma* Lyle D. GR 1993, Baker. 254 p. $15 [RelStR 21,151, D.K. *McKim*].

14514 **Hesselink** I, John, Calvin's concept of the Law [< 1961 Basel diss.]: Allison Park PA 1992, Pickwick. 311 p. ➤ 9,16458: $28: ᴿEurJT 3,2 (1994) 175 (-8 Eng. A. *Sell*); JRel 74 (1994) 396s (Jane E. *Strohl*); TZBas 50 (1994) 174 (U. *Gäbler*); WestTJ 55 (1993) 168-171 (M.W. *Karlberg*).

14515 *a) Jeschke* Dieter, 'Gott schwört bei seinem Leben; er dich nicht lassen will'; die Prädestinationslehre in Johannes Calvins Seelsorgepraxis: – *b) Stoevesandt* Hinrich, Prädestination und Geschichte: ➤ 34d, ᶠFANGMEIER J., Das Wort 1994, 45-54 / 55-74.

14515* *Leithart* Peter J., Stoic elements in Calvin's doctrine of the Christian life, 2. Mortification: WestTJ 55 (1993) 191-208.

14516 **McGrath** A. E., Life of Calvin 1990 ⇒ 6,k866... 9,16461: ᴿCritRR 5 (1992) 339-341 (Elsie *McKee*); ExpTim 105 (1993s) 160 (C. S. *Rodd*, 'profoundly worthy of study' though not much on Calvin's own life); ScotJT 45 (1992) 563-6 (W. P. *Stephens*); ZKG 105 (1994) 427s (W. H. *Neuser*).

14517 **Millet** Olivier, Calvin et la dynamique de la parole; étude de rhétorique réformée [diss.]: BtLitRen 3/28, 1992 ⇒ 9,16465: ᴿBuHumRen 56 (1994) 223-8 (M. *Engammare*); ÉTRel 69 (1994) 81-87 (H. *Bost*); RivStoLR 30 (1994) 397-400 (Roberta *Burdese*).

14518 **Naphy** William G., Calvin and the consolidation of the Genevan Reformation. Manchester UK 1994, Univ. [NY St. Martin's]. 272 p. 0-7190-4141-4 [RelStR 21,245, D. K. *McKim*].

14518* *Oberman* Heiko A., Via Calvini; zur Enträtselung der Wirkung Calvins: Zwingliana 21 (1994) 29-58.

14519 **Parker** T. H. I., Calvin's OT/NT² commentaries 1986/93. LVL 1993, W-Knox. 239 p.; 257 p. $17 each. 0-664-25490-X; -89-6 [TDig 41,377]. – ᴿPrincSemB 15 (1994) 297-9 (G. N. *Hansen*).

14520 **Parker** T. H. L., Calvin's preaching 1992 ⇒ 8,m329; 9,16467: ᴿJEH 45 (1994) 732s (E. *Cameron*); JRel 74 (1994) 395s (R. A. *Muller*).

14521 **Reist** Benjamin A., A reading of Calvin's Institutes. LVL 1991, W-Knox. 124 p. $8 pa. – ᴿCritRR 6 (1993) 525 (D. G. *Danner* gives an unconvincing sample of his 'aggravating' style).

14522 *Thorson* Stephen, Tensions in Calvin's view of faith; unexamined assumptions in B. T. KENDALL's Calvin and English Calvinism to 1649 [Ox 1979]: JEvTS 37 (1994) 413-424.

14523 **Thompson** J. L., J. Calvin and... women in exceptional roles 1992 ⇒ 9, 16471: ᴿWestTJ 56 (1994) 208-210 (R. *Letham*); Zwingliana 21 (1994) 193-5 (E. J. *Furcha*).

14523* **Zillenbiller** Anette, Die Einheit der katholischen Kirche; Calvins CYPRIANrezeption in seinen ekklesiologischen Schriften [Diss. Wü, ᴰ*Ganoczy* A.]: InstEurG 151. Mainz 1993, von Zabern. x-182 p. DM 58 [TR 91,491, H. *Schützeichel*].

14524 CAMPANELLA: *Sievernich* Michael, The idea of interreligious dialogue in Tommaso Campanella [1618; (re-)published Firenze (1s) 1939; vol. 3 (1955) is on Jews; 4 (1960) on Muslims]: JIntRD 3 (1993) 138-149.

14524* CERVINI: **Hudon** William V., [3-week Pope 1555] Marcello Cervini and ecclesiastical government in Tridentine Italy. DeKalb IL 1992, Northern Illinois Univ. ix-261 p. $32 [RelStR 21,150, D. R. *Janz*: very informative].

14525 CHEMNITZ: **Preus** Jacob A. O., The second Martin; the life and theology of Martin Chemnitz. St. Louis 1994, Concordia. 411 p. $35. 0-570-04645-9 [TDig 42,287].

14525* CHYTRAEUS: **Keller** Rudolf, Die Confessio Augustana im theologischen Wirken des Rostocker Professors David Chytraeus (1530-1600): ForKDg 60. Gö 1994. Vandenhoeck &R. 239 p. DM 74 [RelStR 21,150, R. *Kolb*: a momentous document meticulously researched].

14526 CISNEROS: **García Oro** José, El Cardenal Cisneros, vida y empresas: BAC 520.528, 1992s ⇒ 9,16475: ᴿEstE 69 (1994) 395-400 (I. *Arranz Roa*); Hispania Sacra 46 (1994) 385s (J. *Goñi Gaztambide*).

14526* CRANMER: ᴱ**Ayris** Paul, *Selwyn* David, Thomas Cranmer, churchman and scholar. Woodbridge 1993, Boydell. xx-355 p.; 1 pl. £35. 0-85115-249-9. – ᴿJEH 45 (1994) 511-3 (D. *MacCulloch*).

14527 CRESPIN: **Parker** C. H., French Calvinists as the Children of Israel; an OT self-consciousness in Jean Crespin's Histoire des martyrs before the Wars of Religion: SixtC 24 (1993) 227-248 [< RHE 89,233*].

14528 DUMOULIN: *Bavaud* Georges, La doctrine de l'Eucharistie selon le pasteur Pierre Dumoulin (1568-1658); étude pour dépasser la polémique: NVFr 68 (1993) 93-106.

14529 DUNGERSHEIM: **Freudenberger** Theobald, H. Dungersheim... Leben und Schriften: RgST 126, 1988 ➤ 5,k176*; 9,16484: ᴿZKG 105 (1994) 236s (H. *Klueting*).

14530 ECK: ᴱ**Iserloh** Erwin, Johannes Eck (1486-1543) im Streit der Jahrhunderte... Ingolstadt/Eichstätt 13.-16. Nov. 1986: RefGStT 127. Münster 1988, Aschendorff. 274 p. DM 84. – ᴿTR 90 (1994) 306-8 (J. *Wicks*, ᵀ*Richter* Annegret).

14531 **Ziegelbauer** Max, Johannes Eck, Mann der Kirche im Zeitalter der Glaubensspaltung 1987 ➤ 6,k688: ᴿTR 90 (1994) 308s (H.-J. *Gerste*).

14532 ERASMUS: **Brady** James F., *Olin* John C., Erasmus, the edition of JEROME etc. Collected Works 61. Toronto 1992, Univ. xxxvii-293 p. $85. – ᴿChH 63 (1994) 96s (P. I. *Kaufman*).

14532* **Augustijn** C., Erasmus 1991 (Eng.) ➤ 7,g579*... 9,16485: ᴿCritRR 6 (1993) 345-7 (Elizabeth *McCutcheon*).

14533 *a*) *Gielis* M., L'augustinisme anti-érasmien des premiers controversistes de Louvain; – *b*) *Vercruysse* J. E., Die Stellung AUGUSTINs in Jacobus LATOMUS' Auseinandersetzung mit Luther: ➤ 366, Augustinisme 1994, 19-61 / 7-18.

14534 **Halkin** Léon-E., Erasmus, a critical biography, ᵀ*Tonkin* John 1993 ➤ 9,16489: ᴿAmHR 99 (1994) 1307s (H. A. *Oberman*); JEH 45 (1994) 506s (D. *Baker-Smith*).

14534* **Hoffmann** Manfred, Rhetoric and theology; the hermeneutic of Erasmus. Toronto 1994, Univ. ix-303. $70 [TS 56,164s, J. W. *O'Malley*].

14535 *Loskoutoff* Yvan, La parturition des clercs; figures de la maïeutique dans la correspondance d'Érasme: BtHumRen 56 (1994) 305-326.

14535* *Nuttall* Geoffrey F., Erasmus and Spain; the vision of Marcel BATAILLON: JEH 45 (1904) 105-113.

14536 **[Seidel] Menchi** Silvana, Erasmus als Ketzer: Reformation und Inquisition im Italien des 16. Jahrhunderts 1992 ➤ 8,m357: ᴿRelStR 20 (1994) 66 (M. *Hoffmann*: Italians Lutheranized him by seeking in him answers to their own questions).

14537 *Ozaeta* José M., Erasmo de Rotterdam y fray José de SIGÜENZA: CiuD 206 (1993) 5-45.

14538 **Rummel** Erika, Erasmus and his Catholics critics 1989 ➤ 6,k693... 9,16495: ᴿZKG 105 (1994) 235s (G. *Elton*, Eng.).

14539 **Shantz** Douglas H., CRAUTWALD and Erasmus; a study in humanism and radical reform in sixteenth-century Silesia 1992 ➤ 8,m538; 9,16499: ᴿTorJT 10 (1994) 137s (E. *Rummel*).

14540 ᴱ**Steenbeek** Andrea Wilhelmina, 'Desiderii Erasmi Roterodami apologia ad Iacobum Fabrum STAPULENSEM' edited with... notes: diss. ᴰ*Jonge* H. J. de. Leiden 1994. 484 p. – RTLv 26,545.

14541 FISHER: **Rex** R., The theology of John Fisher 1991 ➤ 8,m362; 9,16501: ᴿAnnTh 8 (1994) 221-4 (T. J. *McGovern*); EngHR 109 (1994) 1001s (J. *Guy*: outstanding); ScotJT 47 (1994) 281s (B. D. *Spinks*).

14542 GAŁKA: *Marinelli* Luigi, Venenum in ecclesia; sull'anticostantinianesimo del polacco Jędrzej GAŁKA [c. 1450] di Dobczyn: Protestantesimo 49 (1994) 41-57.

14543 GROPPER: **Filser** Hubert, Ekklesiologie und Sakramentenlehre des Kardinals Johannes Gropper; eine Glaubenslehre zwischen Irenik und Kontroverstheologie im Zeitalter der Reformation: kath. Diss. ᴰ*Neuner* P. München 1994. – TR 91,99.

14544 GROTIUS: *a) Laplanche* François, Grotius et les religions du paganisme dans les Annotationes in Vetus Testamentum: – *b) Trapman* Johannes, Grotius and Erasmus; – *c) Rabbie* Edwin, Hugo Grotius and Judaism; – *d) Fatio* Olivier, Grotius remplaça-t-il Calvin à Genève?: → 82, ᶠMEYJES G. 1994, 53-64 / 77-98 / 99-120 / 185-194.

14545 HUBMAIER: **Mabry** Eddie L., Balthasar Hubmaier's doctrine of the Church. Lanham MD 1994, UPA. xviii-216 p. $32.50. 0-8191-9472-7 [TDig 42,175].

14546 LAS CASAS: ᵀᴱ**Collo** Paolo, Bartolomé de Las Casas, Brevissima relazione della distruzione delle Indie. Fiesole 1991, S. Domenico. 142 p. Lᵐ 20. – ᴿCC 145 (1994,1) 617s (P. *Vanzan*).

14546* ᴱ**Delgado** Mariano, Bartolomé de Las Casas, Missionstheologische Schriften: Werkauswahl 1. Pd 1994, Schöningh. 456 p. DM 88. 3-506-75121-2 [TR 91,281].

14547 **Pérez Fernández** Isacio, Bartolomé de Las Casas, ¿ Contra los negros? M 1991, Mundo Negro. 268 p. – ᴿScripTPamp 26 (1994) 333 (J. C. *Martín de la Hoz*).

14548 **Poole** Stafford, Bartolomé de Las Casas, In defense of the Indians. De Kalb II 1992, N. Illinois Univ. 385 p. $18. – ᴿChH 63 (1994) 281s (J. *Durán Luzio*).

14549 **Las Casas** Bartolomé de, The only way, ᵀ*Sullivan* F.P., ᴱ*Parish* Helen R. NY c. 1993, Paulist. 282 p. $23. – ᴿCanadCath 12,6(1994)21 (B. *McGrory*).

14549* **Gutiérrez** G., Dieu ou l'or des Indes occidentales 1492-1991 [1989] ᵀ: Théologies, 1992 → 8,8721: ᴿNRT 116 (1994) 619s (N. *Plumat*).

14550 **Gutiérrez** Gustavo, En busca... Las Casas 1993 → 9,16510: ᴿEstE 69 (1994) 274-6 (E. *Aguiluz Milla*); LumenVr 43 (1994) 277-9 (J. *Querejazu*); TLZ 119 (1994) 354s (D. *Ortmann*).

14551 **Gutiérrez** Gustavo, Las Casas; in search of the poor of Jesus Christ [1993 → 9,16510], ᵀ*Barr* R. Mkn 1993, Orbis. xxii-682 p. $35. 0-88344-838-6 [TDig 41,363]. – ᴿChrCent 111 (1994) 657s (F. *Herzog*); JHisp 2,4 (1994s) 69-71 (A. *García-Rivera*).

14552 *Nickoloff* James B., A 'church of the poor' in the sixteenth century; the ecclesiology of Bartolomé de Las Casas' *De unico modo*: JHisp 2,4 (1994s) 26-40.

14553 *Lancha* Charles, Las Casas protecteur des indigènes, défenseur des droits de l'homme: RHist 291 (1994) 51-70.

14553* LÓPEZ DE SOLIS: **Carmona Moreno** Félix, Fray Luis López de Solis O.S.A. [obispo Quito 1594-1606] (figura estelar de la evangelización de América): Historia viva 6. M 1993, RAg. 223 p. 84-86898-23-4 [TLZ 120,190, H.-J. *Prien*].

14554 MADRUZZO: **Steinhauf** Bernhard, Giovanni Ludovico Madruzzo (1532-1600); katholische Reformation zwischen Kaiser und Papst...: RefGStT 132. Münster 1993, Aschendorff. xxxii-269 p.; 1 fig. DM 94. 3-402-03794-7 [TLZ 120,49, E. *Koch*].

14555 MAROT: **Screech** Michael A., Clément Marot – Lutheranism, Fabrism and Calvinism in the royal courts of France and of Navarre and in the Gospel Court of Ferrara; a renaissance poet discovers the Gospel: StMdvRefT 54. Leiden 1994, Brill. [viii-] 181 p. 90-04-09909-3. ⇥ 2883. – ᴿBtHumRen 56 (1994) 59-82 (G. *Defaux*).

14556 MARPECK: **Boyd** Stephen B., Pilgram Marpeck; his life and social theology: MgMdvRen 12, 1992 ⇥ 9,16520: ᴿAmHR 99 (1994) 1710s (W. O. *Packull*).

14557 MELANCHTHON: **Scheible** Heinz, Melanchthons Briefwechsel T-1 [Texte 1-254, 1514-22], ᴱ*Wetzel* Richard; 6. ᴱ*Scheible* [1550-2]. Stu 1991/88, Frommann-Holzboog. 558 p.; 400 p. 3-7728-0631-7; -993-6. – ᴿZKG 105 (1994) 239-241 (M. *Brecht*) & 241s (W. H. *Neuser*).

14558 MELCHIORITES: *Derksen* John, Second generation radicals of the Protestant Reformation; Melchiorites after Melchior Hoffman in Strasbourg: NesTR 15 (1994) 15-36.

14559 MORE T.: **Duch** Lluis, La secularización de la Utopía en el renacimiento (a pesar de...) [Tomás More]: BibFe 20,58 ('El hechizo de la Utopía' 1994) 85-110.

14560 *Guy* John, Morus [More] Thomas, ᵀ*Thurm* Rüdiger: ⇥ 517, TRE 23 (1994) 323-330.

14561 MORÉLY: **Denis** Philippe, *Rott* Jean, Jean Morély (ca 1524 - ca 1594) et l'utopie d'une démocratie dans l'Église: TravHistRel 278. Genève 1993, Droz. 406 p. – ᴿÉTRel 69 (1994) 279-281 (H. *Bost*).

14562 MÜNTZER: **Warnke** Ingo, Wörterbuch zu Thomas Müntzers deutschen Schriften und Briefen: Lexicographica, maior 50. Tü 1993, Niemeyer. ix-470 p. – ᴿBeitNam 29s (1994s) 107 (G. *Lerchner*).

14563 *Seebass* Gottfried, Müntzer, Thomas (ca. 1490-1525): ⇥ 517, TRE 23 (1994) 414-436.

14564 DA PARADISO: *Valerio* Adriana, 'Et io expongo le Scripture'; Domenica da Paradiso e l'interpretazione biblica; un documento inedito nella crisi del Rinascimento fiorentino [1515-45]: RivStoLR 30 (1994) 499-534.

14566 JOHANNES VON RAGUSA: *Sieben* Hermann J., Basler Konziliarismus konkret; der Tractatus... J. von Ragusa: TPhil 69 (1994) 182-210.

14567 SEGOVIA J. de: **Mann** Jesse D., The historian and the truths; Juan de Segovia's Explanatio de tribus veritatibus fidei: diss. ᴰMcGinn B. Chicago 1994. – RelStR 21,256.

14567* SOTO: *Jiménez Patón* Lorenzo, 'De natura et gratia' de Domingo Soto en la controversia luterana: ComSev 27 (1994) 187-270.

14568 TYNDALE: **Daniell** David, William Tyndale, a biography. NHv 1994, Yale Univ. x-429 p.; 16 pl. 0-300-06132-3. £20 [TDig 42,265]. – ᴿTBR 7,3 (1994s) 56 (M. W. *Elliott*).

14569 VALDÉS: *Firpo* Massimo, Juan de Valdés, fra 'alumbrados' e Lutero [*Nieto* J. C., Two catechisms 1993]: RivStoLR 30 (1994) 535-541.

14570 VITORIA: **Méndez Fernández** B., El problema de la salvación de los 'infieles' en Francisco de Vitoria; desafíos humanos y respuestas teológicas en el contexto del descubrimiento de América: Inst. Hist. Ed. Mg. 33. R 1993, Iglesia Nacional. 382 p. – ᴿSalmanticensis 41 (1994) 460-2 (J. I. *Tellechea Idígoras*).

14571 WYCLIFF: *Hargreaves* Henry, The Wycliffite Glossed Gospels as source; further evidence: Traditio 48 (1993) 247-251.

14571* ZWINGLI: **Hauser** Martin, Prophet und Bischof; Huldrych Zwinglis Amtsverständnis im Rahmen der Zürcher Reformation: FrSZ ÖkBeih 21. FrS 1994, Univ. DM 46. 3-7278-0937-X [TLZ 120,542, J. *Rogge*].

14572 **Hoburg** Ralf, Seligkeit und Heilsgewissheit; Hermeneutik und Schriftauslegung bei Huldrych Zwingli bis 1522: Th Mg B-11.   Stu 1994, Calwer.
x-308 p. DM 120.   3-7668-0798-6 [TLZ 120,670-2, J. *Rogge*].
14572* **Wandel** L., Always ... the poor in Zwingli's Zürich 1990 ➤ 7,g640 ...
9,16541:   ᴿEngHR 109 (1994) 425s (B. *Pullan*).

Y4.5   *Exegesis post-reformatoria* – **Historical criticism to 1800.**

14573 **Baird** William, History of NT research 1. From Deism to Tübingen 1992 ➤ 8,m411; 9,16543:   ᴿCBQ 56 (1994) 355-7 (R. *Scroggs*:
exciting, judicious); ÉTRel 68 (1993) 597s (E. *Cuvillier*); JRel 74 (1994)
384s (W. T. *Wilson*: H. *Credner* and F. *Bleek* passed over); Neotestamentica 28 (1994) 610s (G. D. *West*); TorJT 10 (1994) 249s (J. S.
Kloppenborg).
14574 *Barzazi* Antonella, Settecento monastico italiano; ordini, Chiesa e
società tra XVII e XVIII secolo [Atti Cesena 8-12.IX.1986, ᴱ**Farnedi** D.,
al.]:   RivStoLR 30 (1994) 141-173.
14575 **Bontempi** Franco, Il ferro e la stella; Presenza ebraica a Brescia durante
il Rinascimento. Ono S. Pietro 1994, Circolo Culturale S. Alessandro,
xlii-257 p.
14575* *Borzin* Hartmut, Hebraistik im Zeitalter der Philologia Sacra am
Beispiel der Universität Altdorf: ➤ 323*, Syntax 1993, 151-169.
14576 ᴱ**Bury** Emmanuel, **Meunier** Bernd, Les Pères de l'Église au XVIIᵉ
siècle; Actes du colloque de Lyon 2-5 oct. 1991, 1993 ➤ 9,433*:
ᴿArchivScSocR 39/88 (1994) 55 (E. *Goichot*).
14577 *Childs* Brevard S., Biblical scholarship in the seventeenth century; a
study in ecumenics: ➤ 10, ᶠBARR J., Language 1994, 325-333.
14578 **Clifford** Alan C., Atonement and justification; English evangelical
theology 1640-1790; an evaluation. Ox 1990, Clarendon. xvi-268. £30. –
ᴿScotJT 47 (1994) 376s (B. D. *Spinks*).
14579 ᴱ**Drury** John, Critics of the Bible, 1724-1873: 1989 ➤ 5,k224; 7,g650:
ᴿChrLit 41 (Seattle 1991s) 76-78 (Virginia R. *Mollenkott*).
14579* ᴱ**Force** James E., **Popkin** Richard H., The books of nature and
Scripture; recent essays on natural philosophy, theology and biblical
criticism in the Netherlands of SPINOZA's time and the British Isles of
NEWTON's time: ArchHistId 130. Dordrecht 1994, Kluwer. xviii-223 p.
0-7923-2467-6.
14580 **Goffi** T., La spiritualità del settecento; crisi di identità e nuovi percorsi
(1650-1800). Bo 1993, Dehoniane. 282 p. Lᵐ 22. – CC 144 (1993,4) 98s
(M. *Fois*).
14580* ᴱ**Goldman** Shalom, Hebrew and the Bible in America; the first two
centuries: Brandeis Jewish Culture 1993 ➤ 9,281:   ᴿTrinJ 15 (1994)
259-266 (R. C. *Ortlund*: sometimes provocative).
14581 ᴱ**Graham** W. Fred, Later Calvinism [by country, 26 art.]; international
perspectives: Sixteenth Century Essays. Kirksville MO 1994, Northeast
Missouri Univ. xxii-564 p. [RelStR 21,152, D. K. *McKim*].
14582 **Harrison** Peter, 'Religion' and the religions 1990 ➤ 8,m429; 9,16554:
ᴿScotJT 45 (1992) 567s (D. A. *Pailin*: thorough).
14583 **Hartmann** Claus, Der Jesuitenstaat in Süd Amerika, 1609-1768; eine
christliche Alternative zu Kolonialismus und Marxismus. Weissenhorn
1994, Konrald. 174 p. – ᴿRHist 292 (1994) 155-164 (J. *Meyer*).
14584 **Hill** Christopher, The English Bible and the seventeenth-century
revolution 1993 ➤ 9,16555:   ᴿTLond 97 (1994) 213-5 (L. *Houlden*: from

the mid-century when censorship temporarily ceased and all kinds of political views were inventively and confidently found in the Bible).

14585 **Ignatzi** Hans-Joachim, Die Liturgie des Begräbnisses in der katholischen Aufklärung; eine Untersuchung von Reformentwürfen im südlichen deutschen Sprachgebiet: LtgQFor 75. Münster 1994, Aschendorff. xl-353 p. 3-402-04054-9 [TR 91,425, M. *Probst*].

14585* ᴱ**Klueting** H., Katholische Aufklärung; Aufklärung im Katholischen Deutschland: St. XVIII. Jh. 12. Ha 1993, Meiner. 438 p. [RHE 90,73*].

14586 ᴱ**Kroll** Richard, *al.*, Philosophy, science and religious life 1640-1700 [Latitudinarian conference] 1992 ➤ 8,m433 (0-521-41095-9 in BIP): ᴿTBR 7/1 (1994) 51 (F. *Watts*).

ᴱ**Lamberigts** M. (*Kenis* L.), L'Augustinisme à l'ancienne Faculté de théologie de Louvain: BtETL 111, 1994 ➤ 365*e*.

14588 **Laplanche** François, La Bible en France entre mythe et critique (XVIᵉ-XIXᵉ siècle). P 1994, A. Michel. 291 p. [RHE 90,34*]. – ᴿArchivScSocR 39,88 (1994) 83s (Danièle *Hervieu-Léger*).

14589 *Lauriol* Claude, Philosophes et Protestants dans la France du XVIIIᵉ siècle: ÉTRel 69 (1994) 13-27.

14590 **Lombardi** P., La Bibbia contesa; tra umanesimo e razionalismo: Idee 3. Scandieci FI 1992, Nuova Italia. 290 p. – ᴿRivB 42 (1994) 365-8 (C. *Balzaretti*).

14590* *Martín Melquiades* Andrés, ¿Prequietismo en Valencia?: AnVal 20 (1994) 347-365.

14591 **Martina** Giacomo, Storia della Chiesa, da Lutero ai nostri giorni, 2. L'età dell'assolutismo. Brescia 1994, Morcelliana, 371 p. Lᵐ 35. – ᴿCC 145 (1994,4) 513s (S. *Mazzolini*).

14592 **Noll** Mark A., A history of Christianity in the US and Canada 1992 ➤ 9,16561*: ᴿJEvTS 37 (1994) 453s (D. L. *Russell*).

14592* **Olmo Lete** G. del, Semitistas catalanes siglo XVIII, 1988 ➤ 6,k779; 8,m436: ᴿJSS 39 (1994) 302-5 (G. *Khan*).

14593 **Podskalsky** G., Griechische Theologie in der Zeit der Türkenherrschaft (1453-1821) 1988 ➤ 3,g635... 6,k781: ᴿVizVrem 53 (1992) 182-5 (V. G. *Lurie*, ❸).

14593* **Scholdar** Klaus, The birth of modern critical theology... 17th century [1966], ᵀ*Bowden* J. L 1990, SCM. 184 p. £10.50. – ᴿScotJT 47 (1994) 394s (R. P. *Carroll*: excellent).

14594 *Singer* Thomas C., Hieroglyphs, real characters, and the idea of natural language in English seventeenth-century thought: JHistId 51 (1990) 49-70.

14595 **Spurr** John, The Reformation Church of England, 1646-1689. NHv 1991, Yale Univ. xvii-445 p. $45. – ᴿTS 55 (1994) 157-9 (M. J. *Hayman*).

14596 *Sutter* Jacques, L'actualité des Lumières: RechSR 82 (1994) 39-69; Eng. 7 [The Enlightenment is criticized but not rejected by Romantics and Aᴅᴏʀɴᴏ-Frankfurt, and Catholic thought should be more open to it].

14597 ᴱ**Vogler** G., Wegscheiden der Reformation; Alternatives Denken vom 16. bis 18. Jahrhundert [Bautzen 1989; 23 art.]. 553 p. DM 149. 3-7400-0832-6.

14598 **Vovelle** Michel, The [French] revolution against the Church; from reason to the Supreme Being; [1988], ᵀ*José* Alain. C 1991, Polity. vii-214 p. £35. 0-7546-0748-9. – ᴿTBR 7,2 (1994s) 42 (Judith P. *Champ*).

14599 **Walters** Kerry S., Rational infidels; the American Deists. Durango CA 1992, Longwood. xvi-308 p. [RelStR 21,248, P. K. *Goff*].

14599* **Wessels** A., Europe; was it ever truly Christian? The interaction between gospel and culture [Dutch]^T. L 1994, SCM. xi-242 p.; ill. £13 [RHE 90,62*].

Y4.7 Auctores 1600-1800 alphabetice.

14600 BREVINT: a) McAdoo Henry R., A theology of the Eucharist; [Daniel] Brevint and the Wesleys; – b) Irvine Christopher, Celebrating the Eucharist: TLond 97 (1994) 245-256 / 256-265.

14600* ᴱBury E., Meunier B., Les Pères de l'Église au XVIᵉ s.; Actes du colloque de Lyon, 2-5 oct. 1991/1993 ➤ 9,433* [RHE 88,447*].

14601 BUTLER: ᴱCunliffe Christopher, Joseph Butler's moral and religious thought; tercentenary essays 1992 ➤ 8,380b; £37.50: ᴿJTS 45 (1994) 413-7 (D. A. Pailin).

14601* **Butler** Jon, Awash in a sea of faith 1990 ➤ 6,k770 ... 8,m417: ᴿChH 63 (1994) 129s (D. G. Mathews); EngHR 109 (1994) 477s (C. Brooks: vigorous, even brash).

14602 CORRODI: Görg Manfred, Heinrich Corrodi [1752-93] und die Anfänge der historisch-kritischen Arbeit am NT: BibNot 73 (1994) 13-17.

14602* COTTON: **Knight** Janice, Orthodoxies in Massachusetts; rereading American Puritanism. CM 1994, Harvard Univ. iv-201 p. $45. 0-674-64487-5 [TDig 42,172: W. C. Heiser: focuses 'Spiritual Brethren' neglected by Perry MILLER's 'Intellectual Fathers'].

14603 EDWARDS: **Smith** John E., Jonathan Edwards; Puritan, preacher, philosopher 1991 ➤ 9,16584: ᴿHorizons 21 (1994) 354-6 (W.M. Shea); RelStR 20 (1994) 246 (G. R. McDermott: best US philosopher till PEIRCE).

14603* **Daniel** Stephen H., The philosophy of Jonathan Edwards, a study in divine semiotics. Bloomington 1994, Indiana Univ. ix-202 p. $23. 0-253-31609-X [TDig 42,361].

14604 GIBBON: Frend W. H. C., Edward Gibbon (1737-1794) and early Christianity: JEH 45 (1994) 661-672.

14605 HAMANN: **Berlin** Isaiah, The magus of the north; J. G. Hamann and the origins of modern irrationalism, ᵀHard Henry. NY 1994, Farrer-SG. 160 p. $21. 0-374-19657-9. – ᴿFirsT 44 (1994) 56-58 (T. K. Carr).

14605* **Vaughan** Larry, Johann Georg Hamann, metaphysics of language and vision of history: AmerUnivSt 1/. NY 1989, P. Lang. – ᴿZRGg 46 (1994) 188s (C. Schulte).

14606 HERDER: **Bollacher** Martin, J. G. Herder, Geschichte und Kultur. Wü 1994, Königshausen & N. xii-414 p. ᴅᴍ 98. 3-88479-816-2 [TLZ 120, 819-823, U. F. Huss].

14606* ᴱHintzenstern H. von, J. G. Herder, Vom Geist des Christentums; aus den 'Christlichen Schriften' (1793-8): Thüringer KSt 6. Weimar 1994, Wartburg. 186 p. 3-86160-091-9 [TLZ 120,902, E. Koch].

14607 JANSENIUS: Ceyssens Lucien, a) Autour de l'Unigenitus; Armand BAZIN de Besons; – b) Jean-Pierre VERHORST, évêque auxiliaire de Trèves (1657-1708) [... l'antijansénisme]: AugLv 43 (1993) 85-101 / 42 (1992) 213-233.

14608 Hilgar Marie-France, Saint-Nicolas du Chardonnet [17th century Paris parish] et le Jansénisme: Antonianum 69 (1994) 69-77.

14609 **Neveu** Bruno, L'erreur et son juge; remarques sur les censures doctrinales à l'époque moderne [Jansénisme]: Ist. Ital. Filos. N 1993, Bibliopolis. 758 p. Lᵐ 160 [TS 56,371, J. M. Gres-Gayer].

14610 *Quantin* J.-L., Le catholicisme classique et les Pères de l'Église; recherches sur le retour aux sources patristiques en France de la paix clémentine à l'Unigenitus (1669-1713): diss. Sorbonne 1994. – RHE 89 (1994) 822-5 (C. *Grell*).

14611 **Senofonte** C., Ragione moderna e teologia; l'uomo di ARNAULD. N 1989, Guida. 382 p. – ᴿRTPhil 126 (1994) 387-9 (Clotilde *Calabi*).

14611* *Vanneste* A., Pour une relecture critique de l'Augustinus de Jansenius: AugLv 44 (1994) 115-136..

14612 **Vidal** Daniel, La Morte-Raison; ISAAC le Juive, convulsionnaire janséniste de Lyon 1791-1814. Grenoble 1994, Millon. 212 p. F 140. 3-84137-002-X. – ᴿRHPR 74 (1994) 350 (M. *Chevallier*).

14613 JURIEU: *Bavaud* Georges, Pierre Jurieu (1637-1713); un calvinisme mitigé: NVFr 69 (1994) 255-268.

14614 LATOMUS: **Gielis** Marcel, Scholastiek en humanisme; de kritiek van de Leuvense theoloog Jacobus Latomus op de Erasmiaanse theologie-hervorming: diss. ᴰ*Bornewasser* J. Tilburg 1994. 399 p. > Univ. – TvT 35, 72; RTLv 26, p. 544.

14615 LAVATER c. 1770: **Weigelt** Horst, Johann Kaspar Lavater; Leben, Werk, Wirkung. Gö 1991, Vandenhoeck & R. 132 p. – ᴿTZBas 50 (1994) 177s (H. J. E. *Brintker*).

14616 LE CLERC: *Klauber* Martin I., Between Protestant orthodoxy and rationalism; fundamental articles in the early career of Jean Le Clerc: JHistId 54 (1993) 611-636.

14617 LENFANT: **Mourral** Isabelle, La pensée catholique au siècle des Lumières; la vie et l'œuvre d'Alexandre Lenfant [confesseur de Louis XVI, fondée sur ses sermons]: Mémoire chrétienne. P 1993, Desclée. 378 p. – ᴿRHPR 74 (1994) 350s (M. *Arnold*).

14618 LESSING: ᴱ**Bohnen** Klaus, *Schilson* Arno, Gotthold E. Lessing, Werke 1778-1780 [Teil 2. das GOEZE-Streit seit 1774]: Werke 9. Fra 1993, Deutsche Klassiker. 1380 p. DM 178. – ᴿTüTQ 174 (1994) 245-7 (M. *Seckler*).

14619 *Borg* Marcus J., Profiles in scholarly courage; early days of NT criticism [Tom PAINE; Lessing ...]: BR 10,5 (1994) 40-45.

14619* **Quapp** Erwin, Lessings Theologie statt JACOBIS 'Spinozismus'; eine Interpretation der 'Erziehung des Menschengeschlechts' auf der Grundlage der Formel *hèn egō kai pân* I. 1-25. Bern 1992, Lang. 367 p. DM 98. 3-261-04501-9 [TLZ 120,910, H. *Schultze*].

14620 *Willmer* Peter, Lessing und Zinzendorf: AmerUnivSt 1/72. Fra 1989, Lang. vi-224 p. DM 57. – ᴿTR 90 (1994) 145-8 (G. *Pfleiderer*).

14621 LOCKE: *a*) *Vogt* Philip, Seascape with fog; metaphor in Locke's Essay; – *b*) *Paxman* David B., Language and difference; the problem of abstraction in eighteenth-century language study: JHistId 54 (1993) 1-18 / 19-36.

14621* *Jinkins* Michael, Elements of federal theology in the religious thought of John Locke: EvQ 66 (1994) 123-141.

14622 MUHLENBERG: *Strohmidel* Karl O., Henry M. Muhlenberg's European heritage: LuthQ 6,1 (Milwaukee 1992) 5-34 (1-84 *al.*).

14623 NEWTON: *Wiles* Maurice, [Isaac] Newton and the Bible [... The chronology of ancient kingdoms amended 1728; The prophecies of Daniel and the Apocalypse of John 1733]: ➤ 10, ᶠBARR J., Language 1994, 334-350.

14624 PASCAL: *Papasogli* Benedetta,   Letture settecentesche di Pascal: Riv-StoLR 30 (1994) 479-497.

14625 **Kreeft** Peter, Christianity for modern pagans; Pascal's Pensées edited, outlined and explained. SF 1993, Ignatius. 341 p. $15 pa. 0-89870-452-9 [TDig 41,367].

14626 **Martineau** Emmanuel, Blaise Pascal,   Discours sur le religion et sur quelques autres sujets qui ont été trouvés après sa mort parmi ses papiers. P 1992. – ᴿTPhil 69 (1994) 402-410 (A. *Raffelt*).

14627 POIRET: **Chevallier** Marjolaine,   Pierre Poiret (1646-1719); du protestantisme à la mystique [doctorat d'État].   Genève 1994, Labor et Fides. – ᴿETRel 69 (1994) 590s (H. *Bost*); RHPR 74 (1994) 111.

14627* QUICK: *Clifford* Alan C.,   Reformed pastoral theology under the Cross; John Quick [, Synodicon 1692] and Claude BROUSSON [1647-98]: EvQ 66 (1994) 291-306.

14628 REUCHLIN: **Pandžić** Elisabeth & Basilius, Juraj DRAGIŠIĆ und Johannes Reuchlin... Kampf für die jüdischen Bücher. Bamberg 1989, Univ. 144 p. 48 p. phot. 'Defensio'. – ᴿOrChrPer 60 (1994) 270s (I. *Golub*).

14629 ᴱHerzig Arno, *Schoeps* Julius H., Reuchlin und die Juden: Pforzheimer-Reuchlin 3. Sigmaringen 1993, Thorbecke.   255 p. DM 58. – ᴿCathHR 80 (1994) 351s (M. U. *Edwards*).

14629* ROUSSEAU: **Lefebvre** Philippe,   Les pouvoirs de la parole; l'Église et Rousseau 1768-1848:   Histoire.   P 1992, Cerf.   492 p. – ᴿMélSR 51 (1994) 100s (P. *Daubercies*: d'abord apologistes de vue étroite; assez vite après, réception.

14630 SEMLER: **Lüder** Andreas,   Historie und Dogma; ein Beitrag zur Genese und Entfaltung von Johann Salomo Semlers Verständnis des Alten Testaments: Diss. ᴰ*Kaiser* O.   Marburg 1994. – RTLv 26, p. 545; TR 91,99.

14631 TURRETTINI F. 1623-87:   ᴱ**Giger** George M.,   ᵀ*Dennison* James T., Francis Turretin, Institutes of Elenctic theology I, first through tenth topics 1992 → 8,m478:   ᴿJEvTS 37 (1994) 609s (T. R. *Phillips*).

14632 *Klauber* Martin L.,   Francis Turretin [1623-87] on biblical accommodation; loyal Calvinist or reformed scholastic?: WestTJ 55 (1993) 73-86.

14633 **Meijering** E. P.,   Reformierte Scholastik... Väterbeweis/Turrettins 1991 → 8,m479; 9,16606:   ᴿBijdragen 55 (1994) 90s (H. J. *Adriaanse*).

14634 TURRETTINI J.-A. 1671-1737: *Klauber* Martin,   Jean-Alphonse Turrettini (1671-1737) on natural theology; the triumph of reason and revelation in the academy of Geneva: ScotJT 47 (1994) 301-325.

14634* *Pitassi* Maria Cristina,   D'une parole à l'autre; les sermons du théologien genevois Jean-Alphonse Turrettini: AnStoEseg 10 (1993) 71-93; Eng. 4.

14635 WESLEY: **Rataboul** Louis J.,   John Wesley, un anglican sans frontières 1703-1791.   Nancy 1991, PUF.   239 p. – ᴿRTPhil 126 (1994) 83s (Maria Cristina *Pitassi*).

14635* **Oden** Thomas C.,   John Wesley's scriptural Christianity; a plain expression of his teaching on Christian doctrine, 1 [2 will be pastoral, 3 ethics]. GR 1994, Zondervan.   376 p. $23.   0-310-75321-X [TDig 42,284].

14636 **Brown-Lawson** Albert,   John Wesley and the Anglican evangelicals of the eighteenth century; a study in cooperation and separation with special

reference to the Calvinistic controversies. 1994, Pentland.   xvii-410 p.
£11.50 pa. – ᴿTLond 97 (1994) 471s (D. W. *Bebbington*).

Y5   *Saeculum XIX* – **Exegesis** – **19th Century.**

14637 **Addinall** Peter, Philosophy and biblical interpretation ... 19th c. conflict
1991 ⇒ 7,g706 ... 9,16612: ᴿChH 63 (1994) 135s (W. J. *Wilkins*); CritRR
5 (1992) 80s (C. *Brown*); ScotJT 47 (1994) 101-3 (G. *Jones*).
14638 **Azzolin** Giovanni, Manzoni e i Gesuiti della Civiltà Cattolica. R 1992,
UCIIM. 115 p. – ᴿRivStoLR 30 (1994) 662-4 (Anna Maria *Golfieri*).
14639 ᴱ**Baker** Robert, *al.*, The codification of medical morality; historical and
philosophical studies of the formalization of Western medical morality in
the eighteenth and nineteenth centuries [Wellcome Institute 1989; on John
GREGORY and Thomas PERCIVAL]. Dordrecht 1993, Kluwer. viii-230 p.
$87. 0-7923-1921-4 [TDig 42, 159].
14639* ᴱ**Lora** Erminio, *Simonati* Rita, Enchiridion delle encicliche 1. Benedetto XIV... Pio VIII: Strumenti. Bo 1994, Dehoniane. xxxi-1524 p.
Lᵐ 65. 88-10-20571-5 [RHE 90,236, C. *Soetens*].

14640 **BAUER** Bruno, Kritik der evangelischen Geschichte des Johannes
(1840). Hildesheim 1990, Olms. xiv-440 p. – ᴿCiuD 207 (1994) 519s (J.
Gutiérrez).
14640* BAUR: **Andrae** Christian, F. C. Baur als Prediger ᴰ1993 ⇒ 9,16637:
ᴿTLZ 119 (1994) 1135 (Kerstin *Voigt*).
14641 *a*) *Hester* C. E., Baurs Anfänge in Blaubeuren; – *b*) *Graf* F. W.,
Gelungene Bürgertheologie? 'Der alte und der neue Glaube' von D. F.
STRAUSS: ⇒ 365c, Historisch/Baur 1994, 67-82 / 227-244.
14641* ᴱ**Hester** Carl E., Ferdinand C. Baur; die frühen Briefe (1814-1835):
Contubernium 38. Sigmaringen 1993, Thorbecke. 246 p.; 2 fig. DM 78.
3-7995-3232-3 [TLZ 120,51, Kerstin *Voigt*].
14642 **Bechtold** Hans-Joachim, Die historische Bibelkritik im Judentum des
19. Jahrhunderts; ausgewählte Vertreter und ihre Werke: ev. Diss. ᴰ*Mayer*
G. Mainz 1994s. – RTLv 26,534.
14643 *Beckwith* Roger, Essays and Reviews (1860) [manifesto]; the advance
of [Anglican] liberalism: Churchman 108 (1994) 48-58.
14644 BEECHER: **Harding** Vincent, A certain magnificence; Lyman Beecher
and the transformation of American Protestantism, 1775-1963. Brooklyn
1991, Carlson. xi-570 p. $75. – ᴿCritRR 6 (1993) 370-2 (Linda K.
Pritchard).
14645 **Boylan** Anne M., Sunday school; the formation of an American
institution 1790-1880. NHv 1990, Yale Univ. xii-225 p. $12. – ᴿCritRR
6 (1993) 349-351 (Susan D. *Rose*).
14646 BRIGGS: **Sawyer** M. James, Charles Augustus Briggs and tensions in
late nineteenth-century American theology. Lewiston NY 1994, Mellen.
xiii-204 p. $90. 0-7734-9961-X [TDig 42,88].
14647 *Cabanel* Patrick, L'institutionalisation des 'Sciences religieuses' en
France (1879-1908); une entreprise protestante: BHistProt 140,1 (1994)
33-80 [< ZIT 94,288].
14648 **Ciola** Nicola, La crisi del teocentrismo trinitario nel novecento
teologico; il tema nel contesto emblematico della secolarizzazione.
R 1993, Dehoniane. 510 p. Lᵐ 48. 88-396-0482-0. – ᴿAntonianum 69
(1994) 555-561 (V. *Battaglia*); Gregorianum 75 (1994) 356s (J.
O'Donnell).

14649 DERMESTETER: *Malkiel* Yakov, Les frères Darmesteter à l'aube de la philologie française: RÉJ 153 (1994) 383-401.
14650 DELITZSCH 1: **Wagner** S., Franz Delitzsch 1991 ↠ 8,m519: ᴿZAW 106 (1994) 541 (D. *Vieweger*).
14651 DELITZSCH 2: **Lehmann** Reinhard G., Friedrich Delitzsch und der Babel-Bibel-Streit [Diss. Mainz 1989, ᴰ*Michel* D.]: OBO 133. FrS/Gö 1994, Univ./VR. 444 p.; 12 pl. 3-7278-0932-9 [TLZ 120,905, W. *Wiefel*]. – ᴿTüTQ 174 (1994) 241s (W. *Gross*)

14652 **De Luca** Lorraine S., Adult education and the ambivalence of the Catholic Church towards modern American society, in the archdiocese of New York, 1860-1910: diss. Columbia Teachers, ᴰ*Sloan* D. NY 1994. 335 p. 94-24520. – DissA 55 (1994s) p. 832.
14653 **Dowling** Linda, Hellenism and homosexuality in Victorian Oxford. Ithaca 1994, Cornell Univ. xvi-173 p. $26. 0-8014-2960-9 [RelStR 21,50, W. G. *Rusch*).

14654 EMERSON: **Grusin** Richard A., Transcendentalist hermeneutics 1991 ↠ 16646: ᴿChrLit 41 (1991s) 88s (C. E. *Ostwalt*).
14655 **Finke** Roger, **Starr** Rodney, The churching of America, 1776-1990, winners and losers in the religious economy. New Brunswick 1992, Rutgers Univ. 325 p. $23. 0-8135-1837-7. – ᴿAmHR 99 (1994) 288s (J. *Butler*).
14656 **Flegg** C. G., Gathered under apostles 1992 ↠ 8,m497; 9,16618: ᴿJTS 45 (1994) 777-9 (D. M. *Thompson*).
14657 **Franchot** Jenny, Roads to Rome: the American Protestant encounter with Catholicism: New Historicism 28. Berkeley 1994, Univ. California. xxvii-500 p. $55; pa. $18. 0-520-07818-7; -8606-6.
14658 **Gauvreau** Michael, The evangelical century; college and creed in English Canada from the Great Revival to the Great Depression [based on theologization of history; diss.] 1991 ↠ 16620: ᴿTTod 50 (1993s) 486.488 (N. F. *Cornett*).
14659 **Gonzalez** Justo J., *al.*, Poverty and ecclesiology. ColMn 1992, Liturgical. 104 p. $8. – ᴿTorJT 10 (1994) 239-242 (Loraine M. *Shepherd*).
14659* HEBEL: *Reents* Christine, Johann Peter Hebels Biblische Geschichten; ein Longseller 1824-1992: ↠ 34*d*, ᶠFANGMEIER J., Das Wort 1994, 283-292.

14660 HEGEL: **Olson** Alan M., Hegel and the Spirit; philosophy as pneumatology. Princeton 1992, Univ. 223 p. $25. – ᴿJAAR 62 (1994) 208-211 (R. L. *Perkins*).
14660* **Bialas** Wolfgang, Von der Theologie der Befreiung zur Philosophie der Freiheit; Hegel und die Religion [< Diss. Lp. 1983]: FrSZÖkBeit 23. FrS 1993, Univ. 168 p. Fs 28. 3-7278-0905-1 [TLZ 120,1102, F. *Wagner*].
14661 *Bremer* Dieter, Der Begriff des Schicksals bei Hegel und seine griechischen Ursprünge: Antike und Abendland 35 (1989) 24-38 [ArBegG 37 (1994) 352s (*ipse*)].
14662 *Bueno de la Fuente* Eloy, Hegel y el cristianismo; ¿'Aufhebung' o superación?: RET 53 (1993) 449-480.
14662* **Gniosdorsch** Iris, Religion denken, eine kritische Untersuchung der Hegelschen Verwendung in der Religionsphilosophie: kath. Diss. ᴰ*Schrödter*. Frankfurt Goethe-Univ. 1993. – TR 90,82.
14663 **Hodgson** Peter C., Winds of the Spirit; a constructive [Hegelian]

Christian theology. LVL 1994, W-Knox. xv-421 p. $25 [TS 56,387, P. *Lakeland*].
14664 *Secretan* Philibert, Tentations et tentatives hégéliennes [FESSARD G. 1990; BRITO E. 1991]: FrSZ 41 (1994) 252-9.
14665 **Tilliette** Xavier, La cristologia idealista [Hegel]: GdT 221. Brescia 1993, Queriniana. 211 p. – ᴿActuBbg 31 (1994) 300 (E. *Forment*); AnStoEseg 11 (1994) 312s (G. *Coccolini*).

14665* ᴱ**Helmstadter** Richard J., *Lightman* Bernard, Victorian faith in crisis; essays on continuity and change in nineteenth-century religious belief. L 1990, Macmillan. xii-391 p. £45. – ᴿLitTOx 8 (1994) 111s (S. *Prickett*).
14666 **Howsam** Leslie, Cheap Bibles... 19th century 1991 ⇒ 7,1660: ᴿHeythJ 35 (1994) 97s (A. F. *Jesson*).
14667 **Jossua** Jean-Pierre, Pour une histoire religieuse de l'expérience littéraire; Dieu aux XIXᵉ et XXᵉ siècles: Religions 22. P 1994, Beauchesne. 305 p. 2-7010-1907-0.
14668 KÄHLER: **Göll** Hans-Peter, Versöhnung und Rechtfertigung; die Rechtfertigungslehre Martin Kählers. Giessen 1991, Brunnen. 272 p. – ᴿZKG 105 (1994) 393-5 (H. *Assel*).
14669 KANT: **Lichtenberger** Hans P., Wie kommt der Christus in die Philosophie? Gotteslehre und Christologie bei Immanuel Kant: ev. Hab.-Diss. ᴰ*Link* C. Bern 1994. – TR 91,89.
14669* KEIL: **Siemens** Peter, Carl Friedrich Keil 1807-1888); Leben und Werk. Giessen 1994, Brunnen. xi-355 p. 3-7655-9394-X [TLZ 120,996, A. *Hauboldt*].
14670 **Kenis** Leo, De Theologische Faculteit te Leeuven in de negentiende eeuw, 1834-1889 [diss. 1989, ᴰ*Boudens* R.]: VerhAcad lett 14,143. Bru 1992, Acad. 543 p. 90-6569-576-1. – ᴿGregorianum 75 (1994) 579s (J. E. *Vercruysse*, Eng.); JEH 45 (1994) 713-5 (G. *Fransen*, franç.).
14671 **Kerner** Hanns, Reform des Gottesdienstes; von der Neubildung der Gottesdienstordnung und Agende in der evangelisch-lutherischen Kirche in Bayern im 19. Jahrhundert: ThMg C-23. Stu 1994, Calwer. 286 p. DM 68.

14672 KIERKEGAARD: *Bannach* Klaus, Gleichzeitig mit Jesus? Anmerkungen zu Kierkegaard: KerDo 40 (1994) 203-218; Eng. 218.
14672* **Hinskon** Craig Q., Kierkegaard's theology; cross and grace, the Lutheran and idealist traditions in his thought: diss. ᴰ*Berrish* B. Chicago 1994. – RelStR 21,253.
14673 **Law** David R., Kierkegaard as negative theologian. Ox 1993, Clarendon. xiv-231 p. £25. – ᴿTLond 97 (1994) 45s (J. *Macquarrie*).
14674 **Mooney** Edward F., Knights of faith and resignation; reading Kierkegaard's Fear and Trembling 1991, SUNY. $57.50; pa. $19. – ᴿCritRR 6 (1993) 521-3 (R. M. *Green*: first book on what SK said would immortalize him).
14675 **Rosas** L. Joseph, Scripture in the thought of Søren Kierkegaard. Nv 1994, Broadman &H. 219 p. $30. 0-8005-1624-2.
14676 **Torralba Roselló** F., Amor y diferencia; el misterio de Dios en Kierkegaard [diss. ᴰ*Giralt* F.]. Barc 1993, Promociones. 383 p. – ᴿCiuD 206 (1993) 651s (J. M. *Ozaeta*).

14677 KUENEN: ᴱ**Dirksen** P. B., Abraham Kuenen; his major contributions to the study of the OT: OTS 29, 1993 ⇒ 9,77: ᴿETL 70 (1994) 136 (J.

Lust: valuable, though bypassing van HOONACKER); TLZ 119 (1994) 17 (H. *Reventlow*).

14678 LIGHTFOOT: *Pointer* Stephen R., J[oseph] B. Lightfoot [1828-89] as a Christian historian of early Christian literature: ChrSchR 23 (1993s) 426-444.

14679 McGARVEY: *Haynes* Don, 'To honor the God of the Bible': J.W. McGarvey [b. 1829]: LexTQ 29 (1994) 159-187.

14680 VAN MANEN: **Verhoef** Edward, W.C. van Manen, een Hollandse radicale theoloog. Kampen 1994, Kok. 91 p. £22.50.

14680* MARX: *Tran Van Toan*, La religion dans les lectures du jeune Marx: MélSR [50 (1993)...] 51 (1994) 11-40. 181-199 [Eng. 80. 200].

14681 MIGNE: **Bloch** Howard, God's plagiarist; being an account of the fabulous industry and irregular commerce of the Abbé Migne. Ch 1994, Univ. 182 p. $25. 0-226-05970-7 [TDig 42,57].

14682 MÖHLER: *Erb* Peter C., Johann Adam Möhler [† 1838] concerned with the unity of the Church: CanadCath 12,3 (1994) 21-26.

14683 *Wagner* Harald, Möhler, Johann Adam (1796-1838): → 517, TRE 23 (1994) 140-3.

14684 MOULTON: *Turner* Nigel, Moulton, James Hope (1863-1917), T*Balz* Horst: → 517, TRE 23 (1994) 382-4.

14685 NIETZSCHE: *Hoogen* Toine van den, Duster licht; het verlangen naar God en de mystiek van Nietzsche: → 110, F*SCHILLEBEECKX* E., TvT 34 (1994) 385-406; Eng. 406.

14686 *Forte* Bruno, Salvezza e storia in Nietzsche: Asprenas 41 (1994) 323-336.

14687 **O'Neill** J.C., The Bible's authority: LESSING to BULTMANN 1991 → 7,g718; 8,m508: R*CritRR* 6 (1993) 129-131 (S. *Fowl*: too idealizing); IrTQ 60 (1994) 71s (W. *Riley*); ScotJT 47 (1994) 107s (G. *Jones*).

14688 OVERBECK: **Peter** Niklaus, Im Schatten der Modernität; Franz Overbecks Weg zur [1873] 'Christlichkeit unserer heutigen Theologie'. Stu 1992, Metzler. viii-272 p. – R*TZBas* 50 (1994) 84-86 (A.U. *Sommer*).

14689 **Paz** D.G., Popular anti-Catholicism in mid-Victorian England. Stanford 1992, Univ. v-322 p. $42.50. – R*AnglTR* 76 (1994) 529s (D. *Siegenthaler*).

14690 PEIRCE: **Brent** Joseph, Charles Sanders Peirce; a life. Bloomington IN 1993, Univ. 388 p. $35. – R*AmJTP* 15 (1994) 337-342 (M.L. *Raposa*).

14691 REUSS: *Vincent* Jean-Marcel, Le 'rationalisme mystique' d'Édouard Reuss et ses incidences sur *La Bible* [1884-91, 19 vol.]: RHPR 74 (1994) 43-66; Eng. 112.

14691* *Vincent* Jean Marcel, Die Stellung Eduard Reuss' zur BAURschen Tendenzkritik: TZBas 50 (1994) 1-8.

14692 RITSCHL: E*Gisel* P., al., Albrecht Ritschl... en modernité 1991 → 7, g761: R*ScripTPamp* 26 (1994) 330s (P. *Conesa*).

14692* a) **McCulloh** Gerald W., Christ's person... Ritschl munus triplex 1990 → 8,m889: R*CritRR* 6 (1993) 516-8 (C. *Marsh*). – b) **Marsh** Clive, Albrecht Ritschl and the problem of the historical Jesus; a study in the relationship between historical-critical research into the canonical gospel and Christian theology. Lewiston 1992, Mellen. xxiv-236 p. $70. – R*Crit*RR 6 (1993) 264-6 (W. *Baird*).

14693 ROBINSON: **Conser** Walter R.j, God and the natural world [reconciled by Edward Robinson, HODGE, BUSHNELL and 6 contemporaries]. Columbia 1993, Univ. S. Carolina. x-202 p. $35 [RelStR 21,209, Mary *Gerhart*].

14693* ROTHE: *Drehsen* Volker, Vision eines kirchenfreien, ethischen Zeit-alters des modernen Christentums; Richard Rothe (1799-1867): BTZ 11 (1994) 201-218.

14694 SCHELLING: **Maesschalck** Marc, L'anthropologie politique et religieuse de Schelling: BtPhLv 35. LvN 1991, Peeters. xxxviii-330 p. – ᴿScEspr 46 (1994) 249-253 (Suzanne *Foisy*).

14695 SCHLEIERMACHER: *Crouter* Richard, Kierkegaard's not so hidden debt to Schleiermacher: ZnTg 1,2 (1994) 205-225.

14695* **Boekels** Joachim, Schleiermacher als Kirchengeschichtler: Archiv 13. B 1994, de Gruyter. xi-488 p. DM 238.   3-11-014203-1 [TLZ 120,893-5, K. *Nowak*].

14696 **Brito** Émilio, La pneumatologie de Schleiermacher: BtETL 113. Lv 1994, Peeters. xii-649 p. Fb 3000.   90-6186-604-9 [TLZ 120,831, K. *Nowak*].

14697 *Brito* Emilio, La distinction d'Église visible et de l'Église invisible selon Schleiermacher: RevSR 68 (1994) 465-480.

14698 **Christe** Wilhelm, Kirche und Welt; eine Untersuchung zu ihrer Ver-hältnisbestimmung in der Theologie F. Schleiermachers: Diss. ᴰ*Greshake* G. FrB 1993. – TR 90,83.

14699 *Dierken* Jörg, Das zweifältige Absolute; die irreducible Difference zwi-schen Frömmigkeit und Reflexion im Denken Friedrich Schleiermachers: ZnTG 1 (1994) 16-46.

14700 **Fischer** Konrad, Gegenwart Christi und Gottesbewusstsein; drei Stu-dien zur Theologie Schleiermachers: ThBtTöp 55. B 1992, de Gruyter. vii-117 p. DM 48. – ᴿJRel 74 (1994) 399 (W. E. *Wyman*).

14701 *Heesch* Matthias, Transzendentale Individualität? Schleiermacher und sein Schüler ROTHE im Streit um das Wesen des Endlich-Gegebenen: NSys 35 (1993) 259-263; Eng. 264.

14702 *Kvist* Hans-O., Gefühl bei Schleiermacher und seinen Nachfolgern in der Vermittlungstheologie: ArBegG 36 (1993) 196-226.

14703 *Lamm* Julia A., Schleiermacher's post-KANTian Spinozism; the early essays on SPINOZA, 1793-94: JRel 74 (1994) 476-505.

14704 *Nowak* Kurt, Die neue Schleiermacherausgabe: TLZ [I. 109,917 + 110,752] II. 119 (1994) 718-728.

14705 *Pfau* Thomas, Immediacy and the text; F. Schleiermacher's theory of style and interpretation: JHistId 51 (1990) 51-73.

14705* **Schnur** Harald, Schleiermachers Hermeneutik und ihre Vorgeschichte im 18. Jahrhundert; Studien zur Bibelauslegung zu Hamann, Herder und F. Schlegel. Stu 1994, Metzler. viii-248 p. DM 58.   3-476-00995-5 [TLZ 120,460, M. *Obst*].

14706 *Thouard* Denis, Schleiermacher et le langage religieux; sentiment, lan-gage et communauté: RechSR 82 (1994) 335-360; Eng. 360.

14706* *Wyman* Walter E.ᴶ, Rethinking the Christian doctrine of sin; Friedrich Schleiermacher and HICK's 'Irenaean type': JRel 74 (1994) 199-217.

14707 **Sieben** H.J., Die katholische Konzilsidee im 19, und 20, Jahrhundert. Pd 1993, Schöningh. 432 p. 3-506-74725-8: ᴿEstE 69 (1994) 264-6 (S. *Madrigal*).

14708 STUART: **Giltner** John H., Moses Stuart 1988 → 4,k300; 5,k350: ᴿRB 101 (1994) 470s (B. T. *Viviano*).

14709 **Taylor** Marion A., The Old Testament in the Old Princeton School

(1812-1929). SF 1992, Mellen Research Univ. xx-380, $80. – ᴿBL (1994)
20 (R. E. *Clements*); PrincSemB 14 (1993) 288-290 (P. D. *Miller*).
14710 Tocqueville: **Kessler** Sanford, Tocqueville's civil religion; Christianity
and the prospects for freedom: RelCuSoc. Albany 1994, SUNY. xiv-237 p.
$54.50; pa. $18. 0-7914-1929-0; – 30-4 [TDig 42,172].
14711 Wesley: *Bassett* Paul M., Culture and concupiscence; the changing
definition of sanctity in the Wesleyan holiness movement, 1867-1920:
WesleyT 28 (1993) 59-127.
14712 de Wette: **Rogerson** J., W. L. M. de Wette jOsu 126, 1992 ➤ 8,m488;
9,16690: ᴿCBQ 56 (1994) 339s (A. J. *Hauser*); CritRR 6 (1993) 131-2 (W.
Baird); ETL 70 (1994) 452s (F. *Neirynck*); JRelH 18 (1994) 255s (T. A.
Howard); RB 101 (1994) 308s (B. T. *Viviano*); RivB 42 (1994) 363-5 (A.
Minissale); ZAW 106 (1994) 366 (C. *Bultmann*: de W. '1870-1849').
14713 *Vincent* Jean-Marcel, Unpublizierte Quellen zur Wirksamkeit von
W. M. L. de Wette und zur Beziehung von Eduard Reuss zum Basler
Gelehrten: TZBas 50 (1994) 322-335.

14713* **Ward** W. R., The Protestant Evangelical awakening 1992 ➤ 9,16632:
ᴿEvQ 66 (1994) 95s (A. S. *Wood*).
14714 Whitefield: **Stout** Harry S., The divine dramatist, G. Whitefield:
Library of Religious Thought. GR 1991, Eerdmans. 301 p. $15 pa. –
ᴿCritRR 6 (1993) 397s (J. R. *Tyson*).
14715 **Wolffe** John, The Protestant crusade in Great Britain, 1829-1860. Ox
1991, Clarendon. xii-366 p.; 4 fig. £40. 2-19-820199-0. – ᴿJTS 45 (1994)
779 (D. M. *Thompson*).
14716 **Wosh** Peter J., Spreading the Bible business in nineteenth century
America. Ithaca 1994, Cornell Univ. [xiv-]271 p. 0-8014-2928-5.

Y5.5   *Crisis modernistica* – **The Modernist era.**

14717 **Appleby** R. S., 'Church and age unite!' 1992 ➤ 8,m564; 9,16692:
ᴿCritRR 6 (1993) 341-3 (J. M. *O'Toole*); Horizons 21 (1994) 190s (Mary
Jo *Weaver*); JEH 45 (1994) 530-2 (M. S. *Massa*); JRel 74 (1994) 102s
(P. R. *D'Agostino*); TorJT 10 (1994) 270s (Ellen M. *Leonard*); TS 55
(1994) 161-3 (G. P. *Fogarty*).
14718 **Guasco** Maurilio, Dal Modernismo al Vaticano II 1991 ➤ 9,16697:
ᴿArchivScSocR 35,86 (1994) 286s (J.-D. *Durand*).
14719 **Hutchison** William R., The modernist impulse in American Protestantism. Durham NC 1992, Duke Univ. xiv-349 p. – ᴿReligion 24
(1994) 83s (C. C. *Smith*).
14720 **O'Connell** Marvin R., Critics on trial; an introduction to the Catholic
modernist crisis. Wsh 1994, Catholic University of America. xiii-394 p.;
bibliog. 377-385. 0-8132-0799-1; pa. -800-9.
14721 **O'Meara** Thomas F., Church and culture; German Catholic theology
1860-1914: 1991 ➤ 8,m567: ᴿChH 63 (1994) 147s (D. G. *Schultenover*);
LvSt 19 (1994) 83-85 (L. *Kenis*); TorJT 10 (1994) 136s (D. *Donovan*).
14722 *Neuner* Peter, Das anti-modernistische Erbe der Katholischen Kirche
und die Krise der Moderne: UnSa 49 (1994) 19-28.
14723 *Poulat* Émile, *a*) Le renouveau des études patristiques en France et la
crise moderniste: ➤ 359*b*, Patristique 1991/3, 20-29; – *b*) Catholiques sans
église; que reste-t-il aujourd'hui de l' 'intransigeantisme'?: RScSocRel
23,46 (1994) 117-125.
14723* *Reardon* Bernard M. G., Modernismus: ➤ 517, TRE 23 (1994) 129-138.

14724 **Schatz** Klaus, Vaticanum I., 1. Vor der Eröffnung. Pd 1992, Schöningh. xviii-300 p. DM 84. 3-506-74693-6. – ᴿGregorianum 75 (1994)
574-8 (M. *Chappin*, Eng.); HerdKorr 47 (1993) 105 (U. *Ruh*). – 2. bis zur
K. 'Dei Filius'. 480 p. DM 98. 3-506-74694-4.

14725 **Schultenover** David G., A view from Rome on the eve of the modernist crisis 1993 ➤ 9,16699: ᴿCathHR 80 (1994) 390s (L. *Barmann*);
Schultenover rejoinder p. 824-6, reply 826-8); JEH 45 (1994) 522s (O.
Chadwick: an extraordinary book); Tablet 247 (1993) 1006 (M. *Walsh*:
largely from the published diary of Luis MARTIN).

14726 *Winling* Raymond, Nouvelle Theologie [CONGAR Y., BOUILLARD
H. ...], ᵀ*Stöve* Eckehart: ➤ 517, TRE 24 (1994) 668-675.

14727 BLONDEL: *Cacciapuoti* Pierluigi, Attualità di Blondel nell'età postmoderna; nel centenario de L'Action una nuova edizione italiana [CinB 1993,
Paoline]: Asprenas 41 (1994) 97-110.

14728 ᴱ**Forni** Guglielmo, Blondel Maurice, Storia e dogma; le lacune filo-
sofiche dell'esegesi moderna [1904]: GdT 214. Brescia 1992, Queriniana.
139 p. Lᵐ 16. 88-399-0714-9. – ᴿGregorianum 75 (1994) 350 (R. *Fisichella*).

14728* *Forni* Guglielmo, Blondel e la controversia cristologica: AnStoEseg
11 (1994) 229-265; Eng. 6: took some from LOISY and anticipated
LABERTHONNIÈRE.

14729 **Izquierdo** C., Blondel e la crisis modernista; análisis de 'Historia y
dogma'. Pamplona 1990, EUNSA. 396 p. – ᴿAnnTh 7 (1993) 245-7 (A.
Cirillo).

14730 **Letourneau** Alain, Dia-logique et logique de L'Action; épistémologie,
logique herméneutique et théorie de la sociabilité dans la première œuvre
de Maurice Blondel: diss. Sorbonne, ᴰ*Meslin* M. P 1994. – RTLv 26,
p. 529.

14731 *a) Létourneau* Alain, [*Renault* Marc], L'herméneutique de Blondel dans
L'Action de 1893; – *b) Bordeleau* Léo-Paul, Blondel et SCHOPENHAUER;
regards sur le pessimisme: ScEspr 46 (1994) 149-163 [139-148] / 165-177.

14732 *a) Noey* K., Blondel in het licht van Ignatius' Geestelijke oefeningen; –
b) Schrama Martin, Blondel en de traditie van het ingeschapen verlangen
naar God: Bijdragen 55 (1994) 399-411; Eng. 411 / 412-433; Eng. 433s.

14733 *Russo* Antonio, A proposito del rapporto S. TOMMASO-M. Blondel in
H. de LUBAC: Angelicum 71 (1994) 427-444.

14734 **Virgoulay** R., Blondel, L'Action... centenaire 1992 ➤ 9,16708: ᴿGregorianum 75 (1994) 351 (R. *Fisichella*).

14735 *Viscovi* Annalise, Storia e dogma di M. Blondel: Studium 90 (R 1994)
446-451.

14736 DUCHESNE: **Waché** Brigitte, Monseigneur Louis Duchesne (1843-1922),
historien de l'Église, directeur de l'ÉcFR: Coll. ÉFR 167, 1992 ➤ 9,16713:
ᴿRÉLat 72 (1994) 347-9 (J. *Fontaine*); RevSR 68 (1994) 113s (C. *Munier*).

14737 FRACASSINI: *Iozzelli* Fortunato, Modernismo e antimodernismo a Perugia; il caso Fracassini [Umberto, 1862-1950]: RivStoLR 30 (1994)
299-345.

14738 HECKER: **O'Brien** David J., Isaac Hecker, an American Catholic
1992 ➤ 8,m850; 9,16714: ᴿEglT 25 (1994) 455s (L. *Laberge*).

14739 VON HÜGEL: *Leonard* Ellen M., Friedrich von Hügel's spirituality of
empowerment: Horizons 21 (1994) 270-287.

14740 **Zorzi** Giuseppe, Auf der Suche nach der verlorenen Katholizität; die Briefe Friedrich von Hügels and Giovanni SEMERIA: TüStThPh 3. Mainz 1991, Grünewald. I. 301 p.; II. p. 303-618; Bibliog. 573-606. 3-7867-1577-7.

14741 KRAUS: *Reinhardt* Rudolf, Wie 'liberal' war Franz Xaver Kraus?: ZKG 105 (1994) 229-233.

14742 *Reinhardt* Rudolf, Franz Xaver Kraus und das Theologische Literaturblatt (1873) [praktisch Sprachrohr der Döllinger-Theologie] mit Notizen zur Katholisch-Theologischen Fakultät Tübingen und ihrer Theologischen Quartalschrift: TüTQ 174 (1994) 208-213.

14743 *Becker* W., Modernismus und Modernisierung; ein Versuch zur Abgrenzung der Positionen von Franz Xaver KRAUS, Herman SCHELL, Georg von HERTLING und Ludwig WINDTHORST in der Auseinandersetzung um den Katholizismus im Kaiserreich: Zts Bayrische Landesgeschichte 57 (1994) 119-141 [< RHE 89,191*].

14744 KUHN: **Wolf** H., Ketzer oder Kirchenlehrer; der Tübinger Theologe Johannes von Kuhn (1806-1887) in den kirchenpolitischen Auseinandersetzungen seiner Zeit. Mainz 1992, Grünewald. vii-395 p. 3-7867-1624-2. – RTvT 34 (1994) 201s (A. van *Harskamp*).

14745 LABERTHONNIÈRE: ᴱ**Cantone** Carlo, Lucien Laberthonnière, Saggi di filosofia religiosa 1993 ➤ 9,16718: RAsprenas 41 (1994) 618s (A. *Ascione*); CC 145 (1994,3) 325 (X. *Tilliette*: di valore non invecchiato).

14746 LOISY: **Ciappa** Rosanna, Storia e teologia; l'itinerario intellettuale di Alfred Loisy 1993 ➤ 9,16721: RRHPR 74 (1994) 356s (E. *Goichot*).

14747 **Lucien** Bernard, GRÉGOIRE XVI, PIE IX et Vatican II; Études sur la liberté religieuse dans la doctrine catholique. Tours 1990, Forts dans la foi. 350 p. – RRTPhil 126 (1994) 84s (E. *Imbach*: 'Vatican II').

14748 NEWMAN; OXFORD MOVEMENT: *Bedouelle* Guy, Bulletin; Histoire religieuse de l'Angleterre [GRÈS-GAYER J. 1989; NEWMAN, RAMSEY ...]: RThom 94 (1994) 123-132.

14749 *Berranger* Olivier de, Des paradoxes au mystère chez J.H. Newman et H. de LUBAC: RSPT 78 (1994) 45-78; Eng. 79.

14750 **Blehl** Vincent F., The white stone; the spiritual theology of J.H. Newman. Petersham MA 1994, St. Bede's. xi-187 p. $13 pa. 1-879007-03-7 [TDig 41,352].

14750* ᴱ**Blehl** Vincent F., J.H. Newman, Sermons 1824-1843 2. Sermons on biblical history, sin and justification, the Christian way of life, and biblical theology. Ox 1993, Clarendon. xx-472 p. $90. 0-19-920401-2 [TDig 41,375: postulator of Newman's cause].

14751 **Crumb** Laurence N., The Oxford Movement and its leaders; a bibliography of secondary and lesser primary sources: ATLA 24, 1993 ➤ 9,16729: RTBR 7,1 (1994s) 7 (G. *Rowell*: supplements his primary bibliography).

14752 **Deng Shih An**, Idea of the Church in an age of reform; the ecclesiological thoughts of John N. DARBY and J.H. Newman, 1824-1850 diss. Minnesota, ᴰ*Altholz* J. Mp 1994. 273 p. 94-33045. – DissA 55 (1994s) p. 2107.

14753 *Gilley* Sheridan, Newman J.H., ᵀ*Schäferdiek* Knut: ➤ 517, TRE 24 (1994) 416-422.

14754 **Ker** Ian, Healing the wound of humanity; the spirituality of J.H. Newman. L 1993, Darton-LT. 128 p. £8 pa. – RTLond 97 (1994) 219s (B. *Horne*: not what the title promises; first half dogmas of God, second half of ecclesiology; but valuable as such).

14755 **Ker** Ian, Newman, la fede. Mi 1993, Paoline. 214 p. L^m 28. – ^RCC 145 (1994,4) 629 (E. *Baragli*).
14756 *Knight* Christopher, An authentic theological revolution? Scientific perspectives on the development of doctrine: JRel 74 (1994) 524-541.
14757 *Lindon* John, Alessandro Manzoni and the Oxford Movement; his politics and conversion in a new English source: JEH 45 (1994) 297-318.
14758 **Maceri** Francesco, J. H. Newman, pellegrino della verità, Cosenza 1993, Progetto 2000, 160 p. L^m 18. – ^RCC 145 (1994,4) 631s (G. *Ferraro*).
14759 *McManus* E. Leo, Newman's 'great anxiety' [D. ACHILLI libel charge 1852]: CathHR 80 (1994) 457-475.
14760 ^EMagill Gerard, Discourse and context; an interdisciplinary study of J. H. Newman. Carbondale 1993, Southern Illinois Pr. xii-220 p. $35. 0-8093-1836-9. – ^RHeythJ 35 (1994) 462 (J. *Sullivan*); JEH 45 (1994) 523-5 (I. *Ker*).
14761 *Mandle* W. F., 'Witnesses in sackloth'; Newman at Littlemore: JRelH 18 (1994) 159-173.
14762 *Merrigan* Terrence, Newman's Catholic synthesis: IrTQ 60 (1994) 39-48.
14763 **Merrigan** T., Clear heads and holy hearts 1992 → 7,g818... 9,16739: ^RHeythJ 35 (1994) 213s (N. *Lash*); IrTQ 60 (1994) 156s (G. *Collins*).
14764 **Nockles** Peter B., The Oxford Movement in context [debt to 70 years pre-Tractarian High Church]; Anglican High Churchmanship, 1760-1857. C 1994, Univ. xvii-342 p. $50. 0-521-38162-2 [TDig 42,283]. – ^RExpTim 106 (1994s) 216 (Elizabeth *Varley*).
14764* **Page** John R., What will Dr. Newman do? J. H. Newman and papal infallibility, 1865-1875. ColMn 1994, Liturgical/Glazier. vi-458 p. $25. 0-8146-5027-9 [TDig 42,285; TS 56,375, J. *Gaffney*].
14765 **Pattison** Robert, The great dissent ... Newman 1991 → 7,g824 ... 9, 16741: ^RCritRR 6 (1993) 523s (G. *Magill*: stimulating though on too few writings); JRel 74 (1994) 263s (E. J. *Miller*: opinionated, unfair).
14765* **Peterbury** Michael, Divine revelation and the infallible Church; Newman, Vatican II and Arcic: diss. ^DGilley S. Durham UK 1994. 529 p. – RTLv 26, p. 550.
14766 **Thomas** Stephen, Newman and heresy; the Anglican years 1991 → 7,g828 ... 9,16746: ^RJRel 74 (1994) 262s (E. J. *Miller*).
14767 **Vaiss** Paul, Newman, sa vie, sa pensée et sa spiritualité; première période (1801-1832): Chemins de la mémoire. P 1991, L'Harmattan. 510 p. 3-7384-1042-1. – ^RGregorianum 75 (1994) 785 (R. *Fisichella*).
14768 *a*) *Withey* Donald A., J. H. Newman and Dr Charles LLOYD; – *b*) *Ringel* Stacy S., J. H. Newman, human being; – *c*) *Tolhurst* Joseph, The Church of the multitudes; – *d*) *Bussche* J. Vanden, Father Ignatius *Spencer* and Newman: DowR 111 (1993) 235-257 / 258-272 / 273-283 / 284-305.

14769 PIUS IX: *Pedrini* A., Pio IX e l'archeologo Giambattista de Rossi (scienza e fede a servizio della verità): Pio IX 24 (1995) 147-166 [RHE 90,77*].
14769* PIUS X: **Romanato** Gianpaolo, Pio X, la vita di Papa Sarto. Mi 1992, Rusconi. 346 p.; xii pl. – ^RRivStoLR 30 (1994) 223-6 (P. *Marangon*).

14770 RENAN: *Wright* Terence R., The letter and the spirit; deconstructing Renan's Life of Jesus and the assumptions of modernity: RLitND 26,2 (1994) 55-71.

14771 ROSMINI: **Quacquarelli** A.,   Le radici ... di Rosmini 1991 ➤ 8,293: ᴿAsprenas 41 (1994) 126s (L. *Fatica*).
14772 TYRRELL: **Lyons** John R., The fundamental theology of George Tyrrell: diss. Fordham, ᴰ*Heaney* J. NY 1993. – RTLv 26, p. 550.
14773 **Leonard** Ellen, Unresting transformation ... Maude PETRE 1991 ➤ 7, g838; 9,16760: ᴿHorizons 21 (1994) 189s (D. M. *Doyle*).

Y6   *Saeculum XX* – 20th Century Exegesis.

14773* *Asurmendi* Jesús,   Cien años de exégesis católica: Salmanticensis 41 (1994) 67-82.
14774 **Byrskog** Samuel,   Nya testamentet och forskningen; några aktuella tandenser 1992 ➤ 8,4471: ᴿCritRR 6 (1993) 209s (B. A. *Pearson*).
14774* *Ernst* Josef,   Die vielen Stimmen und das eine Wort; 25 Jahre Schriftauslegung auf dem Prüfstand: TGL 84 (1994) 462-473.
14775 *Hengel* Martin, Den nytestamentliga vetenskapens uppgifter [.... LICHTENBERG G.], ᵀ*Fornberg* T.: SvEx 59 (1994) 145-161.
14775* *Moloney* Francis J., Catholic Biblical scholarship, fifty years on: AustralasCR 70 (1993) 275-288.
14776 **Roots** Ivan, Finding strength in biblical tradition.   Ottawa c. 1994, CCCB. $30 each (student/teacher editions). – ᴿCanadCath 12,4 (1994) 26s (D. J. *McLeod*, inadequate data).
14777 **Smith** Theophus H.,   Conjuring culture; biblical formations of black America; Religion in America.   Ox 1994, UP.   xvi-287 p. $32 [< diss; TS 56,380, V. L. *Wimbush*].
14778 **Sperling** S. D., Students of the covenant 1992 ➤ 8,m637: ᴿCBQ 56 (1994) 341s (E. J. *Fisher*); CritRR 6 (1993) 180s (D. *Marcus*); JRel 74 (1994) 120s (N. M. *Sarna*: much of the variegated spectrum of Jewish interpretation would today be called heretical, 'but then heresy, like beauty, is mostly in the eye of the beholder').

14780 BEA: *Cassidy* Edward I., card., Il Cardinale Agostino Bea a 25 anni dalla scomparsa [< (conferenza) Centro Pro Unione 45 (1994) 3-12]: AcPIB 9,10 (1993s) 983-1003.
14781 **Schmidt** Stjepan,   Augustin Bea, the cardinal of unity [1987 ➤ 3,g812], ᵀ*Wearne* Leslie.   New Rochelle 1992, New City.   806 p. $49. – ᴿAmerica 170,5 (1994) 29-31 (B. W. *Westerwelt*); CanadCath 12,11 (1994) 20 (F. *Corley*); Mid-Stream 33 (1994) 483s (J. T. *Ford*; barely a reference to his status as exegete).
14781* *Grootaers* Jan,   I protagonisti del Vaticano II ... Bea [+ 15]. – CinB 1994, Paoline.   279 p. Lᵐ 28 [RHE 90,213-220, C. *Soetens*].
14782 BLOCH: **Roberts** Richard H., Hope and its hieroglyph; a critical decipherment of Ernst Bloch's Principle of hope: AAR StR 57. Atlanta 1990, Scholars.   xv-248 p. $21; sb. pa. $14. – ᴿCritRR 6 (1993) 467-9 (J. A. *Colombo*).
14783 *Bloch* Ernst,   Filosofía de la religión en clave de utopía: BibFe 20,58 ('Hechizos de la utopía' 1994) 111-146.
14784 BUBER: **Retenstreich** Nathan,   Immediacy and its limits; a study in Martin Buber's thought.   Chur 1991, Harwood.   118 p. – ᴿAJS 19 (1994) 104-6 (S. D. *Breslauer*).
14785 **Vetter** Uwe,   Im Dialog mit der Bibel; Grundlinien der Schriftauslegung Martin Bubers: *a*) Diss. Paderborn 1992s, ᴰ*Weinrich*. – TR 90,87; – *b*) Bern 1993, Lang. 353 p. DM 89. – ᴿJudaica 50 (1994) 160s (F. von *Hammerstein*).

14786 **Buber** Martin, Eclipse de Dios; estudios sobre las relaciones entre religión y filosofía, ᴱ*Seltzer* M.; Breviarios 520. México 1993, Fondo de Cultura Económica. 179 p. – ᴿEfMex 12 (1994) 127-132 (Amanda *Porter de Lazo*).

14787 BUDDE: *Smend* Rudolf, Karl Budde (1850-1935): ➤ 10, ᶠBARR J., Language 1994, 351-369.

14789 BULTMANN: **Beyer** Gudrun. Kerygmatheologie als rechtfertigungstheologischer Denkweg; Untersuchung zu Bultmanns Grundlegung der Kerygmatheologie in genetischer, systematisch-theologischer und exegetischer Perspektive: Diss. ᴰ*Hübner* H. Göttingen 1994. – RTLv 26, p. 528.

14790 **Fergusson** David, Bultmann 1992 ➤ 9,16783: ᴿNBlackf 7s (1994) 179s (T. *Williams*); ScotBuEvT 11 (1993) 135s (P. *Ensor* commends highly).

14791 **Gagey** Henri-Jérôme, Jésus dans la théologie de Bultmann. P 1993, Desclée. 386 p. F 225. – ᴿÉtudes 380 (1994) 714s (J. *Sommet*).

14792 *a*) *Grässer* Erich, Notwendigkeit und Möglichkeiten heutiger Bultmannsrezeption; – *b*) *Pöttner* Martin, Die Einheit von Sachkritik und Selbstkritik; semiotische Rekonstruktion der grundlegenden hermeneutischen These R. Bultmanns: ZTK 91 (1994) 272-284 / 396-423.

14793 *Hübner* Hans, Rudolf Bultmann, Her-Kunft und Hin-Kunft: TLZ 120 (1995) 3-22.

14794 **Huppenbauer** M., Mythos und Subjektivität; Aspekte neutestamentlicher Entmythologisierung im Anschluss an R Bultmann und Georg PICHT. Tü 1992, Mohr. xii-226 p. DM 148. 3-16-146015-4. – ᴿTRu 59 (1994) 108s (W. *Schmithals*).

14795 ᴱ**Jaspert** Bernd, Bibel und Mythos [Bultmann] 1991 ➤ 7,442: ᴿEntschluss 48,12 (1993) 37s (M. *Brasser*).

14796 **Jones** Gareth, Bultmann 1991 ➤ 7,g855... 9,16785: ᴿScotJT 47 (1994) 129-141 (D. A. S. *Fergusson*).

14797 **Kay** James F., Christus praesens; a reconsideration of R. Bultmann's Christology. GR 1994, Eerdmans. xii-187 p. $15. 0-8028-0131-5 [TDig 42,72; TS 56, 199s, M. L. *Cook*].

14797* *Sinn* Gunnar, Existenz durch das Wort; R. Bultmanns Paulusdeutung angesichts der theologischen Gegenwart: LuMon 32,9 (1993) 27-30.

14798 **Valerio** Katerina de, Altes Testament und Judentum im Frühwerk Rudolf Bultmanns: *a*) ev. Diss. ᴰ*Merk* O. Erlangen 1994. – RTLv 26, p. 531; TR 91,94; – *b*) BZNW 71. B 1994, de Gruyter. xiv-454 p. 3-11-014201-5 [BL 95,105, J. *Goldingay*; TLZ 120,37s, E. *Lohse*]. – ᴿTüTQ 174 (1994) 318s (W. *Gross*).

14799 CRAIGIE: *Idestrom* Rebecca G. S., Some aspects of Peter C. Craigie's approach to the Old Testament [† 26.10.1985 aet. 47]: SR 23 (1994) 457-467.

14800 ᴱ**Felder** Caine H., Stony the road 1991 ➤ 7,433; 8,m632: ᴿJIntdenom 21 (1993s) 175-8 (Diane *Bergant*) + 22 (1994) 110-117-126-134-147-152 (R. *Chopp*, J. *Grant*, A. *Park Sung*, F. *Segovia*, G. *Yee*) responses 153-169 (T. *Hoyt*).

14801 **Felder** Cain H., Troubling biblical waters; race, class and family; McNeal Black Religion 3. Mkn 1989, Orbis. xix-237 p. $16 pa. – ᴿCritRR 5 (1992) 88s (H. C. *Waetjen*).

14802 **Grelot** Pierre, Combats pour la Bible en Eglise; une brossé de souvenirs. P 1994, Cerf. 415 p. F 175. 2-204-04908-5 [NTAbs 38,

p. 448; NRT 117,457, A. *Toubeau*; TLZ 119,885]. − ᴿRevSR 68 (1994) 509s (B. *Renaud*); RICathP (C. *Perrot*: valait la peine).
14803 KAUFMANN: **Kraft** Thomas, Yehezkel Kaufmann; ein Lebens- und Erkenntnisweg zur Theologie der Hebräischen Bibel: KIsr St 11. B 1990, Institut Kirche und Judentum. 154 p.; 4 pl. − ᴿSefarad 53 (1993) 217-9 (A. *Rofé*).
14804 LAGRANGE: **Gilbert** M., Exégèse à Jérusalem; M.-J. Lagrange: CahRB 29, 1991 ➤ 7,g684 ... 9,16975: ᴿVT 44 (1994) 128 (J. A. *Emerton*).
14805 **Guitton** Jean, Portrait du père Lagrange, celui qui a réconcilié la science et la foi 1992 ➤ 8,m667*; 9,16796: ᴿReligion 24 (1994) 91s (C. *Dickinson*: 'If Pius IX scourged the Church with thongs, Pius X scourged it with scorpions', via compliant Jesuits but also others; Lagrange 'reconciled' by submitting to being 'gagged').
14806 *Montagnes* Bernard, *a*) Marie-Joseph Lagrange; la figure du savant et du croyant: NRT 116 (1994) 715-726; − *b*) L'ultime chagrin du P. Lagrange: RSPT 78 (1994) 3-29.
14807 MARTINI Carlo Maria, interview with *Samway* Patrick: America 170,8 (1994) 8s.
14807* **Martini** Carlo Maria, The new wine; Christian witness of the family. Boston 1994, St. Paul. 319 p. $7 pa. 0-8198-5131-0 [TDig 42,77].
14808 METZGER: *Brooks* James A., Bruce Metzger as textual critic: Princ-SemB 15 (1994) 156-164.
14809 MOFFATT: *Anderson* Hugh, Moffatt, James, 1870-1944, ᵀ*Balz* Horst: ➤ 517, TRE 23 (1994) 196-9.
14810 MOWINCKEL: *Sæbø* Magne, Mowinckel, Sigmund (1884-1965): ➤ 517, TRE 23 (1994) 384-8.

14811 ROSENZWEIG: *Mayer-de Pay* Annemarie, Der gesunde Menschenverstand; zu einem Aspekt der Philosophie Franz Rosenzweigs ['fast alle modernen Menschen haben einen "kranken" Verstand'; ... Erfahrungen mit der Bibel]: Judaica 50 (1994) 122-134.
14812 *Galli* Barbara, Rosenzweig's philosophy of speech-thinking through response to the poetry of Jehuda HALEVI: SR 23 (1994) 413-427.
14813 **Gibbs** Robert, Correlations in Rosenzweig and LEVINAS. Princeton 1992, Univ. xii-281 p. $40. − ᴿJRel 74 (1994) 585 (M. L. *Morgan*).
14813* *Wolzoen* Christoph von, 'Vertauschte Fronten'; HEIDEGGER und Rosenzweig: ZRGg 46 (1994) 109-125.

14814 SANDAY: *Chapman* Mark D., The Socratic subversion of tradition; William Sanday and theology, 1900-1920: JTS 45 (1994) 94-116.
14815 SCATTOLON: *Gioberti* Giuseppe, La biografia di mons. [Gioacchino] Scattolon [1901-1986: *due* biografie, di *Tafi* Angelo 1990 e di *Pesenti* Gaetano G. 1993]: RivB 42 (1994) 209-212.
14816 SCHOLEM: *Shapira* Abraham, Historisches Gedächtnis und Utopie bei Gerschom Scholem: ᵀ*Schatz* Andrea: KIsr 9 (1994) 107-125.

14817 SCHWEITZER: **Müller** Erich W., Albert Schweitzers Kulturphilosophie im Horizont säkulärer Ethik. B 1993, de Gruyter. 331 p. − ᴿFrSZ 41 (1994) 576-8 (J.-C. *Wolf*).
14818 *Zager* Werner, Albert Schweitzers Anleitung zu selbständiger exegetischer Arbeit [aus seinen] Kolleghegten: ZNW 85 (1994) 286-9.
14819 **Schweitzer** Albert, Gespräch über das Neue Testament²ʳᵉᵛ [=

1988]: Beck'sche Reihe 1071. Mü 1994, Beck. 217 p. DM 19,80. 3-406-37461-1.

14820 SMYTH: *Farthing* John L., Ecumenical hermeneutics; Newman Smyth [1843-1925] and the Bible: AmJTP 11 (1990) 215-232.

14821 STRATHMANN: **Hass** Otto, Hermann Strathmann [NT Erlangen 1918-65; christliches Denken und Handeln in bewegter Zeit. Bamberg 1993, Wiss.-Vg. [xii-] 505 p.; portr. 3-927392-41-3. – ᴿTR 90 (1994) 319s (E. *Lohse*).

14822 VERMES Geza, Escape and rescue; an Oxford don's peregrinations (interview): BR 10,3 (1994) 30-37.

14823 WESTERMANN: *Berge* Kåre, Rettung und Segen; Beurteilung eines heilsgeschichtlichen Strukturelements der Theologie Claus Westermanns: ➤ 108, ᶠSÆBØ M. 1994, 49-66 [< OTAbs 17, p. 289].

Y6.3   *Influxus Scripturae saeculo XX* – surveys of current outlooks.

14824 **Alexandre** Bobby C., Televangelism reconsidered; ritual in the search for human community: [J]AAR 68. Atlanta 1994, Scholars. x-205 p. $40; pa. $25. 1-55540-906-7; -7-5 [TDig 42,153].

14825 **Altermatt** Urs, [schweiz.] Katholizismus und Moderne 1989 ➤ 7,g883 [8,m932 nicht Alterman, pardon!]: ᴿTGL 84 (1994) 108s (R. M. *Bucher*).

14826 **Avella** Steven M., The confident Church; Catholic leadership and life in Chicago 1940-1965. ND 1992, Univ. xviii-410 p. $30. – ᴿNewTR 7,1 (1994) 12-7 (E. *Marciniak*).

14827 ᴱ**Badone** Ellen, Religious orthodoxy and popular faith in European society. Princeton 1990, Univ. vii-230 p. $40; pa. $13. – ᴿCritRR 5 (1992) 312-5 (L. N. *Primiano*).

14828 **Balthasar** H. U. von, Gottbefreites Leben; der Laie und der Rätestand; Nachfolge Christi in der heutigen Welt. Fr 1993, Johannes. 244 p. DM 28. 3-89411-318-9 [TLZ 120,81, F. *Hoffmann*].

14828* **Bastian** J. P., Les Protestants en Amérique Latine. Genève 1994, Labor et Fides. 324 p. FF 178. 0-8307-0684-5. – ᴱÉTRel 69 (1994) 591s (M. *Müller*).

14829 **Berkhof** Hendrikus, Two hundred years of theology, ᵀ*Vriend* J. 1989 ➤ 6,m109*; 7,g956: ᴿRTPhil 126 (1994) 176s (K. *Blaser*: 'Vreind').

14830 **Berkhof** Hendrik, 200 anni di teologia e filosofia, da Kant a Rahner. Torino 1992, Claudiana. 462 p. – ᴿAngelicum 71 (1994) 115-8 (A. *Wilder*).

14831 **Beyer** Paul, When time shall be no more; prophecy belief in modern American culture 1992 ➤ 9,16817: ᴿChrC 110 (1994) 48-50 (G. *Wacker*); ChrSchR 24 (1994) 314-6 (P. *Wilt*).

14832 **Brereton** Virginia L., Training God's army; the American Bible school 1880-1940: 1990 ➤ 6,1233*; 8,1114: ᴿCritRR 6 (1993) 351-3 (J. L. *Seymour*); JEvTS 37 (1994) 458s (D. L. *Russell*).

14833 *Bruggink* Donald J., Contemporary context and the biblical and theological roots of Reformed worship: RefR 48 (1994s) 77-90.

14834 **Burns** Gene, The frontiers of Catholicism; the politics of ideology in a liberal world. Berkeley 1992, Univ. California. – ᴿMonth 255 (1994) 171s (P. *Lakeland*).

14835 *Calver* Clive, Red herrings and hot potatoes; the real issues for evangelicals today [London Bible College Jubilee 1993]: VoxEvca 24 (1994) 43-54 (responses 55-57 *Wroe* Martin, 59-61 *Tidball* Derek).

14836 **Calvez** Jean-Yves, Tiers monde; un monde dans le monde; aspects

sociaux, politiques, internationaux. P 1989, Ouvrières. 204 p. – ᴿBro-téria 137 (1993) 354 (F. *Pires Lopes*).
14837 **Cannuyer** Christian, Les catholiques français: Fils d'Abraham. Turn-hout 1992, Brepols. 291 p. – ᴿEsprVie 104 (1994) 171s (R. *Epp*).
14838 **Carroll** Jackson, *Roof* Wade C., Beyond establishment; Protestant identity in a post-Protestant age 1993 ➤ 9,16821: ᴿQRMin 14 (1994) 337-340 (C. F. *Guthrie*); RefR 48 (1994s) 52 (H. *Buis*: depressing).
14839 **Carter** Stephen L., The culture of disbelief; how American law and politics trivialize religious devotion 1993 ➤ 9,16822: ᴿChurch 10,2 (1994) 50-55 (J. R. *Kelly*, also on four cognates); Mid-Stream 33 (1994) 498-507 (W. J. *Nottingham*).
14840 ᴱ**Casper** B., *Sparn* W., Alltag und Transzendenz; Studien zur religiösen Erfahrung in der gegenwärtigen Gesellschaft [19 art.]. FrB 1992, Alber. 434 p. DM 118. 3-495-47739-X. – ᴿAntonianum 69 (1994) 393-5 (Lluis *Oviedo*).
14841 *Chiavaro* Francesco, Wo stehen die Katholiken Westeuropas heute?: TGgw 37 (1994) 124-125.
14842 *Cholvy* Gérard, L'evangélisation [... terme protestant]: des Lumières au New Age: NRT 116 (1994) 701-714.
14843 **Clark** Henry, The Church under Thatcher. L 1993, SPCK. viii-166 p. £13. – ᴿTLond 97 (1994) 389-391 (J. *Gladwin*: the facts are accurate; Thatcher undoubtedly achieved a totally different approach to a government which included — and here comes an inescapable dilemma and anxiety — a Church).
14844 **Crabtree** Harriet, The Christian life; traditional metaphors and con-temporary theologies: HarvDissRel. Mp 1991, Fortress. 193 p. $15 pa. – ᴿCritRR 6 (1993) 502-4 (D. L. *Alexander*); TorJT 10 (1994) 287s (D. A. *Read*).
14846 **Crews** Clyde F., American and Catholic; a popular history of Catholicism in the United States. Cincinnati 1994, St. Anthony. v-167 p. $12 pa. 0-86716-173-2 [TDig 42,160].
14848 **D'Agostino** Peter R., Missionaries in Babylon; the adaptation of Italian priests to Chicago's Church, 1870-1940: diss. ᴰ*Marty* M. Chicago 1994. – RelStR 21,257.
14850 **Day** Thomas, Where have you gone Michelangelo? The loss of soul in Catholic culture. NY 1993, Crossroad. v-240 p. [RelStR 21,41, P. D. *Molnar* queries his 'nobody in the congregation, no theologian, really *understands* the mysteries of faith'].
14852 **De-la-Noy** Michael, The Church of England, a portrait. NY 1993, Simon & S. 341 p. £17. – ᴿTLond 97 (1994) 222s (J. *Pridmore*: Ramsey's press-of-ficer admires many *ordained* Anglicans, but finds chiefly ridiculous many wielders of considerable power, and nothing funny in bishops' gay-lesbian hedging, mismanagement of church finances, only one black bishop).
14855 **Delgado** Mariano, Die Metamorphosen des Messianismus in den ibe-rischen Kulturen; eine religionsgeschichtliche Studie: NZMisss Schr 34. Immensee 1994. 133 p. Fs 21,80. 3-85824-075-3 [TLZ 120,1139, Margit *Eckholt*].
14857 **Dickson** Kwesi A., Uncompleted mission; Christianity and exclusivism 1991 ➤ 8,b36: ᴿCritRR 6 (1993) 358s (S. M. *Heim*).
14858 *Drehsen* Volker, Neuprotestantismus: ➤ 517, TRE 24 (1994) 363-383 [327-341 al., Neuluthertum].
14859 *Dulles* Avery, The four faces of American Catholicism: LvSt 18 (1993) 99-109.

14860 **Dunn** Joseph, The rest of us Catholics; the loyal opposition [= No lions in the hierarchy]. Springfield IL 1994, Templegate, 314 p. $15 [RelStR 21,316, J.J. *Buckley*].

14861 **Dupront** Alphonse, Puissances et latences de la religion catholique: Le Débat. P 1993, Gallimard. 118 p. – RArchivScSocR 39,88 (1994) 63s (É. *Poulat*: livre étrange mais substantiel).

14862 **Dyrness** William A., How does America hear the Gospel? 1989 ➤ 8,m691; 9,16830: RChH 63 (1994) 168-170 (W.L. *Vinz*).

14863 **Ellwood** Robert S., The sixties spiritual awakening; American religion moving from modern to postmodern. New Brunswick 1994, Rutgers Univ. viii-369 p. $25. 0-6135-2093-2 [TDig 42,163].

14863* *Engel* Ulrich, Bourgeois priests, proletarian priests; a paradigm from the history of the conflict between the Church and the workers [... Vatican 'disciplinary action' against CONGAR, CHENU, and Cerf director P. BOISSELOT]. – RVidyajyoti 58 (1994) 168-174 [< Orientierung 1993, T*Clausen* F.].

14864 a) *Fackre* Gabriel, Zur Lage der systematischen Theologie in den USA; – b) *Welker* Michael, Entwicklungstendenzen... USA; – c) *Sauer* Gerard, *Schröder* Caroline, Was bewegt die nordamerikanische Theologie?: VerkF 38,1 (1993) 1-20 / 20-35 / 35-55 [38,2 (1993) 1-85, Osteuropa].

14865 **Falcke** Heino, Die unvollendete Befreiung; die Kirchen, die Umwälzung in der DDR und die Vereinigung Deutschlands: ÖkExistenzHeute 9. Mü 1991, Kaiser. DM 16,80. – RIkiZ 83 (1993) 187-9 (E.H. *Kessler*).

14866 EFord David F., Theologen der Gegenwart; eine Einführung in die christliche Theologie das zwanzigsten Jhts. [1989], TESchwöbel Christoph. Pd 1993, Schöningh. 359 p. DM 98; pa. 48. 3-506-72598-X; -9-8 [TLZ 120,356, Annette *Weidhas*]. – RTGL 84 (1994) 252s (W. *Beinert*).

14867 **Fouilloux** Étienne, Au cœur religieux du XXe siècle: Églises/Sociétés. P 1993, Ouvrières. 317 p. F 150. – REsprVie 104 (1994) 59-62 (G. *Cholvy*).

14867* *Frankl* K.H., Wie sieht die katholische Kirche heute die Gegenreformation?: ➤ 14458*, 1994, 709-716.

14868 **Frei** Hans, Types 1992 ➤ 8,m695; 9,16838: RPersRelSt 21 (1994) 167-9 (M.E. *Deal*).

14869 *Geffré* Claude, L'approche de Dieu par l'homme d'aujourd'hui: RevSR 68 (1994) 489-508.

14870 **Gelpi** Donald, The turn to experience in contemporary theology. NY 1994, Paulist. iii-170 p. $10 pa. 0-8091-3452-7 [TDig 42,66].

14871 **Gibellini** Rosino, La teologia del XX secolo 1992 ➤ 9,16839: RAsprenas 41 (1994) 129 (P. *Pifano*); Gregorianum 75 (1994) 770s (R. *Fisichella*).

14872 **Gibellini** Rosino, Panorama de la théologie au XXe siècle (La teologia 1992): Théologies. P 1994, Cerf. 684 p. 2-204-04910-7. – RRET 54 (1994) 368-370 (M. *Gesteira*).

14873 **Gill** Robin, The myth of the empty Church 1993 ➤ 9,16841: L 1993, SPCK. £20. – RTLond 97 (1994) 143s (L.J. *Francis*: 'subsidy to mission rather than maintenance').

14873* **Goethals** Gregor T., The electronic golden calf; images, religion, and the making of meaning. CM 1990, Crowley. 225 p. $12 [RelStR 21,98, C. *Arthur*, also on BIERNATZKI W. 1991 and 5 other cognates].

14874 **González** Justo L., A Mañana; Theologie aus der Sicht der Hispanics Nordamerikas, TGensichen A. & H.: ThÖk 25. Gö 1994, Vandenhoeck & R. 162 p. DM 38. 3-525-56329-9 [TLZ 120,912, H.-J. *Prien*].

14874* *Gous* I. G. P., OT theology of reconstruction: socio-cultural anthropology, OT theology and a changing South Africa: OTEssays 6 (1993) 175-189

14875 **Grenz** Stanley J., Revisioning Evangelical theology. DG 1993, InterVarsity. 208 p. – ᴿRefR 48 (1994) 154s (J. C. *Koedyker*).

14875* **Grenz** Stanley J., *Olson* Roger E., 20 th century theology; God and the world in a transitional age 1992 → 9,16842*: ᴿBtS 151)1994) 489-491 (J. L. *Burns*).

14876 *Grenz* Stanley J., Twentieth-century theology; the quest for balance in a transitioned age: Persp[Ref] 8,6 (1993) 10-13.

14876* ᴱ**Greschat** M., *Guerriero* E., Storia dei Papi. CinB 1994, Paoline. 1015 p.; 24 pl. [RHE 90,113s, R. *Aubert*: les sept pontificats récents, p. 629-949].

14877 **Gritsch** Eric W., Fortress introduction to Lutheranism. Mp 1994, Fortress. ix-158 p. $10 pa. 0-8006-2780-6 [TDig 41,362].

14878 ᴱ**Hastings** Adrian, Modern Catholicism 1991 → 7,358*a*: ᴿChH 63 (1004) 156-8 (Paula M. *Kane*).

14879 **Hastings** Adrian, The theology of a protestant Catholic 1990 → 6,244; 7,9629: ᴿScotJT 46 (1993) 426-8 (G. S. *Wakefield*).

14880 **Hatch** N., Democratization 1989 → 6,m69... 9,16846: ᴿAmJTP 14 (1993) 74-74 (J. R. *Wimmer*).

14881 *Hellwig* Monika K., What are the theologians saying now? 1992 → 9,16847: ᴿMonth 255 (1994) 21s (P. *Gallagher*, also on H. KÜNG Credo).

14882 **Holmes** David L., A brief history of the Episcopal Church, with a chapter on the Anglican Reformation and an appendix on the quest for an annulment of Henry VIII. Ph 1993, Trinity. xiii-239 p. $17. 1-56338-060-9 [TDig 41,364].

14883 ᶠ**Hornig** Gottfried: Theologie und Aufklärung 1992 → 8,87: ᴿTGL 84 (1994) 123s (A. *Schilson*).

14884 **Horton** Michael S., Made in America; the shaping of modern American evangelicalism. GR 1991, Baker. 198 p. $14. – ᴿJEvTS 37 (1994) 454-6 (D. L. *Russell*).

14885 ᴱ**Hutchison** William R., Between the times; the travail of the Protestant Establishment in America, 1900-1960: 1989 → 5,679... 8,m706: ᴿCritRR 5 (1992) 327-9 (D. N. *Williams*).

14886 **Hylson-Smith** Kenneth, High Churchship in the Church of England from the sixteenth century to the late twentieth century. E 1993, Clark. xvi-424 p. £30. – ᴿTLond 97 (1994) 468s (G. *Russell*: companion to his Anglican Evangelicalism survey but limited by the sources available or chosen).

14887 **Keck** Leander E., The [mainline Protestant] Church confident [Yale Beecher lectures]. Nv 1993, Abingdon. 128 p. $10. 0-687-08151-3 [NTAbs 38, p. 476]. – ᴿTorJT 10 (1994) 292s (R. C. *Mathewson*).

14888 *a) Kelly* Tony, Praxis and pragmatism in an Australian theology [...*Hamilton* Alexander]; – *b) Wilcken* John, KIERKEGAARD and Australian society: AustralasCR 71 (1994) 261-274 [275-285] / 314.

14889 **Klöcker** Michael, Katholisch – von der Wiege bis zur Bahre; eine Lebensmacht im Zerfall? Mü 1991, Kössl. 520 p.; 24 col. pl. – ᴿZRGg 46 (1994) 366-8 (C. *Weber*).

14890 **Kosmin** Barry A., *Lachman* Seymour P., One nation under God; religion in contemporary American society. NY 1993, Crown-Harmony. 312 p. $25. 0-517-58789-0 [TDig 42,73].

14891 *a*) **Lamb** Matthew L., Modernism and Americanism revisited dialectically; a challenge for evangelization; – *b*) *Schindler* David L., Religious freedom, truth, and American liberalism; another look at John Courtney MURRAY: ComWsh 21 (1994) 631-662 / 696-741.

14892 ᴱ**Lamberigts** M., *Soetens* C., À la veille de Vat. II 1992 ➤ 8,576*: ᴿGregorianum 75 (1994) 373-5 (M. *Chappin*).

14893 **Lee** Philip J., Against the Protestant Gnostics [North America; infiltrate by individualism, elitism, solipsism and antimaterialism]. 1993 (1987) ➤ 3,1342 ... 6,1405: ᴿSR 23 (1994) 507s (D. H. *Shantz*).

14894 **Leech** Kenneth, Subversive orthodoxy 1992 ➤ 8,m711: ᴿTorJT 10 (1994) 293s (Anitra *Hanson*).

14895 **Lefebvre** Jean-Paul, The empty cathedral; an open letter to the Pope, ᵀ*Hébert* Madeleine. ... c. 1993, Davies. 176 p. $15. – ᴿCanadCath 12,11 (1994) 24 (D. J. *Dooley*: should never have been written; follows eccentric WEAKLAND and dissenting HÄRING and McCORMICK).

14896 ᴱ**Lehmann** Karl [Bischof], *Schnackenburg* Rudolf, Brauchen wir noch Zeugen? Die heutige Situation in der Kirche und die Antwort des NTs. FrB 1992, Herder. 116 p. DM 22,80, – ᴿTPQ 142 (1994) 89 (S. *Stahr*).

14897 *Lies* Lothar, Europäische Theologien in neuer Katholizität: ZkT 116 (1994) 270-287.

14898 **Longfield** Bradley J., The Presbyterian controversy 1991 ➤ 7,1138: ᴿCritRR 6 (1993) 378-380 (M. *Massa*).

14899 ᴱ**Loth** Wilfried, Deutscher Katholizismus im Umbruch zur Moderne [11 Art., Tagung Bochum 1990]: Konfession und Gesellschaft 3, 1991 ➤ 7,363*c*; 9,16858; 3-17-011729-7: ᴿZKG 105 (1994) 405-7 (H. *Wolf*).

14900 **MacArthur** John, [evangelicals] Ashamed of the Gospel. Wheaton IL 1993, Crossway. 256 p. $18. 0-89107-729-4: ᴿBtS 151 (1994) 116-8 (A. M. *Malghurs*: controversial, against George BARNA); RExp 91 (1994) 628-630 (J. M. *Terry*: Americans sliding into pragmatism much as the British slid into modernism).

14901 **McBrien** R. P., Report after Vatican II..., 1992 ➤ 8,m976: ᴿTorJT 10 (1994) 308s (Rebecca *McKenna*).

14902 ᴱ**Marsden** George M., *Longfield* Bradley J., Secularization of the Academy 1992 ➤ 8,m506: ᴿChrSchR 24 (1994) 318s (S. R. *Pointer*); TrinJ 14 (1993) 85-88 (T. *Ward*).

14903 **Marsden** George M., The soul of the American university, from Protestant establishment to established nonbelief. NY 1994, Oxford-UP. xiv-462 p. $35. 0-19-507046-1 [TDig 41,177].

14903* **Martin** Ralph, The Catholic Church at the end of an age; what is the Spirit saying? SF 1994, Ignatius. 309 p. $13 pa. 0-89870-524-X [TDig 42,280].

14904 *Martini* Carlo M., [*al.*], Europa e cristianesimo dopo il Sinodo dei Vescovi: ScuolC 122 (1994) 718 [-191].

14904* ᴱ**Marty** Martin E., Protestantism & Social Christianity / & Regionalism / Women & women's issues / Missions and ecumenical expressions: Modern American Protestantism and its world 6.7.12.13. München 1992-2-3-3, Saur. xiii-409 p. xiii-254 p. xiii-566 p. xiii-205 p. – ᴿChH 63 (1994) 646s (-650) (P. A. *Carter, al.*).

14906 **May** Georg, Kirchenkampf oder Katholikenverfolgung? Ein Beitrag zu dem gegenseitigen Verhältnis von Nationalsozialismus und christlichen Bekenntnissen. Stein 1991, Christiana. 700 p. 3-7171-0942-1. – ᴿZKG 105 (1994) 410-2 (K. *Meier*).

14907 ᴱ**Mayeur** Jean-M., Erster und zweiter Weltkrieg; Demokratien und

totalitäre Systeme (1914-1958): Christentum 12, [TE]*Meier* Kurt; 1992
→ 9,16863: [R]TPhil 69 (1994) 299-301 (K. *Schatz*); TPQ 142 (1994) 96s
(R. *Zinnhobler*).
14908 *Meier* John P., Miracles and modern minds [< A marginal Jew II]:
CathW 238 (May) 52-58 ... This issue continues with *Mc Manus* Dennis,
Angels, their importance in our lives p. 68-73 and three other articles on
angels p. 59-67. 74-79.
14908* **Melady** Thomas P., The ambassador's story; the United States and
the Vatican in world affairs. Huntington IN 1994, Our Sunday Visitor.
224 p. $20. 0-87973-702-6 [TDig 42,177].
14909 **Michelin** Étienne, Vatican II et le 'surnaturel' [thème important dans
les documents préparatoires mais non dans les documents finals]; enquête
préliminaire 1959-1962 [diss.]: Théologie 6. Venasque 1993, Carmel.
376 p. – [R]RThom 94 (1994) 326s (G. *Bavaud*).
14910 **Newbigin** Lesslie, Truth to tell; the Gospel as public truth 1991
→ 8,m858: [R]ScripTPamp 26 (1994) 847 (P. *Rodríguez*).
14911 **Nielsen** Kai, *Hart* Hendrik, Search for community in a withering
tradition; conversation between a Marxian atheist and a Calvinian
Christian. Lanham MD 1991, UPA. x-264 p. $39. – [R]WestTJ 55 (1993)
366-8 (R. E. *Otto*).
14912 **Noll** Mark A., A history of Christianity in the U.S. and Canada 1992
→ 8,m723; 9,16870: [R]ChrSchR 23 (1993) 92-94 (D. F. *Anderson*); SR 23
(1994) 85-87 (D. *Lyon*); TorJT 10 (1994) 279s (B. *Hillis*).
14912* **Noll** Mark, The scandal of the evangelical mind. GR 1994, Eerdmans. ix-274 p. [RelStR 21,316, S. M. *Heim*].
14913 **O'Malley** William J., Why be a Catholic? NY 1994, Crossroad.
189 p. $12. – [R]NOxR 61,5 (1994) 26-28 (L. R. *Gómez*: brilliant but
CARNEGIE not CHESTERTON).
14914 **Paul** Robert S.†, Whatever happened to Sherlock Holmes? Detective
fiction, popular theology and society. Carbondale 1991, Southern Illinois
Univ. 305 p. – [R]Mid-Stream 33 (1994) 245s (D. *Belcastro*: detective
fiction appeals directly to the moral and spiritual roots of society
endorsed by the readers, and thus today reflects the spiritual and moral
changes occurring in Western culture).
14915 **Peters** J., *al.*, Kerk op de helling; veranderingen in katholiek Nederland
en gevolgen voor de pastoraal. Kampen 1993, Kok. 102 p. – [R]CollatVL
24 (1994) 102s (W. Van *Soom*).
14916 **Ramet** Sabrina P., Religious policy in the Soviet Union [1917-1991].
C 1993, Univ. – [R]Mid-Stream 33 (1994) 112-121 (Véronique *Lossky*).
14917 **Ravitch** Norman, The Catholic Church and the French nation,
1589-1989. L 1994, Routledge. 214 p. $55. – [R]CanadCath 12,7 (1994) 26
(Colleen *Fitzgerald*).
14917* **Rigault** Georges, Les temps de la 'sécularisation' 1904-1914: ÉtLa-
salliennes 1. R 1991, Frères des Écoles Chrétiennes. 306 p. – [R]MélSR 51
(1994) 458-460 (J.-C. *Mathys*, aussi sur 2s).
14918 **Rogers** Delores J., The American empirical movement in theology:
EurUnivSt 7/70. NY 1990, P. Lang. viii-246 p. $47.50. – [R]CritRR 5
(1992) 484-8 (E. S. *Goldsmith*: 'EurUnivSt').
14919 [E]**Rowell** Geoffrey, The English religious tradition and the genius of
Anglicanism [Keble lectures]. Ox 1992, Ikon. 256 p. £18, pa. £10. –
[R]HeythropJ 35 (1994) 337s (A. *Hamilton*, also on *Hylson-Smyth* K.).
14920 *a) Royal* Robert, Slouching toward suburbia; America and the new
evangelization; – *b) Kereszty* Roch [*al.*], Why a new evangelization; a

study of its theological rationale; – c) *Schmitz* Kenneth L., The language of conversion and the conversion of language: ComWsh 21 (1994) 663-684 / 631-663 / 594-641 [569-817 *al.*].

14921 **Rubin** Julius H., Religious melancholy and Protestant experience in America. Ox 1994, UP. ix-308 p. $35. 0-19-508301-6 [TS 56,378, E. B. *Holifield*; RelStR 21,60, G. M. *Dermott*: fascinating].

14922 *Ruff* Pierre-Jean, Le protestantisme libéral; vers un christianisme d'ouverture. P 1993, Foyer de l'Âme. 135 p. F 100. 3-9507099-1-5. – ᴿÉTRel 69 (1994) 293 (A. *Gounelle*).

14923 *Ruh* Ulrich, [Niederland] In einer missionarischen Situation: HerdKorr 47 (1993) 145-9 [+ 212].

14923* **Ruster** Thomas, Die verlorene Nützlichkeit der Religion; Katholizismus und Moderne in der Weimarer Republik. Pd 1994, Schöningh. 421 p. [RelStR 21,317, R. A. *Krieg*].

14924 **Salmann** Elmar, Der geteilte Logos; zum offenen Prozess von neuzeitlichem Denken und Theologie: StAnselm 111. R 1992, Benedictina. 511 p. – ᴿTPhil 69 (1994) 301-5 (J. *Splett*).

14924* **Schatz** Klaus, Kirchengeschichte der Neuzeit II: LeitfadenT 20, 1989 ➤ 7,g785* [TR 91,412, K. J. *Rivinius*].

14925 **Schneider** A. Gregory, The way of the Cross leads home; the domestication of American Methodism. Bloomington 1992, Indiana Univ. xxviii-257 p. $30 pa. – ᴿJRel 74 (1994) 572s (R. E. *Rickey*).

14926 *Schoof* Ted, Duitse [German] reformatorische theologie in de ban van cultuur en geschiedenis: TvT 34 (1994) 300-5.

14927 **Schwarke** Christian, Jesus kam nach Washington 1991 ➤ 7,g666; 9,16881: ᴿZKG 105 (1994) 407s (J. *Rieger*).

14928 **Schwehn** Paul, Exiles from Eden; religion and the academic vocation in America. Ox 1993, UP. xiv-143 p. $20. – ᴿChrSchR 24 (1994) 316-8 (R. W. *Wall*); Commonweal 120,7 (1993) 26-28 (E. M. *Gaffney*); Horizons 21 (1994) 383-6 (R. *Van Allen*).

14929 *Segovia* Fernando F., Theological education and scholarship as struggle; the life of racial/ethnic minorities in the profession: JHisp 2,2 (1994s) 5-25.

14930 **Shepard** Robert S., God's people in the ivory tower; religion in the early American university [1880-1920]; ChStAmRel 20. Brooklyn 1991, Carlson. xiii-376 p. $50. – ᴿCritRR 6 (1993) 390 (J. W. *Stewart*).

14931 **Sisson** C. H., Is there a Church of England? Manchester 1993, Carcanet. vi-302 p. £25. 1-85754-010-7. – ᴿTBR 7,3 (1994s) 63 (G. *Howes*: malaise of many Anglicans).

14931* **Soper** J. Christopher, Evangelical Christianity in the United States and Great Britain; religious beliefs, political choices. NYU 1994. x-198 p. $40. 0-8147-7987-5 [TDig 42,292].

14932 **Sparr** Arnold, To promote, defend and redeem; the Catholic literary revival and the cultural transformation of American Catholicism, 1920-1960. Westport CT 1990, Greenwood. xiv-240 p. $40. – ᴿCritRR 5 (1992) 347-350 (J. M. *McShane*).

14933 ᴱStroup George W., Reformed reader; a source book in Christian theology [1.] 2. Contemporary trajectories, 1799 to the present. LvL 1993, W-Knox. xxx-369 p. $25. 0-664-21958-6. – ᴿTBR 7,2 (1992s) 23s (M. *Elliott*: merits, flaws).

14934 **Strübind** Andrea, Die unfreie Freikirche; der Bund der Baptistengemeinden im 'Dritten Reich': HThSt 19s. Neuk 1991, V. xv-343 p. DM 48. – ᴿTR 90 (1994) 312-4 (E. *Laubach*).

14935 **Tagliaferri** M., L'unità cattolica; studio di una mentalità: AnGreg 264. R 1993, Pont. Univ. Gregoriana. xxii-376 p. – ᴿRasT 35 (1994) 374-6 (U. *Parente*).
14936 *Thils* Gustave, Le mouvement théologique au XXᵉ siècle; RTLv 25 (1994) 289-309; Eng. 424.
14937 **Türcke** Christoph, Kassensturz; zur Lage der Theologie. Fra 1992, Fischer-Tb. 141 p. DM 16,90. 3-596-11249-4. – ᴿTGL 84 (1994) 109s (R. M. *Bucher*).
14938 **Veith** Gene E.ᴶ, Modern [Nazi] fascism; liquidating the Judeo-Christian worldview. St. Louis 1993, Concordia. 186 p. $16. – ᴿConcordJ 20 (1994) 89-93 (H. A. *Moellering*).
14939 **Watt** David H., A transforming faith; exploration of American evangelism [1925-75] 1991 → 7,g907*a; ᴿCritRR 6 (1993) 399s (R. V. *Pierard*).
14940 WELLS-BERNETT Idea B. (1862-1931): **Townes** Emilie M., Womanist justice, womanist hope: AAR 79. Atlanta 1993, Scholars. 229 p. $20 pa. 1-55540-683-1. – ᴿInterpretation 48 (1994) 333s (Emily Townes *Durham*).
14941 **Wentz** Richard E., Religion in the New World; the shaping of religious traditions in the US 1990 → 7,g907*b... 9,16887: ᴿTR 90 (1994) 254-6 (N. M. *Borengässer*).
14942 *Wilcken* John, Models of Catholic theology, 1950-1990: AustralasCR 70 (1993) 333-341.
14943 **Willaime** Jean-Paul, La précarité protestante 1992 → 9,16889: ᴿÉTRel 68 (1993) (J.-M. *Prieur*); HerdKorr 47 (1993) 376 (K. *Nientiedt*); MélSR 51 (1994) 349s (L. *Debarge*); RevSR 68 (1994) 123s (J. *Werckmeister*).
14944 **Wilshire** Bruce W., The moral collapse of the university; professionalism, purity, and alienation. Albany 1990, SUNY. xxv-287 p. $57.50; pa. $19. – ᴿCritRR 6 (1993) 470-3 (S. C. *Rockefeller*).
14945 **Witten** Marsha C., All is forgiven [Lk 15,11 → 9,5249; but really on] the secular message in American Protestantism. Princeton 1993, Univ. ix-179 p. $20. 0-691-03280-7 [TDig 41,396].
14946 **Wuthnow** Robert, The struggle for America's soul; evangelicals, and secularism 1989 → 7,g909; 8,m737: ᴿChrSchR 24 (1994) 95s (T. D. *Parham*); LuthQ 6 (1992) 443-5 (R. *Benne*).
14947 **Wuthnow** Robert, Producing the sacred; an essay on public religion. Urbana 1994, Univ. Illinois. x-181 p. $25; pa. $13. 0-252-01920-2; -6401-1 [TDig 42,194],
14948 *Yonke* Eric, The Catholic subculture in modern Germany; recent work in the social history of religion: CathHR 80 (1994) 534-545.
14949 **Youngs** J. William, The Congregationalists. NY 1990, Greenwood Pr. xvi-376 p. $41. 0-313-22159-6. – ᴿChH 63 (1994) 165s (A. M. *Steece*).

Y6.5   **Theologi influentes** *in exegesim saeculi XX*.

14949* ALBERTZ: *Mettinger* Tryggve N. D., Israels religion med nya accenter — sociologi och ideologikritik enligt Rainer Albertz: SvEx 59 (1994) 21-32.
14950 ALTHAUS: **Christensen** Kurt, Erkendelsen af Guds vilje; en studie i Paul Althaus' teologi: Menighedsfak. 5. Århus 1994, Kolon. 429 p. Dk 298. 87-87737-09-4 [TLZ 120,166, G. *Hornig*].
14951 ALTIZER: *Fountain* J. Stephen, Ashes to ashes; Kristeva's Jouissance, Altizer's Apocalypse, Byatt's Possession and 'The dream of the rood': LitTOx 8 (1994) 191-208.

14952 ARRUPE: *Pittau* Giuseppe, Pedro Arrupe; un'esplosione nella Chiesa: VConsacr 20 (1994) 244-8 [< ᴱ*Lainet* P. 1993].
14953 BAILLIE: ᴱ**Fergusson** David, Christ, Church and Society ... J. & D. Baillie 1993 ➤ 9,16898: ᴿJTS 45 (1994) 783s (J. *Macquarrie*).

14954 BALTHASAR: *Amiot* Chantal, Esthétique théologique et signes des temps: RevSR 68 (1994) 73-94.
14955 *Bernad* Miguel A., 'A theological phenomenon' [Balthasar on G. M. HOPKINS]: Landas 8 (Manila 1994) 10-26.
14956 **Carvalho** Maria Dias de, A centralidade cristológica do 'eschaton' nos escritos de H. U. v. Balthasar: BtHumT. Porto 1993, Univ. Católica. 344 p. – ᴿEborensia 7 (1994) 151 (T. M.).
14957 *Dumont* Camille, 'Action' et 'dénouement' dans la 'Dramatique' de H. U. von Balthasar: NRT 116 (1994) 727-736.
14958 **Guerriero** Elio. H. U. v. Balthasar 1993 ➤ 9,16899: ᴿTPhil 69 (1994) 605s (W. *Löser*).
14959 ᴱ**McGregor** Bede, *Norris* Thomas. The beauty of Christ; an introduction to the theology of Hans Urs von Balthasar. E 1994, Clark. xv-277. £20. 0-567-09697-1. – ᴿTBR 7,3 (1994s) 33s (M. *Higton*).
14960 **O'Donnell** John, H. U. von Balthasar 1992 ➤ 8,m749; 9,16904: ᴿJRel 74 (1994) 266s (E. T. *Oakes*); TorJT 10 (1994) 311s (D. *Donovan*).
14960* ᴱ**Schindler** David L., Hans Urs von Balthasar; his life and work 1991 ➤ 9,16908: ᴿThomist 58 (1994) 689-694 (C. *Potworowsky*).
14961 **Scola** A., H.U.v. Balthasar, uno stile teologico: 1991 ➤ 9,16909: ᴿNRT 116 (1994) 258 (C. *Dumont*).
14961* **Spangenberg** Volker, Herrlichkeit des Neuen Bundes; die Bestimmung des biblischen Begriffs der 'Herrlichkeit' bei Hans Urs von Balthasar: WUNT 2/55. Tü 1993, Mohr. 280 p. DM 98 [RelStR 21, 211, W. T. *Dickens*].
14962 *Splett* Jörg, Wahrheit in Herrlichkeit; auf Balthasar hören: TPhil 69 (1994) 411-421.
14963 **Wallner** Karl J., Gott als Eschaton ... Balthasar 1992 ➤ 9,16912: ᴿRTLv 25 (1994) 487s (É. *Gaziaux*).
14964 **Balthasar** Hans U. von., La dramatique divine, 4. L'action [➤ 9, 16914]; 5. Le dénouement. Namur 1990-3, Culture et Vérité. 477 p. 481 p. – ᴿBLitEc 95 (1994) 349s (B. de *Guibert*).

14965 BARTH: *Andrews* Stephen, The ambiguity of capacity; a rejoinder to Trevor HART ['Barth misunderstood BRUNNER']: TyndB [44 (1993) 289-305] 45 (1994) 169-179, 289-305 Hart.
14966 *Assel* Heinrich, 'Barth ist entlassen ...'; Emanuel HIRSCHS Rolle im Fall Barth und seine Briefe an Wilhelm STAPEL: ZTK 91 (1994) 444-475.
14967 **Biggar** Nigel, The hastening that waits; Karl Barth's ethics 1993 ➤ 9,16923: ᴿTLond 97 (1994) 139s (G. *Ward*).
14968 *Buckley* James J., A field of living fire; Karl Barth on the Spirit and the Church: ModT 10 (1994) 81-102.
14969 *a) Busch* Eberhard, Die Kirche am Ende ihrer Welt-Geltung; zur Deutung der Ekklesiologie Karl Barths; – *b) Sommer* Dieter, '... ganz und gar nicht mehr sein ...' Sachgemässe Sündenrede als Verheissung für den Sünder bei Karl Barth: ➤ 34*d*, ᶠFANGMEIER J, 1994, 63-98 / 99-106.
14969* *Deddo* Gary, The grammar of Barth's theology of personal relations: ScotJT 47 (1994) 183-222.
14970 *a) Eicher* P., Die Erfahrung der Offenbarung; zum Anfang der Theo-

logie nach K. Barth; – b) *Ritschl* D., Sinn und Grenzen der theologischen Kategorie der Vorsehung: ZdialT 10 (1994) 171-186 / 117-133 (-170, al.).

14971 *Forde* G.O., Does the Gospel have a future? Barth's Romans revisited: WWorld 14,1 (1994) 67-77 [< NTAbs 38, p. 287].

14972 **Hunsinger** G., How to read Barth 1991 ➤ 6,m100* ... 9,16930: ᴿEur-JT 3,2 (1994) 175-7 (T. *Hart*, Eng); 173 franç., dt.: ScripTPamp 26 (1994) 1239s (J. M. *Odero*).

14973 *Hunsinger* George, Karl Barth's The Göttingen Dogmatics: ScotJT 46 (1993) 371-382.

14974 **Küng** Hans, Great Christian thinkers ... Barth. [L 1994, SCM ➤ 14021], p. 185-212.

14975 **Leslie** Benjamin C., Trinitarian hermeneutics; the hermeneutical significance of K. Barth's doctrine of the Trinity 1991 ➤ 7,g944: ᴿJRel 74 (1994) 264-6 (Lois *Malcolm*).

14976 **Macken** John, The autonomy theme 1990 ➤ 6,m104 ... 9,16935: ᴿScotJT 47 (1994) 540-2 (N. *Biggar*).

14977 *a*) *Marshall* Bruce D., Rhetoric and realism in Barth; – *b*) *Webster* John, 'Assured and patient and cheerful expectation'; Barth on Christian hope as the Church's task: TorJT 10 (1994) 9-16 (17s response, *Webb* Stephen H.) / 35-52.

14978 *Neven* G. W., K. Barth und K. H. MISKOTTE als Prediger: ZdialT 10,1 ('Schoorl' 1994) 9-13 (-95, al.).

14979 *Nichols* Aidan, Barth's theology of revelation; I. The setting in life: DowR 112 (1994) 153-163.

14980 *Peter* Niklaus, Karl Barth als Leser und Interpret NIETZSCHES: ZnZg 1 (1994) 251-264.

14981 **Plonz** Sabine, Theologie im veränderten Kontext; eine Relektüre Karl Barths in befreiungstheologischer Perspektive: Diss. ᴰ*Hunger* K. Heidelberg 1994. – TR 91,97.

14982 ᴱ**Reiffen** Hannelotte, Barth, The Göttingen Dogmatics I [1990], ᵀ1991 ➤ 7,g926 ... 9,16937: ᴿWestTJ 56 (1994) 115-132 (R. A. *Muller*).

14983 **Roberts** R. H., A theology on its way? Barth 1991 ➤ 8,m775; 9,16938: ᴿEvQ 66 (1994) 359s (D. A. S. *Ferguson*: 6 hostile reprints); ScotJT 47 (1994) 133-5 (B. L. *McCormack*).

14984 *Smith* Robert S., Scene counter scene; Barth and BRECHT: SR 23 (1994) 25-42.

14985 **Sonderegger** Katherine, 'That Jesus ...' K. Barth's 'Doctrine of Israel' 1992 ➤ 8,a789: ᴿJRel 74 (1994) 104s (J. T. *Pawlikowski*).

14986 ᴱ**Sorrentino** Sergio, Barth in discussione. Potenza 1993, Ermes. – ᴿProtestantesimo 49 (1994) 168-170 (M. C. *Laurenzi*).

14987 **Torrance** Thomas F., Karl Barth, biblical and evangelical theologian 1990 ➤ 6,m100 ... 9,16942: ᴿCritRR 6 (1993) 537s (J. F. *McKenna*).

14988 *Wallace* Mark I., The second naiveté; Barth, RICŒUR and the New Yale Theology 1990 ➤ 6,3123; 8,1196a: ᴿPerspRelSt 21 (1994) 160-5 (R. *Martinez*).

14989 *Weathers* Robert A., Barth's epistemology as a postmodern paradigm; a reconsideration; PerspRelSt 21 (1994) 115-126.

14990 **Webb** Stephen H., Re-figuring theology; the rhetoric of Karl Barth 1991 ➤ 9,16944: ᴿCritRR 6 (1993) 541-3 (G. E. *Paul*); ScotJT 47 (1994) 143s (A. *Wood*).

14991 BERRIGANS: **Gathje** Peter R., The cost of virtue; the theological ethics

of Daniel and Philip Berrigan: diss. Emory; ᴰ*Tipton* S. Atlanta 1994. –
RelStR 21,254.
14991* BOFF: **Goldstein** Horst, Leonardo Boff zwischen Poesie und Politik:
Theologische Profile. Mainz 1994, Grünewald. 136 p. DM 24,80 pa.
[TüTQ 174,255 adv].
14992 *Hortal* Jesus, Tentando comprender o 'caso Boff': Teocomunicaçao
23,102 (1993) 485-492.
14993 **Boff** Leonardo, La nouvelle évangélisation dans la perspective des
opprimés; [+] Lettre du 28 juin 1992; ᵀ*Jarton* Maine & Michèle: Théologie. P 1992, Cerf. 171 p. – ᴿScEspr 46 (1994) 134s (C.-R. *Nadeau*:
thèmes mobilisateurs comme 'Nouvel Âge', 'Post-modernité' reposent sur
une utopie de retour vers une origine insaisissable).

14994 BONHOEFFER: **Clements** Keith W., What freedom? The persistent
challenge of Dietrich Bonhoeffer. Bristol 1990, Baptist College. 189 p.
£8. – ᴿBapQ 34 (1991) 345s (R. *Ellis*).
14995 **Huntemann** G., The other Bonhoeffer; an evangelical assessment of
Dietrich Bonhoeffer, ᵀ*Huizinga* Todd. GR 1993, Baker. 342 p. $25. 0-
8010-4382-4 [TDig 41,364].
14996 **Marsh** Charles, Reclaiming Dietrich Bonhoeffer; the promise of his
theology. NY 1994, Oxford-UP. xvi-195 p. $40. 0-19-508723-2 [TDig
42,77].
14997 *Pangritz* Andreas, Aspekte der 'Arkandisziplin' bei Dietrich Bonhoeffer: TLZ 119 (1994) 755-768.
14998 *Rochelle* Jay C., Bonhoeffer; community, authority, and spirituality:
CurrTM 21 (1994) 117-122.
14999 *a) Schönherr* Albrecht, Being Christian in the GDR, Bonhoeffer's
significance; – *b) Geyer* Alan, Creation and politics in Bonhoeffer's
thought; – *c) Rasmussen* Larry, A theologian for transition: Church &
Society 85,6 (1994s) 58-77 / 93-100 / 101-113 (-123).
15000 *a)* COBB John Bᴶ, A challenge to American theology and philosophy; –
b) Pedersen Ann M., The understanding of... the relationship between
God and the world; a comparison between John B. Cobb Jr.'s and
Bernard LOOMER's theologies; – *c) Soneson* Jerome P., Doing public
theology; Cobb's reconstruction of the concepts of 'world' and 'God' in
the context of the environmental crisis: AmJTP 15,2 (Dayton 1994)
123-136 / 137-151 / 153-161.
15001 **Cone** James H., Martin [Luther KING] and MALCOLM [X.] and
America; a dream or a nightmare 1991 → 9,17000: ᴿAmJTP 14 (1993)
70-74 (T. *Walker*); JIntdenom 18 (1990s) 166-172 (A. *Johnson*). RelStR 20
(1994) 87-90 (P. J. *Paris*) & 90-93 (Katherine *Waller*).
15001* **Baker-Fletcher** Garth, Somebodiness 1993. – ᴿJIntdenom 21 (1993s)
165-8 (R. *Burrow*).
15002 *Cone* James H., The vocation of a theologian [St. Louis University
Bellarmine lecture 1994, unabridged]: TDig 41 (1994) 303-313.
15003 *Scott* Bernard B., From Reimarus to CROSSAN; stages in a quest:
CuRB 2 (1994) 253-280.
15004 CULLMANN: *Moda* Aldo, La recezione della teologia di Oscar
Cullmann in Italia: TItSett 19 (1993) 225-281; Eng. 282.

15005 CUPITT: *Brinkmann* B. R., 'Outsidelessness' [Don *Cupitt*, perhaps
relativized by NIETZSCHE apud *Cousineau* R. 1991] and 'high noon':
HeythJ 35 (1994) 53-58.

15006 **White** Stephen R., Don Cupitt and the future of Christian doctrine. L 1994, SCM. xv-254 p. £15. 0-334-02563-X. – ᴿTBR 7,1 (1994s) 33s (T. *Gray*).

15007 **Cupitt** Don, After all; religion without alienation. L 1994, SCM. 121 p. £10. – ᴿTLond 97 (1994) 447s (Dennis *Nineham*: beautifully written defense of a single 'outsideless' reality, meriting theologians' attention and academic preferment).

15008 **Cupitt** D., The time being 1992 → 8,b865*; 9,16962: ᴿLvSt 18 (1993) 258s (L. *Boeve*: to be discarded).

15008* DELP: **Pope** Michael, Alfred Delp s.J. [1945 hingerichtet] im Kreisauer Kreis; die rechts- und sozialphilosophischen Grundlagen in seinen Konzeptionen für eine Neuordnung Deutschlands: KommZtG B-63. Mainz 1994, Grünewald. xx-233 p. 3-7867-1769-9 [TLZ 120, 900, F. *Schrader*].

15009 FARRER: *Morris* J. N., Religious experience in the philosophical theology of Austin Farrer: JTS 45 (1994) 569-592.

15010 FOSDICK: *May* David M., Harry Emerson Fosdick, a man for the current season: PerspRelSt 21 (1994) 45-57.

15011 GARAUDY Roger, Mon tour di siècle en solitaire 1989 / Mi vuelta al mundo en solitario. Barc 1991, Plaza & J. – ᴿQVidCr 172 (1994) 105-110 (R. *Panikkar*: un document de cristiania).

15012 GILSON: *a*) ᴱ*Donneaud* Henry, Correspondance Étienne Gilson -Michel LABOURDETTE [1950-2]; – *b*) *Bonino* Serge-Thomas, Pluralisme et théologisme [dans cette correspondance]: RThom 94,3 ('Autour d'É. Gilson' 1994) 479-529 / 530-553.

15013 GOGARTEN: *Braun* Dietrich, Carl SCHMITT und Friedrich Gogarten; Erwägungen zur 'eigentlich katholischen Verschärfung' und ihrer protestantischen Entsprechung im Übergang von der Weimarer Republik zum Dritten Reich: BTZ 11 (1994) 219-242.

15014 GORE: *Kollar* René, Charles Gore and Anglican religious communities; an Anglo-Catholic interpretation of conventual life: LvSt 19 (1994) 163-179.

15015 GUILLET Jacques, Habiter les Écritures; entretiens avec Charles *Ehlinger*: Les interviews. P 1993, Centurion. 348 p. – ᴿRivB 42 (1994) 485s (A. *Minissale*: destinato professore del Biblico ma escluso a causa di Gen 1-11 nel suo Thèmes Bibliques).

15016 GUTIÉRREZ G., The truth shall make you free, ᵀ*O'Connell* Matthew J. Mkn c.1993, Orbis. 204 p. $15. – ᴿCanadCath 12,3 (1994) 28 (G. *Judd*).

15017 HABERMAS: ᴱ**Arens** Edmund, Habermas und die Theologie; Beiträge zur theologischen Rezeption 1989 → 6,384: ᴿTR 90 (1994) 58-62 (H. *Fritzsche*).

15018 ᴱ**Browning** Don S., *Schüssler Fiorenza* Francis, Habermas, modernity and public theology 1992 → 8,378c: ᴿJRel 74 (1994) 408s (P. *Lakeland*: Habermas' answer includes positions not adequately presented).

15019 HÄRING B., My witness for the Church, ᵀ*Swidler* L., 1992 → 8,m813; 9,16978: ᴿTablet 247 (1993) 919 (S. *O'Riordan*).

15019* *Häring* B., My participation in the Second Vatican Council: CrNSt 15 (1994) 161-181 [< TR 91, 73].

15020 HARNACK A. von, Histoire des dogmes, ᵀ*Choisy* E., centenaire ᴱ*Nowak* K.: Patrimoines Christianisme. P 1993, Cerf. xxvi-495 p. F 160 [NRT 117,275, L. *Renwart*].

15020* *Boschini* Paolo, 'Cristianesimo e storia'; il pensiero storico come apo-

logia moderna della religione secondo A. von Harnack: AnStoEseg 10 (1993) 127-143; Eng. 4.
15021 HAUERWAS Stanley, Unleashing the Scripture; freeing the Bible from captivity to America. Nv 1994, Abingdon. 159 p. $13. – ᴿChrT 38,5 (1994) 52s (R. *Yarbrough*).

15022 HEIDEGGER: *Brito* Emilio, Le déracinement du vrai et la 'fuite des dieux' d'après les 'Questions fondamentales de philosophie' de Heidegger: RHPR 74 (1994) 171-191; Eng. 229.
15023 *Brito* Emilio, L'être des démi-dieux d'après les leçons heideggeriennes sur 'Le Rhin' de Hölderlin: RTLv 25 (1994) 310-347; Eng. 424.
15024 *a*) *Kolb* David, Heidegger at 100, in America; – *b*) *Lammi* Walter, [Platonist] Hans-Georg GADAMER's 'correction' of Heidegger: JHistId 52 (1991) 140-151 / 487-507.
15025 **Macquarrie** John, Heidegger and Christianity [Henson lectures 1993s]. L 1994, SCM. viii-135 p. £10. 0-334-2564-8. – ᴿTBR 7,3 (1994s) 10 (G. *Pattison*).
15026 *Ott* Heinrich, Four decades of theology in the neighbourhood of Martin Heidegger: ÉglT 25 (1994) 85-103.

15027 JOHN PAUL II., answers to 20 questions of *Messori* Vittorio, Crossing the threshold of hope, ᵀ*McPhee* Jenny & Martha. NY 1994, Knopf. ix-244 p. $20. 0-679-44058-5 [TDig 42,171].
15028 *a*) *Lahidalga Aguirre* J.M., Del libro 'Amor y responsabilidad' (K. WOJTYŁA) a la encíclica 'Veritatis Splendor' (JUAN PABLO II); – *b*) *Granados Temes* José Miguel, Recuperar el sentido de la dignidad humana, reto de Juan Pablo II: LumenVr 42 (1993) 98-423 / 366-397.
15029 *Neuhaus* Richard J., A voice in the relativistic wilderness [Veritatis splendor]; the current pope is crusading for 'moral truth'; we should welcome his help: ChrT 38,2 (1994) 33-35.
15030 **Schmitz** Kenneth L., At the center of the human drama; the philosophical anthropology of Karol Wojtyła / pope John Paul II. Wsh 1993, Catholic University of America. x-170 p. $12. 0-8132-0780-8 [TDig 41,381].
15031 **Vircondelet** Alain, Jean Paul II, biographie. P 1994, Julliard. 632 p. F 145. – ᴿÉtudes 381 (1994) 571s (J.-Y. *Calvez*).
15032 JONAS Hans, Scienza come esperienza personale; autobiografia intellettuale: Dialogo. Brescia 1992, Morcelliana. 81 p. – ᴿScripTPamp 26 (1994) 1233s (J.M. *Odero*).
15033 JOURNET: *a*) *Cottier* Georges, Les rapports du spirituel et du temporel chez C. Journet; – *b*) *Lemière* Emmanuel, Charles Journet, pour en finir avec un mythe; réflexions à l'occasion d'une première lecture du 'Catéchisme ÉC: NVFr 68 (1993) 3-21.

15034 JÜNGEL: **Cislaghi** Alessandra, Interruzione e corrispondenza; il pensiero teologico di Eberhard Jüngel: GdT 225. Brescia 1994, Queriniana. 256 p. 88-399-9735-4. – ᴿEstE 69 (1994) 416s (J.J. *Alemany*).
15035 **Gamberini** Paolo, Nei legami del Vangelo; l'analogia nel pensiero di Eberhard Jüngel: Aloisiana 27. R/Brescia 1994, Univ. Gregoriana/Morcelliana. 217 p. Lᵐ 32.
15036 **Rodríguez Garrapucho** F., La cruz de Jesús y el ser de Dios; la teología del Crucificado en Eberhard JÜNGEL [dis. Pont. Univ. Gregoriana]:

BtSalm 148. S 1992, Univ. Pontificia. 286 p. – RTeresianum 45 (1994) 624s (S. *Cannistrà*).
15036* **Zimany** Roland D., Vehicle for God; the metaphorical theology of Eberhard Jüngel. Macon 1994, Mercer Univ. x-180 p. $25. 0-86554-444-1 [TDig 42,296].
15037 KLEE: *Deneken* Michel, L'église comme sacrement chez Heinrich Klee: RevSR 68 (1994) 197-217.

15038 KÜNG: *Bourden* John, [Küng] Giant among theologians: Tablet 247 (1993) 364s.
15039 **Becker** Rudolf, H. Küngs Modell einer 'Evangelischen Katholizität' als wahrer Katholizität: Diss. D*Krüger* F. Osnabrück 1994. – TR 91,100.
15040 *Kirchner* Hubert, Hans Küngs Theologie des Dialogs; Bilanz und neuer Einsatz: TLZ 119 (1994) 867-876.
15040* **Küng** Hans, Infallible? An unresolved inquiry [new revised English of unrevised German 1989 = 1970, with relevant 1980 and 1981 Küng items in English]. NY 1995, Continuum. xx-289 p. $20 [RelStR 21,317, J.J. *Buckley*].
15041 KUYPER: *Henderson* R. D., How Abraham Kuyper became a Kuyperian: ChrSchR 22,1 (1992) 22-25 [< ZIT 93,332].
15042 LEHMANN: **Duff** Nancy J., Humanization and the politics of God; the koinonia ethics of Paul Lehmann 1992 → 9,17008: RPrincSemB 15 (1994) 71s (W. M. *Alston*).
15043 LEVINAS: *Habbel* Torsten; Emmanuel Levinas; Philosophie im Angesicht des Anderen; ein Forschungsbericht: TR 90 (1994) 187-200.
15044 LEWIS: **Hyatt** Douglas T., C. S. Lewis, a theological assessment of his propagation of the faith: diss. D*Lochmann* J. Basel 1994. – TR 91,92.
15045 LINDBECK George A., Christliche Lehre als Grammatik des Glaubens; Religion und Theologie im postliberalen Zeitalter, T*Müller* M.: TBüch 90. Mü 1994, Kaiser. 212 p. DM 78. 3-579-01943-0 [TLZ 120,368, C. *Albrecht*].

15046 LONERGAN: **Crowe** Frederick F., Lonergan 1992 → 8,m833; 9,17012: RTPhil 69 (1994) 119-122 (G. B. *Sala* auch über ELAWRENCE F., Workshop 8, 1990).
15047 **Dobroczyński** Grzegorz, Einsicht und Bekehrung; Ausgangspunkt der Fundamentaltheologie bei B. Lonergan 1992 → 8,m834; 9,17013: RHeythJ 35 (1994) 80-82 (P. *Endean*, also on H. A. MAHONEY).
Kinberger Mary K., Lonergan on conversion 1992 → 8678.
15048 **Mooney** Hilary A., The liberation of consciousness ... Lonergan, BALTHASAR D1992 → 8,m838; 9,17018: RGregorianum 75 (1994) 168 (R. *Fisichella*).
15049 **Nielsen** Kirsten Busch, Teologi og sandhed [truth]; B. Lonergans teologiske metode fortolket i protestantisk perspektiv: diss. D*Nørgaard-Højen* P. Kopenhagen 1994. – RTLv 26, p. 528 sub Busch.
15050 **Pelzel** Morris W., A historical study of the notion of development 'from above' in the writings of Bernard Lonergan: diss. Catholic Univ., D*Loewe* W. P. Washington 1994. 411 p. 92-21569. – DissA 55 (1994s) p. 614; RTLv 26, p. 530.
15051 **Teevan** Donna Marie, Bernard Lonergan's transcendental method as a hermeneutical approach to theology: diss. St. Michael, D*Doran* R. Toronto 1994. 417 p. – RTLv 26, p. 530.
15052 **Lonergan** Bernard J. F., Comprendere e essere; le lezioni di Halifax su

Insight: ᵀᴱ*Spaccapelo* Natalino, *Muratore* Saturnino: Opere 5, 1993 ➤ 9, 17023; 88-311-73051-7: ᴿAngelicum 71 (1994) 620-2 (C. *Vansteenkiste*).

15053 DE LUBAC: **Berzosa Martínez** R., La teología del sobrenatural en los escritos de Henri de Lubac 1991 ➤ 7,k17; 8,m847: ᴿNRT 116 (1994) 257 (C. *Dumont*); RET 53 (1993) 252-4 (J. *Prades*); Salesianum 56 (1994) 161s (G. *Abbà*).

15054 *a*) *Bolgiani* Franco, Henri de Lubac e l'esegesi spirituale; – *b*) *Pesce* Mauro, Un 'bruit absurde'? Henri de Lubac di fronte alla distinzione tra esegesi storica e esegesi spirituale; – *c*) *Studer* Basil, L'esegesi doppia in ORIGENE: ➤ 330*a*, X-Viverone 1992/3, 283-300 / 301-353 / 427-437; Eng. 275s.

15054* **Ciola** Nicola, Henri de LUBAC e la 'memoria' intorno alle sue opere [ᵀᴱ*Guerriero* E. (Mi 1992, Jaca) xxviii-466 p.]: RasT 35 (1994) 480-6.

15055 **Russo** A., Henri de Lubac; teologia e dogma nella storia; l'influsso di BLONDEL: La cultura 40, 1990 ➤ 8,m842: ᴿNRT 116 (1994) 257 (C. *Dumont*).

McPartlan Paul, The Eucharist makes the Church., H. de LUBAC and J. ZIZIOULAS in dialogue 1993 ➤ 4607.

15056 **Lubac** Henri de, Auf den Wegen Gottes, ᵀ*Scherer* Robert, ᴱ*Capol* Cornelia 1992 ➤ 9,17027 [TR 91,38, K. H. *Neufeld*].

15058 MACHEN: *Hart* D. G., Christianity and liberalism in a postliberal age: WestTJ 56 (1994) 329-343.

15058* **Hart** D. G., Defending the faith; J. Gresham Machen and the crisis of conservative Protestantism in modern America. Baltimore 1994, Johns Hopkins Univ. x-227 p. $35 [RelStR 21,249, T. E. *Fulop*].

15059 *a*) *Klaassen* Walter, 'There were giants on the earth in those days'; Harold S. BENDER and the Anabaptist vision [1943]; – *b*) *Yoder* J. note, J. Gresham Machen's influence...: CGrebel 12,3 (1994) 233-7 / 257-270 [239-319, *al*.).

15059* **McGrath** Alister E., The renewal of Anglicanism. Harrisburg PA 1993, Morehouse. 170 p. $10. 0-8192-1612-7 [TDig 41,371].

15060 MERSCH: **Arraj** James, Mind aflame; the theological vision of one of the world's great theologians, Èmile Mersch. Chiloquin OR 1994, Inner Growth. 100 p. $10. 0-914073-08-7 [TDig 42,255]. – ᴿTBR 7,3 (1994s) 32, no comment.

15061 MERTON: **Kilcourse** George, Ace of freedoms; Thomas Merton's Christ. ND 1993, Univ. xii-273 p. $35; pa. $15. – ᴿHorizons 21 (1994) 332-337 (D. *Burton-Christie*) & 237-340 (Christine M. *Bochen*) & 340-2 (A. T. *Padovano*; 343-7 Kilcourse response); further on Merton, 239-252, *Carr* Anne; 253-269; *Doud* Robert E.

15062 **Shannon** William H., Silent lamp; the Thomas Merton story 1992 ➤ 9,17033; ᴿCritRR 6 (1993) 530s (D. D. *Cooper*: high praise); TLond 97 (1994) 68s (A. *Haggart*).

15063 MURRAY: **Hughson** Thomas, The believer as citizen; John Courtney Murray in a new context. NY 1993, Paulist. 185 p. $15 pa. – ᴿCW 237,3 (1994) 146s (M. E. *Marty*).

15064 **Ferguson** Thomas P., Catholic and American; the political theology of John Courtney Murray. KC 1993, Sheed & W. xii-189 p. $15 pa. 1-55612-650-6 [TDig 41,359].

15065 NEWBIGIN Lesslie, Truth to tell 1991 ➤ 8,m858: – ᴿScotJT 47 (1994) 105s (P. *Avis*).

15066 NICHOLS Aidan,   A grammar of consent; the existence of God in Christian tradition. ND 1991, Univ.   xv-214 p. $32. – ᴿCritRR 6 (1993) 465-7 (R. F. *Repohl*).

15067 NIEBUHR: **Brown** Charles C., Niebuhr and his age; Reinhold Niebuhr's prophetic role in the twentieth century. Ph 1992, Trinity.   xiii-317 p. – ᴿChH 63 (1994) 161s (R. T. *Handy*); ModT 12 (1994) 114-6 (J. H. *Yoder*); WestTJ 56 (1994) 212-4 (R. W. *Vunderink*).

15068 **Ausmus** Harry J.,   The pragmatic God; on the nihilism of Reinhold Niebuhr. NY 1990, P. Lang.   xii-308 p. $58. – ᴿCritRR 6 (1993) 435-7 (R. H. *Stone*: a strange book).

15068* **Clark** Henry B.,   Serenity, courage, and wisdom; the enduring legacy of Reinhold Niebuhr.   Cleveland 1994, Pilgrim.   xii-223 p. $15.   0-8298-1004-8 [TDig 42,262].

15069 **Fackre** Gabriel J.,   The promise of Reinhold Niebuhr[2rev] [[1]1970]. Lanham MD 1994, UPA.   xiv-71 p. $18.50 pa. [TDig 42,164].

15070 *Naveh* Eyal,   The Hebraic foundation of Christian faith according to Reinhold Niebuhr [R. Fox biography 1985]: Judaism 41 (1992) 37-56.

15071 *Gustafson* James M., Niebuhr 'K. P. Reinhold'/H. Richard, ᵀ*Grünkorn* Gertrud: ➤ 517, TRE 24 (1994) 470-3 / 468-470.

15072 **Stone** Ronald H.,   Professor Reinhold Niebuhr 1992 ➤ 9,17043: ᴿChH 63 (1992) 159-161 (J. *Diefenthaler*); Interpretation 48 (1994) 294-6 (D. P. *McCann*).

15073 NYGREN: *Wingren* Gustaf,   Nygren, Anders (1890-1978): ➤ 517, TRE 24 (1994) 711-5.

15074 **Gerhardsson** Birger,   FRIDRICHSEN ODEBERG AULÉN Nygren; fyra theologer. Lund 1994, Novapress.   183 p. 91-7137-002-1. – ᴿSvTKv 70 (1994) 184s (B. *Olsson*).

15075 ONG: *Walhout* Clarence,   Christianity, history, and literary criticism; Walter Ong's global vision: JAAR 62,2 (1994) 435-459. This oversize fascicle, without book-reviews, has a curious resemblance to a festschrift or meeting-acta, but with no specific indication (or relation to Ong).

15075* OVERBECK: *Graf* Friedrich W.,   Theolog und Antitheolog; die Neuentdeckung Franz Overbecks: EvKomm 27 (1994) 678-681.

15076 PANIKKAR: **Ahlstrand** Kajsa,   Fundamental openness; an enquiry into Raimundo Panikkar's theological vision and its presuppositions: diss. Uppsala 1993. 209 p. 91-85424-33-1. – ᴿExchange 22 (1993) 86s.

15077 *Panikkar* Raimon,   Política eclesiàstica, pertinença eclesial i identitat cristiana: QVidCr 172 (1994) 93-98.

15078 PANNENBERG: **Brena** G. L.,   La teologia di Pannenberg; cristianesimo e modernità 1993 ➤ 9,17045; Lᵐ 32:   ᴿRasT 35 (1994) 625s (Virginia d'*Anselmo*).

15079 **Grenz** Stanley, Reason for hope ... Pannenberg 1990 ➤ 7,k28; 8,m867: ᴿBapQ 34 (1991s) 411 (T. *Bradshaw*).

15080 *La Bute* Todd S.,   The ontological motif of anticipation in the theology of Wolfhart Pannenberg: JEvTS 37 (1994) 275-282.

15081 **Martínez Camino** Juan Antonio,   Recibir la libertad; dos propuestas de fundamentación de la teología en la modernidad, W. Pannenberg y E. JÜNGEL. M 1992, UPCO Investing. Liberalismo 3.   192 p. 84-87840-01-9. – ᴿTLZ 119 (1994) 687s (A. *González Montes*).

15082 *Pannenberg* Wolfhart, Christianity and the West; ambiguous past, uncertain future: FirsT 48 (1994) 18-23.

15083 **Pannenberg** Wolfhart, An introduction to [his 3-vol.] systematic theology 1991 ➤ 7,9045 ... 9,8656: – ᴿJEvTS 36 (1993) 413s (T. M. *Dorman*).

15084 PAULUS VI: **Hebblethwaite** Peter, Paul VI, the first modern Pope 1993 ➤ 9,17053: ᴿCommonweal 120,10 (1993) 23s (R. A. *Schroth*); LvSt 19 (1994) 85s (J. A. *Dick*); Tablet 247 (1993) 436s (G. *Fogarty*); TLond 97 (1994) 65s (S. *Norman*).

15084* PETERSON E.: [➤ 11560] **Nichtweiss** Barbara, Erik Peterson, Neue Sicht auf Leben und Werk. FrB 1992, Herder. xvii-966 p. DM 65 [TR 91,238, K. S. *Frank*].

15085 ᴱPINNOCK Clark H., The grace of God, the will of man; a case for Arminianism. GR 1989, Zondervan. – ᴿConcordTQ 58 (1994) 312s (E. F. *Klug*: a normal view of the average man).

15086 RAHNER; *Batlogg* Andreas, Welches Memorandum? Einspruch gegen eine sogenannte Rahner-Edition [1943, ᴱ*Wolf* Hubert 1994]: ZkT 116 (1994) 330-4.

15087 **Berkhof** H., 200 anni di teologia e filosofia; da Kant a Rahner, un itinerario di viaggio [1989 ➤ 6,m109*], ᵀᴱ*Fiorillo* M.: PiccBtT 27. Torino 1992, Claudiana. 462 p. Lᵐ 48. – ᴿAsprenas 41 (1994) 127-9 (P. *Giustiniani*).

15088 *Burke* Patrick J., Conceptual thought in Karl Rahner: Gregorianum 75 (1994) 65-93; franç 93.

15089 **Conway** Eamonn, The anonymous Christian — a relativized Christianity? [diss. Maynooth 1991]: EurUnivSt 23/485. 189 p. DM 59. 3-631-46209-3 [TR 90,262; TDig 42,264].

15090 **Guggenberger** Engelbert, Karl Rahners Christologie und heutige Fundamentaltheologie [Diss.]: InTST 28, 1990 ➤ 7,7460; 8,7524: ᴿÉglT 25 (1994) 142-4 (J. R. *Pambrun*).

15091 *McDermott* John M., Dialectical analogy; the oscillating center of Rahner's thought: Gregorianum 75 (1994) 675-703; franç. 703.

15092 *Metz* Johann B., Karl Rahners Ringen um die theologische Ehre des Menschen: StiZt 212 (1994) 383-393.

15093 **Knoeppfler** Nikolaus, Der Begriff 'transzendental' bei K. Rahner; zur Frage seiner KANTISCHEN Herkunft: InTSt 39. 1993, Tyrolia. 214 p. DM 32. 3-7022-1880-7. – ᴿTPhil 69 (1994) 307s (P. *Knauer*); ZkT 116 (1994) 204-7 (W. *Kern*).

15094 *Muck* Otto, HEIDEGGER und Karl Rahner: ZkT 116 (1994) 257-269.

15095 *a)* **Splett** Jörg, Mystisches Christentum? Karl Rahner zur Zukunft des Glaubens; – *b)* *Hilberath* Bernd J., *Nitsche* Bernhard, Transzendentale Theologie? Beobachtungen zur Rahner-Diskussion der letzten Jahre: TüTQ 174 (1994) 258-271 / 304-315.

15096 RAUSCHENBUSCH: **Beckley** Harlan, Passion for justice ... Rauschenbusch ... 1992 ➤ 8,m887; 9,17070: ᴿChH 63 (1994) 643s (G. A. *Hewitt*); Horizons 21 (1994) 370-2 (N. J. *Rigali*, also on STONE R., Niebuhr); Interpretation 48 (1994) 186-8 (C. E. *Curran*); JRel 74 (1994) 582s (Lois K. *Daly*).

15096* **Smucker** Donovan E., The origins of Walter Rauschenbusch's social ethics ['publishing sensation of 1907']. Montreal 1994, McGill-Queens Univ. x-173 p. $40. 0-7735-1163-6 [TDig 42,291].

15097 RICŒUR: **Mongin** Oliver,   Paul Ricœur.   P 1994, Seuil.   264 p. F 150. –
ᴿÉtudes 381 (1994) 279 (G. *Petitdemange*).
15100 ROBINSON J.A.T.   ᴱ**Bowden** John,   Thirty years of honesty; 'Honest to
God' then and now.   L 1993, SCM.   viii-103 p. £6.   0-334-02362-9. –
ᴿTBR 7,3 (1994s) 36s (M.P.R. *Linskill*).
15101 RUIZ GARCÍA: *Klein* Nikolaus,   Land, Freiheit, Würde; zum Kontext
der Indigena-Pastoral vom Bischof Samuel Ruiz: Orientierung 55 (1994)
15-17.
15102 RUNCIE: **Hastings** Adrian,   Robert Runcie 1991 ➤ 7,k51 ... 9,17077:
ᴿMid-Stream 33 (1994) 247-251 (bp. P. C. *Rodger*).

15103 SCHILLEBEECKX: **Kennedy** P.,   Schillebeeckx 1993 ➤ 9,17079; also L
1993, Chapman: ᴿNBlackf 75 (1994) 333s (G. *D'Costa*).
15104 *a) Schoof* Ted,   Werk van en over Edward Schillebeeckx; – *b) Borgman*
Erik,   Van cultuurtheologie naar theologie als onderdeel van de cultuur;
de toekomst van het theologisch project van E. Schillebeeckx: ➤ 110,
ꜰSchillebeeckx E., TvT 34,4 (1994) 430-8 / 335-360; Eng. 360.
15105 **Schillebeeckx** Edward, (with *Strazzari* Francesco), I am a happy
theologian.   L/NY 1994, SCM / Crossroad.   xv-103 p. $12. – ᴿLvSt 19
(1993) 328s (D. *Rochford*); Tablet 248 (1994) 894 (D. L. *Edwards*).
15106 **Schillebeeckx** E.,   Soy un teólogo feliz.   M 1994, Atenas.   163 p. –
ᴿEstAg 29 (1994) 601 (C. *Morán*).
15107 SCHUSTER: ᴱ**Crippa** L.,   Il servo di Dio A. Ildefonso Card. Schuster
O.S.B.   nell'anniversario della morte (1954): Monastica 8.   R 1994,
Benedictina.   308 p. Lᵐ 30.
15108 TEILHARD: **Carles** Jules, *Dupleix* André,   Teilhard de Chardin.   P 1991,
Centurion.   285 p. – ᴿScEspr 46 (1994) 271s (G. *Novotný*).
15109 **Trennert-Hellwig** Mathias,   Die Urkraft des Kosmos ... Teilhard 1993
➤ 9,17086: ᴿZkT 116 (1994) 513-5 (K. H. *Neufeld*).

15110 TILLICH: *Gounelle* André,   La collaboration de Tillich à [la revue de
gauche] The Protestant (1941-2):   ÉTRel 69 (1994) 213-229.
15111 *Gounelle* André,   Pour ou contre Hitler? le débat entre HIRSCH et Tillich
en 1934:   RHPR 74 (1994) 411-429 [Eng. TDig 42,103-8 ᵀᴱ*Jermann*
Rosemary).
15112 *Higuet* Étienne A.,   Atualidade da teologia da cultura de Paul Tillich:
REB 54 (1994) 50-61 [914-925, *Ribeiro* C.].
15113 *a) Hummel* Gert,   Das früheste System Paul Tillichs, die 'Systematische
Theologie von 1913'; – *b) Scharf* Uwe C.,   The concept of the break-
through of revelation in Tillich's Dogmatik of 1925: NSys 35 (1993)
115-131; Eng. 132 / 36 (1994) 99-115; deutsch 116.
15114 **Tillich** Paul,   Christianisme et socialisme; écrits socialistes allemands
1919-1931: Œuvres 2.   P/Genève/Québec; 1992, Cerf/LF/Univ. Laval.
546 p. – ᴿScEspr 46 (1994) 129s (J.-C. *Petit*).

15115 TRACY: *a) Fortin-Melkevik* Anne,   Le statut de la religion dans
la modernité selon David Tracy et Jürgen HABERMAS; – *b) Lalonde*
Marc P.,   From postmodernity to postorthodoxy, or Charles DAVIS
and the contemporary context of Christian theology; – *c) Voyé* Liliane,   La religion en postmodernité: SR 22 (1993) 417-436 / 437-449 /
503-520.
15116 ᴱ**Jeanrond** W. G., *Rike* Jennifer L.   Radical pluralism and truth, D.˸
Tracy 1991 ➤ 8,m909:   ᴿGregorianum 75 (1994) 352s (J. *Galot*).

15117 TROELTSCH: **Coakley** Sarah, Christ without absolutes ... Troeltsch 1988
➤ 5,7492 ... 7,k58 [pa. 1994: 0-19-826374-0]: ᴿScotJT 46 (1993) 129-131
(M. D. *Chapman*).

15118 **Drescher** Hans-Georg, Ernst Troeltsch, Leben und Werk ➤ 8,m910;
9,17102: ᴿZkG 105 (1994) 396-402 (M. *Wichelhaus*).

15119 **Drescher** Hans-Georg, Ernst Troeltsch, his life and work. ᵀ*Bowden*
John 1993 ➤ 9,17103: ᴿJRel 74 (1994) 260-2 (W. E. *Wyman*).

15120 ᴱ**Gisel** Pierre, Histoire et théologie chez Ernst Troeltsch: Lieux Théologiques 22, 1992 ➤ 8,m911: ᴿRHPR 74 (1994) 453s (M. *Lienhard*).

15121 ᵀᴱ*Paul* Garrett E., **Troeltsch**, The Christian faith 1991 ➤ 8,m918:
ᴿCritRR 6 (1993) 538-541 (S. R. *Gordy*).

15122 **Séguy** Jean, Cristianesimo e società; la sociologia di Ernst Troeltsch,
ᵀ*Prandi* Carlo: Cultura Sociale. Brescia 1994, Morcelliana. 366 p. Lᵐ
36. 88-372-1515-0. – ᴿGregorianum 75 (1994) 792 (W. R. *Suárez*).

15123 *Chapman* Mark D., The 'sad story' of Ernset Troeltsch' [death shortly
before his] proposed British lectures of 1923: ZnTg 1 (1994) 97-122;
deutsch 97.

15124 WEAKLAND Rembert, Wait a moment, now [on NEUHAUS R.]: Tablet
248 (1994) [1116s] 1225s [1255-7, *Chittister* Joan; 1340-2, *Dulles* Avery].

15125 WEIGEL: **Collins** Patrick W., Gustave Weigel S.J., a pioneer of reform.
ColMn 1992, Liturgical. 287 p. $20 pa. – ᴿChH 63 (1994) 155s (R. S.
Appleby).

15126 WITTGENSTEIN: **Kerr** Fergus, La teologia dopo Wittgenstein [1986],
ᵀ*Volpe* Giorgio 1992 ➤ 9,17109; ᴿGregorianum 75 (1994) 351s (R.
Fisichella).

15127 **Galbreath** Paul, An investigation of the Apostles' Creed in light of
Ludwig Wittgenstein: Diss. ᴰ*Ritschl* D. Heidelberg 1994. – TR 91,97.

15128 **Malcolm** Norman †, Wittgenstein; a religious point of view? ᴱ*Winch*
Peter. Ithaca NY 1994, Cornell Univ. xi-140 p. $32.50. 0-8104-2978-1
[TDig 42,279].

Y6.8 *Tendentiae exeuntis saeculi XX* – **Late 20th Century Movements.**

15128* *a*) *Allen* Diogenes, Christianity and the creed of postmodernism; – *b*)
Gay Craig M., Christianity and the 'homelessness' of the modern mind:
ChrSchR 23 (1993s) 117-126 / 127-144.

15129 *Altizer* Thomas J.J., The contemporary challenge of radical
Catholicism [Vatican II inverted reactionary Vatican I and *Lamentabile*
1907]: JRel 74 (1994) 182-198.

15130 *Anderson* Leith, Christian ministry in the 21st century, 1. The Church
at history's hinge; – 2. Theological issues; – 3. Personal challenges; – 4.
Practice of ministry in 21st century churches: BtS 151 (1994) 3-10 / 131-8
/ 259-266 / 387-393.

15131 *Berzosa Martínez* Raúl, ¿Ha muerto la postmodernidad? (A modo de
quasi-memoria bibliográfica): LumenVr 43 (1994) 267-275.

15132 **Biser** Eugen, Pronóstico de la fe; orientación para una época postse-
cularizada, ᵀ*Gancho* Claudio. Barc 1994, Herder. 525 p. – ᴿBibFe 20,58
(1994) 147s (A. *Salas*); LumenVr 43 (1994) 368-370 (U. *Gil Ortega*); RazF
230 (1994) 233s (J. M. *Vallarino*: ¿qué es posmodernismo?).

15133 ᴱ**Burnham** Frederic B., Postmodern theology; Christian faith in a
pluralist world 1984/9 ➤ 7,k85: ᴿJEvTS 37 (1994) 619-623 (R. E. *Otto*,
also on ALLEN D., GRIFFIN D., ODEN C.).

15134 *Boeve* Lieven, Theologie na het christelijke grote verhaal: Bijdragen 55 (1994) 269-294; 294, Postmodern theology after the decline of the master-story of Christianity, inspired by Jean-François LYOTARD, La condition postmoderne 1979.
15135 **Carrier** Hervé, Evangelizing the culture of modernity: Faith and Cultures. Mkn 1993, Orbis. viii-168 p. $17.   0-88344-898-X [TDig 41,353].
15136 **Castiñeira** Ángel, La experiencia de Dios en la postmodernidad 1992 → 9,17118: ᴿSalmanticensis 41 (1994) 150-3 (D. *Borobio*).
15137 **Centore** F. F., Being and becoming; a critique of post-modernism 1991 → 7,186: 8,m940: ᴿCritRR 6 (1993) 497s (G. *Allan*).
15138 *Conti* Martino, Nuovi evangelizzatori per la nuova evangelizzazione: Antonianum 69 (1994) 78-96 [497-528, nei paesi postcomunisti, *Teklak* Czesław].
15139 *Deist* Ferdinand E., Post-modernism and the use of Scripture in theological argument; footnote to the Apartheid theology debate: → 132, ᶠVORSTER W., Neotestamentica 28 (1994) 253-263.
15140 *Dick* John A., American Catholics; accomplishments and challenges at century's end: LvSt 19 (1994) 138-148.
15141 **Dupré** Louis, Passage to modernity; an essay in the hermeneutics of nature and culture, NHv 1993, Yale Univ. x-300 p. $30. – ᴿComWsh 21 (1994) 551-561 (P. *Casarella*); LvSt 19 (1994) 81-83 (P. L. *Levesque*); TS 55 (1994) 555s (J. E. *Thiel*).
15141* **Eagan** Joseph F., Restoration and revewal; the Church in the third millennium. KC c. 1994, Sheed & W. xiii-466 p. $20. 1-55612-763-4 [TDig 42,364].
15142 ᴱ**Engel** Mary Potter, *Wyman* Walter E.ᴶ, Revisioning the past; prospects in historical theology. Mp 1992, Fortress, ix-308 p. $27. 0-8006-2641-1. – ᴿZnTg 1,1 (1994) 201-3 (John *Clayton*).
15142* *Estal* Gabriel del, Nueva Iglesia; postmodernidad y muerte de Dios [... Opus Dei]: CiuD 207 (1994) 101-132.
15143 *Famerée* Joseph, Vers une histoire du concile Vatican II [Comité ALBERIGO G., Bologna]: RHE 89 (1994) 622-643.
15144 *a) Finger* Thomas, Modernity, postmodernity — what in the world are they?; – *b) Sugden* Christopher, Modernity, post modernity and the Gospel; – *c) Guinness* Os, Mission modernity [... No foe in 2000 years has wreaked such havoc on the Church as modernity]; – *c) Samuel* Vinay, Modernity, postmodernity and ethnic minorities [... 80% of British Asians who convert to Christianity give it up within a year]: Transformation 10,4 (1993) 20-26 / 1s / 3-13 / 14-17.
15145 **Gabriel** Karl, Christentum zwischen Tradition und Postmoderne: QDisp 141, 1992 → 8,m952; ᴿTPQ 142 (1994) 82s (M. *Lehner*). TLZ 119 (1994) 66s (H. *Obst*).
15146 *Gehring* Hugo, Wohnt Christus schon im den Herzn der Menschen? Von den Schwierigkeiten, den Glauben an Jesus Christus ins dritte Jahrtausend himein zu vermitteln: Entschluss 49,12 (1994) 4-13.
15147 **González-Carvajal** Luis, Evangelizar en un mundo postcristiano. Sdr 1993, SalTerrae. 174 p. – ᴿRazF 229 (1994) 441s (J. M. *Vallarino*).
15147* *Greinacher* Norbert, Ist die Kirche noch zu retten?: BLtg 67 (1994) 64-71.
15148 **Grenz** Stanley J., Revisioning evangelical theology; a fresh agenda for the 21st century 1993 → 9,17132: ᴿTrinJ 15 (1994) 123-130 (T. J. *Nettles*).

15149 **Griffin** D. R., *Smith* H., Primordial truth and postmodern theology 1989 ⇒ 5,k680 ... 8,m957: ᴿCritRR 5 (1992) 471-3 (B. L. *Whitney*).

15150 ᴱ**Hastings** Adrian, Modern Catholicism; Vatican II and after: 1991 ⇒ 7,348*a*. k100 ... 9,17136: ᴿMissiology 20 (1992) 543s (A. *Dries*).

15150* *a*) *Herrera Aceves* J. Jesús, La teología en la cultura adveniente; – *b*) *Gómez Hinojosa* José F., ¿Tiene futuro la postmodernidad? Algunas perspectivas para América Latina: EfMex 11 (1993) 73-110 / 305-330.

15151 **Hill** W. J., Search for the absent God; tradition in religious understanding and modernity. NY 1992, Crossroad. 192 p. $29. 0-8245-1114-X. – ᴿÉglT 25 (1994) 440s (J. van den *Hengel*).

15152 ᴱ**Höhn** Hans-Joachim, Theologie, die an der Zeit ist; Entwicklungen, Positionen, Konsequenzen 1992 ⇒ 9,17173: ᴿTR 90 (1994) 485s (H. *Wagner*).

15153 **Hughes** Robert D., Talking to the world in the days to come. Nv 1991, Broadman. 159 p. 0-8054-6037-3. – ᴿRExp 91 (1994) 109s (C. *Miller*: we must dismount our dinosaurs; nothing said in church today is different from 50 years ago).

15154 **Jorstad** Erling, Holding fast, pressing on; religion in America in the 1980s, 1990 ⇒ 7,g898*; 8,m962: ᴿCritRR 5 (1992) 331s (K. J. *Christiano*).

15155 ᶠKAUFMAN Gordon; Theology at the end of modernity, ᴱ**Davaney** Sheila G., 1991 ⇒ 7,85*d*: ᴿAmJTP 14 (1993) 336-341 (E. J. *Tarbox*).

15156 *Kevern* John R., A future for Anglican Catholic theology: AnglTR 76 (1994) 246-261.

15157 ᴱ**Kremer** Jacob, Aufbruch des Zweiten Vatikanischen Konzils heute [Ringvorlesung Univ. Wien 1992s]. Innsbruck 1993, Tyrolia. 180 p. DM 28. 3-7022-1907-2 [TLZ 120,86, J. *Wohlmuth*].

15158 *Krieg* Gustav A., Der verstummende Diskurs; praktische Theologie der Postmoderne im Spiegel ihrer Liturgik: ZTK 91 (1994) 346-374.

15159 **Lundin** Roger, The culture of interpretation; Christian faith and the postmodern world 1993 ⇒ 9,17146: ᴿChrSchR 56 (1994) 79-82 (J. M. *Ricks*); RLitND 26,3 (1994) 101s (B. *Hanson*).

15160 **McCarthy** Timothy G., The Catholic tradition, before and after Vatican II, 1878-1993. Ch 1994, Loyola Univ. xvii-427 p. $14 pa. 0-8294-0776-6 [TDig 41,370: '1878'].

15160* **McGrath** Alister, Evangelicalism and the future of Christianity. L 1994, Hodder & S. 195 p. £8. 0-340-60809-9. – ᴿTBR 7,3 (1994s) 60 (Saeed *Hamid-Khani*: optimism to be balanced by WELLS D.).

15161 *Martelli* Stefano, Ragione e religione nell'età post-moderna; note sul fondamentalismo razionalista: Asprenas 41 (1994) 349-366.

15161* **Mudge** Lewis S., The sense of a people 1992 ⇒ 9,17158: ᴿModT 10 (1994) 231-5 (P. D. *Kenneson*).

15162 *Natal* Domingo, La aventura postmoderna; II. La razón y su sombra, el sujeto y la máscara, el hombre contra lo humano y lo divino: EstAg 29 (1994) 97-153.

15163 **Norris** Christopher, The truth about postmodernism. Ox 1993, Blackwell. vi-333 p. £42; pa. £13. – ᴿLitTOx 8 (1994) 428s (H. *Wigh-Poulsen*).

15164 *Parker Gumucio* Cristián, Mutaciones culturales y paradigmas emergentes: Páginas 19,129 (Lima 1994) 40-54.

15164* **Pennington** M. Basil, Vatican II; we've only just begun. NY 1994, Crossroad. xi-167 p. $14. 0-8245-1410-6 [TDig 42,286].

15165 **Pesch** Otto H., Das zweite Vatikanische Konzil (1962-5) 1993 ⇒ 9, 17166: ᴿHerdKorr 47 (1993) 537 (U. *Ruh*).

15166 **Poulat** Émile,   L'ère postchrétienne; un monde sorti de Dieu.   P 1994, Flammarion. – ᴿEsprVie 104 (1994) 408-413 (G. *Cholvy*).

15167 **Rendtorff** Trutz,   Theologie in der Moderne 1991 → 7,g905: ᴿHerdKorr 47 (1993) 105 (A. S. —).

15168 **Routhier** Gilles,   La réception d'un concile [Vat. II]: CogF 174, 1993 → 9,12172;   F 149;   2-204-04654-X: ᴿBrotéria 138 (1994) 482 (Isidro *Ribeiro da Silva*); ÉTRel 69 (1994) 440s (J.-M. *Prieur*); Gregorianum 75 (1994) 775s (A. *Antón*: de gran actualidad; errores tipográficos); RHPR 74 (1994) 442 (A. *Birmelé*); ScEspr 46 (1994) 369-371 (N. *Provencher*).

15169 ᴱ**Scharlemann** Robert P.,   Theology at the end of the century; a dialogue on the postmodern [→ 5784, RUSSELL].   Charlottesville 1990, Univ. Virginia.   160 p. $29,50. – ᴿJEvTS 37 (1994) 585s (J. *Morrison*).

15170 **Sheppard** G. T.,   The future of the Bible; beyond liberalism and literalism.   Toronto 1990, United Church.   147 p. – ᴿAnnTh 8 (1994) 171s (M. A. *Tábet*).

15171 ᴱ**Siebenrock** Roman,   Christliches Abendland — Ende oder Neuanfang?: Theologische Trends 6.   Thaur 1994, Kulturverlag.   251 p.   3-85395-165-1.

15172 **Sraelen** H. Van,   L'Église et les religions non-chrétiennes au seuil du XXIᵉ siècle; étude historique et théologique.   P 1994, Beauchesne.   326 p. F 150. [NRT 117, 405, J. *Masson*: auteur aussi du Zen démystifié].

15173 *Stiver* Dan R.,   Much ado about Athens and Jerusalem; the implications of postmodernism for faith: RExp 91 (1994) 83-102.

15174 **Swidler** Leonard,   Die Zukunft der Theologie, im Dialog der Religionen und Weltanschauungen 1990 → 7,a487],ᵀ.   Gü 1992, Kaiser. ᴿTPQ 142 (1994) 83s (J. *Janda*).

15175 **Taylor** Charles,   *a*) The malaise of modernity.   CM c. 1992, Harvard Univ.   0-674-54384-X. – *b*) Grandeur et malaise de la modernité, ᵀ*Melançon* Charlotte: L'Essentiel.   Montréal 1992, Bellarmin.   152 p. – ᴿSR 22 (1993) 523s (J. P. *Rouleau*).

15176 *Turner* Theodore A.ᴵᴵᴵ,   Speaking in a broken tongue; postmodernism, principled pluralism, and the rehabilitation of public moral discourse: WestTJ 56 (1994) 345-377.

15177 **Vahanian** Gabriel,   L'utopie chrétienne 1992 → 8,322:   ᴿÉTRel 68 (1993) 128 (A. *Gounelle*: impatient avec les trop conservateurs).

15177* **Veith** Gene E.,   Postmodern times; a Christian guide to contemporary thought and culture.   L 1994, Crossway.   256 p. – ᴿEvJ 12 (1994) 94-96.

15178 *a*) *Vorgrimler* Herbert.   Die Volk-Gottes-Theologie des Zweiten Vatikanischen Konzils und die Folgen 30 Jahre 'danach'. – *b*) *Blasberg-Kuhnke* Martina,   Volk Gottes leben lernen; – *c*) *Frevel* Christian,   Die gespaltene Einheit des Gottesvolkes: TLtg 66 (1993) 67-72 / 73-80 / 80-97.

15179 *a*) *Vorländer* Wolfgang,   Perspektiven für eine Kirche von Morgen; – *b*) *Twardella* Günter,   Theologie ohne Gemeinde? Gemeinde ohne Theologie?: → 34d, ᶠFANGMEIER J. 1994, 293-300 / 301-310.

15179* **Wuthnow** Robert,   Christianity in the 21st century; reflections on the challenges ahead.   1993 → 9,17191: ᴿChrCent 111 (1994) 862s (L. J. *Sweet*); Commonweal 120,11 (1993) 23s (P. J. *Murnion*); TvT 34 (1994) 450 (J. *Sloot*).

Y7 (*Acta*) *Congressuum* .2 *biblica*: **nuntii**, rapports, Berichte.

15180 *Barbaglia* Silvio,   V convegno nazionale di studi neotestamentari e antico-cristiani (Vico Equense 15-18 sett. 1993) [L'apocalittica]: RivB 42 (1994) 119-123.

15181 *a) Brasil Pereira* Ney, Santo Domingo — a dimensão biblica; – *b) Martins Terra* João E., A Cristologia de Santo Domingo; – *c) Bellinato* Guillermo, A Pobreza no corpus paulinum [nos proverbios, *Martins Terra*]: RCuBib 36,65s ('Bíblia e Santo Domingo' 1993) 28-41 / 42-52 (3-25) / 128-142 [143-8].

15182 *a) Chmiel* Jerzy, ℗ VII/VIII colloquium biblicum w Wiedniu (1992/4); – *b) Nowak* Władysław, ℗ VI Międzynarodowe sympozjum józefologiczne w Rzymie (1993); – *c) Kapera* Zdzisław J. ℗ IV międzynarodowy kolokwium qumranologiczne (Kraków - Swoszowice 1993): RuBi 47 (1994) 52s.280s / 53-56 / 57.

15183 *De Sandre* Italo, Biblia aperta; per una lettura generativa della Bibbia [Padova dal 1987]: RivB 42 (1994) 249-253.

15184 *Fitych* Tadeusz, ℗ La rencontre des évêques européens avec un propos de la formation biblique des chrétiens (Mü-Freising, 16-18.II.1994): AtKap 123 (1994) 310s.

15185 *Fusco* Vittorio, 49° congresso della 'Studiorum Novi Testamenti Societas' (Edinburgh, 1-5 Agosto 1994): RivB 42 (1994) 503s.

15186 *Matras* Tadeusz, ℗ XXXI spotkanie biblistów polskich (Ożarów Mazowiecki - Ołtarzew 1993): RuBi 47 (1994) 120-3: 124s, postal-addresses of the 66 participants.

15187 *a) Panier* Louis, La dimension figurative dans les textes bibliques; Urbino 14-16 juillet 1994; – *b) Martin* François, La rencontre de Bordeaux [XIeme nationale Sémiotique et Bible, 22-26 août]: SémBib 75 (1994) 53s / 55-57.

15188 E*Neirynck* F., Colloquium Biblicum Lovaniense. Journées Bibliques de Louvain 1949-1993: Annua Nuntia Lovaniensia 29. Lv 1994 Univ. / Peeters, 112 p. Fb 400.

15189 *Savvatos* Chnysostomos, Ⓖ First inter-Christian symposium [Rome Antonianum + Thessaloniki Univ. 8-10 Sept. 1992 in Kolumbari, Crete]: TAth 64 (1993) 323-8.

15190 *a) Steins* Georg, Pentateuchforschung am runden Tisch [Univ. Osnabrück 13.-14.XI. 1992]; – *b) Jüngling* Hans-Winfried, Jeremia und die deuteronomistische Bewegung [AGAT (Arbeitsgemeinschaft der deutschsprachigen katholischen Alttestamentlerinnen und Alttestamentler) Fra St. Georgen 30.VIII.-3.IX.1993]; – *c) Klauck* Hans-J., 48. General Meeting der SNTS 9.-13. Aug. 1993 Chicago: BZ 38 (1994) 155-7 / 157s / 158-160.

15191 *Tuckett* C. M., SNTS 48th general meeting [Chicago] 9-13 August 1993: NTS 40 (1994) 298s; list of members 300-320.

15192 *Walsh* Jerome T., Report on the 57th general meeting of the Catholic Biblical Association of America [San Diego, August 11-13, 1994]: CBQ 56 (1994) 735-742.

Y7.4   (*Acta*) *theologica:* **nuntii.**

15193 *a) Boeve* Lieven, Vlaamse katholieke theologen over de taak van de theolog [Antwerpen 28 feb. 1994]; – *b) Witte* Henk, Nederlandse katholieke theologen over het potentieel aan gewelt in het christendom ['s-Hertogenbosch 11 maart 1994]: TvT 34 (1994) 185 / 186s.

15194 *Bokwa* Ignacy, Sensus fidelium; l'église comme la communauté apprenante et enseignante (symposium des professeurs des pays germanophones, Augsburg 21-25.VIII.1992): AtKap 120 (1993) 160-4.

15195 CARMEL: La première rencontre de la commission internationale car-

mélitaine de théologie: Teresianum 45 (1994) 195-203 (-301, sur les plusieurs pays).
15196 a) *Carroll* Eamon R., 44th annual convention of the Mariological Society of America (Providence RI May 27-28, 1993); – b) *Gendrot* Marcel, 50ème session de la Société française d'Etudes Mariales (Puy/Velay 30.VIII-2.IX.1993); Marianum 55 (1993) 657-9 / 660-3.
15197 *Diestel* Gudrun, Judentum und Christentum in einer säkularisierten Gesellschaft [Jerusalem 1.4. Feb. 1994[: UnSa 49 (1994) 60-65.
15198 a) *Evers* Georg, Conferentie in Hongkong over wijsheid in de joodse en de chinese traditie [nov. 1992]; – b) *Zwan* Rob van der, Congres over fundamentalisme in Tilburg [11 okt. 1993]; – c) *Grond* Agnes, Symposium in Nijmegen over grenzen van de feministische theologie [21 okt. 1993]; – d) *Hoogen* Toine van den, Katholieke theologen over theologie en communicatie [12 nov. 1993; two Amsterdam mentions]: TvT 34 (1994) 67 / 67s / 68s / 69s.
15199 a) *Evers* Georg. Conferentie over christelijke theologie in islamische context; – b) *Anckaert* Luc, *Pattyn* Bart, Colloquium te Leuevn over narrativiteit en toegepaste ethiek; – c) *Kalsky* Manuela, Debat over feministische hermeneutik te Nijmegen; – d) *Brok* Jan, Symposium te Nijmegen over individualisering en religie: TvT 34 (1994) 292 / 293s / 294s / 295s.
15200 *Fernández García* Domiciano, Congresos internacionales; XI mariológico y XVIII mariano [Huelva 18-27 sept. 1992]: EphMar 43 (1993) 461-473.
15201 *Galli* Giuseppe, Riconoscersi in un testo. Colloqui sulla interpretazione 1980-93, Univ. Macerata: RivB 42 (1994) 115-9.
15202 *Gaziaux* É., La foi dans le temps de risque; colloque [LvN 3-4 nov. 1993, ᴰ*Gesché* P.]: RTLv 25 (1994) 135-9.
15203 *Giannoni* Paolo, Male cosmico e male morale; congresso zonale ATI/centr; (Lecceto 26-27 sett. 1994): RasT 35 (1994) 743-9.
15204 *Henn* William, Santiago de Compostela's [5th conference of Faith and Order commission, August 3-14,1993] vision of koinonia in faith: Gregorianum 75 (1994) 623-639; franc. 639.
15205 a) *Janicki* Jan, ℗ De XXIX conventu liturgistarum polonorum (Varsaviae 1993); – b) *Kantor* Maria, ℗ De VI conventu Association of Coordinators of Catholic Schools of Evangelization (Mediolan 1994): RuBi 47 (1994) 125-130 / 130s.
15206 *Kanior* Marian, ℗ XIᵉᵐᵉ congrès mariologique, Huelva 18-27.IX.1992: AtKap 120 (1993) 168-174.
15207 *Liebler* Konrad, Glauben und feiern als ganzer Mensch; 30. internationale altkatholische Theologenkonferenz 24.-29. August 1992 in Leuven: IKiZ 83 (1993) 15-20 [101-127, *Kraft* Sigisbert].
15208 *Mastantuono* Antonio, Il Vangelo della carità per la Chiesa e la società; in margine ad un convegno (Pont. Univ. Lateranense al., Roma 15-17 marzo 1994]: RasT 35 (1994) 338-345.
15209 *Matabosch* Antoni, Vers la *koinonia* en la fe, la vida i el testimoni, cinquena conferència mundial de 'Fe i Constitució'; Santiago de Compostel·la (3-14 d'Agost 1993): RCatalT 18 (1993) 169-175.
15210 *Miranda* Maria de França, Um catolicismo plural? A propósito da 'evangelização inculturada' de Santo Domingo: PerspT 25 (1993) 31-44.
15211 *Muratore* Saturnino, Futuro del cosmo, futuro dell'uomo; un dialogo multidisciplinare; linee della relazione-base per il XV congresso nazionale [Forum ATI]: RasT 35 (1994) 346-362.

15212 *Neuner* Joseph, Paths of mission in India today; national consultation, Pune 4-9 Jan, 1994: VerbumSVD 35 (1994) 259-267.
15213 *Piazza* Orazio F., Sociologia e teologia di fronte al futuro; convegno interdisciplinare Trento 11-12 maggio 1994: RasT 35 (1994) 464-479.
15214 *Przybyłowski* Jan, ❷ XXIV Spotkanie polskich Józefologów 28-29.IV.1993: AtKap 121 (1993) 431-5.
15215 *Uribarri* Gabino, II encuentro de teólogos jesuitas europeos [Varsovia 22-25.IX.1994]: EstE 69 (1994) 529s.
15216 *Vall* Hector, La utopîa ecuménica; 'hacia la koinonia en la fe, la vida y el testimonio' (V Conferencia Mundial de 'Fe y Constitución'; Santiago de Compostela, agosto de 1993): EstE 69 (1994) 203-224. [289-341, desde Montréal a Santiago 1963-93].

Y7.6 *Acta congressuum philologica:* **nuntii.**

15217 *Ankum* Hans, *Michel* Jacques-Henri, La XLVIIᵉ session Soc. Droits de l'Antiquité (Oxford 21-25 sept. 1993): RIDA 41 (1994) 449-489; 490 index des 43 rapports.
15218 *Nörenberg* Heinz-Werner, VIII. internationales HIPPOKRATES -Kolloquium [23.-28. Sept. 1993, Banz-Staffelstein]: Gnomon 66 (1994) 286s.
15218* ᴱ*Scholer* D., Colloquium on women in the ancient Mediterranean world: BRes 39 (1994) 29-30 (-79).
15219 Twentieth St-Louis Conference on manuscript studies [8-9 Oct. 1993]: Manuscripta 37 (1993) 227-241.

Y7.8 *Acta congressuum orientalistica et archaeologica:* **nuntii.**

15220 *Liverani* Mario, Geografia neo-assira [Roma 10-12 nov. 1993]: GeogAnt 3s (1994s) 257s.
15221 *Shanks* Hershel, Capital archaeology; 7200 scholars and two precious artifacts [Israel museum Temple-pomegranate and Caiaphas ossuary] come to Washington for the annual meeting; ASOR is an organization in trouble; should ASOR and SBL have a private chat?: BAR-W 20,2 (1994) 46-49.91.

Y8 *Periti,* **Scholars, Personalia, organizations.**

15222 *Bressolette* Claude, L'Institut Catholique de Paris [1890-1930] et la 'science allemande': RICathP 50 (1994) 109-129.
15223 [Catalunya Fac. Teol.], Memòria del curs acadèmic 1992-1993: RCatalT 18 (1993) 191-9.
15224 *Czajkowski* Michał, 100 lat biblistyki w École Biblique: RuBi 47 (1994) 111-120.
15225 *Dick* John A., Chronicles: LvSt 19 (1994) 352-8; 359-372, doctoral dissertations with summary.
15226 ᴱ**Doré** J., Les cent ans FacT 1991 ➔ 9,17257: ᴿTPhil 69 (1994) 297-9 H. J. *Sieben*).
15227 *Esua* Cornelius F., The 25th anniversary of the Catholic biblical federation: Verbum SVD 35 (1994) 281-5.
15228 ᴱ**Farrugia** Edward G., The Pontifical Oriental Institute; the first 75 years. 1993. – ᴿOrChrPer 60 (1994) 279s (T. *Špidlík*).
15229 *Livingstone* G. Hebert, Bethel Academy 200th anniversary [of founding by Bishop Francis ASBURY]: AsbTJ 49,2 (1994) 115 p.

15230 Lublin: Z życia Uniwersytetu: ZeKUL 35,1 (1992) 115-120; 35,3 (1992) 87-116); 36 (1993) 129-177.
15231 *Merino* José Antonio, Chronica 1994-5: Antonianum 69 (1994) 565-588.
15231* *Olmo Lete* G. del,   Instituto Interuniversitario del Próximo Oriente Antiguo [Barcelona]: AulaO 12 (1994) 121-3.
15232 **Remus** Harold, *al.*,   Religious studies in Ontario; a State-of-the-Art review. Waterloo 1992, W. Laurier. xvii-422 p. – RSR 23 (1994) 499s (P. *Bowlby*).
15233 **Selden** William K.,   Princeton theological seminary of America; a narrative history, 1812-1992. Princeton 1992, Theol.Sem.   xiv-201 p. $12. – RPrincSemB 14 (1993) 287s (R. T. *Handy*).
15233* [*Swetnam* J., *Valentino* C., Acta Pontificii Instituti Biblici 10,1 (1994). 120 p.
15234 *a*) *Szczurek* Jan Daniel,   The 1993-4 academic year in the Cracow Pontifical Academy of Theology [Eng., <]; – *b*) *Wojciechowski* Tadeusz, ℗ Die wissenschaftlichen Beziehungen mit der Fakultät für katholische Theologie der Johannes-Gutenberg Universität Mainz: → 92* FPIERONEK T., AnCracov 26 (1994) 641-652 / 653-9.
15235 **Taft** Robert F., *Dugan* James L.,   Il 75° anniversario del Pontificio Istituto Orientale; Atti delle celebrazioni giubilari, 15-17 ott. 1992: OrChrAnal 244.   R 1994, Pont.Inst.Stud. Orientalium.   318 p.; 2 fig.; 16 pl. [RHE 89,448*]. 88-7210-303-7.
15236 EVesco J.-L. / **Murphy-O'Connor** J., Cent'anni di esegesi – AT/NT – l'École Biblique di Gerusalemme 1992 → 9,17272 / 17262: RCC 145 (1994,4) 206s (D. *Scaiola*); Protestantesimo 49 (1994) 76-78 (C. *Tron* repeated 340s).

Y8.5   *Periti,* **in memoriam.**

15237 Necrologia: REB 53 (1993) 232-6. 469-479 / 718-732 / 974-9 / 54 (1994) 204-224. / 498-506 / 737-748 / 971-983. – RHE 89 (1994) 131* / 304*s / 458*.
15238 Abdulhak, Selim, 1913-1992: Syria 71 (1994) 443s; phot. (E. *Will*).
15238* Åkerberg, Hans, 1935-1994: SvTKv 70 (1994) 200 (N. G. *Holm*).
15239 Aland, Kurt, aet. 79, † 13.IV.1994: ETL 70 (1994) 257 [F. *Neirynck*]; TLZ 119 (1994) 1038s (T. *Holtz*).
15240 Alföldi-Rosenbaum, Elisabeth [→ 9,17275] 1.VIII.1921 - 6.X.1992: AJA 97 (1993) 565s, phot. (Sheila D. *Campbell*, James *Russell*).
15241 Anawati, Georges Chehata, O.P. 1905-1994: BSACopte 33 (1994) 181s (Amin *Abdel Nour*); Islamochristiana 20 (1994) 1-22 (H. *Teissier, al.*).
15242 André, Jacques, 30.VII.1910 - 3.VI.1994: RÉLat 72 (1994) 21s (P. *Flobert*); co-directeur, RPg 68 (1994) 195-7 (aussi P. *Flobert*).
15243 Barry, Coleman J. O.S.B., 21.V.1921 - 7.I.1994: CathHR 80 (1994) 418-420 (V. G. *Tegeder*); RHE 89 (1994) 570 (R. *Aubert*).
15245 Bauer, Heinrich [→ 9,17284] 17.IX.1935 – 14.II.1993: Gnomon 66 (1994) 476s (H. *Drerup*).
15246 Beltritti, Giacomo Giuseppe, aet. 82, 1. nov. 1992; già Patriarca di Gerusalemme: HLand 124,4 (1992) 4; Phot.
15247 Berchem, Denis Van, 19.XII.1908 - 7.V.1994: CRAI (1994) 421s (J. *Marcadé*); MusHelv 51 (1994) 65, phot. (Margarethe *Billerbeck, al.*); p. 3s (ses) Souvenirs d'un fondaterur; Syria 71 (1994) 444s (E. *Will*).
15248 Berg, Roger, XII.1910 ... c. 1994: RÉJ (53 (1994) 429-432 (Eliane *Roos*).
15249 Bertinelli, Roberto, 4.VI.1956 - 3.IV.1994: RSO 68 (1994) 161-4 (P. *Corradini*, bibliog.).

15249* Bertotti, Filippo, 23.VII.1963 - 16.VI.1993: AION 53 (1993) 492-6 (G. M. *D'Erme*, M. *Bernardini*).
15250 Bescapé, Giacomo C., 12.II.1902-3.VIII.1993: RitNum 96 (1994s) 372s (A. *Savio*).
15250* Biedermann, Hermenegild M., O.S.A., 15.XII.1911 - 26.X.1994: OstKSt 43 (1994) 273s (G. *Holmann*).
15251 Böhne, Winfried, 12.II.1926 - 15.III.1991: ArLtgW 33 (1991) 192 (A. *Häussling*); bibliog. 295-301.
15252 Bonora, Antonio, 12.X.1939 - 3.II.1993: TItSett 19 (1993) 99s (G. *Segalla*).
15253 Borovskiy, Yakov Markovič, 21.XI.1896 - 5.III.1994: VDI 211 (1994) 222 (F. K. *Gavrilov*, ⑧).
15254 Bosch, David [➤ 8,r122; 9,17295] 1929-15.IV.1992: ᴿExchange 21 (1992) 84s (J. B. *Jongeneel*).
15255 Bothmer, Bernard V., 13.X.1912 - 24.XI.1993: AJA 98 (1994) 345s, phot. (J. A. *Josephson*); VDI 209 (1994) 217 (A.O. *Bolshakov*).
15256 Bourassa, François, 1912 - 18.XII.1993: ScEspr 46 (1994) 5-13 (R. *Latourelle*; bibliog.).
15256* Braun, Egon, 10.IX.1906 - 14.IX.1993: JbÖsA 63-G (1994) 1-3 (D. *Knibbe*; Bibliog. Maria *Aurenhammer*).
15257 Brommer, Frank [➤ 9,17200] 8.IX.1911 - 21.IV.1993; Klas. Arch. Mainz. Gnomon 66 (1994) 383s (R. *Fleischer*).
15258 Broughton T. Robert S., aet. 94, 17.IX.1993; Mitarbeiter: Historia 43 (1994) vii, portr.
15259 Caminos, Ricardo Augusto [➤ 9,17302], 11.VII.1915 - 26.V.1992: iii-v (J. *Osing*).
15260 Cary-Elwes, Columba, O.S.B., 1903 - 22.I.1994, abbot of Ampleforth: Tablet 248 (1994) 166 (D. *Goodall*).
15261 Charles, Maxime, mgr. 1908 - 29.VIII.1993: Communio 19,11 (P 1994) 57-80 (L. *Bouyer*, J. *Duchesne*, S. *Pruvot*).
15262 Châtillon, François, 20.IX.1908 - 7.I.1994; fondateur de la Revue du Moyen Âge latin 1945: RHE 99 (1994) 342 (J. *Longère*).
15263 Ciavolino, Nicola, mons. 11.II.1943 - 29.VIII.1994: RivArCr 70 (1994) 472-4 (D. *Mazzoleni*).
15264 Ciprotti, Pio c. 1914, † c. 1994: StRom 42 (1994) 91s; phot (L. de *Luca*).
15264* Cohen, Claude, d. 18.IX.1991: JAs 281 (1993) 1-19 (T. *Bianquis*: 'historien de l'Orient arabe médiévale').
15265 Comfort, Howard, 4.VI.1904 - 20.IX.1993; Haverford college: AJA 98 (1994) 561s, phot. (P. M. *Kenrick*).
15266 Cook, John, aet. 85, 2.I.1994: AnSt 44 (1994) 129 (S. *Mitchell*).
15267 Copleston, Frederick, aet 86, 3.II.1994: ChrCent 111 (1994) 412 (a brief review of his recent memoirs in the same volume); Tablet 248 (1994) 187s (B. *Brinkman*).
15268 Cowan, J. Milton, 22.II.1907 - 20.XII.1993; Language 71 (1995) 341-4 (C. F. *Hockett*).
15269 Daniel, William, S.J. † 23.X.1994: Pacifica 7 (1994) 324.
15270 Dantoing Alain, aet. 44, 14.X.1994: RHE 89 (1994) 820 (J. *Lory*).
15271 Deane, Herbert A., 1921-14.II.1991: JHistId 52 (1991) 524 (J. H. *Franklin*).
15272 Della Torre, Paolo, 1910 - 11.XI.1993: StRom 42 (1994) 89s; phot. (C. *Pietrangeli*).
15273 Desroche, Henri, 1914-1994, premier directeur: ArchivScSocR 39,87 (1994) 5-11 (J. *Seguy*).

15274 Dijk-Hemmes, Fokkelien Van, 1943-1994: JStOT 63 (1994) 35-37 (Mieke *Bal*, Athalya *Brenner*).
15275 Dillard, Raymond Bryan, [➤ 9,17216], 7.I.1994 - 1.X.1993: Chron. comm.: WestTJ 55 (1993) 188s, phot.
15276 Eastwood Walter H., 13.IV.1906 - 9.VI.1994: PrincSemB 15 (1994) 287s.
15277 Eilers, Wilhelm, 27.IX.1900 - 3.VII.1989 WZKM 80 (1990) 7-12; portr. (R. *Schmitt*).
15278 Fernández-Miranda, Manuel, 1946 - VII.1994; prehistoriador: BSAA 60 (1994) 542 (J. *Fernández Manzano*); ArEspArq 67 (1994) i-iv (D. *Plácido*, F.-J. *Sánchez-Palencia*, sin fechas); Zephyrus 47 (S 1994) 395; phot. (F. *Bernaldo de Quiros*).
15278* Fichter, Joseph H. aet. 85, 23.II.(1994): ETL 71,291 (R. F. *Collins*).
15279 Flesseman-van Leer, Ellen, [➤ 8,r153], 17.XII.1912 - 18.VI.1991: KerkT 45 (1994) 219-237: 'met de Schrift tussen Kerk en Jodendom'.
15280 *Frostin,* Per, aet. 48, † 8.VI.1992: SvTKv 68 (1992) 143s (P. E. *Persson*).
15280* Fuchs, Anna, 20.I.1939 - 4.VII.1992: Kratylos 38 (1993) 218-220 (H. *Seiler*).
15281 Fürst, Walther, 1911 - 25.III.1991: VerkF 38,2 (1993) 85 (G. *Sauer*).
15282 Gara, Alessandra, 1944 - 26.IV.1993: ArPapFor 40 (1994) 110 (H. *Muehler*); BASP 30 (1993) 79s (R. S. *Bagnall*).
15283 Geense, Adrian, 1931 - 30.I.1994: KerkT 45 (1994) 177-9.
15283* Gening, Vladimir Feodorovitch, 10.V.1924 - 30.X.1993: RossArkh (1994,3) 253s; phot. (E. P. *Bunyatian*).
15284 Gerleman, Gillis, 27.III.1912 - 25.VII.1993: SvTKv 70 (1994) 77 (S. *Hidal*); TsTKi 65 (1994) 63s (M. *Saebø*).
15285 Gimbutas, Marija, 21.I.1921 - 2.II.1994: AJA 98 (1994) 755-7; phot. (Ernestine S. *Elster*); RossArkh (1994,4) 251s, phot. (N. J. *Merpert*; bibliog.).
15286 Gindin, Leonid Aleksandrovič, 25.VII.1928 - 23.IV.1994: VDI 211 (1994) 220s., phot.
15287 Gollwitzer, Helmut, [➤ 9,17335] 1908 - 17,X,1993: Orientierung 58 (1994) 13-15 (K. *Füssel*: 'Anwalt des Rechts der anderen'); EvT 54 (1991) 1 (J. *Moltmann*; 2-7 Predigt, F. W. *Marquardt*).
15288 Grottanelli, Vinigi L., 21.V.1993: RasEtiop 35 (1991!) 171-3 (L. *Ricci*).
15289 Grzegorzewski, Karl, aet. 86, † 10.IX.1994: TLZ 119 (1994) 1040 (H. *Braun*).
15290 Halleux, André de, 18.I.1929 - 30.I.1994: ETL 70 (1994) 235 (J. *Étienne*, bibliog. 236-243 + 1100 recensions, G. van *Belle* 'un des plus féconds collaborateurs': RTLv 25 (1994) 425-8 (J.-M. *Sevrin*) & 429-432 (P. *Duprey*) & 433-7 (S. *Brock*, études syriaques); 438-444, bibliog. RHE 99 (1994) 324-6 (U. *Zanetti*; on attend la bibliographie dans RTLv); RevSR 68 (1994) 403-8 (J. *Lison*).
15291 Hammerschmidt, Ernst, 29.IV.1928 - 16,XII.1993 (Autounfall), Mitherausgeber: IkiZ 84 (1994) 1s (H. A. *Frei*); RasEtiop 35 (1991!) 177-9 (L. *Ricci*).
15292 Hartmann, Josef, 1992: RasEtiop 35 (1991!) 181s (L. *Ricci*).
15293 Hasel, Gerhard Franz, 1935 - 11.VIII.1994 (auto accident): Andr-UnSem 32 (1994) 166-8; phot. ➤ 8934.
15294 Haubst, Rudolph, MFCusan 21 (1994) 7-26 (K. *Kremer*).
15295 Hebblethwaite, Peter † 1994: Tablet 248 (1994) 1676s.
15296 Helck, Wolfgang [➤ 9,17347] 16.IX.1914 - 27.VIII.1993: ZägSpr 121 (1994) vi-ix; portr. (Elke *Blumenthal*, E. *Hornung*).

15297 Hendry, George F., 20.III.1904 - 17.VIII.1993: PrincSemB 15 (1994) 44s
(W. G. *Bodamer*) & 46-51 (D. L. *Migliore*).
15297* Hilmarsson, Jörundur, 15.III.1946 - 13.VIII.1992: Kratylos 39 (1994)
217-220 (G.-J. *Pinault*).
15298 Hirsch-Dyczek, Olga, 24.II.1936 - 15.I.1993: ArchWsz 44 (1993) 155-7
(J. *Śliwa*).
15299 Holth, Sverre, '2. juledag' 1902 − † aet. 90; TsTKi 65 (1994) 67 (N. E.
Bloch-Hoell).
15300 Horn, Siegfried H., 17.III.1908 - 28.XI.1993: BA 57 (1994) 58s (phot.)
& BAR-W 20,2 (1994) 22-24 (L. T. *Geraty*).
15301 Hospers, Johannes Hendrik, 5.II.1921 - 3.V.1993: ZAHeb 7 (1994) 1s
(A. van der *Woude*).
15302 Hubert, Jean, 12.VI.1902 - 1.VII.1994: CRAI (1994) 653s (J. *Marcadé*).
15303 Jacobsen, Thorkild † 2.V.1993: AfO 42s (1995s) 332s (W. *Moran*).
15304 Jakobs, Manfred, 5.XI.1928 - 16.X.1994: TLZ 119 (1994) 1040.
15305 Jakubiec, Czesław, 14.VII.1909 - 15.IV.1993, prof. S. Scr.: RuBi 47
(1994) 59-62 (R. *Rumianek*, bibliog.).
15306 Jean-Nesmy, Claude, 13.VI.1920 - 1.I.1994; EsprVie 104 (1994) 18-couv.
15307 Jobling, William, 1941 - 4.XII.1994: BurHist 30,4 (1994) 115.
15308 Johnson, Sherman, aet. 85, 24.III.1993: ETL 70 (1994) 249 (R. F.
Collins).
15308* Jonas, Hans, aet. 89, 3.II.1994(?): ETL 70 (1994) 249 (R. F.
Collins).
15309 Kempinski, Aharon, 26.I.1939 - 2.VII.1994: BAnglsr 13 (1993s) 63-66,
phot. (Claudine *Dauphin*); BAR-W 20,5 (1994) 20.22 (H. *Shanks*); TAJ 21
(1994) 159-161; phot. (Z. *Herzog*).
15310 Kilian, Klaus [➤ 8,r184] 27.II.1939 - 28.V.1992: MiDAI-A 108 (1993)
1-7; phot. (K. *Fittschen*), 9-27 (S. E. *Jakovidis*).
15311 Knoch, Otto Bernhard, 7.I. 1926 − 17.XI.1993: BiKi 49 (1994) 56; portr.
15311* Knox, David Broughton, 1916- I.1994: RefTR 53 (1994) 1.
15312 Köster, Heinrich Maria 1.VII.1911 − 29.V.1993: Marianum 55 (1993)
429-459 (F. *Courth*; Bibliog.).
15313 Kołkówna, Stanisława, 25.VI.1926 − 26.VI.1993: ArchWsz 44 (1993)
157-160 (Malgorzata *Biernacka-Lubańska*; bibliog.).
15314 Korek, József, 1920-1992; Archäologe, Museologe: AcArchH 46 (1994)
405-7 (N. *Kalicz*).
15315 Kostochkim, Vladimir Vladimirovtch, 1920-1992: RossArkh (1994,1)
249s, phot. (G. K. *Vagdar, al.*, Ⓡ; bibliog.).
15316 Krajcar, Jan, 5.VII.1915 - 24.VI. 1992; storia slavica ecclesiastica:
OrChrPer 60 (1994) 5-19 (V. *Poggi*, bibliog.).
15317 Kraus, Theodor, 27.V.1919 - 13.III.1994: MiDAI-R 101 (1994) 3s.
15318 Krautheimer, Richard, 6.VII.1897 - 1.XI.1994: ByZ 88 (1995) 359-362
(U. *Peschkow*); RivArCr 70 (1994) 463-470 (F. *Guidobaldi*).
15319 Kropotkin, Vladislav Vsevolodovich, 2.II.1922 - 23.VIII.1993: Ross-
Arkh (1994,1) 243-8; phot. (N. Y. *Merpert*, Ⓡ; bibliog.).
15320 Kupiszewski, Henryk 1927-1994: JJurPap 24 (1994) 7-10, phot. (J.
Mélèze-Modrzejewski).
15321 Labande, Edmond-René, [➤ 9,17375 '22.VII.1992 < Speculum'] 1908
- 22.VII.1992: CahCMédv 36 (1993) 3-10; phot; bibliog. 11-25.
15322 Ladner, Gerhart Burian, 3.XII.1905 - 21.IX.1993: CathHR 80 (1994)
415-8 (J. *Van Engen*).
15323 Lahbabi, Mohamed Aziz, 23.VIII.1993: Islamochristiana 20 (1994)
23-28 (M. *Borrmans*).

15324 Lantier, Raymond, 11.VII.1886 - 2.IV.1990: CRAI (1994) 656-663, phot. (R. *Turcan*).
15325 Lauria, Mario, 20.X.1903 - 5.IX.1991: IVRA 42 (1991) 231-3 (F.P. *Casavola*).
15326 Lavagnini, Bruno, aet. 93, 19/20.III.1992: Orpheus 14 (1993) 231-7 (G. *D'Ippolito*).
15327 Le Bonniec, Henri, 11.II.1915 - 28.XII.1994: RÉLat 72 (1994) 23s (J. *Hellegouarc'h*).
15328 Leclercq, Jean, [➤ 9,17380] 31.I.1911 - 27.X.1993: Aevum 68 (1994) 439-444 (G. *Penco*); Benedictina 41 (1994) 317-339 (anche G. *Penco*); MélSR 61 (1994) 201-212 (H. *Platelle*); Revue Mabillon 66 (1994) 5-9 (G. *Constable*).
15329 Lehmann, Paul Louis, 10.IX.1906 - 27.II.1994: PrincSemB 15 (1994) 165-169 (F. *Rutledge*); Princeton, Harvard, NY-Union theology professor: ChrCent 111 (1994) 276 [ETL 71,251, R.F. *Collins*].
15330 Leloir, Louis, O.S.B. [➤ 8,r200], 1911 -15.VIII.1992 ETL 69 (1993) 236 (G. *Thils*).
15331 Lentzen-Deis Fritzleo S.J. [➤ 9,17381] 15.III.1928 -29.III.1993; BZ 38 (1994) 157 (R. *Dillmann*).
15332 Lewis, Alan Edmond, † 19.II.1994, co-editor: ScotJT 47 (1994) 145-7 (J.L. *Stotts*).
15333 Lewison, Anthony, 1921-1993: BAngIsr 13 (1993s) 61s (D.J. *Siddle*).
15334 Lipshits, Elena Emmanuelovna, 9.V.1901 - 22.IV.1990: VizVrem 53 (1992) 216-9, **Ⓑ**, bibliog.
15335 Loposzko, Tadeusz, 15.VI.1929 - 3.VIII.1994; Eos 81 (1993!) 324s.
15336 Lubac H de [➤ 7,k317 ... 9,17387] 20.III.1896-1991: ForKT 10 (1994) 82-96 (M. *Lochbrunner*, 'Leidenschaft für die Theologie').
15337 Ludwig, Wido, 1927-1994; MDOG 126 (1994) 7-10; phot. (Eva *Strommenger*).
15338 Lurker, Manfred, 17.III.1928 - 11.VI.1990: Ges. Symbolforschung 1955: Symbolon 11 (1993) 7s (H. *Jung*).
15339 Maccarrone, mons. Michele [➤ 9,17389], 16.III.1910 - 4.V.1993: AnHistIgl 3 (1994) 467s (J. *Orlandis*).
15340 MacKenzie, Roderick A.F., 15.XI.1911 - 30.IV.1994; Rettore del Pontificio Istituto Biblico 1963-9: AcPIB 9,10 (1993s) 963-8 (T. *Prendergast*); Biblica 75 (1994) 447s (F.E. *Brenk*); CBQ 56 (1994) 309s; also professor in Canada and Berkeley: SR 23 (1994) 228s (T. *Prendergast*; bibliog.).
15340* MacKinnon, Donald M. 1913-1994: TLond 97 (1994) 401s (Ann *Loades*).
15341 Macúch, Rudolf, 16.X.1919 - 23.VII.1993: ArOr 62 (1994) phot., 333s (R. *Voigt*, deutsch) & 334-340 (S. *Segert*, Eng.).
15342 Marlé, René, S.J. 1920 - 17.II.1994: RICathP 50 (1994) 195s - 201 (J. *Joncheray*, J. *Moingt*).
15343 Marsili, Salvatore, abate O.S.B., 10.VIII.1910 - 27.XI.1983, dir.: RivLtg 80 (1993) 259-261 (G. *Sobrero*) 267-372, *al.*, bibliog. 373-388 (M. *Ballatori*, M. *Alberta*).
15344 Marty, François, aet. 89 - 16.II.1994; card. archévêque de Paris: Tablet 248 (1994) 265s (A. *Woodrow*).
15345 Matronola, Martino [Vittorio], O.S.B., vescovo; 2.XI.1903 -20.V.1994. Benedictina 41 (1994) 507s (M. *Dell'Omo*).
15346 Méjan, François, 23.V.1908 - 4.VII.1993; ancien président: BuProtF 140 (1994) 177-180 (R. *Zuber*).

15347 Meyendorff J. F. [➤ 8,r218; 9,17398], 1926 - 22.VII.1992: VizVrem 54 (1993) 220s (A. *Rogov*, ⑬).
15348 Moeller, Eugène, 6.V.1909 - 3.IV.1991: QLtg 73 (1992) 188s (G. *Michiels*).
15349 Monaco, Giusto, sans dates: Orpheus 15 (1994) 277-9 (D. *Romano*).
15350 Moody Joseph N., 18.IV.1904 - 2.IV.1994: CathHR 80 (1994) 420s (F. J. *Murphy*). RHE 89 (1994) 822 (R. *Aubert* '2.III').
15351 Moretti, Athos, 17.XI.1907 - 29.X.1993: RitNum 96 (1994s) 371 (L. *Ferri*).
15352 Mulder, Martin Jan, 25.XII.1923 - 24.VI.1994: JStJud 25 (1994) 175s (A. S. van der *Woude*).
15353 Niederländer, Hubert, 10.II.1921 - 14.XI.1991: IVRA 42 (1991) 233-6 (F. *Sturm*); ZSavR 111 (1994) 765-8 (auch F. *Sturm*).
15354 Nusselein, Ernst Wilhelm, msgr., 2.IX.1908 - 4.V.1992: Mitglied: HLand 194,2 (1992) 4; phot. (H. *Michel*).
15354* Oesterreicher, John, aet. 89, 1993 [➤ 9,17408] 1904 -10.IV.1994 (?): ETL 70 (1994) 249 (R. F. *Collins*).
15355 Oldfield, Kenneth, 1944-1992: BritJRelEd 15,3 (1993) 4s.
15356 Paraicki-Pudełko, Stefan, 10.VII.1914 - 16.IV.1994: Eos 81 (1993!) 323s (L. *Mrożewicz*).
15357 Parker, Richard Anthony, 10.XII.1905 - 3.VI.1993: JAmEg 31 (1994) 1s (L. H. *Lesko*).
15358 Pax, Elpidius (Wolfgang) O.F.M., [➤ 9,17413], 22.IV.1912 - 14.IV.1993; licenziato del Biblico (Roma), esegeta a Gerusalemme: TerraS 69,3 (1993) 53-55; foto; BiKi 48 (1993) 154 (J.-J. *Klauck*).
15359 Peale, Norman Vincent, aet 95. † 1994: ChrC 110 (1994) 41.
15360 Pissarek-Hudelist, Herlinde aet. 62, 19.VI.1994, Theol.-Dekanin: ZkT 116 (1994) 494-503 (G. *Bader*; Bibliog.).
15361 Porada, Edith, 22.VIII.1912 - 24.III.1994: MDOG 126 (1994) 5s (Ruth *Mayer-Opificius*); JPrehRel 8 (1994) 76 (Parvine H. *Merrillees, al.*).
15362 Portillo, Alvaro del, † 23.III.1994: AnnTh 8 (1994) 3-12, portr.; 13-22 (J. L. *Illanes*).
15363 Poulain, Pierre, 29.V.1907 - 6.III.1994: RICathP 50 (1994) 202s (A. *Wartelle*).
15364 Press, Volker, 28.III.1939 - 16.X.1993: HZ 259 (1994) 878-883 (P. *Moraw*).
15365 Preuss, Horst Dietrich. 1.V.1927 - 25.XII.1993 ('1. juledag'): TsT 65 (1994) 65s (M. *Sæbø*).
15366 Pugh, Thomas Jefferson, 25.X.1917 - 9.II.1994: JIntdenom 21 (1993s) ii-iv; portr.
15367 Purdy, William, 1911-1994; Rome correspondent for 25 years: Tablet 248 (1994) 1530.
15368 Rainey, Froelich Gladstone, 1907-1992: AJA 97 (1993) 353s, phot. (W. H. *Goodenough*).
15369 Rennings, Heinrich, 9.VI.1926 - 3.X.1994: HDienst 48 (1994) 251s, phot. (W. *Glade*).
15370 Rexine, John Efstratios [➤ 9,17427], 6.VI.1929 - 23.X.1993: ClasB 70 (1994) 29s; phot. (A. J. *Papalas* '24.XI').
15371 Riet, Simone Van, 12.IV.1919 - 28.XI.1993 [➤ supra 103]: Byzantion 64 (1994) 4-7, phot. (J. *Grand'Henry*).
15372 Rinaldi, Giovanni, 26.IX.1906 - 6.VI.1994; fondatore: BbbOr 36 (1994) 67-70 (G. *Oddone*); 6.VI.1994: Henoch 16 (1994) 127 (anche G. *Oddone*).

15373 Ru, G. de, † 29.VII.1994; secretaris: KerkT 45 (1994) 353 (A. A. *Spijkerboer*).
15374 Rupp, Alfred, 19.XI.1930 - 28.I.1993: MAnthropRg [➤ supra 106] 9 (1994) ix-xx + Bibliog. (M. *Dietrich*).
15375 Schaendlinger, Anton Cornelius, 28.X.1931 - 20.I.1991; Osmanist: ➤ 109, WZKM 82 (1992) 5-14 (M. *Köhbach*, C. *Römer*, Bibliog.).
15376 Schierse, Franz Josef, 1915-19.V.1992: BiKi 48 (1993) 224 (R. *Russ*).
15376* Schmaus, Michael, 17.VII.1897 - 8.XII.1993: MüTZ 45 (1994) 115-127.
15377 Schwartz, Jacques, 5.III.1914 - 17.VI.1992: Orient romain: Ktema 14 (1989!) 3s (J. *Gascou*).
15377* Shelov, Dmitrij Borisovich, 1.III.1919 - 19.XI.1993: VDI 210 (1994) 260-2; phot. **Ⓑ**.
15378 Shofman, Arkadia Semenovich, 1913 - 7.X.1933: VDI 208 (1994) 237.
15378* Smithson, Evelyn Lord, 19.VII.1923 - III.1992: Buffalo SUNY; Athens school: AJA 98 (1994) 563s, phot. (J. K. *Papadopoulos*).
15379 Solà i Carrió, Francesc de Paula, S.J. † 18.V.1993: AnSacTar 66 (1993) 4.
15379* Stamm, Johann Jakob, aet. 83, 3.XI.1993: ZAW 106 (1994) 1-3 (M. A. *Klopfenstein*).
15380 Staniloae, Dumitru [➤ 9,17455], 16.XI.1903 - 5.X.1993: ÖkRu 43 (1994) 190-2 (H. J. *Held*).
15380* Steenberghen, Fernand van, 13.II.1904 - 16.IV.1993: AnHistIgl 3 (1994) 469 (J. *García López*).
15381 Straka, Georges, 1910 - 23.XII.1993: CRAI (1994) 41 (J. *Marcadé*).
15381* Strecker, Georg, 15.III.1929 - 11.VI.1994: ETL 70 (1994) 536-8 (F. W. *Horn*).
15382 Stückelberger, Alfred E., 4.IX.1899 - 8.XI.1993: Pädagogik: Fundamentum (Basel 1994,1) 90-94 (O. *Schaude*).
15383 Stuhlmueller, Carroll, C.P., 2.IV.1923 - 21.II.1994, president CBA 1979; associate editor CBQ, JBL; editor: The Bible Today 32 (1994) 196s; 6 fig. (D. *Senior*); CBQ 56 (1994) 97-98 (unsigned).
15384 Sullivan, John P., 13.VII.1930 - 9.IV.1993: Gnomon 66 (1994) 188s (W. A. *Krenkel*).
15384* Sundén, Hjalmar, (no dates): SvTKv 70 (1994) 144 (O. *Wikström*).
15385 Szwagrzyk, Tadeusz Stanisław, 14.XI.1923 - 7.XII.1992: RuBi 46 (1993) 104-8 (T. *Matras*; bibliog.).
15386 Szyszman, Simon, 30.VI.1909 - 22.II.1993: Judaica 49 (1993) 193-9 (T. *Willi*).
15387 Théodoridès, Aristide, 30.VI.1911 - 4.II.1994: RIDA 41 (1994) IX-XII; phot. (M. *Nuyens*).
15387* Tkatchev, Mikhail Alexandrovich, 10.III.1942 - 1992: RossArkh (1994,3) 250-2; phot. (J. V. *Alekseev*, al.).
15388 Todd, John M., aet. 75, 9.VI.1994; founded Darton-LT 1959: ETL 70 (1994) 245.
15388* Trethowan, Kenneth (Illtyd), 12.V.1907 - 30.X.1993: DowR 112 (1994) 71-87 (A. *Baxter*: 'as thinker').
15389 Treu, Kurt [➤ 7,k377; 8,r283], 15.IX.1928 - 7.VI.1991: Gnomon 66 (1994) 380-3 (J. *Dummer*).
15390 Trilling, Wolfgang, 1925 - 1.VIII.1993: BiKi 48 (1993) 225 (R. *Russ*).
15391 Uhlig, Christian, 27.IX.1942 - 13.I.1994; Redakteur; TRE 23 (1994) v.
15392 Ungerleider-Mayerson, Joy, 1920 - 7.IX.1994: ASOR benefactress: BAR-W 20,6 (1994) 18; phot. (H. *Shanks*).

15392* Valentini, Ubaldo, 20.VIII.1908 - 15.IV.1994: ScuolC 122 (1994) 601-4 (A. *Rimoldi*, bibliog.).
15393 Vallet, Georges, 4.III.1922 - 29.III.1994: MÉF 106 (1994) 7-14, phot. (M. *Gras*); CRAI (1994) 301-3 (J. *Marcadé*); AnPisa 24 (1994) 455-7.
15393* Velkov, Velizar Ivanovich, 18.V.1928 - 21.IV.1993: RossArkh (1994,1) 253 (T. Y. *Blavatskaya*).
15394 Vergote, Joseph [➤ 9,17469 (8,r287 'aet. 82')] 1910 - 8.I.1992: OrLovPer 23 (1992) 5-13; phot. (J. *Quaegebeur*, 'aet. 81'; bibliog. 1931-75 complément).
15394* Vetters, Hermann, 1.VII.1915 - 24.V.1993: JbÖsA 62-B Grabungen (1993) 1-3, phot. (H. *Zabehlicky*).
15395 Vicaire, Marie-Humbert, O.P., 15.XII-1906 - 2.X.1993: RHE 99 (1994) 343s (A. *Duval*).
15396 Vitiello, Alfredo Maria, 23.VII.1931 - 5.XI.1993; socio ATI: RasT 35 (1994) 613.
15397 Weinberg, Saul [➤ 8,r291; 9,17475], 13.XI.1911 - 24.X.1992: AJA 97 (1993) 567-9, phot. (Sharon C. *Herbert*); 98 (1994) 519.
15398 Wieacker, Franz, † 17.II.1994: ZSav-R 111 (1994) 806.
15399 Wiener, Philip P., 1905 - 5.IV.1992: co-founder, editor: JHistId 54 (1993) 329 (Sidney *Axinn*).
15399* Wilder, Amos Niven [➤ 9,17469], aet. 97, 1.V.1994: ETL 70 (1994) 249 (R. F. *Collins*).
15400 Wilkinson, Walter W., † 22.IX.1993: CathHR 80 (1994) 193s (Dorothy M. *Brown*).
15401 Williams, Nigel, 15.VII.1944 - 21.IV.1992, British Museum conservator: JGlass 35 (1993) 158s, phot. (K. S. *Painter*).
15402 Williams, Ronald James, 1917-1993: JAmEg 31 (1994) 2s (R. J. *Leprohon*); OLZ 89 (1994) 530.
15403 Wolff Hans-Walter, [➤ 9,17480 'geb. 1912'] 17.XII.1911 -22.X.1993: TsTKi 65 (1994) 64s (M. *Sæbø*).
15404 Zauner, Franciscus Salesius, aet. 90, 20.II.1994: Bischof, Linz: HDienst 47 (1994) 91-96; portr. (H. *Hollerweger*).
15405 Zilliacus, Henrik, 23.I.1908 - 9.I.1992: Arctos 27 (1993) 7-9, phot. (M. *Kaimio*).

Index Alphabeticus

Auctores – *situs* – (omisso *al-*, *tell*, *abu* etc.).

5469 6027 9676*
Agrigentum 12439
Aguado de Gea G 573
Agudelo Giraldo G 8482
Aguiluz Milla 14550
Aguirre J 7917 **R** 151a
   762 7338 7745 7828
-Monasterio R 4218 4540
Agusta-Boularot S 9280
Ahanotu Austin M 8558
Aharoni Y 13265
Aḥiqar 3211
Ahituv S 10999 12528
Ahlbrecht A 10862
Ahlgrimma E 2678
Ahlstrand K 10232* 15075
Ahlström G 1571 10979
   11484 12199
Aḥmar 12503 12913
Aḥmed Ḥaṭṭu 12095
Ahmed Salaḥ ed-Din
   M 12833
Ahn G 10817
Ahrens M 6283 **T** 6221
AIA 94th/95th 455
Aichele G 4627
Aidonia 13047
Aigner-Foresti L 12432
Aillet M 827
Ain Dara 12501s
Ain Karim 4390
Aïn-Temouchent 9168
Airoldi M 539
Aizanoi 12914
Ajrud 12252
Aka C 8835
Akao J 2394
Akarnia 13048
Akenson D 13531
Åkerberg H →15238*
Åkesson J 9167
Akiyama J 597
Akkad 11128 11139 12607
Akkerman F 14414*
Akmajian A 9486
Akoun A 10479
Akpunonu D 5336
Akpunou D 5096

Alaca 12891
Alagna S 11482
Alalaḫ 487 9165* 12915
Alamein 12769
Alana O 5356
Aland B 303b 1415 5612
   K 1414-6 5057 5592
   †15239
Alarcón Sainz J 9738
   9780 11475
Alasia 13001 13001*
Albaceta L 9267*
Albada A van 13343
Albanese C 1843
Albani M 117* 9595
Albeck C 9843
Albenda P 12550 13391*
Alberigo G 7829 7918
   13892s 13893 15143
Albert B 10068 10088 **H**
   828 **M** 1079
   9239 14222* 14239 **P** 276
Alberta M 15343
Albertus M 4402 14375s
   14411*
Albertz R 2796 3638
   10688-90 10704 14949*
Albini F 10629*
Albisani S 5214
Albrecht A 995 **C** 15045
   F 8 **J** 9496
-Roth M 10050
Albricht 10916
Albus M 1268
Alcalá M 4149 9633*
   10103
Alcock S
   259 11672 12076 13089
   13214
Alcuin 14377
Alderink L 227*
Alderman G 9985 9989
   10003 10028
Alegre
   X 4056 4218 4288 4938 5
   492
Aleixandre D 2029
Alekseev J 15387*

Alemany J 1288 7123
   7137 7590 7949 8940 150
   34
Alencherry F 933
Aleppo 13871
Aleshire S 13051 13476
Alessi A 10287
Aletti J 4215
   4938s 5606 5746 5948 61
   22s
Aleu J 3803 3921
Alexander B 4773 **D** 3824
   14844 **J** 1344 4620 12838
   L 3826 3890 4870 4907 5
   077 11336 **M** 13793
   P 303c 1404 9684* 9739
   T 1593 1638 1814
   2324 4182 **W** 829
Alexandre B 14834 **D** 3343
Alexandria 844 9382 9400
   9614s 10759 11704 12163
   12771-81 13465 13761*
   13950
Alexeev A 12850
Alfano C 11515
Alfaro J 4284
-Asins C 12123 12451
Alföldi-Rosenbaum E
   †15240
Alföldy G 12840
Alfonso Carro E 10864
Algaze
   G 11127 12551 12952
Algeria 12438
Algorta del Castillo J 13989
Alhistur F 5411
Aligan R 4628
Alimirzoev A 9450
Alison J 3922 7746
Alkier S 5097
Alkire S 1099
Alkofer A 207b
Allam S 443
Allan G 15137 **P** 8042
   T 13323
Allara A 12539
Allaz J 5576
Allegri G 14192

Anaximander 13239*
Anbar M 2275 2483 2656
    3752 12529
AnchorBD 495
Ancilli E 538
Ancona G 4681 7159
Andeberhan W 3658
Anderlini G 7830*
Andersen F 8954 8966 Ø
    3805
Anderson B 763 3440
    7386 7621 C 10437
    D 10233 10327* 14912 G
    108a 208c 861 869 1410
    1594 1603 1881 2309
    2921 3379 7395 9030*
    9602 9825 10493s
    H 4802 4861 14809 J 1481
    2878 4299 4734 5980
    8619 11751 13681 L
    15130 M 11921 P 5296
    5300 8788 9534 9573
    11586 R 2028 2884 4653
    5146
Andersson E 13396
Andiñach P 1556 2187
    2875 3151 3720 12184*
Ando C 14139
Andonegui J 7886 14266
Andorlini Marcone I 13521
Andrade P 8399
Andrae C 14640* 14641*
André J 11740 11778
    †15242
Andreae B 11515* 12901 J
    14487*
Andreas SV 3201 3571
    14378
Andreatta E 14429
Andreau J 11717 13687
Andreev Y 13079
Andrés R de 524 4337
Andresen C 539 567 13895
Andrewes L 1035
Andrews C 11962 S 14965
    T 11571
Andrzejewski R 2*
ANE & India 444

Anees M 10865
Anemurium 12017
Angehrn E 11012
Angel H 152 L 10935 M
    152
Angeli Bertinelli M 11416
Angelomo 14379
Angenendt A 8262 8264 J
    14266
Angert-Quilter T 4338
Angiolani S 11369
Anglares M 10434
Angstenberger P 5975
Ankum H 15217
Annas J 10661
Annequin J 6151
Annio V 9621
AnPg 669
ANRW 496
Ansaldi J 1257 2182 7638
    7920 8296 10288 10915
Ansaldo A 8317
Anschütz K 7921
Ansede V 7177 7503
Anselmetto C 8742
Anselmus C 14363 14380-2
Ansulewicz H 14375
Antakya 12917s
Antes P 10918
Antiochia 2860s 5170
-Pisidia 12979
Antón A 4607 5873 7905
    7911 8043s 15168
Antonacci Sanpaolo E 456*
Antonaccio C 12085 M
    8366
Antonelli L 13060 M 7101
Antonetti C 10570*
Antoninus plac 13812*
Antoniotti L 4379
Antonius A 14249
Antoun R 10866
Anziani G 3490
Apameia 12507s
Aparicio A 8694
-Rodríguez A 2987s
Apczyński J 4129 K 7967
Aphraates 7427 14250-51*

Aphrodisias 12145 12919-
    23
Apollinarius 14065
Apollonia 11923*
Apollonius T 4469s 4481
Apophthegmata 14066s
    14252
Apostolos-Cappadona
    D 294a
Appianus 11307 12917
Applebaum H 1099*
Appleby R 935 985s 1024
    1061 14717 15125
Appleton G 5659
Appleyard B 1748
Apponius 3155 3169
Apringio B 5470
apRoberts R 2868
Ap-Thomas D 2963
Apuleius 10673
Aqiba 9789 12286
Aquileia 13205
Aquinas T 827 1665 3088
    4120 4422 5338 7019
    7029 7172 7043* 7180
    7191 7206 7334 7452
    7510 7550 7563s 7581
    7739 7885 8060 8299*
    8387 8532 8732 8747
    9917 9926 14383-96
    14733
Aquino Vargas M 8485
'Araba 13445 1394
Arabia 9167-9191* 9902
    10819-42 12157 12159
    12637*-12642* 13649
Arad 2740 12253 12253*
    12358*
Arafat K 11828
Aram 2438s 2692 2723s
    9114-9137
- Naharaim 2414 12525*
-Ṣobah 1383
Aran G 9783
Aranda G 22a
- Pérez G 524 4714 5406
    7154
'Araq al-Amîr 12380*

Assmann H 8400 **J** 309
340* 10289 10720 10740
12761
Assyria 9147*-9159 10996
11134-49* 9147*-9159
Astarita M 10524 13519*
Astås R 1535
Astell A 14228
Astley J 10234
Aston D 12187
Astor M 14459
Astour M 11158 12486*
13762
Åström P 11548 12177
Asurmendi J 3145 3192*
3609 14773*
Aswan 12796s
As'ad K al- 12536*
Atallah R 5765
Atchison J 9487 9497
Ateek N 13841
Athanasius A 7076 7178
7446 14072-7 14131
Athanassiadi P 10554
11441 11445
Athenae 9414 10586 11834
13051-8 13564 13573*
13603 13628 13650
13672 13697 13729
Athenagoras 13960s
Atherton C 10662 **J** 259*
8401
Atîj 12504 12510
Atiya A 540
Atkinson D 7924 10373
K 11483*
Atlan-Sayag S 9004*
Atlantis 12978 13109
Atlit 11593* 11698
Atrib 12782
Attanasio S 1404
Attfield R 341
Attias J 9668
Attica 13796
Attinger D 5215 7829 **P**
9145
Attridge D 10216 **H** 3826
5437 6138 9687

Attwood D 287c 8337
Atwan R 1191 1193
Auberger J 11718
Aubert J 13644 **R** 34a
152*499 503 14876*
15243 15350
Aubigne A d' 2947
Aubin P 14051
Aubriot D 10571*
-Sévin D 10572
Auchter T 10261
Auckaert L 15199
Audinet J 10222
Audisio G 14456
Auerbach E 12610 **J** 10002
Aufderhaide A 482
Auffarth C 3573 10556
10630* 13276
Auffret P 2932 2974 2989s
3033 3040 3050 3057
Aufrecht W 9090 10719
12386
Aufrère S 11551*
Auf Suche 236b
August R 11719
Augustijn C 8020 14532*
Augustin G 7925 10387 **M**
2771
Augustinus 206 213b 360d
366 497 840 1367 1658
1671 1679 1686 1895
1953 2020 3010 3027
3065 3482* 4425 5235
5237 5238* 5338 5340
5446 5446* 5549 5737
5756 5779 5792 6028s
7072 7160 7176 7284
7754 7877 8715 8869
9340 9386* 10180 11053
13249 13993 14047
14139-90 14193* 14197
14209 14225 14363
14533
-Lexikon 497
Augustinus C 14397
Aujac G 13245 13754
Aukerman D 5534
Auld A 333 2162 2465

2470 2583 2588 2714
Aulén 15074
Aulino F 670
Aulisa I 14126
Aumont M 8046
Aune D 5484 13890 13978
N 6127
Auneau J 573* 5439
Aupert P 13006
Aurelius M 10523s
Aurell M 412d
Aurenche O 13271
Aurenhammer M 15256*
Auro Jorro F 9420
Aus R 153 4865 4985 9771
Ausin S 2036 3668 8398
- Olmos S 9732
Ausmus H 15068
Austad T 5425
Austen J 1205
Austin G 99a **N** 11466
Auth S 13727
Auwers J 181 229e 329*
2879 3032 3380 5443
Auza B 8559*
Avagianou A 10573
Avagliano F bibliog. 613
Avanzini A 10819
'Avdat 99c 10826
Avdia N 13293
Aveling H 14030
Avella S 14825
Avendaño F 8486
Averbeck R 1603 1715
Averintsev S 8667*
Avery P 6 **V** 10459*
-Peck A 3805
Avestisyan K 11074 11440*
Avgustides A 1247
Avicenna 1670 14253
Avigdor V 10715
Avis P 1829 1838 4683*
7138 7672 7838 8047
8944 15065
Avishur Y 2926 8954*
Avi-Yonah M 13265
Avni G 12204 12233 12276
Avril A 764

Ball D 5381 **M** 5020 **R**
  12284 **W** 13290
Balla G 2842 **P** 6080
Ballard B 8438 **P** 8284
Ballatori M 15343
Ballériaux O 10626
Ballet P 12022
Ballhatchett K 8562
Balling J 5149
Balme D 13345
Balmuth M 12449
Baloglou C 13688* 13689
Baloian B 9028
Baltes M 496
Balthasar H von 5849 6152
  7033 7187 7424 7751
  7782 13999 14828 14954-
  64 15048
Balthazar J 11595
Baltrusch E 14229
Balty J 11795 11843 11867
  12007 12192 12507s
  13180 13201 13561
  13664
Baltzer K 3466
Balz H 520 6290 9797
  13809 14684
Balzaretti C 8999 14590
Balzarini M 11380
Balz-Cochois H 10720
Bammel C 5594 14012 **E**
  4103 5389 5407 11259*
Bammer A 12891*
Bammesberger A 9474*
Banana C 8622
Bandera A 7510 8027 8678
  C 10550
Bandini M 92 13960
Bangsund J 2053*
Banks M 1659 **R** 5706
Bankston C 11446 14471*
Bannach K 14672
Banning E 12419* **J** 14270
Banon D 9923
Banterle G 14221
Bañeza Román C 14269
Baqîr M 10898
Barag D 12272

Baragli E 9571 10434
  10438 14755
Barakat A 13393
Baranski G 14407
Bar-Asher M 146* 9168
  9458*
Baratin M 9451
Baratte F 11575 11923
Baraúna L 10889
Baraz D 8669
Barbaglio G 5663 7748 **S**
  2830 15180
Barbàra M 3154
Barber E 11764 **M** 13829
Barbera M 12061
Barberá C 5963
Barberi Squaroni G 29
Barbero A 565
Barbet A 12362
Barbieri E 1374
Barbiero G 2273
Barbin V 13146
Barbour H 14326 **I** 1751s **R**
  260
Barceló P 9363 11323
  11400
Barclay J 4111 5654 5856
  5870 5881 5996 6009 **R**
  5349
Bard K 13565
Bardesanes 14252*
Bardet J 23
Bardwell J 4255
Bares J 12798
Bareş L 11112 11582
  12703 12716 12755
Barford P 13203
Bargebuhr F 13180
Barhebraeus 10215 14253
Barigazzi A 157
Baring A 10574
Barkaï R 261 10845 13478
Bar Kepha M 5739
Barker A 11752* **E** 142
  G 13226 **K** 1562 **M**
  334 3604 4243 5481
  10692s
-Benfield B 2882 14312

Bar-Kochva B 2843s
Bar Koni T 10202
Barkun M 8560* 10055
Barlow B 7926 **J** 457
  12023 12028 **P** 10436
  10469
Barmann L 14725
Barna G 14900
Barnabas 2969 9595*
  13962 14008
Barnes A 8142 **G** 11502 **H**
  12981 **J** 10627 10778 **M**
  1251 7104 7152 10388
  10960 14068 **T** 158a 2677
  11442 11467 13690
  14032 14073 14105*
  14173 **W** 2677
Barnett P 4708 **W** 3985
Barnhardt W 4126
Barnhart P 5258
Barnhouse R 1511
Barnouin M 6176
Bar Nun I 4203
Barolini T 14407
Baron A 6113 **J** 1029 8048
Baroni A 13801
Barquero P 660
Barr J 10 1512 1884 2524
  5660 7639 7686 8955-7
  10992 **M** 8212 **R** 10399
  14551 **W** 342 7543
Barrachina Carbonell
  A 7555
Barrado Fernández P 752
  791 5711 2954 4409 4332
  4728 4938 5230 5745
  7293 8714 8716 8807
  9738* 10989 11500
  13219
Barragán-Ortiz A 14490
Barral-Baron N 8049
Barrandan J 11577*
Barré L 2729* **V** 9349b
Barrett CK 243 268c 5058
  5058* 5070 5085 5191
  5573 5618 **R** 3200
Barricelli J 4871
Barrie J 1728

Bayreuther E Bibliog. 614
Bazerman C 9578
Bazin A 14607
Bea A 14780
Beachem R 11721
Beagon M 10496 13479
Beal T 3751
Beale G 158e 236d 5561
Bealey L 10363*
Bean A 7831
Bear D 12205
Beards A 11012*
Beardslee W 1286 4630
  5843
Beare F 4267
Bearman G 9668
Bearzot C 11224 11248
  13236
Beasley J 715
-Murray G 4856 5296
Beaton R 88a
Beatrice P 13896
Beattie D 304b 1400 2514
Beaucamp É 3442
Beauchamp P 765 905 2015
  4184s 4518 7270 8206
Beaucour F 12669
Beaude P 4186
Beaudean J 5661
Beaudette P 8051
Beaulieu P 12550
  12557 12573
Beaumont D 10909
Beauvais C 832
Beaux N 9192*
Beavis M 4748 4955
Bebbington D 380 11013
  14636
Bec P 672
Becchi F 10663 13347
Becher A 11370
Bechtel D 2267 L 2101
  13567
Bechtler S 4243 5823
Bechtold H 14642
Beck A 7465 F 11 H 7556
  J 5152 N 10056 P 12333
  R 5969 10498 10566 W

1526
Becker A 12634 D
  1585 1589 1611 H 9870 J
  2079 2273 2748 3806
  4487 5099 5676 13951
  M 14217 P 7435 R 15039
  U 808 2673 10703 W
  7751 14743
-Spörl S 2559
Beckerath J von 2158
  11078 12670 12735
Becking B 2719 3538 3544
  3775 10982
Beckley F 14140 H 1509
Beckman G 10707·13479
Beckmann K 5433
Beckwith R 14643
Becquet G 3609
Beda V 191 5068 13498s
Bedford N 8452 P 3779
Bediako K 8561
Bedini E 1122
Bednarik R 11830*
Bednarowski M 10437
Bednarski M 9316
Bedouelle G 14748
Beecher L 14644
Beeck F van 7101 8921
Beek M 716 925 2472 2631
  N 5724
Beeke J 14510
Beeker C 13348
Beentjes P 938 2641 2766
  2775 3180 3298 3340
  3467 3554 7397 9007
  9395 10688 10719 13670
Beer C 11907 J 4736 8133
  M 97
Beers W 7751*
Beersheba 2740 12255s
  12275
Beestermüller G 7334
Beeston A 10821*
Beetham F 9307
Begg C 1 1591 2384 2390
  2392 2395 2413 2417
  2469 2475 2535 2545
  2600 2658 3093 3750

7331 9145 9163 11261
Beggiani S 14240
Begley V 457* 13690
Begrich G 4477 7398
  12420
Beguin D 673
Begzos M 10235
Behlmer H 137*
Behm-Blancke 12943
Behr C 3806
-Sigel E 8811
Behrends O 13421
Beilner S 75 W 4561s
  5457 5620
Beinert W 33c 159 939
  1265 7122 7127 8003
  8262 8679s 8767 8842
  8916 8940 8943 14866
Beinlich H 12726
Bein Ricco E 8272
Beintker H 4444 M 7698
Beisser F 400 8840
Beit-Alpha 12014
Beit-Arié M 1376
Beit-Hallahmi B 13843
Bejczy I 4352
Bejor G 11908 12944
Beker A 10040 J 3808 5621
  5717 5794 6179 8841
Békés G 11*
Bekkenkamp J 3180
Bekkum W van 4298
Belaj V 5008
Belardi W 12* 90a 11687
Belcastro D 14914
Belevi 12927
Belford W 8052
Belier W 10235* 10236
Belke K 11461 12852
Bell 10291 A 3809 11285
  13470 13568 M 13212
  13422 R 5001 10828
  11286 T 7156 14400*
Bellamy J 12549
Bellarmino R 14499-14501
Belle G van 5259 J
  van 15290
Bellebaum A 10347

Berlioz J 1042*
Berlis A 67b
Berman R 906
Bermejo J 7833 10575
- Cabrera E 12207 13816
Bermpohl F 3319
Bermúdez C 7508
Bernabé A 11693
- Ubieta C 8716
Bernabei S 4175
Bernal M 9092 9523 11168
  11845* 14955
Bernaldo de Quiros
  F 15278
Bernand A 10664 É 9251
  9373 M 10869
Bernard É 452 P 11516*
Bernardi J 4991
Bernardini M 15250 P 5490
  10056* 12448 12454
Bernardinus S 7484
Bernardo B 7789
Bernardus C 13* 3190
  14400-14401* 14407b
Bernas C 10 3432 3458
  3808 4549 5058 10989
Bernays I 10029*
Bernbeck R 12504 13269
Berndt R 3201 3246 10145
  14378 14401*
Bernhardt R 7108 10388*
  10389 10389* 13657
Bernier P 8052
Bernstein A 2378 8843 M
  2971 9135 9688
Beroea 13059
Berquist J 2129 2620 7753
  8053
Berranger O de 14749
Berrigan D 14991 14991
Berriot F 14
Berrish B 14672*
Berruto A 14005
Berry D 2991 10354 J
  13194 P 343 T 7202 1866
Berryman P 1011 8565
Bersheh 12798
Bertalot R 304d 2274

Bertelloni F 8405
Berten I 7466 8406
Berthold G 7641 R 11691
Bertholet J 7498
Berthrong J 10938
Berti S 207f
Bertinelli R †15249
Bertolino A 1590 R 9476*
Bertotti F †15250
Bertrac P 11381
Bertrand A 14103 D 3158
  9636 13960 13977*
  14400 G 1717 4372 J
  9374 11240 11242 M
  11361
-Ecanvil E 11288
Bertrandy F 12477
Bertsch L 14*
Bertuletti A 615 841 9536
Berve H 11242
Berz A 8499
Berzosa Martínez R 8491
  15053 15131
Besançon J 12547
Bescapé G †15244
Besserman L 1199 9475
Best E 195 4201 4649 4695
  4724 4774 4785 5212
  5265 5414 5667 5801
  5954 6054 6069 6091
  6185 7433 7895 T 343*
  8201*
Besutti G 616
Bethania 5402
Bethel 2083 10686 12283
  2083
Beth-Hallahmi B 10005s
Bethke H 3159
Bethlehem 12555*
Betori G 5059
Betrò M 13801*
Bet She'an 12310-4
Betsner E 8437
Bettalli M 11652
Bettetini M 14141
Bettocchi S 13958 14112
Betts A 12381 12417
Bet-Yerah 12315

Betz A 10880 H 160 3812
  3925 4250 5698 5746
  5886 5983 6005 10558
  10878 O 4226 7834 9701
  9710-2
-/Riesner 4135
Beukel A van den 1754
Beuken W 305 1290 2607
  3122 7240
Beulay R 14256
Beulin M 1503
Beutel A 833
Beutler J 4248 4428 5115
  5206 5392 5400 5404
  5450
Beutner E 3950
Bevans S 287b 8566
Bevin M 11013*
Bevington D 8319 11235
Bevir M 10939
Bey G 12024
Beydon F 8722
Beyer B 759 D 13394 G
  14789 K 9114 P 14831 R
  2648
Beyerhaus 4210
Beyerle S 2447
Beyerlin W 15 716* 3028
Beylot R 1079 9642*
Beyschlag K 7467
Beyse K 4187 9066 9077
Bezuidenhout L 3125
Bezza D 2088*
Bharati S 7071
Biaggio card. 10905
Bialas W 14660*
Bialik H 1214 9840
Biallas L 10973
Bianchetti S 13124
Bianchi E 766 1660 7835
  8144 8224 F 2972 3288
  3304 3776 L 98* R
  11093 11104 11948
  12673* 12677 12800
  12815 U 15* 344a 10156
Bianchin Citton E 129*
Bianchini W 13802

Blanck H 1346
Blanco S 8741
Blancpain J 8656*
Blancy A 7363 7929
Bland D 3247 **K** 9914 9977
Blank R 5998
Blanke H 6124 11014
Blanquart F 5439
Blasberg-Kuhnke M 10406
　15178
Blasco Martínez A 9881*
Blašek V 143 9255
Blaser K 7085 7973 **R** 7726
Blasi A 13571*
-Birbe F 3815 3926
Blau J 8965 8990 9135
　9169-9171 9178 9254
　9765
Blaufuss D 614
Blavatskaya T 15393*
Blavatsky mme 10939
Blázquez J 16* 455* 3856
　10500 12776 13963 **R**
　7907
-Martínez J 12429
Blecua J 3156s
Bleek F 14573
Bleiberg E 458*
Bleibtreu E 11811 11913
　12556
Bleicken J 11443
Blench J 14359
Blenkinsopp J 1579 1612
　2782* 3779
Bleuchot H 13887
Blevins J 4742 5534 6041
Blickle P 8465
Blidstein G 10011
Bliese J 13838
Blinkenberg C 2771
Bloch A 9172s **E** 14782s **H**
　14681
-Smith E 2664 7378 11645
　12086 12303 12386
Blocher H 7920
Block D 2498 3595 10790
-Hoell N 15299
Blockley R 11372

Blöcher F 11966
Bloedhorn H 12209
Bloedow E 11228
Bloesch D 1059 7080
Blösch D 8933
Blois L de 11289
Blok A 7274
Blomart A 10564
Blomberg C 4269 5013
　5844 **M** 11517
Blomqvist J 1721
Blondé F 13004 13145
Blondel M 14727-35 15055
Bloock C Vander 552*
Bloom J i 1611
Bloomquist L 6100
Blough N 4107
Blount B 4739 4774 4813
　4841 4857
Blowers P 14013 14018
　14128
Blue B 5192
Blümel W 9378
Bluestein J 10015
Blum E 1580 1584 1611
　2159 2330 3712 **F** 2084 **R**
　12780 **W** 1360
Blumenberg H 10480*
Blumenfeld R 14320
Blumenthal D 7002 **E** 9213
　15296 **H** 414 10637
Blumhardt 5923
Blumreich-Moore K 1890
Blumrich R 834
Boada J 1995 3772 3921
　4016 4030 4053 4114
　4170 5636 8141 8541*
　8781* 8952 9564* 9645
　10326*
Boadt L 1716 2750 3471
　3491
Boardman J 11839 13411*
　13544
Boas A 13820
Bobrinskoy B 160*
Boccaccini G 9773s 11274
Boccara E 4031
Bocciolini Palagi L 14193*

Bochen C 15061
Bochet I 859
Bochi P 12689
Bocian M 523a
Bock D 4634 4877 4917
　4921 5552 6047 7364 **E**
　10448 **S** 7003 10984
Bockmuehl K 7081 **M** 269
　1417 3927 9716 9873
Boda M 2809
Bodamer W 15297
Bode E 3860
Bodendorfer-Langer G 835
　3586 9656
Bodéüs R 9622
Bodi D 3227
Bodinger M 2035
Bodoff L 609
Bodrum 12940s
Bodson L 10496 11382
　13349 13360 13389
Böcher O 5211 5521 5524
Böck B 9155
Boecker H 1614 2126 2568
　J 5370
Boeder W 9278
Boeft J den 262* 11441
　11481 11373
Boeglin J 1073
Böhlemann P 4940
Böhlig A 17 10181
　10181* 10199 14252*
Böhm G 10034 **S** 11832* **T**
　7426 7439 14119
Böhmisch F 575 4213 7022
　9647
Böhne W †15251
Boekels J 14695* **K** 9475*
Boëlle C 9421
Boëls-Janssen N 10501
Boeotia 10622 13073-5
　13229
Boer M de 5211 5852 **R**
　2676
Börker-Klähn J 9269 12853
　12881*
Börner-Klein D 2832
Børresen K 236e 8717

Borger K 5538 **R** 12574
Borges P 8495s
Borghesi M 5560
Borghini A 10629*
Borgman E 110 619
  872815104
Borgo A 68a
  11486* 13336
Borgolte M 14274*
Borgonovo C 2904 **G** 3163
Bori P 5338 5349
Boring M 4339 5489 5549
  5914 8343 13905
Bormann L 40 5151
Born A van den 524
Bornewasser J 14614
Bornkamm E 5676
Bornstein D 14366
Borobio D 8497 15136
Borochovski E 9459*
Borochovsky E 9025
Borovskiy Y †15253
Borowitz E 7320
Borowski O 10999 11513
  11617
Borràs A 4358
Borrell A 904 1258 2793
  3811 3856 4223 4814
Borrmans M 161* 190* 393
  4127 10870 13849*
  15323
Borrowdale A 8768
Borse U 5376 5842
Borsippa 12574* 13312
Bortoloni P 12443 12457
Borza E 11229 13077
Borzin H 14575*
Borzsák S 11341
Bosch D 7836 †15254 **G**
  13572 **J** 7931
Boschi B 7383 11483
Boschini P 15020*
Boschung D 11910
Bosenius B 5955
Boshof E 14294
Boshoff P 5269 7468 **W**
  733 3669 3681 10695
Bosica T 8075

Bosio G 13898
Bosman H 237 327 3472
  3748
Bosporus 9779
Boss J 1662
Bosshard E 3398
Bossman D 1572 5805
  7386*
Bossu C 13424
Bossuyt P 5179
Bossy J 14470 14488
Bost H 3161 11014* 14325
  14459* 14468 14476
  14481 14517 14561
  14627
Bostock B 4687 **G** 4707
  8237
-Berger A 11602
Boström L 3248
Boswell J 8275 14275
Bosworth C 697
Botella Cubells V 8769
Botha J 893 5365 5831
  5834 8567 **P** 132h 1314
  2949 2998 3904 4032
  4782 4899 9395 **S** 5949
Bothmer B 11627 †15255
Botrè C 12129
Bottema S 11486 13395
Botterill S 14407b
Bottéro J 1552 10791
  12554-6
Bottini G 4267 4874 5038
  5447 6206 6300 9287
  11550
Bouchard G 8776 **L** 1180
  MA 7052*
Bouclin M 8721
Boudens R 152* 14670
Boudon V 11167 11257
Bouffartigue J 10657 11445
Bougerol J 14403
Boughton L 7046* 8275
Bouillard H 14726
Boulay F Du 14265
Boulding MC 7089
Boulhol P 12948
Boulnois M 7559

Boulogne J 11170
Bouman J 10871
Bouma-Prediger S 7244
Bounni A 12513 12536*
Bourassa F †15256
Bourden J 15038
Bourdillon M 8658
Boureau A 14276
Boureux C 2096
Bourg D 5284
Bourgeois D 8054 **H** 345c
  7534 7643 7789* 7823
  10665
Bourger I 13131
Bourgknecht J de 14301
Bourke S 12401
Bousoño C 9544
Boussac M 415
Boutinon J 7920
Bouttier M 4924 5596 6054
  9283 10583 13978
Boutwell W 8880
Bouwen F 7932 8023
  13845
Bouwman W 8055
Bouyer L 542 8197 9353
  15261
Bouzek J 11803
Bovati P 2276 2380 3690-2
  7320* 9054s
Bover J 1420
- F 572 3885s 4271 4922
  5576 5581 7837 8893
  9639
Bowden H 11208 14360 **J**
  247 746 1107 1754 7666
  8074* 8337 8672 8705
  10690 14593* 15100
  15119 **M** 11551
Bowe B 8197* 13969 **R**
  5412
Bowen A 11171 **N** 3345
Bowering M 8056
Bowersock G 3875 11230
Bowker J 8846
Bowlby P 15232
Bowley J 9852* 11263
Bowman A 294d 11984 **E**

Brichto H 723 2706
Bridges L 5364
Bridler R 13489
Briend J 461 515 2293
    3490* 7004 12248
Brier B 12089
Briese C 12090 **R** 942
Briggs C 14646
Brighenti A 8497*
Bright J 11048*
Brill R 11582
Brilliant R 13152
Brin G 163 163* 3346 9689
Brinkhaus H 230f
Brinkman B 15267 **J** 2306 **K**
    10652 **M** 7623* 7626 7937
Brinkmann B 15005
Brinks J 12763
Brintker H 14615
Briquel D 10235* 11050
    12854
-Chatonnet F 9091 12420
    14252*
Brisco T 11484
Briscoe J 11374 **P** 5805
Brissaud P 12789
Bristow J 8279
Brito E 887 7109 7470 7183
    7501 7697 9578* 14664
    14696s 15022s
Britton J 13239
Brixhe C 9284
Brjusov V 12985
Broadhead E 3888 4740s
    4861
Broadie A 2190
Brock A 9639 **P** 14494 **R**
    13044 13573* **S** 9308
    9620 14240 14242 14246
    14257 15290
Brockelman P 10295
Brocker M 7535
Brockway A 10151
Brodbeck A 11945
Brodersen K 9380 11172
    12917
Brodeur S 5948
Brodie T 4300* 4997 5262

Brody R 1369
Broer D 4259 **I** 4033 4317
    4437 6166 9711
Brogányi B 9492
Brogyanyi B 9470
Brok J 371 15199
Bromiley G 7685 8945
Bromley D 10440
Brommer F †15257
Bron F 10820
Bronner L 1126
Broodbank C 11710 11825
    11851
Brook S 3718
Brooke 1442 **C** 13755 **G**
    231 307 1438 1641 2223
    2826 3558 4091 7383
    8771 9653 9712 9734
    9766 9775 **J** 1757s 9699
    9699* 9744*
Brooks C 14601* **G** 9685
    9751 **J** 1347 9285 14808
    O 5275 **P** 355c **R** 2235
    13419*
Brooten B 1115 5709 7673
Brosend W 4501
Broshi M 9704 9766
Brosius M 11150 11153
Brossier F 5596
Broszio G 4348
Brottier L 7447 11697*
Brotzman E 1378
Broughton T 13574 †15258
Brouquier-Reddé V 12069
    12827
Brousson C 14627*
Brovarski E 12792*
Brown 5262 **B** 7786 **C** 1127
    4113 5725 14637 15067 **D**
    1422 4169 7098 7568
    14195 14207 15400
    E 9260 **F** 19 **G** 9493 **J**
    1160 2980 13335 **L** 8145
    M 576 **P** 8226 8264 11446
    14142 **R** 2382 5126 5512
    RE 272 768s 1576 4360
    4634 4645 4684 5100
    5219 7410 **S** 5692 7034

    12182 12456 12986*
    13545 **W** 1664 3203
-Lawson A 14636
Browne G 1479 9236s
    9237* 14242*
Browning D 15018 **P** 8280
Brownrigg R 775*
Brownson J 5444
Brownstone D 11655
Brox J 6188* **N** 6258 13978
    13990 14294 14337*
Bruce F 5061 8860 **I** 11213
    S 7195
Bruder J 10057*
Brück M von 7957 10431
Brueggemann W 164a 723
    785 1030 2136 2313 2634
    2927 2980 3202 3491
    3546 3793 6132 7004*
    7388 7397 7639 7727
    10688 11016 13764
Bruekelman F 7387
Brümmer V 7196 8864 9539
Brüning C 3051
Bruffey L 597
Bruggink D 14833
Bruggisser P 11450
Bruguès J 8281
Bruijn J de 10849
Bruit L 10579s
Brulin M 2589
Brulotte E 13084
Brun J 12813 **P** 156 11684
    13453 13767 13773
Brunasco P 11793
Brunet M 11623 **P** 10594
Brunfield A 10669
Brunn C 172f 13310
Brunner E 14965 **K** 294f
Bruno G 9946*
Bruns B 14250 **G** 9841 **J**
    5242 5300 **P** 7427 14133
Brunsch W 9381s
Brunswick W 13860
Brusch J 3019
Brusin G 13205
Brustolín L 7472
Bruun C 11655*

Chavalas M 11049 12494
Chavanne M 13004
Chavasse A 8200* 13150
Chavero Blanco F 324c 7153
    7487 7581 8691 14305
Chazan R 10058 14295
Chazelle C 253
Chazon E 9734*
Cheal C 10574
Checinski J 13904
Chédozeau B 1503
Chehayed J 10852
Chelbi F 12457
Chelhod J 13583 13749
Chemnitz M 14525
Cheney M 3090
Chenu 7118 14863*
Cheon S 3323
Chepkwony A 8575
Cheregatti A 2814
Cherix P 9634
Cherpion N 12671 12742
Cherry J 13137 S 5827
Chersonesus 12930
Chesnutt R 1950 4084 9773
Chester A 272 4320 4902
    6286 13634
Chesterton G 1233 14913
Chethimattam J 8612
Cheung V 3634
Cheung Tat-Man A 5898
Chevalier J 10631 14289
Chevallier M 210 503 14612
    14627 R 23* 60a 11202
    11594* 11729 11835
    11958 12039 12158 12896
    12944 13177s 13386
    13771
Chevronneaud J 8067
Chewning R 8414
Cheynet J 446 448
Cheza M 8576
Chianese J 3979
Chiarini G 14183
Chiasson G 13114
Chiavaro F 14841
Chickering H 168e
Chidester D 840 10974

Chiesa B 1370 8954 8961
    8967 9004 9006 9869
    9909 9941 9964 C 9495
ChiesaMag 239
Childe VG 462*
Childs B 71 723 890 3821
    8924s 8947 14577
Chilton B 166* 239b 4020
    4039s 4234 4395 4589s
    7755
Chin C 3133
Chinca M 356*
Ching J 8609 10925
Chiodi S 10629* 10743
Chipman J 163* 7309* 9743
Chippendale C 13133
CHIran 500
Chirichigno G 2346
Chisholm R 2497 2708 2968
    3654
Chistonogova L 11436
Chittister J 15124
CHJud 501
Chmiel J 810 4004 7304*
    9767 15182
Chmielewski P 1101
Cho Byoung-Ha 7430
- Byoung-Son 4382
Choisy E 15020
Chojnacki S 3637
Cholidis N 11643
Cholij R 8063 8129
Cholvy G 14842 14867
    15166
Chopelin N 8774
Chopineau J 774
Chopp R 8926 14800
Choricius G 13325
Chorão J 10059
Chouquer G 13426
Chouraqui A 1541
Chow Kin-Mun 5851
Chow S 4499 T 1537
Choza J 7154
Christ F 3443 G 24a K
    5220 11292 M 11021*
Christe W 14698
Christensen C 14483 D 1643

    2384 K 14950 P 7024
Christes J 6150
Christian C 7164 O 14455
Christiano K 15154
Christians C 1292
Christiansen E 7843*
Christie T 5929
Christofferson O 5296 5735
    5795
Christol A 416c 9284 M
    12104
Christoph J 11968
Christos A 9270
Christou D 13016
Chrostowski W 9321 9699
    10060s
Chrupcala A 4875 L 5006
    7597
Chrysostomus D 11207
    11417 11429 J 1678 3415
    4341 5121 7447 7451
    7792 8912 11697* 14088-
    95 14132 14191
Chryssavgis J 4607
Chudskij Y 11657
Churcher C 13353
Chuvin P 10583s 11450
Chytraeus D 14525*
Chyutin M 12212
Ciafaloni D 64 11841
Ciancio A 12008
Ciappa R 14746
Ciasca E 12444s
Ciavolino N †15263
Ciccarese M 3529
Ciccolo Fabris F 10069
Cicero M 10515 10560s
    11295 11304 13589 14217
Cieślak T 8006*
Cignelli L 9287
Cilia L 5320
Cilicia 12852 12875 12931
Çilingiroğlu A 463
Cimmerii 12862s 13457s
Cimmino F 11081 12728
Cimosa M 309* 753 947
    1672 2152 2276 2946
    3163 3225 3228 3231

10063-5 10354 13268
Cola S 14238
Colao Pellizzari M 3967
Colbow G 11658 11913
   11969 11992
Colchis 12879 12991*
Colditz J 1767 10199
Coldman E 198
Coldstream J 13585
Cole B 8316 **D** 3426 **R** 4716
   5983 11490 **S** 10793
   12597 13312 **T** 11175 **W**
   10945
-Turner R 1768 1840
Coleman J 11024 **K** 13355
   R 5061 14291
Coleridge M 775 4964
Coles R 1130 9372 9386
Colin B 14234 **F** 9374
   10584 11094 11226 13260
Colish M 14369
Coll.Essays 235
Collange J 7161
Collantes J 7647
Colledge M 11843
Colless B 9524
Collet G 7945 8499 **O** 19*
Collier G 4272 5905
Collin M 4056
Collingwood R 10260
Collins A 4635 4722 4724
   4741 4747 4758 4771
   4774 4832 5951 9631 **B**
   13644 **C** 1769 2534 3800
   E 11157* **G** 14763 **J** 913
   1666 2091 2835 3560
   3610 3874 4192 5210
   7366 7383 8064 8106
   9678 9681 9749 10354*
   11084 11454 **N** 1142 2116
   2218 11274 11361 12308
   P 15125 **R** 3822 4433
   5070 5198 5285 5301
   5598 6014 6122 7029
   8924 13633 15278* 15308
   15308* 15329 15354*
   15399* **T** 3349
Collinson P 24c

Collmer R 1215
Collo P 14546
Collombier A 11925*
   12997*
Collon D 11658 11969
   11971 11997 13355*
   13641
Colloq,œc.paulin. 314
Colom E 8372 8412 8412*
- de Llopis M 11270
Colombás G 1349
Colombo 7842 **G** 5377 **P**
   841 5818*
Colomer E 14406*
Colossae 6128 6138
Colpe C 350b 3598 3810
   11463
Colson L 13968
Columbus C 7368
Columella 13432 13797
Colvin H 8854 12093 **S**
   9466
Colwell J 5568
Colzani G 7691 8854*
Comay J 775*
Comba A 184* 14477 **P**
   1757
- Corsani M 5058*
Combès R 8289 11130
Comblin J 5678 7155
Combrink H 1290 4162
   4304s
Combronne P 14144
Comby J 13903
Comes J 3366
Comet G 456 11594*
Comfort H †15265 **P** 1421
   5221 5247
Commagene 10817
Commonweal 666
Communio 264
Compagnani L 12266
Compernolle T van 12057
Compostella C 11913*
Comrie R 9275
Comstock G 8288 **R** 10866
   S 1475
Concilium 265

Concrete Foundation 349c
Cone J 15001s
Conesa F 7098 7104 10240
   10293 10346 10420 14692
Congar Y 1075 7855 8045
   14726 14863*
Congourdeau M 13960
Conn W 358b
Connell D 25
Conniry C 5103
Connolly M 2965
Connor P 416d 12525
Connors R 8137
Conrad J 2537 2633 **L** 446
Conroy C 3644 3664 3762
Conser W 14693
Consolo Langher S 11572
Constable C 4722 **G** 14292
   15328 **T** 6180 6281 7706
Constant B 845
Constantin 9515
Constantinidis A 13688*
Constantinopolis 11626*
   12946
Constas N 7431
Contardo I 10068
Conte G 125 8188 10048
Contegiacomo L 8154
Contenson H de 12480*
   12563* 12345*
Contes Soriano A 949*
Conti G 5119 **M** 2983 3054
   15138
Contini R 9138
Contreras E 7463 13904
   14212 14213* **F** 3856 **P**
   5230
- Molina F 5491s
Contri A 10443*
Conus H 4459
Conway E 15089 **M** 7907
   8775
Conwell D 13058
Conzelmann H 4163 6063
   10066 13905
Coogan M 67a 741 1033
   2672 11484
Cook B 10386 **E** 2597 9092

Couture A 8855
Couturier G 30 3352
Cova P 10496
Covino D 4164
Cowan C 13429* **J** †15268
Coward H 10355
Cowdery A 6244
Cowe S 1478 3611 9273
   9636
Cowey J 9391
Cowley R 843
Cox C 1442 **D** 7292 **H**
   10444 **J** 1555 7648 7758
   8577 **S** 3905 3960 4867
Coxon P 1514 2041 3177
   3179 3616 3630
Coyle J 4475 8123 14146
Coyne G 1784 1859
Cozzo A 13698
Cozzoi M 8371
Crabtree H 3824 14844 **P**
   475
Cracco G 10875
Craddock F 4913 **P** 5854
   11572* 11607
Craemer-Ruegenberg I 149
   266b
Craffert P 3919 6004 13587
Cragg K 7947s 10883 13848
Craghan J 3276
Crahan M 10032
Craig K 2581 3727 **W** 1772
   7271
Craigie P 14799
Craik E 10573
Cramer P 14293
Crane J 7844*
Cranfield C 4189 4584 5782
   5790
Cranford M 6037
Cranmer T 341* 14526*
Crassl H 13466
Crautwald 14539
Craven T 2955
Crawford B 2017 **H** 11129
   11529 12529 **J** 8201* **P**
   8725* 12784 14466
   T 9033

Cray G 7493
Creach J 2928
Credner H 14573
Creegan C 10342
Creeger C 10472
Cremascoli G 3085 3568
   3724 8191 13817 13936
   14176 14231*
Cremonini 1852
Crenshaw J 167* 1294 3092
   3202 3204s 3268 3282
Crespin J 14527
Crespo J 8027
Creta 9423-9435 10609
   11970 12120 13097-13134
   13284
Cretopolis 12934
Crews C 14846 **M** 10445
Cribb R 13745
Cribbs F 4950
Crichton J 1813
Crielaard J 13080
Crijnen T 7201
Criniti N 13430
Criscuolo U 11447 11469
Crist/Latino 351*
Crist/Specif 351
Cristiani M 5338
Cristofani J 3648
Croatto J 3399 3443
Crocco S 217
Crocker P 2138 2806 11085
   13274
Crofts M 6157
Croissant F 13063
Crombie K 10067
Crone P 13588
Crook K 498 **P** 1773
Croonen J 13506
Crosby D 10268 10329
Cross A 4856 **D** 3688 **F**
   9093 10697 11519* 13010
Crossan J 315 3930 3932
   3936-9 3999 4009 4019
   4069 4071 4075 4228
   15003
Crouch D 13313 **W** 3743
Crouter R 14695

Crouwel J 11854
Crouzel H 131h 1898 2493
   4505 14014s 14022 14032
   14089 14128 14202
Crouzet D 14456
Crow P 352a
Crowe F 15046
Crowley J 2968 **P** 7577 8544
   T 9497
Crown A 9735 9756-8
Crowther N 11723
Crozier-Brelot C 9195*
   12760
Crüsemann F 1581 1584
   5819
Crumb L 14751
Crump D 4876 **M** 255d
Crutsinger G 8124 8334 **T**
   8586s
Cruz Andreotti G 13222
- Hernández M 2111
-Uribe E 12672 12698
Cryer F 2602 2621 3350
   3608 10700
Crysdale C 7058
Cuenca Molina J 769 4938
   5139
Cukrowski K 5186 6005
Culbertson D 8884
Culham P 13705
Culianu I 9946*
Cullen M 7863 **T** 11505
Culley R 908 2676 3042
Culligan K 10948
Cullmann O 168a 4358 7949
   15004
Culp J 1831 7025
Culpepper G 7474 **R** 4956
   5199 5280
Cultrera F 8372
Culy M 1542
Cuming G 14243
Cumming A 9461*
Cummings C 7201*
Cummins J 8579 **S** 3860
   4163
Cumpsty J 10297
Cunchillos J 9094-6 12481

14407ab
Dantoing A †15270
Danzger H 10016
Daoud K 12743
Daoust J 1887 3734 4368
  4667 9672 12266s
Da Paradiso D 14564
Dar S 12302* 12335 13747
Darby J 14752
Dardaine S 35*
Dare P 10379 10927
Da Re A 14390
Daris S 445 9289
Darling-Young R 7431 7437
Darr J 4878 4910 K 3400
  3440 3575
Darrical N 4056
D'Arrigo A 11360
Darrow W 10818
Darteville P 417a
Darwin C 1728 1771 1773s
  1781 1800 1812 1820
  1879
Daschner D 2956
Da Silva A 1654 2121* 3525
  12557 I 3843 15168 J de
  5518
Daskyleion 12869
Dassmann E 129 168c 512
  13908 13908* 14148
  14220
Dassow E von 9196
Daszewski A 12774 V
  11498 W 12769 13026
Datsow E von 12574*
D'Atteo F 7847
Dattrino L 7434 11560
Daube D 168d
Daubercies P 8309 14629*
Dauer A 4879 5049
Daugherty K 8880
Daughty M 1807
Daumas F 12799
Dauphin C 12198 12265
  12275 15309
Dautzenberg G 31* 4663
  4791 5673 5846 M 11105
Dauval R 12759*

Daviau P 10701 11645
  12382s
David B 9899 J 8880
  11296s 11483*
Davidman L 1132
Davidovsky M 2502
Davids A 5446* 13895 P
  258c 5932 6285 6302
Davidsen O 4750
Davidson C 168e J 11720 L
  14296 R 32a 34 3236
Davies A 9290 B 14385 C
  1353 E 2432 2694 13531
  G 465 2145 2161 2181
  2287 2434 3585 3661
  3671 5985 9007 9462
  11617 12319 12343
  12369 13661* 15108* H
  7650 7951 J 334 2208
  8580 8857 10111 11449
  13682 13777 K 13701 M
  316 2135 4231 4264 4273
  4290 4589 4774 5108
  5287 P 1209 1302 1611
  2327 2451 2750 2783s
  3351 3574 3727 9655
  9681 9712 9736s 9749
  9751 9767* 10986 11786
  12322 12326 13637 S
  3825 13354* W 501 4274
  12838
Davila J 1636 1664 1716
  9678 9944* 9945
Davis C 7155 8581 10300
  15115 D 1640 2538 E
  1711 3587 G 1237 J
  13215 11810 K 7952 M
  240 580 13804 N 32b P
  3610 7411 R 5543 S 4683*
  4687 W 11724 12672*
  12676
Davoli P 12729 13758
Dawe D 7489
Dawes G 8066 H 9568 S
  717 5916
Dawn M 5827
Dawson D 844 8963 9614
  10587 14149

Dawwara 12247
Day A 528 1555 J 740 1716
  1924 2704 2887 3093
  3678 5547* 9442 10702
  10702* L 12400 M 5125 P
  544 1133 1158 1897
  13116 T 14850
Dayton D 953 J 11581
D'Costa G 343 10379
  10395-7 15103
Deal M 8944 14868 8944 W
  10949
Dean J 14297 O 5991 8356
  W 10271
-Jones L 13487a
-Otting M 3805 4190
Deane A 14297 H †15271
Deanesley M 14329
Dear P 1834
Deardorff J 3891
Dearman J 2572 11009
  11507 S 10703
Debarge L 14943
Debenedetti S 9914*
De Benedetti P 375b 10069
  1963
Debergh J 230a 10562
  11293 11835 13161
De Bernardi A 11615
De Bonfils G 6146
Debono J 4953
Debord P 466 11679
Debru A 11386
Debuyst F 7840
Decapolis 4825 10735
  12365 4825
De Carlo G 3316
De Caro S 13195
De Chazal N 4349
De Chirico L 125
Deck A 8582
Decker W 11725 11728
  11825 12729*
Deckers-Dijs M 3182
Declerck J 3281
De Clerck 10135
Decloux S 8231
De Concini B 4592

14631
Denny F 10356 **W** 11612*
Denon V 13825
De Nonno M 676
Denova R 4880
Denti M 11916 13153
Dentzer J 12537 12546
-Feydy J 12538 12546
Denyer N 10633
Denzinger H 970
Denzler G 539
De Palma L 13
De Piccoli S 7248
   7616 8073* 8074
Depré G 7150
Deproost P 213b
Deptula C 1201
De Puma R 457*
Depuydt L 9197
Derchain P 10745 10779
-Urtel MT 10746
Derda T 13788
Dereck D 128
Deremetz A 8159
Dericquebourg R 5925
Derksen J 3203 3222
Der Manuelian P 11086
   12704
D'Erme G 15249*
Dermesteter 14649
Dermience A 8717
Deroche V 13062
De Rosa G 1252
De Rossi G 1366 11549
Derrett J 3941 4401 5385
   5388 5429   5766 13959
D'Errico F 11588
Derrida J 330b 4780
Derville A 503
Derycke H 1901
De Salvo L 13699
Desan P 2947
De Sandoli S 13831*
De Sandre I 15183
Desanges J 13242 13754
DeSantis P 13183
Descamps S 11676 11911
Descat R 466 12855

Deschamps L 413b 433c
   10517 14418*
Deschuyteneer P 3943
Desclos M 13487c
Descœudres J 13042
Des Courtils J 460
Descy S 7849
Deshen S 9993
Deshman R 1361
De Silva D 1035 5022 5170
   5478 5496 6119 6217
De Simone G 13606
Desjardins M 10175 10177
Deskis S 1515
De Smet R 3095
Desnier J 13154
Desouche M 11026
De Souza W 1063
Despland M 845 10224
Desreumaux A 9138* 9634
   9642* **S** 8223
Desroche H 10244 †15273
Dessel J 12203
Destro A 3847 3892* 4175
   5171 7155*
DeTommaso G 11809
Dettenhofer M 11299 11363
   13057 13092 13566
Dettex P 375c
Detting W 3445
Detweiler R 32c 8858
-Doty 838
Detwiler A 5420
Deun P van 70 1493 4306
Deurloo K 1969 1980* 2026
   2133 2412 2746 3469
Deutsch C 4307 **E** 280 **R**
   9008
Devauchelle D 12744 12805
Develin R 13750
Devenish P 7639 9540
Dever W 295 2751 11492
   11492* 11567* 11645
   11813 12069* 12182
Devereux D 13849
De Veris G 9571
Devijver H 11662
Devillers L 5307 5320 5330

O 11340 11360 11435
Devine P 8450
De Virgilio G 4529 5788
   7087
Devis F 430a 14328
Devoti L 10567
De Vries B 12168* 12418 **D**
   7887
Dewachter M 467 11554*
Dewey 10233 **A** 5821 5837
   5841 **J** 5821 8824* 10327*
De Witt C 1712 7197 7205
Dexinger F 9667 11476
   13935*
Dey L 6013
Dhanaraj D 2929
Dharih 12370
Dharmakirti 10271
Dhavamony M 7850 10396
   10951
DHGE 502
Dhonaraj D 2982
Diahukian G 9274
Dianich S 14448
Dianich S 7907
Díaz → Alonso J 3802
- García G 5733
- Merchán G 33a
- Regañón J 12466
- Rodelas J 5803
- Sánchez-Cid J 5734
- y Díaz M 33b
Dibble H 11588*
Di Berardino A 506 5653
   13909
Dibie P 8067
Dibon 12371s
Di Castro D 11865 13155
Dicenso J 9567
Di Censo J 10301
Dichy J 9174
Dick J 15084 15140 15225
Dickens A 169 **W** 14961*
Dickers A 11970
Dickinson C 14805 **O** 12181
   13128
Dickson D 1225 **G** 7535 **K**
   14857

Doglio C 5473
Dogniez C 2385
Dohan G 1633
Dohm C 10056*
Dohmen C 108d 1064 4191
  1082 1091s 1902 2250
  10752 11831 **T** 1297
  U 2399
Doignon J 3059 5217 6139
  12213 13925* 14176
  14204
D'Oignon G 14139
Dolan J 78 14315*
Dolbeau F 1494 3482* 9643
  14150
Dolbreau F 2695
Dolby Múgica MC 7160
Dolce R 12552
Dolci C 8693
Dolezal M 1481
Dolgopolsky A 9003
Dollfuss G 705
Dombes g 7929
Dombrowski D 7026
Domergue C 11729
Domeris W 3500 5375
  13591
Domingos Casonatto O 9721
Domínguez M 33b
- Monedero A 9363 11303
  12429 9363 13759
Dominik W 10590
Donadoni Roveri A 11568*
Donaghy T 14366
Donahue J 4501 4738 **W**
  1815 1860
Donaldson M 1208 **T** 5818
  6024 13492
Donatus 14155
Donbaz V 12885
Donceel-Voûte P 12009
  12017
Donderer M 12010
Donders J 8641
Donfried K 6158
Dongola 12830
Doniger W 1179
Donne J 1224s

Donneaud H 941 15012
Donnelly JP 3020
Donner H 170 3481 9018
  13243
Donnet D 11419 11763*
Donovan D 4611 7899 8065
  8068 8113 14721 14960
Doña Blanca t 9094
Dool J 7084 11071
Dooley D 14895
Doore G 8861
Doorly W 2459 3401
Dor 11711 12290 12290*
Doran C 8203 **R** 3827 4917
  7084 10172 11027 11037*
  15051
Dorandi T 10633*
Dorcey P 10507
Doré J 4022 7109s 15226
Dorff E 7005
Doriani D 4252
Dorival G 1495 2350 2909
Dorman P 12711 13431 **T**
  15083
Dormeyer D 847* 3864
  3942 4632 4750
Dorner J 12783*
Doron P 1382
Dorph G 813
Dorrell P 12415 13314
Dorsey D 1565
Dorsselaer K van 14143
Dos Santos E 1559 **J** 4461
Dothan 12291
Dothan M 12181 **T** 12181
Doty W 1102 10258
Doucet M 2547
Douch → *Dûs* 12800 13393
Doud R 15061
Dougherty C 417c 13759*
Doughty D 4763 5599
Douglas J 546 **K** 4133 **M**
  2351 2357 8051
Douglass J 4810 **R** 268 355a
Doukhan J 2056 8964
Doumet C 11971
Douramani K 13896
Dournoy S 10987

Dourthe P 11616
Doutreleau L 14100
Dovere E 11478
Dowan D 2139
Dowd M 7204 **S** 8156
Dowden K 10508 10589
  10669
Dowe D 10102
Dowell S 8768 8832
Dowling L 14653
Downey M 547 7562 8157 **S**
  413c
Downing F 3868 3925 4235
  5108 7295 **J** 3826
Dowse E 7130
Doyle A 33d **D** 7898
Dozeman T 1579 7023*
DPA EncEC 506
Drączkowski F 14224
Dräger M 12857
Dragišić J 14628
Dragona-Monachou
  M 7271*
Drake A 866 **H** 12213
Drane J 778 3819 4528 7205
  7624
Draper J 7598 7639
Drasen-Segbers V 1288
Drążek D 14224
Drechsel W 1253
Drechsler E 282* 10451
  10453
Drees W 1776
Dreher L 8483 **M** 11300
Drehsen D 14858 **V** 14693*
Dreifuss G 2023
Dreitcer A 8158
Dreja A 773
Drennan M 7391
Drerup H 15245
Drescher H 15118s
Dresen G 8728 8772
Dresner S 2087* 2088 7322*
Dreuille M de 10951
Drew-Bear M 12794 **T** 9378
  9388
Drewermann E 1249 1254-
  70 2815 4275 4371s 4718

12660
Durkheim É 13631 13656
13676
Durliat J 13433* 13702 R
13487d 13501
Durrwell F 4688 7048s 4688
8862s 8863*
Duru R 12945
Dus J 10988
Dûš 12800
Dussaut L 6220
Dutch-Flemish Wk 333
Dutcher-Walls P 2735
Dutheil J 10111
Duthoy R 13430 13602
Du Toit A 6051
Duval A 625 15395 N 11493
11867 12070 Y 626 2547
4923 14207
Duvall J 6048
Dworakowska A 11624
Dwyer J 547* T 318 4511
4761
Dyakonov I 13457
Dych W 8218
Dyck A 553
Dyer C 21 3527
Dyk P van 1321
Dykema P 356*
Dykstra C 7653 10234 D
12673
Dylan B 4124
Dyrness W 8586 14862
Dyson S 11494 11552*
11561 13592
Dzhaparidze O 11567
Dzharakyan R 12610
Dziobek E 12713s
Dziuba A 7088 8644

Eagan J 15141*
Eames S 12995
Earnshaw D 5785
Easley K 9292
East W 1219 12345
Eastman R 10357
Easton D 11564 11566
Eastwood W †15276

Eaton J 2895 2897* 2920
2955 2974 3007 3014
3142 3205 3268 7292 M
2596 R 10814
-Krauss M 11836 12706s
Ebach J 1904 7005*
Ebane Ango S 3007
Ebeling G 848s 7156 J 33e
Ebenbauer A 357
Eber J 7953
Ebers G 11554
Ebert J 12922 K 896 9562
Ebla 9157 12486-93 13300
13344
Ebner M 4263
Eccles J 1777
ÉcFrançaise Rome 11514
Echánove A 3937
Echeverri A 8482
Echigoya A 3446
Echlin E 7207
Eck 10085 D 10927 J
14530 W 11665
Eckardt A 10042 R 3944
7479
Eckart O 2277 2340
Eckermann W 33f
Eckert G 14035 J 3945
14358*
Eckhardt M 5220
Eckhart M 14413
Eckholt M 8518 14855
Eckstein H 6031
Economou E 14052*
Ecum.Resources 626*
Edbury P 13832 13839*
Edde A 12242
Eddy G 1997 8641 M 2358
Edel E 12882
Edelman D 2570 2606
2746* 11028 11492
Edelstein A 13563 G 12214
Edens C 13429*
Eder B 13593 C 11972 M
813* P 13c W 11303
Edersheim A 2665 3946
Edfou 12805 → *Idfu*
Edgar W 8364

Edgerton R 13594 W 850
Edgeworth R 9451*
Edlund-Berry I 11916*
13308
Edmond D 5215
Edmondson J 11343
Edmunds L 296 11176
Edom 2079 3093 12356*
12358* 12414 12414*
Edwards C 11299 11309
11389 13615 D 179 1778
7050 7208 7675 11265
12317 12329 12834 12921
14466 15105 F 7273 I
12760 12761* J 4754 5735
9890 10858 14603 14603*
M 5384 9623 10178 10510
10634 11373 13898 14017
14430 14629 R 1055 4303
5199 5416 8132 8724s
8752 S 262
Edzard D 309 514 1983
10791 11975 11998 12494
L 9477
Eenigenburg E 8298
Efe T 12925
Effe B 7354
Effenberger A 11519
Effenterre H van 13075
13080 13105
Efferin H 4497
Efron J 2845
Egan K 14308
Egawa K 4572
Egelkrout H 10442
Egeria 12207 13812* 13814-
8
Egetmeyer M 9424
Eggebrecht A 12670
Eggemann I 8680
Eggen W 8588
Egger M 10074
Egmond A van 7594 D
van 8864
Ego B 2091 2230
Egypt 5522 → *Aegyptus*
Ehlinger C 15015
Ehlke R 3237

Endruweit A 12730
Engammare M 1909 3161
    14517
Engberg-Pedersen T 241a
    5665 5856
Engebrecht J 4462
'En Gedi 12256*
Engel D 10107* H 1090 M
    15142 U 14863*
Engelbach E 12668
Engelbert P 34b
Engelbrecht J 4360
Engelken K 9082
Engels O 34b 14337*
Engelsma D 7274
Engelstein L 10082
Engemann W 1036 9501
Engen J Van 15322
England A 7379 J 8589
Englander D 9987*
Englert R 821
English D 357* 4719
Englund G 12760 R 12579s
    12601 R 13357
Ennabli L 12458*
Ennaïfer M 12008
Enns P 2224 3321 6242
Ennulat A 4253s
Eno R 5557
Enomate J 2803
Enrico A 565
Enríquez L 586
Ensor P 5246 5316 14790
Entrich M 4402 14375
Enuwosa J 4636 5039
Ephesus 5342 6192 11785*
    12891*-12900 13806*
Ephraem S 1525 3718
Ephraim f 4044
Ephraim 14254*
Ephratt M 13294
Epictetus 3854 5699 6025
Epicurus 5890 7015 10547
    10657
Epiphanius 4533 14101-3
Epp E 627 1426 R 14837
-Tiessen D 3534
Epperson S 9988

Epstein J 9843 M 1443
    13358
Eran A 11819
Erani 12257
Erasmus D 360d 372 863
    1353 5237 5338 5741
    10384 14194 14503
    14532-40 14614
Erath G 13760
Erb P 14682
Erciyas mons 12871
Erck C 10829
Erdel T 546
Erdemgil S 12892
Erhart H 268*
Ericksen J 1516
Erickson D 1205 M 7419
    7480 10430 V 8729
Ericsson B 6125
Eriksson A 5851 6114 K
    12028 L 851 2921 3007
Eristov H 11843
Eriugena J 213b 368* 14129
Erlemann K 6159
Erler M 496 10670
Erman A 66
Ermatinger J 12134
Ernst A 3207 9059 9061 H
    9057 J 224a 669 4008
    4191 4385 4924 5200
    8929 9701 14774* M 4134
    5498 W 358a
Erskine A 11123 11303
    11390 11414 12917
Erwin J 5555
Escaffre B 6043
Escallier C 3947
Eschweiler P 10749
Escobar Donoso S 7735
Escrivá de Balaguer J 5406
    8090*
Esda C 5336
Eshel E 581 9124 9704*
    9705 9737* H 9737*
    12305
Eskenazi T 317 2618 2785
    7625
Esler P 4405 4870 4878

11274 13595
Eslinger L 2620
Esna 12793
Esolen A 10512
Esparza C 1575
Espeja J 7209
Espinel J 4518 4705 4938
    5230
- Marcos J 7338
Esposito J 10880
Esquiza J 7654
Ess J van 10830 10903
    12641 M van 12635
Esse D 10721 12315 13373
Essen G 4688 4695
Estal G del 8305 15142*
Esteban R 8022
Ester P 2810
Estivill D 2092 11868
Estrada B 897 1199 3907
    4930 J 3991 5711
-Barbier B 4529
Estraikh G 10040
Estruch Tobella J 9970
Esua C 15227
ÉtClas60 34c
Ethiopia → Aeth-
Étienne A 10166 14301 J
    72 287e 417d 7161 10272
    15290 R 412c 417d 13437
Etruria 12854
Ettlinger B 9778 10063 G
    7428
Eubanks L 4844
Euclides 13282
Euler W 14324
Euphrates 2414 12524-6
    12565 12864 13281
Euripides 10571
Eusebius C 3411 7446
    9142* 10183 10212
    14104-6* E 14211
Eutyches 14132*
Euxinus 12993 13411*
    13544
Euzennat M 12459
Evagrius P 3279 8178*
    14107-9

Feagin G 4744
Fear A 11324
Feber H 690
Fecht O 10774
Fechter F 3590
Federici T 781 1964 5012
    8160
Fédou M 3160 3212 7150
    7855 13910* 14018 14225
Fedwick P 14079
Fee G 852 1426 3828 5060
    5845 5981 6041 6087
    6170 7529
Feeney D 10590
Feenstra R 7708
Fehlandt C 5459
Fehling D 11219
Feiertag J 13911
Feig N 11974
Feige G 1914
Feil D 12899
Feinan 12373
Feinberg P 7271 10362
Feingold H 9979 10019*
Feinman G 11510
Feissel D 9400*
Feist U 3796
Feisthauer J 4371
Fekkes J 5499
Felber A 2481 8730 13911*
Feld H 5952 5986
Felder C 8592 14800s
Feldman D 9989 E 10079 L
    2693 2696 2715 2720
    2725 2846 2854 3728
    9843 11263 11266 11331
    11454 S 9843* 11519*
Feldmeier R 241c 270 2728
    6270
Felici S 319* 8073* 8074
    8681 10545 13912 14336
Feliciano J 8531
Felip-Jaud E de 1485
Feliu L 9147*
Felix C 7881
Felle A 9403 13184
Fellner H 11792
Felmy K 7955*

Felosova V 13790
Felten F 12840
Fendri M 10904
Fendrich H 11894 W 5577
    13935*
Fenn R 11267
Fenster T 14331
Fenton J 4273
Ferguson D 363 559 7035
    7275 10446 14683 K 1785
    P 1984 T 15064
Fergusson D 188 10401
    14790 14796 14953
Ferjaoui A 12460
Fernandez J 6066
Fernández C 14372 D 957 E
    8593 10200 S 14154
    V 4642 5224
-Galiano D 9671* 12776
- García D 15200
- Jurado J 12453
- Lago J 1508 14019
- Manzano J 15278
- Marcos N 1386 1444 1506s
    2386 2636 3078 7296
    9338 9781 12071
-Miranda M †15278
- Ramos F 4347 5371 5500
-Rañada A 1786
- Rodríguez P 4110
- Sangrador J 1445 9615
    12777
- Tejero E 1376 1384 1395
    1506 3156 3162 3164
    3377
-/Busto 2546
Fernhout R 10358* 10379
Ferone C 691
Ferrando M 5317 M 7565
Ferrante J 1222
Ferrara Bible 320
Ferrara D 8060 8777 G
    11539
Ferrari A 568 12985 L
    14152s M 5673 5880 S
    13805 13849*
Ferrario F 14454
Ferraro G 5105 5236 5271

    5278 5300 5302 5318
    5329 7112 7561 12895
    13901 14758
Ferrary J 11075
Ferre L 9005
Ferré A 13848 F 7253
Ferreira DS. J 4461
Ferreiro A 2923
Ferrer J 3662
- Iñarata A 8865
Ferrero V 8474
Ferri L 14351
Ferris P 3553
Ferron J 12461
Ferrua A 796 9299 11249
    11391 13205
Fersterer A 2255
Ferwerda T 8074*
Fessard G 9583 14664
Festugière A 4720
Festus R 11302
Feuillet J 9464
Fewell D 911
    1136 1300 2521
Fic L 10464
Fichter J 8581 15278*
Fichtner R 4386
Fiddes P 1174 7732
Fideler D 3829 7435
Fidler R 2660
Fiedler L 11494* P 4033
    4428 11540
Fiema Z 12778
Fiensy D 3830 13598*
Fiey J 34e 14243*
Figueroa P 629
- Deck A 8582
Filigheddu P 418 1961
Filippi A 958 N 4690
- Cappi C 13487b
Fillmore C 9520
Filoramo G 172b 270* 549
    10160 10302* 10591
    11391
Filser H 14543
Finan T 14053
Finance J de 8300
Fincke J 9148

Follet S 11344
Folliet G 14152*
Folry A 484
Fondevila J 8864*
Fong Ko Ha M 4045*
Fontaine J 359b 1046 14048
    14195* 14220 14303
    14328 14736 **P** 10184
Fontana E 14052 **M** 11870
Fontbona i Missè J 7796*
Fonteyn L 8304
Foppa C 1788
Foraboschi D 12167 13707
Foran J 13851
Forbes A 8954 8966 **C**
    11739
Forcano B 8305
Force J 14579*
Forconi M 7157
Ford A 1789 13672* 14460
    C 114 **D** 7022 7117 7485
    14866 **J** 7989* 14781 **L**
    9557 **N** 8305 **S** 3883
Forde G 3482 5756 5757
    14971
Fordyce R 9462*
Forell G 172d
Forestell J 8075
Forey A 172e 13289 13824
Forlizzi G 3805*
Forment E 14665
Formigli E 11791
Formozov A 11567
Fornara C 11477 13217
Fornaro P 11214*
Fornberg T 173 4163 14775
Fornet-Betancourt R 8518
Forni G 172f 11655* 11667
    14728 14728*
Fornis C 11220
Forrest R 334 1992
Forrester D 182* 8477
    10345 13539
Forsbey G 5666
Forsén B 13437 **J** 13037
    13127
Forshey G 1194
Forsthoefel P 1790

Forstner M 10855*
Forsyth N 1905
Forte B 866 7472 7522 7797
    7856 8682 11029 14686
Fortezza/donna 305*
Fortin M 490 9532 11814
    11987 12480* 12504
    12510 12543 12636
Fortin-Melkevik A 10423
    15115
Fortna R 5392
Fortuna M 4256
Foschepoth J 10080
Fosdick H 15010
Foss C 12858*
Fossey J 13074
Fossier R 53*
Fossion A 961
Fossum C 4464 **J**
    10213 10692
Foster B 9165 11130 11637*
    12568 12607 13704 **D**
    14157 14179 **H** 13474 **J**
    1624 7051* **K** 13147
Fotiadis M 12020
Foti Talamanca G 9413
Foucault M 3851 4780
    13629
Fouchard A 467
Foucher L 13202 13486
Fouilloux É 14867
Fouilloy H 13354
Foulkes P 3331 **R** 4717
Fountain J 14951
Fourie L 7394
Fournier K 7655 **M** 5172
Fouts D 11131
Fouture B 12462
Fowden G 11455s
Fowl S 5703 6007 6114
    8307 14687
Fowler A 12688 **D** 10520 **J**
    7653 10234 **R** 4758 4768
    T 1672
Fox E 1540 **G** 5349 **H** 962
    9838 **K** 5540 **M** 2835 3261
    7389 7626 8436 9915
    11393 **R** 10333 11409

14187 **S** 9116
Foxbrunner R 9990
Foxe J 5563
Foxgrover D 3566
Foxvog A 9145
Fraade S 2387
Fraas H 1279
Fracassini U 14737
Fraenkel Y 9845
Fragnelli P 2908
Fragomeni R 359c
Frahier L 4581
Fraisse P 13131
Fraling B 57 1105 8608*
Frame G 11132 12562 **J**
    7136 7279
Frampton M 1827
França Miranda M de 10412
    15210
France J 13833 **R** 271 4741
    8076
Francesconi G 561
Franchot J 14657
Franchthi 13402
Francis L 10234 14873
Franck I 11655
Franco I 10750 **P** 13924 **R**
    33c
- Martínez C 6241
Francovich G de 12859
Frandsen P 9199
Frank D 9769 9929 **H** 9996
    10515 **K** 15084 **R** 1670
Franke C 330c 3463 **T**
    11667* **W** 1223
-Vogt U 11975
Frankel D 2312 2375 13020
    J 241d 9991s
Frankemölle H 2164 4277
    6278 6287 7957
Franken H 12216 12341
    12369
Frankenberry N 9557
Frankfort H 10708*
Frankfurter D 1908 9610
    9610*
Frankl K 14867*
Franklin C 12215 **E** 4870

Fuente A 13930
Füredi F 11029
Fürst A 129 3742 14197 **W**
    †15281
Füssel K 15287
Fuhrmann M 1346 11304
    11457 P 14512
Fujita N 8594
Fulford M 12835
Fulk R 1515
Fulkerson M 8779
Fuller D 953 6228 **G** 5056 **R**
    173* 362 1396 1523 2268
    6058 7480* 10277
Fullerton M 11926 13166
Fulop T 15058*
Fulton R 3187 3201
Fumagalli V 14461
Funari P 13197
Fung R 3488 6172
Fung Sin-Sing 5977
Funk R 3950 4017 4019
    4069 4226-8 10110 **W**
    3881
Funkenstein A 9889 10039
Furcha E 14523
Furger F 8460
Furlong J 125*
Furnari A 12980
Furnish V 4111 5578 5600
    8360
Furnoux A 13080
Furugori T 915
Fusco F 345b 11444 **V** 4263
    4309 4729s 4774 4892
    4922 5035 7616 7619
    10146 15185
Fusi-Rossetti A 12135
Fuss A 2278
Fusṭaṭ 13263
Futterlieb H 782 4759
Fyall R 333

Gabaon 2487 2608 12248
    → *Gibeon*
Gabba E 11293 11309
Gabel H 1064
Gabler D 12030

Gabolde L 12721 **M** 12731
Gaboriau F 7118 **M** 10943
Gabra G 2881
Gabriel A 10706 **K** 15145 **R**
    13488
Gabrieli E 12394
Gabrielsen V 11233
Gabus J 7425 7670 7692*
    8936
Gabutti Roncalli A 13220
    13401
Gadamer H 845 854 1074
    1332 9567 11047 14239
    15024
Gądecki S 2858 11497
Gadel A 12863
Gadeyne J 13779
Gadille J 152* 399
Gäbler U 14514
Gäde G 4193* 4213
Gärtner H 11412
Gaeta G 5338
Gaffin R 5648 7119
Gaffney E 14928 **J** 14764*
    K 909 **P** 10880
Gaffuri A 1367
Gafo J 8313
Gage W 5152
Gagey H 7481 14791
Gagnebin L 7481*
Gagnon R 4453 4919 4995
    5717
Gagos T 11090*
Gagsteiger G 11668 11699*
Gahbauer F 7158 14434
Gaibov V 12128
Gaide F 9452
Gaillard A 1254 10172
    10309 10987
Gain B 14106*
Gaio L 1299 8687
Gaiser F 3482
Gaitzsch W 12902
Gal Z 12185 12446
Galán J 11091 11920 13359
Galantino N 7131 7159
Galas M 9994
Galatia 12866 12877

Galaty J 13746
Galbiati E 529 13289
Galbreath P 15127
Galchinsky M 10021*
Gale M 10516 13708
Galen K 14339
Galenus 13487d 13493
    13499 13501 13506
    13516 13521
Galeota G 14499
Galil G 2476 12217
Galilaea 12021 12185
    13775 13795 13840*
Galileo G 1585 1756 1761
    1770 1783s 1816 1820
    1852s 1860 1867
Galili E 11593*
Galimberti S 10881
Galindo A 360a
-Rodrigo J 7160 7798
Galinsky K 9463 11309
Galitis G 7960
Galizzi M 4045* 4388
Galka J 14542
Gallagher E 177 4919
    10447 13914* **P** 14881 **W**
    3433
Gallant T 13564
Gallares J 1138
Gallart M 524
Gallavotti C 37
Gallego E 4046 7961
Galli B 14812 **C** 8505 **G**
    321 15201
Gallicet E 3065
Gallico A 3605 4527 10618
    14146
Gallinaro R 854
Gallo I 417b 11730
Gallopin M 7258 8005*
Gallorini C 10751
Galloway K 4419
Galonnier A 14382
Galot J 406 499 1293 4595
    5272 6122 6241 7052
    7052* 7188 7511 7544
    7566 8002 8068 8079
    8162 8234 15116

Gitay Y 1650
Gittins A 7859
Giudice F 13023 13027
Giudici M 3208
Giumlia-Mair A 5854
   11572* 12441*
Giustiniani P 15087
Given M 13008
Giveon 11977*
Giversen S 65 10185
Giza 12758-62
Gizewski C 11387
Gizzi E 301d
Glade W 15369
Gladwin J 14843
Glässer A 34a
Glanc A 3724
Glassen E 207c
Glassner G 3055 J 11135
   12649
Glasswell M 4863
Gledhill T 3188
Gleixner H 8294
Glesmer U 1994
Glessmer U 2482 9716
Glinert L 9022s 9467
   12236*
Glück H 569
Glueck N 12367
Glücker J 11506
Gnädinger L 169*
Gnan M 3341
Gneuss H 44
Gnilka C 13913* J 3407
   3954s 4784 6063 7482*
   8929s
Gniosdorsch I 14662*
Gnoli G 10820*
Gnomon Bibliog 674
Gnuse R 935 1611 1614
   2224 2963 7390
Godart L 9426-8 12976
   13134
Godlewski W 9241
Godlove T 10316
Godron G 12033
Godwin J 10520
Goedicke H 10777

Goehring J 8235 10189
Goelet O 9196
Göll H 14668
Göreme 12936
Görg M 511 1975 2127
   2173 2490 3198 3244
   3445 4194 8884* 10752
   11977* 14602
Görgemanns H 14022
Goergen D 4113 8079
Görler W 13319
Görtz H 3895
Gössmann E 551 1921 8737
   8781*
Goethals G 14873*
Goethe 2315
Goetschel R 9978
Goff P 14599
Goffi T 14580
Gogarten F 15013
Gohary J 12700
Goichot E 14576 14746
Goizueta R 8596
Golan 11984 12348 13423
Golan A 11589 13854
Golb N 9684*
Golczewski F 9975
Gold A 7301* D 1746
Goldberg A 9838* H 10023
   10027 13844 S 537
Golden M 13602 13619
Goldenberg G 94 N 1139
   R 2235 9824
Goldhill S 222 11829
   11917
Golding A 3076
Goldingay J 32a 333 727
   1303 2450 3271 3457
   3501 3610 3644 7388
   7391 13539 14798
Goldish M 9972*
Goldman B 11767s E
   13865 H 13604 N 11768
   12062 S 14580* Y 3493
Goldsmith E 14918 M 2404
   3956
Goldstein B 4880 D 9962 H
   8400 14991*

Goldsworthy G 3209 5503
Goldwasser J 3721 U 9201
Goldy R 7392
Goldziher I 10882
Gołębiewski M 910 3479
Golfieri A 14638
Golka F 2119 3210 3236
Goller H 7186
Gollwitzer H †15287
Golomb D 2828
Golovina V 10753
Golub I 1701 14628
Golubtsova E 11033
Golvin J 11731 11749
Gomes A 7712 M 10450*
Gómez L 14913
- Acebo I 7053
- Aranda M 3280 9919
   9930
- Bellard C 12441
- Caffarena J 830
- Fregoso J 8597
- Hinojosa J 15150*
- Pallarès J 14407*
Gonçalves F 3502
Gondal M 345c
Gonella A 4900
Gong Yushu 9149
Gonneaud D 1271
Gonnet D 7964
Gonzalez J 8428 14659
González CI 7463 8427 E
   5226 J 8598 14874 N
   8599 S 7438 14210 Z
   1864
-Carvajal L 15147
-Conde M 11668*
-Conde Fuente M 11685
- de Cardedal O 7162 8236
-Dorado A 8687
- Echegaray J 728 2856
   11500 12169 13219
- Faus J 2867 4429 5422
   7483 7656 8080 8508s
   8543*
- Lamadrid A 10989
- Maeso D 90c
- Montes A 7965 15081

P 10998 T 10264 W 1526
14581
Graindorge-Héreil C 10755
Grainger J 11248 13762
Gramaglia P 14032 14048
Gramcord 597
Gramlich R 10956
Grams R 5647
Granado C 1919 12777
13944 13977*
Granados Temes J 15028
Grand A 15198
Grand'Henry J 103 15371
Grandazzi A 10522 11424
13159
Grandet P 13490
Grandjean Y 13145
Grane L 360e
Granfield P 361 8101
Grant J 1601 14800 M
4545 11180 11401 11459
R 13914* 13954 14073
Grapp G 11520
Grappe C 3911 4394 5140
5686 5786 6033 6213
6270 6301 9283 9716
Gras M 12430 15393
Grassi H 13605 J 1140
4534 5201
Grassinger D 11923
Grassl H 11059
Grasso G 367* 13761 S
4310
Gratien B 12834
Gratseas G 9693*
Grattepanche J 1970
Gratuze B 11577*
Graumann T 4943
Grau Monrós V 630
Graves P 11602 R 1742
Gray D 4047 R 11269 S
4581 T 1938 15006 V 69
6147 9334 11324
-Pov M 11308
Grayson A 11132 12569s
12587
Grayston K 4638
Grayzel S 10084

Greatrex J 14307
Greaves R 1238 S 9100
Grecco R 8292
Grech P 5109 10170
Greco E 13208 13211
- Mauri G 13209
Greef W de 14513*
Green A 12629* B 1149 C
8782 12011 12321 E 7255
7256* 7483* 8750 8827 J
77* 245 532 1560 4674
4886 4965 5045 13231 L
11768* M 2502 9525 P
11235s R 14208 14674 T
10795 12942 W 1582
11034
Greenacre R 127 8083
Greenberg G 11092 M 2950
3577
Greene J 67a 2367
-McCreight K 858 1671
Greenewalt C 12966
Greenfield G 1043 6008 J
8956 9137 9694* R 14219
Greenhalgh S 2352 3124
Greenhut Z 12204 12221
12233
Greenleaf F 8511 R 8538
Greenlee J 6288
Greenman J 8314
Greenspahn F 330d 918
1642 1971 2012 2122
2518 L 10037
Greenspoon L 304b 745
1378 1457 1544 1562
1573 1664 2477
Greenstein E 2215 2334
10705
Greenway R 10414
Greenwood R 8042
Greer R 7844
Gregersen N 1800
Grego I 12220
Grégoire J 3603 4139 4158
4661 5357 12579
Gregorius E 3177 7448* M
2547 3085 3568 4475
10875 14228-32 Naz

2864 7437 14083 14110-
8 14255 Nyss 2169s 2891
3160 3172 3193 8901
14119-26 14160*
Gregorius XVI 14747
Gregory J 14639 R 2697 T
14088
Greif D 9893
Greig J 7929
Greilsammer A 9986
Greinacher N 7968 15147*
Greipl E 1756
Greisch J 839 859 9545
10249
Greive W 4130 7859*
Grell C 14610
Grellier I 10302
Grelot P 573* 1256 1404
1911 3610 3640 3832
4361 5776 5967 7004
7407 9729* 9738 14802
Grenet F 10811
Grenholm C 4195
Grenz H 12482 S 5556
7735 8315 14875 14875*
14876 15079 15148
Greschat H 10263 M 175*
14502 14876*
Grès-Gayer J 14609 14748
Greschake G 14698
Gresham J 7567
Grethlein C 119
Greve A 8
Grey M 7089 7235 7255
7693 8728
Grieb A 4040 5835 7323
Grieco S 14337
Grierson P 12136 12153s
Griesbach 4231 4239 4258
Griesheimer M 11622*
12406
Griffin D 7121 7694 15133
15149 H 6180 M 11389
Griffith S 176 3620 10833
10883 13843
-Jones R 6166
Griffiths B 4123 8612 J
9193 10534 10556 10565

Gurevitch Z 9783
Gurna 12723
Gurney O 11755*
Gurock J 10040*
Gurtler G 10645
Gury F 13363
Guš Ḥalav 12329
Gushee D 785 8388
Gustafson J 1829 7216
  8342 8603 8871 15071
Gustavs K 14438
Gutenberg 1374
Gutenson C 7570
Guthrie C 14838 **G** 6222 **S**
  8526 8932
Gutiérrez G 2663 3344
  8512 14549* 14550s
  15016 **J** 728 1326 1359
  3832 4079 4347 4503
  4542 4692 4721 4737
  4814 4874 5164 5203
  5304 5313 5348 5354
  5366 5435 5489 5500
  5733 5745 6151* 6280
  6301 8382s 8708 9623
  9732 11364 11503*
  14230 14425* 14640
-Behemerid M 11621
Gutman S 9983
Gutmann J 8059 11933*
Guttgemanns E 8931*
Guttmann A 11725
Gutwein D 10024
Guy J 14066 14541 14560
Guyot P 13921* **R** 10267
Guzzetti G 8783
Guzzo P 11501* 13772
Gvozdanović J 9478
Gwaltney W 3551
Gwynne P 4712 7492
Gy P 631 8205
Gyatso Tendsin 10928
Gys-Devic 11345
Gyselen R 20 11821
  13220 13401 13441
  13710
Gythiel A 8730 14244*

Haack F 10451

Haacke R 4276 8054
Haacker K 4434
Haag E 145 3430 3435
  5465 7626* **H** 1141 3152
  8932* 13387 **K** 9320
Haak R 3547 3769
Haaki 12614
Haardt M de 8728 8784
Haarmann L 12240
Haas C 11446 **J** 1801 1872
  P 1142 8785 10140 **R de**
  8028 **V** 10680 12889
Haase R 496 2280 2295
  11601
Hab,/Diss. 1992s 632
Habbe J 13442
Habbel T 15043
Habel N 10370
Habermann J 7414
Habermas J 1304 1332
  5011 15017s 15115
Habermehl P 1905
Habgood J 179
Habichler A 159
Habicht C 180
Habiner T 13457
Habisch A 8431
Habito R 10365
Ḥabur 12524s
Haceldama 12204 12233
Hachlili R 12072*
Hachmann R 12264*
Hackens T 423
Hackett P 741
Hacking P 3383
Hackl U 11240
Hackstein K 13649
Hadar 12330
Hadas G 12256*b
-Lebel M 8969 11264
  11270 11346
Hadaway C 287a
Haddad Y 274b
Hadden B 1220
Hadfield A 1224
Hadjisavvas S 13443
Hadley J 3678 10702
  10729* 12252

Hadot P 10524
Haeckl A 12474
Häfner G 4367
Hägg I 11769 **R** 423 470*
  10599 11521* 12076
Hägglund B 517 4444
Hägler B 10085
Haehling R von 11181
Haelewyck J 2608
Haenckl A 11921
Haendler G 180* 3166 5737
  6029 10180 13910
  13913* 13915 14039*
  14074
- bibliog. 633
Hänsel-Hohenhausen M
  583
Häring B 984 7048 8328
  14895 15019 15019* **H**
  110 7702 10340
Härle W 552 5971
Haers J 409* 7485
Häselhoff R 13806
Häussling A 634 15251
Hafemann I 9203 **S** 5743
  5964
Haffner P 1802
Hafner G 11924
Hafstad K 1143
Haft 12649
Hagan L 8824
Hagara 12801*
Hagarsa 12802
Hage W 14309
Hagedorn D 3080 9389 **U**
  3080
Hagège C 297 9503
Hagelia H 2041
Hagen K 127 966 5988
  5993 **M von** 816
Hagenbuchner A 11165
Hager F 14054
Hagermann D 11600
Haggart A 15062
Haggis D 13123 13127
Hagia Triada 10616
Hagiz M 9984
Hagleitner S 10144

12977
Hanson A 5250 14894 **B**
  363 4443 7520* 15159 **C**
  2025 **G** 12877 **K** 879
  4405 13571* 13655 **P**
  3450 7277 **R** 3722 14005
  14070 **V** 11670 13446
Hanvey J 7111
Happel S 7202 10257
Haquin A 1360 7827 8220
Haquzim 12295
Har Karkom 12845
Haradum 12521
Harakas S 8912
Haran M 1085
Harappa 12665s
Haras E 14020
Harb P 8238
Hardelin A 14308
Harden G 7217
Harding M 3827 4251 6179
  11274
Hardmeier C 3540
Hardwick C 9552 **L** 11210
Hardy D 13147 **F** 3647 **H**
  14605 **T** 1209
Hare D 4281 7600 **R** 8268
Haręzga S 5352
Hargreaves C 1544 8654
Hark H 2090
Harl M 181 1552 2385
Harland P 1646 1662 1664
  1710 2041 3458
Harle D 11554*
Harley J 13247
Harlfinger D 51 118*
Harlow D 3560 **M** 11451
Harman A 2960*
Harmening D 14309*
Harnack A von 15020
  15020*
Harner P 5263
Harnisch W 4509
Harnoncourt P 7970
Harper B 7601 **F** 11522 **W**
  7055
Harpigny G 2253 7692*
Harpur J 13806* **P** 1913 **Y**

12747
Harrak A 12986* 13545
Harran 9123 12942
Harrauer C 9371
Harrell J 11579*
Harrelson W 495 9788
  10087
Harrich W 7302
Harries J 10493 **R** 8433
Harril J 5887
Harrill L 5731
Harrington D 584 3290
  3332 4010 4269 4282-4
  4290 4313 5303 5805
  8320 9773 9823 11454 **H**
  2327 9739 **J** 10558 **W**
  181* 3960 4762 5288
  5476s 5520 7495
Harris D 8530 **E** 1803 5339
  J 5677 9889 9916 10053
  M 1208 7303 7414*
  13587 **R** 7658 9515 **T**
  9026 **W**
  6085 8377 9525* 13608 1
  3711 13793
Harrison C 14157 14173
  14387 **G** 13118 **J** 10238
  10238* 10239 **P** 14582 **R**
  237 531 1976 2352 12429
  12947 **S** 9451* **V** 7796
Harrisville R 2017 5685
  9358
Harrop C 5865
Harskamp A van 14744
Harstine S 4068
Hart A 8321 **D** 967 7659
  15058s 15058* **H** 14911 **J**
  10027* **K** 9578* **S** 8434 **T**
  3290 7523 14965 14972
Hartigan K 13786
Hartin P 4234 5996 6289
  12306
Hartley J 3093
Hartman D 10026 **G** 1179
  L 4782 7475 13975*
Hartmann C 14583 **J**
  †15292 **K** 13917
Hartshorne C 7030*

Hartung U 12253*
Harvengt A 403* 554 2493
  3085 3279 3568 8034
  8102 8697 8737 13913*
  13944 14031* 14091*
Harvey A 5871 8322 10065
  B 4643 **D** 5784 **G** 2335
  4092 10465 **L** 10858 **M**
  14310 **P** 10929 12295
  14208 **S** 9599 9940 9942
  14241 14256
Harviainen T 9768
Harwood B 1230 **W** 10483
Hary B 9178 9184
Ḥasa 12376
Hasel F 4196 8933 9028 **G**
  3646 5919 7394 8934s
  †15293 **M** 1040 2166
  2451
Haṣeva 12260
Hasitschka M 4726 4764
  5304 5482 5544 6246
  7626* 7760
Hasitzka M 9242s 13364*
Haskell F 11841
Hasker W 1812 13594
Haskins S 8734
Haslam M 9392 9416
Hasler V 5696 5908
Hassake 12522
Hassan bin-Talal 10884* **F**
  12709 **S** 10453
Hasse H 14298*
Hassek 12943
Hastings A 14878s 15102
  15150
Hata G 11264
Hatch N 14880
Hatcher H 11541
Hatem J 14256
Hathcock W 5719
Hatigan K 10621
Hatina T 4040 4068 4774
Hatoum H 1254
Ḥatra 12615s
Hatt H 8458
Hattin 13835*
Hattrup D 1870 1915 7443

Heine H 10904 **S** 7070
    13609
Heinemann I 10153
Heinemeyer W 54a
Heinen H 11376
Heininger B 4161 4928
Heinrich J 6209
Heintz F 5150 **H** 1038 **J**
    585 3555 **M** 5340
Heinz P 10795
Heipp-Tamer C 12138
Heiser W 14602*
Heither T 5737 14016
Heitink G 7124
Heitsch E 10601 10639
Helberg J 3636 7395 13535
Helck W 11005 12033
    12422* †15296
Held H 15380 **S** 5557
Helder H 5518
Helderman J 5218 10211
Heldman M 11872
Helewa G 6109
Helfmeyer F 3384
Heliand 1197
Helinand 1057
Heliodorus E 11405
Heliopolis 9603
-Libani 12421
Hellegouarc'h J 167 676
    10497 11374 15327
Helleman W 322 14057
Heller B 10713 **D** 360b
    14401* **J** 519 **M** 9849
-Kallai L 12045
Hellholm D 3598 4750
Hellmann M 2822 11623
Hellmuth L 10904
Hellwig M 7340 14881
Helly D 13873
Helm P 862 7279 10298 **P**
    8884 **R** 2339
Helmstadter R 14665*
Hélou C 5504
Helper M 760
Helsper M 2220
Helton S 4867
Heltzer M 2771 2831 3354

9008 11601
Helvidius 4533
Helyer L 5628 6136 9802
Hemans C 11493
Hemelrijk J 11828 11924
Hemelsoet B 5374
Hemer C 5064
Hempel C 9653 9751 9768*
    J 54b 183 **V** 7602
Hempelmann H 9546 **R**
    4612
Hempton D 13531
Henau E 10406
Henaut B 4821
Hendel R 1656 1664 1716
    8924
Henderson J 6224 **R** 15041
Hendrichs O 877b
Hendricks J 152* **S** 12801
    W 1566 5520 7535 7615
Hendry G †15297
Henein N 12675*
Hengel H 3364 **J van den**
    7040 8489 15151 **M** 246
    322* 323a 1446 3962
    4166 5579s 5582 5686
    7603 8216 13633 14775
Hengsbach F 8518
Henigan T 4690
Henkel W 636
Henker E 10089
Henking S 8790
Henkys J 2962
Henn W 7974 15204
Hennaux J 8325
Henne P 3496 7444 9597
    9599 13980 14378
Hennessy A 4369 12307 **J**
    12354
Hennings R 6029 14200s
Henrich S 5161
Henrichs A 10576
Henrici P 183* 7347 7680
    14386
Henriksen H 7257*
Henrix H 10089*
Hensel P 11387 **S** 11387
Hensell E 203b 1603 9321

Hens-Piazza G 3392 3397
Henten J van 267 323b
    2823 7332 12273
Hentschel G 2539s 2606
    2619 2632 2680 2697
    2726 2729
Henz H 54c
Henze K 590
Hepburn L 8773
Hepper F 13403-5
Heraklēs banca-dati 670
Heran F 10253*
Herbert E 2546 2612 9678
    S 15397
Herbin F 12675
Herbordt S 11995
Herculaneum 11639 11648
    13681
Herder J 334 11017 14606
    14606* 14705*
Heriban J 6096
Herklots H 749
Herman J 13119 **Z** 36
    6052
Herman-Judah 14170
Hermary A 11925* 13002s
    13007
Hermas 7444 10173 13975*
    13978-83
Hermelink J 225* 1051
Hermias 14005
Hermon E 425 13444
Hermon 12335s
Hermopolis 12794 12804
Herms E 8088 10406* **I** 2*
Hernández Ruiz J 7865
Herning S 914
Hernon R 4662
Herodium 13305
Herodotus 9343 11207*
    11209 11212 11219
    13305s 11061 11068
    11146 11151 11154
    11159 11170s 11181
    11186 11191 13078*
    13546
Herr B 2683
Herranz C 9029

Hirunuma T 1428
Hispania 5837 11206
Hitchcock J 1803
Hitchner E 13226
Hittitae 10678-86 11158-65
    12881*-12890 13480
Hitzl I 12099
Hjelde S 10227 10256
    10407
Hjelm R 4102
Hlaváček K 112
Ho A 9050 C 2588
Hobbs H 3555 J 1806 T
    869 2555 2773* 7340*
    10979 13633
Hoberman R 9119 10045
Hobert P 4601
Hobson D 471
Hoburg R 14572
Hoch J 9205 9527 12785 M
    13835
Hochmann E 13444
Hochschild R 4167
Hock R 3826 3834
Hocken P 5921
Hockett C 15268
Hodapp W 10526
Hodder A 10252 I 13104
Hodel-Hoenes S 12100
Hodge 14693 A 13320 C
    6056 P 14621
Hodges L 1065 Z 6279
Hodgson P 7396 7568
    10323 14663
Hodot R 9270
Hoedemaker B 7220
Hödl L 658 9502* 14382
    14411* 14419*
Höffken M 3425
Högemann P 11151 11242
Høgenhaven J 7221
Höghammar K 11926
Höhn H 15152
Hoehner H 5571 11320
Hoek A van den 9619 E
    5811
Hoekstra E 10452
Hölbl G 11245 12893

Hölderlin 15022s
Hölkeskamp K 11181*
    11241 11318
Hoelmer H 3593
Hölscher E 5050
Hölzl R 11927
Hönle A 11140
Hoepe R 7256
Höpfl H 14471*
Hoepfner H 12927 W
    13763
Hörandner W 58
Hörnemann W 2167
Hörnlund B 9658
Hoerth A 246*
Hoesterey I 275*
Höver G 2193
Höyücek 12945
Hoff M 13054
Hoffman B 12971 F 10936
    L 7294s M 14458 14534*
    14536 R 276 Y 330d 2509
    3524
Hoffmann A 472 11624
    12914 14158-60 C 10090
    F 9199 14828 14449* G
    10602 I 112 J 7418 14391
    M 863 P 185 4114 4993
    13198 Y 8393
Hoffmeier J 2486 13386
Hoffner H 9262 10681
Hofius O 186 4050 4811
    5581 6226 7802
Hofmeier J 8012
Hofrichter P 5348
Hofstra J 5341
Hoftijzer J 323c 2365 8970s
Hogan L 13492 M 5818
    7165
Hogg C 14230
Hoglund K 2787s
Hognesius K 2773
Hoheisel K 10456
Hohlfelder R 13025*
Hohnberg I 13379
Hoitenga D 7125
Hoksbergen R 8438
Hokwerda H 4

Holdsworth C 14378
Holenstein E 849
Holer C 9176
Holeton D 7803
Holifield E 14921
Holl A 11842
Holladay C 1568 2140 W
    2961 3493 3495
Holland D 14315* G 5173
    M 2469 R 324d S 912
    7804 T 12612
Hollander H 5877
Hollenbach D 268 355a
Hollerweger H 15404
Holliday P 473 11842*
Hollis A 10584s S
    8736 10778
Holloway R 271 8792 12449
    13042 13095 13162 13212
Hollstein W 12139 12139*
Hollyday J 1145
Holm J 247 277 10361 N
    15238*
-Nielsen L 9653 S 3099
Holman C 6087 J 3131 7393
Holmann G 15250*
Holmberg B 3965
Holmes D 14882 G 570 M
    1084 5063 5995 S 8326
Holmgren F 3729 5026
Holper J 4617
Holt B 8165 E 3793 F
    11252 11255 12662 P
    10613 12242 12767
    13841* 13889
Holtenga D 292
Holth S †15299
Holthuis S 301a
Holtrop P 7280
Holtz G 4051 S 1030 T 3874
    4168 5588 6019
Holtzer M 2808
Holum K 12210
Holwerda D 4197
Holzberg N 11432
Holzhausen J 10160* 10176
    10640*
Hombert P 5875

Hünermann P 57 970 7486
8518 8661 13617 14404*
14405
Huerre D 8206
Hürten H 189*
Hütter R 7580 8055
Huey F 3494
Huffman D 4888
Huffmon H 3220
Huftier M 8119
Hugenberger G 3795
Hughes C 9547 D 7762
10612 F 6024 G 11040 J
10992 13313 13416 13940
K 373 M 4406 P 2142 R
1917 15153 S 8280 14496
Hughson T 15063
Hugo SV 7179* 14417
14417*
Hugolinus 14418
Huizing K 1307
Huizinga T 14995
Hull J 2738 10227*
Hulmes E 10403
Hult G 12542
Hultberg A 6097
Hultgård A 4489*
Hultgren A 3482 3836 3836
3966 4035s 5757 7455*
7715 7805 13919
Hultkranz Å 10974*
Human D 3000
Humans S 13561
Humbach H 9450*
Humbert J 9663-5 11536
Humble B 8037
Hume D 4465 10262 10285
L 8605
Hummel G 15113 H 1096
3077 P 9366 R 8333 S
9238
Humphrey H 4725 S 10393
Humphreys K 14312 R
10830 W 246* 911 1579
1652 2706
Hunger H 58 1429 9227
12588 K 14981
Hunink V 11311

Hunke S 10829
Hunn M 1047
Hunsberger G 932
Hunsinger G 172h 14972s
Hunt A 4374 5881 5893 B
7604 E 13824* L 426
12012 M 1242 8793 P
11184 S 5262
Huntemann G 14995
Hunter A 32a 7057 4303
8606 E 12625* 13272 F
13856 J 1321 2935 3069
3554
Hunyadi M 4451
Huonder V 2962
Huot J 11504 11915 12095
12563 12629* 12637
13763*
Huppenbauer M 4170 14794
Hupper W 586
Huppertz H 7975
Hurault B 1504 L 1504
Hurd J 5902
Hurlet F 11328
Hurley D 59 11348 R 818
Hurowitz V 2128 2563 2662
2666s 10715
Hurritae 12195.13552
Hurst D 14398 H 12456
12464s L 6229 8923
Hurtado L 2091 4774 5624
Hurth E 4141s
Hurvitz A 2892 3267
Huskinson J 11906
Huss U 14606 W 11094
11246 12466 12809
Husser J 1272 3625 10714
Husslein G 13248
Husson G 11812
Hutchinson T 11542
Hutchison W 364* 14719
14885
Hutmacher H 863*
Hutter M 10186 10416
10682 10811 10928 10975
12074 14250 U 14436
Hutton R 13612
Huwyler B 3503

Huyse P 9445
Huÿssteen P van 9151
Huyssteen J van 10326
10329
Hvidberg-Hansen F 10716
Hwang Shin-Ja J 3723
Hyatt D 15043
Hyers C 1750
Hyland A 11671 13367 W
1920
Hylson-Smith
K 14886 14919
Hyman A 9918 P 9982

Iakovidis S 13555
Iamblichus 414 10554 10668
Iamim A 11271
Iammarrone G 7487
Iamnia 9399
Iappolo G 13200
Iasos 12956
Ibañez A 5922
-Arana A 3356 7281 7793
Ibbett J 1074
Iberia-E 12991*
Ibiza 12441
Ibn Bal'am J 3379
Ibn Ezra 1617 3280
3667 9919 9932 9936-8
Ibn Falaquera S 9940-2
Ibn Gabirol 1678 9939
Ibn Ganaḥ 9904
Ibn Hazm 10864
Ibn Massa I 13497
Ibn Tawus 10858*
Ibn Tibbon S 3526*
Icaria 13136
Icaza R 4732 5072
Ickert S 7027*
Idalion 13008-13010
Idel M 9895
Idelsohn A 11757
Idestrom R 14799
Idfu 12805
Idinopulos T 278
Idle C 271
Idu 13298
Iersel A van 7352 7765 **B**

6158 7001 9314 9588
9629 9766 12092
Jacquet-Gordon H 12699
Jacquin F 2240
Jacquinod B 9298
Jaeger M 8092 11430*
Jähne A 13765
Jaffa 12296
Jaffee M 3838 7300 9860
Jagersma H 733 2320 2331
2341 8973 10993
Jagger P 2*
Jagoda M 9604*
Jahndel M 590
Jahnow H 59*
Jaini P 10958
Jaki S 591 1003 1672 1802
1807-9 1873
Jakobielski S 12830
Jakobs M †15304
Jakobson V 1985*
Jakovidis S 15310
Jakubiec C †15305
Jal P 60a 11375 11377
Jambet C 10867
Jamdat Nasr 11987
James F 12311 **L** 8519 **M**
9628 **P** 11122 12187s **S**
11672* **T** 11558 12687 **W**
10269-71
Jameson M 9398 13778 **R**
11799
Jamieson-Drake D 8973*
13613
Jamzadeh P 12644*
Janaki S 60b
Janda J 1249 7007 8617
10188 10245 10380 10431
10892 10953 10967 15174
Janeras S 13818
Janicki J 15205
Jankowskaya N 13712
Jankowski A 5506 7417*
Janni P 13801
Jannot J 11806 11916*
Jánosi P 12684
Janota J 53
Janov M de 14419*

Janowitz N 9858
Janowski B 2316 2975 7695
10718 13368 **J** 8796* 8876
Jans J 287e 8328
Jansen A 13555 **G** 13321 **H**
1865 7028 10358* **L**
10358*
-Winkeln K 9207s
Jansenius C 14607-12
Janssen E 13369 **J** 13614
13712* **R** 11522* 13369
13614
Janssens L 8329
Janvier Y 13250
Janz D 207e 212* 213 286
3020 5988 14315 14389
14414* 14524*
Janzen E 5300 **J** 1620 2438
3459 3465 7324 **W** 9050
Jaoudi M 10888
Jaouen R 7862
Japhet S 63 2059 2754
2787 2800 3300
Jaquette J 5602 5699 6025
6110
Jaramillo R 13894
-Rivas P 3357
Jarczyk G 7689 8897
Járdányi-Paulovics I 60c
Jarick J 3283 3358
Jaritz G 10674 **H** 12723
12797
Jaroš K 11734 11980 13750
M 12623
Jarton M 14993
Jaruzelska I 2282 3695
Jarvis L 5704
Jas M 10182 14471
Jaschke H 13990
Jasink A 12862 12928
Jasnow R 9209 11095
Jasper D 32c 319 879 1180s
1198 1200 1339 7104 **R**
61
Jaspert B 190 14795
Jastrow J 9120
Jastrzębowska E 5395 11491
Jauss H 2936

Jawa-E 12381 **W** 10701
12382s
Jawf 12411
Jay E 9299 **N** 7763 **P** 3089
4112 4119 7052 7086
7407 7424 14391
Jeammet N 2182
Jeanes G 5067
Jeanne d'Arc sr 787 1505
Jean-Nesmy C 1182 2901
†15306
Jeannière A 10642
Jeanrond W 865s 10258
10408 15116
Jeansonne S 1146
Jeauneau A 14129
Jebaraj D 2144
Jedin H 14315*
Jeffers A 1167 2335 2675
Jefferson P 7796
Jefford C 248 13977
Jeffrey D 1199 1210
Jeffreys D 12741 12744
12746
Jefremow N 11979 12034
Jehne M 11185
Jehoschua A 10186*
Jelonek T 10994
Jemdet Nasr 12579
Jeme 12806
Jemielity T 1183 3359
Jenkins G 1497 4237 **J** 552*
13053 **R** 1497
Jenks G 5465
Jenkyns R 11404
Jenner K 1464
Jenni E 3023 9030 9040
9043*
Jennings R 12996 13857
Jens J 8385 **W** 1184
Jensen A 8737 8794 **G** 8534
8566 14450* **H** 1729 7758
J 1200
1519 9786 **K** 342* 14078 **L**
3099 **M** 131b **R** 2061
Jenson P 1603 3737 3787 **R**
620 7978 14437
Jenssen P 7716

José A 14598
Joseph M 8654 **P** 4471
Josephson J 15255
Josephus F 2231 2267 2275
　2600 2693 2696 2715
　2720 2725 2844 2854
　3627 3728 4917 9358
　9624 9749 9755 11259*-
　11281 13237 13500
Joshel S 13615 13715
Josipovici G 734
Jospe R 7281* 9940
Jossa G 7415 11272 11272*
Jossua J 639* 1207 4660
　8069 14667
Jost R 3526
Jostein Å 867
Josuttis M 6223
Jotischky A 12255*
Jouan F 10603
Jouanna J 11735
Jouanna J 13494-6
Joubert J 7717 **S** 3837 7341
Joukowsky M 11465
Joüon P 8974
Jourdain-Annequin C 10577
　12505s
Journet C 10093 15033
Joussot D 14005
Joy M 8795 14167
Joyal M 10643
Joyce P 1167 3349 3517
　3567 3576 3595 9873
　10092
JStOT index 593
Juan P 5139
Jubb'adin 9127
Jucci E 1590 9594*
Judaea 12252-81
Judd G 15016
Judeideh 12268
Judge E 4052
Judisch D 2358
Juel D 4199 4768 4835 7433
　8924 13919*
Jüngel E 332a 846 1539
　7774* 7782 8093 8440
　15034-6* 15081

Jüngling H 7059 15190
Jürgens P 9211
Juliana N 14420 14420*
Julianus Imp 11469 11471*
　11481 14111s 14136
Julianus T 14421
Juncker G 4143
Junco Garza C 2669
Jundt P 3719
Jundzili J 11406
Jung C 1251s 4025 **H** 191*
　15338 **M** 9972 **S** 7223
Junghans H 508 639 7156
　14438
Jungman P 9275
Jungraithmayr H 9485
Junod É 3158 9629* 14104
　14245
Jurgens D 4102
Jurgensen H 6168s
Jurić S 757 780 869 1672
　2614 3490 4421 4280
　4519 4930 5230 5442
Jurieu P 14613
Jursa M 11821*
Jussen B 14316
Just A 5052
Justel B 9179 10894*
Justinus M 2033 2969 3901
　5291 7458 9637* 14000-5
Juvenalis 14191
Juvencus 4386

Kabasele M 3562
-Mukenge A 1583 8608
Kaczynski R 8210
Kadá S 8260
Kaddari M 9011
Kaegi W 11461 12641
　12947 13826
Kähler C 4399 **M** 3888
　14668
Kämmerer T 13616
Kaempf B 2815 3885
Käsemann E 5654
Kaestli J 593* 5203 9634
　13163
Kafafi Z 12374

Kafr Miṣr 12339
Kagan I 9844 **J** 12141
Kahana M 13536 **R** 136
Kahil L 571
Kahl B 5361 7251* **J** 9202
　9212 12121 **O** 13496 **R**
　173* **W** 4466
Kahle W 7980
Kahler C 6103
Kahn P 3730
Kaimakis D 3487
Kaimio M 15405
Kaiser A 7489 7500 **B** 759
　C 1813 2315 **J** 7627 **O**
　61* 735 2818 2977 3134
　3174 4200 5778 7395
　12753 14630 **R** 14316 **W**
　868 2321 4884 7291 7718
　13378
Kajava M 11477*
Kakar S 10314
Kakavas G 11873*
Kaklos M 12106
Kákosy L 10759s 12714
　13519
Kakovkin A 11524* 11776*
　12807
Kakovkine A 11771
Kalamakia 13070
Kalavasos 13011s
Kaleh H 13858
Kalfatovic M 13807
Kaliba J 8568
Kalicz N 15314
Kalimi I 2760 2777 2859
Kalin E 5719
Kalmin R 9845 9851s
Kalogirou J 62
Kalongo J 377
Kalonymos 9942 9944
Kalsky M 15199
Kaltner J 13562
Kaman 12949 13461
Kamaroff L 12646
Kamen C 13872 **H** 14471*
Kamesar A 1622 3381 3725
　9618* 9853 9876 12780
Kamid/Loz 12423*

Keenan J 7696 9337 11331
14100* 14348
Keener C 4222 4433 4435
5700
Keerankeri G 3973 4329
Keesmaat S 5793
Kefaranaya 13293*
Keggler H 11893
Kegler J 3100
Kehl M 5559 7868 8878
8884*
Kehoe D 13447s 13717*
Keil C 14669* **G** 10306
Keim 7475
Keisan 12340
Keiser G 1355 **R** 10257
Keith G 14472
Kekes J 10409
Kelber W 3838 3898 4770
5319
Kellas C 4452 4836
Kellenberger E 2555
Kellens F 9445* 9450* **J**
10813
Keller A 14091 **C** 1905 3652
7002 10194 **H** 52 2848
11874 **M** 1588 9454 **R**
1904 14525* **S** 11484
Kelley C 12514 **P** 8976
Kellia 12807s
Kelliher J 8041
Kellner D 13282 **M** 97
3526* 9920 9934
Kelly B 1918 7029 **C** 7491
F 979 **G** 969 **H** 1220 **J** 554
1482 4407 10894 14128
14216 14280 14839 **K** 984
7868* **T** 990 14888
Kelm C 1166
Kelsay J 10891
Kelsey D 1671 7128 **N** 9245
Kemeza M 8800
Kemmler A 2047
Kemp B 12733 12736 **E**
8057
Kemper C 10604
Kempinski A 11617 12257
12342 †15309

Kempson W 6245
Kendall B 14522 **D** 4866
9352
Kenig É 7368
Kenis L 366 640 1350 8502
14670 14721
Kennedy B 4892 **C** 9700* **D**
12540 12982 **E** 65* 8879
G 1309 11187 **H** 8880
10831 **L** 14439 **P** 15103 **S**
7201* **T** 14385
-Riley 11672
Kennek G 13920*
Kennell S 14223
Kennelly J 11188
Kenneson P 15161*
Kenney G 5204 **J** 10645
Kennicott 1366
Kenny A 10315
Kenrick P 12036 12042
12064 15265
Kent J 284 5931 7944 8501
Keos 13137s
Keown D 10962 **G** 3673
Kepel G 10363 10363*
Képinski-Lecomte C 12521
Kepler 1815
Kepnes S 10295
Keppie L 11662
Ker I 14754s 14760
Kerak 2691 12384-6
Kerameikos 13052 13055
Kerber W 10967
Kerby-Fulton K 1230s
Kerekomouri 13119*
Kerényi G 10126
Kereszty R 7492 14920
Kerma 12833s
Kern B 8520 **U** 1104 **W** 192
1915 5093 7020 7122
-Ulmer B 2125 9786*
Kerner H 14671 **S** 12658
Kerr F 3922 4362 11020
15126
Kertelge K 4727 4768 4854
5636s 5750 6214 8003
8932*
Kertsch M 5737

Kesel J de 7869 8094
Keshishian A 7982
Kessel Blake A 10873
Kessler A 31 14041 **D** 7974
E 14865 **H** 4692 12517 **J**
3777 **K** 12533 **M** 250 2133
2251 2389 **R** 2572 3357
3476 3664 10995 13618 **S**
14710
Ketelaer S 2052*
Kett A 8642
Kettler C 7719
Keulman K 365b
Keur J 9589 **P** 9589
Kevern J 15156
Kevers P 251
Kevorkian R 9276
Khabur 12524s
Khafaga M 66
Khafajah 12612
Khairallah M 8138
Khalid R 13792
Khalîd 12525
Khalidi R 13861
Khan G 8977 9003* 9479
9767 14592* **M** 9528
Kharaz 12390
Khargeh 10764
Khatchadourian H 8881
Kheleifeh 12367
Kholetria 13014
Khorsabad 12586
Khouli A el- 12748
Khoury A 10867 10885
10892 13859 **N** el- 131h **P**
189 13884 14259*
Kible B 658
Kicher-Durand C 77
Kidd I 11439 **R** 6068
Kidder A 3806 8824*
11552* 13951
Kieckhofer R 14459
Kieffer R 3839 13955*
-Pülz P 9526
Kiefner G 50
Kienast B 9152 **D** 11407
Kienzler K 13860
Kierkegaard S 2058 7098*

Klimov G 9480
Kline M 2216 3786
Klingenberg G 137
Klinger J 11752 **S**
  7148 9564*
Klinghardt M 4605 9667
Klingshorn W 14221* 14222
Klock C 14120
Klöcker M 14889
Kloft H 9525* **M** 10097
Kloner A 12223
Klopfenstein M 467* 3258
  10704* 15379
Kloppemborg J 4171 4236
  4240-2 4263 4333 5010
  5870 13824 14573
Klostermaier K 10930
Klotz J 1831
Klueting H 14485 14529
  14585*
Klug E 14473
Kluger R 1988*
Klumbies P 5667
Knabe J 11296
Knapp A 11502 12402
  12998 **M** 7606
Knappert J 1730 10484
  13549
Knauer P 7959 15093
Knauf E 736 2526 2843
  2857 3499 8977* 9090
  10719 10988 12325*
  13649
Knaus H 194
Knebel S 13620
Knecht D 10561 **L** 819 **M**
  819
Knee S 10051
Knell H 13051*
Knellwolf U 1041
Kneppe A 13776
Kniazeff A 7606*
Knibb M 138 2780 6200
  7309* 9596* 9652 9681
  9682 9694 9768*
Knibbe D 12893 15256*
Knierim R 2330 2738 9028
Kniff H de 8952

Knigge U 13055
Knight C 1850 14756 **D**
  2460 2963 7319 **G** 3395
  5558 **J** 14602*
Knights C 3188 3543
Kniss F 7195
Knitter P 8014* 8333 10362
  10396
Knobel P 3082
Knobloch J 1036 9328
Knoch O 880 1520 4408
  4672 6260 †15311
Knoeppfler N 15093
Knöppler T 5306
Knoll I 9739*
Knopf 6273
Knoppers G 2637 2774*
Knossos 9422 9425 9428
  9435 10604* 12019
  13113-8 13371 Knowles
  M 4313 4548
Knox B 10529 **D** †15311* **R**
  498
Knysh A 10858*
Kobusch T 7166
Kobusiewicz M 12786
Koch D 2969 5679 6106 **E**
  14463 14554 14606 **H**
  9449 11153 12142 12645 **I**
  114 **K** 1551 2888 3361
  3618 7331 7607 13304 **P**
  1074 **R** 7325 9313
Kochan L 241d 10018
  13875
Kochanek H 975
Kochavi M 12330
Köckert M 607 1581 1646
  2143 2424 2555 2822
  3213 3420 3675 7378
  9471 10738 11734 12364
  13266
Kocsis I 5942 **L** 11673
Koedyker J 14875
Köhbach M 109 15375
Köhler J 1105
Koehler L 9012
Koeker P 7151
Koelb C 9574 13604

Kölzer T 54a
Koemoth P 13405s
Koen L 5229
Koenen K 3308 3361 9047*
  13372 **L** 10188 11189
König E 3169 **R** 13407
Koenig J 8166 8332
Köpf U 365
Körn M 4891
Körner J 9043* **U** 10098
Körntgen L 14319
Koerrenz R 9994*
Körtner U 870s 7370
Köster H †15312 **R** 12954
Koester C 2301 5243 5250
  5311 5345 6219 6224
  H 3841 3902
  3974 4665 6162 13986
Köszeghy M 3434
Koet B 1907 5001 5701
Kötter R 14508
Köves T 11475*
-Zulauf T 10530
Kogel J 2314 2474
Kogman-Appel K 2171
  11893
Kogut S 8978
Koh S 10721 13373
Kohák E 7225
Kohl M 13674 **P** 12190
  12559
Kohlenberger J 1562
Kohlschein F 2589
Kohn R 579
Kok M 7869*
Kokabi M 459
Kokkinos N 9419* 11313
Kolakowski L 12694
Kolarcik M 3319
Kolars J 12864
Kolataj W 12771
Kolb C 12024 **D** 15022s
  R 5351 14473 14487*
  14492 14525*
Kolbus S 12191
Kolden M 1106
Kolendo J 11638
Kolenkow A 5904

Krekeler A 12796
Kremer J 718 967 4577 4693
  5122 7871 8882* 15157 **K**
  364
Kremers H 4696
Krenkel W 15384
Krenn K 8096
Krentz E 4090 4220 4278
  5661 5717 5991 6058
  6102 6156 8948 10627
  13265
Kress H 8308
Kretzmann N 14389
Kreutz A 13862
Kreuzer B 13144 **M** 9775 **S**
  13622 13751
Kreyenbroek P 10811
Krieg G 1042 15158 **M**
  3796 **R** 14923*
Krieger D 10364 **T** 11273
Kriesch E 12970
Krim K 1527
Krinetzki G 2427
Krings V 11250
Krini 13071
Krispin G 7879
Krist H 5425
Kristeller P 10646
Kristensen A 12863
Kritopoulos M 3850
Kriz J 6151
Krmičková H 14419*
Krochmal N 9916
Krochmalnik D 1629 9794
  10029*
Krodel G 6058 14465
Kroeber K 10485
Kroeger C 6191 **J** 4154 7859
  7872 7985 10399 **R** 6191
Kröker V 2805*
Kroeker P 8442
Kroeze J 8979
Krog A 1228
Kroger M 1422
Krokos J 939
Królikowski J 4375 8677
Kroll E 475 **R** 14586 **S**
  12657 **U** 1913 7583

Kromer K 12749
Krondorfer B 2576
Krone S 10822
Kronfeld C 1226
Kronholm T 9075 10030
  10716 12582
Kropotkin V †15319
Kropp M 843 14246*
Krotkoff G 9141
Kroyanker P 12224
Kruchten J 2158 9214 10762
Krueger D 8434
Krüger F 8096* 14503
  15039 **H** 1310 **P** 10695
  T 2670 2941 3046 3292
  3301 3981
Krümmel A 33f 14163
Kruger H 3427 **P** 3769
Kruisheer D 10202
Krumenacker Y 356
Krundorfer B 916
Krupe M 2060
Krupp M 13863 **R** 14090
Krusche G 8003 10914
Kruse I 5182* **M** 183
Kselman T 8673 8883
Kuan Kah-Jin 2722 10996
Kubo S 5735
Kuchi N 2710
Kuck D 6050
Kudasiewicz J 4987 8688
Kudlien F 6150 13501
  13718
Kübel W 14411*
Küchler U 4144
Kühn F 54b **U** 7720 7985*
Kuehn C 14100*
Kühnel H 11773
Kühnert B 13623
Kühneweg U 14024
Kühschelm R 5404
Kültepe 12000* 12951
  13293 13712
Kümmel W 3976
Kuen A 3977
Kuenen A 14677
Küng H 984 1184 4018
  7130 7664 7664* 8114

8333-7 8609 10101-3
  10237 10410 10960 14021
  14881 14974 15038-40*
Künzl H 11876
Küppers K 2589
Kürze-Göthe E 13052
Küster V 872 8610
Kuftin B 11567
Kugel J 1693 3321
Kugler R 3797 9832s 9854
  9960
Kuhl J 4342 10368
Kuhn J von 14744 **T** 14502
Kuhnen H 12192 13766
Kuhoff W 11408 12213
Kuhrt A 415 11156 11255
Kuijt I 12355
Kuikman J 7011 7294
Kuitert H 7665s
Kuitse R 4145
Kull B 12038 12044
Kullmann 13477
KULublin 15230
Kumme 13302
Kunert G 10486
Kuniholm B 13866
Kunow J 12038
Kunst C 13660
Kuntillet → *'Ajrûd*
Kuntz J 2893 2991
Kunze E 11676 **M** 12904
  -Götte E 12039
Kupczyg-Lewin L 13809
Kuper R 474*
Kupfer M 2882
Kupiszewski H †15320
Kuppers J 12429*
Kurban 12952
Kurisuthara V 7227
Kurke L 417c
Kurochkin G 11001
Kurru 12097
Kurth D 12805
Kurtz M 7346
Kurz W 4892 5072
Kus R 225
Kusche U 9788
Kuschel K 1107 3101 3462

Lambrechts R 571 11803 12069
Lambton A 9444 10859
Lameyre A 1733
Lamm J 14703
Lammi W 15024
Lamouille A 5260
Lamoureux F 10647
Lampe G 7547 **P** 4617
Lampsacus 12164
Lana I 433c 7343
Lanata G 10506
Lancel S 12467
Lancha C 14553
Lanci J 5709
Lançon B 11464
Lanczkowski J 555
Land R 7228 **S** 8167
Landau J 196 10894 13864
Landes G 1183 2748
Landis S 5367
Landmesser C 5801
Ladon C 6306
Landucci Gattinoni F 11677
Landy F 951 2527
Lane B 7229 7601 **D** 1468s 1818 2322 **R** 788 **T** 271 1521 4947 8097 **W** 6210s
- Fox R 11409
Lanfranchi G 12591
Lang B 511 589 826 1257 3258 4590 8884* 10347 10723 13562 **M de** 4256
Langa P 14164*
Langacker R 9133
Langan F 282 **J** 977*
Langdon J 132* **S** 11524
Lange A 581 9668 **D** 7628 8339 **J** 1567 13164 **N de** 90c 9821 9892 9968* 10036* 11889
Langella A 4128 8612*
Langendijk L 7282
Langenhorst G 3101 **H** 2837
Langenhoven P van 1346
Langer G 9826 10104 13622 **M** 282* 10105 **R** 7306 **W** 820* 821

Langevin P 495 5021 5648 7110 7440 7827 12876 13903
Langhade J 9181
Langholf V 13502
Langkammer H 7230 8689
Langlamet F 1 1387 2586 2593 2599 2627
Langland W 1230-2
Langlois L 10262
Langmuir G 9910 10106 10147
Lanne E 978 7873 14074*
Lanpher J 4771
Lanszweert R 9357
Lanternari V 13503
Lantier R †15324
Lanting J 11543
Laperrousaz E 252 12193
Lapide P 197 1547 1972 4055 9711
Lapidge M 14273*
Lapidus I 12767
Lapin H 9827
Laplanche F 14544 14588
Lapointe G 4606 **R** 381
Laporte J 5800
La Potterie I de 255* 979 3979 4640 5460 5468 8168 8690s
Lapp G 10763 **N** 12263 12414
Lapsley J 71
Lara Peinado F 10487
Larché F 12698*
Larcher P 9182
Larchet J 7532 8169 14066 14129*
Lardet P 14202 14207
La Regina A 476
Larere P 7533
Largo G 10399
Larkin D 11627 **K** 3255 3333 3775 3787 877 1 **W** 874
La Rocca E 11932
Laronde A 11702*
La Rosa V 13124

Larouche J 10331 13625
Larrabe J 7807* 7827
Larrañaga T 12207
Larroque L 4331
Larsa 12572 12617
Larsen L 4843 **P** 11529
Larson E 1843 2753 **J** 10605 -Miller L 11628
Larsson E 5073
Lascaris A 7765
Las Casas B de 8546 14546-53
Lash N 2019 7574 8927 14763
La Shell J 1753 7419*
Lasker D 9893 9910
Laskier M 9998
La Soujeole B 941
Lass E 11703
Lasserre G 2283 3442
Lassner J 2675
Læssøe J 12863
Lategan B 875 1321 5456
Lateiner D 10613
Latham J 10844 10858
Lathrop G 4611 7808*
Latomus J 14431 14533 14614
Latorre J 524 2912
LaTorre J de 72 **R de** 4688 7476
Latourelle R 505 4471s 15256
Latti G 7842
Lattimore S 416d
Lattke M 4428 13925
Lau W 3481
Laub F 5559
Laubach E 14934
Laudani C 13351
Laughlin J 12319
Launderville D 1920
Launius R 10459*
Laurence R 13199 13766* **V** 8266
Laurenti J 9922
Laurentin R 8692
Laurenzi M 14986

Le Masters P 8885
Lemay H 13478
Lemche N 124 1449 2455
    2590 2645 3599 10704
    10997* 11062 12387
    13236 13748
Lemière E 15033
Lemke W 7393
Lemoine M 14372
Lemonnier P 11605*
Le Mort F 12101
Lemos B 7049
Lenaerts J 9392 9413
Lenchak T 1197 2441
Lendle O 11182
Lendon J 11446
Lenfant A 14617
Lenhardt P 4056 7310 7754
Lennan R 1778 7875
Lennardi C 14322
Lenoble P 13351*
Lenoir M 11740
Lentacker N 13376
Lentheric B 12799
Lentini G 4949
Lentz J 5164
Lentzen-Deis F 4420 4572
    4992 †15331
Lenzen C 12392 D 13450 V
    2193 4194 10031
Leo I 14132*
León J de 8485 L de 3083
    3156s 5733 7438
Leonard A 12041 E 3935
    14717 14739 14773
Léonard J 2457 9895 9923
    9951 9957 10009 10990
    14498
Leonardi G 304d 478 4310
    L 7990
Léon-Dufour X 372 5245
    5270 5330 5392 5448
Leone A 13377 L 5231
Leong Tien Fock 9153
León-Portilla M 274a 8510
Leontopolis 12790
Lepargneur H 8341
Leperer S 9962

L'Éplattenier C 3843 5074
    5232
Le Poidevin R 1772
Lepori F 428
Leppin H 11059 14207
Leprohon R 11927 15402
Leptiminus 12835
Leptis Magna 9101 11702*
    12825
Lequin Y 9626
Lerberghe T van 12631
Lerchner G 14562
Leriche P 11609 11679
    12515s 12607* 12662
    13006
Le Rider G 12131* 12133
    12143
Lerinensis V 1076
Lerner G 8801 M 10114 R
    14323
Léroi-Gourhan A 11602
Lerot J 9504
Le Roux J 876s 1310 3507
Leroy H 4669
Leśniewski K 13992
Lesbos 13139-41
Lesch D 13866 K 108d
Leschert D 6228
Leschhorn W 13025
Lescow T 917 1973
Lesko L 10778 11168 11844
    12682* 12719 13825 15357
Leslau W 9253-5
Leslie B 14975
Lesnick D 14362
Lessing E 7973 14618-20
    14687
Lessnoff M 13719
Lete G → Olmo 12541*
Letellier B 13378
Letham R 3980 7720* 14523
Lethel F 8170
Létoublon F 429 9346
Letourneau A 14730s L
    1063 P 255 5355
Letti J 10048
Lettinga J 8981
Lettl J 10075

Leuba J 324f 7992
Leung Ka-lun 10963
Leutzsch M 5014
Leven C 1673
Levene J 10562
Levenson A 9857 J 792
    7766 1311 3595
Lévêque J 3139 P 11190
Lever J 77
Levesque P 15141
Levet J 416b
Levey S 9789
Levi d'Ancona M 2519
Levi della Vida G 12440*
Levick B 11351 12852
Levin C 1991 3547 M 9937
Levinas E 1178 7739 8795
    8900 14813 15043
Levine A 1882 4346 8738*
    8825 11451 B 2291 2309
    2330 2353 9159 H 2913*
    10107* L 324g 9790
    12236 12308 R 10032
Levinskaya I 4335 10228
Levinson B 2284 S 8982
Levison J 1922 4146 4895
    9619 P 4146
Levitt L 1160
Levit-Tawil D 1379 12656
Levoratti A 883 999 1150
    3103 3365 3665 3828
    4521 4724 4874 4946
    5224 5296 6241 7748*
    10989 13654
Levy B 253 T 11592*
Lévy E 9358* 11602*
Lewenstein H 13470
Lewis A †15332 B 367
    10896s 14324 C 1233s
    15043 D 13052* G 335c J
    1974 8443 8886 K 8919 N
    13409 P 7493 T 2123
    2364* 2560 10687 10723*
    10731 W 1235
Lewison A †15333
LexÄg 509
LexMA 510
Leyerle M 74

Lippy C 78 10445
Lips H von 4263 6262
Lipschitz O 12334
Lipshits E †15334
Lipson J 10108
Lirb H 13360
Lison J 7532 7537* 15290
Lissarague F 11681 13457
Lissovsky M 12289
List C 1360
List 12762*-12764 13688
Listl J 1012
Litfin D 5871
Litinas N 13296
Littell F 10108*
Little C 11882* **D** 12242
Littleman C 7344
Litton C 11537
Litvinenko Y 13451
Liuzza R 1522
Liverani M 11044 11138s
	11664 12607 13749*
	15220 **P** 12013
Livermore C 4147
Livingstone A 10791 12595
	D 12283 12300 **E** 13925*
	G 15229
Livius T 60a 11374s 11377
	11414 11421 11428
Liwak R 2194 2677 3493
	3537 9080 11009 12249*
Ljung I 1151
Llamas R 10109
Llewelyn S 4496 9401
Lloyd A 12750 **C** 14768 **G**
	199a 13504 **J** 13226
-Davies J 13505 **M** 13505
-Jones D 5460* 5818* 9302
Loader B 9741 **J** 2036 2437
	2528s 3137 3174 3235
	7401 **W** 5307
Loades A 878 7061 7255
	8331 15340*
Lobato A 14326
Lobet B 7994 10467
Lobo G 199b
Lobrichon G 643 14400
Lo Cascio E 13792

Lo Castro G 14138
Lochbrunner M 7995 14091
	15336
Lochbühler W 7233
Locher C 2434
Lochmann J 15044
Lochner von Hüttenbach
	F 11778
Lo Cicero C 207g
Locke J 14621
Lockwood G 1312 4514
	4753 **J** 3860
Lodahl M 5926 7011
Lodge J 6014
Loeben C 12704
Löffler W 25 1797 9572*
Löhr H 246 322* 5903 6230
	6253
Löning K 4263 7767*
Lønning I 7666*
Lönnqvist K 12144
Löser W 7642 14958
Lössl J 14157 14159s 14190
Lövestam E 5176
Löwe H 199c
Loewe R 9930 **W** 3998 7474
	8927
Löwenclau I von 2838
Loewenstamm S 2145
Loewenthal E 13811* **N**
	9990*
Löwy M 10008 10119
	13563
Lof L van der 2020
Loffreda S 11644 12063
	12318
Loftus W 11552
Logan A 10167 10177
	13914*
Logister W 8889
Loh J 1734
Lohfink N 200s 789 1066
	2402s 2415 2442 2484
	2751 2910 2960 2999
	3056 3309 3402 4972
	4977 7283 7347 7707
	9068
Lohmeyer M 4259 5694*

Lohrbächer A 254
Lohrmann K 14327
Lohrum M 14376
Lohse E 195 1430 4037
	7895 8343s 8385 14798
	14820
Loicq-Berger M 13256
Loisy A 14729 14746s
Lolla J 4694
Lomas F 430a 14328 **K**
	11414 13705
Lombardi P 737 14590
Lomtatidze K 9278
Lona H 6072 13970
Londey P 13077
Londoño L 8522
Lonergan B 7084 7202 7576
	8449 8608* 10365 11012*
	11071 15046-52
Long A 7063 **B** 2413 2638
	G 7012 8802 **M** 8292 **T**
	1028 3252 5508s **V** 2573
	2577 11045
Longacre R 914 3723 8982
Longenecker R 76a 4059
	5617 5981 5990 6041
Longère J 15262
Longfellow S 283
Longfield B 967 14898
	14902
Longman T 2894
Longo O 13255
Longobardo L 1076 14233
Longrigg J 13345
Longstreet C 9637
Lonis R 13767
Lonnet A 9182
Lonsdale S 10606 11758
	13379
Loofs F 13999
Loomer B 15000
Loomis R 8408
Loon M van 10682* 12563*
	12653 13337
Loopik M van 9860 9924
Looy H Van 9368
Lopasso V 2232
López J 10487 11862* **R**

2448 2546 2787 3349
3542 3589 3595 3626
3671 3686 3693s 3722
3736 3747 3788 9006
9303 9308 14677
Luther M 158 172d 206*
360d 833 1691 2063 2095
3019 3719 4444 4608
5338 5351 5732 5738
5740 5971 5988 6043
7027* 7032 7436 7538
7816 7826 7984 8077
8461 8465 8483 8674
14400* 14429-49*
Lutski J 9769
Lutterbach H 7806 14274*
14309 14319 14357*
Luttikhuizen G 10163
Luttrell A 202
Lux R 3213 3732 3981
Luxor 9218 12697-12723
Luz U 790 1313 4286-8
4317s 4695 4728 5631
8173
Luzarraga J 4351
Luzbetak L 7876
Luzi A 11515 **P** 5675
Luzzatto A 10010 **M** 9604*
Lyapustin B 13722
Lycia 49 9271 12853
12858* 12859 12867
12880s 12926
Lydamore M 8672
Lydda 12297
Lydia 11159 11162 12854
Lyke L 2047*
Lyman J 7446
Lynch E 8524 **J** 8740 14329
Lyon D 13629 14912 **J** 1470
Lyonnet S 5780
Lyons C 1314 **D** 9607 **E**
4116 7495 **J** 14772
Lyotard J 5784 15134
Lyranus N 14422s
Lys D 1298 1554 2324 7004
7309 13383
Lystra 5168 5171s

Maaluf L 4978
Ma'ani S 13297
Maarsh J Van Der 1504
Ma'arûf 12251
Maas F 8172 **J** 919 **M**
11468
Maass C 13926* **H** 9669 **M**
12458 13063*
-Lindemann G 12458
Mabee C 7759 8611
Mabillon 54a
Mabry E 14545
McAdoo H 8346 14600
Macaliano F 4173 13630
McAllister M 11703*
McAreavey J 8099
MacArthur J 1043 7721
14900
McArthur H 4514
Macaulay R 9505
McAuliffe J 10899
McBeth H 10425
macBible 595
McBride A 983 **D** 10163*
McBrien R 7667 14901
McCagg W 9997
McCall H 11558
McCambley C 2890
McCann D 15072 **J** 2895s
Maccarrone M 8100s
†15339
McCarter P 332d 2655
10991
McCarthy C 2536 6082 **D**
150 2971 **J** 935 6137 7210
7234 13792 **P** 7492 **T**
15159
McCartney D 4242 6210
7609 **G** 4856
McCarus E 9172
McCauley T 10316
Macchi A 13869 **G** 12343*
J 754 1389 1583 2186
2736 2754 9761 12302
Macchia F 5923
Maccini R 5243 5362
Maccise C 8246

McClain T 11414
McClellan M 13011 **T**
12496
McClendon J 8885
McClenon J 4474
McClure M 8347
Maccoby H 4657
McCole J 10489
McComiskey T 3654
McCone K 1204
McConnell B 13211 **R** 8880
McConville G 1603 **J** 68
2037 2393 2404s 3508
McCool G 279 14389*
McCormack B 14983
McCormick F 7630 **R** 203a
8348s 14895 **S** 3982
McCorriston J 13402
MacCoull L 2938 9244*
McCowley J 9500
McCoy A 14384 14394 **C**
14509
McCracken D 3844 4515
McCrady E 1822
McCready D 3932 **W** 4061
4475 5992 9814
McCreesh T 3268
McCreight K 3865
MacCulloch D 169 14526*
McCulloch J 54a
MacCullogh D 14466
McCulloh G 14692*
McCullough C 657 **J**
5013 6225 6231
McCutcheon E 14532*
McDade J 7545 8083
McDaniel J 7251
McDermond J 6190
McDermott B 7496 **G**
14603 14921 **J** 7576
15091
McDonagh F 4153 8550 **J**
9581
Macdonald M 5165 13291
13987
MacDonald B 2615 12356*
12414 **D** 5185 12145
12923 **H** 7169 7722 12609

14086
McWilliams W 7480
Macy G 4611 14333
Madaba 12391-5 13243
Madden N 14053 **P** 4535
Maddox R 1810 8444 8825
Madec G 203c 14165
Madelung W 204 10812
  10848 10859
Madfai M al- 13870
Madges W 969
Madigan D 10837 **P** 7533
  7858
Madras K 14253*
Madrid T 7877s
Madrigal S 14707
Madruzzo G 14554
Maduro O 10114
Maeir A 12327* 13379*
Mänz-Davies R 11496
Märtl C 14267
März C 4243 6208 6232
Maesschalck M 10318
  14694
Maestri G 14097*
Maffeis A 8102
Maffesoli M 13631
Maffre J 13035
Magall M 11503*
Magallón García A 13812*
Magazzù C 14050
Magdalen M 3983
Magdalena J 9005
Magdalino P 11046
Magen U 11933 **Y** 12282
Magesa L 8601*
Maggay M 8580
Maggi R 479
Maggioni B 4517 4639
Magill G 14760 14765
Magnani G 10319
Magnante A 2146* 5689
Magnard P 10649
Magne de la Croix P 6236
Magnelli L 8888
Magness J 4869 12227
  12346 12366
-Gardiner B 487 12403

Magnin T 1823
Magnou-Nortier E 14333*
Magonet J 2914 2937
Magrill P 12059
Magris A 10164
Maguire H 427
Mahdi M 76c 9183
Maher M
  357 1624 2146s 2323 2829
  4094 **R** 4803
Mahlmann T 7720 7725
  10261
Mahmud A al- 12515s
Mahoney E 14427 **H** 15047
  J 8470
Maia P 7504
Maidl L 3190
Maidman M 12592
Maier F 11555 13000 13022
  13024 **G** 535 880 3170 **H**
  7044 13964 14218 **J** 718
  1383 2231 2309 2789s
  4062 7308 7312 8719
  8954 9693* 9726 9792s
  9810* 9820 9925 **K** 9751
Maigret E 10466
Maillot A 8741 **S** 3241
Maimonides M 2190 3526*
  7276 9912-9929 13493
  14396
Main L 12780*
Mainelli H 2354
Mainville O 255 255* 779
  1697 4893 5736 8352
Maire T 2939
Maisels C 11504 13778
Maison-Dieu tables 645
Maissner S 5189
Maitland S 1675
Majercik R 12771
Makarushka I 8819
Makita E 11047
Makkay J 11793
Makowski J 13484
Makrakis M 10320
Makselon J 10296
Maksen K 689
Málaga 12441*

Malaise M 9221 10511
  12800
Malamat A 334 11567*
  12527s 12530 13323*
Malan F 5878
Malandra W 10810
Malaspina F 11878
Malay H 9402*
Malbon E 139 850 1140
  4174 11933*
Malcolm N 15128 **X** 15001
Malcom L 14975
Maldamé J 1676 1824 4148
  7236 8874
Maldonado R 2456
Malek E 1201 **H** 12145* **J**
  11104 11121 11523
Males J 11381
Malghurs A 14900
Malherbe A 76a 160 186
  5186 5583 5615 5701 **J**
  9932 **M** 10262
Malia 11705 13120
Malick D 4966
Malina B 2980 4319 4838
  5429 5511 13632-4 13654s
  J 11505
Malingrey A 7447 14091*
Malinowski B 13673
Malipurathu T 4420 4992
Malki R 9971
Malkiel Y 14649
Malkin J 10673
Mallard W 14165*
Mallat C 10898
Malone J 981 8983
Maloney E 4333 **G** 7811 **H**
  10234 **L** 201 5310 **P**
  12103
Malory 1224
Malschitzky H 8512
Malta 12442 → *Melita*
Maltz M 1154
Mammini S 1782
Mammoottil J 4974
Mamre 13404
Mana K 8611*
Manacorda D 11501*

Mariański J 10317
Marichal R 11984
Marin M 1699
Marinatos N 10609 12076
    13104 13355*
Marinelli E 7016 **G** 8803* **L**
    14542
Marinese L 13352
Marín Heredia F 791 3190*
    3698 13324
- Orenes A 14043*
Marini A 14334
Marinkovic P 2728
Marino A 7514 **L** 12357
    13813
Marinović L 6151
Maristany J 7999
Markham I 7008 8354
    10223 10254
Marki 13020
Markle M 13059
Markoe G 12431
Marks R 11355
Markschies C 10177 10181
    11465 13920* 14044
Marksteiner T 12867 12953
Markus R 206 11446 11455
    14166 14341
Marlé R 1925 14391 †15342
Marlowe J 13849 **W** 8904
Marmoudian M 9507
Marnewick J 3104
Maron G 206*
Maroni 13021
Marot C 2883 14555
Maróti E 11736
Marotta Mannino B 9792
    13896
Marpeck P 14556
Marquardt F 4067 7498
    8889 15287
Marquart K 7879 9518
Marquet J 7091
Márquez Rowe I 13723*
Marquis G 3582
Marra B 8446 10052 13635
Marriage A 7064
Marrow S 4433 7353 7759

Marrs R 89b 3679
Marsch A 13078*
Marsden D 953 **G** 14902s **J**
    8448 **R** 1484
Marsh C 358c 7058 3959
    3985 4068 7058 14692*
    14996 **T** 7577
Marshall B 7525 7989
    14977 **C** 3848 4775 13837
    I 77* 3819 3986 4040
    4403 4554 4870 4936
    5004 5076 5083 6104
    6158 6181 8355 **J** 2262
    8370 **L** 532 **M** 6041 7072*
    7422 7743 7768 8793
    8812 **R** 4553
Marsili S †15343
Marsilius F 14424
Martel G de 8668
Martelet G 8104
Martelli S 13631 15161
Martens G 7725 **J** 5764
Martensen D 172a
Martialis 11432
Martikainen J 14257
Martin 7881 9547 **A** 9289
    9380 11699 13052* 13475
    D 3566 8527 14335 **F**
    7065 8376 15187 **G** 12734
    12751s 12757 **H** 12613 **J**
    1441 3255 7880 8712
    11363 13636 **K** 8612
    12696 **L** 4469 10424
    10556 12943 14398 **P**
    11299 11315 13589 **R**
    1827 5584 5974 6286
    10846 13436 **S** 6199
    13779 **T** 11255 14168
-Achard R 7309
Martín J 2457 5291 13971 **L**
    14725 **M** 14480 **R** 3429 **T**
    14408*
-Bueno M 12375
-Camino M 12439*
- de la Haz J 14547
- Estalayo C 10459
- Juárez M 3703 3955
-Kilcher S 13724

-Lunas T 2169 3172
- Melquiades A 14590*
-Pardey E 12748
- Rodríguez F 7811 8035
- Velasco J 10366
Martina G 14591
Martineau E 14626
Martínez R 14988
- Borobio E 2723 9090
- Camino J 7499 15081
- de Lapera A 8864* **V** 7264
    10103
- de Pisón L.R 1823 7631
    7406 7671 8864 8890
    8915
- Díaz F 7880
- Fresneda F 3803 3955
    3989 4705 7153 7179
    7199 7418 7440 8508
    8549
- García J 7668
- Hernández M 9346*
- Lacy R 11047*
- Maza C 419
- Saura F 13509
- Sierra A 4529
- Z. J 4676
Martini C 792 1433 3105
    4410 5585 8178 10117
    14807 14904 **L** 256 **R**
    12146
Martiniani-Reber M 11524*
    11776
Martins E 11049
- Terra J 15181
Martone C 9698* 9703
    9741* 9773 10056* 11076
Martorana G 13090
Martos B 10468
Marty F 391 †15344 **M** 78
    882 985s 1024 1061 14848
    14904* 15063
Martyn 5262
Marucci C 987 3849
Marx A 2330 7770 **E** 13749
    K 5784 7687 8410 8448
    8455 8520 8534 14680* **S**
    1185 **T** 10118

Meyuhas Ginio A 431a
  10901
Mianbé Bétoudji D 2196
Micaelli C 14045*
Micallella D 11471*
Micelin É 14909
Michael T 1422
Michaelidou-Nicolaou
  I 12151
Michaels J 5513 6170
Michailidou A 9430
Michal 12297*
Michalon P 8000*
Michalowski P 5603 9154
  11139 12607
Michalski S 14483
Michaud J 4642 8694 **R**
  2022 2919
Michel A 3010 **C** 477
  10799* 12561 12590* **D**
  8985 9045 14651 **J** 15217
  M 10249 **P** 10286 **S** 13380
  T 13862 **V** 373 **W** 3131
  3136
Michelet J 845
Michiels G 15348 **R** 7614
  7883
Michniewicz W 3363
Mickel T 4130
Mickelsen A 883
Midant-Reynes B 12793
Middleburgh C 7312 11458*
Middleton J 1704
Midgley M 1829 1860
Midian 2124 2189 12849
Miegge G 7669 **M** 5338
  5349
Mielcarek K 4987
Mielczarek M 11683
Mielgo C 524 1591 2467
  2572 4705 11002
Mieroop M Van De 12526*
  12556 12578 13641 13728
  Z van de 12556
Mierse W 12827
Mieth D 8738*
Migdal J 13861
Migeotte L 13464 13720

Migliardi Zingale L 9405
Migliasso S 1726 5354*
Migliore D 326 374 4443
  7670 8533 8926 15297 **R**
  7884
Miglus P 11631
Migne B 14681
Mignon J 13892
Mignot X 9502 9507 9509
Miguel González J de 7793
Míguez N 4899
Mikasa T 11506
Mikelson T 7044
Mikocki T 11937 12084
Milanese G 10633*
Milanesi G 10321 **S** 11196
Milani C 13105 **M** 3347*
Milano A 4076 8743 **L** 480
  12533
Milavec A 13976
Milazzo F 13779 **G** 7030 **V**
  14203
Milbank J 8450
Milde H 11844
Mildenberg L 12152 12152*
Mildenberger F 7171 7238
  8940s
Mile M 9431
Miles G 3848 **M** 14167 **S**
  1845
Milet J 346 5155
Mileta C 6145
Miletto G 1380
Miletus 12051 12954-6
Milevski I 9670 12214
Milgrom J 907 2324 2327
  2310 2320 2335 2352
  2355 2362 9579 9739
  10715
Milhau M 8257
Milik J 9655 9699 12212
Milikovsky C 2753*
Milikowski H 9795
Milingo a 8658
Milis L 14339
Militello C 375 8695 8742
  8804s
Millar F 11275 11331 11357

  13781 **G** 2495 2522
Millard A 326* 2037 2319
  2664 9008 11049 11049
  11140* 11504 11734
  12217* 12409 12420*
  12589 13548 **M** 2320
  2897* 3108
Millás J 7697
Millefiorini P 1783 1820
Miller B 12105 **C** 918 1917
  5147 7011 15153 **D** 4777
  5264 7837 8538 9530
  9717 **E** 5299 14765s **I** 6 **J**
  216* 1088 1624 4778 7066
  11003 11009 12386 13584
  K 3403 13248 **M** 11812*
  P 597 2391 2706 2942
  2955 2985 3345 4777
  8179 9508* 9769 13981
  14602* 14709 **R** 1084
  1611 4176 4237 7346
  7349s 9620 10123 10271
  10321* 13455 **S** 3614
  10000 11794 11845 13083
  T 10460
  -Collett S 12052
  -McLemore B 7175
Millet A 9147* **L** 7172 **O**
  2063 14517
Millett M 11371 13729
Milligan 9297
Mills G 1879 **J** 988 8321 **W**
  586 598 1573 4322 4779
Milne B 5252 **P** 12105
Milner N 11732 12922
  12959
Milovanović-Barham
  Č 14113
Milton J 1238-40
Mimbu K 10673*
Mimouni S 8696 9635*
  12198 13824*
Mina abu 12791
Minas M 145
Minde H van der 1259
Mindling J 4080 8358
Minear P 1645 1677* 4202
  7632

Mongrovejo T de 8525
Moniclas X de 557
Monloubou L 803
Monloup T 13031
Monnot G 10834 14099
Monreale M 1488
Monro A 4539
Mons Claudianus
 9377 13168
Monsacré H 12554
Monsengwo L 5336
-Pasinya L 5180
Monshouwer D 5374 8211 **J**
 5218
Montagnes B 14806
Montagnini F 2790 5409
 6060 7610
Montague G 4281 7534
 7813
Montan A 5100
Montaut A 430d
Monte Sirai 12443
Montecalvo S 11058
Montefiore H 7672 8047
Monteil P 9279
Monteleone C 1319
Montero S 11600
- Carrión D 9592
Montesi G 208a
Montevecchi O 1434 5023
 9404 12797* 13691
Monti 10087
Montini P 8754*
Montserrat D 9413 10197*
 10674 **J** 7886
-Torrents J 10165
Moo D 3819 5735
Moody J †15350
Mook M 13123 **W** 11544
Moon J 12629
Mooney C 7152 **E** 14674 **H**
 15048
Moor J de 334 2410 2504
 10725s
Moore B 480* **G** 2872 4587
 J 4643 **L** 7228 **M** 1608
 2373 12047 **R** 2719* 3274
 10460 13618 **S** 3851 4177

4734 4780 7135 7771
Moorehead C 12972
Mooren T 10368
Moorey P 11507 11643
 11813 11967* 12302
 12566 12612 12653 11527
Moorhead J 4857 5549 5562
 T 12140
Moormann E 12944 13153·
Moorsel P Van 8698 11528
Moortel A van de 11704
Moortgat-Correns U 9155
Mopsik C 6086 9950-2
Mor M 10036 12305
Mora C 10684 11990
 13801* **F** 10534 10610*
 10766 **V** 3734 4323 7736
-Lomeli R 8597
Moral A 5371 8424
Moraldi L 3388 9630
Morales J 1813 1926 14009
 W 9899
Moran G 10412* **W** 9156
 12727s 15303
Morán C 3989 7473 15106
Morand G 1928
Morandi Bonacorsi
 D 12524*
Morani M 10598
Morano Rodríguez C 1487
 2541 2639
Moranski M 9303
Morant M 35*
Morard F 10218 14245
 14262 **M** 7147
Moraw P 15364
Mordek H 67b
More T 8756 14459s
Moreau A 10674 **D** 1601
Moreh S 11557
Moreland D 84 **J** 1794
 1831-3 **M** 4246
Morely J 14561
Moreno P 11938
-García J 9218*
-Hernández A 2541 2639
-Villa M 7246
Moreos S 11705

Morerod C 7530 14458
Moreschini C 375b 14114
 14126 14204
Moretti A †14351
Morfino M 147* 3173 3404
 9829
Morgado J 5160
Morgan C 11738 **F** 257a **L**
 13148 **M** 208b 10650
 11359 14813 **P** 8432 **R**
 1167 3825 4745 4950
 5242 5287 5305 5584
 5669 5679 5812 5851
 6286 7417
Morgen M 5308 5359
Morgenstern F 14169
Morgenthaler R 4897 **T**
 1272*
Mori M 11506 12949
Moriarty F 1971 3556
Morigi Govi C 11530*
 12817
Morisi L 2038
Moritz T 3871
Morla Asensio V 3214
Morland K 6075
Morley J 12685
Morocco 10881*
Morony M 10840
Morpeth N 11470
Morray D 12965
Morray-Jones C 9955
Morrice W 4510
Morris B 13875 **C** 13b
 10221 13755 14341 **G**
 2115 3673 **I** 300c 481*
 12106 12118 13019 13576
 13603 13644 13697 **J**
 4591 15009 **L** 3819 4289
 6061 6154 **P** 1929 **R**
 7030* **S** 8740 11845*
Morrison C 528 **J** 9567
 11714 15169 **K** 14170
Morrissette J 12557
Morrissey M 11051
Morrisson C 12154
Morscher E 14381
Morse C 5

Munn M 484 11684
Munro I 9219 10767 **J** 334
-Hay S 12157
Munz P 1804
Muñoz J 573
- Iglesias S 4351
- León D 989 3601 3343
  3428 4204 5514
- Nieto J 4970
- Ramírez G 3702
Muoneke B 5336
Mura G 884
Murad A 8529
Muralt L 14340
Muraoka T 1450 1456 8957
  8974 8990 9141 9303
  9308 9678 Muratore
  S 1836 15052 15211
Muratori 1084
Muraviev A 13426*
Murdoch B 145 **I** 8336
  14426
Murnane J 12735
Murnion P 15179*
Murphy A 7734 8802
  14403* **C** 1525 **D** 9558 **F**
  1174 5515 9620 15350
  G 1837 **J** 8622 **N** 1838 **R**
  203b 1544 2177 2898
  2965 3214 3217s 3221
  3224 3236 3254 3281
  3292 7386*
Murphy-O'Connor J 495
  4215 5134 5606s 5668
  5735s 5746 5830 5846
  5860s 5868 5886 5957
  5968 5992 6023 6067
  6122 6125 7410 8739
  12228 12265 13292 13826
  15236
Murray A 990 **D** 2535 2620
  G 4326 **J** 7964
  10651 11175 **JC** 10432
  14891 15063s **L** 7252 **M**
  4450 8237 **O** 10651*
  11449 13411* 13457s
  13732s **P** 2251 14242
  14251* **R** 984 2914 2991

3175 3415 7240
Murre-van den Berg
  H 14257
Murrmann-Kahl M 11056
Murtonen A 9014
Muš 12991
Muscarella O 11156
Musche B 11793 12657
  13512
Musella M 8454
Musgrave J 13116
Mushkat M 10124*
Music D 11756
Musielak M 13064
Mussche H 11918
Mussies G 3835
Mussner F 3864 4191 5577
  6030 7602 8699 10074
  10125
Mustafa 11975
Mustakallio K 11420
Musti D 481* 11176 13081
  13257
Musto R 7351
Muzzolini A 10823
Mveng E 8623
Mwakitwile C 8880
Mycenae 9420-38 10604*
  11762 11193 11693
  12737s 12883 12891*
  13012 13033 13079-82
  13100 13102 13115 13555
  13710*
Myers C 4781 **E** 13107
  13264 **J** 13107 13283
-/Briggs 3956
Myhill M 605
Mylasa 12025
Myllykoski M 4644
Mynatt D 1066 1381
Myos Hormos 12813s
Myre A 3992
Mysliwiec K 12782
Mystique Afr. 377
Myszor W 10206 10219

Na'aman N 2455 2646 2691
  2739 2741 12195

12425*13297
NAB 2965
Nabataea 3543 6023 9411
  12162 12365 12404-12412
  13700*
Nabe C 7142 10322*
Nabratein 12346
Naccache A 11622* 12512*
Nachman B 13803*
Nachmanides 9935 9935*
Nachtergael G 9384
Nacimento Pena A do 11445
Nackaparampil M 4290
Naddaf G 11057
Naddaff R 10652
Nadeau C 14993 **D** 5939
Nadel D 12295 12316
Nadell P 1147
Nadelman Y 12229
Nadolski B 2958
Nador G 9861
Naeh S 9739* 13459
Naerebout F 13601
Nagano S 2304
Naga'/Der 12809*
Nagel P 65 **T** 7026 10835
  W 11695 12633
Nag' Ḥammadi 10181
  10200 10204-10219
Nagler N 5113
Naguib S 14247
Nagy B 11198 **M** 60c
Nahmanides 9932
Nahon G 580 1369 9893
Najjar F 76c **M** 12363
Nakano A 9127
Nakasone S 2750
Nakata I 12531
Nakhai B 12077
Naldini M 87
Nanni C 884
Naphy W 14518
Napiórkowski S 7984 8667
  8700s
Napoleon B 11557
Naqš-i Rustam 12654
Narcisse G 503 1283
Nardi C 2700

Neusch M 378 7754 7772
Neuschäfer B 14024
Neuser W 379 14516 14557
Neusner J 283* 4071-5 4090
    9049 9790 9798-9806
    9824 9830-4 9849 9861*-
    9866 10036* 10127 10229
    10322 11840
Neve P 12886
Neven G 7531 14978
Neveu B 991 14609 L 2943
Neville D 4231 R 7031 7396
    8926 9552
Newbigin L 10396 10415
    14910 15065
Newby G 9902 M 11583
Newell L 10459 W 5668
Newing E 2649
Newlands G 4685
Newman 7104 A 10128
    10858* C 5641 J 14748-
    68 W 13270
Newmeyer S 13462
Newport J 847 7244
Newsom C 742 1574 3109
    3146 3564
Newsome J 721* 3853
    13648
Newton D 8414 I 14623 J
    24c
Neymeyr U 13956
Neyrey J 4319 4899 5363
    5608 11276
Neyton A 4477
Nezlet Batran 12749
Ngayihemhako S 8893
Ngien D 7032
Nibbi A 2173 9220 12779
Niccacci A 1996 3221 3259
    6079 8986 8989* 11994
    12372
Niccum C 5128
Nichol T 7997
Nicholls B 379* 8530
Nichols A 209 3855 4023
    7138 7935 8004 14979
    15066 L 10458* M 10344
    S 5553

Nicholson E 1591 2349* H
    13837* O 11474 12874 P
    11584 13381
Nichtweiss B 11560 15084*
Nickel J 1841
Nickelsburg G 336 3934
    9593
Nickl P 7240*
Nickoloff J 8531 14552
Nicol D 88a G 7013
Nicolai R 11058
Nicolaou I 9407 13025
Nicolas J 7507 M 4148
Nicolaus D 9942 11281
    13420
Nicole J 8005s
Nicolet-Croizat F 11421
-Pierre H 12157*
Nicolini G 11794
Nicomedia 12948
Nida E 1549 9329 9570
Niditch S 908 1739 7352
Niebuhr C 13821 H 15071
    K 4041 4213 5582 5691
    6022 7370 R 15067-72 U
    88a
Niedballa T 9553
Niederländer H †14353
Niederwimmer K 8935
    13976*
Niehaus J 1931 2587 11049
Niehoff M 2030 2116 2531
-Panagiotidis J 9281
Niehr H 2287 9079 10702
    10727s 10738s 12431
    12483
Niekerk M van 3306
Niel J 4139
Nielsen B 2387 13730 E 214
    851 2590 3793 12677 H
    4325 13715 I 2850 11726
    11740 11746 J 2343 5783
    10911 K 1932 2532 4198
    8877 11062 14911 15049
    S 1534
Niemand C 1109 5414s
Niemann F 7094 H 1119
    1698 2648 3708 7776 M

115 R 4658
Niemeyer H 12473
Nientiedt K 8744 9645
    10334 14943
Nieto J 14569
Nietzsche F 221*b 7687
    10251 14685s 14980
    15005
Nieuwenhove J Van 8368
Niewiadomski J 510
    7773 10083 10101 10129
    10416
Niewöhner F 367 14324
Niewonger R 11332
Niger flumen 12836
Nigosian S 10369 10815
Nigro L 11632 12344 12351
Nijenhuis W 210
Nijf O Van 13464
Niklasson K 12107
Nikolakopoulos K 4179
Nikolidaki K 9432
Nikopoulos V 5808
Niland C 10102
Nilsson H 12167
Nilus 13283 13306 13309
    13807
Nilus A 3166
Nimrin 12399
Nimrud 12441* 12619-22
Ninan I 5789
Nineham D 8059 13674
    14341 15007
Ninive 3718 12560* 12561
    12589 12623s
NInterp 1575
Nioku M 3559
Nipkow K 821
Nippa A 13649
Nippel W 300e 11059
    11059* 11387
Nippur 2300 9447 10808
    11986 11977 12625-8
Nishiaki Y 11578
Nisibis 12958
Nispen C van 10902
Nissen H 9525 9531 11128
    11529 12607 J 4944

10752 13266 13570
Oberhäusli-Widmer G 2178
  2200 10186*
Oberhelman S 14219
Oberholzer J 2234
Oberleitner W 12894*
Oberlinner L 4387 6019
  6183
Oberman H 212 212* 356
  14451 14518* 14534
O'Brien D 8458 10166
  14738 J 3798 8097 8459
  11252 M 1306 1589 2462
  P 5513 6077 6096
Obst H 15145 M 7730
  14705*
O'Callaghan J 1420 3277
  4427 4568 4570 5082
  5139 5371 5678 7429
  9719
Ocariz F 7508
O'Carroll M 4117
Ochs C 8181 P 257a 792
  4755 7392
Ochsner I 8810
Ockham G 14425
Ockinga B 10536 10768
O'Collins G 272 559 3936
  3994 4118 4611 4634
  4683* 4700 4707 4866
  5123 7082 7098 7139
  7509 7675 8894 9352
O'Connell K 12262 M 7299
  14720 15016 R 3405 7176
  14172
O'Connor C 11634* D
  12839 F 1241 J 8895 K
  3114 3222 3493 M 9044
Odahl C 14214
Odasso R 7487
O'Day G 5380
Oddone G 15372
Odeberg 15074
Odell D 3148 M 3594
Oden A 8745 C 15133 T
  858 1324 8942 10237
  14635*
Odendaal D 327 M 1310

Odero J 7403 7676 7689
  9923 10275 10321 10910
  14972 15032
Odisho E 9130
Odo T 1938
O'Donnell C 8702 J 7535
  14173 14648 14960
O'Donovan O 8369
Oegema G 7371s 11881
Oehlke H 14486
Oelmüller W 3101
Oelschlaeger M 7241s
Oelsner J 2263 12626
Oeming C 8925 M 1082
  1091 2243 2611 2937
  3121 9058 9081
Oenoanda 11732
Örsy L 993 8005*
Oesch
  J 1387 1396 2118 2544 34
  16 9303 10089
Oesterreicher J 10129
  †15354*
Özfırat A 12913
Özgüç N 89a 12951 T 89a
  12951
Öztuncay B 13285
Özyar A 11941
O'Fahey R 9186
Ó Fearghail F 4972* 5070
Offer Y 8958
Offermann U 14405*
O'Flaherty C 7890*
'Ofrat 12301
Ogawa A 4327
Ogden D 9363 J 11805 S
  8880 10417
Ognibeni B 1366 9015
O'Gorman J 8854
O'Grady J 3995 5108 6011
  8110 R 8656
O'Halloran M 209
Ohalo 12316
O'Hanlon G 7033
O'Hara J 10537
Ohlhafer K 11105
Ohlig K 7806
Ohly F 1678

Ohm Won Shik 1649
Ohnesorge S 3584
Ohr K 13201
Ohrenstein R 13732
OIAc 696
Oikonomou E 7243
Oinoanda 12959
Okambawa W 769
O'Keefe J 13940 M 6275×
O'Keeffe M 7547
O'Kennedy E 7890*
Okure T 5205
Oladipo E 8561
Olafsson S 8987
Olasagasti M 7503
- Gaztellumendi M 4288
Olasky M 8370
Olávarri E 11814
- Goicoechea E 6116
Olbasa 12960
Olbia 12961
Olbricht T 89b 330c
Old H 7815
Oldfield K †15355
O'Leary S 5562
Oleson J 12287 13320
  13700*
Olin J 89c 14194 14532
Oliphant M 13274
Olitzky K 9787
Oliva Mompeán J 9037*
Olivar A 1046 8112
Olivares E 752
Oliveira F de 10497*
-C. J 5518
Olivelle P 10966
Olivera F 5440
Oliver Alcón F 7115 8722
Olivetti O 1509*
Olivier G 12178 H 327
  12358 J 9433s 13101
  13224 13733
Olivieri S 7441
Olivott S 6064
Olkhovski V 12108
Ollenburger B 1082 7352
  7639 8912 R 7639
Ollig H 10640 11012

Otoćnik V 1000
O'Toole J 14717 **R** 4589
  4737 4900 4936 5188
  5703 8030
Ott H 10417 11061* 15026
Ottati D 3998
Otten H 12888s **W** 368*
Otto A 11991 **E** 163* 1889
  2263 2265s 2346 2407
  2421 2428 2480 2982
  3595 3769 7328 9078 **R**
  7815 8583 10265 14911
  15133
Ottosson M 2041 11062
Otzen B 89e 9810*
Ouaknin M 1276
Ourliac P 11384 13838*
  14279
Oury G 651
Overbeck F 14688 15075*
Overholt T 10370
Overman J 4078 4329 12309
Overstreet R 5279
Ovidius 2315 10532 10546
  13318 13435*
Oviedo L 358a 7682 8294
  8419 14840
- Torró L 7246 8943
Owen D 342* 444 2300
  11698 12578 12628 **G**
  12736 **R** 13877
Owens E 12963 13377 **G**
  9432 **J** 9187 **R** 1345
Owst G 14359
Owusi-Antwi B 3646
Oxus 11530 12663s
Oxyrhynchus 2881 9386
  9391s 9410 9413 9416
Oyen G Van 4225 4433
  4785
Ozaeta J 4705 5139 7741
  13946 14537 14676
Ozanne I 13082

Pablo Martín J 9633*
Pacaut M 14282 14338
Pace E 10286 **S** 8831

Pace nella Bibbia 257b
Pacelli D 8034
Pachis P 10199
Pacho E 366*
Pachomius 10968
Pack E 10090
Packer J 13167*
Packull W 14556
Pacomio L 5236 8184
Paczkowski M 13909 13929
  14084
Padgett A 126 5909 7034
Padilla M 10600 **S** 8539
- Monge A 2006
Padovano A 15061
Padovese L 328s 5271
  12895 13929 14231
Paestum 10503* 13206-9
Paffenroth K 4367 6000
Pagan G 12491
Paganelli R 814
Page C 13225 **H** 3688 **J**
  14764* **R** 7061
Pagé J 7891 **N** 381 **R** 995
Pagels E 1936
Paget J 13962
Pagis D 9903
Paglia C 11848
Pagliaro A 90a
Pagoulatos G 12810
Pailin D 409* 7035 7140
  10263 10322* 14582
  14601
Paillard J 4660
Paillerets M de 14391
Pain J 1029 1538 8048
  14160* **T** 4478
Paine T 14619
Painter J 5206 5332 **K**
  11583 11867 15401 **R**
  10569
Pairault-Massa F 11849
Pakoczy S 10371
Pakrasi M 12780*
Pak Yeong-Sik J 5670
Palache J 920 925
Palácio C 7472 8282
Palagia O 11666 13053

Palaima T 13472
Palamas G 7532
Palamidessi S 13352
Palaver B 10083 **W** 1109
  7773
Palazzo E 11882 14345
Paleani M 12065
Palener-Friedrich G 7962*
Palestrina 12008* 13355
Paley S 12622
Palliser M 14420
Pallottino M 11422
Palmaitis M 12358*
Palme B 4979 9337
Palmer A 9142 9642* **D**
  5077 **F** 9510 **M** 7235
Palmyra 12513 12536*-
  12541 13708*
Palomino López S 8533
Pals D 11039 **J** 13419*
Paltiel E 11380
Pałuch K 1111
Palucki J 13966
Paluzzi M 13352
Pambrun J 1707 1759 1803
  7196 15090
Pamminger P 10769s 12751
Pamphylia 13692
Pamukkale 12944
Panagyotou E 14116
Pancaldi N 14048
Panciera S 13160
Panckhurst R 1546
Pandžić B 14628 **E** 14628
Panella F 263
Panessa G 13338
Pang A 7284
Pangallo M 9926
Pangritz A 14487 14997
Pani G 5738 5796 14013 **M**
  11333s
Panier L 4967 15187
Panikkar R 3223 7337 7651
  7947 8182 10232* 10258*
  10323 10372 10967 15011
  15075s
Panimolle S 534
Pankhurst R 13800

3697
Paulien J 1421 5481 5522
    5542
Paulovics I 12030
Paulsen H 6273 6283
    13955*
Paulus A 7475 10912
    14258*
Paulus VI 394 15084
Pauly W 962
Paupert C 11884
Pausanias 11224 13234
    13078* 13236 13240
    13244 13249 13252s
    13257
Pauwels D 13840
Pavan M 91
Paverd A van de 8900 F van
    de 1914
Pavia N 3724
Pavis d'Escurac H 11604*
    13249
Pavolini C 12060
Pawlak M 13447
Pawlas A 8461
Pawlikowski J 359c 2235
    9910 10108 10110* 13804
    14985
Pawlowicz Z 10464
Pawlowski Z 3044*
Pax E †15358
Paximadi G 996
Paxman D 14621
Paxton F 14347 N 8063
Payen P 10603
Payer P 14348
Payne D 2550 G 2874 J
    10882 12818 R 10436
Payton G 3422 R 11545
Paz D 14689
Pazzi R 4661
Pazzini D 5338 M 1465
    2180 9121 9720
Peacock D 12814 13168 S
    10238*
Peacocke A 1844 10311
Peale N †15359
Pearcey N 1845

Pearse M 13923
Pearson A 13038 B 27 3878
    6273 10167 12779 14260
    14774
Peatfield A 12068
Pecchioli Daddi F 10684
Pecci F 734 4641
Pečirková J 12588 12623
Peck A 10012 W 9234
    11558 12700 12707
Peckham B 3709
Pedde F 12635
Peden A 2158 11107s 14285
    W 383 10264
Pedersen A 15000 P 12855
    12940 S 303a 4198
Pedersén O 12587
Pederson A 8416
Pedrini A 14769
Peel D 347*
Peels H 2445 3263
Peinado Muñoz M 14425*
- Peinado M 13930
Peirce C 14603 14690
Pekary T 12109
Peklaj M 3539 4213
Peláez J 3856 5082 5265
    5769
- del Rosal J 9926* 12078
Pelagius 5739
Pelchat M 384
Pelczyński G 3406
Peled R 9680 M 12310
Pelikan J 11885 13931
    14057
Pell M 3735
Pella/Fahil 11994 12400-3
Pella G 8005*
Pelland G 2493 4923 5217
    5737 7141 10243 13973
    13980 14005 14014 14176
    14186 l4349
Pellegrini A 10287 14425
Pellegrino E 365
Pelletier A 3192* M 3724*
    4079
Pelling C 11307
Pellistrandi C 12230

Pelon O 477
Peltenburg E 13015
Pelzel M 15050
Pemberton C 8761 8167
Pena A 11445
Penchansky D 898
Penco G 15328
Pendergast J 10556 14178
Pendlebury J 12823
Penglase C 1743 10614
Penham D 3842
Penkower J 1382s
Penna R 2622 3907 4412
    4517 4932 5587 5608
    5634 5642 5770 5809
    6040 6063 6089 7487
    8371 9344 13653
Pennamen V 10507
Pennant D 2098
Penney D 9744
Pennington B 15164*
Pennock M 997
Pennoyer R 2655
Pentazos E 13067
Pentecost J 4966 6234
Penzenstadler J 3111
Peña R 13904 14212 14212*
Pepuza 14044
Peradotto J 10595
Perani M 164c 1382 1384
    1461 2907 3663 9792s
    9800* 9585* 9835 9835*
    9872 9904
Percival T 14639
Perdue L 3112 3122 3224
    7396*
Perea A 13735
Perea Yébenes S 11690
Pereira Ney B 15181
Perelli L 10538* 11423
Perelmuter H 2944 3062
    4080 10102
Pérès J 4393 7534 8071
    9641* 9642
Peretto C 483
Peretz A 11326 M 11519*
Pereyre A 10131
Perez C 12158 M 3379

Phelps J 349c **M** 2139
Philae 12809-11
Philias G 7817
Philip G 12315 12402 12416
Philipp H 13087* **T** 11063
Philippak-Warburton I 431b
Philippart G 4460 14192*
Philippi 6098 13088
Philippon A 10514
Philistaea 2566 13295*
Phillips A 1605 **D** 4480
  10279 **J** 5237 10491
  13834 **N** 2265 **T** 14631
Philo A 2149 2267 2728
  4089 5933 9613-9627
  13389 13448* -
  Pseud 4907 7381
Philodemus 10633*
Philonenko M 3592 9598
Philostratus 4469 4481
Philoxenus M 1497
Phipps W 1159 4081
Phocylides 3874 3882
Phoenicia 9088-9106
  12420-12454 13010 13703
  17321*
Phokis 13089 13556
Phrygia 9269 12852 12858s
  12924
Piacentini P 12677s
Piaget J 7043
Piaia G 108c
Piana G 7270
Piattelli D 5133 6146
Piazza O 15213
Picard O 13067
Piccirilli L 11416
Piccirillo M 4390 11644
  11974 12016 12172 12232
  12362 12380 12391
  12393-7 12405 12408
  12418* 13275 13813
Piccolomini R 14177
Picht G 4170 14794
Pickering S 1435
Pickstock C 1965 8214*
Pico M 14424 14427
Piehler P 1221

Pienaar D 2692 11508
Piepke J 8629
Pieraccioni D 92
Pieralli L 1429 1626 3281
Pierard R 10425 13902
  14939
Piérart M 484
Pierce R 7285 9226
Pierelli L 1343
Pierini F 567
Pieris A 8110* 8463 8630
Pieronek T 92*
Pierre M 8238 9600 14251*
Piers Plowman 1230-2
Pierucci A 10905
Pietersma A 1475 6200
  9643* 12383
Pietrangeli C 15272
Piette A 10466
Pifano P 561 8859 14871
Pifarré C 7450*
Pighin A 8892
Pigna A 8168
Pijoan J 14428
Pikaza X 1937 3343 7179
  7409 7581 7774*
- Ibarrono X 4786
Pike N 10325 **S** 5562
Pilch J 743 4773 8611
  11648* 11777 13654s
Pilgaard A 3602 3617 4731
Pilhofer P 13956*
Pilhover P 6106
Pilkington C 333
Pillinger R 11886
Pina Polo F 11315
Pinault D 10860 **G** 15297*
Pinch G 10772
Pinches C 7251
Pinckaers S 215 503 8372
Pindarus 3805 9366
Pindel R 5643
Pinder M 11169
Pinellii i Pons J 93
Piñero A 601* 3856s 4149
  9309 9671*
Pingree D 13257*
Pinnock C 953 5915 7743

  8912 10419 15085 **J** 8672
Pinto C 3296 4461 5321*
- León A 2148 9044
Piotrovsky B 12984
Piper H 879 **J** 7892
Piperno M 11589*
Pippin T 330b 2654 5519
Piraeus 13058 13468
Pirart J 9445* 9450*
Piras A 3199
Pirenne-Delforge V 10572
  12428*
Pires Lopes F 7540 7617
  10458 14836
Piret P 1326
Pirola T 3118
Pirzio Biroli Stefanelli
  L 11573 11575 11795
Pisano S 1334* 2535 3660
Pisarek S 9867
Pisarevsky N 11708
Pischikova E 12110
Pisidia 49 12852 13692
Pissarek-Hudelist H †15360
Pitard W 9105
Pitassi M 14634* 14635
Pitcher E 4389
Pitschikjan I 12664
Pitta A 5644 5732 5805
  6014 6120 13651
Pittau G 387 998 8111
  14952
Pitt Rivers A 11551
Pitts R 11569
Pius VIII 14639* **IX** 14769
  14747 14805 **X** 14769*
  14805
Piveteau J 13534
Pixner B 13820
Pizzorni R 8373
Pizzuti C 1248
Places É des 14104
Placher W 172h 1804 3858
  7036
Plácido D 11290 15278
Plag C 5772
Plaice N 9981
Plank B 224b 8007* **P**

Porsch F 1946
Porte D 10539
Porten D 9131
Porter A 8648 **B** 11144 **C**
5761 **D** 823 **G** 4708 **H** 94*
J 1654 1739 2449 2599
8747 11649 13618 **S** 45
257c 330c 909 930 3859
3868 5192 6234 9310-12
9332 9348 9511
- de Lazo A 14786
Portier W 666 1077 7512
Portillo A del †15362
Porton G 9812 9834
Portugali Y 12349
Posadas J 11437
Poseidonia 13206-8
Posidonius S 9752* 10610*
11166
Possehl G 12665s
Possekel U 7179* 14417*
Postgate J 5603 11145
11796 12562* 12568
12582 12626 12636 **N** 486
12597 12601 13794
Potcher O 99c
Potgieter A 3736 10695
Pothoff A 11778
Potin J 3943 4001 4648 **P**
4667
Pottenger J 8536
Potter D 11315 11749
Pottmeyer H 95 1262
Potts A 11849* **B** 12159 **D**
413c 11975 12640 13382
T 9572
Potworsky C 14960*
Poucet J 11301 11424
Pouchet J 14081 14106
Poucouta P 5205
Pouderon B 1081 13914
13960s 14003*
Poulain P †15363
Poulat É 1791 1853 4119
7964 10267 13932 14723
14861 15166
Poulsen H 9052
Pounder R 11917

Pounon 12373
Poupard P 216* 1853
Poupet P 12793
Pourkier A 14103
Poursat J 13080
Pouzet L 10838*
Powell B 9531* **E** 4291
5207 **J** 13839 **M** 486 921
1327 4330 4338 4955
5080 13741 **S** 9017 10414
Powels S 9017
Power D 4611 8059 9556
Powers J 10271 13832*
Poythress V 899 5387 5485
5571 5977
Pozo C 8898
Prachner G 6150
Prades J 7818 10331 13656
15053
Pradines M 10267
Praetorius I 13911*
Prag K 12386
Praglin L 1132
Pralong A 13002 13005
Prandi C 10220 15122
Praschniker C 12927
Prasse K 9257
Pratico D 12291 **G** 12367
Prato G 737 740 1581 2233
2324 2393 2724 3817
9587 9594* 9792 9875
11483 12184
Pratscher W 6291
Pratt K 65* **L** 10633
Prayon F 12859 12870
Prebish C 10932 11741
Precedo Lafuente J 1962 **M**
3262
Preisigke L 9397
Preissler H 12549
Premper W 9517
Premsteller V 3318
Prendergast T 4899 15340
Prenner K 863*
Press V †15364
Pressler C 2407
Preston R 8464
Prete B 4377 **S** 95*

Pretorius E 6015 6292 **M** 84
Pretot P 5053
Preus J 14525 **R** 3403
Preuss C 12708 **H** 2291
2403 7310 7397 †15365 **L**
3225
Prévost J 2916* 5471 5520
8296 10467
Prewitt T 1650
Price C 1776 **G** 606 **J** 8988
11361 **M** 12148 12160
12162 12164 13025 **R**
8237 9389 11449 **S** 12866
13773 **T** 475
Prickett S 838 1186 1302
14665*
Pridmore J 3105 5250 10410
14852
Prien H 7945 8465 14553*
14874
Priene 12962
Prieur A 4905 **J** 7978 8028
10312 13774 14943 15168
Prigent P 1700 11864
Prignaud J 5606
Prijs L 1370 7311
Primavesi A 7251*
Primiano L 14827
Princeton Sem.publ. 653
Principe W 7678 14392*
Pringle D 12338 13839*
Prins J 1001
Prinsloo W 1321 3029 3043
3748
Printzipa G 654
Prinzivalli E 2917s 13957
14025
Prior J 105 8631 **M** 4988
6030
Priotto M 3314
Pritchard L 14644
Pritchett W 11201 13227
13227*
Probst H 5891 **M** 14585
Procházka S 94 110*
124 12258 13297
-Eisl G 20
Prockter L 4082 9593*

Quṣayri 10856
Quseima 12278
Quṣeir 12813
Qustul 12843 13351*

Raab K 1144
Raabe P 1603 5293
Raaflaub K 431c 11317
    13771
Raban A 12287 12447
Rabb T 11067
Rabbie E 372 14544
Rabello A 11475
Rabenau M 2818
Rabenich S 11446
Rabiej S 5309
Rabinovich A 11512 **R**
    12101
Rabinowitz I 744
Raby J 12232
RAC 512
Racca T 6259
Race A 291 7659
Racine J 13774
Rackley S 11247
Rackman J 2082 **M** 97
Rad G von 1627 1680 3236
    3607 4182
Rad Shaqrah 12523
Radak 9936
Radcliffe E 7679 **T** 1167
Radermakers J 5179
Radici Colace P 9313 9339
Radke G 1912 11202
    11287* 11475*
Radl W 4870 5057
Radley L 11888
Radmilli A 98
Radt S 13258 **W** 12906s
    12912
Radtke B 13259
Rae M 389*
Raeck W 12906
Raeder J 12962
Räisänen H 5818 8946
Raepsaet G 11502 11605*
    12046

-Charlier MT 10513 10545
    11379 11394 11408 13659
Raevsky D 13546 13551
Rafailidis N 4224
Raffelt A 14626
Rafferty J 8189
Ragness M 1030
Ragone G 12956 13242
Raguer H 2903
Ragusa J von 14566
Raguse H 1263 5529
Raheb M 13879
Rahmani L 12111
Rahner K 7152 8078* 8191
    8218 8342 10972 15086-
    95
Rahtz S 708
Raineri O 3744 9252
Raines W 741
Rainey A 2740 9158 10982
    11005 12322 13265 12725
    F 11561 †15368
Raison J 13117
Raitt J 14487*
Rajak T 9813 11411 11264
Rakotoharintsifa A 5870
Rakover N 2275 2278 2289
Ralph M 741 794 1651 3905
Ralston H 8633 **T** 1435
Ramâ 3538
Ramage N 11929
Ramakrishna 10957
Ramban 9935 9935*
Rambaux C 14237
Rambo L 10373
Ramelli M 13413*
Ramet S 14916
Raming I 8813
Ramírez Ayala M 1883
    7664*
- Fueyo P 5587
Ramisch H 85
Ramlot L 7383
Rammant-Peeters A 13286
Ramón de Diego J 4970
Ramos F 4347 5371 5500 **L**
    7237
-Lissón D 3193

Ramsaran R 5864
Ramsay W 745 5539
Ramsey 8347 14748 **B**
    10268 11869 **P** 217
Rand J du 5255 5450 5508s
Randall I 10470
Randi E 98*
Randolph D 1213
Randsborg K 12197 12961
Rang J 1329
Ranieri A 3259
Ranke-Heinemann U 795
    4364 8112 8375
Rankema J 3554
Rankin R 8880
Rankov B 11653 11714
Ranzato A 116 5432
Rapa R 6015
Rapalino E 14050
Raphals L 9351
Rapin C 9412
Rapley E 8748
Raposa M 10269 14690
Rappaport U 2843 9652
    11272* 11968*
Rapske B 5164 5191s
Ras Kaimah 13365
Ras Šamra 12482 → *Ugarit*
Ras Abu Ma'arûf 12251
Raschke W 11742
Rasco E 4816 4892 4971
    5038
Rashbam 9932
Rashi 1628 2068 9930-2
Rashkow I 1652 2055
Rasmussen A 8466 **D** 8375*
    L 10300 14999 **N** 99a **S**
    13821
Rassam H 11553
Rassart-Debergh M 9246
    11875* 12458*
Rast W 15108*
Raster 11824*
Rataboul L 14635
Ratcliffe R 9188
Rathbone D 13448 13737
Ratko P 1701
Ratschow C 7629

Reiterer F 13c 3330 3337
    9067
Reites J 7067
Reitsema G 9558
Rejwan N 10908
Reling H 4788
Reller J 5739
Remaud M 7313
Rempel J 4613
Remus H 3862 15232
Remy G 7728 8951
Renan E 4027 14770
Renard J 4150 10861s 10909
    L 538 4115 7643 8169
    8834 9923
Renaud
    B 2233 2625 2650 3493 36
    64 14802
Renault M 14731
Rendsburg G 2130 3197
    3697 8966 8987 9135
    12487
Rendtorff R 746 758 1091
    1330 1593 1606 2199
    2330 2897* 5819 8924
    13860 T 15167
Renek G 8634
Renfrew C 10696 11509 J
    13419*
Rengen W van 12507
Renger J 13738
Renick T 7350
Renkens J 9512
Renner A 10135 L 9596
-Volbach D 11779
Renninger W 2069
Rennings H †15369
Reno B 8388 R 1779
Renoir A 100
Renoux C 5462
Rensberger D 5208 5293
    5455
Rentrop J 2705
Renwart L 1919 7085 7513
    8248 8943 8951 13838*
    13924 15020
Renz J 9018 9085
Rephaim 12214

Repicky R 8111*
Repohl F 15066
Resch A 4556
Rese M 4382 4876 4910
    6188
Resenqvist J 436
Resner A 4272
Resnick I 1938 8124 14360
Resta Barrile A 14047*
Resto A 3972
Resweber J 887
Retenstreich N 14784
Retief C 3661
Rettig J 5238*
Reuchlin J 9947 9970*
    14628s
Reumann J 8116 8764 8948
Reuschel W 453
Reuss E 14713 V 14691
    14691*
Reusser C 12903
Reuter E 2749 T 1361
    14360
Reved 12279*
Revel-Neher E 1372 11889
    11893
Reventlow H 101 257e 330d
    2065 3400 3410 3773
    7354 7775 8393 8935
    9069 13934 14677
Revilla F 11890
Reviv H 13661*
Rex J 10919 R 14453 14541
Rexine J 13136 †15370
Rey B 4001 7514 13924 R
    3943
Reyburn W 3114
Rey-Coquais J 448
Reydams-Schils G 9613
Reyes A 12999
-Mate M 301b
Reymond B 517 S 5159
Reynier C 5402 6054 6072
Reynold E 5522
Reynolds 11354 C 3064 F
    390 P 14351 R 99a 219*
    14352 S 13624 T 182*
Rhamnous 13036

Rheenen G van 8466
Rheidt K 12908 12914
Rheinheimer M 13840*
Rhem R 1028
Rhoads D 4068 4741 4834
    13905
Rhode R 1620
Rhodes P 11204 R 7419
Rhodus 202 11709 11233
    12881 13142s
Riace 11908 11954
Riad H 10759
Ribaut J 1707
Ribeiro C 15112 H 7180 I
    3843 J 4110 7789
- da Silva I 14391 15168
Ribera J 3511 9132
-Florit J 1552 3498
-Mariné R 2900
Ribichini S 10611 12434
    12495 12506 12827
RICathP travaux 664
Ricca P 7941 8705 13935
Riccardino G 7521
Ricci C 8749 L 15288
    15291s
Ricciardi A 15 1028 2360
    3319
Rice C 5111 13924* E 1277
    M 12640 R 11709 T
    11510
Rich A 3180 8468 D 8469 J
    11356 13776s
Richard E 331 4893 J 172e
    5916 10153 11334 11362
    11458 13835 L 4650 M
    10654 R 7728* 10414
    10419 10421
Richards 5649 E 5611 F
    11994 K 317 2875 R 2792
    W 5724
Richardson H 102 J 425*
    3194 8117 L 13170 13201
    M 9012 N 5645 6174 P
    5818 5902 8198 8203
    11895 W 9322 13516
Richer N 12112

-Robles J 8486
-Sierra A 14351*
Robra M 8539
Robson M 8113
Rocca G 8815
Roccati A 9215*
Rocchetta C 7819 9582
Rocha A da 2159
Rochais G 5297
Roche J 8374 **M** 12409*
Rochette B 9223
Rochettes J des 2815
Rochford D 15105
Rock P 54a
Rockefeller S 7252 14944
Rocker S 7102
Roda S 11391
Rodante S 12114
Rodd C 32a 45 54e 141
  230c 337c 1844 1848 1850
  2276 2872 2896 2914s
  2937 3189 3556 3596
  3927 3956 3990 4722
  4736 5030 5953 7245
  7329 7485 7648 7766
  8350 8356 8360 8397
  8757 8884 9006 14516
Roddaz J 11394
Rodger P 15102
Rodgers P 3883
Rodgers V 3573
Rodhe E 13836*
Rodlèy G 9673*
Rodrigue A 10008
-Schwarzwald O 9467
Rodríguez A 172b **L** 8378 **P**
  5406 14910
- Amenábar S 7181
- Carmona A 1007* 5082
  7381
- de Coro F 9905
- Garrapucho F 7774* 7894
  15036
- Izquierdo J 4586
- Panizo P 10325*
Rodziewicz M 12797
Röckelein H 8801
Roeffaers H 7664

Röhm E 10138
Röhser G 7286
Röll W 7316*
Röllig W 10694 11136
  12587 13272*
Römelt J 1264*
Römer C 109 196 10188
  10195 15375 **M** 10774 **T**
  68 1389 1580 1603 1630
  2044 2183 2210 2402
  2408s 2353 3227 3510
  3512 3515 3664 3698
  12325* **W** 9160
Römheld K 581
Røsæg N 4003
Rösel M 1551
Rössler 8977*
-Köhler U 11112
Roest-Crollius A 8593
Röttgers H 1087
Roetzel C 5662 5676
Roey A Van 70 7451*
  14247* 14260*
Rofé A 1594 14803
Rogers C 5124 **D** 7011
  14450 14917 **G** 12540
  12892 12896 **R** 1518
Rogerson D 3686 **J** 229 334
  1302 2906 3719 3755
  13280 14712
Rogge J 54b 191* 5952
  14571* 14572
Rogov A 15347
Rohmann C 11850
Rohr F 11248 **R** 797
Rohrbacher S 9998*
Rohrbaugh R 11267 13633
Rohrhirsch F 9674
Roiné C 5959
Roisel V 2547 2905 3169
  11000 14012 14019
Roitman A 2825
Rojewski A 2260
Rokay Z 3038
Roll S 4611
Rolla A 147* 716* 1680
  2148* 2634 2729 3163
  3276 3288 3328 3369

3490* 3596* 4207 4225
  7353 8709
Rolland P 3915 8119
Rollefson G 12374
Roller D 13075 **L** 463
Rolley C 11943*
Rollinger R 11146 11743
Rolnick P 8815
Roloff B 185 **E** 8952 **J** 77*
  3873 4298 5140 5478
  5523 5605 5836 7895
  13938
Rolston H 1748 7253 7255
Rolwing R 1940
Roma 12840-1 13150-93
  13226 13310 13315s
  13318 13374 13422 13438
  13447 13573 13597-13601
Romaine S 9513
Roman A 9189 **C** 7068
Romanato G 14769*
Romanides J 8008 14132*
Romaniuk K 1008 1048
Romano D 4668 9881*
  9906 10541 11825 12075
  13060* 15349 **E** 13519* **J**
  9914*
Romanos M 14130*
Romarheim A 10395
Romer E 12709 **J** 12709
Romero C 12420
-Pose E 2917 3278 5470
  5734 5470 8872 10171*
  11758* 12777 13896
  13944 13991 14210
- Recio M 11190 13699
Romm J 13260
Rommelaere C 13386
Rompay L Van 9142* 14250
Ronca I 12822
Ronconi L 11068
Roof W 14838
Rooker M 9019s
Roos E 15248
Root M 469* 8024 8059
-Bernstein R 1856
Roots I 14776
Rooy H 3581 **H van** 3674

Sandahl S 123*
Sanday W 14814
Sandberger J 2996
Sande S 11666
Sanders 4916 **D** 5713 7461
 E 4005s 4009 4088-90
 9814 **G** 12115
 14220 **J** 332d 1092 1341
 3418 5679 9836 10421s
 11488 **T** 3066 7644
Sandler W 7760
Sandner K 5114*
Sandnes K 4678
Sands K 8819
Sandt H van de 224a 5169
 5195 5698
Sanford J 13520*
Sanjian A 11880
San José Lera J 3083
Sanks T 7898 13693
Sanlaville P 12509
Sanmartín J 9106 9148*
 10487 12595
Sanna I 7131 7145
Sanneh L 8639s
Sannibale M 12116
Sans I 1926
Sansone P 9708
Sansonetti G 4622
Santa Ana J de 8472
Santana Henríquez G 9346*
Santi F 428 14393
Santiago-Otero H 394*
Santinello G 108c
Santirocco M 11430*
Santmire H 7257*
Santorelli P 2205
Santoro F 11352
Santos B 5292
- Hernández A 642 8497
- Santos D 2487
Sanua V 13881
Sanz E 9665
- Valdivieso R 520 1081
 1396 1583 3145 3241
 3458 3495 3856 3913
 4199 4728 5308 5371
 6014 6273 7736 8495

 9344 10688 13919*
Sanzi E 208a
Sapaugh G 6078
Saperstein M 9977 10058
Saphinaz-Amal N 12705
Sapin J 2967 12184 12263
 12297 12302* 12378*
 13228 13703
Saporetti C 698 2117
Saprikin S 13411*
Šaqab/Manassa 10820*
Saqqara 2114 12741-57
 13381
Saramago J 1510
Sarason R 9841
Sardini D 12290
Sardinia 12448-50 12472
 13041
Sardis 12966
Sarfatti G 9106*
Sarna J 10041 **N** 2970 14778
Sarnowsky J 14371
Sarot M 7039
Sartre M 12194* 13214
 13657
Sass B 11996
Sassmann C 2065 7775
Sasson V 2368
Sassoon D 1390
Satlow M 7330*
Satran D 2797
Satterthwaite P 798 908
 1622 2508 2895 5077
Sattler D 4615 7070 7730
Satzinger H 11532
Saucy M 4336 **R** 5564 6194
Sauer G 2155 2185
 14864 15281 **H** 7682 **J**
 12400 13339 **R** 108d **T**
 175*
Saulnier C 12233*
Saunders S 4329 **T** 10656
Sauron G 10544
Sauser E 8239 14091
Saussure F de 9515
Saussy C 8814*
Sauter G 1301 9559
Sauzeau P 484

Savage A 2947
Savasta C 1980 2070
Savigni R 1944
Savio A 12161 15250
Sàvoca G 3570
Savonarola G 3020
Savran G 2369
Savvatos C 15189
Sawyer B 14355* **D** 1148
 1574 1929 **J** 1172 3400
 3425 9006 9812 **M** 14646
 W 1559
Sax M 11997 11997*
Saxbee J 357*
Saxer V 223 14097*
Sayed A 301c
Sayés J 1945 7820
Ša'ar abu 12792
Sa'id F 12363
Sa'idiya 12415
Sbaffoni F 5467
SBF cron 11534
Sblendorio Cugusi M 9456
Sbrozi M 14448
Scaer D 4236 4274 4320
 7419
Scafa E 9435 11687
Scagliarini F 9177
Scaiola D 228 309* 526 726
 732 3276 3288 3458 3490
 3660 4292 4517 4684
 4932 4959 5223 5226
 5230 5587 5742 6014
 6280 7004 8140* 8929
 15236
Scalise C 889s 8186 14512 **J**
 8228 **P** 1165
Scandone G 12423
- Matthiae G 10708*
Scanlon T 11209
Scannone J 8505
Scarborough J 13494 13521
Scardigli B 10663
Scarfi B 129*
Scarisbrick J 14459
Scarpat G 3320 14031 **J**
 3324
Scarpi P 10178 10618

Schlosser J 2626 3864 5647
Schlott A 9227
Schlueter C 6166
Schlüter M 9837 **R** 8013
Schmalenberg G 31*
Schmaltz B 12950
Schmalz B 11254* **M** 10927
Schmandt-Besserat D 9524*
    9531s
Schmaus M 111 †15376*
Schmeling G 421 12426
    12426*
Schmeller T 4524 4825 5698
    5870 8541
Schmelzer H 10029
Schmid J 11060 **P** 8821
-Tempel U 5612
Schmidinger H 332a 7585
Schmidt A 12117 **B** 10730 **D**
    9311 9511 11781 **E** 111*
    8822 12653 **F**
2668 4091 4638 7488 9745
    10276 **G** 962 **H** 4050 8907
    11606 **J** 10547 **K** 112 649
    L 1608 1611 2083 2214
    8538 **M** 11311 11317
    14423 **R** 11946 **S** 11947
    14781 **T** 46 5468* **W**
    1744 2428 3021 3207
    3518 3535 7018 7384
    8039 10880
-Colinet A 12539
-Dounas B 12909
- Lauber G 5740 **H** 4608
- Leukel P 33c 7108
-Tempel U 5612
Schmied A 7439
Schmithals W 5269 7468
    13938 14794
Schmitt A 3313 3318 3618
    C 82 2118 2370 3425
    3471 15013 **J** 3704 14356*
    R 9294* 9445s 11151
    12644 15277
-Korte K 12162
-Pantel P 684 10579s 13464
Schmitter P 9515*
Schmitz F 1476 **J** 7097 **K**

14920 15030 **P** 8473
    12439 **R** 13810 **S** 8541*
Schmolinsky S 5480
Schnackenburg R 113 258c
    332b 4008 4412 4891
    5230 5409 5414 5453s
    5636 6063 6067 6070
    7420 7874 7895 7899*
    8381s 8385 14896
Schnapp A 11511
Schneck R 4790
Schneemelcher W 9628
    9629* 9631 9636
Schneider A 14925 **G** 520
    5070 7421 13971* **H**
    11600 12225 12741 **M**
    7635 8208 14366 **S** 5950 **T**
    571* 1090 9228 12785 **W**
    8995
-Flume G 8823
Schneiders S 891 3865 5009
    5243 8824
Schnelle U 3866 5248 5310
    5386 7190 7433
Schnider F 6280
Schniedewind W 2766s
    9044*
Schniertshauer R 8884
Schnur H 14705*
Schochet G 1647
Schöllgen G 13977
Schoenbaum D 13882
Schönberger R 658
Schönborn C 1005 **C von**
    14129*
Schoenbrun B 13060*
Schönherr A 14999
Schoep I 11635*
Schöppner L 10143
Schoeps J 536 14629
Schörf R 1988*
Schörner G 11959
Schofield L 12738 **M** 13780
Scholder K 14593*
Scholem G 1178 9954s
    10037 14816
Scholer D 105 107 604 749
    15218* **J** 5345 6227 6236

Scholl R 6144 13737
Scholtissek K 224a 1520
    4727 4768 4777 4790*
    4795 9342
Scholz B 11782 **C** 685 **H**
    10265
Schonberg D 2278 **E** 7881
Schoneveld J 5344
Schoof T 1269 14926 15104
Schoonenberg P 7038 7489
    7500 7547-9
Schoors A 70 1603 1950
    2365 3112 3298 3515
    3554 8998 13299* 14130
Schoot H 7452
Schooyans M 8325
Schopenhauer 14731
Schor R 10144
Schori K 1078
Schork R 4126
Schott E 12690 **F** 7336 **S**
    12690
Schottroff L 5531 8751s
    8824* **W** 2724 3526 4473
Schotz P 13811
Schouten van der Velden
    A 13387
Schouwey J 860
Schoville K 3504
Schowalter D 10548 11479
Schrader F 15008*
Schrage W 5718 5847 8385
Schragl F 75
Schrama M 14732
Schreckenberg H 10145
    11277
Schreiber J 4862
Schreiner J 495 1596 2202
    3409 3591* **P** 553 685 **S** 367
    1604 1705 3084 7373
    9955 9970* 9971 10047*
    10124 **T** 5811 5822
Schreiter C 11641 **R** 8014
    8014* 8641s
Schrenk S 11892
Schretter M 9161s
Schreurs N 4068 7773 8784
Schrier O 9143

Scouteris C 8944
Scranton G 1187
Scribner B 14491*
Scroggs R 1574 5545 7475
  14573
Scullion J 1631 1643 3883
  4080 7283 7778* S 10619
Scully S 10589
Scult A 1325
Scuotto E 9313
Scythia 12850 13380 13428*
  13546s 13551
Scythopolis 12313
SDB 515
Seager R 10277 13566
Seagraves R 14226
Sear F 13171*
Searby D 14308
Searle M 7822
Seasoltz R 7827
Seaver J 11454 P 14359
Seavey W 11171
Sebasta J 488
Sebaste 4390 12302
Sebastian J 7071
Sebastiani L 8754*
Sebeok T 9516
Sebesta J 8725 11783
Sebothoma W 4357
Sebott R 4191 7393 9716
Seckler M 95 1010 14618
Secretan P 14664
Sedgwick C 2317 5183 5973
  8707
Sedlmeier F 3589
Sed-Rajna G 1372 9930
  11840 11893*
Sedulius 14428*
Seebass G 206* 7627 7816
  8077 14563 H 222* 250
  2119 2359 2364 4209
  9083
Seeber D 561
Seebold E 131a
Seefried M 11611
Seeher J 12768
Seeley D 3868 3988 4673
  6117 7332

Seeliger H 14207
Seeman C 13652
Seeskin K 9928
Segal 278 A 4102 9955 E
  2829 9958 L 9969 R
  10282 13666 S 5692
Segalla G 1726 3907 4093
  4584 5313 5327 5463
  6016 8385 8950 15252
Seger J 11617
Segert S 712 2218 2365
  3270 7315 9014 15341
Segovia F 1575 4713* 5201
  5332 5419 14800 14929 J
  de 14567
Segre M 1860
Seguenny A 7454
Segundo J 1011 4337 4413
  8515 8510 8529 8543*
  8544
Segura J 8474
Séguy J 1293 4613 15122
  15273
Seibold J 8545
Seidel B 1609 H 117* 2632
  9595 11760 S 14536
Seidl T 3008 7779 U 11949
  12627
Seidlmeyer S 12691
Seif el-Din M 11940
Seif J 13939
Seifert B 3675 M 12051
Seifrid M 5590 5647 6041
Seijas G 9029
Seiler H 9517 15280* J
  14337 S 11516
Seils M 5351
Seim T 4908
Seitz C 3392 7072 8924 M
  1281
Šekem 1393 12303s
Sekki A 9053
Sekunda N 13791
Sela S 9762
Selavan I 133
Selb W 2299
Selden W 15233
Seldeslachts H 9515*

Seleucia 12630
Selge K 14371*
Seligman J 12251
Selinus 9398 12027
Sell A 8015 14514 M 9518
Sellars M 924*
Sellew P 13988*
Sellin G 4792
Selling J 287e 8016 8385
  8385*
Sellner E 8259
Sellwood D 12142
Selman F 14394 M 2755
Seltzer M 14786
Selva A 8674
Selwyn D 341* 14526*
Selz G 11815* 11985 13741
Semenchenko L 13411*
Semeraro G 5738 M 5100
  8043
Semeria G 14740
Semler J 14630
Semmelink J 9723*
Sen F 9686 9736
Seneca 6019 10525 10538*
  10541
Senff R 13009
Senger H 14405
Senior D 891 4010 4634
  4645 4650 5431s 7499*
  15383
Senn F 8217
Sennett J 7125
Senofonte C 14611
Sense W 1230
Sentis L 7019 7587
Sepe C 387 8111
Sepière M 4679
Sepphoris 12015 12350
  12350*
Sepulcre J 9633*
Serafini A 12946 M 680
Sérandour A 2783 3798
Serapion T 14131
Serbat G 11619
Sered S 10375
Sereis M 10000
Sergent B 12885 13229

Shupak N 2120 3229
Shurman M 12235
Shuruppak 12613
Shute M 11071
Sibley J 8489
Sibony D 10915
Sicari E 13667
Sichem 12303s
Sicherl M 118*
Sicilia 205 9403s 13090
    13124 13210-2 13435
    13714
Sicker M 8475 9837*
Sicking T 287f 8138
Sickinger J 9414
Sicre J 752 1505* 2535
    3365s 4483 10995
Siddle D 15333
Sidebotham S 12792
Sidebottom H 11429 11663
    11671
Sider R 5741 8476 14190
Sidon 12424* 12425 12425*
Sidorov A 14129
Sieben H 1067 4923 4935
    7339 8071 11053 14158
    14566 14707 15226
Siebenrock R 15171
Siebenthal H 8980
Siebers T 229d 288a 10327
Siebesma R 8991
Sieg F 5537
Siegenthaler D 14689
Siegert F 2852 3725 4914
    10514 13492
Siegwalt G 1861 4067 7236
    7629 8855 8951 13924
    14391
Sielepin A 5322
Siemens P 14669*
Siems H 14358*
Siepen W 10968
Sier K 9466
Sierksma F 10253
Sierotowicz T 1862
Sierra S 1963
Sievernich M 288b 8499
    8546 14524

Sievers J 123 2849 10377
    12236
Siewert P 11211 13086
Sigal P 397
-Klagsbald L 11893*
Sigmund P 8547
Signer M 3571
Sigountos J 5936
Sigrist M 2263 9449 10681
    10803 11158 11535*
    11949 11986 12529 12599
    12628
Sigüenza J de 14537
Šijaković B 10490
Sijpesteijn P 9415 13465
Siker J 288c 2025 11274
Sikka S 10315
Sikkenga E 9306
Sikor J 4042
Silanes N 7409
Silberman L 4968 N 4096
    9677 9724 11334* 11567*
Siliotti A 12693
Silius I 12429*
Siller H 119
Sills C 1332
Siloam 334 12219 12234
Šiloh 1981
Silva A da 2121 3525 12557
    I da 3843 15168 J da 5518
    M 46 847 868 1334 5262
    5815 5825 5898 6042
    6097 6119 9120 9511 V da
    6175
Silver M 13742
Silverio F 11680
Silverman D 7 10778
    12798
Sim D 4969
Simek R 13260
Simelon P 11310 13743
Simian-Yofre H 1334* 3367
    3664-6 8548
Simiat B 12541
Simkins
    R 1685 1750 1863 1929 26
    94 3688 7261
Simmel 13631

Simmons A 13014
Simmons B 6008
Simms N 9574
Simoens Y 905 972 1293
    3915 4720 5272 5300
    9344 13541
Simon B 11321 C 2513
    11852 11858 E 10551 L
    6120* M 8115 P 14411* R
    7550 8386 10023 10840 U
    3667 3726
Simón Muñoz A 4983
- Palmer J 8251
Simonati R 14639*
Simonds T 8387
Simonetti M 229e 10171
    10171* 13940 14183
    14220
Simotas P 2376 2780 3633
    7400 11010
Simpson S 11148 12659 W
    10779
-Housley P 13228*
Sinai 2232-4 12845-9 14227
Sinclair M 892 S 5267 T
    12874
Sindima H 8644*
Sindoni C 8019
Singer J 401 P 8380 13495
    T 14594
Singleton K 10273
Siniscalco P 3085
Sinkewicz R 14138*
Sinn G 7455* 14797* U
    11950 13087
Sinope 12034 12976
Sinor D 11137
Sinos S 13017
Sinus arabicus 13327
Sippar 11134 12575 12591*
    12631s
Šiqmîm 12280*
Sirat C 9909
Sirinelli J 10514 11257
Sirinian A 14112 14117
    14255
Sirks A 10552 13466
Sirota I 8710

Soares-Prabhu G 4713*
Sobeczko H 2260 7636
Sobel A 1270
Sobolewski R 12621s
Sobrero G 15343
Sobrino J 229f 4153 7538*
 8503s 8549-8551;
 bibliog.660
Socias I 5528
Socinus F 7712
Socrates 13487c 14424
Soden W von 9021 9146
 9163 10803 11149 11975
 12570 12589 12591 13695
Södergård J 10424
Söding T 809 1087 2680
 4033 4161 4225 4317
 4795 5648 5693 5705
 5717 5866 5892 6232
 6270 7256 8383 13400
Sodini J 12070
Sodom 5522
Soergel P 14459 14492
Soest H van 2647 2746
Soetens C 14639* 14781*
 14892
Soggin JA 754 1387 1632
 2106 2051 2512 3738
 3762 8967 10688 11006s
 13532 13613
Soheir B 12163
Sohn S 7287
Soisalon-Soininen I 1456
Soisson P 10732
So Ki Jong 1538
Sokoloff M 1406 9135
 9140* 9467
Sokolowski R 4618
Sola i Carrió F †15379
Solberg M 7903 8483
Soldan U 12898
Solère J 8159 14400
Soles J 13098 13113 13121
Solin H 9457 9457* 11477*
 12010
Solís Fernández E 1864
Soll W 2915
Sollamo R 11062

Sölle D 1128 1141
Solms É de 2901
Soloff R 1373
Solomon J 13438 N 10042
 10102
Soloveitchik J 9857 10011
Sommer A 14688 B 3454 D
 14969 U 4862
Sommerfeldt J 14b
Sommet J 14791
Somorja A 12
Soncino 1395
Sonderegger K 14985
Soneson J 8416 15000
Song C 4011 7551
Song Choan-Seng 7615
 8619 8646
Songer H 5062
Sonnet J 2441 2747
Sons R 1281
Soom W Van 7869 8127
 14915
Soosten J von 1889
Soper J 14931*
Sordi M 4796 11214 11367
 11400 11478 12854
Soren D 11636
Sorg J 4012
Sorkin D 10107
Sorrentino S 288d 10328
 14986
Soskice J 1167
Sot M 14414
Soto D de 14567*
Sotomayor M 14419
SOTS 69-W 333; 70-S 334
Soulen R 4159
Sourvinou-Inwood C 10620
 13148
Southard S 5650 13633
Southern P 11663 R 14382
Souza P de 11720
Souzenelle A de 1685*
Sowada K 12718
Spaccapelo N 15052
Spadoni Cerroni M 11745
Spaemann H 7903*
Spaeth B 10553

Spaey J 13277
Spalinger A 9229 11110
 11238
Spangenberg I 3150 3298 J
 7400 V 14961*
Spanier K 2610 2774 Y
 12298
Spanner D 764* 1752 1754
 1757 1813 7288 8829
 13993
Spanneut M 7271* 14091*
Spanos P 11637
Spanu D 147*
Spar I 12600
Spariosu M 10621
Sparkes B 11834 11845
 11860 11925 12054 13214
 13313
Sparks B 1561 H 1622
Sparn W 894 5753 14840
Sparr A 14932
Sparta 12112 13091s 13449
Spawforth A 13091 13214
Speck P 11898s
Speelman G 119* H 8020
Speer A 149 266b
Speidel M 10554 11667
 11689s
Speight R 3805
Speigl J 14184
Spek R van der 9156 11255
Spence I 11691
Spencer A 6254 12795 F
 4278 5077 5142 5156 H
 14359 I 14768 J 2364*
 10276 12687 N 302 13140
 R 8924 S 5565 14388
Spera S 13640
Sperber A 1412 D 9818
 13732
Sperl S 4445
Sperling S 14778 U 2949
Sperti L 11620
Speyr A von 5241 5331
Spicer M 12556
Spickard P 13668
Spickermann W 10555
Spicq C 9317-9

Steiert F 3231
Steiger M 5438 **T** 1490
Stein A 11268 **B** 9949 **D**
    11985 11999 **G** 490 **R** 895
    3869s 3891 4936
-Hölkeskamp E 13467
Steinbach W 5993
Steinberg N 2053 2262
Steiner A 11954 13172 **D**
    10621* 11215 **G** 9575 **M**
    12203 12216 12237 12243
    R 10448 10472
Steingrimsson S 3439 11062
Steinhauer G 13468
Steinhauf B 14554
Steinhauser K 7429 14160
Steinkeller P 12601 12607
Steinmann A 754 1618 3395
    3572 **W** 13911
Steinmetz D 1653 2002
Steins G 2307 2768 9036
    15190
Steinsaltz A 10044
Stella P 7041 7156 9894
    14174 14271 14477 14500
Stemberger G 581* 3228
    3606 4098 4574 7369
    9342 9747 9753 9819s
    9835 9872-5 12211 13492
    J 11072 **T** 2250
Stemper R 112
Stendahl K 7666* 9576
Stendebach F 1091 1335
    7397 9065 9075 10727
    11006
Stenger W 3871
Stenhouse J 389*
Stenico T 8128
Stepanenko V 12852
Stephens J 14493* **P** 6073
    W 14516
Sterk A 14084 **H** 8761
Sterling G 2036 2843 4917
    5137 9395 9614 11274
    11454 13956*
Stern E 2743 11711 12000
    12197* 12290 **J** 13841 **N**
    9025 **P** 2997 3460 **S** 9821

9876
Sternberg M 4182 **T** 1335
    2097
Sternberg-el Hotabi H 9230
    10781 12703
Sternberger J 2572 2592
Sternini M 11583
Sternstein J 13846
Stertz S 11372
Stetson B 10324 10414
Steuben H von 11202
Steudel A 7309* 9694
Steudler A 2104
Steuernagel C 2395
Steussy M 3639
Stève M 9449
Stevens C 8129 **G** 5541 **M**
    7520 **W** 191
Stevenson K 61 94* 4611
    4618s 7796 7825 8219
    14345 **W** 7766
-Moessner J 8757
Stewart C 1949 8148 14067
    D 1127 **F** 12848 **J** 7247
    14930
Steymans H 1604 2443
    7767*
Steyn G 5088
Stibbe M 5242 5244 5258
    5273 5280s 5396
Stichel R 1050
Stickler A 8130 8130*
Stieber M 11833
Stiebing W 11513 12183
    13340 13824*
Stiegler S 2796
Stiglmair A 3791
Stillman N 9902 9974 10045
    Y 9974 10019
Stimming M 14450*
·Stimpfle A 4669
Stine R 8880
Stipp H 3516
Stirrat R 8651
Stiver D 15173
Stobbe H 4689
Stock A 4099 4340 4342
    4482 4918 **K** 400 4424

4798 4937 5524 8911
Stockwell C 13784
Stoddart S 300b
Stoebe H 2545 2556;
    Bibliog. 661
Stoeber M 10970
Stoeger W 1859
Stöhr M 13883 **S** 145
Stoellger W 4341
Stöve E 14726
Stoevesandt H 14515
Stoffregen-Pedersen K 9256
Stok F 14028
Stoker W 9560
Stokes M 10637
Stoldt M 3908
Stoll D 8507 8527 8552
Stolle V 7190 7904
Stolper M 12602 12602*
    12644
Stolz E 2885 **F** 309 401
    10704
Stone E 2300 12618 12628
    G 7357 9679 12238 13388
    I 7315* 10152* **J** 7241
    10269 10326 10329 13262
    K 2609 **M** 1881 1950 2797
    2812 9471 9602 9694*
    9705 **R** 15068 15072
    15096 **S** 11783 12406
Stoneburner T 10257
Stoneman R 11258 12540
    13278
Stoof M 12708
Stookey L 4620
Stordalen T 1112 1621 1884
    2748 3007 13941 14195
Storfjell J 9522
Stork H 194
Storkey A 8389
Storme A 12239 **H** 1039
Storniolo I 2863
Storper-Perez D 9986
Storz S 12475
Stott J 3872 4494 5742*
    8853 8896
Stotts J 15332
Stout A 11801 **S** 14714

Suys V 10622
SVDVerbum index 662
Svenbro J 13672*
Svensson J 2488 **T** 83
Sventsitskaya T 11433
Swahnberg A 7255
Swain S 11230 13524
Swan T 9483
Swanepoel C 3232 **M** 1716 3683
Swanson B 13755 **D** 4081 **T** 5324
Swarat U 542*
Swart G 4671* **I** 3531
Swartley W 926 4264 7357*
Swartz M 9134 9960s **S** 4999
Swatos W 290 10278
Sweeney D 953 10783 11802 13469 **L** 125* 7041 **M** 67a 1730 2041 2602 3342 3408 3424s 3431 3463 3472 3481 3567 3766 3795 13618
Sweet A 1920 **J** 5489 5499 **L** 15179*
Sweetland D 6044
Swetnam J 5130 6204 6207 6243 6252 7766 9321 15234*
Swidler L 4016 8023* 10149s 10426 15019 15174
Swift L 13896
Swiggers P 8956
Swimme B 1866
Swinburne R 126 7098 7732
Switek G 8175
Sykes S 7780
Sylva D 2951
Sylwan A 1633
Symmachus 1454
Symonds R 8758
Synan E 9910 10084 **V** 5932
Synek E 8737
Synowiec J 1610 3369*
Syreeni K 4438
Syrén R 1654

Syria 12494-12588 13290s 13762 13839 13853 13866
Sysling H 7385 9929*
Syson L 11841
Syx R 4818
Szabó M 11792
Szczurek J 7592 15234
Szell T 14320
Szemerényi O 9328 9470 9484
Szennay A 12
Szentmartóni M 11*
Szerwiniack O 8994*
Szilágyi J 11803
Szostek A 8390
Szpek H 3087 3130
Szpet J 11008
Szwagrzyk T †15385
Szyszman S 9770* †15386

T aanak 12345 12351
Ṭabari 11008*
Taber B 10230 **C** 10230
Tábet M 768 827 897 1016 1070 3917 8271 13912 15170
Tabgha 12318
Tabor J 2794 4494 7323 9728
Taborda F 7819 7827 8080 8498 8655 8687
Taborelli L 13525
Tabuyo M 8714 8080
Taceva M 41a
Tacitus 430e 6148 11138 11202 11340 11352 11356 11359 11362
Taddei Ferretti C 8804 9587 9774 11757 11761 13897 14315
Tadmor H 11149*
Taeger J 5325 5499 6274
Taels J 8329
Täuber H 9418
Tafi A 5294 14815
Taft R 8198 8219s 14093 15235
Tagliacarne P 2749

Tagliaferri F 5175 **M** 14935
Taglit 12451
Ṭaiyiba 12301
Takenaka M 8656
Tal A 1393 **L** 12280*
Talatinian B 12119 12241
Talbert C 4017 4228 4554 4904 4969 5243 5262 5484 7475
Tallach J 7098*
Tallon F 11814
Talmon S 5003 9667 9711
Talon P 13277
Talshir D 13385 **Z** 9678
Talstra E 1387 1396 2673 3135 8995
Taltavull i Anglada S 7904*
Tamani G 1395 9928*
Tamayo J 7377 7599 8255 -Acosta J 4729 8913 14361
Tambasco A 5649 7348
Tamez E 7734
Tamm W 8795
Tan A 5387
Tånberg K 13300
Tandecki D 11894
Tang-e Qandîl 12656
Tångberg A 108a 2805
Tanimoto C 12759
Tanis 12789
Tannehill R 4723 4915 4955 5029 5090
Tannen D 1168
Tanner G 354 **J** 1240 11839 **K** 290* 7235 8477
Tanzella-Nitti G 1867 7173
Tanzer S 4018
Taormina D 14183
Tappy R 12302
Taq-e Bustan 12657
Taracha P 11163 11676 11691*
Taradach M 1552 9876* 9877
Tarazi P 755 3370 5994
Tarbox E 10271 15155
Tardan-Masquelier Y 402
Tardieu J 8656* **M** 1094

3 1247 7906 5808 7243
7960 8253 8760 9340
9355 11896
Theodorus M 14133-7
Theodotion 2473 3613
Theodotus A 14025* 14138
Théodulf 8994*
Theoleptus 14138*
ThéolRisqHist 403
Theophrastus 13392 13399
Theopompus 11213
Thera 9430 13142 13147-9
13394
Thériault J 8075
Thermos 13092*
Thessalia 13717
Thessalonica 6162
Theuer M 12927
Thévenot X 8094
Thévoz J 8306
Thibaut A 9338
Thiede C 749 9729-30*
Thiel J 566 4709 7146
10427 15141 **W** 1* 101
150 170 2632s 2644 2702
2713 9063 10689 10979
Thiele J 7264 **W** 5128
Thielicke H 7685
Thielman F 5814s 6114
Thieme P 9481
Thierfelder J 10138
Thiering B 4009 8750 9684
9711s 9717 9723* 9727
9731
Thiermeyer A 8219
Thierry N 12938*
Thiessen G 7905 11897
Thils G 8022 14936 15330
Thiselton A 899 930 1188
4177 6203 7686
Thönissen W 4621
Thom C 4344 **J** 4804
13943* **N** 7955
Thoma C 3019 3725 7369
7374 9057 10150* 11272*
Thomas A 7081 **C** 5489
8058 9640 11169 **D** 4485
4719 10841 **E** 10279 **G**

13008 **H** 8295 8336 8862
J 3874 5416 6299 13104
M 10410* **O** 7104 **R** 5485
5548 5937 11218 13328
13675 13848 **S** 5541
14766 **U** 5154
Thompson A 8131 **C** 10279*
14188 **D** 14656 14715 **G**
10427* **H** 3622 7653 **J**
2755 3495 5986 6128
6267 7539 7569 7593
7708 11649 14523 **K**
13631 13676 **L** 8872 **M**
3397 3770 4109 4505
4724 5312s 5431 5451
5705* 12164 **P** 437 **R**
7575 **S** 10381 10784
11005 **T** 403* 2041 2201
11009 13236 14448* **W**
4021 7520* 7769 8189
Thomson R 226 2812 12986
Thorau P 12242
Thordarson F 9446
Thoreau V 5357
Thorion Y 8995*
Thornhill J 1039* 8392
Thornton C 5175 **L** 7025 **M**
11638 **R** 11638
Thorpe S 10382
Thorson S 14522
Thouard D 14706
Thraede K 129
Thrall M 5953
Thrams P 11479
Throntveit M 2697 2719*
2763 2782
Thuburbo 12008
Thucydides 9335 11043
11176 11178 11182s
11201 11209 11216 13210
13481 13514 13524 13757
Thümmel H 4470 11898s
13187 14029* 14068
14421*
Thünen von 13463
Thür G 9418 **H** 12899
Thüsing W 4795
Thughūr 13238

Thunberg L 5229
Thung M 9177
Thurén L 6268
Thurm R 10263
Thurmond D 10507
Thurston B 5117
Thyen D 10917 **H** 5459
Tiberias 11974 12352
Tibi B 10867
Tibiletti C 13906
Tidball D 5931 14835
Tidiman B 3774
Tiede D 4928
Tieleman D 8131*
Tiessen T 7737 13998
Tietze A 9191*
Tiffin L 1868
Tigchelaar E 3784 3787
9596*
Tilborg S van 876 5327s
Tilby A 1869 10221
Tilghman B 10333
Tillard J 7651 7796* 7907
8026-30
Tiller P 9596*
Tilley A 11712 **M** 404
11446 **T** 7146 11027
Tillich P 263 3978 8880
11897 15110-4
Tilliette G 4022 **X** 4155s
4622 7470 7513 7521s
11025 14665
Tillmann N 3031
Tillmans W 7445
Tilsed I 605
Timm A 3486 8511 **H** 900
8810 9564 10334 **S** 10982
11005 12387
Timmer D 8596 **J** 801
Timmermnn P 389
Timmins N 5213
Tincq H 13885
Tinker G 8659 **M** 8076
Tipler F 1870
Tipton S 14991
Tirosh-Rothschild H 9977
Tirumanywa C 8660 10428
Tiryns 9435 13093

Vinay S 5421 **V** 228
Vincent G 10309 10557 **J**
11957* 14691 14691*
14713 **M** 327* 14127
Vincentius L 1076 14239
Vincenzi G 9325
Viney R 10221
Vinogradov Y 12878
Vinson M 2864 **S** 11713
Vinten G 8433
Vinz W 948 14862
Violante C 128
Viparelli V 164d
Vipsanius A 11325
Vircondelet A 15031
Virgilio B 440 12910s
Virgilius 9347 10537
13430* 14028
Virgoulay R 1020 14734
Virgulin S 3486*
Virlouvet C 13471
Virt G 560
Vis J 10280
Visa V 11748
Visca D 10978
Vischer L 1021 8035* 8136
Viscovi A 14735
Visentin P 131g
Visicato G 12596
Visonà P 12122
Visotzky B 1411 3243
9852*
Visser J 9580
Vita J 9095s
Vitelli K 12053
Viterbi ben Horin M 2099
Vitestam G 10842
Vitiello A †15396
Vitoria F de 7283* 8496
14570
Vitruvius 11599 11619
11619* 11638* 13250
Vittmann G 9228 9243
9248
Vitto F 12072*
Vivante A 12081*
Vives J 7578*

Vivian T 8256 14260
Viviani R 11915
Viviano B 3834 3931 4284
4293 4319 4346 4492
4513 4559 4582 4791
4869 5298 7073 7617
10066 10668 14708
14712
Viviers D 11488 11614
11924 11958 13111 **H**
3061 3179
Vlaardingerbroek J 3757
Vlachos C 8924 **K** 11010
VLat Stiftung 1491
Vledder E 4345 4458
Vleeming S 9232
Vliet E van der 11122
Voas D 1528
Voegelin E 11040 11051;
bibliog. 606
Vögtle A 4286 6304 7618
Völker H 10029 **W** 14126
Völling T 11804
Voelz J 9326
Vogels W 908 1683 1689
1706 2022 2413 2889
2919 2943 2974 3122s
3128 3374 4184
Vogelsang W 11156*
12647*
-Eastwood G 11766 11786s
Vogelzang M 453* 9165
Vogler G 14597 **W** 4644
5017 5209 5744 6095
6239 9749 13948
Vogt 5234 5976 7077 **H**
131h 4294 4935 14029 **K**
236e **R** 15341 **T** 4799
Vogthern T 13842
Vogüé A de 8257 14195*
Voicu S 5417 9276 14131*
Voigt K 14640* 14641* **M**
12650
Volanakis J 12936
Volf M 6269
Volgger D 3008 3045 8999
Volk T 12166

Vollenweider S 6111
Vollkommer R 13332
Vollmer D 11323
Vollrath H 34b
Volos 13096
Volp R 8221* 9501
Volpe F 22b **G** 866 11487
13734 15126 **L** 7251 7827
8773 8855
Volschenk G 5011
Voltaire 11002
Volz C 13225 13947
Von Fange E 1874
Voolen E van 7304
Voragine J de 9635
Vorbestimmung 407*
Vorgrimler
H 2097 7740 7824 8840 8
916 15178
Vorländer D 15179
Vorlaufer J 7265
Vorster H 648* **J** 1314
1690 3235 5834 **W** 132
875 3919
Vos H 8362 **J** 7784 **L de**
10280 **R** 12755
Vosloo W* 777
Voss G 8265
Votto S 12497
Vouga F 4175 5119 5456
5891 11335 13948
Voulgarakis É 8479
Vounos 13034
Vovelle M 14598
Voyé L 15115
Vriend J 8212 14829
Vries J de 644 1553 **S de**
10992
Vriezen K 12192
Vroom H 902
Vry S 10735
Vryonis S 132* 442
Vuillaume G 2547
Vulpe N 1991
Vunderink R 7940 15067
Vycichl W 9233
Vyhmeister N 9307

Washington H 3238 3260
7352
Washofsky M 9824 9844
Wassén C 2107
Wasserman N 12004
Wassermann J 9196
Wasserstein A 501 9136
Wasserstrom S 9594
Waterbolk H 11544
Waterfield R 11439
Waterhouse H 12019
Watkins T 12177
Watrous J 13110 L 13119
13137 13284
Watson A 10558s D 608
1338 6102 6173 F 1023
1199 1339 7100 G 9365
14061 J 1210 L 10560 N
5848 P 12603 13429* W
230c 2875 2877 3160
3163 3168 3195 3528
8973* 8991 8994 9111
9136* 10739 12541*
Watt D 14939 J 14254* J
van der 5423 W 230d
10920 13843 13887*
Wattenmaler P 487
Watts F 9565* J 723 2224
2413 3394 3550 8955
9069 9775
Waugh D 11073 E 10886
10899
Wauzzinski R 1875
Waxman C 609 13888
Way D 5654
Weakland R 5120 8218
14895 15124
Wearne L 14781
Weatherhead F 12740
Weatherly J 4920
Weathers R 14989
Weaver D 4493 G 11547 J
912 M 14717 W 312
11488*
Webb E 7785 H 8037 J
1053* 13020 R 4394s S
5754 7129 7525 10321*
10339 14977 14990 W

5561 5568s
Webber R 7662
Weber B 3035 4558 C
14889 D 9449* 9549 G
9397 11123 11443 H
8395 K 4585 10236
10253* 10278 11059
11641 13563 13604
13658 13694* 13719 T
7831 12192
Wéber É 667 4120
Webster D 154 G 10067
11569 13285 13804 J
14977 M 8832
Wechsler A 6030
Wedde M 11715
Wedderburn A 5132 5655s
8946
Weder D 4863 H 870 3877
4416 4527 5343 7420
7619
Weeber K 11440
Weeks N 1843 10703 S
3236
Wees H van 13720
Wegener M 4975
Weger K 10340
Wegman H 7541
Wegner A 3773 I 9261
12889 M 11959 P 3424
Wegs R 13642
Wehnert J 13974
Wehoe D 9419
Wehrle J 3244 3464
Weibel R 8396
Weidhas A 552* 1007
14866
Weidinger E 9594*
Weidmann F 14007
Weier W 7192 10341
Weigel G 15125 V 7266
Weigelt H 385 14615
Weigl M 3763
Weiher E von 12604
Weijers O 14369
Weil L 668* O 9934* S
7203 10339
Weiler I 13623

Weima J 5617 5758
Weinandy T 4023
Weinberg D 10021 J 2670
2769* 3078 9969 S
†15397 W 7316* Z 3445
7003
Weinberger T 7401* 10022
Weiner G 285* R 10040*
Weinfeld M 2393 2986
10686
Weinfurter S 34b
Weingartner P 408 1876
Weinrich W 5256 5303
13947 13949 13954
14785
Weinstein F 11030 J 11994
12768
-Evron M 12288
Weintraub D 136
Weippert H 2462 2521
7345 10738* 12199
12386 M 12386
Weir E 4847
Weis A 11960 13705
Weisbard P 2278
Weisberg D 1398 12605
12617
Weiser A 5081 5174 8953
Weiskopf M 11157
Weismann F 9519
Weiss A 3411 C 11804* H
6213 6230 9763 11128
11273* 12500 12607 M
3043* P 12939* R 9929 Z
12015 12350
Weisshaar H 13046
Weitenberg J 9275
Weitzman M 1468 13459 S
2045 2604
Weitzmann K 7317 12517
Welborn L 4801
Welburn A 3878 10174
Welch A 3701 C 5283 7580
L 7460 S 8833
Welker M 4710 7620 8333
10406* 14864
Wellesley K 11341
Wellhausen J 11011

Wiedemann T 498 11307
  11324 11343 11348
  11354 11749 13601
  13619
Wiedenhöver L 5241
Wiedenhofer S 7911s
Wieder L 1191
Wiederkehr D 409 5019
Wiedler S 13333
Wiefel W 4277 4313 5261
  7362 10029 14651
Wieh H 562
Wieland G 14370
Wiemeyer J 8400 8473
  8520
Wiener P †15398
Wiens S 5148
Wieringen A van 3474 3480
Wierschowski L 13689
  13798
Wiersma S 10624*
Wiertz P 7960
Wiese C 10153
Wiesehöfer J 11153
Wiesel E 1959 4158
Wiessner G 10199
Wietheger C 12756
Wigg D 11516 11715*
Wigger B 7175
Wiggins S 102 309 7324
  10739
Wigh-Poulsen H 15163
Wight F 729*
Wightman G 12245
Wigoder G 537
Wijngaards J 5426
Wikander Ö 13443
Wikström O 15384*
Wilbur K 3790
Wilcken J 7267 8064 14888
  14942
Wilckens U 168a 5745
  5810
Wilcock M 2495
Wilcox D 1794 P 3396
Wild R 6059 8059
Wildavsky A 2108 2129
Wilder A 138 266d 1190

1802 7118 7150 7641
  9576 10313 14830
  †15399*
Wildgen W 928
Wildmann G 7334
Wiles M 290* 337c
  7076 7235 7288 7475 756
  8 8038 10305 14623
Wiley J 7066
Wilflinger C 9816 10428*
Wilfong T 9610
Wilfred F 8664
Wilhelm G 11133 12606
  12890 12989 13302
  13528 13552
Wilk R 2865
Wilken R 262 9619 11411
  13243 13826 13973
Wilkens W 4396
Wilkes J 11916 12944
Wilkin R 6279
Wilkins W 14637
Wilkinson D 1877 J 12246
  13824 L 7637 13529 R
  9234 12110 12695* T
  12952 13745 W †15400
Will E 9815 9823 11535*
  12512 13044 15247 W
  11327
Willaert B 409* 410 F 545
Willaime J 14943
Willard M 2901*
Willems H 12121
Willers D 492* 11624
  11791* 11926 12944
Willesen F 2590
Willets R 13111
Willi T 2769 2798 15386
William D 7814
Williams 13579 B 8948
  12843s C 1224 5227
  10352* 10360 D 3266
  3338 5730 8037 8834
  9584 9755 11280s 11805
  11871 14068 14070
  14885 F 3826 5155 14102
  G 14497 H 13139 I 8554
  J 140 2576 3203 4419

4802 5486 7058 7786
  12139 12147 L 8665
  12849 M 806 3827 9565*
  10169 10219 10343
  11901 12931s N †15401
  R 10818 12168 14071*
  †15402 S 141 7100 7140
  T 7535 14790
Williamson C 3944 10111
  10154 H 597 918 2787
  2835 3175 3385 3389
  3397 3470s 7397 10997*
  11261 R 6219 9626
Willis J 3679 T 68 6256
  13647 W 5860
-Watkins D 2248
Willisch H 12780
Willmer P 14620
Wills É 7526 11069 J 282
  L 2122*
Wilmer J 5567
Wilshire B 14944
Wilson 12235 A 13328
  14185 B 142 5562 10477
  D 7666 13116 E 10807 H
  1789 4376 8666 J 3827
  3880s 10274 13498 14125
  K 12629 M 140 189 5539
  P 1054 R 1573 2298 4810
  6302 9610 9628 9631
  10214 13212 S 5143 5204
  9637 T 1362 W 3874
  3882 5830 14573
Wilt P 14831
Wilton P 2337
Wiltshire C 9541
Wiman I 11806
Wimber J 5934
Wimbush V 5860 8259
  14777
Wimmer J 14880 S 12314
Winand J 9234*
Winands K 131b
Winch P 15128
Winckelmann 11849*
Winckler W 1548
Wind J 78 8137
Windeatt B 14420*

Woodrum E 8536
Woods D 11686* 11692 **F**
 2704 **L** 1140 **T** 10646
Woodward D 13247 **K**
 8267
Woolf G 294d 11449 13214
 13436
Woolfenden G 14248
Woolley L 11552*
Wordsworth W 1205 1245
Worgul G 7804
Worley D 6247 **J** 11692*
Worp K 9419 **R** 11238
Worrall A 1677
Worthen T 1746
Worthington I 302* 1342
Wosh P 14716
Woude A van der 1406
 1604 2448 3633 3643
 3784 7290 9685 11076
 14352 15301
Wouters A 4347 10584
Wray D 1851
Wrede N 11952
Wreen M 10274
Wreide 12548
Wrenn M 1026
Wriedt M 8555
Wright C 1516 2348 **D** 410
 798 2330 3053 8851
 10686 **G** 11617 12304 **J**
 668* 2345 2772* 2782
 7639 9738 11150* 11157*
 M 10561 10648 **N** 3883
 4026 5818 6024 6134
 7914s **P** 2155 2185 12617
 R 5890 5928 9113 **T** 4027
 14770
Wroe M 14835
Wu J 3009
Wuellner W 330 4175
Würthwein E 233 2466
 2500 2709 3021
Wujastyk D 13511
Wujewski T 10511
Wulf G de 227 **U** 12912
Wulff D 10344
Wulfilas 14187

Wunsch C 454
Wurst G 10194*
Wurster W 11642*
Wurz P 14462
Wuthnow R 10345 14946s
 15179*
Wyatt N 1719 2049 2196
 10693 10725 12479* **R**
 1999 **W** 9306
Wybrow C 1711
Wycliff 14571
Wyk K van 12389 **W van**
 1581
Wylin K 9473
Wyman W 7704 10265
 14700 14706* 15119
 15142
Wynia E 10478
Wyper G 5551s
Wypustek A 7787
Wyschogrod E 10231 **M**
 2292 10366

Xanthos flumen 12959
Xella P 350c 12434

Yaacoub A 8138
Yadin Y 3332 9137 9419*
 9679* 9686 11567*
Yaèche M 10007
Yahil J 13478
Yahudiyya 12790
Yalvaç 12979
Yamada M 12004* **S** 1979
Yamaga T 1627
Yamauchi E 8619 9134
 9666 11157* 10205
 11049 13942
Yanai E 12294
Yanartaş 12980
Yandell K 10285
Yang Zhi 12606*
Yanke E 14948
Yannaras C 8040
Yanow D 2068
Yapp M 13891
Yarborough R 4028 4226

Yarbrough R 785 1312
 15021
Yarden L 13175
Yardeni A 9131 9137 9704
 9737* 11716
Yarkho V 9416
Yarmut 12281
Yarnold E 275 5067 7461
 8041 14293
Yasileh 12419
Yates R 5117 6126 **T** 7825
 7916
Yee G 5330 14800 **M** 8836
 9577
Yegül F 11726 11740
 11751
Yeivin I 146*
Yekutieli Y 12277
Yellin J 12327*
Yemen 10825
Yener K 11580
Yeo K 6172
Yeo Khiok-Khng 2203
 5182 5893s
Yerkapı 12881*
Yerushalmi Y 1278
Yerxa D 13902
Yılanlı 12981
Yıldız F 12590
Ynukow S 12034
Yocham V 1999
Yocum G 247 380a **R** 342
Yoder J 1236 4029 7349
 7359 8435 8480 8558
 8885 10921 14472*
 15059 15067
Yoman A 13666
Yon M 494 12485* 12505
Yona S 8992
Yonge C 9627
Yoshimura S 12759
Yoshitako S 10660
Yosippo 11263
Yossi L 12244
You Choon-Ho M 5889*
Young D 1879 4817 9249 **F**
 1495 6188* 6196 13949

VOCES

ordine **graeco**

agróteros 9333
adelphós 5101
adelphótēs 7853
agōgē 11739
agōnistikós 3623
ágrapha dógmata 10626
aidōs 9334
airetis 3320
akēdía 14109
akoúsmata 13943*
amphiktyonía 2464 11217
anánkē 9335
anachōrēsis 13721

anapesōn 11899*
anástasis 4705
*antērēs*9336
antí 5910
apátheia 7025 7271 14109
apaitētēs 9337
apeithéō 9338
argyrion 9339
archisynagōgós 9813
architéktōn 11604*
arotêres 13428*
authentéo 6193

Baítylos 12074
basileía toû theoû 4005
bios 4339

Gár 4843
geōrgoí 13428*
gnôsis 14149
grammatikē 9618*

Dé 306*
despótēs 6306
diaphanē 9339*
díkaios 5047
dikē 9340
dynamis 5966
dys- 9346*b
Egō eimi 5309
eidōlóthyton 5888-5900
eikōn 5487
ekklēsía 5487 9341
eleuthería 5809
en Christō 5639 5646
exousía 9342
epieikēs 9343
epieikeía 14429
epískopos 6196
episynagōgē 6251
érga nómou 6015
ergolabos 11604*
ergonēs 11604*
érchesthai 9344
érōs 13625
erōtapokríseis 14080
éschatos 3455

bar 9031
bar anša †9114*
b^erît 2305 3000
bārak 9032s *birkat ha-mînîm* 9784
bešaggam 1981

Ghimel

gêr 9034-6
m^egûlâ 10039
galût 2044
gôlâ 3469

Daleth

dābār 9349
dw(y)d/dwd 12325*
dwq 9748*
dam 9037
deraš 861 *daršan* 3062
   madrasa °10838*
*d^erôr, *anduraru* 9037*

He

hālak 9732 *halākâ* 4982
   6287
hûn/hîn 9038
ihāyāh 5381 9003*
hubal 9185
hnh hnwmh 3459

Waw

w^e- 9039 *wa-* 333

Zayin

iššâ zārâ 3256s 3260 3264
zazakku *9147
m^ezûzâ 7315

Ḥeth

ḥebel 3295
ḥebra 13661*
ḥādal 9040
maḥzor 7297 7301*

ḥaṭṭat 2333
teḥiyyat ha-metîm 7385
ḥyl 7051*
ḥokmâ 2892 3139 *ḥokmat*
   y^ebanît 3294 *ḥikma*
   °10853
ḥamas w^esad 3531
ḥasâ 2928
ḥerem 2485 7343*

Ṭeth

itebaih 3265
itôb ... min 3244

Yod

tôdôt 2899
yāda' 9041
yehûd 2798 11968 11968*
Yiśrā'ēl 2163 2173
y^ešûrûn, yādîd 9042

Kaph

k^e- 9043*
kudurru 13439
kî 9043
kippûr 2337 6220 7297
kîšôr 3275
kitbê ha-qôdeš 9824*
   ketubbâ 9137

Lamed

l^e- 9044
lô', h^alô' 9044*
lyn 3024
lašûaih 2075
l^ešôn limmûdîm 3454

Mem

mar †9114*
mat`eh 3941
mawtbê, bêt 1079
m^eraihevet 1696
mesith 4205
mêt 7385

min 9089
mpr ‡9113

Nun

neged, haggādâ 4985
niggûn 10043
nepeš 9045
nāqām 3263
n^etînîm 9704

Samech

Saba °12639
sābab 2415
sôd 9046
sukkâ 2344 *sukkat Dawîd*
   12326
sāmānu 13498
simtu *10798
safinâ °9759
ss'gr 12487

'Ayin

'ibrî 1047
'eber, 'ibrâ 13344
'egel 9047*
'iggeret ha'qôdeš 7322
'ôd 9048
'ēd 1961
'êdâ 9899
ma^{'a}lôt 3061s
'im 2368
'olat tamîd 7389
'ôlām 9049 *bêt 'olāmô*
   3307
'almâ 3414
'ê<u>i</u>s 3592
'aqēdâ 2055-68 6013

Pe

Pûrîm 2836 2840 9178
peres 13344
falsafa °10853
pesaḥ 2215
piskin 9049*
pešat 856 861

2 Regum

-: 2638s 2643
1s: 2717-24
2.21s: 13314
3-6: 2725
4: 1729
5: 2726s
5,19: 2728
8,25-10,36: 2729
9-11: 2729*
9,14: 2730
9,25s: 2731
9,33: 2732
10,36: 2734
11s: 2735
14,27: 2735*
16,10: 2332
17,24-41: 2736
18-20: 2738-42
21: 2743
22s: 2744s 2749
22: 2747 2750
22,14: 1746*
22,15-20: 2746
23: 2751
23,8: 2752
24,17: 2753
25,8: 2753*
25,22-26: 11265

1 Chronica

-: 2162 2754-69
1-9: 2770
5,1-10: 2771
5s: 2770*
7,18: 2378
10s: 2771*
11-13: 2772
11,4-8: 2611
27: 2772*

2 Chronica

-: 2759 2764
4,5: 2773
10-13: 2676

11: 2774
11,5-12: 2773*
13,1s: 2689
17,7-19,11: 2774*
20,6-13: 2775
21: 2600 2774 2774
35,32: 2775*
36,6: 2776*
36,9s: 2777

Esdras, Ezra

-: 2778-2800 2810-
12
7-10: 2800-1
9: 2802
4 Esdras -: 2810-2
3601

Nehemias

-: 2778 2781s 2799
2803-5*
3,1-32: 2806
5: 2788
6: 3354
8: 2801
9: 2807
11-24: 2808
12: 2809

Tobias

-: 148 2813-8 4853
9691
12,6-11: 2817
13: 2817*

Judith

-: 2819-26
5,6: 2825
7-13: 2823
7,13: 267

Esther

-: 2778 2781 2827-

30 3174 4855
2,21-23: 2831

1 Machabaeorum

-: 1079 2842-52
4853
4,26-35: 2856
6,28-63: 2856
9,35-4: 2057

2 Machabaeorum

-: 2847 2858
2,7s 2859
4,9: 2860s
7: 2863
13,33: 2865
4 Mcb: 1866

Psalmi

-: 2867-2968 3402
6228
1: 2969s
2: 2971 2971*
3-41: 1453
4: 2972
5: 2973
7-10: 2974
7: 2975s
8: 2976-8
8,2: 2979
8.6: 2979*
9s: 2980
11-14: 2980*
11: 2981
12-18: 2982
12: 2983
13: 2984
15-24: 2985
15; 2986
16; 2987s
17: 2989
18: 2990s 4671
19: 2993
19,3: 2992
20s: 2995

22,2; 108d
23: 2951 2996s
24: 2986 2998
25: 2999s
25,2: 3001
28,6: 3002
30,4: 3066
31: 3003s 3020
33: 3005
33,14: 3006
34: 3007
35: 2974
39: 3008s
40s: 3010
42-49: 3012
42s: 3042
42: 1110 3011
44: 3013
47: 3014s
47.4: 3016
49,12: 3017
50: 3018
50,23: 7767*
51-72: 2960
51: 3019-21
55: 3000 3022
55,14: 3023
58,5: 3023
59,16: 3024
60: 3025
61: 3026
62: 2951
62,9: 3027
63: 3042
67: 3028s
67,1: 3030
69: 3031
70-72; 3032
71: 3033
73-83: 3018
74,8: 3034
77: 3035
77,11: 3036
77,17-19: 3037
79: 3000
82: 3038s
83: 3000
84: 3012 3040-43

23: 3439
24-27: 3436s
24,10: 3438
24,21: 3439
25,6-10: 3439
27,1: 3440
29,1-8: 3425
30,20: 5385
31: 13356
32: 3424
32,15: 3550
34s: 3436
35,5-7: 5385
38,14: 12487
40-55 333
46-48; 3463
40-52: 3441-55
40,1s: 3456
40,6-8: 334
41,1-7: 3457
41.17-20: 3458
41,27: 3459
42,19: 2460
43,8-15: 3461
45.7: 3462
45,15: 333
47: 3464
48-55: 3470-2
51,17-23: 4614
51,9: 3465
52,13-53,12: 5377
52,13: 3466 3469
    3477
52s: 5038 10083
53: 2980 3466 5403
54,1-17: 3478
54,7-10: 2313
55,12-13: 3479
56-66: 3480s
56,1-8: 3482
57,8G: 3482*
57,12; 3483
57.15: 3550
59,1-21: 3484
59,15-20: 3048
61,1: 3485
61,1s: 4989
63,1-8: 3486
63,7-64,11: 3486*

65,17s: 3487
65,20-23; 3488

Jeremias

-: 2311* 2746 3364
    3489-3519 3679
    3698 4313
1,11-19: 3518
1,18: 3521
2-25: 3522
2,21s: 3523
6,16-21: 3524
7,1-15: 3525
7,17s: 3526
7,18: 3547
8,7: 12487
9,22s: 3526*
9,22s: 5979
10,1-16: 3525
11: 3511
13,1-7: 3527
17,1: 3528
17,11: 3529
18,6: 3530
20,8: 3531
20,14-18: 3532
20,14-19: 3126
23: 2753
23,1-4: 3533
23,28: 3535
23,9-29,32: 3534
27,5.15: 3542
27s: 3536
30,12-17: 3533
30s: 3537s
31,15-17: 3538
31,31: 3539
32: 3540s
32,18: 2246
33: 3542
34: 2753
35: 3543 3546
36,29: 2776*
40,14: 3544
43.1-7; 3546
43(50): 3545
44: 3547
44,15-25: 3526

45.4: 2337
45: 3548
46,25: 2337
52.20: 3549
52,12: 2753*

Lamentationes

-: 3174 3294 3551-
    6 3737
2: 3577

Baruch

-: 3546 3559-3561
1,15-3,8: 3562
3,9-44: 3138
2Bar -: 3601
- 6,7s: 2859
3Bar -: 3561

Ezechiel

-: 2311* 3364 3517
    3563-82
1: 3583
11: 3584
13: 3585
18: 3587s
20: 3589
25s: 3590
28,25s: 3591
34: 3591*
36,26: 3550
37,1-4; 3592
37,16-20: 3592*
38s: 3593
39,11-16: 3594
40-48: 3595

Daniel

-: 3364 3608-3633
    5494 11275
1,3-16: 3634
2-7: 3635
2,47: 334
3,17s: 3636
3,20: 3637

4-6: 3638
4,13: 3640
6: 3643
6,1-7,28: 3641
6,11: 3643
6,16: 3642
7: 3644
8: 3645
9: 3617
9,24-27: 3646
9,27: 3647
11,29-35: 3648
12,3: 3649

Amos

-: 334 3652 3654
    3667 3690-3705
1s: 3708
1,3-2,16: 3706s
1,3: 3710
3.8: 3710*
3,9: 3711
5,18.20: 2337
6s: 3712
7,4: 3713
7,10-19: 3714
9,1-4; 3715
9,1: 3716
9,7: 3717

Osee, **Hosea**

-: 3500 3514 3652
    3654 3658-67
    3696 3705
1-3: 334
1s: 3681
1,2: 3670
2.22s: 2313
6,1-6: 3682
6,2: 3683
11: 13356
12: 3684

Jonas

-: 3671 3677 3718-
    41

1,14s: 4808
2,1-12: 4810
2,5: 4811
2,13-17: 4812
2,13: 4323*
2,23: 4814
2,23-28: 4813
3.17: 4815
3,20-30: 4818
3,20-35: 4817
3,20s.31-35: 4816
3,28-30: 4819
4-11: 4820
4: 4821
4,1-34: 4817
4,10-12: 4822
4,21s: 4823
4,26-29: 4824
5,1-20: 4825
5,17: 4826
5,21-24.35-
    43: 4827
5,25-34: 4828
6,1-6: 4985
6,17-29: 4829
6,30-44: 4830
6,45: 4832
6,45-8,22: 4831
6,48: 4831
7,1-23: 4813
7,24-30: 4833
7,24-37: 4825
7,25-30: 4834
8-10: 4835
8,1-4: 4836
8,11; 4837
8,21: 4825
8,29: 4095×
8,31: 4810
8,34: 4838
8,38: 3864
9,1: 4839
9,2-13: 4840
9,14-19: 4840
9,14-29: 4842
9,49: 4843
10,1-2: 4845
10,2-12: 4561

10,13-52: 4846
10,13-16: 4844
10,17-19: 4783
11,12.20: 5037
11,12-21: 4847
11,12-25: 4848
11,12-25: 5029
11.15-19: 4849
11,27-12,34: 4850
12,12: 4851
12,13-17: 4852
12,18-23: 4853
12,28-34:4833
13: 3617 4856-9
    5494
13,1-37: 5035
13,3: 4860
14-16: 4861
14s: 4861-9
14,24: 4599 4864
14,53-72: 4810
15,6-15: 4865
15,21: 4813
15,42-47: 4866
16.3: 4691
16,9-20: 4867

Lucas

-: 1908 4780 4870
    4961 7632
1-3: 4962-84
1s: 4348-80 4964-6
1,1-4: 4870 4962s
1,5-2,52: 4970
1,5-25: 4389 4971
1,13-17: 4972
1,26-38: 4972*
1,28-42: 4973
1,31: 4974
1,46-55: 4975-8
2,1-20: 4975
2,1-5: 4979
2,2: 4980
2,14: 4981
2,22: 4982
2,29-35: 4983
2,32: 4984

2,41-51: 4985
3,15-17.21s: 4975
3,22: 1696
4,1-13; 4391
4,13: 4985*
4,16-30: 4986-8
4,18: 5873
4,18-21: 4989
4,19: 4558
5,16-26: 4990
5,27: 4323*
6,1: 4991
6,17: 4417-26
6,17-49: 4408
6,20-49: 4409
6,20-22: 4417-29
6,20-26: 4423 4992
6,22 (Q); 4993
6,46-49: 4994
7,1-10: 4995 5367
7,18-35: 4996
7,36-50: 4997s
    5413
8.16s: 4823
8,16-18: 4999
9,51-56: 4887
9,51: 5001
10: 5001
10,25-28: 5004
10,41: 5005
10s: 5001
11.29-32: 4499
11,2-4: 4439-46
11,20: 5006
11,33: 4823
11,37-54: 5029
11,40s: 5007
12,8s: 3864
12,10: 4819
13,6-9: 5008 5037
13,22-30: 5009
13,34s: 4555
14,1-24: 5010
14,1-6: 5011
14,25-35: 5012
15: 5013s 5018s
15,1-3: 5015
15,11: 14945

15,11-32: 5015s
15,11s: 5017
16: 5020
16,1-13: 5021
16,1-8: 5022s
16,1-13: 7605
16,16: 4497
17,7-10: 5024
17,11-19: 5025
18,9-14: 5026
18,18-30: 5027
18,18s: 5028
19,1-10: 5029
19,11-27: 5031
19,11-32: 5030
19,28-48: 5032
19,29-44: 5033
19,40: 5034
21,5-36: 5035
21,25-36: 5036
22,14-20: 4607*
22,14-38: 3467
22,19s: 5041
22,24-30: 5042s
22,29s: 5043
22s: 5038-5056
23,26-49: 5044
23,44-49: 5045
23,46: 5046
23,47: 5047
24,11: 5048
24,12: 5049
24,13-32; 5155
24,13-33: 5050-4
24,13-35: 5038
24,35: 4633
24,50-53: 5056
    5122

Johannes

-: 5197-5330 6239
    7632
1.14: 5349-51
1-9: 5249
1,1: 5346
1,1-8: 5331-45
1,3s: 5347

FINIS –Elenchus of Biblica 10, 1994 – END OF INDEX

Finito di stampare il 21 novembre 1997
Tipografia Poliglotta della Pontificia Università Gregoriana
Piazza della Pilotta, 4 – 00187 Roma

1996-1997 TITLES

ANALECTA BIBLICA

109. SKA, Jean-Louis: Le passage de la mer. Étude de la construction, du style et de la symbolique d'Ex 14,1-31. Deuxième édition revue et corrigée.
1997. pp. 204. ISBN 88-7653-109-2. L. 46.000

110. BOVATI, Pietro: Ristabilire la giustizia. Procedure, vocabolario, orientamenti. Prima ristampa, riveduta e corretta.
1997. pp. 448. ISBN 88-7653-110-6. L. 54.000

119. COSTACURTA, Bruna: La vita minacciata. Il tema della paura nella Bibbia Ebraica. Prima ristampa, riveduta e corretta.
1997. pp. 360. ISBN 88-7653-119-X. L. 54.000

136. MANZI, Franco: Melchisedek e l'angelologia nell'Epistola agli Ebrei e a Qumran.
1997. pp. XVIII-434. ISBN 88-7653-136-X. L. 52.000

137. TREMOLADA, Pierantonio: «E fu annoverato fra iniqui». Prospettive di lettura della Passione secondo Luca alla luce di Lc 22,37 (Is 53,12d).
1997. pp. 288. ISBN 88-7653-137-8. L. 36.000

STUDIA POHL: SERIES MAIOR

17. CUNNINGHAM, Graham: 'Deliver me from Evil'. Mesopotamian incantations 2550-1500 BC.
1997. pp. VIII-204. ISBN 88-7653-608-6. L. 37.000

18. VOLK, Konrad: A Sumerian Reader.
1997. pp. 132. ISBN 88-7653-610-8. L. 26.000

SUBSIDIA BIBLICA

14. JOÜON, Paul - MURAOKA, T.: A Grammar of Biblical Hebrew.
Vol. I: Part One: Orthography and Phonetics.
Part Two: Morphology.
Vol. II: Part Three: Syntax. Paradigms and Indices.
Second Reprint. The two volumes cannot be separated.
1996. pp. L-782. ISBN 88-7653-595-0. L. 80.000

19. Lasserre, Guy: Les synopses: élaboration et usage.
1996. pp. VIII-136. ISBN 88-7653-607-8.   L. 20.000

Separate Monographs

PIB BIBLICA: Index Generalis. 1970 - 1994. Volumina 51 - 75.
1997. pp. 140. ISSN 0006-0887.   L. 22.000

PIB Joün, Paul: Grammair de l'hébreu biblique. Deuxième edition
corrigée, Deuxième reproduction.
1996. pp. XII-544-80*. ISBN 88-7653-498-9.   L. 62.000

PIB Zerwick, Max - Grosvenor, Mary: A Grammatical Analysis
of the Greek New Testament. Fifth Revised Edition.
1996. pp. XXXVIII-778-16*. ISBN 88-7653-588-8.   L. 50.000